W9-CDE-192

ley,
ant
we
you
cole
Nicole

Smith and Roberson's
BUSINESS LAW
Eighth Edition

Smith and Roberson's
BUSINESS LAW

Eighth Edition

Richard A. Mann
Professor of Business Law
The University of North Carolina at Chapel Hill
Member of the North Carolina Bar

Barry S. Roberts
Associate Dean and Professor of Business Law
The University of North Carolina at Chapel Hill
Member of the North Carolina and Pennsylvania Bars

WEST PUBLISHING COMPANY
St. Paul   New York   Los Angeles   San Francisco

Cover and Text Design   Lois Stanfield Design Associates
Copy Editor   Mary Hough
Artwork   Printing Arts, Inc.
Composition   Carlisle Communications
Proofreader   Lynn Reichel
Index   David Buskus, Northwind Editorial Services

A study guide has been developed to assist you in mastering concepts presented in this text. Prepared by Peter T. Kahn and Dennis R. Hower of the University of Minnesota, this practical student study guide includes chapter overviews, educational objectives, chapter outlines, key terms, and exercises that match key terms to definitions. Your comprehension can be tested with multiple choice, true/false, short essay problems, and research problems. Answers are provided for all exercises and are keyed to the text material. The study guide is available from your local bookstore under the title *Study Guide to Accompany Smith and Roberson's Business Law, Eighth Edition.* If you cannot locate it in the bookstore, ask your bookstore manager to order it for you.

COPYRIGHT © 1962, 1966, 1971, 1977,
           1982, 1985, 1988   By WEST PUBLISHING COMPANY
COPYRIGHT © 1991   By WEST PUBLISHING COMPANY
                             50 W. Kellogg Boulevard
                             P.O. Box 64526
                             St. Paul, MN 55164–0526

All rights reserved

Printed in the United States of America

98 97 96 95 94 93 92 91   8 7 6 5 4 3 2 1

Library of Congress Cataloging-in-Publication Data

Smith, Len Young, 1901-
    [Business law]
    Smith and Roberson's business law.—8th ed. / Richard A. Mann,
    Barry S. Roberts.
        p.   cm.
    Includes index.
    ISBN 0–314–80190–1 (hard)
        1. Commercial law—United States.   I. Roberson, G. Gale (George
Gale), 1903–   II. Mann, Richard A.   III. Roberts, Barry S.
IV. Title.
KF888.S554   1991
346.73'07—dc20
[347.3067]   90–47792
                                       CIP

ABOUT THE AUTHORS

Richard A. Mann received a B.S. in Mathematics from the University of North Carolina at Chapel Hill and a J.D. from Yale Law School. He is currently Professor of Business Law at the University of North Carolina. Richard Mann is a past President of the Southeastern Regional Business Law Association. He is a member of Who's Who in American Law, Outstanding Young Men of America, and the North Carolina Bar.

Professor Mann has written extensively on a number of legal topics including bankruptcy, sales, secured transactions, real property, insurance law and business associations. He has received the *American Business Law Journal* award for both the best article and the best comment. He has served as a reviewer and staff editor for the *American Business Law Journal*. He teaches in several executive education programs and is a founder, managing director and instructor in the Carolina CPA Review. He is a co-author of *Essentials of Business Law, Third Edition,* as well as *Business Law and the Regulation of Business, Third Edition.*

Barry S. Roberts received a B.S. in Business Administration from Pennsylvania State University, a J.D. from the University of Pennsylvania and an LL.M. from Harvard Law School. He served as a judicial clerk for the Pennsylvania Supreme Court prior to practicing law in Pittsburgh. Barry Roberts is currently Associate Dean and Professor of Business Law at the School of Business Administration, University of North Carolina at Chapel Hill. He is a member of Who's Who in American Law, Outstanding Young Men of America, and the North Carolina Bar.

Professor Roberts has written numerous articles on such topics as antitrust, products liability, constitutional law, banking law, employment law, and business associations. He has been a reviewer and staff editor for the *American Business Law Journal*. Professor Roberts is a founder, managing director and instructor in the Carolina CPA Review. He is a co-author of *Essentials of Business Law, Third Edition,* as well as *Business Law and the Regulation of Business, Third Edition.*

CONTENTS IN BRIEF

Contents

Preface

The format of the Eighth Edition is the same as that of the seven prior editions, in that each chapter contains narrative text, cases consisting of selected court decisions, and problems. This text is designed for use in Business Law and Legal Environment courses generally offered in universities, colleges, and schools of business and commerce. By reason of the broad coverage and variety of the material, this volume may be readily adapted to specially designed courses in Business Law by assigning and emphasizing different combinations of the subject matter. All topics included in the CPA exam are covered by the text.

To improve readability, all unnecessary "legalese" has been eliminated while necessary legal terms are printed in boldface and clearly defined, explained, and illustrated. The text is enriched by numerous illustrative hypothetical and case examples which help students relate material to real life experiences. The end of chapter cases are cross-referenced in the text as are related topics covered in other chapters.

Greater emphasis has been placed upon the regulatory environment of Business Law: the first seven chapters are devoted to introductory coverage of the legal environment of business and Part IX (Chapters 41 to 47) addresses the area of government regulation of business. Two new chapters have been added: Business Ethics and Social Responsibility (Chapter 7) and International Business Law (Chapter 47).

From long classroom experience we are of the opinion that fundamental legal principles can be more effectively learned from text and case materials having at least a degree of human interest. To accomplish this objective a large number of recent cases have been included. Landmark cases, on the other hand, have not been neglected. Cases have been placed at the end of the chapter and are cross-referenced to the text. They have been carefully edited to preserve the actual language of the court and to show the essential facts of the case, the issue or issues involved, the decision of the court, and the reason for its decision.

In this text, we have used approximately 100 classroom tested figures, charts, and diagrams. The diagrams help the student conceptualize the many abstract concepts in the law; the charts not only summarize prior discussions but also aid in pointing out relationships among legal rules. In addition, each chapter begins with highlights which summarize the topics to be covered.

Classroom-proven problems appear at the end of chapters to test the student's understanding of major concepts. We have used the problems and consider them excellent stimulants to classroom discussion. Students have found the problems helpful in enabling them to apply the basic rules of law to factual situations, many of which are taken from reported court decisions. The problems serve as a springboard for discussion and readily suggest other and related problems to the inquiring, analytical mind. We have added discussion questions to the end of all chapters to provide another opportunity for the students to examine their comprehension of the material.

A new feature, Computer Research Problems, has been added to Part Two—Contracts, Part Four—Sales, and Chapters 41 through 44 of Part Nine—Regulation of Business. These problems are based on cases appearing in LEGAL CLERK, which is an interactive software package that introduces students to the basics of computer-aided research and amplifies the principles of business law covered in those chapters. Access to LEGAL CLERK provides the student the opportunity to review the legal principles relating to the facts of the problem and to read an edited version of the court's decision in the case upon which the facts are based. The Computer Research Problems are identified with a logo indicating which of the three versions of LEGAL CLERK contains that case:

 Uniform Commercial Code Article 2 Sales—Version 1.0

 Government Regulation and The Legal Environment of Business—Version 1.0

 Contracts—Version 1.0

The text contains comprehensive appendixes, including the Constitution of the United States (Appendix A); selected provisions of the Restatements of Torts, Contracts and Agency (Appendix B); the Uniform Commercial Code (Appendix C); the Uniform Partnership Act (Appendix D); the Revised Uniform Limited Partnership Act (Appendix E); selected provisions of the 1985 Amendments to the Revised Uniform Limited Partnership Act as amended (Appendix F); the Revised Model Business Corporation Act (Appendix G); and selected provisions of the Model Business Corporation Act (Appendix H). A comprehensive Dictionary of Legal Terms appears in Appendix I.

Classroom use and study of this book should provide for the student the following benefits and skills:

1. Perception and appreciation of the scope, extent, and importance of the law.

2. Basic knowledge of the fundamental concepts, principles, and rules of law that apply to business transactions.

3. Acquisition of knowledge of the function and operation of courts and governmental administrative agencies.

4. Ability to recognize the possibility of potential legal problems which may arise in a doubtful or complicated situation, and the necessity of consulting a lawyer and obtaining competent professional legal advice.

5. Development of analytical skills and reasoning power.

SUPPLEMENTAL MATERIALS

The **Study Guide** by Peter Kahn and Denny Hower provides hints on how to study law for each chapter and a brief statement of purpose, chapter objectives, chapter outlines, key term definitions, true/false and multiple choice questions, and short essays. Each part has optional research questions. The study guide also includes a CPA exam business law review.

The **Instructor's Manual** by Richard Mann, Barry Roberts, and Mark Altieri contains chapter outlines, teaching notes, answers to problems and questions, discussion questions and answers, key terms, recommendations for transparency masters and acetates, and Part Openers which provide suggested research and outside activities for students.

The **Test Bank** by Georgia Holmes is bound in a separate volume and includes true/false, multiple choice, short essay, and challenge test questions.

Computerized Testing—WesTest contains the complete test bank on disk and allows professors the ability to generate a variety of tests using floppy disks for either IBM PC's and compatibles or for Apple II family microcomputers. This is available to qualified adopters.

74 **Transparency Masters** and 72 one- and two-color **Acetates** highlight text illustrations.

LEGAL CLERK Software (Computerized Legal Research Package) is West's software package that introduces students to computerized legal research and black letter law. It is intended to help schools meet AACSB recommendations for using microcomputers in business law courses. The complete package includes copyable disks, a Student User's Guide, and an Instructor's Guide. LEGAL CLERK is available to qualified adopters.

West's Book of Legal Forms by McNutt offers 40 sample business forms.

Computerized Library of Cases contains on computer disk the full text of all cases upon which end of chapter problems have been based.

ACKNOWLEDGMENTS

We express our gratitude to the following professors for their helpful comments: Mark Altieri, Cleveland State University; Joell Bjorke, Winona State University; William Bockanic, John Carroll University; Alex DeVience, DePaul University; William G. Elliott, Saginaw Valley State University; Kurt Erickson, South West Michigan College; James Granito, Youngstown State University; Donald Haley, Cleveland State University; James V. Harrison, St. Peters State College; James Holzinger, Muhlenberg College; Marilee Jones-Confield, California State University—Long Beach; Al Joyner, Eastern Illinois University; Louise Knight, Bucknell University; Michael A. Mass, American University; Cheryl Massingale, University of Tennessee—Knoxville; Bruce McClain, Cleveland State University; James Molloy, University of Wisconsin—Whitewater; Elinor Rahm, Central Missouri State University; Samuel H. Ramsay, Jr., Bryant College; Roger Reinsch, Emporia State University; Janis Stamm, Edinboro University of Pennsylvania; David Steele, University of Wisconsin—Eau Claire; Peter Strohm, Georgian Court College; and Al Talarczyk, Edgewood College.

We are also grateful to those who provided us with comments regarding recent editions of the book: Albert Andrews, Jr., University of Minnesota; William N. Bockanic, John Carroll University; John P. Carnasiotis, University of Missouri; Mitchell F. Crusto, Washington University—St. Louis; Arthur S. Davis, Long Island University; Alex DeVience, Jr., DePaul University; Karla H. Fox, University of Connecticut; Michael J. Garrison, North Dakota State University; Frances J. Hill, University of Wisconsin—Whitewater; Georgia L. Holmes, Mankato State University; Mary C. Keifer, Ohio University; James L. Porter, University of New Mexico; George Roe, University of Illinois—Chicago; Charles H. Walker, University of Mississippi; and James B. Zimarowski, University of Notre Dame; Herbert McLaughlin, Bryant College; Leonard Tripodi, St. Joseph's College; Al Stauber, Florida State University; Donald Boren, Bowling Green University; William Day, Cleveland State University; Donald Nelson, University of Denver; Richard Paxton, San Diego Community College; Richard Luke, Ricks College; Tim Rueth, Marquette University; David Webster, University of South Florida, Tampa; Joe W. Fowler, Oklahoma State University, Stillwater; Wells J. Wright, University of Minnesota; Donald Cantwell, University of Texas, Arlington; Telford F. Hollman, University of Northern Iowa, Cedar Falls; Duane R. Lambert, California State University, Hayward.

We express our thanks and deep appreciation to Carol Courts for typing the manuscript. For their support we extend our thanks to Karlene Fogelin Knebel and Joanne Erwick Roberts. And we are grateful to Richard Fenton, Nancy Hill-Whilton, and Mary Verrill of West Publishing Company for their invaluable assistance and cooperation in connection with the preparation of this text.

This text is dedicated to our children Lilli-Marie Knebel Mann, Justin Erwick Roberts, and Matthew Charles Roberts.

Richard A. Mann
Barry S. Roberts

TABLE OF STATUTES

TABLE OF CASES

Cases in italic are the principal cases included at the ends of the chapters.
References are to pages.

TABLE OF ILLUSTRATIONS

Smith and Roberson's
BUSINESS LAW
Eighth Edition

The Legal Environment of Business

Chapter 1

INTRODUCTION TO LAW

Nature of Law
Classification of Law
Sources of Law
Legal Analysis

LAW concerns the relations of individuals with one another as they affect the social and economic order. It is both the product of civilization and the means by which civilization is maintained. As such, law reflects the social, economic, political, religious, and moral philosophy of society. The laws of the United States affect and influence the life of every American citizen. At the same time, the laws of each State affect and influence the life of each of its citizens as well as a large number of noncitizens. The rights and the duties of all individuals, as well as the safety and security of all people and their property, depend upon the law.

The law is pervasive. It interacts with and influences the political, economic, and social systems of every civilized society. It permits, forbids, and/or regulates practically every known human activity and affects all persons either directly or indirectly. Law is, in part, prohibitory: certain acts must not be committed. For example, one must not steal; one must not murder. Law is also partly mandatory: certain acts must be done or be done in a prescribed way. Taxes must be paid; corporations must make and file certain reports with State authorities; traffic must keep to the right. Finally, law is permissive: certain

acts may or may not be done. Thus, one may or may not enter into a contract; one may or may not dispose of one's estate by will.

Because the law is so highly interrelated, it is helpful to begin the study of the several branches of law known collectively as business law by first considering the nature, classification, and sources of law as a whole. This enables the student not only to comprehend better any given branch of law but also to understand its relation to other areas of law.

NATURE OF LAW

The law has evolved slowly, and it will continue to change. It is not a pure science based upon unchanging and universal truths. Rather, it is a continuous striving to attain a workable set of rules that balance the individual and group rights of a society. In *The Common Law*, Oliver Wendell Holmes writes, "The life of the law has not been logic; it has been experience. The felt necessities of the time, the prevalent moral and political theories, avowed or unconscious, even the prejudices which judges share with their fellowmen, have had a good deal more to do than the syllogism in determining the rules by which men should be governed. The law embodies the story of a nation's development through many centuries, and it cannot be dealt with as if it contained only the axioms and corrollaries of a book of mathematics."

Definition of Law

A fundamental but difficult question regarding law is, What is it? Numerous philosophers and jurists (legal scholars) have attempted to define it. The American jurists and Supreme Court Justices Oliver Wendell Holmes and Benjamin Cardozo defined law as predictions of the way that a court will decide specific legal questions. Blackstone, an English jurist, on the other hand, defined law as "a rule of civil conduct prescribed by the supreme power in a state, commanding what is right, and prohibiting what is wrong." Similarly, Austin, a nineteenth-century English jurist, defined law as a general command of a state or sovereign to those who are subject to its authority by laying down a course of action that is enforced by judicial or administrative tribunals.

Because of its great complexity, many legal scholars have attempted to explain the law by outlining its essential characteristics. Roscoe Pound, a distinguished American jurist and former dean of the Harvard Law School, described law as having multiple meanings:

First, we may mean the legal order, that is, the régime of ordering human activities and relations through systematic application of the force of politically organized society, or through social pressure in such a society backed by such force. We use the term "law" in this sense when we speak of "respect for law" or for the "end of law."

Second, we may mean the aggregate of laws or legal precepts; the body of authoritative grounds of judicial and administrative action established in such a society. We may mean the body of received and established materials on which judicial and administrative determinations proceed. We use the term in this sense when we speak of "systems of law" or of "justice according to law."

Third, we may mean what Mr. Justice Cardozo has happily styled "the judicial process." We may mean the process of determining controversies, whether as it actually takes place, or as the public, the jurists, and the practitioners in the courts hold it ought to take place.

Functions of Law

At a general level the primary function of law is to maintain stability in the social, political, and economic system while at the same time permitting change. The law accomplishes this basic function by performing a number of specific functions, among them dispute resolution, protection of property, and preservation of the state.

Disputes inevitably arise in a society as complex and interdependent as ours. Disputes may involve criminal matters, such as theft, or noncriminal matters, such as an automobile accident. Because disputes threaten the stability of society, the law has established an elaborate and evolving set of rules to resolve disputes. In addition, the legal system has instituted societal remedies, usually administered by the courts, in place of private remedies such as revenge.

The recognition of private ownership of property is fundamental to our economic system, based as it is upon the exchange of goods and services among privately held units of consumption. Therefore, a second crucial function of law is to protect the owner's use of property and to facilitate voluntary agreements (called contracts) regarding exchanges of property and services. Accordingly, a significant portion of law, as well as this text, involves property and its disposition, including the law of property, contracts, sales, commercial paper, and business associations.

A third essential function of the law is preservation of the state. In our system, law ensures that changes in the political structure and leadership are brought about by political action such as elections, legislation, and referenda rather than by revolution, sedition, and rebellion.

Legal Sanctions

A primary function of the legal system is to make sure that legal rules are enforced.

Sanctions are the means by which the law enforces the decisions of the courts. Laws without sanctions would be ineffectual and unenforceable.

An example of a sanction in a civil (non-criminal) case is the seizure and sale of the debtor's property if the debtor fails to pay the court-ordered obligation called a judgment. Moreover, under certain circumstances the court may enforce its orders by finding an offender in contempt of court and sentencing him to jail until he obeys the court's order. In criminal cases, the principal sanctions are the imposition of a fine, imprisonment, and capital punishment.

Law and Morals

Although the law is greatly affected by moral and ethical concepts, morals and law are not the same. They may be considered as two intersecting circles, as shown in Figure 1–1. The shaded area common to both circles includes the vast body of ideas that are both moral and legal. For instance, "Thou shall not kill" and "Thou shall not steal" are both moral precepts and legal constraints.

On the other hand, the part of the legal circle not intersecting the morality circle includes many rules of law that are completely unrelated to morals, such as the rules that you must drive on the right side of the road and that you must register before you can vote. Likewise, the part of the morality circle not intersecting the legal circle includes moral precepts not enforced by law, such as you should not silently stand by and watch a blind man walk off a cliff, or you should not foreclose a poor widow's mortgage.

Law and Justice

Law and justice represent separate and distinct concepts. Without law, however, there can be no justice. Although there are at least as many definitions of justice as there are of law, justice may be defined as fair, equitable, and impartial treatment of competing interests and desires of individuals and groups with due regard for the common good.

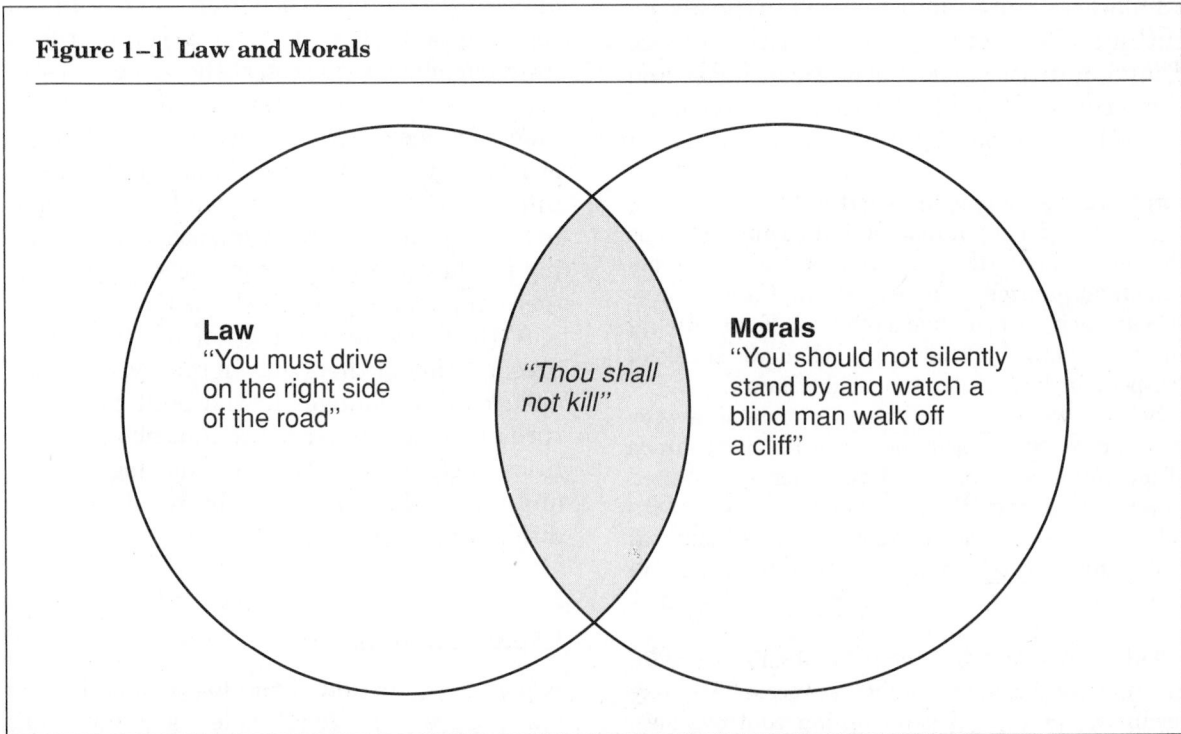

Figure 1–1 Law and Morals

Law
"You must drive on the right side of the road"

"Thou shall not kill"

Morals
"You should not silently stand by and watch a blind man walk off a cliff"

On the other hand, law is no guarantee of justice. Some of history's most monstrous acts have been committed pursuant to "law." For example, recall the actions of Nazi Germany during the 1930s and 1940s. Totalitarian societies have often carefully shaped a formal legal system around the atrocities they have caused to be committed.

CLASSIFICATION OF LAW

Because the law is vast, it is helpful to classify the law into categories. This can be done in a number of ways, but the most useful categories are (1) substantive and procedural, (2) public and private, and (3) civil and criminal (see Figure 1–2).

Basic to understanding these classifications are the terms *right* and *duty*. A **right** is the capacity of a person, with the aid of the law, to require another person or persons to perform, or to refrain from performing, some certain act. Thus, if Alice sells and delivers goods to Bob for the agreed price of $500 payable at a certain date, Alice has the capability, with the aid of the courts, of enforcing the payment by Bob of the $500. A **duty** is the obligation imposed by law upon a person by which he is required to perform a certain act or to refrain from performing a certain act. Duty and right are correlatives: there can be no right in one person without a corresponding duty resting upon some other person, or in some cases, upon all other persons.

Substantive and Procedural Law

Substantive laws create, define, and regulate legal rights and obligations. Thus, the rules of contract law that determine when a binding contract is formed are rules of substantive law. This book is principally concerned with substantive law. On the other hand, **procedural law** establishes the rules for enforcing those rights that exist by reason of the substantive law. Thus, procedural law defines the method by which to obtain a remedy in court.

Public and Private Law

Public law is that branch of substantive law that deals with the government's rights and powers in its political or sovereign capacity and its relation to individuals or groups. Public law consists of constitutional, administrative, and criminal law. **Private law** is that part of substantive law governing individuals and legal entities (such as corporations) in their relations with one another. Business law is primarily private law.

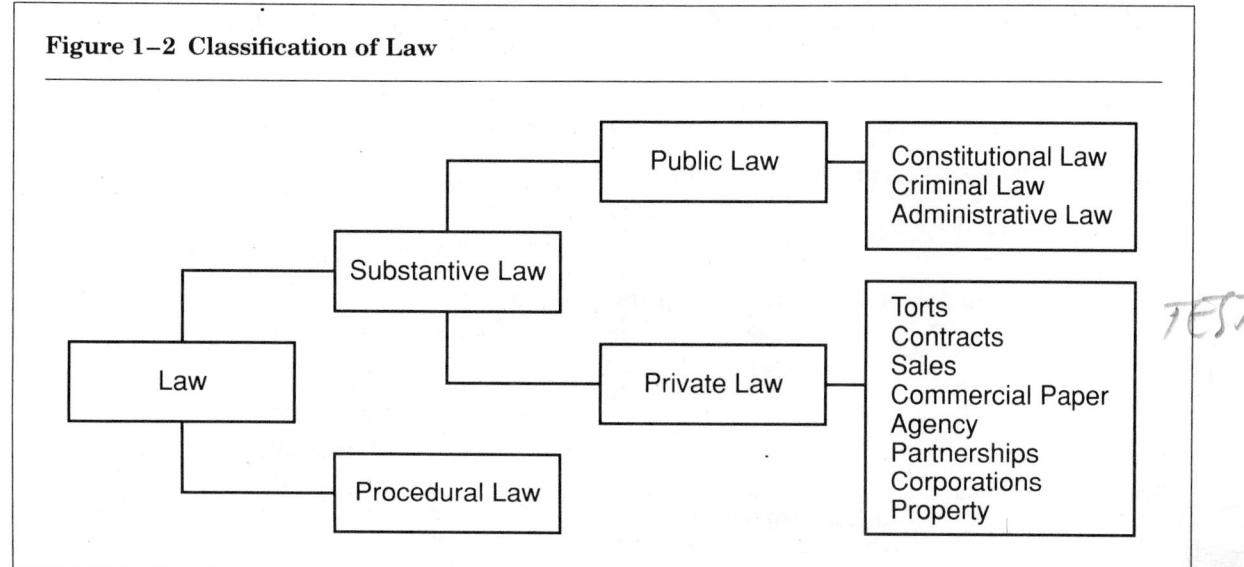

Figure 1–2 Classification of Law

- Law
  - Substantive Law
    - Public Law
      - Constitutional Law
      - Criminal Law
      - Administrative Law
    - Private Law
      - Torts
      - Contracts
      - Sales
      - Commercial Paper
      - Agency
      - Partnerships
      - Corporations
      - Property
  - Procedural Law

Civil and Criminal Law

The **civil law** defines duties the violation of which constitutes a wrong against the party injured by the violation. In contrast, the **criminal law** establishes duties the violation of which is a wrong against the whole community. Civil law is a part of private law, whereas criminal law is a part of public law. In a civil action the injured party **sues** to recover **compensation** for the damage and injury sustained as a result of the defendant's wrongful conduct. The party bringing a civil action (the **plaintiff**) has the burden of proof, which the plaintiff must sustain by a **preponderance** (greater weight) of the evidence. The purpose of the civil law is to compensate the injured party, not to punish the wrongdoer as in the case of criminal law. The principal forms of relief afforded by the civil law are a judgment for money damages and a decree ordering the defendant to specifically perform a certain act or to desist from specified conduct.

A crime is any act or omission prohibited by public law in the interest of protection of the public and made punishable by the government in a judicial proceeding brought (**prosecuted**) by it. The government must prove criminal guilt **beyond a reasonable doubt,** which is a significantly higher burden of proof than that required in a civil action. Crimes are prohibited and punished upon the ground of public policy, which may include the protection and safeguarding of

government, human life, or private property. Additional purposes of the criminal law include deterrence and rehabilitation. A comparison of civil and criminal law is shown in Figure 1–3.

SOURCES OF LAW

The sources of law in the American legal system are the Federal and State constitutions, Federal treaties, interstate compacts, Federal and State statutes, the ordinances of countless local municipal governments, Federal and State executive orders, the rules and regulations of Federal and State administrative agencies, and an ever increasing volume of reported Federal and State court decisions.

The *supreme law* of the land is the United States Constitution. The Constitution also provides that statutes and treaties made under the authority of the United States shall be the supreme law of the land. Federal legislation and treaties are, therefore, paramount to State constitutions and statutes. Federal legislation is of great significance as a source of law. Other Federal actions having the force of law are executive orders by the president and rules and regulations of Federal administrative officials, agencies, and commissions. The Federal courts also contribute considerably to the body of law in the United States.

The same pattern exists in every State. The paramount law of each State is contained

---

Figure 1–3 Comparison of Civil and Criminal Law

	Civil Law	Criminal Law
Commencement of Action	Aggrieved individual (plaintiff) sues	State or Federal government prosecutes
Purpose	Compensation Deterrence	Punishment Deterrence Rehabilitation Preservation of peace
Burden of Proof	Preponderance of the evidence	Beyond a reasonable doubt
Principal Sanctions	Monetary damages Equitable remedies	Capital punishment Imprisonment Fines

in its written constitution. Subordinate to this are the statutes enacted by its legislature and the case law developed by its judiciary. Likewise, State administrative agencies issue rules and regulations having the force of law as do executive orders promulgated by the governor. In addition, cities, towns, and villages have limited legislative powers within their respective municipal areas to pass ordinances and resolutions.

Constitutional Law

A **constitution**—the fundamental law of a particular level of government—serves a number of critical functions. It establishes the governmental structure and allocates power among the levels of government, thereby defining political relationships. One of the fundamental principles on which our government is founded is that of separation of powers. As incorporated into our Constitution, this means that there are three distinct and independent branches of government: the Federal judiciary, the Congress, and the Executive branch.

A constitution also restricts the powers of government and specifies the rights and liberties of the people. For example, the Constitution of the United States not only specifically states what rights and authority are vested in the national government but also specifically enumerates certain rights and liberties of the people. Moreover, the Ninth Amendment to the U.S. Constitution makes it clear that this enumeration of rights does not in any way deny or limit other rights that are retained by the people.

All other law in the United States is subordinate to the Federal Constitution. No law, Federal or State, is valid if it violates the Federal Constitution. Under the principle of **judicial review,** the Supreme Court of the United States determines the constitutionality of *all* laws.

Judicial Law

The American legal system is a **common law system,** first developed in England. It relies heavily on the judiciary as a source of law and on the adversary system for adjudication of disputes. In an **adversary system** the parties, not the court, must initiate and conduct litigation. This approach is based upon the belief that the truth is more likely to emerge from the investigation and presentation of evidence by two opposing parties, both motivated by self-interest, than from judicial investigation motivated only by official duty. The common law system is also used in other English-speaking countries, including England, Canada, and Australia.

In distinct contrast to the common law system are civil law systems, which are based upon Roman law. **Civil law systems** depend upon comprehensive legislative enactments (called codes) and the inquisitorial method of adjudication. In the **inquisitorial system,** the judiciary initiates litigation, investigates pertinent facts, and conducts the presentation of evidence. The civil law system prevails in most of Europe, Scotland, the State of Louisiana, the province of Quebec, Mexico, and South America.

Common Law   The courts in common law systems have developed a body of law that serves as precedent for determination of later controversies. This law is called "case law," "judge-made law," or "common law." In this sense, common law is distinguished from other sources of law such as legislation and administrative rulings.

In order to evolve in a stable and predictable manner, the common law has developed by application of stare decisis. Under the principle of **stare decisis** (to stand by the decisions), rules of law announced and applied by courts in prior decisions are later adhered to and relied upon in deciding cases of a similar nature. Judicial decisions thus have two uses: to determine with finality the case being decided and to indicate how similar cases will be decided if and when they arise. *Stare decisis* does not, however, preclude correction of erroneous decisions or judicial choice among conflicting precedents. Thus, the doctrine allows sufficient flexibility for the common law to change.

The strength of the common law is its ability to adapt to change without losing its sense of direction. As Justice Cardozo said, "The inn that shelters for the night is not the journey's end. The law, like the traveler, must be ready for the morrow. It must have a principle of growth."

Equity As the common law developed in England, it became overly rigid and beset with technicalities. As a consequence, in many cases no remedies were provided because the judges insisted that a claim must fall within one of the recognized forms of action. Moreover, courts of common law could provide only limited remedies; the principal type of relief obtainable was a money judgment. Consequently, individuals who could not obtain adequate relief from monetary awards began to petition the king directly for justice. He, in turn, came to delegate these petitions to his chancellor.

Gradually, there evolved what was in effect a new and supplementary system of needed judicial relief for those who had no adequate remedy at common law. This new system, called **equity,** was administered by a court of chancery presided over by the chancellor. The chancellor, deciding cases on "equity and good conscience," afforded relief in many instances in which the common law judges refused to act or where the remedy at law was inadequate. Thus, there grew up, side by side, two systems of law administered by different tribunals, the common law courts and courts of equity.

An important difference between law and equity is that the chancellor could order a defendant to do or refrain from doing a specific act. If the defendant did not comply with this order, called a **decree,** the defendant could be held in contempt of court and punished by fine or imprisonment. This power of compulsion available in a court of equity opened the door to many needed remedies not available in a court of common law.

Equity jurisdiction, in some cases, recognized rights that were enforceable at common law but equity provided more effective remedies. For example, for breach of a land con-tract the buyer could obtain a decree of **specific performance** in a court of equity. The defendant seller would be commanded to perform his part of the contract by transferring title to the land. Another powerful and effective remedy available only in the courts of equity was the **injunction,** a court order requiring a party to do or refrain from doing a specified act. Another remedy in equity not available elsewhere was the remedy of **reformation,** where, upon the ground of mutual mistake, an action could be brought to reform or change the language of a written agreement to conform to the actual intention of the contracting parties. Another remedy was an action for **rescission** of a contract, which allowed a party to invalidate a contract under certain circumstances.

Although courts of equity provided remedies not available in courts of law, they granted them only at their discretion, not as a matter of right. This discretion was exercised according to the general legal principles, or **maxims,** formulated by equity courts over the years. A few of these familiar maxims of equity are the following. Equity will not suffer a wrong to be without a remedy. Equity regards the substance rather than the form. Equity abhors a forfeiture. Equity delights to do justice and not by halves. He who comes into equity must come with clean hands. He who seeks equity must do equity.

In nearly every jurisdiction in the United States, there has been a union of courts of common law and equity to form a single court that administers both systems of law. Vestiges of the old division continue, however. For example, the right to a trial by jury applies only to actions at law and, under Federal law and in almost every State, not to suits filed in equity.

Restatements of Law The common law of the United States results from the independent decisions of the State and Federal courts. The rapid increase in the number of decisions by these courts led to the establishment of the American Law Institute (ALI) in 1923. The ALI was composed of a distinguished group of lawyers, judges, and law teachers who assumed the task of preparing "an orderly restatement of the general common law of the United States, including in that term not only the law developed solely by judicial decision, but also the law that has grown from the application by the courts of statutes that were generally enacted and were in force for many years." Wolkin, "Restatements of the Law: Origin, Preparation, Availability," 21 *Ohio B.A.Rept.* 663 (1940).

The Restatements cover many of the important areas of the common law, including torts, contracts, agency, property, and trusts. Although not law by themselves, they are highly persuasive and have frequently been utilized by courts in support of their opinions. The Restatements are regarded as the authoritative statement of the common law of the United States. Because they provide a concise and clear statement of much of the common law, relevant portions of the Restatements are frequently relied upon in this book.

Legislative Law

Since the end of the nineteenth century, legislation has become the primary source of new law and ordered social change in the United States. The annual volume of legislative law is enormous. Justice Felix Frankfurter's remarks to the New York City Bar in 1947 are even more appropriate today:

Inevitably the work of the Supreme Court reflects the great shift in the center of gravity of lawmaking. Broadly speaking, the number of cases disposed of by opinions has not changed from term to term. But even as late as 1875 more than 40 percent of the controversies before the Court were common-law litigation, fifty years later only 5 percent, while today cases not resting on statutes are reduced almost to zero. It is therefore accurate to say that courts have ceased to be the primary makers of law in the sense in which they "legislated" the common law. It is certainly true of the Supreme Court that almost every case has a statute at its heart or close to it.

This modern emphasis upon legislative or statutory law has occurred because common law, which develops evolutionarily and haphazardly, is not well suited for making drastic or comprehensive changes. Moreover, courts tend to be hesitant about overruling prior decisions, while it is a common practice for legislatures to repeal prior enactments. In addition, legislatures are independent and able to choose the issues they wish to address, while courts may deal only with those issues presented by actual cases. As a result, legislatures are better equipped to make the dramatic, sweeping, and relatively rapid changes in the law that are needed to respond to the numerous and vast technological, social, and economic innovations that arise.

Some business law topics, such as contracts, agency, property, and trusts, remain governed principally by the common law. Most areas of commercial law, however, have become largely statutory, including partnerships, corporations, sales, commercial paper, secured transactions, insurance, securities regulation, antitrust, and bankruptcy. Because most States enacted their own statutes dealing with these branches of commercial law, a great diversity developed among the States and hampered the conduct of commerce on a national scale. The increased need for greater uniformity brought about the codification of large parts of business and commercial law.

The most successful example is the **Uniform Commercial Code** (UCC), which was prepared under the joint sponsorship and direction of the National Conference of Commissioners on Uniform State Laws and the American Law Institute. The entire Official Text of the Code is set forth in Appendix C of this book. All fifty States (although Louisiana has adopted only part of it), the District of Columbia, and the Virgin Islands have adopted the Uniform Commercial Code. The underlying purposes and policies of the Code are to

1. simplify, clarify, and modernize the law governing commercial transactions;

2. permit the continued expansion of commercial practices through custom, usage, and agreement of the parties;

3. make uniform the law among the various jurisdictions.

Other uniform laws include the Uniform Partnership Act, the Uniform Limited Partnership Act, the Model Business Corporation Act, and the Uniform Probate Code.

Treaties A treaty is an agreement between or among independent nations. The United States Constitution authorizes the president to enter into treaties with the advice and consent of the Senate "providing two thirds of the Senators present concur."

Treaties may be entered into only by the Federal government and not by the States. Examples of treaties include NATO and SALT I. A treaty signed by the President and approved by the Senate has the legal force of a Federal statute. Accordingly, a Federal treaty may supersede a prior Federal statute, while a Federal statute may supersede a prior treaty. As with any statute, treaties are subordinate to the Federal Constitution and subject to judicial review.

Executive Orders In addition to his executive functions, the president of the United States also has authority to issue laws, which are called **executive orders.** This authority typically derives from specific delegation by Federal legislation. An executive order may be amended, revoked, or superseded by a subsequent executive order. An example of an executive order is the one issued by President Johnson in 1965 prohibiting discrimination by Federal contractors on the basis of race, color, sex, religion, or national origin in employment on any work performed by the contractor during the period of the Federal contract.

The governors of the States enjoy comparable authority to issue executive orders.

Administrative Law

Administrative law is the branch of public law that deals with the various regulatory functions and activities of the government in its executive capacity as performed, supervised, and regulated by public officials, departments, boards, and commissions. It also involves controversies arising between individuals and these public officials and agencies. Administrative functions and activities concern such important matters of national safety, welfare, and convenience as the establishment and maintenance of military forces, police, citizenship and naturalization, taxation, coinage of money, elections, environmental protection, the regulation of transportation, interstate highways, waterways, television, radio, trade and commerce, and, in general, public health, safety, and welfare.

Because of the increasing complexity of the social, economic, and industrial life of the nation, the scope of administrative law has expanded enormously. Justice Jackson stated that "the rise of administrative bodies has been the most significant legal trend of the last century, and perhaps more values today are affected by their decisions than by those of all the courts, review of administrative decisions apart." *Federal Trade Commission v. Ruberoid Co.,* 343 U.S. 470 (1952). This is evidenced by the great increase in the number and activities of Federal government boards, commissions, and other agencies. Certainly, agencies create more legal rules and adjudicate more controversies than all the legislatures and all the courts combined.

LEGAL ANALYSIS

Decisions in State trial courts are not generally reported or published. The weight of the precedent set by a trial court is not sufficient to warrant permanent reporting. Except in New York and a few other States where selected opinions of trial courts are published, decisions in trial courts are simply filed in the office of the clerk of the court where they are available for public inspection. Decisions of State courts of appeals are published in volumes called "reports" which are numbered consecutively. Most State court decisions are found in the State reports of that State. In addition, State reports are published in a regional reporter, published by West Publishing Company, called the National Reporter System, comprised of the following: Atlantic

(A. or A.2d); South Eastern (S.E. or S.E.2d); South Western (S.W. or S.W.2d); New York Supplement (N.Y.S. or N.Y.S.2d); North Western (N.W. or N.W.2d); North Eastern (N.E. or N.E.2d); Southern (So. or So.2d); and Pacific (P. or P.2d). After they are published, these opinions or "cases" are referred to ("cited") by giving the name of the case, the volume, name, and page of the official State report, if any, in which it is published; the volume, name, and page of the particular set and series of the National Reporter System; and the volume, name, and page of any other selected case series. For instance, *Lefkowitz v. Great Minneapolis Surplus Store, Inc.*, 251 Minn. 188, 86 N.W.2d 689 (1957) indicates that the opinion in this case may be found in Volume 251 of the official Minnesota Reports at page 188; and in Volume 86 of the Northwestern Reporter, Second Series, at page 689.

The decisions of courts in the Federal system are found in a number of reports. Federal District Court opinions appear in the Federal Supplement (F.Supp.). Decisions of the U.S. Court of Appeals are found in the Federal Reporter (Fed. or F.2d), while the U.S. Supreme Court's opinions are published in the United States Supreme Court Reports (U.S.), Supreme Court Reporter (S.Ct.), and Lawyers Edition (L.Ed.).

In reading the title of a case, such as *"Jones v. Brown,"* the *"v"* or *"vs"* means versus or against. In the trial court, Jones is the **plaintiff,** the person who filed the suit, and Brown is the **defendant,** the person against whom the suit was brought. When the case is appealed, some, but not all, courts of appeal place the name of the party who appeals, or the **appellant,** first, so that *"Jones v. Brown"* in the trial court becomes, if Brown loses and is the appellant, *"Brown v. Jones"* in the appellate court. But because some appellate courts retain the trial court order of names, it is not always possible to determine from the title itself who was the plaintiff and who the defendant. The student must carefully read the facts of each case and clearly identify each party in her mind in order to understand the discussion by the appellate court. In a criminal case the caption in the trial

court will first designate the prosecuting governmental unit and then will indicate the defendant, as in *"State v. Jones"* or *"Commonwealth v. Brown."*

Study of the reported cases requires an understanding and application of legal analysis. Normally, the reported opinion in a case sets forth (a) the essential facts, the nature of the action, the parties, what happened to bring about the controversy, what happened in the lower court, and what pleadings are material to the issues; (b) the issues of law or fact; (c) the legal principles involved; (d) the application of these principles; and (e) the decision.

A serviceable method of analyzing and briefing cases after a careful reading and comprehension of the opinion is for students to write in their own language a brief containing the following:

1. facts of the case

2. issue or question involved

3. decision of the court

4. reasons for the decision

The following excerpt from Professor Karl Llewellyn's *The Bramble Bush* contains several useful suggestions for reading cases:

The first thing to do with an opinion, then, is read it. The next thing is to get clear the actual decision, the judgment rendered. Who won, the plaintiff or defendant? And watch your step here. You are after in first instance the plaintiff and defendant *below,* in the trial court. In order to follow through what happened you must therefore first know the outcome *below;* else you do not see what was appealed from, nor by whom. You now follow through in order to see exactly what *further* judgment has been rendered on appeal. The stage is then cleared of form—although of course you do not yet know all that these forms mean, that they imply. You can turn now to what you want peculiarly to know. Given the actual judgments below and above as your indispensable framework— what has the case decided, and what can you derive from it as to what will be decided later?

You will be looking, in the opinion, or in the preliminary matter plus the opinion, for the following: a statement of the facts the court assumes; a statement of the precise way the question has come before the court—which includes what the plaintiff wanted below, and what the defendant did about it, the judgment below, and what the trial court did that is complained of; then the outcome on appeal, the judgment; and, finally the reasons this court gives for doing what it did. This does not look so bad. But it is much worse than it looks.

For all our cases are decided, all our opinions are written, all our predictions, all our arguments are made, on certain four assumptions. They are the first presuppositions of our study. They must be rutted into you till you can juggle with them standing on your head and in your sleep.

1) *The court must decide the dispute that is before it.* It cannot refuse because the job is hard, or dubious, or dangerous.

2) *The court can decide* only *the particular dispute which is before it.* When it speaks to that question it speaks ex cathedra, with authority, with finality, with an almost magic power. When it speaks to the question before it, it announces *law,* and if what it announces is new, it legislates, it *makes* the law. But when it speaks to any other question at all, it says mere words, which no man needs to follow. Are such words worthless? They are not. We know them as judicial *dicta;* when they are wholly off the point at issue we call them *obiter dicta*—words dropped along the road, wayside remarks. Yet even wayside remarks shed light on the remarker. They may be very useful in the future to him, or to us. But he will not feel bound to them, as to his ex cathedra utterance. They came

not hallowed by a Delphic frenzy. He may be slow to change them; but not so slow as in the other case.

3) *The court can decide the particular dispute only according to a* general *rule which covers a whole class of like disputes.* Our legal theory does not admit of single decisions standing on their own. If judges are free, are indeed forced, to decide new cases for which there is no rule, they must at least make a new rule as they decide. So far, good. But how wide, or how narrow, is the general rule in this particular case? That is a troublesome matter. The practice of our case-law, however, is I think fairly stated thus: it pays to be suspicious of general rules which look too wide; it pays to go slow in feeling *certain* that a wide rule has been laid down at all, or that, if seemingly laid down, it will be followed. For there is a fourth accepted canon:

4) *Everything, everything, everything, big or small, a judge may say in an opinion, is to be read with primary reference to the particular dispute, the particular question before him.* You are not to think that the words mean what they might if they stood alone. You are to have your eye on the case in hand, and to learn how to interpret all that has been said *merely* as a reason for deciding *that* case *that* way.

By way of example, the following edited case of *Caldwell v. Bechtel, Inc.* is presented and then briefed using the suggested format.

CASE

CALDWELL v. BECHTEL, INC.
United States Court of Appeals, District of Columbia Circuit, 1980.
631 F.2d 989.

MacKinnon, J.

We are here concerned with a claim for damages by a worker who allegedly contracted silicosis while he was mucking in a tunnel under construction as part of the [Washington] metropolitan subway system [WMATA]. The basic issue is whether a consultant engineering firm owed the worker a duty to protect him against unreasonable risk of harm.

* * *

In attempting to convince the court that it owes no duty of reasonable care to protect appellant's safety, Bechtel argues that by its contract with WMATA it assumed duties only to WMATA. Appellant has not brought action, however, for breach of contract but rather seeks damages for an asserted breach of the duty of reasonable care. Unlike contractual duties, which are imposed by agreement of the parties to a contract, a duty of due care under tort law is based primarily upon social policy. The law imposes upon individuals certain expectations of conduct, such as the expectancy that their actions will not cause foreseeable injury to another. These societal expectations, as formed through the common law, comprise the concept of duty.

Society's expectations, and the concomitant duties imposed, vary in response to the activity engaged in by the defendant. If defendant is driving a car, he will be held to exercise the degree of care normally exercised by a reasonable person in like circumstances. Or if defendant is engaged in the practice of his profession, he will be held to exercise a degree of care consistent with his superior knowledge and skill. Hence, when defendant Bechtel engaged in consulting engineering services, the company was required to observe a standard of care ordinarily adhered to by one providing such services, possessing such skill and expertise.

A secondary but equally important principle involved in a determination of duty is to whom the duty is owed. The answer to this question is usually framed in terms of the foreseeable plaintiff, in other words, one who might foreseeably be injured by defendant's conduct. This secondary principle also serves to distinguish tort law from contract law. While in contract law, only one to whom the contract specifies that a duty be rendered will have a cause of action for its breach, in tort law, society, not the contract, specifies to whom the duty is owed, and this has traditionally been the foreseeable plaintiff.

It is important to keep these differences between contract and tort duties in mind when examining whether Bechtel's undertaking of contractual duties to WMATA created a duty of reasonable care toward Caldwell. Dean Prosser expressed the relationship in this terse fashion:

[B]y entering into a contract with A, the defendant may place himself in such a relation toward B that the law will impose upon him an obligation, sounding in tort and not in contract, to act in such a way that B will not be injured. The incidental fact of the existence of the contract with A does not negative the responsibility of the actor when he enters upon a course of affirmative conduct which may be expected to affect the interests of another person.

* * *

Analyzing the common law, Prosser noted that courts have found a duty to act for the protection of another when certain relationships exist, such as carrier–passenger, innkeeper–guest, shipper–seaman, employer–employee, shopkeeper–visitor, host–social guest, jailor–prisoner, and school–pupil. These holdings suggest that courts have been eroding the general rule that there is no duty to act to help another in distress, by creating exceptions based upon a relationship between the actors.

* * *

We find that case law provides many such analogous situations from which the principles deserving of application to this case may be culled. The foregoing concepts of duty converge in this case, as the facts include both the WMATA–Bechtel contractual relationship from which it was foreseeable that a negligent undertaking by Bechtel might injure the appellant, and a special relationship established between Bechtel and the appellant because of Bechtel's superior skills, knowledge of the dangerous condition, and ability to protect appellant.

* * *

We reverse the summary judgment of the district court, and hold that as a matter of law, on the record as we are required to view it at this time, Bechtel owed Caldwell a duty of due care to take reasonable steps to protect him from the foreseeable risk of harm to his health posed by the excessive concentration of silica dust in the Metro tunnels. We remand so that Caldwell will have an opportunity to prove, if he can, the other elements of his negligence action.

BRIEF OF CALDWELL v. BECHTEL, INC.

I. FACTS: Caldwell was a laborer who now suffers from silicosis. He claims that he contracted the disease while he was working in a tunnel under construction as part of the Washington Metropolitan Area Transportation Authority (WMATA). He brought this action for damages against Bechtel, Inc., a consultant engineering firm under contract with WMATA for the project.

II. ISSUE: Did Bechtel owe a duty of due care to Caldwell to take reasonable steps to protect him from the foreseeable risk of harm to his health posed by the excessive concentration of silica dust in the subway tunnels?

III. DECISION: In favor of Caldwell. Summary judgment reversed and case remanded to the district court.

IV. REASONS: Caldwell has not brought an action for breach of contract. Rather, he seeks damages for an alleged breach of the duty of reasonable care. Unlike contractual duties, which are imposed by agreement of the parties to a contract, a duty of due care under tort law is based primarily on social policy; that is, the law imposes upon individuals the expectation that their actions will not cause foreseeable injury to another. These societal expectations comprise the concept of duty—a concept that varies in response to the activity engaged in by the individual. Moreover, the duty is owed by anyone who might foreseeably be injured by the conduct of the actor in question. In contrast, under contract law, a duty is owed only to those parties specified in the contract. Here, by entering into a contract with WMATA, Bechtel placed itself in such a relation toward Caldwell that the law will impose upon it an obligation in tort, and not in contract, to act in such a way that Caldwell would not be injured.

QUESTIONS

1. Identify and describe the basic functions of law.

2. Distinguish between law and justice.

3. Distinguish between law and morals.

4. Define and discuss substantive and procedural law.

5. Distinguish between public law and private law.

6. Distinguish between civil and criminal law.

7. Identify and describe the sources of law.

8. Distinguish between law and equity.

9. Explain the principle of *stare decisis*.

10. Identify and define five remedies available in equity.

Chapter 2

LEGAL PROCESS

The Court System
Jurisdiction
Civil Procedure
Alternative Dispute Resolution

A S discussed in Chapter 1, substantive law establishes the rights and duties of individuals and other legal entities while procedural law determines the means by which these rights are asserted. Procedural law attempts to accomplish two competing objectives: (1) to be fair and impartial and (2) to operate efficiently. The judicial process in the United States represents a balance between these two objectives as well as a commitment to the adversary system.

The first part of this chapter describes the structure and function of the Federal and State court systems. The second part deals with jurisdiction; the third part discusses civil dispute resolution, including the procedure in civil lawsuits.

THE COURT SYSTEM

Courts are impartial tribunals (seats of judgment) established by governmental bodies to settle disputes. A court may render a binding decision only when it has jurisdiction over the dispute and the parties to that dispute; that is, when it has a right to hear and make a judgment in a case. The United States has a dual

court system: The Federal government has its own independent system, as does each of the fifty States plus the District of Columbia.

THE FEDERAL COURTS

Article III of the United States Constitution states that the judicial power of the United States shall be vested in one Supreme Court and such lower courts as Congress may establish. Congress has established a lower Federal court system consisting of a number of special courts, district courts, and courts of appeals. The Federal court system is staffed by judges who receive lifetime appointments from the president, subject to confirmation by the Senate. The structure of the Federal court system is illustrated in Figure 2–1.

District Courts

The district courts are the trial courts in the Federal system. Most cases begin in the district court, and it is here that issues of fact are decided. The district court is generally presided over by *one* judge, although in certain cases three judges preside. In a few cases, an appeal from a judgment or decree of a district court is taken directly to the Su-

Figure 2–1 Federal Judicial System

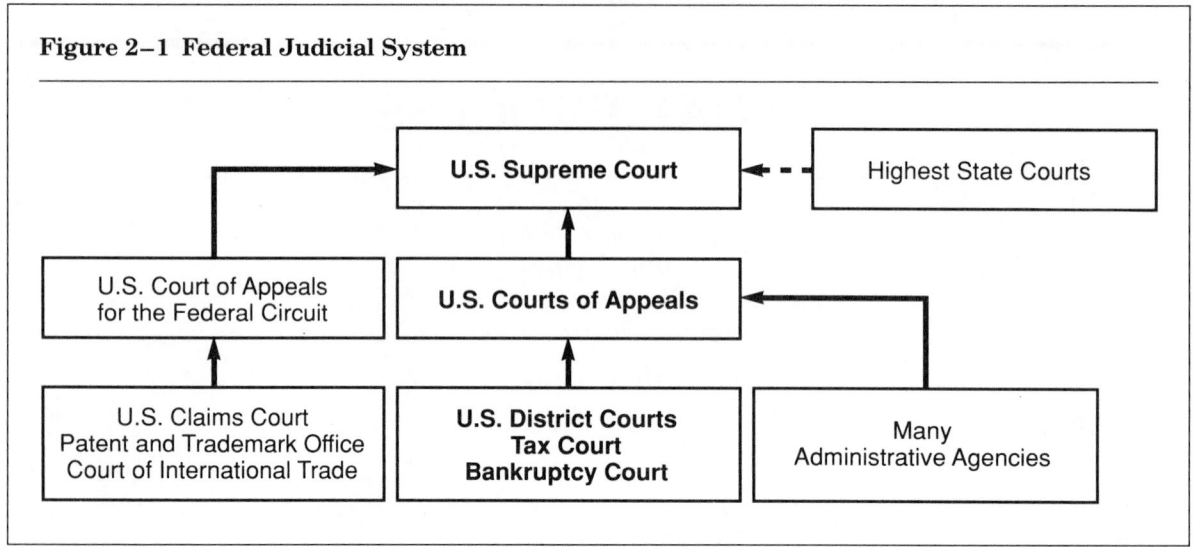

preme Court. In most cases, however, appeals go to the Circuit Court of Appeals of the appropriate circuit, the decision of which is, in most cases, final.

Congress has established judicial districts, each of which is located entirely in a particular State. All States have at least one district, while certain States contain more than one district. For instance, New York has four districts, Illinois has three, and Wisconsin has two, while a number of less populated States comprise a single district (see Figure 2–2).

Courts of Appeals

Congress has established twelve judicial circuits (eleven numbered circuits plus the D.C. Circuit), each having a court known as the Court of Appeals, which primarily hears appeals from the district courts located within its circuit (see Figure 2–2). In addition, they review decisions of many administrative agencies, the Tax Court, and the Bankruptcy Court. Congress has also established the U.S. Court of Appeals for the Federal Circuit, which is discussed below in the section on "Special Courts." The United States Courts of Appeals generally hear cases in panels of *three* judges, although in some instances all of the judges of the circuit will sit *en banc* to decide a case.

The function of appellate courts is to examine the record of a case on appeal and to determine whether the trial court committed prejudicial error. If so, the appellate court will **reverse** or **modify** the judgment of the lower court and if necessary **remand** (or send it back) to the lower court for further proceeding. If there is no prejudicial error, the appellate court will **affirm** the decision of the lower court.

The Supreme Court

The nation's highest tribunal is the United States Supreme Court, which consists of nine justices (a Chief Justice and eight Associate Justices) who sit as a group in Washington, D.C. In certain types of cases the United States Supreme Court has original jurisdiction (the right to hear a case first). The Court's principal function, nonetheless, is to review decisions of the Federal Courts of Appeals and, in some instances, those of the highest State courts or other tribunals. Cases reach the Supreme Court under its appellate jurisdiction by one of two routes. Very few come by way of **appeal by right**—cases the Court must hear if one of the parties requests the review. In 1988, Congress enacted legislation that almost completely eliminated the right to appeal to the U.S. Supreme Court.

Figure 2–2 District and Circuit Courts of the United States

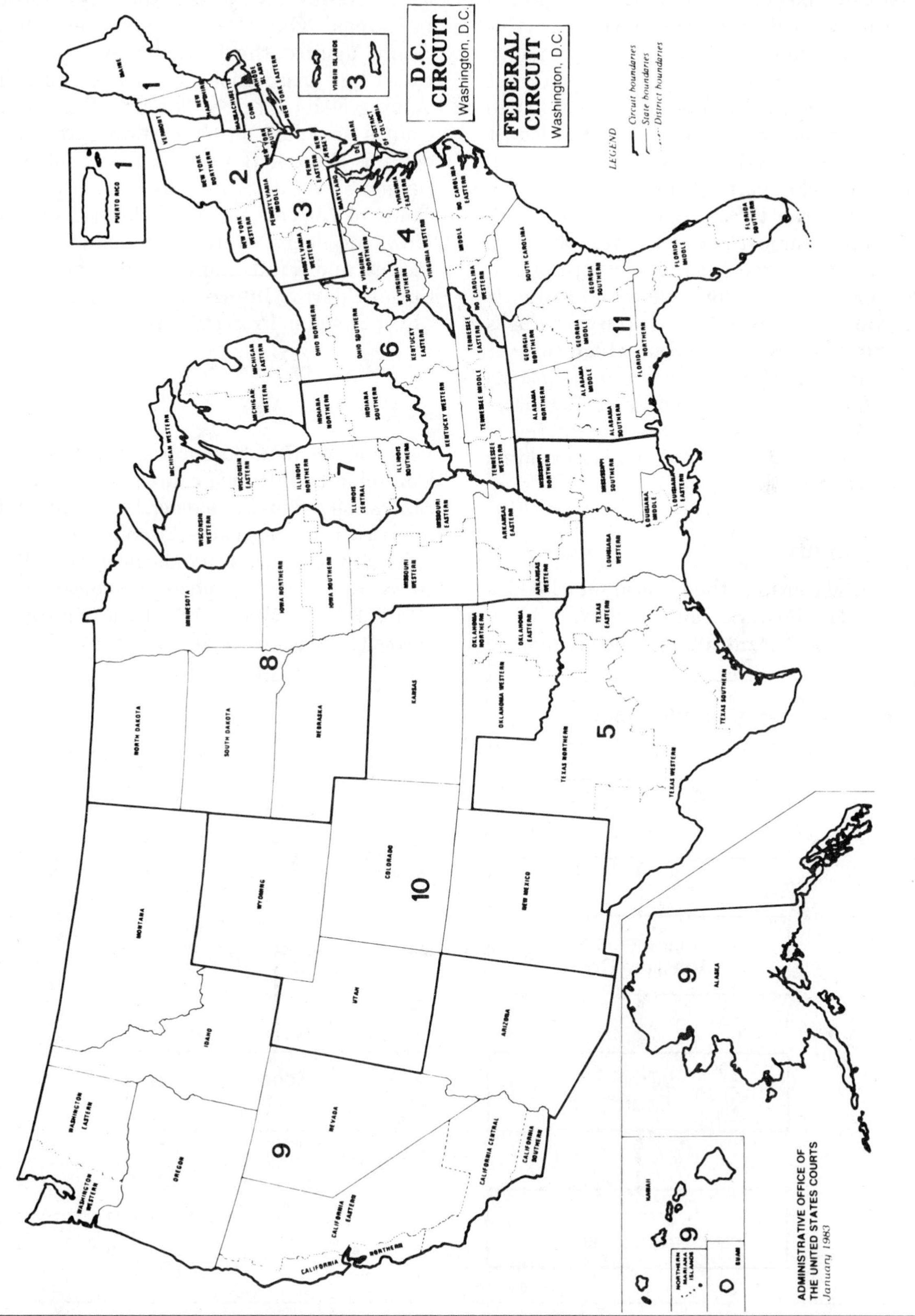

ADMINISTRATIVE OFFICE OF
THE UNITED STATES COURTS
January 1983

The second way in which a decision of a lower court may be reviewed by the Supreme Court is by the discretionary **writ of certiorari,** which requires a lower court to produce the records of a case it has tried. Now almost all cases reaching the Supreme Court come to it by means of writs of *certiorari.* The Court grants writs when there is a Federal question of substantial importance or a conflict in the decisions of the U.S. Circuit Courts of Appeals and if four justices vote to hear the case. Only a small percentage of the petitions to the Supreme Court for review by *certiorari* are granted, however, because the Court uses the writ as a device to choose which cases it wishes to hear. *Maryland v. Baltimore Radio Show, Inc.* describes some of the criteria the Supreme Court uses in deciding whether to grant review by *certiorari;* it also explains the effect of a denial.

Special Courts

The special courts in the Federal judicial system include the U.S. Claims Court, the Tax Court, the U.S. Bankruptcy Courts, and the U.S. Court of Appeals for the Federal Circuit. These courts have jurisdiction over particular areas. The U.S. Claims Court hears claims against the United States. The Tax Court has jurisdiction over certain cases involving Federal taxes. The U.S. Bankruptcy Courts hear and decide certain matters under the Federal Bankruptcy Act, subject to review by the U.S. District Court. The U.S. Court of Appeals for the Federal Circuit reviews decisions of the Claims Court, the Patent and Trademark Office, the United States Court of International Trade, and the Merit Systems Protection Board.

STATE COURTS

Each of the fifty States and the District of Columbia has its own court system. In most States the judges are elected by the voters for a stated term of years. Although the structure of State court systems varies from State to State, Figure 2–3 shows a typical system while Figure 2–4 displays the courts and terms of judges in each of the States.

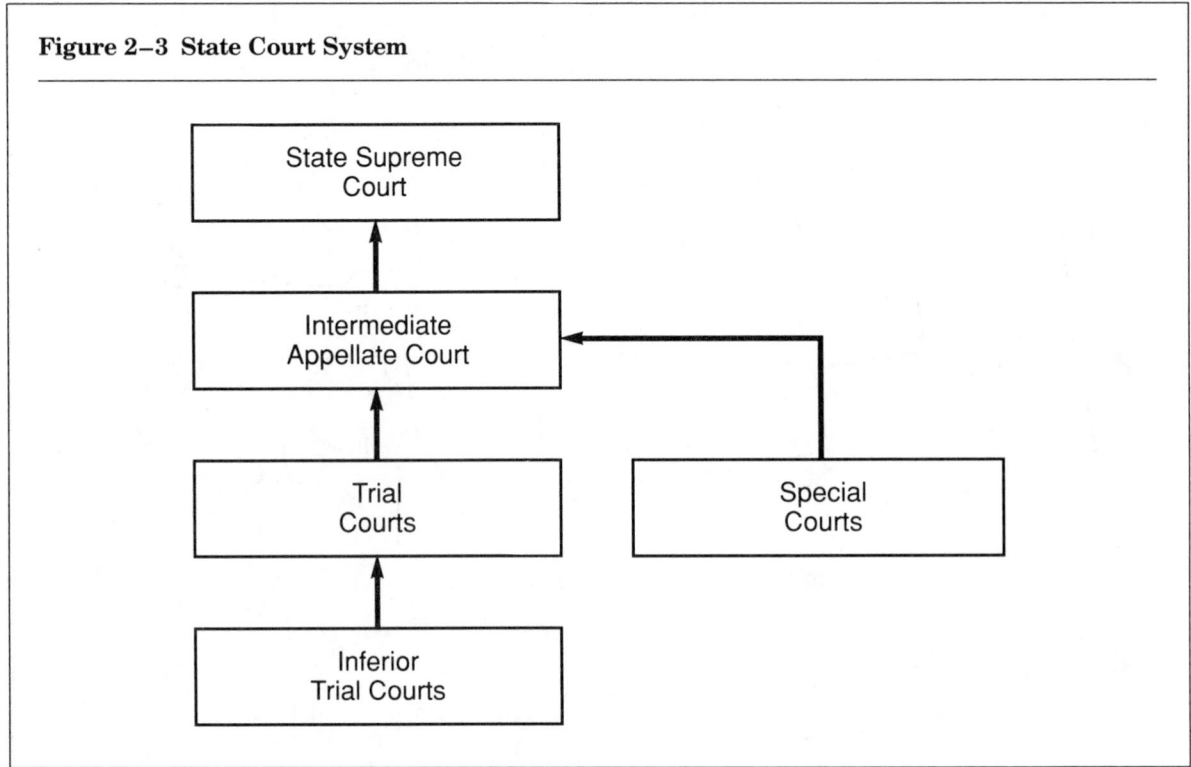

Figure 2–3 State Court System

Inferior Trial Courts

At the bottom of the State court system are the inferior trial courts, which decide the least serious criminal and civil matters. Usually inferior trial courts do not keep a complete written record of the trial proceedings. Minor criminal cases such as traffic offenses are heard in inferior trial courts, which are referred to as municipal courts, justice of the peace courts, or traffic courts. These courts also conduct preliminary hearings in the more serious criminal cases.

Small claims courts are inferior trial courts which hear civil cases involving a limited amount of money. Usually in small claims courts there are no juries, the procedure is informal, and neither side employs an attorney. Appeal from small claims court is taken to the trial court of general jurisdiction, where a new trial (called a trial *de novo*) is begun and in which the small claims court's decision is given no weight.

Trial Courts

Each State has trial courts of general jurisdiction, which may be called county, district,

Figure 2–4 Courts in Each State

State or Other Jurisdiction	Appellate Courts						Major Trial Courts	No. of Judges	Term (In years)
	Court of Last Resort	No. of Judges	Term (in years)	Intermediate Appellate Court	No. of Judges	Term (In years)			
Alabama	Supreme Court	9	6	Court of Criminal Appeals	5	6	Circuit courts	124	6
				Court of Civil Appeals	3	6			
Alaska.	Supreme Court	5	10	Court of Appeals	3	8	Superior courts	29	6
Arizona	Supreme Court	5	6	Court of Appeals	18	6	Superior courts	101	4
Arkansas	Supreme Court	7	8	Court of Appeals	6	8	Chancery courts	30	6
							Circuit Courts	41	4
California	Supreme Court	7	12	Courts of Appeal	77	12	Superior courts	724	6
Colorado.	Supreme Court	7	10	Court of Appeals	10	8	District Court	110	6
Connecticut	Supreme Court	7	8	Appellate Court	9	8	Superior courts	139	8
Delaware.	Supreme Court	5	12	. . . .	. . .	. . .	Superior courts	13	12
							Court of Chancery	4	12
Florida	Supreme Court	7	6	District Court of Appeals	46	6	Circuit courts	362	6
Georgia.	Supreme Court	7	6	Court of Appeals	9	6	Superior courts	135	4
Hawaii.	Supreme Court	5	10	Intermediate Court of Appeals	3	10	Circuit courts	24	10
Idaho.	Supreme Court	5	6	Court of Appeals	3	6	District courts	33	4
Illinois.	Supreme Court	7	10	Appellate Court	34	10	Circuit courts	780	6
Indiana	Supreme Court	5	10	Court of Appeals	12	10	Circuit courts	89	6
Iowa	Supreme Court	9	8	Court of Appeals	6	6	Superior Court	117	6
							District courts	100	6
Kansas	Supreme Court	7	6	Court of Appeals	10	4	District courts	146	4
Kentucky	Supreme Court	7	8	Courts of Appeals	14	8	Circuit courts	91	8
Louisiana	Supreme Court	7	10	Court of Appeals	48	10	District courts	192	6
Maine	Supreme Judicial Court	7	7	. . . .	. . .	. . .	Superior Court	16	7
Maryland.	Court of Appeals	7	10	Court of Special Appeals	13	10	Circuit courts	109	15
Massachusetts . . .	Supreme Judicial Court	7	To age 70	Appeals Court	10	To age 70	Trial Court	281	To age 70
Michigan.	Supreme Court	7	8	Court of Appeals	18	6	Circuit and Recorders courts	196	6
Minnesota.	Supreme Court	7	6	Court of Appeals	13	6	District courts	224	6
Mississippi	Supreme Court	9	8	. . . .	. . .	. . .	Chancery courts	39	4
							Circuit courts	40	4
Missouri	Supreme Court	7	12	Court of Appeals	32	12	Circuit courts	133	6
Montana	Supreme Court	7	8	. . . .	. . .	. . .	District courts	36	6
Nebraska	Supreme Court	7	6	. . . .	. . .	. . .	District courts	48	6
Nevada	Supreme Court	5	6	. . . .	. . .	. . .	District courts	35	6

Figure 2–4 Courts in Each State—Continued

State or Other Jurisdiction	Appellate Courts								
	Court of Last Resort	No. of Judges	Term (in years)	Intermediate Appellate Court	No. of Judges	Term (In years)	Major Trial Courts	No. of Judges	Term (In years)
New Hampshire . .	Supreme Court	5	To age 70	. . . .	. . .	. . .	Superior Court	25	To age 70
New Jersey.	Supreme Court	7	7	Appellate Division of Superior Court	28	7	Superior Court	321	7
New Mexico	Supreme Court	5	8	Court of Appeals	7	8	District courts	59	6
New York	Court of Appeals	7	14	Appellate Division of Supreme Court	47	5	Supreme Court County Court	269 118 .	14 10
North Carolina . . .	Supreme Court	7	8	Court of Appeals	12	8	Superior Court	72	8
North Dakota	Supreme Court	5	10	. . . .	. . .	. . .	District courts	26	6
Ohio	Supreme Court	7	6	Court of Appeals	58	6	Courts of common pleas	339	6
Oklahoma.	Supreme Court Court of Criminal Appeals	9 3	6 6	Court of Appeals	12	6	District Court	71	4
Oregon	Supreme Court	7	6	Court of Appeals	10	6	Circuit courts Tax Court	85 1	6 6
Pennsylvania	Supreme Court	7	10	Superior Court Commonwealth Court	15 9	10 10	Court of common pleas	330	10
Rhode Island	Supreme Court	5	Life	. . . .	. . .	. . .	Superior Court	19	Life
South Carolina . . .	Supreme Court	5	10	Court of Appeals	6	6	Circuit Court	31	6
South Dakota	Supreme Court	5	8	. . . .	. . .	. . .	Circuit courts	35	8
Tennessee	Supreme Court	5	8	Court of Appeals Court of Criminal Appeals	12 9	8 8	Chancery courts Circuit courts	33 92	8 8
Texas	Supreme Court Court of Criminal Appeals	9 9	6 6	Courts of Appeals	80	6	District courts	375	4
Utah	Supreme Court	5	10	Court of Appeals	7	10	District courts	29	6
Vermont	Supreme Court	5	6	. . . .	. . .	. . .	Superior courts District courts	10 15	6 6
Virginia.	Supreme Court	7	12	Court of Appeals	10	8	Circuit courts	122	8
Washington.	Supreme Court	9	6	Court of Appeals	16	6	Superior courts	133	4
West Virginia	Supreme Court of Appeals	5	12	. . . .	. . .	. . .	Circuit courts	60	8
Wisconsin.	Supreme Court	7	10	Court of Appeals	13	6	Circuit courts	197	6
Wyoming	Supreme Court	5	8	. . . .	. . .	. . .	District courts	17	6
Dist. of Col..	Court of Appeals	9	15	. . . .	. . .	. . .	Superior Court	51	15

SOURCE: Court Statistics Project, *State Court Organization 1987*, Williamsburg, Va.: National Center for State Courts, 1988.

superior, circuit, or common pleas court. (In New York the trial court is called the Supreme Court.) These courts do not have a dollar limitation on their jurisdiction in civil cases and hear all criminal cases other than minor offenses. Unlike the inferior trial courts, these trial courts of general jurisdiction maintain formal records of their proceedings as procedural safeguards.

Special Courts

Many States have special courts that have jurisdiction over particular areas. For exam-

ple, many States have probate courts with jurisdiction over the administration of wills and estates. Many States also have family courts, which have jurisdiction over divorce and child custody cases. Appeals from these special courts go to the general State appellate courts.

Appellate Courts

At the summit of the State court system is the State's court of last resort, a reviewing court generally called the Supreme Court of the State. Except for those cases in which review by the U.S. Supreme Court is available, the decision of the highest State tribunal is final. Most States have also created intermediate appellate courts to handle the large volume of cases in which review is sought. Review by such a court is usually by right. Further review is in most cases a matter of the highest court's discretion.

JURISDICTION

Jurisdiction means the power or authority of a court to hear and decide a given case. To resolve a lawsuit, a court must have two kinds of jurisdiction. The first is jurisdiction over the subject matter of the lawsuit. Where a court lacks jurisdiction over the subject matter of a case, any action it takes in the case is without legal effect.

The second kind of jurisdiction is over the parties to a lawsuit. This jurisdiction is required for the court to render an enforceable judgment affecting the rights and duties of the parties to the lawsuit. A court usually may obtain jurisdiction over the defendant in a lawsuit if the defendant lives and is present in the court's territory or the transaction giving rise to the case has a substantial connection to the court's territory. The court obtains jurisdiction over the plaintiff by the plaintiff's voluntary submission to the court's power through filing a complaint with the court.

Even if a court has subject matter jurisdiction and personal jurisdiction over the defendant, the court's exercise of jurisdiction is valid under the Due Process Clause of the U.S. Constitution only if the defendant has sufficient minimum contacts with the State so that the court's assertion of jurisdiction does not offend "traditional notions of fair play and substantial justice." In order for a court constitutionally to assert jurisdiction over a defendant, the defendant must have engaged in either purposeful acts in the State or acts outside the State that are of such a nature that the defendant could reasonably foresee being sued in that State (*see World-Wide Volkswagen v. Woodson*).

As discussed more fully in Chapter 3, the Due Process Clause of the U.S. Constitution requires that parties to a lawsuit be given both adequate notice of the lawsuit and an opportunity to be heard. What notice is due depends on a number of factors but generally must be "notice reasonably calculated, under the circumstances, to apprise interested parties of the pendency of the action and afford them the opportunity to present their objections."

SUBJECT MATTER JURISDICTION

Subject matter jurisdiction refers to the authority of a particular court to adjudicate a controversy of a particular kind. Federal courts have *limited* subject matter jurisdiction, as set forth in the U.S. Constitution, Article III, Section 2. State courts have jurisdiction over *all* matters that have not been given exclusively to the Federal courts or expressly taken away by the Constitution or Congress.

Federal Jurisdiction

The Federal courts have, to the exclusion of the State courts, subject matter jurisdiction over some areas. Such jurisdiction is called **exclusive Federal jurisdiction.** Federal jurisdiction is exclusive only if Congress so provides, either explicitly or implicitly. If Congress does not so provide and the area is one over which Federal courts have subject matter jurisdiction, they share such jurisdiction with the State courts. Such jurisdiction is known as **concurrent Federal jurisdiction.**

Exclusive Federal Jurisdiction   The Federal courts have exclusive jurisdiction over Federal criminal prosecutions, admiralty, bankruptcy, antitrust, patent, trademark and copyright cases, suits against the United States, and cases arising under certain Federal statutes that expressly provide for exclusive Federal jurisdiction.

Concurrent Federal Jurisdiction   There are two types of concurrent Federal jurisdiction: Federal question jurisdiction and diversity jurisdiction. The first arises whenever there is a Federal question over which the Federal courts do not have exclusive jurisdiction. A **Federal question** is any case arising under the Constitution, statutes, or treaties of the United States. In order for a case to be treated as "arising under" Federal law, either Federal law must create the plaintiff's cause of action or the plaintiff's right to relief must depend upon resolution of a substantial question of Federal law in dispute between the parties. There is no minimum dollar requirement in Federal question cases.

Diversity jurisdiction arises where there is "diversity of citizenship" and the amount in controversy exceeds $50,000. Then an action between private litigants may be brought in a Federal district court or a State court. **Diversity of citizenship** exists (1) when the plaintiffs are all citizens of a State or States different from the State or States of which the defendants are citizens; (2) when a foreign country brings an action against citizens of the United States; *or* (3) when the controversy is between citizens of the United States and citizens of a foreign country. The citizenship of an individual litigant is the State of the individual's residence or domicile, whereas that of a corporate litigant is both the State of incorporation and the State where its principal place of business is located. For example, if the amount in controversy exceeds $50,000, then diversity of citizenship jurisdiction would be satisfied if A, a citizen of California, sues B, a citizen of Idaho. If, however, A, a citizen of Virginia, and B, a citizen of North Carolina, sue C, a citizen of Georgia, and D, a citizen of North Carolina, there would *not* be diversity of citizenship because there are citizens of North Carolina as both plaintiff and defendant.

The $50,000 jurisdictional requirement is satisfied if the amount claimed in the complaint is made in good faith, unless it is clear to a legal certainty that the claim does not exceed the required amount.

When a Federal district court hears a case solely under diversity of citizenship jurisdiction, no Federal question is involved, and ac-cordingly the Federal courts must apply substantive State law (*see Erie Railroad Co. v. Tompkins*). Which State's substantive law is determined by the conflict of laws rules of the State in which the district court is located. (Conflict of laws is discussed below.) Federal courts apply Federal procedural rules in diversity cases.

In any case involving concurrent jurisdiction, the plaintiff has the choice of bringing the action in either an appropriate Federal court or State court. If the plaintiff brings the case in a State court, however, the defendant usually may have it *removed* (shifted) to a Federal court for the district in which the State court is located.

State Jurisdiction

Exclusive State Jurisdiction The State courts have exclusive jurisdiction over *all other matters*. All matters not granted to the Federal courts in the Constitution or not exercised by Congress are solely within the jurisdiction of the States. Accordingly, exclusive State jurisdiction would include cases involving diversity of citizenship but where the amount in controversy is $50,000 or less. In addition, the State courts have exclusive jurisdiction over all cases to which the Federal judicial power does not reach. These matters include, but are by no means limited to, property, torts, contract, agency, commercial transactions, and most crimes.

The jurisdiction of the Federal and State courts is illustrated in Figure 2–5.

Choice of Law in State Courts A court in one State may be a proper forum for a case even though some or all of the relevant events occurred in another State. For example, a California plaintiff may sue a Washington defendant in Washington over a car accident that occurred in Oregon. Because of Oregon's connections to the accident, Washington may choose, under its **conflict of laws** rules, to apply the substantive law of Oregon. Conflict of laws rules vary from State to State.

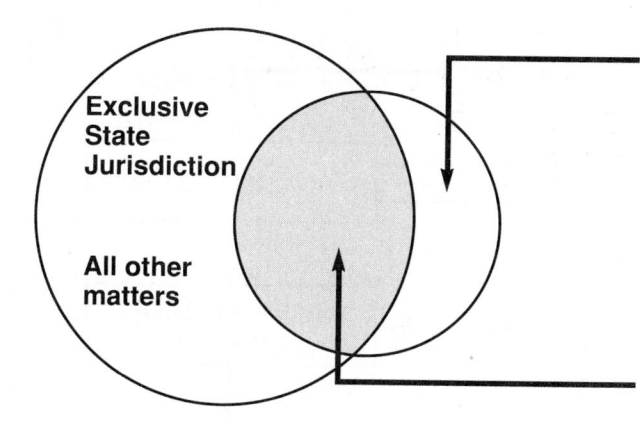

Figure 2–5 Federal and State Jurisdiction

Exclusive State Jurisdiction

All other matters

Exclusive Federal Jurisdiction
1. Federal crimes
2. Bankruptcy
3. Patents
4. Copyright and trademarks
5. Admiralty
6. Antitrust
7. Suits against the United States
8. Specified Federal Statutes

Concurrent Jurisdiction
1. Federal questions
2. Diversity of citizenship

Stare Decisis in the Dual Court System

The doctrine of *stare decisis* presents certain problems when there are two parallel court systems. As a consequence, in the United States *stare decisis* functions approximately as follows (also illustrated in Figure 2–6):

1. The United States Supreme Court has never held itself to be rigidly bound by its own decisions, and lower Federal courts and State courts have followed that course in respect to their own decisions.

2. A decision of the U.S. Supreme Court on Federal questions is binding on all other courts, Federal or State.

3. Although a decision of a Federal court other than the Supreme Court may be persuasive in a State court on a Federal question, it is nevertheless not binding.

4. A decision of a State court may be persuasive in the Federal courts, but it is not binding except where Federal jurisdiction is based on diversity of citizenship. In such a case the Federal courts must apply State law as determined by the highest State tribunal.

5. Decisions of the Federal courts (other than the U.S. Supreme Court) are not binding upon other Federal courts of equal rank or inferior rank, unless the latter owe obedience to the court rendering the decision. For example, a decision of the Fifth Circuit Court of Appeals binds district courts in the fifth circuit but no other Federal court.

6. A decision of a State court is binding upon all courts inferior to it in its jurisdiction. Thus, the decision of the supreme court in a State binds all other courts in that State.

7. A decision of a State court is not binding on courts in other States except where the latter courts are required under their conflict of laws rules to apply the law of the former State as determined by the highest tribunal in that State. For example, if a North Carolina court is required to apply Virginia law, it must follow decisions of the Virginia Supreme Court.

JURISDICTION OVER THE PARTIES

The second essential type of jurisdiction is the power of a court to bind the parties involved in the dispute. This type of jurisdiction is called **jurisdiction over the parties** and its requirements may be met in any of three ways: (1) *in personam* jurisdiction, (2) *in rem* jurisdiction, or (3) attachment jurisdiction. In addition, the exercise of jurisdiction must satisfy the constitutionally imposed requirements of due process: reasonable notification

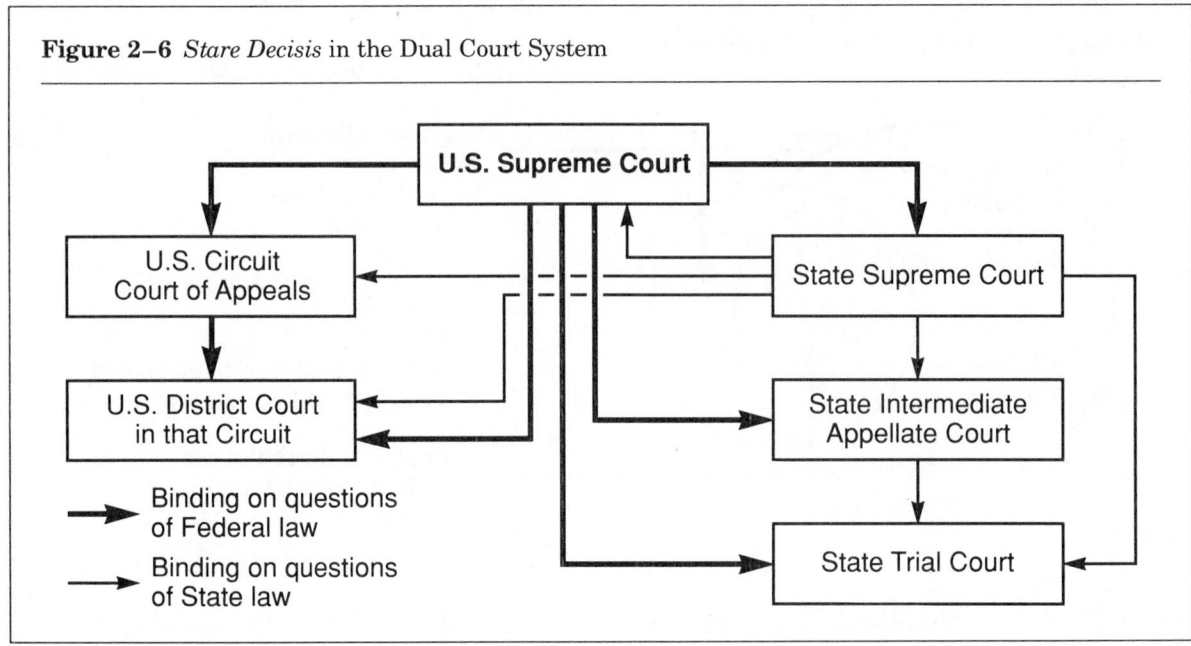

Figure 2–6 *Stare Decisis* in the Dual Court System

In Personam Jurisdiction

In personam jurisdiction, or **personal jurisdiction,** is jurisdiction of a court over the parties to a lawsuit in contrast to jurisdiction over their property. A court obtains *in personam* jurisdiction over a person either (1) by serving process on the party within the State in which the court is located or (2) by reasonable notification to a party outside the State in those instances where a "long-arm statute" applies. To *serve process* means to deliver a summons, which is an order to respond to a complaint lodged against a party. (The terms *summons* and *complaint* are more fully explained later in this chapter.)

Personal jurisdiction may be obtained by personally serving a person within a State if that person is domiciled in that State. Personal jurisdiction may also arise from a party's consent. For example, parties to a contract may agree that any dispute concerning that contract will be subject to the jurisdiction of a specific court. It is unclear whether personal service on a nonresident only temporarily in the State is sufficient to establish a court's personal jurisdiction over that person. Some courts have held that personal service within a State upon such a nonresident must meet the constitutionally imposed requirement that there are sufficient minimum contacts with that State so as not to offend traditional notions of fair play and substantial justice.

Most States have adopted **long-arm statutes** in order to expand their jurisdictional reach beyond those persons who may be personally served within the State. These statutes allow courts to obtain jurisdiction over nonresident defendants when the contacts of the nonresident defendant with the State in which the court is located are such that the exercise of jurisdiction does not offend traditional notions of fair play and substantial justice. The typical long-arm statute permits a court to exercise jurisdiction over a defendant even though process is served beyond its borders if the defendant (1) has committed a tort (civil wrong) within the State, (2) owns property within the State if that property is the subject matter of the lawsuit, (3) has entered into a contract within the State, or (4) has

and a reasonable opportunity to be heard. This overriding limitation on jurisdictional power is imposed upon the Federal and State courts through the U.S. Constitution, as discussed more fully in Chapter 3.

transacted business within the State if that business is the subject matter of the lawsuit.

In Rem Jurisdiction

Courts in a State have the jurisdiction to adjudicate claims to property situated within the State if the plaintiff gives reasonable notice and opportunity to be heard to those persons who have an interest in the property. Such jurisdiction over property is called *in rem* jurisdiction from the Latin word *res,* which means *thing.* For example, if Carpenter and Miller are involved in a lawsuit over property located in Kansas, then an appropriate court in Kansas would have *in rem* jurisdiction to adjudicate claims with respect to this property so long as both parties are given notice of the lawsuit and a reasonable opportunity to contest the claim.

Attachment Jurisdiction

Attachment jurisdiction, or **quasi *in rem*** jurisdiction, is jurisdiction over property rather than over a person. Attachment jurisdiction is invoked by seizing the defendant's property located within the State in order to obtain payment of a claim against the defendant that is *unrelated* to the property seized. For example, Allen, a resident of Ohio, has obtained a valid judgment in the amount of $20,000 against Bradley, a citizen of Kentucky. Allen can attach Bradley's automobile which is located in Ohio to satisfy his court judgment against Bradley.

Venue

Venue, which is often confused with jurisdiction, deals with the location where a lawsuit *should* be brought. The purpose of venue is to regulate the distribution of cases within a specific court system and to identify a convenient forum. In the Federal court system, venue determines the district or districts in a given State in which suit may be brought. State rules of venue typically require that a suit be initiated in a county where one of the defendants resides. In matters involving real estate, most venue rules require that a suit be initiated in the county where the property is situated. A defendant may, however, object to the venue for various reasons. For instance, a defendant may object to venue based on the principle of *forum nonconveniens.* This basically means that the presentation of the case in that court will create a hardship on the defendant or on relevant witnesses because of the great distance the individuals must travel. If the court accepts the defendant's *forum non conveniens* argument, the court does not dismiss the case but instead moves it to a more convenient location.

CIVIL DISPUTE RESOLUTION

As mentioned in Chapter 1, one of the primary functions of law is to provide for the peaceful resolution of disputes. Our legal system has established an elaborate set of governmental mechanisms to settle disputes. The most prominent of these is judicial dispute resolution called *litigation.* Judicial resolution of civil disputes is governed by the rules of civil procedure, which are discussed in the first part of this section. Judicial resolution of criminal cases is governed by the rules of criminal procedure, which are covered in Chapter 4. Dispute resolution by administrative agencies is also very common and is discussed in Chapter 3.

As an alternative to governmental dispute resolution, several nongovernmental methods of dispute resolution such as arbitration have developed. These are discussed in the second part of this section.

CIVIL PROCEDURE

Civil disputes that enter the judicial system must follow the rules of civil procedure. These rules are designed to resolve the dispute in a just, prompt, and inexpensive way.

To acquaint the student with civil procedure, it will be helpful to carry a hypothetical action through the trial court to the highest court of review in the State. Although there are technical differences in trial and appellate procedure among the States and the Federal courts, the following illustration will provide a general understanding of the trial and appeal of cases. Assume that Pam Pederson, a pedestrian, while crossing a street in Chicago, is struck by an automobile driven by David Dryden. Pederson suffers serious personal injuries, incurs heavy medical and hospital expenses, and is unable to work for several months. Pederson desires that Dryden pay her for the loss and damages that she sustained. Attempts at settlement failing, Pederson brings an action at law against Dryden. Pederson is the plaintiff, and Dryden the defendant. Each is represented by a lawyer. Let us follow the progress of the case.

The Pleadings

The purpose of **pleadings** is to give notice and to establish the issues of fact and law presented and disputed. An "issue of fact" is a dispute between the parties regarding the events that gave rise to the lawsuit. In contrast, an "issue of law" is a dispute between the parties as to what legal rules apply to these facts. Issues of fact are decided by the jury, or judge when there is no jury, whereas issues of law are decided by the judge.

A lawsuit is commenced by Pederson, the plaintiff, filing with the clerk of the trial court a **complaint** against Dryden which contains (1) a statement of the claim and supporting facts showing that she is entitled to relief and (2) a demand for that relief. Pederson's complaint alleges that while exercising due and reasonable care for her own safety, she was struck by Dryden's automobile, which was negligently being driven by Dryden, causing personal injuries and damages of $50,000 for which Pederson requests judgment.

The sheriff of the county or a deputy sheriff serves a summons and a copy of the complaint upon Dryden, the defendant, commanding him to file his appearance and answer with the clerk of the court within a specific time, usually thirty days from the date the summons was served. The **summons** has the important function of notifying the defendant that a suit has been brought

against him. If the defendant has sufficient contacts with the State such that the State's assertion of jurisdiction over the defendant is constitutional, proper service of the summons establishes the court's jurisdiction over the person of the defendant.

At this point Dryden, the defendant, has several options. If he fails to respond at all, a **default judgment** will be entered against the defendant for the relief requested in the complaint. He may make **pretrial motions** contesting the court's jurisdiction over him or asserting that the action is barred by the statute of limitations, which requires suits to be brought within a specified time. Dryden may also move that the complaint be made more definite and certain, or Dryden may instead move that the complaint be dismissed for failure to state a claim upon which relief may be granted. Such a motion is sometimes called a **demurrer** and essentially asserts that even if all of Pederson's allegations are true, Pederson would, nevertheless, not be entitled to the relief she seeks, and, therefore, there is no need for a trial of the facts. The court rules on this motion as a matter of law. If it rules in favor of the defendant, the plaintiff may appeal the ruling.

If he does not make any pretrial motions, or if they are denied, Dryden will respond to the complaint by filing an **answer** which may contain admissions, denials, affirmative defenses, and counterclaims. Thus, Dryden might answer the complaint by denying its allegations of negligence and stating, on the other hand, that he, Dryden, was driving his car at a low speed and with reasonable care (a **denial**) when his car struck Pederson (an **admission**), who had dashed across the street in front of Dryden's car without looking in any direction to see whether cars or other vehicles were approaching; that, accordingly, Pederson's injuries were caused by her own negligence (an **affirmative defense**) and therefore she should not be permitted to recover any damages. Dryden might further state that Pederson caused damages to his car and request a judgment for $2,000 (a **counterclaim**). These pleadings create an issue of fact about whether Pederson or Dryden, or both, failed to exercise due and reasonable care under the circumstances and were thus negligent and liable for their carelessness.

If the defendant counterclaims, the plaintiff must respond by a **reply** which may also contain admissions, denials, or affirmative defenses.

After the pleadings, either party may move for **judgment on the pleadings** which requests the judge to rule as a matter of law whether the facts as alleged in the pleadings, which for the purpose of the motion are taken to be as alleged by the nonmoving party, form a sufficient basis to grant the requested relief.

Pretrial Procedure

In preparation for trial and even before completion of the pleadings stage, each party has the right to obtain relevant evidence, or facts that may lead to evidence, from the other party. This procedure is known as **discovery.** It includes (1) pretrial **depositions** consisting of sworn testimony of the opposing party, or other witnesses, taken out of court; (2) sworn answers by the opposing party to **written interrogatories; (3) production** of documents and physical objects in the possession of the opposing party; (4) **examination** by a physician of the physical and/or mental condition of the opposing party, to the extent relevant; and (5) admissions of facts set forth in a **request for admissions** submitted to the opposing party. By proper use of discovery each party may become fully informed of the relevant evidence and avoid surprise at the trial. Another purpose of this procedure is to encourage and facilitate settlements by providing both parties with as much relevant information as possible.

Also furthering these objectives is the pretrial conference between the judge and the attorneys representing the parties. The basic purposes of the **pretrial conference** are (1) to simplify the issues in dispute by amending the pleadings, admitting or stipulating facts, and limiting the number of expert witnesses; and (2) to encourage settlement of the dispute without trial. If no settlement occurs, then the judge will enter an order containing all of the amendments, stipulations, admissions, and other matters agreed to during the pretrial conference. The order supersedes the pleadings and controls the trial.

The evidence disclosed by discovery may be so clear that a trial to determine the facts becomes unnecessary. Thus, after discovery, either party may move for a summary judgment, which requests the judge to rule that, since there are no issues of fact to be determined by trial, as a matter of law that party should prevail. A **summary judgment** is a binding determination on the merits made by the judge before a trial. See *Parker v. Twentieth Century-Fox Film Corp.*

Trial

In all Federal civil cases at common law involving more than twenty dollars, the United States Constitution guarantees the right to a jury trial. In addition, nearly every State constitution provides a similar right. Under Federal law and in almost all States, jury trials are *not* available in equity cases. Even in cases where a jury trial is available, the parties may waive (choose not to have) a trial by jury. When a trial is conducted without a jury, the judge serves as the fact finder and will make separate findings of fact and conclusions of law. When a trial is conducted *with* a jury, the judge determines issues of law and the jury determines questions of fact.

Assuming a timely demand for a jury has been made, the trial begins by selection of a jury. The jury selection process involves an examination by the parties' attorneys (or in some courts by the judge) of the potential jurors called **voir dire.** Each party has an unlimited number of **challenges for cause** that allow a party to prevent a prospective juror from serving if the juror is biased or cannot be fair and impartial. In addition, each party has a limited number of **peremptory challenges** for which no cause is required to disqualify a prospective juror.

After the jury has been selected, both attorneys make an **opening statement** concerning the facts that they expect to prove in the trial. The plaintiff and her witnesses then testify upon **direct examination** by the plaintiff's attorney. Each is subject to **cross-examination** by the defendant's attorney. Thus, in our hypothetical case, the plaintiff and her witnesses testify that the traffic light at the street intersection where Pederson was struck was green for traffic in the direction in which Pederson was crossing but changed to orange when she was about one-third of the way across the street.

During the trial the judge rules on the admission and exclusion of evidence. If the judge does not allow certain evidence to be introduced or certain testimony to be given, the attorney may preserve the question of its admissibility for review on appeal by making an **offer of proof.** The offer of proof is not regarded as evidence, and the offer, which consists of oral statements of counsel or witnesses for the purpose of the record to show the substance of the evidence which the judge has ruled inadmissible, is not heard by the jury.

After cross-examination, followed by redirect examination of each of her witnesses, the plaintiff rests her case. At this point the defendant may move for a directed verdict in his favor. A **directed verdict** is a binding determination on the merits made by the judge after a trial but before the jury renders a judgment. If the judge concludes that the evidence introduced by the plaintiff, which is assumed for the purposes of the motion to be true, would not be sufficient for the jury to find in favor of the plaintiff, then the judge will grant the directed verdict in favor of the defendant.

If the judge denies the motion for a directed verdict, then the defendant has the opportunity to present evidence. The defendant and his witnesses testify that Dryden was driving his car at a low speed when it struck Pederson and that Dryden at the time had the green light at the intersection. After the defendant has presented his evidence and both parties have rested (concluded), then each party may move for a directed verdict. By this motion the party contends that the evidence is so clear that reasonable persons

could not differ as to the outcome of the case. If the judge grants the motion for a directed verdict, the judge takes the case away from the jury and enters a judgment for the party making the motion.

If these motions are denied, then the plaintiff's attorney makes a closing argument to the jury, reviewing the evidence and urging a verdict in favor of Pederson. Dryden's attorney then makes a closing argument, reviewing the evidence and urging a verdict in favor of the defendant. Pederson's attorney is permitted to make a short argument in rebuttal.

The attorneys have previously tendered written **jury instructions** on the applicable law to the trial judge, who gives those he approves to the jury and denies those he considers incorrect. The judge may also give the jury instructions of his own. These instructions (called "charges" in some States) advise the jury of the particular rules of law that apply to the facts as the jury determines them from the evidence.

The jury then retires to the jury room to deliberate and to reach a **general verdict** in favor of one party or the other. If it finds the issues in favor of defendant, its verdict is that the defendant is not liable. If, however, it finds the issues for the plaintiff and against defendant, its verdict is that the defendant is liable and it specifies the amount of plaintiff's damages. In this case the jury found that Pederson's damages were $35,000. Upon returning to the jury box, the foreman either announces the verdict or hands it in written form to the clerk to give to the judge, who reads the general verdict in open court. In some jurisdictions, a **special verdict** is used, by which the jury makes specific written findings on each factual issue. The judge then applies the law to these findings and renders a judgment.

The unsuccessful party may then file a written motion for a new trial or for judgment notwithstanding the verdict. A **motion for a new trial** may be granted if (1) the judge committed prejudicial error during the trial, (2) the verdict is against the weight of the evidence, (3) the damages are excessive, or (4) the trial was not fair. The judge has the discretion to grant a motion for a new trial (on grounds 1, 3, or 4 above) even if the verdict is supported by substantial evidence. On the other hand, the motion for judgment notwithstanding the verdict (also called a judgment n.o.v.) must be denied if there is any substantial evidence supporting the verdict. This motion is similar to a motion for a directed verdict, only it is made after the jury's verdict. To grant the **motion for judgment notwithstanding the verdict,** the judge must decide that the evidence is so clear that reasonable people could not differ as to the outcome of the case.

If these motions are denied, the judge enters judgment on the verdict for $35,000 in favor of the plaintiff. If Dryden does not appeal, or if the reviewing court affirms the judgment if he does appeal, and Dryden does not pay the judgment, the task of enforcement remains. Pederson requests the clerk to issue a **writ of execution,** which is served by the sheriff upon the defendant demanding payment of the judgment. Upon return of the writ "unsatisfied," Pederson may post bond or other security and order a levy on and sale of specific nonexempt property belonging to the defendant which is then seized by the sheriff, advertised for sale, and sold at public sale under the writ of execution. If the proceeds of the sale do not produce sufficient funds to pay the judgment, plaintiff Pederson's attorney may institute a supplementary proceeding in an attempt to locate money or other property belonging to defendant. He may also proceed by **garnishment** against Dryden's employer to collect from Dryden's wages or against a bank in which Dryden has an account in an attempt to collect the judgment.

Appeal

The purpose of an appeal is to determine whether the trial court committed prejudicial error. As a general rule only errors of law are reviewed by an appellate court. Errors of law include the judge's decisions to admit or exclude evidence; the judge's instructions to the jury; and the judge's actions in denying or granting a motion for a demurrer, a summary judgment, a directed verdict, or a judgment notwithstanding the verdict. Errors of fact will only be reversed if they are so clearly erroneous that they are considered to be an error of law.

Assume that Dryden directs his attorney to appeal. A notice of appeal is filed with the clerk of the trial court within the prescribed time. Later Dryden, as appellant, files in the reviewing court the record on appeal, which contains the pleadings, transcript of the testimony, rulings by the judge on motions made by the parties, arguments of counsel, jury instructions, the verdict, post-trial motions, and the judgment from which the appeal is taken. In States where there is an intermediate court of appeals, it will usually be the reviewing court. In States where there are no intermediate courts of appeal, a party may appeal directly from the trial court to the State supreme court.

Dryden, as appellant, is required to prepare a condensation of the record, known as an abstract, or pertinent excerpts from the record which he files with the reviewing court together with a brief and argument. His **brief** contains a statement of the facts, the issues, the rulings by the trial court which Dryden contends are erroneous and prejudicial, grounds for reversal of the judgment, statement of the applicable law, and arguments on his behalf. Pederson, the appellee, files an answering brief and argument. Dryden may, but is not required to, file a reply brief. The case is now ready for consideration by the reviewing court.

The appellate court does not hear any evidence. It decides the case upon the record, abstracts, and briefs. After **oral argument** by the attorneys, if the court elects to hear one, the court takes the case under advisement. The appellate court then makes a decision based upon majority rule. The court prepares a written opinion containing the reasons for its decision, the rules of law which apply, and its judgment. The judgment may **affirm** the judgment of the trial court, or if it finds that reversible error was committed, the judgment may be **reversed,** or the case may be **reversed and remanded** for a new trial. In some instances the appellate court will affirm the lower court's decision in part and will reverse it in part. The losing party may file a petition for rehearing, which is usually denied.

If the reviewing court is an intermediate appellate court, the party losing in that court may decide to seek a reversal of its judgment by filing within a prescribed time a notice of appeal, if the appeal is by right, or a petition for leave to appeal to the State supreme court, if the appeal is by discretion. This petition corresponds to a petition for a writ of *certiorari* in the United States Supreme Court. The party winning in the appellate court may file an answer to the petition for leave to appeal. If the petition is granted, or if the appeal is by right, the record is certified to the higher court, and

each party files a new brief and argument in the supreme court. Oral argument may be held, and the case is taken under advisement. If the supreme court concludes that the judgment of the appellate court is correct, it affirms. If it decides otherwise, it reverses the judgment of the appellate court and enters a reversal or an order of remand. The unsuccessful party may again file a petition for a rehearing which is likely to be denied. Barring the remote possibility of an application for still further review by the United States Supreme Court, the case has either reached its termination or, upon remand, is about to start its second journey through the courts, beginning as originally in the trial court.

The various stages in civil procedure are illustrated in Figure 2–7.

Figure 2–7 Stages in Civil Procedure

Determine what facts are in dispute	**Pleadings**	Complaint Answer Reply
Discover what evidence there is to prove the facts in dispute	**Pretrial**	Discovery Conference Summary Judgment
Determine what facts are proved by the evidence	**Trial**	Jury Selection Opening Statements Introduction of Evidence Closing Arguments Judgment on Verdict
Review the lower court's actions for prejudicial error	**Appeal**	Briefs and Transcript Oral Argument Decision
Implement the court's judgment	**Enforcement**	Execution Garnishment

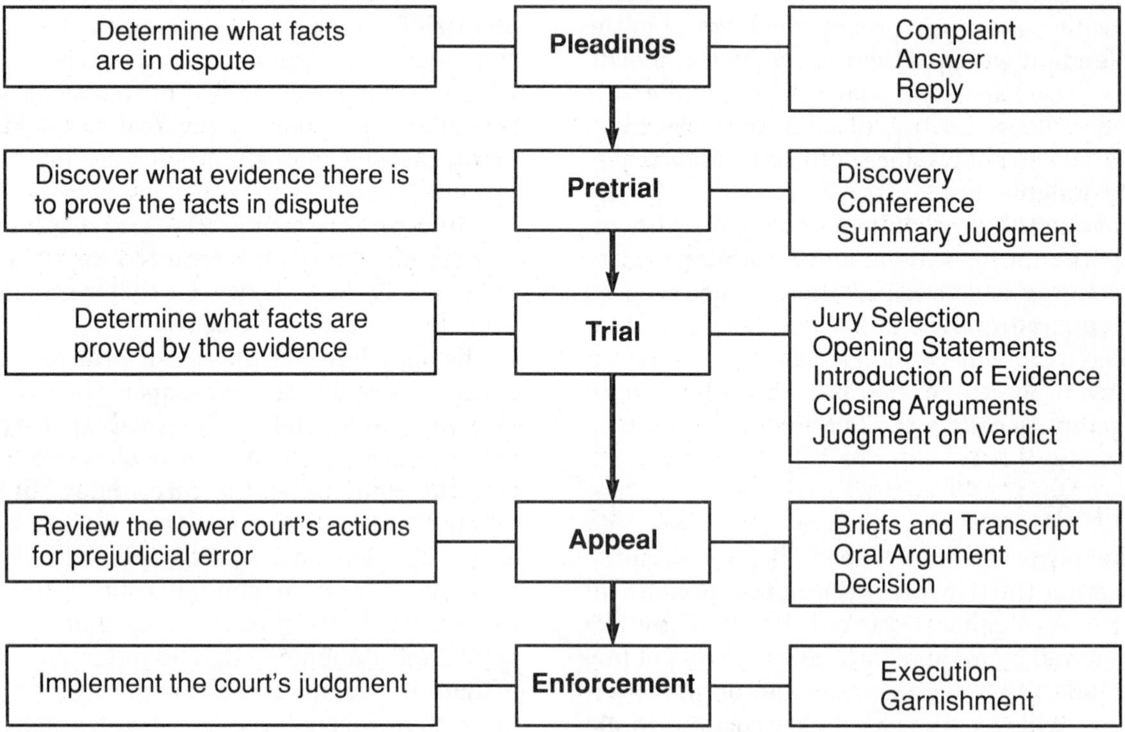

ALTERNATIVE DISPUTE RESOLUTION

Litigation is complex, time-consuming, and expensive. Furthermore, court adjudications involve long delays, lack special expertise in substantive areas, and provide only a limited range of remedies. Additionally, litigation is structured so that one party takes all with little opportunity for compromise and often causes animosity between the disputants. Consequently, several nonjudicial methods of dealing with disputes have developed in an attempt to overcome some of the disadvantages of litigation. The most important of these alternatives to litigation is arbitration. Others include conciliation, mediation, and "mini-trials."

The various techniques differ in a number of ways, including (1) whether the process is voluntary, (2) whether the process is binding, (3) whether the disputants represent themselves or are represented by attorneys, (4) whether the decision is made by the disputants or by a third party, (5) whether the procedure utilized is formal or informal, and (6) whether the basis for the decision is law or some other criteria.

Which method of civil dispute resolution— litigation or one of the nongovernmental methods—is better for a particular dispute depends on a number of factors, including the financial circumstances of the disputants, the nature of the relationship (commercial or personal, ongoing or limited) between the disputants, and the urgency of a quick resolution. Alternative dispute resolution methods are especially suitable where privacy, speed, preservation of continuing relations, and control over the process— including the flexibility to compromise—are important to the parties. Nevertheless, the disadvantages and limitations of using alternative dispute mechanisms may make court adjudication more appropriate. Except for arbitration, only courts can compel participation and provide a binding resolution. In addition, only courts can establish precedents and create public duties. Furthermore, the courts provide greater due process protections and uniformity of outcome. Finally, the courts are independent of the disputants and are publicly funded (see Figure 2–8).

Arbitration

In **arbitration** the parties select a third person or persons (the arbitrator) who render(s)

Figure 2–8 Comparison of Adjudication, Arbitration, and Mediation/Conciliation

	Court Adjudication	Arbitration	Mediation/Conciliation
Advantages	Binding Public norms Precedents Uniformity Publicly funded Compels participation	Binding Parties control process Privacy Special expertise Speedy resolution	Preserves relations Parties control process Privacy Flexible
Disadvantages	Expensive Time-consuming Long delays Limited remedies Lacks special expertise No compromise Disrupts relationships Publicity	No public norms No precedent No uniformity	Not binding Lacks finality No compelled participation No precedent No uniformity

SOURCE: Adapted from Table 4 of *Report of the Ad Hoc Panel on Dispute Resolution and Public Policy,* prepared by the National Institute for Dispute Resolution.

a binding decision after hearing arguments and reviewing evidence. Because the presentation of the case is less formal and the rules of evidence are more relaxed, arbitration usually takes less time and costs less than litigation. Moreover, in many arbitration cases the parties are able to select an arbitrator with special expertise concerning the subject of the dispute. Thus, the quality of the arbitrator's decision may be higher than that available through the court system. In addition, arbitration is normally conducted in private, thus avoiding unwanted publicity. Arbitration is commonly used in commercial and labor management disputes.

There are two basic types of arbitration—consensual, which is by far the most common, and compulsory. **Consensual arbitration** occurs whenever the parties to a dispute agree to submit the controversy to arbitration. They may do this in advance by agreeing in their contract that disputes arising out of their contract will be resolved by arbitration. Or they may do so after a dispute arises by then agreeing to submit the dispute to arbitration. In either instance, such agreements are enforceable under the Federal Arbitration Act and statutes in over forty States. (See *Perry v. Thomas*.) In **compulsory arbitration,** which is relatively infrequent, a Federal or State statute requires arbitration for specific types of disputes, such as those involving public employees like police officers or fire fighters.

The decision of the arbitrators, called an **award,** is binding on the parties. Nevertheless, it is subject to limited judicial review for such matters as illegality, fraud or other misconduct, lack of due process, or excess of the arbitrators' powers. Historically, the courts were unfriendly to arbitration. The courts have dramatically changed their attitude, however, and now favor arbitration.

A growing number of Federal and State courts have experimented with "court-annexed arbitration" in civil cases where limited amounts of damages are sought. The arbitrators are usually attorneys. Appeal from this type of *nonbinding* arbitration is by trial *de novo*.

Conciliation

Conciliation is a nonbinding, informal process in which a third party (the conciliator) selected by the disputing parties attempts to help them reach a mutually acceptable agreement. The functions of the conciliator include improving communications, explaining issues, scheduling meetings, discussing differences of opinion, and serving as an intermediary between the parties when they are unwilling to meet.

Mediation

Mediation is a process in which a third party (the mediator) selected by the disputants helps them to reach a resolution of their disagreement. In addition to employing the techniques of conciliation to improve communications, the mediator, unlike the conciliator, proposes possible solutions for the parties to consider. Like the conciliator, the mediator does not have the power to render a binding decision.

Sometimes the techniques of arbitration and mediation are combined in a procedure called "med-arb." In med-arb, the neutral third party serves first as a mediator and, if all issues are not resolved through such mediation, then serves as an arbitrator authorized to render a binding decision on the remaining issues.

Mini-Trial

A mini-trial typically occurs when both disputants are corporations. In a mini-trial, attorneys for the two corporations conduct limited discovery and then present evidence to a panel consisting of managers from each company as well as a neutral third party, who may be a retired judge or other attorney. After the lawyers complete their presentations, the managers try to negotiate a settlement without the attorneys. The managers may consult the third party on how a court might resolve the issues in dispute.

CASES

Supreme Court: Writs of Certiorari

MARYLAND v. BALTIMORE RADIO SHOW, INC.

Supreme Court of the United States, 1950.
338 U.S. 912, 70 S.Ct. 252, 94 L.Ed. 562.

FRANKFURTER, J.

The Criminal Court of Baltimore City found the respondents guilty of contempt and imposed fines for broadcasting over local radio stations matter relating to one Eugene H. James at a time when he was in custody on a charge of murder. The facts upon which these findings were based are best narrated in the authoritative statement of the trial court:

"A little girl in one of the parks of Washington, D.C., had been murdered under horrible and tragic circumstances. Some ten days later, little Marsha Brill was dragged from her bicycle on one of the public thoroughfares of Baltimore City while in the company, or at least, in the vicinity of two of her playmates, and there stabbed to death. The impact of those two similar crimes upon the public mind was terrific. The people throughout the City were outraged. Not only were they outraged but they were terrified. . . . Mr. Connelly [the announcer] then proceeded to explain that James had been apprehended and that he had been charged with the Brill murder. That was all right. Nobody could quarrel with that, but then he goes on to say that James had confessed to this dastardly crime, that he has a long criminal record, that he went out to the scene with the officers and there re-enacted the crime, and further, dug up from somewhere down in the leaves the knife that he had used to murder the little girl. Now, gentlemen, the Court has no difficulty in concluding that the broadcast was devastating. Anybody who heard it would never forget it. The question then before us is: Did that broadcast and others which were less damaging by the other stations, have a clear and present effect upon the administration of justice? The Court is bound to say that we do not believe that those broadcasts had any appreciable effect to say nothing of constituting a clear and present danger, upon the decision of the Judges who tried the case. . . .

"Now, the Court can not help but feel that the broadcast referred to in these cases must have had an indelible effect upon the public mind and that that effect was one that was bound to follow the members of the panel into the jury room. The Court hardly needs evidence in this factual situation to reach the conclusion that James' free choice to either a court trial on the one hand and a jury trial on the other, has been clearly and definitely interfered with. . . .

"Now, gentlemen, the Court must conclude that these broadcasts did constitute, not merely a clear and present danger to the administration of justice, but an actual obstruction of the administration of justice, in that they deprived the Defendant, James, of his Constitutional right to have an impartial jury trial."

The Court of Appeals of Maryland reversed these convictions. [Citation.] It did so by sustaining "the chief contention of the appellants, that the power to punish for contempt is limited by the First and Fourteenth Amendments to the Federal Constitution, and that the facts in the case at bar cannot support the judgments, in the light of those amendments, as authoritatively construed by the Supreme Court." . . .

Thereupon the State of Maryland asked this Court to issue a writ of certiorari to review the decision of its Court of Appeals. In its petition Maryland urges that while the Court of Appeals was of course bound by the decisions of this Court, that court misconceived our rulings, that the interpretation which it placed upon the [Supreme Court] cases was not correct, with the result that it erroneously reversed the judgments for contempt. . . .

This Court now declines to review the decision of the Maryland Court of Appeals. The sole significance of such denial of a petition for writ of certiorari need not be elucidated to those versed in the Court's procedures. It simply means that fewer than four members of the Court deemed it desirable to review a decision of the lower court as a matter "of sound judicial discretion." [Citation.] A variety of considerations underlie denials of the writ, and as to the same petition different reasons may lead different Justices to the same result. This is especially true of petitions for review on writ of certiorari to a State court. Narrowly technical reasons may lead to denials. Review may be sought too late; the judgment of the lower court may not be final; it may not be the judgment of a State court of last resort; the decision may be supportable as a matter of State law, not subject to review by this Court, even though the State court also passed on issues of federal law. A decision may satisfy all these technical requirements and yet may commend itself for review to fewer than four members of the Court. Pertinent considerations of judicial policy here come into play. A case may raise an important question but the record may be cloudy. It may be desirable to have different aspects of an issue further illumined by the lower courts. Wise adjudication has its own time for ripening.

* * *

Inasmuch, therefore, as all that a denial of a petition for a writ of certiorari means is that fewer than four members of the Court thought it should be granted, this Court has rigorously insisted that such a denial carries with it no implication whatever regarding the Court's views on the merits of a case which it has declined to review. The Court has said this again and again; again and again the admonition has to be repeated.

* * *

It becomes necessary to say that denial of this petition carries no support whatever for concluding that either the majority or the dissent in the court below correctly interpreted the scope of our decisions in [citation]. It does not carry any implication that either, or neither, opinion below correctly applied those decisions to the facts in the case at bar.

Jurisdiction

WORLD-WIDE VOLKSWAGEN CORP. v. WOODSON

Supreme Court of the United States, 1980.
444 U.S. 286, 100 S.Ct. 559, 62 L.Ed.2d 490.

WHITE, J.

The issue before us is whether, consistently with the Due Process Clause of the Fourteenth Amendment, an Oklahoma court may exercise *in personam* jurisdiction over a nonresident automobile retailer and its wholesale distributor in a products-liability action, when the defendants' only connection with Oklahoma is the fact that an automobile sold in New York to New York residents became involved in an accident in Oklahoma.

Respondents Harry and Kay Robinson purchased a new Audi automobile from petitioner Seaway Volkswagen, Inc. (Seaway), in Massena, N.Y., in 1976. The following year the Robinson family, who resided in New York, left that State for a new home in Arizona. As they passed through the State of Oklahoma, another car struck their Audi in the rear, causing a fire which severely burned Kay Robinson and her two children.

The Robinsons subsequently brought a products-liability action in the District Court for Creek County, Okla., claiming that their injuries resulted from defective design and placement of the Audi's gas tank and fuel system. They joined as defendants the automobile's manufacturer, Audi NSU Auto Union Aktiengesellschaft (Audi); its importer, Volkswagen of America, Inc. (Volkswagen); its regional distributor, petitioner World-Wide Volkswagen Corp. (World-Wide); and its retail dealer, petitioner Seaway. Seaway and World-Wide entered special appearances, claiming that Oklahoma's exercise of jurisdiction over them would offend the limitations on the State's jurisdiction imposed by the Due Process Clause of the Fourteenth Amendment.

The facts presented to the District Court showed that World-Wide is incorporated and has its business office in New York. It distributes vehicles, parts, and accessories, under contract with Volkswagen, to retail dealers in New York, New Jersey, and Connecticut. Seaway, one of these retail dealers, is incorporated and has its place of business in New York. Insofar as the record reveals, Seaway and World-Wide are fully independent corporations whose relations with each other and with Volkswagen and

Audi are contractual only. Respondents adduced no evidence that either World-Wide or Seaway does any business in Oklahoma, ships or sells any products to or in that State, has an agent to receive process there, or purchases advertisements in any media calculated to reach Oklahoma. In fact, as respondents' counsel conceded at oral argument, [citation], there was no showing that any automobile sold by World-Wide or Seaway has ever entered Oklahoma with the single exception of the vehicle involved in the present case.

* * *

The Supreme Court of Oklahoma [held] that personal jurisdiction over petitioners was authorized by Oklahoma's "long-arm" statute, [citation]. * * *

* * *

The Due Process Clause of the Fourteenth Amendment limits the power of a state court to render a valid personal judgment against a nonresident defendant. [Citation.] A judgment rendered in violation of due process is void in the rendering State and is not entitled to full faith and credit elsewhere. [Citation.] Due process requires that the defendant be given adequate notice of the suit, [citation], and be subject to the personal jurisdiction of the court, [citation]. In the present case, it is not contended that notice was inadequate; the only question is whether these particular petitioners were subject to the jurisdiction of the Oklahoma courts.

As has long been settled, and as we reaffirm today, a state court may exercise personal jurisdiction over a nonresident defendant only so long as there exist "minimum contacts" between the defendant and the forum State. [Citation.] The concept of minimum contacts, in turn, can be seen to perform two related, but distinguishable, functions. It protects the defendant against the burdens of litigating in a distant or inconvenient forum. And it acts to ensure that the States, through their courts, do not reach out beyond the limits imposed on them by their status as coequal sovereigns in a federal system.

The protection against inconvenient litigation is typically described in terms of "reasonableness" or "fairness." We have said that the defendant's contacts with the forum State must be such that maintenance of the suit "does not offend 'traditional notions of fair play and substantial justice.' " [Citation.] The relationship between the defendant and the forum must be such that it is "reasonable . . . to require the corporation to defend the particular suit which is brought there." [Citation.] Implicit in this emphasis on reasonableness is the understanding that the burden on the defendant, while always a primary concern, will in an appropriate case be considered in light of other relevant factors, including the forum State's interest in adjudicating the dispute, [citation]; the plaintiff's interest in obtaining convenient and effective relief, [citation], at least when that interest is not adequately protected by the plaintiff's power to choose the forum, [citation]; the interstate judicial system's interest in obtaining the most efficient resolution of controversies; and the shared interest of the several States in furthering fundamental substantive social policies, [citation].

* * *

Thus, the Due Process Clause "does not contemplate that a state may make binding a judgment *in personam* against an individual or corporate defendant with which the state has no contacts, ties, or relations." [Citation.]

* * *

Applying these principles to the case at hand, we find in the record before us a total absence of those affiliating circumstances that are a necessary predicate to any exercise of state-court jurisdiction. Petitioners carry on no activity whatsoever in Oklahoma. They close no sales and perform no services there. They avail themselves of none of the privileges and benefits of Oklahoma law. They solicit no business there either through salespersons or through advertising reasonably calculated to reach the State. Nor does the record show that they regularly sell cars at wholesale or retail to Oklahoma customers or residents or that they indirectly, through others, serve or seek to serve the Oklahoma market. In short, respondents seek to base jurisdiction on one, isolated occurrence and whatever inferences can be drawn therefrom: the fortuitous circumstance that a single Audi automobile, sold in New York to New York residents, happened to suffer an accident while passing through Oklahoma.

It is argued, however, that because an automobile is mobile by its very design and purpose it was "foreseeable" that the Robinsons' Audi would cause injury in Oklahoma. Yet "foreseeability" alone has never been a sufficient benchmark for personal jurisdiction under the Due Process Clause. * * *

This is not to say, of course, that foreseeability is wholly irrelevant. But the foreseeability that is critical to due process analysis is not the mere likelihood that a product will find its way into the forum State. Rather, it is that the defendant's conduct and connection with the forum State are such that he should reasonably anticipate being haled into court there. [Citations.] The Due Process Clause, by ensuring the "orderly administration of the laws," [citation], gives a degree of predictability to the legal system that allows potential defendants to structure their primary conduct with some minimum assurance as to where that conduct will and will not render them liable to suit.

When a corporation "purposefully avails itself of the privilege of conducting activities within the forum State," [citation], it has clear notice that it is subject to suit there, and can act to alleviate the risk of burdensome litigation by procuring insurance, passing the expected costs on to customers, or, if the risks are too great, severing its connection with the State. Hence if the sale of a product of a manufacturer or distributor such as Audi or Volkswagen is not simply an isolated occurrence, but arises from the efforts of the manufacturer or distributor to serve, directly or indirectly, the market for its product in other States, it is not unreasonable to subject it to suit in one of those States if its allegedly defective merchandise has there been the source of injury to its owner or to others. The forum State does not exceed its powers under the Due Process Clause if it asserts personal jurisdiction over a corporation that delivers its products

into the stream of commerce with the expectation that they will be purchased by consumers in the forum State. [Citation.]

But there is no such or similar basis for Oklahoma jurisdiction over World-Wide or Seaway in this case. Seaway's sales are made in Massena, N.Y. World-Wide's market, although substantially larger, is limited to dealers in New York, New Jersey, and Connecticut. There is no evidence of record that any automobiles distributed by World-Wide are sold to retail customers outside this tristate area. It is foreseeable that the purchasers of automobiles sold by World-Wide and Seaway may take them to Oklahoma. But the mere "unilateral activity of those who claim some relationship with a nonresident defendant cannot satisfy the requirement of contact with the forum State." [Citation.]

Because we find that petitioners have no "contacts, ties, or relations" with the State of Oklahoma, [citation], the judgment of the Supreme Court of Oklahoma is

Reversed.

Concurrent Federal Jurisdiction

ERIE RAILROAD CO. v. TOMPKINS

Supreme Court of the United States, 1938.
304 U.S. 64, 58 S.Ct. 817, 82 L.Ed. 1188.

BRANDEIS, J.

The question for decision is whether the oft-challenged doctrine of Swift v. Tyson shall now be disapproved.

Tompkins, a citizen of Pennsylvania, was injured on a dark night by a passing freight train of the Erie Railroad Company while walking along its right of way at Hughestown in that state. He claimed that the accident occurred through negligence in the operation, or maintenance, of the train; that he was rightfully on the premises as licensee because on a commonly used beaten footpath which ran for a short distance alongside the tracks; and that he was struck by something which looked like a door projecting from one of the moving cars. To enforce that claim he brought an action in the federal court for Southern New York, which had jurisdiction because the company is a corporation of that state. It denied liability; and the case was tried by a jury.

The Erie insisted that its duty to Tompkins was no greater than that owed to a trespasser. It contended, among other things, that its duty to Tompkins, and hence its liability, should be determined in accordance with the Pennsylvania law; that under the law of Pennsylvania, as declared by its highest court, persons who use pathways along the railroad right of way—that is, a longitudinal pathway as distinguished from a crossing—are to be deemed trespassers; and that the railroad is not liable for injuries to undiscovered trespassers resulting from its negligence, unless it be wanton or willful. Tompkins denied that any such rule had been established by the decisions of the Pennsylvania courts; and contended that, since there was no statute of the state on the subject, the railroad's duty and liability is to be determined in federal courts as a matter of general law.

The trial judge refused to rule that the applicable law precluded recovery. The jury brought in a verdict of $30,000; and the judgment entered thereon was affirmed by the Circuit Court of Appeals, which held [citation], that it was unnecessary to consider whether the law of Pennsylvania was as contended, because the question was one not of local, but of general, law, and that "upon questions of general law the federal courts are free, in absence of a local statute, to exercise their independent judgment as to what the law is; and it is well settled that the question of the responsibility of a railroad for injuries caused by its servants is one of general law. . . . Where the public has made open and notorious use of a railroad right of way for a long period of time and without objection, the company owes to persons on such permissive pathway a duty of care in the operation of its trains. . . . It is likewise generally recognized law that a jury may find that negligence exists toward a pedestrian using a permissive path on the railroad right of way if he is hit by some object projecting from the side of the train."

The Erie had contended that application of the Pennsylvania rule was required, among other things, by section 34 of the Federal Judiciary Act of September 24, 1789. . . .

Because of the importance of the question whether the federal court was free to disregard the alleged rule of the Pennsylvania common law, we granted certiorari, [citation].

Swift v. Tyson, [citation], held that federal courts exercising jurisdiction on the ground of diversity of citizenship need not, in matters of general jurisprudence, apply the unwritten law of the state as declared by its highest court; that they are free to exercise an independent judgment as to what the common law of the state is—or should be. . . .

* * *

Experience in applying the doctrine of Swift v. Tyson had revealed its defects, political and social; and the benefits expected to flow from the rule did not accrue. Persistence of state courts in their own opinions on questions of common law prevented uniformity; and the impossibility of discovering a satisfactory line of demarcation between the province of general law and that of local law developed a new well of uncertainties.

. . . [T]he mischievous results of the doctrine had become apparent. Diversity of citizenship jurisdiction was conferred in order to prevent apprehended discrimination in state courts against those not citizens of the State. Swift v. Tyson introduced grave discrimination by noncitizens against citizens. It made rights enjoyed under the unwritten "general law" vary according to whether enforcement was sought in the state or in the federal court; and the privilege of selecting the court in which the right should be determined was conferred upon the noncitizen. Thus, the doctrine rendered impossible equal protection of the law. In attempting to promote uniformity of law throughout the United States, the doctrine had prevented uniformity in the administration of the law of the state.

* * *

The injustice and confusion incident to the doctrine of Swift v. Tyson have been repeatedly urged as reasons for abolishing or limiting diversity of citizenship jurisdiction. Other legislative relief has been proposed. If only a question of statutory construction were involved, we should not be prepared to abandon a doctrine so widely applied throughout nearly a century. But the unconstitutionality of the course pursued has now been made clear, and compels us to do so.

* * * Except in matters governed by the Federal Constitution or by Acts of Congress, the law to be applied in any case is the law of the State. And whether the law of the State shall be declared by its Legislature in a statute or by its highest court in a decision is not a matter of federal concern. There is no federal general common law. Congress has no power to declare substantive rules of common law applicable in a State whether they be local in their nature or "general," be they commercial law or a part of the law of torts. And no clause in the Constitution purports to confer such a power upon the federal courts. * * *

* * *

Reversed.

Pretrial Procedure: Summary Judgment

PARKER v. TWENTIETH CENTURY–FOX FILM CORP.

Supreme Court of California, 1970.
3 Cal.3d 176, 89 Cal.Rptr. 737, 474 P.2d 689.

BURKE, J.

Defendant Twentieth Century-Fox Film Corporation appeals from a summary judgment granting to plaintiff [Shirley MacLaine Parker] the recovery of agreed compensation under a written contract for her services as an actress in a motion picture. As will appear, we have concluded that the trial court correctly ruled in plaintiff's favor and that the judgment should be affirmed.

Plaintiff is well known as an actress, and in the contract between plaintiff and defendant is sometimes referred to as the "Artist." Under the contract, dated August 6, 1965, plaintiff was to play the female lead in de-fendant's contemplated production of a motion picture entitled "Bloomer Girl." The contract provided that defendant would pay plaintiff a minimum "guaranteed compensation" of $53,571.42 per week for 14 weeks commencing May 23, 1966, for a total of $750,000. Prior to May 1966 defendant decided not to produce the picture and by a letter dated April 4, 1966, it notified plaintiff of that decision and that it would not "comply with our obligations to you under" the written contract.

By the same letter and with the professed purpose "to avoid any damage to you," defendant instead offered to employ plaintiff as the leading actress in another film tentatively entitled "Big Country, Big Man" (hereinafter, "Big Country"). The compensation offered was identical, as were 31 of the 34 numbered provisions or articles of the original contract. Unlike "Bloomer Girl," however, which was to have been a musical production, "Big Country" was a dramatic "western type" movie. "Bloomer Girl" was to have been filmed in California; "Big Country" was to be produced in Australia. Also, certain terms in the proffered contract varied from those of the original. Plaintiff was given one week within which to accept; she did not and the offer lapsed. Plaintiff then commenced this action seeking recovery of the agreed guaranteed compensation.

The complaint sets forth two causes of action. The first is for money due under the contract; the second, based upon the same allegations as the first, is for damages resulting from defendant's breach of contract. Defendant in its answer admits the existence and validity of the contract, that plaintiff complied with all the conditions, covenants and promises and stood ready to complete the performance, and that defendant breached and "anticipatorily repudiated" the contract. It denies, however, that any money is due to plaintiff either under the contract or as a result of its breach, and pleads as an affirmative defense to both causes of action plaintiff's allegedly deliberate failure to mitigate damages, asserting that she unreasonably refused to accept its offer of the leading role in "Big Country."

Plaintiff moved for summary judgment under Code of Civil Procedure section 437c, the motion was granted, and summary judgment for $750,000 plus interest was entered in plaintiff's favor. This appeal by defendant followed.

The familiar rules are that the matter to be determined by the trial court on a motion for summary judgment is whether facts have been presented which give rise to a triable factual issue. The court may not pass upon the issue itself. Summary judgment is proper only if the affidavits or declarations in support of the moving party would be sufficient to sustain a judgment in his favor and his opponent does not by affidavit show facts sufficient to present a triable issue of fact. The affidavits of the moving party are strictly construed, and doubts as to the propriety of summary judgment should be resolved against granting the motion. Such summary procedure is drastic and should be used with caution so that it does not become a substitute for the open trial method of determining facts. The moving party cannot depend upon allegations in his own pleadings to cure deficient affidavits, nor can his adversary rely upon his own pleadings in lieu or in support of affidavits in opposition to a motion; however, a party can rely on his adversary's pleadings to establish facts not contained in his own affidavits. [Citations.] Also, the court may consider facts stipulated to by the parties and facts which are properly the subject of judicial notice. [Citations.]

As stated, defendant's sole defense to this action which resulted from its deliberate breach of contract is that in rejecting defendant's substitute offer of employment plaintiff unreasonably refused to mitigate damages.

The general rule is that the measure of recovery by a wrongfully discharged employee is the amount of salary agreed upon for the period of service, less the amount which the employer affirmatively proves the employee has earned or with reasonable effort might have earned from other employment. [Citations.] However, before projected earnings from other employment opportunities not sought or accepted by the discharged employee can be applied in mitigation, the employer must show that the other employment was comparable, or substantially similar, to that of which the employee has been deprived; the employee's rejection of or failure to seek other available employment of a different or inferior kind may not be resorted to in order to mitigate damages. [Citations.]

In the present case defendant has raised no issue of *reasonableness of efforts* by plaintiff to obtain other employment; the sole issue is whether plaintiff's refusal of defendant's substitute offer of "Big Country" may be used in mitigation. Nor, if the "Big Country" offer was of employment different or inferior when compared with the original "Bloomer Girl" employment, is there an issue as to whether or not plaintiff acted reasonably in refusing the substitute offer. Despite defendant's arguments to the contrary, no case cited or which our research has discovered holds or suggests that reasonableness is an element of a wrongfully discharged employee's option to reject, or fail to seek, different or inferior employment lest the possible earnings therefrom be charged against him in mitigation of damages.

Applying the foregoing rules to the record in the present case, with all intendments in favor of the party opposing the summary judgment motion—here, defendant—it is clear that the trial court correctly ruled that plaintiff's failure to accept defendant's tendered substitute employment could not be applied in mitigation of damages because the offer of the "Big Country" lead was of employment both different and inferior, and that no factual dispute was presented on that issue. The mere circumstance that "Bloomer Girl" was to be a musical review calling upon plaintiff's talents as a dancer as well as an actress, and was to be produced in the City of Los Angeles, whereas "Big Country" was a straight dramatic role in a "Western Type" story taking place in an opal mine in Australia, demonstrates the difference in kind between the two employments; the female lead as a dramatic actress in a western style motion picture can by no stretch of imagination be considered the equivalent of or substantially similar to the lead in a song-and-dance production.

Additionally, the substitute "Big Country" offer proposed to eliminate or impair the director and screenplay approvals accorded to plaintiff under the original "Bloomer Girl" contract . . . and thus constituted an offer of inferior employment. No expertise or judicial notice is required in order to hold that the deprivation or infringement of an employee's rights held under an original employment contract converts the available "other employment" relied upon by the employer to mitigate damages, into inferior employment which the employee need not seek or accept. [Citation.]

Statements found in affidavits submitted by defendant in opposition to plaintiff's summary judgment motion, to the effect that the "Big Country" offer was not of employment different from or inferior to that under the "Bloomer Girl" contract, merely repeat the allegations of defendant's answer to the complaint in this action, constitute only conclusionary assertions with respect to undisputed facts, and do not give rise to a triable factual issue so as to defeat the motion for summary judgment. [Citations.]

In view of the determination that defendant failed to present any facts showing the existence of a factual issue with respect to its sole defense—plaintiff's rejection of its substitute employment offer in mitigation of damages—we need not consider plaintiff's further contention that for various reasons, including the provisions of the original contract, plaintiff was excused from attempting to mitigate damages.

The judgment is affirmed.

Arbitration

PERRY v. THOMAS

Supreme Court of the United States, 1987.
482 U.S. 483, 107 S.Ct. 2520, 96 L.Ed.2d 426.

MARSHALL, J.

In this appeal we decide whether § 2 of the Federal Arbitration Act (Act), [citation], which mandates enforcement of arbitration agreements, pre-empts § 229 of the California Labor Code, which provides that actions for the collection of wages may be maintained "without regard to the existence of any private agreement to arbitrate." [Citation.]

Appellee, Kenneth Morgan Thomas, brought this action in California Superior Court against his former employer, Kidder, Peabody & Co. (Kidder, Peabody), and two of its employees, appellants Barclay Perry and James Johnston. His complaint arose from a dispute over commissions on the sale of securities. Thomas alleged breach of contract, conversion, civil conspiracy to commit conversion, and breach of fiduciary duty, for which he sought compensatory and punitive damages. After Thomas refused to submit the dispute to arbitration, the defendants sought to stay further proceedings in the Superior Court. Perry and Johnston filed a petition in the Superior Court to compel arbitration; Kidder, Peabody invoked diversity jurisdiction and filed a similar petition in Federal District Court. Both petitions sought arbitration under the authority of §§ 2 and 4 of the Federal Arbitration Act.

The demands for arbitration were based on a provision found in a Uniform Application for Securities Industry Registration form, which Thomas completed and executed in connection with his application for employment with Kidder, Peabody. That provision states:

"I agree to arbitrate any dispute, claim or controversy that may arise between me and my firm, or a customer, or any other person, that is required to be arbitrated under the rules, constitutions or by-laws of the organizations with which I register. . . ."

Rule 347 of the New York Stock Exchange, Inc. (1975) (NYSE), with which Thomas registered, provides that

"[a]ny controversy between a registered representative and any member or member organization arising out of the employment or termination of employment of such registered representative by and with such member or member organization shall be settled by arbitration, at the instance of any such party. . . ."

Kidder, Peabody sought arbitration as a member organization of the NYSE. Perry and Johnston relied on Thomas' allegation that they had acted in the course and scope of their employment and argued that, as agents and employees of Kidder, Peabody, they were beneficiaries of the arbitration agreement.

Thomas opposed both petitions on the ground that § 229 of the California Labor Code authorized him to maintain an action for wages, defined to include commissions, despite the existence of an agreement to arbitrate. * * *

The Superior Court denied appellants' petition to compel arbitration. * * *

* * *

In an unpublished opinion, the Court of Appeal affirmed. * * *

The California Supreme Court denied appellants' petition for review.

* * *

"Section 2 is a congressional declaration of a liberal federal policy favoring arbitration agreements, nonwithstanding any state substantive or procedural policies to the contrary. The effect of the section is to create a body of federal substantive law of arbitrability, applicable to any arbitration agreement within the coverage of the Act." [Citation.] Enacted pursuant to the Commerce Clause, U.S. Const. Art. I, § 8, cl. 3, this body of substantive law is enforceable in both state and federal courts. [Citation.] As we stated in [citation], "[i]n enacting § 2 of the federal Act, Congress declared a national policy favoring arbitration and withdrew the power of the states to require a judicial forum for the res-

olution of claims which the contracting parties agreed to resolve by arbitration." [Citation.] "Congress intended to foreclose state legislative attempts to undercut the enforceability of arbitration agreements." [Citation.] Section 2, therefore, embodies a clear federal policy of requiring arbitration unless the agreement to arbitrate is not part of a contract evidencing interstate commerce or is revocable "upon such grounds as exist at law or in equity for the revocation of any contract." [Citation.] "We see nothing in the Act indicating that the broad principle of enforceability is subject to any additional limitations under state law." [Citation.]

* * *

* * * the present appeal addresses the preemptive effect of the Federal Arbitration Act, a statute that embodies Congress' intent to provide for the enforcement of arbitration agreements within the full reach of the Commerce Clause. Its general applicability reflects that "[t]he preeminent concern of Congress in passing the Act was to enforce private agreements into which parties had entered. . . ." [Citation.] We have accordingly held that these agreements must be "rigorously enforce[d]." [Citation.] This clear federal policy places § 2 of the Act in unmistakable conflict with California's § 229 requirement that litigants be provided a judicial forum for resolving wage disputes. Therefore, under the Supremacy Clause, the state statute must give way.

* * *

The judgment of the California Court of Appeal is reversed, and the case is remanded for further proceedings not inconsistent with this opinion.

It is so ordered.

QUESTIONS

1. List and describe the courts in the Federal court system and in a typical State court system.

2. Distinguish between appeal by right and writ of *certiorari.*

3. Distinguish between subject matter jurisdiction and jurisdiction over the parties.

4. Distinguish between exclusive and concurrent Federal jurisdiction. Identify the two types of Federal concurrent jurisdiction.

5. Define and describe a typical long-arm statute.

6. List and distinguish among the three types of jurisdiction over the parties.

7. Describe the purpose of pleadings.

8. List and explain the various stages of a civil proceeding.

9. Compare and contrast the following: demurrer, judgment on the pleadings, summary judgment, directed verdict, and judgment notwithstanding the verdict.

10. Compare and contrast litigation, arbitration, conciliation, and mediation.

PROBLEMS

1. A newspaper columnist predicted that the coast of State X would be flooded on September 1, 1990. Relying on this pronouncement, Gullible quit his job and sold his property at a loss so as not to be financially ruined. When the flooding did not occur, Gullible sued the columnist in a State X court for damages. The court dismissed the case for failure to state a cause of action under applicable State law. On appeal, the State X Supreme Court upheld the lower court. Three months after this ruling, the State Y Supreme Court heard an appeal in which a lower court had ruled that a reader could sue a columnist for falsely predicting flooding.

(a) Must the State Y Supreme Court follow the ruling of the State X Supreme Court as a matter of *stare decisis?*

(b) Should the State Y lower court have followed the ruling of the State X Supreme Court until the State Y Supreme Court issued a ruling on the issue?

(c) Once the State X Supreme Court issued its ruling, could the United States Supreme Court overrule the State X Supreme Court?

(d) If the State Y Supreme Court and the State X Supreme Courts rule in exactly opposite ways, must the United States Supreme Court resolve the conflict between the two courts?

2. State Senator Bowdler convinced the legislature of State Z to pass a law requiring all professors to submit their class notes and transparencies to a board of censors to be sure that no "lewd" materials were presented to students at State universities. Professor Rabelais would like to challenge this law as being violative of his First Amendment rights under the U.S. Constitution.

(a) May Professor Rabelais challenge this law in the State Z courts?

(b) May Professor Rabelais challenge this law in a Federal district court?

3. While driving his car in Virginia, Carpe Diem, a resident of North Carolina, struck Butt, a resident of Alaska. As a result of the accident, Butt suffered over $60,000 in medical expenses. Butt would like to know if he personally serves the proper papers to Diem whether he can obtain jurisdiction against Diem for damages in the following courts:

(a) Alaska State trial court

(b) Federal Circuit Court of Appeals for the Ninth Circuit (includes Alaska)

(c) Virginia State trial court

(d) Virginia Federal district court

(e) Federal Circuit Court of Appeals for the Fourth Circuit (includes Virginia and North Carolina)

(f) Virginia equity court

(g) North Carolina State trial court.

4. Sam Simpleton, a resident of Kansas, and Nellie Naive, a resident of Missouri, each bought $85,000 in stock at local offices in their home States from Evil Stockbrokers, Inc. ("Evil"), a business incorporated in Delaware with its principal place of business in Kansas. Both Simpleton and Naive believe that they were cheated by Evil Stockbrokers and would like to sue Evil for fraud.

Assuming that no Federal question is at issue, assess the accuracy of the following statements:

(a) Simpleton can sue Evil in a Kansas State trial court.

(b) Simpleton can sue Evil in a Federal district court in Kansas.

(c) Naive can sue Evil in a Missouri State trial court.

(d) Naive can sue Evil in a Federal district court in Missouri.

5. The Supreme Court of State A ruled that, under the law of State A, pit bull owners must either keep their dogs fenced or pay damages to anyone bitten by the dogs. Assess the accuracy of the following statements:

(a) It is likely that the United States Supreme Court would issue a writ of *certiorari* in the "pit bull" case.

(b) If a case similar to the "pit bull" case were to come before the Supreme Court of State B in the future, the doctrine of *stare decisis* would leave the court no choice but to rule the same way as the "pit bull" case.

6. The Supreme Court of State G decided that the United States Constitution requires professors to warn students of their right to remain silent before questioning the students about cheating. This ruling directly conflicts with a decision of the Federal Court of Appeals for the circuit which includes State G.

(a) Must the Federal Circuit Court of Appeals withdraw its ruling?

(b) Must the Supreme Court of State G withdraw its ruling?

7. Thomas Clements brought an action to recover damages for breach of warranty against defendant, Signa Corporation. (A warranty is an obligation that the seller of goods assumes with respect to the quality of the goods sold.) Clements had purchased a motor boat from Barney's Sporting Goods, an Illinois corporation. The boat was manufactured by Signa Corporation, an Indiana corporation with its principal place of business in Decatur, Indiana. Signa has no office in Illinois and no agent authorized to do business on its behalf within Illinois. Clements saw Signa's boats on display at the Chicago Boat Show. In addition, literature on Signa's boats was distributed at the Chicago Boat Show. Several boating magazines, delivered to Clements in Illinois, contained advertisements for Signa's boats. Clements had also

seen Signa's boats on display at Barney's Sporting Goods Store in Palatine, Illinois, where he eventually purchased the boat. A written warranty issued by Signa was delivered to Clements in Illinois. Although Signa was served with a summons, it failed to enter an appearance in this case. A default order was entered against Signa and subsequently a judgment of $6,220 was entered against Signa. Signa appealed. Decision?

8. Mariana Deutsch worked as a knitwear mender and attended a school for beauticians. The sink in her apartment collapsed on her foot, fracturing her big toe and making it painful for her to stand. She claims that as a consequence of the injury she was compelled to abandon her plans to become a beautician because that job requires standing for long periods of time. She also asserts that she was unable to work at her current job for a month. She filed a tort claim against Hewes Street Realty for negligence in failing properly to maintain the sink. She brought the suit in Federal district court, claiming damages of $25,000. Her medical expenses and actual loss of salary were less than $1,500; the rest of her alleged damages were for loss of future earnings as a beautician. Hewes Street moved to dismiss the suit on the basis that Deutsch's claim fell short of the jurisdictional requirement, which then was $10,000, and therefore the Federal court lacked subject matter jurisdiction over her claim. Decision?

9. Vette sued Aetna under a fire insurance policy. Aetna moved for summary judgment on the basis that the pleadings and discovered evidence showed a lack of an insurable interest in Vette. An "insurable interest" exists where the insured derives a monetary benefit or advantage from the preservation or continued existence of the property or would sustain an economic loss from its destruction. Aetna provided ample evidence to infer that Vette had no insurable interest in the contents of the burned building. Vette also provided sufficient evidence to put in dispute this factual issue. The trial court granted the motion for summary judgment. Vette appealed. Decision?

10. Mark Womer and Brian Perry were members of the United States Navy and were stationed in Newport, Rhode Island. On April 10, 1978, Womer allowed Perry to borrow his automobile so that Perry could visit his family in New Hampshire. Later that day, while operating Womer's vehicle, Perry was involved in an accident in Manchester,

New Hampshire. As a result of the accident, Tzannetos Tavoularis was injured. Tavoularis brought this action against Womer in a New Hampshire superior court, contending that Womer was negligent in lending the automobile to Perry when he knew or should have known that Perry did not have a valid driver's license. Womer sought to dismiss the action on the ground that the New Hampshire courts lacked jurisdiction over him, citing the following facts: (1) he lived and worked in Georgia; (2) he had no relatives in New Hampshire; (3) he neither owned property nor possessed investments in New Hampshire; and (4) he had never conducted business in New Hampshire. Decision?

Chapter 3

CONSTITUTIONAL AND ADMINISTRATIVE LAW

Basic Principles of Constitutional Law
Powers of Government
Limitations upon Government
Operation of Administrative Agencies
Limits on Administrative Agencies

AS mentioned in Chapter 1, public law is that branch of substantive law that deals with the rights and powers of government in its political or governing capacity and its relation to individuals or groups. Public law consists of constitutional law, administrative law, and criminal law. The first two are discussed in this chapter; criminal law is covered in the next chapter.

Public law continues to increase in importance in the study of business. Large and significant areas of the regulation of business arise from public law. For example, bankruptcy (Chapter 40), antitrust (Chapter 42), employment law (Chapter 44), and securities regulation (Chapter 45) are principally public law. In addition, other areas of the law such as products liability and warranties (Chapter 22), unfair competition (Chapter 41), and consumer protection (Chapter 43) are also greatly affected by public law.

CONSTITUTIONAL LAW

Constitutions are the fundamental and organic law of a particular jurisdiction and serve a number of critical functions. They are the supreme law of that jurisdiction. In addition, they establish the structure of and allocate power among the various levels of government (see Figure 3–2). They also impose restrictions upon the powers of government and enumerate the rights and liberties of the people.

The Constitution of the United States (reprinted in Appendix A) was adopted on September 17, 1787, by representatives of the thirteen newly created States. Its purpose is stated in the preamble:

We the People of the United States, In Order to form a more perfect Union, establish Justice, insure domestic Tranquility, provide for the common defence, promote the general Welfare, and secure the Blessings of Liberty to ourselves and our Posterity, do ordain and establish this Constitution for the United States of America.

Although the framers of the Constitution of the United States enumerated precisely what rights and authority were vested in the new national government, they considered it unnecessary to list those liberties the people reserved to themselves. Alexander Hamilton, a coauthor of *The Federalist,* put it this way: "Here in strictness the people surrender nothing; and as they retain everything, they have no need of particular reservations." Nonetheless, during the State ratifying conventions, people had expressed fear that the Federal government might abuse its powers. To calm these concerns, the first Congress approved ten amendments to the U.S. Constitution, now known as the Bill of Rights, which were adopted on December 15, 1791.

The Bill of Rights serves as a major restriction on the powers and authority of the Federal government and establishes many of the civil and political rights enjoyed in the United States, including the right to due process of law and freedoms of speech, press, religion, assembly, and petition. The Bill of Rights does not apply directly to the States. The Supreme Court has held, however, that the Fourteenth Amendment incorporates many of the principles of the Bill of Rights, thus making them applicable to the States.

This part of the chapter will discuss constitutional law as it applies to business and commerce. It will begin by surveying some of the basic principles of constitutional law. Then it will examine the allocation of power between the Federal and State governments with respect to the regulation of business. Finally, it will discuss the constitutional restrictions imposed upon the power of government to regulate business.

BASIC PRINCIPLES OF CONSTITUTIONAL LAW

The delegates to the constitutional convention desired a stronger national government but feared the accumulation of governmental power in the hands of one person or group. These two concerns underlie a number of the basic principles of the U.S. Constitution: Federalism, Federal supremacy, judicial review, and separation of power. An additional basic principle of constitutional law is state action.

Federalism

Federalism means that governing power is divided between the Federal government and the States. The U.S. Constitution enumerates the powers of the Federal government and

specifically reserves to the States or the people the powers not expressly delegated to the Federal government. Accordingly, the Federal government is a government of enumerated, or limited, powers and each act of the Federal government must be authorized by a specified power. The doctrine of enumerated powers is not, however, a significant limitation on the Federal government because a number of the enumerated powers, in particular the power to regulate interstate and foreign commerce, have been broadly interpreted.

Furthermore, the Constitution grants Congress not only specified powers but also the power "[t]o make all Laws which shall be necessary and proper for carrying into Execution the foregoing Powers, and all other Powers vested by this Constitution in the Government of the United States, or in any Department or Officer thereof." In the Supreme Court's view, the necessary and proper clause enables Congress to legislate in areas not mentioned in the list of enumerated powers as long as such legislation relates in a reasonable way to some enumerated power. As Chief Justice John Marshall noted in the landmark case of *McCulloch v. Maryland,* 17 U.S. (4 Wheat.) 316 (1819): "[l]et the end be legitimate, let it be within the scope of the constitution, and all means which are appropriate, which are plainly adapted to that end, which are not prohibited, but consist with the letter and spirit of the constitution, are constitutional."

Federal Supremacy and Preemption

Although under our Federalist system the States retain significant powers, the **supremacy clause** of the U.S. Constitution provides that within its own sphere, Federal law is supreme and State law must, in case of conflict, yield. Accordingly, any State constitutional provision or law that conflicts with the U.S. Constitution or valid Federal laws or treaties is unconstitutional and may not be given effect. In *McCulloch v. Maryland,* Chief Justice Marshall also stated, "This great principle is, that the Constitution and the laws made in pursuance thereof are supreme;

that they control the Constitution and laws of the respective states, and cannot be controlled by them."

Under the supremacy clause, whenever Congress enacts legislation within its constitutional powers, any conflicting State legislation is **preempted** (overridden) by the Federal action. Even if a State regulation is not obviously in conflict, it must still give way *if* Congress has clearly intended that its enactment should preempt the field. In such an instance, nonconflicting State legislation would be prohibited. This intent may be expressly stated in the legislation or inferred from the pervasiveness of the Federal regulation, the need for uniformity, or the danger of conflict between concurrent Federal and State regulation.

When Congress has *not* intended to displace all State legislation, then nonconflicting State legislation is permitted. *See Silkwood v. Kerr-McGee Corporation.* When Congress has not acted, the fact that Congress has the power to act does not prevent the States from acting. Until Congress exercises its power to preempt, State regulation is permitted.

Judicial Review

Judicial review describes the process by which the courts examine governmental actions to determine whether they conform to the U.S. Constitution. Judicial review extends to legislation, acts of the executive branch, and to the decisions of inferior courts. Judicial review includes actions of both the Federal and State governments and applies the same standards of constitutionality to both governments. The U.S. Supreme Court is the final authority as to the constitutionality of any Federal and State law. Judicial review is not expressly provided for in the U.S. Constitution, but in 1803 Chief Justice John Marshall, speaking for the Court, declared the existence of such authority in the landmark case of *Marbury v. Madison,* 5 U.S. (1 Cranch) 137 (1803).

To reach his conclusion in *Marbury,* Marshall reasoned that (1) in drafting and approving the Constitution, the people intended it to be the supreme law of the land, (2) it was the province and duty of the judiciary to say what the law is, and (3) therefore, the judiciary's interpretation of the Constitution was controlling and bound the executive and legislative branches of government.

Alexander Hamilton forcefully explained the justification for judicial review:

The interpretation of the laws is the proper and peculiar province of the courts. A constitution is, in fact, and must be regarded by the judges, a fundamental law. It therefore belongs to them to ascertain its meaning as well as the meaning of any particular act or proceeding from the legislative body. If there should happen to be an irreconcilable variance between the two, that which has the superior obligation and validity ought of course to be preferred; or, in other words, the Constitution ought to be preferred to the statute, the intention of the people to the intention of their agents. *The Federalist,* No. 78, Lodge Ed., pp. 485–86.

Separation of Powers

Another fundamental principle on which our government is founded is that of separation of powers. As incorporated in our Constitution this means that there are three distinct and independent branches of government, consisting of the executive, legislative, and judicial branches (see Figure 3–2). The purpose of the doctrine of separation of powers is to prevent the concentration of excessive power in any group or branch of government. Basically, the legislative branch is granted the power to make the law, the executive branch to enforce the law, and the judicial branch to interpret the law. The separation of powers is not complete, however, and in some instances two or more branches share power. For example, the executive branch has veto power over legislation enacted by Congress; the legislative branch must approve a great number of executive appointments; and the judicial branch may declare both legislation and executive actions unconstitutional. Nevertheless, where this occurs, the shared powers usually operate as a check and balance on the power of each branch.

State Action

Most of the protections provided by the U.S. Constitution and its amendments apply only to governmental action, Federal or State, collectively referred to as state action. Only the Thirteenth Amendment, which abolishes slavery or involuntary servitude, applies to the actions of private individuals. These other protections may be extended, however, by *statute* to apply to private activity. **State action** includes any actions of the Federal and State governments, as well as their subdivisions, such as city or county governments and agencies. For example, when a legislature, executive officer, or a court takes some official action against an individual, there has been state action.

Additionally, action taken by private citizens may constitute state action if an arm of the state is used to effect the action. For example, the Supreme Court found state action when the Supreme Court of Missouri ordered a lower court to enforce an agreement among white property owners that prohibited the transfer of their property to nonwhites. *Shelley v. Kraemer*, 334 U.S. 1 (1948). Moreover, if "private" individuals or entities engage in public functions, their actions may be considered state action subject to constitutional limitations. For example, in *Marsh v. Alabama*, 326 U.S. 501 (1946), it was held that a company town was subject to the First Amendment because the State had allowed the company to exercise all of the public functions and activities that usually were conducted by a town government. Since that case the Supreme Court has been less willing to find state action based upon private entities performing public functions, now limiting it to those functions "traditionally exclusively reserved to the State." For instance, in *Jackson v. Metropolitan Edison Co.*, 419 U.S. 345 (1974), the Court held that a privately owned electric utility was *not* subject to the due process clause because operating a utility is not state action even though the utility had been granted a monopoly by the State. In reaching this conclusion the Court held that the fact that the State could have operated its own

utilities did not make the activity of providing electric services state action. Also, *see National Collegiate Athletics Ass'n. v. Tarkanian.*

POWERS OF GOVERNMENT

As previously stated, the U.S. Constitution created a Federal government of enumerated powers. Moreover, as the Tenth Amendment declares, "the powers not delegated to the United States by the Constitution, nor prohibited by it to the States, are reserved to the States respectively, or to the people." Consequently, legislation enacted by Congress must be based on a specified power granted to the Federal government by the Constitution or be reasonably necessary for carrying out an enumerated power.

This part of the chapter examines the sources and extent of the powers of the Federal government—as well as the residual power of the States—to regulate business and commerce.

Federal Commerce Power

The U.S. Constitution provides that "The Congress shall have Power . . . To regulate Commerce with foreign Nations, and among the several States . . ." Article I, Section 8. This commerce clause has two important effects: (1) it is a broad source of power for the Federal government to regulate the economy and (2) it operates as a restriction upon State regulations that obstruct or unduly burden interstate commerce. As the U.S. Supreme Court has stated: "The Clause is both a prolific sourc[e] of national power and an equally prolific source of conflict with legislation of the state[s]." This section will discuss the first of these effects; the next section will discuss the second effect.

The U.S. Supreme Court interprets the commerce clause as granting virtually complete power to Congress to regulate the economy and business. A court may invalidate legislation enacted under the commerce clause only if it is clear either (1) that there is no rational basis for a congressional finding that the regulated activity affects interstate commerce or (2) that there is no reasonable connection between the regulatory means selected and the asserted ends.

The civil rights case of *Katzenbach v. McClung,* 379 U.S. 294 (1964), illustrates the operation of this test. The McClungs owned Ollie's Barbecue, a restaurant located a few blocks from the interstate highway in Birmingham, Alabama, with dining accommodations for whites only and a take-out service for blacks. In the year preceding the passage of the Civil Rights Act of 1964, the restaurant had purchased a substantial portion of the food it served from outside the State. The restaurant had refused to serve blacks since its original opening in 1927 and asserted that if it were required to serve blacks, it would lose much of its business. The McClungs argued that the application of the Civil Rights Act to their restaurant was unconstitutional since their admitted racial discrimination did not restrict nor significantly impede interstate commerce. The Supreme Court upheld the constitutionality of the act. The Court stated that the commerce clause of the Constitution empowers Congress to regulate interstate commerce and to make all laws necessary and proper for that purpose. Even if a business' activity is local it may be reached by Congress if the activity directly or indirectly burdens or obstructs interstate commerce. Title II of the Civil Rights Act passed by Congress in 1964 prohibits racial discrimination in a restaurant if it serves or offers to serve interstate travelers or if a substantial portion of the food it serves has moved in interstate commerce.

Because of the broad and permissive interpretation of the commerce power, Congress currently regulates a vast range of activities. Many of the activities discussed in this text are regulated by the Federal government based on the commerce power, including Federal crimes, consumer warranties, consumer credit transactions, electronic fund transfers, trademarks, unfair trade practices, consumer transactions, residential real estate transactions, consumer safety, employee safety, labor relations, civil rights in employment, and transactions in securities.

State Regulation of Commerce

The commerce clause, as previously discussed, specifically grants to Congress the power to regulate commerce among the States. In addition to acting as a broad source of Federal power, the clause also implicitly restricts the States' power to regulate activities if the result obstructs or unduly burdens interstate commerce.

Regulations The Supreme Court ultimately decides the extent of permissible State regulation affecting interstate commerce. In doing so, the Court weighs and balances several factors: (1) the necessity and importance of the State regulation, (2) the burden it imposes upon interstate commerce, and (3) the extent to which it discriminates against interstate commerce in favor of local concerns. The application of these factors involves case-by-case analysis.

Taxation The commerce clause in conjunction with the import-export clause also limits the power of the States to tax. The import-export clause provides: "No State shall, without the Consent of the Congress, lay any Imposts or Duties on Imports or Exports." Article I, Section 10. Together, the commerce clause and the import-export clause exempt from State taxation goods that have entered the stream of commerce, whether they are interstate or foreign and whether as imports or exports. The purpose of this immunity is to protect goods in commerce from both discriminatory and cumulative State taxes. Once the goods enter the stream of interstate or foreign commerce, the power of the State to tax ceases and does not resume until the goods are delivered to the purchaser or the owner terminates the movement of the goods through interstate or foreign commerce.

The due process clause of the Fourteenth Amendment also restricts the power of States to tax. Under the due process clause, for a State tax to be consitutional, there must be sufficient nexus between the State and the person, thing, or activity to be taxed.

Federal Fiscal Powers

The Federal government exerts a dominating influence over the national economy through its control of financial matters. Much of this impact, as previously discussed, results from the exercise of its regulatory powers under the commerce clause. In addition, a substantial portion of its influence derives from powers arising independent of the commerce clause. These include (1) the power to tax, (2) the power to spend, (3) the power to borrow and coin money, and (4) the power of eminent domain.

Taxation   The Federal government's power to tax, although extremely broad, is subject to three major limitations: (1) direct taxes other than income taxes must be apportioned among the States, (2) all custom duties and excise taxes must be uniform throughout the United States, and (3) no duties may be levied upon exports from any State.

Besides raising revenues, taxes also have regulatory and socioeconomic effects. For example, import taxes and custom duties can protect domestic industry from foreign competition. Graduated or progressive tax rates and exemptions may further social policies of redistributing wealth. Tax credits encourage investment in favored enterprises to the disadvantage of unfavored businesses. Even though a tax does more than just raise revenue, it will be upheld "so long as the motive of Congress and the effect of its legislative action are to secure revenue for the benefit of the general government. . . ." *J.W. Hampton Co. v. United States*, 276 U.S. 394 (1928).

Spending Power   The Constitution authorizes the Federal government to pay debts and spend for the common defense and general welfare of the United States. Article I, Section 8. The spending power of Congress is extremely broad and will be upheld so long as it does not violate a specific constitutional limitation upon Federal power.

Furthermore, through its spending power, Congress may accomplish indirectly what it may not do directly. For example, in *South Dakota v. Dole*, 483 U.S. 203 (1987), the Supreme Court held that Congress could condition a State's receipt of Federal highway funds on that State's mandating twenty-one as the minimum drinking age, even though the Twenty-first Amendment grants the States significant powers with respect to alcohol consumption within their respective borders. As the Court noted, "Constitutional limitations on Congress when exercising its spending power are less exacting than those on its authority to regulate directly."

The power to spend is an important way in which the Federal government regulates the economy. In some cases this is accomplished directly as the level and type of government expenditure has a significant impact upon economic cycles and activity. More indirectly, as shown by the *Dole* case, governmental appropriations may be conditioned upon recipients of Federal grants engaging in, or refraining from, specified conduct. Whether directly or indirectly, the power of the Federal government to spend money represents an important regulatory force in the economy and significantly affects the general welfare of the United States.

Borrowing and Coining Money   The U.S. Constitution also grants Congress the power to borrow money on the credit of the United States and to coin money. Article I, Section 8. These two powers have enabled the Federal government to establish a national banking system, the Federal Reserve System, and specialized Federal lending programs such as the Federal Land Bank. Through these and other institutions and agencies, the Federal government wields extensive control over national fiscal and monetary policies and exerts considerable influence over interest rates, the money supply, and foreign exchange rates.

Eminent Domain   The government's power to take private property for public use, known as the power of eminent domain, is recognized as one of the inherent powers of government in the Federal Constitution and in the constitutions of the States. At the same time, however, the power is carefully limited. The Fifth

Amendment to the Federal Constitution contains a "takings clause" that provides: "nor shall private property be taken for public use, without just compensation." Although this amendment applies only to the Federal government, the Supreme Court has held that the takings clause is incorporated through the Fourteenth Amendment and is therefore applicable to the States. Moreover, similar or identical provisions are found in the constitutions of the States.

As the language of the takings clause indicates, the taking must be for a public use. Public use has been interpreted to be synonymous with public purpose. Thus, private entities, such as railroads and housing authorities, may utilize the government's power of eminent domain so long as the entity's use of the property benefits the public. When the government or a private entity properly takes property under the power of eminent domain, the owners of the property must receive just compensation, which has been interpreted as the fair market value of the property.

The Supreme Court has held that the takings clause requires just compensation only if there is a governmental taking of property and not if there is a mere reduction in value because of governmental regulation. If, however, a regulation deprives the owner of all economic use of property, then there has been a taking. Eminent domain is discussed further in Chapter 51.

LIMITATIONS UPON GOVERNMENT

The Constitution of the United States enumerates certain powers which are granted to the Federal government. Other powers, without enumeration, have been reserved to the States. The Constitution and its amendments, however, impose limits on the powers of both the Federal government and the States. This part of the chapter will discuss those limitations most applicable to business: (1) the contract clause, (2) the First Amendment, (3) due process, and (4) equal protection.

None of these restrictions operates as an absolute limitation but instead triggers scrutiny by the courts to determine whether the governmental power exercised encroaches impermissibly upon the interest protected by the Constitution. The U.S. Supreme Court has used different levels of scrutiny depending on the interest affected and the nature of the governmental action. Although the differentiation among levels of scrutiny has been most fully developed in the area of equal protection, it also occurs in other areas including substantive due process and protection of free speech.

The least rigorous level of scrutiny is the **rational relationship test**, which requires that the legislation conceivably bear some rational relationship to a legitimate governmental interest furthered by the legislation. The most exacting level of scrutiny is the **strict scrutiny test**, which requires that the legislation be necessary to promote a compelling governmental interest. Finally, under the **intermediate test,** the legislation must have a substantial relationship to an important governmental objective. These standards will be more fully explained below. (Also see Figure 3–1.)

Contract Clause

Article I, Section 10, of the Constitution provides: "No State shall . . . pass any . . . Law impairing the Obligation of Contracts. . . ." The Supreme Court has used this clause to restrict States from retroactively modifying public charters and private contracts. For example, the contract clause protects the charter of a corporation formed under a State incorporation statute against impairment.

To avoid the restrictions of the contract clause, State incorporation and other enabling statutes commonly reserve to the State the power to prescribe such regulations, provisions, and limitations as it shall deem advisable, and to amend, repeal, or modify the statute at its pleasure. Because such reservations are actually written into the contract between the State and the other party, any amendment or modification does not impair the obligation of contract because it was expressly permitted by the contract or charter.

Figure 3–1 Limitations upon Government

Test/Interest	Equal Protection	Substantive Due Process	Free Speech
Strict Scrutiny	Fundamental Rights Suspect Classifications	Fundamental Rights	Protected Noncommercial Speech
Intermediate	Gender Legitimacy Citizenship		Commercial Speech
Rational Relationship	Economic Regulation	Economic Regulation	Nonprotected Speech

---

Moreover, the Supreme Court has held that the contract clause does **not** preclude the States from exercising eminent domain or their police powers. As the Supreme Court stated: "No legislature can bargain away the public health or the public morals." *Stone v. Mississippi,* 101 U.S. (11 Otto) 814 (1879).

Because State enabling statutes typically provide for amendment and because States retain police powers, the contract clause had seemed to lose most of its significance. Two decisions in the late 1970s, however, suggested that the Supreme Court was reviving the contract clause. In *United States Trust Company v. New Jersey,* 431 U.S. 1 (1977), the Supreme Court held that New Jersey could not retroactively alter a statutory covenant relied on by bond purchasers because it was not "reasonable and necessary to serve an important public purpose." In the following year, the Supreme Court invalidated a Minnesota statute that required certain private employers to pay a pension funding charge if they terminated a pension plan or closed a Minnesota office even though such charge was inconsistent with the employers' obligations under their private pension plans. *Allied Structural Steel Co. v. Spannus,* 438 U.S. 234 (1978). Since these two decisions, however, the Court has generally been unwilling to use the contract clause to invalidate State economic regulation with respect to private contracts, where the legislation reasonably promotes a significant and legitimate public purpose that justifies the impairment of the contractual obligation.

First Amendment

The First Amendment states:

Congress shall make no law respecting an establishment of religion, or prohibiting the free exercise thereof; or abridging the freedom of speech, or of the press; or the right of the people peaceably to assemble, and to petition the Government for a redress of grievances.

The First Amendment's protection of free speech is not absolute. Some forms of speech, such as obscenity, receive no protection. Most forms of speech, however, are protected by strict or exacting scrutiny to determine whether a compelling and legitimate state interest exists. If so, then to achieve this purpose, the legislature must use means that are the least restrictive of free speech. This section will examine the application of the First Amendment's guarantee of free speech to (1) corporate political speech, (2) commercial speech, and (3) defamation.

Corporate Political Speech Freedom of speech is indispensable to the discovery and spread of political truth and "the best test of truth is the power of the thought to get itself accepted in the competition of the market." *Abrams v. United States,* 250 U.S. 616 (1919) (Holmes' dissent). To promote this competition of ideas, the First Amendment's guarantee of free speech applies not only to individuals but also to corporations. Accordingly, corporations may not be prohibited from speaking out on political issues. In *First National Bank v. Bellotti,* 435 U.S. 765 (1978), the Supreme Court held unconstitutional a Massachusetts criminal statute that prohibited banks and business corporations from making contributions and expenditures on most referenda issues. The Court in *Bellotti* held that if speech is otherwise protected, the fact that the speaker is a corporation does not alter the speech's protected status.

Commercial Speech   Commercial speech is expression related to the economic interests of the speaker and its audience, such as advertisements of a product or service. Within the past decade, U.S. Supreme Court decisions have eliminated the doctrine that commercial speech is wholly outside the protection of the First Amendment. Instead the Court has established the principle that speech that does no more than propose a commercial transaction is entitled to a "lesser degree" of constitutional protection. Protection is accorded commercial speech because of interest in the communication by the advertiser, consumer, and general public. Advertising and other such messages provide important information for the proper and efficient distribution of resources in our free market system. At the same time, commercial speech is less valuable and less vulnerable than other varieties of speech and therefore does not merit complete First Amendment protection.

In commercial speech cases, a four-part analysis has developed. First, the court must determine whether the expression is protected by the First Amendment. For commercial speech to come within that provision, it at least must concern lawful activity and not be misleading. Second, the court must determine whether the asserted governmental interest is substantial. If both inquiries yield positive answers, then, third, the court must determine whether the regulation directly advances the governmental interest asserted, and, fourth, whether it is not more extensive than is necessary to serve that interest.

Because the constitutional protection extended to commercial speech is based upon the informational function of advertising, governments may regulate or suppress commercial messages that do not accurately inform the public about lawful activity. "The government may ban forms of communication more likely to deceive the public than to inform it, or commercial speech related to illegal activity." *Central Hudson Gas and Electric Corp. v. Public Service Commission,* 447 U.S. 557 (1980). Therefore, governmental regulation of false and misleading advertising is permissible under the First Amendment.

Defamation   Defamation is a civil wrong or tort consisting of a false communication that injures a person's reputation by disgracing the person and diminishing the respect in which the person is held. An example would be the publication of a statement that a person had committed a crime or had a loathsome disease. For a discussion of defamation see Chapter 5.

Because defamation involves a communication, the protection extended to speech by the First Amendment applies. The case of *New York Times Co. v. Sullivan,* 376 U.S. 254 (1964), held that a public official who was defamed in regard to his conduct, fitness, or role as public official may *not* recover in an action of defamation unless the statement was made with *actual malice,* which requires clear and convincing proof that the defendant had knowledge of the falsity of the communication or acted in reckless disregard of its truth or falsity. This restriction upon the right to recover for defamation is based upon "a profound national commitment to the principle that debate on public issues should be uninhibited, robust and wide-open, and that it may well include vehement, caustic and sometimes unpleasantly sharp attacks on government and public officials." The communication may deal with the official's qualifications for and his performance in office, which would likely include most aspects of character and public conduct.

In addition, the Supreme Court has extended the same rule to candidates for public office and public figures. The court, however, has not precisely defined the term "public figure." Examples of persons held to be public figures include a well-known football coach of a State university and a retired army general who had taken a prominent and controversial position regarding racial segregation. In *Gertz v. Robert Welch, Inc.,* 418 U.S. 323 (1974), the Court has explained:

For the most part [public figures are] those who attain this status [by assuming] roles of especial prominence in the affairs of society. Some occupy positions of such persuasive power and influence that they are deemed public figures for all purposes. More commonly, those classed as public figures have thrust themselves to the forefront of particular public controversies in order to influence the resolution of the issues involved.

Thus, the public official or public figure must prove that the defendant published the defamatory and false comment about him with knowledge or in reckless disregard of the comment's falsity and its defamatory character. In a defamation suit brought by a private person (one who is not a public official and is not a public figure) against a member of the news media, the plaintiff must prove that the defendant published the defamatory and false comment with malice *or* negligence. Where a private person brings suit against a defendant who is *not* a member of the news media, it is currently unresolved whether the plaintiff must prove anything beyond the fact that a defamatory statement had been made.

Due Process

The Fifth and Fourteenth Amendments prohibit the Federal and State governments, respectively, from depriving any person of life, liberty, or property without due process of law. Due process has two different aspects: *substantive* due process and *procedural* due process. As discussed in Chapter 1, substantive law creates, defines, or regulates legal rights whereas procedural law establishes the rules for enforcing rights created by the substantive law. Accordingly, **substantive due process** concerns the compatibility of a law or governmental action with fundamental constitutional rights such as free speech. In contrast, **procedural due process** involves the review of the decision-making process that enforces substantive laws and results in depriving a person of life, liberty, or property.

Substantive Due Process   Substantive due process involves a court's determination of whether a particular governmental action is compatible with individual liberties. Substantive due process addresses the constitutionality of the substance of a legal rule, not the fairness of the process by which the rule is applied. From 1885 until 1937, the Supreme Court viewed substantive due process as authorizing it to act as a "super legislature" and enabling it to invalidate any law it considered unwise. Since 1937, the Court has abandoned this approach and no longer overturns legislation affecting economic and social interests, so long as the legislation is rationally related to legitimate governmental objectives. This drastic shift has been explained as follows:

Legislative bodies have broad scope to experiment with economic problems, and this Court does not sit to "subject the State to an intolerable supervision hostile to the basic principles of our Government and wholly beyond the protection which the general clause of the Fourteenth Amendment was intended to secure." *Ferguson v. Skrupa,* 372 U.S. 726 (1963).

Where fundamental rights of individuals under the Constitution are affected, however, the Court will carefully scrutinize the legislation to determine that it is necessary to promote a compelling or overriding state interest. Included among the fundamental rights that trigger the strict scrutiny standard of substantive due process are (1) the First Amendment rights of freedom of speech, religion, press, peaceful assembly, and petition; (2) the right to engage in interstate travel; (3) the right to vote; (4) the right to privacy; and (5) the right to marry.

Procedural Due Process   Procedural due process pertains to the governmental decision-making process that results in depriving a person of life, liberty, or property. As the Supreme Court has interpreted procedural due process, the government is required to provide persons with a fair procedure if, but only if, the person is faced with deprivation of life, liberty, or property. When governmental action adversely affects an individual but does not deny life, liberty, or property, the government is not required to give the person any hearing at all.

Liberty, for the purposes of procedural due process, generally includes the ability of individuals to engage in freedom of action and choice regarding their personal lives. Any significant physical restraint constitutes a deprivation of liberty which requires procedural safeguards. The most important and common example is criminal proceedings. Chapter 4 discusses these proceedings more fully. In addition, civil proceedings which result in depriving a person of freedom of action are also subject to the requirements of procedural due process. Liberty also includes an individual's right to engage in the fundamental rights described above.

Property, for the purposes of procedural due process, includes not only all forms of real and personal property but also certain entitlements conferred by government, such as social security payments and food stamps. In *Logan v. Zimmerman Brush Co.,* 455 U.S. 422 (1982), the Supreme Court stated: "The hallmark of property . . . is an individual entitlement grounded in state law, which cannot be removed except 'for cause.' " Under this interpretation of property, the Court has, for example, found protected property interests in high school education when attendance is required, welfare benefits when the individual has previously been found to meet the statutory requirements, social security payments, and a driver's license. On the other hand, if a public employee's job is terminable at any time, he has no property interest in his employment and accordingly may lose his job without any procedural due process protections at all.

When applicable, procedural due process requires that the procedure be fundamentally fair and impartial in the resolution of the factual and legal basis for the governmental actions which result in the deprivation of life, liberty, or property. The Supreme Court generally considers three factors in determining which procedures are required: the importance of the individual interest involved; the adequacy of the existing procedural protections and the probable value, if any, of additional safeguards; and the governmental interest in fiscal and administrative efficiency. In this regard see *Board of Curators of the University of Missouri v. Horowitz.*

Equal Protection

The Fourteenth Amendment states that "nor shall any State . . . deny to any person within its jurisdiction the equal protection of the laws." Although this amendment applies only to the actions of State governments, the Supreme Court has interpreted the due process clause of the Fifth Amendment to subject Federal actions to the same standards of review. Basically, the guarantee of equal protection requires that similarly situated persons be treated similarly by governmental actions. Since 1937, when the Supreme Court abandoned substantive due process as a critical check on legislation, the equal protection guarantee has become the most important constitutional concept protecting individual rights. When governmental action involves classification of people, the equal protection guarantee comes into play. In determining whether legislation satisfies the equal protection guarantee, the Supreme Court uses one of three standards of review, depending on the nature of the right involved. The three standards are: (1) the rational relationship test, (2) the strict scrutiny test, or (3) the intermediate test.

Rational Relationship Test The rational relationship test applies to economic legislation and requires that it be *conceivable* that the legislation bears some rational relationship to a legitimate governmental interest furthered by the legislation. Under this standard of review, the legislature is permitted to attack part of the evil to which the legislation is addressed. Moreover, there is a strong presumption that the legislation is constitutional. Therefore, the courts will overturn the legislation *only* if clear and convincing evidence shows that there is *no* reasonable basis justifying the legislation.

For example, in *Minnesota v. Clover Leaf Creamery Co.*, 449 U.S. 456 (1981), a Minnesota statute banning the retail sale of milk in plastic nonreturnable, nonrefillable containers, but permitting such sale in other nonreturnable, nonrefillable containers, such as paperboard milk cartons, was attacked as violating the equal protection clause. It was stipulated by the parties that the purposes of the statute cited by the legislature—promoting resource conservation, easing solid waste disposal problems, and conserving energy—were legitimate State purposes. The Court upheld the statute because those challenging it failed to "convince the court that the legislative facts on which the classification is apparently based could not reasonably be conceived to be true by the governmental decision maker."

Strict Scrutiny Test The strict scrutiny test is far more exacting than the rational relationship test. Under this test the courts do not defer to the legislature; rather they independently determine whether the classification is constitutionally permissible. This determination requires that the legislature's classification is necessary to promote a compelling or overriding governmental interest.

The strict scrutiny test is applied when the legislation affects fundamental rights or involves suspect classifications. Fundamental rights include most of the provisions of the Bill of Rights. Suspect classifications include those made on the basis of race or national origin. A classic and important example of strict scrutiny of classifications based upon race is the 1954 school desegregation case in which the Supreme Court ruled that segregated public school systems violated the equal protection guarantee. *See Brown v. Board of Education of Topeka.* Subsequently, the Court invalidated segre-

gation in public beaches, municipal golf courses, buses, parks, public golf courses, and courtroom seating.

Another important example of strict scrutiny is the "one person, one vote" rule based upon the fundamental right to vote. Chief Justice Warren formulated the rule as follows:

Legislators represent people, not trees or acres. . . . And, if a State should provide that the votes of citizens in one part of the State should be given two times, or five times, or ten times the weight of votes of citizens in another part of the State, it could hardly be contended that the right to vote of those residing in the disfavored areas had not been effectively diluted . . . the Equal Protection Clause requires that the seats in both houses of a bicameral state legislature must be apportioned on a population basis. *Reynolds v. Sims,* 377 U.S. 533 (1964).

Intermediate Test An intermediate test applies to legislation based on gender, legitimacy, and usually alienage (citizenship). Under this test, the legislation must have a substantial relationship to an important governmental objective. The intermediate standard eliminates the strong presumption of constitutionality adhered to by the rational relationship test.

For example, in *Orr v. Orr,* 440 U.S. 268 (1979), the Court invalidated an Alabama law that allowed courts to grant alimony awards only from husbands to wives and not from wives to husbands. Similarly, in *Reed v. Reed,* 404 U.S. 71 (1971), an Idaho statute gave preference to males over females in qualifying for selection as administrators of estates. The Court invalidated the statute because the preference did not bear a fair and substantial relationship to any legitimate objective of the legislation. On the other hand, not all legislation based upon gender is invalid. For example, the Court has upheld a California statutory rape law which imposed penalties only upon males as well as the Federal military selective service act which exempted women from registering for the draft.

ADMINISTRATIVE LAW

Administrative law is the branch of public law that governs the powers and procedures of administrative agencies, as well as judicial review of agency action. **Administrative agencies** are governmental entities—other than courts and legislatures—having authority to affect the rights of private parties through their operations. Administrative agencies are referred to by various names such as commission, board, department, agency, administration, government corporation, bureau, or office. These agencies regulate a vast array of important matters of national safety, welfare, and convenience. For instance, Federal administrative agencies are charged with responsibility for national security, citizenship and naturalization, law enforcement, taxation, currency, elections, environmental protection, consumer protection, regulation of transportation, telecommunications, labor relations, trade, commerce, and securities markets, as well as providing health and social services.

Because of the increasing complexity of the social, economic, and industrial life of the nation, the scope of administrative law has expanded enormously. Justice Jackson stated that "the rise of administrative bodies has been the most significant legal trend of the last century, and perhaps more values today are affected by their decisions than by those of all the courts, review of administrative decisions apart." *Federal Trade Commission v. Ruberoid Co.,* 343 U.S. 470 (1952). This observation is even more true today, as evidenced by the great increase in the number and activities of Federal government boards, commissions, and other agencies. Certainly, agencies create more legal rules and adjudicate more controversies than all the legislatures and all the courts combined.

State agencies also play a significant role in the functioning of our society. Among the more important boards and commissions in the States are those supervising and regulating banking, insurance, communications, transportation, public utilities, pollution control, and workers' compensation.

Much of Federal, State, and local law in this country is established by the countless administrative agencies. These agencies, which many label the "fourth branch of government," possess tremendous power and have long been criticized as being "in reality miniature independent governments. . . [which are] a haphazard deposit of irresponsible agencies. . . ." 1937 Presidential Task Force Report.

Despite this criticism against administrative regulations, it is clear that these agencies play a significant and necessary role in our society. Administrative agencies serve the important function of relieving legislatures from the impossible burden of fashioning legislation which deals with every detail of the specific problem addressed. As a result, Congress can enact legislation, such as the Federal Trade Commission Act, which prohibits unfair and deceptive trade practices, without having to define this phrase or anticipate all the particular problems that may arise. Instead, Congress enacts an **enabling statute** that creates an agency—in this example, the Federal Trade Commission—to which it can delegate the power to issue rules, regulations, and guidelines to carry out the statutory mandate. In addition, the establishment of separate, specialized bodies enables administrative agencies to be staffed by individuals with expertise in the field being regulated. Administrative agencies can thus develop the knowledge and devote the time necessary to provide continuous and flexible solutions to evolving regulatory problems.

In this section of the chapter Federal administrative agencies will be discussed. Federal administrative agencies can be classified as either independent or executive. Executive agencies are those agencies housed within the executive branch of government, while independent agencies are not. Many Federal agencies are discussed in other parts of the text. More specifically, the Federal Trade Commission (FTC) and Department of Justice are discussed in Chapter 42; the FTC and the Consumer Product Safety Commission in Chapter 43; the Department of Labor, National Labor Relations Board (NLRB), and Equal Employment Opportunity Commission (EEOC) in Chapter 44; and the Securities and Exchange Commission (SEC) in Chapters 45 and 46.

OPERATION OF ADMINISTRATIVE AGENCIES

Most administrative agencies perform three basic functions: (1) to make rules, (2) to enforce the law, and (3) to adjudicate controversies. The term **administrative process** refers to the entire set of activities in which administrative agencies engage while carrying out their rulemaking, enforcement, and adjudicative functions. Administrative agencies exercise powers that have been allocated by the Constitution to the three separate branches of government. More specifically, agencies exercise legislative power when they make rules, executive power when they enforce the statute and their rules, and judicial power when they adjudicate disputes. This concentration of power has raised questions regarding the propriety of having the same bodies which establish the rules also act as prosecutor and judge in determining whether the rules have been violated. To address this issue and bring about certain additional procedural reforms, the Administrative Procedure Act (APA) was enacted in 1946.

Rulemaking

Rulemaking is the process by which an administrative agency enacts or promulgates rules of law. Under the APA, a rule is "the whole or a part of an agency statement of general or particular applicability and future effect designed to implement, interpret, or process law or policy." Section 551(4). Once promulgated, rules are applicable to all parties. Moreover, the process of rulemaking puts all parties on notice that the impending rule is being considered and provides concerned individuals with an opportunity to be heard. Three types of rules are promulgated

by administrative agencies: legislative rules, interpretative rules, and procedural rules.

Legislative Rules Legislative rules, often called regulations, are in effect "administrative statutes." **Legislative rules** are those issued by an agency under a legislative delegation of power to make rules having the force and effect of law. For example, the FTC has rulemaking power to elaborate its enabling statute's prohibition of unfair or deceptive acts or practices. Legislative rules are immediately binding and generally receive greater deference from reviewing courts than do interpretative rules.

Legislative rules have the force of law if they are constitutional, within the power granted to the agency by the legislature, and issued according to proper procedure. To be constitutional, regulations must not violate any provisions of the U.S. Constitution, such as due process or equal protection. In addition, they may not involve an unconstitutional delegation of legislative power from the legislature to the agency. To be constitutionally permissible, the enabling statute granting power to an agency must establish reasonable standards guiding the agency in implementing the statute. This requirement has been met by statutory language such as "to prohibit unfair methods of competition," "fair and equitable," "public interest, convenience, and necessity," and other equally broad expressions. In any event, agencies may not exceed the actual authority granted by the enabling statute. See *F.C.C. v. Midwest Video Corp.*

Legislative rules must be promulgated in accordance with the procedural requirements of the APA, although the enabling statute may impose more stringent requirements. Most legislative rules are issued in accordance with the **informal** rulemaking procedures of the APA, which require that the agency provide:

1. prior notice of a proposed rule, usually by publication in the Federal Register;

2. an opportunity for interested parties to participate in the rulemaking; and

3. publication of a final draft containing a concise general statement of its basis and purpose at least thirty days before the rule's effective date. Section 553.

In some instances the enabling statute requires that certain rules be made only after the opportunity for an agency hearing. This formal rulemaking procedure is far more complex than the informal procedures and is governed by the same provisions of the APA as is an adjudication, discussed below. In **formal** rulemaking, the agency must base its rules upon consideration of the record of the trial-type agency hearing and include a statement of "findings and conclusions, and the reasons or basis therefore, on all the material issues of fact, law, or discretion presented on the record." Section 557(c).

Some enabling statutes direct that in making rules the agency use some procedures beyond informal rulemaking but do not require the full hearing required by formal rulemaking. This intermediate procedure has become known as **hybrid rulemaking** and results from combining the informal procedures of the APA with the additional procedures specified by the enabling statute. For example, an agency may be required to conduct a legislative-type hearing (formal) but with no cross-examination permitted (informal).

Interpretative Rules Interpretative rules are statements issued by an agency that explain how the agency construes its governing statute. For instance, the Securities and Exchange Commission "renders administrative interpretations of the law and regulations thereunder to members of the public, prospective registrants and others, to help them decide legal questions about the application of the law and the regulations to particular situations and to aid them in complying with the law." *The Work of the SEC* (1980).

Interpretative rules, which are exempt from the APA's procedural requirements of notice and comment, are *not* automatically binding on private parties regulated by the agency or on the courts, although they are given substantial weight. As the Supreme Court has stated, "the weight of such [an interpretative rule] in a particular case will depend upon the thoroughness evident in its consideration, the validity of its reasoning, its consistency with earlier and later pronouncements, and all those factors which give it power to persuade. . . ." *Skidmore v. Swift & Co.*, 323 U.S. 134 (1944).

Procedural Rules Procedural rules are also exempt from the notice and comment requirements of the APA and are not law. These rules establish rules of conduct for practice before the agency, identify an agency's organization, and describe its method of operation. For example, the Securities and Exchange Commission's Rules of Practice deal with such matters as who may appear before the commission; business hours, notice of proceedings and hearings; settlements, agreements, and conferences; presentation of evidence and taking of depositions and interrogatories; and review of hearings.

Enforcement

Agencies also investigate conduct to determine whether the statute or the agency's legislative rules have been violated. In carrying out this executive function the agencies have traditionally been accorded great discretion to compel the disclosure of information, subject to constitutional limitations. These limitations require that (1) the investigation is authorized by law and undertaken for a legitimate purpose, (2) the information sought is relevant, (3) the demand for information is sufficiently specific and not unreasonably burdensome, and (4) the information sought is not privileged.

For example, the following explains some of the investigating and enforcement functions of the Securities and Exchange Commission:

Most of the Commission's investigations are conducted privately, the facts being developed to the fullest extent possible through informal inquiry, interviewing of witnesses, examination of brokerage records and other documents, reviewing and trading data and similar means. The Commission however, is empowered to issue subpoenas requiring sworn testimony and the production of books, records and other documents pertinent to the subject matter under investigation; in the event of refusal to respond to a subpoena, the Commission may apply to a Federal court for an order compelling obedience thereto. *The Work of the SEC* (1980).

Adjudication

After concluding an investigation the agency may use informal or formal methods to resolve the matter. Since the caseload of administrative agencies is vast and greatly outnumbers that of the judicial system, most matters are informally adjudicated. Informal procedures include advising, negotiating, and settling.

The formal procedure by which an agency resolves a matter (called **adjudication**) involves finding facts, applying legal rules to the facts, and formulating orders. An **order** "means the whole or a part of a final disposition, whether affirmative, negative, injunctive or declaratory in form, of an agency." APA Section 551(6). Adjudication is in essence an administrative trial and is used when required by the enabling statute.

The procedures employed by the various administrative agencies to adjudicate cases are nearly as varied as the agencies themselves. Nevertheless, the APA does establish certain standards which must be followed by those Federal agencies covered by the Act. Notice must be given of the hearing. The APA also requires that the agency give all interested parties the opportunity to submit and consider "facts, arguments, offers of settlement, or proposals of adjustment." Section 554(c). In many cases this involves testimony and cross-examination of witnesses. If no settlement is reached, then a hearing must be held.

The hearing is presided over by an administrative law judge (ALJ) and is prosecuted by the agency. ALJs are appointed by the agency through a professional merit selection system and may be removed only for good cause. There are more than twice as many administrative law judges as there are Federal judges. Juries are never used. Thus, the agency serves as both the prosecutor and decision maker. In order to reduce this conflict of interest, the APA provides for the separation of functions between those engaged in investigation and prosecution from those involved in decision making. Section 544(d).

Oral and documentary evidence may be introduced by either party. All sanctions, rules, and orders must be based upon "consideration of the whole record or those parts cited by a party and supported by and in accordance with the reliable, probative, and substantial evidence." Section 556(d). All decisions must include a statement of findings of fact and conclusions of law and the reasons or basis for them as well as a statement of the appropriate rule, order, sanction, or relief.

If authorized by law and within the jurisdiction delegated to an agency, it may impose in its orders, sanctions such as penalties; fines; seizing property; assessing damages, restitution, compensation, or fees; and requiring, revoking, or suspending a license. Sections 551(10) and 558(b). In most instances orders are final unless appealed, and failure to comply with an order is subject to a statutory penalty. If the order is appealed, the governing body of the agency may decide the case *de novo*. Section 557(b). Thus, the agency may hear additional evidence and arguments in deciding whether to revise the findings and conclusions in the initial decision.

Although administrative adjudications mirror to a large extent the procedures of judicial trials, there are many differences between the two. "Agency hearings tend to produce evidence of general conditions as distinguished from facts relating solely to the respondent. Administrative agencies more consciously formulate policy by adjudicating (and rulemaking) than do courts. Consequently, administrative adjudications may require that the administrative law judge consider more consciously the impact of his decision upon the public interest as well as upon the particular respondent. . . . Even more important is the fact that an administrative hearing is tried to an *administrative law judge* and never to a *jury*. Since many of the rules governing the admission of proof in judicial trials are designed to protect the jury from unreliable and possibly confusing evidence, the rules need not be applied with the same vigor in proceedings solely before an administrative law judge. The administrative judge decides both the facts and the law to be applied." *McCormick on Evidence*, 3d ed., Section 350, p. 1005.

LIMITS ON ADMINISTRATIVE AGENCIES

An important and fundamental part of administrative law is the limits imposed by judicial review upon the activities of administrative agencies. Courts, however, are not supposed to substitute their judgment on matters of policy for the agency's judgment. Additional limitations arise from the legislature and the executive branch, which, unlike the judiciary, may address the wisdom and correctness of an agency's decision or action.

Judicial Review

Judicial review acts as a control or check on a particular rule or order of an administrative agency. Judicial review is available unless a statute precludes judicial review or the agency action is committed to agency discretion by law. Section 701. In exercising judicial review the court may either compel agency action unlawfully withheld or set aside impermissible agency action. In making these determinations the court must review the whole record and may set aside agency action only if the error is prejudicial. In conducting a review, the court decides all relevant questions of law, interprets constitutional and statutory provisions, and determines the meaning or applicability of the terms of an agency action.

This review of questions of law includes determining whether the agency has (1) exceeded its authority, (2) properly interpreted the applicable law, (3) violated any constitutional provision, or (4) acted contrary to the procedural requirements of the law. When reviewing factual determinations, the courts

use one of three different standards. Where there has been informal rulemaking or informal adjudication, then the standard generally is the **arbitrary and capricious** test, which requires only that the agency had a rational basis for reaching its decision. *See Motor Vehicle Mfrs. Ass'n v. State Farm Mutual Automobile Ins. Co.* Where there has been a formal hearing the substantial evidence test usually applies. It also applies to informal or hybrid rulemaking if the enabling statute so requires. The **substantial evidence** test requires that the conclusions reached are supported by "such relevant evidence as a reasonable mind might accept as adequate to support a conclusion." *Consolidated Edison Co. v. NLRB*, 305 U.S. 197 (1938). Finally, in rare instances the reviewing court may apply the **unwarranted by the facts** standard, which permits the court to try the facts *de novo*. This strict review is available only when the enabling statute provides, when the agency has conducted an adjudication with inadequate fact-finding procedures, or when issues that were not before the agency are raised in a proceeding to enforce nonadjudicative agency action.

Legislative Control

The legislature may exercise control over administrative agencies in various ways. Through its budgetary power it may greatly restrict or expand an agency's operations. Congress may amend the enabling statute to increase, modify, or decrease the agency's authority. Even more drastically, it may completely eliminate an agency. Or, Congress may establish general guidelines governing agency action, as it did by enacting the Administrative Procedure Act. Moreover, it may reverse or change an agency rule or decision by specific legislation. In addition, each house of Congress has oversight committees that review the operations of administrative agencies. Finally, the Senate has the power of confirmation over some high-level appointments to administrative agencies.

Figure 3–2 Branches of the Government

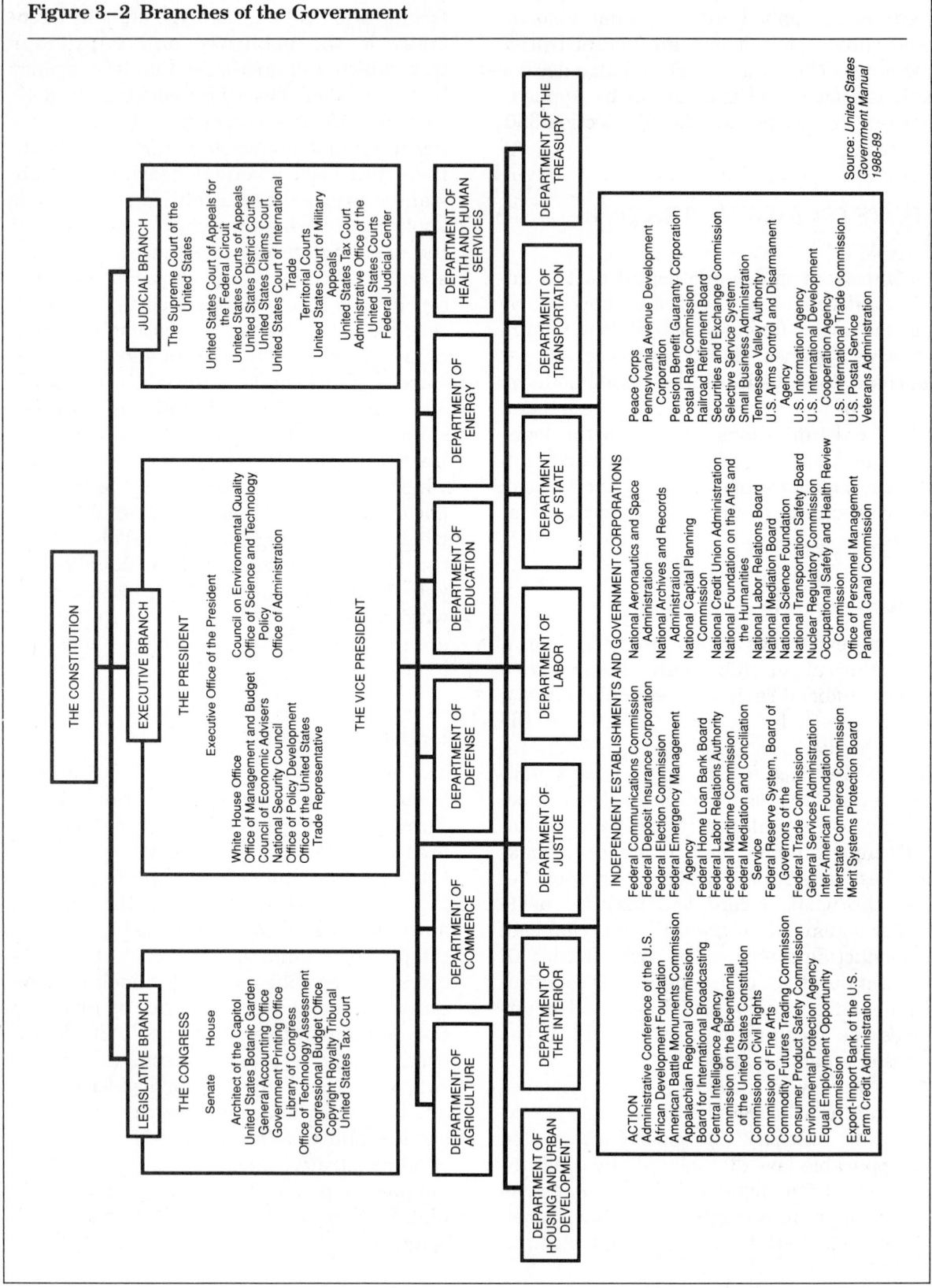

Source: *United States Government Manual 1988–89.*

Control by Executive Branch

The president has significant control over administrative agencies housed within the executive branch by virtue of his power to appoint and remove the chief administrator of these agencies (see Figure 3–2). With respect to independent agencies, the president has less control because commissioners serve for a fixed term that is staggered with the president's term of office. Nevertheless, his power to appoint the chairman and to fill vacancies confers considerable control, as does his power to remove commissioners for statutorily defined cause. The president's central role in the budgeting process of agencies also enables him to exert great control over agency policy and operations. Even more extreme is the president's power to impound monies appropriated to an agency by Congress. In addition, the president may radically alter, combine, or even abolish agencies of the executive branch unless disapproved by either house of Congress within a prescribed time.

CASES

Federal Preemption

SILKWOOD v. KERR–McGEE CORPORATION

Supreme Court of the United States, 1984.
464 U.S. 238, 104 S.Ct. 615, 78 L.Ed.2d 443.

WHITE, J.

This case requires us to determine whether a state-authorized award of punitive damages arising out of the escape of plutonium from a federally-licensed nuclear facility is preempted either because it falls within that forbidden field or because it conflicts with some other aspect of the Atomic Energy Act.

Karen Silkwood was a laboratory analyst for Kerr-McKee at its Cimmaron plant near Crescent, Oklahoma. The plant fabricated plutonium fuel pins for use as reactor fuel in nuclear power plants. Accordingly, the plant was subject to licensing and regulation by the Nuclear Regulatory Commission (NRC) pursuant to the Atomic Energy Act. [Citation.]

During a three-day period of November 1974, Silkwood was contaminated by plutonium from the Cimmaron plant. On November 5, Silkwood was grinding and polishing plutonium samples, utilizing glove boxes designed for that purpose. In accordance with established procedures, she checked her hands for contamination when she withdrew them from the glove box. When some contamination was detected, a more extensive check was performed. A monitoring device revealed contamination on Silkwood's left hand, right wrist, upper arm, neck, hair, and nostrils. She was immediately decontaminated, and at the end of her shift, the monitors detected no contamination. However, she was given urine and fecal kits and was instructed to collect samples in order to check for plutonium discharge.

The next day, Silkwood arrived at the plant and began doing paperwork in the laboratory. Upon leaving the laboratory, Silkwood monitored herself and again discovered surface contamination. Once again, she was decontaminated.

On the third day, November 7, Silkwood was monitored upon her arrival at the plant. High levels of contamination were detected. Four urine samples and one fecal sample submitted that morning were also highly contaminated. Suspecting that the contamination had spread to areas outside the plant, the company directed a decontamination squad to accompany Silkwood to her apartment. Silkwood's roommate, who was also an employee at the plant, was awakened and monitored. She was also contaminated, although to a lesser degree than Silkwood. The squad then monitored the apartment, finding contamination in several rooms, with especially high levels in the bathroom, the kitchen, and Silkwood's bedroom.

The contamination level in Silkwood's apartment was such that many of her personal belongings had to be destroyed. Silkwood herself was sent to the Los Alamos Scientific Laboratory to determine the extent of contamination in her vital body organs. She returned to work on November 13. That night, she was killed in an unrelated automobile accident. [Citation.]

Bill Silkwood, Karen's father, brought the present diversity action in his capacity as administrator of her estate. The action was based on common law tort principles under Oklahoma law and was designed to recover for the contamination injuries to Karen's person and property. Kerr-McGee stipulated that the plutonium which caused the contamination came from its plant, and the jury expressly rejected Kerr-McGee's allegation that Silkwood had intentionally removed the plutonium from the plant in an effort to embarrass the company. However, there were no other specific findings of fact with respect to the cause of the contamination.

* * *

The jury returned a verdict in favor of Silkwood, finding actual damages of $505,000 ($500,000 for personal injuries and $5,000 for property damage) and punitive damages of $10,000,000. The trial court entered judgment against Kerr-McGee in that amount.

* * *

. . . [Upon appeal the Court of Appeals for the Tenth Circuit] held that because of the federal statutes regulating the Kerr-McGee plant, "punitive damages may not be awarded in this case," [citation].

* * *

Silkwood appealed, seeking review of the Court of Appeals' ruling with respect to the punitive damages award. * * *

* * *

As we recently observed in *Pacific Gas & Electric Co. v. State Energy Resources Conservation & Development Comm'n,* [citation], state law can be preempted in either of two general ways. If Congress evidences an in-

tent to occupy a given field, any state law falling within that field is preempted. [Citations.] If Congress has not entirely displaced state regulation over the matter in question, state law is still preempted to the extent it actually conflicts with federal law, that is, when it is impossible to comply with both state and federal law, [citation], or where the state law stands as an obstacle to the accomplishment of the full purposes and objectives of Congress, [citation]. Kerr-McGee contends that the award in this case is invalid under either analysis. We consider each of these contentions in turn.

In *Pacific Gas & Electric,* an examination of the statutory scheme and legislative history of the Atomic Energy Act convinced us that "Congress . . . intended that the federal government regulate the radiological safety aspects involved . . . in the construction and operation of a nuclear plant." [Citation.] Thus, we concluded that "the federal government has occupied the entire field of nuclear safety concerns, except the limited powers expressly ceded to the states." [Citation.]

Kerr-McGee argues that our ruling in *Pacific Gas & Electric* is dispositive of the issue in this case. Noting that "regulation can be as effectively asserted through an award of damages as through some form of preventive relief," [citation], Kerr-McGee submits that because the state-authorized award of punitive damages in this case punishes and deters conduct related to radiation hazards, it falls within the prohibited field. However, a review of the same legislative history which prompted our holding in *Pacific Gas & Electric,* coupled with an examination of Congress' actions with respect to other portions of the Atomic Energy Act, convinces us that the preempted field does not extend as far as Kerr-McGee would have it.

* * *

Congress' decision to prohibit the states from regulating the safety aspects of nuclear development was premised on its belief that the Commission was more qualified to determine what type of safety standards should be enacted in this complex area. As Congress was informed by the AEC, the 1959 legislation provided for continued federal control over the more hazardous materials because "the technical safety considerations are of such complexity that it is not likely that any State would be prepared to deal with them during the foreseeable future." [Citation.] If there were nothing more, this concern over the states' inability to formulate effective standards and the foreclosure of the states from conditioning the operation of nuclear plants on compliance with state-imposed safety standards arguably would disallow resort to state-law remedies by those suffering injuries from radiation in a nuclear plant. There is, however, ample evidence that Congress had no intention of forbidding the states from providing such remedies.

Indeed, there is no indication that Congress even seriously considered precluding the use of such remedies either when it enacted the Atomic Energy Act in 1954 and or when it amended it in 1959. This silence takes on added significance in light of Congress' failure to provide any federal remedy for persons injured by such conduct. It is difficult to believe that Congress would, without comment, remove all means of judicial recourse for those injured by illegal conduct. [Citation.]

More importantly, the only congressional discussion concerning the relationship between the Atomic Energy Act and state tort remedies indicates that Congress assumed that such remedies would be available. After the 1954 law was enacted, private companies contemplating entry into the nuclear industry expressed concern over potentially bankrupting state-law suits arising out of a nuclear incident. As a result, in 1957 Congress passed the Price-Anderson Act, an amendment to the Atomic Energy Act. [Citation.] That Act established an indemnification scheme under which operators of licensed nuclear facilities could be required to obtain up to $60 million in private financial protection against such suits. The government would then provide indemnification for the next $500 million of liability, and the resulting $560 million would be the limit of liability for any one nuclear incident.

Although the Price-Anderson Act does not apply to the present situation, the discussion preceding its enactment and subsequent amendment indicates that Congress assumed that persons injured by nuclear accidents were free to utilize existing state tort law remedies.

* * *

The belief that the NRC's exclusive authority to set safety standards did not foreclose the use of state tort remedies was reaffirmed when the Price-Anderson Act was amended in 1966. The 1966 amendment was designed to respond to concerns about the adequacy of state law remedies.

* * *

* * * Indeed, the entire discussion surrounding the 1966 amendment was premised on the assumption that state remedies were available notwithstanding the NRC's exclusive regulatory authority. For example, the Committee rejected a suggestion that it adopt a federal tort to replace existing state remedies, noting that such displacement of state remedies would engender great opposition. [Citation.] If other provisions of the Atomic Energy Act already precluded the states from providing remedies to its citizens, there would have been no need for such concerns. Other comments made throughout the discussion were similarly based on the assumption that state remedies were available.

* * *

In sum, it is clear that in enacting and amending the Price-Anderson Act, Congress assumed that state-law remedies, in whatever form they might take, were available to those injured by nuclear incidents. This was so even though it was well aware of the NRC's exclusive authority to regulate safety matters. No doubt there is tension between the conclusion that safety regulation is the exclusive concern of the federal law and the conclusion that a state may nevertheless award damages based on its own law of liability. But as we understand what was done over the years in the legislation concerning nuclear energy, Congress intended to stand by both concepts and to tolerate whatever tension there was between them. We can do no less. It may be that the award of damages based on the state law of negligence or strict liability is regulatory in the sense that a nuclear plant will be threatened with damages liability if it does not conform to state standards, but that regulatory consequence was something that Congress was quite willing to accept.

We do not suggest that there could never be an instance in which the federal law would preempt the recovery of damages based on state law. But insofar as damages for radiation injuries are concerned, preemption should not be judged on the basis that the federal government has so completely occupied the field of safety that state remedies are foreclosed but on whether there is an irreconcilable conflict between the federal and state standards or whether the imposition of a state standard in a damages action would frustrate the objectives of the federal law. We perceive no such conflict or frustration in the circumstances of this case.

* * *

We conclude that the award of punitive damages in this case is not preempted by federal law.

* * *

* * * The judgment of the Court of Appeals with respect to punitive damages is therefore reversed, and the case is remanded to the Court of Appeals for proceedings consistent with this opinion.

State Action

NATIONAL COLLEGIATE ATHLETICS ASS'N. v. TARKANIAN
Supreme Court of the United States, 1988.
488 U.S. 179, 109 S.Ct. 454, 102 L.Ed.2d 469.

STEVENS, J.

When he became head basketball coach at University of Nevada, Las Vegas (UNLV) in 1973, Jerry Tarkanian inherited a team with a mediocre 14–14 record. [Citation.] Four years later the team won 29 out of 32 games and placed third in the championship tournament sponsored by the National Collegiate

Athletic Association (NCAA), to which UNLV belongs. [Citation.]

Yet in September 1977 UNLV informed Tarkanian that it was going to suspend him. No dissatisfaction with Tarkanian, once described as "the 'winningest' active basketball coach," [citation], motivated his suspension. Rather, the impetus was a report by the NCAA detailing 38 violations of NCAA rules by UNLV personnel, including 10 involving Tarkanian. The NCAA had placed the University's basketball team on probation for two years and ordered UNLV to show cause why the NCAA should not impose further penalties unless UNLV severed all ties during the probation between its intercollegiate athletic program and Tarkanian.

Facing demotion and a drastic cut in pay, Tarkanian brought suit in Nevada state court, alleging that he had been deprived of his Fourteenth Amendment due process rights in violation of 42 U.S.C. § 1983. [That section provides in part: "Every person who, under color of any statute, ordinance, regulation, custom, or usage, of any State or Territory or the District of Columbia, subjects, or causes to be subjected, any citizen of the United States or other person within the jurisdiction thereof to the deprivation of any rights, privileges, or immunities secured by the Constitution and laws, shall be liable to the party injured in an action at law, suit in equity, or other proper proceeding for redress."] Ultimately Tarkanian obtained injunctive relief and an award of attorney's fees against both UNLV and the NCAA. [Citation.] NCAA's liability may be upheld only if its participation to the events that led to Tarkanian's suspension constituted "state action" prohibited by the Fourteenth Amendment and were performed "under color of" state law within the meaning of § 1983.

* * *

Embedded in our Fourteenth Amendment jurisprudence is a dichotomy between state action, which is subject to scrutiny under the Amendment's Due Process Clause, and private conduct, against which the Amendment affords no shield, no matter how unfair that conduct may be. [Citations.] As a general matter the protections of the Fourteenth Amendment do not extend to "private conduct abridging individual rights." [Citation.]

"Careful adherence to the 'state action' requirement preserves an area of individual freedom by limiting the reach of federal law" and avoids the imposition of responsibility on a State for conduct it could not control. * * *

In this case Tarkanian argues that the NCAA was a state actor because it misused power that it possessed by virtue of state law. He claims specifically that UNLV delegated its own functions to the NCAA, clothing the Association with authority both to adopt rules governing UNLV's athletic programs and to enforce those rules on behalf of UNLV. Similarly, the Nevada Supreme Court held that UNLV had delegated its authority over personnel decisions to the NCAA. Therefore, the court reasoned, the two entities acted jointly to deprive Tarkanian of liberty and property interests, making the NCAA as well as UNLV a state actor.

* * *

This case uniquely mirrors the traditional state action case. Here the final act challenged by Tarkanian—his suspension—was committed by UNLV. A state university without question is a state actor. When it decides to impose a serious disciplinary sanction upon one of its tenured employees, it must comply with the terms of the Due Process Clause of the Fourteenth Amendment to the Federal Constitution. [Citations.] Thus when UNLV notified Tarkanian that he was being separated from all relations with the University's basketball program, it acted under color of state law within the meaning of 42 U.S.C. § 1983.

The mirror image presented in this case requires us to step through an analytical looking glass to resolve it. Clearly UNLV's conduct was influenced by the rules and recommendations of the NCAA, the private party. But it was UNLV, the state entity, that actually suspended Tarkanian. Thus the question is not whether UNLV participated to a critical extent in the NCAA's activities, but whether UNLV's actions in compliance with the NCAA rules and recommendations

turned the NCAA's conduct into state action.

We examine first the relationship between UNLV and the NCAA regarding the NCAA's rulemaking. UNLV is among the NCAA's members and participated in promulgating the Association's rules; it must be assumed, therefore, that Nevada had some impact on the NCAA's policy determinations. Yet the NCAA's several hundred other public and private member institutions each similarly affected those policies. Those institutions, the vast majority of which were located in States other than Nevada, did not act under color of Nevada law. It necessarily follows that the source of the legislation adopted by the NCAA is not Nevada but the collective membership, speaking through an organization that is independent of any particular State.

State action nonetheless might lie if UNLV, by embracing the NCAA's rules, transformed them into state rules and the NCAA into a state actor. [Citation.] UNLV engaged in state action when it adopted the NCAA's rules to govern its own behavior, but that would be true even if UNLV had taken no part in the promulgation of those rules. * * * UNLV retained the authority to withdraw from the NCAA and establish its own standards. The University alternatively could have stayed in the Association and worked through the Association's legislative process to amend rules or standards it deemed harsh, unfair, or unwieldy. Neither UNLV's decision to adopt the NCAA's standards nor its minor role in their formulation is a sufficient reason for concluding that the NCAA was acting under color of Nevada law when it promulgated standards governing athlete recruitment, eligibility, and academic performance.

Tarkanian further asserts that the NCAA's investigation, enforcement proceedings, and consequent recommendations constituted state action because they resulted from a delegation of power by UNLV. UNLV, as an NCAA member, subscribed to the statement in the Association's bylaws that NCAA "enforcement procedures are an essential part of the intercollegiate athletic program of each member institution." [Citation.] It is, of course, true that a state may delegate authority to a private party and thereby make that party a state actor. * * * But UNLV delegated no power to the NCAA to take specific action against any University employee. The commitment by UNLV to adhere to NCAA enforcement procedures was enforceable only by sanctions that the NCAA might impose on UNLV itself.

* * *

The NCAA enjoyed no governmental powers to facilitate its investigation. It had no power to subpoena witnesses, to impose contempt sanctions, or to assert sovereign authority over any individual. Its greatest authority was to threaten sanctions against UNLV, with the ultimate sanction being expulsion of the University from membership. Contrary to the premise of the Nevada Supreme Court's opinion, the NCAA did not— indeed, could not—directly discipline Tarkanian or any other state university employee. The express terms of the Confidential Report did not demand the suspension unconditionally; rather, it requested "the University . . . to show cause" why the NCAA should not impose additional penalties if UNLV declines to suspend Tarkanian. [Citation.] Even the University's vice president acknowledged that the Report gave the University options other than suspension: UNLV could have retained Tarkanian and risked additional sanctions, perhaps even expulsion from the NCAA, or it could have withdrawn voluntarily from the Association.

Finally, Tarkanian argues that the power of the NCAA is so great that the UNLV had no practical alternative to compliance with its demands. We are not at all sure this is true, but even if we assume that a private monopolist can impose its will on a state agency by a threatened refusal to deal with it, it does not follow that such a private party is therefore acting under color of state law. [Citation.]

In final analysis the question is whether "the conduct allegedly causing the deprivation of a federal right [can] be fairly attributable to the State." [Citation.] It would be ironic indeed to conclude that the NCAA's imposition of sanctions aganist UNLV— sanctions that UNLV and its counsel, including the Attorney General of Nevada, steadfastly opposed during protracted adversary proceedings—is fairly attributable to the State of Nevada. It would be more appropriate to conclude that UNLV has conducted its athletic program under color of the policies adopted by the NCAA, rather than that those policies were developed and enforced under color of Nevada law.

The judgment of the Nevada Supreme Court is reversed and the case is remanded to that court for further proceedings not inconsistent with this opinion.

It is so ordered.

Due Process

BOARD OF CURATORS OF THE UNIVERSITY OF MISSOURI v. HOROWITZ

Supreme Court of the United States, 1978.
435 U.S. 78, 98 S.Ct. 948, 55 L.Ed.2d 124.

REHNQUIST, J.

Respondent, a student at the University of Missouri-Kansas City Medical School, was dismissed by petitioner officials of the school during her final year of study for failure to meet academic standards. Respondent sued petitioners . . . alleging, among other constitutional violations, that petitioners had not accorded her procedural due process prior to her dismissal. The District Court, after conducting a full trial, concluded that respondent had been afforded all of the rights guaranteed her by the Fourteenth Amendment to the United States Constitution and dismissed her complaint. The Court of Appeals for the Eighth Circuit reversed. * * *

Respondent was admitted with advanced standing to the Medical School in the fall of 1971. During the final years of a student's education at the school, the student is required to pursue in "rotational units" academic and clinical studies pertaining to various medical disciplines such as obstetrics-gynecology, pediatrics, and surgery. Each student's academic performance at the School is evaluated on a periodic basis by the Council on Evaluation, a body composed of both faculty and students, which can recommend various actions including probation and dismissal. The recommendations of the Council are reviewed by the Coordinating Committee, a body composed solely of faculty members, and must ultimately be approved by the Dean. Students are not typically allowed to appear before either the Council or the Coordinating Committee on the occasion of their review of the student's academic performance.

In the spring of respondent's first year of study, several faculty members expressed dissatisfaction with her clinical performance during a pediatrics rotation. The faculty members noted that respondent's "performance was below that of her peers in all clinical patient-oriented settings," that she was erratic in her attendance at clinical sessions, and that she lacked a critical concern for personal hygiene. Upon the recommendation of the Council on Evaluation, respondent was advanced to her second and final year on a probationary basis.

Faculty dissatisfaction with respondent's clinical performance continued during the following year. For example, respondent's docent, or faculty adviser, rated her clinical skills as "unsatisfactory." In the middle of the year, the Council again reviewed respondent's academic progress and concluded that respondent should not be considered for graduation in June of that year; furthermore, the Council recommended that, absent "radical improvement," respondent be dropped from the school.

Respondent was permitted to take a set of oral and practical examinations as an "appeal" of the decision not to permit her to graduate. Pursuant to this "appeal," respondent spent a substantial portion of time with seven practicing physicians in the area who enjoyed a good reputation among their peers. The physicians were asked to recommend whether respondent should be allowed to graduate on schedule and, if not, whether she should be dropped immediately or allowed to remain on probation. Only two of the doctors

recommended that respondent be graduated on schedule. Of the other five, two recommended that she be immediately dropped from the school. The remaining three recommended that she not be allowed to graduate in June and be continued on probation pending further reports on her clinical progress. Upon receipt of these recommendations, the Council on Evaluation reaffirmed its prior position.

The Council met again in mid-May to consider whether respondent should be allowed to remain in school beyond June of that year. Noting that the report on respondent's recent surgery rotation rated her performance as "low-satisfactory," the Council unanimously recommended that "barring receipt of any reports that Miss Horowitz has improved radically, [she] not be allowed to re-enroll in the . . . School of Medicine." The Council delayed making its recommendation official until receiving reports on other rotations; when a report on respondent's emergency rotation also turned out to be negative, the Council unanimously reaffirmed its recommendation that respondent be dropped from the school. The Coordinating Committee and the Dean approved the recommendation and notified respondent, who appealed the decision in writing to the University's Provost for Health Sciences. The Provost sustained the school's actions after reviewing the record compiled during the earlier proceedings.

To be entitled to the procedural protections of the Fourteenth Amendment, respondent must in a case such as this demonstrate that her dismissal from the school deprived her of either a "liberty" or a "property" interest. Respondent has never alleged that she was deprived of a property interest. Because property interests are creatures of state law, [citation], respondent would have been required to show at trial that her seat at the Medical School was a "property" interest recognized by Missouri state law. Instead, respondent argued that her dismissal deprived her of "liberty" by substantially impairing her opportunities to continue her medical education or to return to employment in a medically related field.

* * *

We need not decide, however, whether respondent's dismissal deprived her of a liberty interest in pursuing a medical career. Nor need we decide whether respondent's dismissal infringed any other interest constitutionally protected against deprivation without procedural due process. Assuming the existence of a liberty or property interest, respondent has been awarded at least as much due process as the Fourteenth Amendment requires. The school fully informed respondent of the faculty's dissatisfaction with her clinical progress and the danger that this posed to timely graduation and continued enrollment. The ultimate decision to dismiss respondent was careful and deliberate. These procedures were sufficient under the Due Process Clause of the Fourteenth Amendment. We agree with the District Court that respondent

was afforded full procedural due process by the (school). In fact, the Court is of the opinion, and so finds, that the school went beyond (constitutionally required) procedural due process by affording (respondent) the opportunity to be examined by seven independent physicians in order to be absolutely certain that their grading of the (respondent) in her medical skills was correct [citation].

In *Goss v. Lopez,* [citation], we held that due process requires, in connection with the suspension of a student from public school for disciplinary reasons, "that the student be given oral or written notice of the charges against him and, if he denies them, an explanation of the evidence the authorities have and an opportunity to present his side of the story." [Citation.] The Court of Appeals apparently read *Goss* as requiring some type of formal hearing at which respondent could defend her academic ability and performance. All that *Goss* required was an "informal give-and-take" between the student and the administrative body dismissing him that would, at least, give the student "the opportunity to characterize his conduct and put it in what he deems the proper context." [Citation.] But we have frequently emphasized that "[t]he very nature of due process negates

any concept of inflexible procedures universally applicable to every imaginable situation." [Citation.] The need for flexibility is well illustrated by the significant difference between the failure of a student to meet academic standards and the violation by a student of valid rules of conduct. This difference calls for far less stringent procedural requirements in the case of an academic dismissal.

* * *

* * * A school is an academic institution, not a courtroom or administrative hearing room. In *Goss,* this Court felt that suspensions of students for disciplinary reasons have a sufficient resemblance to traditional judicial and administrative factfinding to call for a "hearing" before the relevant school authority. While recognizing that school authorities must be afforded the necessary tools to maintain discipline, the Court concluded:

[I]t would be a strange disciplinary system in an educational institution if no communication was sought by the disciplinarian with the student in an effort to inform him of his dereliction and to let him tell his side of the story in order to make sure that an injustice is not done.

* * *

[R]equiring effective notice and informal hearing permitting the student to give his version of the events will provide a meaningful hedge against erroneous action. At least the disciplinarian will be alerted to the existence of disputes about facts and arguments about cause and effect. [Citation.]

Even in the context of a school disciplinary proceeding, however, the Court stopped short of requiring a *formal* hearing since "further formalizing the suspension process and escalating its formality and adversary nature may not only make it too costly as a regular disciplinary tool but also destroy its effectiveness as a part of the teaching process." [Citation.]

Academic evaluations of a student, in contrast to disciplinary determinations, bear little resemblance to the judicial and administrative factfinding proceedings to which we have traditionally attached a full-hearing requirement. In *Goss,* the school's decision to suspend the students rested on factual conclusions that the individual students had participated in demonstrations that had disrupted classes, attacked a police officer, or caused physical damage to school property. The requirement of a hearing, where the student could present his side of the factual issue, could under such circumstances "provide a meaningful hedge against erroneous action." [Citation.] The decision to dismiss respondent, by comparison, rested on the academic judgment of school officials that she did not have the necessary clinical ability to perform adequately as a medical doctor and was making insufficient progress toward that goal. Such a judgment is by its nature more subjective and evaluative than the typical factual questions presented in the average disciplinary decision. Like the decision of an individual professor as to the proper grade for a student in his course, the determination whether to dismiss a student for academic reasons requires an expert evaluation of cumulative information and is not readily adapted to the procedural tools of judicial or administrative decisionmaking.

Under such circumstances, we decline to ignore the historic judgment of educators and thereby formalize the academic dismissal process by requiring a hearing. The educational process is not by nature adversary; instead it centers around a continuing relationship between faculty and students, "one in which the teacher must occupy many roles—educator, adviser, friend, and, at times, parent-substitute." [Citation.] This is especially true as one advances through the varying regimes of the educational system, and the instruction becomes both more individualized and more specialized.

* * *

The judgment of the Court of Appeals is therefore reversed.

Equal Protection

BROWN v. BOARD OF EDUCATION OF TOPEKA

Supreme Court of the United States, 1954.
347 U.S. 483, 74 S.Ct. 686, 98 L.Ed. 873.

WARREN, C.J.

These cases come to us from the States of Kansas, South Carolina, Virginia, and Delaware. They are premised on different facts and different local conditions, but a common legal question justifies their consideration together in this consolidated opinion.

In each of the cases, minors of the Negro race, through their legal representatives, seek the aid of the courts in obtaining admission to the public schools of their community on a nonsegregated basis. In each instance, they have been denied admission to schools attended by white children under laws requiring or permitting segregation according to race. This segregation was alleged to deprive the plaintiffs of the equal protection of the laws under the Fourteenth Amendment. In each of the cases other than the Delaware case, a three-judge federal district court denied relief to the plaintiffs on the so-called "separate but equal" doctrine announced by this Court in *Plessy v. Ferguson,* [citation]. Under that doctrine, equality of treatment is accorded when the races are provided substantially equal facilities, even though these facilities be separate. In the Delaware case, the Supreme Court of Delaware adhered to that doctrine, but ordered that the plaintiffs be admitted to the white schools because of their superiority to the Negro schools.

The plaintiffs contend that segregated public schools are not "equal" and cannot be made "equal" and that hence they are deprived of the equal protection of the laws. Because of the obvious importance of the question presented, the Court took jurisdiction. * * *

Reargument was largely devoted to the circumstances surrounding the adoption of the Fourteenth Amendment in 1868. It covered exhaustively consideration of the Amendment in Congress, ratification by the states, then existing practices in racial segregation, and the views of proponents and opponents of the Amendment. This discussion and our own investigation convince us that, although these sources cast some light, it is not enough to resolve the problem with which we are faced. At best, they are inconclusive. The most avid proponents of the post-War Amendments undoubtedly intended them to remove all legal distinctions among "all persons born or naturalized in the United States." Their opponents, just as certainly, were antagonistic to both the letter and the spirit of the Amendments and wished them to have the most limited effect. What others in Congress and the state legislatures had in mind cannot be determined with any degree of certainty.

An additional reason for the inconclusive nature of the Amendment's history, with respect to segregated schools, is the status of public education at that time. In the South, the movement toward free common schools, supported by general taxation, had not yet taken hold. Education of white children was largely in the hands of private groups. Education of Negroes was almost nonexistent, and practically all of the race were illiterate. In fact, any education of Negroes was forbidden by law in some states. Today, in contrast, many Negroes have achieved outstanding success in the arts and sciences as well as in the business and professional world. It is true that public school education at the time of the Amendment had advanced further in the North, but the effect of the Amendment on Northern States was generally ignored in the congressional debates. Even in the North, the conditions of public education did not approximate those existing today. The curriculum was usually rudimentary; ungraded schools were common in rural areas; the school term was but three months a year in many states; and compulsory school attendance was virtually unknown. As a consequence, it is not surprising that there should be so little in the history of the Fourteenth Amendment relating to its intended effect on public education.

In the first cases in this Court construing the Fourteenth Amendment, decided shortly after its adoption, the Court interpreted it as proscribing all state-imposed discriminations against the Negro race. The doctrine of "separate but equal" did not make its appearance in this Court until 1896 in the case of *Plessy v. Ferguson,* involving not education but transportation. American courts have since labored with the doctrine for over half a century. In this Court, there have been six cases involving the "separate but equal" doctrine in the field of public education. . . . In none of these cases was it necessary to reexamine the doctrine to grant relief to the Negro plaintiff. And in *Sweatt v. Painter,* [citation], the Court expressly reserved decision on the question whether *Plessy v. Ferguson* should be held inapplicable to public education.

In the instant cases, that question is directly presented. Here, unlike *Sweatt v. Painter,* there are findings below that the Negro and white schools involved have been equalized, or are being equalized, with respect to buildings, curricula, qualifications and salaries of teachers, and other "tangible" factors. Our decision, therefore, cannot turn on merely a comparison of these tangible factors in the Negro and white schools involved in each of the cases. We must look instead to the effect of segregation itself on public education.

* * *

Today, education is perhaps the most important function of state and local governments. Compulsory school attendance laws and the great expenditures for education both demonstrate our recognition of the importance of education to our democratic society. It is required in the performance of our most basic public responsibilities, even service in the armed forces. It is the very foundation of good citizenship. Today it is a principal instrument in awakening the child to cultural values, in preparing him for later professional training, and in helping him to adjust normally to his environment. In these days, it is doubtful that any child may reasonably be expected to succeed in life if he is denied the opportunity of an education. Such an opportunity, where the state has undertaken to provide it, is a right which must be made available to all on equal terms.

We come then to the question presented: Does segregation of children in public schools solely on the basis of race, even though the physical facilities and other "tangible" factors may be equal, deprive the children of the minority group of equal educational opportunities? We believe that it does.

In *Sweatt v. Painter,* [citation], in finding that a segregated law school for Negroes could not provide them equal educational opportunities, this Court relied in large part on "those qualities which are incapable of objective measurement but which make for greatness in a law school." In *McLaurin v. Oklahoma State Regents,* [citation], the Court in requiring that a Negro admitted to a white graduate school be treated like all other students, again resorted to intangible considerations: ". . . his ability to study, to engage in discussions and exchange views with other students, and, in general, to learn his profession." Such considerations apply with added force to children in grade and high schools. To separate them from others of similar age and qualifications solely because of their race generates a feeling of inferiority as to their status in the community that may affect their hearts and minds in a way unlikely ever to be undone. The effect of this separation on their educational opportunities was well stated by a finding in the Kansas case by a court which nevertheless felt compelled to rule against the Negro plaintiffs:

"Segregation of white and colored children in public schools has a detrimental effect upon the colored children. The impact is greater when it has the sanction of the law, for the policy of separating the races is usually interpreted as denoting the inferiority of the Negro group. A sense of inferiority affects the motivation of a child to learn. Segregation with the sanction of law, therefore, has a tendency to (retard) the educational and mental development of Negro children and to deprive them of some of the benefits they would receive in a racial(ly) integrated school system."

Whatever may have been the extent of psychological knowledge at the time of *Plessy v. Ferguson,* this finding is amply supported by modern authority. Any language in *Plessy v. Ferguson* contrary to this finding is rejected.

We conclude that in the field of public education the doctrine of "separate but equal" has no place. Separate educational facilities are inherently unequal. Therefore, we hold that the plaintiffs and others similarly situated for whom the actions have been brought are, by reason of the segregation complained of, deprived of the equal protection of the laws guaranteed by the Fourteenth Amendment. This disposition makes unnecessary any discussion whether such segregation also violates the Due Process Clause of the Fourteenth Amendment.

Administrative Law: Legislative Rules

F.C.C. v. MIDWEST VIDEO CORP.
Supreme Court of the United States, 1979.
440 U.S. 689, 99 S.Ct. 1435, 59 L.Ed.2d 692.

WHITE, J.

In May 1976, the Federal Communications Commission promulgated rules requiring cable television systems that have 3,500 or more subscribers and carry broadcast signals to develop, at a minimum, a 20–channel capacity by 1986, to make available certain channels for access by third parties, and to furnish equipment and facilities for access purposes. *Report and Order in Docket No. 20508,* 59 F.C.C.2d 294 *(1976 Order).* The issue here is whether these rules are "reasonably ancillary to the effective performance of the Commission's various responsibilities for the regulation of television broadcasting," [citation], and hence within the Commission's statutory authority.

* * *

As ultimately adopted, the rules prescribe a series of interrelated obligations ensuring public access to cable systems of a designated size and regulate the manner in which access is to be afforded and the charges that may be levied for providing it. Under the rules, cable systems must possess a minimum capacity of 20 channels as well as the technical capability for accomplishing two-way, nonvoice communication. [Citation.] Moreover, to the extent of their available activated channel capacity, cable systems must allocate four separate channels for use by public, educational, local governmental, and leased-access users, with one channel assigned to each. * * *

Under the rules, cable operators are deprived of all discretion regarding who may exploit their access channels and what may be transmitted over such channels. System operators are specifically enjoined from exercising any control over the content of access programming except that they must adopt rules proscribing the transmission on most access channels of lottery information and commercial matter. [Citation.] The regulations also instruct cable operators to issue rules providing for first-come, nondiscriminatory access on public and leased channels. [Citation.]

Finally, the rules circumscribe what operators may charge for privileges of access and use of facilities and equipment. * * *

The Commission's capacity and access rules were challenged on jurisdictional grounds in the course of the rulemaking proceedings. In its *1976 Order,* the Commission rejected such comments on the ground that the regulations further objectives that it might properly pursue in its supervision over broadcasting. * * *

On petition for review, the Eighth Circuit set aside the Commission's access, channel capacity, and facilities rules as beyond the agency's jurisdiction. . . . We granted certiorari, [citation], and we now affirm.

The Commission derives its regulatory authority from the Communications Act of 1934, [citation]. The Act preceded the advent of cable television and understandably does not expressly provide for the regulation of that medium. . . . In [citation], we construed § 2(a) [of the Act] as conferring on the Commission a circumscribed range of power to regulate cable television, and we reaffirmed that determination in [citation]. The question now before us is whether the Act, as construed in these two cases, authorizes the capacity and access regulations that are here under challenge.

* * *

With its access rules, however, the Commission has transferred control of the content of access cable channels from cable operators to members of the public who wish to communicate by the cable medium. Effectively, the Commission has relegated cable systems, *pro tanto,* to common-carrier status. A common-carrier service in the communications context is one that "makes a public offering to provide [communications facilities] whereby all members of the public who choose to employ such facilities may communicate or transmit intelligence of their own design and choosing. . . ." [Citations.] A common carrier does not "make individualized decisions, in particular cases, whether and on what terms to deal." [Citation.]

The access rules plainly impose common-carrier obligations on cable operators. Under the rules, cable systems are required to hold out dedicated channels on a first-come, nondiscriminatory basis. [Citation.] Operators are prohibited from determining or influencing the content of access programming. * * *

* * * The language of § 3(h) [of the Act] is unequivocal; it stipulates that broadcasters shall not be treated as common carriers. As we see it, § 3(h), consistently with the policy of the Act to preserve editorial control of programming in the licensee, forecloses any discretion in the Commission to impose access requirements amounting to common-carrier obligations on broadcast systems. The provision's background manifests a congressional belief that the intrusion worked by such regulation on the journalistic integrity of broadcasters would overshadow any benefits associated with the resulting public access. It is difficult to deny, then, that forcing broadcasters to develop a "nondiscriminatory system for controlling access . . . is precisely what Congress intended to avoid through § 3(h) of the Act." [Citation.]

* * *

* * * In light of the hesitancy with which Congress approached the access issue in the broadcast area, and in view of its outright rejection of a broad right of public access on a common-carrier basis, we are constrained to hold that the Commission exceeded those limits in promulgating its access rules. The Commission may not regulate cable systems as common carriers, just as it may not impose such obligations on television broadcasters. We think authority to compel cable operators to provide common carriage of public-originated transmissions must come specifically from Congress.

Affirmed.

Administrative Law: Judicial Review

MOTOR VEHICLE MFRS. ASS'N v. STATE FARM MUTUAL AUTOMOBILE INS. CO.

Supreme Court of the United States, 1983.
463 U.S. 29, 103 S.Ct. 2856, 77 L.Ed.2d 443.

WHITE, J.

The development of the automobile gave Americans unprecedented freedom to travel, but exacted a high price for enhanced mobility. Since 1929, motor vehicles have been the leading cause of accidental deaths and injuries in the United States. In 1982, 46,300 Americans died in motor vehicle accidents and hundreds of thousands more were maimed and injured. * * * In 1966, Congress decided that at least part of the answer lies in improving the design and safety features of the vehicle itself. * * * This task called for considerable expertise and Congress responded by enacting the National Traffic and Motor Vehicle Safety Act of 1966, (Act), [citation]. The Act, created for the purpose of "reduc[ing] traffic accidents and deaths and injuries to persons resulting from traffic accidents," directs the Secretary of Transportation or his delegate to issue motor vehicle safety standards that "shall be practicable, shall meet the need for motor vehicle safety, and shall be stated in objective terms." [Citation.] In issuing these standards, the Secretary is directed to consider "relevant available motor vehicle safety data," whether the proposed standard "is reasonable, practicable and appropriate" for the particular type of motor vehicle, and the "extent to which such standards will contribute to carrying out the purposes" of the Act.

The Act also authorizes judicial review under the provisions of the Administrative Procedure Act (APA), [citation], of all "orders establishing, amending, or revoking a Federal motor vehicle safety standard," [citation]. Under this authority, we review today whether NHTSA acted arbitrarily and capriciously in revoking the requirement in Motor Vehicle Safety Standard 208 that new motor vehicles produced after September 1982 be equipped with passive restraints to protect the safety of the occupants of the vehicle in the event of a collision. Briefly summarized, we hold that the agency failed to present an adequate basis and explanation for rescinding the passive restraint requirement and that the agency must either consider the matter further or adhere to or amend Standard 208 along lines which its analysis supports.

The regulation whose rescission is at issue bears a complex and convoluted history. Over the course of approximately 60 rulemaking notices, the requirement has been imposed, amended, rescinded, reimposed, and now rescinded again.

As originally issued by the Department of Transportation in 1967, Standard 208 simply required the installation of seatbelts in all automobiles. It soon became apparent that the level of seatbelt use was too low to reduce traffic injuries to an acceptable level. The Department therefore began consideration of "passive occupant restraint systems"— devices that do not depend for their effectiveness upon any action taken by the occupant except that necessary to operate the vehicle. Two types of automatic crash protection emerged: automatic seatbelts and airbags. The automatic seatbelt is a traditional safety belt, which when fastened to the interior of the door remains attached without impeding entry or exit from the vehicle, and deploys automatically without any action on the part of the passenger. The airbag is an inflatable device concealed in the dashboard and steering column. It automatically inflates when a sensor indicates that deceleration forces from an accident have exceeded a preset minimum, then rapidly deflates to dissipate those forces. The life-saving potential of these devices was immediately recognized, and in 1977, after substantial on-the-road experience with both devices, it was estimated by NHTSA that passive restraints could prevent approximately 12,000 deaths and over 100,000 serious injuries annually.

In 1969, the Department formally proposed a standard requiring the installation of passive restraints, thereby commencing a lengthy series of proceedings. In * * *

1972, the agency amended the standard to require full passive protection for all front seat occupants of vehicles manufactured after August 15, 1975. * * *

The effective date for mandatory passive restraint systems was extended for a year until August 31, 1976. But in June 1976, Secretary of Transportation William Coleman . . . suspended the passive restraint requirement. Although he found passive restraints technologically and economically feasible, the Secretary based his decision on the expectation that there would be widespread public resistance to the new systems. He instead proposed a demonstration project involving up to 500,000 cars installed with passive restraints, in order to smooth the way for public acceptance of mandatory passive restraints at a later date. * * *

Coleman's successor as Secretary of Transportation disagreed. Within months of assuming office, Secretary Brock Adams decided that the demonstration project was unnecessary. He issued a new mandatory passive restraint regulation, known as Modified Standard 208. . . . The two principal systems that would satisfy the Standard were airbags and passive belts; the choice of which system to install was left to the manufacturers. In [citation], the Court of Appeals upheld Modified Standard 208 as a rational, nonarbitrary regulation consistent with the agency's mandate under the Act. The standard also survived scrutiny by Congress, which did not exercise its authority under the legislative veto provision of the 1974 Amendments.

Over the next several years, the automobile industry geared up to comply with Modified Standard 208. * * * In February 1981, however, Secretary of Transportation Andrew Lewis reopened the rulemaking due to changed economic circumstances and, in particular, the difficulties of the automobile industry. Two months later, the agency * * * proposed the possible rescission of the entire standard. [Citation.] After receiving written comments and holding public hearings, NHTSA issued a final rule (Notice 25) that rescinded the passive restraint requirement contained in Modified Standard 208.

In a statement explaining the rescission, NHTSA maintained that it was no longer able to find, as it had in 1977, that the automatic restraint requirement would produce significant safety benefits. [Citation.] This judgment reflected not a change of opinion on the effectiveness of the technology, but a change in plans by the automobile industry. In 1977, the agency had assumed that airbags would be installed in 60% of all new cars and automatic seatbelts in 40%. By 1981 it became apparent that automobile manufacturers planned to install the automatic seatbelts in approximately 99% of the new cars. For this reason, the life-saving potential of airbags would not be realized. Moreover, it now appeared that the overwhelming majority of passive belts planned to be installed by manufacturers could be detached easily and left that way permanently.

* * * For this reason, the agency concluded that there was no longer a basis for reliably predicting that the standard would lead to any significant increased usage of restraints at all.

In view of the possibly minimal safety benefits, the automatic restraint requirement no longer was reasonable or practicable in the agency's view. The requirement would require approximately $1 billion to implement and the agency did not believe it would be reasonable to impose such substantial costs on manufacturers and consumers without more adequate assurance that sufficient safety benefits would accrue. * * *

State Farm Mutual Automobile Insurance Co. and the National Association of Independent Insurers filed petitions for review of NHTSA's rescission of the passive restraint standard. The United States Court of Appeals for the District of Columbia Circuit held that the agency's rescission of the passive restraint requirement was arbitrary and capricious. [Citation.]

* * * Both the Motor Vehicle Safety Act and the 1974 Amendments concerning occupant crash protection standards indicate that

motor vehicle safety standards are to be promulgated under the informal rulemaking procedures of § 553 of the Administrative Procedure Act. The agency's action in promulgating such standards therefore may be set aside if found to be "arbitrary, capricious, an abuse of discretion, or otherwise not in accordance with law." [Citation.]

We believe that the rescission or modification of an occupant protection standard is subject to the same test. * * *

* * *

The Department of Transportation accepts the applicability of the "arbitrary and capricious" standard. It argues that under this standard, a reviewing court may not set aside an agency rule that is rational, based on consideration of the relevant factors and within the scope of the authority delegated to the agency by the statute. We do not disagree with this formulation. The scope of review under the "arbitrary and capricious" standard is narrow and a court is not to substitute its judgment for that of the agency. Nevertheless, the agency must examine the relevant data and articulate a satisfactory explanation for its action including a "rational connection between the facts found and the choice made." [Citation.] In reviewing that explanation, we must "consider whether the decision was based on a consideration of the relevant factors and whether there has been a clear error of judgment." [Citations.] Normally, an agency rule would be arbitrary and capricious if the agency has relied on factors which Congress has not intended it to consider, entirely failed to consider an important aspect of the problem, offered an explanation for its decision that runs counter to the evidence before the agency, or is so implausible that it could not be ascribed to a difference in view or the product of agency expertise. The reviewing court should not attempt itself to make up for such deficiencies: "We may not supply a reasoned basis for the agency's action that the agency itself has not given." [Citation.] We will, however, "uphold a decision of less than ideal clarity if the agency's path may reasonably be discerned." [Citation.]

* * *

The ultimate question before us is whether NHTSA's rescission of the passive restraint requirement of Standard 208 was arbitrary and capricious. We conclude, as did the Court of Appeals, that it was. * * *

The first and most obvious reason for finding the rescission arbitrary and capricious is that NHTSA apparently gave no consideration whatever to modifying the Standard to require that airbag technology be utilized. Standard 208 sought to achieve automatic crash protection by requiring automobile manufacturers to install either of two passive restraint devices: airbags or automatic seatbelts. There was no suggestion in the long rulemaking process that led to Standard 208 that if only one of these options were feasible, no passive restraint standard should be promulgated. Indeed, the agency's original proposed standard contemplated the installation of inflatable restraints in all cars. Automatic belts were added as a means of complying with the standard because they were believed to be as effective as airbags in achieving the goal of occupant crash protection. At that time, the passive belt approved by the agency could not be detached. Only later, at a manufacturer's behest, did the agency approve of the detachability feature—and only after assurances that the feature would not compromise the safety benefits of the restraint.
* * *

The agency has now determined that the detachable automatic belts will not attain anticipated safety benefits because so many individuals will detach the mechanism. Even if this conclusion were acceptable in its entirety, standing alone it would not justify any more than an amendment of Standard 208 to disallow compliance by means of the one technology which will not provide effective passenger protection. It does not cast doubt on the need for a passive restraint standard or upon the efficacy of airbag technology. In its most recent rulemaking, the agency again acknowledged the life-saving potential of the airbag:

"The agency has no basis at this time for changing its earlier conclusions in 1976 and 1977 that basic airbag technology is sound and has been sufficiently demonstrated to be effective in those vehicles in current use. . . ." NHTSA Final Regulatory Impact Analysis (RIA) at XI-4 (App. 264).

Given the effectiveness ascribed to airbag technology by the agency, the mandate of the Safety Act to achieve traffic safety would suggest that the logical response to the faults of detachable seatbelts would be to require the installation of airbags. At the very least this alternative way of achieving the objectives of the Act should have been addressed and adequate reasons given for its abandonment. But the agency not only did not require compliance through airbags, it did not even consider the possibility in its 1981 rulemaking. Not one sentence of its rulemaking statement discusses the airbags-only option. * * *

* * *

We do not require today any specific procedures which NHTSA must follow. Nor do we broadly require an agency to consider all pol-icy alternatives in reaching decision. It is true that a rulemaking "cannot be found wanting simply because the agency failed to include every alternative device and thought conceivable by the mind of man . . . regardless of how uncommon or unknown that alternative may have been. . . ." [Citation.] But the airbag is more than a policy alternative to the passive restraint standard; it is a technological alternative within the ambit of the existing standard. We hold only that given the judgment made in 1977 that airbags are an effective and cost-beneficial life-saving technology, the mandatory passive-restraint rule may not be abandoned without any consideration whatsoever of an airbags-only requirement.

* * *

* * * Accordingly, we vacate the judgment of the Court of Appeals and remand the case to that court with directions to remand the matter to the NHTSA for further consideration consistent with this opinion.

So ordered.

QUESTIONS

1. List and distinguish the basic principles of constitutional law.

2. Explain the two effects of the commerce clause.

3. Distinguish the three levels of scrutiny used by the courts to determine the consititutionality of governmental action.

4. Explain the difference between substantive and procedural due process.

5. List and explain the three basic functions of administrative agencies.

PROBLEMS

1. In May, Patricia Allen left her automobile on the shoulder of a road in the city of Erewhon after the car stopped running. A member of the Erewhon city police department came upon the car later that day and placed on the car a sticker which stated that unless the car were moved it would be towed. After a week the car had not been removed and the police department authorized Baldwin Auto Wrecking Co. to tow it away and store it on its property. Allen was told by a friend

that her car was at Baldwin's. Allen asked Baldwin to allow her to take possession of her car but Baldwin refused to relinquish the car until the $70 towing fee was paid. Allen could not afford to pay the fee and the car remained at Baldwin's for six weeks. At that time Baldwin requested the police department for a permit to dispose of the automobile. After the police department tried unsuccessfully to telephone Allen, the department issued the permit. In late July, Baldwin destroyed the automobile. Allen brings an action against the city and Baldwin for damages for loss of the vehicle, arguing that she was denied due process. Decision?

2. In 1967, large oil reserves were discovered in the Prudhoe Bay area of Alaska. As a result the State revenues increased from $124 million in 1969 to $3.7 billion in 1981. In 1980 the State legislature enacted a dividend program that would distribute annually a portion of these earnings to the State's adult residents. Under the plan, each citizen eighteen years of age or older receives one unit for each year of residency subsequent to 1959, the year Alaska became a State. Crawford, a resident since 1978, brings suit challenging the dividend distribution plan as violative of the equal protection guarantee. Decision?

3. Maryland enacted a statute prohibiting any producer or refiner of petroleum products from operating retail service stations within the State. The statute also required that any producer or refiner discontinue operating their company-owned retail service stations. Approximately 3,800 retail service stations in Maryland sell over twenty different brands of gasoline. However, no petroleum products are produced or refined in Maryland and only five percent of the total number of retailers are operated by a producer or refiner. Maryland enacted the statute because a survey conducted by the State Comptroller indicated that gasoline stations operated by producers or refiners had received preferential treatment during periods of gasoline shortage. Seven major producers and refiners bring an action challenging the statute on the ground that it discriminates against interstate commerce in violation of the commerce clause of the United States Constitution. Decision?

4. The Federal Aviation Act of 1958 provides that "The United States of America is declared to possess and exercise complete and exclusive na-

tional sovereignty in the airspace of the United States." The city of Orion adopted an ordinance which makes it unlawful for jet aircraft to take off from its airport between 11:00 P.M. of one day and 7:00 A.M. of the next day. The Jordan Airlines, Inc. is adversely affected by this ordinance and brings suit challenging it under the supremacy clause of the United States Constitution. Decision?

5. The Public Service Commission of State X issued a regulation completely banning all advertising that "promotes the use of electricity" by any electric utility company in State X. The commission issued the order in order to conserve energy. Central Electric Corporation of State X challenges the order in the State courts arguing that the commission had restrained commercial speech in violation of the First Amendment. Decision?

6. E–Z–Rest Motel is a motel with 216 rooms located in the center of a large city in State Y. It is readily accessible from two interstate highways and three major state highways. The motel solicits patronage from outside of State Y through various national advertising media including magazines of national circulation. It accepts convention trade from outside State Y and approximately 75 percent of its registered guests are from out of State Y. An action under the Federal Civil Rights Act of 1964 has been brought against E–Z–Rest Motel alleging that the motel discriminates on the basis of race and color. The motel contends that the statute cannot be applied to it because it is not engaged in interstate commerce. Decision?

7. State Z enacted a Private Pension Benefits Protection Act requiring private employers with 100 or more employees to pay a pension funding charge upon terminating a pension plan or closing an office in State Z. Acme Steel Company closed its offices in State Z, whereupon the State assessed the company $185,000 under the vesting provisions of the Act. Acme challenged the constitutionality of the Act under the contract clause (Article I, Section 10) of the U.S. Constitution. Decision?

8. In 1942 Congress passed the Emergency Price Control Act in the interest of national defense and security. The stated purpose of the Act was "to stabilize prices and to prevent speculative, unwarranted and abnormal increases in prices and rents. . . ." The Act established the office of Price

Administration which was authorized to establish maximum prices and rents which were to be "generally fair and equitable and [were to] effectuate the purposes of this Act." Stark was convicted for selling beef at prices in excess of those set by the agency. Stark appeals on the ground that the Act was an unconstitutional delegation to the agency of the legislative power of Congress to control prices. Decision?

9. A State statute empowered public school principals to suspend students for up to ten days without any notice or hearing. A student who was suspended for ten days challenges the constitutionality of his suspension on the grounds that he was denied due process. Decision?

10. Iowa enacted a statute prohibiting the use of sixty-five-foot double trailer truck combinations. All of the other States in the midwest and west permit such trucks to be used on their roads. Consolidated Freightways is adversely affected by this statute and brings suit against Iowa, alleging that the statute violated the commerce clause. Decision?

Chapter 4

CRIMINAL LAW

Nature of Crimes
White-Collar Crimes
Crimes against Business
Defenses to Crimes
Criminal Procedure

AS discussed in Chapter 1, the civil law defines duties, the violation of which constitutes a wrong against the injured party. The criminal law, on the other hand, establishes duties, the violation of which is a societal wrong against the whole community. Civil law is a part of private law, whereas criminal law is a part of public law. In a civil action the injured party sues to recover compensation for the damage and injury that he has sustained as a result of the defendant's wrongful conduct. The party bringing a civil action (the plaintiff) has the burden of proof, which he must sustain by a preponderance (greater weight) of the evidence. The purpose of the civil law is to compensate the injured party.

Criminal law is designed to prevent harm to society by declaring what conduct is criminal and establishing punishment for such conduct. In a criminal case the defendant is prosecuted by the government. The government must prove the defendant's guilt beyond a reasonable doubt, which is a significantly higher burden of proof than that required in a civil action. Moreover, under our legal system, guilt is never presumed. Indeed, the law presumes the innocence of the accused, and this presumption is not affected by the defendant's failure to testify in her own defense. The government still has the burden of affirmatively proving the guilt of the accused beyond a reasonable doubt.

Of course, the same conduct may, and often does, constitute both a crime and a tort, which is a civil wrong. (Torts are discussed in Chapters 5 and 6.) But an act may be criminal without being tortious, and by the same token, an act may be a tort but not a crime.

Because of the increasing use of criminal sanctions to enforce governmental regulation of business, criminal law is an essential part of business law. Moreover, businesses sustain considerable loss as victims of criminal actions. Accordingly, this chapter covers the general principles of criminal law and criminal procedure as well as specific crimes relevant to business.

NATURE OF CRIMES

A **crime** is any act or omission forbidden by public law in the interest of protecting society and made punishable by the government in a judicial proceeding brought by it. Punishment for criminal conduct includes fines, probation, imprisonment, and death. In addition, some States and the Federal government have enacted victim indemnification statutes which establish funds, financed by criminal fines, to provide indemnification in limited amounts to victims of criminal activity. Crimes are prohibited and punished on grounds of public policy, which may include the protection and safeguarding of government (as in treason), human life (as in murder), or private property (as in larceny). Additional purposes of the criminal law include deterrence, rehabilitation, and retribution.

Historically, criminal law was primarily common law. Today, however, criminal law is almost exclusively statutory. All States have enacted comprehensive criminal-law statutes (or codes) covering most, if not all, of the common law crimes. Moreover, these statutes have made the number of crimes defined in criminal law far greater than the number of crimes defined under common law. Some codes expressly limit crimes to those included in the codes, thus abolishing common-law crimes. Because there are no Federal common law crimes, all Federal crimes are statutory. Nonetheless, some States do not statutorily define all of their crimes and therefore the courts must rely on the common law definitions.

Within recent times the scope of the criminal law has increased greatly. Traditional crimes have been expanded by a large number of regulations and laws which contain criminal penalties. These pertain to nearly every phase of modern living. Typical examples in the field of business law are those laws concerning the licensing and conduct of a business, antitrust laws, and the laws governing the sales of securities.

Essential Elements

In general, a crime consists of two elements: (1) the wrongful or overt act (**actus reus**) and (2) the criminal intent (**mens rea**). For example, to support a larceny conviction it is not enough to show that the defendant stole another's goods; it must also be established that

he intended to steal the goods. Conversely, criminal intent without an overt act is not a crime. For instance, Ann decides to rob the neighborhood grocery store and then really "live it up." Without more, Ann has committed no crime.

Actus reus refers to all the nonmental elements of a crime, including the physical act that must be performed, the consequences of that act, and the circumstances under which it must be performed. The *actus reus* required for specific crimes will be discussed later in this chapter. **Mens rea,** or mental fault, refers to the mental element of a crime. Most common law and some statutory crimes require subjective fault, other crimes require objective fault, while some statutory crimes require no fault at all. The American Law Institute's Model Penal Code and most modern criminal statutes recognize three possible types of **subjective fault:** purposeful, knowing, and reckless. A person acts purposely or intentionally if his conscious object is to engage in the prohibited conduct or to cause the prohibited result. Thus, if Arthur shoots his rifle at Donna, who is seemingly out of gunshot range, with the desire to kill Donna and in fact does kill her, Arthur had the purpose or intent to kill Donna. If Benjamin, desiring to poison Paula, places a toxic chemical in the water cooler in Paula's office and unwittingly poisons Gail and Victor, Benjamin will be found to have purposefully killed Gail and Victor because Benjamin's intent to kill Paula is transferred to Gail and Victor, regardless of Benjamin's feelings toward Gail and Victor.

A person acts **knowingly** if he is aware that his conduct is of the type prohibited or that the prohibited act is practically certain to result. A person acts **recklessly** if he consciously disregards a substantial and unjustifiable risk (1) that his conduct is prohibited, or (2) that it will cause the prohibited result.

Objective fault involves a gross deviation from the standard of care that a reasonable person would observe under the circumstances. Criminal statutes refer to objective fault by such terms as *carelessness* or *negligence.* Such conduct occurs when a person

Figure 4–1 Degrees of Mental Fault

Type	Fault Required	Examples
Subjective Fault	Purposeful Knowing Reckless	Larceny Embezzlement
Objective Fault	Negligent Careless	Careless driving Issuing bad checks (some States)
Liability without Fault	None	Sale of alcohol to a minor Sale of adulterated food

should be aware of a substantial and unjustifiable risk that his conduct is prohibited or will cause the prohibited result. Examples of crimes requiring objective fault are involuntary manslaughter (negligently causing the death of another), carelessly driving an automobile, and, in some States, issuing a bad check.

Many regulatory statutes have totally dispensed with the mental element of a crime. These statutes impose criminal liability without fault. Criminal **liability without fault** makes it a crime for a person to do a specified act or to bring about a certain result without regard to the care exercised by that person. Statutory crimes imposing liability without fault include the sale of adulterated food and the sale of alcoholic beverages to a minor. Most of these crimes involve regulatory statutes dealing with health and safety, and impose only fines for violations (see Figure 4–1).

Classification

Historically, crimes were classified *mala in se* (wrongs in themselves or morally wrong, such as murder) or *mala prohibita* (not morally wrong but declared wrongful by law, such as the prohibition against making a U-turn).

From the standpoint of the seriousness of the offense, crimes are also classified as a **felony** (any crime punishable by death or imprisonment in the penitentiary) or a **misde-**meanor (any crime punishable by a fine or imprisonment in a local jail).

Vicarious Liability

Vicarious liability is liability imposed upon one person for the acts of another person. Employers are vicariously liable for the authorized criminal acts of their employees if the employer directed, participated in, or approved of the act. For example, if an employer directs an employee to fix prices with the employer's competitors, and the employee does so, both the employer and employee have criminally violated the Sherman Antitrust Act. On the other hand, employers are ordinarily not liable for the unauthorized criminal acts of their employees. As previously discussed, most crimes require mental fault, and this element is not present, so far as criminal responsibility of the employer is concerned, where the act of the employee was not authorized.

Employers may, however, be subject to a criminal penalty for the unauthorized act of an advisory or managerial person acting in the scope of employment. Moreover, employers may be criminally liable under liability without fault statutes for certain unauthorized acts of their employees, whether the employee is managerial or not. For example, many States have statutes that punish "every person who by himself or his employee or agent sells anything at short weight," or "whoever sells liquor to a minor and any sale by an employee shall be deemed the act of the employer as well."

The leading case on executive criminal liability without fault is *United States v. Park,* 421 U.S. 658 (1975). John Park, chief executive officer of Acme Markets, a retail supermarket food chain with over 36,000 employees, 874 stores, 12 general warehouses, and 4 special warehouses, was convicted of violating the Federal Food, Drug, and Cosmetic Act. The allegations were based on rodent infestation of Acme's warehouses. In 1970, the FDA informed Acme of rodent infestation in its Philadelphia warehouse and gave notice that the situation must be corrected. In 1971, an FDA inspection discovered unsanitary conditions in Acme's Baltimore warehouse. The FDA notified Park by letter of these findings. After receiving the 1971 letter, Park met with the vice-president for legal affairs, who informed him that the situation was being corrected. When the FDA reinspected the Baltimore facility in March 1972, it again found continued rodent contamination, despite some improvement in sanitary conditions. The FDA charged both Acme, which pleaded guilty, and Park. In upholding the conviction of Park, the U.S. Supreme Court ruled that under the "Federal Food and Drug Act of 1906 knowledge and intent were not required to be proved in prosecutions under its criminal provisions, and that responsible corporate agents could be subjected to the liability thereby imposed." The Court stated that the jury had found that Park had authority and responsibility to deal with the situation, but he had failed to do so.

Liability of the Corporation

Historically, corporations were not held criminally liable because under the traditional view a corporation could not possess the requisite criminal intent and, therefore, was incapable of committing a crime. The dramatic growth in size and importance of corporations has brought about a change in this view. Under the modern approach, a corporation may be liable for violation of statutes imposing liability without fault. In addition, a corporation may be liable where the offense is perpetrated by a high corporate officer or the board of directors. The Model Penal Code provides that a corporation may be convicted of a criminal offense for the conduct of its employees if

1. the legislative purpose of the statute defining the offense is to impose liability on corporations and the conduct is within the scope of the agent's office or employment;

2. the offense consists of an omission to discharge a specific, affirmative duty imposed upon corporations by law; or

3. the offense was authorized, requested, commanded, performed, or recklessly tolerated by the board of directors or by a high managerial agent of the corporation.

Punishment of a corporation for crimes is necessarily by fine and not imprisonment. Nonetheless, individuals bearing responsibility for the criminal act face either or both fines and imprisonment. The Model Penal Code provides that the corporate agent having primary responsibility for the discharge of the duty imposed by law on the corporation is accountable for a reckless omission to perform the required act to the same extent as if the duty were imposed by law directly upon himself. For example, three corporate officials of Film Recovery Systems, Inc., were convicted of murder, while the company and its parent company were found guilty of involuntary manslaughter. The case involved the death of a Film Recovery employee from acute cyanide poisoning. The court found that the conditions at the company facility were "totally unsafe" and that the company officials knew of the danger, since employees were becoming ill, but the officials did nothing to alleviate the situation.

WHITE-COLLAR CRIME

White-collar crime has been defined in various ways. The Justice Department defines it as nonviolent crime involving deceit, corruption, or breach of trust. It has also been defined to include crimes committed by individuals—such as embezzlement and forgery—as well as crimes committed on behalf of a corporation—such as commercial bribery, product safety and health crimes, false advertising, and antitrust violations. A less precise definition is crime "committed by a person of respectability and high social status in the course of his occupation," while a more narrow definition is fraud or deceit practiced through misrepresentation to gain an unfair advantage. Regardless of the definition of white-collar crime, it is clear that such crime costs society billions of dollars; estimates range from $40 billion to over $200 billion per year. Historically, prosecution of white-collar crime was deemphasized because it was not considered violent. Now, however, many contend that white-collar crime often inflicts violence but does so impersonally. For example, unsafe products cause injury and death to consumers while unsafe working conditions cause injury and death to employees.

Computer Crime

One special type of white-collar crime is computer crime. **Computer crime** includes the use of a computer to steal money or services, to remove personal or business information, and to tamper with information. Computer crimes can be broken down into five general categories: (1) theft of computer hardware, software, or secrets; (2) unauthorized use of computer services; (3) theft of money by computer; (4) vandalism of computer hardware or software; and (5) theft of computer data.

Detection of crimes involving computers is extremely difficult. In addition, computer crimes often are not reported because businesses do not want to give the impression that their security is lax. Nonetheless, losses due to computer crimes are estimated to be in the tens of billions of dollars. Moreover, with the ever-increasing societal dependence upon computers, this type of crime will in all likelihood continue to increase.

Already computer crimes have become commonplace. Examples abound: employees of Hitachi and Mitsubishi were indicted for attempting to steal IBM trade secrets. Software piracy (the unauthorized copying of copyrighted software) is now so widespread that it is estimated that two out of every three copies of software are illegally obtained. A computer consultant hired by Security Pacific Bank wrongfully transferred $10 million dollars from the bank to his own Swiss bank account. Six employees stole TRW's credit-rating data and offered to repair poor credit ratings for a fee. Disgruntled or discharged employees have used computer programs called "logic bombs" to destroy software.

As a consequence, enterprises are spending large sums of money to increase computer security. In addition, approximately twenty States have enacted computer crime laws. Despite numerous attempts, the Federal government has not passed comprehensive legislation prohibiting computer crime. The absence of comprehensive Federal legislation has been explained on three grounds: (1) computer crime is not unique and can be addressed under existing criminal law statutes, (2) State legislation can deal with the problem, and (3) writing effective legislation is difficult. Congress has, however, enacted specific legislation (the Counterfeit Access Device and Computer Fraud and Abuse Act) making unauthorized access to a computer a Federal crime.

Racketeering Influenced and Corrupt Organizations Act

The Racketeering Influenced and Corrupt Organizations Act (RICO) was enacted in 1970 with the stated purpose of terminating the infiltration by organized crime into legitimate business. The Act subjects enterprises that engage in a pattern of racketeering to severe civil and criminal penalties. A pattern of racketeering is defined as the commission of two or more predicate acts within a period of ten years. A "predicate act" is any of several criminal offenses listed in RICO. Included are nine major categories of State crimes and twenty-six Federal crimes, such as murder, kidnapping, arson, extortion, drug dealing, securities fraud, mail fraud, and bribery. The most controversial issue concerning RICO is its application to businesses that are not engaged in organized crime but that do meet the "pattern of racketeering" test under the Act. RICO provides for both criminal and civil penalties. *See Sedima, S.P.R.L. v. Imrex Co., Inc.* Criminal conviction under the law may result in a prison term of up to 20 years plus a fine of up to $25,000 per violation. In addition, individuals harmed by RICO violations may invoke the statute's civil remedies, which include treble damage and attorney's fees.

CRIMES AGAINST BUSINESS

Criminal offenses against property greatly affect businesses and amount to losses in the hundreds of billions of dollars each year. This section covers the following crimes against property: (1) larceny, (2) embezzlement, (3) false pretenses, (4) robbery, (5) extortion and bribery, (6) burglary, (7) forgery, and (8) bad checks.

Larceny

The crime of **larceny** is the (1) trespassory (2) taking and (3) carrying away of (4) personal property (5) of another (6) with the intent to deprive the victim permanently of the goods. All six elements must be present for the crime to exist. Thus, if Barbara pays Larry $5,000 for an automobile that Larry agrees to deliver the following week, and Larry does not do so, Larry is *not* guilty of larceny because he has not trespassed on Barbara's property. Larry has not taken anything from Barbara; he has simply refused to turn over the automobile to her. Larceny applies only when a person takes personal property from another without the other's consent. Here Barbara voluntarily paid the money to Larry. Larry has not committed larceny but may have obtained the $5,000 by false pretenses (which is discussed later). Likewise, if Carol takes Dan's 1968 automobile without Dan's permission, intending to

use it for a joyride and then to return it to Dan, Carol has not committed larceny because she did not intend to deprive Dan permanently of the automobile. (Carol has committed the offense of unauthorized use of an automobile, which is a crime in most States.) On the other hand, if Carol left Dan's 1968 car in a junkyard after the joyride, Carol would most likely be held to have committed a larceny because of the high risk that Dan would be permanently deprived of the car. *See People v. Olivo* for a discussion of whether a person may be convicted of larceny for shoplifting if he is arrested before his leaving the store.

Embezzlement

Embezzlement is the fraudulent conversion of another's property by one who was in lawful possession of it. A **conversion** is any act that seriously interferes with the owner's rights in the property such as using it up, selling it, giving it away, or refusing to return it to its rightful owner. This statutory crime was first enacted in response to a 1799 English case in which a bank employee was found not guilty of larceny for taking money given to him for deposit in the bank because the money had been voluntarily handed to him. Thus, embezzlement is a crime intended to prevent individuals who are lawfully in possession of property of another from taking the property for their own use.

The key distinction between larceny and embezzlement, therefore, is whether the thief is in lawful possession of the property. In both there is a misuse of the property of another, but in larceny the thief unlawfully possesses the property, whereas in embezzlement the thief lawfully possesses the property. A second distinction between larceny and embezzlement is that unlike larceny, embezzlement does not require the intent to deprive the owner premanently of his property. Nonetheless, in order to constitute an embezzlement, there must be a serious act of interference with the owner's rights to the property.

False Pretenses

Obtaining property by **false pretenses,** like embezzlement, is a statutory crime enacted to close a loophole in the requirements of larceny. False pretenses is the crime of obtaining title to property of another by means of materially false representations of an existing fact, with knowledge of their falsity, and made with the intent to defraud. Larceny does not cover this situation because the victim voluntarily transfers the property to the thief. For example, a con artist who goes door to door and collects money by saying he is selling stereo equipment, when he is not, is committing the crime of false pretenses. The test of deception is *subjective:* if the victim is actually deceived, the test is satisfied even though a reasonable person would not have been deceived by the defendant's lies. Therefore, gullibility or lack of due care on the part of the victim is no defense.

The great majority of courts hold that a false statement of intention, such as a promise, does not constitute false pretenses. In addition, a false expression of opinion regarding value is usually not considered a misrepresentation of fact and thus will not suffice for false pretenses.

Robbery

Under the common law as well as most statutes, **robbery** is a larceny with the additional elements that (1) the property is taken from the victim or in the immediate presence of the victim and (2) it is accomplished through either force or threat of force. The defendant's force or threat of force need not be against the person from whom the property is taken. For example, a robber threatens Sam that unless Sam opens up his employer's safe, the robber will shoot Maria. Moreover, the victim's presence may be actual or constructive. *Constructive presence* means that the victim is prevented from being present by the defendant's actual or threatened force. For example, if the robber knocks the victim unconscious or ties her up, the victim is considered constructively present.

Many laws distinguish between simple robbery and aggravated robbery. Robbery can be aggravated by any of several factors, including (1) robbery with a deadly weapon, (2) robbery where the robber has the intent to kill or would kill if faced with resistance, (3) robbery that involves serious bodily injury, *or* (4) robbery by two or more persons.

Extortion and Bribery

Although extortion and bribery are frequently confused, they are two distinct crimes. **Extortion,** or blackmail as it is sometimes called, is generally held to be the making of threats for the purpose of obtaining money or property. For example, Lindsey tells Jason that unless Jason pays her $10,000 she will tell Jason's customers that Jason was once arrested for disturbing the peace. Lindsey has committed the crime of extortion. In a few jurisdictions, however, the crime of extortion occurs only if the defendant actually causes the victim to give up money or property.

Bribery, on the other hand, is the offer of money or property to a public official to influence the official's decision. The crime of bribery is committed when the illegal offer is made, whether accepted or not. Thus, if Andrea offered Edward, the mayor of Town Y, a 20-percent interest in Andrea's planned real estate development if Edward would use his influence to have the development proposal approved, Andrea would be guilty of criminal bribery. In contrast, if Edward had threatened Andrea that unless he received a 20-percent interest in Andrea's development he would use his influence to prevent the approval of the development, Edward would be guilty of criminal extortion. Bribery of foreign officials is covered by the Foreign Corrupt Practices Act discussed in Chapter 45.

Some jurisdictions have gone beyond traditional bribery law and have adopted statutes that make commercial bribery illegal. Commercial bribery is the use of bribery to acquire new business, obtain secret information or processes, or obtain kickbacks.

Burglary

At common law, **burglary** was defined as breaking and entering the dwelling of another at night with the intent to commit a felony. Modern statutes differ from the common law definition. Many of them simply require that there be (1) an entry (2) into a building (3) with the intent to commit a felony in the building. Thus, these statutory definitions omit three elements of the common law crime: the building need not be a dwelling house, the entry need not be at night, and the entry need not be a technical breaking. The modern statutes vary so greatly it is impossible to generalize, except that each of the statutes include some, but not all, of the common law elements.

Forgery

Forgery is the intentional falsification or false making of a document with the intent to defraud. Accordingly, if William prepares a false certificate of title to a stolen automobile, he is guilty of forgery. Likewise, if an individual alters some receipts in order to increase her income tax deductions, she has committed the crime of forgery. The most common type of forgery is the signing of another's name to a financial document.

Bad Checks

A statutory crime that has some relation to both forgery and false pretenses is the passing of **bad checks**—that is, writing a check when there is not enough money in the account to cover the check. All jurisdictions have now enacted laws making it a crime to issue bad checks; however, these statutes vary greatly from jurisdiction to jurisdiction. Most jurisdictions simply require that the check be issued; they do not require that the issuer receive anything in return for the check. Also, most jurisdictions require that the defendant issue a check with knowledge that she does not have enough money to cover the check. The Model Penal Code and a number of States provide that knowledge is presumed if the issuer had no account at the bank or if the check was not paid for lack of funds and the issuer failed to pay the check within ten days.

DEFENSES TO CRIMES

Even though a defendant is found to have committed a criminal act, he will not be convicted if he has a valid defense. The defenses most relevant to white-collar crimes and crimes against business include defense of property, insanity, infancy, intoxication, duress, mistake of fact, and entrapment. In some instances, a defense proves the absence of a required element of the crime. For example, insanity, infancy, intoxication, and mistake of fact demonstrate the lack of criminal intent. Other defenses, such as defense of property, duress, and entrapment, provide a justification or excuse that bars criminal liability.

Defense of Person or Property

Individuals may use reasonable force to protect their property. This defense enables a person to commit, without any criminal liability, what would otherwise be considered the crime of assault, battery, manslaughter, or murder. Under the majority rule, deadly force is *never* reasonable to protect property because life is deemed more important than the protection of property. If, however, the defender's use of reasonable force in protecting his property is met with an attack upon his person, then he may use deadly force if the attack threatens him with death or serious bodily harm. For this reason, individuals cannot use a deadly mechanical device, such as a spring gun, to protect their property.

Insanity

The extent to which insanity should be a defense to criminal conduct has long troubled the legal system. The criminal law defense of insanity is directed at those for whom criminal sanctions are not appropriate. Those who are found "not guilty by reason of insanity" are generally not allowed to go free but are typically committed to a mental institution for treatment.

The traditional and most common test for insanity is the *M'Naghten* test. Under this test, defendants are *not* criminally responsible for their conduct if, at the time of committing the act, they did not understand the nature and quality of their act or they could not distinguish between right or wrong. *See State v. Crenshaw.*

Some States have added another test to the *M'Naghten* test—the irresistible impulse test. Under this test, a defendant is freed of criminal responsibility if he had a mental disease that prevented him from controlling his conduct, even though he understood the nature of his act and that it was wrong.

A third test of insanity has been accepted by some States and incorporated into the Model Penal Code. This test provides:

1. A person is not responsible for criminal conduct if at the time of such conduct as a result of mental disease or defect he lacks substantial capacity either to appreciate the criminality (wrongfulness) of his conduct or to conform his conduct to the requirements of law.

2. As used in this Article, the terms "mental disease or defect" do not include an abnormality manifested only by repeated criminal or otherwise antisocial conduct.

This test differs from the other two tests in that it requires only a substantial lack of capacity, whereas the others require a complete impairment of capacity or self-control. This test was universally adopted by the United States Courts of Appeals.

In 1984, Congress adopted the Comprehensive Crime Control Act, which governs the use of the insanity defense in Federal criminal cases. The Act rejects the Model Penal Code's formulation and adopts a variant of the *M'Naghten* test. This statute provides that a defendant is insane if at the time of the commission of the acts the defendant, as a result of a severe mental disease or defect, was unable to appreciate the nature and quality or wrongfulness of his acts. It also

places the burden on the defendant to prove his insanity by clear and convincing evidence.

Infancy

Under the common law and most modern statutes, a child under the age of seven is conclusively presumed to be incapable of committing a crime. From the ages of seven to fourteen, there is a rebuttable presumption that the child is incapable of committing a crime. Above the age of fourteen, there is a rebuttable presumption that the child is capable of committing a crime. The common law defense of infancy has been rendered moot, however, by the enactment of juvenile court acts, which require that all individuals below a certain age—varying among States between fourteen and eighteen—be brought before a juvenile, and not a criminal, court. Juvenile courts are not criminal in nature; rather they attempt to deal with the welfare of the youth and decide if the youth is a delinquent.

Intoxication

The great majority of the States follow what is commonly known as the voluntary/involuntary test. With respect to intoxication, whether brought on by alcohol or narcotic drugs, involuntary intoxication is treated the same as insanity in most jurisdictions. Involuntary intoxication occurs when a person is forced to take the intoxicating substance or he takes it without knowledge or reason to know of its intoxicating nature. In the more common case of voluntary intoxication, in a few States and under the Model Penal Code, it is a defense if it negates a required element of the crime. Thus, if the voluntary intoxication makes the defendant unable to have the knowledge or intent required by the crime, then the defendant is not liable. In the great majority of States, voluntary intoxication is not a defense at all. Where the crime requires negligence, voluntary intoxication is not a defense; where it requires recklessness, the majority of courts and the Model Penal Code provide that it is no defense.

Duress

A person who is threatened with immediate, serious bodily harm to himself or another unless he engages in criminal activity has the valid defense of **duress** to criminal conduct other than murder. For example, Ann threatens to kill Ben if Ben does not assist her in committing larceny. Ben complies. Ben would not be guilty of the larceny because of duress.

Mistake of Fact

If a person reasonably believes the facts to be such that his conduct would not constitute a crime, then the law will treat the facts as he reasonably believed. Accordingly, an honest and reasonable **mistake of fact** will justify the defendant's conduct. For example, if Ann gets into a car that she reasonably believes to be hers—the car is the same color, model, and year as hers, is parked in the same parking lot, and is started by her key—she will be relieved of criminal responsibility for taking Ben's automobile.

Entrapment

The defense of **entrapment** arises when a law enforcement official induces a person to commit a crime when that person would not have done so otherwise. The rationale behind the rule is to prevent law enforcement officials from provoking crime and from engaging in reprehensible conduct. The doctrine is aimed only at government officials and agents and does not apply to private individuals.

CRIMINAL PROCEDURE

Each of the States and the Federal government have procedures for initiating and coordinating criminal prosecutions. In addi-
tion, the first ten amendments to the U.S. Constitution (called the Bill of Rights) guarantee many defenses and rights of an accused. The Fourth Amendment prohibits unreasonable searches and seizures to obtain incriminating evidence. The Fifth Amendment requires indictment for capital crimes by a grand jury, prevents double jeopardy and self-incrimination, and prohibits deprivation of life or liberty without due process of law. The Sixth Amendment requires a speedy and public trial by an impartial jury, and that the accused be informed of the nature of the accusation, be confronted with the witnesses who testify against him, be given the power to obtain witnesses in his favor, and have the right to competent counsel for his defense. The Eighth Amendment prohibits excessive bail, excessive fines, and cruel or unusual punishment (see Figure 4–2).

Most State constitutions have similar provisions protecting the rights of accused persons. In addition, the Fourteenth Amendment prohibits State governments from denying any person of life, liberty, or property without due process of law. Moreover, the U.S. Supreme Court has held that most Constitutional protections just discussed apply to the States through operation of the Fourteenth Amendment.

Although the various jurisdictions differ in details, they have a number of common objectives for their criminal process. The primary purpose is the effective enforcement of the criminal law, but this purpose must be accomplished within the limitations imposed by other goals. These goals include advancing an adversary system of adjudication, requiring the government to bear the burden of proof, minimizing erroneous convictions, minimizing the burdens of defense, respecting individual dignity, maintaining the appearance of fairness, and achieving equality in the administration of the process.

We will first discuss the steps in a criminal prosecution; then we will focus on the major constitutional protections for the accused in our system of criminal justice.

Figure 4–2 Constitutional Protection for the Criminal Defendant

Amendment	Protection Conferred
Fourth	Freedom from unreasonable search and seizure
Fifth	Due process
	Right to indictment by grand jury for capital crimes*
	Freedom from double jeopardy
	Freedom from self-incrimination
Sixth	Right to speedy, public trial by jury
	Right to be informed of accusations
	Right to confront witnesses
	Right to present witnesses
	Right to competent counsel
Eighth	Freedom from excessive bail
	Freedom from cruel and unusual punishment

*This right has *not* been applied to the States through the Fourteenth Amendment.

Steps in Criminal Prosecution

Although the particulars of criminal procedure vary from State to State, the following provides a basic overview. After arrest, the accused is booked and appears before a magistrate, commissioner, or justice of the peace, where formal notice of the charges is given; he is given advice of his rights, and bail is set. Next, a **preliminary hearing** is held to determine whether there is probable cause to believe the defendant is the one who committed the crime. The defendant is usually entitled to be represented by counsel.

If the magistrate concludes that there is probable cause, she will bind the case over to the next stage, which is either an indictment or information, depending upon the jurisdiction. The Federal system and about one-third of the States require indictments for all felony prosecutions (unless waived by the defendant), while the other States permit but do not mandate indictments. A grand jury issues an *indictment* or true bill if it finds sufficient evidence to justify a trial on the charge brought. The grand jury is not bound by the magistrate's decision at the preliminary hearing. Unlike the preliminary hearing, the grand jury does not hear evidence from the defendant, nor does the defendant appear before the grand jury. A grand jury tradition-

ally consisted of not less than sixteen and not more than twenty-three people. An *information* is used in misdemeanor cases and in some felony cases in those States that do not require indictments. An **information** is a formal accusation of a crime brought by a prosecuting officer and not a grand jury.

At the **arraignment,** the defendant is brought before the trial court where he is informed of the charge against him and he enters his plea. The arraignment must be held promptly after the indictment or information has been filed. If his plea is "not guilty," he must stand trial. He is entitled to a jury trial for all felonies and for misdemeanors punishable by more than six months imprisonment. If he chooses, however, he may have his guilt or innocence determined by the court sitting without a jury, which is called a "bench trial."

A criminal trial is somewhat similar to a civil trial but there are some significant differences: (1) the defendant is presumed innocent, (2) the burden of proof on the prosecution is to prove criminal guilt beyond a reasonable doubt, and (3) the defendant is not required to testify. The trial begins with the selection of the jury and the opening statements by the prosecutor and the attorney for the defense. The prosecution presents evidence first; then the defendant presents his.

At the conclusion of the testimony, closing statements are made and the jury is instructed as to the applicable law and retires to arrive at a verdict. If the verdict is "not guilty," the matter ends there. The State has no right to appeal from an acquittal; and the accused, having been placed in "jeopardy," cannot be tried a second time for the same offense. If the verdict is "guilty," the judge will enter a judgment of conviction and set the case for sentencing. The defendant may make a motion for a new trial, asserting that prejudicial error occurred at the trial, thus requiring a retrial of the case. He may appeal to a reviewing court, alleging error by the trial court and asking for either his discharge or a remandment of the case for a new trial.

Fourth Amendment

The Fourth Amendment protects all individuals against unreasonable searches and seizures. This Amendment is designed to protect the privacy and security of individuals against arbitrary invasions by government officials. Although the Fourth Amendment by its terms applies only to the Federal government, the Fourteenth Amendment makes it applicable to the States as well.

When there is a violation of the Fourth Amendment, the general rule prohibits the introduction of the illegally seized evidence. The purpose of this **exclusionary rule** is to discourage illegal police conduct and to protect individual liberty, not to hinder the search for the truth. In *Weeks v. United States,* 232 U.S. 383 (1914), the United States Supreme Court ruled:

If letters and private documents can thus be seized and held and used in evidence against a citizen accused of an offense, the protection of the Fourth Amendment declaring his right to be secure against such searches and seizures is of no value, and, so far as those thus placed and concerned, might as well be stricken from the Constitution. The efforts of the courts and their officials to bring the guilty to punishment, praiseworthy as they are, are not to be aided by the sacrifice of those great principles established by years of endeavor and suffering which have resulted in their embodiment in the fundamental law of the land.

Nonetheless, in recent years the U.S. Supreme Court has limited the exclusionary rule. *See United States v. Leon.*

To obtain a search warrant of a particular person, place, or thing, the law enforcement official must demonstrate to a magistrate that he has probable cause to believe that the search will reveal evidence of criminal activity. **Probable cause** means that "the apparent facts set out in the affidavit [of the requesting authority] are such that a reasonably discreet and prudent man would be led to believe that there was a commission of the offense charged. . . ." *Dumbra v. United States,* 268 U.S. 435 (1925).

Even though the Fourth Amendment requires that a search and seizure generally be made after a valid search warrant has been obtained, in some instances a search warrant is not necessary. For example, it has been held that a warrant is not necessary where (1) there is hot pursuit of a fugitive, (2) voluntary consent is given, (3) an emergency requires such action, (4) there has been a lawful arrest, (5) evidence of a crime is in plain view of the law enforcement officer, or (6) delay would present a significant obstacle to the investigation.

Fifth Amendment

The Fifth Amendment protects persons against self-incrimination, double jeopardy, and being charged with a capital or infamous crime except by grand jury indictment.

The prohibitions against self-incrimination and double jeopardy, but not the grand jury clause, also apply to the States through the Due Process Clause of the Fourteenth Amendment.

The privilege against self-incrimination extends only to testimonial evidence and not to physical evidence. The Fifth Amendment "privilege protects an accused only from being compelled to testify against himself, or otherwise provide the State with evidence of a testimonial or communicative nature." *Schmerber v. California,* 384 U.S. 757 (1966). Therefore, a person can be forced to stand in a lineup for identification purposes, provide a handwriting sample, or take a blood test. Most significantly, the Fifth Amendment does not protect business records of a business entity such as a corporation or partnership; it applies only to papers of individuals. Moreover, the Fifth Amendment does not prohibit examination of an individual's business records as long as the individual is not compelled to testify against himself.

The Fifth Amendment and the Fourteenth Amendment also guarantee due process of law, which is basically the requirement of a fair trial. Every person is entitled to have charges or complaints against him, whether in civil or criminal proceedings, made publicly and in writing, and be given the opportunity to defend against them. In criminal prosecutions, it includes the right to counsel, to confront and cross-examine adverse witnesses, to testify in his own behalf if desired, to produce witnesses and offer other evidence, and to be free from any and all prejudicial conduct and statements.

Sixth Amendment

The Sixth Amendment provides that the Federal government shall provide the accused with a speedy and public trial by an impartial jury, inform her of the nature and cause of the accusation, confront her with the witnesses against her, have compulsory process for obtaining witnesses in her favor, and have the assistance of counsel for her defense. The Fourteenth Amendment extends these guarantees to the States.

The Supreme Court has explained the purpose of guaranteeing the right to a trial by jury as follows: "[T]he purpose of trial by jury is to prevent oppression by the Government by providing a safeguard against the corrupt or overzealous prosecutor and against the compliant, biased, or eccentric judge. . . . [T]he essential factors of a jury trial obviously lie in the interposition between the accused and his accuser of the common sense judgment of a group of laymen." *Apodaca v. Oregon*, 406 U.S. 404 (1972). Nevertheless, a defendant may give up her right to a jury trial.

Historically, juries consisted of twelve jurors, but in the Federal courts and in the courts of certain States, the number has been reduced to six. The Supreme Court has held that the use of a six-member jury in a criminal case does not violate a defendant's right to a jury trial under the Sixth Amendment. The Supreme Court recognized that there was no observable difference between the results reached by a jury of twelve or by a jury of six, nor was there any evidence to suggest that a jury of twelve is more advantageous to a defendant. The jury needs only to be large enough "to promote group deliberation, free from outside attempts at intimidation, and to provide a fair possibility for obtaining a representative cross section of the community." Moreover, State court jury verdicts need not be unanimous provided the vote is sufficient to assure adequate deliberations. Thus, the Supreme Court has upheld jury votes of 11–1, 10–2, and 9–3 but rejected as insufficient a 5–1 vote.

CASES

RICO

SEDIMA, S.P.R.L. v. IMREX CO., INC. (1985)

United States Supreme Court, 1985.
473 U.S. 479, 105 S.Ct. 3275, 87 L.Ed.2d 346.

WHITE, J.

The Racketeer Influenced and Corrupt Organizations Act (RICO) [citation] provides a private civil action to recover treble damages for injury "by reason of a violation of" its substantive provisions. [Citation.] The initial dormancy of this provision and its recent greatly increased utilization are now familiar history. In response to what it perceived to be misuse of civil RICO by private plaintiffs, the court below construed [citation] to permit private actions only against defendants who had been convicted on criminal charges, and only where there had occurred a "racketeering injury." While we understand the court's concern over the consequences of an unbridled reading of the statute, we reject both of its holdings.

RICO takes aim at "racketeering activity," which it defines as any act "chargeable" under several generically described state criminal laws, any act "indictable" under numerous specific federal criminal provisions, including mail and wire fraud, and any "offense" involving bankruptcy or securities fraud or drug-related activities that is "punishable" under federal law. [Citation]. * * *

Congress provided criminal penalties of imprisonment, fines, and forfeiture for violation of these provisions. [Citation.] In addition, it set out a far-reaching civil enforcement scheme [citation]. * * *

In 1979, petitioner Sedima, a Belgian corporation, entered into a joint venture with respondent Imrex Co. to provide electronic components to a Belgian firm. The buyer was to order parts through Sedima; Imrex was to obtain the parts in this country and ship them to Europe. The agreement called for Sedima and Imrex to split the net proceeds. Imrex filled roughly $8 million in orders placed with it through Sedima. Sedima became convinced, however, that Imrex was presenting inflated bills, cheating Sedima out of a portion of its proceeds by collecting for nonexistent expenses.

In 1982, Sedima filed this action in the Federal District Court for the Eastern District of New York.

* * *

While not choosing a precise formulation, the District Court held that a complaint must allege a "RICO-type injury," which was either some sort of distinct "racketeering injury," or a "competitive injury." It found "no allegation here of any injury apart from that which would result directly from the alleged predicate acts of mail fraud and wire fraud" . . . and accordingly dismissed the RICO counts for failure to state a claim.

A divided panel of the Court of Appeals for the Second Circuit affirmed.

* * *

The language of RICO gives no obvious indication that a civil action can proceed only after a criminal conviction. The word "conviction" does not appear in any relevant portion of the statute. [Citations.] To the contrary, the predicate acts involve conduct that is "chargeable" or "indictable," and "offense[s]" that are "punishable," under various criminal statutes.

* * *

Accordingly, the fact that Imrex and the individual defendants have not been convicted under RICO or the federal mail and wire fraud statutes does not bar Sedima's action.

In considering the Court of Appeals' second prerequisite for a private civil RICO action—"injury . . . caused by an activity which RICO was designed to deter"—we are somewhat hampered by the vagueness of that concept. Apart from reliance on the general purposes of RICO and a reference to "mobsters," the court provided scant indication of what the requirement of racketeering injury means. It emphasized Congress' undeniable desire to strike at organized crime, but acknowledged and did not purport to overrule Second Circuit precedent rejecting a requirement of an organized crime nexus. [Citation.]

* * *

We need not pinpoint the Second Circuit's precise holding, for we perceive no distinct "racketeering injury" requirement. Given that "racketeering activity" consists of no more and no less than commission of a predicate act, [citation], we are initially doubtful about a requirement of a "racketeering injury" separate from the harm from the predicate acts. A reading of the statute belies any such requirement. [The Act] authorizes a private suit by "[a]ny person injured in his business or property by reason of a violation of [the Act]." [Further, the Act] makes it unlawful for "any person"—not just mobsters—to use money derived from a pattern of racketeering activity to invest in an enterprise, to acquire control of an enterprise through a pattern of racketeering activity, or to conduct an enterprise through a pattern of racketeering activity. [Citation.] If the defendant engages in a pattern of racketeering activity in a manner forbidden by these provisions, and the racketeering activities injure the plaintiff in his business or property, the plaintiff has a claim. [Citation.] There is no room in the statutory language for an additional, amorphous "racketeering injury" requirement.

* * *

Underlying the Court of Appeals' holding was its distress at the "extraordinary, if not outrageous," uses to which civil RICO has been put. [Citation.] Instead of being used against mobsters and organized criminals, it has become a tool for everyday fraud cases brought against "respected and legitimate 'enterprises.' " [Citation.] Yet Congress wanted wanted to reach both "legitimate" and "illegitimate" enterprises. [Citation.] The former enjoy neither an inherent incapacity for criminal activity nor immunity from its consequences. The fact that [the Act] is used against respected businesses allegedly engaged in a pattern of specifically identified criminal conduct is hardly a sufficient reason for assuming that the provision is being misconstrued. Nor does it reveal the "ambiguity" discovered by the court below. "[T]he fact that RICO has been applied in situations not expressly anticipated by Congress does not demonstrate ambiguity. It demonstrates breadth." [Citation.]

It is true that private civil actions under the statute are being brought almost solely against such defendants, rather than against the archetypal, intimidating mobster. Yet this defect—if defect it is—is inherent in the statute as written, and its correction must lie with Congress. It is not for the judiciary to eliminate the private action in situations where Congress has provided it simply because plaintiffs are not taking advantage of it in its more difficult applications.

We nonetheless recognize that, in its private civil version, RICO is evolving into something quite different from the original conception of its enactors. [Citation.] Though sharing the doubts of the Court of Appeals about this increasing divergence, we cannot agree with either its diagnosis or its remedy. The "extraordinary" uses to which civil RICO has been put appear to be primarily the result of the breadth of the predicate offenses, in particular the inclusion of wire, mail, and securities fraud and the failure of Congress and the courts to develop a meaningful concept of "pattern." * * *

Sedima may maintain this action if the defendants conducted the enterprise through a pattern of racketeering activity. The questions whether the defendants committed the requisite predicate acts, and whether the commission of those acts fell into a pattern, are not before us. The complaint is not deficient for failure to allege either an injury separate from the financial loss stemming from the alleged acts of mail and wire fraud, or prior convictions of the defendants. The judgment below is accordingly reversed, and the case is remanded for further proceedings consistent with this opinion.

Larceny

PEOPLE v. OLIVO

Court of Appeals of New York, 1981.
52 N.Y.2d 309, 438 N.Y.S.2d 242, 420 N.E.2d 40.

COOKE, C.J.

[This case presents] a recurring question in this era of the self-service store which has never been resolved by this court: may a person be convicted of larceny for shoplifting if the person is caught with goods while still inside the store? For reasons outlined below, it is concluded that a larceny conviction may be sustained, in certain situations, even though the shoplifter was apprehended before leaving the store.

In *People v. Olivo,* defendant was observed by a security guard in the hardware area of a department store. Initially conversing with another person, defendant began to look around furtively when his acquaintance departed. The security agent continued to observe and saw defendant assume a crouching position, take a set of wrenches and secret it in his clothes. After again looking around, defendant began walking toward an exit, passing a number of cash registers en route. When defendant did not stop to pay for the merchandise, the officer accosted him a few feet from the exit. In response to the guard's inquiry, denied having the wrenches, but as he proceeded to the security office, defendant removed the wrenches and placed them under his jacket. At trial, defendant testified that he had placed the tools under his arm and was on line at a cashier when apprehended. The jury returned a verdict of guilty on the charge of . . . larceny. The conviction was affirmed by Appellate Term.

* * *

The primary issue * * * is whether the evidence, viewed in the light most favorable to the prosecution, was sufficient to establish the elements of larceny as defined by the Penal Law. To resolve this common question, the development of the common-law crime of larceny and its evolution into modern statutory form must be briefly traced.

Larceny at common law was defined as a trespassory taking and carrying away of the property of another with intent to steal it. The early common-law courts apparently viewed larceny as defending society against breach of the peace, rather than protecting individual property rights, and therefore placed heavy emphasis upon the requirement of a *trespassory taking* [citation]. Thus, a person such as a bailee who had rightfully obtained possession of property from its owner could not be guilty of larceny [citation]. The result was that the crime of larceny was quite narrow in scope.

Gradually, the courts began to expand the reach of the offense, initially by subtle alterations in the common-law concept of possession [citation]. Thus, for instance, it became a general rule that goods entrusted to an employee were not deemed to be in his possession, but were only considered to be in his custody, so long as he remained on the employer's premises [citation]. And, in the case of [citation], it was held that a shop owner retained legal possession of merchandise being examined by a prospective customer until the actual sale was made. In these situations, the employee and the customer would not have been guilty of larceny if they had first obtained lawful possession of the property from the owner. By holding that they had not acquired possession, but merely custody, the court was able to sustain a larceny conviction.

As the reach of larceny expanded, the intent element of the crime became of increasing importance, while the requirement of a trespassory taking became less significant. As a result, the bar against convicting a person who had initially obtained lawful possession of property faded * * *.

Later cases went even further, often ignoring the fact that a defendant had initially obtained possession lawfully, and instead focused upon his later intent. The crime of larceny then encompassed, not only situations where the defendant initially obtained property by a trespassory taking, but many situations where an individual, possessing the requisite intent, exercised control over property inconsistent with the continued rights of the owner. During this evolutionary process, the purpose served by the crime of larceny obviously shifted from protecting society's peace to general protection of property rights.

Modern penal statutes generally have incorporated these developments under a unified definition of larceny [citation]. Case law, too, now tends to focus upon the actor's intent and the exercise of dominion and control over the property [citation]. * * *

This evolution is particularly relevant to thefts occurring in modern self-service stores. In stores of that type, customers are impliedly invited to examine, try on, and carry about the merchandise on display. Thus in a sense, the owner has consented to the customer's possession of the goods for a limited purpose. That the owner has consented to that possession does not, however, preclude a conviction for larceny. If the customer exercises dominion and control wholly inconsistent with the continued rights of the owner, and the other elements of the crime are present, a larceny has occurred. Such conduct on the part of a customer satisfies the "taking" element of the crime.

It is this element that forms the core of the controversy in these cases. The defendants argue, in essence, that the crime is not established, as a matter of law, unless there is evidence that the customer departed the shop without paying for the merchandise.

Although this court has not addressed the issue, case law from other jurisdictions seems unanimous in holding that a shoplifter need not leave the store to be guilty of larceny. This is because a shopper may treat merchandise in a manner inconsistent with the owner's continued rights—and in a manner not in accord with that of prospective purchaser—without actually walking out of the store. Indeed, depending upon the circumstances of each case, a variety of conduct may be sufficient to allow the trier of fact to find a taking. * * *

In many cases, it will be particularly relevant that defendant concealed the goods under clothing or in a container. Such conduct is not generally expected in a self-service store and may in a proper case be deemed an exercise of dominion and control inconsistent with the store's continued rights. Other furtive or unusual behavior on the part of the defendant should also be weighed. Thus, if the defendant surveys the area while secreting the merchandise or abandoned his or her own property in exchange for the concealed goods, this may evince larcenous rather than innocent behavior. Relevant too is the customer's proximity to or movement towards one of the store's exits. Certainly it is highly probative of guilt that the customer was in possession of secreted goods just a few short steps from the door or moving in that direction. Finally, possession of a known shoplifting device actually used to conceal merchandise, such as a specially designed outer garment or false bottomed carrying case, would be all but decisive.

Of course, in a particular case, any one or any combination of these factors may take on special significance. And there may be other considerations, not now identified, which should be examined. So long as it bears upon the principal issue—whether the shopper exercised control wholly inconsistent with the owner's continued rights—any attending circumstance is relevant and may be taken into account.

* * *

Accordingly, . . . the order of the Appellate Term should be affirmed.

Insanity

STATE v. CRENSHAW

Supreme Court of Washington, 1983.
98 Wash.2d 789, 659 P.2d 488.

BRACHTENBACH, J.

Rodney Crenshaw was convicted by a jury of first degree murder. Finding that the trial court committed no reversible error, we affirm the conviction.

Petitioner Rodney Crenshaw pleaded not guilty and not guilty by reason of insanity to the charge of first degree murder of his wife, Karen Crenshaw. A jury found him guilty. Petitioner appealed his conviction. * * *

Before turning to the legal issues, the facts of the case must be recounted. While defendant and his wife were on their honeymoon in Canada, petitioner was deported as a result of his participation in a brawl. He secured a motel room in Blaine, Washington and waited for his wife to join him. When she arrived 2 days later, he immediately thought she had been unfaithful—he sensed "it wasn't the same Karen . . . she'd been with someone else."

Petitioner did not mention his suspicions to his wife, instead he took her to the motel room and beat her unconscious. He then went to a nearby store, stole a knife, and returned to stab his wife 24 times, inflicting a fatal wound. He left again, drove to a nearby farm where he had been employed and borrowed an ax. Upon returning to the motel room, he decapitated his wife with such force that the ax marks cut into the concrete floor under the carpet and splattered blood throughout the room.

Petitioner then proceeded to conceal his actions. He placed the body in a blanket, the head in a pillowcase, and put both in his wife's car. Next, he went to a service station, borrowed a bucket and sponge, and cleaned the room of blood and fingerprints. Before leaving, petitioner also spoke with the motel manager about a phone bill, then chatted with him for awhile over a beer.

When Crenshaw left the motel he drove to a remote area 25 miles away where he hid the two parts of the body in thick brush. He then fled, driving to the Hoquiam area, about 200 miles from the scene of the crime. There he picked up two hitchhikers, told them of his crime, and enlisted their aid in disposing of his wife's car in a river. The hitchhikers contacted the police and Crenshaw was apprehended shortly thereafter. He voluntarily confessed to the crime.

The defense of not guilty by reason of insanity was a major issue at trial. Crenshaw testified that he followed the Moscovite religious faith, and that it would be improper for a Moscovite not to kill his wife if she committed adultery. Crenshaw also has a history of mental problems, for which he has been hospitalized in the past. The jury, however, rejected petitioner's insanity defense, and found him guilty of murder in the first degree.

* * *

Insanity is an affirmative defense the defendant must establish by a preponderance of the evidence. [Citation.] Sanity is presumed, even with a history of prior institutional commitments from which the individual was released upon sufficient recovery.

The insanity defense is not available to all who are mentally deficient or deranged; legal insanity has a different meaning and a different purpose than the concept of medical insanity. [Citation.] A verdict of not guilty by reason of insanity completely absolves a defendant of any criminal responsibility. Therefore, "the defense is available only to those

persons who have lost contact with reality so completely that they are beyond any of the influences of the criminal law." [Citation.]

Petitioner assigned error to insanity defense instruction 10 which reads:

* * *

Insanity existing at the time of the commission of the act charged is a defense.

For a defendant to be found not guilty by reason of insanity you must find that, as a result of mental disease or defect, the defendant's mind was affected to such an extent that the defendant was unable to perceive the nature and quality of the acts with which the defendant is charged or was unable to tell right from wrong with reference to the particular acts with which defendant is charged.

What is meant by the terms "right and wrong" refers to knowledge of a person at the time of committing an act that he was acting contrary to the law.

[Citation.] But for the last paragraph, this instruction tracks the language of [citation], which is the *M'Naghten* test as codified in [Washington State]. Petitioner contends, however, that the trial court erred in defining "right and wrong" as legal right and wrong rather than in the moral sense.

We find this instruction was not reversible error on three, alternative grounds: (1) The *M'Naghten* opinion amply supports the "legal" wrong definition as used in this case, (2) under these facts, "moral" wrong and "legal" wrong are synonymous, therefore the "legal" wrong definition did not alter the meaning of the test, and (3) because Crenshaw failed to prove other elements of the insanity defense, any error in the definition of wrong was harmless.

* * *

Such an interpretation is consistent with Washington's strict application of *M'Naghten*. This court's view has been that "when *M'Naghten* is used, all who might possibly be deterred from the commission of criminal acts are included within the sanctions of the criminal law." [Citation.]

[O]nly those persons "who have lost contact with reality so completely that they are beyond any of the influences of the criminal law," may have the benefit of the insanity defense in a criminal case.

* * *

Alternatively, the statement in instruction 10 may be approved because, in this case, legal wrong is synonymous with moral wrong. This conclusion is premised on two grounds.

First, in discussing the term "moral" wrong, it is important to note that it is society's morals, and not the individual's morals, that are the standard for judging moral wrong under *M'Naghten*. If wrong meant moral wrong judged by the individual's own conscience, this would seriously undermine the criminal law, for it would allow one who violated the law to be excused from criminal responsibility solely because, in his own conscience, his act was not morally wrong. [Citations.]

* * *

We conclude that Crenshaw knew his acts were morally wrong from society's viewpoint and also knew his acts were illegal. His personal belief that it was his duty to kill his wife for her alleged infidelity cannot serve to exculpate him from legal responsibility for his acts.

A narrow exception to the societal standard of moral wrong has been drawn for instances wherein a party performs a criminal act, knowing it is morally and legally wrong, but believing, because of a mental defect, that the act is ordained by God: such would be the situation with a mother who kills her infant child to whom she is devotedly attached, believing that God has spoken to her and decreed the act. [Citation.] Although the woman knows that the law and society condemn the act, it would be unrealistic to hold her responsible for the crime, since her free will has been subsumed by her belief in the deific decree. [Citation.]

This exception is not available to Crenshaw, however. Crenshaw argued only that he followed the Moscovite faith and that Moscovites believe it is their duty to kill an unfaithful wife. This is not the same as acting under a deific command. Instead, it is akin to "[t]he devotee of a religious cult that enjoins ... human sacrifice as a duty [and] is *not*

thereby relieved from responsibility before the law." [Citation.]

* * *

We also find that, under any definition of wrong, Crenshaw did not qualify for the insanity defense under *M'Naghten;* therefore, any alleged error in that definition must be viewed as harmless. * * * Here, any error is harmless for two alternate reasons. First, Crenshaw failed to prove an essential element of the defense because he did not prove his alleged delusions stemmed from a mental defect; second, he did not prove by a preponderance of the evidence that he was legally insane at the time of the crime.

In addition to an incapacity to know right from wrong, *M'Naghten* requires that such incapacity stem from a mental disease or defect. [Citation.] Assuming, arguendo, that Crenshaw did not know right from wrong, he failed to prove that a mental defect was the cause of this inability.

* * *

Finding no reversible error was committed by the trial court, we affirm the judgment.

Fourth Amendment Exclusionary Rule

UNITED STATES v. LEON

Supreme Court of the United States, 1984.
468 U.S. 897, 104 S.Ct. 3405, 82 L.Ed.2d 677.

WHITE, J.

This case presents the question whether the Fourth Amendment exclusionary rule should be modified so as not to bar the use in the prosecution's case-in-chief of evidence obtained by officers acting in reasonable reliance on a search warrant issued by a detached and neutral magistrate but ultimately found to be unsupported by probable cause. To resolve this question, we must consider once again the tension between the sometimes competing goals of, on the one hand, deterring official misconduct and removing inducements to unreasonable invasions of privacy and, on the other, establishing procedures under which criminal defendants are "acquitted or convicted on the basis of all the evidence which exposes the truth." [Citation.]

* * *

In August 1981, a confidential informant of unproven reliability informed an officer of the Burbank Police Department that two persons known to him as "Armando" and "Patsy" were selling large quantities of cocaine and methaqualone from their residence at 620 Price Drive in Burbank, Cal. The informant also indicated that he had witnessed a sale of methaqualone by "Patsy" at the residence approximately five months earlier and had observed at that time a shoebox containing a large amount of cash that belonged to "Patsy." He further declared that "Armando" and "Patsy" generally kept only small quantities of drugs at their residence and stored the remainder at another location in Burbank.

On the basis of this information, the Burbank police initiated an extensive investigation focusing first on the Price Drive residence and later on two other residences as well. Cars parked at the Price Drive residence were determined to belong to respondents Armando Sanchez, who had previously been arrested for possession of marihuana, and Patsy Stewart, who had no criminal record. During the course of the investigation, officers observed an automobile belonging to respondent Ricardo Del Castillo, who had previously been arrested for possession of 50 pounds of marihuana, arrive at the Price Drive residence. The driver of that car entered the house, exited shortly thereafter carrying a small paper sack, and drove away. A check of Del Castillo's probation records led the officers to respondent Alberto Leon, whose telephone number Del Castillo had listed as his employer's. Leon had been arrested in 1980 on drug charges, and a companion had informed the police at that time that Leon was heavily involved in the importation of drugs into this country. Before the current investigation began, the Burbank officers had learned that an informant had told a Glendale police officer that Leon stored a large quantity of methaqualone at his residence in Glendale. During the course of this investigation, the Burbank officers learned that Leon was living at 716 South Sunset Canyon in Burbank.

Subsequently, the officers observed several persons, at least one of whom had prior drug involvement, arriving at the Price Drive residence and leaving with small packages; observed a variety of other material activity at the two residences as well as at a condominium at 7902 Via Magdalena; and witnessed a variety of relevant activity involving respondents' automobiles. The officers also observed respondents Sanchez and Stewart board separate flights for Miami. The pair later returned to Los Angeles together, consented to a search of their luggage that revealed only a small amount of marihuana, and left the airport. Based on these and other observations summarized in the affidavit, Officer Cyril Rombach of the Burbank Police Department, an experienced and well-trained narcotics investigator, prepared an application for a warrant to search 620 Price Drive, 716 South Sunset Canyon, 7902 Via Magdalena, and automobiles registered to each of the respondents for an extensive list of items believed to be related to respondents' drug-trafficking activities. Officer Rombach's extensive application was reviewed by several Deputy District Attorneys.

A facially valid search warrant was issued in September 1981 by a state superior court judge. The ensuing searches produced large quantities of drugs at the Via Magdalena and Sunset Canyon addresses and a small quantity at the Price Drive residence. Other evidence was discovered at each of the residences and in Stewart's and Del Castillo's automobiles. Respondents were indicted by a grand jury in the District Court for the Central District of California and charged with conspiracy to possess and distribute cocaine and a variety of substantive counts.

The respondents then filed motions to suppress the evidence seized pursuant to the warrant. The District Court held an evidentiary hearing and, while recognizing that the case was a close one, granted the motions to suppress in part. It concluded that the affidavit was insufficient to establish probable cause, but did not suppress all of the evidence as to all of the respondents because none of the respondents had standing to challenge all of the searches. In response to a request from the Government, the court made clear that Officer Rombach had acted in good faith, but it rejected the Government's suggestion that the Fourth Amendment exclusionary rule should not apply where evidence is seized in reasonable, good-faith reliance on a search warrant.

The District Court denied the Government's motion for reconsideration and a divided panel of the Court of Appeals for the Ninth Circuit affirmed. The Court of Appeals . . . concluded that Officer Rombach's affidavit could not establish probable cause to search the Price Drive residence. To the extent that the affidavit set forth facts demonstrating the basis of the informant's knowledge of criminal activity, the information included was fatally stale. The affidavit, moreover, failed to establish the informant's credibility.

* * *

The Fourth Amendment contains no provision expressly precluding the use of evidence obtained in violation of its commands, and an examination of its origin and purposes makes clear that the use of fruits of a past unlawful search or seizure "work[s] no new Fourth Amendment wrong." [Citation.] The wrong condemned by the Amendment is "fully accomplished" by the unlawful search or seizure itself, and the exclusionary rule is neither intended nor able to "cure the invasion of the defendant's rights which he has already suffered." [Citation.] The rule thus operates as "a judicially created remedy designed to safeguard Fourth Amendment rights generally through its deterrent effect, rather than a personal constitutional right of the person aggrieved." [Citation.]

Whether the exclusionary sanction is appropriately imposed in a particular case, our decisions make clear, is "an issue separate from the question whether the Fourth Amendment rights of the party seeking to invoke the rule were violated by police conduct." [Citation.] Only the former question is

currently before us, and it must be resolved by weighing the costs and benefits of preventing the use in the prosecution's case-in-chief of inherently trustworthy tangible evidence obtained in reliance on a search warrant issued by a detached and neutral magistrate that ultimately is found to be defective.

The substantial social costs exacted by the exclusionary rule for the vindication of Fourth Amendment rights have long been a source of concern. "Our cases have consistently recognized that unbending application of the exclusionary sanction to enforce ideals of governmental rectitude would impede unacceptably the truth-finding functions of judge and jury." [Citation.] An objectionable collateral consequence of this interference with the criminal justice system's truth-finding function is that some guilty defendants may go free or receive reduced sentences as a result of favorable plea bargains. Particularly when law enforcement officers have acted in objective good faith or their transgressions have been minor, the magnitude of the benefit conferred on such guilty defendants offends basic concepts of the criminal justice system. [Citation.] Indiscriminate application of the exclusionary rule, therefore, may well "generat[e] disrespect for the law and the administration of justice." [Citation.] Accordingly, "[a]s with any remedial device, the application of the rule has been restricted to those areas where its remedial objectives are thought most efficaciously served." [Citation.]

* * *

Close attention to those remedial objectives has characterized our recent decisions concerning the scope of the Fourth Amendment exclusionary rule. The Court has, to be sure, not seriously questioned, "in the absence of a more efficacious sanction, the continued application of the rule to suppress evidence from the [prosecution's] case where a Fourth Amendment violation has been substantial and deliberate. . . ." [Citation.] Nevertheless, the balancing approach that has evolved in various contexts including criminal trials—"forcefully suggest[s] that the exclusionary rule be more generally modified to permit the introduction of evidence obtained in the reasonable good-faith belief that a search or seizure was in accord with the Fourth Amendment." [Citation.]

* * *

Because a search warrant "provides the detached scrutiny of a neutral magistrate, which is a more reliable safeguard against improper searches than the hurried judgment of a law enforcement officer 'engaged in the often competitive enterprise of ferreting out crime,'" [Citations], we have expressed a strong preference for warrants and declared that "in a doubtful or marginal case a search under a warrant may be sustainable where without one it would fail." [Citations.] Reasonable minds frequently may differ on the question whether a particular affidavit establishes probable cause, and we have thus concluded that the preference for warrants is most appropriately effectuated by according "great deference" to a magistrate's determination. [Citations.]

Deference to the magistrate, however, is not boundless.

* * *

If exclusion of evidence obtained pursuant to a subsequently invalidated warrant is to have any deterrent effect, . . . it must alter the behavior of individual law enforcement officers or the policies of their departments. One could argue that applying the exclusionary rule in cases where the police failed to demonstrate probable cause in the warrant application deters future inadequate presentations or "magistrate shopping" and thus promotes the ends of the Fourth Amendment. Suppressing evidence obtained pursuant to a technically defective warrant supported by probable cause also might encourage officers to scrutinize more closely the form of the warrant and to point out suspected judicial errors. We find such arguments speculative and conclude that suppression of evidence obtained pursuant to a warrant should be ordered only on a case-by-case basis and only in those unusual cases in which exclusion will further the purposes of the exclusionary rule.

We have frequently questioned whether the exclusionary rule can have any deterrent effect when the offending officers acted in the objectively reasonable belief that their conduct did not violate the Fourth Amendment. * * *

In short, where the officer's conduct is objectively reasonable,

excluding the evidence will not further the ends of the exclusionary rule in any appreciable way; for it is painfully apparent that . . . the officer is acting as a reasonable officer would and should act under the circumstances. Excluding the evidence can in no way affect his future conduct unless it is to make him less willing to do his duty. [Citation.]

This is particularly true, we believe, when an officer acting with objective good faith has obtained a search warrant from a judge or magistrate and acted within its scope. In most such cases, there is no police illegality and thus nothing to deter. It is the magistrate's responsibility to determine whether the officer's allegations establish probable cause and, if so, to issue a warrant comporting in form with the requirements of the Fourth Amendment. In the ordinary case, an officer cannot be expected to question the magistrate's probable-cause determination or his judgment that the form of the warrant is technically sufficient. "[O]nce the warrant issues, there is literally nothing more the policeman can do in seeking to comply with the law." [Citation.] Penalizing the officer for the magistrate's error, rather than his own, cannot logically contribute to the deterrence of Fourth Amendment violations.

* * *

We conclude that the marginal or nonexistent benefits produced by suppressing evidence obtained in objectively reasonable reliance on a subsequently invalidated search warrant cannot justify the substantial costs of exclusion. . . . Nevertheless, the officer's reliance on the magistrate's probable-cause determination and on the technical sufficiency of the warrant he issues must be objectively reasonable, [citation], and it is clear that in some circumstances the officer will have no reasonable grounds for believing that the warrant was properly issued.

* * *

Accordingly, the judgment of the Court of Appeals is *Reversed.*

QUESTIONS

1. Discuss criminal intent and the various degrees of mental fault.

2. List and define the offenses against property.

3. Identify the significant features of white-collar crimes.

4. List and explain the constitutional amendments affecting criminal procedure.

5. Discuss the defense of criminal insanity and the various tests employed.

PROBLEMS

1. Sam said to Carol, "Kim is going to sell me a good used car next Monday and then I'll deliver it to you in exchange for your microcomputer, but I'd like to have the computer now." Relying on this statement, Carol delivered the computer to Sam. Sam knew Kim had no car, would have none in the future, and had no such arrangement with Kim. The appointed time of exchange passed, and Sam failed to deliver the car to Carol. Has a crime been committed? Discuss.

2. Sara, a lawyer, drew a deed for Robert by which Robert was to convey land to Rick. The deed was correct in every detail. Robert examined and verbally approved it but did not sign it. Sara erased Rick's name and substituted her own. Robert signed the deed with all required legal formalities without noticing the change. Was Sara guilty of forgery? Discuss.

3. Ann took Bonnie's watch before Bonnie was aware of the theft. Bonnie discovered her loss immediately and pursued Ann. Ann pointed a loaded pistol at Bonnie, who, in fear of being shot, allowed Ann to escape. Was Ann guilty of robbery? Of any other crime?

4. Jones and Wilson were on trial, separately, for larceny of a $1,000 bearer bond (payable to the holder of the bond not a named individual) issued by Brown, Inc. The Commonwealth's evidence showed that the owner of the bond had dropped it accidentally in the street enclosed in an envelope bearing his name and address; that Jones found the envelope with the bond in it; that Jones could neither read nor write; that Jones presented the

envelope and bond to Wilson, an educated man, and asked Wilson what he should do with it; that Wilson told Jones that the finder of lost property becomes the owner of it; that Wilson told Jones that the bond was worth $100 but that the money could only be collected at the issuer's home office; that Jones then handed the bond to Wilson, who redeemed it at the corporation's home office and received $1,000; that Wilson gave Jones $100 of the proceeds. What rulings?

5. Truck drivers for a hauling company, while loading a desk, found a $100 bill that fell out of the desk. They agreed to get it exchanged for small bills and divide the proceeds. En route to a bank, one of them changed his mind and refused to proceed with the scheme, whereupon the other pulled a knife and demanded the bill. A police officer intervened. It turned out that the bill was counterfeit money. What crimes have been committed?

6. William was judged legally insane and committed as an inmate of a State hospital. Six months after his commitment he escaped and met his friend Roberta. After Roberta and William had several drinks of hard liquor, they rode to a liquor store in a car driven by William. In accordance with a previous plan William waited in the car while Roberta held up the proprietor of the liquor store. William and Roberta were later apprehended and are now being prosecuted for robbery. William pleaded not guilty by reason of insanity and intoxication and on the further ground that he did not enter the building or receive any part of the stolen property. Discuss and decide.

7. Peter, an undercover police agent, was trying to locate a laboratory where it was believed that methamphetamine or "speed"—a controlled substance—was being manufactured illegally. Peter went to Mary's home and said that he represented a large organization that was interested in obtaining methamphetamine. Peter offered to supply a necessary ingredient for the manufacture of the drug, which was very difficult to obtain, in return for one-half of the drug produced. Mary agreed and processed the chemical given to her by Peter in Peter's presence. Later Peter returned with a search warrant and arrested Mary. Mary was charged with various narcotics law violations. Mary asserted the defense of entrapment. Decision?

8. The police obtained a search warrant based on an affidavit that contained the following allegations: (a) Donald was seen crossing a State line on four occasions during a five-day period and going to a particular apartment; (b) telephone records disclosed that the apartment had two telephones; (c) Donald had a reputation as a bookmaker and as an associate of gamblers; and (d) the FBI was informed by a "confidential reliable informant" that Donald was conducting gambling operations. When a search was made based on the warrant, evidence was obtained that resulted in Donald's conviction of violating certain gambling laws. Donald challenged the constitutionality of the search warrant. Decision?

9. A national bank was robbed by a man with a small strip of tape on each side of his face. An indictment was returned against David. David was then arrested, and counsel appointed to represent him. Two weeks later, without notice to David's lawyer, an FBI agent arranged to have the two bank employees observe a lineup, including David and five or six other prisoners. Each person in the lineup wore strips of tape, as had the robber, and each was directed to repeat the words "Put the money in the bag," as had the robber. Both of the bank employees identified David as the robber. At David's trial he was again identified by the two, in the courtroom, and the prior lineup identification was elicited on cross-examination by David's counsel. David's counsel moved the court either to grant a judgment of acquittal or alternatively to strike the courtroom identifications on the grounds that the lineup had violated David's Fifth Amendment privilege against self-incrimination and his Sixth Amendment right to counsel. Decision?

10. Waronek owned and operated a trucking rig, transporting goods for L.T.L. Perishables, Inc., of St. Paul, Minnesota. He accepted an offer to haul a trailer load of beef from Illini Beef Packers, Inc., in Joslin, Illinois, to Midtown Packing Company in New York City. After his truck was loaded with ninety-five forequarters and ninety-five hindquarters of beef in Joslin, Waronek drove north to his home in Watertown, Wisconsin, rather than east to New York. While in Watertown, he asked employees of the Royal Meat Company to butcher and prepare four hindquarters of beef—two for himself and two for his friends. He also offered to sell ten hindquarters to one employee of the company at an alarmingly reduced rate. The suspicious employee contacted the authorities, who told him to proceed with the deal. When Waronek arrived in New York with his load short nineteen hindquarters, Waronek telephoned L.T.L. Perishables in St. Paul. He notified them "that he was short nineteen hindquarters, that he knew where the beef went, and that he would make good on it out of future settlements." L.T.L. told him to contact the New York police but he failed to do so. Shortly thereafter, he was arrested by the Federal Bureau of Investigation and indicted for the embezzlement of goods moving in interstate commerce. Decision?

11. Four separate cases involving similar fact situations were consolidated since they presented the same constitutional question. In each case, police officers, detectives, or prosecuting attorneys took a defendant into custody and interrogated him in a police station to obtain a confession. In none of these cases did the officials fully and effectively advise the defendant of his rights at the outset of the interrogation. Police interrogations produced oral admissions of guilt from each defendant, as well as signed statements from three of them, which were used to convict them at their trials. The defendants appeal, arguing that the officials should have warned them of their constitutional rights and the consequences of waiving them before the questionings began. It was contended that to permit any statements obtained without such a warning violated their Fifth Amendment privilege against self-incrimination. Decision?

Chapter 5

INTENTIONAL TORTS

Interference with the Person
Interference with Right of Dignity
Interference with Property
Interference with Economic Interests
Defenses to Intentional Torts

ALL forms of civil liability are either (1) voluntarily assumed, as by contract, or (2) involuntarily imposed by law. Tort liability is of the second type. Tort law gives persons redress from civil wrongs or injuries to their person, property, and economic interests. The law of torts therefore reallocates losses caused by human misconduct. In general, a tort is committed when

1. a duty owing by one person to another,

2. is breached, and

3. proximately causes

4. injury or damage to the owner of a legally protected interest.

The law of torts is not static and affords relief against novel forms of misconduct when necessary and appropriate. Over the past decade, the courts have expanded tort law by recognizing new torts to provide additional protection for personal, dignitary, property, and economic interests. At the same time State legislatures and, to a lesser extent, courts have been extremely active in assessing the need for tort reform. In general, the reform has focused on limiting liability by restricting damages or narrowing claims.

Each person is legally responsible for the damages that are proximately caused by his tortious conduct. Moreover, as discussed in Chapter 19, businesses that use employees to conduct their business activities are also liable for the torts committed by their employees in the course of the employees' duties. The tort liability of employers makes the study of tort law essential to business managers.

In a tort action the injured party *sues* to recover *compensation* for the injury sustained as a result of the defendant's wrongful conduct. The primary purpose of tort law is to compensate the injured party, not to punish the wrongdoer as in the case of criminal law. The same conduct may, and often does, constitute both a crime and a tort. An example is an assault and battery committed by Johnson against West. For the commission of this crime, the State may take appropriate action against Johnson. In addition, however, Johnson has violated West's right to be secure in his person, and so has committed a tort against West. West, regardless of the criminal action by the State against Johnson, may bring a civil action against Johnson for damages. On the other hand, an act may be criminal without being tortious and, by the same token, an act may be a tort but not a crime. In certain cases courts may award **punitive** or exemplary damages, which are damages over and above the amount necessary to compensate the plaintiff. Where the defendant's tortious conduct has been intentional and outrageous, exhibiting "malice" or a fraudulent or evil motive, most courts permit a jury to award punitive damages. The allowance of punitive damages is designed to punish and make an example of the defendant and thus deter others from similar conduct.

Injuries may be inflicted intentionally, negligently, or without fault (strict liability). This chapter will discuss intentional torts. The following chapter will cover negligence and strict liability.

Tort law is primarily common law. The Restatement of Torts provides an orderly presentation of this law. The first Restatement was adopted and promulgated by the American Law Institute during the years from 1934 to 1939. Since then, it has served as a vital force in shaping the law of torts. Between 1965 and 1978 the institute adopted and promulgated a revised edition of the Restatement of Torts which supersedes the First Restatement. The revised Restatement will be referred to simply as the Restatement. Selected provisions of the Restatement are included in Appendix B of this book.

INTENT

Intent, as used in tort law, does not require a hostile or evil motive but rather denotes that the actor desires to cause the consequences of his act *or* that he believes that the consequences are substantially certain to result from it. Restatement, Section 8A. Thus, it has been stated:

The three most basic elements of this most common usage of "intent" are that (1) it is a *state of mind* (2) about *consequences* of an act (or omission) and not about the act itself, and (3) it extends not only to having in the mind a purpose (or desire) to bring about given consequences but also to having in mind a belief (or knowledge) that given

consequences are substantially certain to result from the act. Prosser and Keeton on Torts (5th ed.) p. 34.

The following examples should help to clarify the definition of intent: (1) If A fires a gun in the middle of the Mojave Desert, he intends to fire the gun, but when the bullet hits B who is in the desert without A's knowledge, A does not intend that result. (2) A throws a bomb into B's office in order to kill B. A knows that C is in B's office and that the bomb is substantially certain to injure C, although A has no desire to do so. A is, nonetheless, liable to C for any injury caused C. A's intent to injure B is *transferred* to C.

Infants (persons who have not reached the age of majority) are held liable for their intentional torts. The infant's age and knowledge, however, are critical in determining whether the infant had sufficient intelligence to form the requisite intent. Incompetents, like infants, are generally held liable for their intentional torts.

A number of established and specifically named torts protect an individual from intentional interferences with his person, dignity, property, and economic interests. Because the law of torts is dynamic, new forms of relief continue to develop. To provide guidance for determining when liability should be imposed for intentionally inflicted harm that does not fall within the requirements of an established tort, Section 870 of the Restatement provides a general catchall intentional tort:

One who intentionally causes injury to another is subject to liability to the other for that injury, if his conduct is generally culpable and not justifiable under the circumstances. This liability may be imposed although the actor's conduct does not come within a traditional category of tort liability.

This section also provides a unifying principle for both the long-established torts and those that have developed more recently.

INTERFERENCE WITH THE PERSON

The law provides protection against intentional interference with the person. The primary interests protected by these torts are freedom from bodily contact (by the tort of battery), freedom from apprehension (assault), freedom from confinement (false imprisonment), and freedom from mental distress (infliction of emotional distress). Generally, intentional torts to the person entitle the injured party to recover damages for bodily harm, emotional distress, loss or impairment of earning capacity, reasonable medical expenses, and harm to property or business if caused by the tortious conduct.

Battery — *TOUCHING*

Battery is an intentional infliction of harmful or offensive bodily contact. It may cause serious injury, such as a gunshot wound or a blow on the head with a club, or it may cause little or no physical injury, such as knocking a hat off of a person's head or flicking a glove in another's face. Bodily contact is offensive if it would offend a reasonable person's sense of dignity, even if the defendant's conduct was intended only as a joke or a compliment. Restatement, Section 19. For instance, kissing another without permission would constitute a battery. Bodily contact may be accomplished by the use of objects, such as Arthur's throwing a rock at Bea with the intention of hitting her. If the rock hits Bea or any other person, Arthur has committed a battery. Nonetheless, in a densely populated society one cannot expect complete freedom from personal contact with others. Accordingly, neither casual bumping into another in a congested area nor a gentle tap on the shoulder to get one's attention would constitute a battery.

Assault — *FEAR OF TOUCHING*

Assault is intentional conduct by one person directed at another which places him in apprehension of immediate bodily harm or offensive contact. It is usually committed immediately preceding a battery, but if the intended battery fails, the assault remains. Assault is principally a mental rather than a physical intrusion. Accordingly, damages for

it may include compensation for fright and humiliation. The person in danger of immediate bodily harm must have *knowledge* of the danger and be apprehensive of its imminent threat to his safety. For example, Joan aims a loaded gun at Kelly's back but is subdued by Pat before Kelly becomes aware of the danger. Joan has not committed an assault upon Kelly.

Historically, it has been said that words alone do not constitute an assault. Nonetheless, spoken words must be taken in context, and if as taken cause apprehension, these spoken words will constitute an assault. On the other hand, words sometimes will negate an apparent threat so that there is no assault. This does not mean that a defendant can avoid liability for an assault by making his threat conditional. The threat "If you do not give me your book, I will break your arm" constitutes an assault.

False Imprisonment

The tort of **false imprisonment,** or false arrest, is the intentional confining of a person against her will within fixed boundaries if the person is conscious of the confinement or harmed by it. Merely obstructing a person's freedom of movement is not false imprisonment so long as there is a reasonable alternative exit available. *See Peterson v. Sorlien.* The restraint may be brought about by physical force, the threat of physical force (both express and implied), by physical barriers, or by force directed against the plaintiff's property. For instance, an individual who remains in a store after his wallet is confiscated or who remains on a train after the conductor refuses to allow her suitcase to be removed are both examples of false imprisonment by using force against personal property. Damages for false imprisonment may include compensation for loss of time, physical discomfort, inconvenience, physical illness, and mental suffering.

Merchants occasionally have a problem with potential liability for false imprisonment when they seek to question a suspected shoplifter. If the merchant detains an innocent person, she may be facing a lawsuit for false imprisonment. Most States have statutes which protect the merchant, provided she detains the suspect upon probable cause, in a reasonable manner, and for not more than a reasonable time.

Infliction of Emotional Distress

One of the more recently recognized torts is that of intentional infliction of emotional distress. The Restatement, Section 46 states the rule as follows:

One who by extreme and outrageous conduct intentionally or recklessly causes severe emotional distress to another is subject to liability for such emotional distress, and if bodily harm to the other results from it, for such bodily harm.

Under this tort, liability is imposed for conduct exceeding all bounds usually tolerated by society when the conduct intentionally causes serious mental distress. Many courts allow recovery even in the absence of physical injury. *See Agis v. Howard Johnson Company.* This cause of action does not protect a person from abusive language or rudeness, but rather from atrocious, intolerable conduct beyond all bounds of decency. Examples of this tort include leading to a person's home, when he is present, a noisy demonstrating mob yelling threats to lynch him unless he leaves town, or placing a rattlesnake in another's bed as a practical joke. Other examples include sexual harassment on the job and outrageous and prolonged bullying tactics employed by creditors or collection agencies, attempting to collect a debt, or insurance adjusters trying to force a settlement of an insurance claim.

INTERFERENCE WITH RIGHT OF DIGNITY

The law also protects a person against intentional interference with his right of dignity. This right includes a person's reputation, privacy, and freedom from unjustifiable litigation.

Defamation QUASI TORT

The tort of **defamation** is a false communication that injures a person's reputation by disgracing him and diminishing the respect in which he is held. An example would be the publication of a statement that a person had committed a crime or had a loathsome disease. In *Beckman v. Dunn,* 276 Pa.Super. 527, 419 A.2d 583 (1980), the court stated:

A communication is defamatory if it tends to harm the reputation of another so as to lower him in the estimation of the community or deter third persons from associating or dealing with him, and necessarily involves the idea of disgrace.

Elements of Defamation   The burden of proof is on the plaintiff to prove the falsity of the defamatory statement. If the defamatory communication is handwritten, typewritten, printed, pictorial, or by other means with like communicative power, such as television or radio, it is designated **libel.** If it is spoken or oral, it is designated **slander.** Restatement, Sections 568 and 568A. In either case it must be communicated to a person or persons other than the one who is defamed. This is referred to as its *publication.* If Maurice writes a defamatory letter about Pierre's character, which he hands or mails to Pierre, this is not a publication since it is intended only for Pierre.

A new and significant trend affecting business has been the bringing of defamation suits against former employers by discharged employees. It has been reported that such suits comprise approximately one-third of all defamation lawsuits. *See Frank B. Hall & Co., Inc. v. Buck.*

Defenses to Defamation   Truth and privilege are defenses to defamation. In most States, **truth** is a complete defense without regard to the purpose or intent in publishing the defamation. **Privilege** is an immunity from tort liability granted when the defendant's conduct furthers a societal interest of greater importance than the injury inflicted upon the plaintiff. There are three types of

privileges that apply to defamation: absolute, conditional, and constitutional.

As with the defense of truth, **absolute privilege** protects the defendant regardless of his motive or intent. Absolute privilege has been confined to those few situations where public policy clearly favors complete freedom of speech and includes: (1) statements made regarding a judicial proceeding; (2) statements made by members of Congress on the floor of Congress; (3) statements made by certain executive officers in the discharge of their governmental duty; and (4) statements made between spouses when they are alone.

Qualified or **conditional privilege** depends upon proper use of the privilege. A person has conditional privilege to publish defamatory matter to protect his own legitimate interests, or in some cases the interests of another. Conditional privilege also extends to many cases where the publisher and the recipient have a common interest as with letters of reference. Conditional privilege, however, is forfeited by the publisher if she acts in an excessive manner, without probable cause, or for an improper purpose.

The First Amendment to the United States Constitution guarantees freedom of speech and freedom of press. The U.S. Supreme Court has applied these rights to the law of defamation by extending a form of **constitutional privilege** to comment regarding public officials or public figures so long as it is done without *malice*. Restatement, Section 580A. For these purposes "malice" is not ill will but clear and convincing proof of the publisher's knowledge of falsity or reckless disregard of the truth. Thus, under constitutional privilege the public official or public figure must prove that the defendant published the defamatory and false comment with knowledge or in reckless disregard of the comment's falsity and its defamatory character.

In a defamation suit brought by a private person (one who is not a public official and is not a public figure) against a member of the news media, the plaintiff must prove that the defendant published the defamatory and false comment with malice *or* negligence. Where a private person brings suit against a defendant who is *not* a member of the news media, it is currently unresolved whether the plaintiff must prove anything beyond the fact that a false and defamatory statement had been made.

Invasion of Privacy

The invasion of a person's right to privacy actually consists of four distinct torts: (1) appropriation of a person's name or likeness; (2) unreasonable intrusion upon the seclusion of another; (3) unreasonable public disclosure of private facts; or (4) unreasonable publicity which places another in a false light in the public eye. Restatement, Section 652A.

It is entirely possible and not uncommon for a person's right of privacy to be invaded in such a way that two or more of these related torts are committed. For example, Cindy forces her way into Ozzie's hospital room, takes a photograph of Ozzie, and publishes it to promote Cindy's cure for Ozzie's illness along with false statements about Ozzie that would be highly objectionable to a reasonable person. Ozzie would be entitled to recover on any or all of the four torts comprising invasion of privacy.

Appropriation Appropriation is the use of plaintiff's name or likeness for the benefit of the defendant, as for example in promoting or advertising a product or service. Restatement, Section 652C. The tort of appropriation, which is also known as the **right of publicity**, seeks to protect the individual's right to the exclusive use of his identity. In the example above, Cindy's use of Ozzie's photograph to promote Cindy's business constitutes the tort of appropriation. *See Carson v. Here's Johnny Portable Toilets, Inc.*

Intrusion Intrusion is the unreasonable and highly offensive interference with the solitude or seclusion of another. Restatement, Section 652B. Such unreasonable interference would include improper entry into another's dwelling, unauthorized eavesdropping upon another's private conversations, and unauthorized examination of another's private papers and records. The intrusion must be offensive or objectionable to a reasonable person and must involve matters which are private. Thus, there is no liability if the defendant examines public records or observes the plaintiff in a public place. This form of invasion of privacy is committed once the intrusion occurs as publicity is not required.

Public Disclosure of Private Facts Under the tort of public disclosure of private facts, liability is imposed for *publicity* given to private information about another if the matter made public would be highly offensive and objectionable to a reasonable person. As with intrusion, this tort only applies to private, not public, information regarding an individual, but unlike intrusion it requires publicity. Under the Restatement, the publicity required differs in degree from "publication" as used in the law of defamation. Under this tort the private facts must be communicated to the public at large or become public knowledge, whereas publication of a defamatory statement need only be made to a single third party. Section 652D, Comment a. Some courts, however, have allowed recovery where the disclosure was made to only one person. Thus, under the Restatement approach, Kathy, a creditor of Gary, will not invade Gary's privacy by writing a letter to Gary's employer informing the employer of Gary's failure to pay the debt, but Kathy would be liable if she posted in the window of her store a statement that Gary will not pay a debt owed to Kathy. Also, unlike defamation, this tort applies to truthful private information if the matter published would be offensive and objectionable to a reasonable person of ordinary sensibilities.

False Light The tort of false light imposes liability for *publicity* that places another in a false light that is highly offensive if the defendant *knew* or acted in *reckless disregard* that the matter publicized was false. Restatement, Section 652E. For example, Linda includes Keith's name and photograph in a public "rogues' gallery" of convicted criminals. Keith has never been convicted of any crime. Linda is liable to Keith for placing him in a false light. Other examples include publicly and falsely attributing to a person an opinion, statement, or written work as well as the unauthorized use of a person's name on a petition or on a complaint in a lawsuit.

As with defamation, the matter must be untrue, but unlike defamation it must be "publicized," not merely "published." Restatement, Section 652D, Comment a. Although the matter must be objectionable to a reasonable person, it need not be defamatory. In many instances, the same facts will give rise to both an action for defamation and false light.

Defenses *Absolute, conditional,* and *constitutional* privilege apply to publication of any matter that is an invasion of privacy to the same extent as they do to defamation.

Misuse of Legal Procedure

Three torts comprise the misuse of legal procedure: malicious prosecution, wrongful civil proceedings, and abuse of process. Each protects an individual from being subjected to unjustifiable litigation. Malicious prosecution and wrongful civil proceedings impose liability for damages caused by improperly brought proceedings, including harm to reputation, credit or standing, emotional distress, and expenses of defending against the wrongfully brought lawsuit. Abuse of process imposes liability for harm caused by the wrongful conduct.

Malicious Prosecution The tort of malicious prosecution consists in bringing about a criminal proceeding against another person if the proceeding is initiated (1) without probable cause, (2) for an improper purpose, and (3) results in a finding of not guilty. Restatement, Section 653. A public prosecutor acting in her official capacity in bringing about and maintaining a criminal proceeding is cloaked with absolute immunity from liability for malicious prosecution. Restatement, Section 656.

Wrongful Civil Proceedings The tort of wrongful civil proceedings is similar to malicious prosecution except that the legal proceeding is a civil suit instead of a criminal proceeding. It occurs when a person brings a civil action without probable cause, for an improper purpose, and the civil suit results in a judgment for the defendant. Restatement, Section 674. An improper purpose is any purpose other than the adjudication of the claim in the suit, such as initiating litigation in order to prevent an owner from selling his property to another.

Abuse of Process Abuse of process is a tort consisting of the use of a legal proceeding (criminal or civil) in order to accomplish a purpose for which it is not designed. It applies even when there is probable cause or when the plaintiff or prosecution succeeds in the litigation. Typically, the tort involves the use of a legal process to coerce the payment of money or transfer of property. For example, Wilson brings about a criminal prosecution of Janet with reasonable grounds to believe her guilty, but Wilson's primary purpose is to extort payment of a debt. Wilson has commited the tort of abuse of process.

INTERFERENCE WITH PROPERTY

The law also provides protection against invasions of a person's interests in property. Intentional interference with property includes the torts of (1) trespass to real property, (2) nuisance, (3) trespass to personal property, and (4) conversion.

Real Property

Real property is land and anything attached to it, such as buildings, trees, and minerals. The law protects the rights of the possessor of land to its exclusive use and quiet enjoyment. Accordingly, damages for harm to land include compensation for the diminution in value of the land caused by the harm, the loss of use of the land, and the discomfort caused to the possessor of the land. Restatement, Section 929.

Trespass Section 158 of the Restatement provides:

One is subject to liability to another for trespass, irrespective of whether he thereby causes harm to any legally protected interest of the other, if he intentionally
(a) enters land in the possession of the other, or causes a thing or a third person to do so, or
(b) remains on the land, or
(c) fails to remove from the land a thing which he is under a duty to remove.

It is no defense that the intruder acted upon the mistaken belief of law or fact that he was not trespassing. If the intruder intended to be upon the particular property, it is irrelevant that he reasonably believed that he owned the land or had permission to enter upon the land. Restatement, Section 164. An intruder is not liable if his presence on the land of another is not caused by his own actions. For example, if Ralph is thrown onto Tim's land by Carol, Ralph is not liable to Tim for trespass, although Carol is.

A trespass may be committed on, beneath, or above the surface of the land, although the law regards the upper air, above the prescribed minimum altitude of flight, as a public highway. Therefore, there is no trespass unless the aircraft enters into the lower reaches of the air space and substantially interferes with the landowner's use and enjoyment. Restatement, Section 159.

Nuisance A nuisance is a non-trespassory invasion of another's interest in the private use and enjoyment of land. Restatement, Section 821D. In contrast to trespass, nuisance does not require interference with another's right to exclusive possession of land, but rather imposes liability for significant and unreasonable harm to another's use or enjoyment of land. Examples of nuisances include the emission of unpleasant odors, smoke, dust, or gas, as well as the pollution of a stream, pond, or underground water supply. In one case, a computer's serious disturbance of a television retailer's signal reception was considered a nuisance.

Personal Property

Personal property or chattel is any type of property other than an interest in land. The law protects a number of interests in the possession of personal property including an interest in the property's physical condition and usability, an interest in the retention of possession, and an interest in its availability for future use.

Trespass Trespass to personal property consists of the intentional dispossession or unauthorized use of the personal property of another. The interference with the right to exclusive use and possession may be direct or indirect, but liability is limited to instances in which the trespasser (a) dispossesses the other of the property; (b) substantially impairs the condition, quality, or value of the property; or (c) deprives the possessor of the use of the property for a substantial time. Restatement, Section 218. For example, Albert parks his car in front of his house. Ronald pushes Albert's car around the corner. Albert subsequently looks for his car but cannot find it for several hours. Ronald is liable to Albert for trespass.

Conversion Conversion is the intentional exercise of dominion or control over another's personal property which so seriously interferes with the other's right of control as to justly require the payment of full value for the property. Restatement, Section 222A. The Restatement considers the following factors in determining whether justice requires the wrongdoing actor to pay full value:

1. the extent and duration of the actor's exercise of dominion or control;

2. the actor's intent to assert a right in fact inconsistent with the other's right of control;

3. the actor's good faith;

4. the extent and duration of the resulting interference with the other's right of control;

5. the harm done to the chattel; and

6. the inconvenience and expense caused to the other.

Conversion may consist of the intentional destruction of the personal property or the use of the property in an unauthorized manner. For example, Ken entrusts an automobile to Barbara, a dealer, for sale. Barbara drives the car 8,000 miles on her own business. Barbara is liable to Ken for conversion. On the other hand, in the example above in which Ronald pushed Albert's car around the corner, Ronald would *not* be liable to Albert for conversion.

A major distinction between trespass to personal property and conversion is the measure of damages. In trespass, the possessor recovers damages for actual harm to the property or for the loss of possession. In conversion, the possessor recovers the full value of the property, and the convertor takes possession of it upon payment of the judgment.

INTERFERENCE WITH ECONOMIC INTERESTS

A fourth set of interests protected by the law against intentional interference is economic interests. Economic or pecuniary interests include a person's existing and prospective contractual relations, a person's business reputation, a person's name and likeness (previously discussed under appropriation), and a person's freedom from deception. Business torts—those torts that protect a person's economic interests—are discussed in this section under the following headings: (1) interference with contractual relations, (2) disparagement, and (3) fraudulent misrepresentation.

Interference with Contractual Relations

In order to conduct business it is necessary to establish trade relations with employees, suppliers, and customers. These relations may or may not be contractual but those that are, or are capable of being established by contract, receive legal protection against interference. Section 766 of the Restatement provides:

One who intentionally and improperly interferes with the performance of a contract (except a contract to marry) between another and a third person by inducing or otherwise causing the third person not to perform the contract, is subject to liability to the other for the pecuniary loss resulting to the other from the failure of the third person to perform the contract.

Similar liability is imposed for intentional and improper interference with another's prospective contractual relation, such as lease renewals or financing for construction. Restatement, Section 766B.

In either case, the rule requires that a person act with the purpose or motive of interfering with another's contract or with the knowledge that such interference is substantially certain to occur as a natural consequence of her actions. The interference may be by prevention through the use of physical force or by threats. Frequently, it is accomplished by inducement, such as the offer of a better contract. For instance, Edgar may offer Doris, an employee of Frank, a yearly salary of $5,000 per year more than the contractual arrangement between Doris and Frank. If Edgar is aware of the contract between Doris and Frank and that his offer to Doris interferes with that contract, then Edgar is liable to Frank for intentional interference with contractual relations. *See Texaco, Inc. v. Pennzoil Co.*

To be distinguished is the situation where the contract may be terminated at will or there is only the prospect of a contractual relation. In these cases, competition is a proper basis for interference, for if one party is pursuing a contractual relation, others are also free to pursue a similar arrangement. For example, Amos and Brenda are competing distributors of transistors. Amos induces Carter, a prospective customer of Brenda, to buy the transistors from Amos instead of Brenda. Amos has no liability to Brenda because Amos's interference with Brenda's prospective contract with Carter is justified on the basis of competition, so long as Amos does not use predatory means such as physical violence, fraud, civil suits, or criminal prosecution to persuade Carter to deal with Amos.

Damages for interference with contractual relations include the pecuniary loss of the benefits of the contract, consequential losses caused by the interference, and emotional distress or actual harm to reputation. Restatement, Section 774A.

Disparagement

The tort of **disparagement** or injurious falsehood imposes liability for the publication of a false statement that results in harm to another's interests which have pecuniary value if the publisher knows that the statement is false or acts in reckless disregard of its truth or falsity. This tort most commonly involves false statements intended by the party making them to cast doubt upon the title or quality of another's property or products. Thus, Adam, while contemplating the purchase of merchandise which belongs to Barry, reads an advertisement in a newspaper in which Carol falsely asserts she owns the merchandise. Carol has disparaged Barry's property in the goods. Similarly, Marlene, knowing her statement to be false, tells Lionel that Matthew, an importer of wood, does not deal in mahogany. As a result Lionel, who had intended to buy mahogany from Matthew, buys it elsewhere. Marlene is liable to Matthew for disparagement.

Absolute, conditional, and constitutional privilege apply to the same extent to the tort of disparagement as they do to defamation. In addition, a competitor has conditional privilege to compare her products favorably to those of a rival, even though she does not believe that her products are superior. There is no privilege, however, if the comparison contains false assertions of specific unfavorable facts about the competitor's property. For example, a manufacturer advertises that his goods are the best in the market, even though he knows that a competitor's product is better. The manufacturer is not liable for disparagement. If he goes further, however, and falsely states that his product is better because his competitor uses shoddy materials, then his disparagement would not be privileged and he would be liable to his competitor for disparagement.

The pecuniary loss which may be recovered by an injured person is that which directly and immediately results from impairment of the marketability of the property disparaged. Damages may also be recovered for expenses necessary to counteract the false publication, including litigation expenses, the cost of notifying customers, and the cost of publishing denials. Thus, Ursula publishes an untrue statement in a magazine that cranberries grown during the current season in a particular area are unwholesome. Victor is a jobber who has contracted to buy the entire output of cranberries grown in this area. Victor's business falls off 50 percent. If there are no other facts which account for this falling off of Victor's business, Victor is entitled to recover the amount of his loss from Ursula, plus expenses necessary to counteract the misinformation published.

The torts of defamation and disparagement are similar in a number of respects and may overlap in some situations. Both torts involve the imposition of liability for injuries sustained through publication of false statements. Moreover, the defense of truth as well as absolute, conditional, and constitutional privilege apply to the same extent to the tort of disparagement as they do to defamation. Nevertheless, the torts protect two different interests. Defamation protects the *reputation* of the injured party while disparagement protects the *economic interests* of the injured party. Therefore, if the statement reflects solely upon the title or quality of the product sold by the plaintiff, then there is only disparagement. For example, Nathan knowingly states to Olivia that Paula manufactures and sells soap that is gritty. Although Paula's soap is not gritty, her sales of soap fall off as a consequence. Nathan is liable to Paula for disparagement but not defamation. If, on the other hand, the statement implies that the plaintiff lacks integrity or is dishonest, there may also be personal defamation. For instance, Quentin falsely states to a number of people that Rhonda knowingly sells pork that is diseased. Quentin is liable to Rhonda for both defamation and disparagement.

Fraudulent Misrepresentation

With respect to intentional, or fraudulent, misrepresentation, Section 525 of the Restatement provides:

One who fraudulently makes a misrepresentation of fact, opinion, intention, or law for the purpose of inducing another to act or to refrain from action in reliance upon it, is subject to liability to the other in deceit for pecuniary loss caused to him by his justifiable reliance upon the misrepresentation.

For example, Smith represents to Jones that a tract of land in Texas is located in an area where drilling for oil had recently commenced. Smith made this statement knowing it was not true. In reliance upon the statement, Jones purchased the land from Smith. Smith is liable to Jones for fraudulent misrepresentation.

A basic element of fraud is a false representation. There must be some positive statement or conduct that misleads. Another element of fraud is the misrepresentation of a *fact:* actionable fraud can rarely be based on what is merely a statement of opinion. A representation is one of opinion if it expresses only the belief of the representor as to the existence of a fact or his judgment as to quality, value, authenticity, or other matters of judgment. Restatement, Section 538A.

In addition to the requirement that the misrepresentation be one of fact, it is necessary that it be material; it must relate to something of sufficient substance to induce reliance. In the sale of a race horse it may not be material whether the horse was ridden in its most recent race by a certain jockey, but its running time for the race probably would be.

To establish fraud the misrepresentation must have been known by the one making it to be false and must be made with an intention to deceive. This element of fraud is called *scienter.* Knowledge of falsity can consist of (a) actual knowledge, (b) lack of belief in the statement's truthfulness, or (c) reckless indifference as to its truthfulness. Restatement, Sections 526 and 527.

A person is not entitled to damages unless he has justifiably relied upon the misrepresentation to his detriment or injury. Restatement, Section 537. If the complaining party's decision was in no way influenced by the misrepresentation, he must abide by the terms of the contract. He is not deceived if he does not rely. A party who has been induced to enter into a contract by fraud may recover damages in a tort action. Although fraudulent misrepresentation is a tort action, it is closely connected with contractual negotiations and is further discussed in Chapter 10.

Figure 5–1 lists the intentional torts and the interests they protect.

DEFENSES TO INTENTIONAL TORTS

Even though the defendant has intentionally invaded the interests of the plaintiff, the defendant will not be liable if such conduct was privileged. A defendant's conduct is privileged if it furthers an interest of such social importance that the law confers immunity from tort liability for damage to others. Examples of privilege include self-defense, defense of property, and defense of others. In addition, the plaintiff's consent to the defendant's conduct is a defense to intentional torts.

Consent

If one consents to conduct resulting in damage or harm done to his own person, dignity, property, or economic interests, no liability will generally attach to the intentional infliction of injury. **Consent** to an act is the willingness that it shall occur and negates the wrongfulness of the act. It may be manifested expressly or impliedly, by words or by conduct. For example, Jerome states that he wishes to kiss Sally. Although Sally does not wish Jerome to do so, she does not object or resist by word or act. Jerome kisses Sally. Jerome is not liable to Sally for battery since Sally has impliedly consented to Jerome's conduct.

Consent must be given by an individual with capacity to do so. Consent given by a minor, mental incompetent, or intoxicated individual is invalid if he is not capable of appreciating the nature, extent, or probable consequences of the conduct to which he has consented. Consent is not effective if given under duress, which is constraint of another's will by which the other is compelled to give consent unwillingly.

Figure 5–1 Intentional Torts

Interest Protected	Tort
Person	
Freedom from contact	Battery
Freedom from apprehension	Assault
Freedom of movement	False imprisonment
Freedom from distress	Infliction of emotional distress
Dignity	
Reputation	Defamation
Privacy	Appropriation
	Intrusion
	Public disclosure of private facts
	False light
Freedom from wrongful legal actions	Misuse of legal procedure
Property	
Real	Trespass
	Nuisance
Personal	Trespass
	Conversion
Economic	
Contracts	Interference with contractual rights
Good will	Disparagement
Freedom from deception	Fraudulent misrepresentation

Exceeding Consent The defendant's privilege is limited to the conduct to which the plaintiff consents. For example, Vinny consents to an exploratory operation by Michele, a surgeon, but refuses to have any further operation performed. While Vinny is under anesthetic, Michele discovers a condition that indicates an operation is needed and proceeds to operate. Michele is liable to Vinny, even though the operation is properly and successfully performed, because Michele exceeded the consent given. On the other hand, assume that Isiah consents to a particular operation to be performed by Janet. Isiah submits to anesthesia. Upon opening Isiah's body, Janet discovers conditions which make it necessary to extend the operation in order to save Isiah's life. A reasonable man would consent to the operation if he knew of the conditions discovered by Janet. Janet performs the operation. Janet is not liable to Isiah.

By agreeing to participate in a game, a person consents to encounter such bodily contact and limitations upon freedom of movement as is permitted by or general to the game. Such consent does not, however, extend to intentional acts of violence or restrictions beyond the rules and usages of the game. Thus, if Guy participates in a game of ice hockey, he does not consent to an intentional attack by Jacques, another player, wielding his hockey stick as a weapon.

Consent to a Criminal Act The jurisdictions are divided on whether consent to conduct which constitutes a crime is a valid defense to an intentional tort. If conduct is made criminal in order to protect a certain class of persons, however, the consent of members of that class will *not* be effective as a defense to a tort action. For example, a statute makes it a crime to sell alcoholic beverages to a person who is intoxicated. Larry sells liquor to Mark in violation of the statute. Mark consumes the liquor and suffers physical injury from it. Mark's consent in purchasing the liquor does not bar his suit against Larry.

Privilege

A person who would otherwise be liable for a tort is *not* liable if he acts pursuant to and within the limits of a privilege. Restatement, Section 890. Conditional privileges, as discussed in defamation, depend upon the proper use of the privilege. Absolute privilege, on the other hand, protects the defendant regardless of his purpose. Examples of absolute privilege include untrue, defamatory statements made during the course of judicial proceedings, by legislators, by certain governmental executives, and between spouses. Absolute immunity also protects a public prosecutor from civil liability for malicious prosecution.

This section deals with conditional privilege entitling an individual to injure another's person without the other's consent. These privileges are created by law to enable an individual to protect himself, others, or his property against tortious interference. By virtue of these privileges an individual may inflict or impose what would otherwise constitute battery, assault, or false imprisonment. This section covers the following conditional privileges: (1) self-defense, (2) defense of others, and (3) defense of property.

Self-Defense The law permits a person to take appropriate action to prevent harm to himself where time does not allow resort to the law. Section 63 of the Restatement provides:

(1) An actor is privileged to use reasonable force, not intended or likely to cause death or serious bodily harm, to defend himself against unprivileged harmful or offensive contact or other bodily harm which he reasonably believes that another is about to inflict intentionally upon him.

The privilege of self-defense exists whether or not the danger actually exists, provided that the defendant reasonably believed self-defense was necessary. The reasonableness of the defendant's actions is based upon what a person of average courage would have thought under the circumstances.

Self-defense is warranted even if the defendant reasonably believed that she could avoid the threatened contact or confinement by retreating. The defendant is not privileged to retaliate, however, because revenge is not self-defense. The defendant, to protect herself from offensive or nonserious bodily contact, is limited to reasonable force, which is proportionate in extent to the harm from which the defendant is seeking to protect herself.

The defendant is privileged to defend by the use of force intended or likely to cause death or serious bodily harm if she reasonably believes that the plaintiff is about to inflict death, serious bodily harm, or ravishment upon the defendant. Most States limit the right to use deadly force in self-defense to those situations in which the defendant does not have a completely safe means of escape. If the defendant, however, has the slightest doubt, if reasonable, as to the safety of her escape, she may stand her ground. A person may also stand her ground and use deadly force if the attack occurs in her own residence, even though a reasonable means of escape exists. Restatement, Section 65.

Defense of Others An individual is privileged to defend third persons from harmful or offensive contact to the same extent that he is privileged to protect himself, provided that the defendant correctly or reasonably believes that the third person possesses the privilege of self-defense and that the defendant's intervention is necessary for the safety of the third person. Restatement, Section 76. Thus, Alvin sees Bruce about to strike Alvin's friend Connie. Bruce is, in fact, privileged to do so to repel Connie's attack. Alvin has no reason to suspect that Connie is the aggressor and intercedes to assist Connie. Alvin is privileged to use reasonable force to assist Connie against Bruce.

Defense of Property A possessor of property is permitted to use reasonable force, not intended or likely to cause death or serious bodily harm, to protect his real and personal property. Such force can only be employed if the possessor reasonably believes that the intrusion can only be terminated or prevented by use of force and the intruder has disregarded requests to cease. Restatement, Section 77. For example, Wayne sees Sandra walking across his vacant lot. Wayne is not privileged to use even the mildest of force to eject Sandra until Wayne has requested Sandra to leave and Sandra has disregarded the warning. Once reasonable force has been used, the defendant may use such greater force as is necessary to protect himself and his property. The intruder is not entitled to invoke the privilege of self-defense. Nonetheless, there is no privilege to use any force calculated to cause death or serious bodily injury in order to protect property unless there is also a threat to the defendant's personal safety justifying the use of such force.

A person may not through indirect means, such as mechanical devices, employ deadly force to protect his property unless he would, if present, have been privileged to employ such force. Restatement, Section 85. This applies to spring guns, electrified fences, and other traps that are intended or likely to cause death or serious bodily harm. *See Katko v. Briney.*

CASES

False Imprisonment

PETERSON v. SORLIEN
Supreme Court of Minnesota, 1980.
299 N.W.2d 123.

SHERAN, C.J.

This action by plaintiff Susan Jungclaus Peterson for false imprisonment * * * arises from an effort by her parents, in conjunction with other individuals named as defendants, to prompt her disaffiliation from an organization known as The Way Ministry.

* * *

At the time of the events in question, Susan Jungclaus Peterson was 21 years old. For most of her life, she lived with her family on a farm near Bird Island, Minnesota. In 1973, she graduated with honors from high school, ranking second in her class. She matriculated that fall at Moorhead State College. A dean's list student during her first year, her academic performance declined and her interests narrowed after she joined the local chapter of a group organized internationally and identified locally as The Way of Minnesota, Inc.

The operation of The Way is predicated on the fund-raising activities of its members. * * * Recruits must contribute a minimum of 10 percent of their earnings to the organization; to meet the tithe, student members are expected to obtain part-time employment. * * *

* * *

As her junior year in college drew to a close, the Jungclauses grew increasingly alarmed by the personality changes they witnessed in their daughter; overly tired, unusually pale, distraught and irritable, she exhibited an increasing alienation from family, diminished interest in education and decline in academic performance. The Jungclauses, versed in the literature of the youth cults and based on conversations with former members of The Way, concluded that through a calculated process of manipulation and exploitation Susan had been reduced to a condition of psychological bondage.

On May 24, 1976, defendant Norman Jungclaus, father of plaintiff, arrived at Moorhead to pick up Susan following the end of the third college quarter. Instead of returning to their family home, defendant drove with Susan to Minneapolis to the home of Veronica Morgel. Entering the home of Mrs. Morgel, Susan was greeted by Kathy Mills and several young people who wished to discuss Susan's involvement in the ministry. Each of those present had been in some way touched by the cult phenomenon. Kathy Mills, the leader of the group, had treated a number of former cult members, including Veronica Morgel's son. It was Kathy Mills a

self-styled professional deprogrammer, to whom the Jungclauses turned, and intermittently for the next sixteen days, it was in the home of Veronica Morgel that Susan stayed.

The avowed purpose of deprogramming is to break the hold of the cult over the individual through reason and confrontation. Initially, Susan was unwilling to discuss her involvement; she lay curled in a fetal position, in the downstairs bedroom where she first stayed, plugging her ears and crying while her father pleaded with her to listen to what was being said. This behavior persisted for two days during which she intermittently engaged in conversation, at one point screaming hysterically and flailing at her father. But by Wednesday Susan's demeanor had changed completely; she was friendly and vivacious and that night slept in an upstairs bedroom. Susan spent all day Thursday reading and conversing with her father and on Saturday night went roller skating. On Sunday she played softball at a nearby park, afterwards enjoying a picnic lunch. The next week Susan spent in Columbus, Ohio, flying there with a former cult member who had shared with her the experiences of the previous week. While in Columbus, she spoke every day by telephone to her fiance who, playing tapes and songs from the ministry's headquarters in Minneapolis, begged that she return to the fold. Susan expressed the desire to extricate her fiance from the dominion of the cult.

Susan returned to Minneapolis on June 9. Unable to arrange a controlled meeting so that Susan could see her fiance outside the presence of other members of the ministry, her parents asked that she sign an agreement releasing them from liability for their past weeks' actions. Refusing to do so, Susan stepped outside the Morgel residence with the puppy she had purchased in Ohio, motioned to a passing police car and shortly thereafter was reunited with her fiance in the Minneapolis headquarters of The Way. Following her return to the ministry, she was directed to counsel and initiated the present action. [She appealed from the trial court's judgment in favor of her parents.]

* * *

* * * this case marks the emergence of a new cultural phenomenon: youth-oriented religious or pseudo-religious groups which utilize the techniques of what has been termed "coercive persuasion" or "mind control" to cultivate an uncritical and devoted following. Commentators have used the term "coercive persuasion," originally coined to identify the experience of American prisoners of war during the Korean conflict to describe the cult-induction process. * * * Coercive persuasion is fostered through the creation of a controlled environment that heightens the susceptibility of a subject to suggestion and manipulation through sensory deprivation, physiological depletion, cognitive dissonance, peer pressure, and a clear assertion of authority and dominion. The aftermath of indoctrination is a severe impairment of autonomy and the ability to think independently, which induces a subject's unyielding compliance and the rupture of past connections, affiliations and associations. [Citation.] One psychologist characterized the process of cult indoctrination as "psychological kidnapping." [Citation.]

The period in question began on Monday, May 24, 1976, and ceased on Wednesday, June 9, 1976, a period of 16 days. The record clearly demonstrates that Susan willingly remained in the company of defendants for at least 13 of those days. * * * Had Susan desired, manifold opportunities existed for her to alert the authorities of her allegedly unlawful detention * * * At no time during the 13-day period did she complain of her treatment or suggest that defendants were holding her against her will. If one is aware of a reasonable means of escape that does not present a danger of bodily or material harm, a restriction is not total and complete and does not constitute unlawful imprisonment. Damages may not be assessed for any period of detention to which one freely consents. [Citations.]

* * *

* * * the behavior Susan manifested during the initial three days at issue must be considered in light of her actions in the remainder of the period. Because, it is argued, the cult conditioning process induces dramatic and non-consensual change giving rise to a new temporary identity on the part of the individuals whose consent is under examination, Susan's volitional capacity prior to treatment may well have been impaired. Following her readjustment, the evidence suggests that Susan was a different person, "like her old self." As such, the question of Susan's consent becomes a function of time. We therefore deem Susan's subsequent affirmation of defendants' actions dispositive.

* * *

* * * The facts in this case support the conclusion that plaintiff only regained her volitional capacity to consent after engaging in the first three days of the deprogramming process. As such, we hold that when parents, or their agents, acting under the conviction that the judgmental capacity of their adult child is impaired, seek to extricate that child from what they reasonably believe to be a religious or psuedo-religious cult, and the child at some juncture assents to the actions in question, limitations upon the child's mobility do not constitute meaningful deprivations of personal liberty sufficient to support a judgment for false imprisonment. * * * [Judgment for Mr. and Mrs. Jungclaus affirmed.]

Infliction of Emotional Distress

AGIS v. HOWARD JOHNSON COMPANY

Supreme Judicial Court of Massachusetts, 1976.
371 Mass. 140, 355 N.E.2d 315.

Quirico, J.

This case raises the issue, expressly reserved in *George v. Jordan Marsh Co.*, [citation], whether a cause of action exists in this Commonwealth for the intentional or reckless infliction of severe emotional distress without resulting bodily injury. Counts 1 and 2 of this action were brought by the plaintiff Debra Agis against the Howard Johnson

Company and Roger Dionne, manager of the restaurant in which she was employed, to recover damages for mental anguish and emotional distress allegedly caused by her summary dismissal from such employment. . . . This case is before us on the plaintiffs' appeal from the dismissal of their complaint.

* * *

Debra Agis was employed by the Howard Johnson Company as a waitress in a restaurant known as the Ground Round. On or about May 23, 1975, the defendant Dionne notified all waitresses that a meeting would be held at 3 P.M. that day. At the meeting, he informed the waitresses that "there was some stealing going on," but that the identity of the person or persons responsible was not known, and that, until the person or persons responsible were discovered, he would begin firing all the present waitresses in alphabetical order, starting with the letter "A." Dionne then fired Debra Agis.

The complaint alleges that, as a result of this incident, Mrs. Agis became greatly upset, began to cry, sustained emotional distress, mental anguish, and loss of wages and earnings. It further alleges that the actions of the defendants were reckless, extreme, outrageous and intended to cause emotional distress and anguish. In addition, the complaint states that the defendants knew or should have known that their actions would cause such distress.

The defendants moved to dismiss the complaint [citation] on the ground that, even if true, the plaintiffs' allegations fail to state a claim upon which relief can be granted because damages for emotional distress are not compensable absent resulting physical injury. The judge allowed the motion, and the plaintiffs appealed.

1. Our discussion of whether a cause of action exists for the intentional or reckless infliction of severe emotional distress without resulting bodily injury starts with our decision in *George v. Jordan Marsh Co.,* [citation]. While in that case we found it unnecessary to address the precise question raised here, we did summarize the history of actions for emotional distress and concluded that the

law of the Commonwealth should be, and is, "that one who, without a privilege to do so, by extreme and outrageous conduct intentionally causes severe emotional distress to another, with bodily harm resulting from such distress, is subject to liability . . ." [Citation.] The question whether such liability should be extended to cases in which there is no resulting bodily injury was "left until it arises," and that question has arisen here.

In the *George* case, we discussed in depth the policy considerations underlying the recognition of a cause of action for intentional infliction of severe emotional distress with resulting physical injury, and we concluded that the difficulties presented in allowing such an action were outweighed by the unfair and illogical consequences of the denial of recognition of such an independent tort. In so doing, we examined the persuasive authority then recognizing such a cause of action, and we placed considerable reliance on the Restatement (Second) of Torts § 46 (1965). Our examination of the policies underlying the extension of that cause of action to cases where there has been no bodily injury, and our review of the judicial precedent and the Restatement in this regard, lead us to conclude that such extension is both warranted and desirable. [Citation.]

The most often cited argument for refusing to extend the cause of action for intentional or reckless infliction of emotional distress to cases where there has been no physical injury is the difficulty of proof and the danger of fraudulent or frivolous claims. There has been a concern that "mental anguish, standing alone, is too subtle and speculative to be measured by any known legal standard," that "mental anguish and its consequences are so intangible and peculiar and vary so much with the individual that they cannot reasonably be anticipated," that a wide door might "be opened not only to fictitious claims but to litigation over trivialities and mere bad manners as well," and that there can be no objective measurement of the extent or the existence of emotional distress. [Citation.]

While we are not unconcerned with these problems, we believe that "the problems presented are not . . . insuperable" and that "administrative difficulties do not justify the denial of relief for serious invasions of mental and emotional tranquility. . . ." [Citation.] "That some claims may be spurious should not compel those who administer justice to shut their eyes to serious wrongs and let them go without being brought to account. It is the function of courts and juries to determine whether claims are valid or false. This responsibility should not be shunned merely because the task may be difficult to perform." [Citations.]

Furthermore, the distinction between the difficulty which juries may encounter in determining liability and assessing damages where no physical injury occurs and their performance of that same task where there has been resulting physical harm may be greatly overstated. "The jury is ordinarily in a better position . . . to determine whether outrageous conduct results in mental distress than whether that distress in turn results in physical injury. From their own experience jurors are aware of the extent and character of the disagreeable emotions that may result from the defendant's conduct, but a difficult medical question is presented when it must be determined if emotional distress resulted in physical injury. . . . Greater proof that mental suffering occurred is found in the defendant's conduct designed to bring it about than in physical injury that may or may not have resulted therefrom."

* * *

In light of what we have said, we hold that one who, by extreme and outrageous conduct and without privilege, causes severe emotional distress to another is subject to liability for such emotional distress even though no bodily harm may result. However, in order for a plaintiff to prevail in a case for liability under this tort, four elements must be established. It must be shown (1) that the actor intended to inflict emotional distress or that he knew or should have known that emotional distress was the likely result of his conduct, Restatement (Second) of Torts § 46, comment i (1965); [citations]; (2) that the conduct was "extreme and outrageous," was "be-

yond all possible bounds of decency" and was "utterly intolerable in a civilized community," Restatement (Second) of Torts § 46, comment d (1965) [citation]; (3) that the actions of the defendant were the cause of the plaintiff's distress, [citations]; and (4) that the emotional distress sustained by the plaintiff was "severe" and of a nature "that no reasonable man could be expected to endure it." Restatement (Second) of Torts § 46, comment j (1965). [Citation.] These requirements are "aimed at limiting frivolous suits and avoiding litigation in situations where only bad manners and mere hurt feelings are involved," [citation], and we believe they are a "realistic safeguard against false claims. . . ." [Citation.]

Testing the plaintiff Debra Agis's complaint by the rules stated above, we hold that she makes out a cause of action and that her complaint is therefore legally sufficient.

* * *

The judgment entered in the Superior Court dismissing the plaintiffs' complaint is reversed.

Defamation

FRANK B. HALL & CO., INC. v. BUCK

Court of Appeals of Texas, Fourteenth District, 1984.
678 S.W.2d 612.

JUNELL, J.

Larry W. Buck (Buck or appellee) sued his former employer, Frank B. Hall & Co. (Hall or appellant), for damages for defamation of character, . . . By unanimous verdict, a jury found damages for . . . defamation of character and exemplary damages. The court entered judgment for appellee for $1,905,000.00 in damages, plus interest, attorney's fees and costs of court. For the reasons set forth below we affirm.

Appellee, an established salesman in the insurance business, was approached in the spring of 1976 by a representative of Hall with a prospective job offer. Appellee was then an executive vice-president of the insurance firm of Alexander & Alexander, and in the previous year he generated approximately $550,000.00 in commissions for the firm. He was the top producer in Alexander's Houston office and was ranked nationally among the top five salesmen for Alexander. After several meetings, Buck accepted Hall's offer of employment and began working for Hall on June 1, 1976. Hall agreed to pay Buck an annual salary of $80,000.00 plus additional compensation equal to seven and one-half percent of net retained commissions for each year to a maximum commission of $600,000.00, plus fringe benefits. The agreement was to be for a three year period. Several Alexander employees followed Buck to Hall's office. During the next several months Buck generated substantial commission income for Hall and succeeded in bringing several major accounts to the firm.

In October, 1976, Mendel Kaliff, then president of Frank B. Hall & Co. of Texas, held a meeting with Buck and Lester Eckert, Hall's office manager and a former Alexander employee. Kaliff informed Buck his salary was being reduced to $65,000.00 and that Hall was eliminating Buck's incentive and profit sharing benefits. Kaliff told Buck these measures were being taken because of Buck's failure to produce sufficient income for Hall. However, Kaliff added that if Buck could generate $400,000.00 net commission income by June 1, 1977, his salary and benefits would be reinstated retroactively.

On March 31, 1977, at another impromptu meeting, Kaliff and Eckert abruptly fired Buck and instructed him not to return to Hall's offices. Buck sought employment with several other insurance firms, but his efforts were fruitless. Distraught at having lost his job and being unable to find suitable employment in the insurance business, Buck hired an investigator, Lloyd Barber, in an attempt to discover Hall's true reasons for firing him. This suit is based upon statements made by Hall employees to Lloyd Barber and to Charles Burton, a prospective employer, and upon a note written by Virginia Hilley, a Hall employee. Appellant brings eighty points of error, which will be grouped in thirteen categories.

In points one through thirteen, appellant challenges the legal and factual sufficiency of

the evidence to support the jury's findings that the statements to Barber were published. Hall urges the statements were invited as a matter of law.

Lloyd Barber contacted Mendel Kaliff, Lester Eckert and Virginia Hilley and told them that he was an investigator, Buck was being considered for a position of trust and responsibility, and Barber was seeking information about Buck's employment with Frank B. Hall & Co. Barber testified that he had interviewed Kaliff, Eckert and Hilley on separate occasions in September and October of 1977, and had tape recorded the conversations. Appellee introduced into evidence Barber's properly authenticated investigative reports, which were based on these taped interviews. The report shows Kaliff remarked several times that Buck was untrustworthy, and not always entirely truthful; he said Buck was disruptive, paranoid, hostile and was guilty of padding his expense account. Kaliff said he had locked Buck out of his office and had not trusted him to return. He charged that Buck had promised things he could not deliver. Eckert told Barber that Buck was horrible in a business sense, irrational, ruthless, and disliked by office personnel. He described Buck as a "classical sociopath," who would verbally abuse and embarrass Hall employees. Eckert said Buck had stolen files and records from Alexander & Alexander. He called Buck "a zero," "a Jekyll and Hyde person" who was "lacking in compucture (sic) or scruples."

Virginia Hilley told Barber that Buck could have been charged with theft for materials he brought with him to Hall from Alexander & Alexander.

Any act wherein the defamatory matter is intentionally or negligently communicated to a third person is a publication. In the case of slander, the act is usually the speaking of the words. Restatement (Second) Torts § 577 comment a (1977). There is ample support in the record to show that these individuals intentionally communicated disparaging remarks to a third person. The jury was instructed that "Publication means to communicate defamatory words to some third person in such a way that he understands the words to be defamatory. A statement is not published if it was authorized, invited or procured by Buck and if Buck knew in advance the contents of the invited communication." In response to special issues, the jury found that the slanderous statements were made and published to Barber.

Hall argues that Buck could and should have expected Hall's employees to give their opinion of Buck when requested to do so. Hall is correct in stating that a plaintiff may not recover for a publication to which he has consented, or which he has authorized, procured or invited, [citation]; and it may be true that Buck could assume that Hall's employees would give their opinion when asked they do so. However, there is nothing in the record to indicate that Buck knew Hall's employees would defame him when Barber made the inquiries. The accusations made by Kaliff, Eckert and Hilley were not mere expressions of opinion but were false and derogatory statements of fact.

* * *

A defamer cannot escape liability by showing that, although he desired to defame the plaintiff, he did not desire to defame him to the person to whom he in fact intentionally published the defamatory communication. The publication is complete although the publisher is mistaken as to the identity of the person to whom the publication is made. Restatement (Second) of Torts § 577 comment 1 (1977). Likewise, communication to an agent of the person defamed is a publication, unless the communication is invited by the person defamed or his agent. Restatement s 577 comment e. We have already determined that the evidence is sufficient to show that Buck did not know what Kaliff, Eckert or Hilley would say and that he did not procure the defamatory statements to create a lawsuit. Thus, the fact that Barber may have been acting at Buck's request is not fatal to Buck's cause of action. There is absolutely no proof that Barber induced Kaliff, Eckert or Hilley to make any of the defamatory comments.

* * *

When an ambiguity exists, a fact issue is presented. The court, by submission of

proper fact issues, should let the jury render its verdict on whether the statements were fairly susceptible to the construction placed there on by the plaintiff. [Citation.] Here, the jury found (1) Eckert made a statement calculated to convey that Buck had been terminated because of serious misconduct; (2) the statement was slanderous or libelous; (3) the statement was made with malice; (4) the statement was published; and (5) damage directly resulted from the statement. The jury also found the statements were not substantially true. The jury thus determined that these statements, which were capable of a defamatory meaning, were understood as such by Burton.

* * *

We hold that the evidence supports the award of actual damages and the amount awarded is not manifestly unjust. Furthermore, in responding to the issue on exemplary damages, the jury was instructed that exemplary damages must be based on a finding that Hall "acted with ill will, bad intent, malice or gross disregard to the rights of Buck." Although there is no fixed ratio between exemplary and actual damages, exemplary damages must be reasonably apportioned to the actual damages sustained. [Citation.] Because of the actual damages [$605,000] and the abundant evidence of malice, we hold that the award of punitive damages [$1,300,000] was not unreasonable. * * *

The judgment of the trial court is affirmed.

Appropriation

CARSON v. HERE'S JOHNNY PORTABLE TOILETS, INC.

United States Court of Appeals, Sixth Circuit, 1983.
698 F.2d 831.

BROWN, J.

This case involves . . . invasion of the right of privacy and the right of publicity arising from appellee's adoption of a phrase generally associated with a popular entertainer.

Appellant, John W. Carson (Carson), is the host and star of "The Tonight Show," a well-known television program broadcast five nights a week by the National Braodcasting Company. Carson also appears as an entertainer in night clubs and theaters around the country. From the time he began hosting "The Tonight Show" in 1962, he has been introduced on the show each night with the phrase "Here's Johnny." This method of introduction was first used for Carson in 1957 when he hosted a daily television program for the American Broadcasting Company. The phrase "Here's Johnny" is generally associated with Carson by a substantial segment of the television viewing public. In 1967, Carson first authorized use of this phrase by an outside business venture, permitting it to be used by a chain of restaurants called "Here's Johnny Restaurants."

Appellant Johnny Carson Apparel, Inc. (Apparel), formed in 1970, manufactures and markets men's clothing to retail stores. Carson, the president of Apparel and owner of 20% of its stock, has licensed Apparel to use his name and picture, which appear on virtually all of Apparel's products and promotional material. Apparel has also used, with Carson's consent, the phrase "Here's Johnny" on labels for clothing and in advertising campaigns. In 1977, Apparel granted a license to Marcy Laboratories to use "Here's Johnny" as the name of a line of men's toiletries. The phrase "Here's Johnny" has never been registered by appellants as a trademark or service mark.

Appellee, Here's Johnny Portable Toilets, Inc., is a Michigan corporation engaged in the business of renting and selling "Here's Johnny" portable toilets. Appellee's founder was aware at the time he formed the corporation that "Here's Johnny" was the introductory slogan for Carson on "The Tonight Show." He indicated that he coupled the phrase with a second one, "The World's Foremost Commodian," to make "a good play on a phrase."

Shortly after appellee went into business in 1976, appellants brought this action alleging . . . invasion of privacy and publicity rights. They sought damages and an injunction prohibiting appellee's further use of the phrase "Here's Johnny" as a corporate name or in connection with the sale or rental of its portable toilets.

* * *

The appellants . . . claim that the appellee's use of the phrase, "Here's Johnny" violates the common law right of privacy and right of publicity. The confusion in this area of the law requires a brief analysis of the relationship between these two rights.

In an influential article, Dean Prosser delineated four distinct types of the right of privacy: (1) intrusion upon one's seclusion or solitude, (2) public disclosure of embarrassing private facts, (3) publicity which places one in a false light, and (4) appropriation of one's name or likeness for the defendant's advantage. Prosser, *Privacy*, 48 Calif.L.Rev. 383, 389 (1960). This fourth type has become known as the "right of publicity." [Citations.] Henceforth we will refer to Prosser's last, or fourth, category as the "right of publicity."

* * *

The right of publicity has developed to protect the commercial interest of celebrities in their identities. The theory of the right is that a celebrity's identity can be valuable in the promotion of products, and the celebrity has an interest that may be protected from the unauthorized commercial exploitation of that identity. In [citation], we stated: "The famous have an exclusive legal right during life to control and profit from the commercial use of their name and personality." [Citation.]

The district court dismissed appellants' claim based on the right of publicity because appellee does not use Carson's name or likeness. [Citation.] It held that it "would not be prudent to allow recovery for a right of publicity claim which does not more specifically identify Johnny Carson." [Citation.] We believe that, on the contrary, the district court's conception of the right of publicity is too narrow. The right of publicity, as we have stated, is that a celebrity has a protected pecuniary interest in the commercial exploitation of his identity. If the celebrity's identity is commercially exploited, there has been an invasion of his right whether or not his "name or likeness" is used. Carson's identity may be exploited even if his name, John W. Carson, or his picture is not used.

In *Motschenbacher v. R. J. Reynolds Tobacco Co.*, [citation], the court held that the unauthorized use of a picture of a distinctive race car of a well known professional race car driver, whose name or likeness were not used, violated his right of publicity. * * *

In *Ali v. Playgirl, Inc.*, [citation], Muhammad Ali, former heavyweight champion, sued Playgirl magazine under the New York "right of privacy" statute and also alleged a violation of his common law right of publicity. The magazine published a drawing of a nude, black male sitting on a stool in a corner of a boxing ring with hands taped and arms outstretched on the ropes. The district court concluded that Ali's right of publicity was invaded because the drawing sufficiently identified him in spite of the fact that the drawing was captioned "Mystery Man." The district court found that the identification of Ali was made certain because of an accompanying verse that identified the figure as "The Greatest." The district court took judicial notice of the fact that "Ali has regularly claimed that appellation for himself." [Citation.]

* * *

In this case, Earl Braxton, president and owner of Here's Johnny Portable Toilets, Inc., admitted that he knew that the phrase "Here's Johnny" had been used for years to introduce Carson. * * *

* * *

* * * It is our view that, under the existing authorities, a celebrity's legal right of publicity is invaded whenever his identity is intentionally appropriated for commercial purposes. . . . It is not fatal to appellant's claim that appellee did not use his "name." Indeed, there would have been no violation of his right of publicity even if appellee had used his name, such as "J. William Carson Portable Toilet" or the "John William Carson Portable Toilet" or the "J. W. Carson Portable Toilet." The reason is that, though literally using appellant's "name," the appellee would not have appropriated Carson's identity as a celebrity. Here there was an appropriation of

Carson's identity without using his "name."

* * *

The judgment of the district court is vacated and the case remanded for further proceedings consistent with this opinion.

Interference with Contractual Relations

TEXACO, INC. v. PENNZOIL, CO.

Court of Appeals of Texas, First District, 1987.
729 S.W.2d 768.

WARREN, J.

This is an appeal from a judgment awarding Pennzoil damages for Texaco's tortious interference with a contract between Pennzoil and the "Getty entities" (Getty Oil Company, the Sarah C. Getty Trust, and the J. Paul Getty Museum).

The jury found, among other things, that:

(1) At the end of a board meeting on January 3, 1984, the Getty entities intended to bind themselves to an agreement providing for the purchase of Getty Oil stock, whereby the Sarah C. Getty Trust would own 4/7th of the stock and Pennzoil the remaining 3/7th; and providing for a division of Getty Oil's assets, according to their respective ownership if the Trust and Pennzoil were unable to agree on a restructuring of Getty Oil by December 31, 1984;

(2) Texaco knowingly interfered with the agreement between Pennzoil and the Getty entities;

(3) As a result of Texaco's interference, Pennzoil suffered damages of $7.53 billion;

(4) Texaco's actions were intentional, willful, and in wanton disregard of Pennzoil's rights; and,

(5) Pennzoil was entitled to punitive damages of $3 billion.

* * *

Though many facts are disputed, the parties' main conflicts are over the inferences to be drawn from, and the legal significance of, these facts. There is evidence that for several months in late 1983, Pennzoil had followed with interest the well-publicized dissension between the board of directors of Getty Oil

Company and Gordon Getty, who was a director of Getty Oil and also the owner, as trustee, of approximately 40.2% of the outstanding shares of Getty Oil. On December 28, 1983, Pennzoil announced an unsolicited, public tender offer for 16 million shares of Getty Oil at $100 each.

Soon afterwards, Pennzoil contacted both Gordon Getty and a representative of the J. Paul Getty Museum, which held approximately 11.8% of the shares of Getty Oil, to discuss the tender offer and the possible purchase of Getty Oil. In the first two days of January 1984, a "Memorandum of Agreement" was drafted to reflect the terms that had been reached in conversations between representatives of Pennzoil, Gordon Getty, and the Museum.

* * *

The Memorandum of Agreement stated that it was subject to approval of the board of Getty Oil, and it was to expire by its own terms if not approved at the board meeting that was to begin on January 2. Pennzoil's CEO, Liedtke, and Gordon Getty, for the Trust, signed the Memorandum of Agreement before the Getty Oil board meeting on January 2, and Harold Williams, the president of the Museum, signed it shortly after the board meeting began. Thus, before it was submitted to the Getty Oil board, the Memorandum of Agreement had been executed by parties who together controlled a majority of the outstanding shares of Getty Oil.

The Memorandum of Agreement was then presented to the Getty Oil board, which had previously held discussions on how the company should respond to Pennzoil's public tender offer. * * *

The board voted to reject recommending Pennzoil's tender offer to Getty's shareholders, then later also rejected the Memorandum of Agreement price of $110 per share as too low. Before recessing at 3 a.m., the board decided to make a counterproposal to Pennzoil of $110 per share plus a $10 debenture. * * *

When the board reconvened at 3 p.m. on January 3, a revised Pennzoil proposal was presented, offering $110 per share plus a $3 "stub" that was to be paid after the sale of a Getty Oil subsidiary ("ERC"), from the excess proceeds over $1 billion. Each shareholder was to receive a pro rata share of these excess proceeds, but in any case, a minimum of $3 per share at the end of five years. * * *

The Museum's lawyer told the board that, based on his discussions with Pennzoil, he believed that if the board went back "firm" with an offer of $110 plus a $5 stub, Pennzoil would accept it. After a recess, the Museum's president (also a director of Getty Oil) moved that the Getty board should accept Pennzoil's proposal provided that the stub be raised to $5, and the board voted 15 to 1 to approve this counter-proposal to Pennzoil. The board then voted themselves and Getty's officers and advisors indemnity for any liability arising from the events of the past few months. Additionally, the board authorized its executive compensation committee to give "golden parachutes" (generous termination benefits) to the top executives whose positions "were likely to be affected" by the change in management. There was evidence that during another brief recess of the board meeting, the counter-offer of $110 plus a $5 stub was presented to and accepted by Pennzoil. After Pennzoil's acceptance was conveyed to the Getty board, the meeting was adjourned, and most board members left town for their respective homes.

That evening, the lawyers and public relations staff of Getty Oil and the Museum drafted a press release describing the transaction between Pennzoil and the Getty entities. The press release, announcing an agreement in principle on the terms of the Memorandum of Agreement but with a price of $110 plus a $5 stub, was issued on Getty Oil letterhead the next morning, January 4, and later that day, Pennzoil issued an identical press release.

On January 4, Boisi [Getty Oil's investment banker] continued to contact other companies, looking for a higher price than Pennzoil had offered. After talking briefly with Boisi, Texaco management called several meetings with its in-house financial planning group, which over the course of the day studied and reported to management on the value of Getty Oil, the Pennzoil offer terms, and a feasible price range at which Getty might be acquired. Later in the day, Texaco hired an investment banker, First Boston, to represent it with respect to a possible acquisition of Getty Oil. Meanwhile, also on January 4, Pennzoil's lawyers were working on a draft of a formal "transaction agreement" that described the transaction in more detail than the outline of terms contained in the Memorandum of Agreement and press release.

On January 5, the Wall Street Journal reported on an agreement reached between Pennzoil and the Getty entities, describing essentially the terms contained in the Memorandum of Agreement. The Pennzoil board met to ratify the actions of its officers in negotiating an agreement with the Getty entities, and Pennzoil's attorneys periodically attempted to contact the other parties' advisors and attorneys to continue work on the transaction agreement.

The board of Texaco also met on January 5, authorizing its officers to make an offer for 100% of Getty Oil and to take any necessary action in connection therewith. Texaco first contacted the Museum's Lawyer, Lipton, and arranged a meeting to discuss the sale of the Museum's shares of Getty Oil to Texaco. Lipton instructed his associate, on her way to the meeting in progress of the lawyers drafting merger documents for the Pennzoil/Getty transaction, to not attend that meeting, because he needed her at his meeting with Texaco. At the meeting with Texaco, the Museum outlined various issues it wanted resolved in any transaction with Texaco, and then agreed to sell its 11.8% ownership in Getty Oil.

That evening, Texaco met with Gordon Getty to discuss the sale of the Trust's shares. He was informed that the Museum had agreed to sell its shares to Texaco. Gordon Getty's advisors had previously warned him that the Trust shares might be "locked out" in a minority position if Texaco bought, in addition to the Museum's shares, enough of the public shares to achieve over 50% owner-

ship of the company. Gordon Getty accepted Texaco's offer of $125 per share and signed a letter of his intent to sell his stock to Texaco, as soon as a California temporary restraining order against his actions as trustee was lifted.

At noon on January 6, Getty Oil held a telephone board meeting to discuss the Texaco offer. The board voted to withdraw its previous counter-proposal to Pennzoil and unanimously voted to accept Texaco's offer. Texaco immediately issued a press release announcing that Getty Oil and Texaco would merge.

Soon after the Texaco press release appeared, Pennzoil telexed the Getty entities, demanding that they honor their agreement with Pennzoil. Later that day, prompted by the telex, Getty Oil filed a suit in Delaware for declaratory judgment that it was not bound to any contract with Pennzoil. The merger agreement between Texaco and Getty Oil was signed on January 6; the stock purchase agreement with the Museum was signed on January 6; and the stock exchange agreement with the Trust was signed on January 8, 1984.

* * *

The record as a whole demonstraes that there was legally and factually sufficient evidence to support the jury's finding . . . that the Trust, the Museum, and the Company intended to bind themselves to an agreement with Pennzoil at the end of the Getty Oil board meeting on January 3, 1984. * * *

* * *

Texaco's next points of error concern the jury's finding . . . that Texaco knowingly interfered with the agreement . . . between Pennzoil and the Getty entities. Texaco contends that the evidence is legally and factually insufficient to show that Texaco had actual knowledge of any agreement, that it actively induced breach of the alleged contract, and that the alleged contract was valid and capable of being interfered with.

New York law requires knowledge by a defendant of the existence of contractual rights as an element of the tort of inducing a breach of that contract. [Citation.] However, the defendant need not have full knowledge of all the detailed terms of the contract. [Citations.]

There is even some indication that a defendant need not have an accurate understanding of the exact legal significance of the facts giving rise to a contractual duty, but rather may be liable if he knows those facts, but is mistaken about whether they constitute a contract. *Restatement (Second) of Torts* § 766, comment i (1977); [citations].

* * * New York's highest court has followed the principles and precepts embodied in the Restatement in this developing area of tort law. [Citation.]

The element of knowledge by the defendant is a question of fact, and proof may be predicated on circumstantial evidence. [Citation.] Since there was no direct evidence of Texaco's knowledge of a contract in this case, the question is whether there was legally and factually sufficient circumstantial evidence from which the trier of fact reasonably could have inferred knowledge.

Texaco argues that the writings known to Texaco and the verbal assurances it was given are matters of undisputed fact that do not add up to actual knowledge of a binding contract. It states that the only written evidence known to Texaco was the Memorandum of Agreement, the January 4 press release, and the January 2 "Dear Hugh" letter from Gordon Getty to Hugh Liedtke, Pennzoil's CEO. Texaco contends that these writings confirm the absence of a binding agreement.

* * *

Pennzoil responds that there was legally and factually sufficient evidence to support the jury's finding of knowledge, because the jury could reasonably infer that Texaco knew about the Pennzoil deal from the evidence of (1) how Texaco carefully mapped its strategy to defeat Pennzoil's deal by acting to "stop the train" or "stop the signing"; (2) the notice of a contract given by a January 5 Wall Street Journal article reporting on the Pennzoil agreement—an article that Texaco denied anyone at Texaco had seen; (3) the knowledge of an agreement that would arise from comparing the Memorandum of Agreement with the Getty press release; (4) the demands made by the Museum and the Trust for full

indemnity from Texaco against any claims by Pennzoil arising out of the Memorandum of Agreement; and (5) the Museum's demand that, even if the Texaco deal fell through, the Museum would be guaranteed the price Pennzoil had agreed to pay for the Museum's shares. * * *

* * *

We find that an inference could arise that Texaco had some knowledge of Pennzoil's agreement with the Getty entities, given the evidence of Texaco's detailed studies of the Pennzoil plan, its knowledge that some members of the Getty board were not happy with Pennzoil's price, and its subsequent formulation of strategy to "stop the [Pennzoil] train" and "take care of Liedtke."

* * *

The jury was not required to accept Texaco's version of events in this case, and this Court may not substitute its own interpretation of the evidence for the decision of the trier of fact. There was legally and factually sufficient evidence to support an inference by the jury that Texaco had the required knowledge of an agreement. * * *

* * *

A necessary element of the plaintiff's cause of action is a showing that the defendant took an active part in persuading a party to a contract to breach it. [Citation.] Merely entering into a contract with a party with the knowledge of that party's contractual obligations to someone else is not the same as inducing a breach. [Citation.] It is necessary that there be some act of interference or of persuading a party to breach, for example by offering better terms or other incentives, for tort liability to arise. [Citations.] The issue of whether a defendant affirmatively took steps to induce the breach of an existing contract is a question of fact for the jury. [Citation.]

Texaco contends that it did not actively procure the alleged breach and that the required inducement did not occur. Texaco argues that it merely responded to a campaign of active solicitation by Getty Oil and the Museum, who were dissatisfied by the terms of Pennzoil's offer.

* * *

The evidence discussed above on Texaco's calculated formulation and implementation of its ideal strategy to acquire Getty is also inconsistent with its contention that it was merely the passive target of Getty's aggressive solicitation campaign and did nothing more than to accept terms that Getty Oil and the Museum had proposed. The evidence showed that Texaco knew it had to act quickly, and that it had "24 hours" to "stop the train." Texaco's strategy was to approach the Museum first, through its "key person" Lipton, to obtain the Museum's shares, and then to "talk to Gordon." It knew that the Trust instrument permitted Gordon Getty to sell the Trust shares only to avoid a loss, and it knew of the trustee's fear of being left in a powerless minority ownership position at Getty Oil. Texaco notes indicated a deliberate strategy to "create concern that he will take a loss"; "if there's a tender offer and Gordon doesn't tender, then he could wind up with paper"; and "pressure." This evidence contradicts the contention that Texaco passively accepted a deal proposed by the other parties.

* * *

[The judgment of the trial court was affirmed.]

Defense of Property

KATKO v. BRINEY

Supreme Court of Iowa, 1971.
183 N.W.2d 657.

MOORE, C.J.

The primary issue presented here is whether an owner may protect personal property in an unoccupied boarded-up farm house against trespassers and thieves by a spring gun capable of inflicting death or serious injury.

We are not here concerned with a man's right to protect his home and members of his family. Defendants' home was several miles from the scene of the incident to which we refer. * * *

Plaintiff's action is for damages resulting from serious injury caused by a shot from a 20-gauge spring shotgun set by defendants in a bedroom of an old farm house which had been uninhabited for several years. Plaintiff and his companion, Marvin McDonough, had broken and entered the house to find and steal old bottles and dated fruit jars which they considered antiques.

* * * The jury returned a verdict for plaintiff and against defendants for $20,000 actual and $10,000 punitive damages. [The defendants appealed.]

Most of the facts are not disputed. In 1957 defendant Bertha L. Briney inherited her parents' farm land in Mahaska and Monroe Counties. Included was an 80-acre tract in southwest Mahaska County where her grandparents and parents had lived. No one occupied the house thereafter. Her husband, Edward, attempted to care for the land. He kept no farm machinery thereon. The outbuildings became dilapidated.

For about 10 years, 1957 to 1967, there occurred a series of trespassing and housebreaking events with loss of some household items, the breaking of windows and "messing up of the property in general." The latest occurred June 8, 1967, prior to the event on July 16, 1967, herein involved.

Defendants through the years boarded up the windows and doors in an attempt to stop the intrusions. They had posted "no trespass" signs on the land several years before 1967. The nearest one was 35 feet from the house. On June 11, 1967, defendants set "a shotgun trap" in the north bedroom. After Mr. Briney cleaned and oiled his 20-gauge shotgun, the power of which he was well aware, defendants took it to the old house where they secured it to an iron bed with the barrel pointed at the bedroom door. It was rigged with wire from the doorknob to the gun's trigger so it would fire when the door was opened. Briney first pointed the gun so an intruder would be hit in the stomach but at Mrs. Briney's suggestion it was lowered to hit the legs. He admitted he did so "because I was mad and tired of being tormented" but "he did not intend to injure anyone." He gave no explanation of why he used a loaded shell and set it to hit a person already in the house. Tin was nailed over the bedroom window. The spring gun could not be seen from the outside. No warning of its presence was posted.

Plaintiff lived with his wife and worked regularly as a gasoline station attendant in Eddyville, seven miles from the old house. He had observed it for several years while hunting in the area and considered it as being abandoned. He knew it had long been uninhabited. In 1967 the area around the house was covered with high weeds. Prior to July 16, 1967, plaintiff and McDonough had been to the premises and found several old bottles and fruit jars which they took and added to their collection of antiques. On the latter date about 9:30 p.m. they made a second trip to the Briney property. They entered the old house by removing a board from a porch window which was without glass. While McDonough was looking around the kitchen area plaintiff went to another part of the house. As he started to open the north bedroom door the shotgun went off striking him in the right leg above the ankle bone. Much of his leg, including part of the tibia, was blown away. Only by McDonough's assistance was plaintiff able to get out of the house and after crawling some distance was put in his vehicle and rushed to a doctor and then to a hospital. He remained in the hospital 40 days.

Plaintiff's doctor testified he seriously considered amputation but eventually the healing process was successful. Some weeks after his release from the hospital plaintiff returned to work on crutches. He was required to keep the injured leg in a cast for approximately a year and wear a special brace for another year. He continued to suffer pain during this period.

There was undenied medical testimony plaintiff had a permanent deformity, a loss of tissue, and a shortening of the leg.

The record discloses plaintiff to trial time had incurred $710 medical expense, $2,056.85 for hospital service, $61.80 for orthopedic service and $750 as loss of earnings. In addition thereto the trial court submitted to the jury the question of damages for pain and suffering and for future disability.

* * *

The main thrust of defendants' defense in the trial court and on this appeal is that "the law permits use of a spring gun in a dwelling or warehouse for the purpose of preventing the unlawful entry of a burglar or thief." * * *

* * *

The overwhelming weight of authority, both textbook and case law, supports the trial court's statement of the applicable principles of law.

Prosser on Torts, Third Edition, pages 116–118, states:

. . . the law has always placed a higher value upon human safety than upon mere rights in property, it is the accepted rule that there is no privilege to use any force calculated to cause death or serious bodily injury to repel the threat to land or chattels, unless there is also such a threat to the defendant's personal safety as to justify a self-defense. . . . spring guns and other man-killing devices are not justifiable against a mere trespasser, or even a petty thief. They are privileged only against those upon whom the landowner, if he were present in person, would be free to inflict injury of the same kind.

Restatement of Torts, section 85 . . . states: "The value of human life and limb, not only to the individual concerned but also to society, so outweighs the interest of a possessor of land in excluding it from those whom he is not willing to admit thereto that a possessor of land has, as is stated in § 79, no privilege to use force intended or likely to cause death or serious harm against another whom the possessor sees about to enter his premises or meddle with his chattel, unless the intrusion threatens death or serious bodily harm to the occupiers or users of the premises. . . ."

Judgment affirmed.

QUESTIONS

1. Identify and define the torts that protect against intentional interference with personal rights.

2. Explain the application of the various privileges to defamation suits and how they are affected by whether the plaintiff is a (a) public figure, (b) public official, or (c) private person.

3. Distinguish the four torts comprising invasion of privacy.

4. Distinguish by example among interference with contractual relations, disparagement, and fraudulent misrepresentation.

5. Identify and describe the defenses to intentional torts.

PROBLEMS

1. The Penguin intentionally hits Batman with his umbrella. Batman, stunned by the blow, falls backwards, knocking Robin down. Robin's leg is broken in the fall, and he cries out, "Holy broken bat bones! My leg is broken." Who, if anyone, is liable to Robin? Why?

2. CEO is convinced by his employee, M. Ploy, that a coworker, A. Cused, has been stealing money from the company. At lunch that day in the company cafeteria, CEO discharged Cused from her employment, accused her of stealing from the company, searched through her purse over her objections, and finally forcibly escorted her to his office to await the arrival of the police, which he had his secretary summon. Cused is indicted for embezzlement but subsequently is acquitted upon establishing her innocence. What rights, if any, does Cused have against CEO?

3. Ralph kisses Edith while she is asleep but does not waken or harm her. Edith sues Ralph for battery. Decision?

4. Claude, a creditor seeking to collect a debt, calls on Dianne and demands payment in a rude and insolent manner. When Dianne says that she cannot pay, Claude calls Dianne a deadbeat and says that he will never trust Dianne again. Is Claude liable to Dianne? If so, for what tort?

5. Lana, a 10-year-old child, is run over by a car negligently driven by Mitchel. Lana, at the time of the accident, was acting reasonably and without negligence. Clark, a newspaper reporter, photographs Lana while she is lying in the street in great pain. Two years later, Perry, the publisher of a newspaper, prints Clark's picture of Lana in his newspaper as a lead to an article concerning the negligence of children. The caption under the picture reads: "They ask to be killed." Lana, who has recovered from the accident, brings suit against Clark and Perry. What result?

6. In 1963 the *Saturday Evening Post* featured an article entitled "The Story of a College Football Fix," characterized in the subtitle as "A Shocking Report of How Wally Butts and Bear Bryant Rigged a Game Last Fall." Butts was athletic director of the University of Georgia, and Bryant was head coach of the University of Alabama. The article was based on a claim by one George Burnett that he had accidentally overheard a long distance telephone conversation between Butts and Bryant in the course of which Butts divulged information on plays Georgia would use in the upcoming game against Alabama. The writer assigned to the story by the *Post* was not a football expert and did not interview either Butts or Bryant, nor did he personally see the notes Burnett had made of the telephone conversation. Butts admitted that he had a long distance telephone conversation with Bryant but denied that any advance information on prospective football plays was given. Butts brought a libel suit against the *Post*. Decision?

7. Joan is a patient confined in a hospital with a rare disease that is of great interest to the public. Carol, a television reporter, requests Joan to consent to an interview. Joan refuses, but Carol, nonetheless, enters Joan's room over her objection and photographs her. Joan brings a suit against Carol. Decision?

8. Owner has a place on his land where he piles trash. The pile has been there for a period of three months. John, a neighbor of Owner and without Owner's consent or knowledge, throws trash onto the trashpile. Owner learns that John has done this and sues him. What tort, if any, has John committed?

9. Chris leaves her car parked in front of a store. There are no signs that say Chris cannot park there. The store owner, however, needs the car moved to enable a delivery truck to unload. He releases the brake and pushes Chris's car three or four feet, doing no harm to the car. Chris returns and sees that her car has been moved and is very angry. She threatens to sue the store owner for trespass to her personal property. Can she recover?

10. Carr borrowed John's brand new Ford Escort for the purpose of going to the store. He told John he would be right back. Carr then decided, however, to go to the beach while he had the car. Can John recover from Carr the value of the automobile? If so, for what tort?

11. Marcia Samms, a respectable married woman, claimed that David Eccles had repeatedly and persistently called her at various hours, including late at night, from May to December, soliciting her to have illicit sexual relations with him. She also claimed that on one occasion Eccles came over to her residence to again solicit sex and indecently exposed himself to her. Mrs. Samms had never encouraged Eccles but had continuously repulsed his "insulting, indecent, and obscene" proposals. She brought suit against Eccles, claiming she suffered great anxiety and fear for her personal safety and severe emotional distress, demanding actual and punitive damages. Decision?

12. National Bond and Investment Company sent two of its employees to repossess Whithorn's car after he failed to complete the payments. The two repossessors located Whithorn while he was driving his car. They followed him and hailed him down in order to make the repossession. Whithorn refused to abandon his car and demanded evidence of their authority. The two repossessors became impatient and called a wrecker. They ordered the driver of the wrecker to hook Whithorn's car and move it down the street while Whithorn was still inside the vehicle. Whithorn started the car and tried to escape, but the wrecker lifted the car off the road and progressed seventy-five to one hundred feet until Whithorn managed to stall the wrecker. Whithorn sued National Bond for false imprisonment. Decision?

13. In March 1975 William Proxmire, a United States senator from Wisconsin, initiated the "Golden Fleece of the Month Award" to publicize what he believed to be wasteful government spending. The second of these awards was given to the Federal agencies that had for seven years funded Dr. Hutchinson's research on stress levels in animals. The award was made in a speech Proxmire gave in the Senate; the text was also incorporated into an advance press release that was sent to 275 members of the national news media. Proxmire also referred to the research again in two subsequent newsletters sent to 100,000 constituents and during a television interview. Hutchinson then brought this action alleging defamation resulting in personal and economic injury. Decision?

14. Capune was attempting a trip from New York to Florida on an eighteen-foot-long paddleboard. The trip was being covered by various media to gain publicity for Capune and certain products he endorsed. Capune approached a pier by water. The pier was owned by Robbins who had posted signs prohibiting surfing and swimming around the pier. Capune was unaware of these notices and attempted to continue his journey by passing under the pier. Robbins ran up yelling and threw two bottles at Capune. Capune was frightened and tried to maneuver his paddle to go around the pier. Robbins then threw a third bottle that hit Capune on the head. Capune had to be helped out of the water and taken to the hospital. He suffered a physical wound which required twenty-four sutures and as a result had to discontinue his trip. Capune brought suit in tort against Robbins. Is

Robbins liable? If so, for which tort or torts?

15. Ralph Nader has been a critic of General Motors for several years. When General Motors learned that Nader was about to publish a book entitled *Unsafe at any Speed,* criticizing one of its automobiles it decided to conduct a campaign of intimidation against him. Specifically, Nader claims that GMC (1) conducted a series of interviews with Nader's acquaintances, questioning them about his political, social, racial, and religious views; (2) kept him under surveillance in public places for an unreasonable length of time; (3) caused him to be accosted by women for the purpose of entrapping him into illicit relationships; (4) made threatening, harassing, and obnoxious telephone calls to him; (5) tapped his telephone and eavesdropped by means of mechanical and electronic equipment on his private conversations with others; and (6) conducted a "continuing" and harassing investigation of him. Nader brought suit against GMC for invasion of privacy. Which, if any, of the alleged actions would constitute invasion of privacy?

16. Bill Kinsey was charged with murdering his wife while working for the Peace Corps in Tanzania. After waiting six months in jail he was acquitted at a trial that attracted wide publicity. Five years later, while a graduate student at Stanford University, Kinsey had a brief affair with Mary Macur. He abruptly ended the affair by telling Macur he would no longer be seeing her because another woman, Sally Allen, was coming from England to live with him. A few months later, Kinsey and Allen moved to Africa and were subsequently married. Soon after Bill ended their affair, Macur began a letter writing campaign designed to expose Bill and his mistreatment of her. Macur sent several letters to both Bill and Sally Kinsey, their former spouses, their parents, their neighbors, their parents' neighbors, members of Bill's dissertation committee, other faculty, and the president of Stanford University. The letters contained statements accusing Bill of murdering his first wife, spending six months in jail for the crime, being a rapist, and other questionable behavior. The Kinseys brought an action for invasion of privacy, seeking damages and a permanent injunction. Decision?

Chapter 6

NEGLIGENCE AND STRICT LIABILITY

Requirements of Negligence Actions
Defenses to Negligence
Activities Giving Rise to Strict Liability
Defenses to Strict Liability

NEGLIGENCE involves conduct that creates an unreasonable risk of harm, whereas intentional torts deal with conduct that has a substantial certainty of causing harm. The basis of liability for negligence is the failure to exercise reasonable care under the circumstances for the safety of another person or his property, which failure proximately causes injury to such person or damage to his property, or both. Thus, if the driver of an automobile runs down a person, intentionally, she has committed the intentional tort of battery. If, on the other hand, the driver hits and injures a person while driving unreasonably for the safety of others, she is negligent.

Strict liability is not based upon the negligence or intent of the defendant but rather upon the nature of the activity in which he is engaging. Under this doctrine, defendants who engage in certain activities, such as keeping animals or maintaining abnormally dangerous conditions, are held liable for injuries they caused even though they exercise the utmost care. The law imposes this liability in order to bring about a just reallocation of loss, given that the defendant engaged in the activity for his own benefit and is in a better position to manage the risk by insurance or otherwise.

NEGLIGENCE

The Restatement defines negligence as "conduct which falls below the standard established by law for the protection of others against unreasonable risk of harm." Restatement, Section 282. The standard established by law is the conduct of a reasonable person acting prudently and with due care under the circumstances.

A person is not liable for injury caused to another by an **unavoidable accident**—an occurrence which was not intended and could not have been prevented by the exercise of reasonable care. Thus, no liability results from the loss of control of an automobile because the driver is suddenly and unforeseeably stricken with a heart attack, stroke, or fainting spell. If the driver, however, had warning of the imminent heart attack or other infirmity, it would be negligent for him to drive at all.

An action for negligence consists of three elements, each of which must be proved by the plaintiff:

1. **Breach of duty of care:** that a legal duty required the defendant to conform to the standard of conduct established for the pro-

tection of others, and that the defendant failed to conform to the required standard of conduct;

2. **Proximate cause:** that the injury and harm sustained by the plaintiff was proximately caused by the defendant's failure to conform to the required standard of conduct; and

3. **Injury:** that the injury and harm is protected against negligent interference.

BREACH OF DUTY OF CARE

Negligence consists of conduct that creates an unreasonable risk of harm. In determining whether a given risk of harm is unreasonable the following factors are considered: (1) the probability that the harm will occur, (2) the gravity or seriousness of the resulting harm, (3) the utility of the conduct creating the risk, and (4) the cost of taking precautions that will reduce the risk. Thus, the standard of conduct, which is the basis of the law of negligence, is usually determined by a cost-benefit analysis.

Reasonable Person Standard

The duty of care imposed by law is measured by the degree of carefulness that a reasonable person would exercise in a given situation. The reasonable person is a fictitious individual who is always careful, prudent, and never negligent. What the judge or jury determines that a reasonable person would have done in the light of the facts brought out by the evidence in a particular case sets the standard of conduct for that case. The reasonable person standard is thus external and *objective,* as described by Justice Holmes:

If, for instance, a man is born hasty and awkward, is always hurting himself or his neighbors, no doubt his congenital defects will be allowed for in the courts of Heaven, but his slips are no less troublesome to his neighbors than if they sprang from guilty neglect. His neighbors accordingly require him, at his peril, to come up to their standard, and the courts which they establish decline to take his personal equation into account. Holmes, *The Common Law.*

Children The standard of conduct to which a child must conform to avoid being negligent is that of a reasonable person of like age, intelligence, and experience under like circumstances. Restatement, Section 283A. For example, Alice, a five-year-old girl, while walking with her father on the crowded sidewalk along Main Street, was told by her father that he was going to take her to Disneyworld for her birthday next week. Upon hearing the news, Alice became so excited that she began to jump up and down and run around. During this fit of exuberance, Alice accidentally ran into and knocked down an elderly woman who was passing by. Alice's liability, if any, would be determined by whether she had the capacity and judgment to understand the increased risk caused to others by her enthusiastic display of joy.

The law applies an individualized test because children are incapable of exercising the judgment, intelligence, knowledge, and experience of an adult. Moreover, children as a general rule do not engage in activities entailing high risk to others, and their conduct does not involve the same magnitude of harm. A child who engages in an adult activity, however, such as flying an airplane or driving a boat or car, is held in about half the States to the standard of care applicable to adults. Finally, some States modify this individualized test by holding that under a minimum age, most commonly the age of seven, a child is incapable of committing a negligent act.

Physical Disability If a person is ill or otherwise physically disabled, the standard of conduct to which he must conform to avoid being negligent is that of a reasonable person under like disability. Thus, a blind man must act as a reasonable man who is blind and a woman with multiple sclerosis must act as a reasonable woman with multiple sclerosis.

Mental Deficiency The law makes no allowance for the insanity or other mental deficiency of the defendant in a negligence case, and the defendant is held to the standard of conduct of a reasonable person who is *not* mentally deficient even though it is, in fact, beyond his capacity to conform to the standard. The Restatement, Section 283B, Comment b, justifies this rule as follows:

1. The difficulty of drawing any satisfactory line between mental deficiency and those variations of temperament, intellect, and emotional balance which cannot, as a practical matter, be taken into account in imposing liability for damage done.
2. The unsatisfactory character of the evidence of mental deficiency in many cases, together with the ease with which it can be feigned, the difficulties which the triers of fact must encounter in determining its existence, nature, degree, and effect, . . .
3. The feeling that if mental defectives are to live in the world, they should pay for the damage they do, and that it is better that their wealth, if any, should be used to compensate innocent victims than that it should remain in their hands.
4. The belief that their liability will mean that those who have charge of them or their estates will be stimulated to look after them, keep them in order, and see that they do not do harm.

Thus, an adult with the mental acumen of a six-year-old will be held liable for his negligent conduct if he fails to act as carefully as a reasonable adult of normal intelligence. In this case the law may demand more of the individual than his mental limitations permit him to accomplish.

Superior Skill or Knowledge   Persons who are qualified and who practice a profession or trade which calls for special skill and expertise are required to exercise that care and skill which are normally possessed by members in good standing of their profession or trade. This standard applies to such professionals as physicians, surgeons, dentists, attorneys, pharmacists, architects, accountants, and engineers and to such skilled trades as airline pilots, electricians, carpenters, and plumbers. If a member of a profession or skilled trade possesses greater skill than that common to the profession or trade, she is required to exercise that skill.

Emergencies   An emergency is a sudden and unexpected event which calls for immediate action and does not permit time for deliberation. In determining whether a defendant's conduct is reasonable, the fact that he was at the time confronted with a sudden emergency is taken into consideration. Restatement, Section 296. The standard is still that of a reasonable person under the circumstances—the emergency is simply part of the circumstances. Where, however, the defendant's own negligent or tortious conduct has created the emergency, he is liable for the consequences of this conduct even if he acts reasonably in the emergency situation.

Violation of Statute   The reasonable person standard of conduct may be established by legislation. Restatement, Section 285. Some statutes expressly impose civil liability upon violators. Absent such a provision, courts may adopt the requirements of the statute as the standard of conduct if the statute is intended to protect a class of persons, which includes the plaintiff, against the particular hazard and kind of harm which resulted.

If the statute is found to be applicable, the majority of the courts hold that an unexcused violation is **negligence *per se;*** that is, it is conclusive on the issue of negligent conduct. In a minority of States, the violation is considered merely evidence of negligence. In either event, the plaintiff must also prove legal causation and injury.

For example, a statute enacted to protect employees from injuries requires that all factory elevators be equipped with specified safety devices. Arthur, an employee in Freya's factory, and Carlos, a business visitor to the factory, are injured when the elevator falls because of the failure to install the safety devices. The court may adopt the statute as a standard of conduct as to Arthur, and hold Freya negligent *per se* to Arthur, but not as to Carlos, because Arthur, and not Carlos, is within the class of persons intended to be protected by the statute. Carlos would have to establish that a reasonable person in the position of Freya under the circumstances would have installed the safety device. *See Walz v. City of Hudson.*

On the other hand, compliance with a legislative enactment or administrative regulation does not prevent a finding of negligence if a reasonable person would have taken additional precautions. Restatement, Section 288C. For instance, driving at the speed limit may not constitute due care when traffic or road conditions require a lesser speed. The legislative or administrative standard normally establishes a *minimum* standard.

Duty to Act

Except in special circumstances, no one is required to aid another in peril. As Prosser has stated, "the law has persistently refused to recognize the moral obligation of common decency and common humanity, to come to the aid of another human being who is in danger, even though the outcome is to cost him his life." For example, Toni, an adult standing along the edge of a steep cliff, observes a baby carriage with a crying infant in it slowly heading toward the edge and certain doom. Toni could easily prevent the baby's fall at no risk to her own safety. Nonetheless, Toni does nothing, and the baby falls to his death. Toni is under no legal duty to act and, therefore, incurs no liability for failing to do so. *But see Soldano v. O'Daniels.*

Section 314 of the Restatement reflects this position: "The fact that the actor realizes or should realize that action on his part is necessary for another's aid or protection does not of itself impose upon him a duty to take such action." Special relations between the parties may exist, however, that impose a duty upon the defendant to aid or protect the other. Thus, if in the example above, Toni were the baby's mother or babysitter, Toni would be under a duty to act and would therefore be liable for not taking action. The special relations giving rise to the duty to aid or protect another include: common carrier–passenger, innkeeper–guest, employer–employee, and parent—child. Restatement, Sections 314A and 314B. *See Caldwell v. Bechtel, Inc.* in Chapter 1.

A duty of affirmative action is also imposed upon those whose conduct, whether tortious or innocent, has injured another and left him helpless and in danger of further harm. For example, Dale drives her car into Bob, who is rendered unconscious. Dale leaves Bob lying in the middle of the road, where he is run over by a second car driven by Chen. Dale is liable to Bob for the additional injuries inflicted by Chen. Moreover, a person incurs a duty to exercise care by voluntarily coming to the assistance of another in need of aid. In such instance, the actor is liable if his failure to exercise reasonable care increases the risk of harm, causes harm, or leaves the other in a worse position. For example, Ann finds Ben drunk and stumbling along a dark sidewalk. Ann leads Ben halfway up a steep and unguarded stairway, where she abandons him. Ben attempts to climb the stairs but trips and falls, suffering serious injury. Ann is liable to Ben for having left him in a worse position.

A parent is not liable for the torts of his minor child simply because of the parental relationship. Where, however, the parent authorizes, encourages, or participates in, the tort of his child, or ratifies it by knowingly participating in the benefits, he is liable. So, also, tort liability may be attributed to the parents on the grounds of their negligence, as where the parent places a dangerous instrumentality, such as a gun or knife, in the hands of the child, and the child thereby causes injury to another. For example, "A is informed that his six-year-old child is shooting at a target in the street with a .22 rifle, in a manner which endangers the safety of those using the street. A fails to take the rifle away from the child, or to take any other action. The child unintentionally shoots B, a pedestrian, in the leg. A is subject to liability to B." Restatement, Section 316, Illustration 1.

Duties of Possessors of Land

The right of possessors of land to use that land for their own benefit and enjoyment is limited by their duty to do so in a reasonable manner. They cannot cause unreasonable risks of harm to others by the use of their land.

Liability for breach of this obligation may arise from conduct in any of the three areas of torts discussed in this and the preceding chapter: intentional harm, negligence, or strict liability. The great majority of these cases falls within the classification of negligence.

The possessor of land is required to exercise reasonable care in carrying on activities on her land in order to protect others who are *not* on her property. For example, a property owner must use reasonable care in constructing a factory on her premises so that it is not unreasonably dangerous to people off the site.

The duty of a possessor of land to persons who come *upon* the land depends upon whether that person is a trespasser, a licensee, or an invitee. A few States have abandoned these distinctions and apply ordinary negligence principles of foreseeable risk and reasonable care.

Duty to Trespassers A trespasser is a person who enters or remains on the land of another without permission or privilege to do so. The lawful possessor of the land is *not* liable to adult trespassers for her failure to maintain the land in a reasonably safe condition. Nonetheless, trespassers are not criminals, and the lawful possessor is not free to inflict intentional injury on them. Moreover, some courts have held that upon discovery of the presence of trespassers on the land, the lawful possessor is required to exercise reasonable care for their safety.

The law extends greater protection to a child who trespasses by imposing upon a possessor of land liability for physical harm caused by artificial conditions upon the land if:

(a) the place where the condition exists is one upon which the possessor knows or has reason to know that children are likely to trespass, and
(b) the condition is one of which the possessor knows or has reason to know and which he realizes or should realize will involve an unreasonable risk of death or serious bodily harm to such children, and
(c) the children because of their youth do not discover the condition or realize the risk involved in intermeddling with it or in coming within the area made dangerous by it, and

(d) the utility to the possessor of maintaining the condition and the burden of eliminating the danger are slight as compared with the risk to children involved, and
(e) the possessor fails to exercise reasonable care to eliminate the danger or otherwise to protect the children. Restatement, Section 339.

The Restatement provides the following illustration: "A has on his land a small artificial pond full of goldfish. A's land adjoins a nursery in which children from two to five years of age are left by their parents for the day, and such children are, as A knows, in the habit of trespassing on A's land and going near the pond. A could easily prevent this by closing and locking his gate. A does not do so. B, a child three years of age, trespasses, enters the pond to catch goldfish, and is drowned. A is subject to liability for the death of B." Section 339, Illustration 7.

Duty to Licensees A licensee is a person who is privileged to enter or remain upon land only by virtue of the consent of the lawful possessor. Restatement, Section 330. Licensees include members of the possessor's household, *social guests,* and salespersons calling at private homes. A licensee, however, will become a trespasser if he enters a portion of the land to which he is not invited or remains upon the land after his invitation has expired.

The possessor owes a higher duty of care to licensees than to trespassers. The possessor must warn the licensee of dangerous activities and conditions of which the possessor has knowledge and which the licensee does not and is not likely to discover. If he is not warned, the licensee may recover if the activity or dangerous condition resulted from the possessor's failure to exercise reasonable care to protect him from the danger. Restatement, Section 342. To illustrate: Jose invites a friend, Julia, to his place in the country at eight o'clock on a winter evening. Jose knows that a bridge in his driveway is in a dangerous condition that is not noticeable in the dark. Jose does not inform Julia of this fact. The bridge gives way under Julia's car, causing serious harm to Julia. Jose is liable to Julia.

Duty to Invitees An invitee is either a public invitee or a business visitor. Restatement, Section 332. A **public invitee** is a person who is invited to enter or remain on land as a member of the public for a purpose for which the land is held open to the public, such as a public park, beach, or swimming pool, or a governmental facility where business with the public is transacted openly, such as a post office or office of the Recorder of Deeds. A **business visitor** is a person invited to enter or remain on the premises for a purpose directly or indirectly connected with business dealings with the possessor of the land, such as one who enters a store or a workman who enters a residence to make repairs.

The duty of the possessor of land to invitees with respect to the condition of the premises is to exercise reasonable care to protect them against dangerous conditions they are unlikely to discover. This liability extends not only to those conditions the possessor knows of but also to those conditions of which he should reasonably know. Restatement, Section 343. For example, supermarket A has in its store a large, glass front door which is well lighted and plainly visible. Johnson, a customer, mistakes the glass for an open doorway and walks into the glass, injuring himself. A is not liable to Johnson. If, on the other hand, the glass was difficult to see and it was foreseeable that a person might mistake the glass for an open doorway, then A would be liable to Johnson if Johnson crashed into the glass while exercising reasonable care.

For a case involving a "bizarre and most unusual circumstance," *see Yania v. Bigan.*

These three categories of duties are illustrated in Figure 6–1.

Res Ipsa Loquitur

A rule has developed that permits the jury to infer *both* negligent conduct and causation from the mere occurrence of certain types of events. This rule is called ***res ipsa loquitur,*** which means "the thing speaks for itself," and applies when the event is of a kind which ordinarily does not occur in the absence of negligence and other possible causes are sufficiently eliminated by the evidence. Section 328D of the Restatement provides as follows:

(1) It may be inferred that harm suffered by the plaintiff is caused by negligence of the defendant when

    (a) the event is of a kind which ordinarily does not occur in the absence of negligence;

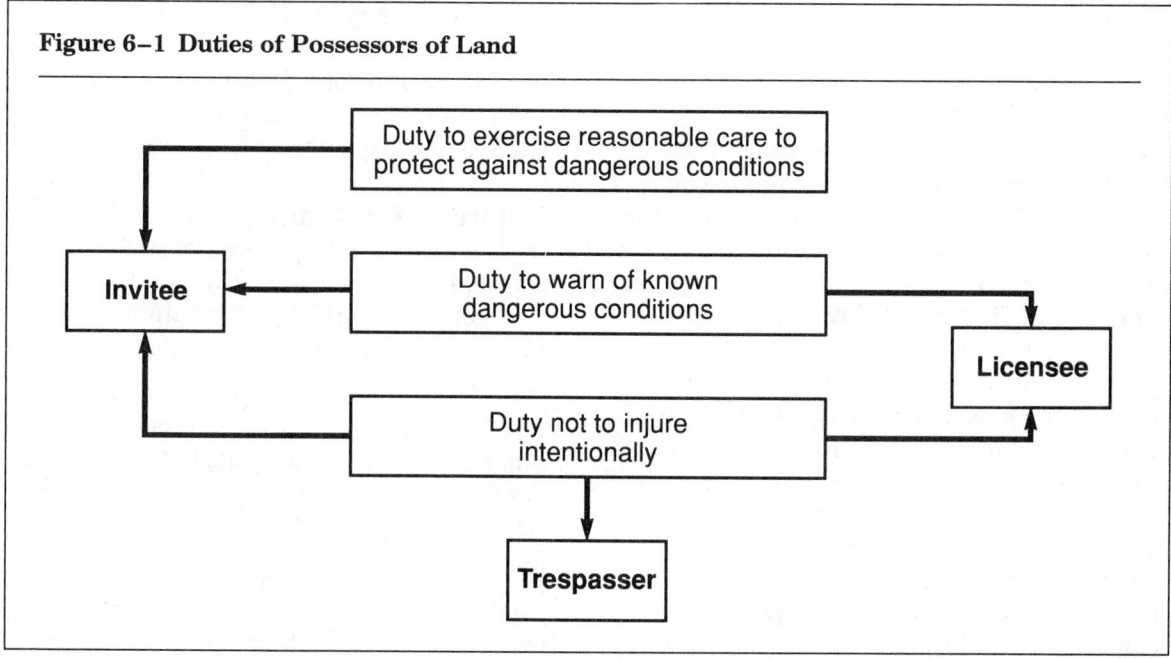

Figure 6–1 Duties of Possessors of Land

(b) other responsible causes, including the conduct of the plaintiff and third persons, are sufficiently eliminated by the evidence; and

(c) the indicated negligence is within the scope of the defendant's duty to the plaintiff.

For example, Abrams rents a room in Brown's motel. During the night a large piece of plaster falls from the ceiling and injures Abrams. In the absence of other evidence, the jury may infer that the harm resulted from Brown's negligence in permitting the plaster to become defective. Brown is permitted, however, to introduce evidence to contradict the inference of negligence.

PROXIMATE CAUSE

Liability for the negligent conduct of a defendant requires not only that the conduct in fact caused injury to the plaintiff, but also that it was the proximate cause of the injury. Most simply expressed, proximate cause consists of the judicially imposed limitations upon a person's liability for the consequences of his or her negligence. As a matter of social policy, legal responsibility has not been permitted to follow all the consequences of a negligent act. Responsibility has been limited—to a greater extent than with intentional torts—to those persons and results which are closely connected with the negligent conduct.

Causation in Fact

In order to support a finding that the defendant's negligence was the proximate cause of the plaintiff's injury, it is first necessary that the defendant's conduct was the *actual cause* of the injury. A widely applied test for causation in fact is the **but for rule:** A person's conduct is a cause of an event if the event would not have occurred *but for* the person's negligent conduct. Under this test, an act or omission to act is *not* a cause of an event if that event would have occurred regardless of the act or omission. For instance, Arnold fails to erect a barrier around an excavation. Doyle is driving a truck when its accelerator becomes stuck. Arnold's negligence is not a cause in fact of Doyle's death if the runaway

truck would have crashed through the barrier even if it had been erected. Similarly, failure to install a proper fire escape to a hotel is not the cause in fact of the death of a person who is suffocated by the smoke while sleeping in bed.

The "but for" test, however, is not useful where there are two or more forces actively operating, each of which is sufficient to bring about the harm in question. For example, Wilson accidentally stabs Kennedy with a knife while Hart negligently fractures Kennedy's skull with a rock. Either wound would be fatal, and Kennedy dies from both. Under the "but for" test, either Wilson or Hart, or both, could argue that Kennedy would have died from the wound inflicted by the other and therefore he is not liable. The **substantial factor** test addresses this problem by stating that negligent conduct is a legal cause of harm to another if the conduct is a substantial factor in bringing about the harm. Restatement, Section 431. Under this test the conduct of both Wilson and Hart would be found to be a cause in fact of Kennedy's death.

Limitations on Causation in Fact

As a matter of policy, the law imposes limitations on the causal connection between the defendant's negligence and the plaintiff's injury. Two of the principal factors that are taken into consideration in determining such limitations are (a) unforeseeable consequences and (b) superseding causes.

Unforeseeable Consequences   The liability of a negligent defendant for unforeseeable consequences has proved to be troublesome and controversial. The Restatement and a majority of the courts have adopted the following position:

(1) If the actor's conduct is a substantial factor in bringing about harm to another, the fact that the actor neither foresaw nor should have foreseen the extent of the harm or the manner in which it occurred does not prevent him from being liable.
(2) The actor's conduct may be held not to be a legal cause of harm to another where after the event and looking back from the harm to the ac-

tor's negligent conduct, it appears to the court highly extraordinary that it should have brought about the harm. Section 435.

Even if the defendant's negligent conduct is a cause in fact of harm to the plaintiff, the defendant is *not* liable to the plaintiff *unless* the defendant could have reasonably anticipated injuring the plaintiff or a class of persons of which the plaintiff is a member. Restatement, Section 281, Comment c. Proximate cause involves a recognition of the risk of harm to the plaintiff individually or to a class of persons of which the plaintiff is a member. *See Palsgraf v. Long Island Railroad Co., and Petition of Kinsman Transit Co.*

For example, Albert, while negligently driving an automobile, collides with a car carrying dynamite. Albert is unaware of the contents of the other car and has no reason to know about it. The collision causes the dynamite to explode, shattering glass in a building a block away. The shattered glass injures Betsy, who is inside the building. The explosion also injures Calvin, who is walking on the sidewalk near the collision. Albert would be liable to Calvin because Albert should have realized that his negligent driving might result in a collision that would endanger pedestrians nearby, and the fact that the actual harm resulted in an unforeseeable manner does not affect his liability. Betsy, however, was beyond the zone of danger, and Albert, accordingly, is not liable to Betsy. Albert's negligent driving is not deemed to be the "proximate cause" of Betsy's injury because, looking back from the harm to Albert's negligence, it appears highly extraordinary that Albert's conduct should have brought about the harm to Betsy.

Superseding Cause An intervening cause is an event or act that occurs after the defendant's negligent conduct and together with the defendant's negligence causes the plaintiff's harm. If the intervening cause is deemed a superseding cause, then it relieves the defendant of liability for harm to the plaintiff caused in fact by both the defendant's negligence and the intervening event or act. Sec-

tion 442 of the Restatement provides the following list of considerations in determining whether an intervening force is a superseding cause that relieves the defendant of liability:

(a) the fact that its intervention brings about harm different in kind from that which would otherwise have resulted from the actor's negligence;
(b) the fact that its operation or the consequences thereof appear after the event to be extraordinary rather than normal in view of the circumstances existing at the time of its operation;
(c) the fact that the intervening force is operating independently of any situation created by the actor's negligence, or, on the other hand, is or is not a normal result of such a situation;
(d) the fact that the operation of the intervening force is due to a third person's act or to his failure to act;
(e) the fact that the intervening force is due to an act of a third person which is wrongful toward the other and as such subjects the third person to liability to him;
(f) the degree of culpability of a wrongful act of a third person which sets the intervening force in motion.

For example, Adams negligently runs down a cow which is left lying stunned in the road. Several minutes later the cow regains consciousness, takes fright, and charges into Bogues, a bystander. The cow's conduct is an intervening, but not a superseding, cause of harm to Bogues because it is a normal consequence of the situation caused by Adams' negligence. Therefore, Adams is liable to Bogues. In contrast, Adams negligently leaves an excavation in a public sidewalk into which Bogues intentionally hurls Carson. Adams is not liable to Carson because Bogues' conduct is a superseding cause that relieves Adams of liability.

When an intervening cause is a foreseeable or normal consequence of the defendant's negligence, it is *not* a superseding cause. Thus, a person who negligently places another in imminent danger is liable for injury sustained by a third party rescuer who attempts to aid the imperilled victim. The same is true of attempts by the endangered person to escape the peril as, for example, when a person swerves off the road to avoid a head-on collision with an automobile driven negligently on the wrong side of the road. It is commonly held that a negligent defendant is liable for the results of necessary medical treatment of the injured party, even if the treatment is negligent.

INJURY

The plaintiff must prove that the defendant's negligent conduct proximately caused harm to a legally protected interest. Certain interests receive little or no protection from negligent interference, while others receive full protection. The extent of protection for a particular interest is determined by the courts as a matter of law on the basis of social policy and expediency. For example, negligent conduct that is the proximate cause of harmful contact with the person of another is actionable. Thus, if Bob negligently runs into Julie, a pedestrian, who is carefully crossing the street, Bob is liable for physical injuries sustained by Julie as a result of the collision. On the other hand, if Bob's careless conduct causes only offensive contact with Julie's person, Bob is not liable. "In general, however, it may be said that the law gives protection against negligent acts to the interest in security of the person, and to the various interests in tangible property. In other words, negligence may result in liability for personal injury or property damage." *Prosser and Keeton on the Law of Torts,* p. 359.

The courts have traditionally been reluctant to allow recovery for negligently inflicted emotional distress. This view has gradually changed during this century, and the majority of courts now hold a person liable for negligently causing emotional distress if bodily harm results from the distress. Restatement, Section 436. In the great majority of States, if the defendant's conduct merely results in emotional disturbance without resultant bodily harm, the defendant is not liable. Restatement, Section 436A. A few courts, however, have recently allowed recovery of damages for negligently inflicted emotional distress in the absence of resultant physical harm.

Most courts do not award damages for mental distress suffered by those who have witnessed injury to a closely related person caused by the negligence of another. A number of courts, however, have recently done so.

DEFENSES TO NEGLIGENCE

Although a plaintiff has established by the preponderance of the evidence all the required elements of a negligence action, he may, nevertheless, be denied recovery if the defendant proves a valid defense. As a general rule, any defense to an intentional tort is also available in an action in negligence. In addition, there are defenses available in negligence cases that are not defenses to intentional torts. These are contributory negligence, comparative negligence, and assumption of risk.

Contributory Negligence

Contributory negligence is defined as "conduct on the part of the plaintiff which falls below the standard to which he should conform for his own protection, and which is a legally contributing cause co-operating with the negligence of the defendant in bringing about the plaintiff's harm." Restatement, Section 463.

In those few States where it is still recognized, the contributory negligence of the plaintiff prevents him from recovering *any* damages from the defendant. It does not matter whether the plaintiff's contributory negligence was slight or extensive.

Notwithstanding the contributory negligence of the plaintiff, if the defendant had a **last clear chance** to avoid injury to the plaintiff but did not avail himself of such chance, the contributory negligence of the plaintiff does not bar his recovery of damages. Restatement, Section 479. For example, Terry negligently stops his car on the highway. Janice, who is driving along, sees Terry's car in sufficient time to stop. Janice, however, negligently puts her foot on the accelerator instead of the brake and runs into Terry's car. Because Janice had the last clear chance to stop her car before striking Terry's car, Terry's contributory negligence does not bar his recovery from Janice.

Comparative Negligence

The harshness of the contributory negligence doctrine has caused all but a few States to reject the all-or-nothing rule of contributory negligence and to substitute the doctrine of comparative negligence. Under **comparative negligence,** damages are apportioned between the parties in proportion to the degree of fault or negligence found against the parties. For instance, Matthew negligently drives his automobile into Nancy, who is crossing against the light. Nancy sustains damages in the amount of $10,000 and sues Matthew. If the trier of fact determines that Matthew's negligence contributed 70 percent to Nancy's injury and that Nancy's contributory negligence contributed 30 percent to her injury, then Nancy would recover $7,000.

Most States that have adopted the doctrine of comparative negligence have enacted statutes that do not permit the plaintiff any recovery if her contributory negligence was "as great as" or "greater than" that of the defendant. Thus, in the example above, if the trier of fact determined that Matthew's negligence contributed 40 percent to Nancy's injury and Nancy's contributory negligence contributed 60 percent to her injury, then Nancy would not recover anything from Matthew.

Assumption of Risk

A plaintiff who has *voluntarily* and *knowingly* assumed the risk of harm arising from the negligent or reckless conduct of the defendant cannot recover from such harm. Basically, **assumption of risk** is the plaintiff's express or implied consent to encounter a known danger. Thus, a spectator entering a baseball park may be regarded as consenting that the players may proceed with the game without taking precautions to protect him from being hit by the ball. *See Falgout v. Wardlaw.*

Considerable confusion has arisen by reason of the use of the term "assumption of risk" in several different senses. Comment c to Section 496A of the Restatement explains four of these meanings:

1. In its simplest form, assumption of risk means that the plaintiff has given his express consent to relieve the defendant of an obligation to exercise care for his protection, and agrees to take his chances as to injury from a known or possible risk. The result is that the defendant, who would otherwise be under a duty to exercise such care, is relieved of that responsibility, and is no longer under any duty to protect the plaintiff. . . .
2. A second, and closely related, meaning is that the plaintiff has entered voluntarily into some relation with the defendant which he knows to involve the risk, and so is regarded as tacitly or impliedly agreeing to relieve the defendant of responsibility, and to take his own chances. . . .
3. In a third type of situation, the plaintiff, aware of a risk created by the negligence of the defendant, proceeds or continues voluntarily to encounter it. . . . The same policy of the common law which denies recovery to one who expressly consents to accept a risk will, however, prevent his recovery in such a case. . . .
4. To be distinguished from these three situations is the fourth, in which the plaintiff's conduct in voluntarily encountering a known risk is itself unreasonable, and amounts to contributory negligence. There is thus negligence on the part of both plaintiff and defendant; and the plaintiff is barred from recovery, not only by his implied consent to accept the risk, but also by the policy of the law which refuses to allow him to impose upon the defendant a loss for which his own negligence was in part responsible.

A number of States have abolished or modified the defense of assumption of risk. Some have merged one or all of the types of assumption of risk into their comparative negligence or comparative fault system.

Figure 6–2 illustrates the defenses to a negligence action.

STRICT LIABILITY

In some instances, people may be held liable for injuries they have caused even though they have not acted intentionally or negligently. Such liability is called strict liability, absolute liability, or liability without fault.

The law has determined that certain types of otherwise socially desirable activities pose sufficiently high risks of harm regardless of how carefully they are conducted, and, therefore, those who carry on these activities should bear the cost of all harm they cause. The doctrine of strict liability is *not* predicated upon any particular fault of the defendant, but rather upon the nature of the activity in which he is engaging. In effect, strict liability makes those who conduct these activities insurers of all who may be harmed by the activity.

ACTIVITIES GIVING RISE TO STRICT LIABILITY

The following activities giving rise to strict liability will be discussed in this section: (1) maintaining abnormally dangerous activities, (2) keeping animals, and (3) selling defective, unreasonably dangerous products. In addition, strict liability is also imposed upon other activities. All States have enacted Workers' Compensation statutes which make employers liable to employees for injuries arising out of the course of employment. Because this liability is imposed without regard to the employer's negligence it is a form of strict liability. Workers' compensation is discussed in Chapter 44. Moreover, the liability imposed upon an employer for torts committed by employees in the scope of their employment is also a type of strict liability, as discussed in Chapter 19. Additional instances of strict liability include carriers and innkeepers (Chapter 49), innocent misrepresentation (Chapter 10), and some violations of the securities laws (Chapter 45).

Abnormally Dangerous Activities

Strict liability is imposed for harm resulting from extraordinary, unusual, abnormal, or exceptional activities, as determined in light of the place, time, and manner in which the

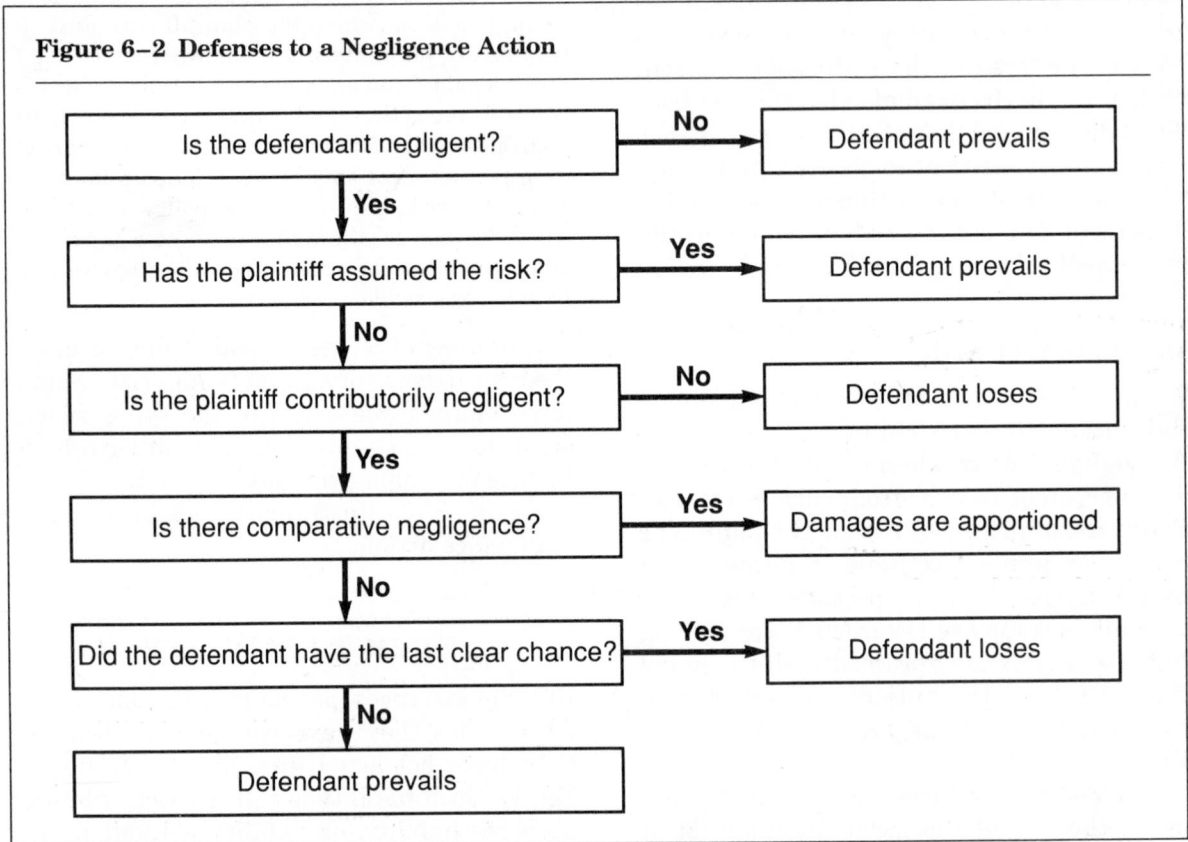

Figure 6–2 Defenses to a Negligence Action

activity is conducted. An **abnormally dangerous activity** is one which (1) necessarily involves a high degree of risk of serious harm to the person and/or chattels of others, which risk cannot be eliminated by the exercise of reasonable care, *and* (2) is not a matter of common usage. Activities to which the rule has been applied include collecting water in such quantity and location as to make it dangerous; storing explosives or flammable liquids in large quantities; blasting or pile driving; crop dusting; drilling for or refining oil in populated areas; and emitting noxious gases or fumes into a settled community. On the other hand, courts have refused to apply the rule where the activity is a "natural" use of the land, such as drilling for oil in the oil fields of Texas, collecting water in a stock watering tank, and transmitting gas through a gas pipe or electricity in electric wiring.

Keeping of Animals

Strict liability for harm caused by animals existed at common law and continues today with some modification. As a general rule, those who possess animals for their own purposes do so at their peril and must protect against harm to people and property.

Trespassing Animals   Keepers of animals are generally held liable for any damage done if their animals trespass on the property of another. There are three exceptions to this rule: (1) keepers of cats and dogs are liable only for negligence; (2) keepers of animals are not strictly liable for animals straying from a highway on which they are being lawfully driven, although the owner may be liable for negligence if he fails to properly control them; and (3) keepers of farm animals, typically cattle, in some Western states are not strictly liable for harm caused by their trespassing animals which are allowed to graze freely. Statutes in many States have imposed strict liability for all damages done by dogs.

Nontrespassing Animals   Keepers of wild animals are strictly liable for harm caused by such animals, whether or not they are trespassing. **Wild animals** are defined as those which in the particular region are known to be likely to inflict serious damage and cannot be considered safe no matter how domesticated. Animals included in this category are bears, lions, elephants, monkeys, tigers, wolves, zebras, deer, and raccoons.

Domestic animals are those which are traditionally devoted to the service of mankind and as a class are considered safe. Examples of domestic animals are dogs, cats, horses, cattle, and sheep. Keepers of domestic animals are liable if they knew, or should have known, of the animal's dangerous propensity. Restatement, Section 509. The dangerous propensity of the animal must be the cause of the harm. For example, a keeper is not liable for a dog which bites a human merely because he knows that the dog has a propensity to engage in combat with other dogs. On the other hand, if a person's 150-pound sheep dog has a propensity to jump enthusiastically on visitors, the animal's keeper would be liable for any damage done by the dog's playfulness. *See Allen v. Whitehead.*

Products Liability

A recent and important trend in the law is the imposition of a limited form of strict liability upon manufacturers and merchants who sell goods in a *defective condition* unreasonably dangerous to the user or consumer. Restatement, Section 402A. Liability is imposed regardless of the seller's due care and applies to all merchant sellers. Nearly all States have adopted some version of strict product liability. This topic is covered in Chapter 23.

DEFENSES TO STRICT LIABILITY

This section will discuss the availability in a strict liability action of the following defenses: (1) contributory negligence, (2) comparative negligence, and (3) assumption of risk.

Contributory Negligence

Because the strict liability of one who carries on an abnormally dangerous activity, keeps animals, or sells products is not based on his negligence, the ordinary contributory negligence of the plaintiff is *not* a defense to such liability. The law in imposing strict liability places the full responsibility for preventing harm on the defendant. For example, Adrian negligently fails to observe a sign on a highway warning of a blasting operation conducted by Benjamin. As a result Adrian is injured by these operations. Adrian may nonetheless recover from Benjamin.

Comparative Negligence

Despite the rationale that disallows contributory negligence as a defense to strict liabil-ity, some States apply the doctrine of comparative negligence to some types of strict liability, in particular, products liability.

Assumption of Risk

Voluntary assumption of risk *is* a defense to an action based upon strict liability. If the owner of an automobile knowingly and voluntarily parks the vehicle in a blasting zone, he may not recover for harm to his automobile. The assumption of risk, however, must be voluntary. If blasting operations are established, the possessor of nearby land is not required to move away and may recover for harm suffered.

CASES

Violation of Statute

WALZ v. CITY OF HUDSON

Supreme Court of South Dakota, 1982.
327 N.W.2d 120.

FOSHEIM, C.J.

Lela Walz (appellant), as special administrator of the estate of Guy William Ludwig, sued the City of Hudson, South Dakota (appellee), doing business as the Hudson Municipal Liquor Store, for the wrongful death of Mr. Ludwig. Appellant's complaint alleged that appellee sold Larry VanEgdom intoxicating beverages when appellee knew or could have ascertained by observation that Mr. VanEgdom was intoxicated; that immediately thereafter Mr. VanEgdom, while driving a car, collided with Mr. Ludwig who was stopped on his motorcycle at a stop sign; and that Mr. Ludwig's resulting death was caused by appellee's negligence in selling alcoholic beverages to Mr. VanEgdom. . . . [The trial court dismissed the complaint for failure to state a cause of action.]

Appellant urges that we overrule our decision in *Griffin v. Sebek,* [citation], thus affording her a cause of action against appellee.

In *Griffin* the plaintiffs brought a negligence action against defendants, licensed tavernkeepers, seeking damages for personal injury resulting from defendants' unlawful sale of alcoholic beverages. Our decision, affirming the trial court's order granting defendants' motion to dismiss for failure to state a claim, said the issue was whether, in the absence of a dram shop act, "the common law now authorizes or should be liberalized to afford a remedy." We determined that no such cause of action exists in South Dakota and declined to expand the common law to afford a remedy. We also did not extend SDCL 35–4–78(2) to impose a civil liability duty. [SDCL 35–4–78(2) reads: "No licensee shall sell any alcoholic beverage, except low-point beer . . . (t)o any person who is intoxicated at the time, or who is known to the seller to be an habitual drunkard. A violation of this section is a Class 1 misdemeanor."] We take judicial notice that since *Griffin* was decided, alcohol has been involved in 50.8% of this state's traffic fatalities from 1976 to 1981; in 1981 alone 62% of South Dakota's traffic fatalities were alcohol-related. [Citation.] This tragic waste of life prompts us to review our conclusions in *Griffin*. If the Legislature does not concur with our application of SDCL 35–4–78(2), as now announced, it is the prerogative of the Legislature to so assert. We fully realize this decision, while hopefully helpful, certainly cannot resolve the problems of alcohol-related deaths or injuries.

Negligence is the breach of a legal duty imposed by statute or common law. [Citation.] *Griffin* recognized that a liquor licensee is not liable at common law for damages resulting from a patron's intoxication. The common law is in force in South Dakota except where it conflicts with federal or state constitutions and laws. [Citation.] SDCL 35–4–78(2) makes it a crime to sell intoxicating beverages to one in Mr. VanEgdom's inebriated state and violation of a statute is negligence as a matter of law if the statute "was intended to protect the class of persons in which plaintiffs are included against risk of the type of harm which has in fact occurred." [Citations.]

The reason for this rule is that the statute or ordinance becomes the standard of care or conduct to which the reasonably prudent person is held. Failure to follow the statute involved constitutes a breach of the legal duty imposed and fixed by such statute. Since negligence is a breach of a legal duty, the violator of a statute is then negligent as a matter of law.

* * *

We believe that statute [SDCL 35–4–78(2)] was enacted to include the protection of the class of people in Mr. Ludwig's position from the risk of being killed or injured "as a result of the drunkenness to which the particular sale of alcoholic liquor contributes." [Citation.] Since SDCL 35–4–78(2) must be liberally construed "with a view to effect its objects and to promote justice," [citations], we conclude that SDCL 35–4–78(2) establishes a standard of care or conduct, a breach of

which is negligence as a matter of law. [Citation.] It follows that such negligence must be a proximate cause of any resulting injury and defenses, such as contributory negligence, are available when appropriate.

We therefore reverse the trial court's order dismissing appellant's complaint for failure to state a claim upon which relief may be granted.

* * *

Duty to Act

SOLDANO v. O'DANIELS

California Court of Appeal, Fifth District, 1983.
141 Cal. App.3d 443, 190 Cal. Rptr. 310.

ANDREEN, J.

Does a business establishment incur liability for wrongful death if it denies use of its telephone to a good samaritan who explains an emergency situation occurring without and wishes to call the police?

This appeal follows a judgment of dismissal of the second cause of action of a complaint for wrongful death upon a motion for summary judgment. The motion was supported only by a declaration of defense counsel. Both briefs on appeal adopt the defense averments:

"This action arises out of a shooting death occurring on August 9, 1977. Plaintiff's father [Darrell Soldano] was shot and killed by one Rudolph Villanueva on that date at defendant's Happy Jack's Saloon. This defendant owns and operates the Circle Inn which is an eating establishment located across the street from Happy Jack's. Plaintiff's second cause of action against this defendant is one for negligence.

"Plaintiff alleges that on the date of the shooting, a patron of Happy Jack's Saloon came into the Circle Inn and informed a Circle Inn employee that a man had been threatened at Happy Jack's. He requested the employee either call the police or allow him to use the Circle Inn phone to call the police. That employee allegedly refused to call the police and allegedly refused to allow the patron to use the phone to make his own call. Plaintiff alleges that the actions of the Circle Inn employee were a breach of the legal duty that the Circle Inn owed to the decedent."

We were advised at oral argument that the employee was the defendant's bartender. The state of the record is unsatisfactory in that it does not disclose the physical location of the telephone—whether on the bar, in a private office behind a closed door or elsewhere. The only factual matter before the trial court was a verified statement of the defense attorney which set forth those facts quoted above. Following normal rules applicable to motions for summary judgment, we strictly construe the defense affidavit. [Citation.] Accordingly, we assume the telephone was not in a private office but in a position where it could be used by a patron without inconvenience to the defendant or his guests. We also assume the call was a local one and would not result in expense to defendant.

There is a distinction, well rooted in the common law, between action and nonaction. [Citation.] It has found its way into the prestigious Restatement Second of Torts (hereafter cited as "Restatement"), which provides in section 314:

"The fact that the actor realizes or should realize that action on his part is necessary for another's aid or protection does not of itself impose upon him a duty to take such action."

* * *

Defendant argues that the request that its employee call the police is a request that it *do* something. He points to the established rule that one who has not created a peril ordinarily does not have a duty to take affirmative action to assist an imperiled person. [Citation.] It is urged that the alternative request of the patron from Happy Jack's Saloon that he be allowed to use defendant's telephone so that he personally could make the call is again a request that the defendant do something—assist another to give aid. Defendant points out that the Restatement sections which impose liability for negligent interference with a third person giving aid to another do not impose the additional duty to *aid* the good samaritan.

The refusal of the law to recognize the moral obligation of one to aid another when he is in peril and when such aid may be given without danger and at little cost in effort has been roundly criticized. Prosser describes the case law sanctioning such inaction as a "refus[al] to recognize the moral obligation of common decency and common humanity" and characterizes some of these decisions as "shocking in the extreme. . . . Such decisions are revolting to any moral sense. They have been denounced with vigor by legal writers." [Citation.] A similar rule has been termed "morally questionable" by our Supreme Court. [Citation.]

Francis H. Bohlen, in his article *The Moral Duty to Aid Others as a Basis of Tort Liability,* commented:

"Nor does it follow that because the law has not as yet recognized the duty to repair harm innocently wrought, that it will continue indefinitely to refuse it recognition. While it is true that the common law does not attempt to enforce all moral, ethical, or humanitarian duties, it is, it is submitted, equally true that all ethical and moral conceptions, which are not the mere temporary manifestations of a passing wave of sentimentalism or puritanism, but on the contrary, find a real and permanent place in the settled convictions of a race and become part of the normal habit of thought thereof, of necessity do in time color the judicial conception of legal obligation. * * *

As noted in [citation], the courts have increased the instances in which affirmative duties are imposed not by direct rejection of the common law rule, but by expanding the list of special relationships which will justify departure from that rule.* * *

* * *

Section 314A of the Restatement lists other special relationships which create a duty to render aid, such as that of a common carrier to its passengers, an innkeeper to his guest, possessors of land who hold it open to the public, or one who has a custodial relationship to another. A duty may be created by an undertaking to give assistance. [Citation.]

Here there was no special relationship between the defendant and the deceased. It would be stretching the concept beyond recognition to assert there was a relationship between the defendant and the patron from Happy Jack's Saloon who wished to summon aid. But this does not end the matter.

It is time to re-examine the common law rule of nonliability for nonfeasance in the special circumstances of the instant case.

* * *

We turn now to the concept of duty in a tort case. The [California] Supreme Court has identified certain factors to be considered in determining whether a duty is owed to third persons. These factors include:

"the foreseeability of harm to the plaintiff, the degree of certainty that the plaintiff suffered injury, the closeness of the connection between the defendant's conduct and the injury suffered, the moral blame attached to the defendant's conduct, the policy of preventing future harm, the extent of the burden to the defendant and consequences to the community of imposing a duty to exercise care with resulting liability for breach, and the availability, cost, and prevalence of insurance for the risk involved." [Citation.]

We examine those factors in reference to this case. (1) The harm to the decedent was abundantly foreseeable; it was imminent. The employee was expressly told that a man had been threatened. The employee was a bartender. As such he knew it is foreseeable that some people who drink alcohol in the milieu of a bar setting are prone to violence. (2) The certainty of decedent's injury is undisputed. (3) There is arguably a close connection between the employee's conduct and the injury: the patron wanted to use the phone to summon the police to intervene. The employee's refusal to allow the use of the phone prevented this anticipated intervention. If permitted to go to trial, the plaintiff may be able to show that the probable response time of the police would have been shorter than the time between the prohibited telephone call and the fatal shot. (4) The employee's conduct displayed a disregard for human life that can be characterized as morally wrong: he was callously indifferent to the possibility that Darrell Soldano would die as the result of his refusal to allow a person to

use the telephone. Under the circumstances before us the bartender's burden was minimal and exposed him to no risk: all he had to do was allow the use of the telephone. It would have cost him or his employer nothing. It could have saved a life. (5) Finding a duty in these circumstances would promote a policy of preventing future harm. A citizen would not be required to summon the police but would be required, in circumstances such as those before us, not to impede another who has chosen to summon aid. (6) We have no information on the question of the availability, cost, and prevalence of insurance for the risk, but note that the liability which is sought to be imposed here is that of employee negligence, which is covered by many insurance policies. (7) The extent of the burden on the defendant was minimal, as noted.

The consequences to the community of imposing a duty, the remaining factor mentioned in [citation] is termed "the administrative factor" by Professor Green in his analysis of determining whether a duty exists in a given case. [Citation.] The administrative factor is simply the pragmatic concern of fashioning a workable rule and the impact of such a rule on the judicial machinery. It is the policy of major concern in this case.

* * *

Many citizens simply "don't want to get involved." No rule should be adopted which would require a citizen to open up his or her house to a stranger so that the latter may use the telephone to call for emergency assistance. As Mrs. Alexander in Anthony Burgess' A Clockwork Orange learned to her horror, such an action may be fraught with danger. It does not follow, however, that use of a telephone in a public portion of a business should be refused for a legitimate emergency call. Imposing liability for such a refusal would not subject innocent citizens to possible attack by the "good samaritan," for it would be limited to an establishment open to the public during times when it is open to business, and to places within the establishment ordinarily accessible to the public. Nor would a stranger's mere assertion that an "emergency" situation is occurring create the duty to utilize an accessible telephone because the duty would arise if and only if it were clearly conveyed that there exists an imminent danger of physical harm. [Citation.]

Such a holding would not involve difficulties in proof, overburden the courts or unduly hamper self-determination or enterprise.

A business establishment such as the Circle Inn is open for profit. The owner encourages the public to enter, for his earnings depend on it. A telephone is a necessary adjunct to such a place. It is not unusual in such circumstances for patrons to use the telephone to call a taxicab or family member.

We acknowledge that defendant contracted for the use of his telephone, and its use is a species of property. But if it exists in a public place as defined above, there is no privacy or ownership interest in it such that the owner should be permitted to interfere with a good faith attempt to use it by a third person to come to the aid of another.

* * *

We conclude that the bartender owed a duty to the plaintiff's decedent to permit the patron from Happy Jack's to place a call to the police or to place the call himself.

It bears emphasizing that the duty in this case does not require that one must go to the aid of another. That is not the issue here. The employee was not the good samaritan intent on aiding another. The patron was.

It would not be appropriate to await legislative action in this area. The rule was fashioned in the common law tradition, as were the exceptions to the rule. [Citation.] To the extent this opinion expands the reach of section 327 of the Restatement, it represents logical and needed growth, the hallmark of the common law. It does not involve the sacrifice of other respectable interests.

The courts have a special responsibility to reshape, refine and guide legal doctrine they have created. * * *

* * *

The possible imposition of liability on the defendant in this case is not a global change in the law. It is but a slight departure from the "morally questionable" rule of nonliability for inaction absent a special relationship. It is one of the predicted "inroads upon the older rule." (Rest.2d Torts, *supra*, § 314, com. c.) It is a logical extension of Restatement Section 327 which imposes liability for negligent interference with a third person who the defendant knows is attempting to render necessary aid. However small it may be, it is a step which should be taken.

We conclude there are sufficient justiciable issues to permit the case to go to trial and therefore reverse.

Duty to Invitees

YANIA v. BIGAN

Supreme Court of Pennsylvania, 1959.
397 Pa. 316, 155 A.2d 343.

JONES, J.

A bizarre and most unusual circumstance provides the background of this appeal.

On September 25, 1957 John E. Bigan was engaged in a coal strip-mining operation in Shade Township, Somerset County. On the property being stripped were large cuts or trenches created by Bigan when he removed the earthen overburden for the purpose of removing the coal underneath. One cut contained water 8 to 10 feet in depth with side walls or embankments 16 to 18 feet in height; at this cut Bigan had installed a pump to remove the water.

At approximately 4 P.M. on that date, Joseph F. Yania, the operator of another coal strip-mining operation, and one Boyd M. Ross went upon Bigan's property for the purpose of discussing a business matter with Bigan, and, while there, were asked by Bigan to aid him in starting the pump. Ross and Bigan entered the cut and stood at the point where the pump was located. Yania stood at the top of one of the cut's side walls and then jumped from the side wall—a height of 16 to 18 feet—into the water and was drowned.

Yania's widow, in her own right and on behalf of her three children, instituted wrongful death and survival actions against Bigan contending Bigan was responsible for Yania's death.

* * *

The complaint avers negligence in the following manner: (1) "The death by drowning of . . . (Yania) was caused entirely by the acts of (Bigan) . . . in *urging, enticing, taunting and inveigling* (Yania) to jump into the water, which (Bigan) knew or ought to have known was of a depth of 8 to 10 feet and dangerous to the life of anyone who would jump therein"; (2) ". . . (Bigan) violated his obligations to a business invitee in not having his premises reasonably safe, and not warning his business invitee of a dangerous condition and to the contrary urged, induced and inveigled (Yania) into a dangerous position and a dangerous act, whereby (Yania) came to his death"; (3) "After (Yania) was in the water, a highly dangerous position, having been induced and inveigled therein by (Bigan), (Bigan) failed and neglected to take reasonable steps and action to protect or assist (Yania) or extradite (Yania) from the dangerous position in which (Bigan) had placed him". Summarized, Bigan stands charged with three-fold negligence: (1) by urging, enticing, taunting and inveigling Yania to jump into the water; (2) by failing to warn Yania of a dangerous condition on the land, i.e. the cut wherein lay 8 to 10 feet of water; (3) by failing to go to Yania's rescue after he had jumped into the water.

* * *

The complaint does not allege that Yania slipped or that he was pushed or that Bigan made any *physical* impact upon Yania. On the contrary, the only inference deducible from the facts alleged in the complaint is that Bigan, by the employment of cajolery and inveiglement, caused such a *mental* impact on Yania that the latter was deprived of his volition and freedom of choice and placed under a compulsion to jump into the water. Had Yania been a child of tender years or a person mentally deficient then it is conceivable that taunting and enticement could constitute actionable negligence if it resulted in harm. However, to contend that such conduct directed to an adult in full possession of all his mental faculties constitutes actionable negligence is not only without precedent but completely without merit. * * *

* * * Yania was a business invitee in that he entered upon the land for a common business purpose for the mutual benefit of Bigan and himself (Restatement, Torts, § 332; [citation.]) As possessor of the land, Bigan would become subject to liability to Yania for any physical harm caused by any artificial or natural condition upon the land (1) if, and only if, Bigan knew or could have discovered the condition which, if known to him he should have realized involved an unreasonable risk of harm to Yania, (2) if Bigan had no reason to believe Yania would discover the condition or realize the risk of harm and (3) if he invited or permitted Yania to enter upon the land without exercising reasonable care to make the condition reasonably safe or give adequate warning to enable him to avoid the harm. [Citations.] The inapplicability of this rule of liability to the instant facts is readily apparent.

The *only* condition on Bigan's land which could possibly have contributed in any manner to Yania's death was the water-filled cut with its high embankment. Of this condition there was neither concealment nor failure to warn, but, on the contrary, the complaint specifically avers that Bigan not only requested Yania and Boyd to assist him in starting the pump to remove the water from the cut but "led" them to the cut itself. If this cut possessed any potentiality of danger, such a condition was as obvious and apparent to Yania as to Bigan, both coal strip-mine operators. Under the circumstances herein depicted Bigan could not be held liable in this respect.

Lastly, it is urged that Bigan failed to take the necessary steps to rescue Yania from the water. The mere fact that Bigan saw Yania in a position of peril in the water imposed upon him no legal, although a moral, obligation or duty to go to his rescue unless Bigan was legally responsible, in whole or in part, for placing Yania in the perilous position. Restatement, Torts, § 314.

[Citations.] . . . The complaint does not aver any facts which impose upon Bigan legal responsibility for placing Yania in the dangerous position in the water and, absent such legal responsibility, the law imposes on Bigan no duty of rescue.

* * *

Recognizing that the deceased Yania is entitled to the benefit of the presumption that he was exercising due care and extending to appellant the benefit of every well pleaded fact in this complaint and the fair inferences arising therefrom, yet we can reach but one conclusion: that Yania, a reasonable and prudent adult in full possession of all his mental faculties, undertook to perform an act which he knew or should have known was attended with more or less peril and it was the performance of that act and not any conduct upon Bigan's part which caused his unfortunate death.

Proximate Cause

PALSGRAF v. LONG ISLAND RAILROAD CO.

Court of Appeals of New York, 1928.
248 N.Y. 339, 162 N.E. 99.

CARDOZO, C.J.

Plaintiff was standing on a platform of defendant's railroad after buying a ticket to go to Rockaway Beach. A train stopped at the station, bound for another place. Two men ran forward to catch it. One of the men reached the platform of the car without mishap, though the train was already moving. The other man, carrying a package, jumped aboard the car, but seemed unsteady as if about to fall. A guard on the car, who had held the door open, reached forward to help him in, and another guard on the platform pushed him from behind. In this act, the package was dislodged, and fell upon the rails. It was a package of small size, about fifteen inches long, and was covered by a newspaper. In fact it contained fireworks, but there was nothing in its appearance to give notice of its contents. The fireworks when they fell exploded. The shock of the explosion threw down some scales at the other end of the platform many feet away. The scales struck the plaintiff, causing injuries for which she sues.

The conduct of the defendant's guard, if a wrong in its relation to the holder of the package, was not a wrong in its relation to the plaintiff, standing far away. Relatively to her it was not negligence at all. Nothing in the situation gave notice that the falling package had in it the potency of peril to persons thus removed. Negligence is not actionable unless it involves the invasion of a legally protected interest, the violation of a right. "Proof of negligence in the air, so to speak, will not do." [Citations.] "Negligence is the absence of care, according to the circumstances." [Citations.]

* * *

If no hazard was apparent to the eye of ordinary vigilance, an act innocent and harmless, at least to outward seeming, with reference to her, did not take to itself the quality of a tort because it happened to be a wrong, though apparently not one involving the risk of bodily insecurity, with reference to someone else. "In every instance, before negligence can be predicated of a given act, back of the act must be sought and found a duty to the individual complaining, the observance of which would have averted or avoided the injury." [Citations.]

* * *

A different conclusion will involve us, and swiftly too, in a maze of contradictions. A guard stumbles over a package which has been left upon a platform. It seems to be a bundle of newspapers. It turns out to be a can of dynamite. To the eye of ordinary vigilance, the bundle is abandoned waste, which may be kicked or trod on with impunity. Is a passenger at the other end of the platform protected by the law against the unsuspected hazard concealed beneath the waste? If not, is the result to be any different, so far as the distant passenger is concerned, when the guard stumbles over a valise which a truckman or a porter has left upon the walk? The passenger far away, if the victim of a wrong at all, has a cause of action, not derivative, but original and primary. His claim to be protected against invasion of his bodily security is neither greater nor less because the act resulting in the invasion is a wrong to another far removed. In this case, the rights that are said to have been violated, the interests said to have been invaded, are not even of the same order. The man was not injured in his person nor even put in danger. The purpose of the act, as well as its effect, was to make his person safe. If there was a wrong to him at all, which may very well be doubted, it was a wrong to a property interest only, the safety of his package. Out of this wrong to property, which threatened injury to nothing else, there has passed, we are told, to the plaintiff by derivation or succession a right of action for the invasion of an interest of another order, the right to bodily security. The diversity of interests emphasizes the futility of the effort to build the plaintiff's right upon the basis of a wrong to someone else. . . . One who jostles one's neighbor in a crowd does not invade the rights of others standing at the outer fringe when the unintended contact casts a bomb upon the ground. The wrongdoer as to them is the man who carries the bomb, not the one who explodes it without suspicion of the danger. Life will have to be made over, and human nature transformed, before prevision so extravagant can be accepted as the norm of conduct, the customary standard to which behavior must conform.

* * *

The judgment of the Appellate Division and that of the Trial Term should be reversed, and the complaint dismissed, with costs in all courts.

Proximate Cause

PETITION OF KINSMAN TRANSIT CO.

United States Court of Appeals, Second Circuit, 1964.
338 F.2d 708.

FRIENDLY, J.

[The MacGilvray Shiras was a ship owned by the Kinsman Transit Company. During the winter months when Lake Erie was frozen, the ship and others moored at docks on the Buffalo River. As oftentimes happened, one night an ice jam disintegrated upstream, sending large chunks of ice downward. Chunks of ice began to pile up against the Shiras which at that time was without power and manned only by a shipman. The ship broke loose when a negligently constructed "deadman" to which one mooring cable was attached pulled out of the ground. The "deadman" was operated by Continental Grain Company. The ship began moving down the S-shaped river stern first and struck another ship, the Tewksbury. The Tewksbury also broke loose from its mooring, and the two ships floated down the river together. Although the crew manning the Michigan Avenue Bridge downstream had been notified of the runaway ships, they failed to raise the bridge in time to avoid the collision because of a mixup in the shift changeover. As a result, both ships crashed into the bridge and were wedged against the bank of the river. The two vessels substantially dammed the flow of the river, causing ice and water to back up and flood installations as far as three miles upstream. The injured parties brought this action for damages against Kinsman, Continental, and the City of Buffalo.]

The very statement of the case suggests the need for considering *Palsgraf v. Long Island RR.*, [citation], and the closely related problem of liability for unforeseeable consequences.

* * *

We see little similarity between the Palsgraf case and the situation before us. The point of Palsgraf was that the appearance of the newspaper-wrapped package gave no notice that its dislodgement could do any harm save to itself and those nearby, and this by impact, perhaps with consequent breakage, and not by explosion. In contrast, a ship insecurely moored in a fast flowing river is a known danger not only to herself but to the owners of all other ships and structures downriver, and to persons upon them. No one would dream of saying that a shipowner who "knowingly and willfully" failed to secure his ship at a pier on such a river "would not have threatened" persons and owners of property downstream in some manner. The shipowner and the wharfinger in this case having thus owed a duty of care to all within the reach of the ship's known destructive power, the impossibility of advance identification of the particular person who would be hurt is without legal consequences. [Citations.] Similarly the foreseeable consequences of the City's failure to raise the bridge were not limited to the Shiras and the Tewksbury. Collision plainly created a danger that the bridge towers might fall onto adjoining property, and the crash of two uncontrolled lake vessels, one 425 feet and the other 525 feet long, into a bridge over a swift ice-ridden stream, with a channel only 177 feet wide, could well result in a partial damming that would flood property upstream.

* * *

All the claimants here met the Palsgraf requirement of being persons to whom the actors owed a "duty of care," . . . . But this does not dispose of the alternative argument that the manner in which several of the claimants were harmed, particularly by flood damage, was unforeseeable and that recovery for this may not be had—whether the argument is put in the forth-right form that unforeseeable damages are not recoverable or is concealed under a formula of lack of "proximate cause."

So far as concerns the City, the argument lacks factual support. Although the obvious risks from not raising the bridge were damage to itself and to the vessels the danger of a fall of the bridge and of flooding would not have been unforeseeable under the circumstances to anyone who gave them thought. And the same can be said as to the failure of Kinsman's shipkeeper to ready the anchors after the danger had become apparent. * * *

Continental's position on the facts is stronger. It was indeed foreseeable that the improper construction and lack of inspection of the "deadman" might cause a ship to break loose and damage persons and property on or near the river—that was what made Continental's conduct negligent. With the aid of hindsight one can also say that a prudent

man, carefully pondering the problem, would have realized that the danger of this would be greatest under such water conditions as developed during the night of January 21, 1959, and that if a vessel should break loose under those circumstances, events might transpire as they did. But such *post hoc* step by step analysis would render "foreseeable" almost anything that has in fact occurred; if the argument relied upon has legal validity, it ought not be circumvented by characterizing as foreseeable what almost no one would in fact have foreseen at the time.

* * *

Foreseeability of danger is necessary to render conduct negligent; where as here the damage was caused by just those forces whose existence required the exercise of greater care than was taken—the current, the ice, and the physical mass of the Shiras, the incurring of consequences other and greater than foreseen does not make the conduct less culpable or provide a reasoned basis for insulation. [Citation.] The oft encountered argument that failure to limit liability to foreseeable consequences may subject the defendant to a loss wholly out of proportion to his fault seems scarcely consistent with the universally accepted rule that the defendant takes the plaintiff as he finds him and will be responsible for the full extent of the injury even though a latent susceptibility of the plaintiff renders this far more serious than could reasonably have been anticipated. [Citation.]

The weight of authority in this country rejects the limitation of damages to consequences foreseeable at the time of the negligent conduct when the consequences are "direct," and the damage, although other and greater than expectable, is of the same general sort that was risked.

* * *

Here it is surely more equitable that the losses from the operators' negligent failure to raise the Michigan Avenue Bridge should be ratably borne by Buffalo's taxpayers than left with the innocent victims of the flooding; yet the mind is also repelled by a solution that would impose liability solely on the City and exonerate the persons whose negligent acts of commission and omission were the precipitating force of the collision with the bridge and its sequelae. We go only so far as to hold that where, as here, the damages resulted from the same physical forces whose existence required the exercise of greater care than was displayed and were of the same general sort that was expectable, unforeseeability of the exact developments and of the extent of the loss will not limit liability. Other fact situations can be dealt with when they arise.

* * *

[Judgment for plaintiffs.]

Assumption of Risk

FALGOUT v. WARDLAW

Court of Appeal of Louisiana, Second Circuit, 1982.
423 So.2d 707.

MARVIN, J.

Ms. Falgout appeals a judgment rejecting her demands for personal injury damages arising out of her fall on a partially decked pier on Lake Bistineau.

The factual and legal issues relate to the trial court's finding that Ms. Falgout's recovery was barred by her fault. We affirm.

The pier is supported by posts or pilings. . . . Each pair of posts is about six feet from the next pair. Ms. Falgout was the social guest of defendant William Wardlaw, who partially decked the pier and frequented the camp with the tacit permission of his brother, Glenn, who owned the once community camp and began construction of the pier. Glenn Wardlaw and his wife, divorced co-owner, were also made defendants in this action.

Ms. Falgout accompanied William to the camp on a Saturday afternoon, arriving there from Shreveport about 3:30 p.m. After the two had consumed an eight-pack of "little" beers purchased on the way to the camp, Ms. Falgout also drank some vodka she found in the kitchen of the camp, according to William.

While it was still daylight about 7:00 p.m., Ms. Falgout, with a drink in hand, went with William outside the camp while he checked on the camp utilities. William says that he told her not to go on the pier and that she told him, "don't tell me what to do, . . . [I have] walked on every pier on Lake Bistineau. . . ."

William said that Ms. Falgout went all the way to the end of the pier and sat there. Ms. Falgout was returning toward the camp when she fell near post four. William said that after she got on the pier he told her not to go past where the boards were close together ($25/32$ inch spacing between posts one and three almost to post four). In any event Ms. Falgout says that her shoe "got caught between two boards under a board . . ." and she fell, suspended by her foot with her head and arms in the water. She suffered serious injuries to her knee and leg.

William, who at one time went on the pier . . . by this time was back on the ground and heard, but did not see, Ms. Falgout hit the water. He went to her aid and later helped her obtain medical attention.

Notwithstanding that the trial court found the pier, because of its partially constructed state, to be defective and to pose an unreasonable risk of harm to anyone who might walk on it, Ms. Falgout's demands were rejected because the circumstances constituted [plaintiff fault.]

* * *

As a defense to . . . liability, [plaintiff] fault in some circumstances may encompass either or both assumption of the risk and contributory negligence. * * *

Knowledge is the mainstay of assumption of risk and is imputed to a plaintiff, not because he was in a position to make observations, but only when he actually made the observations and it is found that plaintiff should reasonably have known that a particular risk existed. [Citation.] Assumption of risk is a subjective inquiry. [Citation.]

Contributory negligence is conduct which falls below the reasonable man standard and is determined by objective inquiry on a case to case basis. As a defense to liability, it is applied only where the policy considerations imposing the liability on the defendant in the first place are not present, such as where the defendant's conduct is not ultra hazardous, not abnormally dangerous, is not that of a manufacturer whose product causes injury, and is not commercial in the sense that it is designed to render a profit. Where these policy considerations are not present, [plaintiff] fault includes contributory negligence. [Citation.] Some circumstances which may not constitute assumption of risk, may constitute contributory negligence. [Citation.]

Here Ms. Falgout was told by her host not to go on the pier and, after she was on it, she was effectively told not to walk on the area where the decking boards were widely spaced. She had knowledge and, having traversed the pier to its end, she admittedly observed the variance in spacing of the decking. She was returning to the safer area where the decking was more closely and uniformly spaced when her foot or shoe got caught. The trial court's conclusions that she *saw* and *understood* the risk are supported by competent evidence which the trial court could believe. We find no error in the ultimate conclusion that Ms. Falgout assumed the risk because she *observed* and she was effectively told of the risk. Under these circumstances she should reasonably have known of the existence of the particular risk of getting her foot or her shoe caught in the wider spacing. [Citation.]

These circumstances also constitute contributory negligence. [Citation.] The defendants here were not engaged in an ultra hazardous or abnormally dangerous activity and were not engaged in a commercial enterprise. While the Wardlaw brothers manufactured or constructed the partially completed pier, they cannot be deemed to have been manufacturers of a product to gain a profit. The policy considerations or factors which impose strict liability to which contributory negligence is not a defense are sorely lacking and, in such circumstances, contributory negligence is encompassed in the defense of [plaintiff] fault. [Citation.]

[Judgment for defendant affirmed.]

Keeping of Animals

ALLEN v. WHITEHEAD

Supreme Court of Alabama, 1982.
423 So.2d 835.

PER CURIAM.

On November 22, 1978, David Allen, then two years old, was playing on a porch at the Allen residence when a dog attacked him. The dog that bit David was later identified as the dog which had taken up at the home of Whitehead, the defendant and appellee herein, approximately one and a half years prior to the incident in question. As a result of the attack, David suffered facial cuts, a severed muscle in his left eye, a hole in his left ear, and scarring over his forehead.

After the attack, the dog was picked up by the Humane Society and placed in quarantine. Whitehead subsequently had the dog placed in a private veterinary clinic, from which the dog allegedly escaped. Following the dog's escape, David underwent rabies treatment. Whitehead later found the dog and placed it in another veterinary hospital for the duration of the quarantine period.

On July 10, 1981, David, through his father, appellant herein, filed a complaint against Whitehead, the alleged owner of the dog. The complaint alleged that "as a proximate result of defendant's negligence and violation of various state and municipal ordinances plaintiff's child was injured. . . ." On November 5, 1981, Whitehead filed an affidavit and a motion for summary judgment based on the ground that there was no genuine issue as to whether Whitehead had any reason to believe his dog had vicious propensities at the time of the attack.

A hearing on the motion for summary judgment was scheduled for December 10, 1981. * * *

On December 22, 1981, the trial court granted Whitehead's motion for summary judgment and, further, dismissed plaintiff's amended complaint. We affirm the trial court's order granting summary judgment directed to the claim in appellant's original complaint and reverse the trial court's order dismissing the claims of appellant's amended complaint.

This court in *Kershaw v. McKown,* [citation], reiterated the common law rule that the owner of a dog is not liable for acts of the dog unless the owner had knowledge of the vicious propensities of the dog that resulted in the injury complained of. In *McCullar v. Williams,* [citation], the court stated, "[p]revious knowledge of the animal's vicious habits must be alleged and proved," although positive proof is not always necessary. [Citation.] This court held in *Owen v. Hampson,* [citation], that the common law rule was still applicable in Alabama: . . . that previous knowledge of the animal's dangerous propensity, whether it be shown by positive proof or inferred from the circumstances, must be alleged and proved.

* * *

Appellant Allen asserts that there is a genuine issue of material fact relating to the alleged vicious propensities of the dog and the knowledge of appellee as to such propensities. Our examination of the record in its factual context reveals the following. In answers to interrogatories propounded by appellee, appellant stated in substance that (1) the dog was large and mean looking and frequently barked at neighbors; (2) the dog was allowed to run wild; and (3) the dog frequently chased cars and barked at them. On the other hand, appellee, by way of affidavit and also in answers to interrogatories propounded by appellant to him, in effect, stated: (1) the dog was friendly and "enjoyed" playing with his children and other children in the neighborhood; (2) appellee had never received any complaints from anyone nor had any reason to believe that the dog represented any kind of threat to anyone; (3) there was nothing aggressive or threatening about the dog's manner or behavior, but on the contrary, his disposition was quiet and gentle, and the dog was affectionate and enjoyed being petted; and (4) that to the best of the knowledge and belief of appellee, the dog had never bitten anyone prior to the instance in question. Appellee admitted that the dog was not confined.

Considering the evidence submitted to the trial court on appellee's motion for summary judgment most favorably to appellant, the nonmoving party, we cannot find that there existed a genuine issue of material fact. Accordingly, we hold as a matter of law that evidence that a dog was large and mean looking, chased and barked at cars, and frequently barked at neighbors is not sufficient to present an issue of fact as to the dangerous propensities of such an animal.

In support of his contention that Whitehead had notice of the dog's dangerous propensities, appellant also points out that Whitehead had admitted in an affidavit that the dog had a playful nature. * * *

* * * In his treatise, Professor Prosser has also stated that notice of the character of the animal "must extend to the trait or propensity which caused the damage." [Citation.] Accordingly, notice of an animal's playful character is not notice that it will viciously attack and bite a person. Liability is limited to the particular risk known to the defendant.

In *Owen v. Hampson,* [citation], the defendant's dog ran out and overturned plaintiff's motorcycle while plaintiff was riding on a public street. This court stated that the law makes no distinction between an animal dangerous from playfulness and one dangerous from viciousness, but places on the owner a burden of restraint when he knows of the animal's dangerous propensities. [Citation.] The crucial issue remains whether the owner knows or has reason to know of the animal's dangerous propensities. This is not a case where the plaintiff was knocked down or injured in a manner traditionally associated with an overly friendly dog. The claim and the evidence is that David was attacked and bitten. Knowledge of an animal's playfulness would not provide sufficient notice that the dog would be likely to act in the harmful manner alleged in this incident.

* * *

* * * The Court concludes that the order dismissing the amended complaint is due to be reversed and the cause remanded for consideration of the claims stated in the amended complaint.

The judgment appealed from, therefore, is affirmed in part, and reversed in part, and the cause remanded.

QUESTIONS

1. List and briefly describe the three required elements of an action for negligence.

2. Explain the duty of care that is imposed upon (a) adults, (b) children, (c) persons with a physical disability, (d) persons with a mental deficiency, (e) persons with superior knowledge, and (f) persons acting in an emergency.

3. Define trespassers, licensees, and invitees. Discuss the duties owed by possessors of land to each of these.

4. Identity the defenses that are available to a tort action in negligence. Identify those that are available in a tort action in strict liability.

5. Identify and discuss those activities giving rise to a tort action in strict liability.

PROBLEMS

1. A statute, which requires railroads to fence their tracks, is construed as intended solely to prevent injuries to animals straying onto the right of way who may be hit by trains. B & A Railroad Company fails to fence its tracks. Two of Calvin's cows wander onto the track. Nellie is hit by a train. Elsie is poisoned by weeds growing beside the track. For which cows, if any, is B & A Railroad liable to Calvin? Why?

2. Martha invites John to come to lunch. Martha knows that her private road is dangerous to travel, having been guttered by recent rains. She doesn't warn John of the condition, reasonably believing that he will notice the gutters and exercise sufficient care. John's attention, while driving over, is diverted from the road by the screaming of his child, who has been stung by a bee. He fails to notice the condition of the road, hits a gutter, and skids into a tree. If John is not contributorily negligent, is Martha liable to John?

3. Nathan is run over by a car and left lying in the street. Sam, seeing Nathan's helpless state, places him in his car for the purpose of taking him to the hospital. Sam drives negligently into a ditch, causing additional injury to Nathan. Is Sam liable to Nathan?

4. Led Foot drives his car carelessly into another car. The second car contains dynamite which Led had no way of knowing. The collision causes an explosion which shatters a window of a building half a block away on another street. The flying glass inflicts serious cuts on Sally, who is working at a desk near the window. The explosion also harms Vic, who is walking on the sidewalk near the point of the collision. Toward whom is Led Foot negligent?

5. A statute requires all vessels traveling on the Great Lakes to provide lifeboats. One of Winston Steamship Company's boats is sent out of port without a lifeboat. Perry, a sailor, falls overboard in a storm so heavy that had there been a lifeboat it could not have been launched. Perry drowns. Is Winston liable to Perry's estate?

6. Lionel is negligently driving an automobile at excessive speed. Reginald's negligently driven car crosses the center line of the highway and scrapes the side of Lionel's car, damaging its fenders. As a result Lionel loses control of his car, which goes into the ditch, where Lionel's car is wrecked and Lionel suffers personal injuries. What, if anything, can Lionel recover?

7. (a) Ellen, the owner of a baseball park, is under a duty to the entering public to provide a reasonably sufficient number of screened seats to protect those who desire it against the risk of being hit by batted balls. Ellen fails to do so. Frank, a customer entering the park, is unable to find a screened seat and, although fully aware of the risk, sits in an unscreened seat. Frank is struck and injured by a batted ball. Is Ellen liable?

(b) Gretchen, Frank's wife, has just arrived from Germany and is viewing baseball for the first time. Without asking any questions, she follows Frank to a seat. After the batted ball hits Frank, it caroms into Gretchen, injuring her. Is Ellen liable to Gretchen?

8. CC Railroad is negligent in failing to give warning of the approach of its train to a crossing, and thereby endangers Larry, a blind man who is about to cross. Mildred, a bystander, in a reasonable effort to save Larry, rushes onto the track to push Larry out of danger. Although Mildred acts as carefully as possible, she is struck and injured by the train.

(a) Can Mildred recover from Larry?

(b) Can Mildred recover from CC Railroad?

9. Vance was served liquor while he was an intoxicated patron of the Clear Air Force Station Non-Commissioned Officers' Club. He later injured himself as a result of his intoxication. An Alaska State statute makes it a crime to give or to sell liquor to intoxicated persons. Vance has brought an action seeking damages for the injuries suffered. He argues that the United States was negligent *per se* by its employee's violation of the statute. Decision?

10. Timothy keeps a pet chimpanzee, which is thoroughly tamed and accustomed to playing with its owner's children. The chimpanzee escapes, despite every precaution to keep it upon its owner's premises. It approaches a group of children. Wanda, the mother of one of the children, erroneously thinking the chimpanzee is about to attack the children rushes to her child's assistance; and in her hurry and excitement, she stumbles and falls, breaking her leg. Can Wanda recover for her personal injuries?

11. Hawkins slipped and fell on a puddle of water just inside of the automatic door to the H. E. Butt Grocery Company's store. The water had been tracked into the store by customers and blown through the door by a strong wind. The store manager was aware of the puddle and had mopped it up several times earlier in the day. Still, no signs had been placed to warn store patrons of the danger. Hawkins brought an action to recover damages for injuries sustained in the fall. Decision?

12. Escola, a waitress, was injured when a bottle of Coca Cola exploded in her hand while she was putting it into the restaurant's cooler. The bottle came from a shipment that had remained under the counter for thirty-six hours after being delivered by the bottling company. The bottler had subjected the bottle to the method of testing for defects commonly used in the industry, and there is no evidence that Escola or anyone else did anything to damage the bottle between its delivery and the explosion. Escola brought an action against the bottler for damages. Since she is unable to show any specific acts of negligence on its part, she seeks to rely on the doctrine of *res ipsa loquitur.* Decision?

13. Hunn injured herself when she slipped and fell on a loose plank while walking down some steps that the hotel had repaired the day before. The night before, while entering the hotel, she had noticed that the steps were dangerous, and although she knew from her earlier stays at the hotel that another exit was available, she chose that morning to leave via the dangerous steps. The hotel was aware of the hazard, as one of three other guests who had fallen that night had reported his accident to the desk clerk then on duty. Still, there were no cautionary signs on the steps to warn of the danger, and they were not roped off or otherwise excluded from use. Hunn brought an action against the hotel for injuries she sustained as a result of her fall. Decision?

14. Fredericks, a hotel owner, had a dog named "Sport" that he had trained as a watch-dog. When Vincent Zarek, a guest at the hotel, leaned over to pet the dog, it bit him. Although Sport had never bitten anyone before, Fredericks was aware of the dog's violent tendencies and, therefore, did not allow it to roam around the hotel alone. Vincent brought an action for injuries sustained when the dog bit him. Decision?

15. An unidentified man was held up by two thugs in an alley in Manhattan. When the thieves departed with his possessions, the man quickly gave chase. He had almost caught one when the thief managed to force his way into an empty taxicab stopped at a traffic light. The cab was owned by the Peerless Transport Company. The thief pointed his gun at the driver's head and ordered him to drive on. The driver started to follow the directions while closely pursued by a posse of good citizens, but then suddenly jammed on the brakes and jumped out of the car to safety. The thief also jumped out, but the car traveled on, injuring Mrs. Cordas and her two children. The Cordases then brought an action for damages, claiming that the cab driver was negligent in jumping to safety and leaving the moving vehicle uncontrolled. Decision?

16. A foul ball struck Marie Uzdavines on the head while she was watching the Metropolitan Baseball Club ("The Mets") play the Philadelphia Phillies at "The Mets" home stadium in New York. The ball came through a hole in a screen designed to protect spectators sitting behind home plate. The screen contained several holes that had been repaired with baling wire, a lighter weight wire than that used in the original screen. Although the manager of the stadium makes no formal inspections of the screen, his employees do try to repair the holes as they find them. Weather conditions, rust deterioration, and baseballs hitting the screen are the chief causes of these holes. The owner of the stadium, the city of New York, leases the stadium to "The Mets" and replaces the entire screen every two years. Uzdavines sued "The Mets" for negligence under the doctrine of *res ipsa loquitur*. Decision?

Chapter 7

BUSINESS ETHICS AND THE SOCIAL RESPONSIBILITY OF BUSINESS

Law versus Ethics
Ethical Theories
Ethical Standards in Business
Ethical Responsibilities of Business

Business ethics is a subset of ethics: there is no special set of ethical principles that applies only to the world of business. Immoral acts are immoral, whether or not a businessperson has committed them. But before a behavior is judged immoral, special attention must be paid to its business circumstances. For example, suppose a company discovers a new cost-effective technology, enabling it to outperform its competitors. Few would condemn the company for using the technology even if it put one or more competitors out of business. After all, the economic benefits derived from the new technology would seem to so outweigh the social costs of unemployment that it would be difficult to conclude that the business acted immorally.

On the other hand, unethical business practices date from the very beginning of business and continue today. As one court stated in connection with a securities fraud, "Since the time to which the memory of man runneth not to the contrary, the human animal has been full of cunning and guile. Many of the schemes and artifices have been so sophisticated as almost to defy belief. But the ordinary run of those willing and able to take unfair advantage of others are mere appren-

tices in the art when compared with the manipulations thought up by those connected in one way or another with transactions in securities." *See U.S. v. Mulheren.* In the last few years, countless business wrongs have been reported almost daily, such as insider trading, the Beech-Nut adulterated apple juice scandal, the Bhopal disaster, the Dalkon Shield tragedy, and the savings and loan industry depredations. *See A. H. Robins: Dalkon Shield Settlement Approval.*

Ethics can be broadly defined as the study of what is right or good for human beings. It pursues the questions of what people ought to do, what goals they should pursue. In *Business Ethics,* 2d ed., Richard T. DeGeorge provides the following explanation of ethics:

Ethics in general can be defined as a systematic attempt, through the use of reason, to make sense of our individual and social moral experience, in such a way as to determine the rules that ought to govern human conduct and the values worth pursuing in life. The attempt is systematic and therefore goes beyond what each reflective person tends to do in his daily life in making sense of his moral experience, organizing it, and attempting to make it coherent and unified. Because it uses reason and not revelation, ethics can be distinguished from a religious or theological approach to morality. Insofar as it attempts to ascertain what rules and values *ought* to be followed and pursued, ethics can be distinguished from anthropology, psychology, and sociology. Those disciplines describe how people behave, but they usually do not prescribe how they should or ought to behave. Ethics concerns itself with human conduct, taken here to mean human activity that is done knowingly and, to a large extent, willingly. It does not concern itself with automatic responses, or with, for example, actions done in one's sleep or under hypnosis.

Business ethics, as a branch of applied ethics, is the study and determination of right and good in business settings. Business ethics seeks to understand the moral issues that arise from business practices, institutions, and decision making and their relationship to generalized human values. Unlike the law, analyses of ethics have no central authority, such as courts or legislatures, upon which to rely nor do they have clear-cut, universal standards. Despite these inherent limitations, it may still be possible to make meaningful ethical judgments. To improve ethical decision making, it is important to understand how others have approached the task.

Some examples of the many business ethics questions illuminate the definition of business ethics. In the employment relationship, countless ethical issues arise regarding the safety and compensation of workers, their civil rights (such as equal treatment, privacy, and freedom from sexual harassment), and the legitimacy of whistle blowing. In the relationship of business with its customers, ethical issues permeate marketing techniques, product safety, and consumer protection. The relationship between business and its owners bristles with ethical questions involving corporate governance, shareholder voting, and management's duties to the shareholders. The relationship among competing businesses involves numerous ethical matters, including fair competition and collusive conduct. The interaction between business and society at large has additional ethical dimensions: pollution of the physical environment, commitment to the communi-

ty's economic and social infrastructure, and depletion of natural resources. Not only do all of these issues recur at the international level, but additional ones present themselves, such as bribery of foreign officials, exploitation of less developed countries, and conflicts among differing cultures and value systems.

This chapter first surveys the most prominent ethical theories, then it examines ethical standards in business and concludes by exploring the ethical responsibilities of business.

LAW VERSUS ETHICS

As discussed in Chapter 1, the law is strongly affected by moral concepts, but law and morality are not the same. Although it is tempting to say that "if it's legal, it's moral," it is generally believed that such a proposition is too simplistic. For example, it would seem gravely immoral to stand by silently while a blind man walks off a cliff if one could prevent the fall by shouting a warning, even though there is no legal obligation to warn the blind man. Similarly, moral questions arise concerning "legal" business practices, such as failing to fulfill a promise that is not legally binding; exporting products banned in the United States to third world countries, where they are not prohibited; manufacturing and selling tobacco or alcohol products; or slaughtering baby seals for fur coats. The mere fact that these practices are legal does not prevent them from being challenged on moral grounds.

Just as it is possible for acts that are legal to be immoral, it is equally possible for acts that are illegal to be considered morally preferable to following the law. It is the moral conviction of the great majority of people that those who sheltered Jews in violation of Nazi edicts during World War II and those who committed acts of civil disobedience in the 1950s and 1960s to challenge racist segregation laws in the United States were acting properly and that the laws themselves were immoral.

Therefore, although legality is often a reliable guide to moral behavior, it cannot be relied upon blindly as an infallible standard for action. The individual must engage in independent determinations of both the legal requirements *and* the moral ⸱equirements of a course of action.

ETHICAL THEORIES

Philosophers have sought for centuries to develop dependable and universal methods for making ethical judgments. In earlier times, some thinkers analogized the discovery of ethical principles with the derivation of mathematical proofs. They asserted that people could discover fundamental ethical rules by applying careful reasoning *a priori*. (*A priori* reasoning is based on theory rather than experimentation and deductively draws conclusions from cause to effect and from generalizations to particular instances.) In more recent times, many philosophers have concluded that although careful reasoning and deep thought assist substantially in moral reasoning, experience reveals that the complexities of the world defeat most attempts to fashion precise, *a priori* guidelines. Nevertheless, it is useful to review the most significant ethical theories to help analyze issues of business ethics.

Ethical Fundamentalism

Under **ethical fundamentalism** or absolutism, individuals look to a central authority or set of rules to guide them in ethical decision making. Some look to the Bible; others look to the Koran or the writings of Karl Marx or to any number of living or deceased prophets. The essential characteristic of this approach is a reliance upon a central repository of wisdom. In some cases, reliance is total. In others, it occurs to a lesser degree: followers of a religion or a spiritual leader may believe that all members of the group have an obligation to assess moral dilemmas independently, according to each person's understanding of the dictates of the fundamental principles. Even this more restrained approach, however, retains the essential belief that universal, revealed truths derive from a central moral authority. Ethical fundamentalism has had numerous devotees in every society throughout history.

Ethical Relativism

Ethical relativism is a doctrine asserting that actions must be judged by what individuals feel is right or wrong for themselves. It holds that when any two individuals or cultures differ regarding the morality of a particular issue or action, they are both correct because morality is relative. While ethical relativism promotes open-mindedness and tolerance, it has limitations. If each person's actions are always correct for that person, then his behavior is, by definition, moral and no one can truly criticize it. If a child abuser truly felt it right to molest children, a relativist would accept the proposition that the child abuser acted properly. Since almost no one would accept the proposition that child abuse could ever be ethical, few can truly claim to be relativists. Once a person concludes that it is appropriate to criticize or punish behavior in some cases, he abandons ethical relativism and faces the task of developing a broader ethical methodology.

Although bearing a surface resemblance to ethical relativism, situational ethics actually differs substantially. **Situational ethics** holds that it is difficult to develop precise ethical guidelines that effectively guide people through many ethical dilemmas because real-life decision making is so complex. To judge the morality of someone's behavior, the person judging must actually put herself in the other person's shoes to understand what motivated him to choose a particular course of action. In this respect, situational ethics shares with ethical relativism the notion that we must judge actions from the perspective of the person who actually made the judgment. From that point on, however, the two ethical approaches differ dramatically. Ethical relativism passes no judgment on what the person did other than to determine that the person truly believed the decision was right for him. Situational ethics is much more judgmental. It insists that once the decision is viewed from the actor's perspective, then a judgment can be made on whether or not what the person did was ethical. Situational ethics does not cede the ultimate judgment of the propriety of an action to the actor; rather, it insists that before evaluating a person's decision or act, it must be viewed from the perspective of a person in the actor's shoes.

Utilitarianism

Utilitarianism is a doctrine that assesses good and evil in terms of the consequences of actions. Those that produce the greatest net pleasure compared to the net pain are better in a moral sense than those that produce less net pleasure. As Jeremy Bentham, one of the most influential proponents of utilitarianism, proclaimed, a good or moral act is one that results in "the greatest happiness for the greatest number."

The two major forms of utilitarianism are act utilitarianism and rule utilitarianism. **Act utilitarianism** assesses each separate act according to whether it maximizes pleasure over pain. For example, if telling a lie in a particular situation produces more overall pleasure than pain, then an act utilitarian would support lying as the moral thing to do. Rule utilitarians, disturbed by the unpredictability and possibility for abuse of act utilitarianism, follow a different approach. **Rule utilitarianism** holds that general rules must be established and followed even though, in some instances, following rules may produce less overall pleasure than not following them. It applies utilitarian principles in developing rules; thus, it supports rules that on balance produce the greatest satisfaction. Whether telling a lie in a given instance would produce greater pleasure than telling the truth is less important to the rule utilitarian than deciding if a general practice of lying would maximize society's pleasure. If lying would not maximize pleasure generally, then one should follow a rule of not lying even though on occasion telling a lie would produce greater pleasure than would telling the truth.

Utilitarian notions underlie cost-benefit analysis, an analytical tool used by many

business and government managers today. **Cost-benefit analysis** first quantifies in monetary terms and then compares the direct and indirect costs and benefits of program alternatives for meeting a specified objective. The primary purpose of cost-benefit analysis is to choose from alternative courses of action the program that maximizes society's wealth. For example, based on cost-benefit analysis, an auto designer might choose to devote more effort to perfecting an air bag that would be quite expensive but would save hundreds of lives and prevent thousands of disabling injuries than to developing an improved latching mechanism for a car hood that would produce a less favorable cost-benefit ratio.

Cost-benefit analysis seeks the greatest economic efficiency. The underlying notion for doing so is that acts achieving the greatest output at the least cost promote the greatest marginal happiness over less efficient acts, other things being equal.

The chief criticism of utilitarianism is that in some important instances it ignores justice. A number of situations would maximize the pleasure of the majority but at a great sacrifice by a minority. Slavery, for example, might well produce such an abundance of pleasure for slaveowners that the misery of the slaves would be substantially outweighed by the owners' satisfaction. Similarly, under a strict utilitarian approach, it would be ethical to compel a few citizens to undergo painful, even fatal medical tests to develop cures for the rest of the nation. For most people, however, such actions would be unacceptable.

Another major criticism of utilitarianism is that measuring pleasure and pain in the fashion advocated by its supporters is extremely difficult, if not impossible. For example, the dollar value of increased pleasure due to a 10 percent reduction in industrial pollution cannot be compared with the dollar cost of the increased pain of industry clean-up efforts. Although analysts attempt to perform such calculations by converting pleasure and pain into monetary terms, serious questions arise: Are they providing true insight into the decision process or are they arbitrarily assigning values? It is extremely difficult to measure the monetary value of a human life or a lost limb and compare it with the cost of safety measures necessary to avoid these harms. Such calculations make some sense when comparing alternative actions but make less sense in deciding whether to take the action in the first place. For example, a cost-benefit calculation might provide valuable assistance in choosing among competing technologies to implement a decision to spend $100 million on enhanced safety in auto design. But such a calculation would be much less help in deciding whether or not to spend the extra $100 million on safety. The decision to spend the $100 million would require qualitative judgments about the value of a human life, which cannot be reduced to quantitative terms.

Although utilitarianism seems intuitively appealing to many people and provides useful guidance in many situations, it does not provide definitive answers to all moral dilemmas because some moral issues are not easily addressed by this philosophy.

Deontology

Deontological theories (from the Greek word *deon,* meaning duty or obligation) address the practical problems of utilitarianism by holding that certain underlying principles are right or wrong irrespective of any pleasure or pain calculations. Deontologists believe that actions cannot be measured simply by their results but must be judged by the means and motives as well.

Our criminal laws apply deontological reasoning. Knowing that John shot and killed Marvin is not enough to tell us how to judge John's act. We must know whether John shot Marvin in anger, self-defense, or by mistake. Although under any of these motives Marvin is just as dead, we judge John quite differently depending on the mental process that led him to commit the act. Similarly, deontologists judge the morality of acts, not so much by the consequences of the acts but by the motives that lead to them. A person not only must achieve just results but also must employ the proper means.

The best-known deontological theory was proffered by the eighteenth-century philosopher Immanuel Kant. Kant asserted what he called the **categorical imperative**, which has been summarized by Bowie and Duska in *Business Ethics,* 2d ed., as follows:

1. Act only according to that maxim by which you can, at the same time, will that it should become a universal law.
2. Act as never to treat another human being merely as a means to an end.

Thus, for an action to be moral it must (1) be possible for it to be made a universal law to be applied consistently and (2) be respectful of the autonomy and rationality of all human beings and not treat them as an expedient. That is, one should not do anything that he or she would not have everyone do in a similar situation. For example, you should not lie to colleagues unless you support the right of all colleagues to lie to one another. Similarly, you should not cheat others unless you advocate everyone's right to cheat. We apply Kantian reasoning when we challenge someone's behavior by asking, What if everybody acted that way?

Kant did not assert that the categorical imperative stemmed from a direct pronouncement from God or any other absolute authority. Rather, he believed that it arose from man's ability, through the application of his rational faculties, to reach logical, consistent principles and to see the desirability of following those principles. In this sense, Kant's approach differed from ethical fundamentalism since it was premised on man's rationality—not on principles handed down from above.

Under Kant's approach, it would be improper to assert a principle to which one claimed an exception, such as insisting that it was acceptable for you to cheat but not for anyone else to do so. This principle could not be universalized since everyone would then insist on similar rules that excepted only themselves.

Kant's philosophy also rejects notions of the ends' justifying the means. To Kant, every person is an end in himself or herself. Each person deserves respect simply because of his or her humanity. Thus, any sacrifice of a person for the greater good of society would be unacceptable to Kant.

In many respects, Kant's categorical imperative is a variation of the Golden Rule. Like the Golden Rule, the categorical imperative appeals to the self-centeredness of individuals. As one writer on business ethics notes, this is what makes the Golden Rule so effective:

It is precisely this self-centeredness of the Golden Rule that makes it so valuable, and so widely acknowledged, as a guide. To inquire of yourself, "How would I feel in the other fellow's place?" is an elegantly simple and reliable method of focusing in on the "right" thing to do. The Golden Rule works not in spite of selfishness, but because of it. Tuleja, *Beyond the Bottom Line.*

As with every theory, Kantian ethics has its critics. Just as deontologists criticize utilitarians for excessive pragmatism and flexible moral guidelines, utilitarians and others criticize deontologists for rigidity and excessive formalism. For example, if one inflexibly adopts as a rule to tell the truth, one ignores situations in which lying might well be justified. A person hiding a terrified wife from her angry, abusive husband would seem to be acting morally by falsely denying that the wife is at the person's house. Yet, a deontologist, feeling bound to tell the truth, might ignore the consequences of truthfulness, tell the husband where his wife is, and create the possibility of a terrible tragedy. Less dramatically, one wonders whether the world would effect a higher ethical code if "white lies" concerning friends' appearance, clothing, or choice of spouse were considered immoral.

Another criticism of deontological theories is that the proper course may be difficult to determine when values or assumptions conflict. To one person, abortion may be the murder of an innocent human being while to another it may be a personal decision made in private that society has no right to question. Without consensus regarding the rules to be universalized, one finds it difficult to apply Kantian analysis, even though it may be useful under many circumstances.

Social Ethics Theories

Social ethics theories assert that special obligations arise from the social nature of human beings. They focus not only on each person's obligations to other members of society but also on the individual's rights and obligations within the society. For example, **social egalitarians** believe that society should provide all persons with equal amounts of goods and services irrespective of the contribution each makes to increase society's wealth.

Two other ethics theories have received widespread attention in recent years. One is the theory of **distributive justice** proposed by Harvard philosopher John Rawls, which seeks to analyze the type of society that people in a "natural state" would establish if they could not determine in advance whether they would be talented, rich, healthy, or ambitious, relative to other members of society. Thus, it is argued that the society contemplated through this "veil of ignorance" is the one that should be developed because it considers the needs and rights of all members. Rawls did not argue that such a society would be strictly egalitarian. That would unfairly penalize those who turned out to be the most talented and ambitious. Instead, Rawls suggested that such a society would stress equality of opportunity, not of results. On the other hand, Rawls stressed that society would pay heed to the least advantaged to ensure that they did not suffer unduly and that they participated meaningfully in society's benefits. To Rawls, society must be premised on justice. Everyone is entitled to his or her fair share in society, which all must work to guarantee.

In contrast to Rawls, another Harvard philosopher, Robert Nozick, stressed liberty, not justice, as the most important obligation that society owes its members. **Libertarians** stress market outcomes as the basis for distributing society's rewards. Only to the extent that one meets the demands of the market does one deserve society's benefits. Libertarians oppose interference by society in their lives as long as they do not violate the rules of the marketplace, that is, as long as they do not cheat others and they disclose meaningfully the nature of their transactions with others. The fact that some end up with fortunes while others accumulate little simply proves that some can play in the market effectively while others cannot. To libertarians, this is not unjust. What is unjust to them is any attempt by society to take wealth earned by citizens and then distribute it to those who did not earn it.

These theories and others (e.g., Marxism) judge society in moral terms by how it is organized and how it distributes goods and services. They demonstrate the difficulty of ethical decision making in the context of a social organization: behavior that is consistently ethical from individual to individual may not necessarily produce a just society.

Other Theories

The preceding theories do not exhaust the possible approaches to evaluating ethical behavior but represent the most commonly cited and most intuitively appealing theories advanced over the years. Several other theories also deserve mention. **Intuitionism** holds that a rational person possesses inherent powers to assess the correctness of actions. An individual may refine and strengthen these powers, but they are just as basic to humanity as our instincts for survival and self-defense. Just as some people are better artists or musicians, some people have more insight into ethical behavior than others. Consistent with intuitionism is the philosophy of **good persons,** which declares that if individuals wish to act morally, they should seek out and emulate the behavior of those individuals who always seem to know what the right choice is in any given situation and who always seem to do the right thing. One variation of these ethical approaches is the "**Television Test,**" which directs us to imagine that every ethical decision we make is being broadcast on nationwide television. Adherents of this approach believe a decision is appropriate if we would be comfortable with our decision and its broadcast on national television for all to witness.

ETHICAL STANDARDS IN BUSINESS

This section will explore the application of the theories of ethical behavior to the world of business.

Choosing an Ethical System

Philosophers and other thinkers have struggled for years to refine the various systems discussed above in their efforts to resolve the moral dilemmas facing mankind. All of the systems have limited precision, however, and tend to produce unacceptable prescriptions for action in some circumstances. But to say that each system has some limits is not to say it is useless. To the contrary, a number of systems provide insight into ethical decision making and help us formulate issues and resolve moral dilemmas. Furthermore, concluding that moral standards are difficult to articulate and that the boundaries are imprecise is not the same as concluding that moral standards are unnecessary or nonexistent.

Research by the noted psychologist Lawrence Kohlberg provides some insight into ethical decision making and lends credibility to the notion that moral growth, like physical growth, is part of the human condition. Kohlberg observed that people progress through stages of moral development according to two major variables: age and education. During the first level—the **preconventional level**—a child's conduct is a reaction to the fear of punishment and, later, to the pleasure of reward. Although people who operate at this level may behave in a moral manner, they do so without understanding why their behavior is moral. The rules are imposed upon them. During adolescence—Kohlberg's **conventional level,** people conform their behavior to meet the expectations of groups, such as family, peers, and eventually society. The motivation for conformity is loyalty, affection, and trust. Most adults operate at this level. According to Kohlberg, some reach the third level—the **postconventional level**—where they accept and conform to moral principles because they understand *why* the principles are right and binding. At this level, moral principles are voluntarily internalized, not externally imposed. Moreover, these individuals develop their own universal ethical principles and even question the laws and values that society and others have adopted (see Figure 7–1).

Kohlberg believed that these stages were sequential and that not all people reach the second or third stages. He therefore argued that essential to the study of ethics was the exploration of ways to get people to develop to the advanced stage of postconventional thought. Other psychologists assert that individuals do not pass from stage to stage but rather function in all three stages simultaneously.

Whatever the source of our ethical approach, we cannot avoid facing moral dilemmas that challenge us to recognize and to do the right thing. Moreover, for those who plan business careers, such dilemmas will necessarily have implications for many others—employees, shareholders, suppliers, customers, and society at large.

Corporations as Moral Agents

Corporations are not persons but artificial entities created by the State, so it is not obvious whether they can or should be held morally accountable. As Lord Chancellor Thurlow lamented two hundred years ago, "A company has no body to kick and no soul to damn, and by God, it ought to have both." Clearly, individuals within corporations can be held morally responsible, but the corporate entity presents unique problems.

Commentators are divided on the issue. Some, like philosopher Manuel Velasquez, insist that only people can engage in behavior that can be judged in moral terms. Opponents of this view, like philosophers Kenneth Goodpaster and John Matthews, Jr., concede that corporations are not persons in any literal sense but insist that a sufficient number of attributes of responsibility inhere in corporations to permit judging corporate behavior from a moral perspective.

In assessing the merits of the debate, it is useful to note the law's approach to corporate criminal responsibility. The early common law, as discussed in Chapter 4, held that a corporation could not commit crimes because it could not develop a criminal intent. Under the modern view, if high corporate officers or the board of directors commit improper acts for the corporation, they and the corporation may be criminally liable. Although corporations cannot be imprisoned, sanctions such as fines can be imposed on them. In fact, several recent proposals would penalize corporations that flagrantly violate the law by barring violators from conducting business for defined periods of time (analogous to a jail sentence) or if a corporate "death penalty" is in order, by dissolving the corporate charters of offenders.

Figure 7–1 Kohlberg's Stages of Moral Development

LEVELS	PERSPECTIVE	JUSTIFICATION
Preconventional (Childhood)	Self	Punishment/Reward
Conventional (Adolescent)	Group	Group Norms
Postconventional (Adult)	Universal	Moral Principles

Although the debate over the *legality* of imposing criminal liability on corporations has more or less been settled, the wisdom of doing so continues to be argued along somewhat the same lines as the controversy about holding corporations *morally* responsible for their behavior. Those who support criminal penalties for corporations argue the following: that such penalties help deter illegal behavior by encouraging shareholders to insist that management act properly; that these penalties punish illegal behavior otherwise not easily punishable because the behavior cannot readily be traced to specific individuals within an organization; that some offenses result from a tainted corporate culture, which must be attacked broadly; that fines should be borne by the corporation, which otherwise might profit from its illegal behavior; and that imposing criminal liability on a corporation effectively and appropriately stigmatizes the corporation.

On the other hand, those who oppose criminal penalties for corporations cite these arguments: that fines often are simply passed on to a company's customers; that some large, publicly held corporations have so many shareholders that fines do not affect their interests significantly; that prosecutors may simply seek the "easy way out" by obtaining a conviction against a corporation rather than against culpable corporate officers or directors; and that corporate images, in fact, do not suffer from criminal convictions.

ETHICAL RESPONSIBILITIES OF BUSINESS

Many people assert that the only responsibility of business is to maximize profit and that this obligation overrides any ethical or social responsibility. Although our economic system of modified capitalism is based on the pursuit of self-interest, it also contains other components to keep in check this motivation of greed. Our system has always recognized the need for some form of regulation, whether it be by the "invisible hand" of competition, the self-regulation of business, or government regulation.

Regulation of Business

As explained and justified by Adam Smith in *The Wealth of Nations* (1776), the capitalistic system is composed of six "institutions": economic motivation, private productive property, free enterprise, free markets, competition, and limited government. Economic motivation assumes that a person will work harder if he receives an economic return for his effort; therefore, the economic system should provide greater economic rewards for those who work harder. Private property is the means by which economic motivation is exercised. It permits individuals to innovate and produce while securing to them the fruits of their efforts. Jack Behrman, a professor of business ethics, has described how the four other institutions combine with these two to bring about industrialized capitalism:

Free enterprise permits the combination of properties so people can do things together that they can't do alone. Free enterprise means a capitalistic combination of factors of production under decisions of free individuals. Free enterprise is the group expression of the use of private property, and it permits greater efficiency in an industrial setting through variation in the levels and kinds of production.

. . . The free market operates to equate supply and demand—supply reflecting the ability and willingness to offer certain goods or services, and demand reflecting the consumer's *ability* and *willingness* to pay. Price is adjusted to include the maximum number of *both* bids and offers. The market, therefore, is *the* decisionmaking mechanism outside of the firm. It is the *means* by which basic decisions are made about the use of resources, and all factors are supposed to respond to it, however they wish.

. . . Just in case it doesn't work out that way, there is one more institution—the *Government*—which is supposed to set rules and provide protection for the society and its members. That's all, said Smith, that it should do: it should set the rules, enforce them, and stand aside. J. Behrman, *Discourses on Ethics and Business* (1981), 25–29.

As long as all these constituent institutions continue to exist and operate in a balanced manner, the factors of production—land, capital, and labor—combine to produce an efficient allocation of resources for individual consumers and for the economy as a whole. For this outcome to succeed, however, Smith's model requires that a number of conditions be satisfied: "standardized products, numerous firms in markets, each firm with a small share and unable by its actions alone to exert significant influence over price, no barriers to entry, and output carried to the point where each seller's marginal cost equals the going market price." E. Singer, *Antitrust Economics and Legal Analysis* (1981), 2.

History has demonstrated that almost all of these assumptions have not been satisfied by the actual operation of the economy. More specifically, the actual competitive process falls considerably short of the assumptions of the classic economic model of perfect competition:

Competitive industries are never perfectly competitive in this sense. Many of the resources they employ cannot be shifted to other employments without substantial cost and delay. The allocation of those resources, as between industries or as to relative proportions within a single industry, is unlikely to have been made in a way that affords the best possible expenditure of economic effort. Information is incomplete, motivation confused, and decision therefore ill informed and often unwise. Variations in efficiency are not directly reflected in variations of profit. Success is derived in large part from competitive selling efforts, which in the aggregate may be wasteful, and from differentiation of products, which may be undertaken partly by methods designed to impair the opportunity of the buyer to compare quality and price. C. Edwards, *Maintaining Competition* (1964), 7.

In addition to capitalism's failure to accomplish its objective of efficient resource allocation, it cannot be relied on to achieve all of the social and public policy objectives required by a pluralistic democracy. For example, equitable distribution of wealth, national defense, conservation of natural resources, full employment, stability in economic cycles, protection against economic dislocations, health and safety, social security, and other important social and economic goals are simply not comprehended or addressed by the free enterprise model. Increased governmental intervention has occurred not only to preserve the competitive process in our economic system but also to achieve social goals extrinsic to the efficient allocation of resources because the invisible hand and self-regulation by business have failed to bring about these desired results. Such intervention attempts (1) to regulate both "legal" monopolies, such as those conferred by law through copyrights, patents, and trade symbols, and "natural" monopolies such as utilities, transportation, and communications; (2) to correct imperfections in the market system to preserve competition; (3) to protect specific groups from failures of the marketplace, especially labor and agriculture; and (4) to promote other social goals. Successful government regulation involves a delicate balance between regulations that attempt to preserve competition and those that attempt to advance other social objectives. The latter should not undermine the basic competitive processes that are relied on for an efficient allocation of economic resources.

Corporate Governance

In addition to the broad demands of maintaining a competitive and fair marketplace, another factor demanding the citizenship of business is generated by the sheer size and power of individual corporations. The five thousand largest U.S. firms currently produce over half of the nation's gross national product. Statutorily, their economic power should be delegated by the shareholders to the board of directors, who in turn appoint the officers of the corporation. "In reality, this legal image is virtually a myth. In nearly every large American business corporation, there exists a management autocracy. One man—variously titled the President, or the Chairman of the Board, or the Chief Executive Officer—or a small coterie of men rule the corporation. Far from being chosen by the directors to run the corporation, this chief executive or executive clique chooses the board of directors and, with the acquiescence of the board, controls the corporation." R. Nader, M. Green, and J. Seligman, *Taming the Giant Corporation* (1976), 75–76.

In a classic study published in 1932, Adolf Berle and Gardner Means concluded that great amounts of economic power had been concentrated in a relatively few large corporations, that the ownership of these corporations had become widely dispersed, and that the shareholders had become far removed from active participation in management. Since their original study, these trends have steadily continued. The five hundred largest U.S. industrial corporations have combined sales of approximately $2 trillion, profits of $100 billion, assets over $1 trillion, and more than fifteen million employees.

Thus, vast amounts of wealth and power are now controlled by a small number of corporations, which are in turn controlled by a small group of corporate officers. In fact, the separation of ownership and control has widened so far that Myles Mace, a leading scholar in this area, has stated that boards of directors are so reluctant to discharge ineffective management that they fire a chief executive only when "the leadership of the [chief executive] was so unsatisfactory that even his mother thought he ought [to be removed] for the good of the company . . . before the board [of directors] reluctantly moved." Testimony before the Securities and Exchange Commission, 30 September 1977.

These developments raise a large number of social, policy, and ethical issues about the governance of large, publicly owned corporations. Many observers insist that companies playing such an important role in economic life should have a responsibility to undertake projects that benefit society in ways that go beyond mere financial efficiency in producing goods and services. In some instances, the idea of corporate obligations come from industrialists themselves. Andrew Carnegie, for example, advocated philanthropy throughout his life and contributed much of his fortune to educational and social causes. *See A. P. Smith Mfg. Co. v. Barlow.*

Arguments against Social Responsibility

A number of arguments oppose business involvement in socially responsible activities: profitability, unfairness, accountability, and expertise.

Profitability   As Milton Friedman and others have argued, businesses are artificial entities established to permit people to engage in profit-making, not social, activities. Without profits, they assert, there is little reason for a corporation to exist and no real way to measure the effectiveness of corporate activities. Businesses are not organized to engage in social activities; they are structured to produce goods and services for which they receive money. Their social obligation is to return as much of this money to their direct stakeholders as possible. In a free market with significant competition, the selfish pursuits of corporations will lead to maximizing output, minimizing costs, and establishing fair prices. All other concerns distract companies and interfere with achieving these goals.

Unfairness   Whenever companies stray from their designated role of profit-maker, they take unfair advantage of company employees and shareholders. For example, a company may support the arts or education or spend excess funds on health and safety; however, these funds rightfully belong to the shareholders or employees. The company's decision to disburse these funds to others who may well be less deserving than the shareholders and employees is unfair. Furthermore, consumers can express their desires through the marketplace, and shareholders and employees can decide independently if they wish to make charitable contributions. In most cases, senior management consults the board of directors about supporting social concerns but does not seek the approval of the company's major stakeholders. Thus, these shareholders are effectively disenfranchised from actions that reduce their benefits from the corporation.

Accountability   Corporations, as previously noted, are private institutions that are subject to a lower standard of accountability than are public bodies. Accordingly, a company may decide to support a wide range of social causes and yet submit to little public scrutiny. But a substantial potential for abuse exists in such cases. For one thing, a company could provide funding for a variety of causes not supported by its employees or shareholders. It could also provide money "with strings attached," thereby controlling the recipients' agendas for less than socially beneficial purposes. For example, a drug company that contributes to a consumer group might implicitly or explicitly condition its assistance on the group's agreement never to criticize the company or the drug industry.

This lack of accountability warrants particular concern because of the enormous power wielded by corporations in modern society. Many large companies, like General Motors or IBM, generate and spend more money in a year than all but a handful of the world's countries. If these companies suddenly began to vigorously pursue their own social agendas, their influence might well rival, and perhaps undermine, that of their own governments. In a country like the United States, founded on the principles of limited government and the balance of powers, too much corporate involvement in social affairs might well present substantial problems. Without clear guidelines and accountability, companies' pursuing their private visions of socially responsible behavior might well distort the entire process of governance.

There is a clear alternative to corporations' engaging in socially responsible action. If society wishes to increase the resources devoted to needy causes, it has the power to do so. Let the corporations seek profits without the burden of a social agenda, let the consumers vote in the marketplace for the desired products and services, and let the government tax a portion of the profits for socially beneficial causes.

Expertise Even though a corporation has an expertise in producing and selling its product, it may not possess a talent for recognizing or managing socially useful activities. Corporations become successful in the market because they can identify and meet the needs of its customers. Nothing suggests that this talent spills over into nonbusiness arenas. In fact, critics of corporate engage-

ment in social activities worry that corporations will prove unable to distinguish the true needs of society from their own narrow self-interests.

Arguments in Favor of Social Responsibility

First, it should be recognized that even the critics of business acknowledge that the prime responsibility of business is to make a reasonable return on its investment by producing a quality product at a reasonable price. They do not suggest that business entities be charitable institutions. They do assert, however, that business has certain obligations beyond making a profit or not harming society. Critics contend that business must help to resolve societal problems and they offer a number of arguments in support of their position.

The Social Contract Society creates corporations and gives them a special social status, including the grant of limited liability, which insulates the owners from liability for debts incurred by the organization. Supporters of social roles for corporations assert that limited liability and other rights granted to companies carry a responsibility: corporations, just like other members of society, must contribute to its betterment. Therefore, companies owe a moral debt to society to contribute to its overall well-being. Society needs a host of improvements, such as pollution controls, safe products, a free marketplace, quality education, cures for illness, and freedom from crime. Corporations can help in each of these areas. Granted, deciding on which social needs deserve corporate attention is difficult; however, this challenge does not lessen a company's obligation to choose a cause. Corporate America cannot ignore the multitude of pressing needs that still remain, despite the efforts of government and private charities.

Less Government Regulation According to another argument in favor of corporate social responsibility, the more responsibly companies act, the less the government must regulate. This idea, if accurate, would likely appeal to those corporations that typically view regulation with distaste, perceiving it as a crude and expensive way of achieving social goals. To them, regulation often imposes inappropriate, overly broad rules that hamper productivity and require extensive record-keeping procedures to document compliance. If companies can use more flexible, voluntary methods of meeting a social norm such as pollution control, then government will be less tempted to legislate norms.

The argument can be taken further. Not only does anticipatory corporate action lessen the likelihood of government regulation, but social involvement by companies creates a climate of trust and respect that reduces the overall inclination of government to interfere in company business. For example, a government agency is much more likely to show some leniency toward a socially responsible company than toward one that ignores social plights.

Long-Run Profits   Perhaps the most persuasive argument in favor of corporate involvement in social causes is that such involvement actually makes good business sense. *See A. P. Smith Manufacturing Co. v. Barlow.* Consumers often support good corporate images and avoid bad ones. For example, consumers generally prefer to patronize stores with "easy return" policies. Even though such policies are not required by law, companies institute them because they create goodwill—an intangible though indispensable asset for ensuring repeat customers. In the long run, enhanced goodwill often redounds to stronger profits. Moreover, corporate actions to improve the well-being of their communities make these communities more attractive to citizens and more profitable for business.

CASES

Throughout this book the authors have included cases dealing with ethical or social issues. Every chapter has at least one case relating to ethical or social issues; in a number of chapters all of the cases discuss these issues.

Business Ethics

U.S. v. MULHEREN

U.S. District Court, Southern District of New York, 1990.

Excerpts from Ivan Boesky's testimony as reported in *The New York Times,* 28 May 1990, p. 21. Copyright © 1990 by The New York Times Company. Reprinted by permission.

Direct Examination by E. Scott Gilbert, Assistant U.S. Attorney

MR. GILBERT: Your honor, the Government calls Ivan Boesky.

* * *

Q. Do you know a man named John Mulheren?

A. Yes, I do.

* * *

Q. After you met him, what if any relationship did you form with John Mulheren?

A. We established a business relationship and also a friendship.

* * *

Discussions With Levine

Q. Do you know a man named Dennis Levine?

A. Yes, I do.

Q. To the best of your recollection, when did you meet him for the first time?

A. In the early 80's.

Q. At the time that you met Mr. Levine . . ., where was he employed?

A. The firm of Drexel Burnham Lambert. . . . He was an investment banker.

Q. After you met with Mr. Levine, what was the nature of your relationship with him?

* * *

A. We had a commonality of interest and communication, and we did speak from time to time on various transactions that were pending.

* * *

Q. Now at the time that you had discussions with Mr. Levine, eventually did there come a time when you believed that some of the information that was being provided to you was being provided in breach of some confidential relationship?

A. Yes.

Q. And at that time was there a term commonly used to describe information about securities that is being provided in breach of confidential relationships?

A. Inside information.

* * *

Q. Did there come a time, Mr. Boesky, when you agreed to pay Dennis Levine for the information which he was providing to you?

A. Yes.

Q. What was your understanding of the agreement that you reached with Mr. Levine?

A. That to the extent he was very helpful in the transaction he would receive 5 percent of the profits that our firm might derive. To the extent that he was only minimally helpful he might receive 1 percent of the profits that our firm might derive.

Q. Did you ever pay, actually pay, Mr. Levine pursuant to that agreement?

A. No.

Q. Do you know a person named Martin Siegel?

A. Yes.

* * *

Relationship With Siegel

Q. What was the nature of the relationship between you and Mr. Siegel?

A. Investment banker to arbitrager. Pretty much the same relationship that I outlined with Mr. Levine.

* * *

Q. In your discussions with Mr. Siegel you and he exchanged information?

A. We did.

Q. Did you believe that some of the information that Mr. Siegel was providing to you was, in fact, inside information?

A. Yes.

* * *

Q. Did there come a time when you agreed to pay Mr. Siegel for the information he was providing to you?

A. Yes.

Q. How did that agreement come about?

A. Mr. Siegel suggested that he felt that his continued communications had a value that he would like to derive.

Q. And how did you respond to that?

A. Eventually I agreed to provide that to him as he wished.

* * *

Q. Did you in fact pay Mr. Martin Siegel for information he provided to you?

A. Yes.

Q. How many times did you arrange for him to be paid?

A. Three times.

Q. And how much money did you arrange for him to be paid?

A. Approximately $800,000.

Q. In what form were the payments made, Mr. Boesky?

A. Cash in a briefcase.

Q. How did you arrange for this cash to be delivered?

A. It was assembled by a colleague, put into a briefcase and presented by an intermediary who handed the briefcase to Mr. Siegel.

* * *

Investment in Gulf and Western

Q. Mr. Boesky, are you familiar with a company called Gulf and Western?

A. Yes, I am.

Q. And did the company for which you purchased stock invest in Gulf and Western?

A. Yes, they did.

* * *

Q. Now based upon what did you cause the companies whose portfolios you managed to invest in Gulf and Western?

A. My initial interest, I think, began with the suggestion of Mr. Icahn [Carl C. Icahn].

Q. Who was Mr. Icahn?

A. Mr. Icahn was an arbitrager at the time and a well-known corporate acquirer.

* * *

Meeting With Icahn at G. & W.

Q. Would you be a little more specific about the type of proposal that you intended to make along with Mr. Icahn?

A. Well, let me differentiate. I was going to make that proposal. Mr. Icahn was going to be present. It was not going to be a joint proposal.

* * *

Q. Where did you meet?

A. At the Gulf and Western Building.

Q. Who was present at that meeting?

A. Mr. Martin Davis, myself, Mr. Icahn.

Q. And could you tell us what you said at the meeting and what was said to you?

A. I simply, after having a very cordial meal together, proposed the notion that I thought Gulf and Western was a very exceptional company and that perhaps everyone would be served well if management would consider a leveraged buyout. . . . Mr. Icahn indicated that sounded like an interesting proposal to him also.

Q. What, if anything, did Mr. Davis say in response?

A. He listened carefully and he said that his inclination was to maintain Gulf and Western as . . . a public company.

* * *

Q. Did you have any discussion with Carl Icahn about what you would do with your respective blocks of shares?

A. Yes.

Q. What did you say to him and what did he say to you?

A. Basically I'd said to him that I had possibly two ways to go. One way would be to consider selling my stocks. . . .

Q. Did you agree with him at a price that you both wanted to get for your shares?

A. Well, I told him—I think he agreed—that a price of $45 at the time seemed reasonable.

Q. Did you have any discussion with Carl Icahn with respect to the willingness of the company to buy back the shares at $45 a share?

A. Yes.

Q. What did Mr. Icahn tell you?

A. Mr. Icahn told me that he felt the company would be willing to buy back the shares at $45—however, would not be willing to buy back the shares at a premium over the market, so if the market were not $45 they would not pay $45.

* * *

Q. Did you have any discussion with John Mulheren concerning Gulf and Western?

A. Yes.

Q. Would you tell us what you said to John Mulheren and what Mr. Mulheren said to you?

A. Mr. Mulheren asked me if I liked the stock on that particular day, and I said yes. I said I liked it. . . . However, I would not pay more than $45 for it and it would be great if it traded at $45.

* * *

Q. What, if anything, did he say to you?

A. "I understand."

Cross-Examination by Thomas Puccio, Lawyer for Mr. Mulheren

* * *

Q. Have you violated that oath [to tell the truth] before and have you lied under oath?

A. I have.

Q. How many times have you lied under oath prior to your appearance in this case, Mr. Boesky?

A. Several times. I cannot tell you the number.

* * *

Q. Do you like money, Mr. Boesky?

A. Of course, don't you?

* * *

Authorship of Book on Mergers

Q. By the way Mr. Boesky, did you at one point write a book, co-author a book on mergers?

A. I am familiar with the book.

Q. Well it has your picture on the front, the cover, isn't that right?

A. That is right.

Q. And the name of the book, forgive me, is "Merger Mania"—is that right?

A. I don't forgive you. It's accurate; it's nothing to apologize for, sir.

Q. You were the author, Ivan F. Boesky, "Merger Mania." Is that right?

A. That's correct.

* * *

Q. You stand by whatever you wrote in this book, isn't that right?

A. No, it's incomplete and inaccurate.

Q. And false as well, isn't that right?

A. By omission of certain information, I think you have to make that conclusion.

Q. As a matter of fact, . . . you described the ingenuity of an arbitrager in doing great research and making these wonderful transactions. Isn't that correct?

A. Absolutely true.

Q. And did you tell the readers of your book, Mr. Boesky, that your transaction in Getty Oil that you described here was based upon inside information?

A. That was a significant omission, in part.

* * *

Agreement With Government

Q. Mr. Boesky, did you understand as part of your agreement with the Government that you would have to give complete and truthful information and testimony at all times? Did you understand that?

A. Absolutely.

* * *

Q. Did you understand that to mean, Mr. Boesky, that you had to reveal to the Government every crime that you committed?

A. About which they may have inquired.

* * *

Q. Did you believe that if it didn't inquire about it, you didn't have to admit it?

A. We volunteered much information about which they did not inquire.

Q. Mr. Boesky, that is an answer to the question I didn't ask. The question I'm asking, did you believe, if they didn't inquire about it, you didn't have to admit it?

A. I do not remember my state of mind at the time, sir.

* * *

Q. Were you given advice at the time concerning the disposition of your assets in contemplation of cooperation with the Government?

A. My counsel is meticulous in advising me as to functioning in a totally appropriate manner, which I did.

* * *

Q. Well, did you dispose of assets or did you put assets in somebody else's name in contemplation of cooperating with the Government, Mr. Boesky?

A. I do not remember what I did in terms of financial affairs in 1986.

* * *

Personal Finances

Q. Let me ask you this. At the time you were sentenced, Mr. Boesky, were you nearly bankrupt?

A. Most probably correct, yes.

Q. Now I ask you, sir, bearing in mind that in the summer of 1986, according to your testimony, you were worth over $100 million but less than a billion. How were you virtually wiped out?

A. Well, I think you know that I paid a substantial fine, did I not, sir, to the United States Government?

Q. Was that every cent you had at the time?

A. No.

Q. How much did you have over and above $100 million?

A. I don't recall. I would have to see a financial statement, sir.

* * *

Q. Can you tell me now?

A. I don't round off to the nearest $100 million or $200 million. I would like to see a financial statement, sir.

* * *

Sources of Inside Information

Q. Did you tell the United States Government, Mr. Boesky, about every illegal insider trading transaction with Mr. Siegel? Yes or no?

A. I believe that they have requested me. . . .

Q. Yes or no, Mr. Boesky.

* * *

A. It's not a yes or no question, I believe. But the answer to your question really is that I think the answer is yes. But I would need documents to refresh my recollection.

* * *

Q. The only two people you've indicated that you received inside information from are Siegel and Levine, is that right?

A. That's not right.

* * *

Q. Who else did you receive inside information from?

A. Mr. Milken [Michael R. Milken] comes to mind.

* * *

Q. Mr. Milken from Drexel Burnham Lambert. Is that correct?

A. That's correct.

Q. Are you saying that the only three people that you've ever received inside information from are Mr. Siegel, Mr. Levine and Mr. Milken?

A. I have no recollection of anyone else, sir.

* * *

Business Ethics

A. H. ROBINS: DALKON SHIELD SETTLEMENT APPROVAL

U.S. District Court, Minnesota, 1984.

LORD, J.

Mr. Robins [President of A. H. Robins], Mr. Forrest [vice-president and general counsel], and Dr. Lunsford [vice-president for research and development]: After months of reflection, study, and cogitation—and no small amount of prayer—I have concluded that it is perfectly appropriate to make this statement, which will constitute my plea to you to seek new horizons in corporate consciousness and a new sense of personal responsibility for the activities of those who work under you in the name of the A. H. Robins Company.

It is not enough to say, "I did not know." "It was not me," "Look elsewhere." Time and again, each of you has used this kind of argument in refusing to acknowledge your re-

sponsibility and in pretending to the world that the chief officers and directors of your gigantic multinational corporation have no responsibility for its acts and omissions.

Today as you sit here attempting once more to extricate yourselves from the legal consequences of your acts, none of you has faced up to the fact that more than 9000 women claim they gave up part of their womanhood so that your company might prosper. It has been alleged that others gave their lives so you might prosper. And there stand behind them legions more who have been injured but who have not sought relief in the courts of this land.

I dread to think what would have been the consequences if your victims had been men rather than women—women, who seem, through some quirk of our society's mores, to be expected to suffer pain, shame, and humiliation.

If one poor young man were, without authority or consent, to inflict such damage upon óne woman, he would be jailed for a good portion of the rest of his life. Yet your company, without warning to women, invaded their bodies by the millions and caused them injuries by the thousands. And when the time came for these women to make their claims against your company, you attacked their characters. You inquired into their sexual practices and into the identity of their sex partners. You ruined families and reputations and careers in order to intimidate those who would raise their voices against you. You introduced issues that had no relationship to the fact that you had planted in the bodies of these women instruments of death, of mutilation, of disease.

Gentlemen, you state that your company has suffered enough, that the infliction of further punishment in the form of punitive damages would cause harm to your business, would punish innocent shareholders, and could conceivably depress your profits to the point where you could not survive as a competitor in this industry. When the poor and downtrodden commit crimes, they too plead that these are crimes of survival and that they should be excused for illegal acts that helped them escape desperate economic straits. On a few occasions when these excuses are made and remorseful defendants promise to mend their ways, courts will give heed to such pleas. But no court will heed the plea when the individual denies the wrongful nature of his deeds and gives no indication that he will mend his ways. Your company, in the face of overwhelming evidence, denies its guilt and continues it monstrous mischief.

Mr. Forrest, you have told me that you are working with members of the Congress of the United States to find a way of forgiving you from punitive damages that might otherwise be imposed. Yet the profits of your company continue to mount. Your last financial report boasts of new records for sales and earnings, with a profit of more than $58 million in 1983. And, insofar as this court has been able to determine, you three men and your company are still engaged in a course of wrongdoing. Until your company indicates that it is willing to cease and desist this deception and to seek out and advise the victims, your remonstrances to Congress and to the courts are indeed hollow and cynical. The company has not suffered, nor have you men personally. You are collectively being enriched by millions of dollars each year. There is no evidence that your company has suffered any penalty from these litigations. In fact, the evidence is to the contrary.

The case law suggests that the purpose of punitive damages is to make an award that will punish a defendant for his wrongdoing. Punishment has traditionally involved the principles of revenge, rehabilitation, and deterrence. There is no evidence I have been able to find in my review of these cases to indicate that any of these objectives has been accomplished.

Mr. Robins, Mr. Forrest, Dr. Lunsford: You have not been rehabilitated. Under your direction, your company has continued to allow women, tens of thousands of them, to wear this device—a deadly depth charge in their wombs, ready to explode at any time. Your attorney denies that tens of thousands of these devices are still in women's bodies. But

I submit to you that he has no more basis for denying the accusation than the plaintiffs have for stating it as truth. We simply do not know how many women are still wearing these devices because your company is not willing to find out. The only conceivable reasons that you have not recalled this product are that it would hurt your balance sheet and alert women who have already been harmed that you be liable for their injuries. You have taken the bottom line as your guiding beacon and the low road as your route. That is corporate irresponsibility at its meanest. Rehabilitation involves an admission of guilt, a certain contrition, an acknowledgment of wrongdoing, and a resolution to take a new course toward a better life. I find none of this in you or your corporation. Confession is good for the soul, gentlemen. Face up to your misdeeds. Acknowledge the personal responsibility you have for the activities of those who work under you. Rectify this evil situation. Warn the potential victims and recompense those who have already been harmed.

Mr. Robins, Mr. Forrest, Dr. Lunsford: I see little in the history of this case that would deter others. The policy of delay and obfuscation practiced by your lawyers in courts throughout this country has made it possible for you and your insurance company to put off the payment of these claims for such a long period that the interest you earned in the interim covers the cost of these cases. You, in essence, pay nothing out of your own pockets to settle these cases. What corporate officials could learn a lesson from this? The only lesson they might learn is that it pays to delay compensating victims and to intimidate, harass, and shame the injured parties.

Your company seeks to segment and fragment the litigation of these cases nationwide. The courts of this country are burdened with more than 3000 Dalkon Shield cases. The sheer number of claims and the dilatory tactics used by your company's attorneys clog court calendars and consume vast amounts of judicial and jury time. Your company settles those cases out of court in which it finds itself in an uncomfortable position, a handy device for avoiding any proceeding that would give continuity or cohesiveness to this nationwide problem. The decision as to which cases are brought to trial rests almost solely at the whim and discretion of the A. H. Robins Company. In order to guarantee that no plaintiff or group of plaintiffs mounts a sustained assault upon your system of evasion and avoidance, you have time after time demanded that, as the price of settling a case, able lawyers agree not to bring a Dalkon Shield case again and not to help less experienced lawyers with cases against your company.

Another of your callous legal tactics is to force women of little means to withstand the onslaughts of your well-financed attorneys. You target your worst tactics at the meek and the poor.

If this court had the authority, I would order your company to make an effort to locate each and every woman who still wears this device and recall your product. But this court does not. I must therefore resort to moral persuasion and a personal appeal to each of you. Mr. Robins, Mr. Forrest, and Dr. Lunsford: You are the people with the power to recall. You are the corporate conscience.

Please, in the name of humanity, lift your eyes above the bottom line. You, the men in charge, must surely have hearts and souls and consciences.

Please, gentlemen, give consideration to tracing down the victims and sparing them the agony that will surely be theirs.

Corporate Governance/Social Responsibility

A. P. SMITH MFG. CO. v. BARLOW

Supreme Court of New Jersey, 1953.
13 N.J. 145, 98 A.2d 581.

JACOBS, J.

The Chancery Division, in a well-reasoned opinion by Judge Stein, determined that a donation by the plaintiff The A. P. Smith Manufacturing Company to Princeton University was *intra vires*. * * *

The company was incorporated in 1896 and is engaged in the manufacture and sale of valves, fire hydrants and special equipment, mainly for water and gas industries. Its plant is located in East Orange and Bloomfield and it has approximately 300 employees. Over the years the company has contributed regularly to the local community chest and on occasions to Upsala College in East Orange and Newark University, now part of Rutgers, the State University. On July 24, 1951 the board of directors adopted a resolution which set forth that it was in the corporation's best interests to join with others in the 1951 Annual Giving to Princeton University, and appropriated the sum of $1,500 to be transferred by the corporation's treasurer to the university as a contribution towards its maintenance. When this action was questioned by stockholders the corporation instituted a declaratory judgment action in the Chancery Division and trial was had in due course.

Mr. Hubert F. O'Brien, the president of the company, testified that he considered the contribution to be a sound investment, that the public expects corporations to aid philanthropic and benevolent institutions, that they obtain good will in the community by so doing, and that their charitable donations create favorable environment for their business operations. In addition, he expressed the thought that in contributing to liberal arts institutions, corporations were furthering their self-interest in assuring the free flow of properly trained personnel for administrative and other corporate employment. Mr. Frank W. Abrams, chairman of the board of the Standard Oil Company of New Jersey, testified that corporations are expected to acknowledge their public responsibilities in support of the essential elements of our free enterprise system. He indicated that is was not "good business" to disappoint "this reasonable and justified public expectation," nor was it good business for corporations "to take substantial benefits from their membership in the economic community while avoiding the normally accepted obligations of citizenship in the social community." Mr. Irving S. Olds, former chairman of the board of the United States Steel Corporation, pointed out that corporations have a self-interest in the maintenance of liberal education as the bulwark of good government. He stated that "Capitalism and free enterprise owe their survival in no small degree to the existence of our private, independent universities" and that if American business does not aid in their maintenance it is not "properly protecting the long-range interest of its stockholders, its employees and its customers." Similarly, Dr. Harold W. Dodds, President of Princeton University, suggested that if private institutions of higher learning were replaced by governmental institutions our society would be vastly different and private enterprise in other fields would fade out rather promptly. Further on he stated that "democratic society will not long endure if it does not nourish within itself strong centers of non-governmental fountains of knowledge, opinions of all sorts not governmentally or politically originated. If the time comes when all these centers are absorbed into government, then freedom as we know it, I submit, is at an end."

The objecting stockholders have not disputed any of the foregoing testimony nor the showing of great need by Princeton and other private institutions of higher learning and the important public service being rendered by them for democratic government and industry alike. Similarly, they have acknowledged that for over two decades there has been state legislation on our books which expresses a strong public policy in favor of corporate contributions such as that being questioned by them. Nevertheless, they have taken the position that the plaintiff's certificate of incorporation does not expressly authorize the contribution and under common-law principles the company does not possess any implied or incidental power to make it   *   *   *

In his discussion of the early history of business corporations Professor Williston refers to a 1702 publication where the author stated flatly that "The general intent and end of all civil incorporations is for better government." And he points out that the early corporate charters, particularly their recitals, furnish additional support for the notion that the corporate object was the public one of managing and ordering the trade as well as the private one of profit for the members.

*   *   *

When the wealth of the nation was primarily in the hands of individuals they discharged their responsibilities as citizens by donating freely for charitable purposes. With the transfer of most of the wealth to corporate hands and the imposition of heavy burdens of individual taxation, they have been unable to keep pace with increased philanthropic needs. They have therefore, with justification, turned to corporations to assume the modern obligations of good citizenship in the same manner as humans do. Congress and state legislatures have enacted laws which encourage corporate contributions, and much has recently been written to indicate the crying need and adequate legal basis therefor. . . . In actual practice corporate giving has correspondingly increased. Thus, it is estimated that annual corporate contributions throughout the nation aggregate over 300 million dollars with over 60 million dollars thereof going to universities and other educational institutions. Similarly, it is estimated that local community chests receive well over 40% of all their contributions from corporations; these contributions and those made by corporations to the American Red Cross, to Boy Scouts and Girl Scouts, to 4-H Clubs and similar organizations have almost invariably been unquestioned.

During the first world war corporations loaned their personnel and contributed substantial corporate funds in order to insure survival; during the depression of the '30s they made contributions to alleviate the desperate hardships of the millions of unemployed; and during the second world war they again contributed to insure survival. They now recognize that we are faced with other, though nonetheless vicious, threats from abroad which must be withstood without impairing the vigor of our democratic institutions at home and that otherwise victory will be pyrrhic indeed. More and more they have come to recognize that their salvation rests upon sound economic and social environment which in turn rests in no insignificant part upon free and vigorous nongovernmental institutions of learning. It seems to us that just as the conditions prevailing when corporations were originally created required that they serve public as well as private interests, modern conditions require that corporations acknowledge and discharge social as well as private responsibilities as members of the communities within which they operate. Within this broad concept there is no difficulty in sustaining, as incidental to their proper objects and in aid of the public welfare, the power of corporations to contribute corporate funds within reasonable limits in support of academic institutions. But even if we confine ourselves to the terms of the common-law rule in its application to current conditions, such expenditures may likewise readily be justified as being for the benefit of the corporation; indeed, if need be the matter may be viewed strictly in terms of actual survival of the corporation in a free enterprise system. The genius of our common law has been its capacity for growth and its adaptability to the needs of the times. Generally courts have accomplished the desired result indirectly through the molding of old forms. Occasionally they have done it directly through frank rejection of the old and recognition of the new. But whichever path the common law has taken it has not been found wanting as the proper tool for the advancement of the general good. [Citations.]

* * *

In the light of all of the foregoing we have no hesitancy in sustaining the validity of the donation by the plaintiff. There is no suggestion that it was made indiscriminately or to a pet charity of the corporate directors in furtherance of personal rather than corporate

ends. On the contrary, it was made to a preeminent institution of higher learning, was modest in amount and well within the limitations imposed by the statutory enactments, and was voluntarily made in the reasonable belief that it would aid the public welfare and advance the interests of the plaintiff as a private corporation and as part of the community in which it operates. We find that it was a lawful exercise of the corporation's implied and incidental powers under common-law principles and that it came within the express authority of the pertinent state legislation. As has been indicated, there is now widespread belief throughout the nation that free and vigorous non-governmental institutions of learning are vital to our democracy and the system of free enterprise and that withdrawal of corporate authority to make such contributions within reasonable limits would seriously threaten their continuance. Corporations have come to recognize this and with their enlightenment have sought in varying measures, as has the plaintiff by its contribution, to insure and strengthen the society which gives them existence and the means of aiding themselves and their fellow citizens. Clearly then, the appellants, as individual stockholders whose private interests rest entirely upon the well-being of the plaintiff corporation, ought not be permitted to close their eyes to present-day realities and thwart the long-visioned corporate action in recognizing and voluntarily discharging its high obligations as a constituent of our modern social structure.

The judgment entered in the Chancery Division is in all respects

Affirmed.

QUESTIONS

1. Describe the differences between law and ethics.

2. List and contrast the various ethical theories.

3. Describe cost-benefit analysis and explain when it should be used and when it should be avoided.

4. Explain Kohlberg's stages of moral development.

5. Explain the ethical responsibilities of business.

PROBLEMS

1. You have an employee who has a chemical imbalance in the brain that causes her to be severely unstable. The medication that is available to deal with this schizophrenic condition is extremely powerful and decreases the taker's life span by one to two years for every year that the user takes it. You know that her doctors and family believe that it is in her best interest to take the medication. What course of action should you follow?

2. You have an employee who is from another country and is very shy. After a period of time, you notice that the quality of her performance is deteriorating rapidly. You find an appropriate time to speak with her and determine that she is extremely distraught. She informs you that her family has arranged a marriage for her and that she refuses to obey their contract. She further informs you that she is contemplating suicide. Two weeks later, after continued poor performance, you determine that she is on the verge of a nervous breakdown, and once again she informs you that she is going to commit suicide. What should you do? Consider further that you can petition a court to have her involuntarily committed to a mental hospital. You know, however, that such a commitment would be considered an extreme insult by her family and they might seek retribution. Does this alter your decision?

3. You receive a telephone call from a company you never do business with requesting a reference on an employee, Mary Sunshine. You believe Mary performs in a generally incompetent manner and would be delighted to see her take another job. You give her a glowing reference. Is this right? Explain.

4. You have just received a report suggesting that a chemical your company uses in its manufacturing process is very dangerous. You have not read the report, but you are generally aware of its contents. You believe that the chemical can be replaced fairly easily, but that if word gets out panic may set in among employees and community members. A reporter asks if you have seen the report, and you say no. Is your behavior right or wrong? Explain.

5. Joe Jones, your neighbor and friend, and you bought lottery tickets at the corner drug store. While watching the lottery drawing on TV with you that night, Joe leaped from the couch, waved his lottery ticket, and shouted, "I've got the winning number!" Suddenly, he clutched his chest, keeled over, and died on the spot. You are the only living person who knows that Joe, not you, bought the winning ticket. If you substitute his ticket for yours, no one will know of the switch and you will be $10 million richer. Joe's only living relative is a rich aunt whom he despised. Will you switch his ticket for yours? Explain.

6. Omega, Inc., a publicly held corporation, has assets of $100 million and annual earnings in the range of $13–15 million. Omega owns three aluminum plants, which are profitable, and one plastics plant, which is losing $4 million a year. The plastics plant shows no sign of ever becoming profitable, because of its very high operating costs, and there is no evidence that the plant and the underlying real estate will increase in value. Omega decides to sell the plastics plant. The only bidder for the plant is Gold, who intends to use the plant for a new purpose, introduce automation, and replace all existing employees. Would it be ethical for Omega to turn down Gold's bid and keep the plastics plant operating indefinitely, for the purpose of preserving the employees' jobs? Explain.

7. You are the sales manager of a two year old electronics firm. At times, the firm has seemed on the brink of failure, but recently has begun to be profitable. In large part, the profitability is due to the aggressive and talented sales force you have recruited. Two months ago, you hired Alice North, an honors graduate from the State University who decided that she was tired of the Research Department and wanted to try sales.

Almost immediately after you sent Alice out for training with Brad West, your best salesman, he began reporting to you an unexpected turn of events. According to Brad, "Alice is terrific: she's confident, smooth and persistent. Unfortunately, a lot of our buyers are good old boys, who just aren't comfortable around young, bright women. Just last week, Hiram Jones, one of our biggest customers, told me that he simply won't continue to do business with 'young chicks' who think they invented the world. It's not that Alice is a know-it-all. She's not. It's just that these guys like to booze it up a bit, tell some off-color jokes and then get down to business. Alice doesn't drink and, although she never objects to the jokes, it's clear she thinks they're offensive." Brad felt that several potential deals had fallen through "because the mood just wasn't right with Alice there." Brad added, "I don't like a lot of these guys' styles myself, but I go along to make the sales. I just don't think Alice is going to make it."

When you call Alice in to discuss the situation, she concedes the accuracy of Brad's report, but indicates that she's not to blame and insists that she be kept on the job. You feel committed to equal opportunity, but don't want to jeopardize your company's ability to survive. What should you do?

PART TWO

Contracts

Chapter 8

INTRODUCTION TO CONTRACTS

Development of the Law of Contracts
Definition of a Contract
Essentials of a Contract
Classification of Contracts
Promissory Estoppel
Quasi Contracts

IT is impossible to over-estimate the importance of contracts in the field of business. Every business, whether large or small, must enter into contracts with its employees, its suppliers, and its customers in order to conduct its business operations. Contract law is, therefore, an important subject for the business manager. Contract law is also basic to other fields of law treated in other parts of this book, such as agency, partnerships, corporations, sales of personal property, commercial paper, and secured transactions.

Even the most common transaction may involve a multitude of contracts. In a typical contract for the sale of land, the seller promises to transfer title to the land, and the buyer promises to pay an agreed-upon purchase price. In addition, the seller may promise to pay certain taxes or assessments; the buyer may promise to assume a mortgage on the property or may promise to pay the purchase price to a creditor of the seller. A portion of the purchase price may consist of the buyer's check, which is a contract containing the buyer's written order to his bank to pay a sum certain in money to the seller. If the parties are represented by counsel, they very likely have contracts with their attorneys. If the seller deposits the proceeds of the sale in a bank, he enters into a contract with the bank. If the buyer leases the property, he enters into a contract with the tenant. When one of the parties leaves his car in a parking lot to attend to any of these matters, he assumes a contractual relationship with the proprietor of the lot. In short, nearly every business transaction is based upon contract and the expectations created by the agreed-upon promises. It is, therefore, essential to know the legal requirements for making a promise or set of promises binding.

DEVELOPMENT OF THE LAW OF CONTRACTS

Law arises from social necessity. This is clearly true of the law of contracts. The vast and complicated institution of business can be conducted efficiently and successfully only upon the certainty of fulfillment of promises. Business must have assurances of supplies of raw materials or manufactured goods, as well as of labor, management, capital, insurance, and so forth. Common experience has shown that promises based solely on personal honesty or integrity will not suffice. Such promises do not have the reliability essential to business. Hence the development of the law of contracts, which is the law of enforceable promises.

Contract law, like law as a whole, is not static. It has undergone—and is still undergoing—enormous changes. In the nineteenth century virtually absolute autonomy in forming contracts was the rule. Contract liability was imposed only where the parties strictly complied with the required formalities. The same principle also dictated that once a contract was formed it should be enforced according to its terms and neither party should be lightly excused from performance.

During the twentieth century, contract law has experienced tremendous changes. As will be discussed in the next ten chapters, many of the formalities of contract formation have been relaxed. Today contractual obligations are usually recognized whenever the parties manifest an intent to be bound. In addition, an increasing number of promises are now enforced in certain circumstances even though they do not comply strictly with the basic requirements of a contract. While in the past contract liability was absolute and there were few, if any, escapes from liability once assumed, presently the law allows a party to be excused from contractual duties where fraud, duress, undue influence, mistake, unconscionability, or impossibility is present. Last century's narrow view of contract damages has been expanded to grant equitable remedies and restitution as remedies for breach of contract. The older doctrine of privity of contract which sharply restricted which parties could enforce contracts rights, has given way to the current view that permits intended third party beneficiaries to sue in their own right.

In brief, the twentieth century has left its mark on contract law by limiting the absolute freedom of contract and, at the same time, by relaxing the requirements of contract formation. Accordingly, it is accurate to say that now it is considerably easier to get into a contract and correspondingly less difficult to get out of one.

Common Law

Contracts are primarily governed by State common law. An orderly presentation of this law is found in the Restatements of the Law of Contracts. The first Restatement was adopted and promulgated on May 6, 1932, by the American Law Institute. On May 17, 1979, the institute adopted and promulgated a revised edition of the Restatement—the Restatement, Second, Contracts—which will be referred to as the Restatement. Provisions of the Restatement cited in the text are included in Appendix B of this book. For more than fifty years the Restatements have been regarded as a valuable authoritative reference work and have been extensively relied upon and quoted in reported judicial opinions.

The Uniform Commercial Code

The sale of personal property forms a substantial portion of commercial activity. Article 2 of the Uniform Commercial Code (the Code or U.C.C.) governs sales in all States except Louisiana. (The U.C.C. is set forth in Appendix C of this text.) A **sale** is a contract involving the transfer of title to goods from a seller to a buyer for a price. Section 2–106. The Code essentially defines goods as movable personal property. Section 2–105(1). **Personal property** is any type of property other than an interest in real property (land). For example, the purchase of a television set, automobile, or textbook is considered a sale of goods. All such transactions are governed by Article 2 of the Code, but, where general contract law has not been specifically modified by the Code, the common law of contracts continues to apply. Section 1–103. In other words, the law of sales is a specialized part of the general law of contracts, and the law of contracts governs unless specifically displaced by the Code (see Figure 8–1).

Prior to the U.C.C., sales of personal property were governed by State laws, which varied from State to State. Since such sales are an important part of commercial activity, and since much of that activity takes place across State lines, the diversity of laws created difficulties. The Code has been successful in bringing considerable uniformity to the commercial laws of forty-nine of the fifty States.

See Colorado Carpet Installation, Inc. v. Palermo.

Types of Contracts outside the Code

General contract law governs all contracts outside the scope of the Code. Such contracts play a significant role in commercial activities. For example, the Code does *not* apply to employment contracts, service contracts, insurance contracts, contracts involving **real property** (land and anything attached to it, including buildings), and contracts for the sale of intangibles such as patents and copyrights. These transactions continue to be governed by general contract law. (See Figure 8–1).

DEFINITION OF A CONTRACT

The true nature of a contract lies in the fact that it is not a physical thing, but a relationship existing between the parties to the contract. The elements of this relationship are the mutual rights and duties of the parties. A contract is essentially a certain type of agreement or promise or set of promises. And contractual agreements and promises, while not physical realities, are nevertheless very important legal realities.

A **contract** is a set of promises that the courts will enforce. Section 1 of the Restatement more precisely defines a contract as "a promise or a set of promises for the breach of which the law gives a remedy, or the performance of which the law in some way recognizes as a duty." The Restatement provides further insight by defining a **promise** as follows: "A promise is a manifestation of the intention to act or refrain from acting in a specified manner." Restatement, Section 2.

Those promises that meet *all* of the essential requirements of a binding contract are contractual and will be enforced. All other promises are *not* contractual and usually no legal remedy is available for a **breach** (a failure to perform properly) of these promises. Thus, a promise may be contractual and therefore binding or noncontractual. In other words, all contracts are promises, but not all promises are contracts.

For example, if Andy promises to pay Brenda $5,000 in return for Brenda's promise to burn down Carl's factory, neither promise is contractual and neither is binding because

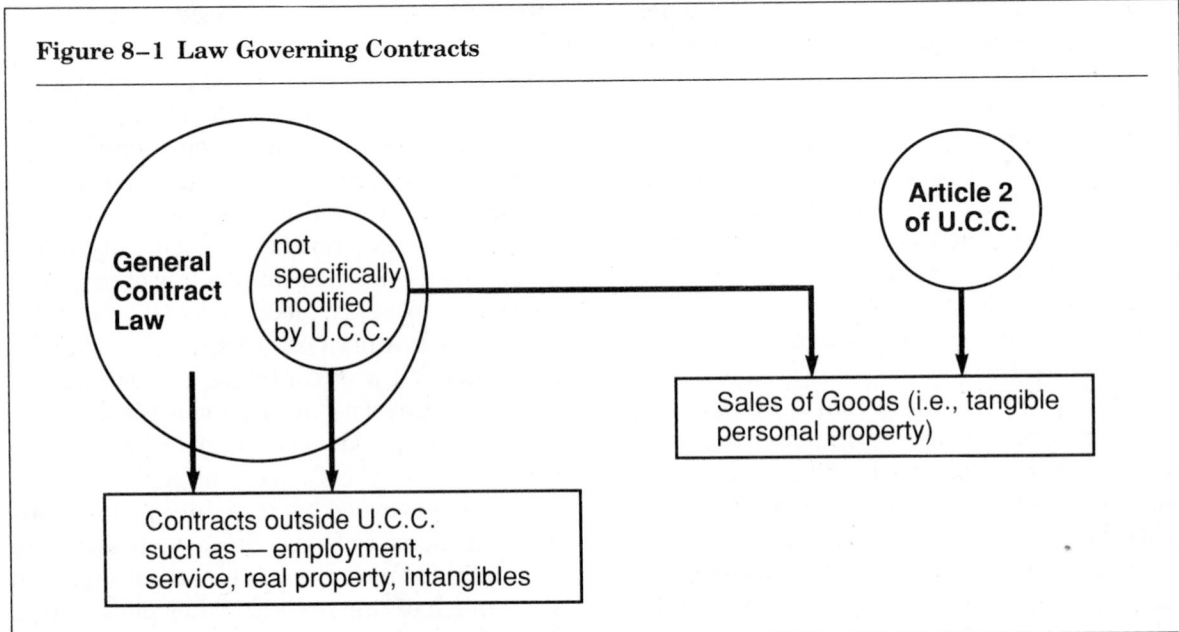

Figure 8–1 Law Governing Contracts

General Contract Law — not specifically modified by U.C.C.

Article 2 of U.C.C.

Contracts outside U.C.C. such as — employment, service, real property, intangibles

Sales of Goods (i.e., tangible personal property)

each is for an illegal purpose. As a result, the law will not provide a remedy to Brenda for Andy's failure to fulfill his promise. The law will also not provide a remedy to Andy for Brenda's failure to perform her promise.

See Steinberg v. Chicago Medical School for a discussion of the definition of a contract.

ESSENTIALS OF A CONTRACT

The four basic requirements of a contract are as follows:

1. **Mutual Assent.** The parties to a contract must manifest by words or conduct that they have agreed to enter into a contract. The usual way parties show mutual assent is by offer and acceptance.

2. **Consideration.** Each party to a contract must intentionally exchange something of value as an inducement to the other party to make a return exchange.

3. **Legality of Object.** The purpose of a contract must not be criminal, tortious, or otherwise against public policy.

4. **Capacity.** The parties to a contract must have contractual capacity. Certain persons have no legal capacity to contract (adjudicated incompetents), while others have limited capacity to contract (minors, incompetent persons, and intoxicated persons). All others have full contractual capacity. *See Steinberg v. Chicago Medical School.*

In addition, in a limited number of instances, a contract must be in writing to be enforceable, although in most cases an oral contract is binding and enforceable. If all of these essentials are present, the promise is contractual and legally binding. If any of them is lacking, the promise is noncontractual. These essentials will be separately considered in succeeding chapters.

CLASSIFICATION OF CONTRACTS

Contracts can be classified from various standpoints such as their method of formation, their content, and their legal effect. The standard classifications are: (1) express or implied contracts; (2) unilateral or bilateral contracts; (3) valid, void, voidable, or unenforceable contracts; (4) executed or executory contracts; and (5) formal or informal contracts. These classifications are not mutually exclusive. For example, a contract may be express, bilateral, valid, executory, and informal.

Express and Implied Contracts

Parties to a contract may indicate their assent either by express language or by conduct which implies such willingness. Thus, a contract may be (1) entirely oral; (2) partly oral and partly written; (3) entirely written; (4) partly oral or written and partly implied from the conduct of the parties; and (5) wholly implied from the conduct of the parties. The first three are known as express contracts, and the last two as implied contracts. Both express and implied contracts are genuine contracts, equally enforceable. The difference between them is merely the manner in which assent is manifested. *See Richardson v. J.C. Flood Co.*

An **express contract** is therefore one in which the agreement of the parties has been manifested by oral or written language, or both.

An **implied contract** is one which is inferred from the parties' conduct and not from the expression of words. Implied contracts are also called implied in fact contracts. Thus, if Elizabeth orders and receives a meal in Bill's restaurant, a promise is implied on Elizabeth's part to pay Bill the price stated in the menu, or, if none is stated, Bill's customary price. Likewise, when a person boards a bus as a passenger, a wholly implied contract is formed, by which the passenger undertakes to pay the customary fare, and the bus company undertakes to provide the passenger transportation.

Unilateral and Bilateral Contracts

In the typical contractual transaction, each party makes at least one promise. For example, Ali says to Ben, "If you promise to mow my lawn, I will pay you ten dollars," and Ben agrees to mow Ali's lawn. Ali and Ben have made mutual promises, each undertaking to do something in exchange for the promise of the other. When a contract comes into existence by the exchange of promises, each is under a duty to the other. This kind of contract is called a **bilateral contract,** because each party is both a *promisor* (a person making a promise) and a *promisee* (the person to whom a promise is made).

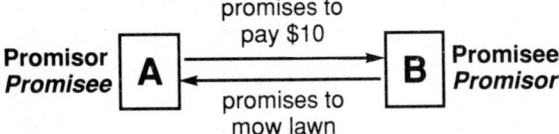

But suppose that only one of the parties makes a promise. Ali says to Ben, "If you will mow my lawn, I will pay you ten dollars." A contract will be formed when Ben has finished mowing the lawn and not before. At that time Ali becomes contractually obligated to pay ten dollars to Ben. Ali's offer was in exchange for Ben's act of mowing the lawn, and not for the promise of Ben to mow it. Ben was under no duty to mow the lawn. This is a **unilateral contract** because only *one* of the parties made a promise.

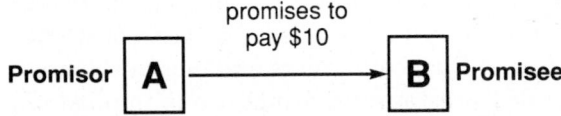

Thus, a bilateral contract results from the exchange of a promise for a return promise. A unilateral contract results from the exchange of a promise either for an act or for a forbearance (refraining) from acting. Where it is not clear whether a unilateral or bilateral contract has been formed, the courts presume that the parties intended a bilateral contract. Thus, in the above example, if Ali says to Ben, "I will pay you ten dollars, if you will mow my lawn," and Ben replies, "O.K., I will mow your lawn," a bilateral contract is formed.

Valid, Void, Voidable, and Unenforceable Contracts

By definition a **valid contract** is one that meets all of the requirements of a binding contract. It is an enforceable promise or agreement.

A **void contract** is an agreement that does not meet all of the requirements of a binding contract. Thus, it is no contract at all; it is merely a promise or agreement which has no legal effect. An example of a void agreement is an agreement entered into by an *adjudicated* (judicially declared) incompetent.

A voidable contract, on the other hand, is not wholly lacking in legal effect. A **voidable contract** is a contract, but because of the manner in which it was formed or a lack of capacity of a party to it, the law permits one or more of the parties to avoid the legal duties created by the contract. Restatement, Section 7. If the contract is avoided, both of the parties are relieved of their legal duties under the agreement. For instance, through intentional misrepresentation of a material fact (*fraud*), Thomas induces Regina to enter into a contract. Regina may, upon discovery of the fraud, notify Thomas that by reason of the misrepresentation she will not perform her promise, and the law will support Regina. The contract induced by fraud is not void, but is voidable at the election of Regina, the defrauded party. Thomas, the fraudulent party, has no such election. If Regina elects to avoid the contract, Thomas will be released from his promise under the agreement although he may be liable for damages under tort law for fraud.

Although a contract may be neither void nor voidable, it may be unenforceable. An **unenforceable contract** is one for the breach of which the law does not provide a remedy. Restatement, Section 8. For example, a contract may be unenforceable because of a failure to satisfy the requirements of the Statute of Frauds, which requires certain kinds of contracts to be in writing in order to be enforceable. Also, the right to bring a lawsuit for breach of contract may be barred by running of the time within which such a suit may be filed, as provided in the Statute of Limitations. After that period of time has run, the contract is referred to as unenforceable, rather than void or voidable.

Executed and Executory Contracts

These terms pertain to the state of performance of a contract. If a contract has been fully performed by all of the parties, it is an **executed contract.** Strictly, an executed contract is no contract in the present tense, as all duties under it have been performed, but it is useful to have a term for the completed contract. (The word "executed" is also used to mean signed, as in to execute or sign a certain document.)

The term **executory** contract means unperformed and applies to situations where there are one or more unperformed promises by any party to the contract, or the contract is wholly unperformed by one or more of the parties. Thus, David and Carla make a contract under which David is to sell and deliver certain goods to Carla in ten days and Carla is to pay the agreed price in thirty days. Prior to the delivery of the goods by David on the tenth day, the contract is wholly executory. Upon David's delivery of the goods to Carla, the contract is executed as to David and executory as to Carla. When Carla duly pays for the goods the contract is wholly executed, and thereby completely fulfilled.

Formal and Informal Contracts

A **formal contract** depends upon a particular form, or mode of expression, for its legal existence. For example, at common law a promise under seal, a particular symbol which serves to authenticate an instrument, is enforceable without anything more. Another formal contract is a negotiable instrument, such as a check, which has certain legal attributes resulting solely from the special form in which it is made. A letter of credit (a promise to honor drafts or other demands for payment) is also a formal contract. Recogni-

zances, formal acknowledgments of indebtedness made in court, are another example of formal contracts. All other contracts, whether oral or written, are simple or **informal contracts** since they do not depend upon formality for their legal validity.

PROMISSORY ESTOPPEL

As a general rule promises are not enforceable if they do not meet all the requirements of a contract. Nevertheless, in certain circumstances noncontractual promises are enforced under the doctrine of promissory estoppel in order to avoid injustice. A noncontractual promise is enforceable when it is made under circumstances that should lead the promisor reasonably to expect that the promisee will be induced by the promise to take definite and substantial action or forbearance in reliance on the promise, and the promisee does take such action or forbearance. Section 90 of the Restatement provides:

A promise which the promisor should reasonably expect to induce action or forbearance on the part of the promisee or a third person and which does induce such action or forbearance is binding if injustice can be avoided only by enforcement of the promise. The remedy granted for breach may be limited as justice requires.

For example, Gordon promises Constance not to foreclose on a mortgage Gordon owns on Constance's land for a period of six months. Constance then expends $100,000 on a building constructed on the land. Gordon's promise not to foreclose is binding on Gordon under the doctrine of promissory estoppel.

QUASI CONTRACTS

In addition to implied in fact contracts, there are implied in law contracts or quasi contracts which were not included in the foregoing classification of contracts for the reason that a quasi (meaning "as if") contract is not a contract at all.

A quasi contract is *not* a contract because it is based upon neither an express nor an implied promise. A **contract implied in law** or **quasi contract** is an obligation imposed by law to avoid injustice. For example, Anna by mistake delivers to Robert a plain, unaddressed envelope containing $100 intended for Claudia. Robert is under no contractual obligation to return it. However, Anna is permitted to recover the $100 from Robert. The law imposes a quasi-contractual obligation upon Robert in order to prevent his unjust enrichment at the expense of Anna. The elements of such a recovery are: (1) a benefit conferred upon the defendant (Robert) by the plaintiff (Anna); (2) an appreciation or knowledge by the defendant (Robert) of the benefit; and (3) acceptance or retention by the defendant (Robert) of the benefit under circumstances making it inequitable for the defendant (Robert) to retain the benefit without payment of its value.

One court has summarized the doctrine of quasi contract in the following manner:

Quasi contracts are not contracts at all, although they give rise to obligations more akin to those stemming from contract than from tort. The contract is a mere fiction, a form imposed in order to adapt the case to a given remedy. . . . Briefly stated, a quasi-contractual obligation is one imposed by law where there has been no agreement or expression of assent, by word or act, on the part of either party involved. The law creates it, regardless of the intention of the parties, to assure a just and equitable result. *Bradkin v. Leverton,* 26 N.Y.2d 192, 309 N.Y.S.2d 192, 257 N.E.2d 643 (1970).

Not infrequently, quasi contracts are used to provide a remedy when the parties enter into a void contract, an unenforceable contract, or a voidable contract that is avoided. In such a case, the law of quasi contracts will determine what recovery is permitted for any performance rendered by the parties under the invalid, unenforceable, or invalidated agreement. *See also Nursing Care Services, Inc. v. Dobos.*

CASES

UCC: Sale of Goods

COLORADO CARPET INSTALLATION, INC. v. PALERMO

Supreme Court of Colorado, 1983.
668 F.2d 1384.

QUINN, J.

In July 1980 Colorado Carpet Installation, Inc., doing business as Sierra Range Carpets, Inc. (Colorado Carpet), commenced an action in the District Court of Adams County against Fred and Zuma Palermo for breach of contract. The claim was based on an alleged oral agreement in which the Palermos agreed to pay $4,775.75 to Colorado Carpet for the purchase and installation of carpeting, other flooring materials, and bathroom tile for the Palermo home in Thornton, Colorado. The Palermos in their answer denied the existence of a contract and affirmatively asserted that the statute of frauds, [UCC] § 2–201(1), rendered any such agreement unenforceable.

The controversy was tried to the court and arose as follows. Colorado Carpet is a Colorado corporation engaged in the business of selling and installing carpeting, tile and other flooring materials. In April 1980, Jack Duran, the president of Colorado Carpet, began negotiations with the Palermos for the sale and installation of carpeting, carpet padding, tile and vinyl floor covering in the downstairs and upstairs areas of their home. Colorado Carpet did not maintain an actual retail store or warehouse for these materials, but arranged to purchase them from other distributors. In the course of his negotiations with the Palermos, Duran delivered carpet samples to the Palermo home, measured the home, and assisted Mrs. Palermo in locating at local retail outlets the type and brand of flooring materials that she wanted. Further negotiations ensued, including a written proposal from Duran.

This written proposal, which referred to Colorado Carpet as "the seller" and to the

Palermos as "the customer," stated that Colorado Carpet offered for the Palermos' acceptance the following items: a total of 195 square yards of Seduction and Amaretto carpeting, along with padding, at $15.95 per square yard, for a total price of $3110.45; 48 square yards of kitchen carpeting at $8.50 per square yard, for a total price of $399.50; 55 square yards of deck carpeting at $7.50 per square yard, for a total price of $412.50; approximately 220 square feet of ceramic tile at $3.50 per square foot, for a total price of $770; and 9 square yards of vinyl floor covering at $9.50 per square yard, for a total price of $85.50. The proposal expressly included all labor. According to Duran, the source of Colorado Carpet's profit from such a transaction would be the markup on the sale of the materials and not their installation, the latter being provided at cost. He estimated the labor cost at $2.00 per square yard for installing the upstairs, downstairs and kitchen carpeting, and $1.50 per square foot for installing the tile.

Although the Palermos never made a written acceptance of Colorado Carpet's proposal, Duran testified that Mrs. Palermo orally accepted the proposal on or about April 25, 1980, shortly after he submitted it to her. Mrs. Palermo, in contrast, denied accepting the written proposal. It was her testimony that neither she nor her husband ever agreed to purchase any carpeting from Colorado Carpet and that she had contacted Duran only about a tiling job for the upstairs and downstairs bathrooms.

On April 30 and May 1, 1980, Colorado Carpet placed orders with Georgia and California manufacturers for the Seduction (downstairs) and the Amaretto (upstairs) carpeting. These orders called for both carpets to be cut into segments measuring 12 feet by 73 feet in order to permit effective installation in the upstairs and downstairs sections of the Palermo home. The orders were filled in due course, and the carpets were eventually delivered to a Denver warehouse. Colorado Carpet deferred ordering the carpet padding and kitchen carpet at this time because these were stock items and could be purchased immediately before the installation was to commence.

Colorado Carpet purchased and delivered the ceramic tile to the Palermo home for eventual installation in the upstairs and downstairs bathrooms. Mrs. Palermo, however, had a disagreement with Colorado Carpet's tile man over some repair work in connection with the tile installation and arranged with some other contractor to supply and install other tile. Duran, on behalf of Colorado Carpet, attempted unsuccessfully to renegotiate with the Palermos but to no avail. Colorado Carpet removed its tile from the home, returned half of it to the supplier for a refund and sold the other half. It also shipped the Seduction carpeting back to the California manufacturer in exchange for some credit and was able to sell the Amaretto carpeting to a local purchaser.

The trial court found that Colorado Carpet's proposal for the sale and installation of the carpeting and other materials had been orally accepted by the Palermos, thereby resulting in a contract, and determined that the contract was enforceable for two reasons: first, the agreement constituted a service contract for the performance of labor, rather than a contract for the sale of goods, and thus was not subject to the "writing" requirement of the statute of frauds section of the Uniform Commercial Code, § 2–201(1), and second, even if the entire agreement was construed as a contract for the sale of goods, that part of the agreement relating to the purchase and installation of carpeting fell within the "specially manufactured goods" exception to the statute of frauds, [UCC] § 2–201(3) (a), and thus was enforceable on that basis. The court awarded damages to Colorado Carpet in the amount of $1,356.50, based upon lost profits, labor, and storage and shipping costs in connection with all the carpeting and padding ordered under the contract, not just the upstairs and downstairs carpeting. The court of appeals reversed the judgment, reasoning that although the agreement was a contract for the sale of goods, it did not satisfy the "specially manufactured goods" exception to the statute of frauds. We granted certiorari to consider whether the oral agreement in question constituted a contract for the sale of goods within the meaning of § 2–201(1) of the Uniform Commercial Code, and, if so, whether it qualified for the "specially manufactured goods" exception of [UCC] § 2–201(3) (a).

We first address the court of appeals' determination that the contract was one for the sale of goods, rather than for the performance of labor or services. We conclude that the agreement in question involved a contract for the sale of goods as contemplated by [UCC] Section 2–201(1).

This section prohibits the enforcement of contracts "for the sale of goods for the price of $500 or more . . . unless there is some writing sufficient to indicate that a contract for sale has been made between the parties and signed by the party against whom enforcement is sought. . . ." By its terms, the statute applies only to contracts for the sale of goods, and not to contracts for labor or services. [Citations.] The Uniform Commercial Code defines "goods" to mean " all things (including specially manufactured goods) which are movable at the time of identification to the contract for sale other than the money in which the price is to be paid, investment securities . . . and things in action." [UCC] Section 2–105(1). [Citation.] *   *   *

In this case the subject of the contract involved "goods" because the carpeting and other materials were movable at the time that Colorado Carpet procured them for installation pursuant to the agreement. Since the agreement contemplated that title to the carpeting and other materials would pass to the Palermos, it constituted a "contract for sale." The scope of the contract, however, included not only the sale of goods but also the performance of labor or service. Thus, we must determine whether such a mixed contract qualified as a contract for the sale of goods or, instead, constituted a contract for labor or service outside the scope of [UCC] Section 2–201(1).

The performance of some labor or service frequently plays a role in sales transactions. "Goods," however, are not the less "goods" merely because labor or service may be essential to their ultimate use by the purchaser. The mere furnishing of some labor or service, in our view, should not determine the ultimate character of a contract for purposes of . . . the Uniform Commercial Code. Rather, the controlling criterion should be the primary purpose of the contract—that is, whether the circumstances underlying the formation of the agreement and the performance reasonably expected of the parties demonstrates the primary purpose of the contract as the sale of goods or, in contrast, the sale of labor or service.

*   *   *

This "primary purpose" test, we believe, is designed to promote one of the expressed statutory policies of the Uniform Commercial Code—"[t]o simplify, clarify, and modernize the law governing commercial transactions." [Citation.] Useful factors to consider in determining whether "goods" or "service" predominates include the following: the contractual language used by the parties [citations]; whether the agreement involves one overall price that includes both goods and labor or, instead, calls for separate and discrete billings for goods on the one hand and labor on the other [citations]; the ratio that the cost of goods bears to the overall contract price [citations]; and the nature and reasonableness of the purchaser's contractual expectations of acquiring a property interest in goods.*   *   *

Considering the contract under these guidelines, we are satisfied that, as a matter of law, its primary purpose was the sale of goods and not the sale of labor or service. The language in Colorado Carpet's proposal referred to the parties as "seller" and "customer." In addition, the agreement called for an overall contract price that included both the cost of goods and labor, and, as the trial evidence established, the charge for labor was slight in relation to the total contractual price. Finally, the carpeting and other materials were movable when Colorado Carpet procured them for the purpose of selling them to the Palermos.

*   *   *

The judgment of the court of appeals is affirmed.

Definition and Essentials of a Contract

STEINBERG v. CHICAGO MEDICAL SCHOOL

Illinois Court of Appeals, 1976.
41 Ill.App.3d 804, 354 N.E.2d 586.

DEMPSEY, J.

In December 1973 the plaintiff, Robert Steinberg, applied for admission to the defendant, the Chicago Medical School, as a first-year student for the academic year 1974–75 and paid an application fee of $15. The Chicago Medical School is a private, not-for-profit educational institution, incorporated in the State of Illinois. His application for admission was rejected and Steinberg filed a[n] . . .action against the school, claiming that it had failed to evaluate his application . . . according to the academic entrance criteria printed in the school's bulletin. Specifically, his complaint alleged that the school's decision to accept or reject a particular applicant for the first-year class was primarily based on such nonacademic considerations as the prospective student's familial relationship to members of the school's faculty and to members of its board of trustees, and the ability of the applicant or his family to pledge or make payment of large sums of money to the school. The complaint further alleged that, by using such unpublished criteria to evaluate applicants, the school had breached the contract which Steinberg contended was created when the school accepted his application fee.

* * *

The defendant filed a motion to dismiss, arguing that the complaint failed to state a cause of action because no contract came into existence during its transaction with Steinberg inasmuch as the school's informational publication did not constitute a valid offer. The trial court sustained [ruled in favor of] the motion to dismiss and Steinberg appeals from this order.

* * *

A contract is an agreement between competent parties, based upon a consideration sufficient in law, to do or not do a particular thing. It is a promise or a set of promises for the breach of which the law gives a remedy, or the performance of which the law in some way recognizes as a duty. [Citation.] A contract's essential requirements are: competent parties, valid subject matter, legal consideration, mutuality of obligation and mutuality of agreement. Generally, parties may contract in any situation where there is no legal prohibition, since the law acts by restraint and not by conferring rights. [Citation.] However, it is basic contract law that in order for a contract to be binding the terms of the contract must be reasonably certain and definite. [Citation.]

A contract, in order to be legally binding, must be based on consideration. [Citation.] Consideration has been defined to consist of some right, interest, profit or benefit accruing to one party or some forbearance, disadvantage, detriment, loss or responsibility given, suffered, or undertaken by the other. [Citation.] Money is a valuable consideration and its transfer or payment or promises to pay it or the benefit from the right to its use, will support a contract.

In forming a contract, it is required that both parties assent to the same thing in the same sense [citation] and that their minds meet on the essential terms and conditions. [Citation.] Furthermore, the mutual consent essential to the formation of a contract, must be gathered from the language employed by the parties or manifested by their words or acts. The intention of the parties gives character to the transaction, and if either party contracts in good faith he is entitled to the benefit of his contract no matter what may have been the secret purpose or intention of the other party. [Citation.]

Steinberg contends that the Chicago Medical School's informational brochure constituted an invitation to make an offer; that his subsequent application and the submission of his $15 fee to the school amounted to an offer; that the school's voluntary reception of his fee constituted an acceptance and because of these events a contract was created between the school and himself. He contends that the school was duty bound under the terms of the contract to evaluate his application according to its stated standards and that the deviation from these standards not only breached the contract, but amounted to an arbitrary selection which constituted a violation of due process and equal protection. He concludes that such a breach did in fact take place each and every time during the past ten years that the school evaluated applicants according to their relationship to the school's faculty members or members of its board of trustees, or in accordance with their ability to make or pledge large sums of money to the school. Finally, he asserts that he is a member and a proper representative of the class that has been damaged by the school's practice.

The school counters that no contract came into being because informational brochures, such as its bulletin, do not constitute offers, but are construed by the courts to be general proposals to consider, examine and negotiate. The school points out that this doctrine has been specifically applied in Illinois to university informational publications.

* * *

We agree with Steinberg's position. We believe that he and the school entered into an enforceable contract; that the school's obligation under the contract was stated in the school's bulletin in a definitive manner and that by accepting his application fee—a valuable consideration—the school bound itself to fulfill its promises. Steinberg accepted the school's promises in good faith and he was entitled to have his application judged according to the school's stated criteria.

* * *

[Reversed and remanded.]

Implied Contracts

RICHARDSON v. J.C. FLOOD CO.

District Court of Appeals, 1963.
190 A.2d 259.

MYERS, J.

This is an appeal by a property owner from a judgment against her for costs of labor and material furnished by appellee plumbing company.

Appellant contends there was error in the findings of the trial court that all work done by appellee was authorized by her and that

there was sufficient competent evidence to substantiate the amount of recovery.

Appellant requested appellee to correct a stoppage in the sewer line of her house. In the course of the work a "snake" used to clear the line leading to the main sewer became caught and to secure its release a portion of the sewer line in the backyard was excavated. It was then discovered that the instrument was embedded in pieces of wood which had become lodged in a sewer trap from surface debris. At this time numerous leaks were found in a rusty, defective water pipe which ran parallel with the sewer line. In order to meet District regulations, the water pipe, of a type no longer approved for such service, had to be replaced then or at a later date when the yard would have to be redug for that purpose. Appellee's agent testified he so informed appellant's agent. Appellant testified she had requested appellee to clear the sewer line but denied she was told about the need for replacement of the water line and contested the total amount of the charges for all the work done by appellee.

In the absence of a written contract, but with appellant admitting she had requested correction of a sewer obstruction but denying she had agreed to replace the water pipe, the existence of an implied agreement between the parties to replace the water pipe at the same time became an issue for the trial court.

It seems clear from the record that there was evidence to support a finding that appellant and her agent through daily inspections of the repairs knew of the magnitude of the work required and made no objection to the performance of the extra work in replacing the water pipe until after the entire job was finished when appellant refused to pay any part of the total bill submitted.

Contracts for work to be done are either express or implied—*express* when their terms are stated by the parties, *implied* when arising from a mutual agreement and promise not set forth in words. Direct evidence is not essential to prove a contract which may be presumed from the acts and conduct of the parties as a reasonable man would view them under all the circumstances. The testimony was conflicting but we cannot say that the trial court was wrong in holding that the burden of proving its right to recover had been carried by appellee.

With respect to the costs of both jobs the record reveals that no testimony was offered by appellant to show that itemized amounts for labor and materials furnished by appellee were wrong or excessive and unreasonable or that the work performed was either unnecessary or unsatisfactory. Appellee produced testimony that the charges were fair and reasonable and that the work on both the sewer and the water lines was fully completed. We find no merit in appellant's claim of error that the evidence on the costs of labor and material was insufficient to support the finding on this point.

[Affirmed.]

Quasi Contracts

NURSING CARE SERVICES, INC. v. DOBOS

District Court of Appeal of Florida, Fourth District, 1980. 380 So.2d 516.

HURLEY, J.

Plaintiff, Nursing Care Services, Inc., appeals from that part of a final judgment which disallowed compensation for certain nursing care services. Our review of the record reveals substantial uncontradicted testimony supporting plaintiff's theory of recovery and thus we remand for entry of an amended final judgment.

Mary Dobos, the defendant, was admitted to Boca Raton Community Hospital with an abdominal aneurysm. Her condition was sufficiently serious to cause her doctor to order around-the-clock nursing care. The hospital implemented this order by calling upon the plaintiff, which provides individualized nursing services.

Mrs. Dobos received care which in retrospect can be divided into three periods: (1) two weeks of in-hospital care; (2) forty-eight-hour post-release care; and (3) two weeks of at-home care. The second period of care (the forty-eight-hour post-release care) was removed as an issue at trial when Mrs. Dobos

conceded that she or her daughter authorized that period of care. The total bill for all three periods came to $3,723.90; neither the reasonableness of the fee, the competency of the nurses, nor the necessity for the services was contested at trial.

The gist of the defense was that Mrs. Dobos never signed a written contract nor orally agreed to be liable for the nursing services. Testifying about the in-hospital care, she said, "Dr. Rosen did all the work. I don't know what he done (sic), and he says, I needed a nurse." It is undisputed that Mrs. Dobos was mentally alert during her at-home recuperation period. Asked if she ever tried to fire the nurses or dispense with their care, she replied, "I didn't. I didn't know who I thought maybe if they insist, the doctors insist so much, I thought the Medicare would take care of it, or whatever. I don't know."

After a non-jury trial, the court granted judgment for the plaintiff in the sum of $248.00, the cost of the forty-eight hour post-release care. It declined to allow compensation for the first and third periods of care, saying,

". . . (T)here certainly was a service rendered, but based on the total surrounding circumstances, I don't think there is sufficient communications and dealings with Mrs. Dobos to make sure that she knew that she would be responsible for those services rendered. . . ."

We concur in the trial court's determination that the plaintiff failed to prove an express contract or a contract implied in fact. It is our view, however, that the uncontradicted testimony, provided by plaintiff and defendant alike, clearly established a contract implied in law which entitles the plaintiff to recover.

Contracts implied in law, or as they are more commonly called, "quasi contracts," are obligations imposed by law on grounds of justice and equity. Their purpose is to prevent unjust enrichment. Unlike express contracts or contracts implied in fact, quasi contracts do not rest upon the assent of the contracting parties. [Citation.]

One of the most common areas in which recovery on a contract implied in law is allowed is that of work performed or services rendered. The rationale is that the defendant would be unjustly enriched at the expense of the plaintiff if she were allowed to escape payment for services rendered or work performed. There is, however, an important limitation. Ordinarily liability is imposed to pay for services rendered by another only when the person for whose benefit they were rendered requested the services or knowingly and voluntarily accepted their benefits. [Citations.]

The law's concern that needless services not be foisted upon the unsuspecting has led to the formulation of the "officious intermeddler doctrine." It holds that where a person performs labor for another without the latter's request or implied consent, however beneficial such labor may be, he cannot recover therefor. [Citation.] A notable exception to this rule, however, is that of emergency aid:

A person who has supplied things or services to another, although acting without the other's knowledge or consent, is entitled to restitution therefor from the other if he acted unofficiously and with intent to charge therefor, and the things or services were necessary to prevent the other from suffering serious bodily harm or pain, and the person supplying them had no reason to know that the other would not consent to receiving them, if mentally competent, and it was impossible for the other to give consent or, because of extreme youth or mental impairment, the other's consent would have been immaterial. [Citation.]

In the case at bar it is unclear whether Mrs. Dobos, during the period of in-hospital care, understood or intended that compensation be paid. Her condition was grave. She had been placed in the hospital's intensive care unit and thereafter had tubes and other medical equipment attached to her body which necessitated special attention. She was alone, unable to cope and without family assistance. It is worthy of note that at no point during the litigation was there any question as to the propriety of the professional judgment that the patient required special nursing care. To the contrary, the record demonstrates that the in-hospital care was essential to Mrs. Dobos' health and safety. Given these circumstances it would be unconscionable to deny the plaintiff recovery for services which fall squarely within the emergency aid exception. [Citation.]

The third period of care is less difficult. It is unquestioned that during the at-home recuperation, Mrs. Dobos was fully aware of her circumstances and readily accepted the benefits conferred. Given such facts, we believe the rule set down in [citation] must govern:

It is well settled that where services are rendered by one person for another which are knowingly and voluntarily accepted, the law presumes that such services are given and received in expectation of being paid for, and will imply a promise to pay what they are reasonably worth.

A patient's unannounced misconception that the cost of accepted services will be paid by an insurer or Medicare does not absolve her of responsibility to bear the cost of the services.

* * *

Accordingly, we remand the cause to the trial court with instructions to enter an amended final judgment for the plaintiff in the sum of $3,723.90 plus interest and court costs. It is so ordered.

QUESTIONS

1. Distinguish between contracts that are covered by the U.C.C. and those covered by common law.

2. Define the terms *contract* and *breach*.

3. List the essential elements of a contract.

4. Distinguish between express and implied contracts.

5. Distinguish between unilateral and bilateral contracts.

6. Explain the differences among valid, void, voidable, and unenforceable agreements.

7. Distinguish between executed and executory contracts.

8. Distinguish between formal and informal contracts.

9. Explain the doctrine of promissory estoppel.

10. Identify the three elements of an enforceable quasi contract and how it differs from a contract.

PROBLEMS

1. Owen telephones an order to Hillary's store for certain goods which Hillary delivers to Owen. Nothing is said by either party about the price or payment of the price. What are the legal obligations of Owen and Hillary?

2. Minth is the owner of the Hiawatha Supper Club, which he leased during 1972 and 1973 to Piekarski. During the period of the lease, Piekarski contracted with Puttkammer for the resurfacing of the access and service areas of the supper club. The work, including labor and materials, had a reasonable value of $2,540, but Puttkammer was never paid because Piekarski went bankrupt. Puttkammer brought an action against Minth to recover the amount owed to him by Piekarski. Decision?

3. Jonathan writes to Willa, stating "I'll pay you $150 if you reseed my lawn." Willa reseeds Jonathan's lawn as requested. Has a contract been formed? If so, what kind?

4. Calvin uses fraud to induce Maria to promise to pay money in return for goods delivered by Calvin to Maria. Has a contract been formed? If so, what kind? What are the rights of Calvin and Maria?

5. Anna is about to buy a house on a hill. Prior to the purchase she obtains a promise from Betty, the owner of the adjacent property, that Betty will not build any structure that would block Anna's view. In reliance on this promise Anna buys the house. Is Betty's promise binding? Why or why not?

COMPUTER RESEARCH PROBLEMS

 1. St. Charles Drilling Co. contracted with Osterholt to install a well and water system that would produce a specified quantity of water. The water system failed to meet its warranted capacity and Osterholt sued for breach of contract. Does the U.C.C. apply to this contract?

 2. On March 4, 1970, Helvey brought suit against REMC for breach of implied and express warranties. He alleged that REMC furnished electricity in excess of 135 volts to Helvey's home, causing damage to his 110-volt household appliances. This incident occurred on January 10, 1966. In defense, REMC pleads that the Uniform Commercial Code's Article 2 statute of limitations of four years has passed thereby barring Helvey's suit. Helvey argues that providing electrical energy is not a transaction in goods under the U.C.C. but rather a furnishing of services that would make applicable the general contract statute of limitations of six years. Decision?

Chapter 9

MUTUAL ASSENT

Essentials of an Offer
Duration of Offers
Communication of Acceptance
Variant Acceptances

ALTHOUGH each of the requirements for the formation of a contract is essential to its existence, mutual assent is so basic that frequently a contract is referred to as the agreement between the parties. The Restatement, Section 3, provides this definition: "An agreement is a manifestation of mutual assent on the part of two or more parties." When the contract is enforced, it is the agreement that is enforced. The agreement between the parties is the very core of the contract.

The manner in which parties usually show mutual assent is by **offer** and **acceptance.** One party makes a proposal (offer) by words or conduct to the other party who agrees by words or conduct to the proposal (acceptance). A contractual agreement always involves either a promise exchanged for a promise (*bilateral contract*) or a promise exchanged for an act or forbearance to act (*unilateral contract*) as manifested by what the parties communicated to one another.

An implied contract may be formed by conduct. Thus, there may be no definite offer and acceptance, or definite acceptance of an offer, yet a contract exists if both of the parties have acted in a manner that manifests a recognition by each of them of the existence of a contract. Thus, it may be impossible to determine the exact moment when such a contract formed by conduct was made.

To form the contract the agreement must be objectively manifested. The important thing is what the parties indicate to one another by spoken or written words or by conduct. The law applies an **objective** standard and is, therefore, concerned only with the assent, agreement, or intention of a party as it reasonably appears from his words or actions. The law of contracts is not concerned with what a party may have actually thought or the meaning that he intended to convey, insofar as his subjective understanding or intention differed from the meaning objectively manifested. For example, if Leslie offers to sell to Sam her Chevrolet automobile but intends to offer and believes that she is offering her Ford automobile, and Sam accepts the offer reasonably believing it was for the Chevrolet, a contract has been formed for the sale of the Chevrolet. Subjectively, there is no agreement as to the subject matter, but objectively there is a manifestation of agreement, and this is binding.

The Code's treatment of mutual assent is covered in greater detail in Chapter 20.

OFFER

An offer is a definite proposal or undertaking made by one person to another which manifests a willingness to enter into a bargain. The person making the proposal is the **offeror.** The person to whom it is made is the **offeree.** Upon receipt, the offer confers on the offeree the power of acceptance, which is an expression of willingness to comply with the terms of the offer.

The communication of an offer to an offeree does not of itself confer any rights or impose any duties on either of the parties. The offeror, by making his offer, simply confers upon the offeree a power to create a contract between the parties by accepting the offer. Until the offeree exercises this power, the outstanding offer creates neither rights nor liabilities.

An offer may take several forms: (1) It may propose a promise for a promise. An example is an offer to sell and deliver goods in thirty days in return for the promise to pay a stipulated amount upon delivery of the goods. If this offer is accepted, the resulting contract consists of the mutual promises of the parties, each made in exchange for the other. (2) An offer may be a promise for an act. A common example is an offer of a reward for certain information or for the return of lost property. Such an offer can be accepted only by the performance of the act requested. (3) An offer may be in the form of an act for a promise. For example, Maria offers the stated price to a clerk in a theater ticket office and asks for a ticket for a certain performance. This offer of an act can be accepted only by the delivery of the requested ticket, which amounts, in effect, to the theater owner's promise to admit Maria to the designated performance.

ESSENTIALS OF AN OFFER

An offer need not take any particular form to have legal validity. To be effective, however, it must (1) be communicated to the offeree, (2) manifest an intent to enter into a contract, and (3) be sufficiently definite and certain. If these essentials are present, an offer which has not terminated gives the offeree the power to form a contract by accepting the offer.

Communication

In order to have the mutual assent required to form a contract the offeree must have knowledge of the offer, because he cannot agree to something of which he has no knowledge. Accordingly, the offer must have been communicated to the offeree by the offeror.

For example, Andy signs a letter containing an offer to Bonnie and leaves it on top of the desk in his office. Later that day, Bonnie, without prearrangement, goes to Andy's office, discovers that Andy is away, notices the letter on Andy's desk, reads it, and then writes on it an acceptance which she dates and signs. No contract is formed because the offer never became effective for the reason that it was never communicated by Andy to Bonnie. If Andy had mailed the letter, and it had gone astray in the mail, the offer would likewise never have become effective.

Not only must the offer be communicated to the offeree, but the communication must also be made or authorized by the offeror. For instance, if Joanne tells Karlene that she is going to offer $600 to Larry for his piano, and Karlene promptly informs Larry of this proposal, no offer has been made. There was no authorized communication of any offer by Joanne to Larry. By the same token, if Lance should offer to sell his diamond ring to Ed, an acceptance of this offer by Dianne would not be effective, because Lance made the offer to Ed and not to Dianne.

An offer need not be stated or communicated by words. Conduct from which a reasonable person may infer a proposal in return for either an act or a promise amounts to an offer.

An offer may be made to the general public. No person, however, can accept such an offer until and unless he has knowledge that the offer exists. For example, if a person, without knowledge of the existence of an advertised reward for information leading to the return of a lost watch, gives information that leads to its return, he is not entitled to the reward. His act was not an acceptance of the offer because he could not accept something of which he had no knowledge.

Intent

To have legal effect an offer must manifest an intent to enter into a contract. The intent of an offer is determined objectively from the manifestation of the parties. The meaning of the manifestation is based upon what a reasonable person in the position of the other party would have believed. *See City of Everett v. Estate of Sumstad* and *Newman v. Schiff.*

Occasionally, a person exercises her sense of humor by speaking or writing words which—taken literally and without regard to context or surrounding circumstances—could be construed as an offer. The promise is intended as a joke, however, and the promisee as a reasonable person should understand it to be such. Therefore it is not an offer. It should not create a reasonable expectation in the mind of the person to whom it is made because he realizes or should realize that it is not made in earnest. There is no contractual intent on the part of the promisor, and the promisee is or reasonably ought to be aware of that fact. If, however, the intended jest is so successful that the promisee as a reasonable man under all the circumstances reasonably believes that it has been made as an offer, and so believing accepts, the objective standard applies and the parties have entered into a contract.

A promise made under circumstances of obvious excitement or emotional strain is likewise not an offer. For example, Charlotte, after having her month-old Cadillac break down for the third time in two days, screams in disgust, "I will sell this car to anyone for $10.00!" Lisa hears Charlotte and hands her a ten-dollar bill. Under the circumstances, Charlotte's statement was not an offer, if a reasonable person in Lisa's position would not have considered it one.

It is important to distinguish language that constitutes an offer from that which merely solicits or invites offers. Such proposals, although made in earnest, lack intent and are therefore not deemed offers. As a result, a purported acceptance does not bring about a contract but operates only as an offer. These proposals include preliminary negotiations, advertisements, and auctions.

Preliminary Negotiations Communications between the parties in many cases take the form of preliminary negotiations. The parties are either requesting or supplying the terms of an offer that may or may not be given. A statement that may indicate a willingness to make an offer is not itself an offer. If Terri writes to Susan, "Will you buy my automobile for $3,000?" and Susan replies "Yes," there is no contract. Terri has not made an offer to sell her automobile to Susan for $3,000.

The offeror must manifest an intent to enter into a contract and not merely a willingness to enter into negotiation. For example, in the landmark case of *Owen v. Tunison,* 131 Me. 42, 158 A. 926 (1932), Owen sent a letter to Tunison asking him to sell his property in Bucksport, Maine for $6,000. Tunison replied with a letter to Owen, stating: "Because of improvements [to the property] . . . it would not be possible for me to sell it unless I was to receive $16,000 in cash." Owen quickly wired Tunison the following message: "Accept your offer for [the property] Terms sixteen thousand cash send deed to Eastern Trust and Banking Co. Bangor Maine Please Acknowledge." Four days later, Tunison notified Owen that he did not wish to sell the property. Owen sued for damages, claiming Tunison unjustifiably refused to complete the sale after his written offer and Owen's acceptance. In ruling in favor of Tunison, the court held that Tunison's response to Owen's offer of $6,000 for his property merely indicated his interest to open negotiations that might lead to a sale. It was not a clear offer or proposal to sell, such as "I offer to sell to you."

Advertisements Merchants desire to sell their merchandise and thus are interested in informing potential customers about the goods, the terms of sale, and the price. But if they make widespread promises to sell to each person on their mailing list, it is conceivable that the number of acceptances and resulting contracts might exceed their ability to perform. Consequently, a merchant might refrain from making offers by merely announcing that he has goods for sale, describing the goods, and quoting prices. He is inviting his customers and, in the case of published advertisements, the public, to make offers to him to buy the goods. His advertisements, circulars, quotation sheets, and display of merchandise are *not* offers because (1) they do not contain a promise and (2) they leave unexpressed many terms which would be necessary to the making of a contract. Accordingly, the responses are not acceptances because no offer to sell has been made.

Nonetheless, a seller is not free to advertise goods at one price and then raise the price once demand has been stimulated. Although as far as contract law is concerned no offer has been made, such conduct is prohibited by the Federal Trade Commission as well as by legislation in many States. (See Chapter 43.)

Moreover, in some circumstances a public announcement or advertisement may constitute an offer. This is so if the advertisement or announcement contains a definite promise of something in exchange for something else and confers a power of acceptance upon a specified person or class of persons. The typical offer of a reward is an example of a definite offer as is *Lefkowitz v. Great Minneapolis Surplus Store, Inc.* In this case, the court held that a newspaper advertisement was an offer because it contained a promise of performance in definite terms in return for a requested act.

Auction Sales The auctioneer at an auction sale does not make offers to sell the property that is being auctioned but invites offers to buy. The classic statement by the auctioneer is, "How much am I offered?" The persons attending the auction may make progressively higher bids for the property, and each bid or statement of a price or a figure is an offer to buy at that figure. If the bid is accepted, which is customarily by the fall of the hammer in the hands of the auctioneer, a contract results. A bidder is free to withdraw his bid at any time prior to its acceptance. The auctioneer is likewise free to withdraw the goods from sale *unless* the sale is advertised or announced to be without reserve.

If the auction sale is advertised or announced in explicit terms to be **without reserve,** the auctioneer may not withdraw an article or lot put up for sale unless no bid is made within a reasonable time. Unless so advertised or announced the sale is with reserve. Whether with or without reserve, a bidder may retract his bid at any time prior to acceptance by the auctioneer. Such retraction does not revive any previous bid.

Definiteness

The terms of a contract, all of which are usually contained in the offer, must be reasonably certain so as to provide a court with a basis for determining the existence of a breach and for giving an appropriate remedy. It is a fundamental policy that contracts should be made by the parties and not by the courts; accordingly, remedies for breach must have a basis in the parties' contract.

However, where the parties have intended to form a contract, the courts will attempt to find a basis for granting a remedy. Missing terms may be supplied by course of dealing, usage of trade, or by inference. Thus, uncertainty as to incidental matters will seldom be fatal so long as the parties intend to form a contract. Nevertheless, the more terms the parties leave open, the less likely it is that they have intended to form a contract. What terms must be included in all contracts cannot be stated because of the great variety of contracts. In most cases, however, material terms would include the subject matter, price, quantity, quality, terms of payment, and duration.

Open Terms With respect to agreements for the sale of goods, the Code provides standards by which omitted terms may be determined, provided the parties intended to enter into a binding contract. The Code provides missing terms in a number of instances, such as where the contract fails to specify the price or the time or place of delivery or payment. Sections 2–204(3), 2–305, 2–308, 2–309, and 2–310. The Restatement, Section 34, has adopted an approach similar to the Code's in supplying terms omitted in the parties' contract.

Under the Code, an offer for the purchase or sale of goods may leave open particulars of performance to be specified by one of the parties. Any such specification must be made in good faith and within limits set by commercial reasonableness. Section 2–311(1). **Good faith** is defined as honesty in fact in the conduct or transaction concerned. Section 1–201(19). **Commercial reasonableness** is a standard measured by the business judgment of reasonable persons familiar with the customary practices in the type of transaction involved and with regard to the facts and circumstances of the case.

If the price is to be fixed otherwise than by agreement and is not so fixed through the fault of one of the parties, the other party has an option to treat the contract as cancelled or to fix a reasonable price in good faith for the goods. However, where the parties intend not to be bound unless the price is fixed or agreed upon as provided in the agreement, and it is not so fixed or agreed upon, the Code provides in accordance with the parties' intent that there is no contractual liability. In such case the seller must refund to the buyer any portion of the price received, and the buyer must return the goods to the seller or, if unable to do so, pay the reasonable value of the goods. Section 2–305(4).

Output and Requirements Contracts An agreement of a buyer to purchase the entire output of a seller's factory for a stated period, or an agreement of a seller to supply a buyer with all his requirements for certain goods may appear to lack definiteness and mutual-

ity of obligation. The exact quantity of goods is not specified; moreover, the seller may have some degree of control over her output and the buyer over his requirements. Under the Code and the Restatement such agreements are enforceable by the application of an objective standard based upon good faith of both parties. Thus, the seller cannot operate her factory twenty-four hours a day and insist that the buyer take all of the output when she had operated it only eight hours a day before the agreement was made. Nor can the buyer expand his business abnormally and insist that the seller supply all of his requirements.

DURATION OF OFFERS

An offer confers upon the offeree a power of acceptance, which continues until the offer terminates. The ways in which an offer may be terminated, other than by acceptance, are: (1) lapse of time; (2) revocation; (3) rejection; (4) counter-offer; (5) death or incompetency of the offeror or offeree; (6) destruction of the subject matter to which the offer relates; and (7) subsequent illegality of the type of contract proposed by the offer.

Lapse of Time

The offeror may specify the time within which the offer is to be accepted, just as he may specify any other term or condition in the offer. It may be provided that the offer is to be accepted immediately or within a specified period, such as a week or ten days. Unless otherwise terminated, the offer remains open for the **specified** time period. Upon the expiration of that time, the offer no longer exists and cannot be accepted. *See Newman v. Schiff.* Any subsequent purported acceptance will serve as a new offer.

If no time is stated in the offer within which the offeree must accept, the offer will terminate after a **reasonable** period of time. What is a reasonable period of time is a question of fact, depending on the nature of the contract proposed, the usages of business, and other circumstances of the case. Restatement, Section 41. For instance, an offer to sell a perishable good would be open for a far shorter period of time than an offer to sell undeveloped real estate.

Revocation

An offeror may generally withdraw an offer at any time before it has been accepted, even though he has definitely promised to keep it open for a stated time. To be effective, notice of revocation of the offer must actually reach the offeree before he has accepted. If the offeror originally promises that the offer would be open for thirty days, but after five days wishes to terminate it, he may do so merely by giving the offeree notice that he is withdrawing the offer. Notice may be given by any means of communication and effectively terminates the offer when **received** by the offeree. An offer made to the general public is revoked only by giving publicity to the revocation equivalent to that given the offer.

Notice of revocation may be indirectly communicated to the offeree, as where he receives reliable information from a third person that the offeror has disposed of the goods which he has offered for sale or has otherwise placed himself in a position which indicates an unwillingness or inability to perform the promise contained in the offer. Restatement, Section 43. For example, Jane offers to sell her portable television set to Bruce and tells Bruce that he has ten days in which to accept. One week later Bruce observes the television set in Carl's house and is informed that Carl had purchased it from Jane. The next day Bruce sends to Jane an acceptance of the offer. There is no contract, since Jane's offer was effectively revoked when Bruce learned of Jane's inability to sell the television set to him because she had sold it to Carl.

Certain limitations, however, have been imposed upon the offeror's power to revoke the offer at any time prior to its acceptance. These limitations apply to the following five situations.

Option Contracts   An **option** is a contract by which the offeror is bound to hold open an offer for a specified period of time. It must comply with all of the requirements of a contract, including *consideration* being given to the offeror by the offeree. (Consideration is discussed in Chapter 11.) For example, if Ann, in return for the payment of $500 to her by Bobby, grants Bobby an option to buy Blackacre at a price of $80,000 exercisable at any time within thirty days, Ann's offer is irrevocable. Ann is legally bound to keep the offer open for thirty days, and any communication by Ann to Bobby of notice of withdrawal of the offer is ineffective. Bobby is not bound to accept the offer, but the option contract entitles him to thirty days in which to accept. *See Ryder v. Wescoat.*

Firm Offers under the Code   The Code provides that a *merchant* is bound to keep an offer to buy or sell **goods** open for a stated period (or if no time is stated for a reasonable time) but not in excess of three months, if the merchant gives assurance in a **signed writing** that it will be held open. Section 2–205. The Code, therefore, makes a merchant's written promise not to revoke an offer for a stated period of time enforceable even though no consideration is given the offeror for that promise. A **merchant** is defined as a person (1) who is a dealer in goods of that kind, (2) who by his occupation holds himself out as having knowledge or skill peculiar to the goods or practices involved, or (3) who employs an agent or broker whom he holds out as having such knowledge or skill. Section 2–104.

Statutory Irrevocability   Certain offers are made irrevocable by statute, such as bids made to the State, municipality, or other governmental body for the construction of a building or some other public work. Another example is preincorporation stock subscription agreements, which are irrevocable for a period of six months under many State corporation statutes. See Section 17 of the Model Business Corporation Act (Appendix G).

Irrevocable Offers of Unilateral Contracts   Where an offer contemplates a unilateral contract, that is, a promise for an act, injustice to the offeree may result if revocation is permitted after the offeree has started to perform the act requested in the offer and has substantially but not completely accomplished it. Traditionally, such an offer is not accepted and no contract is formed until the offeree has *completed* the requested act. By commencing performance the offeree does not bind himself to complete performance and historically did not bind the offeror to keep the offer open. Thus, the offeror could revoke the offer at any time prior to the offeree's completion of performance. For example, Linda offers Tom $300 if Tom will climb to the top of the flagpole in the center of campus. Tom commences his ascent, and when he is five feet from the top, Linda yells to him, "I revoke."

Some courts have attempted to solve this difficulty by treating the offer as if it were an offer for a bilateral contract (a promise for a promise), which is accepted by the offeree's commencing performance. Such construction, however, is inconsistent with the terms of the offer, and causes the offeree as well as the offeror to become bound, which may not have been the intent of the parties.

The Restatement deals with this problem by providing that where the performance of the requested act necessarily requires time and effort to be expended by the offeree, the offeror is obligated not to revoke the offer for a reasonable time. This obligation arises when the offeree begins the invited performance and the offeror's duty of performance is conditional on completion of the invited performance according to the terms of the offer. If, however, the offeror does not know of the offeree's performance and has no adequate means of learning of it within a reasonable period of time, the offeree must exercise reasonable diligence to notify the offeror.

Promissory Estoppel As discussed in the previous chapter, a noncontractual promise may be enforced when it is made under circumstances that should lead the promisor reasonably to expect that the promisee will be induced by the promise to take action in reliance on the promise. This doctrine has been used in some cases to prevent an offeror from revoking an offer prior to its acceptance. The Restatement provides the following rule:

An offer which the offeror should reasonably expect to induce action or forbearance of a substantial character on the part of the offeree before acceptance and which does induce such action or forbearance is binding as an option contract to the extent necessary to avoid injustice. Restatement, Section 87(2).

Thus, Ramanan Plumbing Co. submits a written offer for plumbing work to be used by Resolute Building Co. as part of Resolute's bid as a general contractor. Ramanan knows that Resolute is relying on Ramanan's bid and in fact Resolute submits Ramanan's name as the plumbing subcontractor in the bid. Ramanan's offer is irrevocable until Resolute has a reasonable opportunity to notify Ramanan that Resolute's bid has been accepted.

Rejection

An offeree is at liberty to accept or reject the offer as he sees fit. If he decides not to accept it, he is not required to reject it but may simply do nothing and eventually the offer will terminate by the lapse of time. A **rejection** of an offer is a manifestation by the offeree of his unwillingness to accept. The power of acceptance is terminated by a communicated rejection. From the effective moment of rejection, which is the **receipt** of the rejection by the offeror, the offeree may no longer accept the offer. Rejection by the offeree may consist of express language or may be implied from language or from conduct.

Counter-offer

A **counter-offer** is a counter-proposal from the offeree to the offeror and indicates a willingness to contract but upon terms or conditions different from those contained in the offer. It is not an unequivocal acceptance and, by indicating an unwillingness to agree to the terms of the offer, it operates as a rejection. It also operates as a new offer. For instance, assume that Jordan writes Chris a letter stating that he will sell to Chris a secondhand color television set for $300. Chris replies that she will pay Jordan $250 for the set. This is a counter-offer which, upon **receipt** by Jordan, terminates the original offer. Jordan may, if he wishes, accept the counter-offer and thereby create a contract for $250. If, on the other hand, Chris states in her reply that she wishes to consider the $300 offer but is willing to pay $250 at once for the set, that is a counter-offer which does *not* terminate Jordan's original offer. In the first instance, after making the $250 counter-offer, Chris may not accept the $300 offer. In the second instance she may do so, as the counter-offer was stated in such a manner as not to indicate an unwillingness to accept the original offer, and Chris therefore did not terminate it. *See Zeller v. First National Bank & Trust.* In addition, a mere inquiry about the possibility of obtaining different or new terms is not a counter-offer and does not terminate the offer.

Another common type of counter-offer is the **conditional acceptance.** A conditional acceptance purports to accept the offer but expressly makes the acceptance conditional upon the offeror's assent to additional or different terms. Nonetheless, it is a counter-offer and terminates the original offer. The Code's treatment of acceptances containing terms that vary from the offer are discussed later in this chapter.

Death or Incompetency

The death or incompetency of either the offeror or the offeree ordinarily terminates an offer. Upon his death or incompetency the offeror no longer has the legal capacity to enter into a contract, and thus all outstanding offers are terminated. Death or incompetency of the offeree likewise terminates the offer because an ordinary offer is not assignable (transferable) and may be accepted only by the person to whom it was made. When the offeree dies or ceases to have legal capability to enter into a contract, there is no one who has the power to accept the offer. Therefore, the offer terminates.

The death or incompetency of the offeror or offeree, however, does *not* terminate an offer contained in an option. The effect of death or incompetence upon an option contract is determined by the general rules of discharge that apply to contracts, as discussed in Chapter 16.

Destruction of Subject Matter

Destruction of the specific subject matter of an offer terminates the offer. The impossibility of performance prevents a contract from being consummated and thus terminates all outstanding offers with respect to the destroyed property. Suppose that Martina, owning a Buick automobile, offers to sell the car to Worthy and allows Worthy five days in which to accept. Three days later the car is destroyed by fire. On the following day Worthy, without knowing about the destruction of the car, notifies Martina that he accepts Martina's offer. There is no contract. Martina's offer was terminated by the destruction of the car.

Subsequent Illegality

One of the four essential requirements of a contract, as previously mentioned, is legality of purpose or subject matter. If performance of a valid contract is subsequently made illegal, the obligations of both parties under the contract are discharged. Illegality taking effect after the making of an offer but prior to acceptance has the same effect. The offer is legally terminated.

ACCEPTANCE

The acceptance of an offer is essential to the formation of a contract. Once an acceptance has been given, the contract is formed. An acceptance can only be made by an offeree. Acceptance of an offer for a bilateral contract requires some overt act by the offeree which manifests his assent to the terms of the offer, such as speaking or sending a letter, a tele-gram, or other explicit or implicit communica-tion to the offeror. If the offer is for a unilateral contract, acceptance is the performance of the requested act (or refraining from acting as re-quested) with the intention of accepting. For example, if Joy publishes an offer of a reward to anyone who returns the diamond ring which she has lost (a unilateral contract offer), and Steven, with knowledge of the offer, finds and returns the ring to Joy, Steven has accepted the offer. If, however, Steven returns the ring to Joy but in doing so disclaims the reward and says that he does not accept the offer, there is no contract. Merely doing the act requested by the offeror is not sufficient to form a contract where it is not done with the intention of ac-cepting the offer.

A late acceptance or defective acceptance does not create a contract. After the offer has expired, it cannot be validly accepted. A late or defective acceptance, however, does mani-fest a willingness on the part of the offeree to enter into a contract and therefore constitutes a new offer. In order to create a contract based upon this offer, the original offeror must ac-cept the new offer by manifesting his assent.

COMMUNICATION OF ACCEPTANCE

General Rule

Since acceptance is the manifestation of the offeree's assent to the offer, it must necessar-ily be communicated to the offeror. This is the rule as to all bilateral offers. In the case of unilateral offers, however, notice of accep-tance to the offeror is usually not required. Where, however, in a unilateral contract the offeree has reason to know that the offeror has no adequate means of learning of the per-formance with reasonable promptness and certainty, then the offeree must make reason-able efforts to notify the offeror of acceptance or lose the right to enforce the contract. Re-statement, Section 54.

Silence as Acceptance

An offeree is generally under no legal duty to reply to an offer. Silence or inaction is there-fore *not* an acceptance of the offer. By custom, usage, or course of dealing, however, silence or inaction by the offeree may operate as an acceptance.

Thus, silence or inaction of an offeree who fails to reply to an offer operates as an accep-tance and causes a contract to be formed where by previous dealings the offeree has given the offeror reason to understand that the offeree will accept all offers unless the offeree sends notice to the contrary. Another example of silence operating as an accep-tance is the various purchase-by-mail clubs which a person joins by agreeing that his fail-ure to return a notification card rejecting of-fered goods constitutes acceptance of the club's offer to sell the goods.

Furthermore, if an offeror sends unordered or unsolicited merchandise to a person stat-ing that the goods may be purchased at a specified price, and that unless the goods are returned within a stated period of time the offer will be deemed to have been accepted, the offer is one for an inverted unilateral con-tract (i.e., an act for a promise). This practice led to abuse, however, which has prompted the Federal government as well as most States to enact statutes which provide that in such cases the offeree-recipient of the goods may keep them as a gift and is under no ob-ligation either to return them or to pay for them.

Effective Moment

As previously discussed, an offer, a revoca-tion, a rejection, and a counter-offer are effec-tive when they are *received*. An acceptance, on the other hand, is generally effective upon **dispatch.** *See Cushing v. Thomson.* This is true unless the offer specifically provides oth-erwise, the offeree uses an unauthorized means of communication, or the acceptance follows a prior rejection.

Stipulated Provisions in the Offer   If the offer specifically stipulates the means of com-munication to be utilized by the offeree, the acceptance to be effective must conform to that specification. Thus, if an offer states that acceptance must be made by registered mail, any purported acceptance not made by registered mail would be ineffective. Moreover, the rule that an acceptance is effective when dispatched or sent does not apply where the offer provides that the acceptance must be received by the offeror. If the offeror states that a reply must be received by a certain date or that he must hear from the offeree or uses other language indicating that the acceptance must be received by him, the effective moment of the acceptance is when it is received by the offeror and not when it is sent or dispatched by the offeree.

Authorized Means Historically, an authorized means of communication was the means expressly authorized by the offeror in the offer, or, if none was authorized, it was the means utilized by the offeror. For example, if in reply to an offer by mail, the offeree places in the mail a letter of acceptance properly stamped and addressed to the offeror, a contract is formed at the time and place that the offeree mails the letter. This assumes, of course, that the offer at that time was open and had not been terminated by any of the methods previously discussed. The reason for this rule is that the offeror, by using the mail, impliedly authorized the offeree to use the same method of communication. It is immaterial if the letter of acceptance goes astray in the mails and is never received.

The Restatement, Section 30, and the Code, Section 2–206(1) (a), both now provide that where the language in the offer or the circumstances do not otherwise indicate, an offer to make a contract shall be construed as authorizing acceptance in any **reasonable** manner. These provisions are intended to allow flexibility of response and the ability to keep pace with new modes of communication.

Unauthorized Means When the method of communication used by the offeree is unauthorized, the traditional rule is that acceptance is effective when and if received by the offeror, provided that it is received within the time the authorized means would have arrived. The Restatement, Section 67, provides that if these conditions are met the effective time for the acceptance relates back to the moment of dispatch.

Acceptance Following a Prior Rejection If an acceptance is sent after a prior rejection, the acceptance is not effective when sent by the offeree, but is only effective when and if **received** by the offeror before he receives the rejection. Thus, when an acceptance follows a prior rejection, the first communication to be received by the offeror is the effective one. For example, Anna in New York sends by mail to Fritz in San Francisco an offer which is expressly stated to be open for one week. On the fourth day Fritz sends to Anna by mail a letter of rejection which is delivered on the morning of the sixth day. At noon on the fifth day Fritz dispatches a telegram of acceptance which is received by Anna before the close of business on that day. A contract was formed when Fritz's telegram of acceptance was received by Anna as it was received before the letter of rejection.

Figure 9–1 Offer and Acceptance

	Time Effective	Effect
Communications by Offeror		
Offer	Received by offeree	Creates power to form a contract
Revocation	Received by offeree	Terminates offer
Communications by Offeree		
Rejection	Received by offeror	Terminates offer
Counter-offer	Received by offeror	Terminates offer
Acceptance	Sent by offeree	Forms a contract
Acceptance after prior rejection	Received by offeror	If received before rejection, forms a contract

VARIANT ACCEPTANCES

A variant acceptance—one that contains terms different from or additional to those in the offer—receives distinctly different treatment by the common law and the Code.

Common Law

An acceptance must be *positive* and *unequivocal*. It may not change, add to, subtract from, or qualify in any way the provisions of the offer. It must be the **mirror image** of the offer. Any communication by the offeree which attempts to modify the offer is not an acceptance but is a counter-offer, which does not create a contract.

Code

The common law "mirror image" rule, by which the acceptance cannot vary or deviate from the terms of the offer, is modified by the Code. This modification is necessitated by the realities of modern business practices. A vast number of business transactions use standardized business forms. For example, a merchant buyer sends to the merchant seller on the buyer's order form a purchase order for 1,000 dozen cotton shirts at $60.00 per dozen with delivery by October 1 at the buyer's place of business. On the reverse side of this standard form are twenty-five numbered paragraphs containing provisions generally favorable to the buyer. When the seller receives the buyer's order, he sends to the buyer on his acceptance form an unequivocal acceptance of the offer. However, despite the fact that the seller agrees to the buyer's quantity, price, and delivery terms, on the back of his acceptance form, the seller has thirty-two numbered paragraphs generally favorable to himself and in significant conflict with the buyer's form. Under the common law's *mirror image* rule no contract would exist, for there has not been an unequivocal acceptance of all of the material terms of the buyer's offer.

The Code in Section 2–207 attempts to alleviate this **Battle of the Forms** problem by focusing upon the intent of the parties. If the offeree expressly makes her acceptance conditioned upon assent to the additional or different terms, no contract is formed. If the offeree does not expressly make her acceptance conditional upon the offeror's assent to the additional or different terms, a contract is formed. The issue then becomes whether the offeree's different or additional terms become part of the contract. If both offeror and offeree are merchants, *additional* terms will be part of the contract provided they do not materially alter the agreement and are not objected to either in the offer itself or within a reasonable period of time. If both parties are not merchants or if the additional terms materially alter the offer, then the additional terms are merely construed as proposals to the contract. *Different* terms proposed by the *offeree* will not become part of the contract unless accepted by the offeror. The courts are divided over what terms are included when the terms differ or conflict. Most courts hold that the offeror's terms govern; other courts hold that the terms cancel each other out and look to the Code to provide the missing terms. (See Figure 19–4 in Chapter 19.)

To apply Section 2–207 to the example above: since both parties are merchants and the acceptance was not conditional upon assent to the additional or different terms, then (1) the contract will be formed without the *seller's* different terms unless they are specifically accepted by the buyer, (2) the contract will be formed without the *seller's* additional terms unless (a) they are specifically accepted by the buyer or (b) they do not materially alter the offer and the buyer does not object, and (3) depending upon the jurisdiction either (a) the *buyer's* conflicting terms are included in the contract or (b) the Code provides the missing terms since the conflicting terms cancel each other out.

CASES

Objective Standard

CITY OF EVERETT v. ESTATE OF SUMSTAD

Supreme Court of Washington, 1981.
95 Wn.2d 853, 631 P.2d 366.

DOLLIVER, J.

The City of Everett commenced an . . . action against the seller (the Sumstad Estate) and the buyer (Al and Rosemary Mitchell) of a safe to determine who is entitled to a sum of money found in the safe. Both the Estate and the Mitchells moved for summary judgment. The trial court entered summary judgment in favor of the Estate. The Court of Appeals affirmed. [Citation.]

Petitioners, Mr. and Mrs. Mitchell, are the proprietors of a small secondhand store. On August 12, 1978, the Mitchells attended Alexander's Auction, where they frequently had shopped to obtain merchandise for their own use and for use as inventory in their business. At the auction the Mitchells purchased a used safe with an inside compartment for $50. As they were told by the auctioneer when they purchased the safe, the Mitchells found that the inside compartment of the safe was locked. The safe was part of the Sumstad Estate.

Several days after the auction, the Mitchells took the safe to a locksmith to have the locked compartment opened. The locksmith found $32,207 inside. The Everett Police Department, notified by the locksmith, impounded the money.

. . . The issue is whether there was in fact a sale of the safe and its unknown contents at the auction. In contrast to the Court of Appeals, we find that there was.

A sale is a consensual transaction. The subject matter which passes is to be determined by the intent of the parties as revealed by the terms of their agreement in light of the surrounding circumstances. [Citation.] The objective manifestation theory of contracts, which is followed in this state [cita-tion] lays stress on the outward manifestation of assent made by each party to the other. The subjective intention of the parties is irrelevant.

A contract has, strictly speaking, nothing to do with the personal, or individual, intent of the parties. A contract is an obligation attached by the mere force of law to certain acts of the parties, usually words, which ordinarily accompany and represent a known intent. If, however, it were proved by twenty bishops that either party, when he used the words, intended something else than the usual meaning which the law imposes upon them, he would still be held, unless there were some mutual mistake, or something else of the sort. [Citation.]

As stated in *Washington Shoe Mfg. Co. v. Duke* [citation.]

The apparent mutual assent of the parties, essential to the formation of a contract, must be gathered from their outward expressions and acts, and not from an unexpressed intention.

The inquiry, then, is into the outward manifestations of intent by a party to enter into a contract. We impute an intention corresponding to the reasonable meaning of a person's words and acts. [Citation.] If the offeror, judged by a reasonable standard manifests an intention to agree in regard to the matter in question, that agreement is established. [Citation.]

* * *

In the case before us, . . . the Mitchells were aware of the rule of the auction that all sales were final. Furthermore, the auctioneer made no statement reserving rights to any contents of the safe to the estate. Under these circumstances, we hold reasonable persons would conclude that the auctioneer manifested an objective intent to sell the safe and its contents and that the parties mutually assented to enter into that sale of the safe and the contents of the locked compartment.

* * *

This matter is remanded to the trial court for entry of the summary judgment in favor of the Mitchells.

Invitations Seeking Offers

LEFKOWITZ v. GREAT MINNEAPOLIS SURPLUS STORE, INC.

Supreme Court of Minnesota, 1957.
251 Minn. 188, 86 N.W.2d 689.

MURPHY, J.

This is an appeal from an order of . . . judgment award[ing] the plaintiff the sum of $138.50 as damages for breach of contract.

This case grows out of the alleged refusal of the defendant to sell to the plaintiff a certain fur piece which it had offered for sale in a newspaper advertisement. It appears from the record that on April 6, 1956, the defendant published the following advertisement in a Minneapolis newspaper:

Saturday 9 A.M. Sharp
3 Brand New
Fur
Coats
Worth to $100.00
First Come
First Served
$1
Each

On April 13, the defendant again published an advertisement in the same newspaper as follows:

Saturday 9 A.M.
2 Brand New Pastel
Mink 3–Skin Scarfs
Selling for $89.50
Out they go
Saturday. Each . . . $1.00
1 Black Lapin Stole
Beautiful,
worth $139.50 . . . $1.00
First Come
First Served

The record supports the findings of the court that on each of the Saturdays following the publication of the above-described ads the plaintiff was the first to present himself at the appropriate counter in the defendant's store and on each occasion demanded the coat and the stole so advertised and indicated his readiness to pay the sale price of $1. On both occasions, the defendant refused to sell the merchandise to the plaintiff, stating on the first occasion that by a "house rule" the offer was intended for women only and sales would not be made to men, and on the second visit that plaintiff knew defendant's house rules. . . .

The defendant contends that a newspaper advertisement offering items of merchandise for sale at a named price is a "unilateral offer" which may be withdrawn without notice. He relies upon authorities which hold that, where an advertiser publishes in a newspaper that he has a certain quantity or quality of goods which he wants to dispose of at certain prices and on certain terms, such advertisements are not offers which become contracts as soon as any person to whose notice they may come signifies his acceptance by notifying the other that he will take a certain quantity of them. Such advertisements have been construed as an invitation for an offer of sale on the terms stated, which offer, when received, may be accepted or rejected and which therefore does not become a contract of sale until accepted by the seller; and until a contract has been so made, the seller may modify or revoke such prices or terms. [Citations.] . . .

On the facts before us we are concerned with whether the advertisement constituted an offer, and, if so, whether the plaintiff's conduct constituted an acceptance.

* * *

The test of whether a binding obligation may originate in advertisements addressed to the general public is "whether the facts show that some performance was promised in positive terms in return for something requested."

* * *

Whether in any individual instance a newspaper advertisement is an offer rather than an invitation to make an offer depends on the legal intention of the parties and the surrounding circumstances. [Citations.] We are of the view on the facts before us that the offer by the defendant of the sale . . . was clear, definite, and explicit, and left nothing open for negotiation. The plaintiff, having successfully managed to be the first one to appear at the seller's place of business to be served, as requested by the advertisement, and having offered the stated purchase price of the article, was entitled to performance on the part of the defendant. We think the trial court was correct in holding that there was in the conduct of the parties a sufficient mutuality of obligation to constitute a contract of sale.

* * *

Affirmed.

Duration of Offers/Objective Manifestation

NEWMAN v. SCHIFF

United States Court of Appeals, Eighth Circuit, 1985.
778 F.2d 460.

BRIGHT, J.

John A. Newman, an attorney practicing law in St. Louis, Missouri, brought this action against Irwin Schiff of Hamden, Connecticut, alleging breach of contract. Newman claimed that Schiff had made a public offer of reward to anyone who could cite any section of the Internal Revenue Code that says an individual is required to file an income tax return. Newman asserted that he accepted Schiff's offer, and that Schiff breached the contract by failing to pay him the reward. The district court ruled in favor of Schiff by finding that Newman's acceptance was not timely, and Newman appeals. We affirm the judgment of the district court.

* * *

Irwin Schiff is a self-styled "tax rebel," who has made a career and substantial profits out of his tax protest activities. Schiff's basic contention is that the federal income tax is a voluntary tax which no one is required to pay. * * *

On February 7, 1983, Irwin Schiff appeared live on CBS News Nightwatch (Nightwatch), a nighttime television program with a viewer participation format. Schiff was interviewed by host Karen Stone from approximately 3:00 a.m. to 4:00 a.m. Eastern Time. The words "Nightwatch Phone-In" and telephone number (212) 955–9555 were flashed on the screen periodically during Schiff's appearance. In addition, Ms. Stone repeated the telephone number and encouraged viewers to call and speak directly with Schiff on the air.

During the course of the Nightwatch program, Schiff repeated his long-standing position that, "there is nothing in the Internal Revenue Code which I have here, which says anybody is legally required to pay the tax." Following a discussion of his rationale for that conclusion, Schiff stated: "If anybody calls this show—I have the Code—and cites any section of this Code that says an individual is required to file a tax return, I will pay them $100,000."

Newman did not see Schiff's live appearance on Nightwatch. He did, however, see a two-minute taped segment of the original Nightwatch interview that was rebroadcast several hours later on the CBS Morning News. The CBS Morning News rebroadcast included Schiff's reward proposal.

Newman felt certain that Schiff's statements regarding the Internal Revenue Code were incorrect. Upon arriving at work that day, he researched the issue and located several sections of the Code that to his satisfaction demonstrated the mandatory nature of the federal income tax system. The next day Newman telephoned CBS Morning News and cited . . . provisions of the Internal Revenue Code as authority for his position that individuals are required to pay federal income tax. [Citation.] Newman placed his call to (212) 975–4321, the number given him by the long distance operator for CBS in New York. He then reduced this conversation to writing and sent it to the CBS Morning News. Newman's letter stated that it represented "performance of the consideration requested by Mr. Schiff in exchange for his promise to pay $100,000."

* * *

On April 20, 1983, Schiff wrote to Newman and stated that: "[y]our letter to Mr. O'Regan at CBS Morning News was forwarded to me. I did make an offer on the February 7, 1983 news (which was actually part of an interview conducted earlier in the week)." Schiff said, however, that Newman had not properly accepted his offer for both substantive and procedural reasons.

Newman then sued Schiff in federal district court for breach of contract. The district court decided that: (1) Schiff intended for his offer to remain open only until the conclusion of the live Nightwatch broadcast; (2) the rebroadcast on CBS Morning News did not renew or extend Schiff's offer; and therefore (3) Newman's acceptance of the offer was untimely.

* * *

A. The Requirement of Mutual Assent

It is a basic legal principle that mutual assent is necessary for the formation of a contract. A significant doctrinal struggle in the development of contract law revolved around whether it was a party's actual or apparent assent that was necessary. This was a struggle between subjective and objective theorists. The subjectivists looked to actual assent. Both parties had to actually assent to an agreement for there to be a contract. External acts were merely necessary evidence to prove or disprove the requisite state of mind. The familiar cliche was that a contract required a "meeting of the minds" of the parties. [Citation.] The objectivists, on the other hand, looked to apparent assent. The expression of mutual assent, and not the assent itself, was the essential element in the formation of a contract. * * *

By the end of the nineteenth century the objective approach to the mutual assent requirement had become predominant, and courts continue to use it today. [Citation.]

* * *

B. The Mechanics of Mutual Assent: Offer and Acceptance

Courts determine whether the parties expressed their assent to a contract by analyzing their agreement process in terms of offer and acceptance. An offer is the "manifestation of willingness to enter into a bargain, so made as to justify another person in understanding that his assent to that bargain is invited and will conclude it." [Citations.]

The present case concerns a special type of offer: an offer for a reward. . . . [C]ourts have enforced public offers to pay rewards.

* * *

1. The Nightwatch Offer

In the present case, Schiff's statement on Nightwatch that he would pay $100,000 to anyone who called the show and cited any section of the Internal Revenue Code "that says an individual is required to file a tax return" constituted a valid offer for a reward. In our view, if anyone had called the show and cited the code sections that Newman produced, a contract would have been formed and Schiff would have been obligated to pay the $100,000 reward, for his bluff would have been properly called.

2. The CBS Morning News Rebroadcast

Newman, however, never saw the live CBS Nightwatch program upon which Schiff appeared and this lawsuit is not predicated on Schiff's Nightwatch offer. Newman saw the CBS Morning News rebroadcast of Schiff's Nightwatch appearance. This rebroadcast served not to renew or extend Schiff's offer, but rather only to inform viewers that Schiff had made an offer on Nightwatch. The rebroadcast constituted a newsreport and not a renewal of the original offer. An offeror is the master of his offer and it is clear that Schiff by his words, "If anybody calls this show * * *", limited his offer in time to remain open only until the conclusion of the live Nightwatch broadcast. A reasonable person listening to the news rebroadcast could not conclude that the above language—"calls this show"—constituted a new offer; rather than what it actually was, a newsreport of the offer previously made, which had already expired.

* * *

We affirm the judgment of the district court for the reasons discussed above.

Although Newman has not "won" his lawsuit in the traditional sense of recovering a reward that he sought, he has accomplished an important goal in the public interest of unmasking the "blatant nonsense" dispensed by Schiff. * * *

* * *

Revocation—Option Contracts

RYDER v. WESCOAT

Missouri Court of Appeals, 1976.
535 S.W.2d 269.

TURNAGE, J.

This case poses the problem of a rejection on the part of an option holder and a subsequent acceptance within the time limited. The trial court held the rejection terminated all rights under the option. This court holds the option rights were not terminated.

Wescoat, for a valuable consideration, gave Ryder an option to purchase a 120 acre farm upon which Wescoat held an option. The parties agree the deadline for Ryder to exercise the option was September 1. This was prior to the time within which Wescoat had to exercise his option so that in the event Ryder exercised his option with Wescoat, Wescoat would have time in turn to exercise his option and acquire title to convey to Ryder.

The parties do not clash on any factual issue, but rather strongly disagree as to the effect of a rejection Ryder made of his right to purchase the farm.

It is tacitly agreed that on August 20, before Ryder's option expired on September 1, Ryder said he was going to "pass" on the 120 acre farm. Wescoat testified he took this to

mean Ryder was not going to exercise his option to purchase such farm, and thereupon talked with a bank about obtaining the necessary financing to purchase the farm himself under his option. Wescoat also stated he talked with a bulldozer operator and obtained a price for doing some work on the farm, and in addition, arranged to do some liming. Wescoat admitted he had not legally obligated himself under any of these arrangements, and stated if Ryder had actually purchased the farm on September 1, he would not have been obligated for any expenditure on the land.

On August 30, Ryder caused a contract to be prepared by which he agreed to purchase the 120 acre farm from Wescoat. This contract along with a down-payment was given to Wescoat on that day. Wescoat refused to sign the contract and stated he did not sell the land to Ryder because of Ryder's previous rejection of his right to purchase on August 20.

The trial court made findings of fact in which it was found Ryder had informed Wescoat on August 20 that he would not exercise his option to purchase and Ryder had thereby rejected and relinquished his option and right to purchase. The court further found on August 30 Ryder undertook to exercise his option but that Wescoat refused to honor the same or to comply with the terms of the option.

* * *

No case has been cited, and diligent research on the part of this court has failed to locate any case involving this precise issue. However, text writers have dealt with the problem. In Simpson on Contracts, [citation] the author states:

Where an offer is supported by a binding contract that the offeree's power of acceptance shall continue for a stated time, will a communicated rejection terminate the offeree's power to accept within the time? On principle, there is no reason why it should. The offeree has a contract right to accept within the time. . . . So an option holder may complete a contract by communicating his acceptance despite the fact that he has previously rejected the offer. Where, however, before the acceptance the offeror has materially changed his position in reliance on the communicated rejection, as by selling or contracting to sell the subject matter of the offer elsewhere, the subsequent acceptance will be inoperative. . . .

* * *

It must be kept in mind Ryder had purchased for a valuable consideration the right to purchase this farm. This removes this case from the rule applied in those cases where an offer has been made, but the offeree has not paid any consideration for the making of the offer. In those cases, it is uniformly held that a rejection of the offer terminates the offer. Likewise, the making of a counter-offer terminates the original offer and places it beyond the power of the offeree to thereafter accept the offer.

However, the courts treat options which are purchased for a valuable consideration in a different manner. . . .

Since an option stands on a different footing from an offer which is made without consideration being paid therefor, and since it has been held that an option is irrevocable for the time stated, and that a counter-offer does not effect a rejection, it necessarily follows that a rejection standing alone would not end the rights of the option holder. This court adopts the rule . . . that a rejection of an option which has been purchased for a valuable consideration does not terminate the rights of the option holder unless the optionor has materially changed his position prior to a timely acceptance.

This rule fully protects the rights of both parties. It extends to the optionor the protection he requires in the event a rejection of the option is communicated to him and he thereafter changes his position in reliance thereon to his detriment. At the same time it protects the right of the option holder to have the opportunity to exercise his option for the full period for which he paid, absent the material change in position.

To apply this rule in this case, it must be held Ryder retained his right to exercise the option for the reason Wescoat has not shown any material change in his position between the time of the rejection and the later accep-

tance. The material change required by the rule . . . requires that a party must suffer a legal detriment or change his position for the worse and be prejudiced. [Citation.]

Wescoat did not show that he had suffered any detriment, had changed his position for the worse, or had been prejudiced by any action he took between the time of Ryder's rejection and acceptance. Wescoat talked about obtaining a loan, doing bulldozing and spreading lime on the farm, but actually took no action which obligated him to pay prior to Ryder exercising his option to purchase. In that situation, Wescoat did not materially change his position prior to the acceptance by Ryder, and Ryder's acceptance prior to September 1 was a valid exercise of his right to purchase the farm.

Wescoat's position on this appeal is based solely on the proposition that a rejection once communicated terminated all Ryder's rights under the option. In taking this position, Wescoat relies on cases involving continuing offers for which no valuable consideration was paid. . . .

* * *

The judgment in favor of Wescoat is reversed and the cause is remanded with directions to enter a judgment in favor of Ryder. The court shall direct specific performance of the agreement between Ryder and Wescoat for the purchase and sale of the 120 acre farm. The court is also directed to enter judgment in favor of Wescoat and against Ryder for $1500 admittedly due Wescoat under the option.

All concur.

Counter-offer

ZELLER v. FIRST NATIONAL BANK & TRUST

Appellate Court of Illinois, First District, 1979.
79 Ill.App.3d 170, 34 Ill.Dec. 473, 398 N.E.2d 148.

McNAMARA, J.

Plaintiff filed a complaint . . . alleging a contract to sell real estate to him. . . . The trial court entered summary judgment against plaintiff . . . and he appeals.

The property in question is held in trust. Defendant First National Bank and Trust Company of Evanston was trustee. William Jennings, who is not party to these proceedings, was beneficiary of the trust and executor of the estate containing the trust property. Austin L. Wyman, Jr., an attorney, and the law firm of Tenney & Bentley represented the estate.

In November, 1977, plaintiff and Jennings began negotiations with respect to the sale of the property. On December 23, 1977, Wyman wrote plaintiff, stating that he had been instructed by his principals to offer plaintiff the building for $240,000. The letter also recited interest rates and loan fees. Following receipt of this letter, plaintiff met with his attorney, Roger Jamma, and instructed him to communicate a counter-offer to Wyman. Accordingly, on January 10, 1978, Jamma sent Wyman a written counter-offer offering $230,000 and suggesting varying interest and loan arrangements.

On the same day, Jamma telephoned Wyman, and the two men discussed the offer and counter-offer. In his discovery deposition, Jamma stated that he might have mentioned the contents of the counter-offer to Wyman. Wyman testified at his deposition that Jamma informed him that a counter-offer of $230,000 had been sent and detailed the substance of the counter-offer.

* * *

On review, we deem it necessary to consider only the finding that the contract under which relief is sought was never properly formed.

It is elementary that for a contract to exist, there must be an offer and acceptance. [Citations.] Moreover, to create a binding contract, an acceptance must comply strictly with the terms of the offer. An acceptance requesting modification or containing terms which vary from those offered constitutes a rejection of the original offer, and becomes a counterproposal which must be accepted by the original offeror before a valid contract is formed. [Citations.]

On December 23, 1977, Wyman offered to sell plaintiff the property for $240,000. In a telephone conversation with Wyman on January 10, 1978, plaintiff's attorney discussed the counter-offer of $230,000. This counter-offer, containing terms varying from the original offer, operated as a rejection and terminated plaintiff's power to accept Wyman's offer. There was no suggestion that Wyman, the offeror, assented to the price modification in plaintiff's counter-offer so as to create a contract. Once having rejected Wyman's offer, plaintiff could not revive the offer by later telegraphing acceptance. [Citation.]

* * *

Plaintiff urges, however, that the counter-offer which was disclosed in the telephone conversation had no legal significance because it was oral rather than written. We do not agree. It is clear that the language of an offer may govern the mode of acceptance required. [Citation.] Where an offer requires a written acceptance, no other mode of acceptance may be used. [Citation.] Since the offer in the present case did not require acceptance or other communications regarding the sale to be in writing, verbal communication of the counter-offer was an effective rejection. Thus, contrary to plaintiff's contention, it is not determinative that the subsequent written acceptance arrived prior to the written counter-offer. In view of plaintiff's rejection prior to acceptance, no binding contract was created.

* * *

Judgment affirmed.

Effective Moment of Acceptance

CUSHING v. THOMSON

Supreme Court of New Hampshire, 1978.
118 N.H. 292, 386 A.2d 805.

Per Curiam.

This is a bill in equity brought by five members of an antinuclear protest group called the Portsmouth Area Clamshell Alliance against Governor Meldrim Thomson, Jr., and John Blatsos, adjutant general of the State of New Hampshire. The bill seeks specific performance of a contract allegedly entered into by the parties for the use of the New Hampshire National Guard armory in Portsmouth.

* * *

The [trial] court ruled that a binding contract existed, granted the plaintiffs specific performance, and enjoined the defendants from any and all acts that would impede performance.

* * *

On or about March 30, 1978, the adjutant general's office received an application from plaintiff Cushing for the use of the Portsmouth armory to hold a dance on the evening of April 29, 1978. On March 31 the adjutant general mailed a signed contract offer agreeing to rent the armory to the Portsmouth Clamshell Alliance for the evening of April 29. The agreement required acceptance by the renter affixing his signature to the accompanying copy of the agreement and returning the same to the adjutant general within five days after its receipt. On Monday, April 3, plaintiff Cushing received the contract offer and signed it on behalf of the Portsmouth Clamshell Alliance. At 6:30 on the evening of Tuesday, April 4, Mr. Cushing received a telephone call from the adjutant general advising him that the governor had ordered withdrawal of the rental offer, and accordingly the offer was being withdrawn. During that conversation Mr. Cushing stated that he had already signed the contract. A written confirmation of the withdrawal was sent by the adjutant general to the plaintiffs on April 5.

On April 6 defendants received by mail the signed contract dated April 3, postmarked April 5.

The first issue presented is whether the trial court erred in determining that a binding contract existed. Neither party challenges the applicable law. "To establish a contract of this character . . . there must be . . . an offer and an acceptance thereof in accordance with its terms. . . . [W]hen the parties to such a contract are at a distance from one another and the offer is sent by mail . . . the reply accepting the offer may be sent through the same medium, and the contract will be complete when the acceptance is mailed . . . properly addressed to the party making the offer and beyond the acceptor's control." [Citation.] Withdrawal of the offer is ineffectual once the offer has been accepted by posting in the mail. [Citation.]

* * *

Plaintiffs introduced the sworn affidavit of Mr. Cushing in which he stated that on April 3, he executed the contract and placed it in the outbox for mailing. Moreover plaintiffs' counsel represented to the court that it was customary office practice for outgoing letters to be picked up from the outbox daily and put in the U.S. mail. . . . Thus the representation that it was customary office procedure for the letters to be sent out the same day that they are placed in the office outbox, together with the affidavit, supported the implied finding that the completed contract was mailed before the attempted revocation. [Citation.]

[Judgment for plaintiff.]

QUESTIONS

1. Identify the three essentials of an offer and discuss briefly the requirements associated with each.

2. Identify and discuss briefly seven ways by which an offer may be terminated other than by acceptance.

3. Compare briefly the traditional and modern theories of definiteness of acceptance of an offer as

shown by the common law "miror image" rule and by the rule of the Uniform Commercial Code.

4. Discuss the five situations limiting an offeror's right to revoke her offer.

5. Explain the various rules that determine when an acceptance takes effect.

PROBLEMS

1. Ames, seeking business for his lawn maintenance firm, posted the following notice in the meeting room of the Antlers, a local lodge: "To the members of the Antlers—Special this month. I will resod your lawn for two dollars per square foot using Fairway brand sod. This offer expires July 15."

The notice also included Ames's name, address, and signature and specified that the acceptance was to be in writing.

Bates, a member of the Antlers, and Cramer, the janitor, read the notice and became interested. Bates wrote a letter to Ames saying he would accept the offer if Ames would use Putting Green brand sod. Ames received this letter July 14 and wrote to Bates saying he would not use Putting Green sod. Bates received Ames's letter on July 16 and promptly wrote Ames that he would accept Fairway sod. Cramer wrote to Ames on July 10, saying he accepted Ames's offer.

By July 15, Ames had found more profitable ventures and refused to resod either lawn at the specified price. Bates and Cramer brought an appropriate action against Ames for breach of contract. Decision as to the respective claims of Bates and Cramer?

2. Garvey owned four speedboats named Porpoise, Priscilla, Providence, and Prudence. On April 2, Garvey made written offers to sell the four boats in the order named for $4,200 each to Caldwell, Meens, Smith, and Braxton, respectively, allowing ten days for acceptance. In which, if any, of the following four situations described was a contract formed?

(a) Five days later, Caldwell received notice from Garvey that he had contracted to sell Porpoise to Montgomery. The next day, April 8, Caldwell notified Garvey that he accepted Garvey's offer.

(b) On the third day, April 5, Meens mailed a rejection to Garvey which reached Garvey on the morning of the fifth day. But at 10:00 A.M., on the fourth day, Meens sent an acceptance by telegram to Garvey who received it at noon on the same day.

(c) Smith, on April 3, replied that she was interested in buying Providence but declared the price asked appeared slightly excessive and wondered if, perhaps, Garvey would be willing to sell the boat for $3,900. Five days later, having received no reply from Garvey, Smith, by letter, accepted Garvey's offer and enclosed a certified check for $4,200.

(d) Braxton was accidentally killed in an automobile accident on April 9. The following day, the executor of Braxton's estate mailed an acceptance of Garvey's offer to Garvey.

3. Alpha Rolling Mill Corporation, by letter dated June 8, offered to sell Brooklyn Railroad Company 2,000 to 5,000 tons of fifty-pound iron rails upon certain specified terms adding that, if the offer was accepted, Alpha Corporation would expect to be notified prior to June 20. Brooklyn Company, on June 16, by telegram, referring to Alpha Corporation's offer of June 8, directed Alpha Corporation to enter an order for 1,200 tons of fifty-pound iron rails on the terms specified. The same day, June 16, Brooklyn Company, by letter to Alpha Corporation, confirmed the telegram. On June 18, Alpha Corporation by telegram, declined to fulfill the order. Brooklyn Company, on June 19, telegraphed Alpha Corporation: "Please enter an order for 2,000 tons rails as per your letter of the eighth. Please forward written contract. Reply." To Brooklyn Company's repeated inquiries whether the order for 2,000 tons of rails had been entered, Alpha denied the existence of any contract between Brooklyn Company and itself. Thereafter, Brooklyn Company sues Alpha Corporation for breach of contract. Decision?

4. On April 8, Burchette received a telephone call from Bleluck, a truck dealer, who told Burchette that a new model truck in which Burchette was interested would arrive in one week. Although Bleluck initially wanted $10,500, the conversation ended after Bleluck agreed to sell and Burchette to purchase the truck for $10,000, with $1,000 down payment and the balance upon delivery. The next day, Burchette sent Bleluck a check for $1,000 which Bleluck promptly cashed.

One week later, when Burchette called Bleluck and inquired about the truck, Bleluck informed Burchette he had several prospects looking at the truck and would not sell for less than $10,500. The following day Bleluck sent Burchette a properly executed check for $1,000 with the following notation thereon: "Return of down payment on sale of truck."

After notifying Bleluck that she will not cash the check, Burchette sues Bleluck for damages. Decision?

5. On November 15, I. Sellit, a manufacturer of crystalware, mailed to Benny Buyer a letter stating that Sellit would sell to Buyer 100 crystal "A" goblets at $100 per goblet and that "the offer would remain open for fifteen (15) days." On November 18, Sellit, noticing the sudden rise in the price of crystal "A" goblets, decided to withdraw her offer to Buyer and so notified Buyer. Buyer chose to ignore Sellit's letter of revocation and gleefully watched as the price of crystal "A" goblets continued to skyrocket. On November 30, Buyer mailed to Sellit a letter accepting Sellit's offer to sell the goblets. The letter was received by Sellit on December 4. Buyer demands delivery of the goblets; what result?

6. On May 1, Melforth Realty Company offered to sell Greenacre to Dallas, Inc., for $1,000,000. The offer was made by telegraph and stated that the offer would expire on May 15. Dallas decided to purchase the property and sent a registered letter to Melforth on May 10, accepting the offer. Due to unexplained delays in the postal service, the letter was not received by Melforth until May 22. Melforth wishes to sell Greenacre to another buyer, who is offering $1,200,000 for the tract of land. Has a contract resulted between Melforth and Dallas?

7. Rowe advertised in newspapers of wide circulation and otherwise made known that she would pay $5,000 for a complete set consisting of ten volumes of certain rare books. Ford, not knowing of the offer, gave Rowe all but one of the set of rare books as a Christmas present. Ford later learned of the offer, obtained the one remaining book, tendered it to Rowe, and demanded the $5,000. Rowe refused to pay. Is Ford entitled to the $5,000?

8. Scott, manufacturer of a carbonated beverage, entered into a contract with Otis, owner of a baseball park, whereby Otis rented to Scott a large signboard on top of the center field wall. The contract provided that Otis should letter the sign as desired by Scott and would change the lettering from time to time within forty-eight hours after receipt of written request from Scott. As directed by Scott, the signboard originally stated in large letters that Scott would pay $100 to any ball player hitting a home run over the sign.

In the first game of the season, Hume, the best hitter in the League, hit one home run over the sign. Scott immediately served written notice on Otis instructing Otis to replace the offer on the signboard with an offer to pay fifty dollars to every pitcher who pitched a no hit game in the park. A week after receipt of Scott's letter, Otis had not changed the wording on the sign, and on that day Perry, a pitcher for a scheduled game, pitched a no hit game while Todd, one of his teammates, hit a home run over Scott's sign.

Scott refuses to make any payment to any of the three players. What are the rights of Scott, Hume, Perry, and Todd?

9. Barnes accepted Clark's offer to sell to him a portion of Clark's coin collection. Clark forgot that his prized $20 gold piece at the time of the offer and acceptance was included in the portion which he offered to sell to Barnes. Clark did not intend to include the gold piece in the sale. Barnes, at the time of inspecting the offered portion of the collection, and prior to accepting the offer, saw the gold piece. Is Barnes entitled to the $20 gold piece?

10. Small, admiring Jasper's watch, asked Jasper where and at what price he had purchased it. Jasper replied: "I bought it at West Watch Shop about two years ago for around $85, but I am not certain as to that." Small then said: "Those fellows at West are good people and always sell good watches. I'll buy that watch from you." Jasper replied: "It's a deal." The next morning Small telephoned Jasper and said he had changed his mind and did not wish to buy the watch.

Jasper sued Small for breach of contract. In defense, Small has pleaded that he made no enforceable contract with Jasper (a) because the parties did not agree on the price to be paid for the watch, and (b) because the parties did not agree on the place and time of delivery of the watch to Small. Are either, or both, of these defenses good?

11. Jeff says to Brenda, "I offer to sell you my IBM PC for $900." Brenda replies, "If you do not hear otherwise from me by Thursday, I have accepted your offer." Jeff agrees, and does not hear from Brenda by Thursday. Does a contract exist between Jeff and Brenda? Explain.

12. On November 19, 1949, Hoover Motor Express Company sent to Clements Paper Company a written offer to purchase certain real estate. Some time in December, Clements authorized Williams to accept. Williams, however, attempted to bargain with Hoover to obtain a better deal, specifically that Clements would retain easements on the property. In a telephone conversation on January 13, 1950, Williams first told Hoover of his plan to obtain the easements. Hoover replied: "Well, I don't know if we are ready. We have not decided, we might not want to go through with it." On January 20 Clements sent a written acceptance of Hoover's offer. Hoover refused to buy, claiming it had revoked its offer through the January 13 phone conversation. Clements then brought suit to compel the sale or obtain damages. Decision?

13. Walker leased a small lot to Keith for ten years at one hundred dollars a month, with a right for Keith to extend the lease for another ten-year term under the same terms except as to rent. The renewal option provided:

rental will be fixed in such amount as shall actually be agreed upon by the lessors and the lessee with the monthly rental fixed on the comparative basis of rental values as of the date of the renewal with rental values at this time reflected by the comparative business conditions of the two periods.

Keith sought to exercise the renewal right and, when the parties were unable to agree on the rent, brought suit against Walker. Who prevails? Why?

COMPUTER RESEARCH PROBLEMS

 1. The Brewers contracted to purchase Dower House from McAfee. Then, several weeks before the May 7 settlement date for the purchase of the house, the two parties began to negotiate for the sale of certain items of furniture in the house. On April 30 McAfee sent the Brewers a letter containing a list of the furnishings to be purchased at specified prices; a payment schedule including a $3,000 payment due on acceptance; and a clause reading: "If the above is satisfactory please sign and return one copy with the first payment."

On June 3 the Brewers sent a letter to McAfee stating that enclosed was a $3,000 check; that the original contract had been misplaced and could another be furnished; that they planned to move into Dower House on June 12; and that they wished that the red desk be included in the contract. McAfee then sent a letter dated June 8 to the Brewers listing the items of furniture purchased.

The Brewers moved into Dower House in the middle of June. Soon after they moved in, they tried to contact McAfee at his office to tell him that there had been a misunderstanding relating to their purchase of the listed items. They then refused to pay him any more money, and he brought this action to recover the balance outstanding. Decision?

 2. The Thoelkes were owners of real property located in Orange County, which the Morrisons agreed to purchase. The Morrisons signed a contract for the sale of that property and mailed it to the Thoelkes in Texas on November 26. The next day the Thoelkes executed the contract and placed it in the mail addressed to the Morrisons' attorney in Florida. After the executed contract was mailed but before it was received in Florida, the Thoelkes called the Morrisons' attorney in Florida and attempted to repudiate the contract. Decision?

3. On December 20, 1952, Lucy and Zehmer met while having drinks in a restaurant. During the course of their conversation, Lucy apparently offered to buy Zehmer's 471.6-acre farm for $50,000 cash. Although Zehmer claims that he thought the offer was made in jest, he wrote the following on the back of a pad: "We hereby agree to sell to W. O. Lucy the Ferguson Farm complete for $50,000, title satisfactory to buyer." Zehmer then signed the writing and induced his wife Ida to do the same. She claims, however, that she signed only after Zehmer assured her that it was only a joke. Finally, Zehmer claims that he was "high as a Georgia pine" at the time but admits that he was not too drunk to make a valid contract. Decision?

4. On July 31, Lee Calan Imports advertised a used Volvo station wagon for sale in the Chicago *Sun-Times* newspaper. As part of the information for the advertisement, Lee Calan Imports instructed the newspaper to print the price of the car as $1,795. However, due to a mistake made by the newspaper, without any fault on the part of Lee Calan Imports, the printed ad listed the price of the car as $1,095. After reading the ad and then examining the car, O'Brien told a Lee Calan Imports salesman that he wanted to purchase the car for the advertised price of $1,095. Calan Imports refuses to sell the car to O'Brien for $1,095. Is there a contract? If so, for what price?

5. On May 20 cattle rancher Oliver visits his neighbor Southworth, telling him "I know you're interested in buying the land I'm selling." Southworth replies "Yes, I do want to buy that land, especially since it adjoins my property." Although the two men did not discuss the price, Oliver told Southworth he would determine the value of the property, and send that information to him so that Southworth would have "notice" of what Oliver "wanted for the land." On June 13, Southworth called Oliver to ask if he still planned to sell the land. Oliver answered "Yes, and I should have the value of the land determined soon." On June 17 Oliver sent a letter to Southworth listing a price quotation of $324,000. Southworth then responded to Oliver by letter on June 21 stating that he accepted Oliver's offer. However, on June 24 Oliver wrote back to Southworth saying "There has never been a firm offer to sell, and there is no enforceable contract between us." Oliver maintains that a price quotation alone is not an offer. Southworth claims a valid contract has been made. Who wins? Discuss.

Chapter 10

CONDUCT INVALIDATING ASSENT

Duress
Undue Influence
Fraud
Nonfraudulent Misrepresentation
Mistake

THE preceding chapter considered one of the essential requirements of a contract, namely, the objective manifestation of mutual assent by each party to the other. In addition to requiring that the offer and acceptance be satisfied, the law also demands that the agreement be voluntary and knowing. If both of these requirements are not met, then the agreement is either voidable or void. This chapter deals with situations in which the manifested consent by one of the parties to the contract is not effective because it was not knowingly and voluntarily given. These situations are considered under the headings of duress, undue influence, fraud, nonfraudulent misrepresentation, and mistake.

DURESS

A person should not be held to an agreement into which she has not entered voluntarily. Accordingly, the law will not enforce any contract induced by **duress,** which in general is any wrongful act or threat that overcomes the free will of a party.

Physical Compulsion

There are two basic types of duress. The first occurs when a party is compelled to manifest assent to a contract through actual **physical force,** such as pointing a gun at a person or taking a person's hand and compelling him to sign a written contract. This type of duress is extremely rare, but it renders the agreement **void.** Restatement, Section 174(1).

Improper Threats

The second type of duress involves the use of **improper threats** or acts, including economic and social coercion, to compel a person to enter into a contract. The threat may be explicit or inferred from words or conduct, but in either case it must leave the victim with no reasonable alternative. This type of duress makes the contract **voidable** at the option of the coerced party. Restatement, Section 175(2). For example, if Lance, a landlord, induces Tamara, an infirm bedridden tenant, to enter into a new lease on the same apartment at a greatly increased rent by wrongfully threatening to terminate Tamara's lease and evict her, Tamara can escape or *avoid* the new lease by reason of the duress exerted upon her. *See International Underwater Contractors, Inc. v. New England Telephone and Telegraph Co.*

With respect to the second and more common type of duress, the fact that the act or threat would not affect a person of average strength and intelligence is not determinative if it places the particular person in fear and induces an action against his will. The test is *subjective,* and the question is, did the threat actually induce assent on the part of the person claiming to be the victim of duress? Threats that would suffice to induce assent by one person may not suffice to induce assent by another. All circumstances must be considered, including the age, background, and relationship of the parties. Restatement, Section 175. Indeed, as comment c to this section of the Restatement states:

Persons of a weak or cowardly nature are the very ones that need protection; the courageous can usually protect themselves. Timid and inexperienced persons are particularly subject to threats, and it does not lie in the mouths of the unscrupulous to excuse their imposition on such persons on the ground of their victims' infirmities.

Ordinarily, the acts or threats constituting duress are themselves crimes or torts. But this is not true in all cases. The acts need not be criminal or tortious in order to be *wrongful;* they merely need be contrary to public policy or morally reprehensible. For example, if the threat involves a breach of a contractual duty of good faith and fair dealing or the use of the civil process in bad faith it is improper.

Moreover, it has generally been held that contracts induced by threats of criminal prosecution are voidable, regardless of whether the coerced party had committed an unlawful act. Likewise, a threat of criminal prosecution of a near relative, as a son or husband, is duress, regardless of the guilt or innocence of the relative. *See Haumont v. Security State Bank.*

To be distinguished are threats to resort to ordinary civil remedies in order to recover a debt due from another. It is not wrongful to threaten to bring a civil suit against an individual to recover a debt. What is prohibited is the use of a threat of civil suit when bringing such a suit would be abuse of process.

UNDUE INFLUENCE

Undue influence is the unfair persuasion of a person by a party in a dominant position based upon a **confidential relationship.** The law very carefully scrutinizes contracts between those in a relationship of trust and confidence that is likely to permit one party to take unfair advantage of the other. Examples are the relationships of guardian-ward, trustee-beneficiary, principal-agent, spouses to each other, parent-child, attorney-client, physician-patient, and clergy-parishioner.

A transaction induced by unfair persuasion on the part of the dominant party is induced by undue influence and is **voidable.** The ultimate question in undue influence cases is whether the transaction was induced by influencing a freely exercised and competent judgment or by dominating the mind or emotions of a submissive party. The weakness or dependence of the person persuaded is a strong circumstance tending to show that persuasion may have been unfair. For example, Ronald, a person without business experience, has for years relied in business matters on the advice of Nancy, who is experienced in business. Nancy, without making any false representations of fact, induces Ronald to enter into a contract with Nancy's confederate, George, that is disadvantageous to Ronald as both Nancy and George know. The transaction is voidable on the grounds of undue influence.

Undue influence, as previously mentioned, generally arises in the context of the relationships in which one person is in a position of dominance over another, or is likely to be. Where such a relationship exists at the time of the transaction and it appears that the dominant party has gained at the expense of the other party, the transaction is presumed to be voidable. For example, in a legally challenged contract between a guardian and his ward, the law presumes that advantage was taken by the guardian. It is, therefore, incumbent upon the guardian to rebut this presumption. Important factors in determining whether the contract is fair are (1) whether the dominant party made full disclosure of all relevant information known to him, (2) whether the consideration was adequate, and (3) whether the dependent party had competent and independent advice before completing the transaction. Without limitation, in every situation in which a confidential relationship exists the dominant party is held to utmost good faith in his dealings with the other. *See Schaneman v. Schaneman.*

FRAUD

Another factor affecting the validity of consent given by a contracting party is fraud. Fraud prevents the assent from being knowingly given. There are two distinct types of fraud: fraud in the execution and fraud in the inducement.

Fraud in the Execution

Fraud in the execution, which is extremely rare, consists of a misrepresentation that deceives the defrauded person as to the very nature of the contract. Fraud in the execution occurs when a person does not know or have reasonable opportunity to know the character or essence of a proposed contract because the other party misrepresents its character or essential terms. Fraud in the execution renders the transaction **void.**

For example, Abigail delivers a package to Boris, requests that Boris sign a receipt for it, holds out a simple printed form headed "Receipt," and indicates the line on which Boris is to sign. This line appears to Boris to be the bottom line of the receipt, but instead it is the signature line of a promissory note cleverly concealed underneath the receipt. Boris signs where directed without knowing that he is signing a note. This is fraud in the execution. The note is void and of no legal effect. The reason is simply that, although the signature is genuine and appears to be a manifestation of assent to the terms of the note, there is no actual assent. The nature of Abigail's fraud precluded consent to the signing of the note

because it prevented Boris from reasonably knowing what he was signing.

Fraud in the Inducement

Fraud in the inducement, generally referred to as fraud or deceit, is an intentional misrepresentation of material fact by one party to the other who consents to enter into a contract in justifiable reliance upon the misrepresentation. Fraud in the inducement renders the contract **voidable** by the defrauded party. For example, Ada, in offering to sell her dog to Ben, tells Ben that the dog won first prize in its class in the recent national dog show. In fact, the dog had not even been entered in the show. This statement induces Ben to accept the offer and pay a high price for the dog. There is a contract, but it is voidable by Ben because of Ada's fraud, which induced his assent.

The requisite elements of fraud in the inducement are:

1. a false representation
2. of a fact
3. that is material and
4. made with knowledge of its falsity and the intention to deceive and
5. which representation is justifiably relied upon.

False Representation A basic element of fraud is a false representation or misrepresentation, i.e., an assertion not in accord with the facts. There must be some positive statement or conduct that misleads. Active **concealment** can form the basis for fraud, as where the seller puts heavy oil or grease in a car engine to conceal a knock. **Concealment** is an action intended or known to be likely to keep another from learning of a fact of which he would otherwise have learned. Truth may be suppressed by concealment as much as by active misrepresentation. An express denial of knowledge of a fact which a party knows to exist is a misrepresentation if its effect on the other party is to lead him to believe that the facts do not exist or cannot be discovered.

Moreover, a statement of misleading half-truth is considered the equivalent of a false representation.

As a general rule, **silence** or nondisclosure alone does *not* amount to fraud. There is generally no obligation on the part of a seller to tell a purchaser everything he knows about the subject of the sale. Thus, it is not fraud when a buyer possesses advantageous information about the seller's property, of which he knows the seller to be ignorant, and does not disclose such information to the seller. A buyer is under no duty to inform the seller of the greater value or other advantages of his property. Assume that Sid owns a farm which, as a farm, is worth $10,000. Brenda knows that there is oil under Sid's farm, and knows that Sid is ignorant of this fact. Brenda, without disclosing this information to Sid, makes an offer to Sid to buy the farm for $10,000. Sid accepts the offer and a contract is duly made. Sid, on later learning the facts, can do nothing about the matter, either at law or in equity. As one case puts it, "a purchaser is not bound by our laws to make the man he buys from as wise as himself."

Although nondisclosure usually does not constitute a misrepresentation, in certain situations it does. One such situation arises when (1) a person fails to disclose a fact known to him, (2) he knows that the disclosure of that fact would correct a mistake of the other party as to a basic assumption on which that party is making the contract, and (3) nondisclosure of the fact amounts to a failure to act in a good faith and in accordance with reasonable standards of fair dealing. Restatement, Section 161. Accordingly, if there is a latent (hidden) defect of a substantial character, one that would not be discovered by an ordinary examination, the seller may be obliged to reveal it. Suppose, for example, that Judith owns a valuable horse, which Judith knows is suffering from a disease discoverable only by a competent veterinary surgeon. Judith offers to sell this horse to Curt, but does not inform Curt about the condition of her horse. Curt makes a reasonable examination of the horse and, finding it in apparently normal condition, purchases it from Judith. Curt, on later discovering the disease in question, can have the sale set aside. Judith's silence, under the circumstances, was a misrepresentation.

There are other situations in which the law imposes a duty of disclosure. For example, one may have a duty of disclosure because of prior representations innocently made but which are later discovered to be untrue before entering into the contract. Another instance in which silence may constitute fraud is a transaction involving a fiduciary. A **fiduciary** is a person in a confidential relationship, who owes a duty of trust, loyalty, and confidence to another. For example, an agent owes a fiduciary duty to his principal as does a trustee to the beneficiary of the trust and a partner to her copartners. A fiduciary may not deal at *arm's length* but rather owes a duty to make full disclosure of all relevant facts when entering into a transaction with the other party to the relationship. In contrast, in most everyday business or market transactions, the parties are said to deal at "arm's length." This expression means that the parties deal with each other on equal terms.

Fact   The basic element of fraud is the misrepresentation of a material fact. A **fact** is an event that actually took place or a thing that actually exists. Suppose that Dale induces Mike to purchase shares in a company unknown to Mike at a price of $100 per share by representing that she had the preceding year paid $150 per share for them, when in fact she had paid only $50. This representation of a past event is a misrepresentation of fact.

Actionable fraud can rarely be based upon what is merely a statement of opinion. A representation is one of **opinion** if it expresses only the uncertain belief of the representor as to the existence of a fact or his judgment as to quality, value, authenticity, or other matters of judgment.

The line between fact and opinion is not an easy one to draw and in close cases presents an issue for the jury. The solution will often turn upon the superior knowledge of the person making the statement and the information available to the other party. Thus, if Dale said to Mike that the shares were "a good investment," she is merely stating her opinion, and in the usual case Mike ought to regard it as no more than that. Other common examples of opinion are statements of value, such as "This is the best car for the money in town" or "This deluxe model will give you twice the wear of a cheaper model." Such exaggerations and commendations of articles offered for sale are to be expected from dealers who are merely puffing their wares with "sales talk." If the representor is a professional advising a client, the courts are more likely to regard an untrue statement of opinion as actionable. When the expression of opinion is of one holding himself out as having expert knowledge, the tendency is to grant relief to those who have sustained loss by reasonable reliance upon the expert evaluation. *See Vokes v. Arthur Murray, Inc.*

Also to be distinguished from a representation of fact is a **prediction** of the future. Predictions are similar to opinions, as no one can know with certainty what will happen in the future, and normally they are not regarded as factual statements. Likewise, promissory statements ordinarily do not constitute a basis of fraud, as a breach of promise does not necessarily indicate that the promise was fraudulently made. A promise that the promisor, at the time of making, had no intention of keeping, however, is a misrepresentation of fact. Most courts take the position that the state of a person's mind, which is being misrepresented, "is as much a fact as the state of a person's digestion." *Edgington v. Fitzmaurice*, 29 Ch.D. 459 (1885). If a dealer promises, "I will service this machine free for the next year," but at the time has no intention of doing so, his conduct is actionable if the other elements of fraud are present.

Historically, courts held that representations of **law** were not statements of fact but rather of opinion. The present trend is to recognize that a statement of law may have either the effect of a statement of fact or a statement of opinion. Restatement, Torts, Section 545. For example, it has the effect of a statement of fact if it asserts that a particular statute has been enacted or repealed. On the other hand, a statement as to the legal consequences of a particular set of facts is a statement of opinion. Nonetheless, such a statement may carry the implication that the facts known to the maker are consistent with the legal conclusion stated. For example, an assertion that a company has the legal right to do business in a State may include the assurance that the company has taken all the steps required to be duly qualified. Moreover, a statement by one who is learned in the law, as a practicing attorney, may be considered one of fact.

Materiality In addition to the requirement that the misrepresentation be one of fact, it is necessary that it be material. A misrepresentation is **material** if (1) it would be likely to induce a reasonable person to manifest his assent or (2) the maker knows that it would be likely to induce the recipient to do so. Restatement, Section 162. In the sale of a race horse, it may not be material whether the horse was ridden in its most recent race by a certain jockey, but its running time for the race probably would be. The Restatement of Contracts provides that a contract justifiably induced by a misrepresentation is voidable if the misrepresentation is either fraudulent *or* material. Therefore, a fraudulent misrepresentation does not have to be material to obtain rescission but it must be to recover damages. Restatement, Section 164; Restatement, Torts, Section 538.

See Reed v. King for an unusual factual situation involving the duty to disclose a "material" fact.

Knowledge of Falsity and Intention to Deceive To establish fraud, the misrepresentation must have been known by the one making it to be false and must be made with an intent to deceive. This element of fraud is known as *scienter*. Knowledge of falsity can consist of (a) actual knowledge, (b) lack of belief in the statement's truthfulness, or (c) reckless indifference as to its truthfulness.

Justifiable Reliance A person is not entitled to relief unless he has justifiably relied upon the misrepresentation. If the complaining party's decision was in no way influenced by the misrepresentation, he must abide by the terms of the contract. He is not deceived if he does not rely. What is required is that the misrepresentation substantially contributes to the misled party's decision to enter into the contract. If the complaining party knew or it was obvious that the representation of the defendant was untrue, but still entered into the contract, he has not justifiably relied. Moreover, where the misrepresentation is fraudulent, the party who relies on it is entitled to relief even though he does not investigate the statement or he is contributorily negligent in relying on it. Restatement, Torts, Sections 540, 545A. A recipient's fault in not knowing or discovering the facts before making the contract does not make his reliance unjustified unless it amounts to a failure to act in good faith and in accordance with reasonable standards of fair dealing. Restatement, Section 172.

NONFRAUDULENT MISREPRESENTATION

Nonfraudulent misrepresentation is a material, false statement that induces another to rely justifiably but is made *without* scienter.

Negligent misrepresentation is a false representation that is made without due care in ascertaining its truthfulness. **Innocent misrepresentation** is a false representation made without knowledge of its falsity but with due care. To obtain relief for nonfraudulent misrepresentation, all of the other elements of fraud must be present *and* the misrepresentation must be material. The remedies that may be available for nonfraudulent misrepresentation are rescission and damages (see Chapter 17).

MISTAKE

A **mistake** is a belief that is not in accord with the facts. Where the mistaken facts relate to the basis of the parties' agreement, the law permits the adversely affected party to avoid the contract under certain circumstances. But because permitting avoidance for mistake undermines the objective approach to mutual assent, the law has experienced considerable difficulty in specifying those circumstances that justify permitting the subjective matter of mistake to invalidate an otherwise objectively satisfactory agreement. As a result, establishing clear rules governing the effect of mistake has proven elusive.

The Restatement and a number of States treat mistakes of law in existence at the time of making the contract *no* differently than mistakes of fact. For example, Susan contracts to sell a parcel of land to James with the mutual understanding that James will build an apartment house on the land. Both Susan and James believe that such a building is lawful, but unknown to them the town had enacted an ordinance precluding such use of the land three days before they entered into their contract. This mistake of law would be treated as a mistake of fact with consequences discussed below.

Mutual Mistake

Mutual mistake occurs when *both* parties are mistaken as to the same set of facts. If the mistake relates to a basic assumption on which the contract is made and has a material effect on the agreed exchange, then it is **voidable** by the adversely affected party unless he bears the risk of the mistake. Restatement, Section 152.

Usually market conditions and the financial situation of the parties are not considered basic assumptions. Thus, if Gail contracts to purchase Pete's automobile under the belief that she can sell it at a profit to Jesse, she is not excused from liability if she is mistaken in this belief. Nor can she rescind the agreement simply because she was mistaken as to her estimate of what the automobile was worth. These are the ordinary risks of business, and courts do not undertake to relieve against them. But suppose that the parties contract upon the assumption that the automobile is a 1991 Cadillac with fifteen thousand miles of use, when, in fact, the engine is that of a cheaper model and has been run in excess of fifty thousand miles. Here, a court would likely allow a rescission because of mutual mistake of a material fact. Another example of mutual mistake of fact was presented in a California case where a noted violinist purchased two violins from a collector for $8,000, the bill of sale reading: ". . . I have on this date sold to Mr. Efrem Zimbalist one Joseph Guarnerius violin and one Stradivarius violin dated 1717." Actually, unknown to either party, neither violin was genuine. Taken together they were worth no more than $300. The sale was voidable by the purchaser for mutual mistake. In a New Zealand case, the plaintiff purchased a "stud bull" at an auction. There were no express warranties as to "sex, condition, or otherwise." Actually, the bull was sterile. Rescission was allowed, the court observing that it was a "bull in name only."

Unilateral Mistake

Unilateral mistake occurs when only one of the parties is mistaken. Courts have been hesitant to grant relief for unilateral mistake even though it relates to a basic assumption on which the party entered into the contract and has a material effect on the agreed exchange. Nevertheless, relief will be granted where the nonmistaken party knows, or reasonably should know, that such a mistake has been made or where the mistake was caused by the fault of the nonmistaken party. For example, suppose a building contractor submits a bid on a job that is one-half the amount it should be because he made a serious error in his computations. If the other party knows that he made such an error, or reasonably should have known of it, she cannot, as a general rule, take advantage of the other's mistake by accepting the offer. In addition, some courts and the Restatement allow rescission where the effect of the unilateral mistake makes enforcement of the contract unconscionable. Section 153.

Assumption of Risk of Mistake

If a party has undertaken to bear the risk of a mistake, then he will not be able to avoid the contract even though the mutual or unilateral mistake would have otherwise permitted the party to do so. This allocation of risk may occur by agreement of the parties. For instance, a ship at sea may be sold "lost or not lost." In such case the buyer is liable whether the ship was lost or not lost at the time of the making of the contract. There is no mistake; instead, there is a conscious allocation of risk.

The risk of mistake may also be allocated by conscious ignorance when the parties recognize that they have limited knowledge of the facts. For example, the Supreme Court of Wisconsin refused to set aside the sale of a stone for which the purchaser paid one dollar, but which was subsequently discovered to be an uncut diamond valued at $700. The parties did not know at the time of sale what the stone was and knew they did not know. Each consciously assumed the risk that the value might be more or less than the selling price.

Effect of Fault upon Mistake

The Restatement provides that a mistaken party's fault in not knowing or discovering a fact before making the contract does not prevent him from avoiding the contract "unless his fault amounts to a failure to act in good faith and in accordance with reasonable standards of fair dealing." Restatement, Section 157. This rule does not, however, apply to a failure to read a contract. As a general proposition, a party is held to what she signs. Her signature authenticates the writing, and she cannot repudiate that which she has voluntarily approved. Generally, one who assents to a writing is presumed to know its contents and cannot escape being bound by its terms merely by contending that she did not read them; her assent is deemed to cover unknown as well as known terms. Restatement, Section 157, Comment b.

Mistake in Meaning of Terms

Somewhat related to mistakes of facts is the situation where the parties have a misunderstanding regarding the meaning of their manifestations of mutual assent. A famous case involving this problem is *Raffles v. Wichelhaus,* 2 Hurlstone & Coltman 906 (1864), popularly known as the *"Peerless* Case." A contract of purchase was made for 125 bales of cotton to arrive on the Peerless from Bombay. It happened, however, that there were two ships by the name of "Peerless," each sailing from Bombay, one in October and the other in December. The buyer had in mind the ship that sailed in October, while the seller reasonably believed the agreement referred to the Peerless sailing in December. Neither party was at fault, but both believed in good faith that a different ship was intended. The English court held that no contract existed. The Restatement, Section 20 is in accord.

There is no manifestation of mutual assent where the parties attach materially different meanings to their manifestations and neither party knows or has reason to know the meaning attached by the other. If blame can be ascribed to either party, however, that party will be held responsible. Thus, if the seller knew of the sailing from Bombay of two ships by the name of Peerless, then he would be at fault, and the contract would be for the ship sailing in October as the buyer expected. If neither is to blame or both are to blame, there is no contract at all; that is, the agreement is void.

CASES

Duress

INTERNATIONAL UNDERWATER CONTRACTORS, INC. v. NEW ENGLAND TELEPHONE AND TELEGRAPH CO.

Massachusetts Court of Appeals, 1979.
8 Mass.App.Ct. 340, 393 N.E.2d 968.

BROWN, J.

The plaintiff, International Underwater Contractors, Inc. (IUC), appeals from the entry of summary judgment for the defendant, New England Telephone and Telegraph Company (NET).

The plaintiff, which had entered into a written contract with the defendant to assemble and install certain conduits under the Mystic River for a lump sum price of $149,680, to be paid semimonthly in installments in proportion to the progress of the work, seeks additional compensation in a total amount of $811,816.73 for a major change in the system from that specified in the contract. The plaintiff asserts that the change, which was necessitated by delays caused by the defendant, forced the work to be performed in the winter months instead of during the summer, as originally bid, making the equipment originally specified unusable. This major change was made, the plaintiff alleges, at the direction of the defendant, and upon the defendant's assurances that it would pay the resulting additional costs.

The defendant moved for summary judgment with a supporting affidavit, wherein it argued in defense a release signed by the plaintiff settling the additional claim for a total sum of $575,000. The plaintiff, which submitted countervailing affidavits in opposition to the motion, argues that the release is not binding because it was signed under economic duress.

A special master appointed to hear summary judgment motions found that "as a matter of law, the economic duress required to vitiate the subject release was not present." Summary judgment was entered for the defendant, and the plaintiff's motions for reconsideration and to vacate judgment were denied. The instant appeal ensued.

* * *

A release signed under duress is not binding. [Citation.] "Coercion sufficient to avoid a contract need not, of course, consist of physical force or threats of it. Social or economic pressure illegally or immorally applied may be sufficient." [Citations.]

To show economic duress (1) a party "must show that he has been the victim of a wrongful or unlawful act or threat, and (2) such act or threat must be one which deprives the victim of his unfettered will." [Citation.] "As a direct result of these elements, the party threatened must be compelled to make a disproportionate exchange of values." [Citation.]

The elements of economic duress have also been described as follows: "(1) that one side involuntarily accepted the terms of another; (2) that circumstances permitted no other alternative; and (3) that said circumstances were the result of coercive acts of the opposite party." [Citations.] "Merely taking advantage of another's financial difficulty is not duress. Rather, the person alleging financial difficulty must allege that it was contributed to or caused by the one accused of coercion." [Citation.] Thus "[i]n order to substantiate the allegation of economic duress or business compulsion . . . [t]here must be a showing of acts on the part of the defendant which produced [the financial embarrassment]. The assertion of duress resulted from defendant's wrongful and oppressive conduct and not by plaintiff's necessities." [Citation.]

. . . Here, if the plaintiff's allegations are true, the defendant's acts in (1) insisting on a deviation from the contract and repeatedly assuring the plaintiff that it would pay the additional cost, which was substantially greater than the original, if the plaintiff would complete the work and (2) then refusing to make payments for almost a year caused the plaintiff's financial difficulties. Such acts could be considered "wrongful" acts and indications of bad faith.

* * *

The unequal bargaining power of the two parties (both in terms of their comparative size and resources as well as the financial difficul-

ties into which the plaintiff had fallen, allegedly because of the defendant's acts) is a factor to be considered in determining whether the transaction involved duress. [Citations.] In addition, the disparity between not only the plaintiff's alleged costs ($811,816) but also the amount NET's engineers had recommended in November, 1974, to the board for settlement ($775,000) and the amount offered on a "take-it-or-leave-it" basis in December and accepted in settlement ($575,000) raises the possibility there may have been a disproportionate exchange of values and should be considered in determining whether the release was signed under duress. [Citation.]

The defendant argues that it did not have to settle the case but could have "exercised its lawful right to litigate the rights of the parties under the agreement" and that "[d]oing or threatening to do what a party has a legal right to do cannot form the basis of a claim of economic duress." [Citation.] However, if the assertions of the plaintiff are true, the defendant did more than assert a legal right, as its acts created the financial difficulties of the plaintiff, of which it then took advantage.

* * *

In summary, we are therefore unable to say as matter of law that the signing of the release was voluntary. Accordingly, it was error to enter summary judgment.

Judgment reversed.

Duress

HAUMONT v. SECURITY STATE BANK

Supreme Court of Nebraska, 1985.
220 Neb. 809, 374 N.W.2d 2.

HASTINGS, J.

This is an appeal by the defendant, Security State Bank, from a judgment of the district court granting equitable rescission of a guaranty agreement, note, and mortgage executed by the plaintiffs, Lee P. and Letha Haumont.

* * *

The plaintiffs are husband and wife living in Broken Bow and have been farming their own 1,500 acres of land in Custer County for over 40 years. Glen Haumont is their son, and he had operated M & G Implement, Inc., in Broken Bow since the summer of 1977.

M & G Implement ran into financial difficulties in the fall of 1981. As a result the plaintiffs arranged a loan for the company in the approximate amount of $75,000 with the defendant bank. This was the first that either of the plaintiffs knew of their son's financial difficulties.

During the early part of January 1982, the defendant bank and the Broken Bow Production Credit Association (hereinafter PCA) became aware of installment sales contracts originated by Glen which were irregular. After meeting with Glen and investigating further, it was discovered that six contracts, totaling some $324,000, were improperly handled by M & G. On two contracts Glen had resold machinery and failed to pay off the lienholder; on three contracts he had financed the same machinery more than once; and on one contract he had simply forged and subsequently financed. This was in addition to the $251,932.60 that was owed to the defendant on M & G's line of credit. During this time Glen and his attorneys were trying to work with the bank to refinance his business.

On January 20, 1982, Glen was at his parents' home, and, after speaking with his attorney on the phone, he told his father that he, Glen, could be prosecuted and sent to jail. He went on to describe jail conditions, including his fear of drugs and prostitution. Glen did not say specifically why he could go to jail, only that he had financial troubles, and his father was unaware of his business dealings.

On February 8 Glen arranged for his parents to meet with him and his accountant to see if they would be willing to financially back his business. According to the plaintiffs and the accountant, the Haumonts refused to back the business. The next morning Glen spoke to David Schweitz, president of the defendant bank, who had been looking after the interests of the bank with regard to M & G. Glen indicated that his parents were willing to back the long-term financing of the business. According to Schweitz, Glen had claimed all along that his parents were definitely going to help him out.

As a result of that phone call, Schweitz, the bank's attorney, and the president of the PCA determined that they needed written confirmation of the plaintiffs' commitment to M & G and Glen. The bank's attorney contacted Glen's attorney, who drew up a document for Lee Haumont to sign, which reads as follows:

I, Lee Haumont, intend to pursue a course of action which is reasonably calculated to result in the refinancing of M & G Implement, Inc. I intend to do this by pledging my real estate (in Custer County) as collateral for a sufficient loan to cover the debts of M & G Implement with an appropriate financial institution.

On February 12, 1982, Glen went to see his father and asked him to sign the statement. Lee insisted on seeing his lawyer, Howard Spencer, who advised him not to sign. Eventually, however, Spencer added a paragraph which allowed his client to withdraw the letter of intent until February 26, 1982, and Lee signed it. Lee testified that he signed it because his son told him it would give Glen 10 more days to straighten up his business before the bank closed him up. Upon receipt, the bank refused the statement and demanded that the original document, without qualification, be signed.

On February 15 Glen went out to his parents' home and tried to convince his father to sign the original statement of intent. Lee refused to sign. Glen stayed approximately 3 to 4 hours, and as he pulled out to leave he met David Schweitz just arriving. The two returned to the plaintiffs' home and found Lee in his garage.

According to Lee, both his son and Schweitz told him that Glen had past due notes, and if he did not sign the statement of intent, Glen would be prosecuted and would go to jail. The three went into the kitchen, where Lee signed the paper. He stated that he signed it because he did not want to be responsible for sending his son to jail. Contrarily, Schweitz testified that no threats were made and that Glen asked his father to sign and he agreed.

* * *

Schweitz and Glen went out to the plaintiffs' home at approximately 11:30 on that morning, February 16. According to the plaintiffs, Schweitz had Lee read the guaranty agreement and mortgage. Schweitz then threatened to prosecute Glen, through his Omaha attorneys, if the plaintiffs did not sign the documents by 3 o'clock that afternoon. Lee signed both documents because it "[s]eemed like sending Glen to jail blanked out anything else and so I signed it." He was unaware that he had encumbered his previously debt-free land in the amount of $628,708.99.

Subsequently, Letha read both documents and did not understand them. She told Schweitz that she wanted her lawyer to look at them. In response he offered to, and in fact did, read the papers to her. She told him she still did not understand and wanted to wait for her lawyer. Schweitz said that he did not have time to wait for the lawyer to read it. He once again indicated that the guaranty agreement and mortgage had to be signed or Glen would be prosecuted. Letha also signed both documents and did so because "I was like his dad I couldn't lose another son and so I signed it."

* * *

"To constitute duress, there must be an application of such pressure or constraint as compels a man to go against his will, and takes away his free agency, destroying the power of refusing to comply with the unjust demands of another." [Citation.]

And in [citation] this court said: "In Nebraska the law is well established that where a parent or other relative is induced to execute an instrument by threats and fear of criminal punishment of a child or relative, the instrument is the result of duress and the contract may be voided."

* * *

The judgment of the district is affirmed.

Undue Influence

SCHANEMAN v. SCHANEMAN

Supreme Court of Nebraska, 1980.
206 Neb. 113, 291 N.W.2d 412.

CLARK, J.

This is an action in equity to set aside and cancel a deed executed by Conrad Schaneman, Sr., hereinafter called Conrad, in favor of his eldest son, the defendant, Laurence Schaneman.

* * *

By his answer, the defendant admitted the execution of the deed but alleged that the conveyance was pursuant to an oral understanding and agreement between Conrad and the defendant.

The District Court of Scotts Bluff County, Nebraska, found that the execution of the deed was a result of fraud and undue influence, set aside the deed, and quieted title in Conrad. Defendant appeals.

* * *

We affirm the judgment of the District Court.

The property in question was purchased in January 1945 for a price of $23,500. Defendant helped arrange the purchase and loaned his father $10,500 toward the purchase price. The grantees were Conrad and the defendant as joint tenants. There is some testimony that another son, Conrad, Jr., loaned his father $2,500 toward the purchase price also. In any event, it is agreed that Conrad was the real purchaser. By October 1946, Conrad had repaid the loans to his sons. . . .

Conrad, who was born in Russia, could not read or write the English language. He was the father of eight sons and five daughters, ...

Over the years, the family had been closeknit, especially the father and the sons. It had been customary for Conrad and his sons to help one another financially in the purchase of farms. Conrad helped his sons; the sons helped Conrad; and the brothers helped one another in this fashion.

After Conrad's retirement from farming, all the children had frequent contact with Conrad and helped him with his personal needs, although defendant, as the oldest son, perhaps had more contact and a closer relationship with Conrad.

* * *

[T]he defendant was the primary person who advised Conrad and handled Conrad's business matters, although the other sons did continue to help Conrad to some extent.

On March 18, 1975, Conrad deeded the farm in question to the defendant for a stated consideration of $23,500, which was the original purchase price of the property in 1945. The value of the farm in March 1975 was between $145,000 and $160,000.

In March of 1975, Conrad was a man 82 years of age whose health had been deteriorating since at least 1971. He had numerous periods of hospitalization and suffered from heart problems, diabetes with extremely high and uncontrollable blood sugar levels at times, and obesity. He weighed between 325 and 350 pounds, had difficulty breathing, could not walk more than 15 feet, and was no longer able to drive an automobile. He was unable to shave himself and a special jack-hoist had to be utilized to get him in and out of the bathtub. He was, for all intents and purposes, an invalid, completely dependent on others for most of his personal needs and for transportation, banking, and other business matters.

Conrad's children, other than the defendant, testified that during early 1975 Conrad had some days when he was sharper and more alert mentally than on other days, that at times he was confused, had difficulty communicating, and, on occasion, seemed to lapse into times long past. . . .

In about the spring of 1977, one of Conrad's sons discovered by accident that defendant's name was on Conrad's bank account as a joint tenant with right of survivorship. At about the same time, it was discovered that defendant had bought, with Conrad's money, a $20,000 certificate of deposit and that this also listed defendant as joint owner with right of survivorship. It was also later discovered that Conrad had executed a power of attorney in favor of defendant on August 20, 1975.

* * *

At trial, defendant testified that in March 1975 his father trusted and relied on the defendant; that defendant held a "special place" with his father, and that Conrad had complete trust and confidence in defendant. He did not recall any period that he and Conrad were not speaking and said that he and his father had never had a falling out. He further stated that, in March 1975, he was handling Conrad's business affairs generally.

* * *

An examination of the evidence reflects, in our opinion, that from the fall of 1974 until the conservatorship proceedings were commenced, there existed between the defendant and Conrad a confidential relationship and that, during that period, Conrad relied on the defendant for advice in his business affairs.

"[A confidential] relationship exists between two persons if one has gained the confidence of the other and purports to act or advise with the other's interest in mind." [Citation.]

"In a confidential or fiduciary relationship in which confidence is rightfully reposed on one side and a resulting superiority and opportunity for influence is thereby created on the other, equity will scrutinize the transaction critically, especially where age, infirmity, and instability are involved, to see that no injustice has occurred." [Citation.]

Here the evidence reflects that, due to age and physical infirmities, Conrad was, for all intents and purposes, an invalid at the time of the conveyance. It further supports a finding that Conrad's mental acuity was impaired at times and that he sometimes suffered from disorientation and lapse of memory. Considering all the evidence, we find that, in March 1975, Conrad was subject to the influence of the defendant, who was acting in a confidential relationship; that the opportunity to exercise undue influence existed; that there was a disposition on the part of the defendant to exercise such undue influence; and that the conveyance appears to be the effect of such influence. These findings establish a *prima facie* case of undue influence and cast upon the defendant the burden of going forward with the evidence.

A *prima facie* case of undue influence is made out in case of a deed where it is shown by clear and satisfactory evidence (1) that the grantor was subject to such influence; (2) that the opportunity to exercise it existed; (3) that there was a disposition to exercise it; and (4) that the result appears to be the effect of such influence. . . . In an action based on undue influence, when a confidential relationship exists between the parties, and a *prima facie* case is established, the burden of proof remains on the plaintiff, but the burden of going forward with the evidence shifts to the defendant.

* * *

We find that the defendant has not rebutted the presumption of undue influence which was raised by the plaintiff's *prima facie* case.

The judgment of the trial court was correct and is affirmed.

Affirmed.

Fraud: False Representation of Fact

VOKES v. ARTHUR MURRAY, INC.

Florida Court of Appeals, 1968.
212 So.2d 906.

PIERCE, J.

[Audrey E. Vokes, plaintiff, appeals from a final order dismissing her complaint, for failure to state a cause of action.]

Defendant Arthur Murray, Inc., a corporation, authorizes the operation throughout the nation of dancing schools under the name of "Arthur Murray School of Dancing" through local franchised operators, one of whom was defendant J.P. Davenport whose dancing establishment was in Clearwater.

Plaintiff Mrs. Audrey E. Vokes, a widow of 51 years and without family, had a yen to be "an accomplished dancer" with the hopes of finding "new interest in life." So, on February 10, 1961, a dubious fate, with the assist of a motivated acquaintance, procured her to attend a "dance party" at Davenport's "School of Dancing" where she whiled away the pleasant hours, sometimes in a private room, absorbing his accomplished sales technique, during which her grace and poise were elaborated upon and her rosy future as "an excellent dancer" was painted for her in vivid and glowing colors. As an incident to this interlude, he sold her eight ½–hour dance lessons to be utilized within one calendar month therefrom, for the sum of $14.50 cash in hand paid, obviously a baited "come-on."

Thus she embarked upon an almost endless pursuit of the terpsichorean art during which, over a period of less than sixteen months, she was sold fourteen "dance courses" totalling in the aggregate 2,302 hours of dancing lessons for a total cash outlay of $31,090.45, all at Davenport's dance emporium.

* * *

These dance lesson contracts and the monetary consideration therefor of over $31,000 were procured from her by means and methods of Davenport and his associates which went beyond the unsavory, yet legally permissible, perimeter of "sales puffing" and intruded well into the forbidden area of undue influence, the suggestion of falsehood, the suppression of truth, and the free exercise of rational judgment, if what plaintiff alleged in her complaint was true. From the time of her first contact with the dancing school in February, 1961, she was influenced unwittingly by a constant and continuous barrage of flattery, false praise, excessive compliments, and panegyric encomiums, to such extent that it would be not only inequitable, but unconscionable, for a court exercising inherent chancery power to allow such contracts to stand.

She was incessantly subjected to overreaching blandishment and cajolery. She was assured she had "grace and poise"; that she was "rapidly improving and developing in her dancing skill"; that the additional lessons would "make her a beautiful dancer, capable of dancing with the most accomplished dancers"; that she was "rapidly progressing in the development of her dancing skill and gracefulness"; etc. She was given "dance aptitude tests" for the ostensible purpose of "determining" the number of remaining hours of instruction needed by her from time to time.

At one point she was sold 545 additional hours of dancing lessons to be entitled to the award of the "Bronze Medal" signifying that she had reached "the Bronze Standard," a supposed designation of dance achievement by students of Arthur Murray, Inc.

Later she was sold an additional 926 hours in order to gain the "Silver Medal," indicating she had reached "the Silver Standard," at a cost of $12,501.35.

At one point, while she still had to her credit about 900 unused hours of instructions, she was induced to purchase an additional 24 hours of lessons to participate in a trip to Miami at her own expense, where she would be "given the opportunity to dance with members of the Miami Studio."

She was induced at another point to purchase an additional 126 hours of lessons in order to be not only eligible for the Miami trip but also to become "a life member of the Arthur Murray Studio," carrying with it certain dubious emoluments, at a further cost of $1,752.30.

At another point, while she still had over 1,000 unused hours of instruction she was induced to buy 151 additional hours at a cost of $2,049.00 to be eligible for a "Student Trip to Trinidad," at her own expense as she later learned.

Also, when she still had more than 1,000 unused hours to her credit, she was prevailed upon to purchase an additional 347 hours at a cost of $4,235.74 to qualify her to receive a "Gold Medal" for achievement, indicating she had advanced to "the Gold Standard."

On another occasion, while she still had over 1,200 unused hours, she was induced to buy an additional 175 hours of instruction at a cost of $2,472.75, to be eligible "to take a trip to Mexico."

Finally, sandwiched in between other lesser sales promotions, she was influenced to buy an additional 481 hours of instruction at a cost of $6,523.81 in order to "be classified as a Gold Bar Member, the ultimate achievement of the dancing studio."

All the foregoing sales promotions, illustrative of the entire fourteen separate contracts, were procured by defendant Davenport and Arthur Murray, Inc., by false representations to her that she was improving in her dancing ability, that she had excellent potential, that she was responding to instructions in dancing grace, and that they were developing her into a beautiful dancer, whereas in truth and in fact she did not develop in her dancing ability, she had no "dance aptitude," and in fact had difficulty in "hearing the musical beat." The complaint alleged that such representations to her "were in fact false and known by the defendant to be false and contrary to the plaintiff's true ability, the truth of plaintiff's ability being fully known to the defendants, but withheld from the plaintiff for the sole and specific intent to deceive and defraud the plaintiff and to induce her in the purchasing of additional hours of dance lessons." It was averred that the lessons were sold to her "in total disregard to the true physical, rhythm, and mental ability of the plaintiff." In other words, while she first exulted that she was entering the "spring of her life," she finally was awakened to the fact there was "spring" neither in her life nor in her feet.

* * *

It is true that "generally a misrepresentation, to be actionable, must be one of fact rather than of opinion." [Citation.] But this rule has significant qualifications, applicable here. . . . As stated by Judge Allen of this court [citation]: "A statement of a party having . . . superior knowledge may be regarded as a statement of fact although it would be considered as opinion if the parties were dealing on equal terms."

It could be reasonably supposed here that defendants had "superior knowledge" as to whether plaintiff had "dance potential" and as to whether she was noticeably improving in the art of terpsichore. And it would be a reasonable inference from the undenied averments of the complaint that the flowery eulogiums heaped upon her by defendants as a prelude to her contracting for 1,944 additional hours of instruction in order to attain the rank of the Bronze Standard, thence to the bracket of the Silver Standard, thence to the class of the Gold Bar Standard, and finally to the crowning plateau of a Life Member of the Studio, proceeded as much or more from the urge to "ring the cash register" as from any honest or realistic appraisal of her dancing prowess or a factual representation of her progress.

Even in contractual situations where a party to a transaction owes no duty to disclose facts within his knowledge or to answer inquiries respecting such facts, the law is if he undertakes to do so he must disclose the *whole truth*. [Citations.] From the face of the complaint, it should have been reasonably apparent to defendants that her vast outlay of cash for the many hundreds of additional hours of instruction was not justified by her slow and awkward progress, which she would have been made well aware of if they had spoken the "whole truth."

* * *

Reversed.

Fraud: Materiality

REED v. KING

California Court of Appeals, 1983.
145 Cal.App.3d 261, 193 Cal.Rptr. 130.

BLEASE, J.

In the sale of a house, must the seller disclose it was the site of a multiple murder?

Dorris Reed purchased a house from Robert King. Neither King nor his real estate agents (the other named defendants) told Reed that a woman and her four children were murdered there 10 years earlier. However, it seems "truth will come to light; murder cannot be hid long." (Shakespeare, Merchant of Venice, act II, scene II.) Reed learned of the gruesome episode from a neighbor after the sale. She sues seeking rescission and damages. King and the real estate agent defendants successfully demurred to her first amended complaint for failure to state a cause of action. Reed appeals the ensuing judgment of dismissal. We will reverse the judgment.

* * * King and his real estate agent knew about the murders and knew the event materially affected the market value of the house when they listed it for sale. They represented to Reed the premises were in good condition and fit for an "elderly lady" living alone. They did not disclose the fact of the murders. At some point King asked a neighbor not to inform Reed of that event. Nonetheless, after Reed moved in neighbors informed her no one was interested in purchasing the house because of the stigma. Reed paid $76,000, but the house is only worth $65,000 because of its past.

* * *

Does Reed's pleading state a cause of action? Concealed within this question is the nettlesome problem of the duty of disclosure of blemishes on real property which are not physical defects or legal impairments to use.

Reed seeks to state a cause of action sounding in contract, i.e., rescission, or in tort, i.e., deceit. In either event her allegations must reveal a fraud. [Citation.] "The elements of actual fraud, whether as the basis of the remedy in contract or tort, may be stated as follows: There must be (1) a *false representation* or concealment of a material fact (or, in some cases, an opinion) susceptible of knowledge, (2) made with *knowledge* of its falsity or without sufficient knowledge on the subject to warrant a representation, (3) with the *intent* to induce the person to whom it is made to act upon it; and such person must (4) act in *reliance* upon the representation (5) to his *damage*." (Original italics.) [Citation.]

The trial court perceived the defect in Reed's complaint to be a failure to allege concealment of a material fact. . . .

Concealment is a term of art which includes mere nondisclosure when a party has a duty to disclose. [Citation.] Rest.2d Contracts, § 161; Rest.2d Torts, § 551; Reed's complaint reveals only nondisclosure despite the allegation King asked a neighbor to hold his peace. There is no allegation the attempt at suppression was a cause in fact of Reed's ignorance. (See Rest.2d Contracts, §§ 160, 162–164; Rest.2d Torts, § 550; Rest., Restitution, § 9.) Accordingly, the critical question is: does the seller have a duty to disclose here? Resolution of this question depends on the materiality of the fact of the murders.

In general, a seller of real property has a duty to disclose: "where the seller knows of facts *materially* affecting the value or desirability of the property which are known or accessible only to him and also knows that such facts are not known to, or within the reach of the diligent attention and observation of the buyer, the seller is under a duty to disclose them to the buyer. [Citation.] This broad statement of duty has led one commentator to conclude: "The ancient maxim *caveat emptor* ('let the buyer beware.') has little or no application to California real estate transactions." [Citation.]

Whether information "is of sufficient materiality to affect the value or desirability of the property . . . depends on the facts of the particular case." [Citation.] Materiality "is a question of law, and is part of the concept of right to rely or justifiable reliance." [Citation.] * * * Three considerations bear on this legal conclusion; the gravity of the harm inflicted by nondisclosure; the fairness of imposing a duty of discovery on the buyer as an alternative to compelling disclosure, and the impact on the stability of contracts if rescission is permitted.

Numerous cases have found nondisclosure of physical defects and legal impediments to use of real property are material. [Citation.] However, to our knowledge, no prior real estate sale case has faced an issue of nondisclosure of the kind presented here.

* * *

The murder of innocents is highly unusual in its potential for so disturbing buyers they may be unable to reside in a home where it has occurred. This fact may foreseeably deprive a buyer of the intended use of the purchase. Murder is not such a common occurrence that *buyers* should be charged with anticipating and discovering this disquieting possibility. Accordingly, the fact is not one for which a duty of inquiry and discovery can sensibly be imposed upon the buyer.

Reed alleges the fact of the murders has a quantifiable effect on the market value of the premises. We cannot say this allegation is inherently wrong and, in the pleading posture of the case, we assume it to be true. If information known or accessible only to the seller has a significant and measurable effect on market value and, as is alleged here, the seller is aware of this effect, we see no prin-

cipled basis for making the duty to disclose turn upon the character of the information. Physical usefulness is not and never has been the sole criterion of valuation. * * *

Reputation and history can have a significant effect on the value of realty. "George Washington slept here" is worth something, however physically inconsequential that consideration may be. Ill-repute or "bad will" conversely may depress the value of property. * * *

Whether Reed will be able to prove her allegation the decade-old multiple murder has a significant effect on market value we cannot determine. If she is able to do so by competent evidence she is entitled to a favorable ruling on the issues of materiality and duty to disclose. Her demonstration of objective tangible harm would still the concern that permitting her to go forward will open the floodgates to rescission on subjective and idiosyncratic grounds.

* * *

The judgment is reversed.

Mistake

STATE OF FLORIDA, DEPARTMENT OF STATE v. TREASURE SALVORS, INC.

United States Court of Appeals, Fifth Circuit, 1980.
621 F.2d 1340.

JOHNSON, J.

* * *

The facts underlying the merits of this case are quite simple. Beginning in 1971, Treasure Salvors and the State of Florida entered into a series of annual contracts governing the salvage of the *Atocha*. [The *Atocha* is a Spanish galleon that sank in 1622 carrying a treasure now worth well over $250 million.] Both parties entered into these agreements under the impression that the seabed on which the *Atocha* lay was state land. Treasure Salvors agreed to relinquish 25% of the items recovered in return for the right to salvage on state lands. In accordance with these contracts, Treasure Salvors delivered to Florida its share of the successfully salvaged artifacts. In 1975 the [United States] Supreme Court, in *United States v. Florida,* [citation], held that the part of the continental shelf on which the *Atocha* was resting had never been owned by Florida. It was at this point that Treasure Salvors sought to be declared owner of the *Atocha.*

Even the briefest of glances at these facts cannot help but invoke thoughts of the doctrine of mutual mistake and call to mind the seminal case of *Sherwood v. Walker,* [citation]. *Sherwood* involved the classic remedy, "replevin for a cow." Plaintiff had agreed to purchase Rose 2d of Aberlone from defendants for $80. When the plaintiff tendered the money, the sellers refused to accept it and declined to yield Rose. At trial the sellers introduced evidence establishing that at the time of the agreement both parties thought

Rose was barren and could not breed. Only in the interim, between the agreement to sell and the buyer's tender of the funds, was it discovered that Rose was with calf. This mistake, sellers argued, went to the root of the parties' agreement. The Michigan Supreme Court agreed and allowed the sellers to avoid their contractual obligation.

The case at bar presents another example of mutual mistake. The parties entered into the salvage contracts under the mistaken assumption that the State of Florida owned the land. But for this belief, the Division of Archives and Treasure Salvors would not have executed the agreements. The trial court correctly held that the parties made a mutual mistake.

* * *

Affirmed.

QUESTIONS

1. Identify the types of duress and discuss the legal effect of each.

2. Identify the types of fraud and the elements that must be shown to establish the existence of each.

3. Discuss undue influence and identify some of the situations giving rise to a confidential relationship.

4. Identify and discuss the situations involving voidable mistakes.

5. Define the two types of nonfraudulent misrepresentation.

PROBLEMS

1. Anita and Barry were negotiating, and Anita's attorney prepared a long and carefully drawn contract, which was given to Barry for examination. Five days later and prior to its execution, Barry's eyes became so infected that it was impossible for him to read. Ten days thereafter and during the continuance of the illness Anita called upon Barry and urged him to sign the contract, telling him that time was running out. Barry signed the contract despite the fact he was unable

to read it. In a subsequent action by Anita, Barry claimed that the contract was not binding upon him because it was impossible for him to read and he did not know what it contained prior to his signing it. Decision?

2. (a) Johnson tells Davis that he paid $150,000 for his farm in 1984, and that he believes it is worth twice that at the present time. Relying upon these statements, Davis buys the farm from

Johnson for $225,000. Johnson did pay $150,000 for the farm in 1984, but its value has increased only slightly, and it is presently not worth $300,000. On discovering this, Davis offers to reconvey the farm to Johnson and sues for the return of his $225,000. Result?

(b) Modify the facts in (a) by assuming that Johnson had paid $100,000 for the property in 1984. What result?

3. On September 1, Adams in Portland, Oregon, wrote a letter to Brown in New York City offering to sell to Brown one thousand tons of chromite at $48.00 per ton, to be shipped by *S.S. Malabar* sailing from Portland, Oregon, to New York City via the Panama Canal. Upon receiving the letter on September 5, Brown immediately mailed to Adams a letter stating that she accepted the offer. There were two ships by the name of *S.S. Malabar* sailing from Portland to New York City via the Panama Canal, one sailing in October and the other sailing in December. At the time of mailing her letter of acceptance Brown knew of both sailings and further knew that Adams knew only of the December sailing. Is there a contract? If so, to which *S.S. Malabar* does it relate?

4. Adler owes Panessi, a police captain, $500. Adler threatens Panessi that unless Panessi gives him a discharge from the debt, Adler will disclose the fact that Panessi has on several occasions become highly intoxicated and has been seen in the company of certain disreputable persons. Panessi, induced by fear that such a disclosure would cost him his position or in any event lead to social disgrace, gives Adler a release but subsequently sues to set it aside and recover on his claim. Decision?

5. Harris owned a farm that was worth about $600 an acre. By false representations of fact, Harris induced Pringle to buy the farm at $1,500 an acre. Shortly after taking possession of the farm, Pringle discovered oil under the land. Harris, on learning this, sues to have the sale set aside on the ground that it was voidable because of fraud. Decision?

6. On February 2, Phillips induced Miller to purchase from her fifty shares of stock in the XYZ Corporation for $10,000, representing that the actual book value of each share was $200. A certificate for fifty shares was delivered to Miller. On February 16, Miller discovered that the book value was only $50 per share on February 2. Thereafter, Miller sues Phillips. Decision?

7. Doris mistakenly accused Peter's son, Steven, of negligently burning down her barn. Peter believed that his son was guilty of the wrong, and that he, Peter, was personally liable for the damage since Steven was only fifteen years old. Upon demand made by Doris, Peter paid Doris $2,500 for the damage to her barn. After making this payment, Peter learned that his son had not caused the burning of Doris's barn and was in no way responsible for its burning. Peter then sued Doris to recover $2,500, which he had paid Doris. Decision?

8. Jones, a farmer, found an odd-looking stone in his fields. He went to Smith, the town jeweler, and asked him what he thought it was. Smith said he did not know but thought it might be a ruby. Jones asked Smith what he would pay for it, and Smith said two hundred dollars; whereupon Jones sold it to Smith for $200. The stone turned out to be an uncut diamond worth $3,000. Jones brought an action against Smith to recover the stone. On trial, it was proved that Smith actually did not know the stone was a diamond when he bought it, but he thought it might be a ruby. Decision?

9. Decedent Judith Johnson, a bedridden, lonely woman of eighty-six years, owned outright Greenacre, her ancestral estate. Ficky, her physician and friend, visited her weekly and was held in the highest regard by Johnson. Johnson was extremely fearful of pain and suffering and depended upon Ficky to ease her anxiety and pain. Several months before her death, she deeded Greenacre to Ficky for $5,000. The fair market value of Greenacre at this time was $125,000. Johnson was survived by two children and six grandchildren. Johnson's children challenged the validity of the deed. Decision?

10. Dorothy and John Huffschneider listed their house and lot for sale with C. B. Property. The asking price was $165,000, and the owners told C. B. that the size of the property was 6.8 acres. Dean Olson, a salesman for C. B., advertised the property in local newspapers as consisting of six acres. James and Jean Holcomb signed a contract to purchase the property through Olson after first inspecting the property with Olson and being assured by Olson that the property was at least 6.6 acres. The Holcombs never asked for nor received a copy of the survey. In actuality, the lot was only 4.6 acres. The Holcombs now seek to rescind the contract. Decision?

11. In February, Gardner, a school teacher with no experience in running a tavern, entered into a contract to purchase for $40,000 the Punjab Tavern from Meiling. The contract was contingent upon Gardner's obtaining a five-year lease for the tavern's premises and a liquor license from the State. Prior to the formation of the contract, Meiling had made no representations to Gardner concerning the gross income of the tavern. Approximately three months after the contract was signed, Gardner and Meiling met with an inspector from the Oregon Liquor Control Commission (OLCC) to discuss transfer of the liquor license. Meiling reported to the agent, in Gardner's presence, that the tavern's gross income figures for February, March, and April were $5,710, $4,918, and $5,009, respectively. The OLCC granted the required license, the transaction was closed, and Gardner took possession on June 10. After discovering that the tavern's income was very low, and that the tavern had very few female patrons, Gardner contacted Meiling's bookkeeping service and learned that the actual gross income for those three months had been approximately $1,400 to $2,000. Gardner then sued for rescission of the contract. Decision?

12. Christine Boyd was designated as the beneficiary of a life insurance policy issued by Aetna Life Insurance Company on the life of Christine's husband, Jimmie Boyd. The policy insured against Jimmie's permanent total disability and also provided for a death benefit to be paid on Jimmie's death.

Several years after the policy was issued, Jimmie and Christine separated. Jimmie began to travel extensively, and therefore, Christine was unable to keep track of his whereabouts or his state of health. Jimmie, however, continued to pay the premiums on the policy until Christine tried to cash in the policy to alleviate her financial distress. A loan had previously been made on the policy, however, so that its cash surrender value, and thus the amount received by Christine, was only $4.19. Shortly thereafter, Christine learned that Jimmie had been permanently and totally disabled before the surrender of the policy. Aetna also

was unaware of Jimmie's condition, and Christine requested the surrendered policy be reinstated and that the disability payments be made. Jimmie died soon thereafter, and Christine then requested that Aetna pay the death benefit. Decision?

13. Plaintiff, Gibson, entered into negotiation with W. S. May, president of Home Folks Mobile Home Plaza, Inc., to buy Home Plaza Corporation. Plaintiff visited the mobile home park on several occasions, at which time he noted the occupancy, visually inspected the sewer and water systems, and asked May numerous questions concerning the condition of the business. Plaintiff, however, never requested to see the books, nor did May try to conceal them. May admits making the following representations to the plaintiff: (1) the water and sewer systems were in good condition and no major short-term expenditures would be needed; (2) the park realized a 40 percent profit on natural gas sold to tenants; and (3) usual park vacancy was 5 percent. Additionally, May gave plaintiff the park's accountant-prepared income statement, which showed a net income of $38,220 for the last eight months. Based on these figures, plaintiff projected an annual net profit of $57,331.20. Upon being asked whether this figure accurately represented income of the business for the last three years, May stated by letter that indeed it did.

Plaintiff purchased the park for $275,000. Shortly thereafter, plaintiff spent $5,384 repairing the well and septic systems. By the time plaintiff sold the park three years later, he had expended $7,531 on the wells and $8,125 on the septic systems. Furthermore, in the first year park occupancy was nowhere near 95 percent. Even after raising rent and the charges for natural gas, plaintiff still operated at a deficit.

Plaintiff sued defendant, alleging that May, on behalf of defendant, made false and fraudulent statements on which plaintiff relied when he purchased the park. Defendant moved for summary judgment. Decision?

14. Columbia University brought suit against Jacobsen on two notes signed by him and his parents, representing the balance of tuition he owed the University. Jacobsen counterclaimed for money damages due to Columbia's deceit or fraudulent misrepresentation. Jacobsen argues that Columbia fraudulently misrepresented that it would teach wisdom, truth, character, enlightenment, and similar virtues and qualities. He specifically cites as support the Columbia motto: *"in lumine tuo videbimus lumen"* ("In your light we shall see light"); the inscription over the college chapel: "Wisdom dwelleth in the heart of him that hath understanding"; and various excerpts from its brochures, catalogues, and a convocation address made by the University's president. Jacobsen, a senior who was not graduated because of poor scholastic standing, claims that the University's failure to meet its promises made through these quotations constituted fraudulent misrepresentation or deceit. Decision?

15. Frank Berryessa stole funds from his employer, the Eccles Hotel Company. His father, W. S. Berryessa, learned of his son's trouble and, thinking the amount involved was about $2000, gave the hotel a promissory note for $2,186 to cover the shortage. In return, the hotel agreed not to publicize the incident or notify the bonding company. (A bonding company is an insurer that is paid a premium for agreeing to reimburse an employer for thefts by an employee.) Before this note became due, however, the hotel discovered that Frank had actually misappropriated $6,865. The hotel then notified its bonding company, Great American Indemnity Company, to collect the entire loss. W. S. Berryessa claims that the agent for Great American told him that unless he paid them $2,000 in cash and signed a note for the remaining $4,865, Frank would be prosecuted. Berryessa agreed, signed the note, and gave the agent a cashier's check for $1,500 and a personal check for $500. He requested that the agent not cash the personal check for about a month. Subsequently, Great American sued Berryessa on the note. He defends against the note on the grounds of duress and counterclaims for the return of the $1,500 and the cancellation of the uncashed $500 check. Decision?

COMPUTER RESEARCH PROBLEMS

 1. Jane Francois married Victor H. Francois in 1984. At the time of the marriage, Victor was a fifty-year-old bachelor living with his elderly mother, and Jane was a thirty-year-old, twice-divorced mother of two. Victor had a relatively secure financial portfolio; Jane, on the other hand, brought no money or property to the marriage.

The marriage deteriorated quickly over the next couple of years, with disputes centered on financial matters. During this period, Jane systematically gained a joint interest in and took control of most of Victor's assets. Then, in September of 1987, Jane contracted Harold Monoson, an attorney, to draw up divorce papers. Victor was unaware of Jane's decision until he was taken to Monoson's office where Monoson presented for Victor's signature a "Property Settlement and Separation Agreement." Monoson told Victor that he would need an attorney, but Jane vetoed Victor's choice. Monoson then asked another lawyer, Gregory Ball, to come into the office. Ball read the agreement and strenuously advised Victor not to sign it because it would commit him to financial suicide. The agreement transferred most of Victor's remaining assets to Jane. Victor, however, signed it because Jane and Monoson persuaded him that it was the only way that his marriage could be saved. In October of 1988, Jane informed Victor that she had sold most of his former property and that she was leaving him permanently. Victor brought this action to have the agreement set aside as a result of undue influence. Decision?

2. Iverson owned Iverson Motor Company, an enterprise engaged in the repair as well as the sale of Oldsmobile, Rambler, and International Harvester Scout automobiles. Forty percent of the business's sales volume and net earnings came from the Oldsmobile franchise.

Whipp contracted to buy Iverson Motors, which Iverson said included the Oldsmobile franchise. After the sale, however, General Motors refused to transfer the franchise to Whipp. Whipp then returned the property to Iverson and brought this action seeking rescission of the contract. Decision?

3. On February 10, Mrs. Sunderhaus purchased a diamond ring from Perel & Lowenstein for $6,990. She was told by the company's salesman that the ring was worth its purchase price, and she also received at that time a written guarantee from the company attesting to the diamond's value, style, and trade-in value. When Mrs. Sunderhaus went to trade the ring for another, however, she was told by two jewelers that the ring was valued at $3,000 and $3,500, respectively. Mrs. Sunderhaus knew little about the value of diamonds and claims to have relied on the oral representation of the Perel & Lowenstein's salesman and the written representation as to the ring's value. She seeks rescission of the contract or damages in the amount of the sales price over the ring's value. Decision?

4. Division West Chinchilla Ranch advertised on television that a five figure income could be earned by raising chinchillas with an investment of only $3.75 per animal per year and only thirty minutes of maintenance per day. The minimum investment was $2,150 for one male and six female chinchillas. Division West represented to plaintiffs that chinchilla ranching would be easy and that no experience was required to make ranching profitable. Plaintiffs, who had no experience raising chinchillas, each invested $2,150 or more to purchase Division's chinchillas and supplies. After three years without earning a profit, plaintiffs sue Division for fraud. Decision?

5. William Schmalz entered into an employment contract with Hardy Salt Company. The contract granted Schmalz six months' severance pay for involuntary termination but none for voluntary separation or termination for cause. Schmalz was asked to resign from his employment. He was informed that if he did not resign he would be fired for alleged misconduct. When Schmalz turned in his letter of resignation, he signed a release prohibiting him from suing his former employer as a consequence of his employment. Schmalz consulted an attorney before signing the release and upon signing it received $4,583.00 (one month's salary) in consideration. Schmalz now sues his former employer for the severance pay claiming that he signed the release under duress. Decision?

Chapter 11

CONSIDERATION

Legal Sufficiency
Illusory Promises
Pre-existing Obligation
Bargained for Exchange
Contracts without Consideration

CONSIDERATION is the primary—but not only—basis for the enforcement of promises in our legal system. Consideration is the "price" paid to make a promise enforceable. The doctrine of consideration ensures that promises are enforced only where the parties have exchanged something of value in the eye of the law. Gratuitous (gift) promises, accordingly, are not legally enforceable, except under certain circumstances, which are discussed later in the chapter.

Consideration is that which is exchanged for a promise and is present only when the parties intend an exchange. The consideration exchanged for the promise may be an act, a forbearance to act, or a promise to do either of these. In like manner, Section 71 of the Restatement defines consideration for a promise as (a) an act other than a promise, (b) a forbearance, (c) the creation, modification, or destruction of a legal relation, or (d) a return promise if any of these are bargained for and given in exchange for the promise.

Thus, there are two basic elements to consideration: (1) legal sufficiency (something of value) and (2) bargained for exchange. Both must be present to satisfy the requirement of consideration. The consideration may be given to the promisor or to some other person; likewise, it may be given by the promisee or by some other person.

LEGAL SUFFICIENCY

To be legally sufficient, the consideration exchanged for the promise must be either a legal detriment to the promisee *or* a legal benefit to the promisor. In other words, has the promisor received something of legal value, or has the promisee given up something of legal value in return for the promise.

Legal detriment means (1) the doing (or undertaking to do) that which the promisee was under no prior legal obligation to do *or* (2) the refraining from doing (or undertaking to refrain from doing) that which he was previously under no legal obligation to refrain from doing. On the other hand, **legal benefit** means the obtaining by the promisor of that which he had no prior legal right to obtain. In most, if not all, cases where there is legal detriment to the promisee, a legal benefit to the promisor will also be found. Nonetheless, the presence of **either** one is sufficient. *See State ex rel. Ludwick v. Bryant.*

Adequacy

Legal sufficiency has nothing to do with adequacy of consideration. Restatement, Section 79. The subject matter that the parties agree to exchange does not need to have the same or equal value. The law will regard consideration as adequate if the parties have freely agreed to the exchange. The requirement of legally sufficient consideration is, therefore, *not* at all concerned with whether the bargain was good or bad, or whether one party received disproportionately more or less than what he gave or promised in exchange for it. Such an inquiry may be relevant to the availability of certain defenses (such as fraud, duress, or undue influence) or certain remedies (such as specific performance). The requirement of legally sufficient consideration is simply (1) that the parties have agreed to an exchange and (2) that with respect to each party the subject matter exchanged, or promised in exchange, either imposed a legal detriment upon the promisee or conferred a legal benefit upon the promisor. *See State ex rel. Ludwick v. Bryant.*

Unilateral Contracts

In a unilateral contract a promise is exchanged for an act or a forbearance to act. Since only one promise exists, one party is the promisor and the other party is the promisee. For example, A promises to pay B $1,500 if B paints A's house. B paints A's house.

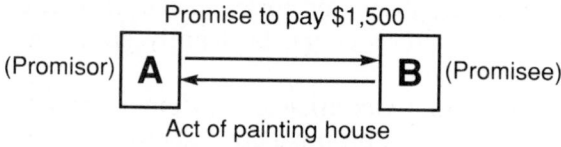

Promise to pay $1,500

(Promisor) **A** ← **B** (Promisee)

Act of painting house

In order for A's promise to be binding, it must be supported by consideration consisting of either a legal detriment to B, the promisee, or a legal benefit to A, the promisor. B's having painted the house is a legal detriment to B, the promisee, because she was under no prior legal duty to paint A's house. Also, B's painting A's house is a legal benefit to A, the promisor, because A had no prior legal right to have his house painted by B.

A unilateral contract may also consist of a promise exchanged for a forbearance. To illustrate, A negligently injures B, for which B may recover damages in a tort action. A promises to pay B $5,000 if B forbears from bringing suit. B accepts by not filing suit.

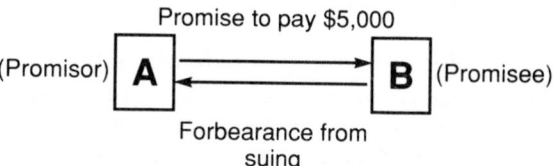

Promise to pay $5,000

(Promisor) **A** ⇄ **B** (Promisee)

Forbearance from suing

A's promise to pay B $5,000 is binding because it is supported by consideration; B, the promisee, has incurred a legal detriment by refraining from bringing suit which he was under no prior legal obligation to refrain from doing. A, the promisor, has received a legal benefit because she had no prior legal right to B's forbearance from bringing suit.

To illustrate further, suppose that Alice promises Kristi, a high school graduate, that if Kristi will attend and graduate from Reed College, Alice will pay to Kristi upon graduation the entire cost of her college education. Kristi enters Reed College and duly graduates. The college education that she received is an actual benefit to Kristi, but legally she suffered a detriment in graduating from Reed College in that she gave up her freedom to attend any other college, or not to attend college at all, in consideration for Alice's promise. Consequently, the consideration that Kristi, the promisee, gave for Alice's promise, although not actually detrimental, was a legal detriment to the promisee Kristi. It is therefore legally sufficient, and Alice's promise is enforceable by Kristi.

Bilateral Contracts

In a bilateral contract there is an exchange of promises. Thus, each party is *both* a promisor and a promisee. For example, if A promises to purchase an automobile from B for $15,000 and B promises to sell the automobile to A for $15,000, the following relationship exists:

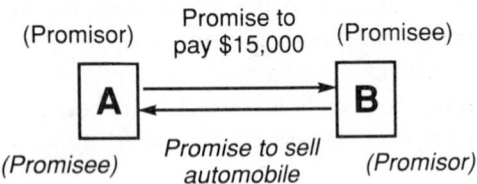

A's promise to pay B $15,000 is binding and therefore enforceable by B, if that promise is supported by legal consideration, which may consist of either a legal detriment to B, the promisee, or a legal benefit to A, the promisor. B's promise to sell A the automobile is a legal detriment to B because he was under no prior legal duty to sell the automobile to A. Moreover, B's promise is also a legal benefit to A because A had no prior legal right to that automobile. Consequently, A's promise to pay $15,000 to B *is* supported by consideration and is enforceable.

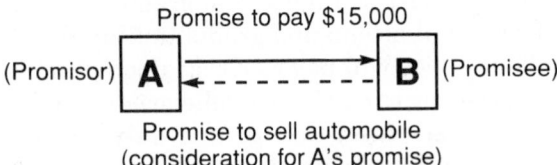

For **B's promise** to sell the automobile to A to be binding, it likewise must be supported by consideration, which may be either a legal detriment to A, the promisee, or a legal benefit to B, the promisor. A's promise to pay B $15,000 is a legal detriment to A because he was under no prior legal duty to pay $15,000 to B. At the same time, A's promise is also a legal benefit to B because B had no prior legal right to the $15,000. Thus, B's promise to sell the automobile is supported by consideration and *is* enforceable.

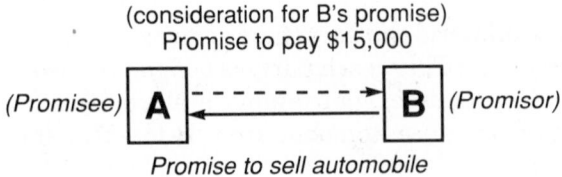

To summarize, in order for A's promise to B to be binding, it must be supported by legally sufficient consideration, which requires that the promise received from B in exchange provide either a legal benefit to A (the promisor) or a legal detriment to B (the promisee). B's return promise to A must also be supported by consideration for it to be binding on B. *See Collins v. Parsons College.*

Thus, in a bilateral contract each promise is the consideration for the other, a relationship that has been referred to as **mutuality of obligation.** A general consequence of mutuality of obligation is that each promisor in a bilateral contract must be bound or neither is bound. There is an important exception to this principle: voidable promises. An obligation under a contract may be voidable because of lack of capacity, misrepresentation, duress, undue influence, or mistake. The promise of the party with the power of avoidance, nevertheless, serves as consideration for the other party's promise. Restatement, Section 78. Until the power of avoidance is exercised, both promises are deemed supported by consideration and therefore binding.

Illusory Promises

Words of promise that make performance entirely optional with the purported promisor do not constitute a promise at all. Consequently, they cannot serve as consideration. In this section, such illusory promises will be distinguished from other promises that do impose obligations of performance upon the promisor and thus can be legally sufficient consideration.

An **illusory promise** is a statement that is in the form of a promise but imposes no obligation upon the maker of the statement. An illusory promise is not consideration for a return promise. Thus, a statement committing to purchase such quantity of goods as the promisor may "desire" or "want" or "wish to buy" is an illusory promise because its performance is entirely optional. For example, if Ames, Inc. offers to sell to Barnes Co. as many barrels of oil as Barnes shall choose at forty dollars per barrel, there is no contract for lack of consideration. Barnes may wish or desire to buy none of the oil, yet in buying none it would fulfill its promise. An offer containing such a promise, although accepted by the offeree, does not create a contract because the promise is illusory—performance by Barnes is entirely optional and no constraint is placed upon its freedom. It is not bound to do anything nor can Ames reasonably expect to receive any performance. Thus, Barnes, by its promise, suffers no legal detriment and confers no legal benefit. Consequently, Barnes' promise does not provide legally sufficient consideration for Ames' promise and thus Ames' promise is not binding upon Ames.

Many courts have transformed otherwise illusory promises into actual promises by implying an obligation of good faith or fair dealing. Under this approach, courts have held to be nonillusory a promise "to spend such time as he personally sees fit in developing" a business and a clause "specifying that leases 'satisfactory' to plaintiff must be secured before he would be bound to perform."

Output and Requirement Contracts An agreement to sell the entire production of a particular seller is called an **output contract.** It affords the seller an assured market for her product. An agreement to purchase all the materials of a particular kind that the purchaser needs is called a **requirements contract.** It assures the buyer of a ready source of inventory or supplies. These contracts may or may not be accompanied by an estimate of the quantity to be sold or to be purchased. Nevertheless, these promises are *not* illusory. The buyer under a requirements contract does not promise to buy as much as she desires to buy, but rather to buy as much as is *needed.* Similarly, under an output contract the seller promises to sell to the buyer the seller's entire production, not merely as much as the seller desires.

Furthermore, the Code, Section 2–306(1), imposes a good faith limitation upon the quantity to be sold or purchased under an output or requirements contract. Thus, an output or requirements contract means such

actual output or requirements as may occur in good faith, except that no quantity unreasonably disproportionate to any stated estimate or, in the absence of a stated estimate, to any normal prior output or requirements may be tendered or demanded. Therefore, after contracting to sell to Adler, Inc. its entire output, Benevito Company cannot increase its production from one eight-hour shift per day to three eight-hour shifts per day.

Exclusive Dealing Contracts Where a manufacturer of goods grants an exclusive right to a distributor to sell its products in a designated territory, unless otherwise agreed, an implied obligation is imposed on the manufacturer to use its best efforts to supply the goods and on the distributor to use his best efforts to promote their sale. U.C.C. Section 2–306(2). The obligations that arise upon acceptance of the **exclusive dealing agreement** are sufficient consideration to bind both parties to the contract.

Conditional Promises A conditional promise is a promise the performance of which depends upon the happening or non-happening of an uncertain event (the condition). A conditional promise is sufficient consideration *unless* the promisor knows at the time of making the promise that the condition cannot occur. Restatement, Section 76.

Thus, if Debbie offers to pay John $8,000 for John's automobile, provided that Debbie receives such amount as an inheritance from the estate of her deceased uncle, and John accepts the offer, the duty of Debbie to pay $8,000 to John is *conditioned* upon her receiving $8,000 from her deceased uncle's estate. The consideration moving from John to Debbie is the promise to transfer title to the automobile. The consideration moving from Debbie to John is the promise of $8,000 subject to the condition.

Pre-existing Obligation

The law does not regard the performance of or promise to perform a pre-existing legal duty, public or private, as either a legal detriment to the party under the prior legal obligation or a benefit to the other party. A **public duty** is one that does not arise out of a contract but is imposed upon members of society by force of the common law or by statute. Illustrations are found in the law of torts, such as the duty not to commit an assault, battery, false imprisonment, or defamation. The criminal law also imposes numerous duties of a public nature. Thus, if Cleon promises to pay Spike, the village ruffian, $100 not to abuse him physically, Cleon's promise is unenforceable since Spike is under a pre-existing public obligation imposed by both tort and criminal law to refrain from so acting.

Public officials, such as the mayor of a city, members of a city council, police officers, and fire fighters, are under a pre-existing obligation to perform their duties by virtue of their public office. *See Denney v. Reppert.*

The performance of or the promise to perform a **pre-existing contractual duty,** which is neither doubtful nor the subject of honest dispute, is also legally insufficient consideration because the doing of what one is legally bound to do is neither a detriment to the promisee nor a benefit to the promisor. For example, Leigh and Associates employs Jason for one year at a salary of $2,000 per month, and at the end of six months promises Jason that in addition to the salary it will pay him $3,000 if he remains on the job for the remainder of the period originally agreed upon. Leigh's promise is not binding because Jason's promise does not constitute legally sufficient consideration. If Jason's duties were changed in nature or amount, however, Leigh's promise would be binding because Jason's new duties are a legal detriment. *See Denney v. Reppert.*

Modification of a Pre-existing Contract

A modification of a contract occurs when the parties to the contract mutually agree to change one or more of its terms. Under the common law, a modification of an existing contract must be supported by mutual consideration to be enforceable. For example, Fred and Jodie agree that Fred shall put in a gravel driveway for Jodie at a cost of $2,000. Subse-

quently, Jodie agrees to pay an additional $1,000 if Fred will blacktop the driveway. Since Fred was not bound by the original contract to provide blacktopping, he would incur a legal detriment in doing so and is therefore entitled to the additional $1,000. *See Brenner v. Little Red School House, Limited.*

The Code has modified the common law rule by providing that a contract for the sale of goods can be effectively modified by the parties without new consideration. The Comments to this section make the modification subject to the requirement of good faith. Moreover, the Restatement has moved toward this position by providing that a modification of an executory contract is binding if it is fair and equitable in light of the surrounding facts that were not anticipated by the parties when the contract was made. Restatement, Section 89.

Substituted Contracts

A substituted contract occurs when the parties to a contract mutually agree to rescind their original contract and enter into a new contract. In this situation, there are three separate contracts: the original contract, the agreement of rescission, and the substitute contract. Substituted contracts are perfectly valid and effective to discharge the original contract and to impose obligations under the new contract. The rescission is binding in that each party, by giving up his rights under the original contract, has provided consideration to the other, as long as each party still has rights under the original contract. Where the rescission and new agreement are simultaneous, the effect is the same as a contractual modification. The Restatement takes the position that the substitute contract is *not* binding unless it is fair and equitable in view of circumstances not anticipated by the parties when the original contract was made. Section 89, Comment b.

Settlement of an Undisputed Debt

An **undisputed debt** is an obligation that is not contested as to its existence or its amount. Under the common law, the partial payment of a sum of money in consideration of a promise to discharge a fully matured, undisputed debt is legally *insufficient* to support the promise of discharge. To illustrate, assume that Pamela owes Julie $100, and in consideration of Pamela's paying Julie $50, Julie agrees to discharge the debt. In a subsequent suit by Julie against Pamela to recover the remaining $50, at common law Julie is entitled to judgment for $50 on the ground that Julie's promise of discharge is not binding because Pamela's payment of $50 was no legal detriment to the promisee, Pamela, as she was under a *pre-existing legal obligation* to pay that much and more. Consequently, the consideration for Julie's promise of discharge was legally insufficient, and Julie is not bound on her promise. If, however, Julie had accepted from Pamela any new or different consideration, such as the sum of $40 and a fountain pen worth $10 or less, or even the fountain pen with no payment of money, in full satisfaction of the $100 debt, the consideration moving from Pamela would be legally sufficient inasmuch as Pamela was under no legal obligation to give a fountain pen to Julie. In this example, consideration would also exist if Julie had agreed to accept $50 *before* the debt became due, in full satisfaction of the debt. Pamela was under no legal obligation to pay any of the debt before its due date. Consequently, Pamela's early payment is a legal detriment to Pamela as well as a legal benefit to Julie. The law is not concerned with the amount of the discount, as that is simply a question of adequacy. Likewise, Pamela's payment of a lesser amount on the due date at an agreed-upon different place of payment would be legally sufficient consideration. The Restatement requires that the new consideration "differs from what was required by the duty in a way which reflects more than a pretense of bargain." Section 73.

Settlement of a Disputed Debt A disputed debt is an obligation that is either contested as to its existence or as to its amount. A promise to settle a validly disputed claim in exchange for an agreed payment or other performance is supported by consideration. Where

the dispute is based upon contentions which are non-meritorious or not made in good faith, however, giving up such a claim by the debtor is no legal detriment. The Restatement adopts a different position by providing that the settlement of a claim that proves invalid is consideration if at the time of the settlement (1) the claimant honestly believed that the claim was valid *or* (2) the claim was in fact doubtful because of uncertainty as to the facts or the law. Section 74.

For example, where a person has requested professional services from an accountant or a lawyer and no agreement was made with respect to the amount of the fee to be charged, the accountant or lawyer is entitled to receive from her client a reasonable fee for the services rendered. As no definite amount has been agreed upon, the obligation of the client is uncertain. The legal obligation of the client is to pay the reasonable worth of the services performed. When the accountant or lawyer sends the client a bill for her services, the amount stated in the bill is her estimate of the reasonable value of the services, but the debt does not in this manner become undisputed until and unless the client agrees to pay the amount of the bill. If the client honestly disputes the amount that is owing and tenders in full settlement an amount less than the bill, acceptance of the lesser amount by the creditor discharges the debt. Thus, if Ted sends to Betty, an accountant, a check for $120 in payment of his debt to Betty for services rendered, which services Ted considered worthless but for which Betty billed Ted $600, Betty's acceptance of the check releases Ted from any further liability. Ted has given up his right to dispute the billing further, while Betty has forfeited her right to further collection. Thus, there is mutuality of consideration.

BARGAINED FOR EXCHANGE

The central idea behind consideration is that the parties have intentionally entered into a bargained exchange with one another and have each given to the other something in exchange for his promise or performance. "A performance or return promise is bargained for if it is sought by the promisor in exchange for his promise and is given by the promisee in exchange for the promise." Restatement, Section 71. Thus, a promise to give someone a birthday present is without consideration, as the promisor received nothing in exchange for his promise of a present.

Past Consideration

Consideration is the inducement for a promise or performance. The element of bargained for exchange is absent where a promise is given for a past transaction. Therefore, unbargained for past events are not consideration, despite their designation as "past consideration." A promise made on account of something that the promisee has already done is not enforceable. For example, Noel gives emergency care to Tim's adult son while the son is ill. Tim subsequently promises to pay Noel for her services. Tim's promise is not binding because there is no bargained for exchange. *See Feinberg v. Pfeiffer Co.*

Third Parties

Consideration to support a promise may be given to a person other than the promisor if the promisor bargains for that exchange. For example, A promises to pay B $15 if B delivers a specified book to C.

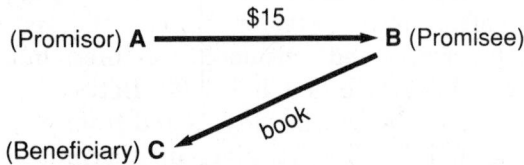

A's promise is binding because B incurred a legal detriment by delivering the book to C, as B was under no prior legal obligation to do so, and A had no prior legal right to have the book given to C. A and B have bargained for A to pay B $15 in return for B's delivering to C the book. A's promise to pay $15 is also consideration for B's promise to give the book to C.

Conversely, consideration may be given by some person other than the promisee. For example, A promises to pay B $25 in return for D's promise to give A a radio.

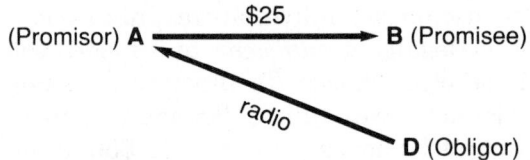

A's promise to pay $25 to B is consideration for D's promise to give A a radio and vice versa.

CONTRACTS WITHOUT CONSIDERATION

Certain transactions are enforceable, even though they are not supported by consideration. These transactions include the following: (1) promises to perform prior unenforceable obligations, (2) promises which induce detrimental reliance (promissory estoppel), (3) promises made under seal, and (4) promises made enforceable by statute.

Promises to Perform Prior Unenforceable Obligations

In certain circumstances the courts will enforce new promises to perform an obligation that originally was not enforceable or has become unenforceable by operation of law. These situations include promises to pay debts barred by the statute of limitations, debts discharged in bankruptcy, and voidable obligations. In addition, as previously indicated, some courts will enforce promises to pay moral obligations.

Promise to Pay Debt Barred by the Statute of Limitations Every State has a statute of limitations, which provides that legal actions must be initiated within a prescribed period of time after the right to bring the action arose. Actions not commenced within the specified time period will be dismissed. The time periods vary among the States and also vary with the nature of the legal action.

An exception to the past consideration rule extends to promises to pay all or part of a contractual or quasi-contractual debt barred by the statute of limitations. The new promise is binding according to its terms without consideration for a second statutory period. Any recovery under the new promise is limited to the terms contained in the new promise. For example, Hazen owes Broome a contractual debt of $1,000, which is barred by the statute of limitation. Hazen then promises to pay Broome $20 a week until the debt is fully paid. Broome has no right to insist upon a lump sum payment of $1,000 because Hazen's obligation is to pay in weekly installments of $20. If instead Hazen's promise had been to pay $20 per week for twenty weeks, Hazen's total obligation would be to pay for $400 in weekly installments of $20 but not to pay the full $1,000 owed on the original debt.

The following facts operate as a sufficient promise unless circumstances indicate otherwise: (1) a voluntary, unqualified admission that the debt is owing; (2) a partial payment of the debt; or (3) a statement that the statute of limitations will not be pleaded as a defense. Restatement, Section 82. Most States require that new promises falling under this rule, except where the new promise is indicated by part payment, be in writing to be enforceable.

Promise to Pay Debt Discharged in Bankruptcy

Another exception to the requirement that consideration be given in exchange for a promise in order to make it binding is a promise to pay a debt that has been discharged in bankruptcy. Restatement, Section 83. The Bankruptcy Act, however, imposes a number of requirements before a promise to pay a debt discharged in bankruptcy may be enforced. These requirements are discussed in Chapter 40.

Voidable Promises

Another promise that is enforceable without new consideration is a new promise to perform a voidable obligation that has not previously been avoided. Restatement, Section 85. The power of avoidance may be based on lack of capacity, fraud, misrepresentation, duress, undue influence, or mistake. For instance, a promise to perform an antecedent obligation made by a minor upon reaching the age of majority is enforceable without new consideration. To be enforceable, the promise itself must not be voidable. For example, if the new promise is made without knowledge of the original fraud or by a minor before reaching the age of majority, then the new promise is not enforceable.

Moral Obligation

Under the common law, a promise made in order to satisfy a pre-existing moral obligation is made for past consideration and therefore is unenforceable for lack of consideration. Instances involving such moral obligation include promises to pay for board and lodging previously furnished to a needy relative of the promisor, promises to pay debts owed by a relative of the promisor, and promises of an employer to pay a completely disabled former employee a sum of money in addition to the amount of an award made under a worker's compensation statute. Although in many cases the moral obligation may be strong by reason of the particular facts and circumstances, no liability generally attaches to the promise.

The Restatement and a minority of States give considerable recognition to moral obligations as consideration. The Restatement provides that a promise made for "a benefit previously received by the promisor from the promisee is binding to the extent necessary to prevent injustice." Section 86. For instance, a promise following the rendering of emergency services is binding even though it is not supported by new consideration.

The Restatement also provides for enforcement of a moral obligation when a person promises to pay for a mistakenly conferred benefit. For example, Pam hires Elizabeth to pave her driveway and Elizabeth mistakenly paves Chuck's driveway next door. Chuck subsequently promises to pay Pam $1,000 for the benefit conferred. Under the Restatement, Chuck's promise to pay the $1,000 is binding.

Promissory Estoppel

As discussed in Chapter 9, in certain circumstances noncontractual promises are enforced where there has been detrimental reliance under the doctrine of promissory estoppel. When applicable, the doctrine makes gratuitous promises enforceable to the extent necessary to avoid injustice. The doctrine applies when a promise that the promisor should reasonably expect to induce detrimental reliance does induce such action or forbearance.

Promissory estoppel does not mean that every gratuitous promise is binding simply because it is followed by a change of position on the part of the promisee. Liability is created by the change of position in justifiable reliance on the promise. For example, Smith promises to Barclay not to foreclose on a mortgage Smith holds on Barclay's factory for a period of six months. Barclay then expends $900,000 on expanding the factory. Smith's promise not to foreclose is binding on Smith under the doctrine of promissory estoppel. *See Feinberg v. Pfeiffer Co.*

The most common application of the doctrine of promissory estoppel is to charitable subscriptions. Numerous churches, memorials, college buildings, hospitals, and other structures used for religious, educational, and charitable purposes have been built with the assistance of contributions made through fulfillment of pledges or promises to contribute to particular worthwhile causes. Although the pledgor regards herself as making a gift for a charitable purpose and gift promises are generally not enforceable, the courts have generally enforced charitable subscription promises. Although a variety of reasons and theories have been advanced in support of liability, the one most accepted is that the subscription has induced a change of position by the promisee (the church, school, or charitable organization) in reliance on the promise. The Restatement, moreover, has relaxed the reliance requirement for charitable subscriptions so that actual reliance need not be shown; the probability of reliance is sufficient.

Contracts under Seal

Under the common law, when a person desired to bind himself by bond, deed, or solemn promise, he executed his promise under seal. He did not have to sign the document. His delivery of a document to which he had affixed his seal was sufficient. No consideration for his promise was necessary. In some States a promise under seal is still binding without consideration.

Nevertheless, most States have abolished by statute the distinction between contracts under seal and written unsealed contracts. In these States, the seal is no longer recognized as a substitute for consideration. The Code has also adopted this position and specifically eliminates the use of seals in contracts for the sale of goods.

Promises Made Enforceable by Statute

Some gratuitous promises that would otherwise be unenforceable have been made binding by statute. Most significant among these are (1) contract modifications, (2) renunciations, and (3) irrevocable offers.

Contract Modifications As mentioned previously, the Uniform Commercial Code has abandoned the common law rule requiring that a modification of an existing contract be supported by consideration in order to be valid. The Code provides that a contract for the sale of goods can be effectively modified without new consideration, provided the modification is made in good faith. Section 2–209.

Renunciation Under the Code, Section 1–107, any claim or right arising out of an alleged breach of contract can be discharged in whole or in part without consideration by a written waiver or renunciation signed and delivered by the aggrieved party.

Irrevocable Offers Under the Code, a written offer signed by a merchant offeror promising to keep open an offer (*firm offer*) to buy or sell goods is not revocable for lack of consideration during the time stated, not to exceed three months, or if no time is stated, for a reasonable time. Section 2–205.

CASES

Legal Sufficiency

COLLINS v. PARSONS COLLEGE

Supreme Court of Iowa, 1973.
203 N.W.2d 594.

UHLENHOPP, J.

This appeal involves the enforceability of an employment agreement between a teacher and Parsons College.

Ben L. Collins holds bachelor and master of arts degrees and a doctor of philosophy degree. He studied at Harvard University in addition and taught for a number of years. In the spring of 1966 he was a full professor with tenure at Wisconsin State University at Whitewater.

In March of 1966, Collins was invited to confer with Dr. W.B. Munson, vice president for academic affairs of Parsons College. Collins testified that the following transpired at that conference:

Dr. Munson asked me to his office and told me he was prepared to offer me a contract for $25,000.00, that he would give me the rank of full professor and that I would be on full tenure.

Further regarding the conference, Collins testified concerning salary increments:

Yes, he told me there would be annual increments of $1,000.00 per year until I reached $30,000.00 in 1971.

The college introduced no evidence contradicting Collins' testimony about the conference.

Munson tendered Collins a written contract for the first year incorporating the terms stated at the conference. Collins was to teach two trimesters in the academic year beginning October 1, 1966, at a salary of $25,000, with the academic rank of "Professor of English and Humanities with tenure." The contract covered the 1966–1967 school year and incorporated Parsons' faculty bylaws by reference. The last two paragraphs of the contract stated:

4. You are hereby placed on tenure.

5. You will receive annual increments of $1,000.00 to the level of $30,000.00 by 1971.

The faculty bylaws provided in part:

The service of a Faculty member on permanent tenure shall be terminated before retirement or his rank reduced only for just cause. Charges which may lead to the dismissal or reduction in rank of Faculty members with permanent tenure shall be made in writing through the Professional Problems Committee whose recommendation will be presented to a meeting of the tenured Faculty.

* * *

After considering the offer of the college, Collins accepted it and gave up his teaching position in Wisconsin. He signed the contract covering the first year and Munson signed it on behalf of the college.

* * *

In February 1968, however, Collins was tendered a different contract, to cover the following year. He was still to have the rank of "Professor of English with tenure," but at a salary of $15,000 with no provision for increment. The tendered contract also stated:

By accepting this contract, the Faculty member agrees that it shall constitute the only contract of employment with the College for the period set forth above and that he waives any rights or claims arising from any other contract of employment with the College, save and except any rights he may have to any unpaid salary or fringe benefits for service performed by him under any previous contract with the College.

* * *

Collins did not sign this contract and in due course the college notified him that he would not be employed the following year. He desired to teach at the college under the original agreement, but in view of the action of the college he sought employment elsewhere. He secured a position at the University of North Dakota and taught there at a salary of $15,000 for the academic year commencing in the fall of 1968, $15,800 commencing in 1969, $16,400 commencing in 1970, and $16,700 commencing in 1971.

No one suggests that Collins did not perform his work properly at Parsons College or that the college had grounds to discharge him or to depart from the original agreement. No written charge was made against him before the tenured faculty, or before anyone else for that matter.

In Collins' present action against the college, he asks as damages the difference between the amount he was promised by the college to 1971 and the amount he was able to earn elsewhere. The trial court tried the case by ordinary proceedings without a jury and held for the college. The controlling facts on liability are really uncontroverted. The dispute is over the legal conclusions to be drawn from the facts.

* * *

Consideration. We have considerable doubt that an agreement for tenure such as this one requires mutuality in any event, *as to duration of the employment.* Tenured teachers in institutions of higher learning have permanent positions as spelled out in the bylaws of their institutions, just as civil servants have permanent positions as spelled out in statutes. Yet such teachers and servants are free to resign if they wish. But a different situation exists *as to compensation to be paid.* This case presents both the duration and compensation aspects.

We do not place the decision, however, on the issue of whether mutuality is required in the case of tenured positions such as the present one. The contention of the college that mutuality of obligation is essential is not strictly an accurate statement of the law. Promises must be mutually obligatory if they constitute the only consideration for each other. But if a promise is supported by other consideration, it is enforceable although the promisee has the right to terminate his undertaking or indeed makes no promise at all, as in the case of unilateral contracts. Speaking for the court, Judge Evans stated the principle thus:

If the lack of mutuality amounts to a lack of consideration, then the contract is invalid. But mere lack of mutuality in and of itself does not render a contract invalid. If mutual promises be the mu-

tual consideration of a contract, then each promise must be enforceable in order to render the other enforceable. Though consideration is essential to the validity of a contract, it is not essential that such consideration consist of a mutual promise. A promissory note for a consideration is valid, though no mutuality appear thereon. This is true of all unilateral contracts which are supported by a consideration.

[Citations.]

The question before us, then, becomes one of consideration. Collins did not promise to serve permanently or even until 1971, and so we have no promise from him in exchange for the promise of the college to employ him permanently at a specified salary with increments to 1971. Did he provide other consideration?

Collins points to his surrender of his tenured position at Wisconsin State University to accept this position, to the knowledge of Parsons College. The evidence shows that he had good academic credentials as well as experience in teaching, and evidently the college believed he would be a valuable addition and would lend stature to its staff. The college appeared eager to get him and was aware that he was surrendering a secure position to accept its offer. Once Collins left Wisconsin, he lost his tenure there. Did his surrender of that position constitute consideration for the agreement of Parsons College?

Courts are divided on such a question, some holding yes and some no. [Citations.] This court has adverted to the question but does not appear to have decided it squarely. [Citations.] Some courts hold the surrender of employment to take a new job constitutes consideration if the new employer is aware that the employee is giving up the other position. [Citations.] Generally consideration may, of course, consist of a detriment to the promisee. [Citations.] Consideration need not move to the promisor. Restatement, Contracts § 75, Comment *e:* "It matters not from whom the consideration moves or to whom it goes."

After considering the question, we think the better rule to be that an employee who gives up other employment to accept an offer of a permanent job provides independent consideration—at least, when as here the employment surrendered was itself permanent and the new employer is aware of the facts. [Citations.]

The result is that the college agreed to employ Collins permanently and at the salary and increments promised to 1971, and that Collins provided consideration for the agreement of the college.

* * *

Reversed and remanded with directions.

Legal Sufficiency/Adequacy

STATE EX REL. LUDWICK v. BRYANT

Supreme Court of Kansas, 1985.
237 Kan. 47, 697 P.2d 858.

HERD, J.

This is a suit on a guarantee executed by Virginia Anne Bryant in which she personally guaranteed payment of a debt of Tender Loving Care, Inc., a corporation which she owned and operated. Bryant moved for summary judgment on the grounds the guarantee lacked consideration. The trial court sustained the motion and the State Department of Human Resources appeals.

Tender Loving Care, Inc., (TLC) was a Kansas corporation organized in October, 1977. * * * On February 15, 1982, the corporate charter was cancelled by the Secretary of State for failure to correct and return the 1980 corporate annual report.

On July 31, 1981, TLC filed its second-quarter wage report with the Kansas Department of Human Resources (Human Resources). Its check drawn by Bryant on the corporate account for $231.79 was returned for insufficient funds.

TLC stopped all operations in August, 1981. It has not been reopened and Bryant testified she has no intention of reopening the business.

On October 21, 1981, Virginia Bryant individually filed a petition in bankruptcy. Human Resources was listed as a creditor. It filed a proof of claim in Virginia Bryant's bankruptcy. On April 29, 1982, appellee Bry-

ant received a discharge in bankruptcy. The debt owed by TLC to Human Resources was not allowed in the bankruptcy action since Bryant was held not to be personally liable to the State for the taxes of TLC. Thus, after the discharge of Bryant, Human Resources had still not been paid. In their motions arguing summary judgment, both parties agreed that the debt was owed by TLC and Bryant had no personal liability for its payment.

On July 12, 1982, Bryant was contacted by a representative of Human Resources. She was asked to come to its offices, which she did. When she arrived at the offices of Human Resources she was told she needed to pay the $231.79 debt of TLC. Bryant advised the department she had been discharged in bankruptcy. Department officials told her that State unemployment taxes cannot be discharged by the bankruptcy court and she needed to pay the debt.

Bryant advised Human Resources three or four times that she wished to check with her attorney. She placed a telephone call to him, but she was unable to reach him. Bryant made no attempt to leave the offices of the department or to terminate the conversation as a result of her inability to speak with her lawyer. The discussion continued.

Another Human Resources official then spoke with Bryant. The man advised Bryant the debt of TLC was not excused or discharged and she needed to sign a personal guarantee to set up a payment plan. Bryant was then presented with a typed guarantee. After further urging by Human Resources officials, Bryant signed the personal guarantee agreement.

* * *

After signing the agreement, Bryant contacted her attorney. On July 14, 1982, her attorney wrote to the Department of Human Resources stating the debt covered by the personal guarantee was discharged in bankruptcy and, further, the guarantee was without consideration. On April 15, 1983, the department filed an action in state court against Bryant for $267.02.

* * *

The first issue raised is whether the trial court erred in holding there was not consideration to support the guarantee of Virginia Bryant.

It is a longstanding rule of law that for a contract to be enforceable it must be supported by consideration. [Citation.] The parties agree no consideration is stated on the face of the guarantee involved in this case.

* * *

We have held consideration is sufficient if there is a benefit to the debtor or an inconvenience or deprivation to the creditor, such as a promise by the creditor to refrain from legal proceedings or an extension of time within which the debtor may pay the creditor. [Citation.]

Appellant argues there was a benefit to the guarantor, Virginia Bryant, because the agreement allowed her to make monthly payments rather than one payment. Clearly there is no benefit to Bryant. By the guarantee agreement she agreed to pay a debt which she had no obligation to pay.

The next question is whether there was consideration in the form of a benefit to the debtor, TLC. Appellant contends TLC was benefited by having its debt paid, by being allowed to pay its debt in installments, and by not being sued for its debt by Human Resources.

Appellee argues there was no benefit to TLC. First, the agreement on its face does not relieve the corporation of its obligation to pay. * * * Additionally, appellant argues it does not want to release TLC from its debt and rely only upon Bryant. Rather, it wants Bryant in a traditional guarantor status where she pays the debt only if TLC defaults. Despite the seeming logic of this argument, it is important to note TLC is already in default. Its debt is long overdue. It is no longer operating and receiving fees. Its charter has been cancelled and it has no assets and many liabilities. Therefore, there is no benefit to TLC since it was in default and unable to pay the debt prior to the guarantee. The guarantee serves only to create a new obligation, that of requiring Bryant to pay a debt she did not owe. Hence, the benefit to TLC is illusory

since the corporation cannot pay the debt and Bryant clearly received no benefit from the agreement.

* * *

The question then turns to whether there was an inconvenience to Human Resources by forbearing from suing TLC and agreeing to accept payment in installments, rather than suing for the full amount to which it was entitled in one payment. Bryant argues there was no such benefit.

The crux of Bryant's argument is that the agency's claim against the corporation was worthless, and as such it provides no consideration to support the contract.

* * *

Appellant Human Resources . . . argues that the claim was not worthless since it was a debt legally owed. The issue is not the validity of the debt, but whether the entity which owes the debt is viable. Substantiating this, Professor Corbin in his treatise on contracts states: "[I]t is said that even though a claim is perfectly valid, forbearance to press it is not a sufficient consideration if there is no possibility of enforcement and collection, making both the claim and the forbearance valueless." [Citation.] This issue is without merit.

* * *

Hence, the debt owed by TLC, despite its validity, was unenforceable and Human Resources' agreement to forbear was without consideration due to the worthlessness of its claim against TLC.

We hold there was no consideration to support appellee's execution of the guarantee. The judgment of the trial court is affirmed.

Pre-existing Obligation

DENNEY v. REPPERT

Court of Appeals of Kentucky, 1968.
432 S.W.2d 647.

MYRE, SPECIAL COMMISSIONER.

The sole question presented in this case is which of several claimants is entitled to an award for information leading to the apprehension and conviction of certain bank robbers.

* * *

On June 12th or 13th, 1963, three armed men entered the First State Bank, Eubank, Kentucky, and with a display of arms and threats robbed the bank of over $30,000. Later in the day they were apprehended by State Policemen Garret Godby, Johnny Simms, and Tilford Reppert, placed under arrest, and the entire loot was recovered. Later all of the prisoners were convicted and Garret Godby, Johnny Simms, and Tilford Reppert appeared as witnesses at the trial.

The First State Bank of Eubank was a member of the Kentucky Bankers Association which provided and advertised a reward of $500.00 for the arrest and conviction of each bank robber. Hence the outstanding reward for the three bank robbers was $1,500.00. Many became claimants for the reward and the Kentucky State Bankers Association, being unable to determine the merits of the claims for the reward, asked the circuit court to determine the merits of the various claims and to adjudge who was entitled to receive the reward or share in it. All of the claimants were made defendants in the action.

At the time of the robbery the claimants Murrell Denney, Joyce Buis, Rebecca McCollum, and Jewell Snyder were employees of the First State Bank of Eubank and came out of the grueling situation with great credit and glory. Each one of them deserves approbation and an accolade. They were vigilant in disclosing to the public and the peace officers the details of the crime, and in describing the culprits, and giving all the information that they possessed that would be useful in capturing the robbers. Undoubtedly, they performed a great service. It is in the evidence that the claimant Murrell Denney was conspicuous and energetic in his efforts to make known the robbery, to acquaint the officers as to the personal appearance of the criminals, and to give other pertinent facts.

The first question for determination is whether the employees of the robbed bank are eligible to receive or share in the reward?

The great weight of authority answers in the negative. *In Re Waggoner* [citation] states the rule thusly:

To the general rule that, when a reward is offered to the general public for the performance of some specified act, such reward may be claimed by any person who performs such act, is the exception of agents, employees, and public officials who are acting within the scope of their employment or official duties. . . .

Or, as the rule was set forth in *Forsythe v. Murnane et al.,* [citation]:

". . . The defendant Delaney is and during all the times herein mentioned has been, employed by defendant Great Northern Railway Company . . . and by virtue of such employment it was his duty to do and perform all the things that were done and performed by him in the matter of the arrest, identification, and prosecution . . . .

"It is clear that defendant Delaney is not, in view of . . . his contractual relations and the duties in the premises . . . entitled to any part of the reward. . . ."

In *Stacy v. President, etc., of State Bank of Ill.* [citation] it was held that a director of a bank was not entitled to share in the reward offered by the bank for the arrest of a robber because it was his duty as a director to further the best interests of the bank, and apprehending one who had robbed the bank was in the best interest of the bank. [Citations.]

At the time of the robbery the claimants Murrell Denney, Joyce Buis, Rebecca McCollum, and Jewell Snyder were employees of the First State Bank of Eubank. They were under duty to protect and conserve the resources and moneys of the bank, and safeguard every interest of the institution furnishing them employment. Each of these employees exhibited great courage and cool bravery, in a time of stress and danger. The community and the county have recompensed them in commendation, admiration, and high praise, and the world looks on them as heroes. But in making known the robbery and assisting in acquainting the public and the officers with details of the crime and with identification of the robbers, they performed a duty to the bank and the public, for which they cannot claim a reward.

The claims of Corbin Reynolds, Julia Reynolds, Alvie Reynolds, and Gene Reynolds also must fail. According to their statements they gave valuable information to the arresting officers. However, they did not follow the procedure as set forth in the offer of reward in that they never filed a claim with the Kentucky Bankers Association. It is well established that a claimant of a reward must comply with the terms and conditions of the offer of reward. [Citation.]

State Policemen Garret Godby, Johnny Simms, and Tilford Reppert made the arrest of the bank robbers and captured the stolen money. All participated in the prosecution. At the time of the arrest, it was the duty of the state policemen to apprehend the criminals. Under the law they cannot claim or share in the reward and they are interposing no claim to it.

This leaves the defendant, Tilford Reppert the sole eligible claimant. The record shows that at the time of the arrest he was a deputy sheriff in Rockcastle County, but the arrest and recovery of the stolen money took place in Pulaski County. He was out of his jurisdiction, and was thus under no legal duty to make the arrest, and is thus eligible to claim and receive the reward. In *Kentucky Bankers Ass'n et al. v. Cassady* [citation], it was said:

It is . . . well established that a public officer with the authority of the law to make an arrest may accept an offer of reward or compensation for acts or services performed outside of his bailiwick or not within the scope of his official duties. . . .

The claimant Tilford Reppert was present with Garret Godby and Johnny Simms at the time of the arrest and all cooperated in its consummation. The claimant Tilford Reppert personally recovered the stolen money. He recovered $2,000.00 more than the bank records show was stolen. This record does not reveal what became of the $2,000.00 excess.

It is manifest from the record that Tilford Reppert is the only claimant qualified and eligible to receive the reward. Therefore, it is

the judgment of the circuit court that he is entitled to receive payment of the $1,500.00 reward now deposited with the clerk of this court.

The judgment is affirmed.

Modification of a Pre-existing Contract

BRENNER v. LITTLE RED SCHOOL HOUSE, LIMITED

Court of Appeals of North Carolina, 1982.
59 N.C.App. 68, 295 S.E.2d 607.

ARNOLD, J.

[The plaintiff, Brenner, entered into a contract with the defendant, Little Red School House, Ltd., which stated that in return for payment of nonrefundable tuition of $1,080, Brenner's son could attend defendant's school for a year. When Brenner's ex-wife refused to enroll their son, plaintiff sought and received a verbal promise of a refund. Defendant now refuses to refund plaintiff's money for lack of consideration.]

* * *

Before a contract modification is effective there must be consideration to support it. [Citation.] Consideration can be found in benefit to the promisor or detriment to the promisee.

[T]here is a consideration if the promisee, in return for the promise, does anything legal which he is not bound to do, or refrains from doing anything which he has a right to do, whether there is any actual loss or detriment to him or actual benefit or not. [Citation.]

The defendant argues that there was no consideration given by the plaintiff because the plaintiff as promisee suffered no detriment. But as the Supreme Court observed [in a prior case]:

[I]n return for the defendant's promise to refund the tuition paid, plaintiff would relinquish his right to have his child educated in defendant school . . . . It is well established that any benefit, right, or interest bestowed upon the promisor, or any forbearance, detriment, or loss undertaken by the promisee, is sufficient consideration to support a contract. [Citation.]

The record shows that plaintiff was relinquishing the opportunity to have his child educated by the defendant when he testified "From the time . . . [the defendant] first told me that she would refund the tuition to me and from that point on, I did not expect the school to do anything else in regard to providing services or anything else on behalf of Russ Brenner." [Citation.] . . . [Thus,] the record as quoted above shows sufficient consideration to support the modification in this case.

* * *

[Judgment for plaintiff.]

Past Consideration/Promissory Estoppel

FEINBERG v. PFEIFFER CO.

Saint Louis Court of Appeals, Missouri, 1959.
322 S.W.2d 163.

DOERNER, COMMISSIONER.

This is a suit brought in the Circuit Court of the City of St. Louis by plaintiff, a former employee of the defendant corporation, on an alleged contract whereby defendant agreed to pay plaintiff the sum of $200 per month for life upon her retirement. A jury being waived, the case was tried by the court alone. Judgment below was for plaintiff for $5,100, the amount of the pension claimed to be due. . . .

The parties are in substantial agreement on the essential facts. Plaintiff began working for the defendant, a manufacturer of pharmaceuticals, in 1910, when she was but 17 years of age. By 1947 she had attained the position of bookkeeper, office manager, and assistant treasurer of the defendant, and owned 70 shares of its stock out of a total of 6,503 shares issued and outstanding. * * *

On December 27, 1947, the annual meeting of the defendant's Board of Directors was held at the Company's offices in St. Louis, presided over by Max Lippman, the then president and largest individual stockholder. * * * At the meeting the Board of Directors adopted the following resolution, which, because it is the crux of the case, we quote in full:

"The Chairman thereupon pointed out that the Assistant Treasurer, Mrs. Anna Sacks Feinberg, has given the corporation many years of long and faithful service. Not only has she served the corporation devotedly, but with exceptional ability and skill. The President pointed out that although all of the officers and directors sincerely hoped and desired that Mrs. Feinberg would continue in her present position for as long as she felt able, nevertheless, in view of the length of service which she has contributed provision should be made to afford her retirement privileges and benefits which should become a firm obligation of the corporation to be available to her whenever she should see fit to retire from active duty, however many years in the future such retirement may become effective. It was, accordingly proposed that Mrs. Feinberg's salary which is presently $350.00 per month, be increased to $400.00 per month, and that Mrs. Feinberg would be given the privilege of retiring from active duty at any time she may elect to see fit so to do upon a retirement pay of $200.00 per month for life, with the distinct understanding that the retirement plan is merely being adopted at the present time in order to afford Mrs. Feinberg security for the future and in the hope that her active services will continue with the corporation for many years to come. After due discussion and consideration, and upon motion duly made and seconded, it was—

"Resolved, that the salary of Anna Sacks Feinberg be increased from $350.00 to $400.00 per month and that she be afforded the privilege of retiring from active duty in the corporation at any time she may elect to see fit so to do upon retirement pay of $200.00 per month, for the remainder of her life."

* * * Plaintiff testified on cross-examination that she had no prior information that such a pension plan was contemplated, that it came as a surprise to her, and that she would have continued in her employment whether or not such a resolution had been adopted. It is clear from the evidence that there was no contract, oral or written, as to plaintiff's length of employment, and that she was free to quit, and the defendant to discharge her, at any time.

Plaintiff did continue to work for the defendant through June 30, 1949, on which date she retired. In accordance with the foregoing resolution, the defendant began paying her the sum of $200 on the first of each month. Mr. Lippman died on November 18, 1949, and was succeeded as president of the company by his widow. Because of an illness, she retired from that office and was succeeded in October, 1953, by her son-in-law, Sidney M. Harris. Mr. Harris testified that while Mrs. Lippman had been president she signed the monthly pension check paid plaintiff, but fussed about doing so, and considered the payments as gifts. After his election, he stated, a new accounting firm employed by the defendant questioned the validity of the payments to plaintiff on several occasions, and in the Spring of 1956, upon its recommendation, he consulted the Company's then attorney, Mr. Ralph Kalish. Harris testified that both Ernst and Ernst, the accounting firm, and Kalish told him there was no need of giving plaintiff the money. He also stated that he had concurred in the view that the payments to plaintiff were mere gratuities rather than amounts due under a contractual obligation, and that following his discussion with the Company's attorney plaintiff was sent a check for $100 on April 1, 1956. Plaintiff declined to accept the reduced amount, and this action followed. * * *

* * *

Appellant's next complaint is that there was insufficient evidence to support the court's findings that plaintiff would not have quit defendant's employ had she not known and relied upon the promise of defendant to pay her $200 a month for life, and the finding that, from her voluntary retirement until April 1, 1956, plaintiff relied upon the continued receipt of the pension installments. The trial court so found, and, in our opinion, justifiably so.

* * *

It is defendant's contention, in essence, that the resolution adopted by its Board of Directors was a mere promise to make a gift, and that no contract resulted either thereby, or when plaintiff retired, because there was no consideration given or paid by the plaintiff. It urges that a promise to make a gift is not binding unless supported by a legal consideration; that the only apparent consider-

ation for the adoption of the foregoing resolution was the "many years of long and faithful service" expressed therein; and that past services are not a valid consideration for a promise. Defendant argues further that there is nothing in the resolution which made its effectiveness conditional upon plaintiff's continued employment, that she was not under contract to work for any length of time but was free to quit whenever she wished, and that she had no contractual right to her position and could have been discharged at any time.

Plaintiff concedes that a promise based upon past services would be without consideration, but contends that there were two other elements which supplied the required element: First, the continuation by plaintiff in the employ of the defendant for the period from December 27, 1947, the date when the resolution was adopted, until the date of her retirement on June 30, 1949. And, second, her change of position, i.e., her retirement, and the abandonment by her of her opportunity to continue in gainful employment, made in reliance on defendant's promise to pay her $200 per month for life.

We must agree with the defendant that the evidence does not support the first of these contentions. There is no language in the resolution predicating plaintiff's right to a pension upon her continued employment. She was not required to work for the defendant for any period of time as a condition to gaining such retirement benefits. She was told that she could quit the day upon which the resolution was adopted, as she herself testified, and it is clear from her own testimony that she made no promise or agreement to continue in the employ of the defendant in return for its promise to pay her a pension. Hence there was lacking that mutuality of obligation which is essential to the validity of a contract. [Citations.]

But as to the second of these contentions we must agree with plaintiff.

* * *

Section 90 of the Restatement of the Law of Contracts states that: "A promise which the promisor should reasonably expect to induce action or forbearance of a definite and substantial character on the part of the promisee and which does induce such action or forbearance is binding if injustice can be avoided only by enforcement of the promise." This doctrine has been described as that of "promissory estoppel," . . .

* * *

Was there such an act on the part of plaintiff, in reliance upon the promise contained in the resolution, as will estop the defendant, and therefore create an enforceable contract under the doctrine of promissory estoppel? We think there was *   *   * At the time she retired plaintiff was 57 years of age. At the time the payments were discontinued she was over 63 years of age. It is a matter of common knowledge that it is virtually impossible for a woman of that age to find satisfactory employment, much less a position comparable to that which plaintiff enjoyed at the time of her retirement.

* * *

PER CURIAM.

The foregoing opinion by DOERNER, C., is adopted as the opinion of the court. The judgment is, accordingly, affirmed.

QUESTIONS

1. Define consideration and what is meant by legal sufficiency.

2. Discuss illusory promises, output contracts, requirements contracts, exclusive dealing contracts, and conditional contracts.

3. Explain whether pre-existing public and contractual obligations satisfy the legal requirement of consideration.

4. Explain the concept of bargained for exchange. Is this element present with past consideration or third-party beneficiaries? Explain.

5. Identify and discuss those contracts that are enforceable even though they are not supported by consideration.

PROBLEMS

1. In consideration of $800 paid to him by Joyce, Hill gave Joyce a written option to purchase his house for $80,000 on or before April 1. Prior to April 1, Hill verbally agreed to extend the option until July 1. On May 18, Hill, known to Joyce, sold the house to Gray, who was ignorant of the unrecorded option. Joyce brought suit against Hill. Decision?

2. (a) Ann owed $500 to Barry for services Barry rendered to Ann. The debt was due June 30, 1989. In March 1990, the debt was still unpaid. Barry was in urgent need of ready cash and told Ann that if she would pay $150 of the debt at once, Barry would release her from the balance. Ann paid $150 and stated to Barry that all claims had been paid in full. In August 1990, Barry demanded the unpaid balance and subsequently sued Ann for $350. Decision?

(b) Modify the facts in (a) by assuming that Barry gave Ann a written receipt stating that all claims had been paid in full. Result?

(c) Modify the facts in (a) by assuming that Ann owed Barry the $500 on Ann's purchase of a motorcycle from Barry. Result?

3. (a) Judy orally promises her daughter, Liza, that she will give her a tract of land for her home.

Liza, as intended by Judy, gives up her homestead and takes possession of the land. Liza lives there for six months and starts construction of a home. Is Judy bound to convey the real estate?

(b) Ralph, knowing that his son, Ed, desires to purchase a tract of land, promises to give him the $25,000 he needs for the purchase. Ed, relying on this promise, buys an option on the tract of land. Ralph now seeks to rescind his promise. Decision?

4. George owed Keith $800 on a personal loan. Neither the amount of the debt nor George's liability to pay the $800 was disputed. Keith had also rendered services as a carpenter to George without any agreement as to the price to be paid. When the work was completed, an honest and reasonable difference of opinion developed between George and Keith with respect to the value of Keith's services. Upon receiving Keith's bill for the carpentry services for $600, George mailed in a properly stamped and addressed envelope his check for $800 to Keith. In an accompanying letter, George stated that the enclosed check was in full settlement of both claims. Keith indorsed and cashed the check. Thereafter, Keith unsuccessfully sought to collect from George an alleged unpaid balance of $600. Keith then sued George for $600. Decision?

5. The Snyder Mfg. Co., being a large user of coal, entered into separate contracts with several coal companies, in each of which it was agreed that the coal company would supply coal during the year 1989 in such amounts as the manufacturing company might desire to order, at a price of $49 per ton. In February 1989, the Snyder Company ordered 1,000 tons of coal from Union Coal Company, one of the contracting parties. Union Coal Company delivered 500 tons of the order and then notified Snyder Company that no more deliveries would be made and that it denied any obligation under the contract. In an action by Union Coal to collect $49 per ton for the 500 tons of coal delivered, Snyder files a counterclaim, claiming damages of $1,500 for failure to deliver the additional 500 tons of the order and damages of $4,000 for breach of agreement to deliver coal during the balance of the year. Decision?

6. On February 5, Devon entered into a written agreement with Gordon whereby Gordon agreed to drill a well on Devon's property for the sum of $5,000 and to complete the well on or before April 15. Before entering into the contract, Gordon made test borings and had satisfied himself as to the character of the subsurface. After two days of drilling, Gordon struck hard rock. On February 17, Gordon removed his equipment and advised Devon that the project had proved unprofitable and that he would not continue. On March 17, Devon went to Gordon and told Gordon that he would assume the risk of the enterprise and would pay Gordon $100 for each day required to drill the well, as compensation for labor, the use of Gordon's equipment, and Gordon's services in supervising the work, provided Gordon would furnish certain special equipment designed to cut through hard rock. Gordon said that the proposal was satisfactory. The work was continued by Gordon and completed in an additional fifty-eight days. Upon completion of the work, Devon failed to pay, and Gordon brought an action to recover $5,800. Devon answered that he had never become obligated to pay $100 a day and filed a counterclaim for damages in the amount of $500 for the month's delay based on an alleged breach of contract by Gordon. Decision?

7. Discuss and explain whether there is valid consideration for each of the following promises:

(a) A and B entered into a contract for the purchase and sale of goods. A subsequently promised to pay a higher price for the goods when B refused to deliver at the contract price.

(b) A promised in writing to pay a debt, which was due from B to C, on C's agreement to extend the time of payment for one year.

(c) A executed a promissory note to her son, B, solely in consideration of past services rendered to A by B, for which there had been no agreement or request to pay.

8. Alan purchased shoes from Barbara on open account. Barbara sent Alan a bill for $10,000. Alan wrote back that 200 pairs of the shoes were defective and offered to pay $6,000 and give Barbara his promissory note for $1,000. Barbara accepted the offer, and Alan sent his check for $6,000 and his note in accordance with the agreement. Barbara cashed the check, collected on the note, and one month later sued Alan for $3,000. Decision?

9. Nancy owed Sharon $1,500, but Sharon did not initiate a lawsuit to collect the debt within the time period prescribed by the statute of limitations. Nevertheless, Nancy promises Sharon that she will pay the barred debt. Thereafter, Nancy refuses to pay. Sharon brings suit to collect on this new promise. Decision?

10. Anthony lends money to Frank. Frank dies without having paid the loan. Frank's widow, Carol, promises Anthony to repay the loan. Upon Carol's refusal to pay the loan, Anthony brings suit against Carol for payment of the loan. Decision?

11. The parties entered into an oral contract in June 1969, under which plaintiff agreed to construct a building for defendant on a time and materials basis, at a maximum cost of $56,146, plus sales tax and extras ordered by defendant. When the building was 90 percent completed, defendant told plaintiff he was unhappy with the whole job as "the thing wasn't just being run right." The parties then on October 17 signed a written agreement lowering the maximum cost to $52,000 plus sales tax. Plaintiff thereafter completed the build-

ing at a cost of $64,155. The maximum under the June oral agreement, plus extras and sales tax, totalled $61,040. Defendant contended that he was obligated to pay only the lower maximum fixed by the October 17 agreement. Decision?

12. Taylor assaulted his wife, who then took refuge in Ms. Harrington's house. The next day, Mr. Taylor entered the house and began another assault on his wife. Taylor's wife knocked him down and, while he was lying on the floor, attempted to cut his head open or decapitate him with an axe. Harrington intervened to stop the bloodshed, and was hit by the axe as it was descending. The axe fell upon her hand, mutilating it badly, but sparing Taylor his life. Afterwards, Taylor orally promised to compensate Harrington for her injury. He paid a small sum but nothing more. Harrington sued to enforce Taylor's promise. Decision?

COMPUTER RESEARCH PROBLEMS

1. Jonnel Enterprises, Inc., contracted to construct a student dormitory at Clarion State College. On May 6, Jonnel entered into a written agreement with Graham and Long as electrical contractors to perform the electrical work and to supply materials for the dormitory. The contract price was $70,544.66. Graham and Long claim that they believed the May 6 agreement obligated them to perform the electrical work on only one wing of the building, but that three or four days after work was started, a second wing of the building was discovered. At that time Graham and Long informed Jonnel that they would not wire both wings of the building under the present contract, so a new contract was orally agreed upon by the parties. Under the new contract Graham and Long were obligated to wire both wings and were to be paid only $65,000, but they were relieved of the obligations to supply entrances and a heating system. Graham and Long resumed their work, and Jonnel made seven of the eight progress payments called for. When Jonnel did not pay the final payment, Graham and Long brought this action. Jonnel claims that the May 6 contract is controlling. Decision?

2. Baker entered into an oral agreement with Healey, the State distributor of Ballantine & Sons's liquor products, that Ballantine would supply Baker with its products on demand and that Baker would have the exclusive agency for Ballantine within a certain area of Connecticut. Shortly thereafter the agreement was modified to give Baker the right to terminate at will. Eight months later, when Ballantine & Son's revoked its agency, Baker sued to enforce the oral agreement. Decision?

3. PLM, Inc. entered into an oral agreement with Quaintance Associates, an executive "headhunter" service, for the recruitment of qualified candidates to be employed by PLM. As agreed, PLM's obligation to pay Quaintance did not depend on PLM actually hiring a qualified candidate presented by Quaintance. After several months Quaintance sent a letter to PLM, admitting that it had so far failed to produce a suitable candidate, but included a bill for $9,806.61, covering fees and expenses. PLM responded that Quaintance's services were only worth $6,060.48, and that payment of the lesser amount was the only fair way to handle the dispute. Accordingly, PLM enclosed a check for $6,060.48, writing on the back of the check "IN FULL PAYMENT OF ANY CLAIMS QUAINTANCE HAS AGAINST PLM, INC." Quaintance cashed the check, and then sues PLM for the remaining $3,746.13. Decision?

4. Red Owl Stores told the Hoffman family that, upon the payment of approximately $18,000, a grocery store franchise would be built for them in a new location. Upon the advice of Red Owl, the Hoffmans bought a small grocery store in their hometown in order to get management experience. After three months of operating at a profit, Red Owl advised the Hoffmans to sell the small grocery, assuring them that Red Owl would find them a larger store elsewhere. Although selling at that point would cost them much profit, the Hoffmans followed Red Owl's directions. Additionally, to raise the required money for the deal, the Hoffmans sold their bakery business in their hometown. The Hoffmans also sold their house, and moved to a new home in the city where their new store was to be located. Red Owl then informed the Hoffmans that it would take $24,100, not $18,000, to complete the deal. The family scrambled to find the additional funds. However, when told by Red Owl that it would now cost them $34,000 to get their new franchise, the Hoffmans decided to sue instead. Decision?

Chapter 12

ILLEGAL BARGAINS

Violations of Statutes
Violations of Public Policy
Effect of Illegality

AN essential requirement of a binding promise or agreement is legality of objective. When the formation or performance of an agreement is criminal, tortious, or otherwise contrary to public policy, the agreement is illegal and **unenforceable**. The law does *not* provide a remedy for the breach of an unenforceable agreement and thus "leaves the parties where it finds them." It is preferable to use the term "illegal bargain" or "illegal agreement" rather than "illegalcontract," because the word "contract," by definition, denotes a legal and enforceable agreement. The illegal bargain is made unenforceable (1) to discourage such undesirable conduct and (2) to avoid the inappropriate use of the judicial process in carrying out the socially undesirable bargain.

The Restatement avoids defining the term "illegal bargain" and instead focuses upon whether public policy should bar enforcement of the agreement. By relying upon the concept of public policy the Restatement provides the courts with greater flexibility in determining the enforceability of questioned agreements by weighing the strength of legally recognized policies against the effect upon the contracting parties and on the pub-

lic of declaring a particular bargain to be against public policy.

This chapter will discuss (a) agreements in violation of a statute, (b) agreements contrary to public policy, and (c) the effect of illegality upon agreements.

VIOLATIONS OF STATUTES

An agreement declared illegal by statute will not be enforced by the courts. For example, wagering or gambling contracts are specifically declared unenforceable in most States. In addition, an agreement to violate a statute prohibiting crimes, such as murder, robbery, embezzlement, forgery, and price fixing, is unenforceable. Likewise, an agreement that is induced by criminal conduct will not be enforced. For example, if Alice enters into an agreement with Brent Co. through the bribing of Brent Co.'s purchasing agent, the agreement would be unenforceable.

Licensing Statutes

Every jurisdiction has laws requiring a license for those who engage in certain trades, professions, or businesses. Common examples are licensing statutes which apply to lawyers, doctors, dentists, accountants, brokers, plumbers, and contractors. Some licensing statutes mandate schooling and/or examination, while others only require financial responsibility and/or good moral character. Whether a person may recover for services rendered if he has failed to comply with a licensing requirement depends upon the terms or type of licensing statute. This rule only pertains to the rights of the unlicensed party to enforce the obligations of the other party.

The statute itself may expressly provide that an unlicensed person engaged in a business or profession for which a license is required shall not recover for services rendered. Where there is no such statutory provision, the courts commonly distinguish between those statutes or ordinances that are regulatory in character and those that are enacted merely to raise revenue. If the statute is regulatory, a person cannot recover for professional services unless he has the required license, as long as the public policy behind the regulatory purpose clearly outweighs the person's interest in being paid for his services. Restatement, Section 181. Some courts have gone further by balancing the penalty suffered by the unlicensed party against the benefit received by the other party. In contrast, if the law is for revenue purposes only, agreements for such services are enforceable.

A **regulatory license** is a measure designed to protect the public against unqualified persons, such as statutes prescribing standards for those who seek to practice law or medicine. *See Brady v. Fulghum.* A **revenue license,** on the other hand, does not seek to protect against the incompetent or unqualified but simply to furnish revenue. An example is a statute requiring a license of plumbers but not establishing standards of competence for those who seek to follow the trade. It is regarded as a taxing measure and lacking in any expression of legislative intent to preclude unlicensed plumbers from enforcing their business contracts.

Gambling Statutes

In a **wager** the parties stipulate that one shall win and the other lose depending upon the outcome of an event in which they have no "interest" other than that arising from the possibility of such gain or loss. All States have legislation pertaining to gambling or wagering, and American courts generally refuse to recognize the enforceability of a gambling agreement. Thus, if Arnold makes a bet with Bernice on the outcome of a ball game, the agreement is unenforceable by either party. Some States, however, now permit certain kinds of regulated gambling. Wagering conducted by governmental agencies, principally State-operated lotteries, has come to constitute an increasingly important source of public revenues.

To be distinguished from wagers are ordinary insurance contracts in which the insured, having an "insurable interest" (discussed in Chapter 53), pays a certain sum of money or premium in exchange for a promise of the company to pay a larger amount upon the occurrence of some event such as a fire which causes loss to the insured. Here, the agreement compensates for loss under an existing risk; it does not create an entirely new risk. In a wager the parties contemplate gain through mere chance, whereas in an insurance contract they seek to distribute possible loss. Furthermore, most fast-food games and grocery store drawings have been upheld because the participants need not make a purchase to be eligible for the prize.

Sunday Statutes

The common law does not prohibit entering into contracts on Sunday. In the absence of a statutory prohibition, a valid contract may be entered into on Sunday as on any other day. Some States, however, have legislation, referred to as **Blue Laws,** modifying this common law rule and prohibiting certain types of commercial activity on Sunday. Even in a State which prohibits contracts on Sunday, a court will enforce a subsequent weekday ratification of a loan made on Sunday or a promise to pay for goods sold and delivered on Sunday. Blue Laws usually do not apply to activities of "necessity" and "charity."

Usury Statutes

A **usury statute** is a law establishing a maximum rate of permissible interest that may be contracted for between a lender and borrower of money. Historically, every State had a usury law. Recently, however, there has been a trend to limit or relax usury statutes. Maximum rates permitted vary greatly from State to State and among types of transactions. These statutes typically are general in their application, although certain specified types of transactions are exempted. For example, numerous States impose no limit on the rate of interest that may be charged on loans to corporations. Furthermore, some States permit the parties to contract for any rate of interest on loans made to individual proprietorships or partnerships for the purpose of carrying on a business.

In addition to the exceptions accorded certain designated types of borrowers, a number of States have exempted specific lenders. For example, the majority of the States have enacted installment loan laws, which permit eligible lenders a higher return on installment loans than would otherwise be permitted under the applicable general interest statute. These *specific* lender usury statutes, which have all but eliminated the general usury statute, vary greatly but have generally included small consumer loans, corporate loans, loans by small lenders, real estate mortgages, and numerous other transactions.

General usury statutes have traditionally been interpreted to exempt credit terms granted by vendors under the judicially created time-price doctrine. The **time-price doctrine** provides that sellers may have two prices for their merchandise—a cash price and a credit or "time-price," and that the credit price may exceed the cash price by more than the statutorily allowed interest on the cash price. Today, most States have rendered the time-price doctrine moot by adopting State retail installment sales acts, which apply specific usury statutes to specific consumer transactions and are beyond the scope of the general usury statutes.

For a transaction to be usurious, courts usually require evidence of the following factors: (a) a loan or forbearance (b) of money (c) which is repayable absolutely and in all events (d) for which an interest charge is exacted in excess of the interest rate allowed by law. Transactions that are really loans may not be clothed with the trappings of a sale for the purpose of avoiding the usury laws.

Assuming that it is established that the arrangement is for a loan, certain expenses or charges are permitted in addition to the maximum legal interest. Payments made by a borrower to the lender for expenses incurred or for services rendered in good faith in making a loan or in obtaining security for its repayment are generally not included in determining whether the loan is usurious. Ordinary expenses by the lender that are permissible include costs of examining title, investigating the credit rating of the borrower, drawing necessary documents, and inspecting the property. If not excessive, they are not considered in determining the rate of interest with respect to usury statutes. Nonetheless, payments made to the lender or from which she derives an advantage are included if they exceed the reasonable value of services actually rendered. *See Abramowitz v. Barnett Bank of West Orlando.*

The legal effect to be given a usurious loan varies from State to State. In a few States the lender forfeits both principal and interest. In some jurisdictions, the lender can recover the principal but forfeits all interest. In other States, only that portion of interest exceeding the maximum permitted is forfeited. In several States, the amount forfeited is a multiple (double or treble) of the interest charged. Disposition of usurious interest already paid also varies. Some States do not allow any recovery of usurious interest paid; others allow a recovery of the usurious interest paid or a multiple of it.

VIOLATIONS OF PUBLIC POLICY

The reach of a statute may extend beyond its language. Sometimes, the courts, by analogy, use the statute and the policy sought to be served by it as a guide in determining the private contract rights of one harmed by a violation of the statute. In addition, the courts must frequently articulate the "public policy" of the State without significant help from statutory sources. This judicially declared public policy is very broad in scope, it often being said that agreements which have "a tendency to be injurious to the public or the public good" are contrary to public policy. Thus, the term "public policy" is broad and general, and not subject to precise definition. *See Marvin v. Marvin* for a general overview of the nature and extent of public policy. Contracts raising questions of public policy include agreements that (1) involve tortious conduct, (2) restrain trade, (3) tend to obstruct the administration of justice, (4) tend to corrupt public officials or impair the legislative process, (5) exempt or exculpate a party from liability for his own tortious conduct, or (6) are unconscionable.

Tortious Conduct

"A promise to commit a tort or to induce the commission of a tort is unenforceable on grounds of public policy." Restatement, Section 192. The courts will not permit contract law to violate the law of torts. Any agreement attempting to do so is considered contrary to public policy. For example, Andrew and Barlow Co. enter into an agreement under which Andrew promises Barlow that in return for $5,000 he will disparage the product of Barlow Co.'s competitor Cosmo, Inc. in order to provide Barlow Co. with a competitive advantage. Andrew's promise is to commit the tort of disparagement and is unenforceable as contrary to public policy.

Common Law Restraint of Trade

A **restraint of trade** is any contract or agreement that eliminates or tends to eliminate competition or otherwise obstructs trade or commerce. One type of restraint is a **covenant not to compete,** which is an agreement to refrain from entering into a competing trade, profession, or business.

At early common law any restraint upon an individual's right to engage in his trade or calling was illegal. Such restraints were viewed with disfavor because of the belief that they would diminish the individual's means of earning a living, deprive the public of useful services, adversely affect competition, and otherwise be harmful to the welfare of the community. But this strict view has been modified so that **reasonable** restraints of trade are enforceable. Restatement, Section 186.

Today an agreement to refrain from a particular trade, profession, or business is enforceable if (1) the purpose of the restraint is to protect a property interest of the promisee and (2) the restraint is no more extensive than is reasonably necessary to protect that interest. Restraints typically arise in two situations: the sale of a business and employment contracts.

It is important to distinguish between a contract that has for its **primary purpose** the imposition of a restraint of trade upon one of the parties and a contract in which the agreement in restraint of trade is merely **ancillary** or subordinate to some other major purpose of the contract. A common example of the latter is a contract for the sale of a business in which the seller agrees to refrain from engaging in the same business in a specified territory for a stipulated time. A contract in which the agreement in restraint of trade is primary and not ancillary is illegal, regardless of the possible reasonableness of the restraint. Suppose, for example, that Karen and Steven each own a drug store in the city of Wye. They make a contract under which, in consideration of $50,000 paid by Karen to Steven, Steven closes his store and also agrees to refrain from engaging in the drug store business in Wye. This contract is opposed to public policy and unenforceable. Steven is not bound by it and may re-enter the drug store business in Wye as and when he sees fit. Assume instead that Karen sells her drug store and business to Cindy, and that, as part of the transaction, Karen agrees not to engage in the drug store business in the city of Wye at any time. In this case, the agreement in restraint of trade is ancillary to the primary purpose of the contract: the sale of Karen's store. The only question raised by this contract is whether the restraint is reasonable or not. If the restraint is reasonable, Karen is bound by her agreement. If it is not, the restraint is not enforceable.

Sale of a Business As part of an agreement to sell a business, the seller frequently promises not to compete in the particular business in a *defined area* for a stated period of *time*. To protect the business's good will (an asset that the buyer has purchased) the buyer must be allowed to enforce such a covenant (promise) by the seller not to compete with the purchaser within reasonable limitations. *See McCart v. H & R Block, Inc.* Most litigation on this subject has involved the requirement that the restraint be no greater than is reasonably necessary. The reasonableness of the restraint depends on the geographic area covered, the time period for which the restraint is to be effective, and the hardship imposed on the promisor and the public.

For example, the promise of a person selling a service station business in Detroit not to enter the service station business in Michigan for the next twenty-five years is unreasonable, both as to area and time. The business interest to be protected would not include the entire State, so it is not necessary to the protection of the purchaser that the seller be prevented from engaging in the service station business in the entire State or perhaps, for that matter, in the entire city of Detroit. Limiting the area to the neighborhood or within a radius of a few miles would probably be adequate protection.

The same type of inquiry must be made about time limitations. In the sale of a service station, twenty-five years would be unreasonable, but one year probably would not. Each case must be considered on its own facts, with the court determining what is reasonable under the particular circumstances.

Employment Contracts Salespeople, management personnel, and other employees are frequently required to sign employment contracts prohibiting them from competing with their employers during the time of employment and for some additional stated period after termination. The same is also frequently true among professional partnerships or corporations, such as accountants, lawyers, investment brokers, stockbrokers, or doctors. The courts readily enforce a covenant not to compete during the period of employment. But the promise not to compete after termination of employment is subjected to an even stricter test of reasonableness than that applied to noncompetition promises included in a contract for the sale of a business. One reason for this is that the employer is in a stronger bargaining position than the employee.

A court order enjoining the former employee from competing in a described territory for a stated period of time is the usual method by which the employer seeks enforcement of the promise not to compete made by the employee. Before granting such injunctions, the courts insist that the employer demonstrate that the restriction is *necessary* to protect his legitimate interests, such as trade secrets or customer lists. Because issuance of the injunction may have the practical effect of placing the employee out of work, the courts must carefully balance the public policy favoring the employer's right to protect his business interests against the public policy favoring full opportunity for individuals to gain employment. *See McCart v. H & R Block, Inc.*

Thus, one court has held that a covenant in a contract that a travel agency employee after termination of her employment would not engage in a like business in any capacity in either of two named towns or within a radius of sixty miles of the towns for a period of two years was unreasonable. There was no indication that the employee had enough influence over customers to cause them to move their business to her new agency, nor was it shown that any trade secrets were involved. *United Travel Service, Inc. v. Weber,* 108 Ill.App.2d 353, 247 N.E.2d 801 (1969). Some courts, instead of refusing to enforce an unreasonable covenant, will if considered justifiable under the circumstances of the particular case reform the agreement to make it reasonable and enforceable.

Obstructing the Administration of Justice

Agreements harmful to the administration of justice are illegal and unenforceable. For example, a promise by an employer not to press criminal charges against an embezzling employee who restores the stolen funds is not enforceable. Similarly, a promise to conceal evidence or to give false testimony tends to obstruct the administration of justice and for that reason is illegal and unenforceable.

Corrupting Public Officials

Agreements that may adversely affect the public interest through the corruption of public officials or the impairment of the legislative process are unenforceable. Examples include using improper means to influence legislation, to secure some official action, or to procure a government contract. To be distinguished from illegal influence peddling agreements are contracts to pay lobbyists for services to obtain or defeat official action by means of persuasive argument.

To illustrate, a bargain by a candidate for public office to make a certain appointment following his election is illegal. In addition, an agreement to pay a public officer something extra for performing her official duty, such as a promise to a police officer for strictly enforcing the traffic laws on her beat, is illegal. The same is true of an agreement in which a citizen promises to perform, or to refrain from performing, duties imposed upon her by citizenship. Thus, a promise by Jones to pay fifty dollars to Sandler if she will register and vote is opposed to public policy and unenforceable.

Exculpatory Clauses

Some contracts contain an **exculpatory clause** that excuses one party from liability for her own tortious conduct. There is general agreement that exculpatory clauses relieving a person from tort liability for harm caused intentionally or recklessly are unenforceable as violating public policy. On the other hand, exculpatory clauses that excuse a party from liability for harm caused by negligent conduct are scrutinized carefully by the courts, which often require that the clause be conspicuously placed in the contract and clearly written. Accordingly, an exculpatory clause on the reverse side of a parking lot claim check, which attempts to relieve the parking lot operator of liability for negligently damaging the customer's automobile, will generally be held unenforceable as against public policy.

The Restatement provides that exculpatory clauses excusing negligent conduct are unenforceable on grounds of public policy if they exempt (1) an employer from liability to an employee, (2) a public service business (such as a common carrier) from liability to a customer, or (3) a person from liability to a party who is a member of a protected class. Restatement, Section 195.

A similar rule applies to a contractual provision unreasonably exempting a party from the legal consequences of a misrepresentation. Restatement, Section 196. Such a term is unenforceable on the grounds of public policy with respect to both fraudulent and nonfraudulent misrepresentations.

Further, where one party has a superior bargaining position that has enabled him to impose upon the other party such a provision, the courts are inclined to nullify the provision. Such a situation may arise in residential leases exempting a landlord from liability for his negligence. *See Henrioulle v. Marin Ventures, Inc.* Moreover, an exculpatory clause may be unenforceable for unconscionability.

Unconscionable Contracts

Every contract of sale may be scrutinized by the court to determine whether in its commercial setting, purpose, and effect, it is **unconscionable.** The court may refuse to enforce an unconscionable contract or any part of the contract found to be unconscionable. Section 2–302 provides:

If the court as a matter of law finds the contract or any clause of the contract to have been unconscionable at the time it was made the court may refuse to enforce the contract, or it may enforce the remainder of the contract without the unconscionable clause, or it may so limit the application of any unconscionable clause as to avoid any unconscionable result.

Similarly, Section 208 of the Restatement provides:

If a contract or term thereof is unconscionable at the time the contract is made, a court may refuse to enforce the contract, or may enforce the remainder of the contract without the unconscionable term, or may so limit the application of any unconscionable term as to avoid any unconscionable result.

Neither the Code nor the Restatement defines the word *unconscionable;* however, the term is defined in the *New Webster's Dictionary* (Deluxe Encyclopedic Edition) as: "contrary to the dictates of conscience; unscrupulous or unprincipled; exceeding that which is reasonable or customary; inordinate, unjustifiable."

The doctrine of unconscionability has been justified on the basis that it permits the courts to resolve issues of unfairness explicitly on that basis without recourse to formalistic rules or legal fictions. In policing contracts for fairness, the courts have again demonstrated their willingness to limit freedom of contract in order to protect the less advantaged from overreaching by dominant contracting parties. The doctrine of unconscionability has evolved through its applica-

tion by the courts to include both procedural and substantive unconscionability.

Procedural unconscionability involves scrutiny for the presence of "bargaining naughtiness." In other words, was the negotiation process fair, or were there procedural irregularities, such as burying important terms of the agreement in fine print or obscuring the true meaning of the contract with impenetrable legal jargon?

Substantive unconscionability deals with the actual terms of the contract and involves oppressive or grossly unfair provisions, such as an exorbitant price or an unfair exclusion or limitation of contractual remedies. An all-too-common example is that involving a necessitous buyer in an unequal bargaining position with a seller who has obtained an exorbitant price for his product or service. In one case, a price of $749 ($920 on time) for a vacuum cleaner that cost the seller $140 was held unconscionable. In another case the buyers, welfare recipients, purchased by time payment contract a home freezer unit for $900 which, added to time credit charges, credit life insurance, credit property insurance, and sales tax, amounted to $1,235. The purchase resulted from a visit to the buyer's home by a salesman representing Your Shop At Home Service, Inc., and the maximum retail value of the freezer unit at time of purchase was $300. The court held the contract unconscionable and reformed it by reducing the price to the total payment ($620) made by the buyers. *See also Williams v. Walker-Thomas Furniture Co.*

Closely akin to the concepts of unconscionability is the doctrine of contracts of adhesion. An **adhesion contract** is a standard-form contract prepared by one party and generally involves the preparer offering the other party the contract on a "take-it-or-leave-it" basis. Such contracts are not automatically unenforceable but are subject to greater scrutiny for procedural or substantive unconscionability.

EFFECT OF ILLEGALITY

As a general rule, illegal contracts are unenforceable. In a few instances, however, one of the parties may be permitted to enforce all or part of the contract. Under other circumstances, one party will be allowed to recover in restitution for his performance of the illegal contract.

General Rule: Unenforceability

In most cases when an agreement is illegal, neither party can successfully sue the other for breach nor recover for any performance rendered. Whichever party is plaintiff is immaterial to the courts. As is frequently said in these cases, the court will leave the parties where it finds them.

Exceptions

There are several exceptions to the general rule as to the effect of illegality on a contract. The circumstances surrounding the particular contract may be such that the courts will grant relief to one of the parties although not to the other. These exceptions will now be considered.

Party Withdrawing before Performance
A party to an illegal agreement may, prior to performance, withdraw from the transaction and recover whatever she has contributed, if the party has not engaged in serious misconduct. Restatement, Section 199. A common example is recovery of money left with a stakeholder pursuant to a wager before it is paid over to the winner.

Party Protected by Statute Sometimes an agreement is illegal because it violates a statute designed to protect persons in the position of one of the parties. *See Brady v. Fulghum.* For example, State "Blue-Sky Laws" prohibiting the sale of unregistered securities are designed primarily for the protection of investors. In such case, even though there is an unlawful agreement, the statute usually expressly gives the purchaser a right to rescind the sale and recover the money paid.

Party Not Equally at Fault Where one of the parties is less at fault than the other, he will be allowed to recover payments made or property transferred. Restatement, Section 198. For example, this exception would apply where one party is induced to enter into an illegal bargain through the fraud, duress, or undue influence of the other party.

Excusable Ignorance An agreement that appears to be entirely permissible on its face may, nevertheless, be illegal by reason of facts and circumstances of which one of the parties is completely unaware. For example, a man and woman make mutual promises to marry, but unknown to the woman, the man is already married. This is an agreement to commit the crime of bigamy. It is illegal, and the marriage, if entered into, is void. In such case the courts permit the party who is ignorant of the illegality to maintain a lawsuit against the other party for damages.

A party may also be excused of ignorance of legislation of a minor character. Restatement, Section 180. For instance, Jones and Old South Building Co. enter into a contract to build a factory that contains specifications in violation of the town's building ordinance. Jones did not know of the violation and had no reason to know. Old South's promise to build would not be rendered unenforceable on grounds of public policy and Jones would have a claim against Old South for damages for breach of contract.

Partial Illegality A contract may be partly unlawful and partly lawful. In such case there are two possibilities. First, the partial illegality may be held to taint the entire contract with illegality, so that it is wholly unenforceable. Second, it may be possible to separate the illegal from the legal part, in which case the illegal part only will be held unenforceable, while the legal part will be enforced. For example, if a contract contains an illegal covenant not to compete, the covenant will not be enforced but the rest of the contract may be.

CASES

Licensing Statutes/Party Protected by Statute

BRADY v. FULGHUM

Supreme Court of North Carolina, 1983.
308 S.E.2d 327.

EXUM, J.

Plaintiff brought this action for monies allegedly due under a contract for construction of a private dwelling. In affirming summary judgment for defendants, the Court of Appeals concluded that plaintiff, a general contractor, had not complied "substantially" with the statutory licensing requirements. [Citation.] We agree with the result reached by the Court of Appeals, but we reject the substantial compliance doctrine which that court has developed in earlier licensing cases and which formed the basis of its analysis in this case.

In February 1980, plaintiff agreed with defendants by written contract to construct their house for a price of approximately $106,850. Plaintiff began construction on or about 13 March 1980. Neither during the negotiation of this contract nor when he began performance was plaintiff licensed as a general contractor as required by North Carolina law. [Citation.] * * * Plaintiff was awarded his builder's license on 22 October 1980. Having passed the examination on his second attempt. At that time, he had completed two-thirds of the work on defendants' house. Defendants paid plaintiff $104,000. Plaintiff by this action seeks an additional $2,850 on the original contract and $28,926.41 for "additions and changes" requested by defendants during construction.

* * *

The legislature has provided a mechanism for certification of general construction contractors. [Citation.] This process * * * protects the public by insuring confidence and integrity within the construction industry. [Citation.] Although the statute does not expressly preclude an unlicensed contractor's suit against an owner for breach of contract,

Builders Supply v. Midyette, [citation], held the contractor may not recover on the contract or *in quantum meruit* when he has ignored the protective statute.

After *Midyette,* the Court of Appeals determined several cases, including the one at bar, in terms of whether the contractor had "substantially" complied with the licensing statutes.

* * *

A majority of the [Court of Appeals] concluded [in this case] that because [Brady] did not have a license at the time the contract was made and "was not licensed during at least 66 percent of the construction, which comprised the major portion of the work," plaintiff had not substantially complied with the licensing requirements of the statute. * * * [T]he division on the Court of Appeals in this case [however] demonstrates that the doctrine of substantial compliance is sometimes difficult to apply. By generating skewed results, it leaves uncertain the rights of parties, which tends to promote litigation. We now reject the doctrine and end its application in this state.

Generally, contracts entered into by unlicensed construction contractors, in violation of a statute passed for the protection of the public, are unenforceable by the contractor. [Citation.] A majority of jurisdictions adhere to this interpretation. [Citation.] Reading these statutes as being designed to protect the public from irresponsible contractors, [citation], most state courts find "no legal remedy for that which is illegal itself." [Citation.] General contractors have been precluded from maintaining actions if they must rely on their illegal act to justify their recovery. [Citation.] The unenforceability of such contracts by the contractor stems directly from their conception in the contractor's illegal act.

The express language of the North Carolina licensing statute indicates that it is designed to insure competence within the construction industry. * * * (T)he legislature seeks to guarantee "skill, training and ability to accomplish such construction in a safe and workmanlike fashion." [Citation.] In tandem, these requirements "protect members of the general public without regard to the impact upon individual contractors." [Citation.]

In examining the licensing statute in question, we recognize the distinction between legislation designed to produce revenue and to protect the public. In the former situation, the legislature exercises its taxing authority. In the latter, it exercises its police power. Accordingly, when a legislature invokes its police power to provide statutory protection to the public from fraud, incompetence, and irresponsibility, as ours has done with the contractor licensing statutes, courts impose greater penalties on violators. [Citation.] Making contracts unenforceable by the violating contractor produces "a salutary effect in causing obedience to the licensing statute." [Citation.] These public policy considerations militate against permitting unlicensed general construction contractors to enforce their contracts.

* * *

In recognition of the essential illegality of an unlicensed contractor's entering into a construction contract for which a license is required and in order to give full effect to the legislative intent to furnish protection to the public by strict licensing requirements, we reject the doctrine of substantial compliance, cognizant that harsh consequences may sometimes fall on those who do contracting work without a license. [Citation.]

We do recognize the minority rule, adhered to by our Court of Appeals, is not without some support. California applies the doctrine of substantial compliance in certain cases to avoid unnecessarily harsh results on unlicensed contractors who perform well. [Citations.] * * *

We agree that the existence of a license at the time the contract is signed is determinative and attach "great weight to the significant moment of the entrance of the parties into the relationship." [Citation.] Accordingly, we adopt the rule that a contract ille-

gally entered into by an unlicensed general construction contractor is unenforceable by the contractor. It cannot be validated by the contractor's subsequent procurement of a license. [Citation.] In this circumstance there can be no substantial compliance with the licensing statutes. Neither may the contractor recover for extras, additions or changes made during construction commenced pursuant to the contract. Such a contract is not, however, void. Others not regulated by the licensing statutes passed for their protection do not act illegally in becoming parties to such a contract. The policy underlying the licensing statutes would not be served by preventing enforcement by those for whose protection the statutes were passed. These parties may enforce the contract against the unlicensed contractor. [Citation.] Further, if a licensed contractor's license expires, for whatever reason, during construction, he may recover for only the work performed while he was duly licensed. If, in that situation, the contractor renews his license during construction, he may recover for work performed before expiration and after renewal. If, by virtue of these rules, harsh results fall upon unlicensed contractors who violate our statutes, the contractors themselves bear both the responsibility and the blame.

Plaintiff was unlicensed at the time he negotiated and contracted with defendants to construct their house. He illegally entered into the contract; it is, therefore, unenforceable by him. His subsequent procurement of a valid license cannot validate or make legal that which was illegal in its inception. * * *

Usury Statutes

ABRAMOWITZ v. BARNETT BANK OF WEST ORLANDO

Florida Court of Appeals, 1981.
394 So.2d 1033.

SHARP, J.

Abramowitz appeals from a judgment denying him any relief in his suit against the Barnett Bank of West Orlando, appellee, in which he sought damages for an allegedly "usurious" loan.

* * *

The record established that Abramowitz filed three or more loan applications with the bank from February 1973 through October 1973. Originally he sought a construction loan to build a building to be leased to Ford Motor Company on land he owned near the John Young Parkway. C. Lee Maynard, president of the bank, wanted the loan for his bank, although the $300,000 to $400,000 loan requests considerably exceeded the bank's lending limits. In anticipation of making the loan, Maynard made "inspections" of the site and building being constructed, although Ford was financing the construction itself and the bank had made no loan commitment.

When the building was completed in November of 1973, the parties rushed into a mortgage loan closing without the benefit of a written loan commitment and without a carefully prepared loan closing statement. Maynard had verbally promised Abramowitz a $400,000 loan for one year, at 9% interest, with a 1% "point" or "service fee." The $4,000 "service fee" was shown on the closing statement as a "discount," but everyone agreed no "discount" was involved because the bank was not purchasing a mortgage loan from another party at less than face value.

The $4,000 service fee was deducted in full from the loan proceeds, and it was immediately received by the bank as income. During the one year term of this loan, Abramowitz was charged and he paid $36,347.78 in "interest." If the $4,000 charge was also "interest," Abramowitz paid more than $40,000 or 10% of his $400,000 loan in total interest charges. If viewed as a "discount" loan where interest is paid in advance, the rate should be properly gauged on the amount of principal actually disbursed to the borrower plus legitimate expenses—($396,000 or a somewhat larger figure if any part of the $4,000 were attributable to a legitimate expense of the lender).

Maynard testified that the $4,000 charge was meant to be a "service charge" or "points." He was the only mortgage loan officer at his bank, so he made "in-house" inspections of the construction of the building and a final inspection. He reported verbally to the bank's loan committee. He admitted that part of the $4,000 went to pay the bank's normal overhead expenses, such as salaries and utilities. Another expense attributed to this loan was Maynard's contacting other Barnett banks to obtain the participation of other lenders, and the preparation of loan participation agreements.

The other banker witnesses at trial testified that their banks normally imposed "service fees" or "points" on real estate loans in addition to interest, but they were careful not to exceed the usury limits when the two amounts were combined. Sometimes inspection fees were paid to architects or engineers for which the customer was charged; sometimes the inspections were done "in-house," and the borrower was charged a small amount, or was not charged at all.

* * *

A lender will not be allowed to impose any miscellaneous fees or service charges on the front end of a loan when that sum, added to the interest charged, exceeds the maximum legal rate of interest allowable. [Citations.] Application of such fees to pay the general overhead of a lender or the cost of participating out the loan are not sufficient to alter the characterization of these charges as interest. [Citation.]

It is also well established that a borrower can be charged the actual reasonable expenses of making a particular loan. [Citations.] However "bogus" charges for services not actually rendered will not be allowed to cloak the extraction of illegal interest. [Citation.]

The only basis to characterize the "service fee" in this case as something other than interest, is to allocate part of it as an "inspection" fee performed "in-house" by the bank's president. Such fees are usually paid to third-parties, and are documented on the mortgage loan closing statement. We are not prepared to say, however, that in all cases the inspection must be done by a third-person or that it must be documented on the closing statement, although that obviously is the better practice. The fact that Maynard himself performed the inspection does not flaw the charges although any charge for this "service" is inconsistent with his testimony that he did the inspection "in-house" to save the borrower money.

It is fundamental that the charges must be "reasonable." [Citations.] This loan was not a "construction" loan which requires more inspections to insure the lender's construction funds are being properly used as the building progresses. Rather, it was a loan on a completed building, and similar to a "take-out" loan for a permanent lender, only a final inspection fee is required. The only testimony in the record on this point established that $300 was the maximum a third party expert would have charged.

The conclusion thus follows inescapably that Abramowitz was charged in excess of 10% interest on this one year loan.

"Service Fee"	$ 4,000.00
Less "Reasonable Expenses"	− 300.00
"Hidden Interest"	$ 3,700.00
Principal of Loan	$ 400,000.00
Less Prepaid Interest	− 3,700.00
Actual Principal	$ 396,300.00
Maximum legal amount of interest collectible on this loan (10%) of actual principal	$ 39,630.00
Actual interest charged and billed	36,347.78
Plus "hidden interest"	+ 3,700.00
	$ 40,047.78
Amount of over-charge	$ 40,047.78
	− 39,630.00
	$ 417.78

The lower court found there was no "corrupt" intent on the part of the bank to charge a usurious rate of interest because the bank did not deliberately charge more than 10%. It charged 9% on the loan plus 1% in points only. The difficulty here was that the 1% was taken up-front, resulting in a reduction in principal received, and an increase in the rate paid. [Citation.] The "intent" to exceed the legal rate of interest need not be to consciously decide to charge a borrower greater than the legal rate, when the lender consciously intends and

does in fact make the charges which add up to usury. [Citations.]

In this case, the closing statement showing a 1% point of service fee was prepared by the bank; and it calculated and billed the borrower interest throughout the year. No errors were shown to have occurred in the billing. In fact during two quarters, the lender billed on a 360–day year basis, which for a 10% or maximum rate loan, was usurious in and of itself. [Citation.] We conclude the bank had the requisite intent to make the usurious charges. [Citation.]

Accordingly, the judgment is reversed and this case is remanded for imposition of damages against the bank. . . .

Reversed and remanded.

Public Policy

MARVIN v. MARVIN

Supreme Court of California, 1976.
18 Cal.3d 660, 134 Cal.Rptr. 815, 557 P.2d 106.

Tobriner, J.

During the past 15 years, there has been a substantial increase in the number of couples living together without marrying. Such nonmarital relationships lead to legal controversy when one partner dies or the couple separates. Courts of Appeal, faced with the task of determining property rights in such cases, have arrived at conflicting positions. * * *

In the instant case plaintiff and defendant lived together for seven years without marrying; all property acquired during this period was taken in defendant's name. When plaintiff sued to enforce a contract under which she was entitled to half the property and to support payments, the trial court granted judgment on the pleadings for defendant, thus leaving him with all property accumulated by the couple during their relationship. * * *

Plaintiff avers that in October of 1964 she and defendant "entered into an oral agreement" that while "the parties lived together they would combine their efforts and earnings and would share equally any and all property accumulated as a result of their efforts whether individual or combined." Furthermore, they agreed to "hold themselves out to the general public as husband and wife" and that "plaintiff would further render her services as a companion, homemaker, housekeeper and cook to . . . defendant."

Shortly thereafter plaintiff agreed to "give up her lucrative career as an entertainer (and) singer" in order to "devote her full time to defendant . . . as a companion, homemaker, housekeeper and cook"; in return defendant agreed to "provide for all of plaintiff's financial support and needs for the rest of her life."

Plaintiff alleges that she lived with defendant from October of 1964 through May of 1970 and fulfilled her obligations under the agreement. During this period the parties as a result of their efforts and earnings acquired in defendant's name substantial real and personal property, including motion picture rights worth over $1 million. In May of 1970, however, defendant compelled plaintiff to leave his household. He continued to support plaintiff until November of 1971, but thereafter refused to provide further support.

* * *

In *Trutalli v. Meraviglia* (1932), [citation], we established the principle that nonmarital partners may lawfully contract concerning the ownership of property acquired during the relationship. We reaffirmed this principle in *Vallera v. Vallera* (1943), [citation], stating that "If a man and woman (who are not married) live together as husband and wife under an agreement to pool their earnings and share equally in their joint accumulations, equity will protect the interests of each in such property."

* * *

Defendant first and principally relies on the contention that the alleged contract is so closely related to the supposed "immoral" character of the relationship between plaintiff and himself that the enforcement of the contract would violate public policy. He points to cases asserting that a contract between nonmarital partners is unenforceable if it is "involved in" an illicit relationship, [citations], or made in "contemplation" of such a relationship. [Citations.]

A review of the numerous California decisions concerning contracts between nonmarital partners, however, reveals that the courts have not employed such broad and uncertain standards to strike down contracts. The decisions instead disclose a narrower and more precise standard: a contract between nonmarital partners is unenforceable only *to the extent* that it *explicitly* rests upon the immoral and illicit consideration of meretricious sexual services.

* * *

In summary, we base our opinion on the principle that adults who voluntarily live together and engage in sexual relations are nonetheless as competent as any other persons to contract respecting their earnings and property rights. Of course, they cannot lawfully contract to pay for the performance of sexual services, for such a contract is, in essence, an agreement for prostitution and unlawful for that reason. But they may agree to pool their earnings and to hold all property acquired during the relationship in accord with the law governing community property; conversely they may agree that each partner's earnings and the property acquired from those earnings remains the separate property of the earning partner. So long as the agreement does not rest upon illicit meretricious consideration, the parties may order their economic affairs as they choose, and no policy precludes the courts from enforcing such agreements.

In the present instance, plaintiff alleges that the parties agreed to pool their earnings, that they contracted to share equally in all property acquired, and that defendant agreed to support plaintiff. The terms of the contract as alleged do not rest upon any unlawful consideration. We therefore conclude that the complaint furnishes a suitable basis upon which the trial court can render . . . relief. [Citation.] The trial court consequently erred in granting defendant's motion for judgment on the pleadings.

Restraint of Trade

McCART v. H & R BLOCK, INC.

Court of Appeals of Indiana, Third District, 1984.
70 N.E.2d 756.

GARRARD, J.

* * * After a full hearing on the merits of a complaint filed by H & R Block, Inc. (Block), the Fulton Circuit Court entered its order enjoining Robert and June McCart: ". . . from participating in any business, either directly or indirectly, or by acting individually, to file, prepare, or assist in preparing income tax returns within fifty (50) miles of the City of Rochester, Indiana."

The injunction entered on January 18, 1983 was to dissolve on December 15, 1983, two years after June terminated her satellite franchise agreement with Block.

The McCarts now appeal raising . . . [these] issues:

I. Did the covenant not to compete contained in the agreement signed by June apply to Robert so that he could be enjoined from competing with Block?

II. Was the covenant unenforceable as a restraint of trade?

Robert first engaged in the preparation of tax returns in 1955 in Kokomo. He opened a tax preparation business in Rochester in 1964 or 1965. In Rochester in 1968, Robert executed a contract with Block because he "felt there was some money to be made in it." In 1969, Robert became a district manager for Block, a position which precluded him from retaining the Rochester office in his name. Accordingly, Robert, as district manager, executed a contract in behalf of Block issuing the Rochester franchise to June. In 1975, June signed a new franchise agreement with Block which continued in force until December 15, 1981 when June terminated the agreement. Robert was familiar with that agreement.

From 1972 until 1979, Robert was involved in the operation of a satellite franchise for Block in Rensselaer. After August 1979, Robert worked at 900 Main Street, the location of the Block franchise in Rochester. While there he performed management tasks, represented to others that he was the manager of the office, conferred with representatives of Block, attended meetings held by Block, and prepared tax returns on forms furnished by Block. At the office at 900 Main Street, Robert also engaged in an accounting business separate from that related to Block. However, the McCarts' own joint income tax returns for the years 1978 through 1981 show that nearly all of their income was from the Block business. For the years 1978 and 1979, Robert reported on his Schedule C that his business was tax preparation under the business name of H & R Block at 900 Main Street. June used that description on her Schedule C for 1980 and 1981.

On December 15, 1981, June wrote a letter to Kathy Heise, district manager for Block, giving notice that, due to arthritis, she would not be able to continue the satellite operation in Rochester after December 31, 1981. Earlier in December, the McCarts had picked up supplies ordered from Block in September for the preparation of tax returns in early 1982.

Shortly after sending her letter of cancellation, June sent the following letter to people who had been clients of the Block office in Rochester:

DEAR CLIENT:
After being associated with H & R Block in the Rochester locality for 15 years, I have arrived at a decision which I feel I must make—dissociate (sic) myself from H & R Block.

In the past the company has issued a standard schedule of charges which we were told to go by and these charges have been increasing at a rate I did not feel was warranted. * * *

This, I feel, is out of order with the economic and unemployment situation in our area, and, I am cancelling my contract. I will assist my husband in his tax service in the future.
Thank you,
/s/ June McCart
June McCart

June sent each letter in an H & R Block envelope with the name "H & R Block" blacked out but with Block's slogan "The Income Tax People," remaining. The name "Community Tax Service" appeared on each envelope.

A letter written by Robert also was enclosed in each envelope reading as follows:

* * * On January 2, 1982, I will open my tax preparation office . . . [900 Main Street, Rochester] using the name Community Tax Service.

We will continue to offer the same competent service, guarantee, etc., and, at the same location with the same personnel. About the only change that is being made is the name.

Our prices will not increase this year, in fact, we are offering a discount of 10% off what you may have paid last year. * * *

After the cancellation of the agreement, Robert spoke to employees of the post office, requesting that all mail addressed to 900 Main Street be delivered there even if addressed to Block. Block opened a separate office for tax preparation at 802 Main Street. Paula Garcia was the new franchisee. When she called "Information" to check the telephone number for Block that was being given, she was asked whether she wanted the 900 or 802 Main Street address. * * *

Robert contends that because he did not sign the satellite agreement with Block containing the covenant not to compete, the trial court erred by enjoining him from competing with Block. We disagree.

* * *

Robert's argument is a logical one: he did not sign the satellite agreement; he therefore should not be bound by its restrictive covenant, especially in light of our courts' disfavor with restraints on trade. [Citation.] While we find no Indiana cases directly addressing this issue, our search of the law in other states reveals: ". . . that the rule that a stranger to a covenant may be enjoined from aiding and assisting the covenanter in violating his covenant is supported by an overwhelming weight of authority." [Citations.]

* * *

Robert knowingly participated and aided June in the violation of her contract with Block. [Citation.] Their cooperative conduct amounted to mere subterfuge designed to avoid June's obligation under the contract. The court did not err by including Robert within the scope of the injunction.

* * *

Paragraph 11 of the satellite franchise agreement signed by June provides, in relevant part:

"11. FRANCHISEE'S COVENANT NOT TO COMPETE.

Franchisee covenants that (i) during the term hereof he will not compete, directly, indirectly, whether as an owner, stockholder, partner, officer, director or employee, with Block or Block's franchisees in the business of preparing tax returns or performing related services in, or within 250 miles of, the franchise territory, and (ii) for a period of two years after the termination, or the transfer or other disposition of the franchise, he will not so compete as aforesaid in, or within 50 miles of, the franchise territory, but if Franchisee does so compete (whether by reason of the unenforceability of such covenant not to so compete or otherwise), Franchisee shall pay Block royalties. * * * The parties expressly acknowledge and agree that such payments shall not affect the rights or remedies Block may have, at law or in equity (including the right to seek injunctive relief), against Franchisee by reason of such competition by Franchisee."

June contends the covenant is void as a restraint on trade and unreasonable as to its territorial limitation. She contends that, because she did not learn any of Block's trade secrets, confidential information or customer lists during the term of the agreement, Block had no recognizable, protectible interest that could be covered by the covenant consistent with public policy.

It is true that a covenant in general restraint of trade is void as against public policy. [Citations.] However, a restraint which is clear and specific carries no such presumption of disfavor [citation] and will be enforced if reasonable with respect to the convenantee, the covenantor and the public interest. [Citation.] The enforceability of the covenant depends upon the facts and circumstances surrounding each case including the legitimate interests of the covenantee and the protection provided in terms of the duration and geographical limitation of the covenant.

* * *

Before we can affirm the enforcement of this covenant not to compete, we first must determine the nature of Block's protectible interest. In the satellite franchise agreement, Block granted to June "exclusively, the right to operate an income tax return preparation service and to perform 'related services' under the name and service mark 'H & R Block' in Rochester. A service mark is a form of property and has property rights associated with it. [Citation.] In exchange for the property right granted to her by Block, June agreed, . . . to pay Block a percentage of the gross receipts from the preparation of income tax returns during the term of the agreement and to not compete with Block for two years thereafter.

The rationale for entering a contract for the use of a service mark is to draw on the reputation associated with the name in order to attract customers by identifying the services of one person and distinguishing them from services of another.

* * *

When a person sells a business to another, the seller often will agree not to compete with the buyer for a certain period of time within a certain area. Such agreements reflect the value of the customers' affiliation with the particular business which is part of the bargain sought by the buyer. This "good will" is the protectible interest upon which the covenant not to compete focuses. [Citation.] If the seller competed with the buyer for customers, the buyer would not receive all that had been sold to him or her. [Citation.]

A similar concept of customer affiliation prevails here. Block has a valuable property right in its service mark. The value is reflected by customers' name recognition and resultant use of the service offered under the Block name. June was willing to pay for that customer affiliation as would a buyer of a business. In return, Block gave June the right to use that service mark and benefit from the customers it drew as long as the contract terms were met. By including the covenant not to compete in the agreement, Block preserved the value of the property right to itself alone after the termination of the agreement.

* * *

While we conclude Block did have a protectible interest in the customers June serviced under the Block name, we still must determine the reasonableness of the covenant. The subject of area limitations in such covenants has been discussed in this state in the context of employment contracts. The law developed from these cases is instructive here. Restrictive covenants in employment contracts are invalid if they restrict the employee from competing in an area greater than necessary to protect the good will of the employer; conversely, ". . . such covenants will be upheld, if limited to the area in which operation of the employee's activity was related to the good will of the employer's business." [Citation.] * * *

The evidence here shows that 22 miles was as far as any customer had traveled to use June's services at the H & R Block office in Rochester. June argues that the 50 mile limitation imposed upon her is therefore unreasonable. However, focusing again on Block's protectible interest . . ., we cannot agree with her. * * * Here Block's protectible interest was the customer recognition of its service mark and the year to year affiliation those customers might develop with a particular office. * * * It was not unreasonable to recognize Block's protectible interest and to enforce the covenant against the McCarts as it was written restricting competition for two years within a 50 mile radius of Rochester.

* * *

Affirmed.

Exculpatory Clauses

HENRIOULLE v. MARIN VENTURES, INC.

Supreme Court of California, 1978.
20 Cal.3d 512, 573 P.2d 465, 143 Cal.Rptr. 247.

BIRD, C.J.

Appellant, John Henrioulle, seeks to set aside orders of the superior court granting his landlord, respondent Marin Ventures, Inc., a judgment notwithstanding the jury's verdict and a new trial. Appellant contends that the exculpatory clause in his lease could not relieve the landlord of liability for the personal injuries appellant sustained in a fall on a common stairway in the apartment building. This court agrees.

* * *

From the record, it appears that on April 3, 1974, appellant entered into a lease agreement with respondent for an apartment in San Rafael, California. At that time, appellant was an unemployed widower with two children who received public assistance in the form of a rent subsidy from the Marin County Department of Social Services. There was also evidence of a shortage of housing accommodations for persons of low income in Marin County.

The printed form lease agreement which appellant signed contained the following exculpatory clause: "INDEMNIFICATION: Owner shall not be liable for any damage or injury to Tenant, or any other person, or to any property, occurring on the premises, or any part thereof, or in the common areas thereof, and Tenant agrees to hold Owner harmless from any claims for damages no matter how caused."

On May 22, 1974, appellant fractured his wrist when he tripped over a rock on a common stairway in the apartment building. At the time of the accident the landlord had been having difficulty keeping the common areas of the apartment building clean. An on-site manager, whose duties included keeping these areas clean, had proven unsatisfactory and had been terminated in the month prior to the accident. The landlord had also employed an additional person to do maintenance work, but he had worked only a few hours at the apartment building in the month preceding the accident.

* * *

In *Tunkl v. Regents of the University of California*, [citation], this court held invalid a clause in a hospital admission form which released the hospital from liability for future negligence. This court noted that although courts have made "diverse" interpretations of [California] Civil Code section

1668, which invalidates contracts which exempt one from responsibility for certain wilful or negligent acts, all the decisions were in accord that exculpatory clauses affecting the public interest are invalid. [Citation.]

In *Tunkl*, six criteria are used to identify the kind of agreement in which an exculpatory clause is invalid as contrary to public policy. "(1) It concerns a business of a type generally thought suitable for public regulation. (2) The party seeking exculpation is engaged in performing a service of great importance to the public, which is often a matter of practical necessity for some members of the public. (3) The party holds himself out as willing to perform this service for any member of the public who seeks it, or at least any member coming within certain established standards. (4) As a result of the essential nature of the service, in the economic setting of the transaction, the party invoking exculpation possesses a decisive advantage of bargaining strength against any member of the public who seeks his services. (5) In exercising a superior bargaining power, the party confronts the public with a standardized adhesion contract of exculpation, and makes no provision whereby a purchaser may pay additional fees and obtain protection against negligence. (6) Finally, as a result of the transaction, the person or property of the purchaser is placed under the control of the seller, subject to the risk of carelessness by the seller or his agents." [Citation.]

The transaction before this court, a residential rental agreement, meets the *Tunkl* criteria.

* * *

In holding that exculpatory clauses in residential leases violate public policy, this court joins an increasing number of jurisdictions. [Citations.]

* * *

The orders of the superior court granting respondent's motions for judgment notwithstanding the jury's verdict and a new trial are reversed, and the cause is remanded with direction to enter judgment for appellant on the verdict.

Unconscionable Contracts

WILLIAMS v. WALKER–THOMAS FURNITURE CO.

Court of Appeals, District of Columbia, 1965.
350 F.2d 445.

WRIGHT, C.J.

Appellee, Walker-Thomas Furniture Company, operates a retail furniture store in the District of Columbia. During the period from 1957 to 1962 each appellant in these cases purchased a number of household items from Walker-Thomas, for which payment was to be made in installments. The terms of each purchase were contained in a printed form contract which set forth the value of the purchased item and purported to lease the item to appellant for a stipulated monthly rent payment. The contract then provided, in substance, that title would remain in Walker-Thomas until the total of all the monthly payments made equaled the stated value of the item, at which time appellants could take title. In the event of a default in the payment of any monthly installment, Walker-Thomas could repossess the item.

The contract further provided that "the amount of each periodical installment payment to be made by [purchaser] to the Company under this present lease shall be inclusive of and not in addition to the amount of each installment payment to be made by [purchaser] under such prior leases, bills, or accounts; *and all payments now and hereafter made by [purchaser] shall be credited pro rata on all outstanding leases, bills, and accounts* due the Company by [purchaser] at the time each such payment is made." (Emphasis added.) The effect of this rather obscure provision was to keep a balance due on every item purchased until the balance due on all items, whenever purchased, was liquidated. As a result, the debt incurred at the time of purchase of each item was secured by the right to repossess all the items previously purchased by the same purchaser, and each new item purchased automatically became subject to a security interest arising out of the previous dealings.

On May 12, 1962, appellant Thorne purchased an item described as a Daveno, three tables, and two lamps, having total stated value of $391.10. Shortly thereafter, he defaulted on his monthly payments and appellee sought to replevy all the items purchased since the first transaction in 1958. Similarly, on April 7, 1962, appellant Williams bought a stereo set of stated value of $514.95. She too defaulted shortly thereafter, and appellee sought to replevy all the items purchased since December 1957. The Court of General Sessions granted judgment for appellee. The District of Columbia Court of Appeals affirmed, and we granted appellants' motion for leave to appeal to this court.

Appellants' principal contention, rejected by both the trial and the appellate courts . . ., is that these contracts, or at least some of them, are unconscionable and, hence, not enforceable. * * *

Unconscionability has generally been recognized to include an absence of meaningful choice on the part of one of the parties together with contract terms which are unreasonably favorable to the other party. Whether a meaningful choice is present in a particular case can only be determined by consideration of all the circumstances surrounding the transaction. In many cases the meaningfulness of the choice is negated by a gross inequality of bargaining power. The manner in which the contract was entered is also relevant to this consideration. Did each party to the contract, considering his obvious education or lack of it, have a reasonable opportunity to understand the terms of the contract, or were the important terms hidden in a maze of fine print and minimized by deceptive sales practices? Ordinarily, one who signs an agreement without full knowledge of its terms might be held to assume the risk that he has entered a one-sided bargain. But when a party of little bargaining power, and hence little real choice, signs a commercially unreasonable contract with little or no knowledge of its terms, it is hardly likely that his consent, or even an objective manifestation of his consent, was ever given to all the terms. In such a case the usual rule that the terms of the agreement are not to be questioned should be abandoned and the court should consider whether the terms of the contract are so unfair that enforcement should be withheld.

In determining reasonableness or fairness, the primary concern must be with the terms of the contract considered in light of thecircumstances existing when the contract was made. The test is not simple, nor can it be mechanically applied. The terms are to be considered "in the light of the generalcommercial background and the commercial needs of the particular trade or case." Corbin suggests the test as being whether the terms are "so extreme as to appear unconscionable according to the mores and business practices of the time and place." [Citation.] We think this formulation correctly states the test to be applied in those cases where no meaningful choice was exercised upon entering the contract.

Because the trial court and the appellate court did not feel that enforcement could be refused, no findings were made on the possible unconscionability of the contracts in these cases. Since the record is not sufficient for our deciding the issue as a matter of law, the cases must be remanded to the trial court for further proceedings.

Reversed and remanded.

QUESTIONS

1. Define unenforceable. Why are illegal agreements unenforceable? What are the major exceptions to this rule?

2. Identify and distinguish between the two types of licensing statutes.

3. Distinguish between general and specific usury laws.

4. Describe when a covenant not to compete will be enforced and discuss the two situations in which these types of covenants most frequently arise.

5. Distinguish between procedural and substantive unconscionability.

PROBLEMS

1. Johnson and Wilson were the principal shareholders in XYZ Corporation located in the city of Jonesville, Wisconsin. This corporation was engaged in the business of manufacturing paper novelties, which were sold over a wide area in the Middle West. The corporation was also in the business of binding books. Johnson purchased Wilson's shares of the XYZ Corporation and, in consideration thereof, Wilson agreed that for a period of two years he would not: (a) manufacture or sell in Wisconsin any paper novelties of any kind that would compete with those sold by the XYZ Corporation or (b) engage in the book binding business in the city of Jonesville. Discuss the validity and effect, if any, of this agreement.

2. Wilkins, a resident of and licensed by the State of Texas as a certified public accountant, rendered service in his professional capacity in Louisiana to Coverton Cosmetics Company. He was not registered as a certified public accountant in Louisiana. His service under his contract with the cosmetics company was not the only occasion on which he had practiced his profession in that State. The company denied liability and refused to pay him relying upon a Louisiana statute declaring it unlawful for any person to perform or offer to perform services as a CPA for compensation until he has been registered by the designated agency of the State and holds an unrevoked registration card. Provision is made for issuance of a certificate as a CPA without examination to any applicant who holds a valid unrevoked certificate as a CPA under the laws of any other State. The statute provides further that rendition of services of the character performed by Wilkins, without registration, is a misdemeanor punishable by a fine or imprisonment in the county jail, or by both fine and imprisonment. Wilkins brought an action against Coverton seeking to recover a fee in the amount of $1,500 as the reasonable value of his services. Decision?

3. Michael is interested in promoting the passage of a bill in the State legislature. He agrees with Christy, an attorney, to pay Christy for her services in drawing the required bill, procuring its introduction in the legislature and making an argument for its passage before the legislative committee to which it will be referred. Christy renders these services. Subsequently, upon Michael's refusal to pay Christy, Christy sues Michael for damage for breach of contract. Decision?

4. Anthony promises to pay McCarthy $10,000 if McCarthy reveals to the public that Washington is a Communist. Washington is not a Communist and never has been. McCarthy successfully persuades the media to report that Washington is a Communist and now seeks to recover the $10,000 from Anthony, who refuses to pay. McCarthy initiates a lawsuit against Anthony. What result?

5. The Dear Corporation was engaged in the business of making and selling harvesting machines. It sold everything pertaining to the business to the ABC Company agreeing "not again to go into the manufacture of harvesting machines anywhere in the United States." The seller had national and international goodwill in its business. It now begins the manufacture of such machines contrary to its agreement. Should the court enjoin it?

6. Charles Leigh, engaged in the industrial laundry business in Central City, employed Tim Close, previously employed in the home laundry business, as a route salesman on July 1, 1984. Leigh rents linens and industrial uniforms to commercial customers; the soiled linens and uniforms are picked up at regular intervals by the routemen and replaced with clean ones. Every employee is assigned a list of customers whom he

services. The contract of employment stated that in consideration of being employed, upon termination of the employment, Close would not "directly or indirectly engage in the linen supply business or any competitive business within Central City, Illinois, for a period of one year from the date when his employment under this contract ceases." On May 10 of the following year, Close's employment was terminated by Leigh for valid reasons. Thereafter, Close accepted employment with Ajax Linen Service, a direct competitor of Leigh in Central City. He commenced soliciting former customers whom he had called on for Leigh, and obtained some of them as customers for Ajax.

Leigh brings an action to enforce the provisions of the contract. Decision?

7. On July 5, 1988, Barbara and Kitty entered into a bet on the outcome of the 1988 presidential election. On January 28, 1989, Barbara, who bet on the winner, approached Kitty, seeking to collect the $3,000 Kitty had wagered. Kitty paid Barbara the wager and now seeks to recover the funds from Barbara. Result?

8. Carl, a salesman for Smith, comes to Benson's home and sells him a complete set of "gourmet cooking utensils" that are worth approximately $300. Benson, an eighty-year-old man, lives alone in a one-room efficiency apartment. Benson signs a contract to buy the utensils for $1,450 plus a credit charge of $145 and to make payment in ten equal monthly installments. Three weeks after Carl leaves with the signed contract, Benson decides he cannot afford the cooking utensils and has no use for them. What can Benson do? Explain.

9. Consider the same facts as in problem 8, but assume that the price was $350. Benson, nevertheless, wishes to avoid the contract based on the allegation that Carl befriended and tricked him into the purchase. Decision?

10. Adrian rents a bicycle from Barbara. The bicycle rental contract Adrian signed provides that Barbara is not liable for any injury to the renter caused by any defect in the bicycle or the negligence of Barbara. Adrian is injured when she is involved in an accident due to Barbara's improper maintenance of the bicycle. Adrian sues Barbara for her damage. Decision?

COMPUTER RESEARCH PROBLEMS

 1. Merrill Lynch employed Post and Maney as account executives beginning on April 20, 1959, and May 15, 1961, respectively. Both men elected to be paid a salary and to participate in the firm's pension and profit-sharing plans rather than take a straight commission. Merrill Lynch terminated the employment of both Post and Maney on August 30, 1974. On September 4, 1974, both began working for Bache & Company, a competitor of Merrill Lynch. Merrill Lynch then informed them that all of their rights in the company-funded pension plan had been forfeited pursuant to a provision of the plan that permitted forfeiture in the event an employee directly or indirectly competed with the firm. Decision?

 2. Tovar applied for the position of resident physician in Paxton Community Memorial Hospital. The hospital examined his background and licensing and assured him that he was qualified for the position. Relying upon the hospital's promise of permanent employment, Tovar resigned from his job and began work at the hospital. He was discharged two weeks later, however, because he did not hold a license to practice medicine in Illinois as required by State law. He had taken the examination but had never passed it. Tovar claims that the hospital promised him a position of permanent employment and that by discharging him it breached their employment contract. Decision?

3. Carolyn Murphy, a welfare recipient with four minor children, responded to an advertisement that offered the opportunity to purchase televisions without a deposit or credit history. She entered into a rent-to-own contract for a twenty-five-inch console color television set that required seventy-eight weekly payments of $16 (a total of $1,248, which was two and one-half times the retail value of the set). Under the contract, the renter could terminate the agreement by returning the television and forfeiting any payments already made. After Murphy had paid $436 on the television, she read a newspaper article critical of the lease plan. She stopped payment and sued the television company. The television company has attempted to take possession of the set. Decision?

4. Albert Bennett, an amateur cyclist, participated in a bicycle race conducted by the United States Cycling Federation. During the race Bennett was hit by an automobile. Bennett claims that employees of the Federation improperly allowed the car onto the course. The Federation claims that it cannot be held liable to Bennett because Bennett signed a release exculpating the Federation from responsibility for any personal injury resulting from his participation in the race. Decision?

Chapter 13

CONTRACTUAL CAPACITY

Minors
Incompetent Persons
Intoxicated Persons

A binding promise or agreement requires that the parties to the agreement have contractual capacity. Everyone is regarded as having such capacity unless the law for reasons of public policy holds that the individual lacks such capacity. This essential ingredient of a contract will be discussed by considering those classes and conditions of persons who are legally limited in their capacity to contract: (1) minors, (2) incompetent persons, and (3) intoxicated persons.

MINORS

A **minor,** also called an infant, is a person who has not attained the age of legal majority. At common law, a minor was a person who was under twenty-one years of age. Today the age of majority has been changed in nearly all jurisdictions by statute, usually to age eighteen. Almost without exception a minor's contract, whether executory or executed, is **voidable** at his option. Restatement, Section 14. Even an "emancipated" minor, one who because of marriage or other reason is no longer subject to strict parental control, may avoid contractual liability in most jurisdictions. Consequently, business people deal with minors at their peril and in situations of consequence generally require an adult to co-sign or guarantee the performance of the contract. Nevertheless, most States recognize special categories of contracts that either cannot be avoided (such as student loans or contracts for medical care) or have a lower age for capacity (such as bank accounts, marriage, and insurance contracts).

Liability on Contracts

A minor's contract is not entirely void and of no legal effect, but rather it is *voidable* at the minor's option. He has a power of avoidance. This exercise of power is called a **disaffirmance,** and the minor is ordinarily released from any liability on the contract. On the other hand, after the minor becomes of age, she may choose to adopt or **ratify** the contract, in which case she surrenders her power of avoidance and becomes bound.

Disaffirmance   As previously stated, a minor's contract is voidable at his option, conferring upon him a power to avoid liability. He, or in some jurisdictions his guardian, may exercise the power to disaffirm through words or conduct manifesting an intention not to abide by it.

In general, a minor's disaffirmance must come either during his minority or within a reasonable time after reaching majority as long as he has not already ratified the contract. In most States, what is a reasonable time depends upon such circumstances as the nature of the transaction, whether either party has caused the delay, and the extent to which either party has been injured by the delay. Some States, however, statutorily prescribe a time period, generally one year, in which the minor may disaffirm the contract.

A notable exception is that a sale of land by a minor cannot be disaffirmed until after he reaches his majority. But must he disaffirm immediately upon becoming an adult? In the case of a sale of land, there is a strong precedent that the minor may wait until the expiration of the period of the statute of limitations if there are no questions of fairness and equity involved.

Disaffirmance may be either *express* or *implied*. No particular form of words is essential, so long as they show an intention not to be bound. This intention may be manifested by acts or by conduct. For example, a minor agrees to sell property to Alice and then sells that property to Brian. The sale to Brian would constitute a disaffirmance of the contract with Alice.

A troublesome yet important problem in this area pertains to the minor's duty upon a disaffirmance. The courts are not in agreement on this question. The majority hold that the minor must return any property he has received from the other party, provided he has it in his possession at the time of disaffirmance. Nothing more is required. If the minor disaffirms the purchase of an automobile and the vehicle has been wrecked, he need only return the wrecked vehicle. Other States require at least the payment of a reasonable amount for the use of the property or the amount of its depreciation while in the hands of the minor. A few States, either by statute or court ruling, recognize a duty upon the part of the minor to make *restitution,* i.e., return an equivalent of what has been received in order to place the seller in approximately the same position she would have occupied had the sale not occurred.

Finally, can a minor disaffirm and recover property that has been transferred by his buyer to a good faith purchaser for value? Traditionally, the minor could avoid the contract and recover the property, despite the fact that the third person gave value for it and had no notice of the minority. Thus, in the case of the sale of real estate, a minor's deed of conveyance may be rescinded even against a good faith purchaser of the land who did not know of the minority. This, however, has been changed regarding sales of goods by Section 2–403 of the U.C.C., which provides that a person with voidable title (e.g., the person buying goods from a minor) has power to transfer valid title to a good faith purchaser for value. For example, a minor sells his car to an individual who resells it to a used car dealership, a good faith purchaser for value. The used car dealer would acquire legal title even though he bought the car from a seller who had only voidable title.

For a good overview of the rights of a minor to avoid a contract, *see Parrent v. Midway Toyota.*

Ratification   A minor has the option of ratifying a contract after reaching the age of majority. Ratification makes the contract binding *ab initio* (from the beginning). That is, the result is the same as if the contract had been valid and binding from the beginning. Ratification, once effected, is final and cannot be withdrawn. Ratification must be in total; it must validate the entire contract. The minor can ratify the contract only as a whole, both as to burdens and benefits. He cannot, for example, ratify so as to retain the consideration he received and escape payment or other performance on his part, nor can he retain part of the contract and disaffirm the rest.

Ratification can occur in three ways: express, implied from conduct, and failure to make a timely disaffirmance. Suppose that a minor makes a contract to buy property from an adult. The contract is voidable by the minor, and she can escape liability. But suppose that after reaching her majority, she promises to go through with the purchase. Her promise is binding, and the adult can recover for breach upon her failure to perform. She has *expressly* ratified the contract entered into when she was a minor. In the absence of a statute an express ratification may be oral.

Note that a minor has *no* power to ratify a contract while he remains a minor. A ratification *cannot* be based on words or conduct occurring while he is still under age, for his ratification at that time would be no more effective than his original contractual promise. The ratification must take place after the individual has acquired contractual capacity by attaining his majority.

Ratification, as previously stated, need not be express; it may be *implied* from the minor's conduct. Suppose that the minor, after attaining her majority, uses the property, undertakes to sell it to someone else, or performs some other act showing an intention to affirm the contract. She may not thereafter disaffirm the contract but is bound by it. Perhaps the most common form of implied ratification occurs when the minor, after attaining her majority, continues to use the property which she purchased as a minor. This use is obviously inconsistent with the nonexistence of the contract, and whether the contract is performed or still partly executory, it will amount to a ratification and prevent a disaffirmance by the minor. Simply keeping the goods for an unreasonable time after attaining majority has also been construed as a ratification. Although the courts are divided on the issue, payments by the minor upon reaching majority either on principal or interest or on the purchase price of goods have been held to amount to a ratification. Some courts require some additional evidence of an intention to abide by the contract, such as an express promise to that effect or the actual use of the subject matter of the contract.

Liability for Necessaries

Contractual incapacity does not excuse a minor from an obligation to pay for necessaries, those things that suitably and reasonably supply his personal needs, such as food, shelter, medicine, and clothing. Even here, however, the minor is liable not for the agreed price but for the *reasonable* value of the items furnished. Recovery is based on quasi contract. Thus, if a clothier sells a minor a suit that the minor needs, the clothier can successfully sue the minor and recover the reasonable value of the suit. The clothier is limited to this amount even if it is much less than the agreed-upon selling price.

Determining what are necessaries is a difficult problem. In general, the States regard as **necessary** those things that the minor needs to maintain himself in his particular station in life. Items necessary for subsistence and health, such as food, lodging, clothing, medicine, and medical services, are obviously included. But other less essential items, such as textbooks, school instruction, and legal advice, may be included as well. Further, some States enlarge the concept of necessaries to include articles of property and services that a minor needs to earn the money required to provide the necessities of life for himself and his dependents. *See Gastonia Personnel Corp. v. Rogers.* Nevertheless, many States limit necessaries to items that are not provided to the minor. Thus, if a minor's guardian provides her with an adequate wardrobe, a blouse the minor purchased would *not* be considered a necessity. In addition, a minor is not liable for anything on the ground that it is necessary unless it has been actually furnished to him and used or consumed by him. In other words, a minor may disaffirm his executory contracts for necessaries and refuse to accept the clothing, lodging, or other necessaries.

Ordinarily, luxury items, such as cameras, tape recorders, stereo equipment, television sets, and motor boats, seldom qualify as necessaries. Whether automobiles and trucks are necessaries has caused considerable controversy, but some courts have recognized that under certain circumstances an automobile may be a necessary where it is used by the minor for his business activities.

Liability for Misrepresentation of Age

The States do not agree on whether a minor who has fraudulently misrepresented her age when entering into contract has the power to disaffirm. Suppose a minor says that she is eighteen years of age (or twenty-one if that is the year of attaining majority) and actually looks that old or even older. By the prevailing view in this country, the minor may nevertheless disaffirm the contract. Some States, however, prohibit disaffirmance if a minor misrepresents her age and the adult, in good faith, reasonably relied upon the misrepresentation. Other States not following the majority rule either (a) require the minor to restore the other party to the position she occupied before the making of the contract or (b) allow the defrauded party to recover damages against the minor in tort. *See Keser v. Chagnon* for a case following the minority position.

Liability for Tort Connected with Contract

It is well settled that minors are generally liable for their torts. There is, however, a doctrine in the law that if a tort and a contract are so connected or "interwoven" that to enforce the tort action the court must enforce the contract, the minor is not liable in tort. Thus, if a minor rents an automobile from an adult, he enters into a contractual relationship obliging him to exercise reasonable care and diligence to protect the property from injury. By negligently damaging the automobile, he breaches that contractual undertaking. But his contractual immunity protects him from an action by the adult based on the contract. However, can the adult recover damages on a tort theory? By the majority

view he cannot. For, it is reasoned, a tort recovery would, in effect, be an enforcement of the contract and would defeat the protection that contract law affords the minor.

There is a different result, however, when the minor departs from the terms of the agreement, as by using a rental automobile for an unauthorized purpose and in so doing negligently causes damage to the automobile. In that event most courts would hold that the tort is independent, and the adult can collect from the minor. This would not involve the breach of a contractual duty, but rather the commission of a tort during the course of an activity that is a complete departure from the rental agreement.

INCOMPETENT PERSONS

This section discusses incompetent persons who are under court-appointed guardianship and those who are not adjudicated incompetents.

Person under Guardianship

If a person is under guardianship by court order, her contracts are **void** and of no legal effect. *See First State Bank of Sinai v. Hyland.* Restatement, Section 13. A *guardian* is appointed by a court, generally under the terms of a statute, to control and preserve the property of a person (the *ward*) with impaired capacity to manage her own property. Nevertheless, a party dealing with an individual under guardianship may be able to recover the fair value of any necessaries provided to the incompetent. Moreover, the contracts of the ward may be ratified by her guardian or by herself upon termination of the guardianship.

Mental Illness or Defect

A contract is a consensual transaction, therefore, it is necessary to a valid contract that the parties have a certain level of mental capacity. If a person lacks such capacity (is mentally incompetent), he may avoid liability under the agreement (because the contract is **voidable**).

Under the traditional, cognitive ability test, a person who is lacking in sufficient mental capacity to enter into a contract is one unable to comprehend the subject of the contract, its nature, and probable consequences. To avoid the contract it is not necessary that he be proved permanently incompetent; but his mental defect must be something more than a weakness of intellect or a lack of average intelligence. In short, a person is competent unless he is unable to understand the nature and effect of his act. Restatement, Section 15.

A second type of mental incompetence that is recognized by the Restatement and some States is a mental condition that impairs a person's ability to act in a reasonable manner. Section 15. In other words, the person understands what he is doing but cannot control his behavior in order to act in a reasonable and rational way.

As with a minor and persons under guardianship, an incompetent person is liable for *necessaries* furnished on the principle of quasi contract, the amount of recovery being the reasonable value of the goods or services. Moreover, an incompetent person's voidable contracts may be *ratified* or *disaffirmed* by him when he becomes competent, or during a lucid period.

According to the predominant view in this country, an incompetent person's responsibility on disaffirmance varies somewhat from that of a minor. If the contract is entirely executory or grossly unfair it is voidable. If, however, the contract is executed, fair, and the competent party had no reason to suspect the incompetency of the other, the incompetent must restore the competent party to the *status quo* by a return of the consideration received by the incompetent or its equivalent in money. But if restoration to the *status quo* is not possible avoidance will depend upon the equities of the situation.

INTOXICATED PERSONS

A person may *avoid* any contract that he enters into if the other party has reason to know that, because of intoxication, he is unable to understand the nature and consequences of his actions or that he is unable to act in a reasonable manner. Restatement, Section 16. Such contracts are voidable, although they may be ratified when the intoxicated person regains his capacity. Slight intoxication will not destroy one's contractual capacity, but neither is it essential that one be so drunk as to be totally without reason or understanding.

The effect of intoxication on contractual capacity is similar to that given to contracts that are voidable because of incompetency, although the courts are even more strict with intoxication due to its voluntary nature. The courts, therefore, require that the intoxicated person on regaining his capacity must act promptly to disaffirm and must generally offer to restore the consideration received. *See First State Bank of Sinai v. Hyland.* As with incompetent persons, intoxicated persons are liable in quasi contract for necessaries furnished during their incapacity.

Figure 13–1 illustrates the various types of contractual incapacities and the resulting effects.

Figure 13–1 Contractual Incapacity

Incapacity	Effect
Minority	Voidable
Mental illness or defect	Voidable
Guardianship for incompetency	Void
Intoxication	Voidable

CASES

Minors: Liability for Necessaries

GASTONIA PERSONNEL CORP. v. ROGERS

Supreme Court of North Carolina, 1970.
276 N.C. 279, 172 S.E.2d 19.

BOBBITT, C.J.

[Rogers (defendant) was a nineteen-year-old (the age of majority being twenty-one) high school graduate pursuing a civil engineering degree when he learned that his wife was expecting a child. As a result he quit school and sought assistance from Gastonia Personnel Corporation (plaintiff) in finding a job. Rogers signed a contract with the employment agency providing that he would pay the agency a service charge if it obtained suitable employment for him. The employment agency found him such a job, but Rogers refused to pay the service charge asserting that he was a minor when he signed the contract. Plaintiff sued to recover the agreed upon service charge from Rogers.]

Under the common law, persons, whether male or female, are classified and referred to as *infants* until they attain the age of twenty-one years. [Citations.]

"By the fifteenth century it seems to have been well settled that an infant's bargain was in general void at his election (that is voidable), and also that he was liable for necessaries." [Citation.]

An early commentary on the common law, after the general statement that contracts made by persons (infants) before attaining the age of twenty-one "may be avoided," sets forth "some exceptions out of this generality," to wit: "*An infant may bind himself to pay for his necessary meat, drinke, apparell, necessary physicke, and such other necessaries,* and likewise for his good teaching or instruction, whereby he may profit himself afterwards." [Citations.] . . . If the infant married, "necessaries" included necessary food and clothing for his wife and child. [Citation.]

In accordance with this ancient rule of the common law, this Court has held an infant's contract, unless for "necessaries" or unless authorized by statute, is voidable by the infant, at his election, and may be disaffirmed during infancy or upon attaining the age of twenty-one. [Citations.]

* * *

In general, our prior decisions are to the effect that the "necessaries" of an infant, his wife and child, include only such necessities of life as food, clothing, shelter, medical attention, etc. In our view, the concept of "necessities" should be enlarged to include such articles of property and such services as are reasonably necessary to enable the infant to earn the money required to provide the necessities of life for himself and those who are legally dependent upon him.

The evidence before us tends to show that defendant, when he contracted with plaintiff, was nineteen years of age, emancipated, married, a high school graduate, within "a quarter or 22 hours" of obtaining his degree in applied science, and capable of holding a job at a starting annual salary of $4,784.00. To hold, as a matter of law, that such a person cannot obligate himself to pay for services rendered him in obtaining employment suitable to his ability, education, and specialized training, enabling him to provide the necessities of life for himself, his wife and his expected child, would place him and others similarly situated under a serious economic handicap.

In the effort to protect "older minors" from improvident or unfair contracts, the law should not deny to them the opportunity and right to obligate themselves for articles of property or services which are reasonably necessary to enable them to provide for the proper support of themselves and their dependents. The minor should be held liable for the reasonable value of articles of property or services received pursuant to such contract.

Applying the foregoing legal principles, which modify *pro tanto* the ancient rule of the common law, we hold that the evidence offered by plaintiff was sufficient for submission to the jury for its determination of issues substantially as indicated below.

To establish liability, plaintiff must satisfy the jury by the greater weight of the evidence that defendant's contract with plaintiff was an appropriate and reasonable means for defendant to obtain suitable employment. If this issue is answered in plaintiff's favor, plaintiff must then establish by the greater weight of the evidence the reasonable value of the services received by defendant pursuant to the contract. Thus, plaintiff's recovery, if any, cannot exceed the reasonable value of its services to defendant.

[Judgment for plaintiff awarding a new trial in accordance with legal principles stated in this opinion.]

Minors: Disaffirmance

PARRENT v. MIDWAY TOYOTA

Supreme Court of Montana, 1981.
626 P.2d 848.

HARRISON, J.

This is an appeal from the Workers' Compensation Court's denial of claimant's petition to reopen a final compromise settlement agreement entered into after claimant injured himself in the course of his employment.

The issue raised on this appeal is whether the Workers' Compensation Court erred in refusing to allow claimant, who is a minor, to disaffirm the "petition for final settlement" and reopen his workers' compensation case.

On August 18, 1975, claimant, who was then fifteen years old, injured his lower back while in the employ of Midway Toyota, Inc., of Great Falls, Montana. At the time he was engaged in lifting heavy objects.

Notice was properly and timely given by all parties in the dispute. Defendant accepted liability and paid claimant the appropriate amount of biweekly temporary total disability payments from August 18, 1975, through November 15, 1976, at the weekly rate of $53.36. On October 6, 1975, a lumbar myelography was performed on claimant which demonstrated a herniated disk at the L4–5 level. Claimant underwent surgery in October 1975 performed by Dr. Robert Chambers. The herniated disk was removed and the posterolateral fusion from the fifth lumbar vertebrae to the sacrum was performed.

On February 1977 claimant and defendant entered into a final settlement of the claim for 150 weeks of permanent partial disability benefits totaling $6,136.40, less credit in the amount of $640.32 for the permanent partial payments made after November 16, 1976.

Claimant has been employed in the oil fields of Montana since his graduation from high school in June 1978. In the performance of his work, he occasionally experienced low back pain when engaged in heavy lifting or straining, but he has been able to perform all work.

Tom Mazurek, an adjuster, represented defendant in the settlement negotiations. He negotiated with the claimant's mother (natural guardian) and claimant directly. The petition for final settlement, based on a 23 percent impairment rating, was signed by claimant only and was witnessed by a friend. Claimant's mother was present at the time he signed the agreement. She did not object to the signing, nor did she or any other person of legal age or of "legal guardian status" cosign the agreement. Later, claimant and his mother requested that the money be paid in a lump sum amount. The Workers' Compensation Division denied the request.

Claimant later filed a petition to reopen his claim pursuant to [citation]. At the hearing, the Workers' Compensation Court found no evidence to indicate that there was any increase in claimant's disability from the time of the final settlement to the date of this hearing. The Workers' Compensation Court found no evidence of fraud, misrepresentation or deceit by defendant in the settlement.

The Workers' Compensation Court concluded:

"The claimant's guardian participated fully in consideration of the offered final settlement and though did not actually sign the final settlement petition, she nevertheless ratified and approved it on behalf of her ward, the claimant, to the same legal effect as if she had actually signed the petition . . ."

Claimant argues this conclusion is contrary to the law.

Claimant was a minor at the time the final compromise settlement agreement was entered into between the parties. The petition for final settlement is a contract, and contract principles, therefore, must be applied to determine the petition's validity and enforceability. [Citation.]

The pertinent statutes are:

Section 28–2–201, MCA:

"Who may contract. All persons are capable of contracting except minors, persons of unsound mind, and persons deprived of civil rights. Minors and persons of unsound mind have only such capacity as is defined by this part, [citation]."

Section 28–10–104, MCA:

"Who may appoint an agent, who may be an agent. Any person having capacity to contract, except a minor, may appoint an agent, and any person may be an agent."

Section 41–1–302, MCA:

"Contracts of minors disaffirmance. A minor may make a conveyance or other contract in the same manner as any other person, subject only to his power of disaffirmance under the provisions of this chapter. . . ."

Section 41–1–304, MCA:

"When minors may disaffirm. . . . the contract of a minor may, upon restoring the consideration to the party from whom it was received, be disaffirmed by the minor himself, either before his majority or within a reasonable time afterwards, or in case of his death within that period, by his heirs or personal representatives."

Section 41–1–304, MCA, allows a minor to disaffirm his contract. Because the sixteen-year-old claimant signed the petition for final settlement in his own behalf, he alone was the contracting party.

Tom Mazurek chose to contract with the claimant; he must, therefore, be prepared to accept the consequences of claimant's disaffirmance of the petition. The person who deals with an infant does so at his own peril. [Citation.]

Defendant claims that the mother, Hermoine Parrent, was present at all times during the signing of the contract; that the mother approved of the contract; that there was no objection to the contract; that the adjuster negotiated with the mother and the claimant during the weeks prior to the signing of the contract and that after the contract was signed, the mother was still aware of the contract rights of claimant and did not object to the same. Because of this close relation and continuous awareness of the mother, the contract is enforceable. We disagree.

It is immaterial that Hermoine Parrent may have advised and counseled claimant with respect to his workers' compensation claim. The mother is the natural guardian of the minor claimant, but this relation only affects her right to the custody of the minor and does not enlarge her rights to the property of the minor. Claimant was the sole contracting party. He is the only party that bound himself legally to the contract. As a minor, he is entitled to disaffirm and rescind the final settlement.

Contrary to defendant's argument in this area is *Gage v. Moore* [citation.] In *Gage* a fourteen-year-old boy brought an action to rescind a contract. The defendant refused, and suit was brought. The defendant contended that the plaintiff's father had acquiesced in and ratified the purchase and, for that reason, the contract should not be rescinded and avoided by the plaintiff. In rejecting this contention and finding for the fourteen-year-old plaintiff, the court, quoting from [citation], stated:

"The right of an infant to rescind his contract is unaffected by the fact that his father was present advising and approving the transaction. The assent of the father adds nothing to the binding force of an infant's promise . . ." [Citation.]

It is the policy of the law to discourage adults from contracting with a minor. Tom Mazurek testified he knew claimant was a minor at the time claimant signed the petition for final settlement; yet, Mazurek was not discouraged from obtaining claimant's signature on the petition.

The insurer, adjuster Mazurek and the Workers' Compensation Division have much greater expertise and knowledge in the area of workers' compensation law than have claimant and his mother. We are dismayed that these knowledgeable parties overlooked simple contract law. Defendant erred in not requiring claimant's legal guardian to sign the petition for final settlement on behalf of and in place of claimant himself.

The final compromise settlement is set aside, and we remand this case to the Workers' Compensation Court for proceedings consistent with this Opinion.

Liability for Misrepresentation of Age

KESER v. CHAGNON

Supreme Court of Colorado, 1966.
159 Colo. 209, 410 P.2d 637.

McWILLIAMS, J.

This writ of error concerns the purchase of an automobile by a minor and his efforts to thereafter avoid the contract of purchase. The salient facts are as follows:

1. on June 11, 1964, Chagnon bought a 1959 Edsel from Keser for the sum of $1025, payment therefor[e] being in cash which Chagnon obtained by borrowing a portion of the purchase price from the Cash Credit Company on a signature note, with the balance of the money being obtained from the Public Finance Corporation, the latter loan being secured by a chattel mortgage [security interest] upon the automobile;

2. as of June 11, 1964, Chagnon was a minor of the age of twenty years, ten months and twenty days, although despite this fact Chagnon nonetheless falsely advised Keser that he was then over the age of twenty-one; and

3. on about September 25, 1964, when Chagnon was then of the age of twenty-one years, two months and four days, Chagnon formally advised Keser of his desire to disaffirm the contract theretofore entered into by the parties, and thereafter on October 5, 1964 Chagnon returned the Edsel to Keser.

Based on this sequence of events Chagnon brought an action against Keser wherein he sought to recover the $1025 which he had allegedly theretofore paid Keser for the Edsel. By answer Keser alleged, among other things, that he had suffered damage as the direct result of Chagnon's false representation as to his age.

A trial was had to the court, sitting without a jury, all of which culminated in a judgment in favor of Chagnon against Keser in the sum of $655.78. This particular sum was arrived at by the trial court in the following manner: the trial court found that Chagnon initially purchased the Edsel for the sum of $995 . . . and that he was entitled to the return of his $995; and then by way of set-off the trial court subtracted from the $995 the sum of $339.22, this latter sum apparently representing the difference between the purchase price paid for the vehicle and the reasonable value of the Edsel on October 5, 1964, which was the date when the Edsel was returned to Keser.

* * *

Before considering each of these several matters, it is deemed helpful to allude briefly to some of the general principles pertaining to the longstanding policy of the law to protect a minor from at least some of his childish foibles by affording him the right, under certain circumstances, to avoid his contract, not only during his minority but also within a reasonable time after reaching his majority. In [citation] we held that when a minor elects to disaffirm and avoid his contract, the "contract" becomes invalid *ab initio* and that the parties thereto then revert to the same position as if the contract had never been made. In that case we went on to declare that when a minor thus sought to avoid his contract and had in his possession the specific property received by him in the transaction, he was in such circumstance required to return the same as a prerequisite to any avoidance.

In [citation] it is said that a minor failing to disaffirm within a "reasonable time" after reaching his majority loses the right to do so and that just what constitutes a "reasonable time" is ordinarily a question of fact. As regards the necessity for restoration of consideration, in [citation] it is stated that the minor after disaffirming is "usually required . . . to return the consideration, if he can, or the part remaining in his possession or control."

* * *

Keser's . . . contention that Chagnon upon attaining his majority ratified the contract by his failure to disaffirm within a reasonable time after becoming twenty-one and by his retention and use of the Edsel prior to its return to the seller is equally untenable. In this connection it is pointed out that Chagnon did not notify Keser of his desire to disaffirm until 66 days after he became twenty-one and that he did not return the Edsel until 10 days after his notice to disaffirm, during all of which time Chagnon had the possession and use of the vehicle in question. As already noted, when an infant attains his majority he has a reasonable time within which he may thereafter disaffirm a contract entered into during his minority. And this rule is not as strict where, as here, we are dealing with an executed contract. There is no hard and fast rule as to just what constitutes a "reasonable" time within which the infant may disaffirm. In [citation] we held that the failure to disaffirm for a period of five years after a minor reached his majority, together with other acts recognizing the validity of the contract, constituted ratification. In [citation] disaffirmance four months after reaching majority was held to be within a reasonable time. . . . Suffice it to say, that under the circumstances disclosed by the record we are not prepared to hold that as a matter of law Chagnon ratified the contract either by his actions or by his alleged failure to disaffirm within a reasonable time after reaching his majority. In other words, there is competent evidence to support the conclusion of the trial court that Chagnon disaffirmed the contract within a reasonable time after reaching his majority and such finding of fact cannot be disturbed by us on review.

Finally, error is predicated upon the trial court's finding in connection with Keser's set-off for the damage occasioned him by Chagnon's admitted false representation of his age. In this regard the trial court apparently found that the reasonable value of the Edsel when it was returned to Keser by Chagnon was $655.78, and accordingly went on to allow Keser a set-off in the amount of $339.22, this latter sum representing the difference between the purchase price, $995, and the value of the vehicle on the date it was returned. Finding, then, that Chagnon was entitled to the return of the $995 which he had theretofore paid Keser for the Edsel, the trial court then subtracted therefrom Keser's set-off in the amount of $339.22, and accordingly entered judgment for Chagnon against Keser in the sum of $655.78. Whether it was by accident or design we know not, but $655.78 is apparently the exact amount which Chagnon "owed" the Public Finance Corporation on his note with that company.

* * *

The judgment is reversed and the cause remanded with direction that the trial court determine Keser's set-off in accord with the rule in [citation] [in order to determine damages caused by Chagnon's misrepresentation of age], and once this set-off has been thus determined, to then enter judgment for Chagnon in an amount equal to the difference between $995 and the amount of such set-off.

Intoxicated Persons/Incompetent Persons

FIRST STATE BANK OF SINAI v. HYLAND

Supreme Court of South Dakota, 1987.
399 N.W.2d 894.

HENDERSON, J.

Plaintiff-appellant First State Bank of Sinai (Bank) sued defendant-appellee Mervin Hyland (Mervin) seeking to hold him responsible for payment on a promissory note which he cosigned. . . . [T]he circuit court entered . . . judgment holding Mervin not liable for the note's payment. Bank appeals advocating that the court erred when it ruled that

(1) Mervin was incompetent to transact business when he signed the note;

(2) Mervin's obligation to Bank was void; and

(3) Mervin did not subsequently accept/ratify the obligation.

* * *

On March 10, 1981, Randy Hyland (Randy) and William Buck (Buck), acting for Bank, executed two promissory notes. One note was for $6,800 and the other note was for $3,000. Both notes became due on September 19, 1981.

The notes remained unpaid on their due date and Bank sent notice to Randy informing him of the delinquencies. On October 20, 1981, Randy came to the Bank and met with Buck. Buck explained to Randy that the notes were past due. Randy requested an extension. Buck agreed, but on the condition that Randy's father, Mervin, act as cosigner. One $9,800 promissory note dated October 20, 1981 (the two notes of $6,800 and $3,000 were combined) was created. Randy was given the note for the purpose of obtaining his father's signature. According to Randy, Mervin signed the note on October 20 or 21, 1981.

Mervin had transacted business with Bank since 1974. Previously, he executed approximately 60 promissory notes with Bank. Mervin was apparently a good customer and paid all of his notes on time. Buck testified that he knew Mervin drank, but that he was unaware of any alcohol-related problems.

Randy returned to the Bank about one week later. Mervin had properly signed the note. In Buck's presence, Randy signed the note, which had an April 20, 1982 due date.

On April 20, 1982, the note was unpaid. Buck notified Randy of the overdue note. On May 5, 1982, Randy appeared at the Bank. He brought a blank check signed by Mervin with which the interest on the note was to be paid. Randy filled in the check amount at the Bank for $899.18 (the amount of interest owing). Randy also requested that the note be extended. Buck agreed, but required Merv-in's signature as a prerequisite to any extension. A two-month note for $9,800 with a due date of July 2, 1982, was prepared and given to Randy.

Randy did not secure his father's signature on the two-month note, and Mervin testified that he refused to sign that note. On June 22, 1982, Randy filed for bankruptcy which later resulted in the total discharge of his obligation on the note.

On July 14, 1982, Buck sent a letter to Randy and Mervin informing them of Bank's intention to look to Mervin for the note's payment. On December 19, 1982, Bank filed suit against Mervin, requesting $9,800 principal and interest at the rate of 17% until judgment was entered. Mervin answered on January 14, 1983. His defense hinged upon the assertion that he was incapacitated through the use of liquor when he signed the note. He claimed he had no recollection of the note, did not remember seeing it, discussing it with his son, or signing it.

Randy testified that when he brought the note home to his father, the latter was drunk and in bed. Mervin then rose from his bed, walked into the kitchen, and signed the note. Later, Randy returned to the Bank with the signed note.

The record reveals that Mervin was drinking heavily from late summer through early winter of 1981. During this period, Mervin's wife and son accepted responsibilities for managing the farm. Mervin's family testified that his bouts with liquor left him weak, unconcerned with regard to family and business matters, uncooperative, and uncommunicative. When Mervin was drinking, he spent most of his time at home, in bed.

Mervin's problems with alcohol have five times resulted in his involuntary commitment to hospitals. Two of those commitments occurred near the period of the October 1981 note. On September 10, 1981, Mervin was involuntarily committed to the Human Services Center at Yankton. He was released on September 19, 1981. On November 20, 1981, he was involuntarily committed to River Park at Pierre.

Between the periods of his commitments, September 19, 1981 until November 20, 1981, Mervin did transact some business himself. * * *

A trial was held on October 4, 1985. Mervin was found to be entirely without understanding (as a result of alcohol consumption) when he signed the October 20, 1981 promissory note. The court pointed to Mervin's lack of personal care and nonparticipation in family life and farming business as support for finding the contractual relationship between the parties void at its inception. It was further held that Bank had failed to show Mervin's subsequent ratification of the contract. Bank appeals.

* * *

Historically, the void contract concept has been applied to nullify agreements made by mental incompetents who have contracted . . . after a judicial determination of incapacity had been entered. [Citations.]* * *

Mervin had numerous and prolonged problems stemming from his inability to handle alcohol. However, he was not judicially declared incompetent during the note's signing.

* * *

Contractual obligations incurred by intoxicated persons may be voidable. [Citation.] Voidable contracts (contracts other than those entered into following a judicial determination of incapacity, . . . may be rescinded by the previously disabled party. [Citation.] However, disaffirmance must be prompt, upon the recovery of the intoxicated party's mental abilities, and upon his notice of the agreement, if he had forgotten it. [Citation.] * * *

A voidable contract may also be ratified by the party who had contracted while disabled. Upon ratification, the contract becomes a fully valid legal obligation. [Citation.] Ratification can either be express or implied by conduct. [Citations.] In addition, failure of a party to disaffirm a contract over a period of time may, by itself, ripen into a ratification, especially if rescission will result in prejudice to the other party. [Citations.]

Mervin received both verbal notice from Randy and written notice from Bank on or about April 27, 1982, that the note was overdue. On May 5, 1982, Mervin paid the interest owing with a check which Randy delivered to Bank. This by itself could amount to ratification through conduct. If Mervin wished to avoid the contract, he should have then exercised his right of rescission. We find it impossible to believe that Mervin paid almost $900 in interest without, in his own mind, accepting responsibility for the note. His assertion that paying interest on the note relieved his obligation is equally untenable in light of his numerous past experiences with promissory notes.

* * *

We conclude that Mervin's obligation to Bank as not void. . . . Mervin's obligation on the note was voidable and his subsequent failure to disaffirm (lack of rescission) and his payment of interest (ratification) then transformed the voidable contract into one that is fully binding upon him.

We reverse and remand.

QUESTIONS

1. Define a necessary and explain how it affects the contracts of a minor.

2. How and when may a minor ratify a contract?

3. What is the liability of a minor who disaffirms a contract?

4. Distinguish between the legal capacity of a person under guardianship and a mentally incompetent person who is not under guardianship.

5. What is the rule governing an intoxicated person's capacity to enter into a contract?

PROBLEMS

1. Michael, a minor, operates a one-man automobile repair shop. Anderson, having heard of Michael's good work on other cars, takes her car to Michael's shop for a thorough engine overhaul. Michael, while overhauling Anderson's engine, carelessly fits an unsuitable piston ring on one of the pistons, with the result that Anderson's engine is seriously damaged. Michael offers to return the sum which Anderson paid him for his work, but refuses to make good the damage. Anderson sues Michael in tort for the damage to her engine. Decision?

2. (a) On March 20, Andy Small became seventeen years old, but he appeared to be at least twenty-one. On April 1, he moved into a rooming house in Chicago where he orally agreed to pay the landlady $300 a month for room and board, payable at the end of each month for services and room during that month.

(b) On April 4, he went to Honest Hal's Carfeteria and signed a contract to buy a used car on time with a small down payment. He made no representation as to his age, but Honest Hal represented the car to be in A–1 condition, which it subsequently turned out not to be.

(c) On April 7, Andy sold and conveyed to Adam Smith a parcel of real estate which he owned.

On April 30, he refused to pay his landlady for his room and board for the month of April; he returned the car to Honest Hal and demanded a refund of his down payment; and he demanded that Adam Smith reconvey the land although the purchase price, which Andy received in cash, had been spent in riotous living. Decisions as to each claim?

3. Jones, a minor, owned a 1982 automobile. She traded it to Stone for a 1983 car. Jones went on a three-week trip and found that the 1983 car was not as good as the 1982 car. She asked Stone to return the 1982 car but was told that it had been sold to Tate. Jones thereupon sued Tate for the return of the 1982 car. Decision?

4. On May 7, Roy, a minor, a resident of Smithton, purchased an automobile from Royal Motors, Inc., for $12,750 in cash. On the same day he bought a motor scooter from Marks, also a minor, for $750 and paid him in full. On June 5, two days

before attaining his majority, Roy disaffirmed the contracts and offered to return the car and the motor scooter to the respective sellers. Royal Motors, Inc., and Marks each refused the offers. On June 16, Roy brought separate appropriate actions against Royal Motors, Inc., and Marks to recover the purchase price of the car and the motor scooter. By agreement on July 30, Royal Motors, Inc., accepted the automobile. Royal filed a counterclaim against Roy for the reasonable rental value of the car between June 5 and July 30. The car was not damaged during this period. Royal knew that Roy lived twenty-five miles from his place of employment in Smithton and that he would probably drive the car, as he did, to provide himself transportation. Decision as to (a) Roy's action against Royal Motors, Inc., and its counterclaim against Roy; (b) Roy's action against Marks?

5. George Jones on October 1, being then a minor, entered into a contract with Johnson Motor Company, a dealer in automobiles, to buy a car for $10,850. He paid $1,100 down and, under the agreement, was to make monthly payments thereafter of $325 each. After making the first payment on November 1, he failed to make any more payments. Jones was seventeen years old at the time he made the contract. He represented to the company that he was twenty-one years old, and the reason he made the representation was because he was afraid that if the company knew his real age, it would not sell the car to him. His appearance was that of a man of twenty-one years of age. On December 15, the company repossessed the car under the terms provided in the contract. At that time, the car had been damaged and was in need of repairs. On December 20, George Jones became of age and at once disaffirmed the contract and demanded the return of the $1,425 paid on the contract. On refusal of the company to do so, George Jones brought an action to recover the $1,425, and the company set up a counterclaim for $1,500 for expenses to which it was put in repairing the car. Decision?

6. Rebecca entered into a written contract to sell certain real estate to Mary, a minor, for $80,000, payable $4,000 on the execution of the contract and $800 on the first day of each month thereafter until paid. Mary paid the $4,000 down payment and eight monthly installments before attaining her majority. Thereafter, Mary made two additional monthly payments and caused the contract to be recorded in the county where the real estate was located. Mary was then advised by her attorney that the contract was voidable. After being so advised, Mary immediately tendered the contract to Rebecca, together with a deed reconveying all of Mary's interest in the property to Rebecca. Also, Mary demanded that Rebecca return the money she had paid under the contract. Rebecca refused the tender and declined to repay any portion of the money paid to her by Mary. Mary then brought an action to cancel the contract and recover the amount paid to Rebecca. Decision?

7. Anita sold and delivered an automobile to Marvin, a minor. Marvin, during his minority, returned the automobile to Anita, saying that he disaffirmed the sale. Anita accepted the automobile and said she would return the purchase price to Marvin the next day. Later in the day, Marvin changed his mind, took the automobile without Anita's knowledge, and sold it to Chris. Anita had not returned the purchase price when Marvin took the car. On what theory, if any, can Anita recover from Marvin? Explain.

8. Ira, who in 1989 had been found innocent of a criminal offense because of insanity, was released from the hospital for the criminally insane during the summer of 1990 and since that time has been a reputable and well-respected citizen and businessman. On February 1, 1991, Ira and Shirley entered into a contract in which Ira would sell his farm to Shirley for $100,000. Ira seeks to void the contract. Shirley insists that Ira is fully competent and has no right to avoid the contract. Who will prevail? Why?

9. Daniel, while under the influence of alcohol, agreed to sell his 1988 automobile to Belinda for $8,000. The next morning when Belinda went to Daniel's house with the $8,000 in cash, Daniel stated that he did not remember the transaction but "a deal is a deal." One week after completing the sale, Daniel decides that he wishes to avoid the contract. What result?

10. Langstraat, age seventeen, owned a motorcycle that he insured against liability with Midwest Mutual Insurance Company. He signed a notice of rejection attached to the policy indicating that he did not desire to purchase uninsured motorists' coverage from the insurance company. Later he was involved in an accident with another motorcycle owned and operated by a party who was uninsured. Langstraat now seeks to recover from the insurance company, asserting that his rejection was not a valid rejection because he is a minor. Decision?

11. G.A.S. married his wife, S.I.S., on January 19, 1957. His mental health problems began in 1970 when he was hospitalized at the Delaware State Hospital for eight weeks. Similar illnesses occurred in 1972 and the early part of 1974, with G.A.S. suffering from such symptoms as paranoia and loss of a sense of reality. In early 1975, G.A.S. was still committed to the Delaware State Hospital, attending a regular job during the day and returning to the hospital at night. It was during this time that he entered into a separation agreement prepared by his wife's attorney. G.A.S., however, never spoke with the attorney about the contents of the agreement, nor did he read it prior to signing. Moreover, G.A.S. was not independently represented by counsel when he executed this agreement. G.A.S. brings this action to disaffirm the separation agreement. Decision?

COMPUTER RESEARCH PROBLEMS

1. Rose, a minor, bought a new Buick Riviera from Sheehan Buick. Seven months later, while still a minor, he attempted to disaffirm the purchase. Sheehan Buick refused to accept the return of the car or to refund the purchase price. Rose, at the time of the purchase, gave all the appearance of being of legal age. The car had been used by him to carry on his school, business, and social activities. Decision?

2. L. D. Robertson bought a pickup truck from King and Julian, doing business as the Julian Pontiac Company. Robertson, at the time of purchase was seventeen years old, living at home with his parents, and driving his father's truck around the county to different construction jobs. According to the sales contract, he traded in a passenger car for the truck and was given $723 credit toward the truck's $1,743 purchase price, agreeing to pay the remainder in monthly installments. After he paid the first month's installment, the truck caught fire and was rendered useless. The insurance agent, upon finding that Robertson was a minor, refused to deal with him. Consequently, Robertson sued to exercise his right as a minor to rescind the contract and to recover the purchase price he had already paid ($723 credit for the car plus the one month's installment). The defendants argue that Robertson, even as a minor, cannot rescind the contract since it was for a necessary item. Decision?

3. Haydocy Pontiac sold Jennifer Lee an automobile for $1,552, of which $1,402 was financed with a note and security agreement. At the time of the sale Lee, age twenty, represented to Haydocy that she was twenty-one years old, the age of majority, and capable of contracting. After receiving the car, Lee allowed John Roberts to take possession of it. Roberts took the car and has not returned. Lee has failed to make any further payments on the car. Haydocy has sued to recover on the note. Lee disaffirms the contract claiming that she was too young to enter into a valid contract. Decision?

4. Carol White ordered a $225.00 pair of contact lenses through an optometrist. White, an emancipated minor, paid $100.00 by check and agreed to pay the remaining $125.00 at a later time. The doctor ordered the lenses incurring an indebtedness of $110.00. After the lenses were ordered, White called to cancel her order and stopped payment on the $100.00 check. The lenses could be used by no one but White. The doctor sued White for the value of the lenses. Decision?

5. Williamson, her mortgage in default, was threatened with foreclosure on her home. She decided to sell the house. The Matthewses learned of this and contacted her about the matter. Williamson claims that she offered to sell her equity for $17,000, and that the Matthewses agreed to pay off the mortgage. The Matthewses contend that the asking price was $1,700. On September 27, 1978, the parties signed a contract of sale, which stated the purchase price to be $1,800 ($100 increase regarding furniture in the house) plus the unpaid balance of the mortgage. The parties met again on October 10 to sign the deed. Later that day, Williamson, concerned that she had not received her full consideration, contacted an attorney. On October 12, Williamson filed for injunctive relief, seeking to set aside the sale based upon inadequate consideration and mental weakness due to intoxication. Decision?

6. Halbman, a minor, purchased a 1968 Oldsmobile from Lemke for $1,250. Under the terms of the contract, Halbman would pay $1,000 down and the balance in $25 weekly installments. Upon making the down payment, Halbman received possession of the car, but Lemke retained the title until the balance was paid. After Halbman had made his first four payments, a connecting rod in the car's engine broke. Lemke denied responsibility, but offered to help Halbman repair it if Halbman would provide the parts. Halbman, however, placed the car in a garage where the repairs cost $637.40. Halbman never paid the repair bill.

Hoping to avoid any liability for the vehicle, Lemke transferred title to Halbman even though Halbman never paid the balance owed. Halbman returned the title with a letter disaffirming the contract and demanded return of the money paid. Lemke refused. Since the repair bill remained unpaid, the garage removed the car's engine and transmission and towed the body to Halbman's father's house. Vandalism during the period of storage rendered the car unsalvageable. Several times Halbman requested Lemke to remove the car. Lemke refused. Halbman sued Lemke for the return of his consideration, and Lemke countersued for the amount still owed on the contract. Decision?

Chapter 14

CONTRACTS IN WRITING

Contracts within the Statute of Frauds
Compliance with Statute of Frauds
Effect of Noncompliance
Parol Evidence Rule
Interpretation of Contracts

A N **oral** contract, that is one not written, is in every way as enforceable as a written contract unless otherwise provided by statute. Although most contracts are not required to be in writing to be enforceable, it is highly desirable that significant contracts be written. Written contracts avoid the numerous problems inevitably involved in proving the terms of oral contracts. The process of setting down the contractual terms in a written document also tends to clarify the terms and bring to light a number of problems the parties might not otherwise foresee. Moreover, the terms of a written contract do not change over time, while the parties' recollections of the terms might.

When the parties do reduce their agreement to a complete and final written expression, the law (the parol evidence rule) honors this document by not allowing the parties to introduce any evidence in a lawsuit that would alter, modify, or vary the terms of the written contract. Nevertheless, the parties may differ as to the proper or intended meaning of language contained in the written agreement where such language is ambiguous or susceptible to different interpretations. To ascertain the proper meaning requires an interpretation, or construction, of the contract. The rules of construction permit the introduction of evidence in order to resolve ambiguity and to show the meaning of the language employed and the sense in which both parties used it.

This chapter will examine (1) the types of contracts that must be in writing to be enforceable, (2) the parol evidence rule, and (3) the rules of contractual interpretation.

STATUTE OF FRAUDS

The statute of frauds requires that certain designated types of contracts be in a particular form to be enforceable. The original statute became law in 1677 when the English Parliament adopted "An Act for Prevention of Frauds and Perjuries," commonly referred to as the statute of frauds. From the early days of American history practically every State had and continues to have a statute of frauds patterned upon the original English statute.

The statute of frauds has no relation whatever to any kind of fraud practiced in the making of contracts. The rules relating to such fraud are rules of common law and are discussed in Chapter 10. For example, Adam claims that Brenda fraudulently misrepresented a material fact and thereby induced Adam to make a certain contract. Adam cannot rely upon the statute of frauds in support of his claim. It has been frequently stated that the word "frauds" in the title of this statute is misleading. The purpose of the statute is to prevent fraud in the proof of certain oral contracts by perjured testimony in court. This purpose is accomplished by the requirement that certain contracts be proved by a signed writing. On the other hand, the statute does not prevent the performance of oral contracts if the parties are willing to perform. In brief, the statute relates only to the proof or evidence of a contract. It has nothing to do with the circumstances surrounding the making of a contract or with the validity of a contract.

CONTRACTS WITHIN THE STATUTE OF FRAUDS

Many more types of contracts are *not* subject to the statute of frauds than are subject to it. Most oral contracts, as previously indicated, are as enforceable and valid as a written contract. If, however, a given contract is subject to the statute of frauds, the contract is said to be **within** the statute, and to be enforceable it must comply with the requirements of the statute. All other types of contracts are said to be "not within" or "outside" the statute and need not comply with its requirements to be enforceable.

The following kinds of contracts are within the original English statute and remain within most State statutes. Compliance requires a writing signed by the party to be charged (the party seeking to avoid the contract).

1. Promises to answer for the duty of another

2. Promises of an executor or administrator to answer personally for a duty of the decedent whose funds he is administering

3. Agreements upon consideration of marriage

4. Agreements for the sale of an interest in land

5. Agreements not to be performed within one year

A sixth type of contract within the statute applied to contracts for the sale of goods. Section 2–201 of the U.C.C. now governs the enforceability of contracts of this kind.

The various provisions of the statute of frauds apply independently of each other. Accordingly, a contract for the sale of an interest in land may also be a contract in consideration of marriage, a contract not to be performed in one year, *and* a contract for the sale of goods.

In addition to those contracts specified in the original statute, some modern statutes require that others be written; for example, a contract to make a will, to authorize an agent to sell or purchase real estate, or to pay a commission to a real estate broker. Moreover, the U.C.C. requires that a contract for the sale of securities and contracts creating certain types of security interests be in writing as well as contracts for the sale of other personal property for more than $5,000.

Suretyship Provision

The **suretyship** provision applies to a contractual promise by a **surety** (*promisor*) to a **creditor** (*promisee*) to perform the duties or obligations of a third person (**principal debtor**) if the principal debtor does not perform. Thus, if a mother tells a merchant to extend $1,000 worth of credit to her son and says, "If he doesn't pay, I will," the promise must be in writing to be enforceable. The factual situation can be reduced to the simple "If X doesn't pay, I will." The promise is said to be **collateral,** in that the promisor is not the one who is primarily liable. The mother does not promise to pay in any event; her promise is to pay only if the one primarily obligated, her son, defaults.

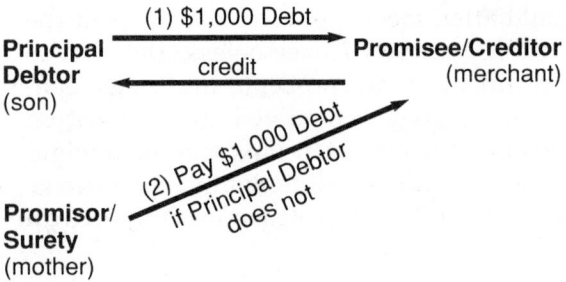

The rule applies only to cases where three parties and two contracts are involved. The primary contract is between the principal debtor and the creditor and creates the indebtedness. The collateral contract is made by the third person (surety) directly with the creditor, whereby she promises to pay the debt to the creditor in case the principal debtor (son) fails to do so. For a complete discussion of suretyship see Chapter 39.

Original Promise If the promisor makes an **original promise** by undertaking to become primarily liable, then the statute of frauds does not apply. For example, a father tells a merchant to deliver certain items to his daughter and says, "I will pay $400 for them." The father is not promising to answer for the debt of another, but rather he is making the debt his own. It is to the father, and the father alone, that the merchant extends credit and may look for payment. The statute of frauds does not apply, and the promise may be oral.

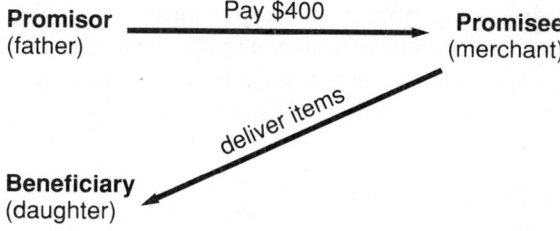

Promisor (father) — Pay $400 → Promisee (merchant)

deliver items

Beneficiary (daughter)

See Shane Quadri v. Goodyear Service Stores.

Main Purpose Doctrine The courts have developed an exception to the suretyship provision based on the purpose or object of the promisor, called the "main purpose doctrine" or "leading object rule." Where the object or purpose of the promisor is to obtain an economic benefit for himself, the promise is *not* within the statute. Restatement, Section 116. The expected benefit to the surety "must be such as to justify the conclusion that his main purpose in making the promise is to advance his own interest." Restatement, Section 116, Comment b. The fact that the surety received consideration for his promise or that he might receive a slight and indirect advantage

is insufficient to bring the promise within the main purpose doctrine.

Suppose that a supply company has refused to furnish materials upon the credit of a building contractor. Faced with a possible slow down in construction of his building, the owner of the land promises the supplier that if he will extend credit to the contractor, the owner will pay if the contractor does not. Here, the primary purpose of the promisor was to serve an economic interest of his own, even though the performance of the promise would discharge the duty of another. The intent to benefit the contractor was at most incidental, and courts will uphold oral promises of this type. *See Stuart Studio, Inc. v. National School of Heavy Equipment, Inc.*

Promise Made to Debtor The suretyship provision has been interpreted *not* to include promises made to a *debtor*. For example, D owes a debt to C. S promises D to pay her debt. Since the promise of S was made to the debtor (D), not the creditor, the promise may be oral. The promise is not a collateral promise to pay C if D fails to pay and thus is not a promise to discharge the obligation of another.

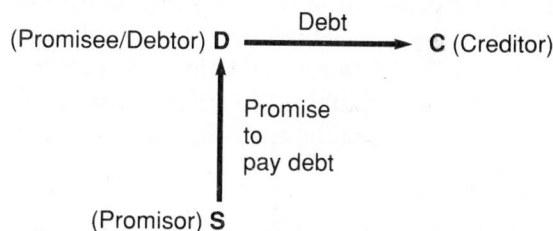

(Promisee/Debtor) D — Debt → C (Creditor)

Promise to pay debt

(Promisor) S

Executor-Administrator Provision

The executor-administrator provision applies to promises of an executor of a decedent's will, or the administrator of his estate if he dies without a will, to answer personally for a duty of the decedent. An **executor** or **administrator** is a person appointed by a court to carry on, subject to order of court, the administration of the estate of a deceased person. If the will of a decedent nominates a certain person as executor, the court customarily appoints that person. (For a more detailed discussion of executors and administrators see Chapter 52.)

If an executor or administrator promises to pay personally a debt of the decedent, the promise must be in writing to be enforceable. For example, Brian, who is Ann's son and executor of her will, recognizes that Ann's estate will not have sufficient funds to pay all of her debts and orally promises Curtis, one of Ann's creditors, that he, Brian, will *personally* pay all of his mother's creditors in full. Brian's oral promise is not enforceable. This provision does not apply to promises to pay debts of the deceased out of assets of the estate.

The executor-administrator provision is thus a specific application of the suretyship provision. Accordingly, the exceptions to the suretyship provision also apply to this provision.

Marriage Provision

The notable feature of the marriage provision is that it does *not* apply to mutual promises to marry. If, for example, Greg and Betsy each orally promise and agree to marry each other, the agreement is *not* within the statute and is a binding contract between the parties. The provision only applies if a promise to marry is made in consideration for some promise other than a reciprocal promise to marry. Restatement, Section 124. Therefore, this provision covers a promise to convey title to a certain farm to one individual if the other individual accepts the proposal of marriage.

Land Contract Provision

The land contract provision covers promises to transfer "any interest in land," which includes any right, privilege, power, or immunity in real property. Restatement, Section 125. Thus, all promises to transfer, buy, or pay for an interest in land, including ownership interests, leases, mortgages, options, and easements, are within the provision.

The land contract provision does not include contracts to transfer an interest in personal property. It also does not cover short-term leases which by statute in most States are those for one year or less, contracts to build a building on a piece of land, contracts to do work on the land, or contracts to insure a building on the land.

An oral contract for the transfer of an interest in land may be enforced if the party seeking enforcement has so changed his position in reasonable reliance upon the contract, that injustice can only be prevented by enforcing the contract. Restatement, Section 129. In applying this **part performance** exception, many States require that the transferee have paid a portion or all of the purchase price *and* either have taken possession of the real estate or have started to make valuable improvements on the land. For example, Aaron orally agrees to sell land to Barbara for $30,000. With Aaron's consent, Barbara takes possession of the land, pays Aaron $10,000, builds a house on the land, and occupies it. Several years later Aaron repudiates the contract. The courts will enforce the contract against Aaron. On the other hand, courts will not enforce the promise unless equity so demands.

An oral promise by a purchaser is also enforceable if the seller fully performs by conveying the property to the purchaser. As previously indicated, however, payment of part or all of the price is not sufficient itself to take the contract outside of the statute.

One-Year Provision

The statute of frauds requires all contracts that **cannot** be fully performed within one year of the making of the contract to be in writing. Restatement, Section 130.

The Possibility Test   The test to determine whether a contract can be performed within a year is whether it is *possible* for its performance to be completed within a year. The **possibility test** is not whether the agreement is likely to be performed within one year from the date it was formed nor whether the parties think that performance will be within the year. The enforceability of the contract does *not* depend on probabilities or on the actuality of subsequent events. For example, an oral contract between Alice and Bill for Alice to build a bridge, which should reasonably take three years, is enforceable if it is possible, although extremely unlikely and difficult, for Alice to perform the contract in one year. Similarly, if Alice agrees to employ Bill for life, the contract is not within the statute of frauds. It is possible that Bill may die within the year, in which case the contract would be completely performed. The contract is therefore one that is *fully performable* within a year. Contracts of indefinite duration are likewise excluded from the provision. *See Price v. Mercury Supply Co., Inc.* On the other hand, an oral contract to employ another person for thirteen months could not possibly be performed within a year and is unenforceable.

Computation of Time   The year runs from the time the *agreement is made,* not from the time when the performance is to begin. For example, on January 1, 1990, A orally hires B to work for eleven months starting on May 1, 1990. That contract will be fully performed on March 31, 1991, which is more than one year after January 1, 1990, the date the contract was made. Consequently, it is *within* the statute of frauds and unenforceable since it is oral.

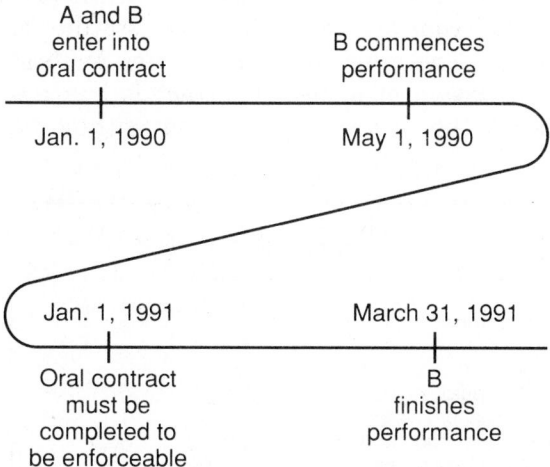

Similarly, a contract for a year's performance which is to begin three days after the date of the making of the contract is within the statute and if oral, is unenforceable. If, however, the performance is to begin the following day or under the terms of the agreement could have begun the following day, it is

not within the statute and need not be in writing, as the one year's performance would be completed on the anniversary date of the making of the contract.

Full Performance by One Party   Where a contract has been fully performed by one party, most courts hold that the promise of the other party is enforceable even though by its terms its performance was not possible within the period of a year. Restatement, Section 130. For example, Vince borrows $4,800 from Julie. Vince orally promises to pay Julie $4,800 in three annual installments of $1,600. Vince's promise is enforceable, notwithstanding the one-year provision because Julie has fully performed by making the loan.

Sales of Goods

The original statute of frauds applied to contracts for the sale of goods and has been used as a prototype for the U.C.C. Article 2 statute of frauds provision. Section 2–201 of the U.C.C. provides that a contract for the sale of goods for the price of **$500 or more** is not enforceable unless there is some writing sufficient to indicate that a contract for sale has been made between the parties. **Goods,** as previously indicated, are defined as movable personal property. Section 2–105(1). The definition expressly includes growing crops and unborn animals.

Admission   The Code permits an oral contract for the sale of goods to be enforced against a party who in his pleading, testimony, or otherwise in court admits that a contract was made, but limits enforcement to the quantity of goods so admitted. Section 2–201(3)(b). The language "otherwise in court" may include pretrial deposition and written interrogatories of the defendant. Some courts are now employing this exception to other statute of frauds provisions.

Specially Manufactured Goods   The Code permits enforcement of an oral contract for goods specially manufactured for the buyer but only if there is evidence indicating that the goods were made for the buyer and the seller can show that he has made a *substantial beginning* of their manufacture prior to receipt of any notice of repudiation. Section 2–201(3)(a). If the goods, although manufactured on special order, are readily marketable in the ordinary course of the seller's business, this exception does not apply.

If Jim brings an action against Robin alleging breach of an oral contract under which Robin agreed to purchase from Jim three million balloons with Robin's trademark imprinted on them at a price of $30,000, the action is not subject to the defense of the statute of frauds unless Robin can show (1) that the balloons are suitable for sale to other buyers, which is highly improbable in view of the trademark, or (2) that notice of repudiation was received by Jim before he had made a substantial start on the production of the balloons or had otherwise substantially committed himself for their procurement.

Delivery or Payment and Acceptance

Prior to the Code, delivery and acceptance of part of the goods or payment of part of the price made enforceable the entire oral contract against the buyer who had received part delivery or against the seller who had received part payment. Under the Code, such "partial performance," validates the contract only for the goods that have been accepted or for which payment has been accepted. Section 2–201(3)(c). To illustrate, Johnson orally agrees to buy 1,000 watches from Barnes for $15,000. Barnes delivers 300 watches to Johnson, who receives and accepts the watches. The oral contract is enforceable to the extent of 300 watches ($4,500)—those received and accepted—but is unenforceable to the extent of 700 watches ($10,500).

But what if the contract is indivisible, such as one for the sale of an automobile, so that if part payment is made there is only a choice between not enforcing the contract or enforcing the contract as a whole? Presently, there is a division of authority on this issue although the better rule appears to be that such part payment and acceptance makes the entire contract enforceable.

Figure 14–1 summarizes the contracts within and the exceptions to the statute of frauds.

Modification or Rescission of Contracts within the Statute of Frauds

Oral contracts modifying previously existing contracts are unenforceable if the resulting contract is within the statute of frauds. The reverse is also true: an oral modification of a prior contract is enforceable if the new contract is not within the

---

Figure 14–1 The Statute of Frauds

Contracts within the Statute of Frauds	Exceptions
Suretyship—a promise to answer for the duty of another	• Main purpose rule • Original promise • Promise made to debtor
Executor-Administrator—a promise to answer personally for debt of decedent	• Main purpose rule • Original promise • Promise made to debtor
Agreements made upon consideration of marriage	• Mutual promises to marry
Agreements for the sale of an interest in land	• Part performance plus detrimental reliance • Seller conveys property
Agreements not to be performed within one year	• Full performance by one party • Possibility of performance within one year
Sale of goods for $500 or more	• Admission • Specially manufactured goods • Delivery or payment and acceptance

statute of frauds. Thus, examples of unenforceable oral contractual modifications include an oral promise to guarantee additional duties of another, an oral agreement to substitute different land for that described in the original contract, and an oral agreement to extend an employee's contract for six months to a total of two years. On the other hand, an oral agreement to modify an employee's contract from two years to six months at a higher salary is not within the statute of frauds and is enforceable.

By extension, an oral rescission is effective and discharges all unperformed duties under the original contract. For example, Linda and Donald enter into a written contract of employment for a two-year term. Later they orally agree to rescind the contract. The oral agreement is effective and the written contract is rescinded. Where, however, land has been transferred, an agreement to rescind the transaction is a contract to retransfer the land and is within the statute of frauds.

Under the U.C.C., the decisive point is the contract price *after* the modification. Section 2–209(3). If the parties enter into an oral contract to sell a motorcycle for $450 to be delivered to the buyer and later, prior to delivery, orally agree that the seller shall paint the motorcycle and install new tires and the buyer shall pay a price of $550, the modified contract is unenforceable. Conversely, if the parties have a written contract for the sale of 200 bushels of wheat at a price of $4.00 per bushel and later orally agree to decrease the quantity to 100 bushels at the same price per bushel, the agreement, as modified, is for a total price of $400 and thus is enforceable.

COMPLIANCE WITH STATUTE OF FRAUDS

Even though a contract is within the statute of frauds, it will be enforced if there is a sufficient *writing* or *memorandum*. The writing need not be in any specific form nor be an attempt by the parties to enter into a binding contract nor represent the entire agreement of the parties. The writing must merely comply with the requirements of the statute of frauds.

General Contracts Provisions

The English statute of frauds and most modern statutes of frauds require that the agreement be in writing to be enforceable. The note or memorandum, which may be formal or informal, must:

1. specify the parties to the contract;

2. specify with reasonable certainty the subject matter and the essential terms of the unperformed promises; and

3. be signed by the party to be charged or by his agent.

The statute's purpose in requiring a writing is to make sure that the parties have entered into a contract. It is, therefore, not necessary that the writing be in existence at the time of the litigation; it is sufficient to show that the memorandum existed at one time.

The memorandum may be a receipt, a check, or a telegram. It may be such that the parties view it as having no legal significance whatever, as for example, a personal letter between the parties, an interdepartmental communication, an advertisement, or the record books of a business. The writing need not have been delivered to the party who seeks to take advantage of it, and it may even contain a repudiation of the oral agreement. For example, Adrian and Joseph enter into an oral agreement that Adrian will sell Blackacre to Joseph for $5,000. Adrian subsequently receives a better offer and sends Joseph a signed letter, which begins by reciting all the material terms of the oral agreement. The letter concludes: "Since my agreement to sell Blackacre to you for $5,000 was oral, I am not bound by my promise. I have since received a better offer and will accept that one." Adrian's letter constitutes a sufficient memorandum for Joseph to enforce Adrian's promise to sell Blackacre. It should be recognized that since Joseph did not sign the memorandum, the writing does not bind Joseph. Thus, a contract may be enforceable against only one of the parties.

The "signature" may be by initials or even typewritten or printed so long as the party intended it to authenticate the writing. Furthermore, the signature need not be at the bottom of the page or at the customary place for a signature.

The memorandum may consist of *several* papers or documents, none of which would be sufficient by itself. The several memoranda, however, must together satisfy all of the requirements of a writing to comply with the statute of frauds and must clearly indicate that they relate to the same transaction. Restatement, Section 132. The latter requirement can be satisfied if (1) the writings are physically attached, (2) the writings refer to each other, or (3) an examination of the writings shows them to be in reference to each other. *See Gittes v. Cook International.*

Sale of Goods

The Article Two statute of frauds provision is more liberal. For a sale of goods, Section 2–201 of the Code requires merely some writing

1. sufficient to indicate that a contract has been made between the parties;

2. to specify the quantity of goods to be sold; and

3. signed by the party against whom enforcement is sought or by her authorized agent or broker.

The writing is sufficient even if it omits or incorrectly states a term agreed upon, but where the quantity term is misstated the contract can be enforced only to the extent of the quantity stated in the writing.

As with general contracts, several related documents may satisfy the writing requirement. Moreover, the signature may be by initials or even typewritten or printed so long as the party intended thereby to authenticate the writing.

In addition, the Code provides relief to a merchant who, within a reasonable period of time after entering into the oral contract, confirms the agreement for the sale of goods by letter or signed writing to the other party if he too is a merchant. As between **merchants,** the **written confirmation,** if sufficient against the sender, is also sufficient against the recipient of the confirmation unless the recipient gives written notice of his objection within ten days after receiving the confirmation. Section 2–201(2). This means that if these requirements have been met, the recipient of the writing is in the same position as if he had signed it, and therefore, it is enforceable against him.

For example, Brown Co. and ATM Industries enter into an oral contract which provides that ATM will deliver one thousand dozen shirts to Brown at $6.00 per shirt. Brown sends a letter to ATM acknowledging the agreement. The letter is signed by Brown's president, containing the quantity term but not the price, and is mailed to ATM's Vice President for sales. Brown is bound by the contract once its authorized agent signed the letter; ATM is bound by the oral contract ten days after receiving the letter if it does not object within that time period. Therefore, as further illustrated by *Thomson Printing Machinery Co. v. B.F. Goodrich Co.,* it is extremely important for merchants to examine their mail carefully and promptly to make certain that any written confirmations conform to their understanding of their outstanding contractual agreements.

EFFECT OF NONCOMPLIANCE

The English statute provided that "no action shall be brought" upon a contract to which the statute of frauds applied *and* which did not comply with its requirements. The Code states that the contract "is not enforceable by way of action or defense." Despite the difference in language the basic legal effect is the same: a contracting party has a defense to an action by the other party for enforcement of an oral contract which is within the statute and does not comply with its requirements. In short, the oral contract is **unenforceable.**

If Tia, a painter, and James, a homeowner, make an oral contract under which James is to give Tia a certain tract of land in return for the painting of his house, the contract is unenforceable under the statute of frauds. It is a contract for the sale of an interest in land. Either party can repudiate and has a defense to an action by the other to enforce the contract.

Full Performance

After *all* the promises of an oral contract have been *performed* by all the parties, the statute of frauds no longer applies. Accordingly, neither party can have the contract set aside on the ground that it should have been in writing. The purpose of the statute is simply to exclude oral evidence of contracts within its provisions, and not to prohibit the performance of oral contracts. Courts, in other words, will not "unscramble" a fully performed contract merely because it was not in writing. In short, the statute applies to executory contracts only.

Restitution

A party to a contract that is unenforceable because of the statute of frauds may have, nonetheless, acted in reliance upon the contract. In such a case the party may recover in restitution the benefits conferred upon the other in relying upon the unenforceable contract. Thus, if Wilton makes an oral contract to furnish services to Rochelle that are not to be performed within a year and Rochelle discharges Wilton after three months, Wilton may recover as restitution the value of the services rendered during the three months. Most courts require that the party seeking restitution not be in default.

Promissory Estoppel

In recent years a number of courts have used the doctrine of promissory estoppel to displace the requirement of a writing. Oral con-

tracts within the statute of frauds have been enforced where the party seeking enforcement has reasonably and foreseeably relied upon a promise in such a way that injustice can only be avoided by enforcement of the promise. Restatement, Section 139. This section is essentially identical to Section 90 of the Restatement, which as discussed in Chapter 11, dispenses with the requirement of consideration, although the comments to Section 139 state that "the requirement of consideration is more easily displaced than the requirement of a writing." The remedy granted is limited as justice requires and depends upon such factors as the availability of other remedies, the foreseeability, reasonableness, and substantiality of the reliance, and the extent to which reliance corroborates evidence of the promise.

The use of promissory estoppel to avoid the writing requirement of the statute of frauds has been less accepted in cases involving the sale of goods. A dispute has arisen among the courts as to whether the "except as otherwise provided in this section" language of the statute of frauds provision (Section 2–201) precludes the application of the equitable doctrine of promissory estoppel. Some courts have been persuaded by this argument, while others have concluded that promissory estoppel is applicable to sales of goods.

PAROL EVIDENCE RULE

A contract reduced to writing and signed by the parties is frequently the result of many conversations, conferences, proposals, counterproposals, letters, and memoranda and sometimes is the product of negotiations conducted, or partly conducted, by agents of the parties. At some stage in the negotiations tentative agreements may have been reached on a certain point or points that were superseded (or so regarded by one of the parties) by subsequent negotiations. Offers may have been made and withdrawn, either expressly or by implication, or lost sight of in the give-and-take of negotiations. Ultimately a final draft of the written contract is prepared and signed by the parties. It may or may not include all of the points that were discussed and agreed upon in the course of the negotiations. By signing the agreement, however, the parties have declared it to be their contract, and the terms as contained in it represent the contract they have made. As a rule of substantive law, neither party is later permitted to show that the contract they made is different from the terms and provisions that appear in the written agreement. This rule is called the parol evidence rule.

THE RULE

When a contract is expressed in a writing that is intended to be the complete and final expression of the rights and duties of the parties, parol evidence of **prior** oral or written negotiations or agreements of the parties, or their **contemporaneous** oral agreements that **vary** or **change** the written contract, are not admissible. The word *parol* means literally "speech" or "words." The term **parol evidence** refers to any evidence, whether oral or in writing, which is outside the written contract and not incorporated into the contract either directly or by reference.

The parol evidence rule applies only to an **integrated** contract; that is, one in which the parties have assented to a certain writing or writings as the statement of the *complete* agreement or contract between them. When there is such an integration of a contract, parol evidence of any prior or contemporaneous agreement will not be permitted to vary, change, alter, or modify any of the terms or provisions of the written contract. Restatement, Section 213.

A writing may contain a **merger clause,** which states that the writing is intended to be the complete and final expression of the agreement between the parties. Most courts consider a merger clause to be conclusive proof of an integration, while a few courts view a merger clause as only evidence of an integration.

The reason for the parol evidence rule is that the parties, by reducing their entire agreement to writing, are regarded as having intended the writing that they signed to include the whole of their agreement. The terms and provisions contained in the writing are there because the parties intended them to be in their contract. Any provision not in the writing is regarded as having been omitted because the parties intended that it should not be a part of their contract. The rule excluding evidence that would tend to change, alter, vary, or modify the terms of the written agreement safeguards the contract as made by the parties. *See Continental Life & Acc. Co. v. Songer.* The rule applies to all integrated written contracts and deals with what terms are part of the contract. The rule differs from the statute of frauds, which governs what contracts must be in writing to be enforceable.

SITUATIONS TO WHICH THE RULE DOES NOT APPLY

The parol evidence rule, in spite of its name, is not an exclusionary rule of evidence, nor is it a rule of construction or interpretation. It is a rule of substantive law that defines the limits of a contract. Bearing this in mind, as well as the reason underlying the rule, it will be readily understood that the rule does **not** apply to any of the following:

1. A contract that is *partly written* and partly oral; that is, the parties do not intend the writing to be their entire agreement.

2. A clerical or *typographical error* that obviously does not represent the agreement of the parties. Where a written contract for the services of a skilled mining engineer provides that his rate of compensation be $7.00 per day, a court of equity would permit reformation (correction) of the contract to correct the mistake upon a showing that both parties intended the rate to be $700 per day.

3. The lack of *contractual capacity* of one of the parties, such as proof of minority, intoxication, or mental incompetency. Such evidence would not tend to vary, change, or alter any of the terms of the written agreement, but rather would show that the written agreement was voidable or void.

4. A *defense* of fraud, misrepresentation, duress, undue influence, mistake, illegality, or unconscionability. Evidence establishing any of these defenses would not purport to vary, change, or alter any of the terms of the written agreement, but rather would show such agreement to be voidable, void, or unenforceable.

5. A *condition precedent* agreed upon orally at the time of the execution of the written agreement and to which the entire agreement was made subject. Such evidence does not tend to vary, alter, or change any of the terms of the agreement, but rather shows whether the entire written agreement, unchanged and unaltered, ever became effective. For example, if John signs a subscription agreement to buy stock in a corporation to be formed and delivers it to Thompson with the mutual understanding that the agreement is not to be binding unless the other financially responsible persons shall each agree to buy at least an equivalent amount of such stock, John is permitted to show by parol evidence this condition.

6. A *subsequent mutual rescission or modification* of the written contract. Parol evidence of a later agreement does not tend to show that the integrated writing did not represent the contract between the parties at the time it was made. Parties to an existing contract, whether written or oral, may agree to change the terms of their contract as they see fit, or to cancel it completely, if they so desire.

7. Parol evidence is admissible to explain *ambiguous* terms in the contract. To enforce a contract, it is necessary to understand its intended meaning. Such interpretation is not to alter, change, or vary the terms of the contract.

SUPPLEMENTAL EVIDENCE

Although a written agreement may not be contradicted by evidence of a prior agreement or of a contemporaneous agreement, under the Restatement, Section 216, and the Code, Section 2–202, a written contract may be explained or supplemented by (1) course of deal-

ing between the parties, (2) usage of trade, (3) course of performance, or (4) evidence of consistent additional terms unless the writing was intended by the parties as a complete and exclusive statement of their agreement.

A **course of dealing** is a sequence of previous conduct between the parties to an agreement that may be fairly regarded as establishing a common basis of understanding for interpreting their expressions and other conduct.

A **usage of trade** is a practice or method of dealing, regularly observed and followed in a place, vocation, or trade.

Course of performance refers to the manner and extent to which the respective parties to a contract have accepted successive tenders of performance by the other party without objection.

The Restatement and the Code permit *supplemental consistent evidence* to be introduced into a court proceeding. Such evidence is admissible only if it does not contradict a term or terms of the original agreement and would probably not have been included in the original contract.

Figure 14–2 illustrates the parol evidence rule.

INTERPRETATION OF CONTRACTS

Although the written words or language in which the parties embodied their agreement or contract may not be changed by parol evidence, the ascertainment (determination) of the meaning to be given to the written language is outside the scope of the parol evidence rule. The written words embody the terms of the contract. Words are but symbols, however. If their meaning is not clear, it may be made clear by the application of rules of interpretation or construction and by the use of extrinsic (external) evidence for this purpose where necessary.

The Restatement, Section 200, defines **interpretation** as the ascertainment of the meaning of a promise or agreement or a term of the promise or agreement. Where the language in a contract is clear and unambiguous, extrinsic evidence tending to show a meaning different from that which the words clearly convey will not be accepted by a court. It is the function of the court to interpret and construe written contracts and documents. The court adopts rules of interpretation to apply a legal standard to the words contained in the agreement by which to determine their sense or meaning. Among the rules that aid interpretation are the following:

1. Words and other conduct are interpreted in the light of all the circumstances, and if the principal purpose of the parties is ascertainable, it is given great weight.

2. A writing is interpreted as a whole, and all writings that are part of the same transaction are interpreted together.

3. Unless a different intention is manifested, where language has a commonly accepted meaning, it is interpreted in accordance with that meaning.

Figure 14–2 Parol Evidence Rule

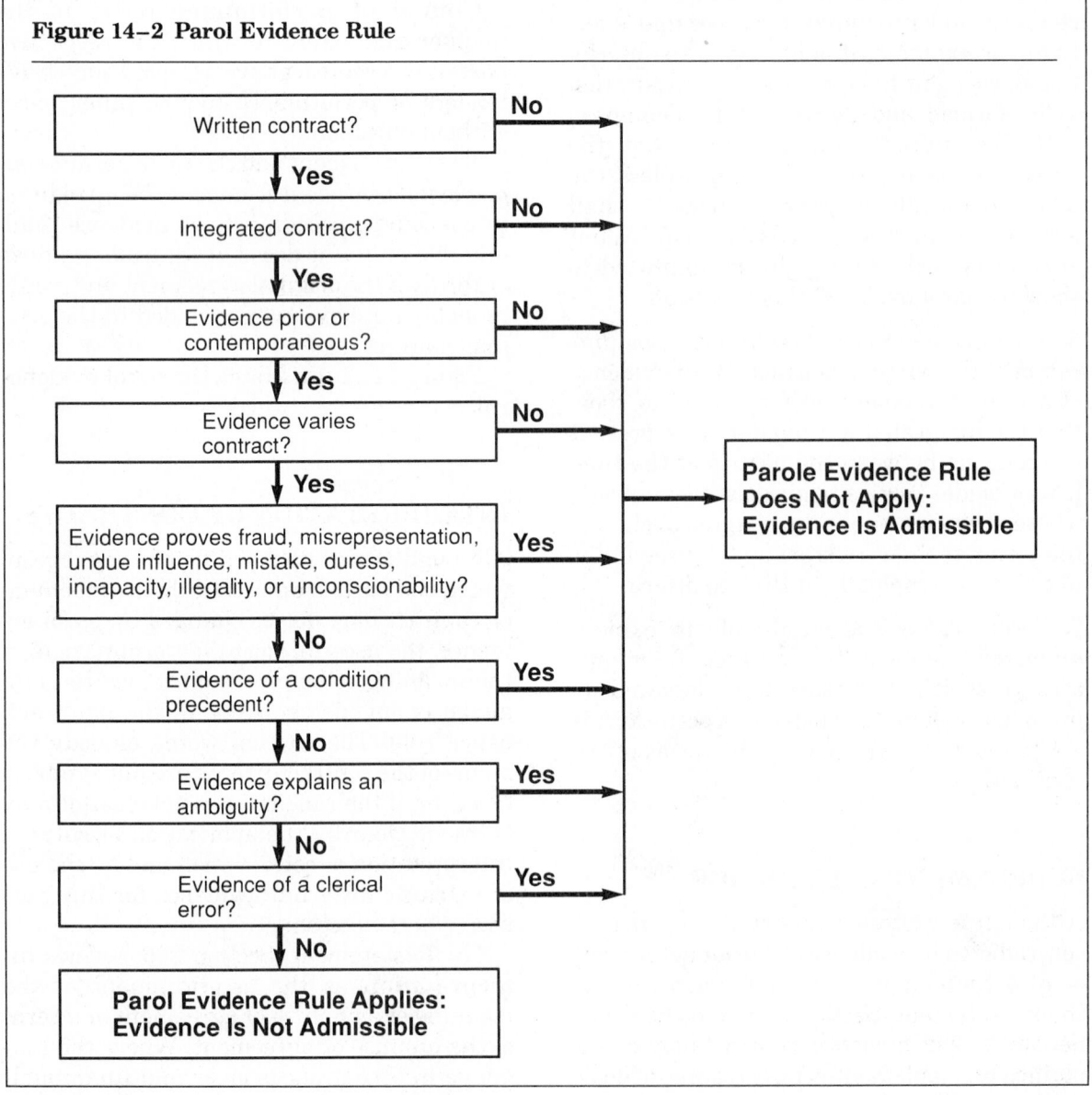

4. Unless a different intention is manifested, technical terms and words of art are given their technical meanings.

5. Wherever reasonable, the manifestations of intention of the parties to a promise or agreement are interpreted as consistent with each other and with any relevant course of performance, course of dealing, or usage of trade.

6. An interpretation that gives a reasonable, lawful, and effective meaning to all the terms is preferred to an interpretation that leaves a part unreasonable, unlawful, or of no effect.

7. Specific terms and exact terms are given greater weight than general language.

8. Separately negotiated or added terms are given greater weight than standardized terms or other terms not separately negotiated.

9. Express terms, course of performance, course of dealing, and usage of trade are weighted in that order.

10. Where a term or promise has several possible meanings, it will be interpreted against the party who supplied the contract or the term. Restatement, Sections 201, 202, and 203.

Through the application of the parol evidence rule, where it is properly applicable, and the above rules of interpretation and construction, it may be observed that the law not only enforces a contract but in doing so exercises great care that the contract being enforced is the one the parties made and that the sense and meaning of the intentions of the parties are carefully ascertained and given effect.

CASES

Suretyship Provision

SHANE QUADRI v. GOODYEAR SERVICE STORES

Court of Appeals of Indiana, Third District, 1980.
412 N.E.2d 315.

HOFFMAN, J.

[The defendant, Shane Quadri, contacted Don Hoffman, employee of defendant Al J. Hoffman & Co., to procure car insurance. Later, Quadri's car was stolen on October 25 or 26, 1977. Quadri contacted Hoffman who arranged with Budget Rent-a-Car, a plaintiff in this case, for a rental car for Quadri until his car was recovered. Hoffman authorized Budget Rent-a-Car to bill the Hoffman Agency. Later, when the stolen car was recovered, Hoffman telephoned plaintiff, Goodyear, and arranged to have four new tires put on Quadri's car to replace those damaged during the theft. The plaintiffs (Budget and Goodyear) sued the defendants (Quadri and Hoff-

man) for payment for the car rental and tires, respectively.]

* * *

The Hoffman Agency's liability must be based on Don Hoffman's oral promises. The Hoffman Agency asserts that these promises are promises to pay the debts of Shane Quadri and are therefore made unenforceable by the Statute of Frauds. [Citation.]

The Hoffman Agency is correct in the theoretical statement of the law but errs in its application in this case. Although the statute makes unenforceable contracts to pay the debts of a third person, it does not affect the enforceability of oral contracts between two parties for the benefit of a third party. [Citation.] The statute therefore does not apply to original promises to pay for services rendered to a third person. [Citation.] The evidence in the present case is clear that Don Hoffman made original promises to both Budget and Goodyear that the Hoffman Agency would pay for goods and services rendered to Quadri.

* * *

The evidence discloses that Don Hoffman initiated the transactions with both Goodyear and Budget through a telephone call. Hoffman indicated that Quadri was insured and authorized the billing of the Hoffman Agency. Hoffman also gave both Goodyear and Budget a claim number to use in their records. Quadri merely went to Goodyear and Budget to obtain the benefits as negotiated by Hoffman. Although Quadri's signature appears on the Budget rental agreement and the Goodyear invoice, both documents indicate that Don Hoffman authorized the transaction. Based on this evidence it cannot be said that the trial court erred in determining that credit was extended solely to the Hoffman Agency. Don Hoffman's oral promises are not within the Statute of Frauds.

* * *

[Judgment of the trial court in favor of Budget and Goodyear against Hoffman and in favor of Quadri affirmed.]

Main Purpose Doctrine

STUART STUDIO, INC. v. NATIONAL SCHOOL OF HEAVY EQUIPMENT, INC.

Court of Appeals of North Carolina, 1975.
25 N.C.App. 544, 214 S.E.2d 192.

CLARK, J.

In this action plaintiff seeks to recover from the defendant, National School of Heavy Equipment, Inc., (hereafter School), and the individual defendants the sum of $18,010.02 under a contract whereby it produced catalogues for use by the School in promoting its services. The School has been adjudged a bankrupt corporation, and plaintiff has obtained a judgment against the School in the sum claimed, plus interest. By amended complaint plaintiff seeks to recover from individual defendant, Gilbert S. Shaw, the sum of $17,828.02 for purchasing and supervising the printing of the catalogues, claiming that

Shaw promised, when the contract was made on 6 March 1972, to stand behind or guarantee payment.

It was stipulated that all work pursuant to the contract was completed and catalogues delivered to and accepted by the School on 7 July 1972.

It appeared from the evidence that Gilbert S. Shaw was Chairman of the Board of Directors of the School and drew a salary of $2,000 per month. He held 100% of the voting stock and 49% of the Class B stock of the School; he employed various members of his family in the operation of the School, including his son, Donald T. Shaw, as President.

Plaintiff is an art studio. Its president, Keith Stuart, had a conversation with Gilbert Shaw and Donald Shaw in August 1971, about the preparation of a new catalogue for the School, and in September 1971, all agreed that plaintiff was to produce the camera-ready art for the catalogue. Plaintiff completed this work and the School accepted the format. There was a discussion between Stuart and the Shaws about the printing. Plaintiff does not do printing but in some cases purchased the printing for its clients. In a meeting on 6 March 1972, when the camera-ready art work was virtually finished, Gilbert Shaw requested Stuart to purchase and supervise the printing of 25,000 catalogues. They discussed payment of printing costs, and Gilbert Shaw told Stuart that payment would be made within ten days after billing and that if the *National School could not pay the full total that he would stand good for the entire bill.*

Plaintiff then contracted in its name for the printing. The School made an advance payment of $2,000 to plaintiff on 23 March 1972. Plaintiff delivered the catalogues to the School on 7 July 1972 with its invoice. To requests for payment thereafter, Donald T. Shaw, Gilbert S. Shaw being overseas, replied that the School did not have the money but expected to get it.

At the completion of plaintiff's evidence, the individual defendants moved for directed verdicts, and from judgment granting the motions, the plaintiff appeals. It appears from the amended complaint, filed after entry of judgment, that plaintiff has elected to proceed only against the individual defendant, Gilbert S. Shaw.

* * *

The North Carolina Statute of Frauds, a substantial prototype of the historic English statute [citation] contains the provision that "no action shall be brought . . . upon a special promise to answer the debt . . . of another person, unless the agreement upon which such action shall be brought, or some memorandum or note thereof, shall be in writing, and signed by the party charged therewith or some other person thereunto by him lawfully authorized." [Citations.]

The promise of Gilbert S. Shaw to stand good for the debt of National School of Heavy Equipment, Inc., to be incurred for the printing of catalogues was not in writing and was within the Statute of Frauds unless plaintiff has offered evidence to invoke the application of the "main purpose rule," which is a well-known exception to the rule requiring that such promises be evidenced by a written memorandum.

The "main purpose rule" is . . . as follows:

. . . [W]henever the main purpose and object of the promisor is not to answer for another, but to subserve some pecuniary or business purpose of his own, involving either a benefit to himself, or damage to the other contracting party, his promise is not within the statute, although it may be in form a promise to pay the debt of another, and although the performance of it may incidentally have the effect of extinguishing that liability.

* * *

Shaw's personal and pecuniary interest in the transaction was evident; he was the founder of the School, owned 100% of the Class A voting stock and 49% of the Class B stock, was Chairman of the Board of Directors, and as an officer drew a monthly salary of $2,000. At this time, 6 March 1972, it is reasonable to assume that the School was facing financial difficulty; Shaw personally advanced $12,000 to the School during this period of financial distress. The School went into receivership in December 1972, and bankruptcy in March 1973. Apparently, Shaw sought, in a final effort to avoid the School's financial ruin, to attract new students through an advertising campaign, which included the production and circulation of new catalogues.

Burlington Industries v. Foil [citation] a 1974 decision, culminates a line of cases which have developed the "main purpose rule" and prescribed its limitations. The *Foil* case holds that the benefit accruing to a party merely by virtue of his position as a stockholder, officer, or director is not alone such personal, immediate, and pecuniary benefit as to invoke the main purpose rule, and that Foil's evidence failed to establish the required *direct interest* on the part of Foil.

In *Foil*, the court cited with approval the cases of *May v. Haynes*, [citation] and *Warren v. White*, [citation]. In *Warren v. White*, defendant promisor was the principal investor and owned most of the capital stock, and during a period of financial difficulty advanced in excess of $23,000 to the corporation. In *May v. Haynes*, the defendant and his wife owned the entire capital stock of the corporation, and he was its president, managing officer, and controlling stockholder. In both of these cases it was held that the evidence was sufficient to invoke the main purpose rule and in doing so it is obvious that the significant, if not controlling, factor was the extent of the promisor's control over the corporation.

In this case the evidence offered by the plaintiff tends to show that Gilbert S. Shaw had a personal and direct interest in the School; and the evidence is clearly sufficient to raise an issue for jury determination. We find that the trial court improvidently granted defendant's motion for directed verdict and the judgment is modified and the cause remanded for trial on the issue of the liability of Gilbert S. Shaw on the printing contract of 6 March 1972.

Modified and Remanded.

One-Year Provision

PRICE v. MERCURY SUPPLY CO., INC.

Court of Appeals of Tennessee, 1984.
682 S.W.2d 924.

Koch, J.

Mr. Richard P. Price was discharged from his position as vice president in charge of sales for Mercury Supply Company, Inc. He filed this action against his former employers alleging breach of an oral employment contract. * * * [T]he Chancery Court. . . granted the defendants' motion for a summary judgment. * * * This appeal follows. For the reasons stated herein, we hold that the defendants were entitled to a summary judgment based upon the undisputed facts presented in this record.

* * *

For many years prior to 1970, Mr. Leonard Weil operated a business known as Mercury Supply Company. This business sold cleaning materials and janitorial supplies in the Nashville and Middle Tennessee area. Mr. Weil had complete charge of the business, although his wife was a nominal partner.

In July, 1970, Mr. Price applied for and obtained a job as a salesman with Mercury Supply Company. On July 6, 1970, Mr. Price and Mr. Weil signed a written employment contract of indefinite duration which could be cancelled by either party for any reason upon fifteen days notice. Under this contract, Mr. Price was employed as a salesman, and his compensation consisted of a straight weekly salary as well as a commission based on the sales he actually made. This contract specifically provided that Mr. Price's compensation could be altered from time to time without affecting the validity of the rest of the contract.

The company prospered during the years immediately after 1970. * * * In accordance with the contract, Mr. Price received annual salary increases in recognition of his performance.

In August, 1972, Mr. Price was given the title of sales coordinator. While he was still acting as a salesman, he also took on the responsibility to hire and train other salesmen.

Later, in 1973, Mr. Price's title was changed to sales manager. His duties were still the same as they had been when he was the company's sales coordinator. Again, as permitted by the 1970 employment contract, the basis for Mr. Price's salary was changed so that in addition to his weekly salary and commissions based upon his personal sales, Mr. Price was entitled to receive an annual bonus based upon the company's annual profits as contained in the annual profit and loss statement. On June 30, 1974, Mr. Price received his first such bonus.

* * *

In March, 1975, Mr. Price's title was changed to vice president for sales. There was no change in his compensation at that time. His duties remained the same as they had been when he was sales manager and sales coordinator.

* * *

[In 1977] both parties agree that they were experiencing difficulties. Mr. Weil went so far as to hire an industrial psychologist to help resolve these problems. In September, 1978, in the presence of this psychologist, Mr. Weil told Mr. Price that his performance was not satisfactory and gave him an ultimatum that if the situation did not improve, Mr. Price would be discharged.

The relationship between the two did not improve. Following a disagreement in February, 1981, concerning the manner in which Mr. Price conducted a sales meeting, Mr. Weil called Mr. Price into his office on March 2, 1981, and discharged him. * * *

The linchpin of Mr. Price's entire claim is his assertion that on March 5, 1975, the parties entered into a valid oral employment contract wherein Mr. Price was hired as the vice president for sales of Mercury Supply Company for the rest of his life or until he retired. If this contract is found not to exist or to be unenforceable, then Mr. Price has no basis for relief because as an employee-at-will, he could be discharged at any time for any reason upon receiving fifteen days notice.

After reviewing the proof, the trial court found that the oral contract allegedly entered into on March 5, 1975 was barred by . . . the provision of Tennessee's statute of frauds providing that no action shall be brought on a contract "which is not to be performed within the space of one (1) year from the making thereof" unless the contract itself is in writing and signed by the party to be charged. Relying upon [citation], the trial court found that the oral employment contract was unenforceable because Mr. Price's retirement would take place beyond one year from the making of the contract.

We disagree with the trial court's legal conclusion in this regard.

A defense predicated upon the statute of frauds must, of necessity, presume that the parties had an agreement but that [statute of frauds] renders this agreement unenforceable because it is one of those species of agreements required to be in writing: Tennessee's version of the statute of frauds, [citation.], was originally enacted in 1801. Like those existing in all other states except Louisiana, Tennessee's statute of frauds is patterned after the English Statute of Frauds and Perjuries enacted in 1677. Its purpose is to prevent frauds based upon oral testimony and to deter the formation of contracts based upon loose statements or innuendoes long after witnesses have become unavailable or when memories of the precise agreement have been dimmed by the passage of time. [Citations.]

The portion of the statute of frauds at issue in this case, [citation] which proscribes oral contracts not to be performed in one year from the time they are made is generally referred to as the *infra annum* provision. Of all the provisions of the statute of frauds, it is generally construed very narrowly by the courts, [citation], because courts generally attempt to give effect to contracts rather than defeating them. Accordingly, our courts have declined to construe a contract to require performance over more than one year if to do so would render the contract unenforceable because of the statute of frauds. [Citation.]

* * * It is now well-settled that the determination concerning whether a particular agreement is included within the statute of frauds depends upon the terms of the agreement itself and the intentions of the parties at the precise moment the contract is made. [Citations.]

* * *

The Tennessee Supreme Court has specifically held that an oral employment contract for an unspecified term is not subject to the statute of frauds because it is capable of complete, *bona fide* performance within one year of its making should the employee die within that time. [Citations.] * * *

This is in accord with the view expressed by most courts and commentators. Succinctly stated, the majority rule is that an oral employment contract for an indefinite term that can be terminated at any time at the will of the parties is not within the statute of frauds because it is capable of being fully performed within one year either through the employee's death or by either party's decision to terminate the contract. [Citations.]

When the disputed facts in this case are viewed in light of these precedents, it is clear that any oral contract between Mr. Price and Mercury Supply Company, if indeed there is a contract, would not be barred by the statute of frauds. Mr. Price himself stated that the term of this contract would be for life or until he decided to retire. Thus, it could be performed within one year because Mr. Price could have died or could have elected to retire within a year after the alleged contract was made. The fact that neither contingency occurred is not sufficient to bring the agreement within [the statute of frauds].

However, even if Mr. Price is able to avoid the statute of frauds, he will not necessarily be able to recover for a breach of contract unless he can show that a contract existed. The normal rules of contracts must still apply even if an agreement does not come within the statute of frauds. [Citation.]

* * *

Thus, even if this Court were to agree with Mr. Price's premise that an oral contract was formed on March 5, 1975, the undisputed facts in this record require the legal conclusion that this contract was not breached when Mr. Price was discharged because he was an employee-at-will. Thus, the defendants could discharge Mr. Price at any time without breaching the contract.

A Writing or Memorandum

GITTES v. COOK INTERNATIONAL

United States District Court, S.D. New York, 1984.
598 F.Supp. 717.

KREM, J.

* * *

Plaintiff Enrique Foster Gittes ("Gittes") is a businessman and financial consultant. In 1981, his services as a consultant were retained by an English company, NNC [sic] Energy plc ("NCC"), of which he was also a director. NCC's principal business was as a holding company, investing its capital in other businesses in return for a stake in those businesses. Gittes' activities for NCC were not made clear at trial; however, NCC believed his services to be useful and worthwhile, and compensated him at the rate of $100,000 per year for his consultancy work.

One of NCC's investments was a substantial holding of the shares of an American company, Simplicity Pattern Co. ("Simplicity"). For reasons which are not relevant here, Gittes' contract to perform consulting services for NCC was assigned to Simplicity. Prior to that assignment, Gittes was elected to the Board of Directors of Simplicity. It is this dual relationship between Gittes and Simplicity which led to this lawsuit.

In April, 1982, NCC found itself in difficult financial condition and decided to sell its holdings in Simplicity as a means of realizing badly needed cash. To that end, NCC began a search for a purchaser of the Simplicity shares, in which search Gittes was an active participant. The search led to offers to buy from at least two sources, one in New York and one in Europe. NCC apparently decided to accept the offer from the New York purchaser, while holding the European offer in reserve in the event the New York purchaser withdrew or otherwise failed to close the sale.

The sale by NCC of its Simplicity stock apparently made more urgent shortly before the agreement to sell the shares was to be consummated, by the threat of various financial sources to call outstanding debt, thereby forcing NCC into receivership. On May 7, 1982, the sale of the shares to the New York purchaser was scheduled to take place in the offices of the law firm Debevoise & Plimpton. Gittes and the individual defendant, Edward W. Cook, arrived together. At some point after the closing began, it came to Gittes' attention that the purchaser apparently required the resignation of the four directors of Simplicity who had been elected by NCC as a shareholder of Simplicity. These directors included Gittes and three other directors of NCC; of the four, only Gittes had failed to tender his resignation prior to the closing. Apparently, in fact, only Gittes had not been informed that these resignations were considered a necessary prerequisite to consummation of the purchase of the shares by the New York purchaser. When informed of this fact, Gittes initially flatly refused to tender his resignation from the Simplicity board. * * *

Gittes' refusal to resign created serious problems, jeopardizing the closing. Clearly, some accommodation needed to be made, and eventually one was agreed upon; Gittes would resign from his position on the Simplicity board and his consultancy with Simplicity in return for a five year, $50,000 per year, consultancy contract with Cook International, Inc. ("Cook International"). Cook International, headed by Edward W. Cook and the largest shareholder of NCC, stood to be the greatest loser if the sale of the Simplicity shares failed to occur and resulted in NCC's going into receivership. Cook International, through its chairman Edward W. Cook, offered to employ Gittes as a financial consultant, an offer which Gittes accepted. Subsequently, however, Gittes was given no responsibilities and was never paid, and on October 12, 1982, Cook International repudiated the contract by letter to Gittes. Shortly thereafter, Gittes commenced this action.

* * *

The issues in this case tend to overlap. Plaintiff claims that Cook's offer to employ him as a consultant was accepted by him and was sufficiently definite to constitute a contract. Defendants, in response, claim that any alleged contract based on the undisputed facts fails to satisfy the Statute of Frauds because it was never reduced to a writing signed by the party to be charged. * * * In reply, plaintiff points to several subsequent writings issuing from defendants in which reference is made to the consultancy agreement between Cook International and Gittes, and that these writings satisfy the Statute of Frauds.

* * *

The agreement in question here falls within the [statute of frauds] since it was "not to be performed within one year [of its] making." From this conclusion the issue becomes whether there was a sufficient writing or memorandum of the agreement and whether it was subscribed by the party to be charged.

Both parties agree that, notwithstanding Cook's assent to Gittes' suggestion that the agreement be reduced to a written contract, and Gittes' submission to Cook of a form consulting contract, there was never executed a document which would serve as a formal agreement between the parties. This fact is only the beginning of the inquiry, however. As case law demonstrates, several writings other than a formal contract can suffice to satisfy the requirement of the Statute of Frauds. In the instant case, plaintiff proposes that at least two other writings promulgated by the defendant fill this requirement: a Prospectus issued by Cook International, the text of which was approved by Cook and refers to Cook's agreement to employ Gittes as a consultant for five years at an annual compensation of $50,000 per year; and a memorandum signed by Cook which contains substantially the same terms and states flatly that Cook agreed to them as a necessary condition to Gittes' resignation from the Simplicity Board of Directors. Defendant contends that these documents do not satisfy the threshold requirements of the New York Statute of Frauds, that a writing must contain the essential terms of the agreement.

"The concept of essentiality is relative. A term is 'essential,' and must thus appear in the 'memorandum,' if it seriously affects the rights and obligations of the parties and there is a significant evidentiary dispute as to its content." [Citations.] In the instant case, the writings each contain the duration of the agreement (five years) and the annual compensation (fifty thousand dollars). The Cook International Prospectus makes further reference to employment of Gittes "as a consultant to Cook . . ." Two of these terms, duration and compensation, are essential within the requirements of the Statute of Frauds because they seriously affect the rights and obligations of the parties.

* * * The defendants do, however, take issue with whether the nature of the plaintiff's duties under the alleged contract are an essential term and if so whether those duties are adequately described or are sufficiently determinable by reference to existing external facts as to eliminate any significant evidentiary dispute as to that term of the contract.

Plaintiff argues that his duties under the agreement are not essential terms of a contract within the context of this lawsuit because the significant evidentiary issue is not whether plaintiff performed adequately but rather whether the parties were obligated to perform at all. This argument is well taken and I hold that plaintiff's duties are not an essential term and therefore need not be reduced to writing.

Furthermore, were the nature of plaintiff's duties properly before this Court, it appears from the aforementioned writings and a third document introduced at trial that both parties had a clear idea as to plaintiff's skills and abilities and the work for which he held himself out as equipped. * * * In sum, then, there are no missing material terms from the writings memorializing the agreement in question. The writings are either subscribed to or signed by the parties to be charges, to wit, Edward Cook, individually and Cook International, Inc., by Edward Cook, its chairman. The agreement therefore satisfies the Statute of Frauds.

* * *

Written Confirmation

THOMSON PRINTING MACHINERY CO. v. B.F. GOODRICH CO.

United States Court of Appeals, Seventh Circuit, 1983.
714 F.2d 744.

CUDAHY, J.

Appellant Thomson Printing Company ("Thomson Printing") won a jury verdict in its suit for breach of contract against appellee B.F. Goodrich Company ("Goodrich"). The district court concluded, however, that as a matter of law the contract could not be enforced against Goodrich because it was an oral contract, the Statute of Frauds applied and the Statute was not satisfied. Because we conclude that the contract was enforceable on the basis of the "merchants" exception to the Statute of Frauds, we reverse.

Thomson Printing buys and sells used printing machinery. On Tuesday, April 10, 1979, the president of Thomson Printing, James Thomson, went to Goodrich's surplus machinery department in Akron, Ohio to look at some used printing machinery which was for sale. James Thomson discussed the sale terms, including a price of $9,000, with Goodrich's surplus equipment manager, Ingram Meyers. Four days later, on Saturday, April 14, 1979, James Thomson sent to Goodrich in Akron a purchase order for the equipment and a check for $1,000 in part payment.

Thomson Printing sued Goodrich when Goodrich refused to perform. Goodrich asserted by way of defense that no contract had been formed and that in any event the alleged oral contract was unenforceable due to the Statute of Frauds. . . .

A modern exception to the usual writing requirement is the "merchants" exception to the Uniform Commercial Code (U.C.C. § 2–201(2)), which provides:

Between merchants if within a reasonable time a writing in confirmation of the contract and sufficient against the sender is received and the party receiving it has reason to know its contents, it satisfies the |writing requirement| against such party unless written notice of objection to its contents is given within 10 days after it is received.

We must emphasize that the only effect of this exception is to take away from a merchant who receives a writing in confirmation of a contract the Statute of Frauds defense if the merchant does not object. The sender must still persuade the trier of fact that a contract was in fact made orally, to which the written confirmation applies.

In the instant case, James Thomson sent a "writing in confirmation" to Goodrich four days after his meeting with Ingram Meyers, a Goodrich employee and agent. The purchase order contained Thomson Printing's name, address, telephone number and certain information about the machinery purchase. . . .

Goodrich argues, however, that Thomson's writing in confirmation cannot qualify for the 2–201(2) exception because it was not received by anyone at Goodrich who had reason to know its contents. Goodrich claims that Thomson erred in not specifically designating on the envelope, check or purchase order that the items were intended for Ingram Meyers or the surplus equipment department. Consequently, Goodrich contends, it was unable to "find a home" for the check and purchase order despite attempts to do so, in accordance with its regular procedures, by sending copies of the documents to several of its various divisions. Ingram Meyers testified that he never learned of the purchase order until weeks later when James Thomson called to arrange for removal of the machines. By then, however, the machines had long been sold to someone else.

We think Goodrich misreads the requirements of 2–201(2). First, the literal requirements of 2–201(2), as they apply here, are that a writing "is received" and that Goodrich "has reason to know its contents." There is no dispute that the purchase order and check were received by Goodrich, and there is at least no specific or express requirement that the "receipt" referred to in 2–201(2) be by any Goodrich agent in particular.

These issues are not resolved by [2–201(2)], but it is probably a reasonable projection that a delivery at either the recipient's principal place of business, a place of business from which negotiations were conducted, or to which the sender may have transmitted previous communications, will be an adequate receipt. [Citation.]

* * *

Even if we go beyond the literal requirements of 2–201(2) and read into the "receipt" requirement the "receipt of notice" rule of 1–201(27), we still think Thomson Printing satisfied the "merchants" exception. Section 1–201, the definitional section of the U.C.C., provides that notice received by an organization

is effective for a particular transaction . . . from the time when it would have been brought to [the attention of the individual conducting that transaction] if the organization had executed *due diligence.*

U.C.C. § 1–201(27) (emphasis supplied). The Official Comment states:

reason to know, knowledge, or a notification, although "received" for instance by a clerk in Department A of an organization, is effective for a transaction conducted in Department B only from the time when it was *or should have been* communicated to the individual conducting that transaction.

U.C.C. § 1–201(27), Official Comment.

Thus, the question comes down to whether Goodrich's mailroom, given the information it had, should have notified the surplus equipment manager, Ingram Meyers, of Thomson's confirmatory writing. At whatever point Meyers should have been so notified, then at that point Thomson's writing was effective even though Meyers did not see it. [Citations.]

The definitional section of the U.C.C. also sets the general standard for what mailrooms "should do":

An organization exercised due diligence if it maintains reasonable routines for communicating significant information to the person conducting the transaction and there is reasonable compliance with the routines.

U.C.C. § 1–201(27). One cannot say that Goodrich's mailroom procedures were reasonable as a matter of law: if Goodrich had exercised due diligence in handling Thomson Printing's purchase order and check, these items would have reasonably promptly come to Ingram Meyers' attention. First, the purchase order on its face should have alerted the mailroom that the documents referred to a purchase of used printing equipment. Since Goodrich had only one surplus machinery department, the documents "home" should not have been difficult to find. Second, even if the mailroom would have had difficulty in immediately identifying the kind of transaction involved, the purchase order had Thomson Printing's phone number printed on it and we think a "reasonable routine" in these particular circumstances would have involved at some point in the process a simple phone call to Thomson Printing. Thus, we think Goodrich's mailroom mishandled the confirmatory writings. This failure should not permit Goodrich to escape liability by pleading nonreceipt. [Citations.]

* * *

The district court's order granting judgment for Goodrich is reversed and the cause is remanded for further proceedings consistent with this opinion.

Reversed and Remanded.

Parol Evidence

CONTINENTAL LIFE & ACC. CO. v. SONGER

Court of Appeals of Arizona, 1979.
124 Ariz. 294, 603 P.2d 921.

CONTRERAS, J.

This appeal and cross-appeal present a substantial number of issues concerning the legal remedies available to a medical insurance applicant whose injury occurs prior to the date the application is either accepted or rejected by the insurance company's home office. The issues arose out of an action brought by appellees and cross-appellants David and Nancy Songer (Songers) against appellant and cross-appellee Continental Life and Accident Company (Continental), two other insurance companies, and two insurance agents. The action involves an effort to recover damages including benefits allegedly due under a medical insurance policy.

* * *

With the exception of the testimony concerning a "binder", the facts giving rise to the Songers' action are not in substantial dispute. In the summer of 1973, the Songers were planning an extended visit to the Island of Ponape. Anticipating difficulties they might encounter in procuring insurance coverage once they left the States, the Songers wanted to obtain medical insurance before departure which would cover them on their trip. With these thoughts in mind, on August 6, 1973, they discussed major medical coverage with insurance agents, including an agent of Continental, and began to fill out an application. In the course of filling out the application, Nancy Songer mentioned that she had been advised by one of her physicians that she had an "innocent" heart murmur. Arrangements were made for her to have a medical examination, which she promptly received. After her medical examination, on August 13, 1973, the agents returned to complete the application. On that date, David Songer signed the completed application, gave the Continental agent a check in the amount of $133 for the first six months' premium, and received a receipt signed by the agent.

The record reflects a sharp conflict in the testimony concerning the contemporaneous statements by Continental's agent regarding the effective date of coverage and the conditions and terms affecting that coverage. The Songers testified that, during their discussion with the agents, they were assured there was a "binder", and that they were immediately covered unless and until they heard otherwise from the company. Although Continental's agent admitted he used the word "binder" in both meetings, he claimed that he intended the term to be taken in its slang sense rather than in the sense which imparts

a legal significance and obligation on the part of Continental. The agent testified that he did not tell the Songers that there was immediate coverage, but instead explained to them that coverage would begin as of the date of application if the application was later accepted by the company.

Approximately one week after the application was submitted and the check received by Continental, the Songers left for the Island of Ponape. After being gone from the United States for about 60 days, and since the Songers had not heard anything from Continental about their application, Nancy Songer wrote a letter to her mother, Mrs. Knowles, asking her to inquire into the matter. On the day she received the letter—October 23, 1973—Mrs. Knowles phoned Continental's agent and asked the reason for the delay of over two months. The agent replied that the delay was due to the fact that Continental was having difficulty in obtaining necessary medical records from Mrs. Songer's doctor, apparently because the records were filed under her maiden name. On October 24, 1973, this problem was resolved and the doctor's office forwarded the necessary information to Continental.

On October 30, 1973, Mrs. Songer was involved in a motor vehicle accident on the Island of Ponape and was severely injured. A few days later, Continental gave written notice that the Songer's application for medical insurance was being declined for medical and other reasons. This notice was by means of a letter written and mailed on November 3, 1973, by Continental's agent to Mrs. Knowles. Accompanying the notice was a refund check from Continental dated October 29, 1973. The Songers never endorsed the check or accepted the refund.

* * *

One of the primary issues presented to the jury for resolution in this case was whether a temporary contract for insurance arose on the basis of alleged statements by Continental's agent that the Songers would immediately be covered by temporary insurance upon payment of the first premium and issuance of the receipt. The jury was instructed to determine whether an oral contract did in fact exist. Appellant contends that the trial court erred in instructing on an oral contract because such instruction erroneously allowed the jury to alter the written terms of the application and receipt on the basis of inadmissible parol evidence.

* * *

We next consider, . . . whether an oral contract for temporary insurance arose on the basis of the statements by Continental's agents that a "binder", effective immediately, was created when the Songers submitted the completed application. The oral representations made by Continental's agents could only have been considered to establish a temporary contract if such evidence did not violate the parol evidence rule. This rule, in essence, provides that "[i]n the absence of fraud or mistake, parol evidence is inadmissible to change, alter or vary the express terms in a written contract." [Citation.] The express terms of the health insurance application filled out by the Songers specified that "the insurance applied for will not become effective until this application has been accepted by the Company at its Home Office." Appellees argue that, because this provision is ambiguous, or was made so by the representations of Continental's agent, the parol evidence rule does not apply to bar consideration of the representations. We disagree.

It is well settled that parol evidence is admissible to clarify and explain a document where an ambiguity exists on the face of the document or the language admits of differing interpretations. [Citation.] The Songers contend that the acceptance provision in their application was so uncertain that its meaning could not be determined from the language of the document. Although the legal effect of a given provision is dependent on the specific terms of the application and receipt used in a particular transaction, this court has, in *Pawelczyk v. Allied Life Insurance Co.,* [citation], a case factually similar to the instant case, provided some guidance as to the

interpretation of a similar provision in an application for life insurance.

* * *

In holding that the provision presented no ambiguity, the court [in *Pawelczyk*] stated: "Courts must give effect to agreements as they are written, however, and ambiguities will not be found or created where they do not exist in order to avoid a harsh result." [Citation.] The court in upholding the enforcement of the parol evidence rule, concluded that:

. . . the [oral] representation in question would clearly vary the terms of the application and the contemplated contract of which it would form a part, and that its admission would be, therefore, in violation of the parol evidence rule. [Citations.]

It is our opinion that the same conclusion reached in *Pawelczyk* obtains in the instant case. The quoted language in the Songers' application for health insurance is too clear to admit of any doubt. The only difference between the application in *Pawelczyk* and the application of the Songers is that the *Pawelczyk* application requires that is (*sic*) be "approved" (at the home office), whereas the Songers' application requires that it be "accepted" (at the home office). This is a distinction without substantive difference. There could be no insurance in effect until the application was "accepted *by* the Company *at* its Home Office." [Citation.]

In view of our conclusion that there was no ambiguity in the application, the parol evidence rule necessarily bars consideration of the oral representations of the agent. The representation by Continental's agent that the insurance would take effect immediately upon completion of the application and payment of the premium clearly varies the terms of the application and the contemplated contract of which it would form a part. Therefore, admission and consideration of such representations as evidence of a contract would be in violation of the parol evidence rule. [Citations.]

* * *

For the reasons stated, this case is reversed and remanded for retrial.

QUESTIONS

1. Identify and discuss the five types of general contracts covered by the statute of frauds and the contracts covered by the U.C.C. statute of frauds provision.

2. Describe the writing that is required to satisfy the general contract and U.C.C. statute of frauds provisions.

3. Identify and discuss the exceptions to the various statute of frauds provisions.

4. Explain the parol evidence rule and identify the situations to which the rule does not apply.

5. Discuss the rule that aids in the interpretation of a contract.

PROBLEMS

1. Rafferty was the principal shareholder in Continental Corporation, and, as a result, he received the lion's share of Continental's dividends. Continental Corporation was eager to close an important deal for iron ore products to use in its business. A written contract was on the desk of Stage Corporation for the sale of the iron ore to Continental. Stage Corporation, however, was cautious about signing the contract, and it was not until Rafferty called Stage Corporation on the telephone and stated that if Continental Corporation did not pay for the ore, he would, that Stage Corporation signed the contract. Business reverses struck Continental Corporation and it failed. Stage Corporation sues Rafferty. What defense, if any, has Rafferty? Decision?

2. Green was the owner of a large department store. On Wednesday, January 26, he talked to Smith and said, "I will hire you as sales manager in my store for one year at a salary of $28,000; you are to begin work next Monday." Smith accepted and started work on Monday, January 31. At the end of three months, Smith was discharged by Green. On May 15, Smith brings an action against Green to recover the unpaid portion of the $28,000 salary. Decision?

3. Rowe was admitted to the hospital suffering from a critical illness. He was given emergency treatment and later underwent surgery. On at least four occasions Rowe's two sons discussed with the hospital the payment for services to be rendered by the hospital. The first of these four conversations took place the day after Rowe was admitted. The sons informed the treating physician that their father had no financial means but that they themselves would pay for such services. During the other conversations, the sons authorized whatever treatment their father needed, assuring the hospital that they would pay for the services. After Rowe's discharge, Dr. Peterson brought this action against the sons to recover the unpaid bill for the services rendered to their father. Decision?

4. Ames, Bell, Cain, and Dole each orally ordered color television sets from Marvel Electronics Company, which accepted the orders. Ames's set was to be specially designed and encased in an ebony cabinet. Bell, Cain, and Dole ordered standard sets described as "Alpha Omega Theatre." The price of Ames's set was $1,800 and of the sets ordered by Bell, Cain, and Dole, $700 each. Bell paid the company seventy-five dollars to apply on his purchase; Ames, Cain, and Dole paid nothing. The next day, Marvel sent Ames, Bell, Cain, and Dole written confirmations captioned "Purchase Memorandum," numbered 12345, 12346, 12347, and 12348, respectively, containing the essential terms of the oral agreements. Each memorandum was sent in duplicate with the request that one copy be signed and returned to the company. None of the four purchasers returned a signed copy. Ames promptly sent the company a repudiation of the oral contract, which it received before beginning manufacture of the set for Ames or making commitments to carry out the contract. Cain sent the company a letter reading in part, "Referring to your Contract No. 12347, please be advised I have cancelled this contract. Yours truly, (Signed) Cain." The four television sets were duly tendered by Marvel to Ames, Bell, Cain, and Dole, all of whom refused to accept delivery. Marvel brings four separate actions against Ames, Bell, Cain, and Dole for breach of contract.

Decide each claim.

5. Moriarity and Holmes enter into an oral contract by which Moriarity promises to sell and Holmes promises to buy Blackacre for $10,000. Moriarity repudiates the contract by writing a letter to Holmes in which she states accurately the terms of the bargain, but adds "our agreement was oral. It, therefore, is not binding upon me, and I shall not carry it out." Thereafter, Holmes sues Moriarity for specific performance of the contract. Moriarity interposes the defense of the statute of frauds, arguing that the contract is within the statute and, hence, unenforceable. Decision?

6. On March 1, Lucas called Craig on the telephone and offered to pay him $90,000 for a house and lot which Craig owned. Craig accepted the offer immediately on the telephone. Later in the same day, Lucas told Annabelle that if she would marry him, he would convey to her the property then owned by Craig which was the subject of the earlier agreement. On March 2, Lucas called Penelope and offered her $15,000 if she would work for him for the year commencing March 15, and she agreed. Lucas and Annabelle were married on June 25. By this time Craig had refused to convey the house to Lucas. Thereafter, Lucas renounced his promise to convey the property to Annabelle. Penelope, who had been working for Lucas, was discharged without cause on July 5; Annabelle left Lucas and instituted divorce proceedings in July 1984.

What rights, if any, have (a) Lucas against Craig for his failure to convey the property; (b) Annabelle against Lucas for failure to convey the house to her; (c) Penelope against Lucas for discharging her before the end of the agreed term of employment?

7. Clay orally promises Trent to sell him five crops of potatoes to be grown on Blackacre, a farm in Minnesota, and Trent promises to pay a stated price for them on delivery. Is the contract enforceable?

8. Grant leased an apartment to Epstein for the term May 1, 1990, to April 30, 1991, at $550 a month "payable in advance on the first day of each and every month of said term." At the time the lease was signed, Epstein told Grant that he received his salary on the 10th of the month, and that he would be unable to pay the rent before that date each month. Grant replied that would be satisfactory. On June 2, due to Epstein's not having paid the June rent, Grant sued Epstein for such rent. At the trial, Epstein offered to prove the oral agreement as to the date of payment each month. Decision?

9. Rachel bought a car from the Beautiful Used Car Agency under a written contract. She purchased the same in reliance on Beautiful's agent's oral representations that the car had never been in a wreck and could be driven at least two thousand miles without adding oil. Thereafter Rachel discovered that the car had, in fact, been previously wrecked and rebuilt, that it used excessive quantities of oil, and that Beautiful's agent was aware of these facts when the car was sold. Rachel brings an action to rescind the contract and recover the purchase price. Beautiful objects to the introduction of oral testimony concerning representations of its agent, contending that the written contract alone governed the rights of the parties. Decision on the objection?

10. In a contract drawn up by Booke Company, it agreed to sell and Yermack Contracting Company agreed to buy wood shingles at $6.50. After the shingles were delivered and used, Booke Company billed Yermack Company at $6.50 per bunch of 900 shingles. Yermack Company refused to pay because it thought the contract meant $6.50 per thousand shingles. Booke Company brought action to recover on the basis of $6.50 per bunch. The evidence showed that there was no applicable custom or usage in the trade and that each party held its belief in good faith. Decision?

11. Halsey, a widower, was living without family or housekeeper in his house in Howell, New York. Burns and his wife claim that Halsey invited them to give up their house and business in Andover, New York, to live in his house and care for him. In return, they allege, he promised them the house and its furniture upon his death. Acting upon this proposal, the Burnses left Andover, moved into Halsey's house, and cared for him until he died five months later. No deed, will, or memorandum exists to authenticate Halsey's promise. McCormick, the administrator of the estate, claims the oral promise is unenforceable under the statute of frauds. Decision?

12. Amos orally agrees to hire Elizabeth for an eight-month trial period. Elizabeth performs the job magnificently, and after several weeks Amos orally offers Elizabeth a six-month extension at a salary increase of twenty percent. Elizabeth accepts the offer. At the end of the eight-month trial period Amos discharges Elizabeth. Elizabeth brings suit against Amos for breach of contract. Is Amos liable? Why?

13. Ethel Greenberg acquired the ownership of the Carlyle Hotel on Miami Beach but had little experience in the hotel business. She asked Miller to participate in and counsel her operation of the hotel, which he did. Because his efforts produced a substantial profit, he claims that Ethel made an oral agreement for the continuation of his services. Miller alleges that in return for his services, Ethel promised to marry him and to share the net income resulting from the operation of the hotel. Miller agreed and rendered his services to Ethel in reliance upon her promises, and the couple planned to wed in the fall of 1955. Ethel, due to physical illness, decided not to marry. Miller sued for damages for Ethel's breach of their agreement. Decision?

14. Dean was hired on February 12, 1962, as a sales manager of the Co-op Dairy for a minimum period of one year with the dairy agreeing to pay his moving expenses. By February 26, 1962, Dean had signed a lease, moved his family from Oklahoma to Arizona, and reported for work. After he worked for a few days, he was fired. Dean then brought this action against the dairy for his salary for the year, less what he was paid. The dairy argues that enforcement of the oral contract is barred by the statute of frauds because the contract was not to be performed within one year. Decision?

15. Alice solicited an offer from Robett Manufacturing Company to manufacture certain clothing that Alice intended to supply to the government. Alice contends that in a telephone conversation Robett made an oral offer that he immediately accepted. He then received the following letter from Robett, which, he claims confirmed their agreement:

Confirming our telephone conversation, we are pleased to offer the 3,500 shirts at $4.00 each and the trousers at $3.80 each with delivery approximately ninety days after receipt of order. We will try to cut this to sixty days if at all possible.

This, of course, as quoted f.o.b. Atlanta and the order will not be subject to cancellation, domestic pack only.

Thanking you for the opportunity to offer these garments, we are

Very truly yours,

ROBETT MANUFACTURING CO., INC.

Alice sued to enforce this agreement. Decision?

COMPUTER RESEARCH PROBLEMS

 1. Yokel, a grower of soybeans, had sold soybeans to Campbell Grain and Seed Company and other grain companies in the past. Campbell entered into an oral contract with Yokel to purchase soybeans from him. Promptly after entering into the oral contract, Campbell signed and mailed to Yokel a written confirmation of the oral agreement. Yokel received the written confirmation but did not sign it or object to its content. Campbell now brings this action against Yokel for breach of contract upon Yokel's failure to deliver the soybeans. The trial court ruled in favor of the defendant, Yokel, on the ground that the defendant is not a "merchant" within the meaning of the Code. Decision?

2. Presti claims that he reached an oral agreement with Wilson by telephone in October 1970 to buy a horse for $60,000. Presti asserts that he sent Wilson a bill of sale and a postdated check, which was retained by Wilson. Presti also claims that Wilson told him that he

wished not to consumate the transaction until January 1, 1971, for tax reasons. The check was neither deposited nor negotiated. Wilson denies that he ever agreed to sell the horse or that he received the check and bill of sale from Presti. Presti's claim is supported by a copy of his check stub and by the affidavit of his executive assistant, who says that he monitored the telephone call and prepared and mailed both the bill of sale and the check. Wilson argues that the statute of frauds governs this transaction, and since there was no writing, the contract claim is barred. Decision?

3. Louie E. Brown worked for the Phelps Dodge Corporation under an oral contract for approximately twenty-three years. In 1967 he was suspended from work for unauthorized possession of company property. In 1968 Phelps Dodge fired Brown after discovering that he was using company property without permission and building a trailer on company time. Brown sued Phelps Dodge for benefits under an unemployment benefit plan. According to the plan, "in order to be eligible for unemployment benefits, a laid-off employee must: (1) Have completed 2 or more years of continuous service with the company, and (2) Have been laid off from work because the company had determined that work was not available for him." The trial court held that the wording of the second condition was ambiguous and should be construed against Phelps Dodge, the party who chose the wording. A reading of the entire contract, however, indicates that the plan was not intended to apply to someone who was fired for cause. Decision?

4. Katz offered to purchase land from Joiner, and after negotiating the terms, Joiner accepted. On October 13, over the telephone, both parties agreed to extend the time period for completing and mailing the written contract until October 20. Although the original paperwork deadline in the offer was October 14, Katz stated he had inserted that provision "for my purpose only." All other provisions of the contract remained unchanged. Accordingly, Joiner completed the contract and mailed it on October 20. Immediately after, however, Joiner sends Katz a telegram stating that "I have signed and returned contract, but have changed my mind. Do not wish to sell property." Joiner now claims an oral modification of a contract within the statute of frauds is unenforceable. Katz counters that the modification is not material, and therefore does not affect the underlying contract. Decision?

5. When Mr. McClam died, he left the family farm, heavily mortgaged, to his wife and children. In order to save the farm from foreclosure, Mrs. McClam planned to use insurance proceeds and her savings to pay off the debts. She was unwilling to do so, however, unless she had full ownership of the property. Mrs. McClam wrote her daughter, stating that the daughter should deed over her interest in the family farm to her mother. Mrs. McClam promised that upon her death all the children would inherit the farm from their mother equally. The letter further explained that if foreclosure occurred, each child would receive very little, but if they complied with their mother's plan, each would eventually receive a valuable property interest upon her death. Finally, the letter stated that all the other children had agreed to this plan. The daughter also agreed. Years later, Mrs. McClam tries to convey the farm to her son Donald. The daughter challenges, arguing that the mother is contractually bound to convey the land equally to all children. Donald says this was an oral agreement to sell land, and is unenforceable. Daughter says the letter satisfies the statute of frauds, making the contract enforceable. Who gets the farm? Explain.

6. Butler Brothers Building Company sublet all of the work in a highway construction contract to Ganley Brothers, Inc. Soon thereafter, Ganley brought this action against Butler for fraud in the inducement of the contract. The contract, however, provided: "The contractor [Ganley] has examined the said contracts . . ., knows all the requirements, and is not relying upon any statement made by the company in respect thereto." Decision?

Chapter 15

THIRD PARTIES TO CONTRACTS

Assignment of Rights
Delegation of Duties
Intended Beneficiary
Incidental Beneficiary

PRIOR chapters considered situations in which essentially only two parties were involved. This chapter deals with the rights or duties of third parties, namely, persons who are not parties to the contract but have a right to, or obligation for, its performance. These rights and duties arise either by (1) an assignment of the rights of a party to the contract, (2) a delegation of the duties of a party to the contract, or (3) the express terms of a contract entered into for the benefit of a third person. In an assignment or delegation, the third-party's rights or duties arise *after* the contract is made, whereas in the third situation the third-party beneficiary's rights arise *at* the time the contract was formed. We consider these three situations in that order.

ASSIGNMENT OF RIGHTS

Every contract creates both rights and duties. A person who owes a duty under a contract is an **obligor** while a person to whom a duty is owed under a contract is an **obligee.** For instance, Ann promises to sell to Bart an automobile for which Bart promises to pay $10,000 in monthly installments over the next three years. Ann's right under the con-

tract is to receive payment from Bart, whereas Ann's duty is to deliver the automobile. Bart's right is to receive the automobile; his duty is to pay for the automobile.

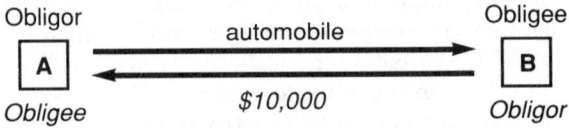

An **assignment of rights** is the voluntary transfer to a third party of the rights arising from the contract. In the above example, if Ann were to transfer her right under the contract (the installment payments due from Bart) to Clark for $8,500 in cash, this would constitute a valid assignment of rights. In this case, Ann would be the **assignor,** Clark would be the **assignee,** and Bart would be the **obligor.**

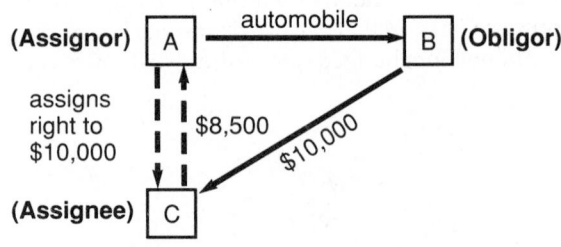

An effective assignment terminates the assignor's right to receive performance by the obligor. After an assignment *only* the assignee has a right to the obligor's performance.

On the other hand, if Ann and Doris agree that Doris should deliver the automobile to Bart, this would constitute a delegation, not an assignment, of duties between Ann and Doris. A **delegation of duties** is a transfer to a third party of a contractual obligation. In this instance, Ann would be the **delegator,** Doris would be the **delegatee,** and Bart would be the **obligee.** Delegations of duties are discussed later in this chapter.

Law Governing Assignments

The law governing assignments arises principally from the common law of contracts, Article 2 of the U.C.C., and Article 9 of the U.C.C. Article 2 applies to assignments of rights under a contract for the sale of goods. Article 9 covers all assignments made to secure the performance of an obligation *and* all assignments involving rights to payment for goods sold or leased or for services rendered.

Requirements of an Assignment

The Restatement defines an assignment of a right as a "manifestation of the assignor's intention to transfer it by virtue of which the assignor's right to performance by the obligor is extinguished in whole or in part and the assignee acquires the right to such performance." Section 317(1). No special form or particular words are necessary to create an assignment. Any words that fairly indicate an intention to make the assignee the owner of the right are sufficient. For instance, Eve delivers to Harold a writing addressed to Mary stating, "Pay Harold for his own use $1,000 out of the amount you owe me." This writing is a legally sufficient assignment. Restatement, Section 325, Illustration 1.

Unless otherwise provided by statute, an assignment may be oral. In addition, consideration is *not* required for an effective assignment. Consequently, gratuitous assign-ments are valid and enforceable. When the assignee gives value for the assignment, the assignee manifests his assent to the assignment as part of the bargained for exchange. On the other hand, when the assignment is gratuitous, the assignee's assent is not always required. Any assignee who has not assented to an assignment, however, may disclaim the assignment within a reasonable time after learning of its existence and terms. Restatement, Section 327. No particular formality is required for the disclaimer, which renders the assignment inoperative from the beginning.

There cannot be an assignment of rights under a contract that is yet to be made. Such a purported assignment "operates only as a promise to assign the right when it arises and as a power to enforce it." Restatement, Section 321.

Revocability of Assignments When the assignee gives consideration in exchange for an assignment, there is a contract between the assignor and the assignee. Consequently, the assignor may not revoke the assignment without the assent of the assignee. A gratuitous assignment is revocable by the assignor and is terminated by the assignor's death, incapacity, or subsequent assignment of the right, *unless* an effective delivery of the assignment has been made by the assignor to the assignee. Such delivery can be accomplished by transferring a deed or other document evidencing the right, such as a stock certificate or savings passbook. Delivery may also consist of physically delivering a signed, written assignment of the contract right.

A gratuitous assignment is also rendered irrevocable if, prior to the attempted revocation, the donee-assignee receives payment of the claim from the obligor, obtains a judgment against the obligor, or obtains a new contract with the obligor. For example, Nancy owes Howard $50,000. Howard signs a written statement granting Paul a gratuitous assignment of his rights from Nancy. Howard dies prior to delivering to Paul the signed, written assignment of the contract right. The assignment is terminated and therefore ineffective.

On the other hand, had Howard delivered the signed, written assignment to Paul before Howard died, the assignment would have been effective and irrevocable.

Partial Assignments A partial assignment is a transfer of a portion of the contractual rights to one or more assignees. Although at early common law, partial assignments were not enforceable, today partial assignments are permitted and are enforceable. The obligor, however, may require all the parties entitled to the promised performance to litigate the matter in one action. This insures that all parties are present and avoids the undue hardship of multiple lawsuits. For example, Jack owes Richard $2,500. Richard assigns $1,000 to Mildred. Neither Richard nor Mildred can maintain an action against Jack if Jack objects, unless the other is joined in the lawsuit against Jack.

Rights That Are Assignable

As a general rule, most contract rights, including rights under an option contract, are assignable. *See Munchak Corporation v. Cunningham.* The most common contractual right that may be assigned is the right to the payment of money, such as an account receivable or interest due or to be paid. The right to property other than money, such as goods or lands, is also frequently assignable.

Rights That Are Not Assignable

In order to protect the obligor or the public interest, some contract rights are not assignable. These nonassignable contract rights include those that (1) materially change the obligor's duty or materially increase the risk or burden upon the obligor, (2) transfer highly personal contract rights, (3) are validly prohibited by the contract, or (4) are prohibited by statute or public policy. Restatement, Section 317(2).

Assignments that Materially Increase the Duty, Risk, or Burden An assignment is ineffective where performance by the obligor

to the assignee would be materially different from performance to the assignor; that is, where the assignment would significantly change the nature or extent of the *obligor's duty.* Thus, an automobile liability insurance policy issued to Alex is not assignable by Alex to Betty. The risk assumed by the insurance company was liability for Alex's negligent operation of the automobile. Liability for operation of the same automobile by Betty would be an entirely different risk and one that the insurance company had not assumed. Similarly, Alex would not be allowed to assign his contractual right to have Betty paint his small, two-bedroom house to Cynthia, the owner of a twenty-five room mansion. Clearly, such an assignment would materially increase Betty's duty of performance. By comparison, the right to receive monthly payments under a contract may be assigned, for it costs no more to mail the check to the assignee than it does to mail it to the assignor.

Assignments of Personal Rights Where the rights under a contract are of a highly personal nature, in that they are limited to the person of the *obligee,* then such rights are not assignable. An extreme example of such a contract is an agreement of two persons to marry one another. The prospective groom obviously cannot transfer the prospective bride's promise to marry him to some third party. A more typical example of a contract of a personal character would be a contract between a teacher and a school. The teacher could not assign her right to another teacher. Similarly, a student who is awarded a scholarship cannot assign his right to some other person.

Express Prohibition against Assignment Contract terms prohibiting assignment of rights under the contract are strictly construed. Most courts interpret a general prohibition against assignments as a mere promise not to assign. As a consequence, the prohibition, if violated, gives the obligor a right to damages for breach of the terms forbidding assignment but does *not* render the assignment ineffective.

U.C.C. Section 2–210(2) provides that a right to damages for breach of the whole contract or a right arising out of the assignor's due performance of his entire obligation can be assigned despite a contractual provision to the contrary. U.C.C. Section 9–318(4) makes ineffective any term in a contract prohibiting the assignment of any right to payment for goods sold or leased or for services rendered. Section 322(1) of the Restatement and Section 2–210(3) of the Code provide that, unless circumstances indicate the contrary, a contract term prohibiting assignment of the *contract* bars only the delegation to the assignee (delegatee) of the assignor's (delegator's) *duty* of performance and not the assignment of *rights*. Thus, Abe and Bill contract for the sale of land by Bill to Abe for $30,000 and provide in their contract that Abe may not assign his rights under it. Abe pays Bill $30,000 and thereby fully performs his obligations under the contract. Abe then assigns his rights to Cheryl. Cheryl is entitled to receive the land from Bill (the obligor) despite the contractual prohibition of assignment.

Assignments Prohibited by Law Various Federal and State statutes, as well as public policy, prohibit or regulate the assignment of certain types of contract rights. For instance, assignments of future wages are subject to statutes, some of which prohibit them altogether while others require them to be in writing and subject to certain restrictions. An assignment that violates public policy will be unenforceable even in the absence of a prohibiting statute.

Rights of the Assignee

Obtains Rights of Assignor The general rule is that an assignee **stands in the shoes** of the assignor. He acquires the rights of the assignor, but *no* new rights, and takes the assigned right with all of the defenses, defects, and infirmities to which it would be subject in an action against the obligor by the assignor. Thus, in an action brought by the assignee against the obligor, the obligor

may plead fraud, duress, undue influence, failure of consideration, breach of contract, or any other defense arising out of the original contract against the assignor. The obligor may assert rights of setoff or counterclaim arising out of entirely separate matters that he may have against the assignor, provided they arose prior to his receiving notice of the assignment.

The Code permits the buyer under a contract of sale to agree as part of the contract that he will not assert against an assignee any claim or defense that the buyer may have against the seller if the assignee takes the assignment for value and in good faith. U.C.C. Section 9–206. Such a provision in an agreement affords greater marketability to the rights of the seller. The Federal Trade Commission, however, has invalidated such waiver of defense provisions in consumer credit transactions. This rule is discussed more fully in Chapter 27.

Notice To be valid, notice of an assignment does not have to be given to the obligor. Nonetheless, it is advisable that such notice be given because an assignee will lose his rights against the obligor if the obligor pays the assignor without notice of the assignment. This is because it would be unfair to compel an obligor to pay a claim a second time when she was not notified that a new party was entitled to payment. For example, Donald owes Gary $1,000 due on September 1. Gary assigns the debt to Paula on August 1 but neither Gary nor Paula inform Donald. On September 1 Donald pays Gary. Donald is fully discharged from his obligation while Gary is liable for $1,000 to Paula. On the other hand, if Paula had given notice of the assignment to Donald before September 1 and Donald had nevertheless paid Gary, Paula would then have the right to recover the $1,000 from either Donald or Gary.

Furthermore, as already indicated, notice cuts off any defenses based on subsequent agreements between the obligor and assignor, as well as subsequent setoffs and counterclaims of the obligor that arise out of entirely separate matters.

Implied Warranties of Assignor

An **implied warranty** is an obligation imposed by law upon the transfer of property or contract rights. In the absence of an express intention to the contrary, an assignor who receives value makes the following implied warranties to the assignee with respect to the assigned right:

1. that he will do nothing to defeat or impair the assignment;

2. that the assigned right actually exists and is subject to no limitations or defenses other than those stated or apparent at the time of the assignment;

3. that any writing evidencing the right delivered to the assignee or exhibited to him as an inducement to accept the assignment is genuine and what it purports to be; and

4. that he has no knowledge of any fact that would impair the value of the assignment.

Thus, Eric has a right against Julia and assigns it for value to Gwen. Later Eric gives Julia a release. Gwen may recover damages from Eric for breach of the first implied warranty.

The assignor is further bound by any express warranties he makes to the assignee with respect to the right assigned. Unless explicitly stated, however, the assignor does *not* guarantee that the obligor will pay the assigned debt or otherwise perform.

Successive Assignments of the Same Right

The owner of a right could conceivably make successive assignments of the same claim to different persons. Assume that B owes A $1,000. On June 1, A for value assigns the debt to C. Thereafter, on June 15, A assigns it to D, who in good faith gives value and has no knowledge of the prior assignment by A to C. If the assignment is subject to Article 9, then its priority rules will control, as discussed in Chapter 38. Otherwise, the priority is determined by the common law. The majority rule in the United States is that the **first assignee in point of time** (here, C) prevails over subsequent assignees. In England and in a minority of the States, the first assignee that notifies the obligor prevails. *See Boulevard National Bank of Miami v. Air Metal Industries.*

The Restatement adopts a third view: a prior assignee is entitled to the assigned right and its proceeds to the exclusion of a subsequent assignee, *except* where the prior assignment is revocable or voidable by the assignor or the subsequent assignee in good faith and without knowledge of the prior assignment gives value and obtains one of the following: (1) payment or satisfaction of the obligor's duty, (2) a judgment against the obligor, (3) a new contract with the obligor, or (4) possession of a writing of a type customarily accepted as a symbol or as evidence of the right assigned. Restatement, Section 342.

DELEGATION OF DUTIES

As already indicated, contractual **duties** are *not* assignable, but their performance may generally be *delegated* to a third person. A **delegation of duties** is a transfer to a third party of a contractual obligation. For example, A promises to sell B a new automobile for which B promises to pay $10,000 by monthly installments over the next three years. If A and D agree that D should deliver the automobile to B, this would not constitute an assignment but would be a delegation of duties between A and D. In this instance, A would be the **delegator,** D would be the **delegatee,** and B would be the **obligee.**

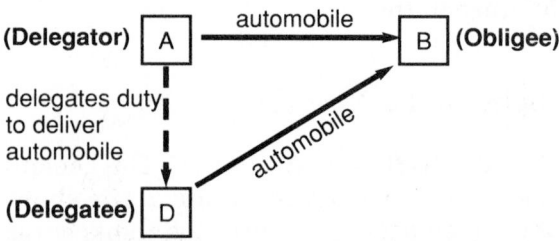

A delegation of duty does *not* extinguish the delegator's obligation to perform, because A remains liable to B. When the delegatee accepts or **assumes** the delegated duty, **both**

the delegator and delegatee are held liable for performance of the contractual duty to the obligee.

Delegable Duties

Contractual duties are generally delegable. Nevertheless, a delegation will not be permitted if

1. the nature of the duties are personal in that the obligee has a substantial interest in having the delegator perform the contract;

2. the performance is expressly made nondelegable; or

3. the delegation is prohibited by statute or public policy.

The courts will examine a delegation more closely than an assignment because, with a delegation, the nondelegating party to the contract (the obligee) is being compelled to receive performance from a party with which she has not dealt.

For example, a school teacher may not delegate her performance to another teacher, even if the substitute is equally competent, for this is a contract that is personal in nature. In the frequently quoted words of an English case: "You have a right to the benefit you contemplate from the character, credit and substance of the person with whom you contract." On the other hand, where performance by a party involves no peculiar or special skill, and where no personal trust or confidence is involved, the party may delegate the performance of his duty. For example, the duty to pay money, to deliver fungible goods such as corn, or to mow a lawn is usually delegable. *See Macke Company v. Pizza of Gaithersburg, Inc.*

Duties of the Parties

Even when permitted, a delegation of a duty to a third person still leaves the delegator bound to perform. If the delegator desires to be discharged of the duty, it may be possible for her to enter into an agreement obtaining the consent of the obligee to substitute a third person (the delegatee) in her place. This is a

novation whereby the delegator is discharged and the third party becomes directly bound upon his promise to the obligee.

A delegation authorizes a third party to perform the duty for the delegator. A delegatee becomes liable for performance only if he assents to perform the delegated duties. Thus, if Frank owes a duty to Grace, and Frank delegates that duty to Henry, Henry is not obligated to perform the duty to either Frank or Grace unless Henry agrees to do so. If Henry promises either Frank (the delegator) or Grace (the obligee) that he will perform Frank's duty, Henry is said to have **assumed the delegated duty** and becomes liable for nonperformance to both Frank and Grace. Accordingly, when there has been a delegation of duties *and* an assumption of the delegated duties, **both** the delegator and the delegatee are liable to the obligee for proper performance of the original contractual duty.

The question of whether the delegatee has assumed the delegated duties has frequently arisen when Marty and Carol agree to an assignment of Marty's *contract* with Bob. The common law rule is unclear as there is a division of authority among the jurisdictions. The Code clearly resolves this conflict by providing that, unless the language or circumstances indicate the contrary, an assignment of "the contract," or of "all my rights under the contract," or an assignment in similar general terms is an assignment of rights *and* a delegation of performance of the duties of the assignor, and its acceptance by the assignee constitutes a promise by her to perform those duties. Section 2–210(4). The Restatement, Section 328, has also adopted this position. For example, Cooper Oil Co. has a contract to deliver oil to Halsey. Cooper Oil Co. delivers to Lowell Oil Co. a writing assigning to Lowell Oil Co. "all Cooper Oil Co.'s rights and duties under the contract." Lowell Oil Co. is under a duty to Halsey to deliver the oil called for by the contract, and Cooper Oil Co. is liable to Halsey if Lowell Oil Co. does not perform. It should also be recalled that the Restatement and the Code provide that a clause prohibiting an assignment of "the contract" is to be construed as barring only the delegation to the assignee (delegatee) of the assignor's (delegator's) performance, unless the circumstances indicate the contrary.

THIRD-PARTY BENEFICIARY CONTRACTS

A contract in which a party (the **promisor**) promises to render a certain performance not to the other party (the **promisee**) but to a third person (the **beneficiary**) is called a third-party beneficiary contract. The third person is not a party to the contract but is merely a beneficiary of the contract. Such contracts may be divided into two types: (1) intended beneficiary and (2) incidental beneficiary. An **intended beneficiary** is intended by the two parties to the contract (the promisor and promisee) to receive a benefit from the performance of their agreement. Accordingly, the courts generally enforce intended beneficiary third-party contracts. For example, Abbott promises Baldwin to deliver an automobile to Carson if Baldwin promises to pay $10,000. Carson is the intended beneficiary.

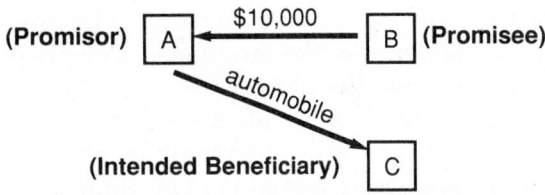

In an **incidental beneficiary** contract, the third party is not intended to receive a benefit under the contract. Accordingly, courts do not enforce the third party's right to the benefits of the contract. For example, Abbott promises to purchase and deliver to Baldwin an automobile for $10,000. In all probability Abbott would acquire the automobile from Davis. Davis would be an incidental beneficiary.

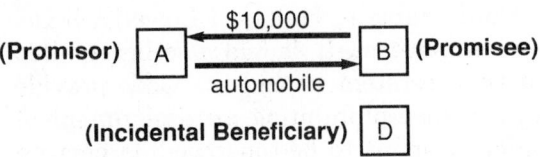

Intended Beneficiary

There are two types of intended beneficiaries: (1) donee beneficiaries and (2) creditor beneficiaries.

Donee Beneficiary   A third party is an **intended donee beneficiary** if the promisee's purpose in bargaining for and obtaining the agreement with the promisor were to make a gift to the beneficiary. The ordinary life insurance policy is an illustration of this type of intended beneficiary third-party contract. The insured (the promisee) makes a contract with an insurance company (the promisor) that promises, in consideration of premiums paid to it by the insured, to pay upon the death of the insured a stated sum of money to the named beneficiary, who is an intended donee beneficiary.

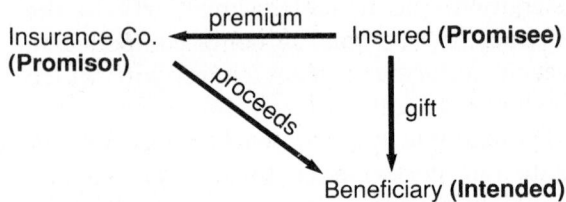

Creditor Beneficiary   A third person is also an intended beneficiary if the promisee intends the performance of the promise to satisfy a legal duty owed to the beneficiary, who is a creditor of the promisee. The contract involves consideration moving from the promisee to the promisor in exchange for the promisor's engaging to pay some debt or discharge some obligation of the promisee to the third person.

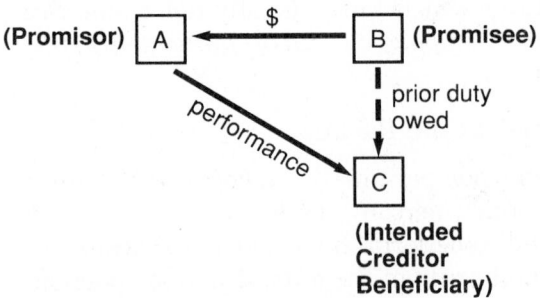

To illustrate, in the contract for the sale by Wesley of his business to Susan, Susan promises Wesley that she will pay all of Wesley's outstanding business debts, as listed in the contract. Here, Wesley's creditors are creditor beneficiaries. Similarly, in the classic *Lawrence v. Fox*, 20 N.Y.268 (1859), Holly loaned Fox $300 in consideration for Fox's promise to pay that sum to Lawrence, a creditor of Holly. Fox failed to pay Lawrence, who sued Fox for the $300. The court held for Lawrence, who was permitted to recover as a third-party creditor beneficiary to the contract between Holly and Fox.

Rights of Intended Beneficiary An intended *donee* beneficiary may enforce the contract against the promisor only. He cannot maintain an action against the promisee, since the promisee was under no legal obligation to him. An intended *creditor* beneficiary, however, may enforce the contract against either or both parties. If Willard owes Lola $500, and Julie contracts with Willard to pay this debt to Lola, Willard is not thereby relieved of his liability to Lola. If Julie breaks the contract, Lola, as a creditor beneficiary, may sue her. In addition, Lola may sue Willard as her debtor. If Lola should obtain judgments against both Julie and Willard, she is, of course, entitled to collect only one judgment. If Lola recovers against Willard, Willard has a right of reimbursement from Julie, the promisor. Restatement, Section 310.

In an action by the intended beneficiary of a third-party contract to enforce the promise, the promisor may assert any defense that would be available to him if the action had been brought by the promisee. The rights of the third party are based upon the promisor's contract with the promisee. Thus, the absence of mutual assent or consideration, lack of capacity, fraud, mistake, and the like may be asserted by the promisor against the intended beneficiary. *See Brown v. National Supermarkets, Inc.*

Vesting of Rights A contract for the benefit of an intended beneficiary confers upon that beneficiary rights that the beneficiary may enforce. Until these rights **vest** (take effect), however, the promisor and promisee

may, by later agreement, vary or completely discharge these rights. The States vary considerably as to when vesting takes place. Some States hold that vesting takes place immediately upon making the contract. In other States, vesting occurs when the third party learns of the contract and assents to it. In another group of States, vesting requires the third party to change his position in reliance upon the promise made for his benefit. The Restatement has adopted the following position: If the contract between the promisor and promisee provides that its terms may not be varied without the consent of the beneficiary, such a provision is effective. Otherwise, the parties to the contract may rescind or vary the contract unless the intended beneficiary (1) has brought an action upon the promise, (2) has changed her position in reliance upon it, or (3) has assented to the promise at the request of the promisor or promisee. Restatement, Section 311.

On the other hand, the promisor and promisee may provide that the benefits will *never* vest. For example, Mildred purchases an insurance policy on her own life, naming her husband as beneficiary. Her policy, as is common with such policies, reserves to Mildred the right to change the beneficiary or even to cancel the policy entirely.

Incidental Beneficiary

An incidental third-party beneficiary is a person whom the parties to a contract did not intend to benefit, but who nevertheless would derive some benefit by its performance. For instance, a contract to raze an old, unsightly building and replace it with a costly, modern house would benefit the owner of the adjoining property by increasing his property's value. He would have no rights under the contract, however, as the benefit to him is unintended and incidental.

A third person who may be incidentally benefited by the performance of a contract to which he is not a party has no rights under the contract. It was not the intention of either the promisee or the promisor that the third person be benefited. Assume that for a stated consideration George promises Kathy that he will purchase and deliver to Kathy a brand new Sony television of the latest model. Kathy performs. George does not. Cosmos Appliances, Inc., the local exclusive Sony dealer, has no rights under the contract although performance by George would produce a sale from which Cosmos Appliances, Inc. would derive a benefit. Cosmos Appliances, Inc. is only an incidental beneficiary. *See Jackson, Lewis, Schnitzler & Krupman v. Local 100, Transport Workers Union of America.*

CASES

Rights That Are Assignable

MUNCHAK CORPORATION v. CUNNINGHAM

United States Court of Appeals, Fourth Circuit, 1972.
457 F.2d 721.

Winter, J.

Plaintiffs, the owners and operators of the basketball club "The Carolina Cougars" (the "Cougars"), sued to enjoin defendant, William John Cunningham ("Cunningham"), a professional basketball player, from performing services as a basketball player for any basketball club other than the Cougars in violation of a contract between the Cougars and Cunningham. The district court, finding that Cunningham had contracted to play for the Cougars, nevertheless concluded that even if Cunningham had failed and refused to perform his contract, plaintiffs had unclean hands and had breached their contract with Cunningham. It, therefore, denied injunctive relief.

In this appeal, we conclude that plaintiffs did not have unclean hands, that any breach of contract on the part of plaintiffs was too insubstantial to justify the denial of injunctive relief, and that Cunningham's additional argument that his contract was not assignable is lacking in merit. Accordingly, we reverse and remand the case for entry of an injunction restraining Cunningham from playing for any team, other than the Cougars, for the duration of his contract with that club.

* * *

The district judge made detailed findings of fact to support his opinion and conclusions of law that plaintiffs were not entitled to injunctive relief, [citation], and, consequently, we need not repeat all of the facts. It suffices to say that Cunningham is a basketball player of special, exceptional, and unique knowledge, skills, and ability. For the period October 1, 1969, until October 1, 1970, as well as for four earlier seasons, he had contracted to play professional basketball for the Philadelphia 76ers. For the period October 1, 1969, to October 1, 1970, Cunningham received $40,000.00 compensation under the contract, together with a bonus of $15,000.00, a total of $55,000.00. The contract contained a "reserve clause," which gave that club the right on or before September 1, 1970, to tender a contract to Cunningham to play the next season. If Cunningham failed, neglected, or omitted to sign the tendered contract and to return it by October 1, 1970, the existing contract would be continued for another year, but at the rate of compensation fixed in the tendered contract, provided that that compensation was not less than 75% of the compensation being paid Cunningham under the contract then in force.

During May or early June of 1969, the Cougars, with knowledge that Cunningham was under contract with the Philadelphia 76ers, and that that club had an option to Cunningham's services for the 1970–71 basketball season, through intermediaries, entered into contract negotiations with Cunningham. On August 5, 1969, the negotiations ripened into a three-year contract *commencing on the 2nd day of October, 1971.* For the first year of the contract Cunningham was to receive a salary of $100,000.00, for the second year $110,000.00, and for the third year $120,000.00. Additionally, Cunningham was to receive

$125,000.00 as a bonus for signing the contract. The bonus was payable $45,000.00 on August 5, 1969, and the balance of $80,000.00 was evidenced by a promissory note wherein the Cougars promised to pay Cunningham $80,000.00 not later than May 15, 1970. The contract contained a provision which recited that Cunningham had special, exceptional and unique knowledge, skill and ability as a basketball player, the loss of which was not readily translatable into money damages; and, therefore, Cunningham agreed that the Cougars could enjoin him from playing basketball for another team during the term of his contract with the Cougars. The validity and enforceability of this provision in a proper case is not disputed. The litigation revolves about whether Cunningham has meritorious defenses to obviate plaintiffs' equitable remedy.

* * *

Cunningham's contention that his contract was not assignable and that by reason of a purported assignment he is excused from performance arises from these facts. Cunningham's contracts with the Cougars were made at a time when Southern Sports Corporation, owned and operated primarily by James C. Gardner, was the owner of the Cougars' franchise. His contract with Southern Sports Corporation prohibited its assignment to another "*club*" without his consent, but it contained no prohibition against its assignment to another owner of the same club. In 1971, Southern Sports Corporation assigned its franchise and Cunningham's contracts to the plaintiffs, who, as joint venturers, operate the franchise. Cunningham was not asked to consent, nor has he consented, to this assignment. While Cunningham's contracts require him to perform personal services, the services were to the club.

We recognize that under North Carolina law the right to performance of a personal service contract requiring special skills and based upon the personal relationship between the parties cannot be assigned without the consent of the party rendering those services. [Citation.] But, as discussed in [citation], some of such contracts may be assigned when the character of the performance and the obligation will not be changed. To us it is inconceivable that the rendition of services by a professional basketball player to a professional basketball club could be affected by the personalities of successive corporate owners. Cf. Washington Capitols Basketball Club, Inc. v. Barry, [citation]. Indeed, Cunningham had met only Gardner of Southern Sports Club, and had not met, nor did he know, the other stockholders. If Gardner had sold all or part of his stock to another person, Cunningham could not seriously contend that his consent would be required.

The policy against assignability of certain personal service contracts is to prohibit an assignment of a contract in which the obligor undertakes to serve only the original obligee. [Citations.] This contract is not of that type, since Cunningham was not obligated to perform differently for plaintiffs than he was obligated to perform for Southern Sports Club. We, therefore, see no reason to hold that the contract was not assignable under the facts here.

For the reasons stated, we reverse the judgment of the district court and remand the case for entry of appropriate equitable relief.

Reversed and remanded.

Successive Assignments of Same Right

BOULEVARD NATIONAL BANK OF MIAMI v. AIR METAL INDUSTRIES

Supreme Court of Florida, 1965.
176 So.2d 94.

WILLIS, J.

The suit commenced as an action at law by the plaintiff bank against several defendants, including the respondent Tompkins-Beckwith, Inc., in whose favor the summary final judgment involved here was rendered.

Tompkins-Beckwith was the contractor on a construction project which had entered into a subcontract with a division of Air Metal Industries, Inc. Air Metal procured American

Fire and Casualty Company to be surety on certain bonds in connection with contracts it was performing for Tompkins-Beckwith and others. As security for such bonds, Air Metal executed, on January 3, 1962, a "Contractor's General Agreement of Indemnity" which contains an assignment to American Fire of [all accounts receivable under the Tompkins-Beckwith contract].

On November 26, 1962, the petitioner bank lent money to Air Metal and to secure the loans Air Metal purported to assign to the bank certain accounts receivable it had with Tompkins-Beckwith which arose out of subcontracts being done for that contractor.

In June, 1963 Air Metal defaulted on various contracts bonded by American Fire. On July 1, 1963 American Fire served formal notice on Tompkins-Beckwith of Air Metal's assignment. Tompkins-Beckwith acknowledged the assignment and agreed to pay. On August 12, 1963, the petitioner bank notified Tompkins-Beckwith of its assignment and claim thereunder. The claim was not recognized and on September 26, 1963, this action was filed in the trial court. On October 9, 1963 Tompkins-Beckwith paid all remaining funds which had accrued to Air Metal to American Fire.

* * * The "question" . . . is whether the law of Florida requires recognition of the so-called "English" rule or "American" rule of priority between assignees of successive assignments of an account receivable or other similar chose in action. Stated in its simplest form, the American rule would give priority to the assignee first in point of time of assignment, while the English rule would give preference to the assignment of which the debtor was first given notice. Both rules presuppose the absence of any estoppel or other special equities in favor of or against either assignee. The English rule giving priority to the assignee first giving notice to the debtor is specifically qualified as applying "unless he takes a later assignment with notice of a previous one or without a valuable consideration." [Citations.]

* * *

The American rule for which petitioner contends is based upon the reasoning that an account or other chose in action may be assigned at will by the owner; that notice to the debtor is not essential to complete the assignment; and that when such assignment is made the property rights become vested in the assignee so that the assignor no longer has any interest in the account or chose which he may subsequently assign to another. [Citations.]

* * *

It is undoubted that the creditor of an account receivable or other similar chose in action arising out of contract may assign it to another so that the assignee may sue on it in his own name and make recovery. Formal requisites of such an assignment are not prescribed by statute and it may be accomplished by parol, by instrument in writing, or other mode, such as delivery of evidences of the debt, as may demonstrate an intent to transfer and an acceptance of it. * * *

It seems to be generally agreed that notice to a debtor of an assignment is necessary to impose on the debtor the duty of payment to the assignee, and that if before receiving such notice he pays the debt to the assignor, or to a subsequent assignee, he will be discharged from the debt. [Citation.] To regard the debtor as a total nonparticipant in the assignment by the creditor of his interests to another is to deny the obvious. An account receivable is only the right to receive payment of a debt which ultimately must be done by the act of the debtor. For the assignee to acquire the right to stand in the shoes of the assigning creditor he must acquire some "delivery" or "possession" of the debt constituting a means of clearly establishing his right to collect. The very nature of an account receivable renders "delivery" and "possession" matters very different and more difficult than in the case of tangible personalty and negotiable instruments which are readily capable of physical handling and holding. However, the very principles which render a sale of personal property with possession remaining in the vendor unexplained fraudulent and void as to creditors applies with equal urgency to choses in action which are the subject of assignment. It would seem to follow that the mere private dealing between the creditor and his assignee unaccompanied by any manifestations discernable to others having or considering the acquiring of an interest in the account would not meet the requirement of delivery and acceptance of possession which is essential to the consummation of the assignment. Proper notice to the debtor of the assignment is a manifestation of such delivery. It fixes the accountability of the debtor to the assignee instead of the assignor and enables all involved to deal more safely.

We thus find that the so-called English rule which the trial and appellate court approved and applied is harmonious with our jurisprudence, whereas the so-called American rule is not. * * *

[Judgment for Air Metal.]

Delegation of Duties

MACKE COMPANY v. PIZZA OF GAITHERSBURG, INC.

Court of Appeals of Maryland, 1970.
259 Md. 479, 270 A.2d 645.

SINGLEY, J.

The appellees and defendants below, Pizza of Gaithersburg, Inc.; Pizzeria, Inc.; The Pizza Pie Corp., Inc.; and Pizza Oven, Inc., four corporations under the common ownership of Sidney Ansell, Thomas S. Sherwood, and Eugene Early and the same individuals as partners or proprietors (the Pizza Shops) operated at six locations in Montgomery and Prince George's Counties. The appellees had arranged to have installed in each of their locations cold drink vending machines owned by Virginia Coffee Service, Inc., and on 30 December 1966, this arrangement was formalized at five of the locations, by contracts for terms of one year, automatically renewable for a like term in the absence of 30 days' written notice. A similar contract for the sixth location, operated by Pizza of Gaithersburg, Inc., was entered into on 25 July 1967.

On 30 December 1967, Virginia's assets were purchased by The Macke Company (Macke) and the six contracts were assigned to Macke by Virginia. In January, 1968, the Pizza Shops attempted to terminate the five contracts having the December anniversary date, and in February, the contract which had the July anniversary date.

Macke brought suit in the Circuit Court for Montgomery County against each of the Pizza Shops for damages for breach of contract. From judgments for the defendants, Macke has appealed.

* * *

In the absence of a contrary provision—and there was none here—rights and duties under an executory bilateral contract may be assigned and delegated, subject to the exception that duties under a contract to provide personal services may never be delegated, nor rights be assigned under a contract where *delectus personae* [choice of person] was an ingredient of the bargain. [Citations.] Crane Ice Cream Co. v. Terminal Freezing & Heating Co., [citation], held that the right of an individual to purchase ice under a contract which by its terms reflected a knowledge of the individual's needs and reliance on his credit and responsibility could not be assigned to the corporation which purchased his business. In [citation], our predecessors held that an advertising agency could not delegate its duties under a contract which had been entered into by an advertiser who had relied on the agency's skill, judgment and taste.

The six machines were placed on the appellees' premises under a printed "Agreement-Contract" which identified the "customer," gave its place of business, described the vending machine, and * * *

We cannot regard the agreements as contracts for personal services. They were either a license or concession granted Virginia by the appellees, or a lease of a portion of the appellees' premises, with Virginia agreeing to pay a percentage of gross sales as a license or concession fee or as rent, [citations], and were assignable by Virginia unless they imposed on Virginia duties of a personal or unique character which could not be delegated, [citation].

The appellees earnestly argue that they had dealt with Macke before and had chosen Virginia because they preferred the way it conducted its business. Specifically, they say that service was more personalized, since the president of Virginia kept the machines in working order, that commissions were paid in cash, and that Virginia permitted them to keep keys to the machines so that minor adjustments could be made when needed. Even if we assume all this to be true, the agreements with Virginia were silent as to the details of the working arrangements and contained only a provision requiring Virginia to "install . . . the above listed equipment and . . . maintain the equipment in good operating order and stocked with merchandise." We think the Supreme Court of California put the problem of personal service in proper focus a century ago when it upheld the assignment of a contract to grade a San Francisco street:

All painters do not paint portraits like Sir Joshua Reynolds, nor landscapes like Claude Lorraine, nor do all writers write dramas like Shakespeare or fiction like Dickens. Rare genius and extraordinary skill are not transferable, and contracts for their employment are therefore personal, and cannot be assigned. But rare genius and extraordinary skill are not indispensable to the workmanlike digging down of a sand hill or the filling up of a depression to a given level, or the construction of brick sewers with manholes and covers, and contracts for such work are not personal, and may be assigned. [Citation.]

. . . Moreover, the difference between the service the Pizza Shops happened to be getting from Virginia and what they expected to get from Macke did not mount up to such a material change in the performance of obligations under the agreements as would justify the appellees' refusal to recognize the assignment, [citation].

* * *

* * * Modern authorities . . . hold that, absent provision to the contrary, a duty may be delegated, as distinguished from a right which can be assigned, and that the promisee cannot rescind, if the quality of the performance remains materially the same. * * *

As we see it, the delegation of duty by Virginia to Macke was entirely permissible under the terms of the agreements.

* * *

[Judgment reversed.]

Rights of Intended Beneficiary

BROWN v. NATIONAL SUPERMARKETS, INC.

Missouri Court of Appeals, Eastern District, Division Three, 1984.
679 S.W.2d 307.

KAROHL, J.

Plaintiff-appellants Pauline and George Brown appeal from a summary judgment in favor of the three defendants, National Super Markets (National), Sentry Security Agency (Sentry) and T.G. Watkins, a security guard, employed by Sentry. The issue is whether defendants as a matter of law had a duty to protect the plaintiff from an assault by an unknown third party on defendant National's parking lot.

Pauline and George Brown brought a negligence action against the defendants after Pauline was shot and seriously injured by an unknown assailant in National's parking lot. The Browns allege that the defendants have a duty to protect National's patrons both in the store and in the parking lot and that they breached that duty. Defendants denied that they have such a duty and filed a motion for summary judgment. The trial court granted the motion.

* * *

The question as to Sentry and its employee is whether they assumed a duty to plaintiff if, as alleged, they contracted with National to provide protection National may owe to its patrons. The cases do not clearly establish whether a security company or security guard working for a business owner under contract have a duty to protect patrons from crime. It is the general rule that a private person has no duty to protect another from a deliberate criminal attack by a third person. [Citation.] We find that Sentry may or may not have assumed such a duty when it entered into the security contract. [Citation.] The existence of a duty will turn on the terms of the contract and the circumstances.

Plaintiffs allege in their amended petition that Sentry contracted with National to provide security against criminal activities for National *and its patrons*. (our emphasis). In

effect plaintiffs claim that the contract between National and Sentry is an attempt to
perform National's previously established
duty. The provisions of the contract are not in
evidence. However, the National store manager testified by deposition that although he
had never seen the contract he understood it
to cover the area both inside and outside the
store. T.G. Watkins, the security guard, stated
in his deposition that he was never told to pa-
trol the parking lot. As it is unclear whether
the security company assumed any duty
through the contract an issue of facts remain
and summary judgment was error.

Plaintiffs may be third party beneficiaries
to this contract. As such they may sue in tort
or contract for any contract breach by Sentry
or its employees.

Third party beneficiary is the nomenclature given
to one who is not privy to a contract nor its consideration but to whom the law gives the right to
maintain a cause of action for breach of contract.
. . . Only those third parties for whose primary
benefit the contracting parties intended to make
the contract may maintain an action. . . . The intention of the parties is to be gleaned from the four
corners of the contract, and if uncertain or ambiguous from the circumstances surrounding its execution.

[Citation.]

Privity of contract is no longer always necessary to maintain a suit for breach of contract. [Citation.]

[T]here are situations in which the making of the
contract creates a relation between the defendant
and the promise, which is sufficient to impose a
tort duty of reasonable care . . .
. . . Where an agent or servant has accepted the
control of property under a contract with his principal, and under circumstances where there is an
obvious risk of harm to outsiders if he does not use
reasonable care, the obligation of affirmative conduct has been imposed upon him.

W. Prosser, Law of Torts 623–624 (1971).

As a matter of law both National and Sentry *may* have a duty to protect National patrons from criminal assaults. Summary judgment was inappropriate because questions of
fact remain.

We reverse the trial court decision for summary judgment and remand the cause for an
action consistent with this opinion.

Incidental Beneficiary

BURNS, JACKSON, MILLER, SUMMIT & SPITZER v. LINDNER

Supreme Court, Special Term, Queens County,
New York, 1981.
108 Misc.2d 458, 437 N.Y.S.2d 895.

KASSOFF, J.

This action arises out of an 11–day strike
by the members of the unions representing
the employees of the Transit Authority and
MaBSTOA [Manhattan & Bronx Surface Operating Authority]. The five union organizations and their respective officers in their respective individual capacities are named as
defendants.

Plaintiffs are engaged in the practice of
law as a profession, maintaining offices in
Manhattan. Plaintiffs sue both individually
and on behalf of all other professional and
business entities (the class) that were damaged as a consequence of the defendants' wilful disruption of the service provided by the
public transportation system of the City of
New York.

On April 1, 1980, in violation of an injunction, the members of the defendants unions
commenced the strike which halted all mass
transit in, and paralyzed the life and commerce of, the City of New York. On the eighth
day of the strike, the court entered an order
finding the unions and certain of their principal officers guilty of criminal contempt for
having wilfully disobeyed the court's preliminary injunction by, among other things, "engaging in, causing, instigating, encouraging,
condoning, aiding and abetting a strike by
employees (of the Transit Authority and
MaBSTOA)" and wilfully and intentionally
failing to instruct the unions' members not to
engage in any strike or other act prohibited
by the injunction. Although heavy fines were
imposed and the officers were personally adjudged in contempt, and in the face of a fur-

ther order that the defendant officers instruct their members that they return to work forthwith, the strike continued until April 11, 1980.

By the time the members of the defendant unions had reported to work, the strike had caused widespread disruption of the lives of the citizens of New York City and severe economic damage to its professional and business community.

* * *

Plaintiffs ... seek recovery as a third-party beneficiary of the collective bargaining agreement between defendant unions and the public employers. Plaintiffs particularly claim the benefit of the no-strike clauses contained in those agreements. Historically, New York has been in the vanguard of the development of the third-party beneficiary doctrine. The doctrine itself had its American genesis in *Lawrence v. Fox,* 20 N.Y. 268 [1859]. Subsequent cases have applied this principle to contracts where one of the parties was a governmental entity. [Citations.] Extensive research by the court has failed to disclose any New York case where a public sector union breached an explicit no-strike clause of a contract which explicitly referred to protecting the interests of those who utilize the public service. In this regard, the facts before the court are highly unusual.

The critical inquiry in third-party beneficiary claims is whether the contracting parties intended their contract to benefit third parties. The best evidence of such intent is language in the agreement to that effect. The TWU's agreement states one of its purposes is "[t]o assure to the people of the State of New York efficient, economic, sufficient and dependable transportation service . . . and to protect the interests of the public" (Agreement, Article 1A). The TWU has also agreed "to cooperate with the authorities in a joint effort to place and keep the transit system on a safe, efficient, economical operating basis" (Agreement, Article 4).

As a member of the public which depends on the public transit system and which employs dozens of persons who need the public transit system to get to and from work, plaintiffs argue that they are within the class of persons for whose benefit the TWU has promised to provide "dependable transportation service". [Citation.]

A person not a party to a contract may sue for damages resulting from non-performance if the contract demonstrates that its primary intent was to benefit that person. [Citations.] Such cannot be said to be the case here. Where, as here, the government agency contracts for services which it bears no obligation to provide to the public, no duty can be found against the promisor on behalf of the member of the public unless the contract clearly makes the promisor answerable to that person for the breach. This, the court does not find. [Citation.]

[Judgment for the Transport Workers Union.]

QUESTIONS

1. Distinguish between an assignment of rights and a delegation of duties.

2. Identify (a) the requirements of an assignment of contract rights and (b) those rights that are *not* assignable.

3. Identify those situations in which a delegation of duties is not permitted.

4. Distinguish between an intended beneficiary and an incidental beneficiary.

5. When do the rights of an intended beneficiary vest?

PROBLEMS

1. On December 1, Euphonia, a famous singer, contracted with Boito to sing at Boito's theatre on December 31st for a fee of $25,000 to be paid immediately after the performance.

(a) Euphonia, for value received, assigns this fee to Carter.

(b) Euphonia, for value received, assigns this contract to sing to Dumont, an equally famous singer.

(c) Boito sells his theatre to Edmund and assigns his contract with Euphonia to Edmund.

State the effect of each of these assignments.

2. The Smooth Paving Company entered into a paving contract with the city of Chicago. The contract contained the clause "contractor shall be liable for all damages to buildings resulting from the work performed." In the process of construction, one of the bulldozers of the Smooth Paving Company struck and broke a gas main, causing an explosion and a fire that destroyed the house of John Puff. Puff brought an appropriate action against the Smooth Paving Company to recover damages for the loss of his house. Decision?

3. Anne, who was unemployed, registered with the Speedy Employment Agency. A contract was then made under which Anne, in consideration of such position as the Agency would obtain for Anne, agreed to pay the Agency one-half of her first month's salary. The contract also contained an assignment by Anne to the Agency of one-half of her first month's salary. Two weeks later, the Agency obtained a permanent position for Anne with the Bostwick Co. at a monthly salary of $900. The agency also notified the Bostwick Co. of the assignment by Anne. At the end of the first month, the Bostwick Co. paid Anne her salary in full. Anne then quit and disappeared. The Agency now sues the Bostwick Co. for $450 under the assignment. Decision?

4. Georgia purchased an option on Blackacre from Pamela for $1,000. The option contract contained a provision by which Georgia promised not to assign the option contract without Pamela's permission. Georgia, without Pamela's permission, assigns the contract to Michael. Michael seeks to exercise the option, and Pamela refuses to sell Blackacre to him. Decision?

5. Julia contracts to sell to Hayden, an ice cream manufacturer, the amount of ice Hayden may need in his business for the ensuing three years to the extent of not more than 250 tons a week at a stated price per ton. Hayden makes a corresponding promise to Julia to buy such an amount of ice. Hayden sells his ice cream plant to Clark and assigns to Clark all Hayden's rights under the contract with Julia. Upon learning of the sale, Julia refused to furnish ice to Clark. Clark sues Julia for damages. Decision?

6. Brown enters into a written contract with Ideal Insurance Company under which, in consideration of the payment of the premiums, the insurance company promises to pay XYZ College the face amount of the policy, $100,000, on Brown's death. Brown pays the premiums until her death. Thereafter, XYZ College makes demand for the $100,000 of the insurance company, which refuses to pay upon the ground that XYZ College was not a party to the contract. Decision?

7. Grant and Debbie enter into a contract binding Grant personally to do some delicate cabinet work. Grant assigns his rights and delegates performance of his duties to Clarence.

(a) On being informed of this, Debbie agrees with Clarence, in consideration of Clarence's promise to do the work, that Debbie will accept Clarence's work, if properly done, instead of the performance promised by Grant. Later, without cause, Debbie refuses to allow Clarence to proceed with the work, though Clarence is ready to do so, and makes demand on Grant that Grant perform. Grant refuses. Can Clarence recover damages from Debbie? Can Debbie recover from Grant?

(b) Instead, assume that Debbie refuses to permit Clarence to do the work, employs another carpenter, and brings an action against Grant claiming as damages the difference between the contract price and the cost to employ the other carpenter. Decision?

8. Rebecca owes Lewis $2,500 due on November 1. On August 15 Lewis assigns this right for value received to Julia, who gives notice on September 10 of the assignment to Rebecca. On August 25 Lewis assigns the same right to Wayne, who in good faith gives value and has no prior knowledge of the assignment by Lewis to Julia. Wayne gives Rebecca notice of the assignment on August 30. What are the rights and obligations of Rebecca, Lewis, Julia, and Wayne?

9. Lisa hired Jay in the spring, as she had for many years, to set out in beds the flowers Lisa had grown in her greenhouses during the winter. The work was to be done in Lisa's absence for $300. Jay became ill the day after Lisa departed and requested his friend, Curtis, to set out the flowers, promising to pay Curtis $250 when he was paid. Curtis agreed. Upon completion of the planting, an agent of Lisa's, who had authority to dispense the money, paid Jay, and Jay paid Curtis. Within two days it became obvious that the planting was a disaster. Everything set out by Curtis had died of water rot because he did not operate Lisa's automatic watering system properly.

May Lisa recover damages from Curtis? May Lisa recover damages from Jay, and, if so, does Jay have an action against Curtis?

10. Caleb, operator of a window washing business, dictated a letter to his secretary addressed to Apartments, Inc. stating: "I will wash the windows of your apartment buildings at $4.10 per window to be paid upon completion of the work." The secretary typed the letter, signed Caleb's name, and mailed it to Apartments, Inc. Apartments, Inc. replied: "Accept your offer."

Caleb wrote back: "I will wash them during the week commencing July 10 and direct you to pay the money you will owe me to my son, Bernie. I am giving it to him as a wedding present." Caleb sent a signed copy of the letter to Bernie.

Caleb washed the windows during the time stated and demanded payment to him of $8,200 (2,000 windows at $4.10 each), informing Apartments, Inc. that he had changed his mind about having the money paid to Bernie.

What are the rights of the parties?

11. McDonald's granted to Copeland a franchise in Omaha, Nebraska. In a separate letter, it also granted him a right of first refusal for future franchises to be developed in the Omaha-Council Bluffs area. Copeland then sold all rights in his six McDonald's franchises to Schupack. When McDonald's offered a new franchise in the Omaha area to someone other than Schupack, he attempted to exercise the right of first refusal. McDonald's would not recognize the right in Schupack, claiming that it was personal to Copeland and, therefore, nonassignable without its consent. Schupack brought an action for specific performance, requiring McDonald's to accord Schupack the right of first refusal. Decision?

12. In 1952, the estate of George Bernard Shaw granted to Gabriel Pascal Enterprises, Limited, the exclusive rights to produce a musical play and a motion picture based on Shaw's play *Pygmalion.* The agreement contained a provision terminating the license if Gabriel Pascal Enterprises did not arrange for well-known composers, such as Lerner and Loewe, to write the musical and produce it within a specified period of time. George Pascal, owner of 98 percent of the Gabriel Pascal Enterprise's stock, attempted to meet these requirements but died in July 1954 before negotiations had been completed. In February 1954, however, while the license had two years yet to run, Pascal sent a letter to Kingman, his executive secretary, granting to her certain percentages of his share of the profits from the expected stage and screen productions of *Pygmalion.* Subsequently, Pascal's estate arranged for the writing and production of the highly successful *My Fair Lady,* based on Shaw's *Pygmalion.* Kingman then sued to enforce Pascal's gift assignment of the future royalties. Decision?

13. Northwest Airlines leased space in the terminal building at the Portland Airport from the Port of Portland. Crosetti entered into a contract with the Port to furnish janitorial services for the building, which required Crosetti to keep the floor clean, to indemnify the Port against loss due to claims or lawsuits based upon Crosetti's failure to perform, and to provide public liability insurance for the Port and Crosetti. A patron of the building who was injured by a fall caused by a foreign substance on the floor at Northwest's ticket counter brought suit for damages against Northwest, the Port, and Crosetti. Upon settlement of this suit, Northwest sued Crosetti to recover the amount of its contribution to the settlement and other expenses on the grounds that Northwest was a third-party beneficiary of Crosetti's contract with the Port to keep the floors clean and, therefore, within the protection of Crosetti's indemnification agreement. Decision?

COMPUTER RESEARCH PROBLEMS

 **1.** The International Association of Machinists (the union) was the bargaining agent for the employees of Powder Power Tool Corporation. On August 24, 1953, the union and the corporation executed a collective bargaining agreement providing for retroactively increased wage rates for the corporation's employees effective as of April 1, 1953. Three employees were working for Powder before and for several months after April 1, 1953, but were not employed by the corporation when the agreement was executed on August 24, 1953. They were paid to the time their employment terminated at the old wage scale. The three employees assigned their claims to Springer who brought this action against the corporation for the extra wages. Decision?

 2. In March 1962, Adrian Saylor sold government bonds owned exclusively by him and with $6,450 of the proceeds opened a savings account in a bank in the name of "Mr. or Mrs. Adrian M. Saylor." In June 1963, Saylor deposited the additional sum of $2,132 of his own money in the account. There were no other deposits and no withdrawals prior to the death of Saylor in May 1964. Is the balance of the account on Saylor's death payable wholly to Adrian Saylor's estate, wholly to his widow, or half to each?

 3. Linda King was found liable to Charlotte Clement as the result of an automobile accident. King, who was insolvent at the time, declared bankruptcy and directed her attorney, Prestwich, to list Clement as an unsecured creditor. The attorney failed to carry out this duty, and consequently King sued him for legal malpractice. When Clement pursued her judgment against King, she received a written assignment of King's legal malpractice claim against Prestwich. Clement has attempted to bring the claim, but Prestwich alleges that a claim for legal malpractice is not assignable. Decision?

 4. Rensselaer Water Company contracted with the city of Rensselaer to provide water to the city for use in homes, public buildings, industry, and fire hydrants. During the term of the contract a building caught fire. The fire spread to a nearby warehouse and destroyed it and its contents. The water company knew of the fire but failed to supply adequate water pressure at the fire hydrant to extinguish the fire. The warehouse owner sued the water company for failure to fulfill its contract with the city. Decision?

Chapter 16

PERFORMANCE, BREACH, AND DISCHARGE

Conditions
Discharge by Performance
Discharge by Breach
Discharge by Agreement
Discharge by Operation of Law

THE subject of discharge of contracts concerns the termination of contractual duties. In earlier chapters we have seen how parties may become contractually bound by their promises. It is also important to know how a person may become unbound from a contract. Contractual promises are made for a purpose, and the parties reasonably expect this purpose to be fulfilled by performance. But performance of a contractual duty is only one method of discharge.

Whatever causes a binding promise to cease to be binding is a discharge of the contract. In general, there are four kinds of discharge: (1) performance of the parties, (2) breach of one or both of the parties, (3) agreement of the parties, and (4) operation of law. Moreover, many contractual promises are not absolute promises to perform but rather are conditional promises that are dependent upon the happening or non-happening of a specific event. After a discussion of conditions, the four kinds of discharge will be covered.

CONDITIONS

A **condition** is an event whose happening or non-happening affects a duty of performance under a contract. Some conditions must be satisfied before any duty to perform arises; others terminate the duty to perform; still others either limit or modify the duty to perform. A condition is inserted into a contract for the protection and benefit of the promisor. The more conditions to which a promise is subject, the less content the promise has. A promise to pay $8,000, provided that such sum is realized from the sale of an automobile, provided the automobile is sold within sixty days, and provided that the automobile which has been stolen can be found, is clearly different from, and worth considerably less than, an unconditional promise by the same promisor to pay $8,000.

There is a fundamental difference between the breach or non-performance of a promise and the failure or non-happening of a condition. A breach of contract subjects the promisor to liability. It may or may not, depending upon its materiality, excuse non-performance by the non-breaching party of his duty under the contract. The happening or non-happening of a condition, on the other hand, either prevents a party from acquiring a right or deprives him of a right, but subjects neither party to any liability.

Conditions may be classified by *how* they are imposed: express conditions, implied-in-fact conditions, or implied-in-law conditions (also called constructive conditions). They may also be classified by *when* they affect a duty of performance: conditions concurrent, conditions precedent, or conditions subsequent. These two ways of classifying conditions are not mutually exclusive; for example, a condition may be constructive and concurrent, or express and precedent.

Express Conditions

An **express condition** is explicitly set forth in language. Although no particular form of words is necessary to create an express condition, the event to which the performance of the promise is made subject is in some manner clearly expressed. An express condition is usually preceded by such words as "provided that," "on condition that," "if," "while," "after," "upon," or "as soon as."

The basic rule applied to express conditions is that they must be fully and literally performed before the conditioned duty arises. Where a forfeiture would result, however, the courts usually apply a *substantial satisfaction* test, as discussed below under substantial performance.

Satisfaction of a Contracting Party The parties to a contract may agree that performance by one of them will be to the **satisfaction** of the other, who will not be obligated to pay for it unless he is satisfied. This is an express condition to the duty to pay for the performance. Assume that tailor Melissa contracts to make a suit of clothes to Brent's satisfaction, and that Brent promises to pay Melissa $350 for the suit if he is satisfied with it when completed. Melissa completes the suit using materials ordered by Brent. The suit fits Brent beautifully, but Brent tells Melissa that he is not satisfied with it and refuses to accept or pay for it. Melissa is not entitled to recover $350 or any amount from Brent by reason of the non-happening of the express condition. This is so if the

dissatisfaction of Brent is honest and in good faith, even if it is unreasonable. Where satisfaction relates to a matter of personal taste, opinion, or judgment, the law applies the **subjective satisfaction** standard, and the condition has not occurred if the promisor is in good faith dissatisfied.

If the contract does not clearly indicate that satisfaction is subjective, or if the performance contracted for relates to mechanical fitness or utility, the law assumes an **objective satisfaction** standard. For example, the objective standard would apply to the sale of a building or standard goods, such as steel, coal, or grain. In such cases, the question would not be whether the promisor was actually satisfied with the performance by the other party, but whether as a reasonable man, he ought to be satisfied.

Satisfaction of a Third Party A contract may provide that the duty to accept and pay for the performance of the other party is subject to the condition that the performance be approved by a third party. For example, a provision frequently found in building contracts is that before the owner is required to pay, the builder shall furnish a certificate of the architect that the building has been constructed according to the plans and specifications. The price is being paid for the building, not for the certificate, yet before the owner is obliged to pay, he must have both the building and the certificate. The duty of payment was made expressly conditional upon the presentation of the certificate. This condition is excused if the architect dies, becomes insane, capriciously refuses to give a certificate, or if there is collusion between the owner and the architect.

Implied-in-Fact Conditions

Implied-in-fact conditions are similar to express conditions, in that they must fully and literally occur and are understood by the parties to be part of the agreement. They differ in that they are not stated in express language. They are necessarily inferred from the terms of the contract, the nature of the transaction, or the conduct of the parties. Thus, if Fernando, for $750, contracts to paint Peggy's house any color desired by Peggy, it is necessarily implied in fact that Peggy will inform Fernando of the desired color before Fernando begins to paint. The notification of choice of color is an implied-in-fact condition, an operative event that must occur before Fernando is subject to the duty of painting the house.

Implied-in-Law Conditions

A **condition implied-in-law,** or a **constructive condition,** is imposed by law in order to accomplish a just and fair result. It differs from an express condition and a condition implied-in-fact in two ways: (1) it is not contained in the language of the contract or necessarily implied from the contract and (2) it need only be substantially performed. For example, Melinda contracts to sell a certain tract of land to Kelly for $18,000 and the contract is silent as to the time of delivery of the deed and payment of the price. The law will imply that the respective performances are not independent of one another. The courts will treat the promises as mutually dependent and will therefore hold that a delivery or tender of the deed by Melinda to Kelly is a condition to the duty of Kelly to pay the price. Conversely, payment or tender of $18,000 by Kelly to Melinda is a condition to the duty of Melinda to deliver the deed to Kelly. If the contract specifies a sale on credit, however, giving Kelly thirty days after delivery of the deed within which to pay the price, these conditions are not implied by law because the parties have expressly agreed to make their respective duties of performance independent of each other.

Concurrent Conditions

Concurrent conditions occur when the mutual duties of performances are to take place at the same time. As indicated in the previous section, in the absence of an agreement to the contrary, the law assumes that the respective performances under a contract are concurrent conditions. *See K & G Construction Co. v. Harris.*

Conditions Precedent

A **condition precedent** is an event that must occur before performance under a contract is due. For instance, if Gail is to deliver shoes to Mike on June 1, with Mike's duty to pay for the shoes on July 15, Gail's delivery of the shoes is a condition precedent to Mike's performance. Similarly, if Seymour promises to buy Edna's land for $50,000, provided Seymour can obtain financing in the amount of $40,000 at 10½ percent or less for thirty years within sixty days of signing the contract, Seymour's obtaining the specified financing is a condition precedent to his duty. If the condition is met, Seymour is bound to perform; if it does not occur, he is not bound to perform. Seymour, however, is under an implied-in-law duty to use his best efforts to obtain financing under these terms.

Conditions Subsequent

A **condition subsequent** is an event that terminates an existing duty. Where goods are sold under terms of "sale or return," the buyer has the right to return the goods to the seller within a stated period but is under an immediate duty to pay the price unless credit has been agreed upon. The duty to pay the price is terminated by a return of the goods, which operates as a condition subsequent. Conditions subsequent occur very infrequently in contract law, while conditions precedent are quite common.

DISCHARGE BY PERFORMANCE

Discharge by performance is undoubtedly the most frequent method of discharging a contractual duty. If a promisor exactly performs his duty under the contract he is no longer subject to that duty.

Tender is an offer by one party, who is ready, willing, and able to perform, to the other party to perform his obligation according to the terms of the contract. Where the contract is bilateral, the refusal or rejection of a tender of performance may be treated as a repudiation, excusing or discharging the tendering party from further duty of performance under the contract. For example, on the due date of contractual performance George arrives at Thelma's house prepared to do the plumbing work under the contract. Thelma refuses to allow George to enter the premises. George is discharged from performing the contract and has a legal claim against Thelma for material breach of contract.

A tender of payment of a debt past due, however, does not discharge the debt if the creditor refuses to accept the tender; instead, further accumulation of interest on the debt will cease. Thus, Peter owes Paul $10,000 which was due last month and upon which $1,000 of interest has accrued. Peter sees Paul and offers to pay Paul the money owed. Paul tells Peter to pay him the next day. Peter is not discharged from payment of the principal ($10,000) plus interest due up until the time of tender ($1,000) but is relieved of any further interest.

If a debtor owes money on several accounts and tenders to his creditor less than the total amounts due, the debtor has the right to designate the account or debt to which the payment is to be applied. This direction by the debtor must be accepted by the creditor. If the debtor does not direct the application of the payment, the creditor may apply it to any account owing to him by the debtor or distribute it among several such accounts.

DISCHARGE BY BREACH

Breach of contract is the unexcused failure of a party to perform her promise. Breach of contract always gives rise to a cause of action for damages by the aggrieved (injured) party. It may, however, have a more important effect: an uncured (uncorrected) *material* breach by one party operates as an excuse for nonperformance by the other party and discharges the aggrieved party from any further duty under the contract. If the breach, on the

other hand, is not material, the aggrieved party is not discharged from the contract, although she may recover money damages. Under the Code *any* deviation discharges the aggrieved party.

Material Breach

An unjustified failure to perform *substantially* the obligations promised in a contract constitutes a **material breach.** The key is whether the aggrieved party obtained substantially what he bargained for or whether his rights under the contract were significantly impaired by the breach. A material breach discharges the aggrieved party from his duty of performance. For instance, Esta orders a specially made, tailored suit from Stuart to be made of wool, but Stuart instead makes the suit of cotton. Stuart has materially breached the contract. Consequently, Esta is discharged from her duty to pay for the suit. Esta may also recover money damages from Stuart due to Stuart's breach.

Although there are no clear-cut rules as to what constitutes a material breach, the Restatement, Section 241, lists a number of factors that are relevant:

In determining whether a failure to render or to offer performance is material, the following circumstances are significant:

(a) the extent to which the injured party will be deprived of the benefit which he reasonably expected;
(b) the extent to which the injured party can be adequately compensated for the part of that benefit of which he will be deprived;
(c) the extent to which the party failing to perform or to offer to perform will suffer forfeiture;
(d) the likelihood that the party failing to perform or to offer to perform will cure his failure, taking account of all the circumstances including any reasonable assurances;
(e) the extent to which the behavior of the party failing to perform or to offer to perform comports with standards of good faith and fair dealing.

An *intentional* breach of contract is generally held to be material. Moreover, a failure to perform a promise promptly is a material breach if time is of the essence, that is, if the parties have clearly indicated that a failure to perform by the stated time is material; otherwise the aggrieved party may recover damages only for the loss caused by the delay. Finally, the parties to a contract may, within limits, specify what breaches are to be considered material. *See K & G Construction Co. v. Harris.*

Prevention of Performance   One party's substantial interference with or **prevention of performance** by the other generally constitutes a material breach that discharges the other party to the contract. For instance, Craig prevents an architect from giving a certificate, which is a condition to Craig's liability to pay Maud a certain sum of money. Craig may not set up Maud's failure to produce a certificate as an excuse for Craig's nonpayment. Likewise, if Harold has contracted to grow a certain crop for Rafael, and after Harold has planted the seed, Rafael plows the field and destroys the seedling plants, his interference with Harold's performance discharges Harold from his duty under the contract. It does not, however, discharge Rafael from his duty under the contract.

Perfect Tender Rule   The Code greatly alters the common law doctrine of material breach by adopting what is known as the **perfect tender rule.** This rule, which is discussed more fully in Chapter 21, essentially provides that *any* deviation from the promised performance in a sales contract under the Code constitutes a material breach of the contract and discharges the aggrieved party of his duty of performance. Thus, if a seller of camera accessories delivers to buyer ninety-nine of the hundred ordered pieces, or ninety-nine correct accessories and one incorrect accessory, the buyer may rightfully reject the improper delivery.

Substantial Performance

If a party substantially, but not completely, performs her obligations under a contract, the common law will generally allow that party to obtain the other party's performance less any damages caused by the partial performance. Thus, in the specially ordered suit illustration discussed in the previous section, if Stuart, the tailor, improperly used black buttons instead of blue, Stuart would be permitted to collect from Esta the contract price of the suit less the damage, if any, caused to Esta by the substitution of the wrongly colored buttons. The doctrine of substantial performance assumes particular importance in the construction industry in cases where the structure is being built on the aggrieved party's land. Consider the following: Kent Construction Co. builds a $300,000 house for Martha but deviates from the specifications, causing Martha $10,000 in damages. If this breach were considered material, then Martha would not have to pay for the house that is now on her land. This would clearly be an unjust forfeiture. Therefore, because Kent's performance is substantial, the courts would probably not deem the breach material. As a result, Kent would be able to collect $290,000 from Martha.

    See Mayor & City of Douglasville v. Hildebrand.

Anticipatory Repudiation

A breach of contract, as previously discussed, is a failure to perform the terms of the contract. It is logically and physically impossible to fail to perform a duty before the date that performance is due. A party, however, may announce before the due date that she will not perform, or she may commit an act that makes her unable to perform. Either of these acts is a repudiation of the contract, which notifies the other party that a breach is imminent. Such repudiation before the date fixed by the contract for performance is called an **anticipatory repudiation.** The courts, as shown in the leading case of *Hochster v. De La Tour,* allow it to be treated as a breach, discharging the nonrepudiating party's duty to perform and permitting her to bring suit immediately as if it were a breach. Nonetheless, the nonbreaching party may wait until the time of performance to see if the repudiator will retract his repudiation and perform his contractual duties. If the repudiator does perform, then there is a discharge by performance; if he does not perform, there is a material breach.

Material Alteration of Written Contract

An unauthorized alteration or change of *any* of the material terms or provisions of a written contract or document is a discharge of the *entire* contract. To be a discharge, the alteration must be material and fraudulent and must be the act of a party to the contract or someone acting on his behalf. An alteration is material if it would vary any party's legal relations with the maker of the alteration or adversely affect that party's legal relations with a third person. Restatement, Section 286. An unauthorized change in the terms of a written contract by a person who is not a party to the contract does not discharge the contract.

DISCHARGE BY AGREEMENT OF THE PARTIES

The parties to a contract may by agreement discharge each other from performance under the contract. They may do this by rescission, substituted contract, accord and satisfaction, or novation.

Mutual Rescission

A **mutual rescission** is an agreement between the parties to terminate their respective duties under the contract. It is a contract to end a contract. All of the essentials of a contract must be present. In an executory, bilateral contract, each party furnishes consideration in giving up his rights under the contract in exchange for the other party's relinquishment of his rights under the contract. *See Watts Construction Co. v. Cullman County.* Where one party has already fully performed, a mutual rescission may not be binding at common law because of lack of consideration.

Substituted Contracts

A **substituted contract** is a new contract accepted by both parties in satisfaction of the parties' duties under the original contract. Restatement, Section 279. A substituted contract immediately discharges the original duty and imposes new obligations. For example, the Restatement, Section 279, gives the following illustration:

A and B make a contract under which A promises to build on a designated spot a building, for which B promises to pay $100,000. Later, before this contract is performed, A and B make a new contract under which A is to build on the same spot a different building, for which B is to pay $200,000. The new contract is a substituted contract and the duties of A and B under the original contract are discharged.

Accord and Satisfaction

An **accord** is a contract by which an obligee promises to accept a stated performance in *satisfaction* of the obligor's *existing* contractual duty. Restatement, Section 281. The performance of the accord is called a **satisfaction** and it discharges the original duty. Thus, if Ted owes Alan $500 and the parties agree that Ted shall paint Alan's house in satisfaction of the debt, the agreement is an accord. The debt, however, is not discharged until Ted performs the accord by painting Alan's house.

Novation

A **novation** is a substituted contract that involves an agreement among *three* parties to substitute a new promisee for the existing promisee, or to replace the existing promisor with a new one. Restatement, Section 280. A novation discharges the old obligation by creating a new contract in which there is either a new promisee or a new promisor. Thus, if B owes A $500 and A, B, and C agree that C will pay the debt and B will be discharged, the novation is the substitution of the new promisor C for B. Alternatively, if the three parties agree that B will pay $500 to D instead of to A, the novation is the substitution of a new promisee D for A. In each instance the debt owed by B to A is discharged.

DISCHARGE BY OPERATION OF LAW

This chapter has considered various ways by which contractual duties may be discharged. In all of these cases, the discharge resulted from the action of one or both of the parties to the contract. This section examines discharge brought about by the operation of law.

Impossibility

"Contract liability is strict liability . . . [and an] obligor is therefore liable for breach of contract even if he is without fault and even if circumstances have made the contract more burdensome or less desirable than he had anticipated." Restatement, Introductory Note to Chapter 11. Historically, the common law excused a party from contractual duties for **objective impossibility;** that is, where the performance could not be done by anyone. If a particular contracting party is unable to perform because, for instance, of financial inability or lack of competence, this is **subjective impossibility** and does not excuse the promisor from liability for breach of contract. For example, the Christys entered into a written contract to purchase an apartment house from Pilkinton for $30,000. Pilkinton tendered a deed to the property and demanded payment of the unpaid balance of $29,000 due on the purchase price. As a result of a decline in Christy's used car business, the Christys did not possess and could not borrow the unpaid balance and, thus, asserted that it was impossible for them to perform their contract. The court held for Pilkinton, stating that there is an important distinction between objective impossibility, which amounts to saying, "the thing cannot be done," and subjective impossibility—"I cannot do it." The latter, which is illustrated by a promisor's financial inability to pay, does not discharge the con-

tractual duty. *Christy v. Pilkinton,* 224 Ark. 407, 273 S.W.2d 533 (1954).

The **death** or **incapacity** of a person who has contracted to render *personal services* is a discharge of his contractual duty due to objective impossibility. For example, a singer, unable to perform her contractual engagement because of a severe cold, is excused from performance, as is a pianist or violinist who is unable to perform because of an injury to his hand.

Destruction of the **subject matter** or of the agreed upon means of performance of a contract, without the fault of the promisor, is also excusable impossibility. Subject matter here means specific subject matter. Suppose that Alice contracts to sell to Gary five office chairs at an agreed price. Alice has 100 of these chairs in stock, out of which she expects to deliver five to Gary. Before she can do so, the entire 100 chairs are destroyed by fire without Alice's fault. Alice is not excused from performance. This was not a contract for the sale of specific goods. Alice can perform this contract by delivering to Gary any five chairs of the kind and grade specified in the contract. Her failure to do so will render her liable to Gary for breach of contract. Suppose now that Alice and Gary make a contract for Alice to manufacture these five chairs in her factory but prior to their manufacture the factory is destroyed by fire without Alice's fault. Although the chairs are available from other manufacturers, Alice's duty to deliver the chairs is discharged by the destruction of the factory. Suppose further that Alice and Gary enter into a contract for the sale by Alice to Gary of the particular desk that Alice uses in her private office. This desk and no other is the specific subject matter of the contract. If, before the sale is completed, this desk is destroyed by fire without Alice's fault, it is then impossible for Alice to perform. The contract is therefore discharged.

If the performance of a contract which was legal when formed, becomes **illegal** or impractical by reason of a subsequently enacted law, the duty of performance is discharged. Restatement, Section 264. For example, Jill contracts to sell and deliver to Fred ten cases of a certain whiskey each month for one year. A subsequent prohibition law makes the manufacture, transportation, or sale of intoxicating liquor unlawful. The duties in the contract that are still unperformed by Jill are discharged.

Frustration of Purpose Where, after a contract is made, a party's principal purpose is substantially frustrated without his fault by the occurrence of an event the non-occurrence of which was a basic assumption on which the contract was made, his remaining duties to render performance are discharged, unless the party has assumed the risk. Restatement, Second 265. This rule developed from the so-called coronation cases. When Edward VII became King of England upon the death of his mother Queen Victoria, impressive coronation ceremonies were planned, including a procession along a designated route through certain streets in London. Contracts were made by owners and lessees of buildings along the route to permit the use of rooms with a view on the date scheduled for the procession. The King became ill, and the procession did not take place. The purpose for using the rooms having failed, the rooms were not used. Numerous suits were filed, some by landowners seeking to hold the would-be viewers liable on their promises, and some by the would-be viewers seeking to recover money paid in advance for the rooms. The principle involved was novel, but from these cases evolved the frustration of purpose doctrine under which a contract is discharged if supervening circumstances make impossible the fulfillment of the purpose that both parties had in mind, unless one of the parties contractually assumed that risk.

Commercial Impracticability The Restatement, Section 261, and the Code, Section 2–615, have relaxed the traditional test of objective impossibility by providing that performance need not be actually or literally impossible, but that commercial impracticability will excuse non-performance. This does not mean mere hardship or that the cost of performance would be more than expected. A party will be discharged from performing his duty only when his performance is made impracticable by a supervening event not caused by his fault. Moreover, the non-occurrence of the subsequent event must have been a "basic assumption" upon which both parties made when entering into the contract, and neither party had assumed the risk that the event would occur. Commercial impracticability could include "a severe shortage of raw materials or of supplies due to a contingency such as war, embargo, local crop failure, unforeseen shutdown of major sources of supply or the like, which either causes a marked increase in cost or altogether prevents the seller from securing supplies necessary to his performance. . . ." U.C.C. Section 2–615, Comment 4. *See Northern Corp. v. Chugach Electrical Association.*

Bankruptcy

Bankruptcy is a discharge of a contractual duty by operation of law available to a debtor who, by compliance with the requirements of the Bankruptcy Code, obtains an order of discharge by the bankruptcy court. It is applicable only to obligations that the Code provides are dischargeable in bankruptcy. The subject of bankruptcy is treated in Chapter 40.

Statute of Limitations

At common law a plaintiff was not subject to any time limitation within which to bring an action. Now, however, all States have statutes providing such a limitation. The majority of courts holds that the running of the period of the statute of limitations does not operate to discharge the obligation, but only to bar the creditor's right to bring an action.

For a summary of discharge of contracts, see Figure 16–1.

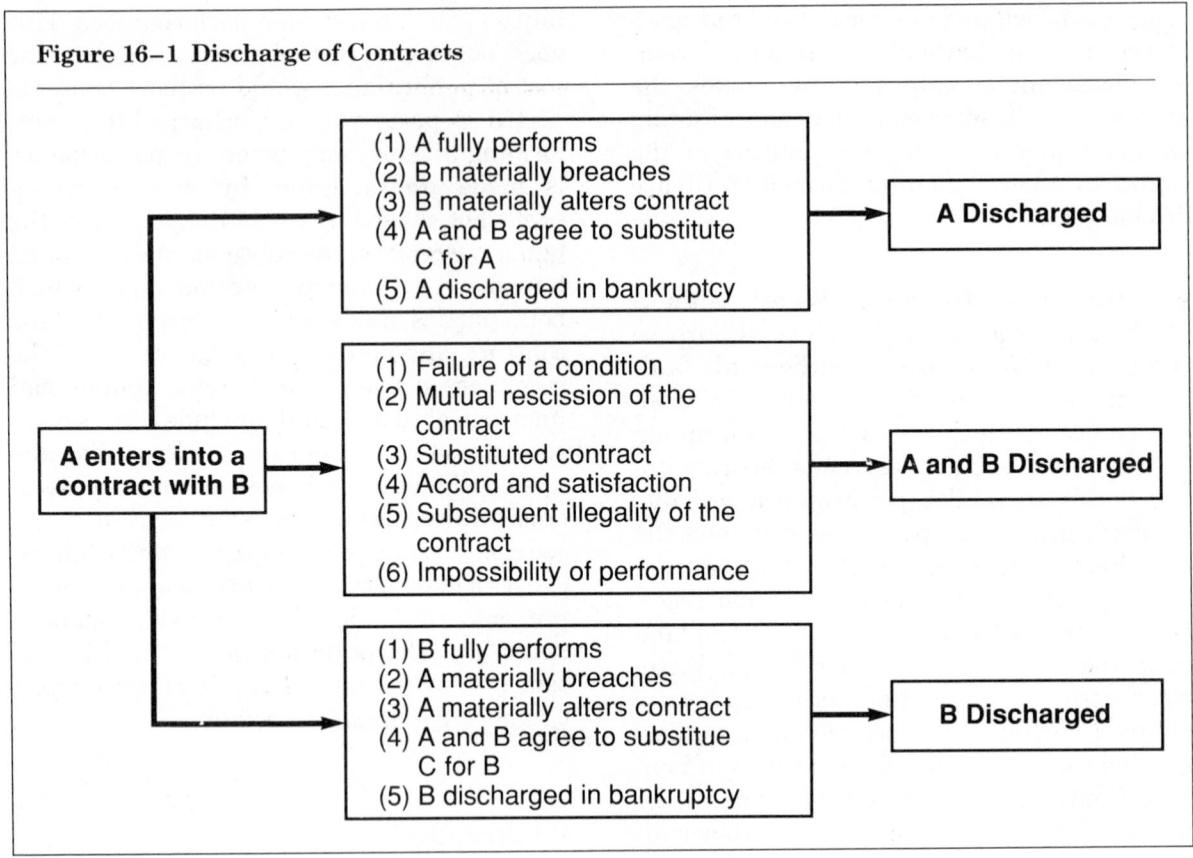

Figure 16–1 Discharge of Contracts

A enters into a contract with B

(1) A fully performs
(2) B materially breaches
(3) B materially alters contract
(4) A and B agree to substitute C for A
(5) A discharged in bankruptcy

→ **A Discharged**

(1) Failure of a condition
(2) Mutual rescission of the contract
(3) Substituted contract
(4) Accord and satisfaction
(5) Subsequent illegality of the contract
(6) Impossibility of performance

→ **A and B Discharged**

(1) B fully performs
(2) A materially breaches
(3) A materially alters contract
(4) A and B agree to substitue C for B
(5) B discharged in bankruptcy

→ **B Discharged**

CASES

Concurrent Conditions/Material Breach

K & G CONSTRUCTION CO. v. HARRIS

Court of Appeals of Maryland, 1960.
223 Md. 305, 164 A.2d 451.

PRESCOTT, JUDGE.

Feeling aggrieved by the action of the trial judge of the Circuit Court for Prince George's County, sitting without a jury, in finding a judgment against it in favor of a subcontractor, the appellant, the general contractor on a construction project, appealed.

The principal question presented is: Does a contractor, damaged by a subcontractor's failure to perform a portion of his work in a workmanlike manner, have a right, under the circumstances of this case, to withhold, in partial satisfaction of said damages, an installment payment, which, under the terms of the contract, was due the subcontractor, unless the negligent performance of his work excused its payment?

* * *

The statement, in relevant part, is as follows:
"... K & G Construction Company, Inc. (hereinafter called Contractor), plaintiff ... and appellant herein, was owner and general contractor of a housing subdivision project being constructed (herein called Project). Harris and Brooks (hereinafter called Subcontractor), defendants ... and appellees herein, entered into a contract with Contractor to do excavating and earth-moving work on the Project. Pertinent parts of the contract are set forth below:

"Section 3. The Subcontractor agrees to complete the several portions and the whole of the work herein sublet by the time or times following:

"(a) Without delay, as called for by the Contractor.

"(b) It is expressly agreed that time is of the essence of this contract, and that the Contractor will have the right to terminate this contract and employ a substitute to perform the work in the event of delay on the part of Subcontractor, and Subcontractor agrees to indemnify the Contractor for any loss sustained thereby, provided, however, that nothing in this paragraph shall be construed to deprive Contractor of any rights or remedies it would otherwise have as to damage for delay.

"Section 4. (b) Progress payments will be made each month during the performance of the work. Subcontractor will submit to Contractor, by the 25th of each month, a requisition for work performed during the preceding month. Contractor will pay these requisitions, less a retainer equal to ten per cent (10%), by the 10th of the months in which such requisitions are received.

* * *

"Section 8. . . . All work shall be performed in a workmanlike manner, and in accordance with the best practices.

"Section 9. Subcontractor agrees to carry, during the progress of the work, . . . liability insurance against . . . property damage, in such amounts and with such companies as may be satisfactory to Contractor and shall provide Contractor with certificates showing the same to be in force."

"While in the course of his employment by the Subcontractor on the Project, a bulldozer operator drove his machine too close to Contractor's house while grading the yard, causing the immediate collapse of a wall and other damage to the house. The resulting damage to contractor's house was $3,400.00. Subcontractor had complied with the insurance provision (Sec. 9) of the aforesaid contract. Subcontractor reported said damages to their liability insurance carrier. The Subcontractor and its insurance carrier refused

to repair damage or compensate Contractor for damage to the house, claiming that there was no liability on the part of the Subcontractor.

* * *

The aforesaid bulldozer accident damaging Contractor's house occurred on August 9, 1958. Contractor refused to pay Subcontractor's requisition due on August 10, 1958, because the bulldozer damage to Contractor's house had not been repaired or paid for. Subcontractor continued to work on the project until the 12th of September, 1958, at which time they discontinued working on the project because of Contractor's refusal to pay the said work requisition and notified Contractor by registered letters of their position and willingness to return to the job, but only upon payment. At that time, September 12, 1958, the value of the work completed by Subcontractor on the project for which they had not been paid was $1,484.50.

"Contractor later requested Subcontractor to return and complete work on the Project which Subcontractor refused to do because of nonpayment of work requisitions of July 25 and thereafter. Contractor's house was not repaired by Subcontractor nor compensation paid for the damage.

* * *

". . . Contractor filed suit against the Subcontractor in two counts: (1) for the aforesaid bulldozer damage to Contractor's house, alleging negligence of the Subcontractor's bulldozer operator, and (2) for the $450.00 costs above the contract price in having another excavating subcontractor complete the uncompleted work in the contract. Subcontractor filed a counter-claim for recovery of work of the value of $1,484.50 for which they had not received payment and for loss of anticipated profits on uncompleted portion of work in the amount of $1,340.00. By agreement of the parties, the first count of Contractor's claim, i.e., for aforesaid bulldozer damage to Contractor's house, was submitted to jury who found in favor of Contractor in the amount of $3,400.00. Following the finding by the jury, the second count of the Contractor's claim and the counter-claims of the

Subcontractor, by agreement of the parties, were submitted to the Court for determination, without jury. All of the facts recited herein above were stipulated to by the parties to the Court. Circuit Court Judge Fletcher found for counter-plaintiff Subcontractor in the amount of $2,824.50 from which Contractor has entered this appeal."

The $3,400 judgment has been paid.

* * *

The vital question, more tersely stated, remains: Did the contractor have a right, under the circumstances, to refuse to make the progress payment due on August 10, 1958?

The answer involves interesting and important principles of contract law. Promises and counter-promises made by the respective parties to a contract have certain relations to one another, which determine many of the rights and liabilities of the parties. Broadly speaking, they are (1) independent of each other or (2) mutually dependent, one upon the other. They are independent of each other if the parties intend that *performance* by each of them is in no way conditioned upon *performance* by the other. [Citation.] In other words, the parties exchange promises for promises, not the *performance* of promises for the *performance* of promises. [Citation.] A failure to perform an independent promise does not excuse non-performance on the part of the adversary party, but each is required to perform his promise, and, if one does not perform, he is liable to the adversary party for such non-performance. (Of course, if litigation ensues questions of set-off or recoupment frequently arise.) Promises are mutually dependent if the parties intend *performance* by one to be conditioned upon *performance* by the other, and, if they be mutually dependent, they may be (a) precedent, i.e., a promise that is to be performed before a corresponding promise on the part of the adversary party is to be performed, (b) subsequent, i.e., a corresponding promise that is not to be performed until the other party to the contract has performed a precedent covenant, or (c) concurrent, i.e., promises that are to be performed at the same time by each of the

parties, who are respectively bound to perform each. [Citation.]

* * * The modern rule, which seems to be of almost universal application, is that there is a presumption that mutual promises in a contract are dependent and are to be so regarded, whenever possible. [Citations.] * * *

* * * It would, indeed present an unusual situation if we were to hold that a building contractor, who has obtained someone to do work for him and has agreed to pay each month for the work performed in the previous month, has to continue the monthly payments, irrespective of the degree of skill and care displayed in the performance of work, and his only recourse is by way of suit for ill-performance. If this were the law, it is conceivable, in fact, probable, that many contractors would become insolvent before they were able to complete their contracts. As was stated by [citation]: "Covenants are to be construed as dependent or independent according to the intention of the parties and the good sense of the case."

We hold that when the subcontractor's employee negligently damaged the contractor's wall, this constituted a breach of the subcontractor's promise to perform his work in a "workmanlike manner, and in accordance with the best practices." [Citations.] And there can be little doubt that the breach was material: the damage to the wall amounted to more than double the payment due on August 10. [Citation.] Corbin, [citation], says: "The failure of a contractor's (in our case, the subcontractor's) performance to constitute 'substantial' performance may justify the owner (in our case, the contractor) in refusing to make a progress payment . . . If the refusal to pay an installment is justified on the owner's (contractor's) part, the contractor (subcontractor) is not justified in abandoning work by reason of that refusal. His abandonment of the work will itself be a wrongful repudiation that goes to the essence, even if the defects in performance did not." [Citations.] Professor Corbin, in § 954, states further: "The unexcused failure of a contractor to render a promised performance when it is due is always a breach of contract. . . . Such failure may be of such great importance as to constitute what has been called herein a 'total' breach, ... For a failure of performance constituting such a 'total' breach, an action for remedies that are appropriate thereto is at once maintainable. Yet the injured party is not required to bring such action. He has the option of treating the nonperformance as a 'partial' breach only. . . ." In permitting the subcontractor to proceed with work on the project after August 9, the contractor, obviously, treated the breach by the subcontractor as a partial one. As the promises were mutually dependent and the subcontractor had made a material breach in his performance, this justified the contractor in refusing to make the August 10 payment; hence, as the contractor was not in default, the subcontractor again breached the contract when he, on September 12, discontinued work on the project, which rendered him liable (by the express terms of the contract) to the contractor for his increased cost in having the excavating done—a stipulated amount of $450.

* * *

Judgment against the appellant reversed; and judgment entered in favor of the appellant against the appellees for $450, the appellees to pay the costs.

Substantial Performance

MAYOR & CITY OF DOUGLASVILLE v. HILDEBRAND

Court of Appeals of Georgia, 1985.
175 Ga.App. 434, 333 S.E.2d 674.

BEASLEY, J.

This appeal involves an action for breach of contract brought against the Mayor and City of Douglasville. On August 20, 1981, plaintiff and the city entered into a written agreement whereby the plaintiff agreed to serve as Community Development Project Engineer for a period of three years at an "annual fee" of $19,000. The contract provided that the "annual fee" could be changed by the parties without affecting the other terms. The contract contained three provisions for its termi-

nation. The only one which has any application to the circumstances of this case reads: "Either party may terminate this agreement at any time by giving notice in writing to the other party at least ninety (90) days prior to the date said party intends to terminate this agreement." The services and duties plaintiff was to perform for the city were listed under sixteen designated subparagraphs.

The plaintiff worked for the city under the contract for over two years and received two 10% increases of his annual fee so that it became $1,915.83 per month. On September 20, 1983, the city sent a letter to plaintiff: "You are hereby notified that, because of certain material breaches by you of the referenced agreement [of August 20, 1981], your services thereunder are no longer desired, effective upon your receipt of this notice."

By suit, Hildebrand sought damages for loss of his annual fee * * *. After the city answered, plaintiff moved for summary judgment based on the terms of the contract and his affidavit which recited that his monthly salary was $1,915.83 and that he was entitled to $5,747.49 because of the city's failure to give him ninety days notice prior to the termination of the contract. The city offered an affidavit by plaintiff's supervisor, the Director of Community Development, that plaintiff did not perform all the services enumerated in the contract.

* * *

The two contractual provisions as to which there was alleged noncompliance are: 1) a portion of paragraph 7 which recites that plaintiff "agrees that he will at all times keep the Community Development Director knowledgeable of his whereabouts and how he may be contacted," and 2) subparagraph 2(p) which required that plaintiff attend "necessary meetings, etc., if requested, which may relate to the program. . . ."

After a hearing, the trial court found that the plaintiff should have been given ninety days notice prior to termination of the contract and thus was entitled to damages equalling compensation for ninety days under the contract. Summary judgment was granted to plaintiff and judgment entered in the amount of $5,747.49 plus interest and costs. The defendant appealed.

Assuming the city could repudiate the contract without giving ninety days notice, the requirement for such termination must be based on a material breach, a substantial failure to perform. A breach which is "incidental and subordinate to the main purpose of the contract, and which may be compensated in damages, does not warrant a rescission . . ." or termination nor does "a mere breach of contract not so substantial and fundamental as to defeat the object of the parties in making the agreement." In order to trigger the right to rescission, "the act failed to be performed must go to the root of the contract. . . ." [Citation.]

* * *

Here there were broad conclusions in the affidavit for the city as to plaintiff's "continuous failure to comply" with the contractual terms. Since mere legal conclusions and allegations present no issue of fact on motion for summary judgment, [citation] we need consider only the two specific charges involving plaintiff's alleged noncompliance. Neither alone nor collectively do either rise to the level necessary to warrant termination, i.e., constituting noncompliance, so substantial and fundamental as to defeat the contract's object. That being true, the city was obliged to give plaintiff the ninety-day notice of termination to which it had agreed in the contract.

* * *

A wrongful discharge in violation of a contract right to continued employment gives an employee the right to recover damages. Even though there is a repudiation of the promise of future earnings, the injured party is not necessarily entitled to the sum for the complete contract term. [Citation.] "Where a contract of employment expressly empowers an employer to terminate the contract upon giving notice, recovery for wrongful breach is limited to the notice period." [Citation.] Here plaintiff is limited to 90 days, to his actual contractual loss, as a measure of liquidated damages.

Judgment affirmed.

Anticipatory Breach

HOCHSTER v. DE LA TOUR
Queen's Bench of England, 1853.
2 Ellis and Blackburn Reports 678.

LORD CAMPBELL, C.J.

[On April 12, 1852, Hochster contracted with De La Tour to serve as a guide for De La Tour on his three-month trip to Europe, beginning on June 1 at an agreed upon salary. On May 11, De La Tour notified Hochster that he would not need Hochster's services. He also refused to pay Hochster any compensation. Hochster brings this action to recover damages for breach of contract.]

On this motion . . . the question arises, Whether, if there be an agreement between A. and B., whereby B. engages to employ A. on and from a future day for a given period of time, to travel with him into a foreign country as a [guide], and to start with him in that capacity on that day, A. being to receive a monthly salary during the continuance of such service, B. may, before the day, refuse to perform the agreement and break and renounce it, so as to entitle A. before the day to commence an action against B. to recover damages for breach of the agreement; A. having been ready and willing to perform it, till it was broken and renounced by B.

* * *

If the plaintiff has no remedy for breach of the contract unless he treats the contract as in force, and acts upon it down to the 1st June, 1852, it follows that, till then, he must enter into no employment which will interfere with his promise "to start with the defendant on such travels on the day and year" and that he must then be properly equipped in all respects as a [guide] for a three months' tour on the continent of Europe. But it is surely much more rational, and more for the benefit of both parties, that, after the renunciation of the agreement by the defendant, the plaintiff should be at liberty to consider himself absolved from any future performance of it, retaining his right to sue for any damage he has suffered from the breach of it.

Thus, instead of remaining idle and laying out money in preparations which must be useless, he is at liberty to seek service under another employer, which would go in mitigation of the damages to which he would otherwise be entitled for a breach of the contract. It seems strange that the defendant after renouncing the contract, and absolutely declaring that he will never act under it, should be permitted to object that faith is given to his assertion, and that an opportunity is not left to him of changing his mind. * * *

* * * The man who wrongfully renounces a contract into which he has deliberately entered cannot justly complain if he is immediately sued for a compensation in damage by the man whom he has injured: and it seems reasonable to allow an option to the injured party, either to sue immediately, or to wait till the time when the act was to be done, still holding it as prospectively binding for the exercise of this option, which may be advantageous to the innocent party, and cannot be prejudicial to the wrongdoer.

Judgment for plaintiff.

Mutual Rescission

WATTS CONSTRUCTION CO. v. CULLMAN COUNTY

Supreme Court of Alabama, 1980.
382 So.2d 520.

SHORES, J.

This is a contract case. Appellant Watts Construction Company submitted the low bid on a County Water Works Improvement Project and was awarded the contract in May of 1976. In July, Robert L. Harbison, chairman of the Cullman County Commission, executed a construction contract for the project, separate copies of which had earlier been executed by Watts. Item V, Section II, of the contract provides that "[t]his contract shall not be effective unless and until approved by the State Director of the Farmers Home Administration, U.S. Department of Agriculture or his delegated representative."

FHA approval for the project was not obtained. However, when a portion of the project which was being funded by the city, rather than the county, was deleted during the summer, the change order was signed by a representative of the State Director of the FHA.

Construction on the project was delayed until the fall, allegedly due to the lowering of the county's debt limit. In September, construction still had not been authorized, and Watts requested a 5 percent increase in the contract price due to seasonal and inflational price increases. The county countered with an offer of 3.5 percent. By a letter dated September 21, 1976 . . ., Watts notified the commission that he could not accept less than a 5 percent increase, and concluded: "If this is not agreeable with you, please consider this letter a withdrawal of our bid." This letter was discussed at a meeting of the county commission on September 24, 1976, where it was agreed that the county could not pay a 5 percent increase. Negotiations were begun with the next lowest bidder to take the project on at the low bid price. On October 4, 1976, the commission re-awarded the contract to Tucker Brothers Construction Company at the low bid made by Watts. Watts alleges that the award to Tucker Brothers included project specification changes which reduced the cost of the project and which were not offered to Watts. He was notified by letter dated October 14, 1976, that his withdrawal of the bid had been accepted by the commission. On October 19, 1976, Watts informed the commission that he was willing to perform the contract at bid price with certain modifications in specifications. His offer was not accepted.

Watts then brought this action to recover damages for breach of contract. . . . The trial court granted the county's motion for summary judgment, and this appeal followed. For the reasons discussed herein, we affirm.

* * *

We find it unnecessary to discuss the issue of whether FHA approval was a condition precedent to creation of a valid contract. Watt's letter of September 21 withdrawing his bid and the commission's letter of October 14 accepting that withdrawal effectively rescinded any contract that might have existed. Parties to a written contract may by mutual consent and without other consideration rescind the contract. [Citation.] Where the acts and conduct of one party inconsistent with the existence of a contract are acquiesced in by the other, such contract will be treated as abandoned or rescinded. [Citation.] Watt's demand for an increase in the contract price demonstrated his intention not to be bound by the original contract. The commission acquiesced in his desire not to be so bound, and the contract was rescinded. Once a party to a contract has repudiated or broken it, he cannot reinstate the contract by an offer to perform. [Citation.] Where the parties have by mutual agreement rescinded a contract, one of the parties thereto cannot recover damages in an action for breach of contract. [Citation.] Where parties agree to rescind the contract, each gives up the provisions for its benefit, and the parties are then competent to contract with others. [Citation.]

* * *

The judgment appealed from is affirmed.

Impossibility

NORTHERN CORP. v. CHUGACH ELECTRICAL ASSOCIATION

Supreme Court of Alaska, 1974.
518 P.2d 76.

BOOCHEVER, J.

[Northern Corporation entered into a contract with Chugach in August 1966 to repair and upgrade the upstream face of Cooper Lake Dam in Alaska. The contract required Northern to obtain rock from a quarry site at the opposite end of the lake and to transport the rock to the dam during the winter across the ice on the lake. In December 1966, Northern cleared the road on the ice to permit deeper freezing, but thereafter water overflowed on the ice preventing its use.

Northern complained of unsafe conditions of the lake ice, but Chugach insisted on performance. In March 1967, one of Northern's loaded trucks broke through the ice and sank. Northern continued to encounter difficulties and ceased operations with the approval of Chugach. On January 8, 1968 Chugach notified Northern that it would be in default unless all rock was hauled by April 1. After two more trucks broke through the ice, causing the deaths of the drivers, Northern ceased operations and notified Chugach that it would make no more attempts to haul across the lake. Northern advised Chugach it considered the contract terminated for impossibility of performance and commenced suit to recover the cost incurred in attempting to complete the contract.]

* * *

The focal question is whether the . . . contract was impossible of performance. The September 27, 1966 directive specified that the rock was to be transported "across Cooper Lake to the dam site when such lake is frozen to a sufficient depth to permit heavy vehicle traffic thereon," and . . . specified that the hauling to the dam site would be done during the winter of 1966–67. It is therefore clear that the parties contemplated that the rock would be transported across the frozen lake by truck. Northern's repeated efforts to perform the contract by this method during the winter of 1966–67 and subsequently in February 1968, culminating in the tragic loss of life, abundantly support the trial court's findings that the contract was impossible of performance by this method.

Chugach contends, however, that Northern was nevertheless bound to perform, and that it could have used means other than hauling by truck across the ice to transport the rock. The answer to Chugach's contention is that . . . the parties contemplated that the rock would be hauled by truck once the ice froze to a sufficient depth to support the weight of the vehicles. The specification of this particular method of performance presupposed the existence of ice frozen to the requisite depth. Since this expectation of the parties was never fulfilled, and since the provisions relating to the means of performance was clearly material, Northern's duty to perform was discharged by reason of impossibility.

There is an additional reason for our holding that Northern's duty to perform was discharged because of impossibility. It is true that in order for a defendant to prevail under the original common law doctrine of impossibility, he had to show that no one else could have performed the contract. However, this harsh rule has gradually been eroded, and the Restatement of Contracts has departed from the early common law rule by recognizing the principle of "commercial impracticability". Under this doctrine, a party is discharged from his contract obligations, even if it is technically possible to perform them, if the costs of performance would be so disproportionate to that reasonably contemplated by the parties as to make the contract totally impractical in a commercial sense. . . . Removed from the strictures of the common law, "impossibility" in its modern context has become a coat of many colors, including among its hues the point argued here—namely, impossibility predicated upon "commercial impracticability." This concept—which finds expression both in case law . . . and in other authorities . . . is grounded upon the assumption that in legal contemplation something is impracticable when it can only be done at an excessive and unreasonable cost. As stated in *Transatlantic Financing Corp. v. United States* [Citation]

. . . The doctrine ultimately represents the ever-shifting line, drawn by courts hopefully responsive to commercial practices and mores, at which the community's interest in having contracts enforced according to their terms is outweighed by the commercial senselessness of requiring performance . . .

* * *

In the case before us the detailed opinion of the trial court clearly indicates that the appropriate standard was followed. There is ample evidence to support its findings that "[t]he ice haul method of transporting riprap ultimately selected was within the contemplation of the parties and was part of the basis of the agreement which ultimately resulted in amendment No. 1 in October 1966," and that that method was not commercially feasible within the financial parameters of the contract. We affirm the court's conclusion that the contract was impossible of performance.

* * *

QUESTIONS

1. Identify and distinguish among the various types of conditions.

2. Distinguish between full performance and tender of performance.

3. Explain the difference between material breach and substantial performance. Explain how the U.C.C. perfect tender rule differs from these rules.

4. Distinguish among a mutual rescission, substituted contract, accord and satisfaction, and novation.

5. Identify and discuss the ways discharge may be brought about by operation of law.

PROBLEMS

1. A–1 Roofing Co. entered into a written contract with Jaffe to put a new roof on the latter's residence for $1,800 with a specified type of roofing, and to complete the job without unreasonable delay. A–1 undertook the work within a week thereafter, and when all the roofing material was at the site and the labor 50 percent completed, the premises were totally destroyed by fire caused by lightning. A–1 submitted a bill to Jaffe for $1,200 for materials furnished and labor performed up to the time of the destruction of the premises. Jaffe refused to pay the bill, and A–1 sued Jaffe. Decision?

2. By contract dated January 5, Rebecca agreed to sell to Nancy and Nancy agreed to buy from Rebecca a certain parcel of land then zoned commercial. The specific intent of Nancy, which was known to Rebecca, was to erect a storage plant on the land. The contract stated that the agreement was conditioned upon Nancy's ability to construct a storage plant upon the land. The closing date for the transaction was set for April 1. On February 15, the city council rezoned the land from commercial to residential, which precluded the erection of the storage plant intended by Nancy. As the closing date drew near, Nancy made it known to Rebecca that she did not intend to go through with the purchase because the land could no longer be used as intended. On April 1, Rebecca tendered the deed to Nancy, who refused to pay Rebecca the agreed purchase price. Rebecca brought an action against Nancy for breach of their contract. Decision?

3. The Perfection Produce Company entered into a written contract with Hiram Hodges for the purchase of 300 tons of potatoes to be grown on Hodge's farm in Maine at a stipulated price per ton. The land would ordinarily produce 1,000 tons. Although the planting and cultivation were properly done, Hodges was able to deliver only 100 tons because of a partial crop failure owing to an unprecedented drought. Hodges sued the produce company to recover an unpaid balance of the agreed price for 100 tons of potatoes. The produce company, by an appropriate counterclaim against Hodges, sought damages for his failure to deliver the additional 200 tons. Decision?

4. On November 23, Sylvia agreed to sell to Barnett her Pontiac automobile for $7,000, delivery and payment to be made on December 1. On November 26, Barnett informed Sylvia that he wished to rescind the contract and would pay Sylvia $350 if Sylvia agreed. She agreed and took the $350 cash. On December 1, Barnett tendered to Sylvia $6,650 and demanded that she deliver the automobile. Sylvia refused and Barnett initiated a lawsuit. Decision?

5. Webster, Inc. dealt in automobile accessories at wholesale. Although manufacturing a few items in his own factory, among them windshield wipers, Webster purchased most of his supplies from a large number of other manufacturers. In January, Webster entered into a written contract to sell Hunter 2,000 windshield wipers for $4,900, delivery to be made June 1. In April Webster's factory burned to the ground, and Webster failed to make delivery on June 1. Hunter, forced to buy windshield wipers elsewhere at a higher price, brings an action against Webster for breach of contract. Decision?

6. Erwick Construction Company contracted to build a house for Charles. The specifications called for the use of Karlene Pipe for all plumbing. Erwick, however, got a better price on Boynton Pipe and substituted the equally good Boynton Pipe for Karlene Pipe. Charles's inspection discovered the change and Charles now refuses to make the final payment. The contract price was for $200,000 and the final payment is $20,000. Erwick now brings suit seeking the $20,000. Decision?

7. Green owed White $3,500, which was due and payable on June 1. White owed Brown $3,500, which was due and payable on August 1. On May 25, White received a letter signed by Green stating: "If you will cancel my debt to you, in the amount of $3,500, I will pay, on the due date, the debt you owe Brown, in the amount of $3,500." On May 28, Green received a letter signed by White stating: "I received your letter and agree to the proposals recited therein. You may consider your debt to me cancelled as of the date of this letter." On June 1, White, needing money to pay his income taxes, made a demand upon Green to pay him the $3,500 due on that date. Is Green obligated to pay the money demanded by White?

8. By written contract Ames agreed to build a house on Bowen's lot for $65,000 commencing within ninety days of the date of the contract. Prior to the date for beginning construction, Ames informed Bowen that he was repudiating the contract and would not perform. Bowen refused to accept the repudiation and demanded fulfillment of the contract. Eighty days after the date of the contract, Bowen entered into a new contract with Curd for $62,000. The next day, without knowledge or notice of Bowen's contract with Curd, Ames began construction. Bowen ordered Ames from the premises and refused to allow him to continue. Ames sued Bowen for damages. Decision?

9. Judy agreed in writing to work for Northern Enterprises, Inc. for three years as Superintendent of Northern's manufacturing establishment and to devote herself entirely to the business, giving it her whole time, attention, and skill, for which she was to receive $24,000 per annum, in monthly installments of $2,000. Judy worked and was paid for the first twelve months, when through no fault of her own or Northern's, she was arrested and imprisoned for one month. It became imperative for Northern to employ another, and it treated the contract with Judy as breached and abandoned, refusing to permit Judy to resume work upon her release from jail. What rights, if any, does Judy have under the contract?

10. The Park Plaza Hotel awarded the valet and laundry concession to Larson for a three-year term. The contract contained the following provision: "It is distinctly understood and agreed that the services to be rendered by Larson shall meet with the approval of the Park Plaza Hotel, which shall be the sole judge of the sufficiency and propriety of the services." After seven months, the hotel gave a month's notice to discontinue services based on the failure of the services to meet its approval. Larson brought an action against the hotel, alleging that its dissatisfaction was unreasonable. The hotel defended upon the ground that subjective or personal satisfaction may be the sole justification for termination of the contract. Decision?

11. Schlosser entered into an agreement to purchase a cooperative apartment from Flynn Company. The written agreement contained the following provision:

This entire agreement is conditioned on Purchaser's being approved for occupancy by the board of directors of the Cooperative. In the event approval of the Purchaser shall be denied, this agreement shall thereafter be of no further force or effect.

When Schlosser unilaterally revoked her "offer," Flynn sued for breach of contract. Schlosser claims the approval provision was a condition precedent to the existence of a binding contract and, thus, she was free to revoke. Decision?

12. Jacobs, owner of a farm, entered into a contract with Earl Walker in which Walker agreed to paint the buildings on the farm. Walker purchased the paint from Jones. Before the work was completed, Jacobs ordered Walker to stop because she was dissatisfied with the results. Offers were made by Jones and Walker to complete the job, but Jacobs declined to permit Walker to fulfill his contract. Jones and Walker bring an action against Jacobs for breach of contract. Decision?

COMPUTER RESEARCH PROBLEMS

1. Walker & Co. contracted to provide a sign for Harrison to place above his dry cleaning business. According to the contract, Harrison would lease the sign from Walker, making monthly payments for thirty-six months. In return, Walker agreed to maintain and service the sign at its own expense. Walker installed the sign in July 1953 and Harrison made the first rental payment. Shortly thereafter, someone hit the sign with a tomato. Harrison also claims he discovered rust on its chrome and little spider webs in its corners. Harrison repeatedly called

Walker for the maintenance work promised under the contract, but Walker did not respond. Harrison then telegraphed Walker that due to Walker's failure to perform the maintenance services, he held Walker in material breach of the contract. Decision?

 **2.** Barta entered into a written contract to buy the K&K Pharmacy, located in the local shopping center. Included in the contract was a provision stating that "this Agreement shall be contingent upon Buyer's ability to obtain a new lease from Landlord for the premises presently occupied by Seller. In the event Buyer is unable to obtain a lease satisfactory to Buyer, this Agreement shall be null and void." Barta planned to sell "high traffic" grocery items, such as bread, milk, and coffee in order to attract customers to his drugstore. A grocery store in the local shopping center, however, had the exclusive right to sell grocery items there. Barta, therefore, could not obtain a leasing agreement meeting his approval. When Barta refused to close the sale, K&K Pharmacy sued him for breach of contract. Decision?

 3. Victor Packing Co. contracted to supply Sun Maid Raisin Growers 1,800 tons of raisins from the current year's crop. After delivering 1,190 tons of raisins by August, Victor refused to supply any more. Although Victor had until the end of the crop season to ship the remaining 610 tons of raisins, Sun Maid treated Victor's repeated refusals to ship any more raisins as a repudiation of the contract. In order to prevent breaching its own contracts, Sun Maid went into the market place to "cover" and bought the raisins needed. Unfortunately, between the time Victor refused delivery and Sun Maid went into the market, disastrous rains had caused the price of raisins to skyrocket. May Sun Maid recover from Victor the difference between the contract price and the market price before the end of the current crop year?

Chapter 17

REMEDIES

Monetary Damages
Remedies in Equity
Restitution
Limitations on Remedies

WHEN one party to a contract breaches the contract by failing to perform his contractual duties, the law provides a remedy for the injured party. The primary objective of contract remedies is to compensate the injured party for the loss resulting from the breach, but it is impossible for any remedy to equal the promised performance. The relief that a court can give an injured party is what it regards as an equivalent of the promised performance.

This chapter will examine the most common judicial remedies available for breach of contract: (1) monetary damages, (2) the equitable remedies of specific performance and injunction, and (3) restitution. Sales of goods are governed by Article 2 of the Uniform Commercial Code, which provides specialized remedies that are discussed in Chapter 24.

INTERESTS PROTECTED BY CONTRACT REMEDIES

Contract remedies are available to protect one or more of the following interests of the injured party:

1. the **expectation interest,** which is his interest in having the benefit of his bargain by being put in as good a position as he would have been in, had the contract been performed;

2. the **reliance interest,** which is his interest in being reimbursed for loss caused by reliance on the contract by being put in as good a position as he would have been in, had the contract not been made; or

3. the **restitution interest,** which is his interest in having restored to him any benefit that he has conferred on the other party. Restatement, Section 344.

The expectation interest is protected by the contract remedies of compensatory damages, specific performance, and injunction. The reliance interest is protected by the contractual remedy of reliance damages, while the restitution interest is protected by the contractual remedy of restitution.

MONETARY DAMAGES

A judgment awarding monetary damages is the most frequently granted judicial remedy for breach of contract. Monetary damages, however, will only be awarded for losses that are foreseeable, established with reasonable certainty, and not avoidable. The equitable remedies discussed in this chapter are discretionary and available only if monetary damages are not adequate.

Compensatory Damages

The right to recover compensatory money damages for breach of contract is always available to the injured party. Restatement, Section 346. The purpose in allowing **compensatory damages** is to place the injured party in as good a position as if the other party had performed under the contract. These damages are intended to protect the injured party's expectation interest, which is the value he expected to derive from the contract. Thus, the amount of damages is generally the loss of value to the injured party caused by the other party's failure to perform or by his deficient performance.

In general, **loss of value** is the *difference between the value of the promised performance* of the breaching party *and the value of the actual performance* rendered by the breaching party.

> Value of promised performance
> − Value of actual performance
> Loss of value

If no performance is rendered at all, then the loss of value is the value of the promised performance. If defective or partial performance is rendered, the loss of value is the difference between the value that full performance would have had and the value of the performance actually rendered. Thus, where there has been a breach of warranty, the injured party may recover the difference between the value of the goods if they had been as warranted and the value of the goods in their actual condition when received by the buyer. To illustrate, Victor sells an automobile to Joan and expressly warrants that it will get forty-five miles per gallon, but the automobile gets only twenty miles per gallon. The automobile would have been worth $8,000 if as warranted but is worth only $6,000 as delivered. Joan would recover $2,000 in damages for loss of value.

In addition to loss of value, the injured party may *also* recover for all other losses actually suffered, subject to the limitation of foreseeability discussed below. These damages include incidental and consequential damages. **Incidental damages** are damages that arise directly out of the breach, such as costs incurred to acquire the non-delivered performance from some other source. For example, Agnes employs Benton for nine months for $20,000 to supervise construction of a factory. Agnes fires Benton without cause after three weeks. Benton spends $350 in reasonable fees attempting to find comparable employment. Benton may recover $350 in incidental damages in addition to any other actual loss suffered.

Consequential damages include lost profits and injury to person or property resulting from defective performance. Thus, if Tracy leases to Sean a defective machine that causes $4,000 in property damage and $12,000 in personal injuries, Sean may recover, in addition to damages for loss of value and incidental damages, $16,000 as consequential damages.

The recovery by the injured party, however, is reduced by any cost or loss she has avoided by not having to perform. For example, Clinton agrees to build a hotel for Debra for $1,250,000 by September 1. Clinton breaches by not completing construction until October 1. As a consequence, Debra loses revenues for one month in the amount of $10,000 but saves operating expenses of $6,000. Debra may recover damages for $4,000. Similarly, in a contract in which the injured party has not fully performed, the injured party's recovery is reduced by the value to the injured party of the performance promised by the injured party but not rendered. For example, Clinton agrees to convey land to Debra in return for Debra's promise to work for Clinton for two years. Debra repudiates the contract before Clinton has conveyed the land to Debra. Clinton's recovery for loss from Debra is reduced by the value to Clinton of the land.

To summarize, the amount of **compensatory damages** an injured party may recover for breach of contract is computed as follows:

Loss of value
+ Incidental damages
+ Consequential damages
− Loss or cost avoided by injured party
Compensatory damages

Nominal Damages

An action to recover damages for breach of contract may be maintained even though the plaintiff has not sustained or cannot prove any injury or loss resulting from the breach. Restatement, Section 346. In such a case he will be permitted to recover **nominal damages**—a small sum fixed without regard to the amount of loss. For example, Edward contracts to sell and deliver goods to Florence for $1,000. Edward refuses to deliver the goods as agreed, and so breaks the contract. Florence, however, is able to purchase goods of the same kind and quality elsewhere for $1,000 without incurring any incidental damages. As a result, although Edward has violated Florence's rights under the contract, Florence has suffered no actual loss. Consequently, if Florence, as she may, should sue Edward for breach of contract, she would recover a judgment for nominal damages only. Nominal damages are also available where loss is actually sustained but cannot be proved with reasonable certainty.

Reliance Damages

As an alternative to compensatory damages, the injured party may seek reimbursement for foreseeable loss caused by his reliance upon the contract. The result of **reliance damages** is to place the injured party in as good a position as he would have been in, had the contract *not been made*. Reliance damages include expenses incurred in preparing to perform, in actually performing, or in foregoing opportunities to enter into other contracts. An injured party may prefer damages for reliance to compensatory damages when he is unable to establish his lost profits with reasonable certainty or when the contract is itself unprofitable. For example, Donald agrees to sell his retail store to Gary. Gary spends $50,000 in acquiring inventory and fixtures. Donald then repudiates the contract, and Gary sells the inventory and fixtures for $35,000. Neither party can establish with reasonable certainty what profit Gary would have made. Gary may recover from Donald as damages the loss of $15,000 he sustained on the sale of the inventory and fixtures plus any other costs he incurred in entering into the contract.

Damages for Misrepresentation

The basic remedy for misrepresentation is rescission (avoidance) of the contract. When appropriate, restitution will also be required. At common law, an alternative remedy to rescission is a suit for damages. The Code liberalizes the common law by not restricting a defrauded party to an election of remedies. That is, the injured party may both rescind the contract by restoring the status quo and recover damages or obtain any other remedy available under the Code. U.C.C. Section 2–721. In most States the measure of damages for misrepresentation depends upon whether the misrepresentation is fraudulent or nonfraudulent.

Fraud A party who has been induced to enter into a contract by fraud may recover general damages in a tort action. The minority of States allows the injured party to recover under the **"out-of-pocket"** rule, general damages equal to the difference between the value of what she has received and the value of what she has given for it. The great majority of States, however, under the **"benefit-of-the-bargain"** rule, permits the intentionally defrauded party to recover general damages that are equal to the difference between the value of what she has received and the value of the fraudulent party's performance as represented. The Restatement of Torts provides the fraudulently injured party with the option of either out-of-pocket or benefit-of-the-bargain damages. Section 549. To illustrate, Emily intentionally misrepresents the capabilities of a printing press and thereby induces Melissa to purchase the machine for

$20,000. The value of the press as delivered is $14,000, but if the machine had performed as represented, it would be worth $24,000. Under the out-of-pocket rule, Melissa would recover $6,000, whereas under the benefit-of-the-bargain rule she would recover $10,000.

In addition to a recovery of general damages under one of the measures just discussed, consequential damages may be recovered to the extent they are proved with reasonable certainty and they do not duplicate general damages. Moreover, where the fraud is gross, oppressive, or aggravated, punitive damages are permitted.

Nonfraudulent Misrepresentation Where the misrepresentation is negligent, the deceived party may recover general damages, under the out-of-pocket measure, and consequential damages. Restatement of Torts, Section 552B. Some States, however, permit the recovery of general damages under the benefit-of-the-bargain measure. Where the misrepresentation is neither fraudulent nor negligent, the Restatement limits damages to the out-of-pocket measure. Section 552C.

Punitive Damages

Punitive damages are monetary damages in addition to compensatory damages awarded to a plaintiff in certain situations involving willful, wanton, or malicious conduct. Their purpose is to punish the defendant and thus discourage him and others from similar wrongful conduct. The purpose of allowing contract damages, on the other hand, is to compensate the plaintiff for the loss that he has sustained because of the defendant's breach of contract. Accordingly, the Restatement provides that punitive damages are *not* recoverable for a breach of contract unless the conduct constituting the breach is also a tort for which punitive damages are recoverable. Restatement, Section 355.

One of the most common examples of the allowance of punitive damages is for an insurance company's tortious conduct in its bad faith refusal to pay a legitimate claim. For

example, Frank, a roofer, purchased disability insurance from Wholewide Insurance Co. While working at a job, Frank fell off a ladder and seriously injured his back. Frank was physically unable to continue working and filed a claim for total disability with Wholewide. Wholewide's claims adjuster refused to honor the claim despite the overwhelming medical evidence Frank presented. Wholewide's adjuster called Frank a fraud and a malingerer in an attempt to have Frank settle the claim for 60 percent disability. Wholewide was aware that Frank's finances would not last very long without some recovery for disability. In a suit by Frank against Wholewide, many courts would award Frank punitive damages in addition to compensatory damages for his actual disability.

Liquidated Damages

A contract may contain a **liquidated damages** provision by which the parties agree in advance to the damages to be paid in event of breach. Such a provision will be enforced if it amounts to a reasonable forecast of the loss that may or does result from the breach. If, however, the sum agreed upon as liquidated damages does not bear a reasonable relationship to the amount of probable loss that may or does result from breach, it is unenforceable as a penalty. A penalty is a contractual provision designed to deter a party from breaching her contract and to punish her if she does breach it. Restatement, Section 356, Comment a states:

The parties to a contract may effectively provide in advance the damages that are to be payable in the event of breach as long as the provision does not disregard the principle of compensation. The enforcement of such provisions for liquidated damages saves the time of courts, juries, parties and witnesses and reduces the expense of litigation. This is especially important if the amount in controversy is small. However, the parties to a contract are not free to provide a penalty for its breach. The central objective behind the system of contract remedies is compensatory, not punitive.

The courts will look at the substance of the provision, the nature of the contract, and the extent of probable harm to the promisee that may reasonably be expected to be caused by a breach in order to determine whether the agreed amount is proper as liquidated damages or unenforceable as a penalty. If a liquidated damage provision is not enforceable, the injured party is nevertheless entitled to the ordinary remedies for breach of contract. *See California and Hawaiian Sugar Co. v. Sun Ship, Inc.*

To illustrate, Reliable Construction Company contracts with Equerry to build a grandstand at Equerry's race course at a cost of $1,330,000, to have it completed by a certain date, and to pay Equerry, as liquidated damages, $1,000 per day for every day's delay beyond that date in completing the grandstand. The stipulated sum for delay is liquidated damages and not a penalty because the amount is reasonable. If, instead, the sum stipulated had been $10,000 per day, it would obviously have been unreasonable and therefore a penalty. Provisions for liquidated damages are sometimes found in contracts for the sale of a business, in which the seller agrees not to re-enter the same business within a reasonable geographic area and time period. Actual damages resulting from the seller's breach of his agreement would ordinarily be difficult to ascertain, and the sum stipulated, if reasonable, would be held to be liquidated damages.

Limitations on Damages

In order to accomplish the basic purposes of contract remedies, the limitations of foreseeability, certainty, and mitigation have been imposed upon monetary damages. These limitations are intended to ensure that damages can be taken into account at the time of contracting, that damages are compensatory and not speculative, and that damages do not include loss that could have been avoided by reasonable efforts.

Foreseeability of Damages A contracting party is generally expected to consider those risks that are foreseeable at the time she entered into the contract. Therefore, compensa-

tory or reliance damages are recoverable only for loss that the party in breach had reason to foresee as a *probable* result of such breach when the contract was made. The breaching party is not liable in the event of a breach for loss that was not foreseeable at the time of entering into the contract. The test of foreseeability is *objective,* based upon what the breaching party had reason to foresee. Loss may be foreseeable as a probable result of a breach because it follows from the breach (a) in the ordinary course of events or (b) as a result of special circumstances, beyond the ordinary course of events, which the party in breach had reason to know. Restatement, Section 351(2). Moreover, "a court may limit damages for foreseeable loss by excluding recovery for loss of profits, by allowing recovery only for loss incurred in reliance, or otherwise if it concludes that in the circumstances justice so requires in order to avoid disproportionate compensation." Restatement, Section 351(3).

The leading case on the subject of foreseeability of damages is *Hadley v. Baxendale,* decided in England in 1854. In this case the plaintiffs operated a flour mill at Gloucester. Their mill was compelled to cease operating because of a broken crankshaft attached to the steam engine that furnished power to the mill. It was necessary to send the broken shaft to a foundry located at Greenwich so that a new shaft could be made. The plaintiffs delivered the broken shaft to the defendants, who were common carriers, for immediate transportation from Gloucester to Greenwich, but did not inform the defendants that operation of the mill had ceased because of the nonfunctioning crankshaft. The defendants received the shaft, collected the freight charges in advance, and promised the plaintiffs to deliver the shaft for repairs the following day. The defendants did not make delivery as promised, and as a result the resumption of the operation of the mill was delayed for several days, causing the plaintiffs to lose profitable sales. The defendants contended that the loss of profits was too remote, and therefore unforeseeable, to be recoverable. In awarding damages to the plaintiffs, the jury was permitted to take into consideration the loss of these profits. The appellate court reversed the decision and ordered a new trial on the ground that the special circumstances that caused the loss of profits, namely, the continued stoppage of the mill while awaiting the return of the repaired crankshaft, had never been communicated by the plaintiffs to the defendants. A common carrier would not reasonably foresee that the plaintiff's mill would be shut down as a result of delay in transporting the broken crankshaft.

On the other hand, if the defendants in *Hadley v. Baxendale* had been informed that the shaft was necessary for the operation of the mill, or otherwise had reason to know this fact, they would be liable to the plaintiffs for loss of profit during the period of shutdown caused by their delay. Under these circumstances the loss would be the "foreseeable" and "natural" result of the breach.

But what if a plaintiff's expected profit should be extraordinarily large? The general rule is that the breaching party will be liable for such extraordinary loss only if he had reason to know of the special loss. In any event, the plaintiff may recover for any ordinary loss resulting from the breach. Thus, if Madeline breaches a contract with Jane, causing Jane, due to special circumstances, $10,000 in damages where ordinarily such a breach would only result in $6,000 of damages, Madeline would be liable to Jane for $6,000, not $10,000, provided Madeline was unaware of the special circumstances causing Jane the unusually large loss.

Certainty of Damages Damages are not recoverable for loss beyond an amount that the injured party can establish with reasonable certainty. Restatement, Section 352. If the injured party cannot prove a particular element of her loss with reasonable certainty, she will nevertheless be entitled to recover the portion of her loss that she can prove with reasonable certainty. The main impact of the requirement of certainty is upon the recovery of consequential damages for lost profits on related transactions. Similar difficulty arises

in proving lost profits caused by breach of a contract to produce a sporting event or to publish a new book.

Mitigation of Damages Under the doctrine of mitigation of damages, the injured party may not recover damages for loss that he could have avoided by reasonable effort and without undue risk, burden, or humiliation. Restatement, Section 350. Thus, where James is under a contract to manufacture goods for Kathy, and Kathy repudiates the contract after James has commenced performance, James will not be allowed to recover for losses he sustains by continuing to manufacture the goods, if to do so would increase the amount of damages. The amount of loss that could reasonably have been avoided is deducted from the amount that would otherwise be recoverable as damages. On the other hand, if the goods were almost completed when Kathy repudiated the contract, the completion of the goods might mitigate the damages, because the finished goods may be resalable whereas the unfinished goods may not. U.C.C. Section 2–704(2).

Similarly, if Harvey contracts to work for Olivia for one year for a weekly salary and after two months is wrongfully discharged by Olivia, Harvey must use reasonable efforts to mitigate his damages by seeking other employment. If he cannot obtain other employment of the same general character, he is entitled to recover full pay for the contract period that he is unemployed. He is not obliged to accept a radically different type of employment or to accept work at a distant place. For example, a person employed as a school teacher or accountant who is wrongfully discharged is not obliged, in order to mitigate damages, to accept available employment as a chauffeur or truck driver. *See Parker v. Twentieth Century-Fox Film Corp.* in Chapter 2.

REMEDIES IN EQUITY

Instances occur when damages (based on the expectation interest, reliance interest, or the restitution interest) will not adequately compensate an injured party. In these cases, equitable relief in the form of specific performance or an injunction may be available to protect the injured party's interest.

The remedies of specific performance and an injunction are not a matter of right but rest in the discretion of the court. Consequently, they will not be granted where:

1. there is an adequate remedy at law;

2. it is impossible to enforce them, as where the seller has already conveyed the subject matter of the contract to an innocent third person;

3. the contract is without consideration;

4. the consideration is grossly inadequate or the terms of the contract are otherwise unfair;

5. the contract is tainted with fraud, duress, undue influence, mistake, or unfair practices;

6. the terms of the contract are not sufficiently certain; or

7. the relief would cause unreasonable hardship.

See Tamarind Lithography Workshop v. Sanders.

A court may grant specific performance or an injunction even though there is a provision for liquidated damages. Restatement, Section 361. Moreover, a court will grant specific performance or an injunction despite a term of the contract prohibiting equitable relief, if denying such relief would cause unreasonable hardship to the injured party. Restatement, Section 364(2).

Another equitable remedy is **reformation,** which is a process whereby the court "rewrites" or "corrects" a written contract to make it conform to the true agreement of the parties. The purpose of reformation is *not* to make a new contract for the parties but rather to express adequately the contract they have made for themselves. The remedy of reformation is granted when the parties agree on a contract but write it down in a way that does not reflect their actual agreement. For example, Acme Insurance Co. and Bell

agree that for good consideration Acme will issue an annuity paying $500 per month. Because of a clerical error, the annuity policy is issued for $50 per month. A court of equity, upon satisfactory proof of the mistake, will reform the policy to provide for the correct amount—$500 per month.

Specific Performance

Specific performance is the equitable remedy that compels the performance by the defaulting party of her contractual obligations. Ordinarily, in case of breach by the seller of her contract for the sale of personal property, the buyer has a sufficient remedy at law. Where, however, the **personal property** contracted for is rare or *unique,* this remedy is inadequate. Examples are a famous painting or statue, an original manuscript or a rare edition of a book, a patent, a copyright, shares of stock in a closely held corporation, or an heirloom. Articles of this kind cannot be purchased elsewhere. Accordingly, on breach by the seller of her contract for the sale of any such article, money damages will not adequately compensate the buyer. Consequently, in these instances she may avail herself of the equitable remedy of specific performance.

While it is only in exceptional circumstances that courts of equity will grant specific performance in connection with contracts for the sale of personal property, they will always grant it in case of breach of contract for the sale of **real property.** The reason for this is that any parcel of land is regarded as unique and different from any other parcel. Consequently, if the seller refuses to convey title to the real estate contracted for, the buyer may seek the aid of a court of equity to compel the seller to convey the title. Most courts of equity will likewise compel the buyer in a real estate contract to perform at the suit of the seller.

Courts of equity will not grant specific performance of contracts for personal services. In the first place, there is the practical difficulty, if not impossibility, of enforcing such a decree. In the second place, it is against the policy of the courts to force one person to work for or serve another against his will, even though he has contracted to do so. Such enforcement would probably amount to involuntary servitude. For example, if Carmen, an accomplished concert pianist, agrees to appear at a certain time and place to play a specified program for Rudolf, upon Carmen's refusal to appear, a court would not issue a decree of specific performance.

Injunctions

The **injunction,** as used as a contract remedy, is a formal court order enjoining (commanding) a person to refrain from doing a specific act or engaging in specified conduct. A court of equity, at its discretion, may grant an injunction against breach of a contractual duty where damages for a breach would be inadequate. For example, Clint enters into a written agreement to give Janice the right of first refusal on a tract of land owned by Clint. Clint, however, subsequently offers the land to Blake without first offering it to Janice. A court of equity may properly enjoin Clint from selling the land to Blake. Similarly, valid covenants not to compete may be enforced by an injunction.

An employee's promise of exclusive personal services may be enforced by an injunction against serving another employer as long as the probable result will not be to leave the employee without other reasonable means of making a living. Restatement, Section 367. Suppose, for example, that Allan makes a contract with Marlene, a famous singer, under which Marlene agrees to sing at Allan's theater on certain dates for an agreed fee. Before the date of the first performance, Marlene makes a contract with Craig to sing for Craig at his theater on the same dates. Allan cannot secure specific performance by Marlene of his contract, as already discussed. A court of equity will, however, on suit by Allan against Marlene, issue an injunction against Marlene, ordering Marlene not to sing for Craig. *See Madison Square Garden Corp., Ill. v. Carnera.*

Where the services contracted for are *not* unusual or extraordinary in character, the injured party cannot obtain injunctive relief. His only remedy is an action at law for damages.

RESTITUTION

One of the remedies that may be available to a party to a contract is restitution. **Restitution** is a return to the aggrieved party of the consideration, or its value, which he gave to the other party. The purpose of restitution is to restore the injured party to the position he was in before the contract was made. Therefore, the party seeking restitution must return what he has received from the other party.

Restitution is available in several contractual situations: (1) as an alternative remedy for a party injured by breach; (2) for a party in default; (3) for a party who may not enforce the contract because of the statute of frauds; and (4) upon rescission (avoidance) of a voidable contract.

Party Injured by Breach

A party is entitled to restitution if the other party totally breaches the contract by non-performance or repudiation. Restatement, Section 373. For example, Benedict agrees to sell land to Beatrice for $60,000. Beatrice makes a partial payment of $15,000. Benedict wrongfully refuses to transfer title. As an alternative to damages or specific performance, Beatrice may recover the $15,000 in restitution.

Party in Default

Where a party, after having partly performed, commits a breach by non-performance or repudiation that discharges the other party's duty to perform, the party in default is entitled to restitution for any benefit she has conferred in excess of the loss she has caused by her breach. Restatement, Section 374. For example, Nathan agrees to sell land to Lilly for $60,000, and Lilly makes a partial payment of

$15,000. Lilly then repudiates the contract. Nathan sells the land to Murray in good faith for $55,000. Lilly may recover from Nathan in restitution the part payment of the $15,000 *less* the $5,000 damages Nathan sustained because of Lilly's breach, which equals $10,000.

Statute of Frauds

A party to a contract that is unenforceable because of the statute of frauds may have, nonetheless, acted in reliance upon the contract. In such a case that party may recover in restitution the benefits conferred upon the other in relying upon the unenforceable contract. In most States the party seeking restitution must not be in default. Thus, if Wilton makes an oral contract to furnish services to Rochelle that are not to be performed within a year, and Rochelle discharges Wilton after three months, Wilton may recover as restitution the value of the services rendered during the three months.

Voidable Contracts

A party who has rescinded or avoided a contract for lack of capacity, duress, undue influence, fraud, misrepresentation, or mistake is entitled to restitution for any benefit he has conferred upon the party. Restatement, Section 376. For example, Samuel fraudulently induces Edith to sell land for $60,000. Samuel pays the purchase price, and Edith conveys the land. Edith then discovers the fraud. Edith may disaffirm the contract and recover as restitution the land. Generally, the party seeking restitution must return any benefit that he has received under the agreement; however, this is not always the case as discussed in Chapter 13 dealing with contractual capacity.

LIMITATIONS ON REMEDIES

Election of Remedies

If a party is injured by a breach of contract and has more than one remedy available to him, his manifestation of a choice of one of them, such as bringing suit, does not prevent him from seeking another remedy unless the remedies are inconsistent and the other party materially changes his position in reliance on the manifestation. Restatement, Section 378. For example, a party who seeks specific performance, an injunction, or restitution may be entitled to incidental damages for delay in performance. Damages for *total breach* are inconsistent with the remedies of specific performance, injunction, and restitution. Likewise, the remedy of specific performance or an injunction is inconsistent with that of restitution. *See Head & Seemann, Inc. v. Gregg.*

With respect to contracts for the sale of goods, the Code rejects any doctrine of election of remedies. Thus, the remedies it provides are essentially cumulative in nature and include all of the available remedies for breach. Whether one remedy precludes another depends on the facts of the individual case. U.C.C. Section 2–703, Comment 1.

Loss of Power of Avoidance

A party with a power of avoidance for lack of capacity, duress, undue influence, fraud, misrepresentation, or mistake may lose that power if (1) she affirms the contract; (2) she delays unreasonably in exercising the power of disaffirmance; or (3) the rights of third parties intervene.

Affirmance   A party who has the power to avoid a contract for lack of capacity, duress, undue influence, fraud, misrepresentation, or mistake will lose that power by affirming the contract. Affirmance occurs where the party, with full knowledge of the facts, either declares his intention to proceed with the contract or takes some other action from which such intention may reasonably be inferred. Thus, suppose that Pam was induced to purchase a ring from Sally through Sally's fraudulent misrepresentation. If, after learning the truth, Pam undertakes to sell the ring to Janet or else does something that is consistent only with her ownership of the ring, she may no longer rescind the transaction. In the case of incapacity, duress, or undue influence, affirmance is effective only after the circumstances that made the contract voidable cease to exist. Where there has been fraudulent misrepresentation, the defrauded party may affirm only after he knows of the misrepresentation. If the misrepresentation is nonfraudulent or there is a mistake, the defrauded or mistaken party may affirm only after he knows or should know of the misrepresentation or mistake.

Delay The power of avoidance may be lost if the party who has the power does not rescind within a reasonable time. What is a reasonable time depends upon all the circumstances, including the extent to which the delay enables the party with the power of avoidance to speculate at the other party's risk. To illustrate, a defrauded purchaser of stock cannot wait unduly to see if the market price or value of the stock appreciates sufficiently to justify retaining the stock. A reasonable time does not begin until the circumstances that made the contract voidable have ceased to exist.

Rights of Third Parties The power of avoidance and the accompanying right to restitution are further limited by the intervening rights of third parties. If A transfers property to B in a transaction that is voidable by A, and B sells the property to C (a good faith purchaser for value) before A exercises her power of avoidance, A will lose the right to recover the property.

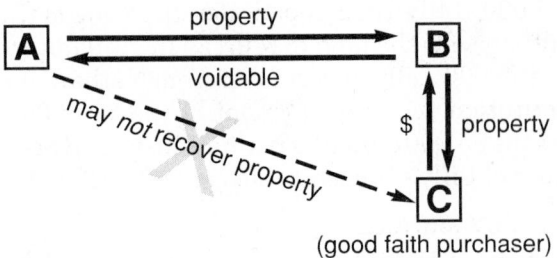

(good faith purchaser)

Thus, if C, a third party who is a good faith purchaser, acquires an interest in the subject matter of the contract before A has elected to rescind, no rescission is permitted. Because the transaction is voidable, B acquires a voidable title to the property. Upon a sale of the property by him to C, who is a purchaser in good faith and for value, C obtains good title and is allowed to retain the property. Since both A and C are innocent, the law will not disturb the title held by C, the good faith purchaser. In this case, as in all cases where rescission is not available, A's only recourse is against B.

The one notable exception to this rule is the situation involving a sale by a minor who subsequently wishes to avoid a transaction, *other than for a sale of goods,* from a good faith purchaser. Under this special rule, a good faith purchaser is deprived of the protection generally provided. Therefore, the third party in a transaction not involving goods is no more protected from the minor's disaffirmance than is the person dealing directly with the minor.

CASES

Liquidated Damages

CALIFORNIA AND HAWAIIAN SUGAR CO. v. SUN SHIP, INC.

United States Court of Appeals, Ninth Circuit, 1986.
794 F.2d 1433.

NOONAN, J.

Jurisdiction in this case is based on the diversity of citizenship of California and Ha-

waiian Sugar Company (C and H), a California corporation; Sun Ship, Inc. (Sun), a Pennsylvania corporation; and Halter Marine, Inc. (Halter), a Louisiana corporation. Interpreting a contract which provides for construction by the law of Pennsylvania, we apply Pennsylvania law. The appeal is from a judgment of the district court in favor of C and H and Halter on the main issues. Reviewing the district court's interpretation of the contract anew as a matter of law and respecting the findings of fact of the district court when not clearly erroneous, we affirm the judgment in all respects.

C and H is an agricultural cooperative owned by fourteen sugar plantations in Hawaii. Its business consists in transporting raw sugar—the crushed cane in the form of coarse brown crystal—to its refinery in Crockett, California. Roughly one million tons a year of sugar are harvested in Hawaii. A small portion is refined there; the bulk goes to Crockett. The refined sugar—the white stuff—is sold by C and H to groceries for home consumption and to the soft drink and cereal companies that are its industrial customers.

To conduct its business, C and H has an imperative need for assured carriage for the raw sugar from the islands. Sugar is a seasonal crop, with 70 percent of the harvest occurring between April and October, while almost nothing is harvestable during December and January. Consequently, transportation must not only be available, but seasonably available. Storage capacity in Hawaii accommodates not more than a quarter of the crop. Left stored on the ground or left unharvested, sugar suffers the loss of sucrose and goes to waste. Shipping ready and able to carry the raw sugar is a priority for C and H.

In 1979 C and H was notified that Matson Navigation Company, which had been supplying the bulk of the necessary shipping, was withdrawing its services as of January 1981. While C and H had some ships at its disposal, it found a pressing need for a large new vessel, to be in service at the height of the sugar season in 1981. It decided to commission the building of a kind of hybrid—a tug of catamaran design with two hulls and, joined to the tug, a barge with a wedge which would lock between the two pontoons of the tug, producing an "integrated tug barge." In Hawaiian, the barge and the entire vessel were each described as a Mocababoo or push boat.

C and H relied on the architectural advice of the New York firm, J.J. Henry. It solicited bids from shipyards, indicating as an essential term a "preferred delivery date" of June

1981. It decided to accept Sun's offer to build the barge and Halter's offer to build the tug.

In the fall of 1979 C and H entered into negotiations with Sun on the precise terms of the contract. Each company was represented by a vice-president with managerial responsibility in the area of negotiation; each company had a team of negotiators; each company had the advice of counsel in drafting the agreement that was signed on November 14, 1979. This agreement was entitled "Contract for the Construction of One Oceangoing Barge for California and Hawaiian Sugar Company by Sun Ship, Inc." The "Whereas" clause of the contract identified C and H as the Purchaser, and Sun as the Contractor; it identified "one non-self-propelled oceangoing barge" as the Vessel that Purchaser was buying from Contractor. Article I provided that Contractor would deliver the Vessel on June 30, 1981. The contract price was $25,405,000.

* * * Article 17 [of the agreement] "Delivery" provided that "the Vessel shall be offered for delivery fully and completely connected with the Tug." Article 8, "Liquidated Damages for Delay in Delivery" provided that if "Delivery of the Vessel" was not made on "the Delivery Date" of June 30, 1981, Sun would pay C and H "as per-day liquidated damages, and not as a penalty" a sum described as "a reasonable measure of the damages"—$17,000 per day.

On the same date C and H entered into an agreement with Halter to purchase "one oceangoing catamaran tug boat" for $20,350,000. The tug (the "Vessel" of that contract) was to be delivered on April 30, 1981 at Sun's shipyard. Liquidated damages of $10,000 per day were provided for Halter's failure to deliver.

Halter did not complete the tug until July 15, 1982. Sun did not complete the barge until March 16, 1982. Tug and barge were finally connected under C and H's direction in mid-July 1982 and christened the Moku Pahu. C and H settled its claim against Halter. Although Sun paid C and H $17,000 per day from June 30, 1981 until January 10, 1982, it ultimately denied liability for any damages, and this lawsuit resulted.

376 CONTRACTS PART TWO

* * *

Sun contends, however, that * * * the $17,000 per day is a penalty, not to be enforced by the court. The barge, Sun points out, was useless to C and H without the tug. Unconnected, the barge was worse than useless—it was an expensive liability. C and H did not want the barge by itself. To get $17,000 per day as "damages" for failure to provide an unwanted and unusable craft is, Sun says, to exact a penalty. C and H seeks to be "paid according to the tenour of the bond"; it "craves the law." And if C and H sticks to the letter of the bond, it must like Shylock end by losing; a court of justice will not be so vindictive. Breach of contract entitles the wronged party only to fair compensation.

Seductive as Sun's argument is, it does not carry the day. Represented by sophisticated representatives, C and H and Sun reached the agreement that $17,000 a day was the reasonable measure of the loss C and H would suffer if the barge was not ready. Of course they assumed that the tug would be ready. But in reasonable anticipation of the damages that would occur if the tug was ready and the barge was not, Article 8 was adopted. As the parties foresaw the situation, C and H would have a tug waiting connection but no barge and so no shipping. The anticipated damages were what might be expected if C and H could not transport the Hawaiian sugar crop at the height of the season. Those damages were clearly before both parties. As Joe Kleschick, Sun's chief negotiator, testified, he had "a vision" of a "mountain of sugar piling up in Hawaii"—a vision that C and H conjured up in negotiating the damage clause. Given the anticipated impact on C and H's raw sugar and on C and H's ability to meet the demands of its grocery and industrial customers if the sugar could not be transported, liquidated damages of $17,000 a day were completely reasonable.

The situation as it developed was different from the anticipation. The barge was not ready but neither was the tug. C and H was in fact able to find other shipping. The crop did not rot. The customers were not left sugarless. Sun argues that, measured by the ac-

tual damages suffered, the liquidated damages were penal.

We look to Pennsylvania law for guidance. Although no Pennsylvania case is square on point, it is probable that Pennsylvania would interpret the contract as a sale of goods governed by the Uniform Commercial Code. [Citation.] The governing statute provides that liquidated damages are considered reasonable "in the light of the anticipated or actual harm." [U.C.C.] 2-718(1).

The choice of the disjunctive appears to be deliberate. The language chosen is in harmony with the Restatement (Second) of Contracts § 356 (1979), which permits liquidated damages in the light of the anticipated or actual loss caused by the breach and the difficulties of proof of loss. Section 356, Comment b declares explicitly: "Furthermore, the amount fixed is reasonable to the extent that it approximates the loss anticipated at the time of the making of the contract, even though it may not approximate the actual loss."

Despite the statutory disjunctive and the Restatement's apparent blessing of it, the question is not settled by these authorities which must be read in the light of common law principles already established and accepted in Pennsylvania. [Citation.] Prior to the adoption of the Uniform Commercial Code, Pennsylvania enforced liquidated damage clauses that its courts labeled as nonpenal, but equitable considerations relating to the actual harm incurred were taken into account along with the difficulty of proving damages if a liquidated damage clause was rejected, [citation]. We do not believe that the U.C.C. overrode this line of reasoning. Indeed, in a lower court case, decided after the U.C.C.'s enactment, it was stated that if liquidated damages appear unreasonable in light of the harm suffered, "the contractual provision will be voided as a penalty." [Citation.] * * *

The Restatement § 356 Comment b, after accepting anticipated damages as a measure, goes on to say that if the difficulty of proof of loss is slight, then actual damage may be the measure of reasonableness: "If, to take an extreme case, it is clear that no loss at all has occurred, a provision fixing a substantial sum as damages is unenforceable. * * *

* * *

* * * Sun contends that the actual damages suffered by C and H for lack of the integrated tug boat were slight. Actual damages were found by the district court to consist of "interest on progress payments, unfavorable terms of conversion to long-term financing, and additional labor expense." No dollar amount was determined by the district court in finding that these damages "bore a reasonable relationship to the amount liquidated in the Barge Contract."

The dollar value of the damages found by the district judge is, to judge from C and H's own computation, as follows:

Additional Construction Interest	$1,486,000
Added Payments to J.J. Henry	161,000
Added Vessel Operating Expenses	73,000
C and H Employee Costs	109,000
	$1,829,000

But "actual damages" have no meaning if the actual savings of C and H due to the nondelivery of the integrated tug barge are not subtracted. It was clearly erroneous for the district judge to exclude these savings from his finding. These savings, again according to C and H's own computation, were:

Transportation savings	$ 525,000
Lay-up Costs	936,000
	$1,461,000

The net actual damages suffered by C and H were $368,000. As a matter of law, Sun contends that the liquidated damages are unreasonably disproportionate to the net actual damages.

* * *

* * * Contracts are contracts because they contain enforceable promises, and absent some overriding public policy, those promises are to be enforced. "Where each of the parties is content to take the risk of its turning out in a particular way" why should one "be released from the contract, if there were no misrepresentation or other want of fair dealing?" [Citation.] Promising to pay

damages of a fixed amount, the parties normally have a much better sense of what damages can occur. Courts must be reluctant to override their judgment. Where damages are real but difficult to prove, injustice will be done the injured party if the court substitutes the requirements of judicial proof for the parties' own informed agreement as to what is a reasonable measure of damages. Pennsylvania acknowledges that a seller is bound to pay consequential damages if the seller had reason to know of the buyer's special circumstances. [Citation.] The liquidated damage clause here functions in lieu of a court's determination of the consequential damages suffered by C and H.

* * *

* * * [T]he exact damages caused [to C and H's] manifold operations by lack of the integrated tug boat are difficult of ascertainment. C and H claimed that it suffered $3,732,000 in lost charter revenues. Testimony supported the claim, but the district court made no finding as to whether the claim was proved or unproved. The district court did not find that the loss of charter revenues had not been anticipated by the parties. But that finding has no bearing on whether the loss occurred. Within the general risk of heavy losses forecast by both parties when they agreed to $17,000 per day damages, a particular type of loss was pointed to by C and H as having happened.

Proof of this loss is difficult—as difficult, perhaps, as proof of loss would have been if the sugar crop had been delivered late because shipping was missing. Whatever the loss, the parties had promised each other that $17,000 per day was a reasonable measure. The court must decline to substitute the requirements of judicial proof for the parties' own conclusion. The Moku Pahu, available on June 30, 1981, was a great prize, capable of multiple employments and enlarging the uses of the entire C and H fleet. When sophisticated parties with bargaining parity have agreed what lack of this prize would mean, and it is now difficult to measure what the lack did mean, the court will uphold the parties' bargain. C and H is entitled to keep the liquidated damages of $3,298,000 it has already received and to receive additional liquidated damages of $1,105,000 with interest thereon, less setoffs determined by the district court.

Affirmed.

Specific Performance

TAMARIND LITHOGRAPHY WORKSHOP v. SANDERS

Court of Appeal of California, Second District, 1983.
143 Cal.App.3d 571, 193 Cal.Rptr. 409.

STEPHENS, J.

The essence of this appeal concerns the question of whether an award of damages is an adequate remedy at law in lieu of specific performance for the breach of an agreement to give screen credits. Our saga traces its origin to March of 1969, at which time appellant, and cross-complainant below, Terry Sanders (hereinafter "Sanders" or "appellant"), agreed in writing to write, direct and produce a motion picture on the subject of lithography for respondent, Tamarind Lithography Workshop, Inc. (hereinafter referred to as "Tamarind" or "respondent").

Pursuant to the terms of the agreement, the film was shot during the summer of 1969, wherein Sanders directed the film according to an outline/treatment of his authorship, and acted as production manager by personally hiring and supervising personnel comprising the film crew. Additionally, Sanders exercised both artistic control over the mixing of the sound track and overall editing of the picture.

After completion, the film, now titled the "Four Stones for Kanemitsu," was screened by Tamarind at its tenth anniversary celebration on April 28, 1970. Thereafter, a dispute arose between the parties concerning their respective rights and obligations under the original 1969 agreement. Litigation ensued and in January 1973 the matter went to trial. Prior to the entry of judgment, the parties entered into a written settlement agreement, which became the premise for the instant action. Specifically, this April 30, 1973, agreement provided that Sanders would be entitled to a screen credit entitled "A Film by Terry Sanders."

Tamarind did not comply with its expressed obligation pursuant to that agreement, in that it failed to include Sanders' screen credits in the prints it distributed. As a result a situation developed wherein Tamarind and co-defendant Wayne filed suit for declaratory relief, damages due to breach of contract, emotional distress, defamation and fraud.

Sanders cross-complained, seeking damages for Tamarind's breach of contract, declaratory relief, specific performance of the contract to give Sanders screen credits, and defamation. Both causes were consolidated and brought to trial on May 31, 1977. A jury was impaneled for purposes of determining damage issues and decided that Tamarind had breached the agreement and awarded Sanders $25,000 in damages.

The remaining claims for declaratory and injunctive relief were tried by the court. The court made findings that Tamarind had sole ownership rights in the film, that "both June Wayne and Terry Sanders were each creative producers of the film, that Sanders shall have the right to modify the prints in his personal possession to include his credits." All other prayers for relief were denied.

It is from the denial of appellant's request for specific performance upon which appellant predicates this appeal.

* * *

The availability of the remedy of specific performance is premised upon well established requisites. These requisites include: A showing by plaintiff of (1) the inadequacy of his legal remedy; (2) an underlying contract that is both reasonable and supported by adequate consideration; (3) the existence of a mutuality of remedies; (4) contractual terms which are sufficiently definite to enable the court to know what it is to enforce; and (5) a substantial similarity of the requested performance to that promised in the contract. [Citation.]

It is manifest that the legal remedies available to Sanders for harm resulting from the future exhibition of the film are inadequate as a matter of law. The primary reasons are twofold: (1) that an accurate assessment of damages would be far too difficult and require much speculation, and (2) that any future exhibitions might be deemed to be a continuous breach of contract and thereby create the danger of an untold number of lawsuits.

There is no doubt that the exhibition of a film, which is favorably received by its critics and the public at large, can result in valuable advertising or publicity for the artists responsible for that film's making. Likewise, it is unquestionable that the nonappearance of an artist's name or likeness in the form of screen credit on a successful film can result in a loss of that valuable publicity. However, whether that loss of publicity is measurable dollar wise is quite another matter.

By its very nature, public acclaim is unique and very difficult, if not sometimes impossible, to quantify in monetary terms. Indeed, courts confronted with the dilemma of estimating damages in this area have been less than uniform in their disposition of same. Nevertheless, it is clear that any award of damages for the loss of publicity is contingent upon those damages being reasonably certain, specific, and unspeculative. [Citation.]

* * *

Accordingly, where the jury in the matter sub judice was fully apprised of the favorable recognition Sanders' film received from the Academy of Motion Picture Arts and Sciences, the Los Angeles International Film Festival, and public television, and further, where they were made privy to an assessment of the value of said exposure by three experts, it was reasonable for the jury to award monetary damages for that ascertainable loss of publicity. However, pecuniary compensation for Sanders' future harm is not a fully adequate remedy. [Citation.]

We return to the remaining requisites for Sanders' entitlement to specific performance. The need for our finding the contract to be reasonable and supported by adequate consideration is obviated by the jury's determination of respondent's breach of that contract. The requisite of mutuality of remedy has been satisfied in that Sanders had fully performed his obligations pursuant to the agreement (i.e., release of all claims of copyright to the film and dismissal of his then pending action against respondents). [Citation.] Similarly, we find the terms of the agreement sufficiently definite to permit enforcement of the respondent's performance as promised.

In the present case it should be obvious that specific performance through injunctive relief can remedy the dilemma posed by the somewhat ambiguous jury verdict. The injunction disposes of the problem of future damages, in that full compliance by Tamarind moots the issue. Of course, violation of the injunction by Tamarind would raise new problems, but the court has numerous options for dealing with the situation and should choose the one best suited to the particular violation.

In conclusion, the record shows that the appellant is entitled to relief consisting of the damages recovered, and an injunction against future injury.

Injunctions

MADISON SQUARE GARDEN CORP., ILL. v. CARNERA

Circuit Court of Appeals, Second Circuit, 1931.
52 F.2d 47.

CHASE, J.

Suit by plaintiff, Madison Square Garden Corporation, against Primo Carnera, defendant. From an order granting an injunction against defendant, defendant appeals.

On January 13, 1931, the plaintiff and defendant by their duly authorized agents entered into the following agreement in writing:

1. Carnera agrees that he will render services as a boxer in his next contest (which contest, hereinafter called the "First Contest," shall be with the winner of the proposed Schmeling-Stribling contest, or, if the same is drawn, shall be with Schmeling, and shall be deemed to be a contest for

the heavyweight championship title; provided, however, that, in the event of the inability of the Garden to cause Schmeling or Stribling, as the case may be, to perform the terms of his agreement with the Garden calling for such contest, the Garden shall be without further liability to Carnera,) exclusively under the auspices of the Garden, in the United States of America, or the Dominion of Canada, at such time, not, however, later than midnight of September 30, 1931, as the Garden may direct. . . .

9. Carnera shall not, pending the holding of the First Contest, render services as a boxer in any major boxing contest, without the written permission of the Garden in each case had and obtained. A major contest is understood to be one with Sharkey, Baer, Campolo, Godfrey, or like grade heavyweights, or heavyweights who shall have beaten any of the above subsequent to the date hereof. If in any boxing contest engaged in by Carnera prior to the holding of the First Contest, he shall lose the same, the Garden shall at its option, to be exercised by a two weeks' notice to Carnera in writing, be without further liability under the terms of this agreement to Carnera. Carnera shall not render services during the continuance of the option referred to in paragraph 8 hereof for any person, firm or corporation other than the Garden. Carnera shall, however, at all times be permitted to engage in sparring exhibitions in which no decision is rendered and in which the heavyweight championship title is not at stake, and in which Carnera boxes not more than four rounds with any one opponent. . . .

Thereafter the defendant, without the permission of the plaintiff, written or otherwise, made a contract to engage in a boxing contest with the Sharkey mentioned in paragraph 9 of the agreement above quoted, and by the terms thereof the contest was to take place before the first contest mentioned in the defendant's contract with the plaintiff was to be held.

The plaintiff then brought this suit to restrain the defendant from carrying out his contract to box Sharkey, and obtained the preliminary injunction order, from which this appeal was taken. Jurisdiction is based on diversity of citizenship and the required amount is involved.

The District Court has found on affidavits which adequately show it that the defen-

dant's services are unique and extraordinary. A negative covenant in a contract for such personal services is enforceable by injunction where the damages for a breach are incapable of ascertainment. [Citations.]

The defendant points to what is claimed to be lack of consideration for his negative promise, in that the contract is inequitable and contains no agreement to employ him. It is true that there is no promise in so many words to employ the defendant to box in a contest with Stribling or Schmeling, but the agreement read as a whole binds the plaintiff to do just that, providing either Stribling or Schmeling becomes the contestant as the result of the match between them and can be induced to box the defendant. The defendant has agreed to "render services as a boxer" for the plaintiff exclusively, and the plaintiff has agreed to pay him a definite percentage of the gate receipts as his compensation for so doing. The promise to employ the defendant to enable him to earn the compensation agreed upon is implied to the same force and effect as though expressly stated. . . . [Citations.]

As we have seen, the contract is valid and enforceable. It contains a restrictive covenant which may be given effect. Whether a preliminary injunction shall be issued under such circumstances rests in the sound discretion of the court. [Citations.] The District Court, in its discretion, did issue the preliminary injunction and required the plaintiff as a condition upon its issuance to secure its own performance of the contract in suit with a bond for $25,000 and to give a bond in the sum of $35,000 to pay the defendant such damages as he may sustain by reason of the injunction. Such an order is clearly not an abuse of discretion.

Order affirmed.

Election of Remedies

HEAD & SEEMANN, INC. v. GREGG

Court of Appeals of Wisconsin, 1981.
104 Wis.2d 156, 311 N.W.2d 667.

Voss, P.J.

Bettye Gregg fraudulently induced Head & Seemann, Inc. to sell her a home in Brookfield. She occupied the home for five months but was subsequently ejected by a court order. In the action on the claim from which this appeal comes, Head & Seemann sought damages for the five months lost use of the property. At issue was whether a defrauded party who obtains rescission and restitution of real estate may also recover rental value and out-of-pocket expenses for the period of lost possession. The trial court held that the election of remedies doctrine barred an additional action for rental value and out-of-pocket expenses. Because we do not believe that rescission and an action for damages are inconsistent remedies, we reverse.

Defendant Bettye J. Gregg offered to buy a Brookfield home from plaintiff corporation. She represented, verbally and in writing, that she had $15,000 to $20,000 of equity in another home and would pay this amount to plaintiff after selling the other home. She knew, however, that she had no such equity. Relying on these intentionally fraudulent representations, plaintiff accepted defendant's offer to buy, and the parties entered into a land contract. After taking occupancy, defendant failed to make any of the contract payments. Plaintiff's investigation then revealed the fraud.

* * *

Plaintiff contends that it is entitled to recover for the lost use of the property and out-of-pocket expenses during defendant's possession of the property. It contends that recovery for these items, in addition to the rescission and return of the real estate, is necessary to restore plaintiff to his status before the fraud and execution of the contract. Since these "damages" would only restore plaintiff to its previous position and would not give plaintiff the purchase price or the benefit of the bargain, plaintiff argues that the remedies are not inconsistent, and the doctrine of election of remedies should not be applied. We agree.

The election of remedies doctrine is an equitable principle barring one from maintaining inconsistent theories or forms of relief.

[Citation.] Its underlying purpose is to prevent double recovery for the same wrong. [Citations.] * * *

The classic application of the election of remedies doctrine is that a defrauded party has the election of either rescission or affirming the contract and seeking damages. [Citation.] The choice is forced with respect to alternative theories in a single lawsuit because of inconsistency of both rescinding and affirming the contract. [Citation.]

Thus, it superficially appears that if a claimant chooses to seek rescission, he may not sue for damages. But the word "damages," like the label "election of remedies," impedes rather than aids the inquiry into the types of relief appropriate in a given case. Rescission is always coupled with restitution: the parties return the money, property or other benefits so as to restore each other to the position they were in prior to the transaction. In the case of fraud or misrepresentation, the victim has the priority of restoration, and if a loss must be borne, the wrongdoer bears it. [Citation.]

This case presents a crucial question dealing with the nature of restitution. At issue is whether restitution to a rescinding fraud victim includes everything he has reasonably paid out or given up in the transaction or only includes what the other party has actually received.

* * *

Many . . . cases recognize that "disaffirmance" of damages [rescission] only rules out "expectation" damages—the benefit of the bargain—and distinguish restitutionary "damages."

Damages for restitution are different from damages for breach of contract; and the former are permissible to restore the plaintiff to his former position when rescission is granted because of fraud. [Citation.] Several other states allow the recovery of restitutionary damages along with rescission when fraud or misrepresentation is the cause of the claim. [Citations.] We believe that restitutionary damages conform with the purpose of rescission, which is to put the defrauded party back in as good a position as he occupied before entering the contract. Consequently, we hold that such damages may be awarded along with rescission.

[Citation.] In equity, the court makes the calculated adjustments necessary to do complete justice. If complete justice requires that damages be awarded with the rescission, the court will award them. [Citations.]

Two clear forms of restitutionary awards are recoverable when coupled with rescission: The first is "reasonable expenditures in reliance on the bargain." [Citations.] The second is the rent or use value of the real estate during the other's possession. [Citations.]

Even in situations where the buyer is defrauded and entitled to the rescission, he or she must ordinarily pay rental value to the seller. This provides *a fortiori* support for the above authorities. [Citations.]

In the instant case, plaintiff seeks rental value and incidental expenses as part of restitution, items clearly recoverable under the great weight of authority. We believe that [citation] recognized the position that rescission and restorative damages are consistent remedies which work together to restore the injured party to his precontract position. For this reason, restorative damages, which in this case is rent, should be allowed in addition to rescission. The two are not inconsistent remedies.

Order reversed.

QUESTIONS

1. Explain how compensatory damages are computed.

2. Explain how reliance damages are computed.

3. Define (a) nominal damages, (b) incidental damages, (c) consequential damages, (d) foreseeability of damages, (e) punitive damages, (f) liquidated damages, and (g) mitigation of damages.

4. Discuss when the courts will grant equitable relief and define the various types of equitable relief.

5. Identify and discuss the situations in which restitution is available as a contractual remedy.

PROBLEMS

1. Edward contracted to buy 1,000 barrels of sugar from Marcia. Marcia failed to deliver, and because Edward could not buy any sugar in the market, he was compelled to shut down his candy factory.

(a) What damages is Edward entitled to recover?

(b) Would it make any difference if Marcia had been told by Edward that he wanted the sugar to make candies for the Christmas trade and that he had accepted contracts for the delivery by certain dates?

2. Daniel agreed to erect an apartment building for Steven for $2 million, Daniel to suffer deduc-

tion of $2,000 per day for every day of delay. Daniel was twenty days late in finishing the job, losing ten days because of a strike and ten days because the material suppliers were late in furnishing Daniel with materials. Daniel claims that he is entitled to payment in full (a) because the agreement as to $2,000 a day is a penalty; (b) because Steven had not shown that he has sustained any damage. Discuss each contention and decide.

3. Sharon contracted with Jane, a shirtmaker, for 1,000 shirts for men. Jane manufactured and delivered 500 shirts, which were paid for by Sharon. At the same time, Sharon notified Jane that she could not use or dispose of the other 500 shirts and directed Jane not to manufacture any more under the contract. Nevertheless, Jane proceeded to make up the other 500 shirts and tendered them to Sharon. Sharon refused to accept the shirts and Jane then sued for the purchase price. Decision?

4. Stuart contracts to act in a comedy for Charlotte and to comply with all theater regulations for four seasons. Charlotte promises to pay Stuart $800 for each performance and to allow Stuart one benefit performance each season. It is expressly agreed that "Stuart shall not be employed in any other production for the period of the contract." During the first year of the contract, Stuart and Charlotte have a terrible quarrel. Thereafter, Stuart signs a contract to perform in Elaine's production and ceases performing for Charlotte. Charlotte seeks (a) to prevent Stuart from performing for Elaine, and (b) to require Stuart to perform his contract with Charlotte. What result?

5. Louis leases a building to Pam for five years at a rental of $1,000 per month, commencing July 1, 1986, Pam depositing $10,000 as security for performance of all her promises in the lease, to be retained by Louis in case of any breach on Pam's part, otherwise to be applied in payment of rent for the last ten months of the term of the lease. Pam defaulted in the payment of rent for the months of May and June 1991. After proper notice to Pam of the termination of the lease for nonpayment of rent, Louis sued Pam for possession of the building and recovered a judgment for possession. Thereafter, Pam sues Louis to recover the $10,000 less the amount of rent due Louis for May and June 1991. Decision?

6. (a) Mary and Anne enter into a written agreement under which Mary agrees to sell and Anne agrees to buy for ten dollars per share 100 shares of the 300 shares outstanding of the capital stock of the Infinitesimal Steel Corporation, whose shares are not listed on any exchange and are closely held. Mary refused to deliver when tendered the $1,000, and Anne sues in equity for specific performance, tendering the $1,000. Decision?

(b) Modifying (a) above, assume that the subject matter of the agreement is stock of the United States Steel Corporation, which is traded on the New York Stock Exchange. Decision?

(c) Modifying (a) above, assume that the subject matter of the agreement is undeveloped farm land of little commercial value. Decision?

7. On March 1, Joseph sold to Sandra fifty acres of land in Oregon, which Joseph at the time represented to be fine, black loam, high, dry, and free of stumps. Sandra paid Joseph the agreed price of $40,000 and took from Joseph a deed to the land. Sandra subsequently discovered that the land was low, swampy, and not entirely free of stumps. Sandra, nevertheless, undertook to convert the greater part of the land into cranberry bogs. After one year of cranberry culture, Sandra became entirely dissatisfied, tendered the land back to Joseph, and demanded from Joseph the return of the $40,000. Upon Joseph's refusal to repay the money, Sandra brings an action against him to recover the $40,000. What judgment?

8. James contracts to make repairs to Betty's building in return for Betty's promise to pay $12,000 upon completion of the repairs. After partially completing the repairs, James is unable to continue. Betty hires another builder who completes the repairs for $5,000. The building's value to Betty has increased by $10,000 as a result of the repairs, but Betty has lost $500 in rents because of the delay caused by James's breach. James sues Betty. How much, if any, may James recover in restitution from Betty?

9. Linda induced Sally to enter into a purchase of a stereo amplifier by intentionally misrepresenting the power output to be sixty watts R.M.S. at rated distortion when in fact it only delivered twenty watts. Sally paid $450 for the amplifier. Amplifiers producing twenty watts generally sell for $200. Amplifiers producing sixty watts generally sell for $550. Sally decides to keep the amplifier and sue for damages. How much may Sally recover in damages from Linda?

10. Virginia induced Charles to sell his boat to her by misrepresentation of material fact upon which Charles reasonably relied. Virginia promptly sold the boat to Donald, who paid fair value for it and knew nothing concerning the transaction between Virginia and Charles. Upon discovering the misrepresentation, Charles seeks to recover the boat. What are Charles's rights against Virginia and Donald?

11. Felch was employed as a member of the faculty of Findlay College on a continuing basis. He was dismissed by action of the president and board of trustees without compliance with a contractual provision for dismissal that requires a hearing. Felch requested the court to enjoin Findlay College to continue Felch as a member of the faculty and to pay him the salary agreed upon. Decision?

COMPUTER RESEARCH PROBLEMS

1. Copenhaver, the owner of a laundry business, contracted with Berryman, the owner of a large apartment complex, to allow Copenhaver to own and operate the laundry facilities within the apartment complex. Berryman terminated the contract with Copenhaver when forty-seven months remained in the five-year contract. Within six months, Copenhaver placed the equipment into use in other locations. Copenhaver filed suit, claiming that he was entitled to conduct the laundry operations for an additional forty-seven months and, by such, would have earned a profit of $13,886.58, after deducting Berryman's share of the gross receipts and other operating expenses. Decision?

2. Billy Williams Builders and Developers entered into a contract with Hillerich under which Williams agreed to sell to Hillerich a certain lot and to construct on it a house according to submitted plans and specifications. The house built by Williams was defectively constructed. Hillerich brought suit for specific performance of the contract and for damages resulting from the defective construction and delay in performance. Williams argued that Hillerich was not entitled to have both specific performance and damages for breach of the contract because the remedies were inconsistent and Hillerich had to make an election between them. Decision?

3. Developers under a plan approved by the city of Rye had constructed six luxury cooperative apartment buildings and were to construct six more. In order to obtain certificates of occupancy for the six completed buildings, the developers were required to post a bond with the city to insure completion of the remaining buildings. The developers posted a $100,000 bond upon which the defendant, Public Service Mutual Insurance Company, as guarantor or surety, agreed to pay $200 for each day after April 1, 1971, that the remaining buildings were not completed. More than 500 days passed without completion of the buildings within the time limit. The city sued the developers and the insurance company to recover $100,000 on the bond. Decision?

4. Kerr Steamship Company sent a telegram to the Philippines through the Radio Corporation of America. The telegram contained instructions for loading cargo on one of Kerr's ships. The telegram was mislaid and never delivered. Consequently, the ship was improperly loaded and the cargo was lost. Kerr sued the Radio Corporation for $6,675.29 in profits lost on the cargo caused by the Radio Corporation's failure to deliver the telegram. Decision?

5. El Dorado Tire Company fired Bill Ballard, a sales executive. Ballard had a five year contract with El Dorado but was fired after only two years of employment. Ballard sued El Dorado for breach of contract. El Dorado claims that any damages due to breach of the contract should be mitigated because of Ballard's failure to seek other employment after he was fired. Decision?

Agency

Chapter 18

RELATIONSHIP OF PRINCIPAL AND AGENT

Nature of Agency
Creation of Agency
Duties of Agent to Principal
Duties of Principal to Agent
Termination of Agency

BY using agents, one person (the principal) may enter into any number of business transactions as though he had personally carried them out. A person may thus multiply and expand his business activities. The law of agency, like the law of contracts, is basic to almost every other branch of business law. Practically every type of contract or business transaction can be created or conducted through an agent. Therefore, the place and importance of agency in the practical conduct and operation of business cannot be overemphasized.

This is particularly true in the case of partnerships and corporations. Partnership is founded on the agency of the partners. Each partner is an agent of the partnership and as such has the authority to represent and bind the partnership in all usual transactions pertaining to the partnership business. A corporation, being an artificial legal entity, must function through the agency of its officers and employees. Thus, practically and legally, agency is an integral part of partnerships and corporations. Agency, however, is not limited to these business associations. Sole proprietors may also employ agents in the op-

erations of their business. Business, therefore, is very largely conducted, not by the owners of the business, but by their representatives or agents.

Although there is some overlap, the law of agency divides broadly into two main parts: the internal and external parts. An agent functions as an agent by dealing with third persons. It is in this way that legal relations are established between the principal and third persons. These relations constitute the external part of agency law and are discussed in the next chapter. This chapter will cover the internal relationship between principal and agent, including the nature of agency, the creation of an agency, the duties of agent to principal, the duties of principal to agent, and the termination of agency.

Agency is primarily governed by State common law. An orderly presentation of this law is found in the Restatement of the Law of Agency. The Restatement has been regarded as a valuable authoritative reference work and is extensively cited and quoted in reported judicial opinions. Selected provisions of the Restatement cited in the text are included in Appendix B of this book.

NATURE OF AGENCY

Agency is the relation existing between two persons, known as principal and agent, through which the agent is authorized to act for and on behalf of the principal. Restatement, Section 1. An agent, therefore, is one who represents another, the principal, in business dealings with third persons. Three persons are involved in the operation of agency: the principal, the agent, and a third person. In dealing with a third person, the agent acts for and in the name and place of the principal. The parties to the transaction, which is usually contractual if properly entered into, are the principal and the third person. If the existence and identity of the principal is disclosed, the agent is not a party but simply an intermediary. The result of the agent's functioning is exactly the same as if the principal had dealt directly with the third person and without the intervention of an agent. When the agent is dealing with the third person, the principal, in legal effect, is present in the person of the agent.

Within the scope of the authority granted to her by her principal, the agent may negotiate the terms of contracts with others and bind her principal to such contracts. Moreover, the negligence of an agent who is an employee in conducting the business of her principal exposes the principal to tort liability for injury and loss to third persons. The old maxim *"Qui facet per alium, facet per se"* (Who acts through another, acts himself) accurately describes the relationship between principal and agent. *See Hanson v. Kynast.* The rights and liabilities of the parties where an agent enters into a contract with a third party or commits a tort against a third party are discussed in the next chapter.

Scope of Agency Purposes

As a general rule, whatever business activity a person may accomplish personally, he may do through an agent. Conversely, whatever he cannot legally do himself, he cannot authorize another to do for him. Thus, a person may not validly authorize another to commit an illegal act or crime. Any such agreement is illegal and therefore unenforceable. Restatement, Section 19. Also, a person may not appoint an agent to perform acts that are so personal that their performance may not be delegated to another, as in the case of a contract for personal services. Restatement, Section 17. For example, Howard, a painter, contracts to paint a portrait of Doris. But Howard has one of his students execute the painting and tenders it to Doris. This is not a valid tender because the duty to paint Doris's portrait is not delegable.

Other Legal Relations

Two other legal relationships overlap with agency: employer–employee and principal–independent contractor. In the **employment relationship** (historically referred to as the master–servant relationship), the employer has the right to *control* the physical conduct of the employee. Restatement, Section 2. In contrast, a person who engages an **independent contractor** to do a specific job does *not* have the right to control the conduct and activities of the independent contractor in the performance of his contract. Restatement, Section 2(3). The latter simply contracts to do a job and is free to choose the method and manner to perform the job. For example, a full-time chauffeur is an employee, while a taxicab driver hired to carry a person to the airport is an independent contractor of the passenger.

Although all employees are agents not all agents are employees. Agents who are not employees are independent contractors. For instance, an attorney retained to handle a particular transaction would be an independent contractor–agent regarding that particular transaction. Other examples are auctioneers, brokers, and factors. Finally, not all independent contractors are agents. For example, the taxicab driver in the example above is not an agent. Likewise, if Pam hires Bill to build a stone wall around her property, Bill is an independent contractor who is not an agent.

The distinction between employee and independent contractor has a number of important legal consequences. *See Massey v. Tube Art Display, Inc.* As discussed in the next chapter, a principal is liable for the torts committed by an employee within the scope of his employment but ordinarily is not liable for torts committed by an independent contractor. In addition, the obligations of a principal under numerous Federal and State statutes apply only to agents who are employees. Examples of these statutes are the Social Security Act, the National Labor Relations Act, and Workers' Compensation Acts. These and other statutory enactments affecting the employment relationship are discussed in Chapter 44.

CREATION OF AGENCY

Agency is a **consensual** relationship that may be formed by contract *or* agreement between the principal and agent. The Restatement provides that "an agency relation exists only if there has been a manifestation by the principal to the agent that the agent may act on his account, and consent by the agent so to act." Section 15. Thus, whether an agency relationship has been created is determined by an *objective* test. If the principal requests another to act for him with respect to a matter, and indicates that the other is to act without further communication and the other consents to act, the relation of principal and agent exists. For example, Paula writes to Austin, a factor whose business is purchasing goods for others, telling him to select described goods and ship them at once to Paula. Before answering Paula's letter, Austin does as directed, charging the goods to Paula. Austin is authorized to do this because there is an agency relationship between Paula and Austin.

The relationship of principal and agent is consensual and not necessarily contractual; therefore, it may exist without consideration. Restatement, Section 16. An agency created without consideration is a **gratuitous agency.** A gratuitous agent has the same power to affect the principal's relations with third persons as if he were paid, and his liabilities to and rights against third persons are the same. Nonetheless, agency by contract is the most usual method of creating the relationship and must satisfy all of the requirements of a contract.

Formalities

As a general rule, no particular formality is required in a contract of agency. The contract may be express or inferred from the conduct of the principal. In some cases, however, the contract must be in writing. The appointment of an agent for a period of more than a year comes within the one-year clause of the statute of frauds, and thus must be in writing to be enforceable. In some States, the authority of an agent to sell land must be in writing and signed by the principal.

A **power of attorney** is a formal appointment of an agent who is known as an attorney in fact. Under a power of attorney, for example, a principal may appoint an agent not only to execute a contract for the sale of the principal's real estate, but also to execute the deed conveying title to the real estate to the third party.

Capacity

The capacity to be a principal, and thus to act through an agent, depends upon the capacity of the principal to do the act herself. For example, contracts entered into by a minor or an incompetent not under a guardianship are voidable. Consequently, the appointment of an agent by a minor or an incompetent not under a guardianship—and any resulting contracts—are voidable, regardless of the agent's contractual capacity. *See Goldfinger v. Doherty* in Chapter 19.

On the other hand, because the act of the agent is considered the act of the principal, the incapacity of an agent to bind himself by contract does *not* disqualify him from making a contract that is binding on his principal. Thus, any person has the capacity to be an agent. Restatement, Section 21. Although the contract of agency may be voidable, an authorized contract between the principal and the third person who dealt with the agent is valid. Nonetheless, some mental capacity is necessary in an agent; therefore, minors and mental incompetents may not have the capacity to act as agents in certain situations.

DUTIES OF AGENT TO PRINCIPAL

Since the relationship of principal and agent is ordinarily created by contract, the duties of the agent to the principal are primarily determined by the provisions of the contract. In addition to the contractual duties assumed by the agent, he is subject to various other duties imposed by law, unless the parties agree otherwise. Restatement, Section 376. Normally, a principal selects an agent based on the agent's ability, skill, and integrity. Moreover, the principal not only authorizes and empowers the agent to bind him on contracts with third persons, but in many cases he also places the agent in possession of his money and other property. As a result, the agent is in a position, either through negligence or dishonesty, to injure the principal. Accordingly, an agent as a **fiduciary** (a person in a position of trust and confidence) owes his principal the duties of obedience, diligence, providing information, providing an accounting, and loyalty. Moreover, the agent "is subject to liability for loss caused to the principal for any breach of duty." Restatement, Section 401.

A gratuitous agent is subject to the same duty of loyalty that is imposed upon a paid agent and is liable to the principal for harm caused by his careless performance. Although a gratuitous agent is usually under no duty to perform for the principal because of the lack of consideration, he may be liable to the principal for failing to perform a promise on which the principal has relied.

Duty of Obedience

The duty of obedience requires the agent to act in the principal's affairs only as authorized by the principal and to obey all reason-able instructions and directions of the principal. Restatement, Sections 383 and 385. The agent may be subject to liability to his principal for breach of this duty (1) because he entered into an unauthorized contract for which his principal is liable, (2) because he has improperly delegated his authority, or (3) because he has committed a tort for which the principal is liable. Thus, if an agent sells on credit in violation of the explicit instructions of the principal, the agent has breached the duty of obedience and is liable to the principal for any amounts not paid by the purchaser. Moreover, an agent who breaches his duty of obedience loses his right to compensation. Restatement, Section 469.

Duty of Diligence

An agent must act with reasonable care and skill in performing the work for which she is employed. She must also exercise any special skill that she may have. Restatement, Section 379. If an agent does not exercise the required care and skill, she is liable to the principal for any resulting loss.

Comment c to Restatement, Section 379 provides:

The paid agent is subject to a duty to exercise at least the skill which he represents himself as having. Unless the circumstances indicate otherwise, a paid agent represents that he has at least the skill and undertakes to exercise the care which is standard for that kind of employment in the community. A business agent represents that he understands the usages of the business and undertakes to conduct transactions in accordance with them; one undertaking a matter involving special knowledge represents that he has the special knowledge required.

For example, Peg appoints Alvin as her agent to sell goods in markets where the highest price can be obtained. Alvin sells goods in a market that is glutted and obtains a low price, although a higher price would have been obtained in a nearby market if Alvin had used care in obtaining information. Alvin is subject to liability to Peg for breach of the duty of diligence. *See F.W. Myers & Co. v. Hunter Farms.*

Duty to Inform

An agent must use reasonable efforts to give the principal information that is relevant to the affairs entrusted to her and that, as the agent knows or should know, the principal would desire to have. Restatement, Section 381. This duty is made imperative by the rule of agency that provides that notice to an agent is notice to his principal. Some examples of information which an agent has been held under a duty to communicate to his principal are: that a customer of the principal has become insolvent; that a debtor of the principal has become insolvent; that one of the partners of a firm with which the principal has previously dealt, and with which the principal or agent is about to deal, has withdrawn from the firm; or that the principal's property which the principal has authorized the agent to sell at a specified price can be sold at a higher price. *See F.W. Myers & Co. v. Hunter Farms.*

Duty to Account

The agent is under a duty to maintain and provide the principal with a true and complete account of money or other property that the agent has received or expended on behalf of the principal. Restatement, Section 382. An agent must also keep the principal's property separate from his own.

Fiduciary Duty

A fiduciary duty is one that arises out of a relationship of trust and confidence. It is a duty imposed by law and is owed by an agent to his principal and an employee to his employer. It is also owed by a trustee to a beneficiary of a trust, an officer or director of a corporation to the corporation and its shareholders, and a lawyer to his clients. Fiduciary duties are not limited to these situations but exist in every relationship where the law authorizes one person to place trust and confidence in another.

The **fiduciary duty** is one of utmost loyalty and good faith. Although the fiduciary duty is not limited to the following situations, they occur most frequently.

Conflicts of Interest An agent must act solely in the interest of his principal and not in his own interest or in the interest of another. An agent may not represent his principal in any transaction in which he has a personal interest. Nor may the agent act on behalf of adverse parties to a transaction without the approval of both principals to the dual agency. An agent may take a position in conflict with the interest of his principal only if the principal, with full knowledge of all of the facts, consents. For example, A, an agent of P who desires to purchase land, agrees with C, who represents B, a seller of land, that A and C will endeavor to effect a transaction between their principals and will pool their commissions. A and C have committed a breach of fiduciary duty to P and B.

Transactions between an agent and her principal are closely scrutinized. The agent may not deal at arm's length with her principal. The agent thus owes her principal the duty of full disclosure of all relevant facts affecting the transaction. Moreover, the transaction must be fair. *See Detroit Lions, Inc. v. Argovitz.*

Duty Not to Compete An agent cannot compete with his principal or act on behalf of a competitor. Moreover, an agent who is employed to buy may not buy from himself without the principal's consent. Restatement, Section 389. Thus, Penny employs Albert to purchase for her a site suitable for a shopping center. Albert owns one that is suitable and sells it to Penny at the fair market value. Albert does not disclose to Penny that Albert had owned the land. Penny may rescind the transaction. An agent who is employed to sell may not become the purchaser nor may he act as agent for the purchaser without the consent of the principal. The agent's loyalty must be undivided, and his actions must be devoted exclusively to represent and promote the interests of his principal.

After termination of the agency, unless otherwise agreed, the agent may compete with his former principal. A contractual agreement by the agent not to compete with the principal after termination of the agency will be enforced by injunction if the restriction is reasonable as to time and place and necessary to protect the principal's legitimate interest. Contractual agreements not to compete are discussed in Chapter 12.

Confidential Information An agent may not use or disclose confidential information obtained in the course of the agency for his own benefit or contrary to the interest of his principal. Confidential information is information which, if disclosed, would harm the principal's business, or which has a value because it is not generally known. Confidential information includes unique business methods, trade secrets, business plans, and customer lists. After termination of the agency, unless otherwise agreed, the agent may not use or disclose to third persons confidential information. The agent, however, is entitled to use skill, knowledge, and general information acquired during the agency relationship. Restatement, Section 396.

Duty to Account for Financial Benefits Unless otherwise agreed, an agent is under a duty to account to the principal for any financial benefit received by her as a direct result of transactions conducted on behalf of the principal. This would include bribes, kickbacks, and gifts. Moreover, an agent is not permitted to make a secret profit out of any transaction subject to the agency. All such profits belong to the principal to whom the agent must account. Thus, if an agent, authorized to sell certain property of his principal for $1,000, sells it for $1,500, he may not secretly pocket the additional $500. Further, suppose Peabody employs real estate broker Anderson to sell his land for a commission of 6 percent of the sale price. Anderson, knowing that Peabody is willing to sell for $20,000, agrees secretly with a prospective buyer who is willing to pay $22,000 for the land that he will endeavor to obtain the consent of Peabody to sell for $20,000 in which event the buyer will pay Anderson $1,000, or one-half

of the amount that the buyer believes she is saving on the price. The broker has violated his fiduciary duty and must pay to Peabody the secret profit of $1,000. Furthermore, Anderson loses the right to any commission on the transaction.

Principal's Remedies An agent who violates his fiduciary duty is liable to his principal for breach of contract, in tort for losses caused, and in restitution for profits made or property received in breach of the fiduciary duty. Moreover, he loses the right to compensation. Restatement, Section 469. The principal may avoid a transaction in which the agent breached his fiduciary duty, even though the principal suffered no loss. A breach of fiduciary duty may also constitute just cause for discharge of the agent.

DUTIES OF PRINCIPAL TO AGENT

Although both principal and agent have rights and duties arising out of the agency relationship, more emphasis is placed on the duties of the agent. This is necessarily so because of the nature of the agency relationship. First, the acts and services to be performed, both under the agency contract and as may be required by law, are to be performed mostly by the agent. Second, the agent is a fiduciary and is subject to the duties discussed earlier. Nonetheless, an agent has certain rights against the principal, both under the contract and by the operation of law. Correlative to these rights are certain duties that the principal owes to the agent. The duties are based in contract and tort law.

Contractual Duties

The contractual duties owed by a principal to an agent are the duties of compensation, reimbursement, and indemnification; each may be excluded or modified by agreement between the principal and agent. Although a gratuitous agent is not owed a duty of compensation, she is entitled to reimbursement and indemnification.

As with any party to a contract, a principal is under a duty to perform his part of the contract according to its terms. The most important duty of the principal, from the standpoint of the agent, is to compensate the agent as specified in the contract. It is also the duty of the principal not to terminate the agency wrongfully. Whether the principal must furnish the means of employment or opportunity for work will depend upon the particular case. A principal who employs an agent to sell his goods must supply the agent with conforming goods. In other cases, the agent must create his own opportunity for work, as in the case of a broker employed to procure a buyer for his principal's house. How far, if at all, the principal must assist or cooperate with the agent will depend on the particular agency. Usually, cooperation on the part of the principal is more necessary where the agent's compensation is contingent upon the success of his efforts than where the agent is paid a fixed salary regularly over a period of permanent employment.

Compensation   A principal has a duty to compensate her agent unless the agent has agreed to serve gratuitously. If the agreement does not specify a definite compensation, a principal is under a duty to pay the reasonable value of authorized services performed for her by her agent. Restatement, Section 443. When an agent's compensation is dependent upon her accomplishing a specific result, she is entitled to the agreed compensation only if she achieves the result in the time specified, or in a reasonable time if no time is stated. A common example is a listing agreement between a seller and a real estate broker providing for a commission to the broker if he finds a buyer ready, willing, and able to buy the property on the terms specified in the listing agreement. A principal also has a duty to maintain and provide the agent a true and complete account of money or property due to the agent.

Reimbursement   A principal is under a duty to reimburse his agent for authorized payments made by the agent on behalf of the principal and for authorized expenses incurred by the agent. Restatement, Section 438. For example, an agent who reasonably and properly pays a fire insurance premium for the protection of her principal's property is entitled to reimbursement for the payment. "The authority to pay money to third persons on account of the principal or to incur liabilities in the course of the principal's business may be created by specific directions or may be the result of the course of business between the principal and the agent, or of the customs of the business in which the agent is engaged for the principal." Section 439, Comment c.

Indemnification   The principal is under a duty to indemnify the agent for losses incurred or suffered while acting as directed by the principal in a transaction that is not illegal or not known by the agent to be wrongful. Restatement, Sections 438 and 439. To indemnify is to make good or pay a loss. Suppose that Perry, the principal, has in his possession goods belonging to Margot. Perry directs Alma, his agent, to sell these goods. Alma, believing Perry to be the owner, sells the goods to Turner. Margot then sues Alma for the conversion of her goods and recovers a judgment, which Alma pays to Margot. Alma is entitled to payment from Perry for her loss, including the amount reasonably expended by Alma in defense of the action brought by Margot. *See F.W. Myers & Co. v. Hunter Farms.*

Tort Duties

A principal owes to any agent the same duties under tort law that the principal owes to all parties. Restatement, Section 470. Moreover, a principal is under a duty to disclose to an agent those risks involved in the agency, of which the principal knows or should know, if the principal should realize that the agent is unaware of these risks. For instance, if a principal directs his agent to collect rent from a tenant who is known to have assaulted rent collectors, the principal has a duty to warn the agent of that fact.

Where the agent is an employee, the principal owes the employee additional duties. Among these is the duty to provide an employee with reasonably safe conditions of employment and to warn the employee of any unreasonable risk involved in the employment. An employer is also liable to her employees for injury caused by the negligence of other employees and of other agents doing work for her. The tort duties owed by an employer to an employee are discussed more fully in Chapter 44.

TERMINATION OF AGENCY

Because the authority of an agent is based upon the consent of the principal, the agency is terminated when such consent is withdrawn or otherwise ceases to exist. Upon termination of the agency the agent's actual authority ends, and he is not entitled to compensation for services subsequently rendered, although the agent's fiduciary duties may continue. Termination may take place by the acts of the parties or by operation of law.

Acts of the Parties

Termination by the acts of the parties may occur by the provisions of the original agreement, by the subsequent acts of both principal and agent, or by the subsequent act of either one of them.

Lapse of Time Authority conferred upon an agent for a specified time terminates at the expiration of that period. If no time is specified, authority terminates at the end of a reasonable period. Restatement, Section 105. For example, Palmer authorizes Avery to sell a tract of land for him. Ten years pass without communication between Palmer and Avery. Avery purports to sell the tract. Avery's authorization has terminated due to lapse of time, and the purported sale is not binding upon Palmer.

Fulfillment of Purpose The authority of an agent to perform a specific act or to accomplish a particular result is terminated when the act is performed or the result is accomplished by the agent. Restatement, Section 106. Thus, if Porter authorizes Alford to sell or lease Alford's land, and Alford leases the land to Taft, Alford's authority is terminated and he may not thereafter sell or lease the land without receiving new authorization.

Mutual Agreement of the Parties The agency relationship is created by agreement and may be terminated at any time by mutual agreement of the principal and the agent.

Revocation of Authority A principal may revoke an agent's authority at any time. Restatement, Section 119. Moreover, the principal may manifest her termination of consent either expressly or implicitly; that is, by conduct inconsistent with its continuance. Examples include where the principal indicates that the agent is to do an act different from that originally authorized, retakes the goods that she had authorized the agent to sell, sells or disposes of the goods, or voluntarily causes their loss or destruction. Restatement, Section 119, Comment b.

If, however, such revocation constitutes a breach of contract by the principal, the agent may recover damages from the principal. For example, Patrick, in consideration of Alice's agreement to advertise and give her best energies to the sale of Patrick's property, Blackacre, grants to Alice "a power of attorney, irrevocable for one year." Alice advertises and spends time trying to sell Blackacre. At the end of three months, Patrick informs Alice that he revokes the power of attorney. Alice's authority is terminated, but Alice may recover damages from Patrick. Restatement, Section 118, Illustration I. *See Hilgendorf v. Hague.* Nonetheless, where the agent has seriously breached the agency contract, willfully disobeyed, or violated the fiduciary duty, the principal is not liable for revocation. In addition, if the agency is gratuitous, then the principal ordinarily may revoke it without liability to the agent.

Renunciation by the Agent The agent also has the power to put an end to the agency by notice to the principal that she renounces the authority given her by the principal. If the parties have contracted that the agency continue for a specified time, an unjustified renunciation prior to the expiration of the time is a breach of contract. If the agency is gratuitous, then the agent ordinarily may renounce it without liability to the principal.

Operation of Law

The occurrence of certain events will automatically terminate an agency relationship by the operation of law. These events either make it impossible for the agent to perform or unlikely that the principal would want the agent to act. As a matter of law, agency is ordinarily terminated by the occurrence of any of the following events.

Bankruptcy Bankruptcy is a proceeding in a Federal court affording relief to financially troubled debtors. The filing of the petition in bankruptcy, which initiates the proceedings, also usually terminates all the debtor's existing agency relationships. The trustee in bankruptcy, however, may assume an executory contract of agency unless under State law the contract is not assignable. If the credit standing of the agent is important to the agency relationship, then it will be terminated by the bankruptcy of the agent. Restatement, Section 113. Thus, Arnold is appointed by Pacific Securities, Inc., an investment house, to act as its agent in advising Pacific's local clients as to investments. Arnold becomes bankrupt. Arnold is no longer authorized to act for Pacific.

Death The death of the principal terminates the authority of the agent. For example, Polk employs Allison to sell Polk's line of goods under a contract that specifies Allison's commission and that the employment is to continue for a year. Without Allison's knowledge Polk dies. Allison has no authority to sell Polk's goods, even though the contract specified that Allison would be employed for one year. The death of Polk, the principal, terminated the authority of the agent and voided the contract. Similarly, the authority given to an agent by a principal is strictly personal, and the agent's death terminates the agency.

Incapacity Incapacity of the principal that occurs after the formation of the agency terminates the agent's authority. To illustrate, Powell authorizes Anna to sell in the next ten months an apartment complex for not less than $2 million. Powell is adjudicated incompetent two months later without Anna's knowledge. Anna's authority to sell the apartment complex is terminated. Likewise, subsequent incapacity of an agent to perform the acts authorized by the principal terminates the agent's authority.

Almost all of the States have statutes providing for a durable power of attorney. If made in compliance with one of these statutes, an appointment of an agent survives the incapacity of the *principal*.

Change in Business Conditions The authority of an agent is terminated by notice or knowledge of a change in the value of the subject matter, or of a change in business conditions from which the agent should reasonably infer that the principal would not consent to an exercise of the authority given him. Restatement, Section 109. Thus, Patricia authorizes Aaron to sell her eighty acres of farm land for $800 per acre. Subsequently, oil is discovered on nearby land, which causes Patricia's land to increase greatly in value. Aaron knows of this, but Patricia does not. Aaron's authority to sell the land is terminated.

Loss or Destruction of the Subject Matter Where the authority of the agent relates to a specific subject matter that becomes lost or destroyed, her authority is thereby terminated. This corresponds to the rule that loss or destruction of the subject matter of an offer terminates the offer. For example, Paul authorizes Allan to make a contract for the sale of Paul's residence. The next week the residence burns completely, as Allan is aware. Allan's authority is terminated.

Loss of Qualification of Principal or Agent   When the authority given the agent relates to the conduct of a certain business, the operation of which requires a license from the government or a regulatory agency, the failure to acquire or the loss of such license terminates the authority of the agent. Restatement, Section 111. Thus, Paine, who holds a retail liquor license, employs Adrian to sell liquor at retail in Paine's store. Paine's license is revoked. Adrian's authority to sell Paine's liquor at retail is terminated.

Disloyalty of Agent   If an agent, without the knowledge of her principal, acquires interests adverse to those of the principal or otherwise breaches her duty of loyalty to the principal, her authority to act on behalf of the principal is terminated. Restatement, Section 112. Thus, Parker employs Agnes, a realtor, to sell Parker's land. Unknown to Parker, Agnes has been authorized by Trent to purchase this land from Parker. Agnes is not authorized to sell the land to Trent.

Change of Law   A change in the law that takes place after the employment of the agent may cause the performance of the authorized act to be illegal or criminal. Such a change in the law terminates the authority of the agent. Restatement, Section 116. Thus, Pablo directs his agent Arp to ship young elm trees from State X to State Y. In order to control elm disease, a quarantine is established by State X upon the shipment of elm trees into any other State, and any such shipment

is punishable by fine. Arp's authority to ship the elm trees is terminated.

Outbreak of War   Where the outbreak of war places the principal and agent in the position of alien enemies, the authority of the agent is terminated because its exercise is illegal. Otherwise, the outbreak of war of which the agent has notice terminates his authority if the conditions are so changed that the agent should infer that the principal would not consent to further exercise of the authority. Restatement, Section 115.

Irrevocable Agencies

In the foregoing discussion of the various ways in which the authority of an agent may be terminated, the agency relationship was assumed to be the ordinary one in which the agent does not have a security interest in the power conferred upon him by the principal. Where the **agency is coupled with an interest** of the agent in the subject matter, as where the agent has advanced funds on behalf of the principal and his power to act is given as security for the loan, the authority of the agent may *not* be revoked by the principal. In addition, neither the incapacity nor bankruptcy of the principal terminates the authority or the power of the agent. The death of the principal also will not terminate the agency unless the duty for which the security was given terminates with the death of the principal. Restatement, Section 139. Illustration 4 to that section provides the following example:

P desires to borrow money from A, who requires security. P delivers to A certain chattels [personal property] and gives to A a writing by which he gives A the power, in case of nonpayment of the money, to sell the chattels as P's agent at a public or private sale for the best price that can be obtained, and out of the proceeds to retain the amount of the loan, paying the surplus to P. Having obtained the money upon these terms, P tells A that he revokes the power to sell. The power is not revoked. P dies. The power is not affected.

CASES

Creation of Agency

HANSON v. KYNAST

Supreme Court of Ohio, 1986.
24 Ohio St.3d 171, 494 N.E.2d 1091.

PARRINO, J.

On May 1, 1982, appellee, Brian K. Hanson, sustained a paralyzing injury while playing in a lacrosse game between Ohio State University ("OSU") and Ashland University, Inc. ("Ashland") at the Ashland lacrosse field. During the game Roger Allen, an OSU player, intercepted an Ashland player's pass and scored a goal. As Allen was scoring the goal, he was body-checked from behind by Ashland defender William D. Kynast. Allen fell and Kynast allegedly stood over Allen taunting him. Brian Hanson saw the contact and Kynast's subsequent behavior. Concerned for Allen's welfare, Hanson grabbed Kynast from the side or back and held him in a bear hug. Kynast immediately twisted and threw Hanson off his back. Hanson's head struck the ground and he sustained serious injuries.

The trainers for both teams came onto the field to attend Hanson. After discovering the seriousness of his injury (Hanson was numb and could not move), an assistant trainer for Ashland was sent to telephone the fire department for an ambulance.

Upon arriving on the scene, the ambulance driver discovered that the main entrance to the playing field was blocked by an illegally parked automobile. As a result, the ambulance driver had to find another entrance.

After immobilizing Hanson, the attendants transported him to Ashland Samaritan Hospital where he remained for almost an hour. He was then transferred to Mansfield General Hospital for surgery. The operation took place at approximately 11:00 p.m., more than five hours after he was taken from the first hospital. The surgery successfully relieved vascular compression thus preventing possible brain damage. Hanson, however, had sustained a serious spinal cord injury on impact. It was determined that he had suffered a compression fracture of his sixth vertebra and, as a result, Hanson is now an incomplete quadriplegic.

On December 13, 1983, Brian Hanson filed an amended complaint in the Court of Common Pleas of Ashland County against William Kynast and Ashland University, Inc. Hanson maintained, in relevant part, that because Kynast was acting as the agent of Ashland, the university was therefore liable for Kynast's alleged wrongful acts under the doctrine of *respondeat superior*. Hanson also alleged that Ashland was directly liable for negligently failing to have an ambulance or emergency vehicle present at the site of the game, and in permitting a motor vehicle to be parked in such a manner that the main entrance to the playing field was blocked. Ashland filed a timely answer denying the material allegations of the complaint.

On April 11, 1984, Ashland filed a motion for summary judgment. * * * The trial court granted Ashland's motion on November 16, 1984. The court held that no agency relationship existed between Kynast and Ashland, and that Ashland did not have a legal duty to have an ambulance at the game. In a split decision, the court of appeals reversed the trial court's judgment, holding that genuine issues of fact existed on the question of agency and upon Ashland's duty to provide medical personnel at the game.

* * *

The first issue to be decided is whether the relationship of principal and agent existed between Kynast and Ashland. Because of the absence of proof as to the existence of a principal-agent relationship, the trial court essentially found as a matter of law that Ashland was not bound by Kynast's conduct under the doctrine of *respondeat superior*. We agree.

This court has held that the relationship of principal and agent or master and servant exists only when one party exercises the right of control over the actions of another, and those actions are directed toward the attainment of an objective which the former seeks. [Citations]; see, also, Restatement of the Law 2d, Agency (1958) 7, Section 1. Therefore, a principal-agent relationship can be found in the instant case only if Kynast was under the control of Ashland, and if he took some action directed toward the attainment of Ashland's objective.

In order to make this determination we must examine the relevant documentary evidence produced before the trial court. A review of the evidence reveals that William Kynast expressed an interest in Ashland when he was in high school. He requested and received written information from the university and he spoke with Ashland lacrosse coach Dick Fahrney. In his deposition Kynast testified that he chose Ashland because it had a good business school, he could live away from home, and he would be able to play lacrosse. He also testified that no promises were made to him by any Ashland official to induce him to attend the university.

Kynast attended Ashland for three semesters, starting in August 1981. He financed his education through bank loans and with the assistance of his parents. While at Ashland, Kynast decided to play lacrosse; however, he was never obligated to play lacrosse for the university. In addition, Kynast did not receive a scholarship, he used his own equipment while playing, and he was not compensated for his participation.

Lacrosse was instituted at Ashland in an effort to meet the needs of students, especially those coming from the East Coast where lacrosse is a popular sport. Ashland provides a coach and the players are each given a game shirt which displays the university's name. The players also received free transportation to games at other schools, and on one occasion while Kynast played for Ashland, they received overnight lodging on a road trip. No admission fee is charged at the home games.

This court is of the opinion that this relationship between Kynast and Ashland is a relationship common to many students attending universities. A university offers a diversified educational experience which includes classroom instruction in a great variety of subjects as well as optional participation in events such as school clubs, and intramural and intercollegiate sports. All of these offerings are designed to expand and enrich a student's overall educational experience. Students evaluate and determine which university best meets their needs, and then pay a fee to attend that university. The relationship formed under these conditions has previously been characterized as contractual. [Citation.] The student pays a fee and agrees to abide by the university rules. In exchange, the university provides the student with a worthwhile education.

This relationship does not constitute a principal-agent relationship. The student is a buyer of education rather than an agent. Restatement of the Law 2d, Agency (1958) 73, Section 14 J, states that a buyer retains goods primarily for his own benefit, while an agent is one who retains goods primarily for the benefit of the one who delivers those goods. In the instant case, the "goods" to be delivered is an education and the university delivers that education to the student for a fee. It is clear that a student retains the benefit of that education for himself rather than for the university.

* * *

In summary, the relationship discussed above constitutes a contractual one between the student and his university. The university is selling and the student is buying an education, and the formation of a principal-agent relationship was not intended, nor was one established, between the parties.

The appellee, however, maintains that Kynast's participation in lacrosse converted his status from the usual university-student relationship to that of principal-agent due to the control exercised by the lacrosse coach over Kynast, and because his participation in lacrosse resulted in beneficial publicity for Ashland. We disagree. In applying the law of agency to the facts of this case, we must conclude that Kynast was not controlled by Ashland, and that he was not playing the game for the school's benefit.

The degree of control necessary to establish agency has not been clearly defined. See, *e.g.,* Restatement of the Law 2d, Agency (1958) 485, Section 220. Instead, courts have generally examined various factors in determining whether the requisite amount of control exists. One such factor is whether the individual is performing in the course of the principal's business rather than in some ancillary capacity. [Citation.] In the case at bar, Kynast was not performing in the course of the principal's business, *i.e.,* he was not educating students. On the contrary, he was participating in one of the educationally related opportunities offered by the university. Another factor to be considered is whether the individual was receiving any compensation from the principal. [Citation.] It is undisputed that Kynast was never compensated for playing on the Ashland lacrosse team. A third factor is whether the principal supplied the tools and the place of work in the normal course of the relationship. [Citation.] Kynast supplied his own equipment in order to play lacrosse. The university did, however, provide the playing field.

A review of these factors clearly shows that Kynast was not controlled by Ashland for the purpose of establishing an agency relationship. The control exerted over Kynast by the university, *i.e.,* the Ashland coach running the lacrosse team, was merely incidental to the educational opportunity in which Kynast *voluntarily* participated. A limited amount of control is necessary to assure that each student is afforded a fair opportunity to benefit from the activity. The athletic guidance that was exercised by Ashland in this case does not satisfy the control element required to establish agency.

Further, the documentary evidence considered in determining appellee's motion for summary judgment clearly establishes that Kynast's activity was not directed toward the attainment of an objective by Ashland. Lacrosse at Ashland is not an income-producing sport. In fact, as previously noted, an admission fee is not charged to attend the games.

The evidence established that Ashland initiated lacrosse for the benefit of the students wishing to play that game; it is simply one of the many educational opportunities offered to any Ashland student.

The appellee's claim that Ashland derived a benefit through the publicity the team generated is not persuasive. * * * In the instant case, there is no evidence that Ashland derived a benefit from publicity; nor is there evidence that Kynast participated in lacrosse so that Ashland could benefit from publicity. Kynast engaged in lacrosse voluntarily, and for *his own* enjoyment. Under such a circumstance no agency relationship is created.

To summarize, we conclude that a student who attends a university of his choice, receives no scholarship or compensation, voluntarily becomes a member of the university lacrosse team that engages in intercollegiate contests with other universities for which games no attendance fee is charged, who purchases his own equipment and who receives instructions from a coach while preparing for and playing such games, but is not otherwise controlled by the coach, and who participates in the game as a part of his total educational experience while attending school, is not the agent of the university at the time he is playing the game of lacrosse. Thus, appellee's claim that Ashland was liable for Kynast's wrongful acts through the doctrine of *respondeat superior* was properly rejected and the trial court properly entered summary judgment for appellant on this issue.

* * *

Accordingly, the judgment of the court of appeals is reversed.

Judgment reversed.

Other Legal Relations: Independent Contractor

MASSEY v. TUBE ART DISPLAY, INC.

Court of Appeals of Washington, Division 1, 1976.
15 Wn.App. 782, 551 P.2d 1387.

SWANSON, J.

Tube Art Display, Inc. (Tube Art) appeals from a judgment entered on a jury verdict awarding $143,000 in damages to John Massey, doing business as Olympic Research & Design Associates (Massey). Tube Art also appeals from an order denying a motion for judgment n.o.v. or for a new trial.

The facts leading to the initiation of this action are not in substantial dispute. A recently opened branch office of McPherson's Realty Company desired to move a reader board sign from its previous location to a site adjacent to its new quarters in a combination commercial-apartment building. An agreement was reached with Tube Art, the owner of the sign, to transport and re-install it on the northwest corner of the building's parking lot. On February 15, 1972, Tube Art obtained a permit from the City of Seattle for installation of the sign. On the following morning Tube Art's service manager and another employee went to the proposed site and took photographs and measurements. Later, a Tube Art employee laid out the exact size and location for the excavation by marking a 4 by 4 foot square on the asphalt surface with yellow paint. The dimensions of the hole, including its depth of 6 feet, were indicated with spray paint inside the square. After the layout was painted on the asphalt, Tube Art engaged a backhoe operator, defendant Richard F. Redford, to dig the hole.

In response to Tube Art's desire that the job be completed on the 16th of February, 1972, Redford began digging in the early evening hours at the location designated by Tube Art. At approximately 9:30 p.m. the bucket of Redford's backhoe struck a small natural gas pipeline. After examining the pipe and finding no indication of a break or leak, he concluded that the line was not in use and left the site. Shortly before 2 a.m. on the following morning, an explosion and fire occurred in the building serviced by that gas pipeline. As a result, two people in the building were killed and most of its contents were destroyed.

Massey and his associates, as tenants of the building, brought an action against Tube Art, Richard Redford and others, alleging the total destruction of drawings, plans, sketches, prototype machine components, castings, and other work products. The jury rendered its

verdict on the liability issue in favor of plaintiffs and against both defendants, Tube Art and Redford. A verdict in favor of Massey was returned, motions for judgment n.o.v. or for a new trial were denied, and judgment on the verdict was entered. Tube Art now appeals.

Tube Art's appeal presents two issues: (1) whether the trial court erred in declaring as a matter of law that an agency relationship existed between Tube Art and Redford, the person it chose to excavate the hole; and (2) whether the trial court erred in instructing the jury on the issue of damages.

* * *

Traditionally, servants and non-servant agents have been looked upon as persons employed to perform services in the affairs of others under an express or implied agreement, and who, with respect to physical conduct in the performance of those services, is subject to the other's control or right of control. [Citations.]

An independent contractor, on the other hand, is generally defined as one who contracts to perform services for another, but who is not controlled by the other nor subject to the other's right to control with respect to his physical conduct in performing the services. [Citations], Restatement (Second) of *Agency* § 2(3) (1958).

In determining whether one acting for another is a servant or independent contractor, several factors must be taken into consideration. These are listed in Restatement (Second) of *Agency* § 220(2) (1958), as follows:

(a) the extent of control which, by the agreement, the master may exercise over the details of the work;
(b) whether or not the one employed is engaged in a distinct occupation or business;
(c) the kind of occupation, with reference to whether, in the locality, the work is usually done under the direction of the employer or by a specialist without supervision;
(d) the skill required in the particular occupation;
(e) whether the employer or the workman supplies the instrumentalities, tools, and the place of work for the person doing the work;
(f) the length of time for which the person is employed;

(g) the method of payment, whether by the time or by the job;

(h) whether or not the work is a part of the regular business of the employer;

(i) whether or not the parties believe they are creating the relation of master and servant; and

(j) whether the principal is or is not in business.

All of these factors are of varying importance in determining the type of relationship involved and, with the exception of the element of control, not all the elements need be present. [Citation.] It is the right to control another's physical conduct that is the essential and oftentimes decisive factor in establishing vicarious liability whether the person controlled is a servant or a non-servant agent. [Citation.]

In discussing the actual extent to which the element of control must be exercised, we pointed out in [citation], that the plaintiff need not show that the principal controlled or had the right to control every aspect of the agent's operation in order to incur vicarious liability. Rather,

[i]t should be sufficient that plaintiff present substantial evidence of . . . control or right to control over those activities from whence the actionable negligence flowed. If the rule were otherwise, then a person wishing to accomplish a certain result through another could declare the other to be an independent contractor generally, and yet retain control over a particularly hazardous part of the undertaking without incurring liability for acts arising out of that part. Such a result would effectively thwart the purpose of the rule of vicarious liability. [Citations.]

In the recent case of [citation], we stated:

In this regard, it may be emphasized that it is not de facto control nor actual exercise of a right to interfere with or direct the work which constitutes the test, but rather, the *right to control* the negligent actor's physical conduct in the performance of the service. (Citations omitted.)

In making his ruling that Tube Art was responsible as a matter of law for Redford's actions the trial judge stated,

I think that under the undisputed evidence in this case they not only had the right to control, but they did control. They controlled the location of the spot to dig. They controlled the dimensions. They controlled the excavation and they got the building permits. They did all of the discretionary work that was necessary before he started to operate. They knew that the method of excavation was going to be by use of a backhoe rather than a pick and shovel which might have made a little difference on the exposure in this situation. They in effect created the whole atmosphere in which he worked. And the fact that even though he did not work for them all of the time and they paid him on a piece-work basis for the individual job didn't impress me particularly when they used him the number of times they did. Most of the time they used him for this type of work. So I am holding as a matter of law that Redford's activities are the responsibility of Tube Art.

Our review of the evidence supports the trial court's evaluation of both the right and exercise of control even though Redford had been essentially self-employed for about 5 years at the time of trial, was free to work for other contractors, selected the time of day to perform the work assigned, paid his own income and business taxes and did not participate in any of Tube Art's employee programs. The testimony advanced at trial, which we find determinative, established that during the previous 3 years Redford had worked exclusively for sign companies and 90 percent of his time for Tube Art. He had no employees, was not registered as a contractor or subcontractor, was not bonded, did not himself obtain permits or licenses for his jobs, and dug the holes at locations and in dimensions in exact accordance with the instructions of his employer. In fact, Redford was left no discretion with regard to the placement of the excavations that he dug. Rather, it was his skill in digging holes pursuant to the exact dimensions prescribed that caused him to be preferred over other backhoe operators. We therefore find no disputed evidence of the essential factor—the right to control, nor is there any dispute that control was exercised over the most significant decisions—the size and location of the hole. Consequently, only one conclusion could reasonably be drawn from the facts presented. In such a circumstance, the nature of the relationship becomes a question of law. [Citation.] We find no error.

* * *

[The court held that the trial court had not erred in giving its instructions on the issue of damages.]

Affirmed.

Duty of Diligence

F.W. MYERS & COMPANY v. HUNTER FARMS

Supreme Court of Iowa, 1982.
319 N.W.2d 186.

LARSON, J.

Hunter Farms was involved in farming in Greene County, and in the sale of chemicals to other farmers. It sought to obtain a large supply of Sencor, a farm herbicide not then readily available in the area, for resale. In response to its newspaper advertisement, Hunter was contacted by Petrolia Grain & Feed Company of Petrolia, Canada, which offered to fill Hunter's order for Sencor. A representative of Petrolia's supplier contacted an "import specialist" with the United States Customs Service to determine the import duty. The specialist advised it the rate would be five percent but the final rate could only be determined upon an examination of the herbicide at the time of importation. This information was forwarded to Hunter, which continued negotiations to purchase the Sencor and retained Myers [an import broker] to assist in moving it through customs, which Myers did.

The "qualified" opinion of the customs specialist was later rescinded; customs determined there were chemicals in the herbicide, not listed on its label, which would increase the duty from approximately $30,000 to over $128,000. Myers, fearing a forfeiture of its security bond for the duty, paid the additional amount under protest and sought indemnity from Hunter. Hunter, however, refused to pay, arguing Myers had breached its duty of care as an import broker in failing to advise Hunter the five-percent duty rate was only

tentative and was subject to being increased. This action was then brought by Myers, which contended it was not retained to give advice to Hunter, especially since it was never informed Hunter was a neophyte in the import business. It averred its duties as an import broker were merely to prepare the forms for importation and satisfy the bonding requirements; advice on matters of importation would be given only if requested. The trial court found Myers did not breach its duty of care to Hunter.

The right of indemnity under such circumstances is clear: If one is compelled to pay sums which another ought to pay, he is entitled to indemnity. [Citations.] Although Hunter does not challenge the general right of an agent to indemnity under such circumstances, it claims Myers had breached a concomitant duty of disclosure, thus precluding its recovery.

An agent is required to exercise such skill as is required to accomplish the object of his employment. If he fails to exercise reasonable care, diligence, and judgment under the circumstances, he is liable to his principal for any loss or damage resulting. [Citation.] Thus,

[u]nless otherwise agreed, a paid agent is subject to a duty to the principal to act with standard care and with the skill which is standard in the locality for the kind of work which he is employed to perform and, in addition, to exercise any special skill that he has.

Restatement (Second) of Agency, § 379(1), at 177 (1958).

We believe there was substantial evidence, [citation], to support the trial court's finding there was no breach of duty by Myers. Evidence was presented that the standard of care for import brokers did not include a special duty to render advice to the importer unless requested to do so. Expert testimony showed such brokers are basically involved in drafting the necessary papers, arranging for the necessary bonds, and actual forwarding of the duty payment. There was no evidence of a request to advise Hunter on import law, nor was there any evidence Myers was advised that Hunter was new in the import business.

Hunter contends, however, Myers had a special duty of disclosure to advise Hunter the five-percent figure was advisory or only an estimate. It claims the trial court erred in failing to recognize and apply such duty of care.

The scope of an agent's duty to disclose is explained by the *Restatement* in this manner:

Unless otherwise agreed, an agent is subject to a duty to use reasonable efforts to give his principal information which is relevant to affairs entrusted to him and which, as the agent has notice, the principal would desire to have and which can be communicated without violating a superior duty to a third person.

Restatement, supra § 381, at 182. This standard requires that the agent have notice the principal would desire to have the relevant information. In this case there was evidence the open-ended nature of an initial duty assessment was widely known and understood by importers. Myers was never informed of the need to convey this information to Hunter which, it could reasonably presume, possessed the fundamental knowledge of an importer. Myers was never advised of Hunter's lack of experience in the business, nor was it aware of the problem in labeling the herbicide which caused the increase in the duty charged. Absent knowledge of Hunter's special need for advice and of the circumstances which might give rise to the additional importation fees, there was no special duty on Myers to advise Hunter of the tentative nature of the assessment. Accordingly, it was not error for the trial court to refuse to recognize such a duty.

Affirmed.

Fiduciary Duty

DETROIT LIONS, INC. v. ARGOVITZ

United States District Court, Eastern District of Michigan, 1984.
580 F.Supp. 542.

DeMascio, J.

The plot for this Saturday afternoon serial began when Billy Sims, having signed a contract with the Houston Gamblers on July 1, 1983, signed a second contract with the Detroit Lions on December 16, 1983. On December 18, 1983, the Detroit Lions, Inc. (Lions) and Billy R. Sims filed a complaint in the Oakland County Circuit Court seeking a judicial determination that the July 1, 1983, contract between Sims and the Houston Gamblers, Inc. (Gamblers) is invalid because the defendant Jerry Argovitz (Argovitz) breached his fiduciary duty when negotiating the Gamblers' contract and because the contract was otherwise tainted by fraud and misrepresentation. * * *

For the reasons that follow, we have concluded that Argovitz's breach of his fiduciary duty during negotiations for the Gamblers' contract was so pronounced, so egregious, that to deny recision would be unconscionable.

Sometime in February or March 1983, Argovitz told Sims that he had applied for a Houston franchise in the newly formed United States Football League (USFL). In May 1983, Sims attended a press conference in Houston at which Argovitz announced that his application for a franchise had been approved. The evidence persuades us that Sims did not know the extent of Argovitz's interest in the Gamblers. He did not know the amount of Argovitz's original investment, or that Argovitz was obligated for 29 percent of a $1.5 million letter of credit, or that Argovitz was the president of the Gamblers' Corporation at an annual salary of $275,000 and 5 percent [of] the yearly cash flow. The defendants could not justifiably expect Sims to comprehend the ramifications of Argovitz's interest in the Gamblers or the manner in which that interest would create an untenable conflict of interest, a conflict that would inevitably breach Argovitz's fiduciary duty to Sims. Argovitz knew, or should have known, that he could not act as Sims' agent under any circumstances when dealing with the Gamblers. Even the USFL Constitution itself prohibits a holder of any interest in a member club from acting "as the contracting agent or representative for any player."

Pending the approval of his application for a USFL franchise in Houston, Argovitz continued his negotiations with the Lions on behalf of Sims. On April 5, 1983, Argovitz offered Sims' services to the Lions for $6 million over a four-year period. The offer included a demand for a $1 million interest-free loan to be repaid over 10 years, and for skill and injury guarantees for three years. The Lions quickly responded with a counter offer on April 7, 1983, in the face amount of $1.5 million over a five-year period with additional incentives not relevant here. The negotiating process was working. The Lions were trying to determine what Argovitz really believed the market value for Sims really was. On May 3, 1983, with his Gamblers franchise assured, Argovitz significantly reduced his offer to the Lions. He now offered Sims to the Lions for $3 million over a four-year period, one-half of the amount of his April 5, 1983, offer. Argovitz's May 3rd offer included a demand for $50,000 to permit Sims to purchase an annuity. Argovitz also dropped his previous demand for skill guarantees. The May 10, 1983 offer submitted by the Lions brought the parties much closer.

On May 30, 1983, Argovitz asked for $3.5 million over a five-year period. This offer included an interest-free loan and injury protection insurance but made no demand for skill guarantees. The May 30 offer now requested $400,000 to allow Sims to purchase an annuity. On June 1, 1983, Argovitz and the Lions were only $500,000 apart. We find that the negotiations between the Lions and Argovitz were progressing normally, not laterally as Argovitz represented to Sims. The Lions were not "dragging their feet." . . . The evidence establishes that on June 22, 1983, the Lions and Argovitz were very close to reaching an agreement on the value of Sims' services.

Apparently, in the midst of his negotiations with the Lions and with his Gamblers franchise in hand, Argovitz decided that he would seek an offer from the Gamblers. Mr.

Bernard Lerner, one of Argovitz's partners in the Gamblers agreed to negotiate a contract with Sims. Since Lerner admitted that he had no knowledge whatsoever about football, we must infer that Argovitz at the very least told Lerner the amount of money required to sign Sims and further pressed upon Lerner the Gamblers' absolute need to obtain Sims' services. In the Gamblers' organization, only Argovitz knew the value of Sims' services and how critical it was for the Gamblers to obtain Sims. In Argovitz's words, Sims would make the Gamblers' franchise.

On June 29, 1983, at Lerner's behest, Sims and his wife went to Houston to negotiate with a team that was partially owned by his own agent. When Sims arrived in Houston, he believed that the Lions organization was not negotiating in good faith; that it was not really interested in his services. His ego was bruised and his emotional outlook toward the Lions was visible to Burrough and Argovitz. Clearly, virtually all the information that Sims had up to that date came from Argovitz. . . . The negotiations began on the morning of June 30, 1983, and ended that afternoon. At the morning meeting, Lerner offered Sims a $3.5 million five-year contract, which included three years of skill and injury guarantees. The offer included a $500,000 loan at an interest rate of 1 percent over prime. It was from this loan that Argovitz planned to receive the $100,000 balance of his fee for acting as an agent in negotiating a contract with his own team. Burrough testified that Sims would have accepted that offer on the spot because he was finally receiving the guarantee that he had been requesting from the Lions, guarantees that Argovitz dropped without too much quarrel. Argovitz and Burrough took Sims and his wife into another room to discuss the offer. Argovitz did tell Sims that he thought the Lions would match the Gamblers financial package and asked Sims whether he (Argovitz) should telephone the Lions. But, it is clear from the evidence that neither Sims nor Burrough believed that the Lions would match the offer. . . . Sims . . . agreed to become a Gambler on the terms offered. At that moment, Argovitz irreparably breached his fiduciary duty. As agent for Sims he had the duty to telephone the Lions, receive its final offer, and present the terms of both offers to Sims. Then and only then could it be said that Sims made an intelligent and knowing decision to accept the Gamblers' offer.

During these negotiations at the Gamblers' office, Mr. Nash of the Lions telephoned Argovitz, but even though Argovitz was at his office, he declined to accept the telephone call. Argovitz tried to return Nash's call after Sims had accepted the Gamblers' offer, but it was after 5 p.m. and Nash had left for the July 4th weekend. When he declined to accept Mr. Nash's call, Argovitz's breach of his fiduciary duty became even more pronounced.* * *

During the evening of June 30, 1983, Burrough struggled with the fact that they had not presented the Gamblers' offer to the Lions. He knew, as does the court, that Argovitz now had the wedge that he needed to bring finality to the Lions' negotiations. Burrough was acutely aware of the fact that Sims' actions were emotionally motivated and realized that the responsibility for Sims' future rested with him. We view with some disdain the fact that Argovitz had, in effect, delegated his entire fiduciary responsibility on the eve of his principal's most important career decision. On July 1, 1983, it was Lerner who gave lip service to Argovitz's conspicuous conflict of interest. It was Lerner, not Argovitz, who advised Sims that Argovitz's position with the Gamblers presented a conflict of interest and that Sims could, if he wished, obtain an attorney or another agent. Argovitz, upon whom Sims had relied for the past four years, was not even there. Burrough, conscious of Sims' emotional responses, never advised Sims to wait until he had talked with the Lions before making a final decision. Argovitz's conflict of interest and self-dealing put him in the position where he would not even use the wedge he now had to negotiate with the Lions, a wedge that is the dream of every agent. Two expert witnesses testified that an agent should telephone a team that he has been negotiating with once he has an offer in hand. . . . The evidence here convinces us that Argovitz's negotiations with the Lions were ongoing and it had not made its final offer. Argovitz did not follow the common practice described by both expert witnesses. He did not do this because he knew that the Lions would not leave Sims without a contract and he further knew that if he made that type of call Sims would be lost to the Gamblers, a team he owned.

On November 12, 1983, when Sims was in Houston for the Lions game with the Houston Oilers, Argovitz asked Sims to come to his home and sign certain papers. He represented to Sims that certain papers of his contract had been mistakenly overlooked and now needed to be signed. Included among those papers he asked Sims to sign was a waiver of any claim that Sims might have against Argovitz for his blatant breach of his fiduciary duty brought on by his glaring conflict of interest. Sims did not receive independent advice with regard to the wisdom of signing such a waiver. Despite having sold his agency business in September, Argovitz did not even tell Sims' new agent of his intention to have Sims sign a waiver. Nevertheless, Sims, an unsophisticated young man, signed the waiver. This is another example of the questionable conduct on the part of Argovitz who still had business management obligations to Sims. In spite of his fiduciary relationship he had Sims sign a waiver without advising him to obtain independent counseling.

* * *

The relationship between a principal and agent is fiduciary in nature, and as such imposes a duty of loyalty, good faith, and fair and honest dealing on the agent. [Citation.]

A fiduciary relationship arises not only from a formal principal-agent relationship, but also from informal relationships of trust and confidence. [Citations.]

In light of the express agency agreement, and the relationship between Sims and Argovitz, Argovitz clearly owed Sims the fiduciary duties of an agent at all times relevant to this lawsuit.

An agent's duty of loyalty requires that he not have a personal stake that conflicts with the principal's interest in a transaction in which he represents his principal. As stated in [citation]:

(T)he principal is entitled to the best efforts and unbiased judgment of his agent. . . . (T)he law denies the right of an agent to assume any relationship that is antagonistic to his duty to his principal, and it has many times been held that the agent cannot be both buyer and seller at the same time nor connect his own interests with property involved in his dealings as an agent for another.

A fiduciary violates the prohibition against self-dealing not only by dealing with himself on his principal's behalf, but also by dealing on his principal's behalf with a third party in which he has an interest, such as a partnership in which he is a member.* * *

Where an agent has an interest adverse to that of his principal in a transaction in which he purports to act on behalf of his principal, the transaction is voidable by the principal unless the agent disclosed all material facts within the agent's knowledge that might affect the principal's judgment. [Citation.]

The mere fact that the contract is fair to the principal does not deny the principal the right to rescind the contract when it was negotiated by an agent in violation of the prohibition against self-dealing.* * *

Once it has been shown that an agent had an interest in a transaction involving his principal antagonistic to the principal's interest, fraud on the part of the agent is presumed. The burden of proof then rests upon the agent to show that his principal had full knowledge, not only of the fact that the agent was interested, but also of every material fact known to the agent which might affect the principal and that having such knowledge, the principal freely consented to the transaction.

It is not sufficient for the agent merely to inform the principal that he has an interest that conflicts with the principal's interest. Rather, he must inform the principal "of all facts that come to his knowledge that are or may be material or which might affect his principal's rights or interests or influence the action he takes." [Citation.]

Argovitz clearly had a personal interest in signing Sims with the Gamblers that was adverse to Sims' interest—he had an ownership interest in the Gamblers and thus would profit if the Gamblers were profitable, and would incur substantial personal liabilities should the Gamblers not be financially successful. Since this showing has been made, fraud on Argovitz's part is presumed, and the Gamblers' contract must be rescinded unless Argovitz has shown by a preponderance of the evidence that he informed Sims of every material fact that might have influenced Sims' decision whether or not to sign the Gamblers' contract.

We conclude that Argovitz has failed to show by a preponderance of the evidence either: 1) that he informed Sims of the [material] facts, or 2) that these facts would not have influenced Sims' decision whether to sign the Gamblers' contract.* * *

As a court sitting in equity, we conclude that recision is the appropriate remedy. We are dismayed by Argovitz's egregious conduct. The careless fashion in which Argovitz went about ascertaining the highest price for Sims' service convinces us of the wisdom of the maxim: no man can faithfully serve two masters whose interests are in conflict.

Judgment will be entered for the plaintiffs rescinding the Gamblers' contract with Sims.

Termination of Agency by Revocation

HILGENDORF v. HAGUE

Supreme Court of Iowa, 1980.
293 N.W.2d 272.

Uhlenhopp, J.

[Harvey Hilgendorf was a licensed real estate broker acting as the agent of the Hagues in the sale of eighty acres of farmland. The Hagues, however, terminated Hilgendorf's agency before the expiration of the listing contract when they encountered financial difficulties and decided to liquidate their entire holdings of land at one time. Hilgendorf brought this action for breach of the listing contract. The Hagues maintain that Hilgendorf's duty of loyalty requires him to give up the listing contract.]

* * *

Since agency is a consensual relationship, a principal has *power* to terminate an agency which is not coupled with an interest [where the agent has an ownership interest in the subject matter of the agency], although the contract is for a period which has not expired. Ordinarily the agent's authority thereupon ceases. Absent some legal ground, however, the principal does not have a *right* to terminate an unexpired agency contract, and may subject himself to damages by doing so. [Citations.]

The whole question regarding liability here turns on whether the Hagues had a legal ground for terminating Hilgendorf's agency before the expiration of the year. All agree that they had power to terminate, but they contend they also had a right to do so. They say PCA [Hagues' principal creditor] would not renew their loan, they had to sell the 80 acres in addition to their other land, and the best way to sell the 80 acres was with the 160 acres. Did these circumstances give them a "right" to terminate the listing contract they had signed and cast on Hilgendorf a "duty" to give up his listing contract as a matter of an agent's loyalty to his principal?

The Hagues appear to confuse the two roles an agent occupies. In performing agency functions for the principal an agent does indeed occupy a fiduciary position, and his duty of loyalty requires him to place the principal's interest first. Restatement (Second) of Agency § 387. But in the contract of agency itself between the agent and principal, neither of the parties is acting for the other; each is acting for himself.

This case involves the latter role. * * *

* * *

Several circumstances are given in the texts as grounds for terminating fixed-term agencies, but coming upon hard times is not among them. [Citations.] We agree with the trial court that the Hagues did not have a right to terminate the one-year listing con-

tract . . . and that Hilgendorf did not have a duty to give up his listing contract.

* * *

Hague terminated the listing on August 13, 1976. Since Hague had the power to do so, Hilgendorf no longer had authority to sell the . . . parcel. For that reason, he cannot recover a commission *as such*, although he thereafter and within the year produced a ready, willing, and able buyer for the price in the listing. Nonetheless, since Hague breached the listing agreement by terminating it, Hilgendorf can recover damages. [Citation.]

The question here relates to the *measure* of damages Hilgendorf is entitled to *recover*. The editors state the measure thus in [citation]:

The courts generally support the principle that a broker whose employment or authority is wrongfully revoked may consider his contract of employment as rescinded and sue for damages, in which event he is entitled to have his recovery include the value of the services he has already rendered, his disbursements, and *such prospective profits as he can establish would have been his but for such revocation. . . .*

* * *

Where as here the principal terminates an exclusive listing within the term, the agent may endeavor to show that he would, but for the termination have sold the property within the unexpired period at the listed price. If he is successful in his proof, his lost profits are ordinarily measured by the commission he would have earned. He does not recover the commission itself, but his damages are measured by the commission. As stated in section 445 of the Restatement, Comment *a:*

If the principal, in breach of contract, prevents the agent from accomplishing the result upon which the agreed compensation is conditioned, the agent is entitled to damages for such breach or, as an alternative, the fair value of his services in attempting to accomplish it. The amount of recovery for damages in such a case is not the specified compensation as such, but the damages which the agent suffers by reason of the breach of contract. *Such damages may coincide in amount with the agreed compensation*; if, however, the agent would have had to incur further expense in order to earn such compensation, and these expenses have been saved to him, he is entitled only to a sum equal to the agreed compensation minus the expenses he has thereby saved. (Emphasis added.)

* * *

Here Hilgendorf proceeded on the damage issue by showing "the gains prevented" by Hague's breach of the listing contract. He established beyond question that he would have sold the . . . parcel for the full asking price within the listing period. His lost profit was the offered price times the six percent commission rate, and this is the amount the trial court allowed him.

We agree with the trial court's decision. Affirmed.

QUESTIONS

1. Distinguish among the following relationships: (a) agency, (b) employment, and (c) independent contractor.

2. Discuss the requirements for creating an agency relationship.

3. Discuss the duties owed by an agent to her principal.

4. Discuss the duties owed by a principal to his agent.

5. Identify the ways in which an agency relationship may be terminated.

PROBLEMS

1. Parker, the owner of certain unimproved real estate in Chicago, employed Adams, a real estate agent, to sell the property for a price of $25,000 or more and agreed to pay Adams a commission of 6 percent for making a sale. Adams negotiated with Turner who was interested in the property and willing to pay as much as $28,000 for it. Adams made an agreement with Turner that if Adams could obtain Parker's signature to a contract to sell the property to Turner for $25,000, Turner would pay Adams a bonus of $1,000. Adams prepared and Parker and Turner signed a contract for the sale of the property to Turner for $25,000. Turner refuses to pay Adams the $1,000 as promised. Parker refuses to pay Adams the 6 percent commission. In an action by Adams against Parker and Turner, what judgment?

2. Perry employed Alice to sell a parcel of real estate at a fixed price without knowledge that David had previously employed Alice to purchase the same property for him. Perry gave Alice no discretion as to price or terms, and Alice entered into a contract of sale with David upon the exact terms authorized by Perry. After accepting a partial payment, Perry discovered that Alice was employed by David and brought an action to rescind. David resisted on the ground that Perry had suffered no damage for the reason that Alice had been given no discretion and the sale was made upon the exact basis authorized by Perry. Decision?

3. Packer owned and operated a fruit cannery in Southton, Illinois. He stored a substantial amount of finished canned goods in a warehouse in East St. Louis, Illinois, owned and operated by Alden, in order to have goods readily available for the St. Louis market. On March 1, he had 10,000 cans of peaches and 5,000 cans of apples in storage with Alden. On the day named, he borrowed $5,000 from Alden, giving Alden his promissory note for this amount due June 1 together with a letter authorizing Alden, in the event the note was not paid at maturity, to sell any or all of his goods in storage, pay the indebtedness, and account to him for any surplus. Packer died on June 2 without having paid the note. On June 8, Alden told Taylor, a wholesale food distributor, that he had for sale as agent of the owner 10,000 cans of peaches and 5,000 cans of apples. Taylor said he would take the peaches and would decide later about the apples. A contract for the sale of 10,000 cans of peaches for $6,000 was thereupon signed. "Alden, agent for Packer, seller; Taylor, buyer." Both Alden and Taylor knew of the death of Packer. Delivery of the peaches and payment were made on June 10. On June 11, Alden and Taylor signed a similar contract covering the 5,000 cans of apples, delivery and payment to be made June 30. On June 23, Packer's executor, having learned of these contracts, wrote Alden and Taylor stating that Alden had no authority to make the contracts, demanding that Taylor return the peaches, and directing Alden not to deliver the apples. Discuss the correctness of the contentions of Packer's executor.

4. Green, a licensed real estate broker in Illinois, and Jones, also an Illinois resident, while both were in New York, signed a contract whereby Green agreed to endeavor to find a buyer for certain real estate located in Illinois owned by Jones who agreed to pay Green a commission of $10,000 in the event of a sale. Green found a buyer, a resident of New York, to whom the land was sold. Thereafter, Jones refused to pay the commission. Green commenced an action in Illinois to recover the commission. Jones defended on the sole ground that the brokerage contract was unenforceable because Green was not a licensed real estate broker in New York. Relevant provisions of the applicable New York statute forbid any person from holding himself out or acting temporarily as a real estate broker or salesman without first procuring a license. A violation is declared to be a misdemeanor, and the commission of a single prohibited act is a violation for which the statute provides a penalty. For whom should judgment be rendered?

5. Palmer made a valid contract with Ames under which Ames was to sell Palmer's goods on commission during the period from January 1 to June 30. Ames made satisfactory sales up to May 15 and was then about to close an unusually large order when Palmer suddenly and without notice revoked Ames's authority to sell. Can Ames continue to sell Palmer's goods during the unexpired term of her contract?

6. Piedmont Electric Co. gave a list of delinquent accounts to Alexander, an employee, with instructions to discontinue electric service to delinquent customers. Among those listed was Todd Hatchery, which was then in the process of hatching chickens in a large, electrically heated incubator. Todd Hatchery told Alexander that it did not consider its account delinquent, but Alexander nevertheless cut the wires leading to the hatchery. Subsequently, Todd Hatchery recovered a judgment of $5,000 against Alexander in an action brought against Alexander for the loss resulting from the interruption of the incubation process. Alexander has paid the judgment and brings a cause of action against Piedmont Electric Co. Decision?

7. In October 1986, Black, the owner of the Grand Opera House, and Harvey entered into a written agreement leasing the Opera House to Harvey for five years at a rental of $30,000 a year. Harvey engaged Day as manager of the theatre at a salary of $175 per week plus 10 percent of the profits. One of Day's duties was to determine the amount of money taken in each night and, after deducting expenses, to divide the profits between Harvey and the manager of the particular attraction which was playing at the theatre. In September 1991, Day went to Black and offered to rent the opera house from Black at a rental of $37,500 per year, whereupon Black entered into a lease with Day for five years at this figure. When Harvey learned of and objected to this transaction, Day offered to assign the lease to him for $60,000 per year. Harvey refused and brought an appropriate action seeking to have Day declared a trustee of the opera house lease on behalf of Harvey. Decision?

8. Timothy retains Cynthia, an attorney, to bring a lawsuit upon a valid claim against Vincent. Recently enacted legislation has shortened the statute of limitations for this type of legal action. Cynthia fails to make herself aware of this new statute. Consequently, she filed the complaint after the statute of limitations had run. As a result the lawsuit is dismissed. What rights, if any, does Timothy have against Cynthia?

9. Wilson engages Ruth to sell Wilson's antique walnut chest to Harold for $2,500. The next day Ruth learns that Sandy is willing to pay $3,000 for Wilson's chest. Ruth nevertheless sells the chest to Harold. Wilson then discovers these facts. What are Wilson's rights, if any, against Ruth?

10. Morris is a salesman for Acme, Inc., a manufacturer of household appliances. Morris received a commission on all sales made, and no further compensation. He drove his own automobile and paid his own expenses. Morris calls on whom he pleases. While driving to make a call on a potential customer, Morris negligently collided with Hudson. Hudson sued (a) Acme and (b) Morris. Who should be held liable?

11. Sierra Pacific Industries purchased various areas of timber and six other pieces of real property, including a ten-acre parcel on which five duplexes and two single-family units were located. Sierra Pacific requested the assistance of Joseph Carter, a licensed real estate broker, in selling the nontimberland properties. It commissioned him to sell the property for an asking price of $85,000, of which Sierra Pacific would receive $80,000 and Carter would receive $5,000 as a commission. Carter was unable to find a prospective buyer, and finally he sold the property to his daughter and son-in-law for $85,000 and retained the $5,000 commission without informing Sierra Pacific of his relationship to the buyers. After learning of these facts, Sierra Pacific brought an action for breach of fiduciary duty against Carter. Decision?

12. Murphy, while a guest at a motel operated by the Betsy-Len Motor Hotel Corporation, sustained injuries from a fall allegedly caused by negligence in maintaining the premises. At that time, Betsy-Len was under a license agreement with Holiday Inns, Inc. The license contained provisions permitting Holiday Inns to regulate the architectural style of the buildings as well as the type and style of the furnishings and equipment. The contract, however, did not grant Holiday Inns the power to control the day-to-day operations of Betsy-Len's motel, to fix customer rates, or to demand a share of the profits. Betsy-Len could hire and fire its employees, determine wages and working conditions, supervise employee work routine, and discipline its employees. In return, Betsy-Len used the trade name, "Holiday Inns," and paid a fee for use of the license and Holiday Inns' national advertising. Murphy sued Holiday Inns, claiming Betsy-Len was its agent. Decision?

Chapter 19

RELATIONSHIP WITH THIRD PARTIES

Contract Liability of the Principal
Tort Liability of the Principal
Criminal Liability of the Principal
Contract Liability of Agent
Tort Liability of Agent
Rights of Agent against Third Person

THE purpose of an agency relationship is to allow the principal to extend his business activities by authorizing agents to enter into contracts with third persons on the principal's behalf. Accordingly, it is important that the law balance the competing interests of principals and third persons. The principal wants to be liable *only* for those contracts he actually authorized the agent to make for him. On the other hand, the third party wishes the principal bound on *all* contracts that the agent negotiates on the principal's behalf. As this chapter discusses, the law has adopted an intermediate outcome: the principal and the third party are bound to those contracts the principal *actually* authorizes *plus* those the principal has *apparently* authorized.

While pursuing her principal's business, an agent may tortiously injure third parties, who may seek to hold the principal personally liable. Under what circumstances should the principal be held liable? Similar questions arise concerning the criminal liability of a principal for an agent's violation of the criminal law. The law of agency has established rules to determine when the principal is liable for the torts and crimes committed by her agents. These rules are discussed in this chapter.

Finally, what liability to the third party should the agent incur, and what rights should she acquire against the third party? Usually, the agent has no liability for, or rights under, contracts made on behalf of a principal. As discussed in this chapter, however, in some situations the agent has contractually created obligations or rights or both.

RELATIONSHIP OF PRINCIPAL AND THIRD PERSONS

This section will first consider the contract liability of the principal; then it will examine the principal's potential tort liability.

CONTRACT LIABILITY OF THE PRINCIPAL

The **power** of an agent is his ability to change the legal status of his principal. An agent has the power to bind his principal whenever he has actual *or* apparent authority. Thus, whenever an agent, acting within his authority, makes a contract for his principal, he creates new rights or liabilities of his principal, changing his principal's legal status. This power of an agent to act for his principal in business transactions is the basis of agency.

The contract liability of a principal also depends upon whether the principal is disclosed, partially disclosed, or undisclosed. The principal is a **disclosed principal** if at the time of a transaction conducted by an agent, the other party has notice that the agent is acting for a principal and of the principal's identity. The principal is a **partially disclosed principal** if at the time of the transaction conducted by the agent, the other party has notice that the agent is or may be acting for a principal but has no notice of the principal's identity. The principal is an **undisclosed principal** if the other party has no notice that the agent is acting for a principal. Restatement, Section 4.

Types of Authority

There are two basic types of authority: actual and apparent. **Actual authority** depends upon consent manifested by the principal to the agent. It may be either express or implied. In either case, it is binding and confers upon the agent both the power and the right to create or affect legal relations of the principal with third persons. Where the principal is undisclosed, an agent acting with actual authority in making the contract will contractually bind the principal and the third party unless the principal is excluded from being a party by the terms of the contract or her existence is fraudulently concealed from the third party.

Apparent authority is based upon acts or conduct of the principal which manifests to a third person that the agent has actual authority and upon which the third person *justifiably* relies. This manifestation confers upon the agent the power to create a legal relationship between the principal and a third party. It may consist of words or actions of the principal as well as other facts and circumstances that induce the third person reasonably to rely upon the existence of an agency relationship.

Actual Express Authority The express authority of an agent is found in the words of the principal, spoken or written, and communicated to the agent. It is actual authority stated in language directing or instructing the agent to do something specific. Thus, if Perkins, orally or in writing, requests his agent Abbott to sell Perkins's automobile for $6,500, Abbott's authority to sell the car for this sum is actual and express.

Actual Implied Authority Implied authority is not found in express or explicit words of the principal but is inferred from words or conduct manifested to the agent by the principal. The agent has implied authority to do what she reasonably infers that the principal desires her to do in light of the principal's manifestations to her and all other facts she knows or should know. Restatement, Section 33. Implied authority may arise from customs and usages of the business. In addition, authority granted to an agent to accomplish a particular purpose necessarily includes authority to employ means reasonably required for its accomplishment. Restatement, Section 35. For example, Pearson authorizes Arlington to manage her eighty-two-unit apartment complex. Nothing is said by Pearson about expenses. In order to manage the building, however, Arlington must employ a janitor, purchase fuel for heating, and arrange for ordinary maintenance. The authority to incur these expenses, while not expressly granted, is implied from the express authority to manage the building because they are required for its proper management.

Unless otherwise agreed, authority to make a contract is inferred from authority to conduct a transaction, if the making of such a contract is incidental to the transaction, usually accompanies such a transaction, or is reasonably necessary to accomplish it. Restatement, Section 50. Thus, Paragon, Inc. appoints Astor as the general manager of Paragon's manufacturing business. Astor's authority is interpreted as including authority to make contracts for the employment of necessary employees. On the other hand, suppose Paige employs Arthur, a real estate broker, to find a purchaser for her residence at a stated price. Arthur has no authority to contract for its sale.

Certain rules have been developed to determine what authority is implied in particular types of agencies. Unless otherwise agreed, authority to acquire or convey property for the principal includes authority to agree upon the terms, to demand or make the usual representations and warranties, to receive or execute the instruments usually required, to pay or receive as much of the purchase price as is to be paid at the time of the transfer, and to receive possession of the goods if a buying agent, or to surrender possession of them if a selling agent.

General authority to manage or operate a business for a principal confers implied authority upon the agent to buy and sell property for the principal to the extent usual and customary in such operation; to make contracts which are incidental to the business, are usually made in it, or are reasonably necessary in conducting it; to employ, supervise, or discharge employees; to receive payment due the principal and to pay debts due from the principal arising out of the business enterprise; and to direct the ordinary operations of the business. Restatement, Section 73.

Apparent Authority Apparent authority is power that arises out of words or conduct of a disclosed or partially disclosed principal manifested to third persons by which they are reasonably induced to rely upon the assumption that actual authority exists. Restatement, Sections 27 and 159. Apparent authority confers upon the agent or supposed agent the power to bind the disclosed or partially disclosed principal in contracts with third persons and precludes the principal from denying the existence of actual authority. Thus, when there is apparent authority but not actual authority, the disclosed or partially disclosed principal is nonetheless bound by the act of the agent. By exceeding his actual authority, however, the agent has violated his duty of obedience and is liable to the principal for any loss suffered as a result

of the agent's acting beyond his actual authority (see Figures 19–1 and 19–2).

Since apparent authority is the power which results from acts that appear to the third party to be authorized by the principal, there can be no apparent authority where the principal is undisclosed (see Figure 19–3).

Comment *a* to Section 27 compares apparent and actual authority as follows:

Apparent authority is created by the same method as that which creates [actual] authority, except that the manifestation of the principal is to the third person rather than to the agent. For apparent authority there is the basic requirement that the principal be responsible for the information which comes to the mind of the third person, similar to the requirement for the creation of [actual] authority that the principal be responsible for the information which comes to the agent. Thus, either the principal must intend to cause the third person to believe that the agent is authorized to act for him, or he should realize that his conduct is likely to create such belief. The information received by the third person may come directly from the principal by letter or word of mouth, from authorized statements of the agent, from documents or other indicia of authority given by the principal to the agent, or from third persons who have heard of the agent's authority through authorized or permitted channels of communication. Likewise, as in the case of [actual] authority, apparent authority can be created by appointing a person to a position, such as that of manager or treasurer, which carries with it generally recognized duties; to those who know of the appointment there is apparent authority to do the things ordinarily entrusted to one occupying such a position, regardless of unknown limitations which are imposed upon the particular agent. So, too, a person who permits another to do an act in such a way as to establish in a community a reputation for having authority to act, either by directing the agent so to represent, or by directing him to act and doing nothing to prevent the spread of such information by the agent or by others, creates apparent authority with respect to those who learn of the reputation. Third persons who are aware of what a continuously employed agent has done are normally entitled to believe that he will continue to have such authority for at least a limited period in the future, and this apparent authority continues until the third person has been notified or learns facts which should lead him to believe that the agent is no longer authorized.

Figure 19–1 Contract Liability of Disclosed Principal

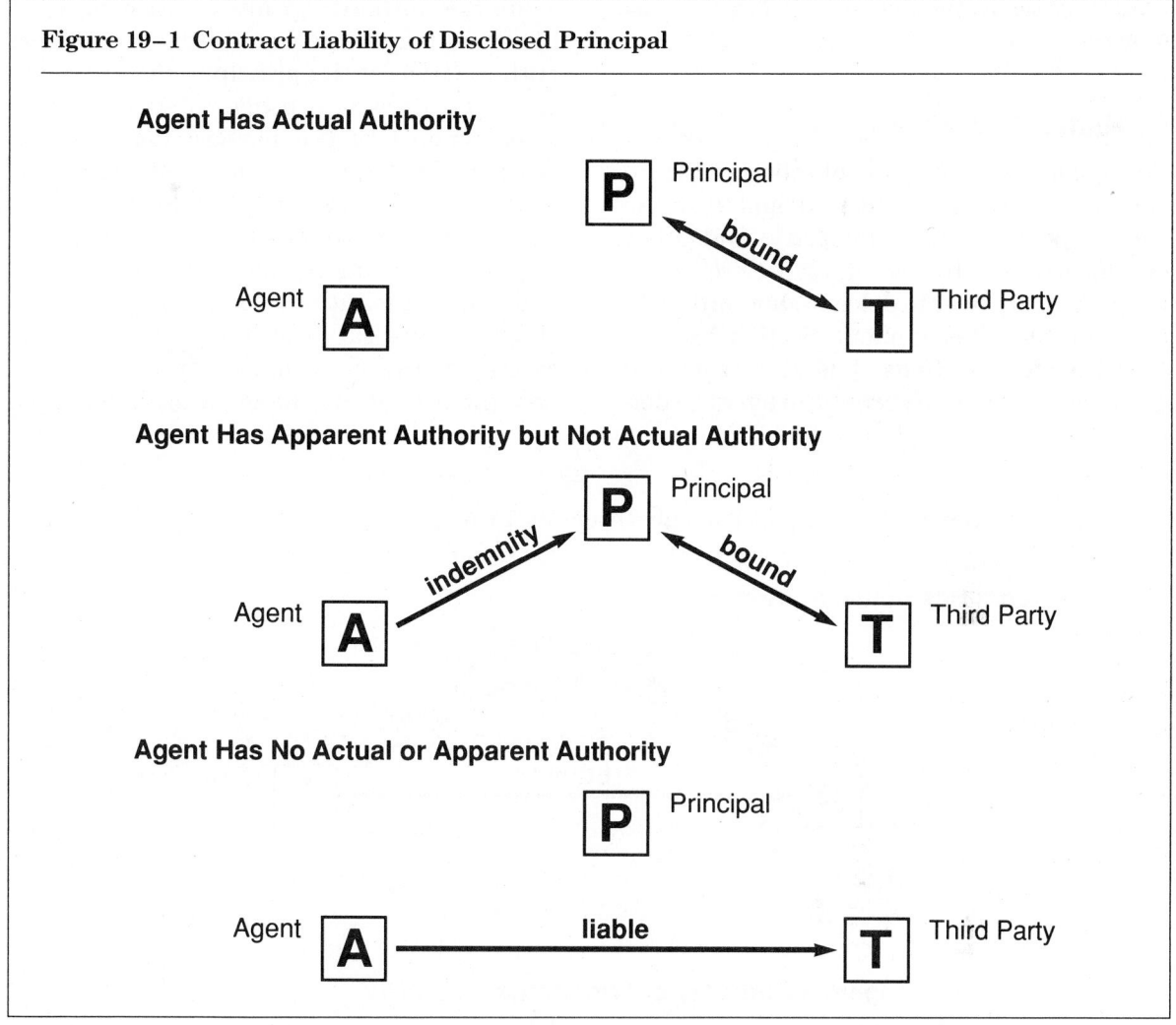

Agent Has Actual Authority

P Principal

Agent A

bound

T Third Party

Agent Has Apparent Authority but Not Actual Authority

P Principal

Agent A

indemnity

bound

T Third Party

Agent Has No Actual or Apparent Authority

P Principal

Agent A   liable   T Third Party

In addition, there may be apparent authority created by the principal's acquiescence in the agent's conduct when this is known to the third party. Likewise, if the principal manifests to the third person that the agent is authorized to conduct a transaction, there is apparent authority in the agent to conduct it in accordance with the ordinary usages of business, unless the third person has notice that the agent's authority is limited.

For example, Peter writes a letter to Alice authorizing her to sell his automobile and sends a copy of the letter to Thomas, a prospective purchaser. On the following day, Peter writes a letter to Alice revoking the authority to sell the car but does not send a copy of the second letter to Thomas, who is not oth-

erwise informed of the revocation. Although Alice has no actual authority to sell the car, she continues to have apparent authority with respect to Thomas. Or, suppose that Arlene, in the presence of Polly, tells Thad that Arlene is Polly's agent to buy lumber. Although this statement is not true, Polly does not deny it, as she could easily have done. Thad, in reliance upon the statement, ships lumber to Polly on Arlene's order. Polly is obligated to pay for the lumber because Arlene had apparent authority to act on Polly's behalf. This apparent authority of Arlene exists only with respect to Thad. If Arlene were to give David an order for a shipment of lumber to Polly, David would not be able to hold Polly liable. No actual authority existed, and as to David there was no apparent authority.

See Schoenberger v. Chicago Transit Authority.

Delegation of Authority

The appointment of an agent reflects the confidence and reliance of the principal upon the agent's personal skill, integrity, and other qualifications. The agent, therefore, ordinarily has no power to delegate her authority to a subagent. Restatement, Section 18.

In certain situations it is clear that the principal intended to permit the agent to delegate the authority granted to her. Such an intention may be gathered from the express authorization of the principal, the character of the business, the usages of trade, or the prior conduct of the parties. Restatement, Sections 78–81. For example, if a check is deposited in a bank for collection at a distant place, the bank is impliedly authorized to employ another bank at the place of payment.

If an agent is authorized to appoint or select other persons, called **subagents,** to perform or assist in the performance of the agent's duties, the acts of the subagent are binding on

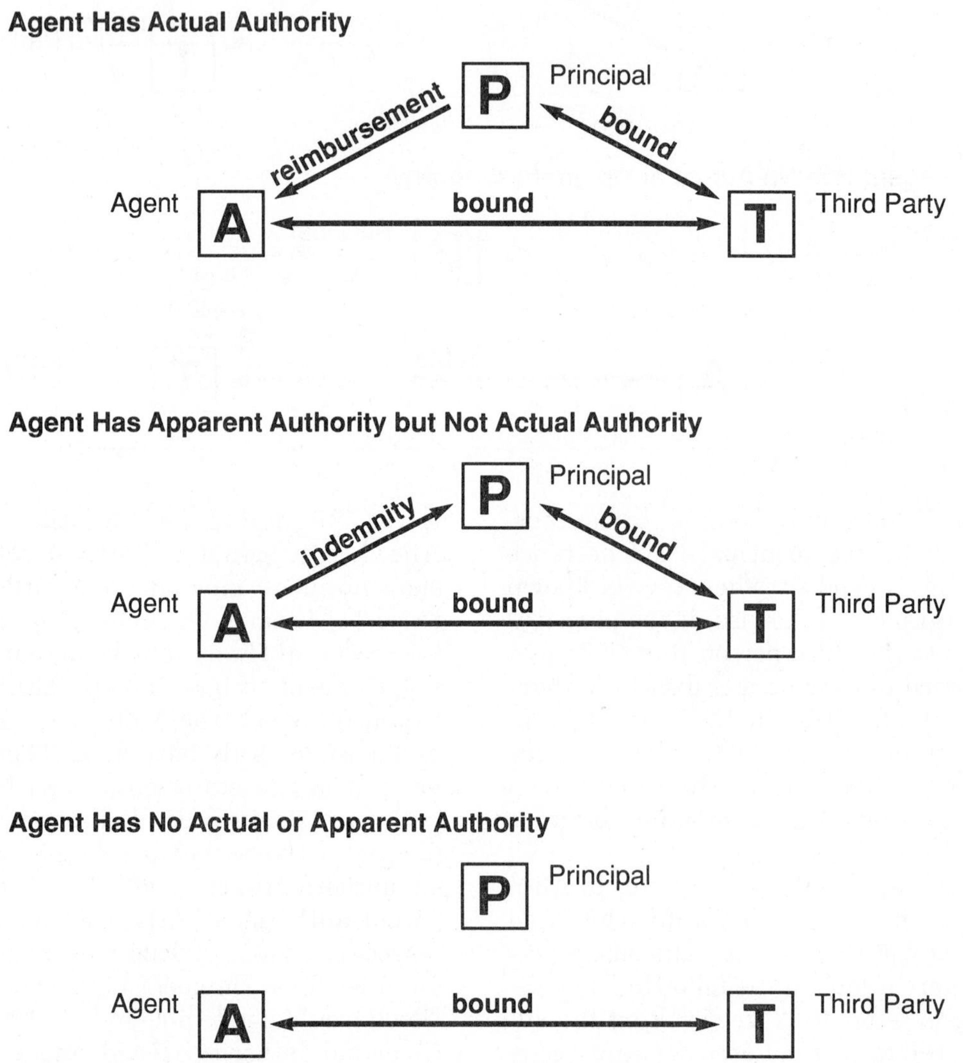

Figure 19–2 Contract Liability of Partially Disclosed Principal

the principal to the same extent as if they had been done by the agent. The subagent is an agent of both the principal and the agent and owes a fiduciary duty to both.

If no authority exists to delegate the agent's authority, but the agent nevertheless does so, the acts of the subagent do not impose upon the principal any obligations or liability to third persons. Likewise, the principal acquires no rights against such third persons.

Effect of Termination of Agency upon Authority

Upon the termination of an agency, the agent's *actual authority* ceases. When the termination is by death or incapacity of the principal or agent, the agent's *apparent authority* also expires as notice of such termination to third persons is *not* required. Thus, in a case where Thomas, a tenant of the principal, Plato, paid rent to Plato's agent, Augustus, in ignorance of Plato's death, and Augustus failed to account for the payment, Thomas is liable to Plato's estate for payment of the amount of the rent. The same holds where an authorized transaction is made im-

possible of performance, such as where the subject matter of the transaction is destroyed or the transaction is made illegal. Restatement, Section 124.

In other cases, apparent authority continues until the third party has actual knowledge or receives actual notice, if that third party is one (1) with whom the agent had previously dealt on credit, (2) to whom the agent has been specially accredited, or (3) with whom the agent has begun to deal. Restatement, Section 136(2). **Actual notice** requires a communication to the third party, either oral or written. If notice is given by mail it is effective as actual notice upon delivery not upon dispatch. All other third parties as to whom there was apparent authority must have actual knowledge or be given **constructive notice** such as publication in a newspaper of general circulation in the area where the agency is regularly carried on. Restatement, Section 136(3).

To illustrate: Alfred is the general agent of Pace, who carries on business in Chicago. Carol knows of the agency but has never dealt with Alfred. Daphne sells goods on credit to Alfred, as agent of Pace. Pace revokes Alfred's authority and publishes a

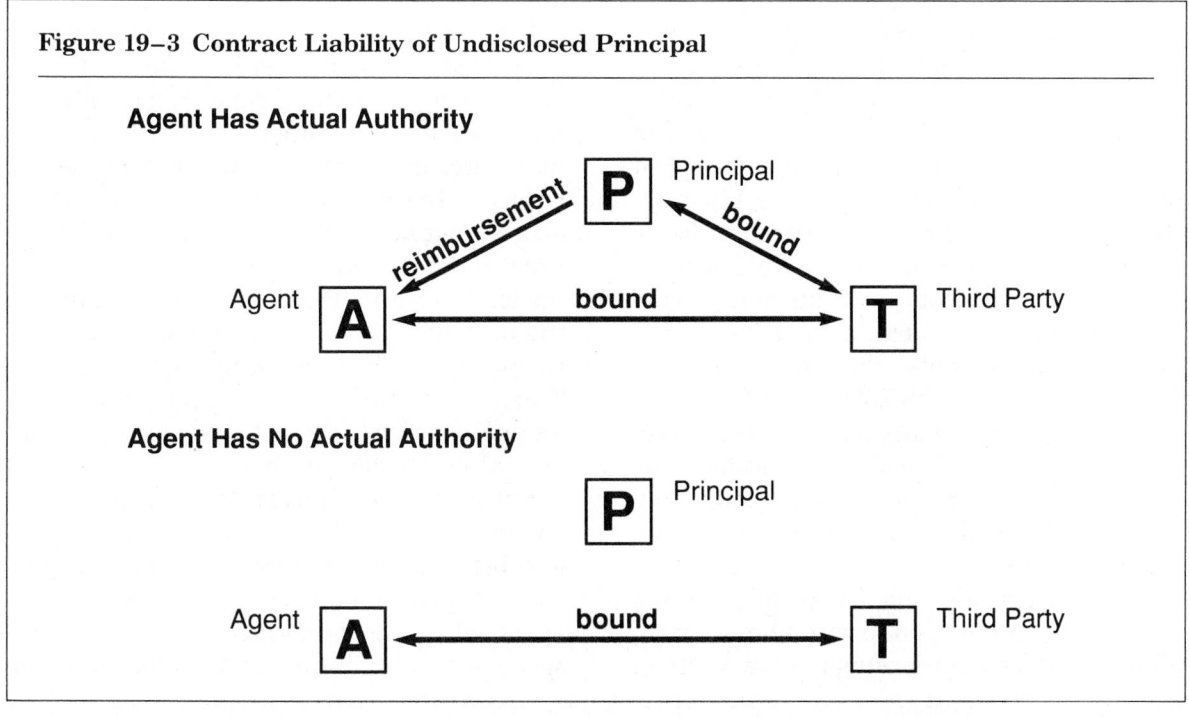

Figure 19–3 Contract Liability of Undisclosed Principal

statement to that effect in a newspaper of general circulation published in Chicago. Carol does not see the statement and deals with Alfred in accordance with and in reliance upon the former agency. Daphne also does not see the statement and has no knowledge of the revocation. Daphne sells more goods to Alfred, as the agent of Pace. Pace has given sufficient notice of revocation as to Carol and, therefore, Alfred's apparent authority has terminated with respect to Carol. On the other hand, Pace has not given sufficient notice of revocation as to Daphne, and Pace is bound to Daphne by the contract of sale made on Pace's behalf by Alfred.

See Zukaitis v. Aetna Casualty and Surety Co.

Ratification

Ratification is the confirmation or affirmance by one person of a prior unauthorized act that another has done as his agent or purporting to be his agent. The ratification of such act or contract binds the principal and the third party as if the agent or purported agent had been initially authorized. Restatement, Section 82. Once made, a valid ratification is irrevocable.

Ratification may relate to the acts of an agent that have exceeded the authority granted to him, as well as to acts that a person without any authority makes on behalf of an alleged principal. The actor, however, must have indicated to the third person that he was acting on behalf of a principal in order that the act may be ratified. There can be no ratification by a principal who is undisclosed. Thus Archie, without any authority, contracts to sell to Tina an automobile belonging to Pierce. Archie states that the auto is his. Tina promises to pay $5,500 for the automobile. Pierce subsequently learns of the agreement and affirms. Pierce's affirmation of Archie's action would *not* be a ratification because Archie did not purport to act on Pierce's behalf.

To effect a ratification, the principal must manifest an intent to do so with knowledge of all material facts concerning the transaction.

Restatement, Section 91. The principal does not need to communicate this intent either to the purported agent or to the third person. It may be manifested by express language or implied from conduct of the principal. Thus, if Amanda, without authority, contracts in Penelope's name for the purchase of goods from Tate on credit, and Penelope, having learned of Amanda's unauthorized act, accepts the goods from Tate, she thereby impliedly ratifies the contract and is bound on the contract. In any event, the principal must ratify the entire act or contract. Restatement, Section 96.

To be effective, ratification must occur before the third person gives notice to the principal or agent of his withdrawal. Restatement, Section 88. If the affirmance of a transaction occurs at a time when the situation has so materially changed that it would be inequitable to subject the third party to liability on the transaction, the third party may elect to avoid liability. For example, Alex has no authority but, purporting to act for Penny, Alex contracts to sell Penny's house to Taylor. The next day the house burns down. Penny then affirms. Taylor is not bound. Moreover, the power to ratify is terminated by the death or loss of capacity of the third party and by the lapse of a reasonable time.

Finally, for ratification to be effective, the purported principal must have been in existence when the act was done. For example, a promoter of a corporation not yet in existence may enter into contracts on behalf of the corporation. In the vast majority of States, these acts cannot be *ratified* by the corporation because it did not exist when the contracts were made. A contract that is voidable because of the principal's incapacity may be ratified by the principal after the incapacity is removed. Thus, a principal who is a minor may ratify an unauthorized contract made on her behalf only after she reaches majority.

Ratification is equivalent to prior authority, which means that the effect of ratification is substantially the same as though the purported agent had been a duly authorized agent when she performed the act. The respective rights, duties, and remedies of the principal and the third party are the same as if the agent had originally possessed due authority. Both the principal and the agent are in the same position as they would have been if the act had been originally authorized by the principal. The agent is entitled to her due compensation. Moreover, the agent is freed from liability to the principal for acting as his agent without authority or for exceeding her authority, as the case may be. Between the agent and the third party, the agent is released from any liability she may have been under to the third party by reason of her having induced the third party to enter into the contract without the principal's authority.

See Bradshaw v. McBride.

Fundamental Rules of Contractual Liability

The following rules summarize the contractual relations between the principal and the third party:

1. A disclosed principal and the third party are contractually bound if the agent acts within her *actual* or *apparent* authority in making the contract (see Figure 19–1).

2. A partially disclosed principal and the third party are contractually bound if the agent acts within her *actual* or *apparent* authority in making the contract (see Figure 19–2).

3. An undisclosed principal and the third party are contractually bound if the agent acts within her *actual* authority in making the contract unless (a) the principal is excluded by the terms of the contract or (b) his existence is fraudulently concealed (see Figure 19–3).

4. No principal is contractually bound to a third party if the agent acts *without* any authority unless a disclosed or partially disclosed principal ratifies the contract.

TORT LIABILITY OF THE PRINCIPAL

In addition to contract liability to third persons, a principal may be liable in tort to third persons as a consequence of the acts of her agent. Tort liability may arise directly or indirectly (vicariously) from authorized or unauthorized acts of the agent. Also, a principal is liable for the unauthorized torts committed by an agent in connection with a transaction that the purported principal, with full knowledge of the tort, subsequently ratifies. Restatement, Section 218. Cases involving unauthorized but ratified torts are extremely rare. Of course, in all of these situations the wrongdoing agent is personally liable to the injured persons because he committed the tort. See Figure 19–4.

Direct Liability of Principal

A principal is liable for his *own* tortious conduct involving the use of agents. There are two primary ways in which liability may result. First, a principal is directly liable in damages for harm resulting from directing an agent to commit a tort. Second, the principal is directly liable if he fails to exercise care in employing competent agents.

Authorized Acts of Agent A principal who authorizes his agent to commit a tortious act with respect to the property or person of another is liable for the injury or loss sustained by that person. Restatement, Section 212. The authorized act is that of the principal. Thus, if Phillip directs his agent, Anthony, to enter upon Clark's land and cut timber, which neither Phillip nor Anthony has any right to do, the cutting of the timber is a trespass, and Phillip is liable to Clark. Or, suppose Phillip instructs his agent, Anthony, to make certain representations as to Phillip's property, which Anthony is authorized to sell. Phillip knows these representations are false, but Anthony does not. Such representations by Anthony to Dryden, who buys the property in reliance on them, is a deceit for which Phillip is liable to Dryden.

Unauthorized Acts of Agent A principal who conducts activities through an employee or other agent is liable for harm resulting from his negligent or reckless conduct. A

Figure 19–4 Tort Liability

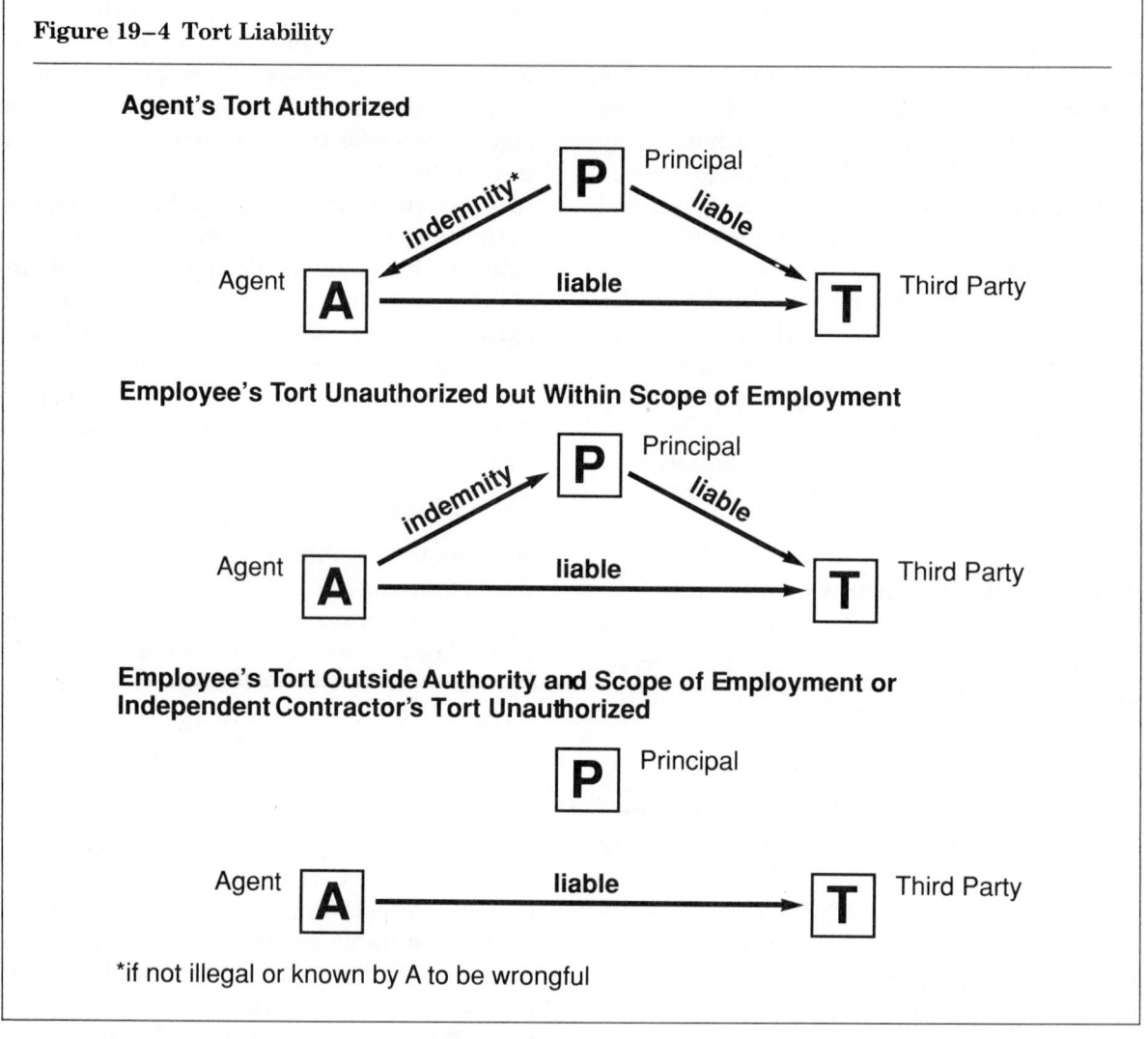

Agent's Tort Authorized

Agent — liable → Third Party
Principal — indemnity* → Agent
Principal — liable → Third Party

Employee's Tort Unauthorized but Within Scope of Employment

Agent — liable → Third Party
Agent — indemnity → Principal
Principal — liable → Third Party

Employee's Tort Outside Authority and Scope of Employment or Independent Contractor's Tort Unauthorized

Agent — liable → Third Party

*if not illegal or known by A to be wrongful

principal is liable if he negligently or recklessly (1) gives improper or ambiguous instructions, (2) fails to make proper regulations, (3) employs improper persons as agents, (4) provides improper instruments, tools, or materials to agents, (5) supervises the activities of agents, or (6) fails to prevent tortious acts by persons on his premises or with instrumentalities under his control. Restatement, Section 213.

For example, if Patricia lends to her employee, Art, a company car to run a business errand knowing that Art is incapable of driving the vehicle, Patricia would be liable for her own negligence to anyone injured by Art's negligent driving. *See Rubin v. Yellow Cab Co.*

Vicarious Liability of Principal for Unauthorized Acts of Agent

The liability of a principal for unauthorized torts by an agent depends primarily on whether the agent is an employee or not. An employee is an agent, employed to perform services for the principal–employer and whose physical conduct in the performance of the service is controlled or subject to the right to control by the principal. If the agent's physical conduct is not controlled or subject to the control of the principal, then the agent is not an employee but is an independent contractor. The general rule is that a principal is *not* liable for physical harm caused by the tortious conduct of an agent who is an independent contractor if the principal did not intend nor authorize the result nor the manner of performance. Restatement, Section 250. Conversely, a principal is liable for an unauthorized tort committed by an employee in the course of his employment. Restatement, Sections 216 and 219. *See Massey v. Tube Art Display, Inc.* in Chapter 18.

On the other hand, if an agent makes an unauthorized yet tortious **misrepresentation**, the principal's liability does not depend upon whether the agent is an employee. A principal is liable for loss caused to another who relies upon a tortious representation made by an agent (whether an employee or an independent contractor) if the representation is apparently authorized. Restatement, Section 257. For example, Adams is an agent of Pillsbury engaged to sell some land owned by Pillsbury. While negotiating with Trent, Adams states that a stream running through the property has not overflowed its banks onto the land during the past ten years. Adams knows that this is false. In reliance upon this false statement, Trent purchases the land. Pillsbury is liable to Trent for fraudulent misrepresentation.

Respondeat Superior An employer may be liable for an unauthorized tort committed by his employee, even one that is in flagrant disobedience of his instructions, if the tort was committed by the employee in the course of his employment. This is a form of liability without fault for the employer and is based upon the doctrine of *respondeat superior* (let the superior respond). The rationale of this doctrine is that a person who carries out his business activities through the use of employees should be liable for their tortious conduct in carrying out those business purposes. It does not matter how carefully the employer selected the employee, if in fact the latter tor-

tiously injured a third person while engaged in the business of the employer. Moreover, an undisclosed principal–employer is liable for the torts committed by her employee within the scope of employment. Restatement, Section 222.

The liability of the principal under *respondeat superior* is vicarious or derivative and depends upon proof of wrongdoing by the employee *in the course of his employment*. Restatement, Section 219. Frequently both principal and employee are joined as defendants in the same suit. If the employee is not held liable, the principal is not liable because the liability of the employer is based upon the employee's tortious conduct. A principal who is held liable for her employee's tort has a right of **indemnification** against the employee, which is the right to be reimbursed for the amount that she was required to pay as a result of the employee's wrongful act. Frequently an employee is not able to reimburse his employer, who must bear the brunt of the liability.

The wrongful act of the employee must be connected with his employment and within its scope if the principal is to be held liable for resulting injuries or damage to third persons. Section 228 of the Restatement provides a general rule for determining whether the conduct of an employee ("servant") is within the scope of employment:

(1) Conduct of a servant is within the scope of employment if, but only if:
    (a) it is of the kind he is employed to perform;
    (b) it occurs substantially within the authorized time and space limits;
    (c) it is actuated, at least in part, by a purpose to serve the master [employer]; and
    (d) if force is intentionally used by the servant against another, the use of force is not unexpectable by the master.
(2) Conduct of a servant is not within the scope of employment if it is different in kind from that authorized, far beyond the authorized time or space limits, or too little actuated by a purpose to serve the master.

For example, Eugene is delivering gasoline for Packer Oil Co. He lights his pipe and negligently throws the blazing match into a pool of gasoline which has dripped upon the ground during the delivery and which ignites. Packer is subject to liability for the resulting harm because the negligence of the employee delivering the gasoline relates directly to the manner in which he is handling the goods in his custody. But if a chauffeur, while driving his employer's car on an errand for his employer, suddenly decided to use his pistol and shoot at pedestrians on the sidewalk for target practice, the employer would not be liable to the pedestrians. This willful and intentional misconduct is not related to the performance of the services for which the chauffeur was employed nor is it expectable by the employer.

To further illustrate, if Page employs Earl to deliver merchandise to Page's customers in a given city, and while driving a delivery truck in going to or returning from a place of delivery Earl negligently causes the truck to hit and injure Fred, Page is liable to Fred for injuries sustained. But if, after making the scheduled deliveries, Earl drives the truck to a neighboring city to visit a friend and while so doing negligently causes the truck to hit and injure Dottie, Page is not liable. In such case, Earl is said to be on a "frolic of his own." He has deviated from the purpose of his employment and was using Page's truck to accomplish his own purposes and not those of his employer.

A principal may be held liable for the intentional torts of his employee if the commission of the tort is so reasonably connected with the employment as to be within its scope. For example, a principal would be liable if his employee makes fraudulent statements about the products she is selling or defames a competitor or disparages the competitor's product. *See Rubin v. Yellow Cab Co.*

Torts of Independent Contractor As previously indicated, an independent contractor is not the employee of the person for whom he is performing work or rendering services. Hence, the doctrine of *respondeat superior* does not apply to torts committed by an independent contractor. For example, Parnell authorizes Bob, his broker, to sell land

for him. Parnell, Teresa, and Bob meet in Teresa's office. Bob arranges the sale to Teresa. While Bob is preparing a deed for Parnell to sign, he negligently knocks over an inkstand and ruins a valuable rug belonging to Teresa. Bob, but *not* Parnell, is liable to Teresa. Similarly, Patty employs Igor, a roofer, as an independent contractor to repair Patty's roof. Igor drops a hammer upon Wanda, a pedestrian walking by on the public sidewalk. Igor, but not Patty, is liable to Wanda.

Under some circumstances a principal will be liable for torts committed by an independent contractor. Certain duties imposed by law are non-delegable, and a person may not escape the consequences of their non-performance by contracting with an independent contractor. For example, a landowner who permits an independent contractor to maintain a dangerous condition on his premises, such as an excavation adjoining a public sidewalk, which is unprotected by a guard rail or by lights at night, is liable to a member of the public who is injured as a result of falling into the excavation.

Moreover, the principal may be directly liable if she should know that there is an undue risk that the independent contractor will be negligent and harm others. Thus, Melanie employs Gordon as an independent contractor to repair her roof. Melanie knows that Gordon is an alcoholic. Gordon attempts the repairs while heavily intoxicated and drops a fifty-pound bundle of shingles upon Eric, a pedestrian walking on the public sidewalk. Both Gordon and Melanie are liable to Eric.

A principal is also liable for an independent contractor's conduct in carrying on an ultrahazardous activity. Finally, a principal is liable if an independent contractor negligently conducts an inherently dangerous activity, such as excavating a public road, demolishing a building, or spraying crops.

CRIMINAL LIABILITY OF THE PRINCIPAL

A principal is liable for the authorized criminal acts of his agents only if the principal directed, participated in, or approved of the acts. For example, if an agent, at his principal's direction or with his principal's knowledge, fixes prices with the principal's competitors, both the agent and the principal have criminally violated the antitrust laws. Otherwise, a principal is not ordinarily liable for the unauthorized criminal acts of his agents. One of the elements of a crime is mental fault, and this element is not present, so far as criminal responsibility of the principal is concerned, where the act of the agent was not authorized.

An employer may, nevertheless, be subject to a criminal penalty for the act of an advisory or managerial person acting in the scope of employment. Restatement, Section 217D, Comment d. Moreover, an employer may be criminally liable under liability without fault statutes for certain unauthorized acts of his employees, whether the employee is managerial or not. These statutes are usually regulatory statutes and do not require mental fault. For example, many States have statutes that punish "every person who by himself or his employee or agent sells anything at short weight," or "whoever sells liquor to a minor and any sale by an employee shall be deemed the act of the employer as well." Another example is a statute prohibiting the sale of unwholesome or adulterated food. See Chapter 4 for a more detailed discussion of this topic.

RELATIONSHIP OF AGENT AND THIRD PERSONS

The function of an agent is to assist in the conduct of the principal's business by carrying out his orders. Generally, the agent acquires no rights against third parties and likewise incurs no liabilities to them. There are, however, several exceptions to this general proposition. In certain instances, an agent may become personally liable to the third party for contracts she made on behalf of a principal. In some of these situations, the agent may also acquire rights against the third party. In addition, an agent who commits a tort is personally liable to the

injured third party. These circumstances involving the personal liability of an agent, as well as those under which an agent may acquire rights against third persons, will be covered in this section.

CONTRACT LIABILITY OF AGENT

The agent is not normally a party to the contract he makes with a third person on behalf of a disclosed principal. If the agent exceeds his actual and apparent authority, however, he may be personally liable to the third party. In addition, an agent acting for a disclosed principal may become liable if he expressly assumes liability on the contract. When an agent enters into a contract on behalf of a partially disclosed principal or an undisclosed principal, the agent becomes personally liable to the third party on the contract. Furthermore, an agent who knowingly enters into a contract on behalf of a nonexistent or incompetent principal is personally liable to the third party on that contract.

Disclosed Principal

As explained earlier, an agent acts for a disclosed principal when at the time of the transaction the other party has notice that the agent is acting for a principal and of the principal's identity. The agent is not normally a party to the contract she makes with a third person on behalf of a disclosed principal. The third person is on notice that he is transacting business with an agent who is acting for an identified principal and that the agent is not personally undertaking to perform the contract, but that she is simply negotiating on behalf of her principal. The resulting contract, if within the agent's actual authority, is between the third person and the principal. The agent ordinarily incurs no liability on the contract to either party. Restatement, Section 320. Thus, Angela, who has actual authority to sell circuit boards manufactured by Pinter, writes to Toni: "On behalf of Pinter, I offer to sell you 5,000 circuit boards for $15,000." Toni accepts. There is a contract between Toni and Pinter. Angela is not a party to that contract and has no liability to Pinter or Toni. See Figure 19–1. This is also true of unauthorized contracts that are subsequently ratified by the principal. If the agent has apparent authority but no actual authority, the agent has no liability to the third party but is liable to the principal for any loss caused by the agent's exceeding his actual authority.

Unauthorized Contracts   If an agent exceeds his actual *and* apparent authority, the principal is not bound. The fact that the principal is not bound, however, does not make the agent a party to the contract. The agent's liability, if any, arises from express or implied representations about his authority that he makes to the third party. An agent may **expressly warrant** that he has authority. For example, the agent may state that he has authority and that he will be personally liable to the third party if he does not have the authority to bind his principal.

Moreover, a person who undertakes to make a contract on behalf of another gives an **implied warranty** that he is in fact authorized to make the contract on behalf of the party whom he purports to represent. If the agent does not have authority to bind the principal, the agent is liable to the third party for damages unless the principal ratifies the contract or the third party knew that the agent was unauthorized. No implied warranty exists, however, if the contract expressly provides that the agent shall not be responsible for any lack of authority or if the agent, acting in good faith, discloses to the third person all of the facts upon which his authority rests. For example, agent Larson has received an ambiguous letter of instruction from his principal, Dan. Larson shows it to Carol stating that it represents all of the authority that he has to act, and both Larson and Carol rely upon its sufficiency. In this case, there is no implied or express warranty by Larson to Carol of his authority.

If a purported agent **misrepresents** to a third person that he has authority to make a contract on behalf of a principal whom he has no power to bind, he is liable in a tort action to the third person for the loss sustained in reliance upon the misrepresentation. If the third party, however, knows that the representations are false, then the agent is not liable.

Agent Assumes Liability   An agent may agree to become liable on a contract between the principal and the third party. She may do this by making the contract in her own name or by co-making the contract with the principal. Or she may guarantee that the principal will perform the contract between the third party and the principal. In all of these situations, the agent's liability is separate unless the parties agree otherwise. Therefore, the third party may sue the agent separately without joining the principal. The third party may obtain a judgment against either the principal or the agent or both. If the principal satisfies the judgment, then the agent is discharged. If the agent pays the judgment, he will usually have a right of reimbursement from the principal. This right is based upon principles of suretyship discussed in Chapter 39.

Partially Disclosed Principal

An agent, as previously discussed, acts for a partially disclosed principal if the third party has notice that the agent is acting for a principal but has no notice of the principal's identity. Thus, the third person is aware that the agent is acting on behalf of another, but he is not informed of the name or identity of the principal. The use of partially disclosed principals may be helpful where the third party might inflate the price of property he was selling if he knew the identity of the principal. It also occurs when the agent fails through neglect to inform the third party of the principal's identity.

Unless otherwise agreed, an agent making a contract for a partially disclosed principal is a party to the contract. Restatement, Section 321. For example, Ashley writes to Terrence offering to sell a rare painting on behalf of its owner, who wishes to remain unknown. Terrence accepts. Ashley is a party to the contract.

Whether the particular transaction is authorized or not, an agent for a partially disclosed principal is liable on the contract to the third party (see Figure 19–2). If the agent is actually authorized to make the contract, then both the agent and the partially disclosed principal are liable. In any event, the agent is separately liable and may be sued individually without joining the principal. The third party may obtain a judgment against either the principal or the agent or both. If the principal satisfies the judgment, then the agent is discharged. If the agent pays the judgment, he has the right to be reimbursed by the principal.

See Van D. Costas, Inc. v. Rosenberg.

Undisclosed Principal

An agent acts for an undisclosed principal when she appears to be acting in her own behalf and the third person with whom she is dealing has no knowledge that she is acting as an agent. The instructions of the principal to the agent are to conceal not only the identity of the principal but also the agency relationship. This can also occur if the agent simply neglects to disclose the existence and identity of her principal. Thus, the third person is dealing with the agent as though she were a principal.

The agent is personally liable upon a contract she enters into with a third person on behalf of an undisclosed principal, unless the third person, after discovering the existence and identity of the principal, elects to hold the principal to the contract (see Figure 19–3). The reason for the liability of the agent is that the third person has placed reliance upon the agent individually and has accepted the agent's personal undertaking to perform the contract. Obviously, where the principal is undisclosed, the third person does not know of the interest of anyone in the contract other than himself and the agent.

After the third person has become informed of the identity of the undisclosed principal, he may hold either the principal or the agent to performance of the contract, but not both. Having once made an election, he is irrevocably bound by it. The third person, however, may bring suit against both the principal and agent so that he does not incur the risk that in a trial the evidence may fail to establish the agency relationship. In most States, bringing suit and proceeding to trial against both is not an election, but before the entry of any judgment, the third person is compelled to make an election because he is not entitled to a judgment against both. A judgment against the agent by a third party who knows the identity of the previously undisclosed principal discharges the liability of the principal. Restatement, Section 210. In this case, the agent would have the right to be reimbursed by the principal. If the third party obtains a judgment against the agent before learning the identity of the principal, then the principal is not discharged. Finally, the agent is discharged from liability if the third party gets a judgment against the principal. Restatement, Section 337.

See Van D. Costas, Inc. v. Rosenberg.

Nonexistent or Incompetent Principal

A person who purports to act as agent for a principal, whom both the agent and the third party know to be nonexistent or wholly incompetent, is personally liable on a contract entered into with a third person on behalf of such a principal. Restatement, Section 326. For example, a promoter of a corporation who enters into contracts with third persons in the name of a corporation to be organized is personally liable on such contracts. The corporation is not liable because it did not authorize the contracts since it was not yet in existence. If the corporation, after coming into existence, affirmatively adopts a preincorporation contract made on its behalf, it becomes bound in addition to the promoter. If the corporation enters into a new contract with such a third person, however, the prior contract between the promoter and the third person is discharged, and the liability of the promoter is terminated. This is a novation. See Figure 34–2 in Chapter 34.

An agent who makes a contract for a disclosed principal whose contracts are voidable for lack of contractual capacity is *not* liable to the third party. Restatement, Section 332.

There are two exceptions to this rule: (1) if the agent warrants or represents that the principal has capacity or (2) if the agent has reason to know both of the principal's lack of capacity and of the third party's ignorance of that incapacity. *See Goldfinger v. Doherty.*

TORT LIABILITY OF AGENT

An agent is personally liable for his tortious acts that injure third persons, whether or not such acts are authorized by the principal and whether or not the principal may also be liable. Restatement, Section 343. For example, an agent is personally liable if he converts the goods of a third person to his principal's use. An agent is also liable for making representations that he knows to be fraudulent to a third person who in reliance sustains a loss.

RIGHTS OF AGENT AGAINST THIRD PERSON

An agent who makes a contract with a third person on behalf of a disclosed principal usually has no right of action against the third person for breach of contract. Restatement, Section 363. The agent is not a party to the contract. An agent for a disclosed principal may sue on the contract, however, if it provides that the agent is a party to the contract. An agent for an undisclosed principal or a partially disclosed principal may maintain in her own name an action against the third person for breach of contract. Restatement, Section 364.

CASES

Types of Authority

SCHOENBERGER v. CHICAGO TRANSIT AUTHORITY

Appellate Court of Illinois, First District, First Division, 1980.
84 Ill.App.3d 1132, 39 Ill.Dec. 941, 405 N.E.2d 1076.

CAMPBELL, J.

The plaintiff, James Schoenberger, brought a small claims action pro se in the Municipal Department of the circuit court of Cook County against the defendant, Chicago Transit Authority (hereinafter C.T.A.) to recover contract damages. The trial court ruled in favor of the defendant and against the plaintiff. The plaintiff appeals from this judgment. At issue is whether the C.T.A. may be held liable under agency principles of a promise allegedly made by an employee of the C.T.A. to the plaintiff at the time that he was hired to the effect that he would receive a $500 increase in salary within a specified period of time. We affirm.

Schoenberger was employed by the C.T.A. from August 16, 1976, to October, 1976, at a salary of $19,300. The facts surrounding his employment with the C.T.A. are controverted. The plaintiff's position at the trial was that he took the job with the C.T.A. at a salary of $19,300 upon the condition that he would receive a $500 salary increase, above and beyond any merit raises, within a year. Schoenberger testified at trial that, after filling out a job application and undergoing an initial interview with a C.T.A. Placement Department interviewer, he met several times with Frank ZuChristian, who was in charge of recruiting for the Data Center. At one of the meetings with ZuChristian, the Director of Data Center Operations, John Bonner, was present. At the third meeting held between ZuChristian and the plaintiff, ZuChristian informed the plaintiff that he desired to employ him at $19,800 and that he was making a recommendation to this effect. Schoenberger told ZuChristian that he would accept the offer. ZuChristian informed him that a formal offer would come from the Placement Department within a few days. However, when the offer was made, the salary was stated at $19,300. Schoenberger did not accept the offer immediately. Rather, he called ZuChristian for an explanation of the salary difference. After making inquiries, ZuChristian informed Schoenberger that a clerical error had been made and that it would take a number of weeks to have the necessary paperwork reapproved because several people were on vacation. To expedite matters, ZuChristian suggested Schoenberger take the job at the $19,300 figure and that he would see that the $500 would be made up to him at the April, 1976, October, 1976, or at the latest, the April, 1977, performance and salary review. The $500 increase was to be prospective and not retroactive in nature. John Hogan, the head of the Data Center, was aware of this promise, ZuChristian informed Schoenberger. Because the defendant was found to be ineligible for the October, 1976 performance evaluation and the April, 1976 review was cancelled, the April, 1977 evaluation was the first evaluation at which the issue of the salary increase was raised. When the increase was not given at that time, the plaintiff resigned and filed this suit.

* * *

The trial court, after hearing the evidence and reviewing the exhibits, ruled in favor of the defendant. The trial court ruled: (1) that it was inconceivable that the plaintiff thought ZuChristian had final authority in regard to employment contracts; and (2) that it was not shown that a commitment or promise was made to the plaintiff by an authorized agent of the C.T.A.

* * *

The main question before us is whether ZuChristian, acting as an agent of the C.T.A., orally contracted with Schoenberger for $500 in compensation in addition to his $19,300 salary. The authority of an agent may only come from the principal and it is therefore necessary to trace the source of an agent's authority to some word or act of the alleged principal. [Citations.] The authority to bind a principal will not be presumed, but rather, the person alleging authority must prove its source unless the act of the agent has been ratified. [Citations.] Moreover, the authority must be founded upon some word or act of the

principal, not on the acts or words of the agent. [Citations.]

* * * Both Hogan and Bonner, ZuChristian's superiors, testified that ZuChristian had no actual authority to either make an offer of a specific salary to Schoenberger or to make any promise of additional compensation. Furthermore, ZuChristian's testimony corroborated the testimony that he lacked the authority to make formal offers. From this evidence, it is clear that the trial court properly determined that ZuChristian lacked the actual authority to bind the C.T.A. for the additional $500 in compensation to Schoenberger.

Nor can it be said that the C.T.A. clothed ZuChristian with the apparent authority to make Schoenberger a promise of compensation over and above that formally offered by the Placement Department. The general rule to consider in determining whether an agent is acting within the apparent authority of his principal was stated in [citation] in this way:

Apparent authority in an agent is such authority as the principal knowingly permits the agent to assume or which he holds his agent out as possessing—it is such authority as a reasonably prudent man, exercising diligence and discretion, in view of the principal's conduct, would naturally suppose the agent to possess.

* * *

Here, Schoenberger's initial contact with the C.T.A. was with the Placement Department where he filled out an application and had his first interview. There is no evidence that the C.T.A. did anything to permit ZuChristian to assume authority nor did they do anything to hold him out as having the authority to hire and set salaries. ZuChristian was not at a management level in the C.T.A. nor did his job title of Principal Communications Analyst suggest otherwise. The mere fact that he was allowed to interview prospective employees does not establish that the C.T.A. held him out as possessing the authority to hire employees or set salaries. Moreover, ZuChristian did inform Schoenberger that the formal offer of employment would be made by the Placement Department.

* * *

Our final inquiry concerns the plaintiff's contention that irrespective of ZuChristian's actual or apparent authority, the C.T.A. is bound by ZuChristian's promise because it ratified his acts. Ratification may be express or inferred and occurs where "the principal, with knowledge of the material facts of the unauthorized transaction, takes a position inconsistent with nonaffirmation of the transaction." [Citations.] Ratification is the equivalent to an original authorization and confirms that which was originally unauthorized. [Citation.] Ratification occurs where a principal attempts to seek or retain the benefits of the transaction. [Citations.]

Upon review of the evidence, we are not convinced that the C.T.A. acted to ratify ZuChristian's promise. According to Bonner's testimony, when he took over the supervision of ZuChristian's group in the fall of 1976 and was told of the promise, he immediately informed ZuChristian that the promise was unauthorized and consequently would not be honored. Subsequently, he informed Schoenberger of this same fact. Mere delay in telling Schoenberger does not, as the plaintiff contends, establish the C.T.A.'s intent to ratify. [Citations.]

* * *

For the reasons we have indicated, the judgment of the circuit court of Cook County granting judgment in favor of the defendant, C.T.A., is affirmed.

Effect of Termination of Agency upon Authority

ZUKAITIS v. AETNA CASUALTY AND SURETY CO.

Supreme Court of Nebraska, 1975.
195 Neb. 59, 236 N.W.2d 819.

BLUE, J.

This is an action for a declaratory judgment brought to determine whether defendant-appellee, the Aetna Casualty and Surety Company, was obligated under its professional liability insurance policy to defend plaintiff-appellant, Raymond R. Zukaitis, in a medical malpractice suit.

The case was tried to the court under a stipulation of facts which can be summarized as follows: Raymond R. Zukaitis was a physician practicing medicine in Douglas County, Nebraska. Aetna issued Dr. Zukaitis a policy of professional liability insurance through its agent, the Ed Larsen Insurance Agency, Inc. This policy was for a period from August 31, 1969, to August 31, 1970.

On August 7, 1971, Dr. Zukaitis received a written notification of a claim for malpractice which allegedly occurred on September 27, 1969. On August 10, 1971, Dr. Zukaitis telephoned the Ed Larsen Insurance Agency. At the request of the agency the written claim was forwarded to it by Dr. Zukaitis. This was received on August 11, 1971, and was erroneously referred to the St. Paul Fire and Marine Insurance Company on that date by the agency.

Dr. Zukaitis was insured with St. Paul Fire and Marine Insurance Company from August 31, 1970, to August 31, 1971. But on the date of the alleged malpractice, he was insured with Aetna. Apparently without notice to Dr. Zukaitis, the agency contract between Ed Larsen Insurance Agency and Aetna had been canceled effective August 1, 1970. At that time the agency placed Dr. Zukaitis' insurance with St. Paul.

On November 22, 1971, a malpractice action was brought against Dr. Zukaitis based on the alleged malpractice of September 27, 1969. Attorneys for St. Paul undertook the defense of the lawsuit. On January 25, 1974, St. Paul discovered that it was not the insurance carrier for Dr. Zukaitis on September 27, 1969, the date of the alleged malpractice, and advised Aetna of this at that time. Dr. Zukaitis was also advised of this, and the attorney retained for St. Paul to represent Dr. Zukaitis withdrew. Dr. Zukaitis made demand upon Aetna on May 28, 1974, for it to undertake the defense of Dr. Zukaitis, but this demand was refused.

Dr. Zukaitis retained his own attorney to represent him in the malpractice case. A motion for summary judgment was filed by Dr.

Zukaitis in that case, which motion was sustained. This action for a declaratory judgment against Aetna therefore resolved itself into an effort to recover attorney's fees and costs. The District Court found for Aetna. Dr. Zukaitis' motion for new trial was overruled, and this appeal followed.

Aetna contends that it is relieved from its obligation to Dr. Zukaitis since notice was not given as required by paragraph 4(b) of the policy which provides: "If claim is made or suit is brought against the insured, the insured shall immediately forward to the company every demand, notice, summons or other process received by him or his representative."

Dr. Zukaitis contends that under the circumstances, notice to Aetna was given within a reasonable period in that the agent who wrote the policy was given notice, and further that a delay in giving notice does not defeat policy obligations unless the insurer is prejudiced by the delay.

* * *

Ordinarily notice to a soliciting agent who countersigns and issues policies of insurance is notice to the insurance company. [Citations.] This is also true even if the agent forwards the notice to the wrong company. * * *

* * *

The question then is whether this is true after the agency contract between the insurance company and the agent has been terminated as it was in this case. To answer this, it is necessary to refer to the general law of agency.

The rule is that a revocation [by agreement of the principal and agent] of the agent's authority does not become effective as between the principal and third persons until they receive [actual] notice of the termination. [Citations.]

Here, Dr. Zukaitis did what most reasonable persons would do in this situation; he notified the agent who sold him the policy. There is no evidence that notice of the termination was sent to him or that he knew the agency contract has been canceled.

"When the insurer terminates the agency contract, it is its duty to notify third persons, such as the insureds with whom the agent dealt, and inform them of such termination. If it does not so notify and such third persons or insureds deal with the agent without notice or knowledge of the termination, and in reliance on the apparently continuing authority of the agent, the insurer is bound by the acts of the former agent." [Citation.]

"The principle of the carrying over of the authority of an agent after termination with respect to third persons having no notice or knowledge thereof has been applied so as to bind the insurer when the third person dealt with the apparent agent by contracting with him, or by forwarding or delivering to him suit papers and proofs of loss." [Citation.]

* * *

Reversed and remanded with directions.

Ratification

BRADSHAW v. McBRIDE

Supreme Court of Utah, 1982.
649 P.2d 74.

Stewart, J.

Defendants appeal from a lower court ruling ordering specific performance of an oral contract to sell plaintiffs two parcels of land and appurtenant water rights. Defendants seek reversal of the order. * * *

Aretta J. Parkinson originally owned the property in dispute (hereinafter the Parkinson farm). Prior to her December 23, 1976 death, she deeded a one-eighth undivided interest in the farm to each of her eight children as tenants in common. The deed was not recorded until January 14, 1977. Aretta Parkinson's children are the defendants in this action. Annabelle Lister, one of Aretta Parkinson's daughters, died shortly after her mother's death. John Parkinson Lister, Annabelle Lister's son, was named administrator of her estate and is a named defendant in this suit.

The Parkinson farm consists of four tracts containing 200 acres. Three adjoining tracts constitute 160 acres; one 40–acre tract is a short distance away. For several years the Bradshaws cared for and used the 40–acre tract with the Parkinson's permission. The Bradshaw property completely surrounds the 40–acre tract and borders the 160–acre tract on several sides.

On January 15, 1977, Roma Funk, one of Aretta's daughters, visited Barbara Bradshaw to ascertain her interest in purchasing the Parkinson farm. They talked about the farm generally and the separate 40–acre tract specifically. Both knew of an appraisal of all Aretta Parkinson's property and agreed to a selling price of $33,000, the approximate appraised value of the 200 acre farm. Bradshaw gave Funk a check for $5,000, with $28,000 payable in cash as soon as a clear title to the property was conveyed.

The testimony of Funk and Bradshaw conflicts as to whether Funk brought with her to the meeting the appraisal and the warranty deed by which Aretta Parkinson conveyed the Parkinson farm to her children. Bradshaw testified that she thumbed through the documents Funk gave her, including the appraisal and the warranty deed. Funk testified that she did not bring these papers, and that neither she nor Bradshaw knew the number of acres included in the farm or the exact lands they were talking about. Funk also stated that the sale was contingent on the approval of her family and that she had no authority to act for them in negotiations or sales. Bradshaw claimed that she asked Funk several times during the meeting whether the Parkinson children gave her authority to act for them and that Funk answered affirmatively.

It is undisputed that there was no written real estate contract. However, the trial court found that the parties had entered into an oral contract of sale. The essential facts are that after the meeting Funk contacted her sisters, notified them of the agreement to sell the farm and advised them of the $5,000 check she had received from Bradshaw. She later contacted Bryant Hansen, a real estate broker, to help her complete the details of the transaction. Hansen prepared an earnest money agreement which the Bradshaws signed and returned to him. The provisions of the unexecuted earnest money agreement corresponded to Barbara Bradshaw's version

of what transpired at the initial meeting. Funk had provided Hansen with a copy of the appraisal which he used for the legal descriptions in the earnest money agreement. Mrs. Funk had not seen the earnest money agreement before her deposition and none of the defendants signed it. Hansen, the real estate agent, also prepared warranty deeds which were signed by three of Aretta's children and returned to him, but not delivered to the Bradshaws. Several defendants later refused to convey their interests in the Parkinson farm despite the Bradshaws' willingness to pay an additional $2,000 to clear a title problem on the property.

Subsequent to the oral agreement between the Bradshaws and Roma Funk, the Bradshaws claim they took possession of the 160–acre parcel by grazing cattle and repairing fences. * * *

* * *

Defendants next contend that Funk was not authorized to act as agent for the other defendants. The general rule is that one who deals with an agent has the responsibility to ascertain the agent's authority despite the agent's representations. [Citation.] The Bradshaws in effect concede this point, but argue that the defendants subsequently ratified the oral contract. The trial court found ratification in the defendants' failure to come forward and repudiate or disaffirm Mrs. Funk's agreement to sell the property or her authority to act for them.

* * *

A principal may impliedly or expressly ratify an agreement made by an unauthorized agent. Ratification of an agent's acts relates back to the time the unauthorized act occurred and is sufficient to create the relationship of principal and agent. [Citations.] A deliberate and valid ratification with full knowledge of all the material facts is binding and cannot afterward be revoked or recalled. [Citation.] However, a ratification requires the principal to have knowledge of all material facts and an intent to ratify. [Citation.] Under some circumstances failure to disaffirm may constitute ratification of the agent's acts. In [citation]:

Ratification like original authority need not be express. Any conduct which indicates assent by the purported principal to become a party to the transaction or which is justifiable only if there is ratification is sufficient. Even silence with full knowledge of the facts may manifest affirmance and thus operate as a ratification. The person with whom the agent dealt will so obviously be deceived by assuming the professed agent was authorized to act as such, that the principal is under a duty to undeceive him. . . . So a purported principal may not be wilfully ignorant, nor may he purposely shut his eyes to means of information within his possession and control and thereby escape ratification 'if the circumstances are such that he could reasonably have been expected to dissent unless he were willing to be a party to the transaction.' . . .

The trial court found that the defendants other than Funk had ratified the Funk-Bradshaw agreement, in part, by their knowledge and acceptance of the agreement. This finding, however, is clearly not supported by the evidence in the record as to two defendants who were not notified of the agreement until receipt of the warranty deeds prepared by Hansen. Funk testified that she did not contact her brother Foch or John Lister, the administrator of Annabelle Lister's estate. At trial, Foch testified that when he first learned of the agreement he was opposed to it, but was willing to go along with the agreement only if the court found it enforceable. Foch attempted to determine the validity of the contract by meeting with his attorney and Ron Bradshaw in his attorney's office. He continually stated his objection to the agreement, and his actions cannot be interpreted as ratification. John Lister testified that he did not become aware of the agreement until he received the real estate documents from Hansen. Lister did not sign the documents and did nothing to ratify the agreement between Funk and Bradshaw. When presented with a writing to convey ownership in property, Lister had no duty to disavow any putative agreement. On the contrary, his failure to sign is evidence of rejection. It is clear that neither Foch nor Lister in fact ratified the agreement.

Furthermore, as to all defendants, there was no ratification as a matter of law because

the Utah statute of frauds requires that any agent executing an agreement conveying an interest in land on behalf of his principal must be authorized in writing. [Citation.] In order to enforce an oral agreement, the same kind of authorization that is required to clothe an agent initially with authority to contract must be given by the principal to constitute a ratification of an unauthorized act. Where the law requires the authority to be given in writing, the ratification must also generally be in writing. [Citations.] There was, therefore, no ratification in this case.

* * *

Reversed.

Tort Liability of Principal

RUBIN v. YELLOW CAB CO.

Appellate Court of Illinois, First District, Fifth Division, 1987.
154 Ill.App.3d 336, 107 Ill.Dec.450, 507 N.E.2d 114.

Lorenz, J.

Plaintiff filed a nine-count complaint against defendants after suffering an alleged battery in the hands of defendant cab driver. The trial court dismissed Counts VII, VIII and IX of plaintiff's fourth amended complaint for failure to state a cause of action against defendant cab company. On appeal, plaintiff argues that the trial court's dismissal was improper as (1) Count IX alleged sufficient facts to render defendant cab company vicariously liable for battery under a theory of *respondeat superior;* and (2) Counts VII and VIII each stated a cause of action for negligent or willful and wanton supervision.

We affirm.

Plaintiff was driving on one of the city's streets when he inadvertently obstructed the path of a taxi, causing the latter to swerve and come into contact with plaintiff's vehicle. Angered by plaintiff's sudden blocking of his traffic lane, defendant driver proceeded to exit his cab, approach plaintiff and strike him about the head and shoulder with a metal pipe.

Plaintiff subsequently filed suit against Robert C. Ball ("Ball"), the cab driver, and Yellow Cab Company ("Yellow Cab"), the owner of the taxi, to recover damages for bodily injuries sustained as a result of the altercation. On defendant Yellow Cab's motion, the trial court dismissed seven of nine counts included in plaintiff's fourth amended complaint for failure to state a cause of action. Counts VII, VIII and IX charged Yellow Cab with vicarious liability for battery and with negligent and/or willful and wanton failure to supervise and inspect. This appeal concerns only the sufficiency of these three counts as they pertain to defendant Yellow Cab.

We initially consider whether the subject complaint states a cause of action under the doctrine of *respondeat superior.*

It is well established that an employer may be held liable for the negligent, willful, malicious or criminal acts of its employees where such acts are committed in the course of employment and in furtherance of the business of the employer. [Citation.] However, where the acts complained of are committed solely for the benefit of the employee, the employer will not be held liable to an injured third party. [Citation.]

Plaintiff in the instant case maintains that his fourth amended complaint alleges sufficient facts to show that Ball committed the battery within the course and scope of his duties as a cab driver. According to plaintiff, Ball's acts were designed to further the business purposes of Yellow Cab by virtue of the fact that they: (1) fulfilled his obligation to investigate and report any accidents damaging property owned by Yellow Cab; (2) were performed pursuant to his obligation to protect property owned by Yellow Cab; and (3) were meant to prevent plaintiff and others from delaying his progress to obtain fares. We disagree.

First, the complaint in question contains no allegation that plaintiff was interfering with Ball's investigation or attempt to report the accident or, for that matter, that Ball was even attempting to investigate or report the incident at the time he struck plaintiff with the pipe. Rather, the subject complaint merely

states that Ball got out of his cab, walked over to plaintiff and proceeded to hit him over the head with a pipe. This act patently has no relation to the business of driving a cab. In view of their duties, cab drivers are not expected to strike individuals on the street with metal pipes. Second, the battery could have no relation to Yellow Cab's interest in protecting its property since the contact between the two vehicles had already occurred. Lastly, the battery could not have prevented plaintiff from delaying Ball's progress to the airport to obtain passengers as a delay had already occurred before Ball got out of his cab to strike plaintiff.

While we accept the principles stated in the cases primarily relied on by plaintiff, their factual inappositeness makes their application improper in the resolution of the instant case. [Citations], all present situations in which bartenders or bouncers endeavored to maintain order or protect the property of their employees. The nature of a bartender's or bouncer's job makes the use of force during the course of his employment highly probable. A cab driver, on the other hand, is basically relegated to transporting individuals from one destination to another and, as such, it is unlikely that he will undertake to attack a person that is neither a passenger nor is connected with the cab company. In [citation], an employee holding the position of office manager in a finance company mistakenly shot plaintiff while in the pursuit of robbers. Likewise, the court found the employee to have acted within his managerial capacity and in accordance with his duty to protect the property and business of his employer.

The assault on plaintiff in the instant case amounted to a deviation from the conduct generally associated with the enterprise of cab driving. Accordingly, we find the facts before us to be more akin to those in *Webb by Harris, v. Jewel Companies, Inc.,* [citation] and *Awe v. Striker,* [citation]. In *Webb by Harris,* plaintiff sought to hold Jewel liable for a sexual assault committed by one of its security guards. This court held at that time that it was impossible to interpret such act as one undertaken for the purpose of furthering Jewel's business. Similarly, plaintiff in *Awe* sought to hold the operators of a carnival liable for the battery committed on his person by several employees. Upon losing a carnival game, plaintiff had complained to the employees of crookedness and threatened to notify the Sheriff. Angered by the threats, the employees proceeded to jump on plaintiff and beat him with their fists and a hammer. In dismissing the counts brought under the doctrine of *respondeat superior* for failure to state a cause of action, the court held that since the game played by plaintiff had been completed and the carnival employees had performed the duties for which they had been hired, the subsequent attack was outside the scope and not in furtherance of their employment.

As Ball's assault on plaintiff was clearly not an act undertaken to further Yellow Cab's business but rather one propelled singularly by anger and frustration, the trial court properly dismissed Count IX of plaintiff's fourth amended complaint for failure to state a cause of action under the doctrine of *respondeat superior.*

Counts VII and VIII of the subject complaint were also correctly dismissed. Said counts seek to charge Yellow Cab with a breach of their duty to supervise Ball on account of his alleged vicious disposition and to inspect the taxicab for the presence of weapons. With respect to the duty to supervise, however, plaintiff in the instant case fails to allege that Yellow Cab had knowledge that one of its drivers was assaulting plaintiff and stood by without taking any action to stop such conduct. Instead, plaintiff pleads bare conclusions regarding Ball's supposedly vicious disposition. Furthermore, charging Yellow Cab with a breach of duty to inspect cabs to ensure that weapons are never present in the vehicles is nonsensical when there is no allegation that the object with which plaintiff was hit was ever within the taxicab. Absent such an allegation, it is difficult to conclude that any failure on the part of Yellow Cab to inspect for weapons could have caused plaintiff's injuries.

* * * Under the circumstances presented in the instant case, the trial court correctly dismissed Counts VII and VIII of plaintiff's fourth amended complaint.

The judgment of the trial court is affirmed. Affirmed.

Agent's Implied Warranty of Authority

GOLDFINGER v. DOHERTY

Supreme Court, Appellate Term, First Department, 1934.
153 Misc. 826, 276 N.Y.S. 289.

SHIENTAG, J.

The plaintiff sued the defendant Doherty, disaffirming certain purchases of stock, made in her behalf by her duly authorized agent, alleging that she was an infant at the time of the transactions, and that she now elected to rescind and offered to return the stock, together with the stock and cash dividends received thereon. The defendant Doherty thereupon obtained an order permitting him to serve a supplemental summons and complaint on the agent Samuel Goldfinger. . . . The supplemental pleading alleged, in substance, that the agent purchased the stock from Doherty on behalf of the alleged infant "without disclosing the infancy of his principal." It further alleged that, if plaintiff should recover against Doherty, then the defendant Goldfinger, plaintiff's agent, will be liable to defendant Doherty for damages sustained through the rescission of the contracts by plaintiff, "on the ground that defendant Samuel Goldfinger has breached his implied warranty that he was authorized to enter into binding contracts for the plaintiff."

* * *

An infant's appointment of an agent is not void; it is merely voidable, like any other contract he makes. * * *

There is, therefore, no basis for the contention of the appellant that disaffirmance by the infant of a contract entered into on his behalf by his agent renders the transaction void ab initio, so that the agent is deemed to have acted without any authority. The infant, without questioning the authority of his agent, may disaffirm the contract entered into on his behalf, in the same manner as if he had made the contract directly. The infant may disaffirm the contract of agency; he may disaffirm the contract entered into by his agent. Either contract is voidable; neither is void.

* * *

"The agent does not warrant the capacity of the principal." [Citation.] "An agent does not warrant that his principal has full contractual capacity, any more than he warrants that his principal is solvent. Thus an agent for one not of legal age is not necessarily liable if the infant avoids the obligation of the contract made on his account." Comment (a) on section 332, Restatement of the Law of Agency. An agent who misrepresents the capacity of his principal to contract is liable as for any other misrepresentation, and this whether he misrepresents tortiously or innocently.

In the absence of misrepresentation, under what circumstances, if any, is an agent acting for an infant, who subsequently disaffirms, not the agency, but the transaction of the agent, liable to the other contracting party? It must appear that the agent knew or had reason to know of his principal's lack of full capacity, and it must further appear that the other contracting party was in ignorance thereof. The theory of breach of warranty of authority is that one dealing with an agent has been misled by him. * * *

Assuming that the agent knows or has reason to know of his principal's lack of full capacity, and of the other party's ignorance thereof, what, if any, is the agent's liability? * * *

The basis of the liability of an agent in a situation such as we are here considering, is that he has produced "a false impression upon the mind of the other party; and, if this result is accomplished, it is unimportant whether the means of accomplishing it are words or acts of the defendant, or his concealment or suppression of material facts not equally within the knowledge or reach of the plaintiff." [Citation.] We believe that the correct rule is that set forth in the Restatement of the Law of Agency as follows:

par. 332. Agent of partially incompetent principal. An agent making a contract for a disclosed principal whose contracts are voidable because of lack of full capacity to contract, or for a principal who, although having capacity to contract generally, is incompetent to enter into the particular transaction, is not thereby liable to the other party. He does not become liable by reason of the failure of the principal to perform, unless he contracts or represents that the principal has capacity or unless he has reason to know of the principal's lack of capacity and of the other party's ignorance thereof. . . .

If, therefore, the liability of the agent is to be based on his failure to disclose facts in connection with his principal's lack of full capacity to the other contracting party, it must appear (1) that the agent knew or had reason to know the facts indicating his principal's lack of full capacity; (2) that the other contracting party was in ignorance thereof and the agent had reason so to believe; (3) that the transaction is one in which lack of full capacity was a material fact.

* * *

The order dismissing the supplemental complaint is affirmed.

Undisclosed or Partially Disclosed Principal

VAN D. COSTAS, INC. v. ROSENBERG

District Court of Appeal of Florida, Second District, 1983.
432 So.2d 656.

GRIMES, J.

This is an appeal from a final judgment denying appellant's claims for mechanic's lien foreclosure and breach of contract.

Gilbert Rosenberg owned a parcel of real property on Siesta Key upon which the Magic Moment Restaurant was located. Seascape Restaurants, Inc., operated the restaurant and paid a monthly rental to Rosenberg for use of the property. Gilbert Rosenberg, his son Jeff Rosenberg, and Chris Moore each owned one third of Seascape. Jeff was president of Seascape and Moore was vice president, and the two of them operated the restaurant. Gilbert was not an officer of the corporation and was not actively involved in the management of the restaurant.

In November of 1980, appellant's president, Van D. Costas, met with Gilbert and Jeff to discuss the creation of a "magical entrance" for the restaurant. The following month, appellant entered into a contract to remodel the entrance. Jeff Rosenberg signed the contract on a line under which appeared "Jeff Rosenberg, The Magic Moment." After the work commenced, the parties became involved in a dispute over performance and payment, and appellant filed a claim of lien on the real estate. Appellant thereafter sued Gilbert to foreclose the lien and in a second count of the complaint sued Jeff Rosenberg for breach of contract. Jeff counterclaimed for damages for faulty performance and other relief. Following a trial, the court entered a final judgment against the appellant which stated in pertinent part:

. . . On the claim against Jeff Rosenberg, individually, the contract was addressed to "The Magic Moment Restaurant." It was drawn on plaintiff's stationery and referred to "Subject: Design and Creation of Mystical Entrance to 'The Magic Moment Restaurant.' " Under the prepared signature line for defendant's signature was typed "Jeff Rosenberg, The Magic Moment." Jeff Rosenberg signed his name on the line provided. Obviously he signed for "The Magic Moment," and there is no dispute that the plaintiff knew he was contracting with "The Magic Moment Restaurant." Plaintiff did testify that he thought the Rosenbergs owned the restaurant. However, there is also no dispute that the business was owned by Seascape Restaurants, Inc. who were doing business under the trade name of "The Magic Moment Restaurant." Under all these circumstances, there is no individual responsibility and the proper party to this suit, as to both claims and counterclaims, is Seascape Restaurants, Inc.

* * *

Appellant bases its claim against Jeff upon the contention that he signed the contract as agent for an undisclosed principal. It is well settled that where one enters into a contract as agent for an undisclosed principal, he may be held individually liable on the contract. [Citations.] The extent to which an agent must make disclosure of his principal in or-

der to avoid personal liability is explained in 3 Am.Jur.2d *Agency* § 320 (1962):

In order for an agent to avoid personal liability on a contract negotiated in his principal's behalf, he must disclose not only that he is an agent but also the identity of his principal, regardless of whether the third person might have known that the agent was acting in a representative capacity. It is not the third person's duty to seek out the identity of the principal; rather, the duty to disclose the identity of the principal is on the agent. The disclosure of an agency is not complete for the purpose of relieving the agent from personal liability unless it embraces the name of the principal; without that, the party dealing with the agent may understand that he intended to pledge his personal liability and responsibility in support of the contract and for its performance. Furthermore, the use of a tradename is not necessarily a sufficient disclosure of the identity of the principal and the fact of agency so as to protect the agent against personal liability.

Section 321 of the Restatement (Second) of the Law of Agency (1957) discusses the liability of the agent under circumstances in which it appears that he is acting for someone else but the identity of his principal is unknown to the other party.

§ 321. Principal Partially Disclosed
Unless otherwise agreed, a person purporting to make a contract with another for a partially disclosed principal is a party to the contract.
Comment:
    a. A principal is a partially disclosed principal when, at the time of making the contract in question, the other party thereto has notice that the agent is acting for a principal but has no notice of the principal's identity. See § 4. The fact that, to the knowledge of the agent, the other party does not know the identity of the principal is of great weight in ascribing to the other party the intention to hold the agent liable either solely, or as a surety or co-promisor with the principal. The inference of an understanding that the agent is a party to the contract exists unless the agent gives such complete information concerning his principal's identity that he can be readily distinguished. If the other party has no reasonable means of ascertaining the principal, the inference is almost irresistible and prevails in the absence of an agreement to the contrary.

Restatement (Second) of Agency § 321, at 70.

In view of the contractual reference to the Magic Moment trade name, the annotation at 150 A.L.R. 1303 (1944) entitled "Use of trade name in connection with contract executed by agent as sufficient disclosure of agency or principal to protect agent against personal liability" is directly on point. The annotator points out that with the possible exception of a single decision, all of the prior cases on the subject have held that the use of a trade name is not a sufficient disclosure of the identity of the principal so as to eliminate the liability of the agent.

* * *

Of course, if the contracting party knows the identity of the principal for whom the agent purports to act, the principal is deemed to be disclosed. [Citation.] A dispute concerning such knowledge presents an issue of fact. [Citation.] Here, however, nothing indicates that appellant had ever heard of Seascape at the time the contract was signed. Subsequent knowledge of the true principal is irrelevant where performance of an indivisible contract has commenced. [Citation.] The trial court emphasized that Costas drafted the contract. However, it was not incumbent upon him to ferret out the record ownership of the Magic Moment when he had every reason to believe that one of the owners was signing the contract. Jeff knew that the owner was Seascape, and he had it within his power to avoid personal liability by properly disclosing his principal. Since there is no evidence that the appellant knew or should have known the true principal, the law holds Jeff legally responsible.

That portion of the judgment exonerating Jeff Rosenberg from liability is reversed, and the case is remanded for further proceedings. Since Jeff's counterclaim was also dismissed on the premise that only Seascape was bound on the contract, this ruling must also be reversed. If Jeff can be held personally liable on the contract, he also has a right to prosecute a claim for breach of that contract or for other relief which relates to the contract. In all other respects, the judgment is affirmed.

QUESTIONS

1. Distinguish among actual express authority, actual implied authority, and apparent authority.

2. Discuss the contractual liability of the principal, agent, and third party when the principal is (a) disclosed, (b) partially disclosed, and (c) undisclosed.

3. Distinguish between actual and constructive notice.

4. Discuss the doctrine of ratification.

5. Discuss the tort liability of a principal for the (a) authorized acts of agents, (b) unauthorized acts of employees, and (c) unauthorized acts of independent contractors.

PROBLEMS

1. Alice was Peter's traveling salesperson and was also authorized to collect accounts. Before the agreed termination of the agency, Peter wrongfully discharged Alice. Alice then called on Tom, an old customer, and collected an account from Tom. She also called on Laura, a new prospect, as Peter's agent, secured a large order, collected the price of the order, sent the order to Peter, and disappeared with the collections. Peter delivered the goods to Laura per the order.

(a) Peter sues Tom for his account. Decision?

(b) Peter sues Laura for the agreed price of the goods. Decision?

2. Paula instructed Alvin, her agent, to purchase a quantity of hides. Alvin ordered the hides from Ted in his own (Alvin's) name and delivered the hides to Paula. Ted, learning later that Paula was the principal, sends the bill to Paula, who refuses to pay Ted. Ted sues Paula and Alvin. Decision?

3. Stan sold goods to Bill in good faith, believing him to be a principal. Bill in fact was acting as agent for Nancy and within the scope of his authority. The goods were charged to Bill, and on his refusal to pay, Stan sued Bill for the purchase price. While this action was pending, Stan learned of Bill's relationship with Nancy. Nevertheless, thirty days after learning of that relationship, Stan obtained judgment against Bill and had an execution issued that was never satisfied. Three months after rendition of the judgment, Stan sued Nancy for the purchase price of the goods. Decision?

4. Green Grocery Company employed Jones as its manager. Jones was given authority by Green Company to purchase supplies and goods for resale and had conducted business for several years with Brown Distributing Company. Purchases by Jones from Brown Distributing Company had been limited to groceries. Jones then contacted Brown Distributing Company and had it deliver a color television set to her house, informing Brown Company the set was to be used in promotional advertising to increase Green Grocery Company's business. The advertising did not develop. Jones disappeared from the area, taking the television set with her. Brown Company sued Green Company for the purchase price of the set. Decision?

5. Stone was the authorized agent to sell stock of the Turner Company at $10 per share and was authorized in case of sale to fill in the blanks in the certificates with the name of the purchaser, the number of shares, and the date of sale. He sold 100 shares to Barrie, and without the knowledge or consent of the company and without reporting to the company, he endorsed on the back of the certificate the following:

"It is hereby agreed that Turner Company shall, at the end of three years after the date, repurchase the stock at $11 per share on thirty days' notice. Turner Company, by Stone."

After three years, demand was made on Turner Company to repurchase, which was refused, and the company repudiated the agreement on the ground that the agent had no authority to make the agreement for repurchase. Barrie sued Turner Company. Decision?

6. Helper, a delivery boy for Gunn, delivered two heavy packages of groceries to Reed's porch. As instructed by Gunn, Helper rang the bell to let Reed know the groceries had arrived. Mrs. Reed came to the door and asked Helper if he would deliver the groceries into the kitchen because the bags were heavy. Helper did so, and upon leaving he observed Mrs. Reed having difficulty in moving a cabinet in the dining room. He undertook to assist her, but being more interested in watching Mrs. Reed than the cabinet, he failed to observe a small, valuable antique table, which he smashed into with the cabinet and totally destroyed. Does Reed have a cause of action against Gunn for the value of the destroyed antique?

7. Driver picked up Friend to accompany him on an out-of-town delivery for his employer, Speedy Service. A "No Riders" sign was prominently displayed on the windshield of the truck, and Driver violated specific instructions of his employer by permitting an unauthorized person to ride in the vehicle. While discussing a planned fishing trip with Friend, Driver ran a red light and collided with an automobile driven by Motorist. Both Friend and Motorist were injured. Is Speedy Service liable to either Friend or Motorist for the injuries they sustained?

8. Cook's Department Store advertises that it maintains a barber shop in its store managed by Hunter. Actually, Hunter is not an employee of the store but merely rents space in the store. Hunter, while shaving Jordon in the barber shop, negligently puts a deep gash into one of Jordon's ears, requiring ten stitches. Jordon sues Cook's Department Store for damages. Decision?

9. The following contract was executed on August 22:

Ray agrees to sell and Shaw, the representative of Todd and acting on his behalf, agrees to buy 10,000 pounds of $0.32 \times 1\frac{5}{8}$ stainless steel strip type 410.

(signed) Ray
(signed) Shaw

On August 26, Ray informs Shaw and Todd that the contract was in reality signed by him as agent for Upson. What are the rights of Ray, Shaw, Todd, and Upson, in the event of a breach of the contract?

10. Harris, owner of certain land known as Red Bank, mailed a letter to Byron, a real estate broker in City X, stating: "I have been thinking of selling Red Bank. I have never met you, but a friend has advised me that you are an industrious and honest real estate broker. I therefore employ you to find a purchaser for Red Bank at a price of $35,000." Ten days after receiving the letter, Byron mailed the following reply to Harris: "Acting pursuant to your recent letter requesting me to find a purchaser for Red Bank, this is to advise that I have sold the property to Sims for $35,000. I enclose your copy of the contract of sale signed by Sims. Your name was signed to the contract by me as your agent." Is Harris obligated to convey Red Bank to Sims?

11. While crossing a public highway in the city, Joel was struck by a horse-drawn cart driven by Morison's agent. The agent was traveling between Burton Crescent Mews and Finchley on his employer's business and was not supposed to go into the city at all. Apparently, the agent was on a detour to visit a friend when the accident occurred. Joel brought this action against Morison for the injuries sustained as a result of the agent's negligence. Morison argues that he is not liable for his agent's negligence because the agent had strayed from his assigned path. Decision?

12. Serges is the owner of a retail meat marketing business. His managing agent borrowed $3,500 from David on Serges's behalf and for use in Serges's business. Serges paid $200 on the alleged loan and on several other occasions told David that the full balance owed would eventually be paid. He then disclaimed liability on the debt, asserting that he had not authorized his agent to enter into the loan agreement. David brought this action to collect on the loan. Decision?

13. Sherwood negligently ran into the rear of Austen's car, which was stopped at a stoplight. As a result, Austen received bodily injuries and her car was damaged. Sherwood, arts editor for the *Mississippi Press Register,* was en route from a Louis Armstrong concert he had covered for the newspaper. When the accident occurred he was on his way to spend the night at a friend's house. Austen sued Sherwood and—under the doctrine of *respondeat superior*—Sherwood's employer, the *Mississippi Press Register.* Decision?

PART FOUR

Sales

Chapter 20

INTRODUCTION TO SALES

Definition
Fundamental Principles of Article 2
Manifestation of Mutual Assent
Consideration
Form of the Contract
Leases

SALES are the most common and important of all commercial transactions. In an exchange economy such as ours, sales are the essential means by which the various units of production exchange their outputs, thereby providing the opportunity for specialization and enhanced productivity. An advanced, complex, industrialized economy with highly coordinated manufacturing and distribution systems requires a reliable mechanism for assuring that *future* exchanges can be entered into today and fulfilled at a later time. The critical role of the law of sales is to establish a framework in which these present and future exchanges may take place in a predictable, certain, and orderly fashion with a minimum of transaction costs. The manufacture and distribution of goods involve numerous sales transactions and practically everyone in our economy is a purchaser of both durable and consumable goods.

Until the early 1900s, sales transactions were completely governed by general contract law. In 1906, the Uniform Sales Act was promulgated and eventually adopted by thirty-six States. By the end of the 1930s, however, dissatisfaction with this and other uniform commercial statutes brought about the development of the Uniform Commercial Code. Article 2 of the Code deals with transactions in sales and has been adopted in all States (except Louisiana) plus the District of Columbia and the Virgin Islands. The Uniform Commercial Code appears in Appendix C.

This chapter will discuss the nature and formation of sales contracts as well as the fundamental principles of new Article 2A–Leases.

NATURE OF SALES CONTRACTS

The law of sales, which governs contracts involving the sale of goods, is a specialized branch of both the law of contracts (discussed previously in Chapters 8–17) and the law of personal property (discussed later in Chapter 48). See Figure 20–1. This section will cover the definition of a sales contract and the fundamentals of Article 2.

DEFINITION

The Code defines a **sale** as the transfer of title to goods from seller to buyer for a price. Section 2–106. The price can be money, other goods, real estate, or services. **Goods** are essentially defined as movable, tangible personal property. For example, the purchase of a bicycle, stereo set, or this textbook is considered a sale of goods. "Goods" also include the unborn young of animals, growing crops, and, if removed by the seller, timber, minerals, or a building attached to real property. Section 2–105(1).

Governing Law

Sales transactions are governed by Article 2 of the Code, but, where general contract law has not been specifically modified by the Code, contract law continues to apply. In other words, the law of sales is a specialized part of the general law of contracts, and the law of contracts continues to govern unless specifically displaced by the Code.

General contract law also continues to govern all contracts outside the scope of the Code. Transactions not within the scope of Article 2 include employment contracts, service contracts, insurance contracts, contracts involving real property, and contracts for the sale of intangibles such as stocks, bonds, patents, and copyrights. For an illustration of this relationship see Figure 8–1. In determining whether a contract containing both a sale of goods and a service is a U.C.C. contract or general contract, the majority of States follows the predominant purpose test. This test holds that if the predominant purpose of the whole transaction is a sale of goods, then Article 2 applies to the entire transaction. If, on the other hand, the predominant purpose is the non-good or service portion, then Article 2 does not apply at all. *See Kline Iron & Steel, Inc. v. Gray Communications Consultants, Inc.* and in Chapter 8 *Colorado Carpet Installation, Inc. v. Palermo.* A few States apply Article 2 only to the goods part of a transaction and general contract law to the non-goods or service part of the transaction.

Nonsales Transactions in Goods

There are a number of transactions that are not sales yet significantly affect goods. For

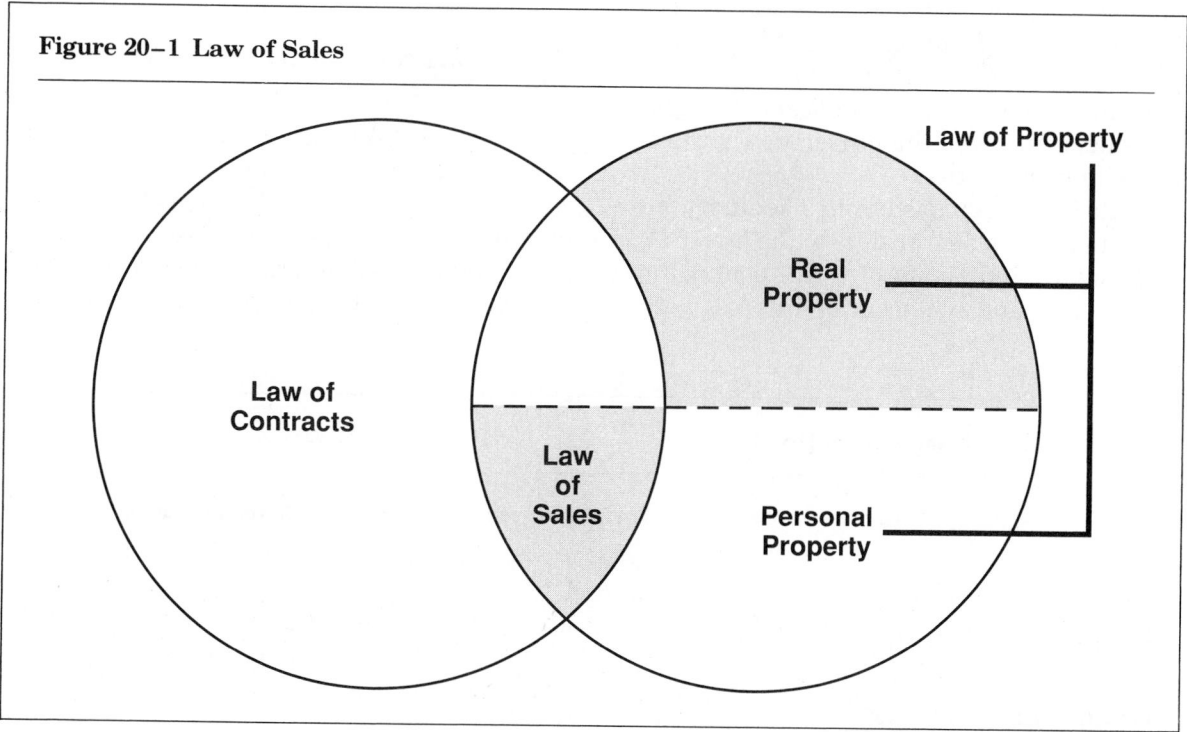

Figure 20–1 Law of Sales

example, a **bailment** is a transfer of the possession of personal property by the owner or rightful possessor (*bailor*) to another (*bailee*) for a determinable period of time *without* a transfer of title. To illustrate, Arnold (the bailor) creates a bailment when he delivers his soiled laundry to the XYZ Laundry Company (the bailee) for cleaning. Other examples of bailments include delivery of goods to a repairman, a carrier, or a warehouseman. In contrast, transfer of title is essential to a sale, although transfer of possession is not.

A **lease** of goods is a contract whereby the owner of the goods (the *lessor*) agrees with another person (the *lessee*) that she will transfer to the lessee the possession and right to use the goods for a period of time in consideration of a specified payment. A lease of goods does not involve a transfer of title to the goods.

A **gift** is a transfer of property from one person to another without consideration. The lack of any consideration is the basic distinction between a gift and a sale. Because a gift involves no consideration or compensation, to be effective it must be completed by delivery of the gift; a promise to make a gift is not binding. There must be intent on the part of the maker (the *donor*) of the gift to make a present transfer, and there must be acceptance by the recipient (the *donee*) of the gift. In a sale, delivery of the property is not necessary to transfer title.

A sale is distinguished from a **security interest** in that a sale transfers to the buyer all of the ownership rights of the seller in the goods, while under a security interest both the *creditor* and the *debtor* have ownership rights in the goods. The right of the secured creditor in the goods is to take possession of the goods in the event of default by the debtor.

Although Article 2 governs sales, the drafters of the Article have invited the courts to extend Code principles to nonsale transactions in goods. To date a number of courts have accepted this invitation and have applied Code provisions by analogy to other transactions in goods not expressly included within the act, most frequently to leases and bailments. The Code has also greatly influenced the revision of the Restatement, Second, Contracts which, as previously discussed, has great effect upon all contracts. In these ways the policies and principles of the Code have been extended to nonsales transactions. In 1987 the drafters of the Code went further and approved Article 2A, Uniform Commercial Code—Leases. This Article is an analogue of Article 2 and adopts many of the rules contained in that Article. The last section of this chapter covers the fundamentals of Article 2A.

Figure 20–2 summarizes the various transactions in goods.

FUNDAMENTAL PRINCIPLES OF ARTICLE 2

The purpose of Article 2 is to modernize, clarify, simplify, and make uniform the law of sales. Furthermore, the Article is to be interpreted in accordance with these underlying principles and not according to some abstraction such as the passage of title. The Code "is

---

Figure 20–2 Transactions in Goods

	Transfer of Title	Transfer of Possession	Governing Law
Sale	Yes	Usually, but not necessarily	Article 2
Gift	Yes	Yes	Common Law
Bailment	No	Yes	Common Law and Article 7
Lease	No	Yes	Common Law or Article 2A
Security Interest	No	No	Article 9

drawn to provide flexibility so that, since it is intended to be a semi-permanent piece of legislation, it will provide its own machinery for expansion of commercial practices. It is intended to make it possible for the law embodied in this Act to be developed by the courts in the light of unforeseen and new circumstances and practices. However, the proper construction of the Act requires that its interpretation and application be limited to its reason." Section 1–102, Comment 1. This open-ended drafting includes the following fundamental concepts.

Good Faith

All parties who enter into a contract or duty within the scope of the Code must perform their obligations in good faith. *See Empire Gas Corp. v. American Bakeries.* The Code defines **good faith** as "honesty in fact in the conduct or transaction concerned." Section 1–201(19). In the case of a merchant (defined below), good faith also requires the observance of reasonable commercial standards of fair dealing in the trade. Section 2–103(1)(b). For instance, if the parties agree that the seller is to set the price term, the seller must establish the price in good faith.

Unconscionability

Every contract of sale may be scrutinized by the court to determine whether in its commercial setting, purpose, and effect it is unconscionable. The court may refuse to enforce an unconscionable contract or any part of it found to be unconscionable or may limit its application to prevent an unconscionable result. Section 2–302. The Code does not define *unconscionable.* The term is defined, however, in the *New Webster's Dictionary* (Deluxe Encyclopedic Edition) as "contrary to the dictates of conscience; unscrupulous or unprincipled; exceeding that which is reasonable or customary; inordinate, unjustifiable."

The Code denies or limits enforcement of an unconscionable contract for the sale of goods in the interest of fairness and decency, and to correct harshness or oppression in contracts resulting from inequality in the bargaining positions of the parties.

The doctrine of unconscionability has been justified on the basis that it permits the courts to resolve issues of unfairness explicitly on that basis without recourse to formalistic rules or legal fictions. In policing contracts for fairness, the courts have again demonstrated their willingness to limit freedom of contract in order to protect the less advantaged from overreaching by dominant contracting parties. Accordingly, most of the cases have involved low-income consumers.

The doctrine of unconscionability has evolved through its application by the courts to include both procedural and substantive unconscionability. **Procedural unconscionability** involves scrutiny for the presence of "bargaining naughtiness." In other words, was the negotiation process fair, or were there procedural irregularities such as burying important terms of the agreement in fine print or obscuring the true meaning of the contract with impenetrable legal jargon?

Substantive unconscionability deals with the actual terms of the contract and looks for oppressive or grossly unfair provisions such as an exorbitant price or an unfair exclusion or limitation of contractual remedies. An all too common example is that involving a necessitous buyer in an unequal bargaining position with a seller who has obtained an exorbitant price for his product or service. In one case, a price of $749 ($920 on time-payments) for a vacuum cleaner that cost the seller $140 was held unconscionable. In another case, the buyers, welfare recipients, purchased by time payment contract a home freezer unit for $900 plus time credit charges, credit life insurance, credit property insurance, and sales tax for a total price of $1,235. The purchase resulted from a visit to the buyer's home by a salesman representing Your Shop At Home Service, Inc., and the maximum retail value of the freezer unit at the time of purchase was $300. The court held the contract unconscionable and reformed it by changing the price to the total payment ($620) made by the buyers. *Jones v. Star Credit Corp.,* 59 Misc.2d 189, 298 N.Y.S.2d 264 (1969).

See Construction Asso., Inc. v. Fargo Water Equip. Co., and in Chapter 12 *Williams v. Walker-Thomas Furniture Co.*

Expansion of Commercial Practices

An underlying policy of the Code is "to permit the continued expansion of commercial practices through custom, usage and agreement of the parties." Section 1–102(2)(b). In particular, the Code places great emphasis upon course of dealings and usage of trade in interpreting agreements.

A **course of dealing** is a sequence of previous conduct between the parties that may fairly be regarded as establishing a common basis of understanding for interpreting their expressions and agreement. Section 1–205(1). For example, Plaza, a sugar company, enters into a written agreement with Brown, a grower of sugar beets, by which Brown agrees to raise and deliver and Plaza to purchase specified quantities of beets during the coming season. No price is fixed. The agreement is on a standard form used by Plaza for Brown and many other growers in prior years. Plaza's practice is to pay all growers uniformly on a formula based on Plaza's established accounting system. Unless otherwise agreed, the established pricing pattern is part of the agreement between Plaza and Brown as a course of dealing.

A **usage of trade** is a practice or method of dealing regularly observed and followed in a place, vocation, or trade. Section 1–205(2). To illustrate: Tamara contracts to sell Seth one thousand feet of San Domingo mahogany. By usage of dealers in mahogany, known to Tamara and Seth, good mahogany of a certain density is known as San Domingo mahogany, though it does not come from San Domingo. Unless otherwise agreed, the usage is part of the contract.

Sales by and between Merchants

The Code establishes separate rules that apply to transactions between merchants or involving a merchant as a party. A **merchant** is defined as a person who (1) is a dealer in the goods, (2) by his occupation holds himself out as having knowledge or skill peculiar to the goods or practices involved, or (3) employs an agent or broker whom he holds out as having such knowledge or skill. Section 2–104(1). These rules exact a higher standard of conduct from merchants because of their knowledge of trade and commerce, and because merchants as a class generally set the standards. The most significant of these merchant rules are listed in Figure 20–3.

Liberal Administration of Remedies

Section 1–106 of the Code provides that its remedies shall be liberally administered in order to place the aggrieved party in as good a position as if the defaulting party had fully performed. The Code does make it clear, however, that remedies are limited to compensation and do not include consequential or punitive damages, unless specifically provided by the Code. Nevertheless, the Code provides that even in cases where the Code does not expressly provide a remedy for a right or obligation, the courts should provide an appropriate remedy. Remedies are discussed in Chapter 24.

Freedom of Contract

Most of the Code's provisions are not mandatory but permit the parties by agreement to vary or displace them altogether. The obligations of good faith, diligence, reasonableness, and care prescribed by the Code, however, may not be disclaimed by agreement, but the parties may by agreement determine the standards by which the performance of these obligations is to be measured so long as such standards are not obviously unreasonable. Section 1–102(3). This approach of the Code not only maximizes freedom of contract but also permits the continued expansion of commercial practices through private agreement.

Figure 20–3 Selected Rules Applicable to Merchants

Section of UCC	Merchant Rules	Chapter in Text Where Discussed
2–103(1)(b)	Good faith	20
2–201	Confirmation of oral contracts	14, 20
2–205	Firm offers	9, 20
2–207(2)	Battle of the forms	9, 20
2–312(3)	Warranty of title	23
2–314(1)	Warranty of merchantability	23
2–327(1)(c)	Sales on approval	22
2–402(2)	Retention of possession of goods by seller	22
2–403(2)	Entrusting of goods	22
2–509(3)	Risk of loss	22
2–603(1)	Duties after rightful rejection	21

Validation and Preservation of Sales Contracts

One of the requirements of commercial law is the establishment of rules that determine when an agreement is valid. The Code's approach to this is to reduce formal requisites to the bare minimum and attempt to preserve agreements whenever the parties manifest an intent to enter into a contract.

FORMATION OF A SALES CONTRACT

The Code's basic approach to validation is to recognize contracts whenever the parties manifest such an *intent*. This is so whether or not the parties can identify a precise moment at which the contract was formed. Section 2–204(2).

As already noted, the law of sales is a subset of the general law of contracts and is governed by general contract law unless particular provisions of the Code displace the general law. Although the Code leaves the great majority of issues of contract formation to general contract law, it has modified the general law of contract formation in several

significant respects. These modifications were made in order to modernize contract law, to relax the validation requirements of contract formation, and to promote fairness.

MANIFESTATION OF MUTUAL ASSENT

In order for a contract to exist, there must be an objective manifestation of mutual assent: an offer and an acceptance. This section examines the U.C.C. rules that impact offers and acceptances.

Definiteness of an Offer

At common law, the terms of a contract were required to be definite and complete. The Code has rejected the strict approach of the common law by recognizing an agreement as valid, despite missing terms, if there is any reasonably certain basis for granting a remedy. Accordingly, the Code provides that even though one or more terms to a contract have been omitted, a contract need not fail for indefiniteness. Section 2–204(3). It provides standards by which omitted essential terms may be ascertained and supplied, provided the parties intended to enter into a binding agreement. Nevertheless, the more terms the parties leave open, the more likely they do not intend to enter into a binding contract.

Open Price The parties may enter into a contract for the sale of goods even though they have reached no agreement on the price. Under the Code, the price is a reasonable one at the time for delivery where the agreement: (1) says nothing as to price, (2) provides that the parties shall agree later as to the price and they fail to so agree, or (3) fixes the price in terms of some agreed market or other standard or as set by a third person or agency and the price is not so set. Section 2–305(1).

An agreement that the price is to be fixed by the seller or buyer means that it must be fixed in good faith. If the price is to be fixed otherwise than by agreement and is not so fixed through the fault of one of the parties, the other party has an option to treat the contract as canceled or to fix a reasonable price in good faith for the goods. Where the parties intend not to be bound unless the price is fixed or agreed upon as provided in the agreement, and it is not so fixed or agreed upon, the Code, in accordance with the parties' intent, provides that there is no contract. Section 2–305(4).

Open Delivery Unless otherwise agreed, the place of delivery is the seller's place of business. Moreover, the delivery, if unspecified, must be made within a reasonable time period and in a single delivery. Section 2–308.

Open Quantity: Output and Requirement Contracts An agreement of a buyer to purchase the entire output of a seller for a stated period, or an agreement of a seller to supply a buyer with all her requirements of certain goods used in her business operations, may appear to lack definiteness and mutuality of obligation. In either case the exact quantity of goods is not specified, and the seller may have some degree of control over his output, and the buyer over her requirements. Nonetheless, such agreements are enforceable by the application of an objective standard based

upon the good faith of both parties, and the quantities may not be disproportionate to any stated estimate or the prior output or requirements. Section 2–306(1). *See Empire Gas Corp. v. American Bakeries, Co.* For example, the seller cannot operate his factory twenty-four hours a day and insist upon the buyer's taking all of the output when the seller operated the factory only eight hours a day at the time the agreement was made. Nor can the buyer unilaterally triple the size of her business and insist that the seller supply all of her requirements.

Other Open Terms The Code further provides rules, where the parties do not agree, as to the terms of payment, duration, and the particulars of performance. Sections 2–310, 2–309, 2–307, 2–311.

Irrevocable Offers

An offeror may generally withdraw an offer at any time prior to its acceptance. To be effective, notice of revocation of the offer must reach the offeree before he has accepted.

An **option** is a *contract* by which the offeror is bound to hold open an offer for a specified period of time. It must comply with all the requirements of a contract, including consideration. Option contracts apply to all types of contracts, including sales of goods.

The Code has made certain offers—called **firm offers**—irrevocable without any consideration being given for the promise to keep the offer open. The Code provides that a merchant is bound to keep an offer open, for a maximum of three months, if the merchant gives assurance in a signed writing that it will be held open. Section 2–205. The Code, therefore, makes a merchant's written promise not to revoke an offer for a stated period of time enforceable even though no consideration is given the merchant–offeror for that promise. Any firm offer on a form supplied by the offeree must be separately signed by the offeror.

For example, Ben's Brewery approached Flora Flooring, Inc. to replace the tile on Ben's floor. On June 6, Flora sent Ben a written, signed offer to provide and install the tile according to Ben's specifications for $26,000 and promised "that the offer would remain open until July 17." Flora is bound by her firm offer to keep the offer open until July 17. The result, however, would differ if Flora had merely stated that the "offer terminated on July 17," or that "the offer will terminate if not accepted on or before July 17." In both of these instances, there is no assurance to keep the offer open because the offer is not a firm offer and thus could be revoked by Flora at any time prior to Ben's acceptance.

Variant Acceptances

The common law's **"mirror image"** rule, by which the acceptance cannot vary or deviate from the terms of the offer, has been modified by the Code. This modification is necessitated by the realities of modern business practices. A vast number of business transactions use standardized business forms, resulting in what has been termed the **battle of the forms.** For example, a merchant buyer sends to the merchant seller on the buyer's order form a purchase order for 1,000 dozen cotton shirts at $60 per dozen with delivery by October 1 at the buyer's place of business. On the reverse side of this standard form are twenty-five numbered paragraphs containing provisions generally favorable to the buyer. When the seller receives the buyer's order, he sends to the buyer an unequivocal acceptance of the offer on his acceptance form. Although the seller agrees to the buyer's quantity, price, and delivery terms, on the back of his acceptance form the seller has thirty-two numbered paragraphs generally favorable to himself and in significant conflict with the buyer's form. Under the common law's "mirror image" rule, no contract would exist, for there has not been an unequivocal acceptance of all of the material terms of the buyer's offer.

Section 2–207 of the Code applies to variant acceptances and provides:

(1) A definite and seasonable expression of acceptance or a written confirmation which is sent within a reasonable time operates as an acceptance even though it states terms additional to or different from those offered or agreed upon, unless acceptance is expressly made conditional on assent to the additional or different terms.

(2) The additional terms are to be construed as proposals for addition to the contract. Between merchants such terms become part of the contract unless:

(a) the offer expressly limits acceptance to the terms of the offer;

(b) they materially alter it; or

(c) notification of objection to them has already been given or is given within a reasonable time after notice of them is received.

(3) Conduct by both parties which recognizes the existence of a contract is sufficient to establish a contract for sale although the writings of the parties do not otherwise establish a contract. In such case the terms of the particular contract consist of those terms on which the writings of the parties agree, together with any supplementary terms incorporated under any other provisions of this Act.

Thus, the Code addresses the battle of the forms problem by focusing upon the intent of the parties. If the offeree expressly makes his acceptance conditioned upon assent to the additional or different terms, no contract is formed. If the offeree does not expressly make his acceptance conditional upon the offeror's assent to the additional or different terms, a contract is formed. The issue then becomes whether the offeree's different or additional terms become part of the contract. If both offeror and offeree are merchants, **additional** terms will be part of the contract provided they do not materially alter the agreement and are not objected to either in the offer itself or within a reasonable period of time. If either or both of the parties are not merchants, or if the terms materially alter the offer, then the additional terms are merely construed as proposals for addition to the contract. **Different** terms proposed by the offeree also will not become part of the contract unless specifically accepted by the offeror. The courts are divided over what terms are included when the terms conflict. Some courts hold that the offeror's terms govern; other courts hold that the terms cancel each other out and look to the Code to provide the missing terms. See Figure 20–4.

Figure 20–4 Battle of the Forms

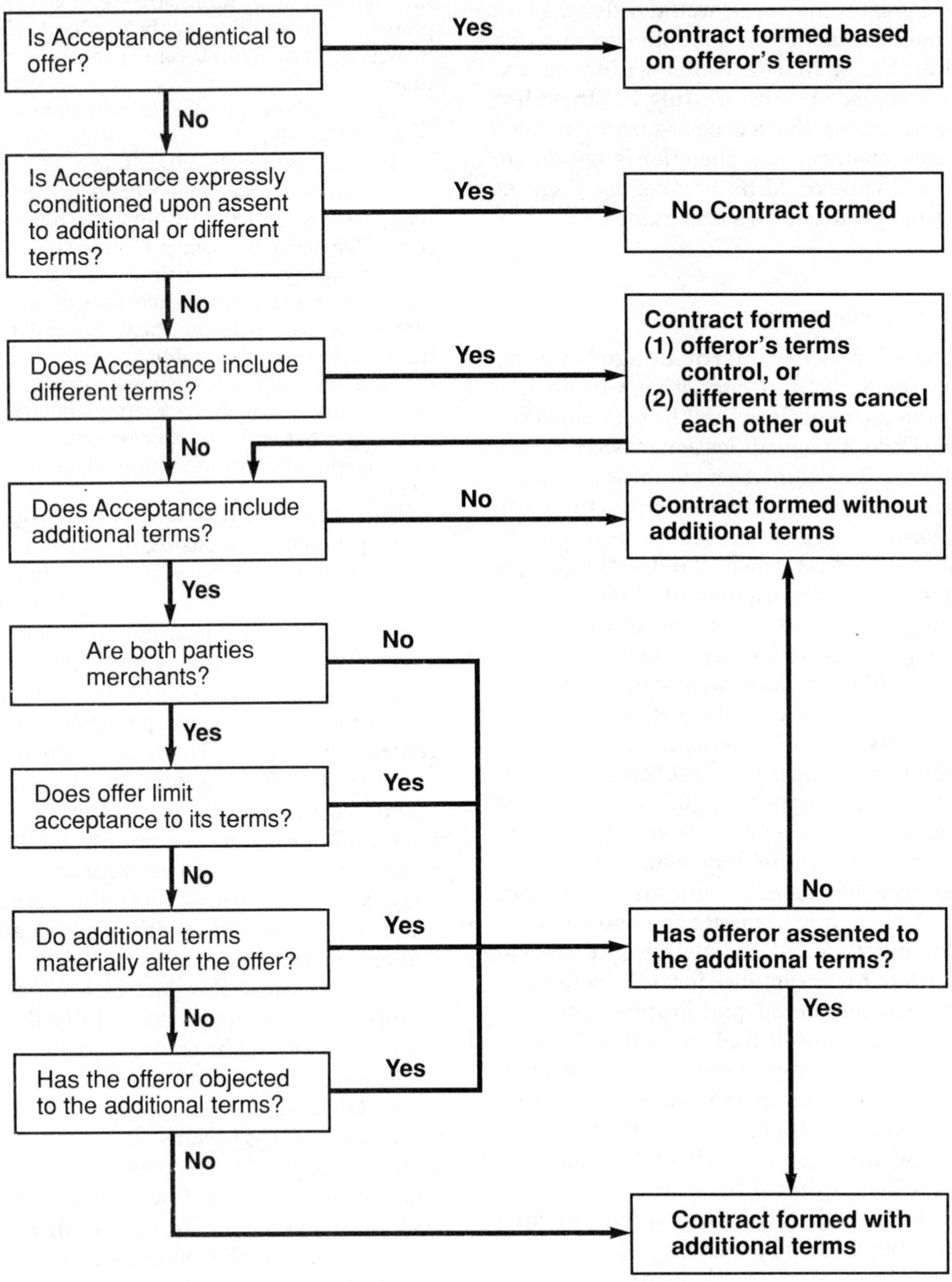

Is Acceptance identical to offer? — **Yes** → **Contract formed based on offeror's terms**

No

Is Acceptance expressly conditioned upon assent to additional or different terms? — **Yes** → **No Contract formed**

No

Does Acceptance include different terms? — **Yes** → **Contract formed (1) offeror's terms control, or (2) different terms cancel each other out**

No

Does Acceptance include additional terms? — **No** → **Contract formed without additional terms**

Yes

Are both parties merchants? — **No**

Yes

Does offer limit acceptance to its terms? — **Yes**

No

Do additional terms materially alter the offer? — **Yes** → **Has offeror assented to the additional terms?**

No

Has the offeror objected to the additional terms? — **Yes**

No

Has offeror assented to the additional terms? — **No** → **Contract formed without additional terms**

Yes → **Contract formed with additional terms**

Applying Section 2–207 to the example above: since both parties are merchants and the acceptance was not conditional upon assent to the additional or different terms, then (1) the contract will be formed without the *seller's different terms* unless they are specifically accepted by the buyer; (2) the contract will be formed without the *seller's additional terms* unless (a) they are specifically accepted by the buyer or (b) the additional terms do not materially alter the offer and they are not objected to by the buyer; and (3) depending upon the jurisdiction either (a) the *buyer's conflicting terms* are included in the contract or (b) the *conflicting terms* cancel each other out and the Code provides the missing terms. *See Dorton v. Collins & Aikman Corp.*

Finally, subsection 3 of 2–207 deals with those situations in which the writings do not form a contract but the conduct of the parties recognizes the existence of one. For instance, Ernest makes an offer to Gwen, who replies with a conditional acceptance. Although no contract has been formed, Gwen ships the ordered goods and Ernest accepts the goods. Subsection 3 provides that in this instance the contract consists of the written terms to which both parties agreed together with supplementary provisions of the Code.

Manner of Acceptance

As with the common law, the offeror may specify the manner in which the offer must be accepted. If the offeror does not and the circumstances do not otherwise clearly indicate, an offer to make a contract invites acceptance in any manner and by any medium reasonable under the circumstances. Section 2–206(1)(a). The Code, therefore, allows flexibility of response and the ability to keep pace with new modes of communication.

An offer to buy goods for prompt or current shipment may be accepted either by a prompt promise to ship or by prompt shipment. Section 2–206(1)(b). Acceptance by performance requires notice within a reasonable time, or the offer may be treated as lapsed.

Auctions

The Code provides that if an auction sale is advertised or announced in explicit terms to be **without reserve,** the auctioneer may not withdraw the article put up for sale unless no bid is made within a reasonable time. Unless the sale is advertised as being without reserve, the sale is **with reserve,** and the auctioneer may withdraw the goods at any time until he announces completion of the sale. Whether with or without reserve, a bidder may retract his bid at any time prior to acceptance by the auctioneer. Such retraction, however, does not revive any previous bid. Section 2–328.

If the auctioneer knowingly receives a bid by or on behalf of the seller, and notice has not been given that the seller reserves the right to bid at the auction sale, the bidder to whom the goods are sold can either avoid the sale or take the goods at the price of the last good faith bid.

CONSIDERATION

The Code has abandoned the common law rule requiring that a modification of an existing contract be supported by consideration in order to be valid. The Code provides that a contract for the sale of goods can be effectively modified without new consideration, provided the modification is made in good faith. Section 2–209.

In addition, (1) any claim of right arising out of an alleged breach of contract can be discharged in whole or in part without consideration by a written waiver or renunciation signed and delivered by the aggrieved party, Section 1–107, and (2) as previously noted, a firm offer is not revocable for lack of consideration.

FORM OF THE CONTRACT

Statute of Frauds

The original statute of frauds applied to contracts for the sale of goods and has been used as a prototype for the Article 2 statute of frauds provision. Section 2–201 of the Code provides that a contract for the sale of goods costing **$500 or more** is not enforceable unless there is some writing sufficient to evidence the existence of a contract between the parties.

Modification of Contracts An agreement modifying a contract must be in writing if the resulting contract is within the statute of frauds. Section 2–209(3). Conversely, if a contract that was previously within the statute of frauds is modified so as to no longer fall within it, the modification is enforceable even if it is oral. Thus, if the parties enter into an oral contract to sell a dining room table for $450 to be delivered to the buyer and later, prior to delivery, *orally* agree that the seller shall stain the table and the buyer pay a price of $550, the modified contract is unenforceable. In contrast, if the parties have a written contract for the sale of 150 bushels of wheat at a price of $4.50 per bushel and later, upon oral agreement, decrease the quantity to 100 bushels at the same price per bushel, the agreement, as modified, is enforceable.

Written Compliance The statute of frauds compliance provisions under the Code are more liberal than the rules under general contract law. The Code requires merely some writing (1) sufficient to indicate that a contract has been made between the parties, (2) signed by the party against whom enforcement is sought or by her authorized agent or broker, and (3) includes a term specifying the quantity. Whereas general contract law requires that all essential terms be included in the writing, under the Code a writing may be sufficient even if it omits or incorrectly states a term agreed upon. This is consistent with other provisions of the Code that contracts may be enforced, even though material terms are omitted. Nevertheless, the contract is enforceable only to the extent of the quantity stated. Given proof that a contract was intended and a signed writing describing the goods, the quantity of goods, and the names of the parties, under the Code the court can supply omitted terms such as price and particulars of performance. Moreover, several related documents may satisfy the writing requirement.

Between merchants, if within a reasonable time a writing in confirmation of the contract is received, the **written merchant confirmation,** if sufficient against the sender, is also sufficient against the recipient of the confirmation unless the recipient gives written notice of his objection within ten days after receiving the confirmation. Section 2–201(2). For example, Brown Co. and ATM Industries enter into an oral contract providing that ATM will deliver 1,000 dozen shirts to Brown at $6.00 per shirt. The next day Brown sends a letter signed by Brown's president to ATM confirming the agreement. The letter contains the quantity term but does not mention the price. Brown is bound by the contract when its authorized agent sent the letter whereas ATM is bound by the oral contract ten days after receiving the letter unless it objects in writing within that time period. Therefore, as further illustrated by *Thomson Printing Machinery Co. v. B.F. Goodrich Co.* in Chapter 14, it is extremely important for merchants to examine their mail carefully and promptly to make certain that any written confirmations conform to their understanding of their outstanding contractual agreements. Where one or both of the parties is not a merchant, however, this rule does not apply.

See Kline Iron & Steel Co., Inc. v. Gray Communications Consultants, Inc.

Exceptions A contract that does not satisfy the writing requirement but is otherwise valid is enforceable in the following instances.

The Code permits an oral contract for the sale of goods to be enforced against a party who in his pleading, testimony, or otherwise in court **admits** that a contract was made, but the Code limits enforcement to the quantity of goods so admitted. Section 2–201(3)(b). This provision recognizes that the policy behind the statute of frauds does not apply when the party seeking to avoid the oral contract admits under oath the existence of the contract.

The Code also permits enforcement of an oral contract for goods **specially manufactured** for the buyer. Section 2–201(3)(a). Nevertheless, if the goods, although manufactured on special order, are readily marketable in the ordinary course of the seller's business, the contract is not enforceable unless in writing.

In most States, prior to the Code, delivery and acceptance of part of the goods or payment of part of the price and acceptance of the payment made the entire oral contract enforceable against the buyer who had received part delivery or against the seller who had received part payment. Under the Code such "partial performance" validates the contract only for the goods that have been **delivered and accepted** or for which **payment** has been **accepted.** Section 2–201(3)(c). To illustrate, Debra orally agrees to buy 1,000 watches from Brian for $15,000. Brian delivers 300 watches to Debra, who receives and accepts the watches. The oral contract is enforceable to the extent of 300 watches ($4,500)—those received and accepted; but is unenforceable to the extent of 700 watches ($10,500).

But what if the contract is indivisible, such as one for the sale of an automobile, so that if part payment is made there is only a choice between not enforcing the contract or enforcing the contract as a whole? Presently, there is a division of authority on this issue although the better rule appears to be that such part payment and acceptance makes the entire contract enforceable.

Parol Evidence

Contractual terms that are set forth in a writing intended by the parties as a final expression of their agreement may not be contradicted by evidence of any prior agreement or of a contemporaneous agreement but, under the Code, the terms may be explained or supplemented by (1) course of dealing, usage of trade, or course of performance; and (2) evidence of consistent additional terms unless the writing was intended as the complete and exclusive statement of the terms of the agreement. Section 2–202.

Seal

The Uniform Commercial Code makes seals inoperative with respect to contracts for the sale of goods or an offer to buy or sell goods. Section 2–203.

For a comparison of general contract and sales of goods, see Figure 20–5.

Figure 20–5 Contract Law Compared with Law of Sales

	Contract Law	Law of Sales
Definiteness	Contract must include all material terms.	Open terms permitted if parties intend to make a contract. Section 2–204.
Counteroffers	Acceptance must be a mirror image of offer. Counteroffer and conditional acceptance are rejections.	Battle of Forms. Section 2–207. See Figure 20–4.
Modification of Contract	Consideration is required.	Consideration is not required. Section 2–209.
Irrevocable Offers	Options.	Options. Firm offers up to three months binding without consideration. Section 2–205.
Statute of Frauds	Writing must include all material terms.	Writing must include quantity term. Specially manufactured goods. Confirmation by merchants. Delivery or payment and acceptance. Admissions. Section 2–201.

FUNDAMENTALS OF ARTICLE 2A—LEASES

Leases of personal property are of great economic significance and exceed $100 billion annually. Leases range from a consumer's renting an automobile or a lawnmower to a Fortune 500 corporation's leasing heavy industrial machinery. Despite the frequent and widespread use of personal property leases, the law governing these transactions had been patched together from the common law of personal property, real estate leasing law, and the Uniform Commercial Code (Articles 2 and 9). Except for several provisions, the U.C.C. did not directly apply to leases. Some courts, nevertheless, have held that the U.C.C. is applicable to leases of goods because a lease is a transaction in goods, while other courts have refused to apply the Code to leases because actual title to the goods never passed. A number of other courts have applied the Code by analogy to leases. Even in States where Article 2 was extended to leases, however, which provisions were to be applied remained unclear. In any event, there had been no unified or uniform statutory law governing the leases of personal property.

To fill this void, in 1987 the drafters of the Code approved Article 2A—Leases. This Article is an analogue of Article 2 and adopts many of the rules contained in Article 2. Article 2A is an attempt to codify in one statute all the rules governing the leasing of personal property. A number of States have already enacted Article 2A.

Definition of a Lease

A lease of goods is defined as a "transfer of the right to possession and use of goods for a term in return for consideration, but . . . retention or creation of a security interest is not a lease." Section 2A–103(1)(j). If a transaction is within this definition of a lease it is governed by Article 2A, but if the transaction is a security interest disguised as a lease it is governed by Article 9. The categorization of a transaction as a lease has significant implications not only for the parties to the lease

but also for third parties. If the transaction is deemed to be a lease, then the residual interest in the goods belongs to the lessor, who need not file publicly to protect this interest. On the other hand, if the transaction is a security interest, then the provisions of Article 9 regarding enforceability, perfection, priority, and remedies apply.

Warranties

Article 2A carries over the warranty provisions of Article 2 with relatively minor revision to reflect differences in style, leasing terminology, or leasing practices. The creation of express warranties and, except for finance leases (discussed below), the imposition of the implied warranties of merchantability and fitness for a particular purpose are virtually identical to their Article 2 analogues. Article 2 and Article 2A diverge somewhat in their treatment of the warranties of title and infringement as well as in their provisions for the exclusion and modification of warranties.

Default and Remedies

The approach to default and remedies within Article 2A is a synthesis of the treatments found in Article 2 and Article 9. Provisions are made for both lessor's remedies upon the lessee's default and for lessee's remedies upon the lessor's default. This is a substantial departure from Article 9, which provides remedies only for the secured party. As is true elsewhere in Article 2A, emphasis is placed on the freedom of the parties to contract among themselves. The lease agreement may include rights and remedies for default in addition to, or in substitution for, those provided in Article 2A. Section 2A–503(1). Article 2A explicitly rejects the notion of election of remedies and provides that its remedies are cumulative. Whether one remedy bars another is a function of whether the injured party has been placed in as good a position as though the lease agreement has been fully performed. Access may be had to both the rights and remedies provided under the lease agreement as well as to those provided by Article 2A. Sections 2A–508(3) and 2A–523(2). In addition, the parties are free to define the circumstances that will trigger a default.

Consumer Leases

Article 2A affords special treatment for consumer leases. The definition of a consumer lease requires that (1) the transaction meet the definition of a lease under Article 2A; (2) the lessor be regularly engaged in the business of leasing *or* selling goods; (3) the lessee be an individual, not an organization; (4) the lessee take the lease interest primarily for a personal, family, or household purpose; and (5) the total payments under the lease do not exceed $25,000. Section 2A–103(1)(e). Although consumer protection for lease transactions is primarily left to other State and Federal law, Article 2A does contain a number of provisions that apply to consumer leases and may *not* be varied by agreement of the parties.

As to *all* leases, a court faced with an unconscionable contract or clause may refuse to enforce the entire contract or just the unconscionable clause, or the court may limit the application of the unconscionable clause to avoid an unconscionable result. This is similar to Article 2's treatment of unconscionable clauses in sales contracts. A lessee under a consumer lease, however, is provided with additional protection against unconscionability. In the case of a consumer lease, if a court as a matter of law finds that any part of a lease contract has been *induced* by unconscionable conduct, the court is expressly empowered to grant appropriate relief. Section 2A–108(2). The same results when unconscionable conduct occurs in the collection of a claim arising from a consumer lease contract. The *explicit* availability of relief for consumers subjected to unconscionable conduct (procedural unconscionability)—in addition to an unconscionable contract provision (substantive unconscionability)—is a departure from Article 2.

An additional remedy provided by Article 2A for consumers is the award of attorney's fees. If the court finds unconscionability with respect to a consumer lease, it shall award reasonable attorney's fees to the lessee. Section 2A–108(4)(a).

Finance Leases

A finance lease is a special type of lease transaction generally involving three parties instead of two. Whereas in the typical lease situation the lessor is also the supplier of the goods, in a finance lease arrangement the lessor is a separate party from the supplier. The lessor's primary function in a finance lease is to provide financing to the lessee for a lease of goods provided by the supplier. For example, under a finance lease arrangement a manufacturer supplies goods pursuant to the lessee's instructions or specifications. The party functioning as the lessor will then either purchase those goods from the supplier or lease them as the prime lessee from the supplier. In turn, the lessor enters into a lease or sublease of the goods to the lessee. Comment g to Section 2A–103. Because the finance lessor functions merely as a source of credit, it will typically have no special expertise as to the goods. Due to the limited role usually played by the finance lessor, Article 2A treats finance leases differently from ordinary leases.

The lessee looks almost exclusively to the supplier for warranties and other promises. Accordingly, the benefit of the warranties and promises made by the supplier to the lessor under the supply contract is extended to the lessee under the finance lease. Section 2A–209(1). In return for extending the benefits of the supplier's warranties to the lessee, the Code makes the finance lessee's promise to pay the finance lessor binding whether or not the goods are defective or the lessor performs as required by the lease agreement. Section 2A–407(1). Finance leases that are consumer leases are not subject to this provision. The general warranty provisions of Article 2A have limited application between the lessor and lessee in a finance lease transaction. Although the finance lessor is liable for breach of any express warranties she makes and for the warranty of quiet possession, she is relieved from the other warranties that are statutorily imposed on ordinary lessors.

CASES

Governing Law/Statute of Frauds

KLINE IRON & STEEL CO., INC. v. GRAY COMMUNICATIONS CONSULTANTS, INC.

United States District Court, South Carolina, 1989.
715. F. Supp. 135.

HENDERSON, J.

This matter is before the court on the defendant's motion for summary judgment * * * Because the court finds that there is no genuine issue of material fact and that the defendant is entitled to judgment as a matter of law, it grants the defendant's motion and orders that judgment be entered in the defendant's favor.

* * *

In early 1986, the defendant contacted various television tower builders, including the plaintiff, concerning manufacture and erection of a television tower near Huttig, Arkansas. The plaintiff and defendant subsequently conducted substantial negotiation by telephone, through correspondence and in person, culminating in a meeting of their representatives in Albany, Georgia, on June 20, 1986. According to the plaintiff, they reached an oral agreement during that meeting that the plaintiff was to provide the defendant's tower for a total price of $1,485,368.

On June 24, B.H. Kline, the plaintiff's chairman, wrote the defendant a letter which stated as follows:

"Thank you for the order for the subject project.
"Separately the contract is being mailed today by United Parcel Service.
"We look forward to full release on or about August 1, 1986."

On the same day, David E. Monts, sales manager for the plaintiff's tower division, sent the defendant a written "proposal" accompanied by the following letter:

"Attached are an original and two (2) carbon copies of our Proposal No. 620–M–86R covering the subject as agreed upon in your office last Friday, June 20, 1986. Please sign the original and one (1) copy on the lower left corner of page 9 and return to us for our execution. We will return one (1) executed copy for your file.
"Again we thank you for selecting us for this project. We assure you it is receiving our best attention. Our Engineering Department is proceeding with the designs, fabrication drawings, and material orders.
"We look forward to your receiving the necessary permits."

The "proposal" consists of five pages of typewritten terms, setting forth specifications for the manufacture, assembly and erection of a television tower and related items and four pages of preprinted "Terms and Conditions of Sale." The printed portion includes the following relevant terms:

"Acceptance of Proposal
"This proposal is for immediate acceptance and prior to such acceptance is subject to modification or withdrawal without notice.
"Acceptance of this proposal will evidence Buyer's intent that the sale be governed solely by the terms and conditions of this proposal.
"Any modifying, inconsistent or additional terms and conditions of Buyer's acceptance shall not become a part of any contract resulting from this proposal unless agreed to in writing by Kline.
"Any order or offer by Buyer as a result of this proposal shall not be binding upon Kline until accepted by Kline in writing by an officer of Kline. If accepted by Kline, this proposal shall constitute the agreement between the Buyer and Kline."

On June 30, Russ Abernathy, the defendant's then Director of Engineering, telephoned David Monts advising him that the defendant had received a lower quote from another tower company and asking that the plaintiff justify its higher price. In this and other calls between June 30 and July 14, 1986, the defendant's representatives indicated they felt there was no contract. Finally, on July 14, Perley E. Eppley, Sr., the defendant's Vice President of Engineering, wrote the plaintiff a letter which stated in part:

"As there is no contract or money has transferred and your competition is discussing the tower situation with our people, it has gotten into a very embarrassing situation as you have elected not to address this particular problem. If this continues much longer, a decision will have to be made and I feel it will not be favorable to Kline."

In a subsequent letter dated August 7, 1988, Mr. Eppley informed the plaintiff: "At this time senior management has made a decision to go another direction and not go with your proposal."

* * *

It is undisputed that no writing exists memorializing the alleged oral agreement and satisfying the requirements of § 2–201(1). The plaintiff asserts, however, that the agreement is not rendered unenforceable by this provision because the contract is not for the sale of goods and therefore not subject to the writing requirement of § 2–201(1), . . . and the contract falls within the "merchant's exception" to the statute of frauds set forth in § 2–201(2).

* * *

The UCC definition of "goods" is very broad. [Citations.] * * * Construing this language, the South Carolina Supreme Court has held that a contract for the sale of a mobile home was a transaction in goods because the mobile home was "movable at the time of sale." [Citation.] This court perceives no reason not to characterize the television tower and other items to be provided under the contract as goods under § 2–105(1) since they would be movable at the time of identification to the contract. Nevertheless, the plaintiff asserts this particular contract is an agreement to provide services rather than to

sell goods. In support of its argument, the plaintiff stresses the "importance of the specialized knowledge and skill required to design, fabricate and erect such a product." . . .

* * *

In considering whether a hybrid contract is for the sale of goods under the UCC, courts generally employ the "predominant thrust" or "predominant factor" test. [Citations.] Under this test, particular transactions are "for the sale of goods" if "their predominant factor, their thrust, their purpose, reasonably stated, is the rendition of service, with goods incidentally involved (e.g., contract with artist for painting) or is a transaction of sale, with labor incidentally involved (e.g., installation of a water heater in a bathroom)." [Citation.] The court finds that the primary thrust of the alleged contract is for the sale of goods.

* * *

First, the transaction by its very nature appears to be one for the sale of a television tower. The plaintiff itself admits that "[t]he contract between Plaintiff and Defendant was to furnish a tower for a fixed price."

Second, the terms and language of the proposal show that the alleged agreement is predominantly for the sale of goods. Throughout the proposal, the defendant is referred to as the "Buyer," a term indicative of a transaction for the sale of goods. [Citation.] The warranty language of the proposal is also peculiar to goods, not services. [Citations.] Further, more than two of the proposal's five typewritten pages are taken up with a detailed description of the tower and various accessories to be provided by the plaintiff and shipped "F.O.B. jobsite." By contrast, the erection services to be provided are listed in summary fashion in approximately one page. Finally, the proposal cites only the total contract price without allocating a particular amount to services. [Citations.]

* * * According to [plaintiff], the price of the assembly and erection services is at most $390,702 or approximately 26% of the total contract price. This price allocation is consistent with the proposal's requirement that 75% of the total price be paid "when tower materials are ready for shipment." That so little of the total contract price is attributable to the services to be performed demonstrates that those services are merely incidental to the sale of the tower and accessory products. [Citation.]

In light of these facts, the court concludes that the predominant thrust of the alleged agreement is to provide goods for the defendant and the contract is one for the sale of goods subject to the writing requirement of § 2–201.

* * *

Next, the plaintiff asserts that, even if the contract is for the sale of goods and therefore subject to the requirements of § 2–201, the statute of frauds is satisfied under the "merchant's exception" in § 2–201(2). * * * The plaintiff contends that the proposal and the letters its agents sent to the defendant on June 24, 1986, constitute a confirmation of the oral contract which satisfies the requirements of this section. The defendant argues, however, that those documents do not bring the alleged oral agreement within the merchant's exception because (1) the defendant is not a "merchant," (2) the writings require the defendant to take further action to accept the proposal's terms, (3) the writings impose no binding obligations on the plaintiff and (4) written notice of objection was given within ten days. The court agrees with the defendant that the alleged oral agreement does not come within the merchant's exception to the statute of frauds because the June 26 writings expressly require further action by the defendant and because they are not binding against the plaintiff.

Although Monts's letter of June 26, 1986, states that the terms of the proposal are "as agreed upon" at the June 20, 1986, meeting, both letters, and especially the proposal, expressly require that the plaintiff take further action for the agreement to be consummated. B.H. Kline's letter thanks the defendant for its "order" and advises that a written contract is being sent separately. Monts's letter directs the defendant to sign and return one copy of the proposal for the plaintiff's "execution." The proposal itself provides that it is for

the defendant's "immediate acceptance" and that its terms can be modified or withdrawn without notice prior to such acceptance. In order to be a "confirmation" under § 2–201(1), a writing must "at least 'indicate that a binding or completed transaction has been made.' " [Citations.]

* * *

Because the oral agreement alleged by the plaintiff is a contract for the sale of goods and because no writing exists sufficient to satisfy the UCC statute of frauds, the court holds that as a matter of law there is no enforceable contract between the parties and directs that summary judgment be entered in the defendant's favor.

Good Faith/Requirements Contract

EMPIRE GAS CORP. v. AMERICAN BAKERIES CO.

United States Court of Appeals, Seventh Circuit, 1988.
5 UCC Rep. Serv.2d 545.

POSNER, J.

This appeal in a diversity contract case presents a fundamental question—surprisingly little discussed by either courts or commentators—in the law of requirements contracts. Is such a contract essentially a buyer's option, entitling him to purchase all he needs of the good in question on the terms set forth in the contract, but leaving him free to purchase none if he wishes provided that he does not purchase the good from anyone else and is not acting out of ill will toward the seller?

Empire Gas Corporation is a retail distributor of liquefied petroleum gas, better known as "propane." It also sells converters that enable gasoline-powered motor vehicles to operate on propane. The sharp rise in gasoline prices in 1979 and 1980 made American Bakeries Company, which operated a fleet of more than 3,000 motor vehicles to serve its processing plants and bakeries, interested in the possibility of converting its fleet to propane, which was now one-third to one-half less expensive than gasoline. Discussions between the companies resulted in an agreement in principle. Empire Gas sent American Bakeries a draft of its standard "Guaranteed Fuel Supply Contract," which would have required American Bakeries to install a minimum number of conversion units each month and to buy all the propane for the converted vehicles from Empire Gas for eight years. American Bakeries rejected the contract and Empire Gas prepared a new one, which was executed on April 17, 1980, and which was "for approximately three thousand (3,000) [conversion] units, more or less depending upon requirements of Buyer, consisting of Fuel Tank, Fuel Lock Off Switch, Converter & appropriate Carburetor & Small Parts Kit," at a price of $750 per unit. American Bakeries agreed "to purchase propane motor fuel solely from EMPIRE GAS CORPORATION at all locations where EMPIRE GAS has supplied carburetion and dispensing equipment as long as EMPIRE GAS CORPORATION remains in a reasonably competitive price posture with other major suppliers." The contract was to last for four years.

American Bakeries never ordered any equipment or propane from Empire Gas. Apparently within days after the signing of the contract American Bakeries decided not to convert its fleet to propane. No reason has been given for the decision.

Empire Gas brought suit against American Bakeries for breach of contract and won a jury verdict for $3,254,963, representing lost profits on 2,242 conversion units (the jury's estimate of American Bakeries' requirements) and on the propane fuel that the converted vehicles would have consumed during the contract period. The judge added $581,916 in prejudgment interest.

* * *

The heart of this case is the instruction concerning American Bakeries' obligation under the contract. If there were no legal category of "requirements" contracts and no provision of the Uniform Commercial Code governing such contracts, a strong argument could be made that American Bakeries agreed to buy 3,000 conversion units or *slightly* more or

slightly less, depending on its actual needs, and hence that it broke the contract by taking none. This is not only a semantically permissible reading of the contract but one supported by the discussions that the parties had before the contract was signed . . . in which American Bakeries assured Empire Gas that it was planning to convert its entire fleet. American Bakeries insisted on adding the phrase "more or less depending upon requirements of Buyer" just in case its estimate of 3,000 was off, and this is quite different from supposing that the phrase was added so that American Bakeries would have no obligation to buy any units at all.

The parties agree, however, that despite the negotiating history and the inclusion in the contract of a specific estimate of quantity, the quoted phrase sorted the contract into the legal bin labeled "requirements contract" and thereby brought it under the governance of § 2–306(1) of the Uniform Commercial Code, which provides:

"A term which measures the quantity by the output of the seller or the requirements of the buyer means such actual output or requirements as may occur in good faith, except that no quantity unreasonably disproportionate to any stated estimate or in the absence of a stated estimate to any normal or otherwise comparable prior output or requirements may be tendered or demanded."

* * *

The interpretive question involves the proviso dealing with "quantity unreasonably disproportionate to any stated estimate." This limitation is fairly easy to understand when the disproportion takes the form of the buyer's demanding more than the amount estimated. If there were no ceiling, and if the price happened to be advantageous to the buyer, he might increase his "requirements" so that he could resell the good at a profit. [Citations.] This would place him in competition with the seller—a result the parties would not have wanted when they signed the contract. So the "unreasonably disproportionate" proviso carries out the likely intent of the parties. The only problem is that the same result could easily be reached by interpretation of the words "good faith" in the preceding clause of § 2–306(1), thus making the proviso redundant. * * *

The proviso does not distinguish between the buyer who demands more than the stated estimate and the buyer who demands less, and therefore if read literally it would forbid a buyer to take (much) less than the stated estimate. Since the judge did not attempt to interpret the statute the jury may have read it literally, and if so the judge in effect directed a verdict for Empire Gas. The stated estimate was for 3,000 units; American Bakeries took none; if this was not unreasonably disproportionate to the stated estimate, what buyer shortfall could be?

So we must decide whether the proviso should be read literally when the buyer is demanding less rather than more than the stated estimate. There are no cases on the question in Illinois, and authority elsewhere is sparse, considering how often (one might think) the question must have arisen. But the clearly dominant approach is not to construe the proviso literally, but instead to treat the overdemanding and underdemanding cases differently. [Citations.]

* * *

More important is the fact that the entire proviso is in a sense redundant given the words "good faith" in the main clause of the statute. The proviso thus seems to have been designed to explicate the term "good faith" rather than to establish an independent legal standard. And the aspect of good faith that required explication had only to do with disproportionately *large* demands. If the buyer saw an opportunity to increase his profits by reselling the seller's goods because the market price had risen above the contract price, the exploitation of that opportunity might not *clearly* spell bad faith; the proviso was added to close off the opportunity. There is no indication that the draftsmen were equally, if at all, concerned about the case where the buyer takes less than his estimated requirements, provided, of course, that he does not buy from anyone else. We conclude that the Illinois courts would allow a buyer to reduce his requirements to zero if he was acting in good faith, even though the contract contained an estimate of those requirements.

This conclusion would be greatly strengthened—too much so, as we shall see—if the only purpose of a requirements contract were to give the seller a reasonably assured market for his product *by forbidding the buyer to satisfy any of his needs by buying from another supplier.* (An output contract, also dealt with in § 2–306(1), gives the buyer a reasonably assured source of supply by forbidding the seller to sell any of his output to any other buyer.) The buyer's undertaking to deal exclusively with a particular seller gives the seller some, although far from complete, assurance of having a market for his goods; and of course he must compensate the buyer for giving up the opportunity to shop around for a better deal from competing sellers.

There was no breach of *this* obligation, or, at most, a trivial one. (American Bakeries did convert 229 of its vehicles to propane, using equipment bought from another company; but the record is silent on how many, if any, of these purchases occurred while the contract with Empire Gas was in force.) If the obligation were not just to refrain from buying a competitor's goods but to buy approximately the stated estimate (or, in the absence of any estimate, the buyer's "normal" requirements), the contract would be altogether more burdensome to the buyer. Instead of just committing himself not to buy from a competitor even if the competitor offered a better product or terms of sale, he would be committing himself to go through with whatever project generated the estimate of required quantity, no matter what happened over the life of the project save those exceptional events that would excuse performance under the related excuses of force majeure, impossibility, impracticability, or frustration. This would be a big commitment to infer from the inclusion in the contract of an estimated quantity, at least once the parties concede as they do here that their contract really is a requirements contract and not a contract for the estimate itself—not, in other words, a fixed-quantity contract.

Both extreme interpretations—that the buyer need only refrain from dealing with a competitor of the seller, and that the buyer cannot go significantly beneath the estimated quantity except in dire circumstances—must be rejected, as we shall see. * * *

The Uniform Commercial Code does not contain a definition of "good faith" that seems applicable to the buyer under a requirements contract. Compare § 2–104(1) with § 2–103(1)(b). Nor has the term a settled meaning in law generally; it is a chameleon. [Citations.] Clearly, American Bakeries was acting in bad faith if during the contract period it bought propane conversion units from anyone other than Empire Gas, or made its own units, or reduced its purchases because it wanted to hurt Empire Gas (for example because they were competitors in some other market). Equally clearly, it was not acting in bad faith if it had a business reason for deciding not to convert that was independent of the terms of the contract or any other aspect of its relationship with Empire Gas, such as a drop in the demand for its bakery products that led it to reduce or abandon its fleet of delivery trucks. A harder question is whether it was acting in bad faith if it changed its mind about conversion for no (disclosed) reason. There is no evidence in the record on why it changed its mind beyond vague references to "budget problems" that, so far as appears, may have been nothing more than a euphemism for a decision by American Bakeries not to allocate funds for conversion to propane.

If no reason at all need be given for scaling back one's requirements even to zero, then a requirements contract is from the buyer's standpoint just an option to purchase up to (or slightly beyond, i.e., within the limits of reasonable proportionality) the stated estimate on the terms specified in the contract, except that the buyer cannot refuse to exercise the option because someone offers him better terms. This is not an unreasonable position, but it is not the law.

* * *

It is a nice question how exigent the buyer's change of circumstances must be to allow him to scale down his requirements from either the estimated level or, in the absence of estimate, the "normal" level. Obviously it need not be so great as to give him a defense under the doctrines of impossibility, impracticability, or frustration, or under a force majeure clause. Yet, although more than whim is required, [citation], how much more is unclear. * * *

The essential ingredient of good faith in the case of the buyer's reducing his estimated requirements is that he not merely have had second thoughts about the terms of the contract and want to get out of it. [Citations.] Whether the buyer has any greater obligation is unclear, but need not be decided here. Once it is decided (as we have) that a buyer cannot arbitrarily declare his requirements to be zero, this becomes an easy case, because American Bakeries has never given any reason for its change of heart.

* * *

The judgment is affirmed except for the award of prejudgment interest. Modified and affirmed.

Unconscionability

CONSTRUCTION ASSOCIATES, INC. v. FARGO WATER EQUIPMENT CO.

North Dakota Supreme Court, 1989.
446 N.W.2d 237.

ERICKSTAD, J.

Johns-Manville Sales Corporation (J-M) appealed from a district court judgment entered upon a jury verdict finding it liable for $140,000 in damages for defective pipe. We affirm.

In 1977 Construction Associates, Inc., was the successful bidder to construct a water supply line for the city of Breckenridge, Minnesota. Construction Associates purchased from Fargo Water Equipment (Fargo Water) a large supply of polyvinyl chloride (PVC) pipe manufactured by J-M. The Breckenridge pipeline was completed during the summer of 1978.

The line eventually developed numerous leaks. J-M sent a technical field specialist to

Breckenridge in August 1978. On his recommendation, the line was pumped to a high pressure using a fire engine in an attempt to set the rubber gaskets in the joints. This temporarily remedied the problem, but additional leaks soon occurred. Fargo Water recommended repairs using bell clamps, which Construction Associates attempted without success. Finally, Construction Associates repaired the leaks as they were discovered by removing the defective joints and replacing them with stainless steel sleeves. At the time of trial in 1981, seventy leaks had been discovered and repaired.

Construction Associates brought this action against J-M and Fargo Water, asserting that the pipe was defective and that the defects caused the leaks in the Breckenridge line. * * * The jury awarded Construction Associates $140,000 for its expenses in repairing the line against J-M * * * J-M appealed.

* * *

J-M asserts that the trial court erred in concluding that a clause limiting the remedies available upon breach of its warranty and specifically excluding liability for consequential damages was unconscionable.

Construction Associates purchased the pipe from Fargo Water, and at the time of contracting had no direct contact with J-M. J-M shipped the pipe directly to the job site in Breckenridge. Included with each shipment of pipe was an installation guide, which expressly stated that it was "written especially for the installer and those who direct the actual handling and installation of Johns-Manville PVC Pressure Rated Pipe." On page three of the installation guide J-M expressly warranted the pipe to be free from defects in workmanship and materials. A limitation of liability clause was also included:

"Limitation of Liability

"It is expressly understood and agreed that the limit of J-M's liability shall be the resupply of a like quantity of nondefective Product and that J-M shall have no such liability except where the damage or claim results solely from breach of J-M's warranty. It is also agreed that J-M shall not be liable for any incidental, consequen-

tial or other damages for any alleged negligence, breach of warranty, strict liability, or any other theory, other than the limited liability set forth above."

The first sentence of the clause is essentially a limitation of remedies. The second sentence is a specific exclusion of consequential or incidental damages.

J-M asserted the provisions of the clause as a defense, arguing that it could only be held liable for replacement of defective pipe. The trial court determined that the limitation of remedies and exclusion of damages were unconscionable and therefore unenforceable.* * *

[U.C.C. § 2–719] specifically allows the parties to an agreement to limit the remedies available upon breach and to exclude consequential damages:

* * *

By its terms, § 2–302 [unconscionable contract or clause] applies to any clause of the contract. Courts thus have construed §§ 2–302 and 2–719 together in holding that a general limitation of remedies clause, including those limiting liability to repair or replacement, may be subject to unconscionability analysis under the Code. [Citations.]

The determination whether a particular contractual provision is unconscionable is a question of law for the court. [Citations.] The court is to look at the contract from the perspective of the time it was entered into, without the benefit of hindsight. * * *

Courts and commentators have generally viewed the Code's unconscionability provisions within a two-pronged framework: procedural unconscionability, which encompasses factors relating to unfair surprise, oppression, and inequality of bargaining power, and substantive unconscionability, which focuses upon the harshness or onesidedness of the contractual provision in question. [Citations.]

A) Procedural Unconscionability We initially note that this case presents a commercial, rather than a consumer, transaction.

Although courts have generally been more reluctant to find unconscionability in purely commercial settings, [citation], under appropriate circumstances a contractual provision may be found unconscionable even in a commercial setting. [Citations.]

Courts' general skepticism of unconscionability claims in purely commercial transactions stems from the presumption that businessmen possess a greater degree of commercial understanding and substantially stronger economic bargaining power than the ordinary consumer. [Citation.] Some courts, however, have recognized that disparity of bargaining power may exist even in traditional commercial transactions: * * *

The circumstances presented in this case demonstrate a substantial inequality in bargaining power between J-M and Construction Associates. Construction Associates is a relatively small local construction firm, while J-M is part of an enormous, highly diversified, international conglomerate. The limitation of remedies and exclusion of damages were part of a pre-printed installation guide included with all shipments of J-M Pipe. J-M has continually stressed on appeal that those limitations and exclusions are included in all of its brochures and guides. It is obvious that there is no room for bargaining or negotiation as to the warranty provisions.

We also note that the facts in this case demonstrate an actual lack of negotiation coupled with elements of unfair surprise. * * *

"To be a part of the bargain, a provision limiting the defendant's liability must, unless incorporated into the contract through prior course of dealings or trade usage, have been bargained for, brought to the purchaser's attention or be conspicuous. . . . If not, the seller has no reasonable expectation that the remedy was being so restricted and the restriction cannot be said to be part of the agreement of the parties. . . . Nor does the mere fact that both parties are businessmen justify the utilization of unfair surprise to the detriment of one of the parties since the Code specifically provides for the recovery of consequential damages and an individual should be able to rely on their existence in the absence of being informed to the contrary

either directly or constructively through prior course of dealings or trade usage. * * *

The limitations and exclusions clause in this case can hardly be described as "bargained for." The clauses were included on page three of a pre-printed installation guide expressly directed to the worker in the field, rather than to officers of Construction Associates. Construction Associates was not apprised at the time of contracting that their remedies under the Code were being limited or excluded. It would be within J-M's control to do so by, for example, requiring its dealers to accept orders for pipe only upon a J-M form which included the limitations and exclusions and which required the purchaser's signature. Clearly an element of procedural unconscionability is present where through a pre-printed guide which was not provided to Construction Associates (and then only to field workers) until long after the sales contract had been finalized.

B) Substantive Unconscionability Substantive unconscionability focuses upon the harshness of the particular contractual terms:

"Substantive unconscionability concerns the question whether the terms themselves are commercially reasonable. . . . While the Code permits the limitation of remedies, it must be remembered that it disfavors them and specifically provides for their deletion if they would act to deprive a contracting party of reasonable protection against a breach. . . . The Code (§ 1–106(1)) specifically provides that the remedies provided by it shall be liberally construed to the end that the aggrieved party may be put in as good a position as if the other party had fully performed." Frank's Maintenance & Engineering, Inc. v. C.A. Roberts Co. [citation].

Similarly, the Official Comment to § 2–719 of the Code stresses that contractual provisions which would deprive a party of "minimum adequate remedies" for breach will not be enforced:

* * *

The clause at issue here would limit Construction Associates' remedy for J-M's breach to a like quantity of replacement pipe, with no recovery of consequential damages. Construction Associates argues, with support in the evidence, that replacement pipe is not used when making repairs to leaking joints on a completed underground water pipeline. Because the accepted method of repair is to cut out the leaking joint and repair it with a stainless steel sleeve, Construction Associates argues, the replacement pipe would be useless in effecting repairs upon the line. The trial court determined that J-M's limited remedy "amount[ed] to nothing whatsoever." J-M has not pointed to any evidence in the record which refutes Construction Associates' contention or which in any manner suggests that replacement PVC pipe could be used to effect the necessary repairs on the leaking joints.

Numerous courts, in a variety of commercial and consumer contexts, have held limitations and exclusions unconscionable when they leave the non-breaching party with no effective remedy. [Citations.] This is particularly true where the defect in the product is latent, so that the buyer is unable to discover the defect until additional damages are incurred. [Citations.] In this case, Construction Associates did not discover the defects until the pipe was assembled and placed underground.

The concept of unconscionability must necessarily be applied in a flexible manner, taking into consideration all of the facts and circumstances of a particular case. [Citation.] The circumstances of this case demonstrate elements of procedural and substantive unconscionability which, when viewed in totality, adequately support the trial court's conclusion that the clause limiting remedies and excluding consequential damages was unconscionable under the relevant statutory provisions. * * *

The judgment of the district court is affirmed.

Variant Acceptances: Battle of the Forms

DORTON v. COLLINS & AIKMAN CORP.

United States Court of Appeals, Sixth Circuit, 1972.
453 F.2d 1161.

CELEBREZZE, J.

[Plaintiffs-Appellees, Frank E. Dorton and J.A. Castle] (hereinafter The Carpet Mart), carpet retailers in Kingsport, Tennessee, purchased carpets from Defendant-Appellant (hereinafter Collins & Aikman), incorporated under the laws of the State of Delaware, with its principal place of business in New York, New York, and owner of a carpet manufacturing plant (formerly the Painter Carpet Mills, Inc.) located in Dalton, Georgia. The Carpet Mart originally brought this action in a Tennessee state trial court, seeking compensatory and punitive damages in the amount of $450,000 from Collins & Aikman for the latter's alleged fraud, deceit, and misrepresentation in the sale of what were supposedly carpets manufactured from 100% Kodel polyester fiber. The Carpet Mart maintains that in May, 1970, in response to a customer complaint, it learned that not all of the carpets were manufactured from 100% Kodel polyester fiber but rather some were composed of a cheaper and inferior carpet fiber. After the cause was removed to the District Court on the basis of diversity of citizenship, Collins & Aikman moved for a stay pending arbitration, asserting that The Carpet Mart was bound to an arbitration agreement which appeared on the reverse side of Collins & Aikman's printed sales acknowledgment forms. Holding that there existed no binding arbitration agreement between the parties, the District Court denied the stay. For the reasons set forth below, we remand the case to the District Court for further findings.

* * *

The primary question before us on appeal is whether the District Court, in denying Collins & Aikman's motion for a stay pending arbitration, erred in holding that The Carpet Mart was not bound by the arbitration agreement appearing on the back of Collins & Aikman's acknowledgment forms. . . .

* * *Under the common law, an acceptance or a confirmation which contained terms additional to or different from those of the offer or oral agreement constituted a rejection of the offer or agreement and thus became a counter-offer. The terms of the counter-offer were said to have been accepted

by the original offeror when he proceeded to perform under the contract without objecting to the counter-offer. Thus, a buyer was deemed to have accepted the seller's counter-offer if he took receipt of the goods and paid for them without objection.

Under Section 2–207 the result is different. This section of the Code recognizes that in current commercial transactions, the terms of the offer and those of the acceptance will seldom be identical. Rather, under the current "battle of the forms," each party typically has a printed form drafted by his attorney and containing as many terms as could be envisioned to favor that party in his sales transactions. Whereas under common law the disparity between the fine-print terms in the parties' forms would have prevented the consummation of a contract when these forms are exchanged, Section 2–207 recognizes that in many, but not all, cases the parties do not impart such significance to the terms on the printed forms. [Citation.] Subsection 2–207(1) therefore provides that "[a] definite and seasonable expression of acceptance or a written confirmation . . . operates as an acceptance even though it states terms additional to or different from those offered or agreed upon, unless acceptance is expressly made conditional on assent to the additional or different terms." Thus, under Subsection (1), a contract is recognized notwithstanding the fact that an acceptance or confirmation contains terms additional to or different from those of the offer or prior agreement, provided that the offeree's intent to accept the offer is definitely expressed, *see* Sections 2–204 and 2–206, and provided that the offeree's acceptance is not expressly conditioned on the offeror's assent to the additional or different terms. When a contract is recognized under Subsection (1), the additional terms are treated as "proposals for addition to the contract" under Subsection (2), which contains special provisions under which such additional terms are deemed to have been accepted when the transaction is between merchants. Conversely, when no contract is recognized under Subsection 2–207(1)—either because no definite expression of acceptance exists or, more specifically, because the offer-

ee's acceptance is expressly conditioned on the offeror's assent to the additional or different terms—the entire transaction aborts at this point. If, however, the subsequent conduct of the parties—particularly, performance by both parties under what they apparently believe to be a contract—recognizes the existence of a contract, under Subsection 2–207(3) such conduct by both parties is sufficient to establish a contract, notwithstanding the fact that no contract would have been recognized on the basis of their writings alone. Subsection 2–207(3) further provides how the terms of contracts recognized thereunder shall be determined.

* * *

Assuming, for purposes of analysis, that the arbitration provision was an addition to the terms of The Carpet Mart's oral offers, we must next determine whether or not Collins & Aikman's acceptances were "expressly made conditional on assent to the additional . . . terms" therein, within the proviso of Subsection 2–207(1). . . . [T]he provision appearing on the face of Collins & Aikman's acknowledgment forms stated that the acceptances (or orders) were "subject to all of the terms and conditions on the face and reverse side thereof, including arbitration, all of which are accepted by buyer." . . . Although Collins & Aikman's use of the words "subject to" suggests that the acceptances were conditional to some extent, we do not believe the acceptances were "expressly made conditional on [the buyer's] assent to the additional or different terms," as specifically required under the Subsection 2–207(1) proviso. In order to fall within this proviso, it is not enough that an acceptance is expressly conditional on additional or different terms; rather, an acceptance must be *expressly* conditional on the offeror's *assent* to those terms. Viewing the Subsection (1) proviso within the context of the rest of that Subsection and within the policies of Section 2–207 itself, we believe that it was intended to apply only to an acceptance which clearly reveals that the offeree is unwilling to proceed with the transaction unless he is assured of the offeror's assent to the additional or different terms therein.

* * *

Because Collins & Aikman's acceptances were not expressly conditional on the buyer's assent to the additional terms within the proviso of Subsection 2–207(1), a contract is recognized under Subsection (1), and the additional terms are treated as "proposals" for addition to the contract under Subsection 2–207(2). Since both Collins & Aikman and The Carpet Mart are clearly "merchants" as that term is defined in Subsection 2–104(1), the arbitration provision will be deemed to have been accepted by The Carpet Mart under Subsection 2–207(2) unless it materially altered the terms of The Carpet Mart's oral offers. [UCC § 2–207(2)(b)]. We believe that the question of whether the arbitration provision materially altered the oral offer under Subsection 2–207(2)(b) is one which can be resolved only by the District Court on further findings of fact in the present case. If the arbitration provision did in fact materially alter The Carpet Mart's offer, it could not become a part of the contract "unless expressly agreed to" by The Carpet Mart. [UCC § 2–207], Official Comment No. 3.

We therefore conclude that if on remand the District Court finds that Collins & Aikman's acknowledgments were in fact acceptances and that the arbitration provision was additional to the terms of The Carpet Mart's oral orders, contracts will be recognized under Subsection 2–207(1). The arbitration clause will then be viewed as a "proposal" under Subsection 2–207(2) which will be deemed to have been accepted by The Carpet Mart unless it materially altered the oral offers.

QUESTIONS

1. Distinguish a sale from other kinds of transactions that affect goods.

2. Identify and discuss the fundamental principles of Article 2 and Article 2A.

3. Discuss the significant changes Article 2 has made in the need for an offer to include all material terms.

4. Distinguish between the common law's mirror image rule and the Code's provisions for dealing with variant acceptances.

5. Discuss (a) the Code's approach to the requirement that certain contracts must be in writing and (b) the alternative methods of compliance.

PROBLEMS

1. Adams orders one thousand widgets at $5 per widget from International Widget to be delivered within sixty days. After the contract is consummated and signed, Adams requests that International deliver the widgets within thirty days rather than sixty days. International agrees. Is the contractual modification binding?

2. In question 1 what effect, if any, would the following telegram have:

International Widget:

In accordance with our agreement of this date you will deliver the 1,000 previously ordered widgets within thirty days. Thank you for your cooperation in this matter.

(signed) Adams

3. Browne & Assoc., a San Francisco company, orders from U.S. Electronics, a New York company, ten thousand electronic units. Browne & Assoc.'s order form provides that any dispute would be resolved by an arbitration panel located in San Francisco. U.S. Electronics executes and delivers to Browne & Assoc. its acknowledgment form, which accepts the order and contains the following provision: "All disputes will be resolved by the State courts of New York." Browne & Assoc. dispute arose concerning the workmanship of the parts, and Browne & Assoc. wishes the case to be arbitrated in San Francisco. What result?

4. Would the result change in problem 3 if the U.S. Electronics' form contained any of the following provisions?

(a) "The seller's acceptance of the purchase order to which this acknowledgment responds is expressly made conditional on the buyer's assent to any or different terms contained in this acknowledgment"

(b) "The seller's acceptance of the purchase order is subject to the terms and conditions on the face and reverse side hereof and which the buyer accepts by accepting the goods described herein"

(c) "The seller's terms govern this agreement—this acknowledgment merely constitutes a counteroffer"

5. Reinfort executed a written contract with Bylinski to purchase an assorted collection of shoes for $3,000. A week before the agreed shipment date, Bylinski called Reinfort and said, "We cannot deliver at $3,000; unless you agree to pay $4,000, we will cancel the order." After considerable discussion, Reinfort agreed to pay $4,000 if Bylinski would ship as agreed in the contract. After the shoes had been delivered and accepted by Reinfort, Reinfort refused to pay $4,000 and insisted on paying only $3,000. Decision?

6. On November 23, Acorn, a dress manufacturer, mailed to Bowman a written and signed offer to sell one thousand sun dresses at $50 per dress. The offer stated that "it would remain open for ten days and that it could not be withdrawn prior to that date."

Two days later, Acorn, noting a sudden increase in the price of sun dresses, changed his mind. Acorn therefore sent Bowman a letter revoking the offer. The letter was sent on November 25 and received by Bowman on November 28.

Bowman chose to disregard the letter of November 25; instead, she happily continued to watch the price of sun dresses rise. On December 1, Bowman sent a letter accepting the original offer. The letter, however, was not received by Acorn until December 9, due to a delay in the mails.

Bowman has demanded delivery of the goods according to the terms of the offer of November 23, but Acorn has refused. Decision?

7. Henry and Wilma, an elderly immigrant couple, agree to purchase from Brown a refrigerator with fair market value of $450 for twenty-five monthly installments of $60 per month. Henry and Wilma now wish to void the contract asserting that they did not realize the exorbitant price they were paying. Result?

8. The Courts Distributors needed two hundred compact refrigerators on a rush basis. It contacted Eastinghouse Corporation, a manufacturer of refrigerators. Eastinghouse said it would take some time to quote a price on an order of that size. Courts replied, "Send the refrigerators immediately and bill us later." The refrigerators were delivered three days later, and the invoice ten days after that. The invoice price was $140,000. Courts believes that the wholesale market price of the refrigerators is only $120,000. Discuss.

COMPUTER RESEARCH PROBLEMS

1. While adjusting a television antenna beside his mobile home and underneath a high voltage electric transmission wire, Prince received an electric shock resulting in personal injury. He claims the high voltage electric current jumped from the transmission wire to the antenna. The wire, which carried some 7,200 volts of electricity, did not serve his mobile home but ran directly above it. Prince sued the Navarro County Electric Co-Op, the owner and operator of the wire, for breach of implied warranty of merchantability under the Uniform Commercial Code. He contends that the Code's implied warranty of merchantability extends to the container of a product—in this instance the wiring—and that the escape of the current shows that the wiring was unfit for its purpose of transporting electricity. The electric company argues that the electricity passing through the transmission wire was not being sold to Prince and, therefore there was no sale of goods to Prince. Decision?

2. HMT, already in the business of marketing agricultural products, decides to try its hand at marketing processing potatoes. Nine months before the potato harvest, HMT contracted to supply Bell Brand with 100,000 sacks of potatoes. At harvest time, Bell Brand would only accept 60,000 sacks. HMT sues for breach of contract. Bell Brand argues that custom and usage in marketing processing potatoes allows buyers to give *estimates* in contracts, not fixed quantities, since the contracts are established so far in advance. HMT responds that the quantity term in the contract was definite and unambiguous. Can custom and trade usage be used to interpret an unambiguous contract? Discuss.

3. Schreiner, a cotton farmer, agreed over the telephone to sell 150 bales of cotton to Loeb & Co. Schreiner had sold cotton to Loeb & Co. for the past five years. Written confirmation of the date, parties, price, and conditions was mailed to Schreiner, who neither signed nor returned it, nor responded to the confirmation in any way. Four months later, when the price of cotton had doubled, Loeb & Co. sought to enforce the contract. Is the contract enforceable?

4. American Sand & Gravel Inc. agreed to sell sand to Clark at a special discount if 20,000–25,000 tons were ordered. The discount price was 45¢ per ton, compared to the normal price of 55¢ per ton. Two years later, Clark orders, and receives, 1,600 tons of sand from American Sand & Gravel. Clark refuses to pay more then 45¢ per ton. American Sand & Gravel sues for the remaining 10¢ per ton. Decision?

5. In September 1973, Auburn Plastics (defendant) submitted price quotations to CBS (plaintiff) for the manufacture of eight cavity molds to be used in making parts for CBS's toys. Each quotation specified that the offer would not be binding unless accepted within fifteen days. Furthermore, CBS would be subject to an additional 30 percent charge for engineering services upon delivery of the molds. In December 1973 and January 1974, CBS sent detailed purchase orders to Auburn Plastics for cavity molds. The purchase order forms stated that CBS reserved the right to remove the molds from Auburn Plastics without an additional or "withdrawal" charge. Auburn Plastics acknowledged the purchase order and stated that the sale would be subject to all conditions contained in the price quotation. CBS paid Auburn for the molds, and Auburn began to fabricate toy parts from the molds for CBS. Later, Auburn announced a price increase, and CBS demanded delivery of the molds. Auburn refused to deliver the molds unless CBS paid the additional charge for engineering services. CBS claimed that the contract did not provide for a withdrawal charge. Decision?

6. Terminal Grain Corporation brought an action against Glen Freeman, a farmer, to recover damages for breach of an oral contract to deliver grain. According to the company, Freeman orally agreed to two sales of wheat to Terminal Grain of 4,000 bushels each at $1.65½ a bushel and $1.71 a bushel, respectively. Dwayne Maher, merchandising manager of Terminal Grain, sent two written confirmations of the agreements to Freeman. Freeman never made any written objections to the confirmations. After the first transaction had occurred, the price of wheat rose to between $2.25 and $2.30 per bushel, and Freeman refused to deliver the remaining 4,000 bushels at the agreed upon price. Freeman denies entering into any agreement to sell the second 4,000 bushels of wheat to Terminal Grain but admits that he received the two written confirmations sent by Maher. Decision?

7. Frank's Maintenance and Engineering, Inc., orally ordered steel tubing from C. A. Roberts Co. for use in the manufacture of motorcycle front fork tubes. Since these front fork tubes bear the bulk of the weight of a motorcycle, the steel used must be of high quality. Roberts Co. sent an acknowledgment with conditions of sale including one that limited consequential damages and restricted remedies available upon breach by requiring claims for defective equipment to be promptly made upon receipt. The conditions were located on the back of the acknowledgment. The legend "conditions of sale on reverse side" was stamped over so that on first appearance it read "No conditions of sale on reverse side." Roberts delivered the order in December 1975. The steel had no visible defects; however, when Frank's Maintenance began using the steel in its manufacture in the summer of 1976, it discovered that the steel was pitted and cracked beyond repair. Frank's Maintenance informed Roberts Co. of the defects, revoked its acceptance of the steel, and sued for breach of warranty of merchantability. Decision?

Chapter 21

PERFORMANCE

Performance by the Seller
Performance by the Buyer
Obligations of Both Parties

PERFORMANCE is the carrying out of a contract's obligations according to its terms so that the obligations are discharged. The basic obligation of the seller in a contract for the sale of goods is to transfer and deliver goods that conform to the contract. The basic obligation of the buyer is to accept and pay for conforming goods in accordance with the contract. Unless the parties have agreed otherwise, a tender (offer) of performance by one party is a condition to performance by the other party. A contract of sale also requires that each party not impair the other party's expectation of having the contract performed.

The obligations of the parties are determined by their contractual agreement. Thus, the contract of sale may expressly provide whether the seller must deliver the goods before receiving payment of the price or whether the buyer must pay the price before receiving the goods. If the contract does not sufficiently cover the particulars of performance, these terms will be supplied by the Code, common law, course of dealing, usage of trade, and course of performance. In all events, both parties to the sales contract must perform their contractual obligations in good faith.

This chapter will examine the performance obligations of the seller and the buyer as well as the contractual obligations that apply to both of them.

PERFORMANCE BY THE SELLER

Tender of conforming goods by the seller entitles him to acceptance of them by the buyer and to payment of the contractually agreed upon price. Nonetheless, the rights of the parties may be otherwise fixed by the terms of the contract. For example, if the seller has agreed to sell goods on sixty or ninety-days' credit, he is required to perform his part of the contract before the buyer performs.

Tender of delivery requires that the seller put and hold goods that conform to the contract at the buyer's disposition and that he give the buyer reasonable notification to enable him to take delivery. Section 2–503. Tender must also be made at a reasonable time and be kept open for a reasonable period of time. For example, Robert agrees to sell Barbara a stereo system composed of a CD player, receiver, tape deck, and two speakers. Each component is specified by manufacturer and model number, and delivery is to be at Robert's store. Robert obtains the ordered equipment in accordance with the contractual specifications and notifies Barbara that she may pick up the system at her convenience. Robert has now tendered and thus performed his obligations under the sales contract: he holds goods that conform to the contract, he has reasonably placed them at the buyer's disposal, and he has notified the buyer of their readiness.

Time and Manner of Tender

Tender must be at a *reasonable* time, and the goods tendered must be kept available for the period reasonably necessary to enable the buyer to take possession of them. Unless otherwise agreed, the buyer must furnish facilities reasonably suited to the receipt of the goods tendered by the seller. Section 2–503.

If no definite time for delivery is fixed by the terms of the contract, the seller is allowed a reasonable time after entering into the contract within which to tender the goods to the buyer. Likewise, the buyer has a reasonable time within which to accept delivery. What length of time is reasonable depends upon the facts and circumstances of each case. If the goods can be delivered immediately, a reasonable time would be very short. Where the goods must be constructed or manufactured, a reasonable time would be longer and would depend on all the circumstances including the usual length of time required to make the goods.

A contract may not be performed piecemeal or in installments unless the parties specifically agree. If not so specified, all of the goods called for by a contract must be tendered in a single delivery, and payment is due on such tender.

Place of Tender

If the contract does not specify the place for delivery of the goods, the place for delivery is the *seller's place of business* or, if he has none, his residence. The seller must hold the goods for buyer's disposition and notify her that the goods are being held for her to pick up. Section 2–308(a). If the contract is for the sale of identified goods that the parties know at the time of making the contract are located elsewhere than the seller's place of business or residence, the *location* of the goods is then the place for delivery. Section 2–308. For example, George, a boat builder in Chicago, contracts to sell to Chris a certain yacht which both parties know is anchored at Milwaukee. The place of delivery would be Milwaukee. On the other hand, if the contract provides that George shall overhaul the motor at George's shipyard in Chicago, George would have to return the yacht to Chicago, and the place of delivery would be George's Chicago shipyard.

The parties frequently agree expressly upon the place of tender, typically by use of one of the various *delivery terms*. These terms specify whether the contract is a shipment or destination contract and determine the place where the seller must tender delivery of the goods.

Shipment Contracts The delivery terms F.O.B. place of shipment, F.A.S. seller's port, C.I.F., and C. & F. are all "shipment contracts." Under a shipment contract the seller is required or authorized to send the goods to the buyer, but the contract does not obligate her to deliver them at a particular destination. In these cases the seller's tender of performance occurs at the point of shipment, provided the seller meets certain specified conditions, which are designed to protect the interests of the absent buyer. A contract is assumed to be a shipment contract unless otherwise indicated.

The initials *"F.O.B."* mean "free on board" and *"F.A.S."* mean "free alongside." Under the Code these are delivery terms even though used only in connection with the stated price. Section 2–319(1)(a). When the contract provides that the sale is **F.O.B. place of shipment** or **F.A.S. port of shipment,** then the contract is a shipment contract. For example, Linda, whose place of business is in New York, enters into a contract with Holly, the buyer, who is located in San

Francisco. The contract calls for delivery of the goods F.O.B. New York. This would be a shipment contract. The initials **"C.I.F."** mean "cost, insurance, and freight" and **"C. & F."** mean simply "cost and freight." Under a C.I.F. contract, in consideration for an agreed unit price for the goods, the seller pays all costs of transportation, insurance, and freight to the destination. The amount of the agreed unit price of the goods will, of course, reflect these costs. The unit price in a C. & F. contract is understandably less than in a C.I.F. contract since it does not include the cost of insurance.

Under a shipment contract, the seller is required to: (1) *deliver* the goods to a carrier; (2) make a contract for their transportation that is reasonable according to the nature of the goods and other circumstances; (3) obtain and promptly deliver or tender to the buyer any document necessary to enable the buyer to obtain possession of the goods from the carrier; and (4) promptly notify the buyer of the shipment. Section 2–504. Failing either to make a proper contract for transportation or to notify the buyer of the shipment is a ground for rejection *only* if material loss or delay results. Section 2–504.

Destination Contracts   The delivery terms "F.O.B. city of buyer," "ex-ship," and "no arrival, no sale" are destination contracts. Since a destination contract requires the seller to *tender* delivery of conforming goods at a *specified destination,* the seller must place the goods at the buyer's disposition and give the buyer reasonable notice to enable him to take delivery. In addition, if the destination contract involves documents of title, the seller must tender the necessary documents. Section 2–503.

Where the contract provides that the sale is **F.O.B. place of destination,** the seller must at his own expense and risk transport the goods to that place and there tender delivery of them to the buyer. Section 2–319(1)(b). For example, if the buyer is in Boston and the seller in Chicago, a contract providing F.O.B. Boston is a destination contract under which the seller must tender the goods at the designated place in Boston at his own expense

and risk. Where the contract provides for delivery **"ex-ship,"** or from the ship, it is also a destination contract requiring the seller to unload the goods from the carrier at the named destination. Finally, where the contract contains terms **"no arrival, no sale,"** the title and risk of loss do not pass to the buyer until the seller makes a tender of the goods after their arrival at destination. The major significance of the "no arrival, no sale" term is that it excuses the seller from any liability to the buyer for failure of the goods to arrive, unless the seller has caused their nonarrival.

Goods Held by Bailee   Where goods are in the possession of a bailee and are to be delivered without being moved, in most instances the seller may either tender a document of title or obtain an acknowledgment by the bailee of the buyer's right to possess the goods. Section 2–503(4). This permits the buyer to obtain the goods directly from the bailee.

For a summary of performance by the seller see Figure 21–1.

Perfect Tender Rule

The Code imposes upon the seller the obligation that her tender of goods conform *exactly* to the requirements of the contract. The seller's tender cannot deviate in any way from the terms of the contract. Thus, a buyer may rightfully reject the delivery of 110 dozen shirts under an agreement calling for delivery of 100 dozen shirts. The size or extent of the breach does *not* affect the right to reject. *See Moulton Cavity & Mold Inc. v. Lyn-Flex Ind.*

If the goods or the tender of delivery fail in any respect to conform to the contract, the buyer may (1) reject the whole lot, (2) accept the whole lot, or (3) accept any commercial unit or units and reject the rest. Section 2–601. A **commercial unit** means such a unit of goods as by commercial usage is a single unit and which, if divided, would materially impair its character or value. A commercial unit may be a single item (as a machine) or a set of articles (as a suite of furniture or

Figure 21–1 Tender of Performance by Seller

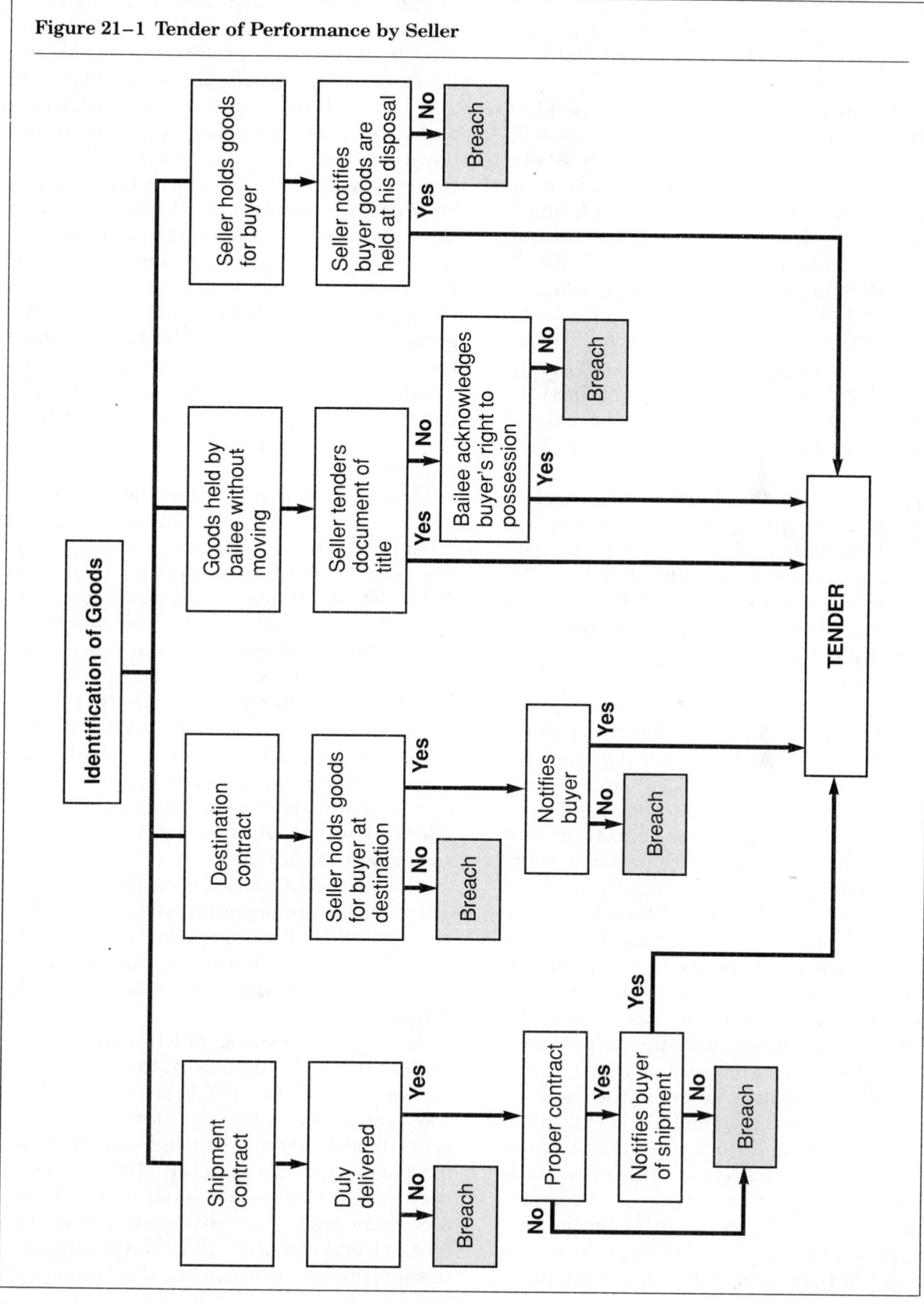

an assortment of sizes) or a quantity (as a bale, gross, or carload) or any other unit treated in use or in the relevant market as a whole. Section 2–105(6).

There are three basic qualifications of the buyer's right to reject the goods upon the seller's failure to comply with the perfect tender rule: (1) agreement between the parties limiting the buyer's right to reject non-conforming goods, (2) cure by the seller, and (3) installment contracts. In addition, as previously discussed, the perfect tender rule does not apply to a seller's breach of her obligation under a shipment contract to make a proper contract for transportation or to give proper notice of the shipment. A failure to perform either of these obligations is a ground for rejection only if material loss or delay results. Section 2–504.

Agreement by the Parties The parties may contractually agree to limit the operation of the perfect tender rule. For example, they may agree that the seller shall have the right to repair or replace any defective parts or goods. Such contractual limitations are discussed in Chapter 24.

Cure by the Seller The Code recognizes two situations in which a seller may cure or correct a nonconforming tender of goods. This relaxation of the seller's obligation to make a perfect tender gives the seller an opportunity to make a second delivery or a substitute tender. The first opportunity for cure occurs when the time for performance under the contract has not expired. The second opportunity for cure is available after the time for performance has expired but only if the seller had reasonable grounds to believe that the nonconforming tender would be acceptable to the buyer with or without monetary adjustment.

Where the buyer refuses to accept a tender of goods that do not conform to the contract, the seller, by acting promptly and within the time allowed for performance, may make a proper tender or delivery of conforming goods and cure his defective tender or performance. Section 2–508. Upon notice of the buyer's rightful rejection, the seller must first give the buyer reasonable notice of her intention

to cure the defect and then must make a proper tender according to the *original* contract. This rule, which was recognized before the Code, is fair to both parties. It gives the seller the full contractual period in which to perform but does not cause any harm to the buyer, who receives full performance within the time agreed to in the contract. For example, Conroy is to deliver to Elizabeth twenty-five blue shirts and fifty white shirts by October 15. On October 1, Conroy delivers twenty-nine blue shirts and forty-six white shirts, which Elizabeth rejects as not conforming to the contract. Elizabeth notifies Conroy of her rejection and the reasons for it. Conroy has until October 15 to cure the defect by making a perfect tender, provided he seasonably notifies Elizabeth of his intention to do so.

The Code also provides the seller an opportunity after the time for performance has expired to cure a nonconforming tender, which the seller had reasonable grounds to believe would be acceptable to the buyer with or without money allowance. Section 2–508(2). This Code-created opportunity to cure a nonconforming tender after the date set for performance is conditioned on the seller's satisfying the following requirements: (1) the seller had reasonable grounds for believing the nonconforming tender would be acceptable to the buyer, (2) the seller, after being informed of the buyer's rightful rejection, seasonably notifies the buyer of his intention to cure the defect, and (3) the seller cures the defect within a reasonable period of time. The principal difficulty in applying this rule, as demonstrated in *Wilson v. Scampoli,* is whether or not the first requirement has been satisfied.

For example, Vanessa orders from Gary a model 110X S.C.A. television to be delivered on January 20. The 110X is unavailable, but Gary can obtain a model 110, which is last year's model of the same television and lists for five percent less than the 110X. On January 20, Gary delivers to Vanessa the 110 at a discount price of ten percent less than the contract price for the 110X. Vanessa rejects the substituted television set. Gary promptly notifies Vanessa that he will obtain and deliver a model 110X. Gary will most likely have a reasonable time beyond the January 20 deadline in which to deliver the 110X television set to Vanessa because under these facts Gary appeared to have reasonable grounds to believe the model 110 would be acceptable with the money allowance.

Installment Contracts Unless the parties have otherwise agreed, the buyer does not have to pay any part of the price of the goods until the entire quantity specified in the contract has been delivered or tendered. Section 2–307. An installment contract is an instance in which the parties have otherwise agreed. It expressly provides for delivery of the goods in separate lots or installments and usually for payment of the price in installments. If the contract is silent about payment, the Code provides that the price, if it can be apportioned, may be demanded for each lot. Section 2–307.

The buyer may reject any nonconforming installment if the nonconformity *substantially* impairs the value of that *installment* and cannot be cured. Section 2–612(2). When, however, the installment does substantially impair the value of the installment but not the value of the entire contract, if the seller gives adequate assurance of the installment's cure, then the buyer cannot reject the installment. Section 2–612(2). Whenever the nonconformity or default with respect to one or more of the installments substantially impairs the value of the *whole contract,* the buyer can treat the breach as a breach of the whole contract. Section 2–612(3).

For example, Kevin makes a contract to deliver to Janet fifty tons of coal each month for one year, delivery to be made on the first day of each month commencing with January; Janet agrees to pay a certain price for each installment on the twentieth day of the month of delivery. Kevin delivers to Janet fifty tons of coal on January 1. Janet does not pay for this coal on January 20. May Kevin on January 21 treat this breach of contract by Janet as completely excusing Kevin from any further duty to perform under the contract and entitling him to recover damages against Janet for breach of the entire contract? A one-day delay in making payment would not substantially impair the value of the whole contract and therefore would not be a material breach. A delay of a week or ten days in payment of the January installment might well be a material breach substantially impairing the value of the whole contract and thereby excuse the seller from any further duty under the contract, whereas an equal delay in payment of the July installment, by which time the contract has been one-half performed on both sides, would probably not be a material breach.

The test of substantial impairment is the materiality of the breach. This involves a weighing of all relevant factors among which are the terms of the contract, its subject matter, the nature and extent of the breach, the reason for delay in performance, the time when the breach occurred, whether in the beginning or after partial or substantial performance on both sides, and the effect of the delay upon the party from whom performance has been withheld.

PERFORMANCE BY THE BUYER

The obligation of the buyer is to accept conforming goods and to pay for them according to the contract terms. Payment or tender of payment by the buyer, unless otherwise agreed, is a condition to the seller's duty to tender and to complete delivery. Section 2–507.

The buyer is not obliged to accept a tender or delivery of goods that do not conform to the contract. Upon determining that the tender or delivery is nonconforming, the buyer has three choices. He may (1) reject all of the goods, (2) accept all of the goods, or (3) accept any commercial unit or units of the goods and reject the rest. Section 2–601. The buyer must pay the contract rate for the commercial units he accepts.

Inspection

Unless otherwise agreed between the parties, the buyer has a right to inspect the goods before payment or acceptance. Section 2–513(1). This **inspection** enables him to satisfy himself that the goods tendered or delivered conform to the contract. If the contract requires payment before acceptance, such as where the contract provides for shipment C.O.D. (collect on delivery), payment must be made prior to inspection unless the nonconformity appears without inspection. Section 2–512. Payment, however, in such a case is *not* an acceptance of the goods and does not impair the buyer's right to inspect nor any of his remedies.

The buyer is allowed a reasonable time to inspect the goods. He may, however, lose the right to reject or revoke acceptance of nonconforming goods by failing to inspect them in a timely manner. The expenses of inspection must be borne by the buyer but may be recovered from the seller if the goods do not conform and are rejected. Section 2–513(2).

Rejection

Rejection is a manifestation by the buyer of his unwillingness to become owner of the goods. It must be made within a reasonable time after the goods have been tendered or delivered. It is not effective unless the buyer seasonably notifies the seller. Section 2–602(1).

Rejection of the goods may be rightful or wrongful, depending on whether the goods tendered or delivered conform to the contract. The buyer's rejection of nonconforming goods or tender is rightful under the perfect tender rule. If the buyer refuses a tender of goods or rejects it as nonconforming without disclosing to the seller the nature of the defect, she may not assert such defect as an excuse for not accepting the goods or as a breach of contract by the seller if the defect is one which is curable. Section 2–605.

After the buyer has rejected the goods, any exercise of ownership of the goods by her is wrongful as against the seller. If the buyer has possession of the rejected goods but does not have a security interest in them, she is obliged to hold them with reasonable care for a time sufficient to permit the seller to re-

move them. The buyer who is not a merchant is under no further obligation with regard to goods rightfully rejected. Section 2–602(2). A merchant buyer of goods who has rightfully rejected them is obligated to follow reasonable instructions from the seller with respect to the disposition of the goods in her possession or control when the seller has no agent or business at the place of rejection. Section 2–603(1). If the merchant buyer receives no instructions from the seller within a reasonable time after notice of the rejection, and the rejected goods are perishable or threaten to decline in value speedily, she is obligated to make reasonable efforts to sell them for the seller's account. Otherwise, she may (1) store the goods for the seller's account, (2) reship them to the seller, or (3) resell them for the seller's account. Such action is not an acceptance or conversion of the goods. Section 2–604.

When the buyer sells the rejected goods, she is entitled to reimbursement for the reasonable expenses of caring for and selling them and a reasonable selling commission not to exceed ten percent of the gross proceeds. Section 2–603(2).

Acceptance

Acceptance of goods means a willingness by the buyer to become the owner of the goods tendered or delivered to him by the seller. Acceptance of the goods precludes any rejection of the goods accepted. Section 2–607(2). It includes overt acts or conduct which manifest such willingness. Acceptance may be indicated by express words, by the presumed intention of the buyer through his failure to act, or by conduct of the buyer inconsistent with the seller's ownership of the goods. More specifically, acceptance occurs when the buyer, after a reasonable opportunity to inspect the goods, (1) signifies to the seller that the goods conform to the contract, (2) signifies to the seller that he will take the goods or retain them in spite of their nonconformity to the contract, or (3) fails to make an effective rejection of the goods. Section 2–606(1). *See Im-*

port Traders, Inc. v. Frederick Manufacturing Corp.

Acceptance, as previously noted, of any part of a commercial unit is acceptance of the entire unit. Section 2–606(2). The buyer must pay at the contract rate for those commercial units he accepts. After giving the seller timely notice of the breach, he is entitled to recover from the seller, or to deduct from the purchase price, the amount of damages for nonconformity of the commercial units accepted and for nondelivery of the commercial units rejected. Sections 2–714 and 2–717. For example, Nancy agrees to deliver to Paul 500 light bulbs of 100 watts each for $300 and 1,000 light bulbs of 60 watts each for $500. Nancy delivers on time but the shipment contains only 400 of the 100-watt bulbs and 750 of the 60-watt bulbs. If Paul accepts the shipment, he must pay Nancy $240 for the 100-watt bulbs accepted and $375 for the 60-watt bulbs accepted less the amount of damages caused Paul by Nancy's nonconforming delivery.

When goods are rejected by the buyer, the burden is on the seller to establish their conformity to the contract, but the burden is on the buyer to establish any breach of contract (including warranty) with regard to goods accepted. Section 2–607(4).

Revocation of Acceptance

A buyer may have accepted goods that contain a defect because it was difficult to discover the defect by inspection or because the buyer reasonably assumed that the seller would correct the defect. In such an instance the buyer may revoke his acceptance of the goods if the uncorrected defect substantially impairs the value of the goods to him. **Revocation of acceptance** gives the buyer the same rights and duties with respect to the goods as if he had rejected them. Section 2–608(3).

More specifically, the buyer may revoke his acceptance of goods that do not conform to the contract when such nonconformity *substantially* impairs the value of the goods to him, provided that his acceptance was:

(1) premised on the reasonable assumption that the nonconformity would be cured by the seller, and it was not seasonably cured; or (2) made without discovery of the nonconformity, and such acceptance was reasonably induced by the difficulty of discovery before acceptance or by assurances of the seller. The test of substantial impairment of the value to the buyer of nonconforming goods is subjective rather than objective. Section 2–608(1).

Revocation of acceptance is not effective until notification is given to the seller. This must be done within a reasonable time after the buyer discovers or should have discovered the grounds for revocation and before the goods have undergone any substantial change that was not caused by their own defects. Section 2–608(2).

See McCullough v. Bill Swad Chrysler-Plymouth, Inc.

Obligation of Payment

The terms of the contract may expressly state the time and place that the buyer is obligated to pay for the goods. If so, these terms are controlling. Thus, if the buyer has agreed to pay for the goods in advance of delivery either to the seller or to a carrier, his duty to pay is not conditioned upon performance or a tender of performance by the seller. Where the sale is on credit, the buyer is not obligated to pay for the goods when he receives them. The credit provision in the contract will control the time of payment. In the absence of agreement, payment is due at the time and place at which the buyer is to receive the goods, even though the place of shipment is the place of delivery. Section 2–310(a). This rule is understandable in view of the right of the buyer to inspect the goods before being obliged to pay for them in the absence of agreement to the contrary.

Tender of payment in the ordinary course of business is sufficient when made by any means or in any manner current, such as a check, unless the seller demands cash and allows the buyer a reasonable time within which to obtain it. Payment by personal check, however, is defeated as between seller and buyer if the check is not paid when the seller attempts to cash it. Section 2–511(3).

For a summary of performance by the buyer see Figure 21–2.

OBLIGATIONS OF BOTH PARTIES

Contracts for the sale of goods necessarily involve risks that future events may or may not occur. In some instances, the parties explicitly allocate these risks; in most instances

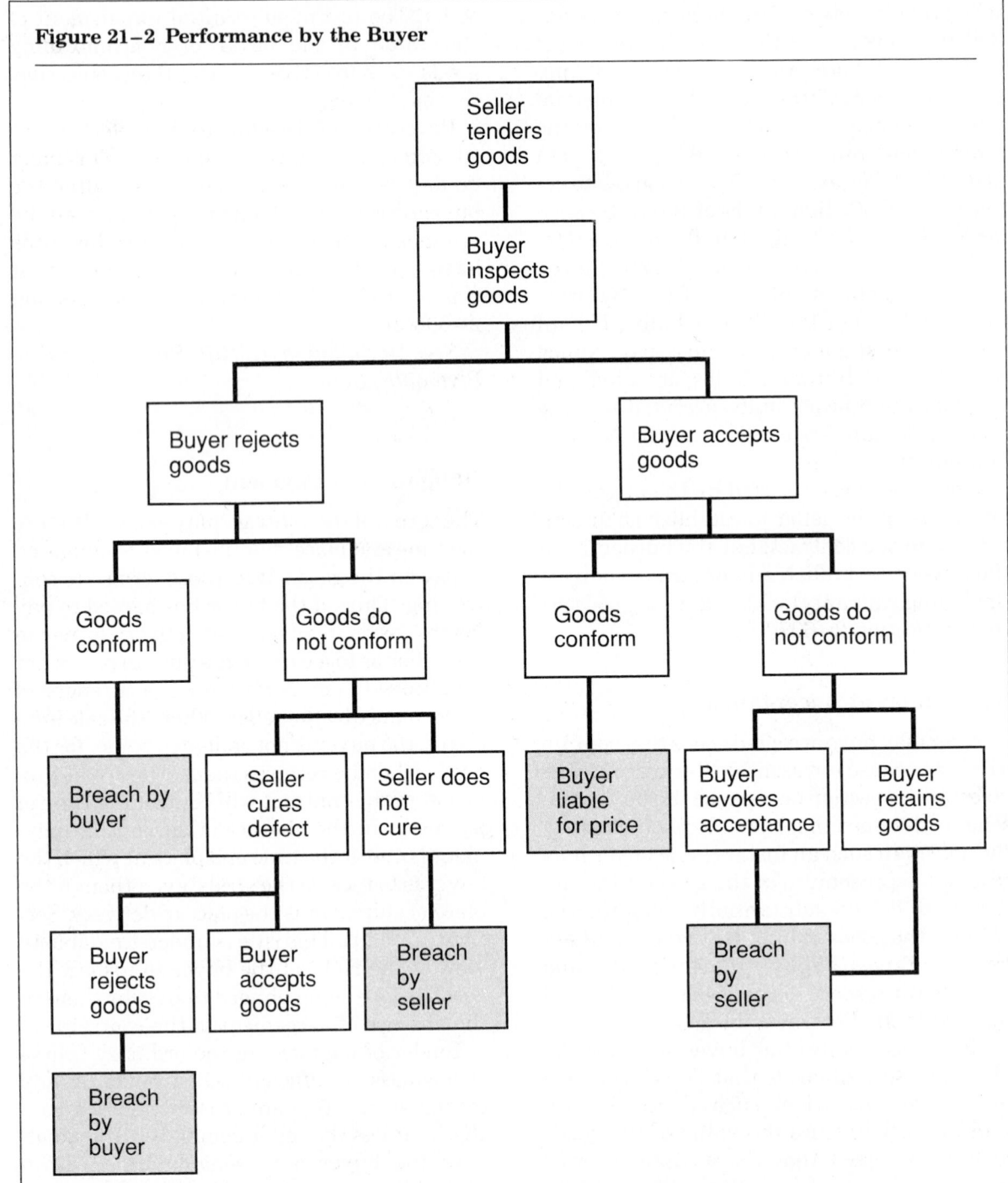

Figure 21–2 Performance by the Buyer

they do not. The Code contains three sections that allocate these risks when the parties fail to do so. Each provision, when applicable, relieves the parties from the obligation of full performance under the sales contract. The first section deals with casualty to identified goods, the second with the non-happening of presupposed conditions, and the third with substituted performance.

Related to the subject of whether performance will be excused is the problem that one of the parties will be unable or unwilling to perform. In such instances, the Code allows the insecure party to seek reasonable assurance from the potentially defaulting party of her willingness and ability to perform. In addition, if one of the parties clearly indicates an unwillingness or inability to perform, the Code protects the other party.

Casualty to Identified Goods

If goods are destroyed before an offer to sell or buy them is accepted, the offer is terminated by general contract law. But what if the goods are destroyed after the sales contract is formed? The rules for the passage of risk of loss (as discussed in Chapter 22) apply with one exception: if the contract is for goods that are identified when the contract was made, and these goods are totally lost or damaged without fault of either party and *before* the risk of loss passes to the buyer, the contract is avoided. Section 2–613(a). This means that the seller is no longer obligated to deliver and the buyer need not pay the price. Each party is excused from his performance obligation under the contract.

In the case of a partial destruction or deterioration of the goods, the buyer has the option to avoid the contract or to accept the goods with due allowance or deduction from the contract price for the deterioration or deficiency. Section 2–613(b). Thus, Adams agrees to sell to Taylor a specific lot of wheat containing 1,000 bushels at a price of $4 per bushel. Without the fault of Adams or Taylor, fire destroys 300 bushels of the wheat. Taylor does not have to take the remaining 700 bushels of wheat,

but he has the option to do so upon paying $2,800, the price of 700 bushels.

If the destruction or casualty to the goods, whether total or partial, occurs *after* risk of loss has passed to the buyer, the buyer has no option but must pay the entire contract price of the goods.

Non-Happening of Presupposed Condition

The ability to perform a contract for the sale of goods is subject to a number of possible hazards, such as strikes, lockouts, unforeseen shutdown of sources of supply, or loss of plant or machinery by fire or other casualty. Ordinarily these do not operate as an excuse on the ground of impossibility of performance, unless the contract expressly so provides. Both parties may have understood at the time the contract was made, however, that its performance depended upon the existence of certain facilities, or that the purpose of the contract and the value of performance depended entirely upon the happening of a specific future contemplated event. In such a case, the seller is excused from her duty of performance upon the non-occurrence of presupposed conditions, which were a basic assumption of the contract, unless the seller has expressly assumed the risk. Section 2–615(a).

Central to the Code's approach to impossibility is the concept of **commercial impracticability.** The Code excuses performance even when performance may not be actually or literally impossible, but where it is commercially impracticable. This, however, requires more than mere hardship or increased cost of performance. In order for a party to be discharged, performance must be rendered impracticable as a result of an unforeseen supervening event not within the contemplation of the parties at the time of contracting. Moreover, the non-occurrence of the subsequent event must have been a "basic assumption" that both parties made when entering into the contract. *See Northern Corp. v. Chugach Electrical Association* in Chapter 16.

Increased production cost alone does not excuse performance by the seller, nor does a collapse of the market for the goods excuse the buyer. But a contract for the sale of programs for a scheduled yacht regatta, which is called off, or for the sale of tin horns for export, which become subject to embargo, or for the production of goods at a designated factory, which becomes damaged or destroyed by fire, would be an excuse for non-performance.

Although the seller may be relieved of her contractual duty by the non-happening of presupposed conditions, if the contingency affects only a part of the seller's capacity to perform, she must, to the extent of her remaining capacity, allocate delivery and production in a fair and reasonable manner among her customers. Section 2–615(b).

Substituted Performance

The Code provides that where neither party is at fault and the agreed manner of delivery of the goods becomes commercially impracticable, as by reason of the failure of loading or unloading facilities or unavailability of an agreed type of carrier, a substituted manner of performance, if commercially reasonable, must be tendered and accepted. Section 2–614(1). Neither seller nor buyer is excused on the ground that delivery in the express manner provided in the contract is impossible where a practical alternative or substitute exists.

If the means or manner in which the buyer is to make payment becomes impossible by reason of supervening governmental regulation, the seller may withhold or stop delivery of the goods unless the buyer provides payment which is commercially a substantial equivalent to that required by the contract. If delivery has already been made, payment as provided by the governmental regulation discharges the buyer unless the regulation is discriminatory, oppressive, or predatory. Section 2–614(2).

Right to Adequate Assurance of Performance

A contract of sale also requires that each party not impair the other party's expecta-

tion of having the contract performed. The essential purpose of a contract is actual performance but an important feature is a continuing sense of reliance and security that peformance will occur when due. If either the willingness or ability of a party to perform is put in doubt after contracting but before the time for performance, the other party is threatened with the loss of a substantial part of what he has bargained for. Therefore, when reasonable grounds for insecurity arise regarding either party's performance, the other party may demand written assurance and suspend his own performance until he receives that assurance. If adequate assurance of performance is not received within a reasonable time not exceeding thirty days, there is a repudiation of the contract. Section 2–609.

Anticipatory Repudiation

A repudiation is a clear indication by either party to a contract that he is unwilling or unable to perform his obligations under the contract. An **anticipatory repudiation** is a repudiation made *before* the time to perform occurs. It may occur by express communication or by the repudiating party's taking an action that makes performance impossible, such as selling unique goods to a third party. A repudiation also results from the failure of a party to give timely assurance of performance after a justifiable demand. If an anticipatory repudiation substantially impairs the value of the contract, the aggrieved party may (1) await performance for a commercially reasonable time or (2) resort to any remedy for breach. In either case, he may suspend his own performance. Section 2–610. The repudiating party may retract his anticipatory repudiation and thereby reinstate the contract unless the aggrieved party has cancelled the contract, materially changed his position, or otherwise indicated that she considers the anticipatory repudiation final. Section 2–611. *See Neptune Research & Development, Inc. v. Teknics Industrial Systems, Inc.*

CASES

Perfect Tender Rule

MOULTON CAVITY & MOLD, INC. v. LYN–FLEX IND.

Supreme Court of Maine, 1979.
396 A.2d 1024.

DELAHANTY, J.

Defendant, Lyn-Flex Industries, Inc., appeals from a judgment entered after a jury trial by the Superior Court, York County, in favor of plaintiff, Moulton Cavity & Mold, Inc. The case concerns itself with an oral contract for the sale of goods which, as both parties agree, is governed by Article 2 of the Uniform Commercial Code. . . . For the reasons set forth below, we agree with defendant that the presiding Justice committed reversible error by instructing the jury that the doctrine of substantial performance applied to a contract for the sale of goods.

* * *

An examination of the record discloses the following sequence of events: On March 19, 1975, Lynwood Moulton, president of plaintiff, and Ernest Sturman, president of defendant, orally agreed that plaintiff would produce, and defendant purchase, twenty-six innersole molds capable of producing saleable innersoles. The price was fixed at $600.00 per mold. Whether or not a time for delivery had been established was open to question. In his testimony at trial, Mr. Moulton admitted that he was fully aware that defendant was in immediate need of the molds, and he stated that he had estimated that he could provide suitable molds in about five weeks' time. * * *

In apparent conformity with standard practice in the industry, plaintiff set about constructing a sample mold and began a lengthy series of tests. These tests consisted of bringing the sample mold to defendant's plant, fitting the mold to one of defendant's plastic-injecting machines, and checking the innersole thus derived from the plaintiff's mold to determine if it met the specifications imposed by defendant. After about thirty such tests over a ten-week period, several problems remained unsolved. * * *

It was plaintiff's contention at trial, supported by credible evidence, that at one point during the testing period officials of defendant signified that in their judgment plaintiff's sample mold was turning out innersoles correctly configured so as to fit the model last supplied by defendant's customer. Allegedly relying on this approval, plaintiff went ahead and constructed the full run of twenty-six molds.

For its part, defendant introduced credible evidence to rebut the assertion that it had approved the fit of the molds. It also noted that Moulton's allegation of approval extended only to the fit of the mold; as Moulton conceded, defendant had never given full approval since it considered the flashing problem, among others, unacceptable.

* * *

At trial, plaintiff's basic theory of recovery was that it had received approval with regard to the fit of the sample mold, that in reliance on that approval it had constructed a full run of twenty-six molds, and that defendant had, in effect, committed an anticipatory breach of contract within the meaning of Section 2–610 by demanding that the fit of the molds be completely redesigned. On its counterclaim, and in response to plaintiff's position, defendant advanced the theory that plaintiff had breached the contract by failing to tender conforming goods within the five-week period mentioned by both parties.

After the presiding Justice had charged the jury, counsel for plaintiff requested at side bar that the jury be instructed on the doctrine of substantial performance. Counsel for defendant entered a timely objection to the proposed charge which objection was overruled. The court then supplemented its charge as follows:

The only point of clarification that I'll make, ladies and gentlemen, is that I've referred a couple of times to performance of a contract and you, obviously, have to determine no matter which way you view the contract to be, and there might even be a possible third way that I haven't even considered, whether the contract whatever it is has been performed and there is a doctrine that you should be aware of in considering that. That is the doctrine of substantial performance.

It is not required that performance be in any case one hundred percent complete in order to entitle a party to enforcement of their contractual rights. That is not to say within the confines of this case that the existence of flashing would be excused or not be excused. It is just a recognition on the part of the law when we talk about performance, probably if we took any contract you could always find something of no substance that was not completed one hundred percent. It is for you to determine that whether it has been substantially performed or not and what in fact constitutes substantial performance.

In your consideration, and as I say in this case, that's not to intimate that something like flashing is to be disregarded or to be considered. It's up to you based upon facts.

The jury returned a verdict in favor of plaintiff in the amount of $14,480.82.

In *Smith, Fitzmaurice Co. v. Harris,* [citation], a case decided under the common law, we recognized the then-settled rule that with respect to contracts for the sale of goods the buyer has the right to reject the seller's tender if in any way it fails to conform to the specifications of the contract. We held that "[t]he vendor has the duty to comply with his order in kind, quality and amount." [Citation.] Thus, in *Smith,* we ruled that a buyer who had contracted to purchase twelve dozen union suits could lawfully refuse a tender of sixteen dozen union suits. Various provisions of the Uniform Sales Act, enacted in Maine in 1923, codified the common-law approach. [Citation.] The so-called "perfect tender" rule came under considerable fire around the time the Uniform Commercial Code was drafted. No less an authority than Karl Llewellyn, recognized as the primum mobile of the Code's tender provisions, [citations] attacked the rule principally on the ground that it al-

lowed a dishonest buyer to avoid an unfavorable contract on the basis of an insubstantial defect in the seller's tender. Llewellyn, *On Warranty of Quality and Society,* 37 Colum. L.Rev. 341, 389 (1937). Although Llewellyn's views are represented in many Code sections governing tender, the basic tender provision, Section 2–601, represents a rejection of Llewellyn's approach and a continuation of the perfect tender policy developed by the common law and carried forward by the draftsmen of the Uniform Sales Act. [Citations.] Thus, Section 2–601 states that, with certain exceptions not here applicable, the buyer has the right to reject "if the goods or the tender of delivery fail *in any respect* to conform to the contract . . ." (emphasis supplied). Those few courts that have considered the question agree that the perfect tender rule has survived the enactment of the Code. [Citations.] We, too, are convinced of the soundness of this position.

In light of the foregoing discussion, it is clear that the presiding Justice's charge was erroneous and, under the circumstances, reversibly so.

* * *

Appeal sustained. New trial ordered.

Cure by the Seller

WILSON v. SCAMPOLI

District of Columbia Court of Appeals, 1967.
228 A.2d 848.

Myers, J.

This is an appeal from an order of the trial court granting rescission of a sales contract for a color television set and directing the return of the purchase price plus interest and costs.

Appellee purchased the set in question on November 4, 1965, paying the total purchase price in cash. The transaction was evidenced by a sales ticket showing the price paid and guaranteeing ninety days' free service and replacement of any defective tube and parts for a period of one year. Two days after purchase the set was delivered and uncrated, the antennae adjusted and the set plugged into an electrical outlet to "cook out." When the set was turned on, however, it did not function properly, the picture having a reddish tinge. Appellant's delivery man advised the buyer's daughter, Mrs. Kolley, that it was not his duty to tune in or adjust the color but that a service representative would shortly call at her house for that purpose. After the departure of the delivery men, Mrs. Kolley unplugged the set and did not use it.

On November 8, 1965, a service representative arrived, and after spending an hour in an effort to eliminate the red cast from the picture advised Mrs. Kolley that he would have to remove the chassis from the cabinet and take it to the shop as he could not determine the cause of the difficulty from his examination at the house. He also made a written memorandum of his service call, noting that the television "Needs Shop Work (Red Screen)." Mrs. Kolley refused to allow the chassis to be removed, asserting she did not want a "repaired" set but another "brand new" set. Later she demanded the return of the purchase price, although retaining the set. Appellant refused to refund the purchase price, but renewed his offer to adjust, repair, or, if the set could not be made to function properly, to replace it. Ultimately, appellee instituted this suit against appellant seeking a refund of the purchase price. After a trial, the court ruled that "under the facts and circumstances the complaint is justified. Under the equity powers of the Court I will order the parties put back in their original status, let the $675 be returned, and the set returned to the defendant."

Appellant does not contest the jurisdiction of the trial court to order rescission in a proper case, but contends the trial judge erred in holding that rescission here was appropriate. He argues that he was always willing to comply with the terms of the sale either by correcting the malfunction by minor repairs or, in the event the set could not be made thereby properly operative, by replacement; that as he was denied the opportunity to try to correct the difficulty, he did not breach the contract of sale or any warranty

thereunder, expressed or implied.

[U.C.C.] 2–508 provides:

(1) Where any tender or delivery by the seller is rejected because nonconforming and the time for performance has not yet expired, the seller may seasonably notify the buyer of his intention to cure and may then within the contract time make a conforming delivery.

(2) Where the buyer rejects a non-conforming tender which the seller had reasonable grounds to believe would be acceptable with or without money allowance the seller may if he seasonably notifies the buyer have a further reasonable time to substitute a conforming tender.

A retail dealer would certainly expect and have reasonable grounds to believe that merchandise like color television sets, new and delivered as crated at the factory, would be acceptable as delivered and that, if defective in some way, he would have the right to substitute a conforming tender. The question then resolves itself to whether the dealer may conform his tender by adjustment or minor repair or whether he must conform by substituting brand new merchandise. The problem seems to be one of first impression in other jurisdictions adopting the Uniform Commercial Code as well as in the District of Columbia.

* * *

While these cases provide no mandate to require the buyer to accept patchwork goods or substantially repaired articles in lieu of flawless merchandise, they do indicate that minor repairs or reasonable adjustments are frequently the means by which an imperfect tender may be cured. In discussing the analogous question of defective title, it has been stated that:

The seller, then, should be able to cure [the defect] under subsection 2–508(2) in those cases in which he can do so without subjecting the buyer to any great inconvenience, risk, or loss. [Citations.]

Removal of a television chassis for a short period of time in order to determine the cause of color malfunction and ascertain the extent of adjustment or correction needed to effect full operational efficiency presents no great inconvenience to the buyer. In the instant case, [Scampoli's] expert witness testified that this was not infrequently necessary with new televisions. Should the set be defective in workmanship or parts, the loss would be upon the manufacturer who warranted it free from mechanical defect. Here the adamant refusal of Mrs. Kolley . . . to allow inspection essential to the determination of the cause of the excessive red tinge to the picture defeated any effort by the seller to provide timely repair or even replacement of the set if the difficulty could not be corrected. The cause of the defect might have been minor and easily adjusted or it may have been substantial and required replacement by another new set— but the seller was never given an adequate opportunity to make a determination.

We do not hold that appellant [Scampoli] has no liability to appellee [Wilson], but as he was denied access and a reasonable opportunity to repair, appellee has not shown a breach of warranty entitling him either to a brand new set or to rescission. We therefore reverse the judgment of the trial court granting rescission and directing the return of the purchase price of the set.

Reversed.

Acceptance

IMPORT TRADERS, INC. v. FREDERICK MANUFACTURING CORP.

Civil Court of the City of New York, Kings County, 1983.
117 Misc.2d 305, 457 N.Y.S.2d 742.

DIAMOND, J.

Defendant-buyer ordered the goods in question on August 7, 1981 after earlier conversations with plaintiff-seller. It was clear that buyer wanted a relatively "soft" pad. The agreed purchase price was $2,580 for 500 dozen units (43¢ per unit). The goods were delivered on November 19, 1981. They were not paid for. Demand for payment was made in a timely manner. Buyer still has the goods.

Both parties knew there would be a question about exactly how soft the pads would be, when delivered.

Buyer had two samples (# 221 and # 222). His order indicated that he wanted a pad "as soft as possible—like the sample no. 222 . . ."

Both buyer and seller could have waited for an exact sample before ordering, or confirming the order. Neither did so. Buyer's order asked for delivery "as soon as possible."

The # 221 and # 222 samples were not in evidence, but the delivered pads were harder than what buyer really wanted.

Buyer did not inspect the goods in a timely manner, especially since he was aware that there was a question about how "soft" the pads would be at the time he ordered them, and during earlier discussions.

Buyer did not advise seller of his disapproval of merchandise until April, 1982— and only then after seller contacted him at that time about payment.

Buyer desired the imported pads from Taiwan because they would be less expensive than comparable pads manufactured in the United States.

* * *

The remedies available to a seller for the breach of a sales contract, by a buyer, are provided in UCC § 2–703. In the present case, the seller has brought an action for the price pursuant to UCC § 2–709. The contract price may be recovered by seller when buyer accepts the goods. UCC § 2–709(1)(a). Acceptance occurred when buyer failed to make an effective rejection [UCC § 2–602(1)] after having had a reasonable opportunity to inspect the goods. UCC § 2–606(1)(b). Official Comment 1 to this section states, "Under this Article 'acceptance' as applied to goods means that the buyer takes particular goods which have been appropriated to the contract as his own, whether or not he is obligated to do so, and whether he does so by words, action or silence when it is time to speak." The goods were delivered to buyer in November, 1981 and it was not until April, 1982, when seller contacted buyer about payment, did buyer first complain about the non-conformity of the rubber pads. Buyer had a reasonable opportunity to inspect and reject the goods. It was his silence for five months that constituted the acceptance.

The acceptance of goods precludes their subsequent rejection. UCC § 2–607(2). Once accepted, return of the goods can only be made by way of revocation of acceptance. UCC § 2–608. "Revocation of acceptance must occur within a reasonable time after the buyer discovers or should have discovered the ground for it. . . . It is not effective until the buyer notifies the seller of it." UCC § 2–608(2). Although this assertion was not made by defendant, he failed to act within a reasonable time to revoke acceptance of the goods.

* * *

Judgment for plaintiff-seller in the amount of $2,580, plus interest from January 1, 1982, plus costs.

Revocation of Acceptance

McCULLOUGH v. BILL SWAD CHRYSLER–PLYMOUTH, INC.

Supreme Court of Ohio, 1983.
5 Ohio St.3d 181, 449 N.E.2d 1289.

LOCHER, J.

On May 23, 1978, appellee, Deborah A. McCullough (then Deborah Miller), purchased a 1978 Chrysler LeBaron from appellant, Bill Swad Chrysler-Plymouth, Inc. (now Bill Swad Datsun, Inc.). The automobile was protected by both a limited warranty and a Vehicle Service Contract (extended warranty). Following delivery of the vehicle, appellee and her (then) fiance informed appellant's sales agent of problems they had noted with the car's brakes, lack of rustproofing, paint job and seat panels. Other problems were noted by appellee as to the car's transmission and air conditioning. The next day, the brakes failed, and appellee returned the car to appellant for the necessary repairs.

When again in possession of the car, appellee discovered that the brakes had not been fixed properly and that none of the cosmetic work was done. Problems were also noted with respect to the car's steering mechanism. Again, the car was returned for repair and again new problems appeared, this time as to

the windshield post, the vinyl top and the paint job. Only two weeks later, appellant was unable to eliminate a noise appellee complained of that had developed in the car's rear end.

On June 26, 1978, appellee returned the car to appellant for correction both of the still unremedied defects and of other flaws that had surfaced since the last failed repair effort. Appellant retained possession of the vehicle for over three weeks in order to service it, but even then many of the former problems persisted. Moreover, appellant's workmanship had apparently caused new defects to arise affecting the car's stereo system, landau top and exterior. Appellee also experienced difficulties with vibrations, the horn, and the brakes.

The following month, while appellee was on a short trip away from her home, the automobile's engine abruptly shut off. The car eventually had to be towed to appellant's service shop for repair. A few days later, when appellee and her husband were embarked on an extensive honeymoon vacation, the brakes again failed. Upon returning from their excursion, the newlyweds, who had prepared a list of thirty-two of the automobile's defects, submitted the list to appellant and again requested their correction. By the end of October 1978, few of the enumerated problems had been remedied.

In early November 1978, appellee contacted appellant's successor, Chrysler-Plymouth East ("East"), regarding further servicing of the vehicle. East was not able to undertake the requested repairs until January 1979. Despite the additional work which East performed, the vehicle continued to malfunction. After May 1979, East refused to perform any additional work on the automobile, claiming that the vehicle was in satisfactory condition, appellee's assertions to the contrary notwithstanding.

On January 8, 1979, appellee, by letter addressed to appellant, called for the rescission of the purchase agreement, demanded a refund of the entire purchase price and expenses incurred, and offered to return the automobile to appellant upon receipt of shipping instructions. Appellant did not respond to appellee's letter, and appellee continued to operate the car.

On January 12, 1979, appellee filed suit. . . . By the time of trial, June 25, 1980, the subject vehicle had been driven nearly 35,000 miles, approximately 23,000 of which were logged after appellee mailed her notice of revocation. The trial court . . . entered judgment for appellee against appellant in the amount of $9,376.82, and ordered the return of the automobile to appellant. The court of appeals subsequently affirmed, determining that appellee had properly revoked her acceptance of the automobile despite her continued use of the vehicle, which use the appellate court found reasonable.

* * *

The case at bar essentially poses but a single question: Whether appellee, by continuing to operate the vehicle she had purchased from appellant after notifying the latter of her intent to rescind the purchase agreement, waived her right to revoke her initial acceptance. After having thoroughly reviewed both the relevant facts in the present cause and the applicable law, we find that appellee, despite her extensive use of the car following her revocation, in no way forfeited such right.

The ultimate disposition of the instant action is governed primarily by [U.C.C. 2–608] which provides, in pertinent part:

"(A) The buyer may revoke his acceptance of a lot or commercial unit whose nonconformity substantially impairs its value to him if he has accepted it:
"(1) on the reasonable assumption that its nonconformity would be cured and it has not been seasonably cured; . . .

* * *

"(B) Revocation of acceptance must occur within a reasonable time after the buyer discovers or should have discovered the ground for it and before any substantial change in condition of the goods which is not caused by their own defects. It is not effective until the buyer notifies the seller of it."

* * *

Appellant essentially argues that appellee's revocation of her initial acceptance of the automobile was ineffective as it did not comply with the mode prescribed for revocation in U.C.C. 2–608. Specifically, appellant asserts that appellee's continued operation of the vehicle after advising appellant of her revocation was inconsistent with her having relinquished ownership of the car, that the value of the automobile to appellee was not substantially impaired by its alleged nonconformities, and that the warranties furnished by appellant provided the sole legal remedy for alleviating the automobile's defects. Each of appellant's contentions must be rejected.

Although the legal question presented in appellant's first objection is a novel one for this bench, other state courts which have addressed the issue have held that whether continued use of goods after notification of revocation of their acceptance vitiates such revocation is solely dependent upon whether such use was reasonable. [Citations.] * * *

The genesis of the "reasonable use" test lies in the recognition that frequently a buyer, after revoking his earlier acceptance of a good, is constrained by exogenous circumstances— many of which the seller controls—to continue using the good until a suitable replacement may realistically be secured. Clearly, to penalize the buyer for a predicament not of his own creation would be patently unjust.

* * *

It is manifest that . . . appellee acted reasonably in continuing to operate her motor vehicle even after revocation of acceptance. First, the failure of the seller to advise the buyer, after the latter has revoked his acceptance of the goods, how the goods were to be returned entitles the buyer to retain possession of them. [Citations.] Appellant, in the case at bar, did not respond to appellee's request for instructions regarding the disposition of the vehicle. Failing to have done so, appellant can hardly be heard now to complain of appellee's continued use of the automobile.

Secondly, appellee, a young clerical secretary of limited financial resources, was scarcely in position to return the defective automobile and obtain a second in order to meet her business and personal needs. A most unreasonable obligation would be imposed upon appellee were she to be required, in effect, to secure a loan to purchase a second car while remaining liable for repayment of the first car loan.

* * *

Finally, it is apparent that appellant was not prejudiced by appellee's continued operation of the automobile. Had appellant retaken possession of the vehicle pursuant to appellee's notice of revocation, the automobile, which at the time had been driven only 12,000 miles, could easily have been resold. Indeed, the car was still marketable at the time of trial, as even then the odometer registered less than 35,000 miles. In any event, having failed to reassume ownership of the automobile when requested to do so, appellant alone must bear the loss for any diminution of the vehicle's resale value occurring between the two dates.

* * *

Appellant maintains, however, that even if appellee's continued operation of the automobile after revocation was reasonable, such use is "prima facie evidence" that the vehicle's nonconformities did not substantially impair its value to appellee, thus precluding availability of the remedy of revocation. Such an inference, though, may not be drawn. As stated earlier, external conditions beyond the buyer's immediate control often mandate continued use of an item even after revocation of its acceptance. Thus, it cannot seriously be contended that appellee, by continuing to operate the defective vehicle, intimated that its nonconformities did not substantially diminish its worth in her eyes.

We must similarly dismiss appellant's assertion that, as appellee's complaints primarily concerned cosmetic flaws, the defects were trivial. First, the chronic steering, transmission and brake problems which appellee experienced in operating the vehicle could hardly be deemed inconsequential. Moreover, even purely cosmetic defects, under the proper set of circumstances, can significantly affect the buyer's valuation of the good. [Citation.]

* * *

Clearly, no error was committed in finding that the fears occasioned by the recurrent brake failings, steering malfunctions and other mechanical difficulties, as well as the utter frustration caused by the seemingly endless array of cosmetic flaws, constituted nonconformities giving rise to the remedy of revocation.

* * *

Judgment affirmed.

Anticipatory Repudiation

NEPTUNE RESEARCH & DEVELOPMENT, INC. v. TEKNICS INDUSTRIAL SYSTEMS, INC.

New Jersey Superior Court, Appellate Division, 1989. 235 N.J. Super. 522, 563 A.2d 465.

KING, J.

The buyer sued in the Law Division, demanding return of its $3,000 deposit plus interest and costs, alleging proper cancellation because the seller failed to make timely delivery. The seller answered and counterclaimed seeking the balance of a 15% contractually-established cancellation price. After a bench trial, Judge Russell found for the buyer and dismissed the counterclaim.

These are the facts. The evidence in this case consisted principally of the written contract and the testimony of Akos Sule, buyer's founder, president and majority shareholder, of Paul Ng, buyer's general manager and Sule's second-in-command, and of Dave Robertson, one of seller's owners. The facts were not in substantial dispute, although there was one minor difference of opinion.

Buyer manufactured solar-operated valves used in scientific instruments. The machine involved is a Model RC-520 triple access Precision Vertical Machining Center which is used to drill holes in components with the very high degree of accuracy required by buyer. Sule saw the machine advertised in a trade journal and, believing that it was ideal for buyer's needs, contacted seller in late

March or early April 1986. Following negotiations with seller's president, Ed Shepler, and an inspection of seller's facility, Sule placed an order on April 22, 1986.

The purchase price was approximately $55,000. The parties agreed to a mid-June 1986 delivery date, Shepler believing at the time that the machine was then in transit from Japan. Although the writing specified a mid-June delivery date; there was no clause stating that time was of the essence of the contract.* * *

In early June, Sule instructed Ng to call seller about the delivery date. Ng testified that from June onwards he made a number of telephone calls and got noncommittal or evasive responses. Robertson testified that after the sale was negotiated seller discovered a design deficiency in the machine and redesigned it in order to make a better product. However, there was no evidence that Robertson informed Sule or Ng of the alleged reasons for the delay.

By late August, buyer was in desperate need of the machine, although it is not clear whether this was communicated to seller. On August 29, Sule went to seller's place of business to examine the product, which was then in the process of being assembled. The machine was essentially the same as that ordered by Sule, except that it no longer had a linear ballbearing raise which Sule had thought was an attractive aspect.

Nonetheless, Sule agreed to take it. He, Shepler and Robertson agreed that seller would have the machine ready on September 5. Robertson promised to call Sule on September 3 so that Sule could have two days to arrange for his truckers to pick up the product.

Robertson did not call Sule on September 3. The next day, September 4, Sule told Ng to find out what was happening. Ng testified that he had three conversations with Robertson. According to Ng, during the first conversation Robertson told him that under "no circumstances" would seller be able to get the machine ready for pickup on September 5. Rather, the machine could be picked up at the earliest on September 9 or September 10. Ng reported this information to Sule, who then decided to cancel because he was "fed up" with the course of dealing and no longer had faith in seller. At Sule's direction, Ng telephoned seller and he informed Robertson and the office manager, Lorraine Mercier, that buyer was cancelling the order and that the contract was void because of the extraordinary delay in delivery and seller's failure to be truthful with buyer. Ng also asked for the return of the deposit. The third phone call took place about an hour later, when Robertson stated that the machine could be ready by the next day. Ng responded, "Thank you, but no thanks."

* * *

By letter dated September 4, 1986, addressed to seller's office manager, Sule confirmed that buyer no longer wanted the machine and expected the return of its $3,000 deposit. Robertson claimed that the machine was in fact ready to be picked up on September 5. The parties thereafter attempted to resurrect the transaction, but the terms proposed by buyer and its attorney were not acceptable to seller. Buyer then filed this law suit a few weeks later.

* * *

We disagree with seller that it had a right to cure.* * *

* * * In the present case, buyer cancelled the contract before seller got around to tendering or delivering the goods. Buyer never rejected the machine. Buyer here simply claims that there was no contract in existence at the time seller was supposed to deliver.

What we then have is a repudiation by seller that allegedly amounted to an anticipatory breach, followed by a retraction. The Code prescribes specific rules for this kind of situation which are similar in many respects to the rejection-cure provisions, but which in some respects are different. [U.C.C.] 2–610, entitled "Anticipatory Repudiation," states that when "either party repudiates the contract with respect to a performance not yet due the loss of which will substantially impair the value of the contract to the other, the aggrieved party may . . . resort to any remedy for breach." One of the remedies available to a buyer is cancellation, [U.C.C.]

2–711(1), which occurs "when either party puts an end to the contract for breach by the other." [U.C.C.] 2–106(4). However, the Code permits a party to retract an anticipatory repudiation under some circumstances. Specifically, [U.C.C.] 2–611(1) states:

"Until the repudiating party's next performance is due he can retract his repudiation unless the aggrieved party has since the repudiation cancelled or materially changed his position or otherwise indicated that he considers the repudiation final."

In our opinion, § 2–610 and § 2–611 govern here. The key questions are: (1) did seller in fact repudiate when Robertson stated that the machine could not possibly be ready by September 5, and (2) should seller be allowed to retract its repudiation because buyer did not change its position for the worse?

Implicated in the first question are whether a statement that the seller cannot deliver on time is a repudiation, and, on these facts, whether such a statement substantially impaired the value of the contract to buyer. The Uniform Commercial Code comment to § 2–610 states that the "most useful test of substantial value is to determine whether material inconvenience or injustice will result if the aggrieved party is forced to wait and receive an ultimate tender minus the part or aspect repudiated." Section 2–610 expresses preexisting New Jersey case law. See New Jersey study comment to [U.C.C.] 2–610. There are some helpful, though not dispositive, extant cases.

Our Supreme Court offered a useful definition of anticipatory repudiation in Ross Systems v. Linden Dari Delite, Inc., [citation], as follows:

"An anticipatory breach is a definite and unconditional declaration by a party to an executory contract—through word or conduct—that he will not or cannot render the agreed upon performance. [Citation omitted.] If the breach is material, i.e., goes to the essence of the contract, the nonbreaching party may treat the contract as terminated and refuse to render continued performance. [Citation omitted.]"

We find no modern support for the trial judge's view that defendant's failure to make delivery in mid-June 1986 in itself constituted a repudiation, or material breach, and immediately entitled plaintiff to cancel. The contract had no "time-of-the-essence" clause and there was nothing in the surrounding circumstances to indicate that the initial time of performance was essential.

The Code leaves it to the parties to agree on time requirements; in the absence of an agreement the Code will imply a provision in the contract requiring delivery within a reasonable time. [U.C.C.] 2–309(1). A court's function is to determine whether and when it was the intention of the parties to make timely performance a vital feature of the contract. [Citation.] If time was of the essence then the breach was material and plaintiff had a right to cancel. [Citations.]

A contract does not need to expressly state that time is of the essence in order for timely delivery to be deemed essential. [Citation.] A failure to deliver within the prescribed time may justify the buyer in cancelling. Likewise, an announcement by the seller to the buyer that he cannot deliver in time may be a repudiation under § 2–610. [Citation.]

* * *

We think under the circumstances here one could reasonably find that seller's repudiation went to the essence of the contract. Defendant had agreed to a mid-June delivery. Throughout the summer it not only failed to deliver, but it refused to explain its reasons for non-delivery or to give plaintiff adequate assurances that the machine would be delivered soon. [U.C.C.] 2–609(1) (entitling a party to cancel under some circumstances if the other party fails to give adequate assurances). By late August buyer, according to Sule, was in desperate need of the machine. On August 29, Sule learned that the machine buyer bought was no longer available because seller had changed the design. We conclude that buyer readily could have cancelled at that point but it did not. Rather, Sule agreed to accept the modified machine but only on the express condition that seller have the product available by September 5.

While Sule did not expressly state to any of seller's representatives that time had now become of the essence, we conclude this condition can fairly be implied, from the surrounding circumstances. Buyer had already waited a long time, seller had not been candid with buyer, and Sule had good reason to believe that seller would not perform. In essence, the events of August 29 can be viewed as Sule giving seller "one last chance." Seller's failure to call buyer on September 3, as seller had promised to do, could have only deepened buyer's suspicion that seller was not going to perform. In light of these circumstances, Robertson's unequivocal statement on September 4, that under no circumstances would the machine be ready by the promised delivery date, September 5, was a repudiation going to the essence of the contract.

* * *

We conclude that Robertson's statement on September 4 constituted an anticipatory repudiation within the meaning of § 2–610. The remaining question is whether Robertson's offer later that day to make the machine available for delivery on the agreed-upon September 5 date amounted to an effective retraction within the meaning of § 2–611(1). That section allows a repudiating party to retract if performance is not yet due unless the nonbreaching party has "since the repudiation cancelled or materially changed his position or otherwise indicated that he considers the repudiation final."

The disjunctive language of § 2–611(1) is key. Pre-Code authority is somewhat ambiguous on whether a buyer must change his position for the worse in order to preclude a seller from retracting a repudiation. * * *

* * *

We have found no helpful cases construing § 2–611(1), but we assume that the drafters intentionally used the disjunctive: that is, the breaching party loses the right to retract if the nonbreaching party materially changes his position or cancels. . . . The Comment [to the cognate provision of the Restatement of Contracts] explains:

"Once the injured party has materially changed his position in reliance on the repudiation, nullification would clearly be unjust. In the interest of certainty, however, it is undesirable to make the injured party's rights turn exclusively on such a vague criterion, and he may therefore prevent subsequent nullification by indicating to the other party that he considers the repudiation [sic] final." [Id., Comment c. at 294–295.]

In the present case buyer did not change its position for the worse prior to retraction, at least in the sense of either filing suit or getting a replacement machine. Buyer clearly had no time to do that, since seller attempted to retract its repudiation within an hour. The question before us is whether buyer's cancellation stands despite the absence of prejudice and seller's nearly immediate retraction. We can find no case which addresses a similar situation.

Under the facts before us, we give effect to buyer's cancellation. We reach this result for three reasons. First, the express language of § 2–611(1) permits cancellation and bars retraction even in the absence of prejudice. Second, the certainty interest expressed and found in the Restatement is, in this instance, persuasive. Third, we cannot ignore seller's previous, less-than-exemplary conduct. Corbin makes the point that if "substantial performance of the contract requires the maintenance of a relation of trust and confidence between the parties and the repudiation is of such a character as to shatter this relation beyond repair, the repudiation in itself creates such a change of position as to prevent retraction." [Citation.]

This was such a relationship. Seller was supplying an expensive, complex "high-tech" machine which, presumably, was important, if not essential, for the success of buyer's business enterprise. Seller was to supply installation services and train two operators as part of the contract. The machine was sold with express warranties. Such a machine would require periodic maintenance and repair, services which seller must perform under the terms of the express warranty. Indeed, the written contract itself contains a statement that seller looked forward to a "long and prosperous relationship." Seller's repudiation, which followed a series of deviations from the terms of the contract, was in a real sense "the straw that broke the camel's back." We find buyer reasonably concluded that it could no longer rely upon seller. The cancellation by buyer was justified.

Affirmed.

QUESTIONS

1. Explain the requirements of tender of delivery with respect to time, manner, and place of delivery.

2. Explain the perfect tender rule and the three limitations upon it.

3. Explain when the buyer has the right to reject the goods and what obligations the buyer has upon rejection.

4. Discuss the buyer's right to revoke acceptance.

5. Identify and discuss the excuses for non-performance.

PROBLEMS

1. Tammie contracted with Kristine to manufacture, sell, and deliver to Kristine and put in running order a certain machine. Tammie set up the machine and put it in running order. Kristine found it unsatisfactory and notified Tammie that she rejected the machine. She continued to use it for three months, but continually complained of its defective condition. At the end of the three months she notified Tammie to come and get it. Has Kristine lost her right (a) to reject the machine? (b) to revoke acceptance of the machine?

2. Smith, having contracted to sell to Beyer thirty tons of described fertilizer, shipped to Beyer by carrier thirty tons of fertilizer which he stated conformed to the contract. Nothing was stated in the contract as to time of payment, but Smith demanded payment as a condition of handing over the fertilizer to Beyer. Beyer refused to pay unless he were given the opportunity to inspect the fertilizer. Smith sues Beyer for breach of contract. Decision?

3. Benny and Sheree entered into a contract for the sale of one hundred barrels of flour. No mention was made of any place of delivery. Thereafter, Sheree demanded that Benny deliver the flour at her place of business, and Benny demanded that Sheree come and take the flour from his place of business. Neither party acceded to the demand of the other. Has either one a right of action against the other?

4. Johnson, a manufacturer of air conditioning units, made a written contract with Maxwell to sell to Maxwell forty units at a price of $200 each and to deliver them at a certain apartment building owned by Maxwell for installation by Maxwell. Upon the arrival of Johnson's truck for delivery at the apartment building, Maxwell examined the units on the truck, counted only thirty units, and asked the driver if this was the total delivery. The driver replied that it was as far as he knew. Maxwell told the driver that she would not accept delivery of the units. The next day Johnson telephoned Maxwell and inquired why delivery was refused. Maxwell stated that the units on the truck were not what she ordered; that she ordered forty units, that only thirty were tendered, and that she was going to buy air conditioning units elsewhere. In an action by Johnson against Maxwell for breach of contract, Maxwell defends upon the ground that the tender of thirty units was improper, as the contract called for delivery of forty units. Is this a valid defense?

5. Edwin sells a sofa to Jack for $800. Edwin and Jack both know that the sofa is in Edwin's warehouse located approximately ten miles from Jack's home. The contract did not specify the place of delivery, and Jack insists that the place of delivery is either his house or Edwin's store. Is Jack correct?

6. On November 4, Kim contracted to sell to Lynn 500 sacks of flour at $4 each to be shipped in November to Lynn. On November 27, Kim shipped the flour. By December 5, when the car arrived, containing only 450 sacks, the market price of flour had fallen. The usual time required for shipment was five to twelve days. Lynn refused to accept delivery or to pay. Kim shipped fifty more sacks of flour, which arrived December 10. Lynn refused delivery. Kim resold the flour for $3 per sack. What are Kim's rights against Lynn?

7. Farley and Trudy enter into a written contract whereby Farley agrees to sell and Trudy to buy 6,000 bushels of wheat at $3.75 per bushel, deliverable at the rate of 1,000 bushels a month commencing June 1, the price for each installment being payable ten days after delivery thereof. Farley delivered and received payment for the June installment. But Farley defaulted by failing to deliver the July and August installments. By August 15, the market price of wheat had increased to $4 per bushel. Trudy thereupon entered into a contract with Albert to purchase 5,000 bushels of wheat at $4 per bushel deliverable over the ensuing four months. In late September, the market price of wheat commenced to decline and by December 1 was $3.25 per bushel. Trudy brings an action against Farley for breach of contract. Decision?

8. Bain ordered from Marcum a carload of lumber, which he intended to use in the construction of small boats for the U.S. Navy pursuant to contract. The order specified that the lumber was to be free from knots, wormholes, and defects. The lumber was shipped, and immediately upon receipt Bain looked into the door of the fully loaded car, ascertained that there was a full carload of lumber, and acknowledged to Marcum that the carload had been received. On the same day Bain moved the car to his private siding and sent to

Marcum full payment in accordance with the terms of the order.

A day later, the car was moved to the work area and unloaded in the presence of the navy inspector, who refused to allow three-fourths of it to be used because of excessive knots and wormholes in the lumber. Bain then informed Marcum that he was rejecting the order and requested refund of the payment and directions on disposition of the lumber. Marcum replied that since Bain had accepted the order and unloaded it, he was not entitled to return of the purchase price. Bain thereupon brought an action against Marcum to recover the purchase price. Decision?

9. Plaintiff, a seller of milk, had for ten years bid on contracts to supply milk to defendant school district and had supplied milk to other school districts in the area. On June 15, 1987, plaintiff contracted to supply defendant's requirements of milk for the school year 1987–1988, at a price of $.0759 per half pint. The price of raw milk delivered from the farm had been for years controlled by the U.S. Department of Agriculture. On June 15, 1987, the department's administrator for the New York–New Jersey area had mandated a price for raw milk of $8.03 per hundredweight. By December 1987, the mandated price had been raised to $9.31 a hundredweight, an increase of nearly 20 percent. If required to complete deliveries at the contract price, plaintiff would lose $7,350.55 on its contract with defendant and would face similar losses on contracts with two other school districts. Plaintiff sued for a judgment that its performance had become impracticable through unforeseen events, particularly unanticipated grain crop failures and the huge amounts of grain sold to Russia in mid–1987. Decision?

10. In April F. W. Lang Company purchased an ice cream freezer and refrigeration compressor unit from Fleet for $2,160. Although the parties agreed to a written installment contract providing for an $850 down payment and eighteen installment payments, Lang made only one $200 payment upon receipt of the goods. One year later, Lang moved to a new location and took the equipment along without notifying Fleet. Two years after the sale, Lang disconnected the compressor from the freezer and used it to operate an air conditioner. Lang continued to use the compressor for that purpose until the sheriff seized the equipment and returned it to Fleet pursuant to a court order. Fleet then sold the equipment for $500 in what both parties conceded was a fair sale. Lang then brought an action charging that the equipment was defective and unusable for the intended purpose and sought to recover the down payment and expenses incurred in repairing the equipment. Fleet counterclaimed for the balance due under the installment contract less the proceeds from the sale. Decision?

COMPUTER RESEARCH PROBLEMS

1. On March 17, Peckham bought a new car from Larsen Chevrolet for $6,400.85. During the first one and one-half months after the purchase, Peckham discovered that the car's hood was dented, its gas tank contained no baffles, its emergency brake was inoperable, the car did not have a jack or a spare tire, and neither the clock nor the speedometer worked. Larsen claimed that Peckham knew of the defects at the time of the purchase. Peckham, on the other hand, claimed that despite his repeated efforts the defects were not repaired until June 11. Then, on July 15, the car's dashboard caught fire, leaving the car's interior damaged and the car itself inoperable. Peckham then returned to Larsen Chevrolet and told Larsen that he had to repair the car at his own expense or he, Peckham, would either rescind the contract or demand a new automobile. Peckham also claimed that at the end of their conversation he notified Larsen Chevrolet that he was electing to rescind the contract and demanded the return of the purchase price. Larsen denied having received that oral notification. On October 12, Peckham sent a written notice of rescission to Larsen. Decision?

2. Joc Oil bought a cargo of fuel oil for resale. The certificate from the foreign refinery stated the sulphur content of the oil was 0.5 percent. Joc Oil entered into a written contract with Con Ed for the sale of this oil. The contract specified a sulphur content of 0.5 percent. Joc Oil knew, however, that Con Ed was authorized to buy and burn oil of up to 1 percent sulphur content, and that Con Ed often bought and mixed oils of varying contents to stay within this limit. The oil under contract was delivered to Con Ed, but independent testing revealed a sulphur content of 0.92 percent. Con Ed promptly rejected the nonconforming shipment. Joc Oil immediately offered to substitute a conforming shipment of oil, although the time for performance had expired after the first shipment of oil. Con Ed refused to accept the substituted shipment. Joc Oil sues Con Ed for breach of contract. Judgment?

3. Plaintiff West German wine producer and exporter contracted to ship 620 cases of wine to the defendant distributor in North Carolina. The contract was silent as to the shipment destination. During the next several months, defendant called repeatedly to find out the status of the shipment. Later, without notifying defendant, plaintiff delivered the wine to a shipping line in Rotterdam, destined for Wilmington, N.C. The ship and the wine were lost at sea en route to Wilmington. When defendant refused to pay on the contract, plaintiff sued. Decision?

4. Can-Key Industries, Inc., manufactured a turkey-hatching unit, which it sold to Industrial Leasing Corporation (ILC), which leased it to Rose-A-Linda Turkey Farms. ILC conditioned its obligation to pay on Rose-A-Linda's acceptance of the equipment. Rose-A-Linda indicated its dissatisfaction with the equipment, and ILC refused to perform its obligations under the contract. Can-Key then brought suit against ILC for breach of contract. It argued that Rose-A-Linda accepted the equipment, since it used it for fifteen months between March 1976 and May 1977. ILC contended that the equipment was unacceptable and asked that it be removed. It claimed that Can-Key refused and failed to instruct Rose-A-Linda to refrain from using the equipment. Therefore, ILC argued, Rose-A-Linda effectively rejected the turkey-hatching unit, relieving ILC of its contractual obligations. Decision?

Chapter 22

TRANSFER OF TITLE AND RISK OF LOSS

Transfer of Title
Risk of Loss
Sales of Goods in Bulk

HISTORICALLY, title governed nearly every aspect of the rights and duties of the buyer and seller arising out of a sales contract. In an attempt to add greater precision and certainty to sales contracts, the Code has abandoned the common law's reliance upon title. Instead, the Code approaches each legal issue arising out of a sales contract on its own merits and provides separate and specific rules to control the various transactional situations. This chapter covers the Code's approach to the transfer of title and other property rights, the passage of risk of loss, and the transfer of goods sold in bulk.

TRANSFER OF TITLE

As previously stated, a sale of goods is defined as the transfer of title from the seller to the buyer for a consideration known as the price. Section 2–106. Transfer of title is, therefore, fundamental to the existence of a sale of goods. Title, however, cannot pass under a contract for sale until existing goods have been identified to the contract. Section 2–401(1). Future goods (goods that are not both existing and identified) cannot constitute a present sale. Section 2–105. *See O'Brien v. Chandler.*

If the buyer rejects the goods, whether justifiably or not, title revests to the seller. Section 2–401(4).

Identification

After formation of the contract it is normal for the seller to take steps to obtain, manufacture, prepare, or select goods with which to fulfill her obligation under the contract. At some stage in the process the seller will have identified existing goods which she intends to ship, deliver, or hold for the buyer. Identification may be made by either the seller or the buyer and can be made at any time and in any manner agreed upon by the parties. In the absence of explicit agreement, **identification** takes place as provided in Section 2–501(1):

1. upon the making of the contract if it is for goods already existing and identified;

2. if the contract is for all other future goods, when the seller ships, marks, or otherwise designates existing goods as those to which the contract refers; or

3. if the contract is (a) for crops to be grown within twelve months or the next normal harvest when the crops are planted or start

growing, or (b) for the offspring of animals to be born within twelve months, when the young animals are conceived.

To illustrate, suppose Barringer contracts to purchase a particular Buick automobile from Stevenson's car lot. Identification occurs as soon as the contract is entered into. If, however, Barringer agreed to purchase a television set from Stevenson, who has his storeroom filled with such televisions, identification will not occur until either Barringer or Stevenson selects a particular television to fulfill the contract.

If the goods are **fungible** (the equivalent of any other unit), identification of a share of undivided goods occurs when the contract is entered into. Thus, if Barringer agreed to purchase 1,000 gallons of gasoline from Stevenson, who owns a 5,000 gallon tank of gasoline, identification occurs as soon as the contract is formed.

Where the goods have been identified to the contract by the seller alone he may substitute other goods for those so identified until such time as he (1) defaults, (2) becomes insolvent, or (3) notifies the buyer that the identification is final. Section 2–501(2).

Insurable Interest   In order for a contract or policy of insurance to be valid, the insured must have an insurable interest in the subject matter. At common law only a person with title or a lien (a legal claim of a creditor on property) could insure his interest in specific goods. The Code extends this right to a buyer's interest in goods that have been identified as goods to which the contract refers. Section 2–501(1). This **special property interest** of the buyer enables her to purchase insurance protection on goods that she does not presently own but that she will own upon delivery by the seller.

So long as he has title to them or any security interest in them, the seller also has an insurable interest in the goods. Section 2–501(2). Nothing prevents both seller and buyer from simultaneously carrying insurance on goods in which they both have a property interest, whether it be title, a security interest, or a special property interest.

Security Interest   A security interest is defined in the Code as an interest in personal property or fixtures that ensures payment or performance of an obligation. Section 1–201(37). Any reservation by the seller of title to goods *delivered* to the buyer is limited in effect to a reservation of a security interest. Section 2–401(1). As mentioned above, the seller retains an insurable interest in goods provided he has title to or any security interest in the goods. Section 2–501(2). Security interests in goods are governed by Article 9 of the Code (discussed in Chapter 38), except that so long as the buyer does not have or lawfully obtain possession of the goods (1) no security agreement is necessary, (2) no filing is required, and (3) the rights of the seller on default by the buyer are governed by Article 2. Section 9–113.

Passage of Title

Title passes when the parties *intend* it to pass, provided the goods are in existence and have been identified. Where the parties have no explicit agreement as to transfer of title, the Code provides rules that determine when title passes to the buyer. Section 2–401.

Physical Movement of the Goods   When delivery is to be made by moving the goods, title passes at the time and place the seller completes his performance with reference to delivery of the goods. Section 2–401(2). When and where delivery occurs depends on whether the contract is a shipment contract or a destination contract.

A **shipment contract** requires or authorizes the seller to send the goods to the buyer but does not require the seller to deliver them to a particular destination. Under a shipment contract, title passes to the buyer at the time and place that the seller *delivers* the goods to the carrier for shipment to the buyer.

A **destination contract** requires the seller to deliver the goods to a particular destination. Under a destination contract, title passes to the buyer upon *tender* of the goods at that destination. **Tender,** as discussed in Chapter 21, requires that the seller (1) put and hold conforming goods at the buyer's disposition, (2) give notice to the buyer that the goods are available, and (3) do so at a reasonable time and keep the goods available for a reasonable period of time. Section 2–503.

No Movement of the Goods When delivery is to be made without moving the goods, unless otherwise agreed, title passes: (1) upon delivery of a document of title where the contract calls for delivery of such document (documents of title are documents that evidence a right to receive specified goods—they are discussed more fully in Chapter 49); or (2) at the time and place of contracting where the goods at that time have been identified and no doc-

uments are to be delivered. Section 2–401(3). Where the goods are not identified at the time of contracting, title passes when the goods are identified.

For a summary of passage of title in the absence of an agreement by the parties, see Figure 22–1.

Power to Transfer Title

It is important to understand under what circumstances a seller has the right or power to transfer title to a buyer. If the seller is the rightful owner of goods or is authorized to sell the goods for the rightful owner, then the seller has the **right** to transfer title. But when a seller is in possession of goods that he neither owns nor has authority to sell, then the sale is not rightful. In some situations,

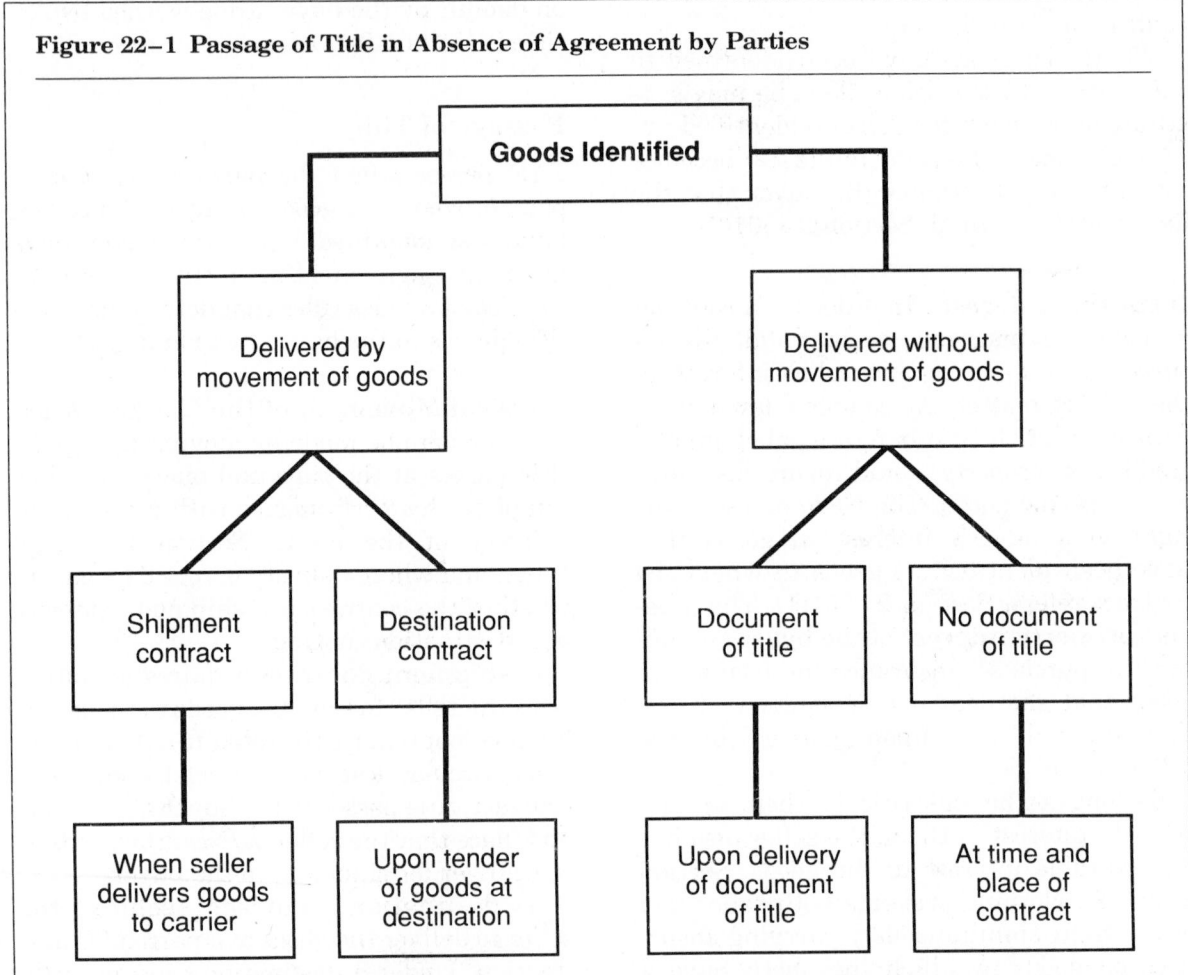

Figure 22–1 Passage of Title in Absence of Agreement by Parties

however, these unauthorized sellers may have the **power** to transfer good title to certain buyers. This section pertains to such sales by a person in possession of goods that he neither owns nor has authority to sell.

The fundamental rule of property law protecting existing ownership of goods is the starting point and background in any discussion of a sale of goods by a nonowner. It is basic that a purchaser of goods obtains such title as his transferor had or had power to transfer, and the Code expressly so states. Section 2–403. Likewise, the purchaser of a limited interest in goods acquires rights only to the extent of the interest that he purchased. By the same token, no one can transfer what he does not have. A purported sale by a thief or finder or ordinary bailee of goods does not transfer title to the purchaser.

The principal reason underlying the policy of the law in protecting existing ownership of goods is that a person should not be required to retain possession at all times of all the goods that he owns in order to maintain his ownership of them. One of the valuable incidents of ownership of goods is the freedom of the owner to make a bailment of his goods as he pleases, and the mere possession of goods by a bailee does not authorize the bailee to sell them.

Another policy of the law, however, conflicts with the policy protecting existing ownership of goods. It is the protection of the good faith purchaser based on the importance in trade and commerce of protecting the expectations of good faith transactions in goods. To encourage and make safe good faith acquisitions of goods it is necessary that *bona fide* (good faith) purchasers for value under certain circumstances be protected. A **good faith purchaser** is defined as one who acts honestly, gives value, and takes the goods without notice or knowledge of any defect in the title of his transferor.

The problems presented in this section and the rules for their solution should be considered in the light of these two competing policies of the law. Both policies are sound, beneficial, and worthy of enforcement. One protects existing property rights; the other protects good faith transactions in the marketplace.

Void and Voidable Title to Goods A **void title** is no title. A person claiming ownership of goods by an agreement that is void obtains no title to the goods. Thus, a person who acquires goods by physical duress or from someone under guardianship as well as a thief or a finder of goods has no title to them and can transfer none.

A **voidable title** is one acquired under circumstances that permit the former owner to rescind the transfer and revest herself with title, as in the case of mistake, common duress, undue influence, fraud in the inducement, misrepresentation, mistake, or sale by a person without contractual capacity (other than an individual under guardianship). In these situations, the buyer has acquired legal title to the goods, which may be divested by action of the seller. If, however, before the seller has rescinded the transfer of title, the buyer were to resell the goods to a good faith purchaser for value, the right of rescission in the seller is cut off, and the good faith purchaser for value acquires good title. *See O'Brien v. Chandler.* The Code defines good faith as "honesty in fact in the conduct or transaction concerned" and value to include a consideration sufficient to support a simple contract. Section 1–201.

The distinction between a void and voidable title is, therefore, extremely important in determining the rights of good faith purchasers of goods. *See Robinson v. Durham.* The good faith purchaser for value always believes that she is buying the goods from the owner or from one with authority to sell. Otherwise she would not be acting in good faith. In each situation, the party selling the goods appears to be the owner whether his title is valid, void, or voidable. Between two innocent persons—the true owner who has done nothing wrong and the good faith purchaser for value who has done nothing wrong—the law will not disturb the *legal title* but will rule in favor of the one who has it. Thus, where A transfers possession of goods to B

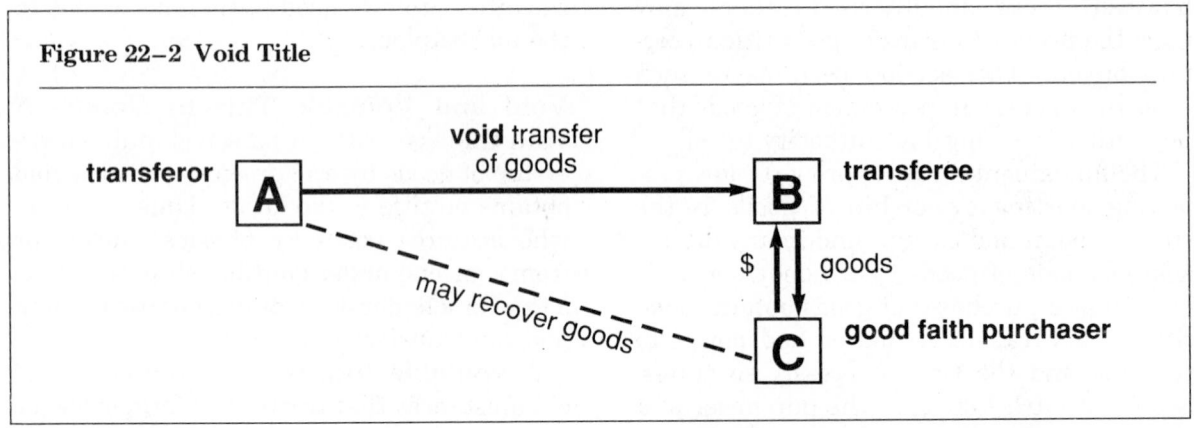

Figure 22–2 Void Title

under such circumstances that B acquires no title or a void title, and B thereafter sells the goods to C, a good faith purchaser for value, B has nothing except possession to transfer to C. In a lawsuit between A and C involving the right to the goods, A will win because she has the legal title. See Figure 22–2. C's only recourse is against B for breach of warranty of title, discussed in Chapter 23.

If, however, B acquired voidable title from A and resold the goods to C, in a suit between A and C over the goods, C would win. In this case, B had title, although it was voidable, which she transferred to the good faith purchaser for value. The title thus acquired by C will be protected. The voidable title in B is title until it has been avoided. After transfer to a good faith purchaser, it may not be avoided. See Figure 22–3. A's only recourse is against B for restitution or damages.

The Code has enlarged this common law doctrine by providing that a good faith purchaser for value obtains valid title from one possessing voidable title even if that person's voidable title was obtained by (1) fraud as to that person's identity, (2) exchange for a subsequently dishonored check, (3) an agreement that the transaction was to be a cash sale and the sale price has not been paid, or (4) criminal fraud punishable as larceny. Section 2–403(1).

In addition, the Code has expanded the rights of good faith purchasers with respect to sales by **minors.** The common law permitted a minor seller of goods to disaffirm the sale and to recover the goods from a third person who had purchased them in good faith from the party who acquired the goods from the minor. The Code has changed this rule and does not permit a minor seller of goods to prevail over a good faith purchaser for value. Section 2–403.

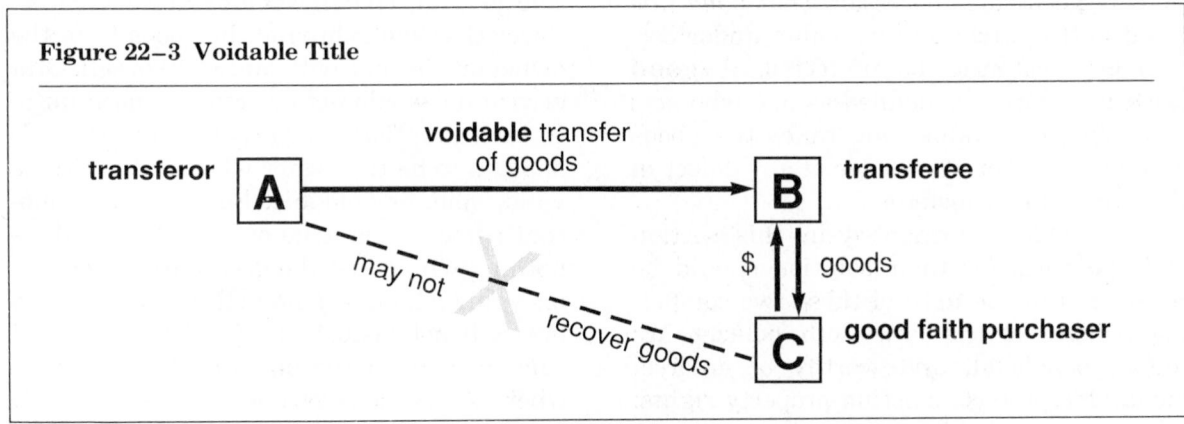

Figure 22–3 Voidable Title

Entrusting of Goods to a Merchant

Frequently, an owner of goods **entrusts** (transfers possession) the goods to a bailee for resale, repair, cleaning, or some other use of the goods. In some instances this entrusting is violated by the bailee selling the goods to a third party. Although the "true" owner has a right of recourse against the bailee for the value of the goods, what right, if any, should the true owner of the goods have against the third party? Once again the law must balance the right of ownership against the rights of market transactions.

The Code takes the position of protecting buyers of goods in the ordinary course of business from merchants who deal in goods of that kind, where the owner has entrusted possession of the goods to the merchant. The Code defines **buyer in ordinary course of business** as a person who in good faith and without knowledge that the sale to him is in violation of the ownership rights or security interest of another buys the goods in the ordinary course of business from a person in the business of selling goods of that kind, other than a pawnbroker. Section 1–201(9). *See Mattek v. Malofsky.* Because the merchant who deals in goods of that kind is cloaked with the appearance of ownership or apparent authority to sell, the Code seeks to protect the innocent third-party purchaser. Any such entrusting of possession bestows upon the merchant the power to transfer all rights of the entruster to a buyer in the ordinary course of business. Section 2–403(2). For example, A brings her stereo for repair to B, who also sells both new and used stereo equipment. C purchases A's stereo from B in the ordinary course of business. The Code protects the rights of C and defeats the rights of A. See Figure 22–4. A's only recourse is against B.

The Code, however, does not go so far as to protect the buyer in the ordinary course of business from a merchant to whom the goods have been entrusted by a thief or finder or by a completely unauthorized person. It merely grants the buyer in the ordinary course of business the rights of the entruster.

Where a buyer of goods to whom title has passed leaves the seller in possession of the goods, the buyer has "entrusted the goods" to the seller. Section 2–403(3). If that seller is a merchant and resells and delivers the goods to a buyer in the ordinary course of business, this second buyer acquires good title to the goods. Thus, Marianne sells certain goods to Martin who pays the price but allows possession to remain with Marianne. Marianne thereafter sells the same goods to Carla, a buyer in the ordinary course of business. Carla takes delivery of the goods. Martin does not have any rights against Carla or to the goods. Martin's only remedy is against Marianne.

RISK OF LOSS

Risk of loss, as the term is used in the law of sales, addresses the question of allocation of loss between seller and buyer where the goods have been damaged, destroyed, or lost *without the fault* of either the seller or the buyer. If the loss is placed on the buyer, he is

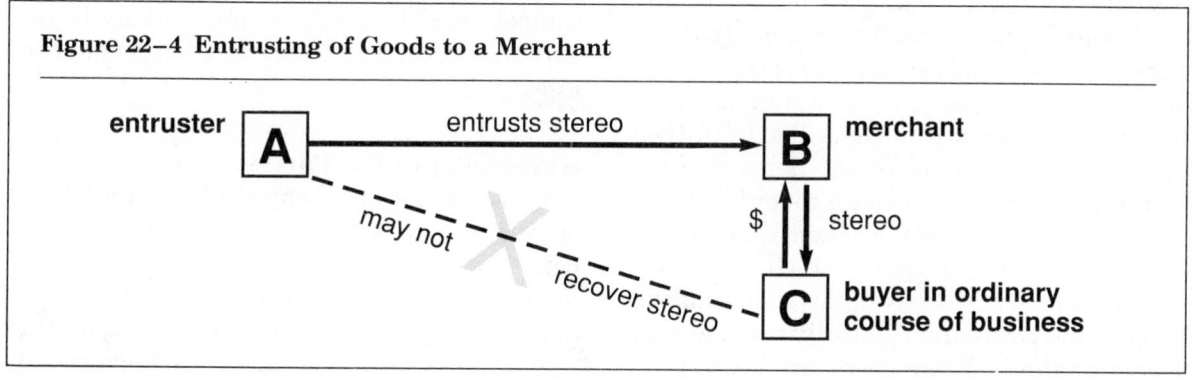

Figure 22–4 Entrusting of Goods to a Merchant

under a duty to pay the price for the goods even though they were damaged or he never received them. If placed upon the seller, he has no right to recover the purchase price from the buyer and is usually liable to the buyer for damages for non-delivery unless he tenders a performance in replacement for the lost or destroyed goods.

In determining the location of risk of loss, the Code provides definite rules for specific situations, a sharp departure from the common law concept of risk of loss, which was determined by ownership of the goods and depended upon whether title had been transferred. In its transactional approach, the Code is necessarily detailed and for this reason is probably more understandable and meaningful than the common law's reliance upon the abstract concept of title. The Code has adopted separate rules for determining the risk of loss in the absence of breach from those that apply where there has been a breach of the sales contract.

Risk of Loss Where There Is a Breach

Where one party breaches the contract, the Code places the risk of loss on the party who breaches the contract. Nevertheless, where the non-breaching party is in control of the goods, the Code places the risk of loss on him to the extent of his insurance coverage.

Breach by the Seller If the seller ships nonconforming goods to the buyer, the risk of loss remains on the seller until the buyer has accepted the goods or the seller has remedied the defect. Section 2–510(1).

Where the buyer has accepted non-conforming goods, and thereafter by timely notice to the seller rightfully revokes his acceptance (discussed in Chapter 21), he may treat the risk of loss as resting on the seller from the beginning to the extent of any deficiency in the buyer's effective insurance coverage. Section 2–510(2). For example, Heidi delivers to Gary nonconforming goods, which Gary accepts. Subsequently, Gary discovers a hidden defect in the goods and rightfully revokes his prior acceptance. If the goods are destroyed

through no fault of either party, and Gary has insured the goods for 60 percent of their fair market value of $10,000, then the insurance company will cover $6,000 of the loss and Heidi will bear the loss of $4,000. If the buyer's insurance coverage had been $10,000, then the seller would not bear any of the loss.

Breach by the Buyer Where conforming goods have been *identified* to a contract that the buyer repudiates or breaches before risk of loss has passed to him, the seller may treat the risk of loss as resting on the buyer "for a commercially reasonable time" to the extent of any deficiency in the seller's effective insurance coverage. Section 2–510(3). For example, Susan agrees to sell 40,000 pounds of plastic resin to Bernie, F.O.B. Bernie's factory, delivery by March 1. On February 1, Bernie wrongfully repudiates the contract by telephoning Susan and telling her that he does not want the resin. Susan immediately seeks another buyer, but before she is able to locate one, and within a commercially reasonable time, the resin is destroyed by a fire through no fault of Susan. The fair market value of the resin is $35,000. Susan's insurance only covers $15,000 of the loss. Bernie is liable for $20,000.

Risk of Loss in Absence of a Breach

Where there is no breach of contract, risk of loss may be allocated by the agreement of the parties. Where there is no breach, and the parties have not otherwise agreed, the Code places the risk of loss, for the most part, upon the party who is more likely to have greater control over the goods, is more likely to insure the goods, or is better able to prevent the loss.

Agreement of the Parties The parties, by agreement, not only may shift the allocation of risk of loss but also may divide the risk between them. Section 2–303. Such agreement is controlling. Thus, the parties may agree that a seller shall retain the risk of loss even though the buyer is in possession of the goods or has title to them. Or, the agreement may provide that the buyer bears 60 percent of the risk and the seller bears 40 percent.

Trial Sales Some sales are made on the understanding that the buyer can return the goods even though they conform to the contract. These trial sales permit the buyer to try the goods for a period of time in order to determine if she wishes to keep them or to try to resell them. Under the Code there are two types of trial sales: a sale on approval and a sale or return. The Code provides a test for distinguishing between the two types of trial sales: unless otherwise agreed, if the goods are delivered primarily for the buyer's use, the transaction is a sale on approval; if they are delivered primarily for resale by the buyer, it is a sale or return. Section 2–326(1).

In a **sale on approval,** possession of, but not title to, the goods is transferred to the buyer for a stated period of time or, if none is stated, for a reasonable time, during which period the buyer may use the goods to determine whether she wishes to buy them. Both title and risk of loss remain with the *seller* until "approval" or acceptance of the goods by the buyer. Section 2–327(1)(a). Until acceptance by the buyer, the sale is a bailment with an option to purchase.

Use of the goods consistent with the purpose of approval by the buyer is not acceptance, but failure of the buyer within a reasonable period of time to notify the seller of her election to return the goods is an acceptance. The buyer's approval may also be manifested by exercising any dominion or control over the goods inconsistent with the seller's ownership. Upon approval, risk of loss and title passes to the buyer who then becomes liable to the seller for the purchase price of the goods. If the buyer elects to return the goods and notifies the seller, the return is at the seller's risk and expense.

In a **sale or return,** the goods are sold and delivered to the buyer with an option to return them to the seller. The risk of loss is on the *buyer* who also has title until she revests

it in the seller by a return of the goods. The return of the goods is at the buyer's risk and expense.

A **consignment** is a delivery of possession of personal property to an agent for sale by the agent. Under the Code, a sale on consignment is regarded as a sale or return. Therefore, creditors of the consignee (the agent who receives the merchandise for sale) prevail over the consignor and may obtain possession of the consigned goods, provided the consignee maintains a place of business where he deals in goods of the kind involved under a name other than the name of the consignor. Nevertheless, under Section 2–326(3) the consignor will prevail if he (a) complies with applicable State law requiring a consignor's interest to be evidenced by a sign, or (b) establishes that the consignee is generally known by his creditors to be substantially engaged in selling the goods of others, or (c) complies with the filing provisions of Article 9 (Secured Transactions). Section 2–326(3).

Contracts Involving Carriers Sales contracts frequently contain terms that indicate the agreement of the parties as to delivery by a carrier. These terms designate whether the contract is a shipment contract or a destination contract and, by implication, when the risk of loss passes. If the contract does not require the seller to deliver the goods at a particular destination but merely to the carrier **(a shipment contract),** risk of loss passes to the buyer upon *delivery* of the goods to the common carrier. If the seller is required to deliver them to a particular destination **(a destination contract),** risk of loss passes to the buyer at destination upon *tender* of the goods to the buyer. Section 2–509(1).

Pestana v. Karinol deals with the question of when the risk of loss passes where the parties have no specific provision or any delivery term. The case demonstrates that if it is unclear whether the contract is a destination or shipment contract, the law assumes that it is a shipment contract.

Goods in Possession of Bailee

In some sales, the goods at the time of the contract are held by a bailee and are to be delivered without being moved. For instance, a seller may contract with a buyer to sell grain which is located in a grain elevator and which the buyer intends to leave in the same elevator. In such situations, Section 2–509(2) provides that the risk of loss passes to the buyer when one of the following occurs:

1. If a negotiable document of title (discussed in Chapter 49) is involved, upon the buyer's *receipt* of the document.

2. If a non-negotiable document of title is involved, when the document is tendered to the buyer.

3. If no documents of title are employed, upon either (a) the seller's tender to the buyer of written directions to the bailee to deliver the goods to the buyer; or (b) the bailee's acknowledgment of the buyer's right to possession of the goods.

In situations 2 and 3(a), if the buyer seasonably objects, the risk of loss remains upon the seller until the buyer has had a reasonable time to present the document or direction to the bailee.

All Other Sales

If the buyer possesses the goods when the contract is formed, risk of loss passes to the buyer at that time. Section 2–509(3). All other sales not involving breach are covered by Section 2–509(3). This catch-all provision applies to those instances in which the buyer picks up the goods at the seller's place of business or the goods are delivered by the seller using the seller's own transportation. In these cases, risk of loss depends on whether or not the seller is a merchant. If the seller is a **merchant,** risk of loss passes to the buyer upon the buyer's *receipt* of the goods. If the seller is **not a merchant,** it passes on *tender* of the goods from the seller to the buyer. Section 2–509(3). The policy behind this rule is that so long as the merchant seller is making delivery at her place of business or with her own vehicle, she continues to control the goods and can be expected to insure them. The buyer, on the other hand, has no control over the goods and is not likely to have insurance on them.

Suppose Belinda goes to Sidney's furniture store, selects a particular set of dining room furniture, and pays Sidney the agreed price of $800 for it upon Sidney's agreement to stain the set a darker color and deliver it. Sidney stains the furniture and notifies Belinda that she may pick up the furniture. That night it is accidentally destroyed by fire. Belinda can recover from Sidney the $800 payment. The risk of loss is on seller Sidney as he is a merchant and the goods were not received by Belinda but were only tendered to her.

On the other hand, suppose Georgia, an accountant, prior to moving to a different city, contracts to sell her household furniture to Nina for $3,000. Georgia notifies Nina that the furniture is available for her to pick up. Nina delays picking up the furniture for several days and in the interim the furniture is stolen from Georgia's residence without Georgia's fault. Georgia may recover from Nina the $3,000 purchase price. The risk of loss is on the buyer (Nina) as the seller is not a merchant and tender is sufficient to transfer the risk. *See Martin v. Melland's Inc.*

See Figure 22–5 for a summary of risk of loss in absence of breach by one of the parties.

SALES OF GOODS IN BULK

Creditors have an obvious interest in a merchant's disposal of the bulk of his merchandise not in the ordinary course of business. The danger to creditors is that the debtor may secretly liquidate all or a major part of his tangible assets by a bulk sale and conceal or divert the proceeds of the sale without paying his creditors. The central purpose of bulk sales law is to deal with two common forms of commercial fraud, namely: (1) the merchant, owing debts, who sells out his stock in trade to a friend for a low price, pays his creditors less than he owes them, and hopes to come back into the business through the back door some time in the future; and (2) the merchant, owing debts, who sells out his stock in trade to anyone for any price, pockets the proceeds, and disappears without paying his creditors.

Article 6 of the Code applies to such sales and defines a **bulk transfer** as "any transfer in bulk and not in the ordinary course of the transferor's business of a major part of the materials, supplies, merchandise, or other inventory." Section 6–102. The transfer of a substantial part of equipment is a bulk trans-

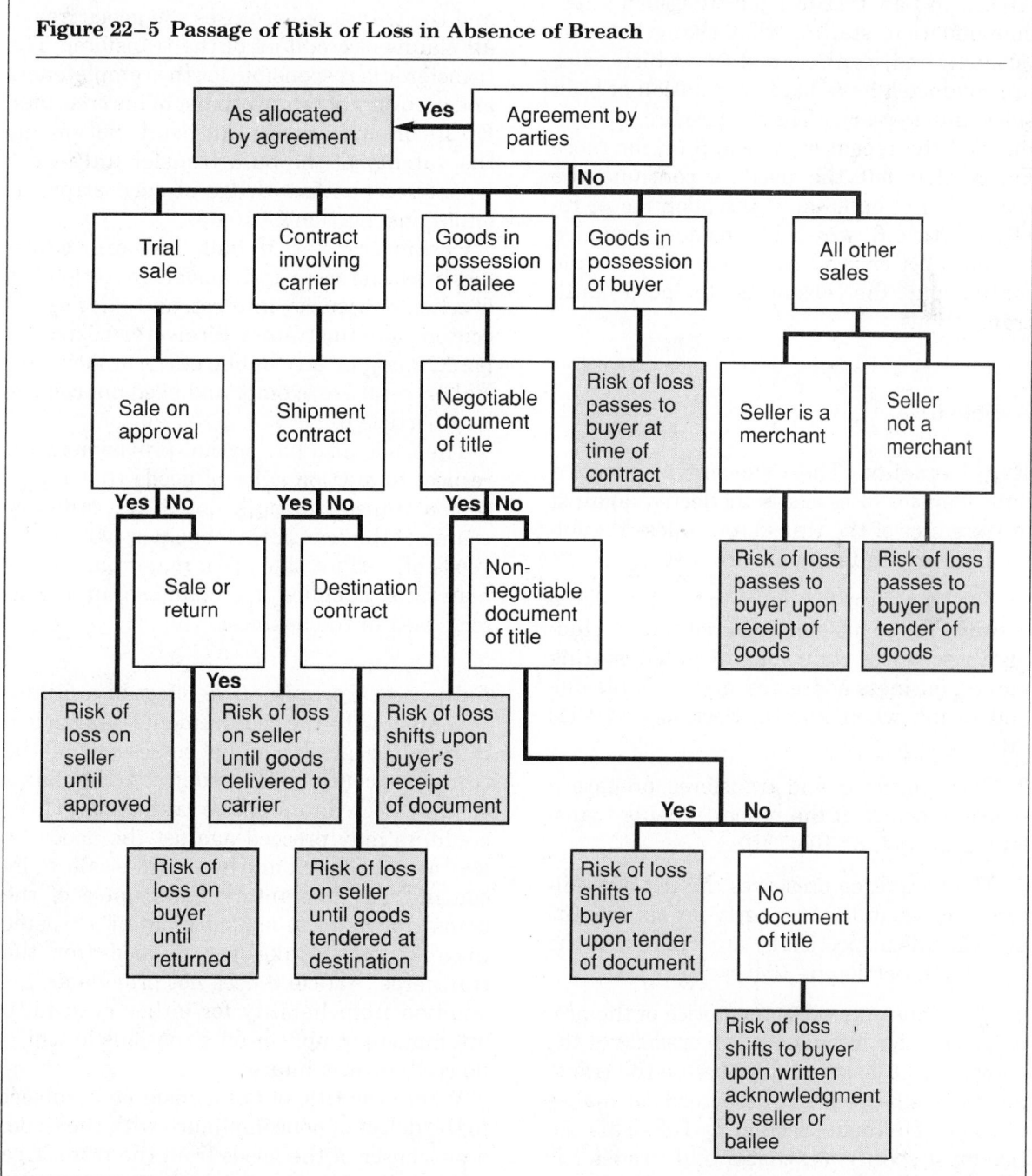

Figure 22–5 Passage of Risk of Loss in Absence of Breach

fer only if made in connection with a bulk transfer of inventory. The enterprises subject to Article 6 of the Code are those whose principal business is the sale of merchandise from stock, including those who manufacture what they sell.

In 1988, the National Conference of Commissioners on Uniform State Laws and the American Law Institute jointly issued a recommendation, stating "that changes in the business and legal contexts in which sales are conducted have made regulation of bulk sales unnecessary." They, therefore, recommended the repeal of Article 6 or, for those States that felt the need to continue the regulation of bulk sales, the adoption of revised Article 6, which it considers designed to afford better protection to creditors while minimizing the obstacles to good faith transactions.

Article 6

Requirements The Code provides that a bulk transfer of assets is ineffective against any creditor of the transferor, unless the following four requirements are met:

1. The transferor furnishes to the transferee a sworn list of his existing creditors, including those whose claims are disputed, stating names, business addresses, and amounts due and owing when known. Section 6–104(1) (a).

2. The transferor and transferee prepare a schedule or list of the property being transferred. Section 6–104(1)(b).

3. The transferee preserves the list of creditors and schedule of property for six months and permits inspection by any creditor of the transferor. Section 6–104(1)(c).

4. The transferee gives the notice of the proposed transfer in bulk to each creditor of the transferor at least ten days before the transferee takes possession of the goods or makes payment for them. Section 6–105. This notice must specify: (a) that a bulk transfer is about to be made; (b) the names and business addresses of the transferor in bulk and transferee in bulk; and (c) whether all debts of the transferor in bulk are to be paid in full as a result of the transaction, and if so, the address to which creditors should send their bills. Section 6–107(1).

If all of the above steps are taken, the transfer in bulk complies with the statute and the transferee acquires the goods free of all claims of creditors of the transferor. The transferor is responsible for the completeness and accuracy of the sworn list of his creditors. Errors or omissions in this list do not impair the validity of the bulk transfer unless the transferee has knowledge of such errors or omissions. Section 6–104(3).

Certain transfers in bulk (including transfers by way of security, transfers in settlement of a lien or security interest, and sales by executors, administrators, receivers, trustees in bankruptcy, or any public officer under judicial process) are exempt and need not comply with Article 6.

The Code also has special provisions with respect to auction sales of goods that represent a transfer in bulk not in the ordinary course of the transferor's business where the goods offered for sale are a major part of the materials, supplies, merchandise, or inventory used in the business.

Failure to Comply The effect of a failure to comply with the requirements of Article 6 is that the goods in the possession of the transferee continue to be subject to the claims of unpaid creditors of the transferor. These creditors may proceed against the goods by levy or attachment and by sheriff's sale, or by causing the involuntary bankruptcy of the transferor and the appointment of a trustee in bankruptcy to take over the goods from the transferee. Article 6 does not provide an exemption from liability for either good faith attempts to comply or for situations in which no creditor was injured.

Where the title of the transferee is subject to the defect of noncompliance with the Code, a purchaser of the goods from the transferee who pays value in good faith and takes the property without notice of such defect acquires the goods free of any claim of creditors of the transferor. A purchaser of the property from the transferee who pays no value or who takes them with notice of noncompliance acquires the goods subject to the claims of creditors of the transferor.

Revised Article 6

As previously noted, revised Article 6 was promulgated in response to the perceived inadequacy of the existing Article 6. The principal, identified shortcomings are that compliance with existing Article 6 is (1) time-consuming and expensive, especially when the seller has a large number of creditors, and (2) over-inclusive by applying to transferors even when there is no reason to believe that they are engaged in a fraudulent transfer.

The major changes made in revised Article 6 include the following:

1. The buyer is only subject to the Article when he has notice, or should have had notice, that the seller will not continue to operate the same or a similar type business. Section 6–102(1)(c).

2. When the seller is indebted to two hundred or more persons, the buyer may give notice by filing and need not send individual notices. Sections 6–105(2) and 6–104(2).

3. The notice requirement is extended from ten to forty-five days. Section 6–105(5).

4. A buyer who makes a good faith attempt to comply with the requirements of the Article, or who in good faith does not believe the Article applies to him, is relieved of liability for noncompliance. Section 6–107(3).

5. A buyer's failure to comply with the requirements of the Article does not render the sale void or otherwise affect the buyer's title to the goods, but the buyer's liability is limited to the damages caused by the noncompliance. Section 6–107(1)(b).

CASES

Identification/Power to Transfer Title

O'BRIEN v. CHANDLER
New Mexico Supreme Court, 1988.
765 P.2d 1165.

RANSOM, J.

This action arose out of an oral agreement between Dennis McCoy, an Oklahoma cattle dealer doing business as T.C. Cattle Co., and William Chandler, a cattle broker from Texas. McCoy agreed to ship cattle to New Mexico Cattle, Inc. (feedlot) in Union County, New Mexico, for delivery to Chandler. The cattle consisted of four lots of steers and two lots of heifers with a combined total value of $119,122.30. They were delivered to the feedlot in March 1986, after which time McCoy provided invoices to Chandler, which described the cattle and set out the sales price. Subsequently, McCoy demanded payment. Chandler refused.

Without McCoy's knowledge, Chandler obtained a loan from First National Bank in Clayton (bank) and pledged as collateral the subject cattle. * * * The bank claims that it had no knowledge of any interest McCoy may have had in the cattle when it made the loan to Chandler.

McCoy sued to recover the cattle, claiming he was to retain title until payment was made by Chandler. * * * McCoy subsequently filed a motion for partial summary judgment. . . . The bank filed a counter motion for partial summary judgment, arguing that it had perfected a security interest in the livestock superior to any claim of McCoy. The court entered judgment for the bank, relying upon the facts specifically pled in McCoy's complaint and certain provisions of the Uniform Commercial Code (U.C.C.), [citation].

* * *

Intention to Conclude a Contract: Identification of the Cattle to the Contract; Price Left to Be Agreed   McCoy argues that, because the cattle had not been identified to the contract, title to these cattle had not passed to Chandler under [U.C.C.] § 2–401(1). He asserts that Chandler's interest was consequently too slight to permit attachment of the bank's security interest. We disagree. Section 2–401(1) states:

"[T]itle to goods cannot pass under a contract for sale prior to their identification to the contract (Section 2–501), and unless otherwise explicitly agreed the buyer acquires by their identification a special property as limited by this act. Any retention or reservation by the seller of the title (property) in goods shipped or deliverd to the buyer is limited in effect to a reservation of a security interest. Subject to these provisions and to the provisions of the article on secured transactions (Article 9), title to goods passes from the seller to the buyer in any manner and on any conditions explicitly agreed on by the parties. . . ."

The clause on which McCoy relies refers to § 2–501. This section provides: "The buyer obtains a special property and an insurable interest in goods by identification of existing goods as goods to which the contract refers even though the goods so identified are non-conforming and he has an option to return or reject them." § 2–501(1). The subject cattle in this case both were in existence and were the goods to which the oral agreement referred. The allegations that McCoy shipped the cattle to Chandler in New Mexico subject to Chandler's right to return some or all of the cattle and subject to further negotiations on the price do not raise material issues of fact as to whether a contract existed. The fact that the transaction was a "sale or return" does not negate the existence of the contract. See § 2–326. The buyer and seller may enter into a binding sales contract notwithstanding that they have yet to agree on a price. See § 2–305.

Effect of Delivery   Because McCoy delivered the cattle under the contract, title passed to Chandler even though McCoy may have retained certain security interests in the cattle, as discussed below. Section 2–401(2) provides:

"[U]nless otherwise explicitly agreed title passes to the buyer at the time and place at which the seller completes his performance with reference to the physical delivery of the goods, despite any reservation of a security interest and even though a document of title is to be delivered at a different time or place; and in particular and despite any reservation of a security interest by the bill of lading. . . ."

* * *

The Buyer's Power to Create a Security Interest in a Third Party under Article 2   Because the goods were delivered to Chandler under the contract, he had the power to create a security interest in a third party. This interest attached even though Chandler was found to have committed a fraud against McCoy and thus only had voidable title to the cattle. Section 2–403(1) allows certain transferors to pass greater title than they themselves claim. [Citations.] "Section [2–403(1)] gives good faith purchasers of even fraudulent buyers-transferors greater rights than the defrauded seller can assert. This harsh rule is designed to promote the greatest range of freedom possible to commercial vendors and purchasers." [Citation.] Section 2–403(1) provides:

"A purchaser of goods acquires all title which his transferor had or had power to transfer except that a purchaser of a limited interest acquires rights only to the extent of the interest purchased. A person with voidable title has power to transfer a good title to a good faith purchaser for value. When goods have been delivered under a transaction of purchase the purchaser has such power even though: . . . (d) the delivery was procured through fraud punishable as larcenous under the criminal law."

Given our discussion above, it is clear that the cattle had been delivered under a "transaction of purchase" and hence that Chandler was a "purchaser." See § 1–201(33). The court in [citation] held that under the comparable section of the Texas U.C.C. it is transfer of *possession* to the defaulting buyer which gives him the power to transfer good title to a good faith purchaser for value. Once McCoy deliverd the cattle pursuant to his agreement with Chandler, under § 2–403(1) Chandler had the power to transfer good title to a good faith purchaser for value.

* * *

Comment 2 to § 2–403 notes that the policy underlying the section as a whole is the protection of good faith purchasers such as Article 9 secured parties against "hidden interest[s]." Whether McCoy shipped the cattle to Chandler under a title-retention contract as alleged in his complaint, or whether he shipped the cattle to the feedlot pursuant to the agreement described in his deposition testimony, his retained interest in the cattle was indeed "hidden" from the view of the bank as a "good faith purchaser" within the meaning of Section 2–403.

* * *

The Seller's Security Interests under Articles 2 and 9. The next question is therefore whether McCoy, by virtue of his status as seller, had a superior interest to that of the bank or Chandler's other creditors in the subject collateral.

* * *

In addition to an Article 2 security interest created as a matter of law under the U.C.C., a seller may create an Article 9 security interest by express agreement. [Citation.] McCoy's oral title retention contract with Chandler may have constituted an attempt to create such a security interest. However, such an interest . . . must be evidenced by a written agreement and filed before it could take priority over the perfected security interest of the bank. An oral agreement fails to meet this standard on both counts. The trial court therefore properly concluded that the bank, as a secured party, took priority over McCoy.

Based upon the foregoing, we therefore affirm the district court's entry of summary judgment.

Void and Voidable Title to Goods

ROBINSON v. DURHAM

Alabama Court of Civil Appeals, 1988.
537 So.2d 966.

WRIGHT, J.

Ronald Robinson, Wyman Robinson, and Friendly Discount Auto Sales (appellants) appeal from the granting of summary judgment in favor of appellee Mike Durham (Durham).

The facts material to this appeal and dispositive of this case are undisputed. Appellants, who are in car sales, purchased a 1968 Chevrolet Camaro. At the time of the purchase, a female transferred to the appellants tag receipts in her name and in the name of the previous owner. Wyman Robinson then registered the automobile in his name. In September 1986 Durham purchased the automobile from appellants, and all prior documentation was transferred to him. Shortly thereafter, the F.B.I. seized the automobile. The automobile had been reported stolen in Florida. It was subsequently returned to the original owner.

Durham filed a suit against appellants alleging fraud, breach of contract, and breach of warranty. Durham moved for summary judgment against appellants on all counts. The trial court granted Durham's motion on the count alleging that appellants made a statement to Durham as true without knowledge of its truth and on the issue of breach of warranty of title. Durham was awarded $5,200, the amount he paid for the car. Appellants appeal.

Appellants assert that the grant of summary judgment was in error because there was a "a scintilla of evidence, if not substantial evidence" from which the trial court could have concluded that appellants held good title "or at least voidable title" on the automobile, thereby conveying actual title to Durham at the time of the purchase.

Appellants' argument is without merit. It is unequivocable that "a person who has stolen goods of another cannot pass title thereto to another, whether such other knew, or did not know, that the goods were stolen." [Citations.] A thief gets only void title and without more cannot pass any title to a subsequent purchaser, even a good faith purchaser. [Citation.] It is undisputed that the automobile had been stolen. Therefore, at the time of purchase appellants obtained no title. In other words, the title was void. Appellants could not convey good title to Durham; therefore, the subsequent sale to Durham constituted a breach of warranty of good title.

Relying on § 2–403(1), [U.C.C.], appellants contend that they at least acquired a voidable title when they purchased the automobile. Section 2–403 recognizes that a person with voidable title has power to transfer a good title to a good faith purchaser for value. Voidable title can only arise from a voluntary transfer, and the rightful owner must assent to the transfer. "A possessor of goods does not have voidable title unless the true owner has consented to the transfer of title to him." [Citation.] In this case the rightful owner did not consent or assent to the transfer of the automobile. Appellants obtained no title. * * *

Affirmed. All the Judges concur.

Entrusting of Goods to a Merchant

MATTEK v. MALOFSKY

Supreme Court of Wisconsin, 1969.
42 Wisc.2d 16, 165 N.W.2d 406.

HALLOWS, C.J.

[Mattek entrusted a car to Frakes, a used car dealer. Malofsky, another automobile dealer, subsequently purchased the car from Frakes without obtaining or inquiring about the certificate of title to the car. Although Frakes did not have to secure a certificate of title for cars held in stock or acquired for stock purposes, he did have a duty under State law to deliver the certificate on the subsequent sale to Malofsky. Mattek brought suit against Malofsky to recover the car.]

Two issues are presented on this appeal: (1) Whether the provisions of [U.C.C.] 2.403 are applicable to sales between merchants; and

(2) whether an automobile dealer who buys a used car from another automobile dealer, who has lawful possession of the car, without obtaining or inquiring about the certificate of title to the used car is a "buyer in the ordinary course of business" within the meaning of [U.C.C.] 2.403.

We think the provisions of [U.C.C.] 2.403 are applicable to sales between merchants. We come to this conclusion because the purpose of [U.C.C.] 2.403(2) and (3) is to protect a person from a third-party interest in goods purchased from the general inventory of a merchant regardless of that merchant's actual authority to sell those goods. This section does not expressly or by implication restrict such protection of a sale by a merchant to a member of the consumer public. If the policy of negotiability of goods held in the inventory of a merchant is to be promoted, it would seem to apply between merchants where merchants buy from one another in the ordinary course of business. The protection is afforded to "a buyer in the ordinary course of business," and by other provisions of the Uniform Commercial Code the term "buyer" includes a merchant.

In [U.C.C.] 1.201(9) a buyer in the ordinary course of business is defined as "a person who in good faith and without knowledge that the sale to him is in violation of the ownership rights or security interest of a third party in the goods buys in ordinary course from a person in the business of selling goods of that kind but does not include a pawn broker." Good faith is defined in [U.C.C.] 1.201(19) to mean "honesty in fact in the conduct or transaction concerned." This definition applies to a member of the consumer public only, because in [U.C.C.] 2.103(1)(b) " 'good faith' in the case of a merchant" is defined to mean "honesty in fact and the observance of reasonable commercial standards of fair dealing in the trade." In addition, [U.C.C.] 2.104(3), relating to the general standard applicable to transactions between merchants charges each merchant with the "knowledge or skill of merchants."

Consequently, a merchant may be a buyer in the ordinary course of business under

[U.C.C.] 2.403 from another merchant if he meets four elements: (1) be honest in fact, (2) be without knowledge of any defects of title in the goods, (3) pay value, and (4) observe reasonable commercial standards. In the observance of reasonable commercial standards, however, a merchant is chargeable with the knowledge or skill of a merchant.

We think Malofsky was not the buyer in the ordinary course of business within the meaning of [U.C.C.] 2.403. Although the delivery of the automobile to Frakes, a used-car dealer, constituted an entrustment, Frakes could by subsequent sale pass title to a buyer in the ordinary course of business. However, Malofsky as a merchant was not a buyer in the ordinary course of business because he was chargeable with the knowledge that the registration law, [citation], which provides that while a dealer need not apply for a certificate of title for a vehicle in stock or acquired for stock purposes, he shall upon the transfer of such vehicle give the transferee evidence of title, and in the case of a vehicle which has a certificate of title, the certificate of title shall be reassigned and delivered to the transferee. Malofsky should have known the used automobile had a certificate of title outstanding and that Frakes was required to give him such certificate of title. Under the standards set forth in [U.C.C.] 2.104(3) applicable to transactions between merchants, Malofsky is chargeable with this knowledge and his failure to procure a certificate of title or some evidence of title was unreasonable as a matter of law. Evidence of custom or usage of automobile dealers contrary to the statute cannot be used to defeat the rights of a third party whatever the value of such evidence may be in adjusting disputes between dealers.

* * *

[Judgment for Mattek affirmed.]

Shipment Contracts

PESTANA v. KARINOL CORP.

District Court of Appeals of Florida, Third District, 1979. 367 So.2d 1096.

HUBBART, J.

This is an action for damages based on a contract for the sale of goods. The defendant seller and others prevailed in this action after a non-jury trial in the Circuit Court for the Eleventh Judicial Circuit of Florida. The plaintiff buyer appeals.

The central issue presented for review is whether a contract for the sale of goods, which stipulates the place where the goods sold are to be sent by carrier but contains (a) no explicit provisions allocating the risk of loss while the goods are in the possession of the carrier and (b) no delivery terms such as F.O.B. place of destination, is a shipment contract or a destination contract under the Uniform Commercial Code. We hold that such a contract, without more, constitutes a shipment contract wherein the risk of loss passes to the buyer when the seller duly delivers the goods to the carrier under a reasonable contract of carriage for shipment to the buyer. Accordingly, we affirm.

The critical facts of this case are substantially undisputed. On March 4, 1975, Nahim Amar B. (the plaintiff Pedro P. Pestana's decedent herein) who was a resident of Mexico entered into a contract through his authorized representative with the Karinol Corporation (the defendant herein) which is an exporting company licensed to do business in Florida and operating out of Miami. The terms of this contract were embodied in a one-page invoice written in Spanish and prepared by the defendant Karinol. By the terms of this contract, the plaintiff's Amar agreed to purchase 64 electronic watches from the defendant Karinol for $6,006. A notation was printed at the bottom of the contract which, translated into English, reads as follows: "Please send the merchandise in cardboard boxes duly strapped with metal bands via air parcel post to Chetumal. Documents to Banco de Commercio De Quintano Roo S.A." There were no provisions in the contract which specifically allocated the risk of loss on the goods sold while in the possession of the carrier; there were also no F.O.B., F.A.S., C.I.F. or C. & F. terms contained in the contract. See [U.C.C. §§ 2-319, 2-320]. A 25% downpayment on the purchase price of the goods sold was made prior to shipment.

On April 11, 1975, there is sufficient evidence, although disputed, that the defendant Karinol delivered the watches in two cartons to its agent American International Freight Forwarders, Inc. (the second defendant herein) for forwarding to the plaintiff's decedent Amar. The defendant American insured the two cartons with Fidelity & Casualty Company of New York (the third defendant herein) naming the defendant Karinol as the insured. The defendant American as freight forwarder strapped the cartons in question with metal bands and delivered them to TACA International Airlines consigned to one Bernard Smith, a representative of the plaintiff's decedent, in Belize City, Belize, Central America. The shipment was arranged by Karinol in this manner in accord with a prior understanding between the parties as there were no direct flights from Miami, Florida to Chetumal, Mexico. Mr. Smith was to take custody of the goods on behalf of the plaintiff's decedent in Belize and arrange for their transport by truck to the plaintiff's decedent Amar in Chetumal, Mexico.

On April 15, 1975, the cartons arrived by air in Belize City and were stored by the airline in the customs and air freight cargo room. Mr. Smith was duly notified and thereupon the plaintiff's decedent made payment on the balance due under the contract to the defendant Karinol. On May 2, 1975, Mr. Smith took custody of the cartons after a certain delay was experienced in transferring the cartons to a customs warehouse. Either on that day or shortly thereafter, the cartons were opened by Mr. Smith and customs officials as was required for clearance prior to the truck shipment to Chetumal, Mexico. There were no watches contained in the cartons. The defendant Karinol and its insurance carrier the defendant Fidelity were duly notified, but both eventually refused to make good on the loss.

* * *

There are two types of sales contracts under Florida's Uniform Commercial Code wherein a carrier is used to transport the goods sold: a shipment contract and a destination contract. A shipment contract is considered the normal contract in which the seller is required to send the subject goods by carrier to the buyer but is not required to guarantee delivery thereof at a particular destination. Under a shipment contract, the seller, unless otherwise agreed, must: (1) put the goods sold in the possession of a carrier and make a contract for their transportation as may be reasonable having regard for the nature of the goods and other attendant circumstances, (2) obtain and promptly deliver or tender in due form any document necessary to enable the buyer to obtain possession of the goods or otherwise required by the agreement or by usage of the trade, and (3) promptly notify the buyer of the shipment. On a shipment contract, the risk of loss passes to the buyer when the goods sold are duly delivered to the carrier for shipment to the buyer. [Citations.]

A destination contract, on the other hand, is considered the variant contract in which the seller specifically agrees to deliver the goods sold to the buyer at a particular destination and to bear the risk of loss of the goods until tender of delivery. This can be accomplished by express provision in the sales contract to that effect or by the use of delivery terms such as F.O.B. (place of destination). Under a destination contract, the seller is required to tender delivery of the goods sold to the buyer at the place of destination. The risk of loss under such a contract passes to the buyer when the goods sold are duly tendered to the buyer at the place of destination while in the possession of the carrier so as to enable the buyer to take delivery. The parties must explicitly agree to a destination contract; otherwise the contract will be considered a shipment contract. [Citations.]

Where the risk of loss falls on the seller at the time the goods sold are lost or destroyed, the seller is liable in damages to the buyer for non-delivery unless the seller tenders a performance in replacement for the lost or destroyed goods. On the other hand, where the risk of loss falls on the buyer at the time the goods sold are lost or destroyed, the buyer is liable to the seller for the purchase price of the goods sold. [Citation.]

In the instant case, we deal with the normal shipment contract involving the sale of goods. The defendant Karinol pursuant to this contract agreed to send the goods sold, a shipment of watches, to the plaintiff's decedent in Chetumal, Mexico. There was no specific provision in the contract between the parties which allocated the risk of loss on the goods sold while in transit. In addition, there were no delivery terms such as F.O.B. Chetumal contained in the contract.

All agree that there is sufficient evidence that the defendant Karinol performed its obligations as a seller under the Uniform Commercial Code if this contract is considered a shipment contract. Karinol put the goods sold in the possession of a carrier and made a contract for the goods [sic] safe transportation to the plaintiff's decedent; Karinol also promptly notified the plaintiff's decedent of the shipment and tendered to said party the necessary documents to obtain possession of the goods sold.

The plaintiff Pestana contends, however, that the contract herein is a destination contract in which the risk of loss on the goods sold did not pass until delivery on such goods had been tendered to him at Chetumal, Mexico—an event which never occurred. He relies for this position on the notation at the bottom of the contract between the parties which provides that the goods were to be sent to Chetumal, Mexico. We cannot agree. A "send to" or "ship to" term is a part of every contract involving the sale of goods where carriage is contemplated and has no significance in determining whether the contract is a shipment or destination contract for risk of loss purposes. [Citations.] As such, the "send to" term contained in this contract cannot, without more, convert this into a destination contract.

It therefore follows that the risk of loss in this case shifted to the plaintiff's decedent as buyer when the defendant Karinol as seller duly delivered the goods to the defendant freight forwarder American under a reasonable contract of carriage for shipment to the plaintiff's decedent in Chetumal, Mexico. The defendant Karinol, its agent the defendant American, and its insurer the defendant Fidelity could not be held liable to the plaintiff in this action. The trial court properly entered judgment in favor of all the defendants herein.

Affirmed.

Risk of Loss: Seller Not a Merchant

MARTIN v. MELLAND'S INC.

Supreme Court of North Dakota, 1979.
283 N.W.2d 76.

ERICKSTAD, C.J.

The narrow issue on this appeal is who should bear the loss of a truck and an attached haystack mover that was destroyed by fire while in the possession of the plaintiff, Israel Martin (Martin), but after certificate of title had been delivered to the defendant, Melland's Inc. (Melland's). The destroyed haymoving unit was to be used as a trade-in for a new haymoving unit that Martin ultimately purchased from Melland's. Martin appeals from a district court judgment dated September 28, 1978, that dismissed his action on the merits after it found that at the time of its destruction Martin was the owner of the unit pursuant to [Section 2-401 U.C.C.]. We hold that Section 2-401 is inapplicable to this case, but we affirm the district court judgment on the grounds that risk of loss had not passed to Melland's pursuant to [Section 2-509 U.C.C.].

On June 11, 1974, Martin entered into a written agreement with Melland's, a farm implement dealer, to purchase a truck and attached haystack mover for the total purchase price of $35,389. Martin was given a trade-in allowance of $17,389 on his old unit, leaving a balance owing of $18,000 plus sales tax of $720 or a total balance of $18,720. The agreement provided that Martin "mail or bring title" to the old unit to Melland's "this week." Martin mailed the certificate of title to Melland's pursuant to the agreement, but he was allowed to retain the use and possession of the old unit "until they had the new one ready." The new unit was not expected to be ready for two to three months because it required certain modifications. During this interim period, Melland's performed minor repairs to the trade-in unit on two occasions without charging Martin for the repairs.

Fire destroyed the truck and the haymoving unit in early August, 1974, while Martin was moving hay. The parties did not have any agreement regarding insurance or risk of loss on the unit and Martin's insurance on the trade-in unit had lapsed. Melland's refused Martin's demand for his new unit and Martin brought this suit. The parties subsequently entered into an agreement by which Martin purchased the new unit, but they reserved their rights in any lawsuit arising out of the prior incident.

The district court found "that although the Plaintiff [Martin] executed the title to the . . . [haymoving unit], he did not relinquish possession of the same and therefore the Plaintiff was the owner of said truck at the time the fire occurred pursuant to Section 2-401."

Martin argues that the district court erroneously applied Section 2-401 regarding passage of title, to this case and that Section 2-509, which deals with risk of loss in the absence of breach, should have been applied instead. Martin argues further that title (apparently pursuant to Section 2-401) and risk of loss passed to Melland's and the property was then merely bailed back to Martin who held it as a bailee. Martin submits that this is supported by the fact that Melland's performed minor repairs on the old unit following the passage of title without charging Martin for the repairs. Melland's responds that Section 2-401(2), governs this case and that the district court's determination of the issue should be affirmed.

One of the hallmarks of the pre-Code law of sales was its emphasis on the concept of title. The location of title was used to determine, among other things, risk of loss, insurable interest, place and time for measuring damages, and the applicable law in an interstate transaction. This single title or "lump" title concept proved unsatisfactory because of the different policy considerations involved in each of the situations that title was made to govern. Furthermore, the concept of single title did not reflect modern commercial practices, *i.e.* although the single title concept worked well for "cash-on-the-barrelhead sales," the introduction of deferred payments, security agreements, financing from third parties, or delivery by carrier required a fluid concept of title with bits and pieces held by all parties to the transaction.

Thus the concept of title under the U.C.C. is of decreased importance. The official comment to Section 2-101 U.C.C. provides in part:

The arrangement of the present Article is in terms of contract for sale and the various steps of its performance. The legal consequences are stated as following directly from the contract and action taken under it without resorting to the idea of when property or title passed or was to pass as being the determining factor. The purpose is to avoid making practical issues between practical men turn upon the location of an intangible something, the passing of which no man can prove by evidence and to substitute for such abstractions proof of words and actions of a tangible character.

[§ 2-401 U.C.C.], which the district court applied in this case, provides in relevant part:

Each provision of this chapter with regard to the rights, obligations and remedies of the seller, the buyer, purchasers or other third parties applies irrespective of title to the goods except where the provision refers to such title. Insofar as situations are not covered by the other provisions of this chapter and matters concerning title become material the following rules apply . . .

[§ 2-509 U.C.C.], is an "other provision of this chapter" and is applicable to this case without regard to the location of title. Comment one to Section 2-509 U.C.C. provides that "the underlying theory of these sections on risk of loss is the adoption of the contractual approach rather than an arbitrary shifting of the risk with the 'property' in the goods."

The position that the Code has taken, divorcing the question of risk of loss from a determination of title, is summed up by Professor Nordstrom in his hornbook on sales:

No longer is the question of title of any importance in determining whether a buyer or seller bears the risk of loss. It is true that the person with title will also (and incidentally) often bear the risk that the goods may be destroyed or lost; but the seller may have title and the buyer the risk, or the seller may have the risk and the buyer the title. In short, title is not a relevant consideration in deciding whether the risk has shifted to the buyer. R. Nordstrom, Handbook of the Law of Sales, 393 (1970).

* * *

Thus, the question in this case is not answered by a determination of the location of title, but by the risk of loss provisions in [§ 2-509 U.C.C.]. Before addressing the risk of loss question in conjunction with [§ 2-509 U.C.C.], it is necessary to determine the posture of the parties with regard to the trade-in unit, *i.e.* who is the buyer and the seller and how are the responsibilities allocated. It is clear that a barter or trade-in is considered a sale and is therefore subject to the Uniform Commercial Code. [Citations.] It is also clear that the party who owns the trade-in is considered the seller. [§ 2-304 U.C.C.], provides that the "price can be made payable in money or otherwise. If it is payable in whole or in part in goods each party is a seller of the goods which he is to transfer." [Citations.]

Martin argues that he had already sold the trade-in unit to Melland's and, although he retained possession, he did so in the capacity of a bailee (apparently pursuant to [§ 2-509(2) U.C.C.]). White and Summers in their hornbook on the Uniform Commercial Code argue that the seller who retains possession should not be considered bailee within Section 2-509.

* * *

The courts that have addressed this issue have agreed with White and Summers. [Citations.]

It is undisputed that the contract did not require or authorize shipment by carrier pursuant to Section [2-509(1)] therefore, the residue section, subsection 3, is applicable:

In any case not within subsection 1 or 2, the risk of loss passes to the buyer on his receipt of the goods if the seller is a merchant; otherwise the risk passes to the buyer on tender of delivery.

Martin admits that he is not a merchant; therefore, it is necessary to determine if Martin tendered delivery of the trade-in unit to Melland's. Tender is defined in [§ 2-503 U.C.C.], as follows:

Manner of seller's tender of delivery.—1. Tender of delivery requires that the seller put and hold conforming goods at the buyer's disposition and give the buyer any notification reasonably necessary to enable him to take delivery. The manner, time and place for tender are determined by the agreement and this chapter, and in particular

a. tender must be at a reasonable hour, and if it is of goods they must be kept available for the period reasonably necessary to enable the buyer to take possession; but
b. unless otherwise agreed the buyer must furnish facilities reasonably suited to the receipt of the goods.

It is clear that the trade-in unit was not tendered to Melland's in this case. The parties agreed that Martin would keep the old unit "until they had the new one ready."

* * *

We hold that Martin did not tender delivery of the trade-in truck and haystack mover to Melland's pursuant to [§ 2-509 U.C.C.]; consequently, Martin must bear the loss.

We affirm the district court judgment.

QUESTIONS

1. Explain the relative importance of title under the common law and Article 2.

2. Distinguish between a shipment and a destination contract. When does title and risk of loss pass under each?

3. When does the seller have a right or power to transfer title? When is the transfer void or voidable? By whom? Against whom?

4. Discuss the rules covering (a) risk of loss in the absence of a breach, and (b) risk of loss when there is a breach.

5. What is a bulk transfer? When is it effective? What does revised Article 6 attempt to accomplish?

PROBLEMS

1. Stein, a mechanic, and Beal, a life insurance agent, entered into a written contract for the sale of Stein's tractor to Beal for $2,800 cash. It was agreed that Stein would tune the motor on the tractor. Stein fulfilled this obligation and on the night of July 1 telephoned Beal that the tractor was ready to be picked up upon making payment. Beal responded, "I'll be there in the morning with the money." On the next morning, however, Beal was approached by an insurance prospect and decided to get the tractor at a later date. On the night of July 2, the tractor was destroyed by fire of unknown origin. Neither Stein nor Beal had any fire insurance. Who must bear the loss?

2. Regan received a letter from Chase, the material portion of which stated: "Chase hereby places an order with you for fifty cases of Red Top Tomatoes, ship them C.O.D." Promptly upon receipt of the letter Regan shipped the tomatoes to Chase. While en route, the railroad car carrying the tomatoes was wrecked. Upon Chase's refusal to pay for the tomatoes, Regan commenced an action to recover the purchase price. Chase defended on the ground that as the shipment was C.O.D., neither title to the tomatoes nor risk of loss passed until their delivery to Chase. Decision?

3. On May 10, the Apple Company, acting through one Brown, entered into a contract with Crane for the installation of a milking machine at Crane's farm. Following the enumeration of the articles to be furnished, together with the price of each article, the written contract provided: "This outfit is subject to thirty-days free trial and is to be installed about June 1." Within thirty days after installation the entire outfit, excepting the double utility unit, was destroyed by fire through no fault of Crane. The Apple Company sued Crane to recover the value of the articles destroyed. Decision?

4. Brown, located in Knoxville, contracted to buy sixty cases of Lovely Brand canned corn from Clark in Toledo at a contract price of $600. Pursuant to the contract, Clark selected and set aside sixty cases of Lovely Brand canned corn and tagged them "For Brown." The contract required Clark to ship the corn to Brown via T Railroad, F.O.B. Toledo. Before Clark delivered the corn to the railroad, the sixty cases were stolen from Clark's warehouse.

(a) Who is liable for the loss of the sixty cases of corn, Brown or Clark?

(b) Suppose Clark had delivered the corn to the railroad in Toledo. After the corn had been loaded on a freight car, but before the train left the yard, the car was broken open and its contents, including the corn, stolen. As between Brown and Clark, who is liable for the loss?

(c) Would your answer in question (b) be the same if this was an F.O.B. Knoxville contract, all other facts remaining the same?

5. Gardner owned a quantity of corn which was contained in a corn crib located on Gardner's farm. On March 12, Gardner wrote a letter to Bassett stating that he would sell to Bassett all of the corn in this crib, which he estimated at between 900 and 1,000 bushels, for $5.60 per bushel. Bassett received this letter on March 13 and immediately wrote and mailed on the same day a letter to Gardner stating that he would buy the corn. The corn crib and its contents were accidentally destroyed by fire which broke out about 3 o'clock a.m. on March 14.

What are the rights of the parties?

What difference, if any, in result if Gardner were a merchant?

6. Anita, a New York dealer, purchased twenty-five barrels of specially graded and packed apples from a producer at Hood River, Oregon. Afterwards she resold the apples to Benji under a contract which specified an agreed price on delivery at Benji's place of business in New York. The apples were shipped to Anita from Oregon but, through no fault of either Anita or Benji, were totally destroyed before reaching New York. Is there any liability resting upon Anita?

7. Smith was approached by a man who introduced himself as Brown of Brown and Co. Brown was not known to Smith, but Smith asked Dun & Bradstreet for a credit report and obtained a very favorable report on Brown. He thereupon sold Brown some expensive gems and billed Brown & Co. "Brown" turned out to be a clever jewel thief, who later sold the gems to Brown & Co. for valuable consideration. Brown & Co. was unaware of "Brown's" transaction with Smith. Smith sued Brown & Co. for the return of the gems or the price as billed to Brown & Co. Decision?

8. Charlotte, the owner of a new Cadillac automobile, agreed to loan the car to Ellen for the month of February while she (Charlotte) went to Florida for a winter vacation. It was understood that Ellen, who was a small-town Cadillac dealer, would merely place Charlotte's car in her showroom for exhibition and sales promotion purposes. While Charlotte was away, Ellen sold the car to Robert. Upon Charlotte's return from Florida, she sued to recover the car from Robert. Decision?

9. Brilles offered to sell his used automobile to Nevarro for $2,600 cash. Nevarro agreed to buy the car, gave Brilles a check for $2,600, and drove away in the car. The next day Nevarro sold the car for $3,000 to Hough, a *bona fide* purchaser. The $2,600 check was returned to Brilles by the bank in which he had deposited it because of insufficient funds in Nevarro's account. Brilles brings an action against Hough to recover the automobile. What judgment?

10. Yount told Lewis he wished to buy Lewis's automobile. He drove the car for about ten minutes, returned to Lewis, stated he wanted to take the automobile to show it to his wife, and then left with the automobile and never returned. Yount sold the automobile in another State to Turner and gave him a bill of sale. Lewis sued Turner to recover the automobile. Decision?

11. On February 7, Pillsbury purchased eight thousand bushels of wheat from Landis. The wheat was being stored at the Greensville Grain Company. Pillsbury also intended to store the wheat with Greensville. On February 10, the wheat was destroyed. Landis demands payment for the wheat from Pillsbury. Who prevails? Who has title? Who has the risk of loss? Explain.

12. Johnson, who owns a hardware store, was indebted to Hutchinson, one of his suppliers. Johnson sold her business to Lockhart, one of Johnson's previous competitors. Lockhart combined the inventory from Johnson's store with his own and moved them to a new, larger store. Hutchinson claims that Lockhart must pay Johnson's debt because the sale of the business had been made without complying with the requirements of the bulk sales law. Decision?

13. Seller had manufactured 40,000 pounds of plastic resin pellets specially for the buyer, who agreed to accept them at the rate of 1,000 pounds per day upon his issuance of shipping instructions. Despite numerous requests by the seller, the buyer issued no such instructions. On August 18, the seller, after warehousing the goods for forty days, demanded by letter that the buyer issue instructions. The buyer agreed to issue them beginning August 20 but never did. On September 22, a fire destroyed the seller's plant containing the goods, which were not covered by insurance. Who bears the risk of loss? Why?

14. Harrison, a men's clothing retailer located in Westport, Connecticut, ordered merchandise from Ninth Street East, Ltd., a Los Angeles-based clothing manufacturer. Ninth Street delivered the merchandise to Denver Chicago Trucking Company in Los Angeles, and then sent four invoices to Harrison that bore the notation "F.O.B. Los Angeles." Denver subsequently transferred the merchandise to a connecting carrier, Old Colony Transportation Company, for final delivery to Harrison's Westport store. When Old Colony tried to deliver the merchandise, Harrison's wife asked the truck driver to deliver the boxes inside the store, but the driver refused. The dispute remained unresolved, and the truck departed with Old Colony still in possession of the goods. Harrison then notified Ninth Street by letter of the nondelivery, but Ninth Street was unable to locate the shipment. Ninth Street then sought to recover the contract purchase price from Harrison. Harrison refused, contending that risk of loss remained with Ninth Street because of its refusal to deliver the merchandise to Harrison's place of business. Decision?

15. United Road Machinery Company, a dealer in heavy road equipment (including truck scales supplied by Thurman Scale Company), received a telephone call on July 21, from James Durham, an officer of Consolidated Coal Company, seeking to acquire truck scales for his coal mining operation. United and Consolidated entered into a twenty-four-month lease-purchase arrangement. United then notified Thurman that Consolidated would take possession of the scales directly. United paid for the scales and Consolidated took possession of them, but the latter never signed and returned the contract papers forwarded to it by United. Consolidated also never made any of the rental payments ($608/month) due under the lease. On September 20, Consolidated, through its officer Durham, sold the scales to Kentucky Mobile Homes for $8,500. Kentucky's president, Ethard Jasper, checked the county records prior to the purchase and found no lien or encumbrance on the title; likewise, he denied knowledge of the dispute between Consolidated and United. On September 22, Kentucky sold the scales to Clyde Jasper, individually, for $8,500. His search also failed to disclose any lien on the title to the scales, and he denied knowledge of the dispute between Consolidated and United. United brought suit to recover the scales from Jasper. Decision?

COMPUTER RESEARCH PROBLEMS

1. Porter, the owner of a collection of artworks, had a number of art transactions with Harold Von Maker who used, among other names, that of Peter Wertz. Porter permitted Von Maker to have temporarily a painting by Maurice Utrillo, *Chateau de Lionsure-Mer,* and to hang it in his home until he decided whether to purchase it. A few months later, Porter sought the return of the Utrillo painting but was unable to reach Von Maker. Porter subsequently discovered that he was not dealing with Peter Wertz but with Harold Von Maker, a man with an etensive criminal record, including a conviction for defrauding the Chase Manhattan Bank. When Porter finally reached him, Von Maker claimed that Utrillo was on consignment with a client. Von Maker then agreed in writing either to return the painting to Porter within ninety days or to make compensation for it. At the time he entered this agreement, Von Maker had already sold the painting. He had used the real Peter Wertz, a delicatessen employee and acquaintance, to effect the sale of the Utrillo to Feigen for $20,000. Feigen, an art dealer, then sold the painting to Brenner, and it is now somewhere in Venezuela. Porter brought suit against Feigen and the others involved to recover possession of the Utrillo or its value. Decision?

2. Home Indemnity, an insurance company, paid one of its insureds after the theft of his car. The car reappeared in another State and was sold to Michael Schrier for $4,300 by a used car dealer. The dealer promised to give Mr. Schrier a certificate of title. One month later the car was seized by the police on behalf of Home Indemnity. Mr. Schrier sued for the return of the car and won. Home Indemnity seeks reversal of that decision and possession of the car. Decision?

3. Fred Lane sells boats, motors, and trailers. Lane sold a boat, motor, and trailer to John Willis in exchange for a check for $6,285.00. The check was not honored when Lane attempted to use the funds. Willis subsequently left the boat, motor, and trailer with John Garrett. Garrett sold the boat, motor, and trailer to Jimmy Honeycutt for $2,500.00. Honeycutt was surprised at how inexpensive the boat was considering its quality. He did not know where Garrett got the boat, but he had dealt with Garrett before and described him as a "sly businessman." Garrett did not sell boats but rather sold fishing tackle and provisions. Honeycutt also received a forged certificate for the boat on which he observed Garrett forge the purported owner's signature. Lane sues Honeycutt for return of the boat, motor, and trailer. Decision?

 4. Mike Moses purchased a mobile home, including installation, from Gary Newman. Newman delivered the home to Moses' lot. Upon inspection of the home, Moses' fiancée found a broken window and water pipe. Moses also had not received keys to the front door. Before Newman corrected these problems, a windstorm destroyed the home. Moses sued Newman for loss of the home. Decision?

Chapter 23

PRODUCTS LIABILITY: WARRANTIES AND STRICT LIABILITY IN TORT

Types of Warranties
Obstacles to Warranty Actions
Nature of Strict Liability
Obstacles to Strict Liability

THIS chapter considers the liability of manufacturers and sellers of goods to buyers, users, consumers, and bystanders for damages caused by defective products. The rapid and expanding development of case law has established products liability as a separate and distinct field of law, combining and enforcing rules and principles of contracts, sales, negligence, strict liability in tort, and statutory law.

One reason for the expansion of this liability is the modern method of distributing goods. Today retailers serve principally as conduits of prepackaged goods that are widely advertised by the manufacturer or distributor. This has brought about the extension of product liability coverage to include manufacturers and other parties along the chain of distribution. The extension of product liability to manufacturers, however, has not lessened the liability of the retailer to his immediate purchaser. Rather, it has broadened and extended the base of liability by the development and application of new principles of law.

Currently, the entire area of product liability has attracted a great deal of public attention. According to the U.S. Consumer Prod-

uct Safety Commission, thirty-six million Americans are injured each year in consumer product-related accidents. Of those injured, twenty-eight thousand die while many others are permanently disabled. The resultant cost of maintaining product liability insurance has skyrocketed, causing great consternation in the business community. In response to the clamor over this insurance crisis, over forty States have revised their tort laws to make it more difficult to successfully bring product liability lawsuits.

The liability of manufacturers and other sellers of goods for a defective product, or its failure to perform adequately, may be based upon one or more of the following: (1) negligence, (2) misrepresentation, (3) violation of statutory duty, (4) warranty, and (5) strict liability in tort. The first three causes of actions have been covered in Chapters 6 and 10. This chapter will explore the last two.

WARRANTIES

The liability of a seller for the quality of goods she sells has long presented numerous legal problems. In its formative period of development, the law of sales was influenced more by the pressures and demands of sellers as a class rather than by those of buyers as a class. The traditional concept of **caveat emptor**—let the buyer beware—was premised on the principle that the buyer and seller were each attempting to obtain the best bargain possible. Because each wielded relatively equal bargaining power, the law did not interfere. Today, however, this is not the case; the consumer generally possesses far less bargaining power. Consequently, the law of sales has abandoned the doctrine of *caveat emptor* and has become more protective of the buyer through the use of warranties. The liability of a seller for breach of warranty has been codified by the Uniform Commercial Code.

A **warranty** creates a duty on the part of the seller that the goods she sells will conform to certain qualities, characteristics, or conditions. A seller, however, is not required to warrant the goods, and in general she may, by appropriate words, disclaim, exclude, negate, or modify a particular warranty or even all warranties.

In bringing a warranty action, the buyer must prove that (1) a warranty existed, (2) the warranty had been breached, (3) the breach of the warranty proximately caused the loss suffered, and (4) notice of the breach of warranty was given to the seller. The seller has the burden of proving defenses based on the buyer's conduct. This section will examine the various types of warranties as well as the obstacles to a cause of action for breach of warranty.

TYPES OF WARRANTIES

A warranty may arise out of the mere existence of a sale (a warranty of title), any affirmation of fact or promise made by the seller to the buyer (an express warranty), or the circumstances under which the sale is made (an implied warranty). In a contract for the sale of goods it is possible to have all three types of warranties. All warranties are construed as consistent with each other and cu-

mulative, unless such a construction is unreasonable. If the seller breaches his warranty, the buyer may reject or revoke acceptance of the goods. Moreover, whether the goods have been accepted or rejected, the buyer may recover a judgment against the seller for damages. Harm for which damages are recoverable include personal injury, damage to property, and economic loss. Economic loss most commonly involves damages for loss of bargain and consequential damages for lost profits. Damages for breach of warranty are discussed in the next chapter.

Warranty of Title

Under the Code's warranty of title, the seller implicitly warrants that (1) the title conveyed is good and its transfer rightful, and (2) the goods have no security interest or other lien (a claim on property by another for payment of debt), which the buyer was not aware of at the time of purchase. Section 2–312.

For example, Iris acquires goods from Sherman in a transaction that is void and then sells the goods to Brenda. Sherman brings an action against Brenda and recovers the goods. Iris has breached the warranty of title because she did not have good title to the goods and her transfer of the goods to Brenda was not rightful. Accordingly, Iris is liable to Brenda for damages.

The Code does *not* label the warranty of title as an implied warranty, even though it arises out of the sale and not from any particular words or conduct. This is done in order to make the Code's general disclaimer provision for implied warranties inapplicable and instead to have the warranty of title subject to its own disclaimer provision. Nevertheless, a seller of goods does implicitly warrant title to those goods.

A seller who is a merchant makes an additional warranty in sales of goods of the kind in which he regularly deals: that such goods shall be delivered free of the rightful claim of any third person by way of infringement (unauthorized use) of any existing patent. Section 2–312(3).

Express Warranties

An express warranty is an explicit undertaking by the seller with respect to the quality, description, condition, or performability of the goods. The undertaking may consist of an affirmation of fact or a promise that relates to the goods, a description of the goods, or a sample or model of the goods. In each of these instances, the undertaking must become or be made part of the basis of the bargain in order for an express warranty to be created. It is not necessary, however, that the seller have a specific intention to make a warranty or use formal words such as "warrant" or "guarantee." Moreover, it is not necessary that a seller have knowledge of the falsity of a statement made by her in order to be liable for breach of express warranty; the seller may be acting in good faith. For example, if John mistakenly asserts to Sam that a rope will easily support 300 pounds and Sam is injured when the rope breaks while supporting only 200 pounds, John is liable for breach of an express warranty.

Creation An express warranty can be created by the seller either orally or in writing. The buyer, however, may have practical problems in establishing the existence of an oral warranty if the seller denies having made one. Moreover, a buyer's assertion that the seller made an oral express warranty may be difficult to establish because of the parol evidence rule, which bars the introduction of prior or contemporaneous oral agreements that contradict the written contract. For a discussion of the parol evidence rule, see Chapter 14.

One of the ways an express warranty can be created is by an **affirmation of fact** or a **promise** that relates to goods and becomes part of the basis of the bargain. The statement can be in regard to the quality, condition, capacity, performability, or safety of the goods. For example, a statement made by a seller that an automobile would get 42 miles to the gallon of gasoline or that a camera has automatic focus is an express warranty.

The Code further provides that an affirmation of the **value** of the goods or a statement purporting merely to be the seller's **opinion** or recommendation of the goods does not create a warranty. Section 2–313(2). Such statements are not factual and do not deceive the ordinary buyer. They are accepted merely as opinions or as puffery (sales talk). For example, a statement by a salesman that "this is one terrific deal" would likely be considered puffery. On the other hand, a statement that "this car gets 30 miles to the gallon" would be considered to be an express warranty given its level of specificity. A statement of value, moreover, may be an express warranty where the seller states the price at which the goods were purchased from a former owner, or where she gives market figures relating to sales of similar goods. These are affirmations of facts. They are statements of events and not mere opinions, and the seller is liable for breach of warranty if they are untrue. Although a statement of opinion by the seller is not ordinarily a warranty, if the seller is an expert and gives her opinion as such, she may be liable for breach of warranty. Thus, if an art expert states that a certain painting is a genuine Rembrandt, and this becomes part of the basis of the bargain, then the expert warrants the accuracy of her professional opinion.

An express warranty can also be created by the use of a **description** of the goods that becomes a part of the basis of the bargain. If so, the seller expressly warrants that the goods shall conform to the description. Examples include statements regarding a particular brand or type of goods, technical specifications, and blueprints.

The use of a **sample** or model is another means of creating an express warranty. If a sample or model is a part of the basis of the bargain, the seller expressly warrants that the entire lot of goods sold shall conform to the sample or model. A sample is a good that is actually drawn from the bulk of goods that is the subject matter of the sale. A model is offered for inspection when the subject matter is not at hand; it is not drawn from the bulk. Section 2–313, Comment 6.

Basis of Bargain The Code does not require that the affirmations, promises, descriptions, samples, or models made or used by the seller be relied on by the buyer but only that they constitute a part of the basis of the bargain. If they are part of the buyer's assumption underlying the sale, then reliance by the buyer is presumed. Some courts merely require that the buyer know of the affirmation of fact or promise for it to be presumed to be part of the basis of the bargain, while others require some showing of reliance. *See Cipollone v. Liggett Group, Inc.* Relaxing the reliance requirement more often has the effect of forcing sellers to live up to their express warranties than does a rule requiring reliance.

Statements or promises made by the seller to the buyer prior to the sale may be express warranties since they may form a part of the basis of the bargain just as much as statements in advertisements, catalogs, and the like may constitute an express warranty. Under the Code, statements or promises made by the seller subsequent to the contract of sale may become express warranties even though no new consideration is given. Section 2–209(1) provides that "an agreement modifying a contract within this Article needs no consideration to be binding." Thus, a statement or promise or assurance with respect to the goods made by the seller to the buyer at the time of delivery may be a binding modification of the prior contract of sale and held to be an express warranty basic to the bargain.

Implied Warranties

An implied warranty, unlike an express warranty, is not found in the language of the sales contract or in a specific affirmation or promise by the seller. Instead, an **implied warranty** is an obligation imposed by operation of law upon the transfer of property or contract rights. An implied warranty arises out of the circumstances under which the parties enter into their contract and depends on such factors as the type of contract or sale entered into, whether the seller is a mer-

chant, the conduct of the parties, and the applicability of other statutes. Implied warranties have been developed by the law, not as something to which the parties have agreed but as a departure from the early rule of *caveat emptor*.

Merchantability At early common law, a seller was not held to any implied warranty as to the quality of the goods. Under the Code, however, a **merchant seller** impliedly warrants the merchantability of goods that are of the kind in which she deals. The implied warranty of **merchantability** is a warranty by a merchant seller that the goods are reasonably fit for the ordinary purposes for which they are manufactured and sold and also that they are of fair, average quality. *See Duford v. Sears, Roebuck & Co.* The warranty arises as a matter of law so there is no need for the buyer to prove that she relied on the warranty or that the warranty formed a basis of the bargain. The warranty applies automatically unless disclaimed by the seller.

Under Section 2–314 of the Code, the minimum requirements of merchantability are that the goods must

1. be fit for the ordinary purposes for which the goods are used;

2. be adequately contained, packaged, and labeled as the agreement may require;

3. pass without objection in the trade under the contract description;

4. in the case of fungible goods, be of fair, average quality within the description;

5. be within variations permitted by the agreement; *and*

6. conform to the promises or affirmations of fact made on the container or label, if any.

In order to satisfy the implied warranty of merchantability the goods must meet all of the above standards. The most common examples of breach of the implied warranty of merchantability are goods that do not function properly or unexpectedly cause harm because of improper manufacturing or labeling. Thus, a bottled drink with broken glass inside, an electric heater that shocks the user, and a new automobile with defective brakes would breach the implied warranty of merchantability.

The Code in Section 2–314(3) expressly provides that implied warranties may arise from course of dealing or usage of trade. Thus, where the seller of a new automobile failed to lubricate it before delivery to the buyer, and the evidence established that it was the regular custom and usage of new car dealers to do so, the seller was held liable to the buyer for the resulting damages to the automobile in an action for breach of implied warranty.

The official Comments to the Code further provide that a contract for the sale of second-hand goods "involves only such obligation as is appropriate to such goods for that is their description." It has been held that "such obligation" includes an implied warranty of merchantability. In defining this warranty the price, age, and condition of the goods are considered. For example, in June 1970, the defendant purchased a used 1965 model automobile from the plaintiff retail dealer. The day after the purchase, the transmission fell out of the car while being driven by the defendant on an expressway. A week after repairs were made, the brakes went out completely on another expressway. The court held that any car without adequate transmission and proper brakes is not fit for the ordinary purpose of driving, that the implied warranty of merchantability was therefore breached, and that the defendant had justifiably revoked his acceptance of the car. *Overland Bond & Investment Corp. v. Howard,* 9 Ill.App.3d 348, 292 N.E.2d 168 (1972).

The Code further provides that the serving for value of food or drink to be consumed on the premises or elsewhere is a sale. Section 2–314(1). Where injuries have been caused by a nonedible substance in food, however, an implied warranty may not exist if the substance is natural to the food. A minority of jurisdictions distinguish between natural objects in food, such as fish bones in fish, and foreign objects such as a pebble, piece of wire, or glass. The modern and majority test is the

reasonable expectation of the consumer. That a substance is natural to a product in one stage of preparation does not necessarily imply that the consumer will reasonably anticipate or expect it to be in the final product served. In one case the plaintiff, upon being served a martini cocktail, removed the olive, observed that it had a hole in the end, and bit down upon it thereby breaking a tooth upon the olive pit. The court held it was a question of fact whether he had acted reasonably in expecting that the olive did not contain a pit. If this was a reasonable expectation, he was entitled to recover damages. *Hochberg v. O'Donnell's Restaurant, Inc.,* 272 A.2d 846 (D.C.App.1971).

Fitness for Particular Purpose Unlike the warranty of merchantability, the implied warranty of fitness for a particular purpose applies to *any* seller, whether or not he is a merchant. The **implied warranty of fitness for a particular purpose** arises if at the time of sale the seller had reason to know the buyer's particular purpose and that the buyer was relying upon the seller's skill and judgment to select suitable goods. Section 2–315.

In contrast to the implied warranty of merchantability, the implied warranty of fitness for a particular purpose pertains to the *specific* purpose, rather than the ordinary purpose, of the goods. *See Duford v. Sears, Roebuck & Co.* Goods that are fit for ordinary purposes, and therefore are merchantable, may nonetheless be unfit for a particular purpose. A particular purpose may be a specific use or relate to a special situation in which the buyer intends to use the goods. Thus, if Miller has reason to know that Levine is purchasing a pair of shoes for mountain climbing and that Levine is relying upon Miller's judgment to furnish suitable shoes for this purpose, an implied warranty of fitness for a particular purpose would arise in this sale. If Miller sold Levine shoes suitable only for ordinary walking purposes, Miller would breach this implied warranty. Likewise, a buyer indicates to a seller that she needs a stamping machine to stamp 10,000 packages in an eight-hour period and relies on the seller to select an appropriate machine. By selecting the machine, the seller impliedly warrants that the machine selected will stamp 10,000 packages in an eight-hour period.

The implied warranty of fitness for a particular purpose does not require any specific statement by the seller. Rather, the warranty of fitness for a particular purpose requires only that the seller know that the buyer is relying on the seller's expertise in selecting a product for the buyer's specific purpose. The buyer need not specifically inform the seller of her particular purpose; it is sufficient if the seller has reason to know it. On the other hand, the implied warranty of fitness for a particular purpose would not arise in a situation where the buyer insists on a particular product and the seller simply conveys it to her.

Reliance is therefore required for this warranty, unlike an express warranty, which requires only that the affirmation meet the broad "basis of the bargain" test, or the implied warranty of merchantability, which requires no proof of reliance. In order to prevail in a case involving an implied warranty of fitness for a particular purpose, the buyer must be able to demonstrate specifically that she relied on the seller's skill or judgment in selecting or furnishing suitable goods.

Frequently, as in *Vlases v. Montgomery Ward and Company,* a sale involves both implied warranties.

OBSTACLES TO WARRANTY ACTIONS

In certain respects, warranty claims offer many advantages to injured persons. Generally, a plaintiff need only establish the existence of a warranty, the breach of the warranty, an injury resulting from the breach, and the giving of notice in order to recover in a warranty action. This makes warranty claims easier to bring than negligence cases, which require a showing by the plaintiff that the defendant failed to act with due care—often a difficult task. A number of technical obstacles, however, limit the effectiveness of warranty as a basis for recovery. These in-

clude disclaimers of warranties, limitations or modifications of warranties, privity, notice of breach, and the conduct of the plaintiff. These obstacles vary considerably from jurisdiction to jurisdiction.

Disclaimer of Warranties

The Code calls for a reasonable construction of words or conduct to **disclaim** (negate) or limit warranties. Section 2–316. The Code makes clear that the seller should not rely on a time-honored formula of words and expect to obtain a disclaimer that may go unnoticed by the buyer. To be effective, disclaimers must be positive, explicit, unequivocal, and conspicuous.

Express Exclusions A **warranty of title** may be excluded only by specific language or by certain circumstances, including judicial sales or sales by sheriffs, executors, or foreclosing lienors. Section 2–312(2). In the latter cases the seller is manifestly offering to sell only such right or title as he or a third person might have in the goods, as it is apparent that the goods are not the property of the person selling them.

In general, a seller cannot provide an **express warranty** and then disclaim it. A seller can avoid making an express warranty by carefully refraining from making any promise or affirmation of fact relating to the goods, refraining from making a description of the goods, or refraining from using a sale by means of a sample or model. Section 2–313. *See Trans-Aire International, Inc. v. Northern Adhesive Co., Inc.* It may be possible that a seller can also negate an express warranty by *clear, specific, unambiguous* language. The Code, however, provides that words or conduct relevant to the creation of an express warranty and words or conduct negating a warranty shall be construed wherever reasonable as consistent with each other and that a negation or limitation is inoperative to the extent that such construction is unreasonable. Section 2–316. For example, a seller and a buyer enter into a written contract in which the seller warrants that the camera being sold is free of defects. This express warranty renders inoperative another provision in the contract that attempts to disclaim liability for any repairs required by any defects in the camera. The inconsistency between the two contractual provisions makes the disclaimer ineffective. Moreover, if the seller's disclaimer attempts to negate "all express warranties" this general disclaimer would be ineffective against the specific express warranty providing that the camera is free of all defects. Finally, oral warranties made prior to the execution of a written agreement that contains an express disclaimer are subject to the parol evidence rule. Thus, as discussed in Chapter 14, if the written contract is intended to be the final and *complete* statement of the agreement between the parties, oral evidence of warranties that *contradict* the terms of the written contract is inadmissible.

To exclude an **implied warranty of merchantability,** the language of disclaimer must mention *merchantability* and, in the case of a writing, must be *conspicuous.* Section 2–316(2). For example, Bart wishes to buy a used refrigerator from Ben's Used Appliances Store for $100. Given the low purchase price, Ben is unwilling to guarantee the refrigerator's performance. Bart agrees to buy it with no warranty protection. To exclude the warranty, Ben writes on the contract in conspicuous language, "This refrigerator carries no warranties, including no warranty of MERCHANTABILITY." Ben has effectively disclaimed the implied warranty of merchantability.

To exclude or to modify an **implied warranty of fitness** for the particular purpose of the buyer, the disclaimer must be in *writing* and *conspicuous.* Section 2–316(2). A term or clause is conspicuous when it is written such that a reasonable person against whom it is to operate should have noticed it. Section 1–201(10).

All implied warranties, unless the circumstances indicate otherwise, are excluded by expressions like *as is, with all faults,* or other language plainly calling the buyer's attention to the exclusion of warranties. Section 2–316(3)(a). Most courts require the "as is" clause to be conspicuous. Implied warranties may also be excluded by course of dealing, course of performance, or usage of trade.

Disclaimers that are viewed as being unconscionable will be invalidated by the courts. Section 2–302 of the Code, as previously discussed in Chapter 20, permits a court to limit the application of any contract or provision of a contract that it finds unconscionable.

Buyer's Examination or Refusal to Examine If the buyer inspects the goods before entering into the contract, *implied warranties* do not apply to defects that are apparent upon examination. The particular buyer's skill and the normal method of examining goods in the circumstances determine what defects are excluded by examination. Section 2–316, Comment 8. Moreover, there is no implied warranty as to defects which an examination ought to have revealed, not only where the buyer has examined the goods as fully as she desired, but also where the buyer has *refused* to examine the goods. Section 2–316(3)(b). *See Trans-Aire International, Inc. v. Northern Adhesive Co., Inc.*

A mere failure or omission to examine the goods is not a refusal to examine them. It is not enough that the goods were available for inspection and the buyer did not see fit to inspect them. In order for the buyer to have "refused to examine the goods," the seller *must* first have demanded that the buyer examine them.

Federal Legislation Relating to Warranties of Consumer Goods To protect purchasers of **consumer goods** (defined as "tangible personal property normally used for personal, family, or household purposes"), Congress enacted the **Magnuson-Moss Warranty Act.** The purpose of the act is to prevent deception and to make available to consumer purchasers adequate information with respect to warranties.

Administration and enforcement of the act is by the Federal Trade Commission. The commission's guidelines about the type of information required to be set forth in warranties of consumer products are aimed at providing the consumer with clear and useful information. More significantly, the act provides that a seller who makes a written warranty cannot disclaim *any* implied warranty. For a complete discussion of the act, see Chapter 43.

For a review of the types of warranties and the way in which they can be disclaimed, see Figure 23–1.

Limitation or Modification of Warranties

Sometimes a seller is willing to give some warranty protection but wishes to limit the scope or type of protection she gives. For example, although she is willing to repair or replace a defective product, she is not willing to pay consequential damages, such as the buyer's lost profits, arising from any product defects. Section 2–719 of the Code permits a seller to **limit** or **modify** the buyer's remedies for breach of warranty. One important exception to the seller's right is Section 2–719(3), which prohibits "unconscionable" limitations or exclusions of consequential damages. Specifically, the "[l]imitation of consequential damages for injury to the person in the case of consumer goods is prima facie unconscionable. . . ."

In some cases, a seller may choose not to limit the buyer's rights to seek damages for breach of warranty but to impose time limits within which the warranty is effective. Except for instances of unconscionability, such clauses are permitted by the Code, but any

---

Figure 23–1 Warranties

Type of Warranty	How Created	What Is Warranted	How Disclaimed
Title (2-312)	Seller contracts to sell goods	• Good title • Rightful transfer	• Specific language • Circumstances giving buyer reason to know that seller does not claim title
Express (2-313)	• Affirmation of fact • Promise • Description • Sample or model	• Conform to affirmation • Conform to promise • Conform to description • Conform to sample or model	• Specific language (extremely difficult)
Merchantability (2-314)	Merchant sells goods	• Fit for ordinary purpose • Adequately contained, packaged, and labeled	• Must mention "merchantability" • If in writing must be conspicuous • As-is sale • Buyer examination • Course of dealing, course of performance, usage of trade
Fitness for a particular purpose (2-315)	Seller knows buyer is relying upon seller to select goods suitable for buyer's particular purpose	Fit for particular purpose	• No "buzz" words necessary • Must be in writing and conspicuous • As-is sale • Buyer examination • Course of dealing, course of performance, usage of trade

attempt to shorten the time period for filing an action for personal injury to a period of less than one year is not permitted under the Code.

Privity of Contract

Because of the association of warranties with contracts, a principle of law became established in the nineteenth century that a plaintiff could not recover for breach of warranty unless he was in a contractual relationship with the defendant. This relationship is known as privity of contract.

Horizontal privity pertains to noncontracting parties who are injured by the defective goods; this group would include users, consumers, and bystanders who are not the contracting purchaser. Horizontal privity concerns who benefits from a warranty and may, therefore, sue for its breach.

Under this rule, a warranty by seller Ingrid to buyer Sylvester, who resells the goods to purchaser Lyle under a similar warranty, gives Lyle no rights against Ingrid. There is no privity of contract between Ingrid and Lyle. In the event of breach of warranty, Lyle may recover only from his seller, Sylvester, who in turn may recover from Ingrid.

The Code relaxes the requirement of horizontal privity of contract by permitting, at a minimum, members of the family or household of the buyer or guests in his home recovery on a seller's warranty. Section 2–318 of the Code provides three alternative sections from which the States may select. *Alternative A*, the least comprehensive and most widely adopted of these legislative alternatives, provides: a seller's warranty whether express or implied extends to any natural person who is in the family or household of his buyer or who is a guest in his home if it is reasonable to expect that such person may use, consume, or be affected by the goods and who is injured in person by breach of the warranty. *Alternative B* extends Alternative A to any natural person who may reasonably be expected to use, consume, or be affected by the goods. *Alternative C* further expands the coverage of the section to any person, not just natural persons, and to property damage as well as per-

sonal injury. (A natural person would not include artificial entities such as corporations.) A seller may not exclude or limit the operation of this section for injury to a person.

Nonetheless, the Code merely sets a minimum standard that the States may expand through case law. Most States have judicially accepted the Code's invitation to relax the requirements of horizontal privity and, for all practical purposes, have *eliminated* horizontal privity in warranty cases.

Vertical privity pertains to remote sellers within the chain of distribution, such as manufacturers and wholesalers, with whom the consumer purchaser has not entered into a contract. Vertical privity determines who is liable for breach of warranty. Although the Code adopts a neutral position regarding vertical privity, the courts in most States have eliminated the requirement of vertical privity in warranty actions.

Notice of Breach of Warranty

When a buyer has accepted a tender of goods that are not as warranted by the seller, she is required to notify the seller of any breach of warranty within a reasonable time after she has discovered or should have discovered it. If the buyer fails to notify the seller of any breach within a reasonable time, she is barred from any remedy against the seller. Section 2–607(3)(a).

The purpose of the reasonable notice requirement is (1) to enable the seller to cure the defect or to minimize the buyer's loss, (2) to provide the seller an opportunity to prepare for conflict resolution and litigation, and (3) to provide the seller with an end point to liability. In determining whether notice was provided in a reasonable period of time, commercial standards apply to a merchant buyer, while different standards apply to a retail consumer so as not to deprive a good faith consumer of his remedy. Section 2–607, Comment 4.

Plaintiff's Conduct

Because warranty liability developed in the law of sales and contracts, in most States contributory negligence of the buyer is *no defense* to an action against the seller for breach of warranty. In some States, comparative negligence statutes apply to warranty actions. (Comparative negligence is discussed more fully later in this chapter.)

If the buyer discovers a defect in the goods that may cause injury and then proceeds to make use of the goods, he will not be permitted to recover damages from the seller for loss or injuries caused by such use. This is not contributory negligence but **voluntary assumption** of a known risk.

Thus, a buyer may not recover damages for breach of an implied warranty of fitness for a particular purpose where he uses the goods after discovering their unfitness. For example, a contractor planning to lay a water pipeline gave plans for the job to defendant supplier who prescribed the needed materials, which the contractor purchased from him. Through an error, the supplier delivered sewer pipe glue instead of glue for water pipeline. Upon commencing the work, the man in charge reported to the contractor his dissatisfaction with the glue as it "didn't bond" the pipe sections. The project supervisor telephoned the supplier who checked his records and said they had shipped the right material. Use of the glue was then continued and after completion of the pipeline, tests disclosed numerous leaks. The contractor had to dig up the line and reconstruct it at a cost of $9,000. The court held that the seller was not liable as the buyer's continued use of the glue after knowledge of its unfitness for the purpose was unreasonable. *Davis v. Pumpco, Inc.,* 519 P.2d 557 (Okl.App.1974).

STRICT LIABILITY IN TORT

The most recent and far-reaching development in the field of products liability is that of strict liability in tort. All but a very few States have now accepted the concept, which is embodied in **Section 402A** of the Restatement, Second, Torts.

Section 402A imposes **strict liability in tort** on merchant sellers for both personal in-

juries and property damage resulting from selling a product in a **defective condition, unreasonably dangerous** to the user or consumer. Section 402A applies even though "the seller has exercised all possible care in the preparation and sale of his product." Thus, negligence is not the basis of liability in strict liability cases. The essential distinction between the two doctrines is that actions in strict liability do not require the plaintiff to prove that the injury-producing defect resulted from any specific act of negligence of the seller. Strict liability actions focus on the *product* not on the *conduct* of the manufacturer. Courts in strict liability cases are interested in the fact that a product defect arose—not in *how* it arose. Thus, even an "innocent" manufacturer—one who has not been negligent—may be liable if his product turns out to contain a defect that injures a consumer.

The reasons asserted in support of imposing strict liability in tort upon manufacturers and assemblers of products include the following: (1) maximum protection should be given consumers against dangerous defects in products; (2) manufacturers are in the best position to prevent or reduce the hazards to life and health in defective products; (3) manufacturers realize the most profit from the total sales of their goods and are best able to carry the financial burden of such liability by distributing it among the public as a cost of doing business; (4) manufacturers utilize wholesalers and retailers merely as conduits in the marketing of their products and should not be permitted to avoid liability simply because they have no contract with the user or consumer; and (5) since the manufacturer is liable to his purchaser who may be a wholesaler who in turn is liable to the retailer who in turn is liable to the ultimate purchaser, time and expense would be saved by making the liability a direct one rather than a chain reaction.

Although liability for personal injuries caused by the defective condition of goods which makes them unreasonably dangerous is usually associated with sales of goods, such liability also exists with respect to **leases** and

bailments of defective goods. The extension of liability to lessors and bailors of goods is not surprising in view of the rationale developed by the courts in imposing strict liability in tort upon manufacturers and sellers of products. The danger to which the public is exposed by defectively manufactured cars and trucks traveling on the highways is not greatly different from the hazards of defective cars and trucks leased to operators.

REQUIREMENTS OF STRICT LIABILITY

Section 402A imposes strict liability in tort on merchant sellers for both personal injuries and property damage resulting from selling a product in a defective condition unreasonably dangerous to the user or consumer. Specifically, this section provides:

1. One who sells any product in a defective condition unreasonably dangerous to the user or consumer or to his property is subject to liability for physical harm thereby caused to the ultimate user or consumer, or to his property, if (a) the seller is engaged in the business of selling such a product, and (b) it is expected to and does reach the user or consumer without substantial change in the condition in which it is sold.
2. The rule stated in Subsection (1) applies although (a) the seller has exercised all possible care in the preparation and sale of his products, and (b) the user or consumer has not bought the product from or entered into any contractual relation with the seller.

Negligence, as previously stated, is not the basis of this liability; it applies even though "the seller has exercised all possible care in the preparation and sale of his product." The seller is not an insurer of the goods which he manufactures or sells, however, and the essential requirements for strict product liability are that: (1) the defendant was engaged in the business of selling such a product; (2) the defendant sold the product in a defective condition; (3) the defective condition was one which made the product unreasonably dangerous to the user or consumer or to his property; (4) the defect in the product existed at the time it left the hands of the defendant; (5)

the defective condition was attributable to the defendant; (6) the plaintiff sustained physical harm or property damage by use or consumption of the product; and (7) the defective condition was the proximate cause of such injury or damage. *See Duford v. Sears, Roebuck & Co.*

This liability is imposed by law as a matter of public policy and does not depend upon contract, either express or implied. It does not require reliance by the injured user or consumer upon any statements made by the manufacturer or seller. The liability is not limited to persons in a relationship of buyer and seller; thus neither vertical nor horizontal privity is required. No notice of the defect is required to have been given by the injured user or consumer. The liability, furthermore, is generally not subject to disclaimer, exclusion, or modification by contractual agreement. The liability is solely in tort and arises out of the common law; it is not governed by the provisions of the Uniform Commercial Code. The majority of courts considering the question have held that Section 402A imposes liability only for injury to person and damage to property but not for commercial loss (such as loss of bargain or profits), which loss is recoverable in an action for breach of warranty.

Merchant Sellers

Section 402A imposes liability only upon a person who is in the *business* of selling the product involved. It does not apply to an occasional seller who is not in the business of selling the product, such as a person who trades in his used car or who sells his lawn mower to a neighbor. It is similar in this respect to the implied warranty of merchantability, which applies only to sales by a merchant with respect to goods of the type in which he deals.

There are a growing number of jurisdictions that recognize the applicability of strict liability in tort to merchant-sellers of *used* goods. One court has stated in a case involving the sale of a used automobile that "the safety of the general public demands that when a used motor vehicle, for example, is sold for use as a *serviceable motor vehicle* (and not as junk parts), absent special circumstances, the seller be responsible for safety defects whether known or unknown at the time of sale, present while the machine was under his control."

Defective Condition

In an action against a defendant manufacturer or other seller to recover damages under the rule of strict liability in tort, the plaintiff must prove a defective condition in the product, but she is not required to prove how or why the product became defective. In an action based on Section 402A, the reason or cause of the defect is not material, although it would be in an action based on negligence. Under a strict liability approach, a manufacturer will be held liable even though it acted in a non-negligent manner. For example, if the Quality Bottling Company, despite the most stringent quality control program in the industry and through no negligence of its own, manufactures a bottle that explodes in the hands of a consumer, the company would be liable to the consumer under Section 402A. Whether or not Quality Bottling Company acted negligently is irrelevant. The plaintiff, however, must show that at the time she was injured the condition of the product was not substantially changed from what it had been at the time it was sold by the manufacturer or seller. In general, defects may arise through faulty manufacturing, through faulty product design, or through inadequate warning, labeling, packaging, or instructions.

Manufacturing Defect A **manufacturing defect** occurs when the product is not properly made; that is, it fails to meet its own manufacturing specifications. For instance, suppose a chair is manufactured with legs designed to be attached by four screws and glue. If such a chair were produced without inserting the appropriate screws, this would constitute a manufacturing defect.

Design Defect A product contains a design defect when it is produced as specified but is dangerous or hazardous because its design is inadequate. Design defects can result from a number of causes, including poor engineering and poor choice of materials. An example of a design defect that received great notoriety was the Ford Pinto. A number of courts found the car to be inadequately designed because its fuel tank had been placed too close to its rear axle, causing the fuel tank to rupture upon impact from the rear. *See also Heckman v. Federal Press Co.*

Section 402A provides no guidance in determining which injury-producing designs should give rise to strict liability and which should not. The courts have adopted widely varying approaches in applying 402A to defective design cases.

At one extreme, a few courts have taken a very literal approach to Section 402A. They have ruled that a manufacturer is strictly liable for injuries caused by a design that a reasonable person would not have produced if he had knowledge of the design's harmful character at the time it was made. Whether the manufacturer *did* or *could have known* of the risk associated with the design, or of an alternative design that could have avoided the risk, is deemed irrelevant for purposes of strict liability. Manufacturers, in effect, are held liable for hazards that were unknowable at the time they manufactured their products.

A slightly larger number of courts, although still a minority, have taken the opposite approach. They have indicated that they see no difference between negligence and strict liability principles in defective design cases and apply negligence principles to such cases. Unless the plaintiff can demonstrate that the manufacturer knew, or should have known, of a safer, cost-effective design, the manufacturer will not be held liable.

The majority of courts have ostensibly adopted a middle-of-the-road approach. They have stated that strict liability cases should be viewed differently from negligence cases, but they have not clarified what that means beyond reciting that strict liability cases focus on the product, not on the manufacturer's conduct. Nevertheless, virtually none of the courts has upheld a judgment in a strict liability case in which the defendant demonstrated that the **"state-of-the-art"** was such that the manufacturer (1) neither knew nor could have known of a product hazard, or (2) if he knew of the product hazard, could have designed a safer product given existing technology. Thus, almost all courts evaluate the design of a product on the basis of the dangers that could have been known at the time of producing the product.

In deciding design defect cases, courts identify any government safety standards applicable to the design involved in the product liability lawsuit. If such a standard exists and the manufacturer's failure to follow it caused the plaintiff's injury, the courts tend to impose liability automatically. On the other hand, courts do not automatically relieve a manufacturer from liability simply because the manufacturer complied with a government safety standard. If a plaintiff can demonstrate that a safer, cost-effective design was available to the manufacturer, the plaintiff can still prevail in a product liability lawsuit even though the manufacturer complied with a government safety standard.

Failure to Warn   A seller is under a duty to provide adequate warning of possible danger, to provide appropriate directions for safe use, and to package the product in a safe manner. Warnings do not, however, always protect sellers from liability. A seller who could have designed or manufactured a product in a cost-effective manner, but who instead chooses to provide a warning of the product's hazards, cannot escape liability simply by the warning. Warnings usually will avoid liability only if there are no cost-effective designs or manufacturing processes available to reduce a risk of injury.

The duty to give a warning arises out of a foreseeable danger of physical harm from the normal or probable use of the product and the likelihood that unless warned, the user or consumer will not ordinarily be aware of such danger or hazard. *See Toups v. Sears, Roebuck and Company.* For example, a seller

may reasonably assume that those with allergies to products such as eggs or strawberries will know of their allergies and therefore need not be warned of this risk. On the other hand, if a product contains an ingredient to which a substantial number of persons are allergic, and the ingredient is one whose danger is not generally known, or if known, is one which the consumer would not reasonably expect to find in the product, the seller is required to give a warning about it. Under strict liability principles, sellers are generally required to provide warnings against product uses for which the product is not marketed, including certain instances of consumer misuse, if the uses are foreseeable by the manufacturer and the hazard is unlikely to be recognized by the consumer.

Section 402A imposes liability in failure-to-warn cases only where the seller "has knowledge, or by the application of reasonable, developed human skill and foresight should have knowledge, of the . . . danger." Comment j. In effect, the seller is held to the knowledge and skill of an expert in the field. Some courts have ruled that this means a manufacturer not only must keep abreast of scientific knowledge, discoveries, and advances, but also must conduct research to determine whether his product contains hazards. Most courts today require proof that the manufacturer knew, or could have known, of a product hazard before imposing liability for a failure to warn.

Unreasonably Dangerous

Section 402A liability applies only if the defective product is unreasonably dangerous to the user or consumer. An **unreasonably dangerous** product is one which contains a danger beyond that which would be contemplated by the ordinary consumer who purchases it with the common knowledge of its characteristics. Thus, "good whiskey is not unreasonably dangerous merely because it will make some people drunk, and is especially dangerous to alcoholics; but bad whiskey, containing a dangerous amount of fuel oil, is unreasonably dangerous. Good tobacco is not unreasonably dangerous merely because the effects of smoking may be harmful; but tobacco containing something like marijuana may be unreasonably dangerous. Good butter is not unreasonably dangerous merely because, if such be the case, it deposits cholesterol in the arteries and leads to heart attacks; but bad butter, contaminated with poisonous fish oil, is unreasonably dangerous." Comment i to Section 402A. Most courts have left the question of what a consumer reasonably expects to find to the jury.

OBSTACLES TO RECOVERY

Few of the obstacles to recovery in warranty cases present serious problems to plaintiffs in strict liability actions brought pursuant to Section 402A because this section was drafted in large part to avoid the obstacles in warranty actions.

Disclaimers and Notice

Comment m to Section 402A provides that the basis of strict liability rests solely in tort and, therefore, is not subject to contractual defenses. The comment specifically states that strict product liability is not governed by the Code, that it is not affected by contractual limitations or disclaimers, and that it is not subject to any requirement that notice be given to the seller by the injured party within a reasonable time. Nevertheless, most courts have *allowed* clear and specific disclaimers of Section 402A liability in *commercial* transactions between merchants of relatively equal economic power.

Privity

With respect to **horizontal privity,** the strict liability in tort of manufacturers and other sellers extends not only to buyers, users, and consumers, but also to injured bystanders. Illustrative cases are: the occupants of an automobile injured in a collision with another car due to the other car's having defective brakes; a golfer killed by a runaway golf cart that started due to a faulty transmission system; a bystander injured by a runaway truck started by a short circuit; a bystander injured by the explosion of a defective beer keg; a neighbor injured by the explosion of a propane gas tank; and a bystander injured by the explosion of a shotgun barrel caused by a defective shell.

In terms of **vertical privity,** strict liability in tort imposes liability on any seller who is engaged in the business of selling the product, including a wholesaler or distributor as well as the manufacturer and retailer. The rule of strict liability in tort also applies to the manufacturer of a defective component part that has been incorporated into the larger product where no essential change has been made in it by the manufacturer of the finished product.

Plaintiff's Conduct

Many product liability defenses relate to the conduct of the plaintiff. The element common to all of them is the defendant's contention that the plaintiff's improper conduct played such a contributing role in the plaintiff's injury that it would be unfair to blame the product or its seller.

Contributory Negligence   Contributory negligence is conduct on the part of the plaintiff that falls below the standard to which he should conform for his own protection and that is the legal cause of the plaintiff's harm. Under traditional negligence law principles, if the negligence of the plaintiff together with the negligence of the defendant proximately caused the plaintiff's injury, the plaintiff could not recover *any* damages from the defendant. It did not matter whether the plaintiff's contributory negligence was slight or extensive. Because strict liability is designed to assess liability without fault, Section 402A rejects contributory negligence as a defense. Thus, a seller cannot defend a strict liability lawsuit on the basis of a plaintiff's negligent failure to discover a defect or to guard against its possibility. But, as discussed below, contributory negligence in the form of an assumption of the risk can bar recovery under Section 402A.

Comparative Negligence The harshness of the contributory negligence doctrine has caused all but a few States to reject the all-or-nothing rule of contributory negligence and to substitute the doctrine of comparative negligence. Under **comparative negligence,** damages are apportioned between the parties in proportion to the degree of fault or negligence found against the parties.

Despite Section 402A's bar of contributory negligence in strict liability cases, most courts apply comparative negligence to strict liability cases. (Some courts use the term **comparative responsibility** rather than comparative negligence.) There are two basic types of comparative negligence or comparative responsibility. One is **pure comparative responsibility,** which simply reduces the plaintiff's recovery in proportion to her fault, whatever that may be. Thus, if a plaintiff is found to be 80 percent at fault in causing an accident in which she suffered a $100,000 loss, her recovery would be limited to 20 percent of her damages, or $20,000. The other type is **modified comparative responsibility** in which the plaintiff recovers according to the general principles of comparative responsibility *unless* she is more than 50 percent responsible for her injuries. If her responsibility exceeds 50 percent, she recovers nothing. The majority of comparative negligence States follows the modified comparative responsibility approach.

Voluntary Assumption of the Risk Assumption of risk is a defense in an action based on strict liability in tort. Basically, **assumption of risk** is the plaintiff's express or implied consent to encounter a known danger. The user or consumer who voluntarily uses the goods in an unusual, inappropriate, or improper manner for which they were not intended, and which use under the circumstances is unreasonable, assumes the risk of injuries that result from such use. Thus, a person who drives an automobile after realizing that the brakes are not in working order or an

employee who attempts to remove a foreign object from a high-speed roller press without shutting off the power has assumed the risk of his own injury. In a comparative negligence or comparative responsibility State, assumption of the risk would either reduce or bar recovery depending on the degree to which it contributed to the plaintiff's injury.

To establish such defense the burden is on the defendant to show that (1) the plaintiff actually knew and appreciated the particular risk or danger created by the defect, (2) the plaintiff voluntarily encountered the risk while realizing the danger, and (3) the plaintiff's decision to encounter the known risk was unreasonable.

Misuse or Abuse of the Product Closely connected to voluntary assumption of the risk is the valid defense of misuse or abuse of the product by the injured party. **Misuse** or **abuse** occurs when the injured party knows, or should know, that he is using the product in a manner not contemplated by the seller. The major difference is that misuse or abuse includes actions which the injured party does not know to be dangerous, while assumption of the risk does not include such conduct. Instances of such misuse or abuse include standing on a rocking chair to change a light bulb or using a lawn mower to trim hedges.

The courts, however, have significantly limited this defense by requiring that the misuse or abuse not be foreseeable by the seller. If a use is foreseeable, then the seller must take measures to guard against it. For example, if William stands on a rocking chair to change a light bulb and is injured when it tilts forward, he would be unable to recover because of his misuse of the chair. Similarly, if Jenny hammers a nail with a hairdryer and suffers an eye injury when a chip flies from the dryer, she will be unsuccessful in a claim against the manufacturer.

Subsequent Alteration

Section 402A provides that liability only exists if the product reaches "the user or consumer without substantial change in the condition in which it is sold." Accordingly, most, but not all, courts would not hold a manufacturer liable for a faulty carburetor if the retailer were to remove the part and make significant changes in it prior to reinserting it into the automobile.

Statute of Repose

Numerous lawsuits have been brought against manufacturers many years after the product had first been sold. In one case, a manufacturer was successfully sued twenty-two years after a defective water meter was first purchased and fourteen years after it was installed in the plaintiff's home. In another case, Volkswagen of America was ordered to pay $1.8 million in damages for a missing door latch costing 35 cents. The accident occurred ten years after the car had been manufactured and nine years after Volkswagen had informed its dealers about the defect.

In response, many States have adopted **statutes of repose.** These enactments limit the time period—typically between six to twelve years—for which a manufacturer is liable for injury caused by its product. After

---

Figure 23–2 Products Liability

	Merchantability*	Strict Liability in Tort
Condition of Goods Creating Liability	Not fit for ordinary purposes	Defective condition, unreasonably dangerous
Type of Transaction Covered	Sales; some courts apply to leases and bailments of goods	Sales, leases, and bailments of goods
Disclaimer	Must mention "merchantability" If in writing, must be conspicuous Must not be unconscionable Subject to Magnuson-Moss Act	Not possible in consumer transactions; may be permitted in commercial transactions
Notice to Seller	Required within reasonable time	Not required
Causation	Required	Required
Who May Sue	In some States, buyer and the buyer's family or guests in home; in other States, any person who may be expected to use, consume, or be affected by goods	Any user or consumer of product; also, in most States, any bystander
Compensable Harms	Personal injury, property damage, economic loss	Personal injury, property damage
Who May Be Sued	Seller who is a merchant with respect to the goods sold	Seller who is engaged in business of selling such a product

*The warranty of fitness for a particular purpose differs from the warranty of merchantability in the following respects: (1) the condition that triggers liability is the failure of the goods to perform according to the particular purpose of the warranty and (2) a disclaimer need not mention "fitness for a particular purpose."

the statutory time period has elapsed, a manufacturer ceases to be liable for harm caused by its defective products.

For a summary of products liability, see Figure 23–2.

CASES

Express Warranties

CIPOLLONE v. LIGGETT GROUP, INC.
United States Court of Appeals, Third Circuit, 1990.
10 UCC Rep. Serv. 625.

BECKER, J.

This appeal is from a final judgment in a protracted products liability case in which the plaintiff, Antonio Cipollone, seeks to hold Liggett Group, Inc., Lorillard, Inc., and Philip Morris, Inc., three of the leading firms in the tobacco industry, liable for the death from lung cancer of his wife, Rose Cipollone, who smoked cigarettes from 1942 until her death in 1984. * * * In an earlier opinion in the case, Cipollone v. Liggett Group, Inc., [citation], we held that the Federal Cigarette Labeling and Advertising Act ("Labeling Act"), [citation], which became effective January 1, 1966, preempted claims arising from smoking after January 1, 1966 (hereinafter post–1965) based upon the cigarette companies' advertising or promotion of cigarettes or upon the adequacy of their warnings as to the hazards of smoking.

At the conclusion of the trial, the jury, answering a series of special interrogatories, returned a verdict in the sum of $400,000.00 for the plaintiff in his individual capacity on the breach of express warranty claim. The jury also found the defendants strictly liable for failing to warn adequately of the hazards of their products, but returned a verdict in their favor on that claim because of Mrs. Cipollone's comparative fault. More precisely, the jury apportioned 80% of the responsibility for Mrs. Cipollone's injuries to her because of its finding that she knew and appreciated the damages of cigarette smoking and voluntarily chose to smoke.

Both sides have appealed, raising a plethora of issues.

* * *

The only way to give effect to our preemption decision and yet ensure fairness in the trial is to limit the evidence going to Mrs. Cipollone's comparative fault to her pre–1966 conduct. * * * Thus, Mr. Cipollone is entitled to a new trial on his failure to warn claim.

Liggett's appeal on the express warranty claim presents an abstruse question pertaining to the nature of the reliance interest required by U.C.C. § 2–313. The attention we pay to this issue on appeal is somewhat ironic, given that the extensive trial focused on other theories of liability, particularly strict liability. The jury's verdict for the plaintiff on an express warranty theory makes our analysis necessary, however.

We conclude that the express warranty charge was flawed and that that portion of the verdict must also be set aside. Primarily, the district court erred to the extent that it prevented Liggett from proving, by a preponderance of the evidence, that Mrs. Cipollone did not believe the advertisements. The advertisements constitute an express warranty as long they constitute a basis of the bargain, that is, as long as Mr. Cipollone can prove that Mrs. Cipollone was aware of the advertisements and as long as Liggett does not prove that she disbelieved them.

* * *

Rose Cipollone was born in 1925 and began to smoke in 1942. She smoked Chesterfield brand cigarettes, manufactured by Liggett, until 1955. In her deposition, introduced into evidence at the trial, she stated that she smoked the Chesterfield brand to be "glamorous," to "imitate" the "pretty girls and movie stars" depicted in Chesterfield advertisements, and because the advertisements stated that Chesterfield cigarettes were "mild." Mrs. Cipollone stated that she understood the description of Chesterfield cigarettes as "mild" to mean that the cigarettes were safe.

Mrs. Cipollone also testified that she was an avid reader of a variety of magazines, frequently listened to the radio, and often watched television during the years that she smoked the Chesterfield brand. Although she could not specifically remember which Chesterfield advertisements she saw or heard during those years, Chesterfield advertisements appeared continuously in those media during that period. Several of these advertisements were introduced into evidence. The following copy appeared commonly in Chesterfield magazine advertisements during the year 1952:

"PLAY SAFE Smoke Chesterfield.

"NOSE, THROAT, and Accessory Organs not Adversely Affected by Smoking Chesterfields. First such report ever published about any cigarette. A responsible consulting organization has reported the results of a continuing study by a competent medical specialist and his staff on the effects of smoking Chesterfield cigarettes. * * * The medical specialist, after a thorough examination of every member of the group, stated: 'It is my opinion that the ears, nose, throat and accessory organs of all participating subjects examined by me were not adversely affected in the six-month period by smoking the cigarettes provided.' "

Television advertisements for the Chesterfield brand were also introduced into evidence. The Chesterfield cigarette was described as having "ingredients that make Chesterfield the best possible smoke as tested and approved by scientists from leading universities." [Citation], and being manufactured with "electronic miracle" technology that makes "cigarettes . . . more better [sic] and safer for you." [Citation.] One advertisement stated "[n]ow Chesterfield is the first cigarette to present this scientific evidence on the effects of smoking—a medical specialist * * * reports that he observed no adverse effects to the nose, throat and sinuses of the group who were smoking Chesterfield. I'd say that means real mildness." [Citation.]

* * *

In 1955, Mrs. Cipollone stopped smoking Chesterfield cigarettes and began to smoke L&M filter cigarettes, also made by Liggett. In response to a question as to why she switched to the L&M brand, Mrs. Cipollone stated that "[w]ell, they were talking about the filter tip, that it was milder and a miracle it would keep the stuff inside a trap, whatever." When asked why she desired the filter tip, she testified that "it was the new thing and I figured, well, go along[, and that] it was better [because t]he bad stuff would stay in the filter then."

* * *

Mrs. Cipollone also stated that she "recall[ed] seeing an ad that said doctors recommend you smoke . . . I think it was L&M's. . . . [T]hrough advertising, I was led to assume that they were safe and they wouldn't harm me. . . . There was lots of advertising. There was advertising everywhere. There was advertising in magazines, on billboards, in newspapers."

Mr. Cipollone also introduced evidence as to how the L&M brand was marketed during the years that Mrs. Cipollone smoked that brand. One series of advertisements that appeared on television and in magazines at the outset of L&M's introduction to the public stated that L&M "miracle tip" filters were "just what the doctor ordered! "; the "just what the doctor ordered" phrase often appeared in a large bold typescript in magazine advertisements. The "miracle tip" was advertised as "remov[ing] the heavy particles, leaving you a Light and Mild smoke."

In 1968, Mrs. Cipollone stopped smoking the L&M brand and started smoking the Virginia Slims brand, manufactured by Philip Morris. * * *

From 1942 until the early 1980's, Mrs. Cipollone smoked between one pack and two packs of cigarettes per day. The only exception to this pattern was that, at the urging of her husband, Mrs. Cipollone substantially reduced her smoking during her first pregnancy in the 1940's. In 1981, Mrs. Cipollone was diagnosed as having lung cancer, but even though her doctors advised her to stop smoking, she was unable to do so. Mrs. Cipollone continued to smoke until June of 1982 when her lung was removed. Even after that, she smoked occasionally, in secret. She testified that she was "addicted" to cigarette smoking and that it was terribly difficult for her to give it up. She stopped smoking in 1983 after her cancer had spread widely and she had become terminally ill. Mrs. Cipollone died on October 21, 1984.

Evidence was also introduced on the subject of Mrs. Cipollone's awareness of the health consequences of smoking cigarettes. * * * In addition, from the beginning of the Cipollones' marriage in 1947, Mr. Cipollone repeatedly told his wife that she should stop smoking because it was unlady-like and bad for her health. When reports linking smoking with cancer and heart disease began to appear in the media, Mr. Cipollone repeatedly brought them to his wife's attention. Other members of the Cipollone family also told her that cigarette smoking was dangerous to her health and could cause cancer. After January 1, 1966, every package of cigarettes purchased by Mrs. Cipollone bore the Congressionally mandated warning labels.

* * *

Authority on the question whether reliance is a necessary element of § 2–313 is divided. Although a few courts have held that reliance is not a necessary element of § 2–313, the more common view has been that it is, and that either a buyer must prove reliance in order to recover on an express warranty or the seller must be permitted to rebut a presumption of reliance in order to preclude recovery. Some treatise writers support this interpretation. No New Jersey court or panel of this court has squarely addressed the question. The history of § 2–313(1)(a), although informative, fails to give a clear answer as to whether reliance is required.

* * *

Liggett argues that reliance must have some place in the "basis of the bargain" determination. Thus, even if reliance should be assumed, based on what "would reasonably induce the purchase of a product," a defendant must have an opportunity to prove non-reliance. This position finds some support in the U.C.C. comments. U.C.C. Official Comment 3 states:

"In actual practice affirmations of fact made by the seller about the goods during a bargain are regarded as part of the description of those goods; hence no particular reliance on such statements need be shown in order to weave them into the fabric of the agreement. Rather, *any fact which is to take such affirmations, once made, out of the agreement requires clear affirmative proof*. The issue normally is one of fact".

Moreover, comment 8 states that "all of the statements of the seller (become part of the basis of the bargain) *unless good reason is shown to the contrary*." The plain language of these comments supports Liggett's position, at least to the extent it indicates that a defendant must be given some opportunity to show that the seller's statements were not meant to be part of the basis of the bargain.

* * *

A final argument in support of a reliance requirement is found in the amicus brief. Without a reliance requirement, one runs the risk of draining the term "basis of the bargain" of all meaning, because the buyer's subjective state of mind becomes completely irrelevant. The district court instructed the jury that a statement could be considered part of the basis of the bargain if it "would naturally induce the purchase of the products." This instruction is completely objective and would permit a buyer to sue for breach of express warranty even if the seller's warranties were advertisements made in another state or country, and even if the buyer did not hear of the claims in these advertisements until the day that she walked into an attorney's office to bring suit for personal injury. It strains the language to say that a statement is part of the "basis" of the buyer's "bargain," when that buyer had no knowledge of the statement's existence.

The above arguments notwithstanding, it is possible to read the "basis of the bargain" requirement as requiring some subjective inducement of the buyer, without requiring a reliance finding. Requiring that the buyer *rely* on an advertisement, whether by imposing this burden initially on the buyer bringing suit, or by allowing the seller to rebut a presumption of reliance, puts a heavy burden on the buyer—a burden that is arguably inconsistent with the U.C.C. as a whole, with other comments to § 2–313 in particular, and with several commentators' suggestions in this area.

* * *

In light of these seemingly inconsistent mandates on the reliance question, some might argue that it is foolish to try to reconcile what is patently inconsistent. We reject this suggestion however, because we find it feasible to reconcile the competing arguments, and we believe that the New Jersey Supreme Court would want us to try. We believe that the most reasonable construction of § 2–313 is neither Liggett's reliance theory, which fails to explain how reliance can be relevant to "what a seller agreed to sell," or the district court's purely objective theory, which fails to explain how an advertisement that a buyer never even saw becomes part of the "basis of the bargain." Instead, we believe that the New Jersey Supreme Court would hold that a plaintiff effectuates the "basis of the bargain" requirement of § 2–313 by proving that she read, heard, saw or knew of the advertisement containing the affirmation of fact or promise. Such proof will suffice "to weave" the affirmation of fact or promise "into the fabric of the agreement," U.C.C. Comment 3, and thus make it part of the basis of the bargain. We hold that once the buyer has become aware of the affirmation of fact or promise, the statements are presumed to be part of the "basis of the bargain" unless the defendant, by "clear affirmative proof," shows that the buyer knew that the affirmation of fact or promise was untrue.* * *

As indicated above, Comment 4 and Comment 7, as well as the largely dominant objective theory of contracts, militate in favor of an interpretation of express warranty that ignores the buyer's subjective state of mind. Under the extreme version of this theory apparently adopted by the district court, all the buyer should have to show is what the seller agreed to sell.* * *

Much of the case law supports this "belief" principle.

* * *

Applying our interpretation of § 2–313 to the case at bar, we conclude that the district court's jury instructions were erroneous for two reasons. First, they did not require the plaintiff to prove that Mrs. Cipollone had read, seen, or heard the advertisements at issue. Second, they did not permit the defendant to prove that although Mrs. Cipollone had read, seen, or heard the advertisements, she did not believe the safety assurances contained therein. We must therefore reverse and remand for a new trial on this issue.

* * *

Liggett contends that New Jersey law permits a manufacturer to assert a comparative fault defense to an express warranty products liability suit and that the district court consequently erred in failing to so instruct the jury. We agree that comparative fault principles may be applicable in some express warranty cases, but we do not believe that they are applicable here.

* * *

In sum, we find that a comparative fault defense is available in an express warranty action, but only to the extent that the defendant can show that the buyer misused or abused the product or used the product after learning that the warranty was false. We do not think that that would be possible in this case. There is no evidence that Mrs. Cipollone misused cigarettes. To the extent that she knew cigarettes were bad for her and hence did not believe Liggett's advertisements to the contrary, she cannot collect on an express warranty theory, but not because she assumed the risk of the cigarettes. If she did not believe the advertisements, then they could not have formed a basis of the bargain in the first place, and the jury could not find an express warranty.

* * *

Liggett contends that it is entitled to judgment n.o.v. on the express warranty claim because the record contains insufficient evidence to support a jury verdict for Mr. Cipollone on this point. At the outset, we note that the express warranty provision of the Uniform Commercial Code, § 2–313, makes clear that no formality or magic words are required to create an express warranty. "It is not necessary to the creation of an express warranty that the seller use formal words such as 'warrant' or 'guarantee' or that he have a specific intention to make a warranty. . . ." § 2–313(2). The seller may be liable if its representation regarding the goods takes the form of newspaper, magazine, radio or television advertisements. [Citation.] Consequently, Mr. Cipollone was free to rely, as he did, on advertisements to prove the existence and scope of Liggett's warranty.

* * *

Many Chesterfield and L&M advertisements were submitted to the jury. Liggett contends that "[n]one of them could constitute to a reasonable person a warranty covering serious health effects in the future from long term use of cigarettes." [Citation.] We disagree. * * *

We hold that a reasonable jury could conclude from these advertisements, and the many others entered into evidence, that Liggett had represented to the consumer that the long-term smoking of Chesterfield or L&M cigarettes would not endanger the consumer's health, and that these warranties were untrue. Liggett cannot successfully defend on the ground that the advertisements represented only that short-term smoking was safe. A reasonable jury could infer that an unqualified representation that smoking is safe creates a warranty that smoking for a long period of time is safe.

* * *

Neither do we find, as Liggett contends, that there was insufficient evidence to prove

that Mrs. Cipollone's smoking caused her cancer. * * *

The statistical correlation between heavy smoking and lung cancer is well-documented. * * *

For the foregoing reasons we will: * * * remand for a new trial.

Merchantability/Strict Liability

DUFORD v. SEARS, ROEBUCK & CO.

United States Court of Appeals, First Circuit, 1987.
4 UCC Rep. Serv. 1374.

CAMPBELL, C.J.

* * * In December of 1979, plaintiffs Raymond and Sandra Duford of Sanbornton, New Hampshire, lost their house and many of their belongings in a fire. It is uncontested that the fire began in the chimney pipe that ran from the Dufords' wood-burning stove up through the roof. The Dufords contend that the fire was attributable to the defective design of the chimney pipe. Thus, they brought this diversity action against the pipe's seller, Sears, Roebuck & Co., and its manufacturer, Preway, Inc., under the following theories of recovery: 1) strict liability, 2) negligence, 3) breach of implied warranties of merchantability and fitness for a particular purpose, and 4) negligent infliction of emotional distress.

The allegedly defective product is known as a "triple wall pipe." It is part of a woodstove chimney kit that is sold by Sears and manufactured by Preway. The pipe is supposed to be a solution to the problem confronted by people with a woodstove but no built-in chimney: getting the smoke out of the house without igniting the combustible materials adjacent to the chimney apparatus where it sticks through the roof. The triple wall pipe is designed to achieve this end by virtue of its operation on a "heat exchanger basis." Because of its triple wall design (it is basically a pipe within a pipe within a pipe), cold air from outside the house is channeled down around the inner flue pipe, thus lowering the temperature of the chimney pipe's outer walls. The evidence at trial indicated that Raymond Duford inadvertently installed the chimney pipe upside down. Witnesses on both sides agreed that such installation negated the purpose of the triple wall design, and rendered a fire virtually inevitable.

The Dufords alleged in their complaint that the pipe had no markings indicating which end was up. Their primary theory of recovery, therefore, was that Preway was tortiously liable because of its failure to warn of the latent danger of incorrect installation. During discovery, Preway lent credence to this theory by making an admission . . . that there were no markings on the pipe itself. * * * So the Dufords were nonplussed when, well into the trial, Preway employee Roy Northwood, who had earlier inspected the pipe and noticed some markings on it, testified that at one end of the pipe, stamped in the metal, were the word "up" with two little arrows. His testimony was confirmed by close examination of the pipe itself, which had been introduced by plaintiffs as an exhibit. The pipe contained embossed markings approximately one-eighth inch high; the markings were not only tiny but also quite faint. Their indistinctness, plus the pipe's sooty condition as a result of the fire, apparently accounted for the fact the markings were overlooked not only by the Dufords and their attorney but also—until Northwood discovered them—by Preway's representatives.

Subsequent to this revelation the plaintiffs proceeded at trial on the theory that the markings, instead of being nonexistent, had been inadequate. This new tack was complicated by the prior testimony of plaintiffs' own expert witness, one Rand, who—testifying before Northwood's disclosure that markings in fact existed—opined that an embossed direction would constitute satisfactory guidance on proper installation of the pipe.

In light of the collapse of plaintiffs' main line of attack, coupled with the self-inflicted wound from their own expert, the district court concluded, following two days of trial, that the Dufords' case was inadequate as a matter of law. The court thus dismissed the emotional distress claim and granted defendants' motion for a directed verdict on all other counts. * * *

We hold that a verdict for defendants should not have been directed—as appears to have happened—largely because plaintiffs' case on the "no markings" theory self-destructed. We believe that plaintiffs were entitled to have the court treat the *adequacy* of the warnings as having been tried with "implied consent of the parties." [Citation.] Thus, in now reviewing the correctness of directing a verdict, we must inquire whether there was sufficient evidence for plaintiffs to have gone to the jury on an "adequacy" of warning theory. We believe there was, in respect to the strict liability and warranty of merchantability claims. We therefore vacate and remand as to these claims and affirm as to all others.

A. Strict Liability We begin with an inquiry into the pertinent substantive law of New Hampshire. * * *

1) Products liability actions can be brought under either of two theories: defective manufacture and defective design. Under the former, a plaintiff attempts to show a product defect caused by a mistake or accident in the manufacturing process; under the latter, a plaintiff tries to prove that the product's design itself rendered the product "unreasonably dangerous" to consumers.

2) A court's inquiry into whether a product's design renders it "unreasonably dangerous" is a "multifaceted balancing process involving evaluation of many conflicting factors." [Citation.] One factor is the product's "social utility," a consideration that must be weighed against the danger posed by the product. In making this calculation,

"courts should also consider whether the risk of danger could have been reduced without significant impact on product effectiveness and manufacturing cost. For example, liability may attach if the manufacturer did not take the available and reasonable steps to lessen or eliminate the danger of even a significantly useful and desirable product." [Citation.]

3) Another factor in the "unreasonable danger" calculus is whether the product was accompanied by a warning of any latent dangers. (Under this analysis, an inadequate warning constitutes a design "defect.") This "duty to warn," however, extends only to dangers that are reasonably foreseeable: "Manufacturers cannot foresee and warn of all absurd and dangerous uses of their product." [Citation.] But a suitable warning is not necessarily a conclusive defense in a defective design case, for liability may still attach if the danger "could have been eliminated without excessive cost or loss of product efficiency." [Citation.]

4) The New Hampshire comparative negligence statute applies to products liability actions. Thus, if the jury finds that a plaintiff's proof is sufficient, it must weigh any "plaintiff misconduct," i.e., contributory negligence or assumption of risk, and discount the amount of damages by the percentage of the loss or injury caused by the misconduct. If the plaintiff's misconduct is more than 50 percent responsible, the statute requires a verdict for the defendant.

5) New Hampshire explicitly rejects the outer limits of section 402A liability, namely, liability based solely upon a theory of cost redistribution, [citation], or the theory of liability recognized in cases requiring a manufacturer to warn against even bizarre uses of its product. [Citation.]

To sustain the court's direction of a verdict for defendants here, we must determine that the evidence produced at trial, viewed in the light most favorable to plaintiffs, would not have permitted a rational jury to reach any conclusion other than that the defendants were not liable. [Citation.] We are unable to make that determination.

*   *   *

We underscore our conclusion that the jury *could* have found defendants liable pursuant to the evidence we have described and the reasonable inferences therefrom. We of course do not suggest that it was required to do so, nor do we mean to indicate that any such outcome was preferable. We hold only

that the issues were not suitable for disposition by the court, as a matter of law. *   *   *

B. Implied Warranty of Merchantability
For the same reasons outlined in Part IIA, we find that it was error for the district court to have directed a verdict for defendants on the Dufords' claim that Sears breached its warranty of merchantability. The same evidence that would have permitted the jury to find that the chimney pipe was defectively designed under section 402A would also have permitted a conclusion that the pipe was not "fit for the ordinary purposes for which such goods are used," the legal standard under the warranty of merchantability statute, [UCC] 2–314(2)(c). The New Hampshire Supreme Court has stated that "when . . . any merchant places a defective product in commerce, the plaintiff may plead alternative theories of tort or contract or both." [Citation.] And the reasoning of the [citation] suggests that either a product unaccompanied by an adequate warning or a product designed without a cheap and available safety device are tantamount to a "defective" product. [Citation.]

*   *   *

We also affirm the district court's entry of a directed verdict for defendants on the claim of a breach of the implied warranty of fitness for a particular purpose. It is beyond cavil that the Dufords intended to use the chimney pipe for its ordinary purpose—as a chimney pipe—and not for the sort of "particular" or "peculiar" purpose contemplated by the statute that affords this particular protection to the purchasers of goods. [UCC] 2–315.

We vacate and remand the direction of a verdict on the claim against Preway for strict liability and the claim against Sears for breach of implied warranty of merchantability. We affirm the district court's judgment in respect to all other claims.

Implied Warranties

VLASES v. MONTGOMERY WARD & COMPANY

United States Court of Appeals, Third Circuit, 1967.
377 F.2d 846.

McLAUGHLIN, J.

This case revolves around the charge that defendant-appellant, Montgomery Ward, was liable for the breach of implied warranties in the sale of one day old chickens to the plaintiff-appellee, Paul Vlases. The latter came to this country from Greece when he was sixteen and until 1954 his primary occupation was that of a coal miner. He had always raised chickens but because of his job as a miner his flocks were small, ranging from between twenty-five to one hundred chicks. In 1958 plaintiff began the construction of a two story chicken coop large enough to house 4,000 chickens and a smaller side building where he could wash, grade and sell the eggs. Vlases worked alone on the coop, twelve hours a day, fifty-two weeks a year, until its completion in 1961. In November of 1961 plaintiff placed an order at defendant's outlet store in Brownsville, Pennsylvania for the purchase of 2,000 one day old chicks. The chickens selected by the plaintiff from Ward's catalogue were hybrid Leghorns and were noted for their excellent egg production. On December 21, 1961 plaintiff received the 2,200 chickens [200 bonus chickens for the large order] and placed them on the first floor of the coop which had been equipped with new brooders, feeders and within a short time, waterers. As a further hygienic precaution wire and sugar cane were placed on the ground so the chickens would not come in contact with the dirt floor. For the first six months Vlases slept in the coop in order to give the new chicks his undivided attention.

During the first few weeks after delivery the chickens appeared to be in good health but by the third week plaintiff noticed that their feathers were beginning to fall off. This condition was brought to the attention of Mr. Howard Hamilton who represented the Agway Corporation which was supplying the plaintiff with feed on credit. In February of 1962 Mr. Hamilton took . . . chickens to the Bureau of Animal Industry Diagnostic Laboratory where they were examined by Dr. Daniel P. Ehlers. The examination revealed signs of drug intoxication, . . . hemorrhagic disease involving the weakening of blood vessels [and visceral and ocular leukosis.] Vis-

ceral and ocular leukosis are two types of avian leukosis complex or bird cancer which disease infected plaintiff's flock either killing the chicks or causing those remaining to be destroyed.

Plaintiff in this . . . suit charged . . . breach of warranty. . . .

The two implied warranties before us are the implied warranty of merchantability, [U.C.C.] § 2–314, and the implied warranty of fitness for a particular purpose, [U.C.C.] § 2–315. Both of these are designed to protect the buyer of goods from bearing the burden of loss where merchandise, though not violating a promise expressly guaranteed, does not conform to the normal commercial standards or meeting the buyer's particular purpose, a condition upon which he had the right to rely.

Were it to be assumed that the sale of 2,000 chickens infected with avian leukosis transgressed the norm of acceptable goods under both warranties, appellant's [Ward's] position is that the action will not lie in a situation where the seller is unable to discover the defect or cure the damage if it could be ascertained. That theory does not eliminate the consequences imposed by the Code upon the seller of commercially inferior goods. It is without merit.

The fact that avian leukosis is nondetectable could be an important issue but only as bearing on the charge of negligence, which is no longer in this suit. . . . The entire purpose behind the implied warranty sections of the Code is to hold the seller responsible when inferior goods are passed along to the unsuspecting buyer. What the Code requires is not evidence that the defects should or could have been uncovered by the seller but only that the goods upon delivery were not of a merchantable quality or fit for their particular purpose. If those requisite proofs are established the only exculpatory relief afforded by the Code is a showing that the implied warranties were modified or excluded by specific language under Section 2–316. Lack of skill or foresight on the part of the seller in discovering the product's flaw was never meant to bar liability. The gravamen here is not so much with what precautions were taken by the seller but rather with the quality of the goods contracted for by the buyer. Even a provision specifically disclaiming any warrant against avian leukosis would not necessarily call for the defendant's freedom from liability. Section 1–102(3) of the Code's General Provisions states that standards which are manifestly unreasonable may not be disclaimed and prevents the enforcement of unconscionable sales where, as in this instance, the goods exchanged are found to be totally worthless.

Appellant contends that plaintiff failed to meet the burden of proof that the chickens were delivered with avian leukosis and further asserts that the verdict is against the weight of the evidence. The argument advanced is founded on the fact that avian leukosis may be contracted in two ways, either inherited through the egg or acquired by reason of an unhealthy environment. Appellant urges that since the disease was first diagnosed when the chickens were nine months of age and since there was evidence indicating the existence of other maladies aside from leukosis, that plaintiff failed to show the presence of avian leukosis at delivery and also that the disease was the cause of the inability of the chicks to produce eggs and of their deaths. Upon consideration of all the trial testimony, appellant's argument must be rejected.

It was firmly established by the evidence that with reference to inherited as opposed to environmental leukosis, incidents of the latter are minimized where proper care and health standards are strictly observed. Testimony revealed that environmental infection will more than likely occur where the chicks are housed in a coop previously occupied by a diseased flock, where leukosis is present in nearby chickens or where the young chicks come in contact with contaminated equipment. On behalf of the plaintiff it was shown that the chicks were placed by him in a newly constructed coop with new equipment. There was no evidence that the disease was then present on the farm or had ever affected other chickens raised by Vlases. Plaintiff's expert witness, Dr. Frank A. Bartus, had examined the chickens six or seven months after the first diagnosis of the disease and testified that at that time "this disease [avian leukosis complex] was just running rampant through the whole flock." In the opinion of Dr. Bartus the leukosis found in plaintiff's chickens was transmitted through the egg. That opinion was based on the witness' expertise and factually supported by the consideration that ". . . he [Vlases] has raised chickens in the past, and the fact that he was a fairly good husbandry man, and the fact that he had a new coop I think are very important features in this case." . . .

The judgment of the District Court [in favor of the plaintiff] will be affirmed.

Disclaimer of Warranties

TRANS-AIRE INTERNATIONAL, INC. v. NORTHERN ADHESIVE CO., INC.

United States Court of Appeals, Seventh Circuit, 1989. 882 F.2d 1254.

KANNE, J.

Trans-Aire International, Inc. purchased a contact adhesive from Northern Adhesive Company, Inc. to laminate various materials during the process of converting standard automotive vans to recreational vehicles. The adhesive failed to perform during the summer months as Trans-Aire had hoped, and it sued Northern under a wide variety of legal theories. The district court entered summary judgment in favor of Northern, and Trans-Aire appeals. We affirm.

Trans-Aire International, Inc. converts ordinary automotive vans into recreational vehicles. Prior to October of 1982, Trans-Aire installed interior carpet and ceiling fabrics with an adhesive product, "3M 4500," manufactured by 3M Company. However, Trans-Aire experienced problems with that adhesive. Apparently, when the temperature rose inside a van, the adhesive often would fail to hold the fabrics in place.

Trans-Aire contacted Northern Adhesive Company, Inc., a manufacturer of a wide range of adhesive products, to find a replacement for the 3M product. Trans-Aire never requested a specific adhesive by name and instead merely informed Northern of the purposes for which Trans-Aire needed an adhesive. In response, Northern sent several adhesive samples to Trans-Aire for experimental purposes. Allegedly, Northern told Trans-Aire that one of their adhesives, Adhesive 7448, was a "match" for the 3M product which had failed previously.

Trans-Aire tested the sample adhesives by putting them into its application equipment and applying them in the same manner in which Trans-Aire had been applying the 3M adhesive. The tests were conducted in a cool plant, rather than under the warmer weather conditions which had caused the 3M product to fail. Nevertheless, Trans-Aire's chief engineer, Stephen Fribley, determined that Northern's Adhesive 7448 was better than the 3M product.

Fribley summarized the results of the various test applications to Robert Higgins, Trans-Aire's president. Fribley suggested to Higgins that they test Northern's adhesive under summer-like conditions. However, Higgins stated that he was satisfied that Adhesive 7448 was better than the 3M product.

When Higgins asked, Fribley told Higgins that to his knowledge Adhesive 7448 had no warranty. A Northern representative confirmed Fribley's belief, stating that "there was no warranty on [Adhesive 7448] other than that—what they would ship would be like the sample. It would be the same chemistry." Fribley informed Higgins of this conversation.

Between November of 1982 and May of 1983, Trans-Aire ordered several shipments of Adhesive 7448. Trans-Aire placed each order by telephone and subsequently confirmed its request by sending a written purchase order.

Trans-Aire began to use Adhesive 7448 in late 1982 after placing its initial order. Beginning sometime in the spring of 1983, Trans-Aire learned of numerous delamination problems in the interiors of the RVs in which Adhesive 7448 had been used—the same problems experienced previously with the 3M product. As a result, Trans-Aire was forced to repair well over 500 vans.

* * *

A. Implied Warranties of Fitness for a Particular Purpose and of Merchantability Section 2–314 of the [Uniform] Commercial Code provides that every sale of goods by a merchant includes an implied warranty that the goods are fit for the ordinary purposes for which they are used unless the warranty is modified or excluded. Section 2–315 of the code states that a sale of goods also includes an implied warranty of fitness for a particular purpose if a seller knows of the buyer's particular purpose for the goods and the buyer relies upon the seller's skill or judgment to select suitable goods. However, § 2–316 of the code states that no implied warranties apply when a buyer examines the goods or a sample as fully as he desires, or refuses to examine the goods, prior to the purchase.

The district court first held that no warranty of fitness for a particular purpose arose under the facts and circumstances of this case because Trans-Aire did not rely upon Northern's skill or judgment to select an adhesive. Nevertheless, the court also held that even if such a warranty existed, it and any implied warranty of merchantability were excluded or waived under § 2–316, as a matter of law, when Trans-Aire examined Adhesive 7448 "as fully as it desired" prior to placing its purchase orders. Trans-Aire challenges the court's legal conclusions under § 2–316 as well as the court's holding that no implied warranty of fitness for a particular purpose arose.

Initially, we hold that the district court correctly concluded that no warranty of fitness for a particular purpose existed. We agree with the district court that Trans-Aire cannot demonstrate that it relied upon Northern's skill or judgment in deciding to purchase Adhesive 7448, even assuming that Northern knew of the purpose for which Trans-Aire needed the adhesive.

* * *

However, we need not dwell upon this issue because we agree with the district court that Trans-Aire excluded all implied warranties by its actions. Under § 2–316 of the [Uniform] Commercial Code, implied warranties are excluded when a party examines a product or sample "as fully as it desires" or "refuses to examine" the product or sample in a reasonable manner given the circumstances of the case. The undisputed facts and circumstances of this case preclude Trans-Aire's attempts to maintain an action based upon breaches of any existing implied warranties of fitness for a particular purpose or of merchantability.

* * *

Upon the facts, we must agree with the district court's finding that Trans-Aire clearly tested the samples as fully as it desired and refused to conduct further tests which would have confirmed a characteristic of contact adhesives which they already knew to be true, that they soften with heat. Trans-Aire attempts to argue that it did not have the means to discover the "latent defects" of the adhesive, because of the cool plant conditions at the time the tests were performed, and that § 2–316 does not exclude the implied warranties under these circumstances. See . . . Section 2–316 Comment 8 ("an examination under circumstances which do not permit chemical or other testing of the goods would not exclude defects which could be ascertained only by such testing"). We agree with the district court that this argument is without merit.

* * *

B. Express Warranty Trans-Aire next argues that the district court erroneously concluded that an express warranty was not created in this case. Trans-Aire contends that by sending specific adhesive samples to Trans-Aire in response to a general statement of need to find a new adhesive for the inadequate 3M product Northern expressly warranted that those samples would meet Trans-Aire's production needs. Trans-Aire apparently did not make this specific argument below, but it certainly would not have fared any better than it does here.

The record indicates that Trans-Aire requested product information from Northern and stated that it wished to purchase a "suitable" product. According to Fribley's undisputed testimony, a Northern representative did not state that any of its adhesives were "suitable" for Trans-Aire's purposes and instead merely commented that Northern manufactured various adhesives, one or more of which "might be applicable." At best (or perhaps worst), Northern stated that its Adhesive 7448 product was a "match" for the 3M product with which Trans-Aire had experienced lamination failures in warmer settings. Thereafter, Northern sent several adhesive samples to Trans-Aire for testing purposes in hopes that Trans-Aire would find an adhesive which it could use. With these facts, Trans-Aire cannot now claim that Northern provided a specific product in response to its needs which amounted to an "affirmation of fact" that the adhesive would meet Trans-Aire's manufacturing needs. See 2–313(1)(a).

* * *

The district court's decision is affirmed.

Design Defect

HECKMAN v. FEDERAL PRESS CO.

United States Court of Appeals, Third Circuit, 1978.
587 F.2d 612.

WEIS, J.

In this products liability case, a jury found that a power press manufactured by defendant without a guarding device was unreasonably dangerous, and awarded plaintiff damages for the injuries he sustained while operating the machine. Although the question of liability was for the jury, the judgment must be vacated because of error in permitting expert testimony that included a "growth factor" in projecting future loss of earnings. Admission of such evidence being impermissible under applicable Pennsylvania law, we grant a new trial.

Plaintiff's left hand was severely injured when it was caught in a power press he was operating in the course of his employment with the Clark Equipment Company. He brought suit against The Federal Press Company, the manufacturer of the machine, alleging defective design because of the lack of an adequate safety device. A jury returned a verdict in favor of the plaintiff in the amount of $750,000 against Federal, with a verdict over [for Federal] against the employer Clark, joined [sued] by Federal on a claim for contribution.

The accident occurred on September 24, 1972, at the Clark factory in Reading, Pennsylvania as Heckman was using a foot pedal to operate the press. The machine functions by dropping a heavy ram onto a die, cutting or shaping the metal which resets on the lower surface. As plaintiff placed a piece of metal in the machine to be cut, the ram came down on his hand, resulting in the amputation of several fingers and other damage.

The press had been purchased by Clark in 1970. It could be operated in two different ways: with hand controls requiring the use of both hands on switches away from the point of operation, or, alternatively, by the use of a foot pedal, an optional item ordered by Clark. When the manual operation was used, the employee's hands necessarily were protected. However, when the foot pedal was utilized without a guard, there was nothing to prevent the hands from being placed in the operating area directly under the descending ram.

Federal did not provide safety appliances other than the dual buttons for manual operation except upon the customer's specific request and at its expense. When ordered, the guards were secured from other sources and attached by Federal. On delivery of the equipment to Clark, Federal sent a letter suggesting that the customer "obtain, install, and use 'point of operation' guarding for greater operator safety." In addition, the press itself had a warning plate with similar instructions for use.

Various types of safeguards designed to protect the operator were available on the market, including some designed to accommodate specific uses of the multi-purpose machine. Clark did in fact purchase a point-of-operation guard for $100, but it was not on the press at the time the injury occurred, and,

in any event, its efficacy was challenged. Plaintiff produced expert testimony to establish that at least one type of appliance would be effective in about 95% of the customary uses of the press, and that the failure to supply such a device made the press defective within the meaning of Restatement (Second) of Torts § 402A (1965).

Federal contended it was not customary in the trade to furnish guards except upon request, and the multitude of uses to which the machine could be put made it impracticable to designate any one device as standard equipment. Moreover, Clark's failure to heed Federal's warning was said to be a superseding cause absolving defendant from all liability. Finally, Federal relied upon state regulations placing responsibility for the safe operation of presses upon employers and employees.

* * *

. . . [T]he jury found that Federal had sold a press in a defective condition . . . and plaintiff Heckman had not assumed a risk. It awarded Heckman damages of $750,000. [Citation.]

*   *   * In *Webb v. Zern*, [citation] Pennsylvania adopted the strict liability provisions of § 402A of the Restatement (Second) of Torts. Cases interpreting this section have held that lack of proper safety devices can constitute a defective design which may subject the manufacturer of machinery to liability. [Citations.]

We find the present case quite similar on its facts to *Capasso v. Minster Machine Co.*, [citation], which also discussed a power press injury. There, as here, a two-button system provided protection in manual operation, but no guard was provided when the optional foot control pedal was used. The manufacturer failed to provide any proposals for a safety guard and a device of the customer's own design proved to be ineffective. We held that since the original purchase included the optional foot switch, its use did not as a matter of law constitute a "substantial change" in the machinery within the scope of § 402(A)(1)(b) absolving the manufacturer; nor did the use of the inadequate shield act as a superseding cause as a matter of law. [Citations.] We concluded that the issue of a defect in the press at delivery was for the jury.

Similarly here, plaintiff's expert maintained that the defendant should have provided safeguards to be used in connection with the foot pedal operation, and that effective implements were available at a reasonable cost. [Citation.]

Federal asserts that the bolster plate which Clark had installed blocked the operator's view of the machine's warning plate, and that this screening constituted a superseding cause insulating the manufacturer from liability. Thus, Federal's theory is that when Clark obscured the warning sign it effected a substantial change that became a superseding cause of the accident. But it cannot be said that as a matter of law the decreased visibility of the plaque was such a major departure from the original design of the machine as to cut off the manufacturer's obligations. [Citation.] Particularly is this so when the sign was addressed to a condition that was not latent. We are unwilling to accept the proposition that the warning plate in and of itself absolved Federal as a matter of law. As we observed in *Schell v. AMF, Inc.*, [citation]:

[A]s a matter of policy, it is questionable whether a manufacturer which produces a machine without minimal available safeguards is entitled to escape liability by warning of a dangerous condition which could reasonably have been avoided by a better design.

In the circumstances here, the warning issue was for the jury as was the defense of assumption of the risk. [Citation.]

Federal also maintains that it was exculpated as a matter of law because regulations of the Pennsylvania Department of Labor and Industry requiring the use of point-of-operation devices placed the responsibility upon the employer and employee. We do not accept this premise. Whatever effect the regulations might have as between employer and employee does not extend to relieve the manufacturer of its liability under § 402A as a matter of law. If a manufacturer fails to provide reasonable safety devices for a product and thus creates an

unreasonable risk of harm to the user, the fact that the manufacturer may expect the user to provide a protective appliance is not sufficient to preclude liability in most circumstances. [Citations.] The issue is one which should be decided by a jury in light of such matters as the feasibility of incorporating safety features during manufacture of the machine, the likelihood that users will not secure adequate devices, whether the machinery is of a standard make or built to the customer's specifications, the relative expertise of manufacturer and customer, the extent of risk to the user, and the seriousness of injury which may be anticipated.

* * *

We conclude that the questions of liability were for the jury's consideration and it was not error to deny Federal's motion for judgment n.o.v.

[A new trial is granted due to a reversible error in the award of damages.]

Inadequate Warning

TOUPS v. SEARS, ROEBUCK AND CO.

Supreme Court of Louisiana, 1987.
507 So.2d 809.

WATSON, J.

Although there were no witnesses to the actual accident other than the three-year-old victim, there is little question about what occurred. The evidence establishes that gasoline leaked from the gasoline-powered lawnmower which had been used earlier in the day by twelve-year-old Richard Toups, Jr., and a friend to cut the grass. The vapors from the gasoline accumulated under the hot water heater. When the burner ignited, the vapors were sucked into its air intake system to cause a flash-back explosion. There was ample testimony about the characteristic sound of such an explosion, described by expert Mandell as a "woosh."

Despite defendants' suggestion that young Shawn Toups was playing with gasoline, neither the palms of his hands nor the soles of his feet were burned, which negates any possibility that he was handling gasoline or kicked over the gas can to cause the fire. Had Shawn been pouring gasoline, his hands would have been burned. Had he been standing in a pool of gasoline, the soles of his feet would have been burned. After the explosion, the gas can was upright on the floor and virtually undamaged. Apparently Richard Toups, Jr. left the gasoline can on the floor, but the lay and expert testimony proves that the gas can was not the source of the fire. It did not explode, which would almost certainly have occurred had it been sitting in a pool of burning gasoline. According to the disinterested testimony of Captain Dauterive, leakage from overfilling the lawnmower caused the explosion.

The physical evidence, including the pattern of Shawn's injuries, plus the pattern of the damage to the gas can and the lawnmower, all implicate the hot water heater as the source of a flash-back explosion.

The jury apparently concluded that this hot water heater was not defective because it was a standard model similar to countless others on the market at the time. Because of erroneous trial rulings, the jury did not have the benefit of the manufacturer/vendor's knowledge of the hidden danger inherent in this hot water heater. The jury was unaware that precautionary warnings were not only needed but were subsequently added to later Sears' models and manuals, proving that they were feasible. In addition, the jury was not specifically asked about Sears' failure to warn its consumers of the danger involved in having gasoline appliances within fifteen feet of the hot water heater. [Citation.]

* * *

The jury was instructed at length about negligence and assumption of the risk and was charged: "A defense to liability in a case of this type may be assumption of the risk or contributory negligence."

The jury was also charged: "As a general rule, a seller or vendor of a product is not presumed to know of any latent defects in the product he sells."

In pertinent part, the interrogatories submitted to the jury only asked if the water heater was defective. No interrogatories were submitted to the jury on the issues of failure to warn or failure to adopt an alternative design.

Plaintiffs objected to the trial court's failure to submit a jury interrogatory on failure to warn and also objected to the jury being charged that a design is not defective if reasonable care is taken in its adoption.

"[I]n order to recover from a manufacturer, the plaintiff must prove that the harm resulted from the condition of the product, that the condition made the product unreasonably dangerous to normal use, and that the condition existed at the time the product left the manufacturer's control. The plaintiff need not prove negligence by the maker in its manufacture or processing, since the manufacturer may be liable even though it exercised all possible care in the preparation and sale of its product." [Citations.]

"Although a product is not unreasonably dangerous per se or flawed by a construction defect, it may still be an unreasonably dangerous product if the manufacturer fails to adequately warn about a danger related to the way the product is designed. A manufacturer is required to provide an adequate warning of any danger inherent in the normal use of its product which is not within the knowledge of or obvious to the ordinary user." [Citations.]

Even if the utility of a product outweighs its danger, if the product could feasibly be designed to be less hazardous, the manufacturer is liable. [Citation.]

A manufacturer is presumed to know of the defects in its product and is therefore required to protect persons against foreseeable risks of injury by adequate warnings.

In general, remedial measures taken after an incident of negligent conduct are not admissible in evidence because such evidence would discourage people from taking steps to prevent future harm. [Citations.] Because of this exclusionary rule, the trial court here did not allow evidence of subsequent warnings added to Sears' water heaters and users' manuals.

The policy considerations which exclude evidence of remedial measures in negligence cases are not applicabl e where strict liability is involved. [Citations.]

In a strict product liability case, evidence of such remedial measures should be allowed insofar as they are relevant in establishing what the manufacturer knew or should have known at the time of the injury.

* * *

"Contributory negligence does not apply in strict products liability cases. The principle of comparative fault may be applied in some products cases . . ." [Citation.]

* * *

The trial court erred in instructing the jury that: "a seller or vendor of a product is not presumed to know of any latent defects in the product he sells." There was no question at trial that Sears, which marketed the product under its brand name, was a professional vendor, with the same responsibility as the manufacturer. In this factual context, the instruction, even though later corrected and qualified, was erroneous.

The phrase "duty to warn" can be misleading because it tends to focus attention on the reasonableness of defendants in failing to give a warning and strict liability should not focus on the question of fault. This is the basis for the distinction in [citation] between products which are "unreasonably dangerous per se" and those strict liability cases based on failure to warn of foreseeable dangers. In the latter, a balancing test is used to determine whether the manufacturer could have reasonably known of the danger and should have issued a warning. [Citation.] The simplistic jury charge that a design is not defective if reasonable care is taken in its adoption was inaccurate, it did not explain the balancing test required in failure to warn cases.

The jury interrogatories failed to inquire whether the hot water heater was defective for lack of a warning, a trial error which must have influenced the jury's verdict.

In sum, the numerous trial errors here resulted in a jury verdict that was clearly wrong. [Citations.] When Sears' prior knowledge is considered in conjunction with adoption of later warnings, the inescapable conclusion is a breach of the duty to warn.

* * *

For the foregoing reasons, the judgment of the court of appeal is reversed, and the matter is remanded to the court of appeal to fix the quantum of damages.

Reversed and remanded.

QUESTIONS

1. Identify and describe the types of warranties.

2. Discuss the various defenses that may be successfully raised to a warranty action.

3. Describe the elements of an action based upon strict liability in tort.

4. Discuss the obstacles to an action based upon strict liability in tort.

5. Compare strict liability in tort with the implied warranty of merchantability.

PROBLEMS

1. At the advent of the social season, Aunt Lavinia purchased a hula skirt in Sadie's dress shop. The saleslady told her: "This superior garment will do things for a person." Aunt Lavinia's house guest, her niece, Florabelle, asked and obtained her aunt's permission to wear the skirt to a masquerade ball. In the midst of the festivity at which there was much dancing, drinking, and smoking, the long skirt brushed against a glimmering cigarette butt. Unknown to Aunt Lavinia and Florabelle, its wearer, the garment was made of a fine unwoven fiber that is highly flammable. It burst into flames, and Florabelle suffered severe burns. Aunt Lavinia notified Sadie of the accident and of Florabelle's intention to recover from Sadie. Florabelle seeks to recover damages in an action against Sadie, the proprietor of the dress shop, and Exotic Clothes, Inc., the manufacturer from which Sadie purchased the skirt. Decision?

2. The Talent Company, manufacturer of a widely advertised and expensive perfume, sold a quantity of this product to Young, a retail druggist. Dentley and Bird visited the store of Young, and Dentley, desiring to make a gift to Bird, purchased from Young a bottle of this perfume, asking for it by its trade name. Young wrapped up the bottle and handed it directly to Bird. The perfume contained an injurious foreign chemical substance which, upon the first use of the perfume by Bird, severely burned her face and caused a permanent facial disfigurement. What are the rights of Bird, if any, against Dentley, Young, and the Talent Company, respectively?

3. John Doe purchased a bottle of "Bleach-All," a well-known brand, from Roe's combination service station and grocery store. When John used the "Bleach-All," the clothes severely deteriorated due to an error made in mixing the chemicals during manufacture of "Bleach-All." John brings an action against Roe to recover damages. Decision?

4. A route salesman for Ideal Milk Company delivered a one-half gallon glass jug of milk to Allen's home. The next day when Allen grasped the milk container by its neck to take it out of his refrigerator, it shattered in his hand and caused serious injury. Allen paid Ideal on a monthly basis for the regular delivery of milk. Ideal's milk bottles each contained the legend "Property of Ideal—to be returned," and the route salesman would pick up the empty bottles when he delivered milk. Allen brought an action against Ideal Milk Company. Decision?

5. While Butler and his wife Wanda were browsing through Sloan's used car lot, Butler told Sloan that he was looking for a safe but cheap family car. Sloan said, "That old Cadillac hearse ain't

hurt at all, and I'll sell it to you for $3,950." Butler said, "I'll have to take your word for it because I don't know a thing about cars." Butler asked Sloan whether he would guarantee the car, and Sloan replied, "I don't guarantee used cars." Then Sloan added, "But I have checked that Caddy over, and it will run another 10,000 miles without needing any repairs." Butler replied, "It has to because I won't have an extra dime for any repairs." Butler made a downpayment of $400 and signed a printed form contract furnished by Sloan which contained a provision, "Seller does not warrant the condition or performance of any used automobile."

As Butler drove the car out of Sloan's lot, the left rear wheel fell off, and Butler lost control of the vehicle. It veered over an embankment, causing serious injuries to Wanda. What is Sloan's liability to Butler and Wanda?

6. John purchased for cash a Revenge automobile manufactured by Japanese Motors, Ltd., from an authorized franchised dealer in the United States. The dealer told John that the car had a "24 months—24,000 miles warranty." Two days after John accepted delivery of the car, he received an eighty-page fine print manual which stated, among other things, on page 72:

The warranties herein are expressly in lieu of any other express or implied warranty, including any implied warranty of merchantability or fitness, and of any other obligation on the part of the company or the selling dealer.

Japanese Motors, Ltd., and the selling dealer warrant to the owner each part of this vehicle to be free under use and service from defects in material and workmanship for a period of twenty-four months from the date of original retail delivery of first use, or until it has been driven for 24,000 miles, whichever first occurs.

Within nine months after the purchase, John was forced to return the car for repairs to the dealer on thirty different occasions, and the car has been in the dealer's custody for over seventy days during these nine months. The dealer has been forced to make major repairs of the engine, transmission, and steering assembly. The car is now in the custody of the dealer for further major repairs, and John has demanded that it keep the car and refund his entire purchase price. The dealer has refused on the ground that it has not breached its contract and is willing to continue repairing the car during the remainder of the "24–24" period.

What are the rights and liabilities of the dealer and John?

7. Fred Lyon of New York, while on vacation in California, rented a new model Home Run automobile from Hart's Drive-A-Car. The car was manufactured by the Dumars Motor Company and was purchased by Hart's from Jammer, Inc., an automobile importer. Lyon was driving the car on a street in San Jose when, due to a defect in the steering mechanism, it suddenly became impossible to steer. The speed of the car at the time was thirty miles per hour, but before Lyon could bring it to a stop, the car jumped a low curb and struck Peter Wolf standing on the sidewalk, breaking both of his legs and causing other injuries. Wolf sues Hart's Drive-A-Car, the Dumars Motor Company, Jammer, Inc., and Lyon. Decisions?

8. Plaintiff brings this cause of action against a manufacturer for the loss of one leg below the hip. The leg was lost when caught in the gears of a screw auger machine sold and installed by the defendant. Shortly before the accident, plaintiff's co-employees had removed a covering panel from the machine by use of sledgehammers and crowbars in order to do repair work. When finished, they replaced the panel with a single piece of cardboard instead of restoring the equipment to its original condition. The plaintiff stepped on the cardboard in the course of his work and fell, catching his leg in the moving parts. Decision?

9. The plaintiff, while driving a van manufactured by the defendant, was struck in the rear by another motor vehicle. Upon impact, the plaintiff's head was jarred backward against the rear window of the cab, causing the plaintiff serious injury. The van was not equipped with a headrest, and none was required at the time. Should the plaintiff prevail on a cause of action based upon strict liability in tort? Why?

10. Plaintiff, while dining at defendant's restaurant, ordered a chicken pot pie. While she was eating the food, she swallowed a sliver of chicken bone which became lodged in her throat, causing her serious injury. Plaintiff brings a cause of action. Should she prevail? Why?

11. Salem Supply Co. sells new and used gardening equipment. Ben Buyer purchased a slightly used, riding lawnmower for $1,500. The price was considerably less than comparable mowers. The sale was clearly indicated to be "as is." Two weeks after Ben purchased the mower, the police arrived at his house with Owen Owner, the true owner of the lawnmower which was stolen from his yard, and reclaimed the mower. What recourse, if any, does Ben have?

12. Seigel, a seventy-three-year-old man, was injured at one of Giant Food's retail food stores when a bottle of Coca-Cola exploded as he was placing a six-pack of Coke into his shopping cart. The explosion caused him to lose his balance and fall, with injuries resulting. Seigel brought suit against Giant Food for damages allegedly caused by Giant's breach of its implied warranty of merchantability. The trial court granted judgment in favor of Giant, and Seigel brought this appeal. Decision?

13. Guarino and two others (plaintiffs) died of gas asphyxiation and five others were injured when they entered a sewer tunnel without masks to answer the cries for help of their crew leader, Rooney. Rooney had left the sewer shaft and entered the tunnel to fix a water leakage problem. Having corrected the problem, Rooney was returning to the shaft when he apparently was overcome by gas because of a defect in his oxygen mask manufactured by Mine Safety Appliance Company (defendant). Plaintiffs brought this action against the defendant for breach of warranty, and defendant raised the defense of plaintiffs' voluntary assumption of the risk. Decision?

14. Green Seed Company packaged, labeled, and marketed a quality tomato seed known as "Green's Pink Shipper" for commercial sale. Brown Seed Store, a retailer, purchased the seed from Green Seed and then sold it to Guy Jones. Jones was an individual engaged in the business of growing tomato seedlings for sale to commercial tomato growers. Williams purchased the seedlings from Jones and then transplanted and raised them in accordance with accepted farming methods. The plants, however, produced not the promised "Pink Shipper" tomatoes but rather an inferior variety that spoiled in the field. Williams then brought an action against Green Seed for $900, claiming that his crop damage had been caused by Green Seed's breach of an express warranty. Green Seed argued in defense that its warranty did not extend to remote purchasers and that the company did not receive notice of the claimed breach of warranty. Decision?

15. Shell Oil Company leased to Flying Tiger Line a gasoline tank truck with a movable ladder for refueling certain types of aircraft. Under the terms of the lease, Flying Tiger was to maintain the equipment in safe operating order, but Shell was obligated to make most of the repairs at Flying Tiger's request. Four years after the lease was entered into, Shell, at Flying Tiger's request, replaced the original ladder with a new one built by an undisclosed manufacturer. Both Flying Tiger and Shell inspected the new ladder. Two years later, however, Price, an aircraft mechanic employed by Flying Tiger, was seriously injured when the ladder's legs split while he was climbing onto an airplane wing. Decision?

COMPUTER RESEARCH PROBLEMS

1. Mrs. Embs went into Stamper's Cash Market to buy soft drinks for her children. She removed five bottles from an upright soft drink cooler, placed them in a carton, and then turned to move away from the display when a bottle of Seven-Up in a carton at her feet exploded, cutting her leg. Apparently, several other bottles had exploded that same week. Stamper's Cash Market received its entire stock of Seven-Up from Arnold Lee Vice, the area distributor. Vice in turn received his entire stock of Seven-Up from Pepsi-Cola Bottling Co. Decision?

2. Catania wished to paint the exterior of his house. He went to Brown, a local paint store owner, and asked him to recommend a paint for the job. Catania told Brown that the exterior walls were stucco, and in a chalky, powdery condition. Brown suggested Pierce's shingle and shake paint. Brown then instructed Catania how to mix the paint, and to use a wire brush to prepare the surface. Five months later the paint began to peel, flake, and blister. Catania brings an action against Brown. Decision?

3. Robinson, a truck driver for a moving company, decided to buy a used truck from the company. Branch, the owner, told Robinson that the truck was being repaired, and that Robinson should wait and inspect the truck before signing the contract. Robinson, who had driven the truck before, felt that inspection was unnecessary. Again, Branch suggested Robinson wait to inspect the truck, and again Robinson declined. Branch then told Robinson he was buying the truck "as is." Robinson then signed the contract. After the fourth time that the truck broke down, Robinson sued. Decision?

4. Perfect Products manufactures balloons, which are then bought and resold by wholesale novelty distributors. Mego Corp. manufactures a doll called "Bubble Yum Baby." A balloon is inserted in the doll's mouth with a mouthpiece, and the doll's arm is pumped to inflate the balloon, simulating the blowing of a bubble. Mego Corp. used Perfect Products balloons in the dolls, bought through the independent distributors. Plaintiff's infant daughter dies after swallowing a balloon removed from the doll. Plaintiff sues Perfect Products, and others, on a theory of strict liability. Decision?

5. Patient was injured when the footrest of an adjustable X-ray table collapsed, causing Patient to fall to the floor. G.E. manufactured the X-ray table and the footrest. At trial evidence was introduced that G.E. had manufactured for several years another model footrest complete with safety latches. However, there was no evidence that the footrest involved was manufactured defectively. The action is based on a theory of strict liability. Who wins? Why?

Chapter 24

REMEDIES

Remedies of the Seller
Remedies of the Buyer
Contractual Provisions Affecting Remedies

A contract for the sale of goods may require total performance at one time or part performance in stages, according to the agreement of the parties. At any stage, one of the parties may breach or repudiate the contract, or become insolvent. Breach is the failure of a party to perform his obligations under the contract. In a sales contract, breach may consist of the seller's delivering defective goods, too few goods, the wrong goods, or no goods. The buyer may breach by not accepting conforming goods or by failing to pay for conforming goods that he has accepted. Breach may occur when the goods are in the possession of the seller, in the possession of a bailee, in transit to the buyer, or in the possession of the buyer.

Remedies, therefore, need to address not only the type of breach of contract but also the situation with respect to the goods. Consequently, the Code provides separate and distinct remedies for the seller and for the buyer, each specifically keyed to the factual situation.

In all events, the purpose of the Code is to put the aggrieved party in as good a position as if the other party had fully performed. Therefore, the Code has provided that its remedies should be liberally administered to accomplish this purpose. Moreover, damages do not have to be "calculable with mathematical precision": they must be proved with "whatever definiteness and accuracy the facts permit, but no more." Comment 1 to Section 1–106. The purpose of remedies under the Code is compensation; therefore, punitive damages are generally not available.

Finally, the Code has rejected the doctrine of election of remedies. Essentially, the Code provides that remedies for breach are cumulative in nature. Whether one remedy bars another depends entirely on the facts of the individual case.

REMEDIES OF THE SELLER

When a buyer defaults in performing any of his contractual obligations, the seller has been deprived of the rights for which he bargained. The buyer's default may consist of any of the following acts: the buyer wrongfully rejects the goods, the buyer wrongfully revokes acceptance of the goods, the buyer fails to make a payment due on or before delivery, or the buyer repudiates (indicates that he does not intend to perform) the contract in whole or in part. Section 2–703 of the Code catalogs the seller's remedies for each of these defaults. These remedies allow the seller to

1. withhold delivery of the goods;

2. stop delivery of the goods by a carrier or other bailee;

3. identify conforming goods to the contract not already identified;

4. resell the goods and recover damages;

5. recover damages for non-acceptance of the goods or repudiation of the contract;

6. recover the price;

7. recover incidental damages;

8. cancel the contract; and

9. reclaim the goods on the buyer's insolvency (Section 2–702).

It is useful to note that the first three and the ninth remedies indexed above are **goods oriented**—that is, they relate to the seller's exercising control over the goods. The fourth through seventh remedies are **money oriented** because they provide the seller with the opportunity to recover monetary damages. The eighth remedy is **obligation oriented** because it allows the seller to avoid his obligation under the contract.

Moreover, if the seller delivers goods on credit and the buyer fails to pay the price when due, the seller's sole remedy, unless the buyer is insolvent, is to sue for the unpaid price. If, however, the buyer received the goods on credit while insolvent, the seller may be able to reclaim the goods. **Insolvency** is defined by the Code to include both its equity meaning and its bankruptcy meaning. Section 1–201(23). The **equity** meaning of **insolvency** is the inability of a person to pay his debts in the ordinary course of business or as they become due. The **bankruptcy** meaning of **insolvency** is that total liabilities exceed the total value of all assets.

As noted above, the Code's remedies are *cumulative*. Thus, by way of example, an ag-

grieved seller may (1) identify goods to the contract; *and* (2) withhold delivery; *and* (3) resell or recover damages for non-acceptance or recover the price; *and* (4) recover incidental damages; *and* (5) cancel the contract.

To Withhold Delivery of the Goods

A seller may withhold delivery of the goods to a buyer who has wrongfully rejected or revoked acceptance of the goods, who has failed to make a payment due on or before delivery, or who has repudiated the contract. Section 2–703. This right is essentially that of a seller to withhold or discontinue performance of her side of the contract because of the buyer's breach.

Where the contract calls for installments, any breach of an installment that impairs the value of the *whole* contract will permit the seller to withhold the entire undelivered balance of the goods. In addition, upon discovery of the buyer's insolvency, the seller may refuse to deliver the goods except for cash, including payment for all goods previously delivered under the contract. Section 2–702.

To Stop Delivery of the Goods

An extension of the right to withhold delivery is the right of an aggrieved seller to stop delivery of the goods in transit to the buyer or in the possession of a bailee. If the seller discovers that the buyer is insolvent, then the seller may stop *any* delivery. If the buyer is not insolvent but repudiates or otherwise breaches the contract, the seller may stop carload, truckload, planeload, or larger shipments. Section 2–705. To stop delivery the seller must notify the carrier or other bailee soon enough for the bailee to prevent delivery of the goods. After this notification the carrier or bailee must hold and deliver the goods according to the directions of the seller, who is liable to the carrier or bailee for any charges or damages incurred. If a negotiable document of title has been issued for the goods, the bailee need not obey a notification until the document is provided. Section 2–705(3).

The right of the seller to stop delivery ceases when (1) the buyer receives the goods; (2) the bailee of the goods, except a carrier, acknowledges to the buyer that he holds them for the buyer; (3) the carrier acknowledges to the buyer that he holds them for the buyer by reshipment or as warehouseman; or (4) a negotiable document of title covering the goods is negotiated to the buyer. Section 2–705(2).

To Identify Goods to the Contract

Upon a breach of the contract by the buyer, the seller may proceed to identify to the contract conforming goods in her possession or control that were not so identified at the time she learned of the breach. Section 2–704(1). This enables the seller to exercise the remedy of resale of goods (discussed below). Furthermore, the seller may resell any unfinished goods that have been demonstrably intended for fulfillment of the particular contract. The seller may either complete the manufacture of unfinished goods and identify them to the contract or cease their manufacture and resell the unfinished goods for scrap or salvage value. Section 2–704(2). In so deciding, the seller must exercise reasonable commercial judgment to minimize her loss.

For example, if at the time of the buyer's breach or repudiation the goods in the process of manufacture are 90 percent finished, in order to avoid loss and obtain maximum realization of value a seller may be justified in completing their manufacture and reselling them as finished goods. On the other hand, if at the time of breach the manufacturing process has only just commenced, sound business judgment may require that the manufacture be halted in order to mitigate loss and damage.

To Resell the Goods and Recover Damages

Under the same circumstances that permit the seller to withhold delivery of goods to the buyer (i.e., wrongful rejection or revocation, repudiation, or failure to make timely pay-

ment), the seller may resell the goods concerned or the undelivered balance of the goods. If the resale is made in good faith and in a commercially reasonable manner, the seller may recover from the buyer the **difference between the contract price and the resale price,** *together* with any incidental damages (discussed below), *less* expenses saved because of the buyer's breach. Section 2–706(1). For example, Floyd agrees to sell goods to Beverly for a contract price of $8,000 due on delivery. Beverly wrongfully rejects the goods and refuses to pay Floyd anything. Floyd resells the goods in strict compliance with the Code for $6,000 and incurs incidental damages for sales commissions of $500 but saves $200 in transportation costs. Floyd would recover from Beverly the difference between the contract price ($8,000) and the resale price ($6,000) plus incidental damages ($500) minus expenses saved ($200), which equals $2,300.

The resale may be a public or private sale, and the goods may be sold as a unit or in parcels. The goods resold must be identified as those related to the contract, but where there has been an anticipatory repudiation, for example, it is not necessary that the goods be in existence or that they be identified to the contract before the buyer's breach. Section 2–706(2).

Where the resale is a private sale, the seller must give the buyer reasonable notice of his intention to resell. Section 2–706(3). A private sale may be carried out by negotiations or solicitations by the seller or a broker. Where the resale is at a public sale (such as an auction), only identified goods can be sold, except where there is a recognized market for a public sale of future goods of the kind involved. The public sale must be made at a usual place or market for public sale if one is reasonably available. The seller must give the buyer reasonable notice of the time and place of the resale unless the goods are perishable or threaten to decline in value speedily. Prospective bidders at the sale must be given an opportunity for reasonable inspection of the goods before the sale. The seller may be a purchaser of the goods at the public sale. Section 2–706(4). In choosing between a public and private sale, the seller must observe relevant trade practices and usages and take into account the character of the goods.

The seller is not accountable to the buyer for any profit made on any resale of the goods. Moreover, a *bona fide* purchaser at a resale takes the goods free of any rights of the original buyer, even though the seller has failed to comply with one or more of the requirements of the Code in making the resale. Section 2–706(5).

Failure to act in good faith and in a commercially reasonable manner deprives the seller of this remedy and relegates him to the remedy of recovering damages for non-acceptance or repudiation (discussed below).

To Recover Damages for Non-Acceptance or Repudiation

In the event of the buyer's wrongful rejection or revocation, repudiation, or failure to make timely payment, the seller may recover damages from the buyer measured by the **difference between the unpaid contract price and the market price** at the time and place of tender of the goods, *plus* incidental damages, *less* expenses saved in consequence of the buyer's breach. Section 2–708(1). This remedy is an alternative to the remedy of reselling the goods.

For example, Joan in Seattle agrees to sell goods to Nelson in Chicago for $20,000 F.O.B. Chicago, delivery on June 15. Nelson wrongfully rejects the goods. The market price would be ascertained as of June 15 in Chicago because F.O.B. Chicago is a destination contract in which the place of tender would be Chicago. The market price of the goods on June 15 in Chicago is $15,000. Joan incurred $1,000 in incidental expenses while saving $500 in expenses. Joan's recovery from Nelson would be the difference between the contract price ($20,000) and the market price ($15,000), plus incidental damages ($1,000), minus expenses saved ($500), which equals $5,500.

If the difference between the contract price and the market price will not place the seller in as good a position as performance would have, then the measure of damages is the **profit,** including reasonable overhead, which the seller would have realized from full performance by the buyer, plus any incidental damages, less expenses saved in consequence of the buyer's breach. Section 2–708(2). For example, Green, an automobile dealer, enters into a contract to sell a large, fuel-inefficient, luxury car to Holland for $22,000. The price of gasoline increases 20 percent, and Holland repudiates. The market value of the car is still $22,000, but because Green cannot sell as many cars as he can obtain, Green's sales volume has decreased by one as a result of Holland's breach. Therefore, Green would be permitted to recover the profits he lost on the sale to Holland (computed as the contract price minus what the car costs Green, plus an allocation of overhead), plus any incidental damages. *See Teradyne, Inc. v. Teledyne Industries, Inc.*

To Recover the Price

The Code permits the seller to recover the price plus incidental damages in only three situations: (1) where the buyer has accepted the goods; (2) where conforming goods have been lost or damaged after the risk of loss has passed to the buyer; and (3) where the goods have been identified to the contract and there is no ready market available for their resale at a reasonable price. Section 2–709(1). For example, Kelly, in accordance with her agreement with Sally, prints ten thousand letterheads and envelopes with Sally's name and address on them. Sally wrongfully rejects the stationery, and Kelly is unable to resell them at a reasonable price. Kelly is entitled to recover the price plus incidental damages from Sally.

A seller who sues for the price must hold for the buyer any goods that have been identified to the contract and are still in her control. If resale becomes possible, the seller may resell the goods at any time prior to the collection of the judgment, and the net proceeds of such resale must be credited to the buyer. Payment of the judgment entitles the buyer to any goods not resold. Section 2–709(2).

To Recover Incidental Damages

In addition to recovering damages for the difference between the contract price and the resale price, or recovering damages for non-acceptance or repudiation, or recovering the price, the seller may also recover in the same action her **incidental damages** in order to reimburse the seller for expenses reasonably incurred by her as a result of the buyer's breach. Incidental damages are defined by Section 2–710 as follows:

Incidental damages to an aggrieved seller include any commercially reasonable charges, expenses or commissions incurred in stopping delivery, in the transportation, care and custody of goods after the buyer's breach, in connection with return or resale of the goods or otherwise resulting from the breach.

To Cancel the Contract

Where the buyer wrongfully rejects or revokes acceptance of the goods, or fails to make a payment due on or before delivery, or repudiates the contract in whole or in part, the seller may cancel the contract with respect to the goods directly affected. If the breach is of an installment contract and it substantially impairs the whole contract, the seller may cancel the entire contract. Section 2–703(f).

The Code defines **cancellation** as putting an end to the contract by one party by reason of a breach by the other. Section 2–106. The obligation of the canceling party for any future performance under the contract is discharged, although she retains any remedy for breach of the whole contract or any unperformed balance. Thus, if the seller has the right to cancel, she may recover damages for breach without having to tender any further performance.

To Reclaim the Goods upon the Buyer's Insolvency

In addition to the right of an unpaid seller to withhold and stop delivery of the goods, he may reclaim them from an insolvent buyer by demand upon the buyer within *ten days* after the buyer has received the goods. Section 2–702(2). Where, however, the buyer has committed fraud by a misrepresentation of her solvency made to the seller in writing within three months prior to delivery of the goods, the ten-day limitation does not apply.

The seller's right to reclaim the goods is subject to the rights of a buyer in ordinary course of business or other good faith purchaser. Upon a successful reclamation of the goods from an insolvent buyer, the seller is excluded from all other remedies with respect to those goods. Section 2–702(3).

REMEDIES OF THE BUYER

There are basically three different ways in which a seller may default: he may repudiate, he may fail to deliver the goods, or he may deliver or tender goods that do not conform to the contract. The Code provides remedies for each of these breaches. Some remedies are available for all of these breaches, while others are available only for certain types. Moreover, some remedies must be triggered by certain actions taken by the buyer. For example, if the seller tenders nonconforming goods, the buyer may reject or accept them. If the buyer rejects them, he can choose from a number of remedies. On the other hand, if the buyer accepts the nonconforming goods and does not justifiably revoke his acceptance, he limits himself to recovering damages.

Where the seller fails to make delivery or repudiates, or the buyer rightfully rejects or justifiably revokes acceptance, the buyer may, with respect to any goods involved, or with respect to the whole if the breach goes to the whole contract, (1) cancel *and* (2) recover payments made. In addition, the buyer may (3) "cover" and obtain damages *or* (4) recover damages for non-delivery. Where the seller fails to deliver or repudiates, the buyer, where appropriate, may also (5) recover identified goods if the seller is insolvent, *or* (6) replevy the goods, *or* (7) obtain specific performance. Moreover, upon rightful rejection or justifiable revocation of acceptance, the buyer (8) has a security interest in the goods.

Where the buyer has accepted goods and given notification to the seller of their nonconformity, the buyer may (9) recover damages for breach of warranty. Finally, in addition to the remedies listed above, the buyer may, where appropriate, (10) recover incidental damages, and (11) recover consequential damages.

It may be observed that the first remedy catalogued above is **obligation oriented;** the second through fourth and ninth through eleventh are **money oriented;** while the fifth through eighth are **goods oriented.**

To Cancel the Contract

Where the seller fails to make delivery or repudiates the contract or where the buyer rightfully rejects or justifiably revokes acceptance of goods tendered or delivered to him, the buyer may cancel the contract with respect to any goods involved, and if the breach by the seller concerns the whole contract, the buyer may cancel the entire contract. Section 2–711(1). The buyer must give the seller notice of his cancellation of the contract and is excused from further performance or tender on his part.

To Recover Payments Made

The buyer, upon the seller's breach, may also recover as much of the price as he has paid. Section 2–711(1). For example, Jonas and Sheila enter into a contract for a sale of goods for a contract price of $3,000, and Sheila, the buyer, has made a down payment of $600. Jonas delivers nonconforming goods to Sheila who rightfully rejects them. Sheila may cancel the contract and recover the $600 plus whatever other damages she can prove.

To Cover

Upon the seller's breach, the buyer may protect himself by obtaining cover. **Cover** means that the buyer may in good faith and without unreasonable delay proceed to purchase goods or make a contract to purchase goods in substitution for those due under the contract from the seller. Section 2–712(1). This right enables the buyer to obtain the needed goods.

Upon making a reasonable contract of cover, the buyer may recover from the seller the **difference between the cost of cover and the contract price,** *plus* any incidental and consequential damages (discussed below) *less* expenses saved in consequence of the seller's breach. Section 2–712(2). For example, Doug, whose factory is in Oakland, agrees to sell goods to Velda, in Atlanta, for $22,000 F.O.B. Oakland. Doug fails to deliver and Velda covers by purchasing substitute goods in Atlanta for $25,000, incurring $700 in sales commissions. Velda suffered no other damages as a consequence of Doug's breach. Shipping costs from Oakland to Atlanta for the goods are $1,300. Velda would recover the difference between the cost of cover ($25,000) and the contract price ($22,000), plus incidental damages ($700 in sales commissions), plus consequential damages ($0 in this example), minus expenses saved ($1,300 in shipping costs Velda need not pay under the contract of cover), which equals $2,400. *See Bigelow-Sanford, Inc. v. Gunny Corp.*

The buyer is not required to obtain cover, and his failure to do so does not bar him from any other remedy provided by the Code. Section 2–712(3). The buyer, however, may *not* recover consequential damages that he could have prevented by cover. Section 2–715(2)(a).

To Recover Damages for Non-Delivery or Repudiation

If the seller repudiates the contract or fails to deliver the goods, or if the buyer rightfully rejects or justifiably revokes acceptance of the goods, the buyer is entitled to recover damages from the seller measured by the **difference between the market price** at the time when the buyer learned of the breach **and the contract price,** together *with* incidental and consequential damages, *less* expenses saved in consequence of the seller's breach. Section 2–713(1). This remedy is a complete alternative to the remedy of cover and is available only to the extent the buyer has not covered. As previously indicated, the buyer who elects this remedy may not recover consequential damages that could have been avoided by cover.

The market price is to be determined as of the place for tender, or, in the event that the buyer has rightfully rejected the goods or has justifiably revoked his acceptance of them, the market price is to be determined as of the place of arrival. Section 2–713(2). For example, Janet agrees to sell goods to Laura for $7,000 C.O.D. with delivery by November 15. Janet fails to deliver. As a consequence Laura suffered incidental damages of $1,500 and consequential damages of $1,000. In the case of non-delivery or repudiation, market price is determined as of the place of tender. Since C.O.D. is a shipment contract, the place of tender would be the seller's city. Therefore, the market price must be determined in the seller's city and on November 15, the date when Laura learned of the breach. At this time and place the market price is $8,000. Laura would recover the difference between the market price ($8,000) and the contract price ($7,000), plus incidental damages ($1,500), plus consequential damages ($1,000), less expenses saved ($0 in this example), which equals $3,500.

In the example above, if Janet had instead delivered nonconforming goods that Laura rejected, then the market price would be determined at Laura's place of business. If Janet had repudiated the contract on November 1, then the market price would be determined on that date.

To Recover Identified Goods upon the Seller's Insolvency

Where existing goods are identified to the contract of sale, the buyer acquires a *special property interest* in the goods. Section 2–501. This special property interest exists even though the goods are nonconforming and the buyer has the right to return or reject them. Identification of the goods to the contract may be made either by the buyer or by the seller.

The Code gives the buyer a right, which does not exist at common law, to recover from an insolvent seller the goods in which the buyer has a special property interest and for which he has paid a part or all of the price. This right exists where the seller, who is in possession or control of the goods, becomes insolvent within ten days after receipt of the first installment of the price. To exercise it, the buyer must tender to the seller any unpaid portion of the price. If the special property interest exists by reason of an identification made by the buyer, he may recover the goods only if they conform to the contract for sale. Section 2–502.

To Sue for Replevin

Replevin is an action at law to recover specific goods in the possession of a defendant that are being unlawfully withheld from the plaintiff. The buyer may maintain against the seller an action for replevin for goods that have been identified to the contract where the seller has repudiated or breached the contract if (1) the buyer after a reasonable effort is unable to effect cover for such goods or (2) the goods have been shipped under reservation of a security interest in the seller and satisfaction of this security interest has been made or tendered. Section 2–716(3).

To Sue for Specific Performance

Specific performance is an equitable remedy compelling the party in breach to perform the contract according to its terms. At common law, specific performance is available only if the legal remedies are inadequate. For example, where the contract is for the purchase of a unique item, such as a work of art, a famous racehorse, or an heirloom, money damages may not be an adequate remedy. In such a case, a court of equity has the discretion to order the seller specifically to deliver to the buyer the goods described in the contract upon payment of the price.

The Code not only has continued the availability of specific performance but also has sought to further a more liberal attitude towards its use. Accordingly, it does not expressly require that the remedy at law be inadequate. Instead, the Code states that "specific performance may be decreed where the goods are unique or in other proper circumstances." Section 2–716(1). As the Comment to that section explains, the test of uniqueness under the Code must be made in view of the total situation that characterizes the contract.

To Enforce a Security Interest in the Goods

A buyer who has rightfully rejected or justifiably revoked acceptance of goods that remain in his possession or control has a security interest in these goods to the extent of any payment of the price that he has made and for any expenses reasonably incurred in their inspection, receipt, transportation, care, and custody. The buyer may hold such goods and resell them in the same manner as an aggrieved seller may resell goods. Section 2–711(3). In the event of resale the buyer is required to account to the seller for any excess of the net proceeds of the resale over the amount of his security interest. Section 2–706(6).

To Recover Damages for Breach in Regard to Accepted Goods

Where the buyer has accepted nonconforming goods and has given timely notification to the seller of the breach of contract, the buyer is entitled to recover from the seller the damages resulting in the ordinary course of events from the seller's breach, as determined in any reasonable manner. Section 2–714(1). Nonconformity includes breaches of warranty as well as any failure of the seller to perform according to her obligations under the contract. Thus, even if a seller cures a nonconforming tender, the buyer may recover under this section for any injury suffered because the original tender was nonconforming.

In the event of breach of warranty, the measure of damages is the **difference** at the time and place of acceptance **between the value of the goods which have been accepted and the value** that the goods would have had

if they had been **as warranted,** unless special circumstances show proximate damages of a different amount. Section 2–714(2). *See Barr v. S–2 Yachts, Inc.* In addition, incidental and consequential damages, where appropriate, may also be recovered.

The contract price of the goods does not figure in this computation because the buyer is entitled to the benefit of his bargain, which is to receive goods that are as warranted. For example, Max agrees to sell goods to Stanley for $1,000. The value of the goods accepted is $800, but if they had been as warranted, their value would have been $1,200. The buyer's damages for breach of warranty are $400, which he may deduct from any unpaid balance due on the purchase price upon notice to the seller of his intention to do so. Section 2–717.

To Recover Incidental Damages

In addition to such remedies as covering, recovering damages for non-delivery or repudiation, or recovering damages for breach in regard to accepted goods, including breach of warranty, the buyer may recover incidental damages. **Incidental damages** provide reimbursement for the buyer who incurs reasonable expenses in handling rightfully rejected goods or in effecting cover. Section 2–715(1) of the Code defines the buyer's incidental damages as follows:

Incidental damages resulting from the seller's breach include expenses reasonably incurred in inspection, receipt, transportation and care and custody of goods rightfully rejected, any commercially reasonable charges, expenses or commissions in connection with effecting cover and any other reasonable expense incident to the delay or other breach.

For example, the buyer of a racehorse justifiably revokes acceptance because the horse does not conform to the contract. The buyer will be allowed to recover as incidental damages the cost of caring for the horse from the date the horse was delivered until it is returned to the seller.

To Recover Consequential Damages

In many cases, the remedies discussed above will not fully compensate the aggrieved buyer for her losses. For example, nonconforming goods that are accepted may explode and destroy the buyer's warehouse and its contents. Goods that are not delivered may have been the subject of a lucrative contract of resale, the profits from which are lost. The Code responds to this problem by providing the buyer with the opportunity to recover **consequential damages** resulting from the seller's breach including (1) any loss resulting from the buyer's requirements and needs of which the seller at the time of contracting had reason to know and which could not reasonably be prevented by cover or otherwise; and (2) injury to person or property proximately resulting from any breach of warranty. Section 2–715(2).

With respect to the first type of consequential damages, *particular* needs of the buyer usually must be made known to the seller whereas *general* needs usually need not be made known to the seller. In the case of a buyer who is in the business of reselling goods, resale is one of the requirements of which the seller has reason to know. For example, Supreme Machine Co., a manufacturer, contracts to sell Allied Sales Inc., a dealer in used machinery, a used machine that Allied plans to resell. Supreme repudiates and Allied is unable to obtain a similar machine elsewhere. Allied's damages include the net profit that it would have made on resale of the machine. A buyer may not, however, recover consequential damages he could have prevented by cover. Section 2–715(2). For instance, Supreme Machine Co. contracts for $10,000 to sell Capitol Manufacturing Co. a used machine to be delivered at Capitol's factory by June 1. Supreme repudiates the contract on May 1. By reasonable efforts, Capitol could buy a similar machine from United Machinery Inc. for $11,000 in time to be delivered by June 1. Capitol fails to do so and loses a profit of $5,000 that it would have made from the resale of the machine. Capitol's damages do *not* include the loss of the $5,000 profit, but it can recover $1,000 from Supreme.

An example of the second type of consequential damage is: Federal Machine Co. sells a machine to Southern Manufacturing Co., warranting its suitability for Southern's purpose. The machine is not suitable for Southern's purpose and causes $10,000 in damage to Southern's property and $15,000 in personal injuries. Southern can recover the $25,000 consequential damages in addition to any other loss suffered.

For a summary and classification of the remedies available to both the buyer and the seller for breach of a sales contract, see Figure 24–1. This figure shows which remedies are available for each type of breach.

CONTRACTUAL PROVISIONS AFFECTING REMEDIES

Within specified limits, the Code permits the parties to a sales contract to modify, exclude, or limit by agreement the remedies or damages that will be available for breach of that contract. Two basic types of contractual provisions affect remedies: (1) liquidation or limitation of damages and (2) modification or limitation of remedy.

Liquidation or Limitation of Damages

The parties may provide for **liquidated damages** in their contract by specifying the amount or measure of damages that either party may recover in the event of a breach by the other party. The amount of such damages must be reasonable in light of the anticipated or actual loss resulting from a breach, the difficulties of proof of loss, and the inconvenience or lack of feasibility of otherwise obtaining an adequate remedy. *See California and Hawaiian Sugar Co. v. Sun Ship, Inc.* in Chapter 17. A provision in a contract fixing unreasonably large liquidated damages is void as a penalty. Section 2–718(1). An unreasonably small amount might be stricken on the grounds of unconscionability. Comment 1 to Section 2–718.

Figure 24–1 Remedies for Breach

	Buyer's Breach		Seller's Breach	
	1) B wrongfully rejects		1) B rightfully rejects	
	2) B wrongfully revokes acceptance		2) B justifiably revokes acceptance	
	3) B fails to make payment		3) S fails to deliver	
	4) B repudiates		4) S repudiates	
			5) B accepts nonconforming goods	
	Seller's Remedy		**Buyer's Remedy**	
		Obligation Oriented		
(1–4)	Cancel		Cancel	(1–4)
		Goods Oriented		
(1–4)	Withhold delivery of goods		Recover identified goods if S is insolvent	(3, 4)
(3)	Reclaim goods upon B's insolvency		Replevy goods	(3, 4)
(1–4)	Stop delivery of goods by carrier or bailee		Obtain specific performance	(3, 4)
(1–4)	Identify conforming goods to contract		Have security interest	(1, 2)
		Money Oriented		
(1–4)	Resell and recover damages		Recover payments made	(1–4)
(1–4)	Recover damages for non-acceptance		Cover and recover damages	(1–4)
(1–4)	Recover price		Recover damages for non-delivery	(1–4)
			Recover damages for breach of warranty	(5)

To illustrate, Sterling Cabinetry Company contracts to build and install shelves and cabinets for an office building being constructed by Baron Construction Company. The contract price is $120,000, and the contract provides that Sterling would be liable for $100 per day for every day's delay beyond the completion date specified in the contract. The stipulated sum of $100 per day is reasonable and commensurate with the anticipated loss. Therefore, it is enforceable as liquidated damages. If, instead, the sum stipulated had been $5,000 per day, it would be unreasonably large and therefore void as a penalty.

Modification or Limitation of Remedy by Agreement

The contract between the seller and buyer may expressly provide for remedies in addition to or instead of those provided in the Code and may limit or change the measure of damages recoverable in the event of breach. Section 2–719(1). For instance, the contract may validly limit the remedy of the buyer to a return of the goods and a refund of the price, or to the replacement of nonconforming goods or parts.

A remedy provided by the contract, however, is deemed optional unless it is expressly agreed to be exclusive of other remedies, in which event it is the sole remedy. Moreover, where circumstances cause an exclusive or limited remedy to fail of its essential purpose, resort may be had to the remedies provided by the Code. Section 2–719(2). *See Wilson Trading Corp. v. David Ferguson, Limited.*

The contract may expressly limit or exclude consequential damages unless such limitation or exclusion would be unconscionable. Limitation of consequential damages for personal injuries resulting from breach of warranty in the sale of consumer goods is *prima facie* unconscionable, whereas limitation of such damages where the loss is commercial is not. Section 2–719(3). For example, Ace Motors, Inc., sells a pickup truck to Brenda, a consumer. The contract of sale excludes liability for all consequential damages.

The next day the truck explodes, causing serious personal injury to Brenda. Brenda would recover for her personal injuries unless Ace could prove that the exclusion of consequential damages was *not* unconscionable.

CASES

Seller's Damages for Non-Acceptance or Repudiation

TERADYNE, INC. v. TELEDYNE INDUSTRIES, INC.

United States Court of Appeals, First Circuit, 1982.
676 F.2d 865.

WYZANSKI, J.

The following facts, derived from the master's report, are undisputed.

On July 30, 1976 Teradyne, Inc. ("the seller"), a Massachusetts corporation, entered into a Quantity Purchase Contract ("the contract") which, though made with a subsidiary, binds Teledyne Industries, Inc., a California corporation ("the buyer"). That contract governed an earlier contract resulting from the seller's acceptance of the buyer's July 23, 1976 purchase order to buy at the list price of $98,400 (which was also its fair market value) a T–347A transistor test system ("the T–347A"). One consequence of such governance was that the buyer was entitled to a $984 discount from the $98,400 price.

The buyer canceled its order for the T–347A when it was packed ready for shipment scheduled to occur two days later. The seller refused to accept the cancellation.

The buyer offered to purchase instead of the T–347A a $65,000 Field Effects Transistor System ("the FET") which would also have been governed by "the contract." The seller refused the offer.

After dismantling, testing, and reassembling at an estimated cost of $614 the T–347A, the seller, pursuant to an order that was on hand prior to the cancellation, sold it for $98,400 to another purchaser (hereafter "resale purchaser").

Teradyne would have made the sale to the resale purchaser even if Teledyne had not broken its contract. Thus if there had been no breach, Teradyne would have made two sales and earned two profits rather than one.

The seller was a volume seller of the equipment covered by the July 23, 1976 purchase order. The equipment represented standard products of the seller and the seller had the means and capacity to duplicate the equipment for a second sale had the buyer honored its purchase order.

* * *

The parties are agreed that § 2–708(2) applies to the case at bar. Inasmuch as this conclusion is not plain from the text, we explain the reasons why we concur in that agreement.

Section 2–708(2) applies only if the damages provided by § 2–708(1) are inadequate to put the seller in as good a position as performance would have done. Under § 2–708(1) the measure of damages is the difference between unpaid contract price and market price. Here the unpaid contract price was $97,416 and the market price was $98,400. Hence no damages would be recoverable under § 2–708(1). On the other hand, if the buyer had performed, the seller (1) would have had the proceeds of two contracts, one with the buyer Teledyne and the other with the "resale purchaser" and (2) *it seems* would have had in 1976–7 one more T–347A sale.

A literal reading of the last sentence of § 2–708(2)—providing for "due credit for payments or proceeds of resale"—would indicate that Teradyne recovers nothing because the proceeds of the resale exceeded the price set in the Teledyne-Teradyne contract. However, in light of the statutory history of the subsection, it is universally agreed that in a case where after the buyer's default a seller resells the goods, the proceeds of the resale are not to be credited to the buyer if the seller is a lost volume seller—that is, one who had there been no breach by the buyer, could and would have had the benefit of both the original contract and the resale contract.

Thus, despite the resale of the T–347A, Teradyne is entitled to recover from Teledyne what § 2–708(2) calls its expected "profit (including reasonable overhead)" on the broken Teledyne contract.

Teledyne not only "does not dispute that damages are to be calculated pursuant to § 2–708(2)" but concedes that the formula used in Jericho Sash & Door Co. v. Building Erectors Inc., [citation], for determining lost profit including overhead—that is, the formula under which direct costs of producing and selling manufactured goods are deducted from the contract price in order to arrive at "profit (including reasonable overhead)" as that term is used in § 2–708(2)— "is permissible provided all variable expenses are identified."

* * *

Teledyne's more significant objection to Teradyne's and the master's application of the Jericho formula in the case at bar is that neither of them made deductions on account of the wages paid to testers, shippers, installers, and other Teradyne employees who directly handled the T–347A, or on account of the fringe benefits amounting in the case of those and other employees to 12 per cent of wages. Teradyne gave as the reason for the omission of the wages of the testers, etc. that those wages would not have been affected if each of the testers, etc. handled one product more or less. However, the work of those employees entered as directly into producing and supplying the T–347A as did the work of a fabricator of a T–347A. Surely no one would regard as "reasonable overhead" within § 2–708(2) the wages of a fabricator of a T–347A even if his wages were the same whether he made one product more or less.

We conclude that the wages of the testers, etc. likewise are not part of overhead and as a "direct cost" should have been deducted from the contract price. A fortiori fringe benefits amounting to 12 per cent of wages should also have been deducted as direct costs. Taken together we cannot view these omitted items as what Jericho called "relatively insignificant items." We, therefore, must vacate the district court's judgment. [Citations.] [We] remand this case so that with respect to the omitted direct labor costs specified above the parties may offer further evidence and the court may make the findings "with whatever definiteness and accuracy the facts permit, but no more." [Citation.]

* * *

The district court's judgment is vacated and the case is remanded to the district court to proceed in accordance with this opinion.

Buyer's Remedy of Cover

BIGELOW–SANFORD, INC. v. GUNNY CORP.

United States Court of Appeals, Fifth Circuit, Unit B, 1981. 649 F.2d 1060.

KRAVITCH, J.

[The plaintiff, Bigelow-Sanford, Inc., contracted with defendant Gunny Corp. for the purchase of 100,000 linear yards of jute at $0.64 per yard. Gunny delivered 22,228 linear yards in January 1979. The February and March deliveries required under the contract were not made, and 8 rolls (each roll containing 66.7 linear yards) were delivered in April. With 72,265 linear yards undelivered Gunny told Bigelow-Sanford that no more would be delivered. In mid-March Bigelow-Sanford then turned to the jute spot market to replace the balance of the order at a price of $1.21 per linear yard. Since several other companies had also defaulted on their jute contracts with Bigelow-Sanford, the plaintiff purchased a total of 164,503 linear yards on the spot market. Plaintiff sues defendant to recover losses sustained as a result of the breach of contract.]

* * *

Gunny contends that appellee's [Bigelow-Sanford] alleged cover purchases should not have been used to measure damages in that they were not made in substitution for the contract purchases, were not made seasonably or in good faith and were not shown to be due to Gunny's breach. [W]e disagree. Again, we quote UCC § 2–711 providing in part for cover damages where the seller fails to make delivery or repudiates the contract:

(1) Where the seller fails to make delivery or repudiates or the buyer rightfully rejects or justifiably revokes acceptance then with respect to any goods involved, and with respect to the whole if the breach goes to the whole contract (2–612), the buyer may cancel and whether or not he has done so may in addition to recovering so much of the price as has been paid

(a) "cover" and have damages under the next section as to all the goods affected whether or not they have been identified to the contract; or

(b) recover damages for non-delivery as provided in this Article (2–713).

UCC § 2–712 defines cover:

(1) After a breach within the preceding section the buyer may "cover" by making in good faith and without unreasonable delay any reasonable purchase of or contract to purchase goods in substitution for those due from the seller.

(2) The buyer may recover from the seller as damages the difference between the cost of cover and the contract price together with any incidental or consequential damages as hereinafter defined (2–715), but less expenses saved in consequence of the seller's breach.

(3) Failure of the buyer to effect cover within this section does not bar him from any other remedy.

In addition, the purchaser may recover under 2–713:

(1) Subject to the provisions of this Article with respect to proof of market price (2–723), the measure of damages for non-delivery or repudiation by the seller is the difference between the market price at the time when the buyer learned of the breach and the contract price together with any incidental and consequential damages provided in this Article (2–715), but less expenses saved in consequence of the seller's breach.

(2) Market price is to be determined as of the place for tender or, in cases of rejection after arrival or revocation of acceptance, as of the place of arrival.

Most importantly, "whether a plaintiff has made his cover purchases in a reasonable manner poses a classic jury issue." [Citation.] The district court thus acted properly in submitting the question of cover damages to the jury, which found that Gunny had breached, appellee had covered, and had done so in good faith without unreasonable delay by making reasonable purchases, and was therefore entitled to damages under § 2–712. Gunny argues Bigelow is not entitled to such damages on the ground that it failed to make cover purchases without undue delay and that the jury should not have been permitted to average the cost of Bigelow's spot market purchases totalling 164,503 linear yards in order to arrive at the cost of cover for the 72,265 linear yards Gunny failed to deliver. Both arguments fail. Gunny notified Bigelow in February that no more jute would be forthcoming. Bigelow made its first spot market purchases in mid-March. Given that it is within the jury's province to decide the reasonableness of the manner in which cover purchases were made, we believe the jury could reasonably decide such purchases, made one month after the date the jury assigned to Gunny's breach, were made without undue delay. The same is true with respect to Gunny's second argument: Bigelow's spot market purchases were made to replace several vendors' shipments. Bigelow did not specifically allocate the spot market replacements to individual vendors' accounts, however, nor was there a requirement that they do so. The jury's method of averaging such costs and assigning them to Gunny in proportion to the amount of jute if [sic] failed to deliver would, therefore, seem not only fair but well within the jury's permissible bounds.

Gunny also argues that the court erroneously charged the jury regarding damages

under both §§ 2–712 and 2–713. We disagree. Whether Bigelow covered was a question of fact submitted to the jury. In the event
that it had not, alternative damages were
available to Bigelow under § 2–713. [Cita-
tion.] The jury found that Bigelow had covered and awarded damages under § 2–712;
§ 2–713 then became irrelevant. Since either
was applicable until that time, the court's
charge as to both sections was not error.

* * *

[Judgment for Bigelow is affirmed.]

Damages for Breach of Warranty

BARR v. S–2 YACHTS, INC.

United States District Court, Eastern District of Virginia,
1988.
7 UCC Rep. Serv. 2d 1431.

WILLIAMS, J.

The parties waived trial by jury and submitted the matter to the court. In the order
on final pretrial conference, the parties stipulated that plaintiff purchased a 31-foot Ti-
ara pleasure yacht from Crow's Nest in July
1987; that S–2 manufactured the yacht; that
the yacht was sold with full manufacturer's
warranties; that on or about November 2,
1986, the yacht had been completely submerged in salt water while tied to the dock at
Crow's Nest, Atlantic Beach, North Carolina;
and that neither Crow's Nest or S–2, nor anyone on behalf of either of them advised plaintiff prior to his purchase of the yacht that it
had been submerged in salt water.

There is little conflict in the evidence in
this case. Plaintiff had observed a 31 foot Ti-
ara and liked it. He contacted S–2 and was
given the names of two dealers. He contacted
Crow's Nest and located the style and type
yacht he wanted. He was told that the retail
price was $102,000.00, but that he could pur-
chase it for $80,000.00. When plaintiff in-
quired of [sic] why the reduction, he was told
Crow's Nest had to move it because there was
a change in model and it had new ones coming in. Plaintiff thereupon asked if the yacht
was new, and if there was anything wrong

with it. He was told by Crow's Nest there was
nothing wrong with it and it only had 20
hours on the engines. Plaintiff agreed to buy.
The yacht was delivered, and a trial run
made. Plaintiff then noticed some rust on the
screws in or near the dash. Shortly thereafter, and after closing the purchase, plaintiff
found the stove was rusted, the seals on some
of the hatches had to be replaced, the helm
seat fell apart and the electrical wiring was
faulty, as well as other things. Plaintiff was
furnished, without cost, a new helm seat assembly, a new stove and was told Crow's Nest
would pay for some other work done. Plaintiff
converted the engines from salt water to
fresh water cooling, and installed a considerable amount of electronic and other equipment. On the first two occasions when plaintiff used the yacht, he traveled a considerable
distance off shore. On each of these occasions,
he experienced tremendous difficulty, and severe hazard. While attempting to cure these
defects, plaintiff was advised that there was
evidence the yacht had been sunk in salt water. Upon inquiry to S–2, plaintiff then
learned this was true. On the last occasion
when plaintiff used the yacht, the alternator
failed. Plaintiff thereupon became afraid to
use the yacht and after unsuccessfully trying
to adjust the matter, instituted this action.

A survey was made of the condition of the
yacht by a marine expert. He found salt crys-
tals in the locks, the cloth had water stains,
the joints had opened up so that one could see
the dowels, the hardware had rusted, the
panels were stained from rust, nails in the
draw[er]s of the cabinets were rusty, the electrical cable had oxidized, the stainless steel
sink showed evidence of rusting, the windshield wipers were heavily rusted, the foil insulation showed evidence of salt water, many
other metal parts were rusted, the interior
light fixtures were rusted and many other
metal parts and stainless steel were rusting,
and so on. The expert said you would not see
such a condition in a new yacht, and its condition was consistent with that of one which
had sunk in salt water. The expert testified
that all electrical systems, wiring and fixtures would need to be replaced, all cloth re-

placed, panels would have to be replaced and that in fact it would cost a great deal to get to the concealed places. He said the alternator, motor, cables and electrical equipment should all be replaced; that the yacht new had a value of between $93,700.00 to $103,000.00, and that the yacht in question, following the sinking, had a value of only one-half the new value.

In addition to Allan F. Fife, a highly experienced marine surveyor, Ernest Moore, President of Virginia Marine Services, examined the yacht. He corroborated Mr. Fife. He was of the opinion the engines would have only 25% of their normal expected life. Stephen Townsend, a fifty percent owner of Crow's Nest, said there was a stigma attached to a boat that had sunk. Ernest Moore, in agreeing with Townsend, said you cannot have the same dependability in a boat that had previously sunk.

* * *

Where a buyer orders and purchases an article from a manufacturer or dealer by specific sample or serial number, there is an implied warranty it is new.

* * *

Any contention that plaintiff examined the yacht and waived any implied warranty of merchantability is without merit. * * *

The evidence is clear and convincing that Crow's Nest fraudulently misrepresented the facts by statements and silence; that it was guilty of knowingly making false statements and in its failure to inform where it had the duty to do so. S–2 acquiesced in this conduct.

A compensable misrepresentation or fraud occurs when the defendant knowingly makes a false statement concerning a material fact to a purchaser who justifiably relies thereon to his detriment. [Citation.]

The evidence is equally as clear that Crow's Nest and S–2 are guilty of breach of warranties.

* * *

The measure of damages under the Uniform Commercial Code for breach of warranty is the difference at the time and place of acceptance between the value of the goods accepted and the value they would have had if they had been as warranted, unless special circumstances show proximate damage of a different amount. This formula was essentially the measure in Virginia prior to adoption of the Commercial Code. [Citations.] For goods bought and sold on the open market, in proving damages for breach of warranty of the goods, a party must present evidence of the fair market value at the time and place of acceptance of the goods accepted and what the value they would have had if they had been as warranted. [Citations.]

Each of the defendants seems to agree that the measure of plaintiff's damage is the difference in the value of the yacht as it was received and its value had it been as represented. That is, the fair market value.

Fife testified the value of the yacht was between $93,700.00 and $103,000.00; that after the sinking it was worth only fifty percent of its cost. Rockhold stated in his letter, Exhibit 1, that the retail price, plus freight, was $103,570.00, and that he was allowing a 22.7% discount as "a year end discount" as the new models were coming out and he needed to move this yacht. Crow's Nest sold a similar yacht in 1987 for $91,000.00.

Considering all the evidence on the issue of damages, the court is of the opinion that plaintiff is entitled to recover $46,850.00 representing the difference between what the market value of the yacht would have been if it had been as warranted and represented and its market value at the time of sale. Plaintiff is also entitled to recover $1,531.00 in warranty repairs without which it would not be worth the fifty percent value.

* * *

Plaintiff is entitled to judgment against each defendant for the sum of $48,381.00.

Limitation of Remedies

WILSON TRADING CORP. v. DAVID FERGUSON, LIMITED

Court of Appeals of New York, 1968.
23 N.Y.2d 398, 297 N.Y.S.2d 108, 244 N.E.2d 685.

Jasen, J.

The plaintiff, Wilson Trading Corporation, entered into a contract with the defendant, David Ferguson, Ltd., for the sale of a specified quantity of yarn. After the yarn was delivered, cut, and knitted into sweaters, the finished product was washed. It was during this washing that it was discovered that the color of the yarn had "shaded"—that is, "there was a variation in color from piece to piece and within the pieces." This defect, the defendant claims, rendered the sweaters "unmarketable."

This action for the contract price of the yarn was commenced after the defendant refused payment. As a defense to the action and as a counterclaim for damages, the defendant alleges that "[p]laintiff has failed to perform all of the conditions of the contract on its part required to be performed, and has delivered . . . defective and unworkmanlike goods."

The sales contract provides in pertinent part:

2. No claims relating to excessive moisture content, short weight, count variations, twist, quality or shade shall be allowed *if made after weaving, knitting, or processing,* or more than 10 days after receipt of shipment. . . . The buyer shall within 10 days of the receipt of the merchandise by himself or agent examine the merchandise for any and all defects. (Emphasis supplied.)

* * *

Special Term granted plaintiff summary judgment for the contract price of the yarn sold on the ground that "notice of the alleged breach of warranty for defect in shading was not given within the time expressly limited and is not now available by way of defense or counterclaim." The Appellate Division affirmed, without opinion.

The defendant on this appeal urges that the time limitation provision on claims in the contract was unreasonable since the defect in the color of the yarn was latent and could not be discovered until after the yarn was processed and the finished product washed.

Defendant's affidavits allege that its sweaters were rendered unsaleable because of latent defects in the yarn which caused "variation in color from piece to piece and within the pieces." . . . Indeed, the plaintiff does not seriously dispute the fact that its yarn was unmerchantable, but instead, like Special Term, relies upon the failure of defendant to give notice of the breach of warranty within the time limits prescribed by paragraph 2 of the contract.

Subdivision (3) (par. [a]) of section 2–607 of the Uniform Commercial Code expressly provides that a buyer who accepts goods has a reasonable time after he discovers or should have discovered a breach to notify the seller of such breach. . . . Defendant's affidavits allege that a claim was made immediately upon discovery of the breach of warranty after the yarn was knitted and washed, and that this was the earliest possible moment at which the defects could reasonably be discovered in the normal manufacturing process .* * *

However, the Uniform Commercial Code allows the parties, within limits established by the code, to modify or exclude warranties and to limit remedies for breach of warranty.* * *

We are, therefore, confronted with the effect to be given the time limitation provision in . . . the contract .* * *

Parties to a contract are given broad latitude within which to fashion their own remedies for breach of contract (Uniform Commercial Code, § 2–316, subd. [4]; §§ 2–718– 2–719). Nevertheless, it is clear from the official comments to section 2–719 of the Uniform Commercial Code that it is the very essence of a sales contract that at least minimum adequate remedies be available for its breach. "If the parties intend to conclude a contract for sale within this Article they must accept the legal consequence that there be at least a fair quantum of remedy for breach of the obligations or duties outlined in the contract. Thus any clause purporting to modify or limit the remedial provisions of this Article in an *unconscionable manner* is subject to deletion and in that event the remedies made available by this Article are applicable as if the stricken clause had never existed." [Citation.]

It follows that contractual limitations upon remedies are generally to be enforced unless unconscionable .* * *

However, it is unnecessary to decide the issue of whether the time limitation is unconscionable on this appeal for section 2–719 (subd. [2]) of the Uniform Commercial Code provides that the general remedy provisions of the code apply when "circumstances cause an exclusive or limited remedy to fail of its essential purpose." As explained by the official comments to this section: "where an apparently fair and reasonable clause because of circumstances fails in its purpose or operates to deprive either party of the substantial value of the bargain, it must give way to the general remedy provisions of this article." [Citation.] Here . . . the contract bars all claims for shade and other specified defects made after knitting and processing. Its effect is to eliminate any remedy for shade defects not reasonably discoverable within the time limitation period. It is true that parties may set by agreement any time not manifestly unreasonable whenever the code "requires any action to be taken within a reasonable time" [citation], but here the time provision eliminates all remedy for defects not discoverable before knitting and processing and section 2–719 (subd. [2]) of the Uniform Commercial Code therefore applies.

* * * The time limitation clause of the contract, therefore, insofar as it applies to defects not reasonably discoverable within the time limits established by the contract, must give way to the general code rule that a buyer has a reasonable time to notify the seller of breach of contract after he discovers or should have discovered the defect. [Citation.]

* * *

The order of the Appellate Division should be reversed, with costs, and plaintiff's motion for summary judgment should be denied.

QUESTIONS

1. Identify and discuss the goods oriented remedies of the seller and the buyer.

2. Identify and discuss the obligation oriented remedies of the seller and the buyer.

3. Identify and discuss the money oriented damages of the seller and the buyer.

4. Identify and discuss the "specific performance" remedies of the seller and buyer.

5. Describe the basic types of contractual provisions affecting remedies and the limitations the Code imposes upon these provisions.

PROBLEMS

1. Mae contracts to sell one thousand bushels of wheat to Lloyd at $4 per bushel. Just before Mae was to deliver the wheat, Lloyd notified her that he would not receive or accept the wheat. Mae sold the wheat for $3.60 per bushel, the market price, and later sued Lloyd for the difference of $400. Lloyd claims he was not notified by Mae of the resale and, hence, is not liable. Decision?

2. On December 15, Judy wrote a letter to David stating that she would sell to David all of the mine run coal that David might wish to buy during the next calendar year for use at David's factory, delivered at the factory at a price of $40 per ton. David immediately replied by letter to Judy, stating that he accepted the offer, that he would purchase all of his mine run coal from Judy, and that he would need 200 tons of coal during the first week in January. During the months of January, February, and March, Judy delivered to David a total of 700 tons of coal, for all of which David made payment to Judy at the rate of $40 per ton.

On April 10, David ordered 200 tons of mine run coal from Judy who replied to David on April 11 that she could not supply David with any more coal except at a price of $48 per ton delivered. David thereafter purchased elsewhere at the market price, namely $48 per ton, all of his factory's requirements of mine run coal for the remainder of the year, amounting to a total of 2,000 tons of coal. David now brings an action against Judy to recover damages at the rate of $8 per ton for the coal thus purchased, amounting to $16,000. Decision?

3. On January 10, Betty, of Emanon, Missouri, visited the show rooms of the Forte Piano Company in St. Louis and selected a piano. A sales memorandum of the transaction signed both by Betty and by the salesman of the Forte Piano Company read as follows: "Sold to Betty one new Andover piano, factory number 46832, price $3,300 to be shipped to the buyer at Emanon, Missouri, freight prepaid, before February 1. Prior to shipment seller will stain the case a darker color in accordance with buyer's directions and will make the tone more brilliant." On January 15, Betty repudiated the contract by letter to the Forte Piano Company. The company subsequently stained the case, made the tone more brilliant, and offered to ship the piano to Betty on January 26. Betty persisted in her refusal to accept the piano. In an action by the Forte Piano Company against Betty to recover the contract price, what judgment?

4. Sims contracted in writing to sell Blake 100 electric motors at a price of $100 each, freight prepaid to Blake's warehouse. By the contract of sale, Sims expressly warranted that each motor would develop 25-brake horsepower. The contract provided that the motors would be delivered in lots of twenty-five per week beginning January 2, that Blake should pay for each lot of twenty-five motors as delivered, but that Blake was to have right of inspection upon delivery. Immediately upon delivery of the first lot of twenty-five motors on January 2, Blake forwarded Sims a check for $2,500, but upon testing each of the twenty-five motors Blake determined that none of the twenty-five motors would develop more than 15-brake horsepower. State all of the remedies available to Blake.

5. Henry and Mary entered into a written contract whereby Henry agreed to sell and Mary agreed to buy a certain automobile for $3,500.

Henry drove the car to Mary's residence and properly parked it on the street in front of her house where Henry tendered it to Mary and requested payment of the price. Mary refused to take the car or pay the price. Henry informed Mary that he would hold her to the contract; but before Henry had time to enter the car and drive it away, a fire truck, answering a fire alarm and traveling at a high speed, crashed into the car and demolished it. Henry brings an action against Mary to recover the price of the car. Who is entitled to judgment? Would there be any difference in result if Henry were a dealer in automobiles?

6. James sells and delivers to Gerald on June 1 certain goods and receives from Gerald at the time of delivery Gerald's check in the amount of $900 for the goods. The following day Gerald is petitioned into bankruptcy, and the check is dishonored by Gerald's bank. On June 5, James serves notice upon Gerald and the trustee in bankruptcy that he reclaims the goods. The trustee is in possession of the goods and refuses to deliver them to James. What are the rights of the parties?

7. The ABC Company, located in Chicago, contracted to sell a carload of television sets to Dodd in St. Louis, Missouri, on sixty days' credit. ABC Company shipped the carload to Dodd. Upon arrival of the car at St. Louis, Dodd paid the freight charges, and reshipped the car to Hines of Little Rock, Arkansas, to whom he had previously contracted to sell the television sets. While the car was in transit to Little Rock, Dodd went bankrupt. ABC Company was informed of this at once and immediately telegraphed XYZ Railroad Company to withhold delivery of the television sets. What should the XYZ Railroad Company do?

8. Robert in Chicago entered into a contract to sell certain machines to Terry in New York. The machines were to be manufactured by Robert and shipped F.O.B. Chicago not later than March 25. On March 24, when Robert is about to ship the machines, he receives a telegram from Terry wrongfully repudiating the contract. The machines cannot readily be resold for a reasonable price because they are a special kind used only in Terry's manufacturing processes. Robert sues Terry to recover the agreed price of the machines. What are the rights of the parties?

9. Calvin purchased a log home construction kit manufactured by Boone Homes, Inc., from an authorized dealer of Boone. The sales contract stated that Boone would repair or replace defective materials and that this was the exclusive remedy available against Boone. The dealer assembled the house, which was defective in several respects. The knotholes in the logs caused the walls and ceiling to leak. A support beam was too small and therefore cracked, causing the floor to crack also. These defects could not be completely cured by repair. Calvin sues Boone for breach of warranty to recover damages for the loss in value. Decision?

10. Margaret contracted to buy a 1973 Rolls Royce Corniche from Paragon Motors, Inc. Only 100 Corniches are built each year. She paid a $3,000 deposit on the car, but Paragon sold the car to Gluck. What remedy, if any, does Margaret have against Paragon?

11. Technical Textile agreed by written contract to manufacture and sell 20,000 pounds of yarn to Jagger Brothers at a price of $2.15 per pound. After Technical had manufactured, delivered, and been paid for 3,723 pounds of yarn, Jagger Brothers by letter informed Technical that it was repudiating the contract and that it would refuse any further yarn deliveries. On August 12, the date of the letter, the market price of yarn was $1.90 per pound.

Technical was awarded $4,069.25 in damages by the trial court, an amount equal to 16,277 times the difference between the contract price ($2.15) and the market price ($1.90) of the yarn on the repudiation date. Jagger Brothers appealed, contending that the proper measure of damages was the difference between the contract price and the cost of manufacture, and that, because no ev-

idence was offered as to the cost of manufacture, Technical was entitled only to nominal damages. Decision?

12. Sherman Burrus, a job printer, purchased a printing press from the Itek Corporation for a price of $7,006.08. Before making the purchase, Burrus was assured by an Itek salesman, Mr. Nessel, that the press was appropriate for the type of printing Burrus was doing. Burrus encountered problems in operating the press almost continuously from the time he received it. Burrus, his employees, and Itek representatives spent many hours in an unsuccessful attempt to get the press to operate properly. Burrus requested that the press be replaced, but Itek refused. Burrus then brought an action against Itek for (1) damages for breach of the implied warranty of merchantability and (2) consequential damages for losses resulting from the press's defective operation. The trial court awarded damages of $10,435 to Burrus, and Itek appealed. Decision?

13. A farmer made a contract in April to sell a grain dealer 40,000 bushels of corn to be delivered in October. On June 3, the farmer unequivocally informed the grain dealer that he was not going to plant any corn, that he would not fulfill the contract, and that if the buyer had commitments to resell the corn he should make other arrangements. The grain dealer awaited in vain for performance of the repudiated contract until October. Then he bought corn at a greatly increased price on the market in order to fulfill commitments to his purchasers. The grain dealer sued for damages. Decision?

COMPUTER RESEARCH PROBLEMS

 1. Lee Oldsmobile sells Rolls-Royce automobiles. Mrs. Kaiden sent Lee a $5,000 deposit on a $29,500, 1973 Rolls-Royce. Although Lee informed Mrs. Kaiden that the car would be delivered in November, the order form did not indicate the delivery date and contained a disclaimer for delay or failure to deliver due to circumstances beyond the dealer's control. On November 21, Mrs. Kaiden purchased another car from another dealer and cancelled her car from Lee. When Lee attempted to deliver a Rolls-Royce to Mrs. Kaiden on November 29, Mrs. Kaiden refused to accept delivery. Lee later sold the car for $26,495.00. Mrs. Kaiden sued Lee for her $5,000 deposit plus interest. Lee counterclaims, based on the terms of the contract, for liquidated damages of $5,000 (the amount of the deposit) as a result of Mrs. Kaiden's breach of contract. Decision?

2. Servebest contracted to sell Emessee 200,000 pounds of 50 percent lean beef trimmings for $105,000. Upon a substantial fall in the market price, Emessee refused to pay the contract price and informed Servebest that the contract was cancelled. Servebest sues Emessee for breach of contract including (a) damages for the difference between the contract price and the resale price of the trimmings and (b) incidental damages. Decision?

 3. Mrs. French was the highest bidder on eight antique guns at an auction held by Sotheby & Company. When Sotheby's billed Mrs. French $24,886.27 for the guns, she refused to pay. Sotheby's sued Mrs. French for the price of the guns. Decision?

Commercial Paper

Chapter 25

FORM AND CONTENT

Negotiability
Types of Commercial Paper
Form of Commercial Paper

COMMERCIAL paper includes checks, promissory notes, drafts, and certificates of deposit. These instruments are crucial to the sale of goods and services as well as to the financing of most businesses. The use of commercial paper has increased to such an extent that payments made with these instruments, in particular checks, are now many times greater than payments made with cash. In fact, currency is now primarily used for smaller transactions. Accordingly, the vital importance of commercial paper as a method of payment cannot be overstated.

To accomplish these social and economic objectives, the payment system must be quick, sure, and efficient. The use of cash can never satisfy all of these requirements because (1) it is inconvenient to maintain large quantities of cash; (2) the risk of loss or theft is far too great; (3) the risk in sending cash is likewise too high as is the cost of postage and insurance in shipping cash over long distances; and (4) the costs to the Federal government of maintaining an adequate supply of currency would be prohibitive. In addition, commercial paper used for payment provides a convenient receipt as well as a record for accounting and tax purposes. Although com-

mercial paper acts as a very close approximation of cash for the purpose of payment, it is not the exact equivalent of cash because, for example, commercial paper may be forged, it may be drawn on insufficient funds, payment may be stopped, or the instrument may be materially altered. Nevertheless, these risks (which are real but very infrequent—over 99 percent of all checks are paid) assume small proportions compared to the advantages that commercial paper provides for payment. Consequently, a major objective of the law of commercial paper and the bank collection process is to reduce these risks by increasing the safety, soundness, and operating efficiency of the entire payment system.

Moreover, the credit function of commercial paper is indispensable. Promissory notes and drafts serve an important business purpose, not only in areas of high finance but also at the level of the small business and individual consumer. In recent years, certificates of deposit have been used increasingly by individuals instead of savings accounts.

The various types of commercial paper may or may not possess the unique characteristic of negotiability, although the term "commercial paper" is generally used to refer to instruments that are negotiable. The way rights and obligations are acquired in commercial paper is important because of the huge volume of daily transactions in promissory notes, certificates of deposit, drafts, and checks.

NEGOTIABILITY

Negotiability is a legal concept that makes written instruments a readily accepted form of payment in substitution for money. The concept of negotiability applies not only to commercial paper, which is governed by **Article 3** of the Code, but also to documents of title (governed by Article 7 and discussed in Chapter 49) and investment securities (governed by Article 8 and discussed in Chapter 35).

Development of Law of Negotiable Instruments

The starting point for an understanding of negotiable instruments is recognizing that four or five centuries ago in England a contract right to the payment of money was not assignable because a contractual promise ran to the promisee. Performance could be rendered to him and to no one else. This was a hardship on the owner of the right because it prevented him from selling or disposing of it. Eventually, the law permitted recovery upon an assignment by the assignee against the obligor.

An innocent assignee bringing an action against the obligor was subject to all defenses available to the obligor. Such an action would result in the same outcome whether it was brought by the assignee or assignor. Thus, a contract right became assignable but not very marketable because merchants had little interest in buying into a possible lawsuit. This remains the law of **assignments:** the *assignee stands in the shoes of his assignor.* For a discussion of assignments, see Chapter 15.

With the flourishing of trade and commerce, it became essential to develop a more effective means for exchanging contractual

rights for money. For example, a merchant who sells goods for cash may use the cash to buy more goods for resale. If he makes a sale on credit in exchange for a promise to pay money, why should he not be permitted to sell that promise to someone else for cash with which to carry on his business. One difficulty was that the buyer of the goods gave the seller only a promise to pay money to him. The seller was the only person to whom performance or payment was promised. If, however, the seller obtained from the buyer a promise in writing to pay money to anyone in possession (*bearer*) of the writing (*paper* or *instrument*) or to anyone the seller (*payee*) designated, then the duty of performance would run directly to the **holder** (the bearer of the paper or to the person to whom the payee ordered payment to be made). This is one of the essential distinctions between negotiable and non-negotiable instruments. Although there are other formal requirements of a negotiable instrument, this particular one eliminates the limitations of a promise to pay money only to a named promisee.

Moreover, if the promise to pay were not subject to all of the defenses available against the assignor, then a transferee would not only be more willing to acquire the promise but also would pay more for it. Accordingly, the law of negotiable instruments developed the concept of the **holder in due course,** whereby certain good faith transferees who gave value acquired the right to be paid, freed of most of the defenses to which an assignee would be subject. Thus, by reason of this doctrine, such a transferee of a negotiable instrument could acquire *greater* rights than his transferor, whereas an assignee would acquire *only* the rights of his assignor. With these basic innovations, negotiable instruments enabled merchants to sell their contractual rights more readily and thereby keep their capital working.

Assignment Compared with Negotiation

Negotiability invests commercial paper with a high degree of marketability and commercial utility. It allows commercial paper to be freely transferable and enforceable by a person with the rights of a holder in due course against any person obligated on the paper, subject only to a limited number of defenses. To illustrate, assume that George sells and delivers goods to Elaine for $50,000 on sixty days' credit and that, a few days later, George assigns this account to Marsha. Unless Elaine is duly notified of this assignment, she may safely pay the $50,000 to George on the due date without incurring any liability to Marsha, the assignee. Assume next that the goods were defective and that Elaine, accordingly, has a defense against George to the extent of $20,000. Assume also that Marsha duly notified Elaine of the assignment. The result is that Marsha can recover only $30,000 from Elaine and not $50,000 because Elaine's defense against George is equally available against George's assignee, Marsha. In other words, an assignee of contractual rights merely "steps into the shoes" of her assignor and, hence, acquires only the same rights as her assignor—and no more.

Assume instead, that upon the sale by George to Elaine, Elaine executed and delivered her negotiable note to George for $50,000 payable to George's order in sixty days and that, a short time later, George duly negotiates (transfers) the note to Marsha. In the first place, Marsha is not required to notify Elaine that she has acquired the note from George. One who issues a negotiable instrument is held to know that the instrument may be negotiated and is obligated to pay the holder of the instrument. In the second place, Elaine's defense is not available against Marsha if Marsha acquired the note in good faith and for value and had no knowledge of Elaine's defense against George. Marsha, therefore, is entitled to hold Elaine at maturity for the full face amount of the note, namely, $50,000. In other words, Marsha, by the negotiation of the negotiable note to her, acquired greater rights than George had, since George, had he kept the note, could have recovered only $30,000 on it because Elaine could have successfully asserted the defense in the amount of $20,000 against George.

To have the full benefit of negotiability, commercial paper not only must meet the requirements of negotiability but also must be acquired by a holder in due course. This chapter discusses the formal requirements instruments must satisfy to be negotiable. Chapter 26 deals with the manner in which a negotiable instrument must be negotiated to preserve its advantages. Chapter 27 covers the requisites and rights of a holder in due course. Finally, Chapter 28 examines the liability of all the parties to a negotiable instrument.

Revised Article 3

In July 1990, the American Law Institute and the National Conference of Commissioners on Uniform Laws approved a Revised Article 3. The new Article, which will now be proposed for enactment by the individual states, maintains the basic scope and content of Article 3. The Article is renamed "Negotiable Instruments" rather than "Commercial Paper." The major changes to Article 3 will be covered in Chapters 25–28. Revised Article 3 appears at the end of Appendix C.

TYPES OF COMMERCIAL PAPER

There are four types of commercial paper: drafts, checks, notes, and certificates of deposit. Section 3–104(2). The first two each contain **orders** or directions to pay money; the last two involve **promises** to pay money.

Drafts

A **draft** involves three parties, each in a distinctly different capacity. One party, the **drawer,** *orders* a second party, the **drawee,** to pay a sum certain in money to a third party, the **payee.** See Figure 25–1. The drawee is ordinarily a person or entity who either is in possession of money belonging to the drawer or owes money to him. A sample draft is reproduced as Figure 25–2. The same party may appear in more than one capacity; for instance, the drawer may also be the payee.

Figure 25–1 Order to Pay: Draft or Check

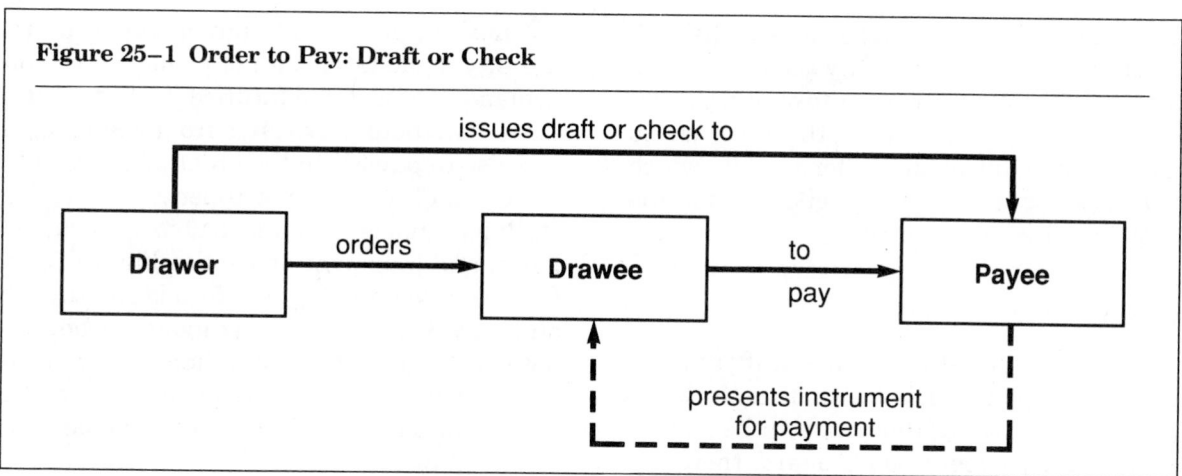

Drafts may be either "time" or "sight." A **time draft** is one payable at a specified future date, whereas a **sight draft** is payable on demand (that is, immediately upon presentation to the drawee).

A form of time draft, known as a trade acceptance, is frequently used as a credit device in a commercial transaction. A **trade acceptance** is a time draft drawn by the seller (drawer) on the buyer (drawee) and names the seller or some third party as the payee. For example, Ben Buyer wishes to purchase goods from Sam Seller. Seller needs cash immediately, but Buyer cannot pay for the goods until he has resold them. Therefore, Seller draws a draft on Buyer ordering Buyer to pay the amount of the purchase price to the order of Seller at a specified future date.

Seller presents this draft to Buyer, who "accepts" it thereby agreeing to make payment according to its terms, and returns the accepted draft to Seller, who can then sell the draft to a third party.

A sight draft, sometimes called a customer's draft, is used by the seller of goods who desires immediate payment for the goods upon delivery of a bill of lading (a document issued by a carrier evidencing receipt of goods shipped, which may also stipulate that the goods will be delivered to its holder). Upon shipment of the goods, the seller would obtain from the carrier an order bill of lading, which he would attach to a customer's draft drawn on the buyer and would send to his local bank for handling. The local bank would send the paper to a bank located in the

Figure 25–2 Draft

St. Louis, Missouri
May 1, 1991

Two years from date pay to the order of Percy Payee
$50,000 Fifty Thousand . . . Dollars

(Signed) Donald Drawer
DONALD DRAWER

To: DAWN DRAWEE
50 Main St.
Louisville, Kentucky

city where the goods were to be delivered. That bank would then notify the buyer upon arrival of the goods. In order to obtain the bill of lading and thus the goods, the buyer would pay the amount of the seller's draft, which would be forwarded to the seller's bank and there credited to his account.

Checks

A **check** is a specialized form of draft; namely, an order to pay money drawn on a *bank* and payable on *demand;* that is, upon the payee's request for payment. Once again, there are parties involved in three distinct capacities: the **drawer,** who orders the **drawee,** a bank, to pay the **payee** on demand. See Figure 25–3. Checks are by far the most widely used form of commercial paper. Each year over ten billion checks are written in the United States for over five trillion dollars.

A **cashier's check** is a check drawn by a bank upon itself to the order of the named payee.

Notes

A **promissory note** is an instrument involving two parties in two capacities. One party,

the **maker,** promises to pay a second party, the **payee,** a stated sum of money, either on demand or at a stated future date. See Figure 25–4. The note may range from a simple, "I promise to pay $X to the order of Y," form to more complex legal instruments such as installment notes, collateral notes, mortgage notes, and judgment notes. See Figure 25–5 for a sample note. Figure 25–5 is a note payable at a definite time—six months from the date of April 7, 1991—and hence is referred to as a **time note.** A note payable upon the request or demand of the payee or holder is a **demand note.**

Certificates of Deposit

A certificate of deposit, or C.D. as it is frequently called, is a specialized form of *promise* to pay money given by a *bank.* A **certificate of deposit** is a written acknowledgment by a bank of the receipt of money that it promises to repay on demand or at a stated future date, with interest at a stated rate. The issuing party, the **maker,** which is always a bank, promises to pay a second party, the **payee,** who is named in the C.D. See Figure 25–6.

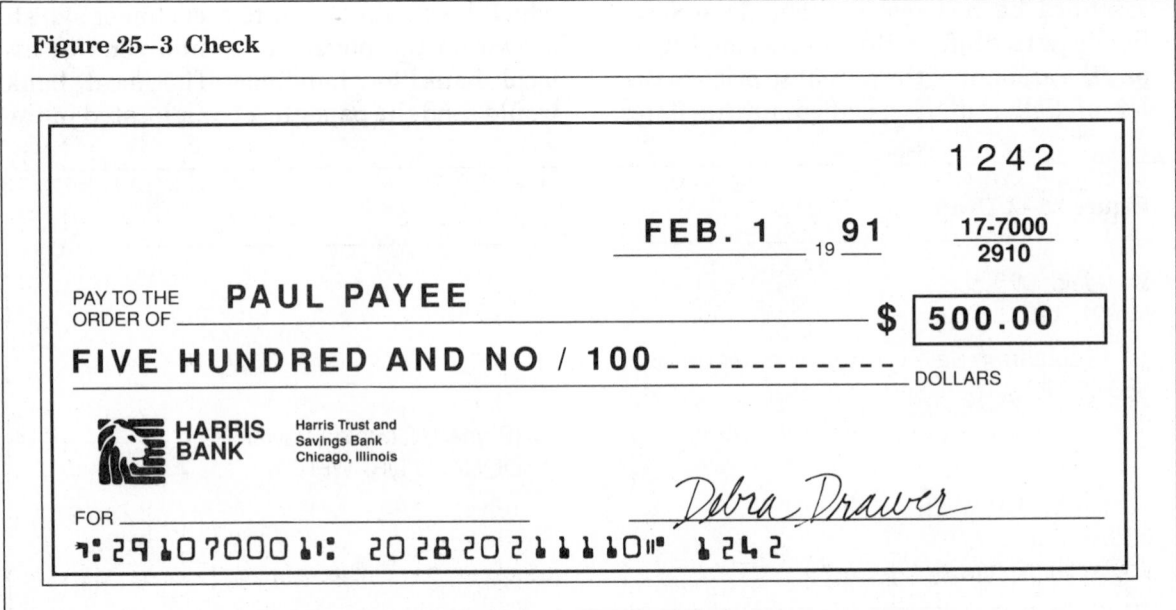

Figure 25–3 Check

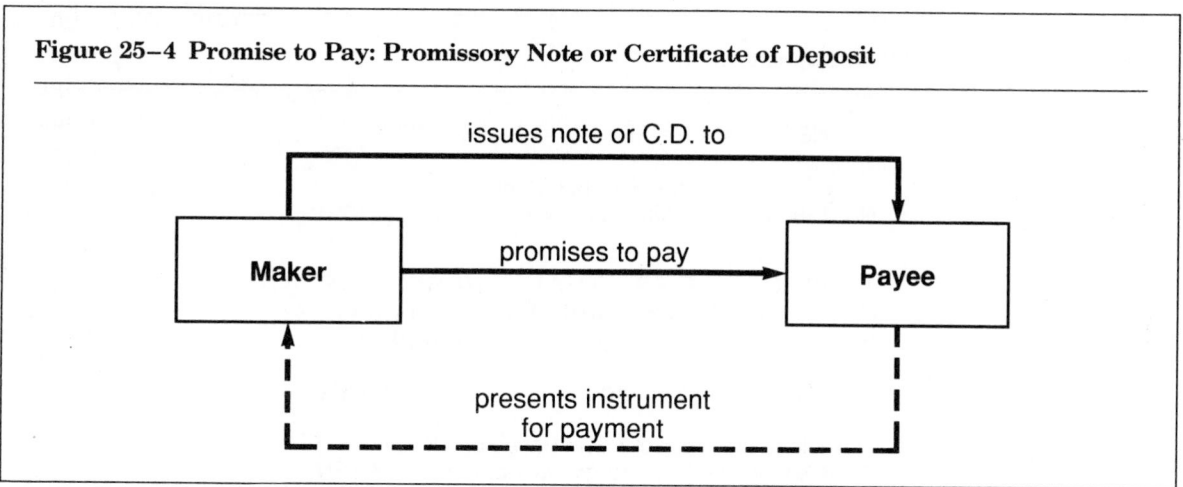

Figure 25–4 Promise to Pay: Promissory Note or Certificate of Deposit

FORM OF COMMERCIAL PAPER

To perform its function in the business community effectively, commercial paper must be capable of passing from person to person freely. This is made possible because *negotiability* is wholly a matter of form. The instrument must contain within its "four corners" all the information required to determine whether it is negotiable. No reference to any other source is permitted. For this reason a negotiable instrument is called a "courier without luggage." In addition, indorsements *cannot* create nor destroy negotiability.

In order to be negotiable, the **instrument** must

1. be in writing,

2. be signed,

3. contain a promise or order to pay,

4. be unconditional,

5. be for a sum certain in money,

6. contain no other promise or order,

7. be payable on demand or at a definite time, and

8. be payable to order or to bearer.

Section 3–104(1). See *First State Bank at Gallup v. Clark.* If these requirements are not met, the instrument is not negotiable, and the rights of the parties are governed by the law of contract (assignment).

Writing

The requirement that the instrument be a writing is broadly construed. Printing, typewriting, handwriting, or any other tangible expression is sufficient to satisfy the requirement. Section 1–201(46). Most negotiable instruments, of course, are written on paper, but this is not required. In one instance, a check was reportedly written on a coconut.

Figure 25–5 Note

$10,000   Albany, N.Y.   April 7, 1991

Six months from date I promise to pay to the order of Pat Payee ten thousand dollars.

(signed) Matthew Maker

Figure 25–6 Certificate of Deposit

NEGOTIABLE CERTIFICATE OF DEPOSIT

The Mountain Bank
No. 13900   Mountain, N.Y.   June 1, 1991

THIS CERTIFIES THAT THERE HAS BEEN DEPOSITED with the undersigned the sum of $200,000.00

Two hundred thousand . . . . Dollars

Payable to the order of Pablo Payee on December 1, 1993 with interest only to maturity at the rate of TEN percent (10%) per annum upon surrender of this certificate properly indorsed.

The Mountain Bank

By (Signature) Malcolm Maker, Vice-President

Authorized Signature

Signed

A note or certificate of deposit must be signed by the maker; a draft or check must be signed by the drawer. As in the case of a writing, extreme latitude is granted in determining what constitutes a **signature**, which is any symbol executed or adopted by a party with the *intent* to validate a writing. Section 1–201(39). Moreover, it may consist of any word or mark used in place of a written signature, Section 3–401(2), such as initials, an X, or a thumb-print. It may be a trade name or assumed name. Even the location of the signature on the document is unimportant. Normally, a maker or drawer signs in the lower right-hand corner of the instrument, but this is not required. Negotiable instruments are frequently signed by an agent for her principal. For a discussion of the appropriate way in which an agent should sign a negotiable instrument, see Chapter 28.

Promise or Order to Pay

A negotiable instrument must contain a promise to pay money, in the case of a note or certificate of deposit, or an order to pay, in the case of a draft or check.

A **promise to pay** is an undertaking and must be more than the mere acknowledgment or recognition of an existing obligation or debt. Section 3–102(1)(c). The so-called due bill or I.O.U. is not a promise, but a mere acknowledgment of indebtedness. Accordingly, an instrument reciting, "due Adam Brown $100" or "I.O.U., Adam Brown, $100" is not negotiable because it does not contain a promise to pay.

An **order to pay** is a direction or command to pay. It must be more than an authorization or request and must identify the person to pay with reasonable certainty. Section 3–102(1)(b). The usual way to express an order is by use of the word *pay:* "*Pay* to the order of John Jones" or "*Pay* bearer." The addition of words of courtesy, such as *please pay* or *kindly pay,* will not destroy the negotiability. Nonetheless, caution should be exercised in employing words modifying the prototypically correct "*Pay.*" For example, it has been held that the use of the words "I wish you would pay" destroyed the negotiability of an instrument and rendered its transfer a contractual assignment.

Unconditional

The requirement that the promise or order be unconditional is to prevent the inclusion of any term that could reduce the promisor's obligation to pay. The payment and credit functions of negotiable instruments would be diminished by conditions limiting the promise, since costly and time-consuming investigations would become necessary to determine the degree of risk imposed by the condition. Moreover, if the holder (transferee) had to take an instrument subject to certain conditions, her risk factor would be substantial, and this would lead to limited transferability. Substitutes for money must be capable of rapid circulation at minimum risks.

A promise or order to pay is **unconditional** if it is absolute and not subject to any contingencies or qualifications. Thus, an instrument would not be negotiable if it stated that "ABC Corp. promises to pay $100,000 to the order of Johnson provided the helicopter sold meets all contractual specifications." On the other hand, suppose that when Meeker, president of ABC, delivered an instrument that provided, "ABC Corp. promises to pay $100,000 to the order of Johnson," Meeker stated that the money would be paid only if the helicopter met all contractual specifications. The instrument would be negotiable because negotiability is determined solely by examining the instrument itself and is not affected by matters beyond the face of the instrument.

An instrument is not made conditional by the fact that it is subject to implied or constructive conditions. Section 3–105(1). Implications of law or fact are not to be considered in deciding whether an instrument is negotiable. Thus, a statement in an instrument that it is given for an executory promise does *not* imply that the instrument is conditioned upon performance of that promise.

A promise or order is conditional if (a) the instrument states that it is subject to or governed by any other agreement or (b) the instrument states that it is to be paid only out of a particular fund or source. Section 3–105(2).

Reference to Other Agreements The restriction against reference to another agreement is to enable any person to determine the right to payment provided by the instrument without having to look beyond its four corners. If such right is made subject to the terms of another agreement, the instrument is non-negotiable. See *Holly Hill Acres, Ltd. v. Charter Bank of Gainesville.*

A distinction is to be made between a mere recital of the *existence* of a separate agreement (this does not destroy negotiability) and a recital that makes the instrument *subject* to the terms of another agreement (this does destroy negotiability).

A statement in a note such as

This note is given in partial payment for a color T.V. set to be delivered two weeks from date in accordance with a contract of this date between the payee and the maker

does not impair negotiability. It merely is a description of the transaction giving rise to the note and describes the consideration. It does not place any restriction or condition on the maker's obligation to pay. The promise is not made subject to any other agreement. Added words that *would* impair negotiability are

This note is subject to all the terms of said contract.

These added words make the promise to pay conditional upon the adequate performance of the television set in accordance with the terms of the contract and thus render the instrument non-negotiable.

The Particular Fund Doctrine An order or promise to pay only out of a particular fund is conditional and destroys negotiability because payment depends upon the existence and sufficiency of the particular fund. On the other hand, a promise or order to pay, coupled with a mere indication of a particular fund out of which reimbursement is to be made or a particular account to be debited with the amount, does not impair negotiability since the drawer's or maker's general credit is relied on and charging a particular account is merely a bookkeeping entry to be followed after payment.

Thus, there is a difference between an instrument that says, "Sixty days after date pay to the order of John Jones $500, payment will be limited to the proceeds of the sale of the contents of freight car No. 1234," and one stating, "Sixty days after date pay to the order of John Jones $500 and charge to proceeds of sale of the contents of freight car No. 1234." In the first case, payment would be made only if such contents were sold and then only to the extent of the proceeds. In the second case, the instrument contains an unqualified order to pay with merely bookkeeping instructions to the drawee of the draft.

The U.C.C. creates two exceptions to the particular fund rule, however, in the interest of promoting marketability of instruments. The first exception permits governmental agencies to draw short-term commercial paper in which payment is restricted to a particular fund. Statutes in many States and ordinances in municipalities may authorize the issuance of instruments to pay for public improvements, and these instruments are generally payable only out of funds raised from special assessments levied against the property benefited. To aid municipalities and States, and to prevent investors from disappointment, Section 3–105(1)(g) provides that an instrument is not rendered non-negotiable solely because it is payable out of a particular fund "if the instrument is issued by a government or governmental agency or unit."

The other exception is in favor of trusts and unincorporated associations. Trustees, executors, and administrators commonly limit payment to the assets of the trust or estate they are administering. Partnerships and other unincorporated organizations, such as joint stock companies and business trusts, issue instruments limited to payment from the entire assets of the organization, expressly providing that the members are not to be personally liable. Section 3–105(1)(h) of the Code specifies that none of these limitations impairs negotiability of an instrument despite the fact that its payment is limited to a particular fund.

Revised Article 3 eliminates the particular fund doctrine and provides that a promise or order is *not* made conditional because payment is to be made only out of a particular fund. Rev. Section 3–106(b)(ii).

Sum Certain in Money

The purpose of the requirement of a sum certain in money is to enable the holder to determine from the instrument itself the amount that he is entitled to receive.

Money The term **money** means a medium of exchange authorized or adopted by a sovereign government as part of its currency. Section 1–201(24). Consequently, even though local custom may make gold or diamonds a medium of exchange, an instrument payable in such commodities would be non-negotiable because of the lack of governmental sanction of such media as legal tender. On the other hand, an instrument paying a sum certain in French francs, German marks, Italian lira, Japanese yen, or other foreign currency is negotiable.

Sum Certain The requirement that payment be of a "sum certain" must be considered from the point of view of the holder, not the maker or drawer. The holder must be assured of a determinable minimum payment, although provisions of the instrument may increase the recovery under certain circumstances. Thus, a frequent provision of a note is that the maker will pay, in addition to the face amount and specified interest, costs of collection and attorney's fees upon default in payment. Such provision is designed to make the paper more attractive without lessening the certainty of the amount due and therefore does not destroy its negotiability.

An instrument payable with a stated rate of interest is an obligation for a sum certain because the amount payable may be computed from the terms of the instrument itself. The rates may be different before and after default, or before and after a specified date. Section 3–106. If interest is payable "at the current rate" (which means current banking rate), however, it is non-negotiable because this is *not* a matter that can be determined without reference to any outside source.

Most courts have held that variable interest rate provisions destroy negotiability because the interest rate is tied to a published index external to the instrument. The legislatures of a number of States, however, have amended Article 3 in their States to permit variable interest rates. Revised Section 3 also takes this approach by providing that the requirement of a "fixed amount" (Revised Article 3's term for a sum certain) applies only to principal and not to interest. Rev. Section 3–104. Moreover, Revised Article 3–112 specifically states that interest in an instrument may be at a fixed or variable rate.

If an instrument omits to provide for any interest, no interest accrues until after maturity, at which time the unpaid principal will begin to bear interest at the legal rate of interest. If an instrument states that it is payable "with interest" but does not designate any rate, the judgment rate of interest applies from the date of the instrument, or if it is undated from the date of issue. Section 3–118.

A sum payable is a sum certain even though it is payable in installments, or with a fixed discount if paid before maturity, or a fixed addition if paid after maturity. This is because it is always possible to make the necessary computations from the face of the instrument to determine the amount due at any given time.

No Other Promise or Order

A negotiable instrument must contain a promise or order to pay money, but it may not contain any other promise, order, obligation or power given by the maker or drawer, except as otherwise specifically authorized under the Code. Section 3–104(1)(b). Accordingly, if an instrument contains an order or promise to do an act in addition to or in lieu of the payment of money, it is not negotiable. For example, a promise to pay $100 "and a ton of coal" would be non-negotiable.

The Code sets out a list of terms and provisions that may be included in instruments without adversely affecting negotiability. Among these are (1) a statement that collateral has been given to secure obligations on the instrument; (2) a promise or power to maintain, protect, or increase collateral and to sell it in case of a default in payment of the instrument; (3) a term authorizing confession of judgment (written authority by the debtor to allow the holder to enter judgment against the debtor in favor of the holder) on the instrument if it is not paid when due; (4) a term purporting to waive the benefit of any law intended for the advantage or protection of any obligor; and (5) a term in a draft providing that the payee, by indorsing or cashing it, acknowledges full satisfaction of an obligation of the drawer. Section 3–112. It is important to note that the U.C.C. does not render any of these terms legal or effective; it merely provides that their inclusion will not affect negotiability.

Payable on Demand or at a Definite Time

A negotiable instrument must "be payable on demand or at a definite time." Section 3–104(1)(c). This requirement, like the other formal requirements of negotiability, is designed to promote certainty in determining the present value of a negotiable instrument.

Demand paper always has been considered sufficiently certain as to time of payment to satisfy the requirements of negotiability because it is the holder who makes the demand and thus sets the time for payment. An instrument payable upon demand means that the money owed under the instrument must be paid upon the holder's request. An instrument, such as a check in which no time for payment is stated, is payable on demand. An instrument qualifies as being payable on demand if it is payable "at sight" or "on presentment." Section 3–108.

Instruments payable at a definite time are called **time paper.** Section 3–109(2) of the Code provides that an instrument which by its terms is otherwise payable only upon an act or event whose time of occurrence is uncertain is *not* payable at a definite time, even though the act or event has occurred. Examples include notes providing for payment to the payee or order "thirty days after my marriage" or "when the payee is twenty-one years old." Such promises in otherwise negotiable instruments destroy their negotiability because they are not payable at a definite time. Nor does the fact that the maker of the note marries or the payee becomes twenty-one years of age after the execution of the note change the result. Negotiability is determined solely from the face of the instrument.

Various types of provisions that are regarded as fixing a definite time for payment of an instrument are detailed in Section 3–109(1) and will now be considered.

"On or Before" Clauses   An instrument is payable at a definite time if it is payable "on or before" a stated date. Section 3–109(1)(a). *See Bottrell v. American Bank.* The holder is thus assured that she will have her money by the maturity date at the latest, although she may receive it sooner. This right of anticipation enables the obligor, at his option, to pay before the stated maturity date (pre-payment) and thereby stop the further accrual of interest or, if interest rates have gone down, to refinance at a lower rate of interest. Nevertheless, it constitutes sufficient certainty so as not to impair negotiability.

At a Fixed Period after a Stated Date   Frequently, instruments are made payable at a fixed period after a stated date. For example, the instrument may be made payable "thirty days after date." This means it is payable thirty days after the date of issuance, which is recited on the instrument. Such an instrument is payable at a definite time, for its exact maturity date can be determined by simple arithmetic.

An undated instrument payable "thirty days after date" is not payable at a definite time, since the date of payment cannot be determined from its face. It is therefore non-negotiable until it is completed.

At a Fixed Period after Sight   This clause is frequently used in drafts. An instrument payable in a fixed period after sight is negotiable, for it means a fixed period after acceptance, and therefore a simple mathematical calculation makes the maturity date certain.

At a Definite Time Subject to Acceleration   An instrument payable at a fixed time subject to acceleration by the holder satisfies the requirement of being payable at a definite time. Indeed, such an instrument would seem to have a more certain maturity date than a demand instrument because it at least states a definite maturity date. In addition, the acceleration may be upon the happening of some act or event.

At a Definite Time Subject to Extension   A provision in an instrument granting the *holder* an option to extend the maturity of the instrument for a definite *or* indefinite period does not impair its negotiability. Section 3–109(1)(d). A provision permitting the *obligor* of an instrument to extend the maturity date to a further *definite* time does not affect negotiability. For example, a provision in a note, payable one year from date, that the maker may extend the maturity date six months does not impair negotiability. If the obligor is given an option to extend the maturity of the instrument for an *indefinite* period of time, however, his promise is illusory, and there is no certainty of time of payment. Such an instrument is non-negotiable. If the obligor's right to extend is limited to a definite time, the extension clause is no more indefinite than an acceleration clause with a time limitation.

In addition, extension may be made automatic upon or after a specified act or event, provided a definite time limit is stated. An example of such an extension clause is, "I promise to pay to the order of John Doe the sum of $2,000 on December 1, 1991, but it is agreed that if the crop of sections 25 and 26 of Twp. 145 is below eight bushels per acre for the 1991 season, this note shall be extended for one year."

Payable to Order or to Bearer

A negotiable instrument must contain words indicating that the maker or drawer intends that it may pass into the hands of someone other than the payee. The "magic words" of negotiability are thus *to the order of* or *to bearer*, but other words which are clearly equivalent to these may be regarded as fulfilling this requirement. The use of synonyms, however, only invites trouble. *See Cooperatieve Centrale Raiffeisen-Boerenleenbank B.A. v. Bailey.* Moreover, as noted above, indorsements cannot create or destroy negotiability and negotiability must be determined from the "face" of the instrument.

Revised Article 3 provides that a *check* which meets all of the requirements of being a negotiable instrument except that it is not payable to bearer or order is nevertheless a negotiable instrument. Rev. Section 3–104(c). This rule does *not* apply to instruments other than checks.

Payable to Order   In addition to the eminently correct "Pay to the order of Jane Jones," the maker or drawer of **order paper** may state: "Pay to Jane Jones or her order" or "Pay to Jane Jones or her assigns." Section 3–110. Moreover, in every instance the person to whose order the instrument is payable must be designated with reasonable certainty. Within this limitation a broad range of payees are possible, including an individual, the maker or drawer, the drawee, two or more payees, an office, an estate, trust or fund, a partnership or unincorporated association, and a corporation.

This requirement should not be confused with the requirement that the instrument contain an order or promise to pay. An order to pay is a direction to a third party to pay the instrument as drawn. An "order instrument," on the other hand, pertains to the transferability of the instrument rather than instructing a specific party to pay.

Payable to Bearer   Section 3–111 of the Code states that an instrument fulfills the requirements of being **payable to bearer** if by its terms it does not designate a specific payee or is payable (1) to bearer or the order of bearer, (2) to a specified person or "bearer," or (3) to "cash" or to the order of "cash." An

instrument made payable both to order and to bearer, that is, "pay to the order of Mildred Courts or bearer," is payable to order. If the words "or bearer" were handwritten or typewritten, then the instrument would be payable to bearer.

Terms and Omissions and Their Effect on Negotiability

The negotiability of an instrument may be questioned because of an omission of certain provisions or ambiguity of language. Problems may also arise in connection with interpretation of instruments, whether or not negotiability is called into question. Accordingly, the Code contains rules of construction that apply to every instrument.

Omissions   The negotiability of an instrument is *not* affected by the omission of a statement of consideration or of the place where the instrument is drawn or payable. Section 3–112(1)(a).

Sealed Instruments   The fact that an instrument is under seal has no effect on its negotiability, despite whatever other effect the seal might have under common law. Section 3–113.

Dating of the Instrument   The negotiability of an instrument is not affected by the fact that it is antedated, postdated, or undated. Section 3–114.

If the instrument is *antedated*, that is, it carries a date prior to its actual issue, the stated date controls. Hence, a note dated October 1, 1991, payable thirty days after date, and issued on November 1, 1991, is due and payable the day before its issue.

If the instrument is *postdated*, that is, carries a date later than the day on which it was issued, the date stated on the instrument is conclusive. A demand instrument, therefore, by postdating becomes a time instrument. For example, if on January 2, 1991, the drawer issues a check and dates it January 21, 1991, the drawer's bank is not authorized to pay the instrument until January 21. The instrument therefore is a time draft.

Incomplete Instruments Occasionally, a party will sign a paper that clearly is intended to become an instrument but that, either by intention or through oversight, is incomplete in some necessary respect, such as the omission of a promise or order, designation of the payee, amount payable, or time for payment. Section 3–115 provides that such an instrument is not negotiable until completed.

If an undated instrument is delivered on November 1, 1991, payable "thirty days after date," the payee has implied authority to fill in "November 1, 1991." Until he does so, however, the instrument is not negotiable because it is not payable at a definite time. If the payee completes the instrument by inserting an erroneous date, the rules as to material alteration, covered in Chapter 28, apply.

Ambiguous Instruments Rather than commit the parties to the use of parol evidence to establish the interpretation of an instrument, Section 3–118 establishes rules to resolve common ambiguities. This promotes negotiability by providing added certainty to the holder.

Where it is doubtful whether the instrument is a draft or note, the holder may treat it as either and present it for payment to the drawee or the person signing it. For example, an instrument reading

To X: On demand I promise to pay $500 to the order of Y.

Signed, Z

may be presented for payment to X as a draft or to Z as a note.

An instrument naming no drawee but stating

On demand, pay $500 to the order of Y.

Signed, Z

although in the form of a draft, may be treated as a note and presented to Z for payment.

If a printed form of note or draft is used and the party signing it inserts handwritten or typewritten language that is inconsistent with the printed words, the handwritten words control the typewritten and the printed words, and the typewritten words control the printed. *See Bottrell v. American Bank.*

If the amount payable is set forth on the face of the instrument in both figures and words which differ, the words control the figures. It is presumed that the maker or drawer would be more careful with words. If the words are ambiguous, then the figures control.

CASES

Form of Commercial Paper

FIRST STATE BANK AT GALLUP v. CLARK

Supreme Court of New Mexico, 1977.
91 N.M. 117, 570 P.2d 1144.

EASLEY, J.

First State Bank of Gallup (First State), Plaintiff-Appellee sued M.S. Horne (Horne), Defendant-Appellant on a promissory note. The trial court granted summary judgment against defendant and we affirm.

Horne had executed a $100,000 note in favor of R. C. Clark which contained a restriction that the note could not be transferred, pledged or assigned without the written consent of Horne. As part of the transaction between Horne and Clark, Horne gave Clark a separate letter authorizing Clark to pledge the note as collateral for a loan of $50,000 which Clark anticipated making with First State. Clark did make the loan and pledged the note, which was accompanied by Horne's letter authorizing the note to be used as collateral. First State also called Horne to verify that he was in agreement that his note could be accepted as collateral. First State attempted to collect from Horne on Horne's note to Clark which had been pledged as collateral. Horne refused to pay and this suit resulted.

The issues raised on appeal include (1) whether the note was a negotiable instrument for purposes of Article 3 of the Uniform Commercial Code (U.C.C.). . . . Article 3 of the U.C.C. defines a certain type of readily transferable instrument and lays down certain rules for the treatment of that instrument and rules concerning the rights, remedies and defenses of persons dealing with it.

In order to be a "negotiable instrument" for Article 3 purposes the paper must precisely meet the definition set out in § 3–104, since § 3–104 itself states that, to be a negotiable instrument, a writing "must" meet the definition therein set out. Moreover, it is clear that in order to determine whether an instrument meets that definition *only the instrument itself* may be looked to, *not* other documents, even when other documents are referred to in the instrument. [Citations.] As [citation] points out in its text and in footnote 3:

The applicability of Article 3 must be determined from the instrument itself, without reference to other documents or oral agreements. The "four-corners test" is still applicable: the determination of negotiability under Article 3 must be made by inspecting only the instrument itself. . . .

This is clear from the mandatory language of U.C.C. § 3–104, and from the following language from the Official Comment to U.C.C. § 3–105 found under the heading "Purposes of Changes": "The section is intended to make it clear that, so far as negotiability is affected, the conditional or unconditional character of the promise or order is to be determined by what is expressed in the instrument itself. . . .

We recognize the Official Comments to the U.C.C. as persuasive, though they are not controlling authority. [Citation.]

Section 3–104 thus requires that, in order to be a negotiable instrument for Article 3 purposes, one must be able to ascertain without reference to other documents that the instrument:

(a) [is] signed by the maker or drawer; and (b) contain[s] an unconditional promise or order to pay a sum certain in money and no other promise, order, obligation or power given by the maker or drawer except as authorized by [Article 3]; and (c) [is] payable on demand or at a definite time; and (d) [is] payable to order or to bearer.

The note in question here failed to meet the requirements of § 3–104, since the promise to pay contained in the note was not unconditional. Moreover, the note was expressly drafted to be non-negotiable since it stated:

This note may not be transferred, pledged, or otherwise assigned without the written consent of M. S. Horne.

These words, even though they appeared on the back of the note, effectively cancelled any implication of negotiability provided by the words "Pay to the order of" on the face of the note. Notations and terms on the back of a note, made contemporaneously with the execution of the note and intended to be part of the note's contract of payment, constitute as much a part of the note as if they were incorporated on its face. [Citation.]

* * *

The whole purpose of the concept of a negotiable instrument under Article 3 is to declare that transferees in the ordinary course of business are only to be held liable for information appearing in the instrument itself and will not be expected to know of any limitations on negotiability or changes in terms, etc., contained in any separate documents. The whole idea of the facilitation of easy transfer of notes and instruments requires that a transferee be able to trust what the instrument says, and be able to determine the validity of the note and its negotiability from the language in the note itself. [Citation.] * * *

Since the note in question is not negotiable for Article 3 purposes, First State cannot be a holder in due course under Article 3, and we need not discuss that issue.

* * *

The summary judgment of the district court is hereby affirmed for the stated reasons.

Reference to Other Agreements

HOLLY HILL ACRES, LTD. v. CHARTER BANK OF GAINESVILLE

Court of Appeals of Florida, 1975.
314 So.2d 209.

SCHEB, J.

Appellant/defendant appeals from a summary judgment in favor of appellee/plaintiff Bank in a suit wherein the appellee sought to foreclose a note and mortgage given by appellant.

The appellee Bank was the assignee from appellees Rogers and Blythe of a promissory note and purchase money mortgage executed and delivered by the appellant. The note, executed April 28, 1972, contains the following stipulation:

This note with interest is secured by a mortgage on real estate, of even date herewith, made by the maker hereof in favor of the said payee, and shall be construed and enforced according to the laws of the State of Florida. *The terms of said mortgage are by this reference made a part hereof.* (Emphasis supplied.)

* * *

The note having incorporated the terms of the purchase money mortgage was not negotiable. * * *

The note, incorporating by reference the terms of the mortgage, did not contain the unconditional promise to pay required by [U.C.C. §] 3–104(1)(b). Rather, the note falls within the scope of [U.C.C. §] 3–105(2)(a). Although negotiability is now governed by the Uniform Commercial Code, this was the Florida view even before the U.C.C. was adopted. * * *

Appellee Bank relies upon *Scott v. Taylor,* [citation], as authority for the proposition that its note is negotiable. *Scott,* however, involved a note which stated: "this note secured by mortgage." Mere reference to a note being secured by mortgage is a common commercial practice and such reference in itself does not impede the negotiability of the note. There is, however, a significant difference in a note stating that it is "secured by a mortgage" from one which provides, "the terms of said mortgage are by this reference made a part hereof." In the former instance the note merely refers to a separate agreement which does not impede its negotiability, while in the latter instance the note is rendered non-negotiable. *See* [U.C.C. §] 3–105(2)(a); [U.C.C. §] 3–119. [In a footnote the court stated] Official Comment 5 to [U.C.C.] § 3–119 provides: Subsection (2) rejects decisions which have carried the rule that contemporaneous writings must be read together to the length of holding that a clause in a mortgage affecting a note destroyed the negotiability of the note. The negotiability of an instrument is always to be determined by what appears on the face of the instrument alone, and if it is negotiable in itself a purchaser without notice of a separate writing is in no way affected by it. *If the instrument itself states that it is subject to or governed by any other agreement, it is not negotiable under this Article*; but if it merely refers to a separate agreement or states that is arises out of such an agreement, it is negotiable. (Emphasis supplied.)

As a general rule the assignee of a mortgage securing a non-negotiable note, even though a bona fide purchaser for value, takes subject to all defenses available as against the mortgagee. [Citation.] Appellant raised the issue of fraud as between himself and other parties to the note, therefore, it was incumbent on the appellee Bank, as movant for a summary judgment, to prove the non-existence of any genuinely triable issue. [Citation.]

Accordingly, the entry of a summary final judgment is reversed and the cause remanded for further proceedings.

Demand or Definite Time/Ambiguous Instruments

BOTTRELL v. AMERICAN BANK

Montana Supreme Court, 1989.
773 P.2d 694.

SHEEHY, J.

Northern Line Layers, Inc. was awarded a judgment of $500,000.00 compensatory damages and $100,000.00 punitive damages against American Bank, based on a jury verdict, in the District Court, . . .

In the same cause, on the same day, the district court granted a separate judgment in favor of American Bank against Donald G. Bottrell, in the sum of $22,126.31, . . .

In the same cause, on the same day, the district court granted judgment in favor of American Bank, and against Northern Line Layers, Inc. (NLL), in the sum of $239,629.43, . . .

*   *   *

As of June 6, 1983, NLL had six outstanding loans in American Bank, identified as follows:

Loan Number	Amount	Origination Date
8355	$ 6,006.00	9/4/81
8455	4,000.00	11/9/81
8462	13,004.00	11/9/81
9470	3,000.00	1/31/83
14077	71,770.49	2/15/83
14463	$ 140,000.00	6/6/83

In the years subsequent to July 31, 1981, NLL had over 25 loans in American Bank which had never been delinquent nor was any payment missed. Generally, the loans were for purchase of equipment or operating capital.

*   *   *

On July 18, 1983, Bottrell and Reeve [representatives of NLL] went to the Bank to discuss note No. 14463, for $140,000.00, which originated on June 6, 1983. The note was not due until October 4, 1983. Bottrell and Reeve were concerned that they might have problems repaying the entire note when it came due and wanted to make the bankers aware of their concerns at an early date.

Bottrell and Reeve had personally guaranteed the $140,000.00 note with the Bank. They met with Derrig [a bank officer] on July 18, 1983. They discussed work coming up for bid, the company's chances for picking up some of that work and how they were going to handle the note. *   *   *

At the meeting of July 20, 1983, at the Bank, Beaton [a bank officer] discussed the steps which the Bank would take to address the NLL concerns about the note due in October. He outlined the loans on a blackboard.

He indicated that a $12,000.00 indebtedness would be renewed when it came due in September, 1983, and also indicated the Bank would rewrite loan No. 14077 on which there was a principal balance due of $64,323.93 at that time. This was the note on which NLL was paying $3,500.00 a month. Beaton indicated that the Bank would rewrite this note to reduce the interest by 1 percent. *   *   *

There was no discussion in this morning meeting about NLL's performance at the Bank or that it was unsatisfactory in any manner nor was there any discussion about other debts owed by NLL to other entities. *   *   *

There was no further contact between the Bank and NLL during July 20, 1983, until Bottrell and Reeve returned at 3:15 P.M., with additional documents and serial numbers that Derrig had requested. At the Bank, they were approached by Derrig who said that Beaton wanted to talk to them.

Bottrell and Reeve went into Beaton's office. Derrig was present. Beaton said, "We have a problem." He told Reeve and Bottrell that the Bank had set off $66,000.00 from NLL's checking and savings accounts against the $140,000.00 loan which was not due until October 4, 1983. The bankers said they felt insecure and that NLL would have to "shore up" its debts. Beaton demanded that NLL either provide additional collateral or pay down the debt before the Bank would release the setoff money.

*   *   *

The first and principal issue raised by the American Bank, is whether, when it exercises a right of setoff existing in the statute and in written agreements with its borrower, it is then subject to tort liability for so doing.

American Bank contended at the trial that the $140,000.00 note of June 6, 1983, was a demand note, and that within the instrument there was language to the effect that the borrower waived demand for payment. The bank officers testified that because of the language in the note, they could declare the demand note immediately due without notice to the borrower, that the debt then matured, and that the Bank had a right to setoff against the matured indebtedness such deposits of NLL as it had in its possession at the time. * * *

NLL answers that the note was not in fact a demand note; that the right of setoff may only apply to matured debts; and that under the terms of the note, the entire amount of the unpaid principal and accrued interest could be declared immediately due and payable, without notice, only upon default of the borrower.

The district court instructed the jury that the $140,000.00 note was not a demand note. * * *

A copy of the note is attached to this opinion for the convenience of the reader [Figure 25–7].

In summary, we hold that the note in question was not a demand note; that the Bank's right to setoff applies only to a mature debt or one that is due and payable; and that in this case, the Bank could accelerate payment or performance by the borrower under the note only if the borrower was in default, under the terms of the note.

Let us first address the problem of whether the note for $140,000.00 was a demand note.

It will be seen that under the column "due date" are inserted the figures "10–4–83" and that in the body of the note, after the square in which the double x has been inserted, appears the language, "[i]f no demand is made. Borrower shall pay 120 days after the date of this note." Those terms take this note out of the category of a demand note.

Section 3–108 [U.C.C.] provides:

"Payable on demand. Instruments payable on demand include those payable at sight or on presentation and those in which no time for payment is stated."

Here, the instrument states a time for payment. The legal effect of a note which contains language as here, "upon demand, borrower promises to pay to bank or order . . . If no demand is made, Borrower shall pay 120 days after the date of this note," is that an actual demand is necessary to mature the promissory note prior to the date set. In [citation], the Arizona Supreme Court discussed demand notes:

". . . As a general rule, notes payable on demand are due and payable immediately upon execution, and no further demand is necessary to mature them. But an exception to this rule applies when the terms of the instrument disclose an intention by the parties that the notes would not become due and payable immediately after the time of delivery. (Citing authority.) In such circumstances, an actual demand is necessary to mature the promissory notes. The terms of the notes in the present case provided one interest rate for the date of execution until maturity, and a higher interest rate after maturity. This discloses a clear intention by the parties that the notes not be due and payable immediately. To hold otherwise would be inconsistent with the express terms of the note, and render these provisions meaningless."

In the note here before us, 15 percent per annum is the rate of interest if paid when due and 22 percent per annum for amounts paid after the due date.

* * *

* * * It is on its face a promissory note payable at a time certain, unless a previous demand is made, and under the language of the note the Bank had no power to declare the entire unpaid principal and accrued interest believed due and payable without notice except "upon default." No default existed with respect to any of the notes due and payable to the Bank when it attempted its "setoff."

WEBER, J.

I dissent because I . . . conclude that the Bank properly exercised its right of set-off.

* * *

I will now discuss the $140,000 demand note. The district court determined as a matter of law that the note was not a demand note, and the majority has reached the same conclusion. I do not agree. The language of the $140,000 note clearly states, "Upon demand, Borrower promises to pay to Bank." The instrument also states, "If no demand is made, Borrower shall pay 120 days after the date of this note." It also recites an actual due date of 10–4–83. These statements are consistent with each other. To state that payment is due in 120 days does not mean that the financial institution could not demand payment prior to the 120 days.

Figure 25–7 Commercial Note (*Bottrell v. American Bank*)

COMMERCIAL NOTE
Single Advance

(simple Interest)

Account Number	Loan Number	Disbursement Date	Due Date	Principal Amount	Call Code	Collateral Code	Officer Number	Officer's Initials
	14463	6-6-83	10-4-83	140,000.00	H			MD

Borrower: Northern Line Layers, Inc.   Bank: Western State Bank

P.O. Box 30643   P.O. Box 50400

Billings, M. 59107   Billings, MT 59105

Upon demand, Borrower promises to pay to Bank, or order,
One hundred forty thousand and no/100-- DOLLARS
($ 140,000.00), together with interest on the unpaid principal balance outstanding from time to time at the rate set out below. Interest will accrue on the outstanding unpaid principal balance for each day that any amount is outstanding and will continue to accrue until this note is paid in full. Interest will be at the rate of:

☒   15 percent per annum.

☐   A rate of _____ point(s) over the prime rate, adjusted _____, based upon the prime rate quoted by _____.
That prime rate currently is _____ percent per annum, and the rate on this note currently is _____ percent per annum.

☐   _____
     _____
     _____

Borrower will pay interest: ☐ Monthly   ☐ Quarterly   ☒ At Maturity   ☐ _____

☒   If no demand is made, Borrower shall pay 120 days after the date of this note.

☐   If no demand is made, Borrower will pay under the following schedule: _____
     _____
     _____

The interest rate shall not exceed the maximum rate permitted by applicable law. If Borrower does not pay as agreed, or if Borrower or any guarantor of this note breaches any other agreement with the Bank, Borrower will be in default. Upon default, the Bank may declare the entire unpaid principal and accrued interest immediately due, without notice, and Borrower will then pay that amount. Upon default Bank also may increase the interest rate ------ points, and include any unpaid interest as of the date of acceleration or maturity as part of the sum due and subject to the higher rate.

Any payment not paid when due shall bear interest at the rate of 22 percent per annum until paid. Borrower will pay Bank at the address named above, or such other place as Bank may designate in writing.

The Bank may pay someone else to help collect this note if Borrower does not pay. Borrower also will pay the Bank that amount. This includes the Bank's lawyers' fees whether or not there is a lawsuit, including any fees on appeal. Borrower also will pay any court costs. The Bank may delay enforcing any of its rights under this note without losing them. If there is a lawsuit, Borrower agrees venue may be in the county in which Bank is located.

Borrower waives presentment, demand for payment, protest, notice of dishonor, and notice of every other kind. The obligations of the Borrower are joint and several.

                                                                Northern Line Layers, Inc.

Date: June 6, 1983   By ✓ Edward R Mee

© 1981 CFI Management Services, Inc.

SOURCE: Reprinted with permission from *Uniform Commercial Code Reporting Service*, 2nd Series (p. 596, Vol. 9, 1990), published by Callaghan & Company, 155 Pfingsten Road, Deerfield, Ill., 60015.

The majority finds that the due date takes this note out of the § 3–108 [U.C.C.] definition of a demand note. However, the statutory definition is not this narrow. In referring to this same definition the [citation] stated, "The drafters obviously felt no need to state the obvious, that demand instruments also include instruments made expressly payable 'on demand'." Initially therefore the note in question meets the definition of a demand note.

Courts have held as a matter of law that a note with similar language is a demand note. * * *

The majority also calls attention to the language in the note which calls for an increase in the interest rate upon default. This however, does not take the note out of demand status, but may mean that an actual demand is necessary. [Citations.]

The majority goes on to state that no actual demand was made. I disagree with that conclusion. Initially, it should be emphasized that no demand is necessary to mature a demand note. "As a general rule, notes payable on demand are due and payable immediately after execution, and no further demand is necessary to mature them." [Citation.] Further, the note signed by NLL specifically stated, "Borrower waives presentment, demand for payment, protest, notice of dishonor, and notice of every other kind." Thus under the wording of the note, demand was unnecessary. The majority disregards this express contractual provision.

However, even if actual demand were necessary, the set-off itself constituted a demand. * * *

SHEEHY, J., concurring specially: * * * The very heart of NLL's case against the Bank is that the instrument in question was not a demand note. Recognizing this, the dissenters, giving no regard to the language of the note, the decisions of courts interpreting that exact language, and the provisions of the Uniform Commercial Code persist in calling the instrument here a demand note.

It is clear that the instrument, a copy of which is affixed to the majority opinion, does not fit the definition of a demand instrument in § 3–108 [U.C.C.].

* * *

The instrument at bar is clearly a note payable at a definite time under the foregoing definition. It contains a stated date when it is due and that definite time is subject to an acceleration by the Bank, by making a demand.

Typewritten into the note are the due date "10–4–83," and the figures "120," setting the days after the date of the note when it is payable if no demand is made. The dissenters claim that the note is ambiguous. Yet, if it were ambiguous, under the UCC, handwritten terms control typewritten and printed terms, and typewritten control printed. Section 3–118(b) [U.C.C.].

The dissenters ignore the language contained in the note, "upon default, the bank may declare the entire unpaid principal and accrued interest immediately due, without notice, and borrower must then pay that amount." An acceleration clause is completely inconsistent with a demand instrument.

Because this instrument provides that "if no demand is made, borrower shall pay *120* days after the date of this note" by the very terms of the note, an actual demand is necessary to mature the promissory note.

Payable to Order or to Bearer

COOPERATIEVE CENTRALE RAIFFEISEN-BOERENLEENBANK B.A. v. BAILEY

United States District Court, Central District California, 1989.
9 UCC Rep. Serv.2d 145.

REA, J.

This matter comes before the court on the motion of both parties to this action for partial summary adjudication and on plaintiff's motion for summary judgment. * * *

This is an action for collection on a promissory note brought by plaintiff, Cooperatieve Centrale Raiffeisen-Boerenleenbank, B.A. ("the Bank"), against the maker of the note, William Bailey, M.D. ("Bailey"). Bailey executed the note in December, 1982, in favor of

"California Dreamstreet," a joint venture which solicited investments in a cattle-breeding operation. California Dreamstreet negotiated the note in 1986 to the Bank, which in turn filed this action on August 29, 1988.

The note states in relevant part:

"DR. WILLIAM H. BAILEY . . . hereby promises to pay to the order to CALIFORNIA DREAM-STREET . . . the sum of Three Hundred Twenty Nine Thousand Eight Hundred ($329,800.00) Dollars. . . ."

* * *

By this motion for partial summary adjudication, the parties seek to determine, as a threshold matter, whether the subject promissory note is a negotiable instrument. * * * [The parties] agree that the sole issue is whether the unusual language in the note obliging Bailey to "pay to the order *to* California Dreamstreet" renders the note non-negotiable.

Whether an instrument is negotiable is a question of law to be determined solely from the face of the instrument, without reference to the intent of the parties. See Official UCC Comment 5 to Code § 3119(2). To be negotiable, an instrument must "be payable to order or bearer." Code § 3104(1)(d). "Payable to order" is further defined by Code § 3110(1), as follows:

"(1) An instrument is payable to order when by its terms it is payable to the order or assigns of any person therein specified with reasonable certainty, or to him or his order, or when it is conspicuously designated on its face as 'exchange' or the like and names a payee."

It is well established that a promissory note is non-negotiable if it states only: "payable to (payee)," rather than "payable to the order of [payee]." [Citations.] Bailey claims that the instant note, which states "pay to the order to [payee]," falls between these two alternatives and should therefore be deemed non-negotiable.

The authorities are unhelpful. There is apparently no case on record in which a variance this small from the language of the Code has been called into question. Both parties direct the Court's attention to Official UCC Comment 5 to Code § 3104, which states:

"5. This Article omits the original Section 10, which provided that the instrument need not follow the language of the act if it 'clearly indicates an intention to conform' to it. The provision has served no useful purpose, and it has been an encouragement to bad drafting and to liberality in holding questionable paper to be negotiable. The omission is not intended to mean that the instrument must follow the language of this section, or that one term may not be recognized as clearly the equivalent of another, as in the case of 'I undertake' instead of 'I promise,' or 'Pay to holder' instead of 'Pay to bearer.' It does mean that either the language of the section or a clear equivalent must be found, and that in doubtful cases the decision should be against negotiability."

In the court's opinion, the Comment fails to persuasively support either party's position. Rules of grammar belie the Bank's argument that the preposition "to" is an apt substitute for "of" since the resulting sentence, read literally, is not just ambiguous but incomplete. On the other hand, the Comment expressly disavows Bailey's argument that the Code drafters intended to set forth certain "magic words," the absence of which precludes negotiability.

What does emerge from the Comment is the need for certainty in determining negotiability. Though sensitive to this goal and to the potentially harsh result of such a finding, the court does not find the instant facts to present the kind of "doubtful" case which should be resolved against negotiability. In this context, the phrase "pay to the order to" can plausibly be construed only to mean "pay to the order of." While other explanations are possible, none are realistic. To hold otherwise would, in this court's opinion, set an overly technical standard that could unexpectedly frustrate legitimate expectations of negotiability in commercial transactions.

* * *

For all the above reasons, It Is Hereby Adjudged that the promissory note which is the subject of this action is a negotiable instrument. It is further Ordered that plaintiff's motion for summary judgment is denied without prejudice to its being renewed upon the completion of discovery.

QUESTIONS

1. Discuss the concept and importance of negotiability.

2. Identify and discuss the types of commercial paper involving an order to pay.

3. Identify and discuss the types of commercial paper involving a promise to pay.

4. List and discuss the formal requirements that an instrument must meet in order to be negotiable.

5. Discuss the effect on the negotiability of an instrument of (1) the absence of a statement of consideration, (2) the absence of a statement of when the instrument is payable, (3) an undated, antedated, or postdated instrument, (4) the lack of completion of an instrument, and (5) an ambiguous instrument.

PROBLEMS

1. State whether the following provisions impair or preclude negotiability, the instrument in each instance being otherwise in proper form. Answer each statement with either the word "Negotiable" or "Non-negotiable," and explain why.

(a) A note for $2,000 payable in twenty monthly installments of $100 each, providing: "In case of death of maker all payments not due at date of death are canceled."

(b) A note stating, "this note is secured by a mortgage of even date herewith on personal property located at 351 Maple Street, Smithton, Illinois."

(c) A certificate of deposit reciting, "June 6, 1988, John Jones has deposited in the Citizens Bank of Emanon, Illinois, Two Thousand Dollars, to the credit of himself, payable upon the return of this instrument properly indorsed, with interest at the rate of 12¾ percent per annum from date of issue upon ninety days written notice. Signed, Jill Crystal, President, Citizens Bank of Emanon."

(d) An instrument reciting "I.O.U., Mark Noble, $1,000.00."

(e) A note stating "In accordance with our contract of December 13, 1991, I promise to pay to the order of Sam Stone $100 on March 13, 1992."

(f) A draft drawn by Brown on the Acme Publishing Company for $500, payable to the order of the Sixth National Bank of Erehwon, directing the bank to "Charge this draft to my royalty account."

(g) A note executed by Pierre Janvier, a resident of Chicago, for $2,000, payable in Swiss francs.

(h) An undated note for $1,000 payable "six months after date."

(i) A note for $500 payable to the order of Ray Rodes six months after the death of Albert Olds.

(j) A note of $500 payable to the assigns of Levi Lee.

2. State whether the following provisions in a note impair or preclude negotiability, the instrument in each instance being otherwise in proper form. Answer each statement with either the word "Negotiable" or "Non-negotiable" and explain why.

(a) A note signed by Henry Brown in the trade name of the Quality Store.

(b) A note for $450, payable to the order of TV Products Company, "If, but only if, the color television set for which this note is given proves entirely satisfactory to me."

(c) A note executed by Adams, Burton, and Cady Company, a partnership, for $1,000, payable to the order of Davis, payable only out of the assets of the partnership.

(d) A note promising to pay $500 to the order of Leigh and to deliver ten tons of coal to Leigh.

(e) A note for $10,000 executed by Eaton payable to the order of the First National Bank of Emanon in which Eaton promises to give additional collateral if the bank deems itself insecure and demands additional security.

(f) A note reading, "I promise to pay to the order of Richard Roe $2,000 on January 31, 1992, but it is agreed that if the crop of Blackacre falls below ten bushels per acre for the 1991 season, this note shall be extended indefinitely."

(g) A note payable to the order of Ray Rogers fifty years from date but providing that payment shall be accelerated by the death of Silas Hughes to a point of time four months after his death.

(h) A note for $4,000 calling for payments of installments of $250 each and stating, "In the event any installment hereof is not paid when due this note shall immediately become due at the holder's option."

(i) An instrument dated September 17, 1992, in the handwriting of John Henry Brown which reads in full: "Sixty days after date, I, John Henry Brown, promise to pay to the order of William Jones $500."

(j) A note reciting, "I promise to pay Ray Reed $100 on December 24, 1991."

3. On March 10, Tolliver Tolles, also known as Thomas Towle, delivered to Alonzo Craig and Abigail Craig the following instrument, written by him in pencil:

For value received, I, Thomas Towle, promise to pay to the order of Alonzo Craig or Abigail Craig One Thousand Seventy-Five ($1,000.75) Dollars six months after my mother, Alma Tolles, dies with interest at the rate of 9 percent from date to maturity and after maturity at the rate of 9¾ percent. I hereby waive the benefit of all laws exempting real or personal property from levy or sale.

Is this instrument negotiable? Explain.

4. Henry Hughes, who operates a department store, executed the following instrument:

$2,600   Chicago, March 5, 1992
On July 1, 1992, I promise to pay Daniel Dalziel, or order, the sum of Twenty-Six Hundred Dollars for the privilege of one framed advertising sign, size 24 × 36 inches, at one end of each of two hundred sixty motor coaches of the New Omnibus Company for a term of three months from May 15, 1992.

         Henry Hughes.

Is this instrument negotiable? Explain.

5. Paul agreed to lend Marsha $500. Thereupon Marsha made and delivered her note for $500 payable to Paul or order "ten days after my marriage."

Shortly thereafter Marsha was married. Is the instrument negotiable? Explain.

6. Mary employs Ann to work for her for one year from January 1, 1991, to December 31, 1991, at a salary of $800 a month payable monthly. On January 2, Mary delivers to Ann twelve promissory notes in otherwise negotiable form, maturing respectively on the last day of successive calendar months throughout the year 1991. On the first note there is the statement "For January 1991 salary"; on the second note "For February 1991 salary"; and so on for each note. On January 3, 1991, Ann sold and endorsed the twelve notes to XYZ Bank and on January 4, 1991, quit work. Are these notes negotiable? Explain.

7. For the balance due on the purchase of a tractor Henry Brown executed and delivered to Jane Jones his promissory note containing the following language:

January 1, 1992, I promise to pay to the order of Jane Jones the sum of $7,000 to be paid only out of my checking account at the XYZ National Bank in Pinckard, Illinois, in two installments of $3,500 each, payable on May 1, 1992, and on July 1, 1992, provided that if I fail to pay the first installment on the due date, the entire sum shall become immediately due. (Signed) Henry Brown.

Is the note negotiable? Explain.

8. Sam Sharpe executed and delivered to Don Dole the following instrument:

         Knoxville, Tennessee
         May 29, 1992
Thirty days after date I promise to pay Don Dole or order, Five Thousand Dollars. The holder of this instrument shall have the election to require the assignment and delivery to him of my 100 shares of Brookside Iron Works Corporation stock in lieu of the payment of Five Thousand Dollars in money.

         (Signed) Sam Sharpe.

Is this instrument negotiable? Explain.

9. Is the following instrument negotiable?

         March 1, 1991
One month from date, I, James Jimson, hereby promise to pay Edmund Edwards: Six thousand, Seven hundred Fifty ($6,750.00) dollars, plus 8¾% interest. Payment for cutting machines to be

delivered on March 15, 1991. To be charged against Garment Sales Account.

James Jimson

10. Broadway Management Corporation obtained a judgment against Briggs. The note on which the judgment was based reads in part: "<u>Ninety Days</u> after date, I, we, or either of us, promise to pay to the order of <u>Three Thousand Four Hundred Ninety Eight and 45/100</u>------------ Dollars." (The underlined words and symbols were typed in; the remainder was printed.) There were no blanks on the face of the instrument, any unused space having been filled in with hyphens. The note contains clauses permitting acceleration in the event the holder deems itself insecure and authorizes judgment "if this note is not paid at any stated or accelerated maturity." Briggs appeals, claiming that the note is not negotiable order paper. Decision?

11. Sandra and Thomas McGuire entered into a purchase and sale agreement for "Becca's Boutique" with Pascal and Rebecca Tursi. The agreement provided that the McGuires would buy the store for $75,000, with a down payment of $10,000 and the balance of $65,000 to be paid at closing on October 5, 1979. The settlement clause stated that the sale was contingent upon the McGuires obtaining a Small Business Administration loan of $65,000. On September 4, 1979, Mrs. McGuire signed a promissory note in which the McGuires promised to pay to the order of the Tursis and the Green Mountain Inn the sum of $65,000. The note specified that interest payments of $541.66 would become due and payable on the fifth days of October, November, and December 1979. The entire balance of the note, with interest, would become due and payable at the option of the holder if any installment of interest was not paid according to that schedule.

The Tursis had for several months been negotiating with Parker Perry for the purchase of the Green Mountain Inn in Stowe, Vermont. On September 7, 1979, the Tursis delivered to Perry a $65,000 promissory note payable to the order of Green Mountain Inn, Inc. This note was secured by transfer to the Green Mountain Inn of the McGuires' note to the Tursis. Subsequently, Mrs. McGuire learned that her Small Business Administration loan had been disapproved. On December 5, 1979, the Tursis defaulted on their promissory note to the Green Mountain Inn. On June 11, 1980, PP, Inc., formerly Green Mountain Inn, Inc., brought an action against the McGuires to recover on the note held as security for the Tursis' promissory note. Decision?

12. On September 2, 1976, Levine executed a mortgage bond under which she promised to pay the Mykoffs a preexisting obligation of $54,000. On October 14, 1979, the Mykoffs transferred the mortgage to Bankers Trust Co., indorsing the instrument with the words "Pay to the Order of Bankers Trust Company Without Recourse." The Lincoln First Bank, N.A., brought this action asserting that the Mykoffs' mortgage is a nonnegotiable instrument because it is not payable to order or bearer; thus it is subject to Lincoln's defense that the mortgage was not supported by consideration since an antecedent debt is not consideration. Decision?

Chapter 26

TRANSFER

Negotiation
Kinds of Indorsements
Requirements of Indorsements

THE principal advantage of commercial paper is its ease of transferability. Both negotiable and non-negotiable instruments are transferable by assignment, but only negotiable instruments can result in the transferee becoming a holder. This distinction is highly significant. If the transferee of a negotiable instrument is entitled to payment by the terms of the instrument, he is a holder of the instrument. Only holders may be holders in due course and thus entitled to greater rights in the instrument than the transferor may have possessed. These rights are discussed in the next chapter and are the reason why negotiable instruments move freely in the marketplace. This chapter discusses the methods by which commercial paper may be transferred.

NEGOTIATION

Negotiation is the transfer of a negotiable instrument in such a manner that the transferee becomes a holder. Section 3–202(1). The transfer of a non-negotiable instrument operates as an assignment as does the transfer of a negotiable instrument by a means which does not render the transferee a holder.

As discussed in Chapter 15, an **assignment** is the voluntary transfer to a third party of the rights arising from a contract.

Whether a transfer is by *assignment* or *negotiation,* the transferee acquires the rights his transferor had. Section 3–201(1). The transfer need not be for value: if the instrument is transferred as a gift, the donee acquires all the rights of the donor. If the transferor was a holder in due course, the transferee acquires the rights of a holder in due course, which rights he in turn may transfer. This rule, which is sometimes referred to as the shelter rule, existed at common law and exists under the U.C.C. The shelter rule is discussed more fully in Chapter 27.

Requirements of Negotiation

The requirements for negotiation depend upon whether the instrument is bearer paper or order paper. As noted above, negotiation is defined as a transfer such that the transferee becomes a holder. A **holder** is broadly defined in Section 1–201(20) as "a person who is in possession of an instrument drawn, issued or indorsed to him or to his order or to bearer or in blank." Accordingly, to qualify as

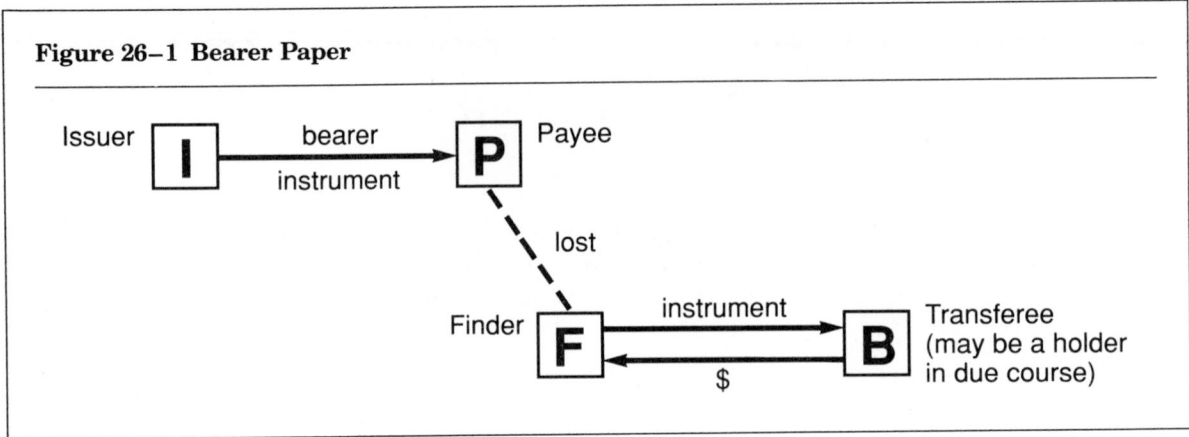

Figure 26–1 Bearer Paper

a holder a person must have possession of an instrument that runs to him.

Bearer Paper Because bearer paper (an instrument payable to bearer) runs to whoever is in possession of it, a finder or a thief of bearer paper would be a holder even though he did not receive possession by voluntary transfer. For example, P loses an instrument payable to bearer that I had issued to her. F finds it and sells and delivers it to B, who thus receives it by negotiation and is a holder. F also qualifies as a holder because he is in possession of bearer paper. As a holder, F has the power to negotiate the instrument (Section 3–301), and the transferee may be a holder in due course if he meets the Code's requirements for such a holder. See Figure 26–1 for an illustration of this example. Thus, a bearer instrument is transferred by

mere *possession* and is therefore comparable to cash.

Order Paper If the instrument is **order paper** (an instrument payable to order), both *possession* and *indorsement* (signature) by the appropriate parties are necessary for the transferee to become a holder. Figure 26–2 compares the negotiation of bearer and order paper.

Any transfer for *value* of an instrument not payable to bearer gives the transferee the specifically enforceable right to have the unqualified indorsement of the transferor, unless the parties otherwise agreed. Section 3–201(3). The parties may agree that the transfer is to be an assignment rather than a negotiation, in which case no indorsement is required. Absent such agreement, the courts presume that negotiation was intended when

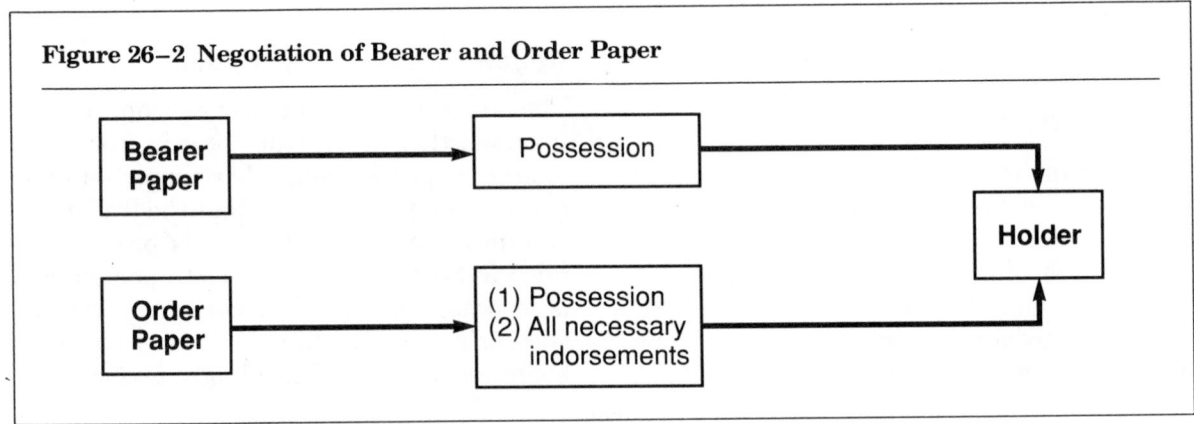

Figure 26–2 Negotiation of Bearer and Order Paper

value is given. Where a transfer is not for value, the transaction is normally not commercial in nature; thus, the courts do not make such a presumption.

Until the necessary indorsement has been supplied, the transferee has nothing more than the contract rights of an assignee. Negotiation takes effect only when a proper indorsement is made, at which time the transferee becomes a holder of the instrument.

If a customer deposits a check or other instrument for collection without properly indorsing the item, the depository bank has the right to supply any indorsement of its customer that is necessary to title unless the item contains the words "payee's indorsement required" or the equivalent. Section 4–205. In the alternative, the bank need not provide the customer's indorsement but may indicate on the item that it was deposited by the customer and credited to her account. Such an indication is effective as the customer's indorsement. Section 4–205. In either case, the bank becomes a holder.

Partial Transfer An indorsement conveying less than the entire instrument or any unpaid balance does not operate as a negotiation, but operates only as a partial assignment. Section 3–202(3). For example, an indorsement containing a direction to pay Guillan "one-half of the note" or "$500 of the note," or to pay "two-thirds to Guillan, one-third to Kittle" constitutes only a partial assignment and neither Guillan nor Kittle becomes a holder. But an indorsement "to Fisk and Fletcher" is effective as a negotiation because it transfers the entire interest to Fisk and Fletcher. Words such as "I hereby assign all my right, title, and interest in the within note" are also sufficient as a negotiation. Section 3–202(4).

Negotiations Subject to Rescission

If a negotiation conforms to the requirements discussed above, it is effective to transfer the instrument even if it is

1. made by an infant, a corporation exceeding its powers, or any other person without capacity; or

2. obtained by fraud, duress, or mistake of any kind; or

3. part of an illegal transaction; or

4. made in breach of a duty. Section 3–207(1).

Thus, a negotiation is valid even though the transaction in which it occurs is voidable or even void. For example, Margaret issues a promissory note to the order of Mustafa, a minor. Mustafa indorses the instrument to Helen. Mustafa's negotiation is effective and makes Helen a holder upon her obtaining possession. Likewise, if Mustafa had indorsed and delivered the instrument to Helen under the threat of death, Helen would nonetheless be a holder. This results from the basic principle of negotiable instruments that a transferee in possession of an instrument that by its terms runs to him is a holder.

In all of these instances, the transferor loses all rights in the instrument until he regains possession of it. The transferor's right to do so is determined by State law. This right is valid against the immediate transferee and all subsequent holders, but not against a subsequent holder in due course. Therefore, in the examples above, Mustafa would be able to reclaim the note from Helen.

INDORSEMENTS

An **indorsement** is the signature of a payee, drawee, accommodation indorser, or holder of an instrument. Revised Article 3, unlike present Article 3, provides a definition of indorsement. An indorsement is "a signature, other than that of a maker, drawer, or acceptor, that alone or accompanied by other words, is made on an instrument for the purpose of (i) negotiating the instrument, (ii) restricting payment of the instrument, or (iii) incurring indorser's liability on the instrument, but regardless of the intent of the signer, a signature and its accompanying words is an indorsement unless the accompanying words, the terms of the instrument, the place of the signature, or other circumstances unambiguously indicate that the signature was made for a purpose other than indorsement." Rev. Section 3–204.

An indorsement may be complex or simple. It may be dated and may indicate where it is made, but neither date nor place is required to be shown. The simplest type is merely the signature of the indorser. Since the indorser undertakes certain obligations, as explained later, an indorsement consisting of merely a signature may be said to be the shortest contract known to the law. A forged or otherwise unauthorized signature necessary to negotiation is inoperative and thus breaks the chain of title to the instrument. Section 3–404(1).

The type of indorsement used in negotiating an instrument affects its subsequent negotiation. Every indorsement is (1) either blank or special, (2) either restrictive or nonrestrictive, and (3) either qualified or unqualified. These indorsements are not mutually exclusive. Indeed, all indorsements may be sorted into three of these six categories because all indorsements disclose three things: (1) the method to be employed in making subsequent negotiations (this depends upon whether the indorsement is blank or special); (2) the kind of interest that is being transferred (this depends upon whether the in-

dorsement is restrictive or nonrestrictive); and (3) the liability of the indorser (this depends upon whether the indorsement is qualified or unqualified). For instance, an indorser who merely signs her name on the back of an instrument is making a blank, nonrestrictive, unqualified indorsement. See Figure 26–3 for further illustrations.

Revised Article 3 identifies an additional type of indorsement—an anomalous indorsement. An anomalous indorsement is "an indorsement made by a person that is not the holder of the instrument." Rev. Section 3–205(d). The only effect of an anomalous indorsement is to make the signer liable on the instrument as an indorser. An anomalous indorsement does not affect the manner in which the instrument may be negotiated.

The effectiveness of an indorsement as well as the rights of the transferee and transferor depend upon whether the indorsement meets the formal requirements of indorsements. This section will cover the different kinds of indorsements and the formal requirements of each.

Blank Indorsements

A **blank indorsement** is one specifying no indorsee and may consist of merely the signature of the indorser or her authorized agent. Section 3–204(2). A blank indorse-

Figure 26–3 Indorsements

Indorsement	Type of Indorsement	Interest Transferred	Liability of Indorser
1. "John Doe"	Blank	Nonrestrictive	Unqualified
2. "Pay to Richard Roe, John Doe"	Special	Nonrestrictive	Unqualified
3. "Without recourse, John Doe"	Blank	Nonrestrictive	Qualified
4. "Pay to Richard Roe in trust for John Roe, without recourse, John Doe"	Special	Restrictive	Qualified
5. "For collection only, without recourse, John Doe"	Blank	Restrictive	Qualified
6. "Pay to XYZ Corp., on the condition that it delivers goods ordered this date, John Doe"	Special	Restrictive	Unqualified

ment converts order paper into bearer paper and leaves bearer paper as bearer paper. Thus, an instrument indorsed in blank may be negotiated by delivery alone without further indorsement. Hence, the holder should treat it with the same care as cash. *See Palmer & Ray Dental Supply of Abilene, Inc. v. First Nat'l. Bank.*

Special Indorsements

A **special indorsement** specifically designates the person to whom or to whose order the instrument is to be payable (order paper). Section 3–204(1). Thus, if Peter, the payee of a note, indorses it "Pay to the order of Andrea," or even "Pay Andrea," the indorsement is special because it names the transferee. Words of negotiability—payable to order or bearer—are *not* required in an indorsement. Thus, an indorsement reading "Pay Edward" is interpreted as meaning "Pay to the order of Edward." Any further negotiation of the instrument would require Edward's indorsement. *See Casarez v. Garcia.*

Moreover, a holder of an instrument with a blank indorsement may protect himself by converting the blank indorsement to a special indorsement by writing over the signature of the indorser any contract consistent with the character of the indorsement. For example, on the back of a negotiable instrument appears the blank indorsement "Sally Seller." Harry Holder, who received the instrument from Seller, may convert this bearer instrument into order paper by inserting above Seller's signature "Pay Harry Holder" or other similar words.

Restrictive Indorsements

As the term implies, a **restrictive indorsement** attempts to restrict the rights of the indorsee in some fashion. The Code defines four types of indorsements as restrictive: conditional indorsements, indorsements prohibiting further transfer, indorsements for deposit or collection, and indorsements in trust. Section 3–205. An **unrestrictive indorse-**

ment does not attempt to restrict the rights of the indorsee.

Conditional Indorsements A conditional indorsement is one by which the indorser makes the rights of the indorsee subject to the happening or non-happening of a specified event. Suppose Marcin makes a note payable to Parker's order. Parker indorses it "Pay Rodriguez, but only if the good ship Jolly Jack arrives in Chicago harbor by November 15, 1991." If Marcin had used this language in the instrument, it would be non-negotiable because her promise to pay must be unconditional to satisfy the formal requisites of negotiability. But indorsers *are* permitted to condition the rights of their indorsees without destroying negotiability.

If the good ship Jolly Jack does not arrive in Chicago harbor by November 15, 1991, Rodriguez has no rights in the instrument. If he presents the instrument to Marcin for payment, Marcin must dishonor the instrument or be required to pay it again to Parker. Marcin is not discharged when she pays an instrument which has been restrictively indorsed, unless she pays in a manner consistent with the indorsement. Section 3–603(1)(b).

Revised Article 3 nullifies the effect of conditional indorsements by providing that an indorsement that states a condition to the right of a holder to receive payment is ineffective to condition payment. Rev. Section 3–206(b).

Indorsements Prohibiting Further Transfer An indorsement may by its express terms attempt to prohibit further transfer, such as an indorsement stating, "Pay Tom Thomas only." Such indorsements, or any other purporting to prohibit further transfer, are designed to be a restriction on the rights of the indorsee. To remove any doubt as to the effect of such a provision, the Code provides that *no* restrictive indorsement prevents further transfer or negotiation of the instrument. Section 3–206(1). As a result of this provision, an indorsement which purports to *prohibit* further transfer of the instrument is given the same effect as an unrestricted indorsement.

Indorsements for Deposit or Collection

The most frequently used form of restrictive indorsement is that designed to place the instrument in the banking system for deposit or collection. Indorsements of this type include "for collection," "for deposit," and "pay any bank." Such an indorsement *effectively limits* further negotiation to those consistent with its limitation and puts all nonbanking persons on notice as to who has a valid interest in the paper. Compare *Fultz v. First Nat'l Bank in Graham* with *Palmer & Ray Dental Supply of Abilene, Inc. v. First National Bank.*

Indorsements in Trust

Another common kind of restrictive indorsement is that in which the indorser creates a trust for the benefit of himself or others. If an instrument is indorsed "Pay Thelma in trust for Barbara" or "Pay Thelma for Barbara" or "Pay Thelma for account of Barbara" or "Pay Thelma as agent for Barbara," Thelma is a fiduciary, subject to liability for any breach of her obligation to Barbara. Trustees commonly and legitimately sell trust assets, and as a consequence, a trustee has power to negotiate an instrument. The first taker under an indorsement to her in trust (Thelma in the above examples) is under the duty to pay or apply all funds given by her consistently with the indorsement or risk having to pay twice. Section 3–206(4). Subsequent indorsees or transferees are not bound by such indorsement *unless* they have knowledge that the trustee negotiated the instrument for her own benefit or otherwise in breach of her fiduciary duty.

Qualified Indorsements

Unqualified indorsers promise that they will pay the instrument according to its terms at the time of their indorsement to the holder or to any subsequent indorser who pays the instrument. Section 3–414(1). In short, an unqualified indorser guarantees payment of the instrument if certain conditions are met.

An indorser may disclaim her liability on the contract of indorsement, but only if the indorsement so declares and the disclaimer is written on the instrument. The customary manner of disclaiming an indorser's liability is to add the words **"without recourse,"** either before or after her signature. A "without recourse" indorsement is called a **qualified** indorsement. A qualified indorsement, however, does not eliminate all liability of an indorser. As discussed in Chapter 28, a qualified indorsement does disclaim contract liability but it does not remove the warranty liability of the indorser, although it slightly modifies transferor's warranties. A qualified indorsement and delivery is a negotiation and transfers legal title to the indorsee, but the indorser does *not* guarantee payment of the instrument. A qualified indorsement does not destroy negotiability or prevent further negotiation of the instrument. For example, assume that an attorney receives a check payable to her order in payment of a client's claim. She may indorse the check to the client without recourse, thereby disclaiming liability as a guarantor of payment of the check. The qualified indorsement plus delivery would transfer title to the client.

Formal Requirements of Indorsements

Place of Indorsement An indorsement must be written on the instrument or on a paper, called an **allonge,** so firmly affixed to the instrument as to become a part of it. The use of an allonge is required when there are so many indorsements that there is no room for additional signatures or when the indorsement is too lengthy to fit on the instrument. A purported indorsement on a separate piece of paper, clipped or pinned to the instrument, is not valid, whereas a piece of paper stapled to the instrument generally is valid. *See Adams v. Madison Realty & Development, Inc.*

Customarily, indorsements are made on the back or reverse side of the instrument, starting at the top and continuing down. Under Federal Reserve Board guidelines, indorsements of checks must be in appropriate color ink such as blue or black and must be made within 1-½ inches of the trailing (left) edge of the back of the check. (See Figure 26–4.) The remaining space is reserved for bank indorsements. Nevertheless, failure to comply with the guidelines does not destroy negotiability and there are no penalties for violation of the standard.

The order of the indorsement and the liability of indorsers, unless otherwise agreed, is presumed to be the order in which their sig-

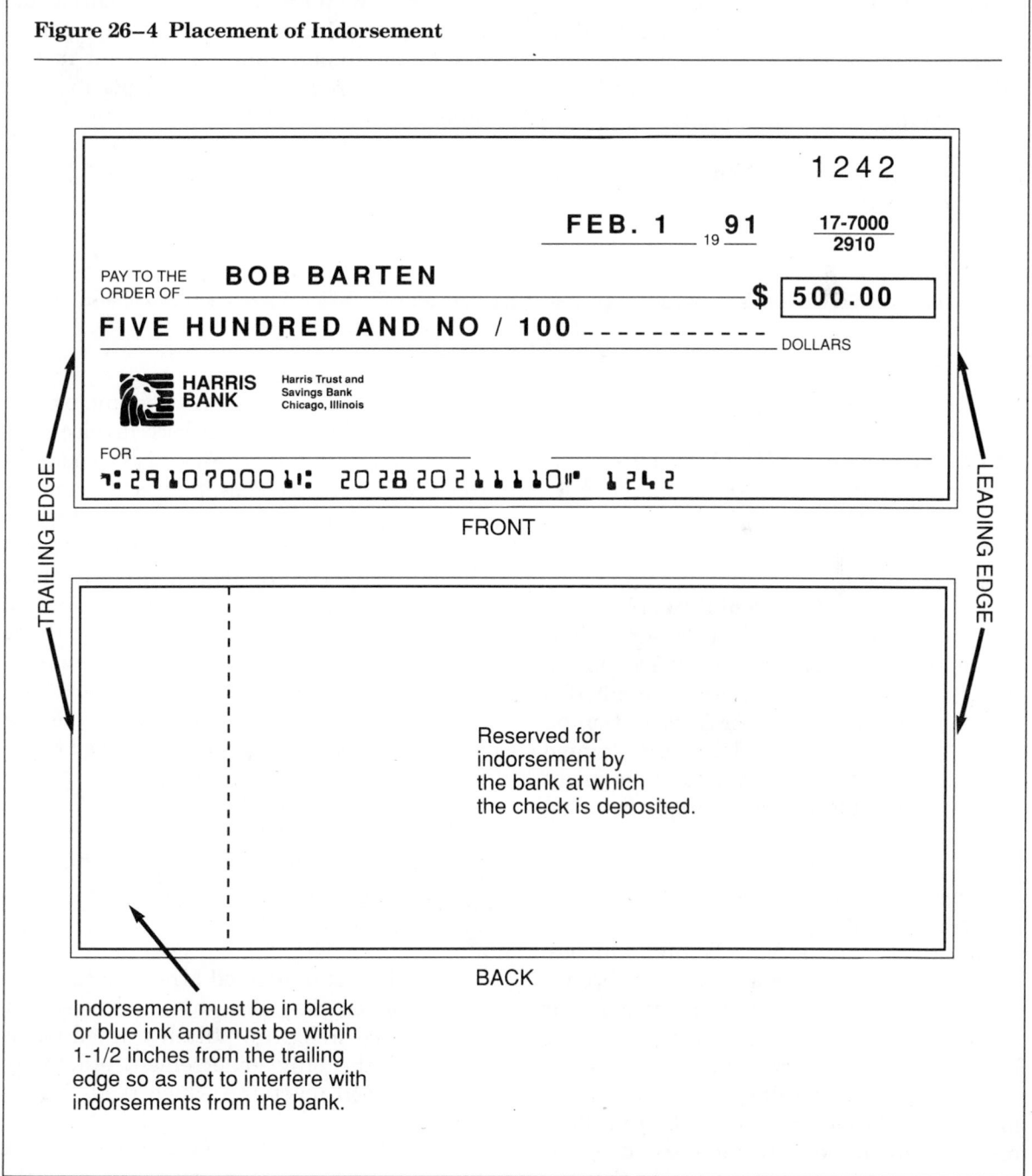

Figure 26–4 Placement of Indorsement

1 2 4 2

FEB. 1   19 91   17-7000 / 2910

PAY TO THE ORDER OF   **BOB BARTEN** $ 500.00

FIVE HUNDRED AND NO / 100 - - - - - - - - - - DOLLARS

HARRIS BANK   Harris Trust and Savings Bank Chicago, Illinois

FOR

⑂:2910 7000 ⑈:   20 2B 20 2 ⑈⑈⑈10‖"   1 242

FRONT

TRAILING EDGE

LEADING EDGE

Reserved for indorsement by the bank at which the check is deposited.

BACK

Indorsement must be in black or blue ink and must be within 1-1/2 inches from the trailing edge so as not to interfere with indorsements from the bank.

natures appear. Section 3–414(2). Occasionally, however, a signature may appear on an instrument in such a way that it is impossible to tell with certainty the nature of the liability undertaken by the signer. In such an event, the Code specifies the signer is to be treated as an indorser. Section 3–402. In keeping with the rule that a transferee must be able to determine her rights from the face of the instrument, the person who signed in an ambiguous capacity may not introduce parol evidence to establish that she intended to be something other than an indorser.

Incorrect or Misspelled Indorsement   If the name of the payee or indorsee is mis-

spelled, or is a name different from the holder, as for example, a trade name, he may indorse the instrument in that name or in his own or both. Section 3–203. A check payable to "Crescent Pizza Palace," a sole proprietorship, may be quite properly indorsed by the owner in either his own name, John Doe, or in that of his business, Crescent Pizza Palace. To assure the highest degree of security and to facilitate subsequent negotiation, a person paying or giving value for such an instrument may require indorsement in both names. Section 3–203.

CASES

Blank Indorsements

PALMER & RAY DENTAL SUPPLY OF ABILENE, INC. v. FIRST NAT'L BANK
Court of Civil Appeals of Texas, 1972.
477 S.W.2d 954.

WALTER, J.

. . . Palmer and Ray Dental Supply Company of Abilene, Inc. filed suit against First National Bank of Abilene for conversion of the proceeds of thirty-five checks presented to the Bank by its bookkeeper Mrs. Wilson on which she received cash. The court granted the Bank's motion for summary judgment and Palmer and Ray Dental Supply have appealed.

* * *

James Frank Ray, President and manager of the dental supply company testified substantially as follows: Mrs. Wilson was employed as our office manager. In February 1970, our auditor found a discrepancy in our inventory and we started looking for the leak. After we had worked on it for about two weeks, Mrs. Wilson called me one Saturday night and told me she would like to talk to me. I met her at the office and she told me she had been stealing by cashing checks that she

was supposed to deposit. She was employed to answer the phone, take orders, invoice merchandise, order merchandise and to perform the general office duties. She also made deliveries and looked after the internal workings of the office. We do a credit business and the customers pay by check. I generally take the checks from the mail and place them in Mrs. Wilson's desk and she deposited them. We try to do our banking business everyday. She made out the deposit slips in our office. At the time Mrs. Wilson was working for us we had a rubberstamp which we used to endorse our checks. The stamp read:

Palmer & Ray Dental Supply
Inc. of Abilene
Box 2894
3110 B N. 1st
Abilene, Texas 79603

I authorized and directed Mrs. Wilson to endorse the checks with this rubber stamp. During the time Mrs. Wilson worked for us this was the only endorsement stamp we used. We had no stamp which read "for deposit only".

Most of the time she would go to the bank in our van. All deposits were made at the

First National Bank and she would bring the deposit slips back to the office. She made the deposits about 75% of the time.

* * *

In its trial petition appellant alleges that Mrs. Wilson made the deposits for it at First National Bank but instead of depositing the thirty-five checks which are listed in appellant's petition as she was instructed to do, she drew cash on them and did not account to the company for such money. It further alleged: "and by means of an unauthorized endorsement by said Dinah Wilson, the defendant First National paid cash to the *plaintiff* (Mrs. Wilson?) for the amount of the checks". It further alleged that by giving Mrs. Wilson cash instead of depositing the checks to its account the Bank converted its funds. Its cause of action against the Bank was predicated on the theory of wrongful conversion.

Section 3–204, Tex. Uniform Commercial Code, defines a blank endorsement as one that specifies no particular endorsee and may consist of a mere signature. Section 3–205 of the U.C.C. defines a restrictive endorsement to include one that uses the words "for deposit". Section 1.201(43), U.C.C., defines an unauthorized signature or endorsement as one made without actual implied or apparent authority and includes a forgery.

The summary judgment proof establishes that each of the checks has affixed thereto the blank rubber stamp endorsement of the appellant. We hold that such blank endorsement constitutes an authorized endorsement. When the Bank delivered cash to Mrs. Wilson instead of depositing the proceeds from the checks to appellant's account, the Bank was not guilty of conversion [wrongdoing]. [Citation].

The judgment is affirmed.

Special Indorsements

CASAREZ v. GARCIA

Court of Appeals of New Mexico, 1983.
99 N.M. 508, 660 P.2d 598.

DONNELLY, J.

The plaintiffs filed suit against the Garcias and the Estate of Oakley P. Guillory, deceased, alleging that the defendants had breached a written contract to properly construct a home for them in Jemez Springs. The first amended complaint asserted that Blas Garcia falsely represented he was acting through a licensed contractor, and that, after commencing the construction, defendants Blas Garcia and Guillory performed the work in a negligent and unworkmanlike manner so that the project was "red-tagged" and halted by state building inspectors. * * *

The plaintiffs also alleged for their cause of action against the Bank that the defendants Garcia and Guillory conspired to defraud plaintiffs with a false loan for $25,000 and to wrongfully deprive plaintiffs of the loan proceeds. Plaintiffs alleged they specially indorsed a cashier's check owned by them to Albuquerque Fence Company and that Blas Garcia forged the company's name thereon. Plaintiffs further allege that the Bank wrongfully and negligently failed to make adequate inquiry or investigation before making payment of the cashier's check in the sum of $25,000. Plaintiffs allege the check was signed by Blas Garcia, without authorization, on behalf of Albuquerque Fence Company and the instrument was then fraudulently delivered to Cecil Garcia, who presented it to the Bank for payment.

* * *

Following a jury trial, the trial court granted the Bank's motion for directed verdict against the plaintiffs.

The single issue raised by the plaintiffs on appeal challenges the propriety of the trial court's order granting a directed verdict in favor of the Bank. The plaintiffs contend that the Bank negligently cashed a cashier's check in the sum of $25,000 without properly investigating the indorser and without requiring a proper indorsement.

* * *

Plaintiffs contend that Blas Garcia represented to them that he was a representative of Albuquerque Fence Company and that relying upon such representation they entered into a written contract dated July 4, 1979, with the company with the understanding that the company would construct a home for them in Jemez Springs for the sum of $48,875.66, plus tax. Blas Garcia later introduced the plaintiffs to Cecil Garcia who agreed to make a loan to plaintiffs to be used as a down payment under the construction contract.

George Martinez, Sr., the president of Albuquerque Fence Company, testified that his company was a domestic corporation and had never been licensed as a general contractor in New Mexico. He further testified that neither Blas Garcia nor Cecil Garcia were ever officers or directors of the corporation or in any way affiliated or employed by it. Albuquerque Fence Company makes no claim to the check.

As shown by the record, Cecil Garcia obtained a $25,000 loan from the Bank in the form of a $25,000 cashier's check payable to himself. Cecil Garcia took the check to a title company, arranged to loan $25,000 to the plaintiffs, and obtained a promissory note from them to evidence this indebtedness. Cecil Garcia then indorsed the cashier's check: "Pay to the order of Lucy N. Casarez, Cecil Garcia". Upon delivery of the check to Lucy Casarez, she indorsed the check: "Pay to the order of Albuquerque Fence Co., Lucy N. Casarez". Lucy Casarez then handed the check to Blas Garcia. Blas Garcia testified that after obtaining the check from Lucy Casarez, he followed the instructions of Cecil Garcia and indorsed the check: "Alb. Fence Co." Thereafter, Blas Garcia gave the check to Cecil Garcia, who signed his own name under the words "Alb. Fence Co." and later presented the check to the Bank in exchange for $5,000 in cash and four $5,000 cashier's checks.

The plaintiffs contend that the language placed on the check by Lucy Casarez, "Pay to the order of Albuquerque Fence Co.", preceding her signature constituted a special indorsement and that the check could be further negotiated only by a proper indorsement by an authorized representative of the company. Because of the special indorsement,

plaintiffs argue, the action of the Bank in cashing the check without investigating or verifying the authority of Cecil Garcia to negotiate the check on behalf of Albuquerque Fence Company was sufficient to raise an issue as to negligence on the part of the Bank. The plaintiffs further assert that the writing of the words "Alb. Fence Co." by Blas Garcia and the signature thereafter by Cecil Garcia amounted to an unauthorized signature or indorsement which invalidated the lawful negotiation of the check and rendered the Bank liable to the plaintiffs for the amount of the check.

* * *

Since the plaintiff Lucy Casarez specially indorsed the cashier's check "Pay to the order of Albuquerque Fence Co., Lucy N. Casarez," and purportedly without authority, Blas Garcia placed the indorsement of "Alb. Fence Co." thereon, the indorsement, if unauthorized, was inoperative to pass title to the instrument to Cecil Garcia. A special indorsement specifies to whom or to whose order it makes the instrument payable; it becomes payable to the order of the special indorsee and may be further negotiated only by his indorsement. [U.C.C.] § 3–204. As stated in the Official Comment to U.C.C. § 3–204, "The principle here adopted is that a special indorser, as the owner even of a bearer instrument, has the right to direct the payment and to require the indorsement of his indorsee as evidence of the satisfaction of own obligation." Under the Uniform Commercial Code, a "person" includes an individual or an organization. § 1–201(30).

* * *

As between the plaintiff Lucy Casarez, and Cecil Garcia, the plaintiff remained the owner of the check until the designated special indorsee indorsed the instrument. The unauthorized signature of the special indorsee rendered that signature inoperative under § 3–404(1) and prevented the further negotiation of the check since negotiation requires the proper indorsement of all special indorsees.

As noted in [citation], "when a bank pays on an instrument bearing a forged indorsement, the owner of the instrument may sue the drawee . . . or drawer. . . ." The plaintiff as the true owner of the cashier's check had a right to bring an action for conversion or negligence against the Bank as drawee when it paid on the unauthorized indorsement of Albuquerque Fence Company. § 3–419(1)(c) [citation].

* * *

The order granting a directed verdict in favor of the Bank was error.

Indorsements for Deposit or Collection

FULTZ v. FIRST NAT'L BANK IN GRAHAM

Supreme Court of Texas, 1965.
388 S.W.2d 405.

STEAKLEY, J.

This suit was brought by W.B. Fultz, Petitioner here, against the First National Bank in Graham, Respondent, to recover the sum of $13,060.00 representing "less cash" sums, in amounts ranging between $50.00 and $300.00, paid by the bank to Mrs. Fern McCoy, an employee of Fultz, in "for deposit only" transactions to the account of Fultz over a period of time between February, 1960, and April, 1963. The sums so paid to Mrs. McCoy were misappropriated to her personal use. Mrs. McCoy had not signed a signature card at the bank and was not authorized by Fultz either to check on his account or to withhold cash amounts from the deposits made for him. The full endorsement which was stamped on each of the checks read: "Pay to the order of the First National Bank, Graham, Texas—For deposit only—W.B. Fultz."

Both parties moved for summary judgment and the trial court granted the motion of Fultz. The Court of Civil Appeals held that the alleged negligence on the part of Fultz in not examining his bank statements and other records and discovering the defalcations so as to notify the bank would, if found to be true, constitute a defense to his suit against, the bank. Consequently, that Court held that in these respects there were issues of fact to be determined by the trier of facts

and the summary judgment for Fultz was improper. . . . We reverse the judgment of the Court of Civil Appeals and affirm that of the trial court.

The key to the first problem is the undisputed fact that the bank violated the written instructions of Fultz, and hence breached its deposit contract with him in each deposit transaction. In the exercise of care by Fultz, all of the checks which were deposited were endorsed "For Deposit Only." This was an unqualified direction to the bank to place the full amount of the checks to the account of Fultz. This instruction was violated when part of the amount of the checks was paid to Mrs. McCoy in cash. The bank had knowledge of its acts in violation of the instruction. Fultz as a depositor had the right to rely on the bank to honor the "For Deposit Only" instructions he had established as the regular deposit routine for his employee and the bank to follow; he was under no duty to exercise further care to ascertain if the bank had followed his instructions, and it is not asserted that Fultz had actual knowledge that the bank had not done so. The instruction carried in the restricted endorsement, "For Deposit Only," if followed, afforded absolute protection to both the bank and the depositor in the check deposit transactions and would have rendered the misappropriations impossible. The bank was in no way misled. Fultz had not filed a signature card for his defalcating employee and had not authorized his employee to sign checks on his account or make cash withdrawals in connection with deposits to his account. The "For Deposit Only" endorsements in the latter transactions were positively to the contrary. The decisions which consider the question of the liability of a bank for the payment of forged checks recognize the principle stated by the Supreme Court of the United States . . . that "If the bank's officers, before paying forged or altered checks, could by proper care and skill have detected the forgeries, then it cannot receive a credit for the amount of these checks, even if the depositor omitted all examination of his account."

So it is here. The Respondent bank had only to exercise proper care by following the specific instructions of Fultz, the depositor, the doing of this required no skill. Its course of action in failing to do so resulted in liability to Fultz "even if" he "omitted all examination of his account." This distinguishes the decisions in the cases which are premised upon a duty of the depositor to examine his statements from the bank, which examination would have revealed the defalcations. [Citations.]

* * *

Since Fultz owed no duty to the bank to examine his bank statements and other records, he was, for that reason, not guilty of negligence in not doing so, and in not discovering the defalcations of his employee. For the same reason he is not estopped to assert the liability of the bank. There existed no genuine issue of fact between the parties in such respects.

The judgment of the Court of Civil Appeals is reversed and that of the trial court is affirmed.

Place of Indorsement

ADAMS v. MADISON REALTY & DEVELOPMENT, INC.

United States Court of Appeals, Third Circuit, 1988.
6 UCC Rep. Serv. 2d 732.

WEIS, J.

The district court entered summary judgments in favor of the purported indorsee of promissory notes. . . . The issue presented on this appeal is whether a good faith purchaser is a holder in due course of promissory notes containing indorsements on separate sheets of paper loosely inserted within each note. We answer in the negative and will vacate the judgments.

The saga of this litigation is extensive and quite complicated. However, the question certified to us is narrow, and the essential facts are easily summarized.

Plaintiffs executed promissory notes in payment for investments in Madison Part-

nerships, a series of tax shelters formed to acquire and operate residential real estate properties. Each of the promissory notes were made payable to one of three originator banks: Tri-County Savings & Loan Association of New Jersey, Community Federal Savings & Loan Association of Connecticut, and First Northern Cooperative Bank of New Hampshire. After a series of transfers, the notes came into the possession of defendant Empire of America Federal Savings Bank.

Charging fraud in connection with the investment scheme, plaintiffs filed suit against numerous defendants who allegedly participated in the wrongdoing. Also named as a defendant was Empire, from whom plaintiffs sought rescission of the notes now in the bank's possession. The discrete issue before us is the legal effect of purported indorsements not physically attached to the notes.

* * *

The promissory notes are each two-page, fold-over documents. The front page names the originator bank and sets forth the repayment schedule. The reverse side contains printed agreement conditions and signature lines. Inserted loosely within the fold, lacking any physical attachment to the note, are two sheets of paper containing purported indorsements, the last of which is the transfer . . . to Empire. * * *

The district court acknowledged that the use of a separate, unattached sheet of paper to carry the indorsements failed to comply with Uniform Commercial Code § 3–202(2), which reads: "An indorsement must be written by or on behalf of the holder and on the instrument or on a paper so firmly affixed thereto as to become a part thereof." [UCC] § 3–202.

The court commented that the object of this statutory provision was "to protect subsequent purchasers from the risk that the present holder or a previous holder has negotiated the instrument to someone outside the apparent chain of title through a separate document." In view of this purpose, the court reasoned, even if the indorsee had been exposed to some risks, "that is no reason to absolve the notemakers, who are in no way injured by the use of an unattached indorsement, or their obligations."

The court observed that the makers of the notes in this case were not threatened with double liability because there "is no reasonable basis to fear that there are other indorsees to the notes in question other than Empire." Failure to properly attach the indorsements, therefore, was excused as "hypertechnical." * * *

Whether a separate, unattached indorsement page can constitute a proper indorsement of a negotiable instrument is a question of state law. The parties concede there is no controlling precedent in any of the three relevant jurisdictions, but each state has adopted the Uniform Commercial Code. The briefs have not cited any case recounting facts close to those presented here, nor has our independent research uncovered any such authority. We are left, therefore, largely to the wording of the Code itself.

Article 3 of the Uniform Commercial Code incorporated many portions of its predecessor, the Uniform Negotiable Instruments Law (NIL), drafted in 1896 by the National Conference of Commissioners on Uniform State Laws. * * * When it was transplanted into the 1956 draft of the Uniform Commercial Code, the indorsements provision was altered in only a minor respect. Section 31 of the NIL had specified that a proper indorsement "must be written on the instrument itself or upon a paper attached thereto." The Code substituted the words "so firmly affixed as to become a part thereof" for the phrase "upon a paper attached thereto."

Indorsement constitutes one step in the process of establishing the highly advantageous position of holder in due course, a status which cuts off certain defenses of previous parties to the instrument and which offers a procedural means for obtaining a judgment on the note promptly and inexpensively. See U.C.C. § 3–305. As a condition for conferring this privileged position, the Code not unreasonably imposes a number of prerequisites. * * *

In explaining the requirement that the indorsement be on or firmly affixed to the instrument, the Official Comment states that the Code "follows decisions holding that a purported indorsement on a mortgage or other separate paper pinned or clipped to an instrument is not sufficient for negotiation. The indorsement must be on the instrument itself or on a paper intended for the purpose which is so firmly affixed to the instrument as to become an extension or part of it. Such a paper is called an allonge." U.C.C. § 3–202 Official Code Comment (3).

We may assume, without actually deciding, that the loose indorsement sheets accompanying Empire's notes would have been valid allonges had they been stapled or glued to the notes themselves. [Citation.] Nevertheless, the fact remains that the indorsement sheets here were not physically attached to the instruments in any way, and thus patently fail to comply with the explicit Code prerequisite. Conceding the requirement's formalistic nature, we explore the arguments in support of its enforcement here.

The Code's requirement that an indorsement be "firmly affixed" to its instrument is a settled feature of commercial law, adopted verbatim by every American state, the District of Columbia, and the Virgin Islands. * * *

When the drafters of the Uniform Commercial Code replaced the term "attached" in the NIL with the phrase "firmly affixed," they intended to make the use of allonges more difficult. [Citations.] Courts have advanced two justifications for the firmly-affixed requirement. The California Court of Appeals reasoned that the provision serves to prevent fraud, remarking that a signature innocently placed upon an innocuous sheet of paper could be fraudulently attached to a negotiable instrument in order to stimulate [sic] an indorsement. [Citation.]

The affixation requirement has also been cited for its utility in preserving a traceable chain of title, thus furthering the Code's goal of free and unimpeded negotiability of instruments. Nearly a century ago, the Supreme Court of Georgia declared it "indispensably necessary" that negotiable instruments "should carry within them the indicia by which their ownership is to be determined; otherwise, their value as a circulating medium would be largely curtailed, if not entirely destroyed." [Citation.] * * *

Defendant here argues that these considerations warrant enforcement of the requirement only against those persons who acquire the notes after issuance, not against the makers who undertook to repay the amount loaned by the bank. This argument overlooks the rights which pass to an indorsee. Through effective negotiation, the indorsee becomes a holder, acquiring the authority to discharge the obligation on the note by accepting payment. See U.C.C. § 3–301. Until the maker pays a holder, he will not be discharged from his obligation. Thus, "if the primary party pays an instrument bearing an improper indorsement, he will not have paid a holder, and the true owner of the instrument may recover against the primary party." [Citation.]

From the maker's standpoint, therefore, it becomes essential to establish that the person who demands payment of a negotiable note, or to whom payment is made, is the duly qualified holder. Otherwise, the obligor is exposed to the risk of double payment, or at least to the expense of litigation incurred to prevent duplicative satisfaction of the instrument. These risks provide makers with a recognizable interest in demanding proof of the chain of title. Consequently, plaintiffs here, as makers of the notes, may properly press defendant to establish its holder status.

* * * Notwithstanding these concerns, defendant maintains that mere "clerical oversight" should not obscure its right to recover as a holder in due course on notes it purchased for value. There is some equitable appeal to this line of reasoning, but overriding considerations militate against it.

* * *

When interpreting the attachment requirement, the courts "have been of one mind" that the lack of an indorsing signature on the instrument itself, or on a sheet "firmly affixed" to the instrument, is fatal to holdership. [Citations.] * * *

Where the state courts, the scholarly commentators, and the unambiguous language of the statute all admit of but one result, only an overwhelming equitable ground would warrant a departure from what is unquestionably settled law. Absent such a circumstance, the Code's express goal of national uniformity must prevail. See U.C.C. § 1–102(2).

* * *

At this stage of the litigation, we cannot anticipate what course the bank may choose to follow in light of our decision here, nor can we predict the responses defendant may interject. We hold only that, on the present state of the record, Empire is not entitled to the status of a holder in due course.

The judgments in favor of Empire will be vacated and the case remanded for further proceedings consistent with this opinion.

QUESTIONS

1. Distinguish among (1) transfer, (2) negotiation, and (3) assignment.

2. What is necessary to become a holder of an instrument?

3. Distinguish between a blank and a special indorsement.

4. Distinguish between a qualified and an unqualified indorsement.

5. Discuss the various types of restrictive indorsements.

PROBLEMS

1. Roy Rand executed and delivered the following note to Sue Sims: "Chicago, Illinois, June 1, 1991; I promise to pay to Sue Sims or bearer, on or before July 1, 1991, the sum of $7,000. This note is given in consideration of Sim's transferring to the undersigned title to her 1988 Buick automobile. (signed) Roy Rand." Rand and Sims agreed that delivery of the car be deferred to July 1, 1991. On June 15, Sims sold and delivered the note, without indorsement, to Karl Kaye for $6,200. What rights, if any, has Kaye acquired?

2. Lavinia Lane received a check from Wilmore Enterprises, Inc., drawn on the Citizens Bank of Erehwon, in the sum of $10,000. Mrs. Lane indorsed the check "Mrs. Lavinia Lane for deposit only, Account of Lavinia Lane," placed it in a "Bank by Mail" envelope addressed to the First National Bank of Emanon, where she maintained a checking account, and placed the envelope over a tier of mailboxes in her apartment building along with other letters to be picked up by the postman the next day.

Flora Fain stole the check, went to the Bank of Omaha, where Mrs. Lane was unknown, represented herself to be Lavinia Lane, and cashed the check. Has Bank of Omaha taken the check by negotiation? Why or why not?

3. What types of indorsements are the following:

(a) "Pay to Monseen without recourse."

(b) "Pay to Allinore for collection."

(c) "I hereby assign all my rights, title, and interest in this note to Fullilove in full."

(d) "Pay to the Southern Trust Company."

(e) "Pay to the order of the Farmers Bank of Nicholasville for deposit only."

Indicate whether the indorsement is (1) blank or special, (2) restrictive or nonrestrictive, and (3) qualified or unqualified.

4. Explain whether the following transactions result in a valid negotiation:

(a) Arnold gives a negotiable check payable to bearer to Betsy without indorsing it.

(b) Golden indorses a negotiable, promissory note payable to the order of Golden, "Pay to Chambers and Rambis, (signed) Golden."

(c) Porter lost a negotiable check payable to his order. Kersey found it and indorsed the back of the check: "Pay to Drexler, (signed) Kersey."

(d) Thomas indorsed a negotiable promissory note payable to the order of Thomas, "(signed) Thomas," and delivered it to Sally. Sally then wrote above Thomas's signature, "Pay to Sally."

5. Alpha issues a negotiable check to Beta payable to the order of Beta in payment of an obligation Alpha owed Beta. Beta delivers the check to Gamma without indorsing it in exchange for 100 shares of General Motors stock owned by Gamma. How has Beta transferred the check? What rights, if any, does Gamma have against Beta?

6. Melvin executed and delivered to Dawkins a negotiable promissory note payable to the order of Dawkins as payment for 100 bushels of wheat Dawkins had sold to Melvin. Dawkins indorsed the note "Pay to Hersey only, (signed) Dawkins" and sold it to Hersey. Hersey then sold the note to Smith after indorsing it "Pay to Smith, (signed) Hersey." What rights, if any, does Smith acquire in the instrument?

7. Simon Sharpe executed and delivered to Ben Bates a negotiable promissory note payable to the order of Ben Bates for $500. Bates indorsed the note, "Pay to Carl Cady upon his satisfactorily repairing the roof of my house, (signed) Ben Bates," and delivered it to Cady as a downpayment on the contract price of the roofing job. Cady then indorsed the note and sold it to Timothy Tate for $450. What rights, if any, does Tate acquire in the promissory note?

8. Debbie Dean issued a check to Betty Brown payable to the order of Cathy Cain and Betty Brown. Betty indorsed the check "Payable to Elizabeth East, (signed) Betty Brown." What rights, if any, does Elizabeth acquire in the check?

9. Triplett attempted to arrange a $2,850,000 loan through Meyer Rabin and his Consumer's Investment Company (CIC). CIC issued a commitment letter conditioned on the payment of a $14,250 commitment fee and the personal guarantee of C. D. Wyche. Triplett sought an additional loan from E. S. Tubin to cover the commitment fee. Tubin agreed to provide the $14,250 if the money would be "safe" pending the closing of the $2,850,000 loan and if he would receive $4,500 for the use of his money. Triplett agreed, and Tubin purchased a $14,250 cashier's check payable to Melvin Rueckhaus, his attorney. Rueckhaus typed the following indorsement on the back of the check: "PAY TO THE ORDER—CONSUMERS INVESTMENT CO. and CHARLES D. WYCHE, SR . . ."

Rabin presented the check to Fair Park National Bank for immediate credit to CIC's account. Not knowing that Wyche's signature had been forged by Rabin, the bank complied, and Rabin subsequently depleted CIC's account. The loan was never closed, and the $14,250 was never returned to Tubin. Tubin then brought this suit against Fair Park National Bank. Decision?

10. The drawer Commercial Credit Corporation issued two checks payable to Rauch Motor Company. Rauch indorsed the checks in blank, deposited them to its account in University National Bank and received a corresponding amount of money. The Bank stamped "pay any bank" on the checks and initiated collection. However, the checks were dishonored and returned to the Bank with the notation "payment stopped." Rauch, through subsequent deposits, repaid the bank. Later, to compromise a lawsuit, the Bank executed a special two-page indorsement of the two checks to Lamson. Lamson then sued the Corporation for the face value of the checks, plus interest. The Corporation contends that Lamson was not a holder of the checks because the indorsement was not in conformity with the UCC in that it was stapled to the checks. Decision?

Chapter 27

HOLDER IN DUE COURSE

Requirements
Holder in Due Course Status
Preferred Position
Limitations upon Rights

THE unique and most significant aspect of negotiability is the concept of the holder in due course. While a mere holder acquires a negotiable instrument subject to all claims and defenses to it, a holder in due course, *except* in *consumer* credit transactions, takes the instrument free of all claims of other parties and free of all defenses to the instrument except for a very limited number specifically set forth in the Code. The law has conferred this preferred position upon the holder in due course in order to encourage the free negotiability of commercial paper by minimizing the risks assumed by an innocent purchaser of the instrument. The transferee of a negotiable instrument wants payment for it; he does not want to be subject to any dispute between the obligor and the obligee (generally the original payee). This chapter discusses the requirements of becoming a holder in due course and the benefits conferred upon a holder in due course.

REQUIREMENTS OF A HOLDER IN DUE COURSE

To acquire the preferential rights of a holder in due course, a person must meet the re-

quirements of Section 3–302 of the Code or must "inherit" these rights under the shelter rule, Section 3–201 (discussed later in this chapter). To satisfy the requirements of Section 3–302, a transferee must

1. be a holder of a negotiable instrument;

2. take it for value;

3. take it in good faith; and

4. take it without notice
    (a) that it is overdue or has been dishonored, or
    (b) of any defense against or claim to it on the part of any person.

Figure 27–1 illustrates the various requirements of becoming a holder in due course and the consequence of meeting or not meeting these requirements.

Holder

In order to become a holder in due course, the transferee must first be a holder. A holder is a person who is in possession of a negotiable instrument (1) issued to his order, (2) issued to bearer, (3) indorsed to him, or (4) indorsed in blank. In other words, a holder is a person

Figure 27–1 Rights of Transferees

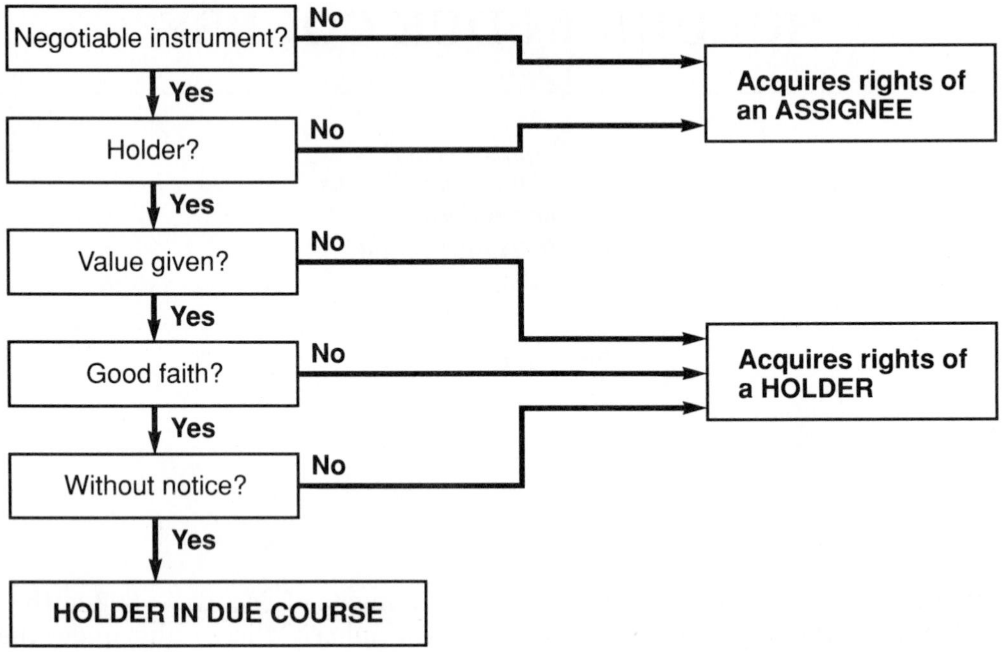

Negotiable instrument? — **No** → **Acquires rights of an ASSIGNEE**

↓ **Yes**

Holder? — **No** → **Acquires rights of an ASSIGNEE**

↓ **Yes**

Value given? — **No** → **Acquires rights of a HOLDER**

↓ **Yes**

Good faith? — **No** → **Acquires rights of a HOLDER**

↓ **Yes**

Without notice? — **No** → **Acquires rights of a HOLDER**

↓ **Yes**

HOLDER IN DUE COURSE

who has both possession of an instrument and all necessary indorsements. Whether or not the holder is the owner of the instrument, he may transfer it, negotiate it, enforce payment of it (subject to valid claims and defenses), or with certain exceptions, discharge it. Section 3–301.

The significance of being a holder is brought out in the following factual situation, which is illustrated in Figure 27–2.

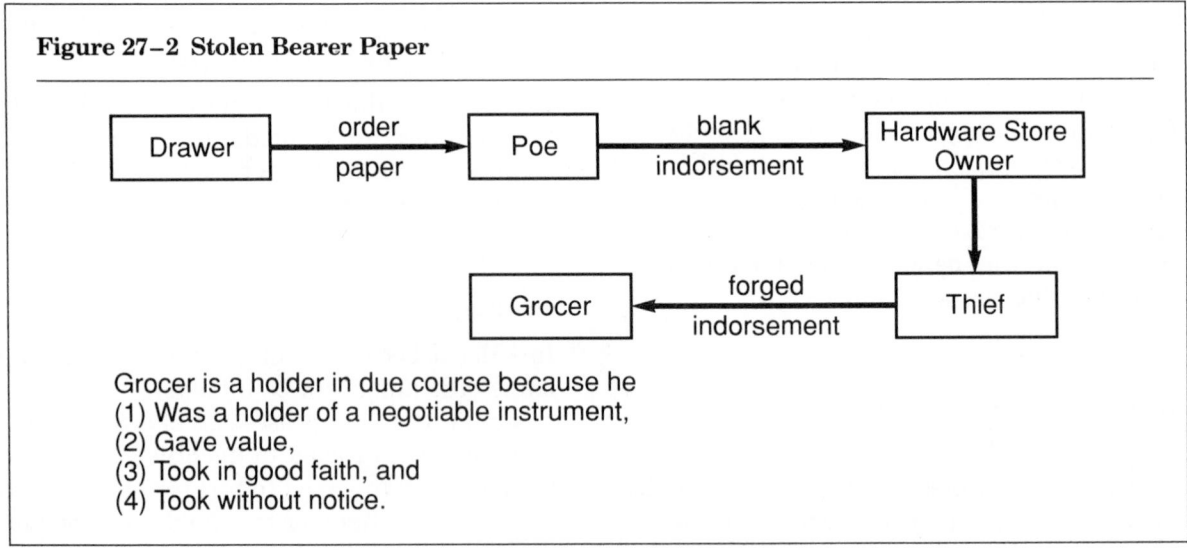

Figure 27–2 Stolen Bearer Paper

Drawer → *order paper* → Poe → *blank indorsement* → Hardware Store Owner

Hardware Store Owner ↓

Grocer ← *forged indorsement* ← Thief

Grocer is a holder in due course because he
(1) Was a holder of a negotiable instrument,
(2) Gave value,
(3) Took in good faith, and
(4) Took without notice.

Poe indorsed her paycheck in blank and cashed it at a hardware store where she was a well-known customer. Shortly thereafter, a burglar stole the check from the hardware store. The owner of the hardware store immediately notified Poe's employer who gave the drawee bank a stop payment order (an order not to pay the instrument). The burglar indorsed the check in a false name and transferred it to a grocer who took it in good faith and for value. The check was dishonored (not paid) when presented to the drawee bank. The paycheck became bearer paper when Poe indorsed it in blank. It retained this character in the hands of the owner of the hardware store, in the hands of the burglar, and in the hands of the grocer, who became a holder in due course even though he had received it from a thief who had indorsed it with a false name. Because an indorsement is not necessary to the negotiation of bearer paper, the forged indorsement was immaterial. The thief was a "holder" of the check within the definition of Section 1–201(20) and under Section 3–301 a holder may negotiate an instrument "whether or not he is the owner." Accordingly, one who, like the grocer, takes from a holder for value, in good faith, and without notice, becomes a holder in due course. Furthermore, in the absence of a real defense, discussed later in this chapter, the grocer will be entitled to payment from the drawer.

This rule does not apply to a stolen order instrument. In the above example, assume that the thief had stolen the paycheck from Poe prior to indorsement. The thief then forged Poe's signature and transferred the check to the grocer who again took it in good faith, for value, and without notice. Negotiation of an order instrument requires a valid indorsement by the person to whose order the instrument is payable, in this case Poe. A forged indorsement is not valid. Consequently, the grocer has not taken the instrument with all necessary indorsements, and, therefore, he could not be a holder or a holder in due course. The grocer's only recourse would be to collect the amount of the check from the thief. Figure 27–3 illustrates this example.

Value

The law requires a holder in due course to give value. An obvious case of failure to give value is where the holder makes a gift of the instrument to a third person.

The concept of value in the law of negotiable instruments is not the same as that of consideration under the law of contracts. **Value,** for purposes of negotiable instruments, is defined as: (1) the actual *performing* of the agreed consideration (executory promises are excluded since they have not been performed); (2) the acquiring of a security in-

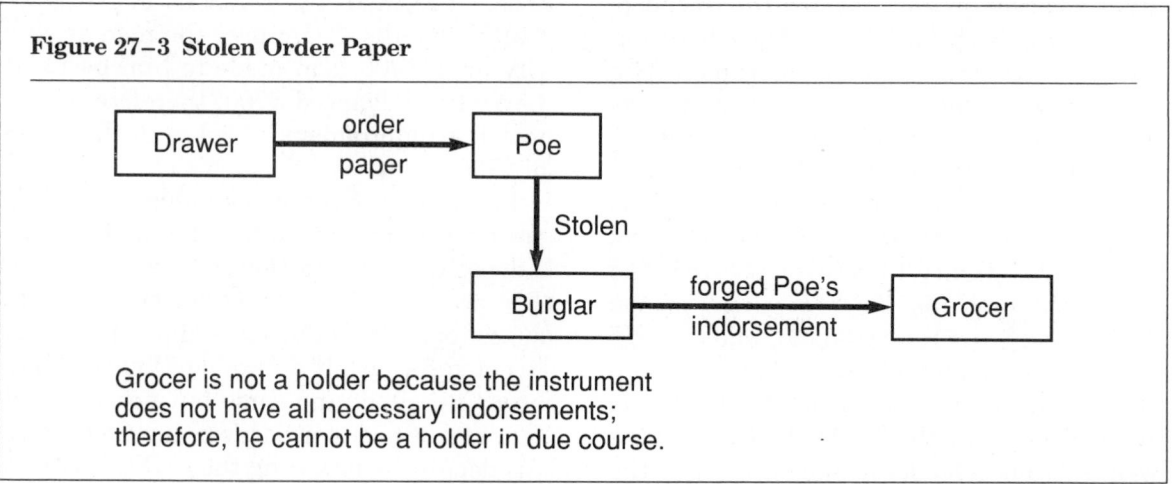

Figure 27–3 Stolen Order Paper

Drawer → order paper → Poe

Poe → Stolen → Burglar

Burglar → forged Poe's indorsement → Grocer

Grocer is not a holder because the instrument does not have all necessary indorsements; therefore, he cannot be a holder in due course.

terest or a consensual lien on the instrument; (3) the taking of the instrument in payment of or as security for an antecedent debt; (4) the giving of a negotiable instrument; or (5) the giving of an irrevocable commitment to a third party. Section 3–303.

Executory Promise An executory promise, clearly valid consideration to support a contract, is *not* the giving of value to support holder in due course status because it has not been performed. A purchaser of a note or draft who has not yet given value may rescind the transaction if she learns of a defense to the instrument. A person who has given value, however, cannot do this and therefore needs the protection given to a holder in due course.

For example, Mike executes and delivers a $1,000 note payable to the order of Pat, who negotiates it to Henry who promises to pay Pat for it a month later. During the month, Henry learns that Mike has a defense against Pat. Henry can rescind the agreement with Pat and return or tender the note back to her. This makes him whole. He has no need to cut off Mike's defense. Assume, on the other hand, that Henry has paid Pat for the note before he learns of Mike's defense. Henry may not be able to recover his money from Pat so Henry needs the holder in due course protection, which permits him to recover on the instrument from Mike.

A holder therefore takes an instrument for value to the extent that the agreed consideration has been *given*, provided the consideration was given prior to the holder's learning of any defense or claim to the instrument. *See Korzenik v. Supreme Radio, Inc.* Assume that in the previous example Henry had agreed to pay Pat $900 for the note. If Henry had paid Pat $600, he could be a holder in due course to the extent of $600 (a number of courts would allow Henry to recover $666.67: the $600 paid plus his *pro rata* share of the discount—$\frac{600}{900} \times 100 or 66.67), and if a defense were available, it would be valid against him only to the extent of the balance. When Henry paid the $300 balance to Pat, he would become a holder in due course as to the full $1,000 face value of the note, provided

payment was made prior to Henry's discovery of Mike's defense. If the $300 payment was made after discovery of the defense or claim, Henry would be a holder in due course only to the extent of $600 (or possibly $666.67). A holder in due course, to give value, is not required to pay the face amount of the instrument, but only the amount he agreed to pay. Section 3–303(a).

The Code provides an exception to the executory promise rule in two situations: (1) the giving of a negotiable instrument and (2) the making of an irrevocable commitment to a third party. Section 3–303(c). Suppose that Molly issues a note for $1,000 payable to the order of Preston, which Preston indorses and delivers to Hillary. Hillary gives her personal check for $1,000 in exchange for it. Hillary met the requirement of giving value for the note when she gave Preston her check, not when the check was paid by the drawee bank. Hillary's check is considered value because it may be negotiated to a holder in due course whom Hillary would have to pay. Value would likewise be given if Hillary made any other irrevocable commitment, if the commitment was to a *third party* rather than to Preston.

Security Interest Where an instrument is given as security for an obligation, the lender is regarded as having given value to the extent of his security interest. Sections 3–302(4) and 3–303(a). For example, Pedro is the holder of a $1,000 note payable to his order, executed by Monica, and due in twelve months. Pedro uses the note as security for a $700 loan made to him by Larry. Larry has advanced $700; therefore, he has met the requirement of value to the extent of $700.

Likewise, a *bank* gives value when a depositor is allowed to withdraw funds against a deposited item. Sections 4–208 and 4–209. The provisional or temporary crediting of a depositor's account (discussed in Chapter 29) is not sufficient. If a number of checks have been deposited, and some but not all of the funds have been withdrawn, the Code traces the deposit by following the "FIFO" or "first-in, first-out" method of accounting.

Antecedent Debt Under general contract law, an antecedent debt (preexisting obligation), is not sufficient consideration to support a promise to pay the debt or a lesser amount in full satisfaction. Under Section 3–303(b) of the Code, however, a holder gives value when she takes an instrument in payment of or as security for an antecedent debt. Thus, Martha makes and delivers a note for $1,000 to the order of Penny. Penny indorses the instrument and delivers it to Howard in payment of an outstanding debt of $970 which Penny owes Howard. Howard has given value. *See St. Paul Fire and Marine Ins. Co. v. State Bank of Salem.*

Good Faith

The Code defines **good faith** as "honesty in fact in the conduct or transaction concerned." Section 1–201(19). The test is **subjective:** it measures good faith by what the purchaser knows or believes. He may be empty-headed, but if his heart is pure, he can pass muster on good-faith grounds. Under this test, if the purchaser were actually innocent, he is held to have bought the instrument in good faith, even though a prudent person under the circumstances would have known that something was wrong. Buying an instrument at a discounted price does not demonstrate lack of good faith.

Revised Article 3 eliminates the subjective standard of good faith and adopts an objective standard. Revised Section 3–103(4) defines good faith as "honesty in fact and the observance of reasonable commercial standards of fair dealing." This objective definition is comparable to the definition of good faith applicable to *merchants* under Article 2.

Lack of Notice

To become a holder in due course, a holder must also take the instrument without notice that it is (1) overdue, (2) dishonored, or (3) subject to any claim or defense. Notice of any of these matters should alert the purchaser that she may be buying a lawsuit and therefore should not be accorded the favored position of a holder in due course. **Notice** is de-

fined in Section 1–201(25) as: "A person has 'notice' of a fact when (a) he has actual knowledge of it; or (b) he has received a notice or notification of it; or (c) from all the facts and circumstances known to him at the time in question he has reason to know that it exists." The first two clauses of this definition impose a wholly subjective standard. The last clause provides a partially objective one: the fact that suspicious circumstances are present does not adversely affect the purchaser, unless he has reason to recognize them as suspicious. Since the applicable standard is "actual notice," "notice received," or "reason to know," constructive notice through public filing or recording is not of itself sufficient notice to prevent a person from being a holder in due course.

To be effective, notice must be received at such a time and way that will give the recipient a reasonable opportunity to act on it. Section 3–304(6).

Notice an Instrument Is Overdue To be a holder in due course, the purchaser must take the instrument without notice that it is overdue. This requirement is based on the idea that overdue paper conveys a suspicion that something is wrong. **Time paper** is due on its stated due date if the stated date is a business day or, if not, on the next business day. Thus, if an instrument is payable on July 1, a purchaser cannot become a holder in due course by buying it on July 2, provided that July 1 was a business day. In the case of an installment note, or of several notes issued as part of the same transaction with successive specified maturity dates, the purchaser has notice that an instrument is overdue if he has reason to know that any part of the principal amount is overdue or that there is an uncured default in payment of another instrument of the same series. Section 3–304(3)(a).

Demand paper is overdue for purposes of preventing one from becoming a holder in due course if the purchaser has notice that she is taking it after demand had been made or after it has been outstanding an unreasonable length of time. Section 3–304(3)(c). Although the Code does not state what constitutes a reasonable time, in the case of a demand note, it is usually about sixty days. The time is somewhat shorter for drafts. The Code also provides that for checks a reasonable time is *presumed* to be thirty days after issuance, but this presumption is rebuttable. Thus, the particular situation, business custom, and other relevant factors must be considered in making the determination: no hard-and-fast rules are possible.

Acceleration clauses have caused problems. If an instrument's maturity date has been accelerated, the holder may be unaware that it is past due. A prospective purchaser may also be unaware of this fact and may qualify as a holder in due course, unless she has reason to know that the acceleration has occurred. Section 3–304(3)(b).

Notice an Instrument Has Been Dishonored **Dishonor** is the refusal to pay or accept an instrument when it has become due. If a transferee has notice that an instrument has been dishonored, he cannot become a holder in due course. For example, if a person takes a check stamped "NSF" (not sufficient funds) or "no account," then she has notice of dishonor and will not be a holder in due course.

Notice of a Claim or Defense A purchaser of an instrument cannot become a holder in due course if he purchases it with notice of a defense or claim to it. A **defense** to an instrument is a justification or shield protecting a person from liability on it, whereas a **claim** to an instrument is an assertion of ownership of it. Defenses to negotiable instruments are discussed below. Claims to negotiable instruments are generally made by a person contending that he is the rightful owner of the instrument. Claims may be made against thieves, finders, or possessors with voidable or void title. In many instances, both a defense and a claim will be involved. For example, Donna is fraudulently induced to issue a check to Pablo. Donna has a claim to ownership of the instrument as well as a defense to Pablo's demand for payment.

A purchaser has notice of a claim or defense if the instrument is so incomplete, bears such visible evidence of forgery or alteration, or is otherwise so irregular as to call its validity into question. Section 3–304(1)(a). For example, Donna draws a check on the First National Bank for $100, payable to the order of Pamela. Pamela crudely raises the amount of the check to $1,000 and negotiates it to Howard. Howard cannot be a holder in due course. He is charged with information which he can learn from the face of the instrument. The instrument is irregular, and the alteration is so obvious that Howard would be held to have notice of it. Nonetheless, as shown in *St. Paul Fire and Marine Ins. Co. v. State Bank of Salem,* courts differ greatly as to how irregular an alteration must be for a holder to have notice of it.

It is unclear under Section 3–304(1) whether the claim or defense must be related to the irregularity or incompleteness which gave notice of that claim or defense. Revised Article 3 eliminates this ambiguity by providing that a party may become a holder in due course only if the instrument "does not bear such apparent evidence of forgery or alteration or is not otherwise so irregular or incomplete as to call into question its authenticity." Rev. Section 3–302(a)(1). According to the comments to this section, the term "authenticity" is used to make it clear that the irregularity or incompleteness must indicate that the instrument may not be what it purports to be. The revision takes the position that persons who purchase such instruments should do so at their own risk and should not be protected against defenses of the obligor or claims of prior owners.

Suppose, however, there is an obvious change on the face of the instrument that does not indicate wrongdoing. For instance, the date is changed from January 2, 1991 to January 2, 1992, on an instrument issued on January 2, 1992. It would be reasonable to assume that the drawer, out of force of habit, wrote "1991" rather than "1992." This would not be considered a material alteration that would give notice of a defense or claim.

A purchaser has notice of a claim or defense if the purchaser has notice that the obligation of any party is **voidable** or that *all* parties to the instrument have been discharged. Section 3–304(1)(b). An obligation by a party that is **void** is a real defense and, as discussed below, may be asserted against any transferee, including a holder in due course. The fact that the holder knows that one or more but not all the parties have been discharged does not prevent the holder from being a holder in due course with respect to the non-discharged parties. For example, Macon issues a negotiable promissory note to Percival, who indorses it in blank and delivers it to Adams. The instrument then passes by blank indorsements to Busjia, Crenshaw, and Dearborn. Dearborn strikes out Crenshaw's indorsement and negotiates it for value to Houghton. Houghton would have notice that Crenshaw's liability had been discharged. This would not prevent Houghton from being a holder in due course with respect to Macon, Percival, Adams, Busjia, and Dearborn because their liability is not discharged. Section 3–304(1) applies only when a purchaser has notice that all the parties have been discharged.

In addition, a purchaser has notice of a claim when he has knowledge that a fiduciary has used the instrument for his own benefit or otherwise in breach of his fiduciary duty. Section 3–304(2). The purchaser's knowledge that the person negotiating the instrument is or was a fiduciary is not notice of a claim or defense; there must also be knowledge of the improper conduct by the fiduciary. Section 3–304(4)(e).

Buying an instrument at a discount less than face value does not mean that the buyer had notice of any defense or claim against the instrument. Nonetheless, an unusually large discount may be construed by a court to indicate notice of a claim or defense.

Section 3–304(4) provides a listing of facts the knowledge of which does not of itself give the purchaser notice of a defense or claim. Subparagraph (4)(a) provides that knowledge of the fact that the instrument is antedated or postdated does not of itself give the purchaser notice of a defense or claim. This accords with Section 3–114(1) that antedating or postdating does not affect negotiability. Subparagraph (b) of Section 3–304(4) provides that the mere fact that the purchaser of an instrument knows that it was originally given or negotiated for an executory promise or was accompanied by a separate agreement does not of itself give notice of a defense or claim, unless he knows that the promise has not been kept. Subparagraph (c) states that mere knowledge of the fact that one party has signed for the accommodation of another does not give the purchaser notice of any claim or defense. Subparagraph (d) provides that knowledge of the fact that an incomplete instrument has been completed does not of itself constitute notice of a defense or claim unless the purchaser also has knowledge that the completion was improper.

HOLDER IN DUE COURSE STATUS

A holder who meets the requirements discussed in the previous section obtains the preferred position of holder in due course status. This section discusses the question of whether a payee may become a holder in due course. It also addresses the rights of a transferee from a holder in due course—the shelter rule. Finally, it identifies those special circumstances that prevent a transferee from acquiring holder in due course status.

A Payee May Be a Holder in Due Course

The Code provides that a payee may be a holder in due course. Section 3–302(2). This does not mean that the payee will always be a holder in due course but merely that he *may* if he satisfies all the requirements for a holder in due course. For example, if a seller delivers goods to a buyer and accepts a current check in payment, the seller will be a holder in due course if he acted in good faith and had no notice of defenses or claims. The seller, however, takes the check *subject* to all claims and defenses because a holder in due course takes the instrument free of defenses only as to persons with whom he had *not* dealt. Section 3–305(2).

In some situations, the payee is not an immediate party to the transaction and therefore will not be subject to any claims and most defenses if he meets the requirements of a holder in due course. In each of the situations, there are three parties involved in the transaction, and the defense exists between the parties other than the payee. *See John Deere Co. v. Boelus State Bank.* For example, after purchasing goods from Punky, Robin fraudulently obtains a check from Clem payable to the order of Punky and forwards it to Punky. Punky takes it for value and without any knowledge that Robin had defrauded Clem into issuing the check. In such a case, the payee, Punky, is a holder in due course and takes the instrument free and clear of Clem's defense of fraud in the inducement.

The Shelter Rule

Through operation of the **shelter rule,** the transferee of an instrument acquires the *same* rights in the instrument as the transferor had. Section 3–201. Therefore, even if a holder does not comply with all the requirements for being a holder in due course, she, nevertheless, acquires all the rights of a holder in due course if some previous holder of the instrument had been a holder in due course. For example, Prosser induces Mundheim, by fraud in the inducement, to make a note payable to her order and then negotiates it to Henn, a holder in due course. After the note is overdue, Henn gives it to Corbin, who has notice of the fraud. Corbin is not a holder in due course, since he has taken the instrument when overdue, did not pay value, and has notice of Mundheim's defense. Nonetheless, through the operation of the shelter rule Corbin acquires Henn's rights as a holder in due course, and Mundheim cannot successfully assert his defense against Corbin. The purpose of the shelter provision is not to benefit the transferee but to assure the holder in due course a free market for commercial paper he acquires.

The shelter rule, however, provides that a transferee (1) who has himself been a party to any fraud or illegality affecting the instrument or (2) who as a prior holder had notice of a claim or defense cannot wash the paper clean by later *reacquiring* it from a subsequent holder in due course or person having the rights of one. For example, Parker induces Miles, by fraud in the inducement, to make an instrument payable to the order of Parker. Parker subsequently negotiates the instrument to Henson, a holder in due course, and later reacquires it from Henson. Parker does not succeed to Henson's rights as a holder in due course and remains subject to the defense of fraud.

Special Circumstances Denying Holder in Due Course Status

In keeping with the theory that the purpose of negotiability is to facilitate the flow of commerce, when an instrument is acquired in a way other than the ordinary flow of commerce, there is no reason to accord the transferee holder in due course status. Section 3–302(3) defines the situations to which this rule applies:

A holder does not become a holder in due course of an instrument:
(a) by purchase of it at judicial sale or by taking it under legal process; or
(b) by acquiring it in taking over an estate; or
(c) by purchasing it as a part of a bulk transaction not in regular course of business of the transferor.

In each of these situations, the transferee takes under unusual circumstances which indicate she is merely a successor in interest to the prior holder. As such, she should acquire no better rights. If her transferor was a holder in due course, however, under the shelter provision of Section 3–201, the transferee acquires the rights of a holder in due course.

THE PREFERRED POSITION OF A HOLDER IN DUE COURSE

In a **nonconsumer transaction** a holder in due course takes the instrument (1) free from all *claims* on the part of any person, and (2) free from all *defenses* of any party with whom he has not dealt except for a limited number of defenses that are available against anyone, including a holder in due course. Such defenses are referred to as **real defenses,** as opposed to defenses which may not be asserted against a holder in due course, which are referred to as **personal** or **contractual defenses.**

Real Defenses

The real defenses available against **all** holders, including holders in due course, are

1. minority, to the extent that it is a defense to a simple contract, Section 3–305(2)(a);

2. any other incapacity, duress, or illegality of the transaction that renders the obligation void, Section 3–305(2)(b);

3. fraud in the execution, Section 3–305(2)(c);

4. discharge in insolvency proceedings, Section 3–305(2)(d);

5. any other discharge of which the holder has notice when he takes the instrument, Section 3–305(2)(e);

6. unauthorized signature, Section 3–404; and

7. material alteration, Section 3–407.

Minority All States have a firmly entrenched public policy of protecting minors from persons who might take advantage of them through contractual dealings. The Code does not state when minority is available as a defense or the conditions under which it may be asserted. Rather, it provides that minority is a defense available against a holder in due course to the extent that it is a defense to a contract under the laws of the State involved. See Chapter 13.

Void Obligations Where the obligation on an instrument originates in such a way that under the law of the State involved it is *void,* the Code authorizes the use of this defense against a holder in due course. This follows from the fact that where the party was never obligated, it is unreasonable to permit an event over which he has no control—negotiation to a holder in due course—to convert a nullity into a valid claim against him.

Incapacity, duress, and illegality of the transaction are defenses that may render the obligation of a party voidable or void, depending upon the law of the State involved as applied to the facts of a transaction. To the extent the obligation is rendered void (duress by physical force, person under guardianship, some illegal contracts) the defense may be asserted against a holder in due course. To the extent it is voidable, which is generally the case, the defense (other than minority, discussed above) is not effective against a holder in due course. *See Bankers Trust Co. v. Litton Systems, Inc.*

Fraud in the Execution Fraud in the execution of the instrument renders the instrument void and therefore is a defense valid against a holder in due course. The Code describes this type of fraud as misrepresentation that induced the party to sign the instrument with neither knowledge nor reasonable opportunity to obtain knowledge of its character or its essential terms. For example, Francis is asked to sign a receipt and does so without realizing or having the opportunity of learning that her signature is going on a promissory note cleverly concealed under the receipt. Francis's signature has been obtained by fraud in the execution, and Francis would have a valid defense against a holder in due course.

Discharge in Insolvency Proceedings If a party's obligation on an instrument is discharged in a bankruptcy or any other insolvency proceeding, he has a valid defense in any action brought against him on the instrument, including one by a holder in due course. Thus, a debtor whose obligation on a negotiable instrument is discharged in an insolvency proceeding is relieved of payment, even to a holder in due course.

Discharge of Which the Holder Has Notice Any holder, including a holder in due course, takes the instrument subject to *any* discharge of which she has notice when she takes the instrument. As previously noted, if a holder acquires an instrument with notice that *all* prior parties have been discharged, she cannot become a holder in due course. Section 3–304(1)(b). If only some, but not all, of the parties to the instrument have been discharged, the purchaser can still become a holder in due course. The discharged parties, however, have a real defense against a holder in due course who had notice of their discharge. For example, Harris, who is in possession of a negotiable instrument, strikes out the indorsement of Jones. The instrument is subsequently negotiated to Stephen, a holder in due course. Jones has a real defense against Stephen.

Unauthorized Signature A person's signature on an instrument is unauthorized when it is made without express, implied, or apparent authority. A person whose signature is unauthorized or forged cannot be held liable on the instrument in the absence of estoppel or ratification, even if the instrument is negotiated to a holder in due course. He has not made a contract. Similarly, if Joan's signature were forged on the back of an instrument, Joan could not be held as an indorser. Joan has not made a contract. Thus, any unauthorized signature is totally invalid as that of the person whose name is signed unless she ratifies it or is precluded from denying it; the unauthorized signature operates only as the signature of the unauthorized signer. Section 3–404(1).

A person may be **estopped** or prevented from asserting a defense because his conduct in the matter has caused reliance by a third party to his loss or damage. Suppose Neal's son forges Neal's name to a check, which the drawee bank cashes. When the returned check reaches Neal, he learns of the forgery. Rather than subject his son to trouble, possibly criminal prosecution, Neal says nothing. Thereafter, Neal's son continues to forge checks and cashes them at the drawee bank. The bank may be suspicious of the signature, but the fact that Neal has not complained may induce it to believe that the signatures are proper. Finally, Neal does complain, seeking to compel the bank to recredit his account for all the forged checks. Neal will not succeed because he is estopped by his conduct from denying that his son had authority to sign his name.

A party is similarly precluded from denying the validity of his signature if his **negligence** substantially contributes to the making of the unauthorized signature. The most obvious case is that of the drawer who makes use of a mechanized or other automatic signing device and is negligent in safeguarding it. In such an instance, the drawer would not be permitted to assert the unauthorized signature as a defense against a holder in due course.

An unauthorized signature may be **ratified** and thereby become valid so far as its effect as a signature. Thus, Kathy forges Laura's indorsement on a promissory note and negotiates it to Allison. Laura subsequently ratifies Kathy's act. As a result, Kathy is no longer liable to Allison on the note although Laura is liable. Nonetheless, Laura's ratification does *not* relieve Kathy from civil liability to Laura, nor does it in any way affect Kathy's criminal liability for the forgery.

Material Alteration Any alteration that changes the contract of any party to the instrument in any way is a material alteration. Against any person *other* than a subsequent holder in due course

1. an alteration by the holder which is *both* fraudulent and material discharges any party whose contract is thereby changed, unless that party assents or is precluded from asserting the defense;

2. no other alteration discharges any party, and the instrument may be enforced according to its original tenor (that is, its terms as initially written) or, if an incomplete instrument, according to the authority given to the holder by the issuing party. Section 3–407(2).

A subsequent holder in due course may always enforce the instrument according to its original tenor, and when an incomplete instrument has been completed, she may enforce it as completed. Section 3–407(3).

An alteration is material only as it changes the contract of a party to the instrument; therefore, the addition or deletion of words which do not in any way affect the contract of any previous signer is not material. For example, where there is a discrepancy between words and figures on a check, the words being "twenty-five hundred dollars" and the figures "$25," a change of the figures to $2,500 is not a material change because words control figures. But even a slight change in the *contract* of a party is a material alteration; the addition of one cent to the amount payable or an advance of one day in the date of payment will operate as a discharge if it is fraudulent.

Where an instrument contains blanks or is otherwise incomplete, it may be completed in accordance with the authority given and is then valid and effective as completed. If, however, the completion is unauthorized and has the effect of changing the contract of any previous signer, it is considered a material alteration.

A material alteration does not discharge any party unless it is made for a *fraudulent* purpose. Thus, there is no discharge where a blank is filled in the honest belief that it is as authorized. Likewise, if the alteration is not material, there is no discharge, and the instrument may be enforced according to its original tenor. Where blanks are filled or an incomplete instrument is otherwise completed, there is no original tenor, but the instrument may be enforced according to the authority actually given.

Thus, a party is discharged from liability on a negotiable instrument to any holder other than a holder in due course by an alteration if the alteration is (1) made by a holder, (2) with fraudulent intent, and (3) is material. If any of these requirements are not met, no party is discharged, and a holder may recover the original tenor of the altered instrument or the authorized amount where the instrument was incomplete. In keeping with the preferential position accorded a holder in due course, he may enforce any altered instrument according to its original terms and may enforce an incomplete instrument as completed. See Figure 27–4.

Material alterations frequently are made possible by the *negligent* manner in which the instrument is drawn or made. Suppose that Maria makes a note, writing it out in pencil. A party increases the amount. Against a holder in due course *or* other good-faith payor, Maria will be precluded from raising the defense of material alteration because her own negligence allowed the alteration. Section 3–406. Assent to an alteration given before or after it is made also prevents the party from asserting the defense. The following illustrates the operation of these rules.

1. M executes and delivers a note to P for $2,000, which P subsequently indorses and transfers to A for $1,900. A intentionally and skillfully increases the note to $20,000 and then negotiates it to B who takes it in good faith and without notice of any wrongdoing for $19,000. B is a holder in due course and, therefore, can collect the original amount of the note ($2,000) from M or P and the full amount ($20,000) from A, less any amount paid by the other parties.

2. Assume the facts in (1) except that B is not a holder in due course. M and P are both discharged by A's fraudulent and material alteration. B's only recourse is against A for the full amount ($20,000).

3. Assume the facts in (1) except that A steals the note from P before P indorsed the instrument. After altering the instrument, A forges P's signature and transfers the note to B. A is not a holder, and therefore B can be neither a holder nor a holder in due course. P is entitled to recover the instrument or its value from B or anyone in possession of it. Moreover, because A was not a holder, his alteration of the instrument does not discharge M. Therefore, if P recovers the note he may enforce it against M.

4. M issues his blank check to P, who is to complete it when the exact amount is deter-

mined. P fraudulently fills in $4,000 when the correct amount should be $2,000. P then negotiates the check to T. If T is a holder in due course, she can collect the amount as completed ($4,000) from either M or P. If T is not a holder in due course, however, she has no recourse against M but may recover the full amount ($4,000) from P.

5. Assume the facts in (4) except that P filled in the amount of $4,000 in good faith. No party is discharged from liability on the instrument because the alteration was not fraudulent. If T is not a holder in due course, M is liable for the correct amount ($2,000). If T is a holder in due course, T is entitled to receive $4,000 from M because she can enforce an incomplete instrument as completed. Whether or not T is a holder in due course, T may recover $4,000 from P.

See Figure 27–5 for a summary of these examples.

Personal Defenses

Defenses to an instrument may arise in many ways, either at the time it is issued or later. In general, defenses to liability on a negotiable instrument are similar to those that may be raised in the case of any action for breach of contract. They are numerous and are available against any holder of the instrument unless he has the rights of a holder in due course. Among the personal defenses are: (1) lack of consideration; (2) failure of consideration; (3) breach of contract; (4) fraud in the inducement; (5) illegality which does not render the transaction void; (6) duress, undue influence, mistake, misrepresentation, or inca-

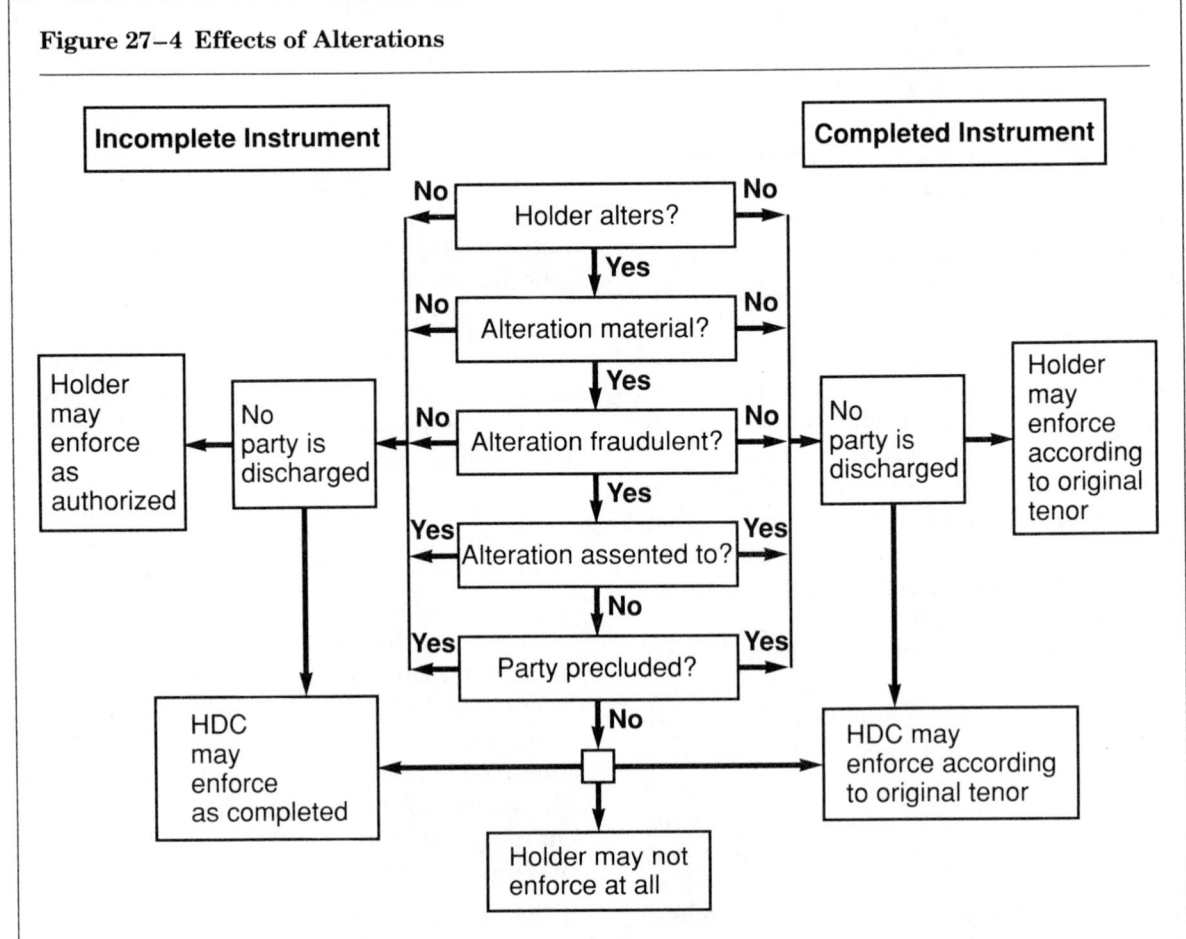

Figure 27–4 Effects of Alterations

Figure 27–5 Material Alteration

(1,2)

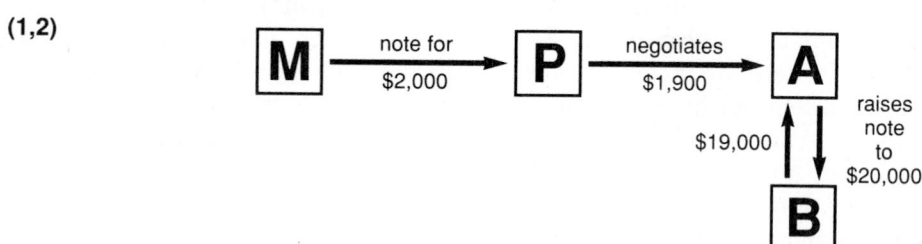

versus	M	P	A
Illustration 1 B = HDC	$2,000	$2,000	$20,000
Illustration 2 B = H	0	0	$20,000

(3)

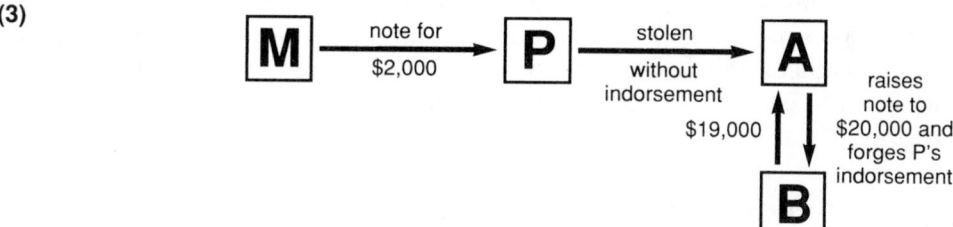

	versus	M	P	A	B
Illustration 3	B	0	0	$20,000	—
	P	$2,000	—	$2,000	$2,000

(4)

M → blank check authorized for $2,000 → P → fraudulently completed for $4,000 → T

	versus	M	P
Illustration 4	T = HDC	$4,000	$4,000
	T = H	0	$4,000

(5)

M → blank check authorized for $2,000 → P → in good faith completed for $4,000 → T

	versus	M	P
Illustration 5	T = HDC	$4,000	$4,000
	T = H	$2,000	$4,000

pacity which does not render the transaction void; (7) setoff or counterclaim; (8) discharge of which the holder in due course does not have notice; (9) non-delivery of an instrument, whether complete or incomplete; (10) unauthorized completion of an incomplete instrument; (11) payment without obtaining surrender of the instrument; (12) theft of a bearer instrument or an instrument payable to him; (13) lack of authority of a corporate officer or an agent or partner as to the particular instrument, where such officer, agent, or partner had general authority to issue negotiable paper for his principal or firm.

These situations are the most common examples, but others exist. Indeed, the Code does not attempt to detail defenses that may be cut off. It is content to state that a holder in due course takes free and clear of all claims to the instrument and defenses except those listed as real defenses (Figure 27–6). *See John Deere Co. v. Boelus State Bank.*

LIMITATIONS UPON HOLDER IN DUE COURSE RIGHTS

The preferential position enjoyed by a holder in due course has been severely limited by a Federal Trade Commission rule restricting the rights of a holder in due course of an instrument concerning a debt arising out of a **consumer credit contract**, which includes negotiable instruments. The rule, entitled "Preservation of Consumers' Claims and Defenses," applies to sellers and lessors of consumer goods, which are goods for personal, household, or family use. It also applies to lenders who advance money to finance the consumer's purchase of consumer goods or services. The rule is intended to prevent situations in which consumer purchase transactions have been financed in such manner that the purchaser is legally obligated to make full payment of the price to a third party, even though the dealer from whom she bought the goods committed fraud or the goods were defective. This occurs when the purchaser executes and delivers to the seller her negotiable instrument which the seller negotiates to a holder in due course. The buyer's defense that the goods were defective or that the seller committed fraud, although valid against the seller, is not valid against a holder in due course of the instrument.

In order to correct this situation, the Federal Trade Commission rule preserves claims and defenses of consumer buyers and borrowers against holders in due course. The rule states that no seller or creditor can take or receive a consumer credit contract unless the contract contains this conspicuous provision:

NOTICE: ANY HOLDER OF THIS CONSUMER CREDIT CONTRACT IS SUBJECT TO ALL CLAIMS AND DEFENSES WHICH THE DEBTOR COULD ASSERT AGAINST THE SELLER OF

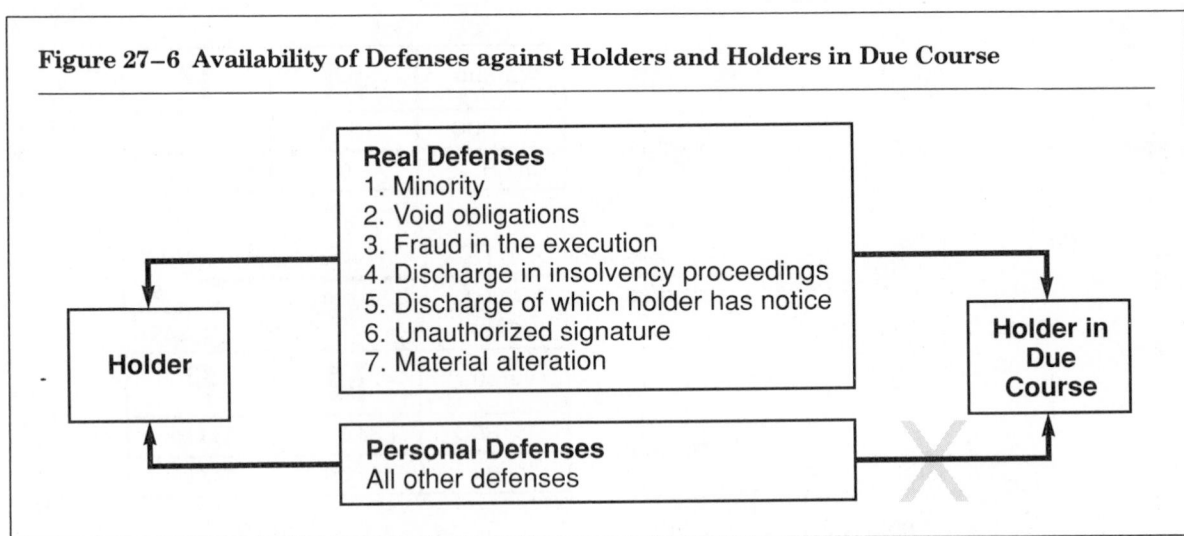

Figure 27–6 Availability of Defenses against Holders and Holders in Due Course

Real Defenses
1. Minority
2. Void obligations
3. Fraud in the execution
4. Discharge in insolvency proceedings
5. Discharge of which holder has notice
6. Unauthorized signature
7. Material alteration

Personal Defenses
All other defenses

Holder

Holder in Due Course

THE GOODS OR SERVICES OBTAINED PURSU-
ANT HERETO OR WITH THE PROCEEDS
HEREOF. RECOVERY HEREUNDER BY THE
DEBTOR SHALL NOT EXCEED AMOUNTS PAID
BY THE DEBTOR HEREUNDER.

The purpose of this conspicuous notice is to
inform any holder that he takes the instru-

ment subject to all claims and defenses which
the buyer could assert against the seller. The
effect of the rule is to place a holder in due
course of the paper or negotiable instrument
in the position of an assignee. See Figure
27–7. *See also Jefferson Bank & Trust Co. v.
Stamatiou.*

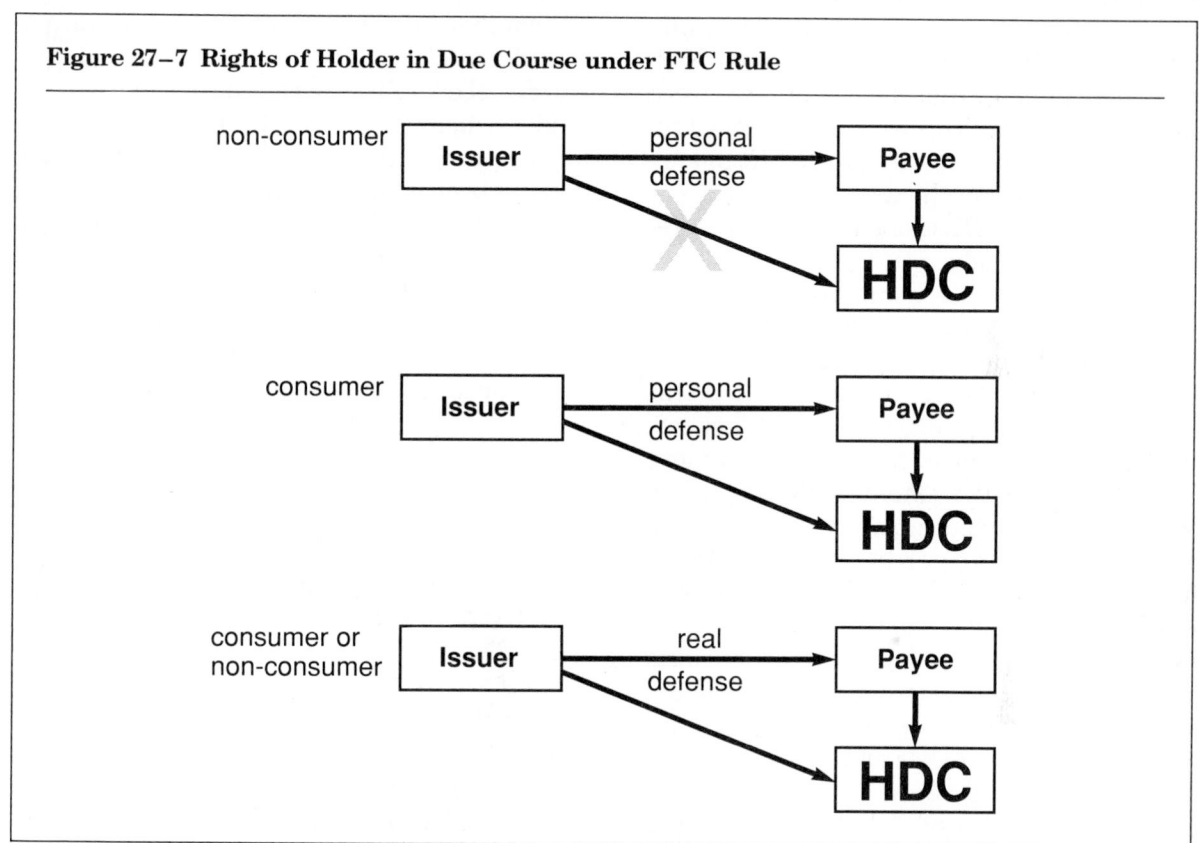

Figure 27–7 Rights of Holder in Due Course under FTC Rule

CASES

Value

KORZENIK v. SUPREME RADIO, INC.

Supreme Judicial Court of Massachusetts, 1964.
347 Mass. 309, 197 N.E.2d 702.

WHITTEMORE, J.

The plaintiffs, as indorsees, brought an action in the District Court of Western Hampden
to recover $1,900 on two "note[s] in the form

of . . . trade acceptance[s]" given by Supreme
Radio, Inc. (Supreme), to Southern New England Distributing Corporation (Southern),
dated October 16, 1961, and due, respectivly,
on November 1, 1961, and December 1, 1961.
The plaintiffs are partners in the practice of
law. The trade acceptances in suit and others,
all of a total face value of about $15,000, were
transferred to them on October 31, 1961, by

their client Southern "as retainer for services to be performed" by the plaintiff Korzenik. The trade acceptances in suit and two others given by Supreme had been obtained by fraud. Southern had retained Korzenik on October 25, 1961, in connection with certain anti-trust litigation. Korzenik did some legal work between October 25 and October 31, but there was no testimony as to the value of the services and the trial judge was unable to determine their value. He found for the defendant. Korzenik did not know that the acceptances were obtained by fraud. "He has paid co-counsel retained in the antitrust case part of the money he has collected" on the assigned items.

The Appellate Division dismissed the report of the trial judge.

Decisive of the case, as the Appellate Division held, is the correct ruling that the plaintiffs are not holders in due course under . . . § 3–302; they have not shown to what extent they took for value under § 3–303. That section provides: "A holder takes the instrument for value (a) to the extent that the agreed consideration has been performed or that he acquires a security interest in or a lien on the instrument otherwise than by legal process; or (b) when he takes the instrument in payment of or as security for an antecedent claim against any person whether or not the claim is due; or (c) when he gives a negotiable instrument for it or makes an irrevocable commitment to a third person."

Under clause (a) of § 3–303 the "agreed consideration" was the performance of legal services. It is often said that a lawyer is "retained" when he is engaged to perform services, and we hold that the judge spoke of "retainer" in this sense. The phrase that the judge used, "retainer *for services* " (emphasis supplied), shows his meaning as does the finding as to services already performed by Korzenik at the time of the assignments. Even if the retainer had been only a fee to insure the attorney's availability to perform future services [citation] there is no basis in the record for determining the value of this commitment for one week.

The Uniform [U.C.C.] Laws Comment to § 3–303 points out that in this article "value

is divorced from consideration" and that except as provided in paragraph (c) "[a]n executory promise to give value is not . . . value. . . . The underlying reason of policy is that when the purchaser learns of a defense . . . he is not required to enforce the instrument, but is free to rescind the transaction for breach of the transferor's warranty."

[U.C.C.] § 3–307(3), provides: "After it is shown that a defense exists a person claiming the rights of a holder in due course has the burden of establishing that he or some person under whom he claims is in all respects a holder in due course." The defense of fraud having been established this section puts the burden on the plaintiffs. The plaintiffs have failed to show "the extent . . . [to which] the agreed consideration . . . [had] been performed."

* * *

Order dismissing report affirmed.

Value/Notice

ST. PAUL FIRE AND MARINE INSURANCE CO. v. STATE BANK OF SALEM

Court of Appeals of Indiana, First District, 1980.
412 N.E.2d 103.

NEAL, J.

On November 26, 1975, Stephens, a farmer, delivered and sold 184 bushels of corn to Aubrey for $478.23. Aubrey was engaged at the time in the sale and distribution of feed and grain in Louisville, Kentucky, under the name of Aubrey Feed Mills, Inc. The following day, Aubrey prepared its check payable to Stephens in payment for the corn and mailed it to Stephens. The check was prepared in the following fashion: the amount "478.23" was typewritten upon the line customarily used to express the amount of the check in numbers, abutting the printed dollar sign. On the line customarily used to express the amount in words there appeared "The sum of $100478 and 23 cts," which was imprinted in red by a checkwriting machine; the line ended with the printed word "Dollars."

On December 9, 1975, Stephens appeared at the Bank's branch in Hardinsburg, Indiana, and presented the Aubrey check and two other items totalling $5,604.51 to the branch manager Charles Anderson. Stephens told Anderson that he wished to apply these funds to the amount of his indebtedness to the Bank, to withdraw $2,000.00 in cash, and to deposit the balance in his checking account. During the interval between November 27, 1975, and December 9, 1975, someone had typed on the check the figures "100" immediately before the typed figures "478.23." This was rather crudely done, and involved typing the "100" in an uneven line; the second "0" was typed directly over the printed dollar sign on the check.

Anderson questioned Stephens about the Aubrey check since Stephens's prior dealings with the Bank had not involved transactions in the amount represented by the Aubrey check. Anderson also knew that Stephens had filed a voluntary petition in bankruptcy several months prior, but had subsequently reaffirmed his obligations to the Bank. Stephens explained that he had purchased a large quantity of corn in Northern Indiana and had sold it in Kentucky at a higher price. Evidently satisfied with his explanation, Anderson stamped nine promissory notes, of which Stephens was maker, "paid" and returned them to Stephens. Anderson then directed a teller at the Bank to fill out a deposit slip for the transaction. At that point, neither Anderson nor the teller noticed the typewritten modification on the check. The transaction consisted of applying the funds represented by the three items in the deposit ($106,082.74) to Stephens's debt represented by the nine promissory notes ($31,851.81), an installment payment of which Stephens was a joint obligor, of $27,559.27, accrued interest owed the Bank by Stephens in the amount of $5,265.65, and the $2,000 cash given to Stephens. The balance was credited to Stephens's account. Stephens then left the Bank.

Later that afternoon, Anderson began thinking about the transaction and examined the items in the deposit. He noted that Aubrey's check bore signs of possible tampering and contacted Aubrey's office in Louisville to inquire about the validity of the check. An Aubrey representative told Anderson that a check in that amount was suspicious, and Anderson then "froze" the transaction. The next day, Aubrey stopped payment on the check.

Thereafter, the Bank attempted to recover possession of the nine promissory notes from Stephens but was unsuccessful. Stephens subsequently left Hardinsburg and his present whereabouts are unknown.

After freezing Stephens's account, the Bank reversed the December 9, 1979, transaction by applying the $5,604.51 then on deposit in Stephens's account (said sum representing the amount of the two checks deposited on December 9, 1979 with Aubrey's check) against the $2,000 paid to Stephens in cash on December 9, 1979, and crediting the remaining $3,604.51 against the aggregate principal balance of the nine promissory notes delivered to Stephens on that date. As a result, the Bank claimed a loss of $28,193.91 and made demand therefor upon Aubrey. * * *

We think the only issue dispositive of Aubrey's appeal is whether the trial court could rightfully have found on the evidence that the Bank was a holder in due course of the Aubrey check under the Uniform Commercial Code (UCC) as adopted in Indiana. * * *

The Bank's right to recover on the check is conditioned upon its status as a holder in due course of the check. Section 3–305 states in part:

To the extent that a holder is a holder in due course he takes the instrument free from
(1) all claims to it on the part of any person; and
(2) all defenses of any party to the instrument with whom the holder has not dealt except . . .

Assuming without presently deciding, that Aubrey showed the existence of a defense, the burden was on the Bank to prove by a preponderance of the evidence that it was in all respects a holder in due course of the check § 3–307(3).

* * *

There is no contention on appeal, and there was none at trial, that the Bank did not take the Aubrey check in good faith, which means honesty in fact in the transaction concerned. [Citation.] There is also no question that the Bank was a holder of the instrument, as it was in possession of the check indorsed by the payee Stephens in blank. See § 1–204(20).

We initially consider whether the Bank took the Aubrey check for value. The Bank contends that it gave value for the check to the extent that it (a) acquired a security interest in the instrument under §§ 3–303(a), 4–208, and 4–209; and (b) took the check in payment of an antecedent claim under § 3–303(b). Aubrey contends that the Bank did not take the check for value since it immediately froze Stephens's account upon apprisal that the validity of the check was suspect and cancelled the amounts it had credited against Stephens's debt. Aubrey considers that the Bank's action in crediting Stephens's debt on the notes merely constituted a bookkeeping procedure and the Bank did not change its position by doing so, particularly since the Bank could still maintain an action against Stephens on the notes. Finally, Aubrey maintains that general principles of law and equity render the UCC provisions relied on by the Bank inapplicable.

We are of the opinion that the Bank took the check for value. The issue is most readily resolved by § 3–303(b) which states in part:

A holder takes the instrument for value

* * *

(b) when he takes the instrument in payment of or as security for an antecedent claim against any person whether or not the claim is due; . . .

The statute [U.C.C.] plainly states that value is given for an instrument when the instrument is taken in payment for an antecedent debt not yet due. The statute contains no provision precluding application of the rule when fraud is exercised by the presenter of the instrument, as Aubrey would have us find.

While this section has not been construed in Indiana, an examination of authorities from other jurisdictions lends support to the Bank's position that the application of funds made available by the Aubrey check to Stephens's indebtedness and the surrender of the notes constituted taking the instrument for value.

Further, we believe that the Bank gave value for the check under §§ 4–208(1) and 4–209, in that it acquired a security interest in the check to the extent funds represented thereby were applied to Stephens's debt. Section 4–208(1)(a) states in part:

(1) A bank has a security interest in an item and any accompanying documents or the proceeds of either

    (a) in case of an item deposited in an account to the extent to which credit given for the item has been withdrawn or applied; . . .

Section 4–209 provides:

For the purposes of determining its status as a holder in due course, the bank has given value to the extent that it has a security interest in an item provided that the bank otherwise complies with the requirements of § 3–302 on what constitutes a holder in due course.

We find no support for Aubrey's argument that the Bank did not give value since it did not change its position vis-a-vis Stephens and made a bookkeeping entry only of the credit given Stephens. . . . Official Comment 3 to § 3–303 states that it is not necessary to give holder in due course status to one who has not actually paid value, and cites as illustration "the bank credit not drawn upon, which can be and is revoked when a claim or defense appears." [Citation.] When the credit is drawn upon, however, value is given to that extent § 4–208(1)(a). Further, if the depositor's account is overdrawn at the time the check is taken, and funds represented thereby are applied to the overdrawal by way of set-off, value is given to that extent if the check is later dishonored. [Citation.]

* * *

Aubrey vigorously contends the Bank was not a holder in due course of the check because, under the objective standard imposed upon the Bank by § 3–304(1), the Bank took the check with notice of a defense to the check on the part of Aubrey. Aubrey argues the evidence of alteration on the face of the check and the irregular circumstances attending the transaction were such as to put a reasonably prudent banker, exercising normal commercial standards, on notice. The circumstances alleged to have imparted notice to Bank include the small size of Stephens's farming operations, Stephens's banking history including frequent indebtedness and overdrawals, the Bank's knowledge of Stephens's petition in bankruptcy, the size of the Aubrey check in relation to typical transactions undertaken by the Bank, and the implausibility of Stephens's explanation to Anderson, himself familiar with farming, of the transaction underlying Stephens's receipt of the check. The Bank concedes the UCC imposed an objective standard of conduct upon it in the transaction. The essence of the Bank's contention is that the matter of the Bank's notice is a question of fact, and the trial court's implicit finding that the Bank took the check without notice of Aubrey's defense was not erroneous.

The general notice provision of the UCC is stated in § 1–201(25), which provides in part:

A person has 'notice' of a fact when (a) he has actual knowledge of it; or (b) he has received a notice or notification of it; or (c) from all the facts and circumstances known to him at the time in question he has reason to know that it exists.

Section 3–304, titled "Notice to Purchasers," states in part:

(1) The purchaser has notice of a claim or defense if

(a) the instrument is so incomplete, bears such visible evidence of forgery or alteration, or is otherwise so irregular as to call into question its validity, terms or ownership or to create an ambiguity as to the party to pay; . . .

The Bank is a "purchaser" within the meaning of § 3–304. [Citation.]

Section 1–201(25) imposes subjective and quasi-objective standards; § 3–304 imposes an objective standard. [Citation.] An irregularity on the face of an instrument is sufficient to import notice under § 3–304(1)(a) where,

A reasonably prudent person exercising normal commercial standards would immediately be put

on notice that there was something very irregular about the terms of the [instrument.]

[Citation.]

The gist of Aubrey's argument is that the alleged "alteration" on the face of the check, i.e., the typed figure "100," was "such visible evidence" of alteration as to call into question its validity or terms.

We do not think that the trial court erred as a matter of law in finding that the Bank took the Aubrey check without notice of a defense.

The Bank's branch manager, Anderson, with whom Stephens dealt in the transaction, admitted that he took the check without comparing the amount expressed in typewritten figures; indeed, he testified that he did not even look at the figures. He relied, instead, upon the amount expressed by the checkwriter that was entered upon the line generally used to express the amount of a check in words.

Section 3–118, captioned "Ambiguous terms and rules of construction," states in part:

The following rules apply to every instrument:

* * *

(b) Handwritten terms control typewritten and printed terms, and typewritten control printed.

(c) Words control figures except that if the words are ambiguous figures control.

* * *

As the section makes clear, in the event of an ambiguity between printed terms and typewritten terms, the latter would control. We do not consider the impressions made by the check imprinter to be "printed" terms under this section. [Citation.]

A conflict between the two amounts on a check would be resolved by § 3–118(c) which states that words control figures. Arguably, the amount imprinted by the checkwriting machine upon the line customarily expressing the amount in words, is expressed in figures. (Recall that the entry reads: "The sum of $100478 and 23 cts.") We think, however, that the purposes of the U.C.C. are best served by considering an amount imprinted by a checkwriting machine as "words" for the purpose of resolving an ambiguity between that amount and an amount entered upon the line usually used to express the amount in figures.

* * *

We cannot say as a matter of law that the bank acted unreasonably in relying upon the amount expressed by the checkwriting machine. Aubrey presented no evidence that customary banking standards require a bank to closely examine and compare the two amounts on the check, and it was Aubrey's burden to prove the existence of such custom. [Citation.] The issue of the Bank's constructive knowledge of any defense Aubrey may have had to the check, based on the alleged irregularity on the face of the check, was a question of fact for the trial court to determine. It was not error for the court to have determined that the Bank acted reasonably in relying on the amount imprinted by the checkwriting machine and took the check without notice, actual or constructive, of a defense thereto.

Aubrey further argues that the circumstances surrounding the transaction were so irregular as to put a reasonably prudent banker on notice of a defense to Aubrey's check. Aubrey directs us to no cases in which a holder was denied holder in due course status because of its knowledge of the questionable general financial position of the presenter of the instrument. Our research reveals such knowledge is not sufficient in itself to defeat holder in due course status. * * *

The only knowledge the Bank had concerning the transaction underlying the issue of the Aubrey check to Stephens, and thus the only knowledge relevant to the issue of Bank's notice of a possible defense to the check, grew out of Stephens's explanation to Anderson of how the check came into his hands. This was not sufficient to call into question the integrity of the Aubrey check.

We therefore hold that the evidence supports the trial court's determination that the Bank was a holder in due course of the Au-

brey check. Since Aubrey has not shown a "real defense" under § 3–305(2) the Bank may enforce the check against Aubrey to the extent it gave value therefor, and we shall not disturb the trial court's award of that amount.

Payee as Holder in Due Course/Personal Defense

JOHN DEERE CO. v. BOELUS STATE BANK

Nebraska Supreme Court, 1989.
233 Neb. 818, 488 N.W.2d 163.

BOSLAUGH, J.

This is a suit by the plaintiff, John Deere Company, against the Boelus State Bank on a cashier's check issued by the defendant bank and payable to the plaintiff. The trial court found that the plaintiff was a holder in due course and entitled to recover $8,455.85. The defendant has appealed. * * *

Taking the view of the evidence most favorable to the plaintiff, the record shows that on October 8, 1982, Walter Duester entered into a "variable rate loan contract security agreement" in connection with the purchase of a John Deere combine and grain platform from St. Paul Equipment, Inc. (St. Paul). John Deere was the lender and secured party under the agreement, and the combine was pledged as collateral. When Duester failed to pay the balance of his contract ($8,455.84) by January 1986, the manager of St. Paul was instructed to repossess the combine.

On January 14, 1986, Randy Hansen, an employee of St. Paul, went to Duester's farm to repossess the combine. Duester told Hansen that he had received some payments for custom combining and would purchase a cashier's check and pay the debt to John Deere. Hansen followed Duester to the defendant bank at about 11 a.m. and waited outside for Duester to return.

Five or ten minutes later, Duester came out of the bank and gave Hansen a cashier's check in the amount of $8,455.84. The check was drawn on defendant Boelus State Bank, payable to the order of John Deere Company, and was signed by an authorized bank employee, Judy Jensen.

* * *

On or about January 22, 1986, John Deere presented the cashier's check for payment, but payment was refused.

A cashier's check is a draft drawn by a bank upon itself. [Citations.] U.C.C. § 3–118(a) provides that a draft drawn on the drawer is effective as a note.

* * *

U.C.C. § 3–306 provides:

"Unless he has the rights of a holder in due course any person takes the instrument subject to . . ."
"(c) the defenses of want or failure of consideration, nonperformance of any condition precedent, nondelivery, or delivery for a special purpose . . . and
"(d) the defense that he or a person through whom he holds the instrument acquired it by theft. . . ."

Section 3–305 provides:

"To the extent that a holder is a holder in due course he takes the instrument free from . . . .
"(2) all defenses of any party to the instrument with whom the holder has not dealt except . . . .
"(b) such other incapacity, or duress, or illegality of the transaction, as renders the obligation of the party a nullity . . . ."

Although the bank alleged that Duester had acquired the cashier's check by theft and that the check had not been delivered, if the plaintiff was a holder in due course it is unnecessary to consider the defenses alleged by the bank.

"A holder in due course is a holder who takes the instrument (a) for value; and (b) in good faith; and (c) without notice that it is overdue or has been dishonored or of any defense against or claim to it on the part of any person." U.C.C. § 3–302(1) In this case the check had been drawn payable to the order of the plaintiff, John Deere. A holder is defined as a "person who is in possession of . . . an instrument . . . *drawn,* issued or indorsed to him or to his order or to bearer or in blank." U.C.C. § 1—201(20).

The payee of an instrument may be a holder in due course if he meets the requirements of § 3–302. Section 3–302 and comment 2 thereto. A holder takes an instrument for value when he takes the instrument in payment of an antecedent claim against any person. U.C.C. § 3–303(b).

The record shows that John Deere was in possession of the cashier's check drawn on the defendant bank and which was payable to the order of John Deere. In obtaining the cashier's check, John Deere did not deal with the bank, and took the instrument in payment of the debt due it from Duester. There was no defect apparent on the face of the instrument. Duester did not tell Hansen what had happened while he was in the bank, did not tell Hansen that there might be a problem with the cashier's check, and did not discuss the subject of his bank loan with anyone from St. Paul. The record supports the trial court's conclusion that John Deere's agent, Hansen, had no knowledge of any defense against the instrument when he received the cashier's check in payment of Duester's debt to St. Paul. Although John Deere subsequently was informed that the bank intended to dishonor the check, subsequent knowledge of an alleged infirmity does not impair its holder in due course status. [Citations.] * * *

Since the plaintiff was a holder in due course, it is unnecessary to discuss the evidence relating to the bank's claim that the check had been stolen by Duester. Under § 3–306, a holder in due course takes the instrument not subject to "the defense that he or a person through whom he holds the instrument acquired it by theft. . . ."

In § 3–306, comment 5, it is stated: "The exception made in the case of theft is based on the policy which refuses to aid a proved thief to recover, and refuses to aid him indirectly by permitting his transferee to recover *unless the transferee is a holder in due course.*" [Citation.]

The judgment is affirmed.

Affirmed.

Void/Voidable Obligation

BANKERS TRUST COMPANY v. LITTON SYSTEMS, INC.

United States Court of Appeals, Second Circuit, 1979.
599 F.2d 488.

MOORE, J.

This is an appeal by defendant Litton Systems, Inc. from a monetary judgment against it and in favor of plaintiffs Bankers Trust Company (Bankers Trust) and Chemical Bank (Chemical) in the sums of $113,495.55 (Bankers Trust) and $126,371.55 (Chemical).

* * *

In 1973 and 1974 Litton decided to purchase photocopiers for use in the branch offices of its private telephone business. A Royal [a division of Litton] salesman, Angelo Buquicchio, recommended that Litton lease the photocopiers from Regent Leasing Corporation, a business entirely independent of Litton or Royal. Unbeknownst to Royal or Litton, Buquicchio was to receive from Regent certain "service fees" which may arguendo be called bribes. Regent was to purchase the equipment from Royal and then lease it to Litton.

In order to finance its purchases Regent borrowed from Bankers Trust and Chemical, ... [transfering] to them the Litton leases [promises to pay] as security. A clause in the leases permitted [transfer] and provided that the [transferee's] rights would be independent of any claims or offsets of Litton as against Regent.

Litton in early 1976 defaulted in meeting its obligations to the Banks under the leases. * * *

In June 1977, plaintiffs moved for summary judgment. . . . The burden of the opposition was that Regent's bribery of Royal's employees renders Litton's obligations a nullity and a defense against the banks as holders in due course.

The trial court, after a review of the facts pertaining to the lease transactions, put to one side the factual issue as to whether the alleged kickbacks were illegal and addressed the only relevant question of whether the banks had notice of the payments and were holders in due course.

* * *

That the alleged service fee payments were illegal. This defense goes to the heart of this appeal and constitutes the main portion of appellant's argument. In sum, it is that the alleged kickbacks to Buquicchio rendered the leases between Regent and Litton so utterly void that they became nullities, never to have any legal validity even for bona fide holders in due course without notice of the side deal Buquicchio made for his own benefit.

Buquicchio's conduct was arguably illegal under New York Penal Law which declares commercial bribery to be a criminal offense. Litton claims that the bribes were such "illegality of the transaction, as renders the obligation of the party a nullity ..." and that, therefore, the leases were unenforceable even by a holder in due course. U.C.C. § 3–305(2)(b).

The court carefully analyzed the New York cases on the subject and concluded that whereas "such payments could constitute a defense as against Regent . . . the making of such payments could not be asserted against a holder in due course. . . ." Accordingly, it granted the banks' motions for summary judgment.

* * *

The court concluded that

"(I)n using the term 'nullity' the Legislature intended to provide a defense against a holder in due course only in cases where the obligation sued upon is void on its face (e.g., a wagering contract or a contract to perform an illegal act), and was not intended to provide a defense against such a holder where one of the parties to the original contract might have an option to declare it void because some illegal conduct in which the other party may have engaged in the course of the negotiations which gave rise to the contract."

There is a distinction here which should be preserved: the lease contracts for photocopiers were not themselves illegal; the contract to bribe a person in connection with those contracts was illegal.

* * *

The illegality defense under U.C.C. § 3–305(2)(b) is available only if under the applicable state law the effect of the illegality is to make the obligation entirely null and void; the defense is ineffective against a holder in due course if the illegality causes the contract to be merely voidable. Official Comment 6, U.C.C. § 3–305.

* * *

The problems and consequences of using the terms "void" and "voidable" were recognized by the Restatement of Contracts:

"Confusion in the use of the words 'void' and 'voidable' is common, chiefly because it frequently makes no difference whether a contract is void or voidable. In either event the injured party can usually escape liability, and in most cases that is the only question involved. The difference becomes important, however, where property is transferred and subsequently passes to a bona fide purchaser for value. If the original transfer is Voidable the innocent purchaser acquires an indefeasible title. A similar consequence follows the negotiation of a negotiable instrument that is Voidable. Furthermore, a contract which is Voidable may be ratified while a Void transaction cannot be." Restatement of Contracts § 475, Comment b.

Bribery which induces the making of a contract is much like a fraud which has the same result. The bribery of a contracting party's agent or employee is, in effect, a fraud on that party. See Restatement of Contracts § 577, Illustrations 4 & 11. Inasmuch as the New York Uniform Commercial Code allows a holder in due course to enforce a contract induced by fraud, § 3–305(2), the same treatment should be given to a contract induced by bribery. The result ought not be changed by the additional fact that commercial bribery is a criminal offense in New York.

Finally, it would be poor policy for courts to transform banks and other finance companies into policing agents charged with the responsibility of searching out commercial bribery committed by their [transferors]. We doubt that denying recovery to holders in due course would have an appreciable effect on the frequency of commercial bribery. Moreover, the holder in due course concept embodies important policies which must be weighed

against the policy of holding void contracts induced by bribery. To paraphrase Professor Gilmore, the holder in due course is protected not because of his praiseworthy character, but to the end that commercial transactions may be engaged in without elaborate investigation of the process leading up to the contract or instrument and in reliance on the contract rights of one who offers them for sale or to secure a loan. [Citation.] Abrogation of the rights of a holder in due course is not warranted in this case.

The appellant's other arguments are without merit and were adequately answered by the district court. For the reasons stated above, the decision of the district court is affirmed.

Limitations upon Holder in Due Course Rights

JEFFERSON BANK & TRUST CO. v. STAMATIOU

Supreme Court of Louisiana, 1980.
384 So.2d 388.

CALOGERO, J.

Defendant's [answer] asserting a defense to plaintiff's suit on a promissory note given plaintiff's assignor for the purchase of a truck was dismissed. The trial judge held in favor of the plaintiff bank, granting its exception of no cause of action upon finding the bank to be a holder in due course. The Court of Appeal affirmed the trial court judgment. [Citation.] We granted writs upon application of defendant, vendee and maker of the promissory note.

Defendant, Christos G. Stamatiou, purchased a truck from Key Dodge, Inc. At the time of purchase, defendant and an agent of Key Dodge signed an instrument designated Sale and Chattel Mortgage. The instrument or contract is on a single sheet of paper, front and back. It consists of provisions relative to the Sale and Chattel Mortgage with a promissory note at the bottom of this same page. The note portion of the contract bears language indicating that it is an unconditional promise to pay $10,774.44 on prescribed terms. The preceding Sale and Chattel Mortgage portion of the instrument has numerous provisions including the following which preserves for the purchaser his defenses against a future holder:

NOTICE: ANY HOLDER OF THIS CONSUMER CREDIT CONTRACT IS SUBJECT TO ALL CLAIMS AND DEFENSES WHICH THE DEBTOR COULD ASSERT AGAINST THE SELLER OF GOODS OR SERVICES OBTAINED PURSUANT HERETO OR WITH THE PROCEEDS HEREOF. RECOVERY HEREUNDER SHALL NOT EXCEED AMOUNTS PAID BY THE DEBTOR HEREUNDER.

Defendant's signature appears twice on the instrument, once following the sale and chattel mortgage and once at the conclusion of the promissory note. The purchaser is shown on the contract as "Christos G. Stamatiou" and no provision of the sale and chattel mortgage/promissory note indicates the purpose of the purchase, or the use to which the truck is to be put. Nor does any provision of the instrument indicate that Stamatiou purchased anything other than an ordinary truck. Near the top of the contract there is a "Disclosure Statement" by which "Buyer acknowledges that the Promissory Note secured by Sale and Chattel Mortgage will be assigned to JEFFERSON BANK, as Assignee and CREDITOR within the meaning of the Federal Truth-In-Lending Act."

Key Dodge assigned this contract to plaintiff, Jefferson Bank and Trust Co., as contemplated. Defendant alleges that the truck became inoperable and unusable a short time after purchase and that he notified Key Dodge and Jefferson Bank of the problem and demanded rescission of the sale. . . . Later, Jefferson Bank filed an ordinary petition against Stamatiou for the unpaid balance on the note (after separating or cutting the note off from the remainder of the contract).

Defendant answered the suit . . . seeking rescission of the sale and judgment for return of the purchase price.

Plaintiff bank filed an exception of no cause of action . . . contending that because defendant purchased the truck for use in his tow truck business, the instrument is not a "consumer credit contract" and that therefore the above quoted language of the contract is not applicable.

* * *

Our [decision to review this case] requires that we determine whether the inclusion of the preservation of defenses language (federally required in all "consumer credit contracts") in a contract which is not a consumer credit contract, allows the defendant to present his defense against a party who would otherwise be a holder in due course; in effect, whether the language, specifically countering the primary effect of holder in due course status is applicable to this holder, Jefferson Bank.

Under authority of [Federal statute], the Federal Trade Commission, a United States regulatory agency, requires the inclusion of the exact same language as was included in the present contract in all "consumer credit contracts" for the sale of goods or services. [Citation.] The federal regulations define a consumer as "a natural person who seeks or acquires goods or services for *personal, family or household use.*" Therefore in any contract for the sale of goods or services where credit is being extended to the purchaser, and the purchaser is acquiring the item for personal, family, or household use, . . . language identical to that language used in the contract and quoted above, must be contained in the contract.

* * *

The express purpose of the FTC regulation is to prevent the seller, in a consumer credit transaction, from separating the buyer's duty to pay from the seller's duty to perform as promised, by the seller's assigning the buyer's promissory note to a financing institution, as against whom, because of holder in due course status, defenses would otherwise not be available.

Plaintiff makes the following argument: that the preservation of defenses language is included in all credit contracts to insure compliance with federal regulations but is only intended to apply to the appropriate transactions even though there is no notation to the effect that the clause is possibly inapplicable; absent inclusion in all credit contracts, the vendor and/or finance company would be required to have two different forms and to hire a staff attorney to instruct them each time which to use; and that the sale of the truck to defendant for use in his tow truck business takes the transaction out of the consumer credit contract category as defined by the FTC, and thus the provision, although there in the contract, was not applicable to this transaction and should be ignored.

Defendant on the other hand claims that the preservation of defenses language (whether federally required in this contract or not) was included in the contract and as such becomes a part of that contract.

* * *

We conclude that defendant's argument is the more persuasive and is more supported by the law. . . ., parties are free to govern their relationships through their contracts, and the contractural provisions have the effect of law on the parties. The contract between Stamatiou and Key Dodge, as assigned to plaintiff, provided "Any holder of this . . . contract is subject to all claims and defenses which the debtor could assert against the seller." That the parties to the contract mistakenly asserted that it was a consumer credit contract ("any holder of this consumer credit contract") is of little consequence. In looking at the contract, there was nothing on the face of the instrument to indicate that this was not a "consumer contract." The assignee/holder was put on notice that all defenses were available to the buyer against him at the time he acquired the instrument. In looking at the face of the instrument, plaintiff could not have expected to be a holder in due course, and is not now entitled to be so treated. At best the contract is ambiguous and is surely not to be construed against the purchaser who did not confect it. [Citations.]

* * *

For these reasons we conclude that the preservation of defenses language is applicable to the contract. Plaintiff bank is subject to defendant purchaser's claims or defenses and the contract provision takes precedence over the right plaintiff would otherwise have been legally entitled to under [U.C.C.] 3–305 as a holder in due course.

Reversed; remanded to District Court.

QUESTIONS

1. Discuss the requirements of becoming a holder in due course.

2. Discuss (a) the shelter rule and (b) the rights of a payee.

3. Define, identify, and discuss the real defenses.

4. Define and discuss personal defenses.

5. Discuss the limitations upon the rights of a holder in due course imposed by the Federal Trade Commission.

PROBLEMS

1. On November 1, Perkins installed a burglar alarm system in Mercer's store. Mercer executed and delivered to Perkins a negotiable promissory note payable to the order of Perkins for $1,100, the purchase price, due on December 1. On November 8, Perkins returned to Mercer's store and told Mercer that he needed money and would accept $1,000 as payment in full. Mercer immediately paid Perkins $1,000 but forgot to obtain the note from Perkins.

On November 10, Perkins indorsed the note in blank and transferred it to Harris for value. Two days later, Harris learned that Mercer had already paid Perkins for the note, whereupon he gave the note to Shopin, his mother-in-law, as a going-away present without further indorsement. Shopin was not aware of Mercer's prior payment of the note.

What are the rights of Shopin, if any, against Mercer? Explain.

2. Moore issues a negotiable promissory note payable to the order of Parish for the amount of $3,000. Parish raises the amount to $13,000 and negotiates it to Holton for $12,000.

(a) If Holton is a holder in due course, how much can she recover from Moore? How much from Parish? If Moore's negligence substantially contributed to the making of the alteration, how much can Holton recover from Moore and Parish, respectively?

(b) If Holton is not a holder in due course, how much can she recover from Moore? How much from Parish? If Moore's negligence substantially contributed to the making of the alteration, how much can Holton recover from Moore and Parish, respectively?

3. On December 2, 1991, Miles executed and delivered to Proctor a negotiable promissory note for $1,000, payable to Proctor or order, due March 2, 1992, with interest at 14 percent from maturity, in partial payment of a printing press. On January 3, 1992, Proctor, in need of ready cash, indorsed and sold the note to Hughes for $800. Hughes paid $600 in cash to Proctor on January 3 and agreed to pay the balance of $200 one week later, namely, on January 10. On January 6, Hughes learned that Miles claimed a breach of warranty by Proctor and, for this reason, intended to refuse to pay the note when it matured. On January 10, Hughes paid Proctor $200, in conformity with their agreement of January 3. Following Miles's refusal to pay the note on March 2, 1992, Hughes sues Miles for $1,000. Decision?

4. Thornton fraudulently represented to Daye that he would obtain for her a new car to be used in Daye's business for $7,800 from Pennek Motor Company. Daye thereupon executed her personal check for $7,800 payable to the order of Pennek Motor Company and delivered the check to Thornton, who immediately delivered it to the motor company in payment of his own prior indebtedness. The motor company had no knowledge of the representations made by Thornton to Daye. Pennek Motor Company now brings an action on the check against Daye, who defends on the ground of failure of consideration. Decision?

5. Adams reads with difficulty. He arranged to borrow $200 from Bell. Bell prepared a note, which Adams read laboriously. As Adams was about to sign it, Bell diverted Adams's attention and substituted the following paper, which was identical to the note Adams had read except that the amounts were different:

On June 1, 1991, I promise to pay Ben Bell or order Two Thousand Dollars with interest from date at 16 percent. This note is secured by certificate No. 13 for 100 shares of stock of Brookside Mills, Inc.

Adams did not detect the substitution, signed as maker, handed the note and stock certificate to Bell, and received from Bell $200. Bell indorsed and sold the paper to Fore, a holder in due course, who paid him $1,800. Fore presented the note at maturity to Adams who refused to pay. What are Fore's rights, if any, against Adams?

6. On January 2, 1991, Martin, seventeen years of age, as a result of Dealer's fraudulent misrepresentation, bought a used motorboat to use in his fishing business for $2,000 from Dealer, signed an installment contract for $1,500, and gave Dealer the following instrument as down payment:

Dated: ___ 1991
I promise to pay to the order of Dealer, six months after date, the sum of $500 without interest. This is given as a down payment on an installment contract for a motorboat.

(signed) Martin

Dealer, on July 1, sold his business to Henry and included this note in the transaction. Dealer indorsed the note in blank and handed it to Henry. Henry left the note in his office safe. On July 10, Sharpie, an employee of Henry, without authority stole the note and sold it to Bert for $300, indorsing the note "Sharpie." At the time, in Bert's presence, Sharpie filled in the date on the note as February 2, 1991. Bert demanded payment from Martin, who refused to pay.

What are Bert's rights against Martin? Please discuss.

7. McLaughlin borrowed $1,000 from Adler. Adler, disturbed about McLaughlin's ability to pay, demanded security. McLaughlin indorsed and delivered to Adler a negotiable promissory note executed by Topping for $1,200 payable to McLaughlin's order in twelve equal monthly installments. The note did not contain an acceleration clause, but it recited that the consideration for the note was McLaughlin's promise to paint and shingle Topping's barn. At the time McLaughlin transferred the note to Adler, the first installment was overdue and unpaid. Adler was unaware that the installment had not been paid. Topping did not pay any of the installments on the note. When the last installment became due, Adler presented the note to Topping for payment. Topping refused upon the ground that McLaughlin had not painted or reshingled her barn.

What are Adler's rights, if any, against Topping on the note?

8. McEnally purchased a refrigerator for his home from Peircault Appliance Store for $700. McEnally paid $200 in cash and signed an installment contract for $500, which in its entirety stated:

January 15, 1991

I promise to pay to the order of Peircault Appliance Store the sum of $500 in ten equal monthly installments.

(Signed) McEnally

Peircault negotiated the installment contract to Hughes, who took the instrument for value, in good faith, and without notice of any claim or defense of any party. After paying two installments, the refrigerator ceased operating, and McEnally wishes to recover his down payment, his first two monthly payments, and to discontinue further payments. What outcome?

9. Joseph Higbee executed and delivered to Robert Dudley, the following instrument:

On September 19, 1992, I promise to pay $15,000 to Robert Dudley.

(signed) Joseph Higbee.

This note was secured by a mortgage on Higbee's real property. Dudley altered the note and mortgage by changing the amount to $25,000 and the date to September 17, 1992, Dudley then sold the note and mortgage for $25,000 less 2 percent discount to Citizens Bank, which was unaware of the alterations. Dudley assigned the mortgage to Citizens Bank and signed the reverse side of the note as follows:

I hereby assign this note to the order of Citizens Bank. (signed) Robert Dudley.

On September 8, 1992, Citizens Bank demanded payment of the note from Higbee. Higbee refused. On September 22, Citizens Bank notified Higbee that the note was in default and demanded payment from him. Higbee again refused. Citizens Bank thereupon brought an action against Higbee to recover $25,000 on the note. No action was taken by Citizens Bank to foreclose the mortgage.

What defenses, if any, may Higbee properly assert in this action?

10. Adams, by fraudulent representations, induced Barton to purchase 100 shares of the capital stock of the Evermore Oil Company. The shares were worthless. Barton executed and delivered to Adams a negotiable promissory note for $5,000 dated May 5, in full payment for the shares, due six months after date. On May 20, Adams indorsed and sold the note to Cooper for $4,800. On October 21, Barton, having learned that Cooper now held the note, notified Cooper of the fraud and stated he would not pay the note. On December 1, Cooper negotiated the note to Davis who, while not a party, had full knowledge of the fraud perpetrated on Barton. Upon refusal of Barton to pay the note, Davis sues Barton for $5,000. Decision?

11. Donna gives Peter a check for $50,000 in return for a personal computer. The check is dated December 2. Peter transfers the check for value to Howard on December 14, and Howard deposits it in his bank on December 20. In the meantime, Donna has discovered that the personal computer is not what was promised and has stopped payment on the check. If Peter and Howard disappear, may the bank recover from Donna notwithstanding her defense of failure of consideration? What will be the bank's cause of action?

12. Eldon's Super Fresh Stores, Inc., is a corporation engaged in the retail grocery business.

William Drexler was the attorney for and the corporate secretary of Eldon's and was also the personal attorney of Eldon Prinzing, the corporation's president and sole shareholder. From January 1989 through January 1990, Drexler maintained an active stock trading account in his name with Merrill Lynch. Eldon's had no such account. On August 12, 1989, Drexler purchased 100 shares of Clark Oil & Refining Company stock through his Merrill Lynch stockbroker. He paid for the stock with a check drawn by Eldon's made payable to Merrill Lynch and signed by Prinzing. On August 15, 1989, Merrill Lynch accepted the check as payment for Drexler's stock purchase. There was no communication between Eldon's and Merrill Lynch until November 1990, fifteen months after the issuance of the check. At that time Eldon's inquired of Merrill Lynch as to the whereabouts of the stock certificate and asserted a claim to its ownership. It then brought this action, claiming that it gave the check to Drexler to be delivered to Merrill Lynch for Eldon's benefit. Decision?

13. Consolidated Business Forms leased a Phillips business computer from Benchmark. Benchmark subsequently transferred the lease and promissory note to Exchange International Leasing Corporation. Consolidated stopped making rental payments when the computer malfunctioned, and Exchange International brought this suit to recover the payments due on the promissory note. Consolidated defends on the grounds that Benchmark prevented its agent, Mr. Spohn, from examining the contents of the agreement between the two companies and further represented that the computer would be removed with a complete refund if it failed to operate properly. Decision?

Chapter 28

LIABILITY OF PARTIES

Primary Contractual Liability
Secondary Contractual Liability
Warranties on Transfer
Warranties on Presentment

THE preceding chapters discussed the negotiability of commercial paper, the transfer of negotiable instruments, and the preferred position of a holder in due course. When parties issue negotiable instruments they do so with the expectation that they, either directly or indirectly, will satisfy their obligation under the instrument. Likewise, when a person accepts, indorses, or transfers an instrument, he incurs liability for the instrument under certain circumstances. This chapter examines the liability of parties arising out of negotiable instruments and the ways in which liability may be terminated.

Two types of potential liability are associated with commercial paper: contractual liability and warranty liability. The law imposes **contractual liability** on those who **sign** a negotiable instrument. Some parties to a negotiable instrument never sign it, so they never assume contractual liability. Section 3–401(1).

Warranty liability, on the other hand, is not based on signature; thus it may be imposed on both signers and nonsigners. **Warranty liability** applies (1) to persons who transfer an instrument and (2) to persons who obtain payment or acceptance of an instrument.

CONTRACTUAL LIABILITY

All parties whose signatures appear on a negotiable instrument incur certain contractual obligations, unless they disclaim liability. The *maker* of a promissory note and the *acceptor* of a draft assume primary liability, subject to valid claims and defenses, to pay according to the tenor of the instrument at the time they sign it or as completed according to the rules discussed in Chapter 27 for incomplete instruments. **Primary liability** means that a party is legally obligated to pay without the holder's having to resort first to another party. *Drawers* of drafts and checks and *indorsers* of all instruments incur secondary liability if the instrument is not paid. **Secondary liability** means that a party is legally obligated to pay only after another party, who is expected to pay, fails to do so. A *drawee* has **no** liability on the instrument until he *accepts* it. The contractual obligations of the maker, drawer, drawee, indorser, and acceptor are codified by the U.C.C. as illustrated in Figure 28–1.

A signature showing that the signer is not in the chain of title is notice of its accommodation character. Section 3–415. An **accom-**

| Figure 28–1 Contractual Liability | | | | |
Maker	Acceptor	Drawee	Drawer	Indorser
Primary	Primary	None	Secondary	Secondary

modation party signs the instrument to lend her credit to another party to the instrument. An accommodation party may sign as a maker, acceptor, drawer, or indorser and her liability is determined by the capacity in which she signed. If she signs as a maker or acceptor, she incurs primary liability; if she signs as a drawer or indorser, she incurs secondary liability. Typically, accommodation parties sign as indorsers or co-makers.

SIGNATURE

The word *signature,* as discussed in Chapter 25, is broadly defined to include any name, word, or mark, whether handwritten, typed, printed, or in any other form, if it is done with the intention of authenticating the instrument. Sections 3–401(2) and 1–201(39). *See Azalea City Motels, Inc. v. First Alabama Bank of Mobile.* The signature may be made by the individual herself or on her behalf by the individual's authorized agent.

Authorized Signatures

Authorized agents often execute negotiable instruments on behalf of their principals. The agent is not liable if the instrument is executed properly (e.g., "Prince, principal, by Adams, agent") and the agent is authorized to execute the instrument. If these two conditions are met, then only the principal is liable on the instrument. (For a comprehensive discussion of the principal–agent relationship see Chapters 18 and 19.)

Occasionally, however, the agent, although fully authorized, uses an inappropriate form of signature, and holders or prospective holders may be misled as to the identity of the obligor. Although there are many incorrect forms of signatures by agents, they can be conveniently sorted into three groups.

The first type occurs when an agent signs only his own name to an instrument. He does not indicate that he is signing in a representative capacity and he does not state the name of the principal. For example, Adams, the agent of Prince, makes a note on behalf of Prince but signs it "Adams." The signature does not indicate that Adams has signed in a representative capacity nor that he has made the instrument on behalf of Prince. In this situation, only the agent is liable on the instrument; Prince is not liable on the instrument because his name does not appear on it. Prince may be liable to Adams or a third party, however, on the basis of contract or agency law.

The second type of incorrect form occurs when an authorized agent indicates that he is signing in a representative capacity but does not disclose the name of his principal. For example, Adams, executing an instrument on behalf of Prince, merely signs it "Adams, agent." In this situation, Prince is liable if the payee is an immediate party to the instrument and knows that Adams represents Prince. But as to any subsequent party, and as to the payee if he does not know that Adams represents Prince, Prince is not liable on the instrument; Adams alone is liable. As with the first situation, Prince may be liable to Adams or to a third party, based on contract or agency law.

The third type of inappropriate signature occurs when an agent reveals both her name and her principal's name, but does not indicate that she has signed in a representative capacity. For example, Adams, signing an instrument on behalf of Prince, signs it "Adams and Prince." Because a subsequent holder might reasonably believe that Adams and Prince were co-makers, both are fully liable. But if the party who dealt with Adams knew or should have known that Adams was acting on behalf of Prince without intending to incur personal liability, Adams may prove this fact by parol evidence and avoid liability to this immediate party. *See Valley National Bank, Sunnymead v. Cook.*

Unauthorized Signatures

Unauthorized signatures include both forgeries and signatures made by an agent without authority. The unauthorized signature is generally not binding on the person whose name appears on the instrument. It is binding, however, upon the unauthorized signer, whether or not her own name appears on the instrument, to any person who in good faith pays or gives value for the instrument. Section 3–404(1). Thus, if Adams, without authority, signed Prince's name to an instrument, Adams, and not Prince, would be liable on the instrument. The rule, therefore, is an exception to the principle that only those whose names appear on a negotiable instrument can be liable on it.

Negligence Contributing to Unauthorized Signature Any person who by his **negligence** substantially contributes to the making of an unauthorized signature may *not* assert the lack of authority as a defense against a holder in due course or a person who pays the instrument in good faith and according to reasonable commercial standards. Section 3–406. For example, Ingrid employs a signature stamp to sign her checks and carelessly leaves it accessible to third parties. Lisa discovers the stamp and uses it to write a number of checks without Ingrid's authorization. Norman, a subsequent holder in due course of one of the checks, will *not* be subject to Ingrid's defense of unauthorized signature and will be able to recover the amount of the check from Ingrid due to Ingrid's negligence in storing the signature stamp.

Revised Section 3–406(b) differs from the present Section 3–406 in that it adopts a comparative negligence standard. For example, if a drawer is negligent in allowing an employee to sign the drawer's name but the drawee is also negligent in failing to detect the awkward forgery, the relative negligence of each party can be weighed by the trier of fact.

Ratification of Unauthorized Signature In addition, an unauthorized signature may be **ratified** by the person whose name appears on the instrument. Section 3–404(2). The ratification relieves the actual signer from liability on the instrument but does not of itself affect any rights the person ratifying the signature may have against the actual signer. Moreover, a party may be precluded from denying the unauthorized signature. Section 3–404(1). This estoppel rule may be available based on a representation by or the negligence of the person whose name is signed.

LIABILITY OF PRIMARY PARTIES

There is a primary party on every note: the *maker.* The maker's commitment is unconditional. No one, however, is primarily liable on a draft or check as issued. The *drawee* is *not* liable on the instrument unless he accepts it. He is free to pay or accept it as he sees fit. If, on the other hand, the drawee accepts the draft, after which he is known as the *acceptor,* he becomes primarily liable on the instrument. **Acceptance,** or in the case of a check, certification, is the drawee's signed promise to pay the draft as presented. Section 3–410(1).

Since the maker of a note and the acceptor of a draft are primarily liable, presentment (that is, a demand for payment) is not a condition to the right of the holder to recover from them. While the holder usually makes a demand, there is no such requirement, nor need one be timely.

Makers

If an instrument is complete, a maker engages that he will pay the instrument according to its terms at the time of making his promise. Section 3–413(1). If an incomplete instrument is completed as authorized, the maker is liable for the amount as completed. Sections 3–413(1) and 3–115. If the completion of an incomplete instrument is unauthorized, (1) a holder in due course may recover from the maker as completed, (2) a holder of an incomplete instrument that has been materially and fraudulently completed may not recover anything, and (3) a holder of an incomplete instrument that has not been materially and fraudulently completed may collect the amount actually authorized. Section 3–407.

Acceptors

A drawee has no liability on the instrument until she accepts it, at which time she becomes an acceptor and, like a maker, primarily liable. The acceptor becomes liable on the draft according to its terms at the time of acceptance or as completed according to the rules for incomplete instruments. Sections 3–413(1) and 3–115.

An acceptance must be written on the draft. Section 3–410(1). No writing separate from the draft and no oral statement or conduct of the drawee will convert the drawee into an acceptor. The acceptance may take many forms. It may be printed on the face of the draft, ready for the drawee's signature. It may consist of a rubber stamp, with the signature of the drawee added. It may be the drawee's signature, preceded by a word or phrase such as "Accepted," "Certified," or "Good." It may consist of nothing more than the drawee's signature. Normally, but by no means necessarily, an acceptance is written vertically across the face of the draft. It must not, however, contain any words indicating an intent to refuse to honor the draft.

Checks, when accepted, are said to be certified. **Certification** is a special type of acceptance consisting of the drawee bank's promise to pay the check when subsequently presented for payment.

If the drawee refuses to accept or pay the instrument, he may be liable to the drawer for breach of contract. For example, a bank is not obligated to accept or pay any check drawn upon it. To do so would be to obligate a bank to pay an instrument regardless of whether the drawer had an account at that bank or sufficient funds in his account. If the drawer does have sufficient funds to cover the check, the drawee may, nevertheless, refuse to honor the instrument, but this would constitute a breach of its contract of deposit with the drawer. The refusal of the drawee to pay or accept the draft causes the *drawer* to become liable on the instrument upon receiving proper notice of dishonor. (This contingent or secondary liability of the drawer will be discussed in the next section.)

LIABILITY OF SECONDARY PARTIES

Parties with secondary liability do not unconditionally promise to pay the instrument; they engage to pay the instrument if the party expected to pay does not do so. The drawer and indorsers (including the payee if he indorses) of an instrument are secondarily liable; their liability is subject to the conditions of presentment, dishonor, notice of dishonor, and, in some instances, protest.

Indorsers and Drawers

If the instrument is *not* paid by a primary party and the conditions precedent to the liability of secondary parties are satisfied, a secondary party is liable unless he has disclaimed his liability or he possesses a valid defense to the instrument. *See Azalea City Motels, Inc. v. First Alabama Bank of Mobile.* The **drawer's** secondary liability is to pay the amount of the draft to the holder, or any indorser who pays it, unless she has disclaimed this liability by drawing without recourse. Section 3–413(2). *See also Davis v. Watson Brothers Plumbing, Inc.* Unless the indorsement otherwise specifies (as by using such words as *without recourse*), every **indorser's** secondary liability is to pay the instrument according to its tenor at the time of her indorsement to the holder or any subsequent indorser who pays it. Section 3–414(1).

Contract of Guarantor   Any indorser who adds the words **payment guaranteed** to her signature promises that if the instrument is not paid when due she will pay it immediately as if she were a *co-maker*. Thus, the use of the words "payment guaranteed" waives not only presentment, notice of dishonor, and protest but also all demand upon the maker or drawer. A **collection guaranteed** indorsement also waives presentment, notice of dishonor, and protest, *provided* that (1) the holder has obtained a legal judgment against the maker or acceptor and the judgment has not been satisfied, or (2) the maker or acceptor has become insolvent, or (3) it is otherwise useless to pursue the maker or acceptor. Section 3–416.

Effect of Certification   Where a **check** is certified at the request of the **holder,** the drawer and all prior indorsers are discharged. The liability of indorsers subsequent to certification is not affected. When the bank certifies a check, it should withhold sufficient funds from the drawer's account to pay the instrument. Since the bank is primarily liable on its certification and has the funds and the drawer does not, the discharge is reasonable.

Certification at the request of the **drawer** does *not,* however, relieve the drawer of secondary liability on the instrument. For example, the drawer may have a check certified before using it to close a business transaction, such as the purchase of a house. Since the drawer is then obtaining the benefit of the transaction, she should bear the risk of the bank's credit, rather than the payee.

Revised Article 3 changes this rule. A certification obtained by *either* a holder or a drawer relieves the drawer of liability on the check for dishonor. Rev. Section 3–414(b).

Disclaimer of Liability by Secondary Parties

Both drawers and indorsers *may* disclaim their normal secondary liability by drawing or indorsing instruments **"without recourse."** Sections 3–413(2) and 3–414(1).

The use of the qualifying words *without recourse* is understood to place purchasers on notice that they may not rely on the credit of the person using this language. A person drawing or indorsing an instrument in this manner does not incur the normal contractual liability of a drawer or indorser to pay the instrument, but he may nonetheless be liable for breach of warranty.

Under Revised Article 3 "[t]he liability of the drawer of an unaccepted draft is treated as a primary liability." Rev. Section 3–414(a), Comment 1. An exception to this more extensive liability of a drawer occurs when a draft has been accepted. If it is accepted by a bank, then the drawer is relieved of all liability for dishonor. If it is accepted by an acceptor who is *not* a bank, the drawer's liability is secondary, the same as an indorser. Rev. Section 3–414(c). The Revision changes current law by not permitting the drawer of a check to avoid liability by drawing without recourse. Rev. Section 3–414(d). A drawer of a draft that is not a check, however, may continue to disclaim all liability by drawing without recourse.

Conditions Precedent to Liability

A **condition precedent** is an event or events that must occur before liability arises. Conditions precedent to the liability of secondary parties are presentment, dishonor, notice of dishonor, and, in some situations, protest. The consequences of failing to comply with the conditions precedent, however, vary greatly between indorsers and drawers.

Presentment   Presentment is a demand for acceptance or payment made by the holder on the maker, acceptor, or drawee. Section 3–504(1). If there are two or more makers, acceptors, or drawees, presentment to one is sufficient. Presentments are of two kinds: presentment for acceptance and presentment for payment.

Presentment of a *draft* for **acceptance** is necessary to hold secondary parties liable on the instrument where (1) the draft so provides, (2) it is payable elsewhere than at the residence or place of business of the drawee, or (3) its date of payment depends on such presentment, as in the case of a draft providing: "Seven days after acceptance pay. . . ." Presentment for acceptance is also authorized in the case of any other time draft, although it is not required. Section 3–501(1)(a). Unless a draft must be presented for acceptance or is payable at a stated date, a drawee's refusal to accept the draft is not a dishonor of the instrument. The distinction made between a time draft and a demand draft or check is that with a demand instrument the holder is entitled to immediate payment, while with a time draft the holder is not entitled to payment until the due date, but may by presentment for acceptance determine whether the drawer will honor it. Thus, a drawee bank's refusal to certify a check for the holder does not constitute a dishonor of the instrument. A bank, unless otherwise agreed, has no obligation to certify a check. Section 3–411(2). The order on the bank is to *pay* the check, and if the bank is willing to pay, refusal to certify is not a dishonor of the check.

Presentment of *any* instrument for **payment** is necessary to charge any *indorser,* unless he indorsed after maturity. Thus, an indorser is completely discharged from liability on an instrument if due presentment for payment has not been made. Failure, however, to present for payment does not discharge the **drawer** except to the extent that there was unreasonable delay in presenting a draft to a drawee–bank where funds were available for its payment and the bank became insolvent in the interim. Section 3–502(1)(b). The difference in treatment between indorsers and drawers is based on the fact that the drawer always expects to have to pay the check, while the indorser expects that the instrument will be paid by the maker or drawee.

The date when presentment is to be made is set forth in detail in Section 3–503. An instrument with a specified maturity date is due for presentment on that date, or if the due date is not a full business day, on the next full business day. In any other case presentment is due within "a reasonable time." The definition of "a reasonable time" depends upon all the facts of the particular case, including the nature of the instrument and any usage of banking or trade.

For an uncertified check, the Code is specific: a reasonable time for presentment for payment or to initiate the bank collection process is *presumed* to be (a) with respect to the liability of the *drawer, thirty days* after date or issue, whichever is later; and (b) with respect to the liability of an *indorser, seven days* after his indorsement. Section 3–503(2).

The discharge of one indorser does not mean that all are discharged. Assume that Donna draws and issues a check payable to the order of Phillip on March 1. Phillip indorses it to Audrey on March 3, and Audrey indorses it to Beatrice on March 6. Beatrice must present the check by March 10 to hold Phillip liable on the instrument, and she must present it by the 13th to hold Audrey liable on the check. If she waits until *after* the 13th, both indorsers are discharged unless Beatrice can show that the presentment was made within a reasonable time. Nevertheless, Beatrice has thirty days (until March 31) to present the check to hold Donna liable because, with regard to a drawer, a reasonable time for presentment of a check is presumed to be thirty days. If Beatrice did not present the check for payment until after March 31, Donna would be discharged *only* to the extent of any loss she might have suffered as the result of the drawee's becoming insolvent during Beatrice's delay, but not otherwise. The indorsers Phillip and Audrey, however, would be completely discharged by Beatrice's failure to make presentment within a reasonable time, whether or not they had any loss.

Presentment may be made in any reasonable manner. The only specific requirement is that an accepted draft or a note made payable at a bank in the United States must be presented at such bank. Section 3–504(4). Otherwise, presentment may be made by mail, through a clearing house in a proper case, or at the place specified in the instrument, or if none is specified, at the place of business or residence of the acceptor or payor. Section 3–504(2).

Dishonor An instrument is dishonored when (1) presentment has been duly made, and acceptance or payment is refused or cannot be obtained within the prescribed time; or (2) presentment is excused and the instrument is not duly accepted or paid. Section 3–507(1). *See Oak Park Currency Exchange, Inc. v. Maropoulos.* Return for lack of a proper indorsement is not a dishonor.

Although the drawee may be willing to accept or pay the draft in strict accordance with its terms, he nevertheless has certain rights that he is entitled to exercise before he commits himself. These rights, the exercise of which does not constitute dishonor, are set out in Sections 3–505 and 3–506. He may require the presenter to produce the instrument at a proper place. In addition, he may require reasonable identification of the person making presentment, and upon payment, a signed receipt, with surrender of the instrument if it is paid in full. The presenter's failure to comply with any of these requests invalidates the presentment; consequently, there can be no dishonor. The person making presentment, however, is entitled to a reasonable opportunity to comply with any such requests, and the time for making presentment is extended accordingly.

Acceptance may be deferred until the close of the next business day following a proper presentment, thereby giving the drawee the opportunity to check with the drawer or to take any other steps he may desire to assure himself of the propriety of acceptance. Conversely, the holder is authorized to allow postponement of acceptance for an additional business day in a good faith effort to obtain acceptance. For example, the drawee may refuse to accept without verification from the drawer and be unable to get in touch with him. He would either have to dishonor the instrument or ask the holder for an additional day. If the holder grants it, there is no dishonor.

Payment of an instrument may be deferred without dishonor pending reasonable examination to determine whether the instrument is properly payable, but payment must be made in any event before the close of business on the day of presentment.

Notice of Dishonor Upon proper presentment and dishonor, and subject to any necessary notice of protest, the holder has an immediate right of recourse against drawers and indorsers after giving them timely notice of dishonor. If due notice is not given, the effect is the same as if there had been undue delay in presentment.

Notice of dishonor is normally given by the holder or by an indorser who has himself received notice. For example, Michael makes a note payable to the order of Phyllis; Phyllis indorses it to Arthur; Arthur indorses it to Bambi; and Bambi indorses it to Henry, the last holder. Henry presents it to Michael within a reasonable period of time, but Michael refuses to pay. Henry may give notice of dishonor to all secondary parties: Phyllis, Arthur, and Bambi. If he is satisfied that Bambi will pay him or he does not know how to contact Phyllis or Arthur, he may only notify Bambi. Bambi then must see to it that Arthur or Phyllis is notified, or Bambi will have no recourse. Bambi may notify either or both. If she notifies Arthur only, Arthur will have to see to it that Phyllis is notified, or Arthur will have no recourse. When notice is properly given it benefits all parties who have rights on the instrument against the party notified. Section 3–508(8). Thus, Henry's notification to Phyllis operates as notice to Phyllis by both Arthur and Bambi. Likewise, if Henry notifies only Bambi and Bambi notifies Arthur and Phyllis, then Henry has the benefit of Bambi's notification of Arthur and Phyllis. Nonetheless, it would be advisable for Henry to give notice to all prior parties because Bambi may be insolvent and thus she may not bother to notify Arthur or Phyllis.

If, in the above hypothetical problem, Henry notifies Phyllis alone, Arthur and Bambi are discharged. Phyllis cannot complain because she has no claim against Arthur or Bambi who indorsed after she did. It cannot matter to Phyllis that she is compelled to pay Henry rather than Arthur.

Therefore, subsequent parties are permitted to skip intermediate indorsers if they want to discharge them and are willing to look solely to prior indorsers for recourse.

Any necessary notice must be given by a **bank** before midnight on the *next* banking day following the banking day when it receives notice of dishonor. Any **nonbank** must give notice before midnight of the third business day after dishonor or receipt of notice of dishonor. Section 3–508(2). For instance, Donna draws a check on Youngstown Bank payable to the order of Pablo; Pablo indorses it to Andrea; Andrea deposits it to her account in Second Chicago National Bank; Second Chicago National Bank properly presents it to Youngstown Bank, the drawee; Youngstown dishonors it because the drawer, Donna, has insufficient funds on deposit to cover it. Youngstown has until midnight of the following day to notify Second Chicago National, Andrea, Pablo, or Donna of the dishonor. Second Chicago National has until midnight of the day after receipt of notice of dishonor to notify Andrea, Pablo, or Donna of the dishonor. That is, if Second Chicago National received the notice of dishonor on Monday, it would have until midnight of Tuesday to notify Andrea, Pablo, or Donna. If it failed to notify Andrea, it could not charge the item back to her. But Andrea has until midnight of the third business day after receipt of notice of dishonor to notify Pablo or Donna. If she received notice on Tuesday, she would have until midnight on Friday to notify Pablo or Donna. Pablo would also have three business days in which to notify Donna.

Revised Article 3 changes the notice of dishonor for a nonbank from three days to 30 days following the day on which the person receives notice of dishonor. Rev. Section 3–503(c).

Frequently, notice of dishonor is given by returning the unpaid instrument with a stamp, ticket, or memorandum attached stating that the item was not paid and requesting that the recipient make good on it. But since the purpose of notice is to give knowledge of dishonor and to inform the secondary party that he may be held liable on the instrument, any kind of notice which informs the recipient of his potential liability is sufficient. No formal requisites are imposed—notice may be given in any reasonable manner. Written notice, however, is effective when sent regardless of whether it is received. Section 3–508(4). An oral notice is sufficient, but is inadvisable because it may be difficult to prove.

If the person notified is not misled, a misdescription of the instrument does not defeat the notice. Section 3–508(3). Thus, if a payee of a promissory note executed on January 3 by Mike Maker is told that the "note of January 5 made by Mike Maker" has been dishonored, this would constitute a sufficient notice if the recipient knew that the dishonor related to Mike Maker's note dated January 3.

Protest   Protest is required only if the draft is drawn or payable *outside* the United States. A **protest** is a certificate of dishonor made under the hand and seal of a United States consul or vice-consul or a notary public or other person authorized to certify to a dishonor by the law of the place where the dishonor occurred. It must identify the instrument and certify either that due presentment has been made or the reason why it is excused and that the instrument has been dishonored by non-acceptance or nonpayment. The protest may also certify that notice of dishonor has been given to all parties or to specified parties. Protest, or the noting for protest, must be made within the time allowed for giving notice of dishonor.

Delay in Presentment, Notice, or Protest Excused   The Code excuses a *delay* in presentment, notice, or protest in two situations. Section 3–511(1). The first excuses a delay where the holder does not have notice that the instrument is due; for example, an instrument may provide that its maturity shall be automatically accelerated upon the happening of a particular event. If the holder does not know that this event has happened, she is excused from presentment until she learns of the acceleration, and secondary parties are not discharged because of the delay. Once the holder learns that the event has occurred, she must present the note within a reasonable time and give prompt notice of dishonor to hold the indorsers liable.

The second situation excuses the holder's delay where it is caused by circumstances beyond his control. For example, suppose the holder cannot present the instrument to the primary party because a storm has disrupted all means of communication and transportation. The circumstances need not make presentment impossible, but the holder must act with reasonable diligence after the cause of delay has ceased.

Presentment, Notice, or Protest Excused

The Code *entirely* excuses the holder from presentment, notice, or protest if the party to be charged: (a) has expressly or implicitly waived the right; or (b) has himself dishonored the instrument or has countermanded payment, or if the holder otherwise has no reason to expect the instrument to be accepted or paid. Section 3–511(2). For example, if Dwight draws a check on a bank where he has no account, he has closed his account, or he has stopped payment on the check, he is not entitled to a due presentment and notice of dishonor. These matters are entirely excused so far as he is concerned. But they would not be excused for intermediate indorsers who did not have any reason to expect that the instrument would not be accepted or paid.

Section 3–511(2) also entirely excuses presentment, notice, or protest, as the case may be, if these things cannot be accomplished by reasonable diligence. For example, if the maker of a note has "departed for places unknown" and cannot be located by reasonable diligence, the holder has no way of making a presentment to him. In such case, presentment is entirely excused, and the holder should treat the instrument as dishonored and give prompt notice of dishonor to the indorsers. Likewise, if one of the indorsers cannot be located by reasonable diligence, notice of dishonor would not have to be given to him—it would be entirely excused.

Presentment Excused

The Code sets out some other specific situations in which only presentment is *entirely* excused. These situations, which do not excuse notice or protest, include the following: (1) the maker, acceptor, or drawee is dead or in insolvency proceedings; or (2) payment or acceptance is refused for reasons not relating to proper presentment, making it clear that a subsequent presentment would be useless. Section 3–511(3).

SPECIAL SITUATIONS AFFECTING LIABILITY

If a drawee pays an instrument, the drawer is generally under a duty to make reimbursement. Usually the drawer has funds in the hands of the drawee, and the drawee, honoring a draft or check, reimburses itself immediately by charging the drawer's account or her funds. The drawee can be reimbursed, however, only if it acts in accordance with the drawer's *order* as it appears on the instrument. Thus, if Davis draws a check to the order of Jones, the drawee bank to whom the instrument is addressed acquires no right of reimbursement by paying Roe, unless Jones has indorsed the check to Roe. In short, it is up to the drawee to determine whether the one presenting the item for payment or acceptance has rights in it, for if it pays the wrong party, it is the drawee's loss and not the drawer's. Two situations involving these principles have been especially troublesome and have been specifically addressed by the Code. A third situation—one giving rise to tort liability for conversion—is also discussed in this section.

The Impostor Rule

Usually, the impostor rule comes into play in situations involving a confidence man who impersonates a respected citizen and who deceives a third party into delivering a negotiable instrument to the impostor in the name of the respected citizen. For instance, John Doe, falsely representing himself as Richard Roe, a prominent citizen, induces Ray Davis to loan him $10,000. Davis draws a check payable to the order of Richard Roe and delivers it to Doe. Doe then forges Roe's name to the check and presents it to the drawee for payment. The drawee pays it. Subsequently, the drawer denies the drawee's right of reimbursement upon the ground that the drawee did not pay in accordance with his order: the drawer ordered payment to Roe or to Roe's order. Roe did not order payment to anyone; therefore, the drawee would not acquire a right of reimbursement against the drawer Davis. This is the argument in favor of the drawer and is supported by the general rule governing unauthorized signatures.

Nevertheless, Section 3–405(1)(a) provides that the indorsement of the impostor (Doe) or of any other person in the name of the named payee is **effective** if the impostor has induced the maker or drawer (Davis) to issue the instrument to him or his confederate using the name of the payee (Roe). It is as if the named payee had indorsed the instrument. The reason for this rule is that the drawer or maker is to blame for failing to detect the impersonation by the impostor. Thus, in the above example, the drawee would be able to debit the drawer's account. *See also Philadelphia Title Ins. Co. v. Fidelity-Philadelphia Trust Co.*

Revised Article 3 expands the impostor rule by extending its coverage to include an impostor who is impersonating an agent. Rev. Section 3–404(a). Under current law and the Revision, if an impostor impersonates Jones and induces the drawer to draw a check to the order of Jones, the impostor can negotiate the check. Under the Revision, but *not* under current law, if an impostor impersonates Jones, the president of Jones Corporation, and the check is to the order of Jones Corporation, the impostor can negotiate the check. Comment to Rev. Section 3–404.

The Fictitious Payee Rule

The second situation is similar, but it involves a disloyal agent rather than an impostor. For instance, the drawer's agent falsely tells the drawer that money is owed to Leon, and the drawer writes a check payable to the order of Leon and hands it to the agent for delivery to him. The agent forges Leon's name to the check and obtains payment from the drawee bank. The drawer then denies the bank's claim to reimbursement upon the ground that the bank did not comply with her order; that the drawer had ordered payment to Leon or order; that the drawee did not make payment either to Leon or as ordered by him, inasmuch as the forgery of Leon's signature is wholly inoperative; and that the drawee paid in accordance with the scheme of the faithless agent and not in compliance with the drawer's order.

Once again, the drawee bank will be able to debit the drawer's account. "An indorsement by any person in the name of a named payee is **effective** if . . . an agent or employee of the maker or drawer has supplied him with the name of the payee intending the latter to have no such interest." Section 3–405(1)(c). (Emphasis supplied.) The Code places the risk of employee fraud upon the party employing the agent.

The same rule also applies to the analogous situation in which a person signs as or on behalf of a maker or drawer and does not intend the payee to have an interest in the instrument. Section 3–405(1)(b). In such situations, any person's indorsement in the name of the named payee is **effective.** For instance, Palmer gives Albrecht, her employee, authority to write checks in order to pay Palmer's debts. Albrecht writes a check for $2,000 to Foushee, a fictitious payee, which Albrecht takes and indorses in Foushee's name to Albrecht. Albrecht cashes the check at Palmer's bank. Palmer's bank can debit Palmer's account because Albrecht's signature in the name of Foushee is effective against Palmer. Palmer should bear the risk of her unscrupulous employees.

Liability for Conversion

Conversion is a **tort** by which a person becomes liable in damages because of his wrongful control over the personal property of another. A negotiable instrument is the property of the holder. Accordingly, the Code provides that a conversion occurs in three situations: (1) when a drawee to whom a draft is delivered for acceptance refuses to return it on demand; (2) when any person to whom an instrument is delivered for payment refuses on demand either to pay or to return it; and (3) when an instrument is paid on a forged indorsement. Section 3–419(1). Situations (1) and (2) involve willful action on the part of the party guilty of the conversion, whereas in situation (3) the payor's action was in all probability completely innocent because his control over the instrument resulted from an unrecognized break in the chain of title. Nevertheless, liability is the same in all three cases. Good faith is immaterial and the person wrongfully exercising dominion over the instrument is liable for damages in a tort action for conversion.

LIABILITY BASED ON WARRANTY

The Code imposes two types of implied warranties on the transfer of commercial paper: (a) transferor's warranties and (b) presenter's warranties. These warranties are effective whether or *not* the transferor or presenter signs the instrument although, as will be seen, the extension of the warranty to subsequent holders does depend upon whether they have indorsed the instrument. *See Oak Park Currency Exchange, Inc. v. Maropoulos.* Like other warranties, these may be disclaimed by agreement between immediate parties. In the case of an indorser, his disclaimer of transfer warranties must appear in the indorsement itself.

WARRANTIES ON TRANSFER

Any person who transfers an instrument, whether by negotiation or assignment, and receives **consideration** makes certain **transferor's warranties.** Section 3–417(2). Any consideration sufficient to support a contract will support a transfer warranty. If transfer is by delivery alone, warranties on transfer run only to the immediate transferee. If the transfer is made by indorsement, whether qualified

or unqualified, the transfer warranty runs to "any subsequent holder who takes the instrument in good faith." See Figure 28–2. The warranties of the transferor are as follows.

Good Title

The first warranty that the Code imposes on a transferor is that the transferor has good title to the instrument or is authorized to obtain payment or acceptance on behalf of one who has good title and the transfer is otherwise rightful. Section 3–417(2)(a). The following example illustrates this rule. Mitchell makes a note payable to the order of Penelope. A thief steals the note from Penelope, forges Penelope's indorsement, and sells the instrument to Aaron. Aaron does not have good title because the break in the indorsement chain prevents him from acquiring title. If Aaron indorses the instrument to Judith for consideration, Judith can hold Aaron liable for breach of warranty. The warranty action is important to Judith because it enables her to hold Aaron liable, even if Aaron indorsed the note "without recourse."

Signatures Genuine

The second warranty imposed by the Code is that **all** signatures are genuine or authorized. In the example presented above, this warranty would also be breached. Section 3–417(2)(b). If the signature of a maker, drawer, drawee, acceptor, or indorser not in the chain of title is unauthorized, there is a breach of this warranty but no breach of the warranty of good title.

No Material Alteration

The third warranty is the warranty against material alteration. Section 3–417(2)(c). Suppose that Maureen makes a note payable to the order of the payee in the amount of $100. The payee, without authority, alters the note so that it appears to be drawn for $1,000 and negotiates the instrument to Lois, who buys it without knowledge of the alteration. Lois, indorsing "without recourse," negotiates the instrument to Kyle for consideration. Kyle presents the instrument to Maureen, who refuses to pay more than $100 on it. Kyle can collect the difference from Lois. Although Lois is not liable to Kyle on the indorsement contract because of her qualified indorsement, she is liable to him for breach of warranty. If Lois had not qualified her indorsement, Kyle would be able to recover against Lois on the basis of either warranty or the indorsement contract.

No Defenses

The fourth transferor's warranty imposed by the Code is that *no defense* of any party is

good against the transferor. Section 3–417(2)(d). Under this warranty, a transferor who indorses "without recourse" stands in a better position than an unqualified indorser. His warranty is only that he has *no knowledge* of any such defense. Section 3–417(3). Suppose that Madeline, a minor and a resident of a State where minors' contracts for non-necessaries are voidable, makes a note payable to bearer in payment of a motorcycle. Pierce, the first holder, negotiates it to Iola by mere delivery. Iola indorses it "without recourse" (qualified indorsement) and negotiates it to Justin, and Justin unqualifiedly indorses it to Hector. All negotiations are made for consideration. Hector can-

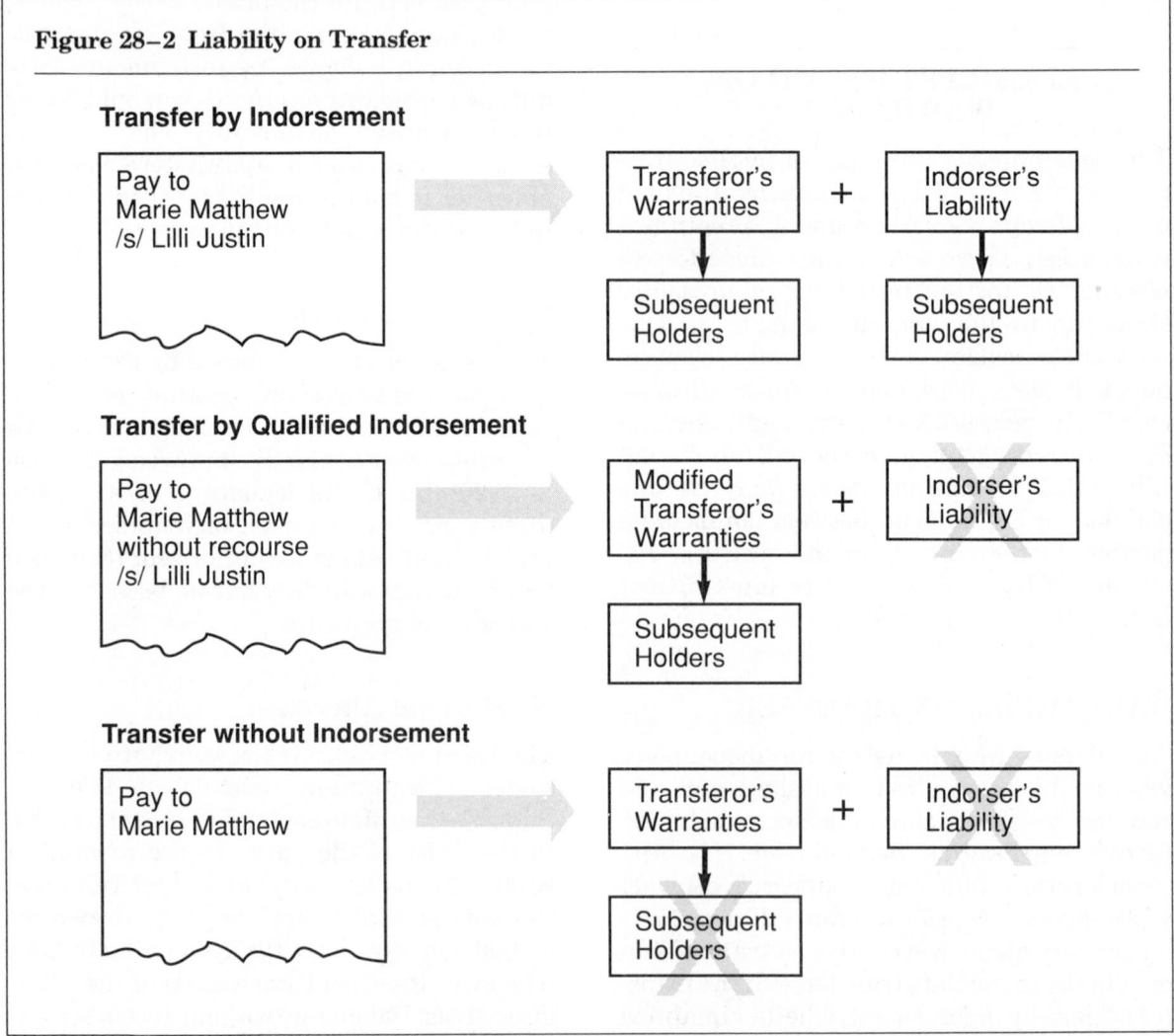

Figure 28–2 Liability on Transfer

Transfer by Indorsement

Pay to
Marie Matthew
/s/ Lilli Justin

Transferor's Warranties + Indorser's Liability

Subsequent Holders   Subsequent Holders

Transfer by Qualified Indorsement

Pay to
Marie Matthew
without recourse
/s/ Lilli Justin

Modified Transferor's Warranties + Indorser's Liability

Subsequent Holders

Transfer without Indorsement

Pay to
Marie Matthew

Transferor's Warranties + Indorser's Liability

Subsequent Holders

not recover upon the instrument against Iola because of Madeline's minority (a real defense). Hector therefore recovers against Justin on either the breach of warranty that no valid defenses exist to the instrument or the indorsement contract, provided Hector gave Justin prompt notice of dishonor. Justin cannot recover against Iola upon Iola's qualified indorsement. Can Justin hold Iola for breach of warranty? Because Iola indorsed without recourse, she does not warrant that the instrument is without defense; she only warrants that she knows of no defense that is good against her. Assuming that Iola did not know that Madeline was a minor, Justin cannot hold Iola for breach of warranty. Can Justin hold Pierce? Pierce is not liable as an indorser because he did not indorse the instrument. Although Pierce, as a transferor, warrants that there are no defenses good against him, this warranty only extends to his immediate transferee, Iola. Therefore, Justin cannot hold Pierce liable. This illustration shows the interplay between indorsement and warranty liability. It also shows the relationship between the liability imposed under the various warranties and the individuals who can or cannot claim protection under a particular warranty.

No Knowledge of Insolvency

Any person who transfers a negotiable instrument warrants that he has no knowledge of any insolvency proceedings instituted with respect to the maker, acceptor, or drawer of an unaccepted instrument. Section 3–417(2)(e). Thus, if Marcia makes a note payable to bearer, and the first holder, Taylor, negotiates it for consideration without indorsement to Ursula, who then negotiates it for consideration by qualified indorsement to Valerie, both Taylor and Ursula make a warranty that they do not know that Marcia is in bankruptcy. Valerie could not hold Taylor liable for breach of warranty, however, because Taylor's warranty runs only in favor of her immediate transferee, Ursula, since Taylor transferred the instrument without indorsement. If Valerie could hold Ursula liable on her warranty,

Ursula could thereupon hold Taylor, her immediate transferor, liable.

Figure 28–2 summarizes liabilities on transfer.

WARRANTIES ON PRESENTMENT

Any party who pays or accepts an instrument must do so in strict compliance with the orders contained in that instrument. For example, the payment or acceptance must be made to a person entitled to receive payment or acceptance, the amount paid or accepted must be the correct amount, and the instrument must be genuine and not altered. If payment or acceptance is not correct, then the payor or acceptor will potentially incur a loss. In the case of a note, a maker who pays the wrong person will not be discharged from his obligation to pay the correct person. If the maker pays too much, he is out of pocket for the excess. If a drawee pays the wrong person, he generally cannot charge the drawer's account. If the drawee pays too much, he generally cannot charge the drawer's account for the excess. Similar incorrect payments can be made by indorsers who pay an instrument.

After paying or accepting an instrument to the wrong person, for the wrong amount, or in some other incorrect way, does the person who incorrectly paid or accepted have any recourse against the person *receiving* payment or acceptance? Section 3–418 addresses this critical question by providing that payment or acceptance of any instrument is final in favor of a (1) holder in due course or (2) a person who has in good faith changed his position in reliance on the payment unless there has been a breach of the implied **warranties of presentment,** which relate to (1) the title of the presenter, (2) the signature of the issuing party, and (3) material alterations. The presenter's warranties run not only *from* the person who obtains payment or acceptance but also from all prior transferors. The presenter's warranties run *to* any person who in good faith pays or accepts the instrument. The presentment warranties are codified in Section 3–417(1) and are discussed below.

If the party receiving payment or acceptance is *not* a holder in due course or a person who has in good faith changed his position in reliance on the payment, then the doctrine of finality under Section 3–418 does not apply and the payor or acceptor may seek recovery under restitution. In most instances, the equities will favor the mistaken payor or acceptor because the other party has not given value or has not taken the instrument in good faith, or has taken with notice that it is overdue, that it has been dishonored, or that there is a defense against or claim to it.

Good Title

Presenters give the same warranty of good title to persons who pay or accept as is granted to transferees under the transferor's warranty. As explained above, this warranty extends to the genuineness of the indorser's signatures but not to the signature of the drawer or maker.

For example, if Donnese draws a check to Peter or order, and Peter's indorsement is forged, the bank does not follow Donnese's order in paying such an item and therefore cannot charge her account (except in the impostor or fictitious payee situations discussed above). The bank, however, can recover from the person who obtained payment of the check from the bank for breach of the presenter's warranty of good title. The bank should not be required to bear this loss because it should not be expected to know the signature of payees or other indorsers of checks, although it should know the signatures of its own customers. The same outcome results if the maker of a note pays on a forged indorsement. The maker, like the drawee, cannot know everyone's signature, and where the indorser's signature is forged, the maker can recover any money paid to the presenting party.

Genuineness of Signature of Maker and Drawer

Presenters warrant that they have no knowledge that the signature of the maker or drawer is unauthorized. To protect a person who takes an instrument in good faith and without knowledge of an unauthorized signature and later learns it was forged, certain exceptions to this warranty are specified in the Code. A holder in due course acting in good faith does not give such a warranty to (1) the maker with respect to his own signature; (2) the drawer with respect to his own signature; and (3) an acceptor of a draft with respect to the drawer's signature if such holder took the draft after acceptance or obtained the acceptance without knowledge of the unauthorized signature. These exceptions are available only to a holder in due course.

For example, suppose Donnese's name is forged to a check making it appear that it was drawn by her. If the bank pays this check, it cannot charge Donnese's account and it cannot recover from a holder in due course or a person who in good faith has changed his position in reliance on the payment or acceptance if neither has knowledge of the unauthorized drawer's signature. The justification for the rule is that the drawee is supposed to know the drawer's signature. The same results apply to the maker of a note who pays a note with his signature forged: he should know his own signature.

No Material Alteration

Presenters also give a warranty against material alteration, but again it is not given by a holder in due course acting in good faith to a maker or drawer, whether or not the drawer is also the drawee. Further, the holder in due course acting in good faith does not give this warranty to the acceptor of a draft or check with respect to an alteration made *prior* to acceptance if such holder took after acceptance, even though the acceptance included a term such as "payable as originally drawn." The acceptor had the first opportunity to detect the alteration. To permit the acceptor to shift the responsibility for a prior material alteration to a subsequent party would defeat the entire purpose of acceptance and certification. An acceptance or certification constitutes a definite commitment to honor a definite instrument.

This rule should not be confused with that which applies where the alteration is made *after* the acceptance or certification. In such a situation, the drawee knows the amount of the original acceptance or certification, and she should not be able to charge back against an innocent party if she pays out more than that amount. Hence, a holder in due course does not warrant against alterations made after acceptance.

For example, if Dolores makes a check to Porter's order in the amount of $3 and it is raised so as to appear to be in the amount of $300, the bank cannot charge the $300 it pays out on such an item to the drawer's account. It can charge the account only $3 because that is all the drawer ordered it to pay. Nonetheless, the bank can collect the difference from the presenting party who received payment because the presenter's warranty of no material alteration has been breached. But suppose that the maker issues a note in the amount of $300, and it is raised to $3,000. If he pays this note, he is not permitted to recover from a holder in due course acting in good faith because the maker—unlike a drawee—has a way of knowing the original amount of the instrument. Similarly, suppose that a check or draft is raised after it has been accepted or certified by the drawee. If the acceptor pays the raised amount to a holder in due course acting in good faith, the acceptor is not entitled to recover the amount by which the instrument was raised because the innocent holder has no way of knowing the proper amount, while the acceptor does.

Figure 28–3 summarizes liability based on warranty.

TERMINATION OF LIABILITY

Eventually, every commercial transaction must end, with the potential liabilities of the parties to the instrument terminated. The Code specifies the various methods and extent by which the liability of *any* party, primary or secondary, is discharged. Section 3–601. It also specifies when the liability of *all* parties is discharged. No discharge of a party is effective against a subsequent holder in due course, however, unless she has knowledge of the discharge when she takes the instrument. Section 3–602.

PAYMENT OR SATISFACTION

The most obvious and common way for a party to discharge liability on an instrument is to pay the holder. Section 3–603. Such a payment results in a discharge even though it is made with knowledge of the claim of another person to the instrument, unless such other person either supplies adequate indemnity or obtains an injunction in a proceeding to which the holder is made a party. The person making payment is not required to decide at his peril whether the claim to the instrument is valid or not. Such a claim may arise, for example, where the prior holder contends the instrument was stolen from him.

The person making payment should, of course, take the instrument or have it cancelled—marked "paid" or "cancelled"—so that it cannot pass into the hands of a subsequent holder in due course against whom his discharge would not be effective.

TENDER OF PAYMENT

Any party liable on an instrument who makes tender of full payment to a holder when or after payment is due is discharged from all subsequent liability for interest, costs, and attorney's fees. Section 3–604(1). Her tender does not relieve her of liability for the face amount of the instrument or any interest accrued until the time of tender. The maker or acceptor may, however, have no way of seeking out a holder so as to make tender to stop the running of interest. Subsection (3) of Section 3–604 solves this problem by providing that if such party is ready and able to pay a time instrument when it is due at the place of payment specified in the instrument, it is the equivalent of tender. This remedy is not available in the case of

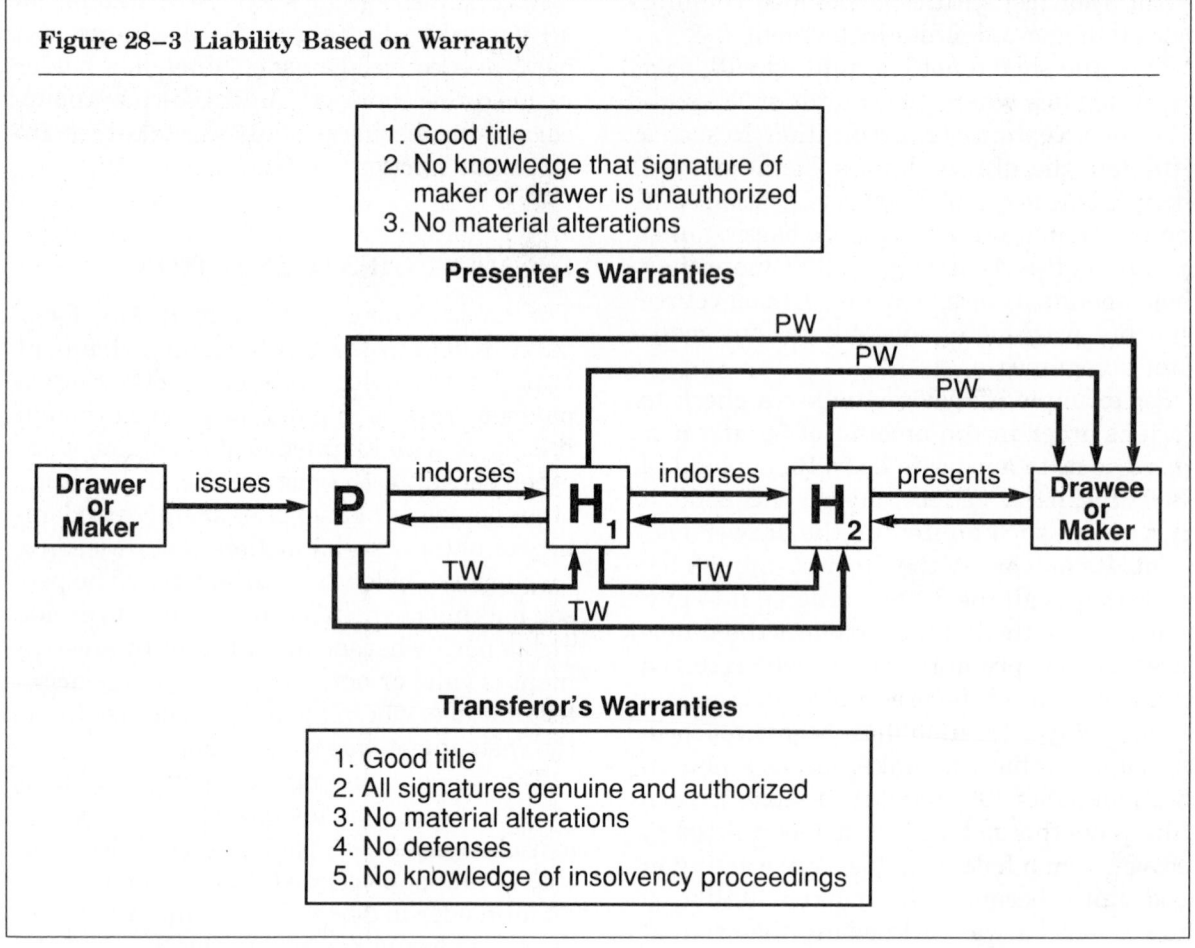

Figure 28–3 Liability Based on Warranty

Presenter's Warranties
1. Good title
2. No knowledge that signature of maker or drawer is unauthorized
3. No material alterations

Transferor's Warranties
1. Good title
2. All signatures genuine and authorized
3. No material alterations
4. No defenses
5. No knowledge of insolvency proceedings

demand paper or paper that does not specify a place of payment.

Occasionally a holder will refuse a tender of payment for reasons known only to himself. It may be that he believes he has rights over and beyond the amount of the tender, or because he desires to enforce payment against another party. In any event, his refusal of the tender has the effect of wholly discharging every party who has a right of recourse against the party making tender. Section 3–604(2). For example, a note executed by Mayer in favor of Peggy is negotiated by indorsement successively to Abraham, Belinda, and Caroline. Mayer defaults, and Caroline asserts her rights against indorsers Peggy, Abraham, and Belinda. If Peggy tenders full payment to Caroline and Caroline refuses to accept it, desiring to collect from Mayer, then Abraham and Belinda are wholly discharged. The reason is that both Abraham and Belinda would have rights of recourse against Peggy if they were required to pay.

CANCELLATION AND RENUNCIATION

Section 3–605 provides that a holder may discharge the liability of any party to an instrument in any manner apparent on the face of the instrument or the indorsement, such as by cancelling the instrument or the signature of the party or parties to be discharged by destruction or mutilation or by striking out a party's signature.

Since the instrument itself constitutes the obligation, intentional cancellation of it by the holder results in a discharge of all parties. Accidental destruction of an instrument does not have such an effect, nor does cancellation in any form by anyone other than the holder.

If the holder wishes to discharge one, but not all parties, he may merely strike out that party's signature. He must be careful, however, that he does not also discharge other parties by impairing their rights of recourse, as discussed below.

A holder may also renounce his rights by a writing, signed and delivered, or by surrendering the instrument to the party to be discharged. As in the case of other discharges, however, a written renunciation is of no effect against a subsequent holder in due course who takes without knowledge of the renunciation.

Cancellation or renunciation is effective even without consideration.

IMPAIRMENT OF RECOURSE OR COLLATERAL

If the holder collects the amount of an instrument from an indorser, the indorser normally has a right of recourse against parties primarily liable, prior indorsers (if any), the drawer (in the case of a draft or check), or any one or more of them. At the time the indorser acquired the instrument, she relied upon the credit of the prior parties, the strict nature of their liability, and in the case of an instrument secured by collateral, on the value of that collateral.

If any of these rights is adversely affected by the action or inaction of the holder, the indorser should not be required to pay the instrument because when she subsequently seeks reimbursement, she will not possess the rights she bargained for when she acquired the instrument. The same rule applies to an accommodation maker or acceptor known to the holder to be such.

Section 3–606 of the Code, therefore, provides that the holder discharges any party to the instrument to the extent that without her consent the holder

1. releases or agrees not to sue any person against whom such party, to the knowledge of the holder, has a right of recourse;

2. agrees to suspend the right to enforce the instrument or collateral against such person;

3. otherwise discharges such person; or

4. unjustifiably impairs any collateral for the instrument given by or on behalf of the party or any person against whom such party has a right of recourse.

The holder may, however, take any of the first three of these actions without discharging a party with a right of recourse if at the same time he expressly reserves his rights against such party. In so doing, he cannot impair any rights of recourse which such party may possess against others.

As indicated above, striking out the signature of a prior indorser discharges subsequent indorsers who have a right of recourse against the indorser discharged. Similarly, if the holder suspends the right to enforce the instrument, as by granting an unauthorized extension of time to pay, the subsequent indorsers are discharged. Their undertaking is only to pay if the maker or drawee does not pay on demand or on the date specified in a time instrument. They have not contracted for any extension of time for payment.

REACQUISITION

When an instrument is returned to or reacquired by a prior party to the instrument, any intervening party is discharged from liability as against the reacquiring party and against any subsequent parties who are not holders in due course without notice of the discharge. Section 3–208. The liability of all parties is discharged when any party who has no right of action or recourse on the instrument reacquires the instrument in his own right. Section 3–601(3)(a).

OTHER METHODS OF DISCHARGE

As discussed earlier, other methods by which a party's liability may be discharged include

1. fraudulent and material alteration (Section 3–407);

2. discharge of the drawer and prior indorsers by certification of a check procured by a holder (Section 3–411); and

3. unexcused delay in presentment, notice of dishonor, or protest (Section 3–502).

Also, any party may be discharged from liability as against another party agreeing to pay money in exchange for the discharge. Section 3–601(2).

CASES

Signature/Condition Precedents to Liability

AZALEA CITY MOTELS, INC. v. FIRST ALABAMA BANK OF MOBILE

Alabama Supreme Court, 1989.
9 UCC Rep. Serv. 2d 1009.

SHORES, J.

Defendants, Azalea City Motels, Inc., W. C. Greene, and Paul M. Jackson, appeal a judgment in a nonjury trial in favor of the plaintiff, First Alabama Bank (hereinafter "FAB").

I. The Facts Azalea City Motels, Inc. (hereinafter "Azalea City"), is a corporation primarily engaged in the business of buying, managing, and selling hotel and motel properties. The corporation was, during the majority of the period relevant to this litigation, exclusively owned and operated by W. C. Greene and Paul M. Jackson. Azalea City maintained at least one checking account at FAB (formerly the Merchants National Bank of Mobile) under the name "Azalea City Motels, Inc." In 1984, Mr. Greene and Mr. Jackson opened an additional account at FAB under the name "Azalea Management Company" (hereinafter "Azalea Management"). Although Greene and Jackson argue that this account was a trade account for Azalea City, the account's signature card indicates that Greene and Jackson owned the account individually, that they were both authorized signatories for the account, and that the account was listed neither as a corporate account nor as a partnership account.

On October 23, 1984, William Hannah, an associate of Greene and Jackson, issued a check for $100,000 drawn on a trust account at the First National Bank of Livingston, Tennessee (FNBL). The check was made payable to Azalea City Motels, Inc., but was not indorsed by Azalea City. Instead, the check bore the indorsement of Azalea Management Company and was deposited to the Azalea Management Company account at FAB on October 24, 1984. A day later, an FAB employee incorrectly encoded the check to reflect a $10,000 item rather than a $100,000 item. Consequently, the Azalea Management Company account was provisionally credited $10,000 instead of $100,000.

FAB then sent the check to the New Orleans branch of the Federal Reserve Bank of Atlanta for collection through the normal check collection process. Relying upon the misencoded information on the check, the New Orleans branch provisionally credited FAB with $10,000 and forwarded the check to the Nashville Federal Reserve branch so that it could present the check to FNBL. Both the Nashville Federal Reserve Bank and FNBL processed the check as a $10,000 item. FNBL received the check on October 26, 1984, paid the item as if it were a $10,000 draft, and deducted a corresponding $10,000 from Hannah's account. On the same day, Hannah issued a stop payment order on the check in the amount of the original instrument. Despite the stop payment order, the check went through the normal sorting and filing procedures at FNBL. Without correcting the encoding error or honoring the stop payment order, FNBL returned the original $100,000 check to Hannah with his statement on October 30, 1984. The evidence fails to indicate whether Hannah entered the stop payment order before or after the Federal Reserve presented the check to FNBL for payment.

Sometime prior to November 5, 1984, the defendants became aware that FAB had miscredited their account. On that date, FAB provisionally credited the Azalea Management account for $90,000, the difference between the original check and the miscoded item. On November 6, 1984, FAB presented a $90,000 adjustment and a photocopy of the check to the Federal Reserve Branch in New Orleans. On November 7, 1984, the Federal Reserve Branch in New Orleans submitted the adjustment to the Federal Reserve Branch in Nashville. The Federal Reserve Branch in Nashville received the adjustment on November 8, 1984. While awaiting final payment of the adjustment, FAB allowed Greene and Jackson to withdraw funds against the $100,000 provisional credit. By November 19, 1984, Greene and Jackson had withdrawn virtually all of the funds from the Azalea Management account.

Meanwhile, the Federal Reserve Branch in Nashville allowed almost 30 days to elapse before it presented the adjustment to FNBL. FNBL received the entry of adjustment on December 4, 1984, and, at that time, informed FAB that it was charging back (debiting FAB) the $100,000 item. The same day, FAB notified the defendants that FNBL had dishonored the item, 41 days after the initial deposit. FAB put a hold on the Azalea Management account on December 5, 1984, but released the hold on December 7, 1984. During the interim, FAB neither returned nor dishonored any items presented for payment against the Azalea Management account.

In March 1985, FAB sued Hannah, individually and d/b/a Southern Properties; Southern Properties, Inc.; Azalea City Motels, Inc.; Azalea City d/b/a Azalea Management; and W. C. Greene. Jackson was not named in the original complaint. In December 1985, FAB obtained a default judgment against Hannah, but was unable to enforce the judgment because the whereabouts of Hannah were unknown. After a lengthy period of relative inactivity in the Azalea Management account,

Jackson procured new signature cards on February 14, 1986, and his wife, Barbara, replaced Greene as an owner of and signatory on the account. In April 1986, after the Jacksons had deposited a substantial amount of money to the account, FAB seized the assets and offset them against the $100,000 check from Hannah. In May, FAB amended its complaint, adding Paul Jackson as a defendant in this action. Jackson counterclaimed, alleging that FAB had wrongfully frozen his account and had wrongfully set off assets in the account against the $100,000 check.

Following a nonjury trial on the merits, the trial court, without articulating any findings of fact or conclusions of law, entered a judgment in favor of FAB in the amount of $73,419.46, which sum represents the $100,000 check, less $26,580.54 seized from the Azalea Management account. In addition, the court entered judgment for FAB on Jackson's counterclaim. Azalea City Motels, Inc., W. C. Greene, and Paul M. Jackson appealed.

* * *

FAB alleges in its complaint . . . indorsement liability under Alabama's version of the Uniform Commercial Code (hereinafter "UCC"), and * * * that the defendants, as customers, are liable to it based upon their UCC engagement to honor checks deposited to their account. We address the UCC claims together.

II. Indorsement Liability and Engagement to Honor

The first claim alleged by FAB upon which the trial court may have found the defendants liable is based upon Code 1975, § 3–414. Section 3–414, entitled "Contract of indorser; order of liability," provides:

"(1) Unless the indorsement otherwise specifies (as by such words as 'without recourse') every indorser engages that upon dishonor and any necessary notice of dishonor and protest he will pay the instrument according to its tenor at the time of his indorsement to the holder or to any subsequent indorser who takes it up, even though the indorser who takes it up was not obligated to do so.

"(2) Unless they otherwise agree indorsers are liable to one another in the order in which they indorse, which is presumed to be the order in which their signatures appear on the instrument."

Greene and Jackson first argue that the trial court erred in holding them personally liable for the $100,000 check because their individual signatures do not appear on the check as indorsers. It is true that, despite the fact that the named payee was Azalea City, the only indorsement registered on the check was Azalea Management Company. In fact, Azalea City never indorsed the check. Citing § 3–401, Greene and Jackson argue that, as a general rule, people are not held liable for checks they did not indorse. They reason, therefore, that because the check does not bear their indorsements, the trial court erred in holding them liable.

FAB responds to this reasoning by pointing out that § 3–401(2) defines the term "signature" as "made by use of any name, *including any trade or assumed name,* upon an instrument." (Emphasis added.) The official comment to § 3–401(2) explains that "[a signature] may be made in any name, including any trade name or assumed name, however false and fictitious, which is adopted for the purpose." Hence, FAB argues that Azalea Management Company is either the trade name or the assumed name of Greene and Jackson and that Azalea Management's indorsement serves as both Greene's and Jackson's indorsements.

* * *

Although we conclude that the Azalea Management indorsement served as both an authorized signature of Azalea City and as indorsements of Greene and Jackson, proving the existence of an indorsement is not the only prerequisite to a finding of indorsement liability. The UCC makes it clear that indorsers of checks or other drafts are only secondarily liable to the maker of the note. § 3–102(1)(d). "Secondary liability means that the holder may not sue the drawer or indorsers on a check or other draft until certain procedural conditions—presentment, dishonor and notice of dishonor—have been

met." [Citation.] See § 3–501(1)(b), (1)(c), (2)(a), and (2)(b). The appellants argue that neither dishonor nor timely notice of dishonor is present under the facts of this case. Thus, before we may affirm the trial court's judgment in favor of FAB upon these grounds, we must determine whether the prerequisites to indorsement liability exist.

While appellants concede that the threshold requirement of presentment was established at trial, they take issue with the trial court's apparent finding that the second prerequisite was met. Contrary to what the trial court must have found, appellants argue that the check was never dishonored. They suggest, instead, that the partial payment of the check by FNBL constituted final payment under the UCC, and that final payment precludes any later attempt by FNBL to dishonor the check. Alternatively, appellants argue that even if partial payment of the check by FNBL did not constitute final payment, then FNBL's retention of the check beyond its midnight deadline did constitute final payment. In either instance, they reason, the necessary prerequisite of dishonor never occurred, and, thus, the trial court erred in its judgment if its holding was based upon a theory of indorsement liability.

* * *

We hold, therefore, that under the express provisions of the UCC, FAB has failed to establish and prove a claim of indorsement liability, because it has failed to prove an essential element of that claim: dishonor of the check involved.

* * * FAB would have this court hold banking customers strictly liable for any item that they deposit, regardless of whether the banks handling the items are negligent and regardless of whether final payment has occurred (thus precluding proof of dishonor of the item, a necessary element of a claim for indorsement liability). The customers in this case did what all banking customers do: they accepted a check from its maker; they indorsed the check; they deposited the check to their account. From that point, there occurred a series of events, all of which were outside the control of the customers: FAB misencoded the item; the collecting banks failed to identify FAB's mistake; FNBL failed to compare the encoded amount with the actual amount of the check; FNBL returned the draft to its maker; and when the mistake was found and the adjustment entered, the Federal Reserve delayed almost 30 days before presenting the adjustment to FNBL.

When we apply . . . , the common law, and the Code to the present case, it becomes apparent that the defendants may not be held liable under a theory of indorsement liability. The UCC provides that every indorser engages that upon dishonor he will pay the instrument according to its tenor at the time of his indorsement to any subsequent indorser who takes it up. § 3–414. FAB took up and indorsed an instrument previously indorsed by Azalea Management on its own behalf, its owners Jackson and Greene, and Azalea City. The Code provides further that an instrument is dishonored when presentment is made and either acceptance or payment is refused or cannot be obtained within the prescribed time, or, in the case of bank collections, when the instrument is not seasonably returned by the midnight deadline. § 3–507(1)(a). Here, FAB transferred the instrument to collecting banks, which in turn presented the instrument to FNBL. FNBL made payment on the instrument within the prescribed time and retained the instrument beyond its midnight deadline. Therefore dishonor, as specifically defined in the UCC, did not occur.

The UCC provides that the payor bank becomes accountable for an item upon paying the item. § 4–213(1). * * * we hold that the partial payment of the item by FNBL constituted final payment within the meaning of § 4–213(3), so that the drawee bank was rendered accountable for the full and proper amount of the item. Moreover, even if the partial payment of the $100,000 check did not constitute final payment, FNBL's retention of the item beyond its midnight deadline discharged the appellants' indorsement liability. §§ 4–302, 3–507(1)(a).

* * *

For the foregoing reasons, the judgment of the trial court must be reversed and the cause remanded. Reversed and remanded.

Signature

VALLEY NATIONAL BANK, SUNNYMEAD v. COOK

Arizona Court of Appeals, Division One, 1983.
136 Ariz. 232, 665 P.2d 576.

CORCORAN, J.

The issue raised in this appeal is whether an individual who signs a check without indicating her representative capacity is personally liable on the obligation evidenced by the check when the check has the name of the corporate principal printed on it. We adopt the minority rule and hold that the individual is not personally liable. [Citation.]

On October 21, 1977, appellee J.M. Cook (Cook), the treasurer of Arizona Auto Auction and R.V. Center, Inc., (Arizona Auto Auction, Inc.) issued three corporate checks to Central Motors Company. Central Motors deposited these checks in its corporate account which was held by appellant Valley National Bank, Sunnymead, a California corporation (Bank). The Bank then sent each of these checks for payment to Arizona Auto Auction, Inc.'s, drawee bank, First National Bank of Arizona. However, a stop payment order had been put on these checks, and the First National Bank dishonored each of the checks. The checks were returned to the Bank, and the account of Central Motors was charged back for the amount of the checks which totaled $9,795. The bank was unable to recover this amount from Central Motors. The Bank demanded payment from Arizona Auto Auction, Inc., but the demand was not honored. On March 27, 1978, the Bank commenced suit against Arizona Auto Auction, Inc., and J.M. Cook and her spouse.

The case was tried to the court on August 1, 1979. After trial the court found that the Bank was a holder in due course and that the Arizona Auto Auction, Inc., was obligated as drawer for the face amount of the checks, $9,795. However, the judgment provided that Cook was not personally liable on the checks. * * *

The question of whether Cook signed in her individual or representative capacity is governed by § 3–403 of the Uniform Commercial Code (UCC) as adopted in this state. [§ 3–403] provides:

(1) A signature may be made by an agent or other representative, and his authority to make it may be established as in other cases of representation. No particular form of appointment is necessary to establish such authority.

(2) An authorized representative who signs his own name to an instrument:

    (a) Is personally obligated if the instrument neither names the person represented nor shows that the representative signed in a representative capacity;

    (b) Except as otherwise established between the immediate parties, is personally obligated if the instrument names the person represented but does not show that the representative signed in a representative capacity, or if the instrument does not name the person represented but does show that the representative signed in a representative capacity.

(3) Except as otherwise established the name of an organization preceded or followed by the name and office of an authorized individual is a signature made in a representative capacity.

The Bank argues that this section conclusively establishes Cook's personal liability on the checks. We do not agree. Admittedly, the checks fail to specifically show the office held by Cook. However, we do not find that this fact conclusively establishes liability, since [§ 3–403(2)(b)] imposes personal liability on an agent who signs his or her own name to an instrument only "if the instrument . . . does not show that the representative signed in a representative capacity." Thus, we must look to the entire instrument for evidence of the capacity of the signer. [Citations.]

The checks are in evidence and are boldly imprinted at the top "Arizona Auto Auction, Inc." and also "Arizona Auto Auction, Inc." is imprinted above a signature line appearing at the lower right-hand corner. Under the im-

printed name of the corporate defendant appears the signature of appellee Cook without any designation of office or capacity on each of the checks before us on appeal. Appellee Cook did not endorse the checks on the back. The record does not reflect appellee Cook made any personal guaranty of these checks or any other corporate obligation.

* * *

The Superior Court of Pennsylvania was confronted with a similar situation in *Pollin v. Mindy Mfg. Co., Inc.* There the court denied recovery by a third party endorsee against one who affixed his signature to a payroll check directly beneath the printed corporate name without indicating his representative capacity. In Pollin the checks were boldly imprinted at the top with the corporate name, address, and appropriate check number. The printed name of the drawee bank appeared in the lower lefthand corner of the instrument and the corporate name was imprinted in the lower righthand corner. Directly beneath the corporate name were two blank lines. The defendant-appellant had signed the top line without any designation of office or capacity. Pointing out that the code imposes liability on the individual only when the instrument controverts any showing of representative capacity, the court considered the instrument in its entirety. The court in Pollin held that disclosure on the face of the instrument that the checks were payable from a special payroll account of the corporation over which the appellant had no control as an individual negated any contention that appellant intended to make the instrument his own order to pay money to the payee.

The difference in outcome in the Pollin case and the cases cited by the Bank in which corporate agents were held liable for failing to show a corporate title reflects the Pollin court's emphasis on *business expectations,* an emphasis which is proper and entirely consistent with the spirit of UCC § 3–403. [Citation.] In determining what these expectations might be, it is important to draw a distinction between a check and a note:

The payee of a corporate check with the corporate name imprinted on its face probably expects less from the individual drawer than the payee of a corporate note may, where both the corporate name and the maker's name may be either hand-written or typewritten. Further, it is common for creditors to demand the individual promise of officers on corporate promissory notes, specially in the case of small corporations. Thus, we think a court should be more reluctant to find an agent personally liable who has signed a corporate check than in the case of a similar indorsement of a corporate note. This does not mean that the drawer of a corporate check will never be personally liable; indeed, more than a few have been stuck. Rather, we hope that courts will be more conscious of differences in business practices with respect to different types of instruments when they evaluate the extrinsic evidence presented by the parties.

[Citation.] Thus, while it may be common for creditors of small corporations to demand that corporate officers personally obligate themselves on corporate notes, it would be most unusual to demand the individual obligation of an officer on corporate checks.

* * *

The judgment of the trial court and the award of attorneys' fees are affirmed.

Drawer's Liability

DAVIS v. WATSON BROTHERS PLUMBING, INC.

Court of Civil Appeals of Texas, Dallas, 1981.
615 S.W.2d 844.

AKIN, J.

Defendant was the drawer of a check for $152.38 payable to its employee Arnett Lee. Lee, in turn, endorsed the check over to plaintiff, who operated a liquor store. After Lee endorsed the check to plaintiff and after plaintiff had placed cash on the counter, Lee stated that he wanted to buy a six-pack of beer and a bottle of scotch. When plaintiff turned to obtain the requested merchandise, a thief grabbed approximately $110.00 of the $150.88 ($152.38 less a $1.50 check cashing fee) for which plaintiff cashed the check. Lee took the remainder of the $150.88, approximately $40.88, and notified defendant of the

theft. Defendant issued Lee a second check for $152.38 and stopped payment on the first check. Plaintiff sued defendant based on the dishonor of the first check.

The county court rendered judgment for plaintiff for the $40.88 that Lee actually received from plaintiff [after the robbery]. Plaintiff, as appellant, asserts that since he proved that he was the holder of the check and since defendant failed to raise any valid defenses, defendant was liable to him for the full face value of the check, $152.38. We agree.

"Holder" is defined in *Tex. Bus. & Com. Code Ann.* [U.C.C.] § 1.201(20) as: "[A] *person who is in possession of* a document of title or *an instrument* or an investment security drawn, issued or *indorsed to him* or to his order or to bearer or *in blank*." Under the undisputed facts, Lee, the payee endorsed the check in blank to plaintiff, who is now in possession of the check. Thus, as a matter of law, plaintiff is a "holder" under the code [U.C.C.] § 3.413(b), which sets forth the rights of a holder, provides, in pertinent part, that: "The drawer engages that upon dishonor of the draft . . . *he will pay the amount of the draft to the holder* or to any indorser who takes it up." Thus, the defendant is liable to the holder of the dishonored check unless the defendant has raised a valid defense against the holder.

The rights of a holder not in due course are subject to the defenses specified in § 3.306, which provides:

Unless he has the rights of a holder in due course any person takes the instrument subject to

(1) all valid claims to it on the part of any person; and

(2) all defenses of any party which would be available in an action on a simple contract; and

(3) *the defenses of want or failure of consideration,* non-performance of any condition precedent, non-delivery, or delivery for a special purpose (Section 3.408); and

(4) the defense that he or a person through whom he holds the instrument acquired it by theft, or that payment or satisfaction to such holder would be inconsistent with the terms of a restrictive indorsement. *The claim of any third person to the instrument is not otherwise available*

as a defense to any party liable thereon unless the third person himself defends the action for such party.

Defendant here asserts that it may raise want or failure of consideration in the transaction between *plaintiff and Lee,* its payee, as a defense to plaintiff's enforcement of the instrument against it. We disagree.

[U.C.C.] § 3.408 provides, in pertinent part that: "Want or failure of consideration is a defense against any person not having the rights of a holder in due course . . ." The comments to § 3.408 provide that: " 'Consideration' refers to what the obligor has received for his obligation, and is important only on the question of whether his obligation can be enforced against him." Thus, any holder can enforce the obligation of a draft against the drawer regardless of whether the holder gave anything in consideration for the draft to his endorser. The drawer can assert as a defense to enforcement of the draft want or failure of consideration only to the extent such defense lies against the payee of the draft. Thus, the fact that a holder remote to the drawer's transaction with the payee did not give full consideration for the draft is not a defense available to the drawer. [Citation.]

This is true because the drawer's sole obligation on the check is to pay it according to its tenor. Consequently, the fact that the transfer of the check by the payee to the transferee is without consideration is immaterial to the drawer's obligation and is not a defense available to the drawer against the holder. A similar conclusion was reached in [citation.] In that case the court held that a defendant maker was not the proper party to raise as a defense that the transfer of the note to the holder was void. Consequently, that court concluded that the maker could not assert the defense that the equitable ownership of the instrument was in someone other than the holder-plaintiff.

The rationale of this, and other decisions, reaching the same conclusion, is that the maker or drawer of an instrument admittedly owes the money and he should not be permitted to bring into the controversy equi-ties of parties with which he has no connection. [Citation.] Furthermore, if the drawer or maker is permitted to assert the defense of another party such as the payee, the judgment on that issue would not be binding on the third party claimant who is not a party to the suit. [Citation.]

Because defendant here may not assert want or failure of consideration in the transaction between plaintiff and Lee, and because defendant has asserted no other defense against plaintiff, plaintiff is entitled to recover the full face value of the check under § 3.413(b) of the Texas Uniform Commercial Code. Accordingly, the judgment of the trial court is reversed and judgment is rendered that plaintiff recover judgment against defendant for $152.38 and all costs.

The Impostor Rule

PHILADELPHIA TITLE INSURANCE CO. v. FIDELITY–PHILADELPHIA TRUST CO.

Supreme Court of Pennsylvania, 1965.
419 Pa. 78, 212 A.2d 222.

COHEN, J.

[Edmund Jezemski, estranged and living apart from his wife, Paula, was administrator and sole heir-at-law of his deceased mother's estate, one asset of which was real estate in Philadelphia. Without Edmund's knowledge or consent, and with the assistance of John M. McAllister, an attorney, and Anthony DiBenedetto, a real estate broker, Paula arranged for a mortgage on the property through Philadelphia Title Insurance Company. Shortly before settlement, Paula represented to McAllister and DiBenedetto that her husband would be unable to attend the closing on the mortgage. She appeared at McAllister's office in advance of the closing, accompanied by a man, whom she introduced to McAllister and DiBenedetto as her husband. She and this man, in the presence of McAllister and DiBenedetto, executed a deed conveying the property from the estate to her husband and herself as tenants by the entireties and also executed the mortgage. McAllister and DiBenedetto were witnesses. Thereafter, McAllister, DiBenedetto, and Paula met at the office of the Title Company on the closing date, produced the signed deed and mortgage, and Paula obtained from Title Company its check for the mortgage loan proceeds of $15,640.82, payable to the order of Edmund Jezemski and Paula Jezemski, individually, and to Edmund as administrator.

Paula cashed the check, bearing the purported indorsements of all the payees, at Penns Grove National Bank and Trust Company. Edmund received none of the proceeds, either individually or as administrator. His purported indorsements were forgeries. In the collection process the check was presented to and paid by the drawee bank, Fidelity-Philadelphia Trust Company and charged against the drawer Title Company's account. Upon discovery of the existence of the mortgage, Edmund brought an action which resulted in the setting aside of the deed and mortgage and the repayment of the amount advanced by the mortgagee. Title Company thereupon sued the drawee bank (Fidelity) to recover the amount of the check, $15,640.82.]

The complaint alleged that the endorsement of one of the payees had been forged and that, therefore, Fidelity should not have paid the check. . . . By way of defense all of the banks asserted that none of them were liable because the issuance of the check by the Title Company was induced by an impostor and delivered by the Title Company to a confederate of the impostor thereby making the forged endorsement effective.

*   *   * Judgment was entered against the Title Company and in favor of the banks.

*   *   *

"There is no question that the man whom Mrs. Jezemski introduced to McAllister and DiBenedetto was not Edmund Jezemski, her husband. It was sometime later that Edmund Jezemski, when he tried to convey the real estate, discovered the existence of the mortgage. When he did so he instituted an action in equity which resulted in the setting aside of the deed and mortgage and the repayment of the fund advanced by the mortgagee."

The parties do not dispute the proposition that as between the [drawee] bank (Fidelity-Philadelphia) and its customer (Title Company), ordinarily, the former must bear the loss occasioned by the forgery of a payee's endorsement (Edmund Jezemski) upon a check drawn by its customer and paid by it. Uniform Commercial Code § 3–404. The latter provides . . . that "(1) Any unauthorized signature [Edmund Jezemski's] is wholly inoperative as that of the person whose name is signed unless he ratifies it or is precluded from denying. . . ."

However, the banks argue that this case falls within an exception to the above rule, making the forged indorsement of Edmund Jezemski's name effective so that Fidelity-Philadelphia was entitled to charge the account of its customer, the Title Company, who was the drawer of the check. The exception asserted by the banks is found in § 3–405(1)(a) of the Uniform Commercial Code—Commercial Paper which provides:

"An indorsement by any person in the name of a named payee is effective if (a) an impostor by use of the mails, or otherwise has induced the maker or drawer to issue the instrument to him or his confederate in the name of the payee. . . ."

The lower court found and the Title Company does not dispute that an impostor appeared before McAllister and DiBenedetto, impersonated Mr. Jezemski, and, in their presence, signed Mr. Jezemski's name to the deed, bond, and mortgage; that Mrs. Jezemski was a confederate of the impostor; that the drawer, Title Company, issued the check to Mrs. Jezemski naming her and Mr. Jezemski as payees; and that some person other than Mr. Jezemski indorsed his name on the check. In effect, the only argument made by the Title Company to prevent the applicability of Section 3–405(1)(a) is that the impostor, who admittedly played a part in the swindle, did not "by the mails or otherwise" induce the Title Company to issue the check within the meaning of Section 3–405(1)(a). The argument must fail.

*   *   *

Both the words of Section 3–405(1)(a) and the official Comment thereto leave no doubt that the impostor can induce the drawer to issue him or his confederate a check within the meaning of the section even though he does not carry out his impersonation before the very eyes of the drawer. Section 3–405(1)(a) says the inducement might be by "the mails or otherwise."

* * * For purposes of imposing the loss on one of two "innocent" parties, either the drawer who was defrauded or the drawee bank which paid out on a forged indorsement, we see no reason for distinguishing between the drawer who is duped by an impersonator communicating directly with him through the mails and a drawer who is duped by an impersonator communicating indirectly with him through third persons. Thus, both the language of the Code and common sense dictate that the drawer must suffer the loss in both instances.

* * *

Judgment affirmed.

Dishonor/Liability of Accommodation Parties/Liability Based on Warranty

OAK PARK CURRENCY EXCHANGE, INC. v. MAROPOULOS

Appellate Court of Illinois, First District, First Division, 1977.
48 Ill.App.3d 437, 6 Ill.Dec. 525, 363 N.E.2d 54.

GOLDBERG, J.

Oak Park Currency Exchange, Inc. (plaintiff) brought action against James Maropoulos (defendant). Plaintiff's theory was that a check for $3,564 had been endorsed by defendant and cashed by plaintiff and that the prior endorsement of the payee was a forgery. After all of the evidence was presented, the trial court directed a jury verdict for defendant. Plaintiff appeals.

Defendant testified that on several occasions, his friend John Bugay had asked for assistance in cashing checks. On these occasions, defendant had accompanied Bugay to a bank where defendant transacted his busi-

ness and had endorsed the check as a favor. On July 24, 1971, Bugay again requested assistance in cashing a check. Defendant suggested that they go to plaintiff currency exchange where defendant often transacted business and was known to plaintiff's employees. The check in question was a certified check drawn on American National Bank payable to the order of "Henry Sherman, Inc." and endorsed "Henry Sherman" on the reverse side.

Defendant testified that at the currency exchange he identified himself and asked the clerk if she would cash his friend's check. Though she was not the woman with whom he usually dealt, she recognized him. She answered that she would cash the check if defendant would endorse it. He endorsed the check and handed it to the clerk. He observed that she examined both sides of the check. She then handed him the money. He did not count this but gave it immediately to Bugay. Defendant testified unequivocally that he received no money from Bugay in return for his help.

Jacqueline Panveno, plaintiff's clerk, testified to essentially the same facts. She stated that she was under the impression that defendant's friend was Henry Sherman, though no one had told her that. She was told by defendant that the check was a commission check and his friend needed the money. She testified that defendant had offered to endorse the check. She watched him endorse it, handed him the money, and saw him give the money to Bugay. She further testified that after the two men turned away from her, she saw Bugay hand defendant some money. When questioned as to the amount, she stated that it was none of her business and, "I wasn't paying that close attention to it." On cross-examination she testified that defendant initially asked her to cash the check as a favor for his friend. When asked why she continued to watch the two men rather than return to her duties, she answered "I didn't continue to watch them." She went on to say that she had looked up to see why the men had stopped walking.

Some time later a claim was made against plaintiff by Belmont National Bank where plaintiff had deposited the check because the endorsement "Henry Sherman" had been forged. Plaintiff determined that it was liable to the bank and paid the claim. Subsequently plaintiff filed this action.

In its judgment order directing the verdict, the trial court found that defendant was an accommodation endorser and as such made no warranty to defendant under the Uniform Commercial Code (§ 3–417(1)) and that payment of the check discharged all endorsers so that defendant was not liable to plaintiff on his endorsement.

In this court, plaintiff urges that defendant breached his warranty of good title when he obtained payment of a check on which the payee's endorsement was forged and that there was sufficient evidence to support a directed verdict in favor of plaintiff. Plaintiff's contentions are based exclusively on section 3–417(1) of the Code. Defendant contends that an accommodation endorser does not make warranties under § 3–417(1) and that the trial court properly directed a verdict for defendant.

A party who signs an instrument "for the purpose of lending his name to another party to . . ." that instrument is an accommodation party. (§ 3–415(1)). [Citation.] Such a party "is liable in the capacity in which he has signed. . . ." (§ 3–415(2).) Therefore defendant is an accommodation endorser and would be liable to plaintiff under his endorser's contract, provided that he had received timely notice that the check had been presented to the drawee bank and dishonored. (§ 3–414.) Because these conditions precedent to the contractual liability of an endorser have not been met, defendant is not liable on his contract as an accommodation endorser.

Furthermore, the drawee bank, American National, did not dishonor the check but paid it. This operated to discharge the liability of defendant as an accommodation endorser. [Citation.]

The portion of the Code upon which plaintiff seeks to hold defendant liable is section 3–417 entitled "Warranties on Presentment and Transfer." As shown above, the parties both confine their arguments to subsection 3–417(1) of the Code and the judgment order refers specifically thereto. Section 3–417(1) sets out warranties which run only to a party who "pays or accepts" an instrument upon presentment. We note that presentment is defined as "a demand for acceptance or payment made upon the maker, acceptor, drawee or other payor. . . ." (§ 3–504(1).) As applied to the instant case, the warranties contained in section 3–417(1) are limited to run only to the payor bank and not to any other transferee who acquired the check. In the case before us, plaintiff is not a payor or acceptor of the draft. This interpretation is strongly supported by the official comment which details the reasons for distinguishing warranties made to a payor or acceptor of an instrument from those made to a transferee. The case before us involves a transferee, not a party who paid or accepted the instrument. Thus it appears that reliance by plaintiff upon subsection 3–417(1) was misplaced. The authorities cited by plaintiff do not support its contention as all of these cases were decided before the effective date of the Code.

* * *

An additional theory requires affirmance of the judgment appealed from. Subsection 3–417(2) of the Code provides that one "who transfers an instrument and receives consideration warrants to his transferee . . ." that he has good title. (§ 3–417(2).) The Illinois comments to this portion of the Code confirm that this warranty is made only by any party who transfers an instrument for consideration. In [citation], the court noted the presence of the phrase "and receives consideration" in this subsection of the Code.

The evidence presented in the case at bar establishes that defendant received no consideration for his endorsement. Though Mrs. Panveno testified that she saw Bugay hand defendant some money as the two left the currency exchange, she also testified that defendant stated that he was doing a favor for his friend; that she was not paying close attention to the two men and that she did not watch them as they walked away from her. Thus her testimony was considerably weakened by her own qualifying statements and it was strongly and directly contradicted by the positive and unshaken testimony of defendant that he received nothing in return for his assistance. The simple fact standing alone that this witness saw Bugay hand some money to defendant, even if proved, would have no legal significance without additional proof of some type showing that the payment was consideration for defendant's endorsement.

* * *

Judgment affirmed.

QUESTIONS

1. Discuss contractual liability, warranty liability, and liability for conversion.

2. Discuss the liability of makers, acceptors, drawees, drawers, indorsers, and accommodation parties.

3. Discuss the conditions precedent to the liability of secondary parties.

4. Compare the warranties on transfer with the warranties on presentment.

5. Discuss the methods by which liability on an instrument may be terminated.

PROBLEMS

1. $800.00   Smalltown, Illinois
                                    November 15, 1991
The undersigned promises to pay to the order of John Doe, Nine Hundred Dollars with interest from date of note. Payment to be made in five monthly installments of One Hundred Eighty Dollars, plus accrued interest beginning on December 1, 1991. In the event of default in the payment of any installment or interest on installment date, the holder of this instrument may declare the entire obligation due and owing and proceed forthwith to collect the balance due on this instrument.
                                    (Signed) Acton, agent.

On December 18, no payment having been made on the note, Doe indorsed and delivered the instrument to Todd to secure a pre-existing debt in the amount of $800.

On January 18, 1992, Todd brought an action against Acton and Phi Corporation, Acton's principal, to collect the full amount of the instrument with interest. Acton defended on the basis that he signed the instrument in a representative capacity and that Doe had failed to deliver the consideration for which the instrument had been issued. Phi Cor-

poration defended on the basis that it did not sign the instrument and that its name does not appear on the instrument.

For what amount, if any, are Acton and Phi Corporation liable?

2. Cole was supervisor of the shipping department of Machine Mfg. Inc. In February, Cole found herself in need of funds and, at the end of that month, submitted to Ames, the treasurer of the corporation, a payroll listing that showed as an employee, among others, "Ben Day," to whom was allegedly owed $800 for services rendered during February. Actually, there was no employee named Day. Relying upon the word of Cole, Ames drew and delivered to her a series of corporate payroll checks, drawn upon the corporate account in the Capital Bank, one of which was made payable to the order of "Ben Day" for $800. Cole took the check, indorsed on its back "Ben Day," cashed it at the Capital Bank, and pocketed the proceeds. She repeated the same procedure at the end of March, April, and May. In mid-June, Machine Mfg. Inc. learned of Cole's fraudulent conduct, fired her, and brought an appropriate action against Capital Bank seeking a judgment for $3,200. Decision?

3. While employed as a night watchman at the place of business of A.B. Cate Trucking Company, Fred Fain observed that the office safe had been left unlocked. It contained fifty payroll checks, which were ready for distribution to employees two days later. The checks had all been signed by the sole proprietor, Cate. Fain removed five of these checks and took two blank checks, which were also in the safe. Fain forged the indorsements of the payees on the five payroll checks and cashed them at local supermarkets. He then filled out one of the blank checks, making himself payee, and forged Cate's signature as drawer. After cashing that check at a supermarket, Fain departed by airplane to Jamaica. The six checks were promptly presented for payment to the drawee bank, the Bank of Emanon, which paid each of the checks. Shortly thereafter, Cate learned about the missing payroll checks and forgeries and demanded that the Bank of Emanon credit his account with the amount of the six checks.

Must the Bank comply with Cate's demand? What are the Bank's rights, if any, against the supermarkets? You may assume that the supermarkets cashed all of the checks in good faith.

4. A negotiable promissory note executed and delivered by B to C passed in due course to and was indorsed in blank by C, D, E, and F. G, the present holder, strikes out D's indorsement. What is the liability of C, D, E, and F on their respective indorsements?

5. On June 15, 1987, Justin, for consideration, executed a negotiable promissory note for $10,000, payable to Reneé on or before June 15, 1992. Justin subsequently suffered financial reverses. In January of 1992, Reneé on two occasions told Justin that she knew that Justin was having a difficult time and that she, Reneé, did not need the money and the debt should be considered as completely cancelled with no other act or payment being required. These conversations were witnessed by three persons, including Larry. On March 15, 1992, Reneé changed her mind and indorsed the note for value to Larry. The note was not paid by June 15, 1992, and Larry sued Justin for the amount of the note. Justin defended upon the ground that Reneé had cancelled the debt and renounced all rights against Justin and that Larry had notice of this fact. Decision?

6. Tate and Fitch were longtime friends. Tate was a man of considerable means; Fitch had encountered financial difficulties. In order to bolster his failing business, Fitch desired to borrow $6,000 from Farmers Bank of Erehwon. To accomplish this, he persuaded Tate to aid him in the making of a promissory note by which it would appear that Tate had the responsibility of maker, but with Fitch's agreeing to pay the instrument when due. Accordingly, they executed the following instrument:

> December 1, 1991
>
> Thirty days after date and for value received, I promise to pay to the order of Frank Fitch the sum of $6,600.
>
> /s/ Timothy Tate

On the back of the note, Fitch indorsed, "Pay to the order of Farmers Bank of Erehwon /s/ Frank Fitch" and delivered it to the bank in exchange for $6,000.

With the note's not having been paid at maturity, the bank, without first demanding payment by Fitch, brought an action on the note against Tate. (a) Decision? (b) If Tate voluntarily pays the note to the bank, may he then recover on the note against Fitch, who appears as an indorser?

7. Alpha orally appointed Omega as his agent to find and purchase for him a 1930 Dodge automobile in good condition. Omega located such a car. The car's owner, Roe, agreed to sell and deliver the car on January 10, 1992, for $9,000. To evidence the purchase price, Omega mailed to Roe the following instrument:

> December 1, 1991
>
> $9,000.00
>
> We promise to pay to the order of bearer Nine Thousand Dollars with interest from date of this instrument on or before January 10, 1992. This note is given in consideration of John Roe's transferring title to and possession of his 1930 Dodge automobile.
>
> (Signed) Omega, agent.

Smith stole the note from Roe's mailbox, indorsed Roe's name on the note, and promptly discounted it with Sunset Bank for $8,700. Not having received the note, Roe sold the car to a third party. On January 10, 1992, the bank, having discovered all the facts, demanded payment of the note from Alpha and Omega. Payment was refused by both.

What are Sunset Bank's rights with regard to Omega? Its rights with regard to Roe and Smith?

8. In payment of the purchase price of a used motorboat, which had been fraudulently misrepresented, Young signed and delivered to Armstrong his negotiable note in the amount of $2,000 due October 1, with Selby as an accommodation co-maker. Young intended to use the boat for his fishing business. Armstrong indorsed the note in blank preparatory to discounting it. Tillman stole the note from Armstrong and delivered it to McGowan on July 1 in payment of a past due debt owing by Tillman to McGowan in the amount of $600, with McGowan making up the difference by giving Tillman his check for $800 and an oral promise to pay Tillman an additional $600 on October 1.

When McGowan demanded payment of the note on December 1, both Young and Selby refused to pay the note because it had not been presented for payment on its due date and because Armstrong had fraudulently misrepresented the motorboat for which the note had been executed.

What are McGowan's rights, if any, against Young, Selby, Tillman, and Armstrong, respectively?

9. On July 1 Anderson sold D'Aveni, who is a jeweler, a necklace containing imitation gems, which Anderson fraudulently represented to be diamonds. In payment for the necklace, D'Aveni executed and delivered to Anderson her promissory note for $25,000 dated July 1 and payable on December 1 to Anderson's order with interest at 12 percent per annum.

The note was thereafter successively indorsed in blank and delivered by Anderson to Bylinski, Bylinski to Conrad, and by Conrad to Shearson, who became a holder in due course on August 10. On November 1, D'Aveni discovered Anderson's fraud and immediately notified Anderson, Bylinski, Conrad, and Shearson that she would not pay the note when it became due. Bylinski, a friend of Shearson, requested that Shearson release him from liability on the note, and Shearson, as a favor to Bylinski and for no other consideration, struck out Bylinski's indorsement.

On November 15, Shearson, who was solvent and had no creditors, indorsed the note to the order of Frederick, his father, and delivered it to Frederick as a gift. At the same time, Shearson told Frederick of D'Aveni's statement that

D'Aveni would not pay the note when it became due. Frederick presented the note to D'Aveni for payment on December 1, but D'Aveni refused to pay. Thereafter Frederick gave due notice of dishonor to Anderson, Bylinski, and Conrad.

What are Frederick's rights, if any, against Anderson, Bylinski, Conrad, and D'Aveni on the note?

10. Saul sold goods to Bruce, warranting that the goods were of a specified quality. The goods were not of the quality warranted, and Saul knew this at the time of the sale. Bruce drew and delivered a check payable to Saul and drawn on Third National Bank in the amount of the purchase price. Bruce subsequently discovered the goods were faulty and stopped payment on the check. Saul brings a suit against Bruce. Decision?

11. While assistant treasurer of Travco Corporation, Frank Mitchell caused two checks, each payable to a fictitious company, to be drawn on Travco's account with Brown City Savings Bank. In each case, Mitchell indorsed the check in his own name and then cashed it at Citizens Federal Savings & Loan Association of Port Huron. Both checks were cleared through normal banking channels and charged against Travco's account with Brown City. Travco subsequently discovered the embezzlement, and after its demand for reimbursement was denied, it brought this suit against Citizens. Decision?

12. R&A Concrete Contractors, Inc., executed a promissory note that identifies both R&A Concrete and Grover Roberts as its makers. On the reverse side of the note, the following appears: "X John Ament Sec. & Treas." National Bank of Georgia, the payee, now sues both R&A Concrete and Ament on the note. Decision?

13. On August 10, 1964, Theta Electronic Laboratories, Inc., executed a promissory note to George and Marguerite Thomson. Three other individuals, Gerald Exten, Emil O'Neil, and James Hane, and their wives also indorsed the note. The note was then transferred to Hane by the Thomsons on November 26, 1965. Although a default occurred at this time, it was not until April 1967, eighteen months later, that Hane gave notice of the dishonor and made a demand for payment on the Extens as indorsers. Hane appeals from a judgment in favor of the Extens. Decision?

Chapter 29

BANK DEPOSITS, COLLECTIONS, AND FUNDS TRANSFERS

Collection of Items
Payor Bank and Its Customers
Consumer Funds Transfers
Wholesale Funds Transfers

IN today's society, most goods and services are bought and sold without a physical transfer of "money." Credit cards, charge accounts, and various deferred payment plans have made cash sales increasingly rare. But even credit sales must ultimately be settled— when they are, payment is usually made by check rather than with cash. If the parties to a sales transaction happen to have accounts at the same bank, a transfer of credit is easily accomplished. In the vast majority of cases, however, the parties do business at different banks. Then the buyer's check must journey from the seller-payee's bank (depositary bank), where the check is deposited by the seller for credit to his account, to the buyer-drawer's bank (payor bank) for payment. In this collection process the check frequently passes through one or more other banks (intermediary banks) so that it may be collected and the appropriate entries recorded. Our banking system has developed a network to handle the collection of checks and other instruments.

In recent years, the amount of payment made by electronic funds transfers has increased at an astounding rate. The dollar volume of commercial payments made by wire transfer far exceeds the dollar amount made by checks or credit cards. In addition, electronic funds transfers have become exceedingly popular with consumers. Consumer electronic funds transfers are covered by the Federal Electronic Fund Transfer Act; nonconsumer (wholesale) electronic transfers are covered by proposed Article 4A of the Uniform Commercial Code.

This chapter will cover both the bank deposit–collection system and electronic funds transfers.

BANK DEPOSITS AND COLLECTIONS

Article 4 of the U.C.C., entitled "Bank Deposits and Collections," provides the principal rules governing the bank collection process. Since items in the bank collection process are essentially those covered by Article 3, "Commercial Paper," and to a lesser extent by Article 8, "Investment Securities," these Articles often apply to a bank collection problem. This section will cover the collection of an item through the banking system and the relationship betwen the payor bank and its customer.

COLLECTION OF ITEMS

When a person deposits a check in his bank (the **depositary bank**), the bank credits his account by the amount of the check. This initial crediting is **provisional.** Normally, a bank does not permit a customer to draw funds against a provisional credit, but if it does permit its customer to draw against the credit, it has given *value* and, provided it meets the other requirements, will be a holder in due course. Under the customer's contract with his bank, the bank is obligated to make a reasonable effort to obtain payment of all checks deposited for collection. When the amount of the check has been collected from the payor bank (drawee), the credit becomes a **final credit**.

The Competitive Equality Banking Act of 1987 has expedited the availability of funds by establishing maximum time periods for a bank to hold (not permit a customer access to her funds) various types of instruments. Under the Act: (1) cash deposits, wire transfers, government checks, the first $100 of a day's check deposits, cashier's checks, and checks deposited in one branch of a depositary institution and drawn on the same or another branch of the same institution must clear by the next business day; (2) local checks must clear within one intervening business day; and (3) nonlocal checks must clear in no more than four intervening business days.

If the payor bank (the drawee bank) does not pay the check for some reason, such as a stop payment order or insufficient funds in the drawer's account, the depositary bank reverses the provisional credit to the account, debits his account for that amount, and returns the check to him with a statement of the reason for nonpayment. If, in the meantime, the customer has been permitted to draw against the provisional credit, the bank may recover the payment from him.

In some cases, the bank involved is both the depositary bank and the payor bank. In most cases, however, the depositary and payor banks are different, in which event the bank collection aspects of Article 4 come into play. Where the depositary and payor banks are different, it is necessary for the item to pass from one to the other, either directly through a clearinghouse or through one or more **intermediary banks** (a bank involved in the collection process other than the depositary payor bank, such as one of the twelve Federal Reserve Banks) as illustrated in Figure 29–1. For an excellent overview of the statutory framework governing the collection process *see Pulaski Bank & Trust Co. v. Texas American Bank*. A **clearinghouse** is an association of banks or other payors for the purpose of settling accounts with each other on a daily basis. Each member of the clearinghouse forwards all deposited checks drawn on other members and receives from the clearinghouse all checks drawn on it. Balances are adjusted and settled each day.

Collecting Banks

A **collecting bank** is any bank handling an item for payment other than the payor bank. In the usual situation where the depositary and payor banks are different, the depositary bank gives a provisional credit to its customer, transfers the item to the next bank in the chain, receiving a provisional credit or "settlement" from it, and so on to the payor bank, which gives a provisional settlement to its transferor. When the item is paid, all the provisional settlements given by the respective banks in the chain become final, and the particular transaction has been completed. No adjustment is necessary on the books of any of the banks involved. This procedure simplifies the bookkeeping processes of all the banks involved because only one entry is necessary if the item is paid.

If the payor bank does not pay the check, however, it returns the check and each intermediary or collecting bank reverses the provisional settlement or credit it previously gave to its forwarding bank. Ultimately, the depositary bank will charge the account (remove the provisional credit) of its customer who deposited the item. The customer must then seek recovery from the indorsers or the drawer.

Figure 29–1 Bank Collections

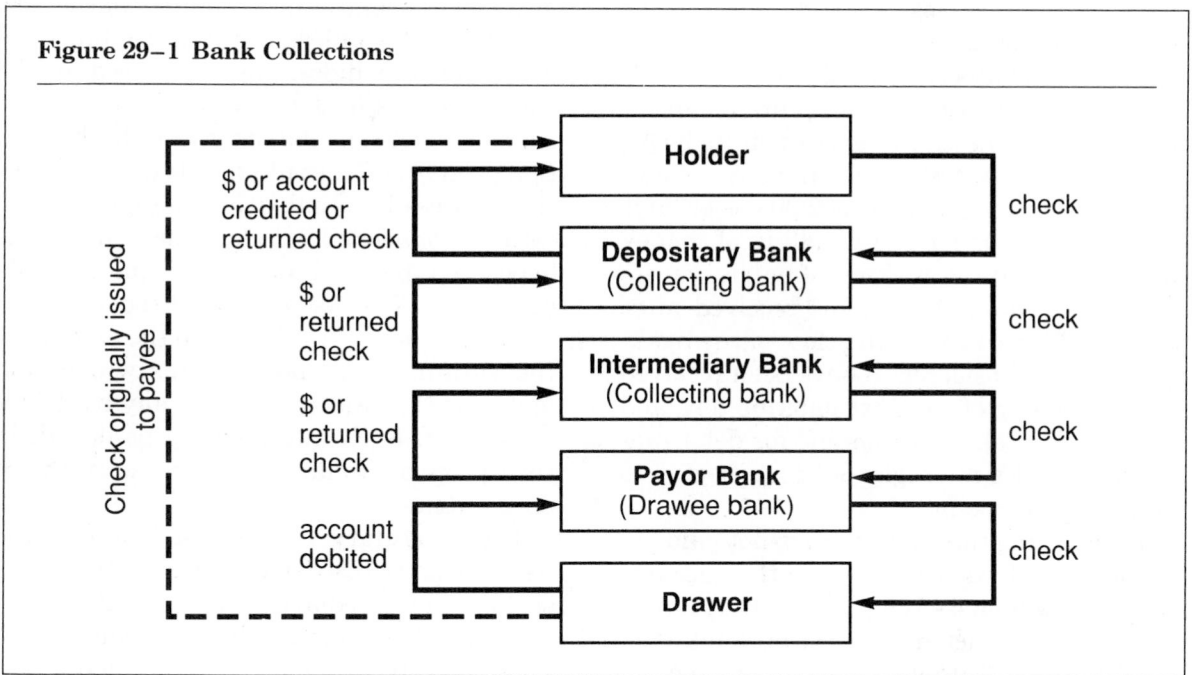

A collecting bank is an **agent** or subagent of the owner of the item until the settlement becomes final. Section 4–201(1). Unless otherwise provided, any credit given for the item initially is provisional. Once it is finally settled, the agency relationship changes to one of **debtor-creditor.** The effect of this agency rule is that the risk of loss remains with the owner and any chargebacks go to her, not to the collecting bank.

All collecting banks have certain responsibilities and duties in collecting checks and other items. These will now be discussed.

Duty of Care A collecting bank must use ordinary care in handling an item transferred to it for collection. Section 4–202(1). The steps it takes in presenting an item or sending it for presentment are of particular importance. It must act within a reasonable time after receipt of the item and must choose a reasonable method of forwarding the item for presentment. It is also responsible for using care in routing and in selecting intermediary banks or other agents.

Duty to Act Seasonably Closely related to the collecting bank's duty of care is its duty

to act seasonably. A collecting bank acts seasonably in any event if it takes proper action, such as forwarding or presenting an item, before its "midnight deadline" following receipt of the item, notice, or payment. *See Pulaski Bank & Trust Co. v. Texas American Bank.* If the bank adheres to this standard, the timeliness of its action cannot be challenged. Although a reasonably longer time may be seasonable, the bank bears the burden of proof. Section 4–202(2). The **midnight deadline** means midnight of the banking day following the banking day on which the bank receives the item or notice. Section 4–104(1)(h). Thus, if a bank receives a check on Monday, it must take proper action by midnight on the next banking day, or Tuesday. A banking day means that part of any day on which a bank is open to the public for carrying on substantially all of its banking functions. Section 4–104(1)(c). *See Wells Fargo Bank v. Hartford Nat'l. Bank & Trust Co.*

The midnight deadline presents a problem because it takes time to process an item through a bank—whether it be the depositary, intermediary, or payor bank. If the various steps involved in a day's transaction are to be completed without overtime work, the bank must either close early or fix an earlier cutoff time for the day's work. Accordingly, the Code provides that for the purpose of allowing time to process items, prove balances, and make the necessary entries on its books to determine its position for the day, a bank may fix an afternoon hour of 2:00 P.M. or later as a cutoff hour for the handling of money and items and the making of entries on its books. Section 4–107. Items received after the cutoff hour fixed as the close of the banking day are considered to have been received at the opening of the next banking day, and the time for taking action and for determining the bank's midnight deadline begins to run from that point.

Recognizing that if an item is not paid everyone involved will be greatly inconvenienced, Section 4–108 provides that unless otherwise instructed a collecting bank in a good faith effort to secure payment may, in the case of specific items, waive, modify, or extend the time limits, but not in excess of one additional banking day. This extension may be made without the approval of the parties involved and without discharging secondary parties. The Code also authorizes delay when communications are interrupted as a result of blizzard, flood, hurricane, other disaster, suspension of payments by another bank, war, emergency conditions, or other circumstances beyond the bank's control. Delay for such causes will be excused only if the bank exercises such diligence as the circumstances require.

Indorsements When an item is restrictively indorsed with words such as "pay any bank," it is locked into the bank collection system, and only a bank may acquire the rights of a holder. When a bank forwards an item for collection, it normally indorses it "pay any bank," irrespective of the type of indorsement, if any, that the item carried at the time of receipt. This serves to protect the collecting bank by making it impossible for the item to stray from regular collection channels.

If the item had no indorsement when received by the depositary bank, it may supply any indorsement of its customer that is necessary to title unless the item contains the words "payee's indorsement required" or the equivalent, as is the case with certain government, pension, and insurance checks. Section 4–205(1). This rule speeds up the collection process by eliminating the necessity of returning checks for indorsement when the depositary bank knows they came from its customers. The usual form of such an indorsement reads "Deposited to the account of the within named payee." This will be followed by the bank's own "pay any bank" indorsement. Each intermediary bank will in turn place a similar restrictive indorsement on the item.

The depositary bank must examine the item for prior restrictive indorsements. Subsequent intermediary banks and the payor bank need examine only one indorsement and may rely on the fact that the depositary bank performed its required function. It would be unnecessarily time-consuming to require each bank to examine all the indorsements on each item.

Warranties Customers and collecting banks give substantially the same warranties as those given by parties under Article 3 upon presentment and transfer, which are discussed in Chapter 28. Each customer or collecting bank who **transfers** an item and receives a settlement or consideration warrants to his transferee and subsequent transferees that (1) he has good title (that is, the transferor is the true owner or is an authorized agent of the owner); (2) *all* signatures are genuine or authorized; (3) the item has not been materially altered; (4) no defense of any party is good against him; and (5) he has no knowledge of any insolvency proceeding involving the maker or acceptor or the drawer of an unaccepted instrument. Moreover, each customer or collecting bank who obtains payment or acceptance, as well as all prior customers and collecting banks, warrants to the *payor* bank on **presentment** that (1) she has good title or is authorized to obtain payment; (2) she has no knowledge that the signature of the maker or drawer is unauthorized; and (3) the item has not been materially altered. Section 4–207.

Final Payment The provisional settlements made in the collection chain are all directed toward final payment of the item by the payor bank. This is one end of the collection process—the turn-around point from which the proceeds of the item begin the return flow and provisional settlements become final. For example, a customer of the California Country State Bank may deposit a check drawn on the State of Maine Country National Bank. The check may then take a course such as follows: from the California Country State Bank to a correspondent bank in San Francisco, to the Federal Reserve Bank of San Francisco, to the Federal Reserve Bank of Boston, to the payor bank. Provisional settlements are made at each step. When the payor bank finally pays the item, the proceeds begin a return flow over the same course.

The critical question, then, is the point in time when the item has been **paid** by the payor bank, since this not only commences the payment process but also has a bearing on questions of priority between the payment of an item and actions such as the filing of a stop payment order against the item. Under the Code, *final payment* occurs when the payor bank does any of the following, whichever happens first: (1) pays an item in cash; (2) settles an item and does not reserve the right to revoke the settlement, or does not have such right through statute, clearinghouse rule, or agreement; (3) makes a provisional settlement and does not revoke it in the time and manner permitted by statute, clearinghouse rule, or agreement; or (4) completes the process of posting the item to the account of the drawer. Section 4–213.

The process of *posting* is normally completed after the following steps have been taken: (a) verifying any signature; (b) ascertaining that sufficient funds are available; (c) affixing a "paid" or other stamp; (d) entering a charge or entry to a customer's account; and (e) correcting or reversing an entry or erroneous action on the item. Section 4–109.

Payor Banks

The **payor** or drawee **bank,** under its contract of deposit with the drawer, agrees to pay to the payee or his order checks issued by the drawer provided the order is not countermanded and that there are sufficient funds in the drawer's account.

Due to the tremendous increase in volume of bank collections, it has become necessary to institute deferred posting procedures whereby items are sorted and proved on the day of receipt, but are not posted to customers' accounts or returned until the next banking day. The U.C.C. not only approves this procedure but also sets up specific standards to govern its application to the actions of payor banks.

When a payor bank that is not also a depositary bank receives a demand item other than for immediate payment over the counter, it must either return the item or give its transferor a provisional settlement before midnight of the banking day on which the item is received. Otherwise it becomes liable to its transferor for the amount of the item, unless it has a valid defense such as breach of a presentment warranty. Section 4–302(a).

If it gives the provisional settlement as required, it then has until its midnight deadline to return the item or, if it is held for protest or is otherwise unavailable for return, to send written notice of dishonor or nonpayment. Section 4–301(1). After doing this, it is entitled to revoke the settlement and recover any payment made. If the payor bank fails to return the item or send notice before its midnight deadline, it becomes accountable for the amount of the item unless it has a valid defense for its inaction.

There are innumerable reasons why a bank may dishonor an item and return it or send notice. The following situations are the most common: the drawer or maker may have no account or may have insufficient funds to cover the item; a signature on the item may be forged; or payment of the item may have been stopped by the drawer or maker.

If a customer's account does not have sufficient funds to pay all items that the bank receives on that account on any given day, the bank may charge them against the account in any order it deems convenient. Items against an account may reach the bank in several different ways on the same day, and it would be unreasonable to require the bank to determine their order of arrival. Items received at the same time but passing through different channels may be posted to the customer's account hours apart. Consequently, a person presenting an item to a payor bank may not object that the bank paid other items received the same day and left his unpaid. His only remedy is to seek recourse against the maker, drawer, or other secondary parties. The owner of the account from which the item was payable also has no basis for complaint that one item rather than another was paid. It is his responsibility to have enough funds on deposit to pay all items chargeable to his account at any time.

RELATIONSHIP BETWEEN PAYOR BANK AND ITS CUSTOMER

The relationship between a payor bank and its checking account customer is primarily the product of their contractual arrangement. Although the parties have relatively broad latitude in establishing the terms of their agreement and in altering the provisions of the Code, a bank may not validly (1) disclaim responsibility for its lack of good faith, (2) disclaim responsibility for its failure to exercise ordinary care, or (3) limit its damages for a breach of such lack or failure. Section 4–103(1). The parties may by agreement however, determine the standards by which such responsibility is to be measured if these standards are not clearly unreasonable.

Payment of an Item

A payor bank owes a duty to its customer, the drawer, to pay checks properly drawn by him on an account that has sufficient funds to cover the items. A check or draft, however, is not an assignment of the drawer's funds that are in the possession of the drawee. Moreover, as discussed in Chapter 28, the drawee

is not liable on an instrument until it accepts the check. Section 3–409(1). Therefore, the *holder* of a check has no right to require the drawee bank to pay it, whether or not there are sufficient funds in the drawer's account. But if an item is presented to a payor bank and the bank improperly refuses payment, it will incur a liability to its *customer* from whose account the item should have been paid. Section 4–402. If the item is not more than six months old, is regular in form, the customer has adequate funds on deposit, and there is no other valid basis for the refusal to pay, the bank is liable to its customer for damages proximately caused by the *wrongful dishonor*. If the dishonor occurs through mistake, liability is limited to actual damages proved, including damages for arrest, prosecution, or other consequential damages. Section 4–402.

When a payor bank receives an item properly payable from a customer's account, but there are insufficient funds in the account to pay it, the bank may (1) dishonor the item and return it or (2) pay the item and charge its customer's account even though an overdraft is created as a result. Section 4–401(1). The item authorizes or directs the bank to make the payment and hence carries with it an enforceable implied promise to reimburse the bank. Further, the customer may be liable to the bank to pay a service charge for the bank's handling of the overdraft or may be liable to pay interest on the amount of the overdraft.

A payor bank is under no obligation to its customer to pay an uncertified check that is over six months old. Section 4–404. This rule reflects the usual banking practice of consulting a depositor before paying a *stale* item (one over six months old) on her account. The bank is not required to dishonor such an item, however, and if payment is made in good faith, the bank may charge the amount of the item to its customer's account.

Stop Payment Orders

A check drawn on a bank is an order to pay a sum of money and an authorization to charge the amount to the drawer's account. The customer may countermand this order, however, by means of a **stop payment order.** Section 4–403. If the order does not come too late, the bank is bound by it. If the bank inadvertently pays a check over a valid stop order, it is *prima facie* liable to the customer, but only to the extent of the customer's loss resulting from the payment. The burden of establishing the fact and amount of loss is on the customer.

To be effective, a stop payment order must be received by the bank in time to give it a reasonable opportunity to act on it. Section 4–403(1). *See Siniscalchi v. Valley Bank of New York.* An oral stop order is binding on the bank for only fourteen calendar days. Section 4–403(2). Therefore, the normal practice is for a customer to confirm an oral stop order in writing, and such an order is effective for six months and may be renewed in writing.

The fact that a drawer has filed a stop payment order does not automatically relieve her of liability. If the bank honors the stop payment order and returns the check, the holder may bring an action against the drawer. If the holder qualifies as a holder in due course, personal defenses that the drawer might have to such an action would be of no avail.

Bank's Right to Subrogation on Improper Payment

If a payor bank pays an item over a stop payment order or otherwise in violation of its contract with the drawer or maker, the payor bank is subrogated to (obtains) the rights of (a) any holder in due course on the item against the drawer or maker, (b) the payee or any other holder against the drawer or maker, and (c) the drawer or maker against the payee or any other holder. Section 4–407. For instance, a bank pays a check over the drawer's stop payment order. The check was presented to the drawee bank by a holder in due course. The drawer's defense is that the check was obtained by fraud in the inducement. The drawee bank is subrogated to the rights of the holder in due course, who would not be subject to the drawer's personal defense and thus can debit the drawer's account. Section 4–407(a). The same would be true if the presenter were the payee against whom the drawer did not have a valid defense. Section 4–407(b).

Customer's Death or Incompetence

The general rule is that death or incompetence revokes all agency agreements. Furthermore, adjudication of incompetency by a court is regarded as notice to the world of that fact. Actual notice is not required. Section 4–405 of the Code modifies these stringent rules with respect to bank deposits and collections in several ways.

First, if a payor or collecting bank does not know of the adjudication of incompetence, its authority to accept, pay, or collect an item or to account for proceeds of its collection is not rendered ineffective by the incompetence of a customer of either bank at the time the item is issued or its collection undertaken. The bank may pay the item without incurring any liability.

Second, neither death nor adjudication of incompetence of a customer revokes a payor or collecting bank's authority to accept, pay, or collect an item until the bank knows of it and has a reasonable opportunity to act on this knowledge.

Finally, even though a bank knows of the death of its customer, it may for ten days after the date of his death pay or certify checks drawn by the customer unless a person claiming an interest in the account, such as an heir, executor, or administrator, orders the bank to stop making such payments. Section 4–405(2).

Customer's Duties

The Code imposes certain affirmative duties on bank customers and fixes time limits within which they must assert their rights. The duties arise and the time starts to run from the time the bank either sends or makes available to its customer a statement of account accompanied by the items paid against the account. The customer is required to exercise reasonable care and promptness to examine the bank statement and items to discover his *unauthorized signature* or any *alteration* on an item. Since he is not presumed to know the signatures of payees or indorsers, this duty of prompt and careful examination applies only to alerations and the customer's own signature, both of which he should be able to detect immediately. If he discovers an unauthorized signature or an alteration, he must notify the bank promptly. Section 4–406(1).

If the customer fails to carry out these duties of prompt examination and notice, he is precluded from asserting against the bank his unauthorized signature or any alteration if the bank establishes that it suffered a loss by reason of such failure. Section 4–406(2).

Furthermore, the customer will lose his rights in a potentially more important situation. Occasionally a forger carries out a series of transactions involving the account of the same individual. Perhaps he is an employee who has access to his employer's checkbook. He may forge one or more checks each month until he is finally detected. The bank, on the other hand, having paid, without objection, one or more of the customer's checks bearing such signatures, may be lulled into a false sense of security. Suddenly the forgery is detected by the customer after many months or even years. Section 4–406(2) of the Code deals with these situations. Once the statement and items become available to him, the customer must examine them within a reasonable period, which in no event may exceed fourteen calendar days and may, under the circumstances, be less, and notify the bank. Any alterations or unauthorized signatures on instruments by the same wrongdoer and paid by the bank during that period will still be the responsibility of the bank, but any paid thereafter but before the customer notifies the bank may not be asserted against it. This rule is based on the concept that the loss involved is directly traceable to the customer's negligence and, as a result, he should stand the loss.

These rules, however, depend on the bank's exercising ordinary care in paying the items involved. If it does not, it properly loses its right to require prompt action on the part of its customer. Section 4–406(3). But whether the bank exercised due care or not, the customer must in all events report any alteration or his unauthorized signature within one year from the time the statement and items were made available to him or be barred from asserting them against the bank. Any *unauthorized indorsement* must be asserted within three years from the time the bank statements and items containing such indorsements are made available to the customer. Section 4–406(4).

See Tally v. American Security Bank.

ELECTRONIC FUND TRANSFER

As previously mentioned, the use of commercial paper for payment has transformed the United States into a virtually "cashless" society. The advent and technological advances of computers make it likely that in the foreseeable future electronic fund transfer systems (EFTS) will bring about a "checkless" society. Financial institutions seek to substitute EFTS for checks for two principal reasons. The first is to eliminate the ever-increasing paperwork involved in processing the billions of checks that are issued annually. The second is to eliminate the "float" that a drawer of a check currently enjoys as a result of maintaining the use of his funds during the check processing period between issuance of the check and final payment.

An electronic fund transfer (EFT) has been defined as "any transfer of funds, other than a transaction originated by check, draft, or similar paper instrument, which is initiated through an electronic terminal, telephonic instrument, or computer or magnetic tape so as to order, instruct or authorize a financial institution to debit or credit an account." For example, with an EFT, William in New York would be able to pay a debt he owes to Yvette in Illinois by entering into his computer an order to his bank to pay Yvette. The drawee bank would then instantly debit William's account and transfer the credit to Yvette's bank, where Yvette's account would immediately be credited in that amount. The entire transaction would be completed in minutes. As to whether an informal telephone conversation to pay a named party constitutes an EFT, *see Kasnanchi v. Texas Commerce Medical Bank.*

Although EFTS are still in their formative stages, their use has generated considerable confusion concerning the legal rights of customers and financial institutions. A partial solution to these legal issues was provided in 1978 by Congress when it enacted the Electronic Fund Transfer Act (EFTA) discussed below. But significant and numerous legal problems remain. In an attempt to resolve some of these questions, the Permanent Editorial Board of the Uniform Commercial Code has promulgated Article 4A—Funds Transfer.

TYPES OF ELECTRONIC FUND TRANSFERS

Although it is highly probable that a number of new EFTS will appear in the coming years, at the moment there are several types of EFTS in use: (1) automated teller machines, (2) point-of-sale systems, (3) direct deposit and withdrawal of funds, (4) pay-by-phone systems, and (5) wholesale wire transfers.

Automated Teller Machines

Automated Teller Machines (ATMs) have become available throughout the country. ATMs permit customers to conduct various transactions with their bank through the use of electronic terminals. After activating an ATM with a plastic identification card and a secret number, customers can deposit and withdraw funds from their accounts, transfer funds between accounts, obtain cash advances, and make payments on loan accounts.

Point-of-Sale Systems

Point-of-sale (POS) systems permit consumers to transfer funds from their bank account to a merchant automatically. The POS machines are located within the merchant's store and are activated by the consumer's identification card and code. The computer will then instantaneously debit the consumer's account and credit the merchant's account.

Direct Deposits and Withdrawals

Another type of EFTS involves direct deposits made to a customer's account through an electronic terminal when the deposit has been authorized in advance by the consumer. Examples include direct payroll deposits, deposits of Social Security payments, and deposits of pension payments. Conversely, automatic withdrawals are preauthorized electronic fund transfers from the customer's account for regular payments to some party other than the financial institution at which the funds are deposited. Automatic withdrawals to pay insurance premiums, utility bills, or automobile loan payments are common examples of this type of EFTS.

Pay-by-Phone Systems

Recently some financial institutions have instituted a service that permits customers to pay bills by telephoning the bank's computer system and directing a transfer of funds to a designated third party. This service also permits customers to transfer funds between accounts.

Wholesale Electronic Funds Transfers

Wholesale electronic funds transfers, commonly called wholesale wire transfers, involve the movement of funds between financial institutions, between financial institutions and businesses, and between businesses. Over one *trillion* dollars is transferred this way each business day over the two major transfer systems—the Federal Reserve wire transfer network system (Fedwire) and the New York Clearing House Interbank Payment System (CHIPS). In addition, a number of private wholesale wire systems exist among the large banks. Limited aspects of wholesale wire transfers are governed by uniform rules promulgated by the Federal Reserve, CHIPS, and the National Automated Clearing House Association.

CONSUMER FUNDS TRANSFERS

In 1978 Congress determined that the use of electronic systems to transfer funds provided the potential for substantial benefits to consumers. But because of the unique characteristics of such systems, the application of existing consumer protection legislation was unclear, leaving the rights and obligations of consumers and financial institutions undefined. Accordingly, Congress enacted Title IX of the Consumer Protection Act, called the Electronic Fund Transfer Act (EFTA), to "provide a basic framework establishing the rights, liabilities, and responsibilities of participants in electronic fund transfers" with primary emphasis upon "the provision of individual consumer rights." Because the EFTA deals exclusively with the protection of **consumers,** it does not govern electronic transfers between financial institutions, between financial institutions and businesses, and between businesses. The act is similar in many respects to the Fair Credit Billing Act (see Chapter 43) which applies to credit card transactions. The Electronic Fund Transfer Act is administered by the Board of Governors of the Federal Reserve System, which is mandated to prescribe regulations to carry out the purposes of the act. Pursuant to this congressional mandate, the Federal Reserve has issued Regulation E.

Disclosure

The act is primarily a disclosure statute and as such requires that the terms and conditions of electronic fund transfers involving a consumer's account be disclosed in readily understandable language at the time the consumer contracts for such services. Included among the required disclosure are the consumer's liability for unauthorized transfers, the kinds of EFTs allowed, the charges for transfers or the right to make transfers, the consumer's right to stop payment of pre-

authorized EFTs, the consumer's right to receive documentation of EFTs, rules concerning disclosure of information to third parties, how account errors can be corrected, and the financial institution's liability to the consumer under the act.

Documentation and Periodic Statements

The act requires the financial institution to provide the consumer with written documentation of each transfer made from an electronic terminal at the time of transfer—a receipt. The receipt must clearly state the amount involved, the date, the type of transfer, the identity of the consumer's accounts involved, the identity of any third party involved, and the location of the terminal involved.

In addition, the financial institution must provide each consumer with a periodic statement for each account of the consumer that may be accessed by means of an EFT. The periodic statement must describe the amount, date, and location for each transfer; the fee, if any, to be charged for the transaction; and an address and phone number for questions and information.

Preauthorized Transfers

A preauthorized transfer *from* a consumer's account must be authorized in advance by the consumer in *writing,* and a copy of the authorization must be provided to the consumer when made. A consumer may stop payment of a preauthorized EFT by notifying the financial institution orally or in writing at any time up to three business days before the scheduled date of the transfer. The financial institution may require the consumer to provide written confirmation within fourteen days of an oral notification.

Error Resolution

The consumer has sixty days after the financial institution sends a periodic statement in which to notify the financial institution of any errors that appear on that statement.

The financial institution is required to investigate and report the results within ten business days. If the financial institution needs more than ten days to investigate, it may take up to forty-five days, provided it recredits the consumer's account for the amount alleged to be in error. If it determines that an error did occur, it must properly correct the error. Failure to investigate in good faith makes the financial institution liable to the consumer for treble damages (that is, three times the amount of provable damages).

Consumer Liability

A consumer's liability for unauthorized electronic fund transfer is limited to a maximum of $50 if the consumer notifies the financial institution within *two days* after he *learns* of the loss or theft. If the consumer does not report the loss or theft within two days, he is liable for losses up to $500. If the consumer fails to report the unauthorized use within *sixty days* of transmittal of a periodic statement, he is liable for losses resulting from *any* unauthorized EFT that appeared on the statement if the financial institution can show that the loss would not have occurred but for the failure of the consumer to report the loss within sixty days.

Liability of Financial Institution

A financial institution is liable to a consumer for all damages proximately caused by its failure to make an EFT in accordance with the terms and conditions of an account, in the correct amount, or in a timely manner when properly instructed to do so by the consumer. There are, however, some exceptions. The financial institution will not be liable if

1. the consumer's account has insufficient funds through no fault of the financial institution,

2. the funds are subject to legal process,

3. the transfer would exceed an established credit limit,

4. an electronic terminal has insufficient cash, or

5. circumstances beyond the financial institution's control prevents the transfer.

The financial institution is also liable for failure to stop payment of a preauthorized transfer from a consumer's account when instructed to do so in accordance with the terms and conditions of the account.

ARTICLE 4A

Article 4A, Funds Transfers, is designed to provide a statutory framework for a payment system that is not covered by existing Articles of the Uniform Commercial Code or the Electronic Fund Transfer Act. The typical wholesale wire transfer is entered into by sophisticated parties who desire great speed in transferring large sums of money.

Article 4A provides that the rights and obligations of the parties to a funds transfer covered by the article are subject to contrary agreement of the parties. Moreover, funds transfer system rules governing banks that use the system may be effective even if the rules conflict with Article 4A. Section 4A–501. Rights and obligations under Article 4A can also be changed by Federal Reserve regulations and operating circulars of Federal Reserve Banks. Section 4A–107.

Scope of Article

Article 4A covers wholesale funds transfers. Article 4A defines a funds transfer as a "series of transactions, beginning with the originator's payment order, made for the purpose of making payment to the beneficiary of the order. The term includes any payment order issued by the originator's bank or an intermediary bank intended to carry out the originator's payment order. A funds transfer is completed by acceptance by the beneficiary's bank of a payment order for the benefit of the beneficiary of the originator's payment order." Section 4A–104(a). The article, therefore, covers the transfers of credit that move from an originator to a beneficiary through the banking system. If any step in the process is governed by the Electronic Fund Transfer Act, however, the entire transaction is excluded from the article's coverage. Section 4A–108.

The following examples illustrate the coverage of the article:

1. Johnson Co. instructs its bank, First National Bank (FNB), to pay $2,000,000 to West Co., also a customer of FNB. FNB executes the payment order by crediting West's account with $2,000,000 and notifying West that the credit has been made and is available.

2. Assume the same facts as the first example except that West's bank is Central Bank (CB). FNB will execute the payment order of Johnson Co. by issuing its own payment order to CB instructing CB to credit the account of West.

3. Assume the facts presented in the second example with the added fact that FNB does not have a correspondent relationship with CB. In this instance, FNB will have to issue its payment order to Northern Bank (NB), a bank that does have a correspondent relationship with CB, and NB will then issue its payment order to CB.

Payment Order   A **payment order** is an instruction of a sender to a receiving bank to pay, or to cause another bank to pay, a fixed or determinable amount of money to a beneficiary. Section 4A–103. The instruction may be communicated orally, electronically, or in writing. To be a payment order the instruction must

(1) contain no condition to payment other than the time of payment;

(2) be sent to a receiving bank that is to be reimbursed by debiting an account of the sender or otherwise receiving payment from the sender; and

(3) be transmitted by the sender directly to the receiving bank or indirectly through an agent, funds-transfer system, or communication system.

The payment order is issued when sent and, if there is more than one payment to be made, each payment is a separate payment

order. Section 4A–104(b)(c). In the examples above, there is one payment order in the first example (from Johnson Co.), two in the second example (from Johnson Co. and from First National Bank), and three in the third example (from Johnson Co., from First National Bank, and from Northern Bank).

Parties   The **originator** is the sender of the payment order or, in a series of payment orders, it is the sender of the first payment order. Section 4A–104(c). A **sender** is the party who gives an instruction to the receiving bank. The bank to which the sender's instruction is addressed is the **receiving bank.** Section 4A–103(4). The receiving bank may be the originator's bank, an intermediary bank, or the beneficiary's bank. The **originator's bank** is either the bank that receives the original payment order or the originator if the originator is a bank. Section 4A–104(d). The **beneficiary's bank** is the bank identified in a payment order to credit the beneficiary's account and is the last bank in the chain of a funds transfer. Section 4A–103(a)(3). The **beneficiary** is the person to be paid by the beneficiary bank. Section 4A–103(a)(2). An **intermediary bank** is any receiving bank, other than an originator's bank or a beneficiary's bank, that receives a payment order. Section 4A–104(b). Thus, in the above examples

(1) Johnson Co. is the *originator* in all three examples;

(2) Johnson Co. is a *sender* in all three examples, FNB is a sender in examples 2 and 3, and NB is a sender in example 3;

(3) FNB is the *receiving bank* of Johnson Co.'s payment order in all three examples; in example 2, CB is the receiving bank of FNB's payment order; and, in example 3, CB is the receiving bank of NB's payment order and NB is the receiving bank of FNB's payment order;

(4) FNB is the *originator's bank* in all three examples;

(5) FNB is the *beneficiary's bank* in example 1; CB is the beneficiary's bank in examples 2 and 3;

Figure 29–2 Parties to a Funds Transfer

	Example 1	*Example 2*	*Example 3*
Originator	Johnson Co.	Johnson Co.	Johnson Co.
Sender(s)	Johnson Co.	Johnson Co.	Johnson Co.
		FNB	FNB
			NB
Receiving Bank(s)	FNB	FNB	FNB
		CB	CB
			NB
Originator's Bank	FNB	FNB	FNB
Beneficiary's Bank	FNB	CB	CB
Beneficiary	West	West	West
Intermediary Bank	—	—	NB

(6) West is the *beneficiary* in all three examples;

(7) NB is an *intermediary bank* in example 3.

See Figure 29–2 for a summary of the parties in these three examples. In some instances, the originator and the beneficiary may be the same party. For example, a corporation may wish to transfer funds from one account to another account that is in the same or a different bank.

Excluded Transactions As previously mentioned, Section 4A–108 provides that if any part of a funds transfer is governed by the Electronic Fund Transfer Act, then the transfer is excluded from Article 4A coverage. In addition, Article 4A covers only credit transactions and excludes debit transactions. If the instruction is given by the person making the payment, the transfer is a credit transfer. See Figure 29–3. If the instruction is given by the person receiving the payment, the transfer is a debit transfer. For example, a seller of goods obtains authority from the purchaser to debit the purchaser's account after the seller ships the goods. Article 4A does not cover this transaction because the instructions to make payment issue from the beneficiary (the seller) and not from the party whose account is to be debited (the purchaser).

Acceptance

Rights and obligations arise as a result of a receiving bank's acceptance of a payment order. The effect of acceptance varies depending upon whether the payment order was issued to the beneficiary's bank or to a receiving bank other than the beneficiary's bank.

If a receiving bank is not the beneficiary's bank, the receiving bank does not subject

Figure 29–3 Credit Transaction

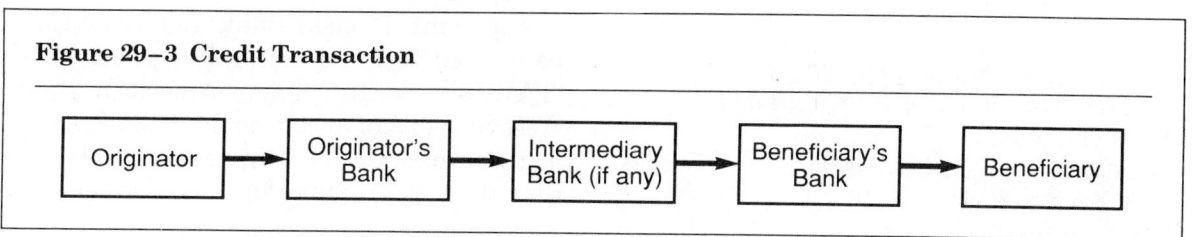

itself to any liability until it accepts the instrument. Acceptance by a receiving bank other than the beneficiary's bank occurs when the receiving bank executes the order. Section 4A–209(a). Execution of the sender's order occurs when the receiving bank "issues a payment order intended to carry out" the sender's payment order. Section 4A–301(a). When the receiving bank executes the sender's payment order, the bank is entitled to payment from the sender and can debit the sender's account. Section 4A–402(c).

The beneficiary's bank may accept an order in any of three ways and acceptance occurs at the earliest of these events: (1) when the bank (a) pays the beneficiary or (b) notifies the beneficiary of receipt of the order or that the beneficiary's account has been credited with the funds; (2) when the bank receives payment of the sender's order; or (3) the opening of the next funds-transfer business day of the bank after the payment date of the order if the order was not rejected and funds are available for payment. Section 4A–209(b).

If a beneficiary's bank accepts a payment order, the bank is obliged to pay the beneficiary the amount of the order. Section 4A–404(a). Acceptance by the beneficiary's bank of the payment order does not create any obligation to either the sender or the originator.

Erroneous Execution of Payment Orders

If a receiving bank mistakenly executes a payment order for an amount greater than the authorized amount, the bank is only entitled to payment of the amount of the sender's correct order. Section 4A–303(a). The receiving bank is then entitled to recover from the beneficiary of the erroneous order the amount in excess of the authorized amount to the extent allowed by the law governing mistake and restitution. If the wrong beneficiary is paid, the bank that issued the erroneous payment order is not entitled to payment from its sender and all prior senders and has the burden of recovering the payment from the improper beneficiary. Section 4A–303(c).

Unauthorized Payment Orders

If a bank establishes commercially reasonable security measures agreed to by the customer for preventing unauthorized transmissions and properly follows its process, the customer must pay the order even if it was unauthorized. Section 4A–202. The customer, however, can avoid liability if it can show that the unauthorized order was *not* caused directly or indirectly by (1) a person acting for the customer with access to confidential security information or (2) a person who obtained that information from a source controlled by the customer. Section 4A–203.

CASES

Collection of Items

PULASKI BANK & TRUST CO. v. TEXAS AMERICAN BANK/FORT WORTH, N.A.

Texas Court of Appeals, Dallas, 1988.
7 UCC Rep. Serv. 2d 335.

THOMAS, J.

Appellant, Pulaski Bank and Trust Company, sued Texas American Bank/Fort Worth (TAB/Fort Worth), Texas American Bank/West Side (TAB/West Side) and Texas American Services, Inc. (TASI), appellees, alleging that they were liable for losses suffered by

Pulaski when notice of dishonor of a $150,000 check drawn upon TAB/West Side was not timely relayed to Pulaski. After a nonjury trial, the trial court entered a take-nothing judgment against TAB/West Side and TASI and further entered judgment in favor of Pulaski against TAB/Fort Worth for $8,202.14. In three points of error, Pulaski contends that the trial court erred: 1) in concluding that TAB/West Side was not liable for Pulaski's loss, because as a matter of law TAB/West Side did not timely return the check; . . .

Statutory Framework

This action is governed by article 4 of the Uniform Commercial Code. Article 4 sets out the method by which a bank in which a check is deposited may be finally paid by the bank upon which the check is drawn. It has been said that article 4 provides the "traffic rules" which keep the bank collection process flowing smoothly. [Citation.] In order to place the facts of this case in context, we must first set out the framework of article 4.

To begin the collection process on a check, the person having possession of the item must transfer it to a bank, but not necessarily the bank through which or upon which the check is drawn. [Citation.] The first bank to which a check is transferred for collection is called the depositary bank. See § 4.105(1); [citation]. After the depositary bank has processed the check and entered a provisional credit to the account of its depositor, the bank will transfer the check to another bank which may be the first of many banks that will handle the check before it reaches the bank upon which it is drawn. [Citations.]

The last bank in the chain—the bank by which an item is payable as drawn—is denominated the payor bank. See § 4.105(2); [citations]. The other banks in the chain are intermediary banks and collecting banks. An intermediary bank is any bank to which an item is transferred in the course of collection, except the depositary or payor bank. See § 4.105(3); [citation]. A collecting bank is one which handles the check for collection, but

not the payor bank. See § 4.105(4); [citation]. These classifications of banks in the collection process are not exclusive. Thus, it is entirely possible that a depositary bank could also be a collecting bank. See § 4.105(1) & (4); [citation].

As the check moves along the chain from the depositary bank to the payor bank, all the banks in the chain enter provisional debits and credits on the account of the bank from which and to which the check is transferred. These provisional credits are termed provisional settlements under article 4. See § 4.104(a)(10); [citation]. As the check passes from the depositary bank to the payor bank through collecting banks, each collecting bank must act seasonably in forwarding the check. A bank acts seasonably if it acts before its midnight deadline following receipt of the check. See § 4.202(b); [citation]. The midnight deadline is midnight on the next banking day following the banking day on which the bank receives the check. See § 4.104(a)(8); [citation].

When the check reaches the payor bank, that bank must decide whether to pay the check or dishonor the check. If the payor bank pays the check, all the provisional settlements among the banks in the collection chain become final. See § 4.213; [citation]. If the payor bank decides to dishonor the check, it must return the item or send notice of dishonor to the intermediary bank from which it received the check. The payor bank must take this step before its midnight deadline. See § 4.301; [citation]. If the payor bank does not return the item or send notice of dishonor before its midnight deadline, the provisional settlements become final. See § 4.213(a)(3); [citation]. Until a check is finally paid, a collecting bank which makes a provisional settlement has the right to charge back the amount of any credit given or to obtain a refund from the bank it credited. See § 4.212. The right of charge-back terminates when a settlement becomes final. [Citations.]

A *payor* bank that does not timely return the check or send notice of dishonor becomes liable to the depositary bank *for the full amount of the check.* See §§ 4.213(a) & 4.302; [citations]. A collecting bank becomes liable if it fails to use ordinary care in returning items or giving notice of dishonor by its midnight deadline. See § 4.202; [citation]. In such instances, the *collecting* bank's liability is measured by the amount of the check reduced by an amount which could not have been realized by the use of ordinary care by the collecting bank. See § 4.103(e); [citations].

Factual Background

On February 5, 1985, Laboratory Management, Inc. deposited into its account at Pulaski, a Little Rock, Arkansas bank, a check in the amount of $150,000. The check was made by Fairway Farms, Inc., and was drawn on TAB/West Side, a Fort Worth bank. Lab Management received a provisional credit in the amount of $150,000 at that time. Pulaski immediately transmitted the check for collection to its correspondent bank, Worthen Bank & Trust Company of Little Rock. Immediately upon receiving the check on February 6th, Worthen sent the check for collection to MBank Dallas, Worthen's corresponding bank in Dallas. MBank Dallas, still on February 6th, delivered the check to MBank Fort Worth.

That same day, MBank Fort Worth delivered the check to the Fort Worth Clearinghouse. Since TAB/West Side is not a "clearing member," it could not participate in the exchange of items at the clearinghouse. Therefore, TAB/Fort Worth, a clearing member, received for collection the $150,000 check payable by TAB/West Side. The clearinghouse sent the check to TASI, an off-premises data processing center used by both TAB/Fort Worth and TAB/West Side.

TASI received the check on February 6th. During the computerized processing procedure, the check was sorted into the TAB/West Side reject pocket and was listed on the TAB/West Side reject list because of insufficient funds in Fairway Farm's account. The rejects list was delivered to TAB/West Side by 8:00 a.m. on February 7th. Barry Smith, the account officer responsible for the Fairway Farms account upon which the $150,000 check was drawn, was notified that there were insufficient funds to cover the check. Smith decided that the check should not be paid and informed the customer service department of TAB/West Side that the check should be returned unpaid. The rejects list was transmitted by courier to TASI between 10:00 a.m. and 11:00 a.m. on February 7th. Thereafter, the check was manually pulled and marked to be returned. The check was then taken to the customer accounting, or bookkeeping, department at TASI. Because of the directions of TAB/West Side that the check should be returned unpaid, the ledger entries previously made were reversed.

The check was then taken to the return item department. The testimony revealed that the return item department represented TAB/Fort Worth in the transaction at this point in time. According to the testimony, once the check was physically pulled and the entries to the general ledgers were reversed, TAB/West Side was "out of the picture." Although it is disputed whether TASI gave MBank Dallas telephone notice of the return on February 7th, it is undisputed that the check was not physically returned to MBank Dallas on February 7th. The check was misrouted by TASI; rather than returning the check to MBank Dallas, TASI sent the check to RepublicBank. After the check was misrouted to RepublicBank, it appears that RepublicBank sent the check to the Federal Reserve Bank of Dallas. On February 14th, TASI received telephone notification from the Federal Reserve Bank that it had the check and was sending it back. The return item department of TASI physically received the check on February 15th, and on that same date telephoned MBank Dallas notifying them of the return of the check. Because of an intervening bank holiday, MBank Dallas did not receive the check itself until February 19th. However, on February 15th, MBank notified Worthen Bank of the return by telephone. MBank sent the check to Worthen on February 19th and Worthen received it on February 21st. Worthen notified

Pulaski by telephone on February 22nd that the check was being returned and Pulaski actually received the check from Worthen on February 23rd.

On February 22nd and 23rd, the balance in Lab Management's checking account at Pulaski was $46,036.65. Pulaski did not freeze the account at that time because it considered the return to be late. It was Pulaski's position that since this was a late return, one of the collecting banks would be required to pay the entire amount of the check. Pulaski sent a late return claim to Worthen. Worthen disclaimed responsibility for the late return, and made a late return claim against MBank Dallas. MBank also disclaimed responsibility, and sent a late return claim to TAB/Fort Worth. TAB/Fort Worth also disclaimed responsibility, relying upon telephonic notice to MBank on February 7th. By March 25th, all of the banks in the collection chain had disclaimed, in writing, liability for late return. The Lab Management account was finally frozen and the $150,000 deposit charged back on April 30, 1985. At that time, the account balance was $1,433.99.

If the check had been returned timely by all the banks in the collection chain, Pulaski should have received notification of dishonor on February 12th. By February 12th, Pulaski had paid out $95,761.21 from the Lab Management account. Between February 12th, the date upon which Pulaski should have received notice of dishonor, and February 23rd, the date upon which the check was returned unpaid, Pulaski paid out $8,202.14 from the Lab Management account.

* * *

Liability of TAB/West Side

Pulaski contends in its first point of error that "[t]he trial court should have found as a matter of law that TAB West Side was liable for Pulaski Bank's loss because it did not timely and adequately revoke settlement and return the check." Pulaski concedes that the U.C.C. does not require TAB/West Side to return directly to Pulaski, but rather requires a

return to its immediate transferor before the midnight deadline. See § 4.301. Pulaski contends, however, that MBank, not TAB/Fort Worth, was TAB/West Side's transferor. Pulaski characterizes TAB/Fort Worth as a "mere agent" of TAB/West Side and a "nominal participant" in the check-handling process. Thus, argues Pulaski, a return to TAB/Fort Worth before TAB/West Side's midnight deadline was ineffective to cut off TAB/West Side's liability.

In the alternative, Pulaski contends that, even if TAB/Fort Worth is the transferor bank, we would frustrate the public policy behind the enactment of article 4 of the U.C.C. if we held that return and revocation of provisional settlements can be achieved through "mere" book entries at TASI. This presents an issue of first impression in this state, and apparently in all jurisdictions that have adopted the U.C.C. * * *

A. TAB/West Side's Midnight Deadline

We must first determine when TAB/West Side's midnight deadline fell. The midnight deadline falls on midnight on the next banking day following the banking day on which TAB/West Side received the check. See § 4.104(a)(8). The $150,000 check reached TASI on February 6th. It is undisputed that TASI functions as the data-processing center for both TAB/Fort Worth and TAB/West Side. It is also undisputed that the check remained at TASI February 6th and 7th and that TAB/West Side's decision to dishonor was not made until February 7th. We need not decide yet whether the delivery of the check to TASI was delivery to TAB/West Side directly or to TAB/West Side only through delivery first to TAB/Fort Worth. TAB/West Side and TAB/Fort Worth concede that, in some fashion, TAB/West Side received the check at TASI at some time on February 6th. This court has held that the midnight deadline calculation begins with the day on which a check is received at an off-premises data-processing center and not the day on which the check or check information is taken to the bank premises from the data-processing center. [Citation.]

Thus, we conclude that the midnight deadline time period must be calculated starting with February 6th, the day TAB/West Side "received" the check by presentment to TASI (Whether that presentment was made by MBank or by TAB/Fort Worth will be addressed later). Therefore, TAB/West Side's midnight deadline was midnight of the next banking day. See § 4.104(a)(8). By midnight of February 7th, TAB/West Side had to return the check to its transferor bank. We must now determine the identity of that transferor bank.

B. TAB/Fort Worth's Status As TAB/West Side's Transferor Bank Pulaski argues that TAB/Fort Worth was acting merely as an agent for presentment of the check and not as a collecting bank. The essence of its argument is that TAB/Fort Worth was involved with this check only because the Fort Worth Clearinghouse rules prohibited TAB/West Side from directly clearing the check. Pulaski alludes to the close relationship between TAB/Fort Worth, TAB/West Side and TASI as proof that TAB/Fort Worth was merely acting as agent for TAB/West Side. We are not persuaded by Pulaski's argument.

Pulaski relies in part on clearinghouse rule 2.03, which provides that a clearing member acts as agent or subagent for the bank for which the clearing member sends or receives items. We do not read this rule to change TAB/Fort Worth's status from a collecting bank to a mere agent. Even the U.C.C. provides that collecting banks are agents. See § 4.201. Because of the similarity in language of clearinghouse rule 2.03 and section 4.201 of the U.C.C., we believe that the clearinghouse rule was enacted for the same reason that § 4.201 was enacted: to end confusion over whether a bank handling an item was a purchaser of the item or merely an agent for collection. See § 4.201 comment 1. Thus, we conclude that any agency status between TAB/West Side and TAB/Fort Worth does not prevent TAB/Fort Worth from being TAB/West Side's transferor bank.

* * *

After reviewing the record, we are constrained to hold that there is ample evidence to support the trial court's finding that TAB/Fort Worth was TAB/West Side's transferor with respect to the $150,000 check. TAB/Fort Worth was authorized by Fort Worth Clearinghouse rules to clear checks for TAB/West Side. TAB/West Side, as an associate member, could not have received the check through the clearinghouse from MBank Fort Worth. TAB/Fort Worth, like any collecting bank, stamped the check with its endorsement. Transferor banks carry accounts for the next bank in the collection chain and will debit the account when it passes the check to that bank. In this case, TAB/Fort Worth carries an account for TAB/West Side. After the check was received at TASI and sorted to TAB/West Side, TAB/Fort Worth charged TAB/West Side's account for the amount of the check. After TAB/West Side notified TASI of its decision to dishonor the check, the ledger entries debiting TAB/West Side's account with TAB/Fort Worth were reversed. These actions are consistent with the relationship of transferor-transferee bank.

* * *

C. Public Policy Pulaski argues that one of the underlying policies of article 4 of the U.C.C. is speed in the collection process. Pulaski contends that we would frustrate this policy encouraging speed if we approved the "legal fiction" of allowing returns and revocations "within the confines of the same data processing center." Pulaski does not explain why it feels speed in collection would suffer by joint use of a data processing center. Its argument appears to be that a bank could extend its midnight deadline by "pretending" that another bank, which shared the data processing center, was involved in the collection chain. Thus, a bank could effectively double the amount of time that the U.C.C. gives it to act.

* * *

While we agree with Pulaski that it would be unfair to allow a bank, through use of a sham transferor bank, to double its midnight deadline, it would be equally unfair to halve the time by requiring separate banks to share the same midnight deadline.

The Code recognizes that each bank is entitled to at least twenty-four hours to process a check. See § 4.104(a)(8). Even closely-related banks have this right; the U.C.C. provides that each branch or separate office of a bank is to be considered a separate bank for purposes of computing the time in which a bank is to act. See § 4.106.

* * *

D. TAB/West Side's Return of the Check to TAB/Fort Worth Before Its Midnight Deadline As we noted previously, TAB/West Side's deadline for return of the check was midnight on February 7th. We have also held that the return had to be made to its transferor bank, which was TAB/Fort Worth. We turn now to the evidence to determine if TAB/West Side returned the $150,000 check to TAB/Fort Worth before midnight on February 7th. The evidence shows that TAB/West Side returned the rejects list with no "pay" notation next to the $150,000 check to TASI between 10:00 a.m. and 11:00 a.m. on February 7th. The lack of a "pay" notation informed TASI that TAB/West Side was returning the check unpaid. At TASI, the check was pulled and routed to the customer accounting department where the ledger entries between TAB/West Side and TAB/Fort Worth were reversed. From that department, the check was taken to the return items department. According to a TASI vice-president, the return between TAB/West Side and TAB/Fort Worth was completed when two events occurred: when the item was physically pulled and the ledger entries were reversed. This occurred before midnight on February 7th. We hold, based upon this evidence, that TAB/West Side met its U.C.C. midnight deadline for returning the check to TAB/Fort Worth.

* * *

F. Conclusion We hold that TAB/West Side timely returned the $150,000 check to its transferor bank, TAB/Fort Worth. Accord-

ingly, we conclude that the trial court was correct in finding that TAB/West Side was not liable for damages to Pulaski. Pulaski's first point of error is overruled.

* * *

Affirmed.

Duty to Act Seasonably

WELLS FARGO BANK v. HARTFORD NAT'L BANK & TRUST CO.

United States District Court, District of Connecticut, 1980. 484 F. Supp. 817.

BLUMENFELD, J.

This is a suit commenced by Wells Fargo Bank, National Association ("Wells Fargo") to recover $25,000 from Hartford National Bank and Trust Company ("HNBT"). Wells Fargo is seeking to reverse the credit it gave to HNBT in the course of handling a check which it had received for collection on which it was later unable to collect. HNBT, in turn, seeks indemnification from the depositary bank, Lincoln First Bank-Central, National Association ("Lincoln"). Each of the parties have (sic) filed for summary judgment on the grounds that no material facts are in dispute, and each claim that Articles 3 and 4 of the U.C.C. entitle them to relief.

Unlike many bank collection cases, this case does not involve the liability of the payor bank, First National Bank of Nevada ("Nevada"), which has not been sued, nor does it involve the liability of the now-bankrupt drawer of the check. The sole question presented by this action is which of these three banks in the chain of collection will have to absorb the loss occasioned by the "bad" check. * * *

Facts

The convoluted facts giving rise to this action are not in dispute, and summary judgment is therefore appropriate. However, before setting forth a detailed description of the intricacies of the bank collection process involved in this case, an overview of the transaction may be useful. On November 22, 1971, the check now in dispute was deposited with Lincoln. Since the check was drawn on the Nevada bank, Lincoln forwarded the check to Nevada via HNBT and Wells Fargo. On December 10, 1971, Nevada received the check and discovered that it was drawn on insufficient funds. Consequently Nevada decided to dishonor the item and sent the check back to Lincoln via Wells Fargo and HNBT. Lincoln received notice of the dishonor in late December of 1971, but it had already allowed the depositor of the check to withdraw funds from his account making it impossible to charge back the amount of the dishonored item. Claiming that the notice of dishonor came too late, Lincoln refused to accept the return of the check and instead sent it back again to Nevada via HNBT and Wells Fargo. When Wells Fargo received the item, however, it conditionally accepted responsibility for the loss and sought to collect from the drawer instead of delivering the check to Nevada. These efforts were unsuccessful and Wells Fargo, who now holds the dishonored item, commenced this action.

A. From Lincoln to Nevada * * * HNBT received the check on November 22, the same day on which it had initially been deposited. After crediting Lincoln's account for $25,000, HNBT indorsed the check and mailed it to its California correspondent bank, Wells Fargo. On November 23, Wells Fargo received and indorsed the check, credited HNBT's account, and then mailed the check to the Las Vegas branch of the Nevada bank.

During this last transfer a substantial delay was encountered. According to the Las Vegas branch bank records, the check inexplicably was not received in the mail until December 8, 1971, 15 days after Wells Fargo sent it. . . . When the check finally arrived . . . the Nevada bank promptly discovered that there were insufficient funds in Great Western's [drawer's] account.

B. From Nevada to Lincoln At 4:45 P.M. on December 10, 1971, Nevada bank personnel sought to inform Wells Fargo by telephone that the check had been dishonored. The call was made to a bank officer in Wells Fargo's San Francisco branch, but it was apparently "rejected" because it was not accompanied by sufficient identifying information. The Nevada bank made a second call, this time to Wells Fargo's Los Angeles branch. At 5:30 P.M. this call was "accepted."

Since December 10, 1971 was a Friday, the next banking day was Monday, December 13, 1971. On Monday, the Nevada bank posted the dishonored check to Wells Fargo, which did not receive it until Friday, December 17. Nevada also reversed the credit which it had given to Wells Fargo.

Upon receiving the check, Wells Fargo immediately wired notice of the dishonor to HNBT. On the same day, Wells Fargo also returned the dishonored item by mail to HNBT and reversed the credit it had previously given. HNBT claims not to have received the telegram on the 17th but admits that it received the check in the mail on Monday, December 21. On that same day, HNBT notified Lincoln by telegram that the check had been dishonored. This notice, however, did not indicate the name of the drawer of the check and therefore failed to give Lincoln effective notice. Lincoln's first opportunity accurately to identify the dishonored item came when it received the check on December 27, 1971. HNBT had mailed the check to Lincoln on December 21 and had at the same time reversed the credit it had given earlier.

C. From Lincoln to Nevada Again For the purpose of ruling on these motions it is not necessary to detail the remaining transfers of the check. Suffice it to say that on December 28, 1971, Lincoln declined to accept the check, claiming that the notice of dishonor had arrived too late. The item was sent back through the chain of collection and ultimately Wells Fargo ended up with both the check and the $25,000 loss. After several unsuccessful efforts at working out repayment from Great Western, Wells Fargo commenced this action.

* * *

The Law

UCC § 3–508(2) provides that "[a]ny necessary notice must be given by a bank before its midnight deadline." "Midnight deadline," in turn, is defined as "midnight on [the bank's] next banking day following the banking day on which it receives the relevant item or notice . . ." UCC § 4–104(1)(h). Thus, in order to determine whether Wells Fargo gave HNBT a timely notice of Nevada's dishonor, it is first necessary to establish "the banking day on which [Wells Fargo received] the relevant item or notice . . ."

As indicated above, Wells Fargo received a notice of Nevada's dishonor by telephone on Friday afternoon, December 10, 1971. It sent no notice to HNBT before the midnight deadline on its next banking day, Monday, December 13. Wells Fargo first received written notice from Nevada on Friday, December 17, when the dishonored check arrived in the mail. Notice of dishonor was then sent to HNBT prior to midnight on Monday, December 21, the next banking day following receipt of the *written* notice. Therefore, the first question this court must decide is whether oral notice from the payor bank, Nevada, can trigger the obligation of the collecting bank, Wells Fargo, to give notice to its customer, HNBT.

At first reading, Section 3–508(3) would seem to resolve this question. That section provides, "Notice may be given in any reasonable manner. It may be oral or written . . ." By virtue of Section 4–102(1), § 3–508(3) applies to bank collections unless it conflicts with a specific provision of Article 4. In such a case, the Article 4 provision governs the transaction.

Wells Fargo argues that Section 4–301 supersedes § 3–508 with respect to notice from payor banks and that therefore only written notice from such banks triggers the presenting bank's obligation to pass the notice of dishonor down through the chain of collection. This position appears to be meritorious and has been adopted by several courts. This court, however, need not rule on the specific question.

* * *

Lincoln has raised an issue which dispenses with the need to determine whether oral or written notification is required by the terms of the statute itself. In an introductory section to Article 4, the UCC provides:

"The effect of the provisions of this article may be varied by agreement except that no agreement can disclaim a bank's responsibility for its own lack of good faith or failure to exercise ordinary care or can limit the measure of damages for such lack or failure; but the parties may by agreement determine the standards by which such responsibility is to be measured if such standards are not manifestly unreasonable.

"Federal reserve regulations and operating letters, clearing house rules, and the like, have the effect of agreements under subsection (1), whether or not specifically assented to by all parties interested in items handled." UCC § 4–103(1), (2).

In its affidavits, Lincoln established that the transaction in question was governed by the terms of the Federal Reserve Operating Circular No. 6. At the time of the transaction this operating circular provided that payor banks can—in fact, must—give notice by "wire" when they dishonor items with values in excess of $1,000. "Wire" is expressly defined to include "telephonic" notices. Thus, since this operating circular governed the transaction here in dispute, it is clear that Nevada's telephonic notice was an adequate notice of dishonor, and Wells Fargo was not entitled to wait for written notice.

As is indicated above, Wells Fargo's failure to give timely notice essentially precludes it from prevailing under any of the three counts in its complaint.

* * *

Conclusion

For the foregoing reasons, Wells Fargo's motion for summary judgment against HNBT and HNBT's motion for summary judgment against Lincoln are denied. HNBT's motion for summary judgment against Wells Fargo and Lincoln's motion for summary judgment against HNBT are granted.

So ordered.

Stop Payment Order

SINISCALCHI v. VALLEY BANK OF NEW YORK

District Court, Nassau County, Second District, 1974.
79 Misc.2d 64, 359 N.Y.S.2d 173.

MELLAN, J.

This action was tried before me in a Small Claims Part of this Court and involved a claim by the plaintiff against the defendant bank for the sum of $200 based upon the fact that he had issued a check dated June 11, 1974, which incidentally was a Tuesday, and that on Monday following, namely, on June 17, 1974, bright and early as he testified, at 9 A.M. he appeared at the bank and asked them to place a stop payment on the check. The plaintiff testified that in speaking to the employee of the bank when he appeared in person as stated, the bank's employee detained the plaintiff for approximately 25 minutes or more while she checked the records to see if in fact this instrument had cleared the bank and, thereafter, at 9:45 A.M. gave him a printed notice confirming his request to stop payment and charging his account $5 for this stop payment. * * *

Nevertheless, it appears from the testimony in this matter that this bank has evening hours on Fridays and morning hours on Saturdays so that on June 14, 1974, Friday evening the bank was open for business, received deposits, made payments on checks and similarly on Saturday morning June 15, 1974. The bank transacted such business, but those transactions were not recorded or processed through the bookkeeping system of the bank until Monday June 17, 1974, the date on which the plaintiff appeared to stop payment the first thing in the morning. Thus, although the bank employee checked early that morning, the activities of Saturday morning had not yet been reflected and it appeared at that time that the check had not yet cleared.

The testimony shows that on Saturday morning, June 15, 1974, the check had been cashed so that the cashing of the check preceded the actual stop order. It is significant that the check was outstanding for nearly a full week before the stop order payment came in.

Section 4–403 of the Uniform Commercial Code provides for the customer's right to stop payment on a check, but specifically provides that the stop payment order must be received at such time and in such manner as to afford the bank a reasonable opportunity to act on the stop payment order prior to other action normally taken by the bank as described in Section 4–303 of the Uniform Commercial Code. Furthermore, the law thus provides that the burden is upon the depositor or customer of the bank to establish the amount of loss which may result from the payment by the bank of an item contrary to a binding stop payment order.

A payment in violation of an effective direction to stop payment is an improper payment even though it is made by mistake or inadvertence. This, however, does not appear to have been the case in this instance since the payment actually anteceded the stop payment order.

It may have been difficult for most depositors without special knowledge of banking practices to realize the multiple details involved in the handling of checks and other banking instruments, but it is clear that the bank must have a reasonable opportunity to act upon stop payment orders. [Citation.] In the case of knowledge, notice and stop orders the effective time for determining whether they were received too late to affect the payment of an item and a charge to the customer's account by reason of such payment is receipt plus a reasonable time for the bank to act on any of these communications. Usually a relatively short time is required to communicate to the bookkeeping department advice of these specific notices, but certainly some time is necessary. In the instant case with the weekend activities all being reflected on the records on the Monday following, the bank certainly did not have a reasonable time to act upon the plaintiff's stop payment order. [Citation.]

Under Section 4–303 of the Uniform Commercial Code a stop payment order comes too late to modify the bank's right or duty to pay a check after the bank has already paid the item in cash. Such is the case in the instant matter and for these reasons I find that the defendant is entitled to judgment.

Customer's Duties

TALLY v. AMERICAN SECURITY BANK

United States District Court, District of Columbia, 1982.
355 U.C.C.R.S. 215.

GREENE, J.

In this breach of contract action a customer sues his bank to recover money allegedly paid to a forger out of three accounts maintained or controlled by the plaintiff. Before the court is a motion by the bank for partial summary judgment. * * *

The background of the case is straightforward. The plaintiff contends that he was swindled out of $52,825 by the once-trusted personal secretary who managed his Washington, D.C. law office. Her job and his trust were lost to the secretary when he discovered, sometime after the employee's confession in February, 1980, that . . . in seven instances she had signed his name on savings account withdrawal slips that she then presented to the defendant American Security Bank. As custodian of the plaintiff's passbook, and recipient of his bank statements, the secretary had avoided detection for some four years.

* * *

§ 4–406(1) . . . establishes the duty of a bank customer to review promptly a "statement and items" sent to him or made available to him "in a reasonable manner." Subsection (4) provides that "a customer who does not within one year from the time the statement and items are made available to the customer (subsection (1)) discover and report his unauthorized signature . . . on the face or back of the item . . . is precluded from asserting against the bank such unauthorized signature. . . ." The issue is whether subsection (4) applies when the "item," here a savings withdrawal order, is made available to the customer not through the mail but upon the customer's request.

The U.S. Court of Appeals for this Circuit recently decided that § 4–406 applies to savings as well as checking accounts. *Boutros v. Riggs National Bank* [citation.] Boutros also held that savings withdrawal slips are "items" within the meaning of § 4–406. Subsection (4), however, was not in issue in Boutros, and the plaintiff urges first, that it is not applicable to savings accounts even if the other subsections are, and second, if the subsection is applicable, the one-year time bar attaches only when the savings statements sent to the customer are accompanied by the negotiated items supporting the statement's entries. The court rejects both contentions.

In order to hold that subsections (2) and (3) were applicable to allegedly unauthorized savings withdrawal orders, the Court of Appeals in Boutros necessarily had to find that when banks send periodic statements to savings customers while keeping the withdrawal orders on file they are "mak[ing] the statement and items available to the customer" within the meaning of § 4–406(1). No reason is apparent from the face of § 4–406 or from the comments to it to suspect that subsection (1) and subsection (4) apply to different kinds of banking transactions. Indeed, subsection (4) expressly incorporates subsection (1) by reference. It is not illogical to suppose that the drafters of the UCC expected a customer to make inquiries of his bank if his savings account balance, as stated on the mailed statement, appeared inexplicably low. Upon these inquiries, the savings withdrawal slips would then be "made available."

It is not necessary now to decide whether the one year should run from the time the customer receives his statement, or from the time the slips are made available for inspection. If the appropriate starting point were the latter, the law would have to require that the request for the items be made reasonably promptly after issuance of the statement, or the objective of finality would be undermined. In the instant case, the last allegedly wrongful savings withdrawal took place over three years before the plaintiff notified the bank that his account was awry. It is unclear whether he asked to see the withdrawal orders at this time, but even if he did so, it was too late to fall within a reasonable interpretation of § 4–406(4).

The court is mindful that § 4–406 should not be interpreted so as to give banks more protection than was intended by the drafters of the UCC or by Congress when it adopted the provision for the District of Columbia. [Citation.] It is this court's view, however, that if § 4–406 is to be segmented into subsections that apply to checking accounts and subsections that apply to savings accounts, it is for the legislating body to do. The court holds, therefore, that subsection (4) bars assertion of the savings account claims as the bank was not notified of the irregularities until over three years after the last withdrawal was effected.

Therefore, upon consideration of the defendant's motion for partial summary judgment, it is this 14th day of December, 1982,

Ordered That said motion be and it is hereby granted. The court dismisses with prejudice that portion of the plaintiff's claim based on allegedly forged . . . savings withdrawal orders paid by defendant. . . .

Electronic Fund Transfer

KASHANCHI v. TEXAS COMMERCE MEDICAL BANK, N.A.

United States Court of Appeals, Fifth Circuit, 1983.
703 F.2d 936.

RANDALL, J.

The plaintiff, Morvarid Paydar Kashanchi, appeals from a final judgment. . . . The issue on appeal is whether the term "electronic fund transfer" as used in the Electronic Fund Transfer Act ("EFTA" or "the Act"), [citation], includes a transfer of funds from a consumer's account, initiated by a telephone conversation between someone other than the owner of the account and an employee of a financial institution, when that transfer is not made pursuant to a prearranged plan or agreement under which periodic transfers

are contemplated. For the reasons set forth below, we affirm.

On or about February 9, 1981, the plaintiff and her sister, Firoyeh Paydar, were the sole owners of a savings account at Texas Commerce Medical Bank in Houston, Texas. On or about that date, $4900 was transferred from their account. The transfer was allegedly initiated by a telephone conversation between an employee of the bank and someone other than the plaintiff or her sister. Upon receipt of a March 31, 1981, bank statement showing the $4900 withdrawal, Firoyeh Paydar sent a letter to the bank, dated April 15, 1981, notifying the bank that the withdrawal was unauthorized.

After the bank refused to recredit the account with the amount of the allegedly unauthorized withdrawal, the plaintiff filed this action on December 4, 1981, alleging violations by the bank of the EFTA. * * *

This is apparently the first case in which we have been called upon to interpret any of the substantive provisions of the EFTA. * * *

The parties agree that the telephonic transfer that allegedly occurred in this case falls within the broad definition of "electronic fund transfers" in the Act:

(T)he term "electronic fund transfer" means any transfer of funds, other than a transaction originated by check, draft, or similar paper instrument, which is initiated through an electronic terminal, telephonic instrument, or computer or magnetic tape so as to order, instruct, or authorize a financial institution to debit or credit an account. Such term includes, but is not limited to, point-of-sale transfers, automated teller machine transactions, direct deposits or withdrawals of funds, and transfers initiated by telephone.

[Citation.] Some of what Congress has given, however, it has also taken away. Excluded from the definition of an electronic fund transfer is

any transfer of funds which is initiated by a telephone conversation between a consumer and an officer or employee of a financial institution which is not pursuant to a prearranged plan and under which periodic or recurring transfers are not contemplated. . . .

[Citation.] The plaintiff concedes that the unauthorized transfer of her funds was not made "pursuant to any prearranged plan," and that it was made by an employee of the bank.

* * *

Many aspects of electronic fund transfer systems are undergoing evolutionary changes and, thus, projections about future events necessarily involve a degree of speculation. Consequently, the appropriate approach to those new financial service concepts is, in general, to permit further development in a free market environment and, to the extent possible, in a manner consistent with the nature and purpose of existing law and regulations governing financial services. [Citation.] The absence of discussion about informal personal phone transfers would seem to indicate an intent not to cover these transfers, or at least an absence of congressional concern about them, in light of the extensive discussion throughout the hearings and reports of the other existing types of electronic transfers. It is highly unlikely that this silence was a result of congressional ignorance of the problem since these informal phone withdrawals presumably had been occurring since shortly after the time of Alexander Graham Bell.

* * *

Finally, we note that the EFTA was passed because "(e)xisting law and regulations in the consumer protection area are not applicable to some aspects of the new financial service concepts." [Citations.] The plaintiff suggests in her reply brief that she would have no adequate legal remedy for the wrong she has suffered if she were denied relief under the EFTA. While she conceded at oral argument that she might have an action under state law for conversion or breach of contract (her deposit agreement with the bank), she maintained that a person suffering a loss resulting from the abuse of one of the other electronic fund transfer systems would also have such an action under state law.

The plaintiff ignores the essential difference between electronic fund transfer systems and personal transfers by phone or by check. When the bank employee allegedly agreed to withdraw funds from the plaintiff's account, he or she presumably could have asked some questions to ascertain whether the caller was one of the account holders. The failure to attempt to make a positive identification of the caller might be considered negligence or a breach of the deposit agreement under state law. When someone makes an unauthorized use of an electronic fund transfer system, however, the financial institution often has no way of knowing that the transfer is unauthorized. For example, in order to make a transfer at an automatic teller machine, a person need only possess the machine card and know the correct personal identification number. The computer cannot determine whether the person who has inserted the card and typed in the magic number is authorized to use the system. What might be a withdrawal negligently permitted by the financial institution in one situation might not be a negligent action in the other.

Our analysis of both the language of the EFTA and the legislative history of the Act leads us to conclude that Congress intended to exclude from the Act's coverage any transfer of funds initiated by a phone conversation between any natural person and an officer or employee of a financial institution, which was not made pursuant to a prearranged plan and under which periodic and recurring transfers were not contemplated. Accordingly, we hold that the withdrawal of funds from the plaintiff's account is not covered by the Act even though said withdrawal allegedly was not made by either the plaintiff or her sister. The district court's dismissal of the plaintiff's action for lack of subject matter jurisdiction is AFFIRMED.

QUESTIONS

1. Distinguish among depositary, payor, intermediary, and collecting banks.

2. Discuss the duties of collecting banks.

3. Discuss the obligations between a customer and the drawee bank.

4. Define a consumer electronic fund transfer and outline the major provisions of the Electronic Fund Transfer Act.

5. Define a wholesale funds transfer and identify the parties to such a transfer.

PROBLEMS

1. On December 9, Jane Jones writes a check for $500 payable to Ralph Rodgers in payment for goods to be received later in the month. Before the close of business on the 9th Jane notifies the bank by telephone to stop payment on the check. On Monday, December 19, Ralph gives the check to Bill Briggs for value and without notice. On the 20th, Bill deposits the check in his account at Bank A. On the 21st, Bank A sends the check to its correspondent Bank B. On the 22nd, Bank B presents the check through the clearing house to Bank C. On the 23rd, Bank C presents the check to Bank P, the payor bank. On Wednesday, the 28th of December the payor bank makes payment of the check final. John Jones sues the payor bank. Decision?

2. Howard Harrison, a long-time customer of Western Bank, operates a small department store, Harrison's Store. Since his store has few experienced employees, Harrison frequently travels throughout the United States on buying trips, although he also runs the financial operations of the business. On one of his buying trips, Harrison purchased a gross of sport shirts from Well-Made Shirt Company and paid for the transaction with a check on his store account with Western Bank in the amount of $1,000. Adams, an employee of Well-Made who deposits its checks in Security Bank, sloppily raised the amount of the check to $10,000 and indorsed the check, "Pay to the order of Adams from Pension Plan Benefits, Well-Made Shirt Company by Adams." He cashed the check and he cannot be found. The check was processed and paid by the Western Bank and was sent to

Harrison's Store with the monthly statement. After brief examination of the statement, Harrison left on another buying trip for three weeks.

(a) Assuming the bank acted in good faith and the alteration is not discovered and reported to the bank until an audit conducted thirteen months after the statement was received by Harrison's Store, who must bear the loss on the raised check?

(b) Assume that Harrison, who was unable to examine his statement promptly because of his buying trips, left instructions with the bank to carefully examine and to notify him of any item over $5,000 to be charged to his account; however, the bank paid the item anyway in his absence. Who bears the loss if the alteration is discovered one month after the statement was received by Harrison's Store? If the alteration is discovered thirteen months later?

3. Tom Jones owed Bank of Cleveland $10,000 on a note due November 17, with one percent interest due the bank for each day delinquent in payment. Tom Jones issued a $10,000 check to Bank of Cleveland and deposited it in the night vault the evening of November 17. Several days later, he received a letter saying he owed one day's interest on the payment because of a one day delinquency in payment. Jones refused because he said he had put it in the vault on the 17th of November. Decision?

4. Assume that Dinah draws a check on Oxford Bank, payable to the order of Pam; that Pam indorses it to Amy; that Amy deposits it to her account in Houston Bank; that Houston Bank presents it to Oxford Bank, the drawee; and that Oxford Bank dishonors it because of insufficient funds. Houston Bank receives notification of the dishonor on Monday. Houston Bank, because of an interruption of communication facilities, fails to notify Amy until Wednesday. What result?

5. Jones, a food wholesaler whose company has an account with City Bank in New York City, is traveling in California on business. He finds a particularly attractive offer and decides to buy a carload of oranges for delivery in New York. He gives Saltin, the seller, his company's check for $25,000 to pay for the purchase. Saltin deposits the check, with others he received that day, with his bank, the Carrboro Bank. Carrboro Bank sends the check to Downs Bank in Los Angeles which, in turn, deposits it with the Los Angeles Federal Reserve Bank. The L.A. Fed sends the check, with others, to the N.Y. Fed. The N.Y. Fed forwards the check to City Bank, Jones's bank, for collection.

(a) Is City Bank a depositary bank? A collecting bank? A payor bank?

(b) Is Carrboro Bank a depositary bank? A collecting bank?

(c) Is the N.Y. Fed. an intermediary bank?

(d) Is Downs Bank a collecting bank?

Explain.

6. On April 1, Moore gave Pipkin a check properly drawn by Moore on Zebra Bank for $500 in payment of a painting to be framed and delivered the next day. Pipkin immediately indorsed the check and gave it to Yeager Bank as payment in full of his indebtedness to the bank on a note he previously had signed. Yeager Bank canceled the note and returned it to Pipkin.

On April 2, upon learning that the painting had been destroyed in a fire at Pipkin's studio, Moore promptly went to Zebra Bank, signed a printed form of stop payment order, and gave it to the cashier. Zebra Bank refused payment on the check upon proper presentment by Yeager Bank.

(a) What are the rights of Yeager Bank against Zebra Bank?

(b) What are the rights of Yeager Bank against Moore?

(c) Assuming that Zebra Bank, by inadvertence, had paid the amount of the check to Yeager Bank and debited Moore's account, what are the rights of Moore against Zebra Bank?

7. As payment in advance for services to be performed, Acton signed and delivered the following instrument:

December 1, 1991
LAST NATIONAL BANK
MONEYVILLE, STATE X
Pay to the order of Olaf Owen $1,500.00_____
Fifteen Hundred Dollars _____ For services to be performed by Olaf Owen starting on December 6, 1991.

(signed) Arthur Acton

Owen requested and received Last National Bank's certification of the check even though Acton had only $900 on deposit. Owen indorsed the check in blank and delivered it to Dan Doty in payment of a pre-existing debt.

When Owen failed to appear for work, Acton gave a written stop payment order to the bank ordering the bank not to pay the check. Doty presented the check to Last National Bank for payment. The bank refused payment.

What are the bank's rights and liabilities relating to the transactions described?

8. Jones drew a check for $1,000 on The First Bank and mailed it to the payee, Thrift, Inc. Caldwell stole the check from Thrift, Inc., chemically erased the name of the payee, and inserted the name of Henderson as payee. Caldwell also increased the amount of the check to $10,000 and, by using the name of Henderson, negotiated the check to Willis. Willis then took the check to The First Bank and obtained its certification on the check. Willis then negotiated the check to Griffin who deposited the check in The Second National Bank for collection. The Second National Bank forwarded the check to the Detroit Trust Company for collection from The First Bank which honored the check. Griffin exhausted her account in the Second National Bank, and the account was closed. Shortly thereafter, The First Bank learned that it had paid an altered check.

What are the rights of each of the parties? Assume that all parties (except Caldwell) are respectively holders in due course.

9. Jason, who has extremely poor vision, went to an ATM to withdraw $200 on February 1. Joshua saw that Jason was having great difficulty reading the computer screen and offered to help. Joshua obtained Jason's secret pass number and secretly exchanged one of his old credit cards for Jason's ATM card. Between February 1 and February 15, Joshua withdrew $1,600 from Jason's account. On February 15, Jason discovered that his ATM card was missing and immediately notified his bank. The bank closed Jason's ATM account on February 16, by which time Joshua had withdrawn another $150. What is Jason's liability, if any, for the unauthorized use of his account?

10. On July 21, Boehmer, a customer of Birmingham Trust, secured a loan from that bank for the principal sum of $5,500 in order to purchase a boat allegedly being built for him by A. C. Manufacturing Company, Inc. After Boehmer signed a promissory note, Birmingham Trust issued a cashier's check to Boehmer and A. C. Manufacturing Company as payees. The check was given to Boehmer, who then forged A. C. Manufacturing Company's indorsement and deposited the check in his own account at Central Bank. Central Bank credited Boehmer's account and then placed the legend "P.I.G.," meaning "Prior Indorsements Guaranteed," on the check. The check was presented to and paid by Birmingham Trust on July 22. When the loan became delinquent in March of the following year, Birmingham Trust contacted A. C. Manufacturing Company to learn the location of the boat. They were informed that it had never been purchased, and they soon after learned that Boehmer had died on January 24 of that year. On May 1, Birmingham Trust sought reimbursement from Central Bank under the latter's warranty of prior indorsements. Decision?

11. Advanced Alloys, Inc., issued a check in the amount of $2,500 to Sergeant Steel Corporation. The check was presented for payment fourteen months later to the Chase Manhattan Bank. Chase Manhattan made payment on the check and charged Advanced Alloy's account. Advanced Alloy now seeks to recover the payment made on the check. Decision?

Partnerships

Chapter 30

NATURE AND FORMATION

Nature of Partnership
Formation of a Partnership
Partnership Property
Partners' Ownership Rights

A business enterprise may be operated or conducted by a sole proprietor, a joint venture, a general partnership, a limited partnership, a corporation, or by some other form of business organization. The owner or owners of the enterprise determine which form of business unit to use. Various factors, not the least of which are Federal and State income tax laws, affect the decision to use one medium rather than another. Other factors include ease of formation, capital requirements, flexibility of management and control, extent of external liability, and the duties imposed by law upon management. For a concise comparison of general partnerships, limited partnerships and corporations, see Figure 34–1 in Chapter 34.

Although corporations today outnumber unincorporated business associations (general partnerships, joint ventures, and limited partnerships) by about two to one and generate greater revenues by over twenty to one, unincorporated business associations are widely used in a number of areas. General partnerships have been used principally in finance, insurance, accounting, real estate, wholesale and retail trade, law, and other services. Joint ventures have enjoyed popularity among major corporations planning to engage in cooperative research; in the exploitation of land and mineral rights; in the development, promotion, and sale of patents, trade names, and copyrights; and in manufacturing operations in foreign countries. Limited partnerships have been widely used for enterprises such as real estate investment and development, motion picture and theater productions, oil and gas ventures, and equipment leasing.

This and the following two chapters will examine general partnerships, commonly called partnerships; Chapter 33 discusses limited partnerships and other types of unincorporated business associations. Part Seven covers corporations.

NATURE OF PARTNERSHIP

Partnership is an extremely old form of business association known to have been used in ancient Babylonia, classical Greece, and the Roman Empire. It was also used in Europe and England during the Middle Ages. Eventually the English common law recognized partnerships. In the nineteenth century, partnerships were widely used in England and the United States and the common law of partnership developed considerably during this period. Partnerships are important in that they allow individuals with different expertise, backgrounds, resources, and interests to bring their various skills together to form a more competitive enterprise.

In 1914, the National Conference of Commissioners on Uniform State Laws promulgated the Uniform Partnership Act (UPA). Since then it has been adopted in all States, except Louisiana, and has been adopted by the District of Columbia, the Virgin Islands, and Guam. The UPA is reprinted in Appendix D. Although the UPA is rather comprehensive, it does not cover all legal issues concerning partnerships. Accordingly, Section 5 of the UPA provides that any situation not provided for by the Act shall be governed by the rules of law and equity.

The UPA Revision Subcommittee of the Committee on Partnerships and Unincorporated Business Organizations of the American Bar Association's Section of Corporation, Banking and Business Law has recommended that the UPA be revised. Its report has been submitted to the National Conference of Commissioners on Uniform State Laws, which in August 1986 decided to undertake a complete revision of the Uniform Partnership Act. To date, the revision has not been completed.

Definition

The UPA's definition of a **partnership** is "A partnership is an association of two or more persons to carry on as co-owners a business for profit." Section 6. The UPA broadly defines "person" to include "individuals, partnerships, corporations, and other associations." Section 2. A business is also defined by Section 2 of the UPA and includes every trade, occupation, or profession.

Entity Theory

A **legal entity** is a unit with the capacity of possessing legal rights and being subject to legal duties. A legal entity may acquire, own, and dispose of property. It may enter into contracts, commit wrongs, sue, and be sued. Each business corporation is a legal entity having a distinct legal existence separate from its shareholders.

A partnership was regarded by the common law as a legal aggregate or group of individuals not having a legal existence separate from its members. The UPA, however, has partially rejected the common law view of partnerships. It treats partnerships as a legal entity for some purposes, although for other purposes it still treats them as an aggregate. *See Pate v. Martin.*

Partnership as a Legal Entity The UPA recognizes a partnership as a legal entity distinct from its members in several ways. (1) The assets of the firm are treated as those of the business and are considered separate and distinct from the individual assets of its members. Section 25. (2) Title to real estate may be acquired by a partnership in the partnership name. Section 8(3). (3) A partner is accountable as a fiduciary to the partnership. Section 21. (4) Every partner is considered an agent of the partnership. Section 9(1). (5) Under the doctrine of marshaling of assets—which applies in cases of insolvency administered by a State court of equity—partnership creditors have a prior right to partnership assets, while creditors of the individual members have a prior right to the separate assets of their individual debtors. Section 40(h).

Some States have modified the UPA to recognize a partnership as an entity in additional respects. Moreover, some courts have extended entity treatment to matters not addressed by the UPA.

Partnership as a Legal Aggregate Because a partnership is considered an aggregate for some purposes, it can neither sue nor be sued in the firm name unless a statute specifically allows it. Similarly, the debts of the partnership are ultimately the debts of the individual partners, and any one partner may be held liable for the partnership's entire indebtedness. Section 15. Thus, if Meg and Mike enter into a partnership that becomes insolvent, as does Meg, Mike is fully liable for the debts of the partnership.

In addition, a partnership generally lacks continuity of existence: whenever any partner ceases to be associated with the partnership, it is dissolved. Section 29. Likewise, a partner's interest in the partnership may be assigned, but the assignee does not become a partner without the consent of all the partners. Section 18(g).

Finally, the Internal Revenue Code treats a partnership as an aggregate. A partnership is not required to pay Federal income tax but must file an information return stating the name of each partner and the amount of income derived from the partnership. It is the responsibility of each partner to include his share of partnership income in his individual tax return and to pay the tax on his share. Partnership income is taxed to the individual partners regardless of whether the income is distributed.

Types of Partners

Partners can be classified as either general or limited. A partner may also be silent, secret, or dormant. In addition, nonpartners may be considered ostensible partners or subpartners.

A **general partner** is a partner of either a general or limited partnership whose liability for partnership indebtedness is unlimited, who has full management powers, and who shares in the profits. Most partnerships consist of only general partners and are referred to as "general partnerships" or just "partnerships."

A special or **limited partner** is one who, as a member of a limited partnership, is liable for firm indebtedness only to the extent of the capital he has contributed or agreed to contribute. Limited partnerships are formed by compliance with a number of statutory requirements and are discussed in Chapter 33.

A **silent partner** is a partner who elects to take no part in the partnership business.

A **secret partner** is a partner whose membership in the firm is not disclosed to the public.

A **dormant partner** is a partner who is both a silent and a secret partner.

An **ostensible partner** is one who has consented to be held out as a partner whether he is a real partner or not. The term is more commonly applied to one who is a partner by estoppel: although not an actual partner, he is liable to those who, in good faith, have extended credit on the reasonable assumption that he was a partner.

A **subpartner** is one who is not a partner at all but has a contractual arrangement with a partner which entitles him to a share of the profits realized by such partner. The relationship calls for no continuous acts or the performance of any duty by the subpartner.

FORMATION OF A PARTNERSHIP

The formation of a partnership is relatively simple and may be done consciously or unconsciously. A partnership may result from an oral or written agreement between the parties, from an informal arrangement, or from the conduct of the parties. Persons become partners by associating themselves in business together as co-owners. Consequently, if two or more individuals share the control and profits of a business, the law may deem them partners without regard to how they might characterize their relationship. Thus, associates frequently discover, to their chagrin, that they have inadvertently formed a partnership and have thereby subjected themselves to the duties and liabilities of partners. Whether their agreement is simple or elaborate, definite or indefinite, fully understood and fair or obscure and inequitable is of importance principally to the partners. The legal existence of the relationship depends upon the parties' explicit or implicit agreement and their association in business as co-owners and not upon the degree of care, intelligence, study, or investigation that preceded its formation.

Articles of Partnership

In the interest of achieving a more clear, definite, and complete understanding between the partners, it is preferable, although not usually required, that partners put their agreement in writing. A written agreement creating a partnership is referred to as the partnership agreement or **articles of partnership.** Any partnership agreement *should* include

1. The firm name and the identity of the partners;

2. The nature and scope of the partnership business;

3. The duration of the partnership;

4. The capital contributions of each partner;

5. The division of profits and sharing of losses;

6. The duties of each partner in the management;

7. A provision for salaries if desired;

8. Restrictions, if any, upon the authority of particular partners to bind the firm;

9. The right, if desired, of a partner to withdraw from the firm, and the terms, conditions, and required notice in the event of such withdrawal; and

10. A provision for continuation of the business by the remaining partners, if desired, in the event of the death of a partner or other dissolution, and a statement of the method or formula for appraisal and payment of the interest of the deceased or former partner.

A partnership agreement can provide almost any conceivable arrangement of capital investment, control sharing, and profit distribution that the partners desire. In addition, it can provide for continuity of the partnership in the event of one member's death or retirement.

Figure 30–1 shows a sample partnership agreement.

Statute of Frauds The statute of frauds does not expressly apply to a contract for the formation of a partnership, and therefore no writing is required to create the relationship. A contract to form a partnership to continue for a period longer than one year is within the statute and requires a writing in order to be enforceable. Moreover, a contract for the transfer of an interest in real estate to or by a partnership is governed by the statute of frauds and requires a writing to be enforceable.

Firm Name In the interest of acquiring and retaining good will a partnership should have a firm name. The name selected by the partners may not be identical with or deceptively similar to the name of any other existing business concern. It may be the name of the partners or of any one of them, or the partners may decide to operate the business under a fictitious or assumed name, such as "Peachtree Restaurant" or "Globe Theater" or "Paradise Laundry." A partnership may not use a name that would be likely to indicate to the public that it is a corporation. Nearly all of the States have enacted statutes that require any person or persons conducting any business under an assumed or fictitious name to file in a designated public office a certificate setting forth the name under which the business is conducted and the real names and addresses of all persons conducting the business as partners or proprietors.

Tests of Partnership Existence

Partnerships can be formed without the slightest formality. Consequently, it is important that the law establish a test for determining whether a partnership has been formed. Two situations most often require this determination. The most common is a creditor who has dealt with one person but wants to hold another also liable by asserting that the two were partners. Less frequently, a person seeks to share profits and property held by another by claiming that they are partners.

As previously mentioned, Section 6 of the UPA provides the basic definition of a partnership: an association of two or more persons to carry on as co-owners of a business for profit. Thus, there are three components to this definition, all of which have to be met: (1)

Figure 30–1 Sample Partnership Agreement

PARTNERSHIP AGREEMENT

This agreement, made and entered into as of the [*Date*], by and among [*Names*] (hereinafter collectively sometimes referred to as "Partners").

WITNESSETH:

Whereas, the Parties hereto desire to form a General Partnership (hereinafter referred to as the "Partnership"), for the term and upon the conditions hereinafter set forth;

Now, therefore, in consideration of the mutual covenants hereinafter contained, it is agreed by and among the Parties hereto as follows:

Article I

BASIC STRUCTURE

§ 1.1 **Form**

The Parties hereby form a General Partnership pursuant to the Laws of [*Name of State*].

§ 1.2 **Name**

The business of the Partnership shall be conducted under the name of [*Name*].

§ 1.3 **Place of Business**

The principal office and place of business of the Partnership shall be located at [*Describe*], or such other place as the Partners may from time to time designate.

§ 1.4 **Term**

The Partnership shall commence on [*Date*], and shall continue for [*Number*] years, unless earlier terminated in the following manner:

(a) By the completion of the purpose intended, or

(b) Pursuant to this Agreement, or

(c) By applicable [*State*] law, or

(d) By death, insanity, bankruptcy, retirement, withdrawal, resignation, expulsion, or disability of all of the then Partners.

§ 1.5 **Purpose—General**

The purpose for which the Partnership is organized is _____.

Article II

FINANCIAL ARRANGEMENTS

§ 2.1 **Initial Contributions of Partners**

Each Partner has contributed to the initial capital of the Partnership property in the amount and form indicated on Schedule A attached hereto and made a part hereof. Capital contributions to the Partnership shall not earn interest. An individual capital account shall be maintained for each Partner.

§ 2.2 **Additional Capital Contribution**

If at any time during the existence of the Partnership it shall become necessary to increase the capital with which the said Partnership is doing business, then (upon the vote of the Managing Partner(s)):

Each party to this Agreement shall contribute to the capital of this Partnership within _____ days notice of such need in an amount according to his then Percentage Share of Capital as called for by the Managing Partner(s).

§ 2.3 **Percentage Share of Profits and Capital**

(a) The Percentage Share of Profits and Capital of each Partner shall be (unless otherwise modified by the terms of this Agreement) as follows:

Names	Initial Percentage Share of Profits and Capital

§ 2.4 **Interest**

No interest shall be paid on any contribution to the capital of the Partnership.

Figure 30–1 (*continued*)

§ 2.5 Return of Capital Contributions

No Partner shall have the right to demand the return of his capital contributions except as herein provided.

§ 2.6 Rights of Priority

Except as herein provided, the individual Partners shall have no right to any priority over each other as to the return of capital contributions except as herein provided.

§ 2.7 Distributions

Distributions to the Partners of net operating profits of the Partnership, as hereinafter defined, shall be made at (*least monthly/at such times as the Managing Partner(s) shall reasonably agree.*) Such distributions shall be made to the Partners simultaneously.

For the purpose of this Agreement, net operating profit for any accounting period shall mean the gross receipts of the Partnership for such period, less the sum of all cash expenses of operation of the Partnership, and such sums as may be necessary to establish a reserve for operating expenses.

§ 2.8 Compensation

No Partner shall be entitled to receive any compensation from the Partnership, nor shall any Partner receive any drawing account from the Partnership.

Article III

MANAGEMENT

§ 3.1 Managing Partners

The Managing Partner(s) shall be [*Names*] [*or* "all partners"].

§ 3.2 Voting

The Managing Partner(s) shall have the right to vote as to the management and conduct of the business of the Partnership as follows:

Names   **Vote**

Article IV

DISSOLUTION

§ 4.1 Dissolution

In the event that the Partnership shall hereafter be dissolved for any reason whatsoever, a full and general account of its assets, liabilities, and transactions shall at once be taken. Such assets may be sold and turned into cash as soon as possible and all debts and other amounts due the Partnership collected. The proceeds thereof shall thereupon be applied as follows:

(a) To discharge the debts and liabilities of the Partnership and the expenses of liquidation.

(b) To pay each Partner or his legal representative any unpaid salary, drawing account, interest or profits to which he shall then be entitled and in addition, to repay to any Partner his capital contributions in excess of his original capital contribution.

(c) To divide the surplus, if any, among the Partners or their representatives as follows:

(1) First (to the extent of each Partner's then capital account) in proportion to their then capital accounts.

(2) Then according to each Partner's then Percentage Share of *Capital/Income.*

§ 4.2 Right To Demand Property

No Partner shall have the right to demand and receive property in kind for his distribution.

Witnesses   **Partners**

_____   _____

_____   _____

Dated: _____.

SOURCE: Adapted from *West's Legal Forms*, 2d ed., by Paul Lieberman. Copyright © 1981 by West Publishing Co. Reprinted with permission.

an association of two or more persons, (2) conducting a business for profit, (3) which they co-own. See Figure 30–2.

Association A partnership must have two or more persons who agree to become partners. Any natural person having full *capacity* may enter into a partnership. To the extent that a minor has capacity to act as a principal or agent, she may become a partner, although she has the right both to disaffirm the partnership agreement at any time before reaching majority and to avoid personal liability to partnership creditors. On disaffirmance and withdrawal from the partnership, a minor is entitled to the return of her capital contribution and her accrued and unpaid share of the profits except to the extent that such funds are necessary to pay partnership creditors.

The position of a nonadjudicated incompetent is basically the same as that of a minor except that his incompetency may afford his co-partners a ground for seeking dissolution by court decree. Section 32. Since all contracts of an adjudicated incompetent are void, not voidable, a partnership agreement entered into by such an individual is void.

A corporation is defined as a "person" by Section 2 of the UPA and is, therefore, legally capable of entering into a partnership in those States whose incorporation statutes authorize a corporation to do so. A partnership may be a member of other partnerships. Section 2.

Business for Profit The UPA provides that co-ownership does not of itself establish a partnership, even though the co-owners share the profits derived from use of the property. Section 7(2). For a partnership to exist, there must be a business in addition to the mere co-ownership of property. Moreover, to be a partnership, the business carried on by the association of two or more persons must be "for profit." This requirement excludes social clubs, fraternal orders, civic societies, and charitable organizations from being a partnership.

Where persons are associated together for mutual financial gain on a temporary or limited basis involving a single transaction or relatively few isolated transactions, no partnership results because the parties are not engaged in a continuous series of commercial activities necessary to constitute a business. Co-ownership of the means or instrumentality of accomplishing a single business transaction or a limited series of transactions may result in a joint venture but not a general partnership. Joint ventures are discussed in Chapter 33.

Figure 30–2 Tests for Existence of a Partnership

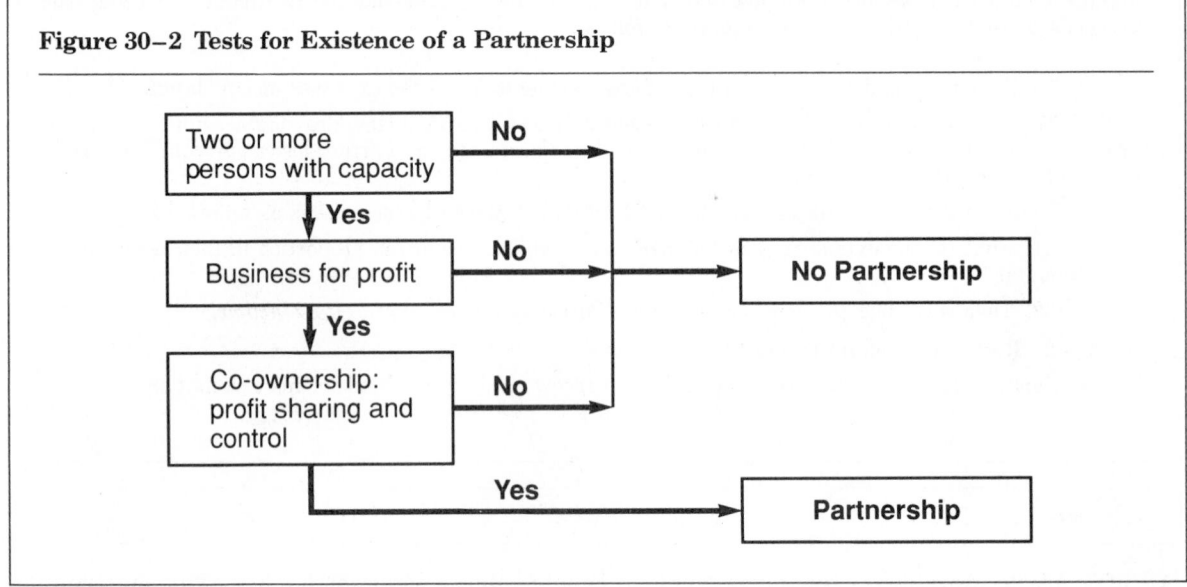

For example, Katherine and Edith are joint owners of shares of the capital stock of a corporation, have a joint bank account, and have inherited or purchased real estate as joint tenants or tenants in common. They share the dividends paid on the stock, the interest on the bank account, and the net proceeds from the sale or lease of the real estate. Katherine and Edith are not partners. Although they are co-owners and share profits, they are not engaged in the carrying on of a business, and hence no partnership results. On the other hand, if Katherine and Edith were engaged in continuous transactions of buying and selling real estate over a period of time and were carrying on a business of trading in real estate, a partnership relation would exist between them, regardless of whether they considered themselves partners.

To illustrate further: Alec, Laura, and Shirley each inherit an undivided one-third interest in a hotel and, instead of selling the property, decide by an informal agreement to continue operation of the hotel. The operation of a hotel is a business, and, as co-owners of a hotel business, Alec, Laura, and Shirley are partners and are subject to all of the rights, duties, and incidents arising from the partnership relation.

Co-ownership Although co-ownership of *property* used in a business is neither a necessary nor a sufficient condition for the existence of a partnership, the co-ownership of a *business* is essential. In determining the element of co-ownership of a business, the two most important factors are sharing of profits and the right to manage and control the business.

The receipt by a person of a share of the **profits** of a business is *prima facie* evidence that he is a partner in the business. Section 7(4) of the UPA, however, provides that no inference of the existence of a partnership relation shall be drawn where such profits are received in payment

1. of a debt by installments or otherwise;

2. of wages of an employee or rent to a landlord;

3. of an annuity to a widow or representative of a deceased partner;

4. of interest on a loan, though the amount of payment may vary with the profits of the business; or

5. as consideration for the sale of the good will of a business or other property by installments, or otherwise.

These transactions do not give rise to a presumption that the party is a partner because the law assumes it more likely that the creditor, employee, landlord, or other recipient of a share of the profits is not a co-owner. It is possible, nonetheless, to establish that such a person was a partner by proof of other facts and circumstances, such as the sharing of control.

The sharing of *gross returns,* in contrast to profits, does *not* of itself establish a partnership. Section 7(3). This is so whether or not the persons sharing the gross returns have a joint or common interest in any property from which the returns are derived. Thus, two brokers who share commissions are not necessarily or even presumed partners. Similarly, an author who receives royalties (a share of gross receipts from the sales of a book) is not a partner with the publisher.

An agreement to share in or contribute to the *losses* of a business, however, affords strong evidence of an ownership interest. Few jurisdictions insist upon an express agreement of loss sharing for a partnership to exist, but all consider such an agreement compelling proof of the existence of a partnership.

By itself, evidence as to participation in the *management* or **control** of a business is not conclusive proof of a partnership relation, but it is persuasive. A voice in management and control of a business may be accorded, in a limited degree, to an employee, a landlord, or a creditor. On the other hand, one who is actually a partner may take no active part in the affairs of the firm and may, by agreement with his co-partners, forego all right to exercise any control over the ordinary affairs of the business. In any event, the right to participate in control is an important factor considered by the courts in conjunction with other factors, profit sharing in particular. *See Chaiken v. Employment Security Commission and Cutler v. Bowen.*

Partnership Capital and Property

The total money and property contributed by the partners and dedicated to use in the enterprise is the **partnership capital**. A partnership is not required to have a minimum amount of capitalization before commencing business. Nonetheless, no partner may withdraw any part of his capital contribution without the consent of all the partners, except when the partnership is dissolved.

Partnership property, on the other hand, is the sum of all of the partnership assets and it may vary in amount, whereas partnership capital is a fixed amount, changed only by an amendment to the articles of partnership. All property originally brought into the partnership or subsequently acquired by the partnership is partnership property. Section 8(1). Unless the contrary intention appears, property acquired with partnership funds is partnership property. Section 8(2).

As discussed later, who owns the property—an individual partner or the partnership—determines (1) who gets it upon dissolution of the partnership, (2) who shares in any loss or gain upon its sale, (3) who shares in income from it, (4) who may sell it or transfer it by will, and (5) whose creditors have a priority against it in satisfying their claims.

Title to real estate which is properly a partnership asset, as where purchased with partnership funds or specifically made a capital contribution, may stand in the name of the partnership, an individual partner, or a third party. The UPA alters the common law by permitting title to real estate to be conveyed to a partnership in the partnership name. Section 8(3). Title so acquired may be conveyed only in the partnership name.

A question may arise whether property owned by a partner before formation of the partnership and used in the partnership business is a capital contribution and hence an asset of the partnership. For example, a partner who owns a store building may contribute to the partnership the use of the building but not the building itself. The building is, therefore, not partnership property, and the amount of capital contributed by this partner is the reasonable value of the rental of the building.

The fact that legal title to property remains unchanged is not conclusive evidence that it has not become a partnership asset. The intent of the partners controls the question of who owns the property. Where there is no express agreement, an intention that property is partnership property may be inferred from any of the following facts: (1) the property was improved with partnership funds; (2) the property was carried on the books of the partnership as an asset; (3) taxes, liens, or expenses, such as insurance or repairs, were paid by the partnership; (4) income or proceeds of the property were treated as partnership funds; or (5) admissions or declarations by the partners. *See Gauldin v. Corn.*

Rights in Specific Partnership Property

A partner's ownership interest in any specific item of partnership property is that of a **tenant in partnership.** Section 25. This type of ownership, which exists only in a partnership, has the following principal characteristics:

1. Each partner has an equal right with his co-partners to possess partnership property for partnership purposes, but he has no right to possess it for any other purpose without the consent of his co-partners.

2. A partner may not make an individual assignment of his right in specific partnership property.

3. A partner's interest in specific partnership property is not subject to attachment or execution by his individual creditors. It is subject

to attachment or execution only on a claim against the partnership.

4. Upon the death of a partner, his right in specific partnership property vests in the surviving partner or partners. Upon the death of the last surviving partner, his right in such property vests in his legal representative.

Partner's Interest in the Partnership

In addition to owning as a tenant in partnership every specific item of partnership property, each partner has an **interest in the partnership,** which is defined as his share of the profits and surplus and is expressly stated to be personal property. Section 26.

Assignability A partner may sell or assign his interest in the partnership. The new owner does *not* become a partner, does not succeed to the partner's rights to participate in the management, and does not have access to the information available to a member of the firm as a matter of right. She is merely entitled to receive the share of profits and rights upon liquidation to which the assigning partner would otherwise be entitled. Section 27. The assigning partner remains a partner with all the other rights and duties of a partner. An assignment does not dissolve the partnership. The other partners may, however, rightfully dissolve the partnership by unanimous agreement. Moreover, the assignee may apply for a court-ordered dissolution. Dissolution is discussed in Chapter 32.

Creditors' Rights A partner's interest is subject to the claims of that partner's creditors who may obtain a **charging order** (a type of judicial lien) against the partner's interest. Section 28. A creditor who has charged the interest of a partner with a judgment debt may apply for the appointment of a receiver. The court may appoint a receiver for the partner's interest who will receive and hold for the benefit of the creditor the share of profits that ordinarily would be paid to the partner. Neither the judgment creditor nor the receiver becomes a partner, and neither is entitled to participate in the management or to have access to information. *See Bohonus v. Amerco.*

Neither the charging order nor its sale upon foreclosure causes a dissolution. The other partners may dissolve the partnership or redeem the charged interest. Sections 32 and 28. The creditor has the same right to a court-ordered dissolution as an assignee.

Figure 30–3 compares a partner's rights in specific partnership property with his interest in the partnership.

Figure 30–3 Partnership Property Compared with Partner's Interest

	Partnership Property	Partner's Interest
Definition	Tenant in partnership	Share of profits and surplus
Possession	For partnership purposes and not for individual purposes	Intangible, personal property right
Assignability	If all other partners assign their rights in the property	Assignee does not become a partner
Attachment	Only for a claim against the partnership	By a charging order
Inheritance	Goes to surviving partner(s)	Passes to the personal representative of deceased partner

CASES

Entity Theory

PATE v. MARTIN

Court of Appeals of Arkansas, Division I, 1985.
13 Ark. App. 182, 681 S.W.2d 410.

CRACRAFT, C.J.

Jimmie Pate brings this appeal from an order of the circuit court denying his motion to quash a writ of garnishment issued on an award from the Arkansas Workers' Compensation Commission and served upon a person having in his hands assets belonging to him. The sole issue presented by this appeal is whether an award of the Workers' Compensation Commission entered against a partnership in its firm name only and which makes no reference to the individual co-partners may be enforced as a judgment by garnishment or execution against a co-partner. We conclude that it cannot.

* * * In April 1978 Troy Martin notified the Arkansas Workers' Compensation Commission by letter that he had been injured within the scope of his employment with "P & P Fabrication." * * * After a hearing the Commission affirmed the findings of the administrative law judge and awarded the appellant all medical expenses and accrued benefits in excess of $7500 against "the respondent." The award and opinion identified the respondent only as "P & P Fabrication." They made no reference as to whether it was a partnership or corporation, or, if a partnership, the identity of the co-partners. * * *

It was undisputed that "P & P Fabrication" was a partnership in which Jimmie Pate and Jimmie Pate, Jr. were equal partners. It was also undisputed that both partners appeared in the hearings before the Workers' Compensation Commission in defense of the claim and admitted that they were equal owners of the firm.

The trial court ruled that because the appellant had notice, appeared and defended before the Commission and was co-owner and partner in P & P Fabrication the circuit court had a right to consider the record before the Commission to determine his legal liability, even though appellant was not named as a party to those proceedings or in the award of the Commission.

* * *

It has long been the rule that in construing a judgment where the identity of a person against whom judgment is rendered is ambiguous or uncertain, resort may be had to the entire judgment or opinion for purposes of identification. In [citation] the body of the award clearly identified the "respondent" against whom that award was being entered. Here, however, the claim was made against "P & P Fabrication" and the award was so styled. The award made no mention of appellant or his son and made no finding that they were the actual employers of the respondent. There was no finding by the Commission that the actual respondent was anyone other than "P & P Fabrication," which was not designated as either a partnership or a corporation. We find it to be error for the circuit court to have made a finding not made by the Commission.

Nor do we find merit in the argument that one may be bound by a judgment even though not a party to the action where he has appeared and actually participated in the proceedings. While we agree that a court may enter a binding judgment against the individual parties under those circumstances, the Commission did not do so here. Nothing in the award or the opinion indicated an intent to make the appellant personally liable for the award.

Both parties agree that at common law a partnership is not an entity separate from its members and is nothing more than the aggregate of the individuals making it up. The partnership was not recognized as a legal entity separate and apart from the individuals owning it and had no capacity to sue or be sued. It was necessary to bring suit by or against a partnership in the names of the individuals comprising it rather than in the name of the partnership itself. The appellee argues, however, that this rule was abrogated by the Uniform Partnership Act and that a partnership may now be sued in the firm name and liability thereby imposed upon the members. We conclude that the enactment of the Uniform Partnership Act * * * did not embrace the entity theory as contended for by the appellee, but retained the common law rule that except in certain specific instances a partnership is not an entity separate and apart from its members and remains no more than the aggregate of the individuals forming it.

In *Mazzuchelli v. Silberberg,* [citation], the court gives a comprehensive history of the partnership act in that respect. In *Mazzuchelli* the court said:

The Uniform Partnership Law, adopted in this State in 1919, did not embrace the so-called "entity" theory. [Citations.] An early draft by Dean Ames for the commissioners was based on the entity theory and accordingly defined a partnership as "a legal person formed by the association of two or more individuals for the purpose of carrying on a business with a view to profits." [Citation.] Dean Lewis, however, advocated the view "that with certain modifications the aggregate or common law theory should be adopted." The history appears in the Commissioners' prefatory note, [citation]. As there revealed, the recommendation of Dean Lewis led to the adoption of a resolution rescinding any prior action which might limit the committee to "what is known as the entity theory." In 1910 the committee and a group of experts recommended that the act "be drawn on the aggregate or common law theory with the modification that the partners be treated as owners of the partnership property holding by a special tenancy which should be called tenancy in partnership." In 1911 Dean Lewis was requested to prepare a draft in "the so-called common law theory," and in 1912 the committee reported a draft "drawn on the aggregate or common law theory, with the modifications referred to." With amendments not negating that basic thesis, the uniform act was recommended for adoption. In harmony with the decision thus reached, a partnership was defined to be "an association of two or more persons to carry on as *co-owners* a business for profit," . . . as con-

trasted with the Ames proposal of "a *legal person* formed by the association of two or more individuals for the purpose of carrying on a business with a view to profits."

In the adoption of our Uniform Partnership Act the legislature followed the recommendation of the drafters to retain the common law or "aggregate" theory. [UPA § 6] defines a partnership as "an association of two or more persons to carry on as co-owners a business for profit." Our legislature did not, as did many other legislatures, accept the Ames definition of "*a legal person* formed by the association of two or more individuals for the purpose of carrying on a business with a view to profits," or make provisions for liability of individual partners sued in the partnership name. Our Uniform Partnership Act adopts the common law approach with modifications consistent with the "entity" approach of the purposes of facilitating the acquisition and transfer of partnership property, marshalling of assets and protecting the business operation against immediate impact of personal involvement of the partners. [Citations.]

* * *

We conclude that the award of the Workers Compensation Commission against the partnership in its firm name only and which makes no reference to the individual partners may not be enforced at law as a judgment by garnishment or execution against a co-partner. This case is reversed and remanded to the circuit court with directions to enter an order not inconsistent with this opinion.

Test of Partnership Existence

CHAIKEN v. EMPLOYMENT SECURITY COMMISSION

Superior Court of Delaware, 1971.
274 A.2d 707.

STOREY, J.

[Chaiken entered into separate but nearly identical agreements with Strazella and Spitzer to operate a barber shop. Under the terms of the "partnership" agreements,

Chaiken would provide barber chairs, supplies, and licenses, while the other two would provide tools of the trade. The agreements also stated that gross returns from the partnership were to be divided on a percentage basis among the three men and that Chaiken would decide all matters of partnership policy. Finally, the agreements stated hours of work and holidays for Strazella and Spitzer and required Chaiken to hold and distribute all receipts. The Delaware Employment Security Commission, however, determined that Strazella and Spitzer were not partners of Chaiken but rather were his employees. The commission then brought this action to assess unemployment compensation contributions against Chaiken for the two barbers. Chaiken contends that they are not employees but partners pursuant to written partnership agreements. As partners, Chaiken would not be liable for unemployment compensation contributions.]

* * *

Chaiken contends that he and his "partners":

(1) properly registered the partnership name and names of partners in the Prothonotary's office, in accordance with [citation],

(2) properly filed federal partnership information returns and paid federal taxes quarterly on an estimated basis, and

(3) duly executed partnership agreements.

Of the three factors, the last is most important. Agreements of "partnership" were executed between Chaiken and Mr. Strazella, a barber in the shop, and between Chaiken and Mr. Spitzer, similarly situated. The agreements were nearly identical. The first paragraph declared the creation of a partnership and the location of business. The second provided that Chaiken would provide barber chair, supplies, and licenses, while the other partner would provide tools of the trade. The paragraph also declared that upon dissolution of the partnership, ownership of items would revert to the party providing them. The third paragraph declared that the income of the partnership would be divided 30% for Chaiken, 70% for Strazella; 20% for

Chaiken and 80% for Spitzer. The fourth paragraph declared that all partnership policy would be decided by Chaiken, whose decision was final. The fifth paragraph forbade assignment of the agreement without permission of Chaiken. The sixth paragraph required Chaiken to hold and distribute all receipts. The final paragraph stated hours of work for Strazella and Spitzer and holidays.

The mere existence of an agreement labeled "partnership" agreement and the characterization of signatories as "partners" does not conclusively prove the existence of a partnership. Rather, the intention of the parties, as explained by the wording of the agreement, is paramount. [Citation.]

A partnership is defined as an association of two or more persons to carry on as co-owners a business for profit. [Citation.] As co-owners of a business, partners have an equal right in the decision making process. [Citation.] But this right may be abrogated by agreement of the parties without destroying the partnership concept, provided other partnership elements are present. [Citation.]

Thus, while paragraph four reserves for Chaiken all right to determine partnership policy, it is not standing alone, fatal to the partnership concept. Co-owners should also contribute valuable consideration for the creation of the business. Under paragraph two, however, Chaiken provides the barber chair (and implicitly the barber shop itself), mirror, licenses, and linen, while the other partners merely provide their tools and labor—nothing more than any barber-employee would furnish. Standing alone, however, mere contribution of work and skill can be valuable consideration for a partnership agreement. [Citations.]

Partnership interests may be assignable, although it is not a violation of partnership law to prohibit assignment in a partnership agreement. [Citation.] Therefore, paragraph five on assignment of partnership interests does not violate the partnership concept. On the other hand, distribution of partnership assets to the partners upon dissolution is only allowed after all partnership liabilities are satisfied. [Citation.] But paragraph two of the agreement, in stating the ground rules for dissolution, makes no declaration that the partnership assets will be utilized to pay partnership expenses before reversion to their original owners. This deficiency militates against a finding in favor of partnership intent since it is assumed Chaiken would have inserted such provision had he thought his lesser partners would accept such liability. Partners do accept such liability, employees do not.

Most importantly, co-owners carry on "a business for profit." The phrase has been interpreted to mean that partners share in the profits and the losses of the business. The intent to divide the profits is an indispensable requisite of partnership. [Citations.] Paragraph three of the agreement declares that each partner shall share in the income of the business. There is no sharing of the profits, and as the agreement is drafted, there are no profits. Merely sharing the gross returns does not establish a partnership. [Citation.] Nor is the sharing of profits prima facie evidence of a partnership where the profits received are in payment of wages. [Citation.]

The failure to share profits therefore, is fatal to the partnership concept here.

Evaluating Chaiken's agreement in the light of the elements implicit in a partnership, no partnership intent can be found. The absence of the important right of decision making or the important duty to share liabilities upon dissolution individually may not be fatal to a partnership. But when both are absent, coupled with the absence of profit sharing, they become strong factors in discrediting the partnership argument. * * *

In addition, the total circumstances of the case taken together indicate the employer-employee relationship between Chaiken and his barbers. The agreement set forth the hours of work and days off—unusual subjects for partnership agreements. The barbers brought into the relationship only the equipment required of all barber shop operators. And each barber had his own individual "partnership" with Chaiken. Furthermore, Chaiken conducted all transactions with suppliers, and purchased licenses, insurance, and the lease

for the business property in his own name. Finally, the name "Richard's Barber Shop" continued to be used after the execution of the so-called partnership agreements.

* * *

[Judgment for Commission.]

Test of Partnership Existence

CUTLER v. BOWEN
Supreme Court of Utah, 1975.
543 P.2d 1349.

CROCKETT, J.

Plaintiff, alleging a partnership with defendant, sued to recover half of $10,000 paid by the Salt Lake City Redevelopment Agency as compensation for the disruption of their tavern business known as The Havana Club at the corner of Second South and West Temple Streets. The district court made findings and entered judgment in favor of the plaintiff. Defendant appeals.

The Havana Club had been operated for some years at the location mentioned under a lease running to defendant Dale Bowen, who owned the equipment, furnishings and inventory. He did not himself work in operating the club. In June, 1968, he discussed with the plaintiff Frances Cutler, who had been working for him as a bartender, that she take over the management of the club. They arrived at an oral agreement which included these conditions: that the plaintiff was to have the authority and the responsibility for the entire active management and operation; to purchase the supplies, pay the bills, keep the books, to hire and fire employees; and do whatever else was necessary to run the business. As to compensation, the arrangement was for a down-the-middle split; each was to receive $100 per week, plus one half of the net profits.

The business was operated under this arrangement for four years, until the lessor's building was taken over by the Redevelopment Agency in 1972. . . . On the basis of the regulations it was ascertained that for such displacement the Havana Club should be entitled to the maximum allowable amount of $10,000. The parties made some effort to find a suitable new location for the Havana Club, but failing to do so, decided to terminate that business in April, 1972.

The dispute giving rise to this lawsuit arose because the defendant contended that he was the sole owner of the entire business; and that the plaintiff's status was merely that of an employee, so defendant was entitled to the whole $10,000. Whereas, plaintiff took the position that, conceding the defendant was the owner of the physical assets of the business as above stated, insofar as the going concern and goodwill value, as a partner in the business, she was entitled to one half of the relocation fund.

One of the primary matters to consider in determining whether a partnership exists is the nature of the contribution each party makes to the enterprise. It need not be in the form of tangible assets or capital, but, as is frequently done, one partner may make such a contribution, and this may be balanced by the other's performance of services and the shouldering of responsibility.

When parties join in an enterprise, it is usually in contemplation of success and making profits, and is often without much concern about who will bear losses. However, when they so engage in a venture for their mutual benefit or profit, that is generally held to be a partnership, in which the law imposes upon them both liability for debts or losses that may occur. This basic principle of partnership law is set forth in our Uniform Partnership Act, [Section 7]:

Rules for determining the existence of a partnership.—In determining whether a partnership exists these rules shall apply:

* * *

(4) The receipt by a person of a share of the profits of a business is prima facie evidence that he is a partner in the business, but no such inference shall be drawn if such profits were received in payment:

* * *

(b) As wages of an employee or rent to a landlord.

On the question whether profits shared should be regarded simply as wages, it is important to consider the degree to which a party participates in the management of the enterprise and whether the relationship is such that the party shares generally in the potential profits or advantages and thus should be held responsible for losses or liability incurred therein.

* * *

It is not shown here that any occasion arose where the plaintiff's responsibility for debts or other liabilities of the business was tested. However, throughout the four years in which she operated and managed the Club, apparently with competence and efficiency, it was her responsibility to see that all bills were paid, including the rental on the lease, employees' salaries, the costs of all purchases, licenses and other expenses of the business. During that time she saw the defendant Bowen only infrequently for the purpose of rendering an accounting and dividing the profits. It is further pertinent that the parties reported their income tax as a partnership.

Under the arrangement as shown and as found by the trial court, a good case can be made out that it was largely through the capability, experience, and efforts of the plaintiff that, in addition to the physical plant, there existed a separate asset in the value of the "going concern and goodwill" of the business, which was being lost by its displacement. On the basis of what has been said above, we see nothing to persuade us to disagree with the view taken by the trial court: that the plaintiff's involvement in this business was such that she would have been liable for any losses that might have occurred in its operation; and that, concomitantly, she was entitled to participate in any profits or advantages that inured to it.

* * *

From the circumstances shown in evidence as discussed herein, there appears to be a reasonable basis for the trial court's view that, except for the physical assets, which belonged to the defendant and to which the plaintiff makes no claim, the further asset of the business: that is, the value of what is called going concern and goodwill belonged to the two of them as partners in the enterprise; and that when the business could not be relocated, the $10,000 should properly be regarded as compensation for the loss by the forced relocation (which turned out to be a termination) of the business; and that the partners having lost their respective equal shares in the going business operation, they should also share equally in the compensation for its loss.

* * *

[Judgment for Cutler affirmed.]

Partnership Property

GAULDIN v. CORN

Court of Appeals of Missouri, Southern District, Division One, 1980.
595 S.W.2d 329.

GREENE, J.

* * *

The following evidence was presented to the trial court. Defendant Joe Corn, testified that in October, 1966, he entered into a 50–50 partnership with plaintiff Claude Gauldin for the purpose of raising cattle and hogs. Defendant and plaintiff contributed equally to getting the business started. The partnership business was carried out on approximately 25 acres of an 83 acre tract of land owned, at the beginning of the partnership, by defendant's parents and later acquired by defendant and his wife.

The bulk of the partnership profits were put back into the business. Some of the profits were used to improve the 25 acres on which the cattle and hogs were raised. Partnership money was used to fence in 10–15 acres and to repair already existing fence. Top dressing and seed, costing $2,000.00, was placed on some of the land. A machine shed, or barn, was built on the land while it was still owned by defendant's father. Defendant testified that the barn cost either $2,487.50 or $2,400.00. He said that a Cargill unit was built on the property in 1975 at a cost of either $8,000.00 or $7,995.00.

At time of trial, both the barn and the Cargill unit were still on the property. Neither could be removed from the land. Defendant testified that neither building could be used for anything other than the raising of cattle and hogs, that he was no longer in the business because of his health, and that the buildings were therefore useless to him and had no value. Defendant admitted, however, that the land was put into better shape by the labors of the partners and that the value of the land was increased thereby.

The partnership never paid any rent on this property either before or after defendant owned it. Nor did plaintiff pay any rent after the partnership was dissolved. However, no rent was ever requested. * * *

* * *

Upon completion of all of the testimony, the case was taken under advisement by the court. On June 13, 1978, the trial court issued its findings of fact and conclusions of law. The court found that the parties had entered into an oral partnership agreement to share costs, labor, losses, and profits equally; that the business was started on land owned by defendant's parents and acquired by defendant and his wife in February, 1971; that no rent was paid for the use of the land and no agreement existed to consider the use of the land as a contribution by defendant; that the machine shed/barn was built in 1970 at a cost of $2,487.50; that the Cargill unit was built in 1975 at a cost of $8,000.00; that $1,167.83 was paid out of partnership funds to seed and fertilize the land between 1969–1975; that fences were improved and new ones built with partnership money; that partnership funds were used to clear or bulldoze the land; that all improvements to the land were made for and used by the partnership; that the partnership was dissolved in January, 1976; that in March, 1977, plaintiff paid defendant $7,500.00 and took a receipt for all "removable assets"; and that plaintiff and defendant had no agreement regarding the distribution of fixed assets upon dissolution of the partnership. The court found for defendant and against plaintiff, who took nothing. This decision was based on reasoning that defendant did not own the land during the period of the partnership, since it was owned either by defendant's parents or by defendant and his wife as an estate by the entirety, and defendant's wife was not made a party to the suit, and by the fact that plaintiff knew that the improvements could not be removed at the time they were constructed.

On appeal, plaintiff's sole point is that the trial court erred, as a matter of law, in awarding judgment against plaintiff in the light of its findings of fact. He contends that since the trial court found that fixed partnership assets were erected on land owned by the defendant after formation of the partnership, which assets were acquired with partnership funds and were used by the partnership, and that there was no agreement regarding the disposition of the fixed assets upon dissolution of the partnership, he was entitled to a judgment, as a matter of law, in the sum of $5,750.00, which he contends is one-half the value of the Cargill unit ($8,000.00) and the barn ($3,500.00).

* * *

We agree that the rule is "well-established" that improvements made upon lands owned by one partner, if made with partnership funds for purposes of partnership business, are the personal property of the partnership, and the non-landowning partner is entitled to his proportionate share of their value. . . . [U.P.A. § 8] states, in part:

1. *All property* originally brought into the partnership stock or *subsequently acquired by purchase or otherwise, on account of the partnership is partnership property.*

2. *Unless the contrary intention appears,* property acquired with partnership funds is partnership property. (emphasis added)

It is clear . . . that the general rule, governing the disposition of improvements upon dissolution of a partnership, is activated only where, as here, there is no agreement between the partners which controls such disposition. It matters not that the landowning partner contributed the use of his land to the partnership, that the non-landowning partner knew

that the improvements, when made, could not be removed from the land, or that a joint owner with the landowning partner was not joined in the suit for dissolution and accounting of the partnership. Thus the trial court, after finding that the partners had no agreement regarding the disposition of fixed assets upon dissolution of the partnership, should have applied the rule that we have approved here, and should have awarded plaintiff his proportionate share of the value of the improvements at the time of dissolution of the partnership.

We therefore reverse the judgment of the trial court awarding plaintiff nothing, and remand with directions to the trial court to determine, from the record, the value of the Cargill unit and the barn at the time of dissolution of the partnership, that the trial court reopen the record for the purpose of hearing testimony on that issue only, and to thereafter enter a judgment awarding plaintiff his proportionate share (one-half) of their value.

Partner's Interest in Partnership Property

BOHONUS v. AMERCO

Supreme Court of Arizona, 1979.
124 Ariz. 88, 602 P.2d 469.

Hays, J.

[Amerco secured a personal judgment against Bohonus. The company now seeks to enforce that judgment by requesting a judicial sale of the assets and property of a partnership of which Bohonus is a member and in which he has an interest.]

* * *

The first issue before us is: *May the trial court order the sale of partnership property to satisfy the individual debt of a partner?*

The appellee, Amerco, after it secured a judgment against the appellant, Bohonus, sought a charging order from the court pursuant to a provision embodied in the Uniform Partnership Act [§ 28]. The court granted the request for a charging order and as a part of that order mandated the sale of appellant's interest in the assets and property of the partnership business, including a spiritous liquor license. The sheriff proceeded with the sale and filed his return.

We now look at the partnership statute. [U.P.A. § 25] says:

A partner's right in specific partnership property is not subject to attachment or execution, except on a claim against the partnership. . . .

[U.P.A. § 24] sets forth the extent of the property rights of the partner:

The property rights of a partner are:
1. His rights in specific partnership property.
2. His interest in the partnership.
3. His right to participate in the management.

[U.P.A. § 26] defines "a partner's interest":

A partner's interest in the partnership is his share of the profits and surplus, and the same is personal property.

[U.P.A. § 28] reads, in pertinent part, as follows:

A. On due application to a competent court by any judgment creditor of a partner, the court which entered the judgment, order, or decree, or any other court, may charge the interest of the debtor partner with payment of the unsatisfied amount of such judgment debt with interest thereon; and may then or later appoint a receiver of his share of the profits, and of any other money due or to fall due to him in respect of the partnership, and make all other orders, directions, accounts and inquiries which the debtor partner might have made, or which the circumstances of the case may require.

With the foregoing statutes in mind, we note that it is only a partner's interest in the partnership which may be charged and, in some jurisdictions, sold. It cannot be overemphasized that "interest in the partnership" has a special limited meaning in the context of the Uniform Partnership Act and hence in the Arizona statutes.

The appellee urges that somehow [U.P.A. § 28(1)] authorizes the sale of partnership assets and property. We note that the record reflects that pursuant to the provisions of the same statute a receiver was appointed in this case. The fact of the receivership provision enforces the conclusion that only the "interest in the partnership" may be charged and we find no provision therein for sale of assets or property of the partnership.

* * *

For the foregoing reasons, we reverse and remand to the trial court for proceedings consistent with this opinion.

QUESTIONS

1. Distinguish between a legal entity and a legal aggregate. Identify those purposes for which a partnership is treated as a legal entity and those purposes for which it is treated as a legal aggregate.

2. List the main provisions that should be included in a partnership agreement.

3. Discuss the tests for the existence of a partnership.

4. Distinguish between partnership capital and partnership property.

5. Distinguish between a partner's rights in specific partnership property and a partner's interest in the partnership.

PROBLEMS

1. Lynn and Jack are joint owners of shares of stock of a corporation, have a joint bank account, and have purchased and own as tenants in common a piece of real estate. They share equally the dividends paid on the stock, the interest on the bank account, and the rent from the real estate. Without the knowledge of Lynn, Jack makes a trip to inspect the real estate and on his way runs over Samuel. Samuel sues Lynn and Jack for his personal injuries, joining Lynn as defendant on the theory that Lynn was Jack's partner. Is Lynn liable as a partner of Jack?

2. Smith, Jones, and Brown were creditors of White, who operated a grain elevator known as White's Elevator. White was heavily involved and about to fail when the three creditors mentioned agreed to take title to his elevator property and pay all the debts. It was also agreed that White should continue as manager of the business at a salary of $1,500 per month and that all profits of the business were to be paid to Smith, Jones, and Brown. It was further agreed that they could dispense with White's services at any time, and he was also at liberty to quit when he pleased. White accepted the proposition and continued to operate the business as before, buying and selling grain, incurring obligations, and borrowing money at the bank in his own name for the business. He did, however, tell the banker of the transaction with Smith, Jones, and Brown, and other former creditors of the business knew of it. It worked successfully and for several years paid substantial profits, enough so that Smith, Jones, and Brown had received nearly all that they had originally advanced. Were Smith, Jones, and Brown partners? Explain.

3. James and Suzanne engaged in the grocery business as partners. In one year they earned considerable money, and at the end of the year they invested a part of the profits in oil land. Title to the land was taken in their names as tenants in common. The investment was fortunate, for oil was discovered near the land, and its value increased many times. Is the oil land partnership property? Why?

4. Sheila owned an old roadside building which she believed could be easily converted into an an-tique shop. She talked to her friend Barbara, an antique fancier, and they executed the following written agreement:

(a) Sheila would supply the building, all utilities, and $10,000 capital for purchasing antiques.

(b) Barbara would supply $3,000 for purchasing antiques, Sheila to repay her at the time the business terminates.

(c) Barbara would manage the shop, make all purchases, and receive a salary of $100 per week plus 5 percent of the gross receipts.

(d) Fifty percent of the net profits would go into the purchase of new stock. The balance of the net profits would go to Sheila.

(e) The business would operate under the name "Roadside Antiques."

Business went poorly, and the result after one year is a debt of $4,000 owing to Old Fashioned, Inc., the principal supplier of antiques purchased by Barbara in the name of Roadside Antiques. Old Fashioned, Inc., sues Roadside Antiques, and Sheila and Barbara as partners. Decision?

5. Clark owned a vacant lot. Bird was engaged in building houses. An oral agreement was entered into between Clark and Bird by which Bird was to erect a house on the lot. Upon the sale of the house and lot, Bird was to have his money first. Clark was then to have the agreed value of the lot, and the profits were to be equally divided. Did a partnership exist?

6. Grant, Arthur, and David formed a partnership for the purpose of betting on boxing matches. Grant and Arthur would become friendly with various boxers and offer them bribes to lose certain bouts. David would then place large bets, using money contributed by all three, and would collect the winnings. After David had accumulated a large sum of money, Grant and Arthur demanded their share, but David refused to make any split. Grant and Arthur then brought suit in a court of equity to compel David to account for the profits of the partnership. What decision?

7. Virginia, Georgia, Carolina, and Louis, residents of State X, were partners doing business under the trade name of Morning Glory Nursery. Virginia owned a one-third interest and Georgia,

Carolina, and Louis, two-ninths each. The partners acquired three tracts of land in State X for the purpose of the partnership. Two of the tracts were acquired in the names of the four partners, "trading and doing business as Morning Glory Nursery." The third tract was acquired in the names of the individuals, the trade name not appearing in the deed. This third tract was acquired by the partnership out of partnership funds and for partnership purposes. Who owns each of the three tracts? Why?

8. Teresa, Peter, and Walker were partners under a written agreement made in January that the partnership should continue for ten years. During the same year, Walker, being indebted to Smith, sold and conveyed his interest in the partnership to Smith. Teresa and Peter paid Smith $5,000 as Walker's share of the profits for that year but refused Smith permission to inspect the books or to come into the managing office of the partnership. Smith brings an action setting forth the above facts and asks for an account of partnership transactions and an order to inspect the books and to participate in the management of the partnership business.

(a) Does Walker's action dissolve the partnership?

(b) To what is Smith entitled with respect to (1) partnership profits, (2) inspection of partnership books, (3) an account of partnership transactions, and (4) participation in the partnership management?

9. Horn's Crane Service furnished supplies and services under a written contract to a partnership engaged in operating a quarry and rock-crushing business. Horn brought this action against Prior and Cook, the individual members of the partnership, to recover a personal judgment against them for the partnership's liability under that contract. Horn has not sued the partnership itself, nor does he claim that the partnership property is insufficient to satisfy its debts. Decision?

10. Richard DeLong and Ken Birch formed Birch-DeLong Construction Company in 1972 as a joint venture. They initially agreed that all disbursements would be only on mutual agreement. Later, though, DeLong agreed to allow Birch to disburse funds solely on Birch's signature. About 1980, DeLong realized that Birch was using partnership funds for personal expenses. Birch admitted this. After the partnership filed for bankruptcy in 1981, DeLong reported the disbursement problems to the State. In 1982, three counts of first degree theft and one count of second degree theft were filed against Birch. The trial court held as a matter of law that a partner could not be charged with embezzling partnership funds because the partner would not be exercising unauthorized control over the property of another. The State appealed. Decision?

11. Smithtown General Hospital was operated as a forty-two-member general partnership. The hospital was criminally indicted for (1) allowing an unauthorized individual to take part in a surgical procedure on an uninformed, nonconsenting patient and (2) falsifying records in an effort to conceal the offense. The partnership moved to dismiss the indictment, claiming that it was not an entity distinct from the aggregate of the forty-two individual partners and thus could not be indicted without a showing of culpable intent on the part of each partner. Decision?

Chapter 31

DUTIES, RIGHTS, AND LIABILITIES

Duties among Partners
Rights among Partners
Contracts of Partnership
Torts and Crimes of Partnership
Liability of Incoming Partner

THE operation and management of a partnership involves interactions among the partners as well as with third persons. This chapter will consider both of these relationships. The first part of the chapter focuses on the rights and duties of the partners among themselves, which are determined by the partnership agreement, the common law, and the Uniform Partnership Act. The second part of the chapter focuses on the relations of partners to third persons dealing with the partnership, which are governed by the laws of agency, contracts, and torts as well as by the UPA.

RELATIONSHIPS AMONG PARTNERS

When parties enter into a partnership, the law imposes certain obligations upon the parties and also provides them with specific rights. So long as the rights of third parties are not affected and standards of fairness are maintained, the parties may, by agreement, vary these rights and obligations.

DUTIES AMONG PARTNERS

The legal duties imposed upon partners in their relationship among themselves are (1) the fiduciary duty (the duty of loyalty), (2) the duty of obedience, and (3) the duty of care. In addition, each partner has a duty to inform his co-partners and a duty to account to the partnership. These additional duties are discussed later in the section covering rights of partners. All of these duties correspond precisely with those duties owed by an agent to his principal and reflect the fact that a large part of the law of partnership is the law of agency.

Fiduciary Duty

A fiduciary relationship exists among the members of a partnership based on the high standard of trust and confidence that they place in one another. Each partner owes a duty of absolute and utmost good faith, fairness, and loyalty to his partners. It is only upon such basis that so intimate a business relationship can function.

The fiduciary duty requires that a partner not make a profit other than his agreed compensation, not compete with the partnership, and not otherwise profit from the relationship at the expense of the partnership. The UPA states that every partner must account to the partnership for any benefit and hold as trustee for it any profits derived by him without the consent of the other partners from any transaction connected with the formation, conduct, or liquidation of the partnership or from any use by him of its property. Section 21. A partner may not prefer himself over the firm, nor may he even deal at arm's length with his partners. His duty is one of undivided and continuous loyalty to his partners. *See Clement v. Clement.* Thus, a partner committed a breach of fiduciary duty when he retained a secret discount on purchases of petroleum which he obtained through acquisition of a bulk plant, and the partnership was entitled to the entire amount of the discount. *Liggett v. Lester,* 237 Or. 52, 390 P.2d 351 (1964).

The extent of this fiduciary duty, which binds all fiduciaries and not just partners, has been most eloquently expressed by the often quoted words of Judge (later Justice) Cardozo:

Joint adventurers, like copartners, owe to one another, while the enterprise continues, the duty of the *finest loyalty.* Many forms of conduct permissible in a workaday world for those acting at arm's length, are forbidden to those bound by fiduciary ties. A trustee is held to something stricter than the morals of the market place. *Not honesty alone, but the punctilio of an honor the most sensitive, is then the standard of behavior.* As to this there has developed a tradition that is unbending and inveterate. Uncompromising rigidity has been the attitude of courts of equity when petitioned to undermine the rule of undivided loyalty by the "disintegrating erosion" of particular exceptions. Only thus has the level of conduct for fiduciaries been kept at a level higher than that trodden by the crowd. It will not consciously be lowered by any judgment of this court. *Meinhard v. Salmon,* 249 N.Y. 458, 459, 164 N.E. 545, 546 (1928) [emphasis added].

A partner cannot acquire for herself a partnership asset or opportunity without the consent of all the partners. Thus, a partner may not renew a partnership lease in her name alone. The fiduciary duty also applies to the purchase of a partner's interest from another partner. Each partner owes the highest duty of honesty and fair dealing to the other partners, including the obligation to disclose fully and accurately all material facts.

A partner cannot, without the permission of her partners, engage in any other business within the scope of the partnership enterprise. Any profit acquired from a competing or similar business must be disgorged by the disloyal partner together with compensation for any damage suffered by the existing partnership as a result of the competition. A partner, however, may enter into any business not in competition with nor within the scope of the partnership's business. For example, a partner in a law firm may, without violating her fiduciary duty, act as an executor or administrator of an estate, and need not account for her fees where it cannot be shown that her partnership suffered by her service in this other capacity such as by her lack of attention.

Duty of Obedience

A partner owes his partners a duty to act in obedience to the partnership agreement and to any business decisions properly made by the partnership. Any partner who violates this duty is individually liable to his partners for any resulting loss. For example, a partner who, in violation of a specific agreement not to extend credit to relatives, advances money from partnership funds and sells goods on credit to an insolvent relative, would be held personally liable to his partners for the unpaid debt.

Duty of Care

Whereas under the fiduciary duty a partner "is held to something stricter than the morals of the market place," he is held to something less than the skill of the market place. Each partner owes a duty to the partnership of faithful service to the best of his ability. Nonetheless, he need not possess the degree of knowledge and skill of an ordinary paid agent.

A partner must manage the partnership affairs without culpable negligence. **Culpable negligence** is something more than ordinary negligence, yet short of gross negligence. Thus, a partner does not breach her duty of care if she makes honest errors of judgment or fails to use ordinary skill in transacting partnership business so long as she is not culpably negligent. For example, a partner assigned to keep the partnership books uses a complicated system of bookkeeping and produces numerous mistakes. Since these errors result simply from poor judgment rather than fraud and are not intended to and do not operate to the personal advantage of the bookkeeping partner, the negligent partner is *not* liable to her co-partners for any resulting loss.

RIGHTS AMONG PARTNERS

The law provides partners with certain rights, which include: (1) their right in specific partnership property, (2) their interest in the partnership, (3) their right to share in distributions, (4) their right to participate in management, (5) their right to choose associates, and (6) their enforcement rights. A partner's ownership of specific partnership property is that of a tenant in partnership. Section 25. In addition, each partner has an interest in the partnership, which is defined as her share of the profits and surplus. Section 26. These two rights were discussed in Chapter 30. The four remaining rights among partners are discussed in this section.

Right to Share in Distributions

A **distribution** is a transfer of partnership property from the partnership to a partner. Distributions include a division of profits, a return of capital contributions, a repayment

of a loan or advance made by a partner to the partnership, and a payment made to compensate a partner for services rendered to the partnership.

Right to Share in Profits

Because a partnership is an association to carry on a business for profit, each partner is entitled, unless otherwise agreed, to a share of the profits. Conversely, each partner must contribute toward any losses sustained by the partnership. Section 18(a). In the absence of an agreement among the partners with regard to the division of profits, the partners share the profits *equally*, regardless of the ratio of their financial contributions or the degree of their participation in the management. Unless the partnership agreement provides otherwise, the partners bear losses in the *same proportion* in which they share profits. The agreement may, however, validly provide for bearing losses in a different proportion than that in which profits are shared.

For example, Alice, Betty, and Carol form a partnership, with Alice contributing $10,000; Betty, $20,000; and Carol, $30,000. They could agree that Alice would receive 20 percent of the profits and assume 30 percent of the losses; that Betty would receive 30 percent of the profits and assume 50 percent of the losses; and that Carol would receive 50 percent of the profits and assume 20 percent of the losses. If their agreement is silent as to the sharing of profits and losses, however, each would have an equal one-third share of both profits and losses.

Right to Return of Capital

After all the partnership creditors have been paid, each partner is entitled to be repaid his capital contribution upon termination of the firm. Section 18(a). *See Felton Investment Group v. Taurman.* Unless otherwise agreed, a partner is not entitled to interest on his capital contribution. If there is a delay in return of his capital contribution, however, he is entitled to interest at the legal rate from the date when it should have been repaid. Section 18(d).

Right to Return of Advances If a partner makes advances (loans) over and above his agreed capital contribution, he is entitled to repayment of the loan plus interest on it. Section 18(c). His position as a creditor of the firm, however, is subordinate to the claims of creditors who are not partners but is superior to the partners' right to the return of capital. In addition, a partner who has reasonably and necessarily incurred personal liabilities in the ordinary and proper conduct of the business of the firm or who has made payments on behalf of the partnership is entitled to indemnification or repayment on equal footing with advances made by partners. Section 18(b).

Right to Compensation The UPA provides that, unless otherwise agreed, *no* partner is entitled to remuneration (payment) for acting in the partnership business. Section 18(f). Even if one partner performs a substantial or disproportionate share of the work of conducting the business, he is entitled to no salary but only his share of the profits. A partner may, however, by agreement among all of the partners, receive a salary. Moreover, a surviving partner is entitled to reasonable compensation for his services in winding up the partnership affairs. Section 18(f).

Right to Participate in Management

Each of the partners, unless otherwise agreed, has an *equal* voice in the management of the business. Section 18(e). The majority generally governs the actions and decisions of the partnership except that *all* the partners must consent to any acts in contravention of the partnership agreement. Section 18(h). In their partnership agreement, the partners may provide for unequal voting rights. For example, Jones, Smith, and Williams form a partnership, agreeing that Jones will have two votes, Smith four votes, and Williams five votes. It is common for large partnerships to concentrate most or all management authority in a committee of a few partners or even in just one partner. Different classes of partners may also be

created with different management rights. This is a common practice in accounting and law firms, which may have two classes (junior and senior partners) or three classes (junior, senior, and managing partners).

Right to Choose Associates

No partner may be forced to accept any person as a partner whom she does not choose. This is because of the fiduciary relationship between the parties, and because each partner has a right to take part in the management of the business, to handle the partnership assets for partnership purposes, and to act as an agent of the partnership. It is possible that a partner, by her negligence, poor judgment, or dishonesty, may bring financial loss or ruin to her co-partners. Because of the close relationship involved, partnerships must necessarily be founded on mutual trust and confidence. All this finds expression in the term *delectus personae,* which literally means "choice of the person" and indicates the right one has to choose or select her partners. This principle is embodied in Section 18(g) of the UPA which provides: "No person can become a member of a partnership without the consent of **all** the partners." [Emphasis added.] It is a consequence of *delectus personae* that when a partner sells her interest to another, the purchaser does not become a partner and is not entitled to participate in the management. The partnership agreement may provide for admission of a new partner by a less than unanimous vote.

Enforcement Rights

As discussed, the partnership relationship creates a number of duties and rights among the partners. Accordingly, partnership law provides the partners with the means to enforce these rights and duties.

Right to Information and Inspection of the Books Each partner may demand to have full information about all partnership matters. Each partner has a duty to supply full and accurate information of all things affecting the partnership. Section 20. The right to demand information extends also to the legal representative of a deceased partner for a reasonable time following the dissolution of the partnership.

Unless the partners agree otherwise, the books of the partnership are to be kept at the principal place of business at all times, and each partner has a right to have access to them, to inspect them, and to copy any of them. Section 19. This right may also be exercised by a duly authorized agent on behalf of a partner.

Right to an Account A **formal account** is a complete review of all financial transactions of the partnership, including financial statements. The UPA grants to each partner the right to an account whenever (1) he is wrongfully excluded from the partnership business or possession of its property by his co-partners, (2) the partnership agreement provides, (3) a partner makes a profit in violation of his fiduciary duty, or (4) other circumstances render it just and reasonable. Section 22.

If a partner does not get a requested account or is dissatisfied with it, she may bring an enforcement action, called an accounting. An **accounting** is an equitable proceeding for a comprehensive and effective settlement of all partnership affairs. An accounting is designed to produce and evaluate all testimony relevant to the various claims of the partners. *See Central Trust & Safe Co. v. Respass.*

RELATIONSHIP BETWEEN PARTNERS AND THIRD PARTIES

In the course of transacting business, partners may also acquire rights and incur duties to third parties. Under the law of **agency** a principal is liable upon contracts made on his behalf by his duly authorized agents and is liable in tort for the wrongful acts of his employees committed in the course of their employment. A large part of the law of partner-

ship is the law of agency, and most problems arising between partners and third persons require the application of principles of agency law. This relationship is made explicit by the UPA which states that "The law of agency shall apply under this act," and "Every partner is an agent of the partnership for the purpose of its business." Sections 4(3) and 9(1). The law of agency is discussed in Chapters 18 and 19.

CONTRACTS OF PARTNERSHIP

The act of every partner binds the partnership to transactions *within* the scope of the partnership business unless the partner does not have actual or apparent authority to so act. See Figure 31–1. If the partnership is bound, then each general partner has **unlimited, personal liability** for that partnership obligation. The UPA provides that partners are jointly liable on all debts and contract obligations of the partnership. Section 15(b). Under **joint liability** a creditor must bring suit against all of the partners as a group and the judgment must be against all of the obligors. Therefore, any suit in contract against the partners must name all the partners as defendants.

Authority to Bind Partnership

A partner may bind the partnership by her act if (1) she has actual authority, express or implied, to perform the act or (2) she has apparent authority to perform the act. If the act is not apparently within the scope of the partnership business, then the partnership is bound only where the partner has actual authority, and the third person dealing with the partner assumes the risk of the existence of such actual authority. Section 9(2). *See Hodge v. Garrett.* Where there is no actual authority and no apparent authority, the partnership is bound only if it ratifies the act. Ratification is discussed in Chapter 19.

Actual Express Authority The actual express authority of partners may be specifically set forth in the partnership agreement

Figure 31–1 Contract Liability

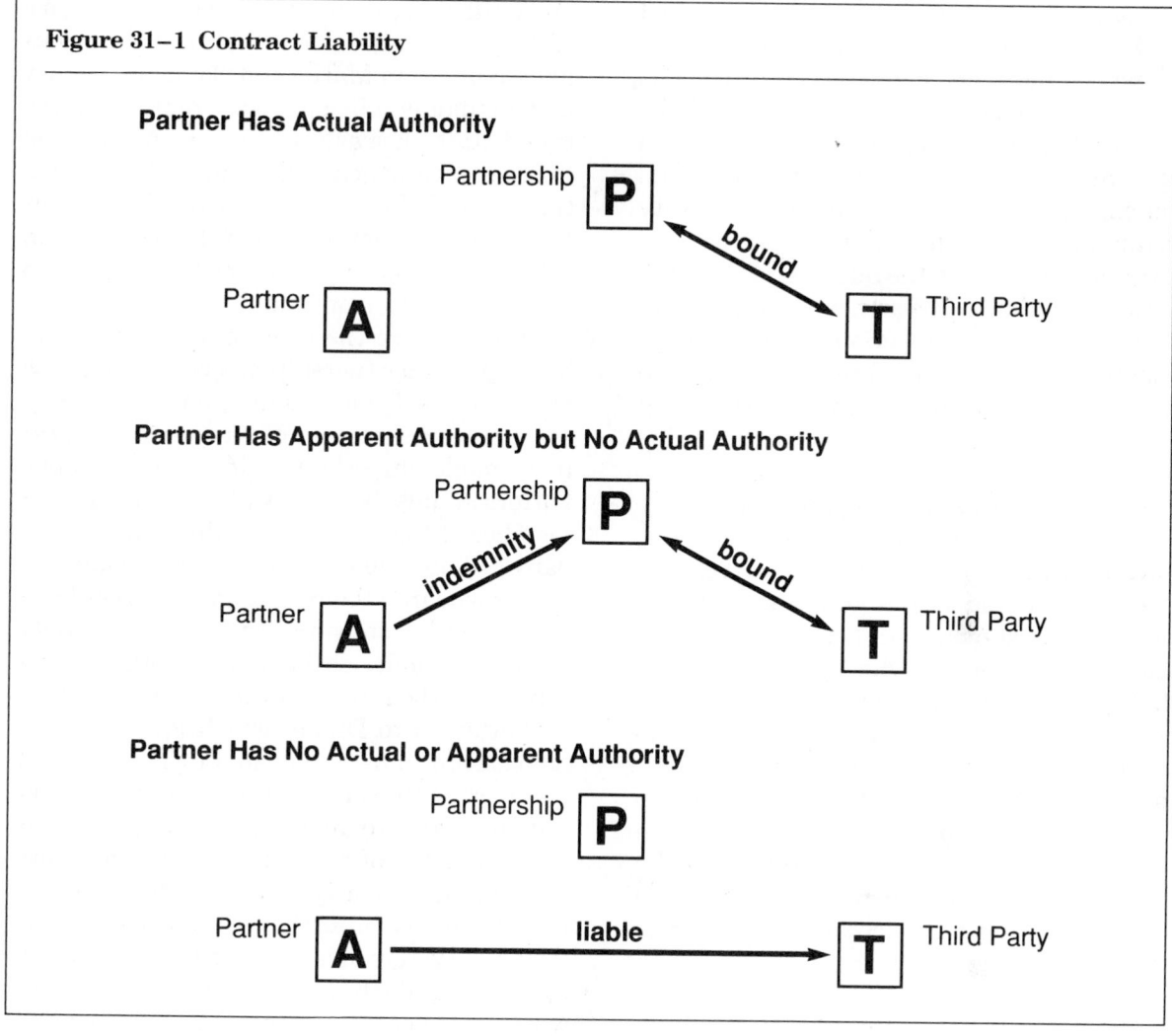

or in an additional agreement between the partners and may be written or oral. In addition, it may arise from decisions made by a majority of the partners regarding ordinary matters connected with the partnership business. Section 18(h).

Section 9(3) of the UPA provides that the following acts do **not** bind the partnership unless authorized by **all** of the partners:

1. assignment of partnership property for the benefit of its creditors;

2. disposal of the good will of the business;

3. any act which would make it impossible to carry on the ordinary business of the partnership;

4. confession of a judgment;

5. submission of a partnership claim or liability to arbitration or reference.

In addition, a partner who does not have actual authority from all of her partners may not bind the partnership by any act that is not apparently for the carrying on of the business of the partnership in the usual way. Section 9(2). This would include the following acts inasmuch as they are clearly outside of the scope of the partnership under ordinary circumstances: (1) execution of contracts of guaranty or suretyship in the firm name, (2) sale of partnership property not held for sale in the usual course of business, and (3) payment of individual debts out of partnership assets.

Actual Implied Authority Actual implied authority is authority that is neither expressly granted nor expressly denied but is reasonably deduced from the nature of the partnership, the terms of the partnership agreement, or the relations of the partners. For example, a partner has implied authority to hire and fire employees whose services are necessary to carry on the business of the partnership. In addition, a partner has implied authority to purchase property necessary for the business, to receive performance of obligations due to the partnership, and to bring legal actions to enforce claims of the partnership.

Apparent Authority Apparent authority (which may or may not be actual) is authority that may, in view of the circumstances and the conduct of the parties, be reasonably considered to exist by a third person who has no knowledge or notice of the lack of actual authority. For example, a partner has apparent authority to indorse checks and notes, to make representations and warranties in selling goods, and to enter into contracts for advertising. A third person may not rely upon apparent authority in any situation where he is put on notice or already knows that the partner does not have actual authority. Sections 9(1) and 9(4).

Partnership by Estoppel

Partnership by estoppel imposes partnership duties and liabilities upon a person who is not a partner but who has either represented himself or consented to be represented as a partner. It extends to a third person to whom such a representation is made and who gives credit to the partnership in justifiable reliance upon the representation.

For example, Marks and Saunders are partners doing business as Marks and Company. Marks introduces Patterson to Taylor, describing Patterson as a member of the partnership. Believing that Patterson is a member of the partnership and relying upon Patterson's good credit standing, Taylor sells goods on credit to Marks and Company. In an action by Taylor against Marks, Saunders, and Patterson as partners to recover the price of the goods, Patterson is liable although he is not a partner in Marks and Company. Taylor had justifiably relied upon the representation that Patterson was a partner in Marks and Company, to which Patterson by his silence consented. If Taylor, at the time, knew that Patterson was not a partner, his reliance on the representation would not have been justified, and Patterson would not be liable.

Except where the representation of membership in a partnership has been made in a public manner, no person is entitled to rely upon a representation of partnership unless it is made directly to him. For example, Patterson falsely tells Dillon that he is a member of the partnership Marks and Company. Dillon casually relays this statement to Taylor who in reliance sells goods on credit to Marks and Company. Taylor cannot hold Patterson liable, as he was not justified in relying on the representation made privately by Patterson to Dillon, which Patterson did not consent to have repeated to Taylor.

Where Patterson, however, knowingly permits his name to appear publicly in the firm name or a list of partners, or used in public announcements or advertisements in a manner which indicates that he is a partner in the firm, Patterson is liable to any member of the public dealing with the partnership whether or not the representations have been made or communicated to such person by or with the knowledge of Patterson. Section 16(1).

TORTS AND CRIMES OF PARTNERSHIP

The UPA provides that a partnership is liable for loss or injury caused by any wrongful act or omission of any partner while acting within the ordinary course of the business of the partnership or with the authority of his co-partners. Section 13. If the partnership is liable then each partner has **unlimited, personal liability** for the partnership obligation. The liability of partners for a tort or breach of trust committed by any partner or by an employee of the firm in the course of partnership business is joint and several. Section 15(a). **Joint and several liability** means that all of the partners may be sued jointly in one action based upon tort liability, or separate actions may be maintained against each of them and separate judgments obtained. Judgments obtained are enforceable only against property of the defendant or defendants named in the suit. Payment of any one of the judgments, however, satisfies all of them.

This liability is comparable to the vicarious liability imposed upon a principal for the torts of an agent by the doctrine of *respondeat superior*. The partner committing the tort is directly liable to the third party and must also **indemnify** the partnership for any damages it pays to the third party. See Figure 31–2. Tort liability of the partnership may include not only the negligence of the partners but also trespass, fraud, defamation, and breach of fiduciary duty, so long as the tort is committed in the course of partnership business. Moreover, the fact that a tort is intentional does not necessarily remove it from the course of business, but it is a factor to be considered. *See Husted v. McCloud.*

A partner is not criminally liable for the crimes of her partners unless she authorized or participated in them. A partnership is not criminally liable for the crimes of individual partners or employees unless there is a statute imposing vicarious liability. Even under such a statute, liability of the partnership usually results only in those States that have adopted the entity theory or the statute itself expressly imposes liability upon partnerships. Otherwise, the vicarious liability statute results in liability of the partners as individuals.

ADMISSIONS OF AND NOTICE TO A PARTNER

An admission or representation by any partner concerning partnership affairs, within the scope of his authority, may be used as evidence against the partnership. Section 11. An admission by one person that a partnership exists does not prove its existence. But once the partnership is established by competent evidence, the admission of one partner may be used against the partnership, provided the partner is acting within the scope of the partnership business.

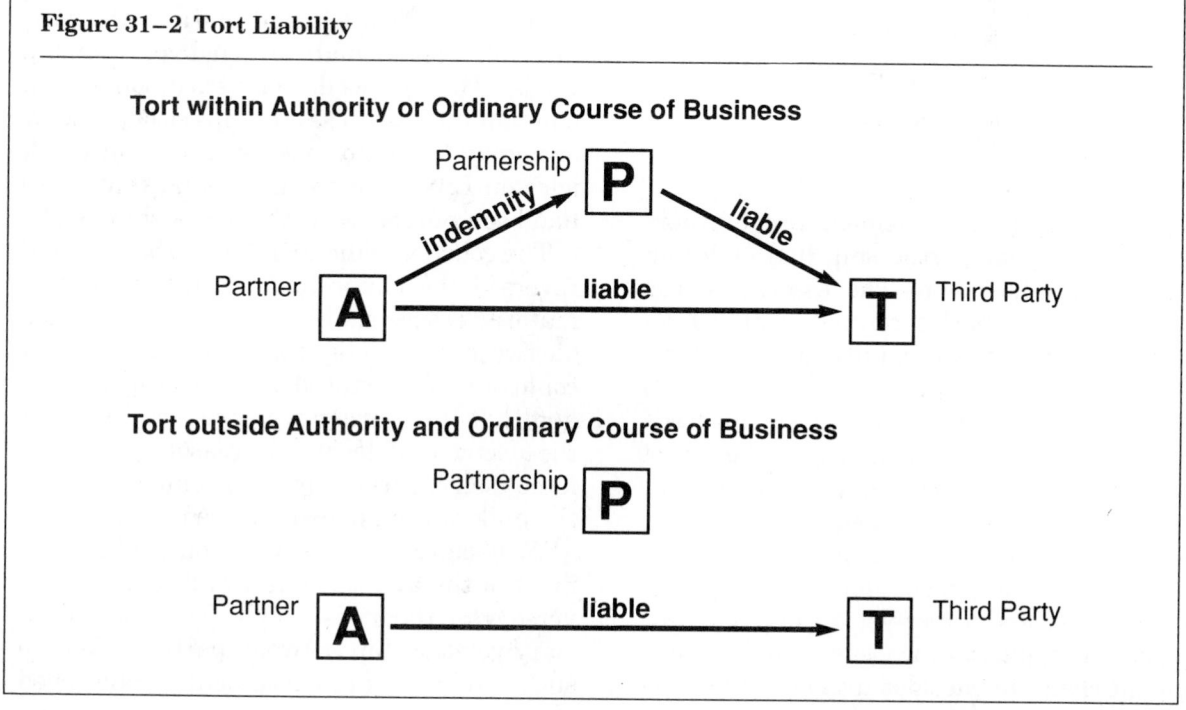

Figure 31–2 Tort Liability

Tort within Authority or Ordinary Course of Business

Partnership **P**

indemnity   liable

Partner **A**   liable   **T** Third Party

Tort outside Authority and Ordinary Course of Business

Partnership **P**

Partner **A**   liable   **T** Third Party

A partnership is bound (1) by notice to any partner of any matter relating to partnership affairs, (2) by the knowledge of the partner acting in a particular matter acquired while he was a partner or then present in his mind, and (3) by the knowledge of any other partner who reasonably could and should have communicated it to the acting partner. Section 12. Notice of a fact occurs when a person states the fact to the partner or delivers a written statement of the fact to the partner. Section 3(2).

A demand upon one partner as representative of the firm constitutes a demand upon the partnership.

LIABILITY OF INCOMING PARTNER

A person admitted as a partner into an existing partnership is liable for **all** of the obligations of the partnership arising before his admission as though he had been a partner when such obligations were incurred, although this liability may be satisfied *only* out of partnership property. Section 17. This means that the liability of an incoming partner for antecedent debts and obligations of the firm is limited to his capital contribution. This restriction does not apply, of course, to obligations arising subsequent to his admission into the partnership as to which his liability is *unlimited*. For example, Nash is admitted to Higgins, Cooke, and White Co., a partnership. Nash's capital contribution is $7,500, which was paid in cash upon her admission to the partnership. A year later the partnership is dissolved when liabilities of the firm exceed its assets by $40,000. Porter had lent the firm $15,000 eight months before Nash was admitted; Skinner lent the firm $20,000 two months after Nash was admitted. Nash has no liability to Porter *except* to the extent of her capital contribution. Nash is *personally* liable to Skinner.

CASES

Fiduciary Duty

CLEMENT v. CLEMENT

Supreme Court of Pennsylvania, 1970.
436 Pa. 466, 260 A.2d 728.

ROBERTS, J.

Charles and L.W. Clement are brothers whose forty year partnership had ended in acrimonious litigation. The essence of the conflict lies in Charles' contention that L.W. has over the years wrongfully taken for himself more than his share of the partnership's profits. Charles discovered these misdeeds during negotiations with L.W. over the sale of Charles' interest in the partnership in 1964. He then filed an action in equity, asking for dissolution of the partnership, appointment of a receiver, and an accounting. Dissolution was ordered and a receiver appointed. After lengthy hearings on the issue of the accounting the chancellor decided that L.W., who was the brighter of the two and who kept the partnership books, had diverted partnership funds. The chancellor awarded Charles a one-half interest in several pieces of property owned by L.W. and in several insurance policies on L.W.'s life on the ground that these had been purchased with partnership assets.

The court en banc then heard the case and reversed the chancellor's decree in several material respects. The reversal was grounded on two propositions: that Charles' recovery could only be premised on a showing of fraud and that this burden was not met, and that the doctrine of laches [unreasonable delay] foreclosed Charles' right to complain about the bulk of the alleged misdeeds.

We disagree with the court en banc's statement of the applicable law and therefore reverse. Our theory is simple. There is a fiduciary relationship between partners. Where such a relationship exists actual fraud need not be shown. There was ample evidence of self-dealing and diversion of partnership assets on the part of L.W.—more than enough to sustain the chancellor's conclusion that several substantial investments made by L.W. over the years were bankrolled with funds improperly withdrawn from the partnership. Further, we are of the opinion that the doctrine of laches is inapplicable because Charles' delay in asserting his rights was as much a product of L.W.'s concealment and misbehavior as of any negligence on his part. In all this we are strongly motivated by the fact that the chancellor saw and heard the various witnesses for exhausting periods of time and was in a much better position than we could ever hope to be to taste the flavor of the testimony.

[U.P.A.] § 21 very simply and unambiguously provides that partners owe a fiduciary duty one to another. [Citation.] One should not have to deal with his partner as though he were the opposite party in an arms-length transaction. One should be allowed to trust his partner, to expect that he is pursuing a common goal and not working at cross-purposes. * * *

It would be unduly harsh to require that one must prove actual fraud before he can recover for a partner's derelictions. Where one partner has so dealt with the partnership as to raise the probability of wrongdoing it ought to be his responsibility to negate that inference. It has been held that "where a partner fails to keep a record of partnership transactions, and is unable to account for them, every presumption will be made against him." [Citation.] Likewise, where a partner commingles partnership funds with his own assets he ought to have to shoulder the task of demonstrating the probity of his conduct.

In the instant case L.W. dealt loosely with partnership funds. At various times he made substantial investments in his own name. He was totally unable to explain where he got the funds to make these investments. The court en banc held that Charles had no claim on the fruits of these investments because he could not trace the money that was invested therein dollar for dollar from the partnership.

Charles should not have had this burden. He did show that his brother diverted substantial sums from the partnership funds under his control. The inference that these funds provided L.W. with the wherewithal to make his investments was a perfectly reasonable one for the chancellor to make and his decision should have been allowed to stand.

* * *

The decree is vacated and the case remanded for further proceedings consistent with this opinion.

Right to Share in Distributions

FELTON INVESTMENT GROUP v. TAURMAN

Supreme Court of Montana, 1986.
722 P.2d 1135.

MORRISON, J.

John Felton is the originator and president of FCC. In 1969 he formed FIG. The purpose of FIG is to provide retirement benefits to certain deserving employees of FCC. Each member of FIG makes weekly contributions which are automatically deducted from the paycheck. The money is then combined and invested. The partners must all agree on the investments to be made.

Initially, FIG was operated as a general partnership, with the only guidelines contained in oral agreements. The October 28, 1969, "Pre-Incorporation Minutes" was the first written document reflecting the purpose behind and terms of FIG. Those minutes state in pertinent part:

ADMITTANCE: Resolved that admittance is available to anyone employed by Felton Construction Company . . .
EMPLOYMENT: . . .
Resolved that if a member ceases employment or is discharged for misconduct, his interest shall be returned in an amount equal to contributions paid into the fund plus 4% simple interest; that the Group shall have a period of one year in which to purchase the stock of such member.
Resolved that involuntary termination caused by disability, death, or retirement shall not affect such member's interest.

Taurman was a charter member of FIG. Paige joined in 1970. They participated in FIG's annual meetings and gave their approval to all decisions until 1974. At that time Felton proposed changing FIG into a limited partnership with Felton as the general and controlling partner. * * *

In the interim, on December 5, 1978, Paige determined his investment in FIG to be in jeopardy due to the proposed limited partnership agreement and ceased contributing to the fund. However, he continued to be employed by FCC until July of 1980. Paige believed himself to still be a member of FIG because he was still employed by FCC. Approximately one year after ceasing to contribute to FIG, Paige received a check from FIG reflecting his contributions to date and interest, $15,040.08. Not wishing to lose his rights in the partnership, Paige refused to endorse and cash the check.

Taurman continued investing in FIG until July of 1980. At that time, he was employed by FCC in Sunburst, Montana. Taurman was told by Felton that once the Sunburst job was completed, there would be a job for him in Aberdeen, Washington. However, FCC had decided to go non-union and the job in Aberdeen was for non-union personnel. Union members would be fined $5,000 by their union for working a non-union project. After considering the choices overnight, Taurman told Felton he would not be quitting the union. Taurman's employment with FCC terminated a week or two later.

Paige was presented with the same decision. He, too, decided to remain union and lost his job with FCC.

Subsequent to Taurman's and Paige's terminations, a meeting of FIG was held and its members voted to expel Taurman from the group. Following his expulsion, Taurman was offered a check by FIG in an amount equal to his contribution plus interest, $21,448.98. Taurman refused to endorse and cash the check.

FIG filed a complaint December 2, 1981, requesting that Taurman, Paige, and a third individual, Thomas Wackler, be ordered to accept the sums previously offered in satisfaction of their entire claims in the partnership. Also on December 2, 1981, Taurman and Paige filed a complaint against FIG seeking the judicial dissolution of FIG; a formal accounting of FIG; and an order that the assets of FIG be sold, applied in full to partnership liabilities and the remainder divided between the partners. Following a bench trial, judgment was entered for Taurman and Paige, awarding them a pro rata share in the partnership's assets.

* * *

Finally, we find no error in the trial court's decision that pursuant to [UPA § 18], Taurman and Paige must be repaid their contributions into the partnership and receive their pro rata share of the assets of the partnership. [UPA § 18] states at the outset that "[t]he rights and duties of the partners in relation to the partnership shall be determined, subject to any agreement between them, by the following rules." The agreement between the partners covers the voluntary termination of a partner's employment with FCC as well as his discharge for misconduct. It also covers involuntary termination caused by disability, death or retirement. However, there is nothing in the partnership agreement concerning the effect of a partner's involuntary termination from FCC absent misconduct. Numerous members of FIG, including its controller, testified that this contingency was not covered in FIG's partnership agreement. Since the rights of partners of FIG who were involuntarily terminated from FCC without cause were not expressed in the agreement, [UPA § 18] controls.

(1) Each partner shall be repaid his contributions whether by way of capital or advances to the partnership property and share equally in the profits and surplus remaining after all liabilities, including those to partners, are satisfied . . .

Taurman and Paige are entitled to receive their pro rata shares of the fair market value of the assets of FIG as of the date their employment with FCC terminated.

Affirmed.

Right to an Accounting

CENTRAL TRUST & SAFE DEPOSIT CO. v. RESPASS

Court of Appeals of Kentucky, 1902.
112 Ky. 606, 66 S.W. 421.

DURELLE, J.

[Action for the settlement of partnership accounts by J.B. Respass against the trust company, as executor of the will of his deceased partner, S.L. Sharp. The partners owned and managed a racing stable and, in addition, were engaged in bookmaking, or accepting wagers on race horses. At the time Sharp died, $4,724, representing the undistributed profits of the bookmaking business, was on deposit in Sharp's personal bank account. The trial court held that Respass was entitled to one-half of the profits from the bookmaking business and the executor appeals.]

* * *

A closer question is presented by the claim for a division of the "bank roll." This $4,724 was, as found by the chancellor, earned by the firm composed of Respass and Sharp in carrying on an illegal business—that of "bookmaking"—in the State of Illinois. But though this amount had been won upon horse races in Chicago, it is claimed that, though secured illegally, "the transaction has been closed, and the appellee Respass is only seeking his share from the realized profits from the illegal contracts, if they are illegal." On the other hand, it is claimed for appellant, the executor, that, as to the bank roll, this proceeding is a bill for an accounting of profits from the business of gambling.

It does not seem to be seriously contended that the business of "bookmaking," whether carried on in Chicago or in this Commonwealth, was legal, for by the common law of this country all wagers are illegal. [Citation.] One of the most interesting cases upon this subject is that of Everet v. Williams—the celebrated Highwaymen's Case—an account of which is given in 9 Law Quart.Rev., 197 [England]. That was a bill for an accounting of a partnership in the business of highwaymen, though the true nature of the partnership

was veiled in ambiguous language. The bill set up the partnership between defendant and plaintiff, who was "skilled in dealing in several sorts of commodities," that they "proceeded jointly in the said dealing with good success on Hounslow Heath, where they dealt with a gentleman for a gold watch," that defendant had informed plaintiff that Finchley "was a good and convenient place to deal in," such commodities being "very plenty" there, and if they were to deal there "it would be almost all gain to them"; that they accordingly "dealt with several gentlemen for divers watches, rings, swords, canes, hats, cloaks, horses, bridles, saddles, and other things, to the value of £2,000 and upwards"; that a gentleman of Blackheath had several articles which defendant thought "might be had for a little or no money in case they could prevail on the said gentleman to part with the same things," and that, "after some small discourse with the said gentleman," the said things were dealt for "at a very cheap rate." The dealings were alleged to have amounted to £ 2,000 and upward. This case, while interesting, from the views it gives of the audacity of the parties and their solicitors, sheds little light upon the legal questions involved, for the bill was condemned for scandal and impertinence; the solicitors were taken into custody, and "fyned" £50 each for "reflecting upon the honor and dignity of this court"; the counsel whose name was signed to the bill was required to pay the costs; and both the litigants were subsequently hanged, at Tyburn and Maidstone, respectively, while one of the solicitors was transported. [Citations.] * * *

In Watson v. Fletcher, [citation], the business of the firm had been the operation of a faro bank. One of the partners having died, the survivor sought an accounting of profits earned. The syllabus reads: "A court of equity will not lend its aid for the settlement and adjustment of the transactions of a partnership for gambling. Nor will it give relief to either partner against the other, founded on transactions arising out of such partnership, whether for profits, losses, expenses, contribution, or reimbursement. . . ."

We conclude that in this country, in the case of a partnership in a business confessedly illegal, whatever may be the doctrine where there has been a new contract in relation to, or a new investment of, the profits of such illegal business, and whatever may be the doctrine as to the rights or liabilities of a third person who assumes obligations with respect to such profits, or by law becomes responsible therefor, the decided weight of authority is that a court of equity will not entertain a bill for an accounting.

The judgment of the chancellor is therefore reversed, and the cause remanded, with directions to enter a judgment in accordance with this opinion.

Authority to Bind Partnership

HODGE v. GARRETT

Supreme Court of Idaho, 1980.
101 Idaho 397, 614 P.2d 420.

BRISTLINE, J.

Following a non-jury trial the court below granted specific performance to the plaintiff-respondent Bill Hodge. All defendants joined in a single notice of appeal, and all defendants joined in a single brief filed in this Court. * * *

Hodge and defendant-appellant Rex E. Voeller, the managing partner of the Pay-Ont Drive-In Theatre, signed a contract for the sale of a small parcel of land belonging to the partnership. That parcel, although adjacent to the theater, was not used in theater operations except insofar as the east 20 feet were necessary for the operation of the theater's driveway. The agreement for the sale of land stated that it was between Hodge and the Pay-Ont Drive-In Theatre, a partnership. Voeller signed the agreement for the partnership, and written changes as to the footage and price were initialed by Voeller.

Voeller testified that he had told Hodge prior to signing that Hodge would have to present him with a plat plan which would have to be approved by the partners before the property could be sold. Hodge denied that a plat plan had ever been mentioned to him, and he testified that Voeller did not tell him that the approval of the other partners was needed until after the contract was signed. Hodge also testified that he offered to pay Voeller the full purchase price when he signed the contract, but Voeller told him that that was not necessary.

The trial court found that Voeller had actual and apparent authority to execute the contract on behalf of the partnership, and that the contract should be specifically enforced. The partners of the Pay-Ont Drive-In Theatre appeal, arguing that Voeller did not have authority to sell the property and that Hodge knew that he did not have that authority.

At common law one partner could not, "without the concurrence of his copartners, convey away the real estate of the partnership, bind his partners by a deed, or transfer the title and interest of his copartners in the firm real estate." [Citation.] This rule was changed by the adoption of the Uniform Partnership Act. The relevant provisions are currently embodied in [U.P.A. §§ 9(1) and 10(1)] as follows:

[U.P.A. § 10(1)]: Where title to real property is in the partnership name, any partner may convey title to such property by a conveyance executed in the partnership name; but the partnership may recover such property unless the partner's act binds the partnership under the provisions of paragraph 1 of section [9] unless such property has been conveyed by the grantee or a person claiming through such grantee to a holder for value without knowledge that the partner, in making the conveyance, has exceeded his authority.

[U.P.A. § 9(1)]: Every partner is an agent of the partnership for the purpose of its business, and the act of every partner, including the execution in the partnership name of any instrument, for apparently carrying on in the usual way the business of the partnership of which he is a member binds the partnership, unless the partner so acting has in fact no authority to act for the partnership in the particular matter, and the person with whom he is dealing has knowledge of the fact that he has no such authority.

The meaning of these provisions was stated in one text as follows:

If record title is in the partnership and a partner conveys in the partnership name, legal title passes. But the partnership may recover the property (except from a bona fide purchaser from the grantee) if it can show (A) that the conveying partner was not apparently carrying on business in the usual way or (B) that he had in fact no authority and the grantee had knowledge of that fact. The burden of proof with respect to authority is thus on the partnership. Crane and Bromburg [sic] on Partnership § 50A (1968) (footnotes omitted).

Thus this contract is enforceable if Voeller had the actual authority to sell the property, or, even if Voeller did not have such authority, the contract is still enforceable if the sale was in the usual way of carrying on the business and Hodge did not know that Voeller did not have this authority.

As to the question of actual authority, such authority must affirmatively appear, "for the authority of one partner to make and acknowledge a deed for the firm will not be presumed. . . ." [Citation.] Although such authority may be implied from the nature of the business, *id.,* or from similar past transactions, [citation], nothing in the record in this case indicates that Voeller had express or implied authority to sell real property belonging to the partnership. There is no evidence that Voeller had sold property belonging to the partnership in the past, and obviously the partnership was not engaged in the business of buying and selling real estate.

The next question, since actual authority has not been shown, is whether Voeller was conducting the partnership business in the usual way in selling this parcel of land such that the contract is binding under [U.P.A. §§ 10(1) and 9(1)], *i.e.,* whether Voeller had apparent authority. Here the evidence showed, and the trial court found:

* * *

That at the inception of the partnership, and at all times thereafter, Rex E. Voeller was the exclusive, managing partner of the partnership and had the full authority to make all decisions pertaining to the partnership affairs, including paying the bills, preparing profit and loss statements, income tax returns and the ordering of any goods or services necessary to the operation of the business.

The court made no finding that it was customary for Voeller to sell real property, or even personal property, belonging to the partnership. Nor was there any evidence to this effect. Nor did the court discuss whether it was in the usual course of business for the managing partner of a theater to sell real property. Yet the trial court found that Voeller had apparent authority to sell the property. From this it must be inferred that the trial court believed it to be in the usual course of business for a partner who has exclusive control of the partnership business to sell real property belonging to the partnership, where that property is not being used in the partnership business. We cannot agree with this conclusion. For a theater, "carrying on in the usual way the business of the partnership," [U.P.A. § 9(1)], means running the operations of the theater; it does not mean selling a parcel of property adjacent to the theater. Here the contract of sale stated that the land belonged to the partnership, and, even if Hodge believed that Voeller as the exclusive manager had authority to transact all business for the firm, Voeller still could not bind the partnership through a unilateral act which was not in the usual business of the partnership. We therefore hold that the trial court erred in holding that this contract was binding on the partnership.

Judgment reversed. Costs to appellant.

Torts of Partnership

HUSTED v. McCLOUD

Supreme Court of Indiana, 1983.
450 N.E.2d 491.

PIVARNIK, J.

This cause comes to us on a Petition to Transfer from the First District Court of Appeals. Appeal was brought to the Court of Appeals by Edgar Husted from that portion of a judgment of the Montgomery Circuit Court awarding Herman McCloud punitive damages in an action involving the conversion of certain funds. The partnership of Husted & Husted also appealed contesting the award of punitive damages and compensatory damages as against itself. The Court of Appeals, [citation], affirmed the trial court in its award of punitive damages against Edgar Husted and in its award of punitive and compensatory damages against Husted & Husted. We now find that the award of punitive damages against Edgar Husted was improper. While the award of compensatory damages against the partnership was proper, we now find that the award of punitive damages was not. Transfer is granted and the opinion of the Court of Appeals is accordingly vacated.

The facts as set out by the Court of Appeals are as follows:

"Herman McCloud was the executor of his mother's estate. The firm of Husted and Husted was retained to act as attorneys for the estate. The partnership consisted of Selwyn and Edgar Husted. After the estate was closed, an Internal Revenue Service (IRS) audit and reappraisal of certain real estate resulted in an additional estate tax liability of $18,006.73. McCloud prepared a check payable to the IRS and a separate check for attorney fees. However, Edgar falsely represented that the exact amount of the tax liability was unknown. He instead took McCloud's check for $18,800.00, payable to the Husted and Husted Trust Account at Edgar's instance, and indicated that he would pay the liability upon exact determination and keep the remainder as his fee. There was no Husted and Husted Trust Account in existence. Edgar instead deposited the check into his own personal account and converted the funds to his own use.

Edgar Husted then induced officials of the First National Bank and Trust Company of Crawfordsville to issue a check from the estate of Walter Fletcher, deceased, in the exact amount needed to pay the additional estate tax liability on the estate of Maude McCloud. This check was credited to the McCloud estate by the IRS. Edgar advised McCloud that the additional taxes had been paid and delivered to McCloud a cash register receipt and computer transcript which purported to show payment. Although McCloud repeatedly asked therefor, Edgar never returned the cancelled check.

In December of 1978, Edgar Husted's misconduct was uncovered. Edgar entered into a plea agreement * * *

The IRS subsequently revoked the satisfaction of the estate tax liability of the McCloud estate, reassessed the additional tax due, and also assessed additional interest of $2,795.24. An additional penalty of $3,034.35 was later dropped. McCloud then paid the additional tax due from his savings and a loan he procured for that purpose.

Edgar pleaded guilty to the four felony charges as agreed and was convicted and sentenced to prison. McCloud subsequently filed a damages action when restitution was not forthcoming.

* * *

On the foregoing basis, the punitive damage award against Edgar Husted should be set aside. The public interest in punishing Husted and in deterring him from such misconduct was fully satisfied by the sentence Husted received. Accordingly, punitive damages are inappropriate. [Citation.] The award of punitive damages against Edgar Husted is set aside.

The trial court relied upon the provisions of Indiana's Uniform Partnership Act, [citation], when it entered judgment against the partnership for both punitive and compensatory damages. The trial court particularly relied upon the following sections of the Uniform Partnership Act which state:

"[§]13. Partnership bound by partner's wrongful act.—Where, by any wrongful act or omission of any partner acting in the ordinary course of the business of the partnership or with the authority of his copartners, loss or injury is caused to any person, not being a partner in the partnership, or any penalty is incurred, the partnership is liable therefore to the same extent as the partner so acting or omitting to act.

[§]14. Partnership bound by partner's breach of trust.—The partnership is bound to make good the loss:

(a) Where one partner acting within the scope of his apparent authority receives money or property of a third person and misapplies it; and

(b) Where the partnership in the course of its business receives money or property of a third person and the money or property so received is misapplied by any partner while it is in the custody of the partnership."

The trial court and the Court of Appeals determined that § 13 required that the partnership be liable to the same extent as Edgar Husted for any civil penalty imposed in this case. The partnership claims that Edgar's criminal acts were not within the ordinary course of partnership business. Furthermore, the partnership claims that it never had possession of the certain funds converted and therefore the partnership cannot be held liable for Edgar's acts with respect to said funds. There were two partners in the partnership law firm, Edgar Husted and Selwyn Husted, Edgar's father. McCloud clearly was a client of the partnership since McCloud dealt with both Selwyn and Edgar on his estate case. In fact, Selwyn was the partner who first brought McCloud's case into the partnership's office. Edgar was acting within the ordinary course of the partnership's business and with apparent authority since Edgar's request for and acceptance of money from McCloud to pay McCloud's estate tax liability was well within the work parameters of an attorney properly handling a decedent's estate. We therefore find that even though fraud and conversion of a client's funds are not part of the ordinary course of a law partnership's business, the trial court correctly found pursuant to § 14 that the partnership was responsible for partner Edgar in taking money entrusted to him and misapplying it. We also find that the trial court was justified in finding that McCloud's money was in the partnership's possession when it was in Edgar's possession since Edgar deviated from McCloud's plan and converted the money to his own use only after he received it in the ordinary course of the partnership's business. Accordingly, the trial court did not err by holding the partnership responsible to McCloud for compensatory damages.

Whether Appellant partnership is liable for punitive damages, however, is another story. Husted & Husted argues that the cases decided under § 13 or its counterpart in other jurisdictions as well as the earlier cases decided under the common law of agency and partnership have generally held that where a partnership is sued for a partner's intentional tort, the partnership's liability turns on whether the purpose or effect of the tortious act was to benefit the partnership's business or whether the tort was so removed from the ordinary course of that business that it could not be considered within the implicit authorization of the copartners. * * *

We accept Appellant's contention that § 13 is the only section by which punitive damages can be imposed against a partnership since § 14 merely limits a partnership's liability to restitution. We further agree with Appellant partnership that the rationale behind punitive damages in Indiana prohibits awarding such damages against an individual who is personally innocent of any wrongdoing. Punitive damages are not intended to compensate a plaintiff but rather are intended to punish the wrongdoer and thereby deter others from engaging in similar conduct in the future. [Citations.] Accordingly, we now hold that the trial court erred by adjudging the innocent partner in this case responsible for punitive damages.

QUESTIONS

1. Discuss the three principal duties owed by a partner to her copartners.

2. Identify and discuss the principal rights of partners (four are discussed in this chapter and two in the previous chapter).

3. Discuss the contract liability of a partnership and the partners.

4. Discuss the tort liability of a partnership and the partners.

5. Distinguish between the liability of an incoming partner for debts arising before his admission and those arising after his admission.

PROBLEMS

1. Albert, Betty, and Carol own and operate the Roy Lumber Company. Each contributed one-third of the capital, and they share equally in the profits and losses. Their partnership agreement provides that all purchases over $500 must be authorized in advance by two partners and that only Albert is authorized to draw checks. Unknown to Albert or Carol, Betty purchases on the firm's account a $2,500 diamond bracelet and a $5,000 forklift and orders $2,000 worth of logs, all from Doug, who operates a jewelry store and is engaged in various activities connected with the lumber business. Before Betty made these purchases, Albert told Doug that Betty is not the log buyer. Albert refuses to pay Doug for Betty's purchases. Doug calls at the mill to collect, and Albert again refuses to pay him. Doug calls Albert an unprintable name, and Albert then punches Doug in the nose. While Doug is lying unconscious on the ground, an employee of Roy Lumber Company negligently drops a log on Doug's leg, thus breaking three bones. The firm and the three partners are completely solvent.

What are the rights of Doug?

2. Paula, Fred, and Stephanie agree that Paula and Fred will form and conduct a partnership business and that Stephanie will become a partner in two years. Stephanie agrees to lend the firm $5,000 and take 10 percent of the profits in lieu of interest. Without Stephanie's knowledge, Paula and Fred tell Harold that Stephanie is a partner, and Harold, relying on Stephanie's sound financial status, gives the firm credit. Later the firm becomes insolvent, and Harold seeks to hold Stephanie liable as a partner. Should Harold succeed?

3. Anita and Duncan had been partners for many years in a mercantile business. Their relationship deteriorated to the point where Anita threatened to bring an action for an accounting and dissolution of the firm. Duncan then offered to buy Anita's interest in the partnership for $25,000. Anita refused the offer and told Duncan that she would take no less than $36,000. A short time later, James approached Duncan and informed him he had inside information that a proposed street change would greatly benefit the business and that he, James, would buy the entire business for $100,000 or buy a one-half interest for $50,000. Duncan made a final offer of $35,000 to Anita for her interest. Anita accepted this offer, and the transaction was completed. Duncan then sold the one-half interest to James for $50,000. Several months later, Anita learned for the first time of the transaction between Duncan and James.

What rights, if any, does Anita have against Duncan?

4. Anthony and Karen were partners doing business as the Petite Garment Company. Leroy owned a dye plant that did much of the processing for the company. Anthony and Karen decided to offer Leroy an interest in their company in consideration for which Leroy would contribute his dye plant to the partnership. Leroy accepted the offer and was duly admitted as a partner. At the time he was admitted as a partner, Leroy did not know that the partnership was on the verge of insolvency. About three months after Leroy was admitted to the partnership, a textile firm obtained a judgment against the partnership in the amount of $50,000. This debt represented an unpaid balance, which had existed before Leroy was admitted as a partner.

The textile firm brought an action to subject the partnership property, including the dye plant, to the satisfaction of its judgment. The complaint also requested that, in the event the judgment was unsatisfied by sale of the partnership property, Leroy's home be sold and the proceeds applied to the balance of the judgment. Anthony and Karen own nothing but their interest in the partnership property.

What should be the result (a) with regard to the dye plant and (b) with regard to Leroy's home?

5. Jones and Ray formed a partnership on January 1, known as JR Construction Co., to engage in the construction business, each partner owning a one-half interest. On February 10, while conducting partnership business, Jones negligently injured Ware, who brought an action against Jones, Ray, and JR Construction Co. and obtained judgment for $25,000 against them on March 1. On April 15, Muir joined the partnership by contributing $10,000 cash, and by agreement each partner was entitled to a one-third interest. In July, the partners agreed to purchase new construction equipment for the partnership, and Muir was authorized to obtain a loan from XYZ Bank in the partnership name for $20,000 to finance the purchase. On July 10, Muir signed a $20,000 note on behalf of the partnership, and the equipment was purchased. In November, the partnership was in financial difficulty, its total assets amounting to $5,000. The note was in default, with a balance of $15,000 owing to XYZ Bank. Muir has substantial resources, while Jones and Ray each individually have assets of $2,000.

What is the extent of Muir's personal liability and the personal liability of Jones and Ray as to (a) the judgment obtained by Ware and (b) the debt owing to XYZ Bank?

6. ABCD Company is a general partnership organized under the UPA. It consists of Dianne, Greg, Knox, and Laura, whose capital contributions were as follows: Dianne = $5,000, Greg = $7,500, Knox = $10,000, and Laura = $5,000. The partnership agreement provided that the partnership would continue for a three-year period and that no withdrawals of capital were to be made without the consent of all the partners. The agreement also provided that all advances would be entitled to interest at 10 percent per year. Six months after the partnership was formed, Dianne made an advance to the partnership of $10,000. At the end of the first year, net profits were realized in the amount of $11,000 before any monies had been distributed to partners. How should the $11,000 be allocated to Dianne, Greg, Knox, and Laura? Explain.

7. Adams, a consulting engineer, entered into a partnership with three others for the practice of their profession. The only written partnership agreement is a brief document specifying that Adams is entitled to 55 percent of the profits and the others to 15 percent each. The venture is a total failure. Creditors are pressing for payment, and some have filed suit. The partners are in fundamental disagreement as to their future course of action.

How many of the partners must agree to achieve each of the following objectives?

(a) To add Jones, also an engineer, as a partner, Jones being willing to contribute a substantial amount of new capital.

(b) To sell a vacant lot held in the partnership name, which had been acquired as the site of a future office for the partnership.

(c) To move the offices of the partnership to less expensive quarters.

(d) To demand a formal accounting.

(e) To dissolve the partnership.

(f) To agree to submit certain disputed claims to arbitration, which Adams believes will prove less expensive than litigation.

(g) To sell all of the partnership personal property, Adams having what he believes to be a good offer for the property from a newly formed engineering firm.

(h) To alter the respective interests of the parties in the profits and losses by decreasing Adams' share to 40 percent and increasing the others' shares accordingly.

(i) To assign all the assets to a bank in trust for the benefit of creditors, hoping to work out satisfactory arrangements without formal bankruptcy.

8. Charles and Jack orally agreed to become partners in a small tool and die business. Charles, who had experience in tool and die work, was to operate the business. Jack was to take no active part but was to contribute the entire $50,000 capitalization. Charles worked ten hours a day at the plant, for which he was paid nothing. Despite Charles's best efforts, the business failed. The $50,000 capital was depleted, and the partnership owed $50,000 in debts. Prior to the failure of the partnership business, Jack became personally insolvent so that the creditors of the partnership collected the entire $50,000 indebtedness from Charles, who was forced to sell his home and farm to satisfy the indebtedness. Jack later regained his financial responsibility, and Charles brought an appropriate action against Jack for (a) one-half of the $50,000 he had paid to partnership creditors and (b) one-half of $18,000, the reasonable value of Charles's services during the operation of the partnership. Decision?

9. Glenn refuses an invitation to become a partner of Dorothy and Cynthia in the retail grocery business. Nevertheless, Dorothy inserts an advertisement in the local newspaper representing Glenn as their partner. Glenn takes no steps to deny the existence of a partnership between them. Ron, who extended credit to the firm, seeks to hold Glenn liable as a partner. Decision?

10. Hanover leased a portion of his farm to Brown and Black, doing business as the Colorite Hatchery. Brown went upon the premises to remove certain chicken sheds that he and Black had placed there for hatchery purposes. Hanover thought Brown intended to remove certain other sheds, which were Hanover's property, and an altercation occurred between them. Brown willfully struck Hanover and knocked him down. Then, Brown ran to the Colorite truck, which he had previously loaded with chicken coops, and drove back to the hatchery. On the way he picked up George, who was hitchhiking to the city to look for a job. Brown was in a hurry and was driving at seventy miles an hour down the highway. At an open intersection with another highway, Brown ran a stop sign, and struck another vehicle at the intersection. The collision caused severe injuries to George. Immediately thereafter, the partnership was dissolved; Brown was insolvent. Hanover and George each bring separate actions against Black as co-partner for the alleged tort committed by Brown against each.

What judgments as to each?

11. Phillips and Harris are partners in a used car business. Under their oral partnership, each has an equal voice in the conduct and management of the business. Because of the irregular business hours kept by the two, it was further agreed that they could use any partnership vehicle as desired. This includes use for transportation to and from work, even though the vehicles are for sale at all times. While driving a partnership vehicle home from the used car lot, Harris hit a car driven by Cook. Cook brought this action against Harris and Phillips individually and as co-partners for his injuries. Decision?

12. Stroud and Freeman are general partners in Stroud's Food Center, a grocery store. Nothing in the articles of partnership restricts the power or authority of either partner to act in respect to the ordinary and legitimate business of the Food Center. In late 1955, however, Stroud informed National Biscuit that he would not be personally responsible for any more bread sold to the partnership. Then, in February 1956, at the request of Freeman, National Biscuit sold and delivered more bread to the Food Center. When payment was refused, National Biscuit brought this action against the partner Stroud and the partnership to recover the value of the bread delivered to the Food Center. Decision?

Chapter 32

DISSOLUTION, WINDING UP, AND TERMINATION

Causes of Dissolution
Effects of Dissolution
Winding Up
Continuation after Dissolution

THREE stages lead to the extinguishment of a partnership: (1) dissolution, (2) winding up or liquidation, and (3) termination. Dissolution occurs when the partners cease to carry on the business together. Upon dissolution, the partnership is not terminated but continues until the winding up of the partnership affairs is completed. During winding up, unfinished business is completed, receivables are collected, payments are made to creditors, and distribution of the remaining assets is made to the partners. Termination occurs when the process of winding up has been completed.

DISSOLUTION

The Uniform Partnership Act defines **dissolution** as the change in the relation of the partners caused by any partner's ceasing to be associated in the carrying on, as distinguished from the winding up, of the business. Section 29. This section discusses the causes and effects of dissolution.

Causes of Dissolution

Dissolution may be brought about by (1) an act of the partners, (2) operation of law, or (3) court order. Section 31. A number of events that were considered causes of dissolution under the common law are no longer considered so under the UPA. For example, the assignment of a partner's interest, a creditor's charging order (judicial lien) on a partner's interest, and an accounting do *not* cause a dissolution.

Dissolution by Act of the Partners Because a partnership is a personal relationship, a partner always has the *power* to dissolve it by his actions, but whether he has the *right* to do so is determined by the partnership agreement. A partner who has withdrawn from the partnership in violation of the partnership agreement is liable to the remaining partners for damages resulting from the **wrongful dissolution.**

A partnership is **rightfully dissolved,** that is, without violation of the partnership agreement, by the act of the partners:

1. when all the partners who have not assigned their interests or permitted their interest to be charged expressly agree to dissolve the partnership;

2. when the period of time provided in the agreement has ended or the purpose for

which the partnership was formed has been accomplished;

3. when a partner withdraws from a partnership at will, that is, a partnership with no definite term or specific undertaking; or

4. when a partner is expelled in accordance with a power to expel conferred by the partnership agreement. Section 31.

Dissolution by Operation of Law

A partnership is dissolved by operation of law upon (1) the death of a partner, (2) the bankruptcy of a partner or of the partnership, or (3) the subsequent illegality of the partnership, which includes any event that makes it unlawful for the business of the partnership to be carried on or for the members to carry on the business in partnership form. Section 31. For example, a partnership formed to manufacture liquor would be dissolved by a law prohibiting the production and sale of alcoholic beverages. A partnership of lawyers would be dissolved if one of its members were disbarred from the practice of law.

Dissolution by Court Order

Upon application by or for a partner, a court will order a dissolution if it finds that (1) a partner has been adjudicated mentally incompetent or suffers some other incapacity that prevents him from functioning as a partner; (2) a partner is guilty of conduct prejudicial to the business, or a partner has willfully or persistently breached the partnership agreement or has conducted himself so that it is impracticable to carry on business; (3) the business can be carried on only at a loss; or (4) other circumstances render a dissolution equitable. Section 32.

An assignee of a partner's interest or a partner's personal creditor who has obtained a charging order against the partner's interest is entitled to a dissolution by court decree. If the partnership is not at will, however, the partnership will not be dissolved until after the specified term or particular undertaking.

Effects of Dissolution

On dissolution, the partnership is *not* terminated but continues until the winding up of partnership affairs is completed. Section 30. Moreover, dissolution does *not* discharge the existing liability of any partner. Dissolution *does* bring about restrictions upon the authority of partners to act for the partnership.

Authority Upon dissolution, the *actual authority* of a partner to act for the partnership terminates, except so far as may be necessary to wind up partnership affairs. Section 33. Actual authority to wind up includes completing existing contracts, collecting debts, selling partnership assets, and paying partnership obligations.

Although actual authority terminates upon dissolution, *apparent authority* persists and binds the partnership for acts within the scope of the partnership business unless notice of the dissolution is given to the third party. Section 35. A third party who had extended credit to the partnership before dissolution may hold the partnership liable for any transaction that would bind the partnership if dissolution had not taken place, unless the third party has knowledge or actual notice of the dissolution. **Actual notice** requires a verbal statement to the third party or actual delivery of a written statement. Section 3(2). On the other hand, a third party, who knew of or had dealt with the partnership but had not extended credit to it before its dissolution, can hold the partnership liable unless he has knowledge, actual notice, or constructive notice of dissolution. **Constructive notice** consists of advertising a notice of dissolution in a newspaper of general circulation in the places at which partnership business was regularly conducted. Section 35(1)(b)(II). *No* notice need be given to third parties who had no knowledge of the partnership before its dissolution.

Existing Liability The dissolution of the partnership does not of itself discharge the existing liability of any partner. Section

36(1). But in some instances the cause of dissolution may result in discharging an executory contract. For example, if the contract called for the personal services of one of the partners, the death of that partner usually will discharge the contract as well as bring about the dissolution of the partnership.

WINDING UP

Whenever a dissolved partnership is not to be continued, the partnership must be liquidated. The process of liquidation is called **winding up** and involves completing unfinished business, collecting debts, taking inventory, reducing assets to cash, auditing the partnership books, paying creditors, and distributing the remaining assets to the partners. During this period, the fiduciary duties of the partners continue in effect. *See Hooper v. Yoder.*

The Right to Wind Up

Upon dissolution any partner has the right to insist on the winding up of the partnership unless the partnership agreement provides otherwise. A partner who has wrongfully dissolved the partnership or who has been rightfully expelled according to the terms of the partnership agreement cannot force the liquidation of the partnership. Unless otherwise agreed, all non-bankrupt partners who have not wrongfully dissolved the partnership have the right to wind up the partnership affairs. Section 37. A court, upon the petition of a partner, his legal representative, or his assignee, may appoint a receiver of all of the property and assets of the partnership. The receiver has authority to wind up the business under the court's direction. The appointment of a receiver is discretionary with the court based upon a showing of cause.

Distribution of Assets

After all the partnership assets have been collected and reduced to cash, they are then distributed to the creditors and partners. When the partnership has been profitable, the order of distribution is not critical; however, when liabilities are greater than assets, the order of distribution has great importance.

Section 40 of the UPA sets forth the rules to be observed in settling accounts between the parties after dissolution. It states that the liabilities of a partnership are to be paid out of partnership assets in the following order:

1. amounts owing to creditors other than partners;

2. amounts owing to partners other than for capital and profits;

3. amounts owing to partners for capital;

4. amounts owing to partners for profits.

The partners may by agreement among themselves change the internal priorities of distribution (numbers 2, 3, and 4) but not the preferred position of third parties (number 1). The UPA defines partnership assets to include all partnership property as well as the contributions necessary for the payment of all partnership liabilities, which consists of numbers 1, 2, and 3. Section 40(a). *See Langness v. "O" Street Carpet Shop, Inc.*

In addition, the UPA provides that, in the absence of any contrary agreement, each partner shall share equally in the profits and surplus remaining after all liabilities (numbers 1, 2, and 3) are satisfied and must contribute toward the losses, whether capital or otherwise, sustained by the partnership according to his share in the profits. Section 18(a). Thus, the proportion in which the partners bear losses, whether capital or otherwise, does not depend upon their relative capital contributions. Rather, it is determined by their agreement. If there is no specific agreement, losses are borne in the same proportion in which profits are shared.

If the partnership is insolvent, the partners individually must contribute their respective share of the losses in order to pay the creditors. Furthermore, if one or more of the partners is insolvent or bankrupt or is out of the jurisdiction and refuses to contribute, the other partners must contribute the additional amount necessary to pay the firm's liabilities in the relative proportions in which they share the profits. Section 40(d). When any partner has paid an amount in excess of his proper share of the losses, he has a right of contribution against the partners who have not paid their share. Section 40(f).

The following examples illustrate the operation of these rules.

Solvent Partnership   Assume that A, B, and C form the ABC Company, a partnership, with A contributing $6,000 capital, B contributing $4,000 capital, and C contributing services but no capital. A also loaned the partnership $3,000, which has not been repaid. There is no agreement as to the proportions in which profits and losses are to be shared. After a few years of operation, the partnership is liquidated. At this time, the assets of ABC Company are $54,000, and its liabilities to creditors are $26,000. The partnership is thus solvent and has enjoyed a profit of $15,000, which is calculated by subtracting the total liabilities ($39,000) from the total assets ($54,000). The total liabilities consist of the amount owed to creditors ($26,000), the amount owed to partners other than for capital and profits ($3,000 owed to A for his loan), and the capital contributions of the partners ($10,000: $6,000 from A and $4,000 from B). Since A, B, and C have not explicitly agreed upon a profit-sharing ratio, they share the profits equally, in this case each receiving $5,000 ($15,000 ÷ 3). After the creditors have been paid in full, A will receive $14,000 ($3,000 for repayment of the loan, $6,000 for capital, and $5,000 for share of profits); B will receive $9,000 ($4,000 for capital and $5,000 for share of profits); and C will receive $5,000 (for share of profits).

Insolvent Partnership   Assume the same partnership had experienced financial adversity. It still owes creditors $26,000, but its total assets only amount to $12,000. In this case the partnership has sustained an aggregate loss of $27,000, which is calculated by subtracting the total liabilities ($39,000, calculated as in the example above) from the total assets ($12,000). In the absence of a contrary agreement, the losses are shared as are the profits, which in this case is equally. Accordingly, each partner's share of the loss will be $9,000 ($27,000 ÷ 3). After the creditors are paid ($26,000), A will receive nothing ($3,000 owed for the loan plus $6,000 for capital *minus* $9,000 for his share of losses); B must make an additional *contribution* of $5,000 to make good his share of the loss ($4,000 owed for capital *minus* $9,000 for his share of losses); and C must contribute $9,000 (his share of losses).

	Loans	+	Capital Contribution	−	Share of Loss	=	Share of Assets or (Additional Contributions Owed)
A	$3,000		$ 6,000		− $ 9,000		$ 0
B	0		$ 4,000		− $ 9,000		$(5,000)
C	0		0		− $ 9,000		$(9,000)
Total	$3,000		$10,000		− $27,000		$(14,000)

Contribution of Partner upon Insolvency In the insolvent partnership example above, if A were individually insolvent, the results would not be changed because A was not required to contribute any additional monies. If A and B were solvent and C were individually insolvent, C would be unable to pay any of his share of the loss. Then A and B must contribute equally, since that is the relative proportion in which they share profits, in order to make good the amount of C's share. Because C's share of the loss is $9,000, A and B must each contribute an additional $4,500. This means that in total A will have to contribute $4,500 and B $9,500 in order to satisfy the unpaid claims of partnership creditors. On the other hand, if A and C were individually insolvent and B was solvent, B would be required to pay the entire balance of $14,000 due to partnership creditors, representing his unpaid share of the loss plus a contribution of the full amount of C's unpaid share of the loss.

Marshaling of Assets

The doctrine of marshaling of assets applies *only* where the assets of a partnership and of its members are being administered by a court of equity. **Marshaling of assets** means segregating and considering the assets and liabilities of the partnership separately from the respective assets and liabilities of the individual partners. Partnership creditors are entitled to be satisfied first out of partnership assets. They have a right to recover any deficiency out of the individually owned assets of the partners, subordinate, however, to the rights of nonpartnership creditors to those assets. Conversely, the nonpartnership creditors have first claim to the individually owned assets of their respective debtors. Their claims to partnership assets are subordinate to claims of partnership creditors.

When a partner is insolvent, the order of distribution of her assets is as follows: (1) debts and liabilities owing to her nonpartnership creditors, (2) debts and liabilities owing to partnership creditors, and (3) contributions owing to other partners who have paid more than their respective share of the firm's liabilities to partnership creditors. Section 40(i).

This rule, however, is *no longer* followed if the partnership is a debtor under the Bankruptcy Code. In a proceeding under the Federal bankruptcy law, a trustee is appointed to administer the estate of the debtor. If the partnership property is insufficient to pay all the claims against the partnership, then the trustee is directed by the statute to seek recovery of the deficiency first from the general partners who are not bankrupt. The trustee may then seek recovery against the estates of bankrupt partners on the same basis as other creditors of the bankrupt partner. Bankruptcy Code, Section 723. This provision, although contrary to the UPA's doctrine of marshaling of assets, governs whenever the assets of a partnership are being administered by a bankruptcy court.

CONTINUATION AFTER DISSOLUTION

After a partnership has been dissolved, one of two outcomes must follow: either the partnership is liquidated or the remaining partners continue the partnership. When a partnership is liquidated, the value of a going concern is sacrificed. On the other hand, continuation of the partnership after dissolution avoids this loss. The UPA, nonetheless, gives each partner the right to have the partnership liquidated except in a limited number of instances where the partners have the right to continue the partnership. Section 37.

Right to Continue Partnership

After dissolution, the remaining partners have the right to continue the partnership, when (1) the partnership has been dissolved in contravention of the partnership agreement, (2) a partner has been expelled in accordance with the partnership agreement, or (3) all the partners agree to continue the business. Nevertheless, the non-continuing partner, or his legal representative, has a right to an account of his interest against the person or partnership continuing the business as of the date of dissolution, unless otherwise agreed. Section 43. Moreover, when a partner dies or retires and the business is continued by the surviving partners, the retired partner or legal representative of the deceased partner is entitled to be paid the value of his interest as of the date of the dissolution as an ordinary creditor of the partnership. In addition, he is entitled to receive interest on this amount or, at his option, in lieu of interest, the profits of the business attributable to the use of his right in the property of the dissolved partnership. His rights, however, are subordinate to those of creditors of the dissolved partnership. Section 42.

Continuation after Wrongful Dissolution

A partner who wrongfully withdraws cannot force the liquidation of the firm. The aggrieved partners have the option of either liquidating the firm and recovering damages for the breach of the partnership agreement or continuing the partnership by buying out the withdrawing partner. The withdrawing partner is entitled to realize his interest in the partnership less the amount of the damages that the other partners have sustained as the result of his breach. The withdrawing partner's interest is computed without considering the good will of the business. In addition, the remaining partners may use the capital contributions of the wrongdoing partner for the unexpired period of the partnership agreement. They must, however, indemnify the former partner against all present and future partnership liabilities. Section 38(2).

Continuation after Expulsion   A partner expelled pursuant to the partnership agreement cannot force the liquidation of the partnership. He is entitled only to be discharged from all partnership liabilities by either payment or a novation with the creditors and to receive in cash the net amount due him from the partnership. Section 38(1).

Continuation Agreement of the Partners By far the best and most reliable way of assuring the preservation of a partnership business after dissolution is a continuation agreement. Continuation agreements are frequently used to insure continuity in the event of death or retirement of one of the partners. A continuation agreement permits the remaining partners to keep the partnership property, carry on its business, and provide a specified settlement with the outgoing partners.

See McClennen v. Commissioner of Internal Revenue.

Rights of Creditors

Whenever a partnership undergoes any change in membership, it is dissolved, and a new partnership is formed even though a majority of the old partners are present in the new combination. The creditors of the old partnership have claims against the new partnership and may also proceed to hold all of the members of the dissolved partnership personally liable. Section 41. If a withdrawing partner has made arrangements with those who continue the business whereby they assume and pay all debts and obligations of the firm, the withdrawing partner is still liable to creditors whose claims arose before the dissolution. If she is compelled to pay such debts, the withdrawing partner has a right of indemnity against her former partners, who had agreed to pay the debts but failed to do so.

A retiring partner may be discharged from his existing liabilities by a **novation** entered into with the continuing partners and the creditors. A creditor must agree to the novation, although his consent may be inferred from his course of dealing with the partnership after dissolution. Section 36(2). Whether such dealings with the continuing partnership constitute an implied novation is a factual question of intent.

A withdrawing partner may protect herself against liability upon contracts entered into by the firm subsequent to her withdrawal by giving notice that she is no longer a member of the firm. Otherwise, she is liable for debts thus incurred to a creditor who had no notice or knowledge of the partner's having withdrawn from the firm. Actual notice must be given to persons who had extended credit to the partnership prior to its dissolution. Constructive notice by newspaper publication will be sufficient for those who knew of the partnership but had not extended credit to it before its dissolution. Section 35. *See Credit Bureaus of Merced County, Inc. v. Shipman.*

Figure 32–1 summarizes the causes and effects of dissolution.

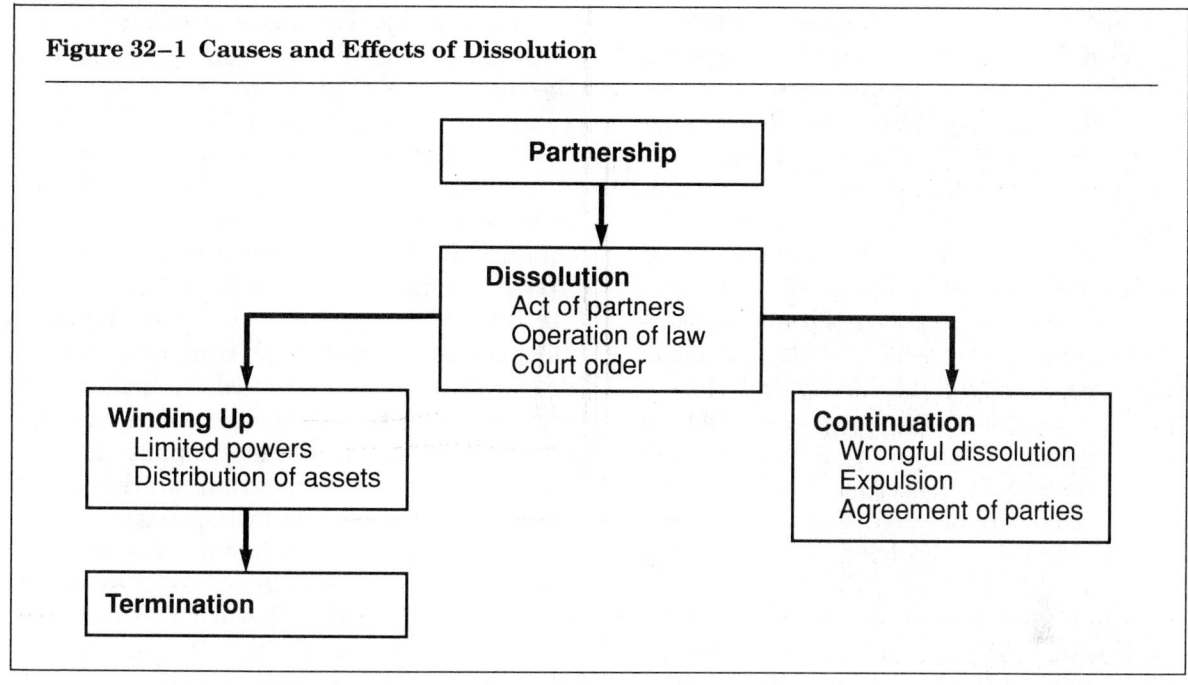

Figure 32–1 Causes and Effects of Dissolution

CASES

Winding Up

HOOPER v. YODER

Supreme Court of Colorado, 1987.
737 P.2d 852.

LOHR, J.

In the fall of 1976, defendant Steven Hooper, a businessman, initiated several meetings with plaintiff David Yoder to discuss business opportunities in the dairy products field. Yoder had experience in that industry, but Hooper had none. After a series of meetings, Yoder and Hooper agreed to work together to develop and market a novelty dairy product, frozen yogurt bars. Yoder testified that they agreed to share equally in the financial risks, the work load and the potential profits of the business. Hooper's contribution was to be his business acumen and Yoder was to contribute his knowledge of the dairy industry. A third individual supplied the initial working capital in consideration of an agreement by Hooper and Yoder to pay that person a commission on sales of frozen yogurt bars. Although Hooper and Yoder agreed upon their respective roles in the business venture, no formal written partnership agreement was drawn. After reaching agreement, both devoted their efforts to the enterprise.

Hooper and Yoder began discussing the possibility of incorporating their business in the early spring of 1977, which corresponded with the time their product was ready to market. After the two parties had consulted several lawyers, both in Colorado and in California where the yogurt bars were being produced, they incorporated their business in California under the name of Beautiful Daydreams, Inc. (Beautiful Daydreams). Hooper became president and treasurer of the corporation and Yoder was named vice-president and secretary. The two men were the only members of the board of directors. They decided to defer the issuance of stock in the corporation.

In May of 1977, Hooper moved to southern California in order to oversee the production and distribution of the frozen yogurt bars. By September of 1978, Hooper had taken over the responsibility of purchasing, shipping, invoicing, and sales in California, while Yoder was responsible for merchandising, distribution, and sales in the Denver area. Yoder worked closely with Market West Brokers (Market West), a Denver-based food brokerage firm engaged by Beautiful Daydreams to help market its product. Yoder and Hooper kept in close contact, talking to each other on the telephone at least daily and sometimes several times a day. Yoder made several trips to California and believed that his business relationship with Hooper was running smoothly.

Market West loaned money to Beautiful Daydreams to alleviate a cash flow problem, and when Beautiful Daydreams was unable to repay the loan promptly, Market West agreed to accept stock in the corporation in partial payment of the debt. In October of 1978, Hooper and Yoder named Brian Bradley, who was Beautiful Daydreams' principal contact at Market West, as an additional member of the board of directors. Market West initiated Bradley's election in order to protect its financial investment in Beautiful Daydreams.

Starting in October of 1978, Yoder began to have difficulty keeping in contact with Hooper. On November 1, 1978, Yoder received a message from Hooper informing him that Hooper had scheduled a meeting of the board of directors of Beautiful Daydreams in Denver for the following week. Yoder immediately attempted to contact Hooper to remind him that Yoder had longstanding plans to attend a business convention in California during the time that the board of directors was scheduled to meet. Yoder was unable to reach Hooper, and Hooper did not return Yoder's calls. After discussing the scheduling conflict with Bradley, Yoder went to the convention in California and did not attend the board meeting. At the meeting and without Yoder's knowledge, the other two directors adopted a resolution for issuance of 100

shares of stock, 95 to Hooper and 5 to Market West in exchange for cancellation of $9500 of the corporation's indebtedness to Hooper and $500 of its indebtedness to Market West.

When Yoder returned from California, he repeatedly tried to reach Hooper, without success. By this time, Hooper had not communicated with Yoder in more than a month. Yoder then flew to California and on November 14, 1978, appeared at a meeting that Hooper had arranged with Bradley and some distributors in San Francisco. After the meeting, the three board members discussed the financial condition of the company. Hooper and Bradley told Yoder that Market West would be taking reduced compensation, that Hooper and Yoder would not be receiving salary, and that no more money would be taken out of the corporation. Hooper testified that Yoder's involvement in the business was terminated at the San Francisco meeting when Hooper told Yoder that Yoder would have to seek another job because Beautiful Daydreams had run out of funds. Yoder, however, testified that he understood the conversation to mean that no one would be able to take money out of the business until it started to generate more income. Yoder expressed to Hooper his frustration at not being kept informed and not being able to help with the business into which he had poured so much of his time and energy.

Yoder and Hooper met once again on November 15, 1978, at the airport immediately prior to Yoder's flight back to Colorado. Yoder testified that at that meeting Hooper was much more cooperative. According to Yoder, the men discussed the need to get part-time jobs and to work on the company's problems. Hooper discouraged Yoder from moving to California when Yoder expressed such an inclination. Yoder testified that at no time did the men discuss a decision to terminate Yoder's employment permanently, nor did Hooper or Bradley mention that a resolution had been adopted for the issuance of 100 shares of stock in Beautiful Daydreams.

On January 15, 1979, by written "Action of Shareholders Without a Meeting," Hooper and Market West, acting through Bradley, removed the entire board of directors of Beautiful Daydreams and elected Hooper and Bradley as the only directors. On that same day these two directors met and elected Hooper as president and treasurer and Bradley as vice president and secretary. Yoder received no advance notice of the meetings or of the nature of the corporate action to be considered on January 15.

After returning to Colorado from the San Francisco meeting in November, Yoder was again unable to reach Hooper by telephone. Yoder then became concerned that he had never seen Beautiful Daydreams' organizational records. On January 19, 1979, he called the California attorney who had helped with the incorporation of the business, and requested a copy of the corporate records.

On February 1, 1979, Yoder received a mailgram from Hooper stating, "For reasons Brian and I discussed with you at our meeting in November we must permanently lay you off. Letter will follow." Yoder again attempted to contact Hooper, without success. Yoder received a letter from Hooper on February 8, 1979, detailing the reasons that his employment had been terminated. On March 16, Yoder received from the California lawyer copies of the minutes of Beautiful Daydreams' board meetings. It was at this time that Yoder first became aware that corporate stock had been issued to Hooper and Market West, and that Yoder was no longer an officer or director of Beautiful Daydreams. Yoder did not learn of the fact that Hooper was receiving a salary from the business, totaling $141,500 for the years beginning in 1978 and continuing into 1982, until much later.

In August of 1979, Yoder filed the present action against Hooper and Beautiful Daydreams in the District Court for Boulder County. In March of 1982 the trial court heard the case without a jury and made the following oral findings of fact and conclusions of law: (1) a partnership was formed between Hooper and Yoder prior to May of 1977 for the purpose of manufacturing and selling frozen yogurt bars; (2) the parties agreed to continue their partnership enterprise in corporate form; (3) the essential term of the

agreement, for the purpose of the present dispute, was that in the event stock were to be issued, it would be issued in equal amounts to Hooper and Yoder; and (4) Hooper breached the agreement and his fiduciary duty by not causing half of Hooper's 95 shares of stock to be issued to Yoder in November 1978, "by freezing him out of the corporation after January 15, 1979 and by drawing a salary for [Hooper]." The trial court also found that Hooper had received $141,500 in salary prior to the time of trial. The court concluded that Hooper should be deemed to hold one-half of the $141,500 salary payments and one-half of the 95 shares of stock in constructive trust for Yoder. It then entered judgment in favor of Yoder for $70,750, and ordered Hooper to transfer 47½ shares of stock in Beautiful Daydreams to Yoder. The court dismissed the complaint against Beautiful Daydreams.

Hooper appealed, and the court of appeals affirmed the judgment. Hooper then petitioned this court for a writ of certiorari, and we granted that petition.

* * *

* * * The trial court found that in the fall of 1976, the parties agreed to engage in the business of manufacturing and selling frozen yogurt bars for the purpose of making a profit. The court found that they agreed to put their money or credit, labor and skills into the enterprise and agreed to share equally in the profits and losses, and in any funds available for salaries. The record contains ample evidence to support these findings, which in turn support the conclusion that Hooper and Yoder entered into a partnership to engage in the frozen yogurt bar business.

The record also establishes without contradiction that the decision to incorporate was mutual. Both parties discussed the possibility of incorporating their business, consulted lawyers in both Colorado and California with respect to incorporation, and upon incorporation, elected themselves as the only members of the board of directors and the only officers of the corporation.

As a general rule, when partners organize a corporation to operate the business of the partnership and transfer the assets to the corporation, the partnership is dissolved. [Citation.] This is so because such action usually reflects the express will of the parties that the partnership be dissolved. [UPA § 31(1)(c).]

* * * Based on this record, we conclude that the partnership between Hooper and Yoder was dissolved upon the incorporation of Beautiful Daydreams.

* * *

The dissolution of a partnership, however, does not automatically terminate the existence of the partnership. The Uniform Partnership Law provides that "[o]n dissolution the partnership is not terminated but continues until the winding up of partnership affairs is completed." [UPA § 30.] "The winding up includes the entire process of settling the partnership affairs after dissolution." [Citations.]

When partners organize a corporation to continue the business of the firm, the winding up of the partnership includes the transfer of the partnership assets to the corporation in exchange for corporate stock. [Citations.] Here, the winding up of the partnership remained incomplete pending issuance of corporate stock to Hooper and Yoder in equal amounts pursuant to the agreement they made as partners prior to incorporation. Because there were no shares of stock issued upon incorporation of Beautiful Daydreams, it cannot be said that the property of the partnership was exchanged for stock in the corporation and that the stock was then distributed to the partners, thereby winding up the partnership affairs. The circumstances of this case bring us to the conclusion that the winding up of the partnership was not accomplished upon incorporation and, therefore, the partnership continued to exist.

* * *

Because the partnership continued to exist, so did the fiduciary duties that one partner owes to another. Partners in a business enterprise owe to one another the highest duty of loyalty; they stand in a relationship of trust and confidence to each other and are bound by standards of good conduct and square dealing. [Citations.] Each partner has the right to demand and expect from the other a full, fair, open and honest disclosure of everything affecting the relationship. [Citations.] During the winding up of partnership affairs, the partners continue to owe to each other the same duty of loyalty and fair dealing. [Citations.]

As the trial court found, Hooper and Yoder initially agreed that partnership profits and losses would be shared equally, as would any funds available for salaries. When they formed the corporation, the "essential term of the agreement" to incorporate was that any stock to be issued to these incorporators would be shared equally. The fiduciary duty of partners to exercise good faith and loyalty, which continued during the winding up of the partnership, required scrupulous adherence to the parties' agreement in winding up the affairs of the partnership as well as full and honest disclosure of everything affecting the relationship. Hooper's actions in causing the issuance of 95 shares of stock to himself and none to Yoder and in drawing a salary from the business without the assent or knowledge of Yoder are the very antithesis of the type of fair dealing required between partners in winding up a partnership. The trial court's conclusion that "Mr. Hooper breached his fiduciary duty by not issuing fifty percent of the shares of stock to Mr. Yoder in November of 1978 and by freezing him out of the corporation after January 15, 1979 and by drawing a salary for himself" is factually supported by the record and is legally correct.

* * *

In the initial partnership agreement in this case, Hooper and Yoder agreed to equal salaries. Yoder was subsequently prevented from participating in the corporate decision-making process when Hooper breached his fiduciary duty by excluding Yoder from stock ownership. Hooper proceeded to take a salary from the business without Yoder's consent or knowledge. Under these circumstances, the trial court's decision to deny compensation to Hooper for his services was a proper exercise of its equitable powers.

* * *

The trial court adopted a proper remedy for Hooper's breach of his fiduciary duties. When a breach of fiduciary duty has been established, the injured party may recover his share of the partnership profits and property through the imposition of a constructive trust. "[Constructive trusts] are raised by equity in respect of property which has been acquired by fraud, or where, though acquired originally without fraud, it is against equity that it should be retained by him who holds it." [Citations.] Hooper's action in acquiring corporate stock and taking a salary without Yoder's consent or knowledge violated Hooper's fiduciary duties to Yoder and can fairly be characterized as fraudulent. The trial court imposed a constructive trust on behalf of Yoder for one-half of the shares of stock issued to Hooper and one-half of the salary received by Yoder as an equitable remedy for Hooper's breach of duty. In doing so, the court properly exercised its equitable powers. [Citation.]

* * *

Judgment affirmed.

Distribution of Assets

LANGNESS v. "O" STREET CARPET SHOP, INC.

Supreme Court of Nebraska, 1984.
217 Neb. 569, 353 N.W.2d 709.

PER CURIAM.

This is an action for an accounting among partners. Defendant-appellant, Herbert J. Friedman, appeals from the decree adjudging that he and a second partner jointly and severally owe the third partner, plaintiff-appellee Strelsa Lee Langness, the sum of $7,290.42. We affirm as modified.

On August 23, 1973, Friedman, The "O" Street Carpet Shop, Inc., through its president, Gerald Neva, and Langness formed a partnership known as NFL Associates. At that time "O" Street Carpet contributed to the partnership a $56,000 purchase agreement on a piece of rental property valued at $65,000. Langness contributed $14,000 in cash, and

Friedman contributed his legal services, upon which no value was placed by the articles of partnership. Of Langness' $14,000, $8,000 went to "O" Street Carpet and $6,000 was used for the downpayment on the purchase agreement and to otherwise fund the partnership operations. The articles of partnership provided that Langness was to receive payments of $116.66 per month. Neva executed a personal guarantee by which he agreed to make the $116.66 monthly payments to Langness if the income of the partnership proved insufficient.

Langness never paid income tax on the monthly payments, nor did the partnership take expense deductions for those payments on its tax return. The partnership's accountant treated the payments as a return to Langness of her capital.

In October of 1978 the partnership sold the rental property which was the subject of the purchase agreement contributed by "O" Street Carpet, and realized $52,001.20 on that transaction. The partnership was wound up; whereupon Neva and Friedman calculated the final distribution of the $48,824.41 in assets remaining, after payment of the $3,176.79 in debts owed by the partnership, to be:

Langness	$16,792.01
"O" Street Carpet	26,808.58
Friedman	5,223.82

Friedman delivered a check for $16,792.01 to Langness, which, although unhappy about the distribution, she cashed.

Langness then brought this action, claiming that she is entitled to a larger share of the partnership assets. The district court found that her final share of the partnership should be $24,082.43, and entered judgment against both Friedman and "O" Street Carpet for $7,290.42, declaring them to be jointly and severally liable thereon.

* * *

Friedman correctly characterizes an action for an accounting between partners to be one grounded in equity. Accordingly, as in all matters of equity, the scope of our review is de novo on the record. [Citations.]

Friedman's first three assignments of error are best analyzed by reviewing the capital contributions made by the parties, the nature of the payments made to Langness, and the distributions made to each of the three partners upon the winding up of the partnership.

As stated earlier, at the time the partnership was formed, "O" Street Carpet contributed a $56,000 purchase agreement on property with a fair market value of $65,000, for a contribution of property worth $9,000. However, $8,000 of the $14,000 contributed by Langness went to "O" Street Carpet, thereby reducing its capital contribution at that time to $1,000. During the life of the partnership, "O" Street Carpet contributed an additional $4,005 in capital. Thus, "O" Street Carpet's total capital contribution is $5,005.

Friedman contributed no money or property. It is the general rule that a partner who contributes only services to the partnership is not deemed to have made a capital contribution to the partnership such as to require capital repayment upon dissolution unless the parties have agreed to the contrary. [Citations.]

Friedman argues that since, by the agreement, he was given 10 percent of the partnership, he was entitled to be credited with a like amount of the partnership capital upon dissolution. While the agreement specifically states that Friedman is entitled to 10 percent of the partnership profits, it mentions nothing concerning his rights to partnership capital upon dissolution. We see nothing in the agreement which indicates the general rule is not to apply. Therefore, Friedman made no capital contribution to the venture.

We next address the nature of the payments made to Langness. The articles of partnership called for the partnership to pay to Langness $116.66 per month for the life of the partnership. While this provision of the articles is found under a section labeled "Distribution of Profits and Losses," the agreement does not state whether it is to be treated as an advance on profits or a capital withdrawal. The personal guarantee executed by Neva labeled it

a "return on the $14,000.00 investment." Both accountants who testified at the trial stated that the payments were treated as capital withdrawals. Langness treated the payments as such when preparing her tax returns. The tax returns of the partnership did not treat them as expenses. Although Friedman argues that they should be treated as advances against Langness' future profits, we do not see any reason to do so when the partnership itself treated them otherwise.

From our review of exhibit 27, a ledger of the payments made by checks issued by NFL Associates, we find that Langness was issued 47 checks for $116.66, 3 checks for $233.32, and 1 check for $117.32. We calculate her total capital withdrawals as $6,300.30, a figure different than that urged upon us by the parties or found by the district court. This $6,300.30 reduced her capital in the partnership to $7,699.70.

We now reach the question of the appropriate amounts of the distribution to each of the partners. The partnership agreement provides: "Upon the dissolution of the partnership after settlement of all of it's (sic) debts, liabilities, and other obligations, the partners are entitled to all remaining assets of the partnership in equal proportions in liquidation of all of their respective interests in the partnership." Amounts owing to partners to reimburse them for capital contributions are liabilities of the partnership and take priority over amounts owing to partners in respect to profits. [UPA § 40.]

Of the $48,824.41 in assets remaining after payment of the partnership's debts, $7,699.70 is to be paid to Langness for her capital contribution and $5,005 to "O" Street Carpet for its capital contribution. The remaining $36,119.71 is to be divided according to the partners' share in the profits, which is on a 45–45–10 basis. This calculation requires $16,253.87 to be paid to Langness for profit, the same amount to "O" Street Carpet, and $3,611.97 to Friedman. At the time of the winding up of the partnership, the distributions should have been as follows:

	Return of Capital	+	Share of Profits	=	Total
Langness	$ 7,699.70		$16,253.87		$23,953.57
"O"	5,005.00		16,253.87		21,258.87
Street Carpet					
Friedman	0.00		3,611.97		3,611.97
	$12,704.70		$36,119.71		$48,824.41

Since Langness was paid only $16,792.01, she is entitled to an additional $7,161.56.

* * *

Therefore, the judgment of the district court is modified as follows: Langness shall have judgment against and recover from Friedman the sum of $1,611.85, the difference between the amount he received, $5,223.82, and the amount he should have received, $3,611.97. Further, Langness shall have judgment against and recover from "O" Street Carpet the amount of $5,549.71, the difference between the amount it received, $26,808.58, and the amount it should have received, $21,258.87.

* * *

AFFIRMED AS MODIFIED.

Continuation per Agreement of the Parties

McCLENNEN v. COMMISSIONER OF INTERNAL REVENUE

United States Court of Appeals, First Circuit, 1942.
131 F.2d 165.

MAGRUDER, J.

[George Nutter was a partner in the law firm of Nutter, McClennen & Fish. The partnership agreement provided that he was entitled to receive 8 percent of the firm's net profits and that on his death or retirement payments in the same percentage of net profits would continue to be made to Nutter or his estate for a period of eighteen months. The agreement expressly stated that the payments would be in full satisfaction of the deceased or retiring partner's interest in the capital, the assets, the receivables, and the good will of the firm.

When Nutter died in 1937, his partners continued the business and made the required payments totaling $34,070 to Nutter's estate, but the Federal estate tax return filed for the estate did not include an amount representing the value of Nutter's interest in the partnership. As a result the Commissioner of Internal Revenue filed this notice of deficiency for taxes due on $34,070, the value of Nutter's partnership interest.]

* * *

In his notice of deficiency the Commissioner determined that $34,069.99 should have been included in the gross estate as the value of decedent's "interest in partnership Nutter, McClennen & Fish." The Board has upheld the Commissioner in this determination. We think the Board was right.

In the absence of a controlling agreement in the partnership articles the death of a partner dissolves the partnership. The survivors have the right and duty, with reasonable dispatch, to wind up the partnership affairs, to complete transactions begun but not then finished, to collect the accounts receivable, to pay the firm debts, to convert the remaining firm assets into cash, and to pay in cash to the partners and the legal representative of the deceased partner the net amounts shown by the accounts to be owing to each of them in respect of capital contributions and in respect of their shares of profits and surplus. The representative of a deceased partner does not succeed to any right to specific partnership property. In substance the deceased partner's interest, to which his representative succeeds, is a chose in action, a right to receive in cash the sum of money shown to be due him upon a liquidation and accounting. These substantive results may be rationalized upon a theory of the partnership "entity." [Citation.] The same substantive results are reached under the Uniform Partnership Act which, in form at least, proceeds on the aggregate theory. [Citation.] That act, which is law in Massachusetts, conceives of the partner as a "co-owner with his partners of specific partnership property holding as a tenant in partnership;" but provides that on the death of a partner "his right in specific partnership property vests in the surviving partner or partners." Another enumerated property right of a partner, "his interest in the partnership," is described as "his share of the profits and surplus, and the same is personal property," regardless of whether the firm holds real estate or personalty or both. [Citations.] * * *

In the case at bar, if there had not been the controlling provision in the partnership articles, above quoted, or if the survivors had not come to some agreement otherwise with the executors of Mr. Nutter, the survivors would have had to proceed to wind up the affairs of the partnership, to conclude all unfinished legal business on hand at the date of the death, or realize upon all of the assets of the firm, tangible or intangible, to pay the debts, to return to Mr. Nutter's estate his contribution of capital, if any, and to pay to his estate in cash the amount shown to be due in respect of his "interest in the partnership," that is, his "share of the profits and surplus", as determined upon an accounting. Among other things to be taken into account, "the earned proportion of the unfinished business" would have had "to be valued to determine the decedent's interest in the partnership assets." [Citations.]

To obviate the necessity of a liquidation, or to eliminate accounting difficulties in determining the value of the deceased partner's interest, partners often make specific provision in the partnership articles.

* * *

In the case at bar the partnership agreement contains another familiar arrangement, whereby no liquidation and final accounting will ever be necessary in order to satisfy the claim of the deceased partner. In place of the chose in action to which Mr. Nutter's executor would have succeeded in the absence of specific provision in the partnership articles, that is, a right to receive payment in cash of the amount shown to be due the deceased partner upon a complete liquidation and accounting, a different right is substituted, a right of the estate to receive a share of the net profits of the firm for 18 calendar months after the partner's death.

The language of the partnership agreement in the present case is couched in terms of a purchase of the deceased partner's interest. What the estate is to receive "shall be in full of the retiring or deceasing member's interest in the capital, the assets, the receivables, the possibilities and the good will of the Firm." There is to be an extinguishment of the decedent's interest in the totality of the firm assets, tangible and intangible, as they stood at the moment of death, and the interests therein of the surviving partners are to be correspondingly augmented. Decision in the estate tax case now before us does not turn on the question whether the effect of the partnership agreement may be characterized with entire accuracy as a "purchase" and "sale" of the deceased partner's interest in the partnership.

[Judgment in favor of the Commissioner is affirmed.]

Rights of Creditors

CREDIT BUREAUS OF MERCED COUNTY, INC. v. SHIPMAN

District Court of Appeal, Third District, California, 1959. 167 Cal.App.2d 673, 334 P.2d 1036.

SCHOTTKY, J.

Donald Davis and Russell Shipman formed a partnership in 1954 under the name of Shipman & Davis Lumber Company. On September 20, 1955, the partnership was dissolved by written agreement. A notice of dissolution was published in a newspaper of general circulation in the county where the business was conducted, and an affidavit of publication was filed with the county clerk. No actual notice of dissolution was given to firms which had extended credit to the partnership at the time of dissolution. By the agreement Shipman, who was to continue the business, was to pay all the debts of the entity. Shipman continued the business as a sole proprietorship for a short time until a successor corporation, Shipman Lumber Servaes Co., was formed. In March, 1955, the partnership had purchased a calculator from the Valley Typewriter Company. The contract of sale provided that the unpaid balance of $457.20 would be paid in twelve installments of $38.10. At the time of dissolution the sum of $255.40 was owing to the Laird Welding & Manufacturing Company. The sum of $255.40 was paid to Laird Welding & Manufacturing Works on November 17, 1955, but this amount did not include the item of $54.48 for repairs made on November 3, 1955, but which was not entered on the books of the Laird Welding & Manufacturing Works until after the payment on November 17th, nor did it cover charges for demurrage on oxygen or acetylene cylinders furnished by Laird Welding & Manufacturing Works, or charges for cylinders which were either lost or not returned, said charges amounting to $135.33.

Commencing in 1956, Merced Hardware & Implement Company, a firm which had previously done business with the partnership, sold merchandise on credit to the successors. The charge for this merchandise, amounting to $538.38, was entered on the books of Merced Hardware & Implement Company in the name of Shipman & Davis Lumber Company.

At the time of dissolution eight payments were due on the calculator. Five were made prior to the institution of this suit. A check in the amount of $76.20 drawn by Shipman Lumber Servaes Co. on June 20, 1956, was accepted by Valley Typewriter Company as was a check of $38.10 dated October 26, 1956, which was also drawn by Shipman Lumber Servaes Co.

The accounts were assigned to the above-named plaintiff, and two separate actions were brought against Davis and Shipman and the partnership. Shipman failed to answer and a default was entered against him. Davis filed an answer denying any indebtedness to plaintiff. The two actions were consolidated for trial; and the court found that plaintiff was entitled to recover from defendant Davis the sum of $189.81 on the Laird account, the sum of $538.38 on the Merced Hardware account, and the sum of $114.30 plus $100 attorney's fees on the Valley Type-

writer account. The court also found that neither plaintiff nor plaintiff's assignors had notice of dissolution of said partnership until after their accounts had been incurred, and that neither plaintiff nor plaintiff's assignors agreed to discharge any of the defendants named herein from liability. In accordance with said findings, judgment for $842.49 principal and attorney's fees in the sum of $100 was entered in favor of plaintiff and defendant has appealed from said judgment.

* * *

As to the repair item incurred on November 3, 1955, which was after the date of the dissolution, appellant [Davis] would not be liable therefor if Laird Welding & Manufacturing Works had notice of the dissolution. While the evidence is conflicting as to whether the Welding Works had notice of the dissolution at the time the repairs were made, it is sufficient to support the finding of the court that the company did not have notice. The burden is on a defendant relying on dissolution to prove notice of dissolution. [Citation.] Appellant cannot rely on the provisions of [citation] to show actual knowledge. This section provides for publication of notice of dissolution of a partnership. However, as to firms having prior credit dealings with the partnership, actual notice of dissolution is necessary. While publication may be evidence from which actual knowledge could be inferred, publication alone would not compel a finding of actual knowledge. A retiring partner is not justified in placing sole reliance upon the publication of notice of dissolution, but should assure himself that existing creditors who have extended credit to the partnership receive actual notice of such dissolution.

As to the Merced Hardware account it is clear that the debt for the items sued upon were all incurred after February, 1956. Appellant contends that he is not liable for these items of debt because they were incurred after the dissolution of the partnership. Respondent in reply points out that [citation] provides that after a dissolution a partner can bind the partnership "By any transaction which would bind the partnership if dissolution had not taken place, provided, the other party to the transaction: I. Had extended credit to the partnership prior to dissolution and had no knowledge or notice of the dissolution." Here again the evidence is conflicting as to whether Merced Hardware & Implement Company had notice of dissolution of the partnership, and we are bound by the court's finding that it did not. There is also evidence that Merced Hardware & Implement Company had previously extended credit to the partnership. The credit reference on the contract on the Shipman & Davis Lumber Company with Valley Typewriter Company, dated March 15, 1955, and signed by Russell C. Shipman, lists Merced Hardware Company; and the items in dispute were charged to Shipman & Davis Lumber Company on the books of Merced Hardware & Implement Company. The evidence supports the implied finding that Merced Hardware & Implement Company had previously extended credit to Shipman & Davis Lumber Company.

As to the Valley Typewriter Company account, the record shows that five payments were made on this account after the date of the dissolution of the partnership. Two checks in favor of Valley Typewriter Company, both signed by Shipman Lumber Servaes Co., one dated June 20, 1956, for $76.20 and one dated October 26, 1956, for $38.10. Appellant contends that this is overwhelming evidence of a novation and conclusive proof that he was discharged from the obligation under [citation] which reads: "(2) A partner is discharged from any existing liability upon dissolution of the partnership by an agreement to that effect between himself, the partnership creditor and the person or partnership continuing the business; and such agreement may be inferred from the course of dealing between the creditor having knowledge of the dissolution and the person or partnership continuing the business." We are unable to agree with this contention. Whether or not there was a novation was a question of fact and conflicting inferences can be drawn from the evidence. The manager of Valley Typewriter Company testified that he had no actual knowledge of the dissolution of the partnership. The checks themselves would not necessarily compel a finding of actual knowledge since the inference appellant seeks to draw is dispelled by the testimony that the creditor had no knowledge. There can be no novation where the creditor testified he had no knowledge of dissolution and such testimony is believed by the trier of the fact.

Appellant also argues that he is entitled to a reversal of the judgment as to the Valley Typewriter account under the following provision of [citation]: "(3) Where a person agrees to assume the existing obligations of a dissolved partnership, the partners whose obligations have been assumed shall be discharged from any liability to any creditor of the partnership who, knowing of the agreement, consents to a material alteration in the nature or time of payment of such obligations." But here again knowledge of the dissolution of the partnership is required, and the court found upon sufficient evidence that none of the creditors here involved had notice or knowledge of the dissolution of the partnership. Furthermore, the fact that the Valley Typewriter Company accepted delayed payments under the contract does not compel a finding in accordance with appellant's argument that the creditor had consented to a material alteration in the nature or time of payment of the obligation.

[Judgment for the Credit Bureaus for all three accounts affirmed.]

QUESTIONS

1. Identify the causes of dissolution of a partnership.

2. Explain the effect of dissolution upon the authority and liability of the partners.

3. Explain the order in which the assets of a partnership are distributed to creditors and partners.

4. Distinguish between the relative rights of partnership creditors and partners' creditors under the UPA and the Bankruptcy Code.

5. Identify and discuss when partners have the right to continue the partnership after dissolution.

PROBLEMS

1. Simmons, Hoffman, and Murray were partners doing business under the firm name of Simmons & Co. The firm borrowed money from a bank and gave the bank the firm's note for the loan. In addition, each partner guaranteed the note individually. The firm became insolvent, and a receiver was appointed. The bank claims that it has a right to file its claim as a firm debt and also that it has a right to participate in the distribution of the assets of the individual partners before partnership creditors receive any payment from such assets.

(a) Explain the principle involved in this case.

(b) Is the bank correct?

2. Lauren, Matthew, and Susan form a partnership, Lauren contributing $10,000; Matthew $5,000; and Susan her time and skill. Nothing was said as to the division of profits. The firm becomes insolvent, and after payment of all firm debts $6,000 is left. Lauren claims that she is entitled to the entire $6,000. Matthew contends that the distribution should be $4,000 to Lauren and $2,000 to Matthew. Susan claims the $6,000 should be divided equally among the partners. Who is correct? Explain.

3. Martin, Mark, and Marvin formed a retail clothing partnership named M Clothiers and conducted a business for many years, buying most of their clothing from Hill, a wholesaler. On January 15, Marvin retired from the business, but Martin and Mark decided to continue it. As part of the retirement agreement, Martin and Mark agreed in writing with Marvin that Marvin would not be responsible for any of the partnership debts, either past or future. A news item concerning Marvin's retirement appeared in the local newspaper on January 15.

Before January 15, Hill was a creditor of M Clothiers to the extent of $10,000, and on January 30, he extended additional credit of $5,000. Hill was not advised and did not in fact know of Marvin's retirement and the change of the partnership. On January 30, Ray, a competitor of Hill, extended credit for the first time to M Clothiers in the amount of $3,000.

On February 1, Martin and Mark left for parts unknown and left no partnership assets with which to pay the described debts. What is Marvin's liability, if any, (a) to Hill and (b) to Ray?

4. Ben, Dan, and Lilli were partners sharing profits in proportions of one-fourth, one-third, and five-twelfths, respectively. Their business failed, and the firm was dissolved. At the time of dissolution, no financial adjustments between the partners were necessary with reference to their respective capital contributions, but the firm's liabilities to creditors exceeded its assets by $24,000. Without contributing any amount toward the payment of the liabilities, Dan moved to a destination unknown. Ben and Lilli are financially responsible. How much must each contribute?

5. Indicate which of the following statements are true and which are false:

(a) Creditors having claims based upon torts committed by partners in the course of business of the partnership are preferred over creditors with claims based upon contracts.

(b) Partners who wish to continue the business have a prior right to purchase the assets.

(c) In the absence of a contract providing otherwise, the distribution to partners of accrued profits should be in equal parts, regardless of the fact that the partners had contributed to the firm unequally.

(d) Advances in the nature of loans made by the various partners to the partnership share in the firm assets on the same basis as debts due other creditors.

(e) Between the partners, the assets of the partnership must be applied to pay the claims of partners with respect to capital ahead of the claims of partners with respect to profits.

(f) Debts owing to partners (other than for the capital and profits) rank ahead of debts owing to partners with respect to capital and profits.

6. Ames, Bell, and Cole were equal partners in the ABC Construction Company. They had no formal or written partnership agreement. Cole died on June 30, and his widow, Cora Cole, qualified as executor of his will. Ames and Bell continued the business of the partnership until December 31, when they sold all of the assets of the partnership. After paying all partnership debts, they distributed the balance equally among themselves and Mrs. Cole as executor.

Subsequently, Mrs. Cole learned that Ames and Bell had made and withdrawn a net profit of $20,000 during the period July 1 to December 31. The profit was made through new contracts using the partnership name and assets. Ames and Bell had concealed from Mrs. Cole the fact of such contracts and profit, and she learned about it from other sources. Immediately after acquiring this information, Mrs. Cole made demand upon Ames and Bell for one-third of the profit of $20,000. They rejected her demand. What are the rights and remedies, if any, of Cora Cole as executor?

7. David and Barbara were partners in Miami. Steven, a traveling salesman for Karen, called on them and on January 14 received from them an order for merchandise. The order was forwarded by Steven to Karen in New York on January 15; the partnership of David and Barbara was dissolved by agreement between the partners on January 18. On January 19, Karen, without knowledge of the dissolution, acknowledged receipt of the order, accepted it, and shipped the goods the next day. Barbara received them on January 23. On January 25, notice of dissolution of the partnership of David and Barbara was duly published. Karen sues David and Barbara for the purchase price of the merchandise sold. Decision?

8. The articles of partnership of the firm of Wilson and Company provide

William Smith to contribute $50,000; to receive interest thereon at 13 percent per annum and to devote such time as he may be able to give; to receive 30 percent of the profits.

John Jones to contribute $50,000; to receive interest on same at 13 percent per annum; to give all of his time to the business and to receive 30 percent of the profits.

Henry Wilson to contribute all of his time to the business and to receive 20 percent of the profits.

James Brown to contribute all of his time to the business and to receive 20 percent of the profits.

There is no provision for sharing losses. After six years of operations, the firm has assets of $400,000 and liabilities to creditors of $420,000. Upon dissolution and winding up, what are the rights and liabilities of the respective parties?

9. Harold Fuller, Mary Warner, and Tom Clardy were co-partners in the operation of a cattle raising partnership. Fuller and Clardy were both killed as the result of a common disaster. Mary Warner took charge of the partnership business and spent considerable time and effort in winding up the partnership business. In a suit brought for an accounting, Mary Warner made a claim for a reasonable allowance for services rendered in winding up the affairs of the partnership. The partnership agreement contained no provision for payment for services rendered in connection with the winding up of partnership affairs. What decision?

10. Adam, Stanley, and Rosalind formed a partnership in State X to distribute beer and wine. Their agreement provided that the partnership would continue until December 31, 1997. Which of the following events would cause the ABC partnership to dissolve? If so, when would the partnership be dissolved?

(a) Rosalind assigns her interest in the partnership to Mary on April 1, 1992.

(b) Stanley dies on June 1, 1997.

(c) Adam withdraws from the partnership on September 15, 1996.

(d) A creditor of Stanley obtains a charging order against Stanley's interest on October 9, 1994.

(e) In 1995 the legislature of State X enacts a statute making the sale or distribution of alcoholic beverages illegal.

(f) Stanley has a formal accounting of partnership affairs on September 19, 1993.

11. Stark, Henning & Co., a partnership formed by Stark and Henning for the purpose of acting as sales representatives for various firms in upstate New York, contracted with Utica Screw Product,

Inc., on June 19, 1975, to act as its sales representative for most of New York State. On October 22, 1976, Stark sent a letter to Henning terminating the partnership. A copy of this letter was also sent to the president of Utica. When Utica refused to pay commissions owed to the partnership for orders the partnership had obtained for Utica between February 10, 1976, and October 20, 1976, Stark brought this action on behalf of the partnership to recover the commissions due. Utica contended that Stark had no standing to sue because he had not received authority from his partner, Henning, to institute this action. Decision?

12. In 1946, Donald Petersen joined his father, William Petersen, in a chicken hatchery business William had previously operated as a sole proprietorship. When the partnership was formed, William contributed the assets of the proprietorship, which included cash, equipment, and inventory having a total value of $41,000. Donald contributed nothing. From 1946 until Donald's death in 1964, Donald took over the operation of the hatchery. This suit was brought on behalf of Donald's estate when William refused to distribute any of the partnership assets to the estate. William contended that the total value of the partnership property at the time of Donald's death was $18,572. He claimed the full amount on the theory that he was entitled to the return of his capital investment of $41,000 before Donald's estate could recover anything. Decision?

Chapter 33

LIMITED PARTNERSHIPS

Formation of Limited Partnerships
Rights and Duties of Partners
Dissolution of Limited Partnerships
Other Unincorporated Business Associations

THIS chapter will consider limited partnerships and other types of unincorporated business associations. These forms of organizations have developed to meet special business and investment needs. Each has its own set of characteristics that make it appropriate for certain purposes.

LIMITED PARTNERSHIPS

The limited partnership has proved itself to be an attractive vehicle for a variety of investments because of its tax advantages and the limited liability it confers upon the limited partners. Unlike general partnerships, limited partnerships are statutory creations. Before 1976 the governing statute in all States except Louisiana was the Uniform Limited Partnership Act (ULPA), which was promulgated in 1916. At that time most limited partnerships were small and had only a few limited partners. Today many limited partnerships are much larger, typically involving a small number of major investors and a relatively large group of widely distributed investors who purchase limited partnership interests. This type of limited partnership has evolved to attract substantial amounts of investment capital. Limited partnerships have been used for investments in real estate, oil and gas, motion pictures, and research and development. The large scale and multistate operations of the modern limited partnership, however, have severely burdened the framework established by the ULPA.

These shortcomings prompted the National Conference of Commissioners on Uniform State Laws to develop a Revised Uniform Limited Partnership Act (RULPA), which was promulgated in 1976. According to its preface, the RULPA is "intended to modernize the prior uniform law while retaining the special character of limited partnerships as compared with corporations." More than forty States have adopted the 1976 RULPA, which appears in Appendix E of this text. In 1985 the National Conference revised the RULPA "for the purpose of more effectively modernizing, improving and establishing uniformity in the law of limited partnerships." The 1985 Act makes almost no change in the basic structure of the 1976 RULPA and is substantially similar to it. The 1985 Act does not alter the underlying philosophy or thrust of the RULPA.

This chapter will discuss the 1976 RULPA and the significant changes made by the 1985 Act. Appendix F of this text contains those provisions of the 1985 Act cited in this book. The ULPA, RULPA, and the 1985 Act are supplemented by the Uniform Partnership Act, which applies to limited partnerships in any case not provided for in the Limited Partnership Act. For a concise comparison of general and limited partnerships, see Figure 34–1 in Chapter 34.

In addition, limited partnership interests are almost always considered to be securities, and their sale is therefore subject to State and Federal regulation as discussed in Chapter 45.

Definition

A **limited partnership** is a partnership formed by two or more persons under the laws of a State and having one or more general partners and one or more limited partners. Section 101(7). A *person* includes a natural person, partnership, limited partnership, trust, estate, association, or corporation. Section 101(11). It differs from a general partnership in several respects, three of which are fundamental:

1. there must be a statute in effect providing for the formation of limited partnerships;

2. the limited partnership must substantially comply with the requirements of that statute; and

3. the **liability** of a *limited* partner for partnership debts or obligations is **limited** to the extent of the capital he has contributed or agreed to contribute.

Formation

Although the formation of a *general* partnership may be accomplished without special procedures, the formation of a *limited* partnership requires substantial compliance with the limited partnership statute. Failure to do so may result in the limited partners' *not* obtaining limited liability.

Filing of Certificate Section 201 of the RULPA provides that two or more persons desiring to form a limited partnership shall file in the office of the Secretary of State of the State in which the limited partnership has its principal office a signed certificate of limited partnership. The certificate must include the following information:

1. the name of the limited partnership;

2. the general character of its business;

3. the address of the office and the name and address of the agent for service of process;

4. the name and the business address of each partner, listing general partners and limited partners separately;

5. the amount of cash and a description and statement of the value of the other property or services contributed by each partner;

6. the times at which, or events on the happening of which, additional contributions are to be made by each partner;

7. any power of a limited partner to make an assignee of his partnership interest a limited partner;

8. the events permitting a partner to withdraw from the partnership;

9. the rights of partners to receive distributions of limited partnership property;

10. the rights of partners to receive a return of their capital contributions; and

11. the time or events upon which the limited partnership is to be dissolved.

Figure 33–1 shows a sample certificate of limited partnership.

The certificate of limited partnership must be amended if a new partner is admitted, a partner withdraws, or the capital contribution of any partner is changed as to amount or character. Section 202. In addition, the certificate may be amended at any time for any other proper purpose as determined by the general partners.

The 1985 Act requires the certificate to include far fewer items. It need only provide the

Figure 33–1 Sample Limited Partnership Certificate

CERTIFICATE OF LIMITED PARTNERSHIP

The undersigned, desiring to form a Limited Partnership under the Limited Partnership Act of the State of _____, make this certificate for that purpose.

§ 1. **Name.** The name of the Limited Partnership shall be "_____."

§ 2. **Purpose.** The business of the Limited Partnership shall be to [*describe*].

§ 3. **Location.** The location of the Limited Partnership's principal place of business is _____ County, _____.

§ 3A. **Agent for Service of Process.** The agent for service of process on the Limited Partnership in the State of _____ shall be _____, whose business address is _____.

§ 4. **Members and Designation.** The names and business addresses of the members, and their designation as General or Limited Partners, are

_____	[*Address*]	General Partner
_____	[*Address*]	General Partner
_____	[*Address*]	Limited Partner
_____	[*Address*]	Limited Partner

§ 5. **Term.** The term for which the Limited Partnership is to exist is indefinite.

§ 6. **Initial Contributions of Partners.** The amount of cash and a description and statement of the agreed value of the other property or services contributed by each Partner are

[*Name*]	[*Describe*]
[*Name*]	[*Describe*]
[*Name*]	[*Describe*]
[*Name*]	[*Describe*]

§ 7. **Subsequent Contributions of Partners.** Each Partner may (but shall not be obliged to) make additional contributions to the capital of the Limited Partnership as follows:

§ 8. **Profit Shares of Partners.** The share of the profits which each Partner shall receive by reason of his contribution is

[*Name*]	_____%
[*Name*]	_____%
[*Name*]	_____%
[*Name*]	_____%

Signed _____, 19_____

_____

_____

_____

_____

name of the limited partnership, the address of its office, the name and address of the agent for service of process, the name and business address of each general partner, and the latest date upon which the limited partnership is to dissolve. Limited partners need not be named and need not sign the certificate. These changes reflect a policy underlying the 1985 Act that the partnership agreement, not the certificate of limited partnership, should be the comprehensive document for limited partnerships.

Name The inclusion of the surname of a limited partner in the partnership name is prohibited unless it is also the surname of a general partner or unless the business had been carried on under that name before the admission of that limited partner. A limited partner who knowingly permits his name to be used in violation of this provision is liable to any creditor who did not know that he was a limited partner. Section 303(d). In addition, a limited partnership cannot use a name that is deceptively similar to any corporation or other limited partnership. Section 102. Finally, the name of the limited partnership must contain, without abbreviation, the words "limited partnership."

Contributions The contribution of a partner may be cash, property, services rendered, a promissory note, or an obligation to contribute cash, property, or to perform services. Section 501. A partner is liable to the partnership for the difference between the contribution actually made and the amount stated in the certificate as having been made. Under the 1985 Amendments a promise by a limited partner to contribute to the limited partnership is not enforceable unless it is in a signed writing.

Defective Formation A limited partnership is formed when the certificate of limited partnership is filed if it substantially complies with the requirements of the statute. Therefore, there is a defective formation if no certificate is filed or if the certificate filed does not substantially meet the statutory

requirements. In either case, the limited liability of limited partners is jeopardized. The RULPA provides that a person who has contributed to the capital of a business (an "equity participant"), erroneously and in good faith believing that he has become a limited partner in a limited partnership, is not liable as a general partner provided that on ascertaining the mistake he either (1) withdraws from the business and renounces *future* profits, or (2) files a certificate or an amendment curing the defect. Section 304. *See In re Westover Hills Ltd.* The equity participant, however, will be liable to any third party who transacted business with the enterprise before the withdrawal or amendment and in good faith believed that the equity participant was a general partner at the time of the transaction.

The 1985 Act does not require that the limited partners be named in the certificate. This greatly reduces the risk that a limited partner would be exposed to liability because of an inadvertent omission of that information from the certificate.

Foreign Limited Partnerships A limited partnership is considered "foreign" in any State in which it has not been formed. The laws of the State under which a foreign limited partnership is organized govern its organization, its internal affairs, and the liability of its limited partners. Section 901. At the same time, the RULPA requires all foreign limited partnerships to register with the Secretary of State before transacting any business in the State. Section 902. Any foreign limited partnership transacting business without so registering may not bring enforcement actions in the State's courts until it registers, although it may defend itself in the State's courts. Section 907.

Rights

Because limited partnerships are organized pursuant to statute, the rights of the parties are usually set forth in the articles of limited partnership. Unless otherwise agreed or provided in the act, a general partner of a limited partnership has all the rights and powers of a partner in a partnership without limited partners. Section 403. A general partner may also be a limited partner and thereby also share in profits, losses, and distributions as a limited partner. Section 404.

Control The general partners of a limited partnership have almost exclusive control and management of the limited partnership. A limited partner, on the other hand, cannot share in the management or control of the association; if he does so, he forfeits his limited liability. *See Alzado v. Blinder, Robinson & Co., Inc.* If the limited partner's participation in control *is* substantially the same as the exercise of the powers of a general partner, then the limited partner assumes the liability of a general partner to *all* third parties who transact business with the partnership. If, however, the limited partner's participation in control of the business is *not* substantially the same as the exercise of the powers of a general partner, he is liable as a general partner for the obligations of the limited partnership *only* to those persons who transact business with the limited partnership *with actual knowledge* of his participation in control. Section 303(a). This approach recognizes the difficulty of determining when the control line has been overstepped and that the purpose of imposing general partner's liability is the protection of creditor's expectations.

The 1985 Act has eliminated the broader liability of a limited partner whose participation is substantially the same as a general partner. Under the 1985 Act, a limited partner who participates in the control of the business is liable only to those persons who transact business with the limited partnership reasonably believing, based upon the limited partner's conduct, that the limited partner is a general partner.

In addition, Section 303(b) of the RULPA provides a "safe harbor" by enumerating certain activities, any or all of which a limited partner may carry on without being deemed to have taken part in control of the business. They are the following:

1. being a contractor for or an agent or employee of the limited partnership or of a general partner;

2. consulting with and advising a general partner with respect to the business of the limited partnership;

3. acting as surety for the limited partnership;

4. approving or disapproving an amendment to the partnership agreement; and

5. voting on one or more of the following matters:

    a. the dissolution and winding up of the partnership;

    b. the sale, exchange, lease, mortgage, pledge, or other transfer of all or substantially all of the assets of the limited partnership other than in the ordinary course of its business;

    c. the incurrence of indebtedness by the limited partnership other than in the ordinary course of its business;

    d. a change in the nature of the business; or

    e. the removal of a general partner.

This listing is nonexclusive: there may be other permissible powers for a limited partner to exercise. The 1985 Amendments have expanded the safe harbor list by adding the following:

1. winding up the partnership;

2. exercising any right or power granted by the act;

3. voting on an amendment to the partnership agreement or certificate;

4. voting on the admission of a general partner;

5. voting on the admission or removal of a limited partner;

6. voting on any matter relating to the business of the limited partnership that the partnership agreement makes subject to the approval or disapproval of the limited partners; or

7. being an officer, director, or shareholder of a general partner that is a corporation.

Choice of Associates   No person may be added as a general partner or a limited partner without the consent of **all** partners. After the formation of a limited partnership, the admission of additional limited partners requires the written consent of all partners unless the partnership agreement provides otherwise. Section 301. The admission of the new limited partner is not effective until the certificate of limited partnership has been amended to reflect that fact. After the formation of a limited partnership, new general partners may be admitted *only* with the specific written consent of *all* partners. Section 401.

The 1985 Act provides that the written partnership agreement determines the procedure for authorizing the admission of additional general partners. The written consent of all partners is required only if the partnership agreement fails to deal with this issue.

Withdrawal   A general partner may withdraw from a limited partnership at any time by giving written notice to the other partners. Section 602. If the withdrawal violates the partnership agreement, the limited partnership may recover damages from the withdrawing general partner. A limited partner may withdraw as provided in the limited partnership certificate or, under the 1985 Act, the written partnership agreement. If the certificate (or written partnership agreement under the 1985 Act) does not specify when a limited partner may withdraw, she may do so upon giving at least six months' prior written notice to each general partner. Section 603. Upon withdrawal, a withdrawing partner is entitled to receive any distribution to which she is entitled under the partnership agreement, subject to the restrictions discussed below on the amount of distributions. If the partnership agreement makes no provision, the partner is entitled to receive the fair value of her interest in the limited partnership as of the date of withdrawal based upon her right to

share in distributions from the limited partnership. Section 604.

Assignment of Partnership Interest   A partnership interest is a partner's share of the profits and losses of a limited partnership and the right to receive distributions of partnership assets. A partnership interest is personal property. Section 701. Unless otherwise provided in the partnership agreement, a partner may assign his partnership interest. An assignment does not dissolve the limited partnership. The assignee does not become a partner and may not exercise any rights of a partner. The assignment only entitles the assignee to receive, to the extent of the assignment, the assigning partner's share of distributions. Except as otherwise provided in the partnership agreement, a partner ceases to be a partner upon assignment of all his partnership interest. Section 702.

An assignee of a partnership interest, including an assignee of a general partner, may become a *limited* partner if all the other partners consent, or if the assigning partner, having such power provided in the certificate (or in the partnership agreement under the 1985 Amendments), grants the assignee this right. Section 704. An assignee who becomes a limited partner is liable for the obligation of his assignor to make or return contributions except for those liabilities unknown to the assignee at the time he became a limited partner. Section 704(b). Upon the death of a partner, her executor or administrator has all the rights of the partner for the purpose of settling her estate, including any power the deceased partner had to make her assignee a substituted limited partner. Section 705.

Profit and Loss Sharing   The profits and losses are allocated among the partners as provided in the partnership agreement. If the partnership agreement does not make such a provision, then the profits and losses are allocated on the basis of the value of contributions actually made by each partner. Section 503. Nonetheless, limited partners are usually not liable for losses beyond their capital contribution. Section 303(a). The 1985 Act requires the agreement sharing profits and losses to be in writing.

Distributions The partners share distributions of cash or other assets of a limited partnership as provided in the partnership agreement. (The 1985 Act requires such agreement to be written.) The RULPA allows partners to share in distributions in a different proportion than they share in profits. If the partnership agreement does not allocate distributions, then distributions are made on the basis of the value of contributions actually made by each partner. Section 504. Unless otherwise provided, a partner has no right to demand a distribution in any form other than cash. Once a partner becomes entitled to a distribution, he has the status of a creditor with respect to that distribution. Section 606. A partner may not receive a distribution from a limited partnership unless there are sufficient assets after the distribution to pay all liabilities of the partnership other than liabilities to partners on account of their partnership interests. Section 607.

Loans Both general and limited partners may be secured or unsecured creditors of the partnership with the same rights as a person who is not a partner, subject to applicable State and Federal bankruptcy and fraudulent conveyance statutes. Section 107.

Information The partnership must continuously maintain within the State an office at which basic organizational and financial records are kept. Section 105. Each limited partner has the right to inspect and copy any of the partnership records. She also may obtain from the general partners upon reasonable demand (1) complete and accurate information regarding the business and financial condition of the limited partnership, (2) a copy of the limited partnership's Federal, State, and local income tax return for each year, and (3) any other reasonable information regarding the affairs of the limited partnership. Section 305.

Derivative Actions A limited partner has the right to bring an action on behalf of a limited partnership to recover a judgment in its favor if the general partners having authority to do so have refused to bring the action. Section 1001. The act also establishes standing and pleading requirements similar to those imposed in shareholder's derivative actions, as well as permitting the court to award reasonable expenses, including attorney's fees, to a successful plaintiff. Section 1002.

Duties and Liabilities

The duties and liabilities of general partners in a limited partnership are quite different from those of a limited partner. A general partner is subject to all the duties and restrictions of a partner in a partnership without limited partners, whereas a limited partner is subject to few, if any, duties and enjoys limited liability.

Duties A *general partner* of a limited partnership has a **fiduciary** relationship to her general and limited partners. This fiduciary duty imposed upon the general partner has extreme importance to the limited partners because of the circumscribed role that a limited partner may play in the control and management of the business enterprise. Conversely, it remains unclear whether a limited partner stands in a fiduciary relationship to his general partners or the limited partnership. Very limited judicial authority on this question exists, but it seems to point towards not placing such a duty on the limited partner.

The RULPA does not distinguish between the duty of care owed by a general partner to a general partnership and that owed by a general partner to a limited partnership. Thus, a general partner owes her partners a duty not to be culpably negligent, as discussed in Chapter 31. Some courts, however, have imposed upon general partners a higher duty of care towards *limited partners*. See *Wyler v. Feuer*. On the other hand, a limited partner owes no duty of care to a limited partnership as long as she remains a limited partner.

Liabilities   One of the most appealing features of a limited partnership is the limited personal liability it offers to limited partners. **Limited liability** means that once a limited partner has paid her contribution she has no further liability to the limited partnership or its creditors. Thus, if a limited partner buys a 25 percent share of a limited partnership for $50,000 and does not forfeit her limited liability, her liability is limited to the $50,000 contributed even if the limited partnership suffers losses of $500,000. This protection is subject to three conditions discussed earlier:

1. that there is substantial compliance in good faith with the requirement that a certificate of limited partnership be filed;

2. that the surname of the limited partner does not appear in the partnership name; and

3. that the limited partner does not take part in control of the business.

In addition, if the certificate contains a false statement, anyone who suffers loss by reliance on that statement may hold liable any party to the certificate who knew the statement to be false when the certificate was executed. Section 207. As long as the limited partner abides by these conditions, his liability for any and all obligations of the partnership is limited to his capital contribution.

At the same time, the general partners of a limited partnership have unlimited external liability. Also, any general partner who knew or *should have known* that the limited partnership certificate contained a false statement is liable to anyone who suffers loss by reliance on that false statement. Moreover, a general partner is liable if he knows or should know that a statement in the certificate has *become* false and he has not amended the certificate within a reasonable time.

Any partner who has received the return of any part of her contribution *without* violation of the partnership agreement or of the limited partnership act is liable for one year to the limited partnership, to the extent necessary to pay creditors who extended credit during the period the partnership held the contribution. Section 608. If a partner has received the return of any part of her contribution *in violation* of the partnership agreement or the limited partnership act, she is liable to the limited partnership for a period of six years for the amount of the contribution wrongfully returned.

See Figure 33–2 for a comparison of general and limited partners.

Dissolution

As with a general partnership, there are three steps involved in the extinguishment of a limited partnership: (1) dissolution, (2) winding up or liquidation, and (3) termina-

---

Figure 33–2 Comparison of General and Limited Partners

	General Partner	Limited Partner
Control	Has all the rights and powers of a partner in a partnership without limited partners	Has no right to take part in management or control
Liability	Unlimited	Limited, unless takes part in control or name used
Agency	Is an agent of the partnership	Is not an agent of the partnership
Fiduciary Duty	Yes	No
Duty of Care	Yes	No

tion. The causes of dissolution and the priorities in the distribution of the assets, however, are somewhat different from those in a general partnership.

Causes In a limited partnership the limited partners do *not* have the right or the power to dissolve the partnership, except by decree of the court. The death or bankruptcy of a limited partner does *not* dissolve the partnership. Section 801 of the RULPA specifies those events that will trigger a dissolution, after which the affairs of the partnership must be liquidated:

1. the expiration of the time period, or the happening of the events specified in the certificate;

2. the unanimous written consent of all the partners;

3. the withdrawal of a general partner, unless all partners agree in writing to continue the business; or

4. a decree of judicial dissolution, which may be granted whenever it is not reasonably practicable to carry on the business in conformity with the partnership agreement.

A general partner's withdrawal includes his retirement, assignment of all his general partnership interest, removal, bankruptcy, death, and adjudication of incompetency.

A certificate of cancellation must be filed upon the dissolution and commencement of winding up of the limited partnership. Section 203.

Winding Up Unless otherwise provided in the partnership agreement, the general partners who have not wrongfully dissolved the limited partnership may wind up the limited partnership's affairs. Section 803. The limited partners may wind up the limited partnership if there are no general partners who have not wrongfully dissolved the partnership. But, any partner, his legal representative, or his assignee may obtain a winding up by court if cause is shown.

Distribution of Assets The priorities in distributing the assets of a limited partnership are set forth in Section 804:

1. to creditors, including partners who are creditors except with respect to liabilities for distributions;

2. to partners and ex-partners in satisfaction of liabilities for unpaid distributions;

3. to partners for the return of their contributions except as otherwise agreed; and

4. to partners for their partnership interests in the proportions in which they share in distributions, except as otherwise agreed.

General and limited partners rank equally unless the partnership agreement provides otherwise.

OTHER TYPES OF UNINCORPORATED BUSINESS ASSOCIATIONS

Joint Venture

A **joint venture** or joint adventure is a form of business association organized to carry out a particular business enterprise for profit. Usually, although not necessarily, it is of short duration. It is an association of persons who combine their property, money, efforts, skill, and knowledge for the purpose of carrying out a single business operation for profit. A joint venture, therefore, differs from a partnership, which is formed to carry on a business over a considerable or indefinite period of time. Except for a few differences, a joint venture is generally governed by the law of partnerships. *See Florida Tomato Packers Inc. v. Wilson.* An example of a joint venture is a securities underwriting syndicate or a syndicate formed to acquire a certain tract of land for subdivision and resale. Other common examples include joint research conducted by corporations, exploitation of mineral rights, and manufacturing operations in foreign countries.

Joint Stock Company

A **joint stock company,** or joint stock association as it is sometimes called, is a form of business association that has some of the characteristics of a corporation and some of the characteristics of a partnership. It is similar to a corporation in that

1. its capital is divided into shares represented by certificates which are transferable;

2. its business and affairs are managed by directors or managers elected by the members, who alone have the authority to represent and bind it;

3. its members are not its agents; and

4. a transfer of shares by a member or his death, insanity, or other incapacity does not dissolve it or afford a ground for dissolution.

It is similar to a partnership but unlike a corporation in that it is formed by contract and not by State authority, and its members generally are personally liable for its debts.

Mining Partnerships

A **mining partnership** is an association of the several owners of the mineral rights in land for the purpose of operating a mine and extracting minerals of economic value for their mutual profit. Although mining partnerships are governed to a considerable extent by the law of general partnerships, there are certain important differences between them. For example, a mining partner has the right to sell his interest in the partnership, the death of a partner does not dissolve a mining partnership, and the members have limited power to bind other members of the partnership.

Limited Partnership Associations

Limited partnership associations are permitted by statute in a few States. This type of organization is a legal hybrid. Although called a partnership association, it closely resembles a corporation. It is a legal entity separate and distinct from its members who are not personally responsible for its debts, their liabilities being limited to their capital contribution, except in the event of violation of some statutory provision. Moreover, un-

like a limited partnership, its members may participate in the management of the business without forfeiting limited liability. An important difference between this kind of association and a corporation pertains to the transfer of shares. Although the shares in a limited partnership association are freely transferable, the transferee does not become a member in the association unless so elected by the other members. If membership is refused, he may recover the value of his shares from the association.

Business Trusts

A trust is a transfer of the legal title to certain specific property to one person for the use and benefit of another. Where an express trust results from contract, the agreement is commonly known as a declaration of trust. It customarily sets forth a designation of the property or trust *res,* the duration of the trust, the exact functions and duties of the trustees concerning the management of the property, the persons to whom the income of the trust is to be paid and the share to be received by each, the method of winding up the trust, and the person or persons entitled to share in the trust property upon termination. See Chapter 52 for a discussion of trusts.

Although trusts are almost as old as the law of equity itself, it was not until late in the nineteenth century that the trust concept was used as a method of conducting a commercial enterprise. The business trust, sometimes called a Massachusetts trust, was devised to avoid the burdens of corporate regulation and particularly the formerly widespread prohibition denying to corporations the power to own and deal in real estate. Like an ordinary trust between natural persons, a business trust may be created by a voluntary agreement without any authorization or consent of the State.

A **business trust** has three distinguishing characteristics: (1) the trust estate is devoted to the conduct of a business; (2) by the terms of the agreement each beneficiary is entitled to a certificate evidencing his ownership of a beneficial interest in the trust which he is free to sell or otherwise transfer; and (3) the trustees must have the exclusive right to manage and control the business free from control of the beneficiaries. If the third condition is not met, the trust may fail, and the beneficiaries would then become personally liable for the obligations of the business as partners.

The trustees are personally liable for the debts of the business unless, in entering into contractual relations with others, it is expressly stated or definitely understood between the parties that the obligation is incurred solely upon the responsibility of the trust estate. In order to escape personal liability on the contractual obligations of the business, the trustee must obtain the agreement or consent of the other contracting party to look solely to the assets of the trust. The personal liability of the trustees for their own torts or the torts of their agents and servants employed in the operation of the business stands on a different footing. While this liability cannot be avoided, the risk involved may be reduced substantially or eliminated altogether by insurance. In most jurisdictions, the beneficiaries of a business trust have no liability for obligations of the business trust.

CASES

Defective Formation

IN RE WESTOVER HILLS LTD.

United States Bankruptcy Court, District of Wyoming, 1985.
46 B.R. 300.

MAI, BKRTCY. J.

[In separate Chapter 11 cases involving the same debtor, one commenced by voluntary petition and the other by involuntary petition, questions arose as to the eligibility of the debtor for relief and as to which of the cases should be maintained. In order to resolve these questions it was necessary to decide whether under State law a limited partnership had been formed.]

Findings of Fact

1. Dale Fullerton was a member of the joint venture, WYORCO. He is also the sole stockholder in Westover Hills Management and is a stockholder in and Chairman of the Board of Envirosearch.

2. On March 17, 1981, in Oregon, Dale Fullerton met with James Anderson, president of AGFC, and James Twedt, the managing joint member of WYORCO. The purpose of the meeting was to discuss the sale of the undeveloped or non-Phase 1 portion of the Westover Hills Subdivision. Anderson and Fullerton agreed to form an organization to purchase the property from WYORCO.

3. On March 18, 1981, Anderson, his attorney Paul Ohallaren, Fullerton, his attorney Michael Was, and all but one of the members of WYORCO met in Denver to arrange the sale. At this March 18 meeting, Anderson and Fullerton agreed, on behalf of their respective companies, to form a limited partnership to purchase the property from WYORCO.

4. The intent of, and the agreement between, the parties was to form a limited partnership with Westover Hills Management as the sole general partner and with Envirosearch and AGFC as limited partners.

5. Anderson, on behalf of AGFC, and Fullerton, on behalf of Westover Hills Management and Envirosearch, executed a certificate of limited partnership. This certificate was filed with the Wyoming Secretary of State on October 16, 1981. This certificate lists the three companies, Envirosearch, Westover Hills Management, and AGFC, as both general and limited partners.

6. Subsequent to the original filing, the parties became aware that the original certificate

as filed did not reflect their intent to form a limited partnership with Envirosearch and AGFC as limited partners only.

7. On May 5, 1984, an amended certificate of limited partnership, executed by James Anderson on behalf of AGFC, and Dale Fullerton on behalf of Westover Hills Management and Envirosearch, was filed with the Wyoming Secretary of State. This amended certificate correctly reflected the intent of the parties to form a limited partnership. It listed Westover Hills Management as the sole general partner and listed Envirosearch and AGFC as limited partners.

8. On February 12, 1984, AGFC assigned all of its right, title, and interest as a limited partner in Westover Hills, Limited to its subsidiary, AGLIC. The assignment purports to be effective as of April 20, 1983.

Discussion

The question of existence of a limited partnership is to be determined by state law. [Citation.]

In 1979, Wyoming adopted the Revised Uniform Limited Partnership Act. [Citation.]

The revised Act has in common with its predecessor, the Uniform Limited Partnership Act, the fundamental assumption that the limited partners are not general partners who secure limited liability by simply filing a certificate. The official comment to Section 1 of the Uniform Limited Partnership Act states this basic assumption.

"(t)he person who contributes the capital, though in accordance with custom called a limited partner, is not in any sense a partner. He is, however, a member of the association."

The official comment further states,

"The limited partner not being in any sense a principal in the business, failure to comply with the requirements of the act in respect to the certificate, while it may result in the nonformation of the association, does not make him a partner or liable as such. The exact nature of his liability in such cases is set forth in Sec. 11."

Thus, if the parties intend to form a limited partnership, the failure to comply with the Wyoming Limited Partnership Act would not, as petitioners argue, result in the formation of a general partnership. Rather, under the theory of the Uniform Act, such noncompliance would result only in the nonformation of the limited partnership.

It is clear that the parties at all times intended to form a limited partnership. However, the original certificate of limited partnership did not correctly reflect their intentions. In such a situation, the Revised Uniform Act provides a remedy to cure such defective compliance with the requirements for Limited Partnership. The applicable Wyoming Statute provides,

"Person Erroneously Believing Himself Limited Partner.

"(a) Except as provided in subsection (b) of this section, a person who makes a contribution to a business enterprise and erroneously but in good faith believes that he has become a limited partner in the enterprise is not a general partner in the enterprise and is not bound by its obligations by reason of making the contribution, receiving distributions from the enterprise, or exercising any rights of a limited partner, if, on ascertaining the mistake, he:

"(i) Causes an appropriate certificate of limited partnership or a certificate of amendment to be executed and filed; or

"(ii) Withdraws from future equity participation in the enterprise." [RULPA § 304.]

Thus, under Wyoming law, an intended limited partner who realizes that a limited partnership has been imperfectly formed, may take either alternative provided in subsection (a) to insure the retention of limited partnership status.

In the present case, when AGFC realized that the certificate of limited partnership had erroneously listed them as a general, rather than as a limited, partner they caused an appropriate certificate of amendment to be executed and filed. Thus, AGFC did not lose its intended status as a limited partner, having corrected the defect in accordance with [citation]. In view of these considerations, the court concludes, without difficulty, that the debtor is a limited partnership. [Citations.]

In deciding that the debtor is a limited partnership for purposes of filing a voluntary Chapter 11 case, the court does not reach the issue of whether, under Wyoming law, the individual limited partners may be liable to third parties in connection with their involvement in the debtor's business and financial affairs.

Although an intended limited partner does not become a general partner by reason of noncompliance with the Act alone, such a limited partner may, by reason of other factors, lose his limited liability and become "liable as" a general partner.

If a limited partner is found to be "liable as" a general partner to third parties, it does not change the fundamental relations of the partners inter se. It is the status of the partners inter se and not their potential liability to third parties that determines the existence of a general partnership or a limited partnership, for the purposes of determining eligibility of relief under the Bankruptcy Code. [Citations.]

[Westover Hills Ltd. held to be a limited partnership for purposes of bankruptcy.]

Control

ALZADO v. BLINDER, ROBINSON & CO., INC.

Supreme Court of Colorado, 1988.
752 P.2d 544.

Kirshbaum, J.

In the spring of 1979, Alzado, Alzado's former accountant, Tinter, and Alzado's former agent, Ronald Kauffman (Kauffman), formed Combat Promotions, Inc. to promote an eight-round exhibition boxing match in Denver, Colorado, between Alzado and Ali. Alzado, Tinter and Kauffman were the directors and sole shareholders of the corporation. Ali had agreed to engage in the match on the condition that prior to the event his attorneys would receive an irrevocable letter of credit guaranteeing payment of $250,000 to Ali.

Combat Promotions, Inc. initially encountered difficulties in obtaining the letter of credit. Ultimately, however, Meyer Blinder (Blinder), President of Blinder-Robinson, expressed an interest in the event. Blinder anticipated that his company's participation would result in a positive public relations image for its recently opened Denver office. Blinder-Robinson ultimately agreed to provide the $250,000 letter of credit.

Blinder-Robinson insisted on several conditions to protect its investment. It required the formation of a limited partnership with specific provisions governing repayment to Blinder-Robinson of any sums drawn against the letter of credit. It also required Alzado's personal secured guarantee to reimburse Blinder-Robinson for any losses it might suffer. Alzado and Combat Promotions, Inc. accepted these conditions.

On June 25, 1979, an agreement was executed by Combat Promotions, Inc. and Blinder-Robinson creating a limited partnership, Combat Associates. Under the terms of the agreement, Combat Promotions, Inc. was the general partner and Blinder-Robinson was the sole limited partner. Blinder-Robinson contributed a $250,000 letter of credit to Combat Associates, and the partnership agreement provided expressly that the letter of credit was to be paid off as a partnership expense.

On the same day, June 25, 1979, Alzado executed a separate guaranty agreement with Blinder-Robinson. This agreement provided that if Ali drew the letter of credit, Alzado personally would reimburse Blinder-Robinson for any amount Blinder-Robinson was unable to recover from Combat Associates under the terms of the limited partnership agreement. As security for his agreement, Alzado placed a general warranty deed to his residence, an assignment of an investment account and a confession of judgment in escrow for the benefit of Blinder-Robinson. Thereafter, a separate agreement was apparently executed by Alzado and Combat Associates providing that Alzado would receive $100,000 in compensation for the exhibition match but subordinating any payment of that sum to the payment of expenses of the match, including, if drawn, the letter of credit.

Approximately one week before the date of the match, Alzado announced that he might not participate because he feared he might lose the assets he had pledged as security for the guaranty agreement. Alzado informed Blinder of this concern, and the two met the next day in Blinder-Robinson's Denver office. Tinter, Kauffman and Ali's representative, Greg Campbell, were also present. Subsequently, on July 14, 1979, the event occurred as scheduled.

Few tickets were sold, and the match proved to be a financial debacle. Ali drew the letter of credit and collected the $250,000 to which he was entitled. Combat Associates paid Blinder-Robinson only $65,000; it did not pay anything to Alzado or, apparently, to other creditors.

In January of 1980, Blinder-Robinson filed this civil action seeking $185,000 in damages plus costs and attorney fees from Alzado pursuant to the terms of the June 25, 1979, guaranty agreement. Alzado denied any liability to Blinder-Robinson and * * * also filed two counterclaims against Blinder-Robinson. The first alleged that because of its conduct Blinder-Robinson must be deemed a general partner of Combat Associates and, therefore, liable to Alzado under the agreement between Alzado and the partnership for Alzado's participation in the match. * * * [The jury returned a verdict of $92,500 in favor of Alzado on this counterclaim. The court of appeals reversed.]

* * *

Alzado next contends that the Court of Appeals erred in concluding that Blinder-Robinson's conduct in promoting the match did not constitute sufficient control of Combat Associates to justify the conclusion that the company must be deemed a general rather than a limited partner. We disagree.

A limited partner may become liable to partnership creditors as a general partner if the limited partner assumes control of partnership business. [Citations]; see also [RULPA] § 303, which provides that a lim-

ited partner does not participate in the control of partnership business solely by doing one or more of the following:

(a) Being a contractor for or an agent or employee of the limited partnership or of a general partner;

(b) Being an officer, director, or shareholder of a corporate general partner;

(c) Consulting with and advising a general partner with respect to the business of the limited partnership;

(d) Acting as surety for the limited partnership or guaranteeing or assuming one or more specific obligations of the limited partnership or providing collateral for an obligation of the limited partnership;

(e) Bringing an action in the right of a limited partnership to recover a judgment in its favor pursuant to part 10 of this article;

(f) Calling, requesting, or participating in a meeting of the partners;

(g) Proposing or approving or disapproving, by voting or otherwise, one or more of the following matters:

(I) The dissolution and winding up or continuation of the limited partnership;

(II) The sale, exchange, lease, mortgage, pledge, or other transfer of any assets of the limited partnership;

(III) The incurrence of indebtedness by the limited partnership;

(IV) A change in the nature of the business;

(V) The admission or removal of a partner;

(VI) A transaction or other matter involving an actual or potential conflict of interest;

(VII) An amendment to the partnership agreement or certificate of limited partnership; or

(VIII) Such other matters as are stated in writing in the partnership agreement;

(h) Winding up the limited partnership; or

(i) Exercising any right or power permitted to limited partners under this article and not specifically enumerated in this subsection (2).

Early determinations regarding whether a limited partner's conduct constituted control of partnership business were largely fact-specific and did not attempt to state general standards for determining what acts evidence such control. [Citation.] More recent decisions construing section 7 of the Uniform Limited Partnership Act [predecessor to Section 303 of the RULPA] have also failed to provide definitive interpretations of what constitutes "control." [Citation.] One commentator has attributed this lack of definitive interpretation to the limited amount of litigation in this area and the tendency of courts to deal with section 7 control issues on an *ad hoc* basis. [Citation.] Any determination of whether a limited partner's conduct amounts to control over the business affairs of the partnership must be determined by consideration of several factors, including the purpose of the partnership, the administrative activities undertaken, the manner in which the entity actually functioned, and the nature and frequency of the limited partner's purported activities.

A judgment notwithstanding the verdict may be entered only if, when viewing the evidence in the light most favorable to the party against whom the motion is directed, reasonable persons could not reach the same conclusion as the jury. [Citations.] The record here reflects that Blinder-Robinson used its Denver office as a ticket outlet, gave two parties to promote the exhibition match and provided a meeting room for many of Combat Associates' meetings. Blinder personally appeared on a television talk show and gave television interviews to promote the match. Blinder-Robinson made no investment, accounting or other financial decisions for the partnership; all such fiscal decisions were made by officers or employees of Combat Promotions, Inc., the general partner. The evidence established at most that Blinder-Robinson engaged in a few promotional activities. It does not establish that it took part in the management or control of the business affairs of the partnership. Accordingly, we agree with the Court of Appeals that the trial court erred in denying Blinder-Robinson's motion for judgment notwithstanding the verdict with respect to Alzado's first counterclaim.

Alzado contends, in the alternative, that the actual management of the partnership's daily business activities is irrelevant to Blinder-Robinson's status for purposes of liability because Blinder-Robinson's power and authority over the partnership assets rendered it liable as a general partner. He finds this alleged unlimited authority in the expense distribution formula contained in section 4.4 of the limited partnership agreement. Alzado cites no authority, and we are aware of none, in support of the theory that provisions of a limited partnership agreement structuring expenses and establishing net profit and loss distribution formulae may themselves render a limited partner liable as a general partner for partnership debts. In theory it may be true that particular provisions of a limited partnership agreement might so circumscribe the general partners' ability to make management decisions as to constitute conclusive evidence of control by the challenged limited partner. We do not view the terms of the Combat Associates limited partnership agreement as constituting such conclusive evidence.

Alzado finally asserts that Blinder–Robinson fostered the appearance of being in control of Combat Associates, that such actions rendered Blinder-Robinson liable as a general partner and that this conduct allowed third parties to believe that Blinder-Robinson was in fact a general partner. The evidence does not support this argument. Certainly, as Vice President of Combat Promotions, Inc., the general partner of Combat Associates, Alzado had no misconception concerning the function and role of Blinder-Robinson as a limited partner only. The Court of Appeals concluded that the evidence failed to establish that Blinder-Robinson exercised control over the business affairs of Combat Associates. We agree with that conclusion.

* * *

We . . . affirm the judgment of the Court of Appeals insofar as it reverses the judgments entered at trial in favor of Alzado on his first counterclaim against Blinder-Robinson.

Duties of General Partner

WYLER v. FEUER

California Court of Appeal, Second District, Division 2, 1978.
85 Cal.App.3d 392, 149 Cal.Rptr. 626.

FLEMING, J.

Defendants Cy Feuer and Ernest Martin, associated as Feuer and Martin Productions, Inc. (FMPI), have been successful producers of Broadway musical comedies since 1948. Their first motion picture, "Cabaret," produced by Feuer in conjunction with Allied Artists and American Broadcasting Company, received eight Academy Awards in 1973. Plaintiff Wyler is president and largest shareholder of Tool Research and Engineering Corporation, a New York Stock Exchange Company based in Beverly Hills. Prior to 1972 Wyler had had no experience in the entertainment industry.

[In 1972, FMPI bought the motion picture and television rights to Simone Berteaut's best-selling books about her life with her half-sister Edith Piaf. To finance a movie based on this novel, FMPI sought a substantial private investment from Wyler. In July 1973, Wyler signed a final limited partnership agreement with FMPI. The agreement stated that Wyler would provide, interest free, 100 percent financing for the proposed $1.6 million project, in return for a certain portion of the profits, not to exceed 50 percent. In addition, FMPI would obtain $850,000 in production financing by September 30, 1973. The contract specifically provided that FMPI's failure to raise this amount by September 30, 1973, "shall not be deemed a breach of this agreement" and that Wyler's sole remedy would be a reduction in the producer's fee.]

Despite their acclaimed success in "Cabaret," defendants at the time of execution of the limited partnership agreement were experiencing difficulties in obtaining distributor commitments and knew it would be unlikely they could obtain any production financing by the September 30 deadline. Their difficulties arose from their overestimation of the attractiveness of the Piaf subject-matter, from the unknown leading actress, and from the scheduling of photography during the summer months when most Europeans go on vacation.

Filming of the motion picture began July 23 and ended October 9. By that time Wyler had advanced $1.25 million and defendants had failed to obtain any production financing. The completed cost of the picture was $1,512,000.

Early in October, Feuer met Wyler in Paris and requested an extension of the deadline for production financing to December 30, so that defendants could take advantage of distributor negotiations in process and recoup their profit percentage and their producer's fee. Wyler said he had already financed the picture and refused to extend the deadline, thereby maintaining his profit percentage at 50 percent.

[A year after its release in 1974, the motion picture proved less than an overwhelming success—costing $1.5 million with total receipts only $478,000. From the receipts, Wyler received $313,500 for his investment. FMPI had failed to obtain an amount even close to the required $850,000 for production financing. Wyler then sued Feuer, Martin, and FMPI for mismanagement of the business of the limited partnership and to recover his $1.5 million as damages.]

A limited partnership affords a vehicle for capital investment whereby the limited partner restricts his liability to the amount of his investment in return for surrender of any right to manage and control the partnership business. [Citation.] In a limited partnership the general partner manages and controls the partnership business. [Citation.] In exercising his management functions the general partner comes under a fiduciary duty of good faith and fair dealing toward other members of the partnership. [Citations.]

These characteristics—limited investor liability, delegation of authority to management, and fiduciary duty owed by management to investors—are similar to those existing in corporate investment, where it has long been the rule that directors are not liable to stockholders for mistakes made in the exercise of honest business judgment [citations], or for losses incurred in the good faith performance of their duties when they have used such care as an ordinarily prudent person would use. [Citation.] By this standard a general partner may not be held liable for mistakes made or losses incurred in the good faith exercise of reasonable business judgment.

According all due inferences to plaintiff's evidence, as we do on review of a nonsuit, we agree with the trial court that plaintiff did not produce sufficient evidence to hold defendants liable for bad business management. Plaintiff's evidence showed that the Piaf picture did not make money, was not sought after by distributors, and did not live up to its producers' expectations. The same could be said of the majority of motion pictures made since the invention of cinematography. No evidence showed that defendants' decisions and efforts failed to conform to the general duty of care demanded of an ordinarily prudent person in like position under similar circumstances. The good faith business judgment and management of a general partner need only satisfy the standard of care demanded of an ordinarily prudent person, and will not be scrutinized by the courts with the cold clarity of hindsight.

[Judgment for Feuer, Martin, and FMPI affirmed.]

Joint Venture

FLORIDA TOMATO PACKERS, INC. v. WILSON

District Court of Appeal of Florida, Third District, 1974. 296 So.2d 536.

RICHARDSON, J.

On or about September 23, 1971, an automobile owned and operated by Willie Floyd Wilson was hit by a farm vehicle owned by George E. Lytton, and driven by Arnold Campbell. The accident occurred in a rural area of Dade County at the intersection of a main highway and a publicly dedicated sand and gravel road.

* * *

Arnold Campbell was employed as a farm hand by Lytton and had been so employed for approximately two or three years. Lytton is a farmer who grows tomatoes in Dade County, Florida. The appellant, Florida Tomato Packers, Inc., is a corporation engaged in the business of packing, selling, wholesaling and distributing tomatoes.

It appears that Lytton and the appellant entered into an arrangement whereby Lytton would do the farming and the Florida Tomato Packers, Inc., would furnish funds and marketing.

The funds of over $100,000.00 supplied by the appellant were placed in a checking account under the name of L & D Farms and Paul DiMare, manager for the appellant, was the only signatory on that account. Lytton was responsible for planting the tomatoes, raising them and getting them to the appellant's warehouse. The appellant paid all of Lytton's farming bills, including for land rental, equipment rental, equipment repair, gasoline and oil, seeds and fertilizer, and all labor from the L & D Farms checking account. When the tomatoes arrived at the packing house, the appellant packed, crated, shipped and sold the crop. After deducting all expenses paid for the Lytton farm operation and the cost of the packing, shipping and selling, any profits were equally divided between Lytton and the appellant. [The Wilsons sued Florida Tomato Packers for the damages caused by the accident with Campbell. The Wilsons] contended that the aforementioned operation was either a partnership or a joint venture between Lytton [whereas the appellant] claims that it was really only a loan and that the appellant had absolutely no control or direction over Lytton's farm operations.

A partnership is usually defined as a voluntary contractual relationship between two or more competent persons to place their money, effects, labor and/or skill in lawful commerce or business, with the understanding that there shall be a communion of profits between them. [Citation.]

A joint venture, although a less formal relationship, partakes of many of the characteristics of a partnership. A joint venture has been defined as a special combination of two or more persons, who, in some specific venture, seek a profit jointly without the existence between them of any actual partnership, corporation, or other business entity. It is an association of persons or legal entities to carry out a single business enterprise for profit. [Citations.] Corporations may be members of a joint venture. [Citations.]

It has been held that as between the parties the existence of a contract is essential to the creation of the relationship of joint venturers. However, it is well established that the contract need not be express or embodied in a formal written agreement specifically defining the rights and duties of the parties. The existence of such a contract—and hence a joint venture—may be implied or inferred from the conduct of the parties or from acts and circumstances which in fact make it appear that they are participants in a joint venture. The courts of Florida have not hesitated to imply the existence of a contract. [Citations.] The Florida courts have held that to create a joint venture relationship, there must be concurrence of the following elements: (1) a community of interest in the performance of the common purpose; (2) joint control or right of control; (3) a joint proprietary interest in the subject matter; (4) a right to share in the profits; and (5) a duty to share in any losses which may be sustained. [Citations.]

In Florida a duty to share in losses actually and impliedly exists as a matter of law in a situation where one party supplies the labor, experience and skill, and the other the necessary capital since in the event of a loss, the party supplying the know-how would have exercised his skill in vain and the party supplying the capital investment would have suffered a diminishment thereof. [Citation.]

Participants in a joint venture are each liable for the torts of the other or of the servants of the joint undertaking committed within the course and scope of the undertaking, without regard to which of the joint venturers actually employed the servant. [Citations.]

This court finds the record contains more than ample evidence to provide the legal predicate for the jury finding that a partnership and/or joint venture relationship existed between George F. Lytton and Florida Tomato Packers, Inc.

[Judgment for the Wilsons affirmed.]

QUESTIONS

1. Distinguish between a general partnership and a limited partnership.

2. Discuss the consequences of defective formation of a limited partnership.

3. Identify those activities in which a limited partner may engage without forfeiting limited liability.

4. Explain the order in which the assets of a limited partnership are distributed to creditors, limited partners, and general partners.

5. Distinguish among (a) joint ventures, (b) joint stock companies, (c) mining partnerships, (d) limited partnership associations, and (e) business trusts.

PROBLEMS

1. John Palmer and Henry Morrison formed the partnership of Palmer & Morrison for the management of the Huntington Hotel and filed an appropriate certificate in compliance with the limited partnership statute. The partnership agreement provided that Palmer would contribute $40,000 and be a general partner and Morrison would contribute $30,000 and be a limited partner. Palmer was to manage the dining and cocktail rooms, and Morrison was to manage the rest of the hotel. Nanette, a popular French singer, who knew nothing of the partnership affairs, appeared for four weeks in the Blue Room at the hotel and was not paid her fee of $8,000. Subsequently, Palmer and Morrison had a difference of opinion, and Palmer bought Morrison's interest in the partnership for $20,000. Palmer later went into bankruptcy. Nanette sued Morrison for $8,000. For how much, if anything, is Morrison liable?

2. A limited partnership was formed consisting of Webster as the general partner and Stevens and Stewart as the limited partners. The limited partnership was organized in strict compliance with the limited partnership statute. Stevens was employed by the partnership as a purchasing agent. Stewart personally guaranteed a loan made to the partnership. Both Stevens and Stewart consulted with Webster with respect to partnership business, voted on a change in the nature of the partnership business, and disapproved an amendment to the partnership agreement proposed by Webster. The partnership experienced serious financial difficulties and its creditors seek to hold Webster, Stevens, and Stewart personally liable for the debts of the partnership. Decision?

3. Fox, Dodge, and Gilbey agreed to become limited partners in Palatine Ventures, a limited partnership. The certificate of limited partnership stated that each would contribute $20,000. Fox's contribution consisted entirely of cash; Dodge contributed $12,000 in cash and gave the partnership her promissory note for $8,000; and Gilbey's contribution was his promise to perform 500 hours of legal services for the partnership. What liability, if any, do Fox, Dodge, and Gilbey have to the partnership by way of capital contribution?

4. Madison and Tilson agree to form a limited partnership with Madison as general partner and

Tilson as the limited partner, each to contribute $12,500 as capital. No papers are ever filed, and after ten months the enterprise fails with liabilities exceeding assets by $30,000. Creditors of the partnership seek to hold Madison and Tilson personally liable for the $30,000. Decision?

5. Kraft is a limited partner of Johnson Enterprises, a limited partnership. As provided in the limited partnership agreement, Kraft decided to leave the partnership and demanded that her capital contribution of $20,000 be returned. At this time, the partnership assets were $150,000 and liabilities to all creditors totaled $140,000. The partnership returned to Kraft her capital contribution of $20,000. What liability, if any, does Kraft have to the creditors of Johnson Enterprises?

6. Gordon is the only limited partner in a limited partnership whose general partners are Daniels and McKenna. Gordon contributed $10,000 for his limited partnership interest and loaned the partnership $7,500. Daniels and McKenna each contributed $5,000 by way of capital. After a year, the partnership is dissolved, at which time it owes $12,500 to its only creditor, Dickel, and has assets of $30,000. How should these assets be distributed?

7. A limited partner has which of the following rights or powers: (a) to assign his interest in the limited partnership, (b) to receive repayment of loans made to the partnership on a *pro rata* basis with general creditors, (c) to manage the affairs of the limited partnership, (d) to receive his share of the profits before the general partners receive their shares of the profits, (e) to dissolve the partnership upon his withdrawing from the partnership.

8. In January, Dr. Vidricksen contributed $25,000 to become a limited partner in a Chevrolet car agency business with Thom, the general partner. Articles of limited partnership were drawn up, but no effort was made to comply with the State's statutory requirement of recording the certificate of limited partnership. In March Vidricksen learned that he may not have formed a limited partnership because of the failure to file. At this time, the business developed financial difficulties and went into bankruptcy on September 11 of that year. Eight days later Vidricksen filed a renunciation of the business's profits. The trustee in bankruptcy now seeks to have Dr. Vidricksen adjudged a general partner for bankruptcy purposes. Decision?

9. Weil organized Diversified Properties as a limited partnership with varying degrees of ownership in several apartment complexes and other real estate located in Maryland. The parties signed a formal written agreement in July 1967, and the partnership was properly registered in the District of Columbia. Weil was the only general partner and managed the partnership's affairs until May 1, 1968. At that time, the partnership encountered cash flow problems, and to help matters, Weil gave up both his office and his salary. At a partnership meeting held the following week, two third parties, Rubenstein and Tempchin, were selected by the limited partners to manage the partnership properties on a commission basis in accordance with a proposal that Weil had advanced earlier. Weil began working for another real estate company as a vice-president, but he remained a general partner of Diversified Properties. Creditors of the partnership, therefore, turned to him with demands for payment of the partnership debts that had not been met. Weil claims that after he surrendered his office and his salary, he remained as the general partner but that his directions were ignored. He also claims that the limited partners at various times gave direct orders to Rubenstein and Tempchin as to how to manage the partnership's affairs. Accordingly, he brings this action seeking to have the limited partners declared general partners. Decision?

Corporations

Chapter 34

NATURE, FORMATION, AND POWERS

Nature of Corporations
Formation of a Corporation
Recognition or Disregard of Corporateness
Corporate Powers

A corporation is an entity created by law that exists separate and distinct from the individuals whose initiative, property, and control enable it to function. In the opinion of the Supreme Court in *Dartmouth College v. Woodward,* 4 U.S. (Wheat.) 518, 4 L.Ed. 629 (1819), Chief Justice Marshall stated:

A corporation is an artificial being, invisible, intangible, and existing only in contemplation of law. Being the mere creature of law, it possesses only those properties which the charter of its creation confers upon it, either expressly or as incidental to its very existence. These are such as are supposed best calculated to effect the object for which it was created. Among the most important are immortality, and, if the expression may be allowed, individuality; properties by which a perpetual succession of many persons are considered as the same, so that they may act as a single individual. A corporation manages its own affairs, and holds property without the hazardous and endless necessity of perpetual conveyances for the purpose of transmitting it from hand to hand.

The corporation is the dominant form of business organization in the United States, accounting for 90 percent of the gross revenues of all business entities. Domestic corporations currently doing business in the United States number over three million, with annual revenues and assets in the trillions of dollars. Approximately thirty million Americans own shares of stock, while more than one hundred million additional people own stock indirectly through institutional investors such as banks, insurance companies, pension funds, and investment companies. Corporations have achieved this dominance because their attributes of limited liability, free transferability of shares, and continuity enabled them to attract great numbers of widespread investors. Moreover, the centralized management of corporations facilitated development of large organizations that could employ great quantities of invested capital to take advantage of economies of scale.

Use of the corporation as an instrument of commercial enterprise has made possible the vast concentrations of wealth and capital that have largely transformed this country from an agrarian to an industrial economy. Due to its size, power, and impact, the business corporation is a key institution not only in the American economy but also in the world power structure.

In 1946, a committee of the American Bar Association, after careful study and research, submitted a draft of a Model Business Corporation Act (MBCA). The Model Act has been amended frequently since then. The provisions of the Model Act do not become law until enacted by a State, but its influence has been widespread, and it was adopted in whole or in part by a majority of the States.

In 1984, the Committee on Corporate Laws of the Section of Corporation, Banking, and Business Law of the American Bar Association approved a Revised Model Business Corporation Act (RMBCA). The Revised Act is the first complete revision of the Model Act in over thirty years, although there had been numerous statutory amendments to it since it was first published. It is "designed to be a convenient guide for revision of state business corporation statutes, reflecting current views as to the appropriate accommodation of the various commercial and social interest involved in modern business corporations." One of the tasks of the revision was to reorganize the provisions of the Model Act more logically and to revise the language to make the act more consistent. In addition, substantive changes were made in a number of areas. Since 1984, several sections of the Revised Act have been amended. The Revised Act as amended will be used throughout the chapters on corporations in this text and referred to as the Revised Act or the RMBCA. Appendix G of this text contains the RMBCA as amended.

NATURE OF CORPORATIONS

It is helpful in understanding corporations to examine their common attributes and the various types of corporations. Both of these topics will be discussed in this section.

CORPORATE ATTRIBUTES

The principal attributes of a corporation are that (1) it is a legal entity; (2) it owes its existence to a State, which also regulates it; (3) it provides limited liability to its shareholders; (4) its shares of stock are freely transferable; (5) it may have perpetual existence; (6) its management is centralized; and it is considered, for some purposes, (7) a person, and (8) a citizen. Figure 34–1 compares the attributes of corporations with those of general partnerships and limited partnerships.

Legal Entity

A corporation is a legal entity separate and apart from its shareholders, with rights and liabilities entirely distinct from theirs. It may sue or be sued by, as well as contract with, any other party including any one of its shareholders. A transfer of stock in the corporation from one individual to another has no effect upon the legal existence of the corporation. Title to corporate property belongs not to the shareholders but to the corporation. Even where a single individual owns all of the stock of the corporation, the shareholder and the corporation are not the same but have separate and distinct existences.

Creature of the State

A corporation may be formed only by substantial compliance with a State incorporation statute. All States have general incorporation statutes authorizing the Secretary of State to issue a certificate of incorporation or charter upon compliance with its provisions.

A corporation's charter and the provisions of the statute under which it is formed constitute a contract between it and the State. Article I, Section 10, of the United States Constitution provides that no State shall pass any law "impairing the obligation of contracts," and this prohibition applies to contracts between a State and a corporation. See Chapter 3.

To avoid the impact of this provision, incorporation statutes reserve to the State the power to establish such regulations, provisions, and limitations as it deems advisable and to amend or repeal the statute at its pleasure. Section 1.02. Because this reservation is a material part of the contract between the State and a corporation formed under the statute, amendments or modifications regulating or altering the structure of the corporation do not impair the obligation of contract because they are expressly permitted by the contract. *See A. P. Smith Mfg. Co. v. Barlow* in Chapter 7.

Limited Liability

A corporation is a legal entity and therefore is liable out of its own assets for its debts. Generally, the shareholders have **limited liability** for the corporation's debts—their liability does not extend beyond the amount of their investment—although, as discussed later in this chapter, under certain circumstances a shareholder may be personally liable.

Free Transferability of Corporate Shares

In the absence of contractual restrictions, shares in a corporation may be freely transferred by way of sale, gift, or pledge. The ability to transfer shares is a valuable right and may enhance their market value. Transfers of shares of stock are governed by Article 8 of

---

Figure 34–1 General Partnership, Limited Partnership, and Corporation Compared

	Partnership	Limited Partnership*	Corporation
Creation	By agreement of the parties	By statutory authorization	By statutory authorization
Entity	A legal entity for some but not all purposes	A legal entity for some but not all purposes	A legal entity
Duration	Dissolved by death, bankruptcy, or withdrawal of a partner	Limited partner may dissolve partnership only by decree of court	May be perpetual
Liability	Partners are subject to unlimited liability upon the contracts, debts, and torts of the partnership	Limited partners are not generally liable for the contracts, debts, or torts of the partnership	Shareholders are not generally liable for the contracts, debts, or torts of the corporation
Transferability	Interest of a partner in a partnership may be assigned, but the assignee does not become a partner	Interest of a limited partner may be assigned and assignee may become a limited partner if all members consent	Shares of stock in a corporation are freely transferable
Management	Each partner is entitled to an equal voice in the management and control of the business	Limited partner may not take part in control of the business	The business of the corporation is managed by a board of directors elected by the shareholders
Agency	Each partner is an agent of the partnership	Limited partner is not an agent of the partnership	A shareholder is not an agent of the corporation
Suits	In actions brought by or against the partnership all partners are generally necessary parties	Limited partners are not a necessary party except where suit is to enforce their rights against or liability to the partnership	The corporation may sue and be sued in its own name

*A general partner of a limited partnership has all the rights, powers, and liabilities of a partner in a general partnership.

the Uniform Commercial Code, Investment Securities, and are discussed in Chapter 35.

Perpetual Existence

A corporation has perpetual existence unless otherwise stated in its articles of incorporation. Section 3.02. As a consequence, the death, withdrawal, or addition of a shareholder, director, or officer does not terminate the existence of a corporation.

Centralized Management

The shareholders of a corporation elect the board of directors, which manages the business of the corporation. The board must then appoint officers to run the day-to-day operations of the business. Since neither the directors nor the officers (collectively referred to as *management*) need be shareholders, it is entirely possible, and in large corporations quite typical, for the ownership of the corporation to be separated from the management of the corporation. The management structure of corporations is discussed in Chapter 36.

As a Person

Whether a corporation is a "person" within the meaning of a constitution or statute is a matter of construction based upon the intent of the lawmakers in using the word. For example, a corporation is considered a person within the provision in the Fifth and Fourteenth Amendments to the Federal Constitution that no "person" shall be "deprived of life, liberty, or property without due process of law"; and in the provision in the Fourteenth Amendment that no State shall "deny to any person within its jurisdiction the equal protection of the laws." A corporation also enjoys the right of a person to be secure against unreasonable searches and seizures, as provided for in the Fourth Amendment. On the other hand, a corporation is not considered to be a person within the clause of the Fifth Amendment, which protects a "person" against self-incrimination.

As a Citizen

A corporation is considered a citizen for some purposes but not for others. A corporation is not deemed to be a citizen as the term is used in the Fourteenth Amendment, which provides "No State shall make or enforce any law which shall abridge the privileges or immunities of citizens of the United States."

A corporation, however, is regarded as a citizen of the State of its incorporation and of the State in which it has its principal office for the purpose of determining whether diversity of citizenship exists between the parties to a lawsuit as a basis for jurisdiction of the Federal courts.

CLASSIFICATION OF CORPORATIONS

Corporations may be classified as public or private, profit or nonprofit, domestic or foreign, publicly held or closely held, and professional. As will be seen, these classifications are not mutually exclusive. For example, a corporation may be a closely held, professional, private, profit, domestic corporation.

Public or Private

A **public corporation** is one that is created to administer a unit of local civil government, such as a county, city, town, village, school district or park district, or one created by the United States to conduct public business, such as the Tennessee Valley Authority or the Federal Deposit Insurance Corporation. A public corporation is usually created by specific legislation, which determines the corporation's purpose and powers. Many public corporations are also referred to as municipal corporations.

A **private corporation** is founded by and composed of private persons for private purposes and has no governmental duties. A private corporation may be for profit or nonprofit.

Profit or Nonprofit

A **profit corporation** is one founded for the purpose of operating a business for profit from which payments are made to its shareholders in the form of dividends.

Although a **nonprofit** (or not-for-profit) **corporation** may make a profit, the profit may not be distributed to its members, directors, or officers but must be used exclusively for the charitable, educational, or scientific purpose for which it was organized. Examples of nonprofit corporations include private schools, library clubs, athletic clubs, fraternities, sororities, and hospitals. Most States have special incorporation statutes governing nonprofit corporations, some of which are patterned after the Model Nonprofit Corporation Act.

Domestic or Foreign

A corporation is a **domestic corporation** in the State in which it is incorporated. It is a **foreign corporation** in every other State or jurisdiction. A corporation may not do business, except for acts in interstate commerce, in a State other than the State of its incorporation without the permission and authorization of the other State. Every State, however, provides for the issuance to foreign corporations of a certificate to do business within its borders and for the taxation of such foreign businesses. Obtaining a certificate (called "qualifying") usually involves filing certain information with the Secretary of State, the payment of prescribed fees, and designation of a resident agent. Doing or transacting of business within a particular State makes the corporation subject to local litigation, regulation, and taxation.

What may constitute doing sufficient business in the State to subject a foreign corporation to the jurisdiction of that State's courts may not be sufficient to require the foreign corporation to obtain a certificate of authority from the State. Furthermore, the qualifying statutes are limited in their application by the constitutional provision that the regulation of commerce between the States is within the power of the Congress of the United States. See Chapter 3.

Doing Business The Revised Act does not attempt to formulate an inclusive definition of what constitutes the transaction of business. Instead, it is defined in a negative manner by stating that certain activities do *not* constitute the transaction of business. Section 15.01. Generally, any conduct more regular, systematic, or extensive than that described in this section constitutes the transaction of business and requires the corporation to obtain a certificate of authority. Conduct typically requiring a certificate of authority includes maintaining an office to conduct local intrastate business, selling personal property not in interstate commerce, entering into contracts relating to local business or sales, and owning or using real estate for general corporate purposes. Section 15.01, Comment.

The Revised Act, as stated, provides a *nonexclusive* list of activities in which a foreign corporation may engage without being considered to have transacted intrastate business:

1. maintaining, defending, or settling any proceeding;

2. holding meetings of the board of directors or shareholders or carrying on other activities concerning its internal corporate affairs;

3. maintaining bank accounts;

4. maintaining offices or agencies for the transfer, exchange, and registration of its own securities, or maintaining trustees or depositaries with relation to its securities;

5. selling through independent contractors;

6. soliciting or obtaining orders, whether by mail or through employees or agents or otherwise, if such orders require acceptance outside the State before they become contracts;

7. creating or acquiring indebtedness, mortgages, and security interests in real or personal property;

8. securing or collecting debts or enforcing mortgages and security interests in property;

9. owning, without more, real or personal property;

10. conducting an isolated transaction that is completed within thirty days and that is not in the course of a number of repeated transactions of like nature; and

11. transacting business in interstate commerce.

See Johnson v. MPL Leasing Corp.

Scope of Regulation It is a common and accepted principle that local courts will not interfere with the internal affairs of a foreign corporation. The Revised Act states that "this Act does not authorize this state to regulate the organization or internal affairs of a foreign corporation." Section 15.05(e).

Sanctions A foreign corporation that transacts business without having first qualified may be subject to a number of penalties. Most statutes provide that an unlicensed foreign corporation doing business in the State shall not be entitled to maintain a suit in the State courts until such corporation shall have obtained a certificate of authority. Failure to obtain a certificate of authority to transact business in the State, however, does not impair the validity of a contract entered into by the corporation nor prevent such corporation from defending any action or proceeding brought against it in the State. Section 15.02. In addition, many States impose fines upon the corporation, while a few States also impose fines upon the corporation's officers and directors as well as holding them personally liable on contracts made within the State.

A State may also specify conditions under which a license or certificate of authority shall be revoked. In general, the statutes provide that a failure to pay taxes, file reports, or maintain a registered agent or registered office in the State will justify revocation of a license. Section 15.30.

Publicly Held or Closely Held

A **publicly held corporation** is one whose shares are owned by a large number of people and are widely traded. There is no accepted minimum number of shareholders, but any corporation required to register under the Federal Securities and Exchange Act of 1934 is considered to be publicly held. In addition, corporations that have issued securities subject to a registered public distribution under the Federal Securities Act of 1933 are also usually considered publicly held. The Federal securities laws are discussed in Chapter 45.

A **corporation** is described as **closely held** when its outstanding shares of stock are held by a small number of persons, frequently family, relatives, or friends. In most closely held corporations, the shareholders are active in the management and control of the business. Accordingly, the shareholders are concerned with who their fellow shareholders are, and therefore they frequently impose restrictions upon the transfer of shares in order to prevent the stock from getting into the hands of persons outside the original group of shareholders. See the discussion in *Galler v. Galler* in Chapter 36. Although a vast majority of corporations in the United States are closely held, they account for only a small fraction of corporate revenues and assets.

In most States, closely held corporations are subject to the general incorporation statute that governs all corporations. The Revised Act includes a number of liberalizing provisions for closely held corporations. Some States have enacted special legislation to accommodate the needs of closely held corporations and a Statutory Close Corporation Supplement to the Model and Revised Acts has been promulgated.

The Supplement applies only to those eligible corporations that elect statutory close corporation status. To be eligible, a corporation must have fewer than fifty shareholders. A corporation may voluntarily terminate statutory close corporation status. Other provisions of the Supplement will be discussed in this and other chapters.

Professional Corporations

All of the States have professional association or corporation statutes that permit the practice of professions by duly licensed individuals in the corporate form. Some statutes apply to all professions licensed to practice within the State, while others apply only to specified professions. There is a Model Professional Corporation Supplement to the MBCA.

FORMATION OF A CORPORATION

The formation of a corporation under a general incorporation statute requires the performance of several acts by various groups, individuals, and State officials. The procedure to organize a corporation begins with the promotion of the proposed corporation by its organizers, also known as promoters, who procure offers by interested persons known as subscribers to buy stock in the corporation when created and who also prepare the necessary incorporation papers. The articles of incorporation are then executed by the incorporators and filed with the Secretary of State who issues the charter or certificate of incorporation. Finally, an organizational meeting is held.

ORGANIZING THE CORPORATION

Promoters

A promoter is a person who brings about the "birth" of a corporation. The **promoter** arranges for the capital and financing of the corporation as well as assembling the necessary assets, equipment, licenses, personnel, leases, and services. He will also attend to the actual legal formation of the corporation. Upon incorporation, the promoter's organizational task is finished.

Promoters' Contracts In addition to procuring subscriptions and preparing the incorporation papers, promoters often enter into contracts in anticipation of the creation of the corporation. The contracts may be ordinary agreements necessary for the eventual operation of the business, such as leases, purchase orders, employment contracts, sales contracts, or franchises. If these contracts are executed by the promoter in her own name and there is no further action, the promoter is liable on such contracts, and the corporation, when created, is not liable. Moreover, a preincorporation contract made by a promoter in the name of the corporation and on its behalf does not bind the corporation, except where so provided by statute. The promoter, in executing such contracts, may do so in the corporate name even though incorporation has not yet taken place. Before its formation, a corporation has no capacity to enter into contracts or to employ agents or representatives. After its formation, it is not liable at common law upon any prior contract, even one made in its name, unless it adopts the contract expressly, impliedly, or by knowingly accepting benefits under it.

A promoter who enters into a preincorporation contract in the name of the corporation usually remains liable on that contract even if the corporation adopts the contract. This results from the rule of agency law that a principal must be in existence at the time a contract is made in order to ratify it. A promoter will be relieved of liability, however, if the contract itself provides that adoption shall terminate the promoter's liability or if the promoter, the third party, and the corporation enter into a novation substituting the corporation for the promoter. *See Coopers & Lybrand v. Fox.*

See Figure 34–2.

Promoters' Fiduciary Duty The promoters of a corporation occupy a fiduciary relationship among themselves as well as with the corporation, its subscribers, and its initial shareholders. This duty requires good faith, fair dealing, and full disclosure to an independent board of directors. If an independent board has not been elected, then full disclosure must be made to all shareholders. Accordingly, the promoters are under a duty to account for any *secret* profit realized by them. Failure to disclose may also constitute a violation of Federal or State securities laws.

Figure 34-2 Promoters' Preincorporation Contracts

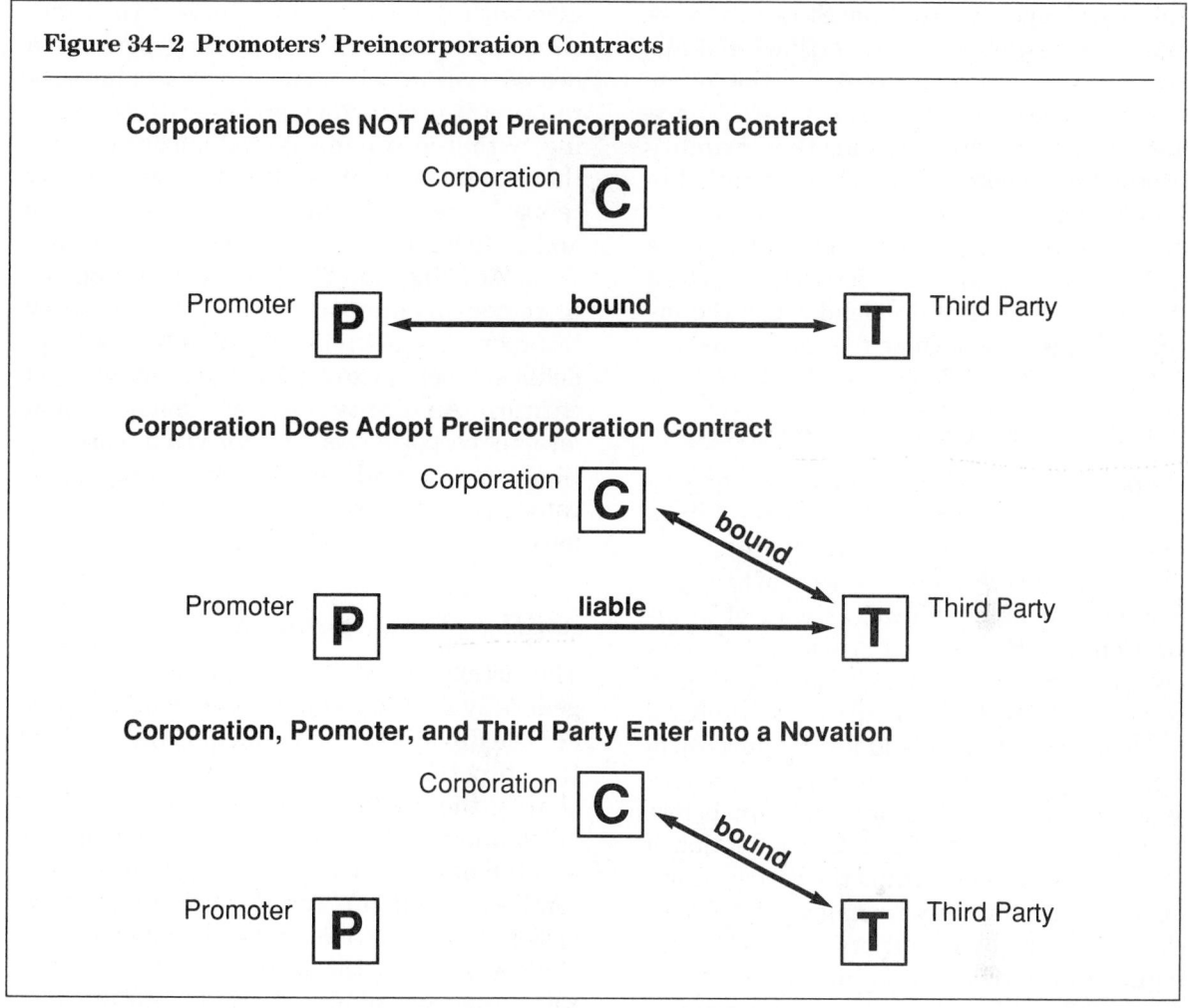

Corporation Does NOT Adopt Preincorporation Contract

Corporation C

Promoter P ←—————— **bound** —————————→ T Third Party

Corporation Does Adopt Preincorporation Contract

Corporation C ←\ **bound**

Promoter P ——————— **liable** ———————→ T Third Party

Corporation, Promoter, and Third Party Enter into a Novation

Corporation C ←\ **bound**

Promoter P   T Third Party

Subscribers

A **preincorporation subscription** is an offer to purchase capital stock in a corporation yet to be formed. The offeror is called a "subscriber." Courts have traditionally viewed subscriptions in two ways. The majority regards a subscription as a continuing offer to purchase stock from a nonexistent entity, which is incapable of accepting the offer until the entity is created. Under this view, a subscription may be revoked at any time prior to its acceptance. A minority of jurisdictions treat a subscription as a contract among the various subscribers, which makes it irrevocable except with the consent of all of the subscribers. Modern incorporation statutes, however, have taken an intermediate position in resolving this issue. The Revised Act pro-

vides that a preincorporation subscription is irrevocable for a period of six months, unless the subscription agreement provides a different period or all of the subscribers consent to the revocation of the subscription. Section 6.20. If the corporation accepts the subscription during the period of irrevocability, the subscription becomes a contract binding on both the subscriber and the corporation.

Selection of State for Incorporation

A corporation is usually incorporated in the State in which it intends to be located and to transact all or the principal part of its business. A corporation may be formed in one State, however, and have its principal place of business and conduct all or most of its operations in another State or States by duly qualifying and obtaining a certificate of authority to transact business in the other States. The principal criteria in selecting a State for incorporation include the flexibility accorded management, the rights granted to shareholders, the protection granted against takeovers, the limitations imposed upon the issuance of shares, the restrictions placed upon the payment of dividends, and the organizational costs such as fees and taxes.

FORMALITIES OF INCORPORATION

Although the procedure involved in organizing a corporation varies to some extent from State to State, typically the incorporators execute and deliver to the Secretary of State, or another designated official, articles of incorporation. The Revised Act provides that after incorporation, an organizational meeting of the board of directors named in the articles of incorporation shall be held for the purpose of adopting bylaws, appointing officers, and carrying on any other business brought before the meeting. Section 2.05. After completion of these organizational details the corporation's business and affairs are managed by its board of directors and by its officers. Several States require that a corporation have a minimum amount of capital before doing any business. Minimum amounts range from $300 to $1,000. The Revised Act and most States have eliminated this requirement.

Selection of Name

Most general incorporation laws require that the name contain a word or words that clearly indicate that it is a corporation, such as "corporation," "company," "incorporated," "limited," "Corp.," "Co.," "Inc.," or "Ltd." Section 4.01. A corporate name must be distinguishable from the name of any domestic corporation or any foreign corporation authorized to do business within the State. Section 4.01.

Incorporators

The **incorporators** are the persons who sign the articles of incorporation, which are filed with the Secretary of State of the State of incorporation. Although they perform a necessary function, their services as incorporators are perfunctory and short-lived, ending with the organizational meeting. Furthermore, modern statutes have greatly relaxed the qualifications of incorporators and reduced the number required. The Revised Act, for example, provides that one or more persons may act as the incorporator or incorporators. Section 2.01. The Revised Act defines a person to include individuals and entities. An entity includes domestic and foreign corporations, not-for-profit corporations, profit and not-for-profit unincorporated associations, business trusts, estates, partnerships, and trusts. Section 1.40.

Articles of Incorporation

The articles of incorporation or **charter** is generally a rather simple document that under the Revised Act *must* include the name of the corporation, the number of authorized shares, the street address of the registered office and the name of the registered agent, and the name and address of each incorporator. Section 2.02(a). The Revised Act permits optional information to be included in the charter, such as the initial directors, corporate purposes, management of internal affairs, powers of the corporation, its board of directors and shareholders, par value of shares, and any provision required or permitted to be set forth in the bylaws.

After the charter is drawn up it must be executed and filed with the Secretary of State in order to form a corporation. The articles of incorporation then become the basic governing document of the corporation, so long as its provisions are consistent with State and Federal law. Figure 34–3 shows a sample charter.

Organizational Meeting

As previously mentioned, the Revised Act requires that an organizational meeting be held to adopt the bylaws, appoint officers, and carry on any other business brought before the meeting. If the initial directors are not named in the articles, the incorporators hold the organizational meeting to elect directors, and either the incorporators or the directors complete the organization of the corporation. Section 2.05. Additional business that may be brought before the meeting typically includes authorization to issue shares of stock, approval of preincorporation contracts made by promoters, selection of a bank, and approval of a corporate seal and the form of stock certificates.

Figure 34–3 Sample Articles of Incorporation

ARTICLES OF INCORPORATION OF [CORPORATE NAME]

The undersigned, acting as incorporator(s) of a corporation under the _____ Business Corporation Act, adopt(s) the following Articles of Incorporation for such corporation:

First: The name of the corporation is _____

Second: The period of its duration is _____

Third: The purpose or purposes for which the corporation is organized are _____

Fourth: The aggregate number of shares which the corporation shall have authority to issue is _____

Fifth: Provisions granting preemptive rights are _____

Sixth: Provisions for the regulation of the internal affairs of the corporation are _____

Seventh: The address of the initial registered office of the corporation is , and the name of its initial registered agent at such address is _____

Eighth: The number of directors constituting the initial board of directors of the corporation is _____, and the names and addresses of the persons who are to serve as directors until the first annual meeting of shareholders or until their successors are elected and shall qualify are

Name	Address
_____	_____
_____	_____
_____	_____

Ninth: The name and address of each incorporator is

Name	Address
_____	_____
_____	_____
_____	_____

Dated _____, 19__.

_____

_____

_____

Incorporator(s)

SOURCE: Reprinted with permission from Henn & Alexander, *Corporations*, 3d ed. Copyright © 1983 by West Publishing Co.

Bylaws

The **bylaws** of a corporation are the rules and regulations that govern its internal management. They are necessary to its organization, and the adoption of bylaws is one of the first items of business at the organizational meeting held promptly after incorporation. Under the Revised Act either the incorporators or the board of directors may adopt the bylaws. Section 2.06.

The bylaws may contain any provision for managing the business and regulating the affairs of the corporation that is not inconsistent with law or the articles of incorporation. Section 2.06. In contrast to the articles of incorporation, the bylaws do not have to be publicly filed. Under the Revised Act, the shareholders may amend or repeal the bylaws. In addition, the board of directors may also amend or repeal the bylaws unless the articles of incorporation or other sections of the RMBCA reserve that power exclusively to the shareholders in whole or in part. Section 10.20.

The Statutory Close Corporation Supplement (Section 22) permits close corporations *not* to adopt any bylaws if all information required to be stated in corporate bylaws is included either in a shareholder agreement or in the articles of incorporation. The comments to the Supplement explain this departure from tradition: "The highly structured formalities in typical bylaws, although necessary in larger corporations with numerous shareholders, can be cumbersome when imposed on closely held corporations."

RECOGNITION OR DISREGARD OF CORPORATENESS

Business associates choose to incorporate to obtain one or more of the corporate attributes—primarily limited liability and perpetual existence. Because a corporation is a creature of the State, such corporate attributes are recognized when the enterprise complies with the State's requirements for incorporation. Although the formal procedures are relatively simple, errors or omissions sometimes occur. In some cases the mistakes may be trivial, such as an incorrect address of an incorporator; in other instances the error may be more significant, such as a complete failure to file the articles of incorporation. The consequences of noncompliance with the statutory incorporation procedure depend upon the seriousness of the error. Conversely, even when a corporation has been formed in strict compliance with the incorporation statute, a court may disregard the corporateness of the enterprise if justice requires. This section addresses these two complementary issues.

DEFECTIVE INCORPORATION

The frequency of defective attempts to incorporate has been greatly reduced by the simplified incorporation procedures of modern corporation statutes. Nonetheless, defective incorporations do occur. The possible consequences of a defective incorporation include the following: (1) the State brings an action against the association for involuntary dissolution, (2) the associates are held personally liable to a third party, (3) the association asserts that it is not liable on an obligation, or (4) a third party asserts that it is not liable to the association. Corporate statutes addressing this issue have taken a considerably different approach from the common law.

Common Law Approach

Under the common law, a defectively formed corporation was, under certain circumstances, accorded corporate attributes. The courts developed a set of doctrines granting corporateness to *de jure* (of right) corporations, *de facto* (of fact) corporations, and corporations by estoppel but denying corporateness to corporations that were too defectively formed. Figure 34–4 illustrates the common law approach to defective formation.

Corporation *de Jure* A corporation *de jure* is one that has been formed in substantial compliance with the incorporation statute and the required organizational procedure.

Once formed, the existence of a *de jure* corporation may not be challenged by anyone, even the State in a direct proceeding for this purpose.

Corporation *de Facto*   A corporation *de facto* is a corporation that is not *de jure* because of a failure to comply substantially with the incorporation statute but nevertheless is recognized for most purposes as a corporation. A failure to form a *de jure* corporation may result in the formation of a *de facto* corporation if the following requirements are met: (1) the existence of a general corporation statute, (2) a *bona fide* attempt to comply with that law in organizing a corporation under the statute, and (3) the actual exercise of corporate power by conducting business in the belief that a corporation has been formed. The existence of a *de facto* corporation can be challenged only by the State. If the corporation sues to collect a debt, it is not a defense that the corporation is not *de jure*. Not even the State can collaterally (in a proceeding involving some other issue) question the *de facto* corporation's existence. The State must bring an independent suit against the corporation for this express purpose, known as an action of *quo warranto* ("by what right").

Corporation by Estoppel   The doctrine of corporation by estoppel is separate and distinct from that of corporation *de facto*. Estoppel does not create a corporation. It operates only to prevent a person or persons under the facts and circumstances of a particular case from raising the question of a corporation's existence or its capacity to act or to own property. Corporation by estoppel requires a holding out and reliance. In addition, application of the doctrine depends on equitable considerations. A person who has dealt with a defectively organized corporation may be precluded or estopped from denying its corporate existence where the necessary elements of holding out and reliance are present. The doctrine can be applied not only to third parties but also to the purported corporation as well as the associates who held themselves out as a corporation. *See Cranson v. International Business Machines Corp.*

Defective Corporation   If the associates who purported to form a corporation fail to comply with the requirements of the incorporation statute to such an extent that neither a *de jure* nor a *de facto* corporation is formed and the circumstances do not justify the application of the corporation by estoppel doc-

---

Figure 34–4 Recognition of Corporate Attributes: Common Law Approach

Requirements		Result
Substantial compliance with incorporation statute	**Corporation *de Jure***	Corporate attributes, insulation from collateral and direct suits
Bona fide attempt to comply with incorporation statute Exercise of corporate powers	**Corporation *de Facto***	Corporate attributes, insulation from collateral suits
Holding out Reliance Equitable considerations	**Corporation by Estoppel**	Corporate existence may not be denied by the parties
Serious failure to comply with incorporation statute	**Defective Corporation**	Unlimited personal liability for associates

trine, then the courts generally deny the associates the benefits of incorporation. This results in the associates being held unlimitedly liable for the obligations of the business.

Statutory Approach

The common law approach is cumbersome in both theory and application. The Revised Act provides that the *filing* of the articles of incorporation by the Secretary of State is conclusive proof that the incorporators have satisfied all conditions precedent to incorporation except in a proceeding brought by the State. Section 2.03(b). The Revised Act imposes liability only on persons who purport to act as or on behalf of a corporation, *knowing that there was no incorporation*. Section 2.04.

The Model Act and many States provide that a "certificate of incorporation shall be conclusive evidence that all conditions precedent required to be performed by the incorporators have been complied with and that the corporation has been incorporated under this Act, except as against this State." Section 56. With respect to the attribute of limited liability, however, the Model Act provides that "all persons who assume to act as a corporation without authority so to do shall be jointly and severally liable for all debts and liabilities incurred or arising as a result thereof." Section 146.

Consider the following two illustrations: First, Smith had been shown executed articles of incorporation some months before he invested in the corporation and became an officer and director. He was also told by the corporation's attorney that the articles had been filed, but in fact they had not been filed because of confusion in the attorney's office. Under the Revised Act and many court decisions, Smith would not be held liable for the obligations of the defective corporation. Second, Jones represents that a corporation exists and enters into a contract in the corporate name when she knows that no corporation has been formed because no attempt has been made to file articles of incorporation. Jones would be held liable for the obligations of the defective corporation under the Model Act, the Revised Act, and most court decisions involving similar situations. RMBCA Section 2.04 and Comment.

Figure 34–5 illustrates the approach to defective incorporation taken by the Model Act and the Revised Act.

PIERCING THE CORPORATE VEIL

If a corporation is formed by substantial compliance with the incorporation statute so that a *de jure* or *de facto* corporation results, the general rule is that corporateness and its attendant attributes including limited liability will be recognized. Nonetheless, the courts will disregard the corporation entity when it is used to defeat public convenience, commit wrongdoing, protect fraud, or circumvent the law. Going behind the corporate entity in order to prevent its use by individuals seeking

---

Figure 34–5 Recognition of Corporate Attributes: Statutory Approach

	No Filing of Articles of Incorporation	**Filing of Articles of Incorporation**
RMBCA Approach	No corporate attributes Joint and several liability for those who act knowing that there was no incorporation	Corporate attributes Limited liability Insulation from collateral suits
	No Certificate Issued	**Certificate Issued**
MBCA Approach	No corporate attributes Joint and several liability for all who assume to act as a corporation	Corporate attributes Limited liability Insulation from collateral suits

to insulate themselves from personal accountability and the consequences of their wrongdoing is referred to as piercing the corporate veil. Courts will pierce the corporate veil where deemed necessary to remedy wrongdoing and have done so most frequently with closely held corporations and in parent-subsidiary relationships.

Closely Held Corporations

The joint and active management by all the shareholders of closely held corporations frequently results in a tendency to forgo adherence to all of the niceties of corporate formalities, such as holding meetings of the board and shareholders, while the small size of close corporations often results in creditors who are unable to satisfy fully their claims against the corporation. Accordingly, the frustrated creditor will likely invoke the court to disregard the organization's corporateness and impose personal liability for the corporate obligations upon the shareholders. Courts have responded by piercing the corporate veil where the shareholders (1) have not conducted the business on a corporate basis, (2) have not provided an adequate financial basis for the business, or (3) have used the corporation to defraud. For example, in *D.I. Felsenthal Co. v. Northern Assurance Co.,* 284 Ill. 343, 120 N.E. 268 (1918), Felsenthal Company sued the Northern Assurance Company to collect on its fire insurance policy. Northern claimed that it was not liable under the policy because Felsenthal's property had been destroyed by a fire instigated by Fox, the president, director, creditor, and principal shareholder of Felsenthal. Judgment for Northern Assurance. The instigator of the fire, Fox, is the beneficial owner of almost all of the corporation's stock as well as the corporation's president and director. Under these circumstances the corporation cannot recover because to allow such a recovery would allow a wrongdoer to benefit from his own illegal act. The corporate form cannot be used in this case to protect Fox and to aid him in his plan to defraud the insurance company.

Conducting the business on a corporate basis involves maintaining the corporation's funds separate from the shareholders' funds, maintaining separate financial records, holding regular directors' meetings, and generally observing corporate formalities. Adequate capitalization requires that the shareholders invest sufficient capital to meet the reasonably anticipated requirements of the enterprise. *See United States v. Healthwin-Midtown Convalescent Hospital.*

The Statutory Close Corporation Supplement validates several arrangements whereby the shareholders may relax the traditional corporate formalities. Section 25 of the Supplement provides: "The failure of a statutory close corporation to observe the usual corporate formalities or requirements relating to the exercise of its corporate powers or management of its business and affairs is not a ground for imposing personal liability on the shareholders for liabilities of the corporation." As the comments observe, the purpose of this section is to prevent a court from holding the shareholders in a statutory close corporation individually liable for the debts and torts of the business because the corporation does not follow the traditional model of a corporation. Courts may still pierce the corporate veil of a statutory close corporation if the same circumstances would justify imposing personal liability on the shareholders of a general business corporation. The Supplement simply prevents a court from piercing the corporate veil just because the corporation is a statutory close corporation.

Parent–Subsidiary

A corporation may choose to risk only a portion of its assets in a particular enterprise by forming a subsidiary corporation. A **subsidiary corporation** is one in which another corporation, **the parent corporation,** owns at least a majority of the subsidiary's shares and therefore has control over the subsidiary corporation. Courts will pierce the corporate veil and hold the parent liable for the debts of its subsidiary if

1. both corporations are not adequately capitalized, *or*

2. the formalities of separate corporate procedures are not observed, *or*

3. each corporation is not held out to the public as separate enterprises, *or*

4. the funds of the two corporations are commingled, *or*

5. the parent corporation completely dominates the operation of the subsidiary to advance solely the parent's own interests.

So long as these pitfalls are avoided, the courts will generally recognize the separateness of the subsidiary even though the parent owns all the stock of the subsidiary and the two corporations have common directors and officers. *See Berger v. Columbia Broadcasting System, Inc.*

CORPORATE POWERS

Because a corporation derives its existence and all of its powers from the State of incorporation, it has only those powers as the State has conferred on it. These powers are those expressly set forth in the statute and articles of incorporation and powers reasonably implied from them. *See A. P. Smith Mfg. Co. v. Barlow* in Chapter 7.

SOURCES OF CORPORATE POWERS

Statutory Powers

Typical of the general powers granted by incorporation statutes are those provided by Section 3.02 of the Revised Act, which include the following:

1. to have perpetual succession;

2. to sue and be sued in its corporate name;

3. to have a corporate seal;

4. to make and amend bylaws for managing the business and regulating the affairs of the corporation;

5. to acquire, own, improve, use, and dispose of real or personal property;

6. to own, vote, and dispose of shares or other interests in, or obligations of, any other entity;

7. to make contracts and guarantees, incur liabilities, borrow money, issue its notes, bonds, and other obligations, and secure any of its obligations;

8. to lend money, invest and reinvest its funds, and receive and hold real and personal property as security for repayment;

9. to be a promoter, partner, member, associate, or manager of any partnership, joint venture, trust, or other entity;

10. to conduct its business, locate offices, and exercise the powers granted by this Act within or without this state;

11. to elect directors and appoint officers, employees, and agents of the corporation, define their duties, fix their compensation, and lend them money and credit;

12. to pay pensions and establish pension plans, pension trusts, profit sharing plans, share bonus plans, share option plans, and benefit or incentive plans for any or all of its current or former directors, officers, employees, and agents;

13. to make donations for the public welfare or for charitable, scientific, or educational purposes;

14. to transact any lawful business that will aid governmental policy; and

15. to make payments or donations, or do any other act, not inconsistent with law, that furthers the business and affairs of the corporation.

The Revised Act also makes a general grant to all corporations of the same powers as an individual to do all things necessary or convenient to carry out its business and affairs. Section 3.02.

Express Charter Powers

The objects or purposes for which a corporation is formed are stated in its articles of incorporation, which delineate in general language the type of business activities in which the corporation proposes to engage. This serves (1) to advise the shareholders of the nature and kind of particular business activity in which their investment is being risked; (2) to advise the officers, directors, and management of the extent of the corporation's authority to act; and (3) to inform any person who may contemplate dealing with the corporation of the extent of its legally authorized power. The express powers must relate to a legitimate business activity or industry within the purview of the general statute.

Implied Powers

A corporation has the authority to take any action that is necessary or convenient to and consistent with the execution of any of its express powers and the operation of the business that it was formed to conduct. This power exists by implication and does not depend upon express language in the charter or statute but upon reasonable inference as to the proper scope and content of such language, taking into consideration the facts and circumstances of the particular case.

The express powers of a corporation may and should be stated in general language, and it is not necessary to set forth in detail every particular type of act which the corporation is empowered to perform. A general statement of corporate purpose or object is sufficient to give rise to all of the powers necessary, incidental, or convenient to accomplish that purpose. Section 3.02. For instance, a corporation organized "to buy and sell goods, wares, and merchandise" has implied power to (a) purchase or lease store premises, (b) employ salesmen, (c) buy or rent trucks, (d) spend money for advertising, (e) open and manage a bank account, (f) employ buyers and pay their salaries and traveling expenses, and (g) purchase insurance on the lives of officers, as well as other powers necessary or incidental to the stated purpose.

ULTRA VIRES ACTS

Since a corporation has authority to act only within the limitation of its express and implied powers, any action taken or contract made by it which goes beyond these powers is *ultra vires*. *Ultra vires* does not mean without power or capability but rather without legal authorization because the act is not within the scope and type of acts which the corporation is legally empowered to perform.

The doctrine of *ultra vires* is of less significance today because modern statutes permit incorporation for any lawful purpose and most articles of incorporation do not limit the powers of the corporation. As a consequence, far fewer acts are *ultra vires*.

Effect of *Ultra Vires* Acts

Traditionally, *ultra vires* contracts were unenforceable as null and void. Under the modern approach courts allow the *ultra vires* defense where the contract is wholly executory on both sides. A corporation having received full performance from the other party to the contract is not permitted to escape liability by a plea of *ultra vires*. Conversely, where a corporation is suing for breach of a contract which has been fully performed on its side, the defense of *ultra vires* is unavailing.

Almost all statutes now have abolished the defense of *ultra vires* in an action by or against a corporation. The Revised Act provides that "the validity of corporate action may not be challenged on the ground that the corporation lacks or lacked the power to act." Section 3.04. This section extends beyond contract actions and includes any corporate action including conveyances of property. Thus, under this section it is not necessary for persons dealing with a corporation to examine its articles of incorporation to discover any limitations upon its purposes or powers that may appear there. The section does not, however, validate illegal corporate actions.

Remedies for *Ultra Vires* Acts

Although *ultra vires* under modern statutes may no longer be used defensively as a shield against liability, corporate activities that are *ultra vires* may be redressed in any of the three following ways, as provided by Section 3.04(b) of the Revised Act:

1. in a proceeding by a shareholder against the corporation to enjoin the act if equitable and if all affected persons are parties to the proceeding, and the court may award damages for loss suffered by the corporation or another party because of enjoining the unauthorized act;

2. in a proceeding by the corporation, or a shareholder derivatively, against the incumbent or former directors or officers for exceeding their authority; or

3. in a proceeding by the Attorney General of the State of incorporation to dissolve the corporation or to enjoin it from the transaction of unauthorized business.

LIABILITY FOR TORTS AND CRIMES

A corporation is liable for the torts committed by its agents in the course of their employment. The doctrine of *ultra vires*, even in those jurisdictions where it is permitted as a defense, has no application to wrongdoing by the corporation. The doctrine of **respondeat superior** imposes full liability upon a corporation for the torts committed by its agents and employees during the course of their employment. For example, Robert, a truck driver employed by the Webster Corporation, while on a business errand, negligently runs over Pamela, a pedestrian. Both Robert and the Webster Corporation are liable to Pamela in an action by her to recover damages for the injuries sustained. A corporation may also be found liable for fraud, false imprisonment, malicious prosecution, libel, and other torts, but some States hold the corporation liable for *punitive* damages only if it authorized or ratified the act of the agent.

Historically, corporations were not held criminally liable because, under the traditional view, a corporation could not possess the requisite criminal intent, and therefore was incapable of committing a crime. The dramatic growth in size and importance of corporations has brought about a change in this view. Under the modern approach, a corporation may be liable for violation of statutes imposing liability without fault. In addition, a corporation may be liable where the offense is perpetrated by a high corporate officer or the board of directors. The Model Penal Code provides that a corporation may be convicted of a criminal offense for the conduct of its employees if:

1. the legislative purpose of the statute defining the offense is to impose liability on corporations and the conduct is within the scope of the agent's office or employment;

2. the offense consists of an omission to discharge a specific, affirmative duty imposed upon corporations by law; *or*

3. the offense was authorized, requested, commanded, performed or recklessly tolerated by the board of directors or by a high managerial agent of the corporation.

Punishment of a corporation for crimes is necessarily by fine and not imprisonment.

CASES

Foreign Corporation

JOHNSON v. MPL LEASING CORP.

Supreme Court of Alabama, 1983.
441 So.2d 904.

TORBERT, C.J.

Defendants Jay Johnson and Jay Johnson Business Products, Inc., ("Johnson") appeal from a judgment in favor of MPL Leasing Corporation arising out of a breach of contract action. We affirm.

The question to be considered by this Court is whether a foreign corporation, not qualified to do business in this state, may nevertheless utilize Alabama courts to enforce a contract which concerns the lease or sale, or both, of products within Alabama to Alabama citizens.

MPL Leasing Corporation ("MPL") is a California corporation organized for the purpose of offering alternative financing plans to dealers of Saxon Business Products. Saxon specializes in the sale of paper copiers which are distributed through independent dealers located throughout the United States, including Alabama. Jay Johnson was a Saxon dealer in Alabama.

Through mailings and telephone calls into the state, MPL solicited Johnson's attendance at a sales seminar in Atlanta. Johnson attended the seminar and entered into an agreement with MPL. The agreement provided for Johnson to lease Saxon copiers with the option to buy. MPL shipped the machines into Alabama and filed a financing statement with the Secretary of State.

Johnson became several months delinquent with his payments to MPL. MPL filed suit in Montgomery Circuit Court. Johnson moved to dismiss, alleging, among other defenses, that MPL was not qualified to do business in Alabama. We find that the trial judge correctly denied the motion.

Section 232 of the Alabama Constitution and § 10–2A–247, Code 1975, bar foreign corporations not qualified to do business in this state from enforcing their contracts through our courts. These laws only come into play "when the business conducted in the state by non-qualified corporations is considered 'intrastate' in nature." [Citations.] MPL's activities within Alabama are limited to (1) delivering copying machines by common carrier and (2) filing this action. This Court has never held previously that contacts as minimal as those of MPL constitute "intrastate business."

For example, in [citation], this Court considered whether the foreign, non-qualifying corporation's contacts were sufficient to constitute "intrastate" business. The facts in [ci-

tation] are indistinguishable from those in this case. The corporation's activities in Alabama were "simply solicitation of orders and delivery incident to that solicitation." [Citation.] This Court held that "[the plaintiff], conducting business in interstate commerce, is justified and welcomed to use the state courts of Alabama to enforce its claim against those who defaulted on payment of an order which was delivered here." [Citation.]

* * *

The appellant cites several cases for the proposition that solicitation of sales constitutes "doing business." [Citation] held that a foreign, non-qualifying corporation (SAR) could not sue on a promissory note against an Alabama co-maker. Unlike MPL, SAR expanded its operation by purchasing a warehouse in Alabama, maintaining two vehicles in Alabama, and employing seven Alabama residents full-time. These factors were "localized enough to easily fall under the ambit of a series of transactions which are primarily intrastate and concomitantly the corporation falls under the satrapy of the qualification statutes. . . ." [Citation.]

In [citation], the Court confused the test for minimum contacts for service of process with the test for determining whether a foreign corporation must qualify to do business in order to sue in state court. The minimum contacts test for service of process protects defendants against the burden of litigating in a distant forum. The doing business test for qualifying foreign corporations is governed by the limits on state regulation inherent in the Commerce Clause of the United States Constitution. [Citations.] As these decisions make clear, it is far easier to find that a foreign corporation is "doing business" for service of process than it is to find that the corporation is conducting intrastate business subject to state regulation in view of the Commerce Clause.

* * *

Therefore, we hold that MPL is welcome to use Alabama courts to enforce rights arising from the agreement with Johnson. The judgment is affirmed.

Affirmed.

Promoters' Contracts

COOPERS & LYBRAND v. FOX

Colorado Court of Appeals, Div. IV, 1988.
758 P.2d 683.

KELLY, C.J.

In an action based on breach of express and implied contracts, the plaintiff, Coopers & Lybrand (Coopers), appeals the judgment of the trial court in favor of the defendant, Garry J. Fox (Fox). Coopers contends that the trial court erred in ruling that Fox, a corporate promoter, could not be held liable on a pre-incorporation contract in the absence of an agreement that he would be so liable, and that Coopers had, and failed to sustain, the burden of proving any such agreement. We reverse.

On November 3, 1981, Fox met with a representative of Coopers, a national accounting firm, to request a tax opinion and other accounting services. Fox informed Coopers at this meeting that he was acting on behalf of a corporation he was in the process of forming, G. Fox and Partners, Inc. Coopers accepted the "engagement" with the knowledge that the corporation was not yet in existence.

G. Fox and Partners, Inc., was incorporated on December 4, 1981. Coopers completed its work by mid-December and billed "Mr. Garry R. (sic) Fox, Fox and Partners, Inc." in the amount of $10,827. When neither Fox nor G. Fox and Partners, Inc., paid the bill, Coopers sued Garry Fox, individually, for breach of express and implied contracts based on a theory of promoter liability.

Fox argued at trial that, although Coopers knew the corporation was not in existence when he engaged the firm's services, it either expressly or impliedly agreed to look solely to the corporation for payment. Coopers argued that its client was Garry Fox, not the corporation. The parties stipulated that Coopers had done the work, and Coopers presented uncontroverted testimony that the fee was fair and reasonable.

The trial court failed to make written findings of fact and conclusions of law. However, in its bench findings at the end of trial, the court found that there was no agreement, either express or implied, that would obligate Fox, individually, to pay Coopers' fee, in effect, because Coopers had failed to prove the existence of any such agreement. The court entered judgment in favor of Fox.

As a preliminary matter, we reject Fox's argument that he was acting only as an agent for the future corporation. One cannot act as the agent of a nonexistent principal. [Citation.]

On the contrary, the uncontroverted facts place Fox squarely within the definition of a promoter. A promoter is one who, alone or with others, undertakes to form a corporation and to procure for it the rights, instrumentalities, and capital to enable it to conduct business. [Citations.]

When Fox first approached Coopers, he was in the process of forming G. Fox and Partners, Inc. He engaged Coopers' services for the future corporation's benefit. In addition, though not dispositive on the issue of his status as a promoter, Fox became the president, a director, and the principal shareholder of the corporation, which he funded, only nominally, with a $100 contribution. Under these circumstances, Fox cannot deny his role as a promoter.

Coopers asserts that the trial court erred in finding that Fox was under no obligation to pay Coopers' fee in the absence of an agreement that he would be personally liable. We agree.

As a general rule, promoters are personally liable for the contracts they make, though made on behalf of a corporation to be formed. [Citation.] The well-recognized exception to the general rule of promoter liability is that if the contracting party knows the corporation is not in existence but nevertheless agrees to look solely to the corporation and not to the promoter for payment, then the promoter incurs no personal liability. [Citations.] In the absence of an express agreement, the existence of an agreement to release the promoter from liability may be shown by circumstances making it reasonably certain that the parties intended to and did enter into the agreement. [Citations.]

Here, the trial court found there was no agreement, either express or implied, regarding Fox's liability. Thus, in the absence of an agreement releasing him from liability, Fox is liable.

Coopers also contends that the trial court erred in ruling, in effect, that Coopers had the burden of proving any agreement regarding Fox's personal liability for payment of the fee. We agree.

Release of the promoter depends on the intent of the parties. As the proponent of an alleged agreement to release the promoter from liability, the promoter has the burden of proving the release agreement. [Citations.]

Fox seeks to bring himself within the exception to the general rule of promoter liability. However, as the proponent of the exception, he must bear the burden of proving the existence of the alleged agreement releasing him from liability. The trial court found that there was no agreement regarding Fox's liability. Thus, Fox failed to sustain his burden of proof, and the trial court erred in granting judgment in his favor.

It is undisputed that the defendant, Garry J. Fox, engaged Coopers' services, that G. Fox and Partners, Inc., was not in existence at that time, that Coopers performed the work, and that the fee was reasonable. The only dispute, as the trial court found, is whether Garry Fox is liable for payment of the fee. We conclude that Fox is liable, as a matter of law, under the doctrine of promoter liability.

Accordingly, the judgment is reversed, and the cause is remanded with directions to enter judgment in favor of Coopers & Lybrand in the amount of $10,827, plus interest to be determined by the trial court pursuant to [citation].

Recognition of Corporateness

CRANSON v. INTERNATIONAL BUSINESS MACHINES CORP.

Court of Appeals of Maryland, 1964.
234 Md. 477, 200 A.2d 33.

HORNEY, J.

* * *

The agreed statement of facts shows that in April 1961, Cranson was asked to invest in a new business corporation which was about to be created. Towards this purpose he met with other interested individuals and an attorney and agreed to purchase stock and become an officer and director. Thereafter, upon being advised by the attorney that the corporation had been formed under the laws of Maryland, he paid for and received a stock certificate evidencing ownership of shares in the corporation, and was shown the corporate seal and minute book. The business of the new venture was conducted as if it were a corporation, through corporate bank accounts, with auditors maintaining corporate books and records, and under a lease entered into by the corporation for the office from which it operated its business. Cranson was elected president and all transactions conducted by him for the corporation, including the dealings with I.B.M., were made as an officer of the corporation. At no time did he assume any personal obligation or pledge his individual credit to I.B.M. Due to an oversight on the part of the attorney, of which Cranson was not aware, the certificate of incorporation, which had been signed and acknowledged prior to May 1, 1961, was not filed until November 24, 1961. Between May 17 and November 8, the Bureau purchased eight typewriters from I.B.M., on account of which partial payments were made, leaving a balance due of $4,333.40, for which this suit was brought.

* * *

The fundamental question presented by the appeal is whether an officer of a defectively incorporated association may be subjected to personal liability under the circumstances of this case. We think not.

Traditionally, two doctrines have been used by the courts to clothe an officer of a defectively incorporated association with the corporate attribute of limited liability. The first, often referred to as the doctrine of *de facto* corporations, has been applied in those cases where there are elements showing: (1)

the existence of law authorizing incorporation; (2) an effort in good faith to incorporate under the existing law; and (3) actual user or exercise of corporate powers. [Citations.] The second, the doctrine of estoppel to deny the corporate existence, is generally employed where the person seeking to hold the officer personally liable has contracted or otherwise dealt with the association in such a manner as to recognize and in effect admit its existence as a corporate body. [Citations.]

It is not at all clear what Maryland has done with respect to the two doctrines. There have been no recent cases in this State on the subject and some of the seemingly irreconcilable earlier cases offer little to clarify the problem.

In one line of cases, the Court, in determining the rights and liabilities of a defectively organized corporation, or a member or stockholder thereof, seems to have drawn a distinction between those acts or requirements which are a condition precedent to corporate existence and those acts prescribed by law to be done after incorporation. In so doing, it has been generally held that where there had been a failure to comply with a requirement which the law declared to be a condition precedent to the existence of the corporation, the corporation was not a legal entity and was therefore precluded from suing or being sued as such. [Citations.] These cases appear to stand for the proposition that substantial compliance with those formalities of the corporation law, which are made a condition precedent to corporate existence, was not only necessary for the creation of a corporation *de jure,* but was also a prerequisite to the existence of a *de facto* corporation or a corporation by estoppel.

* * *

On the other hand, where the corporation has obtained legal existence but has failed to comply with a condition subsequent to corporate existence, this Court has held that such nonperformance afforded the State the right to institute proceedings for the forfeiture of the charter, but that such neglect or omission could never be set up by the corporation itself, or by its members and stockholders, as a defense to an action to enforce their liabilities. [Citations.]

* * *

* * * It seems clear therefore that when a defect in the incorporation process resulted from a failure to comply with a condition subsequent, the doctrine of estoppel may be applied for the benefit of a creditor to estop the corporation, or the members or stockholders thereof, from denying its corporate existence. [Citations.]

In another line of Maryland cases which determined the rights and liabilities of a defectively organized corporation, or a member or stockholder thereof, the Court, apparently disregarding the distinction made between those requirements which are conditions precedent and those which are conditions subsequent to corporate existence, has generally precluded, on the grounds of estoppel or collateral attack, inquiry into the question of corporate existence. [Citations.]

* * *

* * * From these cases it appears that where the parties have assumed corporate existence and dealt with each other on that basis, the Court will apply the estoppel doctrine on the theory that the parties by recognizing the organization as a corporation were thereafter prevented from raising a question as to its corporate existence.

When summarized, the law in Maryland pertaining to the *de facto* and estoppel doctrines reveals that the cases seem to fall into one or the other of two categories. In one line of cases, the Court, choosing to disregard the nature of the dealings between the parties, refused to recognize both doctrines where there had been a failure to comply with a condition precedent to corporate existence, but, whenever such noncompliance concerned a condition subsequent to incorporation, the Court often applied the estoppel doctrine. In the other line of cases, the Court, choosing to make no distinction between defects which were conditions precedent and those which were conditions subsequent, emphasized the course of conduct between the parties and applied the estoppel doctrine when there had been substantial dealings between them on a corporate basis.

* * * There is, as we see it, a wide difference between creating a corporation by

means of the *de facto* doctrine and estopping a party, due to his conduct in a particular case, from setting up the claim of no incorporation. Although some cases tend to assimilate the doctrines of incorporation *de facto* and by estoppel, each is a distinct theory and they are not dependent on one another in their application. [Citations.] Where there is a concurrence of the three elements necessary for the application of the *de facto* corporation doctrine, there exists an entity which is a corporation *de jure* against all persons but the state. On the other hand, the estoppel theory is applied only to the facts of each particular case and may be invoked even where there is no corporation *de facto*. Accordingly, even though one or more of the requisites of a *de facto* corporation are absent, we think that this factor does not preclude the application of the estoppel doctrine in a proper case, such as the one at bar.

I.B.M. contends that the failure of the Bureau to file its certificate of incorporation debarred *all* corporate existence. But, in spite of the fact that the omission might have prevented the Bureau from being either a corporation *de jure* or *de facto*, [citation] supra, we think that I.B.M. having dealt with the Bureau as if it were a corporation and relied on its credit rather than that of Cranson, is estopped to assert that the Bureau was not incorporated at the time the typewriters were purchased. [Citations.] In 1 Clark and Marshall, Private Corporations, § 89, it is stated:

> The doctrine in relation to estoppel is based upon the ground that it would generally be inequitable to permit the corporate existence of an association to be denied by persons who have represented it to be a corporation, or held it out as a corporation, or by any persons who have recognized it as a corporation by dealing with it as such; and by the overwhelming weight of authority, therefore, a person may be estopped to deny the legal incorporation of an association which is not even a corporation *de facto*.

In cases similar to the one at bar, involving a failure to file articles of incorporation, the courts of other jurisdictions have held that where one has recognized the corporate existence of an association, he is estopped to assert the contrary with respect to a claim arising out of such dealings. [Citations.]

Since I.B.M. is estopped to deny the corporate existence of the Bureau, we hold that Cranson was not liable for the balance due on account of the typewriters.

Judgment reversed; the appellee to pay the costs.

Disregard of Corporateness:
Closely Held Corporation

UNITED STATES v. HEALTHWIN–MIDTOWN CONVALESCENT HOSPITAL

United States District Court, Central District of California, 1981.
511 F.Supp. 416.

MALETZ, J.

This is an action by the United States to recover Medicare funds paid to the Healthwin-Midtown Convalescent Hospital and Rehabilitation Center, Inc. (Healthwin). The defendants are Healthwin and Israel Zide, its former president and owner of fifty percent of its stock.

The facts are as follows: On September 14, 1971, Healthwin was organized in California for the purpose of operating a health care facility. From that date, until November 30, 1974, it participated as a provider of services under the Medicare Act, [citation], and received periodic payments from the United States Department of Health, Education and Welfare (HEW). These payments, which were compensation for the services provided Medicare beneficiaries by Healthwin, were only approximations of the exact amount due; the exact amount was determined by periodic audits conducted by Blue Cross of Southern California which was HEW's agent for the purpose of paying Healthwin and auditing its cost reports. It is undisputed that these audits showed that a series of overpayments had been made to Healthwin in 1972, 1973 and 1974 in the total amount of $30,481.55. It is this sum, plus interest, that the United States seeks to recover here.

* * *

Against this background, the issue here is whether defendant Zide is personally liable for the Medicare overpayments to Health-win. As a basis for such liability, plaintiff [United States] first argues that the corporate entity should be disregarded under the *alter ego* theory of liability. . . .

We note at the outset that plaintiff's *alter ego* claim must be analyzed in accordance with state law. [Citation.] And under California law, "[i]ssues of *alter ego* do not lend themselves to strict rules and *prima facie* cases. Whether the corporate veil should be pierced depends upon the innumerable individual equities of each case." [Citation.] Generally, however, the corporate veil may be pierced when it is shown:

(1) that there . . . [is] such unity of interest and ownership that the separate personalities of the corporation and the individual no longer exist and (2) that if the acts are treated as those of the corporation alone, an inequitable result will follow.

[Citation.]

With regard to the "unity of interest and ownership" test, . . . the evidence at trial showed that at all times relevant here, Zide was a fifty percent shareholder of the Healthwin corporation. In addition, Zide had a fifty percent interest in a partnership which owned both the realty in which Healthwin's health care facility was located and the furnishings used at that facility.

Zide was also president of the Healthwin corporation as well as a member of its board of directors and the administrator of its health care facility. While there were other members of the board, they usually did not attend board meetings. Further, only Zide could sign the corporation's checks without the prior approval of another corporate officer, and virtually all the corporation's checks were in fact signed by him. Thus, Zide alone controlled the corporation's operations. Although not dispositive, substantial ownership of a corporation and dominance of its management, as has been shown here, are factors favoring the piercing of the corporate veil. [Citations.]

Other factors the courts consider in determining whether the corporate veil should be pierced include: the inadequacy of the corporation's capitalization or its insolvency; the

failure to observe corporate formalities; the absence of regular board meetings; the non-functioning of corporate directors; the commingling of corporate and noncorporate assets; the diversion of assets from the corporation to the detriment of creditors; and the failure of an individual to maintain an arm's length relationship with the corporation. [Citations.]

All these factors are present here. Zide himself testified that the corporation was undercapitalized. This testimony was confirmed by further evidence which established that although Healthwin consistently had outstanding liabilities in excess of $150,000, its initial capitalization was only $10,000. . . . In 1974 and 1975 the liabilities of the corporation continued substantially to exceed its assets.

The evidence also established that Zide exercised his control over Healthwin so as to cause its finances to become inextricably intertwined with both his personal finances and his other business holdings. * * *

* * *

The necessary conclusion from all this is that Zide handled Healthwin's finances so as to accommodate his own business interests. Treatment of corporate assets in this fashion has long been considered a significant factor supporting the piercing of the corporate veil. [Citations.]

Another factor present here is that the operations of Healthwin were marked by an essential disregard of corporate formalities. [Citation.] Thus board meetings were not regularly held and with the exception of the first board meeting Zide and his wife were the only directors or shareholders present.

There is the final consideration that the court should not pierce the corporation's veil unless necessary to prevent an inequitable result. [Citations.] As to this, it is not necessary that plaintiff prove actual fraud; it is enough if the failure to pierce the corporation's veil would result in an injustice. [Citations.] Given the situation present here, the court must conclude that it would be unjust not to pierce the corporate veil. For one thing, Healthwin's undercapitalization subjected all its creditors, including plaintiff, to inequitable risks regarding Healthwin's obligations to them. [Citations.] Further, the court finds it particularly inequitable that in 1974 Healthwin, though insolvent, paid back to the Zide partnership some $109,000 it had previously borrowed from the partnership leaving a balance due the partnership of only $164.06. What is more, the record indicates that during 1975 Healthwin repaid Zide at least $39,384 on loans he had made to it.

In view of the foregoing considerations, the court holds that Healthwin's corporate entity should be disregarded under the *alter ego* theory of liability.

* * *

For the reasons set forth above, the court holds that Zide is personally liable to plaintiff for the Medicare overpayments to Healthwin. Accordingly, judgment will be entered against defendants in the sum of $30,481.55 plus interest at seven percent from the date of first demand on November 13, 1973.

Disregard of Corporateness:
Parent–Subsidiary

BERGER v. COLUMBIA BROADCASTING SYSTEM, INC.

United States Court of Appeals, Fifth Circuit, 1972.
453 F.2d 991.

GOLDBERG, J.

[Berger was planning to produce a fashion show in Las Vegas. In April 1965, Berger entered into a written licensing agreement with CBS Films, Inc., a wholly owned subsidiary of CBS, for presentation of the show. In 1966 Stewart Cowley decided to produce a fashion show similar to Berger's and entered into a contract with CBS. CBS broadcast Cowley's show and not Berger's show, and Berger brought this action against CBS to recover damages for breach of his contract with CBS Films. Berger claims that CBS is liable because CBS Films is its instrumentality or alter ego, and that the court should disregard the parent-subsidiary form. In support of this claim, Berger has shown that CBS Films' directors are employees of CBS, that CBS's or-

ganizational chart includes CBS Films, and that all lines of employee authority from CBS Films pass through employees of CBS to the chairman of the board of CBS. CBS, in turn, argues that Berger has failed to justify piercing the corporate veil and disregarding the corporate identity of CBS Films in order to hold CBS liable.]

* * *

It is elemental jurisprudence that a corporation is a creature of the law, endowed with a personality separate and distinct from that of its owners, and that one of the principal purposes for legal sanctioning of a separate corporate personality is to accord stockholders an opportunity to limit their personal liability. There does exist, however, a large class of cases in which the separateness of a corporate entity has been disregarded and a parent corporation held liable for the acts of its subsidiary because the subsidiary's affairs had been so controlled as to render it merely an instrument or agent of its parent. [Citation.] But the dual personality of parent and subsidiary is not lightly disregarded, since application of the instrumentality rule operates to defeat one of the principal purposes for which the law has created the corporation. [Citation.] Therefore, to justify judicial derogation of the separateness of a corporate creature, an aggrieved party must prove something more than a parent's mere ownership of a majority or even all of the capital stock and the parent's use of its power as an incident of its stock ownership to elect officers and directors of the subsidiary. [Citations.]

In formulating a basis for predicating liability of a parent corporation for the acts of its subsidiary, courts have developed various legal theories and descriptive terms to explain the relationship between a subsidiary and its dominating parent. For example, under the "identity" theory the separate corporate entity of the dominated subsidiary is disregarded and the parent and subsidiary are treated as one corporation. [Citation.] Furthermore, a dominated subsidiary has been labeled an instrument, agent, adjunct, branch, dummy, department, or tool of the parent corporation. [Citation.] In Lowendahl v. Baltimore & O.R.R., [citation], a New York court analyzed the various terms and legal theories and concluded that the instrumentality rule furnished the most practical theory for toppling a parent corporation's immunity. The court in *Lowendahl* then postulated the following three elements as the quantum of proof necessary to sustain application of the instrumentality rule:

(1) Control, not mere majority or complete stock control, but complete domination, not only of finances, but of policy and business practice in respect to the transaction attacked so that the corporate entity as to this transaction had at the time no separate mind, will or existence of its own; and (2) Such control must have been used by the defendant to commit fraud or wrong, to perpetrate the violation of a statutory or other positive legal duty, or a dishonest and unjust act in contravention of plaintiff's legal rights; and (3) The aforesaid control and breach of duty must proximately cause the injury or unjust loss complained of.

Applying these three elements to the relationship between the defendant and Films in the case at bar, we first turn to the lower court's factual determinations. The district court held that at all relevant times Films was merely an instrumentality of the defendant based on the following findings: (1) the board of directors of Films consisted solely of employees of the defendant; (2) the organization chart of CBS, Inc. included Films; and (3) all lines of employee authority from Films passed through employees of the defendant and other subsidiaries to the chairman of the board of CBS, Inc. In addition, the trial judge was greatly influenced by the fact that several witnesses, including a comptroller of one of the defendant's subsidiaries, testified that Films was a "division" of CBS, Inc. Comparing these several facts to the requisite quantum of proof necessary to satisfy *Lowendahl's* "control" element, we think it is obvious that these factual determinations, standing alone, are insufficient to sustain application of the instrumentality rule. Moreover, an independent examination of the record in this case convinces us that the evidence adduced below concerning the relationship between the defendant and Films could not sustain any finding that the defendant completely dominated not only the finances, but the policy and business practice of Films.

* * * In our opinion complete stock ownership, common officers and directors, and the use of organizational charts illustrating lines of authority are all business practices common to most parent-subsidiary relationships, and such proof of a parent's potential to dominate its subsidiary is precisely the kind of evidence that New York courts have consistently rejected as insufficient in proving a community of management between corporations. [Citations.] Furthermore, with respect to the testimony concerning Films' status as a division of the defendant, we think this evidence under New York law is equally unpersuasive. Affixing labels to corporate relationships for purposes of showing a parent's complete domination of a subsidiary is a dangerous business. As Justice Cardozo, speaking for the New York Court of Appeals [citation], stated:

Metaphors in law are to be narrowly watched, for starting as devices to liberate thought, they end often by enslaving it. We say at times that the corporate entity will be ignored when the parent corporation operates a business through a subsidiary which is characterized as an "alias" or a "dummy." All this is well enough if the picturesqueness of the epithets does not lead us to forget that the essential term to be defined is the act of operation.

. . . But when a lay witness testifies that one corporation is a division of another, then individual thought indeed becomes enslaved for a court to assume that the use of a descriptive term, by some process of testimonial osmosis, automatically introduces into evidence a composite of facts tending to show a community of management. Just as siamesing is a biological fact, so must corporate umbilication be anatomically demonstrated under New York Law. For purposes of application of the instrumentality rule, descriptive characterization is simply not an adequate alternative to a factual showing of the essential "act of operation."

Our prerequisition of the record in this case reveals that the evidence concerning the defendant's "act of operation" is totally insufficient to sustain any possible finding that, with respect to the transaction attacked, Films possessed at the time no separate mind, will, or existence of its own.

* * *

Faced with both this testimony and the total absence of any evidence showing the defendant's actual domination of its subsidiary Films during the period in which the plaintiff's contract was executed and allegedly breached, this court has no alternative but to reverse the decision of the district court on the simple basis that plaintiff has failed to prove, in accordance with New York law, that Films was the alter ego of the defendant. We reiterate that under the substantive law of the State of New York a parent's potential to dominate its subsidiary is insufficient to justify application of the instrumentality rule. New York law respects corporate identity, and its destruction by piercing or surrogation requires substantiation of facts, not just organizational charts and labels. The instrumentality referred to in New York cases requires a specific kinetic result, and muscularity to effectuate such result must be demonstrated. Plaintiff's omission in proving such muscularity constitutes his failing.

[The judgment of the district court in favor of Berger is reversed.]

QUESTIONS

1. Identify the principal attributes of a corporation and explain how these distinguish it from a partnership and a limited partnership.

2. Discuss (a) the liability of promoters on preincorporation contracts and (b) the nature of their fiduciary duty.

3. Distinguish between the common law and the statutory approaches to defective formation of a corporation.

4. Explain how the doctrine of piercing the corporate veil applies to (a) closely held corporations and (b) parent-subsidiary corporations.

5. Distinguish between the common law and statutory approaches to the effect of *ultra vires* acts.

PROBLEMS

1. After part of the shares of a proposed corporation had been successfully subscribed, one of the promoters hired a carpenter to repair a building. The promoters subsequently secured subscriptions to the balance of the shares and completed the organization, but the corporation declined to use the building or pay the carpenter for the reason that it was not suitable to the purposes of the company. The carpenter brought suit against the corporation for the amount that the promoter agreed would be paid to him. Decision?

2. C.A. Nimocks was a promoter engaged in organizing the Times Printing Company. On September 12, on behalf of the proposed corporation, he made a contract with McArthur for her services as comptroller for the period of one year beginning October 1. The Times Printing Company was incorporated October 16, and on that date McArthur commenced her duties as comptroller. No formal action on her employment was taken by the board of directors or by any officer, but all the shareholders, directors, and officers knew of the contract made by Nimocks. On December 1, McArthur was discharged without cause. Has she a cause of action against the Times Printing Company?

3. Todd and Elaine obtained an option on a building that was used for manufacturing pianos. They acted as the promoters for a corporation and turned the building over to the new corporation for $500,000 worth of stock. As a matter of fact, their option on the building called for a purchase price of only $300,000. The other shareholders desire to have $200,000 of the common stock canceled. Can they succeed in this action?

4. Wayne signed a subscription agreement for ten shares of stock having a value of $100 per share of the proposed ABC Company. Two weeks later the company was incorporated. A certificate was duly tendered to Wayne, but he refused to accept it. He was notified of all shareholders' meetings, but he never attended. A dividend check was sent to him, but he returned it. ABC Company brings a legal action against Wayne to recover $1,000. He defends upon the ground that his subscription agreement was an unaccepted offer and that he had done nothing to ratify it and that he was therefore not liable upon it. Decision?

5. Julian, Cornelia, and Sheila petitioned for a corporate charter for the purpose of conducting a retail shoe business. All the statutory provisions were complied with, except that they failed to have their charter recorded. This was an oversight on their part, and they felt that they had fully complied with the law. They operated the business for three years, after which time it became insolvent. The creditors desire to hold the members personally and individually liable. May they do so?

6. Arthur, Barbara, Carl, and Debra decided to form a corporation for bottling and selling apple cider. Arthur, Barbara, and Carl were to operate the business, and Debra was to supply the necessary capital but was to have no voice in the management. They went to Jane, a lawyer, who agreed to organize a corporation for them under the name A–B–C Inc., and sufficient funds were paid to her to accomplish the incorporation. Jane promised that the corporation would definitely be formed by May 3. On April 27, Arthur telephoned Jane to inquire how the incorporation was progressing, and Jane said she had drafted the articles of in-

corporation and would send them to the Secretary of State that very day. She assured Arthur that incorporation would occur before May 3.

Relying on Jane's assurance, Arthur, with the approval of Barbara and Carl, on May 4 entered into a written contract with Grower for the latter's entire apple crop. The contract was executed by Arthur on behalf of "A–B–C Inc." Grower delivered the apples as agreed. Unknown to Arthur, Barbara, Carl, Debra, or Grower, the articles of incorporation were never filed, through Jane's negligence. The business subsequently failed.

What are Grower's rights, if any, against Arthur, Barbara, Carl, and Debra as individuals?

7. The Pyro Corporation has outstanding 20,000 shares of common stock, of which 19,000 are owned by Peter B. Arson, 500 shares are owned by Elizabeth Arson, his wife, and 500 shares are owned by Joseph Q. Arson, his brother. These three individuals are the officers and directors of the corporation. The Pyro Corporation obtained a $250,000 fire insurance policy covering a certain building owned by it. Thereafter, Peter B. Arson set fire to the building, and it was totally destroyed. The corporation now brings an action against the fire insurance company to recover on the $250,000 fire insurance policy. What judgment?

8. A corporation is formed for the purpose of manufacturing, buying, selling, and dealing in drugs, chemicals, and similar products. The corporation, under authority of its board of directors, contracted to purchase the land and building occupied by it as a factory and store. Collins, a shareholder, sues in equity to restrain the corporation from completing the contract, claiming that as the certificate of incorporation contained no provision authorizing the corporation to purchase real estate, the contract was *ultra vires*. Decision?

9. Amalgamated Corporation, organized under the laws of State S, sends traveling salespersons into State M to solicit orders, which are accepted only at the home office of Amalgamated Corporation in State S. Riley, a resident of State M, places an order which is accepted by Amalgamated Corporation in State S. The Corporation Act of State M provides that "no foreign corporation transacting business in this state without a certificate of authority shall be permitted to maintain an action in any court of this state until such corporation shall have obtained a certificate of authority." Riley fails to pay for the goods, and when Amalgamated Corporation sues Riley in a court of State M, Riley defends on the ground that Amalgamated Corporation does not possess a certificate of authority from State M. Result?

10. Dr. North, a surgeon practicing in Georgia, engaged an Arizona professional corporation consisting of twenty lawyers to represent him in a dispute with a Georgia hospital. West, a member of the law firm, flew to Atlanta and hired local counsel with Dr. North's approval. West represented Dr. North in two hearings before the hospital and one court proceeding, as well as negotiating a compromise between Dr. North and the hospital. The total bill for the law firm's travel costs and professional services was $21,000, but Dr. North refused to pay $6,000 of it. The law firm brought an action against Dr. North for the balance owed. Dr. North argued that the action should be dismissed because the law firm failed to register as a foreign corporation in accordance with the Georgia Corporation Statute. Decision?

11. An Arkansas statute provides that if any foreign corporation authorized to do business in the State should remove to the Federal court any suit brought against it by a citizen of Arkansas or initiate any suit in the Federal court against a local citizen, without the consent of the other party, Arkansas's Secretary of State should revoke all authority of the corporation to do business in the State. The Burke Construction Company, a Missouri corporation authorized to do business in Arkansas, has brought a suit in and has removed a State suit brought against it to the Federal court. Burke now seeks to enjoin the Secretary of State from revoking its authority to do business in Arkansas. Burke contends that the Arkansas statute is unconstitutional. Decision?

12. Little Switzerland was incorporated on January 28, 1968. On February 18, Ellison and Oxley were made directors of the company after they purchased some stock. Then, on September 25, Ellison and Oxley signed stock subscription agreements to purchase 5,000 shares each. Under the agreement, they both issued a note which indicated that they would pay for the stock "at their discretion." In March 1970, the board of directors passed a resolution cancelling the stock subscription agreements of Ellison and Oxley. The creditors of Little Switzerland brought suit against Ellison and Oxley to recover the money owed under the subscription agreements. Decision?

13. Oahe Enterprises was formed by the efforts of Emmick, who acted as a promoter and contributed shares of Colonial Manors, Inc., (CM) stock in exchange for stock in Oahe. The CM stock had been valued by CM's directors for internal stock option purposes at $19 per share. One month prior to Emmick's incorporation of Oahe Enterprises, however, CM's board reduced the stock value to $9.50 per share. Although Emmick knew of this reduction prior to the meeting to form Oahe Enterprises, he did not disclose this information to the Morrises, the other shareholders of the new corporation. Oahe Enterprises then brought this action to recover the shortfall. Decision?

Chapter 35

FINANCIAL STRUCTURE

Debt Securities
Equity Securities
Dividends and Other Distributions
Transfer of Investment Securities

CAPITAL is necessary for any business to function. Two of the principal sources for financing corporations involve debt and equity investment securities. Equity securities represent an ownership interest in the corporation and include both common and preferred stock. In addition, corporations finance most of their operations through debt securities. Debt securities, or bonds, do not represent an ownership interest in the corporation but rather create a debtor-creditor relationship between the corporation and the bondholder. The third principal way in which a corporation may meet its financial needs is through retained earnings.

This chapter will discuss debt and equity securities as well as the payment of dividends and other distributions to shareholders. The last part of this chapter will examine the manner in which debt and equity investment securities are transferred.

DEBT SECURITIES

Corporations frequently find it advantageous to use debt as a source of funds. **Debt securities** (also called **bonds**) generally involve the corporation's promise to repay the princi-

pal amount of the *loan* at a stated time and to pay interest, usually at a fixed rate, while the debt is outstanding. Thus, a debt security creates a debtor-creditor relationship between the corporation and the holder of the security. In addition to bonds, a corporation may finance its operations through the use of other forms of debt, such as credit extended by its suppliers and short-term commercial paper.

Some States, but not the Revised Act, permit the articles of incorporation to confer voting rights on debt security holders. A few States allow other rights of shareholders to be conferred on bondholders.

AUTHORITY TO ISSUE DEBT SECURITIES

The Revised Act provides that every corporation has the power "to make contracts and guarantees, incur liabilities, borrow money, issue its notes, bonds, and other obligations (which may be convertible into or include the option to purchase other securities of the corporation), and secure any of its obligations by mortgage or pledge of any of its property, franchises, or income." Section 3.02. The board of directors may issue bonds without the authorization or consent of the shareholders.

TYPES OF DEBT SECURITIES

Debt securities can be classified into various types depending upon their characteristics. There are a great number of variants and combinations of each type, limited only by the ingenuity of the corporation. Debt securities are typically issued under an **indenture** or debt agreement, which specifies in great detail the terms of the loan.

Unsecured Bonds

Unsecured bonds, usually called **debentures,** have only the obligation of the corporation behind them. Debenture holders are thus unsecured creditors and rank equally with other general creditors. To protect the unsecured bondholders, indentures frequently impose limitations on the corporation's borrowing, its payment of dividends, and its redemption and reacquisition of its own shares. They also may require the maintenance of specified minimum reserves.

Secured Bonds

A secured creditor is one whose claim against the corporation not only is enforceable against the general assets of the corporation but also is a lien upon specific property. Thus, **secured** or mortgage **bonds** provide the security of specific corporate property in addition to the general obligation of the corporation. After resorting to the specified security, the holder of secured bonds becomes a general creditor for any unpaid amount of the debt.

Income Bonds

Traditionally, debt securities bear a fixed interest rate that is payable without regard to the financial condition of the corporation. **Income bonds,** on the other hand, condition the payment of interest to some extent upon corporate earnings. This provision lessens the burden of the debt upon the issuer during periods of financial adversity. **Participating bonds** call for a stated percentage of return regardless of earnings, with additional payments dependent upon earnings.

Convertible Bonds

Convertible bonds may be exchanged, usually at the option of the holder, for other securities of the corporation at a specified ratio. For example, a convertible bond may provide that the bondholder shall have the right for a specified time to exchange each bond for twenty shares of common stock.

Callable Bonds

Callable bonds are bonds that are subject to a redemption provision, which permits the corporation to redeem or call (pay off) all or part of the issue before maturity at a specified redemption price. This provision enables the corporation to reduce fixed costs, to improve its credit rating, to refinance at a lower interest rate, to free mortgaged property, or to reduce its proportion of debt.

EQUITY SECURITIES

An **equity security** is a source of capital creating an ownership interest in the corporation. The holders of equity security, as owners of the corporation, occupy a position of greater financial risk than creditors, and bear in greater measure than any other class of investor the impact of changes in the corporation's fortunes and general economic conditions.

Shares of equity securities are a method of describing a proportionate proprietary interest in a corporate enterprise, but they do not in any way vest their owner with title to any property of the corporation. Shares do confer on their owner, however, a threefold interest in the corporation: (1) the right to participate in control, (2) the right to participate in the earnings of the corporation, and (3) the right to participate in the residual assets of the corporation upon dissolution.

The shareholder's interest is usually evidenced by a certificate of ownership and is recorded by the corporation.

ISSUANCE OF SHARES

The State of incorporation regulates the issuance of shares by determining the type of shares that may be issued, the kinds and amount of consideration for which shares may be issued, and the rights of shareholders to purchase a proportionate part of additionally issued shares. Moreover, the issuance and sale of shares are regulated by each State in which the shares are issued or sold and by the Federal government.

Authority to Issue

The initial amount of shares to be issued is determined by the promoters or incorporators and is generally governed by practical business considerations and financial needs. A corporation is limited, however, to selling only the amount of shares that has been authorized in the articles of incorporation. Section 6.03. Unauthorized shares of stock that are purportedly issued by a corporation are void. The rights of parties entitled to these overissued shares are governed by Article 8 of the Uniform Commercial Code (U.C.C.). The Code provides that the corporation must either obtain an identical security, if it is reasonably available, for the person entitled to the security or pay that person the price he (or the last purchaser for value) paid for it with interest. U.C.C. Section 8–104.

Once the amount of shares that the corporation is authorized to issue has been established and specified in the charter, it cannot be increased or decreased without amendment of the articles of incorporation. This means that the shareholders have the residual authority over increases in the amount of authorized capital stock since they must approve any amendment to the articles of incorporation. Consequently, it is common for the articles of incorporation to specify more shares than are to be issued initially.

Qualification of Stock

All States have statutes regulating the issuance and sale of corporate shares and other securities, popularly known as **Blue Sky Laws.** These statutes typically have provisions prohibiting fraud in the sale of securities. In addition, a number of States require the registration of securities, and some States also regulate brokers, dealers, and others who engage in the securities business.

In 1933, Congress passed the first Federal statute providing regulation of securities offered for sale and sold through the use of the mails or otherwise in interstate commerce. This statute, often called the **Truth in Securities Act**, is administered by the Securities and Exchange Commission (SEC). The basic objectives of the statute are (1) to provide investors with relevant information about securities offered to the public and (2) to prevent misrepresentations in the sale of securities. The statute requires corporations to disclose certain information about a proposed security in a registration statement and in their **prospectus** (an offer made by corporations to interest people in buying stock). The SEC does not examine the merits of the proposed security, and registration does not guarantee the accuracy of the facts presented in the registration statement or prospectus. The law does prohibit false and misleading statements under penalty of fine or imprisonment or both.

Under certain conditions, a corporation may receive an exemption from the requirement of registration under the Blue Sky Laws of most States and the Securities Act of 1933. If no exemption is available, a corporation offering for sale or selling its shares of stock or other securities, as well as any person selling such securities, is subject to court injunction, possible criminal prosecution, and civil liability in damages to the persons to whom securities are sold in violation of the regulatory statute. A discussion of Federal regulation of securities appears in Chapter 45.

Preemptive Rights

A shareholder's proportionate interest in the corporation can be changed by either a nonproportionate issuance of additional shares or a nonproportionate reacquisition of outstanding shares. Management is subject to fiduciary duties in both types of transactions. Moreover, when additional shares are issued, a shareholder may have the **preemptive right** to purchase a proportionate part of the new issue. Preemptive rights are used far more frequently in closely held corporations than in publicly traded corporations. In the absence of preemptive rights, a shareholder may be unable to prevent a dilution of his ownership interest in the corporation. For example, Leonard owns 200 shares of stock of the Fordham Company, which has a total of 1,000 shares outstanding. The company decides to increase its capital stock by issuing 1,000 additional shares of stock. If Leonard has preemptive rights, he and every other shareholder will be offered one share of the newly issued stock for every share they own. If he accepts the offer and buys the stock, he will have 400 shares out of a total of 2,000 outstanding, and his relative interest in the corporation will be unchanged. Without preemptive rights, however, he would have only 200 out of the 2,000 shares outstanding and, instead of owning 20 percent of the stock, would own 10 percent.

At common law, shareholders have preemptive rights to the issuance of additionally authorized shares. Preemptive rights do not apply to the reissue of previously issued shares, shares issued for noncash consideration, or shares issued in connection with a merger or consolidation. There is a division among the jurisdictions whether preemptive rights apply to the issuance of unissued shares that were originally authorized.

Modern statutes expressly authorize the articles of incorporation to deny or limit preemptive rights. In some States, preemptive rights exist unless denied by the charter; in others, they do not exist unless the charter so provides.

The Revised Act adopts the latter approach: there are no preemptive rights unless the charter provides for them. Section 6.30. If the charter simply states that "the corporation elects to have preemptive rights," then the shareholders have a preemptive right to

acquire proportional amounts of the corporation's unissued shares but there is no preemptive right with respect to (1) shares issued as compensation to directors, officers, and employees, (2) shares issued within six months of incorporation, and (3) shares issued for consideration other than money. In addition, holders of nonvoting preferred stock have no preemptive rights with respect to *any* class of shares, and holders of voting common shares have no preemptive rights with respect to preferred stock unless the preferred stock is convertible into common stock. Section 6.30(b). The articles of incorporation may expressly provide that any of these limitations does not apply.

Amount of Consideration for Shares

Shares are deemed fully paid and nonassessable when the corporation receives the consideration for which the board of directors authorized the issuance of the shares. Section 6.21(d). The amount of that consideration depends upon the kind of shares being issued.

Par Value Stock   Par value shares may be issued for any amount, not less than par, set by the board of directors or shareholders. The par value of a share of stock can be an arbitrary value selected by the corporation and may or may not reflect either the actual value of the share or the actual price paid to the corporation. It indicates only the *minimum price* that the corporation must receive for it. The par value of stock must be stated in the articles of incorporation.

The consideration received constitutes *stated capital* to the extent of the par value of the shares; any consideration in excess of par value constitutes *capital surplus*.

The Revised Act and the 1980 amendments to the MBCA eliminate the concepts of par values, stated capital, and capital surplus. Under these acts, *all* shares may be issued for such consideration as authorized by the board of directors or, if the charter so provides, the shareholders. Section 6.21. A corporation *may*, however, elect to issue shares with par value. Section 2.02(b)(iv).

No Par Value Stock Shares without par value may be issued for any amount set by the board of directors or shareholders. Under incorporation statutes recognizing par value, stated value, and capital surplus, the entire consideration received constitutes *stated capital* unless the board of directors allocates a portion of the consideration to capital surplus. MBCA Section 21, repealed in 1980. (As noted above, the 1980 amendments to the Model Act and the Revised Act eliminated the concepts of par value, stated value, and capital surplus.) The directors are free to allocate any or all of the consideration received, unless the no par stock has a liquidation preference. In that event, only the consideration in excess of the amount of liquidation preference may be allocated to capital surplus. No par shares provide the directors with great latitude in establishing capital surplus, which can, in some jurisdictions, provide greater flexibility for subsequent distributions to shareholders.

Treasury Stock Treasury stock is shares that have been issued and subsequently reacquired by the corporation. Treasury shares are *issued but not outstanding*, in contrast to shares owned by shareholders, which are issued *and* outstanding. A corporation may sell treasury shares for any amount the board of directors determines, even if the shares have a par value that is more than the sale price. Treasury shares may not be voted, nor may any dividend be paid upon them, nor do they have any preemptive rights.

The Revised Act carries forward the 1980 amendments to the MBCA, which eliminated the concept of treasury shares. Under the Revised Act, all shares reacquired by a corporation constitute authorized but unissued shares, unless the articles of incorporation prohibit reissue, in which event the authorized shares are reduced by the number of shares reacquired. Section 6.31.

Figure 35–1 illustrates the issuance of shares.

Payment for Shares

Two major issues arise regarding payment for shares. First, what type of consideration may be validly accepted in payment for shares? Second, who shall determine the value to be placed upon the consideration received in payment for shares?

Type of Consideration Consideration for the issuance of capital stock is defined in a more limited fashion than it is under contract law. In some States, cash, property, and services actually rendered to the corporation are generally acceptable as valid consideration, but promissory notes and future services are not. *See United Steel Industries, Inc. v. Manhart.* Some States permit shares to be issued for preincorporation services; other States do not.

The Revised Act greatly liberalized these rules by specifically validating for the issuance of shares consideration consisting of any tangible or intangible property or *benefit* to the corporation, including cash, services performed, *contracts for future services,* and *promissory notes.* Section 6.21(b). To guard against possible abuse, the corporation may place the shares in escrow or otherwise restrict their transfer until the services are performed, the note is paid, or the benefits received. If the services are not performed, the note is not paid, or the benefits are not received, the shares escrowed or restricted may be cancelled. Section 6.21(e). Moreover, the Revised Act requires that corporations annually inform in writing shareholders of all shares issued during the previous year for promissory notes or promises of future services. Section 16.21.

Valuation of Consideration The determination of the value to be placed on the consideration exchanged for shares is the responsibility of the directors. The majority of jurisdictions hold that this valuation is a matter of opinion and that, in the absence of fraud in the transaction, the judgment of the board of directors as to the value of the consideration received for shares shall be conclusive. For example, assume that the directors of Elite Corporation authorize the issuance of 2,000 shares of common stock for $5 per share to Kramer for property that the directors value at $10,000. The valuation is fraudulent

Figure 35–1 Issuance of Shares

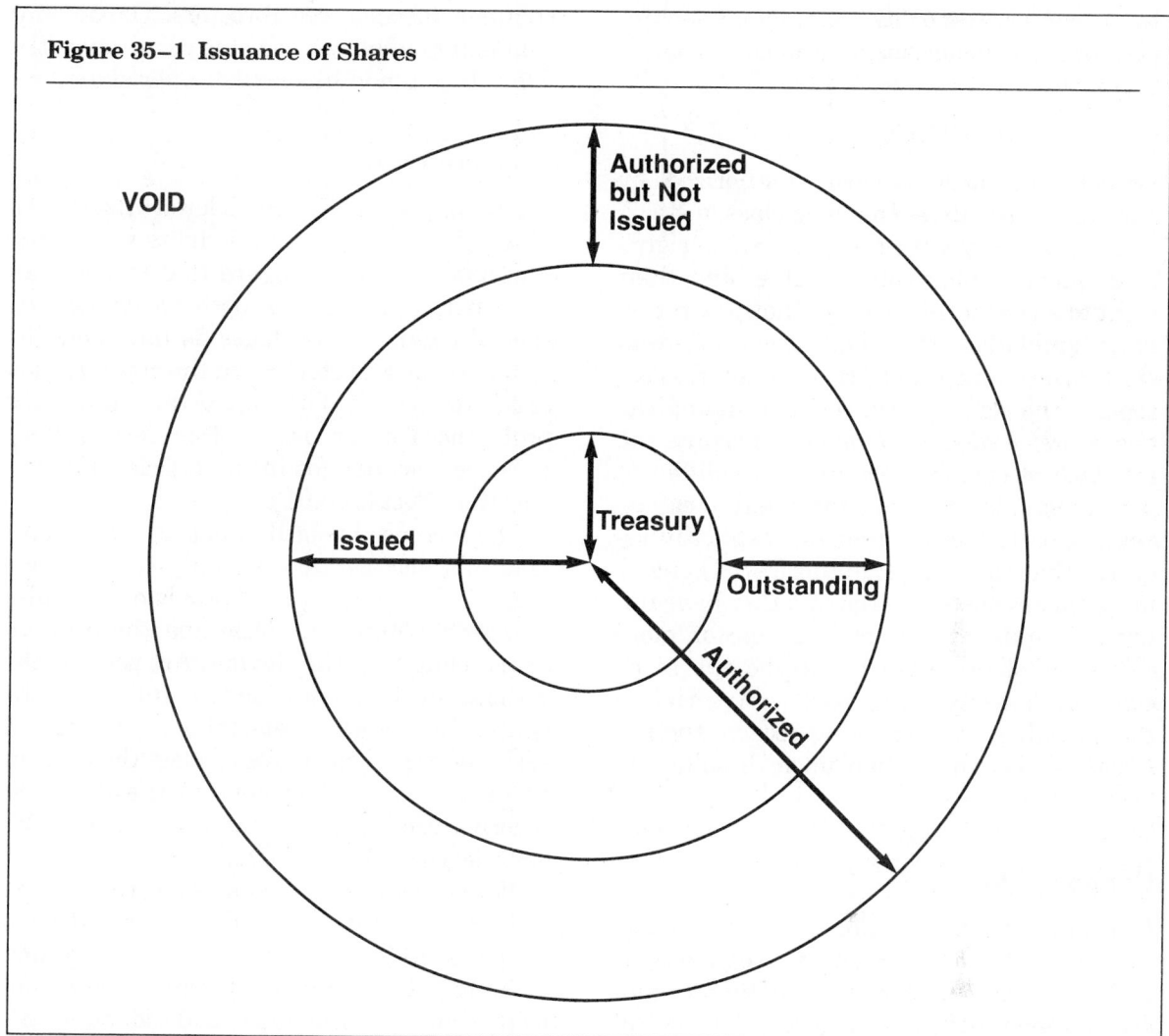

and the property is actually worth $5,000. Kramer is liable to Elite Corporation and its creditors for $5,000. If, on the other hand, the valuation had been made by the directors without fraud and in good faith, Kramer would not be liable, even though the property is actually worth less than $10,000.

Under the Revised Act, the directors simply determine that the consideration received (or to be received) for shares is *adequate*. That determination by the board of directors is "conclusive insofar as the adequacy of consideration for the issuance of shares relates to whether the shares are validly issued, fully paid, and nonassessable." Section 6.21(c). Under the Revised Act, the powers granted to the board regarding the issuance of shares

may be reserved to the shareholders by the articles of incorporation. Section 6.21(a).

Liability for Shares

A purchaser of shares has no liability to the corporation or its creditors with respect to the shares except to pay the corporation the consideration for which the shares were authorized to be issued or specified in the preincorporation stock subscription. Section 6.22(a). When the corporation receives that consideration, the shares are fully paid and nonassessable. Section 6.21(d). A transferee who acquires these shares in good faith and without knowledge or notice that the full consideration had not been paid is *not* personally liable to the corporation or its creditors for the unpaid portion of the consideration.

CLASSES OF SHARES

Corporations are generally authorized by statute to issue more than one class of stock, which may vary with respect to their rights to dividends, their voting rights, and their right to share in the assets of the corporation upon liquidation. The usual classifications of stock are common and preferred shares. Although the Revised Act has eliminated the terms *preferred* and *common*, it permits the issuance of classes of shares with different preferences, limitations, and relative rights. Section 6.01. The Revised Act explicitly requires that the charter authorize "(1) one or more classes of shares that together have unlimited voting rights, and (2) one or more classes of shares (which may be the same class or classes as those with voting rights) that together are entitled to receive the net assets of the corporation upon dissolution." Section 6.01(b).

Common Stock

Common stock does not have any special contract rights or preferences. Frequently, it is the only class of stock outstanding. It generally represents the greatest proportion of the corporation's capital structure and bears the greatest risk of loss in the event of failure of the enterprise.

Common stock may be divided into one or more classes with such designations, limitations, or relative rights as those stated in the articles of incorporation. Section 6.01. The Revised Act and some States permit common stock to be redeemable or convertible. Section 6.01(c)(2). The articles may also limit or deny the voting rights of classes of common shares but there must be at least one or more classes of shares that together have unlimited voting rights. Section 6.01(b). For example, Class A common may be entitled to three times the dividends per share to which Class B common is entitled. Or Class A common may be entitled to elect six directors while Class B

common elects three directors. Or Class A common may have two votes per share while Class B common has no votes per share.

Preferred Stock

Stock is generally considered **preferred stock** if it has contractual rights superior to common stock with regard to dividends, assets upon liquidation, or both. Other kinds of special rights or privileges do not generally remove a class of stock from the classification of common stock. The contractual rights and preferences of an issue of preferred stock must be provided for in the articles of incorporation. Section 6.01(c).

The increased volatility of the capital markets has necessitated not only the development of stock with special provisions but also greater flexibility in designing these provisions. Therefore, the Revised Act permits the articles of incorporation to authorize the board of directors to determine the terms of a series of preferred shares to meet the current financial markets by amending the articles of incorporation without holding a shareholders' meeting. Section 6.02.

Notwithstanding the special rights and preferences that distinguish preferred from common stock, both represent a contribution of capital. Preferred stock is no more a debt than common, and until a dividend is declared, the holder of preferred shares is not a creditor of the corporation. Furthermore, the rights of preferred shareholders are subordinate to the rights of all of the creditors of the corporation.

Dividend Preferences No dividend is payable upon any class of stock, common or preferred, unless it has been declared by the board of directors. An issue of preferred stock with a dividend preference means that its holders will receive full dividends before any dividend may be paid to holders of common stock. The dividend preference may be described in terms of dollars per share ("$3.00 preferred") or as a percentage of par value ("ten percent preferred"). Preferred stock may provide that dividends are cumulative, noncumulative, or cumulative to the extent earned.

For **cumulative** stock, if the board does not declare regular dividends on the preferred stock, such omitted dividends cumulate, and no dividend may be declared on common stock until all dividend arrearages on the preferred stock are declared and paid. For **noncumulative** stock, regular dividends do not cumulate upon failure of the board to declare them, and all rights to a dividend for the period omitted are gone forever. Accordingly, noncumulative stock has a priority over common only in the fiscal period a dividend on common stock is declared. Unless the dividends on preferred stock are made expressly noncumulative, the courts generally hold them to be cumulative. **Cumulative to the extent earned** stock cumulates unpaid dividends only to the extent funds were legally available to pay such dividends in that fiscal period.

Preferred stock may also be **participating**, although generally they are not. The nature and extent of such participation on a specified basis with the common stock must be stated in the articles of incorporation. For example, a class of participating preferred stock could be entitled to share at the same rate with the common in any additional distribution of earnings for a given year *after* provision has been made for payment of the prior preferred dividend and payment of dividends on the common at a rate equal to the fixed rate of the preferred.

Liquidation Preferences   After a corporation has been dissolved, its assets liquidated, and the claims of all of its creditors satisfied, the remaining assets are distributed *pro rata* among the shareholders according to their priority as provided in the articles of incorporation. In the event that a class of stock with a dividend preference does not expressly provide for a preference of any kind upon dissolution and liquidation, the holders of the preferred stock share *pro rata* with the common shareholders.

When a liquidation preference is provided, preferred stock has priority over common to the extent stated in the articles of incorporation. *See Rothschild International Corp. v. Liggett Group, Inc.* In addition, if specified, preferred shares may participate beyond the liquidation preference in a stated ratio with other classes of shares. Such shares are called participating preferred with reference to liquidation. If not so specified, preferred shares do not participate beyond the liquidation preference.

Additional Rights and Limitations   Preferred stock may have additional rights, designations, and limitations. For instance, it may be expressly denied voting rights if permitted by the statute; it may be redeemable by the corporation or convertible into shares of another class. Sections 6.01(c) and 7.21(a). Many States and the Model Act, but not the Revised Act, prohibit "upstream" conversions; that is, conversions of preferred shares into a class of shares having prior or superior rights and preferences as to dividends or distribution of assets upon liquidation. Accordingly, if upstream conversions are prohibited, preferred stock may be converted into common but common may not be converted into preferred.

Stock Rights

A corporation may issue stock rights or **stock options** entitling the holders of them to purchase from the corporation shares of a specified class or classes. A **stock warrant** is a type of stock option that typically has a longer term and is freely transferable. The board of directors determines the terms upon which stock rights, options, or warrants are issued, their form and content, and the consideration for which the shares are to be issued. Section 6.24. One of the uses of share options or warrants is incentive compensation plans for directors, officers, and employees. Another is to assist in raising capital by making one class of securities more attractive by including rights to purchase shares in another class.

Figure 35–2 compares debt and equity securities.

Figure 35-2 Debt and Equity Securities

	Debt	Equity Common	Equity Preferred
Ownership Interest	No	Yes	Yes
Obligation to Repay Principal	Yes	No	No
Fixed Maturity	Yes	No	No
Obligation to Pay Income	Yes	No	No
Preference on Income	Yes	No	Yes
Preference on Liquidation	Yes	No	Yes
Voting Rights	Some States	Yes, unless denied	Yes, unless denied
Redeemable	Yes	In some States	Yes
Convertible	Yes	In some States	Yes

DIVIDENDS AND OTHER DISTRIBUTIONS

The board of directors, in its discretion, determines when to declare distributions and dividends and in what amount. The corporation's working capital requirements, expectations of shareholders, tax consequences, and other factors influence the board in its formation of distribution policy. In addition, the conditions under which the earnings of a business may be paid out in the form of dividends or other distributions of corporate assets will depend upon the contractual rights of the holders of the particular shares involved, the provisions in the charter and bylaws of the corporation, and the provisions of the State incorporation statute designed to protect creditors and shareholders from dissipation of corporate assets. More significant

protection of creditors is provided by contractual restrictions typically included in their loan agreements, as well as by State fraudulent conveyance laws and Federal bankruptcy law.

TYPES OF DIVIDENDS AND OTHER DISTRIBUTIONS

The Revised Act defines a **distribution** as "a direct or indirect transfer of money or other property (except its own shares) or incurrence of indebtedness by a corporation to or for the benefit of its shareholders in respect of any of its shares. A distribution may be in the form of a declaration or payment of a dividend; a purchase, redemption, or other acquisition of shares; a distribution of indebtedness; or otherwise." Section 1.40(6). The comments to this section explain that the term *indirect* is intended to include any other transaction in which the substance is clearly the same as a typical dividend or share repurchase without regard to how it is labeled or structured. Stock dividends and stock splits, which are *not* included in this definition, will also be covered in this section.

Cash Dividends

The most customary type of dividend is a cash dividend, declared and paid at regular intervals from legally available funds. These dividends may vary in amount depending upon the policy of the board of directors and the earnings of the enterprise.

Property Dividends

Although dividends are almost always paid in cash, in a few instances a distribution of earnings has been made to shareholders in the form of property and has been termed a property dividend. On one occasion, a distillery declared and paid a dividend in bonded whiskey.

Stock Dividends

A stock or share dividend is a ratable distribution of additional shares of the capital stock of the corporation to its shareholders. The practical and legal significance of a stock dividend differs greatly from a dividend payable in cash or property. Following the payment of a stock dividend, the assets of the corporation are no less than they were before, and the shareholder does not have any greater relative interest in the net worth of the corporation than he had before, except possibly where the dividend is paid in shares of a different class. His shares will each represent a smaller proportionate interest in the assets of the corporation, but by reason of the increase in the number of shares, his total investment will remain the same. Accordingly, a stock dividend is *not* considered a distribution. For instance, Alice owns 100 shares of Linden Corporation's common stock of which 1,000 shares are issued and outstanding. The board

of directors declares and pays a 15 percent stock dividend. Prior to the stock dividend Alice owned 100 out of a total of 1,000 shares, or 10 percent. Subsequent to the stock dividend Alice owns 115 shares out of 1,150 total shares, or 10 percent. Although Alice owns more shares, her proportionate ownership of the common stock is unchanged by the stock dividend. Under incorporation statutes recognizing par value and stated capital, a stock dividend results in the transfer from surplus to stated capital of an amount equal to the par value of the stock dividend.

The distribution of shares of one class of stock to holders of another class may dilute the equity of the holders of the first class. Therefore, a share dividend may not be issued to holders of another class unless (1) the articles of incorporation expressly provide, (2) a majority of the votes entitled to be cast by the class to be issued approve the issue, or (3) there are no outstanding shares of the class to be issued. Section 6.23(b).

Stock Splits

In a stock split each of the issued and outstanding shares is simply broken up into a greater number of shares, each representing a proportionately smaller interest in the corporation. Under incorporation statutes recognizing par value and stated capital, the par value of the shares to be split are divided among the new shares, and there is no transfer of surplus to stated capital as is done with stock dividends. The usual purpose of a stock split is to lower the price per share to a more marketable price and thus increase the number of potential shareholders. As with a stock dividend, a stock split is *not* a distribution.

Liquidating Dividends

Although dividends are ordinarily identified with the distribution of profits, a distribution of capital assets to shareholders is referred to as a liquidating dividend in some jurisdictions. Incorporation statutes usually require that the shareholder be informed when a distribution is a liquidating dividend.

Redemption of Shares

Redemption is the repurchase by the corporation of its own shares, usually at its own option. The Model Act and the statutes of many States permit preferred shares to be redeemed but do not allow common stock to be redeemed. The Revised Act does not prohibit redeemable common stock. The power of redemption must be expressly provided for in the articles of incorporation.

Acquisition of Shares

A corporation may acquire its own shares. Such shares, unless cancelled, are referred to as treasury shares. Under the Revised Act, such shares are considered authorized but unissued. Section 6.31. As with redemptions, the acquisition of shares is a distribution to shareholders and has an effect similar to a dividend.

LEGAL RESTRICTIONS ON DIVIDENDS AND OTHER DISTRIBUTIONS

Several legal restrictions limit the amount of distributions the board of directors may declare. All States have statutes restricting the funds that are legally available for dividends and other distributions of corporate assets. In many instances, contractual restrictions imposed by lenders provide even more stringent limitations upon the declaration of dividends and distributions.

States restrict the payment of dividends and other distributions in order to protect creditors. All States impose the **equity insolvency test,** which prohibits the payment of *any* dividend or other distribution when the corporation is insolvent or when the payment of the dividend or distribution would render the corporation insolvent. **Insolvent** means the inability of a corporation to pay its debts as they become due in the usual course of business. In addition, each State imposes further restrictions on what funds are legally available to pay dividends and other distributions. These additional restrictions are based upon the corporation's assets, whereas

the equity insolvency test is based upon the corporation's cash flow.

Definitions

The legal, asset-based restrictions upon the payment of dividends or other distributions involve the concepts of earned surplus, surplus, net assets, stated capital, and capital surplus. See Figure 35–3.

Earned surplus consists of the undistributed net profits, income, gains, and losses from the date of incorporation.

Surplus means the excess of the net assets of a corporation over its stated capital.

Net assets are the amount by which the total assets of a corporation exceed the total debts of the corporation.

Stated capital is the sum of the consideration received by the corporation for its issued stock, except that part of the consideration properly allocated to capital surplus, and including any amount transferred to stated capital when a stock dividend is declared. In the case of par value shares, the amount of stated capital is the total par value of all the issued shares. In the case of no par stock, it is the consideration received by the corporation for all the no par shares that have been issued, except that amount allocated to capital surplus or paid-in surplus.

Capital surplus means the entire surplus of a corporation other than its earned surplus. It may result from an allocation of part of the consideration received for no par shares or from any consideration in excess of par value received for par shares or from a higher reappraisal of certain corporate assets.

Legal Restrictions on Cash Dividends

Earned Surplus Test Unreserved and unrestricted earned surplus is available for dividends in all jurisdictions. Some States permit dividends to be paid *only* from earned surplus; dividends in these jurisdictions may not be paid out of capital surplus or stated capital. In addition, dividends may not be paid if the corporation is or would be ren-

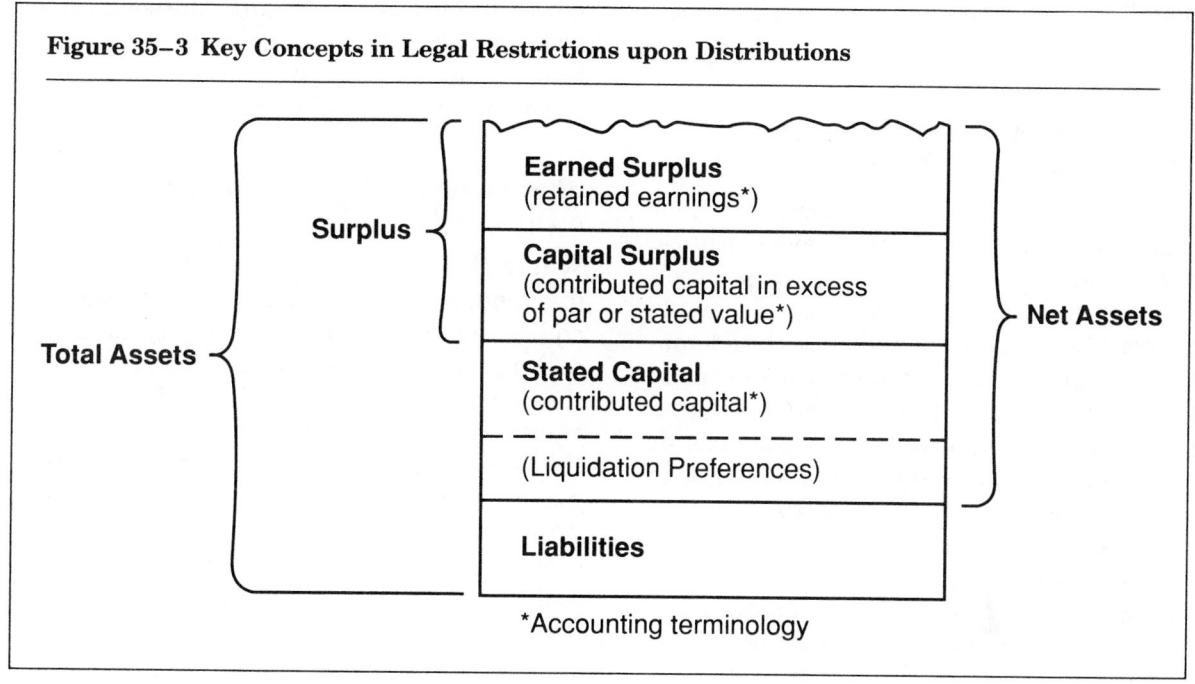

Figure 35–3 Key Concepts in Legal Restrictions upon Distributions

dered insolvent in the equity sense by the payment. The MBCA used this test until 1980.

Surplus Test A number of States are less restrictive and permit dividends to be paid out of any surplus—earned or capital. Some of these States express this test by prohibiting dividends that impair stated capital. Moreover, dividends may not be paid if the corporation is or would be rendered insolvent in the equity sense by the payment.

Net Asset Test The MBCA as amended in 1980 and the Revised Act have adopted a net asset test. Section 6.40 of the Revised Act as amended states:

(c) No distribution may be made if, after giving it effect:

(1) the corporation would not be able to pay its debts as they become due in the usual course of business; or

(2) the corporation's total assets would be less than the sum of its total liabilities plus (unless the articles of incorporation permit otherwise) the amount that would be needed, if the corporation were to be dissolved at the time of the distribution, to satisfy the preferential rights upon disso-

lution of shareholders whose preferential rights are superior to those receiving the distribution.

Legal Restrictions on Liquidating Distributions

Even those States that do not permit cash dividends to be paid from capital surplus usually will permit distributions, or dividends, in partial liquidation from that source. Before 1980, the Model Act had such a provision. A distribution paid out of such surplus is a return to the shareholders of a part of their investment.

No such distribution may be made, however, when the corporation is insolvent or would become insolvent by the distribution. Distributions from capital surplus are also restricted to protect the liquidation preference of preferred shareholders. Unless provided for in the articles of incorporation, a liquidating dividend must be authorized not only by the board of directors but also by the affirmative vote of the holders of a majority of the outstanding shares of stock of each class.

The Revised Act does not distinguish between cash and liquidating dividends and, therefore, imposes the same limitations discussed above under cash dividends. Section 6.40.

Legal Restrictions on Redemption and Acquisition of Shares

To protect creditors and holders of other classes of shares, most States have statutory restrictions upon redemption. A corporation may not redeem or purchase its redeemable shares when insolvent or when such redemption or purchase would render it insolvent or reduce its net assets below the aggregate amount payable upon shares having prior or equal rights to the assets of the corporation upon involuntary dissolution. *See Neimark v. Mel Kramer Sales, Inc.*

A corporation may purchase its own shares only out of earned surplus or, if the articles of incorporation permit or if the shareholders approve, out of capital surplus. As with redemption, no purchase of shares may be made at a time when the corporation is insolvent or when such purchase would make it insolvent.

The Revised Act permits the purchase, redemption, or other acquisition by a corporation of its own shares unless (1) the corporation's total assets after the distribution would be less than the sum of its total liabilities and the maximum amount that then would be payable for all outstanding shares having preferential rights in liquidation, or (2) the corporation would be unable to pay its debts as they become due in the usual course of its business. Section 6.40.

DECLARATION AND PAYMENT OF DISTRIBUTIONS

The declaration of dividends and other distributions is within the discretion of the board of directors of the corporation and may not be delegated. If the charter clearly and expressly provides for mandatory dividends, however, the board must comply with the provision. Nonetheless, such provisions are extremely infrequent and any other attempt by shareholders to usurp the board's power is ineffective, although it is in the shareholders'

power to elect a new board. Moreover, it is well settled that there can be no discrimination in the declaration of dividends among shareholders of the same class.

Shareholders' Right to Compel a Dividend

Where the directors have failed to declare a dividend, a shareholder may bring a suit in equity against them and the corporation seeking a mandatory injunction requiring the directors to declare a dividend. Courts of equity are reluctant to order an injunction of this kind, which involves substituting the business judgment of the court for that of the directors elected by the shareholders. A court of equity will, however, grant an injunction and require the directors to declare a dividend where

1. a demand has been made upon the directors before the suit was brought;

2. corporate earnings or surplus is available out of which a dividend may be legally declared;

3. the earnings or surplus is in the form of available cash; and

4. the directors have acted so unreasonably in withholding a dividend that their conduct clearly amounts to an abuse of discretion.

The existence of a large accumulated surplus does not by itself justify compelling the directors to distribute funds which, in their opinion, should be retained for *bona fide* corporate purposes. Where the evidence shows noncorporate motives or personal animosity as the basis for a refusal to declare dividends, however, a court may require the directors to distribute what appears to be a reasonable portion of the earnings. This is not a frequent occurrence; *Dodge v. Ford Motor Co.* is a landmark example.

The fact that a preferred shareholder has prior rights with respect to dividends does not make her position different from that of the holder of common shares with respect to the directors' discretion regarding the declaration of dividends. The holders of preferred stock, in the absence of special contractual or statutory rights, must likewise abide by the decision of the directors.

Effect of Declaration

Once lawfully and properly declared, a cash dividend is considered a debt owing by the corporation to the shareholders. It follows from the debtor-creditor relationship created by the declaration of a cash dividend that, once declared, a dividend cannot be rescinded against nonassenting shareholders; however, a stock dividend may be revoked unless actually distributed.

The time, place, and manner of payment of dividends are at the discretion of the directors. It is not uncommon for the resolution declaring a dividend to fix a cutoff date by providing that the dividend shall be paid to the shareholders of record as of the close of business on a specified future date, usually about two weeks earlier than the date fixed for payment. Where the resolution declaring a dividend fixes a cutoff date, the shareholder of record as of that date is entitled to the dividend. If the board of directors does not fix a record date, it is the date on which the board authorized the dividend. Section 6.40(b).

LIABILITY FOR IMPROPER DIVIDENDS AND DISTRIBUTIONS

The Revised Act imposes personal liability upon the directors of a corporation who vote for or assent to the declaration of a dividend or other distribution of corporate assets contrary to the incorporation statute or the articles of incorporation. Section 8.33(a). The measure of damages is the amount of the dividend or distribution in excess of the amount that may have been lawfully paid.

A director is not liable if she acted in good faith, with due care, and in a manner she reasonably believed to be in the best interests of the corporation. Sections 8.30 and 8.33. (This standard of conduct is discussed in the next chapter.) In discharging this duty, a director is entitled to rely in good faith upon financial statements presented by the corporation's officers, public accountants, or finance committee. The financial statements must be prepared on the basis of "accounting practices and principles that are reasonable in the circumstances or on a fair valuation or other method that is reasonable in the circumstances." Section 6.40(d). According to the Comments to this section, generally accepted accounting principles *are* always reasonable in the circumstances; other accounting principles *may* be acceptable under a general standard of reasonableness.

The liability of directors is generally to the corporation or to its creditors. The Revised Act expressly provides that the directors who vote for or assent to an illegal dividend or distribution are liable to the corporation. Section 8.33(a).

The obligation of a shareholder to repay an illegally declared dividend depends upon a variety of factors, which may include the good or bad faith on the part of the shareholder in accepting the dividend, his knowledge of the facts, the solvency or insolvency of the corporation, and, in some instances, special statutory provisions. The existence of statutory liability on the part of directors does not relieve shareholders from the duty to make repayment.

A shareholder who receives illegal dividends, with knowledge of their unlawful character, is under a duty to refund them to the corporation. See Section 8.33(b). Where the corporation is insolvent, a dividend may not be retained by the shareholder even though received by him in good faith. The assets of an insolvent corporation are regarded as a trust fund for its creditors. Where an unsuspecting shareholder receives an illegal dividend from a solvent corporation, the majority rule is that he cannot be compelled to make a refund.

TRANSFER OF INVESTMENT SECURITIES

An investor has the right to transfer her securities by sale, gift, or pledge just as she has the inherent right to transfer any other properties she may own. The right to transfer securities is a valuable one and the ease with which it may be done adds to their value and marketability. The availability of a ready market for any security affords liquidity and makes the security attractive to investors and useful as collateral.

The statutory rules applicable to transfers of securities are contained in the Uniform Commercial Code, Article 8, Investment Securities, which establishes rules similar to those in Article 3 concerning commercial paper. Article 8 applies not only to shares but also to bonds, debentures, voting trust certificates, certificates of beneficial interest in business trusts, and any other "interest in property of or an enterprise of the issuer or an obligation of the issuer" which is of a "class or series" and "issued or dealt in as a medium for investment." Section 8–102.

A number of aspects of the transfer of securities are also regulated by the Federal securities laws, discussed in Chapter 45.

OWNERSHIP OF SECURITIES

Record of Ownership

A security is intangible personal property and exists independently of a certificate. Article 8 permits the issuance and transfer of **uncertificated securities,** which are securities not represented by a certificate. The transfer of uncertificated securities is registered on books maintained for that purpose by or on behalf of the issuer. Section 8–102(1)(b).

The Revised Act permits the board of directors to authorize the issue of some or all of any or all of its class of shares without certificates. Section 6.26(a). The rights and obligations of holders of uncertificated shares and certificated shares of the same class and series are identical. Section 6.25.

Duty of Issuer to Register Transfer of Security

The issuing corporation is under a duty to register the transfer of its certificated securities and issue new certificates to the new owner if certain conditions are met:

1. the certificate is indorsed by the appropriate person or persons (Section 8–308);

2. reasonable assurance is given that those endorsements are genuine and effective (Section 8–402);

3. the issuer has no duty as to adverse claims or has discharged the duty (Section 8–403);

4. any applicable law relating to the collection of taxes has been complied with; and

5. the transfer is in fact rightful or is to a *bona fide* purchaser.

The owner or purchaser is entitled to registration in order to vote and to receive dividends, notices, periodic reports of the corporation, and a new certificate because the only way that he can sell or pledge or dispose of the certificated securities is by a transfer of the certificate.

Lost, Destroyed, or Stolen Certificated Securities

If a certificated security has been lost, destroyed, or stolen, the owner is entitled to a new certificate to replace the missing one provided she (1) requests it before the issuer has notice that the "missing" certificate has been acquired by a *bona fide* purchaser, (2) files a sufficient indemnity bond with the issuer, and (3) satisfies other reasonable requirements of the issuer, such as furnishing a sworn statement of the facts in connection with the loss. Section 8–405(2).

The owner of a lost, destroyed, or stolen certificate may be deprived of the right to a replacement certificate by failing to notify the issuing corporation within a reasonable time after learning of the loss, if the corporation has registered a transfer of the certificate before receiving such notification. Section 8–405(1).

TRANSFER OF SECURITIES

Restrictions on Transfer

In the absence of a specific agreement, shares of stock are freely transferable. Although free transferability of shares is usually considered an advantage of the corporate form, in some situations the shareholders prefer to restrict the transfer of shares. In closely held corporations, stock transfer restrictions are used to control who may become shareholders, thereby achieving the corporate equivalent of *delectus personae*. They are also used to restrict the number of persons who may become shareholders in order to maintain statutory close corporation status. In publicly held corporations, restrictions on the transfer of shares are used to preserve exemptions under State and Federal securities laws. (These are discussed in Chapter 45.)

Most incorporation statutes have no provisions governing share transfer restrictions. The common law validates these restrictions if they are adopted for a lawful purpose and do not unreasonably restrain or prohibit transferability. In addition, the U.C.C. provides that an otherwise valid share transfer restriction is ineffective against a person without actual knowledge of it unless the restriction is conspicuously noted on the share certificate or in the initial transaction statement for an uncertificated security. Section 8–204.

The Revised Act and the statutes of a few States permit transfer restrictions to be imposed in the articles of incorporation, bylaws, or a shareholder agreement but require that the restriction be noted conspicuously on the certificate or be contained in the information statement for uncertificated securities. The Revised Act authorizes restrictions for any reasonable purpose including maintaining statutory close corporation status and preserving exemptions under Federal and State securities law. Section 6.27. *See Matter of Estate of Spaziani.*

Statute of Frauds

A contract for the sale of securities is not enforceable unless one of the following conditions is satisfied:

1. a writing signed by the party against whom enforcement is sought and indicating that a contract has been made for sale of a stated quantity of described securities at a defined or stated price;

2. performance, as evidenced by acceptance of delivery or acceptance of payment, but only to the extent of such delivery or payment;

3. failure to object in writing within ten days to a written confirmation binding on the sender; or

4. an admission in pleading, testimony, or otherwise in court that a contract was made. Section 8–319.

Manner of Transfer

Under the Code, a transfer of certificated securities is made by delivery of the certificate alone, if it is in bearer form or indorsed in blank, or, if in registered form, which is more usual, by delivery of the certificate with either (1) the indorsement on it by "an appropriate person," or (2) a separate document of assignment and transfer signed by "an appropriate person." The term "appropriate person" includes the person specified in the certificate or entitled to it by special indorsement, their successors in interest, or the authorized agent of a person so specified or so entitled. Section 8–308. A transfer of uncertificated securities occurs at the time the transfer is registered.

Prior to presentment for registration of transfer of a certificated security in registered form, the corporation may treat the registered owner as the person entitled to vote, to receive notices, and otherwise to exercise all of the rights and powers of the owner. Section 8–207.

The delivery of an unindorsed certificate by the owner with the intention of transferring title to the securities represented thereby gives the intended transferee as against the transferor complete rights in the certificate and in the certificated securities, including the right to compel indorsement. He becomes a *bona fide* purchaser of the certificated securities, however, only as of the time the indorsement is supplied. Section 8–307.

Bona Fide Purchasers

A *"bona fide* purchaser" is a purchaser for value in good faith and without notice of any adverse claim who takes delivery of a certificated security in bearer form or in registered form issued to her or indorsed to her or in blank. Section 8–302. The negotiation and transfer of a security to a *bona fide* purchaser passes title to her free of all adverse claims not conspicuously noted on the certificate. Section 8–204. Adverse claims include a claim that a transfer was or would be wrongful or that a particular adverse person is the owner of or has an interest in the security. Section 8–302(2). Thus, the *bona fide* purchaser from a thief, finder, or other unauthorized person is protected.

Transfer Warranties

As provided by Section 8–306(2), a person by transferring certificated securities to a purchaser for value warrants that

1. the transfer is effective and rightful;

2. the security is genuine and has not been materially altered; and

3. he knows of no fact that might impair the validity of the security.

A person who presents a certificated security for registration of transfer or for payment or exchange warrants to the issuer that he is entitled to the registration, payment, or exchange, but a purchaser for value and without notice of adverse claims who receives a new, reissued, or reregistered certificated security on registration of transfer warrants only that he has no knowledge of any unauthorized signature in a necessary indorsement. Section 8–306(1).

Forged or Unauthorized Indorsement

The owner of securities represented by a certificate is not deprived of his title by a transfer of the certificate bearing a forged or unauthorized indorsement. The purchaser of a security bearing a forged or unauthorized indorsement who resells and transfers it to a *bona fide* purchaser is liable to him for the value of the securities at the time of sale, as he has breached his warranty that the transfer is effective and rightful. Section 8–306(2)(a). Neither party is owner of the securities, as title cannot be transferred through a forged or unauthorized indorsement.

Unless the owner has ratified an unauthorized indorsement or is otherwise precluded from asserting its ineffectiveness, he may assert its ineffectiveness against the issuer and against any purchaser, other than a *bona fide* purchaser who has in good faith received a new, reissued, or reregistered certificated security on registration of transfer. Section 8–311(a). An issuer who registers the transfer of a certificated security upon an unauthorized indorsement is subject to liability for improper registration. Section 8–311(b).

CASES

Payment for Newly Issued Shares

UNITED STEEL INDUSTRIES, INC. v. MANHART

Court of Civil Appeals of Texas, 1966.
405 S.W.2d 231.

McDONALD, C.J.

This is an appeal by defendants, United Steel Industries, Inc., J.R. Hurt, and W.B. Griffitts, from a judgment declaring void and cancelling 5000 shares of stock in United Steel Industries, Inc. issued to Hurt, and 4000 shares of stock in such corporation issued to Griffitts.

Plaintiffs Manhart filed this suit individually and as major stockholders against defendants United Steel Industries, Inc., Hurt, and Griffitts, alleging the corporation had issued

Hurt 5000 shares of its stock in consideration of Hurt agreeing to perform CPA and book-keeping services for the corporation for one year in the future; and had issued Griffitts 4000 shares of its stock in consideration for the promised conveyance of a 5 acre tract of land to the Corporation, which land was never conveyed to the Corporation. Plaintiffs assert the 9000 shares of stock were issued in violation of Article 2.16 Business Corporation Act, V.A.T.S. and prayed that such stock be declared void and cancelled.

Trial was before the Court without a jury which, after hearing, entered judgment declaring the 5000 shares of stock issued to Hurt and the 4000 shares issued to Griffitts, issued without valid consideration, void, and decreeing such stock cancelled.

* * *

The trial court found (on ample evidence) that the incorporators of the Corporation made an agreement with Hurt to issue him 5000 shares in consideration of Hurt's agreement to perform bookkeeping and accounting services for the Corporation for the first year of its operation. The Corporation minutes reflect the 5000 shares issued to Hurt "in consideration of labor done, services in the incorporation and organization of the Corporation." The trial court found (on ample evidence) that such minutes do not reflect the true consideration agreed upon, and that Hurt performed no services for the Corporation prior to February 1, 1965. The Articles of Incorporation were filed on January 28, 1965, and the 5000 shares were issued to Hurt on May 29, 1965. There is evidence that Hurt performed some services for the Corporation between January and May 29, 1965; but Hurt himself testified the "5000 (shares) were issued to me for services rendered or to be rendered for the first year in keeping the books. . . ."

The situation is thus one where the stock was issued to Hurt both for services already performed and for services to be rendered in the future.

The trial court concluded the promise of future services was not a valid consideration

for the issuance of stock under Article 2.16 Business Corporation Act; that the issuance was void; and that since there was no apportionment of the value of future services from the value of services already rendered, the entire 5000 shares were illegally issued and void.

Article 12, Section 6, Texas Constitution, Vernon's Ann.St. provides: "No corporation shall issue stock . . . except for money paid, labor done, or property actually received. . . ." And Article 2.16 Texas Business Corporation Act provides:

Payment for Shares.

A. The consideration paid for the issuance of shares shall consist of money paid, labor done, or property actually received. Shares may not be issued until the full amount of the consideration, fixed as provided by law, has been paid. . . .

B. Neither promissory notes nor the promise of future services shall constitute payment or part payment for shares of a corporation.

C. In the absence of fraud in the transaction, the judgment of the board of directors . . . as to the value of the consideration received for shares shall be conclusive.

* * *

The 5000 shares were issued before the future services were rendered. Such stock was illegally issued and void.

Griffitts was issued 10,000 shares partly in consideration for legal services to the Corporation and partly in exchange for the 5 acres of land. The stock was valued at $1 per share and the land had an agreed value of $4000. The trial court found (upon ample evidence) that the 4000 shares of stock issued to Griffitts was in consideration of his promise to convey the land to the Corporation; that Griffitts never conveyed the land; and the issuance of the stock was illegal and void.

The judgment of the board of directors "as to the value of consideration received for shares" is conclusive, but such does not authorize the board to issue shares contrary to the Constitution, for services to be performed in the future (as in the case of Hurt), or for property not received (as in the case of Griffitts).

The judgment is correct. Defendants' points and contentions are overruled.

Affirmed.

Preferred Stock

ROTHSCHILD INTERNATIONAL CORP. v. LIGGETT GROUP, INC.

Court of Chancery of Delaware, 1983.
463 A.2d 642.

BROWN, CHANCELLOR.

[GM Sub Corporation ("GM Sub"), a subsidiary of Grand Metropolitan Limited, acquired all outstanding shares of Liggett Group, Inc., a Delaware corporation. Rothschild International Corporation ("Rothschild") was the owner of 650 shares of the 7 percent Cumulative Preferred Stock of Liggett Group, Inc. According to Liggett's certificate of incorporation, the holders of the 7 percent Preferred were to receive $100 per share "in the event of any liquidation of the assets of the Corporation." GM Sub had offered $70 per share for the 7 percent Preferred, $158.63 for another class of preferred stock, and $69 for each common stock share. Liggett's board of directors approved the offer as being fair and recommended acceptance by Liggett's shareholders. As a result, 39.8 percent of the 7 percent Preferred shares was sold to GM Sub. In addition, GM Sub acquired 75.9 percent of the other preferred stock and 87.4 percent of the common stock. The acquisition of the overwhelming majority of these classes of stock—coupled with the fact that the 7 percent Preferred shareholders could not vote as a class on the merger proposal—gave GM Sub sufficient voting power to approve a follow-up merger. As a result, all remaining shareholders other than GM Sub were eliminated in return for payment of cash for their shares. These shareholders received the same consideration ($70 per share) as offered in the tender offer.

Rothschild brought suit against Liggett and Grand Metropolitan charging each with a breach of its duty of fair dealing owed to the 7 percent Preferred shareholders. Rothschild based both claims on the contention that the merger was a liquidation of Liggett insofar as the rights of the 7 percent Preferred stockholders were concerned. Therefore, those preferred shareholders were entitled to the liquidation preference of $100 per share, not $70 per share.]

* * *

Quite simply, no liquidation of Liggett occurred here. It still existed as a corporate entity following the tender offer and merger. It still retained shareholder status even though all shares merged in one owner. What happened was that all of its outstanding shares were acquired by a single owner. The corporation did not sell off all of its assets, pay its obligations, distribute the remaining proceeds to its shareholders, and cease to exist as a corporate entity. The fact that the practical effect of the transaction as to the 7% Preferred shareholders may have been similar to the result that would have followed from a liquidation does not make the transaction a liquidation.

The Delaware General Corporation law recognizes the concept of a merger. It is separate and distinct from a liquidation or a sale of assets. Indeed, the argument that a good faith merger is essentially a sale of assets when it suits a plaintiff to view it as such has long since been put to rest. [Citation.] Moreover, it has been held that preference rights of preferred stock can be eliminated legally through the merger process.

Consequently, in a case where a merger of corporations is permitted by law and is accomplished in accordance with the law, the holder of cumulative preference stock as to which dividends have accumulated may not insist that his right to the dividends is a fixed contractual right in the nature of a debt, in that sense vested and, therefore, secure against attack. Looking at the law which is a part of the corporate charter, and, therefore, a part of the shareholder's contract, he has not been deceived nor lulled into the belief that the right to such dividends is firm and stable. On the contrary, his contract has informed him that the right is defeasible; and with that knowledge the stock was acquired.

So here, the merger provisions of the Delaware General Corporation Law necessarily form a part of Liggett's charter. Thus, the liquidation preference given the 7% Preferred under Liggett's restated certificate of incorporation, . . . was always subject to the possibility of defeasance by merger, and the 7% Preferred shareholders were necessarily charged with knowledge of this at the time that they acquired their shares.

The preferential rights attaching to shares of preferred stock are contractual in nature and are governed by the express provisions of a corporation's charter. [Citations.] Nothing is to be presumed in favor of preferences attached to stock, but rather they must be expressed in clear language. [Citations.]

Under the express language of Liggett's charter the holders of the 7% Preferred were entitled to be paid the $100 par value of the shares only in the event of "any liquidation of the assets of the Corporation (whether voluntary or involuntary)." From this there can be no presumption that they would also be paid the par value under other circumstances. The total transfer of the ownership of the stock of the corporation through the tender offer and the follow-up merger was not a "liquidation of the assets" of the corporation, and, I think it fair to say, was never intended to be by either Liggett or by GM Sub. Therefore, no contractual liquidation right of the 7% Preferred shareholders was activated by the combined transaction, and thus no contractual right of the 7% Preferred shareholders was violated by either Liggett or by GM Sub as a result of the payment of the 7% Preferred shareholders of something less than $100 per share.

The contractual aspect of the matter highlights, I think, a significant point of distinction to be made. Closely examined, what Rothschild is arguing is that the 7% Preferred shareholders are entitled to be paid the liquidation value of their shares because *their rights* as preferred shareholders were liquidated as a result of GM Sub's acquisition. As stated by Rothschild in its reply brief, "the *interests of the 7% Preferred* Stockholders were forcibly *liquidated* under any fair and reasonable reading of the terms of Liggett's charter." And also, the "acquisition resulted in the liquidation of *their interests* in Liggett." (Emphasis added.)

In other words, Rothschild is arguing that where the preferred shareholders' rights are liquidated—i.e., their shareholder status terminated in return for the payment of cash— then the transaction by which it is accomplished should be viewed as a liquidation of the corporation itself insofar as those pre-ferred shareholders are concerned even though the corporation continues on as an operating legal entity.

Thus, the argument is not that the corporation has liquidated, or that its assets have been liquidated, but rather it is an argument that the interests of the 7% Preferred shareholders have been liquidated. But under the contractual language of Liggett's charter the right to payment of the par value of the shares springs into being only "[i]n the event of any liquidation of the assets of the Corporation." Thus, as I view Rothschild's argument, it is not based on a right spelled out in the contractual language of the charter.

* * *

Finally, I think it significant to note that Rothschild is making no charge that the $70 price offered in the tender offer and merger was inadequate or unfair in any respect other than it did not meet the stated liquidation price set forth in Liggett's charter. Thus, Rothschild's complaint has nothing to do with the fair value of the 7% Preferred as of the time of the tender offer and merger, or with the intrinsic fairness of the price offered and paid. Rather, its complaint is based strictly on the contention that there was a liquidation within the contemplation of those provisions of Liggett's certificate of incorporation which created the preference rights of the 7% Preferred. On the undisputed facts I find as a matter of law that there was none.

Accordingly, the motion of the plaintiff Rothschild for summary judgment will be denied. The motion of the defendants will be granted and summary judgment will be entered in favor of Liggett and GM Sub.

Legal Restrictions on Distributions

NEIMARK v. MEL KRAMER SALES, INC.

Court of Appeals of Wisconsin, 1981.
102 Wis.2d 282, 306 N.W.2d 278.

DECKER, C.J.

This appeal questions whether the trial court erred in this shareholder's derivative action by ordering specific performance of a stock redemption agreement upon death of the principal shareholder of defendant corporation. We vacate the judgment and remand with directions.

Plaintiff seeks specific performance of an agreement for the redemption of stock owned by the late Mel Kramer (Kramer), founder and majority shareholder of Mel Kramer Sales, Inc. (MKS). MKS is a closely-held Wisconsin corporation engaged in the business of selling automotive parts and accessories. The interests of the shareholders are:

Shareholder	Number of Shares	Percentage
Mel Kramer/Estate of Mel Kramer	1,020	51
Delores Kramer	200	10
Jack Neimark	580	29
Jerome Sadowsky	200	10

Kramer died on December 5, 1976. On May 9, 1977, Delores Kramer, Kramer's widow, was appointed personal representative of his estate. Delores Kramer is president and a director of MKS. Jack Neimark is vice-president and a director. Directors David Gutkin and Sara Lee Begun are relatives of Delores Kramer.

On June 22, 1976, a stock redemption agreement was executed by MKS and its stockholders. The agreement requires MKS to purchase, and a deceased shareholder's estate to sell, all of the deceased shareholder's stock in MKS at $400 per share, less a specified credit. The agreement also provided Delores Kramer with the option to sell her shares to MKS in the event of Kramer's death.

Under the agreement, Kramer's 1,020 shares were to be redeemed by MKS within thirty days after the appointment of his estate's personal representative, Delores Kramer, in the following manner. The redemption price of $408,000, less a specifically provided $50,000 credit, constituting a net price of $358,000, was to be paid in installments of $100,000 at the closing, and the balance in five consecutive annual installments. The first installment after the

closing was to be $43,200, with four remaining installments of $53,700, plus interest at 6%. If Delores Kramer elected to redeem her shares, her stock was to be purchased at the same per-share price payable in two installments of $40,000, on the sixth and seventh anniversaries of the closing, plus interest at 6% after five years.

The agreement provided that the $100,000 payment for Kramer's shares was to be funded by a life insurance policy on Kramer's life. Upon Kramer's death, MKS received the $100,000 proceeds from the life insurance policy, and it was reflected in MKS's retained earnings as of December 31, 1976.

The agreement also provided that if MKS did not have sufficient surplus or retained earnings to purchase the deceased shareholder's stock, the parties would contribute the necessary capital to enable MKS to lawfully redeem the decedent's shares. It was also agreed that the parties would be entitled to specific performance of the agreement.

After Kramer's death, Delores Kramer indicated a reluctance to have MKS redeem the shares owned by her husband's estate. Neimark insisted that MKS redeem the estate's shares, and on May 23, 1977, the board of directors met to consider Neimark's demand. The MKS attorney who was the author of the stock redemption agreement was present at this meeting and explained to the board that redemption of the stock by MKS would violate sec. 180.385(1), Stats. The board voted 3−1 not to purchase the Kramer estate's shares. Neimark, of course, cast the losing vote.

On November 30, 1978, Neimark commenced an action for specific performance of the 1976 agreement and alternatively, sought monetary damages. The first claim was derivative on behalf of MKS, pursuant to sec. 180.405, Stats.; the second claim was personal.

Subsequently, a third party offered to purchase the business for $1,000,000. Neimark conditioned his approval of the sale on the requirement that Delores Kramer and the Kramer estate receive proceeds equal only to the redemption price of the shares which was substantially less than the tendered per-share price. The defendants counterclaimed in Neimark's action and sought an order declaring that Neimark was entitled to receive only his ratable share of the proceeds of any sale of the business, which denied him the redemption agreement benefits. The trial court dismissed Neimark's personal claim, but ordered specific performance of the stock redemption agreement under the derivative claim. The counterclaim was dismissed.

* * *

Section 180.385(1), Stats., prohibits, *inter alia,* acquisition by a corporation of its own stock if the corporation would thereby be rendered insolvent. "Insolvent" is defined in sec. 180.02(14) as the "inability of a corporation to pay its debts as they become due in the usual course of its business." The purpose of prohibiting own stock acquisition by a corporation if it would thereby be rendered insolvent is to protect the creditors, preferred security holders, and in some cases, common stockholders whose stock is not acquired, from director action which would strip funds from the corporation and create a distributive preference to the stockholder whose stock is acquired.

* * *

The trial court's finding of fact, that performance of the stock redemption agreement would not render the corporation insolvent, is supported by ample evidence, and is not contrary to the great weight and clear preponderance of the evidence. The evidence establishes the fact that the corporation had the ability to pay its debts as they became due. In arriving at that conclusion, the trial court is not restricted to analyzing the cash and cash-equivalent assets of the corporation. The flow of cash to maintain solvency can be generated by a multitude of means other than cash generated solely from sales.

In this case, MKS had a $275,000 line of credit with a local bank. Its annual financial statements for 1976, 1977, and 1978, and the May 31, 1979, financial statement, disclose no inability of MKS to pay its debts as they became due if the redemption agreement had been performed.

Upon Kramer's death, it became the obligation of MKS to redeem his stock, provided the corporation could comply with sec. 180.385(1), Stats., with respect to solvency. We agree with the trial court's finding of fact that it could. To the extent that the finding also constitutes a conclusion of law, we also agree.

Contrary to the English rule, American courts at common law generally permit a corporation to acquire its own shares. The American rule has undergone harsh criticism because of the opportunity it affords to prefer selected stockholder/sellers and strip funds from the corporation to the disadvantage of preferred security interest holders, other common stockholders, and creditors. The rule sought protection for those persons by vaguely requiring that the purchase be "without prejudice" to their interests. [Citations.] Additional statutory restrictions resulted and culminated in the two major restraints (for the purposes of this case): the purchase must be made out of earned surplus and cannot be made if insolvency, in the equity sense, is present or would result. "[I]nsolvency in the equity sense has always meant an inability of the debtor to pay his debts as they mature. Under the Bankruptcy Act it means an insufficiency of assets at a fair valuation to pay the debts." [Citation.] The surplus and insolvency tests were incorporated in § 6 of the Model Business Corporation Act which formed the basis of the revision of the Wisconsin Business Corporation Law in the early 1950's. Section 180.385, Stats., adopts surplus and insolvency tests. Purchase of shares is permitted if: "At the time of such acquisition the corporation is not and would not thereby be rendered insolvent." Sec. 180.385(1)(a), Stats.

The self-evident applicability of the insolvency test at the time of acquisition of the stock is not equally self-evident in the case of an installment purchase. Considerations of "corporate flexibility" in the acquisition of its stock for legitimate purposes, balanced by "protection for creditors," led the majority of American courts to apply the insolvency test contemporaneously with each installment payment. The Model Business Corporation Act § 6 has been amended to specifically so provide. Although that specific change has not been incorporated in sec. 180.385(1)(a), Stats., we agree with the reasoning of the majority of American courts that the protection of the corporation's creditors requires that the insolvency limitation be applied both at the time of purchase and when each installment payment is made pursuant to the purchase agreement. When the payment is actually made, the assets leave the corporation and concomitantly the loss of financial protection occurs. If insolvency results or would result, the purchase may constitute a fraudulent conveyance. In any event, the hazard of fraud to creditors is too great to permit the insolvency test to be applied at times remote to payment for the share repurchase.

* * *

When applying the insolvency test at the stage of each payment for a stock repurchase to achieve creditor protection, consistency suggests that the amount of each payment, not the total purchase price, should be a component of the determination of solvency. The weight of authority has so applied the tests and we adopt that method of application. That method is in accord with the equity sense insolvency test expressly prescribed by secs. 180.02(11) and 180.385(1)(a), Stats.

Defendants have not demonstrated insolvency in the equity sense to the trial court or to us. Our review of the corporate financial statements in evidence discloses no arguable claim of insolvency in the equity sense. * * *

The second limitation upon the corporate repurchase of its stock pertinent to this case is the restriction that "the corporation has unreserved and unrestricted earned surplus equal to the cost of such shares." Sec. 180.385(1)(c)2., Stats. In this respect, the Wisconsin Business Corporation Law generally follows its paradigm, the Model Business Corporation Act. Earned surplus is defined in sec. 180.02(11). In this case, the parties do not dispute the amount of earned surplus.

Our review of the record again establishes the following undisputed evidence with respect to paid-up capital stock, retained earnings, and total stockholders' equity.

	12/31 1976	12/31 1977	12/31 1978	5/31 1979
Paid-up Capital Stock	69,400	69,400	69,400	69,400
Retained Earnings	246,409	276,073	317,586	317,584
Current Earnings				31,575
Stockholders' Equity	315,809	345,473	386,986	418,559

We subtract projected payments pursuant to the stock redemption agreement.

Retained and Current Earnings Adjusted to Reflect Deducted Installment Payments	276,073	217,586	205,961
Installment Payments Without Interest	100,000	43,200	53,700
Net Retained Earnings	176,073	174,386	152,261
Credit	50,000		

Historically, the statutory insolvency cutoff test evolved from the "no prejudice to creditors" rule. Dissatisfaction with the limited effectiveness of that test resulted in the formulation of the surplus cutoff test to be applied in conjunction with the insolvency cutoff test.

The same problem arose with the application of the surplus cutoff test that developed in applying the insolvency cutoff test: in the case of an installment purchase, should the surplus test be applied at the time of purchase or at the time cash payment is made? Most cases demonstrate little effort to distinguish between the methods of applying both tests and resolve the question by the easier and more convenient method of applying both tests in the same fashion.

* * *

Professor Herwitz discusses a number of reasons for applying the surplus to the time of purchase rather than at each installment payment. We agree with his view that the statutory surplus cutoff rule should be applied only once, and at the time of purchase. * * *

* * *

Although it is apparent from the MKS financial statements that application of the surplus cutoff test upon an installment basis would not have precluded specific performance as ordered by the trial court, application of the test at the outset will preclude specific performance upon the basis of the facts as presented to us. However, we note that the stock redemption agreement provides:

(f) *Insufficient Corporate Surplus.* If the Corporation does not have sufficient surplus or retained earnings to permit it to lawfully purchase all of such shares, each of the parties shall promptly take such measures as are required to reduce the capital of the Corporation or to take such other steps as may be necessary in order to enable the Corporation to lawfully purchase and pay for the Decedent's shares.

We vacate the judgment of the circuit court and remand for further proceedings consistent with this opinion. The circuit court is directed to apply the surplus cutoff test to the time of specific performance of the stock redemption agreement if it concludes that the evidence justifies specific performance. Because we adopt an application of the statute which has not heretofore been explicated, we think it fair to permit the parties to offer current financial data with respect to MKS and the ability of the parties to the redemption agreement to take the necessary steps to enable the corporation to lawfully purchase and pay for the redeemed stock. Such evidence will enable a current evaluation of the propriety of specific performance. In the event the trial court deems specific performance appropriate, it shall make the necessary findings and requirements with regard to providing sufficient earned surplus and assuring solvency as a condition to specific performance.

Declaration of Dividends

DODGE v. FORD MOTOR CO.

Supreme Court of Michigan, 1919.
204 Mich. 459, 170 N.W. 668.

OSTRANDER, J.

[Action in equity by John F. and Horace E. Dodge, plaintiffs, against the Ford Motor Company and its directors to compel the declaration of dividends and for an injunction restraining a contemplated expansion of the business. The complaint was filed in November, 1916. Since 1909, the capital stock of the company has been $2,000,000, divided into 20,000 shares of the par value of $100 each of which plaintiffs held 2,000. As of the close of business of July 31, 1916, the end of the company's fiscal year, the surplus above capital was $111,960,907.53 and the assets included cash on hand of $52,550,771.92.

For a number of years the company had paid regularly quarterly dividends equal to sixty percent annually on the capital stock of $2,000,000. In addition, from December, 1911, to October, 1915, inclusive, eleven special dividends totalling $41,000,000 had been paid and in November, 1916, after this action was commenced, a special dividend of $2,000,000 was paid.

Plaintiffs' complaint alleged that Henry Ford, president of the company and a member of its board of directors, had declared it to be the settled policy of the company not to pay any special dividends in the future, but to put back into the business all future earnings in excess of the regular quarterly dividend. Plaintiffs sought an injunction restraining the carrying out of the alleged declared policy of Henry Ford and a decree requiring the directors to pay a dividend of at least seventy-five percent of the accumulated cash surplus.

In December, 1917, the trial court entered a decree requiring the directors to declare and pay a dividend of $19,275,385.96 and enjoining the corporation from using its funds for a proposed smelting plant and certain other planned projects. From this decree, defendants have appealed.]

* * *

The case for plaintiffs must rest upon the claim, and the proof in support of it, that the proposed expansion of the business of the corporation involving the further use of profits as capital, ought to be enjoined because inimical to the best interests of the company and its shareholders, and upon the further claim that in any event the withholding of the special dividend asked for by plaintiffs is arbitrary action of the directors requiring judicial interference.

The rule which will govern courts in deciding these questions is not in dispute. . . . In [citation], it is stated:

Profits earned by a corporation may be divided among its shareholders; but it is not a violation of the charter if they are allowed to accumulate and remain invested in the company's business. The managing agents of a corporation are impliedly invested with a discretionary power with regard to the time and manner of distributing its profits. They may apply profits in payment of floating or funded debts, or in development of the company's business; and so long as they do not abuse their discretionary powers, or violate the company's charter, the courts cannot interfere.

But it is clear that the agents of a corporation, and even the majority, cannot arbitrarily withhold profits earned by the company, or apply them to any use which is not authorized by the company's charter. The nominal capital of a company does not necessarily limit the scope of its operations; a corporation may borrow money for the purpose of enlarging its business, and in many instances it may use profits for the same purpose. . . .

When plaintiffs made their complaint and demand for further dividends the Ford Motor Company had concluded its most prosperous year of business. The demand for its cars at the price of the preceding year continued. It could make and could market in the year beginning August 1, 1916, more than 500,000 cars. Sales of parts and repairs would necessarily increase. The cost of materials was likely to advance, and perhaps the price of labor, but it reasonably might have expected a profit for the year of upwards of $60,000,000. It had assets of more than $132,000,000, a surplus of almost $112,000,000, and its cash on hand and municipal bonds were nearly $54,000,000. Its total liabilities, including capital stock, was a little over $20,000,000. It had declared no special dividend during the business year except the October, 1915, dividend. It had been the practice, under similar circumstances, to declare larger dividends. Considering only these facts, a refusal to declare and pay further dividends appears to be not an exercise of discretion on the part of the directors, but an arbitrary refusal to do what the circumstances required to be done. These facts and others call upon the directors to justify their action, or failure or refusal to act. In justification, the defendants have offered testimony tending to prove, and which does prove, the following facts. It had been the policy of the corporation for a considerable time to annually reduce the selling price of cars, while keeping up, or improving their quality. As early as in June 1915 a general plan for the expansion of the productive capacity of the concern by a practical duplication of its plant had been talked over by the executive officers and directors and agreed upon, not all of the details having been settled and no formal action of directors having been taken. The erection of a smelter was considered, and engineering and other data in connection therewith secured. In consequence, it was determined not to reduce the selling price of cars for the year beginning August 1, 1915, but to maintain the price and to accumulate a large surplus to pay for the proposed expansion of plant and equipment, and perhaps to build a plant for smelting ore. It is hoped, by Mr. Ford, that eventually 1,000,000 cars will be annually produced. The contemplated changes will permit the increased output.

The plan, as affecting the profits of the business for the year beginning August 1, 1916, and thereafter, calls for a reduction in the selling price of cars. . . . In short, the plan does not call for and is not intended to produce immediately a more profitable business but a less profitable one; not only less profitable than formerly but less profitable than it is admitted it might be made. The apparent immediate effect will be to diminish the value of shares and the return to shareholders.

It is the contention of plaintiffs that the apparent effect of the plan is intended to be the continued and continuing effect of it and that it is deliberately proposed, not of record and not by official corporate declaration, but nevertheless proposed, to continue the corporation henceforth as a semi-eleemosynary institution and not as a business institution. In support of this contention they point to the attitude and to the expressions of Mr. Henry Ford.

Mr. Henry Ford is the dominant force in the business of the Ford Motor Company. No plan of operations could be adopted unless he consented, and no board of directors can be elected whom he does not favor. One of the directors of the company has no stock. One share was assigned to him to qualify him for the position, but it is not claimed that he owns it. A business, one of the largest in the world, and one of the most profitable, has been built up. It employs many men, at good pay.

"My ambition," said Mr. Ford, "is to employ still more men, to spread the benefits of this industrial system to the greatest possible number, to help them build up their lives and their homes. To do this we are putting the greatest share of our profits back in the business." * * *

The record, and especially the testimony of Mr. Ford, convinces that he has to some extent the attitude towards shareholders of one who has dispensed and distributed to them large gains and that they should be content to take what he chooses to give. His testimony creates the impression, also, that he thinks the Ford Motor Company has made too much money, has had too large profits, and that although large profits might still be earned, a sharing of them with the public, by reducing the price of the output of the company, ought to be undertaken. We have no doubt that certain sentiments, philanthropic and altruistic, creditable to Mr. Ford, had large influence in determining the policy to be pursued by the Ford Motor Company—the policy which has been herein referred to. * * *

These cases, after all, like all others in which the subject is treated, turn finally upon the point, the question, whether it appears that the directors were not acting for the best interest of the corporation. . . . The difference between an incidental humanitarian expenditure of corporate funds for the benefit of the employees, like the building of a hospital for their use and the employment of agencies for the betterment of their condition, and a general purpose and plan to benefit mankind at the expense of others, is obvious. . . . A business corporation is organized and carried on primarily for the profit of the stockholders. The powers of the directors are to be employed for that end. The discretion of directors is to be exercised in the choice of means to attain that end and does not extend to a change in the end itself, to the reduction of profits or to the nondistribution of profits among stockholders in order to devote them to other purposes. * * *

We are not, however, persuaded that we should interfere with the proposed expansion of the business of the Ford Motor Company. In view of the fact that the selling price of products may be increased at any time, the ultimate results of the larger business cannot be certainly estimated. The judges are not business experts. It is recognized that plans must often be made for a long future, for expected competition, for a continuing as well as an immediately profitable venture. The experience of the Ford Motor Company is evidence of capable management of its affairs. * * *

Defendants say, and it is true, that a considerable cash balance must be at all times carried by such a concern. But, as has been stated, there was a large daily, weekly, monthly, receipt of cash. The output was practically continuous and was continuously, and within a few days, turned into cash. Moreover, the contemplated expenditures were not to be immediately made. The large sum appropriated for the smelter plant was payable over a considerable period of time. So that, without going further, it would appear that, accepting and approving the plan of the directors, it was their duty to distribute on or near the first of August, 1916, a very large sum of money to stockholders. * * *

The decree of the court below fixing and determining the specific amount to be distributed to stockholders is affirmed. In other respects, except as to the allowance of costs, the said decree is reversed.

Restrictions on Transfer

MATTER OF ESTATE OF SPAZIANI

Surrogate's Court of New York, Jefferson County, 1984.
125 Misc.2d 901, 480 N.Y.S.2d 854.

GILBERT, J.

Issues of significant concern to practicing attorneys involved in either corporate or estate practice are raised herein. The question is raised herein as to whether a restriction on the transferability of stock binds the personal representative of a deceased stockholder.

The decedent, Vincent Spaziani, was one of the five original subscribers to the certificate of incorporation of Spaziani Bakeries, Inc. Paragraph Eleventh of the certificate states that "No certificate of stock or any interest therein of this corporation shall be transferred to any person, persons, partnership or corporation until it has first been offered for sale in writing by registered mail to this Corporation." The corporation seeks to have such clause enforced while the distributees of Vincent Spaziani demand distribution of the stock to them by his administratrix in equal shares.

A common objective of incorporation, especially in a closely held corporation, is the avoidance of personal liability. [Citations.] Another primary objective is to guarantee and define the continuation of a family business, including the parties who are to be shareholders. [Citation.] Clauses . . . are inserted in the certificate of incorporation to accomplish this latter objective. However, it appears that draftsmen must pay particular attention to the language used in such a clause if it is to be binding upon the estate of a deceased shareholder.

The ownership of stock vests in a person an interest or right in the management, profits and assets of that corporation. [Citation.] The stockholder has basic ownership rights to such stock, including the right to dispose of it as his self-interest dictates. [Citations.] A close corporation generally will seek to define or limit such right of disposition in its certificate of incorporation. [Citation.] As selected herein, one of the common methods of limiting such right of disposition is by requiring the stockholders to offer the stock first to the corporation or by giving it a right of refusal, before transferring the stock to another party. [Citation.] Such restriction is pursuant to the objective of a close corporation to determine "the selection of a particular plan of ownership and classification of the interests of security holders." [Citation.]

Therefore, there has evolved in the law a general principle that the courts will uphold and enforce restrictions on a stockholder's right of disposition of his stock, or his right of alienability, if reasonable and for a valid business purpose. [Citations.] A first option restricting, or right of first refusal, on behalf of the corporation or other stockholders has been determined to be a reasonable and valid business purpose. [Citations.]

Consequently, such a clause, as has been adopted by the incorporators of Spaziani Bakeries, Inc. herein, is valid and enforceable. [Citations.]

The draftsman of such a clause, however, must be very careful if it is the intention of the incorporators to bind the estate of a stockholder with such a clause. In order to bind the estate the restriction must not only be reasonable but must also be clearly expressed as intended to bind the estate. [Citations.] The restriction concerning a "transfer" of stock has generally been held not to include the passing of title by operation of law through a personal representative to the distributees or beneficiaries of a deceased stockholder. [Citations.] The application of such restrictions is limited by the principle "that death would not be presumed to trigger the operation of a repurchase option which did not mention death as a specified contingency." [Citations.] If the certificate of incorporation specifically excludes stock passing by will or intestacy, the restrictive clause will not be applicable to such passage by will or intestacy. [Citation.] If silent as to the contingency of death such a restrictive clause is not valid and enforceable against the estate. [Citations.]

Therefore, the administratrix herein is not required to offer the stock back to the corpo-ration. She may distribute it in kind to the distributees of Vincent Spaziani, since the contingency of death was not specifically referred to in the certificate of incorporation. [Citations.]

QUESTIONS

1. Distinguish between equity and debt securities.

2. Identify and describe the principal kinds of equity and debt securities.

3. Explain what type and amount of consideration may be validly received for shares issued by a corporation.

4. Explain the legal restrictions imposed upon dividends and other distributions.

5. Identify the warranties a person transferring investment securities makes to a purchaser for value.

PROBLEMS

1. Frank McAnarney and Joseph Lemon entered into an agreement to promote a corporation to engage in the manufacture of farm implements. Before the corporation was organized, McAnarney and Lemon solicited subscriptions to the stock of the corporation and presented a written agreement for signatures of the subscribers. The agreement provided that subscribers pay $100 per share for stock in the corporation in consideration of McAnarney and Lemon's agreement to organize the corporation and advance the preincorporation expenses. Thomas Jordan signed the agreement, making application for 100 shares of stock. After filing the articles of incorporation with the Secretary of State, but before the charter was issued to the corporation, Jordan died. The administrator of Jordan's estate notified McAnarney and Lemon that the estate would not honor Jordan's subscription.

After the formation of the corporation, Franklin Adams signed a subscription agreement making application for 100 shares of stock. Before acceptance by the corporation, Adams informed the corporation that he was canceling his subscription.

(a) The corporation brings an appropriate action against Jordan's estate to enforce Jordan's stock subscription. Decision?

(b) The corporation brings an appropriate action to enforce Adams's stock subscription. Decision?

2. The XYZ Corporation was duly organized on July 10. Its certificate of incorporation provides for a total authorized capital of $100,000, consisting of 1,000 shares of common stock with a par value of $100 per share. The corporation issues for cash a total of 50 certificates, numbered 1 to 50 inclusive, representing various amounts of shares in the names of various individuals. The shares were all paid for in advance, so the certificates are all dated and mailed on the same day. The 50 certificates of stock represent a total of 1,050 shares. Certificate 49 for 30 shares was issued to Jane Smith. Certificate 50 for 25 shares was issued to William Jones. Is there any question concerning the validity of any of the stock thus issued? What are the rights of Smith and Jones?

3. Doris subscribed for 200 shares of 12 percent cumulative, participating, redeemable, convertible, preferred shares of the Ritz Hotel Company with a par value of $100 per share. The subscription agreement provided that she was to receive a bonus of one share of common stock of $100 par value for each share of preferred stock. Doris fully paid her subscription agreement of $20,000 and received the 200 shares of preferred and the bonus stock of 200 shares of the par value common. The Ritz Hotel Co. later becomes insolvent. Ronald, the receiver of the corporation, brings suit for $20,000, the par value of the common stock. What judgment?

4. The Hyperion Company has an authorized capital stock of 1,000 shares with a par value of $100 per share, of which 900 shares, all fully paid, are outstanding. Having an ample surplus, the Hyperion Company purchases from its shareholders 100 shares at par. Subsequently, the Hyperion Company, needing additional working capital, issues the 200 shares in question to Alexander at $80 per share. Two years later, the Hyperion Company is forced into bankruptcy. The trustee in bankruptcy now sues Alexander for $4,000. Decision?

5. For five years, Henry and James had been engaged as partners in building houses. They owned the necessary equipment to conduct the business and had an excellent reputation. In March, Joyce, who had previously been in the same kind of business, proposed that Henry, James, and Joyce form a corporation for the purposes of constructing medium-priced houses. They engaged attorney Portia, who did all the work required and caused the business to be incorporated under the name of Libra Corp.

The certificate of incorporation authorized 100 shares of $100 par value stock. At the organizational meeting of the incorporators, Henry, James, and Joyce were elected directors, and Libra Corp. issued a total of 65 shares for its stock. Henry and James each received 20 shares in consideration of transferring to Libra Corp. the equipment and good will of their partnership, which together had a value of over $4,000. Joyce received 20 shares in consideration for promising to work for Libra Corp. in the future, and Portia received 5 shares as compensation for the legal services rendered in forming Libra Corp.

Later that year, Libra Corp. had a number of financial setbacks and in December ceased opera-

tions. What rights, if any, does Libra Corp. have against Henry, James, Joyce, and Portia in connection with the original issuance of its shares?

6. Paul Bunyan is the owner of noncumulative 8 percent preferred stock in the Broadview Corporation, which had no earnings or profits in 1988. In 1989, the corporation had large profits and a surplus from which it might properly have declared dividends. The directors refused to do so but instead used the surplus to purchase goods necessary for the corporation's expanding business. The corporation earned a small profit in 1990. The directors at the end of 1990 declared a 10 percent dividend on the common stock and an 8 percent dividend on the preferred stock without paying preferred dividends for 1989.

(a) Is Bunyan entitled to dividends for 1988? For 1989?

(b) Is Bunyan entitled to a dividend of 10 percent rather than 8 percent in 1990?

7. Alpha corporation has outstanding 400 shares of $100 par value common stock, which has been issued and sold at $105 per share for a total of $42,000. Alpha is incorporated in State X, which has adopted the earned surplus test for all distributions. At a time when the assets of the corporation amount to $65,000 and the liabilities to creditors total $10,000, the directors learn that Rachel, who holds 100 of the 400 shares of stock, is planning to sell her shares on the open market for $10,500. Believing that this will not be in the best interest of the corporation, the directors enter into an agreement with Rachel to buy the shares for $10,500 from her. About six months later, when the assets of the corporation have decreased to $50,000 and its liabilities, not including its liability to Rachel, have increased to $20,000, the directors use $10,000 to pay a dividend to all of the shareholders. The corporation later becomes insolvent.

(a) Does Rachel have any liability to the corporation or its creditors in connection with the reacquisition by the corporation of the 100 shares?

(b) Was the payment of the $10,000 dividend proper?

8. Almega Corporation, organized under the laws of State S, has outstanding 20,000 shares of $100 par value nonvoting preferred stock calling for noncumulative dividends of $5 per year; 10,000 shares of voting preferred stock with $50 par value, calling for cumulative dividends of $2.50 per year; and 10,000 shares of no par common stock. State S has adopted the earned surplus test for all distributions. As of the end of 1985, the corporation had no earned surplus. In 1986, the corporation had net earnings of $170,000; in 1987, $135,000; in 1988, $60,000; in 1989, $210,000; and in 1990, $120,000. The board of directors passed over all dividends during the four years 1986–1989, since the company needed working capital for expansion purposes. In 1990, the directors declared on the noncumulative preferred shares a dividend of $5 per share, on the cumulative preferred stock a dividend of $12.50 per share, and on the common stock a dividend of $30 per share. The board submitted its declaration to the voting shareholders, and they ratified it. Before the dividends were paid, Payne, the record holder of 500 shares of the noncumulative preferred stock, brought an appropriate action to restrain any payment to the cumulative preferred or common shareholders until a full dividend for 1986–1990 was paid to noncumulative preferred shareholders. Decision?

9. Sayre learned that Adams, Boone, and Chase were planning to form a corporation for the purpose of manufacturing and marketing a line of novelties to wholesale outlets. Sayre had patented a self-locking gas tank cap but lacked the financial backing to market it profitably. He negotiated with Adams, Boone, and Chase who agreed to purchase the patent rights for $5,000 in cash and 200 shares of $100 par value preferred stock in a corporation to be formed.

The corporation was formed and Sayre's stock issued to him, but the corporation has refused to make the cash payment. It has also refused to declare dividends, although the business has been very profitable because of Sayre's patent and has a substantial earned surplus with a large cash balance on hand. It is selling the remainder of the originally authorized issue of preferred shares, ignoring Sayre's demand to purchase a proportionate number of these shares. What are Sayre's rights, if any?

10. A bylaw of Betma Corporation provides that no shareholder can sell his shares unless he first offers them for sale to the corporation or its directors. The bylaw also states that this restriction shall be printed or stamped upon each stock certificate and binds all present or future owners or holders. Betma Corporation did not comply with this latter provision. Shaw, having knowledge of the bylaw restriction, nevertheless purchased twenty shares of the corporation's stock from Rice, without having Rice first offer them for sale to the corporation or its directors. When Betma Corporation refused to effectuate a transfer of the shares to her, Shaw sued to compel a transfer and the issuance of a new certificate to her. Decision?

11. Wood, the receiver of Stanton Oil Company, sued Stanton's shareholders to recover dividends paid to them for three years, claiming that at the time these dividends were declared, Stanton was in fact insolvent. Wood did not allege that the present creditors were also creditors when the dividends were paid. Decision?

12. Olympic National Agencies was organized with an authorized capitalization of preferred stock and common stock. The articles of incorporation provided for a 7 percent annual dividend for the preferred stock. The articles further stated that the preferred stock would be given priority interests in the corporation's assets up to the par value of the stock. In 1965, the shareholders voted to dissolve Olympic. Because the assets of Olympic greatly exceeded its liabilities, the liquidating trustee petitioned the court for instructions on the respective rights of the shareholders in the assets of the corporation upon dissolution. Decision?

13. International Distributing Export Company (I.D.E.) was organized as a corporation on September 7, 1948, under the laws of New York and commenced business on November 1, 1948. I.D.E. formerly had been in existence as an individual proprietorship. On October 31, 1948, the newly organized corporation had liabilities of $64,084. Its only assets, in the sum of $33,042, were those of the former sole proprietorship. The corporation, however, set up an asset on its balance sheet in the amount of $32,000 for good will. As a result of this entry, I.D.E. had a surplus at the end of each of its fiscal years from 1949 until 1954. Cano, a shareholder, received $7,144 in dividends from I.D.E. during the period from 1950 to 1955. Fried, the trustee in bankruptcy of I.D.E., brought an action against Cano to recover the amount of these dividends paid to Cano, alleging that they had been paid when I.D.E. was insolvent or when its capital was impaired. Decision?

Chapter 36

MANAGEMENT STRUCTURE

Corporate Governance
Role of Shareholders
Role of Directors
Role of Officers

THE corporate management structure, as required by State incorporation statutes, is pyramidal. At the base of the pyramid are the *shareholders,* who are the residual owners of the corporation. Basic to their role in controlling the corporation is the right to elect representatives to manage the ordinary business matters of the corporation and the right to approve all extraordinary matters.

The *board of directors,* as the shareholders' elected representatives, are delegated the power to manage the business of the corporation. Directors exercise dominion and control over the corporation, hold positions of trust and confidence, and determine questions of operating policy. Directors are not expected to devote full time to the affairs of the corporation and have broad authority to delegate power to officers and agents. The *officers* of the corporation hold their offices at the will of the board. The officers, in turn, hire and fire all necessary operating personnel and run the day-to-day affairs of the corporation. The pyramid structure of corporate management under the statutory model is illustrated in Figure 36–1.

CORPORATE GOVERNANCE

The statutory model of corporate management, although required by most States, accurately describes the actual governance of only a few corporations. A great majority of corporations are closely held; they have a small number of stockholders, no ready market for their shares, and most of the shareholders take an active part in the management of the business. Typically, the shareholders of a closely held corporation are also its directors and officers. Figure 36–2 depicts the actual management structure of a typical, closely held corporation. *See Donahue v. Rodd Electrotype Co., Inc.*

Although the statutory model and the actual governance of closely held corporations diverge, in most States closely held corporations must adhere to the general corporate statutory model. One of the greatest burdens conventional general business corporation statutes impose on closely held corporations is the rigid formalities that they require of corporations. Although these formalities may be necessary and desirable in publicly held corporations whose management and owner-ship have been separated, in a closely held corporation, where the owners are usually the managers, many of these formalities are unnecessary and without meaning. Conse-quently, shareholders in closely held corpora-tions tend to disregard the formalities with the result that limited liability may be for-feited. In response to this problem, the 1969 Amendments to the MBCA included several liberalizing provisions for closely held corpo-rations. The amendments were carried over to the Revised Act. Moreover, some States have enacted special legislation to accommo-date the needs of closely held corporations and, as noted in Chapter 34, a Statutory Close Corporation Supplement (Supplement) to the Model Acts was promulgated.

The Supplement has relaxed most of the nonessential formalities. It permits operation without a board of directors, authorizes broad use of shareholder agreements (including us-ing them instead of bylaws), makes annual meetings optional, and authorizes the execu-tion of documents by one person in more than one capacity. Most importantly, it prevents courts from denying limited liability simply because the corporation is a statutory close corporation. The general incorporation stat-ute applies to closely held corporations except to the extent that it is inconsistent with the Supplement.

In sharp contrast is the large, publicly held corporation with a vast market for its shares. These shares are typically widely dispersed, and very few are owned by management. Ap-proximately one-half of these shares are held by institutional investors (such as insurance companies, pension funds, mutual funds, and trusts), which manage funds for individual investors; the remainder are owned directly by individual investors. A great majority of institutional investors exercise their right to vote their shares, whereas a relatively small percentage of individual investors exercise their right to vote. Nonetheless, virtually all shareholders who vote for the directors do so through the use of a **proxy**—an authoriza-tion by a shareholder to an agent (usually the chief executive officer of the corporation) to vote his shares. The majority of shareholders who return their proxies vote as manage-ment advises. As a result, management pre-vails in nearly all elections and actually de-termines who will be directors. Figure 36–3 illustrates the actual management structure of a typical large, publicly held corporation.

Thus, the 500 to 1,000 large, publicly held corporations—which own the great bulk of the industrial wealth of the United States—are controlled by a small group of corporate officers. This great concentration of control over wealth, and the power that results from it, raises social, policy, and ethical issues con-cerning the governance of these corporations and the accountability of their management. The actions (or inactions) of these powerful corporations greatly affect the national econ-omy, employment policies, the health and safety of the workplace and the environment, the quality of products, and the effects of overseas operations.

Accordingly, the accountability of manage-ment is a critical issue. In particular, what obligations should the large, publicly held corporation and its management have to (1) the corporation's shareholders, (2) its em-ployees, (3) its customers, (4) its suppliers, (5) the communities in which the corporation is located, and (6) the rest of society? For the most part, these critical questions are unan-swered. Some corporate statutes now provide that the board of directors, committees of the board, individual directors, and individual of-ficers *may,* in determining the best interests of the corporation, consider the effects of any action upon employees, suppliers, creditors, and customers of the corporation, communi-ties in which offices or other establishments of the corporation are located, the economy of the State and nation, societal considerations, and all other pertinent factors.

In 1978, the American Law Institute be-gan its Corporate Governance Project to study and formulate recommendations for change in corporate governance. The project has produced several drafts of the *ALI Prin-ciples of Corporate Governance: Analysis and*

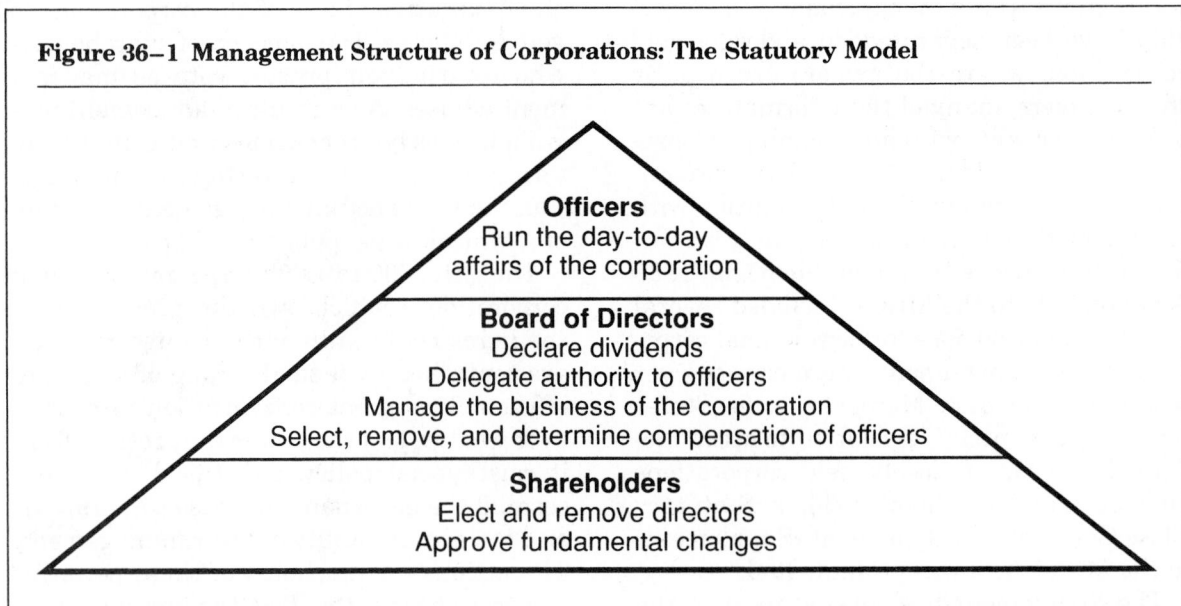

Figure 36–1 Management Structure of Corporations: The Statutory Model

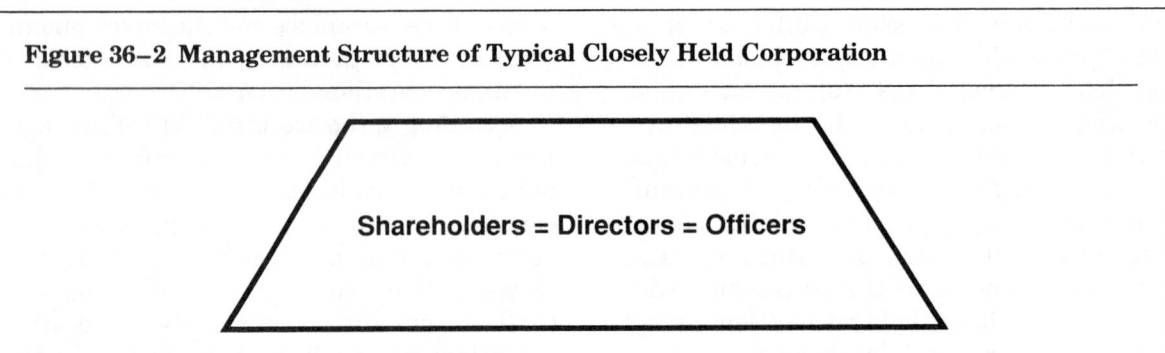

Figure 36–2 Management Structure of Typical Closely Held Corporation

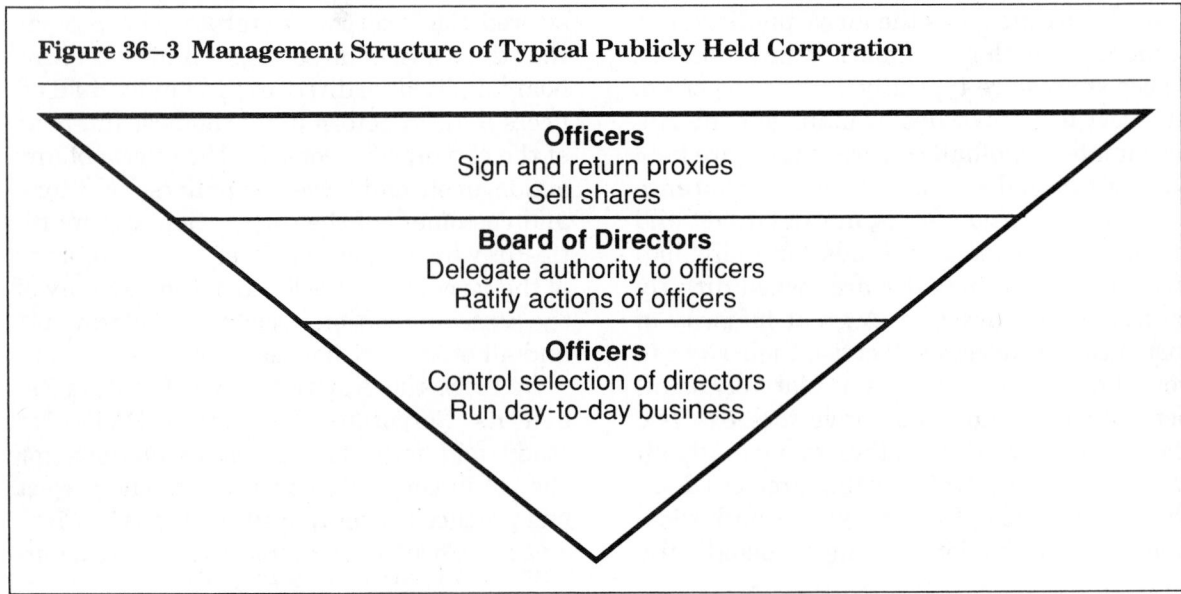

Figure 36–3 Management Structure of Typical Publicly Held Corporation

Recommendations. Although these principles do not have the force of law, they may influence the evolution of law in this area. Section 2.01 of the second tentative draft provides that a business corporation "*may* take into account ethical considerations that are reasonably regarded as appropriate to the responsible conduct of business." With regard to the role of the board of directors in a publicly held corporation, Section 3.02 of the ALI project recommends the following powers and functions for the board:

(1) to elect, evaluate, and, where appropriate, dismiss the principal senior executives;

(2) to oversee the conduct of the corporation's business with a view to evaluating whether the corporation's resources are being managed in a manner consistent with the objectives of the corporation; and

(3) to review and approve corporate plans and actions that the board or the principal senior executives consider major, and changes in accounting principles and practices that the board or the principal senior executives consider material.

The structure and governance of corporations, nevertheless, must adhere to the requirements of the incorporation statutes. Therefore, this chapter will discuss the rights, duties, and liabilities of shareholders, directors, and officers under these statutes.

ROLE OF SHAREHOLDERS

The role of the shareholders in managing the corporation is generally restricted to the election of directors, the approval of certain extraordinary matters, the approval of corporate transactions that are void or voidable unless ratified, and the right to bring suits to enforce these rights. At the same time, as discussed in the previous two chapters, shareholders assume potential personal liability for defective incorporation, disregard of corporateness, and receipt of improper distributions.

VOTING RIGHTS OF SHAREHOLDERS

The shareholder's right to vote is fundamental to the concept of the corporation and its management structure. In most States today, a shareholder is entitled to one vote for each share of stock that she owns, unless the articles of incorporation provide otherwise. In addition, incorporation statutes generally permit the issuance of one or more classes of non-voting stock, so long as at least one class of shares has voting rights. Section 6.01. The articles of incorporation may provide for more or less than one vote for any share. For example, in *Providence & Worcester Co. v. Baker,* 378 A.2d 121 (Del.1977), the court upheld articles of incorporation which provided that each shareholder was entitled to 1 vote per share for each share owned by him not exceeding 50 shares and 1 vote for every 20 shares in excess of 50, but no shareholder was entitled to vote more than one-fourth of the whole number of outstanding shares.

Shareholder Meetings

Shareholders may exercise their voting rights at both annual and special shareholder meetings. **Annual meetings** are required and must be held at a time fixed by the bylaws. Section 7.01. If the annual shareholder meeting is not held within the earlier of six months after the end of the corporation's fiscal year or fifteen months after its last annual meeting, any shareholder may petition and obtain a court order requiring such meeting to be held. Section 7.03. The Revised Act further provides that the failure to hold an annual meeting does not affect the validity of any corporate action. Section 7.01(c). The Close Corporation Supplement provides that no annual meeting of shareholders need be held unless a written request is made by a shareholder at least thirty days in advance of the date specified for the meeting. The date may be established in the articles of incorporation, bylaws, or in a shareholder's agreement. **Special meetings** may be called by the board of directors, holders of at least 10 percent of the shares, or such other persons authorized in the articles of incorporation. Section 7.02.

Written notice, stating the date, time, and place of the meeting and, in the case of a special meeting, the purposes for which it is called, must be given in advance of the meeting. Section 7.05. Notice, however, may be waived in writing by any shareholder entitled to notice. Section 7.06.

A number of States permit shareholders to conduct business without a meeting if all the shareholders consent in writing to the action taken. Section 7.04. Some States have further relaxed the formalities of shareholder action by permitting shareholders to act without a meeting with written consent of only the number of shares required to act on the matter.

Quorum and Voting

In order to effectuate corporate business, a quorum of shares must be represented at the meeting, either in person or by proxy. Unissued shares and treasury stock may not be voted or counted in determining whether a quorum exists. Once a quorum is present at a meeting, it is deemed present for the rest of the meeting despite the withdrawal of shareholders in an effort to break quorum. Unless otherwise provided in the articles of incorporation, a majority of shares entitled to vote constitutes a **quorum.** In many States and under the Model Act, a quorum may not consist of less than one-third of the shares entitled to vote. The Revised Act does not contain a statutory minimum for a quorum. State statutes do not impose an upper limit upon a quorum, so it may be set higher than a majority and even require *all* the outstanding shares.

Most States require shareholder actions to be approved by a majority of shares represented at the meeting and entitled to vote. Nonetheless, many States permit the articles of incorporation to increase the percentage of shares required to take any action that is subject to shareholder approval. Section 7.27.

A provision that increases the voting requirements is usually referred to as a "supermajority provision." Supermajority shareholder voting requirements have been frequently used in close corporations to protect minority shareholders from oppression by the majority. Recently, some publicly held corporations have used them to defend against hostile takeover bids.

Section 7.27 of the Revised Act has added an additional requirement to supermajority provisions:

An amendment to the articles of incorporation that adds, changes, or deletes a greater quorum or voting requirement must meet the same quorum requirement and be adopted by the same vote and voting groups required to take action under the quorum and voting requirement then in effect or proposed to be adopted, whichever is greater.

Section 7.27 thus protects a supermajority requirement for shareholder action from elimination by a simple majority vote generally required for amendments. For example, a supermajority provision requiring a 75 percent affirmative vote may not be deleted from the articles of incorporation or reduced except by a 75 percent affirmative vote. A proposal to increase the 75 percent voting requirement to 90 percent must be approved by a 90 percent affirmative vote.

Election and Removal of Directors

Directors are elected each year at the annual meeting of the shareholders. Most States provide that where the board consists of nine or more directors, the charter or bylaws may provide for a **classification** of directors, that is, a division into two or three classes to be as nearly equal in number as possible to serve for staggered terms. Section 8.06. If the directors are divided into two classes, the members of each class are elected once a year in alternate years for a two-year term; if into three classes, for three-year terms. This permits one-half of the board to be elected every two years or one-third to be elected every three years, thus providing an element of continuity in the membership of the board.

Moreover, where there are two or more classes of shares, it has been generally held that each class may elect a specified number of directors if provided for in the articles of incorporation. The Revised Act makes this explicit. Section 8.04.

Normally, each shareholder has one vote for each share owned, and directors are elected by a *plurality* of the votes. In certain States, however, shareholders have the right of cumulative voting for the election of directors of the corporation. In most of these States and under the Revised Act, cumulative voting is permissive and not mandatory. Section 7.28(b). **Cumulative voting** entitles the shareholders to multiply the number of votes they are entitled to cast by the number of directors for whom they are entitled to vote and cast the product for a single candidate or distribute the product among two or more candidates. Cumulative voting permits a minority shareholder, or group of minority shareholders acting together, to obtain minority representation on the board if they own a certain minimum number of shares. Without cumulative voting, the holder or holders of 51 percent of the voting shares can elect all of the members of the board.

The formula for determining how many shares a minority shareholder with cumulative voting rights must own, or have proxies to vote, in order to secure representation on the board is as follows:

$$X = \frac{ac}{b + 1} + 1$$

a = number of shares voting
b = number of directors to be elected
c = number of directors desired to be elected
X = number of shares necessary to elect the number of directors desired to be elected

For example, Gray Corporation has two shareholders, Stephanie with 64 shares and Thomas with 36 shares. The board of directors of Gray Corporation consists of three directors. Under "straight" or noncumulative voting, Stephanie could cast 64 votes for each of her three candidates, and Thomas could cast 36 votes for his three candidates. As a result, all three of Stephanie's candidates

would be elected. On the other hand, if cumulative voting were in force, Thomas could elect one director:

$$X = \frac{ac}{b + 1} + 1$$

$$X = \frac{100(1)}{3 + 1} + 1 = 26 \text{ shares}$$

Since Thomas has the right to vote more than 26 shares, he would be able to elect one director. Stephanie, of course, with her 64 shares, could elect the remaining two directors:

$$X = \frac{ac}{b + 1} + 1$$

$$X = \frac{100(2)}{3 + 1} + 1 = 51 \text{ shares}$$

To elect all three directors, Stephanie would need 76 shares:

$$X = \frac{100(3)}{3 + 1} + 1 = 76 \text{ shares}$$

The effect of cumulative voting for directors may be diluted by classification or staggered election of the board of directors or by reducing the size of the board. For example, if nine directors are each elected annually, only 11 percent of the shares are needed to elect one director; if the nine directors' elections are staggered and three are elected annually, 26 percent of the shares are required to elect one director.

Shareholders may, by a majority vote, remove, with or without cause, any director or the entire board of directors in a meeting called for that purpose. In the case of a corporation's having cumulative voting, however, removal of a director requires sufficient votes to prevent his election. Section 8.08(c). Removal of directors is discussed more fully later in this chapter.

Approval of Fundamental Changes

The board of directors manages the ordinary business affairs of the corporation. Extraordinary matters involving fundamental changes in the corporation require shareholder approval and include such matters as amendments to the articles of incorporation, a sale or lease of all or substantially all of the corporate assets not in the regular course of business, most mergers, consolidations, compulsory share exchanges, and dissolution. Fundamental changes are discussed in Chapter 37.

Concentrations of Voting Power

A number of devices have been developed to enable groups of shareholders to combine their voting power for such purposes as obtaining or maintaining control or maximizing the impact of cumulative voting. The most important methods of concentrating voting power are proxies, voting trusts, and shareholder agreements.

Proxies A shareholder may vote either in person or by written proxy. Section 7.22(a). A proxy is simply the authorization by a shareholder to an agent to vote his shares at a particular meeting or on a particular question. Generally, proxies must be in writing to be effective. The duration of proxies is typically limited by statute to no more than eleven months, unless the proxy specifically provides otherwise. Section 7.22(c). Since a proxy is the appointment of an agent, it is revocable, as all agencies are, unless conspicuously stated to be irrevocable *and* coupled with an interest, such as when shares are held as collateral. Section 7.22(d). The solicitation of proxies by publicly held corporations is also regulated by the Securities Exchange Act of 1934, as discussed in Chapter 45.

Voting Trusts Voting trusts, which are devices designed to concentrate corporate control in one or more persons, have been used in both publicly held and closely held corporations. A voting trust is a device by which one or more shareholders separate the voting rights of their shares from the ownership of them. Under a voting trust, one or more shareholders confer on a trustee the right to vote or otherwise act for them by signing an agreement setting out the provisions of the trust and transferring their shares to the

trustee. Section 7.30(a). In most States, voting trusts are permitted by statute but are usually limited in duration to ten years. The Revised Act permits all or some of the parties to a voting trust to extend it for an additional term of up to ten years by signing an extension agreement and obtaining the voting trustee's written consent. Section 7.30(c). The extension runs from the time the first shareholder signs the agreement.

Shareholder Voting Agreements In most jurisdictions, shareholders may agree in writing to vote in a specified manner for the election or removal of directors or on any other matter subject to shareholder approval. Section 7.31(a). The Revised Act and some State statutes expressly provide that shareholder agreements are enforceable by a decree of specific performance. Section 7.31(b). Unlike voting trusts, shareholder voting agreements are usually not limited in duration. Shareholder agreements are used frequently in closely held corporations, especially in conjunction with restrictions on the transfer of shares, in order to provide each of the shareholders with greater control and *de-lectus personae* (the right to choose who becomes a shareholder).

A well-known example is *Galler v. Galler,* 32 Ill.2d 16, 203 N.E.2d 577 (1964). In 1927, two brothers, Benjamin and Isadore Galler, incorporated the Galler Drug Co., a wholesale drug business that they had operated as equal partners since 1919. The company continued to grow, and in 1955 the two brothers and their wives, Emma and Rose Galler, entered into a written shareholder agreement to leave the corporation in equal control of each family after the death of either brother. Specifically, the agreement provided for the corporation to continue to provide income for the support and maintenance of their immediate families and for the parties to vote for directors so as to give the estate and heirs of a deceased shareholder the same representation as before. Benjamin died in 1957, and shortly thereafter his widow Emma requested that Isadore, the surviving brother, comply with the terms of the agreement.

When he refused and proposed that certain changes be made in the agreement, Emma brought this action seeking specific performance of the agreement. Isadore and his wife, Rose, defended on the ground that the shareholder agreement was against public policy and the State's corporation law. The court decided in favor of Emma Galler. A close corporation is one in which the stock is held in a few hands and is rarely traded. In contrast to a shareholder in a public corporation, who may easily trade his shares on the open market when he disagrees with its management over corporate policy, the shareholder of a closely held corporation often has no ready market in which to sell his shares should he wish to do so. Moreover, the shareholder in a closely held corporation often has most of his capital invested in the corporation and, therefore, views himself as more than a mere investor, but also as a participant in the management of the business. Without a shareholder agreement subject to specific performance by the courts, the minority shareholder might find himself at the mercy of the controlling majority shareholder. In short, the detailed shareholder voting agreement is the only sound means by which the minority shareholder can protect himself. Therefore, since the agreement was reasonable in its scope and purpose of providing continuing support for the Galler brothers' families, it should be enforced.

Even under modern general incorporation statutes, however, two major obstacles prevent the full and effective utilization of shareholder voting agreements: (1) in many States, contractual terms restricting the discretion of directors may not be valid and (2) in some States, certain types of control arrangements must be contained in the articles of incorporation. The Close Corporation Supplement addresses both of these obstacles. It provides that the shareholders of a statutory closely held corporation may, by unanimous action, enter into written agreements to regulate the exercise of the corporate powers, the management of the business and affairs of the corporation, or the relations among the shareholders of the corporation. The Supple-

ment also provides that any authorized agreement shall be valid and enforceable even if the agreement eliminates the board of directors, restricts the discretion or power of the board of directors, or gives proxy or weighted voting rights to the directors. It also makes shareholder agreements valid even if they result in the business' being operated essentially as a partnership. Shareholder agreements can include provisions regarding the payment of dividends, employment of officers and other employees, selection of directors and officers, arbitration of disagreements, allocation of voting power between shareholders and directors, and the shareholder's right of dissolution.

ENFORCEMENT RIGHTS OF SHAREHOLDERS

To protect a shareholder's interests in the corporation, the law provides shareholders with certain enforcement rights including the right to obtain information, the right to sue the corporation directly or to sue on the corporation's behalf, and the right to dissent.

Right to Inspect Books and Records

Most States have enacted statutory provisions granting shareholders the right to inspect for a *proper purpose* books and records in person or by an agent and to make extracts from them. The Revised Act extends the right to copy records to include, if reasonable, the right to receive copies made by photographic, xerographic, or other means. Section 16.03. The Revised Act provides that *every* shareholder is entitled to examine specified corporate records upon prior written request if the demand is made in good faith, for a proper purpose, and during regular business hours at the corporation's principal office. Section 16.02. A number of States, however, limit this right to shareholders who own a minimum number of shares or have been a shareholder for a minimum period of time. For example, the Model Act requires that a shareholder either must own 5 percent of the outstanding shares or must have owned his shares for at least six months, but a *court* may order an inspection even when neither condition is met.

Proper purpose for inspection means a purpose that is reasonably relevant to that shareholder's interest in the corporation. Proper purpose includes determining the financial condition of the corporation, the value of shares, the existence of mismanagement or improper transactions, or the names of other shareholders in order to communicate with them about corporate affairs. The right of inspection is subject to abuse and will be denied a shareholder who is seeking information for an improper purpose. Examples of improper purpose are obtaining information for use by a competing company or obtaining a list of shareholders in order to offer it for sale. *See Application of Lopez.*

Shareholder Suits

The ultimate recourse of a shareholder, short of selling her shares, is to bring suit against or on behalf of the corporation. Shareholder suits are essentially of two kinds: direct suits or derivative suits. *See Richardson v. Arizona Fuels Corp.*

Direct Suits A direct suit may be brought by a shareholder to enforce a claim that the shareholder has *against* the corporation, based upon his ownership of shares. Any recovery in a direct suit goes to the shareholder plaintiff. Examples of direct suits include actions by a shareholder to compel payment of dividends properly declared, to enforce the right to inspect corporate records, to enforce the right to vote, to protect preemptive rights, and to compel dissolution. Shareholders may also bring a class suit or class action. A **class suit** is a direct suit in which one or more shareholders purport to act as a representative of a class of shareholders to recover for injuries to the entire class. The suit is a direct suit because the representative claims that all similarly situated shareholders were injured by an act that did not injure the corporation.

Derivative Suits A derivative suit is a cause of action brought by one or more shareholders *on behalf* of the corporation to enforce a right belonging to the corporation. It is brought when the board of directors refuses to take such action on behalf of the corporation. Recovery usually goes to the corporation's treasury so that all shareholders can benefit proportionately. Examples of derivative suits are actions to recover damages from management for an *ultra vires* act, to recover damages for a breach of duty by management, and to recover improper dividends. In many such situations, the board of directors may be hesitant to bring suit against the corporation's officers or directors. Consequently, a shareholder derivative suit is the only recourse.

In most States, a shareholder must have owned his shares at the time the transaction complained of occurred in order to bring a derivative suit. Section 7.40. In addition, the shareholder must first make demand upon the board of directors to enforce the corporate right. The Revised Act does not require that such demand be made if circumstances indicate that a demand would be useless. Section 7.40(b) and Comment.

The statutes of many States require a plaintiff to give security for reasonable expenses, including attorneys' fees, if his holdings of shares are not of a specified size or value. Before amendment in 1982, the Model Act required 5 percent of the outstanding shares or a value of $25,000. The Revised Act and the 1982 Amendments to the Model Act have deleted this requirement. Both acts provide that upon termination of a proceeding the court may require the plaintiff to pay the defendants' reasonable expenses, including attorneys' fees, if it finds that the proceeding was brought without reasonable cause. Section 7.40(d). The Revised Act and the statutes of a number of States require that all proposed settlements and discontinuances receive judicial approval. Section 7.40(c).

Shareholder's Right to Dissent

A shareholder has the right to dissent from certain corporate actions that require shareholder approval. These actions include most mergers, consolidations, compulsory share exchanges, and a sale or exchange of all or substantially all the assets of the corporation not in the usual and regular course of business. The shareholder's right to dissent is discussed in Chapter 37.

ROLE OF DIRECTORS AND OFFICERS

Management of a corporation is vested by statute in its board of directors, which determines general corporate policy and appoints officers to execute that policy and to administer the day-to-day operations of the corporation. Both the directors and officers of the corporation owe certain duties to the corporate entity as well as to the corporation's shareholders and are liable for breaching these duties.

The following sections will discuss the role of directors and officers of a corporation. Shareholders who own a sufficient number of shares to have effective control over the corporation are called "controlling shareholders." In some instances controlling shareholders are held to the same duties as directors and officers, which are discussed later in this chapter. Moreover, in close corporations, some courts impose upon *all* the shareholders a fiduciary duty similar to that imposed upon partners. *See Donahue v. Rodd Electrotype Co. Inc.*

FUNCTION OF THE BOARD OF DIRECTORS

Although the directors are elected by the shareholders to manage the corporation, they are neither trustees nor agents of the shareholders or the corporation. They are, however, fiduciaries who must perform their duties in good faith, in the best interests of the corporation, and with due care.

The Revised Act states that "[a]ll corporate powers shall be exercised by or under the authority of, and the business and affairs of the corporation managed under the direction of, its board of directors, subject to any limita-

tion set forth in the articles of incorporation." Section 8.01(b). In some corporations the board is composed of members, all of whom are actively involved in the management of the business. In these cases, the corporate powers are exercised *by* the board of directors. On the other hand, in publicly held corporations a majority of the board members frequently are not actively involved in management. Here, the corporate powers are exercised *under* the authority of the board, which formulates major management policy but does not involve itself in the day-to-day management. In publicly held corporations, the directors who are also officers or employees of the corporation are **inside directors,** while the directors who are not officers or employees of the corporation are **outside directors.** Outside directors who have no business contacts with the corporation are **unaffiliated directors;** outside directors with business contacts with the corporation—such as investment bankers, lawyers, or suppliers— are **affiliated directors.**

The board determines corporate policy in a number of areas, including (1) selecting and removing officers, (2) determining the capital structure, (3) initiating fundamental changes, (4) declaring dividends, and (5) setting management compensation.

Under the Revised Act, a corporation having fifty or fewer shareholders may dispense with or limit the authority of a board of directors by describing in its articles of incorporation who will perform some or all of the duties of a board. Section 8.01(c). The comment to this section explains:

The persons who perform some or all of the duties of the board may be designated "trustees," "agents," or "managers," and they may be selected in ways other than the traditional election by the shareholders. It is necessary, however, that some person or group perform these duties, and the designated persons, while performing them, are subject to the same duties as directors.

Selection and Removal of Officers

In most States, the board of directors has the responsibility to choose the corporate officers and may remove any officer at any time. Sections 8.40 and 8.43. Officers are agents of the corporation and are delegated their responsibilities by the board of directors.

Capital Structure

The board of directors determines the capital structure and financial policy of the corporation. For example, the board of directors has the power to

1. fix the selling price of newly issued shares unless the power to do so is reserved to the shareholders by the articles;

2. determine the value of the consideration received by the corporation in payment for shares issued;

3. purchase, redeem or otherwise acquire shares of the corporation's equity securities;

4. borrow money; issue notes, bonds, and other obligations; and secure any of the corporation's obligations by mortgage or pledge of any or all of the corporation's property; and

5. sell, lease, or exchange assets of the corporation in the *usual* and *regular* course of business.

Fundamental Changes

The board of directors has the power to amend or repeal the bylaws, unless this power is exclusively reserved to the shareholders by the articles of incorporation. Section 10.20. In addition, the board initiates a number of actions that are beyond its powers and require shareholder approval. For instance, the board must initiate proceedings to amend the articles of incorporation; to effect a merger, consolidation, compulsory share exchange, or the sale or lease of all or substantially all of the assets of the corporation *other* than in the usual and regular course of business; and to dissolve the corporation.

Dividends

The board of directors declares the amount and type of dividends, subject to restrictions in the State incorporation statute, the articles of incorporation, and corporate loan and preferred stock agreements. Section 6.40. The board also fixes a record date for the purpose of determining the shareholders who are entitled to receive dividends. Section 6.40(b).

Management Compensation

The board of directors usually determines the compensation of officers. Moreover, a number of States allow the board to fix the compensation of board members. Section 8.11. In addition to fixed salaries, executive compensation may include (1) cash bonuses, (2) share bonuses, (3) share options, (4) share purchase plans, (5) insurance benefits, (6) deferred compensation, (7) retirement plans, and (8) a variety of other fringe benefits.

ELECTION AND TENURE OF DIRECTORS

The incorporation statute, articles of incorporation, and bylaws determine the qualifications that individuals must possess in order to be eligible as directors of the corporation. They also determine the election, number, tenure, and compensation of directors.

Election, Number, and Tenure of Directors

The initial board of directors is generally named in the articles of incorporation and serves until the first meeting of the shareholders at which directors are elected. Section 8.05(a). Thereafter, directors are elected at annual meetings of the shareholders and hold office for one year unless their terms are staggered. If the shares represented at a meeting in person or by proxy are not sufficient to constitute a quorum or the shareholders are deadlocked and unable to elect a new board, the incumbent directors continue in office as "holdover" directors until their successors are duly elected and qualified. Section 8.05(e). State statutes traditionally required that each corporation have three or more directors, although the modern trend is to permit the board to consist of one or more members. Section 8.03(a).

Moreover, the number of directors may be increased or decreased, within statutory limits, by amendment to the bylaws or charter. The Revised Act permits the board of directors, if it has the power to fix or change the number of directors, to increase or decrease its own size by up to 30 percent without shareholder approval. Section 8.03(b). For example, in a board fixed or approved by the shareholders at 15 members, the board may, without shareholder approval, change the size of the board to as few as 11 or as many as 19. A board of 5 may be changed by the board to as few as 4 or as many as 6. Section 8.03(c) of the Revised Act authorizes the articles of incorporation or bylaws to establish a variable range for the size of the board by fixing a minimum and maximum number of directors.

Vacancies and Removal of Directors

The Revised Act provides that a vacancy in the board may be filled either by the shareholders or by the affirmative vote of a majority of the remaining directors, even though they constitute less than a quorum of the board. Section 8.10(a). The term of a director elected to fill a vacancy expires at the next shareholders' meeting at which directors are elected. Section 8.05(d).

Some States have no statutory provision for removal of directors, although a common law rule permits removal for cause by action of the shareholders. The Revised Act and an increasing number of other statutes permit removal of one or more of the directors or of the entire board by the shareholders, with or without cause, at a special meeting called for that purpose, subject to cumulative voting rights, if applicable. Section 8.08. The Revised Act permits the articles of incorporation to provide that directors may be removed only for cause. Section 8.08(a). The Revised Act and a number of States also authorize a court to remove a director in a proceeding brought by the corporation or by shareholders who own at least 10 percent of the outstanding shares of any class of shares, if the court finds

that (1) the director engaged in fraudulent or dishonest conduct or gross abuse of authority or discretion and (2) removal is in the best interests of the corporation. Section 8.09.

Compensation of Directors

Traditionally, directors did not receive salaries for their services as directors, although it was usual for them to be paid a fee or honorarium for attendance at meetings. The Revised Act and a number of incorporation statutes now specifically authorize the board of directors to fix the compensation of directors unless there is a contrary provision in the articles of incorporation. Section 8.11.

EXERCISE OF DIRECTORS' FUNCTIONS

Directors do not have the power to bind the corporation when acting individually but do have the power when acting as a board. The board may act only at a meeting of the directors or by written consent signed by all of the directors, if written consent without a meeting is authorized by the statute and not contrary to the charter or bylaws. Section 8.21.

Meetings are held either at a regular time and place fixed in the bylaws or at special times when they are called. Notice of meetings must be given as prescribed in the bylaws. A director's attendance at any meeting is a waiver of such notice, unless the director attends for the express purpose of objecting to holding the meeting or transacting business and does not vote for or assent to action taken at the meeting. Section 8.23(b). Waiver of notice may also be given in a signed writing. Most modern statutes provide that meetings of the board may be held either in or outside the State of incorporation. Section 8.20(a).

Quorum and Voting

A majority of the members of the board of directors constitute a quorum (the minimum number of members necessary to be present at a meeting in order to transact business). Although most States do not permit a quorum to be set at less than a majority, the Revised Act *allows* the articles of incorporation or the bylaws to authorize a quorum to consist of as few as one-third. Section 8.24(b). The articles of incorporation or bylaws may, however, require a number greater than a simple majority. If a quorum is present at any meeting, the act of a majority of the directors in attendance at such meeting is the act of the board, unless the articles of incorporation or bylaws require the act of a greater number. Section 8.24(c).

Closely held corporations sometimes use supermajority or unanimous quorum requirements. In addition, they may require a supermajority or unanimous vote of the board for some or all matters. The use of either or both of these provisions, however, creates the possibility of deadlock at the director level.

The Revised Act requires a quorum to be present when "a vote is taken," making it clear that the board may act only when a quorum is present. Section 8.24(c) and Comment 2. This rule is in contrast to the rule governing shareholder meetings: once a quorum of shareholders is obtained it *cannot* be broken by the withdrawal of shareholders. In any event, directors may not vote by proxy, although most States permit directors to participate in meetings by means of conference telephones. Section 8.20.

If a director is present at a meeting of the board at which action on any corporate matter is taken, he is deemed to have assented to such action unless, in addition to dissenting from it, he (1) has his dissent entered in the minutes of the meeting, or (2) files his written dissent to such action with the presiding officer before the meeting adjourns, or (3) delivers his written dissent to the corporation immediately after the adjournment of the meeting. Section 8.24(d).

Action Taken without a Meeting

The Revised Act and most States provide that, unless otherwise provided by the articles of incorporation or bylaws, any action required or permitted by the statute to be taken at a meeting of the board may be taken without a meeting if consent in writing is signed by all of the directors. Section 8.21. Such consent has the same effect as a unanimous vote.

Delegation of Board Powers

Unless otherwise provided by the articles of incorporation or bylaws, the board of directors may, by majority vote of the *full* board, appoint one or more committees, all of whose members must be directors. Section 8.25. Many State statutes permit committees to be formed only if the charter or bylaws expressly authorize it. The Revised Act provides that the "creation of a committee and appointment of members to it must be approved by the greater of (1) a majority of all the directors in office when the action is taken or (2) the number of directors required by the articles of incorporation or bylaws to take action." Section 8.25(b). Committees may exercise all of the authority of the board except for certain matters specified in the incorporation statute such as the declaration of dividends and other distributions, filling vacancies on the board of directors or any of its committees, amending the bylaws, recommending fundamental changes to the shareholder, approving a merger or amendment of the charter not requiring shareholder approval, and authorizing the sale or reacquisition of stock. Section 8.25(e). Delegation of authority to a committee does not relieve any board member of his duties to the corporation. Commonly used committees include executive committees, audit committees (to recommend and oversee independent public accountants), compensation committees, finance committees, nominating committees, and investment committees. The New York Stock Exchange requires that companies listed on the exchange have audit committees composed exclusively of outside directors.

Directors' Inspection Rights

Directors have the right to inspect corporate books and records so they can competently and fully perform their duties. This right is considerably broader than a shareholder's right to inspect. Nevertheless, it is subject to some limitations. The American Law Institute's Corporate Governance Project provides that a court may refuse to enforce a director's right of inspection if the information is not reasonably related to the performance of directorial functions and duties or the director is likely to misuse the information and the misuse cannot be prevented by a court order.

OFFICERS

The officers of a corporation are appointed in most States by the board of directors to hold the offices provided in the bylaws that set forth the respective duties of each officer. Statutes generally require as a minimum that the officers consist of a president, one or more vice-presidents as prescribed by the bylaws, a secretary, and a treasurer. A person may hold more than one office, except that the same person may not hold the office of president and secretary at the same time.

The Revised Act permits every corporation to designate whatever officers it wants. Although no particular number of officers is specified, one of the officers must be delegated responsibility for preparing the minutes of directors' and shareholders' meetings and authenticating records of the corporation. The Revised Act permits the same individual to hold *all* of the offices of a corporation. Section 8.40(d).

Selection and Removal of Officers

Most State statutes provide that the officers are appointed by the board of directors and serve at the pleasure of the board. Accordingly, officers may be removed by the board with or without cause. Section 8.43(b). Of course, if the officer has a valid employment contract for a specified period of time, removal of the officer without cause before the contract expires would constitute a breach of the employment contract. The board also determines the compensation of officers.

Role of Officers

The officers are, like the directors, fiduciaries to the corporation. On the other hand, unlike the directors, they are agents of the corporation. The roles of officers are set forth in the corporate bylaws. The following is a typical description drawn from model bylaws:

President   The president is the principal executive officer of the corporation and, subject to the control of the board of directors, in general supervises and controls all of the business and affairs of the corporation. He presides at all meetings of the shareholders and of the board of directors. He may sign for the corporation any deeds, mortgages, bonds, contracts, or other instruments that the board of directors has authorized to be executed.

Vice-President   In the absence of the president or in the event of his death, inability, resignation, or refusal to act, the vice-president performs the duties of the president and, when so acting, has all the powers of and is subject to all the restrictions upon the president.

Secretary   The secretary keeps the minutes of the proceedings of the shareholders and of the board of directors; sees that all notices are duly given; is custodian of the corporate records and of the seal of the corporation; signs with the president certificates for shares of the corporation, the issuance of which has been authorized by resolution of the board of directors; and has general charge of the stock transfer books of the corporation.

Treasurer   The treasurer has charge and custody of and is responsible for all funds and securities of the corporations he receives and gives receipts for and deposits moneys due and payable to the corporation.

Authority of Officers

The Revised Act provides that each officer of the corporation has the authority provided in the bylaws or prescribed by the board of directors to the extent consistent with the bylaws. Section 8.41. As with other agents, the authority of an officer to bind the corporation may be (1) actual express, (2) actual implied, or (3) apparent.

Actual Express Authority Actual express authority results from the manifestation of assent by the corporation to the officer that the officer should act on the behalf of the corporation. Actual express authority arises from the incorporation statute, the articles of incorporation, the bylaws, and resolutions of the board of directors. The principal source of actual express authority is the resolutions of the board of directors.

Actual Implied Authority Officers, as agents of the corporation, have implied authority to do what is reasonably necessary to perform their actual, delegated authority. In addition, the question arises whether officers possess implied authority merely by virtue of their positions. The courts have been circumspect in granting such implied or inherent authority. Traditionally, the courts tended to hold that the president had no implied authority by virtue of his office, although the more recent decisions tend to recognize his authority to bind the corporation in ordinary business transactions. Any act requiring board approval, such as issuing stock, however, is clearly beyond the implied authority of the president or any other officer. In most jurisdictions, implied authority of position does not extend to any officer other than the president.

Apparent Authority Apparent authority arises from acts of the principal that lead third parties to believe reasonably and in good faith that an officer has the required authority. Apparent authority might arise when a third party relies on the fact that an officer has exercised the same authority in the past with the consent of the board of directors.

Ratification A corporation may ratify the unauthorized acts of its officers. Ratification is equivalent to having granted the officer prior authority. Ratification relates back to the original transaction and may be express or implied from the corporation's acceptance of the benefits of the contract with full knowledge of the facts.

DUTIES OF DIRECTORS AND OFFICERS

A corporation may not recover damages from its directors and officers for losses resulting from their poor business judgment or honest mistakes of judgment. The directors and officers are not insurers of business success. They are required only to be obedient, reasonably diligent, and completely loyal. These duties of obedience, diligence, and loyalty are for the most part judicially imposed. State and Federal statutes supplement the common law by imposing liability upon directors and officers for specific acts, but the common law still remains the most significant source of duties.

Duty of Obedience

Directors and officers must act within their respective authority. For any loss resulting to the corporation from their unauthorized acts, they are held strictly liable in some jurisdictions, while in others they are held liable only if they intentionally or negligently exceeded their authority.

Duty of Diligence

In the discharge of their duties, directors and officers must exercise ordinary care and prudence. Some States interpret this standard to mean that directors and officers must exercise "the same degree of care and prudence that men promoted by self-interest generally exercise in their own affairs." *Hun v. Cary,* 82 N.Y. 65. Most States and the Revised Act, however, hold that the test requires that a director or officer discharge his duties

1. in good faith;

2. with the care an ordinarily prudent person in a like position would exercise under similar circumstances; and

3. in a manner he reasonably believes to be in the best interests of the corporation.

Sections 8.30 and 8.42. A director or officer is not liable for any action taken as a director or officer, or any failure to take action, if he performed the duties of his office in compliance with these requirements. Sections 8.30(d) and 8.42(d).

So long as the directors and officers act in good faith and with due care, the courts will not substitute their judgment for the board's or officer's judgment—the so-called **business judgment rule.** Directors and officers will, nonetheless, be held liable for bad faith or negligent conduct. Moreover, they may be liable for failing to act. In one instance, a director of a bank, who in the five-and-one-half years that he had been on the board had never attended a board meeting or made any examination of the books and records, was held liable for the losses resulting from the unsupervised acts of the president and cashier, who had made various improper loans and had permitted large overdrafts. *See Francis v. United Jersey Bank.*

Reliance upon Others   Directors and officers, however, are permitted to entrust important work to others, and if they have selected employees with care, they are not personally liable for the negligent acts or willful wrongs of the employees. A reasonable amount of supervision is required, and an officer or director will be held liable for the losses resulting from an employee's carelessness, theft, or embezzlement if he knew or ought to have known or suspected that such losses were being incurred.

Directors may also rely upon information provided them by officers and employees of the corporation. Section 8.30 of the Revised Act provides:

(b) In discharging his duties a director is entitled to rely on information, opinions, reports, or statements, including financial statements and other financial data, if prepared or presented by:

(1) one or more officers or employees of the corporation whom the director reasonably believes to be reliable and competent in the matters presented;

(2) legal counsel, public accountants, or other persons as to matters the director reasonably believes are within the person's professional or expert competence; or

(3) a committee of the board of directors of which he is not a member if the director reasonably believes the committee merits confidence.

(c) A director is not acting in good faith if he has knowledge concerning the matter in question that makes reliance otherwise permitted by subsection (b) unwarranted.

An officer is also entitled to rely upon this information, but this right may, in many circumstances, be more limited than a director's because of the officer's greater familiarity with the affairs of the corporation. Section 8.42 and Comment.

Business Judgment Rule   Directors and officers are continuously called upon to make decisions that require the balancing of benefits and risks for the corporation. Although hindsight may reveal that some of these decisions were less than optimal, the business judgment rule precludes imposing liability upon the directors or officers for honest mistakes of judgment. To benefit from the business judgment rule, a director or officer must make an informed decision, without any conflict of interests, and have a rational basis for making it. Moreover, when there is a failure to satisfy this standard of conduct, it must be shown that the director's or officer's action (or inaction) is the proximate cause of damage to the corporation.

The fourth tentative draft of Section 4.01(c) of the American Law Institute's Corporate Governance Project provides:

A director or officer who makes a business judgment in good faith fulfills his duty under this Section if:
(1) he is not interested in the subject of his business judgment;
(2) he is informed with respect to the subject of his business judgment to the extent he reasonably believes to be appropriate under the circumstances; and
(3) he rationally believes that his business judgment is in the best interests of the corporation.

Hasty or ill-advised action can also cause directors to be held liable. In a recent case, the Supreme Court of Delaware held the directors liable for approving the terms of a cash-out merger. The court found that the directors did not adequately inform themselves of the company's intrinsic value and were grossly negligent in approving the terms of the merger upon two hours' consideration and without prior notice. *Smith v. Van Gorkom*, 488 A.2d 858 (1985).

Duty of Loyalty

The officers and directors of a corporation owe a duty of loyalty (**fiduciary duty**) to the corporation and to its shareholders. The essence of a fiduciary duty is the subordination of self-interest to the interest of the person or persons to whom the duty is owing. It requires undeviating loyalty on the part of officers and directors to the corporation, which they both serve and control.

An officer or director is required to make full disclosure to the corporation of any financial interest that he may have in any contract or transaction to which the corporation is a party. This is a corollary to the rule that forbids fiduciaries from making secret profits. His business conduct must be insulated from self-interest, and he may not take advantage of opportunities to advance his personal interest at the expense of the corporation. Moreover, he may not represent conflicting interests; his duty is one of strict allegiance to the corporation.

The remedy for breach of fiduciary duty is a suit in equity by the corporation, or more often a derivative suit instituted by a shareholder, to require the fiduciary to pay to the corporation the profits that he obtained through breach of his fiduciary duty. It need not be shown that the corporation could otherwise have made the profits that the fiduciary has realized. The object of the rule is to discourage breaches of duty by a fiduciary, and this is achieved by taking from the fiduciary all of the profits he has made. The enforcement of the rule may result in a windfall to the corporation, but this is incidental to the deterrent effect of the rule. Whenever a director or officer breaches his fiduciary duty, he forfeits his right to compensation during the period he engaged in the breach.

Conflict of Interests   A contract or other transaction between an officer or a director and the corporation inherently involves a conflict of interest. Contracts between officers and the corporation are dealt with by the law of agency. See Chapter 18. Early on, the common law viewed all transactions between a director and the corporation as automatically void or voidable but eventually recognized that this rule was unreasonable because it would prevent directors from entering into contracts that are beneficial to the corporation. Therefore, if such a contract is honest and fair, it will be upheld. In the case of contracts between corporations having an interlocking directorate (corporations having one or more persons who are members of both boards of directors), the courts subject the contracts to scrutiny and will set them aside unless the transaction is shown to have been entirely fair and entered into in good faith.

The Revised Act and most statutes address both of these related problems by providing that such transactions are neither void nor voidable if after full disclosure they are approved by either the board of disinterested directors or the shareholders, or if they are fair and reasonable to the corporation. Section 8.31.

In 1988, the Revised Act was amended to delete Section 8.31 and replace it with a new part (Subchapter F) consisting of Sections 8.60 through 8.63. The new subchapter adopts a more specific approach to director's conflict of interest transactions, which it defines as a transaction between a corporation (or by a subsidiary of it or an entity controlled by it) and one of the corporation's directors or a close relative of the director or a person to whom the director owes a fiduciary duty. Section 8.60. The subchapter establishes more clearly prescribed safe harbors to validate conflict of interest transactions. Section 8.61 provides:

(b) A director's conflicting interest transaction may not be enjoined, set aside, or give rise to an award of damages or other sanctions, in a proceeding by a shareholder or by or in the right of the corporation, because the director, or any person with whom or which he has a personal, economic, or other association, has an interest in the transaction, if:

(1) directors' action respecting the transaction was at any time taken in compliance with section 8.62;

(2) shareholders' action respecting the transaction was at any time taken in compliance with section 8.63;

(3) the transaction, judged according to the circumstances at the time of commitment, is established to have been fair to the corporation.

This section provides two alternative safe harbors, each of which is available before or after the transaction: approval by the directors or approval by the shareholders. In either case, the interested director must make full disclosure to the approving group. Full disclosure requires disclosure of both the existence of the conflicting interest and all material facts known to the director regarding the subject matter of the transaction.

The first safe harbor is satisfied if, after full disclosure, the transaction is approved by the affirmative vote of a majority (but no fewer than two) of those qualified directors. A qualified director is a director who does not have a conflicting interest in the transaction *and* does not have a familial, financial, professional, or employment relationship with a director who does have a conflicting interest in the transaction. Section 8.62(d).

The other safe harbor provision is satisfied if after full disclosure, the transaction was approved by a majority of the votes entitled to be cast by the holders of all qualified shares. Section 8.63(a). Qualified shares means any shares entitled to vote *except* those that are beneficially owned either by a director who has a conflicting interest in the transaction or by a person related to such a director.

If neither of the safe harbor provisions is satisfied, then the transaction is subject to appropriate judicial action *unless* the transaction is fair to the corporation. The comments to Section 8.61 explain that fairness requires that (1) the terms of the transaction, including the price, are fair; (2) the transaction benefits the corporation; and (3) the

course of dealing or process of the transaction is fair.

Loans to Directors The Model Act and some States do not permit a corporation to lend money to its directors without authorization in the particular case by its shareholders. The statutes in most States permit such loans either on a general or on a limited basis. The Revised Act permits such loans if the particular loan is approved (1) by a majority of disinterested shareholders or (2) by the board of directors after determining that the loan benefits the corporation. Section 8.32. The 1988 amendments to the Revised Act deleted this section and made loans to directors subject to the procedure applicable to director's conflicting interest transactions.

Corporate Opportunity Directors and officers may not usurp any corporate opportunity that in all fairness should belong to the corporation. A corporate opportunity is an opportunity in which the corporation has a right, property interest, or expectancy, and it depends on the facts and circumstances of each case. The American Law Institute's *Principles of Corporate Governance* defines a corporate opportunity broadly as including any proposed acquisition of contract rights or other property that is communicated or made available to the officer or director (1) in connection with the performance of his obligations or under circumstances that should reasonably lead him to believe that the person offering the opportunity expects him to offer it to the corporation or (2) through the use of corporate information or property, if the resulting opportunity is one that he should reasonably be expected to believe would be of interest to the corporation. In the case of an officer, an opportunity is a corporate opportunity if it is one that she knows or reasonably should know is closely related to the business in which the corporation is engaged or may reasonably be expected to engage. A corporate opportunity must be promptly offered to the corporation, which should promptly accept or reject the opportunity. Rejection may be based on one or more of several factors, such as lack of interest of the corporation in the opportunity, its financial inability to acquire the opportunity, legal restrictions on its ability to accept the opportunity, or unwillingness of a third party to deal with the corporation. *See Klinicki v. Lundgren.*

For instance, a party proposes a business arrangement to a corporation through its vice-president, who personally accepts it without offering it to the corporation. The vice-president has usurped a corporate opportunity. On the other hand, it generally would not include an opportunity that the corporation was unable to accept or one that the corporation expressly rejected by a vote of disinterested directors after full disclosure. In both of these instances, a director or officer can take personal advantage of the opportunity.

Transactions in Shares The issuance of shares at favorable prices to management by excluding other shareholders will normally constitute a violation of the fiduciary duty. So might the issuance of shares to a director at a fair price if the purpose of the issuance is to perpetuate corporate control rather than to raise capital or serve some other interest of the corporation.

Officers and directors have access to inside advance information not available to the public, which may affect the future market value of the shares of the corporation. Federal statutes have attempted to deal with this trading advantage by prohibiting officers and directors from purchasing or selling shares of stock of their corporation without adequate disclosure of all material facts in their possession that may affect the value or potential value of the stock. Under the Securities Exchange Act of 1934, the Securities and Exchange Commission adopted Rule 10b–5, which requires disclosure in such purchases or sales where use has been made of the mails or an instrumentality of interstate commerce, such as the telephone or telegraph. In addition, Section 16(b) of the same statute requires insiders to disgorge to the corporation any profit realized by their short-swing trading in its stock. In addition, the SEC is au-

thorized by legislation enacted in 1984 and 1988 to bring an action in a U.S. district court to have a civil penalty (of up to three times the profit gained or loss avoided) imposed upon any person who purchases or sells a security while in possession of material nonpublic information. See Chapter 45 for a discussion of these matters.

Although State law has not consistently imposed liability upon officers and directors for secret, profitable use of inside information, the trend is toward holding them liable for breach of fiduciary duty to shareholders from whom they purchase stock without making disclosure to them of facts that give the stock added value potential. They are also held liable to the corporation for profits realized upon a sale of the stock when undisclosed conditions of the corporation make a substantial decline in value practically inevitable.

Duty Not to Compete As fiduciaries, directors and officers owe to the corporation the duty of undivided loyalty, which means they may not compete with the corporation. A director or officer who breaches his fiduciary duty by competing with the corporation is liable for damages caused to the corporation. Although directors and officers may engage in their own business interests, courts will closely scrutinize any interest that competes with the business of the corporation. Moreover, an officer or director may not use corporate personnel, facilities, or funds for her own benefit nor disclose trade secrets of the corporation to others.

Indemnification of Directors and Officers

Directors and officers incur personal liability for breaching any of the duties they owe to the corporation and shareholders. Under many modern incorporation statutes, a corporation *may* indemnify a director or officer for liability incurred if he acted in good faith and in a manner he reasonably believed to be in the best interests of the corporation, so long as he has not been adjudged negligent or liable for misconduct. The Revised Act provides for *mandatory* indemnification of directors and officers for reasonable expenses incurred by them in the wholly successful defense of any proceeding brought against them because they are or were a director or officer. Sections 8.52 and 8.56. These provisions, however, may be limited by the articles of incorporation. In addition, a corporation may purchase insurance to indemnify officers and directors for liability arising out of their corporate activities, including liabilities against which the corporation is not empowered to indemnify directly. Section 8.57.

Liability Limitation Statutes

At least thirty States, including Delaware, have recently enacted legislation authorizing corporations—with shareholder approval—to limit or eliminate the liability of directors for some breaches of duty. A few States permit shareholders to limit the liability of officers. The Delaware statute provides that the articles of incorporation may contain a provision eliminating or limiting the personal liability of a director to the corporation or its stockholders for monetary damages for breach of duty as a director, provided that such provision may not eliminate or limit the liability of a director (1) for any breach of the director's duty of loyalty to the corporation or its stockholders, (2) for acts or omissions not in good faith or that involve intentional misconduct or a knowing violation of law, (3) for liability

for unlawful dividend payments or redemptions, or (4) for any transaction from which the director derived an improper personal benefit.

A handful of States have directly eliminated personal liability for money damages subject to certain exceptions. For example, under the Indiana statute, a director is liable only if the director has breached or failed to perform her duties in compliance with the statutory standard of care and the breach or failure to perform constitutes willful misconduct or recklessness. A third approach consists of imposing a limit or cap on the amount of money damages that may be assessed against a director or officer.

The Committee on Corporate Laws has proposed an amendment to the Revised Act that would authorize the inclusion of a provision in the articles of incorporation eliminating or limiting—with certain exceptions—the liability of a director to the corporation or its shareholders for any action taken, or any failure to take any action, as a director. The exceptions, for which liability would not be affected, are (1) the amount of any financial benefit received by a director to which he is not entitled, such as a bribe, kickback, or profits from a usurped corporate opportunity; (2) an intentional infliction of harm on the corporation or the shareholders; (3) liability under Section 8.33 for unlawful distributions; and (4) an intentional violation of the criminal law. Proposed Section 2.02(b)(4).

CASES

Right to Inspect Books and Records

APPLICATION OF LOPEZ

Supreme Court, Appellate Division, First Department, 1979.
420 N.Y.S.2d 225, 71 A.D.2d 976.

MEMORANDUM DECISION

Order and judgment, Supreme Court, New York County, entered August 30, 1979, denying application for disclosure of respondent's

shareholder lists, unanimously reversed on the law and the facts, with costs, and the petition is granted to the extent of disclosure of all record and beneficial ownership of shares as of September 7, 1979.

Respondent [SCM] is currently defending a multimillion dollar lawsuit brought in federal court by one Muller over the latter's unsuccessful negotiations for purchase of SCM assets abroad. Muller formed the "SCM Corporation Shareholders Committee," consisting of himself, his corporation (MacMuller Industries) and two other officers of his corporation, to challenge the position of respondent's management in this controversy. Up until August 6, 1979, this committee controlled 269,900 of the more than 9½ million outstanding shares of SCM stock. In order to wage a proxy battle for management control at the next meeting for election of directors, scheduled for October 25, 1979, the committee was anxious to obtain the list of shareholders eligible to vote as of the record date of September 7, 1979. However, [the incorporation statute] allows for the availability of such information only to shareholders of record in the corporation for at least six months. As of August 5, 1979, Muller's committee consisted of shareholders of record whose longevity of holdings in the corporation ranged from one month to four months and 23 days. On August 6 petitioner [Lopez], a former SCM executive and record holder of 38 shares of stock since 1977, joined the committee. That same day, petitioner, on behalf of the committee, demanded inspection of minutes of respondent's shareholder proceedings, as well as current lists of shareholders' names and addresses, updated by daily transfer sheets to reflect those eligible to vote at the next election of directors. The stated purpose of the demand was to communicate with shareholders for solicitation of proxies in support of the committee's nominees for directors. Respondent's rejection of this request inspired the instant proceeding.

The purpose of petitioner's demand was clearly set forth in his letter of August 6, so there is no procedural basis for respondent's rejection. [Citation.] Further, the inspection of shareholder lists to facilitate a proxy challenge to incumbent directors is a valid purpose. [Citation.] The burden is on respondent to show an improper purpose for the demand. [Citation.] Petitioner's association with Muller is certainly no indication of impropriety, in light of the otherwise valid stated purpose of the demand. Petitioner alleges without challenge that he has independently concluded that change in the management of

SCM in the interest of its shareholders is warranted, and that in this respect his views and those of the committee are similar. Where the demand is facially valid, good faith is assumed, obviating the necessity for a hearing on this issue. [Citation.] The mere fact that Muller and his companies are engaged in litigation with SCM does not demonstrate lack of good faith. Nor would there be an improper purpose or bad faith if communications with shareholders discussed such litigation. [Citation.]

Petitioner is entitled to access to available transfer sheets, at his expense, showing the daily status of record and beneficial ownership. [Citation.]

Shareholder Suits

RICHARDSON v. ARIZONA FUELS CORP.

Supreme Court of Utah, 1980.
614 P.2d 636.

STEWART, J.

Plaintiffs Donald J. Richardson, Grove L. Cook, and Wayne Weaver are stockholders of Major who brought this action individually and on behalf of all other stockholders of Major. * * *

* * *

* * * The amended complaint describes this action as one brought as a class action pursuant to Rule 23 and as a stockholders' derivative action pursuant to Rule 23.1. Plaintiffs moved for an order certifying this suit as a class action . . . [The] motion [was] granted by the district court.

Defendants attack the order on the grounds . . . that certification of all the claims in the suit as a class action was improper * * *

* * *

A class action and a derivative action rest upon fundamentally different principles of substantive law; to ignore those differences is not a minor procedural solecism. A derivative action must necessarily be based on a claim for relief which is owned by the stockholders' corporation. Indeed, a prerequisite for filing a derivative action is the failure of the corporation to initiate the action in its own name. The stockholder, as a nominal party, has no right, title or interest whatsoever in the claim itself—whether the action is brought by the corporation or by the stockholder on behalf of the corporation.

A class action, on the other hand, is predicated on ownership of the claim for relief sued upon in the representative of the class and all other class members in their capacity *as individuals.* Shareholders of the corporation may, of course, have claims for relief directly against their corporation because the corporation itself has violated rights possessed by the shareholders, and a class action would be an appropriate means for enforcing their claims. A recovery in a class action is a recovery which belongs directly to the shareholders. However, in a derivative action, the plaintiff shareholder recovers nothing and the judgment runs in favor of the corporation.

The difference in the two procedures and their relationship to underlying substantive law has been stated as follows:

Suits which are said to be derivative, and therefore come within the rule, are those which seek to enforce any right which belongs to the corporation and is not being enforced, such as the liability of corporate officers or majority shareholders for mismanagement, to recover corporate assets and related claims, to enforce rights of the corporation by virtue of its contract with a third person, and to enjoin those in charge of the corporation from causing it to commit an ultra vires act. [Citation.]

On the other hand,

[i]f the injury is one to the plaintiff as a stockholder and to him individually, and not to the corporation, as where the action is based on a contract to which he is a party, or on a right belonging severally to him, or on a fraud affecting him directly, it is an individual action. [Citation.]

* * *

The amended complaint states twelve causes of action, the first eight of which allege some fraudulent appropriation of or scheme to appropriate Major's assets by defendants. These causes of action seek to require the defendants to disgorge and return to Major the assets wrongfully obtained. Of the remaining four causes, three seek compensatory or punitive damages for injury attributable to alleged breaches of fiduciary duty implicit in the fraudulent acts enumerated in the first eight causes. The final cause of action seeks appointment of a receiver.

There is no doubt that the first eight causes of action allege injury to the corporation only. The injury alleged can be asserted by plaintiffs only derivatively as stockholders on behalf of the corporation. This leaves the ninth, tenth and eleventh causes of action to be analyzed to determine if they state claims which may be pursued by the stockholders as a class to redress injuries to the stockholders as individuals.

The ninth cause of action alleges initially that the defendants "breached their fiduciary duties to Major Oil and to its stockholders. . . ." As a general rule, directors and other officers of a corporation stand in a fiduciary relation to the corporation. [Citation.] While the statement is made that directors and officers stand in a like relation to the stockholders of the corporation, [citation], in Utah it is clear that that relation is to the stockholders collectively. [Citations.] The distinction between a fiduciary duty owed to the corporation as a whole as opposed to the stockholders collectively does not appear to be one of substance in this case. There is no important issue as to whether the cause of action states a corporate claim. Although plaintiff frames this claim, in the alternative, as one belonging to the shareholders, the claim for relief belongs to the corporation.

The ninth cause of action then goes on to allege that the defendants "mismanaged the corporate and prudential affairs of Major Oil. . . ." The rule in Utah is that mismanagement of the corporation gives rise to a cause of action in the corporation, even if the mismanagement results in damage to stockholders by depreciating the value of the corporation's stock. [Citation.] Therefore, any compensatory damages which may be recovered on account of any breach by defendants of their fiduciary duty as directors and officers or arising as a result of mismanagement of the corporation by defendants belong to the corporation and not to the stockholders individually.

* * *

We therefore reverse the district court's certification of this suit as a class action and remand for further proceedings not inconsistent with this opinion.

Duties of Controlling Shareholders

DONAHUE v. RODD ELECTROTYPE CO., INC.

Massachusetts Supreme Court, 1974.
367 Mass. 578, 328 N.E.2d 505.

TAURO, C. J.

The plaintiff, Euphemia Donahue, a minority stockholder in the Rodd Electrotype Company of New England, Inc. (Rodd Electrotype), a Massachusetts corporation, brings this suit against the directors of Rodd Electrotype, Charles H. Rodd, Frederick I. Rodd and Mr. Harold E. Magnuson, against Harry C. Rodd, a former director, officer, and controlling stockholder of Rodd Electrotype and against Rodd Electrotype (hereinafter called defendants). The plaintiff seeks to rescind Rodd Electrotype's purchase of Harry Rodd's shares in Rodd Electrotype and to compel Harry Rodd "to repay to the corporation the purchase price of said shares, $36,000, together with interest from the date of purchase." The plaintiff alleges that the defendants caused the corporation to purchase the shares in violation of their fiduciary duty to her, a minority stockholder of Rodd Electrotype.

* * * We deem a close corporation to be typified by: (1) a small number of stockholders; (2) no ready market for the corporate stock; and (3) substantial majority stockholder participation in the management, direction and operations of the corporation.

As thus defined, the close corporation bears striking resemblance to a partnership. Commentators and courts have noted that the close corporation is often little more than an "incorporated" or "chartered" partnership. . . . Just as in a partnership, the relationship

among the stockholders must be one of trust, confidence and absolute loyalty if the enterprise is to succeed. Close corporations with substantial assets and with more numerous stockholders are no different from smaller close corporations in this regard. All participants rely on the fidelity and abilities of those stockholders who hold office. Disloyalty and self-seeking conduct on the part of any stockholder will engender bickering, corporate stalemates, and, perhaps, efforts to achieve dissolution. * * *

* * *

Although the corporate form provides . . . advantages for the stockholders (limited liability, perpetuity, and so forth), it also supplies an opportunity for the majority stockholders to oppress or disadvantage minority stockholders. The minority is vulnerable to a variety of oppressive devices, termed "freeze-outs," which the majority may employ. [Citation.] An authoritative study of such "freeze-outs" enumerates some of the possibilities: "The squeezers [those who employ the freeze-out techniques] may refuse to declare dividends; they may drain off the corporation's earnings in the form of exorbitant salaries and bonuses to the majority shareholder-officers and perhaps to their relatives, or in the form of high rent by the corporation for property leased from majority shareholders . . .; they may deprive minority shareholders of corporate offices and of employment by the company; they may cause the corporation to sell its assets at an inadequate price to the majority shareholders. . . ." [Citation.] In particular, the power of the board of directors, controlled by the majority, to declare or withhold dividends and to deny the minority employment is easily converted to a device to disadvantage minority stockholders. * * *

The minority can, of course, initiate suit against the majority and their directors. Self-serving conduct by directors is proscribed by the director's fiduciary obligation to the corporation. [Citation.] However, in practice, the plaintiff will find difficulty in challenging dividend or employment policies. Such policies are considered to be within the judgment of the directors. This court has said: "The courts prefer not to interfere . . . with the sound financial management of the corporation by its directors, but declare as a general rule that the declaration of dividends rests within the sound discretion of the directors, refusing to interfere with their determination unless a plain abuse of discretion is made to appear." * * *

Thus, when these types of "freeze-outs" are attempted by the majority stockholders, the minority stockholders, cut off from all corporation-related revenues, must either suffer their losses or seek a buyer for their shares. Many minority stockholders will be unwilling or unable to wait for an alteration in majority policy. Typically, the minority stockholder in a close corporation has a substantial percentage of his personal assets invested in the corporation. [Citation.] The stockholder may have anticipated that his salary from his position with the corporation would be his livelihood. Thus, he cannot afford to wait passively. He must liquidate his investment in the close corporation in order to reinvest the funds in income-producing enterprises.

At this point, the true plight of the minority stockholder in a close corporation becomes manifest. He cannot easily reclaim his capital. In a large public corporation, the oppressed or dissident minority stockholder could sell his stock in order to extricate some of his invested capital. By definition, this market is not available for shares in the close corporation. In a partnership, a partner who feels abused by his fellow partners may cause dissolution by his "express will . . . at any time" [citation] and recover his share of partnership assets and accumulated profits. . . . To secure dissolution of the ordinary close corporation subject to [citation], the stockholder, in the absence of corporate deadlock, must own at least fifty per cent of the shares [citation] or have the advantage of a favorable provision in the articles of organization [citation]. The minority stockholder, by definition lacking fifty per cent of the corporate shares, can never "authorize" the corporation to file a petition for dissolution under [cita-

tion], by his own vote. He will seldom have at his disposal the requisite favorable provision in the articles of organization.

Thus, in a close corporation, the minority stockholders may be trapped in a disadvantageous situation. No outsider would knowingly assume the position of the disadvantaged minority. The outsider would have the same difficulties. To cut losses, the minority stockholder may be compelled to deal with the majority. This is the capstone of the majority plan. Majority "freeze-out" schemes which withhold dividends are designed to compel the minority to relinquish stock at inadequate prices. . . . When the minority stockholder agrees to sell out at less than fair value, the majority has won.

Because of the fundamental resemblance of the close corporation to the partnership, the trust and confidence which are essential to this scale and manner of enterprise, and the inherent danger to minority interests in the close corporation, we hold that stockholders in the close corporation owe one another substantially the same fiduciary duty in the operation of the enterprise that partners owe to one another. In our previous decisions, we have defined the standard of duty owed by partners to one another as the "utmost good faith and loyalty." [Citations.] Stockholders in close corporations must discharge their management and stockholder responsibilities in conformity with this strict good faith standard. They may not act out of avarice, expediency or self-interest in derogation of their duty of loyalty to the other stockholders and to the corporation.

We contrast this strict good faith standard with the somewhat less stringent standard of fiduciary duty to which directors and stockholders of all corporations must adhere in the discharge of their corporate responsibilities. Corporate directors are held to a good faith and inherent fairness standard of conduct [citation] and are not "permitted to serve two masters whose interests are antagonistic." [Citation.] "Their paramount duty is to the corporation, and their personal pecuniary interests are subordinate to that duty." [Citation.]

The more rigorous duty of partners and participants in a joint adventure, here extended to stockholders in a close corporation, was described by then Chief Judge Cardozo of the New York Court of Appeals in [citation]: "Joint adventurers, like copartners, owe to one another, while the enterprise continues, the duty of the finest loyalty. Many forms of conduct permissible in a workaday world for those acting at arm's length, are forbidden to those bound by fiduciary ties. . . . Not honesty alone, but the punctilio of an honor the most sensitive, is then the standard of behavior."

Application of this strict standard of duty to stockholders in close corporations is a natural outgrowth of the prior case law. In a number of cases involving close corporations, we have held stockholders participating in management to a standard of fiduciary duty more exacting than the traditional good faith and inherent fairness standard because of the trust and confidence reposed in them by the other stockholders. * * *

* * *

Under settled Massachusetts law, a domestic corporation, unless forbidden by statute, has the power to purchase its own shares. When the corporation reacquiring its own stock is a close corporation, the purchase is subject to the additional requirement, in the light of our holding in this opinion, that the stockholders, who, as directors or controlling stockholders, caused the corporation to enter into the stock purchase agreement, must have acted with the utmost good faith and loyalty to the other stockholders.

To meet this test, if the stockholder whose shares were purchased was a member of the controlling group, the controlling stockholders must cause the corporation to offer each stockholder an equal opportunity to sell a ratable number of his shares to the corporation at an identical price. * * *

The benefits conferred by the purchase are twofold: (1) provision of a market for shares; (2) access to corporate assets for personal use. By definition, there is no ready market for shares of a close corporation. The purchase creates a market for shares which previously had been unmarketable. It transforms a previously illiquid investment into a liquid one. If the close corporation purchases shares only from a member of the controlling group, the controlling stockholder can convert his shares into cash at a time when none of the other stockholders can. Consistent with its strict fiduciary duty, the controlling group may not utilize its control of the corporation to establish an exclusive market in previously unmarketable shares from which the minority stockholders are excluded. * * *

The purchase also distributes corporate assets to the stockholder whose shares were purchased. Unless an equal opportunity is given to all stockholders, the purchase of shares from a member of the controlling group operates as a *preferential* distribution of assets. In exchange for his shares, he receives a percentage of the contributed capital and accumulated profits of the enterprise. The funds he so receives are available for his personal use. The other stockholders benefit from no such access to corporate property and cannot withdraw their shares of the corporate profits and capital in this manner unless the controlling group acquiesces. Although the purchase price for the controlling stockholder's shares may seem fair to the corporation and other stockholders under the tests established in the prior case law, the controlling stockholder whose stock has been purchased has still received a relative advantage over his fellow stockholders, inconsistent with his strict fiduciary duty—an opportunity to turn corporate funds to personal use.

The rule of equal opportunity in stock purchases by close corporations provides equal access to these benefits for all stockholders. We hold that, in any case in which the controlling stockholders have exercised their power over the corporation to deny the minority such equal opportunity, the minority shall be entitled to appropriate relief. * * *

The strict standard of duty is plainly applicable to the stockholders in Rodd Electrotype. Rodd Electrotype is a close corporation. Members of the Rodd and Donahue families are the sole owners of the corporation's stock. In actual numbers, the corporation, immediately prior to the corporate purchase of Harry Rodd's shares, had six stockholders. The shares have not been traded, and no market for them seems to exist. Harry Rodd, Charles Rodd, Frederick Rodd, William G. Mason (Phyllis Mason's husband), and the plaintiff's husband all worked for the corporation. The Rodds have retained the paramount management positions.

Through their control of these management positions and of the majority of the Rodd Electrotype stock, the Rodds effectively controlled the corporation. In testing the stock purchase from Harry Rodd against the applicable strict fiduciary standard, we treat the Rodd family as a single controlling group. We reject the defendants' contention that the Rodd family cannot be treated as a unit for this purpose. From the evidence, it is clear that the Rodd family was a close-knit one with strong community of interest. [Citation.] Harry Rodd had hired his sons to work in the family business, Rodd Electrotype. As he aged, he transferred portions of his stock holdings to his children. Charles Rodd and Frederick Rodd were given positions of responsibility in the business as he withdrew from active management. In these circumstances, it is realistic to assume that appreciation, gratitude, and filial devotion would prevent the younger Rodds from opposing a plan which would provide funds for their father's retirement.

* * *

On its face, then, the purchase of Harry Rodd's shares by the corporation is a breach of the duty which the controlling stockholders, the Rodds, owed to the minority stockholders, the plaintiff and her son. The purchase distributed a portion of the corporate assets to Harry Rodd, a member of the controlling group, in exchange for his shares. The plaintiff and her son were not offered an equal opportunity to sell their shares to the corporation. In fact, their efforts to obtain an equal opportunity were rebuffed by the corporate representative. As the trial judge found, they did not, in any manner, ratify the transaction with Harry Rodd.

Because of the foregoing, we hold that the plaintiff is entitled to relief.

Duty of Diligence

FRANCIS v. UNITED JERSEY BANK

Supreme Court of New Jersey, 1981.
87 N.J. 15, 432 A.2d 814.

POLLOCK, J.

[Pritchard & Baird was a reinsurance broker. A reinsurance broker arranges contracts between insurance companies so companies that have sold large policies may sell participations in these policies to other companies in order to share the risks. Pritchard & Baird was controlled for many years by Charles Pritchard, who died in December 1973. Prior to his death, he brought his two sons, Charles Jr. and William, into the business. The pair assumed an increasingly dominant role in the affairs of the business during the elder Charles's later years. Starting in 1970, Charles Jr. and William began to withdraw ever-increasing sums from the corporation account that were designated as "loans" on the balance sheet. These "loans," however, represented a significant misappropriation of funds belonging to the clients of the corporation. By late 1975, Charles Jr. and William had plunged the corporation into hopeless bankruptcy. A total of $12,333,514.47 in "loans" had accumulated by October of that year. Mrs. Lillian Pritchard, the widow of the elder Charles, was a member of the corporation's board of directors during this period until her resignation on December 3, 1975, the day before the corporation filed for bankruptcy. Francis, as trustee in the bankruptcy proceeding, brought suit against United Jersey Bank, the administrator of the estate of Charles Sr. He also charged that Lillian Pritchard, as a director of the corporation, was personally liable for the misappropriated funds on the basis of negligence in discharging her duties as director. The trial court found Lillian Pritchard liable and the appellate court affirmed.]

Individual liability of a corporate director for acts of the corporation is a prickly problem. Generally directors are accorded broad immunity and are not insurers of corporate activities. The problem is particularly nettlesome when a third party asserts that a director, because of nonfeasance, is liable for losses caused by acts of insiders, who in this case were officers, directors and shareholders. Determination of the liability of Mrs. Pritchard requires findings that she had a duty to the clients of Pritchard & Baird, that she breached that duty and that her breach was a proximate cause of their losses.

The New Jersey Business Corporation Act, which took effect on January 1, 1969, was a comprehensive revision of the statutes relating to business corporations. One section, [citation], concerning a director's general obligation had no counterpart in the old Act. That section makes it incumbent upon directors to

discharge their duties in good faith and with that degree of diligence, care and skill which ordinarily prudent men would exercise under similar circumstances in like positions.

* * *

As a general rule, a director should acquire at least a rudimentary understanding of the business of the corporation. Accordingly, a director should become familiar with the fundamentals of the business in which the corporation is engaged. [Citation.] Because directors are bound to exercise ordinary care, they cannot set up as a defense lack of the knowledge needed to exercise the requisite degree of care. If one "feels that he has not had sufficient business experience to qualify him to perform the duties of a director, he should either acquire the knowledge by inquiry, or refuse to act." [Citation.]

Directors are under a continuing obligation to keep informed about the activities of the corporation. Otherwise, they may not be able to participate in the overall management of corporate affairs. [Citations.] Directors may not shut their eyes to corporate misconduct, and then claim that because they did not see the misconduct, they did not have a duty to look. The sentinel asleep at his post contributes nothing to the enterprise he is charged to protect. [Citation.]

Directorial management does not require a detailed inspection of day-to-day activities, but rather a general monitoring of corporate affairs and policies. [Citation.] Accordingly, a director is well advised to attend board meetings regularly. Indeed, a director who is absent from a board meeting is presumed to concur in action taken on a corporate matter, unless he files a "dissent with the secretary of the corporation within a reasonable time after learning of such action." [Citation.] Regular attendance does not mean that directors must attend every meeting, but that directors should attend meetings as a matter of practice. A director of a publicly held corporation might be expected to attend regular monthly meetings, but a director of a small, family corporation might be asked to attend only an annual meeting. The point is that one of the responsibilities of a director is to attend meetings of the board of which he or she is a member. That burden is lightened by [citation], which permits board action without a meeting if all members of the board consent in writing.

While directors are not required to audit corporate books, they should maintain familiarity with the financial status of the corporation by a regular review of financial statements. [Citations.] In some circumstances, directors may be charged with assuring that bookkeeping methods conform to industry custom and usage. [Citation.] The extent of review, as well as the nature and frequency of financial statements, depends not only on the customs of the industry, but also on the nature of the corporation and the business in which it is engaged. Financial statements of some small corporations may be prepared internally and only on an annual basis; in a large publicly held corporation, the statements may be produced monthly or at some other regular interval. Adequate financial review normally would be more informal in a private corporation than in a publicly held corporation.

Of some relevance in this case is the circumstance that the financial records disclose the "shareholders' loans". Generally directors are immune from liability if, in good faith,

they rely upon the opinion of counsel for the corporation or upon written reports setting forth financial data concerning the corporation and prepared by an independent public accountant or certified public accountant or firm of such accountants or upon financial statements, books of account or reports of the corporation represented to them to be correct by the president, the officer of the corporation having charge of its books of account, or the person presiding at a meeting of the board. [Citation.]

The review of financial statements, however, may give rise to a duty to inquire further into matters revealed by those statements. [Citations.] Upon discovery of an illegal course of action, a director has a duty to object and, if the corporation does not correct the conduct, to resign. [Citations.]

In certain circumstances, the fulfillment of the duty of a director may call for more than mere objection and resignation. Sometimes a director may be required to seek the advice of counsel. * * *

A director is not an ornament, but an essential component of corporate governance. Consequently, a director cannot protect himself behind a paper shield bearing the motto, "dummy director." [Citations.] The New Jersey Business Corporation Act, in imposing a standard of ordinary care on all directors, confirms that dummy, figurehead and accommodation directors are anachronisms with no place in New Jersey law. . . . Thus, all directors are responsible for managing the business and affairs of the corporation. [Citations.]

* * *

A director's duty of care does not exist in the abstract, but must be considered in relation to specific obligees. In general, the relationship of a corporate director to the corporation and its stockholders is that of a fiduciary. [Citation.] Shareholders have a right to expect that directors will exercise reasonable supervision and control over the policies and practices of a corporation. The institutional integrity of a corporation depends upon the proper discharge by directors of those duties.

* * *

As a director of a substantial reinsurance brokerage corporation, she should have known that it received annually millions of dollars of loss and premium funds which it held in trust for ceding and reinsurance companies. Mrs. Pritchard should have obtained and read the annual statements of financial condition of Pritchard & Baird. Although she had a right to rely upon financial statements prepared in accordance with [citation], such reliance would not excuse her conduct. The reason is that those statements disclosed on their face the misappropriation of trust funds.

From those statements, she should have realized that, as of January 31, 1970, her sons were withdrawing substantial trust funds under the guise of "Shareholders' Loans." The financial statements for each fiscal year commencing with that of January 31, 1970, disclosed that the working capital deficits and the "loans" were escalating in tandem. Detecting a misappropriation of funds would not have required special expertise or extraordinary diligence; a cursory reading of the financial statements would have revealed the pillage. Thus, if Mrs. Pritchard had read the financial statements, she would have known that her sons were converting trust funds. When financial statements demonstrate that insiders are bleeding a corporation to death, a director should notice and try to stanch the flow of blood.

In summary, Mrs. Pritchard was charged with the obligation of basic knowledge and supervision of the business of Pritchard & Baird. Under the circumstances, this obligation included reading and understanding financial statements, and making reasonable attempts at detection and prevention of the illegal conduct of other officers and directors. She had a duty to protect the clients of Pritchard & Baird against policies and practices that would result in the misappropriation of money they had entrusted to the corporation. She breached that duty.

Nonetheless, the negligence of Mrs. Pritchard does not result in liability unless it is a proximate cause of the loss. . . . Thus, the plaintiff must establish not only a breach of duty, "but in addition that the performance by the director of his duty would have avoided loss, and the amount of the resulting loss." [Citation.]

* * *

Within Pritchard & Baird, several factors contributed to the loss of the funds: comingling of corporate and client monies, conversion of funds by Charles, Jr. and William and dereliction of her duties by Mrs. Pritchard. The wrongdoing of her sons, although the immediate cause of the loss, should not excuse Mrs. Pritchard from her negligence which also was a substantial factor contributing to the loss. [Citation.] Her sons knew that she, the only other director, was not reviewing their conduct; they spawned their fraud in the backwater of her neglect. Her neglect of duty contributed to the climate of corruption; her failure to act contributed to the continuation of that corruption. Consequently, her conduct was a substantial factor contributing to the loss.

Analysis of proximate cause is especially difficult in a corporate context where the allegation is that nonfeasance of a director is a proximate cause of damage to a third party. Where a case involves nonfeasance, no one can say "with absolute certainty what would have occurred if the defendant had acted otherwise." [Citation.] Nonetheless, where it is reasonable to conclude that the failure to act would produce a particular result and that result has followed, causation may be inferred. [Citation.] We conclude that even if Mrs. Pritchard's mere objection had not stopped the depredations of her sons, her consultation with an attorney and the threat of suit would have deterred them. That conclusion flows as a matter of common sense and logic from the record. Whether in other situations a director has a duty to do more than protest and resign is best left to case-by-case determinations. In this case, we are satisfied that there was a duty to do more than object and resign. Consequently, we find that Mrs. Pritchard's negligence was a proximate cause of the misappropriations.

To conclude, by virtue of her office, Mrs. Pritchard had the power to prevent the losses sustained by the clients of Pritchard & Baird. With power comes responsibility. She had a duty to deter the depredation of the other insiders, her sons. She breached that duty and caused plaintiffs to sustain damages.

[Judgment for Francis affirmed.]

Duty of Loyalty

KLINICKI v. LUNDGREN

Supreme Court of Oregon, 1985.
298 Or. 662, 695 P.2d 906.

JONES J.

The factual and legal background of this complicated litigation was succinctly set forth by Chief Judge Joseph in the Court of Appeals opinion as follows:

"In January, 1977, plaintiff Klinicki conceived the idea of engaging in the air transportation business in Berlin, West Germany. He discussed the idea with his friend, defendant Lundgren. At that time, both men were furloughed Pan American pilots stationed in West Germany. They decided to enter the air transportation business, planning to begin operations with an air taxi service and later to expand into other service, such as regularly scheduled flights or charter flights. In April, 1977, they incorporated Berlinair, Inc., as a closely held Oregon corporation. Plaintiff was a vice-president and a director. Lundgren was the corporation's president and a director. Each man owned 33 percent of the company stock. Lelco, Inc., a corporation owned by Lundgren and members of his family, owned 33 percent of the stock. The corporation's attorney owned the remaining one percent of the stock. Berlinair obtained the necessary governmental licenses, purchased an aircraft and in November, 1977, began passenger service.

"As president, Lundgren was responsible, in part, for developing and promoting Berlinair's transportation business. Plaintiff was in charge of operations and maintenance. In November, 1977, plaintiff and Lundgren, as representatives of Berlinair, met with representatives of the Berliner Flug Ring (BFR), a consortium of Berlin travel agents that contracts for charter flights to take sallow German tourists to sunnier climes. The BFR contract was considered a lucrative business opportunity by those familiar with the air transportation business, and plaintiff and defendant had contemplated pursuing the contract when they formed Berlinair. After the initial meeting, all subsequent contacts with BFR were made by Lundgren or other Berlinair employees acting under his directions.

"During the early stages of negotiations, Lundgren believed that Berlinair could not obtain the contract because BFR was then satisfied with its carrier. In early June, 1978, however, Lundgren learned that there was a good chance that the BFR contract might be available. He informed a BFR representative that he would make a proposal on behalf of a new company. On July 7, 1978, he incorporated Air Berlin Charter Company (ABC) and was its sole owner. On August 20, 1978, ABC presented BFR with a contract proposal, and after a series of discussions it was awarded the contract on September 1, 1978. Lundgren effectively concealed from plaintiff his negotiations with BFR and his diversion of the BFR contract to ABC, even though he used Berlinair working time, staff, money and facilities.

"Plaintiff, as a minority stockholder in Berlinair, brought a derivative action against ABC for usurping a corporate opportunity of Berlinair. He also brought an individual claim against Lundgren for compensatory and punitive damages based on breach of fiduciary duty.

"The trial court found that ABC, acting through Lundgren, had wrongfully diverted the BFR contract, which was a corporate opportunity of Berlinair. The court imposed a constructive trust on ABC in favor of Berlinair, ordered an accounting by ABC and enjoined ABC from transferring its assets. The trial court also found that Lundgren, as an officer and director of Berlinair, had breached his fiduciary duties of good faith, fair dealing and full disclosure owed to plaintiff individually and to Berlinair. The court did not award plaintiff any actual damages on the breach of fiduciary duty claim. All the issues were tried to the court, except that a jury was empaneled to try the punitive damages issue. It returned a verdict in favor of plaintiff and assessed punitive damages against Lundgren in the amount of $750,000. Lundgren then moved to dismiss plaintiff's claim for punitive damages. The court granted the motion to dismiss and, *sua sponte,* entered judgment in favor of Lundgren notwithstanding the verdict on the punitive damages claim."

ABC appealed to the Court of Appeals contending that it did not usurp a corporate opportunity of Berlinair. * * *

ABC petitions for review to this court contending that the concealment and diversion of the BFR contract was not a usurpation of a corporate opportunity, because Berlinair did not have the financial ability to undertake that contract. ABC argues that proof of financial ability is a necessary part of a corporate opportunity case and that plaintiff had the

burden of proof on that issue and did not carry that burden.

There is no dispute that the corporate opportunity doctrine precludes corporate fiduciaries from diverting to themselves business opportunities in which the corporation has an expectancy, property interest or right, or which in fairness should otherwise belong to the corporation. [Citation.] The doctrine follows from a corporate fiduciary's duty of undivided loyalty to the corporation. ABC agrees that, unless Berlinair's financial inability to undertake the contract makes a difference, the BFR contract was a corporate opportunity of Berlinair.

* * *

Counsel for defendant, relying on [citation], contends there is no corporate opportunity if there is no capacity to take advantage of the corporate opportunity. We reject this argument. By the same token, we reject plaintiff's contention, relying on [citation], that financial ability is totally irrelevant in an unlawful taking of a corporate opportunity. * * *

On April 13, 1984, the American Law Institute published its "Tentative Draft No. 3" concerning "Principles of Corporate Governance: Analysis and Recommendations." The draft, of course, does not represent the position of the ALI, but it does contain definitions and rules which we find helpful in resolving the main issue in this case. Section 5.12 of the draft, which contains the proposed general rule and definition, reads as follows:

* * *

"A corporate opportunity means any opportunity to engage in a business activity (including acquisition or use of any contract right or other tangible or intangible property) that:

(1) In the case of a principal senior executive or any director, is an opportunity that is communicated or otherwise made available to him either:

(A) in connection with the performance of his obligations as a principal senior executive or director or under circumstances that should reasonably lead him to believe that the person offering the opportunity expects him to offer it to the corporation, or

(B) through the use of corporate information or property, if the resulting opportunity is one that the principal senior executive or director should reasonably be expected to believe would be of interest to the corporation; or

(2) In the case of a principal senior executive or a director who is a full-time employee of the corporation, is an opportunity that he knows or reasonably should know is closely related to the business in which the corporation is engaged or may reasonably be expected to engage."

Section 5.12 presents an approach very similar to that suggested by Chief Judge Joseph in the Court of Appeals decision rendered in this case. Section 5.12 generally would require an opportunity that could be advantageous to the corporation to be offered to the corporation by a director or principal senior executive before he takes it for himself. Section 5.12 declines to adopt the rigid rule expressed in [citation], which precludes a person subject to the duty of loyalty from pursuing a rejected opportunity. The proposed rule permits a director or principal senior executive to deal with his corporation so long as he deals fairly with full disclosure and bears the burden of proving fairness unless the corporate opportunity was rejected by disinterested directors or shareholders.

* * *

Whether the rejection was fair or not includes consideration of whether the corporation was financially or otherwise incapacitated from undertaking the corporate opportunity. We agree with the proposed ALI Principles of Corporate Governance . . . as to the following rules for application in close corporation corporate opportunity cases.

Where a director or principal senior executive of a close corporation wishes to take personal advantage of a "corporate opportunity," as defined by the proposed rule, the director or principal senior executive must comply strictly with the following procedure:

(1) the director or principal senior executive must promptly offer the opportunity and disclose all material facts known regarding the opportunity to the disinterested directors or, if there is no disinterested director, to the disinterested shareholders. If the director or principal senior executive learns of other material facts after such disclosure, the director

or principal senior executive must disclose these additional facts in a like manner before personally taking the opportunity.

(2) The director or principal senior executive may take advantage of the corporate opportunity only after full disclosure and only if the opportunity is rejected by a majority of the disinterested directors or, if there are no disinterested directors, by a majority of the disinterested shareholders. If, after full disclosure, the disinterested directors or shareholders unreasonably fail to reject the offer, the interested director or principal senior executive may proceed to take the opportunity if he can prove the taking was otherwise "fair" to the corporation. Full disclosure to the appropriate corporate body is, however, an absolute condition precedent to the validity of any forthcoming rejection as well as to the availability to the director or principal senior executive of the defense of fairness.

(3) An appropriation of a corporate opportunity may be ratified by rejection of the opportunity by a majority of disinterested directors or a majority of disinterested shareholders, after full disclosure subject to the same rules as set out above for prior offer, disclosure and rejection. Where a director or principal senior executive of a close corporation appropriates a corporate opportunity without first fully disclosing the opportunity and offering it to the corporation, absent ratification, that director or principal senior executive holds the opportunity in trust for the corporation.

Applying these rules to the facts in this case, we conclude:

(1) Lundgren, as director and principal executive officer of Berlinair, owed a fiduciary duty to Berlinair.
(2) The BFR contract was a "corporate opportunity" of Berlinair.
(3) Lundgren formed ABC for the purpose of usurping the opportunity presented to Berlinair by the BFR contract.
(4) Lundgren did not offer Berlinair the BFR contract.

(5) Lundgren did not attempt to obtain the consent of Berlinair to his taking of the BFR corporate opportunity.

(6) Lundgren did not fully disclose to Berlinair his intent to appropriate the opportunity for himself and ABC.

(7) Berlinair never rejected the opportunity presented by the BFR contract.

(8) Berlinair never ratified the appropriation of the BFR contract.

(9) Lundgren, acting for ABC, misappropriated the BFR contract.

Because of the above, the defendant may not now contend that Berlinair did not have the financial ability to successfully pursue the BFR contract. As stated in proposed Section 5.12(c) of the Principles of Corporate Governance, supra. "If the challenging party satisfies the burden of proving that a corporate opportunity was taken without being offered to the corporation, the challenging party will prevail."

[Judgment affirmed.]

QUESTIONS

1. Compare the actual governance of closely held corporations, the actual governance of publicly held corporations, and the statutory model of corporate governance.

2. Distinguish between (a) straight and cumulative voting; (b) proxies and voting trusts; and (c) direct suits and derivative suits.

3. Identify the areas of corporate policy determined by the board of directors.

4. Discuss the business judgment rule.

5. Identify and discuss the most important situations involved in management's duties of loyalty, obedience, and diligence.

PROBLEMS

1. Brown was the president and director of a corporation engaged in owning and operating a chain of motels. Brown was advised, upon what seemed to be good authority, that a superhighway was to be constructed through the town of X, which would be a most desirable location for a motel. Brown presented these facts to the board of directors of the motel corporation and recommended that the corporation build a motel in the town of X at the location described. The board of directors agreed, and the new motel was constructed. It developed that the superhighway plans were changed after the motel was constructed. The highway was never built. Later, a packing house was built on property adjoining the motel, and as a result the corporation sustained a considerable loss. The shareholders brought an appropriate action against Brown, charging that his proposal had caused a substantial loss to the corporation and seeking recovery of that loss from Brown. Decision?

2. A, B, C, D, and E constituted the board of directors of the X Corporation. While D and E were out of town, A, B, and C held a special meeting of the board. Just as the meeting began, C became ill. He then gave a proxy to A and went home. A resolution was then adopted directing and authorizing the purchase by the X Corporation of an adjoining piece of land owned by S as a site for an additional factory building. As was known by S, the purchase required approval by the board of directors. A and B voted for the resolution, and A, as C's proxy, cast C's vote in favor of the resolution. A contract was then made by the X Corporation with S for the purchase of the land.

After the return of D and E, another special meeting of the board was held with all five directors present. A resolution was then unanimously adopted to cancel the contract with S. S was so notified and now sues X Corporation for damages for breach of contract. Decision?

3. Bernard Koch was president of United Corporation, a closely held corporation. Koch, James Trent, and Henry Phillips made up the three-person board of directors. At a meeting of the board of directors, Trent was elected president, replacing Koch. At the same meeting, Trent attempted to have the salary of the president increased. He was unable to obtain board approval of the increase because, although Phillips voted for the increase, Koch voted against it. Trent was disqualified from voting by the corporation's charter. As a result, the directors, by a two-to-one vote, amended the bylaws to provide for the appointment of an executive committee composed of three reputable business persons to pass upon and fix all matters of salary for employees of the corporation. Subsequently, the executive committee, consisting of Jane Jones, James Black, and William Johnson, increased the salary of the president.

Koch brought an appropriate action against the corporation, Trent, and Phillips to enjoin them from paying the increased compensation to the president above that fixed by the board of directors. What decision?

4. Zenith Steel Company operated a prosperous business. In January its president, Roe, who is also a director, was voted a $100,000 bonus by the board of directors for the valuable services he provided to the company during the previous year. Roe received an annual salary of $85,000 from the company. Black, a minority shareholder in Zenith Steel Company, brings an appropriate action to enjoin the payment by the company of the $100,000 bonus. Decision?

5. (a) Smith, a director of the Sample Corporation, sells a piece of vacant land to the Sample Corporation for $50,000. The land cost him $20,000.

(b) Jones, a shareholder of the Sample Corporation, sells a used truck to the Sample Corporation for $8,400, although the truck was worth $6,000.

Raphael, a minority shareholder of the Sample Corporation, claims that these sales are void and should be annulled. Is he correct? Why?

6. The X Corporation manufactures machine tools. The five directors of X Corporation are Black, White, Brown, Green, and Crimson. At a duly called meeting of the board of directors of X Corporation in January, all five directors were present. A contract for the purchase of $1 million worth of steel from the D Company of which Black, White, and Brown are directors was discussed and approved by a unanimous vote. There was a lengthy discussion about entering into negotiations for the purchase of Q Corporation, which allegedly was about to be sold for around $15 million. By a three-to-two vote it was decided not to open such negotiations.

Three months later, Green purchased Q Corporation for $15 million. Shortly thereafter, a new board of directors for X Corporation took office. X Corporation now brings actions to rescind its contract with D Company and to compel Green to assign to X Corporation his contract for the purchase of Q Corporation. Decisions as to each action?

7. Gore had been the owner of one percent of the outstanding shares of the Webster Company, a corporation, since its organization ten years ago. Ratliff, the president of the company, was the owner of 70 percent of the outstanding shares. Ratliff used the shareholders' list to submit to the shareholders an offer of $50 per share for their stock. Gore, upon receiving the offer, called Ratliff and told him that the offer was inadequate and advised that she was willing to offer $60 per share, and for that purpose demanded a shareholders' list. Ratliff knew that Gore was willing and able to supply the funds necessary to purchase the stock, but he nevertheless refused to supply the list to Gore. Further, he did not offer to transmit Gore's offer to the shareholders of record. Gore then brought an action to compel the corporation to make the shareholders' list available to her. Decision?

8. Mitchell, Nelson, Olsen, and Parker, experts in manufacturing baubles, each owned fifteen out of one hundred authorized shares of Baubles, Inc., a corporation of State X, which does not permit cumulative voting. On July 7, 1986, the corporation sold forty shares to Quentin, an investor, for $1,500,000, which it used to purchase a factory building for $1,500,000. On July 8, 1986, Mitchell, Nelson, Olsen, and Parker contracted as follows:

All parties will act jointly in exercising voting rights as shareholders. In the event of a failure to agree, the question shall be submitted to George Yost, whose decision shall be binding upon all parties.

Until a meeting of shareholders on April 17, 1991, when a dispute arose, all parties to the contract had consistently and regularly voted for Nelson, Olsen, and Parker as directors. At that meeting, Yost considered the dispute and decided and directed that Mitchell, Nelson, Olsen, and Parker vote their shares for the latter three as directors. Nelson, Olsen, and Parker so voted. Mitchell and Quentin voted for themselves and Mrs. Quentin as directors.

(a) Is the contract of July 8, 1986, valid, and, if so, what is its effect?

(b) Who were elected directors of Baubles, Inc. at the meeting of its shareholders on April 17, 1991?

9. Acme Corporation's articles of incorporation require cumulative voting for the election of its directors. The board of directors of Acme Corporation consists of nine directors, each elected annually.

(a) Smith owns 24 percent of the outstanding shares of Acme Corporation. How many directors can he elect with his votes?

(b) If Acme Corporation were to classify its board into three classes, each consisting of three directors elected every three years, how many directors would Smith be able to elect?

10. Neese, trustee in bankruptcy for First Trust Company, brings a suit against the directors of the company for losses sustained by the company as a result of the failure of the directors to use due care and diligence in the discharge of their duties. The specific acts of negligence alleged are (1) failure to give as much time and attention to the affairs of the company as its business interests required; (2) abdication of their control of the corporation by turning the entire management of the corporation over to its president, Brown; (3) failure to keep informed as to the affairs, condition, and management of the corporation; (4) taking no action to direct or control the corporation's affairs; (5) permitting large, open, unsecured loans to affiliated but financially unsound companies that were owned and controlled by Brown; (6) failure to examine financial reports that would have shown illegal diversions and waste of the corporation's funds; and (7) failure to supervise properly the corporation's officers and directors. Decision?

11. Minority shareholders of Midwest Technical Institute Development Corporation, a closed-end investment company owning assets consisting principally of securities of companies in technological fields, brought a shareholder derivative suit against officers and directors of Midwest. The shareholders sought to recover on Midwest's behalf the profits realized by the officers and directors through dealings in stock held in Midwest's portfolio in breach of their fiduciary duty. Approximately three years after commencement of the action, a new corporation, Midtex, was organized to acquire Midwest's assets. The shareholders now seek to add Midtex as a party defendant to their suit. Decision?

12. Litton, an officer and the dominant shareholder of Dixie Splint Coal Company, transferred the company's remaining assets to himself when the company came to the verge of bankruptcy. The transfer allegedly was in satisfaction of an accrued salary claim that Litton had not enforced until the company came into financial difficulty. The trustee in bankruptcy seeks to have Litton's claim disallowed. Decision?

13. Riffe, while serving as an officer of Wilshire Oil Company, received a secret commission for work done on behalf of a competing corporation. Wilshire Oil brings this action against Riffe to recover these secret profits and, in addition, to recover the compensation paid to Riffe by Wilshire Oil during the period that he acted on behalf of the competitor. Decision?

Chapter 37

FUNDAMENTAL CHANGES

Charter Amendments
Combinations
Dissolution

CERTAIN extraordinary changes affect a corporation in such a fundamental manner that they are outside the authority of the board of directors and require shareholder approval. Charter amendments, mergers, consolidations, compulsory share exchanges, dissolution, and the sale or lease of all or substantially all of the corporation's assets, other than those in the regular course of business, are fundamental changes because they alter the basic structure of the corporation. Although each of these actions is authorized by State incorporation statutes, which impose specific procedural requirements, they are also subject to equitable limitations imposed by the courts.

Since shareholder approval for fundamental changes does not usually need to be unanimous, such changes frequently will be approved despite opposition by minority shareholders. Shareholder approval means a majority (or some other specified fraction) of *all* votes *entitled* to be cast rather than a majority (or other fraction) of votes represented at a shareholders' meeting at which a quorum is present. In some instances, minority shareholders have the right to dissent and recover the fair value of their shares if they

follow the prescribed procedure. This right is called the appraisal remedy. The legal aspects of fundamental changes will be discussed in this chapter.

CHARTER AMENDMENTS

Shareholders do not have a vested property right resulting from any provision in the articles of incorporation. Section 10.01(b). Accordingly, corporate charters may be amended if proper procedures are followed. The amended articles of incorporation, however, may contain only those provisions that might be lawfully contained in articles of incorporation as of the time of the amendment. Section 10.01(a). For example, provisions in the charter relating to management, control, capital structure, dividend entitlement, purpose, or duration of the corporation may be amended. Common amendments to the capital structure include (1) increasing or decreasing the number of authorized shares, (2) reclassifying shares, (3) changing the preferential rights of shares, (4) creating new classes of shares, (5) changing the voting rights of shares, (6) eliminating the power to vote cumulatively, and (7) eliminating preemptive rights.

Approval by Directors and Shareholders

Under modern statutes the typical procedure for amending the articles of incorporation requires the board of directors to adopt a resolution setting forth the proposed amendment, which must then be approved by a majority vote of the shareholders entitled to vote, although some older statutes require a two-thirds shareholder vote. Moreover, a class of shares is entitled to vote as a class on a proposed amendment, whether or not entitled to vote on it by the articles of incorporation, if that amendment would

(1) increase or decrease the aggregate number of authorized shares of the class;

(2) effect an exchange or reclassification of all or part of the shares of the class into shares of another class;

(3) effect an exchange or reclassification, or create the right of exchange, of all or part of the shares of another class into shares of the class;

(4) change the designation, rights, preferences, or limitations of all or part of the shares of the class;

(5) change the shares of all or part of the class into a different number of shares of the same class;

(6) create a new class of shares having rights or preferences with respect to distributions or to dissolution that are prior, superior, or substantially equal to the shares of the class;

(7) increase the rights, preferences, or number of authorized shares of any class that, after giving effect to the amendment, have rights or preferences with respect to distributions or to dissolution that are prior, superior, or substantially equal to the shares of the class;

(8) limit or deny an existing preemptive right of all or part of the shares of the class; or

(9) cancel or otherwise affect rights to distributions or dividends that have accumulated but not yet been declared on all or part of the shares of the class. Section 10.04(a).

The comment to Section 10.04 provides the following example: "Assume there is a class of preferred shares comprised of three series each with different dividend rights. A proposed amendment would reduce the rate of dividend applicable to Series A preferred and would change the dividend right of Series B preferred from a cumulative to a noncumulative right. The amendment would not affect the dividend right of Series C preferred. Both Series A and B would be entitled to vote as separate classes on the proposed amendment; the holders of Series C preferred, not directly affected by the amendment, would not be entitled to vote at all unless the shares are otherwise voting shares under the articles of incorporation. If the proposed amendment would reduce the dividend right of series A and change the dividend right of both Series B and C from a cumulative to a noncumulative right, the holders of Series A would be entitled to vote as a single class, and the holders of Series B and C would be entitled to vote together as a single separate class."

After the amendment is approved by the shareholders, articles of amendment are executed and delivered to the Secretary of State for filing. Section 10.06. The amendment does not affect the existing rights of nonshareholders. Section 10.09.

Under Section 13.02(a)(4) of the Revised Act *dissenting shareholders* are given the appraisal remedy *only* if an amendment materially and adversely affects the rights of dissenting shareholders because it

1. alters or abolishes a preferential right of the shares;

2. creates, alters, or abolishes a right involving the redemption of the shares;

3. alters or abolishes a preemptive right of the holder of the shares;

4. excludes or limits the right of the holder of the shares to vote on any matter or to cumulate his votes; or

5. reduces the number of shares owned by the shareholder to a fraction of a share if the fractional share is to be acquired for cash.

Under the Revised Act, the required shareholder approval for an amendment depends upon the nature of the amendment. If the amendment would give rise to dissenters' rights, the amendment must be approved by a majority of all votes *entitled* to be cast on the amendment unless the act, the articles of incorporation, or the board of directors require a greater vote. All other amendments must be approved by a majority of all votes *cast* on the amendment at a meeting where a quorum exists, unless the act, the articles of incorporation, or the board of directors require a greater vote. Sections 10.03, 7.25.

Approval by Directors

The Revised Act permits the board of directors to adopt certain amendments without shareholder action unless the articles of incorporation provide otherwise. Section 10.02. These amendments include (1) extending the duration of the corporation if it was incorporated when limited duration was required by law, (2) changing each issued and unissued authorized share of an outstanding class into a greater number of whole shares if the corporation has only one class of shares, and (3) making minor name changes.

COMBINATIONS

It may be desirable and profitable for a corporation to acquire all or substantially all of the assets of another corporation or corporations. This may be accomplished by (1) purchase or lease of the assets, (2) purchase of a controlling stock interest in other corporations, (3) merger with other corporations, or (4) consolidation with other corporations. In 1986, there were more than three thousand mergers and acquisitions, totalling almost $200 billion. In 1988, there were at least one hundred merger and acquisition transactions, each of which exceeded $500 million.

When any of these methods of combination involves the issuance of shares, proxy solicitations, or tender offers, it may be subject to Federal securities regulation, as discussed in Chapter 45. Moreover, when a combination may have a detrimental effect on competition, the Federal antitrust laws, as discussed in Chapter 42, may apply.

Purchase or Lease of All or Substantially All of the Assets

When one corporation purchases or leases all or substantially all of the assets of another corporation, there is no change in the legal personality of either corporation. The purchaser or lessee corporation has simply acquired ownership or control of additional physical assets. The selling or lessor corporation, in exchange for its physical properties, receives cash, other property, or a stipulated rental. Each corporation continues its separate existence with only the form or extent of its assets altered.

Generally, a corporation that purchases the assets of another corporation does not assume the other's liabilities unless (1) the purchaser expressly or impliedly agrees to assume the liabilities of the seller; (2) the transaction amounts to a consolidation or merger of the two corporations; (3) the purchaser is a mere continuation of the seller; or (4) the sale is for the fraudulent purpose of avoiding the liabilities of the seller. Some courts recognize a fifth exception (called the "product line" exception) which imposes strict tort liability upon the purchaser for defects in products manufactured and distributed by the seller corporation when the purchaser corporation continues the product line. *See Ray v. Alad Corporation.*

Regular Course of Business   If the sale or lease of all or substantially all of its assets is in the usual and regular course of business of the selling or lessor corporation, approval by its board of directors is required but shareholder authorization is not. In addition, a mortgage or pledge of any or all of the property and assets of a corporation—whether or *not* in the usual or regular course of business—also requires approval by just the board of directors. Section 12.01. The Revised Act considers a transfer of any or all of a corporation's assets to a wholly owned subsidiary to be a sale in the regular course of business. Section 12.01(a)(3). Under the Revised Act, a sale of assets in the regular course of business does not require shareholder approval unless the articles of incorporation provide otherwise. Section 12.01(b).

Other Than in Regular Course of Business Shareholder approval is necessary only if a sale or lease of all or substantially all of its assets is *not* in the usual and regular course of business. The selling corporation, by liquidation of its assets, or the lessor corporation, by placing its physical assets beyond its control, has significantly changed its position and perhaps its ability to carry on the type of business contemplated by its charter. For this reason, such sale or lease must be approved not only by action of the directors but also by the affirmative vote of the holders of a majority of its shares entitled to vote at a meeting of shareholders called for this purpose. Section 12.02. In most States *dissenting shareholders* of the selling corporation are given an appraisal remedy. Section 13.02(a)(3).

Purchase of Shares

An alternative to the purchase of the assets of another corporation is the purchase of its stock. When one corporation acquires all or a controlling interest of the stock of another corporation, there is no change in the legal existence of either corporation. The acquiring corporation acts through its board of directors, whereas the corporation that becomes a subsidiary does not act at all because the sale of stock is a decision made by the individual shareholders. The capital structure of the subsidiary remains unchanged, and that of the parent is usually not altered unless required in connection with financing the acquisition of the stock. Because no formal shareholder approval of either corporation is required, there is *no* appraisal remedy.

Sale of Control When a controlling interest is owned by one or a few shareholders, a privately negotiated transaction is possible. The courts require that these sales be made with due care. The controlling shareholders must make a reasonable investigation so as not to transfer control to purchasers who wrongfully plan to steal or "loot" the assets of the corporation or to act contrary to the best interests of the corporation. In addition, purchasers are frequently willing to pay a premium for a block of shares that conveys control. Although historically some courts have required that this so-called control premium inure to the benefit of the corporation, today virtually all courts permit the controlling shareholders to retain the full amount of the control premium.

Tender Offer When a controlling interest is not held by one or a few shareholders, acquisition of a corporation by the purchase of shares may take the form of a tender offer. A tender offer is a general invitation to all the shareholders of a target company to tender their shares for sale at a specified price. The offer may be for all of the target company's shares or just for a controlling interest. Tender offers for publicly held companies, which are subject to Federal securities regulation, are discussed in Chapter 45.

Compulsory Share Exchange

The Revised Act and some States provide different procedures where the share acquisition is through a **compulsory share exchange,** which is a transaction by which a corporation becomes the owner of *all* the outstanding shares of one or more classes of another corporation by an exchange that is *compulsory* on *all* owners of the acquired shares. Section 11.02. The shares may be acquired with shares, obligations, or other securities of the acquiring or any other corporation or for cash or other property. For example, if A corporation acquires all of the outstanding shares of B corporation through a compulsory exchange, then B becomes a wholly owned subsidiary of A. In all compulsory share exchanges the separate existence of both corporate parties to the transaction is not affected by the exchange. Although producing results similar to a merger, as discussed below, compulsory share exchanges are used instead of mergers where it is desirable that the acquired corporation does not go out of existence as, for example, in the formation of holding company systems for insurance companies and banks.

A compulsory share exchange requires approval of the board of directors of each corporation and approval by the shareholders of the corporation whose shares are being acquired. Sections 11.02 and 11.03. Separate class voting is required by each class of shares included in the exchange. The transaction need *not* be approved by the shareholders of the corporation acquiring the shares. After the compulsory share exchange plan is adopted and approved by the shareholders, it is binding on all holders of shares of the class to be acquired. Dissenting shareholders of the corporation whose shares are acquired are given an appraisal remedy. Section 13.02(a)(2).

Merger

A **merger** of two or more corporations is the combination of all of their assets. One of the corporations, known as the **surviving corporation,** receives title to all the assets. The other party or parties to the merger, known as the **merged corporation** or corporations, are merged into the surviving corporation and cease to exist as a separate entity. Thus, if A Corporation and B Corporation combine into the A Corporation, A is the surviving corporation and B the merged corporation. The shareholders of the merged corporation may receive stock or other securities issued by the surviving corporation or other consideration, as provided in the merger agreement. All debts and other liabilities of the merged corporation are assumed by the surviving corporation. Section 11.06.

A merger requires the approval of the board of directors of each corporation, as well as the affirmative vote of the holders of a majority of the shares entitled to vote of each corporation. Sections 11.01 and 11.03. If, however, the number of voting or participating shares of the surviving corporation is increased by no more than 20 percent as a result of the merger, the articles of incorporation of the surviving corporation will not differ from its articles before the merger, and the rights of each shareholder will not be altered, the approval of the shareholders of the surviving corporation is *not* required. Section 11.03(g). Dissenting shareholders of each corporation that is a party to the merger have an appraisal remedy if shareholder approval is required and the shareholder is entitled to vote on the merger. Section 13.02(a)(1).

In a **short-form merger,** a corporation that owns at least *90 percent* of the outstanding shares of each class of a subsidiary may merge the subsidiary into itself *without* approval by the shareholders of either corporation. Section 11.04. Requiring the approval of the shareholders or board of directors of the subsidiary is unnecessary because the parent's 90 percent ownership assures that the plan of merger would be approved. All that is required is a resolution by the board of directors of the parent corporation. The dissenting shareholders of the subsidiary have the right to obtain payment from the parent for their shares. Section 13.02(a)(1). The shareholders of the parent do not have this appraisal remedy because the transaction has not materially changed their rights. Instead of indirectly owning 90 percent of the subsidiary's assets, the parent now directly owns 100 percent of the same assets.

Consolidation

A **consolidation** of two or more corporations is the combination of all of their assets, title to which is taken by a newly created corporation known as the **consolidated corporation.** Each of the constituent corporations ceases to exist, and all of their debts and liabilities are assumed by the new corporation. The shareholders of each of the constituent corporations receive stock or other securities, not necessarily of the same class, issued to them by the new corporation, or other consideration provided in the plan of consolidation. A consolidation requires the approval of the boards of directors of each constituent corporation as well as the affirmative vote of the holders of a majority of the shares entitled to vote of each constituent corporation. Dissenting shareholders have an appraisal remedy.

The Revised Act has deleted all references to consolidations as explained by the comment to Section 11.01:

. . . the Model Act also provided for a "consolidation," which was similar to a merger, except that all corporate parties to the transaction disappeared and an entirely new corporation was created. In modern corporate practice consolidation transactions are obsolete since it is nearly always advantageous for one of the parties in the transaction to be the surviving corporation. (If creation of a new entity is considered desirable, a new entity may be created before the merger and the disappearing entities merged into it.)

Going Private Transactions

Corporate combinations are sometimes used to take a publicly held corporation private in order to eliminate minority interests, to reduce the burdens of certain provisions of the Federal securities laws, or both. One method of going private is for the corporation or the majority shareholder to acquire the corporation's shares through purchases on the open market or through a tender offer for the shares. Other methods include a cash-out combination (merger or sale of assets) with a corporation controlled by the majority shareholder. If the majority shareholder is a corporation, it may arrange a cash-out combination with itself or, if it owns enough shares, use a short-form merger. In recent years, a new type of going private transaction—a management buyout—has become much more frequent. This section will examine cash-out combinations and management buyouts.

Cash-out Combinations Cash-out combinations are used to eliminate minority shareholders by forcing them to accept cash or property for their shares. A cash-out combination is often used after a person, group, or company has acquired a large interest in a target company (T) through a tender offer. The tender offeror (TO) then seeks to eliminate all other shareholders, thereby achieving complete control of T. To do so, TO might form a new corporation (Corporation N) and take 100 percent of its stock. A cash-out

merger of T into N is then arranged with all the shareholders of T other than TO to receive cash for their shares. Since TO owns all the stock of N and a controlling interest in T, the merger will be approved by the shareholders of both companies. Alternatively, TO could purchase for cash or notes the assets of T, leaving the minority shareholders with only an interest in the proceeds of the sale. The use of cash-out combinations has raised questions concerning their purpose and their fairness to the minority shareholders. Some States require that cash-out combinations have a valid business purpose and that they are fair to all concerned. Fairness, in this context, includes both fair dealing (which involves the procedural aspects of the transaction) and fair price (which involves the financial considerations of the merger). *See Alpert v. 28 Williams St. Corp.* Other States require only that the transaction is fair.

Management Buy-out A management buy-out is a transaction by which existing management increases its ownership of a corporation and eliminates its public shareholders. The typical procedure is as follows. Management of an existing company (Corporation A) forms a new corporation (Corporation B) in which management owns some of the stock and institutional investors own the rest. Corporation B issues bonds to institutional investors to raise cash with which it purchases the assets or stock of Corporation A. The assets of Corporation A are used as security for the bonds issued by Corporation B. (Because of the extensive use of borrowed funds, a management buy-out is commonly called a **leveraged buyout** (LBO). The result of this transaction is two-fold: the public shareholders of Corporation A no longer have any proprietary interest in the assets of Corporation A, and management's equity interest in Corporation B is greater than its interest was in Corporation A.

In recent years, leveraged buy-outs have become more frequent, and some have involved large, well-known companies. In 1986, Beatrice Foods went private for $6.2 billion, all of which was financed by debt. In the same year, Safeway Stores (the largest supermarket chain in the United States) went private for $4.3 billion, as did Macy's for $3.6 billion. In 1989, the largest LBO in history occurred: Kohlberg Kravis Roberts & Co. acquired RJR Nabisco for $24.53 billion.

A critical issue raised by a management buy-out is its fairness to the shareholders of Corporation A. The transaction inherently places management in a potential conflict of interest because management owes a fiduciary duty to represent the interests of the shareholders of Corporation A. As substantial shareholders of Corporation B, however, management has a personal and probably adverse financial interest in the transaction.

Dissenting Shareholders

The **shareholder's right to dissent** is a statutory right to obtain payment for his shares and is accorded to shareholders who object to certain fundamental changes in the corporation. The Introductory Comment to Chapter 13 of the Revised Act explains the purpose of dissenters' rights:

Chapter 13 deals with the tension between the desire of the corporate leadership to be able to enter new fields, acquire new enterprises, and rearrange investor rights and the desire of investors to adhere to the rights and the risks on the basis of which they invested. Most contemporary corporation codes in the United States attempt to resolve this tension through a combination of two devices. On the one hand, the majority is given an almost unlimited power to change the nature and shape of the enterprise and the rights of its members. On the other hand, the members who dissent from these changes are given a right to withdraw their investment at a fair value.

Transactions Giving Rise to Dissenters' Rights Most States grant dissenters' rights to (1) dissenting shareholders of a corporation *selling* or *leasing* all or substantially all of its property or assets not made in the usual or regular course of business; (2) dissenting shareholders of each corporation that is a party to a *merger*, except in short-form merg-

ers where only the dissenting shareholders of the subsidiary have dissenters' rights; and (3) dissenting shareholders of each corporation that is a party to a *consolidation*. In addition to these three fundamental changes, the Revised Act also provides a right to dissent to (1) any plan of compulsory share exchange to which the corporation is the acquired corporation, (2) any amendment of the articles of incorporation that materially and adversely affects the rights in respect of a dissenter's shares, and (3) any other corporate action taken pursuant to a shareholder vote with respect to which the articles of incorporation, the bylaws, or a resolution of the board of directors provides that shareholders shall have a right to dissent and obtain payment for their shares. Section 13.02.

A number of States have a stock market exception to the appraisal remedy. Under these statutes, there is no right to dissent if an established market, such as the New York Stock Exchange, exists for the shares. The Revised Act does not contain this exception.

Procedure The corporation must notify the shareholders of the existence of dissenters' rights before the vote is taken on the corporate action. If a shareholder dissents and strictly complies with the provisions of the statute, he is entitled to receive the fair value of his shares. In order to perfect his right to payment for his shares, a dissenting shareholder must

1. file with the corporation a written notice of his intent to dissent to the proposed corporate action before the vote of the shareholders;

2. not vote in favor of the proposed corporate action; and

3. make a written demand on the corporation on a form provided by that corporation within the time period set by the corporation, which may not be fewer than thirty days nor more than sixty after the corporation delivers the form. Sections 13.21 and 13.22.

Unless written demand is made within the prescribed time period, the dissenting shareholder is not entitled to payment for his shares.

The purpose of the statutory procedure is to fix a reasonable time in which the corporation may know the number of shares for which it is required to pay cash in order to carry through the proposed corporate action. If enough dissenting shareholders demand to be paid, the lack of sufficient cash or the inability of the surviving or new corporation to raise funds for this purpose may make the proposed corporate action impracticable.

Appraisal Remedy A dissenting shareholder who complies with all of these requirements is entitled to an appraisal remedy, which is payment by the corporation of the fair value of his shares plus accrued interest. The **fair value** means the value immediately before the effectuation of the corporate action to which the dissenter objects, excluding any appreciation or depreciation in anticipation of such corporate action unless such exclusion would be inequitable. *See Endicott Johnson Corp v. Bade.*

A shareholder of a corporation who has a right to obtain payment for his shares does not have the right to attack the validity of the corporate action that gives rise to his right to obtain payment or to have the action set aside or rescinded, except when the corporate action is unlawful or fraudulent with regard to the complaining shareholder or to the corporation. Section 13.02(b). Where the corporate action is not unlawful or fraudulent, the appraisal remedy is exclusive, and the shareholder may not challenge the action. Some States make the appraisal remedy exclusive in all cases while some make it nonexclusive in all cases.

DISSOLUTION

Although a corporation may have perpetual existence, its life may be terminated in a number of ways. Incorporation statutes usually provide for both voluntary dissolution and involuntary dissolution. Dissolution does not terminate the corporation's existence but does require that the corporation wind up its affairs and liquidate its assets.

Voluntary Dissolution

Voluntary dissolution may be brought about by a resolution of the board of directors that is approved by the affirmative vote of the holders of a majority of the shares of the corporation entitled to vote at a meeting of the shareholders duly called for this purpose. Section 14.02. No right to dissent and recover the fair value of shares is usually provided to shareholders objecting to dissolution. The Revised Act, however, grants dissenters' rights in connection with a sale or exchange of all or substantially all the assets not made in the usual or regular course of business, *including* a sale in dissolution, but the act *excludes* such rights in sales by court order and sales for cash on terms requiring that all or substantially all of the net proceeds be distributed to the shareholders within one year. Section 13.02(a)(3).

The Statutory Close Corporation Supplement gives the shareholders, if they elect in the articles of incorporation, the power to dissolve the corporation. Unless the charter specifies otherwise, an amendment to include, modify, or delete a power to dissolve must be approved by *all* of the shareholders. The power to dissolve may be conferred upon any shareholder or holders of a specified number or percentage of shares of any class and may be exercised at will or upon the occurrence of a specified event or contingency.

See Figure 37–1 for a comparison of the types of fundamental changes.

Involuntary Dissolution

A corporation may be involuntarily dissolved by administrative dissolution or by judicial dissolution.

Administrative Dissolution The secretary of state may commence an administrative proceeding to dissolve a corporation if (1) the corporation does not pay within sixty days after they are due any franchise taxes or penalties; (2) the corporation does not deliver its annual report to the secretary of state within sixty days after it is due; (3) the corporation is without a registered agent or registered office in the State for sixty days or more; (4) the corporation does not notify the secretary of state within sixty days that its registered agent or registered office has been changed, that its registered agent has resigned, or that its registered office has been discontinued; or (5) the corporation's period of duration stated in its articles of incorporation expires. Section 14.20.

Judicial Dissolution Judicial dissolution may be brought by the State, a shareholder,

or a creditor. A court may dissolve a corporation in a proceeding brought by the attorney general if it is proved that the corporation obtained its charter through fraud or has continued to exceed or abuse the authority conferred upon it by law. Section 14.30(1).

A court may dissolve a corporation in a proceeding brought by a shareholder if it is established that (1) the directors are deadlocked in the management of the corporate affairs, the shareholders are unable to break the deadlock, and irreparable injury to the corporation is threatened or being suffered; (2) the acts of the directors or those in control of the corporation are illegal, oppressive, or fraudulent; (3) the corporate assets are being

---

Figure 37–1 Fundamental Changes

Change	Board of Director Resolution Required	Shareholder Approval Required	Shareholders' Appraisal Remedy Available
A amends its articles of incorporation	A: Yes	A: Yes	A: No, unless amendment materially and adversely affects rights of shares
B sells its assets in usual and regular course of business to A	B: Yes	B: No	B: No
B sells its assets not in usual and regular course of business to A	B: Yes	B: Yes	B: Yes
A voluntarily purchases shares of B	A: Yes B: No	A: No B: No, individual shareholders decide	A: No B: No
A acquires shares of B through a compulsory exchange	A: Yes B: Yes	A: No B: Yes	A: No B: Yes
A and B merge	A: Yes B: Yes	A: Yes B: Yes	A: Yes B: Yes
A merges its 90% subsidiary B into A	A: Yes B: No	A: No B: No	A: No B: Yes
A and B consolidate	A: Yes B: Yes	A: Yes B: Yes	A: Yes B: Yes
A voluntarily dissolves	A: Yes	A: Yes	A: Not usually

misapplied or wasted; or (4) the shareholders are deadlocked and have failed to elect directors for at least two consecutive annual meetings. Section 14.30(2). *See Matter of Kemp & Beatley, Inc.*

A creditor may bring a court action upon a showing that the corporation has become unable to pay its debts and obligations as they mature in the regular course of its business and either (a) the creditor has reduced his claim to a judgment and an execution issued on it has been returned unsatisfied, or (b) the corporation has admitted in writing that the claim of the creditor is due and owing. Section 14.30(3).

Liquidation

Dissolution does not terminate the corporation's existence but does require that the corporation devote itself to winding up its affairs and liquidating its assets. After dissolution, the corporation must cease carrying on its business except as is necessary to wind up. Section 14.05. When a corporation is dissolved, its assets are liquidated and used first to pay the expenses of liquidation and its creditors according to their respective contract or lien rights. Any remainder is distributed to shareholders proportionately according to their respective contract rights; stock with a liquidation preference has priority over common stock. When liquidation is voluntary, it is usually carried out by the board of directors, who serve as trustees; when liquidation is involuntary, it may be conducted by a court-appointed receiver. Section 14.32.

Protection of Creditors

The statutory provisions governing dissolution and liquidation usually prescribe procedures to safeguard the interests of creditors of the corporation. Such procedures typically include required mailing of notice to known creditors, general publication of notice, and preservation of claims against the corporation. The Revised Act provides a five-year period for (1) a claimant who did not receive notice, (2) a claimant whose timely claim was not acted on, or (3) a claimant whose claim is contingent on an event occurring after dissolution. Section 14.07.

CASES

Purchase of Assets

RAY v. ALAD CORP.

Supreme Court of California, 1977.
19 Cal.3d 22, 136 Cal.Rptr. 574, 560 P.2d 3.

WRIGHT, J.

[On March 24, 1969, Ray fell from a defective ladder while working for his employer. Ray brought suit in strict tort liability against the Alad Corporation (Alad II), which neither manufactured nor sold the ladder to Ray's employer. Prior to the accident, Alad II succeeded to the business of the ladder's manufacturer, the now dissolved "Alad Corporation" (Alad I), through a purchase of Alad I's assets for an adequate cash consideration. Alad II acquired Alad I's plant, equipment, inventory, trade name and good will and continued to manufacture the same line of ladders under the "Alad" name, using the same equipment, designs, and personnel. In addition, Alad II solicited through the same sales representatives with no outward indication of any change in the ownership of the business. The parties had no agreement, however, concerning Alad II's assumption of Alad I's tort liabilities.]

* * *

Our discussion of the law starts with the rule ordinarily applied to the determination of whether a corporation purchasing the principal assets of another corporation assumes the other's liabilities. As typically formulated the rule states that the purchaser does not assume the seller's liabilities unless (1) there is an express or implied agreement of assumption, (2) the transaction amounts to a consolidation or merger of the two corporations, (3) the purchasing corporation is a mere continuation of the seller, or (4) the transfer of assets to the purchaser is for the fraudulent purpose of escaping liability for the seller's debts. [Citations.]

If this rule were determinative of Alad II's liability to plaintiff it would require us to affirm the summary judgment. None of the rule's four stated grounds for imposing liability on the purchasing corporation is present here. There was no express or implied agreement to assume liability for injury from defective products previously manufactured by Alad I. Nor is there any indication or contention that the transaction was prompted by any fraudulent purpose of escaping liability for Alad I's debts.

With respect to the second stated ground for liability, the purchase of Alad I's assets did not amount to a consolidation or merger. This exception has been invoked where one corporation takes all of another's assets without providing any consideration that could be made available to meet claims of the other's creditors [citation] or where the consideration consists wholly of shares of the purchaser's stock which are promptly distributed to the seller's shareholders in conjunction with the seller's liquidation [citation]. In the present case the sole consideration given for Alad I's assets was cash in excess of $207,000. Of this amount Alad I was paid $70,000 when the assets were transferred and at the same time a promissory note was given to Alad I for almost $114,000. Shortly before the dissolution of Alad I the note was assigned to the Hamblys, Alad I's principal stockholders, and thereafter the note was paid in full. The remainder of the consideration went for closing expenses or was paid to the Hamblys for consulting services and their agreement not to compete. There is no contention that this consideration was inadequate or that the cash and promissory note given to Alad I were not included in the assets available to meet claims of Alad I's creditors at the time of dis-

solution. Hence the acquisition of Alad I's assets was not in the nature of a merger or consolidation for purposes of the aforesaid rule.

Plaintiff contends that the rule's third stated ground for liability makes Alad II liable as a mere continuation of Alad I in view of Alad II's acquisition of all Alad I's operating assets, its use of those assets and of Alad I's former employees to manufacture the same line of products, and its holding itself out to customers and the public as a continuation of the same enterprise. However, California decisions holding that a corporation acquiring the assets of another corporation is the latter's mere continuation and therefore liable for its debts have imposed such liability only upon a showing of one or both of the following factual elements: (1) no adequate consideration was given for the predecessor corporation's assets and made available for meeting the claims of its unsecured creditors; (2) one or more persons were officers, directors, or stockholders of both corporations. [Citations.] There is no showing of either of these elements in the present case.

We therefore conclude that the general rule governing succession to liabilities does not require Alad II to respond to plaintiff's claim. . . . We must decide whether the policies underlying strict tort liability for defective products call for a special exception to the rule that would otherwise insulate the present defendant from plaintiff's claim. [Citations.]

The purpose of the rule of strict tort liability "is to insure that the costs of injuries resulting from defective products are borne by the manufacturers that put such products on the market rather than by the injured persons who are powerless to protect themselves." [Citation.] However, the rule "does not rest on the analysis of the financial strength of bargaining power of the parties to the particular action. It rests, rather, on the proposition that '[t]he cost of an injury and the loss of time or health may be an overwhelming misfortune to the person injured, and a needless one, for the risk of injury can be insured by the manufacturer and distributed among the public as a cost of doing business.' [Citations.]" Thus, "the paramount policy to be promoted by the rule is the protection of otherwise defenseless victims of manufacturing defects and the *spreading throughout society* of the cost of compensating them." (Italics added.) [Citation.] Justification for imposing strict liability upon a *successor* to a manufacturer under the circumstances here presented rests upon (1) the virtual destruction of the plaintiff's remedies against the original manufacturer caused by the successor's acquisition of the business, (2) the successor's ability to assume the original manufacturer's risk-spreading rule, and (3) the fairness of requiring the successor to assume a responsibility for defective products that was a burden necessarily attached to the original manufacturer's good will being enjoyed by the successor in the continued operation of the business. We turn to a consideration of each of these aspects in the context of the present case.

We must assume for purposes of the present proceeding that plaintiff was injured as a result of defects in a ladder manufactured by Alad I and therefore could assert strict tort liability against Alad I under the rule of [citation]. However, the practical value of this right of recovery against the original manufacturer was vitiated by the purchase of Alad I's tangible assets, trade name and good will on behalf of Alad II and the dissolution of Alad I within two months thereafter in accordance with the purchase agreement. The injury giving rise to plaintiff's claim against Alad I did not occur until more than six months after the filing of the dissolution certificate declaring that Alad I's "known debts and liabilities have been actually paid" and its "known assets have been distributed to its shareholders." This distribution of assets was perfectly proper as there was no requirement that provision be made for claims such as plaintiff's that had not yet come into existence. Thus, even if plaintiff could obtain a judgment on his claim against the dissolved and assetless Alad I he would face formidable and probably insuperable obstacles in attempting to obtain satisfaction of

the judgment from former stockholders or directors. [Citations.]

* * *

While depriving plaintiff of redress against the ladder's manufacturer, Alad I, the transaction by which Alad II acquired Alad I's name and operating assets had the further effect of transferring to Alad II the resources that had previously been available to Alad I for meeting its responsibilities to persons injured by defects in ladders it had produced. These resources included not only the physical plant, the manufacturing equipment, and the inventories of raw material, work in process, and finished goods, but also the know-how available through the records of manufacturing designs, the continued employment of the factory personnel, and the consulting services of Alad I's general manager. With these facilities and sources of information, Alad II had virtually the same capacity as Alad I to estimate the risks of claims for injuries from defects in previously manufactured ladders for purposes of obtaining insurance coverage or planning self-insurance. [Citation.] Moreover, the acquisition of the Alad enterprise gave Alad II the opportunity formerly enjoyed by Alad I of passing on to purchasers of new "Alad" products the costs of meeting these risks. Immediately after the takeover it was Alad II, not Alad I, which was in a position to promote the "paramount policy" of the strict products liability rule by "spreading throughout society . . . the cost of compensating (otherwise defenseless victims of manufacturing defects)." [Citation.]

Finally, the imposition upon Alad II of liability for injuries from Alad I's defective products is fair and equitable in view of Alad II's acquisition of Alad I's trade name, good will, and customer lists, its continuing to produce the same line of ladders, and its holding itself out to potential customers as the same enterprise. This deliberate albeit legitimate exploitation of Alad I's established reputation as a going concern manufacturing a specific product line gave Alad II a substantial benefit which its predecessor could not have enjoyed without the burden of potential liability for injuries from previously manufactured units. Imposing this liability upon successor manufacturers in the position of Alad II not only causes the one "who takes the benefit (to) bear the burden" [citation] but precludes any windfall to the predecessor that might otherwise result from (1) the reflection of an absence of such successor liability in an enhanced price paid by the successor for the business assets and (2) the liquidation of the predecessor resulting in avoidance of its responsibility for subsequent injuries from its defective products. [Citations.] By taking over and continuing the established business of producing and distributing Alad ladders, Alad II became "an integral part of the overall producing and marketing enterprise that should bear the cost of injuries resulting from defective products." [Citation.]

We therefore conclude that a party which acquires a manufacturing business and continues the output of its line of products under the circumstances here presented assumes strict tort liability for defects in units of the same product line previously manufactured and distributed by the entity from which the business was acquired. * * *

The judgment is reversed.

Cash-out Combinations

ALPERT v. 28 WILLIAMS ST. CORP.

New York Court of Appeals, 1984.
63 N.Y.2d 557, 483 N.Y.S.2d 667, 473 N.E.2d 19.

COOKE, C.J.

The subject of contention in this litigation is a valuable 17-story office building, located at 79 Madison Avenue in Manhattan. In dispute is the propriety of a complex series of transactions that had the net effect of permitting defendants, who were outside investors, to gain ownership of the property and to eliminate the ownership interests of plaintiffs, who were minority shareholders of the corporation that formerly owned the building. This was achieved through what is commonly known as a "two-step" merger: (1) an outside investor purchases control of the majority shares of the target corporation by tender offer or through private negotiations; (2) this newly acquired control is used to arrange for the target and a second corporation controlled by the outside investor to merge, with one condition being the "freeze-out" of the minority shareholders of the target corporation by the forced cancellation of their shares, generally through a cash purchase. This accomplishes the investor's original goal of complete ownership of the target corporation.

Since 1955, the office building was owned by 79 Realty Corporation (Realty Corporation), which had no other substantial assets. About two thirds of Realty Corporation's outstanding shares were held by two couples, the Kimmelmans and the Zauderers, who were also the company's sole directors and officers. Plaintiffs owned 26% of the outstanding shares. The remaining shares were owned by persons who are not parties to this litigation.

Defendants, a consortium of investors, formed a limited partnership, known as Madison 28 Associates (Madison Associates), for the purpose of purchasing the building. * * *

Madison Associates formed a separate, wholly owned company, 28 Williams Street Corporation (Williams Street), to act as the nominal purchaser and owner of the Kimmelman and Zauderer interests. * * *

[T]he partners of Madison Associates approved a plan to merge Realty Corporation with Williams Street, Realty Corporation being the surviving corporation. Together with a notice for a shareholders meeting to vote on the proposed merger, a statement of intent was sent to all shareholders of Realty Corporation, explaining the procedural and financial aspects of the merger, as well as defendants' conflict of interest and the intended exclusion of the minority shareholders from the newly constituted Realty Corporation through a cash buy-out. Defendants also disclosed that they planned to dissolve Realty Corporation after the merger and thereafter to operate the business as a partnership. The merger plan did not require approval by any of the minority shareholders.

The merger proposed by the directors was approved at the shareholders meeting, held on November 7, 1980. As a result, the office building was owned by the "new" Realty Corporation, which, in turn, was wholly owned by Madison Associates. In accordance with the merger plan, Realty Corporation was dissolved within a month of the merger and its principal asset, title to the building, devolved to Madison Associates.

* * *

The plaintiffs instituted this action on October 31, 1980, initially seeking to enjoin the shareholders meeting called to approve the merger. Failing to temporarily enjoin the Realty Corporation's merger with Williams Street, plaintiffs later amended their complaint to include a request for equitable relief in the form of rescission of the merger.

The propriety of the merger was contested on several grounds. It was contended that the merger was unlawful because its sole purpose was to personally benefit the partners of Madison Associates and that the alleged purposes had no legitimate business benefit inuring to the corporation. Plaintiffs argue that the "business judgment" of the directors in assigning various purposes for the merger was indelibly tainted by a conflict of interest because they were committed to the merger prior to becoming directors and were on both sides of the merger transaction when consummated. Further, they assert that essential financial information was not disclosed and that the value offered for the minority's shares was understated and determined in an unfair manner.

* * *

On this appeal, the principal task facing this court is to prescribe a standard for evaluating the validity of a corporate transaction that forcibly eliminates minority shareholders by means of a two-step merger. It is concluded that the analysis employed by the courts below was correct: the majority shareholders' exclusion of minority interests through a two-step merger does not violate the former's fiduciary obligations so long as the transaction viewed as a whole is fair to the minority shareholders and is justified by an independent corporate business purpose. Accordingly, this court now affirms.

* * *

In New York, two or more domestic corporations are authorized to "merge into a single corporation which shall be one of the constituent corporations", known as the "surviving corporation" [citation]. The statute does not delineate substantive justifications for mergers, but only requires compliance with certain procedures: the adoption by the boards of each corporation of a plan of merger setting forth, among other things, the terms and conditions of the merger; a statement of any changes in the certificate of incorporation of the surviving corporation; the submission of the plan to a vote of shareholders pursuant to notice to all shareholders; and adoption of the plan by a vote of two thirds of the shareholders entitled to vote on it [citation].

Generally, the remedy of a shareholder dissenting from a merger and the offered "cash-out" price is to obtain the fair value of his or her stock through an appraisal proceeding [citation]. This protects the minority shareholder from being forced to sell at unfair values imposed by those dominating the corporation while allowing the majority to proceed with its desired merger [citations]. The pursuit of an appraisal proceeding generally constitutes the dissenting stockholder's exclusive remedy [citations]. An exception exists, however, when the merger is unlawful or fraudulent as to that shareholder, in which event an action for equitable relief is authorized [citations]. Thus, technical compliance with the Business Corporation Law's requirements alone will not necessarily exempt a merger from further judicial review.

* * *

Because the power to manage the affairs of a corporation is vested in the directors and majority shareholders, they are cast in the fiduciary role of "guardians of the corporate welfare." * * *

The fiduciary must treat all shareholders, majority and minority, fairly . . . Moreover, all corporate responsibilities must be discharged in good faith and with "conscientious fairness, morality and honesty in purpose" [citation]. Also imposed are the obligations of candor [citation] and of good and prudent management of the corporation [citations].

* * *

* * * In reviewing a freeze-out merger, the essence of the judicial inquiry is to determine whether the transaction, viewed as a whole, was "fair" as to all concerned. This concept has two principal components: the majority shareholders must have followed "a course of fair dealing toward minority holders" . . . and they must also have offered a fair price for the minority's stock. * * *

Generally, the plaintiff has the burden of proving that the merger violated the duty of fairness, but when there is an inherent conflict of interest, the burden shifts to the interested directors or shareholders to prove good faith and the entire fairness of the merger. . . . The interested parties may attempt to establish this element of fair dealing by introducing evidence of efforts taken to simulate arm's length negotiations. Such steps may have included the appointment of an independent negotiating committee made up of neutral directors or of an independent board to evaluate the merger proposal and to oversee the process of its approval. * * *

Fair dealing is also concerned with the procedural fairness of the transaction, such as its timing, initiation, structure, financing, development, disclosure to the independent directors and shareholders, and how the necessary approvals were obtained. . . . Bascially, the courts must look for complete and candid disclosure of all the material facts and circumstances of the proposed merger known to the majority or directors, including their dual roles and events leading up to the merger proposal. * * *

The fairness of the transaction cannot be determined without considering the component of the financial remuneration offered the dissenting shareholders. * * *

In determining whether there was a fair price, the court need not ascertain the precise "fair value" of the shares as it would be determined in an appraisal proceeding. It should be noted, however, that the factors used in an appraisal proceeding are relevant here . . . This would include but would not be limited to net asset value, book value, earnings, market value, and investment value . . . Elements of future value arising from the accomplishment or expectation of the merger which are known or susceptible of proof as of the date of the merger and not the product of speculation may also be considered. * * *

* * *

Fair dealing and fair price alone will not render the merger acceptable. As mentioned, there exists a fiduciary duty to treat all shareholders equally [citation]. This duty arises as a concomitant to the power reposed in the majority over corporate governance [citation]. The fact remains, however, that in a freeze-out merger the minority shareholders are being treated in a different manner: the majority is permitted continued participation in the equity of the surviving corporation while the minority has no choice but to surrender their shares for cash. On its face, the majority's conduct would appear to breach this fiduciary obligation.

* * *

In the context of a freeze-out merger, variant treatment of the minority shareholders— i.e., causing their removal—will be justified when related to the advancement of a general corporate interest. The benefit need not be great, but it must be for the corporation. For example, if the sole purpose of the merger is reduction of the number of profit sharers—in contrast to increasing the corporation's capital or profits, or improving its management structure—there will exist no "independent corporate interest" [citation]. All of these purposes ultimately seek to increase the individual wealth of the remaining shareholders. What distinguishes a proper corporate purpose from an improper one is that, with the former, removal of the minority shareholders furthers the objective of conferring some general gain upon the corporation. Only then will the fiduciary duty of good and prudent management of the corporation serve to override the concurrent duty to treat all shareholders fairly [citation]. We further note that a finding that there was an independent corporate purpose for the action taken by the majority will not be defeated merely by the fact that the corporate objective could have been accomplished in another way, or by the fact that the action chosen was not the best way to achieve the bona fide business objective.

In sum, in entertaining an equitable action to review a freeze-out merger, a court should view the transaction as a whole to determine whether it was tainted with fraud, illegality, or self-dealing, whether the minority shareholders were dealt with fairly, and whether there exists any independent corporate purpose for the merger.

* * *

Without passing on all of the business purposes cited by Supreme Court as underlying the merger, it is sufficient to note that at least one justified the exclusion of plaintiff's interests: attracting additional capital to effect needed repairs of the building. There is proof that there was a good-faith belief that additional, outside capital was required. Moreover, this record supports the conclusion that this capital would not have been available through the merger had not plaintiffs' interest in the corporation been eliminated. Thus, the approval of the merger, which would extinguish plaintiffs' stock, was supported by a bona fide business purpose to advance this general corporate interest of obtaining increased capital.

Accordingly, the order of the Appellate Division should be affirmed.

Dissenting Shareholders

ENDICOTT JOHNSON CORP. v. BADE

Court of Appeals of New York, 1975.
37 N.Y.2d 585, 376 N.Y.S.2d 103, 338 N.E.2d 614.

Fuchsberg, J.

This proceeding was brought pursuant to section 623 of the Business Corporation Law to fix the fair value of the stock of respondent stockholders, who had dissented from a pro-posed merger as a result of which petitioner Endicott Johnson Corporation was to become a wholly-owned subsidiary of McDonough Corporation. Special Term, confirming and adopting the report of the appraiser it had appointed, fixed, *inter alia,* the fair value of the common stock at $45.75. The Appellate Division having modified the order of Special Term by reducing the valuation of the stock to $42.77 per share and having increased the amount of fees allowed to one of respondent's counsel, both sides now appeal.

At the heart of the issues involved are the weight required to be given to the market price of the stock. * * *

The general principles applicable here are clear. Dissenting stockholders were entitled to be paid the "fair value" of their Endicott common stock, excluding any appreciation or depreciation due to the merger or its proposal. [Citation.] Although the statute itself is silent as to how fair value is to be determined, it is well established by case law that, in our State, the elements which are to enter into such an appraisal are net asset value, investment value and market value. [Citation.] While, in order to provide the elasticity deemed necessary to reach a just result, all three factors are to be considered, the weight to be accorded to each varies with the facts and circumstances in a particular case. [Citations.]

* * *

It follows that all three elements do not have to influence the result in every valuation proceeding. It suffices if they are all considered. Compelling the consideration of all of them, including those which may turn out to be unreliable in a particular case, has the salutary effect of assuring more complete justification by the appraiser of the conclusion he reaches. It also provides a more concrete basis for court review.

The three elements are not always discrete: definitionally, they may even flow into one another. For instance, in this very case, by their general concurrence that it would here be inappropriate, no estimation of net asset value was attempted by the parties or the appraiser. Since the corporation was not being liquidated, but was to continue to operate as part of the surviving parent McDonough Corporation, that made business and legal sense. For, in cases of nonliquidation, to the extent that the net asset value might include elements such as good will and potential earnings, these are invariably taken into account, in any event, among the numerous tangible and intangible factors that enter into judgment of the investment value of going concerns, whether by experienced appraisers or prudent investors. [Citations.]

Indeed, in this case investment value, for all practical purposes, became the sole determinant of fair value when the appraiser eliminated market value as a meaningful factor by reporting as follows:

My opinion is that little weight should be given to the past history of market value prior to 1969 because I believe that there was a radical enough change in the management of the company so that it had 'turned around', and that the pre-1969 market is not particularly helpful.

I agree with the thinking of the text writers that a dramatic change in leadership for the good may be valid grounds for disregarding company's [sic] past history of weakness.

Subsequent to 1969 I believe the market became so thin because of the control of McDonough and the subsequent delisting that it is fairly meaningless.

Endicott, pointing to an average market price of $26.25 per share in public trading of the stock for the six months immediately preceding the announcement of the merger, argues that market value was required to be given substantial weight and that the lower courts acted contrary to law in adopting that part of the appraiser's report which had failed to do so. In further support of its position, Endicott, among other things, asserts that, during the pre-merger period it regards as relevant McDonough controlled only 31.8% of the common shares, the remainder constituting a large enough public float in the hands of over two thousand stockholders to ensure a free and active market. On the other hand, the stockholders, relying heavily on such facts as the stock's delisting from the New York Stock Exchange, its relegation for

a year before the merger to being traded on the over-the-counter market and, by then, the ownership by McDonough of 70% of the stock, claim the marketplace was no longer "a fair reflection of the judgment of the buying and selling public" as to Endicott common. [Citation.]

Under the circumstances, the weight of market value, whether great or small or none, was for the fact-finding tribunals, and there is no reason to disturb the Appellate Division's conclusion, on the facts and in its discretion, that in this case the appraiser was not required to rely "to any large degree" on the market value of Endicott's common stock.

* * *

In addition, the right of dissenting stockholders to obtain fair value rather than market value for their stock protects them from being forced to sell at unfair values arbitrarily and unilaterally fixed by those who may dominate a corporation. The obligation to accept fair value is an accepted risk of public stock ownership for, in some instances, market price at the time of a merger may have been pushed to levels in excess of fair value, and the automatic right to it in a valuation proceeding could bring a windfall. Either way, market price is but an ingredient that must enter into the calculation for what it is worth, no more and no less. [Citation.]

* * *

Accordingly, the order should be affirmed.

Involuntary Judicial Dissolution

MATTER OF KEMP & BEATLEY, INC.

Court of Appeals of New York, 1984.
64 N.Y.2d 63, 484 N.Y.S.2d 799, 473 N.E.2d 1173.

COOKE, C.J.

The business concern of Kemp & Beatley, incorporated under the laws of New York, designs and manufactures table linens and sundry tabletop items. The company's stock consists of 1,500 outstanding shares held by eight shareholders. Petitioner Dissin had been employed by the company for 42 years when, in June 1979, he resigned. Prior to resignation, Dissin served as vice-president and a director of Kemp & Beatley. Over the course of his employment, Dissin had acquired stock in the company and currently owns 200 shares.

Petitioner Gardstein, like Dissin, had been a long-time employee of the company. Hired in 1944, Gardstein was for the next 35 years involved in various aspects of the business including material procurement, product design, and plant management. His employment was terminated by the company in December 1980. He currently owns 105 shares of Kemp & Beatley stock.

Apparent unhappiness surrounded petitioners' leaving the employ of the company. Of particular concern was that they no longer received any distribution of the company's earnings. Petitioners considered themselves to be "frozen out" of the company; whereas it had been their experience when with the company to receive a distribution of the company's earnings according to their stockholdings, in the form of either dividends or extra compensation, that distribution was no longer forthcoming.

Gardstein and Dissin, together holding 20.33% of the company's outstanding stock, commenced the instant proceeding in June 1981, seeking dissolution of Kemp & Beatley pursuant to section 1104–a of the Business Corporation Law. Their petition alleged "fraudulent and oppressive" conduct by the company's board of directors such as to render petitioners' stock "a virtually worthless asset." Supreme Court referred the matter for a hearing, which was held in March 1982.

Upon considering the testimony of petitioners and the principals of Kemp & Beatley, the referee concluded that "the corporate management has by its policies effectively rendered petitioners' shares worthless, and . . . the only way petitioners can expect any return is by dissolution". Petitioners were found to have invested capital in the company expecting, among other things, to receive dividends or "bonuses" based upon their stock holdings. Also found was the company's "established buyout policy" by which it would purchase the stock of employee shareholders upon their leaving its employ.

The involuntary-dissolution statute (Business Corporation Law, § 1104–a) permits dissolution when a corporation's controlling faction is found guilty of "oppressive action" toward the complaining shareholders. The referee considered oppression to arise when "those in control" of the corporation "have acted in such a manner as to defeat those expectations of the minority stockholders which formed the basis of [their] participation in the venture." The expectations of petitioners that they would not be arbitrarily excluded from gaining a return on their investment and that their stock would be purchased by the corporation upon termination of employment, were deemed defeated by prevailing corporate policies. Dissolution was recommended in the referee's report, subject to giving respondent corporation an opportunity to purchase petitioners' stock.

Supreme Court confirmed the referee's report. It, too, concluded that due to the corporation's new dividend policy petitioners had been prevented from receiving any return on their investments. Liquidation of the corporate assets was found the only means by which petitioners would receive a fair return. The court considered judicial dissolution of a corporation to be "a serious and severe remedy." Consequently, the order of dissolution was conditioned upon the corporation's being permitted to purchase petitioners' stock. The Appellate Division affirmed, without opinion. [Citation.]

At issue in this appeal is the scope of section 1104–a of the Business Corporation Law. Specifically, this court must determine whether the provision for involuntary dissolution when the "directors or those in control of the corporation have been guilty of . . . oppressive actions toward the complaining shareholders" was properly applied in the circumstances of this case. We hold that it was, and therefore affirm.

* * *

The statutory concept of "oppressive actions" can, perhaps, best be understood by examining the characteristics of close corporations and the Legislature's general purpose in creating this involuntary-dissolution statute. It is widely understood that, in addition to supplying capital to a contemplated or on-going enterprise and expecting a fair and equal return, parties comprising the owner-ship of a close corporation may expect to be actively involved in its management and op-eration. . . . The small ownership cluster seeks to "contribute their capital, skills, ex-perience and labor" toward the corporate enterprise. * * *

As a leading commentator in the field has observed: "Unlike the typical shareholder in a publicly held corporation, who may be simply an investor or a speculator and cares nothing for the responsibilities of management, the shareholder in a close corporation is a co-owner of the business and wants the privi-leges and powers that go with ownership. His participation in that particular corporation is often his principal or sole source of income. As a matter of fact, providing employment for himself may have been the principal reason why he participated in organizing the corpo-ration. He may or may not anticipate an ul-timate profit from the sale of his interest, but he normally draws very little from the corpo-ration as dividends. In his capacity as an of-ficer or employee of the corporation, he looks to his salary for the principal return on his capital investment, because earnings of a close corporation, as is well known, are dis-tributed in major part in salaries, bonuses and retirement benefits." [Citation.]

Shareholders enjoy flexibility in memori-alizing these expectations through agree-ments setting forth each party's rights and obligations in corporate governance [cita-tion]. In the absence of such an agreement, however, ultimate decision-making power respecting corporate policy will be reposed in the holders of a majority interest in the corporation [citation]. A wielding of this power by any group controlling a corporation may serve to destroy a stockholder's vital interests and expectations.

As the stock of closely held corporations generally is not readily salable, a minority shareholder at odds with management poli-cies may be without either a voice in protect-ing his or her interests or any reasonable means of withdrawing his or her investment. This predicament may fairly be considered the legislative concern underlying the provi-sion at issue in this case; inclusion of the cri-teria that the corporation's stock not be traded on securities markets and that the complaining shareholder be subject to op-pressive actions supports this conclusion.

Defining oppressive conduct as distinct from illegality in the present context has been considered in other forums. The ques-tion has been resolved by considering oppres-sive actions to refer to conduct that substan-tially defeats the "reasonable expectations" held by minority shareholders in committing their capital to the particular enterprise [ci-tation]. This concept is consistent with the apparent purpose underlying the provision under review. A shareholder who reasonably expected that ownership in the corporation would entitle him or her to a job, a share of corporate earnings, a place in corporate man-agement, or some other form of security, would be oppressed in a very real sense when others in the corporation seek to defeat those expectations and there exists no effective means of salvaging the investment.

Given the nature of close corporations and the remedial purpose of the statute, this court holds that utilizing a complaining sharehold-er's "reasonable expectations" as a means of identifying and measuring conduct alleged to be oppressive is appropriate. A court consid-ering a petition alleging oppressive conduct must investigate what the majority share-holders knew, or should have known, to be the petitioner's expectations in entering the par-ticular enterprise. Majority conduct should not be deemed oppressive simply because the petitioner's subjective hopes and desires in joining the venture are not fulfilled. Disap-pointment alone should not necessarily be equated with oppression.

Rather, oppression should be deemed to arise only when the majority conduct sub-stantially defeats expectations that, objec-tively viewed, were both reasonable under the circumstances and were central to the pe-titioner's decision to join the venture. It would be inappropriate, however, for us in this case to delineate the contours of the courts' consideration in determining whether directors have been guilty of oppressive conduct. As in other areas of the law, much will depend on the circumstances in the individual case.

The appropriateness of an order of dissolution is in every case vested in the sound discretion of the court considering the application [citation]. Under the terms of this statute, courts are instructed to consider both whether "liquidation of the corporation is the only feasible means" to protect the complaining shareholder's expectation of a fair return on his or her investment and whether dissolution "is reasonably necessary" to protect "the rights or interests of any substantial number of shareholders" not limited to those complaining (Business Corporation Law, § 1104–a, subd. [b], pars. [1], [2]). Implicit in this direction is that once oppressive conduct is found, consideration must be given to the totality of circumstances surrounding the current state of corporate affairs and relations to determine whether some remedy short of or other than dissolution, constitutes a feasible means of satisfying both the petitioner's expectations and the rights and interests of any other substantial group of shareholders [citation].

By invoking the statute, a petitioner has manifested his or her belief that dissolution may be the only appropriate remedy. Assuming the petitioner has set forth a prima facie case of oppressive conduct, it should be incumbent upon the parties seeking to forestall dissolution to demonstrate to the court the existence of an adequate, alternative remedy [citation]. A court has broad latitude in fashioning alternative relief, but when fulfillment of the oppressed petitioner's expectations by these means is doubtful, such as when there has been a complete deterioration of relations between the parties, a court should not hesitate to order dissolution. Every order of dissolution, however, must be conditioned upon permitting any shareholder of the corporation to elect to purchase the complaining shareholder's stock at fair value [citation].

One further observation is in order. The purpose of this involuntary dissolution statute is to provide protection to the minority shareholder whose reasonable expectations in undertaking the venture have been frustrated and who has no adequate means of recovering his or her investment. It would be contrary to this remedial purpose to permit its use by minority shareholders as merely a coercive tool [citation]. Therefore, the minority shareholder whose own acts, made in bad faith and undertaken with a view toward forcing an involuntary dissolution, give rise to the complained-of oppression should be given no quarter in the statutory protection [citation].

* * *

There was sufficient evidence presented at the hearing to support the conclusion that Kemp & Beatley had a long-standing policy of awarding *de facto* dividends based on stock ownership in the form of "extra compensation bonuses." Petitioners, both of whom had extensive experience in the management of the company, testified to this effect. Moreover, both related that receipt of this compensation, whether as true dividends or disguised as "extra compensation", was a known incident to ownership of the company's stock understood by all of the company's principals. Finally, there was uncontroverted proof that this policy was changed either shortly before or shortly after petitioners' employment ended. Extra compensation was still awarded by the company. The only difference was that stock ownership was no longer a basis for the payments; it was asserted that the basis became services rendered to the corporation. It was not unreasonable for the fact finder to have determined that this change in policy amounted to nothing less than an attempt to exclude petitioners from gaining any return on their investment through the mere recharacterization of distributions of corporate income. Under the circumstances of this case, there was no error in determining that this conduct constituted oppressive action within the meaning of section 1104–a of the Business Corporation Law.

Nor may it be said that Supreme Court abused its discretion in ordering Kemp & Beatley's dissolution, subject to an opportunity for a buy-out of petitioners' shares. After the referee had found that the controlling faction of the company was, in effect, attempting to "squeeze-out" petitioners by offering them no return on their investment and increasing other executive compensation, respondents, in opposing the report's confirmation, attempted only to controvert the factual basis of the report. They suggested no feasible, alternative remedy to the forced dissolution. In light of an apparent deterioration in relations between petitioners and the governing shareholders of Kemp & Beatley, it was not unreasonable for the court to have determined that a forced buy-out of petitioners' shares or liquidation of the corporation's assets was the only means by which petitioners could be guaranteed a fair return on their investments.

Accordingly, the order of the Appellate Division should be modified, with costs to petitioners-respondents, by affirming the substantive determination of that court but extending the time for exercising the option to purchase petitioners-respondents' shares to 30 days following this court's determination.

QUESTIONS

1. Which charter amendments (a) do not require shareholder approval and (b) give dissenting shareholders an appraisal remedy?

2. Which combinations (a) do not require shareholder approval and (b) give dissenting shareholders an appraisal remedy?

3. Distinguish between a tender offer and a compulsory share exchange.

4. Compare and contrast a cash-out combination and a management buyout.

5. Identify the ways by which involuntary and voluntary dissolution may occur.

PROBLEMS

1. The stock in Hotel Management, Inc., a hotel management corporation, was divided equally between two families. For several years, the two families had been unable to agree or cooperate in the management of the corporation. As a result, no meeting of shareholders or directors had been held for five years. There had been no withdrawal of profits for five years, and last year the hotel operated at a loss. Although the corporation was not insolvent, such a state was imminent because the business was poorly managed and its properties were in need of repair. As a result, the owners of half the stock brought an action in equity for dissolution of the corporation. What decision?

2. (a) When may a corporation sell, lease, exchange, mortgage, or pledge all or substantially all of its assets in the usual and regular course of its business?

(b) When may a corporation sell, lease, exchange, mortgage, or pledge all or substantially all of its assets other than in the usual and regular course of its business?

(c) What are the rights of a shareholder who dissents from a proposed sale or exchange of all or substantially all of the assets of a corporation otherwise than in the usual and regular course of its business?

3. The Cutler Company was duly merged into the Stone Company. Yetta, a shareholder of the former Cutler Company, having paid only one-half of her subscription, is now sued by the Stone Company for the balance of the subscription. Yetta, who took no part in the merger proceedings, denied liability on the ground that, inasmuch as the Cutler Company no longer exists, all her rights and obligations in connection with the Cutler Company have been terminated. Decision?

4. Smith, while in the course of his employment with the Bee Corporation, negligently ran the company's truck into Williams, injuring him very severely. Subsequently, the Bee Corporation and the Sea Corporation consolidated, forming the SeaBee Corporation. Williams filed suit against the SeaBee Corporation for damages, and the SeaBee Corporation asserted the defense that the injuries sustained by Williams were not caused by any of SeaBee's employees, that SeaBee was not even in existence at the time of the injury, and that the SeaBee Corporation was, therefore, not liable. What decision?

5. The Johnson Company, a corporation organized under the laws of State X, after proper authorization by the shareholders, sold its entire assets to the Samson Company, also a State X corporation. Ellen, an unpaid creditor of the Johnson Company, sues the Samson Company upon her claim. Decision?

6. Zenith Steel Company operates a prosperous business. The board of directors voted to spend $20 million of the surplus funds of the company to purchase a majority of the stock of two other companies—the Green Insurance Company and the Blue Trust Company. The Green Insurance Company is a thriving business whose stock is an excellent investment at the price at which it will be sold to Zenith Steel Company. The principal reasons for Zenith's purchase of the Green Insurance stock are an investment of surplus funds and a diversification of its business. The Blue Trust Company owns a controlling interest in Zenith Steel Company. The main purpose for Zenith's purchase of the Blue Trust Company stock is to enable the present management and directors of Zenith Steel Company to perpetuate their management of the company. Jones, a minority shareholder in Zenith Steel Company, brings an appropriate action to enjoin the purchase by Zenith Steel Company of the stock of either the Green

Insurance Company or of the Blue Trust Company. Decision?

7. Mildred, Deborah, and Bob each own one-third of the stock of Nova Corporation. On Friday, Mildred received an offer to merge Nova into Buyer Corporation. Mildred agreed to call a shareholders' meeting to discuss the offer on the following Tuesday. Mildred telephoned Deborah and Bob and informed them of the offer and the scheduled meeting. Deborah agreed to attend. Bob was unable to attend because he was leaving on a trip on Saturday and asked if the three of them could meet Friday night to discuss the offer. Mildred and Deborah agreed. The three shareholders met informally Friday night and agreed to accept the offer only if they received preferred stock of Buyer Corporation for their shares. Bob then left on his trip. On Tuesday, at the time and place appointed by Mildred, Mildred and Deborah convened the shareholders' meeting. After discussion, they concluded that the preferred stock payment limitation was unwise and passed a formal resolution to accept Buyer Corporation's offer without any such condition. Bob files suit to enjoin Mildred, Deborah, and the Nova Corporation from implementing this resolution. Decision?

8. Tretter alleged that his exposure over the years to asbestos products manufactured by Philip Carey Manufacturing Corporation caused him to contract asbestosis. Tretter brought an action against Rapid American Corporation, which was the surviving corporation of a merger between Philip Carey and Rapid American. Rapid American denied liability, claiming that immediately after the merger it had transferred its asbestos operations to a newly formed subsidiary corporation. Decision?

9. Wilcox was chief executive officer, chairman of the board of directors, and owned 60 percent of the shares of Sterling Corporation. When the market price of Sterling's shares was $22 per share, Wilcox sold all of his shares in Sterling to Conrad for $29 per share. The minority shareholders of Sterling brought suit against Wilcox demanding a portion of the amount Wilcox received in excess of the market price. Decision?

10. All Steel Pipe and Tube is a closely held corporation engaged in the business of selling steel pipes and tubes. Leo and Scott Callier are its two equal shareholders. Leo, Scott's uncle, is one of the company's two directors and is president of the corporation. Scott is the general manager. Scott's father and Leo's grandfather, Felix, is the other director. Over the years, Scott and Leo have had differences of opinion about various aspects of the operation of the business. Despite the deterioration of their relationship, the company flourished. Negotiations aimed at the redemption of Scott's shares by Leo began, but the parties could not reach an agreement. The discussion then turned to voluntary dissolution and liquidation of the corporation, but still no agreement could be reached. Finally, Leo fired Scott and began to wind down All Steel's business and form a new corporation, Callier Steel Pipe and Tube. Leo then brought this action seeking a dissolution and liquidation of All Steel. Decision?

Chapter 38

SECURED TRANSACTIONS IN PERSONAL PROPERTY

Types of Collateral
Attachment
Perfection
Priorities
Default

Today our economy literally runs on borrowed funds. In 1986, $724 billion of consumer installment credit was outstanding, and mortgage debt outstanding in 1988 was estimated to exceed $3 trillion. This extensive use of credit is a relatively recent phenomenon. Shakespeare's well-known lines in *Hamlet* reflect the earlier view of debt: "Neither a borrower nor a lender be; For loan oft loses both itself and friend, And borrowing dulls the edge of husbandry." Over time this attitude has changed dramatically, and today, under our economic system, borrowed funds are absolutely essential and entirely honorable. Without them, units of production would be severely restricted in the goods and services they could provide, and consumers would be greatly limited in the quantities they could afford to purchase.

A lender typically incurs two basic collection risks. The first is that the borrower is unwilling to repay the loan even though he is *able* to do so. The law has provided the lender with a considerable arsenal of collection remedies that significantly reduce this risk, although these remedies are by no means without cost. A number of these remedies are discussed in Chapter 40.

The law has also sought to deal with the second and more significant collection risk: that the borrower may prove to be *unable* to repay the loan. In addition to the remedies just mentioned, the law has developed several devices to maximize the likelihood that the loan will be repaid. The most important of these are consensual security interests. A consensual security interest (secured transaction) is an agreement by the borrower granting the lender the right to reach specified property of the borrower to pay off the debt if the borrower fails to do so.

A secured transaction therefore includes two elements: (1) a debt or obligation to pay money and (2) an interest of the creditor in specific property of the debtor that secures performance of the obligation. An obligation or debt can also exist without security. In fact, a vast amount of indebtedness is unsecured: the integrity, reputation, and net worth of the debtor are deemed adequate by the creditor. In many situations, however, businesses or other individuals cannot obtain credit without giving adequate security. In other cases, an unsecured loan can be obtained, but giving security may result in a lower interest rate.

Financing transactions involving security in personal property are governed by Article 9 of the Uniform Commercial Code, Secured Transactions. This article provides a simple and unified structure within which the tremendous variety of current secured financing transactions can take place with less cost and with greater certainty. Moreover, the article's flexibility and simplified formalities make it possible for new forms of secured financing to fit comfortably under its provisions. This chapter will discuss secured transactions in personal property. Article 9 does not cover secured transactions involving real property; these transactions are discussed in Chapter 51.

ESSENTIALS OF SECURED TRANSACTIONS

Secured transactions in personal property are governed by Article 9 if the debtor *consents* to provide a security interest in personal property to secure the payment of a debt. Article 9 does *not* apply to non-consensual security interests that arise by operation of law, such as mechanics' or landlords' lien. A common type of consensual secured transaction covered by Article 9 occurs when a person who wants to buy goods does not have either the cash or a sufficient credit standing to obtain the goods on open credit. The seller obtains a security interest in the goods to secure payment of all or part of the price. Alternatively, the buyer may borrow the purchase price from a third party and pay the seller in cash. The third party lender may then take a security interest in the goods to secure repayment of the loan.

In every consensual secured transaction there is a debtor, a secured party, collateral, a security agreement, and a security interest. As defined in Section 9–105(1) of the Code, a **debtor** is a person who owes payment or performance of an obligation. A **secured party** is the creditor (lender, seller, or other person) who owns the security interest in the collateral. **Collateral** is the property subject to the security interest. A **security agreement** is the agreement that creates or provides for a

security interest, which Section 1–201(37) defines as "an interest in personal property or fixtures which secures payment or performance of an obligation." A seller of goods who retains a security interest in them by a security agreement has a **purchase money security interest** (PMSI). Similarly, a third party lender who advances funds to enable the debtor to purchase goods has a purchase money security interest if she has a security agreement and the debtor in fact uses the funds to purchase the goods.

Thus, a security interest is created when an automobile dealer sells and delivers a car to an individual (*debtor*) under a retail installment contract (*security agreement*) that provides that the dealer (*secured party*) obtains a *security interest* (*purchase money security interest*) in the car (*collateral*) until the price is paid. A security interest in property cannot exist apart from the debt it secures, and once the debt is discharged in any manner, the security interest in the property is terminated. See Figure 38–1.

CLASSIFICATION OF COLLATERAL

Although most of the provisions of Article 9 apply to all kinds of personal property, some provisions state special rules that apply only to particular kinds of collateral. Under the Code, collateral is classified according to its nature and its use. The classifications according to nature are (a) goods, (b) indispensable paper, and (c) intangibles.

Goods

Goods are tangible personal property that can be moved when the security interest in them becomes enforceable. Section 9–105(1)(h). Goods are subdivided into (1) consumer goods, (2) farm products, (3) inventory, and (4) equipment. Goods that become affixed to real estate are called fixtures. An item of goods may fall into different classifications depending on its primary use or purpose. For example, a refrigerator purchased by a physician to store medicines in his office is classified as equipment, while the same

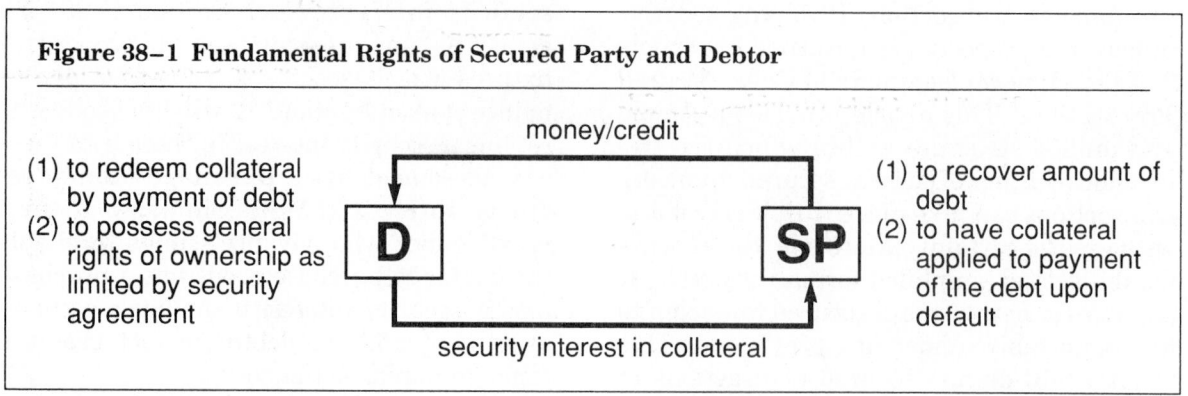

Figure 38–1 Fundamental Rights of Secured Party and Debtor

refrigerator would be classified as consumer goods if it were purchased for use in his home. The refrigerator would be classified as inventory in the hands of a refrigerator dealer or manufacturer.

Consumer Goods Goods are consumer goods if they are used or bought for use primarily for personal, family, or household purposes. Section 9–109(1).

Farm Products The Code defines farm products as "crops or livestock or supplies used or produced in farming operations or if they are products of crops or livestock in their unmanufactured states. . . ." Section 9–109(3). Thus, farm products would include wheat growing on the farmer's land, the farmer's pigs, cows, hens, and the hens' eggs. When such products come into possession of a person not engaged in farming operations, they cease to be farm products.

Inventory The term inventory includes goods held for sale or lease and raw materials, work in process, or materials used or consumed in a business. Section 9–109(4). Thus, a retailer's or wholesaler's merchandise as well as a manufacturer's materials are inventory.

Equipment Goods are classified as equipment if they are used or purchased for use primarily in business (including farming or a profession), provided they are not included in the definition of inventory, farm products, or consumer goods. Section 9–109(2). This cat-

egory is broad enough to include a lawyer's library, a physician's office furniture, or machinery in a factory.

Fixtures Goods and personal property that have become so related to particular *real property* that an interest in them arises under real estate law are called fixtures. Section 9–313(1)(a). Thus, State law other than the Code determines whether and when goods become fixtures. In general terms, goods become fixtures when they are so firmly affixed or attached to real estate in such a manner that they are considered part of the real estate. Examples are furnaces, central air-conditioning units, and plumbing fixtures. See Chapter 48 for a further discussion of fixtures. A security interest under Article 9 may be created in goods that are fixtures, and, under certain circumstances, a perfected security interest in fixtures will have priority over a conflicting security interest or mortgage in the real property to which the goods have been attached.

Indispensable Paper

Three kinds of collateral involve rights evidenced by indispensable paper: (1) chattel paper, (2) instruments, and (3) documents.

Chattel Paper Chattel paper is a writing or writings that evidence both a monetary obligation and a security interest in or a lease of specific goods. Frequently, a secured party may borrow against or sell the security agreement of his debtor along with his interest in the collateral. The collateral provided by the secured party to his lender in this type of transaction is chattel paper. Comment 4 to Section 9–105 of the Code provides the following illustration:

A dealer sells a tractor to a farmer on conditional sales contract or purchase money security interest. The conditional sales contract is a "security agreement," the farmer is the debtor, the dealer is the "secured party" and the tractor is the type of "collateral" defined . . . as "equipment." But now the dealer transfers the contract to his bank either by outright sale or to secure a loan. Since the conditional sales contract is a security agreement relating to specific equipment, the conditional sales contract is now the type of collateral called "chattel paper." In this transaction between the dealer and his bank, the bank is the "secured party," the dealer is the "debtor," and the farmer is the "account debtor."

Instruments   Instruments include negotiable instruments, stocks, bonds, and other investment securities. Section 9–105(1)(i). An instrument is any writing that evidences a right to payment of money, that is transferable by delivery with any necessary indorsement or assignment, and that is not of itself a security agreement or lease.

Documents   The term document includes documents of title, such as bills of lading and warehouse receipts, which may be either negotiable or non-negotiable. Sections 9–105(1)(f), 1–201(15). A document of title is negotiable if by its terms the goods it covers are deliverable to bearer or to the order of a named person. Any other document is non-negotiable. Documents of title are covered in Chapter 49.

Intangibles

The Code also recognizes two kinds of collateral that are neither goods nor indispensable paper, namely, accounts and general intangibles. These types of intangible collateral are not evidenced by any indispensable paper, such as a stock certificate or a negotiable bill of lading.

Accounts   The terms account and accounts receivable refer to the right to payment for goods sold or leased or for services rendered, which is not evidenced by an instrument or chattel paper, whether or not it has been earned by performance. Section 9–106. The 1972 Code deleted the term *contract right* but included contract rights in its expanded definition of account.

General Intangibles   The term general intangibles applies to any personal property other than goods, accounts, chattel paper, documents, instruments, and money. Section 9–106. This is a catchall category for interests not otherwise covered unless they are specifically excluded by Article 9. It leaves room for the use of new kinds of collateral for financing purposes. It includes goodwill, literary rights, and interests in patents, trademarks, and copyrights to the extent they are not regulated by Federal statute.

ATTACHMENT

Attachment is the Code's terminology to describe the creation of a security interest that is *enforceable* against the *debtor*. Attachment is also a prerequisite (and in some instances is sufficient) to a security interest's enforceability against parties other than the debtor. Perfection provides the greatest enforceability against third parties who assert competing interests in the collateral. Perfection is discussed below.

Until a security interest "attaches," it is *ineffective* against the debtor. Under Section 9–203 of the Code, the security interest created by a security agreement attaches to the described collateral once the following events have taken place:

1. the giving of value by the secured party;

2. the debtor's acquiring rights in the collateral; and

3. either the collateral is in the possession of the secured party pursuant to agreement **or** the security agreement is in a writing which

contains a reasonable description of the collateral and is signed by the debtor.

The parties may, however, by explicit agreement postpone the time of attachment. Section 9–203(2).

Value

The term **value** is broadly defined and includes consideration under contract law, a binding commitment to extend credit, and an antecedent debt. Section 1–201(44). For example, Buyer purchases equipment from Seller on credit. When Buyer fails to make timely payment, Seller and Buyer enter into a security agreement under which Seller is granted a security interest in the equipment. Value has been given by the Seller even though he does not provide any new consideration but instead relies upon an antecedent debt—the original transfer of goods to Buyer. Moreover, Seller is not limited to acquiring a security interest in the equipment he sold to Buyer but may also obtain a security interest in other personal property of Buyer.

Debtor's Rights in Collateral

The concept of the debtor's rights in collateral is elusive and not specifically defined by the Code. Before the 1972 amendments, the U.C.C. attempted to provide rules for determining when a debtor acquired rights in certain types of collateral. The 1972 amendments eliminated these provisions because they were considered unnecessary, arbitrary, and confusing. It was decided that such questions were best left for the courts to determine. As a general rule, the debtor is deemed to have **rights in collateral** that he owns or is in possession of as well as those items that he is in the process of acquiring from the seller. For example, if Adrien borrows money from Richard and grants him a security interest in corporate stock that she owns, then Adrien had rights in the collateral before entering into the secured transaction. Likewise, if Sally sells goods to Benjamin on credit and Benjamin provides Sally a security interest

in the goods, Benjamin will acquire rights in the collateral upon identification of the goods to the contract.

Security Agreement

A security interest cannot attach unless there is an agreement between the debtor and creditor granting, creating, or providing the creditor with a security interest in the debtor's collateral. *See In Re Modafferi.* With the exception of pledges (discussed below), the agreement must (1) *be in writing,* (2) *be signed* by the *debtor,* and (3) contain a *reasonable description* of the collateral. Section 9–203(1)(a). In addition, if the collateral is crops growing or to be grown or timber to be cut, the agreement must contain a reasonable description of the land. A sample security agreement is provided as Figure 38–2.

Under the Code, no written security agreement is required when the collateral is pledged or in the possession of the secured party pursuant to an agreement. Section 9–203(1)(a). A **pledge** is the delivery of personal property to a creditor as security for the payment of a debt. A pledge requires that the secured party (the pledgee) and the debtor *agree* to the pledge of the collateral and that the collateral is *delivered* to the pledgee.

Consumer Goods Federal regulation prohibits a credit seller or lender from obtaining a consumer's grant of a nonpossessory security interest in household goods. This rule does not apply to purchase money security interests or to pledges. Household goods are defined to include clothing, furniture, appliances, kitchenware, personal effects, one radio, and one television. Works of art, other electronic entertainment equipment, antiques, and jewelry are specifically excluded from being considered household goods. This rule prevents a lender or seller from obtaining a nonpurchase money security interest covering the consumer's household goods.

After-Acquired Property "A security agreement may provide that any or all obligations covered by the security agreement

Figure 38–2 Sample Security Agreement

SECURITY AGREEMENT

August 22, 1991

Daniel Debtor of 113 Hillsborough Street, City of Raleigh, County of Wake, State of North Carolina, hereinafter called the "Debtor," does hereby grant to S.P. & Assoc., Inc., of Raleigh, North Carolina, hereinafter called "S.P.," its successors and assigns, a security interest in the following described property, hereinafter called the "Collateral," to-wit:

> One (1) Deluxe Personal Computer
>
> Serial number VDL16794321
>
> Manufacturer: Apex Mechanical Equipment Co.
>
> Model 420A

to secure the payment of Debtor's note or notes of even date herewith in the aggregate principal or aggregate face amount of Seven Thousand Five Hundred Dollars ($7,500.00), together with interest and any renewal or extension thereof, in whole or in part, and any and all other debts, obligations, and liabilities of any kind of Debtor to S.P., however created, arising, or evidenced, whether direct or indirect, joint or several, whether as maker, indorser, surety, guarantor or otherwise, whether now or hereafter existing, whether due or not due, and however acquired by S.P. (all hereinafter called the "Obligations").

DEBTOR WARRANTS AND AGREES THAT:

1. Except for the security interest hereby granted, the Debtor will use the proceeds of advances made hereunder, which proceeds may be paid by the S.P. directly to the seller of the Collateral, to become the owner of marketable title to the Collateral free from any prior lien, security interest or encumbrance, and the Debtor will defend the Collateral against all claims and demands of all persons at any time claiming an interest therein.

2. The Collateral is and will be used primarily for personal, family, or household purposes, and the Debtor's residence is that shown at the beginning of this Agreement.

3. The Collateral will be kept at the Debtor's address shown at the beginning of this Agreement.

4. There are no financing statements covering any of the Collateral on file in any public office, and the Debtor has not executed in favor of other secured parties financing statements that could be placed on file prior to any of S.P.'s financing statements.

5. DEBTOR AGREES THAT:

    A. He will pay to S.P. all amounts due on the note or notes mentioned above and the other Obligations secured hereby as and when same shall be due and payable, whether by maturity, acceleration, or otherwise, and will pay to S.P. reasonable attorney's fees incurred by S.P. in collection of said Obligations or enforcement of this Security Agreement.

    B. He will maintain all mechanical equipment and machinery hereby covered in sound and efficient operating condition, including the procurement and installation of such new parts, attachments, and replacements as may be necessary or desirable to maintain said Collateral in proper operating condition.

    C. He will maintain such insurance upon all of the Collateral as S.P. may require, payable to Debtor and S.P. as their interest may appear, in an amount not less than the actual value of the Collateral.

    D. He will pay all insurance premiums and taxes, licenses, or other charges assessed against the Collateral or required to be paid in connection with the use and ownership of the

Figure 38–2 Sample Security Agreement *(continued)*

Collateral. If Debtor shall fail to pay such insurance premiums, taxes, licenses, or other charges when they are due, S.P. at its opinion, may pay the cost thereof, and the amounts so paid and advanced shall be added to the indebtedness secured hereby and shall bear interest at the maximum rate permitted by Law.

E. He will not (a) permit any liens or security interest to attach to any of the Collateral; (b) permit any of the Collateral to be levied upon under any legal process; (c) sell or dispose of any of the Collateral without prior written consent of S.P.; (d) permit anything to be done that may impair the value of the Collateral or the security intended to be afforded by this Agreement.

F. He will immediately notify S.P. in writing of any change of the Debtor's place or residence, place or places of business, or the location of the Collateral.

G. He will not remove the Collateral from the State of North Carolina without prior written consent by S.P.

6. IT IS FURTHER AGREED THAT THE DEBTOR SHALL BE IN DEFAULT UNDER THIS AGREEMENT:

A. If the Debtor uses any of the Collateral in violation of any statute or ordinance or the Debtor is found to have a record or reputation for violating the laws of the United States or any State relating to liquor or narcotics; or

B. If the Debtor shall fail to perform any covenant or Agreement made by him herein; or

C. If the Debtor shall fail to make due and punctual payment of any of the Obligations secured hereby when and as any part or all of such Obligation becomes due and payable; or

D. If any warranty, representation, or statement made or furnished to S.P. by or on behalf of the Debtor in connection with this Agreement proves to have been false in any material respect when made or furnished; or

E. If the Collateral suffers material damage or destruction; or

F. If any bankruptcy or insolvency proceedings are commenced by or against the Debtor or any guarantor or surety for the Debtor; or

G. If the Debtor dies, becomes incompetent, is dissolved, or the Debtor's existence otherwise terminates.

Upon the happening of any of the above events of default or in the event that S.P., in good faith, deems itself insecure, S.P. may at its option, declare all Obligations secured hereby due and payable immediately and have, in addition to other rights and remedies, the rights and remedies of a secured party upon default under the North Carolina Uniform Commercial Code.

The waiver of any particular default of the Debtor hereunder shall not be a waiver of any other or subsequent default of the Debtor.

Any requirement of the North Carolina Uniform Commercial Code of reasonable notification of time and place of public sale, or the time on or after which private sale may be held, may be met by sending written notice by registered or certified mail to the above address of the Debtor at least five (5) days prior to public sale or the date after which private sale may be made.

The Debtor shall be and remain liable for any deficiency remaining after applying the proceeds of disposition of the Collateral first to the reasonable expenses of re-taking, holding, preparing for sale, selling, and the like, including the reasonable attorney's fees, incurred by S.P. in connection therewith, and then to satisfaction of the Obligations secured hereby.

This Agreement and all rights, remedies, and duties hereunder, including matters of construction, shall be governed by the laws of North Carolina.

This Agreement shall apply to, inure to the benefit of, and be binding upon the heirs,

---

Figure 38–2 *(continued)*

---

administrators, executors, and assigns of S.P. and the Debtor. This is the entire agreement of the parties, and no amendment, alteration, deletion, or addition hereto shall be effective and binding unless it is in writing and signed by the parties.

Debtor acknowledges that this Agreement is and shall be effective upon execution by the Debtor and delivery hereof to S.P., and it shall not be necessary for S.P. to execute or otherwise signify its acceptance hereof.

Signed and delivered on the day first above written.

_____ (SEAL)

Daniel Debtor

S.P. & Assoc., Inc.

(Secured Party)

By: _____

---

are to be secured by after-acquired collateral." Section 9–204(1). After-acquired property is property that the debtor does not own or have rights to but may acquire at some time in the future. For example, after-acquired property clauses in a security agreement may include all present and subsequently acquired inventory, accounts, or equipment of the debtor. This clause would provide the secured party with a valid security interest not only in the debtor's presently existing typewriter, desk, and file cabinet, but also in a personal computer subsequently purchased by the debtor. The concept of a "continuing general lien" or a *floating lien* is therefore accepted by Article 9. The Code, however, limits the operation of an after-acquired property clause against *consumers*. No such interest can be claimed as additional security in consumer goods, except accessions, if the goods are acquired more than ten days after the secured party gives value. Section 9–204(2). An *accession* is property installed in or affixed to other property. Section 9–314. For example, a new engine placed in an old automobile is an accession.

Proceeds A secured party is necessarily interested in the use and control of proceeds, which includes whatever is received from the sale, exchange, collection, or other disposition of the collateral. Section 9–306(1). These proceeds may be in the form of money, checks, deposit accounts, promissory notes, or other types of personal property. Unless otherwise agreed, a security agreement gives the secured party rights to proceeds. Section 9–203(3).

Future Advances The obligations covered by a security agreement may include future advances. Section 9–204(3). Frequently, a debtor obtains a line of credit from a creditor for advances to be made at some later time. For instance, a manufacturer may provide a retailer with a $60,000 line of credit of which the retailer initially uses only $20,000. Nevertheless, the manufacturer may enter into a security agreement with the retailer, granting the manufacturer a security interest in the retailer's inventory to secure not only the initial $20,000 advance but also any future advances.

PERFECTION

To be effective against third parties who assert competing interests in the collateral (including other creditors of the debtor, the debtor's trustee in bankruptcy, and transferees of the debtor) the security interest must be perfected. **Perfection** of a security interest occurs when it has attached *and* when all the applicable steps required for perfection have been taken. Section 9–303(1). If these steps are taken before the security interest attaches, it is perfected at the time it attaches. Once a security interest becomes perfected it "may still be or become subordinate to other interests but in general after perfection the secured party is protected against creditors and transferees of the debtor and in particular against any representative of creditors in insolvency proceedings instituted by or against the debtor." Section 9–303, Comment 1.

Depending upon the type of collateral, a security interest may be perfected:

1. by the secured party's filing a financing statement in the designated public office;

2. by the secured party's taking or retaining possession of the collateral;

3. automatically on the attachment of the security interest; or

4. temporarily for a period of time specified by the Code.

Figure 38–3 lists the requisites for enforceability of security interests.

Filing a Financing Statement

Filing a financing statement is the general method of perfecting a security interest under Article 9. Filing may be used to perfect a security interest in any kind of collateral with the *exception* of instruments. The form of the **financing statement,** which is filed to give public notice of the security interest, may vary from State to State. The financing statement does not contain details but must include the names and addresses of the secured party and the debtor, a reasonable description of the types of items of collateral (*See NCR Co. v. Firestone & Co.*), and the signature of the debtor. Section 9–402(1). Figure 38–4 shows a sample financing statement.

In order to determine the terms of a secured transaction between the parties, it is necessary to look at the security agreement or the collateral note or preferably both. It is possible that neither the maturity date of the obligation nor the amount of the obligation secured will appear on the financing statement. Where no maturity date is stated, a financing statement is effective for *five years* from the date of filing. Section 9–403(2). If a **continuation statement** is filed by the secured party within six months prior to expiration, the effectiveness of the filing will be extended for another five-year period. Section 9–403(3).

In most States, security interests in **motor vehicles** must be perfected by a notation on the certificate of title rather than by filing a financing statement.

A **certificate of title** is an official representation of ownership. Nevertheless, in most States, certificate of title laws do not apply to motor vehicles that are held as inventory for sale by a dealer.

Figure 38–3 Requisites for Enforceability of Security Interests

I. Attachment	II. Perfection

A. Agreement
  1. in writing (unless SP has possession)
  2. providing a security interest
  3. in described collateral
  4. signed by debtor,
	A. SP files a financing statement, or

	B. SP takes possession, or
B. Value given by secured party, and	C. Automatically, or
C. Debtor has rights in collateral.	D. Temporarily.

Where to File Section 9–401(1) of the Code provides three alternative provisions regarding the proper place to file a financing statement. The alternatives differ as to which types of collateral are to be filed *locally* (in the county) or *centrally* (with the Secretary of State or another designated State official).

The first alternative, which has been adopted in only a few States, provides that where the collateral is fixtures, timber to be cut, or minerals to be extracted, the financing statement should be filed locally in the office

---

Figure 38–4 Sample Financing Statement

UNIFORM COMMERCIAL CODE—FINANCING STATEMENT
APPROVED FOR USE IN NORTH CAROLINA AND THE FOLLOWING STATES

Alabama	Delaware	Maine	New Jersey	Tennessee	
Alaska	Hawaii	Maryland	New Mexico	Virginia	
Arkansas	Idaho	Massachusetts	North Dakota	West Virginia	UCC-1
Arizona	Indiana	Mississippi	Ohio	Wyoming	
Colorado	Kansas	Montana	Oklahoma	District of Columbia	
Connecticut	Kentucky	New Hampshire	South Carolina		

This FINANCING STATEMENT is presented to a Filing Officer for filing pursuant to the Uniform Commercial Code.	No. of Additional Sheets Presented:	
(1) Debtor(s) (Last Name First) and Address(es):	(2) Secured Party(ies) Name(s) and Address(es):	
(3) (a) ☐ Collateral is or includes fixtures. (b) ☐ Timber, Minerals or Accounts Subject to UCC 9–103(5) are covered (c) ☐ Crops Are Growing Or To Be Grown On Real Property Described in Section (5). If either block 3(a) or block 3(b) applies describe real estate, including record owner(s) in section (5).	(4) Assignee(s) of Secured Party, Address(es):	For Filing Officer

(5) This Financing Statement Covers the Following types [or items] of property.

☐ Products of the Collateral Are Also Covered.

(6) Signatures: Debtor(s)   Secured Party(ies) [or Assignees]

(By) _____   (By) _____

Standard Form Approved by N.C. Sec. of State and other states shown above.   Signature of Secured Party Permitted in Lieu of Debtor's Signature:

(1) Filing Officer Copy—Numerical   (1) Collateral is subject to Security Interest In Another Jurisdiction and ☐

                                     ☐ Collateral Is Brought Into This State

                                     ☐ Debtor's Location Changed To This State

     (2) For Other Situations See: UCC 9–402(2)

                                             UCC-1

where a mortgage on real estate would be filed or recorded. All other filings are to be made centrally with the Secretary of State or another designated State official.

The second alternative, which is the most widely adopted, stipulates local filing for fixtures, farm products, consumer goods, timber, minerals, and farming equipment. All other filings are to be made in the office of the Secretary of State or another designated State official.

The third alternative is the same as the second except that, where central filing is required, the secured party must *also* file locally if the debtor has a place of business in only one county or if the debtor has no place of business in the State but resides in the State.

Improper Filing If a secured party fails to file the financing statement in the proper location or fails to file it in all the required locations, the filing is *ineffective,* subject to two exceptions. First, if the filing is made in good faith, it is nevertheless effective for any collateral for which the filing complied with the requirements of Article 9. Section 9–401(2). This exception applies to situations in which the filing covers a number of different kinds of collateral and is proper with respect to some but not all of the collateral listed. Second, a filing made in good faith is also effective for collateral covered by the financing statement against any person who has knowledge of the contents of that financing statement. Section 9–401(2). This exception has been limited by the 1972 amendments, which give a lien creditor priority over an unperfected security interest without regard to whether the lien creditor knew of the unperfected security interest. Section 9–301(1)(b).

Subsequent Change of Information After a financing statement has been properly filed by a secured party, the debtor may change the place of his residence or business or the location or use of the collateral and thus render the information in the filing in-

correct. In all the States a change in the *use* of the collateral does not impair the effectiveness of the original filing. Most States also provide that the original filing made in the proper place continues to be effective despite any change of location provided the change is **intrastate.** Section 9–401(3). A minority of States have adopted a second alternative provided by Section 9–401(3) limiting the effectiveness of a filing which is made in the proper county to a period of four months after the debtor has moved his residence, place of business, or the collateral to another county. Under the second alternative, if the secured party does not file a financing statement in the new county within the four-month time period, perfection ceases until a new filing is made.

With respect to **interstate** changes, two situations require a new filing: (1) if the collateral is mobile goods, accounts, or general intangibles and the *debtor* moves his residence or place of business to another State or (2) if the *debtor* moves the collateral to another State. Section 9–103. In either case, the security interest perfected in the former State remains in effect for four months or until perfection would have ceased under the laws of the first State, whichever occurs first. *See Exchange Bank of Osceola v. Jarrett.* If the security interest is not perfected within the four-month period, it becomes unperfected and such loss of perfection under the 1972 amendments is retroactive to the time of the change in location of the debtor or collateral. For example, Davis purchases goods in Arizona and grants Sarah Penn a security interest in the goods, which Sarah perfects by filing. Davis then moves to Kansas and immediately sells the goods to Bruce. If Sarah refiles in Kansas within the four-month period, she would have priority over Bruce; however, if Sarah fails to file within the four-month period, Bruce would prevail since the loss of perfection dates back to the time of Davis's move from Arizona to Kansas. Under the 1962 provision, the loss is not retroactive and thus any purchase within the four-month grace period is subordinate to the original perfection in Arizona.

Possession

Possession by the secured party may be used to perfect a security interest in goods (e.g., pawnbrokers), instruments, money, negotiable documents, or chattel paper. Section 9–305. Possession is *not* available as a means of perfecting a security interest in accounts and general intangibles. Subject to the limited exception of the twenty-one-day temporary period of perfection discussed later in this chapter, possession is the *only* way to perfect a security interest in instruments. Section 9–304. In addition, the usual and advisable method of perfecting a security interest in both negotiable documents and chattel paper is by possession. Although both of these types of collateral may be perfected by filing, it is not advisable to rely upon filing because (a) the holder of a negotiable document of title which has been duly negotiated to him takes priority in the goods over an earlier security interest perfected by filing, Section 9–309; and (b) a good faith purchaser in the ordinary course of business of chattel paper takes priority over an earlier security interest perfected by filing. Section 9–308.

A pledge or possessory security interest is the delivery of personal property to a creditor, or to a third party acting as an agent for the creditor, as security for the payment of a debt. Perhaps the most common pledge is that of a borrower who pledges corporate stock by delivery of the certificates to a bank in order to secure a loan. The delivery of the stock certificates (collateral) to the bank (secured party) is the essential element of the pledge. Since *delivery* is made, the security interest is "perfected" without filing. Section 9–302(1)(a). There is no pledge where the debtor retains possession of the collateral. In a pledge the debtor is not legally required to sign a written security agreement; an oral agreement granting the secured party a security interest is sufficient. In any situation other than a pledge, the Code requires a written security agreement. Section 9–203.

One type of pledge is the **field warehouse.** This common arrangement for financing inventory allows the debtor access to the pledged goods while at the same time providing the secured party control over the pledged property. In this arrangement, a professional warehouseman generally establishes a warehouse on the debtor's premises—usually by enclosing a portion of the premises and posting appropriate signs—to store the debtor's unsold inventory. Non-negotiable receipts for the goods are then typically issued by the warehouseman to the secured party. The secured party may then authorize the warehouseman to release a portion of the goods to the debtor as the goods are sold, at a specified quantity per week, or at any rate agreed upon by the parties. Thus, the secured party legally possesses the goods while allowing the debtor easy access to her inventory.

Automatic Perfection

In some situations, a security interest is automatically perfected on attachment. The most important situation to which automatic perfection applies is a purchase money security interest in consumer goods. (Several States either do not permit automatic perfection of purchase money security interests in consumer goods or impose limitations on the purchase price.) In addition, a partial or isolated assignment of accounts that does not transfer a significant part of the outstanding accounts of the assignor is also automatically perfected. Section 9–302(1)(e).

As previously mentioned, a seller of goods who retains a security interest in them by a security agreement has a purchase money security interest (PMSI). Similarly, a third party who advances funds to enable the debtor to purchase goods has a purchase money security interest if she has a security agreement and the debtor in fact uses the funds to purchase the goods. A purchase money security interest in consumer goods, with the exception of motor vehicles, is perfected automatically upon attachment without the necessity of filing a financial statement. Section 9–302(1)(d). For example, Doris purchases a refrigerator from Carol on credit for Doris's own personal, family, or household use. Doris takes possession of the refrigerator and then grants Carol a security interest in the refrigerator pursuant to a written security agreement. Upon Doris's granting Carol the security interest in the refrigerator, Carol's security interest attaches and is automatically perfected. The same is also true if Doris purchased the refrigerator for cash but borrowed the money from Logan, to whom Doris granted a security interest in the refrigerator pursuant to a written security agreement. Logan's security interest attached and was automatically perfected when she received the security agreement from Doris. Because an automatically perfected PMSI in consumer goods does not protect the secured party as fully as a filed PMSI, secured parties do not always rely solely on automatic perfection but frequently file a financing statement.

Temporary Perfection

Security interests in certain collateral are automatically perfected but only for a temporary period of time depending on the type of collateral. After that period expires, the security interest becomes unperfected unless it is perfected by other available means of perfection. A security interest in *negotiable documents* or *instruments* is automatically perfected without filing or taking possession for **twenty-one days** from the time it attaches, to the extent that it arises for new value given under a written security agreement. Section 9–304(4). The secured party, however, runs the risk of loss or impairment of his security interest during the twenty-one-day period, for although his interest is temporarily perfected, a holder in due course of a negotiable instrument or a holder to whom a document has been duly negotiated will take priority over the security interest. Sections 9–308 and 9–309.

The Code further provides that a security interest remains perfected for **twenty-one days** where a secured party, who already has a perfected security interest in an instrument, negotiable document, or goods in possession of a bailee (provided he has not issued a negotiable document for the goods), under certain circumstances delivers the instrument to the debtor, releases the document to him, or makes the goods available to him. Section 9–304(5). Moreover, a security interest in proceeds is automatically perfected for **ten days** after receipt of the proceeds if the security interest in the original collateral was perfected. Section 9–302(1)(b).

Figure 38–5 lists the available methods of perfecting security interests for different types of collateral.

PRIORITIES AMONG COMPETING INTERESTS

As previously noted, a security interest must be perfected to be most effective against other creditors of the debtor, the debtor's trustee in bankruptcy, and transferees of the debtor. Nonetheless, perfection of a security interest does *not* provide the secured party with a **priority** over *all* third parties with an interest in the collateral. On the other hand, even an unperfected security interest that has attached has priority over a limited number of third parties and is enforceable against the debtor. Article 9 establishes a complex set of rules that determine the relative priorities among these parties.

Figure 38–6 on page 911 summarizes these priorities among selected parties who have a competing interest in collateral.

Against Unsecured Creditors

Once a security interest *attaches,* it has priority over claims of other creditors who do not have a security interest or a lien. This priority does not depend upon perfection. If a security interest does not attach, the creditor is merely an unsecured or general creditor of the debtor.

Figure 38–5 Methods of Perfecting Security Interests

| Collateral | Filing | Applicable Method of Perfection | | |
		Possession	Automatic	Temporary
Goods				
Consumer	•	•	PMSI	
Equipment	•	•		
Farm products	•	•		
Inventory	•	•		
Fixtures	•	•		
Indispensable Paper				
Chattel paper	•	•		
Instrument		•		21 days
Document	•	•		21 days
Intangibles				
Account	•		Isolated	
General Intangibles	•		Assignment	

Against Other Secured Creditors

The rights of a secured creditor against other secured creditors depends upon which security interests are perfected, when they are perfected, and the type of collateral. Notwithstanding the rules of priority, it is possible for a secured party entitled to priority to subordinate her interest to that of another secured creditor. This may be done by agreement between the secured parties, and nothing need be filed.

Perfected versus Unperfected A creditor with a *perfected* security interest has greater rights in the collateral than a creditor with an unperfected security interest, whether or not the unperfected security interest has attached.

Perfected versus Perfected If two parties each have a *perfected* security interest, they rank according to priority in *time of filing or perfection*. This general rule is stated in Section 9–312(5)(a), which provides:

Conflicting security interests rank according to priority in time of filing or perfection. Priority dates from the time a filing is first made covering the collateral or the time the security interest is first perfected, whichever is earlier, provided that there is no period thereafter when there is neither filing nor perfection.

This rule gives special treatment to filing since it can occur prior to attachment and thus grants priority from a time that may precede perfection.

For example, Debter Store and Leynder Bank enter into a loan agreement under the terms of which Leynder agrees to lend $5,000 on the security of Debter's existing store equipment. A financing statement is filed, but no funds are advanced. One week later, Debter enters into a loan agreement with Reserve Bank, and Reserve agrees to lend $5,000 on the security of the same store equipment. The funds are advanced, and a financing statement is filed. One week later, Leynder Bank advances the agreed sum of $5,000. Debter Store defaults on both loans. Between Leynder Bank and Reserve Bank, Leynder has priority. When both security interests are perfected by filing, priority is determined in the order of filing. Reserve Bank should have checked the financing statements on file. Had it done so, it would have discovered that Leynder Bank claimed a security interest in the equipment. Once Leynder's financing statement was on file, with no prior secured party of record, Leynder was not required to check the files prior to advancing funds to Debter Store in accordance with its loan commitment.

To further illustrate, assume that Marc grants a security interest in a Chagall painting to Miro Bank, and in accordance with the loan agreement the bank advances funds to Marc. A financing statement is filed. Later Marc wants more money and goes to Brague, an art dealer, who advances funds to Marc upon a pledge of the painting. Marc defaults on both loans. As between Miro and Brague, Miro has priority because its security interest was filed before Brague's perfection by possession. By checking the financing statement on file, Brague would have discovered that Miro had a prior security interest in the painting.

Where there is a **purchase money security interest** in the collateral, the rules vary depending on whether the collateral is non-inventory or inventory.

1. A purchase money security interest in **non-inventory** collateral takes priority over a conflicting security interest if the purchase money security interest is perfected at the time the debtor receives possession of the collateral *or* within *ten days* of receipt. Section 9–312(4). Thus the secured party has a ten-day grace period in which to perfect.

For example, Dawkins Manufacturing Co. entered into a loan agreement with Larkin Bank, which loaned money to Dawkins on the security of Dawkins's existing and future equipment. A financing statement was filed stating that the collateral is "all equipment presently owned and subsequently acquired" by Dawkins. At a later date, Dawkins buys new equipment from Parker Supply Co., paying 25 percent of the purchase price, with Parker retaining a security interest in the equipment to secure the remaining balance. If Parker files a financing statement within ten days of Dawkins's obtaining possession of the equipment, Parker's purchase money security interest in the new equipment purchased from Parker has priority over Larkin's interest. If Parker files on the eleventh day, or later, after Dawkins receives the equipment, Parker's interest is subordinate to Larkin's interest. *Compare In re Ultra Precision Industries, Inc.* with *National Cash Register Co. v. Firestone & Co.*

2. A purchase money security interest in **inventory** has priority over conflicting security interests if the following requirements are met. The purchase money security holder must perfect his interest in the inventory at the time the debtor receives the inventory. He must also give notification in writing of his acquisition of a purchase money security interest and a description of the secured inventory to all holders of conflicting security interests who have filed a financing statement covering the same type of inventory. Section 9–312(3).

For example, Dodger Store and Lyons Bank enter into a loan agreement in which Lyons agrees to finance Dodger's entire inventory of stoves, refrigerators, and other kitchen appliances. A financing statement is filed, and Lyons advances funds to Dodger. Subsequently, Dodger enters into an agreement under which Rodger Stove Co. will supply Dodger with stoves, retaining a purchase money security interest in this inventory. Rodger will have priority as to the inventory it supplies to Dodger provided that a financing statement is filed and Rodger notifies Lyons that it is going to engage in this purchase money financing of the described stoves. If Rodger fails to give the required notice or fails to file a financing statement, Lyons will have priority over Rodger as to the stoves supplied by Rodger to Dodger. The Code adopts a system of notice filing, and secured parties proceed at their peril in failing to check the financing statement on file.

Unperfected versus Unperfected If neither security interest is perfected, then the first to attach has priority. Section 9–312(5)(6). If neither attach, both of the creditors are general, unsecured creditors.

Against Buyers

A security interest continues in collateral even though it is sold, unless the secured party authorizes the sale. The security interest also continues in any identifiable proceeds from the sale of the collateral. Section 9–306(2). In some instances, however, buyers of collateral that was sold without the secured party's authorization take it free of the security interest. Some of these purchasers take the collateral free of even a perfected security interest; others take it free of only an unperfected security interest.

Buyers in the Ordinary Course of Business A buyer in the ordinary course of business takes collateral free of any security interest created by *his* seller, even if the security interest is perfected and the buyer knows of its existence. Section 9–307(1). A buyer in the ordinary course of business is a person who buys in good faith, without knowledge that the sale violates a security interest of a third party, and who buys from a person in the business of selling goods of that kind. Section 1–201(9). Thus, this rule applies primarily to purchasers of inventory. For example, a consumer who purchases a sofa from a furniture dealer and the dealer who purchases the sofa from another dealer are both buyers in the ordinary course of business. On the other hand, a person who purchases a sofa from a dentist who used the sofa in his waiting room or from an individual who used the sofa in his home is not a buyer in the ordinary course of business.

To illustrate further: a buyer in the ordinary course of business of an automobile from an automobile dealership will take free and clear of a security interest created by the dealer from whom she purchased the car. That same buyer in the ordinary course of business will *not* take clear of a security interest created by any person who owned the automobile prior to the dealer. A leading case on this point is *National Shawmut Bank of Boston v. Jones,* 108 N.H. 386, 236 A.2d 484 (1967). In that case Wever bought a 1964 Dodge Dart from Wentworth Motor Company

for his own personal use and granted a security interest in the car to Wentworth. Wentworth later assigned the security interest to National Shawmut Bank, which properly perfected it. Without Shawmut's consent, Wever sold the car to Hanson-Rock, another automobile dealer. Hanson-Rock then sold the car to Jones. Even though Jones is a buyer in the ordinary course of business from Hanson-Rock, he took the automobile subject to Shawmut's security interest since that interest had not been created by Jones's seller, Hanson-Rock. *See also Exchange Bank of Osceola v. Jarrett.*

Buyers in the ordinary course of business of **farm products,** although not protected by Section 9–307, are protected by the Federal Food Security Act. This Act defines a buyer in the ordinary course of business more broadly than does the Code as "a person who, in the ordinary course of business, buys farm products from a person engaged in farming operations who is in the business of selling farm products." The Act provides that such a buyer shall take free of most security interests created by the seller, even if the security interest is perfected and the buyer knows of the existence of the interest. The Act does provide three exceptions that make the security interest effective against the buyer. Two of the exceptions depend upon the State's enacting a central filing system as specified in the Act; the third applies if the creditor gives the buyer written notice of the creditor's interest within one year before the sale in a form specified by the Act.

Buyers of Consumer Goods In the case of consumer goods, a buyer who buys without knowledge of a security interest, for value, and for his own personal, family, or household use takes the goods free of any purchase money security interest **automatically** perfected, but takes the goods subject to a security interest perfected by filing. Section 9–307(2). For example, Ann purchases on credit a refrigerator from Sean for use in her home and grants Sean a security interest in the refrigerator. Sean does not file a financing statement but has a perfected security interest by attachment. Ann subsequently sells the refrigerator to her neighbor, Nick, for use in Nick's home. Nick did not have knowledge of Sean's security interest and therefore takes the refrigerator free of Sean's interest. If Sean had filed a financing statement, however, Sean's security interest would continue in the collateral in the hands of Nick.

Other Buyers An *unperfected* security interest is subordinated to the rights (1) in the case of goods, instruments, documents, and chattel paper, of a purchaser who gives value for the collateral, takes it without knowledge of the existing security interest, and before it is perfected, Section 9–301(1)(c); and (2) in the case of accounts and general intangibles, of a purchaser who takes for value, without knowledge of the security interest, and before perfection. Section 9–301(1)(d). If either of these purchasers has knowledge of the unperfected security interest, he takes the collateral subject to the security interest.

A purchaser of chattel paper or of an instrument, who gives new value and takes possession of it in the ordinary course of his business, has priority over a perfected security interest in the chattel paper or instrument if he acts without knowledge that the specific paper or instrument is subject to a security interest. Section 9–308. A holder in due course of a negotiable instrument, a holder to whom a negotiable document of title has been duly negotiated, and a *bona fide* purchaser of an investment security take priority over an earlier security interest even though perfected. Filing under Article 9 does *not* constitute notice of the security interest to such holders or purchasers. Section 9–309.

Finally, a buyer takes free of any security interest "to the extent that it secures future advances made after the secured party acquires knowledge of the purchase, or more than 45 days after the purchase, whichever first occurs." Section 9–307(3). This rule, therefore, does not apply to advances made pursuant to a commitment entered into without knowledge of the purchase and before expiration of the forty-five-day period.

Against Lien Creditors

A **lien creditor** is a creditor who has acquired a lien in the property by judicial decree *and* includes an assignee for the benefit of creditors, a receiver in equity, as well as a trustee in bankruptcy. Section 9–301(3). A **trustee in bankruptcy** is a representative of the estate in bankruptcy who is responsible for collecting, liquidating, and distributing the debtor's assets. A **perfected** security interest has priority over lien creditors who acquire their lien after perfection. An **unperfected** security interest is subordinate to the rights of a person who becomes a lien creditor before the security interest is perfected. Section 9–301(1)(b). If a secured party files with respect to a *purchase money security interest* within ten days after the debtor receives possession of the collateral, however, the secured party takes priority over the rights of a lien creditor that arise between the time the security interest attaches and the time of filing. Section 9–301(2). Approximately half of the States have expanded the ten-day grace period to twenty days.

Nonetheless, a lien securing claims arising from services or materials furnished in the ordinary course of a person's business with respect to goods (an artisan's or mechanic's lien) "takes priority over a perfected security interest unless the lien is statutory and the statute specifically provides otherwise." Section 9–310.

Against Trustee in Bankruptcy

The Bankruptcy Act empowers a trustee in bankruptcy to invalidate secured claims in certain instances. It also imposes some limitations on the rights of secured parties. This section will examine the power of a trustee in bankruptcy to (a) take priority over an unperfected security interest and (b) avoid preferential transfers.

Priority over Unperfected Security Interest A trustee in bankruptcy may invalidate any security interest that is voidable by a creditor who obtained a judicial lien on the date of the filing of the bankruptcy petition. Bankruptcy Act, Section 544. Under the Code and the Bankruptcy Act, the trustee, as a hypothetical **lien creditor,** has priority over a creditor with a security interest that was not perfected when the bankruptcy petition was filed. A creditor with a purchase money security interest who files within ten days after the debtor receives the collateral will defeat the trustee, even if the petition is filed before the creditor perfects and after the creation of the security interest. For example, David borrowed $5,000 from Cynthia on September 1 and gave her a security interest in the equipment he purchased with the borrowed funds. On October 3, before Cynthia perfected her security interest, David filed for bankruptcy. The trustee in bankruptcy can invalidate Cynthia's security interest because it was unperfected when the bankruptcy petition was filed. If, however, David had filed for bankruptcy on September 8 and Cynthia had perfected the security interest on September 9, Cynthia would prevail because her purchase money security interest was perfected within ten days after David received the equipment.

Avoidance of Preferential Transfers
Section 547 of the Bankruptcy Act provides that a trustee in bankruptcy may invalidate any transfer of property—including the granting of a security interest—from the debtor, provided that the transfer (1) was to or for the benefit of a creditor; (2) was made on account of an antecedent debt; (3) was made at a time the debtor was insolvent; (4) was made on or within ninety days before the filing of the bankruptcy petition, or if made to an insider, was made within one year before the date of the filing; and (5) enabled the transferee to receive more than he would have received in bankruptcy. (An insider includes a relative or general partner of a debtor, as well as a partnership in which the debtor is a general partner or a corporation of which the debtor is a director, officer, or person in control.) In determining whether the debtor is insolvent, the Act establishes a rebuttable presumption of insolvency for the

ninety days prior to the filing of the bankruptcy petition. In order to avoid a transfer to an insider that occurred more than ninety days before bankruptcy, the trustee must prove the debtor's insolvency. If a security interest is invalidated as a preferential transfer, the creditor may still make a claim for the unpaid debt, but the creditor's claim is unsecured.

To illustrate the operation of this rule, consider the following. On May 1 Debra bought and received merchandise from Stuart and gave him a security interest in the goods for the unpaid price of $20,000. On May 20, Stuart filed a financing statement. On August 1, Debra filed a petition for bankruptcy. The trustee in bankruptcy may avoid the perfected security interest as a preferential transfer because (1) the transfer of the perfected security interest on May 20 was to benefit a creditor (Stuart); (2) the transfer was on account of an antecedent debt (the $20,000 owed from the sale of the merchandise); (3) the debtor was insolvent at the time (it is presumed that the debtor is insolvent for the ninety days preceding the filing of the bankruptcy petition—August 1); (4) the transfer was made within ninety days of bankruptcy (May 20 is less than ninety days before August 1); and (5) the transfer enabled the creditor to receive more than he would have received in bankruptcy (Stuart would have a secured claim on which he would recover more than on an unsecured claim).

For the purposes of the voidable preference section, the Bankruptcy Act deems a transfer of a security interest to be made when it is *perfected.* If it is perfected within ten days after attachment, however, the transfer is deemed to be made at the actual time of transfer. Consequently, security interests perfected within ten days of attachment will not be preferential since they are not made for an antecedent debt. This ten-day "grace" period applies to both purchase money and nonpurchase money security interests. Thus, in the example above, if Stuart had filed the financing statement by May 11, the security interest would not be a preferential transfer. Alternatively, if the goods had been consumer goods, the transaction would not be a preferential transfer because the security interest would have been automatically perfected upon attachment, and thus there would not be a transfer for an antecedent debt.

On the other hand, consider the following example. On January 6, Dawn purchases fifty refrigerators from Chad on credit. Dawn grants Chad a security interest in the inventory on January 6, and Chad perfects it on November 15. On December 15, Dawn files a petition in bankruptcy. For purposes of Section 547, the transfer of the security interest will be deemed to have been made on November 15, not on January 6. Thus, the security interest would be held to be within the ninety-day period and for an antecedent debt—the credit sale made on January 6. The trustee in bankruptcy would therefore be able to invalidate Chad's perfected security interest as a preferential transfer.

After-acquired property clauses, called floating liens, as previously discussed, are expressly permitted by Section 9–204 of the Code and are frequently used in financing inventory and accounts. Such clauses, however, may give the floating lien creditor an unfair advantage over other creditors if a debtor accumulates property subject to the after-acquired property clause. The Bankruptcy Act addresses this problem by allowing a trustee in bankruptcy to invalidate any improvement in a creditor's position in inventory, receivables, or proceeds to the extent it occurs during the ninety-day (one year for insiders) period immediately preceding the filing of the bankruptcy petition. The amount of the voidable preference equals:

[Amount of secured debt 90 days prior to bankruptcy —
Amount of collateral available 90 days prior to bankruptcy] —
[Amount of debt on date of bankruptcy —
Amount of collateral available on date of bankruptcy]

To illustrate: at the time of bankruptcy, Dan owes Claudia $100,000 and has inventory valued at $90,000. Ninety days prior to bankruptcy Dan owed Claudia $120,000 and had inventory valued at $60,000. Dan has a security interest in all of Claudia's presently existing and future acquired inventory. In this situation, the trustee in bankruptcy can reduce Claudia's secured claim from $90,000 to $40,000: voidable preference = (120,000 − 60,000) − ($100,000 − $90,000) = $50,000.

DEFAULT

After default, the rights and remedies of the parties are governed by the security agreement and by the applicable provisions of the Code. In general, the secured party may reduce his claim to judgment, foreclose, or otherwise enforce the security interest by available judicial procedure. Section 9–501. Unless the debtor has waived his rights in the collateral after default, he has a right of **redemption** (to free the collateral of the security interest by paying off the loan) at any time before the secured party has disposed of the collateral, entered into a contract to dispose of it, or discharged the obligation by retention of the collateral. Sections 9–506, 9–505(2). The rights and remedies of the creditor are cumulative.

Repossession

Unless the parties have agreed otherwise, the secured party may take possession of the collateral on default. In taking possession, a secured party may proceed without judicial process if it can be done without a breach of the peace. The Code does not define the term "breach of the peace" but leaves it to the courts to define. Some States have defined a breach of the peace to require the use of either violence or threat of violence, while others require merely an entry without consent. Most States require permission for entry to a residence or garage. On the other hand, the courts do permit the repossession of motor vehicles from driveways or streets. Courts usually do not permit a creditor to repossess if the debtor has orally protested against the repossession.

Figure 38–6 Priorities

Vs.	Unsecured creditor	Creditor with unperfected security interest	Creditor with perfected security interest	Creditor with perfected purchase money security interest
Unsecured creditor	=	↑	↑	↑
Creditor with unperfected security interest	←	first to attach	↑	↑
Creditor with perfected security interest — non-inventory	←	←	first to file or perfect	↑ if PMSI perfected within ten days
Creditor with perfected security interest — inventory	←	←	first to file or perfect	↑ if PMSI gives notice and perfects by time debtor gets possession
Buyer in ordinary course of business	←	←	← if created by immediate seller	←
Consumer buyer of consumer goods	←	←	↑	← if not filed
Lien creditor (including trustee in bankruptcy)	←	←	first in time	first in time but PMSI has ten-day grace period
Trustee in bankruptcy — voidable preferences	←	←	↑ if secured party perfects within ten days	↑ if PMSI perfects within ten days

After default, instead of removing the collateral, the secured party may leave it on the debtor's premises and render it unusable until disposing of it. Section 9–503.

Sale of Collateral

The secured party may sell, lease, or otherwise dispose of any collateral in its existing condition at the time of default or following any commercially reasonable preparation or processing. Section 9–504(1). The debtor is entitled to any *surplus* and is liable for any *deficiency,* except that in the case of a sale of accounts or chattel paper, he is not entitled to any surplus or liable for a deficiency unless the security agreement so provides. Section 9–504(2).

The collateral may be disposed of at *public* or *private* sale, so long as all aspects of its disposition are "commercially reasonable." *See In re Modafferi.* Unless the collateral is perishable or threatens to decline speedily in value or is of a type customarily sold on a recognized market, reasonable *notice* must be given to the debtor of a public sale or of the time after which a private disposition will be made and, except in the case of consumer goods, to other secured parties who have filed or who are known by the secured party to have security interests in the collateral. The courts are divided over the effect of a commercially unreasonable disposition of collateral on the debtor's obligation to pay any deficiency. Three theories exist: one absolutely bars the creditor from recovery of a deficiency, a second creates a rebuttable presumption that no deficiency exists, and the third provides that the debtor must establish the harm caused by the unreasonable disposition and then may set the loss off against the debt. *See Connecticut Bank & Trust v. Incendy.*

The secured party may buy at a public sale and at a private sale if the collateral is customarily sold in a recognized market or is the subject of widely distributed standard price quotations. Section 9–504(3).

Retention of Collateral

The secured party may, after default and repossession, send written notice to the debtor and, except in the case of consumer goods, to other secured parties that he proposes to retain the collateral in complete satisfaction of the obligation, and if no objection is received within twenty-one days, the secured party may retain the collateral. If there is objection within this period, however, the collateral must be disposed of as provided in the Code. Section 9–505(2). In the case of *consumer goods, if the debtor has paid 60 percent* of the obligation and has not, after default, signed a statement renouncing his rights, the secured party who has taken possession of the collateral must dispose of it by sale within ninety days after repossession or the debtor may recover, in conversion or under the Code, not less than the credit service charge plus 10 percent of the principal amount of the debt or the time price differential plus 10 percent of the cash price. Sections 9–505(1) and 9–507(1).

CASES

Security Agreement

IN RE MODAFFERI

United States Bankruptcy Court, SDNY, 1985.
40 UCC Rep.Serv. 268.

Schwartzberg, B.J.

This creditor, Peg-Leg Productions, Inc., desires to get a leg up on the unsecured creditors of the above-captioned debtors and asserts that it holds a perfected secured claim by virtue of the debtor's written promissory note and the subsequent filing of UCC-1 forms with the appropriate offices in Rockland County and New York State. On the other hand, the trustee in bankruptcy in this Chapter 7 case argues that Peg-Leg Productions does not have a leg to stand on as a secured claimant because its position is flawed by the absence of a security agreement, as required under Article 9 of the Uniform Commercial Code, § 9–203.

* * *

1. On December 13, 1982, the debtors borrowed $10,000 from Peg-Leg Productions in exchange for their written promissory note to repay that amount. . . . The note was silent as to the existence of any collateral to secure payment.

2. One month later, on January 14, 1983, Peg-Leg Productions filed a financing statement, Form UCC-1, in the appropriate filing office in Rockland County, New York. The financing statement was signed by the debtor, Joseph Modafferi, and the president of Peg-Leg Productions. The debtor listed on the financing statement was Joseph Modafferi, C.P.A. His office address was also specified. Item 5 of form UCC-1 states that the financing statement covers the following property: "All office equipment, furniture and all accounts payable." A similar form UCC-1 was filed by Peg-Leg Productions five months later, on June 21, 1983, with New York State.

3. On December 27, 1983, the debtors filed with this court their joint voluntary petition in bankruptcy * * *.

4. Peg-Leg Productions filed a proof of claim in this case as a secured claimant on the basis of the December 13, 1982 promissory note it received for the $10,000 loan and the subsequent filing of UCC-1 forms, which referred to the office equipment, furniture and accounts receivable of the debtor, Joseph Modafferi.

5. The debtors did not sign any document specifically referred to as a security agreement other than the promissory note and the form UCC-1 which was signed by the debtor, Joseph Modafferi.

* * *

Having failed to obtain from the debtors a signed separate security agreement containing a description of collateral for the purpose of creating a security interest, Peg-Leg Productions has no kick coming when the debtors' trustee in bankruptcy objects that Peg-Leg Productions does not hold a secured claim in this case.

It is fundamental that three requirements must be met for a security interest to be valid and enforceable against both the debtor and third parties: the debtor must sign a document describing the collateral, the security interest must attach and the interest must be perfected. [Citations.] Section 9–203(1) states in pertinent part that "the security interest is not enforceable . . . unless . . . the debtor has signed a security agreement which contains a description of the collateral. . . ." In contrast to a financing statement which merely places creditors on notice that further inquiry is prudent, the security agreement embodies the intentions of the parties. [Citation.] Consequently, "[u]nless the grant of a security interest is contained in the security agreement, there is no security interest." [Citation.]

The foregoing authorities and a literal reading of UCC § 9–203(1) are not dispositive of the issue in this case, namely, whether a financing statement taken together with an earlier signed promissory note, silent as to the existence of collateral, satisfy the writing requirement for the creation of a security interest. The two-fold purpose of the writing requirement was explained by the First Circuit Court of Appeals in [citation], as follows:

"The draftsmen of the UCC ascribed two purposes to [the writing] requirement. One purpose was evidentiary, to prevent disputes as to precisely which items of property are covered by a secured interest. * * * The second purpose of the signed-writing requirement is to serve as a Statute of Frauds, preventing the enforcement of claims based on wholly oral representations. * * *"

The strong weight of authority is of the view that although it is not necessary to present a separate, formal document entitled "security agreement" to establish a valid security interest, [citations], a standard form financing statement, standing alone, does not constitute a security agreement. [Citation.] Indeed, official comment 2 to UCC § 9–402 explains that the financing statement alone "indicates merely that the secured party who has filed *may* have a security interest in the collateral described."

It is clear that where a standard financing statement is presented to establish a valid and enforceable security interest, there must be some further documentation corroborative of the debtor's intent to pledge collateral. * * * It therefore appears that in the absence of a "security agreement" denominated as such, some language reflecting a desire to *grant* a security interest must be contained within the documents offered to establish a security agreement under UCC § 9–203. As the court stated in [citation]:

"The fact that the parties signed and filed a financing statement which covered inventory, accounts receivable and contract rights, in addition to equipment, furniture, and fixtures, is of no consequence to our decision. The function of a financing statement is to put third parties on notice that the secured party who has filed it may have a perfected security interest in the collateral described. *Absent language which would constitute the debtor's grant of a security interest, a financing statement cannot serve as a security agreement.*"

[Citations.]

* * *

An examination of the evidence in this case reveals no written expression by the debtor granting a security interest. The financing statement presented by Peg-Leg Productions, signed by one of the debtors, merely lists the covered collateral; it contains no "granting" language and therefore fails to demonstrate a present intent to pledge collateral. Notwithstanding the policy expressed by the drafters of the UCC that its terms be construed liberally, see § 1–102(1), this court is constrained to find that the debtor did not grant a security interest to Peg-Leg Productions based on the evidence presented. The goal of liberal construction does not dispense with the requirements of UCC § 9–203. * * * The UCC's requirements for the creation of a security interest are simple and clearly set forth. It is not unreasonable to require that a creditor who seeks to obtain priority over other creditors comply with these minimal requirements as a condition for being accorded such favored treatment. [Citation.]

Even if this court were to overlook the lack of "granting" language in the documents proffered by Peg-Leg Productions, there is another reason to deny this creditor secured status. This is not a case where the promissory note refers to collateral or a financing statement so that there are two documents indicative of an intent to create a security agreement. Instead, the promissory note in this case is silent as to the existence of any collateral. Furthermore, the requirement that there be a nexus between the note and financing statement is absent in that the latter fails to state that it secures the indebtedness acknowledged by the debtors in the December 13, 1982 promissory note.

* * *

The bankruptcy trustee's objection to secured status for Peg-Leg Productions under the claim filed by the latter, is sustained.

Filing/Priorities

NATIONAL CASH REGISTER CO. v. FIRESTONE & CO.

Supreme Judicial Court of Massachusetts, 1963.
346 Mass. 255, 191 N.E.2d 471.

WILKINS, C.J.

In this action of tort for conversion of a cash register there was a finding for the plaintiff . . . and the defendant appealed.

. . . The underlying question is the relative standing of two security interests. On June 15, 1960, the plaintiff, a manufacturer of cash registers, and one Edmund Carroll, doing business in Canton as Kozy Kitchen, entered into a conditional sale contract for a cash register. On November 18, 1960, the defendant, which was in the financing business, made a loan to Carroll, who conveyed certain personal property to the defendant as collateral under a security agreement. The defendant filed a financing statement with the Town Clerk of Canton on November 18, 1960, and with the Secretary of State on November 22, 1960. Between November 19 and November 25 the plaintiff delivered a cash register to Carroll in Canton. On November 25, the contract of June 15 was canceled and superseded by a new contract for the same cash register but providing for different terms of payment. The plaintiff filed a financing statement with respect to this contract with the Town Clerk of Canton on December 20 and with the Secretary of State on December 21. Carroll subsequently became in default both on the contract with the plaintiff and on the security agreement with the defendant. In December the defendant took possession of the cash register, and although notified on January 17, 1961, of the plaintiff's asserted right sold it at auction on the following day.

The defendant's security agreement recites that Carroll in consideration of $1,911 paid by it does "hereby grant, sell, assign, transfer and deliver to Grantee the following goods, chattels, and automobiles, namely: The business located at and numbered 574 Washington Street, Canton, Mass. together with all its good-will, fixtures, equipment and merchandise. The fixtures specifically consist of the following: *All contents of luncheonette including equipment such as: booths and tables; stand and counter; tables; chairs; booths; steam tables; salad unit; potato peeler; U.S. Slicer; range; case; fryer; compressor; bobtail; milk dispenser; silex; 100 Class air conditioner; signs; pastry case; mixer; dishes; silverware; tables; hot fudge; Haven Ex.; 2 door stationwagon 1957 Ford A57R107215* together with all property and articles now, and which may hereafter be, used or mixed with, added or attached to, and/or substituted for, any of the foregoing described property."

In the defendant's financing statement the detailed description of the "types (or items) of property" is the same as the words in supplied italics in the security agreement. There is no specific reference to a cash register in either document, and no mention in the defendant's financing statement of property to be acquired thereafter.

Under the Uniform Commercial Code, after-acquired property, such as this cash register, might become subject to the defendant's security agreement when delivered, [UCC], § 9–204(3); and likewise its delivery under a conditional sale agreement with retention of title in the plaintiff would not, in and of itself, affect the rights of the defendant. [UCC] § 9–202. Although the plaintiff could have completely protected itself by perfecting its interest before or within ten days of the delivery of the cash register to Carroll, it did not try to do so until more than ten days after delivery. Thus the principal issue is whether the defendant's earlier security interest effectively covers the cash register.

* * *

Contrary to the plaintiff's contention, we are of opinion that the security agreement is broad enough to include the cash register, which concededly did not have to be specifically described. The agreement covers "All contents of luncheonette including equipment such as," which we think covers all those contents and does not mean "equipment, to wit." There is a reference to "all property and articles now, and which may hereafter be, used . . . with, [or] added . . . to . . . any of the foregoing described property." . . .

We now come to the question whether the defendant's financing statement should have mentioned property to be acquired thereafter before a security interest in the cash register could attach. The Code [UCC], § 9–402(1), reads in part: "A financing statement is sufficient if it is signed by the debtor . . ., gives an address of the secured party from which information concerning the security interest may be obtained, gives a mailing address of the debtor and contains a statement indicating the types, or describing the items, of collateral."

In the official comment to this section appears the following: "2. This Section adopts

the system of 'notice filing' which has proved successful under the Uniform Trust Receipts Act. What is required to be filed is not, as under chattel mortgage and conditional sales acts, the security agreement itself, but only a simple notice which may be filed before the security interest attaches or thereafter. The notice itself indicates merely that the secured party who has filed may have a security interest in the collateral described. Further inquiry from the parties concerned will be necessary to disclose the complete state of affairs. Section 9–208 provides a statutory procedure under which the secured party, at the debtor's request, may be required to make disclosure. Notice filing has proved to be of great use in financing transactions involving inventory, accounts and chattel paper, since it obviates the necessity of refiling on each of a series of transactions in a continuing arrangement where the collateral changes from day to day. Where other types of collateral are involved, the alternative procedure of filing a signed copy of the security agreement may prove to be the simplest solution." [Citation.]

The framers of the Uniform Commercial Code, by adopting the "notice filing" system, had the purpose to recommend a method of protecting security interests which at the same time would give subsequent potential creditors and other interested persons information and procedures adequate to enable the ascertainment of the facts they needed to know. In this respect the completed Code reflects a decision of policy reached after several years' study and discussion by experts. We conceive our duty to be the making of an interpretation which will carry out the intention of the framers of uniform legislation which already has been enacted in twenty-five States. That the result of their policy decision may be asserted to favor certain types of creditors as against others or that a different policy could have been decided upon is quite beside the point.

The case at bar is, for all practical purposes, one of first impression under the Code. There seem to be no decisions anywhere which specifically deal with the situation presented to us.

* * *

The words, "All contents of luncheonette," including, as we have held, all equipment, were enough to put the plaintiff on notice to ascertain what those contents were. This is not a harsh result as to the plaintiff, to which, as we have indicated, § 9–312(4) made available a simple and sure procedure for completely protecting its purchase money security interest.

The order of the Appellate Division is reversed. Judgment for the defendant.

Priorities: Purchase Money Security Interest

IN RE ULTRA PRECISION INDUSTRIES, INC.

United States Court of Appeals, Ninth Circuit, 1974.
503 F.2d 414.

EAST, J.

National Acceptance Company of California (National) appeals from the two several orders of the District Court denying its Petition for Review and affirming the referee's two several rulings or orders that the security interest held by Community Bank (Bank) and Wolf Machinery Company (Wolf) in three large Rigid Hydro Copy Profiling Machines, numbered 5890 and 5910 (Bank) and machine numbered 5934 (Wolf), respectively, had priority over a conflicting security interest held by National. § 9–312(4) of the Uniform Commercial Code of California (Code). We affirm.

* * *

The pertinent facts are:

National loaned Ultra Precision Industries, Inc. (Ultra) $692,000, and to secure the repayment of that sum, Ultra on or about March 7, 1967, executed in favor of National a Chattel Mortgage Security Agreement covering specifically described equipment of Ultra. National perfected its security interest by timely filing a Financing Statement. The Chattel Mortgage Security Agreement and the Financing Statement contained the usual after-acquired equipment security clauses;

however, without reference to any specific property.

Subsequent to the acquisition of National's security interest and during 1967 and 1968, Ultra placed orders with Wolf for two of the machines, later identified as machines numbered 5890 and 5910. It was agreed between Ultra and Wolf that after those machines had been shipped to Ultra and installed, Ultra would be given an opportunity to test them in their operations during a reasonable testing period, and, further, that arrangements satisfactory to Ultra for outside financing was a condition precedent to the ultimate purchase of those machines. The machines were delivered to Ultra on April 30, 1968 and June 20, 1968, respectively, satisfactory testing was accomplished, outside financing obtained, and on July 31, 1968, Ultra and Wolf executed a Purchase Money Security Interest Conditional Sales Agreement (Security Interest Agreement) covering the sale of those two machines by Wolf to Ultra, and as a part of the outside financing arrangement, Wolf in consideration of the payment of $128,122.20 assigned the Security Interest Agreement to Bank. Bank's security interest was perfected by the filing of a Financing Statement on August 5, 1968.

In June, 1968, Ultra placed another order with Wolf for a similar machine, later identified as machine numbered 5934, under identical terms of testing and purchase as those for the purchase of the above numbered machines 5890 and 5910. The machine was delivered to Ultra on August 7, 1968, satisfactory testing was accomplished, outside financing obtained, and on October 23, 1968, Ultra and Wolf executed a similar Security Interest Agreement covering the sale of the machine numbered 5934 by Wolf to Ultra, and as a part of the outside financing arrangement, Wolf, for value received, assigned the Security Interest Agreement to C.I.T. Corporation. C.I.T. Corporation's security interest was perfected by the filing of a Financing Statement on October 30, 1968. On October 7, 1969, C.I.T. Corporation reassigned the Security Interest Agreement to Wolf when Ultra became bankrupt.

* * *

The priorities among the three security interests involved are determined by the application of § 9–312(4), which reads:

A purchase money security interest in collateral other than inventory has priority over a conflicting security interest in the same collateral *if the purchase money security interest is perfected at the time the debtor receives possession of the collateral or within 10 days thereafter.* (Emphasis added).

The sole issue presented by the facts and the contention of the parties on appeal is: On what dates did Ultra become "the debtor [receiving] possession of the collateral [the three respective machines]" within the meaning of § 9–312(4)?

* * *

Briefly stated, National contends that Ultra was its "debtor" in "possession of the collateral" at the moment it received physical delivery of the respective three machines, without regard to any agreement to the contrary between Wolf and Ultra as to the terms and conditions of the ultimate sale and purchase of the machines respectively; hence, the machines were within the grasp of the after-acquired property clause. Since the Security Interest Agreements held by Bank and Wolf were not perfected within ten days "thereafter" as commanded by § 9–312(4), they are unenforceable as against National's perfected security interest.

Bank and Wolf each contend that Ultra did not become their "debtor" in "possession of the collateral" (the three respective machines) until the terms and conditions of the proposed sales and the purchases thereof had been met and the Security Interest Agreement had been executed and delivered. We subscribe to that contention.

Section 9–105(1) of the Code provides:

(1) In this division unless the context otherwise requires:

(d) "Debtor" means the person who owes payment or other performance of the obligation secured. . . .

National urges that the term "debtor" as used in § 9–312(4) means the debtor under its

"conflicting security interest." Such an interpretation does violence to the clear language of the section, and such a thesis is inherently rejected under the rationale and holdings in [citation]. To us, the word "debtor" in § 9–312(4) means the debtor of the seller or holder of the "purchase money security interest in collateral" (the thing sold).

It is manifest that Ultra was not a "debtor" of Wolf and did not owe payment or other performance of the obligation secured unto Wolf until the moment of the execution and delivery of the Security Interest Agreements on July 31, 1968, and October 23, 1968, respectively. Suffice to say that prior to those dates, (a) Wolf held no definitive security interest in the machines which could be perfected by the filing of a Financing Statement, and (b) Ultra held no assignable legal interest in the machines which could fall into the grasp of National's after-acquired property security clause.

We hold that Ultra became the purchase money security interest "debtor [receiving] possession of the collateral [the three respective machines]" at the instant of the execution and delivery of the Security Interest Agreements, respectively, and not before; and, further, that since each of the Security Interest Agreements were timely perfected, the security interests of Wolf and Bank, respectively, are each prior and superior to the conflicting security interest held by National. [Citation.]

* * *

The record as a whole reveals good faith, above board, uninvolved commercial credit transactions, without any withholding on the part of or secret equities among the parties. National was in no way misled by any acts of Wolf or Bank giving rise to an estoppel, and National advanced no money or credit on the strength of Ultra's pre-Security Interest Agreement possession of the machines. Wolf was entitled to abide with the terms and conditions of the proposed sales and purchases of its machines and to perfect its ultimate Security Interest Agreements in accordance with § 9–312(4).

Affirmed.

Priorities: Buyer in the Ordinary Course of Business/Where to File

EXCHANGE BANK OF OSCEOLA v. JARRETT

Supreme Court of Montana, 1979.
180 Mont. 33, 588 P.2d 1006.

SHEEHY, J.

Plaintiff appeals from an order entered by the District Court, Custer County, granting defendant's motion to dismiss for failure to state a claim upon which relief could be granted. We reverse.

The material facts are not in dispute. On September 8, 1976, Daniel F. Holland purchased a Michigan tractor-scraper through the Exchange Bank of Osceola (bank), located in Kissimmee, Florida. The bank retained a security interest in the tractor to insure full payment of the $13,000.00 purchase price. The bank took the necessary steps to perfect its security interest under Florida's Commercial Code.

On February 1, 1977, Daniel F. Holland, without plaintiff's permission and in violation of the security agreement, sold the tractor-scraper to C.B. and O. Equipment Co. of Council Bluffs, Iowa. C.B. and O., an Iowa merchant dealing in farm implements, transported the tractor-scraper from Florida to Council Bluffs, Iowa. The record shows that the tractor arrived in Iowa on February 7, 1977.

On February 21, 1977, defendant, a Montana contractor, purchased the tractor-scraper from C.B. and O. for a good and valuable consideration. Defendant took possession of the tractor-scraper on or about February 21, 1977 and returned to Montana. The record indicates the tractor-scraper arrived in Miles City, Montana on March 9, 1977.

On April 4, 1977 (within four months from the date the tractor arrived in Iowa) the bank filed a financing statement in Iowa, pursuant to Iowa Code § 9–401. Thereafter, plaintiff filed the same financing statement with the Montana Secretary of State.

When Daniel F. Holland defaulted on his obligation to the bank, the bank instituted this action in the District Court, Custer County, to foreclose its security interest.

On November 4, 1977, the District Court entered the following order, dismissing plaintiff's complaint:

* * *

The defendant's motion to dismiss is based upon the following factual premise: An Iowa dealer sold certain equipment to the defendant, a Montana resident. The equipment was supplied to the Iowa dealer by a Florida company, who had given plaintiff a security interest, which was filed in Florida. The security interest agreement of plaintiff was filed in Iowa after the Iowa dealer had sold and delivered the equipment to the Montana purchaser.

The Court agrees with defendant's contention that Sections 9–307(1), 1–201(9) and 2–403(2) control and gives the purchaser title free of the security agreement filed in Iowa.

It is Ordered that defendant's motion to dismiss be granted.

* * *

Judgment finalizing the dismissal was signed on November 29, 1977. This appeal followed.

The sole issue for our determination is whether Spencer Jarrett purchased the tractor-scraper "free of" or "subject to" the bank's security interest.

It is agreed that the bank perfected its security interest in the tractor-scraper by filing the financing statement required by [U.C.C.] § 9–302. The Uniform Commercial Code contemplates the continued perfection of a security interest if there has been no intervening period when it was unperfected. [U.C.C.] § 9–303. A perfected security interest is generally not destroyed by the sale, exchange or other disposition of the collateral:

(2) Except where this chapter otherwise provides, a security interest continues in collateral notwithstanding sale, exchange or other disposition thereof by the debtor unless his action was authorized by the secured party in the security agreement or otherwise, and also continues in any identifiable proceeds including collections received by the debtor. [U.C.C.] § 9–306(2).

Since Daniel Holland sold the tractor without plaintiff's permission and in violation of the security agreement, it is clear that C.B. and O. purchased the tractor-scraper "subject to" the bank's security interest.

When C.B. and O. transported the tractor from Florida to Iowa, the continued existence of the bank's security interest was contingent on the provisions of Iowa's Commercial Code. Iowa Code § 9–103, provides:

d. When collateral is brought into and kept in this state while subject to a security interest perfected under the law of the jurisdiction from which the collateral was removed, the security interest remains perfected, but if action is required by Part 3 of this Article to perfect the security interest,

i. if the action is not taken before the expiration of the period of perfection in the other jurisdiction or the end of four months after the collateral is brought into this state, whichever period first expires, the security interest becomes unperfected at the end of that period and is thereafter deemed to have been unperfected as against a person who became a purchaser after removal;

ii. *if the action is taken before the expiration of the period specified in subparagraph (i), the security interest continues perfected thereafter,*

The courts uniformly hold that Section 9–103 gives a secured party a four-month grace period during which his security interest is protected without any further action on his part. . . .

Applying the provisions of Iowa Code § 9–103 to our fact pattern, it is obvious that the bank's security interest was viable at the time defendant purchased the tractor-scraper from C.B. and O. Equipment Company. The bank fully complied with section 9–103 by filing its financing statement in Iowa on April 4, 1977, well within the four-month period. Therefore, plaintiff's security interest continued unless Article 9 provides otherwise.

Defendant contends that Iowa Code § 9–307 allowed him to purchase the tractor-scraper "free of" plaintiff's security interest. Section 9–307 provides:

Protection of buyers of goods. 1. A buyer in ordinary course of business (subsection 9 of Section 1–201) other than a person buying farm products from a person engaged in farming operations takes free of a security interest *created by his seller* even though the security interest is perfected and even though the buyer knows of its existence.

In the present case, defendant Jarrett purchased in good faith and without knowledge that the sale to him was in violation of the bank's security interest. Defendant also purchased the tractor in the ordinary course from a person in the business of selling tractors, therefore, he was a "buyer in the ordinary course of business". Iowa Code § 1–201(9).

However, section 9–307 contains the further limitation that the security interest must be "created by his [defendant's] seller". This Court has never interpreted the "created by his seller" limitation. However, the landmark case in this area is *National Shawmut Bank of Boston v. Jones* [citation.]

Shawmut was a replevin action instituted to recover possession of a 1964 Dodge station wagon. The station wagon was originally purchased by a man named Robert Wever. To obtain the car, Wever had secured a loan from the plaintiff bank and had executed a security agreement using the car as collateral. Sometime thereafter, Wever traded or sold the wagon to a reputable dealer engaged in the business of selling new and used cars to the public. The dealer then sold the car to defendant. Neither the dealer nor the defendant knew of plaintiff's security interest.

While the defendant in Shawmut was obviously a "buyer in the ordinary course," the Court nonetheless allowed the bank to recover the automobile from him. The Shawmut Court held:

. . . defendant purchased in good faith without knowledge that the sale was in violation of the security interest of another and bought in the ordinary course from a person in the business of selling automobiles, he was a "buyer in the ordinary course of business" . . . . However, 9–307(1) permits him to take free only of "a security interest created by his seller". The security interest of the plaintiff was not created by . . . the defendant's seller, but by Wentworth Motor Co., Inc. *Defendant, therefore, does not take free of the plaintiff's security interest under this section.* [Citation.]

As in Shawmut, defendant's seller *did not* create plaintiff's security interest, therefore, defendant does not take the tractor "free of" plaintiff's security interest under Iowa Code § 9–307.

* * *

This Court recognizes that this is a harsh result, since the purchaser, on the date of purchase in Iowa, had no means to learn in Iowa that the property he purchased was subject to a security interest. It may be that legislative action is necessary to prevent such results in the future. Since we are bound by the enacted laws, and must give full faith and credit to the laws of our sister states, no other course is open to us here.

For the foregoing reasons, this cause is reversed and remanded to the District Court for further proceedings consistent with this decision.

Default

CONNECTICUT BANK & TRUST CO., N.A. v. INCENDY

Connecticut Supreme Court, 1988.
207 Conn. 15.

CALLAHAN, J.

The plaintiff, Connecticut Bank and Trust Company, N.A. (CBT), filed the instant appeal from a judgment of the trial court, * * *. It presents two interrelated issues of first impression for this court. First, whether notice given by a creditor to a debtor of a public sale of repossessed collateral which complies with [UCC] § 9–504(3) is sufficient notice for a subsequent private sale of the same collateral after the public sale has proven unsuccessful. Second, if notice of the sale is not sufficient, what is the effect of such insufficiency on the right of a creditor to obtain a deficiency judgment.

The relevant facts are not in dispute. On June 5, 1974, Connecticut Electric Products, Inc. (CEP), a manufacturer of plastic injected molded products, executed a promissory note in the amount of $103,500, which was made payable to CBT. To secure the note, CEP gave the bank security interests in CEP's inventory, accounts receivable, and machinery and equipment. As part of the financing arrangement, Victor Incendy and Jeanette Incendy, who were the officers and sole owners of the

capital stock in CEP, personally executed a written guaranty to the bank guaranteeing payment of the note and all other moneys advanced to CEP by CBT. To secure the note and as part of their guaranty, the Incendys executed a mortgage deed to the bank on real estate they owned in Norwalk. The mortgage deed was recorded in the Norwalk land records on June 7, 1974.

On June 5, 1974, the same day CEP executed the promissory note, CBT entered into an agreement with Thomas Industries, Inc. (Thomas), a company experienced in liquidating heavy machinery and equipment. Thomas agreed that, in the event of a default by CEP, it would pay to CBT not less than $145,000, minus amounts due to prior lienholders, in return for the right to dispose of the collateral in accordance with the Uniform Commercial Code.

Soon thereafter, CEP defaulted on the note. In November, 1974, CBT took possession of the collateral by a peaceable entry onto CEP's premises and contacted Thomas to effect its disposition. Thomas made arrangements for a public auction of the collateral to be held on January 25, 1975, on CEP's premises and publicly advertised the auction in a trade publication and by circulating brochures within the trade. The Incendys were given proper notice of the public auction and, in fact, attended. All of CEP's machinery and equipment were sold at the auction with the exception of one injection plastic molding machine and three horizontal molding presses. These four machines were withdrawn from the auction block allegedly because the bids received were insufficient to pay prior liens held by the Pennwalt Corporation and ITT Industrial Credit, Inc. The total proceeds realized from the public auction were $46,585.

Sometime after January 25, 1975, Thomas shipped the four unsold machines on consignment to the Gavlick Machinery Corporation (Gavlick), a used machinery dealer located in Bristol, for resale. The first time CBT became aware of the transfer to Gavlick was on April 8, 1975, when it received an accounting from Thomas indicating that two of the four machines had been sold for a total of $41,500.

CBT was informed that the remaining two machines had been sold for a total of $64,500 when it received a final report and accounting from Thomas in February, 1976. It is undisputed that the defendants did not receive any notice from CBT that the four machines had been sent to Gavlick for resale nor did they receive notice of a time after which the machines would be sold. The defendants did not know that a final disposition of the machinery had occurred until after CBT had initiated this lawsuit.

On December 18, 1979, CBT first made a written demand on the Incendys to pay the balance due and owing on the note which they had personally guaranteed. The defendants failed to honor the demand and CBT instituted this action on November 17, 1981, seeking to obtain a deficiency judgment against the Incendys and to foreclose its mortgage on their Norwalk real estate. In response, the defendants asserted . . . that CBT had failed to comply with the Uniform Commercial Code in that it had failed to provide the defendants with reasonable notice of the sale of the machines, and to dispose of the collateral in a commercially reasonable manner. * * * With regard to CBT's action, the referee found that it had failed to comply with the notice requirements of § 9–504(3) regarding the private sale of the four machines remaining unsold after the public auction. The referee further found that the private sale had not been conducted in a commercially reasonable manner and the amount received at the sale was therefore presumed to equal the balance of the debt owed, thus denying CBT a deficiency judgment.

Thereafter, the trial court, Lewis, J., adopted the findings and recommendations of the trial referee and rendered judgment in accordance therewith. On appeal, CBT challenges the trial court's rulings that the notice of the private sale was insufficient, and that the private sale was held in a commercially unreasonably manner. We find no error.

The first issued raised by CBT is whether the court erred in holding that the notice of the public sale was insufficient for purposes of the subsequent private sale of the collateral by Gavlick. It argues generally that notice of the unsuccessful public sale was sufficient notice for the subsequent private sale of the debtor's collateral because it complied with the "Letter and Spirit of the Uniform Commercial Code." We disagree.

The rights of a creditor or secured party to take possession of collateral after default and to dispose of it in a commercially reasonable manner are specifically provided for under the Uniform Commercial Code of this state. See §§ 9–503 and 9–504(1). Prior to disposition, however, the code specifically requires that "[u]nless collateral is perishable or threatens to decline speedily in value or is of a type customarily sold on a recognized market, reasonable notification of the time and place of any public sale or *reasonable notification* of the time after which *any private sale* or other intended disposition is to be made *shall* be sent by the secured party to the debtor. . . ." (Emphasis added [by court].) § 9–504(3). It is thus clear from a reading of § 9–504(3) that a debtor must be given reasonable notice of "any private sale," and not just private sales that occur in the absence of a prior unsuccessful public sale of the same collateral. CBT does not dispute the fact that no notices of the sales by Gavlick were ever given. Rather, it argues that proper notice of the public auction constituted sufficient notice of the subsequent private sale.

* * *

In each case noted, the court held that the creditor's failure to have given notice of a subsequent private sale of unauctioned collateral amounted to noncompliance with the notice requirements of § 9–504(3) of the Uniform Commercial Code, despite the fact that the debtor had received proper notice of a prior unsuccessful public sale. [Citations.] The basic rationales for these holdings are that (a) the mandatory nature of the notice provisions of § 9–504(3) of the Uniform Commercial Code require that when a creditor *elects* the remedy of repossession and subsequent sale, it is the creditor's obligation to notify the debtor and it is the creditor's burden to establish the reasonableness of such notice, and (b) the notice provisions were specifically adopted for the benefit of the debtor, to protect the debtor's interest in his statutory right to redeem the collateral, thereby helping to ensure that the best possible price will be obtained for the collateral, that the sale will be conducted in a commercially reasonable manner, and that the debtor will immediately be placed on notice of the possibility of a deficiency for which he may ultimately be held liable.

* * *

CBT next claims that, despite the absence of a proper notice, the sales of the four machines were, nevertheless, conducted in a commercially reasonable manner, thus entitling it to a deficiency judgment. Specifically, it argues that the sales by Gavlick were commercially reasonable because: (1) CBT made a good faith attempt to dispose of the collateral to the parties' mutual best advantage; (2) the collateral was sold through recognized dealers; and (3) the price obtained for the four machines exceeded the amounts bid at the public auction. These arguments assume that CBT is entitled to a deficiency judgment despite its failure to comply with the notice requirements of the code.

As indicated in the state trial referee's proposed memorandum of decision, there are three divergent views regarding the right to recover a deficiency judgment when the creditor fails to provide the required notice for the disposition of the collateral. * * * The three views are characterized as (1) the set-off rule, (2) the absolute bar rule, and (3) the rebuttable presumption rule. [Citation.]

Under the set-off rule, a minority view, a secured party who fails to give notice to the debtor as required by § 9–504(3) may, nevertheless, obtain a deficiency judgment subject to a reduction or set-off under § 9–507(1) for any loss suffered by the debtor as a result of the secured party's failure to comply with the code. Under this rule, it is the debtor's burden to show that a violation of the code has occurred and that a loss resulted therefrom. [Citations.] It does not seem just, however, to require the debtor to prove that he suffered a loss when it was the creditor who failed to adhere to the code.

The absolute bar rule holds that a secured party who fails to comply strictly with the notice provisions of the code is absolutely barred from recovering a deficiency judgment even when the disposition of the collateral was otherwise made in a commercially reasonable manner. [Citations.] These jurisdictions treat the notification requirements of § 9–504(3) of the Uniform Commercial Code as a mandatory condition precedent to a secured creditor's right to recover a deficiency, and thus require strict statutory compliance. [Citations.]

* * *

In rejecting the application of the absolute bar rule, the Nebraska Supreme Court stated: "No sound policy requires us to inject a drastic punitive element into a commercial context." [Citation.] We agree. * * *

We, therefore, adopt what we think is the better view and that applied by the trial referee below and by two lower courts of this state, which is known as the "rebuttable presumption" rule. [Citations.] Under this rule, a secured party who has failed to give proper notice to the debtor is not absolutely barred from recovering a deficiency judgment. Rather, in the absence of proper notice, a presumption arises in favor of the debtor that the collateral was worth at least the amount of the debt. The burden then shifts to the secured party to establish by a preponderance of the evidence the amount that should reasonably have been obtained through a sale conducted in accordance with the "commercially reasonable" requirements of the code. [Citations.] * * *

To meet this burden the secured party must demonstrate that each and every aspect of the sale was conducted in a "commercially reasonable" manner. See § 9–504(3). Generally, this requires evidence of such things as the amount of advertising done, the number of people contacted, normal commercial practices in disposing of the particular collateral, the length of time between the repossession and the sale, whether any deterioration in the collateral has occurred, the number of bids received, and the price obtained. [Citations.]

The record before this court is devoid of evidence demonstrating that the private sales by CBT through Gavlick were conducted in a commercially reasonable manner. In fact, the record lacks any evidence regarding the actual sales themselves. The only facts apparent from the record are that the four machines were sold by Gavlick, which was a used machinery dealer, sometime between January 25, 1975, and February, 1976, for a total value of $106,000. * * *

CBT argues that it proved that the disposition of the machines was accomplished in a commercially reasonable manner simply because they were sold through Gavlick, which was a recognized used machinery dealer. We disagree. * * *

Accordingly, we find that the trial court did not err in holding that CBT failed to demonstrate that the private sales of the four machines had been conducted in a commercially reasonable manner as required by § 9–504(3).

Alternatively, CBT argues that the details regarding the method and manner of the private sales of the collateral are irrelevant here because the prices ultimately obtained were fair given the fact that they exceeded the amounts bid at the public sale. In addition, CBT argues that "price is the single most important factor in determining whether a section 9–504 sale has been commercially reasonable."

While the price received at the sale of the collateral is important and one of the relevant factors in determining whether the sale was commercially reasonable, alone it is insufficient to establish that the sale was commercially reasonable or to establish the reasonable value of the collateral sold. [Citations.] Rather, " 'it is only where the sale is conducted according to the requirements of the code [i.e., commercially reasonable] that the account received or bid at a sale of collateral is evidence of its true value in an action to recover a deficiency. [Citations.] In any event, the burden rests upon the secured party to establish the fair market value of the collateral at the time of the sale by presenting credible and objective evidence of the value other than the price received or the opinions of its own agents and employees. [Citations.] * * *

After having considered the conflicting evidence regarding the values of the machines, the trial referee held that it "was unable to determine the fair market value of the fair or reasonable value of the collateral at the time of the sale," because the opinions of Gagliardi and Incendy "were not adequately reinforced by independent evidence which would afford them sufficient weight for acceptance by the trier."

* * *

Therefore, we hold that CBT failed to demonstrate what the reasonable value of the machines was at the time of the sales or that the sales of the machines were conducted in a commercially reasonable manner. Thus the trial court properly denied the deficiency judgment sought by CBT.

QUESTIONS

1. Name and define the various kinds of collateral.

2. Define attachment, its purpose, and its requirements.

3. Define perfection and the various methods of perfecting.

4. Discuss the priorities among the various parties who may have competing interests in collateral.

5. Discuss the rights and remedies of the parties to a security agreement after default by the debtor.

PROBLEMS

1. Victor sells to Bonnie a refrigerator under a conditional sales contract for $600 payable in monthly installments of $30 for twenty months. The refrigerator is installed in the kitchen of Bonnie's apartment. There is no filing of any financing statement. Assume that after Bonnie has made the first three monthly payments:

(a) Bonnie moves from her apartment and sells the refrigerator in place to the new occupant for $350 cash. What are the rights of Victor?

(b) Bonnie is adjudicated bankrupt, and her trustee in bankruptcy claims the refrigerator. What are the rights of the parties?

2. On January 2, Burt asked Logan to loan him money "against my diamond ring." Logan agreed to do so. To guard against intervening liens, Logan received permission to record his interest, and Burt and Logan signed a security agreement giving Logan an interest in the ring. Burt also signed a financing statement which Logan properly filed on January 3. On January 4, Burt borrowed money from Tillo pledging his ring to secure the debt. Tillo took possession of the ring and paid Burt the money on the same day. The next day, January 5, Logan loaned Burt the money under the assumption that Burt still had the ring.

Who has priority, Logan or Tillo?

3. Joanna takes a security interest in the equipment in Jason Store and files a financing statement claiming "equipment and all after-acquired equipment." Berkeley later sells Jason Store a cash register on conditional sale and (a) files nine days after Jason receives the register, or (b) files fifteen days after Jason receives the register. If Jason fails to pay both Joanna and Berkeley and they foreclose their security interests, who has priority on the cash register? What would occur if Jason was a consumer and purchased goods for his own personal use?

4. Finley Motor Company sells an automobile to Sara and retains a security interest in the automobile. The automobile is insured, and Finley is named beneficiary. The automobile is totally destroyed in an accident, and three days later Sara files a petition in bankruptcy. As between Finley and Sara's trustee in bankruptcy, who is entitled to the insurance proceeds?

5. On September 5, a widow Wanda who occasionally teaches piano and organ in her home, purchased an electric organ from Murphy's music store for $4,800, trading in her old organ for $1,200 and promising in writing to pay the balance at $120 per month and granting to Murphy a security interest in the property in terms consistent with and incorporating provisions of the UCC. A financing statement covering the transaction was also properly filled out and signed, and Murphy properly filed it. Wanda did not make the December or January payments, and Murphy went to her home to collect the payments or take the organ. Finding no one home and the door unlocked, he went in and took the organ. Two hours later, Tia, a third party and the present occupant of the house who had purchased the organ for her own use, stormed into Murphy's store demanding return of the organ, exhibiting a bill of sale from Wanda to Tia dated December 15, listing the organ and other furnishings in the house.

(a) What are the rights of Murphy, Tia, and Wanda?

(b) Would your answer change if Murphy did not file a financing statement? Why?

(c) Would your answer change if the organ was principally used to give lessons?

6. On May 1, Lincoln lends Donaldson $20,000 and receives from Donaldson his promissory note for this amount due in two years and takes a security interest in the machinery and equipment in Donaldson's factory. A proper financing statement is filed with respect to the security agreement. On August 1, upon Lincoln's request, Donaldson executes an addendum to the security agreement covering after-acquired machinery and equipment in Donaldson's factory. A second financing statement is filed covering the addendum. In September, Donaldson acquires $5,000 worth of new equipment from Thompson which Donaldson installs in his factory. In December Carter, a judgment creditor of Donaldson, causes an attachment to issue against the new equipment. What are the rights of Lincoln, Donaldson, Carter, and Thompson? What can the parties do to best protect themselves?

7. Anita bought a television set from Bertrum for her own personal use. Bertrum was out of conditional sales contracts and showed Anita a form he had executed with Nathan, another consumer. Anita and Bertrum orally agreed to the terms of the form. Anita subsequently defaults on payment, and Bertrum seeks to repossess the television. Decision? Would the result differ if Bertrum had filed a financing statement?

8. Aaron bought a television set for his own personal use from Penny. Aaron properly signed a security agreement and paid Penny twenty-five dollars down as required by their agreement. Penny did not file, and subsequently Aaron sells the television to Clark, Aaron's neighbor, for $300 for Clark to use in his hotel lobby.

(a) When Aaron fails to make the January and February payments, may Penny repossess the television from Clark?

(b) What if instead of Aaron's selling the television set to Clark, a judgment creditor levied (sought possession) on the television? Who would prevail?

(c) What if Clark intended to use the television set in his home? Who would prevail?

9. Jones bought a used car from the A–Herts Car Rental System, who regularly sold its used equipment at the end of its fiscal year. First National Bank of Roxboro had previously obtained a perfected security interest in the car based upon its financing of A–Herts' automobiles. Upon A–Herts' failure to pay, First National is seeking to repossess the car from Jones. Decision?

10. On May 1, Charlie purchased on credit a refrigerator for his own personal use from XYZ for $600 and gave XYZ a security interest in the refrigerator. On May 5, Charlie borrowed $500 from the Friendly Finance Company and gave Friendly a security interest in the refrigerator. Friendly properly perfected its security interest by filing. On May 15, one of Charlie's creditors obtained a judgment lien against Charlie and properly recorded the lien. On May 20th, after Charlie had failed to make his payment on the refrigerator, XYZ properly filed a financing statement. On May 30, Charlie sold the refrigerator at a yard sale to one of his neighbors for $200. All are claiming priority to the refrigerator. Who will prevail? Why?

11. Standridge purchased a 1965 Chevrolet automobile from Billy Deavers, an agent of Walker Motor Company. According to the sales contract,

the balance due after trade-in allowance was $282.50, to be paid in twelve weekly installments. Standridge's version is that he was unable to make the second payment and that Billy Deavers orally agreed that he could make two payments the next week. The day after the double payment was due, Standridge still had not paid. That day, Ronnie Deavers, Billy's brother, went to Standridge's place of employment to repossess the car. Rather than consenting to the repossession, Standridge drove the car to the Walker Motor Company's place of business and tendered the overdue payments. The Deavers refused to accept the late payment and instead demanded the entire unpaid balance. Standridge could not do so. The Deavers therefore "blocked-in" Standridge's car with another car and told him he could just "walk his _____ home." Standridge then brought suit, seeking damages for the Deavers' wrongful repossession of his car. The Deavers deny that they granted Standridge permission to make a double payment; that Standridge tendered the double payment; and that they rejected it. They claim that he made no payment and, therefore, they were entitled to repossess the car. Decision?

12. Plant Reclamation Company sold equipment to Amex-Protein Development Corporation on an open account. Later Plant Reclamation substituted a promissory note for the open account indebtedness and caused a financing statement to be signed and filed that provided notice of the parties' intention to create a security interest in the property sold as collateral for the note. The note stated that it was secured by a security interest in the property "as per invoices." Amex-Protein subsequently declared bankruptcy, and the validity of Plant Reclamation's security interest in the property is now in issue. The trustee asserts that the promissory note does not constitute a valid security agreement and questions the adequacy of the description of the collateral contained in that instrument. Decision?

13. Eggeman and his wife gave Western National Bank a $41,000 promissory note securing the debt by a mortgage on two adjoining tracts of land. Some time later, Eggeman gave the bank an additional $8,625 note, which was secured by "inventory and accounts receivable" described more fully in the security agreement. When Eggeman defaulted on both notes, Western National filed a complaint against Eggeman requesting the sale of the mortgaged land in satisfaction of the balance due on the first note and the sale of the collateral in satisfaction of the balance due on the second note. The judgment authorizing the foreclosure sale provided, with respect to the second note, "that the collateral listed in the security agreement be sold under and pursuant to the judgment of this Court." The inventory and accounts receivable were not listed or itemized in the judgment or at the sale. When the sale was held, both tracts of land, the inventory, and the accounts receivable were offered only as a whole and in one group. They were purchased by James T. Frost for $67,500. Eggeman moved to vacate the sale, claiming that the remedy taken by Western National with reference to the second note was not pursuant to law. Western National countered that the sale was proper as a judicial sale. Decision?

Chapter 39

SURETYSHIP

Nature and Formation
Rights of Surety
Defenses of Surety

IT is common in many business transactions involving the extension of credit for the creditor to require that someone in addition to the debtor promise to fulfill the obligation. This promisor generally is known as a surety. Sureties are commonly used in contracts involving minors, so that there is a party with full contractual capacity responsible for the obligations arising from the contract. Sureties are often used in *addition* to security to reduce further the risks involved in the extension of credit. Sureties are used *instead* of security interests when security is not available or use of a secured transaction is too expensive or inconvenient. Sureties are also frequently utilized by employers to protect against losses caused by defalcations of employees, as well as in construction contracts for commercial buildings to bond the performance of the contract. Similarly, it is commonly required by statute that many contracts for work to be done for governmental entities have the added protection of a surety. Premiums for compensated sureties exceed $1 billion annually in the United States.

NATURE AND FORMATION

A **surety** promises to answer for the payment of a debt or the performance of a duty owed to one person (called the **creditor**) by another (the **principal debtor**) upon the *failure* of the principal debtor to make payment or otherwise perform the obligation. Thus, the suretyship relationship involves three parties—the principal debtor, the creditor, and the surety—and three contractual obligations. When there is more than one person bound for the same debt of a principal debtor they are **cosureties.**

The creditor's rights against the principal debtor are determined by the contract between them. The creditor may also realize upon any collateral securing the principal debtor's performance that the creditor or the surety holds. In addition, the creditor may proceed against the surety if the principal debtor defaults. If the surety is an **absolute surety,** then the creditor may hold the surety liable as soon as the principal debtor defaults. The creditor need *not* first proceed against the principal debtor. If the surety is a **condi-**

tional guarantor of collection he is liable only upon the creditor's *first* exhausting his legal remedies against the principal debtor. Thus, a conditional guarantor of collection is liable if the creditor first obtains a judgment against the principal debtor and is unable to collect upon the judgment.

A surety who is required to pay the creditor for the principal debtor's obligation is entitled to be exonerated (relieved of liability) and reimbursed by the principal debtor. In addition, the surety is subrogated to (assumes) the rights of the creditor and has a right of contribution from cosureties (see Figure 39–1). These rights of sureties are discussed more fully below.

Although in theory a distinction is drawn between a surety and a guarantor, the two terms are used almost synonymously in common usage. Strictly speaking, a surety is bound with the principal debtor as a primary obligor and usually, although not necessarily, on the same instrument, whereas the guarantor is separately or collaterally bound to pay if the principal debtor does not. For convenience, the term *surety* will be used to include both of these terms because the rights

and duties of a surety and a guarantor are almost indistinguishable.

See United States v. Tilleraas.

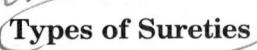

Types of Sureties

A suretyship arrangement is frequently used by creditors seeking to reduce the risk of default by their debtors. For example, Philco Developers, a closely held corporation, applies to Caldwell Bank, a lending institution, for a loan. After scrutinizing the assets and financial prospects of Philco, the lender refuses to extend credit unless Simpson, the sole shareholder of Philco, promises to repay the loan if Philco does not. Simpson agrees and Caldwell Bank makes the loan. Simpson's undertaking is that of a surety. Similarly, Philco wishes to purchase goods on credit from Bird Enterprises, the seller, who agrees to extend credit to Philco only if it obtains an acceptable surety. Simpson agrees to pay Bird Enterprises for the goods if Philco does not. Simpson is a surety. In each of these examples, the effect of the surety's promise is to give the creditor recourse for payment against two persons—the principal debtor

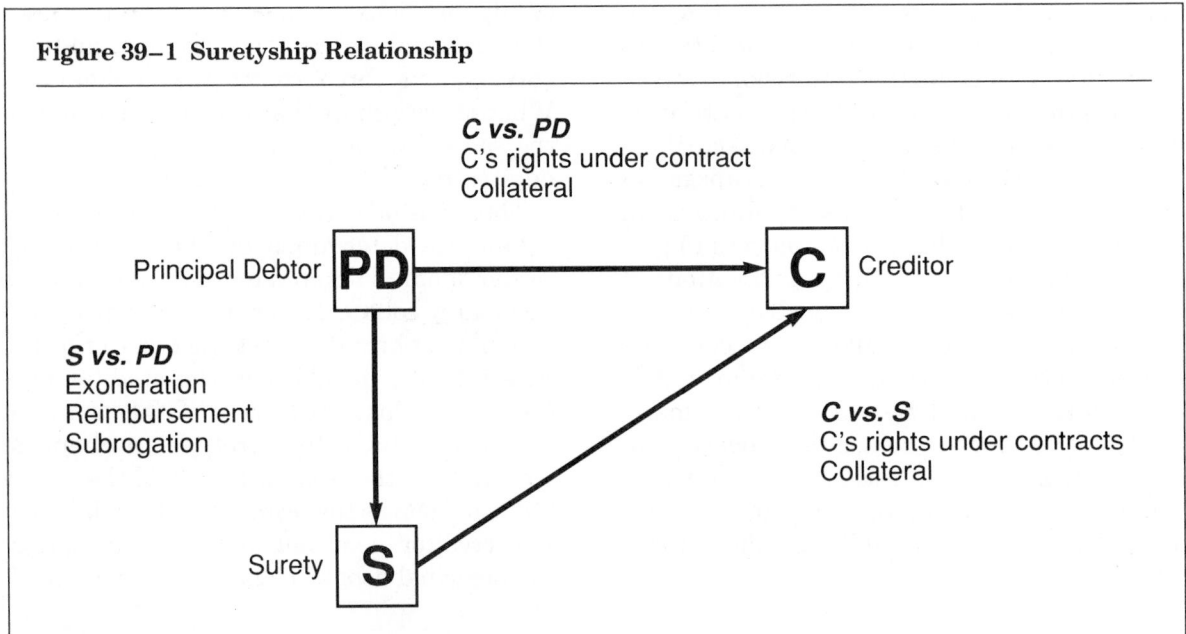

Figure 39–1 Suretyship Relationship

and the surety—instead of one, thereby reducing the creditor's risk of loss.

Another common instance of a suretyship relation arises when an owner of property subject to a mortgage sells the property to a purchaser who expressly **assumes the mortgage.** By assuming the obligation, the purchaser becomes the principal debtor and is personally obligated to pay the seller's debt to the lender. The seller nevertheless remains liable to the lender and is a surety on the obligation assumed by the purchaser (see Figure 39–2). If the purchaser does not assume the mortgage but simply takes the property **"subject to"** the mortgage, the purchaser is not personally liable for the mortgage nor is he a surety for the mortgage obligation. In this case, the purchaser's exposure to loss is limited to the value of the property. Although the mortgagee creditor may foreclose against the property, he may not hold the purchaser personally liable for the debt.

In addition to the more general types of sureties, there are numerous specialized kinds of suretyship, the most important of which are (1) fidelity, (2) performance, (3) official, and (4) judicial. **Fidelity bonds** are undertakings by a surety to protect an employer against the dishonesty of an employee. **Performance bonds** guarantee the performance of the terms and conditions of a contract. These bonds are used frequently in the construction industry to protect the owner

from losses that may result from the contractor's failure to perform the building contract. Statutes commonly require that a public officer furnish a bond for the faithful performance of her duties. Such bonds are called **official bonds** and obligate the surety for all losses caused by the officer's negligence or non-performance of her duties. **Judicial bonds** are provided on behalf of a party to a judicial proceedings to cover losses caused by delay or deprivation of use of property resulting from the institution of the action. In criminal proceedings, the purpose of a judicial bond, called a **bail bond,** is to assure the appearance of the defendant in court.

Formation

The suretyship relationship is contractual and must satisfy all the usual elements of a contract, including offer and acceptance, consideration, capacity of the parties, and legality of object. No particular words are required to constitute a contract of suretyship or guaranty.

As discussed in Chapter 14, the contractual promise of a surety to the creditor must be in writing to be enforceable under the statute of frauds. This requirement applies only to collateral promises and is subject to the exception called the *main purpose doctrine.* Under this doctrine, if the leading object (main purpose) of the promisor (surety) is to

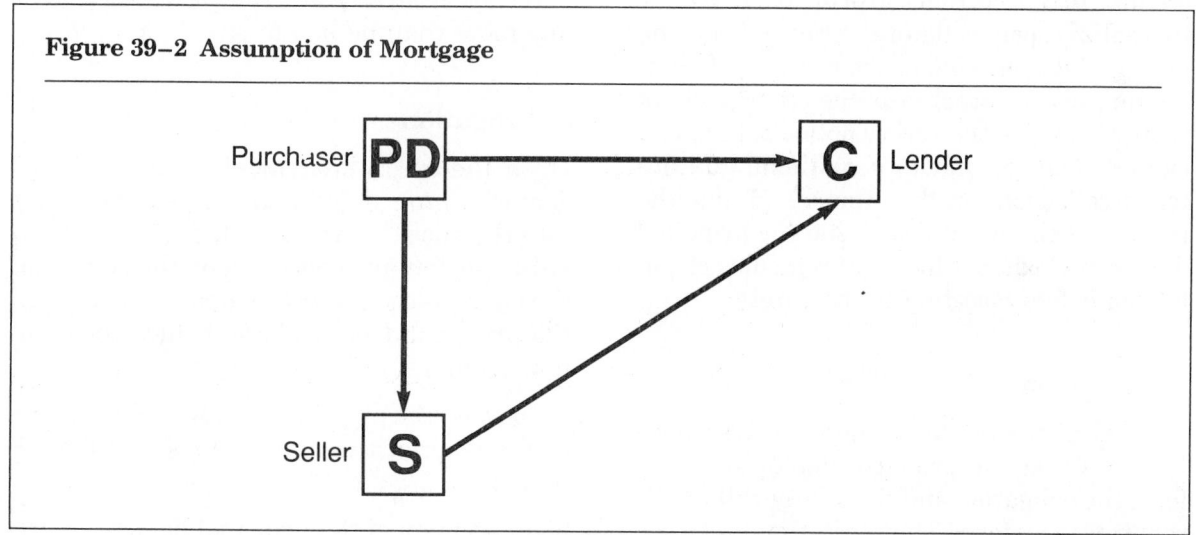

Figure 39–2 Assumption of Mortgage

Purchaser **PD** → **C** Lender

Seller **S**

obtain an economic benefit that he did not previously enjoy, then the promise is *not* within the statute of frauds.

The promise of a surety is *not* binding without consideration. The surety's promise is usually supported by the same consideration that supports the principal debtor's promise because the surety's promise is generally made to induce the creditor to confer a benefit upon the principal debtor. Thus, if Constance lends money to Philip Drake upon Sally's promise to act as a surety, Constance's extension of credit is the consideration to support not only Drake's promise to repay the loan but also Sally's suretyship undertaking. If the surety's promise is made *subsequent* to the principal debtor's receipt of the creditor's consideration, however, the surety's promise must be supported by new consideration. Accordingly, if Constance has already sold goods on credit to Drake, a subsequent guaranty by Sally will not be binding unless new consideration is given.

RIGHTS OF SURETY

Upon the principal debtor's default, the surety has a number of rights against the principal debtor, third parties, and cosureties. These rights include (1) exoneration, (2) reimbursement, (3) subrogation, and (4) contribution. As discussed above, a surety or absolute guarantor has *no* right to compel the creditor to collect from the principal debtor or to realize upon collateral provided by the principal debtor. Unless the contract of suretyship provides otherwise, the creditor is *not* required to give the surety notice of the principal debtor's default. A conditional guarantor of collection, on the other hand, has the right that the creditor first sue the principal debtor and exhaust his legal remedies of collection before resorting to the surety.

Exoneration

The ordinary expectation in a suretyship relation is that the principal debtor will perform the obligation and the surety will not be required to perform. Therefore, the surety has the right to require that his principal debtor pay the creditor when the obligation is due. This right of the surety against the principal debtor is called the right of **exoneration** and is enforceable at equity. If the principal debtor fails to pay the creditor when the debt is due, the surety may obtain a decree ordering the principal debtor to pay the creditor. The surety's remedy of exoneration is against the principal debtor and in no way affects the creditor's right to proceed against the surety.

A surety also has a right of exoneration against his cosureties. When the principal debtor's obligation becomes due, each surety owes every other cosurety the duty to pay her proportionate share of the principal debtor's obligation to the creditor. Accordingly, a surety may bring an action in equity against his cosureties to obtain an order requiring them to pay their share of the debt to the creditor.

Reimbursement

When a surety pays the creditor upon the default of the principal debtor, the surety has the right of **reimbursement** (repayment) against the principal debtor. The surety, however, has no right to reimbursement until he actually has made payment, and then only to the extent of the payment. Thus, if a surety makes an advantageous negotiation of a defaulted obligation and settles it at a compromise figure less than the original sum, he may not recover from the principal debtor any more than he had to pay.

Subrogation

Upon the surety's payment of the principal debtor's *entire* obligation, the surety "steps into the shoes" of the creditor. This is called **subrogation** and confers upon the surety all the rights the creditor has against or through the principal debtor. These include the creditor's rights

1. against the principal debtor, including the creditor's priorities in a bankruptcy proceeding;

2. in security of the principal debtor;

3. against third parties who are also obligated on the principal debtor's obligation, such as co-makers; and

4. against cosureties.

Contribution

When more than one surety exists, the cosureties are *jointly and severally* liable for the principal debtor's default up to the amount of each surety's undertaking. The creditor may proceed against any or all of the cosureties and collect the entire amount of the default from any of them, limited to the amount that surety has agreed to guarantee. As a result, it is possible that one cosurety may pay the creditor the entire amount of the principal debtor's obligation.

When a surety pays her principal debtor's obligation, she is entitled to have her cosureties pay to her their proportionate share of the obligation paid. This right of **contribution** arises when a surety has paid more than her proportionate share of the debt, even though the cosureties originally were not aware of each other or were bound on separate instruments. All that is required is that they are sureties for the same principal debtor and the same obligation. The right and extent of contribution is determined by contractual agreement among the cosureties. If there is no agreement, sureties obligated for equal amounts share equally; where they are obligated for varying amounts, the proportion of the debt that each surety must contribute is determined by proration according to each surety's undertaking. For example, if X, Y, and Z are cosureties for PD to C in the amounts of $5,000, $10,000, and $15,000 respectively, which totals $30,000, then X's contributive share is one-sixth ($5,000/$30,000), Y's share is one-third ($10,000/30,000), and Z's share is one-half ($15,000/$30,000).

See Collins v. Throckmorton.

DEFENSES OF SURETY

The obligations owed to the creditor by the principal debtor and the surety both arise out of contracts. Accordingly, the usual contractual defenses are applicable, such as those that result from (1) the nonexistence of the principal debtor's obligation, (2) a discharge of the principal debtor's obligation, (3) a modification of the principal debtor's contract, or (4) a variation of the surety's risk. Some of these defenses are available only to the principal debtor, some only to the surety, and others are available to both parties. See Figure 39–3.

Personal Defenses of Principal Debtor

Some defenses that a principal debtor may assert against the creditor are available *only* to him and thus are called personal defenses of the principal debtor. The principal debtor's **incapacity** due to infancy or mental incompetency is a defense for the principal debtor but may *not* be used by the surety. If, however, the principal debtor disaffirms the contract *and* returns the consideration he received from the creditor, then the surety is discharged from his liability. A discharge of the principal debtor's obligation in **bankruptcy** also does not discharge the surety's liability to the creditor on that obligation. In addition, the surety may not use as a **setoff** any claim that the principal debtor has against the creditor.

Personal Defenses of Surety

Those defenses that only the surety may assert are called personal defenses of the surety. The surety may use as a defense his own **incapacity,** noncompliance with the **statute of frauds,** and the absence of mutual assent or consideration to support the surety's obligation. **Fraud** or **duress** practiced by the creditor upon the surety is a defense for the surety. Although as a general rule nondisclosure of material facts by the creditor to the surety is not fraud, there are two important exceptions. If the prospective surety requests information, the creditor must disclose it, and concealment of material facts will constitute fraud. Second, if the creditor knows, or should know, that the surety is being deceived, the

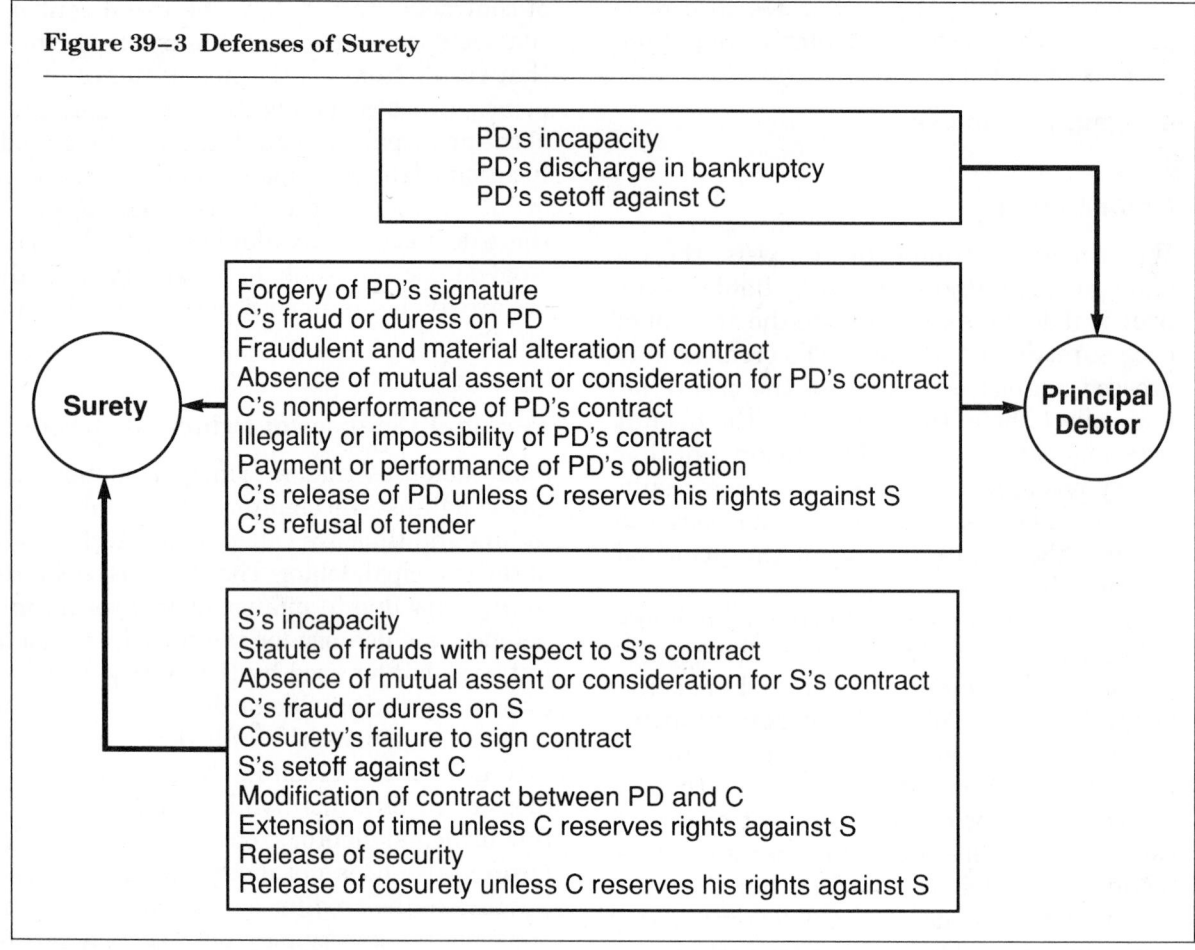

Figure 39–3 Defenses of Surety

PD's incapacity
PD's discharge in bankruptcy
PD's setoff against C

Forgery of PD's signature
C's fraud or duress on PD
Fraudulent and material alteration of contract
Absence of mutual assent or consideration for PD's contract
C's nonperformance of PD's contract
Illegality or impossibility of PD's contract
Payment or performance of PD's obligation
C's release of PD unless C reserves his rights against S
C's refusal of tender

Surety

Principal Debtor

S's incapacity
Statute of frauds with respect to S's contract
Absence of mutual assent or consideration for S's contract
C's fraud or duress on S
Cosurety's failure to sign contract
S's setoff against C
Modification of contract between PD and C
Extension of time unless C reserves rights against S
Release of security
Release of cosurety unless C reserves his rights against S

creditor is under a duty to disclose this information, and nondisclosure is considered fraud on the surety. Fraud on the part of the principal debtor may *not* be asserted against the creditor if the creditor is unaware of the fraud. Similarly, duress exerted by the principal debtor upon the surety is not a defense against the creditor.

A surety is not liable if an intended cosurety, as shown by the contract instrument, does not sign. A surety may **set off** his claims against the creditor if the creditor is solvent. If the creditor is insolvent, then the surety may use his claim against the creditor only if the principal debtor is also insolvent.

If the principal debtor and the creditor enter into a binding **modification** of their contract, the surety may be discharged unless he assents to the modification. The courts vary in their approach to modifications made without the surety's assent. If the surety is uncompensated (an **accommodation surety**), the courts are more likely to discharge him for any material modification, even one that does not prejudice his rights. When a surety is compensated, a number of courts require the alteration to be both material and prejudicial to the interests of the surety. *See United States v. Reliance Insurance Co.*

Such modifications include valid and binding extensions of the time of payment *unless* the creditor expressly reserves his rights against the surety. An extension of time with reservation is construed as only an agreement by the creditor not to sue the principal debtor for the period of the extension. Accordingly, the surety's rights of exoneration, reimbursement, and subrogation are *not* postponed. Thus, the surety's risk is not changed and he is not discharged.

If the creditor releases or impairs the value of the security, the surety is discharged to the extent of the value of the security released or impaired. Similarly, if the creditor releases a cosurety, the other cosureties are discharged to the extent of the contributive share of the surety released. If the creditor reserves his rights against the remaining cosureties, however, the release is considered a promise not to sue. As a result, the remaining cosureties are not discharged.

Defenses of Both Surety and Principal Debtor

A number of defenses are available to both the surety and the principal debtor. Where the principal debtor's signature on an instrument is **forged** or the creditor has exerted **fraud** or **duress** upon the principal debtor, neither the principal debtor nor the surety is liable. Likewise, if the contract instrument is fraudulently and **materially altered** by the creditor, both the principal debtor and the surety are discharged.

The absence of mutual assent or consideration to support the principal debtor's obligation is a defense for both the principal debtor and the surety. In addition, **illegality** and **impossibility** of performance of the principal debtor's contract are also defenses to both the surety and the principal debtor.

Payment or **performance** of the principal debtor's obligation discharges both the principal debtor and the surety. If the principal debtor owes several debts to the creditor and makes a payment to the creditor without directions as to which debt to apply payment, the creditor is free to apply it to any debt. For example, Pam Davis owes Charles two debts, one for $5,000 and another for $10,000. Susan is a surety on the $10,000 debt. Davis sends Charles a payment in the amount of $3,500. If Davis directs Charles to apply the payment to the $10,000 debt, Charles must apply it accordingly. Otherwise Charles may, if he pleases, apply the payment to the $5,000 debt.

If the creditor **releases** the principal debtor, then the surety is also discharged unless the surety consents to the release. If the creditor reserves his rights against the surety, however, the surety is *not* discharged. The release with reservation is construed as a promise not to sue, which leaves the surety's rights against the principal debtor unimpaired. Therefore, the surety is not discharged. This rule has been well explained in *Dean v. Rice*, 63 Kan. 691, 66 P. 992 (1901):

As a general rule an agreement between the creditor and principal for an extension of time to the principal in which to pay the debt, without the knowledge or consent of the surety will operate as a release of the surety. An important exception to the rule is that if the creditor, at the time of the extension, reserves his remedies against the surety the latter will not be discharged from liability.

The principal reason for the release of sureties in such cases is that the postponement of payment varies the contract relation and deprives the surety of the right to pay the debt when it becomes due and to have the immediate recourse on the principal. When a creditor ties his own hands and grants an indulgence which prevents a surety from obtaining that indemnity against a principal which the law gives him, the surety is necessarily prejudiced and should be released. If, however, a creditor explicitly reserves all remedies against the surety, it rebuts the presumption of a purpose to release the surety, and, in effect, it is an agreement between creditor and principal that the creditor may sue the surety, who in turn may then proceed against the principal. If the surety is not deprived of the protection and indemnity which the law affords him against a principal he is not prejudiced and is not entitled to be released from the obligation which he has undertaken.

The creditor's refusal to accept **tender** of payment or performance by either the principal debtor or the surety completely discharges the surety. Tender of payment by the principal debtor refused by the creditor, however, does *not* discharge the principal debtor. The effect of such refusal is to stop further accrual of interest on the debt and to deprive the creditor of court costs on a subsequent suit by him to recover the amount due.

CASES

Nature and Formation

UNITED STATES v. TILLERAAS

United States Court of Appeals, Sixth Circuit, 1983.
709 F.2d 1088.

WELLFORD, J.

Defendant-appellant, Elizabeth Tilleraas, applied for and received three student loans totalling $3,500.00 under the Federal Insured Student Loan Program (FISLP) of the Higher Education Act of 1965, 20 U.S.C. § 1071, *et seq.* These loans were secured by three promissory notes executed, respectively, on September 4, 1969, June 18, 1970, and October 5, 1970, in favor of Dakota National Bank & Trust Co., Fargo, North Dakota. Under terms of these student loans, periodic payments were required commencing twelve months after Tilleraas ceased to carry at least one-half of a full-time academic workload at an eligible institution. 20 U.S.C. § 1077(a)(2)(B). Her student status terminated on January 28, 1971, and the first installment payment thus became due January 28, 1972. Appellant never made any payment on any of her loans. The United States insured to the lender bank the repayment in event of any failure to pay by the borrower under the terms of the FISLP.

Under 20 U.S.C. § 1080(e)(2)(B), it is provided:

the term "default" includes only such defaults as have existed for . . .

(B) one hundred eighty days in the case of a loan which is repayable in less frequent [than monthly] installments.

The first payment due on the loans was in "default" within the meaning of the law on or about July 27, 1972, one hundred and eighty days after the failure to make the first installment payment had continued to exist. It was not until December 17, 1973, that the Dakota National Bank sent notice of its election under the provisions of the loan to accelerate the maturity of the note. The Bank demanded payment in full of the full principal due by December 27, 1973. It then filed FISLP insurance claims against the United States on May 6, 1974, and assigned the three Tilleraas notes to the United States on May 10, 1974. The government, in turn, paid the Bank's claim in full on July 5, 1974. It was not until June 4, 1980, that the appellee government filed suit in Cleveland, Ohio, against the original borrower-recipient of this largess intended to assist students in obtaining a higher education.

The government's suit was met in the trial court by defendant-appellant's motion for a summary judgment based on her contention that the action of the United States was barred by the six year statute of limitations set forth in 28 U.S.C. § 2514(a). The complaint in the cause alleged that the government paid the Bank's insurance claim and was assigned title to the notes after default on the loan and payment by the government pursuant to 45 C.F.R. § 177.48.

* * *

The government argues, however, that it is not limited to assignee status, since it may also rely on its common law right as a surety to bring an action against the principal for reimbursement. Since a surety's or guarantor's cause of action for indemnity does not accrue until payment of the principal's liability [citations], the government claims that it *also* has a cause of action which accrued on the date it paid the lender, July 6, 1974, a cause which was timely when this action was filed.

* * *

The use of the word "insurance" in the statute is not determinative in light of the realities existing between the relevant parties. The nature of the substantive rights and duties among the parties clearly reflects a surety-principal-lender relationship. Insurance is a contract where one undertakes to indemnify another against loss, damage or liability caused by an unknown or contingent event. Since the insured pays the insurer for the promise of indemnity, the insurer benefits to the extent that a contingency never occurs. Where a contingency does occur, the insurer can still be made whole, by virtue of subrogation, to the extent that the insured would be able to recover damages from a third party. Despite the presence of this right of subrogation it is clear that *when the contract is formed* all legal rights and obligations flow between the insurer and the insured. At this initial stage, there is no legal obligation owing from the third party to the insurer. In fact, it is unknown at that stage whether such a third party obligation will ever arise and, if so, who that third party will be.

A surety, on the other hand, promises to assume the responsibility for the payment of a debt incurred by another should he or she fail to repay the creditor. The arrangement is made to induce the creditor to deal with the borrower where there might otherwise be a reluctance to do so. Under this arrangement, the nature, size, and source of the possible loss to the creditor is known from the start. In addition, there is no payment from the creditor to the surety or guarantor for this "insured" payment. Rather, a kind of tripartite relationship is formed. The consideration running from the creditor to the debtor is deemed sufficient to support the surety's promise to make the debt good. In turn, the benefit flowing to the debtor by virtue of the surety's promise places that debtor under an implied legal obligation to make good any loss incurred by any payment the surety must ultimately make to the creditor. [Citation.] It is clear then that the two contracts are materially distinguishable, as are the rights and duties of the parties involved. [Citations.]

Under the FISLP the student contracts to borrow money with no collateral and upon favorable interest and repayment terms. The lender, in turn, contracts with the Department of Education to insure repayment should the student default. This has consistently been interpreted as creating a third-party surety contract, despite its nomenclature. [Citations.] The only possible

"contingency" from which the government protects the lending institution is the possibility that the named student (in this case Tilleraas) may ultimately default on all or part of the designated loan amount. The interdependencies between the three parties, in this case the Dakota National Bank & Trust Co., Tilleraas, and the United States government, "are a situational adaptation of long-recognized principles of guaranty." [Citation.] At common law the nature of the relationship would have undoubtedly given rise to an implied obligation on the part of Tilleraas to make good the loss incurred by the government when forced to satisfy her debt, a loss arising when the monies were paid to the Dakota National Bank & Trust Co.

The courts which have found a surety relationship in the student loan program have, either explicitly or impliedly, determined that § 1080(b) did not prevent the government from enforcing its rights at common law. Changes in or abrogation of the common law must be clearly expressed by the legislature. [Citations.] Even where such an intention is explicit, the scope of the common law will be altered no further than is necessary to give effect to the language of the statute. [Citations.] Where the issue raised is whether or not a given statutory provision is intended to abrogate the common law rights of the government, the presumption against such a reading of the statute is even stronger. The conclusion that the sovereign is to be denied rights which the realities of the relationship would otherwise allow it to exercise is only justified where the language of, and clear implications from, the statute itself command such a construction. [Citations.]

* * *

We conclude, therefore, that the United States in this instance stands in the position of a surety-guarantor, and therefore it may pursue its rights as a surety under FISLP. As pointed out, it was not until July of 1974 that the government paid the Bank's claim and obtained its right to sue the defaulting appellant on the underlying loan. Under the realities of the FISLP, the government is a surety of the borrower and is entitled to its rights as such. This is the position supported by the other Courts of Appeals that have considered the same issue under this law. [Citations.]

* * *

Accordingly, we affirm the thoughtful decision of the district court, concluding that the United States, as surety-guarantor, has six years after paying a claim under FISLP in which to institute suit against a defaulting borrower.

Right of Contribution

COLLINS v. THROCKMORTON

Supreme Court of Delaware, 1980.
425 A.2d 146.

McNEILLY, J.

The defendants below appeal from a money judgment for the plaintiff entered by the Superior Court after a non-jury trial. The basic facts underlying the controversy are as follows:

Plaintiff Philip Throckmorton and defendant Robert Collins were the sole stockholders (as well as the officers and directors) in Central Ceilings, Inc. (hereinafter referred to as "Central"). On March 26, 1973, Central borrowed $10,000 from the Wilmington Trust Company ("the bank"); a demand note therefor was executed by the corporate officers. On the back of the note, the plaintiff, his wife and the defendants (then husband and wife) signed a provision unconditionally guaranteeing payment of the note on behalf of Central. Subsequent to this transaction, relations between Mr. Throckmorton and Mr. Collins deteriorated to the point where, in August, 1973, Mr. Collins left the employ of Central and ceased to be actively involved in the management of the company. Although the Central stockholders discussed terms whereby Mr. Collins was to completely sever his relationship with the company, no agreement was ever reached.

After Mr. Collins' departure from Central, the plaintiff continued to operate the business. However, by mid–1975, Central had become insolvent and simply ceased to do business. The record clearly shows that Central's financial woes, particularly certain problems with the Internal Revenue Service, began before Mr. Collins' departure from the company and continued more or less unabated until the company went out of business.

Apparently Central made no payments on the demand note after 1973. By May, 1975, the bank had become sufficiently concerned about Central's ability to pay the note to institute certain protective actions. Central's assets on deposit with the bank were frozen and demand made on the Throckmortons to satisfy various debts owed by Central to the bank, including the balance on the 1973 note which they and the defendants had guaranteed. On May 30, 1975, pursuant to negotiations between the Throckmortons and the bank, the plaintiff and his wife took out a loan in the amount of $15,402. All of these proceeds were used to satisfy Central's debts to the bank. Of the total, $9,668.73 was paid to satisfy the 1973 note, *i.e.,* $8,800 in unpaid principal plus $868.73 in interest at eight and three-quarters percent per year as specified in the note. In return, the bank assigned its rights under the 1973 note to the plaintiff, individually.

On June 4, 1975, the plaintiff demanded that the defendants reimburse him in full for the amounts he paid in satisfaction of the 1973 note; the defendants refused. The plaintiff subsequently, in his complaint and at trial, reduced his claims against each defendant to one-quarter of the amounts thus paid by him. The Superior court entered judgment against each defendant in the amount of $3,492.86 allocated as follows: $2,417.18 representing the proportionate one-quarter share of each defendant on the demand note as paid by the plaintiff on May 30, 1975; $909.35 representing interest on such proportionate shares at the rate of eight and three-quarters percent per year from June 15, 1975 to November 1, 1979 (the Trial Court order was entered in November, 1979); and $166.33 representing awards of attorney fees at the rate of five percent of the amounts otherwise assessed against each defendant.

* * *

In order to understand the defendants' . . . argument, it is necessary to state the general rule governing contribution rights among coguarantors. The Restatement of the Law of Security . . . § 154 provides in pertinent part:

(1) A surety who has discharged more than his proportionate share of the principal's duty is entitled to contribution from a co-surety.

(a) who has consented to the surety's becoming bound, in the proportionate amount of the net outlay property expended. . . .

[Citations.]

The undisputed facts show that the 1973 note was guaranteed by four persons. Consequently, each was potentially liable for one-quarter of Central's default on the note. See Restatement of the Law of Restitution § 85, Comment (e) (1937). Although the complaint alleged the plaintiff personally satisfied Central's default by paying the entirety of the principal and interest owed on the note in May, 1975, the defendants argue that the trial proofs show that the plaintiff's wife, the fourth co-guarantor, contributed equally with the plaintiff to this satisfaction. Thus, of the $9,668.73 paid to satisfy the 1973 note, the defendants claim the plaintiff contributed only half ($4,834.36). Of that amount the plaintiff was personally liable for half, which constituted one-quarter of Central's total default ($2,417.18). Thus argue the defendants, the maximum amount of contribution which the plaintiff could recover from the two defendants was $2,417.18, i.e. the amount in excess of his share of Central's default which the plaintiff personally paid to satisfy the 1973 note. Therefore, the defendants argue that the Trial Court's decision, which was premised on the assumption that the plaintiff satisfied the entire default by Central (or at least three-quarters thereof), erroneously awarded judgment against each defendant in the amount of $2,417.18, double the excess amount which the plaintiff allegedly paid in satisfaction of the note and, thus, double the total amount of contribution which he was entitled to recover from the defendants collectively.

* * *

Even considering the evidentiary aspect of the argument on the merits, we are not persuaded that the defendants are entitled to appellate relief. Although there was no direct testimony concerning the respective amounts which the plaintiff and his wife contributed to satisfaction of the 1973 note, the bank's assignment of the note to the plaintiff, individually, gives rise to a reasonable inference that, as between the plaintiff and his wife, the plaintiff alone was entitled to seek contribution from the defendants. While it would obviously be desirable to have a more detailed and explicit factual record on this point, the failure to so develop the record must be laid at the defendants' doorstep. Therefore, we will not disturb that portion of the Trial Court's judgment which requires each defendant to pay the plaintiff $2,417.18 for their contributive shares on the demand note as satisfied.

* * *

In conclusion, we modify the judgment below to eliminate the awards of interest and attorney fees, and we affirm the judgment as so modified.

AFFIRMED, as modified.

Defenses

UNITED STATES v. RELIANCE INSURANCE CO. v. ARMY-NAVY '83 FOUNDATION

United States Court of Appeals, Ninth Circuit, 1986.
799 F.2d 1382.

JAMESON, J.

The United States, plaintiff-appellant, brought this action on behalf of the Army Athletic Association (Army) and the Naval Academy Athletic Association (Navy) (collectively the Academies), to recover on a bond issued by defendant-appellee, Reliance Insurance Company (Reliance), securing moneys to be paid the Academies from the proceeds of the 1983 Army-Navy football game by the Army-Navy '83 Foundation (Foundation). Reliance refused to pay a claim made by the Academies, asserting that the underlying contract between the Academies and Foundation was modified to its prejudice. On cross-motions for summary judgment, the district court granted Reliance's motion, holding that the bond was exonerated by material modifications of the contract, at least one of which was prejudicial to the rights of Reliance as surety. We affirm.

On February 18, 1983, the Foundation, a non-profit organization formed to facilitate preparations for the 1983 Army-Navy football game, and the Academies entered into a contract to play the game at the Rose Bowl in Pasadena. Traditionally, the game was played in Philadelphia. The parties drew the contract to ensure that the Academies would receive approximately the same revenue from the 1983 game as they had received from the 1982 game and would not incur additional expenses as a result of the change in location.

The contract followed the basic format used in prior years, with some changes. The Foundation was entitled to "revenue generated from ticket sales, and broadcast rights. . . ." The Foundation was required to pay each academy $875,000—$550,000 from television revenues and $325,000 from ticket sales and concession proceeds. The Foundation agreed to compensate each Academy up to $100,000 for additional costs which were "in excess of those expenses actually incurred by the Army and Navy in conjunction with the 1982 Army-Navy Game." Finally, the Foundation agreed to provide funds to transport cadets, midshipmen and support personnel to Pasadena and to provide housing and meals for them while there.

The contract required the Foundation to obtain two bonds. One bond guaranteed the Foundation's obligation of $650,000 for ticket sales and concession proceeds. The Academies released this bond when they collected the money. The second bond, the subject of this lawsuit, guaranteed the Foundation's obligation to pay up to $200,000 to cover additional expenses incurred by the Academies. When the Foundation failed to pay for the additional expenses, the Academies filed this action to recover their additional expenses from Reliance.

To obtain the bonds, the Foundation had contacted Robert E. Coates, president of the insurance brokerage firm of Ingham, Coates & Payne. Coates, in turn, contacted Dale Dolton of Reliance. Because the Foundation had no assets, Reliance required 100% collateral and indemnification from a financially able person. The Foundation assured Reliance that it was entitled to the television proceeds from the game. In a letter dated February 18, 1983, the Foundation assured Reliance that it would assign the television proceeds to Reliance up to the face amount of the bonds. The television proceeds were initially estimated at $1,100,000. After negotiation with ABC, the television contract amounted to $1,450,000. The Foundation never made the assignment. On their face, the bonds did not mention an assignment of the television proceeds. The bonds contained only two conditions: (1) a force majeure clause; and (2) a six month statute of limitations.

Subsequent to the issuance of the bonds, the Academies and the Foundation executed three modifications of the contract. The first modification changed the date of the game from December 3, 1983 to November 25, 1983, a change required by ABC. The second modification, to comply with the National Collegiate Athletic Association (NCAA) master plan, changed the contract to direct payment of the television proceeds to the Army as the host school, rather than to the Foundation. As a result of the second modification the Foundation was entitled to only $350,000 of the television proceeds. The modification, however, relieved the Foundation of its $1,100,000 obligation to the Academies.

Finally, less than one week before the game, the Academies and the Foundation executed a third modification of the contract. Unexpectedly, the airlines reserved to transport the cadets, midshipmen and supporting personnel to Pasadena, required payment prior to take off. Paragraph 2(d) of the contract required the Foundation to make such payments, but the Foundation was unable to do so prior to the game and consequent receipt of ticket and television revenues. Pursuant to the third modification, the Academies provided the necessary funds. In return, the Foundation waived its rights to ticket revenue already retained by the Academies, which was payable to the Foundation, and to television revenues in excess of $1,100,000 (i.e. $350,000).

Apparently the only persons with knowledge of both the Foundation's assurance that Reliance would receive an assignment of the television proceeds and the three subsequent modifications to the contract were the president and vice-president of the Foundation. Depositions support Reliance's assertion that it knew nothing about the modifications of the contract. The Academies assert they knew nothing about the Foundation's agreement to assign the television proceeds to Reliance.

* * *

The primary issue is whether the modifications of the bonded contract exonerate Reliance. As a general rule a surety will be discharged where the bonded contract is materially altered or changed without the surety's knowledge or consent. [Citations.] In addition, where, as here, a compensated surety seeks exoneration, it must show that the alteration caused prejudice or damage. [Citations.] Thus, Reliance must demonstrate that the modifications were material and that some prejudice resulted.

The parties dispute the effect of the modifications. The Academies argue that the net effect of the modifications was to benefit the Foundation. Although under the second modification the Foundation lost its right to receive $1,100,000 in television revenue, it was also relieved of its obligation to guarantee that amount in television revenue. The Academies argue that the third modification relieved the Foundation of a $1,267,355.63 payment to the airlines for transporting the cadets, midshipmen and supporting personnel. Yet, in exchange, the Foundation gave up its rights to only $350,000 in excess television revenue. Consequently, the Academies argue, the net effect was a $917,355.63 benefit to the Foundation. Reliance, however, contends that the $1,100,000 lost revenue from the second modification and the $350,000 lost revenue

from the third modification coupled with the approximately $1,267,000 decrease in its obligation to the airlines resulted in a net loss of approximately $183,000.

Neither party is entirely correct. First, in monetary terms, the second modification has no net effect. The Foundation lost the rights to $1,100,000 in television revenues, but it was also relieved of its obligation to guarantee that amount. Second, the third modification did not relieve the Foundation of its obligation to pay the airlines. The language of the third modification clearly indicates that the Foundation remained liable for the costs of transportation. The third modification merely shifted from the Foundation to the Academies the immediate burden of providing funds for transportation. In exchange, the Foundation relinquished its sole remaining right of any significance under the contract—the right to receive the excess television revenues.

* * *

Paragraph 2(a) funded the otherwise assetless Foundation with ticket, concession, and television proceeds. These funds provided the Foundation with a means to satisfy its obligations. As evidenced by the Foundation's February 18 letter promising to assign television proceeds, Reliance relied on the Foundation's funding as provided in the original contract. As the district court concluded, "The impact of the third modification on the Foundation was that it was deprived of the excess television revenues on which it depended to meet its contractual obligations, including those secured by (the bond in question)." Absent the provision that the Foundation would receive the television proceeds, Reliance would likely have determined the risk was too great, and declined to issue the bonds. Had there been no third modification, the Foundation may have had funds available to cover its obligations under paragraph 2(c). The prejudice suffered by Reliance is the increased risk resulting from the modifications. As the Court of Appeals for the District of Columbia has stated:

A surety company is not a public utility. It may, for any or no reason, conclude not to furnish its bond with respect to a particular contract. When it has committed itself with respect to one contract, amendments which convert that agreement into a significantly different one should be brought to the attention of the surety so that it may exercise its own business judgment as to whether it wishes to continue its commitment. It is not for the parties to the contract to decide among themselves that their amendments are of no interest to the surety, at least when, as here, those amendments go beyond mere matters of form.

* * *

The modifications of the contract between the Academies and the Foundation were ma-

terial, at least one of which, the third, was prejudicial to the rights of Reliance as surety. Reliance had no knowledge of the modifications and did not consent thereto. Under the circumstances, the bond was exonerated. Reliance was not estopped to raise the defense of material alterations and did not waive its defense or ratify the modifications. The district court did not abuse its discretion in denying further discovery.

AFFIRMED.

QUESTIONS

1. Identify five types of sureties.

2. Explain the requirements for the formation of a suretyship relationship.

3. Explain the rights of a creditor against a surety.

4. Explain the rights of a surety including those of a cosurety.

5. Identify (a) the personal defenses of the principal debtor, (b) the personal defenses of the surety, and (c) the defenses of both the surety and the principal debtor.

PROBLEMS

1. Allen, Barker, and Cooper are cosureties on a $750,000 loan by Durham National Bank to Kingston Manufacturing Co., Inc. The maximum liability of the sureties is as follows: Allen—$750,000, Barker—$300,000, and Cooper—$150,000. If Kingston defaults on the entire $750,000 loan, what is the liability of Allen, Barker, and Cooper?

2. Peter Diamond owes Carter $500,000 secured by a first mortgage on Diamond's plant and land. Stephens is a surety on this obligation in the amount of $250,000. After Diamond defaulted on the debt, Carter demanded and received payment of $250,000 from Stephens. Carter then foreclosed upon the mortgage and sold the property for $375,000. What rights, if any, does Stephens have in the proceeds from the sale of the property?

3. Adams sold his house to Baldwin for $80,000 with Baldwin expressly assuming a mortgage held by Evans on the property in the amount of $60,000. The property has a fair market value of $140,000. Six months later Baldwin defaulted in his payments to Evans on the mortgage.

(a) What are Evans' rights, if any, against Baldwin?

(b) What are Evans' rights, if any, against Adams?

(c) What are Adams' rights, if any, against Baldwin?

4. Paula Daniels purchased an automobile from Carey on credit. At the time of the sale Scott agreed to be a surety for Paula, who is sixteen years old. The automobile's odometer stated 52,000 miles but Carey had turned it back from 72,000 miles. Paula refuses to make any pay-

ments due on the car. Carey proceeds against Paula and Scott. What defenses, if any, are available to (a) Paula and (b) Scott?

5. Stafford Surety Co. agreed to act as the conditional guarantor of collection on a debt owed by Preston Decker to Cole. Stafford was paid a premium by Preston to serve as surety. Preston defaults on the obligation. What are Cole's rights against Stafford Surety Co.?

6. Campbell loaned Perry Dixon $7,000 which was secured by a possessory security interest in stock owned by Perry. The stock had a market value of $4,000. In addition, Campbell insisted that Perry obtain a surety. For a premium, Sutton Surety Co. agreed to act as a surety for the full amount of the loan. Prior to the due date of the loan Perry convinced Campbell to return the stock because its value had increased and he wished to sell it in order to realize the gain. Campbell released the stock and Perry subsequently defaulted. Campbell proceeds against Sutton. Decision?

7. Pamela Darden owed Clark $5,000 on an unsecured loan. On May 1, Pamela approached Clark for an additional loan of $3,000. Clark agreed to make the loan only if Pamela could obtain a surety. On May 5, Simpson agreed to be a surety on the $3,000 loan which was granted that day. Both loans were due on October 1. On June 15, Pamela sent $1,000 to Clark but did not provide any instructions.
  (a) What are Clark's rights?
  (b) What are Simpson's rights?

8. Patrick Dillon applied for a $10,000 loan from Carlton Savings & Loan. Carlton required him to obtain a surety. Patrick approached Sinclair Surety Co., which insisted that Patrick provide it with a financial statement. Patrick did so but the statement was materially false. In reliance upon the financial statement and in return for a premium, Sinclair agreed to act as surety. Upon Sinclair's commitment to act as surety Carlton loaned Patrick the $10,000. After one payment of $400 Patrick defaulted. Patrick then filed a voluntary petition in bankruptcy. Carlton proceeds against Sinclair. Decision?

9. On June 1, Smith contracted with Martin d/b/a Martin Publishing Company to distribute Martin's newspapers and to account for the proceeds. As part of the contract, Smith agreed to furnish Martin a bond in the amount of $10,000

guaranteeing the payment of the proceeds. At the time the contract was executed and the credit extended the bond was not furnished and no mention was made as to the prospective sureties. On July 1, Smith signed the bond with Black and Blue signing as sureties. The bond recited the awarding of the contract for distribution of the newspapers as consideration for the bond.

On December 1, there was due from Smith to Martin the sum of $3,600 under the distributor's contract. Demand for payment was made but Smith failed to make payment. As a result, Martin brought an appropriate action against Black and Blue to recover the $3,600. What decision?

10. Diggitt Construction Company was the low bidder on a well digging job for the Village of Drytown. On April 15, Diggitt signed a contract with Drytown for the job at a price of $40,000. At the same time, pursuant to the notice of bidding, Diggitt prevailed upon Ace Surety Company to execute a performance bond indemnifying Drytown on the contract. On May 1, after having put in three days on the job, the president of Diggitt refigured his bid and realized that if his company were to complete the job it would lose $10,000. Accordingly, Diggitt notified Drytown that it was cancelling the contract, effective immediately. What are the rights and duties of Ace Surety Company?

11. On March 10, 1972, L.R.Z.H. Corporation made and delivered to Langeveld its promissory note in the sum of $57,500. The indebtedness evidenced by the note was secured by a mortgage in the same amount on real property owned by the corporation. By an instrument of guaranty set forth at the bottom of the note, Higgins guaranteed performance of all obligations of the corporation under the note. The note became due on February 15, 1973, and was not paid. At this time, Higgins discovered that Langeveld had never recorded the mortgage securing the note. Langeveld then recorded the mortgage on March 1, 1973. In the intervening year between execution of the mortgage and recordation, another mortgage and two liens in substantial amounts had been filed. Langeveld brought suit against Higgins on the guaranty. Higgins argues that the creditor, Langeveld, owed a duty to him as surety for the debt to protect the security and allow nothing to occur to impair its value. Since Langeveld failed to fulfill this duty, Higgins should be released from all liability on his guaranty. Decision?

Chapter 40

BANKRUPTCY

Liquidation
Reorganization
Adjustment of Debts of Family Farmer
Adjustment of Debts of Individuals
Creditors' Rights Outside of Bankruptcy

A debt is an obligation to pay money owed by a debtor to a creditor. Debts are created daily in countless purchases of goods at the consumer level; by retailers of goods in buying merchandise from a manufacturer, wholesaler, or distributor; by borrowers of funds from various lending institutions; and through the issuance and sale of bonds and other types of debt securities. An enormous volume of business transactions is entered into daily on a credit basis. Commercial activity would be restricted and greatly diminished if credit were not readily obtainable or needed funds not available for lending.

Fortunately, most debts are paid when due, thus justifying the extension of credit and encouraging its continuation. Defaults may create credit and collection problems, but normally the total amount in default represents a very small percentage of the total amount of outstanding indebtedness. Nevertheless, both individuals and corporations encounter financial crises and business misfortune. An individual or a business may be confronted by an accumulation of debts that exceeds total assets. Or, he may have assets in excess of total indebtedness but have the assets in such non-liquid form that the debtor is unable to pay his debts as they become due. Relief from overly burdensome debt and from the threat of impending lawsuits by creditors is frequently necessary for economic survival.

Various solutions to the conflict between creditor rights and debtor relief have developed, such as voluntary adjustments and compromises requiring payment in installments to creditors over a period of time during which they agree to withhold legal action. Other voluntary methods include compositions and assignments of assets by a debtor to a trustee or assignee for the benefit of creditors. Equity receiverships or insolvency proceedings are sometimes filed by creditors in a State court pursuant to statute. Nonetheless, the most adaptable and frequently employed method of debtor relief—one which also affords protection to creditors—is by a proceeding in a Federal court under Federal bankruptcy law.

FEDERAL BANKRUPTCY LAW

The most important method of protecting creditor rights and granting debtor relief is Federal bankruptcy law, which is largely statutory and involves court supervision. The word "bankrupt" is derived from the Latin *banque,* meaning bench or table, and *ruptus,* meaning broken. There is some authority for the legend that, upon bankruptcy, the customary place of business of a merchant in medieval times, his bench or table, was literally broken. In any event, it was figuratively broken since bankruptcy meant commercial failure.

Bankruptcy legislation serves a dual purpose: (1) to effect an *equitable distribution* of the debtor's property among her creditors, and (2) to *discharge* the debtor from her debts and enable her to rehabilitate herself and start afresh. Other purposes are to provide uniform treatment of similarly situated creditors, preserve existing business relations, stabilize commercial usages, and bring about a speedy distribution of the debtor's assets.

The Constitution of the United States provides that "the Congress shall have power . . . to establish . . . uniform Laws on the subject of Bankruptcies throughout the United States." Article I, Section 8, clause 4. Federal bankruptcy law has generally superseded State insolvency laws. Under its constitutional power Congress has enacted or substantially revised Bankruptcy Acts in 1800, 1841, 1867, 1898, and 1938.

In 1978, Congress again enacted a major revision of the Bankruptcy Act. The **Bankruptcy Reform Act of 1978** became effective on October 1, 1979, and was amended in several important respects in 1984 and 1986. The Bankruptcy Reform Act, which will be referred to as the Bankruptcy Code, will be discussed in the first part of this chapter. The Bankruptcy Code consists of eight odd-numbered chapters and one even-numbered chapter (chapter 12, which was added in 1986):

CHAPTER	TITLE
1	General Provisions
3	Case Administration
5	Creditors, the Debtor, and the Estate
7	Liquidation
9	Adjustment of Debts of a Municipality
11	Reorganization
12	Adjustment of Debts of a Family Farmer with Regular Annual Income
13	Adjustment of Debts of an Individual with Regular Income
15	United States Trustees

Chapters 7, 9, 11, 12, and 13 provide five different types of proceedings, while Chapters 1, 3, and 5 apply to all five proceedings. **Straight,** or ordinary, **bankruptcy** (Chapter 7) provides for liquidation and termination of the business of the debtor, whereas the other proceedings provide for **reorganization** and adjustment of the debts of the debtor and the continuance of the debtor's business.

Chapter 7 applies to *all* debtors with the exception of railroads, insurance companies, banks, savings and loan associations, homestead associations, and credit unions. Moreover, Chapter 7 has special provisions for the liquidation of the estates of stockbrokers and commodity brokers. Any person that may be a debtor under Chapter 7 (except stockbrokers and commodity brokers) and railroads may be a debtor under Chapter 11. Chapter 9, however, applies only to a municipality that is generally authorized to be a debtor under that chapter, is insolvent, and desires to effect a plan to adjust its debts. Chapter 12 applies to an individual, or individual and spouse, engaged in farming if 50 percent of their gross income is from farming, their aggregate debts do not exceed $1.5 million, and at least 80 percent of their debts arise out of the farming operation. A corporation or partnership may also qualify for Chapter 12. Chapter 13 applies to individuals with regular income who owe liquidated unsecured debts of less than $100,000 and secured debts of less than $350,000. See Figure 40–1.

The Bankruptcy Code established a new bankruptcy court system but the United States Supreme Court held that this new court system had powers in violation of Article III of the U.S. Constitution. *Northern Pipeline Co. v. Marathon Pipe Line Co.,* 458 U.S. 50 (1982). The Bankruptcy Amendments Act of 1984 thus restructured the bankruptcy court system in an attempt to satisfy the constitutional considerations raised by the *Marathon* case. As amended, the Bankruptcy Code grants to U.S. district courts original and exclusive jurisdiction over all bankruptcy cases and original, but not exclusive, jurisdiction over civil proceedings arising under bankruptcy cases. The district court must, however, abstain from related matters that, except for its relationship to a bankruptcy, could not have been brought in a Federal court. The district court in which a bankruptcy case is commenced has exclusive jurisdiction over all of the debtor's property. In addition, a bankruptcy court staffed by bankruptcy judges is established as a unit of each Federal district court. Bankruptcy courts are authorized to hear certain matters specified by the Bankruptcy Code and to enter appropriate orders and judgments subject to review by the district court, or where established, a panel of three bankruptcy judges. The Federal Circuit Court of Appeals has jurisdiction over appeals from the district court or panel. In all other matters, unless the parties assent, only the district court may issue a final order or judgment that is based upon proposed findings of fact and conclusions of law submitted to the district court by the bankruptcy judge.

CASE ADMINISTRATION—CHAPTER 3

Chapter 3 of the Bankruptcy Code contains provisions dealing with the commencement of the case, the officers who administer the case, the meetings of creditors, and the administrative powers of the various officers.

Commencement of the Case

The jurisdiction of the bankruptcy court and the operation of the bankruptcy laws are begun by the filing of a voluntary or involuntary petition.

Voluntary Petitions More than 99 percent of all petitions are filed voluntarily. Any person eligible to be a debtor under a given bankruptcy proceeding may file a voluntary petition under that chapter. Moreover, the debtor need *not* be insolvent to file the petition. The commencement of a voluntary case by filing a petition constitutes an automatic **order for relief.** The petition must include a list of all creditors (secured and unsecured), a

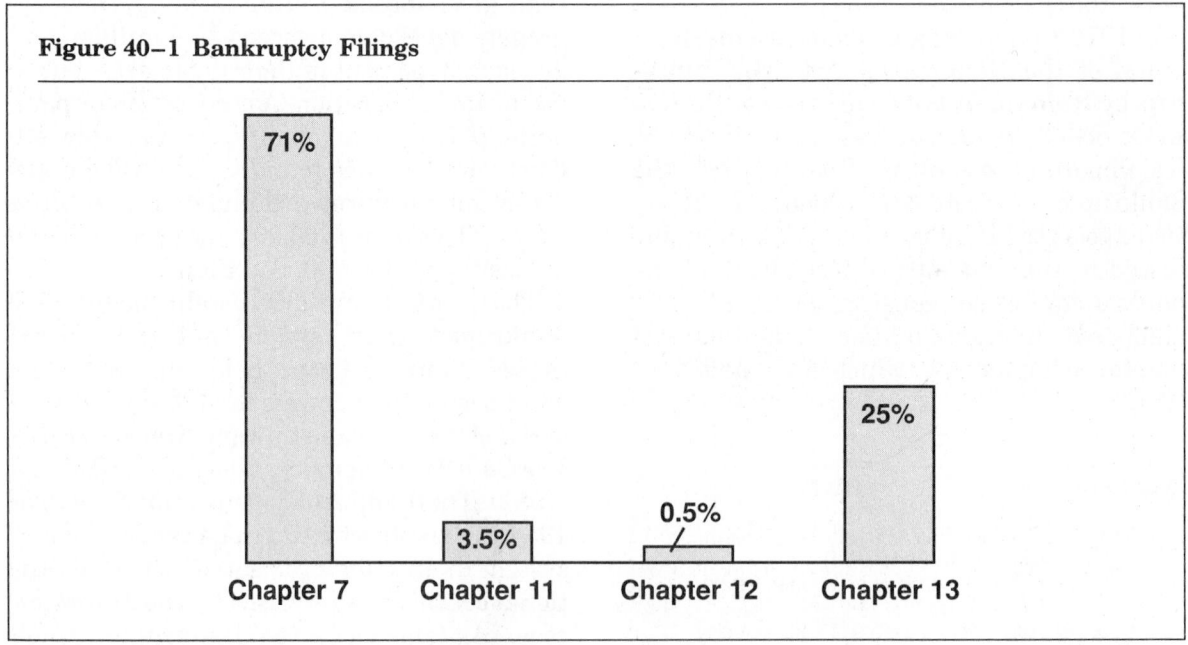

Figure 40–1 Bankruptcy Filings

SOURCE: U.S. Department of Commerce, Bureau of the Census, *Statistical Abstract of the United States* (Washington, D.C.: U.S. Government Printing Office, 1990).

list of all property owned by the debtor, a list of property claimed by the debtor to be exempt, and a statement of the debtor's affairs.

Involuntary Petitions   An involuntary petition in bankruptcy may be filed only under Chapter 7 (liquidation) or 11 (reorganization). It may be filed (1) by three or more creditors who have unsecured claims which total $5,000 or more, or (2) if there are fewer than twelve creditors of the debtor, then by one or more creditors whose total claims equal $5,000 or more. Section 303(b). An involuntary petition may not be filed against a farmer or against a banking, insurance, or nonprofit corporation. Section 303(a).

If the debtor does not contest the involuntary petition, the court will enter an order for relief against the debtor. If the debtor opposes the petition, the court may enter an order of relief only if (1) the debtor is generally not paying his undisputed debts as they become due, or (2) within 120 days before the filing of the petition a custodian or receiver took possession of substantially all of the debtor's property to enforce a lien against that property. Section 303(h).

If an involuntary petition is contested successfully by the debtor and dismissed by the court, Section 303(i) empowers the court to grant a judgment in favor of the debtor against the petitioning creditors for (1) costs, (2) reasonable attorney's fees, and (3) damages proximately caused by the trustee's taking possession of the debtor's property. Moreover, if the petition was filed in bad faith the court may award damages proximately caused by the filing or punitive damages.

If the court orders relief, the debtor must provide the court with the same schedules as those provided by a voluntary petitioner.

Automatic Stays

The filing of a voluntary or involuntary petition operates as a **stay** against (that is, it restrains) all creditors beginning or continuing to recover claims against the debtor, or creating or enforcing liens against property of the debtor. Section 362. This stay applies to both secured and unsecured creditors, although a secured creditor may petition the court to terminate the stay as to her security upon showing that she lacks adequate protection in the secured property.

Trustees

The trustee is the representative of the estate and has the capacity to sue and be sued. In proceedings under Chapter 7, trustees are selected by a vote of the creditors; in all other proceedings the trustee is appointed. The trustee is responsible for collecting, liquidating, and distributing the debtor's estate. The duties and powers of the trustee include the following: (1) to use, sell, or lease property of the estate; (2) to deposit or invest money of the estate; (3) to employ attorneys, accountants, appraisers, or auctioneers; and (4) to assume or reject any executory contract or unexpired lease of the debtor.

Meetings of Creditors

Within a reasonable time after relief is ordered, a meeting of creditors must be held. The court may not attend this meeting. The debtor must appear and submit to an examination by creditors and the trustee with respect to his financial situation. In a proceeding under Chapter 7, qualified creditors at this meeting elect the permanent trustee.

CREDITORS, THE DEBTOR, AND THE ESTATE—CHAPTER 5

Creditors

The Bankruptcy Code defines a **creditor** as any entity that has a claim against the debtor that arose at the time of or before the order for relief. A **claim** means a "right to payment whether or not such right is reduced to judgment, liquidated, unliquidated, fixed, contingent, matured, unmatured, disputed, undisputed, legal, equitable, secured, or unsecured." Section 101(4).

Proof of Claims Creditors that wish to participate in the distribution of the debtor's estate may file a proof of claim. If a creditor does not do so in a timely manner, then the debtor or trustee may file a proof of such claim. Section 501. The debtor may do this to protect himself against a claim's becoming nondischargeable. Claims that are filed are allowed unless a party in interest objects. If an objection to a claim is made, the court determines, after a hearing, the amount and validity of the claim. The court may not allow any claim that (1) is unenforceable against the debtor or his property, (2) is for unmatured interest, or (3) is for services of an insider or attorney in excess of the reasonable value of such services. Section 502. An **insider** includes a relative or general partner of a debtor as well as a partnership in which the debtor is a general partner or a corporation of which the debtor is a director, officer, or person in control. Section 101(28).

Secured Claims An allowed claim of a creditor who has a lien on property of the estate is a secured claim to the extent of the value of the creditor's interest in the property. The creditor's claim is unsecured to the extent to which the value of his secured interest is less than the allowed amount of his claim. Thus, if Andrew has an allowed claim of $5,000 against the estate of debtor Barbara and has a security interest in property of the estate that is valued at $3,000, Andrew has a secured claim in the amount of $3,000 and an unsecured claim for $2,000.

Priority of Claims *After secured claims* have been satisfied the remaining assets are distributed among creditors with unsecured claims. Certain classes of unsecured claims, however, have a **priority,** which means that they must be paid in *full* before any distribution is made to claims of lesser rank. The claims having a priority and the order of their priority, as provided in Section 507, are the following:

1. **Expenses of administration** of the debtor's estate, including the filing fees paid by creditors in involuntary cases; the expenses of creditors in recovering concealed assets for the benefit of the bankrupt's estate; the trustee's necessary expenses; and reasonable compensation to receivers, trustees, and their attorneys as allowed by the court.

2. Unsecured claims of **"gap" creditors**. These are claims in an involuntary case arising in the ordinary course of the debtor's business after the commencement of the case but before the earlier of the appointment of the trustee or the order for relief.

3. Allowed, unsecured claims up to $2,000 for **wages, salaries, or commissions** earned within ninety days before the filing of the petition or the date of cessation of the debtor's business, whichever comes first.

4. Allowed, unsecured claims for contributions to **employee benefit plans** arising from services rendered within 180 days before the filing of the petition or the cessation of the debtor's business, whichever occurs first, but limited to $2,000 multiplied by the number of employees covered by the plan.

5. Allowed, unsecured claims up to $2,000 for **grain** or **fish producers** against a storage facility.

6. Allowed, unsecured claims up to $900 for **consumer deposits,** that is, moneys deposited in connection with the purchase, lease, or rental of property or the purchase of services for personal, family, or household use.

7. Specified income, property, employment, or excise **taxes** owed to governmental units.

After creditors with secured claims and creditors with claims having a priority have been satisfied, creditors with allowed, unsecured claims share proportionately in any remaining assets.

Subordination of Claims In addition to statutory and contract priorities, the bankruptcy court itself can, at its discretion in proper cases, apply equitable priorities. Section 510. This is accomplished through the doctrine of subordination of claims, whereby, assuming two claims of equal statutory priority, the bankruptcy court declares that one claim must be paid in full before the other claim can be paid anything. Subordination is applied in cases where allowing a claim in full would be unfair and inequitable to other creditors, such as to allow the inflated salary claims of officers in closely held corporations. In such cases, the court does not disallow the claim but merely orders it paid after all other claims are paid in full.

The claim of a parent corporation against its bankrupt subsidiary corporation may be subordinated to the claims of other creditors of the subsidiary in cases where the parent has been guilty of mismanaging the subsidiary to the detriment of its innocent creditors in a manner so unconscionable as to preclude the parent from seeking the aid of a bankruptcy court. For example, assume that Stanford Corporation owns all of the capital stock of Drexel Corporation. Assume further that whenever Drexel shows a profit, the profit is taken out of Drexel and transferred to Stanford by means of questionable intercorporate transactions; whenever Drexel shows a loss and Stanford is required to put some money back into Drexel, it does so by "lending" the money to Drexel. Over a period of time, Stanford takes $500,000 out of Drexel and puts $100,000 back. When Drexel goes into bankruptcy, Stanford has a claim of $100,000, while outside creditors have claims aggregating $100,000. Under the general rule of distribution, if the assets total $100,000, Stanford will receive $50,000 and the other creditors $50,000. Since Stanford has already received $500,000, it is clearly unfair for it to receive an additional $50,000 at the expense of the other creditors. The bankruptcy court can exercise its equity power of subordinating claims and subordinate Stanford's claim to that of the other creditors, so that the other creditors will receive the entire $100,000 and Stanford will receive nothing until the prior claims are paid in full.

Debtors

As previously indicated, the purpose of the Bankruptcy Code is to bring about an equi-

table distribution of the debtor's assets and to provide a discharge to the debtor. Accordingly, the Code explicitly subjects the debtor to specified duties while exempting some of his property and discharging most of his debts.

Debtor's Duties Under the Bankruptcy Code, the debtor must file a list of creditors, a schedule of assets and liabilities, and a statement of her financial affairs. In any case in which a trustee is serving, the debtor must cooperate with the trustee and surrender to the trustee all property of the estate and all records relating to property of the estate.

Debtor's Exemptions Section 522 of the Bankruptcy Code exempts specified property of an individual debtor from the bankruptcy proceedings, including the following:

1. up to $7,500 in equity in property used as a residence or burial plot;

2. up to $1,200 in equity in one motor vehicle;

3. up to $200 for any particular item, and not to exceed $4,000 in aggregate value, of household furnishings, household goods, wearing apparel, appliances, books, animals, crops, or musical instruments that are primarily for personal, family, or household use;

4. up to $500 in jewelry;

5. any property up to $400 plus up to $3,750 of any unused amount of the first exemption;

6. up to $750 in implements, professional books or tools of the debtor's trade;

7. unmatured life insurance contracts owned by the debtor other than a credit life insurance contract;

8. professionally prescribed health aids;

9. social security, veteran's, and disability benefits;

10. unemployment compensation;

11. alimony and support payments, including child support;

12. payments from pension, profit sharing, and annuity plans; and

13. payments from an award under a crime victim's reparation law, a wrongful death award, and up to $7,500, not including pain and suffering or compensation for actual pecuniary loss, from a personal injury award.

In addition, the debtor may avoid judicial liens on any exempt property and nonpossessory, non-purchase money security interests on household goods, tools of the trade, and professionally prescribed health aids.

The debtor has the option of using either the exemptions provided by the Bankruptcy Code or those available under State law. Nevertheless, a State may by specific legislative action deny to its citizens the use of the Federal exemptions and limit them to the exemptions provided by State law. More than two-thirds of the States have enacted such "opt out" legislation.

Discharge Discharge relieves the debtor from liability for all dischargeable debts. Certain debts, however, are nondischargeable under the Code. A discharge of a debt voids any judgment obtained at any time with respect to that debt and operates as an injunction against the commencement or continuation of any action to recover that debt. A discharge does not, however, affect a secured creditor to the extent of his security.

No private employer may terminate the employment of, or discriminate with respect to employment against, an individual who is or has been a debtor under the Bankruptcy Code solely because such debtor (1) is or has been a debtor under the Bankruptcy Code; (2) has been insolvent before the commencement of a case or during the case; or (3) has not paid a debt that is dischargeable in a case under the Bankruptcy Code. Section 525(b).

An agreement between a debtor and a creditor permitting the creditor to enforce a discharged debt is enforceable to the extent State law permits but only if (1) the agreement was made before the discharge has been granted; (2) the agreement contains a clear and conspicuous statement which ad-

vises the debtor that the agreement may be rescinded; (3) the agreement has been filed with the court and, if applicable, accompanied by a declaration or an affidavit of the attorney that represented the debtor during the course of negotiating the agreement, which states that such agreement represents a fully informed and voluntary agreement by the debtor, and does not impose an undue hardship on the debtor; (4) the debtor has not rescinded the agreement at any time prior to discharge or within sixty days after the agreement is filed with the court, whichever occurs later; (5) the court has informed a debtor who is an individual that he is not required to enter into such an agreement and has explained the legal effect of the agreement; and (6) in a case concerning an individual who was not represented by an attorney during the course of negotiating the agreement, the court has approved such agreement as not imposing an undue hardship on the debtor and being in the best interests of the debtor. Section 524.

Section 523 provides that the following debts are **not dischargeable** in bankruptcy:

1. certain taxes and customs duties;

2. legal liabilities for obtaining money or property by false pretenses, false representations, or actual fraud;

3. legal liability for willful and malicious injuries to the person or property of another;

4. alimony and support of spouse or child;

5. debts not scheduled, unless the creditor knew of the bankruptcy;

6. debts created by the fraud or defalcation of the debtor while acting in a fiduciary capacity, embezzlement, or larceny;

7. student loans which first became due less than five years before the filing of the petition unless the debt would impose undue hardship;

8. debts that were or could have been listed in a previous bankruptcy in which the debtor waived or was denied a discharge;

9. consumer debts for luxury goods in excess of $500 per creditor if incurred by an individual debtor on or within forty days before the order for relief;

10. cash advances aggregating more than $1,000 obtained by an individual debtor under an open end credit plan within twenty days before the order for relief; and

11. liability for a court judgment based upon the debtor's operation of a motor vehicle while legally intoxicated.

The following illustrates the operation of discharge: Donaldson files a petition in bankruptcy. Donaldson owes Anders $1,500, Boynton $2,500, and Conroy $3,000. Assume that Anders's claim is not dischargeable in bankruptcy while Boynton's and Conroy's claims are. Anders receives $180 from the liquidation of Donaldson's bankruptcy estate, Boynton receives $300, and Conroy receives $360. If Donaldson receives a bankruptcy discharge, Boynton and Conroy will be precluded from pursuing Donaldson for the remainder of their claims ($2,200 and $2,640 respectively). Anders, on the other hand, because his debt is not dischargeable, may pursue Donaldson for the remaining $1,320 subject to the applicable statute of limitations. If Donaldson does *not* receive a discharge, Anders, Boynton and Conroy may all pursue Donaldson for the unpaid portion of their claims.

The Estate

The commencement of a bankruptcy case creates an **estate** consisting of all legal and equitable interests of the debtor in nonexempt property at that time. The estate also includes property that the debtor acquires within 180 days after the filing of the petition by inheritance, by a property settlement, by a divorce decree, or as a beneficiary of a life insurance policy. In addition, property of the estate includes proceeds, rents, and profits from property of the estate and any interest in property that the estate acquires after the commencement of the estate. The estate does *not* include earnings from services performed by an individual debtor after the commencement of the case. Finally, the estate includes property that the trustee recovers under her powers (1) as a lien creditor, (2) to avoid voidable preferences, (3) to avoid fraudulent transfers, and (4) to avoid statutory liens.

Trustee as Lien Creditor The trustee has, as of the commencement of the case, the rights and powers of any creditor with a judicial lien against the debtor or an execution that is returned unsatisfied, whether or not such a creditor exists. Section 544(a). A **judicial lien** is a charge or interest in property to secure payment of a debt or performance of an obligation that is obtained by a judgment, a levy, or some other legal or equitable process. The trustee is made an ideal creditor possessing every right and power conferred by the law of the State upon its most favored creditor who has acquired a lien by legal or equitable proceedings. The trustee does not need to locate an actual existing lien creditor, for the trustee assumes the rights and powers of a purely *hypothetical lien creditor.*

Thus, under the Uniform Commercial Code and the Bankruptcy Code, the trustee, as a hypothetical lien creditor, has priority over a creditor with a security interest that was not perfected when the bankruptcy petition was filed. A creditor with a purchase money security interest who files within ten days of the debtor's receiving the collateral, however, will defeat the trustee, even if the petition is filed before the creditor perfects and after the creation of the security interest (gap filing). For example, Donald borrowed $5,000 from Cathy on September 1 and gave her a security interest in the equipment he purchased with the borrowed funds. On October 3, before Cathy perfected her security interest, Donald filed for bankruptcy. The trustee in bankruptcy can invalidate Cathy's security interest because it was unperfected when the bankruptcy petition was filed. Cathy would be able to assert a claim as an unsecured creditor. If, however, Donald had filed for bankruptcy on September 8 and Cathy had perfected the security interest on

September 9, Cathy would prevail because her purchase money security interest was perfected within ten days after Donald received the equipment.

Voidable Preferences The Bankruptcy Code invalidates certain preferential transfers from the debtor to favored creditors before the date of bankruptcy. If a transfer is invalidated as preferential, the creditor may still make a claim for the unpaid debt, but the property he received from the debtor becomes a part of the debtor's estate to be shared by all creditors. Under Section 547 the trustee may recover any *transfer* of property of the debtor

1. to or for the benefit of a creditor;

2. for or on account of an antecedent debt owed by the debtor before such transfer was made;

3. made while the debtor was insolvent;

4. made on or within ninety days before the date of the filing of the petition, or, if the creditor was an "insider" (as previously defined), within one year of the date of the filing of the petition; **and**

5. that enables such creditor to receive more than he would have received under Chapter 7.

A **transfer** is any mode, direct or indirect, voluntary or involuntary, of disposing of property or an interest in property, including the retention of title as a security interest. Section 101(48). It is presumed that the debtor has been insolvent on and during the ninety days immediately preceding the date of the filing of the petition. **Insolvency** is a financial condition of a debtor such that the sum of its debts is greater than all of its property at fair valuation.

The policy behind the voidable preference provision is explained by the House report as follows:

The purpose of the preference section is two-fold. First, by permitting the trustee to avoid prebankruptcy transfers that occur within a short period before bankruptcy, creditors are discouraged from racing to the courthouse to dismember the

debtor during his slide into bankruptcy. The protection thus afforded the debtor often enables him to work his way out of a difficult financial situation through cooperation with all of his creditors. Second, and more important, the preference provisions facilitate the prime bankruptcy policy of equality of distribution among creditors of the debtor. Any creditor that received a greater payment than others of his class is required to disgorge so that all may share equally. *House of Representatives Report* 95–595 at 177–78 (1977).

For example, on March 3, David borrows $15,000 from Carla and promises to repay the loan on April 3. David repays Carla on April 3 as he promised. On June 1, David files a petition in bankruptcy. His assets are sufficient to pay general creditors only 40 cents on the dollar. David's repayment of the loan is a voidable preference, which the trustee may recover from Carla. The transfer (repayment) on April 3 (1) was to a creditor (Carla); (2) was on account of an antecedent debt (the $15,000 loan made on March 3); (3) was made while the debtor was insolvent (it is presumed that a debtor is insolvent for the ninety days preceding the filing of the bankruptcy petition—June 1); (4) was made within ninety days of bankruptcy (April 3 is less than ninety days before June 1); and (5) enabled the creditor to receive more than she would have received under Chapter 7 (Carla received $15,000; she would have received .40 × $15,000 = $6,000 in bankruptcy). After returning the property to the trustee, Carla would have an unsecured claim of $15,000 against David's estate in bankruptcy for which she would receive $6,000.

To illustrate further, consider the following example. On May 1, Debra bought and received merchandise from Stuart and gave him a security interest in the goods for the unpaid price of $20,000. On May 20 Stuart filed a financing statement. On August 1, Debra filed a petition for bankruptcy. The trustee in bankruptcy may avoid the perfected security interest as a preferential transfer. The transfer of the perfected security interest on May 20 (1) was to benefit a creditor (Stuart); (2) was on account of an antecedent debt (the $20,000 owed from the sale of the merchandise); (3) the debtor was insolvent at the time (it is presumed that the debtor is insolvent for the ninety days preceding the filing of the bankruptcy petition—August 1); (4) the transfer was made within ninety days of bankruptcy (May 20 is less than ninety days before August 1); and (5) the transfer enabled the creditor to receive more than he would have received in bankruptcy (Stuart would have a secured claim, on which he would recover more than on an unsecured claim).

Nevertheless, not all transfers made within ninety days of bankruptcy are voidable. For example, if sixty days before the petition is filed, the debtor purchases an automobile for $9,000, this transfer of property (i.e., the $9,000) is *not* voidable because it was not made for an antecedent debt but rather as a contemporaneous exchange for new value. Similarly, if within ninety days of the filing of the petition, the debtor purchases a refrigerator on credit and grants the seller or lender a security interest in the refrigerator, the transfer of that interest is not voidable if the secured party perfects *within ten days* after the debtor receives possession of the property. In addition; the trustee may *not* avoid a transfer (1) in payment of a debt incurred in the ordinary course of business or financial affairs of the debtor and the transferee, (2) made in the ordinary course of business or financial affairs of the debtor and transferee, and (3) made according to ordinary business terms. Section 547(c). Another exception was added in 1984: if the debtor is an individual whose debts are primarily consumer debts, then the trustee may not avoid any transfer of property valued at less than $600.

See In re Hamilton.

Fraudulent Transfers The trustee may avoid fraudulent transfers made on or within one year before the date of the filing of the petition. Section 548. One type of fraudulent transfer consists of the debtor's transferring property with the actual intent to hinder, delay, or defraud any of her creditors. Another type of a fraudulent transfer is the transfer by the debtor of property for less than a reasonably equivalent consideration while she is insolvent or would become insolvent because of the transfer. For example, Dale, who is in debt, transfers title to her house to Tony, her father, without any payment by Tony to Dale and with the understanding that when the house is no longer in danger of seizure by creditors, Tony will reconvey it to Dale. The transfer of the house by Dale to Tony is a fraudulent transfer.

Statutory Liens A **statutory lien** is a lien that arises solely by force of a statute and does *not* include a security interest or judicial lien. Section 101(45). The trustee may avoid a statutory lien on property of the debtor if the lien (1) first becomes effective when the debtor becomes insolvent *or* (2) is not perfected or enforceable on the date of the commencement of the case against a *bona fide* purchaser. Section 545.

LIQUIDATION—CHAPTER 7

To accomplish its dual goals of equitably distributing the debtor's property and providing the debtor with a fresh start, the Bankruptcy Code has established two approaches: liquidation and adjustment of debts. Chapter 7 uses the first approach of liquidation while Chapters 11, 12, and 13, discussed below, take the second approach of adjusting debts. Liquidation involves the termination of the business of the debtor, distribution of his nonexempt assets, and usually a discharge of all dischargeable debts of the debtor.

Proceedings

Proceedings under Chapter 7 apply to all debtors except railroads, insurance companies, banks, savings and loan associations, homestead associations, and credit unions. A case may be commenced under Chapter 7 by either a voluntary or an involuntary petition. After the order for relief, an interim trustee is appointed, who serves until a permanent trustee is selected by the creditors. If the creditors do not elect a trustee, the interim trustee becomes the permanent trustee. Under Chapter 7, the trustee collects and reduces to money the property of the estate; accounts for all property received; investigates the financial affairs of the debtor; examines and, if appropriate, challenges proofs of claims; opposes, if advisable, the discharge of the debtor; and makes a final report of the administration of the estate.

The creditors may also elect a committee of not fewer than three and not more than eleven unsecured creditors to consult with the trustee, make recommendations to him, and submit questions to the court.

Dismissal

In 1984, Congress amended the Bankruptcy Code to deal with abuses of Chapter 7 by consumer debtors who had the ability to pay their debts. The amendment empowers the court on its own motion, after notice and a hearing, to dismiss a case filed by an individual debtor whose debts are primarily consumer debts if the court finds that granting relief would be a substantial abuse of the provisions of Chapter 7. Section 707(b).

Distribution of the Estate

After the trustee has collected all the assets of the debtor's estate, she distributes them to the creditors and, if any assets remain, to the debtor, in the following order:

1. Secured creditors are paid on their security interests.

2. Creditors entitled to a priority are paid in the order provided.

3. Unsecured creditors who filed their claims on time are paid.

4. Unsecured creditors who filed their claims late are paid.

5. Claims for multiple, exemplary, or punitive damages are paid.

6. Interest at the legal rate from the date of the filing of the petition is paid to all of the above claimants.

7. Whatever property remains is distributed to the debtor.

Claims of the same rank are paid *pro rata*. For example: Donley has filed a petition for a Chapter 7 proceeding. The total value of Donley's estate *after* paying the expenses of administration is $25,000. Evans, who is owed $15,000, has a security interest in property valued at $10,000. Fishel has an unsecured claim of $6,000, which is entitled to a priority of $2,000. The United States has a claim for income taxes of $4,000. Green has an unsecured claim of $9,000 that was filed on time. Hiller has an unsecured claim of $12,000 that was filed on time. Jerdee has a claim of $8,000 that was not filed on time. The distribution would be as follows:

1. Evans receives $11,500

2. Fishel receives $3,200

3. United States receives $4,000

4. Green receives $2,700

5. Hiller receives $3,600

6. Jerdee receives $0

Evans receives $10,000 as a secured creditor and has an unsecured claim of $5,000. Fishel receives $2,000 on the portion of his claim entitled to a priority and has an unsecured claim of $4,000. The United States has a priority of $4,000. After paying $10,000 to Evans, $2,000 to Fishel, and $4,000 to the United States, there remains $9,000 ($25,000 − $10,000 − $2,000 − $4,000) to be distributed *pro rata* to unsecured creditors who filed on time. Their claims total $30,000 (Evans = $5,000, Fishel = $4,000, Green = $9,000 and Hiller = $12,000). Therefore, each will receive $9,000/$30,000 or 30¢ on the dollar. Accordingly, Evans receives an additional $1,500, Fishel receives an additional $1,200, Green receives $2,700, and Hiller receives $3,600. Because there were insufficient assets to pay all unsecured claimants who filed on time, Jerdee, who filed tardily, receives nothing. If Jerdee's claim were not timely filed because Donley had failed to schedule Jerdee's claim, then Donley's debts to Jerdee would not be discharged unless Jerdee knew or had notice of the bankruptcy.

See Figure 40–2.

Discharge

A discharge under Chapter 7 relieves the debtor of all debts that arose before the date of the order for relief, except for those debts that are not dischargeable. After distribution of the estate, the court will grant the debtor a discharge unless the debtor

1. is not an individual (partnerships and corporations may *not* receive a discharge under Chapter 7);

2. has destroyed, falsified, concealed, or failed to keep books of account and records;

3. has knowingly and fraudulently made a false oath or account, presented or used a false claim, or given or received bribes;

4. transferred, removed, destroyed, or concealed any of (a) his property with intent to hinder, delay, or defraud his creditors within twelve months preceding the filing of the bankruptcy petition, or, (b) property of the estate after the date of filing of the petition;

5. has within six years prior to bankruptcy been granted a discharge;

6. refused to obey any lawful order of the court or to answer any question approved by the court;

7. has failed to explain satisfactorily any losses of assets or deficiency of assets to meet his liabilities; or

8. has executed a written waiver of discharge approved by the court.

On the request of the trustee or a creditor and after notice and a hearing, the court may revoke a discharge within one year if it was obtained through the fraud of the debtor.

REORGANIZATION—CHAPTER 11

Reorganization is the means by which a distressed business enterprise and its value as a going concern are preserved through the correction or elimination of the factors that brought about its distress. Chapter 11 of the Bankruptcy Code governs reorganization of eligible debtors, including partnerships and corporations, and permits restructuring of their capital structure. A number of large cor-

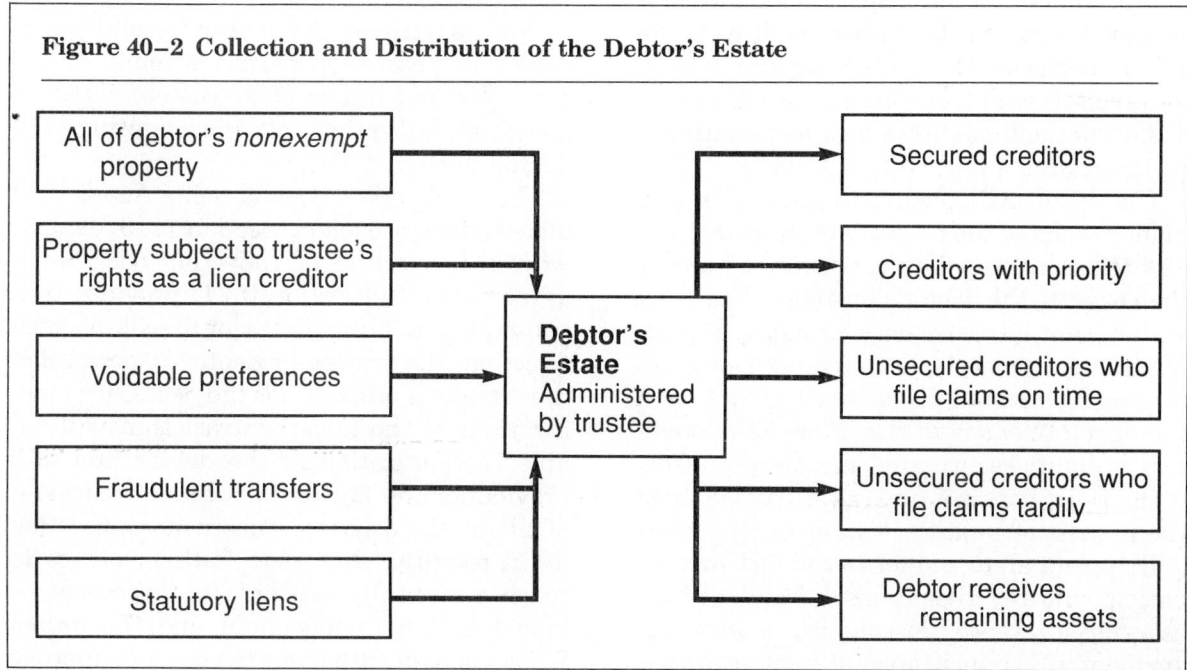

Figure 40–2 Collection and Distribution of the Debtor's Estate

All of debtor's *nonexempt* property

Property subject to trustee's rights as a lien creditor

Voidable preferences

Fraudulent transfers

Statutory liens

Debtor's Estate Administered by trustee

Secured creditors

Creditors with priority

Unsecured creditors who file claims on time

Unsecured creditors who file claims tardily

Debtor receives remaining assets

porations have made use of Chapter 11, including Texaco, A H Robins, Johns-Manville, Allied Stores, and Eastern Airlines. The main objective of a reorganization proceeding is to develop and carry out a fair, equitable, and feasible plan of reorganization. After a plan has been prepared and filed, a hearing is held before the court to determine whether or not it will be confirmed.

Proceedings

Any person that may be a debtor under Chapter 7 (except stockbrokers and commodity brokers) and railroads may be a debtor under Chapter 11. Petitions may be voluntary or involuntary. *See In re Johns-Manville Corp.*

As soon as practicable after the order for relief, a committee of unsecured creditors is appointed. This committee usually consists of persons that hold the seven largest unsecured claims against the debtor. In addition, the court may order the appointment of additional committees of creditors or of equity security holders, if necessary, to assure adequate representation. Section 1102. The committee may, with the court's approval, employ attorneys, accountants, and other agents to represent or perform services for the committee. The committee may consult with the debtor or trustee concerning the administration of the case and may investigate the debtor's affairs and participate in formulating a reorganization plan. Section 1103.

The debtor will remain in possession and management of the property of the estate unless the court appoints a trustee, who may then operate the debtor's business. The court will appoint a trustee *only for cause* (including fraud, dishonesty, incompetence, or gross mismanagement of the debtor's affairs) or if the appointment is in the interests of creditors or equity security holders. Section 1104. If the court does not appoint a trustee upon the request of a party in interest, the court will appoint an examiner to conduct investigations into any allegations of fraud, dishonesty, incompetence, misconduct, or mismanagement if (1) such appointment is in the

interests of creditors or equity security holders or (2) the debtor's fixed, liquidated, unsecured debts exceed $5,000,000.

The duties of a trustee in a case under Chapter 11 include the following:

1. to be accountable for all property received;

2. to examine proofs of claims;

3. to furnish information to all parties in interest;

4. to provide the court and taxing authorities with financial reports of the business operations;

5. to make a final report and account of the administration of the estate;

6. to investigate the financial condition of the debtor and the desirability of the continuance of the debtor's business; and

7. to file a plan or a report as to why there will be no plan or to recommend conversion of the case to Chapter 7.

At any time before confirmation of a plan, the court may terminate the trustee's appointment and restore the debtor to possession and management of the property of the estate and operation of the debtor's business. Section 1105.

When a trustee has not been appointed, the debtor in possession performs many of the functions and duties of a trustee, with the principal exception of investigating the debtor. Section 1107.

The Bankruptcy Amendments Act of 1984 added a new provision (Section 1113) dealing with the rejection of collective bargaining agreements. Subsection (b)(1) provides that subsequent to filing and prior to seeking such rejection, the trustee or debtor-in-possession must make a proposal for the necessary modifications of the labor contract that will enable reorganization of the debtor and also provide for the fair and equitable treatment of all of the parties concerned. Subsection (b)(2) requires that good faith meetings to reach a mutually satisfactory agreement be held between management and the union. Subsection (c) authorizes the court to approve rejection of the collective bargaining agreement only if the court finds that the proposal was made in accordance with these conditions, that the union refused the proposal without good cause, and that the balance of equities clearly favors rejection of such agreement.

Plan of Reorganization

The debtor may file a plan at any time and has the exclusive right to file a plan during the 120 days after the order for relief, unless a trustee has been appointed. Then other parties in interest including the trustee, if a trustee has been appointed, or a creditors' committee may file a plan, if the debtor has not filed a plan within 120 days or the plan has not been accepted within 180 days. Section 1121.

A plan of reorganization must divide creditors' claims and shareholders' interests into classes, specify how each class will be treated, deal with each class equally, and provide adequate means for implementing the plan. After a plan has been filed, the plan and a written disclosure statement approved by the court as containing adequate information must be transmitted to each holder of a claim before seeking acceptance or rejection of the plan. **Adequate information** means information of a kind and in sufficient detail that would enable a hypothetical, reasonable investor to make an informed judgment about the plan. Section 1125.

Acceptance of Plan

Each class of claims and interests has the opportunity to accept or reject the proposed plan. A **class of claims** has accepted a plan if it has been accepted by creditors that hold at least two-thirds in amount and more than one-half of the allowed claims of such class. Acceptance of a plan by a **class of interests,** such as shareholders, requires acceptance by holders of at least two-thirds in amount of the allowed interests of such class.

A class that is not impaired under a plan is conclusively presumed to have accepted the plan. Basically, a class is not impaired if the plan leaves unaltered the legal, equitable, and contractual rights to which such claim or interest entitles the holder of that claim or right. Section 1124. A class that will receive no distribution under a plan is deemed *not* to have accepted the plan.

Confirmation of Plan

A plan must be confirmed, after notice and a hearing, by the court before it is binding on any parties. A court may confirm a plan only if it meets all of the requirements of Section 1129 of the Bankruptcy Code. The most important of these requirements are the following.

Good Faith The plan must have been proposed in good faith and not by any means forbidden by law. Section 1129(a)(3).

Feasibility The court must find that confirmation of the plan is not likely to be followed by the liquidation or the need for further financial reorganization of the debtor. Section 1129(a)(11). The essence of feasibility is that the reorganization entity will be able to operate economically and efficiently, will be able to compete upon fairly equal terms with other companies within the industry, and is not likely to require liquidation or a second reorganization within the foreseeable future.

Cash Payments Certain classes of creditors must have their allowed claims paid in full in cash immediately or, in some instances, upon a deferred basis. Section 1129(a)(9). These classes include the expenses of administration, gap creditors, claims for wages and salaries, and employee benefits and consumer deposits.

Acceptance by Creditors To be confirmed, the plan must be accepted by at least *one* class of claims, and with respect to *each* class, each holder must either accept the plan *or* receive not less than the amount he would have received under Chapter 7. In addition, each class must accept the plan or be unimpaired by the plan. Nonetheless, under certain circumstances the court may confirm a plan that is not accepted by all impaired classes. The court must determine that the plan does not discriminate unfairly and that it is fair and equitable. Section 1129(b)(1). Under these circumstances, a class of claims or interests may, over its objections, be involuntarily subjected to the provisions of a plan.

Fair and equitable with respect to secured creditors requires that they either retain their security interest and receive deferred cash payments at least equal to their claims or that they realize the "indubitable equivalent" of their claims. Fair and equitable with respect to unsecured creditors means that such creditors receive property of value equivalent to the full amount of their claim *or* that no junior claim or interest receive anything at all. With respect to a class of interests, a plan is fair and equitable if the holders receive full value or if no junior interest receives anything at all.

Effect of Reorganization

After confirmation of the plan, the debtor's performance obligations are governed by the plan. The plan binds the debtor and any creditor, equity security holder, or general partner of the debtor. Upon the entry of a final decree closing the proceedings, the debtor is discharged from all of its debts and liabilities that arose before the date of confirmation of the plan except as otherwise provided in the plan, the order of confirmation, or the Bankruptcy Code. Section 1141. The confirmation of a plan does not discharge an *individual* debtor from debts that are not dischargeable under Section 523.

ADJUSTMENT OF DEBTS OF A FAMILY FARMER—CHAPTER 12

In 1986, Congress amended the Bankruptcy Act by adding Chapter 12, which provides for the adjustment of debts of a family farmer with regular annual income. Chapter 12 has a "sunset" provision: it will expire in 1993 unless Congress reenacts it. Its purpose is to provide a proceeding for family farmers who do not qualify for Chapter 13 and find Chapter 11 proceedings overly burdensome.

Proceedings

A family farmer is defined as an individual, or individual and spouse, who are engaged in farming and receive 50 percent of their gross income from farming. Their aggregate debts may not exceed $1.5 million, and at least 80 percent of the debts must arise out of the farming operation. A corporation or partnership may also qualify as a family farmer if, in addition to meeting the requirements just mentioned, 50 percent of the stock or equity is held by one family, and more than 80 percent of the assets of the corporation or partnership are related to the farming operation.

Unlike Chapters 7 and 11, property of the estate in Chapter 12 includes wages earned and other property acquired by the debtor after the Chapter 12 filing. Section 1207. A trustee is appointed in all Chapter 12 cases. The debtor usually remains in possession of all property of the estate. A debtor in possession has the rights, powers, and performs many of the duties of a trustee serving in a case under Chapter 11. At the request of a party in interest and after notice and a hearing, the court shall remove a debtor in possession if cause is shown. Section 1204. Cause includes fraud, dishonesty, incompetence, or gross mismanagement. Upon removal, the trustee performs the duties of the debtor in possession as well as the duties of a trustee under Chapter 12.

The Plan

The debtor is required to file a plan within 90 days after the order for relief, unless the court grants an extension. The debtor may modify the plan at any time before confirmation. The plan must meet three requirements under Section 1222:

1. It must provide for submission of all or any portion of future earnings or income of the debtor, as necessary for the execution of

the plan, to the supervision and control of the trustee.

2. It must provide for full payment on a deferred basis of all claims entitled to a priority, unless a holder of a claim agrees to a different treatment of that claim.

3. If the plan classifies claims, it must provide the same treatment for each claim in the same class.

In addition, the plan *may* modify the rights of unsecured creditors and the rights of secured creditors. A plan may provide for payments on any unsecured claim to be made concurrently with payments on any secured claim.

The plan may *not* provide for payments over a period that is longer than three years, unless the court approves for cause a longer period not to exceed five years.

Confirmation

The plan will be confirmed by the court if certain requirements have been met. First, the plan must comply with applicable law and be proposed in good faith. Second, the value of the property to be distributed to unsecured creditors must not be less than the amount that would be paid them under Chapter 7. Third, either the secured creditors must accept the plan *or* the plan must provide that the debtor will surrender to the secured creditors the collateral *or* the plan must permit the secured creditors to retain their security interest and the value of property to be distributed to them is not less than the allowed amount of their claim. Fourth, the debtor must be able to make all payments and comply with the plan. Fifth, if the trustee or holder of an unsecured claim objects to the confirmation of a plan, then the plan must either provide for payment in full of that claim or provide that all of the debtor's disposable income for three years apply to payments under the plan. Section 1225. Once the plan is confirmed, it binds the debtor, each creditor, each equity security holder, and each general partner in the debtor.

Discharge

After a debtor completes all payments under the plan, the court will grant him a discharge of all debts provided for by the plan except the nondischargeable debts. Even if all payments have *not* been made, the court may, after a hearing, grant a discharge if the debtor's failure to complete such payments is due to circumstances for which the debtor should not justly be held accountable, the value of property actually distributed is not less than what would have been received under Chapter 7, and modification of the plan is not practicable. Section 1228(b). A debtor who receives a discharge under Chapter 7 cannot obtain a discharge again under that chapter for six years, although a debtor discharged under Chapter 12 is not subject to that limitation if payments under the plan totaled at least (1) 100 percent of unsecured claims or (2) 70 percent of such claims *and* the plan was the debtor's best effort. Section 727(a)(9).

ADJUSTMENT OF DEBTS OF INDIVIDUALS—CHAPTER 13

To encourage debtors to pay their debts wherever possible, Congress enacted Chapter 13 of the Bankruptcy Code. This chapter permits an individual debtor to file a repayment plan which, if confirmed by the court, will discharge him from almost all of his debts when he completes his payments under the plan.

Proceedings

Chapter 13 provides a procedure for the adjustment of debts of an *individual* with regular income who owes liquidated, unsecured debts of less than $100,000 and secured debts of less than $350,000. Sole proprietorships are also eligible if the debt limitations are met. A case under Chapter 13 may be initiated *only* by a voluntary petition. A trustee is appointed in every Chapter 13 case. Property of the estate in Chapter 13, as with Chapter 12, includes wages earned and other property acquired by the debtor after the Chapter 13 filing. Section 1306.

The Plan

The debtor files the plan and may modify it at any time before confirmation. The plan must meet three requirements under Section 1322:

1. It must provide for submission of all or any portion of future earnings or income of the debtor, as is necessary for the execution of the plan, to the supervision and control of the trustee.

2. It must provide for full payment on a deferred basis of all claims entitled to a priority unless a holder of a claim agrees to a different treatment of such claim.

3. If the plan classifies claims, it must provide the same treatment for each claim in the same class.

In addition, the plan *may* modify the rights of unsecured creditors and the rights of secured creditors except those secured only by a security interest in the debtor's principal residence. A plan may provide for payments on any unsecured claim to be made concurrently with payments on any secured claim.

The plan may *not* provide for payments over a period that is longer than three years, unless the court approves for cause a longer period not to exceed five years.

Confirmation

The plan will be confirmed by the court if certain requirements have been met. First, the plan must comply with applicable law and be proposed in good faith. Second, the value of the property to be distributed to unsecured creditors must be not less than the amount that would be paid them under Chapter 7. Third, either the secured creditors must accept the plan *or* the plan must provide that the debtor will surrender to the secured creditors the collateral *or* the plan must permit the secured creditors to retain their security interest and the value of property to be distributed to them is not less than the allowed amount of their claim. Fourth,

the debtor must be able to make all payments and comply with the plan. Fifth, if the trustee or holder of an unsecured claim objects to the confirmation of a plan, then the plan must either provide for payment in full of that claim or provide that all of the debtor's disposable income for three years be applied to payments under the plan. For purposes of this provision, *disposable income* means income received by the debtor that is not reasonably necessary for the maintenance or support of the debtor or a dependent of the debtor, or if the debtor is engaged in business, for the payment of expenditures necessary for the continuation, preservation, and operation of the business.

Discharge

After a debtor completes all payments under the plan, the court will grant him a discharge of all debts provided for by the plan except nondischargeable debts for alimony, maintenance, and support. This discharge is considerably more extensive than that granted under Chapter 7. Moreover, a debtor who receives a discharge under Chapter 7 cannot obtain a discharge again under that chapter for six years, although a debtor discharged under Chapter 13 is not subject to that limitation if payments under the plan totaled at least (1) 100 percent of unsecured claims or (2) 70 percent of such claims *and* the plan was the debtor's best effort. Section 727(a) (9). *See In re Jonson.*

Even if all payments have *not* been made, the court may, after a hearing, grant a discharge if the debtor's failure to complete such payments is due to circumstances for which the debtor should not justly be held accountable, the value of property actually distributed is not less than what would have been received under Chapter 7, and modification of the plan is not practicable. Section 1328(b). This discharge, however, is subject to the same exceptions for nondischargeable debts as a discharge under Chapter 7.

CREDITORS' RIGHTS AND DEBTOR RELIEF OUTSIDE OF BANKRUPTCY

The rights and remedies of debtors and creditors outside of bankruptcy are principally governed by State law. Because of the expense and notoriety associated with bankruptcy, it is often in the best interests of both debtor and creditor to resolve their claims outside of a bankruptcy proceeding. Accordingly, bankruptcy is usually viewed as the last resort.

The rights and remedies of creditors outside of bankruptcy are varied. The first part of this section examines the basic right of *all* creditors to pursue their overdue claims to judgment and to satisfy that judgment out of property belonging to the debtor. Other rights and remedies are discussed elsewhere in this book. The rights under Article 2 of the Uniform Commercial Code of an unpaid credit seller to reclaim the goods sold are covered in Chapter 24. The right of a secured creditor to enforce a security interest in personal property is the subject of Chapter 38. Likewise, the right of a creditor to foreclose a mortgage on real property is discussed in Chapter 51. In addition, the right of a creditor to proceed against a surety on the debt is addressed in Chapter 39.

At the same time, the law attempts to protect debtors against overreaching by creditors. This goal has been pursued by a number of means. States have enacted usury laws as discussed in Chapter 12. The Federal Trade Commission has limited the rights of a holder in due course against consumer debtors as explained in Chapter 27. Congress has prohibited abusive, deceptive, and unfair debt collection practices employed by debt collection agencies as discussed in Chapter 43. That chapter also covers other legal protection offered to *consumer* debtors. The second part of this section describes the various forms of nonbankruptcy compromises that have developed to provide relief to debtors who have become overextended and are unable to pay all of their creditors.

CREDITORS' RIGHTS

When a debtor fails to pay a debt, the creditor may file suit to collect the debt owed. The ultimate objective is to obtain a judgment against the debtor and then to collect on that judgment.

Pre-judgment Remedies

Because litigation takes time, a creditor attempting to collect on a claim through the judicial process will almost always experience delay in obtaining judgment. To protect against the debtor's disposing of his assets, the creditor may use, when available, certain pre-judgment remedies. The most important of these is **attachment,** which is the process of seizing property, by virtue of a writ, summons, or other judicial order, and bringing the property into the custody of the court for the purpose of securing satisfaction of the judgment ultimately to be entered in the action. At common law, the main objective was to coerce the defendant debtor to appear in court; today the writ of attachment is statutory and used primarily to seize the debtor's property in the event a judgment is rendered. Most States limit attachment to specified grounds and require the opportunity for a hearing before a judge prior to the issuance of a writ of execution. Generally, attachment is limited to situations in which (a) the defendant cannot be personally served; (b) the claim is based upon fraud or the equivalent; or (c) the defendant has or is likely to transfer his property. In addition, the plaintiff must generally post a bond to compensate the defendant for loss should the plaintiff not prevail in the cause of action.

Similar in purpose is the remedy of pre-judgment **garnishment,** which is a statutory proceeding directed at a third person who owes a debt to the debtor or has property belonging to the debtor. Garnishment is most commonly used against the employer of the debtor and the bank in which the debtor has a savings or checking account. Property garnished remains in the hands of the third party pending the outcome of the suit. For example, Calvin brings an action against Daisy to collect a debt that is past due. Alvin has property belonging to Daisy. Calvin might garnish this property so that if Calvin is successful in his action against Daisy, Calvin's judgment could be satisfied out of that property held by Alvin. If Alvin no longer had the property when Calvin obtained judgment, Calvin could recover from Alvin.

Post-judgment Remedies

If the debtor still has not paid the claim, the creditor may proceed to trial and try to obtain a court judgment against the debtor. Obtaining a judgment, however, is only the first, although necessary, step in collecting the debt. If the debtor does not voluntarily pay the judgment, the creditor will have to take additional steps to collect on the judgment. These steps are called "post-judgment remedies."

First, the judgment creditor will have the clerk issue a **writ of execution,** which is served by the sheriff upon the defendant/debtor demanding payment of the judgment. Upon return of the writ "unsatisfied," the judgment creditor may post bond or other security and order a levy on and sale of specified nonexempt property belonging to the defendant/debtor, which is then seized by the sheriff, advertised for sale, and sold at public sale under the writ of execution.

The writ of execution is limited to property of the debtor that is not exempt. All States restrict creditors from recourse to certain property, the type and amount of which varies greatly from State to State.

If the proceeds of the sale do not produce sufficient funds to pay the judgment, the creditor may institute a **supplementary proceeding** in an attempt to locate money or other property belonging to the defendant. He may also proceed by **garnishment** against the debtor's employer or a bank in which the debtor has an account in an attempt to collect the judgment.

DEBTOR'S RELIEF

There are several inherent conflicts between creditors' rights and debtor relief: (1) the right of diligent creditors to pursue their claims to judgment and to satisfy their judgments by sale of property of the debtor; (2) the right of unsecured creditors who have refrained from suing the debtor; and (3) the social policy of affording relief to a debtor who has contracted debts beyond his ability to pay and who may be confronted by a lifetime burden. Resolving these conflicts necessarily involves a compromise under which the debtor will disclose and surrender all his assets to a trustee or other person for the benefit of his creditors and the creditors will receive fair and equal treatment.

Various forms of nonbankruptcy compromises have been developed to provide relief to debtors, some of which are less formal, such as those offered by credit agencies and adjustment bureaus. Some are founded in common law and involve simple contract and trust principles, such as compositions and assignments; others are statutory, such as statutory assignments. Some involve the intervention of a court and its officers, such as equity receiverships, while others do not.

Compositions

A common law or non-statutory **composition** is an ordinary contract or agreement between the debtor and her creditors, under which the creditors receive *pro rata* a part of their claims and the debtor is discharged from the balance of the claims. As a contract, it requires the formalities of a contract, such as offer, acceptance, and consideration. For example, debtor D owing debts of $5,000 to A, $2,000 to B, and $1,000 to C offers to settle these claims by paying a total of $4,000 to A, B, and C. If A, B, and C accept the offer, a composition results with A receiving $2,500, B $1,000, and C $500. The consideration for the promise of A to forgive the balance of his claim consists of the promises of B and C to forgive the balance of their claims. All the creditors benefit because a race among creditors to obtain the debtor's limited assets is avoided.

It should be noted, however, that the debtor in a composition is discharged from liability only upon the claims of creditors who voluntarily consent to the composition. If, in the illustration above, C had refused to accept the offer of composition and had refused to take the $500, he could attempt to collect the full $1,000 claim. Likewise, if D owed additional debts to X, Y, and Z, these creditors would not be bound by the agreement between D and A, B, and C. Another disadvantage of the composition is the fact that any creditor can attach the assets of the debtor during the usual period of bargaining and negotiation which precedes the execution of the composition agreement. For instance, once D advised A, B and C that he was offering to compose the claims, any one of the creditors could seize D's property.

A variation of the composition is an extension agreement worked out by the debtor with her creditors providing for payment of her debts either in full or proportionately scaled down over a period of time.

Assignments for Benefit of Creditors

A common law or non-statutory assignment for the benefit of creditors, or general assignment as it is sometimes called, is a voluntary transfer by the debtor of some or all of his property to a trustee who applies the property to the payment of all of the debtor's debts. For instance, debtor D transfers title to his property to trustee T, who converts the property into money and pays it to all of the creditors on a *pro rata* basis.

The advantage of the assignment over the composition is that it protects the debtor's assets from attachment and execution, and it halts the race of diligent creditors to attach. On the other hand, the common law assignment does not require the consent of the creditors, and payment by the trustee of part of the claims does not discharge the debtor from the balance of them. Thus, in the previous example, even after T pays A $2,500, B $1,000, and C $500 (and appropri-

ate payments to all other creditors), A, B, and C and the other creditors may still attempt to collect the balance of their claims.

Statutory Assignments

Because assignments benefit creditors by protecting the debtor's assets from attachment, there have been many statutory attempts to combine the idea of the assignment with a corresponding benefit to the debtor by discharging him from the balance of his debts. Since the United States Constitution prohibits a State from impairing the obligation of a contract between private citizens, it is impossible for a State to force all creditors to discharge a debtor upon a *pro rata* distribution of assets, although, as previously discussed, the Federal government *does* have such power and exercises it in the Bankruptcy Act. Accordingly, the States have generally enacted assignment statutes permitting the debtor to obtain *voluntary* releases of the balance of claims from creditors who accept partial payments, thus combining the advantages of common law compositions and assignments.

Equity Receiverships

One of the oldest remedies in equity is the appointment of a receiver by the court. The receiver is a disinterested person who collects and preserves the debtor's assets and income and disposes of them at the direction of the court which appointed her. The court may instruct her (1) to liquidate the assets by public or private sale; (2) to operate the business as a going concern temporarily; or (3) to conserve the assets until final disposition of the matter before the court.

A receiver will be appointed upon the petition (1) of a secured creditor seeking foreclosure of his security; (2) of a judgment creditor after exhausting legal remedies to satisfy the judgment; or (3) of a shareholder of a corporate debtor where it appears that the assets of the corporation will be dissipated by fraud or mismanagement. The appointment of a receiver always rests within the sound discretion of the court. Insolvency, in the equity sense of inability by the debtor to pay his debts as they mature, is one of the factors considered by the court in appointing a receiver.

CASES

Voidable Preferences

IN RE HAMILTON

United States Court of Appeals, Fifth Circuit, 1990.
892 F.2d 1230.

BROWN, C.J.

The question is whether the Texas UCC 20 day grace period or the Federal Bankruptcy § 547(c) 10 day grace period for perfection of a security interest in personal property applies. Not too surprisingly we hold that the bankruptcy law prevails and thus affirm the judgment of the bankruptcy court as affirmed by the district court in favor of the trustee.

* * *

The scenario, unlike the interlocking complex legal issues, is simple. The bankruptcy petition of the vehicle purchaser (Debtor) was filed in Tennessee on May 23, 1985. Well within the 90 day preference period the trustee sought and obtained recovery of a BMW sedan which the Debtor had purchased for his daughter from the Dealer (Howard Thornton Ford, Inc.) in March of that year.

The significant facts, largely undisputed . . . are straightforward and simple. On March 6, 1985 the Debtor, as a then pre-bankruptcy purchaser, negotiated a loan with Interfirst Bank of Dallas, NA (the Bank) and signed a promissory note on that date. The Dealer began processing the necessary documents to transfer title and create a lien in favor of the Bank on March 2d.

* * *

The bankruptcy judge and the district court fixed March 8, 1985 as the date on which the daughter picked up the car little aware that she would shortly lose this luxury as the Bank on August 25, 1985 repossessed it and then surrendered it to the Dealer who sold the car.

. . . The bankruptcy trustee then sought recovery of the vehicle as an asset of the estate claiming the transfer to the Bank was an avoidable preference under § 547(b) of the Bankruptcy Code, [citation]. That section prescribes five requirements for establishing a preference, the first three of which are undisputed: (1) for the benefit of the creditor (Bank-Dealer), (2) made while the Debtor was insolvent, (3) which occurred within 90 days of the date of the filing of the bankruptcy petition. Besides disputing the last two: (4) to be on account of an antecedent debt and (5) enable the creditor to receive more than it would have if proceeding under Chapter 7, the Banker-Dealer contend affirmatively that the transfer was non-avoidable under § 547(c).

* * *

In the analysis of the problem of supremacy/conflict between state and federal (bankruptcy) law it is worthwhile to emphasize that the problem is not accidental. It is indeed the result of a deliberate congressional determination to rely much on the basis of state law, some, if ever, specifically identified and frequently obscure.

For example, Congress in enacting § 547 of the Bankruptcy Act establishing the trustee's power to avoid preferential transfers prescribed in § 547(e)(1)(B) established that "a transfer of . . . property other than real property is perfected when a creditor on a simple contract cannot acquire a judicial lien that is superior to the interest of the transferee." Since the federal law does not prescribe the circumstances under which or when a creditor on a civil contract cannot acquire a judicial lien superior to the interest of the transferee, the source for such definitive standards must be the state law. This automatically sends us to the Texas Business and Commerce Act (hereafter cited as UCC). The transaction involved here comes within the UCC definition of a purchase money security interest, sometimes referred to as enabling loans, and is substantially subject to priorities over an unperfected security interest. Perfection of such a security interest calls ordinarily for the timely filing of a financing statement. * * *

Conflict Between UCC and § 547(c)

All this means is that, most favorable to them, the Banker-Dealer's lien was not perfected until March 19, 1985. . . . Texas law applies to this purchase money security interest the Bank-Dealer's security is saved by §§ 9.301(b), 9.312(d) since perfection occurred within 20 days of the date (March 8, 1985) on which the Debtor or his daughter-agent received possession of the vehicle. [In footnote 14 the court quoted Texas's UCC Section 9–301(b):] "If the secured party files with respect to a purchase money security interest before or within 20 days after the debtor receives possession of the collateral, he takes priority over the rights of a transferee in bulk or of a lien creditor which arise between the time the security interest attaches and the time of filing."

Since Banker-Dealer cannot establish with sufficient force to overcome the trial judge's finding that possession by Debtor-agent (daughter) occurred after the date fixed (March 8) to bring perfection within 10 days their only hope of success depends on establishing that the 20 day Texas grace period, not the 10 day bankruptcy grace period, excuses this 11 day delay. The supremacy of Texas/Federal law must therefore be determined.

Section 547(c) Prevails

This brings us face to face with the conflict raised by § 547(c) of the Bankruptcy Code which provides that the trustee may not avoid a § 547(b) preference . . . of a security interest in property acquired by the debtor

under prescribed conditions if it is perfected on or before 10 days after the debtor has received possession of the collateral. * * *

The relative supremacy of the Texas 20 day versus the federal 10 day grace period has not been widely litigated. Two bankruptcy court decisions reach opposite results. [Citation] holds that the 10 day Bankruptcy Act period controls over the Florida 15 day statute § 679.301, comparable to the requirement of the Texas UCC § 9.301(b). * * * The court applied the Eleventh Circuit statement in [citation] "the establishment of a ten day grace period was an effort to create a national uniform perfection period for enabling loans."

The other case, [citation] on the theory of a continuous perfection throughout the Tennessee 20 day period the court held the state period (20 days) controlled over the § 547(c) 10 day period. The court nevertheless emphasized "that the legislative history shows that Congress intended for ten days to be a uniform grace period." [Citation.]

In this choice we prefer [the 10 day rule] as do treatises commentators. [Citations.]

* * *

Affirmed.

Proceedings in Chapter 11

IN RE JOHNS–MANVILLE CORPORATION

United States Bankruptcy Court, Southern District of New York, 1984.
36 B.R. 727.

LIFLAND, BKRTCY, J.

Whether an industrial enterprise in the United States is highly successful is often gauged by its "membership" in what has come to be known as the "Fortune 500". Having attained this measure of financial achievement, Johns-Manville Corp. and its affiliated companies (collectively referred to as "Manville") were deemed a paradigm of success in corporate America by the financial community. Thus, Manville's filing for protection under Chapter 11 . . . of the United States Code ("the Code or the Bankruptcy

Code") on August 26, 1982 ("the filing date") was greeted with great surprise and consternation on the part of some of its creditors and other corporations that were being sued along with Manville for injuries caused by asbestos exposure. As discussed at length herein, Manville submits that the sole factor necessitating its filing is the mammoth problem of uncontrolled proliferation of asbestos health suits brought against it because of its substantial use for many years of products containing asbestos which injured those who came into contact with the dust of this lethal substance. According to Manville, this current problem of approximately 16,000 lawsuits pending as of the filing date is compounded by the crushing economic burden to be suffered by Manville over the next 20–30 years by the filing of an even more staggering number of suits by those who had been exposed but who will not manifest the asbestos-related diseases until some time during this future period ("the future asbestos claimants"). Indeed, approximately 6,000 asbestos health claims are estimated to have arisen in only the first 16 months since the filing date. This burden is further compounded by the insurance industry's general disavowal of liability to Manville on policies written for this very purpose. * * *

It is the propriety of the filing by Manville which is the subject of the instant decision. Four separate motions to dismiss the petition . . . have been lodged before this Court.

* * *

Preliminarily, it must be stated that there is no question that Manville is eligible to be a debtor under the Code's statutory requirements.

* * *

Moreover, it should also be noted that [no] . . . provision relating to voluntary petitions by companies contains any insolvency requirement.

* * *

Accordingly, it is abundantly clear that Manville has met all of the threshold eligibility requirements for filing a voluntary petition under the Code. This Court will now turn to the issue of whether any of the mo-

vants have demonstrated sufficient "cause" . . . to warrant the dismissal of Manville's petition.

* * *

In determining whether to dismiss . . ., a court is not necessarily required to consider whether the debtor has filed in "good faith" because that is not a specified predicate under the Code for filing. Rather, according to [the] Code . . ., good faith emerges as a requirement for the confirmation of a plan. The filing of a Chapter 11 case creates an estate for the benefit of all creditors and equity holders of the debtor wherein all constituencies may voice their interests and bargain for their best possible treatment. [Citation.] It is thus logical that the good faith of the debtor be deemed a predicate primarily for emergence out of a Chapter 11 case. It is after. confirmation of a concrete and immutable reorganization plan that creditors are foreclosed from advancing their distinct and parochial interests in the debtor's estate.

A "principal goal" of the Bankruptcy Code is to provide "open access" to the "bankruptcy process". [Citation.] The rationale behind this "open access" policy is to provide access to bankruptcy relief which is as "open" as "access to the credit economy." [Citation.] Thus, Congress intended that "there should be no legal barrier to voluntary petitions." [Citation.] Another major goal of the Code, that of "rehabilitation of debtors", requires that relief for debtors must be "timely". [Citation.] * * *

Accordingly, the drafters of the Code envisioned that a financially beleaguered debtor with real debt and real creditors should not be required to wait until the economic situation is beyond repair in order to file a reorganization petition. The "Congressional purpose" in enacting the Code was to encourage resort to the bankruptcy process. *Id.* This philosophy not only comports with the elimination of an insolvency requirement, but also is a corollary of the key aim of Chapter 11 of the Code, that of avoidance of liquidation. The drafters of the Code announced this goal, declaring that reorganization is more efficient than liquidation because "assets that are used for production in the industry for which they were designed are more valuable than those same assets sold for scrap." [Citation.] Moreover, reorganization also fosters the goals of preservation of jobs in the threatened entity. [Citation.]

In the instant case, not only would liquidation be wasteful and inefficient in destroying the utility of valuable assets of the companies as well as jobs, but, more importantly, liquidation would preclude just compensation of some present asbestos victims and all future asbestos claimants. This unassailable reality represents all the more reason for this Court to adhere to this basic potential liquidation avoidance aim of Chapter 11 and deny the motions to dismiss. Manville must not be required to wait until its economic picture has deteriorated beyond salvation to file for reorganization.

* * *

In [this case] it is undeniable that there has been no sham or hoax perpetrated on the Court in that Manville is a real business with real creditors in pressing need of economic reorganization. Indeed, the Asbestos Committee has belied its own contention that Manville has no debt and no real creditors by quantifying a benchmark settlement demand approaching one billion dollars for compensation of approximately 15,500 prepetition asbestos claimants, during the course of negotiations pitched toward achieving a consensual plan. This huge asserted liability does not even take into account the estimated 6,000 new asbestos health claims which have arisen in only the first 16 months since the filing date. The number of post-filing claims increases each day as "future claims back into the present." * * *

Moreover, asbestos related property damage claims present another substantial contingent and unliquidated liability. Prior to the filing date, various schools initiated litigation seeking compensatory and punitive damages from ... Manville for their unknowing use of asbestos-containing products in ceilings, walls, structural members, piping, ductwork and boilers in school buildings.

* * *

Accordingly, it is clear that Manville's liability for compensatory, if not punitive, damages to school authorities is not hypothetical, but real and massive debt. A range of $500 million to $1.4 billion is the total projected amount of Manville's real debt to the school creditors.

In addition, claims of $425 million of liquidated commercial debt have been filed in this proceeding. The filing also triggered the acceleration of more than $275 million in unsecured public and institutional debt which had not been due prior to the filing. Upon a dismissal of this petition, Manville may be liable in the amount of all of the above-described real debts, plus interest. Manville's present holdings of cash and liquid assets would be insufficient to pay these obligations and, as noted above, its insurance carriers have repeatedly expressed their unwillingness to contribute to the payment of this debt. Thus, upon dismissal, Manville would become a target for economic dismemberment, liquidation, and chaos, which would benefit no one except the few winners of the race to the courthouse. The economic reality of Manville's highly precarious financial position due to massive debt sustains its eligibility and candidacy for reorganization.

In short, there was justification for Manville to elect a course contemplating a viable court-supervised rehabilitation of the real debt owed by Manville to its real creditors. Manville's filing did not in the appropriate sense abuse the jurisdiction of this Court and it is indeed, like the debtor in (citation), a "once viable business supporting employees and unsecured creditors (which) has more recently been burdened with judgments (and suits) that threaten to put it out of existence." ... [Citation.] Thus, its petition must be sustained.

* * *

In sum, Manville is a financially beseiged enterprise in desperate need of reorganization of its crushing real debt, both present and future. The reorganization provisions of the Code were drafted with the aim of liquidation avoidance by great access to Chapter 11. Accordingly, Manville's filing does not abuse the jurisdictional integrity of this Court, but rather presents the same kinds of reasons that were present in [citation], for awaiting the determination of Manville's good faith until it is considered . . . as a prerequisite to confirmation or as a part of the cadre of motions before me which are scheduled to be heard subsequently.

[Motions to dismiss the Manville petition denied.]

Confirmation of Chapter 13 Plan

IN RE JONSON

United States Bankruptcy Court, Southern District of Indiana, 1981.
17 B.R. 78.

BAYT, BKRTCY. J.

[The debtor, Jonson, is a single, thirty-five year old male with no dependents. He works as an administrative assistant for a medical doctor and has a net income of $755.00 per month. Jonson received a Master of Music degree from Indiana University and is only 2 courses short of receiving his doctorate. His only indebtedness is a student loan in the amount of $10,250.00 from Indiana University. Jonson has made no payments on this loan which became due and payable two years ago with monthly payments of $98.98. Jonson filed an amended plan under Chapter 13 in which he proposes to make payments to the Trustee of $140.00 per month for 36 months. Jonson's proposed plan would result in a total payment of $4,036.00 to Indiana University for a $10,250.00 loan. The plaintiff, Indiana University, objected to the confirmation of Jonson's Chapter 13 plan, raising the question of "good faith" on the part of Jonson.]

* * *

Before a bankruptcy court can confirm a Chapter 13 plan it must make certain findings. *See* 11 U.S.C. § 1325(a)(3). "In this respect, Chapter 13 differs markedly from Chapter 7 [since] [t]he court has virtually no role to play in straight bankruptcy or liquidation under Chapter 7." [Citation.]

One of the findings that the court must make is whether the "plan has been proposed in good faith. . . ." 11 U.S.C. § 1325(a)(3). The term "good faith", as used in 11 U.S.C. § 1325(a)(3), is not defined in the Code, nor can one look to the legislative history for a definition or a clarification of that term. Therefore, it is the court's duty "to fashion the meaning of that term." [Citation.]

This court is of the opinion that the major purpose of the court's discretion under § 1325 to scrutinize a Chapter 13 plan prior to confirmation, is to prevent debtor abuse of Chapter 13, and to insure that the distinction between Chapter 7 and Chapter 13, as well as the basic and underlying purpose of Chapter 13, is maintained. [Citation.]

A review of the legislative history unmistakably leads to the conclusion that the purpose of a Chapter 13 plan is to enable a debtor to pay either in full or in part, "debts which have become too burdensome to meet without the help of the bankruptcy laws." [Citations.] The purpose of Chapter 13 is not to allow a debtor to discharge a debt or debts which would not be dischargeable under Chapter 7, [citation], without substantial payment by the debtor to the creditor or creditors. To be sure, "the drafters [of the Code] did not intend the liberal provisions of Chapter 13 to be used as a disguised Chapter 7 liquidation. The drafters intended debtors to deal fairly and justly with their creditors." [Citation.] If a debtor is not dealing in such a manner, the court cannot find that the plan was proposed in good faith.

It is the court's opinion that the debtor's plan was not proposed in good faith. It appears that the debtor's sole purpose is to avoid the provisions of Chapter 7 which would not allow a discharge of the debtor's only debt, a student loan. [Citation.] This court does not mean to say, however, that a debtor's use of the liberal discharge provisions of Chapter 13 is *per se* bad faith. [Citation.] "But it may be bad faith to utilize these provisions without a corresponding attempt to repay creditors a meaningful [or substantial] amount." [Citation.] To allow confirmation of debtor's plan would in effect sanction "an abuse of the provisions, purpose and spirit of Chapter 13." [Citation.]

According to the terms of his plan, debtor would pay $140.00 per month for 36 months. At the end of 36 months debtor would have paid approximately $4,036.00 on a $10,250.00 student loan. The court notes that debtor's proposed payment is $41.00 more than the monthly payment of the student loan itself. Debtor's proposed payment is not a meaningful or substantial one. If he is able to pay more under the plan for three years than is required under the terms of his agreement with Indiana University, the court wonders why he should not continue to pay until the entire amount is paid off, particularly in view of the fact that he will earn more money as time passes.

In his Response, debtor maintains that a 39% dividend is a substantial payment, thus warranting confirmation of his plan. Such a dividend may well be substantial in other situations, but it is not so in the instant one, in which the debtor has only one debt and that debt is a student loan.

Given the nature of the debt, public policy should demand that the plan not be confirmed. Student loans serve an important and useful purpose. If a debtor fails to repay a student loan, a loan used to better oneself through higher education, such action by the debtor diminishes the amount that others may borrow.

The court CONCLUDES that debtor's Chapter 13 plan was not filed in good faith and, therefore, should not be confirmed by the court.

QUESTIONS

1. List (a) the priorities of creditors' claims, (b) the debtor's exemptions, and (c) the debts that are not dischargeable in bankruptcy.

2. Discuss the rights of a trustee (a) as a lien creditor, (b) to avoid preferential transfers, (c) to avoid fraudulent transfers, and (d) to avoid statutory liens.

3. State the order in which the debtor's estate is distributed under Chapter 7.

4. Compare the adjustment of debt proceedings under Chapters 11, 12, and 13.

5. Identify and define the nonbankruptcy compromises between debtors and creditors.

PROBLEMS

1. (a) Benson goes into bankruptcy. His estate has no assets. Are Benson's taxes discharged by the proceedings? Why or why not?

(b) Benson obtains property from Anderson on credit by representing that he is solvent when in fact he knows he is insolvent. Is Benson's debt to Anderson discharged by Benson's discharge in bankruptcy?

2. Bradley goes into bankruptcy owing $5,000 as wages to his four employees. There is enough in his estate to pay all costs of administration and enough to pay his employees, but nothing will then be left for general creditors. Do the employees take all the estate? Under what conditions? If the general creditors received nothing at all, would these debts be discharged?

3. Jessica sold goods to Stacy for $2,500 and retained a security interest in them. Three months later Stacy filed a petition in bankruptcy under Chapter 7. At this time Stacy still owed Jessica

$2,000 for the purchase price of the goods, whose value was $1,500.

(a) May the trustee invalidate Jessica's security interest. If so, under what provision?

(b) If the security interest is invalidated, what is Jessica's status in the bankruptcy proceeding?

(c) If the security interest is *not* invalidated, what is Jessica's status in the bankruptcy proceeding?

4. A debtor went through bankruptcy and received his discharge. Which of the following debts were completely discharged, and which remain debts against him in the future:

(a) A claim of $900 for wages earned within three months immediately prior to bankruptcy.

(b) A judgment of $3,000 against the debtor for breach of contract.

(c) $1,000 in past alimony and support money owed to his divorced wife for herself and their child.

(d) A judgment of $4,000 for injuries received because of the debtor's negligent operation of an automobile.

5. Rosinoff and his wife, who were business partners, entered bankruptcy. Objection was made to their discharge in bankruptcy by a creditor, Baldwin, on the grounds that

(a) the partners had obtained credit from Baldwin on the basis of a false financial statement;

(b) the partners had failed to keep books of account and records from which their financial condition could be ascertained; and

(c) Rosinoff had falsely sworn that he had taken $70 from the partnership account when the correct amount was $700.

Were the debtors entitled to a discharge?

6. Ross Corporation is a debtor in a reorganization proceeding under Chapter 11 of the Bankruptcy Code. By fair and proper valuation, its assets are worth $100,000. The indebtedness of the corporation is $105,000, it has outstanding $100 par value preferred stock in the amount of $20,000, and $30 par value common stock in the amount of $75,000. The plan of reorganization submitted by the trustees would give nothing to the common shareholders, bonds of the face amount of $5,000 to the creditors, and common stock in the ratio of 84 percent to the creditors and 16 percent to the preferred shareholders. Should this plan be confirmed?

7. Alex is a wage earner with a regular income. He has unsecured debts of $42,000 and secured debts owing to Betty, Connie, David, and Eunice totaling $120,000. Eunice's debt is secured only by a mortgage on Alex's house. Alex files a petition under Chapter 13 and a plan providing payment as follows: (a) 60 percent of all taxes owed, (b) 35 percent of all unsecured debts, and (c) $100,000 in total to Betty, Connie, David, and Eunice. Should the court confirm the plan? If not, how must the plan be modified and/or what other conditions must be satisfied?

8. John Bunker has assets of $130,000 and liabilities of $185,000 owed to nine creditors. Nonetheless, his cash flow is positive and he is making payment on all of his obligations as they become due. I.M. Flintheart, who is owed $22,000 by Bunker, files an involuntary petition in bankruptcy against Bunker. Bunker contests the petition. Decision?

9. Karen has filed a petition for a Chapter 7 proceeding. The total value of her estate is $35,000. Ben, who is owed $18,000, has a security interest in property valued at $12,000. Lauren has an unsecured claim of $9,000, which is entitled to a priority of $2,000. The United States has a claim for income taxes of $7,000. Steve has an unsecured claim of $10,000 that was filed on time. Sarah has an unsecured claim of $17,000 that was filed on time. Wally has a claim of $14,000 that was not filed on time even though Wally was aware of the bankruptcy proceedings. What should each of the creditors receive in a distribution under Chapter 7?

10. Landmark at Plaza Park, Ltd., filed a plan of reorganization under Chapter 11 of the Bankruptcy Code. Landmark is a limited partnership whose only substantial asset is a 200-unit garden apartment complex. City Federal holds the first mortgage on the property in the face amount of $2,250,000. The mortgage bears an interest rate of 9.5 percent and is due and payable six years from now.

Landmark has proposed a plan of reorganization under which the property now in possession of City Federal would be returned. Landmark will then deliver a nonrecourse note, payable in three years, in the face amount of $2,705,820.31 to City Federal in substitution of all of the partnership's existing liabilities. On the sixteenth month through the thirty-sixth month after the effective date of the plan, Landmark will make monthly interest payments at a rate of 12.5 percent computed on the value of the property of $2,260,000. Finally, the note will be secured by the existing mortgage. Landmark's theory is that the note will be paid off at the end of thirty-six months by a combination of refinancing and accumulation of cash from the project. The key is Landmark's proposal to obtain a new first mortgage in three years in the face amount of $2,400,000.

City Federal is a first mortgagee without recourse that has been collecting rents pursuant to a rent assignment agreement since the default on the mortgage eleven months ago. City Federal is impaired by the plan, has rejected the plan, and seeks to complete its foreclosure action. Decision?

11. Freelin Conn filed a voluntary petition under Chapter 7 of the Bankruptcy Code on September 30, 1980. Conn listed BancOhio National Bank as having a claim incurred in October of 1979 in the amount of $4,000 secured by a 1978 Oldsmobile Omega. The car is listed as having a market value of $3,500. During the period from June 30, 1980, to September 30, 1980, Conn made three payments totaling $439.17 to BancOhio. The net payoff balance on the installment loan was $4,015.91 on September 30 when the bankruptcy petition was filed. The trustee in bankruptcy now seeks to set aside those three payments as voidable preferences. Decision?

Chapter 41

PROTECTION OF INTELLECTUAL PROPERTY

Trade Secrets
Trade Symbols
Copyrights
Patents

THE economic system in the United States is based upon free and fair competition. The law prevents businesses from taking unfair advantage of their competitors. An important part of this area of law is the protection of intellectual property, which includes trade secrets, trade symbols, copyrights, and patents. These interests are protected from **infringement,** or unauthorized use, by others. Such protection is essential to the conduct of business. For example, business would be far less willing to invest considerable resources in research and development unless the resulting discoveries, inventions, and processes were protected by patents and trade secrets. Similarly, business would not be secure in devoting time and money to the marketing of its products and services if its trade symbols and trade names were not protected. Moreover, without copyright protection, the publishing, entertainment, and computer software industries would be vulnerable to having their efforts pirated by competitors. This chapter will discuss the law protecting (1) trade secrets; (2) trade symbols, including trademarks, service marks, certification marks, collective marks, and trade names; (3) copyrights; and (4) patents.

TRADE SECRETS

Every business has secret information, including lists of customers as well as contracts with suppliers and customers. Some have secret formulas, processes, and methods used in the production of goods that are vital to successful operation of the business. This information is considered a protected **trade secret** if it is commercially valuable, secret (guarded from disclosure), and not common knowledge. A trade secret may be disclosed in confidence to an employee with the understanding that the employee will not disclose the information. To the extent the owner of the information obtains a patent on it, then it is no longer a trade secret, but it is protected by patent law.

If a person **misappropriates** (wrongfully uses) a trade secret, the owner of the information may obtain damages and, where appropriate, injunctive relief. Basically, trade secrets are misappropriated in two ways: (1) an employee wrongfully uses or discloses it, or (2) a competitor wrongfully obtains it. *See Ziegler and Company v. Ehren.*

An employee is under a duty of loyalty to his employer, which includes the nondisclosure of trade secrets to competitors. It is wrongful for a competitor to obtain vital secret trade information of this type from an employee by bribery or other means. The faithless employee also commits a tort by divulging secret trade information. In the absence of a contract restriction, an employee is under no duty upon termination of his employment to refrain from competing or working for a competitor of his former employer, but he may not use trade secrets or disclose them to third persons. The employee, however, is entitled to use skill, knowledge, and general information acquired during the employment relationship. For example, Woodrow and Gail, who have been employees of the High Tech Company for fifteen years, have developed in the course of their employment highly specialized knowledge and skills in the manufacture of space suits for astronauts. Few, if any, persons have equivalent skill and knowledge. Low Tech Company, desirous of obtaining a contract with the government for the manufacture of space suits, approaches Woodrow and Gail and offers them employment. There is no contract prohibiting Woodrow and Gail from leaving the High Tech Company and going to work for the Low Tech Company. If they do so, however, the High Tech Company is entitled to an injunction restraining Woodrow, Gail, and the Low Tech Company from the use of trade secrets and methods for manufacturing space suits that were developed by Woodrow and Gail while in the employ of the High Tech Company.

Another improper method of acquiring trade secrets is industrial espionage such as electronic surveillance or spies. In the broadest sense, discovery of another's trade secrets by any means other than one's own independent research efforts or inspection of the finished product is improper unless the other party voluntarily discloses the secret or fails to take reasonable precautions to protect its secrecy.

TRADE SYMBOLS

One of the earliest forms of unfair competition is the fraudulent marketing of one per-

son's goods as those of another. This unlawful practice is sometimes referred to as "passing off" or "palming off." It is basically a "cashing in" on the good will, good name, and reputation of a competitor and of his products. It results in deception of the public and loss of trade by honest businesses. Section 43(a) of the Federal Trademark Act (the Lanham Act) provides protection against the use of a false designation of origin in connection with any goods or services. This section also prohibits false descriptions or representations of a person's own goods and services. In 1988, this section was amended to prohibit misrepresentations of *another* person's goods, services, or commercial activities.

The Lanham Act also established Federal registration of trade symbols and protection against misuse or infringement by injunctive relief and a right of action for damages against the infringer. An infringement is a form of passing off one's goods or services as those of the owner of the mark, is deceptive of the public, and constitutes unfair competition.

Types of Trade Symbols

The Lanham Act recognizes four types of trade symbols or **marks**. A **trademark** is a *distinctive* mark, word, letter, number, design, picture, or combination in any form of arrangement that is adopted or used by a person to identify goods that he manufactures or sells.

Similar in function to the trademark, which identifies tangible goods and products, a **service mark** is used to identify and distinguish the services of one person from those of others. For example, the titles, character names, and other distinctive features of radio and television shows may be registered as service marks.

A **certification mark** is a mark used upon or in connection with goods or services to certify regional or other origin, material, mode of manufacture, quality, accuracy, or other characteristics of the goods or services or that the work or labor in the goods or services were performed by members of a union or other organization. The marks "Good Housekeeping Seal of Approval" and "Underwriter's Laboratory" are examples of certification marks. The owner of the certification mark may *not* be the producer or provider of the goods or services with which the mark is used.

A **collective mark** is a distinctive mark or symbol used to indicate either membership in a trade union, trade association, fraternal society, or other organization or that the goods or services are produced by members of a collective group. As in the case of a certification mark, the owner of a collective mark is not the producer or provider but rather is the group of which the producer or provider is a member. An example of a collective mark is the union mark attached to many products to indicate they were made by a unionized company.

Registration

To be protected by the Lanham Act, a mark must be distinctive so that it identifies the origin of the goods or services. Marks that are fanciful or arbitrary satisfy the distinctiveness requirement, whereas generic or descriptive designations do not. *See Miller Brewing Co. v. G. Heileman Brewing Co.* For example, a word describing the ingredients, quality, purpose, function, or uses of a product may not be monopolized as a mark. Thus, the word *Plow* cannot be a trademark for plows, although it may be a trademark for shoes. A descriptive mark is entitled to protection, however, if it has acquired a secondary meaning by "becoming distinctive" of the goods or services. A mark acquires a **secondary meaning** when it is associated by a substantial number of purchasers with the product or service.

Federal registration is denied to marks that are immoral, deceptive, or scandalous. Marks may not be registered if they disparage or falsely suggest a connection with persons, living or dead, institutions, beliefs, or national symbols. In addition, a trademark may not consist of the flag, coat of arms, or other insignia of the United States, any State, municipality, or any foreign nation.

To obtain Federal protection, the mark must be registered with the Patent and Trademark Office. Registration provides numerous advantages. It gives nationwide constructive notice of the mark to all later users. It permits the registrant to use the Federal courts to enforce the mark. It constitutes *prima facie* evidence of the registrant's exclusive right to use the mark. This right becomes incontestable, subject to certain specified limitations, after five years. Finally, it gives the registrant protection by the Bureau of Customs against imports infringing upon the mark.

Infringement and Remedies

Infringement of a mark occurs when a person without authorization uses an identical or substantially indistinguishable mark that is likely to cause confusion, to cause mistake, or to deceive. Intent to cause confusion among purchasers is not required, nor is proof of actual confusion. Infringement occurs if an appreciable number of ordinarily prudent purchasers are *likely* to be misled or confused as to the source of the goods or services. In deciding whether infringement has occurred, the courts consider various factors, including the strength of the mark, the intent of the unauthorized user, the degree of similarity between the two marks, the relation between the two products or services identified by the marks, and the marketing channels through which the goods or services are purchased.

The Lanham Act provides several remedies for infringement: (1) injunctive relief, (2) an accounting for profits, (3) damages, (4) attorney's fees in exceptional cases, and (5) costs. In assessing profits, the plaintiff has to prove only the gross sales made by the defendant; the defendant has the burden of proving any costs to be deducted in determining profits. If the court finds that the amount of recovery based on profits is either inadequate or excessive, the court may, in its discretion, award an amount it determines to be just. In assessing damages, the court *may* award up to three times the actual damages according to the circumstances of the case.

When an infringement is knowing and intentional, the court *shall* award attorneys' fees plus the greater of treble profits or treble damages, unless there are extenuating circumstances. Moreover, where a *counterfeit* mark is intentionally and knowingly used, criminal sanctions may be imposed, and goods bearing the counterfeit mark may be destroyed. Criminal sanctions include a fine of up to $250,000, imprisonment of up to five years, or both. If the offense is a repeat offense, the limits are $1 million and fifteen years, respectively. If the person infringing is not an individual, such as a corporation, the fine may be up to $1 million for a first offense and up to $5 million for a repeat offense.

TRADE NAMES

A **trade name** is any name used to identify a business, vocation, or occupation. Descriptive and generic words, and personal and generic names, although not proper trademarks, may become protected as trade names upon acquiring a special significance in the trade. This special significance is frequently referred to as a "secondary meaning" of the name acquired as the result of continuing and extended use in connection with specific goods or services whereby the name has lost its primary meaning to a substantial number of purchasers or users of the goods or services. Although trade names may *not* be federally registered under the Lanham Act, trade names are protected, and a person who palms off her goods or services by using the trade name of another is liable in damages and also may be enjoined from doing so.

COPYRIGHTS

Copyright is a form of protection provided by Federal law to authors of original works, which, under Section 102 of the Copyright Act, includes literary works, musical works, dramatic works, pantomimes, choreographic works, pictorial, graphic, and sculptural works, motion picture and other audiovisual works, and sound recordings. This listing is illustrative and not exhaustive, as the act extends **copyright** protection to "original works of authorship in any tangible medium of expression, now known or later developed." Moreover, in 1980 the Copyright Act was amended to extend copyright protection to computer programs. On March 1, 1989, the United States joined the Berne Convention, which is an international treaty protecting copyrighted works.

In no case does copyright protection for an original work of authorship include any idea, procedure, process, system, method of operation, concept, principle, or discovery, regardless of the form in which it is described, explained, illustrated, or embodied in such work. Section 102(b). Copyright protection extends to an *original expression* of an idea. For example, the idea of interfamily feuding cannot be copyrighted, but a particular expression of that idea in the form of a novel, drama, movie, or opera may be copyrighted.

Procedure

Applications for copyright are filed with the Register of Copyrights in Washington, D.C. Registration of the copyright, however, is not required since copyright protection begins as soon as the work is fixed in a tangible medium. Registration is, nonetheless, advisable because it is a condition of certain remedies for copyright infringement. When a work is published, it is advisable, although no longer required, to place a notice of copyright on all publicly distributed copies so as to give notice of the claim of copyright. If proper notice appears on the published copies to which a defendant in a copyright infringement case had access, then the defendant will be unable to assert a defense of innocent infringement in mitigation of actual or statutory damages. Section 401.

Rights

Copyright protection subsists in most instances for a period of the author's life plus an additional fifty years. Section 106 of the Copyright Act gives the owner of the copyright the exclusive right to:

1. reproduce the copyrighted work in copies or recordings;

2. prepare derivative works based upon the copyrighted work;

3. distribute copies or recordings of the copyrighted work to the *public* by sale or other transfer of ownership, or by rental, lease, or lending;

4. perform the copyrighted work *publicly* in the case of literary, musical, dramatic, choreographic, pantomime, motion picture, and other audiovisual works; and

5. display the copyrighted work *publicly* in the case of literary, musical, dramatic, and choreographic works, pantomimes, and pictorial, graphic, or sculptural works, including the individual images of a motion picture or other audiovisual work.

These broad rights are subject, however, to several limitations, the most important of which are "compulsory licenses" and "fair use." **Compulsory licenses** permit certain limited uses of copyrighted material upon the payment of specified royalties and compliance with statutory conditions. Section 107 codifies the common law doctrine of **fair use** by providing that the fair use of a copyrighted work for purposes such as criticism, comment, news reporting, teaching (including multiple copies for classroom use), scholarship, or research is *not* an infringement of copyright. In determining whether the use made of a work in any particular case is a fair use, the following factors are considered: (1) the purpose and character of the use including whether such use is of a commercial nature or is for nonprofit educational purposes; (2) the nature of the copyrighted work; (3) the amount and substantiality of the portion used in relation to the copyrighted work as a whole; and (4) the effect of the use upon the potential market for or value of the copyrighted work. *See Sony Corporation of America v. Universal City Studios, Inc.*

Ownership

The author of a creative work owns the entire copyright. Although usually the actual creator of a work is the author, in two situations under the doctrine of **works for hire,** she is not considered the author. Section 101. First, if a work is prepared by an employee within the scope of her employment, the employer is the author of the work. Second, if a work is specially ordered or commissioned for certain purposes specified in the copyright statute *and* the parties expressly agree in writing that the work shall be considered a work for hire, the person commissioning the work is the author. The kinds of works subject to becoming a work for hire by commission include contributions to collective works, parts of motion pictures or other audiovisual works, translations, supplementary works such as prefaces, illustrations, or afterwords, compilations, instructional texts, and tests.

The ownership of a copyright may be transferred in whole or in part by conveyance, will, or intestate succession. Section 201. A transfer of copyright ownership, other than by operation of law, is not valid unless a note or memorandum of the transfer is in writing and signed by the owner of the rights conveyed or the owner's duly authorized agent. Section 204.

Ownership of a copyright, or of any of the exclusive rights under a copyright, is distinct from ownership of any material object in which the work is embodied. Transfer of ownership of any material object, including the copy or recording in which the work is first fixed, does not of itself convey any rights in the copyrighted work embodied in the object; nor, in the absence of an agreement, does transfer of ownership of a copyright or of any exclusive rights under a copyright convey property rights in any material object. Section 202. Thus, the purchase of this textbook does not affect the publisher's copyright nor does it authorize the purchaser to make and sell copies of the book. The purchaser may, however, rent, lend, or resell the book.

Infringement and Remedies

Infringement occurs whenever somebody exercises the rights exclusively reserved for the copyright owner without authorization. Infringement need *not* be intentional. To prove infringement, the plaintiff must establish that he owns the copyright and that the defendant violated one or more of the plaintiff's exclusive rights under the copyright.

In order to sue for infringement, the copyright must be registered with the Copyright Office. If an infringement occurs *after* registration, the following remedies are available: (1) injunction; (2) impoundment and possible destruction of infringing articles; (3) actual damages plus profits made by the infringer that are additional to those damages *or* statutory damages of at least $500 but no more than $20,000 ($100,000 if the infringement is willful) according to what the court determines to be just; (4) costs and, in the court's discretion, reasonable attorney's fees to the prevailing party; and (5) criminal penalties of a fine of up to $10,000 or up to one year's imprisonment for willful infringement for purposes of commercial advantage or private gain. The Piracy and Counterfeiting Amendments Act of 1982 imposes harsher punishments for large scale piracy: $250,000 fine and five years for pirating 1,000 recordings or 65 films within 180 days.

PATENTS

A **patent** is a grant by the Federal government of a monopoly right to an inventor to make, use, or sell the invention to the absolute exclusion of others for the period of the patent, which currently is 17 years. The owner of the patent may also profit by licensing others to use the patent on a royalty basis. The patent may not be renewed, and upon expiration the invention enters the "public domain" and anyone may then use it.

Patentability

The Patent Act specifies those inventions that may be patented. Section 101 provides:

Whoever invents or discovers any new and useful process, machine, manufacture, or composition of matter, or any new and useful improvement thereof, may obtain a patent therefor, subject to the conditions and requirements of this title.

Thus, naturally occurring substances are not patentable, as the invention must be made or modified by humans. For example, the discovery of an existing bacteria with useful properties is *not* patentable, whereas the manufacture of a human-made, genetically engineered bacterium is patentable. *See Diamond, Commissioner of Patents and Trademarks v. Chakrabarty.* By the same token, laws of nature, principles, systems of bookkeeping, fundamental truths, methods of calculation, and ideas are not patentable. Ac-

Figure 41–1 Intellectual Property

	Trade Secrets	Trade Symbols	Copyright	Patents
What is protected	information	mark	work of authorship	invention
Rights protected	use or sell	use or sell	reproduce, prepare derivative works, distribute, perform, or display	make, use, or sell
Duration	until disclosed	until abandoned	usually author's life plus 50 years	17 years
Federally protected	no	yes	yes	yes
Requirements for protection	valuable secret	distinctive	original and fixed	novel, useful, and nonobvious

cordingly, Einstein could not patent his law that $E = mc^2$, nor could Newton have patented the law of gravity. Similarly, isolated computer programs are not patentable, although, as mentioned above, they may be copyrighted.

To be patentable, the process, machine, manufacture, or composition of matter must meet three criteria:

1. novelty,

2. utility, and

3. nonobviousness.

Procedure

A patent is issued by the United States Patent and Trademark Office upon the basis of a patent application containing a *specification,* which describes how the invention works, and *claims,* which describe the features of the invention that make it patentable. The applicant must be the inventor. Before granting a patent, the Patent Office makes a careful and thorough examination of the prior art and determines whether the submitted invention has novelty (does not conflict with a prior pending application or a previously issued patent), utility, and is nonobvious. An application for a patent is confidential and its contents will not be divulged by the Patent Office. This confidentiality ends upon the granting of the patent.

If the application is rejected, the applicant may apply for reexamination. If the application is again rejected, the applicant may appeal to the Patent and Trademark Office's Board of Appeals, and from there to the Federal courts.

Infringement

Anyone who, without permission, makes, uses, or sells a patented invention is a **direct infringer.** Good faith or ignorance is *not* a defense to direct infringement. A person who actively encourages another to make, use, or sell a patented invention without permission is an **indirect infringer.** A person is a **contributory infringer** if he knowingly sells or supplies a part or component of a patented invention, unless the component is a staple or commodity or it is suitable for a substantial noninfringing use. Good faith and ignorance *are* defenses to contributory infringement.

Remedies

The remedies for infringement under the Patent Act are (1) injunctive relief; (2) damages adequate to compensate the plaintiff but "in no event less than a reasonable royalty for the use made of the invention by the infringer"; (3) treble damages when appropriate; (4) attorney's fees in exceptional cases such as knowing infringement; and (5) costs.

CASES

Trade Secrets

B. C. ZIEGLER AND COMPANY v. EHREN

Court of Appeals of Wisconsin, 1987.
141 Wis. 2d 19, 414 N.W. 2d 48.

BROWN, J.

Lawrence P. Ehren appeals from a grant of summary judgment restraining him from using or disclosing information contained on business papers and records he bought from a scrap paper company but which originated with B. C. Ziegler and Company (Ziegler). The circuit court held that the information was entitled to common law trade secret protection and that Ehren did not acquire title to the information as a good faith purchaser. We affirm those rulings.

Ziegler is an underwriter of securities located in West Bend. Ehren is employed by a scrap dealer, Lynn's Waste Paper Co., Inc.

(Lynn's), where his duties include determining the value for recycling purposes of scrap paper purchased by Lynn's. From 1981 to 1983, Ehren was a licensed securities salesman and worked for two brokerage firms which compete with Ziegler.

Ziegler considered its customer lists confidential and had developed policies for the disposal of scrap paper which were regularly communicated to its employees. Paper containing a customer name was to be burned or shredded on the Ziegler premises before disposal or was to be delivered for shredding to a commercial shredding concern in Appleton, in which case the employee delivering the paper was to wait while it was shredded. Under no circumstances was scrap paper containing names or information about Ziegler customers to leave the possession of its employees in readable form. Scrap paper not containing such information could be disposed of in unshredded form.

On several occasions in late 1985, boxes of scrap paper were delivered to Lynn's by Ziegler maintenance employees. Neither those employees nor Lynn's was aware that these batches of paper scrap contained Ziegler customer names, account summaries and other information on preaddressed envelopes bearing Ziegler's return address, a computer printout, monthly statements and other business records. Lynn's paid scrap rates for the paper. Ehren subsequently purchased from Lynn's six boxes of Ziegler materials in two transactions for a total of $16.75.

In the ensuing months, Ehren's daughter began sorting the Ziegler envelopes alphabetically and by zip code. In December of 1985, Ehren approached a former business associate, Thomas Thorson, a broker with a securities firm in competition with Ziegler, about using the names on the envelopes. There was some evidence that neither was sure of the value of the names, believing they might merely be the names of prospects rather than actual Ziegler customers. However, Ehren suggested compensation of one dollar per name.

Ehren delivered approximately 11,600 envelopes to Thorson. Thorson sent a mailing,

soliciting securities sales, to some of the names and received responses at a rate of eight to ten percent, compared to a normal rate of two or three percent.

Ziegler learned that its customers were receiving solicitations and requested that the West Bend Police Department conduct a quiet investigation to determine whether customer information was being leaked from the company. After learning through the police investigation that Ehren possessed the customer information, Ziegler brought this action seeking injunctive relief and replevin. After granting Ziegler temporary relief, the circuit court granted Ziegler's motion for summary judgment, permanently enjoined Ehren from using or disclosing the information and ordered, subject to a stay pending appeal, that the Washington County Clerk of Courts . . . destroy the materials. * * * This appeal followed.

Ehren first claims the circuit court erred in finding that the information contained in the Ziegler materials was a trade secret belonging to Ziegler.

* * *

Thus, we look to the common law of trade secrets. [The Abbott case (citation)], adopted a six-factor test based on language from the Restatement of Torts. These factors are: (1) the extent to which the information is known outside of the business of the party asserting trade secret status; (2) the extent to which it is known by employees and others involved in his business; (3) the extent or measures taken by him to guard the secrecy of the information; (4) the value of the information to him and to his competitors; (5) the amount of effort or money expended by him in developing the information; and (6) the ease or difficulty with which the information could be properly acquired or duplicated by others. [Citation.] Each of the six factors should indicate that a trade secret exists if the information is to be afforded protection. [Citation.]

* * *

The circuit court found, as essentially undisputed material facts, that: (1) the information was completely confidential and not known outside Ziegler; (2) the information was generally made available only to Ziegler employees who had reason to use it; (3) Ziegler had a policy, which was communicated to its employees, including maintenance personnel, of keeping confidential all material containing customer information; (4) Ziegler took reasonable measures to guard the confidentiality of information about the identity of its customers; (5) the information has substantial value to Ziegler, Ehren and Ziegler's competitors; (6) Ziegler's customer list has been developed through its substantial efforts over the last seventy-five years; (7) the papers in the six boxes contain information about Ziegler's transactions with its customers and contain the names and addresses of persons who have purchased securities from Ziegler in the past and are active prospects for future sales; and (8) the information contained in the six boxes cannot be acquired from sources other than Ziegler. We agree that these findings are not significantly disputed.

Applying these findings to the Abbott factors, we conclude that the Ziegler customer information qualifies for trade secret status.

* * *

Ehren next contends that even assuming trade secret status, this status does not survive an accidental or negligent disclosure. * * *

The rule that accidental disclosure negates trade secret protection has not been expressly adopted in Wisconsin. The determination whether to protect information in a particular case depends upon the circumstances and the nature of the information involved. [Citation.]

Trade secrets law has developed largely in an effort to balance two competing interests— the interest of an employer in precluding others from exploiting specialized knowledge developed in the course of an employment relationship and the interest of the former employee in the general use of his or her skills and training ("know-how"). [Citation.] Our supreme court has narrowly drawn the scope of trade secret protection "to effectuate the public policies of encouraging business competition and facilitating worker mobility." [Citation.]

In the present case, Ehren had no confidential or employment relationship with Ziegler. He purchased materials containing customer information for their scrap value and attempted to sell the information to a Ziegler competitor at an enormous profit. We are not persuaded that he may invoke the same policies which have led to the narrow scope of trade secret protection which applies as between an employer and a former employee. The circumstances are entirely different from those found in the employer-employee cases. No countervailing policy of worker mobility exists here to weigh against Ziegler's interest in the secrecy of extremely valuable and confidential information accidentally disposed of in readable form.

Essentially, we conclude that, even assuming and conceding that Ehren acquired the Ziegler materials through no wrongdoing on his part, it would be inequitable to allow him to make use of the information contained therein. We hold that the trade secret status of the customer information survived its inadvertent disclosure in the present case.

* * *

Judgment affirmed.

Trademarks

MILLER BREWING COMPANY v. G. HEILEMAN BREWING COMPANY, INC.

United States Court of Appeals, Seventh Circuit, 1977. 561 F.2d 75.

Tone, J.

This appeal presents the question whether a misspelled version of the word "light" can become a trademark for a "less filling, low-calorie beer." The District Court answered the question affirmatively and, based on that determination, granted a preliminary injunction, which this court has stayed pending appeal. We hold that, because "light" is a generic or common descriptive word when applied to beer, neither that word nor its phonetic equivalent may be appropriated as a trademark for beer. We therefore reverse the preliminary injunction order.

In May of 1967 a now defunct Chicago brewer, Meister Brau, Inc., began making and selling a reduced calorie, reduced carbohydrate beer under the name "LITE." Late in 1968 that company filed applications for registration of "LITE" as a trademark on the principal register in the United States Patent Office, which ultimately approved three registrations on the principal register of labels containing the name "LITE" for "beer with no available carbohydrates." Meister Brau continued producing and selling beer under the brand name "LITE" in the Chicago area during 1970 and 1971. In 1971 it changed the label used on cans and bottles to eliminate the words "Meister Brau," which had appeared above the word "LITE."

In 1972, with its demise imminent, Meister Brau sold its interest in the "LITE" trademarks, the registrations thereof, and the accompanying goodwill to the plaintiff Miller Brewing Company. For a time Miller continued selling beer under that brand in the Meister Brau marketing area in somewhat smaller quantities than Meister Brau had distributed.

Miller then decided to expand its marketing of beer under the brand "LITE." It developed a modified recipe, which resulted in a beer lower in calories than Miller's regular beer but not without available carbohydrates. The label was revised and one of the registrations was amended to show "LITE" printed rather than in script. In addition, an extensive advertising campaign was undertaken. From 1973 through 1976, Miller expanded its annual sales of "LITE" from 50,000 barrels to 4,000,000 barrels and increased its annual advertising expenditures from $500,000 to more than $12,000,000. In support of its motion for a preliminary injunction in this case, Miller submitted the results of a survey which, as the District Court noted in its opinion and order, showed "that between December, 1975 and March, 1976, a substantial percentage of beer drinkers perceived LITE (43%), Miller LITE (11%), or LITE from or by Miller (1%) as a distinct

brand name indicative of a low-calorie or less-filling beer."

Since early 1975 a number of other brewers have introduced reduced calorie beers labeled or described as "light." One of these, although not the first, was the defendant G. Heileman Brewing Company, Inc., which began using the name on a beer low in calories but containing available carbohydrates in five test markets in 1976. Heileman had long been engaged in the production and sale of other brands of beer, among which were "Old Style" and "Special Export." The small print on the label Heileman has used for many years for its "Old Style" beer describes that product as "light lager beer."

Miller began filing trademark infringement actions against competitors to enjoin the use of the word "light" at least as early as October 1975. * * *

On the basis of affidavits and other written material, the District Court in the case at bar enjoined Heileman from continuing to sell, advertise, and distribute beer "anywhere in the United States, under the brand name incorporating the word 'Light' in the manner of the label attached to the complaint herein . . . and under any colorable imitation of" the labels which had been registered with the Patent Office.

* * *

Miller claims the benefit of [citation], which provides that registration on the principal register

"shall be prima facie evidence of registrant's exclusive right to use the registered mark in commerce on the goods or services specified in the registration subject to any conditions or limitation stated therein. . . ."

The three registrations on which Miller relies specify "beer with no available carbohydrates" as the goods on which the registered mark is to be used. This limitation came about because the Patent Office refused registration on the applications as initially filed, which described the goods as "beer," on the ground that "LITE" was "merely descriptive" and therefore not registerable because of [citation]. In response to this action, Meister

Brau offered evidence of secondary meaning, but in addition its attorney stated that "the beer in connection with which Applicant uses this mark is no-available carbohydrates beer . . ." and also had "one-third less calories than ordinary draft beer," and that "LITE" was suggestive rather than merely descriptive of these qualities. The examiner then required that the applications be amended to describe the goods to which the mark applied as "beer with no available carbohydrates" and they were so amended. We hold that the statute means what it says. The registrations are prima facie evidence of Miller's exclusive right to use the word "LITE" for beer with no available carbohydrates, not for any beer, a breadth of coverage which the applicant disclaimed by amending its applications. Inasmuch as the beer marketed by Heileman as its "Light" beer contains available carbohydrates, as indeed does Miller's "LITE," the registrations are not prima facie evidence of Miller's exclusive right to use the mark on that beer. Thus, although we think the result would be the same whether or not [citation] applied, Miller's brand name "LITE" must be evaluated under the common law of trademarks without the benefit of registration.

* * *

The basic principles of trademark law which are applicable here have often been stated, [citations], and may be briefly summarized. A term for which trademark protection is claimed will fit somewhere in the spectrum which ranges through (1) generic or common descriptive and (2) merely descriptive to (3) suggestive and (4) arbitrary or fanciful. As the ease with which hues in the solar spectrum may be classified on the basis of perception will depend upon where they fall in that spectrum, so it is with a term on the trademark spectrum.

A generic or common descriptive term is one which is commonly used as the name or description of a kind of goods. It cannot become a trademark under any circumstances. [Citations.] Using the phonetic equivalent of a common descriptive word, i.e., misspelling it, is of no avail. [Citation.]

A merely descriptive term specifically describes a characteristic or ingredient of an article. It can, by acquiring a secondary meaning, i.e., becoming "distinctive of the applicant's goods" [citation], become a valid trademark. [Citation.]

A suggestive term suggests rather than describes an ingredient or characteristic of the goods and requires the observer or listener to use imagination and perception to determine the nature of the goods. Such a term can be protected without proof of a secondary meaning. [Citation.]

An arbitrary or fanciful term enjoys the same full protection as a suggestive term but is far enough removed from the merely descriptive not to be vulnerable to possible attack as being merely descriptive rather than suggestive. [Citation.]

* * *

Although Miller argued in the District Court that "LITE" was suggestive, and persuaded the District Court that this was so with respect to the quality of being reduced in calories, it conceded in oral argument before us that the choice is between (1) generic or common descriptive and (2) merely descriptive. Miller argues that light beer is not a "genus," indeed that "light," as an adjective, cannot be a generic or common descriptive term, and that it is a merely descriptive term that has acquired a secondary meaning.

* * *

The fact that "light" is an adjective does not prevent it from being a generic or common descriptive word. [Citations.] This must be the law, given the reason for the rule that precludes appropriation of a common descriptive word, viz., otherwise "a competitor could not describe his goods as what they are." [Citation.] Ordinarily, as here, the adjective which is sought to be appropriated in its generic sense as a trademark will be a part of a name. [Citation.] If "light beer" is a generic name, then "light" is a generic word when used as part of that name.

* * *

The record before us (although less complete than that in at least one of the other pending cases) and facts of which we may take judicial notice, including generally accepted English usage, enable us to conclude that "light" is a generic or common descriptive term when used with "beer."

"Light" has been widely used in the beer industry for many years to describe a beer's color, flavor, body, or alcoholic content, or a combination of these or similar characteristics. The use of that word by Heileman and other brewers long antedated either Miller's or Meister Brau's use of "LITE." The definition given in *Webster's Third New International Dictionary, supra,* at 1308, of "light" as an adjective includes the following:

"10 *of a beverage* a: having a comparatively low alcoholic content ([light] wines and beers) b: having a low concentration of flavoring congenerics: characterized by a relatively mild flavor: not heavy 11a: capable of being easily digested (a [light] soup). . . ."

* * *

Similar definitions and usage are found in reference works on chemical technology, industry publications, and magazines and newspapers generally. Indeed, state statutes even use "light beer" as a generic or common descriptive term. "Light" is clearly a common descriptive word when used with beer.

"Light" is also a common descriptive word in other similar contexts. Miller's president testified in a deposition which has been made part of this record that Miller chose the word "LITE" for its low-calorie beer because of its desire to capitalize on the trend of "consumer products going lighter all over the world, be it foods, be it whiskeys, be it cigarettes," as well as to "convey the message that it would be lighter in taste" and to communicate "the conception of a less filling product." Miller's parent company, Philip Morris, Inc., registered "Light" (Registration No. 878,062) and used that word as a brand name for cigarettes (Marlboro Light). Judge Stewart held the word to be descriptive and ordered the registration cancelled in [citation], a decision from which no appeal was taken. The word is also used by Pepsico, Inc. for "Pepsi Light" a soft drink described as having "half the calories out."

Miller argues that it uses the word as the name for "less filling, low calorie" beer, and that "light" has not heretofore been used in that sense. This argument fails for two reasons. First, "less filling" means essentially light in body and taste and not oppressive to the stomach, which is a common descriptive meaning of "light"; and, as Miller conceded in its brief, the caloric content of beer depends primarily on alcoholic content. Second, even if Miller had given its light beer a characteristic not found in other light beers, it could not acquire the exclusive right to use the common descriptive word "light" as a trademark for that beer. Other brewers whose beers have qualities that make them "light" as that word has commonly been used remain free to call their beer "light." Otherwise a manufacturer could remove a common descriptive word from the public domain by investing his goods with an additional quality, thus gaining the exclusive right to call his wine "rose," his whiskey "blended," or his bread "white."

The word "light," including its phonetic equivalent "lite," being a generic or common descriptive term as applied to beer, could not be exclusively appropriated by Miller as a trademark, "despite whatever promotional effort [Miller] may have expended to exploit it." [Citations.] Because probability of success cannot be established, other issues argued by the parties need not be decided, and the preliminary injunction must be reversed.

REVERSED.

Copyright

SONY CORP. OF AMERICA v. UNIVERSAL CITY STUDIOS, INC.

Supreme Court of the United States, 1984.
464 U.S. 417, 104 S.Ct. 774, 78 L.Ed.2d 574.

STEVENS, J.

Petitioners manufacture and sell home video tape recorders. Respondents own the copyrights on some of the television programs that are broadcast on the public airwaves. Some members of the general public use video tape recorders sold by petitioners to record some of these broadcasts, as well as a large number of other broadcasts. The question presented is whether the sale of petitioners' copying equipment to the general public violates any of the rights conferred upon respondents by the Copyright Act.

Respondents commenced this copyright infringement action against petitioners in the United States District Court for the Central District of California in 1976. Respondents alleged that some individuals had used Betamax video tape recorders (VTR's) to record some of respondents' copyrighted works which had been exhibited on commercially sponsored television and contended that these individuals had thereby infringed respondents' copyrights. Respondents further maintained that petitioners were liable for the copyright infringement allegedly committed by Betamax consumers because of petitioners' marketing of the Betamax VTR's. Respondents sought no relief against any Betamax consumer. Instead, they sought money damages and an equitable accounting of profits from petitioners, as well as an injunction against the manufacture and marketing of Betamax VTR's.

After a lengthy trial, the District Court denied respondents all the relief they sought and entered judgment for petitioners. [Citation.] The United States Court of Appeals for the Ninth Circuit reversed the District Court's judgment on respondent's copyright claim, holding petitioners liable for contributory infringement and ordering the District Court to fashion appropriate relief. [Citation.] We now reverse.

* * *

Article I, Sec. 8 of the Constitution provides that:

The Congress shall have Power . . . to Promote the Progress of Science and useful Arts, by securing for limited Times to Authors and Inventors the exclusive Right to their respective Writings and Discoveries.

The monopoly privileges that Congress may authorize are neither unlimited nor primarily designed to provide a special private benefit. Rather, the limited grant is a means by which an important public purpose may be achieved. It is intended to motivate the creative activity of authors and inventors by the provision of a special reward, and to allow the public access to the products of their genius after the limited period of exclusive control has expired.

* * *

As the text of the Constitution makes plain, it is Congress that has been assigned the task of defining the scope of the limited monopoly that should be granted to authors or to inventors in order to give the public appropriate access to their work product. * * *

* * *

The judiciary's reluctance to expand the protections afforded by the copyright without explicit legislative guidance is a recurring theme. [Citations.] * * *

In a case like this, in which Congress has not plainly marked our course, we must be circumspect in construing the scope of rights created by a legislative enactment which never contemplated such a calculus of interests. * * *

Copyright protection "subsists . . . in original works of authorship fixed in any tangible medium of expression." [Citation.] This protection has never accorded the copyright owner complete control over all possible uses of his work. Rather, the Copyright Act grants the copyright holder "exclusive" rights to use and to authorize the use of his work in five qualified ways, including reproduction of the copyrighted work in copies. Id., § 106. All reproductions of the work, however, are not within the exclusive domain of the copyright owner; some are in the public domain. Any individual may reproduce a copyrighted work for a "fair use;" the copyright owner does not possess the exclusive right to such a use. [Citation.]

"Anyone who violates any of the exclusive rights of the coyright owner," that is, anyone who trespasses into his exclusive domain by using or authorizing the use of the copyrighted work in one of the five ways set forth in the statute, "is an infringer of the copyright." Id., § 501(a). Conversely, anyone who is authorized by the copyright owner to use the copyrighted work in a way specified in the statute or who makes a fair use of the work is not an infringer of the copyright with respect to such use.

The Copyright Act provides the owner of a copyright with a potent arsenal of remedies against an infringer of his work, including an injunction to restrain the infringer from violating his rights, the impoundment and destruction of all reproductions of his work made in violation of his rights, a recovery of his actual damages and any additional profits realized by the infringer or a recovery of statutory damages, and attorney's fees. Id., §§ 502–505.

The two respondents in this case do not seek relief against the Betamax users who have allegedly infringed their copyrights. . . . It is, however, the taping of respondents' own copyrighted programs that provides them with standing to charge Sony with contributory infringement. To prevail, they have the burden of proving that users of the Betamax have infringed their copyrights and that Sony should be held responsible for that infringement.

The Copyright Act does not expressly render anyone liable for infringement committed by another. . . . The absence of such express language in the copyright statute does not preclude the imposition of liability for copyright infringements on certain parties who have not themselves engaged in the infringing activity. For vicarious liability is imposed in virtually all areas of the law, and the concept of contributory infringement is merely a species of the broader problem of identifying the circumstances in which it is just to hold one individual accountable for the actions of another.

* * *

* * * [A]nd the label "contributory infringement" has been applied in a number of lower court copyright cases involving an ongoing relationship between the direct infringer and the contributory infringer at the time the infringing conduct occurred. In such cases, as in other situations in which the imposition of vicarious liability is manifestly

just, the "contributory" infringer was in a position to control the use of copyrighted works by others and had authorized the use without permission from the copyright owner. This case, however, plainly does not fall in that category. The only contact between Sony and the users of the Betamax that is disclosed by this record occurred at the moment of sale. * * *

If vicarious liability is to be imposed on petitioners in this case, it must rest on the fact that they have sold equipment with constructive knowledge of the fact that their customers may use that equipment to make unauthorized copies of copyrighted material. There is no precedent in the law of copyright for the imposition of vicarious liability on such a theory. * * *

* * *

* * * Accordingly, the sale of copying equipment, like the sale of other articles of commerce, does not constitute contributory infringement if the product is widely used for legitimate, unobjectionable purposes. Indeed, it need merely be capable of substantial non-infringing uses.

* * *

* * * In this case, the record makes it perfectly clear that there are many important producers of national and local television programs who find nothing objectionable about the enlargement in the size of the television audience that results from the practice of time-shifting for private home use.

Even unauthorized uses of a copyrighted work are not necessarily infringing. An unlicensed use of the copyright is not an infringement unless it conflicts with one of the specific exclusive rights conferred by the copyright statute. [Citation.] Moreover, the definition of exclusive rights in § 106 of the present Act is prefaced by the words "subject to sections 107 through 118." Those sections describe a variety of uses of copyrighted material that "are not infringements of copyright notwithstanding the provisions of § 106." The most pertinent in this case is § 107, the legislative endorsement of the doctrine of "fair use."

That section identifies various factors that enable a Court to apply an "equitable rule of reason" analysis to particular claims of infringement. * * *

* * *

* * * A challenge to a noncommercial use of a copyrighted work requires proof either that the particular use is harmful, or that if it should become widespread, it would adversely affect the potential market for the copyrighted work.

* * *

When these factors are all weighed in the "equitable rule of reason" balance, we must conclude that this record amply supports the District Court's conclusion that home time-shifting is fair use. In light of the findings of the District Court regarding the state of the empirical data, it is clear that the Court of Appeals erred in holding that the statute as presently written bars such conduct.

In summary, the record and findings of the District Court lead us to two conclusions. First, Sony demonstrated a significant likelihood that substantial numbers of copyright holders who license their works for broadcast on free television would not object to having their broadcasts time-shifted by private viewers. And second, respondents failed to demonstrate that time-shifting would cause any likelihood of non-minimal harm to the potential market for, or the value of, their copyrighted works. The Betamax is, therefore, capable of substantial noninfringing uses. Sony's sale of such equipment to the general public does not constitute contributory infringement of respondent's copyrights.

The direction of Art. I is that *Congress* shall have the power to promote the progress of science and the useful arts. When, as here, the Constitution is permissive, the sign of how far Congress has chosen to go can come only from Congress. Deepsouth Packing Co. v. Laitram Corp., [citation.]

One may search the Copyright Act in vain for any sign that the elected representatives of the millions of people who watch television every day have made it unlawful to copy a program for later viewing at home, or have enacted a flat prohibition against the sale of machines that make such copying possible.

It may well be that Congress will take a fresh look at this new technology, just as it so often has examined other innovations in the past. But it is not our job to apply laws that have not yet been written. Applying the copyright statute, as it now reads, to the facts as they have been developed in this case, the judgment of the Court of Appeals must be reversed.

It is so ordered.

Patents

DIAMOND, COMMISSIONER OF PATENTS AND TRADEMARKS v. CHAKRABARTY

Supreme Court of the United States, 1980.
447 U.S. 303, § 100 S.Ct. 2204, 65 L.Ed.2d 144.

BURGER, C.J.

We granted certiorari to determine whether a live, human-made micro-organism is patentable subject matter under § 101 [of the Patent Act].

* * *

In 1972, respondent Chakrabarty, a microbiologist, filed a patent application, assigned to the General Electric Co. The application asserted 36 claims related to Chakrabarty's invention of "a bacterium from the genus *Pseudomonas* containing therein at least two stable energy-generating plasmids, each of said plasmids providing a separate hydrocarbon degradative pathway." This human-made, genetically engineered bacterium is capable of breaking down multiple components of crude oil. Because of this property, which is possessed by no naturally occurring bacteria, Chakrabarty's invention is believed to have significant value for the treatment of oil spills.

Chakrabarty's patent claims were of three types: first, process claims for the method of producing the bacteria; second, claims for an inoculum comprised of a carrier material floating on water, such as straw, and the new bacteria; and third, claims to the bacteria themselves. The patent examiner allowed the claims falling into the first two categories, but rejected claims for the bacteria. His decision rested on two grounds: (1) that micro-organisms are "products of nature," and (2) that as living things they are not patentable subject matter under § 101 [of the Patent Act].

Chakrabarty appealed the rejection of these claims to the Patent Office Board of Appeals, and the Board affirmed the examiner on the second ground. Relying on the legislative history of the 1930 Plant Patent Act, in which Congress extended patent protection to certain asexually reproduced plants, the Board concluded that § 101 was not intended to cover living things such as these laboratory created micro-organisms.

The Court of Customs and Patent Appeals, by a divided vote, reversed on the authority of [citation], which held that "the fact that micro-organisms . . . are alive . . . [is] without legal significance" for purposes of the patent law. * * *

* * *

The Constitution grants Congress broad power to legislate to "promote the Progress of Science and useful Arts, by securing for limited Times to Authors and Inventors the exclusive Right to their respective Writings and Discoveries." Art. I, § 8, cl. 8. The patent laws promote this progress by offering inventors exclusive rights for a limited period as an incentive for their inventiveness and research efforts. [Citations.] The authority of Congress is exercised in the hope that "[t]he productive effort thereby fostered will have a positive effect on society through the introduction of new products and processes of manufacture into the economy, and the emanations by way of increased employment and better lives for our citizens." [Citation.]

The question before us in this case is a narrow one of statutory interpretation requiring us to construe § 101 [of the Patent Act], which provides:

Whoever invents or discovers any new and useful process, machine, manufacture, or composition of matter, or any new and useful improvement thereof, may obtain a patent therefor, subject to the conditions and requirements of this title.

Specifically, we must determine whether respondent's micro-organism constitutes a "manufacture" or "composition of matter" within the meaning of the statute.

* * *

In cases of statutory construction we begin, of course, with the language of the statute. [Citation.] And "unless otherwise defined, words will be interpreted as taking their ordinary, contemporary, common meaning." [Citation.] We have also cautioned that courts "should not read into the patent laws limitations and conditions which the legislature has not expressed." [Citation.]

Guided by these canons of construction, this Court has read the term "manufacture" in § 101 in accordance with its dictionary definition to mean "the production of articles for use from raw or prepared materials by giving to these materials new forms, qualities, properties, or combinations, whether by hand-labor or by machinery." [Citation.] Similarly, "composition of matter" has been construed consistent with its common usage to include "all compositions of two or more substances and . . . all composite articles, whether they be the results of chemical union, or of mechanical mixture, or whether they be gases, fluids, powders or solids." [Citation.] In choosing such expansive terms as "manufacture" and "composition of matter," modified by the comprehensive "any," Congress plainly contemplated that the patent laws would be given wide scope.

* * *

This is not to suggest that § 101 has no limits or that it embraces every discovery. The laws of nature, physical phenomena, and abstract ideas have been held not patentable. [Citations.] Thus, a new mineral discovered in the earth or a new plant found in the wild is not patentable subject matter. Likewise, Einstein could not patent his celebrated law that $E = mc^2$; nor could Newton have patented the law of gravity. Such discoveries are "manifestations of . . . nature, free to all men and reserved exclusively to none." [Citation.]

Judged in this light, respondent's micro-organism plainly qualifies as patentable subject matter. His claim is not to a hitherto unknown natural phenomenon, but to a non-naturally occurring manufacture or composition of matter—a product of human ingenuity "having a distinctive name, character [and] use." [Citation.] The point is underscored dramatically by comparison of the invention here with that in *Funk*. There, the patentee had discovered that there existed in nature certain species of root-nodule bacteria which did not exert a mutually inhibitive effect on each other. He used that discovery to produce a mixed culture capable of inoculating the seeds of leguminous plants. Concluding that the patentee had discovered "only some of the handiwork of nature," the Court ruled the product nonpatentable:

Each of the species of root-nodule bacteria contained in the package infects the same group of leguminous plants which it always infected. No species acquires a different use. The combination of species produces no new bacteria, no change in the six species of bacteria, and no enlargement of the range of their utility. Each species has the same effect it always had. The bacteria perform in their natural way. Their use in combination does not improve in any way their natural functioning. They serve the ends nature originally provided and act quite independently of any effort of the patentee." [Citation.]

Here, by contrast, the patentee has produced a new bacterium with markedly different characteristics from any found in nature and one having the potential for significant utility. His discovery is not nature's handiwork, but his own; accordingly it is patentable subject matter under § 101.

* * *

We have emphasized in the recent past that "[o]ur individual appraisal of the wisdom or unwisdom of a particular [legislative] course . . . is to be put aside in the process of interpreting a statute." [Citation.] Our task, rather, is the narrow one of determining what Congress meant by the words it used in the statute; once that is done our powers are exhausted. Congress is free to amend § 101 so as to exclude from patent protection organisms produced by genetic engineering. Cf. 42 U.S.C. § 2181(a), exempting from patent protection inventions "useful solely in the utilization of special nuclear material or atomic energy in an atomic weapon." Or it may choose to craft a statute specifically designed for such living things. But, until Congress takes such action, this Court must construe the language of § 101 as it is. The language of that section fairly embraces respondent's invention.

Accordingly, the judgment of the Court of Customs and Patent Appeals is

Affirmed.

QUESTIONS

1. Explain what is protected by trade secrets and how they may be infringed.

2. Distinguish among the various types of trade symbols.

3. Explain the extent to which trade names are protected.

4. Explain what is protected by copyrights and the remedies for infringement.

5. Explain what is protected by patents and the remedies for infringement.

PROBLEMS

1. Keller, a professor of legal studies at Rhodes University, is a diligent instructor. Late one night while reading a newly published, copyrighted treatise of 1800 pages written by Gilbert, he came across a three-page section discussing the subject matter he was going to cover in class the next day. Keller considered the treatment to be illuminating and therefore photocopied the three pages and distributed the copies to his class. One of Keller's students is a second cousin of Gilbert, the author of the treatise, and she showed Gilbert the copies. Instead of being flattered, Gilbert sued Keller for copyright infringement. Decision?

2. A conceived a secret process for the continuous freeze drying of food stuffs and related products and constructed a small pilot plant that practiced the process. A lacked the financing necessary to develop the commercial potential of the process and in hopes of obtaining a contract for its development and the payment of royalties, disclosed it in confidence to B, a coffee manufacturer, who signed an agreement not to disclose it to anyone else. At the same time, A signed an agreement not to disclose the process to any other person as long as A and B were considering a contract for its development. Upon disclosure, B became extremely interested and offered to pay A the sum of $1,750,000 if, upon further development, the process proved to be commercially feasible. While negotiations between A and B were in progress, C, a competitor of B, learned of the existence of the process and requested a disclosure from A, who informed C that the process could not be disclosed to anyone unless negotiations with B were broken off. C offered to pay A $2,500,000 for the process provided it met certain defined objective performance criteria. A contract was prepared and executed between A and C on this basis without any prior disclosure of the process to C. Upon the making of this contract, A rejected the offer of B. The process was thereupon disclosed to C, and demonstration runs of the pilot plant in the presence of representatives of C were conducted under varying conditions. After three weeks of experimental demonstrations, compiling of data, and analyses of results, C informed A that the process did not meet the performance criteria in the contract and that for this reason C was rejecting the process.

Two years later, C placed on the market freeze-dried coffee that resembled in color, appearance, and texture the product of A's pilot plant. What are the rights of the parties?

3. B, a chemist, was employed by A, a manufacturer, to work on a secret process for A's product under an exclusive three-year contract. C, a salesman, was employed by A on a week-to-week basis. B and C resigned the employment with A and accepted employment in their respective capacities with D, a rival manufacturer. C began soliciting patronage from A's former customers whose names he had memorized. What are the rights of the parties in (a) a suit by A to enjoin B from working for D; and (b) a suit by A to enjoin C from soliciting A's customers?

4. Conrad and Darby were competitors in the business of dehairing raw cashmere, the fleece of certain Asiatic goats. Dehairing is the process of separating the commercially valuable soft down from the matted mass of raw fleece which also contains long coarse guard hairs and other impurities. Machinery for this process is not readily available on the open market. Each company in the business designed and built its own machinery and kept the nature of its process secret. Conrad contracted with Lawton, owner of a small machine shop, to build and install new improved dehairing machinery of increased efficiency for which Conrad furnished designs, drawings, and instructions. Lawton knew that the design of the machinery was confidential, and agreed that he would manufacture the machinery exclusively for plaintiff and that he would not reproduce the machinery or any of its essential parts for any one else. Darby purchased from Lawton a copy of the dehairing machinery which Conrad had specially designed. Decision?

5. Jones, having filed locally an affidavit required under the "Assumed Name" statute, has been operating and advertising his exclusive toy store for 20 years in Centerville, Illinois. His advertising has consisted of large signs on his premises reading "The Toy Mart". Lewis, after operating a store in Chicago under the name of "The Chicago Toy Mart" relocated in Centerville, Illinois, and erected a large sign reading "TOY MART" with the word "Centerville" being written underneath in substantially smaller letters. Thereafter, the sales of Jones declined, and many of Jones's customers patronized Lewis's store thinking it to be a branch of Jones's business. What are the rights of the parties?

6. Ryan Corporation manufactures and sells a variety of household cleaning products in interstate commerce. On national television Ryan falsely advertises that its laundry liquid is biodegradable. Has Ryan violated the Lanham Act?

7. Gibbons, Inc. and Marvin Corporation are manufacturers who sell a variety of household cleaning products in interstate commerce. On national television Gibbons states that its laundry liquid is biodegradable and that Marvin's is not.

In fact, both products are biodegradable. Has Gibbons violated the Lanham Act?

8. George McCoy of Florida has been manufacturing and distributing a cheese cake, for over five years, labeling his product with a picture of a cheese cake, which serves as a background for a Florida bathing beauty under which is written the slogan "McCoy All Spice Florida Cheese Cake." George McCoy has not registered his trademark. Subsequently, Leo McCoy of California begins manufacturing a similar product on the West coast using a label in appearance similar to that of George McCoy, containing a picture of a Hollywood star, and the words "McCoy's All Spice Cheese Cake." Leo McCoy begins marketing his products in the Eastern United States, using labels with the word "Florida" added as in George McCoy's label. Leo McCoy has registered his product under the Federal Trademark Act. To what relief, if any, is George McCoy entitled?

COMPUTER RESEARCH PROBLEMS

1. The Coca-Cola Company manufactures a carbonated beverage, Coke, made from coca leaves and cola nuts. The Koke Company of America introduced a similar product into the beverage market named Koke. The Coca-Cola Company brought a trademark infringement action against Koke. Coke claimed unfair competition within the beverage business due to Koke's imitation of the Coca-Cola product and Koke's attempt to reap the benefit of consumer identification with the Coke name. Decision?

2. Vuitton, a French corporation, manufactures high quality handbags, luggage, and accessories. Crown Handbags, a New York corporation, manufactures and distributes ladies' handbags. Vuitton handbags are sold exclusively in expensive department stores and distribution is strictly controlled to maintain a certain retail selling price. The Vuitton bags bear

a registered trademark and a distinctive design. Crown's handbags appear identical to the Vuitton bags but are of inferior quality. Vuitton sues Crown for manufacturing counterfeit handbags and selling them at a discount. Decision?

3. T.G.I Friday's, a New York corporation and registered service mark, entered into an exclusive licensing agreement with Tiffany which allowed Tiffany to open a Friday's restaurant in Jackson, Mississippi. International Restaurant Group, operated by the owners of Tiffany, applied for a license to open a Friday's in Baton Rouge, Louisiana but was refused. International then opened another restaurant, called E.L. Saturday's or Ever Lovin' Saturday's, in Baton Rouge which had the same type of menu and decor as Friday's. Friday's sues International for trademark infringement. Decision?

Chapter 42

ANTITRUST

Sherman Antitrust Act
Clayton Act
Robinson-Patman Act
Federal Trade Commission Act

THE economic community is best served by free competition in trade and industry. It is in the public interest that quality, price, and service in an open, competitive market for goods and services be determining factors in the business rivalry for the customer's dollar. Businesses would prefer to eliminate their competition, so that they would be in a position to dictate price and quantity of their goods. While elimination of competition through production of a better product is the goal of a business, some businesses try to reduce competition through illegitimate means, such as fixing prices and allocating exclusive territories to certain competitors within an industry. The law of antitrust prohibits such illegitimate means and attempts to assure free and fair competition in the marketplace.

The common law has traditionally favored competition and has held agreements and contracts in restraint of trade illegal and unenforceable. In addition, some States during the 1800s had enacted antitrust statutes but in the latter half of the nineteenth century it became apparent that concentrations of economic power in the form of "trusts" and "combinations" were too powerful and widespread to be effectively curbed and controlled by State action. This prompted the Congress to enact the Sherman Antitrust Act in 1890, which was the first Federal statute in this field. Since then, Congress has enacted other antitrust statutes, including the Clayton Act, the Robinson-Patman Act, and the Federal Trade Commission Act. These statutes prohibit anticompetitive practices and seek to prevent unreasonable concentration of economic power that stifles or weakens competition.

SHERMAN ANTITRUST ACT

Section 1 of the Sherman Act prohibits contracts, combinations, and conspiracies that restrain trade, while Section 2 prohibits monopolies and attempts to monopolize. Failure to comply with either section is a criminal felony and subjects the offender to fine or imprisonment, or both. Individual offenders are subject to imprisonment of up to three years and fines up to $100,000, while corporate offenders are subject to fines of up to $1,000,000. Moreover, the Federal district courts are empowered to issue injunctions restraining violations, and anyone injured by a violation is entitled to recover in a civil action **treble damages,** that is, three times the amount of the actual loss sustained. In addition, State Attorney Generals may bring suit for treble damages on behalf of citizens of their State. The United States Justice Department and the Federal Trade Commission have the duty to institute appropriate enforcement proceedings other than treble damage actions.

The Supreme Court stated the purpose of the Sherman Act as follows:

The Sherman Act was designed to be a comprehensive charter of economic liberty aimed at preserving free and unfettered competition as the rule of trade. It rests on the premise that the unrestrained interaction of competitive forces will yield the best allocation of our economic resources, the lowest prices, the highest quality and the greatest material progress, while at the same time providing an environment conducive to the preservation of our democratic political and social institutions. *Northern Pacific Railway Co. v. United States,* 356 U.S. 1 (1958).

Restraint of Trade

Section 1 of the Sherman Act provides that "[e]very contract, combination in the form of trust or otherwise, or conspiracy, in restraint of trade or commerce among the several states, or with foreign nations is hereby declared to be illegal." Because the language of the section is so broad, judicial interpretation has played a significant role in establishing the requirements of a violation.

Standards As just noted, Section 1 prohibits every contract, combination, or conspiracy in restraint of trade. Taken literally, this prohibition would invalidate every unperformed contract. For example, if a seller agrees to supply a buyer with 1000 pounds of grapes, no one else is able to fulfill the buyer's need for those 1000 pounds of grapes and the seller cannot sell those grapes to any other buyer. This agreement would therefore restrain trade. To avoid such a broad and impractical application, the courts have interpreted this section to invalidate only *unreasonable* restraints of trade:

The true test of legality is whether the restraint imposed is such as merely regulates and perhaps thereby promotes competition or whether it is such as may suppress or even destroy competition. To determine that question the courts must ordinarily consider the facts peculiar to the business to which the restraint is applied; its condition before and after the restraint was imposed; the nature of the restraint and its effect, actual or probable. The history of the restraint, the evil believed to exist, the reason for adopting the particular remedy, the purpose or end sought to be attained, are all relevant facts. This is not because a good intention will save an otherwise objectionable regulation or the reverse; but because knowledge of intent may help the court to interpret facts and to predict consequences. *Chicago Board of Trade v. United States,* 246 U.S. 231 (1918).

This standard is known as the **rule of reason test.** The rule of reason test is a flexible standard, under which courts, in determining whether a challenged practice unreasonably restricts competition, consider a variety of factors including the makeup of the relevant industry, the defendants' positions within that industry, the ability of the defendants' competitors to respond to the challenged practice, and the defendants' purpose in adopting the restraint. After reviewing the various factors, a court determines whether the challenged restraint is unreasonably restrictive of competition. By requiring courts to balance the *anticompetitive* effects against the *procompetitive* effects of every questioned restraint, this standard places a substantial burden upon the judicial system. The United States Supreme Court addressed this problem by declaring certain categories of restraints to be unreasonable by their very nature and thus **illegal per se:**

[T]here are certain agreements or practices which because of their pernicious effect on competition and lack of any redeeming virtue are conclusively presumed to be unreasonable and therefore illegal without elaborate inquiry as to the precise harm they have caused or the business excuse for their use. This principle of *per se* unreasonableness not only makes the type of restraints which are proscribed by the Sherman Act more certain to the benefit of everyone concerned, but it also avoids the necessity for an incredibly complicated and prolonged economic investigation into the entire history of the industry involved, as well as related industries, in an effort to determine at large whether a particular restraint has been unreasonable—an inquiry so often wholly fruitless when undertaken. *Northern Pacific Railway Co. v. United States,* 356 U.S. 1 (1958).

The characterization of a type of restraint as *per se* illegal therefore has a significant effect on the prosecution of an antitrust suit. In such a case, the plaintiff is required to show only that the type of restraint occurred and does not need to prove that the restraint limited competition. Furthermore, the defendants may not defend on the basis that the restraint is reasonable. Additionally, as noted in *Northern Pacific Railway,* the court is not required to conduct extensive, and often difficult, economic analysis. Not surprisingly, the ease of applying the *per se* rule has helped to deter those restraints subject to the rule.

Horizontal and Vertical Restraints A restraint of trade may be classified as either horizontal or vertical. A **horizontal restraint** involves collaboration among competitors at the same level in the chain of distribution. For example, an agreement among manufacturers or among wholesalers or among retailers would be horizontal.

On the other hand, an agreement is a **vertical restraint** if it is made by parties that are not in direct competition at the same level of distribution. Thus, an agreement between a manufacturer and a wholesaler is vertical.

Although the distinction between horizontal and vertical restraints can become blurred, it often determines whether a restraint is illegal *per se* or is judged by the rule of reason test. For instance, horizontal market allocations are illegal *per se,* whereas vertical market allocations are not *per se* illegal but are subject to the rule of reason test.

Concerted Action Section 1 does not prohibit unilateral conduct; rather, it forbids **concerted action.** Thus, one person or business by itself cannot violate the section. An organization has the "right to deal, or refuse to deal, with whomever it likes, as long as it does so independently." *Monsanto Co. v. Spray-Rite Service Corporation,* 465 U.S. 752 (1984). For example, if a manufacturer announces its resale prices in advance and refuses to deal with those who fail to comply, there is no violation of Section 1 because the manufacturer has not acted in concert with anyone. On the other hand, if a manufacturer and its retailers together agree that the manufacturer will sell only to those retailers who agree to sell at a specified price, there may be a violation of Section 1.

For purposes of the concerted action requirement, a firm and its employees are viewed as one entity. Furthermore, in 1984 the Supreme Court held that a corporation and its wholly-owned subsidiaries are also viewed as one entity, and thus there is no violation of the Sherman Act when a parent and its wholly-owned subsidiary agree to a restraint in trade. *Copperwald Corp. v. Independence Tube Corp.,* 467 U.S. 752 (1984). The Supreme Court has not yet decided whether a parent and its partially-owned subsidiary may violate Section 1.

The requirement of concerted action may be established by an express agreement. Not surprisingly, however, many times there is no express agreement and the existence of an agreement between the parties must be inferred from circumstantial evidence:

No formal agreement is necessary to constitute an unlawful conspiracy. Often crimes are a matter of inference deduced from the acts of the person accused and done in pursuance of a criminal purpose. Where the conspiracy is proved, as here, from the evidence of the action taken in concert by the parties to it, it is all the more convincing proof of an intent to exercise the power of exclusion acquired through the conspiracy. The essential combination or conspiracy in violation of the Sherman Act may be found in a course of dealings or other circumstances as well as in any exchange of words. * * * Where the circumstances are such as to warrant a jury in finding that the conspirators had a unity of purpose or a common design and understanding, or a meeting of minds in an unlawful arrangement, the conclusion that a conspiracy is established is justified. *American Tobacco Co. v. United States,* 328 U.S. 781 (1946).

Nonetheless, similar patterns of conduct among competitors, called **conscious parallelism,** are not sufficient by themselves to infer a conspiracy in violation of Section 1. There must also be an *additional* factor, such as complex action taken by each competitor that would only benefit each competitor if all of them took similar action or indications of a traditional conspiracy such as identical sealed bids from each competitor.

For an illustration of the difficulty courts face in distinguishing concerted action from unilateral but parallel action *see Matsushita Electric Industrial Co. v. Zenith Radio Corp.*

Price Fixing Price fixing is an agreement with the purpose or effect of inhibiting price competition and includes agreements raising, depressing, fixing, pegging, or stabilizing prices. Price fixing is the primary and most serious example of a *per se* violation under the Sherman Act. As held in *United States v. Socony-Vacuum Oil Co.,* 310 U.S. 150 (1940), *all* **horizontal** price-fixing agreements are illegal *per se*. This prohibition covers any agreement between sellers to establish *maximum* prices at which certain commodities or services are offered for sale as well as *minimum* prices.

The U.S. Supreme Court has condemned not only agreements among horizontal competitors that directly fix prices but also agreements where the effect on price is indirect. For example, in *Catalano, Inc. v. Target Sales, Inc.,* 446 U.S. 643 (1980), the Court held that an agreement among beer wholesalers to eliminate interest-free short-term credit on sales to beer retailers was illegal *per se*. The Court viewed the credit terms "as an inseparable part of price" and concluded that the agreement to eliminate interest-free short-term credit was equivalent to an agreement to eliminate discounts and thus an agreement to fix prices.

Similarly, it is illegal *per se* for a seller to fix the price at which its purchasers must resell the product. This **vertical** form of price fixing—usually called retail price maintenance—is considered a *per se* violation of Section 1.

Despite the U.S. Supreme Court's early and consistent condemnation of resale price maintenance agreements, the Court has found no Section 1 violation when a manufacturer announces in advance that it will not sell to dealers who cut prices and then terminates its dealers who have cut prices. Not surprisingly, courts have sometimes had difficulty distinguishing between an illegal resale price maintenance agreement and a legal refusal to deal with a retailer who refuses to charge a minimum price dictated by the manufacturer.

Market Allocations Direct price fixing is not the only method by which prices can be controlled. Another way is by **market allocation** whereby competitors agree not to compete with each other in specific markets, which may be defined by geographic area, type of customer, or class of product. All **horizontal** agreements to divide markets have been declared illegal *per se,* because their effects give monopoly power in that market to the remaining firm which can then control price. Thus, if Suny and RGE, both manufacturers of color televisions, agree that Suny shall have the exclusive right to sell color televisions in Illinois and Iowa and that RGE shall have the exclusive right in Minnesota and Wisconsin, Suny and RGE have committed a *per se* violation of Section 1 of the Sherman Act. Likewise, if Suny and RGE agree that Suny shall have the exclusive right to sell color televisions to Sears and RGE to J.C. Penney, or that Suny shall have exclusive rights to manufacture 19 inch color televisions and RGE to manufacture 15 inch sets, they are also in *per se* violation of Section 1 of the Sherman Antitrust Act. Horizontal market allocations may be found not only on the manufacturing level but also on the wholesale or retail level.

Vertical territorial and customer restrictions are no longer illegal *per se* but are now judged by the rule of reason. This change in approach resulted from a United States Supreme Court decision that mandated the lower Federal courts to balance the positive effect of vertical market restrictions upon interbrand competition against the negative effects upon intrabrand competition. *See Continental T.V. v. GTE Sylvania*. Consequently, in some situations vertical market restrictions will be found legitimate if they, on balance, do not have an anticompetitive impact on the relevant market.

In 1985, the United States Department of Justice issued a "market structure screen." Under this screen, the Justice Department will not challenge restraints by a firm having less than 10 percent of the relevant market or a "Vertical Restraint Index" (a measure of relative market share) indicating that neither collusion nor exclusion is possible. The concept of relevant market is discussed later in the section on monopolization.

Boycotts   As noted above, Section 1 of the Sherman Act does not apply to unilateral action but only to agreements or combinations. Accordingly, the refusal of a seller to deal with any particular buyer does not violate the act. Thus, a manufacturer can refuse to sell to a retailer who persists in selling below the manufacturer's suggested retail price. On the other hand, when two or more firms agree not to deal with a third party, this is a **concerted refusal to deal** or group boycott, which may violate Section 1 of the Sherman Act. Such a boycott clearly may be anticompetitive, as it may result in eliminating competition or reducing market entry.

Some group boycotts are illegal *per se*, while others are subject to the rule of reason. Group boycotts that are designed to eliminate a competitor or force that competitor to meet a standard of the group are illegal *per se* if the group has market power. On the other hand, cooperative arrangements that are "designed to increase economic efficiency and render markets more, rather than less, competitive" are subject to the rule of reason.

Finally, most courts hold that the *per se* rule of illegality for concerted refusals to deal extends only to horizontal boycotts and not to vertical refusals to deal. Most courts have interpreted *Sylvania* to hold that a rule of reason test should govern all nonprice

vertical restraints, including concerted refusals to deal.

Tying Arrangements   A tying arrangement occurs when a seller of a product, service, or intangible (the "tying" product) conditions its sale on the buyer's purchasing a second product, service, or intangible (the "tied" product) from the seller. For example, assume that Xerox, a major manufacturer of photocopying equipment, were to require that all purchasers of its photocopiers also purchase from Xerox all of the paper they use with the copier. Xerox has tied the sale of its photocopier—the *tying* product—to the sale of paper—the *tied* product.

Because tying arrangements limit the freedom of choice of buyers and may exclude competitors, the law closely scrutinizes such agreements. A tying arrangement exists where a seller exploits its economic power in one market to expand its empire into another market. When the seller has considerable economic power in the tying product and a not insubstantial amount of interstate commerce is affected in the tied product, the tying arrangement will be *per se* illegal. Economic power may be demonstrated by showing that (1) the seller occupied a dominant position in the tying market, (2) the seller's product is sufficiently unique in having some advantage not shared by its competitors in the tying market, or (3) a substantial number of customers have accepted the tying arrangement and there are no explanations for their willingness to comply, other than the seller's economic power in the tying market. If the seller lacks economic power, the tying arrangement is judged by the rule of reason test.

Figure 42–1 summarizes how these restraints on trade are judged under Section 1.

Monopolies

Economic analysis indicates that a monopolist will use its power to limit production and increase prices. Accordingly, a monopolistic market will produce fewer goods at a higher price than a competitive market. In order to address the problem of monopolization, Sec-

Figure 42–1 Restraints of Trade under Sherman Act

	Standard	
Type of Restraint	**Per Se Illegal**	**Rule of Reason**
Price fixing	Horizontal Vertical	
Market allocations	Horizontal	Vertical
Group boycotts or refusals to deal	Horizontal Vertical (minority)	Vertical (majority)
Tying arrangements	If seller has economic power in tying product and a not insubstantial amount of interstate commerce is affected in the tied product	If seller lacks economic power in tying product

tion 2 of the Sherman Act prohibits monopolies, attempts to monopolize, and conspiracies to monopolize. Thus, Section 2 prohibits both agreements among businesses and, unlike Section 1, unilateral conduct by one firm.

Monopolization Although the language of Section 2 appears to prohibit *all* monopolization, the courts have declined to interpret it in that manner. Rather, they have required that in addition to the mere possession of market power there also be either the unfair attainment of the monopoly power or the abusive use of that power once attained. Possession of monopoly power by itself is not considered a violation of Section 2 because a firm may have obtained monopoly power as a result of its skills in developing, marketing, and selling products; that is, the very competitive conduct that the antitrust laws are designed to promote.

It is extremely rare to find an unregulated industry with only one firm, so the issue of monopoly power involves defining what degree of market dominance constitutes monopoly power. **Monopoly power** is the ability to control prices or to exclude competitors from the market place. The courts have grappled with this question of monopoly power and have developed a number of approaches,

but the prevalent test is market share. A market share greater than 75 percent generally indicates monopoly power, while a share less than 50 percent does not. A 50 to 75 percent share is inconclusive.

Market share is the fractional share possessed by a firm of the total relevant product and geographic markets, but defining the relevant markets is often a difficult and subjective task for the courts. The relevant *product market* includes products that are substitutable for the firm's product on the basis of price, quality, and elasticity. For example, although brick and wood siding are both used in buildings as exteriors, it is not likely that they would be considered as part of the same product market. On the other hand, Coca-Cola and Seven-Up are both soft drinks and would be considered part of the same product market. *See United States v. E.I. duPont De Nemours & Co.*

The relevant *geographic market* is that territory in which the firm makes sales of its products or services. This may be at the local, regional, or national level. For instance, the relevant geographic market for the manufacture and sale of aluminum might be national while that of a taxicab operating company would be local. The scope of the relevant geographic market will depend upon such factors as transportation costs, the type of product or services, and the location of competitors and customers.

If sufficient monopoly power has been proved, it must then be shown that the firm has engaged in **unfair conduct.** The courts have not yet agreed upon what constitutes unfair conduct. One judicial approach is that a firm possessing monopoly power has the burden of proving that it acquired such power passively or that it had the power "thrust" upon it. An alternative view is that monopoly power, when coupled with conduct designed to exclude competitors, violates Section 1. A third approach requires monopoly power plus some type of predatory practice, such as pricing below marginal costs. For example, one case that adopted the third approach held that a firm does not violate Section 2 of the Sherman Act if it attained its market share by either (1) research, technical innovation, or a superior product, or (2) ordinary marketing methods available to all. *Telex Corp. v. IBM,* 510 F.2d 894 (10th Cir.1975).

The U.S. Supreme Court decision in *Aspen Skiing Co. v. Aspen Highlands Skiing Corp.,* 472 U.S. 585 (1985), appears to adopt a combination of these approaches. The Court held that "[i]f a firm has been attempting to exclude rivals on some basis other than efficiency, it is fair to characterize its behavior as predatory."

To date, however, the United States Supreme Court has not provided a *definitive* answer to the basic question of exactly what conduct, beyond the mere possession of monopoly power, violates Section 2. To do so, the Court must resolve the complex and conflicting policies involved. On the one hand, condemning fairly acquired monopoly power—that acquired "merely by virtue of superior skill, foresight, and industry"—penalizes firms that compete effectively. On the other hand, permitting firms with monopoly power to continue provides them the opportunity to lower output and raise prices, thereby injuring consumers.

Attempts to Monopolize Section 2 also prohibits attempts to monopolize. As with

monopolization, the courts have experienced difficulty in developing a standard that distinguishes undesirable conduct likely to lead to monopoly from healthy competitive conduct. The standard test applied by the courts requires proof of a specific intent to monopolize plus a dangerous probability of success. This standard leaves numerous questions unanswered, such as what conduct constitutes an attempt and how much power must be achieved. Recent cases suggest that the greater the power acquired, the less flagrant the conduct must be to constitute an attempt. These cases, however, do not specify any threshold level of market power.

Conspiracies to Monopolize Section 2 also condemns conspiracies to monopolize. Few cases involve this offense alone, as any conspiracy to monopolize would also constitute a combination in restraint of trade in violation of Section 1. Because of the overlap between these two provisions, some scholars have stated that the offense of conspiracy to monopolize is "redundant."

CLAYTON ACT

In 1914, Congress strengthened the Sherman Act by adopting the Clayton Act, which was expressly designed "to supplement existing laws against unlawful restraints and monopolies." The Act is intended to stop trade practices before they become restraints of trade or monopolies forbidden by the Sherman Act. The Clayton Act does not provide for criminal penalties but only for civil actions. Civil actions may be brought by private parties in Federal court for *treble* damages and attorneys' fees. In addition, the Justice Department and the Federal Trade Commission are authorized to bring civil actions, including proceedings in equity, to prevent and restrict violations of the Act.

The substantive provisions of the Clayton Act deal with price discrimination, tying contracts, exclusive dealing, mergers, and interlocking directorates. Section 2, which deals with price discrimination, was amended and rewritten by the Robinson-Patman Act, discussed below. In addition, the Clayton Act exempts labor, agricultural, and horticultural organizations from all antitrust laws.

Tying Contracts and Exclusive Dealing

Section 3 of the Clayton Act prohibits tying arrangements and exclusive dealing, selling, or leasing arrangements which prevent purchasers from dealing with the seller's competitors, where the effect *may* be substantially to lessen competition or *tend* to create a monopoly. This section is intended to attack anticompetitive practices in their incipiency before they ripen into violations of Section 1 or 2 of the Sherman Act. Unlike the Sherman Act, however, Section 3 applies only to practices involving commodities and *not* to services, intangibles, or land.

Tying arrangements, which have already been discussed under the Sherman Act, have been labeled by the Supreme Court as serving "hardly any purpose beyond the suppression of competition." While the Supreme Court at one time indicated that different standards applied under the Sherman Act and the Clayton Act, recent lower court cases suggest that the same rules now govern both types of actions.

Exclusive dealing arrangements are agreements by which the seller or lessor of a product conditions the agreement upon the buyer's or lessor's promise not to deal in the goods of a competitor. For example, a manufacturer of razors might require that retailers wishing to sell its line of shaving equipment agree not to carry competing merchandise. Such conduct, although treated more leniently than tying arrangements, violates Section 3 if it tends to create a monopoly or may substantially lessen competition. Exclusive dealing arrangements are treated more leniently because they may be procompetitive to the extent that they benefit buyers, and thus indirectly ultimate consumers, by assuring supplies, protecting against price increases, and enabling long-term planning on the basis of known costs.

Mergers

Corporate mergers have played a significant role in reshaping the structure of both corporations in the United States and our economic system. We have just completed the fourth major wave of mergers in United States history. In 1986, there were 3,336 mergers. The total value of all mergers in 1986 exceeded 173 billion. In 1988, the largest acquisition took place when Philip Morris acquired Kraft for $12.6 billion. Figure 42–2 lists the largest acquisitions from 1985 through 1988.

Mergers are classified as horizontal, vertical, or conglomerate, based upon the relationship between the acquirer and the acquired company. A **horizontal merger** involves the acquisition by a company of all or part of the stock or assets of a competing company. For example, if IBM were to acquire Apple, this would be a horizontal merger. A **vertical merger** is the acquisition by a company of one of its customers or suppliers. A vertical merger is a *forward* merger if the acquiring company purchases a *customer,* such as the purchase of Revco Discount Drug Stores by Procter & Gamble. A vertical merger is a *backward* merger if the acquiring company purchases a supplier; for example, IBM's purchase of a manufacturer of microchips. The third type of merger, the **conglomerate merger,** is a catchall category that covers all acquisitions not involving a competitor, customer, or supplier.

Section 7 of the Clayton Act prohibits the merger or acquisition by a corporation of stock or assets of another corporation where the effect may be to lessen substantially competition or tend to create a monopoly.

Section 7 of the Clayton Act was intended to arrest the anticompetitive effects of market power in their incipiency. The core question is whether a merger may substantially lessen competition, and necessarily requires a prediction of the merger's impact on competition, present and future. The section can deal only with probabilities, not with certainties. And there is certainly no requirement that the anticompetitive power manifest itself in anticompetitive action before § 7 can be called into play. If the enforcement of § 7 turned on the existence of actual anticompetitive practices, the congressional policy of thwarting such practices in their incipiency would be frustrated. *F.T.C. v. Procter & Gamble Co.*, 386 U.S. 568 (1967).

The principal objective of antitrust law governing mergers is to maintain competition. Accordingly, horizontal mergers are scrutinized most stringently. Factors that the courts consider in reviewing the legality of a horizontal merger include the market share of each of the merging firms, the degree of industry concentration, the number of firms in the industry, entry barriers, market trends, the vigor and strength of other competitors in the industry, the character and history of the merging firms, market demand, and the extent of industry price competition. The leading Supreme Court cases on horizontal mergers date from the 1960s and early 1970s. Since that time, lower Federal courts, the Department of Justice, and the FTC have placed a greater emphasis on antitrust's goal of promotion of economic efficiency. Accordingly, while the Supreme Court cases remain the law of the land, recent lower court decisions reflect a greater willingness to tolerate industry concentrations. Nevertheless, the government continues to prosecute, and the courts continue to condemn,

---

Figure 42–2 Largest Acquisitions from 1985 through 1988

Rank*	Acquiring Company	Acquired/Merged Company	Price Paid (millions of dollars)
		1985	
1	Royal Dutch	Shell Oil	$5,700.1
2	Philip Morris	General Foods	5,627.7
3	Allied	Signal Cos.	4,955.0
4	R.J. Reynolds	Nabisco	4,889.1
5	General Motors	Hugh's Aircraft	4,712.5
		1986	
1	General Electric	RCA	$6,406.0
2	Capital Cities	ABC	3,509.0
3	Campeau	Allied Stores	3,505.7
4	Cleveland Electric	Toledo Edison	3,140.5
5	USX	Texas Oil & Gas	2,996.6
		1987	
1	British Petroleum	Standard Oil	$7,564.7
2	National Amusements	Viacom International	3,299.1
3	Unilever	Chesebrough-Pond's	3,095.2
4	Hoechst AG	Celanese Corp.	2,723.5
5	JMB Realty	Cadillac Fairview	1,973.6
		1988	
1	Philip Morris	Kraft	$12,644.2
2	Campeau	Federated Department Stores	6,506.2
3	BAT Industries	Farmers Group	5,168.7
4	Eastman Kodak	Sterling Drug	5.093.1
5	Amoco	Dome Petroleum	3,766.1

*excluding leveraged buyouts

horizontal mergers that are likely to hurt consumers. *See Hospital Corporation of America v. FTC.*

Vertical mergers, which are far less likely to be challenged by the Justice Department or the FTC, have been attacked if the merger was likely to raise entry barriers in the industry or was likely to foreclose other firms in the industry of the acquiring firm from competitively significant customers or suppliers. While the Supreme Court has not decided a vertical merger case since 1972, recent decisions indicate that at least some lower courts have been unwilling to condemn vertical mergers unless anticompetitive effects were clearly shown.

Finally, conglomerate mergers have been challenged only (1) where one of the merging firms is a highly likely entrant into the market of the other firm, or (2) where the merged company would be disproportionately large as compared with the largest competitors in its industry.

The Justice Department and the FTC have both indicated that they will be primarily concerned with horizontal mergers in highly or moderately concentrated industries and that they question the benefits of challenging vertical and conglomerate mergers. Both the Justice Department and the FTC have justified this policy on the basis that the latter two types of mergers are necessary to transfer assets to their most productive use and that any challenge to them would impose costs on consumers without corresponding benefits.

Antitrust law, as currently applied, deals with mergers by focusing on the size of the merged firm in relation to the relevant market and not on the absolute size of the resulting entity. The focus of the Justice Department Guidelines (issued in 1982 and amended in 1984) is that "mergers should not be permitted to create or enhance market power or to facilitate its exercise." The guidelines seek to detect and prevent the use of "market power" by quantifying market concentration using the **Herfindahl-Hirschman Index (HHI)** and by measuring a horizontal merger's impact on the index. This concentration index is calculated by summing the squares of the individual market shares of all firms in the market. An industry with only one firm would have an HHI of 10,000 (100^2). With two firms of equal size it would be 5,000 ($50^2 + 50^2$), with five firms of equal size the result would be 2,000 ($20^2 + 20^2 + 20^2 + 20^2 + 20^2$). The increase in the index caused by any merger is calculated by doubling the product of the market shares of the merging firms. For example, the merger of two firms with market shares of 5 percent and 10 percent respectively would increase the index by 100 ($5 \times 10 \times 2 = 100$).

The guidelines use three categories of market concentration to analyze horizontal mergers and to determine the likelihood of governmental opposition based on the increase in the index caused by the proposed merger. The three categories are classified according to the postmerger HHI. If the postmerger figure is below 1,000, then the department is unlikely to challenge the merger without regard to the increase in the index caused by the merger. For postmerger HHIs between 1,000 and 1,800, the department will examine the increase in HHI due to the merger. Increases less than 100 are unlikely to generate a challenge, but those greater than 100 probably will. When the postmerger HHI is above 1800, the department will look closely at the effects of the merger if the increase is above 50, and it is likely to challenge any merger contributing an increase of more than 100.

In 1987, the National Association of Attorneys General, composed of the attorneys general of the fifty States and five U.S. territories and protectorates, promulgated its own set of guidelines for horizontal mergers. The State attorneys general intended these guidelines to apply to enforcement actions brought by the State attorneys general under Federal and State antitrust statutes. The State guidelines place a greater emphasis on preventing transfer of wealth from consumers to producers than do the Federal guidelines. Accordingly, the State attorneys general may be more likely to challenge some mergers than would the Federal government.

Interlocking Directorates

Section 8 of the Clayton Act prohibits interlocking directorates in competing corporations engaged in interstate commerce (except banks, banking associations, trust companies, and common carriers) where the total capital of the corporations is a million dollars or more.

The broad purposes of Congress are unmistakably clear. Section 8 was but one of a series of measures which finally emerged as the Clayton Act, all intended to strengthen the Sherman Act, which, through the years, had not proved entirely effective. Congress had been aroused by the concentration of control by a few individuals or groups over many gigantic corporations which in the normal course of events should have been in active and unrestrained competition. Instead, and because of such control, the healthy competition of the free enterprise system had been stifled or eliminated. Interlocking directorships on rival corporations had been the instrumentality of defeating the purpose of the antitrust laws. They had tended to suppress competition or to foster joint action against third party competitors. The continued potential threat to the competitive system resulting from these conflicting directorships was the evil aimed at. Viewed against this background, a fair reading of the legislative debates leaves little room for doubt that, in its efforts to strengthen the antitrust laws, what Congress intended by § 8 was to nip in the bud incipient violations of the antitrust laws by removing the opportunity or temptation to such violations through interlocking directorates. The legislation was essentially preventative. *United States v. Sears, Roebuck & Co.,* 111 F.Supp. 14 (S.D.N.Y. 1953).

Since Section 8 of the Clayton Act prohibits interlocking directorships in *competing* corporations, it does not apply to a director who serves on the board of two firms that are vertically associated. Moreover, it has been held that the section does not apply to an individual who is an officer of two corporations or an officer of one corporation and a director of another.

ROBINSON-PATMAN ACT

Section 2 of the Clayton Act originally prohibited only sellers from differentially pricing their products in order to injure local or regional competitors. In 1936, in an attempt to limit the power of large purchasers, the Congress amended Section 2 of the Clayton Act by adopting the Robinson-Patman Act, which further prohibited **price discrimination** in interstate commerce of commodities of like grade and quality. Thus, the Act prohibits both buyers from inducing and sellers from granting discrimination in prices. In order to constitute a violation, the price discrimination must substantially lessen competition or tend to create a monopoly.

Under this Act sellers of goods are prevented from granting discounts to buyers, including allowances for advertisements, counter displays, and samples, unless the same discounts are offered to all other purchasers on proportionately equal terms. The act also prohibits other types of discounts, rebates, and allowances and makes it unlawful to sell goods at unreasonably low prices for the purpose of destroying competition or eliminating a competitor. The Act makes it unlawful for a person knowingly to "induce or receive" an illegal discrimination in price, thus imposing liability on the buyer as well as the seller. Violation of the Robinson-Patman Act, with limited exceptions, is civil and not criminal in nature. Price differentials are permitted when justified by proof of either a cost savings to the seller or a good-faith price reduction to meet the lawful price of a competitor.

Primary-line Injury

In enacting Section 2 of the Clayton Act in 1914, Congress was concerned with sellers who sought to harm or eliminate their competitors through price discrimination. Injuries accruing to competitors of the seller are called "primary-line" injuries. Because the Act forbids price discrimination only where the effect of such discrimination may be substantially to lessen competition or tend to create a monopoly, the plaintiff in a Robinson-Patman primary-line injury case must either show that the defendant has engaged in predatory pricing intending to harm competition or present a detailed market analysis that demonstrates how the defendant's price discrimination actually harmed competition. To prove predatory intent, a plaintiff may rely either on direct evidence of such intent or, more commonly, on inferences drawn from defendant's conduct, such as below-cost or unprofitable pricing for a significant period of time. A predatory pricing scheme may also be challenged under the Sherman Act.

Secondary-line Injury

When Congress amended Section 2 of the Clayton Act in 1936 by adopting the Robinson-Patman Act, Congress was concerned primarily with small buyers who were harmed by discounts granted to large buyers. Injuries accruing to some buyers because of lower prices granted to other buyers are called "secondary-line" injuries. To show the required harm to competition, a plaintiff in a secondary-line injury case must either show substantial and sustained price differentials in a market or offer a detailed market analysis that demonstrates actual harm to competition. Because courts have been willing in secondary-line injury cases to infer harm to competition from a sustained and substantial price differential, it is easier in general for a plaintiff to prove a secondary-line injury than a primary-line injury.

Cost Justification

If a seller can show that it costs less to sell a product to a particular buyer, the seller may lawfully pass along the cost savings. Section 2(a) provides that the Act does not "prevent differentials which make only due allowance for differences in the cost of manufacture, sale, or delivery resulting from the differing methods or quantities in which . . . commodities are . . . sold or delivered." For example, if retailer A orders goods from Seller X by the carload, whereas retailer B orders in small quantities, seller X, who delivers F.O.B. buyer's warehouse, may pass along the transportation savings to buyer A. Nonetheless, although it is possible to pass along

transportation savings, it is extremely difficult to pass along alleged savings in manufacturing or distribution because of the complexity involved in calculating and proving such savings. Therefore, sellers rarely rely upon the defense of cost justification.

Meeting Competition

A seller may lower his price in a good faith attempt to meet competition. To illustrate:

1. Manufacturer X sells its motor oil to retail outlets for 65 cents per can. Manufacturer Y approaches A, one of Manufacturer X's customers, and offers to sell a comparable type of motor oil for 60 cents per can. Manufacturer X will be permitted to lower its price to A to 60 cents per can and need not lower its price to its other retail customers—B, C, and D. Manufacturer X, however, may *not* lower its price to A to 55 cents unless it also lowers its price to B, C, and D.

2. Manufacturer X will not be permitted to lower its price to A without also lowering its price to B, C, and D, in order to allow A to meet the lower price charged by A's competitor N selling Manufacturer Y's oil. The meeting competition defense is available only to meet the competition of the seller and does not extend to the price of a competitor to a specific, individual *purchaser* (see Figure 42–3).

A seller may beat its competitor's price, however, if it does not know the competitor's price, cannot reasonably determine the competitor's price, and acts reasonably in setting its own price.

FEDERAL TRADE COMMISSION ACT

In 1914, Congress enacted the Federal Trade Commission Act, creating the Federal Trade Commission and charging it with the duty to prevent "unfair methods of competition in commerce, and unfair or deceptive acts or practices in commerce." To this end, the five-member Commission is empowered to conduct appropriate investigations and hear-

Figure 42–3 Meeting Competition Defense

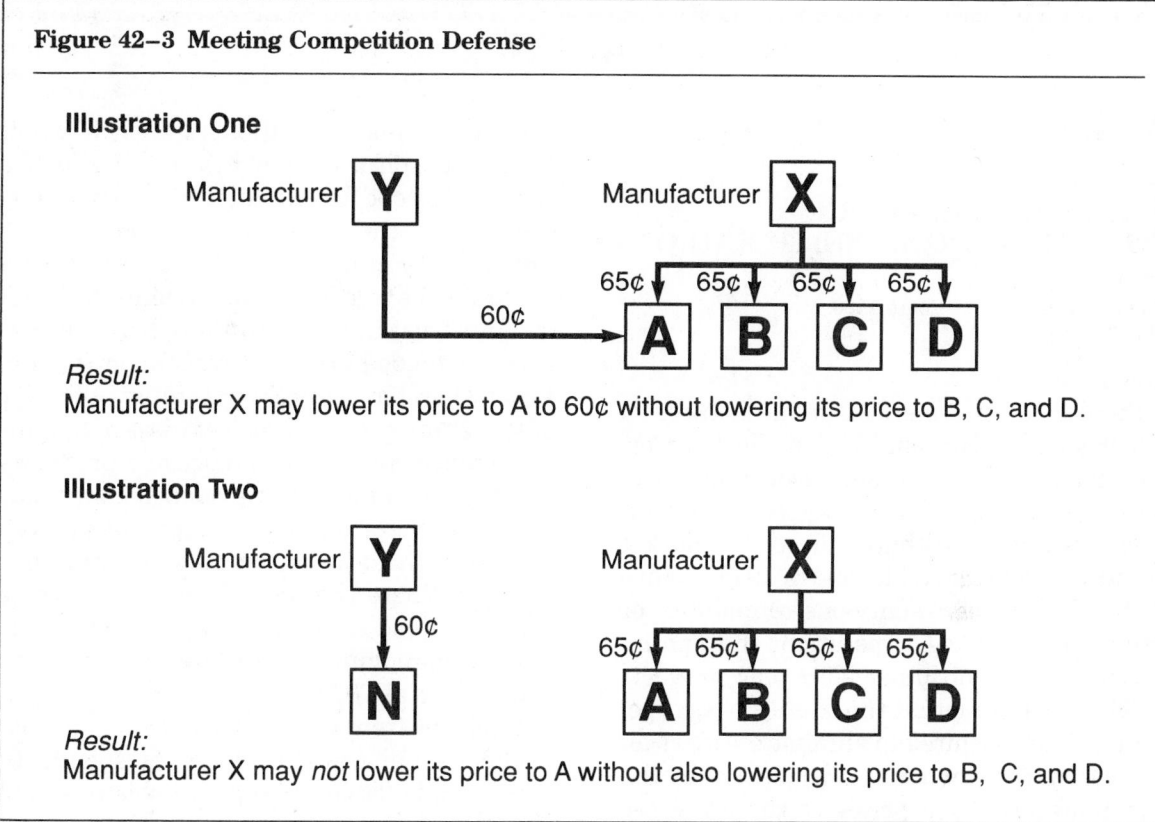

Illustration One

Result:
Manufacturer X may lower its price to A to 60¢ without lowering its price to B, C, and D.

Illustration Two

Result:
Manufacturer X may *not* lower its price to A without also lowering its price to B, C, and D.

ings. It may issue "cease and desist" orders against violators enforceable in the Federal courts. Its broad power has been described by the United States Supreme Court:

The "unfair methods of competition," which are condemned by . . . the Act, are not confined to those that were illegal at common law or that were condemned by the Sherman Act. . . . It is also clear that the Federal Trade Commission Act was designed to supplement and bolster the Sherman Act and the Clayton Act . . . *to stop in their incipiency acts and practices which, when full blown, would violate those Acts. F.T.C. v. Motion Picture Advertising Service Co.,* 344 U.S. 392 (1953). (Emphasis supplied.)

Complaints may be instituted by the Commission, which, after a hearing, "has wide latitude for judgment and the courts will not interfere except where the remedy selected has no reasonable relation to the unlawful practices found to exist." Although the Commission most frequently enters a cease and desist order having the effect of an injunction, it may order other relief, such as affirmative disclosure, corrective advertising, and the granting of licenses to patents on a reasonable royalty basis. *See Warner-Lambert Co. v. Federal Trade Commission* in Chapter 43. Appeals may be taken from orders of the Commission to the United States Courts of Appeals which have exclusive jurisdiction to enforce, set aside, or modify orders of the Commission.

The work of the Federal Trade Commission includes not only investigation of possible violations of the antitrust laws but also unfair methods of competition, such as false and misleading advertisements, false or inadequate labeling of products, passing or palming off goods as those of a competitor, lotteries, gambling schemes, discriminatory offers of rebates and discounts, false disparagement of a competitor's goods, false or misleading descriptive names of products, use of false testimonials, and other unfair trade practices. For a more detailed discussion of the FTC and its powers, see Chapter 43.

CASES

Concerted Action

MATSUSHITA ELECTRIC INDUSTRIAL CO. v. ZENITH RADIO CORP.

United States Supreme Court, 1986.
475 U.S. 574.

POWELL, J.

[Zenith is an American manufacturer of television sets. National Union Electric Corporation ("NUE") is the successor company to an American firm that manufactured television sets until it withdrew from the market because of substantial losses. In 1974, Zenith and NUE sued twenty-one Japanese or Japanese-controlled corporations that manufacture or sell consumer electronic products ("CEP"), claiming that the twenty-one corporations had conspired to eliminate American firms from the American CEP market by fixing artificially high prices in the Japanese market and fixing artificially low prices for the American market in violation of Section 1 of the Sherman Act. The district court granted summary judgment for the defendants, ruling that the evidence that bore directly on the price-cutting conspiracy did not rebut the more plausible inference that the defendants were cutting prices to compete in the American market and not to monopolize it. The Court of Appeals reversed, finding both direct evidence of certain kinds of concerted action and circumstantial evidence that suggested that other types of concerted action may have occurred.]

To survive petitioners' [defendants'] motion for summary judgment, respondents [plaintiffs] must establish that there is a genuine issue of material fact as to whether petitioners entered into an illegal conspiracy that caused respondents to suffer a cognizable injury. [Citations.] This showing has two components. First, respondents must show more than a conspiracy in violation of the antitrust laws; they must show an injury to them resulting from the illegal conduct. Re-

spondents charge petitioners with a whole host of conspiracies in restraint of trade. [Citation.] Except for the alleged conspiracy to monopolize the American market through predatory pricing, these alleged conspiracies could not have caused respondents to suffer an "antitrust injury," [citation], because they actually tended to benefit respondents. [Citation.] Therefore, unless, in context, evidence of these "other" conspiracies raises a genuine issue concerning the existence of a predatory pricing conspiracy, that evidence cannot defeat petitioners' summary judgment motion.

Second, the issue of fact must be "genuine." * * * Where the record taken as a whole could not lead a rational trier of fact to find for the nonmoving party, there is no "genuine issue for trial." [Citation.]

It follows from these settled principles that if the factual context renders respondents' claim implausible—if the claim is one that simply makes no economic sense— respondents must come forward with more persuasive evidence to support their claim than would otherwise be necessary.

* * *

Thus, in *Monsanto Co. v. Spray-Rite Service Corp.,* [citation], we held that conduct as consistent with permissible competition as with illegal conspiracy does not, standing alone, support an inference of antitrust conspiracy. [Citations.]

Petitioners argue that these principles apply fully to this case. According to petitioners, the alleged conspiracy is one that is economically irrational and practically infeasible. Consequently, petitioners contend, they had no motive to engage in the alleged predatory pricing conspiracy; indeed, they had a strong motive *not* to conspire in the manner respondents allege. Petitioners argue that, in light of the absence of any apparent motive and the ambiguous nature of the evidence of conspiracy, no trier of fact reasonably could find that the conspiracy with which petitioners are charged actually existed. This argument requires us to consider the nature of the alleged conspiracy and the practical obstacles to its implementation. * * *

A predatory pricing conspiracy is by nature speculative. Any agreement to price below the competitive level requires the conspirators to forgo profits that free competition would offer them. The forgone profits may be considered an investment in the future. For the investment to be rational, the conspirators must have a reasonable expectation of recovering, in the form of later monopoly profits, more than the losses suffered. * * * [T]he success of such schemes is inherently uncertain: the short-run loss is definite, but the long-run gain depends on successfully neutralizing the competition. Moreover, it is not enough simply to achieve monopoly power, as monopoly pricing may breed quick entry by new competitors eager to share in the excess profits. The success of any predatory scheme depends on *maintaining* monopoly power for long enough both to recoup the predator's losses and to harvest some additional gain. Absent some assurance that the hoped-for monopoly will materialize, *and* that it can be sustained for a significant period of time, "[t]he predator must make a substantial investment with no assurance that it will pay off." [Citation.] For this reason, there is a consensus among commentators that predatory pricing schemes are rarely tried, and even more rarely successful. [Citations.]

These observations apply even to predatory pricing by a *single firm* seeking monopoly power. In this case, respondents allege that a large number of firms have conspired over a period of many years to charge below-market prices in order to stifle competition. Such a conspiracy is incalculably more difficult to execute than an analogous plan undertaken by a single predator. The conspirators must allocate the losses to be sustained during the conspiracy's operation, and must also allocate any gains to be realized from its success. Precisely because success is speculative and depends on a willingness to endure losses for an indefinite period, each conspirator has a strong incentive to cheat, letting its partners suffer the losses necessary to destroy the competition while sharing in any gains if the conspiracy succeeds. The necessary allocation is therefore difficult to accomplish. Yet if conspirators cheat to any substantial extent, the conspiracy must fail, because its success depends on depressing the market price for *all* buyers of CEPs. If there are too few goods at the artificially low price to satisfy demand, the would-be victims of the conspiracy can continue to sell at the "real" market price, and the conspirators suffer losses to little purpose.

Finally, if predatory pricing conspiracies are generally unlikely to occur, they are especially so where, as here, the prospects of attaining monopoly power seem slight. In order to recoup their losses, petitioners must obtain enough market power to set higher than competitive prices, and then must sustain those prices long enough to earn in excess profits what they earlier gave up in below-cost prices. [Citations.] Two decades after their conspiracy is alleged to have commenced, petitioners appear to be far from achieving this goal: the two largest shares of the retail market in television sets are held by RCA and respondent Zenith, not by any of petitioners. [Citation.] Moreover, those shares, which together approximate 40% of sales, did not decline appreciably during the 1970's. [Citation.] Petitioners' collective share rose rapidly during this period, from one-fifth or less of the relevant markets to close to 50%. [Citation.] Neither the District Court nor the Court of Appeals found, however, that petitioners' share presently allows them to charge monopoly prices; to the contrary, respondents contend that the conspiracy is ongoing—that petitioners are still artificially *depressing* the market price in order to drive Zenith out of the market. The data in the record strongly suggest that that goal is yet far distant.

The alleged conspiracy's failure to achieve its ends in the two decades of its asserted operation is strong evidence that the conspiracy does not in fact exist.

* * *

As our [prior] discussion * * * shows, petitioners had no motive to enter into the alleged conspiracy. To the contrary, as presumably rational businesses, petitioners had every incentive *not* to engage in the conduct with which they are charged, for its likely effect would be to generate losses for petitioners with no corresponding gains. * * * [Citation.] Here, the conduct in question consists largely of (i) pricing at levels that succeeded in taking business away from respondents, and (ii) arrangements that may have limited petitioners' ability to compete with each other (and thus kept prices from going even lower). This conduct suggests either that petitioners behaved competitively, or that petitioners conspired to *raise* prices. Neither possibility is consistent with an agreement among 21 companies to price below market levels. Moreover, the predatory pricing scheme that this conduct is said to prove is one that makes no practical sense: it calls for petitioners to destroy companies larger and better established than themselves, a goal that remains far distant more than two decades after the conspiracy's birth. Even had they succeeded in obtaining their monopoly, there is nothing in the record to suggest that they could recover the losses they would need to sustain along the way. In sum, in light of the absence of any rational motive to conspire, * * * [none of the evidence offered] suffice[s] to create a "genuine issue for trial."

On remand, the Court of Appeals is free to consider whether there is other evidence that is sufficiently unambiguous to permit a trier of fact to find that petitioners conspired to price predatorily for two decades despite the absence of any apparent motive to do so.

* * *

The decision of the Court of Appeals is reversed, and the case is remanded for further proceedings consistent with this opinion.

Vertical Market Allocation

CONTINENTAL T.V., INC. v. GTE SYLVANIA, INC.

Supreme Court of the United States, 1977.
433 U.S. 36, 97 S.Ct. 2549, 53 L.Ed.2d 568.

POWELL, J.

Franchise agreements between manufacturers and retailers frequently include provisions barring the retailers from selling franchised products from locations other than those specified in the agreements. This case presents important questions concerning the appropriate antitrust analysis of these restrictions under § 1 of the Sherman Act * * *.

* * *

Respondent GTE Sylvania, Inc. (Sylvania) manufactures and sells television sets. . . . Prior to 1962, like most other television manufacturers, Sylvania sold its televisions to independent or company-owned distributors who in turn resold to a large and diverse group of retailers. Prompted by a decline in its market share to a relatively insignificant 1 to 2% of national television sales Sylvania conducted an intensive reassessment of its marketing strategy, and in 1962 adopted the franchise plan challenged here. Sylvania phased out its wholesale distributors and began to sell its televisions directly to a smaller and more select group of franchised retailers. An acknowledged purpose of the change was to decrease the number of competing Sylvania retailers in the hope of attracting the more aggressive and competent retailers thought necessary to the improvement of the company's market position. To this end, Sylvania limited the number of franchises granted for any given area and required each franchisee to sell his Sylvania products only from the location or locations at which he was franchised. A franchise did not constitute an exclusive territory, and Sylvania retained sole discretion to increase the number of retailers in an area in light of the success or failure of existing retailers in developing their market. The revised marketing strategy appears to have been successful during the period at issue here, for by 1965, Sylvania's share of national television sales had increased to approximately 5%, and the company ranked as the Nation's eighth largest manufacturer of color television sets.

This suit is the result of the rupture of a franchisor-franchisee relationship that had previously prospered under the revised Sylvania plan. Dissatisfied with its sales in the city of San Francisco, Sylvania decided in the spring of 1965 to franchise Young Brothers, an established San Francisco retailer of televisions, as an additional San Francisco retailer. The proposed location of the new franchise was approximately a mile from a retail outlet operated by petitioner Continental T.V., Inc. (Continental), one of the most successful Sylvania franchisees. Continental protested that the location of the new franchise violated Sylvania's marketing policy, but Sylvania persisted in its plans. Continental then cancelled a large Sylvania order and placed a large order with Phillips, one of Sylvania's competitors.

During this same period, Continental expressed a desire to open a store in Sacramento, Cal., a desire Sylvania attributed at least in part to Continental's displeasure over the Young Brothers decision. Sylvania believed that the Sacramento market was adequately served by the existing Sylvania retailers and denied the request. In the face of this denial, Continental advised Sylvania in early September 1965, that it was in the process of moving Sylvania merchandise from its San Jose, Cal., warehouse to a new retail location that it had leased in Sacramento. * * * Shortly thereafter, Sylvania terminated Continental's franchises * * *.

* * * Most important for our purposes was the claim that Sylvania had violated § 1 of the Sherman Act by entering into and enforcing franchise agreements that prohibited the sale of Sylvania products other than from specified locations. At the close of evidence in the jury trial of Continental's claims, Sylvania requested the District Court to instruct the jury that its location restriction was illegal only if it unreasonably restrained or suppressed competition. * * * [T]he District Court rejected the proffered instruction in favor of the following one: "Therefore, if you find by a preponderance of the evidence that Sylvania entered into a contract, combination or conspiracy with one or more of its dealers pursuant to which Sylvania exercised dominion or control over the products sold to the dealer, after having parted with title and risk to the products, you must find any effort thereafter to restrict outlets or store locations from which its dealers resold the merchandise which they had purchased from Sylvania to be a violation of Section 1 of the Sherman Act, regardless of the reasonableness of the location restrictions." In answers to special interrogatories, the jury found that Sylvania had engaged "in a contract, combination or conspiracy in restraint of trade in violation of the antitrust laws with respect to location restrictions alone," and assessed Continental's damages at $591,505, which was trebled. * * *

On appeal, the Court of Appeals for the Ninth Circuit, sitting en banc, reversed by a divided vote. . . . [Concluding that the restraint] should be judged under the "rule of reason" rather than the per se rule.

* * *

We turn first to Continental's contention that Sylvania's restriction on retail locations is a per se violation of § 1 of the Sherman Act. . . .

* * *

The traditional framework of analysis under § 1 of the Sherman Act is familiar and does not require extended discussion. . . . [The "rule of reason" is] the prevailing standard of analysis. [Citation.] Under this rule, the factfinder weighs all of the circumstances of a case in deciding whether a restrictive practice should be prohibited as imposing an unreasonable restraint on competition. Per se rules of illegality are appropriate only when they relate to conduct that is manifestly anticompetitive. As the Court explained in Northern Pac. R. Co. v. United States, 356 U.S. 1, 5 (1958), "there are certain agreements or practices which because of their pernicious effect on competition and lack of redeeming virtue are conclusively presumed to be unreasonable and therefore illegal without elaborate inquiry as to the precise harm they have caused or the business excuse for their use."

* * *

The market impact of vertical restrictions is complex because of their potential for a simultaneous reduction of intrabrand competition and stimulation of interbrand competition.

* * *

Vertical restrictions reduce intrabrand competition by limiting the number of sellers of a particular product competing for the business of a given group of buyers. Location restrictions have this effect because of practical constraints on the effective marketing area of retail outlets. Although intrabrand competition may be reduced, the ability of retailers to exploit the resulting market may be limited both by the ability of consumers to travel to other franchised locations and, perhaps more importantly, to purchase the competing products of other manufacturers. * * *

Vertical restrictions promote interbrand competition by allowing the manufacturer to achieve certain efficiencies in the distribution of his products. These "redeeming virtues" are implicit in every decision sustaining vertical restrictions under the rule of reason. Economists have identified a number of ways in which manufacturers can use such restrictions to compete more effectively against other manufacturers. [Citation.] For example, new manufacturers and manufacturers entering new markets can use the restrictions in order to induce competent and aggressive retailers to make the kind of investment of capital and labor that is often required in the distribution of products unknown to the consumer. Established manufacturers can use them to induce retailers to engage in promotional activities or to provide service and repair facilities necessary to the efficient marketing of their products. Service and repair are vital for many products, such as automobiles and major household appliances. The availability and quality of such services affect a manufacturer's good will and the competitiveness of his product. Because of market imperfections such as the so-called "free rider" effect, these services might not be provided by retailers in a purely competitive situation, despite the fact that each retailer's benefit would be greater if all provided the services than if none did. [Citation.]

* * *

Certainly, there has been no showing in this case, either generally or with respect to Sylvania's agreements, that vertical restrictions have or are likely to have a "pernicious effect on competition" or that they "lack . . . any redeeming virtue." Accordingly, we conclude that the per se rule stated in [citation] must be overruled. In so holding we do not foreclose the possibility that particular applications of vertical restrictions might justify per se prohibition under Northern Pac. R. Co. But we do make clear that departure from the rule of reason standard must be based upon demonstrable economic effect rather than . . . upon formalistic line drawing.

* * * Accordingly, the decision of the Court of Appeals is affirmed.

Monopolization

UNITED STATES v. E.I. Du PONT De NEMOURS & CO.

Supreme Court of the United States, 1956.
351 U.S. 377, 76 S.Ct. 994, 100 L.Ed. 1264.

REED, J.

[In 1923, du Pont was granted the exclusive right to make and sell cellophane in North America. In 1927, the company introduced a moistureproof brand of cellophane that was ideal for various wrapping needs. Although more expensive than most competing wrapping, it was favored for many uses because it offered a desired combination of transparency, strength, and cost. Except as to permeability to gases, however, cellophane had no qualities that were not possessed by a number of competing materials. Cellophane sales increased dramatically, and by 1950, du Pont produced almost 75 percent of the cellophane sold in the United States. Nevertheless, sales of the material constituted less than 20 percent of the sales of "flexible packaging materials."]

The United States brought this action contending that by so dominating cellophane production, du Pont had monopolized a part of trade or commerce in violation of the Sherman Act because it did not have the power to control the price of cellophane or to exclude competitors from the market for flexible wrapping materials.]

* * *

Our cases determine that a party has monopoly power if it has, over "any part of the trade or commerce among the several states," a power of controlling prices or unreasonably restricting competition. * * *

If cellophane is the "market" that du Pont is found to dominate, it may be assumed it does have monopoly power over that "market." Monopoly power is the power to control prices or exclude competition. It seems apparent that du Pont's power to set the price of cellophane has been limited only by the competition afforded by other flexible packaging materials.

* * *

Determination of the competitive market for commodities depends on how different from one another are the offered commodities in character or use, how far buyers will go to substitute one commodity for another. For example, one can think of building materials as in commodity competition but one could hardly say that brick competed with steel or wood or cement or stone in the meaning of Sherman Act litigation; the products are too different. This is the interindustry competition emphasized by some economists. . . . On the other hand, there are certain differences in the formulae for soft drinks but one can hardly say that each one is an illegal monopoly. Whatever the market may be, we hold that control of price or competition establishes the existence of monopoly power under § 2. Section 2 requires the application of a reasonable approach in determining the existence of monopoly power just as surely as did § 1. This of course does not mean that there can be a reasonable monopoly. Our next step is to determine whether du Pont has monopoly power over cellophane: that is, power over its price in relation to or competition with other commodities. The charge was monopolization of cellophane. The defense, that cellophane was merely a part of the relevant market for flexible packaging materials.

* * *

When a product is controlled by one interest, without substitutes available in the market, there is monopoly power. Because most products have possible substitutes, we cannot . . . give "that infinite range" to the definition of substitutes. Nor is it a proper interpretation of the Sherman Act to require that products be fungible to be considered in the relevant market.

* * *

But where there are market alternatives that buyers may readily use for their purposes, illegal monopoly does not exist merely because the product said to be monopolized differs from others. If it were not so, only physically identical products would be a part of the market. To accept the Government's argument, we would have to conclude that the manufacturers of plain as well as moistureproof cellophane were monopolists, and so with films such as Pliofilm, foil, glassine, polyethylene, and Saran, for each of these wrapping materials is distinguishable. These were all exhibits in the case. New wrappings appear, generally similar to cellophane: is each a monopoly? What is called for is an appraisal of the "cross-elasticity" of demand in the trade. . . . In considering what is the relevant market for determining the control of price and competition, no more definite rule can be declared than that commodities reasonably interchangeable by consumers for the same purposes make up that "part of the trade or commerce," monopolization of which may be illegal. As respects flexible packaging materials, the market geographically is nationwide.

* * *

An element for consideration as to cross-elasticity of demand between products is the responsiveness of the sales of one product to price changes of the other. If a slight decrease in the price of cellophane causes a considerable number of customers of other flexible wrappings to switch to cellophane, it would be an indication that a high cross-elasticity of demand exists between them; that the products compete in the same market. The court below held that the "[g]reat sensitivity of customers in the flexible packaging markets to price or quality changes" prevented du Pont from possessing monopoly control over price. The record sustains these findings.

We conclude that cellophane's interchangeability with the other materials mentioned suffices to make it a part of this flexible packaging material market.

The Government stresses the fact that the variation in price between cellophane and other materials demonstrates they are noncompetitive. * * *

[The district court concluded that] "The record establishes plain cellophane and moistureproof cellophane are each flexible packaging materials which are functionally interchangeable with other flexible packaging materials and sold at same time to same customers for same purpose at competitive prices; there is no cellophane market distinct and separate from the market for flexible packaging materials; the market for flexible packaging materials is the relevant market for determining nature and extent of du Pont's market control; and du Pont has at all times competed with other cellophane producers and manufacturers of other flexible packaging materials in all aspects of its cellophane business."

* * * Nor can we say that du Pont's profits, while liberal (according to the Government 15.9% net after taxes on the 1937–1947 average), demonstrate the existence of a monopoly without proof of lack of comparable profits during those years in other prosperous industries. Cellophane was a leader, over 17%, in the flexible packaging materials market. There is no showing that du Pont's rate of return was greater or less than that of other producers of flexible packaging materials.

The "market" which one must study to determine when a producer has monopoly power will vary with the part of commerce under consideration. The tests are constant. That market is composed of products that have reasonable interchangeability for the purposes for which they are produced—prices, use and qualities considered. While the application of the tests remains uncertain, it seems to us that du Pont should not be

found to monopolize cellophane when that product has the competition and interchangeability with other wrappings that this record shows.

Affirmed.

Horizontal Merger

HOSPITAL CORPORATION OF AMERICA v. FTC

United States Court of Appeals, Seventh Circuit, 1986. 807 F.2d 1381.

POSNER, J.

Hospital Corporation of America, the largest proprietary hospital chain in the United States, asks us to set aside the decision by the Federal Trade Commission that it violated section 7 of the Clayton Act, [citation], by the acquisition in 1981 and 1982 of two corporations, Hospital Affiliates International, Inc. and Health Care Corporation. Before these acquisitions (which cost Hospital Corporation almost $700 million), Hospital Corporation had owned one hospital in Chattanooga, Tennessee. The acquisitions gave it ownership of two more. In addition, pursuant to the terms of the acquisitions it assumed contracts, both with four-year terms, that Hospital Affiliates International had made to manage two other Chattanooga-area hospitals. So after the acquisitions Hospital Corporation owned or managed 5 of the 11 hospitals in the area. Later one of the management contracts was cancelled; and one of the lesser issues raised by Hospital Corporation, which we might as well dispose of right now, is whether the Commission should have disregarded the assumption of that contract. We agree with the Commission that it was not required to take account of a post-acquisition transaction that may have been made to improve Hospital Corporation's litigating position. The contract was cancelled after the Commission began investigating Hospital Corporation's acquisition of Hospital Affiliates, and while the initiative in cancelling was taken by the managed hospital, Hospital Corporation reacted with unaccustomed mildness by allowing the hospital to withdraw from the contract. For it had sued three other hospitals that tried to get out of their management contracts—only none of these hospitals was in a market where Hospital Corporation's acquisition of Hospital Affiliates was likely to be challenged. Post-acquisition evidence that is subject to manipulation by the party seeking to use it is entitled to little or no weight. [Citation.] * * *

If all the hospitals brought under common ownership or control by the two challenged acquisitions are treated as a single entity, the acquisitions raised Hospital Corporation's market share in the Chattanooga area from 14 percent to 26 percent. This made it the second largest provider of hospital services in a highly concentrated market where the four largest firms together had a 91 percent market share compared to 79 percent before the acquisitions. These are the FTC's figures, and Hospital Corporation thinks they are slightly too high * * * but the discrepancy is too slight to make a legal difference. Nor would expressing the market shares in terms of the Herfindahl index alter the impression of a highly concentrated market.

* * *

The Commission may have made its task harder (and opinion longer) than strictly necessary, however, by studiously avoiding reliance on any of the [U.S.] Supreme Court's section 7 decisions from the 1960s except [citation], which took an explicitly economic approach to the interpretation of the statute. The other decisions in that decade * * * seemed, taken as a group, to establish the illegality of any nontrivial acquisition of a competitor, whether or not the acquisition was likely either to bring about or shore up collusive or oligopoly pricing. The elimination of a significant rival was thought by itself to infringe the complex of social and economic values conceived by a majority of the Court to inform the statutory words "may . . . substantially . . . lessen competition."

None of these decisions has been overruled. * * *

The most important developments that cast doubt on the continued vitality of such

[1960s] cases as [citations] are found in other cases, where the Supreme Court, echoed by the lower courts, has said repeatedly that the economic concept of competition, rather than any desire to preserve rivals as such, is the lodestar that shall guide the contemporary application of the antitrust laws, not excluding the Clayton Act. * * * Applied to cases brought under section 7, this principle requires the district court (in this case, the Commission) to make a judgment whether the challenged acquisition is likely to hurt consumers, as by making it easier for the firms in the market to collude, expressly or tacitly, and thereby force price above or farther above the competitive level. So it was prudent for the Commission, rather than resting on the very strict merger decisions of the 1960s, to inquire into the probability of harm to consumers. * * *

When an economic approach is taken in a section 7 case, the ultimate issue is whether the challenged acquisition is likely to facilitate collusion. In this perspective the acquisition of a competitor has no economic significance in itself; the worry is that it may enable the acquiring firm to cooperate (or cooperate better) with other leading competitors on reducing or limiting output, thereby pushing up the market price. * * * There is plenty of evidence to support the Commission's prediction of adverse competitive effect in this case. * * *

The acquisitions reduced the number of competing hospitals in the Chattanooga market from 11 to 7. * * *

The reduction in the number of competitors is significant in assessing the competitive vitality of the Chattanooga hospital market. The fewer competitors there are in a market, the easier it is for them to coordinate their pricing without committing detectable violations of section 1 of the Sherman Act, which forbids price fixing. This would not be very important if the four competitors eliminated by the acquisitions in this case had been insignificant, but they were not; they accounted in the aggregate for 12 percent of the sales of the market. As a result of the acquisitions the four largest firms came to control virtually the whole market, and the problem of coordination was therefore reduced to one of coordination among these four.

Moreover, both the ability of the remaining firms to expand their output should the big four reduce their own output in order to raise the market price (and, by expanding, to offset the leading firms' restriction of their own output), and the ability of outsiders to come in and build completely new hospitals, are reduced by Tennessee's certificate-of-need law. Any addition to hospital capacity must be approved by a state agency.

* * *

In showing that the challenged acquisitions gave four firms control over an entire market so that they would have little reason to fear a competitive reaction if they raised prices above the competitive level, the Commission went far to justify its prediction of probable anticompetitive effects. Maybe it need have gone no further [Citations.] But it did. First it pointed out that the demand for hospital services by patients and their doctors is highly inelastic under competitive conditions. This is not only because people place a high value on their safety and comfort and because many of their treatment decisions are made for them by their doctor, who doesn't pay their hospital bills; it is also because most hospital bills are paid largely by insurance companies or the federal government rather than by the patient. The less elastic the demand for a good or service is, the greater are the profits that providers can make by raising price through collusion. * * *

Second, there is a tradition, well documented in the Commission's opinion, of cooperation between competing hospitals in Chattanooga. * * * But a market in which competitors are unusually disposed to cooperate is a market prone to collusion. * * *

Third, hospitals are under great pressure from the federal government and the insurance companies to cut costs. One way of resisting this pressure is by presenting a united front in negotiations with the third-party payors * * *. The fewer the independent competitors in a hospital market, the easier they will find it, by presenting an unbroken phalanx of representations and requests, to frustrate efforts to control hospital costs. This too is a form of collusion that the antitrust laws seek to discourage * * *.

All these considerations, taken together, supported * * * the Commission's conclusion that the challenged acquisitions are likely to foster collusive practices, harmful to consumers, in the Chattanooga hospital market. Section 7 does not require proof that a merger or other acquisition has caused higher prices in the affected market. All that is necessary is that the merger create an appreciable danger of such consequences in the future. A predictive judgment, necessarily probabilistic and judgmental rather than demonstrable [citation].

* * *

The Commission's order is affirmed and enforced.

QUESTIONS

1. Discuss horizontal restraints of trade.

2. Discuss vertical restraints of trade.

3. Discuss monopolization.

4. Discuss the Clayton Act and its rules governing (a) tying contracts, (b) exclusive dealing, (c) vertical mergers, (d) horizontal mergers, and (e) conglomerate mergers.

5. Discuss the Robinson-Patman Act and the various defenses to it.

PROBLEMS

1. Discuss the validity and effect of each of the following:

(a) A, B, and C, manufacturers of stereos, orally agree that due to the disastrous, cutthroat competition in the market, they would establish a reasonable price to charge their purchasers.

(b) D, E, F, and G, newspaper publishers, agree not to charge their customers more than thirty cents per newspaper.

(c) H, a distiller of liquor, and I, H's retail distributor, agree that I should charge a price of five dollars per bottle.

2. Discuss the validity of the following:

(a) An agreement between two manufacturers of the same type of products to allocate territories whereby neither will sell its products in the area allocated to the other.

(b) An agreement between manufacturer and distributor not to sell a dealer a particular product or parts necessary for repair of the product.

3. Universal Video sells $40 million worth of video recording equipment in the United States. The total sales of such equipment in the United States is $100 million. One-half of Universal's sales is to Giant Retailer, a company which possesses 50 percent of the retail market. Giant is presently seeking (1) to obtain an exclusive dealing arrangement with Universal or (2) to acquire Universal. Please advise Giant as to the validity of its alternatives.

4. Z sells cameras to A, B, C, and D for $60 per camera. Y, one of Z's competitor's, sells a comparable camera to A for $58.50. Z, in response to this competitive pressure from Y, lowers its price to A to $58.50. B, C, and D insist that Z lowers its price to them to $58.50, but Z refuses. B, C, and D sue Z for unlawful price discrimination. Decision? Would your answer differ if Z reduced its price to A to $58?

5. Discount is a discount appliance chain store that continually sells goods at a price below the manufacturers' suggested retail prices. A, B, and C, the three largest manufacturers of appliances, agree that unless Discount ceases from its discount pricing, they will no longer sell to Discount. Discount refuses, and A, B, and C refuse to sell to Discount. Discount sues A, B, and C. Decision?

6. Magnum Company produces 77 percent of all the coal utilized in the United States. Coal provides 25 percent of all of the energy used in the United States. In a suit brought by the United States against Magnum for violation of the antitrust laws, what result?

7. Justin Manufacturing Company sells high fashion clothing under the prestigious "Justin" label. The company has a firm policy that it will not deal with any company that sells below its suggested retail price. Justin is informed by one of its customers, XYZ, that its competitor, Duplex, is selling the "Justin" line at a great discount. Justin now demands that Duplex comply with their agreement that they will not sell the "Justin" line below the suggested retail price. Discuss the implications of this situation.

8. Jay Corporation, the largest manufacturer of bicycles in the United States with 40 percent of the market, has recently entered into an agreement with Retail Bike, the largest retailer of bicycles in the United States with 37 percent of the market, under which Jay will furnish its bicycles only to Retail and Retail will sell only Jay's bicycles. The government is now questioning this agreement. Discuss.

9. Whirlpool Corporation manufactured vacuum cleaners under both its own name and under the Kenmore name. Oreck exclusively distributed the vacuum cleaners sold under the Whirlpool name. Sears, Roebuck & Co. exclusively distributed the Kenmore vacuum cleaners. Oreck alleged that its exclusive distributorship agreement with Whirlpool was not renewed because of the existence of an unlawful conspiracy between Whirlpool and Sears. Oreck further contended that a *per se* rule was applicable because the agreement was (a) price fixing or (b) a group boycott, or both. Decision?

10. Indian Coffee of Pittsburgh, Pennsylvania marketed vacuum-packed coffee under the brand name, Breakfast Cheer, in the Pittsburgh and Cleveland, Ohio areas. Later in 1971, Folger Coffee, a leading coffee seller, began selling coffee in Pittsburgh. In order to make inroads into the new territory, Folgers sold its coffee at greatly reduced prices. At first, Indian Coffee met Folger's prices but could not continue operating at such a reduced price and was forced out of the market. Indian Coffee brings an antitrust action. Decision?

11. Von's Grocery, a large retail grocery chain in Los Angeles, sought to acquire Shopping Bag Food Stores, a direct competitor. At the time of the proposed merger, Von's sales ranked third in the Los Angeles area and Shopping Bag's ranked sixth. Both chains were increasing their number of stores. The merger would have resulted in the creation of the second largest grocery chain in Los Angeles, with total sales in excess of $170 million. Prior to the proposed merger, the number of owners operating single stores declined from 5,365 in 1950 to 3,590 by 1963. During this same period,

the number of chains with two or more stores rose from 96 to 150. The United States brought suit against Von's to prevent the merger. It claimed that the proposed merger violated Section 7 of the Clayton Act in that it may result in the substantial lessening of competition or tend to create a monopoly. Decision?

12. Boise Cascade Corporation is a wholesaler and retailer of office products. The Federal Trade Commission issued a complaint charging that Boise had violated the Robinson-Patman Act by receiving a wholesaler's discount from certain suppliers on products that Boise resold at retail, in competition with other retailers that could not obtain wholesale discounts. Decision?

COMPUTER RESEARCH PROBLEMS

1. Great Atlantic and Pacific Tea Company desired to achieve cost savings by switching to the sale of "private label" milk. A&P asked Borden company, its longtime supplier of "brand label" milk to submit a bid to supply certain of A&P's private label dairy products. A&P was not satisfied with Borden's bid, however, and it solicited other offers. Bowman Dairy, a competitor of Borden's, submitted a lower bid. At this point, A&P contacted Borden and asked it to rebid on the private label contract. A&P included a warning that Borden would have to substantially lower its original bid in order to undercut Bowman's bid. Borden offered a bid that doubled A&P's potential annual cost savings. A&P accepted Borden's bid. The Federal Trade Commission then brought this action, charging that A&P had violated the Robinson-Patman Act by knowingly inducing or receiving illegal price discrimination from Borden. Decision?

2. Clorox is the nation's leading manufacturer of household liquid bleach (accounting for 49%—40,000,000—of sales) and is the only brand sold nationally. Clorox and its next largest competitor Purex hold 65% of national sales, and the top four bleach manufacturers control 80% of sales. Since all bleach is chemically identical, Clorox spends over $5,000,000 each year in advertising to attract and keep customers.

Procter & Gamble is the dominant national manufacturer of household cleaning products, with yearly sales of $1.1 billion. Just as with bleach, advertising is vital in the household cleaning products industry. Procter & Gamble spends over $127,000,000 in advertising and promotions. Procter & Gamble decided to diversify into the bleach business, since its household cleaning products and bleach are both low-cost, high-turnover consumer goods, dependent on mass advertising, sold to the same customers at the same stores, by the same merchandising methods. Procter & Gamble decided to merge with Clorox, rather than starting their own bleach division, in order to secure the dominant position in the bleach market immediately. Should the FTC take action against this merger, and if so, what decision?

3. In 1981 the NCAA adopted a plan for televising college football games in order to reduce the adverse effect of TV coverage on spectator attendance. The plan limited the total number of televised intercollegiate football games, and also limited the number of games any one school could televise. No member of the NCAA was permitted to sell any television rights except in accordance with the plan. As part of the plan, the NCAA had agreements with the American Broadcasting Company (ABC) and the Columbia Broadcasting System (CBS) to pay to each

school at least a specified minimum price for televising football games. Several member universities join to bring suit against the NCAA claiming the new plan is a horizontal price fixing agreement and output limitation and as such is illegal *per se*. The NCAA counters that the existence of the product, college football, depends upon member compliance with restrictions and regulations. According to the NCAA its restrictions have a pro-competitive effect, including the TV plan. Is the TV plan valid? Explain.

 4. The National Society of Professional Engineers (Society) had an ethical rule that prohibited member engineers from disclosing or discussing price/fee information with customers until after the customer had hired a particular engineer. This rule against competitive bidding was designed to maintain high standards in the field of engineering. The Society felt that competitive pressure to offer engineering services at the lowest possible price would encourage engineers to design and specify inefficient, unsafe, and unnecessarily expensive structures and construction methods. According to the Society, awarding engineering contracts to the lowest bidder, regardless of quality, would be dangerous to the public health, safety, and welfare. The Society emphasizes that the rule is not an agreement to fix prices. Rather, it claims the rule was drafted by experienced, highly trained professional engineers to prevent public harm and is therefore rea-

sonable. The Government contends that the rule unreasonably restrains trade and thus violates § 1 of the Sherman Act. Decision?

5. In the early 1930s, intense price competition characterized both the retail and the wholesale oil markets. At times, prices in the wholesale market fell below the manufacturer's cost. One cause of the volatile situation was the supply of "distress gasoline" placed on the market by seventeen independent refiners. These independent refiners had no retail sales outlets and little storage capacity, so they were forced to sell it at "distress prices." In spite of their unprofitable operations, they could not afford to shut down, for if they did so, they would be apt to lose their oil connections in the field and their regular customers.

In an attempt to remedy this problem, the major oil companies entered into an informal agreement whereby each selected one or more independent refiners having distress gasoline as its "dancing partner." The major oil company would then assume responsibility for purchasing the independent's distress supply at the "fair going market price." As a result, the market price of oil rose in 1935 and 1936, and the spot market became stable. The United States then brought this criminal action against the companies, charging them with horizontal price fixing in violation of the Sherman Act. Decision?

Chapter 43

CONSUMER PROTECTION

State and Federal Agencies
Unfair and Deceptive Trade Practices
Consumer Purchases
Consumer Credit Transactions

CONSUMER transactions have increased enormously since World War II and today they amount to hundreds of billions of dollars. Although the definition of a consumer transaction varies, it is generally considered one which involves goods, credit, services, or land acquired for personal, household, or family purposes. Historically, consumers were subject to the rule of *caveat emptor*—let the buyer beware. In recent years, however, the law has abandoned this principle in most consumer transactions and has given greater protection to consumers. Most of this protection takes the form of statutory enactments at both the State and Federal levels, and a wide variety of governmental agencies are charged with enforcement of these statutes. This enforcement varies enormously. In some cases, only government agencies have enforcement rights through the imposition of criminal penalties, civil penalties, injunctions, and cease-and-desist orders. In other cases, in addition to government's enforcement rights, consumers are given private rights to seek the rescission of contracts and damages for harm resulting from violations of consumer protection laws. In some instances, such as certain State "lemon laws," consumers alone have rights under consumer protection statutes. This chapter examines State and Federal consumer protection agencies and consumer protection statutes.

STATE AND FEDERAL CONSUMER PROTECTION AGENCIES

Legislatures and administrative bodies at the Federal, State, and local levels all actively seek to protect consumers through the enactment of laws and regulations. These bodies seek to protect consumers from an enormous range of harm. The most common abuses are in the extension of credit, deceptive trade practices, unsafe products, and unfair pricing.

State and Local Consumer Protection Agencies

The many consumer protection agencies at the State and local levels typically deal with fraudulent and deceptive trade practices and fraudulent sales practices, such as false statements about a product's value or quality. In most jurisdictions, consumer protection agencies also help consumers resolve complaints about defective goods or poor service.

Most State attorneys general play an active role in consumer protection by enforcing laws against consumer fraud by means of judicially imposed injunctions and restitution. In recent years, as the Federal government's role in consumer protection has diminished in response to the deregulatory movement, the States have expanded their role. The National Association of Attorneys General (NAAG), has been active in coordinating lawsuits among the States. Under NAAG's guidance, several States often simultaneously file lawsuits against a company that has been engaging in acts of fraud involving more than one State.

In some instances, however, States have not coordinated their efforts. Instead, they have acted inconsistently with respect to consumer protection, especially in health and safety matters. This lack of coordination can present serious problems to companies that sell large numbers of products in interstate commerce. For example, assume that the Glueco Company, which makes and sells glue containing certain toxic chemicals, finds that Connecticut requires warning labels of a certain size and wording while Indiana requires completely different and inconsistent labels. Glueco must incur added expense for placing different labels on different boxes and for making sure that it ships each label type to the correct State. If a large number of States adopt inconsistent approaches, Glueco might be forced to limit the number of States in which it sells or to raise prices to meet the increased labeling costs.

The Federal Trade Commission

At the Federal level, the most significant consumer protection agency is the **Federal Trade Commission** (FTC). Established in 1914, the FTC has two major functions: (1) under its mandate to prevent "unfair methods of competition in commerce," it is responsible for roughly half of the antitrust enforcement at the Federal level (the FTC's role in antitrust enforcement is discussed in Chapter 42); and (2) under its mandate to prevent "unfair and deceptive" trade practices, it is responsible for stopping fraudulent sales techniques.

To address unfair and deceptive trade practices, the five-member commission, no more than three of whose members may be from the same political party, has the power to issue substantive "trade regulation rules" and to conduct appropriate investigations and hearings. Among the rules it has issued so far are those regulating sales of used cars, franchising and business opportunity ventures, funeral home services, and the issuance of consumer credit, as well as those requiring a "cooling-off" period for door-to-door sales (discussed later in this chapter).

In many instances of deceptive trade practices, the agency may seek a cease-and-desist order rather than issue a substantive trade rule. A **cease-and-desist order** directs a party to stop a certain practice or face punishment such as a fine. In a typical situation, the FTC staff discovers a potentially deceptive practice, investigates the matter, files a complaint against the alleged offender (usually referred to as the respondent), and after a hearing in front of an administrative law judge (ALJ) to determine whether a violation of the law has occurred, obtains a cease-and-desist order if the ALJ finds that one is necessary. The respondent may appeal to the FTC commissioners to reverse or modify the order. Appeals from orders issued by the commissioners go to the United States Courts of Appeals, which have exclusive jurisdiction to enforce, set aside, or modify orders of the commission.

Standards The FTC Act does not define the words *unfair* or *deceptive,* and the commission was criticized for many years for its failure to do so. Partly in response to these criticisms and partly in response to Congressional pressure, the commission issued three policy statements in the early 1980s. The first addressed the meaning of **unfairness** and provided the following:

To justify a finding of unfairness the injury must satisfy three tests. It must be substantial; it must not be outweighed by any countervailing benefits to consumers or competition that the practice produces; and it must be an injury that consumers themselves could not reasonably have avoided. The standard, therefore, applies a cost-benefit analysis to the issue of unfairness.

The second policy statement dealt with the meaning of **deception**—the basis of most FTC consumer protection actions. The formulation of this statement generated considerable disagreement among the commissioners, and the statement was approved by a 3–2 vote. The dissenting commissioners issued a minority statement. It is generally accepted that the minority position reflected previous FTC policy, whereas the majority position established new policy.

The majority position provides that "the Commission will find deception if there is a misrepresentation, omission or practice that is likely to mislead the consumer acting reasonably in the circumstances, to the consumer's detriment." Thus, the commission will find an act or practice deceptive if it meets a three-prong test:

First, there must be a representation, omission, or practice that is likely to mislead the consumer. Second, we examine the practice from the perspective of a consumer acting reasonably in the circumstances. Third, the representation, omission, or practice must be a "material" one. The basic question is whether the act or practice is likely to affect the consumer's conduct or decision with regard to a product or service. If so, the practice is material, and consumer injury is likely because consumers are likely to have chosen differently but for the deception.

See In re Cliffdale Associates, Inc. Perhaps the most controversial feature of the new policy is the notion that deception can occur only with respect to "consumers acting reasonably."

Deception may occur by either false representation or material omission. Examples of deceptive practices include advertising that a certain product will save consumers 25 percent on their automotive motor oil while the product simply replaces a quart of oil in the engine (which normally contains four quarts of oil) and is more expensive than the replaced motor oil; placing marbles in a bowl of vegetable soup in order to displace the vegetables from the bottom of the soup and therefore make it appear that the soup had more vegetables; and claiming that a drug provides greater pain relief than another named drug when there is insufficient evidence to prove the claim to the medical community. On the other hand, the FTC will not take action against **puffery** (sales talk that is considered general bragging or overstatement but makes no specific factual representation) if the consumer would recognize it as puffery and not be deceived. For example, a statement by a salesman that "this is one terrific deal" would likely be considered puffery.

Deception can also occur by failing to *disclose* important product information if disclosure is necessary to correct a false and material expectation created in the mind of the consumer by the product or by the circumstances of sale. For example, the FTC has insisted that the failure to disclose a product's country of origin constitutes a deceptive omission, based on the agency's view that consumers assume the United States is the country of origin if no other country's name is listed.

The third policy statement issued by the commission involved **ad substantiation.** This policy requires that advertisers have a reasonable basis for their claims at the time their claims are made. Moreover, in determining the reasonableness of the claim, the commission places great weight upon the cost and benefits of substantiation.

Remedies In addition to the remedies discussed above, the FTC has employed three other potent remedies: (1) affirmative disclosure, (2) corrective advertising, and (3) multiple product orders. **Affirmative disclosure** is frequently employed by the FTC and requires the offender to provide certain information in its advertisement in order for the advertisement not to be considered deceptive.

In ordering such remedial action, however, the commission must be careful not to infringe upon the advertiser's constitutional rights. For instance, the National Commission on Egg Nutrition (NCEN), an egg producers' trade association, was organized in an attempt to combat the damage being done to the egg industry by the anti-cholesterol forces. The Federal Trade Commission alleged that in its attempt to achieve this goal the NCEN had made several false and misleading statements in its advertising campaign. Principally, the FTC contended and subsequently ruled that it was an unfair trade practice for NCEN to represent "that there is no scientific evidence that eating eggs increases the risk of . . . heart and [circulatory] disease. . . ." In addition to ordering the NCEN to cease and desist from this and other representations, the FTC also ordered that (1) any reference made to the relationship between cholesterol (and hence eggs) and circulatory disease be accompanied by a conspicuous statement that many medical authorities believe that eating cholesterol might increase the risk of heart or circulatory disease, and (2) any representation disparaging the scientific evidence connecting cholesterol and heart and circulatory disease is forbidden. The United States Court of Appeals for the Seventh Circuit, however, amended the FTC's affirmative disclosure order on the ground that the order was an overly broad remedial decree. It held that the First Amendment prohibited a remedy "broader than that which is necessary." And, since the order directed NCEN to argue the other side of the issue rather than merely acknowledge the existence of the controversy, the order unduly infringed upon NCEN's freedom of speech. The court, nevertheless, held that: (1) the NCEN cannot disseminate any advertisement that represents that the consumption of eggs or cholesterol does not enhance the risk of heart or circulatory disease unless it conspicuously discloses that a controversy exists surrounding this contention and that the advertisement is merely stating its position, and (2) the NCEN cannot disseminate, any advertisement that presents scientific evidence supporting the position that the consumption of eggs or cholesterol does not increase the consumer's risk of heart or circulatory disease unless it conspicuously discloses that many medical authorities are of the belief that the eating of eggs (cholesterol) does, based on scientific evidence, increase one's risk of heart or circulatory ailments. *National Commission on Egg Nutrition v. FTC,* 570 F.2d 157 (7th Cir. 1977).

Corrective advertising goes beyond affirmative disclosure and requires that the advertiser of a deceptive claim disclose in future advertisements that the deceptive claims made in the prior advertisements were in fact not true. The theory behind this remedy is that the previous deception will continue unless corrected. For a full discussion of this remedy *see Warner-Lambert Co. v. FTC.*

Multiple product orders require that the deceptive advertisers cease and desist from any future deception in regard not only to the product in question but also to all products sold by the company. This remedy is particularly useful in dealing with companies that are repeated violators of the law.

In addition to these traditional remedies, the FTC recently has turned to direct court action rather than administrative proceedings. Legislation enacted in 1973 gave the FTC the right to seek in a Federal district court a preliminary injunction, pending completion of administrative proceedings, whenever the agency had reason to believe that a person was violating FTC laws or rules. First used to stop mergers, this authority is now often invoked in consumer protection cases. The same provision also grants the agency authority to seek a permanent injunction " in proper cases" without a prior administrative finding that FTC law has been violated.

The Consumer Product Safety Commission

In 1967, President Lyndon Johnson, in accordance with a joint resolution of Congress, appointed a study group to examine the level of product safety in the United States. The study group, known as the National Commission on Product Safety, issued its report in 1970 and discovered the following:

Americans—20 million of them—are injured each year in the home as a result of incidents connected with consumer products. Of the total, 110,000 are permanently disabled and 30,000 are killed. A significant number could have been spared if more attention had been paid to hazard reduction. . . . The exposure of consumers to unreasonable consumer product hazards is excessive by any standard of measurement.

Two years later, Congress enacted the Consumer Product Safety Act (CPSA), which established an independent Federal regulatory agency, the Consumer Product Safety Commission (CPSC). The purposes of the CPSA were fourfold:

1. to protect the public against unreasonable risks of injury associated with consumer products;

2. to assist consumers in evaluating the comparative safety of consumer products;

3. to develop uniform safety standards for consumer products and to minimize conflicting State and local regulations; and

4. to promote research and investigation into the causes and prevention of product-related deaths, illnesses, and injuries.

The CPSC consists of five commissioners, no more than three of whom can be from the same political party. Under the authority granted the CPSC, it can: set safety standards for consumer products, ban unsafe products, issue administrative "recall" orders to compel repair, replacement, or refunds for products that have been found to present substantial product hazards, and seek court orders to require the recall of "imminently hazardous" products. In addition, Congress required businesses under CPSC jurisdiction to notify the agency whenever they obtain information indicating that their products contain defects that "could create" substantial product hazards. These reports play a major role in the agency's regulatory activities because they trigger investigations that may lead to product recalls.

The CPSC also enforces four statutes previously enforced by other agencies. These acts, commonly referred to as the "transferred acts," are the Federal Hazardous Substances Act, the Flammable Fabrics Act, the Poison Prevention Packaging Act, and the Refrigerator Safety Act. Whenever the CPSC can regulate a product under one of these specific acts, rather than under the more general CPSA, the agency is directed to do so unless it makes a specific finding that it is in the "public interest" to regulate under the CPSA. Thus, a large number of CPSC regulations, such as those for children's toys, children's flammable sleepwear, and hazard warnings on household chemical products, arise under the transferred acts rather than under the CPSA.

When first established, the CPSC promulgated a number of **mandatory safety standards,** which are rules regarding the design, warning labels, or packaging of a product, which manufacturers either must follow or be faced with legal sanctions. To save time and money, the agency began to rely on industry to write **voluntary safety standards**—rules for which noncompliance does not violate the law—reserving mandatory standards for those instances in which voluntary standards proved inadequate. In 1981, Congress enacted legislation requiring the CPSC to rely on voluntary standards rather than to promulgate mandatory standards "whenever compliance with such voluntary standards would eliminate or adequately reduce the risk of injury addressed and there is substantial compliance with such voluntary standards." Although the 1981 amendments do not bar the CPSC from writing mandatory standards, the CPSC has promulgated few mandatory standards since the law was amended.

Other Federal Consumer Protection Agencies

Among the many other Federal agencies that play a major consumer protection role are the **National Highway Traffic Safety Administration (NHTSA)** and the **Food and Drug Administration (FDA).** Congress established NHTSA in 1966 to reduce the number of deaths and injuries resulting from highway crashes. Each year, roughly 46,000 Americans are killed in highway crashes and 1.8 million suffer disabling injuries. This means that 127 highway deaths occur each day.

NHTSA's authority is similar to the CPSC's. It has the authority to set safety standards for motor vehicles to address crash prevention (e.g., rules for safer tires and brakes) and crashworthiness (e.g., interior padding, safety belts, and collapsible steering columns). As with the CPSC, manufacturers are required to report possible safety defects and the agency is empowered to seek recalls if it determines that a particular automobile model presents a sufficiently great hazard. NHTSA also is authorized to provide grants-in-aid to States to carry out highway safety programs and to conduct research on improving highway safety.

The Food and Drug Administration is the oldest Federal consumer protection agency, dating back to 1906. The FDA enforces the Food Drug and Cosmetic Act, which authorizes the agency to regulate "adulterated and misbranded" products. The agency uses two basic methods of enforcement: it sets standards for products or requires pre-market approval of them. The products most often subject to pre-market approval are drugs. Since 1976, the agency also has had the authority to require medical devices such as pacemakers and intrauterine devices to undergo pre-market approval, and it recently has been requiring an increasing number of such devices to go through this approval process.

Although the FTC, CPSC, NHTSA, and FDA are perhaps the best known Federal consumer protection agencies, numerous other agencies also play important roles in this area. For example, the United States Post Office brings many cases every year to close down mail fraud operations; the Interstate Commerce Commission (ICC) enforces rules to prevent unfair business practices by interstate moving companies; and the Securities and Exchange Commission (SEC) takes action to protect consumers against fraud in the sale of securities. (The SEC is discussed in Chapter 45.) In addition, many other agencies provide assistance to consumers for specific types of problems that come within the scope of an agency.

CONSUMER PURCHASES

Whenever a consumer purchases a product or obtains a service, certain rights and obligations arise. The extent to which these rights and obligations apply to all contracts is discussed more fully in Chapters 8 through 17. The extent to which they apply to a sale of goods under the Uniform Commercial Code is discussed in Chapters 20 through 24. Although a number of consumer protection laws have been enacted in recent years, they still leave large areas of a consumer's rights and duties to State contract law. In particular, Article 2 of the Uniform Commercial Code provides the basic rules governing when a contract for the sale of goods is formed, what constitutes a breach of contract, and what rights an innocent party has against the party who breached a contract. Many consumer protection laws add protections not contained in the U.C.C. but still use it as a basic building block. For example, the Magnuson-Moss Warranty Act builds upon the perceived inadequacy of the U.C.C. in permitting sellers to disclaim or modify warranties. Similarly, many States have passed so-called lemon laws to provide additional contract cancellation rights to dissatisfied automobile purchasers.

Federal Warranty Protection

A **warranty** creates a duty on the part of the seller to assure that the goods or services she sells will conform to certain qualities, characteristics, or conditions. A seller, however, is not required to warrant what she sells, and in general she may, by appropriate words, disclaim (exclude) or modify a particular warranty or all warranties. Because sellers have so much flexibility, consumer protection laws have been enacted to ensure that consumers understand the warranty protection provided them.

To protect and to prevent deception in selling to buyers, Congress enacted the **Magnuson-Moss Warranty Act,** which requires that sellers of consumer products give adequate information about written warranties. The FTC administers and enforces the act. The Magnuson-Moss Warranty Act was enacted to alleviate certain reported warranty problems: (1) most warranties were not understandable; (2) most warranties disclaimed implied warranties; (3) most warranties were unfair; and (4) in some instances the warrantors did not live up to their warranties. The act was Congress's attempt to make consumer product warranties more easily understood and to facilitate the consumer in satisfactorily enforcing her remedies. To accomplish this purpose, the act provides for

1. clear and understandable disclosure of the warranty that is to be offered,

2. a description of the warranty as either "full" or "limited,"

3. a prohibition against disclaiming implied warranties if a written warranty is given, and

4. an optional informal settlement mechanism.

The act applies to consumer products containing a **written warranty.** A consumer product is any item of tangible personal property that is *normally* used for family, household, or personal use and is distributed in commerce. Commercial purchasers are not protected by the act: they are considered to have sufficient knowledge in contracting to protect themselves. Also, they are able to employ their own attorneys to protect themselves and can spread the cost of their injuries in the marketplace.

Pre-sale Disclosure The act contains pre-sale disclosure provisions, which are calculated to avert confusion and deception and to enable purchasers to make educated product comparisons. A warrantor must, "to the extent required by the rules of the [Federal Trade] Commission, fully and conspicuously disclose in simple and readily understood language the terms and conditions of such warranty." When it implemented this requirement, the FTC adopted a rule that the text of the warranties must be accessible to the consumer. Under that rule, the warranty

could be attached to the package, it could be placed on a visible sign, or it could be maintained in a binder. In 1986, the FTC relaxed this rule by permitting stores simply to make warranties available to consumers *upon request*. Retailers using this option, however, must post signs informing the consumer that the warranties are available. Separate rules apply to mail order, catalog, and door-to-door sales.

Labeling Requirements The second major part of the act concerns the labeling requirement. The act divides written warranties into two categories—limited and full—one of which, for any product costing more than ten dollars, must be designated on the written warranty itself. The purpose of this provision is to alert the consumer to the legal rights under a certain warranty for purposes of initial comparison. If a **warranty** is designated as **full,** the warrantor must agree to repair without charge the product to conform with the warranty, no limitation may be placed on the duration of any implied warranty, the consumer must be given the option of a refund or replacement if repair is unsuccessful, and consequential damages may be excluded only if conspicuously noted. A **limited warranty** is any warranty not designated as full.

Limitations on Disclaimers Most significantly, the act provides that a *written* warranty, whether full or limited, cannot *disclaim any implied* warranty. This provision strikes at the heart of the problem, for as revealed in an earlier Presidential task force report, most written warranties gave limited protection but in return took away the more valuable implied warranties. Hence, consumers believed that the warranties they received and the warranty registration cards they promptly returned to the manufacturer were to their benefit. The act, on the other hand, provides that a *full* warranty must not disclaim, modify, or limit any implied warranty, and a *limited* warranty cannot disclaim or modify any implied warranty but can limit its duration to that of the written warranty, provided that such limitation is reasonable, conscionable, and conspicuously displayed. Some States, however, do not allow limitations in the duration of implied warranties.

For example, GE sells consumer goods to Barry for $150 and provides a written warranty regarding the quality of the goods. GE must designate the warranty as full or limited, depending upon the characteristics of the warranty, and cannot disclaim or modify any implied warranty. On the other hand, if GE had not provided Barry with a written warranty, then the Magnuson-Moss Act would not apply, and GE could disclaim any and all implied warranties (see Figure 43–1).

Finally, the act also deals with *remedies* and the establishment, at the option of the warrantor, of an informal settlement procedure. The act does not provide any new or expanded remedies.

State "Lemon Laws"

With the enactment of the Magnuson-Moss Warranty Act, many consumers assumed that automobile manufacturers would feel compelled to offer full warranties to buyers of new cars. This would have given such buyers the option to obtain a refund or replacement without charge for a defective automobile or defective parts. Automobile sellers, however, opted for limited warranties. In response, a number of State legislatures enacted "**lemon laws**" that attempt to provide rights to new

car purchasers that are similar to full warranties under the Magnuson-Moss Warranty Act. There are many different lemon laws, but most define a *lemon* as a car that continues to have a defect substantially impairing the use, value, or safety of a car after a reasonable number of attempts by the manufacturer to repair the defect. In most States, there is a presumption that a manufacturer had a sufficient opportunity to repair a defect if the manufacturer made four unsuccessful attempts to fix it or the consumer's car was out of service for a total of more than thirty days during the year it was sold. If a consumer can prove that her car is a lemon, most lemon laws require the manufacturer either to replace the car or to refund the retail price of the car, less an allowance for the consumer's use of the car. In addition, most lemon laws provide that the consumer may recover attorneys' fees and expenses if the case goes to litigation.

Consumer Right of Rescission

In most cases, a consumer is legally obligated once he has signed a contract. In many States, however, a consumer has by statute a brief period of time—generally two or three days—during which he may **rescind** an otherwise binding credit obligation if the solicitation of the sale occurred in his home. Moreover, the Federal Trade Commission has also promulgated a Trade Regulation applicable to door-to-door sales, leases, or rentals of

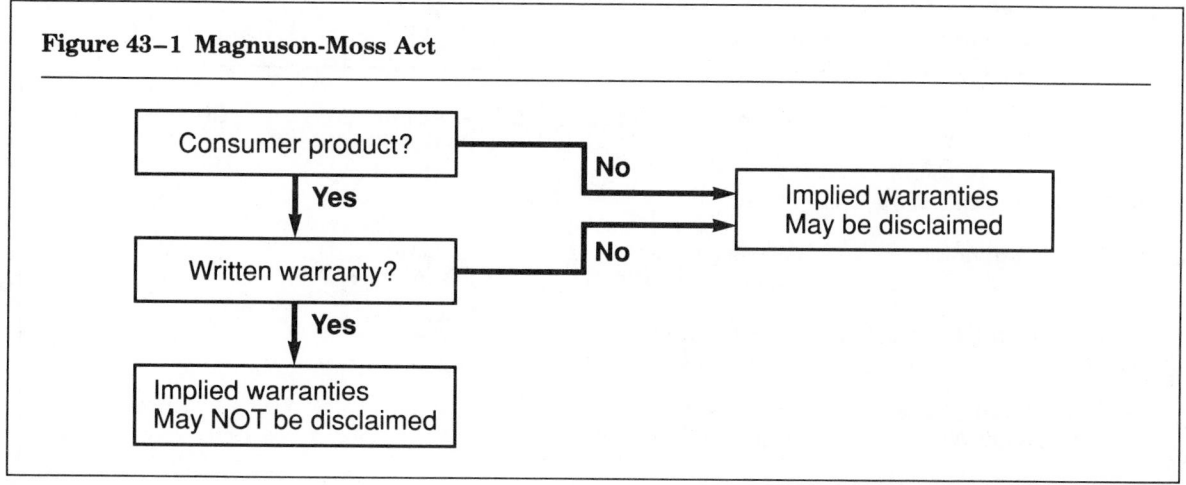

Figure 43–1 Magnuson-Moss Act

goods and services for twenty-five dollars or more, whether the sale is for cash or on credit. The regulation permits a consumer to rescind the contract within *three days* of signing. In order to make the rule effective, the FTC requires sellers to provide a written notice of the buyer's cancellation rights. If the buyer properly cancels, she must make available to the seller, in substantially as good condition as when received, any goods delivered by the seller. The seller must, within ten business days of receiving notice of rescission, return any money paid or any negotiable instrument (such as a personal check or a promissory note) executed by the buyer and cancel any security interest arising out of the transaction. If the seller fails to comply, the FTC will consider the noncompliance to be a violation of the Federal Trade Commission Act and will seek appropriate sanctions, such as a cease-and-desist order and civil penalties. To the extent that State laws on door-to-door sales are directly inconsistent with the FTC rule (for example, if a State provides only two days for rescission) they are unenforceable.

A consumer also has a right of rescission under the **Federal Consumer Credit Protection Act** (discussed more fully below), which allows a consumer three days during which he may withdraw from any credit obligation secured by a mortgage on his home,

unless the extension of credit was made to acquire the dwelling. This right of rescission exists whether or not the contract was the result of a door-to-door sale. If the consumer rescinds, the creditor has twenty days to return any money or property he has received from the consumer.

The **Interstate Land Sales Full Disclosure Act** applies to sales or leases of 100 or more lots of unimproved land as part of a common promotional plan in interstate commerce. The act requires the developer to file a detailed "statement of record" containing specified information about the subdivision and the developer with the Department of Housing and Urban Development (HUD) before offering the lots for sale or lease. The developer must provide a property report, which is a condensed version of the statement of record, to each prospective purchaser or lessee. The act provides that any contract or agreement for sale or lease may be revoked at the option of the purchaser or lessee within seven days of signing the contract, and the contract must clearly provide this right. If the property report has not been given to the purchaser or lessee in advance of signing the contract, the contract may be revoked within two years from the date of signing.

For a summary of consumer rescission rights, see Figure 43–2.

Figure 43–2 Consumer Rescission Rights

Law	Rescission Period	Door-to-Door Solicitation Required?	Credit or Cash
State "cooling-off" laws	Varies	Yes	Varies
FTC trade regulation	Within 3 days of signing the contract	Yes	Both
Consumer Credit Protection Act (CCPA)	Within 3 days of signing the contract	No	Credit only
Interstate Land Sales Full Disclosure Act	Within 7 days of signing of contract	No	Both

CONSUMER CREDIT TRANSACTIONS

A **consumer credit transaction** is customarily defined as any credit transaction the subject matter of which is to be used by one of the parties for their personal, household, or family purposes. The following are illustrative: Atkins borrows $600 from a bank to pay a dentist bill or to take a vacation; Bevins buys a refrigerator for her home from a department store and agrees to pay the purchase price in twelve equal monthly installments; Carpenter has a credit card with an oil company that he uses to purchase gasoline and tires for his family car.

Regulation of consumer credit has increased considerably because of the dramatic expansion of consumer credit since World War II, and the numerous abuses in credit transactions, including misleading credit disclosures, unfair marketing practices, and oppressive collection methods. In response to concerns about consumer credit, Congress passed the **Federal Consumer Credit Protection Act (FCCPA)** in 1968, which requires disclosure of the finance charges (including interest and other charges), credit extension charges, and sets limits on garnishment proceedings. In the years since 1968, Congress has added additional titles to this law. Today, it includes the following laws: (1) Truth-in-Lending Act (including the Fair Credit Billing Act and the Consumer Leasing Act), (2) Restriction on Garnishment, (3) Fair Credit Reporting Act, (4) Equal Credit Opportunity Act, (5) Fair Debt Collection Practices Act, and (6) Electronic Fund Transfer Act. Also in 1968, the National Conference of Commissioners on Uniform State Laws (the group that drafted the Uniform Commercial Code) promulgated the **Uniform Consumer Credit Code (UCCC),** which integrated into one recommended law the regulation of all consumer credit transactions—loans and purchases on credit. The UCCC has been adopted in only nine States, although it has had an impact on the development of consumer credit beyond those States in which it has been adopted.

Consumer credit protection has broadened considerably since the passage of the FCCPA and includes the following areas: (1) access by creditors and consumers to the consumer credit market, (2) disclosure of information to the consumer, (3) regulation of contract terms, (4) regulation of consumer credit card fraud, (5) fair reportage of credit information concerning consumers, and (6) creditors' remedies.

Access to the Market

The **Equal Credit Opportunity Act,** enacted by Congress in 1974 and subsequently revised on a number of occasions, prohibits all businesses that regularly extend credit from discriminating in extending credit on the basis of sex, marital status, race, color, religion, national origin, or age. One of Congress' major concerns in passing the act was the lenders' practice of refusing credit to women based on the assumption that women of childbearing age had a reduced capacity to afford credit because of the likelihood that they would quit work in order to have children. Under **Regulation B,** issued by the Federal Reserve Board to implement the act, and the Women's Business Ownership Act of 1988, creditors cannot inquire into or use information about an applicant's mental status or a woman's likelihood of having children in determining her creditworthiness.

Under the act, creditors have thirty days after receipt of an application for credit to notify the applicant of action taken, and they must give specific reasons for a denial of credit. The act is administered and enforced by several Federal agencies with overall enforcement authority given to the Federal Trade Commission. Credit applicants who are aggrieved by a violation of the act may recover actual and punitive damages plus attorney's fees.

The **Home Mortgage Disclosure Act (HMDA)** was enacted by Congress along with the **Community Reinvestment Act (CRA)** to emphasize to financial institutions the importance of their reinvesting funds in the communities that they serve. Congress therefore outlawed geographic discrimination, or *redlining,* the process by which financial institutions refuse to finance homes to qualified applicants on reasonable terms due to the decline of the geographic area in which the applicant's home is located. In addition, the HMDA requires public disclosure of the financial institution's geographic pattern of mortgage lending. The CRA was intended to encourage financial institutions to meet the credit needs of their local communities. In 1989, Congress adopted a major banking bail-out bill, the **Financial Institutions Reform, Recovery, and Enforcement Act (FIRREA),** which included amendments to the HMDA and the CRA. The amendments expanded the disclosure and reporting requirements of all mortgage lenders and mandated that Federal regulating agencies evaluate and rate CRA performance reports.

Disclosure Requirements

Title One of the FCCPA, also known as the **Truth-in-Lending Act,** has superseded State disclosure requirements relating to credit terms for both *consumer* loans and credit sales under $25,000. The act does not cover credit transactions for business, commercial, or agricultural purposes. Federal disclosure standards must be complied with in every State except those specifically exempted by the Federal Reserve Board. Such an exemption is made only if the State disclosure requirements are substantially the same as the Federal requirements and enforcement is assured. The FCCPA does not eliminate the necessity for creditor compliance with State requirements not covered by, or more stringent than, the requirements of the FCCPA, so long as the State required disclosure is not inconsistent with the FCCPA.

A creditor is required, under both State and Federal statutes, to provide certain information about contract terms to the consumer before he formally incurs the obligation. This information must be provided in a written statement presented to the consumer. Generally, the required disclosure is associated with the cost of credit, i.e., interest, sales charges, finder's fees, mortgage guarantee insurance, or any mandatory credit life insurance. An important requirement in the Truth-in-Lending Act is that sales finance charges and interest rates must be quoted in terms of an *annual percentage rate* (**APR**) and must be calculated on a uniform basis. Congress required disclosure of this information to encourage comparison of credit terms by consumers, to increase competition among financial institutions, and to facilitate economic stability. Enforcement and interpretation of the Truth-in-Lending Act was assigned to several agencies, the two most important being the FTC and the Federal Reserve Board, which issued **Regulation Z** to carry out this responsibility.

Many individuals have claimed that interest rates charged for credit cards are unfairly excessive and should be limited by legislation. In 1988, statutes were proposed in Congress to do this but none was enacted. Instead, Congress passed the **Fair Credit and Charge Card Disclosure Act of 1988.** The act is consistent with other legislation in the field in that it places an emphasis on disclosure of key items. The act adds a new section to the Truth-in-Lending Act requiring all credit and charge card applications and solicitations to include extensive disclosures that vary depending upon the type of card involved and whether the application or solicitation was by mail, telephone, or other means.

Credit Accounts In addition to the cost of the credit, under the Truth-in-Lending Act a creditor must inform consumers who open revolving or open-end credit accounts about how the finance charge is computed and when it is charged, what other charges may be imposed, and whether a security interest is retained or acquired by the creditor. An **open-end** credit account is one that permits the debtor to enter into a series of credit transactions that he may pay off in installments or in a lump sum. Examples of this type of credit include most department store credit cards, most gasoline credit cards, VISA cards, and MASTERCARDs. With this type of credit, the creditor is also required to provide a statement of account for each billing period.

Closed-end credit is credit extended for a specified period of time during which periodic payments are generally made in an amount and at a time agreed upon in advance. Examples of this type of transaction include most automobile financing agreements, most real estate mortgages, and numerous other major purchases. *See Chapman v. Miller.* For non-revolving or closed-end credit accounts, the creditor must provide the consumer with information about the total amount financed; the cash price; the number, amount, and due date of installments; delinquency charges; and a description of the security, if any.

ARMs In 1987, the Federal Reserve amended Regulation Z to deal with variable or adjustable rate mortgages (ARMs). The *ARM disclosure rules* apply to any loan that is (1) a closed-end consumer transaction, (2) secured by the consumer's principal residence, (3) longer than one year in duration, and (4) subject to interest rate variation. This coverage excludes open-end lines of credit secured by the consumer's principal dwelling. The disclosures must be made when an application is furnished to a prospective borrower or before the creditor receives payment of a nonrefundable fee, whichever occurs first. The ARM disclosure rules require that the creditor provide the consumer with a consumer handbook on ARMs and a loan program disclosure statement covering the terms of each ARM that the creditor offers.

Home Equity Loans In recent years a popular method of consumer borrowing has been the home equity loan. In order to regulate the disclosures and advertising of these loans, in 1988 Congress enacted the **Home Equity Loan Consumer Protection Act (HELCPA).** HELCPA amends the Truth-in-Lending Act to require that lenders provide a disclosure statement and consumer pamphlet at (or in some limited instances within three days of) the time they provide an application to a prospective consumer bor-

rower. HELCPA applies to all open-end credit plans for consumer loans that are secured by the consumer's principal dwelling. Unlike other Truth-in-Lending statutes, HELCPA defines a principal dwelling to include second or vacation homes. The disclosure statement must include a statement that (1) a default on the loan may result in the consumer's loss of the dwelling, (2) some conditions must be met, such as time by which an application must be submitted to obtain the specific terms, and (3) the creditor, under certain circumstances, may terminate the plan and accelerate the outstanding balance, prohibit further extension of credit, reduce the plan's credit limit, or impose fees upon the termination of the account. In addition, if the plan contains a fixed rate of interest, the creditor must disclose each APR imposed. If the rate is an ARM, it must include how the rate is computed, the manner in which rates will be changed, the initial rate and how it was determined, the maximum that the rate can change in any one year, the maximum rate that can be charged under the plan, the earliest that the maximum interest can be reached, and an itemization of all fees imposed by the plan. Regulation Z provides the consumer with the right to rescind such a plan until midnight of the third day following the opening of the plan, delivery of a notice of the right to rescind, or delivery of all material disclosures, whichever comes last.

Billing Errors In 1975, the **Fair Credit Billing Act** went into effect to relieve some of the problems and abuses associated with credit card billing errors. The act establishes procedures for the consumer to follow in making complaints about specified errors in billing and requires the creditor to explain or correct such errors. Billing errors are defined to include: (1) extensions of credit that were never made or were not made in the amount indicated on the billing statement; (2) undelivered or unaccepted goods or services; (3) incorrect recording of payments or credits; and (4) accounting or computational errors. Until the creditor responds to the complaint, it may not take any action to collect the disputed amount, restrict the use of an open-ended credit account because the disputed amount is unpaid, or report the disputed amount as delinquent.

In 1974, Congress enacted the **Real Estate Settlement Procedures Act (RESPA)** to provide consumers who purchase a home with greater and more timely information on the nature and costs of the settlement process and with protection from unnecessarily high settlement charges. The act applies to all Federally related mortgage loans and requires advance disclosure to home buyers and sellers of all settlement costs including attorney's fees, credit reports, and title insurance. Nearly all first mortgage loans fall within the scope of the act. RESPA prohibits kickbacks and referral fees and limits the amount home buyers are required to place in escrow accounts to insure payment of real estate taxes and insurance. The act is administered and enforced by the Secretary of Housing and Urban Development.

Contract Terms

Consumer credit is marketed on a mass basis. Contract documents are frequently printed forms containing blank spaces to be filled in by the creditor. These blank spaces relate to matters usually negotiated at the time of the extension of credit. Standardization and uniformity of contract terms facilitate transfer of the rights of the creditor (in most situations a seller) to a third party, which is usually a bank or finance company.

Almost all the States impose statutory ceilings on the amount that may be charged for the extension of consumer credit. Statutes regulating rates also specify what other charges may be made. For example, charges for insurance, official fees, and taxes are usually not considered part of the finance charge. Charges that are incidental to the extension of credit are usually considered part of the finance charge, such as a service charge or a commission for extending credit. Any charge that does not qualify as an authorized additional charge is treated as part of the finance charge and is subject to the statutory rate

ceiling. Other special permitted charges include delinquency and default charges, charges incurred in connection with storing and repairing repossessed goods for sale, reasonable fees for a lawyer who is not a salaried employee of the creditor, and court costs.

Most statutes require a creditor to permit the debtor to pay her obligation in full at any time prior to the maturity date of the final installment. If the interest charge over the period of the loan was computed in advance and added to the principal of the loan, upon making pre-payment in full, the debtor is entitled to a refund of the unearned interest already paid.

Aside from provisions relating to cost, the balance of a credit contract deals with the terms of repayment and the remedies of the creditor if payments are delinquent. Usually, payments must be periodic and substantially equal in amount. Balloon payments (loans in which the final payment is much larger than the regular payments; for example, where the monthly installments are $50 and the final installment is $1,000) may be prohibited. If they are not prohibited, the creditor may be required to refinance the loan at the same rate and with installments in the same amount as the original loan without penalty to the borrower.

In the past, certain consumer purchase transactions were financed in such manner that the purchaser was legally obligated to make full payment of the price to a third party, even though the dealer from whom she bought the goods had committed fraud or the goods were defective. This occurred when the purchaser executed and delivered to the seller a negotiable promissory note which the seller negotiated to a holder in due course, a third party who purchased the note for value, in good faith, and without notice that it was overdue or of any defenses or claims to it. The buyer's defense that the goods were defective or that the seller had committed fraud, although valid against the seller, were not valid against a holder in due course of the note. The Federal Trade Commission, in order to correct this situation by preserving and making available claims and defenses of consumer buyers and borrowers against holders in due course, adopted a rule that limits the rights of a holder in due course of an instrument that evidences a debt arising out of a *consumer credit contract.* The rule applies to sellers and lessors of goods. A discussion of the rule is in Chapter 27.

A similar rule applies to credit card issuers under the **Fair Credit Billing Act.** The act preserves consumers' defenses against the issuer provided the consumer has made a good faith attempt to resolve the dispute with the seller, but only if (1) the seller is controlled by the issuer or under common control with the issuer; or (2) the card issuer included the seller's promotional literature in the monthly billing statement sent to the card holder; or (3) the sale involves more than fifty dollars and the consumer's billing address is in the same State as or within 100 miles of the seller's place of business.

Consumer Credit Card Fraud

Consumer credit card fraud has become an increasingly serious problem and now totals approximately $200 million per year. In 1984, Congress enacted the **Credit Card Fraud Act,** which closed many of the loopholes in prior law. The act prohibits the following practices: (1) possessing unauthorized cards, (2) counterfeiting or altering credit cards, (3) using account numbers alone, and (4) using cards obtained from a third party with his consent, even if the third party conspires to report the cards as stolen. It also imposes stiffer, criminal penalties for violation.

The FCCPA provides protection to the *credit card holder* from loss by limiting the card holder's liability for unauthorized use of a credit card to fifty dollars. The card issuer may collect up to that amount for unauthorized use only if (1) the card has been accepted; (2) the issuer has furnished adequate notice of potential liability to the card holder; (3) the issuer has provided the card holder with a statement of the means by which the card issuer may be notified of the loss or theft of the credit card; (4) the unauthorized use

occurs before the card holder has notified the card issuer of the loss or theft; and (5) the card issuer has provided a method by which the user can be identified as the person authorized to use the card.

Fair Reportage

Whenever an individual applies for credit, it is likely that the lender will run a credit check on the applicant. One of the most common ways for lenders to do this is to purchase a credit report from a credit bureau—a private company that keeps files on consumers and how well they pay their debts. If the file indicates that the applicant fails to repay loans or pays them in an untimely manner, the individual may have difficulty obtaining credit.

Before passage of the Fair Credit Reporting Act, certain unscrupulous creditors took advantage of consumers' fears of bad credit ratings to get them to pay questionable claims. For example, if Barry bought an overpriced, malfunctioning vacuum cleaner from the Ajax Vacuum Company based on the false representations of Ajax's salesman, Barry would have the right to rescind the sale and refuse to pay Ajax. Before the act, if Barry withheld payments, Ajax might have threatened to report him to the credit bureau as delinquent on his account. This would have been a significant threat because such a report might have resulted in Barry's inability to obtain other credit. Accordingly, Barry might have paid Ajax simply to avoid future credit problems. Consumers faced other problems with credit bureaus. In some instances, a credit bureau might simply have made a mistake, such as listing Harry Jones instead of Larry Jones as delinquent, but then have no procedure for, or interest in, correcting mistakes. In other cases, outdated information concerning a consumer's conduct formed the basis for the denial of credit. These and other perceived credit abuses led the Congress to enact the **Fair Credit Reporting Act,** which sets guidelines on credit reports used for purposes of securing employment, insurance, and credit.

The act prohibits consumer reporting agencies from including inaccurate or obsolete (seven years for most information; ten years for bankruptcy) information in consumer reports. The act requires consumer reporting agencies to give written, advance notice to consumers that an investigative report may be made. Consumers have the right to request and receive from any consumer reporting agency (1) the nature and substance of all information on the consumer in the agency's files, (2) the sources of the information, and (3) the names of all recipients of the consumer reports furnished for employment purposes within the preceding two years and for other purposes within the preceding six months.

If the consumer notifies the reporting agency of disagreement with the accuracy and completeness of information in the file, the agency must then reinvestigate the matter within a reasonable period of time unless the complaint is frivolous or irrelevant. If reinvestigation proves that the information is inaccurate, it must be promptly deleted. If the dispute remains unresolved after reinvestigation, the consumer may submit a brief statement setting forth the nature of the dispute which must be incorporated into the report.

Creditors' Remedies

A primary concern of creditors is their rights if a debtor defaults or is tardy in payment. When the credit charge is precomputed, the creditor may impose a delinquency charge for late payments, subject to statutory limits for such charges. If instead of being delinquent, the consumer defaults, the creditor may declare the entire balance of the debt immediately due and payable and may sue on the debt. What other courses of action are open to the creditor depend upon his security. Various security provisions included in consumer credit contracts are: a cosigner, an assignment of wages, a security interest in the goods sold, a security interest in other real or personal property of the debtor, and a confession of judgment clause (that is, an agreement by debtor giving the creditor the authority to enter judgment against the debtor).

Wage Assignments and Garnishment Wage assignments are prohibited by some States. In most States and under the FCCPA, a limitation is imposed on the amount that may be deducted from an individual's wages during any pay period. In addition, the FCCPA prohibits an employer from discharging an employee solely because of a creditor's exercise of an assignment of wages in connection with any one debt.

Even where assignments of wages are prohibited, the creditor may still reach the wages of the consumer through garnishment. But garnishment is only available in a court proceeding to enforce the collection of a judgment. The FCCPA and State statutes contain exemption provisions which limit the amount of wages subject to garnishment.

Security Interests In the case of credit sales, the seller may retain a security interest in the goods sold. Many States impose restrictions on other security the creditor may obtain. Where the debt is secured by property as collateral, the creditor, upon default by the debtor, may take possession of the property and, subject to the provisions of the Uniform Commercial Code (U.C.C.), either retain it in full satisfaction of the debt or sell it and, if the proceeds are less than the outstanding debt, sue the debtor for the balance and obtain a deficiency judgment. The U.C.C. provides that where the buyer of goods has paid 60 percent of the purchase price of the goods or 60 percent of a loan secured by consumer goods, the secured creditor may not retain the property in full satisfaction but must sell the goods and pay to the buyer that part of the sale proceeds in excess of the balance due. In addition, Federal regulation prohibits a credit seller or lender from obtaining a consumer's grant of a nonpossessory security interest in household goods. This rule does not apply to purchase money security interests or to pledges. Household goods include clothing, furniture, appliances, kitchenware, personal effects, one radio, and one television. Works of art, other electronic entertainment equipment, antiques, and jewelry are specifically excluded. This rule prevents a lender or seller from obtaining a nonpurchase money security interest covering the consumer's household goods. Secured transactions are discussed in Chapter 38.

Debt Collection Practices   Abuses by some collection agencies led Congress in 1977 to pass the **Fair Debt Collection Practices Act,** which makes abusive, deceptive, and unfair practices by debt collectors in collecting consumer debts illegal. The act does not apply to creditors who use their own names in trying to collect debts themselves. Rather, the act applies only to those who collect debts for others. This does not mean that creditors are free to use improper methods to collect debts. Most States have laws or common law decisions that prohibit unfair debt collection practices.

Before the act, many debt collectors contacted third parties, such as relatives, neighbors, or employers, to inquire about the whereabouts or financial condition of the debtor. In doing so, the collectors made sure to inform the third parties who they were and why they were calling. In order to avoid the embarrassment resulting from such contacts, many debtors would hasten to pay the debts, even questionable ones. To prevent these often unfair and unnecessary disclosures, the act bars, except in certain narrow circumstances, debt collectors from communicating with third parties about a consumer's debt.

The act does permit debt collectors to contact a third party to ascertain the location of the consumer, but it prohibits them from disclosing that they are debt collectors and from stating that the consumer owes any debt.

The act forbids other abusive collection practices, including (1) communication with the consumer at unusual or inconvenient hours; (2) communication with the consumer if he is represented by an attorney; (3) harassing, oppressive, or abusive conduct, such as threats of violence or the use of obscene language; (4) false, deceptive, or misleading representations, such as false claims that the debt collector is an attorney or a government official, or that the consumer has committed a crime; or (5) other unfair or unconscionable means such as a false threat of a lawsuit to collect or attempt to collect a debt. *See Seabrook v. Onondaga Bur. of Medical Economics.*

The act gives consumers one extremely powerful right in dealing with debt collectors. If a consumer notifies a debt collector in writing that the consumer refuses to pay a debt or that the consumer wishes the debt collector to cease further communication with the consumer, the debt collector must stop further communication except to notify the consumer that the creditor or collector may invoke specified remedies such as filing a lawsuit to collect the debt. Consumers have the right to seek damages from debt collectors for violations of the act. In addition, the FTC has authority for administrative enforcement of its provisions.

CASES

FTC: Standards

IN RE CLIFFDALE ASSOCIATES, INC.
Federal Trade Commission, 1984.
46 Antitrust and Trade Regulation Rep. 703.

COMMISSION:
[The FTC brought this action claiming that Cliffdale Associates engaged in unfair

and deceptive trade practices by advertising its "new air bleed" engine attachment known as the Ball-Matic Gas Save Valve, as an "amazing automobile discovery" and as "the most significant breakthrough in the last ten years." The device was designed to allow more air to enter an automobile's engine and thus increase the automobile's efficiency and gas mileage. The Administrative Law Judge (ALJ) agreed with the FTC and ordered the respondent (Cliffdale) to cease and desist from engaging in these unfair and deceptive practices.]

II. Legal Standard for Deception

[The ALJ] concluded that "any advertising representation that has the tendency and capacity to mislead or deceive a prospective purchaser is an unfair and deceptive practice which violates the Federal Trade Commission Act." [Citations.] We find this approach to deception and violations of Section 5 to be circular and therefore inadequate to provide guidance on how a deception claim should be analyzed. Accordingly, we believe it appropriate for the Commission to articulate a clear and understandable standard for deception.

Consistent with its Policy Statement on Deception, issued on October 14, 1983, the Commission will find an act or practice deceptive if, first, there is a representation, omission, or practice that, second, is likely to mislead consumers acting reasonably under the circumstances, and third, the representation, omission, or practice is material. These elements articulate the factors actually used in most earlier Commission cases identifying whether or not an act or practice was deceptive, even though the language used in those cases was often couched in such terms as "a tendency and capacity to deceive."

The requirement that an act or practice be "likely to mislead," for example, reflects the long established principle that the Commission need not find *actual* deception to hold that a violation of Section 5 has occurred. This concept was explained as early as 1964, when the Commission stated:

In the application of [the deception] standard to the many different factual patterns that have arisen in cases before the Commission, certain principles have been well established. One is that under Section 5 actual deception of particular consumers need not be shown.

Similarly, the requirement that an act or practice be considered from the perspective of a "consumer acting reasonably in the circumstances" is not new. Virtually all representations, even those that are true, can be misunderstood by some consumers. The Commission has long recognized that the law should not be applied in such a way as to find that honest representations are deceptive simply because they are misunderstood by a few. Thus, the Commission has noted that an advertisement would not be considered deceptive merely because it could be "unreasonably misunderstood by an insignificant and unrepresentative segment of the class of persons to whom the representation is addressed." In recent cases, this concept has been increasingly emphasized by the Commission.

The third element is materiality. As noted in the Commission's policy statement, a material representation, omission, act or practice involves information that is important to consumers and, hence, likely to affect their choice of, or conduct regarding, a product. Consumers thus are likely to suffer injury from a material misrepresentation. A review of past Commission deception cases shows that one of the factors usually considered, either directly or indirectly, is whether or not a claim is material.

Although the ALJ in this case used the phrase "tendency and capacity to deceive" in his initial decision, we find after reviewing the record that his underlying analysis shows that the three elements necessary for a finding of deception are present in this case.

III. The Question of Liability

The obvious first step in analyzing whether a claim is deceptive is for the Commission to determine what claim has been made. When the advertisement contains an express claim, the representation itself establishes its meaning. When the claim is implied, the Commission will often be able to determine the meaning through an examination of the representation, including an evaluation of such factors as the entire document, the juxtaposition of various phrases in the document, the nature of the claim, and the nature of the transaction.

In other situations, the Commission will require extrinsic evidence that reasonable consumers interpret the implied claims in a certain way. The evidence can consist of expert opinion, consumer testimony, copy tests, surveys, or any other reliable evidence of consumer interpretation. In all instances, the Commission will carefully consider any extrinsic evidence that is introduced.

A. *Descriptive Claims*

a. *Were the Claims Made?*

1. Important New Invention

Most of respondents' advertisements refer to the Ball-Matic as an "amazing automobile discovery." The same advertisements also describe the products as "the most significant automotive breakthrough in the last ten years." Other ads term the Ball-Matic an "important automobile invention" and a "unique, patented" valve. The Ball-Matic is even compared to a "mini-computer brain."

The ALJ found these advertisements expressly claim that the Ball-Matic is an important, significant, and unique new invention. We agree.

* * *

2. Were the Claims Deceptive?

* * *

a. *Ball-Matic as an Important New Invention*

The evidence presented at trial amply documented that the Ball-Matic is a simple airbleed device similar to many other such devices that have been marketed over the years. Clearly the Ball-Matic is not new. In fact, the Commission has already issued cease and desist orders against various marketers of two such devices, the Albano Air Jet and the G.A. Valve, both of which are virtually identical in design to the Ball-Matic. Airbleed devices have been around a long time and, as the ALJ found, are considered to be of little value by the automobile industry.

The claim that the Ball-Matic was a new invention was expressly made. Having found such a claim to have been made, and that the claim is false, the Commission may infer, within the bounds of reason, that it is material. We therefore conclude that the ALJ was correct in holding that this claim was deceptive.

* * *

B. *Representation that Competent Scientific Tests Prove the Fuel Economy Claims Made for the Ball-Matic*

1. Was the Claim Made?

Most of respondents' advertisements refer to a "controlled, supervised test." The text of some ads details the procedure used in the test, *i.e.*, use of cars equipped with the Ball-Matic driven by non-professional drivers with mileage and fuel consumption monitored by "testers." We find that descriptions of these types of consumer "tests" in advertisements cannot, alone, reasonably be interpreted as representing that the device was tested scientifically.

However, other advertisements simply state that the Ball-Matic was "tested and proven (to yield) up to (a) 20 percent increase in fuel economy." Still other advertisements cite "field tests for over seven years and lab tests at an Accredited Eastern University." Additional tests results are suggested through respondents' invitation that consumers send for test reports if in doubt about the Ball-Matic's performance. These advertisements can be reasonably understood to imply that competent scientific tests support the performance claims made for the Ball-Matic.

2. Was the Claim Deceptive?

Respondents introduced a number of test results with varying evaluations of the Ball-Matic. These include a test conducted by the Vernon, California Emission Test Laboratory, an engine dynomometer test by a University of Bridgeport professor, and a series of tests by Scott Environmental Technology, Industries. However, the ALJ found the tests did not prove the fuel economy claims made for the Ball-Matic. We agree.

First, although the tests did indicate some improvement in fuel economy arguably attributable to the Ball-Matic, none revealed improvement even close to that claimed by respondents. While respondents claim up to 20 percent savings in fuel economy, the highest savings any of the "scientific" tests established was 11 percent. Thus, even assuming that respondents' tests were competent, the claim that they support the representation made for the Ball-Matic's performance is false.

Moreover, the evidence presented by complaint counsel casts serious doubt on the validity of the results obtained in respondent's tests.

* * *

C. *Representations Based on Consumer Endorsements*

1. Were the Claims Made?

* * *

The ALJ concluded, and we agree, that consumers could reasonably interpret these advertisements as claiming that the Ball-Matic would produce significant fuel economy improvement, that the testimonials were unrestrained and unbiased, that the endorsements were from recent or actual users of the Ball-Matic, and that the experiences were typical of all users.

2. Were the Claims Deceptive?

a. *Performance Claims in Testimonials*

By printing the testimonials, respondents implicitly made performance claims similar to those express claims found to be false and deceptive. Thus, irrespective of the veracity of the individual consumer testimonials, respondents' use of the testimonials to make underlying claims that were false and deceptive was, itself, deceptive. Accordingly, we agree with the ALJ that use of these endorsements constituted a law violation.

b. *Unrevealed Relationship of Endorsers to Seller*

The ALJ found that a good number of the testimonials used in the Ball-Matic advertisements were by business associates of the marketers of the product. Nevertheless, he concluded that the failure to disclose these relationships did not constitute either an unfair or a deceptive practice. Complaint counsel appeal from this holding, and we hold for complaint counsel on this issue.

In its "Guides Concerning the Use of Endorsements and Testimonials in Advertising," the Commission's policy is clear that whenever "there exists a connection between the endorser and the seller of the advertised product which might materially affect the weight or credibility of the endorsement" it

should be disclosed. In a case such as this, where it is difficult for a consumer to evaluate the effectiveness of the product on his or her own, the consumer is likely to rely more heavily on endorsements by other users, particularly if the consumer believes such endorsements are independent and unbiased. Failure to disclose the relationship, and therefore the bias, will materially affect the weight given to the endorsement. Thus, having determined that the implied claim of impartiality is false and that the failure to disclose the relationship is a material fact to consumers, we conclude that respondents are guilty of making a deceptive claim.

* * *

[Judgment for FTC.]

FTC: Corrective Advertising

WARNER–LAMBERT CO. v. FEDERAL TRADE COMMISSION

United States Court of Appeals, District of Columbia Circuit, 1977.
562 F.2d 749.

WRIGHT, J.

The Warner-Lambert Company petitions for review of an order of the Federal Trade Commission requiring it to cease and desist from advertising that its product, Listerine Antiseptic mouthwash, prevents, cures, or alleviates the common cold. The FTC order further requires Warner-Lambert to disclose in future Listerine advertisements that: "Contrary to prior advertising, Listerine will not help prevent colds or sore throats or lessen their severity." We affirm but modify the order to delete from the required disclosure the phrase "Contrary to prior advertising."

Background The order under review represents the culmination of a proceeding begun in 1972, when the FTC issued a complaint charging petitioner with violation of Section 5(a)(1) of the Federal Trade Commission Act by misrepresenting the efficacy of Listerine against the common cold.

Listerine has been on the market since 1879. Its formula has never changed. Ever since its introduction it has been represented as being beneficial in certain respects for colds, cold symptoms, and sore throats. Direct advertising to the consumer, including the cold claims as well as others, began in 1921.

* * *

The Commission's Power Petitioner [Warner-Lambert] contends that even if its advertising claims in the past were false, the portion of the Commission's order requiring "corrective advertising" exceeds the Commission's statutory power. The argument is based upon a literal reading of Section 5 of the Federal Trade Commission Act, which authorizes the Commission to issue "cease and desist" orders against violators and does not expressly mention any other remedies. The Commission's position, on the other hand, is that the affirmative disclosure that Listerine will not prevent colds or lessen their severity is absolutely necessary to give effect to the prospective cease and desist order; a hundred years of false cold claims have built up a large reservoir of erroneous consumer belief which would persist, unless corrected, long after petitioner ceased making the claims.

The need for the corrective advertising remedy and its appropriateness in this case are important issues which we will explore. But the threshold question is whether the Commission has the authority to issue such an order. We hold that it does.

Petitioner's narrow reading of Section 5 was at one time shared by the Supreme Court. In *FTC v. Eastman Kodak Co.* the Court held that the Commission's authority did not exceed that expressly conferred by statute. The Commission has not, the Court said, "been delegated the authority of a court of equity."

But the modern view is very different.

* * *

"[W]here the problem lies within the purview of the [Commission], . . . Congress must have intended to give it authority that was ample to deal with the evil at hand. . . . Au-

thority to mold administrative decrees is indeed like the authority of courts to frame injunctive decrees. . . ."

* * *

Thus it is clear that the Commission has the power to shape remedies which go beyond the simple cease and desist order. Our next inquiry must be whether a corrective advertising order is for any reason outside the range of permissible remedies. Petitioner . . . argue(s) that it is because (1) legislative history precludes it, (2) it impinges on the First Amendment, and (3) it has never been approved by any court.

Legislative History. Petitioner relies on the legislative history of the 1914 Federal Trade Commission Act and the Wheeler-Lea amendments to it in 1938 for the proposition that corrective advertising was not contemplated. In 1914 and in 1938 Congress chose not to authorize such remedies as criminal penalties, treble damages, or civil penalties, but that fact does not dispose of the question of corrective advertising.

Petitioner's reliance on the legislative history of the 1975 amendments to the Act is also misplaced. The amendments added a new Section 19 to the Act authorizing the Commission to bring suits in federal District Courts to redress injury to consumers resulting from a deceptive practice. The section authorizes the court to grant such relief as it "finds necessary to redress injury to consumers or other persons, partnerships, and corporations resulting from the rule violation or the unfair or deceptive act or practice," including, but not limited to, rescission or reformation of contracts, the refund of money or return of property, the payment of damages, and public notification respecting the rule violation or the unfair or deceptive act or practice. * * *

* * *

The First Amendment. Petitioner . . . further contends that corrective advertising is not a permissible remedy because it trenches on the First Amendment. Petitioner is correct that this triggers a special responsibility on the Commission to order corrective advertising only if the restriction inherent in its order is no greater than necessary to serve the interest involved. But this goes to the appropriateness of the order in this case.

* * *

The Supreme Court [has] expressly noted that the First Amendment presents "no obstacle" to government regulation of false or misleading advertising. The First Amendment, the Court said, as we construe it today, does not prohibit the State from insuring that the stream of commercial information flow[s] cleanly as well as freely.

* * *

Precedents. According to petitioner, "The first reference to corrective advertising in Commission decisions occurred in 1970, nearly fifty years and untold number of false advertising cases after passage of the Act." In petitioner's view, the late emergence of this "newly discovered" remedy is itself evidence that it is beyond the Commission's authority. This argument fails on two counts. First the fact that an agency has not asserted a power over a period of years is not proof that the agency lacks such power. Second, and more importantly, we are not convinced that the corrective advertising remedy is really such an innovation. The label may be newly coined, but the concept is well established. It is simply that under certain circumstances an advertiser may be required to make affirmative disclosure of unfavorable facts.

* * *

The Remedy Having established that the Commission does have the power to order corrective advertising in appropriate cases, it remains to consider whether use of the remedy against Listerine is warranted and equitable. We have concluded that the order should be modified to delete the phrase "Contrary to prior advertising." With that modification we approve the order.

Our role in reviewing the remedy is limited. The Supreme Court has set forth the standard:

The Commission is the expert body to determine what remedy is necessary to eliminate the unfair or deceptive trade practices which have been dis-

closed. It has wide latitude for judgment and the courts will not interfere except where the remedy selected has no reasonable relation to the unlawful practices found to exist.

The Commission has adopted the following standard for the imposition of corrective advertising:

[I]f a deceptive advertisement has played a substantial role in creating or reinforcing in the public's mind a false and material belief which lives on after the false advertising ceases, there is clear and continuing injury to competition and to the consuming public as consumers continue to make purchasing decisions based on the false belief. Since this injury cannot be averted by merely requiring respondent to cease disseminating the advertisement, we may appropriately order respondent to take affirmative action designed to terminate the otherwise continuing ill effects of the advertisement.

We think this standard is entirely reasonable.

* * *

Accordingly, the order, as modified, is Affirmed.

Federal Truth-in-Lending Act

CHAPMAN v. MILLER

Court of Civil Appeals of Texas, 1978.
575 S.W.2d 581.

KEITH, J.

Defendant below appeals from an adverse judgment rendered in a bench trial of a suit brought under ... the Federal Truth in Lending Act and Regulation Z promulgated thereunder.

Plaintiff entered into a retail installment contract with Don Chapman Motor Sales for the purchase of a used automobile. The contract provided for a down payment of $200, six weekly payments of $25, and eighteen monthly payments of $70.47. Plaintiff made the down payment and the six weekly payments without too much difficulty. The next five monthly installments were accepted even though they were late; but, when the March 1975 payment became overdue, defendant repossessed the car notifying plaintiff that the entire balance was then due and payable. When plaintiff did not pay the balance due, defendant sold the car and determined that plaintiff was entitled to a refund of $19.69. Before the refund was made, plaintiff brought this suit alleging several violations of the cited statute and regulation. The trial court agreed and awarded damages, plus attorney's fees, and the appeal is predicated upon nineteen points of error.

Violation of Federal Regulation. . . . defendant complains that the trial court erred . . . by holding that his contract violated Regulation Z because the description of the security interest is not on the same side of the paper as the buyer's signature.

The cited section requires that all disclosures which must be made thereunder be made together on:

(1) The note or other instrument evidencing the obligation on the same side of the page and above or adjacent to the place for the customer's signature; or (2) One side of a separate statement which identifies the transaction.

Defendant chose to make his disclosures on the retail credit contract. However, he failed to put all the required disclosures on one side of the contract above plaintiff's signature, *i.e.,* the description of his retained security interest is located on the reverse side of the contract. Relying upon the language found in [citation], we are of the opinion that the trial court correctly found a violation of Regulation Z.

Defendant claims that he did not have to make all required disclosures on the front side because of the Interpretive Ruling of the Federal Reserve Board, [citation], which allows the required disclosures to be made on both sides of a combination contract and security agreement. This interpretation, however, has a caveat:

Provided, That the amount of the finance charge and the annual percentage rate shall appear on the face of the document, and, if the reverse side is used, the printing on both sides of the document shall be equally clear and conspicuous, both sides shall contain the statement, "NOTICE: See other side for important information," *and the place for the customer's signature shall be provided following the full content of the document.*

The space provided for the plaintiff's signature is on the front page of the contract only and does not follow "the full content of the document." Therefore, defendant has violated [this] Section. [Citation.]

Defendant rationalizes that his notices at the top and bottom of the front side allow him to incorporate by reference all disclosures and conditions from the reverse side into the front side above the signature. The notice at the top of the page provides:

BUYER HAS ELECTED TO PURCHASE FROM SELLER SUBJECT TO THE TERMS AND CONDITIONS AS SET FORTH BELOW AND UPON THE REVERSE SIDE HEREOF, THE FOLLOWING DESCRIBED MOTOR VEHICLE, WHICH BUYER HAS THOROUGHLY INSPECTED AND WHICH MEETS WITH BUYER'S APPROVAL IN ALL RESPECTS:

The notice at the bottom of the page provides: "NOTICE: SEE REVERSE SIDE FOR IMPORTANT INFORMATION, ALL TERMS OF WHICH ARE HEREBY INCORPORATED BY REFERENCE." However, this notice was below plaintiff's signature.

The Truth in Lending Act was enacted and Regulation Z was issued "to assure a meaningful disclosure of credit terms so that the consumer will be able to compare more readily the various credit terms available to him and avoid the uninformed use of credit. . . ." [Citations.] Their provisions are detailed and explicit.

As noted in [citation]:

Moreover, liability flows from even minute deviations from the requirements of the statute and of Regulation Z. The statute aims to assure a meaningful disclosure of credit terms so that consumers may shop comparatively for credit. . . . [Citations.] Therefore, the defendant may not escape liability by means of incorporation by reference. The line provided for plaintiff's signature should have been at the end of the contract; her signature so located would show that she knew to read the entire contract—front and back—for all important provisions before signing it. The fact that she did not read any of the contract is immaterial. . . .

Finance Charge and Statutory Penalty . . . .
both parties contend that the trial court erred
. . . by holding that the finance charge in this
transaction was $326.99. Defendant claims
the finance charge was $199.99, while plain-
tiff claims it was $423.46. We disagree with
both parties.

[Regulation Z] gives instructions on how to
determine a finance charge. Applying these
rules to the contract before us, we hold that
the finance charge is the sum of the time
price differential and the official fees, or
$249.04. We are not required to include the
premiums for property insurance, credit life
insurance, or health and accident insurance
in the finance charge. *   *   *

The applicable statutory penalty . . . includes twice the amount of the finance
charge, plus court costs and reasonable attorney's fees. [Citations.] In the present case, the
proper statutory penalty would have been
twice of $249.04 or $498.08, plus court costs
and reasonable attorney's fees.

* * *

The judgment of the trial court is reformed
so that the plaintiff will recover of and from
the defendant the sum of $498.08 for the vi-
olation of Regulation Z instead of the excessive amount of $652.98 mistakenly awarded
by the trial court; and, as reformed, the judgment is Affirmed.

Creditors' Remedies

SEABROOK v. ONONDAGA BUR. OF MEDICAL ECONOMICS

U.S. District Court, Northern District New York, 1989.
705 F.Supp. 81.

McCurn, J.

On approximately May 20, 1987, plaintiff,
Michael Seabrook, received a letter from defendant, Onondaga Bureau of Medical Economics, Inc. ("OMBE"), a collection agency
for physicians. That letter dated May 18,
1987, stated:

You have ignored our demands for payment of this
account. If legal action is started by our client and
judgment is obtained against you, *10%* of your

gross weekly wages can be deducted in satisfac-
tion of the judgment. PLEASE DO NOT MAKE
THIS ACTION NECESSARY. PAY THIS CLAIM
DIRECTLY TO THIS OFFICE WITHIN FIVE (5)
DAYS.

The purpose of that letter was to collect a
debt of $198.00, which plaintiff owed Dr.
Scheider. That debt has been outstanding
from 1985 to the present time.

In an effort to collect that debt, OMBE
claims that it sent plaintiff two other letters
demanding payment of the debt before the
May 18, 1987, letter which is the subject of
this litigation. Plaintiff avers, however, that
the May 18, 1987, letter was his only communication from OMBE either prior to or since
May 20, 1987.

On May 17, 1988, plaintiff commenced the
present action seeking statutory damages for
OMBE's alleged violations of the Fair Debt
Collection Practices Act ("FDCPA"). Specifically plaintiff claims that the May 18*th* letter
did not give him the notice required by the
FDCPA and that it threatened legal action in
violation of the Act. OMBE is now moving for
summary judgment on several grounds.
First, OMBE claims that the letter fully complied with the FDCPA. *   *   * Third, OMBE
asserts that even if the court finds that it did
somehow violate the FDCPA, it should not be
held liable because such noncompliance was
unintentional and resulted from bona fide error. Plaintiff has cross-moved for summary
judgment basically claiming that the letter
violated the FDCPA.

*   *   * Plaintiff is claiming that OMBE
violated § 1692e(5); § 1692e(11) and § 1692g
of the FDCPA. Section 1692e(5) states that it
is a violation of the FDCPA to "threat[en] to
take any action that cannot legally be taken
or that is not intended to be taken." [Citation.]
The latter two sections pertain to the content
of communications from debt collectors and
essentially require that debtors be given certain notification in those communications.

* * *

§ 1692g itself, which provides:

(a) *Within five days after the initial communication* with a consumer in connection with the col-

lection of any debt, *a debt collector shall, unless* the following information is contained in the initial communication or the consumer has paid the debt, send the consumer a written notice containing

(1) the amount of the debt;

(2) the name of the creditor to whom the debt is owed;

(3) a statement that unless the consumer, within thirty days after receipt of the notice, disputes the validity of the debt, or any portion thereof, the debt will be assumed to be valid by the debt collector;

(4) a statement that if the consumer notifies the debt collector in writing within the thirty-day period that the debt, or any portion thereof, is disputed, the debt collector will obtain verification of the debt or a copy of a judgment against the consumer and a copy of such verification or judgment will be mailed to the consumer by the debt collector; and

(5) a statement that, upon the consumer's written request within the thirty-day period, the debt collector will provide the consumer with the name and address of the original creditor, if different from the current creditor.

* * *

II. Claimed Violation of § 1692e(5) Section 1692e(5) [of the FDCPA] states, in relevant part:

[T]he following conduct is a violation of this section: . . .

(5) The threat to take any action that cannot legally be taken *or* that is not intended to be taken.

[Citation.] It is OMBE's position that because garnishment is a lawful remedy . . . and because OMBE intended to recommend such action to its client, Dr. Scheider, it did not violate § 1692e(5) as a matter of law; thus summary judgment is proper on this issue. Plaintiff contends, on the other hand, that OMBE could not legally take the garnishment action referred to in the May 18*th* letter, and hence that letter amounts to a *per se* violation of the FDCPA. Therefore, plaintiff asserts that summary judgment should be granted in his favor on this issue.

* * *

In accordance with [N.Y. law], OMBE would only have been legally entitled to what it suggested in the letter *if* plaintiff was earn-

ing more than $100.50 in weekly disposable earnings and if the other limitations on garnishment . . . did not apply. At oral argument, defense counsel asserted that the May 18*th* letter did not violate § 1692e(5) because "in all likelihood" the plaintiff was earning over $85.00 per week. That statement seems highly improbable in light of plaintiff's averments that he has been disabled since October 17, 1986, and thus unable to work since that date. Furthermore, OMBE did not proffer any evidence to establish that it knew the amount of plaintiff's weekly disposable earnings, so that it would have been justified in threatening to garnish plaintiff's gross weekly wages in an amount up to 10%. Consequently, because the May 18, 1988, letter did not accurately reflect the state of New York garnishment law at the time it was sent, the court finds that that letter violated § 1692e(5) in that OMBE was not legally entitled to satisfy any judgment that might have been obtained against plaintiff by executing on his income in an amount up to 10% of his gross weekly wages.

* * *

In sum, OMBE's motion for summary judgment on this issue is denied. Plaintiff's cross-motion is granted, however, because the threat to take legal action which could not legally be taken violates § 1692e(5) and such violation is a *per se* violation of the FDCPA. [Citations.]

III. Claimed Violation of § 1692e(11) It is a violation of the FDCPA to:

[f]ail[] to disclose clearly in *all communications made to collect a debt or to obtain information about a consumer*, that the debt collector is attempting to collect a debt and that any information obtained will be used for that purpose.

[Citation.] Although not expressly articulated, OMBE has two arguments with respect to its claimed violation of this statute. First, OMBE contends that it did comply with the requirements of § 1692e(11) in that the letter "clearly indicates that the debt collector is attempting to collect a debt for Dr.

Scheider," and because the letter states the name of the physician to which plaintiff owes the debt and the amount of the debt. Second, OMBE is apparently contending that even if it did not comply with § 1692e(11) in the May 18*th* letter, it was exempt from doing so because there were prior communications which were in compliance, as is evidenced by the language therein, "you have ignored our demands for payment of this account." OMBE apparently believes the May 18*th* letter was simply a follow-up notice and as such it did not constitute a "communication" for purposes of § 1692e(11).

Turning first to OMBE's contention that it complied with § 1692e(11), there are two requirements of that section. The communication must clearly disclose (1) "that the debt collector is attempting to collect a debt," and (2) "that any information obtained will be used for that purpose." Understandably, OMBE did not address its compliance, or lack thereof, with the second disclosure requirement of § 1692e(11). Nowhere in the May 18*th* letter does it expressly state that "any information obtained will be used for that purpose;" nor is there any language therein even suggestive of that statutory requirement. Therefore, there can be no dispute that OMBE failed to comply with all of the disclosure requirements of § 1692e(11). Although the letter here did not request any information, the failure to include the disclosure language is nonetheless a violation of that section. [Citations.]

Having failed on its compliance argument, OMBE is left with its assertion that it did not have to fully comply with § 1692e(11) because there had been prior communications which were in compliance. In support of that contention, OMBE relies upon *Pressley v. Capital Credit & Collection Service, Inc.*, where the Ninth Circuit held that a "follow up notice" was not a communication within the meaning of § 1692e(11), and consequently the debt collector therein was not required to make the disclosure required by the statute. * * *

As plaintiff correctly points out, the court's holding in *Pressley* has *not* been followed by other courts. [Citations.] The courts in those cases refused to ignore the clear and unambiguous language of § 1692e(11) that "all communications" must contain the disclosure requirements of that statute.

* * *

Given the plain and unambiguous language of the statute, this court follows the majority of courts which have addressed this issue and concludes that debt collectors, such as OMBE, are required to clearly make the statutory disclosures in *every* communication to a debtor. Thus, OMBE's motion for summary judgment on this issue is denied, and plaintiff's cross-motion is granted because OMBE violated § 1692e(11) of the FDCPA by failing to make the required disclosures.

IV. Claimed Violation of § 1692g   The last provision of the FDCPA which plaintiff claims OMBE violated by sending the May 18*th* letter is § 1692g. It is undisputed that the May 18*th* letter did not contain the notice requirements of that statute. * * *

V. "Bona Fide Error" Defense   Perhaps anticipating some liability, OMBE also contends that even if it violated the FDCPA, "any such violation was not international and resulted from a bona fide error." That affirmative defense is codified at 15 U.S.C. § 1692k(c), which states:

A debt collector may not be held liable in any action brought under this subchapter if the debt collector shows by a preponderance of evidence that the violation was not intentional and resulted from a bona fide error notwithstanding the maintenance of procedures reasonably adapted to avoid any such error.

[Citation.] As plaintiff correctly contends, even if OMBE did not intentionally violate the FDCPA, it cannot rely upon § 1692k(c) because it has not come forth with any proof tending to show that the error occurred "notwithstanding the maintenance of procedures reasonably adapted to avoid any such error." [Citations.]

* * *

Accordingly, it is hereby
ORDERED, that:

(1) defendant's motion for summary judgment is denied;

(2) plaintiff's cross-motion for summary judgment is granted * * *

QUESTIONS

1. Discuss the role of the FTC and the major enforcement sanctions that it may use.

2. Discuss the principal provisions of the Magnuson-Moss Act and distinguish between a full and a limited warranty.

3. Discuss what information a creditor must provide a consumer before the consumer incurs the obligation. Distinguish between open-end and close-end credit.

4. Outline the major remedies that are available to a creditor.

5. Discuss the role and workings of the CPSC.

PROBLEMS

1. The Federal Trade Commission brings a deceptive trade practice action against Beneficial Finance Company based on Beneficial's use of its "instant tax refund" slogan. The FTC argues that Beneficial's advertising a tax refund loan or instant tax refund is deceptive in that the loan is not in any way connected with a tax refund but is merely Beneficial's everyday loan based on the applicant's creditworthiness. Decision?

2. Barnes borrows $1000 from Linda for one year. Barnes agreed to pay Linda $200 in interest on the loan and to repay the loan in twelve monthly installments of $100. The contract which Linda provides and Barnes signs specifies that the annual percentage rate is 20 percent. Barnes now contends that the contract violates the FCCPA. Decision?

3. A consumer entered into an agreement with Rent-It Corporation for the rental of a television set at a charge of seventeen dollars per week. The agreement also provided that if the renter chooses to rent the set for seventy-eight consecutive weeks, title would be transferred. The consumer now contends that the agreement was really a sales agreement and not a lease and, therefore, was a credit sale subject to the Truth-in-Lending Act. Decision?

4. Central Adjustment Bureau allegedly threatened Consumer with a lawsuit, service at his office, and attachment and sale of his property in order to collect a debt when it did not intend to do so and when it did not have the authority to commence litigation. On some notices sent to Consumer, Central failed to disclose that it was attempting to collect a debt. In addition, Central, it is charged, sent notices demanding payment that purported to be from attorneys but were written, signed, and sent by Central. Decision?

5. The Giant Development Company undertakes a massive real estate venture to sell 9,000 one-acre unimproved lots in Utah. The company advertises the project nationally. Arrington, a resident of New York, learns of the opportunity and requests information about the project. The company provides Arrington with a small advertising brochure that is devoid of information about the developer and the land. The brochure consists of vague descriptions of the joys of home ownership and nothing else. Arrington purchases a lot. Two weeks after entering into the agreement, Arrington wishes to rescind the contract. Will Arrington prevail?

6. Jane Jones, a married woman, applies for a credit card from Exxon but is refused credit. Jane is bewildered as to why she was turned down. What are her legal rights in this situation?

7. On a beautiful Saturday in October, Francie decides to take the twenty-mile ride from her home in New Jersey into New York City in order to do some shopping. Francie finds that Brown's Retail Sales, Inc., has a terrific sale on television sets and decides to surprise her husband with a new color T.V. She purchases the set from Brown's on her American Express credit card for $450. When the set is delivered, Francie discovers that it does not work. Brown's refuses to repair or replace it or to refund the money. Francie, therefore, refuses to pay American Express for the television. American Express brings this suit against Francie. Decision?

8. Frank finds Thomas's wallet, which contains numerous credit cards and Thomas's identification. By using Thomas's identification and Visa Card, Frank goes on a shopping spree and runs up $5,000 in charges. Thomas does not discover that he has lost his wallet until the following day when he promptly notifies his Visa bank. How much can Visa collect from Thomas?

9. Robert applies to Northern National Bank for a loan. Prior to granting the loan, Northern requests that Callis Credit Agency provide it with a credit report on Robert. Callis reports that three years previously Robert had embezzled money from his employer. Based on this report, Northern rejects Robert's loan application.

(a) Robert demands to know why, but Northern refuses to divulge the information arguing that it is privileged. Is Robert entitled to the information?

(b) Assume that Robert obtains the information and alleges that it is inaccurate. What recourse does Robert have?

10. Colgate-Palmolive Co. produced a television advertisement that dramatically demonstrated the effectiveness of its Rapid Shave shaving cream. The ad purported to show the shaving cream used to shave sandpaper. But because actual sandpaper appeared on television to be regular colored paper, Colgate substituted a sheet of Plexiglass with sand sprinkled on it. The FTC brought an action against Colgate claiming that Colgate's ad was deceptive. Colgate defended on the ground that the consumer was merely being shown a representation of the actual test. Decision?

11. In 1982, several manufacturers introduced into the American market a product known as All-Terrain Vehicles (ATVs). ATVs are motorized bikes that sit on three or four low-pressure balloon tires and are meant to be driven off paved roads. Almost immediately, the Consumer Product Safety Commission began receiving reports of deaths and serious injuries. As the number of injuries and deaths increased, the CPSC began investigating ATV hazards. According to CPSC staff, children under the age of sixteen accounted for roughly half the deaths and injuries associated with this product.

What type of rule, if any, may the CPSC issue for ATVs?

12. In the early 1970s, Sears formulated a plan to increase sales of its top of the line "Lady Kenmore" brand dishwasher. Sears's plan sought to change the Lady Kenmore's image, without the need for reengineering or any mechanical improvements in the dishwasher itself. To accomplish this, Sears undertook a four-year, $8 million advertising campaign that claimed that the Lady Kenmore completely eliminated the need for prerinsing and prescraping dishes. As a result of this campaign, sales rose by more than 300 percent. The "no scraping, no prerinsing" claim was not true, however, and Sears had no reasonable basis for asserting the claim. In addition, the owner's manual that customers received after they purchased the dishwasher contradicted the claim.

After a thorough investigation, the Federal Trade Commission, in 1977, filed a complaint against Sears, alleging that the advertisements were false and misleading. The final FTC order required Sears to stop making the no scraping, no prerinsing claim. The order also prevented Sears from (1) making any "performance claims" for "major home appliances" without first possessing a reasonable basis consisting of substantiating tests or other evidence; (2) misrepresenting any test, survey, or demonstration regarding "major home appliances;" and (3) making any advertising statements not consistent with statements in postpurchase materials supplied to purchasers of "major home appliances." Sears contends the order is too broad, since it covers appliances other than dishwashers, as well as including "performance claims." Decision?

COMPUTER RESEARCH PROBLEMS

1. William Thompson was denied credit based on an inaccurate credit report compiled by the San Antonio Retail Merchant's Association. The Association confused Thompson's credit history with that of another William Thompson and failed to use social security numbers to distinguish the two men. The second Mr. Thompson had a poor credit history. Thompson made numerous attempts to have the Association correct its mistake, but the error was never corrected. Thompson sued the Association for violation of the Fair Credit Reporting Act. Decision?

2. Thompson Medical Company manufactures and sells Aspercreme, a topical analgesic. Aspercreme is a pain reliever that contains no aspirin. Thompson's advertisements strongly suggest that Aspercreme is related to aspirin, however, by claiming that it "provided the strong relief of aspirin right where you hurt." The Federal Trade Commission brought a complaint against Thompson for false and misleading advertising of Aspercreme. Decision?

3. Mary Smith bought a car from Doug Chapman under an installment sales contract. Smith carried the insurance on the car, as required by the contract. Shortly after Smith purchased the car, it was wrecked in an accident. Smith's insurance company paid Chapman the installments still owed on the car as well as Smith's equity in the car. Smith requested a new car from Chapman under the same installment plan as the first car. Chapman refused, claiming that the contract for the first car allowed him to retain the equity amount as security interest and that Smith understood this as a term of the contract. The provision relating to the security interest appeared on the back of the contract although the Truth-in-Lending Act required it to be on the front side. The front side had a notice referring to provisions on the back side. Smith sued Chapman for violation of the Truth-in-Lending Act. Decision?

Chapter 44

EMPLOYMENT LAW

Labor Law
Employment Discrimination Law
Employee Protection

THE common law governs the relationship between employer and employee in terms of tort and contract duties. These rules are a part of the law of agency and are discussed in Chapter 18—Relationship of Principal and Agent. This common law has been supplemented—and in some instances replaced—by statutory enactments, principally at the Federal level. In fact, government regulation affects the balance and working relationship between employers and employees in three areas. First, the general framework in which management and labor negotiate and bargain over the terms of employment is regulated by Federal statutes designed to promote both labor-management harmony and the welfare of society at large. Second, Federal law has been enacted to prohibit discrimination in employment based upon race, sex, religion, age, handicap, or national origin. Finally, Congress, in response to the changing nature of American industry and the tremendous number of industrial accidents, has intervened by mandating that employers provide their employees with a safe and healthy work environment. Moreover, all of the States have adopted worker's compensation acts to provide compensation to employees injured during the course of employment.

This chapter will focus upon these three categories of government regulation of the employment relationship: (1) labor law, (2) employment discrimination law, and (3) employee protection.

LABOR LAW

Traditionally, labor law did not favor concerted activities by workers (such as strikes, picketing, and refusals to deal) to obtain higher wages and better working conditions. At various times these concerted activities were found to constitute criminal conspiracy, tortious conduct, and violation of antitrust law. Subjecting union workers to criminal sanctions, however, became publicly unpopular so employers resorted to civil remedies in an attempt to halt unionization. The primary tool in this campaign was the injunction. Eventually, public pressure in response to the adverse treatment accorded labor forced Congress to intervene.

Norris-LaGuardia Act

The Norris-LaGuardia Act was enacted in 1932 in response to the growing criticism of the use of injunctions in peaceful labor disputes. The act withdrew from the Federal courts the power to issue injunctions in nonviolent labor disputes. Section 1. The term **labor dispute** was broadly defined to include any controversy concerning terms or conditions of employment or union representation, regardless of whether the parties stood in an employer-employee relationship. Section 13(c). More significantly, the act declared it to be the policy of the United States that labor was to have full freedom to form labor unions without interference by the employer. Section 2. Accordingly, the act prohibited the so-called yellow dog contracts by which employers required their employees to promise that they would not join a union.

National Labor Relations Act

The National Labor Relations Act (NLRA), or **Wagner Act,** was enacted in 1935 and marked an affirmative effort by the Federal government to support collective bargaining and unionization. The act provides that "the right to self-organization, to form, join or assist labor organizations, to bargain collectively through representatives of their own choosing, and to engage in concerted activities for the purpose of collective bargaining or other mutual aid or protection" is a Federally protected right. Thus, the act gave employees the right to be represented by a union in their negotiations with their employer concerning terms of employment. Section 7. The act was upheld against constitutional challenge by the Supreme Court in *NLRB v. Jones & Laughlin Steel Corp.*:

[Employees right to bargain collectively] is a fundamental right. Employees have as clear a right to organize and select their representatives for lawful purposes as the respondent [employer] has to organize its business and select its own officers and agents. Discrimination and coercion to prevent the free exercise of the right of employees to

self-organization and representation is a proper subject for condemnation by competent legislative authority. Long ago we stated the reason for labor organizations. We said that they were organized out of the necessities of the situation; that a single employee was helpless in dealing with an employer; that he was dependent ordinarily on his daily wage for the maintenance of himself and family; that if the employer refused to pay him the wages that he thought fair, he was nevertheless unable to leave the employ and resist arbitrary and unfair treatment; that union was essential to give laborers opportunity to deal on an equality with their employer. . . . Fully recognizing the legality of collective action on the part of employees in order to safeguard their proper interests, we said that Congress was not required to ignore this right but could safeguard it. Congress could seek to make appropriate collective action of employees an instrument of peace rather than of strife. We said that such collective action would be a mockery if representation were made futile by interference with freedom of choice. Hence the prohibition by Congress of interference with the selection of representatives for the purpose of negotiation and conference between employers and employees, "instead of being an invasion of the constitutional right of either, was based on the recognition of the rights of both." *NLRB v. Jones & Laughlin Steel Corp.*, 301 U.S. 1 (1937).

Moreover, the act seeks to enforce the right of collective bargaining by prohibiting certain conduct by employers as unfair labor practices. Under the act, the following activities by *employers* are **unfair labor practices:** (1) to interfere with the employees' rights to unionize and bargain collectively; (2) to dominate the union; (3) to discriminate against union members; (4) to discriminate against an employee because he has filed charges or testified under the NLRA; and (5) to refuse to bargain in good faith with the duly established representatives of the employees. Section 8(a). *See National Labor Relations Board v. Berger Transfer & Storage.* The United States Supreme Court has interpreted this section to include as an unfair labor practice conduct by the employer that improves employment conditions or benefits that are being criticized by the union as part of its organizing drive:

The danger inherent in well-timed increases in benefits is the suggestion of a fist inside the velvet glove. Employees are not likely to miss the inference that the source of benefits now conferred is also the source from which future benefits must flow and which may dry up if it is not obliged. *NLRB v. Exchange Parts Co.,* 375 U.S. 405 (1964).

Moreover, the act established the **National Labor Relations Board** (NLRB) to monitor and administer these employee rights. The NLRB is empowered to order employers to remedy their unfair labor practices and to supervise elections by secret ballot so that employees can freely select a representative organization.

Labor-Management Relations Act

Following the passage of the National Labor Relations Act, the country underwent a tremendous increase in union membership and labor unrest. In response to this trend, Congress passed the Labor-Management Relations Act (**LMRA or Taft-Hartley Act**) in 1947. The act prohibits certain unfair union practices and separates the NLRB's prosecutorial and adjudicative functions. More specifically, the act amended the NLRA by declaring the following seven *union* activities to be **unfair labor practices:** (1) coercing an employee to join a union, (2) causing an employer to discharge or discriminate against a non-union employee, (3) refusing to bargain in good faith, (4) levying excessive or discriminatory dues or fees, (5) causing an employer

to pay for work not performed (featherbedding), (6) picketing an employer to require it to recognize an uncertified union, and (7) engaging in secondary activities. NLRA Section 8(b). A **secondary activity** is a boycott, strike, or picketing of an employer with whom a union has no labor dispute in order to persuade the employer to cease doing business with the company that is the target of the labor dispute. For example, a labor union is engaged in a labor dispute with Adams Company. To coerce Adams Company into resolving the dispute favorably for the labor union, the union organizes a strike against Brookings Company, with which the union has no labor dispute. The union agrees to cease striking Brookings Company if Brookings Company agrees to cease doing business with Adams Company. The strike against Brookings Company is a secondary activity prohibited as an unfair labor practice. See Figure 44–1 for a summary of union and employer unfair labor practices.

In addition to prohibiting unfair union practices, the act also limits the scope of employer unfair labor practice in order to foster employer free speech. The act declares that no *employer* unfair labor practice could be based on any statement of opinion or argument that contained no threat of reprisal. NLRA Section 8(c).

The LMRA also prohibits the closed shop, although it permits the existence of union shops, unless union shops are prohibited by a State right-to-work law. A **closed shop** con-

---

Figure 44–1 Unfair Labor Practices

Unfair Employer Practices	**Unfair Union Practices**
• Interfering with right to unionize • Refusing to bargain in good faith • Discriminating against union members • Dominating the union • Discriminating against an employee	• Coercing an employee to join the union • Refusing to bargain in good faith • Causing employer to discriminate against a non-union employee • Featherbedding • Picketing an employer to require recognition of an uncertified union • Engaging in secondary activity • Levying excessive or discriminatory dues

tract requires the employer to hire only union members. A **union shop** contract permits the employer to hire non-union members but requires that the employee must become a member of the union within a specified period of time and must remain a member in good standing as a condition of employment. A **right-to-work** law is a State statute that prohibits union shop contracts. Most States permit the existence of union shops.

Finally, the act reinstates the availability of civil injunctions in labor disputes, if requested of the NLRB in order to prevent an unfair labor practice. The act also grants the President of the United States the power to obtain an injunction for an eighty-day cooling-off period if the strike is likely to endanger the national health or safety.

Labor-Management Reporting and Disclosure Act

The Labor-Management Reporting and Disclosure Act, also known as the **Landrum-Griffin Act,** is aimed at eliminating corruption in labor unions. Section 2(b) of the act provides the following statement in support of the passage of the act:

The Congress further finds, from recent investigations in the labor and management fields, that there have been a number of instances of breach of trust, corruption, disregard of the rights of individual employees, and other failures to observe high standards of responsibility and ethical conduct which require further and supplementary legislation that will afford necessary protection of the rights and interests of employees and the public generally as they relate to the activities of labor organizations, employers, labor relations consultants, and their officers and representatives.

The act was passed in 1959 and attempts to deal with the problem of corruption by establishing an elaborate reporting system and the enactment of a union "bill of rights" designed to make unions more democratic. Section 101. The latter provides union members with the right to nominate candidates for union offices, to vote in elections, to attend membership meetings, to participate in union business, to have free expression at union meetings and conventions, and to be accorded a full and fair hearing before any disciplinary action is taken by the union against them.

EMPLOYMENT DISCRIMINATION LAW

A number of Federal statutes prohibit discrimination in employment on the basis of race, sex, religion, national origin, age, and handicap. The cornerstone of Federal employment discrimination law is Title VII of the 1964 Civil Rights Act, but other statutes and regulations are also significant. In addition, most States have enacted similar laws prohibiting discrimination based on race, sex, religion, national origin, and handicap.

Equal Pay Act

The **Equal Pay Act** prohibits an employer from discriminating between employees on the basis of *sex* by paying unequal wages for the same work. The act forbids an employer from paying wages at a rate less than the rate at which he pays wages to employees of the opposite sex for equal work at the same establishment. Most courts define *equal work* to mean "substantially equal" rather than identical. The burden of proof is on the claimant to make a *prima facie* showing that the employer pays unequal wages for work requiring equal skill, effort, and responsibility under similar working conditions. Once the employee has demonstrated that the employer pays unequal wages for *equal* work to members of the opposite sex, the burden shifts to the employer to prove that the pay differential is based on

1. a seniority system,

2. a merit system,

3. a system that measures earnings by quantity or quality of production, or

4. any factor except sex.

Remedies include recovery of back pay and enjoining the employer from further unlawful conduct. The Department of Labor is the

Federal agency designated by the statute to interpret and enforce the act. In 1979, these functions were transferred to the Equal Employment Opportunity Commission.

Civil Rights Act of 1964

Title VII of the Civil Rights Act of 1964 prohibits employment **discrimination** on the basis of race, color, sex, religion, or national origin in hiring, firing, compensating, promoting, training, or otherwise. The act applies to employers engaged in an industry affecting commerce and having fifteen or more employees.

The enforcement agency for Title VII is the **Equal Employment Opportunity Commission** (EEOC). The EEOC is charged with the responsibility and empowered to (1) file legal actions in its own name or to intervene in actions filed by third parties; (2) to attempt to resolve alleged violations through informal means prior to bringing suit; (3) to investigate all charges of discrimination; and (4) to issue guidelines and regulations concerning enforcement policy.

The act provides three basic defenses: (1) a *bona fide* seniority or merit system; (2) a professionally developed ability test; and (3) a *bona fide* occupational qualification (BFOQ). The BFOQ defense does not apply to discrimination based on race.

Remedies for violation of the act include enjoining the employer from engaging in the unlawful behavior, appropriate affirmative action, and reinstatement of employees and award of back pay from a date not more than two years prior to the filing of the charge with the EEOC. Affirmative action was first employed by an executive order as discussed below. **Affirmative action** generally means the active recruitment of minority applicants, although courts have used the remedy of affirmative action to impose numerical hiring ratios (quotas) and hiring goals based on race and sex. In 1985, the EEOC defined affirmative action in employment as "actions appropriate to overcome the effects of past or present practices, policies, or other barriers to equal employment opportunity."

Discrimination Each of the following constitutes discriminatory conduct prohibited by the act:

1. **Disparate Treatment.** An individual shows that an employer used a proscribed criteria in making an employment decision. The Supreme Court held in *McDonnell Douglas Corp. v. Green,* 411 U.S. 792 (1973), that a *prima facie* case of discrimination would be shown if the plaintiff (a) is within a protected class, (b) applied for an open position, (c) was qualified for the position, (d) was denied the job, and (e) the employer continued to try to fill the position. Once the plaintiff establishes a *prima facie* case the burden shifts to the defendant to "articulate legitimate and non-discriminatory reasons for the plaintiff's rejection."

2. **Present Effects of Past Discrimination.** An employer engages in conduct that on its face is "neutral," that is, non-discriminatory, but nonetheless continues to perpetuate past discriminatory practices. For example, it has been held illegal for a union that had previously limited membership to whites to adopt a requirement that new members be related to or recommended by existing members. *Local 53 of International Association of Heat and Frost Insulators and Asbestos Workers v. Vogler,* 407 F.2d 1047 (5th Cir. 1969).

3. **Disparate Impact.** An employer adopts "neutral" rules that have an adverse impact on a protected class and that are not justified as being necessary to the business. *See Griggs v. Duke Power Co.* In *Wards Cove Packing Co. v. Atonio,* ____ U.S. ____, 109 S.Ct. 2115 (1989), the U.S. Supreme Court placed the burden of proof on the claimant to disprove the employer's defense that the adverse employment decision was based on a legitimate neutral consideration.

Reverse Discrimination A major controversy has arisen over the equality of the use of reverse discrimination in achieving affirmative action. In this context, **reverse discrimination** refers to affirmative action that directs an employer to take the race or sex of an individual into account when hiring or promoting for the purpose of remedying underrepresentation of that race or sex in traditionally segregated jobs. An example would be an employer who discriminates against white males in order to increase the proportion of females or members of a racial minority. This question was presented in the *United Steelworkers of America v. Weber,* 443 U.S. 193 (1979). In *Weber,* the employer and union were implementing a collectively bargained affirmative action plan that granted preference to blacks even though there had been no prior history of proven racial discrimination by that employer. There was, however, a conspicuous racial imbalance in the employer's skilled labor force. The Supreme Court upheld the affirmative action plan against a challenge under Title VII even though it favored black employees with less seniority than white employees. The Court held:

We need not today define in detail the line of demarcation between permissible and impermissible affirmative action plans [under Title VII]. It suffices to hold that the challenged Kaiser-USWA affirmative action plan falls on the permissible side of the line. The purposes of the plan mirror those of the statute. Both were designed to break down old patterns of racial segregation and hierarchy. Both were structured to "open employment opportunities for Negroes in occupations which have been traditionally closed to them." [Citation.]

At the same time, the plan does not unnecessarily trammel the interests of the white employees. The plan does not require the discharge of white workers and their replacement with new black hirees. [Citation.] Nor does the plan create an absolute bar to the advancement of white employees; half of those trained in the program will be white. Moreover, the plan is a temporary measure; it is not intended to maintain racial balance, but simply to eliminate a manifest racial imbalance.

Due to the absence of State action, challenges to affirmative action plans adopted by private employers—those that are not a governmental unit at the local, State, or Federal level—are tested under Title VII of the Civil Rights Act of 1964 and not under the Equal Protection Clause of the U.S. Constitution.

In *Johnson v. Transportation Agency,* 480 U.S. 616 (1987), also an action under Title VII, the United States Supreme Court upheld the employer's right to promote a female employee instead of a white male employee who had higher test scores on the qualifying examination:

In making our decision, we find that the employment decision was justified by the existence of a "manifest imbalance" that reflected underrepresentation of women in "traditionally segregated job categories." The Agency's [employer's] Plan did not authorize such blind hiring but expressly directed that numerous factors be taken into account in making employment decisions. Furthermore, the Plan did not trammel male employee's rights or create a bar to their advancement as it set aside no positions for women. Substantial evidence shows that the Agency has sought to take a moderate, gradual approach to eliminating the imbalance in its work force, one which establishes realistic guidance for employment decisions. Given this fact, as well as the Agency's express commitment to "attain" a balanced work force, there is ample assurance that the Agency does not seek to use its Plan to "maintain" a permanent racial and sexual balance. Thus, we do not find the Agency in violation of Title VII.

When a State or local government adopts an affirmative action plan that is challenged as illegal reverse discrimination, the plan is subject to strict scrutiny under the **Equal Protection Clause** of the Fourteenth Amendment. Under the strict scrutiny test, the subject classification must (1) be justified by a compelling governmental interest and (2) be the least intrusive means available. *See City of Richmond v. J. A. Croson Co.* For a fuller discussion of the Equal Protection Clause and the standards of review see Chapter 3. In a case decided after *Croson,* the United States Supreme Court held that the Federal government had "unique remedial powers" far exceeding those of States and local governments and that Federal programs enacted to address racial discrimination "are subject to a different [and less burdensome] standard than such classifications prescribed by state and local governments." Thus, the Court upheld Federal Communication Commission programs giving preference to minorities applying for licenses to operate television and radio stations. *Metro Broadcasting, Inc., v. FCC,* ____U.S. ____, 58 U.S.L.W. 5053 (1990).

Sexual Harassment In 1980, the EEOC issued a definition of sexual harassment:

Unwelcome sexual advances, requests for sexual favors, and other verbal or physical conduct of a sexual nature constitute sexual harassment when

(1) submission to such conduct is made either explicitly or implicitly a term or condition of an individual's employment,
(2) submission to or rejection of such conduct by an individual is used as the basis for employment decisions affecting such individual, or
(3) such conduct has the purpose or effect of reasonably interfering with an individual's work performance or creating an intimidating, hostile or offensive working environment.

The courts, including the United States Supreme Court, have held that sexual harassment may constitute illegal sexual discrimination in violation of Title VII. Moreover, an employer will be held liable for sexual harassment committed by one of its employees if it does not take immediate action when it knows or should have known of the harassment. When the employee engaging in sexual harassment is an agent of the employer or is in a supervisory position over the victim, the employer may be liable without knowledge or reason to know. *See Meritor Savings Bank v. Vinson.*

Comparable Worth Industrial statistics indicate that women earn approximately two-thirds of the salaries of men. Studies have suggested that between one-third and one-half of the disparity in earnings results from sexual discrimination. Other probable causes for the gap include (1) males and females have different education and job skills, (2) females are employed in lower-paying occupations, and (3) females are more likely to interrupt their careers to raise families.

Because the Equal Pay Act only requires equal pay for equal work, it does not apply to different jobs even if they are comparable. Thus, that statute provides no remedy for women whose traditional jobs have been systematically undervalued and underpaid. As a result, women sought redress under Title VII by arguing that failure to pay comparable worth is discrimination on the basis of sex. The concept of **comparable worth** provides that the relative values to an employer of different jobs should be measured through a rating system or job evaluation that is free of any potential sex bias. Theoretically, all employees will be fairly paid if objective weights are attached consistently across job categories, using such factors as skill, effort, working conditions, responsibility, and mental demands. For example, if under such a system the jobs of truck driver and nurse are evaluated at the same level, then both jobs should receive the same pay.

In 1981, the United States Supreme Court held that a claim of discriminatory undercompensation based on sex may be brought under Title VII, even where the plaintiffs were performing different jobs from their male counterparts. As the Court noted, however, the case involved a situation in which the defendant intentionally discriminated in wages; and the defendant, not the courts, had compared the jobs in terms of value. *County of Washington v. Gunther,* 452 U.S. 161 (1981). The Court also held that the four defenses available under the Equal Pay Act would apply to a Title VII claim. Since *Gunther,* the concept of comparable worth has met with limited success in the courts. Nonetheless, a number of States have legislatively adopted requirements that public and private employers pay equally for comparable work.

Age Discrimination in Employment Act of 1967

The Age Discrimination in Employment Act (ADEA) prohibits discriminating in hiring, firing, compensating, or otherwise on the basis of age. Originally, the act applied the substantive language of Title VII to benefit individuals between the ages of forty and sixty-five. In 1978, the upper age limit was raised from sixty-five to seventy, and finally, in 1986, the upper age limit was eliminated. The act applies to private employers having twenty or more employees and to all governmental units regardless of size. The act also prohibits the mandatory retirement of most employees under the age of seventy.

The major statutory defenses include (1) a *bona fide* occupational qualification; (2) a *bona fide* seniority system; and (3) any other reasonable action. Remedies include back pay, injunctive relief, affirmative action, and liquidated damages equal to the amount of the award for "willful" violations. Unlike discrimination cases brought under Title VII, an ADEA claimant is entitled to a jury trial.

Handicap Discrimination

The **Rehabilitation Act of 1973** attempts to provide assistance to the handicapped in obtaining rehabilitation training, access to public facilities, and employment. The act requires Federal contractors and Federal agencies to take affirmative action to hire qualified handicapped persons. It also prohibits discrimination on the basis of handicap in Federal programs and programs receiving Federal financial assistance.

A **handicapped person** is defined as an individual who (1) has a physical or mental impairment that substantially affects one or more of her major life activities; (2) has a history of major life activity impairment; *or* (3) is regarded as having such an impairment. Major life activities include such functions as caring for oneself, seeing, speaking, or walking. Alcohol and drug abuses are not considered handicapping conditions for the purposes of this statute.

The **Americans with Disabilities Act of 1990** forbids, among other things, all businesses with fifteen or more employees from taking into consideration a person's handicap in hiring decisions. In addition, businesses must make special accommodations available to handicapped workers and customers unless the cost is unduly burdensome.

In addition, the **Vietnam Veterans Readjustment Act of 1974** requires firms having

$10,000 or more in Federal contracts to take affirmative action for disabled veterans and Vietnam era veterans.

Executive Order

In 1965, President Johnson issued an Executive Order that prohibited discrimination by Federal contractors on the basis of race, color, sex, religion, or national origin in employment on *any work* performed by the contractor during the period of the Federal contract. Federal contractors are also required to take affirmative action in recruiting. The Secretary of Labor, **Office of Federal Contract Compliance Programs** (OFCCP) administers enforcement of the program.

The program applies to all contractors who enter into a contract to be performed in the United States with the Federal government and all of their subcontractors in excess of $10,000. Compliance with the affirmative action requirement differs for construction and nonconstruction contractors. All **nonconstruction** contractors with fifty or more employees or with contracts for more than $50,000 must have a written affirmative action plan in order to be in compliance. The plan must include a work force analysis, planned corrective action, if necessary, with specific goals and timetables, and procedures for auditing and reporting. The Director of the OFCCP periodically issues goals and timetables for each segment of the **construction** industry for each region of the country. As a condition precedent to bidding on the Federal contract, the contractor must agree to make a good faith effort to achieve current published goals.

EMPLOYEE PROTECTION

Employees are accorded a number of protections relating to their jobs. These include a limited right not to be unfairly dismissed, a right to a safe and healthy workplace, compensation for injuries sustained in the workplace, and some financial security upon retirement or loss of employment. This section discusses (1) employee termination at will,

(2) occupational safety and health, (3) workers' compensation, (4) Social Security and unemployment insurance, and (5) the Fair Labor Standard Act.

Employee Termination at Will

Under the common law a contract of employment for other than a definite term is terminable at will by either party. Accordingly, under the common law employers may "dismiss their employees at will for good cause, for no cause or even for cause morally wrong, without being thereby guilty of legal wrong." In recent years, however, a growing number of judicial exceptions to the rule have developed based on implied contract, tort, and public policy. A number of Federal and State statutes enacted in the last fifty years also limit the rule. Finally, the rule may be restricted by contractual agreement between employer and employee. In particular, most collective bargaining agreements negotiated through union representatives contain a provision prohibiting dismissal "without cause."

Statutory Limitations   In 1934, as previously discussed, Congress enacted the National Labor Relations Act, which provided employees with the right to unionize free of intimidation or coercion from their employers, including freedom from dismissal for engaging in union activities. Since the enactment of the NLRA, additional Federal legislation has been passed that limits the employer's right to discharge. These statutes fall into three categories: (1) those protecting certain employees from discriminatory discharge; (2) those protecting certain employees in their exercise of statutory rights; and (3) those protecting certain employees from discharge without cause.

An example is Title VII of the Civil Rights Act of 1964, discussed above. Although its primary focus is on hiring, promotion, and seniority practices, this statute has been used in challenging the employer's right to discharge employees for discriminatory reasons. Another example is the Consumer Credit Protection Act, discussed in Chapter 43,

which prohibits an employer from dismissing an employee whose wages have been garnished for indebtedness. Additional Federal statutes protect other categories of employees such as the handicapped, public employees serving jury duty, and the aged.

At the State level, statutes protect workers from discriminatory discharge for filing workers' compensation claims. Also, many State statutes parallel Federal legislation. Some States have adopted statutes similar to the NLRA and many States prohibit discrimination in employment on the basis of such factors as race, creed, nationality, sex, or age. In addition, some States have statutes prohibiting discharge or other punitive actions taken for the purpose of influencing voting or, in some States, political activity.

Judicial Limitations   Judicial limitations on the employment-at-will doctrine have been based on contract law, tort law, and public policy. Cases founded in contract theory have relied on various arguments, including (1) the dismissal was improper because the employee had detrimentally relied on the employer's promise of work for a reasonable period of time; (2) the employment was not at will because of implied-in-fact promises of employment for a specific duration, which meant that the employer could not terminate the employee without just cause; (3) the employment contract contained express or implied provisions that the employee would not be dismissed so long as he satisfactorily performed his work; (4) the employer had assured the employee that he would not be dismissed except for cause; or (5) that, upon entering into the employment contract, the employee gave consideration over and above the performance of services to support a promise of job security.

Cases applying implied contract theory frequently involve reliance by an employee on personnel manuals containing some assurance of job security, often in the form of a provision stating that employees shall be discharged only for "cause." The Supreme Court of Michigan extended this theory in *Toussaint v. Blue Cross & Blue Shield,* 408 Mich.

579, 292 N.W.2d 880 (1980). Toussaint was employed in a middle management position by the defendant and had inquired specifically about job security when he was hired. He testified that the defendant's representatives assured him orally that he would not be fired so long as he did his job. He was at that time given a manual of personnel policies that reinforced the oral assurance of job security. When Toussaint was fired, he brought a cause of action against the defendant, claiming that his discharge violated his employment contract which, pursuant to language in the company's personnel manual, permitted discharge only for cause. The employer argued that Toussaint was merely an employee at will, hired for an indefinite term, and could therefore be dismissed at will. The Supreme Court of Michigan rejected this argument. The court essentially eliminated the at-will doctrine in cases where an employer has given some assurance of job security by holding that

(1) a provision of an employment contract providing that an employee shall not be discharged except for cause is legally enforceable although the contract is not for a definite term—the term is "indefinite," and

(2) such a provision may become a part of the contract either by express agreement, oral or written, or as a result of an employee's legitimate expectations grounded in an employer's policy statements.

Some courts have circumvented the common law at-will doctrine under implied contract theories by finding that contracts of employment contain an implied promise to deal in good faith, including a duty on the part of the employer to terminate only in good faith. These cases provide a remedy for an employee whose discharge was motivated by bad faith, malice, or retaliation.

Courts have also created exceptions to the employment-at-will doctrine by imposing tort obligations on employers with respect to the employment relationship. In particular, the torts of intentional infliction of emotional distress and of interference with employment relations have been used.

The most frequent basis for wrongful discharge is that the discharge violates statutory or other established public policy. In general, these cases involve dismissal for (1) refusing to violate a statute, (2) exercising a statutory right, (3) performing a statutory obligation, (4) reporting an alleged violation of a statute of public interest. *See Novosel v. Nationwide Insurance Co.*

Occupational Safety and Health Act

In 1970, Congress enacted the Occupational Safety and Health Act to assure, as far as possible, every worker a safe and healthful working environment. The act established the **Occupational Safety and Health Administration** (OSHA) to develop standards, conduct inspections, monitor compliance, and institute enforcement actions against those who are not in compliance.

The act imposes upon each employer, who is engaged in a business affecting interstate commerce, a general duty to provide a work environment that is "free from recognized hazards that are causing or likely to cause death or serious physical harm to his employees." Section 119. In addition to this general duty, the employer is required to comply with specific safety rules promulgated by OSHA. The act also requires employees to comply with all OSHA rules and regulations. Finally, the act prohibits any employer from discharging or discriminating against an employee who exercises his rights under the act. Section 11(c)(1). *See Whirlpool Corp. v. Marshall.*

The enforcement of the act generally involves OSHA inspections and citations of employers, if appropriate, for: (1) breach of the general duty obligation; (2) breach of specific safety and health standards; or (3) failure to keep records, make reports, or post notices required by the act.

When a violation is discovered, a written citation, proposed penalty, and correction date are given to the employer. Citations may be contested, and in such cases, administrative law judges are assigned by the Occupational Safety and Health Review Commission to hold hearings. The commission, at its discretion, may grant review of an administrative law judge's decision; review is not a matter of right. If commission review is not undertaken, then the judge's decision becomes the final order of the commission thirty days after receipt and the order may be appealed by the aggrieved party to the appropriate United States Circuit Court of Appeals.

Penalties for violations are both civil and criminal. In cases involving civil penalties, serious violations require that a penalty be proposed, while in nonserious violation cases, penalties are discretionary and rarely proposed. The Secretary of Labor is further empowered by the act to obtain temporary restraining orders in situations where regular OSHA procedures cannot be effective to shut down business operations that create imminent dangers of death or serious injury.

One stated purpose of the act is to encourage State participation in regulating safety and health. The act therefore permits the States to regulate the safety and health of the work environment, provided that OSHA approves the plan. The act sets minimum acceptable standards for the States to impose, but it does not require that the State plan be identical to OSHA. More than one-half of the States have adopted some form of State regulation of health and safety in the workplace.

Workers' Compensation

At common law the basis of most actions by an injured employee against his employer was the failure of the employer to use reasonable care under the circumstances for the safety of the employee. In such an action, however, the employer had several well-established defenses available to him at common law. These defenses included the fellow servant rule, contributory negligence on the part of the employee, and the doctrine of assumption of risk by the employee. If the employer established any of these defenses, the employer was not liable to the injured employee.

The **fellow servant rule** relieved an employer from liability for injuries sustained by an employee caused by the negligence of a fellow employee. Under the common law de-

fense of **contributory negligence,** if an employer established that the negligence of an injured employee contributed to the injury he sustained in the course of his employment, in many jurisdictions the employee could not recover damages from the employer. At common law, an employer was not liable to an employee for harm or injury caused by the unsafe condition of the premises if the employee, with knowledge of the facts and understanding the risks involved, voluntarily entered into or continued in the employment. This is regarded as a **voluntary assumption of risk** by the employee.

In order to provide speedier and more certain relief to injured employees, all States have adopted statutes providing for workers' compensation. Depending upon the State, however, specified employers are exempted from workers' compensation statutes. These statutes create commissions or boards that determine whether an injured employee is entitled to receive compensation and, if so, how much. The basis of recovery under workers' compensation is strict liability; the employee does not have to prove that the employer was negligent. The common law defenses discussed above are *not* available to employers in proceedings under these statutes. Such defenses are *abolished*. The *only* requirement is that the employee be injured and that the injury arise out of and in the course of his employment. The amounts recoverable are fixed by statute for each type of injury and are on a scale less than a court or jury would probably award in an action at common law. The courts, therefore, do not have jurisdiction over such cases except to review decisions of the board or commission, and then only to determine whether such decisions are in accordance with the statute. If a third party causes the injury, however, the employee may bring a tort action against that third party.

Early workers' compensation laws did not provide coverage for occupational disease, and most courts held that occupational injury did not include disease. Today, virtually all States provide general compensation coverage for occupational diseases, although the coverage varies greatly from State to State.

Social Security and Unemployment Insurance

Social Security was enacted in 1935 in an attempt to provide limited retirement and death benefits to certain employees. Since then the Federal Social Security system has expanded to cover almost all employees and to increase greatly the benefits offered. The system now contains four major benefit programs: (1) Old-Age and Survivors Insurance (OASI) (providing retirement and survivor benefits), (2) Disability Insurance (DI), (3) Hospitalization Insurance (Medicare), and (4) Supplemental Security Income (SSI).

The system is financed by contributions (taxes) paid by employers, employees, and self-employed individuals. Employees and employers pay matching contributions. These contributions are calculated by multiplying the Social Security tax (a fixed percentage) times the employee's wages up to a specified maximum. Both the base tax rate and the maximum dollar amount are subject to change by Congress. It is the employer's responsibility to withhold the employee's contribution and to forward the full amount of the tax to the Internal Revenue Service. Contributions made by the employee are not tax deductible by the employee, while those made by the employer are tax deductible.

Self-employed persons are also required to report their own taxable income and pay the Social Security tax. Starting in 1990, the tax paid by a self-employed individual is the same as the combined employer/employee contribution.

Benefits vary greatly depending on the particular program and whether the beneficiary is "fully" insured, "currently" insured, or a dependent. To be **fully insured,** a person must be credited with forty quarters of coverage: a quarter of coverage is received for each $370 of earnings in a year up to a maximum of four quarters per year. An individual is **currently insured** if he has been credited with at least six quarters of coverage in the last three years. In addition, dependents (spouses and children) are also eligible for certain Social Security benefits. Finally, benefits received are tax-free unless the individual receiving benefits under OASI has income in excess of a specified amount, which in 1989 was $25,000 for single persons and $32,000 for married couples.

The Federal **unemployment insurance** system was initially created by Title IX of the Social Security Act of 1935. Subsequently, Title IX was supplemented by the Federal Unemployment Tax Act as well as numerous other Federal statutes. This complex system depends upon the cooperation of State and Federal programs. Federal law provides the general guidelines, standards, and requirements, while the States handle the administration of the program under their own employment laws. The system is funded by taxes imposed on employers with Federal taxes generally paying the administrative costs of the program and State contributions paying for the actual benefits.

Under the Federal Unemployment Tax Act, an employer must pay unemployment tax if (1) he employs one or more persons for some portion of a day in each of twenty weeks in the current or preceding calendar year, or (2) he pays $1,500 or more in wages in any calendar quarter. The employee does not pay any unemployment tax. The tax, like the Social Security tax, is calculated as a fixed percentage of an employee's salary up to a stated maximum. The purpose of the tax is to provide unemployment compensation to workers who have lost their jobs, usually through no fault of their own, and cannot find other employment. Payments generally are made weekly and are based on the particular State's formula.

Fair Labor Standards Act

The Fair Labor Standards Act (FLSA) regulates the employment of child labor outside of agriculture. The act prohibits the employment of anyone under fourteen years in nonfarm work except for newspaper deliverers and child actors. Fourteen- and fifteen-year-olds may be employed for a limited number of hours outside of school hours, under specific conditions, in certain *nonhazardous* occupations. Sixteen- and seventeen-year-olds may work in any *nonhazardous* job while persons eighteen years old or older may work in *any* job whether it is hazardous or not. The Secretary of Labor determines which occupations are considered hazardous.

In addition, the FLSA imposes wage and hour requirements upon covered employers.

The act provides for a minimum hourly wage and overtime pay of time-and-a-half for hours worked in excess of forty hours per week. Certain jobs are exempted from both the FLSA's minimum wage and overtime provisions including the following: professionals, managers, and outside sales persons.

CASES

Unfair Labor Practices

NATIONAL LABOR RELATIONS BOARD v. BERGER TRANSFER & STORAGE

United States Court of Appeals, Seventh Circuit, 1982. 678 F.2d 679.

BAKER, J.

[The defendant, Berger Transfer and Storage, operates a national moving and transfer business employing approximately 40 persons. In May and June of 1979, Local 705 of the International Brotherhood of the Teamsters Union spoke with a number of Berger Employees, obtaining 28 cards signed in support of the Union. The management of Berger, unwilling to work with the Union, attempted to prevent it from representing its employees. The company first assigned all work to those with high seniority, in effect temporarily laying off low seniority employees. The management then threatened permanently to lay off those with low seniority and threatened all employees with a total close down of the plant. The management interrogated several employees about their union involvement and attempted to extract information about other employees' activities. When the Union presented the company the signed cards and Recognition Agreement, Berger refused to acknowledge the Union's existence or right to bargain on behalf of the employees. The Union then called a strike with employees picketing the warehouse. During the picketing, the Company threatened to discharge the picketers if they did not

return to work. Later, one manager on two occasions recklessly drove a truck through the picket line, striking employees. Finally, the company contacted several of the employees and offered them the "grievance procedures and job security" the Union would provide. The employees refused the offer. On June 15, the strike ended with most of the picketers returning to work. Local 705 of the International Brotherhood of Teamsters filed a complaint with the National Labor Relations Board that the defendant is guilty of unfair labor practices by violating Sections 8(a)(1), (3) and (5) of the National Labor Relations Act.]

Sections 8(A) (1), (3) and (5) Violations

The Board adopted the ALJ's [Administrative Law Judge] findings and conclusions that the Company had violated sections 8(a) (1), (3) and (5) of the Act. These findings must be enforced if they are supported by substantial evidence based upon the record as a whole. [Citations.]

(A) Section 8(a)(1) Violations The Board found the Company had committed eighteen independent 8(a)(1) violations which can be divided into six basic categories: (1) interrogating employees about union activities; (2) threatening employees with discharge, layoff and plant closure; (3) creating the impression of surveillance; (4) making promises to redress employees' complaints; (5) assaulting employees; and (6) actual layoff and discharge of employees.

Section 8(a)(1) makes it an unfair labor practice for an employer to interfere with, restrain, or coerce employees in the exercise of their rights to organize and bargain collectively through representatives of their own choosing. [Citation.] The test of interference with the right of self-organization is not whether an attempt at coercion has succeeded or failed, but whether the employer engaged in conduct which reasonably tends to interfere with, restrain, or coerce employees in the free exercise of their section 7 rights. [Citation.]

(1) Interrogation of employees. Section 8(a)(1) does not prohibit all employer questioning of employees about union activities. However, when the questions asked "viewed and interpreted as the employee must have understood the questioning and its ramifications, could reasonably coerce or intimidate the employee with regard to union activities," a violation has been established. [Citation.] An analysis of the employer's conduct should consider: (1) the background of the employer-employee relationship; (2) the questioner's identity; (3) the nature of the information sought; (4) the place and method of the interrogation; and (5) the truthfulness of the reply. [Citations.]

* * *

Applying the[se] consideration[s] . . . it is apparent that the findings of the Board are supported by substantial evidence. *   *   *

(2) Threats to close the plant, discharge and layoff employees. An employer violates section 8(a)(1) when he threatens employees with reprisals or other unfavorable consequences as a result of their union activities. [Citation.] Here the evidence shows that the Company began a campaign of threatened reprisals immediately following the Union's organizational drive. In particular, the Company: (1) informed the employees that if the Union succeeded there would be less work,

smaller crews; (2) told the employees that no work would be booked for Mondays and Tuesdays; (3) emphasized that layoffs would be controlled by seniority; (4) threatened to discharge employees if they continued to participate in the strike; and (5) threatened to close the warehouse if employees continued to support the Union.

Threats to cut back available work in response to employees' exercise of their section 7 rights are classic section 8(a)(1) violations, [citation], as are threats to discharge those employees. [Citation.]

Whether or not threats of plant closure are threats or predictions of the economic consequences of union organization, which fall outside the ambit of section 8(a)(1), turn on the nature of the employer's statement. . . . Here the Company failed to articulate any objective facts to support its "prediction" that the unionization would have dire economic consequences. Instead the record supports the finding that the employees understood the message as a threat of reprisal.

(3) Impressions of surveillance. An employer violates section 8(a)(1) when it conveys to employees the impression that it is engaged in surveillance of their union activities. [Citation.] Here the Company: (1) made it known to employees that the Company was aware of employees signing authorization cards, (2) made notes on a list of employees during an interrogation, and (3) suggested that York and Roesecke [two employees] were the instigators. This course of conduct supports the Board's finding that the Company violated section 8(a)(1) by creating an impression of surveillance.

(4) Solicitation of grievances, implied promises or redress. An employer violates section 8(a)(1) of the Act by soliciting grievances when such solicitation is " 'accompanied by an express or implied promise of benefits specifically aimed at interfering with, restraining, and coercing employees in their organizational effort.' " [Citation.] Here the

Company repeatedly approached employees to determine how differences could be reconciled. On one occasion, Vice-President Goodwin told employee Overton that the Company would give him "basically the same thing" as the Union, and suggested a meeting with the "top guys." Such employer initiated conduct supports a finding that the Company violated section 8(a)(1) by soliciting grievances and impliedly promising redress.

(5) Assaults. The evidence shows that on two occasions, Manager Harris recklessly drove his truck through the picket line. The first incident occurred on May 23, when Harris drove a Company truck through the picket line striking picketers Most and Gocha. He later stated that he hit the picketers both "intentionally and unintentionally." A similar incident occurred on June 6. Although there was testimony that the picketers were inebriated and blocking the Company driveway on that occasion, the Board found that the assaults were connected to the employees' union activity. Considering the active anti-union stand taken by the Company as evidenced in the record, there is substantial support for the Board's finding.

(B) Section 8(a)(3) Violations—Layoffs, Demotions & Discharges Section 8(a)(3) of the Act makes it an unfair labor practice for an employer to discriminate against an employee "in regard to hire or tenure of employment or any term or condition of employment to encourage or discourage membership in any labor organization. . . ." [Citation.] For example, an employer violates section 8(a)(3) when it discharges an employee because of his union activities. [Citation.]

The critical issue in a section 8(a)(3) claim is whether the employer's actions are motivated by anti-union considerations. [Citation.] . . . If a causal relationship between the discharge and protected activity is established, the employer is responsible under the Act unless he sustains his burden of proof. Furthermore, an employer's explanation

need not be accepted if there is a reasonable basis for believing the explanation is a pretext for the retaliatory action. [Citation.]

The evidence shows that Company officials made numerous unlawful threats of discharge, layoff, plant shutdown, together with unlawful interrogations, solicitation of grievances, promises of redress and assaults. Such conduct is a significant factor in determining motive. [Citation.] * * *

(1) Discharges. One of the protected rights of employees under section 7 of the Act is the right to strike. The strike began on May 23 as a recognitional strike. However, after Maierhofer threatened strikers with discharge, the strike was converted to an unfair labor practices strike entitling strikers to unconditional reinstatement. [Citation.] That evening the Company sent the following telegram to striking employees:

We are asking you to report to work at our terminal 2N225 Grace St., Lombard, Illinois at 8 A.M. Thursday, May 24, 1979. If you do not report, we will take this to mean that you have voluntarily terminated your employment with Berger Transfer and Storage, Inc. If you terminate your employment, your hospitalization will be terminated at midnight May 31, 1979. If you contact us, we will advise the procedure to convert your personal policy.

Berger Transfer & Storage, Inc.
2N225 Grace Street
Lombard, Illinois

The Board concluded that the employees were discharged for their union activities and that the Company's follow-up telegram of May 28 did not cure the violation but instead was a factor to consider in any remedial order. Although the Company asserts that the employees "quit," the total atmosphere of hostility promoted by the Company supports the inference of a section 8(a)(3) violation and discredits the Company's argument about the second telegram.

(2) Layoffs. Where anti-union considerations result in the layoff of employees, the

employer has violated section 8(a)(3) of the Act. [Citation.] The testimony before the ALJ established that during the week of May 21, several employees were laid off when the Company failed to book jobs on Mondays and Tuesdays. Furthermore employee Redman testified that he overheard Manager Harris state that he had work for "thirty guys" but was not using them because of the organizational drive. The record therefore supports the finding that the motivation for the threats and actual layoffs was anti-union animus and not economic compulsion.

(3) Demotion of Gocha. The demotion of an employee for engaging in protected union activities is a violation of section 8(a)(3) of the Act. [Citation.] Although there was testimony that Gocha was demoted because of customer complaints, the Board found the claimed justification to be a pretext, citing Harris' explanation that Gocha was no longer warehouse foreman because of his union sympathy. There is substantial evidence in the record to support this finding, particularly since no evidence was introduced that Gocha was aware of the customer complaints or the Company's displeasure with his work.

Section 8(a)(5) Violation The evidence shows that on May 23 the Union had collected signed authorization cards from twenty-eight employees. The Board found that the appropriate unit consisted of forty-two employees, giving the Union majority status. It is well established that the National Labor Relations Act authorized two methods for the confirmation of a binding bargaining relationship between an employer and a labor union. Generally, Board certification of a union's election success is the prevalent and preferred practice, but it is not the only one; and employer may voluntarily recognize the union upon some demonstrable showing of majority status, i.e., union authorization cards.

Although an employer generally has the right to refuse to recognize a card based ma-

jority and to demand an election, an employer who engages in unfair labor practices "likely to destroy the union's majority and seriously impede the election" may not insist that before it bargains an election be held. [Citation.] Therefore, when a union requests recognition and bargaining from an employer which has been presented with cards showing a majority support for the union, and the employer subsequently engages in unfair labor practices which destroy the "laboratory conditions" needed for a fair election, the employer forfeits any right to an election and must bargain with the union or violate section 8(a)(5) of the Act. Whether or not the union maintains majority status in the face of the employer's unfair labor practices is irrelevant to such a violation finding. [Citation.]

The evidence is clear that the Union had valid authorization cards from twenty-eight of the forty-two employees within the bargaining unit and properly requested recognition by the Company. The Company's response was an onslaught of flagrant, unfair labor practices. Under these circumstances there is substantial evidence to support the finding of a section 8(a)(5) violation.

* * *

For the reasons advanced, the order of the National Labor Relations Board is enforced.

Civil Rights Act of 1964: Adverse Impact

GRIGGS v. DUKE POWER CO.

Supreme Court of the United States, 1971.
401 U.S. 424, 91 S.Ct. 849, 28 L.Ed.2d 158.

BURGER, C.J.

We granted the writ in this case to resolve the question whether an employer is prohibited by the Civil Rights Act of 1964, Title VII, from requiring a high school education or passing of a standardized general intelligence test as a condition of employment in or transfer to jobs when (a) neither standard is shown to be significantly related to successful job performance, (b) both requirements operate to disqualify Negroes at a substantially higher rate than white applicants, and (c) the jobs in question formerly had been filled only by white employees as part of a longstanding practice of giving preference to whites.

* * *

The District Court found that prior to July 2, 1965, the effective date of the Civil Rights Act of 1964, the Company openly discriminated on the basis of race in the hiring and assigning of employees at its Dan River plant. The plant was organized into five operating departments: (1) Labor, (2) Coal Handling, (3) Operations, (4) Maintenance, and (5) Laboratory and Test. Negroes were employed only in the Labor Department where the highest paying jobs paid less than the lowest paying jobs in the other four "operating" departments in which only whites were employed. Promotions were normally made within each department on the basis of job seniority. Transferees into a department usually began in the lowest position.

In 1955 the Company instituted a policy of requiring a high school education for initial assignment to any department except Labor, and for transfer from the Coal Handling to any "inside" department (Operations, Maintenance, or Laboratory). When the Company abandoned its policy of restricting Negroes to the Labor Department in 1965, completion of high school also was made a prerequisite to transfer from Labor to any other department. From the time the high school requirement was instituted to the time of trial, however, white employees hired before the time of the high school education requirement continued to perform satisfactorily and achieve promotions in the "operating" departments. Findings on this score are not challenged.

The Company added a further requirement for new employees on July 2, 1965, the date on which Title VII became effective. To qualify for placement in any but the Labor Department it became necessary to register satisfactory scores on two professionally prepared aptitude tests, as well as to have a high school education. Completion of high school alone continued to render employees eligible for transfer to the four desirable departments from which Negroes had been excluded if the incumbent had been employed prior to the time of the new requirement. In September 1965 the Company began to permit incumbent employees who lacked a high school education to qualify for transfer from Labor or Coal Handling to an "inside" job by passing two tests—the Wonderlic Personnel Test, which purports to measure general intelligence, and the Bennett Mechanical Comprehension Test. Neither was directed or intended to measure the ability to learn to perform a particular job or category of jobs. The requisite scores used for both initial hiring and transfer approximated the national median for high school graduates.

The objective of Congress in the enactment of Title VII is plain from the language of the statute. It was to achieve equality of employment opportunities and remove barriers that have operated in the past to favor an identifiable group of white employees over other employees. Under the Act, practices, procedures, or tests neutral on their face, and even neutral in terms of intent, cannot be maintained if they operate to "freeze" the status quo of prior discriminatory employment practices.

The Court of Appeals' opinion, and the partial dissent, agreed that, on the record in the present case, "whites register far better on the Company's alternative requirements" than Negroes. [Court's footnote: In North Carolina, 1960 census statistics show that, while 34% of white males had completed high school, only 12% of Negro males had done so. Similarly, with respect to standardized tests, the EEOC in one case found that use of a battery of tests, including the Wonderlic and Bennett tests used by the Company in the instant case, resulted in 58% of whites passing the tests, as compared with only 6% of the blacks.] This consequence would appear to be directly traceable to race. Basic intelligence must have the means of articulation to manifest itself fairly in a testing process. Because they are Negroes, petitioners have long received inferior education in segregated schools and this Court expressly recognized these differences in [citation]. There, because of the inferior education received by Negroes in North Carolina, this Court barred the institution of a literacy test for voter registration on the ground that the test would abridge the right to vote indirectly on account of race. Congress did not intend by Title VII, however, to guarantee a job to every person regardless of qualifications. In short, the Act does not command that any person be hired simply because he was formerly the subject of discrimination, or because he is a member of a minority group. Discriminatory preference for any group, minority or majority, is precisely and only what Congress has proscribed. What is required by Congress is the removal of artificial, arbitrary, and unnecessary barriers to employment when the barriers operate invidiously to discriminate on the basis of racial or other impermissible classification.

* * *

The Act proscribes not only overt discrimination but also practices that are fair in form, but discriminatory in operation. The touchstone is business necessity. If an employment practice which operates to exclude Negroes cannot be shown to be related to job performance, the practice is prohibited.

On the record before us, neither the high school completion requirement nor the general intelligence test is shown to bear a demonstrable relationship to successful performance of the jobs for which it was used. Both were adopted, as the Court of Appeals noted, without meaningful study of their relationship to job-performance ability. * * *

The evidence, however, shows that employees who have not completed high school or taken the tests have continued to perform satisfactorily and make progress in departments for which the high school and test criteria are now used.

* * *

The facts of this case demonstrate the inadequacy of broad and general testing devices as well as the infirmity of using diplomas or degrees as fixed measures of capability. History is filled with examples of men and women who rendered highly effective performance without the conventional badges of accomplishment in terms of certificates, diplomas, or degrees. Diplomas and tests are useful servants, but Congress has mandated the commonsense proposition that they are not to become masters of reality.

* * *

Nothing in the Act precludes the use of testing or measuring procedures; obviously they are useful. What Congress has forbidden is giving these devices and mechanisms controlling force unless they are demonstrably a reasonable measure of job performance. Congress has not commanded that the less qualified be preferred over the better qualified simply because of minority origins. Far from disparaging job qualifications as such, Congress has made such qualifications the controlling factor, so that race, religion, nationality, and sex become irrelevant. What Congress has commanded is that any tests used must measure the person for the job and not the person in the abstract.

* * *

Reverse Discrimination under Equal Protection Clause

CITY OF RICHMOND v. J. A. CROSON CO.

United States Supreme Court, 1989.
___ U.S. ___ , 109 S.Ct. 706.

O'CONNOR, J.

In this case, we confront once again the tension between the Fourteenth Amendment's guarantee of equal treatment to all citizens, and the use of race-based measures to ameliorate the effects of past discrimination on the opportunities enjoyed by members of minority groups in our society. In *Fullilove v. Klutznick,* [citation] (1980), we held that a congressional program requiring that 10% of certain federal construction grants be awarded to minority contractors did not violate the equal protection principles embodied in the Due Process Clause of the Fifth Amendment. Relying largely on our decision in *Fullilove,* some lower federal courts have applied a similar standard of review in assessing the constitutionality of state and local minority set-aside provisions under the Equal Protection Clause of the Fourteenth Amendment. [Citations.] We noted probable jurisdiction in this case to consider . . . a minority set-aside program adopted by the city of Richmond, Virginia.

* * *

On April 11, 1983, the Richmond City Council adopted the Minority Business Utilitization Plan (the Plan). The Plan required prime contractors to whom the city awarded construction contracts to subcontract at least 30% of the dollar amount of the contract to one or more Minority Business Enterprises (MBEs). [Citation.] The 30% set-aside did not apply to city contracts awarded to minority-owned prime contractors. [Citation.]

The Plan defined an MBE as "[a] business at least fifty-one (51) percent of which is owned and controlled . . . by minority group members." [Citation.] "Minority group members" were defined as "[c]itizens of the United States who are Blacks, Spanish-speaking, Orientals, Indians, Eskimos, or Aleuts." [Citation.] There was no geographic limit to the Plan; an otherwise qualified MBE from anywhere in the United States could avail itself of the 30% set-aside. The Plan declared that it was "remedial" in nature, and enacted "for the purpose of promoting wider participation by minority business enterprises in the construction of public projects." [Citation.] The Plan expired on June 30, 1988, and was in effect for approximately five years. [Citation.]

* * *

The Plan was adopted by the Richmond City Council after a public hearing. [Citation.] * * * Proponents of the set-aside provision relied on a study which indicated that, while the general population of Richmond was 50% black, only .67% of the city's prime construction contracts had been awarded to minority businesses in the 5-year period from 1978 to 1983. It was also established that a variety of contractors' associations, whose representatives appeared in opposition to the ordinance, had virtually no minority businesses within their membership. [Citation.] * * *

There was no direct evidence of race discrimination on the part of the city in letting contracts or any evidence that the city's prime contractors had discriminated against minority-owned subcontractors. [Citation.]

* * *

[A white contractor adversely affected by the ordinance brought] this action . . . , arguing the Richmond ordinance was unconstitutional on its face and as applied in this case.

The District Court upheld the Plan in all respects. * * * [A] divided panel of the Court of Appeals struck down the Richmond set-aside program as violating both prongs of strict scrutiny under the Equal Protection Clause of the Fourteenth Amendment. [Citation.] The majority found that the "core" of this Court's holding in *Wygant* was that, "[t]o show that a plan is justified by a compelling governmental interest, a municipality that wishes to employ a racial preference cannot rest on broad-brush assumptions of historical discrimination." [Citation.] As the court read this requirement, "[f]indings of *societal* discrimination will not suffice; the findings must concern 'prior discrimination *by the government unit involved.*'" [Citation.]

The parties . . . fight an initial battle over the scope of the city's power to adopt legislation designed to address the effects of past discrimination. Relying on our decision in *Wygant*, appellee argues that the city must limit any race-based remedial efforts to eradicating the effects of its own prior discrimination. This is essentially the position taken by the Court of Appeals below. Appellant argues that our decision in *Fullilove* is controlling, and that as a result the city of Richmond enjoys sweeping legislative power to define and attack the effects of prior discrimination in its local construction industry. We find that neither of these two rather stark alternatives can withstand analysis.

* * *

The principal opinion in *Fullilove*, written by Chief Justice Burger, did not employ "strict scrutiny" or any other traditional standard of equal protection review. The Chief Justice noted at the outset that although racial classifications call for close examination, the Court was at the same time, "bound to approach [its] task with appropriate deference to the Congress, a co-equal branch charged by the Constitution with the power to 'provide for the . . . general Welfare of the United States' and 'to enforce by appropriate legislation,' the equal protection guarantees of the Fourteenth Amendment." [Citation.] The principal opinion asked two questions: first, were the objectives of the legislation within the power of Congress? Second, was the limited use of racial and ethnic criteria a permissible means for Congress to carry out its objectives within the constraints of the Due Process Clause? [Citation.]

On the issue of congressional power, the Chief Justice found that Congress' commerce power was sufficiently broad to allow it to reach the practices of prime contractors on federally funded local construction projects. * * *

The Chief Justice next turned to the constraints on Congress' power to employ race-conscious remedial relief. His opinion stressed two factors in upholding the MBE set-aside. First was the unique remedial powers of Congress under § 5 of the Fourteenth Amendment:

* * *

Because of these unique powers, the Chief Justice concluded that "Congress not only may induce voluntary action to assure compliance with existing federal statutory or constitutional antidiscrimination provisions, but also, where Congress has authority to *declare certain conduct unlawful,* it may, as here, authorize and induce state action to avoid such conduct." [Citation.]

* * *

Appellant . . . rely heavily on *Fullilove* for the proposition that a city council, like Congress, need not make specific findings of discrimination to engage in race-conscious relief. Thus, appellant argues "[i]t would be a perversion of federalism to hold that the federal government has a compelling interest in remedying the effects of racial discrimination in its own public works program, but a city government does not."

What appellant ignores is that Congress, unlike any State or political subdivision, has a specific constitutional mandate to enforce the dictates of the Fourteenth Amendment. The power to "enforce" may at times also include the power to define situations which *Congress* determines threaten principles of equality and to adopt prophylactic rules to deal with those situations. * * *

That Congress may identify and redress the effects of society-wide discrimination does not mean that, *a fortiori,* the States and their political subdivisions are free to decide that such remedies are appropriate. Section 1 of the Fourteenth Amendment is an explicit *constraint* on state power, and the States must undertake any remedial efforts in accordance with that provision. To hold otherwise would be to cede control over the content of the Equal Protection Clause to the 50 state legislatures and their myriad political subdivisions. * * *

Thus, if the city could show that it had essentially become a "passive participant" in a system of racial exclusion practiced by elements of the local construction industry, we think it clear that the city could take affirmative steps to dismantle such a system. It is beyond dispute that any public entity, state or federal, has a compelling interest in assuring that public dollars, drawn from the tax contributions of all citizens, do not serve to finance the evil of private prejudice. * * * [Citation.]

* * *

The Richmond Plan denies certain citizens the opportunity to compete for a fixed percentage of public contracts based solely upon their race. To whatever racial group these citizens belong, their "personal rights" to be treated with equal dignity and respect are implicated by a rigid rule erecting race as the sole criterion in an aspect of public decisionmaking.

Absent searching judicial inquiry into the justification for such race-based measures, there is simply no way of determining what classifications are "benign" or "remedial" and what classifications are in fact motivated by illegitimate notions of racial inferiority or simple racial politics. Indeed, the purpose of strict scrutiny is to "smoke out" illegitimate uses of race by assuring that the legislative body is pursuing a goal important enough to warrant use of a highly suspect tool. The test also ensures that the means chosen "fit" this compelling goal so closely that there is little or no possibility that the motive for the classification was illegitimate racial prejudice or stereotype.

Classifications based on race carry a danger of stigmatic harm. Unless they are strictly reserved for remedial settings, they may in fact promote notions of racial inferiority and lead to a politics of racial hostility. [Citation.] We thus reaffirm the view expressed by the plurality in *Wygant* that the standard of review under the Equal Protection Clause is not dependent on the race of those burdened or benefited by a particular classification. [Citation.]

* * *

Even were we to accept a reading of the guarantee of equal protection under which the level of scrutiny varies according to the ability of different groups to defend their interests in the representative process, heightened scrutiny would still be appropriate in the circumstances of this case. One of the central arguments for applying a less exacting standard to "benign" racial classifications is that such measures essentially involve a choice made by dominant racial groups to disadvantage themselves. * * *

In this case, blacks comprise approximately 50% of the population of the city of Richmond. Five of the nine seats on the City Council are held by blacks. The concern that a political majority will more easily act to the disadvantage of a minority based on unwarranted assumptions or incomplete facts would seem to militate for, not against, the application of heightened judicial scrutiny in this case. [Citations.]

* * *

While there is no doubt that the sorry history of both private and public discrimination in this country has contributed to a lack of opportunities for black entrepreneurs, this observation, standing alone, cannot justify a rigid racial quota in the awarding of public contracts in Richmond, Virginia. * * *

These defects are readily apparent in this case. The 30% quota cannot in any realistic

sense be tied to any injury suffered by anyone.

* * *

Finally, the city and the District Court relied on Congress' finding in connection with the set-aside approved in *Fullilove* that there had been nationwide discrimination in the construction industry. The probative value of these findings for demonstrating the existence of discrimination in Richmond is extremely limited. By its inclusion of a waiver procedure in the national program addressed in *Fullilove,* Congress explicitly recognized that the scope of the problem would vary from market area to market area. [Citation.]

* * *

In sum, none of the evidence presented by the city points to any identified discrimination in the Richmond construction industry. We, therefore, hold that the city has failed to demonstrate a compelling interest in apportioning public contracting opportunities on the basis of race. To accept Richmond's claim that past societal discrimination alone can serve as the basis for rigid racial preferences would be to open the door to competing claims for "remedial relief" for every disadvantaged group. The dream of a Nation of equal citizens in a society where race is irrelevant to personal opportunity and achievement would be lost in a mosaic of shifting preferences based on inherently unmeasurable claims of past wrongs. "Courts would be asked to evaluate the extent of the prejudice and consequent harm suffered by various minority groups. Those whose societal injury is thought to exceed some arbitrary level of tolerability then would be entitled to preferential classifications. . . ." [Citation.] We think such a result would be contrary to both the letter and spirit of a constitutional provision whose central command is equality.

* * *

As noted by the court below, it is almost impossible to assess whether the Richmond Plan is narrowly tailored to remedy prior discrimination since it is not linked to identified discrimination in any way. We limit ourselves to two observations in this regard.

First, there does not appear to have been any consideration of the use of race-neutral means to increase minority business participation in city contracting. * * * [Citation.]

Second, the 30% quota cannot be said to be narrowly tailored to any goal, except perhaps outright racial balancing. It rests upon the "completely unrealistic" assumption that minorities will choose a particular trade in lockstep proportion to their representation in the local population. [Citation.]

* * *

Nothing we say today precludes a state or local entity from taking action to rectify the effects of identified discrimination within its jurisdiction. If the city of Richmond had evidence before it that nonminority contractors were systematically excluding minority businesses from subcontracting opportunities it could take action to end the discriminatory exclusion. Where there is a significant statistical disparity between the number of qualified minority contractors willing and able to perform a particular service and the number of such contractors actually engaged by the locality or the locality's prime contractors, an inference of discriminatory exclusion could arise. [Citations.] Under such circumstances, the city could act to dismantle the closed business system by taking appropriate measures against those who discriminate on the basis of race or other illegitimate criteria. [Citation.] In the extreme case, some form of narrowly tailored racial preference might be necessary to break down patterns of deliberate exclusion.

Nor is local government powerless to deal with individual instances of racially motivated refusals to employ minority contractors. Where such discrimination occurs, a city would be justified in penalizing the discriminator and providing appropriate relief to the victim of such discrimination. [Citation.] Moreover, evidence of a pattern of individual discriminatory acts can, if supported by appropriate statistical proof, lend support to a local government's determination that broader remedial relief is justified. [Citation.]

Even in the absence of evidence of discrimination, the city has at its disposal a whole array of race-neutral devices to increase the accessibility of city contracting opportunities to small entrepreneurs of all races.

* * *

Because the city of Richmond has failed to identify the need for remedial action in the awarding of its public construction contracts, its treatment of its citizens on a racial basis violates the dictates of the Equal Protection Clause. Accordingly, the judgment of the Court of Appeals for the Fourth Circuit is AFFIRMED.

Sexual Harassment

MERITOR SAVINGS BANK, FSB v. VINSON

Supreme Court of the United States, 1986.
477 U.S. 57, 106 S.Ct. 2399, 91 L.Ed.2d 49.

REHNQUIST, J.

This case presents important questions concerning claims of workplace "sexual harassment" brought under Title VII of the Civil Rights Act of 1964. [Citation].

* * *

In 1974, respondent Mechelle Vinson met Sidney Taylor, a vice-president of what is now petitioner Meritor Savings Bank (the bank) and manager of one of its branch offices. When respondent asked whether she might obtain employment at the bank, Taylor gave her an application, which she completed and returned the next day; later that same day Taylor called her to say that she had been hired. With Taylor as her supervisor, respondent started as a teller-trainee, and thereafter was promoted to teller, head teller, and assistant branch manager. She worked at the same branch for four years, and it is undisputed that her advancement there was based on merit alone. In September 1978, respondent notified Taylor that she was taking sick leave for an indefinite period. On November 1, 1978, the bank discharged her for excessive use of that leave.

Respondent brought this action against Taylor and the bank, claiming that during her four years at the bank she had "constantly been subjected to sexual harassment" by Taylor in violation of Title VII. She sought injunctive relief, compensatory and punitive damages against Taylor and the bank, and attorney's fees.

At the 11–day bench trial, the parties presented conflicting testimony about Taylor's behavior during respondent's employment. Respondent testified that during her probationary period as a teller-trainee, Taylor treated her in a fatherly way and made no sexual advances. Shortly thereafter, however, he invited her out to dinner and, during the course of the meal, suggested that they go to a motel to have sexual relations. At first she refused, but out of what she described as fear of losing her job she eventually agreed. According to respondent, Taylor thereafter made repeated demands upon her for sexual favors, usually at the branch, both during and after business hours; she estimated that over the next several years she had intercourse with him some 40 or 50 times. In addition, respondent testified that Taylor fondled her in front of other employees, followed her into the women's restroom when she went there alone, exposed himself to her, and even forcibly raped her on several occasions. These activities ceased after 1977, respondent stated, when she started going with a steady boyfriend.

Taylor denied respondent's allegations of sexual activity, testifying that he never fondled her, never made suggestive remarks to her, never engaged in sexual intercourse with her and never asked her to do so. He contended instead that respondent made her accusations in response to a business-related dispute. The bank also denied respondent's allegations and asserted that any sexual harassment by Taylor was unknown to the bank and engaged in without its consent or approval.

The District Court denied relief, . . . It found . . . that

"If (respondent) and Taylor did engage in an intimate or sexual relationship during the time of (respondent's) employment with (the bank), that relationship was a voluntary one having nothing to do with her continued employment at (the bank) or her advancement or promotions at that institution." [Citation.]

Respondent also testified that Taylor touched and fondled other women employees of the bank, and she attempted to call witnesses to support this charge. But while some supporting testimony apparently was admitted without objection, the District Court did not allow her "to present wholesale evidence of a pattern and practice relating to sexual advances to other female employees in her case in chief, but advised her that she might well be able to present such evidence in rebuttal to the defendants' cases." [Citation.] Respondent did not offer such evidence in rebuttal. Finally, respondent testified that because she was afraid of Taylor she never reported his harassment to any of his supervisors and never attempted to use the bank's complaint procedure.

* * *

Although it concluded that respondent had not proved a violation of Title VII, the District Court nevertheless went on to address the bank's liability. After noting the bank's express policy against discrimination, and finding that neither respondent nor any other employee had ever lodged a complaint about sexual harassment by Taylor, the court ultimately concluded that "the bank was without notice and cannot be held liable for the alleged actions of Taylor." [Citation.]

The Court of Appeals for the District of Columbia Circuit reversed. [Citation.] . . . the court stated that a violation of Title VII may be predicated on either of two types of sexual harassment: harassment that involves the conditioning of concrete employment benefits on sexual favors, and harassment that, while not affecting economic benefits, creates a hostile or offensive working environment. The court drew additional support for this position from the Equal Employment Opportunity Commission's Guidelines on Discrimination Because of Sex, [citation], which set out these two types of sexual harassment claims. Believing that "Vinson's grievance was clearly of the (hostile environment) type," [citation] and that the District Court had not considered whether a violation of this type had occurred, the court concluded that a remand was necessary.

The court further concluded that the District Court's finding that any sexual relationship between respondent and Taylor "was a voluntary one" did not obviate the need for a remand. "(U)ncertain as to precisely what the (district) court meant" by this finding, the Court of Appeals held that if the evidence otherwise showed that "Taylor made Vinson's toleration of sexual harassment a condition of her employment," her voluntariness "had no materiality whatsoever." * * * *

As to the bank's liability, the Court of Appeals held that an employer is absolutely liable for sexual harassment practiced by supervisory personnel, whether or not the employer knew or should have known about the misconduct. * * *

* * *

Title VII of the Civil Rights Act of 1964 makes it "an unlawful employment practice for an employer . . . to discriminate against any individual with respect to his compensation, terms, conditions, or privileges of employment, because of such individual's race, color, religion, sex, or national origin." [Citation.] * * *

Respondent argues, and the Court of Appeals held, that unwelcome sexual advances that create an offensive or hostile working environment violate Title VII. Without question, when a supervisor sexually harasses a subordinate because of the subordinate's sex, that supervisor "discriminate(s)" on the basis of sex. Petitioner apparently does not challenge this proposition.

* * *

First, the language of Title VII is not limited to "economic" or "tangible" discrimination. The phrase "terms, conditions, or privileges of employment" evinces a congressional intent "'to strike at the entire spectrum of disparate treatment of men and women'" in employment. * * *

Second, in 1980 the EEOC issued guidelines specifying that "sexual harassment," as there defined, is a form of sex discrimination prohibited by Title VII. As an "administrative interpretation of the Act by the enforcing agency," [citation], these guidelines, "'while not controlling upon the courts by reason of their authority, do constitute a body of experience and informed judgment to which courts and litigants may properly resort for guidance,'" [citation].

The EEOC guidelines fully support the view that harassment leading to noneconomic injury can violate Title VII.

In defining "sexual harassment," the guidelines first describe the kinds of workplace conduct that may be actionable under Title VII. These include "(u)nwelcome sexual advances, requests for sexual favors, and other verbal or physical conduct of a sexual nature." [Citation.] Relevant to the charges at issue in this case, the guidelines provide that such sexual misconduct constitutes prohibited "sexual harassment," whether or not it is directly linked to the grant or denial of an economic quid pro quo, where "such conduct has the purpose or effect of unreasonably interfering with an individual's work performance or creating an intimidating, hostile, or offensive working environment."

* * *

The question remains, however, whether the District Court's ultimate finding that respondent "was not the victim of sexual harassment," [citation], effectively disposed of respondent's claim. The Court of Appeals recognized, we think correctly, that this ultimate finding was likely based on one or both of two erroneous views of the law. First, the District Court apparently believed that a claim for sexual harassment will not lie absent an economic effect on the complainant's employment. . . . Since it appears that the District Court made its findings without ever considering the "hostile environment" theory of sexual harassment, the Court of Appeals' decision to remand was correct.

Second, the District Court's conclusion that no actionable harassment occurred might have rested on its earlier "finding" that "(i)f (respondent) and Taylor did engage in an intimate or sexual relationship . . . , that relationship was a voluntary one." But the fact that sex-related conduct was "voluntary," in the sense that the complainant was not forced to participate against her will, is not a defense to a sexual harassment suit brought under Title VII. The gravamen of any sexual harassment claim is that the alleged sexual advances were "unwelcome."

* * *

Although the District Court concluded that respondent had not proved a violation of Title VII, it nevertheless went on to consider the question of the bank's liability. Finding that "the bank was without notice" of Taylor's alleged conduct, and that notice to Taylor was not the equivalent of notice to the bank, the court concluded that the bank therefore could not be held liable for Taylor's alleged actions. The Court of Appeals took the opposite view, holding that an employer is strictly liable for a hostile environment created by a supervisor's sexual advances, even though the employer neither knew nor reasonably could have known of the alleged misconduct. The court held that a supervisor, whether or not he possesses the authority to hire, fire, or promote, is necessarily an "agent" of his employer for all Title VII purposes, since "even the appearance" of such authority may enable him to impose himself on his subordinates.

* * *

This debate over the appropriate standard for employer liability has a rather abstract quality about it given the state of the record in this case. We do not know at this stage whether Taylor made any sexual advances toward respondent at all, let alone whether those advances were unwelcome, whether they were sufficiently pervasive to constitute a condition of employment, or whether they were "so pervasive and so long continuing . . . that the employer must have become conscious of (them)," [citation].

We therefore decline the parties' invitation to issue a definitive rule on employer liability, but we do agree with the EEOC that Congress wanted courts to look to agency principles for guidance in this area. While such common-law principles may not be transferable in all their particulars to Title VII, Congress' decision to define "employer" to include any "agent" of an employer, [citation], surely evinces an intent to place some limits on the

acts of employees for which employers under Title VII are to be held responsible. For this reason, we hold that the Court of Appeals erred in concluding that employers are always automatically liable for sexual harassment by their supervisors. [Citation.] For the same reason, absence of notice to an employer does not necessarily insulate that employer from liability. [Citation.]

Finally, we reject petitioner's view that the mere existence of a grievance procedure and a policy against discrimination, coupled with respondent's failure to invoke that procedure, must insulate petitioner from liability.

* * *

In sum, we hold that a claim of "hostile environment" sex discrimination is actionable under Title VII, that the District Court's findings were insufficient to dispose of respondent's hostile environment claim, and that the District Court did not err in admitting testimony about respondent's sexually provocative speech and dress. As to employer liability, we conclude that the Court of Appeals was wrong to entirely disregard agency principles and impose absolute liability on employers for the acts of their supervisors, regardless of the circumstances of a particular case.

Accordingly, the judgment of the Court of Appeals reversing the judgment of the District Court is affirmed, and the case is remanded for further proceedings consistent with this opinion.

Termination at Will

NOVOSEL v. NATIONWIDE INSURANCE CO.

United States Court of Appeals, Third Circuit, 1983.
721 F.2d 894.

ADAMS, J.

This appeal presents us with the task of determining under what circumstances a federal court sitting in diversity under Pennsylvania law may intercede in a non-union employment relationship and limit the employer's ability to discharge employees. In his suit against Nationwide Insurance Company, John Novosel brought two separate claims, one sounding in tort, the other in contract. The tort claim turns on whether a cause of action is created by a discharge that contravenes either important public policies or rights conferred on employees as members of the citizenry at large. The contract claim raises the question whether an enforceable contractual right to long-term employment may be read into what has traditionally been termed an employment-at-will position. The district court, concluding that no cause of action was stated, granted the employer's motion to dismiss both claims. . . . [W]e vacate the district court's judgment and remand for further proceedings.

* * *

Novosel was an employee of Nationwide from December 1966 until November 18, 1981. He had steadily advanced through the company's ranks in a career unmarred by reprimands or disciplinary action. At the time his employment was terminated, he was a district claims manager and one of three candidates for the position of division claims manager.

In late October 1981, a memorandum was circulated through Nationwide's offices soliciting the participation of all employees in an effort to lobby the Pennsylvania House of Representatives. Specifically, employees were instructed to clip, copy, and obtain signatures on coupons bearing the insignia of the Pennsylvania Committee for No-Fault Reform. This Committee was actively supporting the passage of House Bill 1285, the "No-Fault Reform Act," then before the state legislature.

The allegations of the complaint charge that the sole reason for Novosel's discharge was his refusal to participate in the lobbying effort and his privately stated opposition to the company's political stand. Novosel contends that the discharge for refusing to lobby the state legislature on the employer's behalf constituted the tort of wrongful discharge on the grounds it was willful, arbitrary, malicious and in bad faith, and that it was contrary to public policy. Alternatively, the complaint avers a breach of an implied contract prom-

ising continued long-term employment so long as Novosel's job performance remained satisfactory. Novosel sought damages, reinstatement and declaratory relief. * * *

* * *

Considerable ferment surrounds the doctrine of employment-at-will. Once the common-law cornerstone of employment relations not covered by either civil service laws or the National Labor Relations Act, the at-will doctrine has been significantly eroded by both tort and contract theories similar to those propounded by appellant in this case. Already 29 states have granted some form of common-law exceptions to the at-will doctrine; in addition, the courts of five other states as well as the District of Columbia have indicated their willingness to do so.

* * *

The circumstances of the discharge presented by Novosel fall squarely within the range of activity embraced by the emerging tort case law. As one commentator has written:

The factual pattern alleged in these cases seldom varies. The employee objects to work that the employee believes is violative of state or federal law or otherwise improper; the employee protests to his employer that the work should not be performed; the employee expresses his intention not to assist the employer in the furtherance of such work and/or engages in "self-help" activity outside the work place to halt the work; and the employer discharges the employee for refusal to work or incompatibility with management. [Citation.]

* * *

[W]e find that Pennsylvania law permits a cause of action for wrongful discharge where the employment termination abridges a significant and recognized public policy. The district court did not consider the question whether an averment of discharge for refusing to support the employer's lobbying efforts is sufficiently violative of such public policy as to state a cause of action. Nationwide, however, now proposes that "the only prohibition on the termination of an employee is that the termination cannot violate a statutorily recognized public policy."

* * *

The key question in considering the tort claim is therefore whether a discharge for disagreement with the employer's legislative agenda or a refusal to lobby the state legislature on the employer's behalf sufficiently implicate a recognized facet of public policy. The definition of a "clearly mandated public policy" as one that "strikes at the heart of a citizen's social right, duties and responsibilities," [citation], appears to provide a workable standard for the tort action. While no Pennsylvania law directly addresses the public policy question at bar, the protection of an employee's freedom of political expression would appear to involve no less compelling a societal interest than the fulfillment of jury service or the filing of a workers' compensation claim.

An extensive case law has developed concerning the protection of constitutional rights, particularly First Amendment rights, of government employees.

* * *

Employment-at-will has long been a major tenet of American contract law. Numerous proposals for statutory protection from arbitrary discharge have come from commentators concerned by the absence of job security for over 60 percent of the American workforce. Legislative proposals extending a "just cause" discharge requirement to all employees regardless of coverage or lack of it under the National Labor Relations Act have been considered in Pennsylvania as well as Colorado, Connecticut, Michigan, New Jersey and Wisconsin.

Novosel concedes that there is no statutory basis at present in Pennsylvania for a just cause requirement for discharges and, in fact, "the case law favoring someone like plaintiff under a breach of contract theory has been sparse." Instead, we are urged to fashion a common-law just cause standard premised primarily on the critical treatment of at-will discharges by the commentaries. Whatever the merits of such a standard, it is not the role of a federal court sitting in diversity to create its own common law.

The absence of a uniform just cause requirement for discharge, however, does not conclude the contractual issue presented here. As with the wrongful discharge tort doctrine, the contractual claims of non-union employees have been the subject of rapidly evolving judicial developments. * * *

Thus, Novosel's allegation that Nationwide's custom, practice or policy created either a contractual just cause requirement or contractual procedures by which defendant failed to abide is a factual matter that should survive a motion to dismiss:

* * *

The judgment and order of the district court will be vacated and the case remanded for discovery and further proceedings consistent with this opinion.

Occupational Safety and Health Act

WHIRLPOOL CORP. v. MARSHALL

Supreme Court of the United States, 1980.
445 U.S. 1, 100 S.Ct. 883, 63 L.Ed.2d 154.

STEWART, J.

The Occupational Safety and Health Act of 1970 (Act) prohibits an employer from discharging or discriminating against any employee who exercises "any right afforded by" the Act. The Secretary of Labor (Secretary) has promulgated a regulation providing that, among the rights that the Act so protects, is the right of an employee to choose not to perform his assigned task because of a reasonable apprehension of death or serious injury coupled with a reasonable belief that no less drastic alternative is available. The question presented in the case before us is whether this regulation is consistent with the Act.

The petitioner company [Whirlpool Corporation] maintains a manufacturing plant in Marion, Ohio, for the production of household appliances. Overhead conveyors transport appliance components throughout the plant. To protect employees from objects that occasionally fall from these conveyors, the petitioner has installed a horizontal wire-mesh guard screen approximately 20 feet above the plant floor. This mesh screen is welded to angle-iron frames suspended from the building's structural steel skeleton.

Maintenance employees of the petitioner spend several hours each week removing objects from the screen, replacing paper spread on the screen to catch grease drippings from the material on the conveyors, and performing occasional maintenance work on the conveyors themselves. To perform these duties, maintenance employees usually are able to stand on the iron frames, but sometimes find it necessary to step onto the steel mesh screen itself.

In 1973, the company began to install heavier wire in the screen because its safety had been drawn into question. Several employees had fallen partly through the old screen, and on one occasion an employee had fallen completely through to the plant floor below but had survived. A number of maintenance employees had reacted to these incidents by bringing the unsafe screen conditions to the attention of their foremen. The petitioner company's contemporaneous safety instructions admonished employees to step only on the angle-iron frames.

On June 28, 1974, a maintenance employee fell to his death through the guard screen in an area where the newer, stronger mesh had not yet been installed. Following this incident, the petitioner effectuated some repairs and issued an order strictly forbidding maintenance employees from stepping on either the screens or the angle-iron supporting structure. An alternative but somewhat more cumbersome and less satisfactory method was developed for removing objects from the screen. This procedure required employees to stand on power-raised mobile platforms and use hooks to recover the material.

On July 7, 1974, two of the petitioner's maintenance employees, Virgil Deemer and Thomas Cornwell, met with the plant maintenance superintendent to voice their concern about the safety of the screen. The superintendent disagreed with their view, but permitted the two men to inspect the screen with their foreman and to point out dangerous areas needing repair. Unsatisfied with the petitioner's response to the results of this inspection, Deemer and Cornwell met on July 9 with the plant safety director. At that meeting, they requested the name, address, and telephone number of a representative of the local office of the Occupational Safety and Health Administration (OSHA). Although the safety director told the men that they "had better stop and think about what [they] were doing," he furnished the men with the information they requested. Later that same day, Deemer contacted an official of the regional OSHA office and discussed the guard screen.

The next day, Deemer and Cornwell reported for the night shift at 10:45 p.m. Their foreman, after himself walking on some of the angle-iron frames, directed the two men to perform their usual maintenance duties on a section of the old screen. Claiming that the screen was unsafe, they refused to carry out this directive. The foreman then sent them to the personnel office, where they were ordered to punch out without working or being paid for the remaining six hours of the shift. The two men subsequently received written reprimands, which were placed in their employment files.

A little over a month later, the Secretary filed suit in the United States District Court for the Northern District of Ohio, alleging that the petitioner's actions against Deemer and Cornwell constituted discrimination in violation of § 11(c)(1) of the Act.

* * *

The Act itself creates an express mechanism for protecting workers from employment conditions believed to pose an emergent threat of death or serious injury. Upon receipt of an employee inspection request stating reasonable grounds to believe that an imminent danger is present in a workplace, OSHA must conduct an inspection. [Citation.] In the event this inspection reveals workplace conditions or practices that "could reasonably be expected to cause death or serious physical harm immediately or before the imminence of such danger can be eliminated through the enforcement procedures otherwise provided by" the Act, [citation], the OSHA inspector must inform the affected employees and the employer of the danger and notify them that he is recommending to the Secretary that injunctive relief be sought. [Citation.] At this juncture, the Secretary can petition a federal court to restrain the conditions or practices giving rise to the imminent danger. By means of a temporary restraining order or preliminary injunction, the court may then require the employer to avoid, correct, or remove the danger or to prohibit employees from working in the area. [Citation.]

To ensure that this process functions effectively, the Act expressly accords to every employee several rights, the exercise of which may not subject him to discharge or discrimination. An employee is given the right to inform OSHA of an imminently dangerous workplace condition or practice and request that OSHA inspect that condition or practice. [Citation.] He is given a limited right to assist the OSHA inspector in inspecting the workplace, [citation], and the right to aid a court in determining whether or not a risk of imminent danger in fact exists. [Citation.] Finally, an affected employee is given the right to bring an action to compel the Secretary to seek injunctive relief if he believes the Secretary has wrongfully declined to do so. [Citation.]

In the light of this detailed statutory scheme, the Secretary is obviously correct when he acknowledges in his regulation that, "as a general matter, there is no right afforded by the Act which would entitle employees to walk off the job because of potential unsafe conditions at the workplace." By providing for prompt notice to the employer of an inspector's intention to seek an injunction against an imminently dangerous condition, the legislation obviously contemplates that the employer will normally respond by voluntarily and speedily eliminating the danger. And in the few instances where this does not occur, the legislative provisions authorizing prompt judicial action are designed to give employees full protection in most situations from the risk of injury or death resulting from an imminently dangerous condition at the worksite.

As this case illustrates, however, circumstances may sometimes exist in which the employee justifiably believes that the express statutory arrangement does not sufficiently protect him from death or serious injury. Such circumstances will probably not often occur, but such a situation may arise when (1) the employee is ordered by his employer to work under conditions that the employee reasonably believes pose an imminent risk of death or serious bodily injury, and (2) the employee has reason to believe that there is not sufficient time or opportunity either to seek effective redress from his employer or to apprise OSHA of the danger.

Nothing in the Act suggests that those few employees who have to face this dilemma must rely exclusively on the remedies expressly set forth in the Act at the risk of their own safety. But nothing in the Act explicitly provides otherwise. Against this background of legislative silence, the Secretary has exercised his rulemaking power [citation] and has determined that, when an employee in good faith finds himself in such a predicament, he may refuse to expose himself to the dangerous condition, without being subjected to "subsequent discrimination" by the employer.

* * *

The regulation clearly conforms to the fundamental objective of the Act—to prevent occupational deaths and serious injuries. The Act, in its preamble, declares that its purpose and policy is "to assure so far as possible every working man and woman in the Nation safe and healthful working conditions and to *preserve* our human resources. . . ." [Citation.]

To accomplish this basic purpose, the legislation's remedial orientation is prophylactic in nature. [Citation]. The Act does not wait for an employee to die or become injured. It authorizes the promulgation of health and safety standards and the issuance of citations in the hope that these will act to prevent deaths or injuries from ever occurring. It would seem anomalous to construe an Act so directed and constructed as prohibiting an employee, with no other reasonable alternative, the freedom to withdraw from a workplace environment that he reasonably believes is highly dangerous.

Moreover, the Secretary's regulation can be viewed as an appropriate aid to the full effectuation of the Act's "general duty" clause. That clause provides that "[e]ach employer . . . shall furnish to each of his employees employment and a place of employment which are free from recognized hazards that are causing or are likely to cause death or serious physical harm to his employees." [Citation.] As the legislative history of this provision reflects, it was intended itself to deter the occurrence of occupational deaths and serious injuries by placing on employers a mandatory obligation independent of the specific health and safety standards to be promulgated by the Secretary. Since OSHA inspectors cannot be present around the clock in every workplace, the Secretary's regulation ensures that employees will in all circumstances enjoy the rights afforded them by the "general duty" clause.

The regulation thus on its face appears to further the overriding purpose of the Act, and rationally to complement its remedial scheme.

QUESTIONS

1. List and briefly discuss the major labor law statutes.

2. Distinguish between the prohibited unfair labor practices that apply to employers and those that apply to unions.

3. Discuss the defenses available to an employer under (1) the Equal Pay Act and (b) the Civil Rights Act of 1964.

4. Discuss (a) the various types of conduct prohibited as employment discrimination, (b) reverse discrimination, (c) sexual harassment, and (d) comparable worth.

5. Discuss the traditional common law, the statutory, and the recent judicial approaches to the termination-at-will doctrine.

PROBLEMS

1. Gooddecade manufactures and sells automobile parts throughout the eastern part of the United States. Among its full-time employees are 220 fourteen- and fifteen-year-olds. These teenagers are employed throughout the company and are paid at an hourly wage rate of $3.00 per hour. Discuss the legality of this arrangement.

2. Janet, a twenty-year-old woman, applied for a position driving a truck for Federal Trucking, Inc. Janet, who is 5'4" tall and weighs 135 lbs., was denied the job because the company requires that all employees be at least 5'6" tall and weigh at least 150 lbs. Federal justified this requirement on the basis that its drivers frequently were forced to move heavy loads in order to make pick-ups and deliveries. Janet brings a cause of action. Decision?

3. N.I.S. promoted John, a 42-year-old employee, to a foreman's position while passing over James, a 58-year-old employee. N.I.S. told James he was too old for the job and preferred a younger man. James brings a cause of action. Decision?

4. Anthony was employed as a forklift operator for Blackburn Construction Company. While on the job, Anthony carelessly and in direct violation of Blackburn's procedure manual operated the forklift and caused himself severe injury. Blackburn now denies liability based on Anthony's (a) gross negligence, (b) disobedience of the procedural manual, and (c) written waiver of liability. Anthony now brings a cause of action. Decision?

5. Hazelwood School District is located in Sleepy Hollow Township. It is being sued by applicants who applied for teaching positions with the school but were rejected. The plaintiffs are all black and produce the following evidence:

(a) 1.8% of the Hazelwood School District's teachers are black, whereas 15.4% of the teachers in Sleepy Hollow Township are black, and

(b) the hiring decisions by Hazelwood School District are based solely on subjective criteria. Will the plaintiffs prevail? Explain.

6. T.W.E., a large manufacturer, prohibited its employees from distributing union leaflets to other employees while on the company's property. Richard, an employee of T.W.E., disregarded the prohibition and passed out the leaflets before his work shift began. T.W.E. discharged Richard for his actions. Has T.W.E. committed an unfair labor practice?

7. Erwick was dismissed from her job at the C & T Steel Company because she was "an unsatisfactory employee." At the time, Erwick was active in an effort to organize a union at C & T. Is the dismissal valid?

8. Johnson, president of the First National Bank of A, believes that it is only appropriate to employ female tellers. Hence, First National refuses to employ Ken Baker as a teller but does make him an offer to be a maintenance man at the same salary. Baker brings a cause of action against First National Bank. Decision?

9. Section 103 of the Federal Public Works Employment Act of 1977 establishes the MBE (Minority Business Enterprise) program and requires that, absent a waiver by the Secretary of Commerce, 10 percent of all Federal grants given by the Economic Development Administration must be used to purchase services or supplies from businesses owned and controlled by U.S. citizens belonging to one of six minority groups: Black, Spanish-speaking, Oriental, Indian, Eskimo, and Aleut. White owners of businesses contend the act constitutes illegal reverse discrimination. Discuss.

10. Worth H. Percivil, a mechanical engineer, was first employed by General Motors in 1947 and remained in their employment until he was discharged in 1973. At the time his employment was terminated, Percivil was head of GM's Mechanical Development Department. Percivil sued GM for wrongful discharge. He contends that he was discharged as a result of a conspiracy among his fellow executives to force him out of his employment because of his age, because he had legitimately complained about certain deceptive practices of GM, because he had refused to give the government false information although urged to do so by his superiors, and because he had, on the contrary, undertaken to correct certain alleged misrepresentations made to the government. General Motors claims that Percivil's employment was terminable at the will of GM for any reason and with or without cause, provided that the discharge was not prohibited by statute. Decision?

11. On May 26, the trial examiner issued his Intermediate Report finding that the Respondent (Sailers' Union) had not engaged in unfair union practice under Section 8(b) in their dispute with Samsoc. With respect to the unfair labor practices, the complaint alleged that the Respondent induced and encouraged employees of Moore to engage in a strike or concerted refusal in the course of their employment to perform services for Moore in connection with the conversion into a bulk gypsum carrier of the SS *Phopho,* a vessel owned by Samsoc, the object being to force Moore to cease doing business with Samsoc and thus force Samsoc to resolve its dispute with Respondent. The General Counsel and Moore Dry Dock Company appealed. Decision?

COMPUTER RESEARCH PROBLEMS

1. Burdine, a female, was hired by the Texas Department of Community Affairs as a clerk in the Public Service Careers Division (PSC). The PSC provides training and employment opportunities for unskilled workers. At the time she was hired, Burdine already had several years experience in employment training. She was soon promoted, and later when her supervisor resigned, she preformed additional duties usually assigned to the supervisor. Burdine applied for the position of supervisor, but that position remained unfilled for six months, and a male from another division was eventually brought in as supervisor. Burdine alleges discrimination violating Title VII of the 1964 Civil Rights Act. The defendant Texas Department of Community Affairs responds that nondiscriminatory evaluation criteria were used to choose the new supervisor. In order to comply with Title VII, must the Texas Department of Community Affairs hire Burdine as supervisor if she and the male candidate are equally qualified? Explain.

 2. Ms. Wise was fired from her job at the Mead Corporation after she was involved in a fight with another co-worker. In four other unrelated occasions fights occurred between male co-workers. Only one of the males was fired, but this was after his second fight in which he seriously injured another employee. There is no dispute that Ms. Wise was qualified and performed her duties adequately. Ms. Wise successfully establishes a *prima facie* case of discrimination; however, defendant Mead Corporation meets its burden to "articulate legitimate and nondiscriminatory reasons" for firing Ms. Wise. Can Ms. Wise prevail? Explain.

Chapter 45

SECURITIES REGULATION

Registration of Public Offerings
Exemptions from Registration
Liability under 1933 Act
Disclosure Requirements of Publicly Held Companies
Liability under 1934 Act

THE primary purpose of Federal securities regulation is to prevent fraudulent practices in the sale of securities and thereby foster public confidence in the securities market. Federal securities law consists principally of two statutes: the Securities Act of 1933, which focuses on the issuance of securities, and the Securities Exchange Act of 1934, which deals mainly with trading in issued securities. Both statutes are administered by the Securities and Exchange Commission (SEC), an independent, quasi-judicial agency. The SEC has the power to seek in a Federal district court civil injunctions against violations of the statutes, to recommend that the Justice Department bring criminal prosecutions, and to issue orders censuring, suspending, or expelling broker-dealers, investment advisors, and investment companies.

The 1933 Act has two basic objectives: (1) to provide investors with material information concerning securities offered for sale to the public and (2) to prohibit misrepresentation, deceit, and other fraudulent acts and practices in the sale of securities generally, whether or not they are required to be registered.

The 1934 Act extends protection to investors trading in securities that are already is-

sued and outstanding. The 1934 Act also imposes disclosure requirements on publicly held corporations and regulates tender offers and proxy solicitations.

In addition to the Federal laws regulating the sale of securities, the States have their own laws regulating such sales within the State, commonly called **Blue Sky Laws.** These statutes all have provisions prohibiting fraud in the sale of securities. In addition, most States require the registration of securities and also regulate brokers and dealers.

Any person who sells securities must comply with the Federal securities laws as well as with those of each State in which he intends to offer his securities. Because the State securities laws vary greatly, this chapter will discuss only the 1933 Act and the 1934 Act.

THE SECURITIES ACT OF 1933

The 1933 Act, also called the "Truth in Securities Act," requires that a registration statement be filed with the Securities and Exchange Commission and become effective before any securities may be offered for sale to the public, unless either the securities or the transaction in which they are offered is exempt from registration. The purpose of registration is to disclose financial and other information about the issuer and those in control of it, so that potential investors may appraise the merits of the securities. The act provides that potential investors must be furnished with a **prospectus** (a document offering the securities for sale) containing the important data set forth in the registration statement. The antifraud provisions of the act apply to *all* sales of securities involving interstate commerce or the mails, even if the securities are exempt from the registration and disclosure requirements of the act. Civil and criminal liability may be imposed for violations of the act.

DEFINITION OF A SECURITY

Section 2(1) of the 1933 Act defines the term **security** to mean:

any note, stock, treasury stock, bond, debenture, evidence of indebtedness, certificate of interest or participation in any profit-sharing agreement, collateral-trust certificate, preorganization certificate or subscription, transferable share, investment contract, voting-trust certificate, certificate of deposit for a security, fractional undivided interest in oil, gas, or other mineral rights, any put, call, straddle, option, or privilege on any security . . . or, in general, any interest or instrument commonly known as a "security," or any certificate of interest or participation in, temporary or interim certificate for, receipt for, guarantee of, or warrant or right to subscribe to or purchase, any of the foregoing.

This definition broadly incorporates the many types of instruments that fall within the concept of a security. Furthermore, the courts have generally interpreted the statutory definition to include nontraditional forms of investments. For the purpose of the securities laws, a security is an investment of money, property, or other valuable consideration made in expectation of receiving a financial return solely from the efforts of others. In *Landreth Timber Co. v. Landreth,* 471 U.S. 681 (1985), the Supreme Court adopted a two-

tier analysis of what constitutes a security. If a financial instrument is denominated a note, stock, bond, or other instrument specifically named in the statute, the financial instrument will presumptively be treated as a security. On the other hand, if a financial transaction does not have the traditional characteristics of an instrument specifically named in the statute, the Court has used a three-part test, derived from *Securities and Exchange Commission v. W. J. Howey Co.,* 328 U.S. 293 (1946), to determine whether that financial transaction constitutes an investment contract and thus a security. Under the *Howey* test, a financial instrument or transaction constitutes an investment contract if there is (1) an investment in a common venture, (2) premised on a reasonable expectation of profit, (3) to be derived from the entrepreneurial or managerial efforts of others. Under this test, investments in limited partnership interests, citrus groves, whiskey warehouse receipts, real estate condominiums, cattle, franchises, and pyramid schemes have been held to be securities in certain circumstances. *See Securities and Exchange Commission v. W. J. Howey Co.*

REGISTRATION OF SECURITIES

The 1933 Act prohibits the offer or sale through the use of the mails or any means of interstate commerce of any security unless a registration statement for that security is in effect or an exemption from registration is secured. Section 5. The purpose of registration is to provide adequate and accurate disclosure of financial and other information upon which investors may appraise the merits of the securities. Registration does not insure investors against loss—the SEC does *not* make any judgment on the financial merits of any security. Moreover, the SEC does *not* guarantee the accuracy of the information presented in the registration statement.

Disclosure Requirements

In general, registration calls for disclosure of such information as (1) a description of the registrant's properties and business, (2) a description of the significant provisions of the security to be offered for sale and its relationship to the registrant's other capital securities, (3) information about the management of the registrant, and (4) financial statements certified by independent public accountants. A company that is not registered under the 1934 Act and is issuing not more than $7.5 million of securities for cash may use a shorter registration form (Form S–18).

Before filing the registration statement, it is unlawful to sell, offer to sell, or offer to buy the securities. Nevertheless, the issuer may give notice that it proposes to make a public offer. The registration statement and prospectus become public immediately on filing with the SEC. The effective date of a registration statement is the twentieth day after filing, although the Commission, at its discretion, may advance the effective date. It is unlawful to sell the securities until the effective date, although after the filing of the registration statement, the securities may be *offered* (1) orally; (2) by certain summaries of the information in the registration statement as permitted by rules of the SEC; (3) by a "tombstone advertisement" that identifies the security, its price, and by whom orders will be executed; or (4) by a preliminary prospectus, called a "red herring," which may contain substantially the same information as a final prospectus but must have a legend in red ink stating that the registration statement has not become effective. After the effective date, the issuer may make sales provided the purchaser has received a final prospectus.

Integrated Disclosure

The disclosure system under the 1933 Act developed independently of that required by the 1934 Act, which is discussed later in this chapter. As a result, issuers subject to both statutes were compelled to provide duplicative or overlapping disclosure. In 1982, the SEC adopted an integrated disclosure system in an effort to reduce or eliminate unnecessary duplication of corporate reporting. Un-

der this system there are three levels of disclosure, depending on the issuer's reporting history and market following. All issuers may use the detailed form (S–1) described previously. Corporations that have continuously reported under the 1934 Act for at least three years are permitted to disclose less detailed information in the 1933 Act registration statement (S–2), and to incorporate some information by reference to reports filed under the 1934 Act. Those corporations that have filed under the 1934 Act continuously for at least three years and also have a "market following" are permitted to disclose even less detail in the 1933 Act registration (S–3) and to incorporate even more information by reference to 1934 Act reports. The SEC's rules establish a test for market following: a minimum market value of voting stock of $150 million (called the "float") or a float of $100 million and a minimum annual trading volume of three million shares.

Shelf Registrations

Shelf registrations permit certain qualified issuers to register securities that are to be offered and sold "off the shelf" on a delayed or continuous basis in the future. This is a departure from the requirement that an issuer must file a registration for *every* new distribution of nonexempt securities. **Rule 415** of the SEC, which governs shelf registrations, requires that the information in the original registration is kept accurate and current. Only companies eligible to use the S–3 short form of registration qualify for shelf registrations. Shelf registrations allow issuers to respond more quickly to market conditions such as changes in stock prices and interest rates.

EXEMPT SECURITIES

The 1933 Act exempts a number of specific securities from its registration requirements. These exemptions apply to the securities themselves so the securities may be resold without registration.

Short-Term Commercial Paper

The act exempts any note, draft, or bankers' acceptance (a draft accepted by a bank) issued for working capital that has a maturity of not more than nine months when issued. Section 3(a)(3). The exemption is not available if the proceeds are to be used for permanent purposes, such as the acquisition of a plant, or if the paper is of a type not ordinarily purchased by the general public.

Other Exempt Securities

The 1933 Act also exempts the following kinds of securities from registration:

1. securities issued or guaranteed by domestic governmental organizations, such as municipal bonds;

2. securities of domestic banks and savings and loan associations;

3. securities of not-for-profit, charitable organizations;

4. certain securities issued by Federally regulated common carriers; and

5. insurance policies and annuity contracts issued by State-regulated insurance companies.

In addition, the Bankruptcy Act exempts securities issued by a debtor if they are offered under a reorganization plan in exchange for a claim or interest in the debtor. Bankruptcy Act, Section 1145(a).

EXEMPT TRANSACTIONS FOR ISSUERS

In addition to the exemptions provided for specific types of securities, the 1933 Act also provides *issuers* with an exemption from the registration requirements for certain kinds of transactions. These exempt transactions include (1) private placements (Rule 506), (2) limited offers not exceeding $5 million (Rule 505), (3) limited offers not exceeding $1 million (Rule 504), and (4) limited offers solely to accredited investors (Section 4(6)). These exemptions from registration apply only to the

transaction in which the securities are issued and not to the securities themselves.

In addition, the 1933 Act identifies a number of exemptions as exempt securities but they are in effect transaction exemptions. These include intrastate issues, exchanges between an issuer and its security holders, and reorganization securities issued and exchanged with court or other governmental approval. These exemptions only apply to the original issuance, and resales may only be made by registration unless the resale qualifies as an exempt transaction.

Another transaction exemption is Regulation A, which permits an issuer to sell a limited amount of securities in an unregistered public offering if certain conditions are met. Unlike other transaction exemptions, there are no restrictions upon the resale of securities issued pursuant to Regulation A.

Limited Offers

The act exempts, or authorizes the SEC to exempt, transactions that do not require the protection of registration because they either involve a small amount of money or are made in a limited manner. Sections 3(b) and 4(2). **Regulation D** was promulgated in 1982 to simplify and clarify the transaction exemptions relating to small issues and small issuers. Regulation D contains three separate exemptions (Rules 504, 505, and 506) each involving limited offers. Section 4(6) is also aimed at small issues and is a companion section to the exemptions under Regulation D.

Securities sold pursuant to these exemptions are considered **restricted securities** and may be resold only by registration or in another transaction exempt from registration. An issuer who uses these exemptions must take reasonable care to assure against nonexempt, unregistered resales of restricted securities. Reasonable care includes, but is not limited to, the following: (a) making a reasonable inquiry to determine if the purchaser is acquiring the securities for herself or for other persons; (b) providing written disclosure prior to the sale to each purchaser that the securities have not been registered and, therefore, cannot be resold unless they are registered or an exemption from registration is available; and (c) placing a legend on the securities certificate stating that the securities have not been registered and that they are restricted securities.

Private Placements The most important transaction exemption for issuers is the so-called private placement provision of the act, which exempts "transactions by an issuer not involving any public offering." Section 4(2). **SEC Rule 506** establishes a nonexclusive safe harbor for limited offers and sales without regard to the dollar amount of the offering. Satisfying the rule assures the exemption, but there is no presumption that the exemption is not available for transactions that do not comply with the rule.

Securities sold under this exemption are restricted securities and may be resold only by registration or in a transaction exempt from registration. General advertising or general solicitation is not permitted. The issue may be purchased by an unlimited number of "accredited investors" and by no more than thirty-five other purchasers. The term **accredited investor** includes banks, insurance companies, investment companies, executive officers or directors of the issuer, savings and loan associations, registered broker-dealers, business entities with total assets in excess of $5 million, any person whose net worth exceeds $1 million, and any person who had an income over $200,000 in each of the last two years and who reasonably expects an income in excess of $200,000 in the current year. If the sale involves any nonaccredited investors, such purchasers must be given before the sale material information about the issuer, its business, and the securities being offered. If all the purchasers are accredited investors, such information is not required to be disclosed. The issuer must reasonably believe that each purchaser who is not an accredited investor has sufficient knowledge and experience in financial and business matters to be capable of evaluating the merits and risks of the investment or has the services of a

representative who has the requisite knowledge and experience to make such an evaluation. The issuer must take precautions against nonexempt, unregistered resales and must notify the SEC of sales made under the exemption.

Limited Offers Not Exceeding $5 Million SEC **Rule 505** exempts from registration offerings by noninvestment company issuers that do not exceed $5 million over twelve months. Securities sold under this exemption are restricted securities and may be resold only by registration or in a transaction exempt from registration. General advertising or general solicitation is not permitted. The issue may be purchased by an unlimited number of accredited investors and by no more than thirty-five other purchasers. If the sale involves any nonaccredited investors, such purchasers must be given before the sale material information about the issuer, its business, and the securities being offered; otherwise, such information is not required to be disclosed. Unlike Rule 506, however, the issuer is *not* required to believe reasonably that each nonaccredited investor, either alone or with his representative, has sufficient knowledge and experience in financial matters to be capable of evaluating the merits and risks of the investment. The issuer must take precautions against nonexempt, unregistered resales and must notify the SEC of sales made under the exemption.

Limited Offers Not Exceeding $1 Million The SEC's **Rule 504** provides private, noninvestment company issuers with an exemption from registration for small issues not exceeding $1 million. The rule permits sales to an unlimited number of investors and does not require any information to be furnished to them. The exemption requires that

1. the securities are offered and sold without general advertising;

2. the aggregate offering price within twelve months does not exceed $1 million;

3. the issuer takes precautions against non-exempt, unregistered resales; and

4. the issuer notifies the SEC of sales under the rule.

No more than $500,000 of securities, however, may be sold in States not requiring registration. The limitations on general advertising do not apply and unregistered resales are permitted if the offering is either (1) made exclusively in compliance with State registration provisions that require the delivery of a disclosure document before sale or (2) made in at least one State requiring such registration and the disclosure document is delivered to all purchasers before sale.

Limited Offers Solely to Accredited Investors In 1980, Congress added **Section 4(6),** which provides an exemption for offers and sales by an issuer made *solely* to accredited investors if not in excess of $5 million. General advertising or public solicitation is not permitted. As with Rules 505 and 506, an unlimited number of accredited investors may purchase the issue; however, unlike these rules, *no* unaccredited investors may purchase. No information is required to be furnished to the purchasers. Securities sold under this exemption are restricted securities and may be resold only by registration or in a transaction exempt from registration. The issuer must take precautions against nonexempt, unregistered resales and must notify the SEC of sales made under the exemption.

Regulation A

Regulation A permits an issuer to offer up to $1.5 million of securities in any twelve-month period without registering them provided that the issuer files a notification and an offering circular with the SEC's regional office prior to the sale of the securities. The circular must also be provided to offerees and purchasers. There are no restrictions regarding the number or qualifications of the investors. Regulation A filings are less detailed and time consuming than full registration

statements, and the required financial statements are simpler and do not need to be audited unless the issuer is a reporting company under the 1934 Act. Securities sold under Regulation A may be freely resold after they are issued even though they are not registered.

Intrastate Issues

The 1933 Act also exempts from registration any security that is a part of an issue offered and sold *only* to persons resident within a single State where the issuer of such security is resident and doing business within such State. Section 3(a)(11). This exemption is intended to apply to local issues representing local financing by local persons and carried out through local investments. The exemption does not apply if *any* offeree, who need not be a purchaser, is not a resident of the State in which the issuer is resident.

The courts and the SEC have interpreted the exemption narrowly. **Rule 147,** promulgated by the SEC, provides a "nonexclusive safe harbor" for securing the intrastate exemption. Rule 147 requires that

1. the issuer is incorporated or organized in the State in which the issuance occurs;

2. the issuer is principally doing business in that State, which means that 80 percent of its gross revenues must be derived from that State, 80 percent of its assets must be located in that State, and 80 percent of the net proceeds from the issue must be used in that State;

3. all of the *offerees* and purchasers are residents of that State;

4. during the period of sale and for nine months after the last sale, no resales to non-residents are made; and

5. precautions are taken against interstate distributions. Such precautions include (a) placing a legend on the certificate evidencing the security stating that the securities have not been registered and that resales can be made only to residents of the State and (b)

obtaining a written statement of residence from each purchaser.

Exempt transactions for issuers are summarized in Figure 45–1.

EXEMPT TRANSACTIONS FOR NON-ISSUERS

The 1933 Act requires registration for any sale by *any* person (including non-issuers) of any nonexempt security unless a statutory exemption can be found for the transaction. The act, however, provides a transaction exemption for any person other than an issuer, underwriter, or dealer. Section 4(1). In addition, the act exempts most transactions by dealers and brokers. Sections 4(3) and 4(4). These three provisions exempt from the registration requirements of the 1933 Act most secondary transactions; that is, the numerous resales that occur on an exchange or in the over-the-counter market. Nevertheless, these exemptions do not extend to some situations involving resales by non-issuers, in particular: (1) resales of restricted securities acquired under Regulation D (Rules 506, 505, or 504) or Section 4(6), and (2) sales of restricted *or* nonrestricted securities by affili-

ates. Such sales must be made pursuant to registration, Rule 144, or Regulation A, subject to the limited exception provided some issuances under Rule 504. An **affiliate** is a person who controls, is controlled by, or is under common control with the issuer. **Control** means the direct or indirect possession of the power to direct the management and policies of a person through ownership of securities, by contract, or otherwise. Rule 405.

Rule 144

Rule 144 of the SEC sets forth conditions, which if met by an affiliate or any person selling restricted securities, exempts her from registering them. The rule requires that there must be adequate current public information about the issuer, that the person selling under the rule must have owned the securities for at least two years, that she sell them only in limited amounts in unsolicited brokers' transactions, and that notice of the sale must be provided to the SEC. A person who is *not* an affiliate of the issuer at the time of sale of the restricted securities and who has owned the securities for at least three years may, however, sell them in unlimited

---

Figure 45–1 Exempt Transactions for Issuers under the 1933 Act

Exemption	Price Limitation	Information Required	Limitations on Purchasers	Resales
Regulation A	$1.5 million	offering circular	none	unrestricted
Intrastate Rule 147	none	none	intrastate only	only to residents before 9 months
Rule 506	none	material information to unaccredited purchasers	unlimited accredited; 35 unaccredited	restricted
Rule 505	$5 million	material information to unaccredited purchasers	unlimited accredited; 35 unaccredited	restricted
Rule 504	$1 million	none	none	restricted with exceptions
Section 4(6)	$5 million	none	only accredited	restricted

amounts and is not subject to *any* of the other requirements of Rule 144. Sales by an affiliate are subject to Rule 144 whether the securities are restricted or nonrestricted; however, compliance with the two-year holding period is not required when an affiliate sells *nonrestricted* securities.

Rule 144A

While Rule 144 permits sales of restricted securities, the requirements of the rule have hampered the liquidity of privately placed securities. To improve the liquidity of such securities, in 1990 the SEC adopted Rule 144A, which provides an additional, nonexclusive safe harbor from registration for resales of restricted securities. Only securities that at the time of issue are *not* of the same class as securities listed on a national securities exchange or quoted in a U.S. automated interdealer quotation system ("nonfungible securities") may be sold under Rule 144A. Such nonfungible securities may be sold only to a qualified institutional buyer, defined generally as an institution that in the aggregate owns and invests on a discretionary basis at least $100 million in securities. Rule 144A also requires the seller of the nonfungible securities to take reasonable steps to ensure that the buyer knows that the seller is relying on Rule 144A. In addition, special requirements apply to securities issued by foreign companies. Securities acquired pursuant to Rule 144A are restricted securities.

Regulation A

Regulation A, in addition to providing issuers an exemption from registration for securities up to $1.5 million, also provides an exemption for non-issuers. Affiliates and non-affiliates are limited to $100,000 in any twelve-month period. There is a $300,000 limit on the total amount of securities sold by all non-affiliates. Use of this exemption requires compliance with all of the conditions imposed upon issuers by Regulation A, as discussed above.

LIABILITY

To implement the statutory objectives of providing full disclosure and preventing fraud in the sale of securities, the 1933 Act imposes a number of sanctions for noncompliance with its requirements. The sanctions include administrative remedies by the SEC, civil liability to injured investors, and criminal penalties.

Unregistered Sales

The act imposes express civil liability for the sale of an unregistered security that is required to be registered, the sale of a registered security without delivery of a prospectus, the sale of a security by use of an outdated prospectus, or the offer of a sale prior to the filing of the registration statement. **Section 12(1).** Liability is strict or absolute because there are no defenses. The person who purchases a security sold in violation of this provision of the act has the right to tender it back to the seller and recover the purchase price. If the purchaser no longer owns the security, he may recover monetary damages from the seller.

False Registration Statements

When securities have been sold subject to a registration statement, **Section 11** of the act imposes express liability for the inclusion in the registration statement of any untrue statement or omission of material fact. **Material** refers to those matters to which there is a substantial likelihood that a reasonable investor would attach importance in determining whether to purchase the security registered. SEC Rule 405. Usually, proof of reliance upon the misstatement or omission is not required. Liability is imposed upon (1) the issuer; (2) all persons who signed the registration statement including the principal executive officer, principal financial officer, and principal accounting officer; (3) every person who was a director or partner; (4) every accountant, engineer, appraiser, or expert who prepared or certified any part of the registration statement; and (5) all underwriters. These persons are jointly and severally liable to any person who acquires the security without knowledge of the untruth or omission for the amount paid for the security less either its value at the time of suit or the price for which it was sold. The court may award attorneys' fees against any party who brings suit or asserts a defense without merit.

An expert is liable only for misstatements or omissions in the portion of the registration that he prepared or certified. Moreover, any defendant, other than the issuer who has strict liability, may assert the affirmative defense of due diligence. This **due diligence** defense generally requires a showing that the defendant had reasonable grounds to believe, and did believe, that there were no untrue statements or material omissions. In some instances, due diligence requires that a reasonable investigation be made. In determining what constitutes a reasonable investigation and reasonable ground for belief, the standard of reasonableness is that required of a prudent man in the management of his own property. Section 11(c). *See Escott v. BarChris Const. Corp.*

Antifraud Provisions

The act also contains two broad antifraud provisions that apply to *all* securities, whether registered or exempt.

Section 12(2) Section 12(2) imposes express liability upon any person who offers or sells a security by means of a prospectus or oral communication that contains an untrue statement of material fact or an omission of a material fact. That liability extends only to the immediate purchaser, provided she did not know of the untruth or omission. The seller may avoid liability by proving that he did not know, and in the exercise of reasonable care could not have known, of the untrue statement or omission. The seller is liable to the purchaser for the amount paid upon tender of the security. If the purchaser no longer owns the security, she may recover damages from the seller.

Section 17(a) Section 17(a) makes it unlawful for any person in the offer or sale of any securities, whether registered or not, to do any of the following when using any means of transportation or communication in interstate commerce or the mails:

1. employ any device, scheme, or artifice to defraud, or

2. obtain money or property by means of any untrue statement of a material fact or any omission to state a material fact without which the information is misleading, or

3. engage in any transaction, practice, or course of business that operates or would operate as a fraud or deceit upon the purchaser.

There is some doubt whether the courts may imply a private right of action for persons injured by violations of this section. The Supreme Court has reserved this question and the lower courts are divided on the issue. The SEC may, however, bring enforcement actions under Section 17(a).

Criminal Sanctions

The 1933 Act imposes criminal sanctions upon any person who willfully violates any of the provisions of the act or the rules and regulations promulgated by the SEC pursuant to the act. Section 24. Conviction may carry a fine of not more than $10,000 or imprisonment of not more than five years or both.

The registration and liability provisions of the 1933 Act are summarized in Figure 45–2.

THE SECURITIES EXCHANGE ACT OF 1934

The Securities Exchange Act of 1934 deals principally with the secondary distribution (resale) of securities. The 1934 Act's definition of a security is substantially the same as the 1933 Act's definition. The act seeks to ensure fair and orderly securities markets by prohibiting fraudulent and manipulative practices and establishing rules for the operation of the securities markets. It provides protection for holders of *all* securities listed on national exchanges as well as for holders of *equity* securities of companies traded over the counter if their assets exceed $5 million and they have a class of equity securities with five hundred or more shareholders. Companies must register such securities and are also subject to the act's periodic reporting requirements, the short-swing profits provision, the tender offer provisions, the proxy solicitation provisions, and the internal control and record keeping requirements of the Foreign Corrupt Practices Act. An over-the-counter issuer may terminate its registration when the registered equity securities have fewer than three hundred shareholders or when there are fewer than five hundred

shareholders *and* assets less than $5 million on the last day of each of the past three years. In addition, issuers of securities, whether registered under the 1934 Act or not, must comply with the antifraud and the antibribery provisions of the act (see Figure 45–3).

DISCLOSURE

The 1934 Act imposes significant disclosure requirements upon reporting companies. These include filing registrations of securities, periodic reports, disclosure statements for proxy solicitations, and disclosure statements for tender offers, as well as compliance with the accounting requirements imposed by the Foreign Corrupt Practices Act.

Figure 45–2 Registration and Liability Provisions of the 1933 Act

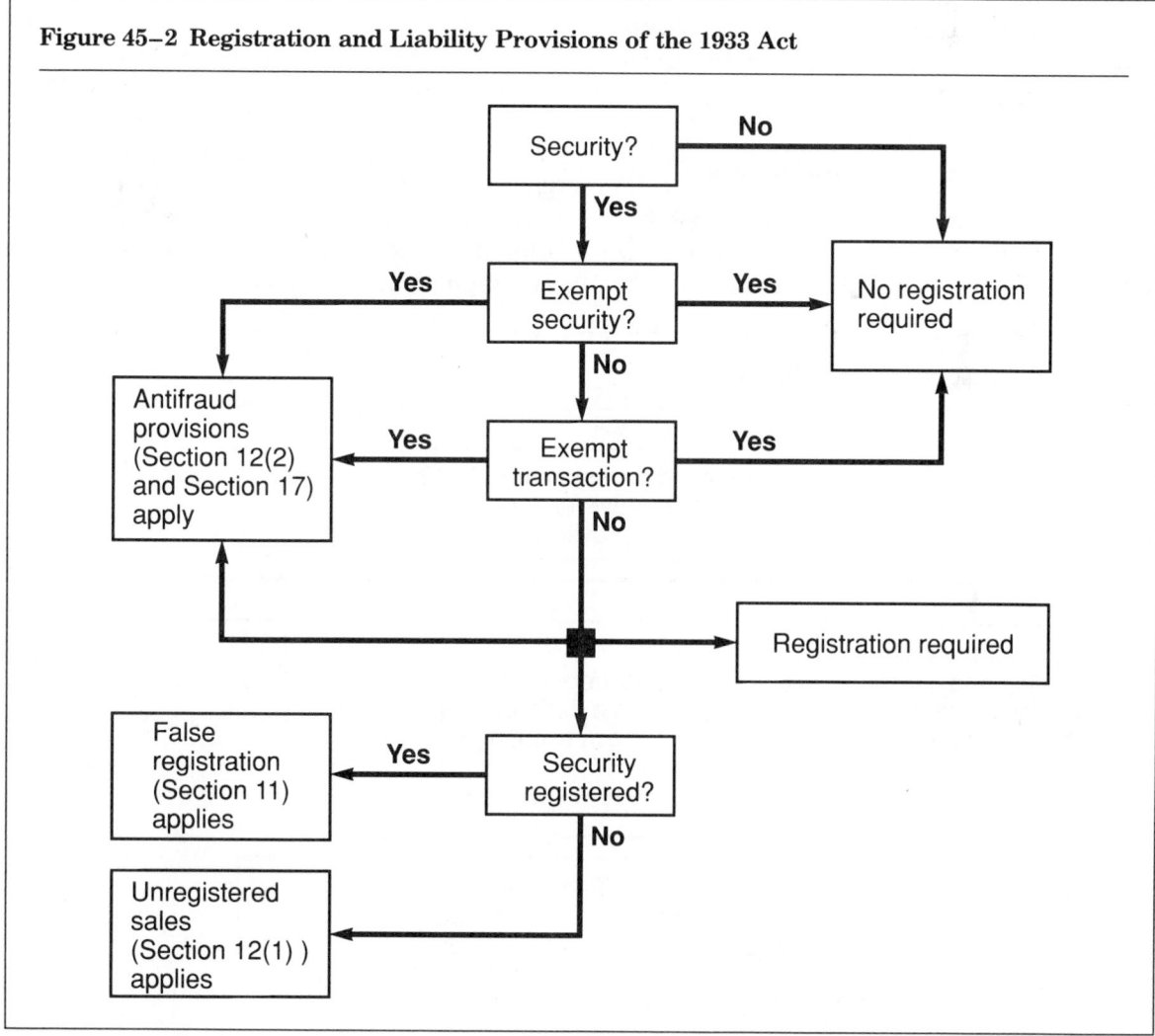

Registration Requirements for Securities

The 1934 Act requires all regulated publicly held companies to register with the SEC. Section 12. These registrations are one-time registrations that apply to an entire class of securities. Thus, they differ from registrations under the Securities Act of 1933, which relate only to securities involved in a specific offering. Registration requires disclosure of such information as the organization, financial structure, and nature of the business; the terms, positions, rights, and privileges of the different classes of outstanding securities; the names of the directors, officers, and underwriters, and each security holder owning more than 10 percent of any class of nonexempt equity security; bonus and profit-sharing arrangements; and balance sheets and profit and loss statements for the three preceding fiscal years.

Periodic Reporting Requirements

Following registration, an issuer must file specified annual (10–K) and periodic (10–Q and 8–K) reports to update the information contained in the original registration. Also subject to the periodic reporting requirements are issuers who have filed a *1933 Act* registration statement with respect to *any* security. Section 15. This duty, however, is suspended in any subsequent year in which the securities registered under the 1933 Act are held by fewer than three hundred persons. The act also requires that each director, officer, and any person who owns more than 10 percent of a registered equity security file reports with the SEC for any month in which there has been any changes in his ownership of such equity securities.

Proxy Solicitations

A **proxy** is a writing signed by a shareholder of a corporation authorizing a named person to vote his shares of stock at a specified meeting of the shareholders. To ensure that shareholders have adequate information with which to vote, the 1934 Act regulates the proxy solicitation process. The act makes it unlawful for any person to solicit any proxy with respect to any registered security "in contravention of such rules and regulations as the Commission may pre-

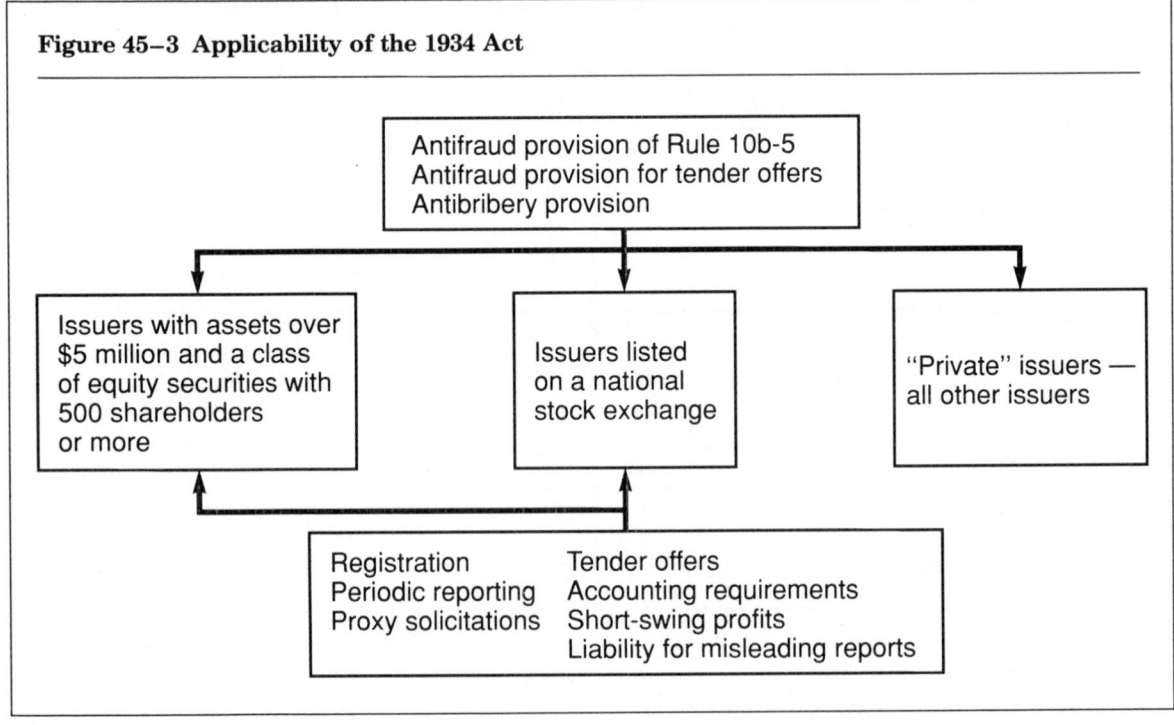

Figure 45–3 Applicability of the 1934 Act

scribe." Section 14. **Solicitation** includes any request for a proxy, any request not to execute a proxy, or any request to revoke a proxy.

Proxy Statements Rule 14a–3 prohibits the solicitation of a proxy unless each person solicited has been furnished with a written proxy statement containing specified information. In the case of solicitations by the issuer, the issuer must furnish security holders with a *proxy statement* describing all material facts concerning the matters being submitted to their vote together with a *proxy form* on which the security holders can indicate their approval or disapproval of each proposal to be presented. Even if a company does not solicit proxies from its shareholders but submits a matter to a shareholder vote, it must provide them with information substantially equivalent to what would appear in a proxy statement. In addition, in an election of directors, solicitations of proxies by a person other than the issuer are subject to similar disclosure requirements. The issuer in such an election also must include an annual report with the proxy statement.

Shareholder Proposals Where management makes a solicitation, any security holder entitled to vote has the opportunity to communicate with other security holders. Upon written request, the corporation must mail the communication at the security holder's expense or, at its option, promptly furnish to that security holder a current list of security holders.

If an eligible security holder entitled to vote submits a timely proposal for action at a forthcoming meeting, management must include the proposal in its proxy statement and provide security holders with an opportunity to vote for or against it. To be eligible, the holder must own the lesser of one percent or $1,000 in market value of the security for at least one year prior to submitting the proposal. If management opposes the proposal, it must include in its proxy materials a supporting statement by the security holder. The aggregate length of the proposal and the supporting statement is limited to a total of five

hundred words. A security holder is limited to submitting one proposal to an issuer each year.

Management may omit a proposal if, among other things, (1) under State law it is not a proper subject for shareholder action, (2) it is not significantly related to the business of the issuer, (3) it is beyond the issuer's power to effectuate, or (4) it relates to the conduct of the ordinary business operations of the issuer.

Tender Offers

A **tender offer** is a general invitation by the buyer (bidder) to the shareholders of a target company to tender their shares for sale at a specified price for a specified time period. In 1968, Congress enacted the Williams Act, which amended the 1934 Act to extend reporting and disclosure requirements to tender offers and other block acquisitions. The purpose of the Williams Act is to provide public shareholders with full disclosure by both the bidder and the target, so that the shareholders may make an informed decision.

Disclosure Requirements The 1934 Act imposes disclosure requirements in three situations: (1) a person or group acquires more than 5 percent of a class of voting securities registered under the 1934 Act, (2) a person makes a tender offer for more than 5 percent of a class of registered equity securities, or (3) the issuer makes an offer to repurchase its own registered shares. Although each of these situations is governed by different rules, the disclosure required is substantially the same. A statement must be filed with the SEC containing (1) the person's background; (2) the source of the funds used to acquire the securities; (3) the purpose of the acquisition, including any plans to liquidate the company or make major changes in the corporate structure; (4) the number of shares owned; and (5) any relevant contracts, arrangements, or understandings. Sections 13(d) and 14(d). This disclosure is also required by anyone soliciting shareholders to accept or reject a tender offer. A copy of the statement must be furnished to each offeree and sent to the issuer.

The target company has ten days in which to respond to the bidder's tender offer by (1) recommending acceptance or rejection, (2) expressing no opinion and remaining neutral, or (3) stating it is unable to take a position. The target company's response must include the reasons for the position taken.

Required Practices   A tender offer by both a third party and the issuer are subject to the following rules. The tender offer must be kept open for at least twenty business days. Shareholders who tender their shares may withdraw them at any time during the offering period. The tender offer must be open to all holders of the class of shares subject to the tender offer. All shares tendered must be purchased for the same price; thus, if an offering price is increased, those who have already tendered receive the benefit of the increase. A tender offeror who offers to purchase less than all of the outstanding securities of the target must accept, on a *pro rata* basis, securities tendered during the offer. During the tender offer, the bidder may buy shares of the target only through that tender offer.

Defensive Tactics   When confronted by an uninvited takeover bid—or by a potential, uninvited bid—management of the target company may decide either to oppose the bid or seek to prevent it. The defensive tactics employed by management to prevent or defend against undesired tender offers have developed into a highly ingenious, and metaphorically named, set of maneuvers, some of which require considerable planning. The tactics continue to evolve, and some of them are of questionable legality. The following excerpt describes most of the commonly used defensive tactics:

When faced with an outsider's attempt to take over the company, target management will frequently respond with a defensive tactic such as seeking a friendly suitor or "white knight." For example, the white knight may be granted a "lock-up" option which gives it an advantage in acquiring the target over other bidders, or the target may arrange to

sell its "crown jewel," or most desirable asset, to the white knight, thereby diminishing the target's attractiveness to others. * * *

Other common alternatives to finding a "white knight" as a defensive tactic include: the issuance of additional shares to dilute any holdings of the would-be acquiring company; stock repurchase programs to strengthen the control of "inside" or "friendly" shareholders; restrictive by-law and charter provisions, (sometimes referred to as "porcupine provisions" or "shark repellent") such as extraordinarily high voting requirements for mergers with other corporations; staggering of directors' terms of office which necessarily increases the time it will take to effect a turnover in management; obligating the corporation to long-term salary or bonus contracts (known as "golden parachutes" or "silver wheel chairs") for top management in the event of a change in control; and using state tender offer statutes to introduce additional delays into the tender offer process. * * * A similar move is for the target company to reincorporate in a state with more onerous antitakeover laws. Other defensive and preventive tactics used in recent years include: the acquisition of another business by the target company, creating a potential antitrust threat to impending tender offers; the purchase of a radio station or some other heavily regulated business to tie up the takeover attempt in administrative proceedings which may be needed to approve any change of ownership in the regulated business; and the "Pac-Man" defense, where the target company makes a tender offer for control of the original tender offeror.

Defensive tactics continue to proliferate. Another recent defensive tactic is the "poison pill" which is a conditional stock right that is triggered by a hostile takeover and makes the takeover prohibitively expensive. The poison pill is a variation of the scorched earth defense whereby the target company prepares itself for self-destruction in the event of a hostile takeover. Another variation on the poison pill is the so-called "flipover" provisions in corporate charters which prohibit combinations with persons who have acquired more than a stated percentage of the issuer's stock without prior approval of the target company's directors. Under such flipover provisions, the shareholders receive rights in the acquiring company's shares for any takeover occurring within a predetermined period. Another device which has survived judicial challenge, but is now prohibited by an SEC rule is the discriminatory issuer self-tender that excludes the hostile bidder from the offer's terms. Greenmail, which consists of target's management buying back the hostile bidder shares at a premium, has also been a widely used tactic. A common charter amendment has been the so-called "fair price" amendment under which all shareholders are guaranteed the best price paid to any one shareholder. Many states have adopted fair price statutes which are to the same effect. Still another approach has been the issuance of preferred shares with extraordinary voting power. Such unequal voting rights have been held to violate state law and also violate the New York Stock Exchange's one share/one vote rule, the enforcement of which was suspended pending SEC reconsideration of the rule. The SEC has since adopted a uniform rule limiting dual class voting. Hazen, *The Law of Securities Regulation,* 2d ed., Section 11.20.

State Regulation More than two-thirds of the States have enacted statutes regulating tender offers. Although they vary greatly, most of them tend to protect the target company from an unwanted tender offer. Some give the State the power to review the merits of the offer or the adequacy of disclosure. Many impose waiting periods before the tender offer is effective. The State statutes generally require more detailed disclosures than the Williams Act requires. Many of them exempt tender offers supported by the target company's management. A number of States have adopted fair price statutes, which require the acquirer to pay to all shareholders the highest price paid to any shareholder. Some States have enacted business combination statutes prohibiting transactions with an acquirer for a specified period of time after change in control unless disinterested shareholders approve.

Some of these statutes have been declared unconstitutional because of Federal preemption by the Williams Act. In 1987, the Supreme Court upheld Indiana's statute, which gave the majority of a target company's shareholders the right to determine whether a controlling block of shares acquired by a bidder would have voting rights. The Court validated the statute because it concluded that the statute was consistent with and fur-

thered a basic purpose of the Williams Act to place shareholders on an equal footing with the takeover bidder. As the Court explained:

The Indiana Act operates on the assumption, implicit in the Williams Act, that independent shareholders faced with tender offers often are at a disadvantage. By allowing such shareholders to vote as a group, the Act protects them from the coercive aspects of some tender offers. If, for example, shareholders believe that a successful tender offer will be followed by a purchase of nontendering shares at a depressed price, individual shareholders may tender their shares—even if they doubt the tender offer is in the corporation's best interest—to protect themselves from being forced to sell their shares at a depressed price. As the SEC explains: "The alternative of not accepting the tender offer is virtual assurance that, if the offer is successful, the shares will have to be sold in the lower priced, second step." [Citations.] In such a situation under the Indiana Act, the shareholders as a group, acting in the corporation's best interest, could reject the offer, although individual shareholders might be inclined to accept it. The desire of the Indiana Legislature to protect shareholders of Indiana corporations from this type of coercive offer does not conflict with the Williams Act. Rather, it furthers the federal policy of investor protection. *CTS Corp. v. Dynamics Corp. of America,* 481 U.S. 69 (1987).

More than one-half of the States with tender offer regulations have adopted similar provisions.

Foreign Corrupt Practices Act

In 1977, Congress enacted the Foreign Corrupt Practices Act (FCPA) as an amendment to the 1934 Act. The FCPA was amended in 1988. The act imposes internal control requirements upon companies with securities registered under the 1934 Act and prohibits all domestic concerns from bribing foreign governmental or political officials, discussed later in this chapter.

The accounting requirements of the FCPA reflect the principle that accurate record keeping is essential for managerial responsibility and that investors should be able to rely on the financial reports they receive. Accordingly, the accounting requirements were enacted (1) to assure that an issuer's books accurately reflect financial transactions, (2) to protect the integrity of independent audits of financial statements, and (3) to promote the reliability of financial information required by the 1934 Act.

The FCPA requires every issuer that has a class of registered securities to

1. make and keep books, records, and accounts which, in reasonable detail, accurately and fairly reflect the transactions and disposition of the assets of the issuer, and

2. devise and maintain a system of internal controls to assure that transactions are executed as authorized and recorded in conformity with generally accepted accounting principles so as to provide accountability for assets and to assure that access to assets is permitted only with management's authorization. Section 13(b).

LIABILITY

To implement its objectives, the 1934 Act imposes a number of sanctions for noncompliance with its disclosure and antifraud requirements. These sanctions include civil liability to injured investors and issuers, civil penalties, and criminal penalties.

Misleading Statements in Reports

Section 18 imposes express civil liability upon any person who makes or causes to be made any false or misleading statement with respect to any material fact in any application, report, document, or registration filed with the SEC under the 1934 Act. Any person who purchased or sold a security in reliance upon that false or misleading statement and without knowing that it was false or misleading may recover under Section 18. A person is not liable, however, if she proves that she acted in good faith and had no knowledge that such statement was false or misleading. The court may award attorneys' fees against either the plaintiff or the defendant.

Short-Swing Profits

Section 16(b) of the 1934 Act imposes express liability upon insiders—directors, officers, and any person owning more than 10 percent of the stock of a corporation listed on a national stock exchange or registered with the SEC—for all profits resulting from their "short-swing" trading in such stock. If any insider sells such stock within six months from the date of its purchase or purchases such stock within six months from the date of a sale of the stock, the corporation is entitled to recover any and all profit realized by the insider from these transactions. The "profit" recoverable is calculated by matching the highest sale price against the lowest purchase price within the relevant six month period. Losses cannot be offset against profits. Suit to recover such profit may be brought by the issuer, or by the owner of any security of the issuer in the name and in behalf of the issuer if the issuer fails or refuses to bring such suit within sixty days after request.

Antifraud Provision

Section 10(b) of the 1934 Act and SEC **Rule 10b–5** make it unlawful for any person to do any of the following when using the mails or facilities of interstate commerce in connection with the purchase or sale of any security:

1. employ any device, scheme, or artifice to defraud;

2. make any untrue statement of a material fact;

3. omit to state a material fact without which the information is misleading; or

4. engage in any act, practice, or course of business that operates or would operate as a fraud or deceit upon any person.

Rule 10b–5 applies to any purchase or sale of **any** security, whether it is registered under the 1934 Act or not, whether it is publicly traded or closely held, whether it is listed on an exchange or sold over the counter, or whether it is part of an initial issuance or a secondary distribution. There are **no** exemptions. The implied liability under Rule 10b–5 applies to misconduct of purchasers as well as sellers and allows both defrauded sellers and buyers to recover.

Requisites of Rule 10b–5 Recovery of damages under Rule 10b–5 requires proof of several elements including (1) a misstatement or omission, (2) that is material, (3) made with *scienter,* and (4) relied upon (5) in connection with the purchase or sale of a security. This rule differs from common law fraud, in that Rule 10b–5 imposes an affirmative duty of disclosure. A misstatement or omission is **material** if there is a substantial likelihood that a reasonable investor would consider it important in deciding whether to purchase or sell the security. Examples of material facts include substantial changes in dividends or earnings, significant misstatements of asset value, and the fact that the issuer is about to become a target of a tender offer. In an action for damages under Rule 10b–5, it must be shown that the violation was committed with **scienter,** which is intentional misconduct. Negligence is not sufficient. Although the Supreme Court has not yet decided whether reckless conduct is sufficient to satisfy the requirement of *scienter,* a great majority of circuit and district courts have held that recklessness is sufficient.

Direct reliance may be difficult to prove in a 10b–5 action because usually there is no face-to-face transaction in which the buyer and seller negotiate the deal. Recognizing the special nature of securities market transactions, the Supreme Court adopted the fraud on the market theory that establishes a rebuttable presumption of reliance based on the premise that the market price of a stock reflects any misstatement or omission and that the fraudulently affected market price has injured the plaintiff. *See Basic Inc. v. Levinson.* By making it significantly easier for many plaintiffs to establish a 10b–5 claim, adoption of the fraud on the market theory has potentially far-reaching consequences.

Remedies for violations of Rule 10b–5 include rescission, damages, and injunctions. The courts are divided over the measure of damages.

Insider Trading Rule 10b–5 applies to sales or purchases of securities made by an "insider" who possesses material information that is not available to the general public. An insider will be liable under Rule 10b–5 if he fails to disclose the material, nonpublic information before trading on the information unless he waits until the information becomes public. **Insiders,** for the purpose of Rule 10b–5, include directors, officers, employees, and agents of the issuer of the security as well as those with whom the issuer has entrusted information solely for corporate purposes, such as underwriters, accountants, lawyers, and consultants. In some instances, persons who receive material, nonpublic information from insiders—tippees—are also precluded from trading on that information. A tippee is under a duty not to trade on inside information when the insider has breached his fiduciary duty to the shareholders by disclosing the information to the tippee who knows or should know that there has been such a breach.

Although both Section 16(b) and Rule 10b–5 address the problem of insider trading and both may apply to the same transaction, they differ in several respects. First, Section 16(b) applies only to transactions involving registered equity securities while Rule 10b–5 applies to all securities. Second, the definition of *insider* is much broader under Rule 10b–5 and extends beyond directors, officers, and owners of more than 10 percent of a company's stock, whereas Section 16(b) is limited to these persons. Third, Section 16(b) does *not* require that the insider possess material, nonpublic information; liability is strict. Rule 10b–5 applies to insider trading only where such information is not disclosed. Fourth, Section 16(b) applies only to transactions within six months of each other; Rule 10b–5 has no such limitation. Fifth, under Rule 10b–5 injured investors may recover damages on their own behalf, while under Section 16(b), although shareholders may bring suit, any recovery is on behalf of the corporation.

Express Insider Trading Liability

In 1988, Congress amended the 1934 Act by adding **Section 20A,** which imposes express civil liability upon any person who violated the act by purchasing or selling a security while in possession of material, nonpublic information. Any person who contemporaneously sold or purchased securities of the same class as persons who improperly traded may bring a private action to recover damages for the violation. The total amount of damages may not exceed the profit gained or loss avoided by the violation diminished by any amount disgorged to the SEC pursuant to a court order. The action must be brought within five years after the date of the last transaction that is the subject of the violation. Tippers are jointly and severally liable with their tippees, if the tippee commits a violation by trading on the inside information.

Civil Penalties for Insider Trading

In addition to the remedies discussed above, the SEC is authorized by legislation enacted in 1984 and 1988 to bring an action in a U.S. district court to have a civil penalty imposed upon any person who purchases or sells a security while in possession of material, nonpublic information. Liability also extends to any person who by communicating material, nonpublic information aids and abets such a violation by another person. Liability may also be imposed on any person who directly or indirectly controlled the person who committed a violation if the controlling person knew or recklessly disregarded the fact that the controlled person was likely to commit a violation and the controlling person failed to take appropriate steps to prevent the violation. The transaction must be on or through the facilities of a national securities exchange or from or through a broker or dealer. Purchases that are part of a public offering by an issuer of securities are not subject to this provision.

The amount of the civil penalty for the person who committed a violation by trading on inside information is determined by the court in light of the facts and circumstances but may not exceed three times the profit gained or loss avoided as a result of the unlawful purchase or sale. The maximum amount of the civil penalty that may be imposed upon a controlling person is the greater of $1 million or three times the profit gained or loss avoided as a result of the controlled person's violation. If the controlled person's violation consists of tipping inside information, then the liability of the controlling person is measured by the profit gained or loss avoided by the person to whom the controlled person directed the tip. For the purpose of this provision, "profit gained" or "loss avoided" is "the difference between the purchase or sale price of the security and the value of that security as measured by the trading price of the security a reasonable period after public dissemination of the nonpublic information."

The penalty is payable into the Treasury of the United States. The SEC is authorized to award bounties of up to 10 percent of the penalty recovered to informants who provide information leading to the imposition of the penalty. An action must be brought within five years after the date of the purchase or sale.

Misleading Proxy Statements

Any person who distributes a materially false or misleading proxy statement may be liable to a shareholder who suffers a loss caused by purchasing or selling a security in reliance upon the statement. In this context, a misstatement or omission is material if there is a substantial likelihood that a reasonable shareholder would consider it important in deciding how to vote. A number of courts have held that negligence is sufficient for an action under the proxy rule's antifraud provisions. In addition, when there have been violations of the proxy disclosure or filing requirement, a court may, if appropriate, enjoin a shareholder meeting or any action taken at that meeting. Other remedies are rescission, damages, and attorneys' fees.

Fraudulent Tender Offers

It is unlawful for any person to make any untrue statement of material fact or omit to state any material fact or to engage in any fraudulent, deceptive, or manipulative practices in connection with any tender offer. Section 14(e). *See Schreiber v. Burlington Northern, Inc.* This provision applies even if the target company is not subject to the 1934 Act's reporting requirements. Insider trading during a tender offer is prohibited by Rule 14e–3.

Some courts have implied civil liability for violations of Section 14(e). Because of the small number of cases, the requirements for such an action are not entirely clear. A target company may seek an injunction and a shareholder of the target may be able to recover damages or obtain rescission. It appears likely that the courts will require *scienter.*

Antibribery Provision of FCPA

The Foreign Corrupt Practices Act makes it unlawful for *any* domestic concern or any of its officers, directors, employees, or agents to offer or give anything of value directly or indirectly to any foreign official, political party, or political official for the purpose of (1) influencing any act or decision of that person or party in his or its official capacity, (2) inducing an act or omission in violation of his or its lawful duty, or (3) inducing such person or party to use his or its influence to affect a decision of a foreign government in order to assist the domestic concern in obtaining or retaining business. An offer or promise to make a prohibited payment is a violation even if the offer is not accepted or the promise is not performed. The 1988 amendments explicitly exclude routine governmental action not involving the discretion of the official, such as obtaining permits or processing applications. They also added an affirmative defense for payments that are lawful under the written laws or regulations of the foreign officials' country.

Violations can result in fines of up to $2 million for companies; individuals may be fined a maximum of $100,000 and imprisoned up to five years or both. Section 32(c). Fines imposed upon individuals may not be paid directly or indirectly by the domestic concern on whose behalf they acted. A civil penalty of up to $10,000 may be imposed.

Criminal Sanctions

Section 32 of the 1934 Act imposes criminal sanctions on any person who willfully violates any of the provisions of the act (except the antibribery provision) or the rules and regulations promulgated by the SEC pursuant to the act. For individuals, conviction may carry a fine of not more than $1 million or imprisonment of not more than ten years or both, except no person is subject to *imprisonment* if he proves he had no knowledge of the rule or regulation. If the person, however, is not a natural person (for example, a corporation), then a fine not exceeding $2.5 million may be imposed.

Figure 45–4 summarizes the civil liability provisions under the 1933 and 1934 Acts.

Figure 45–4 Civil Liability under the 1933 and 1934 Acts

Provision	Conduct	Plaintiffs	Defendants	Standard of Culpability	Reliance Required	Type of Liability	Remedies
Section 12(1) 1933 Act	Unregistered sale or Sale without prospectus	Purchasers from a violator	Sellers in violation	Strict liability	No	Express	Rescission Damages
Section 11 1933 Act	Registration statement containing material misstatement or omission	Purchasers of registered security	Issuer Directors Signers Underwriters Experts	Strict liability for issuer Negligence for others	No	Express	Damages Attorney's fees
Section 12(2) 1933 Act	Material misstatement or omission	Purchasers from violator	Sellers in violation	Negligence	No	Express	Rescission Damages
Section 18 1934 Act	False or misleading statements in a document filed with SEC	Purchasers or sellers	Persons making filing in violation	Knowledge or bad faith	Yes	Express	Damages Attorney's fess
Section 16(b) 1934 Act	Short-swing profit by insider	Issuer Shareholder of issuer	Directors Officers 10 percent shareholders	Strict liability	No	Express	Damages
Rule 10b-5 1934 Act	Deception or Material misstatement or omission	Purchasers or sellers	Purchasers or sellers in violation	Scienter	Yes	Implied	Rescission Damages Injunction
Section 20A 1934 Act	Insider trading	Contemporaneous purchasers or sellers	Inside traders	Scienter	No	Express	Damages
Section 14(a) 1934 Act	Materially false or misleading proxy solicitation	Shareholders	Persons making proxy solicitation in violation	Negligence (probably)	Probably	Implied	Rescission Damages Injunction Attorney's fees
Section 14(e) 1934 Act	Tender offer with: Deception or Manipulation or Material misstatement or omission	Target company Shareholders of target	Persons making tender offer in violation	Scienter (probably)	Probably	Implied	Rescission Damages Injunction

CASES

Definition of a Security

SECURITIES AND EXCHANGE COMMISSION v. W.J. HOWEY CO.

Supreme Court of the United States, 1946.
328 U.S. 293, 66 S.Ct. 1100, 90 L.Ed. 1244.

MURPHY, J.

This case involves the application of § 2(1) of the Securities Act of 1933 to an offering of units of a citrus grove development coupled with a contract for cultivating, marketing and remitting the net proceeds to the investor.

The Securities and Exchange Commission instituted this action to restrain the respondents from using the mails and instrumentalities of interstate commerce in the offer and sale of unregistered and non-exempt securities in violation of § 5(a) of the Act. The District Court denied the injunction, . . . and the Fifth Circuit Court of Appeals affirmed the judgment. * * *

* * *

Most of the facts are stipulated. The respondents, W.J. Howey Company and Howey-in-the-Hills Service, Inc., are Florida corporations under direct common control and management. The Howey Company owns large tracts of citrus acreage in Lake County, Florida. During the past several years it has planted about 500 acres annually, keeping half of the groves itself and offering the other half to the public "to help us finance additional development." Howey-in-the-Hills Service, Inc., is a service company engaged in cultivating and developing many of these groves, including the harvesting and marketing of the crops.

Each prospective customer is offered both a land sales contract and a service contract, after having been told that it is not feasible to invest in a grove unless service arrangements are made. While the purchaser is free to make arrangements with other service companies, the superiority of Howey-in-the-Hills Service, Inc., is stressed. Indeed, 85% of the acreage sold during the 3-year period ending May 31,

1943, was covered by service contracts with Howey-in-the-Hills Service, Inc.

The land sales contract with the Howey Company provides for a uniform purchase price per acre or fraction thereof, varying in amount only in accordance with the number of years the particular plot has been planted with citrus trees. Upon full payment of the purchase price the land is conveyed to the purchaser by warranty deed. Purchases are usually made in narrow strips of land arranged so that an acre consists of a row of 48 trees. During the period between February 1, 1941, and May 31, 1943, 31 of the 42 persons making purchases bought less than 5 acres each. The average holding of these 31 persons was 1.33 acres and sales of as little as 0.65, 0.7 and 0.73 of an acre were made. These tracts are not separately fenced and the sole indication of several ownership is found in small land marks intelligible only through a plat book record.

The service contract, generally of a 10-year duration without option of cancellation, gives Howey-in-the-Hills Service, Inc., a leasehold interest and "full and complete" possession of the acreage. For a specified fee plus the cost of labor and materials, the company is given full discretion and authority over the cultivation of the groves and the harvest and marketing of the crops. The company is well established in the citrus business and maintains a large force of skilled personnel and a great deal of equipment, including 75 tractors, sprayer wagons, fertilizer trucks and the like. Without the consent of the company, the land owner or purchaser has no right of entry to market the crop; thus there is ordinarily no right to specific fruit. The company is accountable only for an allocation of the net profits based upon a check made at the time of picking. All the produce is pooled by the respondent companies, which do business under their own names.

The purchasers for the most part are non-residents of Florida. They are predominantly business and professional people who lack the knowledge, skill and equipment necessary for the care and cultivation of citrus trees. They are attracted by the expectation of substantial profits.

* * *

Section 2(1) of the Act defines the term "security" to include the commonly known documents traded for speculation or investment. This definition also includes "securities" of a more variable character, designated by such descriptive terms as "certificate of interest or participation in any profit-sharing agreement," "investment contract" and "in general, any interest or instrument commonly known as a 'security.' " The legal issue in this case turns upon a determination of whether, under the circumstances, the land sales contract, the warranty deed and the service contract together constitute an "investment contract" within the meaning of § 2(1). An affirmative answer brings into operation the registration requirements of § 5(a), unless the security is granted an exemption under § 3(b). * * *

The term "investment contract" is undefined by the Securities Act or by relevant legislative reports. But the term was common in many state "blue sky" laws in existence prior to the adoption of the federal statute. * * *

By including an investment contract within the scope of § 2(1) of the Securities Act, Congress was using a term the meaning of which had been crystallized by this prior judicial interpretation. It is therefore reasonable to attach that meaning to the term as used by Congress, especially since such a definition is consistent with the statutory aims. In other words, an investment contract for purposes of the Securities Act means a contract, transaction or scheme whereby a person invests his money in a common enterprise and is led to expect profits solely from the efforts of the promoter or a third party, it being immaterial whether the shares in the enterprise are evidenced by formal certificates or by nominal interests in the physical assets employed in the enterprise. Such a definition . . . permits the fulfillment of the statutory purpose of compelling full and fair disclosure relative to the issuance of "the many types of instruments that in our commercial world fall within the ordinary concept of a security." [Citation.] It embodies a flexible rather than a static principle, one that is capable of adaptation to meet the countless and variable schemes devised by those who seek the use of the money of others on the promise of profits.

The transactions in this case clearly involve investment contracts as so defined. The respondent companies are offering something more than fee simple interests in land, something different from a farm or orchard coupled with management services. They are offering an opportunity to contribute money and to share in the profits of a large citrus fruit enterprise managed and partly owned by respondents. They are offering this opportunity to persons who reside in distant localities and who lack the equipment and experience requisite to the cultivation, harvesting and marketing of the citrus products. Such persons have no desire to occupy the land or to develop it themselves; they are attracted solely by the prospects of a return on their investment. Indeed, individual development of the plots of land that are offered and sold would seldom be economically feasible due to their small size. Such tracts gain utility as citrus groves only when cultivated and developed as component parts of a larger area. A common enterprise managed by respondents or third parties with adequate personnel and equipment is therefore essential if the investors are to achieve their paramount aim of a return on their investments. Their respective shares in this enterprise are evidenced by land sales contracts and warranty deeds, which serve as a convenient method of determining the investors' allocable shares of the profits. The resulting transfer of rights in land is purely incidental.

Thus all the elements of a profit-seeking business venture are present here. The investors provide the capital and share in the earnings and profits; the promoters manage, control and operate the enterprise. It follows that the arrangements whereby the investors' interests are made manifest involve investment contracts, regardless of the legal terminology in which such contracts are clothed. The investment contracts in this instance take the form of land sales contracts, warranty deeds and service contracts which respondents offer to prospective investors. And respondents' failure to abide by the statutory and administrative rules in making such offerings, even though the failure result from a bona fide mistake as to the law, cannot be sanctioned under the Act.

This conclusion is unaffected by the fact that some purchasers choose not to accept the full offer of an investment contract by declining to enter into a service contract with the respondents. The Securities Act prohibits the offer as well as the sale of unregistered, nonexempt securities. Hence it is enough that the respondents merely offer the essential ingredients of an investment contract.

* * *

Reversed.

Liability for False Registration Statements

ESCOTT v. BARCHRIS CONSTRUCTION CORP.

United States District Court, Southern District of New York, 1968.
283 F.Supp. 643.

MᴄLᴇᴀɴ, J.

This is an action by purchasers of 5½ per cent convertible subordinated fifteen year debentures of BarChris Construction Corporation (BarChris). * * *

The action is brought under Section 11 of the Securities Act of 1933. Plaintiffs allege that the registration statement with respect to these debentures filed with the Securities and Exchange Commission, which became effective on May 16, 1961, contained material false statements and material omissions.

Defendants fall into three categories: (1) the persons who signed the registration statement; (2) the underwriters, consisting of eight investment banking firms, led by Drexel & Co. (Drexel); and (3) BarChris's au-

ditors, Peat, Marwick, Mitchell & Co. (Peat, Marwick).

* * *

Defendants, in addition to denying that the registration statement was false, have pleaded the defense open to them under Section 11 of the Act,. . . . On the main issue of liability, the questions to be decided are (1) did the registration statement contain false statements of fact, or did it omit to state facts which should have been stated in order to prevent it from being misleading; (2) if so, were the facts which were falsely stated or omitted "material" within the meaning of the Act; (3) if so, have defendants established their affirmative defenses?

* * *

In December 1959, BarChris sold 560,000 shares of common stock to the public at $3.00 per share. This issue was underwritten by Peter Morgan & Company, one of the present defendants.

By early 1961, BarChris needed additional working capital. The proceeds of the sale of the debentures involved in this action were to be devoted, in part at least, to fill that need.

The registration statement of the debentures, in preliminary form, was filed with the Securities and Exchange Commission on March 30, 1961. A first amendment was filed on May 11 and a second on May 16. The registration statement became effective on May 16. The closing of the financing took place on May 24. On that day BarChris received the net proceeds of the financing.

By that time BarChris was experiencing difficulties in collecting amounts due from some of its customers. Some of them were in arrears in payments due to factors on their discounted notes. As time went on those difficulties increased. Although BarChris continued to build [bowling] alleys in 1961 and 1962, it became increasingly apparent that the industry was overbuilt. Operators of alleys, often inadequately financed, began to fail. Precisely when the tide turned is a matter of dispute, but at any rate, it was painfully apparent in 1962.

In May of that year BarChris made an abortive attempt to raise more money by the sale of common stock. It filed with the Securities and Exchange Commission a registration statement for the stock issue which it later withdrew. In October 1962 BarChris came to the end of the road. On October 29, 1962, it filed in this court a petition for an arrangement under Chapter XI of the Bankruptcy Act.

[The court found that the registration statement contained material false statements.]

* * *

The "Due Diligence" Defenses Section 11(b) of the Act provides that:

". . . no person, other than the issuer, shall be liable . . . who shall sustain the burden of proof—

* * *

"(3) that (A) as regards any part of the registration statement not purporting to be made on the authority of an expert . . . he had, after reasonable investigation, reasonable ground to believe and did believe, at the time such part of the registration statement became effective, that the statements therein were true and that there was no omission to state a material fact required to be stated therein or necessary to make the statements therein not misleading; . . . and (C) as regards any part of the registration statement purporting to be made on the authority of an expert (other than himself) . . . he had no reasonable ground to believe and did not believe, at the time such part of the registration statement became effective, that the statements therein were untrue or that there was an omission to state a material fact required to be stated therein or necessary to make the statements therein not misleading. . . ."

Section 11(c) defines "reasonable investigation" as follows:

In determining, for the purposes of paragraph (3) of subsection (b) of this section, what constitutes reasonable investigation and reasonable ground for belief, the standard of reasonableness shall be that required of a prudent man in the management of his own property.

Every defendant, except BarChris itself, to whom, as the issuer, these defenses are not available, and except Peat, Marwick, whose position rests on a different statutory provision, has pleaded these affirmative defenses. * * *

* * *

I turn now to the question of whether defendants have proved their due diligence defenses. The position of each defendant will be separately considered.

* * *

Kircher Kircher was treasurer of BarChris and its chief financial officer. He is a certified public accountant and an intelligent man. He was thoroughly familiar with BarChris's financial affairs. * * *

Moreover, as a member of the executive committee, Kircher was kept informed as to those branches of the business of which he did not have direct charge.

* * *

Knowing the facts, Kircher had reason to believe that the expertised portion of the prospectus, *i.e.*, the 1960 figures, was in part incorrect. He could not shut his eyes to the facts and rely on Peat, Marwick for that portion.

As to the rest of the prospectus, knowing the facts, he did not have a reasonable ground to believe it to be true. On the contrary, he must have known that in part it was untrue. * * *

Kircher has not proved his due diligence defenses.

* * *

Birnbaum Birnbaum was a young lawyer, admitted to the bar in 1957, who, after brief periods of employment by two different law firms and an equally brief period of practicing in his own firm, was employed by BarChris as house counsel and assistant secretary in October 1960. Unfortunately for him, he became secretary and a director of BarChris on April 17, 1961, after the first version of the registration statement had been filed with the Securities and Exchange Commission. He signed the later amendments, thereby becoming responsible for the accuracy of the prospectus in its final form.

Although the prospectus, in its description of "management," lists Birnbaum among the "executive officers" and devotes several sentences to a recital of his career, the fact seems to be that he was not an executive officer in any real sense. He did not participate in the management of the company. As house counsel, he attended to legal matters of a routine nature.

* * *

One of Birnbaums' more important duties, first as assistant secretary and later as fullfledged secretary, was to keep the corporate minutes of BarChris and its subsidiaries. This necessarily informed him to a considerable extent about the company's affairs. * * *

It seems probable that Birnbaum did not know of many of the inaccuracies in the prospectus. He must, however, have appreciated some of them. In any case, he made no investigation and relied on the others to get it right. . . . As a lawyer, he should have known his obligations under the statute. He should have known that he was required to make a reasonable investigation of the truth of all the statements in the unexpertised portion of the document which he signed. Having failed to make such an investigation, he did not have reasonable ground to believe that all these statements were true. Birnbaum has not established his due diligence defenses except as to the audited 1960 figures.

Auslander   Auslander was an "outside" director, *i.e.,* one who was not an officer of BarChris. He was chairman of the board of Valley Stream National Bank. * * *

* * *

In considering Auslander's due diligence defenses, a distinction is to be drawn between the expertised and non-expertised portions of the prospectus. As to the former, Auslander knew that Peat, Marwick had audited the 1960 figures. He believed them to be correct because he had confidence in Peat, Marwick. He had no reasonable ground to believe otherwise.

As to the non-expertised portions, however, Auslander is in a different position. He seems to have been under the impression that Peat, Marwick was responsible for all the figures. This impression was not correct, as he would have realized if he had read the prospectus carefully. Auslander made no investigation of the accuracy of the prospectus. * * *

It is true that Auslander became a director on the eve of the financing. He had little opportunity to familiarize himself with the company's affairs. The question is whether, under such circumstances, Auslander did enough to establish his due diligence defense with respect to the nonexpertised portions of the prospectus.

* * *

Section 11 imposes liability in the first instance upon a director, no matter how new he is. He is presumed to know his responsibility when he becomes a director. He can escape liability only by using that reasonable care to investigate the facts which a prudent man would employ in the management of his own property. In my opinion, a prudent man would not act in an important matter without any knowledge of the relevant facts, in sole reliance upon representations of persons who are comparative strangers and upon general information which does not purport to cover the particular case. To say that such minimal conduct measures up to the statutory standard would to all intents and purposes, absolve new directors from responsibility merely because they are new. This is not a sensible construction of Section 11, when one bears in mind its fundamental purpose of requiring full and truthful disclosures for the protection of investors.

* * *

The Underwriters   The underwriters other than Drexel made no investigation of the accuracy of the prospectus. * * * They all relied upon Drexel as the "lead" underwriter.

Drexel did make an investigation. The work was in charge of Coleman, a partner of the firm, assisted by Casperson, an associate. Drexel's attorneys acted as attorneys for the entire group of underwriters. Ballard did the work, assisted by Stanton.

* * *

The underwriters say that the prospectus is the company's prospectus, not theirs. Doubtless this is the way they customarily regard it. But the Securities Act makes no such distinction. The underwriters are just as responsible as the company if the prospectus is false. And prospective investors rely upon the reputation of the underwriters in deciding whether to purchase the securities.

* * *

The purpose of Section 11 is to protect investors. To that end the underwriters are made responsible for the truth of the prospectus. If they may escape that responsibility by taking at face value representations made to them by the company's management, then the inclusion of underwriters among those liable under Section 11 affords the investors no additional protection. To effectuate the statute's purpose, the phrase "reasonable investigation" must be construed to require more effort on the part of the underwriters than the mere accurate reporting in the prospectus of "data presented" to them by the company. It should make no difference that this data is elicited by questions addressed to the company officers by the underwriters, or that the underwriters at the time believe that the company's officers are truthful and reliable. In order to make the underwriters' participation in this enterprise of any value to the investors, the underwriters must make some reasonable attempt to verify the data submitted to them. They may not rely solely on the company's officers or on the company's counsel. A prudent man in the management of his own property would not rely on them.

It is impossible to lay down a rigid rule suitable for every case defining the extent to which such verification must go. It is a question of degree, a matter of judgment in each case. In the present case, the underwriters' counsel made almost no attempt to verify management's representations. I hold that that was insufficient.

On the evidence in this case, I find that the underwriters' counsel did not make a reasonable investigation of the truth of those portions of the prospectus which were not made on the authority of Peat, Marwick as an expert. Drexel is bound by their failure. It is not a matter of relying upon counsel for legal advice. Here the attorneys were dealing with matters of fact. Drexel delegated to them, as its agent, the business of examining the corporate minutes and contracts. It must bear the consequences of their failure to make an adequate examination.

The other underwriters, who did nothing and relied solely on Drexel and on the lawyers, are also bound by it. It follows that although Drexel and the other underwriters believed that those portions of the prospectus were true, they had no reasonable ground for that belief, within the meaning of the statute. Hence, they have not established their due diligence defense, except as to the 1960 audited figures.

[The decision with respect to the auditors Peat, Marwick is presented in the next chapter.]

Antifraud Provision

BASIC INC. v. LEVINSON

United States Supreme Court, 1988.
485 U.S. 224, 108 S.Ct. 978, 99 L.Ed. 194.

BLACKMUN, J.

Prior to December 20, 1978, Basic Incorporated was a publicly traded company primarily engaged in the business of manufacturing chemical refractories for the steel industry. As early as 1965 or 1966, Combustion Engineering, Inc., a company producing mostly alumina-based refractories, expressed some interest in acquiring Basic, but was deterred from pursuing this inclination seriously because of antitrust concerns it then entertained. In 1976, however, regulatory action opened the way to a renewal of Combustion's interest.

Beginning in September 1976, Combustion representatives had meetings and telephone conversations with Basic officers and directors, including petitioners here, concerning the possibility of a merger. During 1977 and 1978, Basic made three public statements denying that it was engaged in merger negotiations. On December 18, 1978, Basic asked the New York Stock Exchange to suspend trading in its shares and issued a release stating that it had been "approached" by another company concerning a merger. On December 19, Basic's board endorsed Combustion's offer of $46 per share for its common stock, and on the following day publicly announced its approval of Combustion's tender offer for all outstanding shares.

Respondents are former Basic shareholders who sold their stock after Basic's first public statement of October 21, 1977, and before the suspension of trading in December 1978. Respondents brought a class action against Basic and its directors, asserting that the defendants issued three false or misleading public statements and thereby were in violation of section 10(b) of the 1934 Act and of Rule 10b–5. Respondents alleged that they were injured by selling Basic shares at artificially depressed prices in a market affected by petitioners' misleading statements and in reliance thereon.

* * *

The fraud on the market theory is based on the hypothesis that, in an open and developed securities market, the price of a company's stock is determined by the available material information regarding the company and its business. . . . Misleading statements will therefore defraud purchasers of stock even if the purchasers do not directly rely on the misstatements. . . . The causal connection between the defendants' fraud and the plaintiffs' purchase of stock in such a case is no less significant than in a case of direct reliance on misrepresentations. [Citation.]

* * *

Petitioners and their amici complain that the fraud-on-the-market theory effectively eliminates the requirement that a plaintiff asserting a claim under Rule 10b–5 prove reliance. They note that reliance is, and long has been, an element of common-law fraud, [citation], and argue that because the analogous express right of action includes a reliance requirement, see, e.g., section 18(a) of the 1934 Act, as amended, so too must an action implied under section 10(b).

We agree that reliance is an element of a Rule 10b–5 cause of action. [Citation.] Reliance provides the requisite causal connection between a defendant's misrepresentation and a plaintiff's injury. * * *

The modern securities markets, literally millions of shares changing hands daily, differ from the face-to-face transactions contemplated by early fraud cases, and our understanding of Rule 10b–5's reliance requirement must encompass these differences.

In face-to-face transactions, the inquiry into an investor's reliance upon information is into the subjective pricing of that information by that investor. With the presence of a market, the market is interposed between seller and buyer and, ideally, transmits information to the investor in the processed form of a market price. Thus the market is performing a substantial part of the valuation process performed by the investor in a face-to-face transaction. The market is acting as the unpaid agent of the investor, informing him that given all the information available to it, the value of the stock is worth the market price. [Citation.]

* * *

Presumptions typically serve to assist courts in managing circumstances in which direct proof, for one reason or another, is rendered difficult. [Citation.] The courts below accepted a presumption, created by the fraud-on-the-market theory and subject to rebuttal by petitioners, that persons who had traded Basic shares had done so in reliance on the integrity of the price set by the market, but because of petitioners' material misrepresentations that price had been fraudulently depressed. Requiring a plaintiff to show a speculative state of facts, i.e., how he would have acted if omitted material information had been disclosed, [citation], or if the misrepresentation had not been made, [citation], would place an unnecessarily unrealistic evidentiary burden on the Rule 10b–5 plaintiff who has traded on an impersonal market. [Citation.]

Arising out of considerations of fairness, public policy, and probability, as well as judicial economy, presumptions are also useful devices for allocating the burdens of proof between parties. [Citations.] The presumption of reliance employed in this case is consistent with, and, by facilitating Rule 10b–5 litigation, supports, the congressional policy embodied in the 1934 Act. In drafting that Act, Congress expressly relied on the premise that securities markets are affected by information, and enacted legislation to facilitate an investor's reliance on the integrity of those markets:

No investor, no speculator, can safely buy and sell securities upon the exchanges without having an intelligent basis for forming his judgment as to the value of the securities he buys or sells. The idea of a free and open public market is built upon the theory that competing judgments of buyers and sellers as to the fair price of a security brings about a situation where the market price reflects as nearly as possible a just price. Just as artificial manipulation tends to upset the true function of an open market, so the hiding and secreting of important information obstructs the operation of the markets as indices of real value. [Citation.]

The presumption is also supported by common sense and probability. Recent empirical studies have tended to confirm Congress' premise that the market price of shares traded on well-developed markets reflects all publicly available information, and, hence, any material misrepresentations. It has been noted that "it is hard to imagine that there ever is a buyer or seller who does not rely on market integrity. Who would knowingly roll the dice in a crooked crap game?" Indeed, nearly every court that has considered the proposition has concluded that where materially misleading statements have been disseminated into an impersonal, well-developed market for securities, the reliance of individual plaintiffs on the integrity of the market price may be presumed. Commentators generally have applauded the adoption of one variation or another of the fraud-on-the-market theory. An investor who buys or sells stock at the price set by the market does so in reliance on the integrity of that price. Because most publicly available information is reflected in market price, an investor's reliance on any public material misrepresentations, therefore, may be presumed for purposes of a Rule 10b–5 action.

* * *

The Court of Appeals found that petitioners "made public, material misrepresentations and respondents sold Basic stock in an impersonal, efficient market. Thus the class, as defined by the district court, has established the threshold facts for proving their loss." The court acknowledged that petitioners may rebut proof of the elements giving rise to the presumption, or show that the misrepresentation in fact did not lead to a distortion of price or that an individual plaintiff traded or would have traded despite his knowing the statement was false.

Any showing that severs the link between the alleged misrepresentation and either the price received (or paid) by the plaintiff, or his decision to trade at a fair market price, will be sufficient to rebut the presumption of reliance. For example, if petitioners could show that the "market makers" were privy to the truth about the merger discussions here with Combustion, and thus that the market price would not have been affected by their misrepresentations, the causal connection could be broken: the basis for finding that the fraud had been transmitted through market price would be gone. Similarly, if, despite petitioners' allegedly fraudulent attempt to manipulate market price, news of the merger discussions credibly entered the market and dissipated the effects of the misstatements, those who traded Basic shares after the corrective statements would have no direct or indirect connection with the fraud. Petitioners also could rebut the presumption of reliance as to plaintiffs who would have divested themselves of their Basic shares without relying on the integrity of the market. For example, a plaintiff who believed that Basic's statements were false and that Basic was indeed engaged in merger discussions, and who consequently believed that Basic stock was artificially underpriced, but sold his shares nevertheless because of other unrelated concerns, e.g., potential antitrust problems, or political pressures to divest from shares of certain businesses, could not be said to have relied on the integrity of a price he knew had been manipulated.

Fraudulent Tender Offers

SCHREIBER v. BURLINGTON NORTHERN, INC.

Supreme Court of the United States, 1985.
472 U.S. 1, 105 S.Ct. 2458, 86 L.Ed.2d 1.

BURGER, C.J.

On December 21, 1982, Burlington Northern, Inc., made a hostile tender offer for El Paso Gas Co. Through a wholly owned subsidiary, Burlington proposed to purchase 25.1 million El Paso shares at $24 per share. Burlington reserved the right to terminate the offer if any of several specified events occurred. El Paso management initially opposed the takeover, but its shareholders responded favorably, fully subscribing the offer by the December 30, 1982 deadline.

Burlington did not accept those tendered shares; instead, after negotiations with El Paso management, Burlington announced on January 10, 1983, the terms of a new and friendly takeover agreement. Pursuant to the new agreement, Burlington undertook, *inter alia,* to (1) rescind the December tender offer, (2) purchase 4,166,667 shares from El Paso at $24 per share, (3) substitute a new tender offer for only 21 million shares at $24 per share, (4) provide procedural protections against a squeeze-out merger of the remaining El Paso shareholders, and (5) recognize "golden parachute" contracts between El Paso and four of its senior officers. By February 8, more than 40 million shares were tendered in response to Burlington's January offer, and the takeover was completed.

The rescission of the first tender offer caused a diminished payment to those shareholders who had tendered during the first offer. The January offer was greatly oversubscribed and consequently those shareholders who retendered were subject to substantial proration. Petitioner Barbara Schreiber filed suit on behalf of herself and similarly situated shareholders, alleging that Burlington, El Paso, and members of El Paso's board violated § 14(e)'s prohibition of "fraudulent, deceptive or manipulative acts or practices . . . in connection with any tender offer." [Citation.] She claimed that Burlington's withdrawal of the December tender offer coupled with the substitution of the January tender offer was a "manipulative" distortion of the market for El Paso stock. Schreiber also alleged that Burlington violated § 14(e) by failing in the January offer to disclose the "golden parachutes" offered to four of El Paso's managers. She claims that this January nondisclosure was a deceptive act forbidden by § 14(e).

The District Court dismissed the suit for failure to state a claim. * * *

* * *

We are asked in this case to interpret § 14(e) of the Securities Exchange Act, [citation]. The starting point is the language of the statute. Section 14(e) provides:

"It shall be unlawful for any person to make any untrue statement of a material fact or omit to state any material fact necessary in order to make the statements made, in the light of the circumstances under which they are made, not misleading, or to engage in any fraudulent, deceptive or manipulative acts or practices, in connection with any tender offer or request or invitation for tenders, or any solicitation of security holders in opposition to or in favor of any such offer, request, or invitation. The Commission shall, for the purposes of this subsection, by rules and regulations define, and prescribe means reasonably designed to prevent, such acts and practices as are fraudulent, deceptive, or manipulative." [Citation.]

Petitioner relies on a construction of the phrase, "fraudulent, deceptive or manipulative acts or practices." Petitioner reads the phrase "fraudulent, deceptive or manipulative acts or practices" to include acts which, although fully disclosed, "artificially" affect the price of the takeover target's stock. Petitioner's interpretation relies on the belief that § 14(e) is directed at purposes broader than providing full and true information to investors.

Petitioner's reading of the term "manipulative" conflicts with the normal meaning of the term. We have held in the context of an alleged violation of § 10(b) of the Securities Exchange Act:

"Use of the word 'manipulative' is especially significant. It is and was virtually a term of art when used in connection with the securities markets. It connotes intentional or willful conduct *designed to deceive or defraud* investors by controlling or artificially affecting the price of securities." *Ernst & Ernst v. Hochfelder,* [see Chapter 46].

* * * The meaning the Court has given the term "manipulative" is consistent with the use of the term at common law, and with its traditional dictionary definition.

She argues, however, that the term manipulative takes on a meaning in § 14(e) that is different from the meaning it has in § 10(b). Petitioner claims that the use of the disjunctive "or" in § 14(e) implies that acts need not be deceptive or fraudulent to be manipulative. But Congress used the phrase "manipulative or deceptive" in § 10(b) as well, and we have interpreted "manipulative" in that context to require misrepresentation. Moreover, it is a " 'familiar principle of statutory construction that words grouped in a list should be given related meaning.' " [Citation.] All three species of misconduct, i.e., "fraudulent, deceptive or manipulative," listed by Congress are directed at failures to disclose. The use of the term "manipulative" provides emphasis and guidance to those who must determine which types of acts are reached by the statute; it does not suggest a deviation from the section's facial and primary concern with disclosure or Congressional concern with disclosure which is the core of the Act.

* * *

Our conclusion that "manipulative" acts under § 14(e) require misrepresentation or nondisclosure is buttressed by the purpose and legislative history of the provision. Section 14(e) was originally added to the Securities Exchange Act as part of the Williams Act, [citation]. "The purpose of the Williams Act is to insure that public shareholders who are confronted by a cash tender offer for their stock will not be required to respond without adequate information." [Citation.]

* * *

Nowhere in the legislative history is there the slightest suggestion that § 14(e) serves any purpose other than disclosure, or that the term "manipulative" should be read as an invitation to the courts to oversee the substantive fairness of tender offers; the quality of any offer is a matter for the marketplace.

* * *

We hold that the term "manipulative" as used in § 14(e) requires misrepresentation or nondisclosure. It connotes "conduct designed to deceive or defraud investors by controlling or artificially affecting the price of securities." *Ernst & Ernst v. Hochfelder,* [see Chapter 46]. Without misrepresentation or nondisclosure, § 14(e) has not been violated.

Applying that definition to this case, we hold that the actions of respondents were not manipulative. The amended complaint fails to allege that the cancellation of the first tender offer was accompanied by any misrepresentation, nondisclosure or deception. The District Court correctly found, "All activity of the defendants that could have conceivably affected the price of El Paso shares was done openly." [Citation.]

* * *

The judgment of the Court of Appeals is *Affirmed.*

QUESTIONS

1. Distinguish between exempt securities and exempt transactions under the 1933 Act. List four examples of each.

2. Discuss the potential civil liabilities under the 1933 Act.

3. Distinguish between publicly held companies under the 1934 Act and those that are not publicly held. Which provisions of the 1934 Act apply only to publicly held and which apply to all companies?

4. Discuss the requirements and applications of Rule 10b–5.

5. Discuss (a) tender offers and (b) proxy solicitations.

PROBLEMS

1. Acme Realty, a real estate development company, is a limited partnership organized in Georgia. It is planning to develop a 200-acre parcel of land for a regional shopping center and needs to raise $1,250,000. As part of its financing, Acme plans to offer $1,250,000 worth of limited partnership interests to about one hundred prospective investors in the southeastern United States. It anticipates that about forty to fifty private investors will purchase the limited partnership interests.

(a) Must Acme register this offering? Why or why not?

(b) If Acme must register but fails to do so, what are the legal consequences?

2. Bigelow Corporation has total assets of $850,000, sales of $1,350,000, one class of common stock with 375 shareholders, and a class of preferred stock with 250 shareholders, both of which are traded over the counter. Which provisions of the Securities Exchange Act of 1934 apply to Bigelow Corporation?

3. Capricorn, Inc., is planning to "go public" by offering its common stock, which had been previously owned by only three shareholders. The company intends to limit the number of purchasers to twenty-five persons resident in the State of its incorporation. All of Capricorn's business and all of its assets are located in the State of incorporation. Based upon these facts, what exemptions from registration, if any, are available to Capricorn, and what conditions would each of these available exemptions impose upon the terms of the offer?

4. The boards of directors of DuMont Corp. and Epsot, Inc., agreed to enter into a friendly merger with DuMont Corp. to be the surviving entity. The stock of both corporations was listed on a national stock exchange. In connection with the merger both corporations distributed to their shareholders proxy statements seeking approval of the proposed merger. The shareholders of both corporations voted to approve the merger. About three weeks after the merger was consummated, the price of DuMont Corp. stock fell from $25 to $13 as a result of the discovery that Epsot, Inc., had entered into several unprofitable long-term contracts two months before the merger had been proposed. The contracts will result in substantial losses from Epsot's operations for at least the next four years. The existence and effect of these contracts, although known to both corporations at the time of the proposed merger, were not disclosed in the proxy statements of either corporation. Shareholders of DuMont Corp. bring suit against DuMont Corp. under the 1934 Act. Decision?

5. Farthing is a director and vice-president of Garp, Inc., whose common stock is listed on the New York Stock Exchange. Farthing engaged in the following transactions in the same calendar year: on January 1, Farthing sold 500 shares at $30 per share; on January 15, she purchased 300 shares at $30 per share; on February 1, she purchased 200 shares at $45 per share; on March 1, she purchased 300 shares at $60 per share; on March 15, she sold 200 shares at $55 per share; and on April 1, she sold 100 shares at $40 per share. Howell brings suit on behalf of Garp alleging that Farthing has violated the Securities Exchange Act of 1934. Farthing defends on the ground that she lost money on the transactions in question. Decision?

6. Intercontinental Widgets, Inc., had applied for a patent for a new state-of-the-art widget which, if patented, would significantly increase the value of Intercontinental's shares. On September 1, the Patent Office notified Jackson, the attorney for Intercontinental, that the patent application had been approved. After informing Kingsley, the president of Intercontinental, of the good news, Jackson called his broker and purchased 1,000 shares of Intercontinental at $18 per share. He also told his partner, Lucas, who immediately proceeded to purchase 500 shares at $19 per share. Lucas then called his brother-in-law, Mammon, and told him the news. On September 3, Mammon bought 4,000 shares at $21 per share. On September 4, Kingsley issued a press release which accurately reported that a patent had been granted to Intercontinental. On the next day Intercontinental's stock soared to $38 per share. A class action suit is brought against Jackson, Lucas, Mammon, and Intercontinental for violations of Rule 10b–5. Who, if anyone, is liable?

7. Nova, Inc., sought to sell a new issue of common stock. It registered the issue with the Securities and Exchange Commission but included false information in both the registration statement and the prospectus. The issue was under-written by Omega & Sons and was sold in its entirety by Periwinkle, Ramses, and Sheffield, Inc., a securities broker-dealer. Telford purchased 500 shares at $6 per share. Three months later the falsity of the information contained in the prospectus was made public and the price of the shares fell to $1 per share. The following week Telford brought suit against Nova, Inc., Omega & Sons, and Periwinkle, Ramses and Sheffield, Inc. under the Securities Act of 1933.

(a) Who, if anyone, is liable under the act?

(b) What defenses, if any, are available to the various defendants?

8. Tanaka, a director and officer of Deep Hole Oil Company, approached Romani for the purpose of buying 200 shares of Deep Hole Company stock owned by Romani. During the period of negotiations, Tanaka concealed his identity and did not disclose the fact that earlier in the day he had received a report of two rich oil strikes on the oil company's property. Romani sold his 200 shares to Tanaka for $10 per share. Taking into consideration the new strikes, the fair value of the stock was approximately $20 per share. Romani sues Tanaka to recover damages. Decision?

9. Venable Corporation has 750,000 shares of common stock outstanding, which is owned by 640 shareholders. The assets of Venable Corporation are valued at over $5 million dollars. In March, Underhill began purchasing shares of Venable's common stock in the open market. By April, he had acquired 40,000 shares at prices ranging from $12 to $14. Upon discovering Underhill's activities in late April, the directors of Venable had the corporation purchase the 40,000 shares from Underhill for $18 per share. Which provisions of the 1934 Act, if any, have been violated?

10. In 1973, Dirks was an officer of a New York broker-dealer firm who specialized in providing investment analysis of insurance company securities to institutional investors. On March 6, Dirks received information from Ronald Secrist, a former officer of Equity Funding of America. Secrist alleged that the assets of Equity Funding, a diversified corporation primarily engaged in selling life insurance and mutual funds, were vastly overstated as the result of fraudulent corporate practices. Dirks decided to investigate the allegations. He visited Equity Funding's headquarters in Los Angeles and interviewed several officers

and employees of the corporation. The senior management denied any wrongdoing, but certain corporation employees corroborated the charges of fraud. Neither Dirks nor his firm owned or traded any Equity Funding stock, but throughout his investigation he openly discussed the information he had obtained with a number of clients and investors. Some of these persons sold their holdings of Equity Funding securities, including five investment advisers who liquidated holdings of more than $16 million.

While Dirks was in Los Angeles, he was in touch regularly with William Blundell, the *Wall Street Journal*'s Los Angeles bureau chief. Dirks urged Blundell to write a story on the fraud allegations. Blundell did not believe, however, that such a massive fraud could go undetected and declined to write the story. He feared that publishing such damaging hearsay might be libelous.

During the two-week period in which Dirks pursued his investigation and spread word of Secrist's charges, the price of Equity Funding stock fell from $26 per share to less than $15 per share. This led the New York Stock Exchange to halt trading on March 27. Shortly thereafter, California insurance authorities impounded Equity Funding's records and uncovered evidence of the fraud. Only then did the Securities and Exchange Commission (SEC) file a complaint against Equity Funding.

The SEC began an investigation into Dirks's role in the exposure of the fraud. After a hearing by an administrative law judge, the SEC found that Dirks had aided and abetted violations of Section 10(b) of the Securities Exchange Act of 1934 and SEC Rule 10b–5 by repeating the allegations of fraud to members of the investment community who later sold their Equity Funding stock. Recognizing, however, that Dirks "played an important role in bringing Equity Funding's massive fraud to light," the SEC only censured him. Dirks appealed. Decision?

11. Texas Gulf Sulphur Company (TGS) was a corporation engaged in the exploration for and mining of certain minerals. A particular tract of land in Canada looked very promising as a source of desired minerals, and a test hole was drilled by Texas Gulf on November 8, 1963. Because the core sample of the hole contained minerals of amazing quality, Texas Gulf began to acquire surrounding tracts of land. Stevens, the president of Texas Gulf, instructed all on-site personnel to keep the find a secret. Because subsequent test drillings were performed, the amount of activity surrounding the drilling had resulted in rumors as to the size and quality of the find. To counteract these rumors, Stevens authorized a press release denying the validity of the rumors and described them as excessively optimistic. The release was issued on April 12, 1964, though drilling continued through April 15. In the meantime, several officers, directors, and employees had purchased or accepted options to purchase additional Texas Gulf stock on the basis of the information concerning the drilling. They also recommended similar purchases to outsiders without divulging the inside information to the public. At 10 A.M. on April 16, an accurate report on the find was finally released to the American financial press. The SEC brought this action against Texas Gulf Sulphur and several of its officers, directors, and employees to enjoin conduct alleged to violate Section 10(b) of the Securities Act of 1934 and to compel rescission by the individual defendants of securities transactions assertedly conducted in violation of Rule 10b–5. Decision?

Chapter 46

ACCOUNTANTS' LEGAL LIABILITY

Contract Liability
Tort Liability
Criminal Liability
Federal Securities Law

ACCOUNTANTS perform a number of important roles in our business society. One of them is providing reliable financial information to facilitate the effective and efficient allocation of resources in the economy. As Harold M. Williams, former Chairman of the Securities and Exchange Commission, stated: "Obviously, if users of financial data, who often may have little or no contact with the business in question, could not trust in its financial statements, capital formation and lending could not be carried on as they are today."

An accountant is subject to potential civil liability arising from the professional services he provides to his clients and third parties. This legal liability is imposed by both the common law at the State level as well as the securities laws at the Federal level. In addition, an accountant may violate Federal or State criminal law in connection with the performance of his professional activities. This chapter will deal with accountants' legal liability under both State and Federal law.

COMMON LAW

An accountant's legal responsibility under State law may be based upon (1) contract law, (2) tort law, or (3) criminal law. In addition, the common law provides accountants with certain rights and privileges; in particular, ownership of their working papers and, in some States, a limited accountant-client privilege.

Contract Liability

The employment contract between an accountant and her client is subject to the general principles of contract law. All of the requirements of a common law contract must be present for the contract to be binding, including offer and acceptance, capacity, consideration, legality, and a writing if, as is often the case, the agreement falls within the one-year provision of the statute of frauds.

Upon entering into a binding contract (frequently referred to as an *engagement*), the accountant is bound to perform all the duties she **explicitly** agrees to provide under the contract. For example, if an accountant agrees to complete her audit of the client by October 15 to enable the client to release its annual report on time, the accountant is under a contractual obligation to do so. Likewise, if an accountant contractually promises to conduct an audit for the client to detect possible embezzlement, the accountant is under a contractual obligation to provide an audit *beyond* Generally Accepted Auditing Standards (GAAS) and must conduct an expanded audit.

By entering into a contract, an accountant also **implicitly** agrees to perform the contract in a competent and professional manner. By agreeing to render professional services, an accountant is held to those standards that are generally accepted by the accounting profession, such as GAAS and Generally Accepted Accounting Practices (GAAP). Although accountants are not insurers that their work is absolutely accurate, they must exercise the care of a reasonably skilled professional.

If an accountant breaches his contract, he will incur liability not only to his client but also to certain third-party beneficiaries. A **third-party beneficiary** is a noncontracting party whom the contracting parties *intended* to receive the *primary* benefit under the contract. For example, Otis Manufacturing Co. hires Adler, an accountant, to prepare Otis's financial statement for Otis to use in order to obtain a loan from Chemical Bank. Chemical Bank is a third-party beneficiary of the contract between Otis and Adler. For a more detailed discussion of third-party beneficiaries see Chapter 15.

Pursuant to general contract principles, an accountant will not be entitled to any compensation if he *materially breaches* his contract. Thus, if an accountant does not perform his audit on time when time is of the essence, or if the accountant completes only 60 percent of the audit, he has materially breached the contract. On the other hand, if the accountant *substantially performs* his contractual duties, he is generally entitled to be compensated for the contractually agreed upon fee less any damages or loss his nonmaterial breach has caused the client. (See Chapter 17.)

Tort Liability

In performing his professional services, an accountant may incur tort liability to his client or third parties for negligence or fraud. A tort, as discussed in Chapters 5 (intentional torts, including fraud) and 6 (negligence), is a private or civil wrong or injury, other than a breach of contract, for which the courts will provide a remedy in the form of an action for damages.

Negligence An accountant is negligent if she does not exercise the degree of care a reasonably competent accountant would exercise under the circumstances. For example, Arthur, an accountant, is engaged to audit the books of Zebra Corporation. During the course of Arthur's investigation, Arthur is notified by Olivia, an officer of Zebra, that Olivia suspects that Terrence, Zebra's treasurer, is engaged in a scheme to embezzle from the corporation. Arthur does not pursue the matter since she was previously informed that Olivia and Terrence are on bad terms with each other. Terrence, in fact, was engaged in a commonly used scheme of embezzlement. Arthur is negligent for failing to conduct a reasonable investigation of the alleged defalcation. Nonetheless, an accountant is *not* liable for honest inaccuracies or errors of judgment so long as she exercised reasonable care in performing her duties. Moreover, as previously mentioned, an accountant is *not an insurer* of the accuracy of her reports provided she acted in a reasonably competent and professional manner.

Historically, an accountant's liability for negligence extended only to the client and to third-party beneficiaries. Under this view, **privity** of contract was a requirement to a cause of action based upon negligence. This approach was established by the landmark case, *Ultramares Corporation v. Touche*, 255 N.Y. 170, 174 N.E. 441 (1931):

The defendants owed to their employer a duty imposed by law to make their certificate without fraud, and a duty growing out of contract to make it with the care and caution proper to their calling. Fraud includes the pretense of knowledge when knowledge there is none. To creditors and investors to whom the employer exhibited the certificate, the defendants owed a like duty to make it without fraud, since there was notice in the circumstances of its making that the employer did not intend to keep it to himself. [Citations.] A different question develops when we ask whether they owed a duty to these to make it without negligence. If liability for negligence exists, a thoughtless slip or blunder, the failure to detect a theft or forgery beneath the cover of deceptive entries, may expose accountants to a liability in an indeterminate amount for an indeterminate time to an indeterminate class. The hazards of a business conducted on these terms are so extreme as to enkindle doubt whether a flaw may not exist in the implication of a duty that exposes to these consequences.

* * *

Our holding does not emancipate accountants from the consequences of fraud. It does not relieve them if their audit has been so negligent as to justify a finding that they had no genuine belief in its adequacy, for this again is fraud. It does no more than say that, if less than this is proved, if there has been neither reckless misstatement nor insincere profession of an opinion, but only honest blunder, the ensuing liability for negligence is one that is bounded by the contract and is to be enforced between the parties by whom the contract has been made. We doubt whether the average business man receiving a certificate without paying for it, and receiving it merely as one among a multitude of possible investors, would look for anything more.

Today, three different tests are applied to determine accountants' liability for negligence to third parties. The *Ultramares* test has evolved into a **primary-benefit** test, which is followed in only a few States. This test, as explained in *Credit Alliance Corp. v. Arthur Andersen & Co.*, 65 N.Y.2d 536 (1985), is as follows:

Before accountants may be held liable in negligence to noncontractual parties who rely to their detriment on inaccurate financial reports, certain prerequisites must be satisfied: (1) the accountants must have been aware that the financial reports were to be used for a particular purpose or purposes; (2) in the furtherance of which a known party or parties was intended to rely; and (3) there must have been some conduct on the part of the accountants linking them to that party or parties, which evinces the accountants' understanding of that party or parties' reliance.

In recent years a majority of the States has adopted a **foreseen users** or **foreseen class of users** test. This test expands the class of protected individuals to those who the accountant knew would use the work product *or* those who use the accountant's work for a purpose for which the accountant knew the work would be used. For instance, an accountant knows that the client will use the work product to try to obtain a bank loan from NCNB. Even if the client uses the audited financial statements to obtain a loan from a different bank, the auditor would be liable to that bank for any negligent misrepresentations in the financial statements. This class of protected individuals does not, however, include potential investors and the general public.

This approach has also been adopted by the Restatement of Torts. Section 552 provides:

(1) One who, in the course of his business, profession or employment, or in any other transaction in which he has a pecuniary interest, supplies false information for the guidance of others in their business transactions, is subject to liability for pecuniary loss caused to them by their justifiable reliance upon the information, if he fails to exercise reasonable care or competence in obtaining or communicating the information.

(2) Except as stated in Subsection (3), the liability stated in Subsection (1) is limited to loss suffered

(a) by the person or one of a limited group of persons for whose benefit and guidance he intends to supply the information or knows that the recipient intends to supply it; and

(b) through reliance upon it in a transaction that he intends the information to influence or knows that the recipient so intends or in a substantially similar transaction.

(3) The liability of one who is under a public duty to give the information extends to loss suffered by any of the class of persons for whose benefit the duty is created, in any of the transactions in which it is intended to protect them.

Some courts have extended liability to benefit an even broader group: reasonably **foreseeable plaintiffs** who are neither known nor a member of a class of intended recipients. A few States have adopted this test, which requires only that the accountant reasonably foresee that such an individual might use the financial statements. The rationale behind this approach is that a tortfeasor should be fully liable for all reasonably foreseeable consequences of her conduct. *See*

International Mortgage Co. v. John P. Butler Accountancy Corp.

Fraud An accountant who commits a fraudulent act is liable to any person who the accountant *should have* reasonably foreseen would be injured by the misrepresentation and who justifiably relied upon it. The requisite elements of fraud, which are more fully discussed in Chapter 10, are: (1) a false representation (2) of fact (3) that is material, (4) made with *knowledge* of its falsity and with the *intention* to deceive, (5) is justifiably relied upon, and (6) causes injury to the plaintiff. An accountant who commits fraud may be held liable for *both* compensatory and punitive damages.

In recent years, accountants have also been subject to a number of civil lawsuits based on the Racketeering Influenced and Corrupt Organizations Act (RICO). For a discussion of the requirements of this act see Chapter 4.

Criminal Liability

An accountant's potential criminal liability in rendering professional services is primarily based on the Federal law of securities regulation (discussed below) and taxation. Nonetheless, an accountant would violate State criminal law if she knowingly and willfully certified false documents, altered or tampered with accounting records, used false financial reports, gave false testimony under oath, or committed forgery.

Criminal sanctions may be imposed under the Internal Revenue Code for knowingly preparing false or fraudulent tax returns or documents used in connection with a tax return. Such liability also extends to willfully assisting or advising a client or others to prepare a false return. Penalties may be a fine not to exceed $5,000 or three years imprisonment or both.

Client Information

In providing services for his client an accountant necessarily obtains information concerning the client's business affairs. Two legal issues arise concerning this client information: (1) who owns the working papers generated by the accountant, and (2) is the client information privileged.

Working Papers Audit working papers include the records kept by the auditor of the procedures followed, the tests performed, the information obtained, and the conclusions reached pertaining to the audit. All relevant information obtained in connection with the examination should be included in the working papers. An accountant is held to be the owner of his working papers and thus need not surrender them to his client. Nevertheless, the accountant may not disclose the contents of these papers unless either (1) the client consents or (2) a court orders the disclosure.

Accountant-Client Privilege The issue of confidentiality of communication between the accountant and his client is important because, if such information is considered to be privileged, it may not be admitted into evidence over the objection of the person possessing the privilege. The question of a possible accountant-client privilege frequently arises in tax disputes, criminal prosecution, and civil litigation.

Neither the common law nor Federal law recognizes such a privilege. *See United States v. Arthur Young & Company.* Nevertheless, a number of States have adopted statutes granting some form of accountant-client privilege. Most of these statutes grant the privilege to the client, although a few extend the privilege to the accountant. Regardless of whether the privilege exists, it is generally considered to be professionally unethical for an accountant to disclose confidential communications from his client unless the disclosure is in accordance with (1) American Institute of Certified Public Accountants (AICPA) or GAAS requirements, (2) a court order, or (3) the client's request.

FEDERAL SECURITIES LAW

Accountants may be both civilly and criminally liable under provisions of the Securities Act of 1933 and the Securities Exchange Act of 1934. This liability is more extensive and has fewer limitations than liability under the common law.

Securities Act of 1933

Accountants are subject to express **civil** liability under Section 11 if the financial statements they prepare or certify for inclusion in a registration statement contain any untrue statement or omission of material fact. This liability extends to anyone who acquires the security without knowledge of the untruth or omission. Not only is there no requirement of privity between the accountant and the purchasers, but proof of reliance upon the financial statements is also usually not required under Section 11. An accountant will not be liable, however, if he can prove his "due diligence defense." **Due diligence** requires that the accountant had, after reasonable investigation, reasonable ground to believe and did believe, at the *time* the registration statement became *effective,* that the financial statements were true, complete, and accurate. The standard of reasonableness is that required of a prudent man in the management of his own property. Thus, Section 11 imposes liability upon accountants for **negligence** in the conduct of the audit or presentation of the information in the financial statements. *See Escott v. BarChris Construction Corp.*

Moreover, if an accountant *willfully* violates this section, he may be held **criminally** liable for a fine of not more than $10,000 or imprisonment of not more than five years or both. Section 24.

Securities Exchange Act of 1934

Section 18 imposes express **civil** liability upon an accountant if she makes or causes to be made any false or misleading statement with respect to any material fact in any application, report, document, or registration filed with the SEC under the 1934 Act. Liability extends to any person who purchased or sold a security in reliance upon that false or misleading statement without knowing that it was false or misleading. An accountant is not liable, however, if she proves that she acted in good faith and had no knowledge that such statement was false or misleading. Thus, an accountant is *not* liable for false or misleading statements resulting from negligence.

Accountants may also be held **civilly** liable for violations of **Rule 10b–5.** Their liability may be for direct participation in a violation of the rule or for indirect participation resulting from their aiding and abetting others to violate the Rule. Rule 10b–5, as previously discussed in Chapter 45, is extremely broad in that it applies to *both* oral and written misstatements or omissions of material fact, and to *all* securities. This liability extends to purchasers and sellers who rely upon the misstatement or omission of material fact in connection with the purchase or sale of a security. Liability is imposed, however, only if the accountant acted with **scienter**, which is intentional or knowing conduct. *See Ernst & Ernst v. Hochfelder.* Therefore, accountants are not liable under Rule 10b–5 for mere negligence although most courts have held that reckless disregard of the truth is sufficient.

Accountants may also be held **criminally** liable for any willful violation of Section 18 or Rule 10b–5. Conviction may carry a fine of not more than $1 million or imprisonment for not more than ten years or both. Section 32.

CASES

Tort Liability

INTERNATIONAL MORTGAGE COMPANY v. JOHN P. BUTLER ACCOUNTANCY CORP.

Court of Appeal, Fourth District, Division 3, 1986.
177 Cal.App.3d 806, 223 Cal.Rptr. 218.

TROTTER, J.

We are asked to declare for the first time that a certified public accountant ("CPA") owes a duty of care to reasonably foreseeable plaintiffs who rely on alleged negligently prepared and issued unqualified audited financial statements.

* * *

John P. Butler Accountancy Corporation ("Butler") entered into an agreement with Westside Mortgage, Inc. ("Westside") to audit Westside's financial statements for the year ending December 31, 1978. Butler completed its audit and issued unqualified audited financial statements on March 22, 1979.

Westside is a mortgage company that arranges financing for real property. It accepts loan applications, screens qualified buyers, obtains real estate appraisals, and then either lends the funds requested or finds outside lenders. The loans are then sold to other mortgage bankers.

The December 31, 1978 financial statements, as audited by Butler, listed Westside's corporate net worth as $175,036. The primary asset shown on its balance sheet was a $100,000 note receivable secured by a deed of trust on real property in Riverside. The footnotes to the financial statements indicated the fair market value of the property to be $115,000 as determined by a January 13, 1975 appraisal. In reality, the note was worthless. The trust deed had been wiped out by a prior foreclosure of a superior deed of trust at a trustee's sale in August 1977.

International Mortgage Company ("IMC"), a subsidiary of Kaufman & Broad, a major real estate developer, approached Westside in October of 1979 for the purpose of buying and selling loans on the secondary market. In order to demonstrate its financial position, Westside provided IMC with copies of the audited financial statements of March 22, 1979.

After reviewing Westside's financial statements, IMC and Westside negotiated a complex master purchase agreement which they signed on December 13, 1979. Under this agreement, Westside and IMC were to buy and sell various government loans, including Federal Housing Administration ("FHA") loans.

The erroneous valuation of the $100,000 trust deed was material to an accurate representation of Westside's financial condition, since the note constituted 57% of Westside's net worth. Without the note, Westside was capitalized at under $100,000 ($75,035) and, thus, not qualified to do business in FHA in-

sured loans such as those included in Westside's contracts with IMC. Butler was aware at the time of the audit that Westside needed to maintain a net worth of at least $100,000 to qualify for FHA business.

Westside entered into a series of contracts to sell government loans to IMC in April 1980. However, it failed to deliver the promised trust deeds to IMC, causing alleged damage of $475,293. In June of 1980, Westside issued a promissory note to IMC for the $475,293; it paid $40,000 on the note and then defaulted on the balance. After further efforts to obtain payment from Westside and its principal owners failed, IMC brought suit against Westside, its owners, principals, and Butler.

IMC alleged two causes of action against Butler: negligence and negligent misrepresentation, based on Westside's financial statements of December 31, 1978, which Butler had audited and issued without qualification. It allegedly relied on the defective financial statements in deciding to do business with Westside.

It was admitted Butler had no knowledge of IMC at the time of the audit, nor did IMC contact Butler to verify the financial statements' accuracy. Further, Butler was unaware of IMC's receipt of, and reliance upon, Westside's financial statements.

Butler moved for summary judgment, arguing that, as a matter of law, a CPA owes no duty of care to a third party who was not specifically known to the accountant as an intended recipient of the audited financial statement. The trial court granted Butler's motion, finding no duty of care existed. This appeal followed.

* * *

The application of the "duty" doctrine to the accounting profession has been unique. Beginning with Justice Cardozo's seminal opinion in Ultramares Corp. v. Touche [citation], certified public accountants have been shielded from liability for negligence in the preparation and issuance of unqualified audited financial statements when the plaintiff was only a member of a foreseeable class. Liability, based on a "duty" analysis, was limited to those "in privity" with the accountant and more recently to those "intended" recipients of the information. (E.g., Rest.2d Torts (1977) § 552.)

* * *

Even as he was limiting accountants liability by requiring privity before a duty could be found, Justice Cardozo recognized such a holding, even in 1931, was against the flow of the common law. For he observed "(t)he assault upon the citadel of privity is proceeding in these days apace. How far the inroads shall extend is now a favorite subject of juridical discussion." [Citation.]

Yet, the privity requirement in accountant malpractice suits has survived the shifting sands of time and remains relatively intact today in most jurisdictions. That the "citadel" has not been breached, insofar as certified public accountants' liability, may well be due to the reputation of the distinguished author of Ultramares. While we recognize his brilliance and the then compelling logic of Ultramares, we assert that, in light of other decisions . . . and the role of an independent auditor in today's society, the rule of Ultramares is no longer consistent with the fundamental principles of California negligence law.

* * *

Thus, even as Ultramares was being articulated, the tide of precedent had already begun to move against the privity rule. The erosion continued, washing away the protection from all other professions, leaving accountancy as some ennobled species specially protected by the "citadel."

. . . Ultramares was clearly based upon a social utility rationale which has been followed under the privity doctrine or some modification thereof. Section 552 of the Restatement of Torts (Second) adopts a limited approach to liability; however, it rejects Ultramares' requirement of privity, settling instead on the reasoning of [citation] in requiring "knowing reliance." [Citation.] One of the bases for the Restatement rule as stated in the comment and by others is the reluctance of courts to impose liability for pecuniary loss alone absent privity. [Citations.]

* * *

Butler claims that basic differences between the accounting profession and others require a more limited rule of liability, whether it be the rule of Ultramares or the Restatement. While manufacturers, attorneys, architects, doctors, and the like control their products and their records, the accountant does not control his client's records, nor does the accountant control the client's use of the audit product. Further, other professionals do not expose themselves or their services to the public for review and possible reliance. He points out, in reality just the opposite occurs. The lawyer's duty generally is to his or her client only. . . . However, such duty is recognized in ethical as well as legal obligations of confidentiality. Further, an attorney's duty is to represent the client to the best of his or her ability without regard to public opinion; so too the medical practitioner, whose duty of care is easily traced to the patient. The same relationship generally exists between all other professionals and their clients. Not so an accountant. [Citations.]

This criticism seems to misunderstand the role of the accountant. An independent auditor (as opposed to an in-house accountant) is employed to analyze a client's financial status and make public the ultimate findings in accord with recognized accounting principles. Such an undertaking is imbued with considerations of public trust, for the accountant must well realize the finished product, the unqualified financial statement, will be relied upon by creditors, stockholders, investors, lenders or anyone else involved in the financial concerns of the audited client. As stated in the AICPA (American Institute of Certified Public Accountants), Professional Standards, Code of Professional Ethics [citation], "The ethical Code of the American Institute (of Certified Public Accountants) emphasizes the profession's responsibility to the public, a responsibility that has grown as the number of investors has grown, as the relationship between corporate managers and stockholders has become more impersonal, and as government increasingly relies on accounting information." Chief Justice Burger, writing for a unanimous United

States Supreme Court in United States v. Arthur Young & Co. [see below], described the role of the independent auditor, "(a)n independent certified public accountant performs a different role. By certifying the public reports that collectively depict a corporation's financial status, the independent auditor assumes a public responsibility transcending any employment relationship with the client. The independent public accountant performing this special function owes ultimate allegiance to the corporation's creditors and stockholders, as well as to the investing public. This 'public watchdog' function demands that the accountant maintain total independence from the client at all times and requires complete fidelity to the public trust. To insulate from disclosure a certified public accountant's interpretations of the client's financial statements would be to ignore the significance of the accountant's role as a disinterested analyst charged with public obligations." [Citation.]

The auditor must, by necessity, be independent of the client. Unlike a manufacturer who guarantees a product's safety, the accountant does not guarantee that the client's financial statements are completely true and without fault. The accountant's audit certification merely guarantees that the financial statements fairly present the firm's financial position in compliance with generally accepted accounting principles ("GAAP"). The professional standards of the AICPA express the auditor's function as follows: "The objective of the ordinary examination of financial statements by the independent auditor is the expression of an opinion on the fairness with which they present financial position, results of operations, and changes in financial position in conformity with generally accepted accounting principles." [Citation.] * * *

Thus, in issuing an opinion, the auditor is guaranteeing only that the numbers comply with the AICPA's standardized accounting rules and procedures, the GAAP. Further, the auditor is guaranteeing that he tested for GAAP compliance using generally accepted auditing standards ("GAAS"). The auditor is not guaranteeing the client's records and re-

sulting financial statements are perfect; only that any errors which might exist could not be detected by an audit conducted under GAAS and GAAP. Thus, the auditor's degree of control over the client's records is unimportant; the auditor need only control his or her abilities to apply GAAS and GAAP to a given audit situation.

Under a foreseeability standard, the auditor would be liable only to those third parties who reasonably and foreseeably rely on the audited statements. The accountant's lack of control over ultimate users is not prejudicial; the foreseeability standard holds everyone, including accountants, liable to only reasonably foreseeable users. [Citations.] It is only reasonable that the same judicial criteria govern the imposition of negligence liability, regardless of the defendant's profession.

We note that other jurisdictions have already held accountants to the same standard of negligence liability as other professionals. In H. Rosenblum, Inc. v. Adler [citation], faced with almost the exact scenario before us, the Supreme Court of New Jersey stated, "(c)ertified financial statements have become the benchmark for various reasonably foreseeable business purposes and accountants have been engaged to satisfy those ends. In those circumstances accounting firms should no longer be permitted to hide within the citadel of privity and avoid liability for their malpractice. * * * Defendants' ignorance of the precise use to which the statements would be put does not eliminate their obligation. * * * (I)t is necessary only that Giant, the entity for whom the audit was being made, used it for a proper business purpose. There was no limitation in the accountants' opinion. They could reasonably expect that their client would distribute the statements in furtherance of matters relating to its business. Having inserted the audit in that economic stream, the defendants should be responsible for their careless misrepresentations to parties who justifiably relied upon their expert opinions." [Citation.] In Citizens State Bank v. Timm, Schmidt & Co. [citation], the court reversed a summary judgment granted on the basis no duty was owed by the defendant accountant to the unknown third party plaintiff who had relied on an audited financial statement prepared by the defendant. The court rejected defendant's reliance on the Restatement Second of Torts, section 552. "Although the absence of privity does not bar this action, the question remains as to the extent of an accountant's liability to injured third parties. Courts which have examined this question have generally relied upon section 552 of the Restatement to restrict the class of third persons who could sue accountants for their negligent acts. Under section 552(2)(a) and (b), liability is limited to loss suffered. * * * [Citation.] The fundamental principle of Wisconsin negligence law is that a tortfeasor is fully liable for all foreseeable consequences of his act except as those consequences are limited by policy factors. * * * [Citation.] The Restatement's statement of limiting liability to certain third parties is too restrictive a statement of policy factors for this Court to adopt." [Citation.]

* * *

We have determined the protectionist rule of privity announced in Ultramares is no longer viable, for the role of the accountant in our modern society has changed. At the time of Ultramares, the primary obligation of the auditor was to the client who hired him or her to detect fraud or embezzlement by the client's employees. As explained earlier, the accountant (independent auditor) today occupies a position of public trust. [Citation.] We also find the Restatement limitation of liability to those "he intends to supply the information or (to those he) knows that the recipient intends to supply it" (Rest.2d Torts, § 552), does not meet California's concept of tort liability for negligence.

* * *

An innocent plaintiff who foreseeably relies on an independent auditor's unqualified financial statement should not be made to bear the burden of the professional's malpractice. The risk of such loss is more appropriately placed on the accounting profession which is better able to pass such risk to its customers and the ultimate consuming public. By doing so, society is better served; for

such a rule provides a financial disincentive for negligent conduct and will heighten the profession's cautionary techniques.

Thus, we find no societal considerations sufficient to create an exception to California's well established general principles of tort liability. We hold an independent auditor owes a duty of care to reasonably foreseeable plaintiffs who rely on negligently prepared and issued unqualified audited financial statements. Having so determined, the summary judgment must be reversed. A question of fact exists as to whether IMC's reliance was reasonably foreseeable and, if so, whether Butler breached the resulting duty. That determination is for the trial court.

The judgment is reversed.

Accountant-Client Privilege

UNITED STATES v. ARTHUR YOUNG & COMPANY

Supreme Court of the United States, 1984.
465 U.S. 805, 104 S.Ct. 1495, 79 L.Ed.2d 826.

BURGER, C. J.

We granted certiorari to consider whether tax accrual workpapers prepared by a corporation's independent certified public accountant in the course of regular financial audits are protected from disclosure in response to an Internal Revenue Service summons issued under [citation].

* * *

Respondent Arthur Young & Co. is a firm of certified public accountants. As the independent auditor for respondent Amerada Hess Corp., Young is responsible for reviewing the financial statements prepared by Amerada as required by the federal securities laws. In the course of its review of these financial statements, Young verified Amerada's statement of its contingent tax liabilities, and, in so doing, prepared the tax accrual workpapers at issue in this case. Tax accrual workpapers are documents and memoranda relating to Young's evaluation of Amerada's reserves for contingent tax liabilities. Such workpapers sometimes contain information pertaining to Amerada's financial transactions, identify questionable positions Amerada may have taken on its tax returns, and reflect Young's opinions regarding the validity of such positions.

In 1975 the Internal Revenue Service began a routine audit to determine Amerada's corporate income tax liability for the tax years 1972 through 1974. When the audit revealed that Amerada had made questionable payments of $7830 from a "special disbursement account," the IRS instituted a criminal investigation of Amerada's tax returns as well. In that process, pursuant to § 7602, the IRS issued an administrative summons to Young, which required Young to make available to the IRS all its Amerada files, including its tax accrual workpapers. Amerada instructed Young not to comply with the summons.

The IRS then commenced this enforcement action against Young in the United States District Court for the Southern District of New York. Amerada intervened, as permitted by [citation]. The District Court found that Young's tax accrual workpapers were relevant to the IRS investigation within the meaning of § 7602 and refused to recognize an accountant-client privilege that would protect the workpapers. [Citation] Accordingly, the District Court ordered the summons enforced.

* * *

A divided United States Court of Appeals for the Second Circuit affirmed in part and reversed in part. . . . the Court of Appeals fashioned a work-product immunity doctrine for tax accrual workpapers prepared by independent auditors in the course of compliance with the federal securities laws. Because the IRS had not demonstrated a sufficient showing of need to overcome the immunity and was not seeking to prove fraud on Amerada's part, the Court of Appeals refused to enforce the summons insofar as it sought Young's tax accrual workpapers.

* * *

We now turn to consider whether tax accrual workpapers prepared by an independent auditor in the course of a routine review

of corporate financial statements should be protected by some form of work-product immunity from disclosure under § 7602. Based upon its evaluation of the competing policies of the federal tax and securities laws, the Court of Appeals found it necessary to create a so-called privilege for the independent auditor's workpapers.

Our complex and comprehensive system of federal taxation, relying as it does upon self-assessment and reporting, demands that all taxpayers be forthright in the disclosure of relevant information to the taxing authorities. Without such disclosure, and the concomitant power of the Government to compel disclosure, our national tax burden would not be fairly and equitably distributed. In order to encourage effective tax investigations, Congress has endowed the IRS with expansive information-gathering authority; . . .

While § 7602 is "subject to the traditional privileges and limitations," [citation], any other restrictions upon the IRS summons power should be avoided "absent unambiguous directions from Congress." [Citation.] We are unable to discern the sort of "unambiguous directions from Congress" that would justify a judicially created work-product immunity for tax accrual workpapers summoned under § 7602. Indeed, the very language of § 7602 reflects precisely the opposite: a congressional policy choice in favor of disclosure of all information relevant to a legitimate IRS inquiry. In light of this explicit statement by the Legislative Branch, courts should be chary in recognizing exceptions to the broad summons authority of the IRS or in fashioning new privileges that would curtail disclosure under § 7602. [Citation.] If the broad latitude granted to the IRS by § 7602 is to be circumscribed, that is a choice for Congress, and not this Court, to make. [Citation.]

* * *

The Court of Appeals nevertheless concluded that "substantial countervailing policies," [citation], required the fashioning of a work-product immunity for an independent auditor's tax accrual workpapers. To the extent that the Court of Appeals, in its concern for the "chilling effect" of the disclosure of tax accrual workpapers, sought to facilitate communication between independent auditors and their clients, its remedy more closely resembles a testimonial accountant-client privilege than a work-product immunity for accountants' workpapers. But as this Court stated in [citation], "no confidential accountant-client privilege exists under federal law, and no state-created privilege has been recognized in federal cases." In light of [citation], the Court of Appeals' effort to foster candid communication between accountant and client by creating a self-styled work-product privilege was misplaced, and conflicts with what we see as the clear intent of Congress.

Nor do we find persuasive the argument that a work-product immunity for accountants' tax accrual workpapers is a fitting analogue to the attorney work-product doctrine established in [citation]. The ... work-product doctrine was founded upon the private attorney's role as the client's confidential advisor and advocate, a loyal representative whose duty it is to present the client's case in the most favorable possible light. An independent certified public accountant performs a different role. By certifying the public reports that collectively depict a corporation's financial status, the independent auditor assumes a public responsibility transcending any employment relationship with the client. The independent public accountant performing this special function owes ultimate allegiance to the corporation's creditors and stockholders, as well as to the investing public. This "public watchdog" function demands that the accountant maintain total independence from the client at all times and requires complete fidelity to the public trust. To insulate from disclosure a certified public accountant's interpretations of the client's financial statements would be to ignore the significance of the accountant's role as a disinterested analyst charged with public obligations.

We cannot accept the view that the integrity of the securities markets will suffer absent some protection for accountants' tax accrual workpapers. The Court of Appeals apparently feared that, were the IRS to have access to tax accrual workpapers, a corporation might be tempted to withhold from its auditor certain information relevant and material to a proper evaluation of its financial statements. But the independent certified public accountant cannot be content with the corporation's representations that its tax accrual reserves are adequate; the auditor is ethically and professionally obligated to ascertain for himself as far as possible whether the corporation's contingent tax liabilities have been accurately stated. If the auditor were convinced that the scope of the examination had been limited by management's reluctance to disclose matters relating to the tax accrual reserves, the auditor would be unable to issue an unqualified opinion as to the accuracy of the corporation's financial statements. Instead, the auditor would be required to issue a qualified opinion, an adverse opinion, or a disclaimer of opinion, thereby notifying the investing public of possible potential problems inherent in the corporation's financial reports. Responsible corporate management would not risk a qualified evaluation of a corporate taxpayer's financial posture to afford cover for questionable positions reflected in a prior tax return. Thus, the independent auditor's obligation to serve the public interest assures that the integrity of the securities markets will be preserved, without the need for a work-product immunity for accountants' tax accrual workpapers.

We also reject respondents' position that fundamental fairness precludes IRS access to accountants' tax accrual workpapers. Respondents urge that the enforcement of an IRS summons for accountants' tax accrual workpapers permits the Government to probe the thought processes of its taxpayer citizens, thereby giving the IRS an unfair advantage in negotiating and litigating tax controversies. But if the SEC itself, or a private plaintiff in securities litigation, sought to obtain the tax accrual workpapers at issue in this case, they would surely be entitled to do so. In light of the broad congressional command of § 7602, no sound reason exists for conferring lesser authority upon the IRS than upon a private litigant suing with regard to transactions concerning which the public has no interest.

Congress has granted to the IRS "broad latitude to adopt enforcement techniques helpful in the performance of (its) tax collection and assessment responsibilities." [Citation.] Recognizing the intrusiveness of demands for the production of tax accrual workpapers, the IRS has demonstrated administrative sensitivity to the concerns expressed by the accounting profession by tightening its internal requirements for the issuance of such summonses. [Citation.] Although these IRS guidelines were not applicable during the years at issue in this case, their promulgation further refutes respondents' fairness argument and reflects an administrative flexibility that reinforces our decision not to reduce irrevocably the § 7602 summons power.

* * *

Beyond question it is desirable and in the public interest to encourage full disclosures by corporate clients to their independent accountants; if it is necessary to balance competing interests, however, the need of the Government for full disclosure of all information relevant to tax liability must also weigh in that balance. This kind of policy choice is best left to the Legislative Branch. Accordingly, the judgment of the Court of Appeals is affirmed in part and reversed in part, and the case is remanded for proceedings consistent with this opinion.

It is so ordered.

Liability under the 1933 Act: Section 11

ESCOTT v. BARCHRIS CONSTRUCTION CORP.

United States District Court, Southern District of New York, 1968.
283 F.Supp. 643.

McLean, J.

This is an action by purchasers of 5½ per cent convertible subordinated fifteen year de-

bentures of BarChris Construction Corporation (BarChris). * * *

The action is brought under Section 11 of the Securities Act of 1933. Plaintiffs allege that the registration statement with respect to these debentures filed with the Securities and Exchange Commission, which became effective on May 16, 1961, contained material false statements and material omissions.

Defendants fall into three categories: (1) the persons who signed the registration statement; (2) the underwriters, consisting of eight investment banking firms, led by Drexel & Co. (Drexel); and (3) BarChris's auditors, Peat, Marwick, Mitchell & Co. (Peat, Marwick).

[The case against the first two categories was presented in Chapter 45.]

* * *

Defendants, in addition to denying that the registration statement was false, have pleaded the defenses open to them under Section 11 of the Act, ... On the main issue of liability, the questions to be decided are (1) did the registration statement contain false statements of fact, or did it omit to state facts which should have been stated in order to prevent it from being misleading; (2) if so, were the facts which were falsely stated or omitted "material" within the meaning of the Act; (3) if so, have defendants established their affirmative defenses?

* * *

In December 1959, BarChris sold 560,000 shares of common stock to the public at $3.00 per share. This issue was underwritten by Peter Morgan & Company, one of the present defendants.

By early 1961, BarChris needed additional working capital. The proceeds of the sale of the debentures involved in this action were to be devoted, in part at least, to fill that need.

The registration statement of the debentures, in preliminary form, was filed with the Securities and Exchange Commission on March 30, 1961. A first amendment was filed on May 11 and a second on May 16. The registration statement became effective on May 16. The closing of the financing took place on May 24. On that day BarChris received the net proceeds of the financing.

By that time BarChris was experiencing difficulties in collecting amounts due from some of its customers. Some of them were in arrears in payments due to factors on their discounted notes. As time went on those difficulties increased. Although BarChris continued to build [bowling] alleys in 1961 and 1962, it became increasingly apparent that the industry was overbuilt. Operators of alleys, often inadequately financed, began to fail. Precisely when the tide turned is a matter of dispute, but at any rate, it was painfully apparent in 1962.

In May of that year BarChris made an abortive attempt to raise more money by the sale of common stock. It filed with the Securities and Exchange Commission a registration statement for the stock issue which it later withdrew. In October 1962 BarChris came to the end of the road. On October 29, 1962, it filed in this court a petition for an arrangement under Chapter XI of the Bankruptcy Act.

* * *

Summary

For convenience, the various falsities and omissions which I have discussed in the preceding pages are recapitulated here. They were as follows:

1. *1960 Earnings*
   (a) *Sales*

As per prospectus	$9,165,320
Correct figure	8,511,420
Overstatement	$ 653,900

   (b) *Net Operating Income*

As per prospectus	$1,742,801
Correct figure	1,496,196
Overstatement	$ 246,605

   (c) *Earnings per Share*

As per prospectus	$ .75
Correct figure	.65
Overstatement	$ .10

2. *1960 Balance Sheet*
   Current Assets

As per prospectus	$4,524,021
Correct figure	3,914,332
Overstatement	$ 609,689

3. *Contingent Liabilities as of December 31, 1960 on Alternative Method of Financing*

As per prospectus	$ 750,000
Correct figure	1,125,795
Understatement	$ 375,795

Capitol Lanes should have been shown as a direct liability	$325,000

4. *Contingent Liabilities as of April 30, 1961*

As per prospectus	$ 825,000
Correct figure	1,443,853
Understatement	$ 618,853
Capitol Lanes should have been shown as a direct liability	$ 314,166

5. *Earnings Figures for Quarter ending March 31, 1961*
   (a) *Sales*

As per prospectus	$2,138,455
Correct figure	1,618,645
Overstatement	$ 519,810

   (b) *Gross Profit*

As per prospectus	$ 483,121
Correct figure	252,366
Overstatement	$ 230,755

6. *Backlog as of March 31, 1961*

As per prospectus	$6,905,000
Correct figure	2,415,000
Overstatement	$4,490,000

7. *Failure to Disclose Officers' Loans Outstanding and Unpaid on May 16, 1961* — $ 386,615

8. *Failure to Disclose Use of Proceeds in Manner not Revealed in Prospectus Approximately* — $1,160,000

9. *Failure to Disclose Customers' Delinquencies In May 1961 and BarChris's Potential Liability with Respect Thereto Over* — $1,350,000

10. *Failure to Disclose the Fact that BarChris was Already Engaged and was about to be More Heavily Engaged, in the Operation of Bowling Alleys*

* * *

Peat, Marwick

Section 11(b) provides:

"Notwithstanding the provisions of subsection (a) no person . . . shall be liable as provided therein who shall sustain the burden of proof—

* * *

"(3) that . . . (B) as regards any part of the registration statement purporting to be made upon his authority as an expert . . . (i) he had, after reasonable investigation, reasonable ground to believe and did believe, at the time such part of the registration statement became effective, that the statements therein were true and that there was no omission to state a material fact required to be stated therein or necessary to make the statements therein not misleading. . . ."

This defines the due diligence defense for an expert. Peat, Marwick has pleaded it.

The part of the registration statement purporting to be made upon the authority of Peat, Marwick as an expert was, as we have seen, the 1960 figures. But because the statute requires the court to determine Peat, Marwick's belief, and the grounds thereof, "at the time such part of the registration statement became effective," for the purposes of this affirmative defense the matter must be viewed as of May 16, 1961, and the question is whether at that time Peat, Marwick, after reasonable investigation, had reasonable ground to believe and did believe that the 1960 figures were true and that no material fact had been omitted from the registration statement which should have been included in order to make the 1960 figures not misleading. In deciding this issue, the court must consider not only what Peat, Marwick did in its 1960 audit, but also what it did in its subsequent "S–1 review."

* * *

The 1960 Audit Peat, Marwick's work was in general charge of a member of the firm, Cummings, and more immediately in charge of Peat, Marwick's manager, Logan. Most of the actual work was performed by a senior accountant, Berardi, who had junior assistants, one of whom was Kennedy.

Berardi was then about thirty years old. He was not yet a C.P.A. He had had no previous experience with the bowling industry. This was his first job as a senior accountant. He could hardly have been given a more difficult assignment.

After obtaining a little background information on BarChris by talking to Logan and reviewing Peat, Marwick's work papers on its 1959 audit, Berardi examined the results of test checks of BarChris's accounting procedures which one of the junior accountants had made, and he prepared an "internal control questionnaire" and an "audit program." Thereafter, for a few days subsequent to December 30, 1960, he inspected BarChris's inventories and examined certain alley construction. Finally, on January 13, 1961, he began his auditing work which he

carried on substantially continuously until it was completed on February 24, 1961. Toward the close of the work, Logan reviewed it and made various comments and suggestions to Berardi. It is unnecessary to recount everything that Berardi did in the course of the audit. We are concerned only with the evidence relating to what Berardi did or did not do with respect to those items which I have found to have been incorrectly reported in the 1960 figures in the prospectus. More narrowly, we are directly concerned only with such of those items as I have found to be material.

Capitol Lanes First and foremost is Berardi's failure to discover that Capitol Lanes had not been sold. The error affected both the sales figure and the liability side of the balance sheet. Fundamentally, the error stemmed from the fact that Berardi never realized that Heavenly Lanes and Capitol were two different names for the same alley.

* * *

In any case, he never identified this mysterious Capitol with the Heavenly Lanes which he had included in his sales and profit figures. The vital question is whether he failed to make a reasonable investigation which, if he had made it, would have revealed the truth.

Certain accounting records of BarChris, which Berardi testified he did not see, would have put him on inquiry. One was a job cost ledger card for job no. 6036, the job number which Berardi put on his own sheet for Heavenly Lanes. This card read "Capitol Theatre (Heavenly)." In addition, two accounts receivable cards each showed both names on the same card, Capitol and Heavenly. Berardi testified that he looked at the accounts receivable records but that he did not see these particular cards. He testified that he did not look on the job cost ledger cards because he took the costs from another record, the costs register.

The burden of proof on this issue is on Peat, Marwick. Although the question is a rather close one, I find that Peat, Marwick has not sustained that burden. Peat, Marwick has not proved that Berardi made a reasonable investigation as far as Capitol Lanes was concerned and that his ignorance of the true facts was justified.

Howard Lanes Annex   Berardi also failed to discover that this alley was not sold. Here the evidence is much scantier. Berardi saw a contract for this alley in the contract file. No one told him that it was to be leased rather than sold. There is no evidence to indicate that any record existed which would have put him on notice. I find that his investigation was reasonable as to this item.

* * *

The S–1 Review

The purpose of reviewing events subsequent to the date of a certified balance sheet (referred to as an S–1 review when made with reference to a registration statement) is to ascertain whether any material change has occurred in the company's financial position which should be disclosed in order to prevent the balance sheet figures from being misleading. The scope of such a review, under generally accepted auditing standards, is limited. It does not amount to a complete audit.

Peat, Marwick prepared a written program for such a review. I find that this program conformed to generally accepted auditing standards.

* * *

Berardi made the S–1 review in May 1961. He devoted a little over two days to it, a total of 20½ hours. He did not discover any of the errors or omissions pertaining to the state of affairs in 1961 . . ., all of which were material. The question is whether, despite his failure to find out anything, his investigation was reasonable within the meaning of the statute.

What Berardi did was to look at a consolidating trial balance as of March 31, 1961, which had been prepared by BarChris, compare it with the audited December 31, 1960, figures, discuss with Trilling [controller of BarChris] certain unfavorable developments which the comparison disclosed, and read certain minutes. He did not examine any "important financial records" other than the trial balance. As to minutes, he read only what minutes Birnbaum [BarChris's house counsel and secretary] gave him, which consisted only of the board of directors' minutes of BarChris. He did not read such minutes as there were of the executive committee. He did not know that there was an executive committee, hence he did not discover that Kircher [BarChris's treasurer] had notes of executive committee minutes which had not been written up. He did not read the minutes of any subsidiary.

In substance, what Berardi did [was to ask] questions, he got answers which he considered satisfactory, and he did nothing to verify them.

* * *

Accountants should not be held to a standard higher than that recognized in their profession. I do not do so here. Berardi's review did not come up to that standard. He did not take some of the steps which Peat, Marwick's written program prescribed. He did not spend an adequate amount of time on a task of this magnitude. Most important of all, he was too easily satisfied with glib answers to his inquiries.

This is not to say that he should have made a complete audit. But there were enough danger signals in the materials which he did examine to require some further investigation on his part. Generally accepted accounting standards required such further investigation under these circumstances. It is not always sufficient merely to ask questions.

Here again, the burden of proof is on Peat, Marwick. I find that that burden has not been satisfied. I conclude that Peat, Marwick has not established its due diligence defense.

* * *

Defendants' motions to dismiss this action, upon which decision was reserved at the trial, are denied. * * *

Pursuant to Rule 52(a), this opinion constitutes the court's findings of fact and conclusions of law with respect to the issues determined herein.

So ordered.

Liability under the 1934 Act: Rule 10b–5

ERNST & ERNST v. HOCHFELDER

Supreme Court of the United States, 1976.
425 U.S. 185, 96 S.Ct. 1375, 47 L.Ed.2d 668.

POWELL, J.

The issue in this case is whether an action for civil damages may lie under § 10(b) of the Securities Exchange Act of 1934 (1934 Act), . . ., and Securities and Exchange Commission Rule 10b–5, . . . in the absence of an allegation of intent to deceive, manipulate, or defraud on the part of the defendant.

Petitioner, Ernst & Ernst, is an accounting firm. From 1946 through 1967 it was retained by First Securities Company of Chicago (First Securities), a small brokerage firm and member of the Midwest Stock Exchange and of the National Association of Securities Dealers, to perform periodic audits of the firm's books and records. In connection with these audits Ernst & Ernst prepared for filing with the Securities and Exchange Commission (Commission) the annual reports required of First Securities under § 17(a) of the 1934 Act. It also prepared for First Securities responses to the financial questionnaires of the Midwest Stock Exchange (Exchange).

Respondents were customers of First Securities who invested in a fraudulent securities scheme perpetrated by Leston B. Nay, president of the firm and owner of 92% of its stock. * * *

This fraud came to light in 1968 when Nay committed suicide, leaving a note that described First Securities as bankrupt and the escrow accounts as "spurious." Respondents subsequently filed this action for damages against Ernst & Ernst in the United States District Court for the Northern District of Illinois under § 10(b) of the 1934 Act. The complaint charged that Nay's escrow scheme violated § 10(b) and Commission Rule 10b–5, and that Ernst & Ernst had "aided and abetted" Nay's violations by its "failure" to conduct proper audits of First Securities. As revealed through discovery, respondents' cause of action rested on a theory of negligent nonfeasance. The premise was that Ernst &

Ernst had failed to utilize "appropriate auditing procedures" in its audits of First Securities, thereby failing to discover internal practices of the firm said to prevent an effective audit.

* * *

Federal regulation of transactions in securities emerged as part of the aftermath of the market crash in 1929. The Securities Act of 1933 (1933 Act), [citation] was designed to provide investors with full disclosure of material information concerning public offerings of securities in commerce, to protect investors against fraud and, through the imposition of specified civil liabilities, to promote ethical standards of honesty and fair dealing. [Citation.] The 1934 Act was intended principally to protect investors against manipulation of stock prices through regulation of transactions upon securities exchanges and in over-the-counter markets, and to impose regular reporting requirements on companies whose stock is listed on national securities exchanges. [Citation.] Although the Acts contain numerous carefully drawn express civil remedies and criminal penalties, Congress recognized that efficient regulation of securities trading could not be accomplished under a rigid statutory program. As part of the 1934 Act Congress created the Commission, which is provided with an arsenal of flexible enforcement powers. [Citations.]

Section 10 of the 1934 Act makes it "unlawful for any person . . . (b) [t]o use or employ, in connection with the purchase or sale of any security . . . any manipulative or deceptive device or contrivance in contravention of such rules and regulations as the Commission may prescribe as necessary or appropriate in the public interest or for the protection of investors." [Citation.] In 1942, acting pursuant to the power conferred by § 10(b), the Commission promulgated Rule 10b–5.

* * *

Although § 10(b) does not by its terms create an express civil remedy for its violation, and there is no indication that Congress, or the Commission when adopting Rule 10b–5, contemplated such a remedy, the existence of a private cause of action for violations of the statute and the Rule is now well established. [Citation.] During the 30–year period since a private cause of action was first implied under § 10(b) and Rule 10b–5, a substantial body of case law and commentary has developed as to its elements. Courts and commentators long have differed with regard to whether scienter is a necessary element of such a cause of action, or whether negligent conduct alone is sufficient.

* * *

Although the extensive legislative history of the 1934 Act is bereft of any explicit explanation of Congress' intent, we think the relevant portions of that history support our conclusion that § 10(b) was addressed to practices that involve some element of scienter and cannot be read to impose liability for negligent conduct alone.

* * *

The section was described rightly as a "catchall" clause to enable the Commission "to deal with new manipulative [or cunning] devices." It is difficult to believe that any lawyer, legislative draftsman, or legislator would use these words if the intent was to create liability for merely negligent acts of omissions. Neither the legislative history nor the briefs supporting respondents identify any usage or authority for construing "manipulative [or cunning] devices" to include negligence.

* * *

The Commission argues that Congress has been explicit in requiring willful conduct when that was the standard of fault intended * * *

* * *

The structure of the Acts does not support the Commission's argument. In each instance that Congress created express civil liability in favor of purchasers or sellers of securities it clearly specified whether recovery was to be premised on knowing or intentional conduct, negligence, or entirely innocent mistake. [Citations.] For example, § 11 of the 1933 Act unambiguously creates a private action for damages when a registration statement includes untrue statements of material facts or fails to state material facts necessary to make the statements therein not mislead-

ing. Within the limits specified by § 11(e), the issuer of the securities is held absolutely liable for any damages resulting from such misstatement or omission. But experts such as accountants who have prepared portions of the registration statement are accorded a "due diligence" defense. In effect, this is a negligence standard. An expert may avoid civil liability with respect to the portions of the registration statement for which he was responsible by showing that "after reasonable investigation" he had "reasonable ground[s] to believe" that the statements for which he was responsible were true and there was no omission of a material fact. § 11(b)(3)(B)(i). See e.g., Escott v. BarChris Const. Corp. [Citation.] The express recognition of a cause of action premised on negligent behavior in § 11 stands in sharp contrast to the language of § 10(b), and significantly undercuts the Commission's argument.

We also consider it significant that each of the express civil remedies in the 1933 Act allowing recovery for negligent conduct, see §§ 11, 12(2), 15, [citations] is subject to significant procedural restrictions not applicable under § 10(b). * * *

* * *

We have addressed, to this point, primarily the language and history of § 10(b). The Commission contends, however, that subsections (b) and (c) of Rule 10b–5 are cast in language which—if standing alone—could encompass both intentional and negligent behavior. These subsections respectively provide that it is unlawful "[t]o make any untrue statement of a material fact or to omit to state a material fact necessary in order to make the statements made, in the light of the circumstances under which they were made, not misleading . . ." and "[t]o engage in any act, practice, or course of business which operates or would operate as a fraud or deceit upon any person. . . ."

Viewed in isolation the language of subsection (b), and arguably that of subsection (c), could be read as proscribing, respectively, any type of material misstatement or omission, and any course of conduct, that has the effect of defrauding investors, whether the wrongdoing was intentional or not.

We note first that such a reading cannot be harmonized with the administrative history of the Rule, a history making clear that when the Commission adopted the Rule it was intended to apply only to activities that involved scienter. More importantly, Rule 10b–5 was adopted pursuant to authority granted the Commission under § 10(b). The rulemaking power granted to an administrative agency charged with the administration of a federal statute is not the power to make law. Rather, it is " 'the power to adopt regulations to carry into effect the will of Congress as expressed by the statute.' " [Citations.] . . . When a statute speaks so specifically in terms of manipulation and deception, and of implementing devices and contrivances—the commonly understood terminology of intentional wrongdoing—and when its history reflects no more expansive intent, we are quite unwilling to extend the scope of the statute to negligent conduct.

* * *

The judgment of the Court of Appeals is Reversed.

QUESTIONS

1. Explain the contract liability of an accountant to her client.

2. For what and to whom does an accountant have tort liability?

3. Explain who owns the working papers generated by an accountant and whether client information is privileged.

4. Discuss the potential civil and criminal liability of an accountant under the 1933 Act.

5. Discuss the potential civil and criminal liability of an accountant under the 1934 Act.

PROBLEMS

1. Baldwin Corporation made a public offering of $25,000,000 of convertible debentures. It registered the offering with the SEC. The registration statement contained financial statements certified by Adams and Allen, CPAs. The financial statements overstated Baldwin's net income and assets by 20 percent while it understated the company's liability by 15 percent. Because Adams and Allen did not carefully follow GAAS, it failed to detect these inaccuracies, the discovery of which has caused the bond prices to drop from their original selling price of $1,000 per bond to $720. Conrad, who purchased $10,000 of the debentures, has brought suit against Adams and Allen. Decision?

2. Ingram is a CPA employed by Jordan, Keller and Lane, CPAs, to audit Martin Enterprises, Inc., a fast-growing service firm that had gone public two years earlier. The financial statements that were audited by Ingram were included in a proxy statement proposing a merger with several other firms. The proxy statement was filed with the SEC and included several inaccuracies. First, approximately $1 million, or more than 20 per cent, of the previous year's "net sales originally reported" had proven nonexistent by the time the proxy statement was filed and had been written off on Martin's own books. This was not disclosed in the proxy statement in violation of Accounting Board Opinion Number 9. Second, net sales of Martin for the current year were stated as $11,300,000 when they were less than $10,500,000. Third, net profits of Martin for the current year were reported as $700,000 when it had no earnings at all.

(a) What civil liability, if any, does Ingram have?

(b) What criminal liability, if any, does Ingram have?

3. Girard & Company, CPAs, audited the financial statements included in the annual report submitted by PMG Enterprises, Inc., to the SEC. The audit failed to detect numerous false and misleading statements contained in the financial statements.

(a) Investors who subsequently purchased PMG stock have brought suit against Girard under Section 18 of the 1934 Act. What defenses, if any, are available to Girard?

(b) The SEC has initiated criminal proceedings under the 1934 Act against Girard. What must be proven for Girard to be held criminally liable?

4. Dryden, a certified public accountant, audited the books of Elixir, Inc., and certified incorrect financial statements in a form that was filed with the SEC. Shortly thereafter, Elixer, Inc., went bankrupt. Investigation into the bankruptcy disclosed that Kraft, the president of Elixir, had engaged in an intricate and clever embezzlement scheme that siphoned off substantial sums of money that now support Kraft in a luxurious lifestyle in South America. Investors who purchased shares of Elixir have brought suit against Dryden under Rule 10b–5. At the trial Dryden produces evidence that demonstrates that his failure to discover the embezzlements resulted merely from negligence on his part and that he had no knowledge of the fraudulent conduct. Decision?

5. Johnson Enterprises, Inc., contracted with the accounting firm of P, A & E to perform an audit of Johnson. The accounting firm performed its duty in a nonnegligent, competent manner but failed to discover a novel embezzlement scheme perpetrated by Johnson's treasurer. Shortly thereafter, Johnson's treasurer disappeared with $75,000 of the company's money. Johnson now refuses to pay P, A & E its $20,000 audit fee and is seeking to recover $75,000 from P, A & E.

(a) What are the rights and liabilities of P, A & E and Johnson? Explain.

(b) Would your answer to (a) differ if the scheme was a common embezzlement scheme that GAAS should have disclosed? Explain.

6. The accounting firm of T, W & S was engaged to perform an audit of Progate Manufacturing Company. During the course of its investigation T, W & S discovered that the inventory was overvalued by the company in that it was carried on the books at the previous year's prices, which were significantly higher than current prices. When T, W & S approached Progate's president, Lehman, about the improper valuation of inventory, Lehman became enraged and told T, W & S that unless the firm accepted the valuation, Progate would sue T, W & S. Although T, W & S knew that Progate's suit was frivolous and unfounded, it wished to avoid the negative publicity that would arise from any suit brought against it. Therefore, on the assumption that the overvaluation would not harm anybody, T, W & S accepted Progate's inflated valuation of inventory. Progate subsequently went bankrupt, and T, W & S is now being sued by (1) First National Bank, a bank that relied upon T, W & S's statement to loan money to Progate, and (2) Thomas, an investor who purchased 20 percent of Progate's stock after receiving T, W & S's statement. What are the rights and liabilities of First National Bank, Thomas, and T, W & S?

7. J, B & J, CPAs, has audited the Highcredit Corporation for the past five years. Recently, the SEC has commenced an investigation of Highcredit for possible violations of the Federal securities law. The SEC has subpoenaed all of J, B & J's working papers pertinent to the audit of Highcredit. Highcredit insists that J, B & J not turn over the documents to the SEC. What action should J, B, & J take? Why?

8. On February 1, the Gazette Corporation hired Susan Sharp to conduct an audit of its books and to prepare financial statements for the corporation's annual meeting on July 1. Sharp made every reasonable attempt to comply with the deadline but could not finish the report on time due to delays in receiving needed information from Gazette. Gazette now refuses to pay Sharp for her audit and is threatening to bring a cause of action against Sharp. What course of action should Sharp pursue? Why?

Chapter 47

INTERNATIONAL BUSINESS LAW

International Environment
Jurisdiction over Actions of Foreign Governments
Transacting Business Abroad
Forms of Multinational Enterprises

TODAY every aspect of business, including business law, requires some understanding of international business practices. Since World War II, the entire global economy has become increasingly interconnected. Many U.S. corporations now have investments or manufacturing facilities in other countries, while at the same time there is an increase in the number of foreign corporations with business operations in the United States. Furthermore, whether a domestic corporation exports goods or not, it competes with imports from many other countries. For example, U.S. firms face competition from Japanese electronics and automobiles, French wines and fashions, German machinery, and Taiwanese textiles. In order to compete effectively, U.S. firms need to be aware of international business practices and developments.

Laws vary greatly from country to country: what is required by law in one nation may be forbidden by law in another. To make matters more complicated, there is no single authority in international law that can compel countries to act. When the laws of two or more nations conflict, or when one party has violated an agreement and the other party wishes to enforce it or recover damages, it is often very confusing to establish who will adjudicate the matter, which laws will be applied, what remedies are available, or where the matter should be decided. Nonetheless, because of the growing impact of the global economy, it is important to have a basic understanding of international business law.

THE INTERNATIONAL ENVIRONMENT

International law includes the law that deals with the conduct and relations of nation-states and international organizations as well as some of their relations with persons. Unlike domestic law, as a general rule international law cannot be enforced. International courts do not have compulsory jurisdiction to resolve international disputes. These courts, however, have authority to resolve a dispute if the parties to the dispute *accept* the court's jurisdiction over the matter. Furthermore, if an international law has been adopted as law by a sovereign nation, that law will be enforced by that country to the same extent as all of its domestic laws. This section of the chapter examines some of the sources and institutions of international law, including the International Court of Justice, regional trade communities, and international trade agreements.

International Court of Justice

The United Nations, which is probably the most famous international organization, has a judiciary branch called the International Court of Justice (ICJ). The ICJ consists of fifteen judges, no two of whom may be from the same sovereign state, elected for a nine-year term by a majority of both the U.N. General Assembly and the U.N. Security Council. The usefulness of the ICJ is limited, however, because only nations (not private individuals or corporations) may be parties to an action before the court. Furthermore, the ICJ has contentious jurisdiction only if the nations who are parties agree to allow the ICJ to decide the case and agree to be bound by its decision. Moreover, because the ICJ cannot enforce its rulings, countries that do not like a decision by the ICJ may choose to ignore it. Consequently, few nations choose to submit their disputes to the ICJ.

The ICJ also has advisory jurisdiction if requested by a U.N. organ or specialized U.N. agency. Neither sovereign states nor individuals have standing to request an advisory opinion. These opinions are nonbinding, and the requesting U.N. agency usually votes to decide whether to follow the opinion.

Regional Trade Communities

Of much greater significance are international organizations, conferences, and treaties that focus on business and trade regulation. Regional trade communities, such as the European Economic Community (EEC), promote common trade policies among member nations. The EEC, better known as the Common Market, was formed in 1957 by the Treaty of Rome in order to remove trade barriers between the member nations and to unify their economic policies. The EEC now has twelve members (Belgium, France, Italy, Luxemburg, the Netherlands, Germany, Denmark, Ireland, the United Kingdom,

Greece, Portugal, and Spain) with a combined annual gross product of around $3 trillion. The EEC is the largest importer of U.S. made goods. The EEC has the power to make rules that are binding on member nations and that preempt member nations' domestic laws. In order to achieve free movement of goods among member states, the EEC has committed to establishing a truly free trade market by 1992. Some of the other important regional trade communities include the Central American Common Market (CACM), the Caribbean Community (CARICOM), the Association of South East Asian Nations (ASEAN), the Andean Common Market (ANCOM), the Economic Community of West African States (ECOWAS), and the Union Douaniere et Economique et l'Afrique Centrale (UDEAC).

International Treaties

A **treaty** is an agreement between or among independent nations. As discussed in Chapter 1, the U.S. Constitution authorizes the president to enter into treaties with the advice and consent of the Senate "providing two-thirds of the Senators present concur." The U.S. Constitution provides that all valid treaties are "the law of the land," having the legal force of a Federal statute.

Nations have entered into bilateral and multilateral treaties in order to facilitate and regulate trade and to protect their national interests. In addition, treaties have been used to serve as constitutions of international organizations, to establish general international law, to transfer territory, to settle disputes, to secure human rights, and to protect investments. The Treaty Section of the Office of Legal Affairs within the United Nations Secretariat is responsible for registering and publishing treaties and agreements among member nations. Since its inception in 1946, the U.N. Secretariat has registered and published over 30,000 treaties that expressly or indirectly concern international business.

Probably the most important multilateral trade treaty is the General Agreement on Tariffs and Trade (GATT). With almost one hundred participants, the signatories of GATT represent over four-fifths of world trade. The basic purpose of GATT is to facilitate the flow of trade by establishing agreements on potential trade barriers such as import quotas, customs, export regulations, antidumping restrictions (the prohibition against selling goods for less than their fair market value), subsidies, and import fees. This is accomplished by GATT's **most-favored nation provision,** which states that all signatories must treat each other as favorably as they treat any other country. Thus, any privilege, immunity, or favor given to one country must be given to all. Nevertheless, nations may give preferential treatment to developing nations and may also enter into free trade areas with one or more other nations. A free trade area permits countries to discriminate in favor of their free trade partners provided that the agreement covers substantially all trade among the free trade partners. A second important principle adopted by GATT is that where protection is given to domestic industries, it should be in the form of a customs tariff as opposed to other more trade-inhibiting measures.

JURISDICTION OVER ACTIONS OF FOREIGN GOVERNMENTS

This section will focus on the power, and the limits on that power, of a sovereign nation to exercise jurisdiction over a foreign nation or to take over property owned by foreign citizens. More specifically, it will examine state immunities (the principle of sovereign immunity and the act of state doctrine) and the power of a state to take foreign investment property.

Sovereign Immunity

One of the oldest concepts in international law is that every nation has absolute and total authority over what goes on within its own territory. It has also been long recognized, however, that in order to maintain international relations and trade, a host country must refrain from imposing its laws on a foreign sovereign nation present in that host country. This principle of absolute immunity of a foreign sovereign from the courts of the host country is known as **sovereign immunity.** Originally, all acts of a foreign sovereign nation within a host country were considered immune from the host country's laws. In modern times, a distinction is made between public and commercial acts of a foreign nation. Only public acts, such as those concerning diplomatic activity, internal administration, or armed forces, will be granted sovereign immunity by the host country. When a foreign nation engages in trade or commercial activities, that nation subjects itself to the jurisdiction of the courts of the host country with respect to disputes arising out of those commercial activities.

In 1976, Congress enacted the Foreign Sovereign Immunities Act in order to establish legislatively when immunity would be extended to foreign nations. The act specifically provides that a foreign state shall *not* be immune from the jurisdiction of courts of the United States or of the States if the suit is based upon (1) a commercial activity carried on in the United States by the foreign state, (2) an act performed in the United States in connection with a commercial activity of the foreign state carried on elsewhere, or (3) a commercial activity of a foreign state carried on outside the United States that causes a direct effect in the United States. Examples of commercial activities include a contract by a foreign government to buy provisions or equipment for its armed forces; a contract by a foreign government to construct or make repairs on a government building; and a sale of a service or a product by a foreign government or its leasing of property, borrowing money, or investing in a security of a U.S. corporation. Examples of public (noncommercial) activities to which sovereign immunity would extend include nationalizing a corporation, determining the limitations upon the use of natural resources, and granting licenses to export a natural resource. *See Texas Trading & Milling Corp. v. Federal Republic of Nigeria* and *Carey v. National Oil Corp.*

Act of State Doctrine

The **act of state doctrine** provides that the judicial branch of a nation should not question the validity of actions taken by a foreign government within that foreign sovereign's own borders. In 1897, the U.S. Supreme Court described the act of state doctrine in terms that remain valid today: "Every sovereign State is bound to respect the independence of every other sovereign State, and the courts of one country will not sit in judgment on the acts of the government of another done within its own territory." *See United States v. Belmont.*

In the United States, there are several possible exceptions to the act of state doctrine. Some courts hold (1) that a sovereign may waive its right to raise the act of state defense and (2) that the doctrine may be inapplicable to commercial activities of a foreign sovereign. In addition, by Federal statute, the act of state doctrine will not be applied to claims to specific property located in the United States based on the assertion that a foreign state confiscated the property in violation of international law, unless the president of the United States determines that the act of state doctrine should be applied in a particular case.

Taking of Foreign Investment Property

Investing in foreign states involves the risk that the investment property may be taken by the host nation's government. An **expropriation** or nationalization occurs when a government seizes foreign-owned property or assets for a public purpose and pays the owner just compensation for what is taken. **Confiscation** is the term used when no payment (or a highly inadequate payment) is given in exchange for the seized property, or it is seized for a nonpublic purpose. Confiscations violate generally observed principles of international law, whereas expropriations do not. In either case, few remedies are available to injured parties. One precaution that can be taken by U.S. firms is to obtain insurance from a private insurer or the Overseas Private Investment Corporation (OPIC), which is an agency of the U.S. government.

TRANSACTING BUSINESS ABROAD

Transacting business abroad may involve such activities as selling goods, information, or services or investing capital or arranging for the movement of labor. Because these transactions may affect the national security, economy, foreign policy, and national interest of both the exporting and importing countries, nations have imposed measures to restrict or encourage such transactions. This section examines the legal controls imposed upon the flow of trade, labor, and capital across national borders. See also the discussion of the Foreign Corrupt Practices Act in Chapter 45.

Flow of Trade

Advances in modern technology, communication, transportation, and production methods have resulted in an enormous increase in goods flowing across national boundaries. The governments within each country are thereby faced with a dilemma. On the one hand, they want to protect and stimulate domestic industry. On the other hand, they want to provide their citizens with the best quality goods at the lowest possible prices and to encourage exports from their own countries.

Governments have used a variety of trade barriers to protect domestic businesses and to achieve other social and political goals. A frequently applied device is the **tariff**, which is a duty or tax imposed on goods moving into or out of a country. Tariffs raise the price of imported goods, causing some consumers to purchase less expensive, domestically produced items. Governments can also use **nontariff barriers** to give a competitive advantage to local industries. Examples of nontariff barriers include unilateral or bilateral import quotas, import bans, overly restrictive safety or manufacturing standards, complicated and time-consuming customs procedures, and subsidies to local industry.

Governments also exercise control over the flow of some types of goods out of their countries by imposing quotas, tariffs, or total prohibitions. **Export controls** or restrictions usually result from important policy considerations, such as national defense, foreign policy, or protection of scarce national resources. For example, the United States passed the Export Administration Act of 1979, as amended in 1985 and 1988, which imposes restrictions on the flow of technologically advanced goods and data from the United States to other countries. Nonetheless, countries generally encourage exports by the use of **export incentives** and **export subsidies** in order to assist domestic businesses.

Flow of Labor

The flow of labor across national borders generates policy questions involving the employment needs of local workers. Each country has its immigration policies and regulations. Almost all countries require that foreigners obtain valid passports before entering their borders. They also require their citizens to have a passport to leave or reenter the country. In addition, a country may issue visas to foreign citizens permitting them to enter the country for identified purposes or specific periods of time. For example, the U.S. Immigration and Naturalization Service issues various types of visas to persons who are temporarily visiting the United States for pleasure or business, to persons who enter the United States to perform services that the unemployed in this country cannot perform, and to persons who are transferred to the United States by their employers.

Flow of Capital

Multinational businesses frequently have the need to transfer funds to, and receive money from, operations in other countries. Because there is no international currency, nations have sought to ease the flow of capital among themselves. In 1945, the International Monetary Fund (IMF) was established to facilitate the expansion and balanced growth of international trade, to assist in the elimination of foreign exchange restrictions that hamper the growth of international trade, and to shorten the duration and lessen the disequilibrium in the international balance of payments of members. Currently, over 140 countries are members of the IMF.

Nations have also joined to form international and regional banks to facilitate the flow of capital and trade. Such banks include the International Bank for Reconstruction and Development (part of the World Bank), the African Development Bank, the Asian Development Bank, the European Investment Bank, and the Inter-American Development Bank.

International Contracts

The legal issues inherent in domestic commercial contracts also arise in international contracts. Moreover, some additional issues are peculiar to international contracts, such as differences in language, customs, legal systems, and currency. These issues should be addressed by the parties in a carefully drawn contract. The contract should specify the official language of the contract and include definitions of all significant legal terms used. In addition, the acceptable currency or currencies and the method of payment should be specified. The contract should include a choice of law clause designating what law will govern any breach or dispute regarding the contract, and which nation's court will resolve the dispute or whether disputes will be settled by arbitration. Finally, the contract should include a *force majeure* (unavoidable superior force) clause apportioning the liabilities and responsibilities of the parties in the event of an unforeseeable occurrence, such as a typhoon, tornado, flood, earthquake, war, or nuclear disaster.

CISG The United Nations Convention on Contracts for the International Sales of Goods (CISG), which has been ratified by the United States, governs all contracts for the international sales of goods between parties located in different nations that have ratified the CISG. Since treaties are Federal law, the CISG supersedes the U.C.C. whenever the CISG applies. The CISG includes provisions dealing with interpretation, trade usage, contract formation, obligations of sellers and buyers, remedies of sellers and buyers, and risk of loss. Parties to an international sales contract, however, may expressly exclude the CISG in their sales contract. The CISG specifically excludes sales of (1) goods bought for personal, family, or household use; (2) ships or aircraft; and (3) electricity. In addition, it does not apply to contracts in which the preponderant part of the obligations of the party who furnishes the goods consists in the supply of labor or services.

Letters of Credit International trade involves a number of risks not usually created by domestic trade, especially governmental controls over the export or import of goods and currency. The most effective means of managing these risks—as well as the ordinary trade risks of nonperformance by seller and buyer—is the irrevocable documentary letter of credit. Most international letters of credit are governed by the Uniform Customs and Practices, a document drafted by commercial law experts from many countries and adopted by the International Chamber of Commerce. A **letter of credit** is a promise by a buyer's bank to pay the seller, provided certain conditions are met. The letter of credit transaction involves three or four different parties and three underlying contracts. To illustrate: a U.S. business wishes to sell computers to a Belgian company. The U.S. and Belgian firms enter into a sales agreement, including such details as how many computers, what features they will have, and when they will be shipped. The buyer then enters into a second contract with a local bank, called an **issuer,** committing the bank to pay the agreed price upon presentation of specified documents. These documents normally include a bill of lading (proving that the seller has delivered the goods for shipment), a commercial invoice listing the terms of purchase, proof of insurance, and a customs cer-

tificate indicating that the goods have been cleared for export by customs officials. The buyer's bank's commitment to pay is the irrevocable letter of credit. Typically, a **correspondent** or **paying bank** located in the seller's country makes payment to the seller. Here, the Belgian issuing bank arranges to pay to the U.S. correspondent bank the agreed sum of money in exchange for the documents. The issuer then sends the U.S. computer firm the letter of credit. When the U.S. firm obtains all the necessary documents, it presents them to the U.S. correspondent bank. The correspondent bank verifies the documents, pays the computer company in U.S. dollars, and sends the documents to the Belgian issuing bank. Upon receiving the required documents, the issuing bank pays the correspondent bank and then presents the documents to the buyer. In our example, the Belgian buyer pays the issuing bank in Belgian francs for the letter of credit when the buyer receives the specified documents from the bank.

Antitrust Laws

Section 1 of the Sherman Act provides for a broad, extraterritorial reach of the U.S. antitrust laws. As discussed in Chapter 42, contracts, combinations, or conspiracies that restrain trade with foreign nations, as well as among the several States, are deemed illegal. Therefore, agreements among competitors to increase the cost of imports, as well as arrangements to exclude imports from U.S. domestic markets in exchange for not competing in other countries, clearly violate U.S. antitrust laws. The antitrust provisions are also designed to provide protection for U.S. exports in situations where privately imposed restrictions seek to exclude U.S. competitors from foreign markets. Recent amendments to the Sherman Act and the Federal Trade Commission Act limit their application to unfair methods of competition that have a direct, substantial, and reasonably foreseeable effect on U.S. domestic commerce, U.S. import commerce, or U.S. export commerce.

FORMS OF MULTINATIONAL ENTERPRISES

The term **multinational enterprise** refers to any business that engages in transactions involving the movement of goods, information, money, people, or services across national borders. There are a number of business forms in which a multinational enterprise may conduct business: direct sales, foreign agents, distributorships, licensing, joint ventures, and wholly owned subsidiaries. A number of considerations affect the decision of which form of business organization to use in conducting international transactions. These factors include financing, tax consequences, legal restrictions imposed by the host country, and the degree of control over the business sought by the multinational enterprise. *See Bulova Watch Company, Inc. v. K. Hattori & Co.*

Direct Export Sales

Under a direct export sale, the seller contracts directly with the buyer in the other country. This is the simplest and least involved multinational enterprise.

Foreign Agents

An agency relationship is often used by multinational enterprises that want a limited involvement in an international market. The principal firm will appoint a local agent, who may be empowered to enter into contracts in the agent's country on behalf of the principal or may just be authorized to solicit and take orders. The agent generally does not take title to the merchandise.

Distributorships

A commonly used form of multinational enterprise is the distributorship in which a foreign distributor is appointed. Unlike an agent, a distributor takes title to the merchandise it receives, which means that the distributor, not the producer, bears many of the risks connected with commercial sales. The distributorship format, however, is espe-

cially susceptible to antitrust violations. Therefore, special care must be taken to ensure that the antitrust laws of both the producer and distributor's governments are not violated.

Licensing

Multinational enterprises wishing to exploit an intellectual property right, such as a patent, trademark, trade secret, or unpatented but innovative production technology, may choose to sell the right to use such property to a foreign company instead of entering the foreign market itself. The sale of such rights, called licensing, is one of the major means by which technology and information are transferred among nations. Normally, the foreign firm will pay royalties in exchange for the information, technology, or patent. Franchising is a form of licensing in which the owner of intellectual property grants permission to a foreign business under carefully specified conditions.

Joint Ventures

In a joint venture, two or more independent businesses from different countries agree to coordinate their efforts to achieve a common result. The sharing of profits and liabilities, as well as the delegation of responsibilities, is fixed by contract. One of the advantages of the joint venture form is that each company can be assigned responsibility for that which it does best. In order to promote local ownership of investment, a number of developing nations and regional groups have enacted legislation that prohibits foreign businesses from owning more than 49 percent of any business enterprise in that country. In addition, the country may require that its citizens comprise a majority of the management of the enterprise.

Wholly Owned Subsidiaries

By far, wholly owned subsidiaries require the most active participation by the parent firm. The creation of a foreign wholly owned subsidiary corporation, however, can offer numerous advantages to a business, most significantly the opportunity to retain authority and control over all phases of operation. This is especially attractive to businesses wishing to safeguard their technology.

CASES

Sovereign Immunity

TEXAS TRADING & MILLING CORPORATION v. FEDERAL REPUBLIC OF NIGERIA

United States Court of Appeals, Second Circuit, 1981.
647 F.2d 300.

KAUFMAN, J.

[Nigeria, experiencing an economic boom due to exports of high-grade oil, embarked on an infrastructure development plan. Accordingly, Nigeria entered into at least 109 contracts with 68 suppliers for the purchase of cement at a price of almost $1 billion. Among the contracting suppliers were four American corporations, including Texas Trading & Milling Corporation. Nigeria misjudged the cement market (having anticipated only a 20 percent fulfillment rate) and was forced to repudiate most of the contracts. Texas Trading & Milling Corporation and three other American companies brought suit alleging anticipatory breach of contract. Nigeria claimed immunity under the Foreign Sovereign Immunities Act of 1976. In three of the cases the district court held jurisdiction to be present and proceeded to trial. In one of the cases, the district court dismissed for lack of jurisdiction.]

[Section 1605 of the Foreign Sovereign Immunities Act of 1976 (FSIA)] provides, in part:

(a) A foreign state shall not be immune from the jurisdiction of courts of the United States or of the States in any case—

* * *

(2) in which the action is based upon a commercial activity carried on in the United States by the foreign state; or upon an act performed in the United States in connection with a commercial activity of the foreign state elsewhere; or upon an act outside the territory of the United States in connection with a commercial activity of the foreign state elsewhere and that act causes a direct effect in the United States.

Crucial to each of the three clauses of [this section] is the phrase "commercial activity." In it is lodged centuries of Anglo-American and civil law precedent construing the term "sovereign immunity." If the activity is not "commercial," but, rather, is "governmental," then the foreign state is entitled to immunity under [this section], and "original jurisdiction" is not present under [citation].

For the definition of "commercial activity," we turn to subsection 1603(d), which provides:

(d) A "commercial activity" means either a regular course of commercial conduct or a particular commercial transaction or act. The commercial character of an activity shall be determined by reference to the nature of the course of conduct or particular transaction or act, rather than by reference to its purpose.

If "commercial activity" under § 1603(d) is present, and if it bears the relation to the United States required by § 1605(a)(2), then the foreign state is "not entitled to immunity," and the district court has statutory subject matter jurisdiction over the claim through [citation]. And, if the exercise of that jurisdiction falls within the judicial power set forth by Article III of the Constitution, subject matter jurisdiction over the claim exists.

* * *

The determination of whether particular behavior is "commercial" is perhaps the most important decision a court faces in an FSIA suit. This problem is significant because the primary purpose of the Act is to "restrict" the immunity of a foreign state to suits involving a foreign state's public acts. [Citation.] If the activity is not "commercial," it satisfies none of the three clauses of § 1605(a)(2), and the foreign state is (at least under that subsection) immune from suit. Unfortunately, the definition of "commercial" is the one issue on which the Act provides almost no guidance at all. Subsection 1603(d) advances the inquiry somewhat, for it provides: "The commercial character of an activity shall be determined by reference to the nature of the course of conduct or particular transaction or act, rather than by reference to its purpose." No provision of the Act, however, defines "commercial." Congress deliberately left the meaning open and, as noted above, "put [its] faith in the U.S. courts to work out progressively, on a case-by-case basis . . . the distinction between commercial and governmental." [Citations.] We are referred to no less than three separate sources of authority to resolve this fundamental definitional question.

* * *

Under each of these three standards, Nigeria's cement contracts and letters of credit qualify as "commercial activity." Lord Denning, writing in [citation], with his usual erudition and clarity, stated: "If a government department goes into the market places of the world and buys boots or cement—as a commercial transaction—that government department should be subject to all the rules of the marketplace." Nigeria's activity here is in the nature of a private contract for the purchase of goods. Its purpose—to build roads, army barracks, whatever—is irrelevant. Accordingly, courts in other nations have uniformly held Nigeria's 1975 cement purchase program and appurtenant letters of credit to be "commercial activity," and have denied the defense of sovereign immunity. We find defendants' activity here to constitute "commercial activity,"* * *.

* * *

Our rulings today vindicate more than Congressional intent. They affirm the right of all participants in the marketplace of the world to be treated as equals, and to ascribe to principles of trade which found their birth in the law merchant, centuries ago. Corporations can enter contracts without fear that the defense of sovereign immunity will be inequitably interposed, and foreign states can bargain without paying a premium required by a trader in anticipation of a judgment-proof client. Commerce is fostered, and all interests are advanced.

Sovereign Immunity

CAREY v. NATIONAL OIL CORPORATION

Unites States Court of Appeals, Second Circuit, 1979.
592 F.2d 673.

PER CURIAM

This is a contract case which involves several international transactions and attempts to bring into play issues of international concern. The case was dismissed on jurisdictional grounds in the United States District Court for the Southern District of New York, Kevin T. Duffy, *Judge.* For the reasons set out below, we affirm.

The facts may be stated briefly as follows:

Appellant New England Petroleum Corporation ("NEPCO") is a New York company which sells residual fuel oil in the eastern United States. One of the sources for this residual oil is a refinery company located in the Bahamas, the Grand Bahama Petroleum Company, Ltd. ("PETCO"). PETCO is a wholly-owned subsidiary of NEPCO. Appellant Carey is an assignee of PETCO.

In 1968, PETCO entered into a long-term contract to purchase crude oil from Chevron Oil Trading ("COT"), a branch of a petroleum company which held 50 per cent of an oil concession in Libya. The oil obtained under this contract was to be refined and sold to NEPCO. Libyan crude oil was particularly attractive to NEPCO because its low sulphur content aided compliance with United States air pollution standards.

In September 1973, the Socialist People's Libyan Arab Jamahirya ("Libya") nationalized several foreign-owned oil concessions in that country, including that of the company of which COT was a part. This caused COT to suspend all crude oil deliveries to PETCO and to terminate its contract with PETCO.

In order to obtain the oil supplies it needed, PETCO entered into new contracts in September, 1973 with the National Oil Corporation ("NOC"), a company wholly owned by the Libyan government. These new contracts were at a substantially higher price than the canceled one with COT.

The following month, Libya imposed an embargo on oil exports to the United States, the Netherlands, and the Bahamas. Accordingly, NOC canceled its contracts with PETCO. World oil prices rose and available supplies declined. NOC then accepted bids on new contracts to supersede the ones effective until that time. In order to fulfill its contracts for the sale of refined oil in the United States, PETCO entered into a new contract with NOC for crude oil to be refined in Italy (during the embargo) and the Bahamas. In January, 1974 the contract was executed, calling for a price per barrel of oil more than three times the previous price.

In December, 1973 another subsidiary of NEPCO, Antco Shipping Company, agreed to charter two tankers owned by a Libyan government-owned entity. NEPCO claims that these were chartered at excessive rates as a condition of delivering oil to PETCO.

This suit attempts to recover damages for NOC's failure to deliver oil under the September, 1973 contract, for breaches of the 1974 contract, and for overcharges on the charter parties. The damages sought total approximately $1.6 billion. Because we find that this court has no jurisdiction in this case, we do not reach the merits of these claims.

Foreign states are immune from suit in the courts of the United States for many of their acts, and thus federal courts have no jurisdiction in disputes involving such public acts. Specific exceptions to this general grant of immunity were carefully mapped out by Congress in the Foreign Sovereign Immunities Act of 1976 [citation].

Appellants claim, most relevantly, that the events involved in this case come within the exception to immunity which allows U.S. jurisdiction where a claim is based on "an act outside the territory of the United States in connection with a commercial activity of the foreign state elsewhere and that act causes a direct effect in the United States." [Citation.] We find no direct effect in the United States here.

We assume that Congress chose the language in the act purposefully. Section 1605(a)(2) speaks of acts which have a "direct" effect in the United States. The legislative history of this section makes clear that it embodies the standard set out in *International Shoe Co. v. Washington,* [citation], that in order to satisfy due process requirements, a defendant over whom jurisdiction is to be exercised must have "certain minimum contacts with [the forum state] such that the maintenance of the suit does not offend 'traditional notions of fair play and substantive justice.' " That standard has not been met here.

PETCO is a Bahamian corporation. Though a subsidiary of NEPCO, it was a separate corporate entity, and we will not here "pierce the corporate veil" in favor of those who created that veil. The cancellation of the contracts between NOC and PETCO, and the overcharge on the charters, had a direct effect on PETCO as a party to those contracts, but not in the United States. Similarly, while there was an admitted effect on NEPCO, an American company, that effect can only be deemed indirect, through NEPCO's relations with PETCO and Antco, whose dealings with NOC were entirely outside the United States.

At no time did NOC or Libya "purposely avail itself of the privilege" of conducting business in the United States. The product which was destined for the United States, the refined oil, was a different substance than the crude oil sold by NOC to PETCO, so there was no real entering of the marketplace in the United States.

The appellants claim that the Libyan government and NOC were aware that the refineries in the Bahamas were being used primarily to channel oil into the United States. Appellants also contend that the Libyan oil embargo was expressly aimed at affecting the

United States. Even if these allegations are true, they do not fulfill the "minimum contacts" requirement of *International Shoe,* and thus cannot reach the level of "direct" effects described in the statute. The claims concerning the charter parties fail for the same reason.

Act of State

UNITED STATES v. BELMONT

United States Supreme Court, 1937.
301 U.S. 324, 57 S.Ct. 758.

SUTHERLAND, J.

This is an action at law brought by petitioner against respondents in a federal District Court to recover a sum of money deposited by a Russian corporation (Petrograd Metal Works) with August Belmont, a private banker doing business in New York City under the name of August Belmont & Co. August Belmont died in 1924; and respondents are the duly appointed executors of his will. A motion to dismiss the complaint for failure to state facts sufficient to constitute a cause of action was sustained by the District Court, and its judgment was affirmed by the court below. The facts alleged, so far as necessary to be stated, follow.

The corporation had deposited with Belmont, prior to 1918, the sum of money which petitioner seeks to recover. In 1918, the Soviet government duly enacted a decree by which it dissolved, terminated, and liquidated the corporation (together with others), and nationalized and appropriated all of its property and assets of every kind and wherever situated, including the deposit account with Belmont. As a result, the deposit became the property of the Soviet government, and so remained until November 16, 1933, at which time the Soviet government released and assigned to petitioner all amounts due to that government from American nationals, including the deposit account of the corporation with Belmont. Respondents failed and refused to pay the amount upon demand duly made by petitioner.

The assignment was effected by an exchange of diplomatic correspondence between the Soviet government and the United States. The purpose was to bring about a final settlement of the claims and counterclaims between the Soviet government and the United States; and it was agreed that the Soviet government would take no steps to enforce claims against American nationals; but all such claims were released and assigned to the United States, with the understanding that the Soviet government was to be duly notified of all amounts realized by the United States from such release and assignment. The assignment and requirement for notice are parts of the larger plan to bring about a settlement of the rival claims of the high contracting parties. The continuing and definite interest of the Soviet government in the collection of assigned claims is evident; and the case, therefore, presents a question of public concern, the determination of which well might involve the good faith of the United States in the eyes of a foreign government. The court below held that the assignment thus effected embraced the claim here in question; and with that we agree.

That court, however, took the view that the situs of the bank deposit was within the state of New York; that in no sense could it be regarded as an intangible property right within Soviet territory; and that the nationalization decree, if enforced, would put into effect an act of confiscation. And it held that a judgment for the United States could not be had, because, in view of that result, it would be contrary to the controlling public policy of the state of New York. The further contention is made by respondents that the public policy of the United States would likewise be infringed by such a judgment. The two questions thus presented are the only ones necessary to be considered.

First. We do not pause to inquire whether in fact there was any policy of the state of New York to be infringed, since we are of opinion that no state policy can prevail against the international compact here involved.

This court has held, [citation], that every sovereign state must recognize the independence of every other sovereign state; and that the courts of one will not sit in judgment upon the acts of the government of another, done within its own territory.

* * * This court held that the conduct of foreign relations was committed by the Constitution to the political departments of the government, and the propriety of what may be done in the exercise of this political power was not subject to judicial inquiry or decision; that who is the sovereign of a territory is not a judicial question, but one the determination of which by the political departments conclusively binds the courts; and that recognition by these departments is retroactive and validates all actions and conduct of the government so recognized from the commencement of its existence. "The principle," we said, [citation], "that the conduct of one independent government cannot be successfully questioned in the courts of another is as applicable to a case involving the title to property brought within the custody of a court, such as we have here, as it was held to be to the cases cited, in which claims for damages were based upon acts done in a foreign country, for it rests at last upon the highest considerations of international comity and expediency. To permit the validity of the acts of one sovereign state to be reëxamined and perhaps condemned by the courts of another would very certainly 'imperil the amicable relations between governments and vex the peace of nations.' " * * *

* * *

We take judicial notice of the fact that coincident with the assignment set forth in the complaint, the President recognized the Soviet government, and normal diplomatic relations were established between that government and the government of the United States, followed by an exchange of ambassadors. The effect of this was to validate, so far as this country is concerned, all acts of the Soviet government here involved from the commencement of its existence. The recognition, establishment of diplomatic relations, the assignment, and agreements with respect thereto, were all parts of one transaction, resulting in an international compact between the two governments. That the negotiations, acceptance of the assignment and agreements and understandings in respect thereof were within the competence of the President may not be doubted. Governmental power over internal affairs is distributed between the national government and the several states. Governmental power over external affairs is not distributed, but is vested exclusively in the national government. And in respect of what was done here, the Executive had authority to speak as the sole organ of that government. The assignment and the agreements in connection therewith did not, as in the case of treaties, as that term is used in the treaty making clause of the Constitution (article 2,§ 2), require the advice and consent of the Senate.

* * *

Plainly, the external powers of the United States are to be exercised without regard to state laws or policies. The supremacy of a treaty in this respect has been recognized from the beginning. Mr. Madison, in the Virginia Convention, said that if a treaty does not supersede existing state laws, as far as they contravene its operation, the treaty would be ineffective. "To counteract it by the supremacy of the state laws, would bring on the Union the just charge of national perfidy, and involve us in war." [Citations.] And while this rule in respect of treaties is established by the express language of clause 2, article 6, of the Constitution, the same rule would result in the case of all international compacts and agreements from the very fact that complete power over international affairs is in the national government and is not and cannot be subject to any curtailment or interference on the part of the several states. [Citation.] In respect of all international negotiations and compacts, and in respect of our foreign relations generally, state lines disappear. As to such purposes the state of New York does not exist. Within the field of its powers, whatever the United States rightfully undertakes, it necessarily has warrant to consummate. And when judicial authority is involved in aid of such consummation, State Constitutions, state laws, and state policies are irrelevant to the inquiry and decision. It is inconceivable that any of them can be interposed as an obstacle to the effective operation of a federal constitutional power. [Citations.]

Second. The public policy of the United States relied upon as a bar to the action is that declared by the Constitution, namely, that private property shall not be taken without just compensation. But the answer is that our Constitution, laws, and policies have no extraterritorial operation, unless in respect of our own citizens. [Citation.] What another country has done in the way of taking over property of its nationals, and especially of its corporations, is not a matter for judicial consideration here. Such nationals must look to their own government for any redress to which they may be entitled. So far as the record shows, only the rights of the Russian corporation have been affected by what has been done; and it will be time enough to consider the rights of our nationals when, if ever, by proper judicial proceeding, it shall be made to appear that they are so affected as to entitle them to judicial relief. The substantive right to the moneys, as now disclosed, became vested in the Soviet government as the successor to the corporation; and this right that government has passed to the United States. It does not appear that respondents have any interest in the matter beyond that of a custodian. Thus far no question under the Fifth Amendment is involved.

It results that the complaint states a cause of action and that the judgment of the court below to the contrary is erroneous. In so holding, we deal only with the case as now presented and with the parties now before us. We do not consider the status of adverse claims, if there be any, of others not parties to this action. And nothing we have said is to be construed as foreclosing the assertion of any such claim to the fund involved, by intervention or other appropriate proceeding. We decide only that the complaint alleges facts sufficient to constitute a cause of action against the respondents.

Judgment reversed.

Forms of Multinational Enterprises

BULOVA WATCH COMPANY, INC. v. K. HATTORI & CO.

United States District Court, Eastern District of New York, 1981.
508 F.Supp. 1322.

WEINSTEIN, C.J.

This motion to dismiss for lack of personal jurisdiction (F.R.Civ.P. 12(b)(2)), presents a classic problem in adjudicating claims against a multinational corporation using subsidiaries to penetrate the American market.

* * *

Plaintiff Bulova Watch Co., Inc. charges K. Hattori & Co., Ltd. and . . . others with unfair competition and disparagement and with engaging in a conspiracy to raid plaintiff's marketing staff in order to appropriate plaintiff's trade secrets.

Bulova is a New York corporation with its principal place of business in Flushing, New York. It manufactures and sells watches and claims to have the largest direct sales marketing system in the watch business.

Hattori is a company incorporated under the laws of Japan with its principal offices in Tokyo. It owns all the stock of Seiko Corporation of America (SCA), a New York corporation. SCA owns all the stock of Seiko Time Corp., Pulsar Time, Inc. and SPD Precision, Inc., all New York corporations. Hattori contracts in Japan for the manufacture of its watches and sells them under the Seiko, Pulsar and other brand names to its three American sub-subsidiaries. The Japanese parent's annual sales in 1978 were in excess of $1 billion. While the "Hattori group" manufactures many products including computers, measuring instruments, industrial robots, spectacle lenses and electric shavers. . . ., watches and clocks account for approximately ninety percent of Hattori's sales. . . . A very substantial amount of its total revenue is derived from exports of watches and timepieces, the United States being its largest foreign market. In 1980 over four million Hattori timepieces were sold in this country at prices to the consumer of one hundred twenty-five dollars and higher—far more than half a billion dollars at retail. [Citation.]

Hattori sells products to distributors in over one hundred countries around the world. Wholly-owned subsidiaries of Hattori handle distribution of Hattori's products in about ten of those countries, including the United States. In the rest, or the great majority of the countries in which Hattori's products are sold, sales are made by Hattori or its subsidiaries to independent distributors who conduct their own advertising and other marketing activities and maintain their own repair centers pursuant to agreement or arrangements with Hattori. . . . Hattori has never directly marketed its products in any country except Japan.

Hattori's United States subsidiaries sold Seiko-branded products totalling over $50,000,000 in wholesale dollars in 1979 to retail customers and wholesale distributors in the Caribbean, South America and Europe. SCA has also made substantial investments in third countries to assist Hattori in selling its Japanese manufactured timepieces. It owns one hundred percent of the capital stock of Pulsar subsidiaries which it has established in Canada and Europe during the past two years. Seiko Time Canada, Ltd., in 1979, represented an investment of $5,000,000 and accounted for Canadian sales of Hattori products in excess of $35,000,000 in wholesale dollars. In 1980, Seiko Corporation of America also acquired one hundred percent of the stock of a Brazilian corporation, Seiko Time, Ltd., which in turn acquired all the stock of Hase, S. A., a company which sells Hattori's Seiko-branded products in Brazil. [Citation.]

* * *

Between July and December of 1978, six members of Bulova's staff—three regional sales managers and three more senior executive personnel—left Bulova to join either a Seiko subsidiary or a Seiko distributor. During December, 1978 four Bulova salesmen joined SPD Precision's Pulsar division which in January, 1979 was separately incorporated as Pulsar Time, Inc. Sometime during 1979 a number of Bulova salesmen were hired by Pulsar Time. What sharply divides

plaintiff from defendant is the question of whether these hirings were the result of a conspiracy among defendants to appropriate Bulova's trade secrets and marketing system and to damage Bulova and destroy its business and reputation.

* * *

[The N.Y. statute] permits the exercise of such jurisdiction over "persons, property, or status as might have been exercised heretofore." It confers personal jurisdiction over unlicensed foreign corporations that are "doing business" in New York. [Citations.]

The definition of "doing business" has been variously stated, but the common denominator is that the corporation is operating within the state "not occasionally or casually, but with a fair measure of permanence and continuity." [Citations.]

It is no longer a matter of doubt that a foreign corporation can do business in New York through its employees, [citations].

Equally settled is the concept that a corporation may be amenable to New York personal jurisdiction when the systematic activities of a subsidiary in this state may fairly be attributed to the parent. [Citations.]

* * *

When Cardozo enunciated the standard for doing business in New York, [citation], there would have been little need to consider how, or whether, a foreign-based multinational enterprise would be found to be doing business in New York. For one thing, the term "multinational firm," so common in today's parlance, was first used only in 1960. [Citation.] For another, it was not until after World War II that the phenomenon of the multinational enterprise, as we now know it, became a major factor in the world scene. [Citation.] Since then tens of thousands of subsidiaries have been created or acquired by parent enterprises located in other countries. [Citation.] By 1972 it was estimated that in a world that produced about $3,000 billion of goods and services a year, something like one-eighth of the output moved across international boundaries. [Citation.] In that same year the value of American investments abroad was $94 billion. [Citation.]

After the Second World War investment in the United States by foreign parent companies also expanded tremendously so that by the early 1970s non-United States corporations owned more than seven hundred "major manufacturing enterprises" in this country. [Citation.] Direct foreign investment, defined as ownership by foreign parents of at least ten percent of the equity of an American enterprise, was $3.4 billion at the start of the 1950s, $6.6 billion in 1959 and $26.5 billion by 1974. [Citation.] Total assets of foreign-owned affiliates in the United States in 1974 were $174.3 billion, of which more than one-fifth was Japanese-owned. [Citation.] These trends have accelerated.

The vehicles of this modern international economic growth were and are the multinational enterprises. Their size is often awesome: the annual sales of General Motors exceeded the gross national products of Switzerland, Pakistan, or South Africa. [Citation.]

The phenomenon of penetration into the economies of distant areas can be traced through artifacts back into pre-history. But the current situation is in many respects quite different in the sophisticated organizational and legal techniques utilized from even that of earlier periods in American history when foreign financing made so much of our industrial and commercial expansion possible and when American companies like Singer, the American sewing machine company, established manufacturing plants abroad. [Citations.] Aside from their magnitude, today's multinationals are unique in the way vast investments in myriad locations are made to serve the interests of a single organization. Large advantages lie in the possibility of making centralized management and investment decisions on the basis of the situations and opportunities prevailing in various host countries. [Citations.] Such an organization has the resources and scope to plan and to utilize world-wide markets and resources. [Citations.]

The profit motivation for international expansion is common to multinationals. [Citations.] Nevertheless, the means by which the

multinational exercises control over its far-flung elements vary. The degree and nature of control may depend upon the nationality of the corporate parent. [Citations.] The formal structure of the parent's form of ownership also has control implications. Choice among the various corporate modes of entering a market, e.g., by means of licensing arrangement, joint venture, minority-, majority- or wholly-owned subsidiary, has very significant implications for the control exercised by the parent. [Citation.] Utilization of a wholly-owned marketing-based subsidiary is found where "the . . . retention of unambiguous control of foreign operations is critical to the firm's strategy." [Citation.] The decision of marketing-oriented firms to choose wholly-owned subsidiaries means that they can exercise more control over their foreign operation in subtle, indirect ways as well as directly. [Citation.]

Another criterion that will determine the "corporate intimacy" joining a parent and its subsidiary, [citation], is the type and range of products being sold. Enterprises with narrow product lines tend to organize their operations on a highly integrated basis, linking production and marketing into tight strategic patterns. [Citation.] While Hattori manufactures a number of products, the overwhelming concern of its American marketing operation is with its timepieces—constituting ninety percent of its total production by value.

Thus sales subsidiaries tend to be under especially close control where a company produces a limited number of products. In such a case the company has

a higher stake in the maintenance of quality standards, a higher sense of risk in sharing its technology with others, a higher need for a centralized marketing strategy. . . . The strategy of [these] firms, therefore, requires relatively tight controls.

[Citation.]

Finally, a crucial factor in the degree of control over the subsidiary is the age of the subsidiary and the extent to which the subsidiary has been able to develop independently of its parent. A leading scholar of international trade distinguishes multinational firms from national firms with foreign operations: "A multinational firm starts out like a national firm with foreign operations, but after time each national operation takes on a life of its own." [Citation.] The history of modern international business enterprise is largely the history of just this development from a national firm with foreign sales operations, to the truly multinational firm with quasi-independent component entities. [Citation.]

An important question in assessing presence for jurisdictional purposes is whether a multinational has reached a state in its evolution when it can be said that its sales and marketing subsidiaries truly have a "life of their own." [Citation.] * * *

The expanding multinational generally traverses a number of stages. At first it exports its goods to markets abroad, next it establishes sales organizations abroad, then it may license the use of its patents, and finally it may establish foreign manufacturing facilities. At a later stage it may "multinationalize its management and, ultimately, multinationalize the ownership of its stock." [Citation.] While many thousands of corporations are at the first, export stage, only a handful have developed into advanced multinational enterprises each of whose elements can be said to be significant in its own right.

After World War II, foreign companies gained familiarity with the United States market "by first exporting to this country; then, after achieving acceptance for their products, foreign firms set up manufacturing or assembly plants here." [Citation.] As these later stages were reached, the businesses established came to have lives of their own. The "monocentric" enterprise gradually gave way to a polycentric one, with more autonomy in the different elements. Wilkins detects three stages: in the first stage, the firm "reached out to sell or to obtain and in doing so felt the necessity or saw the opportunity to cross over domestic boundaries." [Citation.] The relationship was "monocentric" with the center of operations clearly in the parent's home country. The external activities in a monocentric

relationship were "spokes on a wheel, with the parent company at the hub." [Citation.] In stage two, the functions of the branches broadened. There might, for example, be investment by the subsidiary in a plant for local production or the subsidiary might sell products in third-country markets. "What characterizes stage two is the presence of foreign units that have developed their own separate histories and their own satellite activities." [Citation.] The final, third, stage is characteristic of the most advanced of these entities:

It garbles any chart's attempt to delineate international trade and control lines. The parent company comes to have a number of foreign multifunctional centers, serving overlapping geographical areas with various products. Supply and market lines cross international boundaries in . . . chaotic confusion. . . .

[Citation.]

Over time, certain foreign subsidiaries and affiliates have become full-fledged, fully integrated, multiprocess, multiproduct enterprises, with engineering, product planning and research staffs, with a continuity of employee, supplier, dealer, consumer and banking relationships with their own prominent role in foreign industries, with their own dealings with foreign governments and with their own third-country investments.

[Citation.] At this final stage, complicated, many-faceted relationships have replaced simple bilateral connections. [Citation.]

* * *

It is apparent that Hattori's international activities, large as they may be in terms of sales figures and associated product lines, are essentially akin to Wilkins' stage one "monocentric" export model and not to the much more complex multinationals to which defendants point. What is involved here is a series of relatively young sales and marketing subsidiaries abroad, whose purpose is to market a single product—timepieces. There is no manufacturing or product research done by any of these subsidiaries. They do not seem to have developed third-country trade except for the purpose of selling Hattori's Japanese manufactured goods. Only very recently have they begun to make some investments in third countries, again to produce further outlets for Hattori's factories in Japan. The use of the wholly-owned subsidiary form here reflects the desire for "unambiguous control" over sales and marketing subsidiaries to insure uniform quality and promotion of the product sold. [Citations.]

Hattori and its American subsidiaries do maintain some independence—about as much as the egg and vegetables in a western omelette. Just as, from a culinary point of view, we focus on the ultimate omelette and not its ingredients, so, too, from a jurisdictional standpoint, it is the integrated international operation of Hattori affecting activities in New York that is the primary focus of our concern.

Although with time the Hattori subsidiaries might well evolve, along with their parent, into the later stages of multinational development, today Hattori is a highly effective export manufacturer and not a fully developed multinational. It is monocentric more than polycentric. Large and sophisticated as it may be, it is very much the hub of a wheel with many spokes. It is appropriate, therefore, to look to the center of the wheel in Japan when the spokes violate substantive rights in other countries.

* * *

What is decisive is that at the time this complaint was filed, Hattori, through its American subsidiaries, continued to engage in the market penetration and expansion that are its corporate *raison d'être* and that are the grounds underlying this action. We have no doubt about the validity of an "inference as to the broad scope of the agency" linking Hattori to the activities of its subsidiaries in New York. [Citation.]

* * *

A court might well find substantial unfairness were it to drag a foreign parent into court to defend itself against actions completely unrelated to the subsidiary corporation's purposive activities on behalf of its parent. The holding in this case is simply that while a subsidiary establishes and expands a parent's market position then, so long as that activity is being conducted, and with respect to those activities furthering the parent's ends, the parent is doing business in New York. This is particularly true as to activities directly related to primary steps taken to ensure a place for its subsidiaries, as where action is taken to raid an established competitor's personnel in penetrating the American market.

[Motion to dismiss denied.]

QUESTIONS

1. Discuss the purpose and major provisions of GATT.

2. Discuss and compare the doctrines of sovereign immunity and act of state.

3. Contrast expropriation and confiscation.

4. Briefly discuss the legal controls imposed on the flow of trade, labor, and capital across national borders.

5. List and briefly describe the various forms a multinational enterprise may choose to conduct its business in a foreign country.

PROBLEMS

1. Three banks that are wholly owned by the Republic of Costa Rica had issued promissory notes, payable in U.S. dollars in New York City. The notes are now in default due solely to actions of the Costa Rican government, which had suspended all payments of external debt because of escalating economic problems. Efforts by Costa Rica to curb foreign debt payment difficulties conflicted with U.S. policy for debt resolution procedure as conducted under the auspices of the International Monetary Fund. A syndicate of U.S. banks brought suit to recover on the promissory notes. The three Costa Rican banks assert the act of state doctrine as a defense. Decision?

2. Six U.S. manufacturers of broad spectrum antibiotics derived a large percentage of their sales from overseas markets, including India, Iran, the Philippines, Spain, South Korea, Germany, Colombia, and Kuwait. The manufacturers agreed to a common plan of marketing, whereby territories were divided and prices for products were set. The members of the plan also agreed not to grant foreign producers licenses to the manufacturing technology of any of their "big money" drugs. The above foreign countries bring suit for treble damages for violation of the U.S. antitrust laws. Decision?

3. After reading attractive brochures advertising a package tour of the Dominican Republic, a U.S. family decided to purchase tickets for the family vacation plan. The tour was a product of four different business entities, two domestic (U.S.) and two foreign. Sheraton Hotels & Inns, World Corporation, was to provide food and lodging; Dominicana Airlines, wholly owned by the government of the Dominican Republic, which routinely flew into Miami International Airport and sold tickets within the United States, was to provide round-trip air transportation and "tourist cards" necessary for entry into the Dominican Republic; while two U.S. firms organized and sold the tour. Problems for the family began when their Dominicana flight landed in the Dominican Republic, and immigration officials denied them entry. Forced to leave, the family was shuttled first to Puerto Rico and then to Haiti, where they had to secure their own passage back to the United States at additional expense. The family brings suit against all four different business entities. Decision?

4. A privately owned business in a developing country determines that current computer technology could solve many of the problems faced by its country's private and public sectors. This business, however, lacks the capital resources necessary for research and development to acquire such computer technology, even if trained personnel were available. Furthermore, despite a sense of patriotism, the business concludes that its national government could not efficiently or effectively handle such a development project. What business forms are available to this business for acquiring sophisticated computer technology? What are the advantages and problems inherent in the various options?

5. King Faisal II of Iraq was killed on July 14, 1958, in the midst of a revolution in that country which led to the establishment of a republic subsequently recognized by the U.S. government. On July 19, 1958, the new republic issued a decree that all property of the former ruling dynasty, regardless of location, should be confiscated. Subsequently, the Republic of Iraq brought suit in the United States to obtain possession of money and stocks deposited in the deceased king's U.S. bank account in New York City. Decision?

6. A business entity incorporated under the laws of one of the EEC member nations contracts with the government of a developing nation to form a joint venture for the mining and refining of a scarce raw material used by several developed nations in the manufacture of highly sensitive weapons systems. The contract calls for the investment by the EEC-based corporation of money and technology that will be used to build permanent refinery plants that will eventually revert to the developing nation. The developing nation also reserves the right to set quotas on sales of this scarce resource and to choose the destination of exports. Due to political conflicts, the developing nation refuses to allow any exports of the scarce material to the United States. This causes a sharp price increase in exports to the United States by other suppliers. The United States asserts antitrust violations against the EEC-based corporation for the effects produced within the United States. Decision?

7. A Panamanian corporation lends money to a Turkish enterprise, which issues a promissory note. The loan contract specifies that payment on the interest and principal shall be made to the Chemical Bank of New York City, where both parties maintain accounts. The loan contract contains no choice of law designation, but the Panamanian and Turkish companies have referred to the Chemical Bank in New York as their "legal address." As a result of a contractual performance dispute, the Turkish company has suspended payments on the loan. The Panamanian corporation then brings suit in the United States to recover the balance of the payments due. What possible options for choice of law apply?

PART TEN

Property

Chapter 48

INTRODUCTION TO REAL AND PERSONAL PROPERTY

Kinds of Property
Incidents of Property Ownership
Transfer of Personal Property

IN our democratic and free enterprise society, the concept of property has an importance second only to the idea of liberty. Although many of our rules of property stem directly from English law, in the United States property occupies a unique status because of the protection expressly granted it by the Federal Constitution as well as by most State constitutions. The Fifth Amendment to the Federal Constitution provides that "No person shall be . . . deprived of life, liberty, or property, without due process of law; nor shall private property be taken for public use, without just compensation." A similar requirement is contained in the Fourteenth Amendment: "No State shall . . . deprive any person of life, liberty, or property, without due process of law." This protection afforded to property owners, however, is subject to regulation for the public good under the police power. This chapter will begin with a general introduction to the law governing real and personal property. The second part of this chapter deals specifically with personal property.

INTRODUCTION TO PROPERTY

In spite of the unique place accorded property in our society, uncertainties arise because the term *property* is not easily defined. This is not surprising because property includes almost every right, exclusive of personal liberty, that the law will protect. Property is valuable only because our law provides that certain consequences follow from the ownership of it. The right to use the property, sell it, and control to whom it shall pass on the death of the owner are all included within the term property. Accordingly, **property** is an interest or group of interests that is legally protected. More specifically, property consists of a set of *rights* entitling one person to use and enjoy exclusively some item:

By property we mean an exclusive right to control an economic good.
By private property we mean the exclusive right of a private person to control an economic good.
By public property we mean the exclusive right of a political unit (city, state, nation, etc.) to control an economic good.

* * *

Speaking accurately, then, property is not a thing but the rights which extend over a thing. A less strict use of the word property makes property include the things over which the right extends. We say of a farm, this is my property, meaning the land and improvements on it and not merely the right, or rather, the land and its improvements together with the right. But, strictly speaking, property is the right, and not the object over which the right extends. R. Ely, *Property and Contract in their Relation to the Distribution of Wealth,* 101–02, 08 (1914).

In either sense of the word—the right over the object or the object itself—there is an enormous quantity of property in the United States today. It has been estimated that as of 1988 in the United States there was $9,994 billion of real estate. *Bureau of Economic Analysis Estimates of U.S. Real Estate Aggregate* in 1988. In addition, the total value of assets of just the 500 largest corporations in the United States in 1989 was $2,079 billion, while the stock value of manufacturing companies was $2,398 billion.

KINDS OF PROPERTY

Property may be classified as (1) tangible or intangible property and (2) real or personal property (see Figure 48–1), but these classifications are not mutually exclusive.

Tangible and Intangible

A forty-acre farm, a chair, and a household pet are tangible property. The group of rights or interests referred to as "title" or "ownership" to **tangible property** are embodied in each of these *physical* objects. On the other hand, **intangible property** is property that does *not* exist in a physical form. For example, a stock certificate, a promissory note, and a deed granting Jones a right-of-way over the land of Smith are intangible property. Each represents and stands for certain rights that are not capable of reduction to physical possession but have a legal reality in the sense that they will be protected.

The same item may be the object of both tangible and intangible property rights. Suppose Ann purchases a book published by Brown & Sons. On the first page, there is the statement "Copyright 1990 by Brown & Sons." Ann owns the volume she purchased. She has the right to exclusive physical possession and use of that particular copy. It is a tangible piece of property of which she is the owner. Brown & Sons, however, has the exclusive right to publish copies of the book. This is a right granted it by the copyright laws. The courts will protect this intangible property of Brown & Sons as well as Ann's right to the particular volume.

Real and Personal

The most significant practical distinction between types of property is the classification into real and personal property. A simple definition would be to say that land and all interests in it are **real property** (also called realty), and every other thing or interest identified as property is **personal property** (also called **chattel**). This easy description is adequate for most purposes although certain

---

Figure 48–1 Kinds of Property

	Personal	Real
Tangible	Goods	Land Buildings Fixtures
Intangible	Commercial paper Stock certificates Contract rights Copyrights Patents	Leases Easements Mortgages

physical objects that are personal property under most circumstances may, because of their attachment to land or their use in connection with land, become a form of real property called fixtures.

Fixtures

A **fixture** is an article or piece of personal property that has been attached in some manner to land or a building so that an interest in it arises under *real* property law. For example, materials for a building are clearly personal property; but when worked into a building as its construction progresses, they become real property because buildings are part of the land. Thus, clay in its natural state is, of course, real property; when made into bricks it becomes personal property, and if the bricks are then built into the wall of a house the "clay" once again becomes real property.

Although the question whether various items are personal property or real property may in certain instances be difficult to answer, it is only by obtaining the answer that conflicting claims to their ownership may be determined. Unless otherwise provided by agreement, personal property remains the property of the person who placed it on the real estate. On the other hand, if the property has been affixed so as to become a fixture, an actual part of the real estate, it becomes the property of the owner of the real estate.

These questions affect many persons. The apartment dweller who puts a new chandelier or a bathroom cabinet in his landlord's apartment and the shoe repairman who attaches equipment to the floor of his leased premises will not be entitled to remove them when the lease expires *if* they are held to have become part of the real estate. Thus, if a seller of real estate has installed screens on the premises, the buyer is entitled to them as part of the real estate even though they were not specifically mentioned in the deed.

In determining whether personal property becomes a fixture, the intention of the parties with conflicting claims to the property as expressed in their agreement will control.

Without the binding force of an agreement, the following factors are relevant in determining whether any particular item is a fixture:

1. the physical relationship of the item to the land or building;

2. the intention of the person who attaches the item to the land or building;

3. the purpose served by the item in relation to the land or building and in relation to the person who brought it there; and

4. the interest of that person in the land or building at the time of the attachment of the item.

Although physical attachment is significant, a more important test is whether the item can be removed without material injury to the land or building on the land. If it *cannot* be so removed, it is generally held that the item has become part of the realty. The converse is also true but to a lesser degree. Where the item may be removed without material injury to the land or building, it is generally held that it has not become part of the realty. This test, however, is not conclusive.

Rather, the courts have searched for the answer in the intention of the person who attached the item to the realty. The tests of intention are objective. One of the tests developed has been to inquire into the purpose or use of the item in relation to the land and in relation to the person who brought it there. If the use or purpose of the item is unusual for the type of realty involved (e.g., a small crane in the backyard of a country house) or peculiar to the particular individual who brought it there, then it may be reasonably concluded that the individual intended to remove the item when he left.

An item is not regarded as part of the realty merely because its use or purpose is usual for the kind of realty involved. For example, it is usual to have beds and dressers in bedrooms and dining tables in dining rooms, but these items are not ordinarily part of the realty. The test of purpose or use applies only if the item both (1) is affixed to the realty in some way, and (2) can be removed without material injury to the realty. In such a situation, if the use or purpose of the item is peculiar to the particular owner or occupant of the premises, the courts will tend to let him remove the item when he leaves. Accordingly, in the law of landlord and tenant, it is settled that the tenant may remove **trade fixtures** (that is, items used in connection with his trade) provided that this can be done without material injury to the realty. On the other hand, doors may be removed without injury to the structure, yet because they are necessary to the ordinary use of the building and not peculiar to the use of the occupant, they are considered fixtures and thus part of the real property. *See Sears, Roebuck, and Co. v. Seven Palms Motor Inn, Inc.*

INCIDENTS OF PROPERTY OWNERSHIP

The importance of the distinction between real and personal property stems primarily from very practical legal consequences that follow from the distinction. These consequences include the transfer of property and its taxation.

Transfer of Property

As will be explained in Chapter 51, the transfer of real property during life can be accomplished only by certain formalities, including the execution and delivery of a written instrument known as a deed. Personal property, on the other hand, may be transferred with relative simplicity and informality.

Taxation

Most States levy taxes on the ownership of both real property and personal property. The applicable tax rate, however, usually varies dramatically depending on whether the property is classified as real or personal property.

PERSONAL PROPERTY

The law concerning personal property has been largely codified. The Uniform Commer-

cial Code includes the law of sales of goods (Article 2), as well as the law governing the transfer and negotiation of commercial paper (Article 3) and of investment securities (Article 8). Nonetheless, a number of issues involving the ownership and transfer of title to personal property are not covered by the Code. The remainder of this chapter will address these issues. In addition, personal property may be, and often is, acquired by producing the item.

TRANSFER OF TITLE

The transfer of title to real property is generally a formal affair. In contrast, title to personal property may be acquired and transferred with relative ease and with a minimum of formality. The facility with which personal property may be transferred is required by the demands of a society whose trade and industry is principally based upon transactions in personal property. Stocks, bonds, merchandise, and intellectual property must be sold with a minimum of delay in a free economy. It is only natural that the law will reflect these needs.

By Sale

By definition, a **sale** of *tangible* personal property (goods) is a transfer of title to specified existing goods for a consideration known as the price. Title passes when the parties intend it to pass, and transfer of possession is not required for a transfer of title. For a discussion of this manner of transfer of title see Chapter 21.

Sales of *intangible* personal property also involve the transfer of title. Many of these sales are also governed by provisions of the U.C.C., while some, such as sales of copyrights and patents, are governed by specialized Federal legislation.

By Gift

A **gift** is a transfer of property from one person to another without consideration. The lack of any consideration is the basic distinction between a gift and a sale. Because a gift involves no consideration or compensation, it must be completed by delivery of the gift to be effective. A gratuitous promise to make a gift is not binding. In addition, there must be intent on the part of the maker (the **donor**) of the gift to make a present transfer, and there must be acceptance by the recipient (the **donee**) of the gift.

Delivery Delivery is essential to a valid gift. The term *delivery* has a very special meaning, including but not limited to manual transfer of the item to the donee. There can be "delivery" of a gift sufficient to make it irrevocable if the item is turned over to a third person with instructions to give it to the donee. Frequently, an item, because of its size or location or because it is intangible, is incapable of immediate manual delivery. In such cases, an irrevocable gift may be effected by delivery of something symbolic of dominion over the item. This is referred to as **constructive delivery.** For example, if Joanne declares that she gives an antique desk and all its contents to Barry and hands Barry the key to the desk, in many States a valid gift has been made.

Intent The law is also clear that there must be an intent on the part of the donor to make a present gift of the property. Thus, if Jack leaves a packet of stocks and bonds with Jill, Jill may or may not acquire good title to them, depending on whether Jack intended to make a gift of them or simply to place them in Jill's hands for safekeeping. A voluntary, uncompensated delivery with intent to give the recipient title constitutes a gift when the donee accepts it. If these conditions are met, the donor has no further claim to the property.

Gifts, therefore, cannot be conditional. There is, however, one major exception to this rule: an engagement gift given in anticipation of a marriage. If the marriage does not take place, the donor can generally recover the gift unless the engagement was broken by the donor without justification. But the courts will not apply the exception where the marriage does not take place due to the death of one of the engaged parties. *See Cohen v. Bayside Federal Savings and Loan Association.*

Acceptance The final requirement of a valid gift is acceptance by the donee. In most instances, of course, the donee will accept the gift with gratitude. Accordingly, the law usually presumes that the donee has accepted. But there are situations in which a donee does not wish to accept a gift, such as when the gift imposes a burden upon the donee. In such cases, the law will not require the recipient to accept an unwanted gift. For example, a gift of an elephant or a wrecked car in need of extensive repairs may be prudently rejected by a donee.

Classification Gifts may be either *inter vivos* or *causa mortis*. An *inter vivos* gift is a gift made by a donor during her lifetime. A gift *causa mortis* is a gift made by a donor in contemplation of her imminent death. A gift *causa mortis* is a conditional gift and is contingent upon (1) the donor's death as she anticipated, (2) the donor's refusal to revoke the gift prior to her death, and (3) the donee's surviving the donor.

By Will or Descent

Title to personal property is frequently acquired by inheritance from a person who dies, either with or without a will. This method of acquiring title is discussed in Chapter 52.

By Accession

Many of the practical problems surrounding the title to personal property stem from its principal characteristic—movability. One of these problems is identified by the phrase "title by accession." **Accession,** in its strict sense, means the right of the owner of property to any increase in it, whether caused by natural or man-made means. For example, the owner of a cow acquires title by accession to any calves born to that cow.

Problems arise, however, if David attaches an item of personal property to Timothy's property without Timothy's consent or if

David improves by his labor the property of Timothy without Timothy's consent. For example, David takes lumber belonging to Timothy and without Timothy's consent builds it into a wagon. Or David takes a silver cup belonging to Timothy and without Timothy's consent melts it down into a tray. To whom does the "new" product belong? The material, or part of it, was originally the property of Timothy. The labor and skill necessary to create the new product were David's. Timothy, the owner of the property converted, will be entitled to one of two forms of relief. He will be entitled either to a return of the item or to damages. Which of these two forms of relief he can claim depends on the facts of the case. If the taking was deliberate and with knowledge that the item was the property of another, the general rule is that the original owner can have the improved property returned to him.

The more difficult and frequent problem arises where the person making the improvement mistakenly believes that the property belongs to him. In this case the law is not aided by a sense of punishing a wrongdoer. The law must attempt to reconcile the competing interests of two innocent parties. If there is an innocent taking and the identity of the converted item has changed or the value of the labor is greater than the value of the converted material in its original form, then title passes to the person who applied the labor. In such a case, the original owner will not be entitled to the new item; his only remedy will be an award of money damages for the value of the original article. Otherwise, the original owner may recover the property but must compensate the other party for the reasonable value of the benefits conferred by the improvements.

By Confusion

The basic problem of confusion is somewhat similar to the case of title by accession. **Confusion** arises when identical goods belonging to different people are so *commingled* (mixed) that the owners cannot identify their own property. For example, Hereford cattle belonging to Benton are mixed with Hereford cattle belonging to Armstrong, and neither person's herd can be specifically identified; or grain owned by Courts is combined with similar grain owned by Reichel. Confusion may result from accident, mistake, willful act, or agreement of the parties. If the goods can be apportioned, each owner who proves his proportion of the whole is entitled to receive his share. If, however, the confusion results from the willful and wrongful act of one of the parties, he will lose his entire interest if he cannot prove his share. Frequently, the problem arises not because the original interest cannot be proved but because there is not enough left to distribute a full share to each owner. In such a case, if the confusion was due to mistake, accident, or agreement, the loss will be borne by each in proportion to his share. If caused by an intentional and unauthorized act, the wrongdoer will first bear any loss.

By Possession

In some instances a person may acquire title to movable personal property by taking possession of it. If the property has been intentionally **abandoned** (intentionally disposed of), a *finder* is entitled to the property. Moreover, under the general rule a *finder* is entitled to **lost** (unintentionally left) property as against everyone except the true *owner*. Suppose Zenner, the owner of an apartment complex, leases a kitchenette apartment to Terrell. One night, Waters, Terrell's mother-in-law, is invited to sleep in the convertible bed in the living room. In the course of preparing the bed, Waters finds an emerald ring caught on the springs under the mattress. The ring is turned over to the police, but diligent inquiry does not turn up the true owner. Waters will be entitled to the ring because she is considered the finder.

A different rule applies when the lost property is in the ground. Here, the owner of the land has a claim superior to that of the finder. For example, Josephs employs Kasarda to excavate a lateral sewer. Kasarda uncovers old Indian relics. Josephs, not Kasarda, has the superior claim.

A further exception to the rule gives the finder first claim against all but the true owner. If property is intentionally placed somewhere by the owner, who then unintentionally leaves it, it is called **mislaid property.** Most courts hold that if property has been mislaid, not lost, then the owner of the premises, not the finder, has first claim if the true owner is not discovered. This doctrine is involved frequently in cases where items are found on trains, buses, airplanes, and in restaurants.

Many States now have statutes that provide a means of vesting title to lost property in the finder where a prescribed search for the owner proves fruitless. These statutes generally do not determine the right to possession against any party other than the true owner. *See Paset v. Old Orchard Bank and Trust Co.*

CONCURRENT OWNERSHIP

Real or personal property may be owned by one individual or by two or more persons concurrently. If title is held concurrently by two or more persons, they are generally referred to as **co-tenants,** each entitled to an undivided interest in the entire item and neither having a claim to any specific portion of it. Each may have equal undivided interests or one may have a larger undivided share than the other.

There are four ways in which personal property may be owned concurrently: (1) joint tenancy, (2) tenancy in common, (3) tenancy by the entireties, and (4) community property. The forms of concurrent ownership are discussed in Chapter 50.

CASES

Fixtures

SEARS, ROEBUCK, AND CO. v. SEVEN PALMS MOTOR INN, INC.

Supreme Court of Missouri, 1975.
530 S.W.2d 695.

HENLEY, J.

* * *

It involves a claim by Sears, Roebuck, and Company (respondent) to recover $8,357.49 with interest, and to establish a mechanic's lien, for materials and labor including, among other items, drapes and bedspreads furnished Seven Palms Motor Inn (defendant) in connection with the construction of a motel on land then owned by it. The case was submitted on a stipulation in which ... the only issue to be decided is whether respondent is entitled to a mechanic's lien. The trial court decided this issue for respondent and entered judgment accordingly. The court of appeals affirmed the money judgment but reversed that portion of the judgment imposing the lien, holding that the bedspreads were

not lienable items and their inclusion in the statement vitiated the entire lien. While we determine the case the same as on original appeal, Mo. Const. Art. V, § 10, we ordered the transfer primarily to review the questions presented by the holding that the whole lien was vitiated. We decide that it was not.

* * *

[Missouri law] provides in part: "Every mechanic or other person, who shall do or perform any work or labor upon, or furnish any material [or], fixtures ... for any building ... under or by virtue of any contract with the owner ... shall have for his work or labor done, or materials [or], fixtures ... furnished, a lien upon such building ... and upon the land. ..."

Characterization of an item as a fixture, something otherwise personal but attached to realty under such circumstances as to become part of it, depends upon the finding of three elements: annexation to the realty, adaption to the use to which the realty is devoted, and intent of the annexor that the object become a permanent accession to the freehold [realty]. Missouri cases are uniform in requiring each of these elements to be present in some degree, however slight, before an item may be considered a fixture. [Citations.]

Appellants [Seven Palms] contend that neither the drapes nor the bedspreads are fixtures . . . and therefore not lienable, because they are not annexed or attached to the building.

The purpose of attaching the traverse rods to the realty was to hang drapes therefrom which could be opened or drawn across a window by the motel's guest to control the light in his room or secure his privacy. Of itself, the traverse rod attached to the wall above the window in the room did not accomplish this purpose. To serve this purpose it was essential that the drapes be provided and attached to the rod. They were provided and attached, and became an integral part of the instrument designed for use in connection with the window in the guest's room. As such, the drapes were as much a fixture as the traverse rod itself. It is obvious that the rod and drapes, as a unit, were adapted to the proper use of rooms in a motel and were placed therein with the intent they would form a part of the special purpose for which the building was designed to be used.

Not so the bedspreads. Respondent [Sears] admits that those items are not physically attached to the realty in any way but insists that they have been "constructively annexed." In support of this proposition, respondent argues: the rods are physically fastened to the building; the drapes are affixed to the rods by hooks; the bedspreads match the drapes; a fortiori, the bedspreads "are at least 'constructively annexed' to the rooms . . . by their relationship with the drapes."

The doctrine of constructive annexation recognizes that a particular article, not physically attached to the land, "may be so adapted to the use to which the land is put that it may be considered an integral part of the land" and "constructively annexed" thereto. [Citation.] . . . The rule has not been applied to establishments such as hotels, restaurants, bars, and apartment buildings. Thus, movable fur-

niture, tableware, and similar equipment, although necessary to the operation of a hotel, are generally not considered fixtures. [Citations.]

The bedspreads are not essential to the use of what is clearly a fixture, nor has it been shown that they cannot readily be used independently elsewhere. Respondent asserts that because the bedspreads "were designed to match and to coexist with the drapes" they must be considered part of a matched set which is essential to the use of rods which are clearly fixtures. Respondent seeks support for this contention in cases that have held easily removable parts of machines and other fixtures may not be considered as separate items. [Citations.] However, in each of these cases, the fixture would have been rendered absolutely useless by removal of the items in question, and such items could not readily be used independently elsewhere. There is no indication that the unit of rod and drapes could not serve its function, which respondent says is to "regulate the flow of light and serve the need for privacy," if the bedspreads were removed. That the decor of a guest room in a motel may be more aesthetically pleasing when bedspreads are made of the same material as drapes, falls far short of the functional relationship needed to justify "constructive annexation." Since the bedspreads were not annexed, physically or constructively, they cannot be characterized as fixtures and are, therefore, nonlienable items.

* * * Respondent's argument that both were lienable was not without some substance, even though we have determined that one, the bedspreads, was not a fixture and not lienable. In these circumstances, the inclusion in the lien statement of the nonlienable item, separable as it is from the lienable items, does not vitiate the entire lien.

Appellants do not question the money judgment in favor of respondent and against defendant, Seven Palms Motor Inn. Accordingly, that part of the judgment is affirmed. That part of the judgment imposing a lien on the property for the full amount of the money judgment is reversed and the cause is remanded with directions that the trial court enter judgment in favor of respondent imposing a lien for the amount of the balance due according to the statement after deducting therefrom the amount charged for the bedspreads.

Delivery of Gift

ESTATE OF ROSS v. ROSS

Supreme Court of Utah, 1981.
626 P.2d 489.

HOWE, J.

This action was initiated by the personal representative of decedent David E. Ross to determine whether the decedent had made completed inter vivos gifts of certain shares of corporate stock to his son E. Roderick Ross (hereinafter called Rod) or whether the shares were a part of the decedent's estate and should be distributed equally among his three children, who are his heirs under his will. The District Court held that the decedent had made valid inter vivos gifts of the stock to Rod. David E. Ross II and Betsy Louise Ross Rapps (hereinafter called David and Betsy), the brother and sister of Rod, appeal.

Decedent was the secretary and treasurer of Equitable Life and Casualty Insurance Company and also served as one of its directors and as stock transfer agent. The entire stock was owned by the decedent and his two brothers and their families. Decedent also served in the same capacities in four other family-owned companies, namely, Ross Brothers Corporation, National Housing and Finance Syndicate, Insurance Investment Company, and Equitable Investment Company.

In 1972 Rod began working for Equitable Life. David and Betsy lived out of the state and were not involved in the operations of the various companies. Between 1974 and 1978, decedent told several persons of his desire to reward Rod for his work with Equitable Life by giving him stock which would be in addition to the stock he would later inherit. A number of stock transfers were subsequently made on the corporate books by the decedent.

In November 1974 decedent cancelled a stock certificate representing his ownership of 2440.87 shares of Equitable Life. In its place a certificate for 2210.70 shares was issued in Rod's name and another for 230.17 shares was issued to decedent. These transfers were shown by appropriate entries on the stock ledger sheet of the company. The certificate issued to Rod was placed in an envelope on which was typed his name, the certificate number, the number of shares it represented, and the date. The envelope was placed in a bank safety deposit box with other envelopes that contained stock certificates belonging to other stockholders.

In December 1974 a 25% share dividend was declared and paid to all shareholders of record of Equitable Life. A certificate for 552.67 shares of common stock was issued in Rod's name and was placed in the envelope containing the other certificate already issued to him. A notation on the envelope identified the second certificate. Cash dividends were paid to shareholders in November 1976 and May 1977 and Rod received the amounts of $276.33 and $276.34. He also attended and voted at shareholders' meetings.

In May 1977 Ray Ross, decedent's brother and business associate, died. At that time the decedent and his surviving brother, Galen, transferred the contents of the safety deposit box where the stock certificates of various family members had been kept to a safe located in the company offices. Only the decedent and the president and vice president of Equitable Life had the combination to the safe.

The Ross Brothers Corporation was organized at a meeting held in December 1977 for the purpose of distributing the assets of a former partnership involving the three brothers. Galen Ross issued stock certificates in the new corporation. A certificate for 250 shares, which represented 25% of the shares allotted to his father, was issued in Rod's name and handed to him personally. He delivered the certificate to his father, and it was placed in an envelope identified by his name and kept with the other family stock certificates.

In February 1978 there were several transactions in which stock certificates were issued in Rod's name. These certificates represented shares in Equitable Investment Company, Insurance Investment Company, and the National Housing and Finance Syndicate Corporation. The trial court found that "[a]ll actions necessary to complete the transfer on the books and records of each of the corporations for each of the shares of stock in question were completed. . . ." The certificates were placed in a single envelope with the name of Rod Ross and the certificate numbers written upon it. The envelope was placed with the others in the office safe.

The shares transferred to Rod represented one-fourth of the stock holdings of his father. There was testimony that the decedent had expressed his intention that Rod should receive one-fourth of his stock through lifetime gifts, and that the remaining three-quarters would pass by will and be equally divided among Rod, David and Betsy. This would result in Rod's receiving a total of one-half of his father's stock, and his brother and sister each receiving one-fourth.

A will prepared for the decedent by his brother Galen and dated February 1978 divided the estate equally among the three surviving children. There was no reference in the will to prior gifts of stock to Rod.

After their father's death, on April 19, 1978, David and Betsy challenged the validity of the inter vivos stock transfers. Their position before the trial court was that there had been no completed gifts because Rod did not have possession of the stock certificates issued in his name, he did not know where the certificates were or have access to the safe where they were kept, and no gift tax returns were ever filed by the decedent with respect to the transfers.

* * *

Appellants assert that three elements must be proven for a person to claim valid title to property by inter vivos gift: a clear and unmistakable intention on the part of the donor to pass immediate ownership, an irrevocable delivery, and acceptance. They concede that there is substantial evidence in

the record to support the lower court's conclusion that there was the necessary intent on the part of decedent to make a gift and that Rod "accepted" the stock transfer. They contend, however, that the court's decision was erroneous in that the element of irrevocable delivery was not established by clear and convincing evidence.

An important purpose of the delivery requirement is to avoid the hedging of a would-be donor who wishes to retain certain benefits of ownership, including the control of the gift property, while designating another as the recipient of the property during the donor's lifetime. If a gift is not completed before one's death, of course, it is subject to the formalities of testamentary disposition. In the instant case, therefore, the finding of a gift must be based on the decedent's voluntary parting with the control of the stock during his lifetime.

It is appellants' position that decedent should have parted with his dominion over the certificates by physically delivering them to Rod and that the transfer of ownership on the corporate records was insufficient to meet the requirement of delivery. Other courts have split on this issue, and the question has not been ruled on by this Court.

* * *

We . . . hold that manual delivery of the stock certificates personally to Rod was not a prerequisite to a valid gift.

Viewing the facts of this case in light of the requirements of inter vivos gifts, we find the gifts of stock to Rod were complete and valid. Evidence of decedent's intention that Rod be made the owner of the stock in question during his lifetime was uncontroverted. Appellants do not challenge the sufficiency of the evidence as to donative intent nor the finding of the trial court that the change in ownership was recorded on the corporate books. New certificates were issued in Rod's name. The decedent did not thereafter exercise control over the stocks. On the contrary, Rod voted the stock as its legal owner and received cash and stock dividends.

The fact that the stock certificates were kept in a safe to which decedent, but not Rod, had access is not fatal to the finding of a completed gift. The decedent had physical possession of stock certificates belonging to a number of other Ross family members. There was no assertion or evidence that he exerted control or possessory rights over any of that stock. His custody of Rod's stock was simply consistent with the practice within the family businesses of keeping the stock certificates in a central location clearly identified as to the owners of the shares. Individual envelopes carried owners' names, stock certificate numbers, and the number of shares represented by the certificates.

We find no error in the trial court's interpretation of the evidence or its application of Utah law in reaching the conclusion that the inter vivos gifts to Rod were valid.

* * *

Affirmed.

Gift: Intent

COHEN v. BAYSIDE FEDERAL SAVINGS AND LOAN ASSOCIATION

Supreme Court of New York, Term, 1970.
62 Misc.2d 738, 309 N.Y.S.2d 980.

TESSLER, J.

The fundamental question presented to this court in an agreed statement of facts submitted by the parties is:

Can an engagement ring, given in contemplation of marriage, be recovered from a "donee", by the estate of the "donor", when the contemplated marriage fails to occur because of the death of the "donor"?

The undisputed facts can be summarized as follows: Richard Alan Rothchild became engaged to be married to Carol Sue Cohen, the defendant in this action. Both were over 21 years of age. Richard gave Carol a diamond "engagement" ring which is valued at $1,000. Shortly before the wedding date, Richard was killed in an automobile accident and his estate has instituted this action to recover the ring. The sole question for determination by this court is: "Who is entitled to the ring?"

Actions for return of engagement rings have had an interesting and confusing history in New York. These actions were permitted at common law prior to 1935. However, in 1935 the Legislature of this State enacted . . . (the heart balm statute) which was later interpreted by the courts so as to bar actions for the return of engagement rings in most instances. [Citations.] These results were widely criticized. [Citations.] In response to this criticism, in 1965 the Legislature amended . . . the Civil Rights Law to permit recovery of engagement rings where "justice so requires."

In Lowe v. Quinn, [citation] the Appellate Division, First Department, held that the common law rules formulated before 1935 would again be applicable. * * *

However, reference to these common law rules formulated prior to 1935 is of little help in the present instance since this case appears to be one of first impression in this State. In the absence of any controlling authority, this court has sought help by looking to applicable decisional law in other jurisdictions, the general principles underlying engagement ring cases in general and, finally, to what justice requires in this situation.

An examination of the relevant authorities in other states indicates that they are split.

* * *

Nor does an examination of the principles underlying the gift of engagement ring cases in general clearly point the way to a particular result. The results set forth in the decisions in gift of engagement ring cases are usually predictable and understandable. However, the legal principles and rationales relied upon by the courts are often divergent and muddled. For example, it is settled that where a fiancee breaks an engagement without the fault of the donor, she must return the ring. [Citation.] It is also well settled that where the donor breaks the engagement, the ring may be kept by the donee [citation] and, generally, where the engagement is broken by mutual consent, the ring also goes back to the donor. [Citation.]

While these results are equitable, the various legal theories asserted are not always logical and persuasive. Some courts have propounded a pledge theory. [Citation.] Other courts state that principles of unjust enrichment govern [citation] and the most popular rationale is that the ring is given as a gift on condition subsequent. [Citation.] It is not always clear, however, whether it is the actual marriage of the parties or the donee's not performing any act that would prevent the marriage that is the actual condition of the "transaction."

Thus, a confusing body of law has grown up around the engagement ring and, after careful consideration of these principles, this court has decided that Carol should keep the ring because that result is equitable and because "justice so requires" for the following reasons:

While the engagement ring to some people in the "mod" world of today is just another material possession and while it has not been unknown in some circles for recipients of these rings to flaunt them, to compare their luster, number of carats, etc., with the rings of their friends, for the vast majority the ring still remains a hallowed symbol of the love and devotion that a prospective husband and wife bear for each other. In my judgment, no gift given during a lifetime can approach the meaningfulness and significance of the engagement ring. When Richard gave the ring to Carol, he obviously intended that she have it and keep it unless she affirmatively did something to prevent the marriage of the parties. While it is improbable that at the time of the gift either gave a thought to the consequences that would arise in the event of the death of one of the parties, I firmly believe that had Richard thought of these consequences he would have intended that in the event of his untimely death Carol should keep the ring as a symbol of his love and affection. There appears to be no reason, in logic or morals, to prevent such a result.

This court frankly acknowledges that implicit in this determination is a recognition that the gift of an engagement ring is a special occasion interwoven with romance and mutual love. It is a meaningful act symbolic of much more than the ordinary and usual

business transaction. I am convinced that it is time for a change in our approach to this area. The traditional approach of applying the sound and settled principles of business law and the law of gifts to the giving of an engagement ring has resulted in a myriad of decisional law in this area, which is, to say the least, in much confusion and determinative of little.

I cannot believe that the age-old ritual of giving an engagement ring to bind the mutual premarital vows can be or is intended to be treated as an exchange of consideration as practiced in the everyday market place. Can it be seriously urged that the giving of this ring by the decedent "groom" to his loved one and bride-to-be can be treated as the ordinary commercial or business transaction requiring the ultimate in consideration and payment? I think not. To treat this special and usually once in a lifetime occasion, one as requiring quid pro quo, is a mistake and unrealistic.

Accordingly, the ring shall remain with Carol and judgment shall be entered.

Title to Lost or Misplaced Personal Property

PASET v. OLD ORCHARD BANK AND TRUST CO.

Appellate Court of Illinois, First District, 1978.
62 Ill.App.3d 534, 19 Ill.Dec. 389, 378 N.E.2d 1264.

SIMON, J.

On May 8, 1974, the plaintiff, Bernice Paset, a safety deposit box subscriber at the defendant Old Orchard Bank (the bank), found $6,325 in currency on the seat of a chair in an examination booth in the safety deposit vault. The chair was partially under a table. The plaintiff notified officers of the bank and turned the money over to them. She then was told by bank officials that the bank would try to locate the owner, and that she could have the money if the owner was not located within 1 year.

The bank wrote to everyone who had been in the safety deposit vault area either on the day of, or on the day preceding, the discovery, stating that some property had been found and inviting the customers to describe any property they might have lost. No one reported the loss of currency, and the money remained unclaimed a year after it had been found. However, when the plaintiff requested the money, the bank refused to deliver it to her, explaining that it was obligated to hold the currency for the owner.

The safety deposit vault area of the bank was located on a lower floor of the bank. This area was separated from a lobby by a gate, and . . . entrance to the safety deposit vault area was restricted to bank employees and customers maintaining safety deposit boxes in the vault. . . . The plaintiff sought a declaratory judgment that the Illinois estray statute [citation] was applicable to her discovery and granted her ownership of the $6,325. The circuit court judge, however, found that the money was "deemed mislaid," and concluded that despite the plaintiff's compliance with the requirements of the estray statute, that statute was not applicable.

This appeal, then, requires a determination of whether a finder of cash in an examining booth in a safety deposit vault may be a keeper under the Illinois estray statute and an analysis of the extent to which the common law concepts of lost and mislaid property apply to the statute. . . . The Illinois estray statute's principle purposes are to encourage and facilitate the return of property to the true owner, and then to reward a finder for his honesty if the property remains unclaimed. The statute provides an incentive for finders to report their discoveries by making it possible for them, after the passage of the requisite time, to acquire legal title to the property they have found. [Citation.] By directing the county clerk to publicize and advertise the property, the statute further enhances the opportunity of the owner to recover what he has lost.

Traditionally, the common law has treated lost and mislaid property differently for the purposes of determining ownership of property someone has found. Mislaid property is that which is intentionally put in a certain place and later forgotten; at common law a finder acquires no rights to mislaid property.

The element of intentional deposit present in the case of mislaid property is absent in the case of lost property, for property is deemed lost when it is unintentionally separated from the dominion of its owner. The general rule is that the finder is entitled to possession of lost property against everyone except the true owner. We are not concerned in this case with abandoned property where the owner, intending to relinquish all rights to his property, leaves it free to be appropriated by any other person. Although at common law the finder is entitled to keep abandoned property, the plaintiff has not taken the position that the money here was abandoned. [Citation.]

As is usual in cases involving a determination of whether property is lost or mislaid, this court is not here assisted by direct evidence, for, obviously, the true owner is not available to state what his intent was. Also, because all the evidence here has been presented by affidavit or stipulation, this court is in as advantageous a position as the trial judge to determine whether the money was lost or mislaid. Our conclusion is that the estray statute should be applied, and ownership of the money vested in the plaintiff finder.

Thus, we do not accept the bank's argument that the money was mislaid rather than lost. It is complete speculation to infer, as the bank urges, that the money was deliberately placed by its owner on the chair located partially under a table in the examining booth, and then forgotten. If the money was intentionally placed on the chair by someone who forgot where he left it, the bank's notice to safety deposit box subscribers should have alerted the owner. The failure of an owner to appear to claim the money in the interval since its discovery is affirmative evidence that the property was not mislaid. [Citations.]

Because the evidence, though ambiguous, tends to indicate that the money probably was not mislaid, and because neither party contends that the money was abandoned, we conclude that the ambiguity should, as a matter of public policy, be resolved in favor of the presumption that the money was lost.

This conclusion is in harmony with the above mentioned purposes of the estray statute, for it construes the statute liberally rather than technically, with the result that the statute is brought into play rather than rejected. Such an application of the statute better effectuates the legislature's goal of restoring property to a true owner, it provides incentive for a finder to report his discovery by rewarding him if the true owner does not appear within the statutorily-determined time limit.

* * *

Further, whether the property was discovered in a public or private place should not be permitted to preclude the application of the estray statute. The statute itself makes no distinction between "public" and "private" places of finding.

Accordingly, the judgment of the circuit court is reversed and the case is remanded with directions to enter judgment in favor of the plaintiff finder.

Judgment reversed and remanded with directions.

QUESTIONS

1. Distinguish between (a) tangible and intangible property, and (b) real and personal property.

2. Define and give three examples of a fixture.

3. Identify and discuss the three elements for a valid gift.

4. Distinguish among the rights of a finder to abandoned, mislaid, and lost property.

5. Define and contrast the property rights created by accession and confusion.

PROBLEMS

1. In January, Roger Burke loaned his favorite nephew, Jimmy White, his valuable painting by Picasso. Knowing that Jimmy would celebrate his twenty-first birthday on May 15, Burke sent a letter to Jimmy on April 14 stating:

Dear Jimmy,

Tomorrow I leave on my annual trip to Europe, and I want to make you a fitting birthday gift, which I do by sending you my enclosed promissory note. Also I want you to keep the Picasso, which I loaned you last January, and you may now consider it yours. Happy birthday!

Affectionately,
/s/ Uncle Roger

The negotiable promissory note for $5,000 sent with the letter was signed by Roger Burke, payable to Jimmy White or bearer, and dated May 15. On May 21, Burke was killed in an automobile accident while motoring in France.

First Bank was appointed administrator of Burke's estate. Jimmy presented the note to the administrator and demanded payment, which was refused. Jimmy brought an action against First Bank as administrator seeking recovery on the note. The administrator brought an action against Jimmy seeking return of the painting by Picasso.

(a) What decision in the action on the note?

(b) What decision in the action to recover the painting?

2. Several years ago Pierce purchased a tract of land on which there was an old, vacant house. Recently, Pierce employed Fried, a carpenter, to repair and remodel the house. While Fried was tearing out a partition for the purpose of enlarging one of the rooms, he discovered a metal box hidden in the wall of the house. Fried broke open the box and discovered that it contained $2,000 in gold and silver coins and old-style bills. Fried then took the box and its contents to Pierce and told her where he had found it. When Fried handed the box and the money over to Pierce, he said, "If you do not find the owner, I claim the money." Pierce placed the money in an envelope and deposited it in her safe deposit box, where it is at present. No one has ever claimed the money, but Pierce refuses to give it to Fried.

Fried brings an action against Pierce to recover the money. Decision?

3. Gable, the owner of a lumber company, was cutting trees over the boundary line of his property and property owned by Lane. Although he realized he had crossed onto Lane's property, Gable cut trees on Lane's property of the same kind as those he had cut on his own land. While on Lane's property, he found a diamond ring on the ground, which he took home. All of the timber cut that day by Gable was commingled.

What are Lane's rights, if any, (a) in the timber, and (b) in the ring?

4. Decide each of the following problems.

(a) A chimney sweep found a jewel and took it to a goldsmith, whose apprentice took the stone out and refused to return it. The chimney sweep sues the goldsmith.

(b) One of several boys walking along a railroad track found an old stocking. All started playing with it until it burst in the hands of its discoverer, revealing several hundred dollars. The original discoverer claims it all; the other boys claim it should be divided equally.

(c) A traveling salesman notices a parcel of bank notes on the floor of a store as he is leaving. He picks them up and gives them to the owner of the store to keep for the true owner. After three years they have not been reclaimed, and the salesman sues the storekeeper.

(d) Frank is hired to clean out the swimming pool at the country club. He finds a diamond ring on the bottom of the pool. The true owner cannot be found. The country club sues Frank for possession of the ring.

(e) A customer found a pocketbook lying on a barber's table. He gave it to the barber to hold for the true owner, who failed to appear. The customer sues the barber.

5. Jones had 50 crates of oranges about equally divided between grades A, B, and C, grade A being the highest quality and C the lowest quality. Smith had 1,000 crates of oranges, about 90 percent of which were grade A, but some of them grades B and C, the exact quantity of each being unknown. Smith willfully mixed Jones's crates with his own so that it was impossible to identify any particular crate. Jones seized the whole lot. Smith demanded 900 crates of grade A and 50 each of grades B and C. Jones refused to give them up unless Smith could identify particular crates. This Smith could not do. Smith brought an action against Jones to recover what he demanded or its value. Judgment for whom, and why?

6. Barnes, the owner and operator of Blackacre, decided to cease farming operations and liquidate his holdings. Barnes sold fifty head of yearling Merino sheep to Billing and then sold Blackacre to Clifton. He executed and delivered to Billing a bill of sale for the sheep and was paid for them. It was understood that Billing would send a truck for the sheep within a few days. At the same time, Barnes executed a warranty deed conveying Blackacre to Clifton. Clifton took possession of the farm and brought along one hundred head of his yearling Merino sheep and turned them into the pasture, not knowing the sheep Barnes sold Billing were still in the pasture. After the sheep were mixed, it was impossible to identify the fifty head belonging to Billing. After proper demand, Billing sued Clifton to recover the fifty head of sheep. Decision?

7. Susan permitted Kevin to take her very old grandfather clock on the basis of Kevin's representations that he was skilled at repairing such clocks and restoring them to their original condition and could do the job for $60. The clock had been badly damaged for years. Kevin immediately sold the clock to Fixit Shop for $30. Fixit Shop was in the business of repairing a large variety of items and also sold used articles. Three months later, Susan was in the Fixit Shop and clearly established that a grandfather clock Fixit Shop had for sale was the one she had given Kevin to repair. Fixit Shop had replaced more than half of the moving parts by having exact duplicates custom made; the clock's exterior had been restored by a skilled cabinetmaker; and the clock's face had been replaced by a duplicate. All materials belonged to Fixit Shop, and the work was accomplished by its employees. Fixit Shop asserts it bought the clock in the normal course of business from Kevin who represented that it belonged to him. The fair market value of the clock in its damaged condition was $30, and the value of repairs made is $220.

Susan sued Fixit Shop for return of the clock. Fixit Shop defended that it now had title to the clock and, in the alternative, that Susan must pay the value of the repairs if she is entitled to regain possession. Decision?

8. Hyer rented a vacant lot from Bateman for a filling station under an oral agreement and placed on it a lightly constructed building bolted to a concrete slab and storage tanks laid on the ground in a shallow excavation. Later, a lease was prepared by Hyer, providing that Hyer might remove the equipment at the termination of the lease. This lease was not executed, having been rejected by Bateman because of a renewal clause it contained, but several years later another lease was prepared, which both Hyer and Bateman did sign. This lease did not mention removal of the equipment. At the termination of this lease Hyer removed the equipment, and Bateman brought an action to recover possession of the equipment. What judgment?

9. Elvers sold a parcel of real estate, describing it by its legal description and making no mention of any improvements or fixtures on it. The land had upon it a residence, a barn, a rail fence, a stack of hay, some growing corn, and a windmill. The residence had a mirror built into the panel and a heating system consisting of a furnace, steam pipes, and coils. In the house there were chairs, beds, tables, and other furniture. On the house was a lightning rod. In the basement were screens for the windows. Which of these things passed by the deed and which did not?

10. John Swan rented a safety deposit box at the Tenth Citizens Bank of Emanon, State of X. On December 17, 1990, Swan went to the bank with stock certificates to place in the safety deposit box. After he was admitted to the vault and had placed the stock certificates in the box, Swan found lying on the floor of the vault a $5,000 negotiable bearer bond issued by the State of Wisconsin with coupons attached, due June 30, 1996. Swan picked up the bond and, observing that it did not carry the name of the owner, left the vault and went to the office of the president of the bank. He told the president what had occurred and delivered the bond to the president only after obtaining his promise that, should the owner not call for the bond or become known to the bank by June 30, 1991, the bank would redeliver the bond to Swan. On July 1, 1991, Swan learned that the owner of the bond had not called for it, nor was his identity known to the bank. Swan then asked that the bond be returned to him. The bank refused, stating that it would continue to hold the bond until claimed by the owner. Swan brings an action against the bank to recover possession of the bond. Decision?

Chapter 49

BAILMENTS AND DOCUMENTS OF TITLE

Elements of Bailment
Rights and Duties of Parties
Special Types of Bailments
Documents of Title

A bailment is the relationship created by the transfer by delivery of possession of personal property, without transfer of title, by one person called the bailor to another called the bailee for the accomplishment of a certain purpose, after which the property is to be returned by the bailee to the bailor or disposed of according to the bailor's directions. Unlike such well-known legal terms as contract, agent, sale, partnership, corporation, and insurance, the term *bailment* has not passed into common usage and so is not familiar to many people. Nonetheless, the word *bailment* denotes a transaction that not only is of considerable antiquity but also is one of the most common occurrences in everyday life. It is not an exaggeration to say that practically every person, whether carrying on a business or not, becomes a party to a bailment. This will be readily understood from the following common examples of bailments: keeping a car in a public garage; leaving a car, a watch, or any other article to be repaired; renting a car or truck; checking a hat or coat at a theater or restaurant; leaving clothes to be laundered; delivering jewelry, stocks, bonds, or other valuables to secure the payment of a debt; storing goods in a ware-house; and shipping goods by public or private transportation.

Not only are bailments of common occurrence, but they are also of great commercial importance. As the above examples indicate, bailments include the transportation, storage, repairing, and renting of goods, which together involve billions of dollars in transactions each year.

Documents of title are commonly used in bailment transactions. The most frequently used documents of title are warehouse receipts issued by warehousemen and bills of lading issued by carriers.

BAILMENTS

A **bailment**, as previously mentioned, is the temporary transfer of possession without title of personal property by one party (the **bailor**) to another (the **bailee**). The benefit of a bailment may, by its terms, accrue solely to the bailor or solely to the bailee or may accrue to both parties. A bailment may be with or without compensation. On this basis, bailments are classified as follows.

1. *Bailments for the bailor's sole benefit* include the gratuitous custody of personal property and the gratuitous services that involve custody of personal property, such as repairs or transportation. For example, if Ed stores, repairs, or transports Francis's goods without compensation, this is a bailment for the sole benefit of the bailor, Francis.

2. *Bailments for the bailee's sole benefit* are usually limited to the gratuitous loan of personal property for use by the bailee, as where Francis, without compensation, lends his car, lawnmower, or book to Edith for her use.

3. *Bailments for the mutual benefit of both parties* include the ordinary commercial bailments such as when goods are delivered to a repairman, jewels to a pawnbroker, or an automobile to a parking lot attendant.

ESSENTIAL ELEMENTS OF A BAILMENT

The basic and essential elements of a bailment are (1) delivery of possession by a bailor to a bailee; (2) delivery of personal property and not real property; (3) possession without ownership by the bailee; (4) possession for a determinable period of time; and (5) an absolute duty on the bailee to return the property to the bailor or to dispose of it according to the bailor's directions.

In the great majority of cases, there are two simple tests by which the existence of a bailment can be determined: (1) a separation of ownership and possession of the property (possession without ownership), and (2) a duty on the party in possession to redeliver the identical property to the owner or to dispose of it according to the owner's directions.

Delivery of Possession

The term *bailment* is derived from the French word *bailler,* meaning "to deliver." Possession by a bailee in a bailment relationship involves (1) the bailee's power to control, and (2) an intention to control. Thus, for example, where a customer in a restaurant hangs her hat or coat on a hook furnished for that pur-

pose, the hat or coat is within an area under the physical control of the restaurant owner. But the restaurant owner is not a bailee of the hat or coat unless he clearly signifies that he intends to exercise the power to control the hat or coat. On the other hand, where a clerk in a store helps a customer remove her coat in order to try on a new one, it is generally held that the owner of the store becomes a bailee of the old coat through the clerk, his employee. Here, the clerk has signified an intention to exercise control over the coat by taking it from the customer and a bailment results.

Leaving a car in a commercial parking lot may be a bailment. The parking lot cases fall generally into three categories: (1) Where an owner parks his car in a parking lot, pays a charge, and receives a claim check, but locks the car and takes the keys away. This class of cases is generally held to be a lease or license (a right to use the space). (2) Where an owner leaves his car with an attendant who assumes control of the car and parks it, and the owner pays a charge and receives a ticket as a means of identifying the car on redelivery. This class is held to be a bailment. (3) Where the status of the parties falls in between the above two categories and is controlled by the nature of the circumstances. This class covers cases where, even though the owner parks his car and keeps the keys, the parking lot operator maintains sufficient control to constitute a bailment. In analyzing this third class of cases, the amount of free access permitted by the parking lot operator and how much control the parking lot operator holds himself out to the public to be exercising are crucial. *See Sewall v. Fitz-Inn Auto Parks, Inc.*

Personal Property

The bailment relationship can exist only with respect to personal property. The delivery of possession of real property by the owner to another is not a bailment. It is not necessary that the bailed property be tangible. Intangible property, such as promissory notes, corporate bonds, shares of stock, documents of title, and life insurance policies that are evidenced by written instruments and thus capable of delivery, may be and frequently are the subject matter of bailments.

Possession for a Determinable Time

To establish a bailment relationship, the person receiving possession must be under a duty to return the personal property and must not obtain title to it. Whether a particular transaction constitutes a bailment or a sale must be determined by the particular situation. A sale always involves a transfer to the buyer of *title* to specific property. If the identical property transferred is to be returned, even though in altered form, the transaction is a bailment; however, if other property of equal value or the money value may be returned, there is a transfer of title, and the transaction is a sale.

Whenever a person intentionally abandons her interest in personal property, the relation between her and the person who takes possession of the property will not be that of bailor and bailee. On the other hand, a loser and finder are bailor and bailee because, although the loser may abandon hope that she will ever find the property, she does not abandon her interest in it. For a discussion of abandoned, lost, and mislaid property see Chapter 48.

Restoration of Possession to the Bailor

The bailee is legally obligated to restore possession of the property when the period of the bailment ends. A bailment for the mutual benefit of both parties ordinarily terminates when the purpose of the bailment is fully accomplished or when the time for which the bailment was created expires. The bailment may, of course, be terminated earlier by mutual consent of the parties. A breach by the bailee of any of his obligations gives the bailor the privilege of terminating the bailment. A bailment is also terminated by destruction of the bailed property because there can be no bailment without the subject personal property.

Normally, the bailee is required to return the identical goods bailed, although the goods may be in a changed condition due to the work that the bailee was required to perform on them. An exception to this rule applies to **fungible goods,** such as grain, where, for all practical purposes, every particle is the equivalent of every other particle, and which the bailee is expected to mingle with other like goods during the bailment. In such a case, obviously the bailee cannot be required to return the identical goods bailed. His obligation is simply to return goods of the same quality and quantity.

RIGHTS AND DUTIES OF BAILOR AND BAILEE

The bailment relationship creates rights and duties on the part of the bailor and the bailee. The bailee is under a duty to exercise due care for the safety of the property and to return it to the right person. The bailee has the exclusive right to possess the property for the term of the bailment. Depending on the nature of the transaction, a bailee may have the right to limit its liability and to compensation. The bailor also has certain duties with respect to the condition of the bailed goods.

Bailee's Duty to Exercise Due Care

The bailee must exercise due care not to permit injury to or destruction of the property by himself or third parties. The degree of care depends on the nature of the bailment relationship and the character of the property. *See Mieske v. Bartell Drug Co.* Ordinarily, a bailee is *not* an insurer of the subject of the bailment. Since the failure to exercise due care for the property or intentional wrongdoing is the basis of his liability, in the absence of fault, the bailee is not liable where the property is lost, stolen, or destroyed.

In the context of a **commercial bailment,** from which both parties derive a mutual benefit, the law requires the bailee to exercise the care that a reasonably prudent person would exercise under the same circumstances. Where the bailment is one that benefits the bailee alone, as in the case of one who gratuitously borrows a truck from another, the law requires more than reasonable care of him. On the other hand, where the bailee accepts the property for the sole benefit of the bailor, the law requires a lesser degree of care (see Figure 49–1).

Nevertheless, the amount of care required to satisfy any of the standards will vary with the character of the property. A bailee required to take only slight care under the general rules mentioned above may be liable if he does not take greater care of a $10,000 bracelet than he would have of a $20 watch. In practice, therefore, the distinctions are blurred by the fact that whatever degree of care is required in the abstract, a bailee must respond to the magnitude of the consequences that reasonably ought to have been foreseen if the property were lost or destroyed.

When the property is lost, damaged, or destroyed while in the possession of the bailee, it is often impossible for the bailor to obtain enough information to show that the loss or damage was due to the bailee's failure to exercise the required care. The law aids the bailor in this respect by *presuming* that the bailee was at fault. The bailor is merely required to show that certain property was delivered by way of bailment and that the bailee has failed to return it or that it was returned in damaged condition. The burden then rests upon the bailee to prove that he exercised the degree of care required of him.

Bailee's Absolute Liability

As just discussed, the bailee is free from liability if she has exercised the degree of care required of her under the particular bailment while the property was within her control. This general rule has certain important exceptions that impose an absolute duty upon the bailee to return the property undamaged to the proper person.

Where the bailee has an obligation by express *agreement* with the bailor or by *custom* to insure the property against certain risks but fails to do so, and the property is destroyed or damaged through such risks, she is liable for the damage or nondelivery, even though she has exercised due care.

Where the bailee uses the bailed property in a manner *not* authorized by the bailor or by the character of the bailment, and during the course of such use the property is damaged or destroyed, without fault on the part of the bailee, the bailee is absolutely liable for the damage or destruction. The reason for this is that wrongful use by the bailee automatically terminates her lawful possession, and she becomes a trespasser as to the property. To illustrate, suppose a garage mechanic, after repairing Brown's car, takes it out for a road test, and the car is damaged in an accident that is solely the fault of someone other than the mechanic. The proprietor of the garage will not be liable as bailee for such damage because a road test is a normal incident to this type of bailment. But where the mechanic takes Brown's car for a joy ride or on independent business, and the car is damaged solely through the fault of someone other than the mechanic, the proprietor will be absolutely liable as bailee for the damage.

A bailee has a duty to return the property to the right person. If the bailee, by mistake or intent, *misdelivers* the property to someone other than the bailor, who has no right to

---

Figure 49–1 Bailee's Duty of Care

Type of Bailment	Duty of Care	Liability for
For sole benefit of bailor	Slight	Gross negligence
For sole benefit of bailee	Utmost	Slight negligence
For mutual benefit	Ordinary	Ordinary negligence

its possession, she is guilty of conversion and is liable to the bailor, even when the mistake is caused by negligence on the part of the bailor.

Bailee's Right to Limit Liability

The law does not permit certain bailees— common carriers, public warehousers, and innkeepers—to limit their liability for breach of their duties to the bailor, *except* as provided by statute. Other bailees, however, may vary their duties and liabilities by contract with the bailor. Where liability is limited by contract, the law requires that any such limitation be properly brought to the attention of the bailor before the property is bailed by her. This is especially true in the case of "professional bailees," such as repair garages, who make it their business to act as bailees and who deal with the public on a uniform rather than an individual basis. Thus, a variation or limitation in writing contained in a check or stub given to the bailor or posted on the walls of the bailee's place of business will *not* ordinarily bind the bailor unless the bailee (a) draws the bailor's attention to the writing, and (b) informs the bailor that it contains a limitation or variation of liability.

Bailee's Right to Compensation

A bailee who by express or implied agreement undertakes to perform work on or render services in connection with the bailed goods is entitled to reasonable compensation for those services or work and to reimbursement of expenses. In most cases, the agreement between bailor and bailee fixes the amount of compensation and provides how it shall be paid. In the absence of a contrary agreement, the compensation is payable upon completion of the work or the performance of the services by the bailee. If, after such completion or performance, and before the goods are redelivered to the bailor, the goods are lost or damaged without fault on the part of the bailee, the bailee is still entitled to compensation for his work and services.

Most bailees who are entitled to compensation for work and services performed in connection with bailed goods acquire a possessory lien upon the goods to secure the payment of such compensation. In most jurisdictions, the bailee has a statutory right to obtain a judicial foreclosure of his lien and sale of the goods. Many statutes also provide that the bailee does not lose his lien upon redelivery of the goods to the bailor, as is the case at common law. Instead, the lien continues for a specified period after redelivery by timely recording with the proper authorities an instrument claiming such a lien.

Bailor's Duties

In a bailment for the sole benefit of the bailee, the bailor warrants that she is unaware of any defects in the bailed property. In all other instances, the bailor has a duty to warn the bailee of all defects she knows of or should have discovered upon a reasonable inspection of the bailed property. A number of courts have extended strict liability in tort and the implied warranties under Article 2 of the U.C.C. to leases and bailments. Article 2A, discussed in Chapter 20, imposes implied warranties on the lease of goods.

SPECIAL TYPES OF BAILMENTS

Although pledgees, warehousemen, and safe deposit companies are ordinarily bailees and are subject to the general principles that apply to all ordinary bailees, some special features about the transactions in which they respectively engage deserve further consideration. In addition, innkeepers and common carriers are known as *extraordinary bailees*, while all other bailees are known as *ordinary bailees*. This distinction is based on the character and extent of the liability of these two classes of bailees for loss of or injury to the bailed goods. As has been seen, an **ordinary bailee** is liable for such loss or injury only where it resulted from his failure to exercise ordinary or reasonable care. The liability of the **extraordinary bailee,** on the other hand, is, in general, **absolute.** In other words, the extraordinary bailee is liable to the bailor for any loss or injury to the goods without regard to the question of his care or negligence as to their safety. As it is frequently put, an extraordinary bailee is an insurer of the safety of the goods. This simply means that just as an insurer, in general, becomes automatically liable to the insured upon the happening of the hazard insured against, regardless of the cause, so does the extraordinary bailee become liable to the bailor for any loss or injury to the goods, regardless of the cause.

Pledges

A **pledge** is a bailment for security in which the owner gives possession of her personal property to another (the secured party) to secure a debt or the performance of some obligation. The secured party does not have title to the property involved but merely a possessory interest to secure a debt or some other obligation. Pledges of most types of personal property for security purposes are governed by Article 9 of the Uniform Commercial Code, which is discussed in Chapter 38. In most respects, the secured party's duties and liabilities are the same as those of a bailee for compensation.

Warehousing

A **warehouser** is a bailee who receives goods to be stored in a warehouse for compensation. His duties and liabilities under the common law were in all ways the same as those of the ordinary bailee for compensation. Today, because the activities of warehousers are affected by a strong public interest, they are subject to extensive regulation by State and Federal authorities. Warehousers must also be distinguished from ordinary bailees in that the receipts they issue for storage have acquired a special status in commerce. These receipts are regarded as documents of title, and are governed by Article 7 of the Uniform Commercial Code (U.C.C.), discussed later in this chapter.

Carriers of Goods

In the broadest sense of the term, anyone who transports goods from one place to another, either gratuitously or for compensation, is a **carrier.** Normally, however, a carrier engages in the business of transportation for hire or reward. The delivery of goods to a carrier for shipment creates a bailment; the carrier has the exclusive possession of the goods without ownership and is under a duty to deliver them to the person designated by the shipper. Carriers of goods are by far the most important of all bailees. Not only are their transactions the most numerous and the largest in volume, but also their function in the movement of raw materials and the distribution of manufactured and other goods of every description is of enormous importance in our economic system.

Carriers are classified primarily as common carriers and private carriers. A **common carrier** offers its services and facilities to the public upon terms and under circumstances indicating that the offering is made to all persons. Common carriers of goods include railroad, ship, aircraft, public trucking, and pipeline companies. One who carries the goods of another on isolated occasions or who serves a limited number of customers under individual contracts without offering the same or similar contracts to the public at large is a **private** or **contract carrier**—not a common carrier. Stated somewhat differently, the criteria for determining whether a carrier is subject to the rules applicable to common carriers are (1) the carriage must be part of its business; (2) the carriage must be for remuneration; and (3) the carrier must represent to the general public that it is willing to serve the public in the transportation of property.

The person who delivers goods to a carrier for shipment is known as the **consignor** or **shipper.** The person to whom the goods are to be delivered by the carrier is known as the **consignee.** The instrument containing the terms of the contract of transportation, which the carrier issues to the shipper, is called a *bill of lading* (discussed later in this chapter).

Duty to Carry   A common carrier is under a duty to serve the public to the limits of its capacity and, within those limits, to accept for carriage goods of the kind that it normally transports. A private carrier has no duty to accept goods for carriage except where it agrees to do so by contract.

Duty to Deliver to the Right Person   The carrier is under an absolute duty to deliver the goods to the person to whom they are consigned by the shipper. This duty applies to both common carriers and private carriers. Essentially, this is the duty that renders an ordinary bailee liable for misdelivery. The person to whom delivery must be made is controlled by the form of the bill of lading or other contract of carriage.

Liability for Loss or Damage   A private carrier, in the absence of special contract terms, is liable as a bailee for the goods it undertakes to carry. A common carrier, on the other hand, is under a stricter liability that approaches that of an insurer of the safety of the goods, except where loss or damage is caused by an act of God, an act of a public enemy, the acts or fault of the shipper, the inherent nature of or a defect in the goods, or an act of public authority.

The carrier, however, is permitted to limit its liability by contract with the shipper, provided the carrier gives the shipper notice of this limitation and the opportunity to declare a higher value. UCC Section 7–309. *See Calvin Klein Inc. v. Trylon Trucking Corp.*

Innkeepers

At common law, **innkeepers** (today better known as hotel owners or operators) are held to the same **strict** or **absolute liability** for their guests' belongings as are common carriers for the goods they carry. This rule of strict liability applies only to those who furnish lodging to the public for compensation as a regular business, and liability extends only to the belongings of lodgers who are guests.

Today, in almost all jurisdictions, the old common law strict liability of the innkeeper has been substantially modified by case law and statute. Although the statutes vary as to detail, they all have certain features in common. They provide that the innkeeper may avoid strict liability for loss of his guests' valuables or money by providing a safe where they may be kept and by posting adequate notice of its availability. For articles that are not placed in a safe provided for this purpose, or that are not articles of the kind normally kept in a safe, the statutes often limit recovery to a maximum figure that, although it varies from State to State, is generally insubstantial. These statutory limitations do not apply where the loss is due to the fault of the innkeeper or his employees, in which case the innkeeper is liable for the full value of the lost property.

DOCUMENTS OF TITLE

A **document of title** is a warehouse receipt, bill of lading, or other document evidencing a right to receive, hold, and dispose of the document *and* the goods it covers. To be a document of title, a document must be issued by or addressed to a *bailee* and cover goods in the bailee's possession that are either identified or are fungible portions of an identified mass. UCC Section 1–201(15).

Briefly, a document of title is a symbol of ownership of the goods it describes. Because of the legal characteristics of a document of title, its ownership is equivalent to the ownership or control of the goods it represents, without the necessity of the actual or physical possession of the goods. Likewise, its transfer is a transfer of the ownership or control of the goods without the necessity or inconvenience of the physical transfer of the goods themselves. For these reasons, documents of title are a convenient means of dealing with the billions of dollars of goods transported by carriers or stored with warehousers. Documents of title also serve an important function in facilitating the transfer of title to goods and the creation of a security interest in goods. **Article 7** of the U.C.C. governs documents of title.

TYPES OF DOCUMENTS OF TITLE

Warehouse Receipts

A **warehouse receipt** is a receipt issued by a person engaged in the business of *storing* goods for hire. Section 1–201(45).

Duties of Warehousers A warehouser is liable for damages for loss or injury to the goods caused by his failure to exercise such care in regard to them as a reasonably careful man would exercise under the circumstances. Section 7–204(1). The States and the Federal government may impose more rigid standards of responsibility. Section 7–204(2). Several States have so elected.

The warehouser must deliver the goods to the person entitled to receive them under the terms of the warehouse receipt. If he has already delivered the goods to another, the burden is on him to establish that such delivery was rightful as against the holder of the document. Similarly, if the goods have become damaged, lost, or destroyed, the burden is on the warehouseman to prove by evidence the facts and circumstances which establish her nonliability. Section 7–403(1). *See I.C.C. Metals, Inc. v. Municipal Warehouse Co.*

The liability of a warehouser, however, *may* be limited by a provision in the warehouse receipt fixing a specific maximum liability per article or item or unit of weight. This limitation does not apply in the event of a conversion of the goods by the warehouser to his own use. Section 7–204(2).

A warehouser is not required to keep the goods indefinitely. At the termination of the period of storage stated in the document, the warehouser may notify the person on whose account the goods are held to pay storage charges and remove the goods. If no period of time is stated in the document, the warehouser is required to give thirty days' notice to pay charges and remove the goods. A shorter time, which must be reasonable, is permitted if the goods are about to deteriorate or decline in value to less than the amount of the warehouser's lien, or if the quality or condition of the goods cause them to be a hazard to other property or to persons. Section 7–206.

Lien of Warehouser To enforce the payment of his charges and necessary expenses in connection with keeping and handling the goods, a warehouser has a lien on the goods, which enables him to sell them at public or private sale after notice and to apply the net proceeds of the sale to the amount of his charges. The Code, moreover, provides a definite procedure for enforcement of the lien of a warehouser against the goods stored and in his possession. Section 2–710.

Against the holder of a negotiable warehouse receipt to whom it has been duly negotiated, this lien is limited to charges at the rate specified in the receipt, and if none is specified, to a reasonable charge for storage of the goods subsequent to the date of the receipt. Section 7–209(1).

Bills of Lading

A **bill of lading** is a document issued by a carrier upon receipt of goods for *transportation*. It serves a threefold function: (1) as a receipt for the goods, (2) as evidence of the contract of carriage, and (3) as a document of title. A bill of lading is negotiable if, by its terms, the goods are deliverable to bearer or to the order of a named person. Any other document is non-negotiable. Section 7–104.

Under the Code, bills of lading may be issued not only by common carriers but also by contract carriers, freight forwarders, or any person engaged in the business of transporting or forwarding goods. Section 1–201(6).

Duties of Issuer of Bill of Lading The carrier must deliver the goods to the person entitled to receive them under the terms of the bill of lading. The carrier's duty in this respect is similar to that of the warehouser. Article 7 does not affect any State or Federal law imposing liability upon a common carrier for damages not caused by its negligence. Section 7–309(1). Common carriers of goods are extraordinary bailees under the law of many States and subject to a greater degree of liability than an ordinary bailee.

The Code allows a carrier to limit its liability by contract in all cases where its rates are dependent upon value and the shipper is given an opportunity to declare a higher value. The limitation does not apply to a conversion of the goods by the carrier to its own use. Section 7–309(2). *See Calvin Klein, Inc. v. Trylon Trucking Corp.*

Through Bills of Lading A bill of lading may provide that the issuer deliver the goods to a *connecting* carrier for further transportation to a destination. A bill of lading that specifies one or more connecting carriers is called a **through bill of lading.**

The initial or *originating* carrier, which receives the goods from the shipper and issues a through bill of lading, is liable to the holder of the document for loss or damage to the goods caused by any connecting or delivering carrier. Section 7–302(1). The initial carrier has a right of reimbursement from the connecting or delivering carrier in possession of the goods when the loss or damage occurred. A carrier, however, is not required to issue through bills of lading.

Unlike the initial carrier, the liability of a connecting carrier is limited to the period while the goods are in its possession.

Lien of Carrier The carrier has a lien upon goods in its possession covered by a bill of lading for its charges and expenses necessary for preservation of the goods. Against a purchaser for value of a negotiable bill of lading, this lien is limited to charges stated in the bill or in the applicable published tariff, and if no charges are so stated, to a reasonable charge. Section 7–307(1).

The enforcement of the lien of the carrier is by public or private sale of the goods after notice to all persons known to the carrier to claim an interest in them. The sale must be on terms that are "commercially reasonable" and must be conducted in a "commercially reasonable manner." Section 7–308(1).

A purchaser in good faith of goods sold to enforce the lien takes free of any rights of persons against whom the lien was valid, even though the enforcement of the lien does not comply with the requirements of the Code. This rule applies to both carrier's and warehouser's liens. Sections 7–308(4) and 7–310(5).

NEGOTIABILITY OF DOCUMENTS OF TITLE

The concept of negotiability has long been established in law. It is important not only in connection with documents of title but also in connection with commercial paper and investment securities treated in other chapters of this book.

Negotiability is a characteristic that the law confers upon instruments and documents that comply with the required statutory form. The magic words are *bearer* or *order*. A promise to deliver goods to a named person is manifestly different from a promise to deliver the goods to bearer or to the order of a named person. The first promise may be safely performed by the promisor by delivery of the goods to the person named in the promise. This is typical of a straight bill of lading; that is, one issued by a carrier that undertakes to deliver the goods to a named consignee at a specific destination. In this case it is not necessary for the carrier to obtain the bill of lading upon delivery of the goods at destination. The only concern of the carrier is to make sure that the person to whom it delivers the goods at the specified destination is the person named in the straight bill of lading as the consignee. Such a bill of lading is **non-negotiable.**

If, on the other hand, the promise of the carrier in the bill of lading is to deliver the goods to **bearer** or to the **order** of a person named in the bill, the carrier may not safely deliver the goods to anyone at destination without obtaining surrender of the original bill of lading. Anyone in possession of a bearer form document is entitled to receive the goods from the carrier. Anyone in possession of an order form document, properly indorsed, is likewise entitled to receive possession of the goods from the carrier. A bearer or order form document of title is **negotiable.** By the terms of the promise contained on its face it was intended to go to market, to pass from hand to hand, and to circulate freely through the channels of commerce.

The Code provides that a warehouse receipt, bill of lading, or other document of title is negotiable if, by its terms, the goods are to be delivered to bearer or to the order of a named person or where, in overseas trade, it runs to a named person or assigns. *Any* other document is non-negotiable. Section 7–104.

A non-negotiable document, such as a straight bill of lading or a warehouse receipt under which the goods are deliverable to a person named in the bill and not to the order of any person or to bearer, may be transferred by assignment but may not be negotiated. Only a negotiable document or instrument may be negotiated.

Due Negotiation

The manner in which a negotiable document of title may be negotiated and the requirements of due negotiation are set forth in Section 7–501 of the Code. An order form negotiable document of title running to the order of a named person is negotiated by her indorsement and delivery. After such indorsement in blank or to bearer, the document may be negotiated by delivery alone. A special indorsement by which the document is indorsed over to a specified person requires the indorsement of the special indorsee as well as delivery to accomplish a further negotiation.

The naming in a negotiable document of a person to be notified upon the arrival of the goods does not limit the negotiability of the bill of lading or serve as notice to any purchaser of the document that such person has any interest in the goods.

Due negotiation is a term peculiar to Article 7 and requires not only that the purchaser of the negotiable document must take it in good faith without notice of any adverse claim or defense and pay value, but also that she must take it in the regular course of business or financing and not in settlement or payment of a money obligation. Thus, a transfer for value of a negotiable document of title to a nonbanker or person not in business, such as a college professor or student, would not be a due negotiation.

Rights Acquired by Due Negotiation

Negotiation is a form of transfer in which the transferee acquires not only the rights that the transferor had but also the direct rights based on the language of the promise contained in the instrument or document. Where a property right is merely assigned, the assignee takes only those rights that the assignor had. He stands in the shoes of the assignor, and his rights are subject to all defects and infirmities in the title of the assignor. Where a document is negotiable and is transferred by due negotiation, however, the transferee is one to whom the promise of the issuer runs, and he thereby acquires the direct obligation of the issuer. Thus, if Keith issues a warehouse receipt to Donna in which he promises to deliver the goods to bearer, and subsequently Gail presents the document to Keith and demands the goods, Gail is the bearer and therefore the very person to whom Keith promised to deliver the goods. The same is true for a properly indorsed order form warehouse receipt or bill of lading.

The effect of due negotiation is that it creates new rights in the holder of the document. On due negotiation, the transferee does not stand in the shoes of his transferor. Defects and defenses available against the transferor are not available against the new holder. His rights are newly created by the negotiation and free of such defects and defenses. This enables bankers and businesspersons to extend credit upon documents of title without concern about possible adverse claims or the rights of third parties.

The rights of a holder of a negotiable document of title to whom it has been duly negotiated are that he has (1) title to the document; (2) title to the goods; (3) all rights accruing under the law of agency or estoppel including rights to goods delivered to the bailee after the document was issued; and (4) the direct obligation of the issuer to hold or deliver the goods according to the terms of the document. Section 7–502.

If an order form document of title is transferred without a requisite indorsement, the transferee has the right to compel his transferor to supply any necessary indorsement.

This right is specifically enforceable in a court of equity. The transfer becomes a negotiation only as of the time the indorsement is supplied. Section 7–506.

Rights Acquired in the Absence of Due Negotiation

If a non-negotiable document is transferred or a negotiable document is transferred without due negotiation, the transferee of the document acquires all of the title and rights that the transferor had or had actual authority to convey. Prior to notification received by the bailee of the transfer, the rights of the transferee may be defeated (1) by the creditors of the transferor, who could treat the sale as void; (2) by a buyer from the transferor in the ordinary course of business, if the bailee has delivered the goods to the buyer; or (3) against the bailee by good faith dealings of the bailee with the transferor. Section 7–504.

Warranties

A person who either negotiates or transfers a document of title for value other than a collecting bank or other intermediary incurs certain warranty obligations unless otherwise agreed. Section 7–507. Such transferor warrants to her immediate purchaser (1) that the document is genuine; (2) that she had no knowledge of any fact that would impair its validity or worth; and (3) that her negotiation or transfer is rightful and fully effective with respect to the title to the document and the goods it represents.

Ineffective Documents of Title

It is fundamental that a thief or finder of goods may not deliver them to a warehouser or carrier in return for a negotiable document of title and thus defeat the rights of the owner by a negotiation of the document. Although such a document would be genuine and its indorsement by the thief or finder would not be a forgery, it would not represent title to the goods.

In order for a person to obtain title to goods by a negotiation to him of a document, the goods must have been delivered to the issuer of the document by the owner of the goods or by one to whom the owner has delivered or entrusted them with actual or apparent authority to ship, store, or sell them. Section 7–503(1). A warehouser or carrier, however, may deliver goods according to the terms of the document which it has issued or otherwise dispose of the goods as provided in the Code without incurring liability, even though the document did not represent title to the goods. It must have acted in good faith and complied with reasonable commercial standards in both the receipt and delivery or other disposition of the goods. The bailee has no liability even though the person from whom it received the goods had no authority to obtain the issuance of the document or dispose of the goods, and even though the person to whom it delivered the goods had no authority to receive them. Section 7–404.

Thus, a carrier or warehouser who receives goods from a thief or finder and later delivers them to a person to whom the thief or finder ordered them to be delivered is not liable to the true owner of the goods. Even a sale of the goods by the carrier or warehouser to enforce a lien for transportation or storage charges and expenses would not subject it to liability.

Warehousers and carriers are regarded as furnishing a service necessary to trade and commerce. They are not a link in the chain of title and do not purport to represent the owner in transactions affecting title to the goods. Consequently, this is a sound rule to relieve them from liability upon delivery of the goods pursuant to their contract under the document of title even though the document is ineffective against the true owner of the goods.

Lost or Missing Documents of Title

If a document of title has been lost, stolen, or destroyed, a claimant of the goods may apply to a court for an order directing delivery of the goods or the issuance of a substitute document. Compliance of the carrier or warehouser with the court order relieves it of liability. Section 7–601(1). The claimant must provide security approved by the court if the missing document is negotiable.

If the carrier or warehouser delivers goods to a person claiming them under a missing negotiable document without a court order, it is liable to any person who is thereby injured.

Delivery to such person in good faith is not a conversion of the goods if security is posted in an amount at least double the value of the goods to indemnify any person injured by the delivery who files notice of claim within one year. Section 7–601(2).

CASES

Bailment: Delivery of Possession

SEWALL v. FITZ-INN AUTO PARKS, INC.

Court of Appeals of Massachusetts, 1975.
3 Mass.App.Ct. 380, 330 N.E.2d 853.

ARMSTRONG, J.

The plaintiff seeks recovery of the value of his automobile, which was left by him on the defendant's parking lot early on the morning of April 15, 1970, and was gone when he returned for it early that evening, having apparently been stolen by an unidentified third person. The declaration is in two counts, one based on a theory of breach of the defendant's contractual duty to safeguard the automobile and the other based on principles of ordinary negligence. At the conclusion of the evidence the trial judge directed verdicts for the defendant on both counts. The propriety of that action is the sole issue raised by the plaintiff's bill of exceptions.

The facts do not appear to be in dispute. The defendant's parking lot was approximately 100 by 200 feet in size. A chain link fence had been erected along its rear boundary, separating the lot from a facility of the Massachusetts Bay Transportation Authority. The normal entrance and exit to the lot were located at the front, but it was also possible to leave the lot from the sides, each of which bordered on a small street. Upon entering the lot on the morning of April 15, the plaintiff paid the attendant on duty a fee of twenty-five cents, a flat rate for which he was permitted to park all day or for a shorter period, as he chose. He parked his car in a space designated by the attendant, locked it and

took the keys with him. The attendant remained on duty until 10:30 or 11:00 A.M. on April 15, after which time the lot was unattended, apparently pursuant to a practice followed by the defendant. The plaintiff had never been expressly informed of that practice, but he had regularly parked in the lot for several years and had never seen an attendant when he returned for his car in the evening.

The case turns on whether the facts warranted a finding that the transaction between the parties constituted a bailment for hire of the plaintiff's automobile, rather than a mere letting of parking space. [Citations.] The existence of a bailment is a prerequisite to the plaintiff's right to recover, either in contract or in tort, as the defendant would not otherwise be under any duty to safeguard the plaintiff's car against theft. [Citations.] We are of the opinion that no bailment has been shown and that the trial judge was correct in directing verdicts [in favor of Fitz-Inn Auto Parks].

A bailment, by definition, arises only upon delivery of possession of the property sought to be bailed, and at least some degree of control over that property, to the putative bailee. [Citations.] Once possession and control of an automobile have been transferred to the operator of a parking facility for a fee, the owner (in the absence of any warning or understanding to the contrary) is justified in concluding that the operator has assumed responsibility to safeguard the automobile, and the operator has a legally enforceable duty to exercise reasonable care in the fulfillment of that responsibility. [Citation.] But if there has been no such delivery of possession or control to the operator, nor any acceptance thereof by him, he cannot, without more, be regarded as having undertaken to protect the car and owes the owner no duty to do so. [Citation.]

It has long been held that the surrender of the car keys to the parking facility attendant is a sufficient delivery of possession and control to create a bailment for hire, whether the keys are left at the attendant's request [citation] or with his knowledge and acquiescence in the absence of such a request. [Citation.] The same result has recently been reached where the owner parked and locked his car, without surrendering the keys, in an enclosed parking facility whose sole means of egress was manned by an attendant responsible for stopping and checking each car leaving the facility. [Citation.] * * *

The plaintiff in effect is asking us to extend the principle applied in [citations]. In those cases the garage, while not exercising the degree of control possible through possession of the keys, did exercise (or purport to exercise) control over the departure of vehicles from its facility. In the present case neither type of control was actually or apparently exercised or asserted by the defendant. The role of the attendant, so far as known to the plaintiff, was confined to collecting a uniform twenty-five cent fee from motorists as they entered the lot and directing them to parking spaces. The plaintiff knew that he could remove his car from the lot at any time without interference by any employee of the defendant. Indeed, it should have been obvious to him, because of the open character of the lot and the absence of any attendant on all the evenings when he had removed his car, that any control exercised by the defendant over his car, and any correlative responsibility assumed with respect thereto, came to an end once he had paid the fee and parked the car. [Citation.]

Exceptions overruled.

Bailee's Duty to Return Bailed Property

MIESKE v. BARTELL DRUG CO.

Supreme Court of Washington, 1979.
92 Wn.2d 40, 593 P.2d 1308.

BRACHTENBACH, J.

This case determines the measure of damages for personal property, developed movie film, which is destroyed, and which cannot be replaced or reproduced. It also decides the legal effect of a clause which purports to limit the responsibility of a film processor to replacement of film.

We will detail the facts later, but the heart of the matter is that plaintiffs delivered already developed movie film to a retail store for the sole purpose of having the film spliced onto larger reels. The film was lost or destroyed by the retailer's processing agent. A jury verdict of $7,500 was returned against the retailer and the agent-processor. Those defendants appeal. We affirm.

The facts are that over a period of years the plaintiffs had taken movie films of their family activities. The films started with the plaintiffs' wedding and honeymoon and continued through vacations in Mexico, Hawaii and other places, Christmas gatherings, birthdays, Little League participation by their son, family pets, building of their home and irreplaceable pictures of members of their family, such as the husband's brother, who are now deceased.

Plaintiffs had 32 50–foot reels of such developed film which they wanted spliced together into four reels for convenience of viewing. Plaintiff wife visited defendant Bartell's camera department, with which she had dealt as a customer for at least 10 years. She was told that such service could be performed.

The films were put in the order which plaintiffs desired them to be spliced and so marked. They were then placed in four separate paper bags which in turn were placed in one large bag and delivered to the manager of Bartell. The plaintiff wife explained the desired service and the manner in which the films were assembled in the various bags. The manager placed a film processing packet on the bag and gave plaintiff wife a receipt which contained this language: "We assume no responsibility beyond retail cost of film unless otherwise agreed to in writing." There was no discussion about the language on the receipt. Rather, plaintiff wife told the manager, "Don't lose these. They are my life."

There was no discussion or agreement about who was going to perform the splicing service.

Bartell sent the film package to defendant GAF Corporation, which intended to send them to another processing lab for splicing. Plaintiffs assumed that Bartell did this service and were unaware of the involvement of two other firms.

The bag of films arrived at the processing lab of GAF. The manager of the GAF lab described the service ordered and the packaging as very unusual. Yet it is undisputed that the film was in the GAF lab at the end of one day and gone the next morning. The manager immediately searched the garbage disposal dumpster which already had been emptied. The best guess is that the plaintiff's film went from GAF's lab to the garbage dumpster to a truck to a barge to an up-Sound landfill where it may yet repose.

After several inquiries to Bartell, plaintiff wife was advised to call GAF. Not surprisingly, after being advised of the complete absence and apparent fatality of plaintiffs' films, this lawsuit ensued.

At trial defendants Bartell and GAF denied liability. The janitorial service company which apparently removed the film was a defendant. The verdict was against Bartell and GAF but not against the janitorial service company. It is not a party to the appeal. For purposes of appeal, Bartell and GAF admit liability for negligence.

Two main issues are raised: (1) the measure of damages and (2) the effect of the exclusionary clause appearing on the film receipt.

On damages, the defendants assign error to (a) the court's damages instruction and (b) the court's failure to give their proposed damages instruction.

The standard of recovery for destruction of personal property was summarized in *McCurdy v. Union Pac. R.R.*, [citation]. We recognized in *McCurdy* that (1) personal property which is destroyed may have a market value, in which case that market value is the measure of damages; (2) if destroyed property has no market value but can be replaced or reproduced, then the measure is the cost of replacement or reproduction; (3) if the destroyed property has no market value and cannot be replaced or reproduced, then the value to the owner is to be the proper measure of damages. However, while not stated in *McCurdy,* we have held that in the third *McCurdy* situation, damages are not recoverable for the sentimental value which the owner places on the property. [Citations.]

The defendants argue that plaintiffs' property comes within the second rule of *McCurdy, i.e.,* the film could be replaced and that their liability is limited to the cost of replacement film. Their position is not well taken. Defendants' proposal would award the plaintiffs the cost of acquiring film without pictures imposed thereon. That is not what plaintiffs lost. Plaintiffs lost not merely film able to capture images by exposure but rather film upon which was recorded a multitude of frames depicting many significant events in their lives. Awarding plaintiffs the funds to purchase 32 rolls of blank film is hardly a replacement of the 32 rolls of image which they had recorded over the years. Therefore the third rule of *McCurdy* is the appropriate measure of damages, *i.e.,* the property has no market value and cannot be replaced or reproduced.

The law, in those circumstances, decrees that the measure of damages is to be determined by the value to the owner, often referred to as the intrinsic value of the property. Restatement of Torts § 911 (1939).

Necessarily the measure of damages in these circumstances is the most imprecise of the three categories. Yet difficulty of assessment is not cause to deny damages to a plaintiff whose property has no market value and cannot be replaced or reproduced. [Citations.]

The fact that damages are difficult to ascertain and measure does not diminish the loss to the person whose property has been destroyed. Indeed, the very statement of the rule suggests the opposite. If one's destroyed property has a market value, presumably its equivalent is available on the market and the owner can acquire that equivalent property. However, if the owner cannot acquire the property in the market or by replacement or reproduction, then he simply cannot be made whole.

The problem is to establish the value to the owner. Market and replacement values are relatively ascertainable by appropriate proof. Recognizing that value to the owner encompasses a subjective element, the rule has been established that compensation for sentimental or fanciful values will not be allowed. [Citations.] That restriction was placed upon the jury in this case by the court's damages instruction.

* * *

Under these rules, the court's damages instruction was correct. In essence it allowed recovery for the actual or intrinsic value to the plaintiffs but denied recovery for any unusual sentimental value of the film to the plaintiffs or a fanciful price which plaintiffs for their own special reasons, might place thereon.

* * *

The next issue is to determine the legal effect of the exclusionary clause which was on the film receipt given plaintiff wife by Bartell. As noted above, it read: "We assume no responsibility beyond retail cost of film unless otherwise agreed to in writing."

Is the exclusionary clause valid? Defendants rely upon 2–719(3), a section of the Uniform Commercial Code, which authorizes a limitation or exclusion of consequential damages unless the limitation is unconscionable.

Plaintiffs, on the other hand, argue that the Uniform Commercial Code is not applicable to this transaction. Their theory is that article 2 applies only to sales and not to a bailment as was present in this case. Plaintiffs read article 2 too narrowly. While article 2 is entitled "Sales," the declared scope is more comprehensive. 2–102 sets the parameters of the article by its declaration that it applies to *transactions in goods,* excluding security transactions. If article 2 were limited to sales it would not be directly applicable to this bailment transaction as 2–106(1) defines "Sales" as the passing of title from a seller to a buyer, a factor not present here. Obviously "transactions in goods"—the scope of article 2—is broader than "sales." Had the drafters of the code intended to limit article 2 to sales they could have easily so stated. They did not.

Our analysis seems commonly accepted. See for example [citation] which states:

It is now clearly established that the reach of Article 2 goes considerably beyond the confines of that type transaction which the Code itself defines to be a "sale"; namely, the passing of title from a party called the seller to one denominated a buyer for a price. Chief opportunity for this expansion is found in Section 2–102, which states that the article applies to "transactions in goods." Article 2 sections are finding their way into more and more decisions involving transactions which are not sales, but which are used as substitutes for a sale or which to a court appear to have attributes to which sales principles—or at least some of them—seem appropriate for application. . . .

. . . Most important of these is the application of the Article's warranty provisions to leases, *bailments,* or construction contracts. Of growing importance is the tendency of courts to find the Section on unconscionability, Section 2–302, appropriate to nonsales deals.

[Citations.]

While there are cases to the contrary, [citations] we do not find them persuasive. In fact we have held already that article 2 declares a public policy as to disclaimers and, at least by analogy, applied it to a bailment. *Baker v. Seattle,* 79 Wn.2d 198, 484 P.2d 405 (1971). (Article 2's provisions apply to lease of golf cart.)

We do not think that a distinction can be drawn between a bailment arising from a service transaction, as is the case here, and one arising from a leasing transaction, as was the case in *Baker,* [citation.] Nor do we think, for this purpose, that a proper distinction can be drawn between the lease or rental of a chattel and the sale of a chattel.

* * *

In determining conscionability, the parties are to be provided "a reasonable opportunity to present evidence as to its commercial setting, purpose and effect to aid the court in making the determination." RCW 62A.2–302(2). Defendants concede that there was adequate compliance with that requirement in this case. The court had before it testimony and documents as to each element it was required to consider. * * *

Judgment affirmed.

Liability of Carrier/Duties of Issuer of Bill of Lading

CALVIN KLEIN LTD. v. TRYLON TRUCKING CORP.

United States Court of Appeals, Second Circuit, 1989.
892 F.2d 191.

MINER, J.

Defendant-appellant Trylon Trucking Corp. ("Trylon") appeals from a judgment entered on April 10, 1989 in the United States District Court for the Southern District of New York (Brieant, Ch.J.) in favor of plaintiff-appellee Calvin Klein Ltd. ("Calvin Klein") for the full value of a lost shipment of clothing. The appeal presents a novel issue under New York law: whether a limitation of liability agreement between a shipper and a carrier is enforceable when the shipment is lost as a result of the carrier's gross negligence.

The district court held that the parties' customary limitation of liability agreement did not extend to the shipment at issue, due to the absence of assent and consideration. The court observed that, had there been such an agreement, the liability of the carrier for its gross negligence would be limited. For the reasons that follow, we reverse the judgment of the district court, find that the parties agreed to the limitation of liability, and determine that the agreement limits Trylon's liability for its gross negligence.

* * *

Calvin Klein, a New York clothing company, had used the services of Trylon for at least three years, involving hundreds of shipments, prior to the lost shipment at issue. In past deliveries Calvin Klein, through its customs broker, would contact Trylon to pick up the shipment from the airport for delivery to Calvin Klein's facility. After completing the carriage, Trylon would forward to Calvin Klein an invoice, which contained a limitation of liability provision as follows:

"In consideration of the rate charged, the shipper agrees that the carrier shall not be liable for more than $50.00 on any shipment accepted for delivery to one consignee unless a greater value is declared, in writing, upon receipt at time of ship-

ment and charge for such greater value paid, or agreed to be paid, by the shipper."

A shipment of 2,833 blouses from Hong Kong arrived at John F. Kennedy International Airport for Calvin Klein on March 27, 1986. Calvin Klein arranged for Trylon to pick up the shipment and deliver it to Calvin Klein's New Jersey warehouse. On April 2, Trylon dispatched its driver, Jamahl Jefferson, to pick up this shipment. Jefferson signed a receipt for the shipment from Calvin Klein's broker. By April 2, the parties discovered that Jefferson had stolen Trylon's truck and its shipment. The shipment never was recovered. Calvin Klein sent a claim letter to Trylon for the full value of the lost blouses. * * *

In their stipulation in lieu of a jury trial, the parties agreed that Trylon is liable to Calvin Klein for the loss of the shipment and that Trylon was grossly negligent in the hiring and supervision of Jefferson. They also agreed that "[t]he terms and conditions of [Trylon]'s carriage [were] that liability for loss or damage to cargo is limited to $50 in accordance with the legend on Trylon's invoice forms." Calvin Klein conceded that it was aware of this limitation of liability, and that it did not declare a value on the blouses at the time of shipment.

The parties left at issue whether the limitation of liability clause was valid and enforceable. Calvin Klein argued in the district court, as it does here, that the limitation clause was not enforceable for two reasons: no agreement existed between Calvin Klein and Trylon as to the limitation of liability; and, if such an agreement existed, public policy would prevent its enforcement because of Trylon's gross negligence.

* * *

A common carrier, [citation], under New York law is strictly liable for the loss of goods in its custody. "Where the loss is not due to the excepted causes [that is, act of God or public enemy, inherent nature of goods, or shipper's fault], it is immaterial whether the carrier was negligent or not. . . ." [Citations.] Even in the case of loss from theft by third parties, liability may be imposed upon a negligent common carrier. [Citation.]

A shipper and a common carrier may contract to limit the carrier's liability in cases of loss to an amount agreed to by the parties, [citation], so long as the language of the limitation is clear, the shipper is aware of the terms of the limitation, and the shipper can change the terms by indicating the true value of the goods being shipped. U.C.C. § 7–309(2); [citations.] Such a limitation agreement is generally valid and enforceable despite carrier negligence. [Citation.] The limitation of liability provision involved here clearly provides that, at the time of delivery, the shipper may increase the limitation by written notice of the value of the goods to be delivered and by payment of a commensurately higher fee.

The parties stipulated to the fact that the $50 limitation of liability was a term and condition of carriage and that Calvin Klein was aware of that limitation. This stipulated fact removes the first issue, namely whether an agreement existed as to a liability limitation between the parties, from this case. Calvin Klein's argument that it never previously acknowledged this limitation by accepting only $50 in settlement of a larger loss does not alter this explicit stipulation. * * *

The remaining issue concerns the enforceability of the limitation clause in the light of Trylon's conceded gross negligence. The district court considered that, assuming an agreement between the parties as to Trylon's liability, Trylon's gross negligence would not avoid the enforcement of a limitation clause.

The district court found that New York law, as opposed to federal interstate commerce law, applies in this case.

* * *

Since carriers are strictly liable for loss of shipments in their custody and are insurers of these goods, the degree of carrier negligence is immaterial. [Citation.] The common carrier must exercise reasonable care in relation to the shipment in its custody. U.C.C. § 7–309(1). Carriers can contract with their shipping customers on the amount of liability each party will bear for the loss of a shipment, regardless of the degree of carrier negligence. See U.C.C. § 7–309(2) (allowing limitation of liability for losses from any cause

save carrier conversion). . . . [T]he shipper can calculate the specific amount of its potential damages in advance, declare the value of the shipment based on that calculation, and pay a commensurately higher rate to carry the goods, in effect buying additional insurance from the common carrier.

In this case, Calvin Klein and Trylon were business entities with an on-going commercial relationship involving numerous carriages of Calvin Klein's goods by Trylon. Where such entities deal with each other in a commercial setting, and no special relationship exists between the parties, clear limitations between them will be enforced. [Citation.] Here, each carriage was under the same terms and conditions as the last, including a limitation of Trylon's liability. [Citation.] This is not a case in which the shipper was dealing with the common carrier for the first time or contracting under new or changed terms. Calvin Klein was aware of the terms and was free to adjust the limitation upon a written declaration of the value of a given shipment, but failed to do so with the shipment at issue here. Since Calvin Klein failed to adjust the limitation, the limitation applies here, and no public policy that dictates otherwise can be identified.

Calvin Klein now argues that the limitation is so low as to be void. * * * This amount is immaterial because Calvin Klein had the opportunity to negotiate the amount of coverage by declaring the value of the shipment. [Citation.] Commercial entities can easily negotiate the degree of risk each party will bear and which party will bear the cost of insurance.

* * *

We reverse and remand to the district court with instructions to enter judgment against defendant in the sum of $50.

Duties of Warehousemen

I.C.C. METALS, INC. v. MUNICIPAL WAREHOUSE CO.

Court of Appeals of New York, 1980.
50 N.Y.2d 657, 431 N.Y.S.2d 372, 409 N.E.2d 849.

GABRIELLI, J.

[In the fall of 1974, I.C.C. Metals, Inc., delivered three lots of indium, an industrial metal, to Municipal Warehouse Company for safekeeping. The indium had an aggregate weight of 845 pounds and was worth $100,000. The Warehouse supplied I.C.C. with receipts for each lot. Printed on the back of these receipts were the terms and conditions of the bailment including an exculpatory clause limiting the liability of the Warehouse to a maximum of $50.00. For two years, the Warehouse billed I.C.C. for storage of the indium, and I.C.C. paid each invoice. In 1976, I.C.C. requested the return of the indium. For the first time, the Warehouse told I.C.C. it was unable to locate any of the indium. I.C.C. brought an action in conversion to recover the full value of the indium. The Warehouse defended on the ground that the metal had been stolen through no fault of its own; and that its liability was limited to $50.00 in accordance with the terms of the Warehouse receipts.]

Absent an agreement to the contrary, a warehouse is not an insurer of goods and may not be held liable for any injury to or loss of stored property not due to some fault upon its part (Uniform Commercial Code, § 7–204, subd. [1]). As a bailee, however, a warehouse is required both to exercise reasonable care so as to prevent loss of or damage to the property [citation] and, a fortiori, to refrain from itself converting materials left in its care [citation]. If a warehouse does not convert the goods to its own use and does exercise reasonable care, it may not be held liable for any loss of or damage to the property unless it specifically agrees to accept a higher burden. If, however, the property is lost or damaged as a result of negligence upon the part of the warehouse, it will be liable in negligence. Similarly, should a warehouse actually convert stored property to its own use, it will be liable in conversion. Hence, a warehouse which fails to redeliver goods to the person entitled to their return upon a proper demand, may be liable for either negligence or conversion, depending upon the circumstances. [Citation.]

A warehouse unable to return bailed property either because it has lost the property as a result of its negligence or because it has converted the property will be liable for the full value of the goods at the time of the loss or conversion [citations], unless the parties have agreed to limit the warehouse's potential liability. It has long been the law in this State that a warehouse, like a common carrier, may limit its liability for loss of or damage to stored goods even if the injury or loss is the result of the warehouse's negligence, so long as it provides the bailor with an opportunity to increase that potential liability by payment of a higher storage fee. [Citations.] If the warehouse converts the goods, however, strong policy considerations bar enforcement of any such limitation upon its liability. [Citations.] This rule, which has now been codified in subdivision (2) of section 7–204 of the Uniform Commercial Code, is premised on the distinction between an intentional and an unintentional tort. Although public policy will in many situations countenance voluntary prior limitations upon that liability which the law would otherwise impose upon one who acts carelessly [citations], such prior limitations may not properly be applied so as to diminish one's liability for injuries resulting from an affirmative and intentional act of misconduct (see, generally, Restatement, Torts 2d, § 500; Restatement, Contracts 2d, Tent Draft No. 12, § 337) such as a conversion. Any other rule would encourage wrongdoing by allowing the converter to retain the difference between the value of the converted property and the limited amount of liability provided in the agreement of storage. That result would be absurd. To avoid such an anomaly, the law provides that when a warehouse converts bailed property, it thereby ceases to function as a warehouse and thus loses its entitlement to the protections afforded by the agreement of storage. [Citation.] In short, although the merely careless bailee remains a bailee and is entitled to whatever limitations of liability the bailor has agreed to, the converter forsakes his status as bailee completely and accordingly forfeits the protections of such limitations. Hence, in the instant case, whether defendant is entitled to the benefit of the liability limiting provision of the warehouse receipt turns upon whether plaintiff has proven conversion or merely negligence.

Plaintiff [I.C.C.] has proffered uncontroverted proof of delivery of the indium to defendant [Warehouse], of a proper demand for its return, and of defendant's failure to honor that demand. Defendant has failed to make a sufficient showing in support of its suggested explanation of the loss. . . . [Defendant's] unsupported claim that the metal was stolen does not suffice to raise any issue of fact on this point. Upon this record, it is beyond cavil that plaintiff would be entitled to judgment had it elected to sue defendant in negligence. [Citations]. We now hold that such a record also suffices to sustain plaintiff's action in conversion, thereby rendering inapplicable the contractual limitation upon defendant's liability.

[Judgment for I.C.C.]

QUESTIONS

1. Discuss the essential elements of a bailment.

2. Discuss the rights and duties of the bailor and bailee.

3. Discuss the duties of a (a) warehouser, (b) common carrier, and (c) innkeeper.

4. Define a document of title. Identify and discuss the various types of documents of title.

5. Discuss the negotiability of documents of title, the rights acquired by due negotiation, and the rights acquired in the absence of due negotiation.

PROBLEMS

1. Mercer was the owner of a herd of twenty highly bred dairy cows. He was a prosperous farmer, but his health was very poor. On the advice of his doctor, Mercer decided to winter in Arizona. Before he left, he made an agreement with Freya under which Freya was to keep the cows on her farm through the winter, pay Mercer the sum of $800, and return to Mercer the twenty cows at the close of the winter. For reasons that Freya thought were good farming, she sold six of the cows and replaced them with six other cows. After the winter was over, Mercer returned from Arizona. When he saw that Freya had replaced six cows out of the twenty originally given, he sued Freya for the conversion of the original six cows. Decision?

2. Hines stored her furniture, including a grand piano, in Arnett's warehouse. Needing more space, Arnett stored Hines's piano in Butler's warehouse next door. As a result of a fire, which occurred without any fault of Arnett or Butler, both warehouses and contents were destroyed. Hines sues Arnett for the value of her piano and furniture. Decision?

3. Curtis rented a safe deposit box from Reliable Safe Deposit Company in which he deposited valuable securities and $4,000 in cash. Subsequently, Curtis went to the box and found that $1,000 was missing. Curtis brought an action against Reliable, and at the trial the company showed that its customary procedure was as follows: that there were two keys for each box furnished to each renter; that if a key were lost, the lock was changed; that new keys were provided for each lock each time a box was rented; that there were two clerks in charge of the vault; and that one of the clerks was always present to open the box. Reliable Safe Deposit Company also proved two keys were given to Curtis at the time he rented his box; that his box could not be opened without the use of one of the keys in his possession, and the company had issued no other keys to Curtis's box. Decision?

4. A, B, and C each stored 5,000 bushels of yellow corn in the same bin in X's warehouse. X wrongfully sold 10,000 bushels of this corn to Y. A contends that inasmuch as his 5,000 bushels of corn were placed in the bin first, the remaining 5,000 bushels belong to him. What are the rights of the parties?

5. (a) On April 1, Mary Rich, at the solicitation of Super Fur Company, delivered a $3,000 mink coat to the company at its place of business for storage in its vaults until November 1. On the same day, she paid the company its customary charge of $20 for such storage. After Mary left the store, the general manager of the company, upon finding that its storage vaults were already filled to capacity, delivered Mary's coat to Swift Trucking Company for shipment to Fur Storage Company. En route, the truck in which Mary's coat was being transported was totally damaged by fire caused by negligence on the part of the driver of the truck, and Mary's coat was totally destroyed. Is Super Fur Company liable to Mary for the value of her coat? Why?

(b) Would your answer be the same if Mary's coat had been safely delivered to Fur Storage Company and had been stolen from its storage vaults without negligence on its part? Why?

6. Rich, a club member, left his golf clubs with Bogan, the pro at the Happy Hours Country Club, to be refinished at Bogan's pro shop. The refinisher employed by Bogan suddenly left town, taking Rich's clubs with him. The refinisher had previously been above suspicion, although Bogan had never checked on the man's character references. A valuable sand wedge, which Bogan had borrowed from another member Smith for his own use in an important tournament match, was also stolen by the refinisher, as well as several pairs of golf shoes that Bogan had checked for members without charge as an accommodation. The concerned club members each made claims against Bogan for their losses. Can (a) Rich, (b) Smith, and (c) the other members compel Bogan to make good their respective losses?

7. Bert left his automobile at Tanya's garage in order for Tanya to repair the auto at an agreed upon charge of $125. Bert never returned to re-

claim the automobile, and two months later Caldwell saw it in Tanya's garage. Caldwell claimed it as his own and asserted that it had been stolen from him. Tanya told Caldwell that he could have the automobile if he paid for the repairs and storage. Caldwell paid her, took the automobile, and disappeared. One week later, Owens appeared and proved that the automobile was hers, that it had been stolen from her, and that neither Bert nor Caldwell had any rights in it.

Owens brings an action against Tanya for conversion of the automobile. Decision?

8. On June 1, Cain delivered his automobile to Barr, the operator of a repair shop, for necessary repairs. Barr put the car in his lot on Main Street. The lot, which was fenced on all sides except along Main Street, accommodated one hundred cars and was unguarded at night, although the police made periodic checks. The lot was well lighted. The cars did not have the keys in them when left out overnight. At some time during the night of June 4, the hood, starter, alternator, and gear shift were stolen from Cain's car. The car remained on the lot, and during the evening of June 5 the transmission was stolen from the car. The cost of replacement of the parts stolen in the first theft was $600 and in the second theft $500.

Cain sued Barr to recover $1,100. Decision?

9. Arlington in Phoenix, pursuant to a contract with Rider in New York, ships to Rider goods conforming to the contract and takes from the carrier a shipper's order bill of lading. Arlington indorses the bill of lading in blank and forwards it by mail to Clemson, his agent in New York, with instructions to deliver the bill of lading to Rider upon receipt of payment of the price for the goods. Forest, a thief, steals the bill of lading from Clemson and transfers it for value to Pace, a *bona fide* purchaser. Before the goods arrive in New York, Rider is petitioned into bankruptcy. What are the rights of the parties?

10. Rutger, a Philadelphia merchant, purchased merchandise from Washington in Chicago. The contract of sale provided that the merchandise was sold F.O.B., Chicago, payment to be made sixty days after delivery. Washington delivered the goods to the railroad carrier in Chicago, took an order bill of lading in the name of Rutger, and forwarded it to Rutger. Before the goods arrived in Philadelphia, Washington learned that Rutger had become insolvent and exercised a right of stoppage in transit by proper notice to the railroad company. Thereafter, and before the shipment reached Philadelphia, Rutger indorsed and delivered the bill of lading to Lee, an innocent purchaser for value. Lee claimed the goods by reason of holding the bill of lading. To whom should the goods be awarded?

11. Mrs. Laval was a patient of Dr. Leopold, a practicing psychiatrist. Dr. Leopold shared an office with two associates practicing in the same field. No receptionist or other employee attended the office. Mrs. Laval placed her coat in the clothes closet in the office reception room. Later, when she returned to retrieve the coat to leave, she found it missing. Mrs. Laval then brought this action to recover $1,725, the value of her coat. Decision? Explain.

12. Robert L. Moore, a United States Army sergeant stationed at Fort Benning, Georgia, rented a fourteen-foot aluminum boat from the Fort Benning Morale Support Activities Division, Outdoor Rentals. The manager of the rentals section gave Moore general instructions concerning the use of the craft and provided Moore with a copy of the Fort Benning Boating Safety Rules. He also followed the routine procedure of examining the fuel line of the boat and starting the motor to insure its serviceability. Three days later, while Moore was operating the boat on the Chattahoochee River, the motor stalled, forcing Moore to row the boat back to shore. Later that same day, Moore took six minor children out in the boat to give them a ride on the river. At the time, Moore's blood alcohol level was 0.29 percent, a level that would have made it "extremely difficult to do it [operate a boat] with any type of proficiency." Moore recklessly moved into the swift current and headed toward a concrete dam and spillway. When he finally reversed course, the motor stalled again, and the boat and its occupants were swept over the dam. Juanita Craine and Nancy Brown, parents of four of the drowned children, brought an action against the United States, claiming that the government breached its duty to warn Moore and that the government is liable as the owner of a vessel that was negligently operated. Decision?

Chapter 50

INTERESTS IN REAL PROPERTY

Freehold Estates
Leasehold Estates
Concurrent Ownership
Nonpossessory Interests

INTERESTS in real property may be divided into possessory and nonpossessory interests. Possessory interests in real property are called **estates** and are classified to indicate the quantity, nature, and extent of the rights. The two major categories are freehold estates (those existing for an indefinite time or for the life of a person) and estates less than freehold (those that exist for a predetermined time), called leasehold estates. Both freehold estates and leasehold estates are regarded as possessory interests in property. In addition, there are several nonpossessory interests in property including easements, *profits à prendre,* and licenses. The ownership of interests in property may be held by one individual or concurrently by two or more persons, each of whom is entitled to an undivided interest in the entire property. This chapter will consider these topics.

FREEHOLD ESTATES

A **freehold estate** is a right of ownership of real property for an indefinite time or for the life of a person. Of all the estates in real property, the most valuable are usually those present estates that combine the enjoyment of immediate possession with ownership at least for life. These estates are either some form of fee estates or estates for life. In addition, it is possible that either type of estate may be created without immediate right to possession, called a future interest.

Fee Estates

Fee estates include the right to immediate possession for an indefinite period of time with the right to transfer the interest by deed or will. Fee estates include both fee simple and qualified fee estates.

Fee Simple   When a person says that he has "bought" a house or a corporation informs its shareholders that it has "purchased" an industrial site, the property is generally held in fee simple. **Fee simple** means that the property is owned absolutely and can be sold or passed on at will to heirs or successors. The absolute rights of transferability and of transmitting by inheritance are basic characteristics of a fee simple estate. The estate signifies full control over the property, which is *owned absolutely* and can be sold or disposed of as desired. Fee simple is the largest estate in land; all other estates are derived from it.

A fee simple is created by any words that indicate an intent to convey absolute ownership. "To B in fee simple" will accomplish this, as will "To B forever." The general presumption is that a conveyance is intended to convey full and absolute title in the absence of a clear intent to the contrary.

A practical consequence of a fee simple title is not only that it may be voluntarily transferred, but also that it may be levied on and sold at the insistence of judgment creditors of the fee simple holder (the owner).

Qualified or Base Fee It is possible to convey or will property to a person to enjoy it absolutely, *subject to* its being taken away at a later date if a certain event takes place. The estate thus created is known as a **qualified fee,** base fee, conditional fee, or fee simple defeasible. For example, Abe may provide in his will that his widow is to have his house and lot in "fee simple forever so long as she does not remarry." If his widow dies without remarrying, the property is transferred to her heirs as though she owned it absolutely because the condition did not take place. If Abe's widow remarries or sells the land to Bertha and then remarries, the widow and Bertha would respectively lose their title to the land, and it would revert to the heirs of Abe.

The holder of a qualified fee interest may transfer the property by deed or will, and the property will pass by intestate succession. All transferees, however, take the property subject to the initial condition imposed upon the interest.

Life Estates

By tradition, life estates are divided into two major classes: (1) conventional life estates or those created by voluntary act, and (2) those established by law, the most significant example of which is a wife's dower right in the property of her husband.

Conventional Life Estates A grant or a devise (grant by will) "to Alex for life" creates in Alex an estate that terminates on his death. Such a provision may stand alone, in which case the property will revert to the grantor and his heirs or, as is more likely, it will be followed by a subsequent grant to another party such as "to Alex for life and then to Benjamin and his heirs." Alex is the **life tenant,** and Benjamin is generally described as the **remainderman.** Alex's life, however, need not be the measure of his life estate, as where an estate is granted "to Alex for the life of Dale." Upon Dale's death, Alex's interest terminates, and, if Alex dies before Dale, Alex's interest passes to his heirs or as he directs in his will for the remainder of Dale's life. Thus, a **life estate** is an ownership right in the property for the life of a designated individual, while the **remainder** is the ownership estate that takes effect when the prior life estate terminates.

No particular words are necessary to create a life estate. It is always a matter of determining the intent of the grantor. Life estates arise most frequently in connection with the creation of trusts, a subject considered in Chapter 52.

Generally, a life tenant may make such reasonable use of the property as long as he does not commit "waste." Any act or omission that does permanent injury to the realty or unreasonably changes its characteristics or value constitutes **waste.** For example, the failure to make repairs on a building, the unreasonable cutting of timber, or the neglect of an adequate conservation policy may subject the life tenant to an action by the remainderman to recover damages for waste.

A conveyance by the life tenant passes only his interest. The life tenant and the remainderman may, however, join in a conveyance to pass the entire fee to the property, or the life tenant may terminate his interest by conveying it to the remainderman.

Life Estates Established by Law Under common law, **dower** is a life estate that a *wife* who survives her husband has in one-third of all the real property the husband owned during the marriage. It arises by operation of law and exists irrespective of the intent or wishes of the parties.

At common law, the surviving *husband* had a life estate, known as **curtesy,** in the real property of his wife similar to, although not identical with, the widow's dower. Unlike dower, curtesy did not exist unless a child was born of the marriage.

In almost all States, the estates of dower and curtesy have been substantially modified or entirely abolished, and in lieu of them the surviving spouse in some States is given a statutory share in the estate of the deceased spouse.

Future Interests

Not all interests in property carry the right to immediate possession even though the right and title to the interest are absolute. Thus, where property is conveyed or devised by will "to Anderson during his life and then to Brown and her heirs," Brown has a definite presently existing *interest* in the property, but she is not entitled to immediate *possession*. This right and similar rights are generically referred to as **future interests** of which there are two principal types: reversions and remainders.

Reversions   If Anderson conveys property "to Brown for life" and makes no disposition of the remainder of the estate, Anderson holds the **reversion**—the grantor's right to the property upon the death of the life tenant. Thus, Anderson would regain ownership to the property when Brown dies. A reversion in Anderson is also created if Anderson conveys property "to Caldwell for ten years." Reversions may be transferred by deed or will and pass by intestate succession.

A **possibility of reverter** is a conditional reversionary interest and exists where property *may* return to the grantor or his successor in interest because of the happening of an event upon which a fee simple estate was to terminate. It is the possibility of a reversion that is present in the grant of a base or qualified fee as previously discussed in this chapter. Thus, Ellen has a possibility of reverter if she dedicates property to a public use "so long as it is used as a park." If, in one hundred

years, the city ceases to use the property for a park, the heirs of Ellen would be entitled to the property. A possibility of a reverter may pass by will or intestate succession. In some States it may be transferred by deed.

Remainders   A remainder is an estate in property that, like a reversion, will take effect in possession, if at all, upon the termination of a prior estate created by the *same instrument*. Unlike a reversion, a remainder is held by a person other than the grantor or his successors. A grant from Gwen to "William for his life and then to Charles and his heirs" creates a remainder in Charles. Upon the termination of the life estate, Charles will be entitled to possession as remainderman. Charles takes his title not from William but from the original grantor, Gwen. There are two kinds of remainders: vested remainders and contingent remainders.

A **vested remainder** is a remainder in which the only contingency to the possession by the remainderman is the termination of all preceding estates created by the transferor. When Bruce has a remainder in fee, subject only to a life estate in Carol, the only obstacle to the right of immediate possession by Bruce or his heirs is Carol's life. Carol's death is sufficient and necessary to place Bruce in possession. The law considers this unconditional or vested remainder as a fixed, *present* interest to be enjoyed in the future. It is an interest in property that is transferable just as much as the preceding life estate, and it is characteristic of a vested remainder that the owner of the preceding estate can do nothing to defeat the remainder.

A **contingent remainder** is a remainder in which the right to possession is dependent or conditional on the happening of some event *in addition to* the termination of the preceding estates. The contingent remainder may be conditioned on the existence of some person not yet in being or on the happening of an event that may never occur. A provision in a will "to Sandy for life and then to her children but if she has no children then to Douglas" creates contingent remainders both as to the children and as to Douglas. If Sandy marries and has a child, the remainder then vests in that child, and Douglas's expectancy is closed out. If Sandy dies without having had a child, then and only then will an estate vest in Douglas. It is, of course, possible for a contingent remainder to become vested while possession is still in the preceding life estate, as evidenced by the birth of a child to Sandy in the above example. *See Strickland v. Jackson.* A contingent remainder is transferable by deed in most States. It is inheritable unless it is limited such that it terminates before the death of the remainderman. For a comparison of the different freehold estates see Figure 50–1.

LEASEHOLD ESTATES

A lease is both a contract and a conveyance of an estate in land. It is a contract by which the owner of the land, the **landlord,** grants to another, the **tenant,** an exclusive right to use and possession of the land for a definite or ascertainable period of time or term. The pos-

sessory term thus granted is an estate in land called a **leasehold.** The landlord retains an interest in the property called a *reversion.* The principal characteristics of the leasehold estate are that it continues for a definite or ascertainable term and that it carries with it the obligation on the part of the tenant to pay rent to the landlord. Thus, if Linda, the owner of a house and lot, rents it to Ted for a year, Linda, of course, still holds title to the property but she has sold the right to occupy the property to Ted. During the term of the lease, Ted's right to occupy the property is superior to that of Linda and, as long as Ted occupies in accordance with the lease contract, he does, as a practical matter, have exclusive possession against all the world as though he were the actual owner.

The law of leasehold estates has changed considerably over the past few decades. Traditionally, the common law viewed a leasehold estate principally as a conveyance of the use of land and less as a contract. Today, the landlord-tenant relationship is primarily

Figure 50–1 Freehold Estates

Interest	Complementary Estate	Duration	Transfer by Deed	Transfer by Will or Intestacy
Fee Simple	None	Perpetual	Yes	Yes
Qualified Fee	Possibility of a reverter	Until contingency occurs	Yes	Yes
Life Estate	Reversion or remainder	Life of indicated person	Yes	No, unless measuring life is not life tenant's
Reversion	Life estate	Perpetual	Yes	Yes
Possibility of Reverter	Qualified fee	Perpetual if contingency occurs	In some States	Yes
Vested Remainder	Life estate	Perpetual	Yes	Yes
Contingent Remainder	Life estate	Perpetual if contingency occurs	In most States	Yes, unless it is limited such that it terminates before the death of the remainderman

viewed as a contract, and thus the contract doctrines of unconscionability, implied warranties, and constructive conditions have been applied. Moreover, numerous statutes and ordinances have been enacted to protect tenants, thereby further modifying the relationship, such as the Uniform Residential Landlord and Tenant Act enacted by a number of States.

Creation and Duration

Leaseholds are created by contract and therefore the usual requirements for the formation of a contract apply. By statute, in most jurisdictions, leases for a term longer than a specified period of time must be in writing. The period is generally fixed at either one or three years. A few States require that all leases be in writing.

Definite Term A lease for a definite term automatically expires at the end of the term. Such a lease is frequently termed an estate for years, even though the duration may be for one year or shorter. No notice to terminate is required.

Periodic Tenancy A **periodic tenancy** is a lease of indefinite duration that continues for successive periods unless terminated by notice to the other party. For example, a lease "to Ted from month to month" or "from year to year" creates a periodic tenancy. Periodic tenancies arise frequently by implication. Laura leases to Ted without stating any term in the lease. This creates a tenancy at will. If Ted pays rent to Laura at the beginning of each month and Laura accepts such payments, most courts hold that the tenancy at will has been transformed into a tenancy from month to month.

A periodic tenancy may be terminated by either party at the expiration of any one period but only upon adequate notice to the other party. In the absence of an express agreement in the lease, the common law requires six months' notice in tenancies from year to year. This period has been shortened in most jurisdictions by statute to periods ranging between thirty and ninety days. In periodic tenancies involving periods of less than one year, the notice required at common law is one full period in advance, but, again, this may be subject to regulation by statute.

Tenancy at Will A lease containing a provision that either party may terminate at any time creates a tenancy at will. A lease that does not specify any duration likewise creates a tenancy at will. At common law, such tenancies were terminable without any prior notice, but many jurisdictions now have statutes requiring a notice to terminate, usually of thirty days.

Tenancy at Sufferance A tenancy at sufferance arises when a tenant fails to vacate the premises at the expiration of the lease. The common law gives the landlord the right to elect either to dispossess such tenant or to hold him for another term. Until the landlord makes this election, a tenancy at sufferance exists.

Transfer of Interests

Both the tenant's possessory interest in the leasehold and the landlord's reversionary interest in the property may be freely transferred in the absence of contractual or statutory prohibition. This general rule is subject to one major exception: the tenancy at will. Any attempt by either party to transfer her interest is usually considered as an expression of the intent to terminate the tenancy.

Transfers by Landlord After conveying the leasehold interest, a landlord is left with a reversionary interest in the property plus the right to rent and other benefits acquired under the lease. The landlord may transfer either or both of these interests. The party to whom the reversion is transferred takes the property subject to the tenant's leasehold interest if the transferee has actual or constructive notice of the lease. For example, Linda leases Whiteacre to Tina for five years, and Tina records the lease with the Register of Deeds. Linda then sells Whiteacre to Arthur.

Tina's lease is still valid and enforceable against Arthur whose right to possession of Whiteacre begins only after the expiration of the lease.

Transfers by Tenant A tenant may dispose of his interest either by (1) assignment, or (2) sublease. In the absence of a provision in his lease, both of these rights are available to him. As a consequence, most standard leases expressly require the consent of the landlord to an assignment or subletting of the premises. Under the majority view, a covenant against assignment of a lease does not prohibit the tenant from subleasing the premises. Conversely, a prohibition against subleasing is not considered a restriction upon the right to assign the lease.

If a tenant transfers *all* his interest in the leasehold so that he has no reversionary rights, he has made an **assignment.** Many leases prohibit assignment without the landlord's written consent.

If the tenant assigns the lease without consent, the assignment is not void, but it may be avoided by the landlord. In other words, the prohibition of assignment in a lease is only for the benefit of the landlord and cannot be relied upon by the assignor to terminate an otherwise valid assignment on the ground that the landlord did not consent. If, however, the landlord accepts rent from the assignee, he will be held to have waived the restriction.

The tenant's agreement to pay rent and other contractual **covenants** (express promises) pass to and obligate the assignee of the lease as long as the assignee remains in possession of the leasehold estate. Although the assignee of the lease is thus bound to pay rent, the original tenant is *not* relieved of his contractual obligation to pay rent. If the assignee fails to pay the stipulated rent, the original tenant will have to pay. He will have a right to be reimbursed by the assignee. Thus, after an assignment of a tenant's interest, *both* the original tenant and the assignee are liable to the landlord for failure to pay rent.

A **sublease** differs from an assignment in that it involves the transfer by the tenant to another of *less* than all the tenant's rights in the lease such that the tenant retains a reversion in the leasehold. For example, Mary is a tenant under a lease from Leon which is to terminate on December 31, 1991. If Mary leases the premises to Tony for a shorter period than that covered by her own lease, e.g., until November 30, 1991, Mary has subleased the premises because she has transferred less than her whole interest in the lease.

The legal effects of a sublease are entirely different from those of an assignment. In a sublease, the sublessee (Tony in the example above) has no obligation to Mary's landlord Leon. Tony's obligations run solely to Mary, the original tenant, and Mary is not relieved of any of her obligations under the lease. Thus, Leon has no right of action against Mary's sublessee Tony under any covenants contained in the original lease between him and Mary because that lease has not been assigned to Tony. Mary, of course, remains liable to Leon for the rent reserved and upon all of the other covenants in the original lease between her and Leon. See Figure 50–2.

Tenant's Obligations

While the leasehold estate carries with it an implied obligation upon the part of the tenant to pay reasonable rent, the lease contract almost always contains an express promise or covenant by the tenant to pay rent in specified amounts at specified times. In the absence of a specific covenant providing the amount of rental and the times for payment, the rent is a *reasonable* amount and is *payable only at the end of the term.*

Most leases contain a provision to the effect that if the tenant breaches any of the covenants in the lease, the landlord is entitled to declare the lease at an end and may regain possession of the premises. The tenant's express undertaking to pay rent thus becomes one of the covenants upon which this provision can operate. Where there is no such provision in the lease, at common law the tenant's failure to pay rent when due gives the landlord only the right to recover a

Figure 50–2 Assignment Compared with Sublease

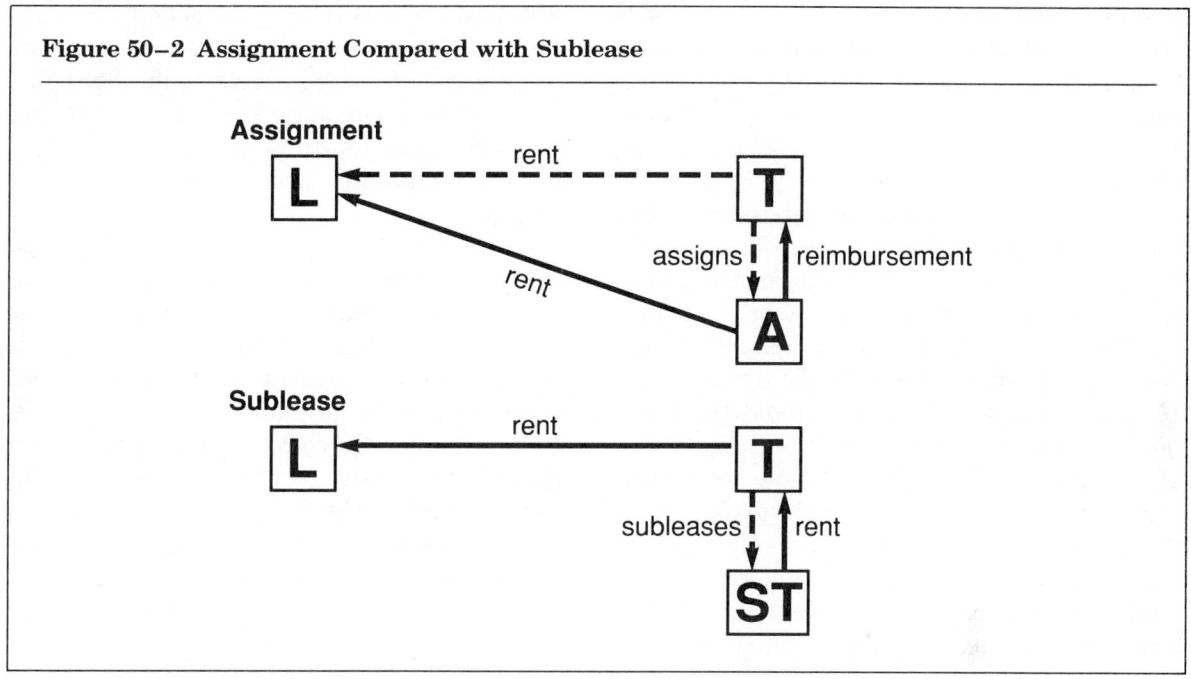

judgment for the amount of such rent; it gives him *no* right to oust the tenant from the premises. In most jurisdictions, however, the common law rule has been changed by statute to give the landlord the right to dispossess the tenant for non-payment of rent, even though there is no provision for this in the lease.

A tenant is under *no* duty to make any repairs to the leased premises, unless the lease expressly so provides. He is not obliged to repair or restore substantial or extraordinary damage occurring without his fault, nor to repair damage caused by ordinary wear and tear. The tenant is obliged to use the premises so that no substantial injury is caused them. The law imposes this duty on him even though it is not expressly stipulated in the lease. For example, a tenant who overloads an electrical connection thereby causing damage to a wiring system is liable to the landlord.

Destruction of the Premises The dual character of a lease as a contract and as a grant of an estate in land is particularly evident when considering the common law rule governing the destruction of the premises by

fire or other cause. Where the tenant leases land together with a building and the building is destroyed by fire or other fortuitous cause, the common law does not relieve him of his obligation to pay rent nor does it permit him to terminate the lease. The common law rule has been modified in most States by statute, and in most States it does not apply to tenants who occupy only a portion of the building and have no interest in the building as a whole, such as apartment tenants. Most leases contain clauses covering the fortuitous destruction of the premises.

Eviction or Abandonment When the tenant breaches one of the covenants in her lease, such as the covenant to pay rent, and the landlord evicts or dispossesses her pursuant to an express provision in the lease or under a statute authorizing her to do so, the lease is terminated. Because the breach of the covenant to pay rent does not involve any injury to the premises and because the landlord's action in evicting the tenant terminates the lease, the tenant is not liable to the landlord for any future installments of the rent after such an eviction. Most long-term leases, however, contain a *survival clause* providing that the eviction of the tenant for non-payment of rent will not relieve her of liability for damages measured by the difference between the rent reserved in the lease and the rent the landlord is able to obtain when reletting the premises.

If the tenant wrongfully abandons the premises before the expiration of the term of the lease and the landlord reenters the premises or relets them to another, a majority of the courts hold that the tenant's obligation to pay rent after reentry terminates. The landlord, if he desires to hold the tenant to his obligation to pay rent, must either leave the premises vacant or must have another "survival clause" in the lease that covers this situation.

If the tenant is wrongfully evicted by the landlord, the tenant's obligations under the lease are terminated, and as discussed below, the landlord is liable for breach of the tenant's right of quiet enjoyment.

Landlord's Obligations

Absent express provisions in the lease, the landlord, under the common law, has few obligations to her tenant. Under the majority rule, at the beginning of the lease, she must give the tenant actual possession. In a minority of States she must only give the tenant the right to possession. Thus, in these States if the previous tenant refuses to move out at the termination of the lease, the landlord must bring dispossession proceedings to oust him, but she is not responsible to the new tenant for the delay thus brought about, and the new tenant is not relieved of the obligation to pay rent from the starting date of the lease.

Quiet Enjoyment The landlord may not interfere with the tenant's right to physical possession, use, and enjoyment of the premises. The landlord is bound to provide the tenant with quiet and peaceful enjoyment. This duty arises by implication and is known as the landlord's covenant of **quiet enjoyment.** The landlord breaches this covenant whenever he wrongfully evicts the tenant. He is

also regarded as having breached this covenant if the tenant is evicted by someone having a better title than the landlord. The landlord is not responsible, however, for the wrongful acts of third parties unless they are done with his assent and under his direction.

Under the doctrine of **constructive eviction** a failure by the landlord in any of her undertakings under the lease, which causes a substantial and lasting injury to the tenant's beneficial enjoyment of the premises, is regarded as being, in effect, an eviction of the tenant. Under such circumstances, the courts permit the tenant to abandon the premises and terminate the lease. The tenant must abandon possession within a reasonable time in order to claim that there was a constructive eviction. *See Colonial Court Apartments, Inc. v. Kern.*

Fitness for Use Unless there is a specific provision in the lease, the landlord, under the common law, is under *no* obligation to provide or maintain the premises in a tenantable (livable) condition or to make them fit for any purpose since the primary value of the lease to the tenant is the land. Most courts, however, have abandoned this rule in residential leases by imposing an **implied warranty of habitability** requiring that the leased premises be fit for ordinary residential purposes. These courts have also held that the covenant to pay rent is conditioned upon the landlord's performance of the implied warranty of habitability. Courts reaching these results have emphasized that the tenant's interest is in a place to live and not merely in the land. The common law assumption that the value of the leasehold is the land may have been valid in an agricultural society and may even be valid in some farm leases, but it is not true in the case of a modern apartment rental.

A number of States have statutes requiring landlords to keep residential premises fit for occupation. Zoning ordinances, health and safety regulations, and building and housing codes may also impose certain duties upon the landlord.

If the landlord violates the warranty of habitability, the tenant may terminate the lease and avoid further liability for rent, sue for damages, and in some States withhold rent.

Repair In the absence of an express provision in the lease or a statutory duty to do so, the landlord has no obligation to repair or restore the premises. The landlord does have, however, a duty to maintain, repair, and keep in safe condition those portions of the premises that remain under her control. For example, an apartment house owner who controls the lobbies, stairways, elevators, and other common areas is liable for their maintenance and repair and is responsible for injuries that occur as a result of her failure to do so. With respect to apartment buildings, the court presumes that any portion of the premises that is not expressly leased to the tenants remains under the landlord's control. Thus, the landlord, in such cases, is liable to make external repairs, including repairs to the roof. The courts have further expanded the "common areas" rule to individual rental unit equipment that is connected to a central system, such as central heating and air conditioning, hot water, and plumbing and electrical systems. For a discussion of the duties and tort liabilities of a landlord to a tenant in common areas see Chapter 6.

While at common law the landlord is under no duty to repair, restore, or keep the premises in a tenantable condition, she may and often does assume those duties in the lease. When she does, her breach of any of these undertakings under the lease does not entitle the tenant to abandon the premises and refuse to pay rent. Unless an express provision in the lease gives the tenant this right, the common law allows him only an action for damages.

CONCURRENT OWNERSHIP

The ownership of property may be held by one individual or by two or more persons concurrently. Two or more persons who hold title concurrently are generally referred to as **co-tenants**. Each is entitled to an undivided interest in the entire property, and neither has a claim to any specific portion of it. Each may have equal undivided interests, or one may have a larger undivided share than the other. Regardless of the particular relationships between the co-tenants, this form of ownership must be carefully distinguished from the separate ownership of specific parts of property by different persons. Thus, it is possible for Anne, Barbara, and Carol to each own distinct and separate parts of Blackstone Manor, or they may each own, as co-tenants, an undivided one-third interest in all of Blackstone Manor. Whether they are co-tenants or owners of specific portions depends on the manner and form in which they acquired their interests.

The two major types of concurrent ownership are tenancy in common and joint tenancy. They both have the characteristics of an undivided interest in the whole, the right of both tenants to possession, and the right of either to sell his interest during life and thus terminate the original relationship. Other forms of co-ownership of real estate are tenancy by the entireties, community property, condominiums, and cooperatives.

Tenancy in Common

Tenancy in common is a form of concurrent ownership in which each co-owner has an undivided interest in the same property, each has the right to possession and use but none claims any specific portion of the property. It is the most frequently used form of concurrent ownership. Tenants in common need not have acquired their interests at the same time or by the same instrument and their interests may differ as to duration and scope. Because there is no right of survivorship, the interest of tenants in common may be devised by will or pass by intestate succession. By statute in all States, a transfer of title to two or more persons is presumed to create a tenancy in common. A tenancy in common may be terminated either by transfer of all the co-interests to one person or by partition of the property among the tenants. **Partition** is a physical division of the property, changing undivided interests into smaller parcels owned by each person individually. The size of individual parcels is based upon the size of the owners' prior share of the undivided interest.

Joint Tenancy

The most significant feature of joint tenancy is the right of *survivorship:* upon the death of one of the joint tenants, title to the entire property passes by operation of law to the survivor or survivors. Neither the heirs of the deceased joint tenant nor his general creditors have a claim to his interest, and a joint tenant cannot transfer his interest by executing a will. Any joint tenant may sever the joint tenancy, however, by conveying or mortgaging his interest to a third party. Further, the interest of either co-tenant is subject to levy and sale upon execution. *Sever* means the right of survivorship is lost, and the tenancy becomes a tenancy in common among the remaining joint tenants and the transferee. *See Hendrickson v. Minneapolis Federal Savings & Loan Association.* A joint tenancy may be terminated by partition of the property among the tenants, making each the exclusive owner of a specific part of the entire property.

To sustain a **joint tenancy,** the common law requires the presence of what are known as the *four unities* of time, title, interest, and possession.

1. The unity of time means that the interest of all tenants must vest at the same time;

2. the unity of title means that all tenants must acquire title by the same instrument;

3. the unity of interest means that all tenants must have identical interests as to duration and scope;

4. the unity of possession means that all tenants have the same right of possession and enjoyment.

The absence of any one of these four unities will prevent the creation of a joint tenancy. A failure of any one of the first three unities will result in the creation of a tenancy in common because the only unity required of a tenancy in common is the unity of possession.

Tenancy by the Entireties

Tenancy by the entireties, which is recognized in some States, is created only by a conveyance to a *husband* and *wife*. It is distinguished from joint tenancy by the inability of either spouse to convey separately his or her interest during life and thus destroy the right of survivorship. Likewise, the interest of either spouse cannot be attached by creditors. By the nature of the tenancy, a divorce terminates the relationship, and partition would then be available as a method of creating separate interests in the property.

Figure 50–3 compares the rights of concurrent owners in joint tenancy, tenancy in common, and tenancy by the entireties.

Community Property

In Arizona, California, Idaho, Louisiana, Nevada, New Mexico, Puerto Rico, Texas, Washington, and Wisconsin, one-half of any property acquired by the efforts of either the

---

Figure 50–3 Rights of Concurrent Owners

	Undivided Interest	Right to Possession	Right to Sell	Right to Mortgage	Levy by Creditors	Right to Will	Right of Survivorship
Joint Tenancy	YES	YES	YES	YES	YES	NO	YES
Tenancy in Common	YES	YES	YES	YES	YES	YES	NO
Tenancy by Entireties	YES	YES	NO	NO	NO	NO	YES

husband or wife belongs to each spouse. This system, known as **community property**, originated in the civil law of continental Europe but it has been modified and affected by the common law as well as by statutes in this country.

In most instances the only property that belongs separately to either spouse is any property acquired prior to the marriage or that acquired subsequent to it if by gift or devise. Upon the death of either spouse, one-half of the community property belongs outright to the survivor, and the interest of the deceased spouse in the other half may go to the heirs of the decedent or as directed by will. Under some conditions in a few jurisdictions, however, the surviving spouse may also claim an interest in the decedent's one-half share of the property.

Condominiums

A form of co-ownership called "condominium" has gained extensive use in the United States. All States have enacted statutes authorizing the use of this form of ownership. The purchaser of a condominium acquires separate ownership to the unit and becomes a tenant in common in the common facilities such as the land upon which the project is built, recreational facilities, hallways, parking areas, and spaces between the units. The common elements are maintained by a condominium association funded by assessments levied on each unit. The transfer of a condominium conveys both the separate ownership of the unit and the share in the common elements.

Cooperatives

Cooperatives involve an indirect form of common ownership. A cooperative, usually a corporation, purchases or constructs the dwelling units. The cooperative then leases the units to its shareholders as tenants, who acquire the right to use and occupy their units.

NONPOSSESSORY INTERESTS

A nonpossessory interest in land entitles the holder to use the land or to take something from the land, but the interest does not give him the right to possess the land. Nonpossessory interests include easements, *profits à prendre,* and licenses.

Definition of Easements

An **easement** is a *limited right* to make use of the land of another in a specific manner, that is created by the acts of the parties or by operation of law and that has all the attributes of an estate in the land itself. For example, a typical easement exists where Liz sells a part of her land to Neal and expressly provides in the same or a separate document that Neal, as the adjoining landowner, shall have a right-of-way over a strip of Liz's remaining parcel of land. Neal's land is said to be the **dominant** parcel (land whose owner has rights in other land), and Liz's land, which is subject to the easement, is the **servient** parcel. Easements may, of course, include a multitude of different types of uses as, for example, a right to run a ditch across another's land, to lay pipe under the surface, to erect power lines, or, in the case of adjacent buildings, to use a stairway or a common or "party" wall.

Because the owner of the entire servient tract retains the title to the servient parcel, she may make any use of or allow others the use of the tract as long as this use does not interfere with the easement. Thus, crops may be grown over an easement for a pipe line, but livestock cannot be pastured on an easement for a driveway. Although it is the duty of the owner of the servient parcel not to interfere with the use of the easement, it is generally the responsibility of the owner of the dominant parcel to maintain the easement and keep it in repair.

Types of Easements

Easements fall into two classes: easements appurtenant and easements in gross. **Appurtenant easements** are by far the more common type, and, as the name indicates, the rights and duties created by such easements pertain to the land itself and not to the particular individuals who may have created them. *See Nelson v. Johnson.* Therefore, the easement usually stays with the land when it is sold. For example, if Liz (from the previous example) sells her servient parcel to Kyle who has actual notice of the easement for the benefit of Neal's land or constructive notice by means of the local recording act, Kyle takes the parcel subject to the easement. Likewise, if Neal conveys his dominant parcel to Daniel, it is not necessary to refer specifically to the easement in the deed from Neal to Daniel in order to give to Daniel, as the new owner of the dominant parcel, the right to use the right-of-way over the servient parcel. Since Neal does not then own the dominant parcel, he has no further right to use the right-of-way. Neal could not, however, transfer the benefit of the easement to a party who did not acquire an interest in the dominant parcel of land. Most frequently, a deed conveying the land "together with all appurtenances" is sufficient to transfer the easement. This characteristic of an appurtenant easement is described by the statement that both the burden and the benefit of an appurtenant easement pass with the land.

The second type of easement is an **easement in gross,** which is personal to the particular individual who received the right. It does not depend on the ownership of land and, in effect, amounts to little more than an irrevocable personal right to use.

Creation of Easements

Easements may be created by (1) express grant or reservation, (2) implied grant or reservation, (3) necessity, (4) dedication, and (5) prescription.

Express Grant or Reservation The most common way to create an easement is to convey it by deed. For example, when Amy conveys part of her land to Robert, she may, in the same deed, expressly grant an easement to Robert over Amy's remaining property. Alternatively, Amy may grant an easement to Robert in a separate document. This document must comply with all the formalities of

a deed. An easement is an interest in land subject to the statute of frauds.

In other instances, when an owner of land transfers it, she may wish to retain certain rights in it. In the example given, Amy may want to "reserve" an easement in favor of the land retained by her over the land granted to Robert. Amy may do this by express words reserving that right to her in the deed of conveyance to Robert.

Implied Grant or Reservation Easements by implied grant or implied reservation arise whenever an owner of adjacent properties establishes an *apparent* and *permanent* use in the nature of an easement, and then conveys one of the properties without mention of any easement. For example, suppose that Andrew owns two adjacent lots, Nos. 1 and 2. There is a house on each lot. Behind each house is a garage. Andrew has constructed a driveway along the boundary between the two lots, partly on lot 1 and partly on lot 2, which leads from the street in front of the houses to the two garages in the rear. Andrew conveys lot 2 to Michael without any mention of the driveway. Andrew is held to have *impliedly granted* an easement to Michael over that portion of the driveway that lies on Andrew's lot 1, and he is held to have *impliedly reserved* an easement over that portion of the driveway that lies on Michael's lot 2.

Necessity If Sharon conveys part of her land to Terry, and the part conveyed to Terry is so situated that Terry would have no access to it except across Sharon's remaining land, the law implies a grant by Sharon to Terry of an easement by necessity across Sharon's remaining land. An easement by necessity will not usually arise if an alternative but circuitous approach to Terry's land is available.

An easement by necessity may also arise by implied reservation. This would be the case where Sharon conveys part of her land to Terry, and Sharon's remaining property would be wholly landlocked unless she is given a right-of-way across the land conveyed to Terry.

Dedication When an owner of land subdivides it into lots and records the plan or plat of the subdivision, she is held, both by common law and now more frequently by statute, to have dedicated *to the public* all of the streets, alleys, parks, playgrounds, and beaches shown on the plat. In addition, when the subdivider sells the lots by reference to the plat, it is now generally recognized that the purchasers acquire easements by implication over the areas shown dedicated to the public.

Prescription An easement may arise by prescription in most States if certain required conditions are met. To obtain an easement by prescription, a person must use a portion of land owned by another in a way (1) that is adverse to the rightful owner's use, (2) that is open and notorious, and (3) that is continuous and uninterrupted for a specific period of time that varies from State to State. *See Nelson v. Johnson.* If the owner gives the claimant permission to use the land, no easement by prescription is acquired.

Profits à Prendre

The phrase a *profit à prendre* comes from the French and means the right to remove the produce of another's land. An example would be the grant by Jack to Roger, an adjoining landowner, of the right to remove coal or fish or timber from Jack's land or to graze his cattle on Jack's land. Like an easement, a *profit à prendre* may arise by prescription, but if it comes by an act of the parties, it must be created with all the formalities of a grant of an estate in real property. Unless the right is clearly designated as exclusive, it is always subject to a similar use by the owner of the land. The right to take profits is frequently held independent of the ownership of other land. Thus, Norman may have a right to remove crushed gravel from John's acreage even though Norman lives in another part of the county.

Licenses

It is not always easy to distinguish such real interests in property as easements or *profits à prendre* from an equally common right of use designated as a license. Permission to make use of one's land generally constitutes a license that creates no interest in the property and is usually exercised only at the will of and subject to revocation by the owner at any time. For example, if Carter tells Karen she may cut across Carter's land to pick hickory nuts, Karen has nothing but a license subject to revocation at any time. It is possible that, upon the basis of a license, Karen may expend funds to exercise the right, and the courts may prevent Carter from revoking the license simply because it would be unfair to penalize Karen under the circumstances. In such a case, Karen's interest is practicably indistinguishable from an easement. *See Bunn v. Offutt.*

A common illustration of a license is a theater ticket or the use of a hotel room. No interest is acquired in the premises; there is simply a right of use for a given length of time, subject to good behavior. No formality is required to create a license; a shopkeeper licenses persons to enter his establishment merely by being open for business.

CASES

Remainders

STRICKLAND v. JACKSON
Supreme Court of North Carolina, 1963.
259 N.C. 81, 130 S.E.2d 22.

RODMAN, J.
[In 1905 a deed for land in Pitt County was executed and delivered by Joel and Louisa Tyson "unto M.H. Jackson and wife Maggie Jackson, for and during the term of their nat-

ural lives and after their death to the children of the said M.H. Jackson and Maggie Jackson that shall be born to their inter-marriage as shall survive them to them and their heirs and assigns in fee simple forever." Thelma Jackson Vester, a daughter of M.H. Jackson and Maggie Jackson, died in 1957, survived by three children. M.H. Jackson, who survived his wife Maggie Jackson, died in 1958, survived by four sons. The children of Thelma Jackson Vester brought this action against M.P. Jackson, a son of and executor of the will of M.H. Jackson. The children of Vester contended that through their deceased mother they were entitled to a ⅕ interest in the land conveyed by the deed of 1905. The executor contended that the deed conveyed a contingent remainder and only those children who survived the parents took an interest in the land.]

* * *

The distinction between a vested and a contingent remainder is the capacity to take upon the termination of the preceding estate. Where those who are to take in remainder cannot be determined until the happening of a stated event, the remainder is contingent. Only those who can answer the roll immediately upon the happening of the event acquire any estate in the properties granted. [Citations.]

Here the estate in remainder was not given to the children of M.H. Jackson and Maggie Jackson, but by clear and express language to those children and only those who survived their parents. Since Mrs. Vester did not survive her parents, there was nothing for her children, plaintiffs, to inherit. [Citations.]

It affirmatively appears from the complaint that plaintiffs acquired no interest in the land by virtue of the deed from Tyson and wife to M.H. Jackson and others.

[Judgment in favor of defendant/executor affirmed.]

Warranty of Habitability

JAVINS v. FIRST NATIONAL REALTY CORP.

United States Court of Appeals, District of
Columbia Circuit, 1970.
428 F.2d 1071.

WRIGHT, J.

These cases present the question whether housing code violations which arise during the term of a lease have any effect upon the tenant's obligation to pay rent. The Landlord and Tenant Branch of the District of Columbia Court of General Sessions ruled proof of such violations inadmissible when proffered as a defense to an eviction action for nonpayment of rent. The District of Columbia Court of Appeals upheld this ruling. [Citation.]

Because of the importance of the question presented, we granted appellants' petitions for leave to appeal. We now reverse and hold that a warranty of habitability, measured by the standards set out in the Housing Regulations for the District of Columbia, is implied by operation of law into leases of urban dwelling units covered by those Regulations and that breach of this warranty gives rise to the usual remedies for breach of contract.

The facts revealed by the record are simple. By separate written leases, each of the appellants rented an apartment in a three-building apartment complex in Northwest Washington known as Clifton Terrace. The landlord, First National Realty Corporation, filed separate actions in the Landlord and Tenant Branch of the Court of General Sessions on April 8, 1966, seeking possession on the ground that each of the appellants had defaulted in the payment of rent due for the month of April. The tenants, appellants here, admitted that they had not paid the landlord any rent for April. However, they alleged numerous violations of the Housing Regulations as "an equitable defense of [a] claim by way of recoupment or set-off in an amount equal to the rent claim," as provided in the rules of the Court of General Sessions. They offered to prove

[t]hat there are approximately 1500 violations of the Housing Regulations of the District of Columbia in the building at Clifton Terrace, where Defendant resides some affecting the premises of this Defendant directly, others indirectly, and all tending to establish a course of conduct of violation of the Housing Regulations to the damage of Defendants. . . .

[Citation.] Appellants conceded at trial, however, that this offer of proof reached only violations which had arisen since the term of the lease had commenced.

* * *

Since, in traditional analysis, a lease was the conveyance of an interest in land, courts have usually utilized the special rules governing real property transactions to resolve controversies involving leases. However, as the Supreme Court has noted in another context, "the body of private property law . . ., more than almost any other branch of law, has been shaped by distinctions whose validity is largely historical." Courts have a duty to reappraise old doctrines in the light of the facts and values of contemporary life— particularly old common law doctrines which the courts themselves created and developed. As we have said before, "[T]he continued vitality of the common law . . . depends upon its ability to reflect contemporary community values and ethics."

The assumption of landlord-tenant law, derived from feudal property law, that a lease primarily conveyed to the tenant an interest in land may have been reasonable in a rural, agrarian society; it may continue to be reasonable in some leases involving farming or commercial land. In these cases, the value of the lease to the tenant is the land itself. But in the case of the modern apartment dweller, the value of the lease is that it gives him a place to live. The city dweller who seeks to lease an apartment on the third floor of a tenement has little interest in the land 30 or 40 feet below, or even in the bare right to possession within the four walls of his apartment. When American city dwellers, both rich and poor, seek "shelter" today, they seek a well known package of goods and services—a package which includes not merely walls and ceilings, but also adequate heat, light and ventilation, serviceable plumbing facilities, secure windows and doors, proper sanitation, and proper maintenance.

* * *

Ironically, however, the rules governing the construction and interpretation of "predominantly contractual" obligations in leases have too often remained rooted in old property law.

Some courts have realized that certain of the old rules of property law governing leases are inappropriate for today's transactions. In order to reach results more in accord with the legitimate expectations of the parties and the standard of the community, courts have been gradually introducing more modern precepts of contract law in interpreting leases. Proceeding piecemeal has, however, led to confusion where "decisions are frequently conflicting, not because of a healthy disagreement on social policy, but because of the lingering impact of rules whose policies are long since dead."

In our judgment the trend toward treating leases as contracts is wise and well considered. Our holding in this case reflects a belief that leases of urban dwelling units should be interpreted and construed like any other contract.

Modern contract law has recognized that the buyer of goods and services in an industrialized society must rely upon the skill and honesty of the supplier to assure that goods and services purchased are of adequate quality. In interpreting most contracts, courts have sought to protect the legitimate expectations of the buyer and have steadily widened the seller's responsibility for the quality of goods and services through implied warranties of fitness and merchantability.

* * *

The rigid doctrines of real property law have tended to inhibit the application of implied warranties to transactions involving real estate. Now, however, courts have begun to hold sellers and developers of real property responsible for the quality of their product. For example, builders of new homes have recently been held liable to purchasers for improper construction on the ground that the builders had breached an implied warranty of fitness. In other cases courts have held builders of new homes liable for breach of an implied warranty that all local building regulations had been complied with. And following the developments in other areas, very recent decisions and commentary suggest the possible extension of liability to parties other than the immediate seller for improper construction of residential real estate.

Despite this trend in the sale of real estate, many courts have been unwilling to imply warranties of quality, specifically a warranty of habitability, into leases of apartments. Recent decisions have offered no convincing explanation for their refusal; rather they have relied without discussion upon the old common law rule that the lessor is not obligated to repair unless he covenants to do so in the written lease contract. However, the Supreme Courts of at least two states, in recent and well reasoned opinions, have held landlords to implied warranties of quality in housing leases. [Citations.] In our judgment, the old no-repair rule cannot coexist with the obligations imposed on the landlord by a typical modern housing code, and must be abandoned in favor of an implied warranty of habitability. In the District of Columbia, the standards of this warranty are set out in the Housing Regulations.

In our judgment the common law itself must recognize the landlord's obligation to keep his premises in a habitable condition. This conclusion is compelled by three separate considerations. First, we believe that the old rule was based on certain factual assumptions which are no longer true; on its own terms, it can no longer be justified. Second, we believe that the consumer protection cases discussed above require that the old rule be abandoned in order to bring residential landlord-tenant law into harmony with the principles on which those cases rest. Third, we think that the nature of today's urban housing market also dictates abandonment of the old rule.

* * *

Today's urban tenants, the vast majority of whom live in multiple dwelling houses, are interested, not in the land, but solely in "a house suitable for occupation." Furthermore, today's city dweller usually has a single, specialized skill unrelated to maintenance work; he is unable to make repairs, like the "jack-of-all-trades" farmer who was the common law's model of the lessee. Further, unlike his agrarian predecessor who often remained on one piece of land for his entire life, urban tenants today are more mobile than ever before.

A tenant's tenure in a specific apartment will often not be sufficient to justify efforts at repairs. In addition, the increasing complexity of today's dwellings renders them much more difficult to repair than the structures of earlier times. In a multiple dwelling repair may require access to equipment and areas in control of the landlord. Low and middle income tenants, even if they were interested in making repairs, would be unable to obtain any financing for major repairs since they have no long-term interest in the property.

* * *

Since a lease contract specifies a particular period of time during which the tenant has a right to use his apartment for shelter, he may legitimately expect that the apartment will be fit for habitation for the time period for which it is rented. We point out that in the present cases there is no allegation that appellants' [lessees'] apartments were in poor condition or in violation of the housing code at the commencement of the leases. Since the lessees continue to pay the same rent, they were entitled to expect that the landlord would continue to keep the premises in their beginning condition during the lease term. It is precisely such expectations that the law now recognizes as deserving of formal, legal protection.

* * *

We follow the Illinois court in holding that the housing code must be read into housing contracts—a holding also required by the purposes and the structure of the code itself. The duties imposed by the Housing Regulations may not be waived or shifted by agreement if the Regulations specifically place the duty upon the lessor.

* * *

In the present cases, the landlord sued for possession for nonpayment of rent. Under contract principles, however, the tenant's obligation to pay rent is dependent upon the landlord's performance of his obligations, including his warranty to maintain the premises in habitable condition.

* * *

The judgment of the District of Columbia Court of Appeals is reversed and the cases are remanded for further proceedings consistent with this opinion.

Constructive Eviction

COLONIAL COURT APARTMENTS, INC. v. KERN

Supreme Court of Minnesota, 1968.
282 Minn. 533, 163 N.W.2d 770.

PER CURIAM

[On January 1, 1966, Mrs. Irene Kern leased an apartment from Colonial Court Apartments, Inc., for a one-year term. When the lease was entered into, Mrs. Kern asked for a quiet apartment, and Colonial assured her that the assigned apartment was in a quiet, well-insulated building. In fact, however, the apartment above Mrs. Kern's was occupied by a young couple, the Lindgrens. From the start of her occupancy, Mrs. Kern complained of their twice-weekly parties and other actions that so disturbed her sleep that she had to go elsewhere for rest. After Mrs. Kern had lodged several complaints, Colonial terminated the Lindgrens' lease effective February 28, 1966. However, the termination of the lease was prolonged and Mrs. Kern vacated her apartment claiming that she was no longer able to endure the continued disturbances. Colonial then brought this action to recover rent owed by Mrs. Kern.]

A constructive eviction is said to occur when the beneficial enjoyment of an apartment by the lessee is so interfered with by the landlord as to justify an abandonment. It does not suppose an actual ouster or dispossession by the landlord. [Citation.] Ordinarily, the rule is that the acts of one tenant do not constitute a constructive eviction of another tenant of the same landlord unless they materially disturb the latter tenant in the use, occupancy, and enjoyment of the demised premises or the natural consequence thereof is to injure the other tenant. [Citations.]

* * *

In fairness it should be said that the trial court could well have found that the landlord

took such reasonable measures as were warranted under the circumstances to correct the conditions of which defendant complained. He might also have found that the landlord's letter to the tenants that their "first possibility to vacate, according to law, will be June 30," referred to liability for rent rather than a requirement to remain in possession. Nevertheless, we are not warranted in making an exception to our well-established rule that in reviewing the record the testimony must be considered in the light most favorable to the prevailing party, and if support for the findings may be found in the evidence as a whole, such findings will not be disturbed. The findings of fact by the trial court and the jury stand on equal footing and are entitled to the same weight and will not be reversed on appeal unless they are manifestly and palpably contrary to the evidence. [Citation.]

"The definition of what constitutes constructive eviction does not get us far. Usually the question whether there is a constructive eviction is one of fact with each case largely dependent upon its particular circumstances."

* * *

[Judgment for Mrs. Kern.]

Concurrent Ownership

HENDRICKSON v. MINNEAPOLIS FEDERAL SAVINGS & LOAN ASSOCIATION

Supreme Court of Minnesota, 1968.
281 Minn. 462, 161 N.W.2d 688.

SHERAN, J.

Appeal from an order and decree of registration of the district court.

The Facts On June 30, 1956, Martin Hendrickson and Solveig Hendrickson were married, and on January 3, 1957, a home previously owned by him was so conveyed as to make them owners of it as joint tenants and not as tenants in common. No part of the consideration for the premises was paid by Mrs. Hendrickson and there is no evidence to show that the creation of the joint tenancy was pursuant to an enforceable agreement.

On August 3, 1964, Martin Hendrickson duly executed a Declaration of Election to Sever Survivorship of Joint Tenancy by which he endeavored to preserve an interest in the premises for Ruth Halbert, his daughter by a previous marriage, appellant in this court. On the same day, he executed his last will and testament, by the terms of which he directed that his wife, Solveig M. Hendrickson, receive the minimum amount to which she was entitled under the laws of the State of Minnesota.

Mr. Hendrickson died testate on October 9, 1964. Thereafter, Solveig M. Hendrickson made application to register title to the premises here involved in her name as fee owner. Ruth Halbert appeared and asserted claim to the interest in the realty to which she would be entitled if the declaration was effective to make Martin Hendrickson and Solveig M. Hendrickson owners of the realty as tenants in common, i.e., an undivided one-half interest subject to the widow's life estate.[1]

Upon reference, the referee found that Martin Hendrickson did not terminate the joint tenancy by his declaration, and that Solveig M. Hendrickson became the owner of an estate in fee simple in the whole of said property as surviving joint tenant. The district court ratified the report of the referee. A decree was entered accordingly and this appeal followed.

The Issue The issue for decision is this: Did the declaration have the effect of severing the joint tenancy, creating a tenancy in common? If it did, Ruth Halbert is the owner of an undivided one-half interest in said real estate subject to the life estate therein of Solveig M. Hendrickson. If it did not, Solveig M. Hendrickson owns the realty in fee simple absolute.

1. Mrs. Hendrickson would be the owner in fee of the other undivided one-half interest in this realty because if the joint tenancy was severed she became with respect to it a tenant in common and owner in fee of an undivided one-half interest therein.

The Decision Under the common law, there were three types of concurrent ownership: Tenancy in common, joint tenancy, and tenancy by the entirety. A joint tenancy is distinguished from a tenancy in common by the fact that a surviving joint tenant succeeds to the person with whom he shared the joint tenancy. A tenancy by the entirety, which can exist only between husband and wife, is like a joint tenancy in that survivorship exists, but is distinguished from the joint tenancy by the fact that there can be no partition, and it cannot be converted into a tenancy in common. [Citations.]

As the common law of property developed during feudal times, there was a presumption in favor of joint tenancy due to reasons related to feudalism. As the age of feudalism ended, the reasons for this presumption also ended and survivorship came to be regarded "as an 'odious thing' that too often deprived a man's heirs of their rightful inheritance." [Citations.]

In Minnesota, the original presumption in favor of joint tenancy has been reversed by Minn.St. 500.19, subd. 2, which provides: "All grants and devises of lands, made to two or more persons, shall be construed to create estates in common, and not in joint tenancy, unless expressly declared to be in joint tenancy." Disfavor for survivorship in Minnesota is also shown by the fact that in this state the estate of tenancy by the entirety, with its indestructible survivorship, is not recognized. [Citations.]

For a joint tenancy to exist, unity of time, title, interest, and possession must concur. [Citations.] Traditionally, the survivorship feature could be destroyed and the joint tenancy converted into a tenancy in common if one of the unities was destroyed. [Citations.] This would result, for example, if one of the joint tenants conveyed his interest to a third party. [Citation.] The common-law lawyer used this principle to enable one joint tenant to unilaterally eliminate the survivorship feature and yet retain ownership in the property. A conveyance would be made to a third party or strawman, thus destroying the joint tenancy. Immediately thereafter the property would be reconveyed to the original owner. A tenancy in common would thus be created because the unities of time and interest would no longer be present. More recently the courts have come to allow joint tenants to convert their estate into a tenancy in common without the ritual of conveyance and reconveyance. It is only necessary for the joint tenants to mutually agree to sever the joint tenancy. [Citations.] We are now asked to allow one joint tenant to do unilaterally that which we allow joint tenants acting in concert to do, i.e., terminate the joint tenancy by declaration without being required to go through the ceremony of a conveyance to a strawman and a reconveyance back again.

* * *

We hold that the method chosen here is sufficient to sever a joint tenancy. Had the property involved been any property other than a homestead, the decedent could have unilaterally severed the joint tenancy. Minn.St. 507.02 and 525.145(1)(b)[7] establish a public policy to protect for the wife the continued occupancy of the place of joint abode. However, this public policy does not necessarily apply to the remainder interest, which can be disposed of without adversely affecting the right of the surviving spouse to continue in possession and enjoyment for so long as she might live. Putting the property into joint tenancy was apparently an estate-planning device. If the decedent had kept title to this real estate in his own name and executed a will by the terms of which it was devised to his wife in fee simple absolute, he would have been free at any time to revoke the will unilaterally. His wife would nevertheless have the right to a life estate in the homestead upon his death, but her right

would be based on the statute and not the will. § 525.145(1)(b). . . .

If the survivor had taken some irrevocable action in reliance upon the creation or existence of the joint tenancy, or if some consideration was given or received when the joint tenancy was created, it would seem reasonable to insist that unilateral action would not be effective to deprive the passive joint tenant of the rights so created. But this is not such a case.

Our conclusion is that the trial court should be reversed.

Types of Easements

NELSON v. JOHNSON

Supreme Court of Idaho, 1984.
106 Idaho 385, 679 P.2d 662.

Huntley, J.

By this appeal we are asked to review the decision of the district court wherein it was determined that two easements in favor of the respondents, Lyle and Loa Nelson, exist. Because the findings of the district court are supported by substantial and competent evidence, we affirm.

In 1956, Robert and Majorie Wake owned certain land in Cassia County. They carried on a dry farming operation on a portion of the land and the rest of the estate was used as a cattle ranch. As part of the cattle ranching operation, each spring and autumn the Wakes would drive their cattle from the home ranch down a county road which bounded the farmland on the west, and then eastward over an access road on the farmland to Butler Springs, also located on the farm. From Butler Springs, the cattle were ranged further eastward onto the adjacent Bureau of Land Management (BLM) property and forest service land, utilizing grazing rights thereon and returning each day to the springs for water. In the summer months, the cattle ranged further up onto forest service land. At the onset of winter they were driven back through Butler Springs, across the access road and down the county road to winter on the home ranch.

7. Minn.St. 525.145(1) provides: "Where there is a surviving spouse the homestead shall descend free from any testamentary or other disposition thereof to which such spouse has not consented in writing or by election to take under the will as provided by law, as follows:
"(b) If there be children or issue of deceased children surviving, then to the spouse for the term of his natural life and the remainder in equal shares to such children and the issue of deceased children by right of representation."

On December 28, 1956, the dry farm was sold to Jesse and Maud Hess. The contract of sale contained the following clause:

It is hereby expressly agreed that the sellers hereby reserve and the purchasers agree to give, the right to the use of water in the Butler Springs located in the NW ¼ of the NE ¼ of said Section 15, for the watering of livestock owned by the sellers, together with an easement and right of way from the said springs Eastward across the NE ¼ of the NE ¼ of said Section 15, and the N ½ of the N ½ of said Section 14, generally along the line near the bottom of Butler Spring Hollow. The said right of way and watering place to consist of approximately 40 acres and the sellers to construct and maintain adequate fences along the right of way and surrounding the water trought (sic). It is agreed that all water not necessary for the watering of the sellers (sic) livestock will be permitted to overflow the water trough and to be used by the purchaser.

The clause defines the Butler Springs area used by the Wakes in the ranching operation, however, it does not describe the access road leading to the springs from the county road.

In 1963, the Hesses sold the farm to Raymond and Wilma Johnson, the appellants herein. The terms of that contract provided that the Johnsons would have uninterrupted possession of the property, "excepting only that permissive use of the premises as is set forth in that certain contract dated the 20th (sic) day of December, 1956, between ROBERT C. WAKE and MARJORIE E. WAKE and the Vendors." The 1956 contract had not been recorded, nor had a deed between the Wakes and Hesses been executed as of 1963; however, the Johnsons had actual notice of the provisions of the Wake-Hess contract. A deed reflecting the terms of the 1956 contract was eventually executed and recorded in 1964.

The Wakes continued the use of the access road, Butler Springs and the federal grazing privileges until they sold the home ranch and cattle operation in 1964. In the sale contract, the Wakes expressly granted to the new owners, "their rights, to the water of Butler Springs . . . consisting of approximately 40 acres which the same was reserved by R. C. Wake and wife, in a Contract for Real Estate with Jean Hess, dated December 26, (sic) 1956." The ranch property and cattle operation were subsequently sold several times. All successors in title to the ranch have utilized the easement in the springs as was reserved in the 1956 contract, as well as the access road leading to the springs from the county road. In 1973, the property was purchased by the Nelsons, the respondents. A corrected warranty deed which included "(r)ight for stock water in Butler Springs located in the NW ¼, NE ¼ of Section 15 and easements on part of Section 15 and 14" was recorded in April of 1979. A second corrected deed containing the same language was recorded in 1981.

The Johnsons have at all times since the purchase from the Hesses in 1964 been the owners of the farmland and Mr. Johnson testified that all owners of the ranch, previous to the Nelsons, had used the easements as a matter of right. Shortly after the Nelsons took possession of the ranch however, the Johnsons purported to grant permission to use the road and Butler Springs to the Nelsons, which "permission" was revoked by a letter sent the Nelsons in 1978. In 1979 the Johnsons placed locks on the gates across the access road.

Access to federal grazing land was subsequently gained by the Nelsons via a circuitous route which required obtaining permission and crossing other private land. The federal grazing land serviced by Butler Springs was not utilized due to its inaccessibility.

The Nelsons filed a complaint in district court alleging that they had easement interests in both the Butler Springs area and the access road. The court ruled for the Nelsons, holding that the easement reserved in the 1956 Wake-Hess contract was appurtenant to the ranch, and that an easement by prescription had arisen in the access road.

I. Butler Springs Easement

In construing an easement in a particular case, the instrument granting the easement is to be interpreted in connection with the intention of the parties, and the circumstances in existence at the time the easement was granted and utilized. [Citation.] The trial court in this case determined that the easement reserved in the 1956 Wake-Hess contract was appurtenant in nature, with a dominant estate in the cattle ranch and a servient estate in the farm, and that the easement had consequently passed with the dominant estate upon each transfer of title. The evidence fully supports that interpretation. The language of the reservation clause in the contract, as well as the established pattern of use of the Butler Springs area, indicate a clear intention by the parties that the easement be for the benefit of the cattle ranch. There is no showing that the parties intended it to be a mere personal right.

The definitions of "appurtenant" and "in gross" further make it clear that the easement is appurtenant. The primary distinction between an easement in gross and an easement appurtenant is that in the latter there is, and in the former there is not, a dominant estate to which the easement is attached. [Citation.] An easement in gross is merely a personal interest in the land of another, [citation]; whereas an easement appurtenant is an interest which is annexed to the possession of the dominant tenement and passes with it. [Citation.] An appurtenant easement must bear some relation to the use of the dominant estate and is incapable of existence separate from it; any attempted severance from the dominant estate must fail. [Citation.] The easement in the Butler Springs area is a beneficial and useful adjunct of the cattle ranch, and it would be of little use apart from the operations of the ranch. Moreover, in case of doubt, the weight of authority holds that the easement should be presumed appurtenant. [Citation.] * * *

II. The Access Road Easement

"A prescriptive easement must be established by open notorious use of the servient property with the actual or imputed knowledge thereof by the owner of the servient tenement. The use must be continuous for a prescriptive period of five years and must be done under a claim of right." [Citation.]

The use of the access road was open and known to both the Hesses and the Johnsons. The Nelsons and their predecessors in interest claimed a right of way in the access road, and no permission was given for such use until Johnson purported to do so in 1978. In fact, Mr. Johnson testified at trial that he believed the ranch owners had driven the cattle over the road by right. These facts established a prescriptive use of the road for the period between 1956 and 1978, at a minimum, which clearly meets the five-year requirement. The finding of the trial court that a prescriptive easement had been established, being supported by substantial and competent evidence, is affirmed.

QUESTIONS

1. Define and discuss the following feehold interests: (a) fee simple, (b) qualified fee, (c) life estate, (d) remainder interest, (e) dower, (f) curtesy, and (g) reversionary interest.

2. Distinguish between a vested and a contingent remainder.

3. Discuss the primary rights and obligations of landlords and tenants.

4. Identify and discuss the various forms of concurrent ownership of real property.

5. Identify and discuss the various ways in which an easement may be created.

PROBLEMS

1. Kirkland conveyed a farm to Adland to have and to hold for and during his life and upon his death to Rubin. Some years thereafter, oil was discovered in the vicinity. Adland thereupon made an oil and gas lease, and the oil company set up its machinery to commence drilling operations. Rubin thereupon filed suit to enjoin the operations. Assuming an injunction to be the proper form of remedy, what decision?

2. Smith owned Blackacre in fee simple. In section 3 of a properly executed will, Smith devised Blackacre as follows: "I devise my farm Blackacre to my son Darwin so long as it is used as a farm." Sections 5 and 6 of the will made gifts to persons other than Darwin. The last and residuary clause of Smith's will provided: "All the residue of my real and personal property not disposed of heretofore in this will, I devise and bequeath to Stanford University."

Smith died in 1991, survived by her son Darwin. Smith's estate has been administered. Darwin has been offered $100,000 for Blackacre if he can convey title to it in fee simple.

What interests in Blackacre were created by Smith's will?

3. Panessi leased to Barnes for a term of ten years beginning May 1 certain premises located at 527–529 Main Street in the City of Cleveland. The premises were improved with a three-story building, the first floor being occupied by stores and the upper stories by apartments. On May 1 of the following year, Barnes leased one of the apartments to Charles for one year. On July 5, a fire destroyed the second and third floors of the building. The first floor was not burned but was rendered untenantable. Neither the lease from Panessi to Barnes, nor the lease from Barnes to Charles contained any provision in regard to the fire loss. Discuss the liability of Barnes and Charles to continue to pay rent.

4. Ames leased an apartment to Boor at $200 a month payable the last day of each month. The term of the written lease was from January 1, 1990 through April 30, 1991. On March 15, 1990, Boor moved out, telling Ames that he disliked all the other tenants. Ames replied: "Well, you are no prize as a tenant; I probably can get more rent from someone more agreeable than you." Ames and Boor then had a minor physical altercation in which neither was injured. Boor sent the keys to the apartment to Ames by mail. Ames wrote Boor, "It will be my pleasure to hold you for every penny you owe me. I am renting the apartment on your behalf to Clay until April 30, 1991 at $175 a month." Boor had paid his rent through February 28, 1990. Clay entered the premises on April 1, 1990.

How much rent, if any, may Ames recover from Boor?

5. Jay signed a two-year lease containing a clause that expressly prohibited subletting. After six months, Jay asked the landlord for permission to sublet the apartment for one year. The landlord refused. This angered Jay, and he immediately assigned his right under the lease to Kay. Kay was a distinguished gentleman, and Jay knew that everyone would consider him a desirable tenant. Is Jay's assignment of his lease to Kay valid?

6. In 1981, Roy Martin and his wife, Alice, their son Hiram, and Hiram's wife, Myrna, acquired title to a 240–acre farm. The deed ran to Roy Martin and Alice Martin, the father and mother, as joint tenants with the right of survivorship, and to Hiram Martin and Myrna Martin, the son and his wife, as joint tenants with the right of survivorship. Alice Martin died in 1986, and in 1989 Roy Martin married Agnes Martin. By his will, Roy Martin bequeathed and devised his entire estate to Agnes Martin. When Roy Martin died in 1991, Hiram and Myrna Martin assumed complete control of the farm.

State the interest in the farm, if any, of Agnes, Hiram, and Myrna Martin immediately upon the death of Roy Martin.

7. In her will, Teressa granted a life estate to Ames in certain real estate, with remainder to Brenda and Clive in joint tenancy. All the residue of Teressa's estate was left to Hillman College. While going to Teressa's funeral, the car in which Ames, Brenda, and Clive were driving was wrecked. Brenda was killed instantly, Clive died a few minutes later, and Ames died on his way to the hospital. Who is entitled to the real estate in question?

8. Otis Olson, the owner of two adjoining city lots, A and B, built a house on each. He laid a drainpipe from lot B across lot A to the main sewer pipe under the alley beyond lot A. Olson then sold and conveyed lot A to Fred Ford. The deed, which made no mention of the drainpipe, was promptly recorded. Ford had no actual knowledge or notice of the drainpipe, although it would have been apparent to anyone making an inspection of the premises because it was only partially buried. Later, Olson sold and conveyed lot B to Luke Lane. This deed also made no reference to the drainpipe and was promptly recorded.

A few weeks thereafter Ford discovered the drainpipe across lot A and removed it. Did he have the right to do so?

9. At the time of his marriage to Ann, Robert owned several parcels of real estate in joint tenancy with his brother Sam. During his marriage, Robert purchased a house and put the title in his name and his wife's name as joint tenants and not as tenants in common. Robert died; within a month of his death, Smith obtained a judgment against the estate of Robert. What are the relative rights of Sam, Smith, and Ann?

10. In 1965, Ogle was the owner of two adjoining lots numbered 6 and 7 fronting at the north on a city street. In that year she laid out and built a concrete driveway along and two feet in front of what she erroneously believed to be the west boundary of lot 7. Ogle used the driveway for access to buildings situated at the southern end of both lots. Later, in 1965 she conveyed lot 7 to Dale, and thereafter in the same year she conveyed lot 6 to Pace. Neither deed made any reference to the driveway, and after the conveyance Dale used it exclusively for access to lot 7. In 1991, a survey by Pace established that the driveway encroached six inches on lot 6, and he brought an appropriate action to establish his lawful ownership of the strip upon which the driveway approaches to enjoin its use by Dale and to require Dale to remove the overlap. Decision?

11. Temco, Inc., conveyed to the Wynns certain property adjoining an apartment complex being developed at that time by Sonnett Realty Company. Although nothing to this effect was contained in the deed, the sales contract gave the purchaser of the property use of the apartment's swimming pool. Temco's sales agent also emphasized that the use of the pool would be a desirable feature in the event that the Wynns decided to sell the property.

Seven years later, the Bunns contracted to buy the property from the Wynns through the latter's agent, Sonnett Realty. Although both the Wynns and Sonnett Realty's agent told the Bunns that the use of the apartment's pool went with the purchased property, neither the contract nor the deed subsequently conveyed to the Bunns so provided. When the Bunns requested passes from Temco and Offutt, the company that owned the apartments, their request was refused. The Bunns then brought this action. Decision?

Chapter 51

TRANSFER AND CONTROL OF REAL PROPERTY

Sales and Deeds
Secured Transactions
Adverse Possession
Zoning
Eminent Domain
Restrictive Covenants

THE law has always been, and is still today, extremely cautious about the transfer of title to real estate. Personal property may, for the most part, be easily and informally passed from owner to owner, but real property can be transferred only in compliance with a variety of formalities. This tendency is apparent in the transfer of property at death, where the strict formalities are relaxed only with respect to personal property, and this attitude of care and formality is most evident in a transfer of land during the lifetime of the owner.

There are three principal ways by which title to land may be transferred: (1) by deed; (2) by will or by the law of descent upon the death of the owner; and (3) by open, continuous, and adverse possession by a nonowner for a statutorily prescribed period of years. This chapter will discuss the first method—transfer by deeds—and the third method of transfer—adverse possession. The second method is covered in Chapter 52.

In addition to the legal restrictions placed on the transfer of real property, a number of other controls apply to the use of privately owned property. Some of these are imposed by governmental units and include zoning and the taking of property by eminent domain. Others are imposed by private parties through restrictive covenants. These three controls are considered in the second part of this chapter.

TRANSFER OF REAL PROPERTY

The most common way in which real property is transferred is by deed. Such transfers usually involve a contract for the sale of the land and the subsequent delivery of the deed and payment of the agreed consideration. The transfer of real estate by deed, however, does not require consideration to be valid; it may be made as a gift. In most cases, the purchase of real estate requires borrowing a part of the purchase price secured by the real property. A far less common method of transfer is called *adverse possession*. This unusual means of transfer of title requires no contract, deed, or other formality.

CONTRACT OF SALE

As indicated in the chapter on contracts, general contract law governs the sale of real property.

Formation

Because an oral agreement for the sale of an interest in land is not enforceable under the statute of frauds, the buyer and seller must reduce the agreement to *writing* and have it signed by the other party in order to be able to enforce the agreement against that party. The simplest agreement should contain (1) the names and addresses of the parties, (2) a description of the property to be conveyed, (3) the time for the conveyance (called the *closing*), (4) the type of deed to be given, and (5) the price and manner of payment. To avoid dispute and to assure adequate protection of the rights of both parties, many other points should be covered by a properly drawn contract for the sale of land.

A majority of the jurisdictions adhere to the common law rule that the risk of loss or destruction of the property, not caused by the fault of the seller, is on the purchaser after the contract is formed. The contract of sale may, of course, provide that the risk of loss or destruction shall remain on the seller until conveyance of the deed to the purchaser, or that the seller must obtain insurance for the benefit of the purchaser, or any other allocation of risk agreed on by the parties.

Marketable Title

It is firmly established in the law of conveyancing that a contract for the sale of land carries with it an *implied* obligation on the part of the seller to transfer marketable title. **Marketable title** means that the title is free from (a) encumbrances (such as mortgages, easements, liens, leases, and restrictive covenants); (b) defects in the chain of title appearing in the land records (such as a prior recorded conveyance of the same property by the seller); and (c) events depriving the seller of title such as adverse possession or eminent domain. The significance of the seller's obligation to convey marketable title is that if the title search reveals any flaw that has not been specifically excepted in the contract, the seller has materially breached the contract. The buy-

er's remedies for breach include specific performance with a price reduction, rescission and restitution, or damages for loss of bargain.

There are two important exceptions to this rule, however. First, most courts hold that the seller's implied or express obligation to convey marketable title does not require him to convey title free from existing zoning restrictions. Second, some courts also hold that the seller's implied or express obligation to convey marketable title does not require him to convey title free from open and visible public rights-of-way or easements such as public roads and sewers.

Implied Warranty of Habitability

The obligation of marketable title deals with the title to the property conveyed and has nothing to do with the quality of any improvements to the land. The traditional common law rule is *caveat emptor*—let the buyer beware. Under the rigid common law rule, the buyer has to inspect the property before the sale is completed. Any undiscovered defect would not be the seller's responsibility. The seller is liable only for any misrepresentation or *express* warranty he may have made about the property.

A majority of States have relaxed the harshness of the common law in sales by the builder of residential dwellings. In such a sale, the builder-seller *impliedly* warrants that a newly constructed house is free of latent defects, that is, those defects not visible or apparent upon a reasonable inspection of the house at the time of the sale. In some States, this implied warranty of habitability benefits only the original purchaser. In other States, the warranty has been extended to subsequent purchasers for a reasonable period of time. *See Gaito v. Auman.* In addition, many jurisdictions now require *all* sellers to disclose hidden defects that materially affect the property's value if the defect would not be discovered by a reasonable examination. See Chapter 10 for a discussion of misrepresentation.

DEEDS

A **deed** is a formal document transferring any interest in land. The party who transfers property by a deed is called the **grantor;** the transferee of the property is the **grantee.**

Types of Deeds

The rights conveyed by a deed vary, depending on the type of deed used. There are three basic types of deeds: warranty, special warranty, and quitclaim.

Warranty By a warranty deed, the grantor promises the grantee that she has a valid title to the property. In addition, under a warranty deed the grantor, either expressly or impliedly, obliges herself to make the grantee whole if the grantee suffers any damage because the grantor's title was defective. Aside from the liability of the grantor for any defects in her title, a distinct characteristic of the general warranty deed is that it will convey after-acquired title. For example, on January 30, Andrea conveys Blackacre by warranty deed to Bob. On January 30, Andrea's title to Blackacre is defective, but by February 14, Andrea has acquired a good title. Without more, Bob has acquired Andrea's good title under the January 30 warranty deed.

Special Warranty Whereas a warranty deed contains a general warranty of title, a special warranty deed warrants only that the title has not been impaired, encumbered, or rendered defective because of any act or omission *of the grantor.* The grantor merely warrants the title so far as acts or omissions of the grantor are concerned. He does *not* warrant that the title may not be defective by reason of the acts or omissions of others.

Quitclaim By a quitclaim deed, the grantor says no more, in effect, than "I make no promise as to what interest I do have in this land, but whatever it is I convey it to you." Quitclaim deeds are used most frequently when it is desired to have persons who appear to have an interest in land release their interest.

Formal Requirements

As previously noted, any transfer of an interest in land is within the statute of frauds if it is an interest of more than a limited duration. The transfer must therefore be in writing. Nearly all deeds, whatever the type, follow substantially the same pattern. Statutes in most States suggest that certain words of conveyance be used to make the deed effective. The words used will vary depending upon whether the instrument is a warranty deed, a special warranty deed, or a quitclaim deed. A common phrase for a warranty deed is "convey and warrant," although in a number of States the phrase "grant, bargain, and sell" is used together with a covenant by the seller later in the deed that she will "warrant and defend the title." A quitclaim deed will generally provide that the grantor "conveys and quitclaims" or, more simply, "quitclaims all interest" in the property.

Description of the Land The description must be sufficiently clear and certain to permit identification of the property conveyed. The test frequently applied is whether a subsequent purchaser or a surveyor employed by him could mark off the land from the description.

Quantity of the Estate After the property has been described, the deed will generally proceed to describe the quantity of estate conveyed to the grantee. Thus, either "to have and to hold to himself and his heirs forever" or "to have and to hold in fee simple" would vest the grantee with absolute title to the land. A deed conveying title to "George for life and to Elliott upon George's death" would grant a life estate to George and a remainder interest to Elliott.

Covenants of Title It is the practice in deeds for the grantor to make certain promises concerning her title to the land. If any one of these promises or covenants is breached, the grantee is entitled to be indemnified. There are a number of these covenants, the most usual of which are **title, against encumbrances, quiet enjoyment,** and **warranty.** These various covenants add up to an assurance that the grantee will have undisturbed possession of the land and will, in turn, be able to transfer it without adverse claims of third parties. In many States, all or many of these covenants are implied from the words of conveyance themselves—for example, "warrants" or "grant, bargain, and sell."

Execution Deeds generally end with the signature of the grantor, a seal, and an acknowledgment before a notary public or other official authorized to attest to the authenticity of documents. The signature can be made by an agent of the grantor if the agent has written authority from the grantor in a form required by law. Today the seal has lost most of its former significance, and in those few jurisdictions where it is required, the seal is sufficient if the word *Seal* or the letters *L.S.* appear next to the signature.

Although the notary public's acknowledgment may not be required to bind the parties to the deed, it is generally a prerequisite to recording the deed, and without an acknowledgment a deed may not be effective against third parties.

Delivery of Deeds

A deed does not transfer title to land until it is delivered. **Delivery** means an *intent* that the deed shall take effect and is evidenced by the acts or statements of the grantor. It is indispensable to the delivery of a deed that the grantor should part with control over it with the intention that it will immediately become operative to convey the estate described. Manual or physical transfer of the deed is usually the best evidence of this intent but it is not necessary. For example, the act of the grantor in placing a deed in a safe deposit box may or may not constitute delivery, depending on such facts as whether the grantee did or did not have access to the box and whether the grantor acts as if the prop-

erty were the grantee's. A deed conceivably may be "delivered" even when kept in the possession of the grantor, just as it would be possible that physical delivery of the deed to the grantee would not transfer title. A deed is frequently turned over to a third party to hold until the grantee performs certain conditions. This is called an **escrow,** and the third party is the escrow agent. Upon the performance of the condition, the escrow agent must turn the deed over to the grantee.

Recordation

In almost all States it is not necessary to record deeds in order to pass title from grantor to grantee. Unless the grantee has the deed recorded, however, a subsequent good faith purchaser for value of the property will acquire superior title to the grantee. Recordation consists of delivery of a duly executed and acknowledged deed to the recorder's office in the county where the property is located. There a copy of the instrument is made and inserted in the current deed book and indexed.

In some States, **notice** States, unrecorded instruments are invalid against any subsequent purchaser without notice. In other States, **notice-race** States, an unrecorded deed is invalid against any subsequent purchaser without notice who records first. Finally, in a few States, **race** States, an unrecorded deed is invalid against any deed recorded before it.

SECURED TRANSACTIONS

The purchase of real estate usually involves a relatively large outlay of money, and few people pay cash for a house or business real estate. Most people must borrow part of the purchase price or defer payment over a period of time. In these cases, the real estate itself is used to secure the obligation, which is evidenced by a note and either a mortgage or a deed of trust. The debtor is referred to as the **mortgagor** and the creditor as the **mortgagee.**

A secured transaction includes two elements: (1) a debt or obligation to pay money, and (2) an interest of the creditor in specific property that secures performance of the obligation. A security interest in property cannot exist apart from the debt it secures, and when the debt is discharged in any manner, the security interest in the property is terminated. Transactions involving the use of real estate as security for a debt are subject to real estate law, which consists of statutes and rules developed by the common law relating to mortgages and trust deeds. The Uniform Commercial Code does *not* apply to real estate mortgages or deeds of trust.

Form of Mortgages

The instrument creating a mortgage is in the form of a conveyance from the *mortgagor* to the *mortgagee* and must meet all the requirements for such documents: it must be in writing, it must contain an adequate description of the property, and it must be executed and delivered. The usual mortgage, however, differs from an outright conveyance of the property by virtue of a provision in the instrument that, upon the performance of the promise by the mortgagor, the conveyance is void and of no effect. This condition is referred to as the "defeasance," and, although it normally appears on the face of the mortgage, it may be in a separate document.

The concept of a **mortgage** as a lien upon real property for the payment of a debt applies with equal force to transactions having the same purpose but under a different name and form. A **deed of trust** is fundamentally identical with a mortgage, the most striking difference being that, under a deed of trust, the property is conveyed not to the creditor as security but to a third person as trustee for the benefit of the creditor. The deed of trust creates rights substantially similar to those created by a mortgage. In some States, it is customary to use a deed of trust in lieu of the ordinary form of mortgage.

As with all interests in realty, the mortgage or deed of trust should be promptly recorded to protect the mortgagee's rights against third persons who acquire an interest in the mortgaged property without knowledge of the mortgage.

Rights and Duties

The rights and duties of the parties to a mortgage may depend upon whether it is viewed as creating a lien or as transferring legal title to the mortgagee. Most States have adopted the **lien** theory. The mortgagor retains title and, even in the absence of any stipulation in the mortgage, is entitled to possession of the premises to the exclusion of the mortgagee, even in the event of default by the mortgagor. Only by foreclosure or sale or court appointment of a receiver can the right of possession be taken from the mortgagor. A minority of States have adopted the common law **title** theory, which gives the right of ownership and possession to the mortgagee. In most cases, as a practical matter, the mortgagor retains possession because the mortgagee has little interest in possession until default occurs.

Even though the mortgagor is generally entitled to possession and to many of the attributes of unrestricted ownership, he has a responsibility to deal with the property in such a manner as not to impair the security. In most instances, *waste* (impairment of the security) results from failure of the mortgagor to prevent the action or threatened action of third parties against the land. Thus, a failure by the debtor to pay taxes or to discharge a prior lien may seriously impair the security of the mortgagee. In such cases, the mortgagee is generally permitted to pay the obligation and add it to his claim against the mortgagor.

The mortgagor has the right to relieve his mortgaged property from the lien of a mortgage by payment of the indebtedness which it secures. This right of **redemption** is characteristic of a mortgage and cannot be extinguished except by operation of law. The right to redeem carries with it the obligation to pay the debt, and payment in full with interest is prerequisite to redemption.

Transfer of Mortgage Interests

The interests of the original mortgagor and mortgagee are capable of being transferred, and the rights and obligations of the assignees will depend primarily upon (1) the agreement of the parties to the assignment, and (2) the legal rules protecting the interest of the one who is party to the mortgage but not to the transfer.

By Mortgagor If the mortgagor conveys the land, the purchaser is *not* personally liable for the mortgage debt unless she expressly assumes the mortgage. If she **assumes the mortgage,** she is personally obligated to pay the mortgagor's debt owing to the mortgagee who can also hold the mortgagor on his promise to pay. A transfer of mortgaged property **subject to the mortgage** does *not* personally obligate the transferee to pay the mortgage debt. In such a case, the transferee's risk of loss is limited to the realty.

By Mortgagee A mortgagee has the right to assign the mortgage to another person without the consent of the mortgagor. An assignee of a mortgage is well advised to obtain the assignment in writing duly executed by the mortgagee and to record it promptly with the proper public official. This will protect her rights against persons who subsequently acquire an interest in the mortgaged property without knowledge of the assignment. Failure to record an assignment may cause an assignee of a mortgage note to lose her security. For example, Dylan buys land from Owen, relying upon a release executed and recorded by the mortgagee Kristi. Kristi, however, had previously assigned the mortgage to Ali who had failed to have her assignment recorded. In the absence of actual knowledge on the part of Dylan of the assignment by Kristi, Ali has no claim against the property.

Foreclosure

The right to foreclose usually arises upon default by the mortgagor. Foreclosure is an action by the mortgage holder to take the property away from the mortgagor, to end the mortgagor's rights in the property, and to sell the property to pay the mortgage debt. The mortgagor's default by non-performance of other promises in the mortgage may also give the mortgagee this right. Thus, a mortgage may provide that failure of the mortgagor to pay taxes is a default that permits foreclosure. It is also a common provision in mortgages that default in payment of an installment of the debt makes the entire unpaid balance of the indebtedness immediately due and payable, permitting foreclosure for the entire amount.

The most general method of terminating the right to redeem is to obtain a judicial decree directing the sale of the property by an officer of the court, the debt being paid out of the proceeds of the sale and the excess, if any, paid to the mortgagor. In some jurisdictions the mortgagor is given a statutory right to redeem from the foreclosure sale within a specified period of time after the sale. This right, in effect, is a second "right of redemption" and should not be confused with the customary right of redemption before foreclosure. In most jurisdictions a foreclosure sale is subject to approval by the court.

In States where foreclosure is not limited to a sale under judicial decree, a clause may be inserted in mortgages permitting the mortgagee to foreclose by a sale without obtaining an order of court. This power of sale is considerably more expedient than a judicial proceeding. The power of sale usually provides for a public auction with published notice, and in some States the mortgagee is forbidden by statute to purchase at the sale.

Whether foreclosure is by sale under judicial proceeding or by grant of power in the mortgage itself, the transaction retains its character of a procedure to obtain satisfaction of a debt. If the proceeds are insufficient to satisfy the debt in full, the debtor-mortgagor remains liable for payment of the balance of the debt. Generally, the mortgagee will obtain a *deficiency judgment* for any unsatisfied balance of the debt and may proceed to enforce payment of this amount out of other assets of the mortgagor.

ADVERSE POSSESSION

It is possible, although very rare, that title to land may be transferred **involuntarily** without any deed or other formality by "adverse possession." In most States, if a person openly and continuously occupies the land of another for a statutorily prescribed period of time, typically ten to twenty years, that person will gain title to the land. The possession must be actual and not merely constructive. Courts have held that living on land, farming it, building on it, or maintaining structures on it are sufficient to constitute possession. Possession, however, must be adverse. This means that any act of dominion by the true owner will stop the period from running. Her entry on the land or assertion of ownership will break the period. In such event the period will commence anew from that time.

In some jurisdictions, shorter periods of adverse possession have been established by statute where there is not only possession but also some other claim such as the payment of taxes or an apparent claim of title, even if it is not valid.

PUBLIC AND PRIVATE CONTROLS

In the exercise of its police power for the benefit of the community, the State can and does place controls upon the use of privately owned land. The State does not pay the owner any compensation for loss or damage sustained by the owner by reason of such legitimate controls. The enforcement of zoning laws, which is a proper exercise of the police power, is not a taking of property but a regulation of its use. The taking of private property for a public use or purpose under the State's power of eminent domain is not, however, an exercise of the police power, and the owners of the property so taken are entitled to be paid its fair and reasonable value.

Also considered in this section are private controls of the use of privately owned property by means of restrictive covenants. In addition, the law of nuisance, as discussed in Chapter 5, imposes controls upon a landowner's use of her property.

ZONING

Zoning is the principal method of public control over *land use*. The validity of zoning is based upon the police power of the State. The police power to provide for the public health, safety, morals, and welfare is one of the inherent powers of government. Police power can be used only to regulate private property, never to "take" it. It is firmly established that regulation which has no reasonable relation to public health, safety, morals, or welfare is unconstitutional as a denial of due process of law.

Enabling Acts and Zoning Ordinances

The power to zone is generally delegated to local authorities by statutes known as "enabling" statutes. A typical enabling statute grants the following powers to municipalities: (1) to regulate and limit the height and bulk of buildings to be erected; (2) to establish, regulate, and limit the building or setback lines on or along any street, trafficway, drive, or parkway; (3) to regulate and limit the intensity of the use of lot areas and to regulate and determine the area of open spaces within and surrounding buildings; (4) to classify, regulate, and restrict the location of trades and industries and the location of buildings designated for specified industrial, business, residential, and other uses; (5) to divide the entire municipality into districts of such number, shape, area, and such different classes as may be deemed best suited to carry out the purposes of the statute; and (6) to fix standards to which buildings or structures must conform.

Under these powers, the local authorities may enact zoning ordinances, which consist of a map and a text. The map divides the municipality into districts, which are designated principally as industrial, commercial, or residential, with possible subclassifications. A well-drafted zoning ordinance will carefully define the uses permitted in each area.

Variance

Enabling statutes provide that the zoning authorities shall have power to grant variances in cases of "unnecessary hardship," which is caused by the application of the zoning ordinance to the property and is unique or peculiar to the property. A **variance** permits a deviation from the zoning ordinance. Special circumstances applicable to the particular property include such matters as its unusual shape, topography, size, location, or surroundings. A variance is not available if the hardship is caused by conditions general to the neighborhood or by the actions of the property owner. It must affirmatively appear that the property as presently zoned cannot yield a reasonable return upon the owner's investment.

Nonconforming Uses

A zoning ordinance may not immediately terminate a lawful use that existed before it was enacted. Such use must be permitted to continue as a nonconforming use—at least for a reasonable time. Most ordinances provide for the elimination of nonconforming uses (1) when the use is discontinued, (2) when a nonconforming structure is destroyed or substantially damaged, or (3) when a nonconforming structure has been permitted to exist for the period of its useful life as fixed by municipal authorities. *See Franklin Planning & Zoning Commission v. Simpson County Lumber Co.*

Judicial Review of Zoning

Although the zoning process is traditionally viewed as legislative in nature, it is subject to judicial review on a number of grounds, including claims that the zoning ordinance is invalid or amounts to a taking of property.

Invalidity of Zoning Ordinance   A zoning ordinance may be invalid as a whole either because it bears no reasonable relation to public health, safety, morals, or welfare, or because it involves an exercise of powers not granted to the municipality by the enabling

act, or it violates the State or U.S. Constitution. *See City of Renton v. Playtime Theatres, Inc.*

Zoning Amounts to a Taking   Another form of attack is to show that the restrictions amount to confiscation or a "taking." It is not sufficient that the owner will sustain a financial loss if the restrictions are not lifted. But when the property owner can show that the restrictions make it impracticable for him to use the property for *any* beneficial purpose, he should prevail. Deprivation of all beneficial use is confiscation.

Subdivision Master Plans

A growing municipality has a special interest in regulating new housing developments so that they will harmonize with the rest of the community; so that streets within the development are integrated with existing streets or planned roads; so that adequate provision is made for open spaces for traffic, recreation, light, and air; and so that adequate provision is made for water, drainage, and sanitary facilities. Accordingly, most States have legislation enabling local authorities to require municipal approval of every land subdivision plat. These enabling statutes provide penalties for failure to secure such approval where required by local ordinance. Some statutes make it a criminal offense to sell lots by reference to unrecorded plats and provide that such plats may not be recorded unless approved by the local planning board. Other statutes provide that building permits will not be issued unless the plat is approved and recorded.

EMINENT DOMAIN

The power to take private property for public use, known as the power of **eminent domain,** is recognized as one of the inherent powers of government in the Federal Constitution and in the constitutions of the States. At the same time, however, the power is carefully circumscribed and controlled. The Fifth Amendment to the Federal Constitution provides, "Nor shall private property be taken for public use without just compensation." Similar or identical provisions are to be found in the constitutions of the States. There is, therefore, a direct constitutional prohibition against taking private property without just compensation and an implicit prohibition against taking private property for other than public use. Moreover, under both Federal and State constitutions, the individual is entitled to due process of law in connection with the taking.

Public Use

As noted, there is an implicit constitutional prohibition against taking private property for other than public use. Most States interpret public use to mean "public advantage." Thus, the power of eminent domain may be delegated to railroad and public utility companies. The reasonable exercise of this power by such companies to enable them to offer continued and improved service to the public is upheld as being for a public advantage. As society grows more complex, other public purposes are accepted as legitimate grounds for exercise of the power of eminent domain. One is in the area of urban renewal. Most States have legislation permitting the establishment of housing authorities with power to condemn slum, blighted, and vacant areas and to finance, construct, and maintain housing projects. Some States have recently gone further and permit the public taking for a private company provided the use is primarily for the benefit of the public, including the alleviation of unemployment or economic decay within the community.

Just Compensation

When the power of eminent domain is exercised, just compensation must be made to the owners of the property taken. The measure of compensation is the fair market value of the property as of the time of taking. *See First English Evangelical Lutheran Church of Glendale v. County of Los Angeles, California.*

The compensation goes to holders of vested interests in the condemned property.

PRIVATE RESTRICTIONS UPON LAND USE

Owners of real property may impose private restrictions, called **restrictive covenants,** on the use of land. Historically, two types of private restrictions developed—real covenants and equitable servitudes. The two had different, although overlapping, requirements. Today, equitable servitudes have nearly replaced real covenants. Accordingly, this section will cover equitable servitudes, which will be referred to by the more general term restrictive covenant.

Requirements for Running Covenants

If certain conditions are satisfied, then a restrictive covenant will bind not only the original parties to it but also remote parties who subsequently acquire the property. If a restrictive covenant binds remote parties, it is said to "run with the land." For a restrictive covenant to run with the land, the covenant must involve promises that are enforceable under the law of contracts. A majority of courts hold that restrictive covenants must be in writing. The parties who agreed to the restrictive covenant must intend that the covenant bind their successors. Moreover, the covenant must "touch and concern" the land. This requirement means that the covenant affects the use, utility, or value of the land. Finally, a restrictive covenant will bind only those successors who have actual or constructive notice of the covenant.

Restrictive Covenants in Subdivisions

Restrictive covenants are widely used in subdivisions. The owners of lots are subject to restrictive covenants which, if actually brought to the attention of subsequent purchasers or recorded by original deed, or by means of a recorded plat or separate agreement, bind purchasers of lots in the subdivision as though the restriction had been inserted in their own deed. If the entire subdivision has been subjected to a general building plan designed to benefit all the lots, any lot owner in the subdivision has the right to enforce the restriction against a purchaser whose title descends from a common grantor. If there is a clear intent that a restriction is to benefit an entire tract, the covenant will be enforced against a subsequent purchaser of one of the lots in the tract if (1) it is apparent that the restriction was intended to benefit the purchaser of any lot in the tract, and (2) that the restriction appears somewhere in the chain of title to which the lot is subject.

Many types of restrictive covenants are used in subdivisions. The more common ones limit the use of property to residential purposes, restrict the area of the lot on which a structure can be built, or provide for a special type of architecture. Frequently a subdivider will specify a minimum size for each house in an attempt to maintain a minimum standard in the neighborhood. *See John J. Walker v. Robert V. Gross.*

Termination of Restrictive Covenants

A restrictive covenant may end by the terms of the original agreement. For example, the developer of a subdivision may provide that the restrictive covenant will terminate after thirty-five years unless a specified majority of the property owners reaffirm the covenant. In addition, a court will not enforce a restrictive covenant if changed circumstances make enforcement inequitable and oppressive. Evidence of *changed conditions* may be found either within the tract covered by the original covenant or within the area adjacent to or surrounding the tract.

Validity of Restrictive Covenants

Although restrictions upon the use of land have never been popular in the law, if it appears that the restriction will operate to the general benefit of the owners of all the land intended to be affected, the restriction will be enforced. The usual method of enforcing such agreements is by an injunction restraining violation.

It has been the law for many years, however, that a State or municipality cannot, under the Fourteenth Amendment to the Federal Constitution, impose any racial restrictions by statute or ordinance. In 1947, the United States Supreme Court held that private racial restrictive covenants cannot be enforced by State courts because the courts are an arm of the State government. This effectively invalidated private racial restrictive covenants.

CASES

Implied Warranty of Habitability

GAITO v. AUMAN

Supreme Court of North Carolina, 1985.
313 N.C. 243, 327 S.E.2d 870.

BRANCH, C.J.

Plaintiffs Sam and Eleanor Gaito brought this action against defendant Howard Frank Auman, Jr. on 19 May 1981, alleging in their complaint that in April 1978 they purchased a home from Auman, its builder, and moved into the home in June 1978. The Gaitos alleged that the purchase price of the home included central air conditioning, but that the air conditioning system in the house never worked properly despite repeated efforts to correct the cooling problems. The plaintiffs alleged that they were damaged in the amount of $3,500 as a result of a breach of warranty on the part of the defendant Auman.

In his answer and amended answer defendant Auman denied liability under a theory of implied warranty of habitability of a recently completed dwelling on grounds that the house was not new at the time plaintiffs purchased it and on grounds that plaintiffs were aware that the house was not new. * * *

The evidence at trial tended to show that the house in dispute was completed by defendant in November 1973 as a speculation house. Defendant was in the business of building houses. The house sat vacant one and one-half years before defendant Auman contracted to sell it to a man named Lee Cole. Although no deed was passed conveying title to him, Cole lived in the house for two months. While living there, Cole bulldozed the area around the house to make a pasture for horses. Cole left the house after he became unable to make a payment and forfeited his down payment.

The house was next rented to a realtor, Jack Vernon, for a period of six months. In 1976 Raymond and Catherine Ashley rented and lived in the house for fifteen months. During the time the Ashleys lived in the house, the air conditioning system did not cool the house properly. During three weeks of 95 degree weather, the Ashleys were unable to get the temperature of the house below 85 degrees. The Ashleys contacted defendant Auman about the problem and defendant LeGrand went to the house to attempt repairs. LeGrand replaced compressors and Freon and did electrical work. Another air conditioning repairman, Metrah Spencer, subsequently replaced the compressor, opened up and rearranged the duct work. He did not change the capacity of the air conditioning unit.

In early 1978 defendant Auman listed the house for sale with a local real estate company, and Thomas Caulk, one of the firm's realtors, showed the house to the Gaitos. Caulk told the Gaitos that the house was four years old and that it had been occupied for two short periods of time. The Gaitos decided to purchase the house and had Caulk inspect it before the closing. The closing on the house was in April 1978 and plaintiffs moved in in June. Plaintiffs first turned on the air conditioning at the end of June 1978 when the temperature outside was in the eighties. Although plaintiffs let the system run two days and nights, the system created only a ten de-

gree difference between outside and inside temperatures. The Gaitos contacted Auman several times during the summer of 1978 and had repairs done. The repairs included the installation of power vents, an exhaust fan, and insulation for the duct work, the changing of filters, and the addition of Freon. The ducting system was reworked, and the compressor was replaced two times. In 1979 the Gaitos converted their garage into an apartment. They had duct work added and attached the apartment to the air conditioning system for the house.

Rod Tripp, who was qualified as an expert in the field of heating and air conditioning, testified for the plaintiffs that in 1973 the accepted standard in the air conditioning industry for the differential between outside and inside temperatures was 20 degrees when the outside temperature was 95 degrees. In 1978 the accepted differential was 15 degrees. Tripp stated that in his opinion a four ton air conditioning system rather than the three and one-half ton system originally installed was the proper size for the Gaitos' house. Tripp testified that the cost of installing a four ton system in a house in 1980 would have been approximately $3,655. At the time of trial the cost would have been $3,955.

At the close of the evidence, Judge Burris granted defendant Alvin LeGrand's motion to dismiss the case against him based on the statute of limitations. Defendant Auman's attorney made a motion to dismiss the case on grounds that the implied warranty of habitability theory was inapplicable. The trial court denied his motion and allowed the jury to deliberate on the question of defendant's liability.

The jury returned with a verdict in favor of the plaintiffs in the amount of $3,655. Defendant appealed to the Court of Appeals, which affirmed the trial court. Judge Hedrick dissented.

The question posed by this appeal is whether the Court of Appeals erred in affirming the judgment in favor of the plaintiffs on a theory of implied warranty of habitability. The majority concluded that a residential structure could be considered new for purposes of the implied warranty within the maximum applicable statute of limitations period. We reject this reasoning.

* * *

The essence of defendant's arguments, however, is that plaintiffs' claim was not cognizable under an implied warranty theory because of the age of the house and its occupation by tenants prior to its purchase by the plaintiffs. Although we held in [citation], that the implied warranty of habitability arises by operation of law, we hold that the applicability of the warranty is to be determined on a case by case basis and that under these facts, plaintiffs presented a legally cognizable claim under a theory of implied warranty of habitability.

The trend of recent judicial decisions has been to invoke the doctrine of implied warranty of habitability or fitness in cases involving the sale of a new house by the builder. [Citations.] The rigid common law rule of *caveat emptor* in the sale of recently completed dwellings was relaxed in this state by this Court's opinion in *Hartley v. Ballou,* [citation]. In *Hartley,* the plaintiffs purchased a "recently" constructed house from defendants. Although they inspected the house prior to moving in, plaintiffs observed nothing amiss. Shortly after moving in the house showed signs of substantial water leakage and insufficient waterproofing in the basement. This Court, in an opinion authored by Chief Justice Bobbitt, concluded that the defendant builder-vendor had an obligation to perform work in a proper, workmanlike and ordinarily skillful manner. Chief Justice Bobbitt then stated the rule as follows:

[I]n every contract for the sale of a recently completed dwelling, and in every contract for the sale of a dwelling then under construction, the vendor, if he be in the business of building such dwellings, shall be held to impliedly warrant to the initial vendee that, at the time of the passing of the deed or the taking of possession by the initial vendee (whichever first occurs), the dwelling, together with all its fixtures, is sufficiently free from major structural defects, and is constructed in a workmanlike manner, so as to meet the standard of workmanlike quality then prevailing at the time and place of construction; and that this implied warranty in the contract of sale survives the passing of the deed or the taking of possession by the initial vendee.

The doctrine recited in *Hartley* is known as an implied warranty of habitability and represents a growing trend in the jurisprudence of our states. An implied warranty of habitability is limited to latent defects—those not visible or apparent to a reasonable person upon inspection of a dwelling. [Citation.]

The relaxing of the rigid rule of *caveat emptor* in *Hartley* is based on a policy which holds builder-vendors accountable beyond the passage of title or the taking of possession by the initial vendee for defects which are not apparent to the purchaser at that time. This policy is justified because the innocent purchaser is often making one of the largest investments of a lifetime from one whose experience and expertise places him in a dominating position in that sale. [Citation.]

Defendant appellant argues that the facts of this case are legally insufficient to support a verdict for the plaintiff because the facts do not fall within the exception to the rule of *caveat emptor* established by *Hartley*. Defendant contends that an implied warranty of habitability is inapplicable because both the pretrial pleadings and evidence at trial show that the house was not "recently completed" or under construction at the time of the passing of the deed; the plaintiff claims and the evidence shows instead that the house was built four and one-half years earlier. Defendant also argues that the previous occupancy by tenants invalidated any implied warranty which may have arisen.

We first consider defendant's argument that he must prevail because the house was built four and one-half years before the plaintiffs received a deed or took possession. Our cases do not address the precise limits of our requirement in *Hartley* that a house be "recently completed." We therefore turn to other jurisdictions for instruction on this question.

A number of courts have established a standard of reasonableness in determining how the age of a house affects the application of the warranty. [Citation.]

* * *

We are persuaded that the reasoning of these courts is sound and that the standard of reasonableness is the appropriate standard for determining whether a dwelling has been recently completed. Thus, under the facts of this case, it was a question of fact for the fact finder to determine whether the house was "recently completed." Among some of the factors which may be considered in determining this question are the age of the building, the use to which it has been put, its maintenance, the nature of the defects and the expectations of the parties. This standard allows extension of the warranty to vary in lengths of time, depending on the nature of the defect and whether the warranty should reasonably be expected to apply. [Citation.]

Even so, defendant argues that the tenancies which intervened between construction and purchase by plaintiffs rendered the warranty inapplicable. We disagree. We note that the purpose of the warranty is to protect homeowners from defects which can only be within the knowledge of vendors. There are many kinds of major structural defects upon which the presence of tenants can have little or no effect. In other cases intervening tenants may contribute to or directly cause major defects in a dwelling's structure. We hold that the effect of occupation by tenants prior to the passage of the deed to the initial vendee is but one of the factors which a fact finder should consider in determining whether defendant is liable for breach of an implied warranty of habitability. [Citation.]

At this point we note that *Hartley* limits the implied warranty of habitability to *initial vendees* at the time of the taking of possession or the passing of the deed. Here plaintiff was an initial vendee and therefore it is unnecessary for us to discuss the applicability of the implied warranty to subsequent purchasers.

* * *

[B]uilders are still accorded substantial protection by the requirement that the defect in a dwelling or its fixtures be latent or not reasonably discoverable at the time of sale or possession. Claimants must also show that structural defects had their origin in the builder-seller and in construction which does not meet the standard of workmanlike quality then prevailing at the time and place of construction. [Citation.] We have also made it clear that the implied warranty falls short of "an absolute guarantee." [Citation.] In regard to this argument we wish to make it clear that the test of reasonableness to determine whether a dwelling is "recently completed" does not affect the relevant statutes of limitation and repose.

Although defendant did not raise the argument at the Court of Appeals level, he now argues that an implied warranty is inapplicable to an air conditioning unit because it is not "an absolute essential utility to a dwelling house." In *Hartley* we held that the builder of a recently completed dwelling impliedly warrants that "the dwelling, *together with all its fixtures,* is sufficiently free from major structural defects and is constructed in a workmanlike manner, so as to meet the standard of workmanlike quality then prevailing at the time and place of construction." [Citation.]

* * *

The test of a breach of an implied warranty of habitability in North Carolina is not whether a fixture is an "absolute essential utility to a dwelling house." The test is whether there is a failure to meet the prevailing standard of workmanship quality. [Citation.] We hold that under the facts of this case, a jury may properly find a defective air conditioning system in a "recently completed dwelling" to be a major structural defect as between an initial vendee and a builder-vendor.

After a review of the evidence we hold that under a theory of implied warranty of habitability, the plaintiff raised questions of fact and a legally cognizable cause of action sufficient to survive defendant's motions for summary judgment, directed verdict and judgment notwithstanding the verdict.

* * *

We therefore do not disturb the jury's award of damages.

For the reasons stated, the decision of the Court of Appeals is affirmed.

Zoning: Nonconforming Uses

FRANKLIN PLANNING & ZONING COMMISSION v. SIMPSON COUNTY LUMBER CO.

Supreme Court of Kentucky, 1965.
394 S.W.2d 593.

HILL, J.

This appeal concerns the propriety of a judgment interpreting the rights of these litigants under a planning and zoning ordinance of the City of Franklin.

Appellee Desford Potts for about seven years owned a six-acre tract of land within the corporate limits of Franklin. It lies between Railroad and Morris Streets. During this period, Potts maintained a livestock barn on the tract in which was stored lumber and other building materials. Outside, and mostly to the rear of the barn, brick was stored in stacks four or five feet high. In 1959 the City of Franklin passed a zoning ordinance by virtue of which Potts' lot was classified as residential (R–2) property.

Shortly before this suit was instituted, Potts moved some saw logs onto his lot back of the barn where he had recently had a bulldozer level the lot. The city complained. Potts sued to enjoin interference by the city. The chancellor decided in favor of Potts.

The city contends the continued use by Potts of his property for storage of building materials is a "nonconforming" use, and under the law cannot be enlarged by storing saw logs thereon. Potts contends it is not an enlargement of the "nonconforming" use and therefore not in violation of the zoning ordinance. We should say here that a "nonconforming use" means simply a use which does not conform to the classification provided for in the ordinance, residential in this instance.

The applicable portion of the ordinance is as follows:

Section 33, Continuance of Non-Conforming Uses. Any use of land or structure existing at the time of enactment or subsequent amendment of this ordinance, but not in conformity with its use provisions may be continued . . .

Regardless of our sadness at seeing the elimination of the "spreading chestnut tree," and the village smith, it must be admitted that in the interest of progress the law favors the gradual elimination of "nonconforming" uses of property in our cities. [Citation.] It naturally follows that such nonconforming uses as are tolerated under the law cannot be enlarged. [Citations.]

So, our question is whether the storage of saw logs in Potts' lot is an enlargement of the "nonconforming use" he enjoyed previously. The chancellor found as a matter of fact the use was not enlarged. We have numerous photographs of the stored logs, and they appear to be stacked higher than the brick, perhaps eight feet high; but it cannot be said they are unsightly, obnoxious, or a health hazard.

Admitting the saw logs were stacked higher than the brick and not so symmetrically, unless they obstruct the view or impede the natural flow of air we cannot see wherein their storage in back of the barn is materially different from the storage of the stacks of brick. Accordingly, we agree with the chancellor that the "nonconforming use" by Potts of his property has not been enlarged by the storage of saw logs on the property. There is no contention Potts plans a sawmill. It goes without saying that a sawmill in such a residential community would be such an enlargement as appellants oppose.

The judgment is affirmed.

Zoning

CITY OF RENTON v. PLAYTIME THEATRES, INC.

Supreme Court of the United States, 1986.
475 U.S. 41.

REHNQUIST, J.

This case involves a constitutional challenge to a zoning ordinance, enacted by appellant city of Renton, Washington, that prohibits adult motion picture theaters from locating within 1,000 feet of any residential zone, single- or multiple-family dwelling, church, park, or school. Appellees, Playtime Theatres, Inc., and Sea-First Properties, Inc., filed an action in the United States District Court for the Western District of Washington seeking a declaratory judgment that the Renton ordinance violated the First and Fourteenth Amendments and a permanent injunction against its enforcement. The District Court ruled in favor of Renton and denied the permanent injunction * * *.

* * *

The Court of Appeals for the Ninth Circuit reversed. The Court of Appeals first concluded, contrary to the finding of the District Court, that the Renton ordinance constituted a substantial restriction on First Amendment interests. Then, using the standards set forth in [citation], the Court of Appeals held that Renton had improperly relied on the experiences of other cities in lieu of evidence about the effects of adult theaters on Renton, that Renton had thus failed to establish adequately the existence of a substantial governmental interest in support of its ordinance, and that in any event Renton's asserted interests had not been shown to be unrelated to the suppression of expression. The Court of Appeals remanded the case to the District Court for reconsideration of Renton's asserted interests.

In our view, the resolution of this case is largely dictated by our decision in [citation]. There, although five Members of the Court did not agree on a single rationale for the decision, we held that the city of Detroit's zoning ordinance, which prohibited locating an adult theater within 1,000 feet of any two other "regulated uses" or within 500 feet of any residential zone, did not violate the First and Fourteenth Amendments. [Citation.] The Renton ordinance, . . . does not ban adult theaters altogether, but merely provides that such theaters may not be located within 1,000 feet of any residential zone, single- or multiple-family dwelling, church, park, or school. The ordinance is therefore properly analyzed as a form of time, place, and manner regulation. [Citation.]

* * *

The District Court's finding as to "predominate" intent, left undisturbed by the Court of Appeals, is more than adequate to establish that the city's pursuit of its zoning interests here was unrelated to the suppression of free expression. The ordinance by its terms is designed to prevent crime, protect the city's retail trade, maintain property values, and generally "protec[t] and preserv[e] the quality of [the city's] neighborhoods, commercial districts, and the quality of urban life," not to suppress the expression of unpopular views. [Citation.] As Justice POWELL observed in [citation], "[i]f [the city] had been concerned with restricting the message purveyed by adult theaters, it would have tried to close them or restrict their number rather than circumscribe their choice as to location." [Citation.]

In short, the Renton ordinance is completely consistent with our definition of "content-neutral" speech regulations as those that "are *justified* without reference to the content of the regulated speech." [Citations.] The ordinance does not contravene the fundamental principle that underlies our concern about "content-based" speech regulations: that "government may not grant the use of a forum to people whose views it finds acceptable, but deny use to those wishing to express less favored or more controversial views." [Citation.]

It was with this understanding in mind that, [citation], a majority of this Court decided that, at least with respect to businesses that purvey sexually explicit materials, zoning ordinances designed to combat the undesirable secondary effects of such businesses are to be reviewed under the standards applicable to "content-neutral" time, place, and manner regulations.

* * *

The appropriate inquiry in this case, then, is whether the Renton ordinance is designed to serve a substantial governmental interest and allows for reasonable alternative avenues of communication. [Citations.] It is clear that the ordinance meets such a standard. As a majority of this Court recognized in [citation], a city's "interest in attempting to preserve the quality of urban life is one that must be accorded high respect." [Citation.] Exactly the same vital governmental interests are at stake here.

The Court of Appeals ruled, however, that because the Renton ordinance was enacted without the benefit of studies specifically relating to "the particular problems or needs of Renton," the city's justifications for the ordinance were "conclusory and speculative." [Citation.] We think the Court of Appeals imposed on the city an unnecessarily rigid burden of proof. The record in this case reveals that Renton relied heavily on the experience of, and studies produced by, the city of Seattle. In Seattle, as in Renton, the adult theater zoning ordinance was aimed at preventing the secondary effects caused by the presence of even one such theater in a given neighborhood.

* * *

We also find no constitutional defect in the method chosen by Renton to further its substantial interests. Cities may regulate adult theaters by dispersing them, as in Detroit, or by effectively concentrating them, as in Renton. "It is not our function to appraise the wisdom of [the city's] decision to require adult theaters to be separated rather than concentrated in the same areas. . . . [T]he city must be allowed a reasonable opportunity to experiment with solutions to admittedly serious problems." [Citation.]

* * *

Finally, turning to the question whether the Renton ordinance allows for reasonable alternative avenues of communication, we note that the ordinance leaves some 520 acres, or more than five percent of the entire land area of Renton, open to use as adult theater sites. The District Court found, and the Court of Appeals did not dispute the finding, that the 520 acres of land consists of "[a]mple, accessible real estate," including "acreage in all stages of development from raw land to developed, industrial, warehouse, office, and shopping space that is criss-crossed by freeways, highways, and roads." [Citation.]

* * *

In sum, we find that the Renton ordinance represents a valid governmental response to the "admittedly serious problems" created by adult theaters. [Citation.] Renton has not used "the power to zone as a pretext for suppressing expression," [citation], but rather has sought to make some areas available for adult theaters and their patrons, while at the same time preserving the quality of life in the community at large by preventing those theaters from locating in other areas. This, after all, is the essence of zoning. Here, as in [citation], the city has enacted a zoning ordinance that meets these goals while also satisfying the dictates of the First Amendment. The judgment of the Court of Appeals is therefore

Reversed.

Eminent Domain

FIRST ENGLISH EVANGELICAL LUTHERAN CHURCH OF GLENDALE v. LOS ANGELES COUNTY, CALIFORNIA

Supreme Court of the United States, 1987.
482 U.S. 304, 107 S.Ct. 2378, 96 L.Ed.2d 250.

CHIEF JUSTICE REHNQUIST delivered the opinion of the Court.

In this case the California Court of Appeal held that a landowner who claims that his property has been "taken" by a land-use regulation may not recover damages for the time before it is finally determined that the regulation constitutes a "taking" of his property. We disagree, and conclude that in these circumstances the Fifth and Fourteenth Amendments to the United States Constitution would require compensation for that period.

In 1957, appellant First English Evangelical Lutheran Church purchased a 21-acre parcel of land in a canyon along the banks of the Middle Fork of Mill Creek in the Angeles National Forest. The Middle Fork is the natural drainage channel for a watershed area owned by the National Forest Service. Twelve of the acres owned by the church are flat land, and contained a dining hall, two bunkhouses, a caretaker's lodge, an outdoor chapel, and a footbridge across the creek. The church operated on the site a campground, known as

"Lutherglen," as a retreat center and a recreational area for handicapped children.

In July 1977, a forest fire denuded the hills upstream from Lutherglen, destroying approximately 3,860 acres of the watershed area and creating a serious flood hazard. Such flooding occurred on February 9 and 10, 1978, when a storm dropped 11 inches of rain in the watershed. The runoff from the storm overflowed the banks of the Mill Creek, flooding Lutherglen and destroying its buildings.

In response to the flooding of the canyon, appellee County of Los Angeles adopted Interim Ordinance No. 11,855 in January 1979. The ordinance provided that "(a) person shall not construct, reconstruct, place or enlarge any building or structure, any portion of which is, or will be, located within the outer boundary lines of the interim flood protection area located in Mill Creek Canyon. . . ." [Citation.] The ordinance was effective immediately because the county determined that it was "required for the immediate preservation of the public health and safety. . . ." [Citation.] The interim flood protection area described by the ordinance included the flat areas on either side of Mill Creek on which Lutherglen had stood.

The church filed a complaint in the Superior Court of California a little more than a month after the ordinance was adopted. As subsequently amended, the complaint alleged two claims against the county and the Los Angeles County Flood Control District. The first alleged that the defendants were liable under Cal.Gov't.Code Ann. [citation] for dangerous conditions on their upstream properties that contributed to the flooding of Lutherglen. As a part of this claim, appellant also alleged that "Ordinance No. 11,855 denies (appellant) all use of Lutherglen." [Citation.] The second claim sought to recover from the Flood District in inverse condemnation and in tort for engaging in cloud seeding during the storm that flooded Lutherglen. Appellant sought damages under each count for loss of use of Lutherglen. * * *

* * *

* * * Appellant asks us to hold that the Supreme Court of California erred in Agins v. Tiburon in determining that the Fifth Amendment, as made applicable to the States through the Fourteenth Amendment, does not require compensation as a remedy for "temporary" regulatory takings—those regulatory takings which are ultimately invalidated by the courts.

* * *

Consideration of the compensation question must begin with direct reference to the language of the Fifth Amendment, which provides in relevant part that "private property (shall not) be taken for public use, without just compensation." As its language indicates, and as the Court has frequently noted, this provision does not prohibit the taking of private property, but instead places a condition on the exercise of that power. [Citations.] This basic understanding of the Amendment makes clear that it is designed not to limit the governmental interference with property rights per se, but rather to secure compensation in the event of otherwise proper interference amounting to a taking. Thus, government action that works a taking of property rights necessarily implicates the "constitutional obligation to pay just compensation." [Citation.]

We have recognized that a landowner is entitled to bring an action in inverse condemnation as a result of " 'the self-executing character of the constitutional provision with respect to compensation.' "

* * *

It has also been established doctrine at least since Justice Holmes' opinion for the Court in [citation] that "(t)he general rule at least is, that while property may be regulated to a certain extent, if regulation goes too far it will be recognized as a taking." [Citation.] While the typical taking occurs when the government acts to condemn property in the exercise of its power of eminent domain, the entire doctrine of inverse condemnation is predicated on the proposition that a taking may occur without such formal proceedings. * * *

While the Supreme Court of California may not have actually disavowed this general rule in Agins, we believe that it has truncated the rule by disallowing damages that occurred prior to the ultimate invalidation of the challenged regulation. The Supreme Court of California justified its conclusion at length in the Agins opinion, concluding that:

"In combination, the need for preserving a degree of freedom in the land-use planning function, and the inhibiting financial force which inheres in the inverse condemnation remedy, persuade us that on balance mandamus or declaratory relief rather than inverse condemnation is the appropriate relief under the circumstances." Agins v. Tiburon.

We, of course, are not mindful of these considerations, but they must be evaluated in the light of the command of the Just Compensation Clause of the Fifth Amendment. The Court has recognized in more than one case that the government may elect to abandon its intrusion or discontinue regulations. [Citations.] Similarly, a governmental body may acquiesce in a judicial declaration that one of its ordinances has affected an unconstitutional taking of property; the landowner has no right under the Just Compensation Clause to insist that a "temporary" taking be deemed a permanent taking. But we have not resolved whether abandonment by the government requires payment of compensation for the period of time during which regulations deny a landowner all use of his land.

In considering this question, we find substantial guidance in cases where the government has only temporarily exercised its right to use private property. * * *

These cases reflect the fact that "temporary" takings which, as here, deny a landowner all use of his property, are not different in kind from permanent takings, for which the Constitution clearly requires compensation. [Citation.] ("Nothing in the Just Compensation Clause suggests that 'takings' must be permanent and irrevocable.") It is axiomatic that the Fifth Amendment's just compensation provision is "designed to bar Government from forcing some people alone to bear public burdens which, in all fairness and justice, should be borne by the public as a whole." [Citations.] In the present case the

interim ordinance was adopted by the county of Los Angeles in January 1979, and became effective immediately. Appellant filed suit within a month after the effective date of the ordinance and yet when the Supreme Court of California denied a hearing in the case on October 17, 1985, the merits of appellant's claim had yet to be determined. The United States has been required to pay compensation for leasehold interests of shorter duration than this. The value of a leasehold interest in property for a period of years may be substantial, and the burden on the property owner in extinguishing such an interest for a period of years may be great indeed. [Citation.] Where this burden results from governmental action that amounted to a taking, the Just Compensation Clause of the Fifth Amendment requires that the government pay the landowner for the value of the use of the land during this period. [Citation.] ("It is the owner's loss, not the taker's gain, which is the measure of the value of the property taken.") Invalidation of the ordinance or its successor ordinance after this period of time, though converting the taking into a "temporary" one, is not a sufficient remedy to meet the demands of the Just Compensation Clause.

* * *

Nothing we say today is intended to abrogate the principle that the decision to exercise the power of eminent domain is a legislative function, " 'for Congress and Congress alone to determine.' " [Citations.] Once a court determines that a taking has occurred, the government retains the whole range of options already available—amendment of the regulation, withdrawal of the invalidated regulation, or exercise of eminent domain. Thus we do not, as the Solicitor General suggests, "permit a court, at the behest of a private person, to require the . . . Government to exercise the power of eminent domain. . . ." [Citation.] We merely hold that where the government's activities have already worked a taking of all use of property, no subsequent action by the government can relieve it of the duty to provide compensation for the period during which the taking was effective.

We also point out that the allegation of the complaint which we treat as true for purposes of our decision was that the ordinance in question denied appellant all use of its property. We limit our holding to the facts presented, and of course do not deal with the quite different questions that would arise in the case of normal delays in obtaining building permits, changes in zoning ordinances, variances, and the like which are not before us. We realize that even our present holding will undoubtedly lessen to some extent the freedom and flexibility of land-use planners and governing bodies of municipal corporations when enacting land-use regulations. But such consequences necessarily flow from any decision upholding a claim of constitutional right; many of the provisions of the Constitution are designed to limit the flexibility and freedom of governmental authorities and the Just Compensation Clause of the Fifth Amendment is one of them. As Justice Holmes aptly noted more than 50 years ago, "a strong public desire to improve the public condition is not enough to warrant achieving the desire by a shorter cut than the constitutional way of paying for the change." [Citation.]

Here we must assume that the Los Angeles County ordinances have denied appellant all use of its property for a considerable period of years, and we hold that invalidation of the ordinance without payment of fair value for the use of the property during this period of time would be a constitutionally insufficient remedy. The judgment of the California Court of Appeals is therefore reversed, and the case is remanded for further proceedings not inconsistent with this opinion.

It is so ordered.

Restrictive Covenants

WALKER v. GROSS

Supreme Court of Massachusetts, 1972.
362 Mass. 703, 290 N.E.2d 543.

Wilkins, J.

The plaintiffs seek a determination, . . . that a deed restriction providing that no part of their premises in Waltham shall be "used for any business purpose" does not prevent the use of their premises for an apartment house. The plaintiffs' land is subject to a restriction, imposed by a 1947 deed to a predecessor in title, which reads as follows: "The premises are conveyed with the benefit of and subject to any easements of record and subject to a permanent restriction that no part of the premises shall be used for any business purpose except for raising, growing and selling live bait and for the sale at retail of fishing tackle and sporting goods, and the grantees for themselves, their heirs, executors, administrators and assigns, covenant and agree with the grantor, his heirs and assigns, not to use the premises or any part thereof in violation of the above restriction, and it is agreed that this covenant shall run with the land."

The plaintiffs contemplate the construction of an apartment building with eighty-three family units and a store. Building permits have been issued for the apartment house by the building inspector of Waltham. The defendants, landowners in the neighborhood of the plaintiffs' premises, are entitled to the benefit of the restriction by which the plaintiffs' premises are burdened.

The restriction itself gives no significant guidance on the question whether an apartment house use is a use for a business purpose. No extrinsic evidence has been presented to assist us in interpreting the intent of the parties in light of the material circumstances and pertinent facts known to the parties to the deed at the time it was executed. We know only that the retail sale of fishing tackle and sporting goods was regarded as a business purpose because those activities were expressly excluded from the prohibition of the restriction. In these circumstances we are guided in reaching our conclusion by the general rule that restrictions in a deed are to be strictly construed against the party seeking to enforce those restrictions. [Citation.] Thus any doubt should be "resolved in favor of the freedom of land from servitude." [Citation.]

We hold that the use of the plaintiffs' premises for apartment house purposes does not violate the deed restriction against the use of those premises for any business purpose. The plaintiffs' apartment building will be used by its occupants for residential purposes. The fact that the apartment house may be owned for income producing purposes does not make the *use* of the premises a use for a business purpose. If we were to accept the view asserted by the defendants, the renting of a single family house and the construction of such a house for sale would seemingly be in violation of this restriction as well. We think that the language of the restriction is concerned with the physical activity carried on upon the premises and not with the presence or absence of a profit making motive on the part of the landowner.

Authority in other jurisdictions supports our view that the use of premises for apartment house purposes does not violate a deed restriction against the use of premises for any business purpose. [Citations.]

The defendants basically object to the construction of an apartment house instead of single family houses. The restriction, however, does not speak in terms of allowing only single family houses, but rather it speaks in words of exclusion to prevent any use for business purposes. If use of an apartment house is, as we hold under the language of the deed restriction, not a use for a business purpose, the scope of the limitation contained in the deed obviously fails to reach the proposed apartment house use. What the grantor might have done if he had anticipated present circumstances need not concern us. Construed, as it must be, strictly against the parties asserting the applicability of the restriction, the restriction simply fails to do what the defendants assert.

Decree affirmed.

QUESTIONS

1. Distinguish among warranty, special warranty, and quitclaim deeds.

2. Distinguish between the obligations of a purchaser who assumes a mortgage and one who buys the property subject to the mortgage.

3. Describe the fundamental requirements of a valid deed.

4. Define and give an example of (a) a variance, and (b) a nonconforming use.

5. Describe the nature and types of restrictive covenants.

PROBLEMS

1. A was the father of B, C, and D and the owner of Redacre, Blackacre, and Greenacre.

A made and executed his warranty deed conveying Redacre to B. The deed provided that "this deed shall only become effective upon the death of the grantor." A retained possession of the deed and died leaving the deed in his safe deposit box.

A made and executed his warranty deed conveying Blackacre to C. The deed provided "this deed shall only become effective upon the death of the grantor." A delivered the deed to C. After A died, C recorded the deed.

A made and executed a warranty deed conveying Greenacre to D. The deed was delivered by A to X with specific instructions to deliver the deed to D upon A's death. Upon the death of A, X duly delivered the deed to D.

(a) What is the interest of B in Redacre, if any?

(b) What is the interest of C in Blackacre, if any?

(c) What is the interest of D in Greenacre, if any?

2. Arkin, the owner of Redacre, executed a real estate mortgage to the Shawnee Bank and Trust Company for $10,000. After the mortgage was executed and recorded, Arkin constructed a dwelling on the premises and planted a corn crop. After default in the payment of the mortgage debt, the bank proceeded to foreclose the mortgage. At the time of the foreclosure sale, the corn crop was mature and unharvested. Arkin contends that the mortgage should not apply to (a) the dwelling and (b) the corn crop. Decision?

3. Robert and Stanley held legal title of record to adjacent tracts of land, each consisting of eighty acres. Stanley fenced his eighty acres in 1966. He placed his east fence fifteen feet onto Robert's property. Thereafter, he was in possession of this fifteen-foot strip of land and kept it fenced and cultivated continuously until he sold his tract of land to Nathan on March 1, 1972. Nathan took possession under deed from Stanley. Nathan continued possession and cultivation of the fifteen-foot strip until May 27, 1991, when Robert, having on several occasions strenuously objected to Nathan's possession, brought suit against Nathan for trespass. Decision?

4. Marcia executed a mortgage on Blackacre to secure her indebtedness to Ajax Savings and Loan Association in the amount of $25,000. Later, Marcia sold Blackacre to Morton. The deed contained the following, "This deed is subject to the mortgage executed by the Grantor herein to Ajax Savings and Loan Association."

The sale price of Blackacre to Morton was $50,000. Morton paid $25,000 in cash, deducting the $25,000 mortgage debt from the purchase price. Upon default in the payment of the mortgage debt, Ajax brings an action against Marcia and Morton to recover a judgment for the amount of the mortgage debt and to foreclose the mortgage. Decision?

5. On January 1, 1990, Davis and Hershey owned Blackacre as tenants in common. On July 1, 1990, Davis made a written contract to sell Blackacre to Grigg for $25,000. Pursuant to this contract, Grigg paid Davis $25,000 on August 1, 1990, and Davis executed and delivered to Grigg a warranty deed to Blackacre. On May 1, 1991, Hershey quitclaimed his interest in Blackacre to Davis. Grigg brings an action against Davis for breach of warranty of title. What judgment?

6. John Doe, for valuable consideration, agreed to convey to Richard Roe eighty acres of land. He delivered a deed, the material portions of which read:

"I, John Doe, grant and convey to Richard Roe eighty acres of land [legal description]: To have and to hold unto Richard Roe, his heirs, and assigns forever.

"I, John Doe, covenant to warrant and defend the premises hereby conveyed against all persons claiming the same or any part thereof by or through me."

Thereafter, Roe conveyed "all my right, title, and interest" in the eighty acres to Paul Poe. It develops that Doe had no title to the land when he conveyed it to Roe. Subsequently, Doe inherited an undivided one-half interest in the property.

What rights, if any, does Poe have against Doe and Roe?

7. Barker operated a retail bakery, Davidson a drugstore, Farrell a food store, Gibson a gift shop, and Harper a hardware store in adjoining locations along one side of a single suburban village block. As the population grew, the business section developed at the other end of the village, and the establishments of Barker, Davidson, Farrell, Gibson, and Harper were surrounded for at least a mile in each direction solely by residences. A zoning ordinance with the usual provisions was adopted by the village, and the area including the five stores was declared to be a "residential district for single-family dwellings." Thereafter, Barker tore down the frame building which housed the bakery and commenced to construct a modern brick bakery. Davidson found her business increasing to such an extent that she began to build an addition to the drugstore in order to extend it to the rear alley. Farrell's building was destroyed by fire, and he started to reconstruct it in order to restore it to its former condition. Gibson changed the gift shop into a sporting goods store and after six months of operation decided to go back into the gift shop business. Harper sold his hardware store to Hempstead.

The village building commissioner brings an action under the zoning ordinance to enjoin the construction work of Barker, Davidson, and Farrell and to enjoin the carrying on of any business by Gibson and Hempstead. Assume the ordinance is valid. What result?

8. Alda and Mattingly are residents of Phase I of Chimney Hills Subdivision. The lots owned by Alda and Mattingly are subject to the following restrictive covenant: "Lots shall be for single-family residence purposes only." Alda intends to convert the interior of her carport into a beauty shop, and Mattingly brings suit against Alda to enjoin her from doing so. Alda argues that the covenant restricts only the type of building that can be constructed, not the incidental use to which residential structures are put. Decision?

9. The City of Boston sought to condemn land in fee simple for use in constructing an entrance to an underground terminal for a subway. The owners of the land contend that no more than surface and subsurface easements are necessary for the terminal entrance and seek to retain air rights above thirty-six feet. The city argues that any building utilizing this airspace would require structural supports that would interfere with the city's plan for the terminal. The city concedes that the properties around the condemned property could be assembled and structures could be designed to span over the condemned property, in which case the air rights would be quite valuable. Decision?

10. In May 1963, Fred Parramore executed four deeds, each conveying a life estate in his land to him and his wife and a remainder interest in one-fourth of his land to each of his four children: Alney, Eudell, Bernice, and Iris. Although Fred executed and acknowledged the four deeds as part of his plan to distribute his estate at his death, he did not deliver them to his children at this time. Instead, he placed the deeds with his will in a safe deposit box and instructed the children to pick up their deeds at his death. Fred later conveyed Alney's deed to Alney, thereby vesting Alney's interest in that parcel, but Eudell, Bernice, and Iris's deeds were never handed over to them during Fred's lifetime. Fred, however, acted as if the land was beyond his control, and on one occasion told a prospective buyer that the land had already been deeded away. When Fred died in November 1974, Alney brought this action, claiming that the deeds to Eudell, Bernice, and Iris were ineffective because they had never been handed over during Fred's lifetime. Accordingly, Alney argued the remaining land should pass in equal shares to each of the four children under the residuary clause of Fred's will. Decision?

11. The Gerwitz family resides on a piece of land known as Lot #24 of the Belleville tract, which they acquired by deed in 1957. Shortly thereafter, the Gerwitzes began to use the adjacent vacant Lot #25. At various times they planted grass seed, flowers, and shrubs on the land and used it for picnics and cookouts. In 1977, Gelsomin acquired Lot #25 and constructed a foundation on it so that he could place a house there. The Gerwitzes then brought this action to stop him, claiming title to Lot #25 by adverse possession. Decision?

12. Leo owned a one-story, one-family dwelling in a single-family residential zoning district in Detroit. He attempted to sell the house with its adjoining lot for $38,500. Houses in the neighborhood generally sold for $20,000 to $25,000. Immediately to the west of Leo's property was a gasoline service station. In addition, Leo's property was located on a corner frequented with heavy traffic. Leo had not received any offers from residence-use buyers during the period of over a year that the property had been listed and offered for sale. He then applied to the board of zoning appeals for a variance to permit the use of the property as a dental and medical clinic and to use the side yard for off-street parking. The variance would be subject to certain conditions, including the preservation of the building's exterior so as to continue to appear to be a one-family dwelling. Puritan-Greenfield Improvement Association, a nonprofit corporation, filed a complaint against Leo's variance request. Decision?

Chapter 52

TRUSTS AND WILLS

Types of Trusts
Creation and Termination
Creation and Revocation of Wills
Special Types of Wills
Intestate Succession
Administration of Estates

IN previous chapters we have seen that real and personal property may be transferred in a number of ways, including by sale and by gift. Another important way in which a person may convey property or allow others to use or benefit from it is through trusts and wills. Trusts may take effect during the transferor's lifetime or, when used in a will, they may become effective upon his death. Wills enable individuals to control the transfer of their property at their death. Upon a person's death, his or her property must pass to someone. It is almost always the best policy for individuals to decide how their property should be distributed and, except for the limitations of dower and curtesy, the law permits individuals to do so by sale, gift, trust, and will. If, however, an individual dies without a will—that is, intestate—State law prescribes who shall be entitled to the property owned by that individual at death. This chapter will examine both trusts and wills, as well as the manner in which property descends when a person dies without leaving a will.

TRUSTS

A **trust** is a *fiduciary relationship* in which *legal title* to property is held by one or more persons while its use, enjoyment, and benefit (*equitable title*) belong to another. A trust may be created by agreement of the parties, by bequest in a will, or by a court decree. However created, the relationship is known as a trust. The party creating the trust is the **creator** or **settlor,** the party holding legal title to the property is the **trustee** of the trust, and the person who receives the benefit of the trust is the **beneficiary** (see Figure 52–1).

TYPES OF TRUSTS

Although there are many varieties of trusts, all trusts may be divided into two major groups: express and implied. Implied trusts, which are imposed upon property by court order, are categorized as either "constructive" or "resulting" trusts.

Express Trusts

An express trust is, as the name indicates, a trust established by voluntary action and is represented by a written document, an oral statement, or conduct of the settlor. In a majority of jurisdictions, an express trust of real property must be in writing to meet the requirements of the statute of frauds. Trusts of

Figure 52–1 Trusts

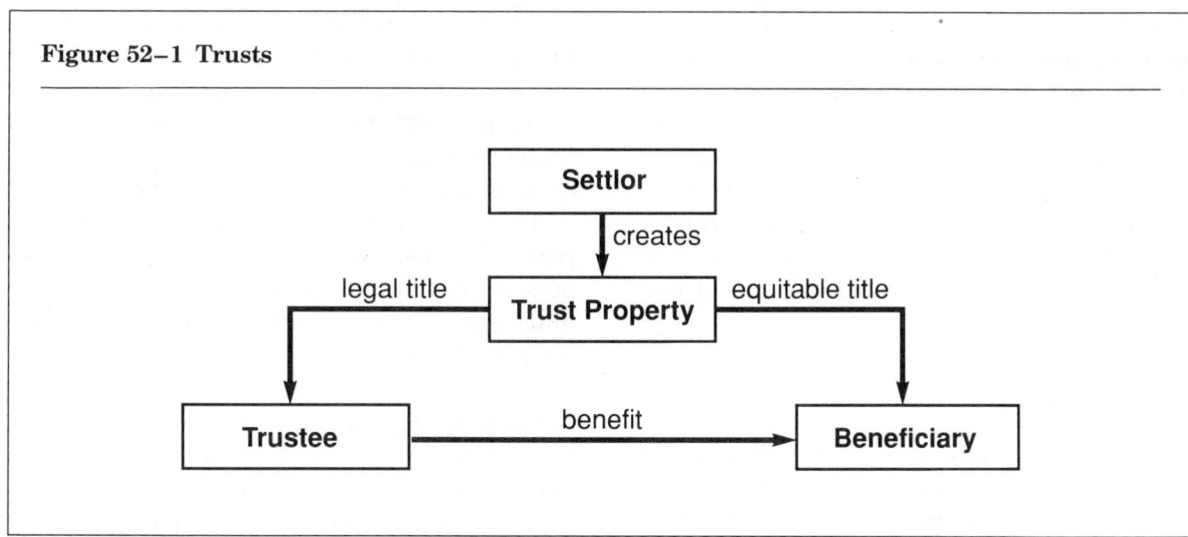

personal property and implied trusts do not fall within the requirements of the statute of frauds.

No particular words are necessary to create a trust, provided that the intent of the settlor to establish a trust is unmistakable. Sometimes words of request or recommendation are used in connection with a gift, implying or hoping that the gift will be used for the purpose stated. Thus, instead of clearly creating a trust by leaving property "to X for the benefit and use of Y," a settlor may leave property to X "in full confidence and with hope that he will care for Y." Such a **"precatory expression"** (words of request) may be so definite and certain as to impose a trust upon the property for the benefit of Y. Whether it creates a trust or is nothing more than a gratuitous wish will depend on whether the court concludes from all the facts that the settlor genuinely intended a trust. Generally, courts view words such as "request," "hope," and "rely" as creating no legal obligation upon the recipient of the gift and therefore do not create a trust.

Charitable Trusts Almost any trust that has for its purpose to benefit the public or a sizeable segment of the public is classified as a **charitable trust,** unless it is so vague and indefinite that it cannot be enforced. Gifts for public museums, upkeep of parks, and to further a particular political doctrine or religious belief have been upheld as "charitable" in character.

Spendthrift Trusts A settlor frequently does not believe that a beneficiary can be relied on to preserve even the limited rights granted her as beneficiary. He may then provide in the trust instrument that the beneficiary cannot, by assignment or otherwise, impair her rights to receive principal or income in the future and that creditors of the beneficiary cannot attach the fund or the income. The term *spendthrift,* as used in connection with **spendthrift trusts,** refers to a provision in a trust instrument under which the trust estate is removed from the beneficiary's control and disposition, and from liability for her individual debts. Spendthrift provisions are valid in most States. Once income from the trust is actually received by the beneficiary, however, creditors may seize it or the beneficiary may use it as she pleases.

Totten Trusts A **totten trust** or **savings account trust** involves a bank account opened by the settlor of the trust. For example, Joanne deposits a sum of money in a savings account in a bank in the name of "Joanne, in trust for Justin." The settlor,

Joanne, may make additional deposits in the account from time to time and may withdraw money from it whenever she pleases. The courts have held this to be a tentative trust that Joanne may revoke by withdrawing the fund or changing the form of the account. Usually the transfer of ownership becomes complete upon the depositor's death when the beneficiary is entitled to the balance of the account.

Implied Trusts

In some cases, the courts, in the absence of any express intent to create a trust, will impose a trust upon property because the acts of the parties appear to call for such a construction. An implied trust owes its existence to the law. As previously stated, implied trusts are generally divided into two classes: constructive trusts and resulting trusts.

Constructive Trusts   A **constructive trust** is created by a court of equity to rectify misconduct or to prevent unjust enrichment. Misconduct includes abuse of a confidential relationship, actual fraud, undue influence, and duress. Justice Cardozo referred to a constructive trust as "the formula through which the conscience of equity finds expression. When property has been acquired in such circumstances that the holder of the legal title may not in good conscience retain the beneficial interest, equity converts him into a trustee." *Beatty v. Guggenheim Exploration Co.*, 225 N.Y. 380, 122 N.E. 378, (1919). A constructive trust is not based on the intent of the parties; it is created by a court in order to achieve an equitable result.

Business and personal affairs provide many examples of constructive trusts. A director of a corporation who takes advantage of a "corporate opportunity" or who makes an undisclosed profit in a deal with the corporation will be treated as a trustee for the corporation with respect to the property or profits he acquires. Likewise, a trustee under an express trust who permits a lease held by the trust to expire and then acquires a new lease of the property in his individual capacity will be required to hold the new lease in trust for the beneficiary. If an agent who is given money by his principal to purchase property in the name of the principal instead uses the funds to acquire title in himself, courts will treat him as a trustee for the principal.

As previously indicated, constructive trusts are also invoked in situations where persons use their positions of friendship or marriage to their unjust advantage. *See Sharp v. Kosmalski.*

Resulting Trusts   A resulting trust does not depend on contract or agreement but is founded on a presumed or inferred intent that arises out of the acts of the parties. Because a resulting trust is created by implication and operation of law, it does not need to be evidenced in writing. A resulting trust is distinguished from a constructive trust in that it serves to carry out the *intent* of the parties in those cases where the intent was inadequately expressed rather than to rectify misconduct.

The most common example of a resulting trust is where Joel pays the purchase price for property and title is taken in the name of Ann. The presumption here is that the parties intended Ann to hold the property for the benefit of Joel, and Ann will be treated as a trustee. The presumption, however, may be rebutted by evidence that Joel intended to make a gift to Ann.

CREATION OF TRUSTS

Each trust has (1) a creator or settlor, (2) a "corpus" or trust property, (3) a trustee, and (4) a beneficiary. As previously mentioned, no particular words are necessary to create a trust, provided that the intent of the settlor to establish a trust is unmistakable. Consideration is not essential to an enforceable trust. In this respect, a trust is more like a conveyance than a contract. Trusts created in wills are known as **testamentary trusts** because they become effective after the death of the settlor. Trusts created during the settlor's lifetime are referred to as ***inter vivos*** or living **trusts.**

Settlor

Any person legally capable of making a contract may create a trust. But if the settlor's contract would be voidable or void because of infancy, incompetency, or some other reason, a declaration of trust is also voidable or void.

Subject Matter

One of the principal characteristics of a trust is the requirement of a trust corpus or *res,* which must be property that is definite and specific. The *res* may be any type of property so long as it is in existence and assignable. A trust cannot be effective immediately for property not yet in existence or to be acquired at a later date. For example, Steven organizes a corporation and executes a trust instrument declaring that he holds all future dividends in trust for his children. When dividends are subsequently declared, Steven may keep them or set them aside as trust property. His prior declaration does not oblige him to hold the *future* unrealized profits in trust. In each succeeding year, a declaration and segregation of dividends received is necessary in order to impose the character of a trust upon them.

The subject matter of the trust must be certain and definite as described or identified in the trust instrument. This requirement is satisfied, for example, by the creation of a testamentary trust in Sari's will, which provides that she leaves to Terri, as trustee, sufficient funds to pay $300 a month to Barbara.

Trustee

Anyone legally capable of holding title to the trust property may be a trustee. The lack of a trustee will not destroy a trust. If the settlor neglects to appoint one, if the named trustee does not qualify, or if the named trustee declines to serve, the court will appoint an individual or institution to act as trustee. A trustee can, of course, decline to serve, and before the property will vest in him it is necessary that he accept the trust.

Duties of the Trustee   A trustee has three primary duties:

1. to carry out the purposes of the trust;

2. to act with prudence and care in the administration of the trust, and

3. to exercise a high degree of loyalty toward the beneficiary.

No special skills are required of a trustee under ordinary circumstances. He is required to act with the same degree of care that a **prudent man** would exercise with respect to his personal affairs. He has a duty to make the trust property productive and thus to invest it in income-producing assets. What constitutes the care of a "prudent man" is, of course, not easy to classify in any particular case. One court has spoken as follows of this responsibility:

. . . trustees are bound in the management of all matters of the trust to act in good faith and employ such vigilance, sagacity, diligence, and prudence as in general prudent men of discretion and intelligence in like matters employ in their affairs. The law does not hold a trustee, acting in accord with such rule, responsible for errors of judgment. *Costello v. Costello,* 209 N.Y. 252, 103 N.E. 148 [1913].

See also Witmer v. Blair.

The duty of loyalty arises out of and illustrates the fiduciary character of the relationship between the trustee and the beneficiary. In all his dealings with the trust property, the beneficiary, and third parties, the trustee must act exclusively in the interest of the beneficiary. Lack of loyalty may arise from obvious self-dealing, or it may be entirely innocent; in either event, the trustee can be charged with lack of loyalty.

Powers of the Trustee   The powers of a trustee are determined by (1) the authority granted him by the settlor in the instrument creating the trust, and (2) the rules of law in the jurisdiction in which the trust is established. State laws affecting the powers of trustees have their greatest impact upon the investments a trustee may make with trust funds. Most States have adopted a prudent investor rule. Some States, however, still follow the historical test, which prescribed a list of types of securities qualified for trust investment. In some jurisdictions this list is permissive; in others it is mandatory. If the list is permissive, the trustee may invest in types of securities not listed although he carries the burden of showing that he made a prudent choice. The trust instrument may give the trustee wide discretion as to investments, and in such an event the trustee is not bound to adhere to the list deemed advisable under the statute.

Allocation of Principal and Income

Trusts often settle a life estate in the trust corpus on one beneficiary and a remainder interest on another beneficiary. For example, on his death, a man leaves his property to trustees who are instructed to pay the income from the property to his widow during her life, and upon her death to distribute the property to his children. In these instances, the trustee must distribute the principal to one party (the remainderman) and the income to another (the life tenant or income beneficiary). The trustee must also allocate receipts and charge expenses between the income beneficiary and the remainderman. If the trust agreement does not specify how the funds should be allocated, the trustee is provided guidance by statute, which in most States is the **Uniform Principal and Income Act.** A trustee who fails to comply with the trust agreement or the statute is personally liable for any loss.

The general rule in allocating benefits and burdens between income beneficiaries and remaindermen is that *ordinary* or current receipts and expenses are chargeable to the income beneficiary while *extraordinary* receipts and expenses are allocated to the remainderman. Ordinary income is money paid for the use of trust property and any gain from the use of the trust property, while any substitute for or change in form of the trust *res* is allocated to the trust principal. Figure 52–2 illustrates these four types of allocations.

Beneficiary

There are very few restrictions on who (or what) may be a beneficiary. Charitable uses are a common purpose of trusts, and if the settlor's object does not outrage public policy or morals, almost any purpose that happens to strike the fancy of a settlor will be upheld.

A person named as a beneficiary of a trust may accept or reject the trust. In the absence of restrictive provisions in the trust instrument such as a spendthrift clause, a beneficiary's interest may be reached by his creditors, or the beneficiary may sell or dispose of his interest. If he held more than a life estate in the trust, his interest upon his death, un-

---

Figure 52–2 Allocation of Principal and Income

	Receipts	Expenses
Ordinary — **Income Beneficiary**	Rents Royalties Cash dividends (regular and extraordinary) Interest	Interest payments Insurance Ordinary taxes Ordinary repairs Depreciation
Extraordinary — **Remainderman**	Stock dividends Stock splits Proceeds from sale or exchange of corpus Settlement of claims for injury to corpus	Extraordinary repairs Long-term improvements Principal amortization Costs incurred in the sale or purchase of corpus

less disposed of by his will, passes to his heirs or personal representatives.

TERMINATION OF A TRUST

Unless a power of revocation is reserved by the settlor, the general rule is that a trust, once validly created, is *irrevocable*. If so reserved, the trust may be terminated at the discretion of the settlor.

Normally the instrument creating a trust establishes a termination date, and the trust terminates at the time stated without complication. A period of years may be specified, or the settlor may provide that the trust shall continue during the life of a named individual. The death of the trustee or beneficiary does not terminate the trust if neither of their lives is the measure of the duration of the trust.

If the purpose for which a trust has been established is fulfilled before the specified termination date, the court may decree a termination of the trust. Most courts will not order the termination of a trust upon the request of all the beneficiaries if any of the trust's purposes has not been accomplished. The court will be governed by the purposes set forth in the trust instrument by the settlor, not by the wishes of the beneficiaries. If the trustee acquires both the equitable and legal title to the trust *res* the *merger doctrine* applies and the trust terminates. In order for a trust to exist, the trustee and beneficiary must be different persons.

DECEDENT'S ESTATES

When a person dies, the title to his property must pass to someone. If the decedent leaves a valid will, his property will pass as he directs, subject only to certain limitations imposed by the State, such as the widow's right to dower discussed in Chapter 50. If, however, no valid will has been executed, the decedent is said to have died "intestate," and the State prescribes who shall be entitled to the property. If a decedent dies having a valid will that does not dispose of all of her net probate estate, the portion that is not effectively devised by the will is governed by intestacy laws. If a

person dies without a will and leaves no heirs or next of kin, her property *escheats* (reverts) to the State. Nonetheless, not all of the decedent's property will pass through the probate estate (the distribution of a decedent's estate to her successors). Certain property will pass outside of the estate as a result of arrangements that are not affected by the distribution of the decedent's estate. For instance, a decedent's life insurance policy or pension plan will pass to the beneficiary of the policy or plan, property the decedent jointly owned with a right of survivorship will pass to the survivor, and property subject to a trust will be governed by the trust instrument.

WILLS

A **will** is a written instrument executed with the formalities required by statutes, whereby a person makes a disposition of his property to take effect after his death. A will is also called a **testament;** the maker of the will is called a testator; and gifts made in a will are called devises or bequests. A **bequest** or **legacy** is a gift by will of personal property; a **devise** is a gift by will of real property.

One major characteristic of a will sets it apart from other transactions such as deeds and contracts: a will is revocable at any time during life. There is no such thing as an irrevocable will. A document binding during life may be a contract (such as a promise to make a will) or a deed (conveying a vested remainder after a life estate in the grantor), but it is not a will. Even if a testator contractually promises not to revoke her will, such as with joint or mutual wills, she retains the power to revoke the will. Nonetheless, the testator may be liable for breach of contract and a constructive trust may be imposed upon the beneficiaries of the estate. A will takes effect only on, and not until, the death of the testator.

In 1969, the National Conference of Commissioners on Uniform State Laws and the American Bar Association approved the Uniform Probate Code (UPC), an attempt to encourage throughout the United States the adoption of a uniform, flexible, speedy, efficient, and, in most cases, less expensive system of settling a decedent's estate. The UPC is based on the major premise that the probate court's appropriate role is to be available to assist in the settlement of an estate when assistance is requested or required rather than to impose its unsolicited supervision to enforce every detailed formality upon completely non-contentious settlements. In the following discussion of decedents' estates, principles and procedures are summarized generally with a notation of the parallel principles and procedures under the UPC.

Mental Capacity

In order to make a valid will, the testator must have both the "power" and the "capacity" to do so. The requisite testamentary intent must always be present to create a valid will.

Testamentary Power and Capacity The *power* to make a will is granted by the State to persons who are of a class believed generally able to handle their affairs without regard to personal limitations of individual members of that class. Thus, in most States, children under a certain age cannot make valid wills.

The *capacity* to make a will refers to the limits placed upon particular persons in the class generally granted the power to make wills because of personal mental deficiencies. Testamentary capacity generally requires that the testator is of sound mind and knows the nature and extent of her property and the objects of her bounty. Underlying the notion of capacity is the premise that, for a will to be valid, a testator must *intend* a document to be his will. This requisite intent is considered absent if he is mentally incompetent or suffers from delusions. Nevertheless, since capacity is an individual matter it is not easy to set down any test that will, in all cases, measure this qualification. A person adjudicated incompetent can, in a lucid period, make a valid will. An aged and enfeebled octogenarian may have the capacity to execute a will. It takes less in the way of mental abilities to meet the test of capacity to make a will than

is required for the independent management of one's affairs during lifetime.

Under the UPC any person eighteen or more years of age who is of sound mind may make a will. Section 2–501.

Conduct Invalidating a Will Any document purporting to be a will, but which has been induced by misconduct negating the testator's voluntary intent is not a valid will. This is the basis for the rule that a will resulting from *duress, undue influence*, or *fraud* is no will at all.

Undue influence is influence that destroys the testator's free will and substitutes another person's will for the testator's will. A general influence over the testator is not sufficient to make a case of improper pressure. The influence must be directed specifically to the act of making the will. A wife urges her husband to leave all his property to her; this influence is not "undue." Most frequently, the charge of undue influence is made when a testator leaves his property to a person who is not a blood relative, such as a friend who took care of the testator in his last illness or during his last years. If the evidence demonstrates that the beneficiary under the will was in close contact with the testator and that natural objects of his bounty are ignored in the will, there is a suggestion of undue influence. *See In re Estate of Hobelsberger.*

Fraud is a misrepresentation of material fact made by a beneficiary of a will with the intent to deceive the decedent and which causes the decedent to write or change a will in reliance upon the misstatement. The charge of fraud can also be used to invalidate a will. For example, Brian dies, leaving all his property to Mark upon the representation by Mark that he is Brian's long-lost son. Mark in fact is not Brian's son. In such a case, the will may be set aside because the misrepresentation was made with the intent to deceive and Brian relied upon it.

Formal Requirements of a Will

By statute in all jurisdictions, a will must comply with certain formalities to be valid.

These formalities are intended both to ensure that the testator understood what she was doing and to help prevent fraud. As discussed later, some States permit specific types of wills that do not meet all of these requirements to be enforced with respect to testamentary dispositions of certain property.

Writing   A basic requirement of a valid will is that it be in writing. UPC, Section 2–502. The writing may be informal, as long as the basic statutory requirements are substantially met. Pencil, ink, typewriter, and mimeograph are equally valid methods, and valid wills have been made on scratch paper and on an envelope.

It is also valid to incorporate into a will by reference another document which in itself is not a will for lack of proper execution. To incorporate a memorandum in a will by reference, the following four conditions must exist: (1) the memorandum must be in writing; (2) it must be in existence when the will is executed; (3) it must be adequately described in the will; and (4) in some States it must be described in the will as being in existence. UPC, Section 2–510.

Signature   A will must be signed by the testator. UPC, Section 2–502. The signature verifies that the will has been executed and is a fundamental requirement in almost all jurisdictions. The initials "A.H.," the word "father," or a mark at the end of a will in the handwriting of the testator are adequate if intended as an execution. *See In re Estate of Hobelsberger.*

Most statutes require the signature to be at the end of the will, and even in jurisdictions where this is not specified, a signature at the end will negate the charge that the portions of a will coming after a signature were written subsequent to the execution and therefore do not have the required signature.

Attestation   A written will must be attested, or certified, by witnesses. The function of witnesses is to acknowledge that the testator did execute the will and that she had the requisite intent and capacity. The number and qualification of witnesses and the manner of attestation are generally set out by statute. Usually two or three witnesses are required. Section 2–502 of the UPC requires that at least two persons, each of whom witnessed either the signing or the testator's acknowledgment of the will, act as witnesses to the will.

The most common restriction is that a witness must not have any interest under the will. This requirement takes at least two forms under statutes. One type of statute disqualifies a witness who is also a beneficiary under the will. The other type voids the bequest or devise to the interested witness, thus making him a disinterested and qualified witness. What constitutes an "interest" sufficient to disqualify a witness is not always easily defined. The spouse of a beneficiary under a will has been held to be "interested" and thus not qualified. Generally, a person is not disqualified simply because he is named as executor in the will. The attorney who drafts the will is generally a qualified witness. Under the UPC no will or any provision thereof is invalid because the will was attested by an interested witness. Section 2–505.

Revocation of a Will

A will is revocable by the testator, and, under certain circumstances, a will may be revoked by operation of law. In most jurisdictions, the methods by which a will is revoked are specified by statute.

Destruction or Alteration   Tearing, burning, or otherwise destroying a will is an effective way of revoking a will unless it can be shown that the destruction was inadvertent. UPC, Section 2–507. In some States, partial revocation of a will may be accomplished by erasure or obliteration of a part of the will. In no case, however, will a substituted or additional bequest by interlineation be effective without reexecution and reattestation.

Courts are occasionally faced with the difficult question of determining whether a will was revoked by destruction or simply mislaid. For a case dealing with this issue, *see Barksdale v. Pendergrass.*

Subsequent Will   The execution of a second will does not in itself constitute a revocation of an earlier will. The first will is revoked only to the extent that the second will is inconsistent with the first. UPC, Section 2–507. The most certain manner of revocation is the execution of a later will containing a declaration that all former wills are revoked. In some but not all jurisdictions, a will may be revoked by a written declaration to this effect in a subsequent document, such as a letter, even though the document does not meet the formal requirements of a will.

Operation of Law   A *marriage* generally revokes a will executed prior to the marriage. *Divorce,* on the other hand, under the general rule, does *not* revoke a provision in the will of one of the parties for the benefit of the other party. Section 2–508 of the UPC takes a different position and provides that a divorce or annulment that occurs after the execution of a will revokes any disposition of property made by the will to the former spouse. No change of circumstances, however, other than divorce or annulment revokes a will. Thus, a subsequent marriage does not revoke a will. Nonetheless, a spouse who marries the testator after the execution of the will is entitled to the same share as though the testator died without a will. UPC, Section 2–301.

The *birth* of a child after execution of a will may revoke a will at least as far as that child is concerned if it appears that the testator omitted to make a provision for the child. In some jurisdictions and under the UPC, the subsequent birth of a child will not revoke the will, but the child is entitled to the same share as though the testator died without a will unless it appears from the will that the omission was intentional. Section 2–302.

Effectiveness of Testamentary Provisions

Renunciation by the Surviving Spouse Statutes generally provide for a right of renunciation of the will by a surviving spouse

and set forth the method of accomplishing it. The purpose of such statutory provisions is to enable the spouse to elect which method of taking—under the will or under intestate succession—would be more advantageous to him or her. The right to renounce a will may be exercised only by persons designated by the statute, and the right conferred on the surviving spouse is personal. Upon renunciation of the will, the law of intestate succession determines the share of the estate taken by the surviving spouse.

Abatement and Ademption of a Bequest Abatement is the reduction or elimination of gifts by category upon the reduction in the value of the estate of the testator after the execution of his will. It can have serious implications. The first items to abate in a will are all the **residue** or remainder after provisions for specific and general gifts. **Specific gifts** are those of a particular identified item. **General gifts** are gifts that do not identify a particular or uniquely identifiable item. Specific gifts must be satisfied first. For example, if John, a widower, after making specific gifts, leaves "all the rest, residue, and remainder of my estate to my daughter, Mary," Mary may receive a great deal less than her deceased father intended. Suppose at the time John executes his will he estimates his worth at $150,000. He leaves $20,000 to his church, $10,000 to the Salvation Army, and his car worth $10,000 to his business partner, and assumes that Mary will receive approximately $110,000. John dies five years later without changing his will but having suffered substantial business and market reverses. His executor reports that there is only $50,000 in the estate. Mary will only receive $10,000 because the specific devise of the car and the general devises of the $20,000 and $10,000 will abate only after the residue is depleted.

Ademption is the removal or extinction of a gift by act of the testator. Ademption occurs when a testator neglects to change his will after changed circumstances have made the performance of a provision in the will impossible. For example, Hope buys the farm, Blackacre, and wants it to go on her death to a favorite nephew who is studying agriculture at college. After so providing in her will, she sells Blackacre and uses the money to buy Greenacre. The general rule is that the nephew will not be entitled to Greenacre. Nonetheless, the courts have sometimes limited this doctrine based upon the perceived intent of the decedent. Where the property in question is missing from the estate because of some involuntary act of the decedent or some event over which he had no control, there is no ademption. This rule, known as the "modified intention theory," is intended to effectuate the decedent's presumed intent.

Special Types of Wills

There are a number of special types of wills. These include nuncupative wills, holographic wills, soldiers' and sailors' wills, conditional wills, joint and reciprocal wills, and living wills.

Nuncupative Wills A **nuncupative will** is an oral declaration made before witnesses without any writing. In the few jurisdictions where authorized, it can usually be made only when the testator is in his last illness. Under most statutes permitting nuncupative wills, only limited amounts of personal property, generally under $1,000, may be passed by such wills. Under the UPC, all wills must be in writing. Section 2–502.

Holographic Wills In a number of jurisdictions, a signed will *entirely* in the handwriting of the testator is a valid testamentary document even though the will is *not* witnessed. Under the UPC, Section 2–503 the signature and *material* provisions must be in the testator's handwriting. Such an instrument is referred to as a **holographic will.** A holographic will must comply strictly with the statutory requirements for such wills.

Soldiers' and Sailors' Wills In the case of soldiers on active service and sailors while at sea, most statutes relax the formal requirements and permit a valid testamentary dis-

position regardless of the informality of the document. In most jurisdictions, however, such a will cannot pass title to real estate.

Conditional Wills A contingent or conditional will is one that takes effect as a will only on the happening of a specified contingency, which is a *condition precedent* to the operation of the will.

Joint and Mutual or Reciprocal Wills A joint will is one where the same instrument is made the will of two or more persons and is signed by them jointly. Mutual or reciprocal wills are separate instruments with reciprocal terms made by two or more persons. Each testator makes a testamentary disposition in favor of the other.

Living Wills Almost all States have adopted statutes that permit an individual to execute a living will. A **living will** is a document that complies with the statutory requirements by which an individual states that she does not wish to receive extraordinary medical treatment in order to preserve her life. The effect of such a document is to reject the use of life prolonging procedures that artificially delay the dying process and permit the person to die naturally when the person has an incurable illness or injury.

Codicils

A **codicil** is a subsequent will that adds to or revises a prior will. Codicils must be executed with all the formal requirements of a will. The most frequent problem raised by codicils is the extent to which their terms, if not absolutely clear, revoke or alter provisions in the will. For the purpose of determining the testator's intent, the codicil and the will are regarded as a single instrument.

INTESTATE SUCCESSION

Property not effectively disposed of before death or by will passes in accordance with the law of intestate succession. The rules set forth in statutes for determining, in case of intestacy, to whom the decedent's property shall be distributed not only assure an orderly transfer of title to property but also purport to carry out what would probably be the wishes of the decedent. Nonetheless, the distribution of the estate is governed by the intestacy statute even if such distribution is contrary to the clear intention of the decedent. *See Ferguson v. Croom.*

The rules of descent vary widely from State to State, but as a general rule and except for the specific statutory or dower rights of the widow, the intestate property passes in equal shares to each child of the decedent living at the time of his death, with the share of any predeceased child to be divided equally among the children of such predeceased child. For example, if Arthur dies intestate leaving a widow and children, the widow will generally receive one-third of his real estate and personal property, and the remainder will pass to his children in the manner stated above. If the wife does not survive Arthur, his entire estate passes to the children. If Arthur dies leaving two surviving children, Belinda and Carl, and two grandchildren, Donna and David, the children of a predeceased child Darwin, the estate will go one-third to Belinda, one-third to Carl, and one-sixth each to Donna and David; the grandchildren dividing equally their parent's one-third share. This result is legally described by the statement that *lineal* descendants of predeceased children take **per stirpes,** or by representation of their parent. If Arthur had executed a will, he may have provided that all his lineal descendants, regardless of generation, would share equally. In that case, Arthur's estate would be divided into four equal parts, and his descendants would be said to take **per capita** (see Figure 52–3).

If no children but only the widow and other relatives survive the decedent, a larger share is generally allotted the widow. She may receive all the personal property and one-half the real estate or, in some States, the entire estate.

At common law, property could not lineally ascend; parents of an intestate decedent did not share in his estate. Today, in many States, if there are no lineal descendants or a surviving spouse, the statute provides that parents are the next to share.

Most statutes make some provision for brothers and sisters in the event no spouse, parents, or children survive the decedent.

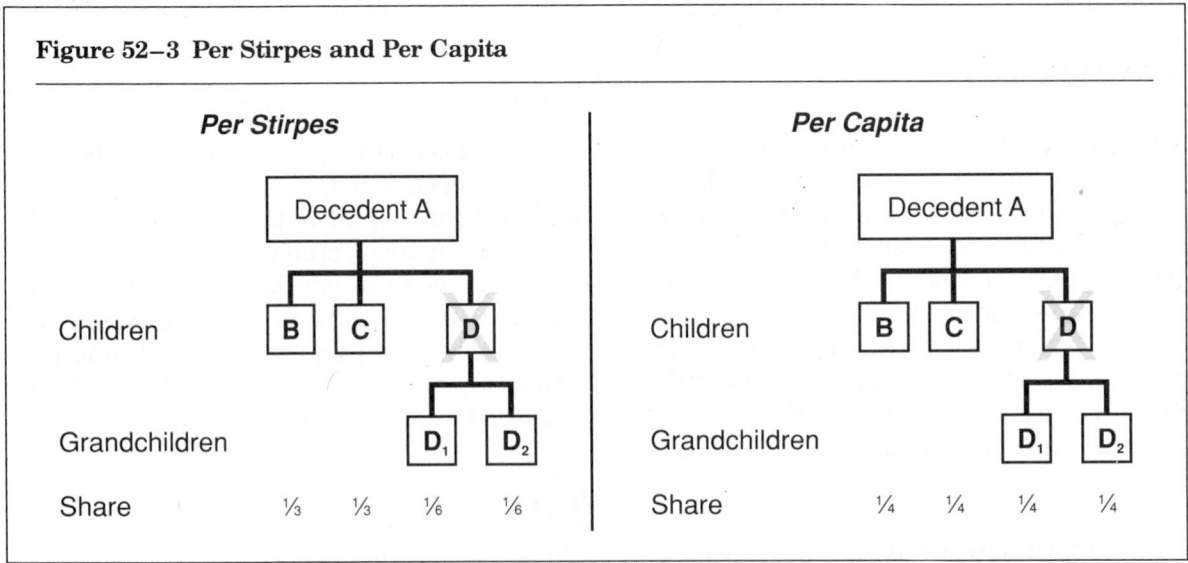

Figure 52–3 Per Stirpes and Per Capita

Per Stirpes				
Decedent A				
Children	B	C	D	
Grandchildren			D₁	D₂
Share	⅓	⅓	⅙	⅙

Per Capita				
Decedent A				
Children	B	C	D	
Grandchildren			D₁	D₂
Share	¼	¼	¼	¼

Brothers and sisters, together with nieces, nephews, aunts, and uncles, are termed *collateral* heirs. Beyond these limits, most statutes provide that, if there are no survivors of the named classes, the property shall be distributed equally among the next of kin in equal degree.

The common law did not consider a *stepchild* as an heir or next of kin, that is, as one to whom property would descend by operation of law, and this rule prevails today. Legally *adopted* children are, however, recognized as lawful heirs of their adopting parents.

These generalities should be accepted as such; few fields of the law of property are so strictly a matter of statute, and the rights of heirs cannot be reasonably predicted without a knowledge of the exact terms of the applicable statute.

Under the UPC, if the decedent dies without a will, the surviving spouse (1) is entitled to the entire estate if there is no issue and no parent surviving; (2) if there is a parent surviving, the spouse is entitled to $50,000 plus one-half of the remaining estate; (3) if there are surviving issue all of whom are issue also of the spouse, the spouse receives $50,000 plus one-half of the remaining estate; and (4) if there are surviving issue one or more of whom are not issue of the spouse, the spouse receives one-half of the estate.

ADMINISTRATION OF ESTATES

The rules and procedures controlling the management of the estate of a deceased are statutory and therefore vary in some respect from State to State. In all jurisdictions, the estate is managed and finally disbursed under the supervision of a court. The procedure of managing the distribution of decedents' estates is referred to as **probate**, and the court that supervises the procedure is often designated as the probate court.

The first legal step after death is usually to determine whether or not the deceased left a will. If a will exists, it is probable that the testator named her executor in it. If there is no will or if there is a will that fails to name an executor, the court will, upon petition, appoint an administrator. The closest adult relative who is a resident of the State is entitled to such appointment.

Once approved or appointed by the court, the **executor** or **administrator** holds title to all the personal property of the deceased and accounts to the creditors and the beneficiaries. The estate is his responsibility.

If there is a will, it must be proved before the court by the witnesses. They will testify to the signing of the will by all signatories and as to the mental condition of the testator at the time of the execution of the will. If the witnesses are dead, proof of their handwriting is necessary. If the court is satisfied that the will is proved, a formal decree will be entered admitting the will to probate.

Soon after the admission of the will to probate, the personal representative of the decedent—the executor or administrator—must file an inventory of the estate. The personal representative will then commence her duties of collecting the assets, paying the debts, and disbursing the remainder. The executor or administrator occupies a *fiduciary* position not unlike that of a trustee, and his responsibility for investing proceeds and otherwise managing the estate is equally demanding.

In the administration of every estate are probate expenses as well as fees to be paid to the executor or administrator and to the attorney who handles the estate. In addition, taxes are imposed at death by both the Federal and State governments. The Federal government imposes an **estate tax** on the transfer of property at death. Most State governments impose an **inheritance tax** on the privilege of an heir or beneficiary to receive the property. These taxes are separate and apart from the basic income tax that the estate must pay on income received during estate administration.

CASES

Constructive Trusts

SHARP v. KOSMALSKI

Court of Appeals of New York, 1976.
40 N.Y.2d 119, 386 N.Y.S.2d 72, 351 N.E.2d 721.

GABRIELLI, J.

Plaintiff commenced this action to impose a constructive trust upon property transferred to defendant on the ground that the retention of the property and the subsequent ejection of the plaintiff therefrom was in violation of a relationship of trust and confidence and constituted unjust enrichment. The Trial Judge dismissed plaintiff's complaint and his decision was affirmed without opinion by the Appellate Division.

Upon the death of his wife of 32 years, plaintiff, a 56-year-old dairy farmer whose education did not go beyond the eighth grade, developed a very close relationship with defendant, a school teacher and a woman 16 years his junior. Defendant assisted plaintiff in disposing of his wife's belongings, performed certain domestic tasks for him such as ironing his shirts and was a frequent companion of the plaintiff. Plaintiff came to depend upon defendant's companionship and, eventually, declared his love for her, proposing marriage to her. Notwithstanding her refusal of his proposal of marriage, defendant continued her association with plaintiff and permitted him to shower her with many gifts, fanning his hope that he could induce defendant to alter her decision concerning his marriage proposal. Defendant was given access to plaintiff's bank account, from which it is not denied that she withdrew substantial amounts of money. Eventually, plaintiff made a will naming defendant as his sole beneficiary and executed a deed naming her a joint owner of his farm. The record reveals that numerous alterations in the way of modernization were made to plaintiff's farmhouse in alleged furtherance of "domestic plans" made by plaintiff and defendant.

In September 1971 while the renovations were still in progress, plaintiff transferred his remaining joint interest to defendant. At the time of the conveyance, a farm liability policy was issued to plaintiff naming defendant and her daughter as additional insureds. Furthermore, the insurance agent was requested by plaintiff, in the presence of defendant, to change the policy to read "J. Rodney Sharp, life tenant. Jean C. Kosmalski, owner." In February 1973 the liaison between the parties was abruptly severed as defendant ordered plaintiff to move out of his home and vacate the farm. Defendant took possession of the home, the farm, and all the equipment thereon, leaving plaintiff with assets of $300.

Generally, a constructive trust may be imposed "[w]hen property has been acquired in such circumstances that the holder of the legal title may not in good conscience retain the beneficial interest" [citation]. In the development of the doctrine of constructive trust as a remedy available to courts of equity, the following four requirements were posited: (1) a confidential or fiduciary relation, (2) a promise, (3) a transfer in reliance thereon and (4) unjust enrichment. [Citations.]

Most frequently, it is the existence of a confidential relationship which triggers the equitable considerations leading to the imposition of a constructive trust. [Citation.] Although no marital or other family relationship is present in this case, such is not essential for the existence of a confidential relation. [Citations.] The record in this case clearly indicates that a relationship of trust and confidence did exist between the parties and, hence, the defendant must be charged with an obligation not to abuse the trust and confidence placed in her by the plaintiff. The disparity in education between the plaintiff and defendant highlights the degree of dependence of the plaintiff upon the trust and honor of the defendant.

Unquestionably, there is a transfer of property here, but the Trial Judge found that the transfer was made "without a promise or understanding of any kind." Even without an express promise, however, courts of equity have imposed a constructive trust upon property transferred in reliance upon a confidential relationship. In such a situation, a promise may be implied or inferred from the very transaction itself. As Judge Cardozo so eloquently observed: "Though a promise in words was lacking, the whole transaction, it might be found, was 'instinct with an obligation' imperfectly expressed." [Citations.] In deciding that a formal writing or express promise was not essential to the application of the doctrine of constructive trust, Judge Cardozo further observed in language that is most fitting in the instant case:

"Here was a man transferring to his sister the only property he had in the world. * * * He was doing this, as she admits, in reliance upon her honor. Even if we were to accept her statement that there was no distinct promise to hold for his benefit, the exaction of such a promise, in view of the relation, might well have seemed to be superfluous" [citation].

* * *

Indeed in the case before us, it is inconceivable that plaintiff would convey all of his interest in property which was not only his abode but the very means of his livelihood without at least tacit consent upon the part of the defendant that she would permit him to continue to live on and operate the farm. I would therefore reject the Trial Judge's conclusion, erroneously termed a finding of fact, that no agreement or limitation may, as a matter of law, be implied from the circumstances surrounding the transfer of plaintiff's farm.

The statutory purpose of the constructive trust remedy is to prevent unjust enrichment and it is to this requirement that I now turn. The Trial Judge in his findings of fact, concluded that the transfer did not constitute unjust enrichment. In this instance also, a legal conclusion was mistakenly labeled a finding of fact. A person may be deemed to be unjustly enriched if he (or she) has received a benefit, the retention of which would be unjust (Restatement, Restitution, § 1, Comment a). A conclusion that one has been unjustly enriched is essentially a legal inference drawn from the circumstances surrounding the transfer of property and the relationship of the parties. It is a conclusion reached through the application of principles of equity. Having determined that the relationship between plaintiff and defendant in this case is of such a nature as to invoke consideration of the equitable remedy of constructive trust, it remains to be determined whether defendant's conduct following the transfer of plaintiff's farm was in violation of that relationship and, consequently, resulted in the unjust enrichment of the defendant. This must be determined from the circumstances of the transfer since there is no express promise concerning plaintiff's continued use of the land. Therefore, the case should be remitted to the Appellate Division for a review of the facts. In so doing I would emphasize that the conveyance herein should be interpreted "not literally or irrespective of its setting, but sensibly and broadly with all its human implications." [Citation.] This case seems to present the classic example of a situation where equity should intervene to scrutinize a transaction pregnant with opportunity for abuse and unfairness. It was for just this type of case that there evolved equitable principles and remedies to prevent injustices. Equity still lives. To suffer the hands of equity to be bound by misnamed "findings of fact" which are actually conclusions of law and legal inferences drawn from the facts is to ignore and render impotent the rich and vital impact of equity on the common law and, perforce, permit injustice. Universality of law requires equity.

Accordingly, the order of the Appellate Division should be reversed and the case remitted to that court for a review of the facts, or, if it be so advised, in its discretion, to order a new trial in the interests of justice.

Duties of the Trustee

WITMER v. BLAIR

Missouri Court of Appeals, Western District, 1979.
588 S.W.2d 222.

WELBORN, J.

Plaintiffs, beneficiaries of a testamentary trust, filed a two-count action against defendant trustee, seeking an accounting, removal of the trustee, and actual and punitive damages for breach of fiduciary duties. After trial to the court, the court ordered an accounting and removal of the defendant as trustee and entered judgment against defendant for $309 for unaccounted-for funds but found against plaintiffs on their claim for damages for breach of fiduciary duties. Plaintiffs appeal from this portion of the decree.

By his Last Will and Testament, Henry F. Nussbaum made a residual bequest and devise of his estate to his niece, Jane Ann Blair, as trustee, "in Trust however, for the education of my grandchildren (children of my daughter, Dorothy Janice Witmer) living at the time of my decease, or born within a period of nine months thereafter." In the event that none of his grandchildren survived to inherit the estate, the residue would revert to plaintiff Dorothy Janice Witmer, his daughter and first cousin of defendant trustee.

Nussbaum died in 1960. The trust estate came into the hands of the trustee in 1961. It consisted of $1,905 in checking and savings accounts, $5,700 in certificates of deposit, and a house valued at $6,000.00. The house was sold in 1962, netting $4,467 to the trust estate. That amount was deposited in a trust checking account. In 1963, $2,000 in certificates of deposit were acquired by the trust and $500 was so invested in 1964. As of December 31, 1970, the trust fund assets consisted of $5,847 in checking account, $506 in savings account, and $8,200 in certificates of deposit. In 1971 and 1972, the checking account balance was reduced by transfers to the savings account and on December 31, 1975, the trust assets consisted of $2,741 checking account, $5,474 savings account, and $8,200 certificates of deposit.

Plaintiff-appellant Marguerite Janice Witmer was the only grandchild of the testator who became a beneficiary of the trust. She was born September 3, 1953. At the time of the trial, she was 23 years of age. She had not attended a college or university. However, various sums of money had been expended from the trust for her benefit, including a typewriter, clothes, glasses, modeling school tuition and expenses, and a tonsillectomy. These expenditures totalled some $1,225.00. The trust also provided $350 for dentures for the mother, Dorothy Witmer.

The trust was handled by appellant rather informally. She kept no books for the trust. The expenditures above mentioned were in most cases advanced by her from her personal account and she reimbursed herself from the trust income. In 1965, the bank erroneously credited the trust account with $560 which should have gone to the trustee's personal account. The mistake was not corrected and that amount remained in the trust account. The trustee received no compensation for her services. Asked at the trial whether she had ever been a trustee before, she responded negatively, adding: "And never again." She explained the large checking account balances in the trust account by the fact that college for Janice "was talked about all the way through high school. . . . [I]n my opinion it was the sensible way to keep the money where I could get it to her without any problems at all in case she needed it quickly."

An accountant testified for plaintiffs that if the sum of $800 had been kept in the checking and savings accounts (the $800 was based upon the maximum disbursement in any year) and the balance of the trust placed in one-year certificates of deposit, $9,138 more interest would have been earned as of September 30, 1976, from the trust estate than had been received under respondent's handling of the trust.

* * *

In this court, appellants contend that the respondent as trustee was bound to comply with the directions of the trust that she "invest the principal and reinvest the same" and that her failure to invest the trust corpus constituted a breach of her fiduciary duty for which she is liable. The respondent answers that inasmuch as the will failed to specify when and what investments were to be made, such matters were left to the discretion of the trustee and that she exercised such discretion honestly, with ordinary prudence and within the limits of the trust and is not liable for damages.

A concise summary of the law applicable in this situation appears in [citation]:

"It is a general power and duty of a trustee, implied if not expressed, at least in the case of an ordinary trust, to keep trust funds properly invested. Having uninvested funds in his hands, it is his duty to make investments of them, where at least they are not soon to be applied to the purposes and objects or turned over to the beneficiaries of the trust. Generally, he cannot permit trust funds to lie dormant or on deposit for a prolonged period, but he may keep on hand a fund sufficient to meet expenses, including contingent expenses, and he need not invest a sum too small to be prudently invested. A trustee ordinarily may not say in excuse of a failure to invest that he kept the funds on hand to pay the beneficiaries on demand."

"The trustee is under a duty to the beneficiary to use reasonable care and skill to make the trust property productive." Restatement (Second) of Trusts § 181 (1959). Comment c to this section states:

"*Money.* In the case of money, it is normally the duty of the trustee to invest it so that it will produce an income. The trustee is liable if he fails to invest trust funds which it is his duty to invest for a period which is under all the circumstances unreasonably long. If, however, the delay is not unreasonable, he is not liable."

"A breach of trust is a violation by the trustee of any duty which as trustee he owes to the beneficiary." Restatement (Second) of Trusts § 201 (1959). Comment b to this section states:

"*Mistake of law as to existence of duties and powers.* A trustee commits a breach of trust not only where he violates a duty in bad faith, or intentionally although in good faith, or negligently, but also where he violates a duty because of a mistake as to the extent of his duties and powers. This is true not only where his mistake is in regard to a rule of law, whether a statutory or common-law rule, but also where he interprets the trust instrument as authorizing him to do acts which the court determines he is not authorized by the instrument to do. In such case, he is not protected from liability merely because he acts in good faith, nor is he protected merely because he relies upon the advice of counsel. [Citation.] If he is in doubt as to the interpretation of the instrument, he can protect himself by obtaining instructions from the court. The extent of his duties and powers is determined by the trust instrument and the rules of law which are applicable, and not by his own interpretation of the instrument or his own belief as to the rules of law."

Under the above rules, there has been a breach of trust by the trustee in this case and her good faith is not a defense to appellants' claim.

* * *

The accountant who testified for appellants calculated that between the opening of the Trust and 1971, when college for Marguerite would have been a realistic possibility, had the trust funds, in excess of $100 checking account and approximately $800–1,000 savings account, been invested in one-year certificates of deposit, the trust would have earned additional interest of $2,840.00. In view of the trustee's transfer of a substantial portion of the checking account balance to savings in 1971 and 1972 and in view of the relatively small difference between the return from savings and what might have been earned from certificates of deposit ($\frac{1}{2}$ % to $1\frac{1}{2}$ %), no damages should be assessed against the trustee for the handling of the estate during that period. However, the trustee should be held liable for the $2,840 which, according to the measure of damages, invoked by appellants, might have been earned by investment of the trust between 1962 and 1971.

Conduct Invalidating a Will/Signature

IN RE ESTATE OF HOBELSBERGER

Supreme Court of South Dakota, 1970.
181 N.W.2d 455.

RENTTO, J.

John Hobelsberger died on July 19, 1967, survived by 27 nieces and nephews and seven grandnieces and grandnephews, his only heirs. In this proceeding the validity of a will which he executed on November 22, 1966, is challenged by nine nieces and nephews. Its admission to probate was sought by his designated executor.

The will in question, after providing for the payment of debts and funeral expenses, left the remainder of his estate to Phyllis Raml, a grandniece. In the event that she did not survive him the property was to go to her husband, Ralph Raml, who was also named executor. If neither of these survived the testator, it would then go to their son Thomas. His estate consisted of 160 acres of farm land in Codington County, South Dakota, appraised at $7,500 and cash, bonds and miscellaneous personal property valued at approximately $9,400.

The challenge of the contestants was based on the following grounds: (1) lack of testamentary capacity; (2) undue influence on the part of the Ramls; and (3) improper execution. The county court, without a jury, held a hearing on the matters in issue and made findings of fact favorable to the proponent and admitted the will to probate. From this the contestants appealed to the circuit court. After hearing testimony for three days and considering the briefs of both parties, the court made similar findings and entered judgment dismissing the appeal and affirming the order of the county court. This appeal is from that judgment.

The testator at the time of executing the will in question was 80 years of age. He had never married and lived alone on his farm near Kranzburg, South Dakota. He had resided in the same general area all of his life. The Ramls lived on and operated a farm about two miles from his. The had made their home there since 1950. Over the years they rented a portion of his farm and for about five years before his death they rented it all, but he continued to reside on it. During these years they pretty much looked after him. Their relations with him seem to have been friendly and cordial and their visits with each other rather frequent. During late years the other heirs had not lived in as close proximity to him nor have they been with him as often as the Ramls.

While attending church on Sunday, October 23, 1966, he became ill during the service and was taken to the St. Ann's hospital in Watertown, South Dakota, by Mr. Raml. It was thought that he had a heart attack. On October 24th he became the patient of Doctor Brevick who diagnosed his indisposition as intermittent cerebral insufficiency. He remained there until November 19th, when he was transferred to the Burgdorf Nursing Home in the same city. During his hospitalization he told the Ramls that he wanted to see an attorney about some legal matters and the preparation of a will. He did not indicate any particular attorney, but suggested that they ask their lawyer to call on him. After several requests they mentioned the matter to Thomas Green who had acted as their attorney.

About a week later Mr. Green went to the hospital and interviewed the testator. This was about the 10th of November. After discussing some apparent defects in the title to his farm which he wanted corrected, the testator told the attorney what provisions he wanted in his will. Their discussion lasted about 45 minutes. After the completion of the interview the attorney returned to his office, with his notes, and prepared a will in compliance with his instructions. About the 17th of November he took the will to the hospital. Because testator's brother, who later predeceased him, was in the same room as a patient it was not discussed or executed. Soon after his transfer to the nursing home he sent word by the Ramls that he wanted to see the attorney about his will.

On November 22nd the attorney and a secretary went to the nursing home. The Ramls were there visiting the testator. They had not known that the will was to be signed that day. It was read to him by the lawyer, after which he indicated that it was the way he wanted it. The testator subscribed it with his mark in the presence of the attorney and secretary as attesting witnesses. It was then taken to the lawyer's office where it remained until after the testator's death. * * *

That the testator was aged and infirm when he executed the will is not questioned. * * *

The matter in issue is the condition of [the testator's] mind when the will was executed. One may be physically weak and aged and still possess a sound mind. [Citation.]

* * *

It was for the trial judge to select from the conflicting evidence that which he would believe. He, not this court, is the trier of the facts. Obviously he chose the proponent's version. From it he found that on the date of executing the will in question "the said John Hobelsberger was of sound and disposing mind and memory, competent and had testamentary capacity to execute a Last Will and Testament." Contestants challenge this finding. On review the successful party is entitled to the benefit of his version of the evidence, and of all favorable inferences fairly deducible therefrom. [Citation.]

* * *

In support of their claim of undue influence the contestants urge that the disposition made by the will is unnatural. If it is subject to reasonable explanation even though apparently unnatural, it becomes understandable. [Citations.] Accepting the evidence of the proponent, the will merely prefers a grandniece and her husband who have been helpful to him during the years when he had need of such concern. [Citation.] Such recognition is not necessarily improper.

What could be more natural in view of his feeling that he did not have enough to remember all of his heirs? Moreover, his nieces, nephews, grandnieces, and grandnephews because of such relationship alone, are not the natural objects of his bounty. [Citation.] Our law does not require that a testator rec-

ognize his relatives equally or at all. [Citation.] In any event it is only a circumstance to be considered with the other evidence bearing on the issue. [Citation.]

Contestants seize on the fact that the Ramls had a motive and the opportunity to exert an undue influence on the testator. These factors alone are not sufficient to invalidate the will. To accomplish that result there must be evidence that they did exert such influence. [Citations.] Here there is none. That the Ramls were provided for in the will and had an opportunity to influence him does not prove that they did. [Citations.] Nor is it alone sufficient to warrant an inference of undue influence. [Citation.]

* * *

They also urge that between the Ramls and the testator there existed a confidential relationship which has a bearing on this issue. Such relationship exists whenever trust and confidence is reposed by the testator in the integrity and fidelity of another. [Citations.] Even if the relationship between them rose to that level, which appears doubtful, it would not require a finding of undue influence nor raise a presumption of such which the beneficiary has the burden of disproving. Its existence, however, may demand close judicial scrutiny and is another item for the court to ponder in deciding the issue. [Citation.]

* * *

In subscribing the will testator did so with a mark. [A South Dakota statute] provides:

" 'Signature or subscription' includes mark, when the person cannot write, his name being written near such mark, and written by a person who writes his own name as a witness;"

It appears that he was a person who was able to write and had signed checks before and after the execution of the will with the help of Mrs. Raml. It is fair to infer that at earlier times he had been able to do so without any help. Contestants argue that because of this he is not one authorized to sign with a mark. It is their only complaint as to the execution of the instrument. This we think is a too restricted view of our statute.

* * *

It appears that at the time of subscribing the will the testator said he could not write because he had trouble with his hands. That this was so becomes apparent on examination of the checks that he had attempted to sign, with the help of others, shortly before and after that occasion. It follows the trial court did not err in holding that the will under attack had been validly executed.

Revocation of a Will

BARKSDALE v. PENDERGRASS

Supreme Court of Alabama, 1975.
294 Ala. 526, 319 So.2d 267.

MERRILL, J.

Mrs. Mamie C. Henry, a widow, died on October 18, 1972. She had no children, but was survived by a number of nieces and nephews.

No duly executed will was found and Joe Barksdale, a nephew of Mrs. Henry, was appointed administrator of her estate.

Later, Rita Jan Pendergrass, formerly Rita Jan Gray, filed a petition in the Probate Court of DeKalb County to probate an alleged lost or destroyed will of Mamie C. Henry. A copy of the will was made an exhibit to the petition. According to its terms, Mrs. Henry left all of her property to Rita Jan Gray and appointed her as executrix.

Joe Barksdale and Olen Barksdale filed a contest and the case was transferred to the circuit court, where it was tried before a jury. The grounds of the contest were that the purported will was never duly executed, or, that if executed, was destroyed by Mrs. Henry prior to her death.

The jury found in favor of the proponent, Rita Jan Gray Pendergrass. Judgment was entered ordering the will admitted to probate.

* * *

In a proceeding to probate an alleged lost or destroyed will, the burden is on the proponent to establish, to the reasonable satisfaction of the judge or jury trying the facts:

(1) The existence of a will—an instrument in writing, signed by the testator or some person in his presence, and by his direction, and attested by at least two witnesses, who must subscribe their names thereto in the presence of the testator. [Citations.]

* * *

(3) The nonrevocation of the instrument by the testator. [Citations.]
(4) The contents of the will in substance and effect. [Citations.]

The first question then is whether there was a validly executed will. It is not necessary that the attestation be at the personal request of the testator. It is sufficient if done in testator's presence with his knowledge and consent expressed or implied. [Citations.]

The testator does not have to tell the subscribing witnesses that the instrument is his will, or to inform them of its contents. [Citations.]

It is not necessary for the witnesses to actually see the testator sign his name. [Citations.] The testator may acknowledge to the subscribing witnesses that it is his signature on the instrument by his express words or by implication from his conduct and from the surrounding circumstances. [Citations.]

* * *

The evidence produced at trial showed that Charles M. Scott, a Ft. Payne attorney, prepared a will for Mrs. Henry in November of 1963. She did not execute the will in Scott's office because she wanted to "get her own witnesses" in Collinsville where she lived. Scott subsequently made several minor changes in the will and mailed her a final version in January of 1964. Rita Jan Gray [Pendergrass] was named a beneficiary in every version of the will.

The evidence also showed that sometime around 1964, Bill Cook, Jack Farmer and Cecil Sharp met at Sharp's funeral home and witnessed Mrs. Henry's signature on a document. The testimony adduced at trial indicated that there was some doubt as to whether each of the witnesses knew that the document was a will. Jack Farmer was deceased at the time of the trial. Witness Bill Cook thought that Mrs. Henry mentioned that the document was a will at some time, but Cecil Sharp could only say that Mrs. Henry wanted him to witness a signature. Nevertheless it is apparent that the requirements of [citation], were met since both Cook and Sharp witnessed a signature which Mrs. Henry acknowledged as her own.

The second thing which the proponent must prove is the loss or destruction of the instrument. Billy McDowell, who rented an apartment from Mrs. Henry between 1967 and 1969, testified that Mrs. Henry showed him a will; that she said Charles M. Scott prepared it, that Cecil Sharp's name was on the will as a witness, and that Rita Jan Gray [Pendergrass] was the sole beneficiary. He also said that Mrs. Henry kept the will in a purse under a mattress in a spare room. Floyd Gray, the father of the beneficiary, testified that he saw one of Mrs. Henry's nephews at her house shortly after her death. Willard Reaves, an employee of the funeral home, testified that several of Mrs. Henry's relatives visited her house that day after she died. There was also an abundance of testimony that the will might have been lost or destroyed by accident. Finally, attorney Scott testified that several weeks after Mrs. Henry's death he searched the house himself. Proponent Rita Jan Gray Pendergrass subsequently filed an application to compel production of the will. Appellant Barksdale responded "That the said purported will, if executed, has been destroyed prior to the death of the Testatrix, and was not found in her possession nor among has [sic] effects at the time of her death, and is presumed, if ever executed, to have been destroyed in accordance with law."

The third element of proof involved the presumption of revocation. When the will is shown to have been in the possession of the testator, and is not found at his death, the presumption arises that he destroyed it for the purpose of revocation; but the presumption may be rebutted, and the burden of rebutting it is on the proponent. [Citations.]

Billy McDowell, attorney Scott, and Mildred Johnson, a former neighbor of Mrs. Henry, testified that Mrs. Henry said that she did not want her nieces and nephews to have anything she had; that she had always made it abundantly clear that she wanted to select somebody other than her nieces and nephews; that she was afraid they were going to get her property; that she knew that her nieces and nephews would get her property if she died intestate; that she wanted Rita to have it, and that this was her fixed opinion.

Finally, proponent offered the copy of the will in evidence as proof of its contents.

A jury question was adequately presented . . . and the jury found for the proponent.

* * *

In the instant case, Billy McDowell testified that Mrs. Henry showed him her will; that he remembered seeing Cecil Sharp's signature; and that Mrs. Henry told him that attorney Scott had written the will, and that Rita Jan Gray was her sole beneficiary. It would appear that there was sufficient evidence from which to identify the copy.

* * *

Affirmed.

Intestate Succession

FERGUSON v. CROOM

Court of Appeals of North Carolina, 1985.
73 N.C.App. 316, 326 S.E.2d 373.

ARNOLD, J.

On 21 June 1983, George Washington Croom died testate. In his will Croom left various bequests of real and personal property to his children and a grandchild. In Item Eight of his will Croom stated "I leave nothing whatsoever to my daughter Kathryn Elizabeth Turner, and my son Ernest Edward Croom." At his death, Croom also left three optional share certificates in Carolina Savings & Loan Association issued to George W. Croom or Kimberly Joyce Croom, the deceased's minor daughter. Each of these certificates had attached to it an "Agreement Concerning Stock in Carolina Savings and Loan Association" which purported to create a joint account with a right of survivorship. Two of these agreements were signed by George Croom only and the third agreement was not signed at all. None of these certificates were specifically devised by Croom's will and the will contained no residuary clause. The plaintiff by this action seeks a determination as to who is entitled to share in these assets. [Kimberly Croom contends the certificates pass to her by right of survivorship.]

* * *

By their appeal, Ernest Edward Croom and Kathryn Elizabeth Turner contend the court erred by concluding that they were not to share in the property which passed by partial intestacy because the deceased's will evidenced an intent that they should be disinherited. We agree, therefore, we reverse.

[North Carolina statute] states: "If part but not all of the estate of a decedent is validly disposed of by his will, the part not disposed of by such will *shall* descend and *be distributed as intestate property.*" [This statute] creates a mandatory plan for disposing of a decedent's property which does not pass by will. It directs that the property pass by intestate succession without regard to the intent expressed by a testator in a will. The statute, which was adopted in 1959, was a codification of our common law. [Citation] (where our Supreme Court held that property not disposed of by will passes as directed by the law regardless of attempts by the testator to disinherit the lawful takers). The rule adopted by [the Statute] is also in accordance with the rule followed by a majority of our sister states. [Citation.]

Under the Intestate Succession Act each of testator's children is entitled to take an equal share of the property not disposed of by his will. [Citation.] Thus, the trial court erred in excluding Kathryn Elizabeth Turner and Ernest Edward Croom from taking a share of the intestate property. The judgment of the court is reversed and the case is remanded for the entry of judgment consistent with this opinion.

Reversed.

QUESTIONS

1. Define the following types of trusts: (a) express, (b) charitable, (c) spendthrift, (d) totten, (e) implied, (f) constructive, and (g) resulting.

2. Describe the powers and duties of a trustee.

3. Discuss the formal requirements of making a valid will and the various ways in which a will may be revoked.

4. Define the following types of wills: (a) nuncupative, (b) holographic, (c) soldiers' and sailors', (d) conditional, (e) joint, and (f) reciprocal.

5. Discuss intestate succession.

PROBLEMS

1. State whether or not a trust is created in each of the following situations.

(a) A declares herself trustee of "the bulk of my securities" in trust for B.

(b) A, the owner of Blackacre, purports to convey to B in trust for C "a small part" of Blackacre.

(c) A orders B, a stockbroker, to buy 2,000 shares of American Steel or any part thereof at $20 per share. After the broker has bought 500 shares but before A knows whether any shares have been bought for him, A declares himself trustee for C of such shares of American Steel as B has bought.

(d) A owns ten bonds. He declares himself trustee for B of such five of the bonds as B may select at any time within a month.

(e) A deposits $1,000 in a savings bank. He declares himself trustee of the deposit in trust to pay B $500 out of the deposit, reserving the power to withdraw from the deposit any amounts not in excess of $500.

2. Testator gives property to Tim in trust for Barney's benefit, providing that Barney cannot anticipate the income by assignment or pledge. Barney borrows money from Linda, assigning his future income under the trust for a stated period. Can Linda obtain any judicial relief to prevent Barney from collecting this income?

3. Collins was trustee for Indolent under the will of Indolent's father. Indolent, a middle-aged doctor, gave little concern to the management of the trust fund, contenting himself with receiving the income paid him by the trustee. Among the assets of the trust were 100 shares of ABC Corporation and 100 shares of XYZ Corporation. About two years before the termination of the trust Collins, at a fair price and after full explanation to Indolent, purchased from the trust the ABC stock. At the same time but without saying anything to Indolent, he purchased the XYZ stock at a price in excess of its then market value. At the termination of the trust, both stocks had advanced in market value well beyond the prices paid by Collins, and Indolent demanded that Collins either account for this advance in the value of both stocks or replace the stocks. What are Indolent's rights?

4. On September 1, 1980, Joe Brown gave to his wife, Mary Brown, $35,000 with which to buy real property. They orally agreed that title to the real property should be taken in the name of Mary Brown but that she should hold the property in trust for Joe Brown. There were two witnesses to the oral agreement, both of whom are still living. Mary purchased the property on September 2, and a deed to it with Mary Brown as the grantee was delivered.

Mary died on October 5, 1990, without a will. The real property is now worth $100,000. Joe Brown is claiming the property as the beneficiary of a trust. Mary's children are claiming that the property belongs to Mary's estate and have pleaded the statute of limitations and the statute of frauds as defenses to the claim of Joe. There is no evidence one way or the other as to whether Mary would have conveyed the property to Joe during her lifetime if she had been requested to do so.

What are Joe's ownership rights to this particular real property?

5. John Carver executed his will on March 10, 1991, which was witnessed by William Hobson and Sam Witt. By his will, Carver devised his farm, Stonecrest, to his nephew Roy White. The residue of his estate was given to his sister Florence Carver.

A codicil to his will executed April 15, 1991, provided that $5,000 be given to Carver's niece Mary Jordan, and $5,000 to Wanda White, Roy White's wife. The codicil was witnessed by Roy White and Harold Brown. John Carver died September 1, 1991, and the will and codicil were admitted to probate.

How should Carver's estate be distributed?

6. Edwin Fuller, a bachelor, prepared his will in his office. The will, which contained no residuary clause, provided that one-third of his estate would go to his nephew Tom Fuller, one-third to the City of Emanon to be used for park improvements, and one-third to his brother Kurt.

He signed the will in his office and then went to the office of his nephew, Tom Fuller, who, at Edwin's request, signed the will as a witness. Since no other persons were available in Tom's office, Edwin then went to the bank where Frank Cash, the cashier, at Edwin's request, also signed as a witness. In each instance Edwin stated that he had signed the document but did not state that it was his will.

Edwin returned to his office where he placed the will in his safe. Subsequently, Edwin died, survived by Kurt, his only heir-at-law. How should the estate be distributed?

7. Arnold executed a one-page will, in which he devised his farm to Burton. Later, as the result of a quarrel with Burton, Arnold wrote the words, "I hereby cancel and revoke this will /s/Arnold," in the margin of the will but did not destroy the will. Arnold then executed a deed to the farm, naming Connie as grantee, and placed the deed and will in his safe. Shortly afterwards, Arnold married Donna, with whom he had one child, Ernest. Thereafter, Arnold died, and the deed and will were found in his safe. Burton, Connie, and Ernest claim the farm, and Donna claims dower. Discuss the validity of each claim.

8. John Walker, a widower, died testate. His will, in part, provided:

"I give and bequeath my piano to my daughter Nancy. I give and bequeath to my daughter Jennifer the sum of $1,000. I give and bequeath to my son John the sum of $1,000 to be paid out of my account at the Tenth National Bank in the city of Erehwon. All the rest and residue of my estate I give to Nancy, Jennifer, and John, share and share alike."

After the will was executed, Walker sold his piano for $2,300 and deposited the proceeds in the Citizens Bank of Erehwon. He withdrew the money he had on deposit in the Tenth National Bank and purchased a new automobile.

At the time of his death, Walker had no debts. The account in the Citizens Bank of Erehwon had a balance of $2,300, which constituted his entire net estate after all expenses of administration were paid. How should Walker's estate be distributed?

9. The validly executed will of John Dane contained the following provision: "I give and devise to my daughter Mary, Redacre for and during her natural life and, at her death, the remainder to go to Wilmore College." The will also provided that the residue of his estate should go to Wilmore College. Thereafter, Dane sold Redacre and then added a validly executed codicil to his will, "Due to the fact that I have sold Redacre which I previously gave to my daughter Mary, I now give and devise Blackacre to Mary in place and instead of Redacre."

Another clause of the codicil provided: "I give my one-half interest in the oil business, which I own in common with William Steele to my son, Henry." Subsequently, Dane acquired all of the interest in the oil business from his partner, Steele,

and, at the time of his death, Dane owned the entire oil business. The will and codicil have been admitted to probate.

(a) What interest, if any, does Mary acquire in Blackacre?

(b) What interest, if any, does Henry acquire in the oil business?

10. Leonard Wolfe was killed in an automobile accident while driving his 1969 Buick Electra automobile. The car was rendered a total loss, and Wolfe's insurance carrier paid his estate $3,550 for damage to the vehicle. Under the terms of Wolfe's will, any car owned at his death was to be given to his brother, David. Wolfe's daughter, Carol, however, brought an action, claiming that the gift of the car to David was adeemed by its total destruction and that she, as the residuary legatee under the will, was entitled to the insurance proceeds. Decision?

11. In April 1961, Grace Peterson, a spinster then aged seventy-four, asked Chester Gustafson, a Minneapolis attorney, to draw a will for her. Gustafson, who had also probated Peterson's sister's estate, drew this first will and six subsequent wills and codicils free of charge because he claimed that she had no money to pay for his services. Over the five-year period during which Gustafson redrew Peterson's will, an increasing amount of property was devised to Gustafson's children until the seventh will, when Peterson's entire estate was so devised. Peterson, however, hardly knew the children except from several chance encounters ten years before. She died on February 1, 1966, without ever having changed the seventh will, and Gustafson, who was named as executor, now seeks to have the will admitted to probate. Decision?

Chapter 53

INSURANCE

Life Insurance
Property Insurance
Other Kinds of Insurance
Nature of Insurance Contracts

INSURANCE covers a vast range of contracts each of which distributes *risk* among a large number of members (the **insured**) through an insurance company (the **insurer**). **Insurance** is a contractual undertaking by the insurer to pay a sum of money or give something of value to the insured or a beneficiary upon the happening of a contingency or fortuitous event that is beyond the control of the contracting parties.

It is impossible to name a commercial activity not affected by insurance coverage of one form or another. Tangible assets of a business can be protected by insurance protecting it against almost any form of damage or destruction, whether from natural causes or from the accidental or improper actions of another. Insurance may also protect a business from tort liability that may be asserted against it including strict liability, negligence, or the intentional act of its representatives. A business may procure credit insurance to protect against losses from poor credit risks and fidelity bonds to protect it against losses incurred through defalcations of employees. If a business hires a famous pianist, it may insure the latter's hands; if it decides to present an outdoor concert, it may insure

against the possibility of rain. A business may purchase life insurance on its key executives to reimburse it for the financial loss arising from their deaths, or it may purchase such life insurance payable to the families of the executives as part of compensation. An additional development of growing importance is the use of insurance to carry out pension commitments arising from bargaining agreements with unions.

The McCarran-Ferguson Act, enacted by Congress in 1945, left the regulation of insurance to the States. Each State has its own statutes that regulate its domestic insurance companies and also set forth standards that foreign (out-of-State) insurance companies must meet if they wish to do business within the State. Most State legislation relates to the incorporation, licensing, supervision, and liquidation of insurers and to the licensing and supervision of agents and brokers.

Because the insurance relationship arises from a contract of insurance between the insurer and the insured, the law of insurance is a branch of contract law. For this reason, the doctrines of offer and acceptance, consideration, and other rules applicable to contracts in general are equally applicable to insurance contracts. Beyond that, however, insurance law, like the law of sales, bailments, negotiable instruments, or other specialized types of contracts, contains numerous modifications of fundamental contract law with which this chapter is concerned.

KINDS OF INSURANCE

There are many kinds of insurance and many kinds of insurance policies. Although the listing that follows is not complete, it contains the most common kinds of insurance.

Life Insurance

Life insurance might be more accurately called "death insurance," since it is a contract by the terms of which the insurer will pay a specified sum of money upon the death of the insured, provided the required premiums have been paid. Most life insurance policies exclude from coverage death that results from a suicide. The payment is made either to a named beneficiary, ordinarily a third-party donee or creditor, or to the estate of the deceased. The naming of a beneficiary is a privilege of the *owner* of the policy, but unless the right to do so is reserved in the policy, the owner has no right to change the beneficiary. Most modern policies, as part of the standard form, reserve to the owner of the policy the express right to change beneficiaries. One person may occupy one or more of these three roles (insured, owner, and beneficiary) or each may be held by a different party. Life insurance includes a number of different types of coverage.

Whole Life Whole life insurance is both a form of insurance and a form of savings or investment because the insured has a right to borrow from the insurer an amount not to exceed the **cash surrender value** of the policy, which value increases the longer the policy is in force. Such a loan generally bears a low interest rate and is secured by an assignment to the insurer of the policy proceeds to the extent necessary to pay the loan in the

event of death, with the remainder going to the beneficiary.

Ordinary life or **straight life** insurance is designed to run for the entire life of the insured and requires the payment of premiums until the insured's death or until the insured reaches a predetermined age. **Limited payment** life policies require the payment of premiums only for a fixed number of years, thus eliminating the duty of paying premiums through the later years of life when such payments may be burdensome. With **single-premium** life insurance, the entire premium is prepaid in one lump sum.

Term Life Term life insurance is issued for a limited period of time, with premiums payable during the period of coverage. The insurance proceeds are paid only if the insured dies within the specified time period. Term insurance, moreover, does not build up any cash surrender value or loan value, and thus the insurer may not be obligated to pay out anything on the policy. Frequently, this type of life insurance carries with it a provision to renew the policy without regard to the state of the insured's health.

Universal Life Universal life insurance is a form of ordinary life, which was first sold in 1979. Universal life divides the whole life contract into two components: life insurance protection and savings. The life insurance protection is provided by renewable term insurance to the end of life. The savings component is the extra portion of the premium, beyond what is necessary to buy term life, which is invested and accumulated.

Endowment and Annuity Contracts

An **endowment contract** is basically an agreement by the insurer to pay a lump sum of money to the insured when she reaches a certain age or to a beneficiary in the event of premature death. An **annuity contract** is an agreement by the insurer to pay fixed sums to the insured at periodic intervals after the insured reaches a designated age. Strictly speaking, endowment and annuity policies are not insurance contracts; but numerous endowment and annuity contracts contain various provisions that are customarily found in life insurance contracts, and thus the contracts are subject to regulation by State insurance departments.

Accident and Health Insurance

Accident and health insurance is insurance against losses due to accidents and sickness and provides for the payment of certain benefits or the reimbursement of specified expenses in the event of illness or accidental injury, within the limits set forth in the policies.

Fire and Property Insurance

Fire and property insurance protects the owner (or another person with an insurable interest such as a secured creditor or mortgagee) of real or personal property against loss resulting from damage to or destruction of the property by fire and certain related perils. Most fire insurance policies also cover damage caused by lightning, explosion, earthquake, water, wind, rain, collision, and riot.

Fire insurance policies are standardized in the United States, either by statute or by order of the State insurance departments, but their coverage is frequently enlarged by an "endorsement" or "rider" to include other perils or to benefit the insured in ways not provided in the standard form. These policies are normally written for periods of one or three years.

Fire insurance policies are generally held to cover damage from "hostile" fires, but do not cover losses caused by "friendly" fires. A **friendly fire** is one that is contained where it is intended to be, for instance, a fire in a fireplace, furnace, or stove. A **hostile fire** is all other fires—any fire outside of where it is intended or is usual. Thus, a friendly fire will be hostile once it escapes from its usual confines. A standard insurance policy therefore will not cover damage to a fireplace from its continual use or damage done to personal property accidentally thrown into a stove. Damages caused by smoke, soot, water, and heat from a hostile fire are covered by the standard fire insurance policy, whereas such damages caused by a friendly fire are generally not covered. Moreover, most policies do not cover recovery for business interruption unless there is a special endorsement covering such loss.

Co-insurance is common in property insurance and is a means of sharing the risk between insurer and insured. For example, under the typical 80 percent co-insurance clause, the insured may recover the full amount of loss not to exceed the face amount of the policy, provided the policy is for an amount not less than 80 percent of the insurable value of the property. If the policy is for less than 80 percent, the insured recovers that proportion of the loss that the amount of the policy bears up to 80 percent of the insurable value. The formula for recovery is as follows: Recovery =

$$\frac{\text{Face Value of Policy}}{\text{Fair Market Value of Property} \times \text{Co-insurance \%}} \times \text{Loss}$$

Thus, if the co-insurance percentage is 80 percent, the value of the property is $100,000, and the policy is for $80,000 or more, the insured is fully protected against loss not to exceed the amount of the policy. If the amount of the policy is less than 80 percent of the value of the property, however, the insured does not receive the full amount of loss but only the above-stated proportion as determined in the formula. Thus, in the above example, if the fire policy was in the amount of $60,000 and the property was 50 percent destroyed, the loss would be $50,000, of which the insurer would pay $37,500, which is 60,000/(100,000 × 80%) of $50,000. On a total loss, the recovery could not, of course, exceed the face amount of the policy. Some States do not favor co-insurance clauses and strictly construe the applicable statute against their validity. *See Surrant v. Grain Dealers Mutual Insurance Co.* In addition, property insurance is not held to be co-insurance unless the policy specifically so provides.

Recovery under property insurance policies is typically also limited by *other insurance* clauses. These clauses generally require that liability be distributed *pro rata* among the various insurers. For example, Alexander insures his $120,000 building with Hamilton Insurance Co. for $60,000 and Jefferson Insurance Co. for $90,000. Alexander's building is partially destroyed by fire, causing Alexander $20,000 in damages. Alexander will collect two-fifths (60,000/150,000) of his damages from Hamilton ($8,000) and three-fifths (90,000/150,000) from Jefferson ($12,000).

Casualty Insurance

Casualty insurance is broad in scope but usually covers loss due to the damage or destruction of personal property by various causes other than fire or the elements and is sometimes applied to personal injury or death or property loss due to accident.

Collision Insurance

Collision insurance protects the owner of an automobile against the risk of loss or damage due to contact with other vehicles or objects, usually subject to a deductibility clause.

Liability Insurance

Liability insurance provides indemnification against loss by reason of liability of the insured for damages resulting from injuries to another's person or property. Although this kind of insurance is usually thought of in connection with automobiles—where it is often of greater interest to the injured person than to the driver who caused the injury—it is also customarily carried by owners and lessees of real property to protect against liability for injuries arising on the premises.

No-Fault Insurance

A number of States have legislatively adopted a system of **no-fault insurance,** which compensates victims of automobile accidents regardless of liability. Generally, coverage is provided for personal injury to the named insured, members of his household, authorized operators of the vehicle, passengers, and pedestrians caused by a motor vehicle accident involving the insured's vehicle.

Fidelity Insurance

Fidelity insurance protects an employer against loss due to the dishonesty or defalcation (embezzlement) of employees.

Group Insurance

Group insurance covers a number of individuals, all with some common interest, under a blanket or single policy. This insurance is usually either life or accident and health insurance. The term *group insurance* simply refers to the method of selling standard types of insurance.

Marine Insurance

Marine insurance was originally restricted to destruction of vessels or cargo due to perils of the sea. Now it is a comprehensive form of all-risk insurance covering ship and cargo against the "perils of the sea." Though it is sometimes divided into ocean marine and inland marine, the distinction is not always made, and marine insurance covers transportation risks generally as well as personal property risks and other personal property coverages of almost all kinds.

Title Insurance

Title insurance is issued in the amount of the purchase price of the property and guarantees the owner against any loss due to defects in the title to the property or due to liens or encumbrances, except for those stated in the policy as existing at the time the policy is issued. Such policies may also be issued to mortgagees or to tenants of property to protect their interests.

NATURE OF INSURANCE CONTRACTS

The basic principles of **contract** law apply to insurance policies. Insurance companies engage in a large volume of business over wide areas, however, and therefore their policies are standardized. In some States, standardization is required by statute. This usually means that the insured must accept a given policy or do without the desired insurance.

Offer and Acceptance

No matter how aggressively a life insurance agent has solicited a person to take out a policy, it is generally true that it is the applicant who makes the offer, and the contract is created when that offer is accepted by the company. The company's acceptance may be conditioned, for instance, upon payment of the premium or delivery of the policy while the insured is in good health. If the company writes a policy that differs from the application, then it is the company that makes a counteroffer which the applicant may or may not choose to accept. This situation arises most frequently where the company is unwilling to write the policy that the agent proposed because of the results of a physical examination of the applicant but is willing to write a different policy based on the particular risk involved.

Life insurance agents, therefore, usually cannot bind the company to a contract with the insured, although on occasion an authorized agent may issue a **binding receipt,** acknowledging payment of the premium and providing for the issuance of a standard policy effective from the date of the medical examination so long as the company has no *bona fide* reason to reject the application. In fire and casualty insurance, agents often have authority to make the insurance effective immediately, when needed, by means of a **binder.** In the event of a loss before the company has actually issued a policy, the binder will be effective on the same terms and conditions the policy would have had if it had been issued.

Insurable Interest

The concept of insurable interest has been developed over many years, primarily to eliminate gambling and to lessen the moral hazard. If a person could obtain an enforceable insurance policy on the life of anyone or a fire insurance policy on property that he did not own or in which he had no interest, he would be in a position to profit by the death of a stranger or the destruction of property which represented no loss to him. An **insurable interest** is such relationship which a person has to another person or with respect to certain property that the happening of a possible, specific, damage-causing contingency would result in direct loss or injury to her. The purpose of insurance is protection against the risk of loss resulting from such happening, not the realization of gain or profit.

Property Insurance Ownership obviously creates an insurable interest in the property, whether the ownership is sole or concurrent. Moreover, a right deriving from a contract concerning the property also gives rise to an insurable interest. *See Butler v. Farmers Insurance Co. of Arizona.* For instance, shareholders in a closely held corporation have been held to have an insurable interest in the corporation's property to the extent of their interest. Likewise, lessees of property have interests that are insurable as do holders of security interests, such as mortgagees or sellers with a purchase money security interest. The insurable interest must exist at the time the property *loss* occurs. Property insurance policies are not assignable before loss occurs but are freely assignable after the loss.

Life Insurance Only close relatives, creditors, and business associates or employers, depending generally on the particular facts involved, may take out insurance on another's life. An insured, however, may take out a policy on her own life and name anyone she chooses as beneficiary, although that particular beneficiary may have no insurable interest in the insured's life. The insurable interest must exist at the time the *policy* is taken out and need not exist at the time of death. *See New York Life Insurance Co. v. Baum.* An insured-owner may assign the life policy proceeds to a third person who has no insurable interest.

Premiums

Premiums are the consideration paid for an insurance policy. Life insurance companies usually receive premiums from insured parties over periods of years. These premiums are fixed in amount and are such that the company will be able to pay the principal sum when the policy matures upon the death of the insured through the accumulation of reserves. Life insurance premiums are calculated on the basis of (1) mortality rates, (2) interest, and (3) expenses.

Casualty insurance policies are written only for periods of a few years at most. Long, continued liability on this type of policy is the exception rather than the rule. The rates that may be charged for fire and various kinds of casualty insurance are regulated by State law. The regulatory authorities are under a duty to require that the companies' rates be reasonable, not unfairly discriminatory, and neither excessively high nor inadequately low.

Double Indemnity

A provision found in some life insurance contracts provides for the recovery of "double indemnity," or twice the face amount of the policy, in the event of accidental death or death which results "directly and independently of all other causes from bodily injuries sustained solely from external, violent, and accidental means." These accidental death provisions are worded in various ways and have given rise to much litigation, frequently involving the question whether a death which resulted from the unexpected consequences of an intentional act was an accidental death.

Defenses of the Insurer

In addition to the ordinary defenses to a contract, the insurer may assert the closely re-lated defenses of misrepresentation, breach of warranty, and concealment.

Misrepresentation   A representation is a statement made by or on behalf of an applicant for insurance to induce an insurer to enter into a contract. The representation is not a part of the insurance contract, but if the application containing the representation is incorporated by reference into the contract the representation becomes a warranty. For a **misrepresentation** to have legal consequences, it must be material, have been relied upon by the insurer as an inducement to enter into the contract and it must have been substantially false when made or it must have become so, to the insured's knowledge, before the contract was created. *See Hawkeye-Security Insurance Co. v. Government Employees Insurance Co.* The principal remedy of the insurer on discovery of the material misrepresentation is rescission of the contract. To rescind the contract, the insurer must tender to the insured all premiums that have been paid, unless the misrepresentation was fraudulent. To be effective, rescission must be made as soon as possible after discovery of the misrepresentation.

Rescission may or may not be available to a *life* insurer, however, because of an **incontestability clause,** which generally makes the life insurance policy incontestable by the insurer after a specified period of time, generally one or two years, after the policy has been in effect. An incontestability clause, which is included in most life insurance contracts (many States statutorily require its inclusion), is designed to prevent stale defenses by insurers. The clause, however, does not prevent the insurer from contesting the policy for failure to pay the premiums, for misrepresentation of age, for lack of an insurable interest by the policy owner, or for false impersonation, as, for example, when the physical examination is taken by another person. If the applicant for insurance *misstates his age,* the amount of insurance is simply reduced to that sum which the premiums paid would have purchased at the insured's correct age.

In most jurisdictions, an innocent misrepresentation of a material fact (not opinion) prior to the running of the incontestability clause is a sufficient ground for avoidance of a policy by the insurer. Whether the fact is material or not depends generally upon whether the policy would have been issued if the truth had been known. An immaterial misrepresentation, even though fraudulently made, is not a ground for avoidance of the policy.

Breach of Warranty Warranties are of great importance in insurance contracts because they operate as conditions that *must* exist before the contract is effective or before the insurer's promise to pay is enforceable. Failure of the condition to exist or to occur relieves the insurer from any obligation to perform its promise. Broadly speaking, a condition is simply an event the happening of which or its failure to happen precedes the existence of a legal relationship or terminates one previously existing. Conditions are either precedent or subsequent. For example, payment of the premium is a condition precedent to the enforcement of the insurer's promise, as is the happening of the insured event. A condition subsequent is an operative event the happening of which terminates an existing matured legal obligation. A provision in a policy to the effect that the insured shall not be liable unless suit is brought within twelve months from the date of the occurrence of the loss is an example of a condition subsequent.

To be a warranty, the provision must be expressly included in the insurance contract or clearly incorporated by reference. Usually, the statements in policies that the insurer considers as express warranties can be identified by the use of such words as *warrant* or *on condition that* or *provided that* or words of similar import. Other statements important to the risk assumed, such as the building address in the case where personal property at a particular location is insured against fire, are sometimes held to be informal warranties.

Generally, the trend is away from allowing an insurer to avoid liability on the policy for *any* breach of a warranty by an insured. For example, a number of States require the breach to be material before the insurer may avoid liability.

Concealment Concealment is the failure of an applicant for insurance to disclose material facts that the insurer does not know. The nondisclosure must normally be fraudulent as well as material to invalidate the policy; the applicant must have had reason to believe the fact was material; and its disclosure must have affected the acceptance of the risk by the insurer.

Waiver and Estoppel

In certain instances, an insurer who normally would be entitled to deny liability under a policy because of a misrepresentation, breach of condition, or concealment, is "estopped" from taking advantage of the defense or else is said to have "waived" the right to rely on it because of other facts.

The terms "waiver" and "estoppel" are used interchangeably, although by definition they are not synonymous. As generally defined, **waiver** is the intentional relinquishment of a known right; and **estoppel** means that a person is prevented by his own conduct from asserting a position that is inconsistent with his acts on which another person justifiably relied.

Because a corporation such as an insurance company can act only by agents, situations involving waiver invariably are based on an agent's conduct. The higher the agent's position in the company's organization, the more likely is his conduct to bind the company, since an agent acting within the scope of his authority binds the principal. Insureds have the right to rely on representations made by the insurer's employees, and where such representations reasonably induce or cause a change of position by the insured or prevent the insured from causing a condition to occur, the insurer may not assert the failure of the condition to occur, whether the term applied to his situation be waiver or estoppel. Companies have tried in many ways to limit the authority of local selling agents to bind the company through waiver or estoppel, but this is difficult to do effectively.

Termination

Most contracts of insurance are performed according to their terms, and due **performance** terminates the insurer's obligation. Normally, the insurer pays the principal sum due and the contract is thereby performed and discharged.

Cancellation of an insurance contract by mutual consent is another way of terminating it. Cancellation by the insurer alone means that the insurer is liable according to the terms of the policy until such time as the cancellation is effective. To cancel a policy, the insurer must tender the unearned portion of the premium to the insured.

CASES

Fire and Property Insurance

SURRANT v. GRAIN DEALERS MUTUAL INSURANCE COMPANY

Court of Appeals of North Carolina, 1985.
74 N.C.App. 288, 328 S.E.2d 16.

WHICHARD, J.

Plaintiffs seek to recover proceeds allegedly due under a homeowner's insurance policy issued by defendant for loss by fire of their home and personal property. The face amount of the policy was $30,000 for loss to the dwelling, $15,000 for personal property loss, and $6,000 for living expenses. Plaintiffs sought to recover the full amount of the policy. Judgment was entered for plaintiffs in the amount of $30,000 for loss of their dwelling. * * *

Defendant contends the court erred in awarding plaintiffs the full amount of the policy for loss of their dwelling. First, defendant argues the court erred in failing to conclude that plaintiffs were underinsured as defined by the replacement cost provisions of the policy and that therefore defendant was only liable for the cost to repair the dwelling minus the amount plaintiffs were underinsured. Under the policy issued by defendant, plaintiffs were insured to the extent of the actual cash value of the property covered therein at the time of loss in an amount not exceeding the limit of liability specified on the face of the policy. [The replacement cost provisions of the policy allowed the Surrants to collect the full repair or replacement costs only if they had insured their home for at least 80 percent of the full replacement cost. In addition, if the insurance was for less than the 80 percent, the Surrants were required to pay the difference between the amount of coverage and 80 percent of the full replacement costs. Based on these replacement provisions, Grain Dealers Mutual contends that the Surrants were underinsured.] * * *

[North Carolina Statute] provides that fire insurance policies issued on property within this State may contain replacement cost provisions. That statute provides, in relevant part:

[A]ny fire insurance company authorized to transact business in this State may, by appropriate riders or endorsements or otherwise, provide insurance indemnifying the insured for the difference between the actual value of the insured property at the time any loss or damage occurs, and the amount actually expended to repair, rebuild or replace on the premises described in the policy, or some other location within the State . . . with new materials of like size, kind and quality, such property as has been damaged or destroyed by fire or other perils insured against.

[North Carolina Statute], however, specifically prohibits the inclusion of coinsurance clauses in insurance policies covering property in this State. That statute provides, in part:

No insurance company or agent licensed to do business in this State may issue any policy or contract of insurance covering property in this State which shall contain any clause or provision requiring the insured to take or maintain a larger amount of insurance than that expressed in such policy, *nor in any way provide that the insured shall be liable as a coinsurer with the company issuing the policy for any part of the loss or damage to the property described in such policy,* and any such clause or provision shall be null and void, and of no effect: Provided, the coinsurance clause or provision may be written in or attached to a policy or policies issued when there is printed or stamped on the filing face of such policy or on the form containing such clause the words "coinsurance contract," and the Commissioner may, in his discretion, determine the location of the words "coinsurance contract" and the size of the type to be used.

Coinsurance has been defined as a relative division of risk between the insurer and the insured, dependent upon the relative amount of the policy and the actual value of the property insured. [Citations.] "Coinsurance clauses in substance require the insured to maintain insurance on the property covered by the policy in a certain amount, and stipulate that upon his failure to do so, the insured shall be a coinsurer and bear his proportionate part of the loss on the deficit." [Citations.] For example, [i]nsurance policies that protect against hazards such as fire or water damage often specify that the owner of the property may not collect the full amount of insurance for a loss unless the insurance policy covers at least some specified percentage, usually about 80 percent of the replacement cost of the property. [Citation.]

Coinsurance clauses are designed to induce the insured to carry full, or nearly full coverage, [citation], and are generally held enforceable unless they are specifically prohibited by statute in the jurisdiction. [Citation.]

Under the replacement cost provisions of the policy here, plaintiffs could only collect the full cost of repair or replacement of their dwelling if they had insured the dwelling for at least 80 percent of its full replacement cost. If the insurance maintained on the dwelling was for less than 80 percent of its full replacement cost, defendant admits that under the policy plaintiffs become coinsurers or self-insurers for the difference between the amount of coverage and 80 percent of the full

replacement cost. Thus, the policy's replacement cost provisions are essentially coinsurance provisions as defined in [the Statute]. The words "coinsurance contract" are not printed or stamped on the policy; therefore, the coinsurance provisions are not allowable under the proviso in [the Statute]. We conclude that to the extent the policy's replacement cost provisions provide for coinsurance they are null and void, and that defendant was not entitled to any reduction of its liability pursuant to those provisions in the event plaintiffs were underinsured. [Citation.]

* * *

Affirmed.

Insurable Interest—Property

BUTLER v. FARMERS INSURANCE COMPANY OF ARIZONA

Supreme Court of Arizona, 1980.
126 Ariz. 371, 616 P.2d 46.

HAYS, J.

This cause was submitted to the trial court upon the following stipulated facts: In 1976, plaintiff-appellant, James Butler, purchased a 1967 Austin-Healy for $3,500. Receiving an Arizona Certificate of Title pursuant to the sale, appellant was unaware that the vehicle had been previously stolen. Approximately two years after the purchase, the automobile was seized by Tucson police and returned to its lawful owner.

At all times relevant hereto, appellant was insured against loss of the vehicle by defendant-appellee, Farmers Insurance Co. of Arizona. It is the insurer's denial of appellant's claim for benefits under the policy which has given rise to the instant dispute.

Citing a lack of insurable interest, appellee declined to reimburse appellant for his loss, tendering instead "$55 to $56" as restitution for premiums paid. Appellant initiated suit, and cross-motions for summary judgment were filed. Although the trial court granted appellee's motion, the Court of Appeals reversed. [Citation], . . . [W]e vacate the opinion of the Court of Appeals and reverse the ruling of the trial court.

Any analysis of the insurable interest principle in Arizona must focus initially upon the language of our statutes. The governing standard is set forth in [Arizona Statute].

"Insurable interest" means any actual, lawful and substantial economic interest in the safety or preservation of the subject of the insurance free from loss, destruction or pecuniary damage or impairment.

We believe that the innocent purchaser of stolen property falls within this protection and reject any construction to the contrary.

Initially, examination of identical circumstances reveals that appellant's interest in conservation of the vehicle was both "lawful" and "substantial." The law is clear that a *bona fide* purchaser of stolen commodities inherits title defeasible by none other than the rightful owner. [Citations.] S/he possesses a valid legal claim to the property which will be given full force and effect in a court of law. Even as against the true owner, moreover, the innocent purchaser may, upon loss or destruction of the illicit merchandise, be held liable in tort for conversion, and therefore has an interest in maintaining the property in an undamaged condition. [Citations.]

In addition, the rule above stated is not only sustained by the authorities, but is in accord with justice and common sense. Among the vices sought to be discouraged by the insurable interest requirement is the intentional destruction of the covered property in order to profit from the insurance proceeds. We believe this purpose will be furthered where the insured has a financial investment in the property and believes him or herself to be in lawful possession. We see no greater risk of illicit activity under these circumstances than where the insured is, in actuality, the rightful owner.

* * *

The opinion of the Court of Appeals is vacated, and this cause is remanded to the trial court for proceedings consistent with this opinion.

Insurable Interest—Life

NEW YORK LIFE INS. CO. v. BAUM

United States Court of Appeals, Fifth Circuit, 1983. 700 F.2d 928.

THORNBERRY, J.

* * * We need not repeat here the facts of this case. *See New York Life Insurance Co. v. Baum,* 617 F.2d 1201, 1201–03 (5th Cir. 1980). [The facts as presented therein are as follows: Noel Baum was a Baton Rouge, Louisiana, field underwriter for the New York Life Insurance Company. In early 1973 Baum and Bill Cook agreed to form a media advertising venture named Media Sales & Marketing, Inc. The business was to be incorporated in Louisiana, but its headquarters were to be in Houston, Texas. Baum was to furnish the starting capital for the corporation, and Cook was to provide the experience for running the business. Another businessman, Carroll Cutler, was later added to the proposed corporate venture.

In late 1973 Cook and Cutler opened an office in Houston and began doing business as Media Sales & Marketing, Inc. Baum helped to arrange a line of credit for the business and personally extended $16,500 to Cook to use for developing the business. By early November, the business had not been formally incorporated, and no operating income was being generated. Baum, to protect his investment, applied to New York Life for an insurance policy on Cook's life with himself as beneficiary and designating Media Sales & Marketing, Inc., as the policy owner. Baum subsequently agreed to change the beneficiary to Media Sales & Marketing, Inc., after New York Life informed him that, as an agent of the company, he could not be named as the beneficiary. The policy was issued on December 8, 1973, at which time Media Sales & Marketing, Inc., had still not been formally incorporated. On December 20, however, Cutler, Cook, and another Houston resident formally incorporated a business of this name in Texas, apparently to protect the participants from personal liability on business debts resulting in part from Baum's failure to provide necessary funds. The evidence whether this incorporation was with Baum's knowledge was conflicting. No stock was ever issued in Media, Inc., and the business never produced any income.

Baum paid all the premiums on Cook's insurance policy from the time of issuance until Cook's death on December 8, 1974. Baum filed a claim for $100,000 in proceeds from the policy, arguing that he was the principal financier of the beneficiary, the proposed corporation in Louisiana, and would have been its principal shareholder. Media, Inc., also filed a claim for the policy proceeds, contending that it was the corporate beneficiary designated in the policy. New York Life moved for summary judgment, alleging that neither contesting beneficiary had an insurable interest in the life of Cook at the time the contract was made. The district court granted summary judgment for New York Life.]

* * *

N.Y.Ins.Law § 146 defines an insurable interest in the person. The statute, derived from a 1909 law and enacted in 1939, is remarkably similar to its Louisiana analogue, [citation]. Section 146 defines an insurable interest in the case of persons not related by blood or by law as follows:

[I]n the case of other persons, a lawful and substantial economic interest in having the life, health or bodily safety of the person insured continue, as distinguished from an interest which would arise only by, or would be enhanced in value by, the death, disablement or injury, as the case may be, of the person insured.

[Citation.]

"It may be generally stated that the reasoning behind legislation requiring an insurable interest . . . is in furtherance of the public policy against wagering or gambling on human lives. This policy has been adopted in most jurisdictions to prevent speculation in human life, since the incentive to shorten the life of the insured would be increased." [Citation.] While discussing the subject of insurable interest between creditors and their debtors another New York court held as follows:

It is now well settled that the bank had an insurable interest in the life of the plaintiff's intestate at the time it made the loan to him and under such circumstances the bank had the right to enter into any agreement with the insurance company so that it would receive a sum of money as indemnity in case its interest in the subject matter should suffer diminution of value by reason of certain specified causes or contingencies. 1 May on Insurance (4th Ed. Sec. 6). The bank with such an insurable interest in the borrower clearly had the right to secure itself against the death of the borrower.

* * *

Applying these principles to our case, we hold that, under New York law, Baum had an insurable interest in the life of Cook, his debtor, as a matter of law. A creditor-debtor relationship existed between Baum and Cook at the time the policy was executed and Baum loaned the majority of the funds to Cook *after* the policy went into effect. The facts fail to show that the policy was taken as a wager. As creditor, Baum had a reasonable ground to expect some benefit or advantage from the continuation of Cook's life, namely, repayment of the loan. Furthermore, there are compelling arguments against allowing the insurer to escape its obligation.

It is surely not a sound policy to permit insurers to contract to insure the lives of persons, receive premiums therefor as long as the * * * beneficiary * * * will continue to pay, and then, when the time comes for the insurers to pay what they agreed to pay, allow them to escape their contract on the ground of want of insurable interest in the life insured, unless it clearly appears that such contracts are pernicious and dangerous to society.

[Citation.]

Regarding Media Texas, the situation is less clear. While it is true that, as a general rule, a corporation has an insurable interest in the life of its key employees, [citation], the district court found that "the record clearly demonstrates that Media Sales (Texas) was nothing more than a nonfunctioning corporate shell." Indeed, no stock was apparently ever issued by Media Texas. The district court also found that "the creation of a Texas corporation was never contemplated by the parties, as evidenced by the representations made by Baum in the application for the life insurance policy."

* * * The evidence shows that, indeed, Baum, Cook, and Cutler at one point contemplated incorporating in Texas, but that on December 19, 1973, Baum instructed his attorney not to incorporate. The next day, Cook, Cutler, and another person formed Media Texas without Baum's knowledge and consent. In fact, Baum stated in his deposition that the Texas incorporation had the effect of cutting him off completely from the venture. Moreover, the articles of incorporation of Media Texas do not list Baum as one of the incorporators of Media Texas. Apparently, attorneys other than the ones Baum or his attorney dealt with in Texas performed the incorporation of Media Texas, and it is fair to conclude that the Texas incorporation envisioned by Baum was different from the actual incorporation that occurred. Finally, the record shows that Cutler was not even aware of the existence of the life insurance policy until after Cook's death.

We consequently cannot say that the district court's findings regarding Baum and his knowledge of Media Texas were clearly erroneous. Indeed, the evidence is clear that Baum paid the original and all subsequent premiums, took out and had possession of the life insurance contract, and sued for the amount of the policy. The district court found that the amendment changing the name of the beneficiary to Media Sales & Marketing, Inc. was made at the insistence of New York Life, and it is clear that New York Life knew that Baum was the real party in interest in the life insurance contract. Moreover, it is clear that Cook, the insured, knew that Baum was to be the designated beneficiary.

* * *

For the reasons stated above, the judgment of the district court is reversed with directions that the proceeds from the life insurance policy be paid to Baum.

Misrepresentation

HAWKEYE–SECURITY INSURANCE CO. v. GOVERNMENT EMPLOYEES INSURANCE CO.

Supreme Court of Virginia, 1967.
207 Va. 944, 154 S.E.2d 173.

SNEAD, J.

On August 18, 1962, Einer Carl Mattson, Jr. was operating an automobile owned by and with consent of his father, Einer Carl Mattson, Sr. It became involved in a collision with another vehicle operated by William Henry Droughn who received personal injuries. Mattson, Sr. reported the accident to Government Employees Insurance Company, appellee, which had issued to him a liability insurance policy on his car involved in the mishap. Under the terms of the policy, Mattson, Jr. was an additional insured. On November 20, 1962, after some investigation, Government Employees wrote Mattson, Sr. advising "[W]e hereby declare the captioned policy null and void and of no effect as of its inception date" because of a material misrepresentation made in his application for the insurance coverage, and it enclosed a check for a refund of premiums paid.

On September 22, 1964, Droughn recovered a judgment in the sum of $2,000 against Mattson, Jr., and on the same day Droughn assigned it to Hawkeye-Security Insurance Company, appellant, for a valuable consideration. Execution on the judgment was returned "unsatisfied."

* * *

Hawkeye, assignee, instituted an action against Government Employees seeking a judgment for $2,000 against it. In its answer and grounds of defense, Government Employees denied that the Mattson vehicle was insured by it, and denied that it was liable to Hawkeye in any amount. A trial by jury was waived, and after hearing all the evidence, the court found that Mattson, Sr. had made a material misrepresentation in his application to Government Employees for the insurance policy and on November 3, 1965, rendered judgment in its behalf. We granted Hawkeye a writ of error.

* * *

The crucial issue presented in this appeal is whether the insurance policy issued to Mattson, Sr. by Government Employees was in full force and effect on August 18, 1962, the date Droughn was injured, or whether it was void ab initio because of an alleged material misrepresentation made by Mattson, Sr. in the procurement of the policy.

The record shows that Mattson, Sr. was insured under an automobile liability policy issued by State Farm Mutual Insurance Company from January 29, 1959, until it was cancelled by the Company on August 5, 1959. Douglas R. Mays, an underwriter for State Farm, testified that the policy was cancelled for "general underwriting reasons" and that Mattson, Sr. was notified of the Company's action by registered mail.

Thereafter, Mattson, Sr. obtained another policy from Home Indemnity Insurance Company which he retained until October 20, 1960 when he was issued the policy here involved by Government Employees. This policy was twice renewed with coverage extending through October 20, 1963. All premiums were duly paid.

Mattson, Sr. testified that he contacted Government Employees by mail for the insurance and was mailed an application for him to complete and return. Above the space for his signature and the questions to be answered the application read:

"I understand and agree that if the answers to questions 7, 8, 9, or 10, or any of them are other than 'No,' the insurance requested will not be effective until approved by the Company. * * * The Company agrees that . . . if the true answers to questions 7, 8, 9, and 10 are 'No', the insurance applied for will be effective as of: postmarked time and date . . .

"IMPORTANT ISSUANCE OF A VALID POLICY IS DEPENDENT UPON YOUR TRUE ANSWERS."

We are here concerned only with question No. 7, which follows:

"7. Has any insurance company (including this Company) ever refused, cancelled, refused to renew, or given notice of intention to cancel or refuse, any automobile insurance for you or any member of your household? . . . If 'yes,' see above (the quoted statement) (Give full information on separate sheet)"

The application which Mattson, Sr. admitted that he himself completed and signed, contained a "No" answer in response to question No. 7. . . .

Gerald T. Jackson, underwriting manager for Government Employees, testified that he had the responsibility of deciding whether a policy should or should not be issued by his Company to an applicant. He said that if question No. 7 had been answered "yes" without elaboration, the application of Mattson, Sr. would have been rejected; . . .

Jackson, on the other hand, testified that when an application contained a "No" answer to question No. 7, and the rest of the application showed no accidents or violations, the answer would be accepted as true and no investigation would be made.

Hawkeye concedes that the answer "No" to question No. 7 was untrue, but contends Government Employees did not clearly prove that such answer was material to the risk when assumed.

"A fact is material to the risk to be assumed by an insurance company if the fact would reasonably influence the company's decision whether or not to issue a policy." [Citations.]

* * *

We have repeatedly held that a misrepresentation of a fact material to the risk when assumed renders an insurance contract void. [Citations.]

Here, Government Employees carried its burden of clearly proving that the untrue answer to question No. 7 in the application for insurance made by Mattson, Sr. was material to the risk when assumed. . . .

Government Employees was entitled to know the whole truth. The false answer ("No") to question No. 7 caused the Company to forego an opportunity to investigate why the State Farm policy was cancelled and to determine whether or not the risk should be assumed as well as the premium rate applicable to the risk in the event the policy was issued. [Citation.]

* * *

Under the evidence adduced, the trial court properly held that the misrepresenta-

tion was material to the risk when assumed and that the policy was null and void *ab initio* for that reason.

Accordingly, the judgment appealed from is

Affirmed.

QUESTIONS

1. Distinguish among ordinary life, term life, and universal life insurance.

2. Discuss (a) an annuity contract, (b) an endowment contract, (c) accident and health insurance, (d) fire and property insurance, (e) casualty insurance, (f) automobile insurance, (g) title insurance, (h) liability insurance, and (i) group insurance.

3. Explain the co-insurance clause in property insurance contracts.

4. Explain an insurable interest. Distinguish between an insurable interest in life insurance and property insurance.

5. Compare the defenses of misrepresentation, concealment, breach of warranty, waiver, and estoppel.

PROBLEMS

1. Lile, an insurance broker, handled all insurance for Tempo Co. Lile purchased a fire policy from Insurance Company insuring Tempo Co.'s factory against fire in the amount of $150,000. Before the policy was delivered to Tempo Co. and while it was still in Lile's hands, Tempo Co. advised Lile to cancel the policy. Prior to cancellation, Tempo Co. suffered a loss. Now Tempo Co. makes a claim against Insurance Company on the policy. The premium had been billed to Lile but was unpaid at the time of loss. In an action by Tempo Co. against Insurance Company, what judgment?

2. On July 15, Adler purchased in Chicago a Buick Sedan intending to drive it that day to St. Louis, Missouri. He telephoned a friend, Maruchek, who was in the insurance business and told him that he wanted liability insurance on the automobile, limited in amount to $50,000 for injuries to one person and $100,000 for any one ac-

cident. Maruchek took the order and told Adler over the telephone that he was covered and that his policy would be written by the Young Insurance Company. Later that same day and before Maruchek had informed the Young Insurance Company of Adler's application, Adler negligently operated the automobile and seriously injured Brown who brings suit against Adler. Is Adler covered by liability insurance?

3. Graham owns a building having a fair market value of $120,000. She takes out a fire insurance policy from the Bentley Insurance Company for $72,000, the policy contains an 80 percent co-insurance clause. The building is damaged by fire to the extent of $48,000. How much insurance is Graham entitled to collect?

4. The Best Automobile Insurance Company issues to Ravenscroft, owner of a Mercury automobile, a liability policy, with $30,000–$60,000 limits. On April 3, as the result of Ravenscroft's negligent operation of his car, Clark, Dawson, and Ernst are injured in a collision. Clark, Dawson, and Ernst sue Ravenscroft and recover judgments of $45,000, $9,000, and $6,000 respectively. To what extent is the Best Company liable?

5. Arthur Heartburn, having knowledge of a bad heart condition, arranges to have his friend, Ira Impostor, represent himself as Heartburn to the medical examiner of the Taken Life Insurance Company. Impostor, posing as Heartburn, is found to be physically sound, and the Insurance Company issues a $75,000 life insurance policy to Heartburn. The policy contains a two-year incontestable clause. Twenty-six months after the issuance of the policy, Heartburn suffers a heart attack and dies. Before paying off the claim of Heartburn's widow, the beneficiary under the policy, the Insurance Company learns about Impostor's actions in helping Heartburn procure the policy. When the Taken Insurance Company refuses to pay the claim, the widow files suit on the policy. Decision?

6. Wiley, an insurance salesman, induces Glutz to purchase a $60,000 life insurance policy on the life of his best friend Doe and at the same time sells a policy to Doe insuring Glutz's life. After ten years Doe dies, and on due proof of death the insurance company denies liability. Glutz sues the company. Decision?

7. Kay was issued a $30,000 life insurance policy by Atlantic Bell Life Insurance Company. In her application, Kay truthfully warranted that she was a professional actress and that she was not engaged in the employ of a railroad company or an airplane company. The policy provided that the company insured "the life of Kay so long as she engaged solely in the business of a professional actress." The policy also provided:

This policy shall be incontestable for any cause after it shall have been in force during the life of the insured for two years from its date.

After the policy had been in effect for three years, Kay was killed while employed as a brakeman by a railroad company. Kay was so employed without the knowledge and consent of the insurance company. The beneficiary of the policy sued the company to recover the face amount of the policy. The company defended, denying liability on the ground that Kay was employed by a railroad company at the time of her death and had been so employed for six months previously. Decision?

8. Paul Poe purchased a life insurance policy in the sum of $100,000. The policy provided: "The proceeds of this policy are payable upon the death of the insured to Penelope Poe, wife of the insured." The policy also provided that Poe had the right to change the name of the beneficiary. Four years after the policy had been purchased, Poe obtained a divorce from his wife, Penelope. One year later, Poe married Dora Doe, and this marriage continued until Poe's death two years later. At Poe's death, the policy remained in its original form. Penelope demanded that the insurance company pay her the proceeds of the policy. Upon its refusal, she brought an action against the company to recover $100,000. Decision?

9. Day had for some time been seeking out Short to "teach him a lesson" for taking out Day's girlfriend, and Day carried a pistol for this purpose. Eventually, Day caught up with Short at a local beer parlor and without warning fired a shot at Short. Day's aim was not too good, for the shot only creased Short's head. Short dove at Day, and a scuffle ensued. During the scuffle, Day fell to the floor, hitting his head upon the bar railing. As a direct result of this blow to his head, Day died. At the time of his death, Day had in effect a policy of accidental death insurance in which the insurance company had agreed to pay the named beneficiary, Day's mother, $70,000 upon the death of Day if the death were "effected solely through external, violent, and accidental means." The insurance company refused to pay the beneficiary. What are the beneficiary's rights, if any?

10. Scarola purchased an automobile for value and without knowledge that it was stolen. After he insured the car with Insurance Company of North America (INA), the car was stolen once again. When INA refused to reimburse for the loss, contending that Scarola did not have an insurable interest in the car, Scarola brought an action. Decision?

11. Pioneer Foundry Company employed Jack Secor for a period of nine years. In the fifth year of employment, Pioneer Foundry obtained a $50,000 insurance policy on his life; Pioneer was the applicant, the owner, and the beneficiary, and it paid the premiums on the policy. After the employment relationship ended, Pioneer Foundry paid the annual premium of $5,625 for the next year. Secor died the following month. Pioneer Foundry had paid over $28,000 in premiums before he died. The insurer paid the proceeds of the policy to Pioneer Foundry. Jack's widow, Florence, sued Pioneer Foundry to recover these proceeds. She contends that after the termination of Secor's employment, Pioneer Foundry lost whatever insurable interest it had in Secor's life. Furthermore, she contended that to pay the insured's former employer violates the public policy against speculation on the life of another. Decision?

APPENDIXES

A   THE CONSTITUTION OF THE UNITED STATES OF AMERICA

B   SELECTED PROVISIONS OF RESTATEMENTS

C   UNIFORM COMMERCIAL CODE

D   UNIFORM PARTNERSHIP ACT

E   REVISED UNIFORM LIMITED PARTNERSHIP ACT

F   SELECTED PROVISIONS OF THE 1985 AMENDMENTS TO THE REVISED UNIFORM LIMITED PARTNERSHIP ACT

G   REVISED MODEL BUSINESS CORPORATION ACT (AS AMENDED THROUGH 1989)

H   SELECTED PROVISIONS OF THE MODEL BUSINESS CORPORATION ACT

I   DICTIONARY OF LEGAL TERMS

THE CONSTITUTION OF THE UNITED STATES OF AMERICA

We the People of the United States, in Order to form a more perfect Union, establish Justice, insure domestic Tranquility, provide for the common defense, promote the general Welfare, and secure the Blessings of Liberty to ourselves and our Posterity, do ordain and establish this Constitution for the United States of America.

Article I

Section 1

All legislative Powers herein granted shall be vested in a Congress of the United States, which shall consist of a Senate and House of Representatives.

Section 2

The House of Representatives shall be composed of Members chosen every second Year by the People of the several States, and the Electors in each State shall have the Qualifications requisite for Electors of the most numerous Branch of the State Legislature.

No Person shall be a Representative who shall not have attained to the Age of twenty five Years, and been seven Years a Citizen of the United States, and who shall not, when elected, be an Inhabitant of that State in which he shall be chosen.

Representatives and direct Taxes shall be apportioned among the several States which may be included within this Union, according to their respective Numbers, which shall be determined by adding to the whole Number of free Persons, including those bound to Service for a Term of Years, and excluding Indians not taxed, three fifths of all other Persons. The actual Enumeration shall be made within three Years after the first Meeting of the Congress of the United States, and within every subsequent Term of ten Years, in such Manner as they shall by Law direct. The number of Representatives shall not exceed one for every thirty Thousand, but each State shall have at Least one Representative; and until such enumeration shall be made, the State of New Hampshire shall be entitled to chuse three, Massachusetts eight, Rhode Island and Povidence Plantations one, Connecticut five, New-York six, New Jersey four, Pennsylvania eight, Delaware one, Maryland six, Virginia ten, North Carolina five, South Carolina five, and Georgia three.

When vacancies happen in the Representation from any State, the Executive Authority thereof shall issue Writs of Election to fill such vacancies.

The House of Representatives shall chuse their Speaker and other Officers; and shall have the sole Power of Impeachment.

Section 3

The Senate of the United States shall be composed of two Senators from each State, chosen by the Legislature thereof, for six Years; and each Senator shall have one Vote.

Immediately after they shall be assembled in Consequence of the first Election, they shall be divided as equally as may be into three Classes. The Seats of the Senators of the first Class shall be vacated at the Expiration of the second Year, of the second Class at the Expiration of the fourth Year, and of the third Class at the Expiration of the sixth Year, so that one third may be chosen every second Year; and if Vacancies happen by

Resignation or otherwise, during the Recess of the Legislature of any State, the Executive thereof may make temporary Appointments until the next Meeting of the Legislature, which shall then fill such Vacancies.

No Person shall be a Senator who shall not have attained to the Age of thirty Years, and been nine Years a Citizen of the United States, and who shall not, when elected, be an Inhabitant of that State for which he shall be chosen.

The Vice President of the United States shall be President of the Senate, but shall have no Vote, unless they be equally divided.

The Senate shall chuse their other Officers, and also a President pro tempore, in the Absence of the Vice President, or when he shall exercise the Office of President of the United States.

The Senate shall have the sole power to try all Impeachments. When sitting for that Purpose, they shall be an Oath or Affirmation. When the President of the United States is tried, the Chief Justice shall preside: And no Person shall be convicted without the Concurrence of two thirds of the Members present.

Judgment in Cases of Impeachment shall not extend further than to removal from Office, and disqualification to hold and enjoy any Office of honor, Trust or Profit under the United States: but the Party convicted shall nevertheless be liable and subject to Indictment, Trial, Judgment and Punishment, according to Law.

Section 4

The Times, Places and Manner of holding Elections for Senators and Representatives, shall be prescribed in each State by the Legislature thereof: but the Congress may at any time by Law make or alter such Regulations, except as to the Places of chusing Senators.

The Congress shall assemble at least once in every Year, and such Meeting shall be on the first Monday in December, unless they shall by Law appoint a different Day.

Section 5

Each House shall be the Judge of the Elections, Returns and Qualifications of its own Members, and a Majority of each shall constitute a Quorum to do Business; but a smaller Number may adjourn from day to day, and may be authorized to compel the Attendance of absent Members, in such Manner, and under such Penalties as each House may provide.

Each House may determine the Rules of its Proceedings, punish its Members for disorderly Behaviour, and, with the Concurrence of two thirds, expel a Member.

Each House shall keep a Journal of its Proceedings, and from time to time publish the same, excepting such Parts as may in their Judgment require Secrecy; and the Yeas and Nays of the Members of either House on any question shall, at the Desire of one fifth of those Present, be entered on the Journal.

Neither House, during the Session of Congress, shall, without the Consent of the other, adjourn for more than three days, nor to any other Place than that in which the two Houses shall be sitting.

Section 6

The Senators and Representatives shall receive a Compensation for their Services, to be ascertained by Law, and paid out of the Treasury of the United States. They shall in all Cases, except Treason, Felony and Breach of the Peace, be privileged from Arrest during their Attendance at the Session of their respective Houses, and in going to and returning from the same; and for any Speech or Debate in either House, they shall not be questioned in any other Place.

No Senator or Representative shall, during the Time for which he was elected, be appointed to any civil Office under the Authority of the United States, which shall have been created, or the Emoluments whereof shall have been encreased during such time; and no Person holding any Office under the United States, shall be a Member of either House during his Continuance in Office.

Section 7

All Bills for raising Revenue shall originate in the House of Representatives; but the Senate may propose or concur with Amendments as on other Bills.

Every Bill which shall have passed the House of Representatives and the Senate, shall, before it become a Law, be presented to the President of the United States; If he approve he shall sign it, but if not he shall return it, with his Objections to that House in which it shall have originated, who shall enter the Objections at large on their Journal, and proceed to reconsider it. If after such Reconsideration two thirds of that House shall agree to pass the Bill, it shall be sent, together with the Objections, to the other House, by which it shall likewise be reconsidered, and if approved by two thirds of that House, it shall become a Law. But in all such Cases the Votes of both Houses shall be determined by Yeas and Nays, and the Names of the Persons voting for and against the Bill shall be entered on the Journal of each House respectively. If any Bill shall not be returned by the President within ten Days (Sundays excepted) after it shall have been presented to him, the Same shall be a Law, in like Manner as if he had signed it, unless the Congress by their Adjournment prevent its Return, in which Case it shall not be a Law.

Every Order, Resolution, or Vote to which the Concurrence of the Senate and House of Representatives may be necessary (except on a question of Adjournment) shall be presented to the President of the United States; and before the Same shall take Effect, shall be approved by him, or being disapproved by him, shall be repassed by two thirds of the Senate and House of Representatives, according to the Rules and Limitations prescribed in the Case of a Bill.

Section 8

The Congress shall have Power to lay and collect Taxes, Duties, Imposts and Excises, to pay the Debts and provide for the common Defence and general Welfare of the United States; but all Duties, Imposts and Excises shall be uniform throughout the United States;

To borrow Money on the credit of the United States;

To regulate Commerce with foreign Nations, and among the several States, and with the Indian Tribes;

To establish an uniform Rule of Naturalization, and uniform Laws on the subject of Bankruptcies throughout the United States;

To coin Money, regulate the Value thereof, and of foreign Coin, and fix the Standard of Weights and Measures;

To provide for the Punishment of counterfeiting the Securities and current Coin of the United States;

To establish Post Offices and post Roads;

To promote the Progress of Science and useful Arts, by securing for limited Times to Authors and Inventors the exclusive Right to their respective Writings and Discoveries;

To constitute Tribunals inferior to the supreme Court;

To define and punish Piracies and Felonies committed on the high Seas, and Offenses against the Law of Nations;

To declare War, grant Letters of Marque and Reprisal, and make Rules concerning Captures on Land and Water;

To raise and support Armies, but no Appropriation of Money to that Use shall be for a longer Term than two Years;

To provide and maintain a Navy;

To make Rules for the Government and Regulation of the land and naval Forces;

To provide for calling forth the Militia to execute the Laws of the Union, suppress Insurrections and repel Invasions;

To provide for organizing, arming, and disciplining, the Militia, and for governing such Part of them as may be employed in the Service of the United States, reserving to the States respectively, the Appointment of the Officers, and the Authority of training the Militia according to the discipline described by Congress;

To exercise exclusive Legislation in all Cases whatsoever, over such District (not exceeding ten Miles square) as may, by Cession of particular States, and the Acceptance of Congress, become the Seat of the Government of the United States, and to exercise like Authority over all Places purchased by the Consent of the Legislature of the State in which the Same shall be, for the Erection of Forts, Magazines, Arsenals, dock-Yards, and other needful Buildings;—And

To make all Laws which shall be necessary and proper for carrying into Execution the foregoing Powers, and all other Powers vested by this Constitution in the Government of the United States, or in any Department or Officer thereof.

Section 9

The Migration or Importation of such Persons as any of the States now existing shall think proper to admit, shall not be prohibited by the Congress prior to the Year one thousand eight hundred and eight, but a Tax or Duty may be imposed on such Importation, not exceeding ten dollars for each Person.

The Privilege of the Writ of Habeas Corpus shall not be suspended, unless when in Cases of Rebellion or Invasion the public Safety may require it.

No Bill of Attainder or ex post facto Law shall be passed.

No Capitation, or other direct, Tax shall be laid, unless in Proportion to the Census or Enumeration herein before directed to be taken.

No Tax or Duty shall be laid on Articles exported from any State.

No Preference shall be given by any Regulation of Commerce or Revenue to the Ports of one State over those of another; nor shall Vessels bound to, or from, one State, be obliged to enter, clear, or pay Duties in another.

No Money shall be drawn from the Treasury, but in Consequence of Appropriations made by Laws; and a regular Statement and Account of the Receipts and Expenditures of all public Money shall be published from time to time.

No Title of Nobility shall be granted by the United States: And no Person holding any Office of Profit or Trust under them, shall, without the Consent of the Congress, accept of any present, Emolument, Office, or Title, of any kind whatever, from any King, Prince, or foreign State.

Section 10

No State shall enter into any Treaty, Alliance, or Confederation; grant Letters of Marque and Reprisal; coin Money; emit Bills of Credit; make any Thing but gold and silver Coin a Tender in Payment of Debts; pass any Bill of Attainder, ex post facto Law, or Law impairing the Obligation of Contracts, or grant any Title of Nobility.

No State shall, without the Consent of the Congress, lay any Imposts or Duties on Imports or Exports, except what may be absolutely necessary for executing its inspection Laws: and the net Produce of all Duties and Imposts, laid by any State on Imports or Exports, shall be for the Use of the Treasury of the United States; and all such Laws shall be subject to the Revision and Controul of the Congress.

No State shall, without the Consent of Congress, lay any Duty of Tonnage, keep Troops, or Ships of War in time of Peace, enter into any Agreement or Compact with another State, or with a foreign Power, or engage in War, unless actually invaded, or in such imminent Danger as will not admit of delay.

Article II

Section 1

The executive Power shall be vested in a President of the United States of America. He shall hold his Office during the Term of four Years, and, together with the Vice President, chosen for the same Term, be elected, as follows:

Each State shall appoint, in such Manner as the Legislature thereof may direct, a Number of Electors, equal to the whole Number of Senators and Representatives to which the State may be entitled in the Congress: but no Senator or Representative, or Person holding an Office of Trust or Profit under the United States, shall be appointed an Elector.

The Electors shall meet in their respective States, and vote by Ballot for two Persons, of whom one at least shall not be an Inhabitant of the same State with themselves. And they shall make a list of all the Persons voted for, and of the Number of Votes for each; which List they shall sign and certify, and transmit sealed to the Seat of the Government of the United States, directed to the President of the Senate. The President of the Senate shall, in the presence of the Senate and House of Representatives, open all the Certificates, and the Votes shall be counted. The Person having the greatest Number of Votes shall be the President, if such Number be a Majority of the whole Number of Electors appointed; and if there be more than one who have such Majority, and have an equal Number of Votes, then the House of Representatives shall immediately chuse by Ballot one of them for President; and if no Person have a Majority, then from the five highest on the List the said House shall in like Manner chuse the President. But in chusing the President, the Votes shall be taken by States, the Representation from each State having one Vote; A quorum for this Purpose shall consist of a Member or Members from two thirds of the States, and a Majority of all the States shall be necessary to a Choice. In every Case, after the Choice of the President, the Person having the greatest Number of Votes of the Electors shall be the Vice President. But if there should remain two or more who have equal Votes, the Senate shall chuse from them by Ballot the Vice President.

The Congress may determine the Time of Chusing the Electors, and the Day on which they shall give their Votes; which Day shall be the same throughout the United States.

No Person except a natural born Citizen, or a Citizen of the United States, at the time of the Adoption of this Constitution, shall be eligible to the Office of President; neither shall any Person be eligible to that Office who shall not have attained to the Age of thirty five Years, and been fourteen Years a Resident within the United States.

In Case of the Removal of the President from Office, or of his Death, Resignation, or Inability to discharge the Powers and Duties of the said Office, the Same shall devolve on the Vice President, and the Congress may by Law provide for the Case of Removal, Death, Resignation or Inability, both of the President and Vice President, declaring what Officer shall then act as President, and such Officer shall act accordingly, until the Disability be removed, or a President shall be elected.

The President shall, at stated Times, receive for his Services, a Compensation, which shall neither be encreased nor diminished during the Period for which he shall have been elected, and he shall not receive within that Period any other Emolument from the United States, or any of them.

Before he enter on the Execution of his Office, he shall take the following Oath or Affirmation:—"I do solemnly swear (or affirm) that I will faithfully execute the Office of President of the United States, and will to the best of my Ability, preserve, protect and defend the Constitution of the United States."

Section 2

The President shall be Commander in Chief of the Army and Navy of the United States, and of the Militia of the several States, when called into the actual Service of the United States; he may require the Opinion, in writing, of the principal Officer in each of the executive Departments, upon any Subject relating to the Duties of their respective Offices, and he shall have Power to grant Reprieves and Pardons for Offences against the United States, except in Cases of Impeachment.

He shall have Power, by and with the Advice and Consent of the Senate, to make Treaties, providing two thirds of the Senators present concur; and he shall nominate, and by and with the Advice and Consent of the Senate, shall appoint Ambassadors, other public Ministers and Consuls, Judges of the supreme Court, and all other Officers of the United States, whose Appointments are not herein otherwise provided for, and which shall be established by Law: but the Congress may by Law vest the Appointment of such inferior Officers, as they think proper, in the President alone, in the Courts of Law, or in the Heads of Departments.

The President shall have Power to fill up all Vacancies that may happen during the Recess of the Senate, by granting Commissions which shall expire at the End of their next Session.

Section 3

He shall from time to time give to the Congress Information of the State of the Union, and recommend to their Consideration such Measures as he shall judge necessary and expedient; he may, on extraordinary Occasions, convene both Houses, or either of them, and in Case of Disagreement between them, with Respect to the Time of Adjournment, he may adjourn them to such Time as he shall think proper, he shall receive Ambassadors and other public Ministers; he shall take Care that the Laws be faithfully executed, and shall Commission all the Offices of the United States.

Section 4

The President, Vice President and all civil Officers of the United States, shall be removed from Office on Impeachment for, and Conviction of, Treason, Bribery, or other high Crimes and Misdemeanors.

Article III

Section 1

The judicial Power of the United States, shall be vested in one supreme Court, and in such inferior Courts as the Congress may from time to time ordain and establish. The Judges, both of the supreme and inferior Courts, shall hold their Offices during good Behaviour, and shall, at Times, receive for their Services, a Compensation, which shall not be diminished during their Continuance in Office.

Section 2

The judicial Power shall extend to all Cases, in Law and Equity, arising under this Constitution, the Laws of the United States, and Treaties made, or which shall be made, under their Authority;—to all Cases affecting Ambassadors, other public Ministers and Consuls;—to all Cases of admiralty and maritime Jurisdiction;—to Controversies to which the United States shall be a Party;—to controversies between two or more States;—between a State and Citizens of another State;—between Citizens of different States;—between Citizens of the same State claiming Lands under Grants of different States; and between a State, or the Citizens thereof, and foreign States, Citizens or Subjects.

In all Cases affecting Ambassadors, other public Ministers and Consuls, and those in which a State shall be Party, the supreme Court shall have original Jurisdiction. In all the other Cases before mentioned, the supreme Court shall have appellate Jurisdiction, both as to Law and Fact, with such Exceptions, and under such Regulations as the Congress shall make.

The Trial of all Crimes, except in Cases of Impeachment, shall be by Jury; and such Trial shall be held in the State where the said Crimes shall have been committed; but when not committed within any State, the Trial shall be at such Place or Places as the Congress may by Law have directed.

Section 3

Treason against the United States, shall consist only in levying War against them, or in adhering to their Enemies, giving them Aid and Comfort. No Person shall be convicted of Treason unless on the Testimony of two Witnesses to the same overt Act, or on Confession in open Court.

The Congress shall have Power to declare the Punishment of Treason, but no Attainder of Treason shall work Corruption of Blood, or Forfeiture except during the Life of the Person attainted.

Article IV

Section 1

Full Faith and Credit shall be given in each State to the public Acts, Records, and judicial Proceedings of every other State. And the Congress may by general Laws prescribe the Manner in which such Arts, Records and Proceedings shall be proved, and the Effect thereof.

Section 2

The Citizens of each State shall be entitled to all Privileges and Immunities of Citizens in the several States.

A Person charged in any State with Treason, Felony, or other Crime, who shall flee from Justice, and be found in another State, shall on Demand of the executive Authority of the State from which he fled, be delivered up, to be removed to the State having Jurisdiction of the Crime.

No Person held to Service or Labour in one State, under the Laws thereof, escaping into another, shall, in Consequence of any Law or Regulation therein, be discharged from such Service or Labour, but shall be delivered up on Claim of the Party to whom such Service or Labour may be due.

Section 3

New States may be admitted by the Congress into this Union; but no new State shall be formed or erected within the Jurisdiction of any other State; nor any State be formed by the Junction of two or more States, or Parts of States, without the Consent of the Legislatures of the States concerned as well as the Congress.

The Congress shall have Power to dispose of and make all needful Rules and Regulations respecting the Territory or other Property belonging to the United States; and nothing in this Constitution shall be so construed as to Prejudice any Claims of the United States, or of any particular State.

Section 4

The United States shall guarantee to every State in this Union a Republican Form of Government, and shall protect each of them against Invasion; and on Application of the Legislature, or of the Executive (when the Legislature cannot be convened) against domestic Violence.

Article V

The Congress, whenever two thirds of both Houses shall deem it necessary, shall propose Amendments to this Constitution, or, on the Application of the Legislatures of two thirds of the several States, shall call a Convention for proposing Amendments, which, in either Case, shall be valid to all Intents and Purposes, as Part of this Constitution, when ratified by the Legislatures of three fourths of the several States, or by Conventions in three fourths thereof, as the one or the other Mode of Ratification may be proposed by the Congress; Provided that no Amendment which may be made prior to the Year One thousand eight hundred and eight shall in any Manner affect the first and fourth Clauses in the Ninth Section of the first Article; and that no State, without its Consent, shall be deprived of its equal Suffrage in the Senate.

Article VI

All Debts contracted and Engagements entered into, before the Adoption of this Constitution, shall be as valid against the United States under this Constitution, as under the Confederation.

This Constitution, and the Laws of the United States which shall be made in Pursuance thereof; and all Treaties made, or which shall be made, under the Authority of the United States, shall be the supreme Law of the Land; and the Judges in every State shall be bound thereby, any Thing in the Constitution or Laws of any State to the Contrary notwithstanding.

The Senators and Representatives before mentioned, and the Members of the several State Legislatures, and all executive and judicial Officers, both of the United States and of the Several States, shall be bound by Oath or Affirmation, to support this Constitution; but no religious Test shall ever be required as a Qualification to any Office or public Trust under the United States.

Article VII

The Ratification of the Conventions of nine States, shall be sufficient for the Establishment of this Constitution between the States so ratifying the Same.

Amendment I [1791]

Congress shall make no law respecting an establishment of religion, or prohibiting the free exercise thereof; or abridging the freedom of speech, or the press; or the right of the people peaceably to assemble, and to petition the Government for a redress of grievances.

Amendment II [1791]

A well regulated Militia, being necessary to the security for a free State, the right of the people to keep and bear Arms, shall not be infringed.

Amendment III [1791]

No Soldier shall, in time of peace be quartered in any house, without the consent of the Owner, nor in time of war, but in a manner to be prescribed by law.

Amendment IV [1791]

The right of the people to be secure in their persons, houses, papers, and effects, against unreasonable searches and seizures, shall not be violated, and no Warrants shall issue, but upon probable cause, supported by Oath or Affirmation, and particularly describing the place to be searched, and the persons or things to be seized.

Amendment V [1791]

No person shall be held to answer for a capital, or otherwise infamous crime, unless on a presentment or indictment of a Grand Jury, except in cases arising in the land or naval forces, or in the Militia, when in actual service in time of War or public danger; nor shall any person be subject for the same offense to be twice put in jeopardy of life or limb; nor shall be compelled in any criminal case to be a witness against himself, nor be deprived of life, liberty, or property, without due process of law; nor shall private property be taken for public use, without just compensation.

Amendment VI [1791]

In all criminal prosecutions, the accused shall enjoy the right to a speedy and public trial, by an impartial jury of the State and district wherein the crime shall have been committed, which district shall have been previously ascertained by law, and to be informed of the nature and cause of the accusation; to be confronted with the Witnesses against him; to have compulsory process for obtaining witnesses in his favor, and to have the Assistance of counsel for his defence.

Amendment VII [1791]

In suits at common law, where the value in controversy shall exceed twenty dollars, the right of trial by jury shall be preserved, and no fact tried by a jury, shall be otherwise re-examined in any Court of the United States, than according to the rules of the common law.

Amendment VIII [1791]

Excessive bail shall not be required, no excessive fines imposed, nor cruel and unusual punishments inflicted.

Amendment IX [1791]

The enumeration in the Constitution, of certain rights, shall not be construed to deny or disparage others retained by the people.

Amendment X [1791]

The powers not delegated to the United States by the Constitution, nor prohibited by it to the States, are reserved to the States respectively, or to the people.

Amendment XI [1798]

The judicial power of the United States shall not be construed to extend to any suit in law or equity, commenced or prosecuted against one of the United States by Citizens of another State, or by Citizens or Subjects of any Foreign State.

Amendment XII [1804]

The Electors shall meet in their respective states and vote by ballot for President and Vice-President, one of whom, at least, shall not be an inhabitant of the same state with themselves; they shall name in their ballots the person voted for as President, and in distinct ballots the person voted for as Vice-President, and they shall make distinct lists of all persons voted for as President, and of all persons voted for as Vice-President, and of the number of votes for each, which lists they shall sign and certify, and transmit sealed to the seat of the government of the United States, directed to the President of the Senate;—The President of the Senate shall, in the presence of the Senate and House of Representatives, open all the certificates and the votes shall then be counted;—The person having the greatest number of votes for President, shall be the President, if such number be a majority of the whole number of Electors appointed; and if no person have such majority, then from the persons having the highest numbers not exceeding three on the list of those voted for as President, the House of Representatives shall choose immediately, by ballot, the President. But in choosing the President, the votes shall be taken by states, the representation from each state having one vote; a quorum for this purpose shall consist of a member or members from two-thirds of the states, and a majority of all the states shall be necessary to a choice. And if the House of Representatives shall not choose a President whenever the right of choice shall devolve upon them, before the fourth day of March next following, then the Vice-President shall act as President, as in the case of the death or other constitutional disability of the President. The person having the greatest number of votes as Vice-President, shall be the Vice-President, if such number be a majority of the

whole number of Electors appointed, and if no person have a majority, then from the two highest numbers on the list, the Senate shall choose the Vice-President; a quorum for the purpose shall consist of two-thirds of the whole number of Senators, and a majority of the whole number shall be necessary to a choice. But no person constitutionally ineligible to the office of President shall be eligible to that of the Vice-President of the United States.

Amendment XIII [1865]

Section 1

Neither slavery nor involuntary servitude, except as a punishment for crime whereof the party shall have been duly convicted, shall exist within the United States, or any place subject to their jurisdiction.

Section 2

Congress shall have power to enforce this article by appropriate legislation.

Amendment XIV [1868]

Section 1

All persons born or naturalized in the United States, and subject to the jurisdiction thereof, are citizens of the United States and of the State wherein they reside. No State shall make or enforce any law which shall abridge the privileges or immunities of citizens of the United States; nor shall any State deprive any person of life, liberty, or property, without due process of law; nor deny to any person within its jurisdiction the equal protection of the laws.

Section 2

Representatives shall be appointed among the several States according to their respective numbers, counting the whole number of persons in each State, excluding Indians not taxed. But when the right to vote at any election for the choice of electors for President and Vice President of the United States, Representatives in Congress, the Executive and Judicial officers of a State, or the members of the Legislature thereof, is denied to any of the male inhabitants of such State, being twenty-one years of age, and citizens of the United States, or in any way abridged, except for participation in rebellion, or other crime, the basis of representation therein shall be reduced in the proportion which the number of such male citizens shall bear the whole number of male citizens twenty-one years of age in such State.

Section 3

No person shall be a Senator or Representative in Congress, or elector of President and Vice President, or hold any office, civil or military, under the United States, or under any State, who, having previously taken an oath, as a member of Congress, or as an officer of the United States, or as a member of any State legislature, or as an executive or judicial officer of any State, to support the Constitution of the United States, shall have engaged in insurrection or rebellion against the same, or given aid or comfort to the enemies thereof. But Congress may by a vote of two-thirds of each House, remove such disability.

Section 4

The validity of the public debt of the United States, authorized by law, including debts incurred for payment of pensions and bounties for services in suppressing insurrection or rebellion, shall not be questioned. But neither the United States nor any State shall assume or pay any debt or obligation incurred in aid of insurrection of rebellion against the United States, or any claim for the loss or emancipation of any slave; but all such debts, obligations and claims shall be held illegal and void.

Section 5

The Congress shall have power to enforce, by appropriate legislation, the provisions of this article.

Amendment XV [1870]

Section 1

The right of citizens of the United States to vote shall not be denied or abridged by the United States or by any State on account of race, color, or previous condition of servitude.

Section 2

The Congress shall have power to enforce this article by appropriate legislation.

Amendment XVI [1913]

The Congress shall have power to lay and collect taxes on incomes, from whatever source derived, without apportionment among the several States, and without regard to any census or enumeration.

Amendment XVII [1913]

The Senate of the United States shall be composed of two Senators from each State, elected by the people thereof, for six years; and each Senator shall have one vote. The electors in each State shall have the qualifications requisite for electors of the most numerous branch of the State legislatures.

When vacancies happen in the representation of any State in the Senate, the executive authority of each State shall issue writs of election to fill such vacancies; *Provided,* That the legislature of any State may empower the executive thereof to make temporary appointments until the people fill the vacancies by election as the legislature may direct.

This amendment shall not be construed as to affect the election or term of any Senator chosen before it becomes valid as part of the Constitution.

Amendment XVIII [1919]

Section 1

After one year from the ratification of this article the manufacture, sale, or transportation of intoxicating liquors within, the importation thereof into, or the exportation thereof from the United States and all territory subject to the jurisdiction thereof for beverage purposes is hereby prohibited.

Section 2

The Congress and the several States shall have concurrent power to enforce this article by appropriate legislation.

Section 3

This article shall be inoperative unless it shall have been ratified as an amendment to the Constitution by the legislatures of the several States, as provided in the Constitution, within seven years from the date of the submission hereof to the States by the Congress.

Amendment XIX [1920]

The right of citizens of the United States to vote shall not be denied or abridged by the United States or by any State on account of sex.

Congress shall have power to enforce this article by appropriate legislation.

Amendment XX [1933]

Section 1

The terms of the President and Vice President shall end at noon on the 20th day of January, and the terms of Senators and Representatives at noon on the 3d day of January, of the years in which such terms would have ended if this article had not been ratified; and the terms of their successors shall then begin.

Section 2

The Congress shall assemble at least once in every year, and such meeting shall begin at noon on the 3d day of

January, unless they shall by law appoint a different day.

Section 3

If, at the time fixed for the beginning of the term of the President, the President elect shall have died, the Vice President elect shall become President. If a President shall not have been chosen before the time fixed for the beginning of his term, or if the President elect shall have failed to qualify, then the Vice President elect shall act as President until a President shall have qualified; and the Congress may by law provide for the case wherein neither a President elect nor a Vice President elect shall have qualified, declaring who shall then act as President, or the manner in which one who is to act shall be selected, and such person shall act accordingly until a President or Vice President shall have qualified.

Section 4

The Congress may by law provide for the case of the death of any of the persons from whom the House of Representatives may choose a President whenever the right of choice shall have devolved upon them, and for the case of the death of any of the persons from whom the Senate may choose a Vice President whenever the right of choice shall have devolved upon them.

Section 5

Sections 1 and 2 shall take effect on the 15th day of October following the ratification of this article.

Section 6

This article shall be inoperative unless it shall have been ratified as an amendment to the Constitution by the legislatures of three-fourths of the several States within seven years from the date of its submission.

Amendment XXI [1933]

Section 1

The eighteenth article of amendment to the Constitution of the United States is hereby repealed.

Section 2

The transportation or importation into any State, Territory, or possession of the United States for delivery or use therein of intoxicating liquors, in violation of the laws thereof, is hereby prohibited.

Section 3

This article shall be inoperative unless it shall have been ratified as an amendment to the Constitution by conventions in the several States, as provided in the Constitution, within seven years from the date of the submission hereof to the States by the Congress.

Amendment XXII [1951]

Section 1

No person shall be elected to the office of the President more than twice, and no person who has held the office of President, or acted as President, for more than two years of a term to which some other person was elected President shall be elected to the office of the President more than once. But this Article shall not apply to any person holding the office of President when this Article was proposed by the Congress, and shall not prevent any person who may be holding the office of President, or acting as President, during the term within which this Article becomes operative from holding the office of President, or acting as President during the remainder of such term.

Section 2

This article shall be inoperative unless it shall have been ratified as an amendment to the Constitution by the legislatures of three-fourths of the several States within seven years from the date of its submission to the States by the Congress.

Amendment XXIII [1961]

Section 1

The District constituting the seat of Government of the United States shall appoint in such manner as the Congress may direct:

A number of electors of President and Vice President equal to the whole number of Senators and Representatives in Congress to which the District would be entitled if it were a State, but in no event more than the least populous State; they shall be in addition to those appointed by the States, but they shall be considered, for the purposes of the election of President and Vice President, to be electors appointed by a State; and they shall meet in the District and perform such duties as provided by the twelfth article of amendment.

Section 2

The Congress shall have power to enforce this article by appropriate legislation.

Amendment XXIV [1964]

Section 1

The right of citizens of the United States to vote in any primary or other election for President or Vice President, for electors for President or Vice President, or for

Senator or Representative in Congress, shall not be denied or abridged by the United States or any State by reason of failure to pay any poll tax or other tax.

Section 2

The Congress shall have power to enforce this article by appropriate legislation.

Amendment XXV [1967]

Section 1

In case of the removal of the President from office or of his death or resignation, the Vice President shall become President.

Section 2

Whenever there is a vacancy in the office of the Vice President, the President shall nominate a Vice President who shall take office upon confirmation by a majority vote of both Houses of Congress.

Section 3

Whenever the President transmits to the President pro tempore of the Senate and the Speaker of the House of Representatives his written declaration that he is unable to discharge the powers and duties of his office, and until he transmits to them a written declaration to the contrary, such powers and duties shall be discharged by the Vice President as Acting President.

Section 4

Whenever the Vice President and a majority of either the principal officers of the executive departments or of such other body as Congress may by law provide, transmit to the President pro tempore of the Senate and the Speaker of the House of Representatives their written declaration that the President is unable to discharge the powers and duties of his office, the Vice President shall immediately assume the powers and duties of the office as Acting President.

Thereafter, when the President transmits to the President pro tempore of the Senate and the Speaker of the House of Representatives his written declaration that no inability exists, he shall resume the powers and duties of his office unless the Vice President and a majority of either the principal officers of the executive department or of such other body as Congress may by law provide, transmit within four days to the President pro tempore of the Senate and the Speaker of the House of Representatives their written declaration that the President is unable to discharge the powers and duties of his office. Thereupon Congress shall decide the issue, assembling within forty-eight hours for that purpose if not in session. If the Congress, within twenty-one days after receipt of the latter written declaration, or, if Congress is not in session, within twenty-one days after Congress is required to assemble, determines by two-thirds vote of both Houses that the President shall continue to discharge the same as Acting President; otherwise, the President shall resume the powers and duties of his office.

Amendment XXVI [1971]

Section 1

The right of citizens of the United States, who are eighteen years of age or older, to vote shall not be denied or abridged by the United States or by any State on account of age.

Section 2

The Congress shall have power to enforce this article by appropriate legislation.

Appendix B

SELECTED PROVISIONS OF RESTATEMENTS

Restatement, Second, of Torts
Restatement, Second, of Contracts
Restatement, Second, of Agency

RESTATEMENT, SECOND, OF TORTS*

§ 8A. Intent

The word "intent" is used throughout the Restatement of this Subject to denote that the actor desires to cause consequences of his act, or that he believes that the consequences are substantially certain to result from it.

§ 46. Outrageous Conduct Causing Severe Emotional Distress

(1) One who by extreme and outrageous conduct intentionally or recklessly causes severe emotional distress to another is subject to liability for such emotional distress, and if bodily harm to the other results from it, for such bodily harm.

(2) Where such conduct is directed at a third person, the actor is subject to liability if he intentionally or recklessly causes severe emotional distress

(a) to a member of such person's immediate family who is present at the time, whether or not such distress results in bodily harm, or

(b) to any other person who is present at the time, if such distress results in bodily harm.

*Copyright 1965–1979 by the American Law Institute. Reprinted with the permission of The American Law Institute.

§ 63. Self-Defense by Force Not Threatening Death or Serious Bodily Harm

(1) An actor is privileged to use reasonable force, not intended or likely to cause death or serious bodily harm, to defend himself against unprivileged harmful or offensive contact or other bodily harm which he reasonably believes that another is about to inflict intentionally upon him.

(2) Self-defense is privileged under the conditions stated in Subsection (1), although the actor correctly or reasonably believes that he can avoid the necessity of so defending himself,

(a) by retreating or otherwise giving up a right or privilege, or

(b) by complying with a command with which the actor is under no duty to comply or which the other is not privileged to enforce by the means threatened.

§ 76. Defense of Third Person

The actor is privileged to defend a third person from a harmful or offensive contact or other invasion of his interests of personality under the same conditions and by the same means as those under and by which he is privileged to defend himself if the actor correctly or reasonably believes that

(a) the circumstances are such as to give the third person a privilege of self-defense, and

(b) his intervention is necessary for the protection of the third person.

§ 164. Intrusions Under Mistake

One who intentionally enters land in the possession of another is subject to liability to the possessor of the land as a trespasser, although he acts under a mistaken belief of law or fact, however reasonable, not induced by the conduct of the possessor, that he

(a) is in possession of the land or entitled to it, or

(b) has the consent of the possessor or of a third person who has the power to give consent on the possessor's behalf, or

(c) has some other privilege to enter or remain on the land.

§ 218. Liability to Person in Possession

One who commits a trespass to a chattel is subject to liability to the possessor of the chattel if, but only if,

(a) he dispossesses the other of the chattel, or

(b) the chattel is impaired as to its condition, quality, or value, or

(c) the possessor is deprived of the use of the chattel for a substantial time, or

(d) bodily harm is caused to the possessor, or harm is caused to some person or thing in which the possessor has a legally protected interest.

§ 282. Negligence Defined

In the Restatement of this Subject, negligence is conduct which falls below the standard established by law for the protection of others against unreasonable risk of harm. It does not include conduct recklessly disregardful of an interest of others.

§ 283A. Children

If the actor is a child, the standard of conduct to which he must conform to avoid being negligent is that of a reasonable person of like age, intelligence, and experience under like circumstances.

§ 286. When Standard of Conduct Defined by Legislation or Regulation Will Be Adopted

The court may adopt as the standard of conduct of a reasonable man the requirements of a legislative enactment or an administrative regulation whose purpose is found to be exclusively or in part

(a) to protect a class of persons which includes the one whose interest is invaded, and

(b) to protect the particular interest which is invaded, and

(c) to protect that interest against the kind of harm which has resulted, and

(d) to protect that interest against the particular hazard from which the harm results.

§ 296. Emergency

(1) In determining whether conduct is negligent toward another, the fact that the actor is confronted with a sudden emergency which requires rapid decision is a factor in determining the reasonable character of his choice of action.

(2) The fact that the actor is not negligent after the emergency has arisen does not preclude his liability for his tortious conduct which has produced the emergency.

§ 314. Duty to Act for Protection of Others

The fact that the actor realizes or should realize that action on his part is necessary for another's aid or protection does not of itself impose upon him a duty to take such action.

§ 314A. Special Relations Giving Rise to Duty to Aid or Protect

(1) A common carrier is under a duty to its passengers to take reasonable action

(a) to protect them against unreasonable risk of physical harm, and

(b) to give them first aid after it knows or has reason to know that they are ill or injured, and to care for them until they can be cared for by others.

§ 328D. Res Ipsa Loquitur

(1) It may be inferred that harm suffered by the plaintiff is caused by negligence of the defendant when

(a) the event is of a kind which ordinarily does not occur in the absence of negligence;

(b) other responsible causes, including the conduct of the plaintiff and third persons, are sufficiently eliminated by the evidence; and

(c) the indicated negligence is within the scope of the defendant's duty to the plaintiff.

(2) It is the function of the court to determine whether the inference may reasonably be drawn by the jury, or whether it must necessarily be drawn.

(3) It is the function of the jury to determine whether the inference is to be drawn in any case where different conclusions may reasonably be reached.

§ 332. Invitee Defined

(1) An invitee is either a public invitee or a business visitor.

(2) A public invitee is a person who is invited to enter or remain on land as a member of the public for a purpose for which the land is held open to the public.

(3) A business visitor is a person who is invited to enter or remain on land for a purpose directly or indirectly connected with business dealings with the possessor of the land.

§ 342. Dangerous Conditions Known to Possessor

A possessor of land is subject to liability for physical harm caused to licensees by a condition on the land if, but only if,

(a) the possessor knows or has reason to know of the condition and should realize that it involves an unreasonable risk of harm to such licensees, and should expect that they will not discover or realize the danger, and

(b) he fails to exercise reasonable care to make the condition safe, or to warn the licensees of the condition and the risk involved, and

(c) the licensees do not know or have reason to know of the condition and the risk involved.

§ 343. Dangerous Conditions Known to or Discoverable by Possessor

A possessor of land is subject to liability for physical harm caused to his invitees by a condition on the land if, but only if, he

(a) knows or by the exercise of reasonable care would discover the condition, and should realize that it involves an unreasonable risk of harm to such invitees, and

(b) should expect that they will not discover or realize the danger, or will fail to protect themselves against it, and

(c) fails to exercise reasonable care to protect them against the danger.

§ 402A. Special Liability of Seller of Product for Physical Harm to User or Consumer

(1) One who sells any product in a defective condition unreasonably dangerous to the user or consumer or to his property is subject to liability for physical harm thereby caused to the ultimate user or consumer, or to his property, if

(a) the seller is engaged in the business of selling such a product, and

(b) it is expected to and does reach the user or consumer without substantial change in the condition in which it is sold.

(2) The rule stated in Subsection (1) applies although

(a) the seller has exercised all possible care in the preparation and sale of his product, and

(b) the user or consumer has not bought the product from or entered into any contractual relation with the seller.

§ 431. What Constitutes Legal Cause

The actor's negligent conduct is a legal cause of harm to another if

(a) his conduct is a substantial factor in bringing about the harm, and

(b) there is no rule of law relieving the actor from liability because of the manner in which his negligence has resulted in the harm.

§ 432. Negligent Conduct as Necessary Antecedent of Harm

(1) Except as stated in Subsection (2), the actor's negligent conduct is not a substantial factor in bringing about harm to another if the harm would have been sustained even if the actor had not been negligent.

(2) If two forces are actively operating, one because of the actor's negligence, the other not because of any misconduct on his part, and each of itself is sufficient to bring about harm to another, the actor's negligence may be found to be a substantial factor in bringing it about.

§ 435. Foreseeability of Harm or Manner of Its Occurrence

(1) If the actor's conduct is a substantial factor in bringing about harm to another, the fact that the actor neither foresaw nor should have foreseen the extent of the harm or the manner in which it occurred does not prevent him from being liable.

(2) The actor's conduct may be held not to be a legal cause of harm to another where after the event and looking back from the harm to the actor's negligent conduct, it appears to the court highly extraordinary that it should have brought about the harm.

§ 442. Considerations Important in Determining Whether an Intervening Force is a Superseding Cause

The following considerations are of importance in determining whether an intervening force is a superseding cause of harm to another:

(a) the fact that its intervention brings about harm different in kind from that which would otherwise have resulted from the actor's negligence;

(b) the fact that its operation or the consequences thereof appear after the event to be extraordinary rather than normal in view of the circumstances existing at the time of its operation;

(c) the fact that the intervening force is operating independently of any situation created by the actor's negligence, or, on the other hand, is or is not a normal result of such a situation;

(d) the fact that the operation of the intervening force is due to a third person's act or to his failure to act;

(e) the fact that the intervening force is due to an act of a third person which is wrongful toward the other and as such subjects the third person to liability to him;

(f) the degree of culpability of a wrongful act of a third person which sets the intervening force in motion.

§ 463. Contributory Negligence Defined

Contributory negligence is conduct on the part of the plaintiff which falls below the standard to which he should conform for his own protection, and which is a legally contributing cause co-operating with the negligence of the defendant in bringing about the plaintiff's harm.

§ 496A. General Principle

A plaintiff who voluntarily assumes a risk of harm arising from the negligent or reckless conduct of the defendant cannot recover for such harm.

§ 509. Harm Done by Abnormally Dangerous Domestic Animals

(1) A possessor of a domestic animal that he knows or has reason to know has dangerous propensities abnormal to its class, is subject to liability for harm done by the animal to another, although he has exercised the utmost care to prevent it from doing the harm.

(2) This liability is limited to harm that results from the abnormally dangerous propensity of which the possessor knows or has reason to know.

§ 549. Measure of Damages for Fraudulent Misrepresentation

(1) The recipient of a fraudulent misrepresentation is entitled to recover as damages in an action of deceit against the maker the pecuniary loss to him of which the misrepresentation is a legal cause, including

(a) the difference between the value of what he has received in the transaction and its purchase price or other value given for it; and

(b) pecuniary loss suffered otherwise as a consequence of the recipient's reliance upon the misrepresentation.

(2) The recipient of a fraudulent misrepresentation in a business transaction is also entitled to recover additional damages sufficient to give him the benefit of his contract with the maker, if these damages are proved with reasonable certainty.

§ 552B. Damages for Negligent Misrepresentation

(1) The damages recoverable for a negligent misrepresentation are those necessary to compensate the plaintiff for the pecuniary loss to him of which the misrepresentation is a legal cause, including

(a) the difference between the value of what he has received in the transaction and its purchase price or other value given for it; and

(b) pecuniary loss suffered otherwise as a consequence of the plaintiff's reliance upon the misrepresentation.

(2) the damages recoverable for a negligent misrepresentation do not include the benefit of the plaintiff's contract with the defendant.

§ 552C. Misrepresentation in Sale, Rental or Exchange Transaction

(1) One who, in a sale, rental or exchange transaction with another, makes a misrepresentation of a material fact for the purpose of inducing the other to act or to refrain from acting in reliance upon it, is subject to liability to the other for pecuniary loss caused to him by his justifiable reliance upon the misrepresentation, even though it is not made fraudulently or negligently.

(2) Damages recoverable under the rule stated in this section are limited to the difference between the value of what the other has parted with and the value of what he has received in the transaction.

§ 568. Libel and Slander Distinguished

(1) Libel consists of the publication of defamatory matter by written or printed words, by its embodiment in physical form or by any other form of communication that has the potentially harmful qualities characteristic of written or printed words.

(2) Slander consists of the publication of defamatory matter by spoken words, transitory gestures or by any form of communication other than those stated in Subsection (1).

(3) The area of dissemination, the deliberate and premeditated character of its publication and the persistence of the defamation are factors to be considered in determining whether a publication is a libel rather than a slander.

§ 580A. Defamation of Public Official or Public Figure

One who publishes a false and defamatory communication concerning a public official or public figure in regard to his conduct, fitness or role in that capacity is subject to liability, if, but only if, he

(a) knows that the statement is false and that it defames the other person, or

(b) acts in reckless disregard of these matters.

§ 623A. Liability for Publication of Injurious Falsehood—General Principle

One who publishes a false statement harmful to the interests of another is subject to liability for pecuniary loss resulting to the other if

(a) he intends for publication of the statement to result in harm to interests of the other having a pecuniary value, or either recognizes or should recognize that it is likely to do so, and

(b) he knows that the statement is false or acts in reckless disregard of its truth or falsity.

§ 652B. Intrusion upon Seclusion

One who intentionally intrudes, physically or otherwise, upon the solitude or seclusion of another or his private affairs or concerns, is subject to liability to the other for invasion of his privacy, if the intrusion would be highly offensive to a reasonable person.

§ 652C. Appropriation of Name or Likeness

One who appropriates to his own use or benefit the name or likeness of another is subject to liability to the other for invasion of his privacy.

§ 652D. Publicity Given to Private Life

One who gives publicity to a matter concerning the private life of another is subject to liability to the other for invasion of his privacy, if the matter publicized is of a kind that

(a) would be highly offensive to a reasonable person, and

(b) is not of legitimate concern to the public.

§ 652E. Publicity Placing Person in False Light

One who gives publicity to a matter concerning another that places the other before the public in a false light is subject to liability to the other for invasion of his privacy, if

(a) the false light in which the other was placed would be highly offensive to a reasonable person, and

(b) the actor had knowledge of or acted in reckless disregard as to the falsity of the publicized matter and the false light in which the other would be placed.

§ 653. Elements of a Cause of Action

A private person who initiates or procures the institution of criminal proceedings against another who is not guilty of the offense charged is subject to liability for malicious prosecution if

(a) he initiates or procures the proceedings without probable cause and primarily for a purpose other than that of bringing an offender to justice, and

(b) the proceedings have terminated in favor of the accused.

§ 766. Intentional Interference with Performance of Contract by Third Person

One who intentionally and improperly interferes with the performance of a contract (except a contract to marry) between another and a third person by inducing or otherwise causing the third person not to perform the contract, is subject to liability to the other for the pecuniary loss resulting to the other from the failure of the third person to perform the contract.

§ 766B. Intentional Interference with Prospective Contractual Relation

One who intentionally and improperly interferes with another's prospective contractual relation (except a contract to marry) is subject to liability to the other for the pecuniary harm resulting from loss of the benefits of the relation, whether the interference consists of

(a) inducing or otherwise causing a third person not to enter into or continue the prospective relation or

(b) preventing the other from acquiring or continuing the prospective relation.

§ 908. Punitive Damages

(1) Punitive damages are damages, other than compensatory or nominal damages, awarded against a person to punish him for his outrageous conduct and to deter him and others like him from similar conduct in the future.

(2) Punitive damages may be awarded for conduct that is outrageous, because of the defendant's evil motive or his reckless indifference to the rights of others. In assessing punitive damages, the trier of fact can properly consider the character of the defendant's act, the nature and extent of the harm to the plaintiff that the defendant caused or intended to cause and the wealth of the defendant.

§ 929. Harm to Land from Past Invasions

(1) If one is entitled to a judgment for harm to land resulting from a past invasion and not amounting to a total destruction of value, the damages include compensation for

(a) the difference between the value of the land before the harm and the value after the harm, or at his election in an appropriate case, the cost of restoration that has been or may be reasonably incurred,

(b) the loss of use of the land, and

(c) discomfort and annoyance to him as an occupant.

(2) If a thing attached to the land but severable from it is damaged, he may at his election recover the loss in value to the thing instead of the damage to the land as a whole.

RESTATEMENT, SECOND, OF CONTRACTS**

§ 1. Contract Defined

A contract is a promise or a set of promises for the breach of which the law gives a remedy, or the performance of which the law in some way recognizes as a duty.

§ 2. Promise; Promisor; Promisee; Beneficiary

(1) A promise is a manifestation of intention to act or refrain from acting in a specified way, so made as to justify a promisee in understanding that a commitment has been made.

(2) The person manifesting the intention is the promisor.

(3) The person to whom the manifestation is addressed is the promisee.

(4) Where performance will benefit a person other than the promisee, that person is a beneficiary.

§ 3. Agreement Defined; Bargain Defined

An agreement is a manifestation of mutual assent on the part of two or more persons. A bargain is an agreement to exchange promises or to exchange a promise for a performance or to exchange performances.

§ 7. Voidable Contracts

A voidable contract is one where one or more parties have the power, by a manifestation of election to do so, to avoid the legal relations created by the contract, or by ratification of the contract to extinguish the power of avoidance.

§ 8. Unenforceable Contracts

An unenforceable contract is one for the breach of which neither the remedy of damages nor the remedy of specific performance is available, but which is recognized in some other way as creating a duty of performance, though there has been no ratification.

§ 12. Capacity to Contract

(1) No one can be bound by contract who has not legal capacity to incur at least voidable contractual duties. Capacity to contract may be partial and its existence in respect of a particular transaction may depend upon the nature of the transaction or upon other circumstances.

(2) A natural person who manifests assent to a transaction has full legal capacity to incur contractual duties thereby unless he is

**Copyright 1981 by The American Law Institute. Reprinted with the permission of The American Law Institute.

(a) under guardianship, or

(b) an infant, or

(c) mentally ill or defective, or

(d) intoxicated.

§ 13. Persons Affected by Guardianship

A person has no capacity to incur contractual duties if his property is under guardianship by reason of an adjudication of mental illness or defect.

§ 14. Infants

Unless a statute provides otherwise, a natural person has the capacity to incur only voidable contractual duties until the beginning of the day before the person's eighteenth birthday.

§ 15. Mental Illness or Defect

(1) A person incurs only voidable contractual duties by entering into a transaction if by reason of mental illness or defect

(a) he is unable to understand in a reasonable manner the nature and consequences of the transaction, or

(b) he is unable to act in a reasonable manner in relation to the transaction and the other party has reason to know of his condition.

(2) Where the contract is made on fair terms and the other party is without knowledge of the mental illness or defect, the power of avoidance under Subsection (1) terminates to the extent that the contract has been so performed in whole or in part or the circumstances have so changed that avoidance would be unjust. In such a case a court may grant relief as justice requires.

§ 16. Intoxicated Persons

A person incurs only voidable contractual duties by entering into a transaction if the other party has reason to know that by reason of intoxication

(a) he is unable to understand in a reasonable manner the nature and consequences of the transaction, or

(b) he is unable to act in a reasonable manner in relation to the transaction.

§ 20. Effect of Misunderstanding

(1) There is no manifestation of mutual assent to an exchange if the parties attach materially different meanings to their manifestations and

(a) neither party knows or has reason to know the meaning attached by the other; or

(b) each party knows or each party has reason to know the meaning attached by the other.

(2) The manifestations of the parties are operative in accordance with the meaning attached to them by one of the parties if

(a) that party does not know of any different meaning attached by the other, and the other knows the meaning attached by the first party; or

(b) that party has no reason to know of any different meaning attached by the other, and the other has reason to know the meaning attached by the first party.

§ 24. Offer Defined

An offer is the manifestation of willingness to enter into a bargain, so made as to justify another person in understanding that his assent to that bargain is invited and will conclude it.

§ 30. Form of Acceptance Invited

(1) An offer may invite or require acceptance to be made by an affirmative answer in words, or by performing or refraining from performing a specified act, or may empower the offeree to make a selection of terms in his acceptance.

(2) Unless otherwise indicated by the language or the circumstances, an offer invites acceptance in any manner and by any medium reasonable in the circumstances.

§ 33. Certainty

(1) Even though a manifestation of intention is intended to be understood as an offer, it cannot be accepted so as to form a contract unless the terms of the contract are reasonably certain.

(2) The terms of a contract are reasonably certain if they provide a basis for determining the existence of a breach and for giving an appropriate remedy.

(3) The fact that one or more terms of a proposed bargain are left open or uncertain may show that a manifestation of intention is not intended to be understood as an offer or as an acceptance.

§ 34. Certainty and Choice of Terms; Effect of Performance or Reliance

(1) The terms of a contract may be reasonably certain even though it empowers one or both parties to make a selection of terms in the course of performance.

(2) Part performance under an agreement may remove uncertainty and establish that a contract enforceable as a bargain has been formed.

(3) Action in reliance on an agreement may make a contractual remedy appropriate even though uncertainty is not removed.

§ 41. Lapse of Time

(1) An offeree's power of acceptance is terminated at the time specified in the offer, or, if no time is specified, at the end of a reasonable time.

(2) What is a reasonable time is a question of fact, depending on all the circumstances existing when the offer and attempted acceptance are made.

(3) Unless otherwise indicated by the language or the circumstances, and subject to the rule stated in § 49, an offer sent by mail is seasonably accepted if an acceptance is mailed at any time before midnight on the day on which the offer is received.

§ 43. Indirect Communication of Revocation

An offeree's power of acceptance is terminated when the offeror takes definite action inconsistent with an intention to enter into the proposed contract and the offeree acquires reliable information to that effect.

§ 45. Option Contract Created by Part Performance or Tender

(1) Where an offer invites an offeree to accept by rendering a performance and does not invite a promissory acceptance, an option contract is created when the offeree tenders or begins the invited performance or tenders a beginning of it.

(2) The offeror's duty of performance under any option contract so created is conditional on completion or tender of the invited performance in accordance with the terms of the offer.

§ 54. Acceptance by Performance; Necessity of Notification to Offeror

(1) Where an offer invites an offeree to accept by rendering a performance, no notification is necessary to make such an acceptance effective unless the offer requests such a notification.

(2) If an offeree who accepts by rendering a performance has reason to know that the offeror has no adequate means of learning of the performance with reasonable promptness and certainty, the contractual duty of the offeror is discharged unless

(a) the offeree exercises reasonable diligence to notify the offeror of acceptance, or

(b) the offeror learns of the performance within a reasonable time, or

(c) the offer indicates that notification of acceptance is not required.

§ 67. Effect of Receipt of Acceptance Improperly Dispatched

Where an acceptance is seasonably dispatched but the offeree uses means of transmission not invited by the offer or fails to exercise reasonable diligence to insure safe transmission, it is treated as operative upon dispatch if received within the time in which a properly dispatched acceptance would normally have arrived.

§ 71. Requirement of Exchange; Types of Exchange

(1) To constitute consideration, a performance or a return promise must be bargained for.

(2) A performance or return promise is bargained for if it is sought by the promisor in exchange for his promise and is given by the promisee in exchange for that promise.

(3) The performance may consist of

(a) an act other than a promise, or

(b) a forbearance, or

(c) the creation, modification, or destruction of a legal relation.

(4) The performance or return promise may be given to the promisor or to some other person. It may be given by the promisee or by some other person.

§ 77. Illusory and Alternative Promises

A promise or apparent promise is not consideration if by its terms the promisor or purported promisor reserves a choice of alternative performances unless

(a) each of the alternative performances would have been consideration if it alone had been bargained for; or

(b) one of the alternative performances would have been consideration and there is or appears to the parties to be a substantial possibility that before the promisor exercises his choice events may eliminate the alternatives which would not have been consideration.

§ 79. Adequacy of Consideration; Mutuality of Obligation

If the requirement of consideration is met, there is no additional requirement of

(a) a gain, advantage, or benefit to the promisor or a loss, disadvantage, or detriment to the promisee; or

(b) equivalence in the values exchanged; or

(c) "mutuality of obligation."

§ 82. Promise to Pay Indebtedness; Effect on the Statute of Limitations

(1) A promise to pay all or part of an antecedent contractual or quasi-contractual indebtedness owed by the promisor is binding if the indebtedness is still enforceable or would be except for the effect of a statute of limitations.

(2) The following facts operate as such a promise unless other facts indicate a different intention:

(a) A voluntary acknowledgment to the obligee, admitting the present existence of the antecedent indebtedness; or

(b) A voluntary transfer of money, a negotiable instrument, or other thing by the obligor to the obligee, made as interest on or part payment of or collateral security for the antecedent indebtedness; or

(c) A statement to the obligee that the statute of limitations will not be pleaded as a defense.

§ 89. Modification of Executory Contract

A promise modifying a duty under a contract not fully performed on either side is binding

(a) if the modification is fair and equitable in view of circumstances not anticipated by the parties when the contract was made; or

(b) to the extent provided by statute; or

(c) to the extent that justice requires enforcement in view of material change of position in reliance on the promise.

§ 90. Promise Reasonably Inducing Action or Forbearance

(1) A promise which the promisor should reasonably expect to induce action or forbearance on the part of the promisee or a third person and which does induce such action or forbearance is binding if injustice can be avoided only by enforcement of the promise. The remedy granted for breach may be limited as justice requires.

(2) A charitable subscription or a marriage settlement is binding under Subsection (1) without proof that the promise induced action or forbearance.

§ 110. Classes of Contracts Covered

(1) The following classes of contracts are subject to a statute, commonly called the Statute of Frauds, forbidding enforcement unless there is a written memorandum or an applicable exception:

(a) a contract of an executor or administrator to answer for a duty of his decedent (the executor-administrator provision);

(b) a contract to answer for the duty of another (the suretyship provision);

(c) a contract made upon consideration of marriage (the marriage provision);

(d) a contract for the sale of an interest in land (the land contract provision);

(e) a contract that is not to be performed within one year from the making thereof (the one-year provision).

(2) The following classes of contracts, which were traditionally subject to the Statute of Frauds, are now governed by Statute of Frauds provisions of the Uniform Commercial Code:

(a) a contract for the sale of goods for the price of $500 or more (Uniform Commercial Code § 2–201);

(b) a contract for the sale of securities (Uniform Commercial Code § 8–319);

(c) a contract for the sale of personal property not otherwise covered, to the extent of enforcement by way of action or defense beyond $5,000 in amount or value of remedy (Uniform Commercial Code § 1–206).

(3) In addition the Uniform Commercial Code requires a writing signed by the debtor for an agreement which creates or provides for a security interest in personal property or fixtures not in the possession of the secured party.

(4) Statutes in most states provide that no acknowledgment or promise is sufficient evidence of a new or continuing contract to take a case out of the operation of a statute of limitations unless made in some writing signed by the party to be charged, but that the statute does not alter the effect of any payment of principal or interest.

(5) In many states other classes of contracts are subject to a requirement of a writing.

§ 111. Contract of Executor or Administrator

A contract of an executor or administrator to answer personally for a duty of his decedent is within the Statute of Frauds if a similar contract to answer for the duty of a living person would be within the Statute as a contract to answer for the duty of another.

§ 116. Main Purpose; Advantage to Surety

A contract that all or part of a duty of a third person to the promisee shall be satisfied is not within the Statute of Frauds as a promise to answer for the duty of another if the consideration for the promise is in fact or apparently desired by the promisor mainly for his own economic advantage, rather than in order to benefit the third person. If, however, the consideration is merely a premium for insurance, the contract is within the Statute.

§ 124. Contract Made Upon Consideration of Marriage

A promise for which all or part of the consideration is either marriage or a promise to marry is within the Statute of Frauds, except in the case of an agreement which consists only of mutual promises of two persons to marry each other.

§ 125. Contract to Transfer, Buy, or Pay for an Interest in Land

(1) A promise to transfer to any person any interest in land is within the Statute of Frauds.

(2) A promise to buy any interest in land is within the Statute of Frauds, irrespective of the person to whom the transfer is to be made.

(3) When a transfer of an interest in land has been made, a promise to pay the price, if originally within the Statute of Frauds, ceases to be within it unless the promised price is itself in whole or in part an interest in land.

(4) Statutes in most states except from the land contract and one-year provisions of the Statute of Frauds short-term leases and contracts to lease, usually for a term not longer than one year.

§ 129. Action in Reliance; Specific Performance

A contract for the transfer of an interest in land may be specifically enforced notwithstanding failure to comply with the Statute of Frauds if it is established that the party seeking enforcement, in reasonable reliance on the contract and on the continuing assent of the party against whom enforcement is sought, has so changed his position that injustice can be avoided only by specific enforcement.

§ 130. Contract Not to Be Performed Within a Year

(1) Where any promise in a contract cannot be fully performed within a year from the time the contract is made, all promises in the contract are within the Statute of Frauds until one party to the contract completes his performance.

(2) When one party to a contract has completed his performance, the one-year provision of the Statute does not prevent enforcement of the promises of other parties.

§ 132. Several Writings

The memorandum may consist of several writings if one of the writings is signed and the writings in the circumstances clearly indicate that they relate to the same transaction.

§ 157. Effect of Fault of Party Seeking Relief

A mistaken party's fault in failing to know or discover the facts before making the contract does not bar him from avoidance or reformation under the rules stated in this Chapter, unless his fault amounts to a failure to act in good faith and in accordance with reasonable standards of fair dealing.

§ 163. When a Misrepresentation Prevents Formation of a Contract

If a misrepresentation as to the character or essential terms of a proposed contract induces conduct that appears to be a manifestation of assent by one who neither knows nor has reasonable opportunity to know of the character or essential terms of the proposed contract, his conduct is not effective as a manifestation of assent.

§ 174. When Duress by Physical Compulsion Prevents Formation of a Contract

If conduct that appears to be a manifestation of assent by a party who does not intend to engage in that conduct is physically compelled by duress, the conduct is not effective as a manifestation of assent.

§ 175. When Duress by Threat Makes a Contract Voidable

(1) If a party's manifestation of assent is induced by an improper threat by the other party that leaves the victim no reasonable alternative, the contract is voidable by the victim.

(2) If a party's manifestation of assent is induced by one who is not a party to the transaction, the contract is voidable by the victim unless the other party to the transaction in good faith and without reason to know of the duress either gives value or relies materially on the transaction.

§ 176. When a Threat Is Improper

(1) A threat is improper if

   (a) what is threatened is a crime or a tort, or the threat itself would be a crime or a tort if it resulted in obtaining property,

   (b) what is threatened is a criminal prosecution,

   (c) what is threatened is the use of civil process and the threat is made in bad faith, or

   (d) the threat is a breach of the duty of good faith and fair dealing under a contract with the recipient.

(2) A threat is improper if the resulting exchange is not on fair terms, and

   (a) the threatened act would harm the recipient and would not significantly benefit the party making the threat,

   (b) the effectiveness of the threat in inducing the manifestation of assent is significantly increased by prior unfair dealing by the party making the threat, or

   (c) what is threatened is otherwise a use of power for illegitimate ends.

§ 177. When Undue Influence Makes a Contract Voidable

(1) Undue influence is unfair persuasion of a party who is under the domination of the person exercising the persuasion or who by virtue of the relation between them is justified in assuming that the person will not act in a manner inconsistent with his welfare.

(2) If a party's manifestation of assent is induced by undue influence by the other party, the contract is voidable by the victim.

(3) If a party's manifestation of assent is induced by one who is not a party to the transaction, the contract is voidable by the victim unless the other party to the transaction in good faith and without reason to know of the undue influence either gives value or relies materially on the transaction.

§ 181. Effect of Failure to Comply with Licensing or Similar Requirement

If a party is prohibited from doing an act because of his failure to comply with a licensing, registration or similar requirement, a promise in consideration of his doing that act or of his promise to do it is unenforceable on grounds of public policy if

   (a) the requirement has a regulatory purpose, and

   (b) the interest in the enforcement of the promise is clearly outweighed by the public policy behind the requirement.

§ 186. Promise in Restraint of Trade

(1) A promise is unenforceable on grounds of public policy if it is unreasonably in restraint of trade.

(2) A promise is in restraint of trade if its performance would limit competition in any business or restrict the promisor in the exercise of a gainful occupation.

§ 187. Non-Ancillary Restraints on Competition

A promise to refrain from competition that imposes a restraint that is not ancillary to an otherwise valid transaction or relationship is unreasonably in restraint of trade.

§ 188. Ancillary Restraints on Competition

(1) A promise to refrain from competition that imposes a restraint that is ancillary to an otherwise valid transaction or relationship is unreasonably in restraint of trade if

   (a) the restraint is greater than is needed to protect the promisee's legitimate interest, or

   (b) the promisee's need is outweighed by the hardship to the promisor and the likely injury to the public.

(2) Promises imposing restraints that are ancillary to a valid transaction or relationship include the following:

(a) a promise by the seller of a business not to compete with the buyer in such a way as to injure the value of the business sold;

(b) a promise by an employee or other agent not to compete with his employer or other principal;

(c) a promise by a partner not to compete with the partnership.

§ 192. Promise Involving Commission of a Tort

A promise to commit a tort or to induce the commission of a tort is unenforceable on grounds of public policy.

§ 195. Term Exempting from Liability for Harm Caused Intentionally, Recklessly or Negligently

(1) A term exempting a party from tort liability for harm caused intentionally or recklessly is unenforceable on grounds of public policy.

(2) A term exempting a party from tort liability for harm caused negligently is unenforceable on grounds of public policy if

(a) the term exempts an employer from liability to an employee for injury in the course of his employment;

(b) the term exempts one charged with a duty of public service from liability to one to whom that duty is owed for compensation for breach of that duty, or

(c) the other party is similarly a member of a class protected against the class to which the first party belongs.

(3) A term exempting a seller of a product from his special tort liability for physical harm to a user or consumer is unenforceable on grounds of public policy unless the term is fairly bargained for and is consistent with the policy underlying that liability.

§ 201. Whose Meaning Prevails

(1) Where the parties have attached the same meaning to a promise or agreement or a term thereof, it is interpreted in accordance with that meaning.

(2) Where the parties have attached different meanings to a promise or agreement or a term thereof, it is interpreted in accordance with the meaning attached by one of them if at the time the agreement was made

(a) that party did not know of any different meaning attached by the other, and the other knew the meaning attached by the first party; or

(b) that party had no reason to know of any different meaning attached by the other, and the other had reason to know the meaning attached by the first party.

(3) Except as stated in this Section, neither party is bound by the meaning attached by the other, even though the result may be a failure of mutual assent.

§ 202. Rules in Aid of Interpretation

(1) Words and other conduct are interpreted in the light of all the circumstances, and if the principal purpose of the parties is ascertainable it is given great weight.

(2) A writing is interpreted as a whole, and all writings that are part of the same transaction are intrepreted together.

(3) Unless a different intention is manifested,

(a) where language has a generally prevailing meaning, it is interpreted in accordance with that meaning;

(b) technical terms and words of art are given their technical meaning when used in a transaction within their technical field.

(4) Where an agreement involves repeated occasions for performance by either party with knowledge of the nature of the performance and opportunity for objection to it by the other, any course of performance accepted or acquiesced in without objection is given great weight in the interpretation of the agreement.

(5) Wherever reasonable, the manifestations of intention of the parties to a promise or agreement are interpreted as consistent with each other and with any relevant course of performance, course of dealing, or usage of trade.

§ 203. Standards of Preference in Interpretation

In the interpretation of a promise or agreement or a term thereof, the following standards of preference are generally applicable:

(a) an interpretation which gives a reasonable, lawful, and effective meaning to all the terms is preferred to an interpretation which leaves a part unreasonable, unlawful, or of no effect;

(b) express terms are given greater weight than course of performance, course of dealing, and usage of trade, course of performance is given greater weight than course of dealing or usage of trade, and course of dealing is given greater weight than usage of trade;

(c) specific terms and exact terms are given greater weight than general language;

(d) separately negotiated or added terms are given greater weight than standardized terms or other terms not separately negotiated.

§ 208. Unconscionable Contract or Term

If a contract or term thereof is unconscionable at the time the contract is made a court may refuse to enforce the contract, or may enforce the remainder of the contract without the unconscionable term, or may so limit the application of any unconscionable term as to avoid any unconscionable result.

§ 213. Effect of Integrated Agreement on Prior Agreements (Parol Evidence Rule)

(1) A binding integrated agreement discharges prior agreements to the extent that it is inconsistent with them.

(2) A binding completely integrated agreement discharges prior agreements to the extent that they are within its scope.

(3) An integrated agreement that is not binding or that is voidable and avoided does not discharge a prior agreement. But an integrated agreement, even though not binding, may be effective to render inoperative a term which would have been part of the agreement if it had not been integrated.

§ 214. Evidence of Prior or Contemporaneous Agreements and Negotiations

Agreements and negotiations prior to or contemporaneous with the adoption of a writing are admissible in evidence to establish

(a) that the writing is or is not an integrated agreement;

(b) that the integrated agreement, if any, is completely or partially integrated;

(c) the meaning of the writing, whether or not integrated;

(d) illegality, fraud, duress, mistake, lack of consideration, or other invalidating cause;

(e) ground for granting or denying rescission, reformation, specific performance, or other remedy.

§ 216. Consistent Additional Terms

(1) Evidence of a consistent additional term is admissible to supplement an integrated agreement unless the court finds that the agreement was completely integrated.

(2) An agreement is not completely integrated if the writing omits a consistent additional agreed term which is

(a) agreed to for separate consideration, or

(b) such a term as in the circumstances might naturally be omitted from the writing.

§ 217. Integrated Agreement Subject to Oral Requirement of a Condition

Where the parties to a written agreement agree orally that performance of the agreement is subject to the occurrence of a stated condition, the agreement is not integrated with respect to the oral condition.

§ 235. Effect of Performance as Discharge and of Non-Performance as Breach

(1) Full performance of a duty under a contract discharges the duty.

(2) When performance of a duty under a contract is due any non-performance is a breach.

§ 241. Circumstances Significant in Determining Whether a Failure Is Material

In determining whether a failure to render or to offer performance is material, the following circumstances are significant:

(a) the extent to which the injured party will be deprived of the benefit which he reasonably expected;

(b) the extent to which the injured party can be adequately compensated for the part of that benefit of which he will be deprived;

(c) the extent to which the party failing to perform or to offer to perform will suffer forfeiture;

(d) the likelihood that the party failing to perform or to offer to perform will cure his failure, taking account of all the circumstances including any reasonable assurances;

(e) the extent to which the behavior of the party failing to perform or to offer to perform comports with standards of good faith and fair dealing.

§ 261. Discharge by Supervening Impracticability

Where, after a contract is made, a party's performance is made impracticable without his fault by the occurrence of an event the non-occurrence of which was a basic assumption on which the contract was made, his duty to render that performance is discharged, unless the language or the circumstances indicate the contrary.

§ 279. Substituted Contract

(1) A substituted contract is a contract that is itself accepted by the obligee in satisfaction of the obligor's existing duty.

(2) The substituted contract discharges the original duty and breach of the substituted contract by the obligor does not give the obligee a right to enforce the original duty.

§ 280. Novation

A novation is a substituted contract that includes as a party one who was neither the obligor nor the obligee of the original duty.

§ 281. Accord and Satisfaction

(1) An accord is a contract under which an obligee promises to accept a stated performance in satisfaction of the obligor's existing duty. Performance of the accord discharges the original duty.

(2) Until performance of the accord, the original duty is suspended unless there is such a breach of the accord by the obligor as discharges the new duty of the obligee to accept the performance in satisfaction. If there is such a breach, the obligee may enforce either the original duty or any duty under the accord.

(3) Breach of the accord by the obligee does not discharge the original duty, but the obligor may maintain a suit for specific performance of the accord, in addition to any claim for damages for partial breach.

§ 286. Alteration of Writing

(1) If one to whom a duty is owed under a contract alters a writing that is an integrated agreement or that satisfies the Statute of Frauds with respect to that contract, the duty is discharged if the alteration is fraudulent and material.

(2) An alteration is material if it would, if effective, vary any party's legal relations with the maker of the alteration or adversely affect that party's legal relations with a third person. The unauthorized insertion in a blank space in a writing is an alteration.

§ 317. Assignment of a Right

(1) An assignment of a right is a manifestation of the assignor's intention to transfer it by virtue of which the assignor's right to performance by the obligor is extinguished in whole or in part and the assignee acquires a right to such performance.

(2) A contractual right can be assigned unless

(a) the substitution of a right of the assignee for the right of the assignor would materially change the duty of the obligor, or materially increase the burden or risk imposed on him by his contract, or materially impair his chance of obtaining return performance, or materially reduce its value to him, or

(b) the assignment is forbidden by statute, or is otherwise inoperative on grounds of public policy, or

(c) assignment is validly precluded by contract.

§ 318. Delegation of Performance of Duty

(1) An obligor can properly delegate the performance of his duty to another unless the delegation is contrary to public policy or the terms of his promise.

(2) Unless otherwise agreed, a promise requires performance by a particular person only to the extent that the obligee has a substantial interest in having that person perform or control the acts promised.

(3) Unless the obligee agrees otherwise, neither delegation of performance nor a contract to assume the duty made with the obligor by the person delegated discharges any duty or liability of the delegating obligor.

§ 322. Contractual Prohibition of Assignment

(1) Unless the circumstances indicate the contrary, a contract term prohibiting assignment of "the contract" bars only the delegation to an assignee of the performance by the assignor of a duty or condition.

(2) A contract term prohibiting assignment of rights under the contract, unless a different intention is manifested,

(a) does not forbid assignment of a right to damages for breach of the whole contract or a right arising out of the assignor's due performance of his entire obligation;

(b) gives the obligor a right to damages for breach of the terms forbidding assignment but does not render the assignment ineffective;

(c) is for the benefit of the obligor, and does not prevent the assignee from acquiring rights against the assignor or the obligor from discharging his duty as if there were no such prohibition.

§ 328. Interpretation of Words of Assignment; Effect of Acceptance of Assignment

(1) Unless the language or the circumstances indicate the contrary, as in an assignment for security, an assignment of "the contract" or of "all my rights under the contract" or an assignment in similar general terms is an assignment of the assignor's rights and a delegation of his unperformed duties under the contract.

(2) Unless the language or the circumstances indicate the contrary, the acceptance by an assignee of such an assignment operates as a promise to the assignor to perform the assignor's unperformed duties, and the obligor of the assigned rights is an intended beneficiary of the promise.

Caveat: The Institute expresses no opinion as to whether the rule stated in Subsection (2) applies to an assignment by a purchaser of his rights under a contract for the sale of land.

§ 333. Warranties of an Assignor

(1) Unless a contrary intention is manifested, one who assigns or purports to assign a right by assignment under seal or for value warrants to the assignee

(a) that he will do nothing to defeat or impair the value of the assignment and has no knowledge of any fact which would do so;

(b) that the right, as assigned, actually exists and is subject to no limitations or defenses good against the assignor other than those stated or apparent at the time of the assignment;

(c) that any writing evidencing the right which is delivered to the assignee or exhibited to him to induce him to accept the assignment is genuine and what it purports to be.

(2) An assignment does not of itself operate as a warranty that the obligor is solvent or that he will perform his obligation.

(3) An assignor is bound by affirmations and promises to the assignee with reference to the right assigned in the same way and to the same extent that one who transfers goods is bound in like circumstances.

(4) An assignment of a right to a sub-assignee does not operate as an assignment of the assignee's rights under his assignor's warranties unless an intention is manifested to assign the rights under the warranties.

§ 342. Successive Assignees from the Same Assignor

Except as otherwise provided by statute, the right of an assignee is superior to that of a subsequent assignee of the same right from the same assignor, unless

(a) the first assignment is ineffective or revocable or is voidable by the assignor or by the subsequent assignee; or

(b) the subsequent assignee in good faith and without knowledge or reason to know of the prior assignment gives value and obtains

(i) payment or satisfaction of the obligation,

(ii) judgment against the obligor,

(iii) a new contract with the obligor by novation, or

(iv) possession of a writing of a type customarily accepted as a symbol or as evidence of the right assigned.

§ 346. Availability of Damages

(1) The injured party has a right to damages for any breach by a party against whom the contract is enforceable unless the claim for damages has been suspended or discharged.

(2) If the breach caused no loss or if the amount of the loss is not proved under the rules stated in this Chapter, a small sum fixed without regard to the amount of loss will be awarded as nominal damages.

§ 350. Avoidability as a Limitation on Damages

(1) Except as stated in Subsection (2), damages are not recoverable for loss that the injured party could have avoided without undue risk, burden or humiliation.

(2) The injured party is not precluded from recovery by the rule stated in Subsection (1) to the extent that he has made reasonable but unsuccessful efforts to avoid loss.

§ 351. Unforeseeability and Related Limitations on Damages

(1) Damages are not recoverable for loss that the party in breach did not have reason to foresee as a probable result of the breach when the contract was made.

(2) Loss may be foreseeable as a probable result of a breach because it follows from the breach

(a) in the ordinary course of events, or

(b) as a result of special circumstances, beyond the ordinary course of events, that the party in breach had reason to know.

(3) A court may limit damages for foreseeable loss by excluding recovery for loss of profits, by allowing recovery only for loss incurred in reliance, or otherwise if it concludes that in the circumstances justice so requires in order to avoid disproportionate compensation.

§ 352. Uncertainty as a Limitation on Damages

Damages are not recoverable for loss beyond an amount that the evidence permits to be established with reasonable certainty.

§ 355. Punitive Damages

Punitive damages are not recoverable for a breach of contract unless the conduct constituting the breach is also a tort for which punitive damages are recoverable.

§ 356. Liquidated Damages and Penalties

(1) Damages for breach by either party may be liquidated in the agreement but only at an amount that is reasonable in the light of the anticipated or actual loss caused by the breach and the difficulties of proof of loss. A term fixing unreasonably large liquidated damages is unenforceable on grounds of public policy as a penalty.

(2) A term in a bond providing for an amount of money as a penalty for non-occurrence of the condition of the bond is unenforceable on grounds of public policy to the extent that the amount exceeds the loss caused by such non-occurrence.

§ 360. Factors Affecting Adequacy of Damages

In determining whether the remedy in damages would be adequate, the following circumstances are significant:

(a) the difficulty of proving damages with reasonable certainty,

(b) the difficulty of procuring a suitable substitute performance by means of money awarded as damages, and

(c) the likelihood that an award of damages could not be collected.

§ 367. Contracts for Personal Service or Supervision

(1) A promise to render personal service will not be specifically enforced.

(2) A promise to render personal service exclusively for one employer will not be enforced by an injunction against serving another if its probable result will be to compel a performance involving personal relations the enforced continuance of which is undesirable or will be to leave the employee without other reasonable means of making a living.

§ 378. Election Among Remedies

If a party has more than one remedy under the rules stated in this Chapter, his manifestation of a choice of one of them by bringing suit or otherwise is not a bar to another remedy unless the remedies are inconsistent and the other party materially changes his position in reliance on the manifestation.

RESTATEMENT, SECOND, OF AGENCY***

§ 1. Agency; Principal; Agent

(1) Agency is the fiduciary relation which results from the manifestation of consent by one person to another that the other shall act on his behalf and subject to his control, and consent by the other so to act.

(2) The one for whom action is to be taken is the principal.

(3) The one who is to act is the agent.

§ 2. Master; Servant; Independent Contractor

(1) A master is a principal who employs an agent to perform service in his affairs and who controls or has the right to control the physical conduct of the other in the performance of the service.

(2) A servant is an agent employed by a master to perform service in his affairs whose physical conduct in the performance of the service is controlled or is subject to the right to control by the master.

(3) An independent contractor is a person who contracts with another to do something for him but who is not controlled by the other nor subject to the other's right to control with respect to his physical conduct in the performance of the undertaking. He may or may not be an agent.

***Copyright 1958 by The American Law Institute. Reprinted with the permission of The American Law Institute.

§ 4. Disclosed Principal; Partially Disclosed Principal; Undisclosed Principal

(1) If, at the time of a transaction conducted by an agent, the other party thereto has notice that the agent is acting for a principal and of the principal's identity, the principal is a disclosed principal.

(2) If the other party has notice that the agent is or may be acting for a principal but has no notice of the principal's identity, the principal for whom the agent is acting is a partially disclosed principal.

(3) If the other party has no notice that the agent is acting for a principal, the one for whom he acts is an undisclosed principal.

§ 15. Manifestations of Consent

An agency relation exists only if there has been a manifestation by the principal to the agent that the agent may act on his account, and consent by the agent so to act.

§ 16. Consideration

The relation of principal and agent can be created although neither party receives consideration.

§ 17. What Acts are Delegable

A person privileged, or subject to a duty, to perform an act or accomplish a result can properly appoint an agent to perform the act or accomplish the result, unless public policy or the agreement with another requires personal performance; if personal performance is required, the doing of the act by another on his behalf does not constitute performance by him.

§ 18. Delegation of Powers Held by Agent

Unless otherwise agreed, an agent cannot properly delegate to another the exercise of discretion in the use of a power held for the benefit of the principal.

§ 19. Appointment to Perform Illegal Acts

The appointment of an agent to do an act is illegal if an agreement to do such an act or the doing of the act itself would be criminal, tortious, or otherwise opposed to public policy.

§ 27. Creation of Apparent Authority: General Rule

Except for the execution of instruments under seal or for the conduct of transactions required by statute to be authorized in a particular way, apparent authority to do an act is created as to a third person by written or spoken words or any other conduct of the principal which, reasonably interpreted, causes the third person to believe that the principal consents to have the act done on his behalf by the person purporting to act for him.

§ 28. Authority to Execute Sealed Instruments

(1) Except as stated in Subsection (2), an instrument executed by an agent as a sealed instrument does not operate as such unless authority or apparent authority to execute it has been conferred by an instrument under seal.

(2) Sealed authority is not necessary to execute an instrument under seal where:

(a) the instrument is executed in the principal's presence and by his direction;

(b) the instrument is authorized by a corporation or partnership in accordance with the rules relating to the authorization of such instruments by such associations; or

(c) a statute deprives seals of their legal significance.

§ 35. When Incidental Authority is Inferred

Unless otherwise agreed, authority to conduct a transaction includes authority to do acts which are incidental to it, usually accompany it, or are reasonably necessary to accomplish it.

§ 50. When Authority to Contract Inferred

Unless otherwise agreed, authority to make a contract is inferred from authority to conduct a transaction, if the making of such a contract is incidental to the transaction, usually accompanies such a transaction, or is reasonably necessary to accomplish it.

§ 73. What Authority is Inferred

Unless otherwise agreed, authority to manage a business includes authority:

(a) to make contracts which are incidental to such business, are usually made in it, or are reasonably necessary in conducting it;

(b) to procure equipment and supplies and to make repairs reasonably necessary for the proper conduct of the business;

(c) to employ, supervise, or discharge employees as the course of business may reasonably require;

(d) to sell or otherwise dispose of goods or other things in accordance with the purposes for which the business is operated;

(e) to receive payment of sums due the principal and to pay debts due from the principal arising out of the business enterprise; and

(f) to direct the ordinary operations of the business.

§ 79. When Authority to Appoint an Agent is Inferred

Unless otherwise agreed, an agent is authorized to appoint another agent for the principal if:

(a) the agent is appointed to a position which, in view of business customs, ordinarily includes authority to appoint other agents; or

(b) the proper conduct of the principal's business in the contemplated manner reasonably requires the employment of other agents; or

(c) the agent is employed to act at a place where or in a business in which it is customary to employ other agents for the performance of such acts; or

(d) an unforeseen contingency arises making it impracticable to communicate with the principal and making such an appointment reasonably necessary for the protection of the interests of the principal entrusted to the agent.

§ 82. Ratification

Ratification is the affirmance by a person of a prior act which did not bind him but which was done or professedly done on his account, whereby the act, as to some or all persons, is given effect as if originally authorized by him.

§ 88. Affirmance after Withdrawal of Other Party or Other Termination of Original Transaction

To constitute ratification, the affirmance of a transaction must occur before the other party has manifested his withdrawal from it either to the purported principal or to the agent, and before the offer or agreement has otherwise terminated or been discharged.

§ 91. Knowledge of Principal at Time of Affirmance

(1) If, at the time of affirmance, the purported principal is ignorant of material facts involved in the original transaction, and is unaware of his ignorance, he can thereafter avoid the effect of the affirmance.

(2) Material facts are those which substantially affect the existence or extent of the obligations involved in the transaction, as distinguished from those which affect the values or inducements involved in the transaction.

§ 96. Effect of Affirming Part of a Transaction

A contract or other single transaction must be affirmed in its entirety in order to effect its ratification.

§ 112. Disloyalty of Agent

Unless otherwise agreed, the authority of an agent terminates if, without knowledge of the principal, he acquires adverse interests or if he is otherwise guilty of a serious breach of loyalty to the principal.

§ 133. Incapacity of Parties or Other Impossibility

The apparent authority of an agent terminates upon the happening of an event which destroys the capacity of the principal to give the power, or an event which otherwise makes the authorized transaction impossible.

§ 136. Notification Terminating Apparent Authority

(1) Unless otherwise agreed, there is a notification by the principal to the third person of revocation of an agent's authority or other fact indicating its termination:

(a) when the principal states such fact to the third person; or

(b) when a reasonable time has elapsed after a writing stating such fact has been delivered by the principal

(i) to the other personally;

(ii) to the other's place of business;

(iii) to a place designated by the other as one in which business communications are received; or

(iv) to a place which, in view of the business customs or relations between the parties is reasonably believed to be the place for the receipt of such communications by the other.

(2) Unless otherwise agreed, a notification to be effective in terminating apparent authority must be given by the means stated in Subsection (1) with respect to a third person:

(a) who has previously extended credit to or received credit from the principal through the agent in reliance upon a manifestation from the principal of continuing authority in the agent;

(b) to whom the agent has been specially accredited;

(c) with whom the agent has begun to deal, as the principal should know; or

(d) who relies upon the possession by the agent of indicia of authority entrusted to him by the principal.

(3) Except as to the persons included in Subsection (2), the principal can properly give notification of the termination of the agent's authority by:

(a) advertising the fact in a newspaper of general circulation in the place where the agency is regularly carried on; or

(b) giving publicity by some other method reasonably adapted to give the information to such third person.

§ 138. Definition

A power given as security is a power to affect the legal relations of another, created in the form of an agency authority, but held for the benefit of the power holder or a third person and given to secure the performance of a duty or to protect a title, either legal or equitable, such power being given when the duty or title is created or given for consideration.

§ 139. Termination of Powers Given as Security

(1) Unless otherwise agreed, a power given as security is not terminated by:

(a) revocation by the creator of the power;

(b) surrender by the holder of the power, if he holds for the benefit of another;

(c) the loss of capacity during the lifetime of either the creator of the power or the holder of the power; or

(d) the death of the holder of the power, or, if the power is given as security for a duty which does not terminate at the death of the creator of the power, by his death.

(2) A power given as security is terminated by its surrender by the beneficiary, if of full capacity; or by the happening of events which, by its terms, discharges the obligations secured by it, or which makes its execution illegal or impossible.

§ 189. Contracts Specifically Excluding Principal

An undisclosed principal does not become liable upon a contract which provides that he or any undisclosed principal shall not be a party to it.

§ 212. Principal Intends Conduct or Consequences

A person is subject to liability for the consequences of another's conduct which results from his directions as he would be for his own personal conduct if, with knowledge of the conditions, he intends the conduct, or if he intends its consequences, unless the one directing or the one acting has a privilege or immunity not available to the other.

§ 213. Principal Negligent or Reckless

A person conducting an activity through servants or other agents is subject to liability for harm resulting from his conduct if he is negligent or reckless:

(a) in giving improper or ambiguous orders of in failing to make proper regulations; or

(b) in the employment of improper persons or instrumentalities in work involving risk of harm to others:

(c) in the supervision of the activity; or

(d) in permitting, or failing to prevent, negligent or other tortious conduct by persons, whether or not his servants or agents, upon premises or with instrumentalities under his control.

§ 216. Unauthorized Tortious Conduct

A master or other principal may be liable to another whose interests have been invaded by the tortious conduct of a servant or other agent, although the principal does not personally violate a duty to such other or authorize the conduct of the agent causing the invasion.

§ 218. Effect of Ratification

Upon ratification, a purported master or other principal becomes subject to liability for injuries caused by the tortious act of one acting or purporting to act as his agent as if the act had been authorized, if there has been no loss of capacity by the principal.

§ 219. When Master is Liable for Torts of His Servants

(1) A master is subject to liability for the torts of his servants committed while acting in the scope of their employment.

(2) A master is not subject to liability for the torts of his servants acting outside the scope of their employment, unless:

(a) the master intended the conduct or the consequences, or

(b) the master was negligent or reckless, or

(c) the conduct violated a non-delegable duty of the master, or

(d) the servant purported to act or to speak on behalf of the principal and there was reliance upon apparent authority, or he was aided in accomplishing the tort by the existence of the agency relation.

§ 222. Servants of Agent of Undisclosed Principal

An undisclosed principal is subject to liability to third persons for conduct within the scope of employment of servants and of subservants employed for him by a servant or other agent empowered to employ them.

§ 228. General Statement

(1) Conduct of a servant is within the scope of employment if, but only if:

(a) it is of the kind he is employed to perform;

(b) it occurs substantially within the authorized time and space limits;

(c) it is actuated, at least in part, by a purpose to serve the master; and

(d) if force is intentionally used by the servant against another, the use of force is not unexpectable by the master.

(2) Conduct of a servant is not within the scope of employment if it is different in kind from that authorized, far beyond the authorized time or space limits, or too little actuated by a purpose to serve the master.

§ 250. Non-liability for Physical Harm by Non-Servant Agents

A principal is not liable for physical harm caused by the negligent physical conduct of a non-servant agent during the performance of the principal's business, if he neither intended nor authorized the result nor the manner of performance, unless he was under a duty to have the act performed with due care.

§ 257. Misrepresentations; in General

A principal is subject to liability for loss caused to another by the other's reliance upon a tortious representation of a servant or other agent, if the representation is:

(a) authorized;

(b) apparently authorized; or

(c) within the power of the agent to make for the principal.

§ 292. General Rule

The other party to a contract made by an agent for a disclosed or partially disclosed principal, acting within his authority, apparent authority or other agency power, is liable to the principal as if he had contracted directly with the principal, unless the principal is excluded as a party by the form or terms of the contract.

§ 320. Principal Disclosed

Unless otherwise agreed, a person making or purporting to make a contract with another as agent for a disclosed principal does not become a party to the contract.

§ 321. Principal Partially Disclosed

Unless otherwise agreed, a person purporting to make a contract with another for a partially disclosed principal is a party to the contract.

§ 326. Principal Known to be Nonexistent or Incompetent

Unless otherwise agreed, a person who, in dealing with another, purports to act as agent for a principal whom both know to be nonexistent or wholly incompetent, becomes a party to such a contract.

§ 343. General Rule

An agent who does an act otherwise a tort is not relieved from liability by the fact that he acted at the command of the principal or on account of the principal, except where he is exercising a privilege of the principal, or a privilege held by him for the protection of the principal's interests, or where the principal owes no duty or less than the normal duty of care to the person harmed.

§ 344. Liability for Directed Conduct or Consequences

An agent is subject to liability, as he would be for his own personal conduct, for the consequences of another's conduct which results from his directions if, with knowledge of the circumstances, he intends the conduct, or its consequences, except where the agent or the one acting has a privilege or immunity not available to the other.

§ 363. Contracts; General Rule

An agent who makes a contract on behalf of a principal cannot maintain an action thereon in his own name on behalf of the principal although authorized by the principal to bring suit, unless the agent is a promisee or transferee.

§ 364. Contracts; Agent a Party Promisee

A person with whom an agent makes a contract on behalf of a principal is subject to liability in an action brought thereon by the agent in his own name on behalf of the principal if the agent is a party promisee.

§ 379. Duty of Care and Skill

(1) Unless otherwise agreed, a paid agent is subject to a duty to the principal to act with standard care and with the skill which is standard in the locality for the kind of work which he is employed to perform and, in addition, to exercise any special skill that he has.

(2) Unless otherwise agreed, a gratuitous agent is under a duty to the principal to act with the care and skill which is required of persons not agents performing similar gratuitous undertakings for others.

§ 381. Duty to Give Information

Unless otherwise agreed, an agent is subject to a duty to use reasonable efforts to give his principal information which is relevant to affairs entrusted to him and which, as the agent has notice, the principal would desire to have and which can be communicated without violating a superior duty to a third person.

§ 382. Duty to Keep and Render Accounts

Unless otherwise agreed, an agent is subject to a duty to keep, and render to his principal, an account of money or other things which he has received or paid out on behalf of the principal.

§ 383. Duty to Act Only as Authorized

Except when he is privileged to protect his own or another's interests, an agent is subject to a duty to the prin-

cipal not to act in the principal's affairs except in accordance with the principal's manifestation of consent.

§ 385. Duty to Obey

(1) Unless otherwise agreed, an agent is subject to a duty to obey all reasonable directions in regard to the manner of performing a service that he has contracted to perform.

(2) Unless he is privileged to protect his own or another's interests, an agent is subject to a duty not to act in manners entrusted to him on account of the principal contrary to the directions of the principal, even though the terms of the employment prescribe that such directions shall not be given.

§ 401. Liability for Loss Caused

An agent is subject to liability for loss caused to the principal by any breach of duty.

§ 438. Duty of Indemnity; the Principle

(1) A principal is under a duty to indemnify the agent in accordance with the terms of the agreement with him.

(2) In the absence of terms to the contrary in the agreement of employment, the principal has a duty to indemnify the agent where the agent

(a) makes a payment authorized or made necessary in executing the principal's affairs or, unless he is officious, one beneficial to the principal, or

(b) suffers a loss which, because of their relation, it is fair that the principal should bear.

§ 439. When Duty of Indemnity Exists

Unless otherwise agreed, a principal is subject to a duty to exonerate an agent who is not barred by the illegality of his conduct to indemnify him for:

(a) authorized payments made by the agent on behalf of the principal;

(b) payments upon contracts upon which the agent is authorized to make himself liable, and upon obligations arising from the possession or ownership of things which he is authorized to hold on account of the principal;

(c) payments of damages to third persons which he is required to make on account of the authorized performance of an act which constitutes a tort or a breach of contract;

(d) expenses of defending actions by third persons brought because of the agent's authorized conduct, such actions being unfounded but not brought in bad faith; and

(e) payments resulting in benefit to the principal, made by the agent under such circumstances that it would be inequitable for indemnity not to be made.

§ 443. Amount of Compensation

If the contract of employment provides for compensation to the agent, he is entitled to receive for the full performance of the agreed service:

(a) the definite amount agreed upon and no more, if the agreement is definite as to amount; or

(b) the fair value of his services, if there is no agreement for a definite amount.

§ 469. Disloyalty or Insubordination as Defense

An agent is entitled to no compensation for conduct which is disobedient or which is a breach of his duty of loyalty; if such conduct constitutes a wilful and deliberate breach of his contract or service, he is not entitled to compensation even for properly performed services for which no compensation is apportioned.

Appendix C

UNIFORM COMMERCIAL CODE*

The Code consists of twelve Articles as follows:
1. General Provisions
2. Sales
2A. Leases
3. Commercial Paper
4. Bank Deposits and Collections
4A. Funds Transfers
5. Letters of Credit
6. Bulk Transfers
7. Warehouse Receipts, Bills of Lading and Other Documents of Title
8. Investment Securities
9. Secured Transactions: Sales of Accounts, Contract Rights and Chattel Paper
10. Effective Date and Repealer

Revised Article 3: Negotiable Instruments is also included in this appendix.

ARTICLE 1: GENERAL PROVISIONS

Part 1—Short Title, Construction, Application and Subject Matter of the Act

§ 1–101. Short Tile.

This Act shall be known and may be cited as Uniform Commercial Code.

*Copyright © 1989 by The American Law Institute and the National Conference of Commissioners on Uniform State Laws. Reproduced with permission.

§ 1–102. Purposes; Rules of Construction; Variation by Agreement.

(1) This Act shall be liberally construed and applied to promote its underlying purposes and policies.

(2) Underlying purposes and policies of this Act are

(a) to simplify, clarify and modernize the law governing commercial transactions;

(b) to permit the continued expansion of commercial practices through custom, usage and agreement of the parties;

(c) to make uniform the law among the various jurisdictions.

(3) The effect of provisions of this Act may be varied by agreement, except as otherwise provided in this Act and except that the obligations of good faith, diligence, reasonableness and care prescribed by this Act may not be disclaimed by agreement but the parties may by agreement determine the standards by which the performance of such obligations is to be measured if such standards are not manifestly unreasonable.

(4) The presence in certain provisions of this Act of the words "unless otherwise agreed" or words of similar import does not imply that the effect of other provisions may not be varied by agreement under subsection (3).

(5) In this Act unless the context otherwise requires

(a) words in the singular number include the plural, and in the plural include the singular;

(b) words of the masculine gender include the feminine and the neuter, and when the sense so indicates words of the neuter gender may refer to any gender.

§ 1–103. Supplementary General Principles of Law Applicable.

Unless displaced by the particular provisions of this Act, the principles of law and equity, including the law merchant and the law relative to capacity to contract, principal and agent, estoppel, fraud, misrepresentation, duress, coercion, mistake, bankruptcy, or other validating or invalidating cause shall supplement its provisions.

§ 1–104. Construction Against Implicit Repeal.

This Act being a general act intended as a unified coverage of its subject matter, no part of it shall be deemed to be impliedly repealed by subsequent legislation if such construction can reasonably be avoided.

§ 1–105. Territorial Application of the Act; Parties' Power to Choose Applicable Law.

(1) Except as provided hereafter in this section, when a transaction bears a reasonable relation to this state and also to another state or nation the parties may agree that the law either of this state or of such other state or nation shall govern their rights and duties. Failing such agreement this Act applies to transactions bearing an appropriate relation to this state.

(2) Where one of the following provisions of this Act specifies the applicable law, that provision governs and a contrary agreement is effective only to the extent permitted by the law (including the conflict of laws rules) so specified:

Rights of creditors against sold goods. Section 2–402.
Applicability of the Article on Bank Deposits and Collections. Section 4–102.
Bulk transfers subject to the Article on Bulk Transfers. Section 6–102.
Applicability of the Article on Investment Securities. Section 8–106.
Perfection provisions of the Article on Secured Transactions. Section 9–103.

§ 1–106. Remedies to Be Liberally Administered.

(1) The remedies provided by this Act shall be liberally administered to the end that the aggrieved party may be put in as good a position as if the other party had fully performed but neither consequential or special nor penal damages may be had except as specifically provided in this Act or by other rule of law.

(2) Any right or obligation declared by this Act is enforceable by action unless the provision declaring it specifies a different and limited effect.

§ 1–107. Waiver or Renunciation of Claim or Right After Breach.

Any claim or right arising out of an alleged breach can be discharged in whole or in part without consideration by a written waiver or renunciation signed and delivered by the aggrieved party.

§ 1–108. Severability.

If any provision or clause of this Act or application thereof to any person or circumstances is held invalid, such invalidity shall not affect other provisions or applications of the Act which can be given effect without the invalid provision or application, and to this end the provisions of this Act are declared to be severable.

§ 1–109. Section Captions.

Section captions are parts of this Act.

Part 2—General Definitions and Principles of Interpretation

§ 1–201. General Definitions.

Subject to additional definitions contained in the subsequent Articles of this Act which are applicable to specific Articles or Parts thereof, and unless the context otherwise requires, in this Act:

(1) "Action" in the sense of a judicial proceeding includes recoupment, counterclaim, set-off, suit in equity and any other proceedings in which rights are determined.

(2) "Aggrieved party" means a party entitled to resort to a remedy.

(3) "Agreement" means the bargain of the parties in fact as found in their language or by implication from other circumstances including course of dealing or usage of trade or course of performance as provided in this Act (Sections 1–205 and 2–208). Whether an agreement has legal consequences is determined by the provisions of this Act, if applicable; otherwise by the law of contracts (Section 1–103). (Compare "Contract".)

(4) "Bank" means any person engaged in the business of banking.

(5) "Bearer" means the person in possession of an instrument, document of title, or certificated security payable to bearer or indorsed in blank.

(6) "Bill of lading" means a document evidencing the receipt of goods for shipment issued by a person engaged in the business of transporting or forwarding goods, and includes an airbill. "Airbill" means a document serving for air transportation as a bill of lading does for marine or rail transportation, and includes an air consignment note or air waybill.

(7) "Branch" includes a separately incorporated foreign branch of a bank.

(8) "Burden of establishing" a fact means the burden of persuading the triers of fact that the existence of the fact is more probable than its non-existence.

(9) "Buyer in ordinary course of business" means a person who in good faith and without knowledge that the sale to him is in violation of the ownership rights or

security interest of a third party in the goods buys in ordinary course from a person in the business of selling goods of that kind but does not include a pawnbroker. All persons who sell minerals or the like (including oil and gas) at wellhead or minehead shall be deemed to be persons in the business of selling goods of that kind. "Buying" may be for cash or by exchange of other property or on secured or unsecured credit and includes receiving goods or documents of title under a pre-existing contract for sale but does not include a transfer in bulk or as security for or in total or partial satisfaction of a money debt.

(10) "Conspicuous": A term or clause is conspicuous when it is so written that a reasonable person against whom it is to operate ought to have noticed it. A printed heading in capitals (as: NON- NEGOTIABLE BILL OF LADING) is conspicuous. Language in the body of a form is "conspicuous" if it is in larger or other contrasting type or color. But in a telegram any stated term is "conspicuous". Whether a term or clause is "conspicuous" or not is for decision by the court.

(11) "Contract" means the total legal obligation which results from the parties' agreement as affected by this Act and any other applicable rules of law. (Compare "Agreement".)

(12) "Creditor" includes a general creditor, a secured creditor, a lien creditor and any representative of creditors, including an assignee for the benefit of creditors, a trustee in bankruptcy, a receiver in equity and an executor or administrator of an insolvent debtor's or assignor's estate.

(13) "Defendant" includes a person in the position of defendant in a cross-action or counterclaim.

(14) "Delivery" with respect to instruments, documents of title, chattel paper, or certificated securities means voluntary transfer of possession.

(15) "Document of title" includes bill of lading, dock warrant, dock receipt, warehouse receipt or order for the delivery of goods, and also any other document which in the regular course of business or financing is treated as adequately evidencing that the person in possession of it is entitled to receive, hold and dispose of the document and the goods it covers. To be a document of title a document must purport to be issued by or addressed to a bailee and purport to cover goods in the bailee's possession which are either identified or are fungible portions of an identified mass.

(16) "Fault" means wrongful act, omission or breach.

(17) "Fungible" with respect to goods or securities means goods or securities of which any unit is, by nature or usage of trade, the equivalent of any other like unit. Goods which are not fungible shall be deemed fungible for the purposes of this Act to the extent that under a particular agreement or document unlike units are treated as equivalents.

(18) "Genuine" means free of forgery or counterfeiting.

(19) "Good faith" means honesty in fact in the conduct or transaction concerned.

(20) "Holder" means a person who is in possession of a document of title or an instrument or a certificated investment security drawn, issued, or indorsed to him or his order or to bearer or in blank.

(21) To "honor" is to pay or to accept and pay, or where a credit so engages to purchase or discount a draft complying with the terms of the credit.

(22) "Insolvency proceedings" includes any assignment for the benefit of creditors or other proceedings intended to liquidate or rehabilitate the estate of the person involved.

(23) A person is "insolvent" who either has ceased to pay his debts in the ordinary course of business or cannot pay his debts as they become due or is insolvent within the meaning of the federal bankruptcy law.

(24) "Money" means a medium of exchange authorized or adopted by a domestic or foreign government as a part of its currency.

(25) A person has "notice" of a fact when

(a) he has actual knowledge of it; or

(b) he has received a notice or notification of it; or

(c) from all the facts and circumstances known to him at the time in question he has reason to know that it exists.

A person "knows" or has "knowledge" of a fact when he has actual knowledge of it. "Discover" or "learn" or a word or phrase of similar import refers to knowledge rather than to reason to know. The time and circumstances under which a notice or notification may cease to be effective are not determined by this Act.

(26) A person "notifies" or "gives" a notice or notification to another by taking such steps as may be reasonably required to inform the other in ordinary course whether or not such other actually comes to know of it. A person "receives" a notice or notification when

(a) it comes to his attention; or

(b) it is duly delivered at the place of business through which the contract was made or at any other place held out by him as the place for receipt of such communications.

(27) Notice, knowledge or a notice or notification received by an organization is effective for a particular transaction from the time when it is brought to the attention of the individual conducting that transaction, and in any event from the time when it would have been brought to his attention if the organization had exercised due diligence. An organization exercises due diligence if it maintains reasonable routines for communicating significant information to the person conducting the transaction and there is reasonable compliance with the routines. Due diligence does not require an individ-

ual acting for the organization to communicate information unless such communication is part of his regular duties or unless he has reason to know of the transaction and that the transaction would be materially affected by the information.

(28) "Organization" includes a corporation, government or governmental subdivision or agency, business trust, estate, trust, partnership or association, two or more persons having a joint or common interest, or any other legal or commercial entity.

(29) "Party", as distinct from "third party", means a person who has engaged in a transaction or made an agreement within this Act.

(30) "Person" includes an individual or an organization (See Section 1–102).

(31) "Presumption" or "presumed" means that the trier of fact must find the existence of the fact presumed unless and until evidence is introduced which would support a finding of its non-existence.

(32) "Purchase" includes taking by sale, discount, negotiation, mortgage, pledge, lien, or re-issue, gift or any other voluntary transaction creating an interest in property.

(33) "Purchaser" means a person who takes by purchase.

(34) "Remedy" means any remedial right to which an aggrieved party is entitled with or without resort to a tribunal.

(35) "Representative" includes an agent, an officer of a corporation or association, and a trustee, executor or administrator of an estate, or any other person empowered to act for another.

(36) "Rights" includes remedies.

(37) "Security interest" means an interest in personal property or fixtures which secures payment or performance of an obligation. The retention or reservation of title by a seller of goods notwithstanding shipment or delivery to the buyer (Section 2–401) is limited in effect to a reservation of a "security interest". The term also includes any interest of a buyer of accounts or chattel paper which is subject to Article 9. The special property interest of a buyer of goods on identification of such goods to a contract for sale under Section 2–401 is not a "security interest", but a buyer may also acquire a "security interest" by complying with Article 9. Unless a lease or consignment is intended as security, reservation of title thereunder is not a "security interest" but a consignment is in any event subject to the provisions on consignment sales (Section 2–326). Whether a lease is intended as security is to be determined by the facts of each case; however, (a) the inclusion of an option to purchase does not of itself make the lease one intended for security, and (b) an agreement that upon compliance with the terms of the lease the leasee shall become or has the option to become the owner of the property for no additional consideration or for a nominal consideration does make the lease one intended for security.

(38) "Send" in connection with any writing or notice means to deposit in the mail or delivery for transmission by any other usual means of communication with postage or cost of transmission provided for and properly addressed and in the case of an instrument to an address specified thereon or otherwise agreed, or if there be none to any address reasonable under the circumstances. The receipt of any writing or notice within the time at which it would have arrived if properly sent has the effect of a proper sending.

(39) "Signed" includes any symbol executed or adopted by a party with present intention to authenticate a writing.

(40) "Surety" includes guarantor.

(41) "Telegram" includes a message transmitted by radio, teletype, cable, any mechanical method of transmission, or the like.

(42) "Term" means that portion of an agreement which relates to a particular matter.

(43) "Unauthorized" signature or indorsement means one made without actual, implied or apparent authority and includes a forgery.

(44) "Value". Except as otherwise provided with respect to negotiable instruments and bank collections (Sections 3–303, 4–208 and 4–209) a person gives "value" for rights if he acquires them

(a) in return for a binding commitment to extend credit or for the extension of immediately available credit whether or not drawn upon or whether or not a chargeback is provided for in the event of difficulties in collection; or

(b) as security for or in total or partial satisfaction of a pre-existing claim; or

(c) by accepting delivery pursuant to a pre-existing contract for purchase; or

(d) generally, in return for any consideration sufficient to support a simple contract.

(45) "Warehouse receipt" means a receipt issued by a person engaged in the business of storing goods for hire.

(46) "Written" or "writing" includes printing, typewriting or any other intentional reduction to tangible form. Amended in 1962, 1972 and 1977.

§ 1–202. Prima Facie Evidence by Third Party Documents.

A document in due form purporting to be a bill of lading, policy or certificate of insurance, official weigher's or inspector's certificate, consular invoice, or any other document authorized or required by the contract to be issued by a third party shall be prima facie evidence of its own authenticity and genuineness and of the facts stated in the document by the third party.

§ 1–203. Obligation of Good Faith.

Every contract or duty within this Act imposes an obligation of good faith in its performance or enforcement.

§ 1-204. Time; Reasonable Time; "Seasonably".

(1) Whenever this Act requires any action to be taken within a reasonable time, any time which is not manifestly unreasonable may be fixed by agreement.

(2) What is a reasonable time for taking any action depends on the nature, purpose and circumstances of such action.

(3) An action is taken "seasonably" when it is taken at or within the time agreed or if no time is agreed at or within a reasonable time.

§ 1-205. Course of Dealing and Usage of Trade.

(1) A course of dealing is a sequence of previous conduct between the parties to a particular transaction which is fairly to be regarded as establishing a common basis of understanding for interpreting their expressions and other conduct.

(2) A usage of trade is any practice or method of dealing having such regularity of observance in a place, vocation or trade as to justify an expectation that it will be observed with respect to the transaction in question. The existence and scope of such a usage are to be proved as facts. If it is established that such a usage is embodied in a written trade code or similar writing the interpretation of the writing is for the court.

(3) A course of dealing between parties and any usage of trade in the vocation or trade in which they are engaged or of which they are or should be aware give particular meaning to and supplement or qualify terms of an agreement.

(4) The express terms of an agreement and an applicable course of dealing or usage of trade shall be construed wherever reasonable as consistent with each other, but when such construction is unreasonable express terms control both course of dealing and usage of trade and course of dealing controls usage of trade.

(5) An applicable usage of trade in the place where any part of performance is to occur shall be used in interpreting the agreement as to that part of the performance.

(6) Evidence of a relevant usage of trade offered by one party is not admissible unless and until he has given the other party such notice as the court finds sufficient to prevent unfair surprise to the latter.

§ 1-206. Statute of Frauds for Kinds of Personal Property Not Otherwise Covered.

(1) Except in the cases described in subsection (2) of this section a contract for the sale of personal property is not enforceable by way of action or defense beyond five thousand dollars in amount or value of remedy unless there is some writing which indicates that a contract for sale has been made between the parties at a defined or stated price, reasonably identifies the subject matter, and is signed by the party against whom enforcement is sought or by his authorized agent.

(2) Subsection (1) of this section does not apply to contracts for the sale of goods (Section 2-201) nor of securities (Section 8-319) nor to security agreements (Section 9-203).

§ 1-207. Performance or Acceptance Under Reservation of Rights.

A party who with explicit reservation of rights performs or promises performance or assents to performance in a manner demanded or offered by the other party does not thereby prejudice the rights reserved. Such words as "without prejudice", "under protest" or the like are sufficient.

§ 1-208. Option to Accelerate at Will.

A term providing that one party or his successor in interest may accelerate payment or performance or require collateral or additional collateral "at will" or "when he deems himself insecure" or in words of similar import shall be construed to mean that he shall have power to do so only if he in good faith believes that the prospect of payment or performance is impaired. The burden of establishing lack of good faith is on the party against whom the power has been exercised.

§ 1-209. Subordinated Obligations.

An obligation may be issued as subordinated to payment of another obligation of the person obligated, or a creditor may subordinate his right to payment of an obligation by agreement with either the person obligated or another creditor of the person obligated. Such a subordination does not create a security interest as against either the common debtor or a subordinated creditor. This section shall be construed as declaring the law as it existed prior to the enactment of this section and not as modifying it. Added 1966.

Note: *This new section is proposed as an optional provision to make it clear that a subordination agreement does not create a security interest unless so intended.*

ARTICLE 2: SALES

Part 1—Short Title, Construction and Subject Matter

§ 2-101. Short Title.

This Article shall be known and may be cited as Uniform Commercial Code—Sales.

§ 2-102. Scope; Certain Security and Other Transactions Excluded From This Article.

Unless the context otherwise requires, this Article applies to transactions in goods; it does not apply to any transaction which although in the form of an unconditional contract to sell or present sale is intended to operate only as a security transaction nor does this Article impair or repeal any statute regulating sales to consumers, farmers or other specified classes of buyers.

§ 2–103. Definitions and Index of Definitions.

(1) In this Article unless the context otherwise requires

(a) "Buyer" means a person who buys or contracts to buy goods.

(b) "Good faith" in the case of a merchant means honesty in fact and the observance of reasonable commercial standards of fair dealing in the trade.

(c) "Receipt" of goods means taking physical possession of them.

(d) "Seller" means a person who sells or contracts to sell goods.

(2) Other definitions applying to this Article or to specified Parts thereof, and the sections in which they appear are:

"Acceptance". Section 2–606.
"Banker's credit". Section 2–325.
"Between merchants". Section 2–104.
"Cancellation". Section 2–106(4).
"Commercial unit". Section 2–105.
"Confirmed credit". Section 2–325.
"Conforming to contract". Section 2–106.
"Contract for sale". Section 2–106.
"Cover". Section 2–712.
"Entrusting". Section 2–403.
"Financing agency". Section 2–104.
"Future goods". Section 2–105.
"Goods". Section 2–105.
"Identification". Section 2–501.
"Installment contract". Section 2–612.
"Letter of Credit". Section 2–325.
"Lot". Section 2–105.
"Merchant". Section 2–104.
"Overseas". Section 2–323.
"Person in position of seller". Section 2–707.
"Present sale". Section 2–106.
"Sale". Section 2–106.
"Sale on approval". Section 2–326.
"Sale or return". Section 2–326.
"Termination". Section 2–106.

(3) The following definitions in other Articles apply to this Article:

"Check". Section 3–104.
"Consignee". Section 7–102.
"Consignor". Section 7–102.
"Consumer goods". Section 9–109.
"Dishonor". Section 3–507.
"Draft". Section 3–104.

(4) In addition Article 1 contains general definitions and principles of construction and interpretation applicable throughout this Article.

§ 2–104. Definitions: "Merchant"; "Between Merchants"; "Financing Agency".

(1) "Merchant" means a person who deals in goods of the kind or otherwise by his occupation holds himself out as having knowledge or skill peculiar to the practices or goods involved in the transaction or to whom such knowledge or skill may be attributed by his employment of an agent or broker or other intermediary who by his occupation holds himself out as having such knowledge or skill.

(2) "Financing agency" means a bank, finance company or other person who in the ordinary course of business makes advances against goods or documents of title or who by arrangement with either the seller or the buyer intervenes in ordinary course to make or collect payment due or claimed under the contract for sale, as by purchasing or paying the seller's draft or making advances against it or by merely taking it for collection whether or not documents of title accompany the draft. "Financing agency" includes also a bank or other person who similarly intervenes between persons who are in the position of seller and buyer in respect to the goods (Section 2–707).

(3) "Between merchants" means in any transaction with respect to which both parties are chargeable with the knowledge or skill of merchants.

§ 2–105. Definitions: Transferability; "Goods"; "Future" Goods; "Lot"; "Commercial Unit".

(1) "Goods" means all things (including specially manufactured goods) which are movable at the time of identification to the contract for sale other than the money in which the price is to be paid, investment securities (Article 8) and things in action. "Goods" also includes the unborn young of animals and growing crops and other identified things attached to realty as described in the section on goods to be severed from realty (Section 2–107).

(2) Goods must be both existing and identified before any interest in them can pass. Goods which are not both existing and identified are "future" goods. A purported present sale of future goods or of any interest therein operates as a contract to sell.

(3) There may be a sale of a part interest in existing identified goods.

(4) An undivided share in an identified bulk of fungible goods is sufficiently identified to be sold although the quantity of the bulk is not determined. Any agreed proportion of such a bulk or any quantity thereof agreed upon by number, weight or other measure may to the extent of the seller's interest in the bulk be sold to the buyer who then becomes an owner in common.

(5) "Lot" means a parcel or a single article which is the subject matter of a separate sale or delivery, whether or not it is sufficient to perform the contract.

(6) "Commercial unit" means such a unit of goods as by commercial usage is a single whole for purposes of sale and division of which materially impairs its character or value on the market or in use. A commercial unit may be a single article (as a machine) or a set of articles (as a suite of furniture or an assortment of sizes) or a quantity (as a bale, gross, or carload) or any other unit treated in use or in the relevant market as a single whole.

§ 2–106. Definitions: "Contract"; "Agreement"; "Contract for Sale"; "Sale"; "Present Sale"; "Conforming" to Contract; "Termination"; "Cancellation".

(1) In this Article unless the context otherwise requires "contract" and "agreement" are limited to those relating to the present or future sale of goods. "Contract for sale" includes both a present sale of goods and a contract to sell goods at a future time. A "sale" consists in the passing of title from the seller to the buyer for a price (Section 2–401). A "present sale" means a sale which is accomplished by the making of the contract.

(2) Goods or conduct including any part of a performance are "conforming" or conform to the contract when they are in accordance with the obligations under the contract.

(3) "Termination" occurs when either party pursuant to a power created by agreement or law puts an end to the contract otherwise than for its breach. On "termination" all obligations which are still executory on both sides are discharged but any right based on prior breach or performance survives.

(4) "Cancellation" occurs when either party puts an end to the contract for breach by the other and its effect is the same as that of "termination" except that the cancelling party also retains any remedy for breach of the whole contract or any unperformed balance.

§ 2–107. Goods to Be Severed From Realty: Recording.

(1) A contract for the sale of minerals or the like (including oil and gas) or a structure or its materials to be removed from realty is a contract for the sale of goods within this Article if they are to be severed by the seller but until severance a purported present sale thereof which is not effective as a transfer of an interest in land is effective only as a contract to sell.

(2) A contract for the sale apart from the land of growing crops or other things attached to realty and capable of severance without material harm thereto but not described in subsection (1) or of timber to be cut is a contract for the sale of goods within this Article whether the subject matter is to be severed by the buyer or by the seller even though it forms part of the realty at the time of contracting, and the parties can by identification effect a present sale before severance.

(3) The provisions of this section are subject to any third party rights provided by the law relating to realty records, and the contract for sale may be executed and recorded as a document transferring an interest in land and shall then constitute notice to third parties of the buyer's rights under the contract for sale.

Part 2—Form, Formation and Readjustment of Contract

§ 2–201. Formal Requirements; Statute of Frauds.

(1) Except as otherwise provided in this section a contract for the sale of goods for the price of $500 or more is not enforceable by way of action or defense unless there is some writing sufficient to indicate that a contract for sale has been made between the parties and signed by the party against whom enforcement is sought or by his authorized agent or broker. A writing is not insufficient because it omits or incorrectly states a term agreed upon but the contract is not enforceable under this paragraph beyond the quantity of goods shown in such writing.

(2) Between merchants if within a reasonable time a writing in confirmation of the contract and sufficient against the sender is received and the party receiving it has reason to know its contents, it satisfies the requirements of subsection (1) against such party unless written notice of objection to its contents is given within ten days after it is received.

(3) A contract which does not satisfy the requirements of subsection (1) but which is valid in other respects is enforceable

(a) if the goods are to be specially manufactured for the buyer and are not suitable for sale to others in the ordinary course of the seller's business and the seller, before notice of repudiation is received and under circumstances which reasonably indicate that the goods are for the buyer, has made either a substantial beginning of their manufacture or commitments for their procurement; or

(b) if the party against whom enforcement is sought admits in his pleading, testimony or otherwise in court that a contract for sale was made, but the contract is not enforceable under this provision beyond the quantity of goods admitted; or

(c) with respect to goods for which payment has been made and accepted or which have been received and accepted (Sec. 2–606).

§ 2–202. Final Written Expression: Parol or Extrinsic Evidence.

Terms with respect to which the confirmatory memoranda of the parties agree or which are otherwise set forth in a writing intended by the parties as a final expression of their agreement with respect to such terms as are included therein may not be contradicted by evidence of any prior agreement or of a contemporaneous oral agreement but may be explained or supplemented

(a) by course of dealing or usage of trade (Section 1–205) or by course of performance (Section 2–208); and

(b) by evidence of consistent additional terms unless the court finds the writing to have been intended also as a complete and exclusive statement of the terms of the agreement.

§ 2–203. Seals Inoperative.

The affixing of a seal to a writing evidencing a contract for sale or an offer to buy or sell goods does not constitute the writing a sealed instrument and the law with respect to sealed instruments does not apply to such a contract or offer.

§ 2–204. Formation in General.

(1) A contract for sale of goods may be made in any manner sufficient to show agreement, including conduct by both parties which recognizes the existence of such a contract.

(2) An agreement sufficient to constitute a contract for sale may be found even though the moment of its making is undetermined.

(3) Even though one or more terms are left open a contract for sale does not fail for indefiniteness if the parties have intended to make a contract and there is a reasonably certain basis for giving an appropriate remedy.

§ 2–205. Firm Offers.

An offer by a merchant to buy or sell goods in a signed writing which by its terms gives assurance that it will be held open is not revocable, for lack of consideration, during the time stated or if no time is stated for reasonable time, but in no event may such period of irrevocability exceed three months; but any such term of assurance on a form supplied by the offeree must be separately signed by the offeror.

§ 2–206. Offer and Acceptance in Formation of Contract.

(1) Unless other unambiguously indicated by the language or circumstances

(a) an offer to make a contract shall be construed as inviting acceptance in any manner and by any medium reasonable in the circumstances;

(b) an order or other offer to buy goods for prompt or current shipment shall be construed as inviting acceptance either by a prompt promise to ship or by the prompt or current shipment of conforming or nonconforming goods, but such a shipment of non-conforming goods does not constitute an acceptance if the seller seasonably notifies the buyer that the shipment is offered only as an accommodation to the buyer.

(2) Where the beginning of a requested performance is a reasonable mode of acceptance an offeror who is not notified of acceptance within a reasonable time may treat the offer as having lapsed before acceptance.

§ 2–207. Additional Terms in Acceptance or Confirmation.

(1) A definite and seasonable expression of acceptance or a written confirmation which is sent within a reasonable time operates as an acceptance even though it states terms additional to or different from those offered or agreed upon, unless acceptance is expressly made conditional on assent to the additional or different terms.

(2) The additional terms are to be construed as proposals for addition to the contract. Between merchants such terms become part of the contract unless:

(a) the offer expressly limits acceptance to the terms of the offer;

(b) they materially alter it; or

(c) notification of objection to them has already been given or is given within a reasonable time after notice of them is received.

(3) Conduct by both parties which recognizes the existence of a contract is sufficient to establish a contract for sale although the writings of the parties do not otherwise establish a contract. In such case the terms of the particular contract consist of those terms on which the writings of the parties agree, together with any supplementary terms incorporated under any other provisions of this Act.

§ 2–208. Course of Performance or Practical Construction.

(1) Where the contract for sale involves repeated occasions for performance by either party with knowledge of the nature of the performance and opportunity for objection to it by the other, any course of performance accepted or acquiesced in without objection shall be relevant to determine the meaning of the agreement.

(2) The express terms of the agreement and any such course of performance, as well as any course of dealing and usage of trade, shall be construed whenever reasonable as consistent with each other; but when such construction is unreasonable, express terms shall control course of performance and course of performance shall control both course of dealing and usage of trade (Section 1–205).

(3) Subject to the provisions of the next section on modification and waiver, such course of performance shall be relevant to show a waiver or modification of any term inconsistent with such course of performance.

§ 2–209. Modification, Rescission and Waiver.

(1) An agreement modifying a contract within this Article needs no consideration to be binding.

(2) A signed agreement which excludes modification or rescission except by a signed writing cannot be otherwise modified or rescinded, but except as between merchants such a requirement on a form supplied by the merchant must be separately signed by the other party.

(3) The requirements of the statute of frauds section of this Article (Section 2–201) must be satisfied if the contract as modified is within its provisions.

(4) Although an attempt at modification or rescission does not satisfy the requirements of subsection (2) or (3) it can operate as a waiver.

(5) A party who has made a waiver affecting an executory portion of the contract may retract the waiver by reasonable notification received by the other party that strict performance will be required of any term waived, unless the retraction would be unjust in view of a material change of position in reliance on the waiver.

§ 2–210. Delegation of Performance; Assignment of Rights.

(1) A party may perform his duty through a delegate unless otherwise agreed or unless the other party has a substantial interest in having his original promisor perform or control the acts required by the contract. No delegation of performance relieves the party delegating of any duty to perform or any liability for breach.

(2) Unless otherwise agreed all rights of either seller or buyer can be assigned except where the assignment would materially change the duty of the other party, or increase materially the burden or risk imposed on him by his contract, or impair materially his chance of obtaining return performance. A right to damages for breach of the whole contract or a right arising out of the assignor's due performance of his entire obligation can be assigned despite agreement otherwise.

(3) Unless the circumstances indicate the contrary a prohibition of assignment of "the contract" is to be construed as barring only the delegation to the assignee of the assignor's performance.

(4) An assignment of "the contract" or of "all my rights under the contract" or an assignment in similar general terms is an assignment of rights and unless the language or the circumstances (as in an assignment for security) indicate the contrary, it is a delegation of performance of the duties of the assignor and its acceptance by the assignee constitutes a promise by him to perform those duties. This promise is enforceable by either the assignor or the other party to the original contract.

(5) The other party may treat any assignment which delegates performance as creating reasonable grounds for insecurity and may without prejudice to his rights against the assignor demand assurances from the assignee (Section 2–609).

Part 3—General Obligation and Construction of Contract

§ 2–301. General Obligations of Parties.

The obligation of the seller is to transfer and deliver and that of the buyer is to accept and pay in accordance with the contract.

§ 2–302. Unconscionable Contract or Clause.

(1) If the court as a matter of law finds the contract or any clause of the contract to have been unconscionable at the time it was made the court may refuse to enforce the contract, or it may enforce the remainder of the contract without the unconscionable clause, or it may so limit the application of any unconscionable clause as to avoid any unconscionable result.

(2) When it is claimed or appears to the court that the contract or any clause thereof may be unconscionable the parties shall be afforded a reasonable opportunity to present evidence as to its commercial setting, purpose and effect to aid the court in making the determination.

§ 2–303. Allocation or Division of Risks.

Where this Article allocates a risk or a burden as between the parties "unless otherwise agreed", the agreement may not only shift the allocation, but may also divide the risk or burden.

§ 2–304. Price Payable in Money, Goods, Realty, or Otherwise.

(1) The price can be made payable in money or otherwise. If it is payable in whole or in part in goods each party is a seller of the goods which he is to transfer.

(2) Even though all or part of the price is payable in an interest in realty the transfer of the goods and the seller's obligations with reference to them are subject to this Article, but not the transfer of the interest in realty or the transferor's obligations in connection therewith.

§ 2–305. Open Price Term.

(1) The parties if they so intend can conclude a contract for sale even though the price is not settled. In such a case the price is a reasonable price at the time for delivery if

    (a) nothing is said as to price; or

    (b) the price is left to be agreed by the parties and they fail to agree; or

    (c) the price is to be fixed in terms of some agreed market or other standard as set or recorded by a third person or agency and it is not so set or recorded.

(2) A price to be fixed by the seller or by the buyer means a price for him to fix in good faith.

(3) When a price left to be fixed otherwise than by agreement of the parties fails to be fixed through fault of one party the other may at his option treat the contract as cancelled or himself fix a reasonable price.

(4) Where, however, the parties intend not to be bound unless the price be fixed or agreed and it is not fixed or agreed there is no contract. In such a case the buyer must return any goods already received or if unable so to do must pay their reasonable value at the time of delivery and the seller must return any portion of the price paid on account.

§ 2–306. Output, Requirements and Exclusive Dealings.

(1) A term which measures the quantity by the output of the seller or the requirements of the buyer means such actual output or requirements as may occur in good faith, except that no quantity unreasonably disproportionate to any stated estimate or in the absence of a stated estimate to any normal or otherwise comparable prior output or requirements may be tendered or demanded.

(2) A lawful agreement by either the seller or the buyer for exclusive dealing in the kind of goods concerned imposes unless otherwise agreed an obligation by the seller to use best efforts to supply the goods and by the buyer to use best efforts to promote their sale.

§ 2–307. Delivery in Single Lot or Several Lots.

Unless otherwise agreed all goods called for by a contract for sale must be tendered in a single delivery and payment is due only on such tender but where the circumstances give either party the right to make or demand delivery in lots the price if it can be apportioned may be demanded for each lot.

§ 2–308. Absence of Specified Place for Delivery.

Unless otherwise agreed

(a) the place for delivery of goods is the seller's place of business or if he has none his residence; but

(b) in a contract for sale of identified goods which to the knowledge of the parties at the time of contracting are in some other place, that place is the place for their delivery; and

(c) documents of title may be delivered through customary banking channels.

§ 2–309. Absence of Specific Time Provisions; Notice of Termination.

(1) The time for shipment or delivery or any other action under a contract if not provided in this Article or agreed upon shall be a reasonable time.

(2) Where the contract provides for successive performances but is indefinite in duration it is valid for a reasonable time but unless otherwise agreed may be terminated at any time by either party.

(3) Termination of a contract by one party except on the happening of an agreed event requires that reasonable notification be received by the other party and an agreement dispensing with notification is invalid if its operation would be unconscionable.

§ 2–310. Open Time for Payment or Running of Credit; Authority to Ship Under Reservation.

Unless otherwise agreed

(a) payment is due at the time and place at which the buyer is to receive the goods even though the place of shipment is the place of delivery; and

(b) if the seller is authorized to send the goods he may ship them under reservation, and may tender the documents of title, but the buyer may inspect the goods after their arrival before payment is due unless such inspection is inconsistent with the terms of the contract (Section 2–513); and

(c) if delivery is authorized and made by way of documents of title otherwise than by subsection (b) then payment is due at the time and place at which the buyer is to receive the documents regardless of where the goods are to be received; and

(d) where the seller is required or authorized to ship the goods on credit the credit period runs from the time of shipment but post-dating the invoice or delaying its dispatch will correspondingly delay the starting of the credit period.

§ 2–311. Options and Cooperation Respecting Performance.

(1) An agreement for sale which is otherwise sufficiently definite (subsection (3) of Section 2–204) to be a contract is not made invalid by the fact that it leaves particulars of performance to be specified by one of the parties. Any such specification must be made in good faith and within limits set by commercial reasonableness.

(2) Unless otherwise agreed specifications relating to assortment of the goods are at the buyer's option and except as otherwise provided in subsections (1)(c) and (3) of Section 2–319 specifications or arrangements relating to shipment are at the seller's option.

(3) Where such specification would materially affect the other party's performance but is not seasonably made or where one party's cooperation is necessary to the agreed performance of the other but is not seasonably forthcoming, the other party in addition to all other remedies

(a) is excused for any resulting delay in his own performance; and

(b) may also either proceed to perform in any reasonable manner or after the time for a material part of his own performance treat the failure to specify or to cooperate as a breach by failure to deliver or accept the goods.

§ 2–312. Warranty of Title and Against Infringement; Buyer's Obligation Against Infringement.

(1) Subject to subsection (2) there is in a contract for sale a warranty by the seller that

(a) the title conveyed shall be good, and its transfer rightful; and

(b) the goods shall be delivered free from any security interest or other lien or encumbrance of which the buyer at the time of contracting has no knowledge.

(2) A warranty under subsection (1) will be excluded or modified only by specific language or by circumstances which give the buyer reason to know that the person selling does not claim title in himself or that he is purporting to sell only such right or title as he or a third person may have.

(3) Unless otherwise agreed a seller who is a merchant regularly dealing in goods of the kind warrants that the goods shall be delivered free of the rightful claim of any third person by way of infringement or the like but a buyer who furnishes specifications to the seller must hold the seller harmless against any such claim which arises out of compliance with the specifications.

§ 2–313. Express Warranties by Affirmation, Promise, Description, Sample.

(1) Express warranties by the seller are created as follows:

(a) Any affirmation of fact or promise made by the seller to the buyer which relates to the goods and becomes part of the basis of the bargain creates an express warranty that the goods shall conform to the affirmation or promise.

(b) Any description of the goods which is made part of the basis of the bargain creates an express warranty that the goods shall conform to the description.

(c) Any sample or model which is made part of the basis of the bargain creates an express warranty that the whole of the goods shall conform to the sample or model.

(2) It is not necessary to the creation of an express warranty that the seller use formal words such as "warrant" or "guarantee" or that he have a specific intention to make a warranty, but an affirmation merely of the value of the goods or a statement purporting to be merely the seller's opinion or commendation of the goods does not create a warranty.

§ 2–314. Implied Warranty: Merchantability; Usage of Trade.

(1) Unless excluded or modified (Section 2–316), a warranty that the goods shall be merchantable is implied in a contract for their sale if the seller is a merchant with respect to goods of that kind. Under this section the serving for value of food or drink to be consumed either on the premises or elsewhere is a sale.

(2) Goods to be merchantable must be at least such as

(a) pass without objection in the trade under the contract description; and

(b) in the case of fungible goods, are of fair average quality within the description; and

(c) are fit for the ordinary purpose for which such goods are used; and

(d) run, within the variations permitted by the agreement, of even kind, quality and quantity within each unit and among all units involved; and

(e) are adequately contained, packaged, and labeled as the agreement may require; and

(f) conform to the promises or affirmations of fact made on the container or label if any.

(3) Unless excluded or modified (Section 2–316) other implied warranties may arise from course of dealing or usage of trade.

§ 2–315. Implied Warranty: Fitness for Particular Purpose.

Where the seller at the time of contracting has reason to know any particular purpose for which the goods are required and that the buyer is relying on the seller's skill or judgment to select or furnish suitable goods, there is unless excluded or modified under the next section an implied warranty that the goods shall be fit for such purpose.

§ 2–316. Exclusion or Modification of Warranties.

(1) Words or conduct relevant to the creation of an express warranty and words or conduct tending to negate or limit warranty shall be construed wherever reasonable as consistent with each other, but subject to the provisions of this Article on parol or extrinsic evidence (Section 2–202) negation or limitation is inoperative to the extent that such construction is unreasonable.

(2) Subject to subsection (3), to exclude or modify the implied warranty of merchantability or any part of it the language must mention merchantability and in case of a writing must be conspicuous, and to exclude or modify any implied warranty of fitness the exclusion must be by a writing and conspicuous. Language to exclude all implied warranties of fitness is sufficient if it states, for example, that "There are no warranties which extend beyond the description on the face hereof."

(3) Notwithstanding subsection (2)

(a) unless the circumstances indicate otherwise, all implied warranties are excluded by expressions like "as is", "with all faults" or other language which in common understanding calls the buyer's attention to the exclusion of warranties and makes plain that there is no implied warranty; and

(b) when the buyer before entering into the contract has examined the goods or the sample or model as fully as he desired or has refused to examine the goods there is no implied warranty with regard to defects which an examination ought in the circumstances to have revealed to him; and

(c) an implied warranty can also be excluded or modified by course of dealing or course of performance or usage of trade.

(4) Remedies for breach of warranty can be limited in accordance with the provisions of this Article on liquidation or limitation of damages and on contractual modification of remedy (Sections 2–718 and 2–719).

§ 2–317. Cumulation and Conflict of Warranties Express or Implied.

Warranties whether express or implied shall be construed as consistent with each other and as cumulative, but if such construction is unreasonable the intention of the parties shall determine which warranty is dominant. In ascertaining that intention the following rules apply:

(a) Exact or technical specifications displace an inconsistent sample or model or general language of description.

(b) A sample from an existing bulk displaces inconsistent general language of description.

(c) Express warranties displace inconsistent implied warranties other than an implied warranty of fitness for a particular purpose.

§ 2–318. Third Party Beneficiaries of Warranties Express or Implied.

Note: If this Act is introduced in the Congress of the United States this section should be omitted. (States to select one alternative.)

Alternative A A seller's warranty whether express or implied extends to any natural person who is in the family or household of his buyer or who is a guest in his home if it is reasonable to expect that such person may use, consume or be affected by the goods and who is injured in person by breach of the warranty. The seller may not exclude or limit the operation of this section.

Alternative B A seller's warranty whether express or implied extends to any natural person who may reasonably be expected to use, consume or be affected by the goods and who is injured in person by breach of the warranty. A seller may not exclude or limit the operation of this section.

Alternative C A seller's warranty whether express or implied extends to any person who may reasonably be expected to use, consume or be affected by the goods and who is injured by breach of the warranty. A seller may not exclude or limit the operation of this section with respect to injury to the person of an individual to whom the warranty extends. As amended 1966.

§ 2–319. F.O.B. and F.A.S. Terms.

(1) Unless otherwise agreed the term F.O.B. (which means "free on board") at a named place, even though used only in connection with the stated price, is a delivery term under which

(a) when the term is F.O.B. the place of shipment, the seller must at that place ship the goods in the manner provided in this Article (Section 2–504) and bear the expense and risk of putting them into the possession of the carrier; or

(b) when the term is F.O.B. the place of destination, the seller must at his own expense and risk transport the goods to that place and there tender delivery of them in the manner provided in this Article (Section 2–503);

(c) when under either (a) or (b) the term is also F.O.B. vessel, car or other vehicle, the seller must in addition at his own expense and risk load the goods on board. If the term is F.O.B. vessel the buyer must name the vessel and in an appropriate case the seller must comply with the provisions of this Article on the form of bill of lading (Section 2–323).

(2) Unless otherwise agreed the term F.A.S. vessel (which means "free alongside") at a named port, even though used only in connection with the stated price, is a delivery term under which the seller must

(a) at his own expense and risk deliver the goods alongside the vessel in the manner usual in that port or on a dock designated and provided by the buyer; and

(b) obtain and tender a receipt for the goods in exchange for which the carrier is under a duty to issue a bill of lading.

(3) Unless otherwise agreed in any case falling within subsection (1)(a) or (c) or subsection (2) the buyer must seasonably give any needed instructions for making delivery, including when the term is F.A.S. or F.O.B. the loading berth of the vessel and in an appropriate case its name and sailing date. The seller may treat the failure of needed instructions as a failure of cooperation under this Article (Section 2–311). He may also at his option move the goods in any reasonable manner preparatory to delivery or shipment.

(4) Under the term F.O.B. vessel or F.A.S. unless otherwise agreed the buyer must make payment against tender of the required documents and the seller may not tender nor the buyer demand delivery of the goods in substitution for the documents.

§ 2–320. C.I.F. and C. & F. Terms.

(1) The term C.I.F. means that the price includes in a lump sum the cost of the goods and the insurance and freight to the named destination. The term C. & F. or C.F. means that the price so includes cost and freight to the named destination.

(2) Unless otherwise agreed and even though used only in connection with the stated price and destination, the term C.I.F. destination or its equivalent requires the seller at his own expense and risk to

(a) put the goods into the possession of a carrier at the port for shipment and obtain a negotiable bill or bills of lading covering the entire transportation to the named destination; and

(b) load the goods and obtain a receipt from the carrier (which may be contained in the bill of lading) showing that the freight has been paid or provided for; and

(c) obtain a policy or certificate of insurance, including any war risk insurance, of a kind and on terms then current at the port of shipment in the usual amount, in the currency of the contract, shown to cover the same goods covered by the bill of lading and providing for payment of loss to the order of the buyer or for the account of whom it may concern; but the seller may add to the price the amount of premium for any such war risk insurance; and

(d) prepare an invoice of the goods and procure any other documents required to effect shipment or to comply with the contract; and

(e) forward and tender with commercial promptness all the documents in due form and with any indorsement necessary to perfect the buyer's rights.

(3) Unless otherwise agreed the term C. & F. or its equivalent has the same effect and imposes upon the seller the same obligations and risks as a C.I.F. term except the obligation as to insurance.

(4) Under the term C.I.F. or C. & F. unless otherwise agreed the buyer must make payment against tender of the required documents and the seller may not tender nor the buyer demand delivery of the goods in substitution for the documents.

§ 2–321. C.I.F. or C. & F.: "Net Landed Weights"; "Payment on Arrival"; Warranty of Condition on Arrival.

Under a contract containing a term C.I.F. or C. & F.

(1) Where the price is based on or is to be adjusted according to "net landed weights", "delivered weights", "out turn" quantity or quality or the like, unless otherwise agreed the seller must reasonably estimate the price. The payment due on tender of the documents called for by the contract is the amount so estimated,

but after final adjustment of the price a settlement must be made with commercial promptness.

(2) An agreement described in subsection (1) or any warranty of quality or condition of the goods on arrival places upon the seller the risk of ordinary deterioration, shrinkage and the like in transportation but has no effect on the place or time of identification to the contract for sale or delivery or on the passing of the risk of loss.

(3) Unless otherwise agreed where the contract provides for payment on or after arrival of the goods the seller must before payment allow such preliminary inspection as is feasible; but if the goods are lost delivery of the documents and payment are due when the goods should have arrived.

§ 2–322. Delivery "Ex-Ship".

(1) Unless otherwise agreed a term for delivery of goods "ex-ship" (which means from the carrying vessel) or in equivalent language is not restricted to a particular ship and requires delivery from a ship which has reached a place at the named port of destination where goods of the kind are usually discharged.

(2) Under such a term unless otherwise agreed

(a) the seller must discharge all liens arising out of the carriage and furnish the buyer with a direction which puts the carrier under a duty to deliver the goods; and

(b) the risk of loss does not pass to the buyer until the goods leave the ship's tackle or are otherwise properly unloaded.

§ 2–323. Form of Bill of Lading Required in Overseas Shipment; "Overseas".

(1) Where the contract contemplates overseas shipment and contains a term C.I.F. or C. & F. or F.O.B. vessel, the seller unless otherwise agreed must obtain a negotiable bill of lading stating that the goods have been loaded on board or, in the case of a term C.I.F. or C. & F., received for shipment.

(2) Where in a case within subsection (1) a bill of lading has been issued in a set of parts, unless otherwise agreed if the documents are not to be sent from abroad the buyer may demand tender of the full set; otherwise only one part of the bill of lading need be tendered. Even if the agreement expressly requires a full set

(a) due tender of a single part is acceptable within the provisions of this Article on cure of improper delivery (subsection (1) of Section 2–508); and

(b) even though the full set is demanded, if the documents are sent from abroad the person tendering an incomplete set may nevertheless require payment upon furnishing an indemnity which the buyer in good faith deems adequate.

(3) A shipment by water or by air or a contract contemplating such shipment is "overseas" insofar as by usage of trade or agreement it is subject to the commercial, financing or shipping practices characteristic of international deep water commerce.

§ 2–324. "No Arrival, No Sale" Term.

Under a term "no arrival, no sale" or terms of like meaning, unless otherwise agreed,

(a) the seller must properly ship conforming goods and if they arrive by any means he must tender them on arrival but he assumes no obligation that the goods will arrive unless he has caused the non-arrival; and

(b) where without fault of the seller the goods are in part lost or have so deteriorated as no longer to conform to the contract or arrive after the contract time, the buyer may proceed as if there had been casualty to identified goods (Section 2–613).

§ 2–325. "Letter of Credit" Term; "Confirmed Credit".

(1) Failure of the buyer seasonably to furnish an agreed letter of credit is a breach of the contract for sale.

(2) The delivery to seller of a proper letter of credit suspends the buyer's obligation to pay. If the letter of credit is dishonored, the seller may on seasonable notification to the buyer require payment directly from him.

(3) Unless otherwise agreed the term "letter of credit" or "banker's credit" in a contract for sale means an irrevocable credit issued by a financing agency of good repute and, where the shipment is overseas, of good international repute. The term "confirmed credit" means that the credit must also carry the direct obligation of such an agency which does business in the seller's financial market.

§ 2–326. Sale on Approval and Sale or Return; Consignment Sales and Rights of Creditors.

(1) Unless otherwise agreed, if delivered goods may be returned by the buyer even though they conform to the contract, the transaction is

(a) a "sale on approval" if the goods are delivered primarily for use, and

(b) a "sale or return" if the goods are delivered primarily for resale.

(2) Except as provided in subsection (3), goods held on approval are not subject to the claims of the buyer's creditors until acceptance; goods held on sale or return are subject to such claims while in the buyer's possession.

(3) Where goods are delivered to a person for sale and such person maintains a place of business at which he deals in goods of the kind involved, under a name other than the name of the person making delivery, then with respect to claims of creditors of the person conducting the business the goods are deemed to be on sale or return. The provisions of this subsection are applicable even though an agreement purports to reserve title to the person making delivery until payment or resale or uses such words as "on consignment" or "on memorandum". However, this subsection is not applicable if the person making delivery

(a) complies with an applicable law providing for a consignor's interest or the like to be evidenced by a sign, or

(b) establishes that the person conducting the business is generally known by his creditors to be substantially engaged in selling the goods of others, or

(c) complies with the filing provisions of the Article on Secured Transactions (Article 9).

(4) Any "or return" term of a contract for sale is to be treated as a separate contract for sale within the statute of frauds section of this Article (Section 2–201) and as contradicting the sale aspect of the contract within the provisions of this Article on parol or extrinsic evidence (Section 2–202).

§ 2–327. Special Incidents of Sale on Approval and Sale or Return.

(1) Under a sale on approval unless otherwise agreed

(a) although the goods are identified to the contract the risk of loss and the title do not pass to the buyer until acceptance; and

(b) use of the goods consistent with the purpose of trial is not acceptance but failure seasonably to notify the seller of election to return the goods is acceptance, and if the goods conform to the contract acceptance of any part is acceptance of the whole; and

(c) after due notification of election to return, the return is at the seller's risk and expense but a merchant buyer must follow any reasonable instructions.

(2) Under a sale or return unless otherwise agreed

(a) the option to return extends to the whole or any commercial unit of the goods while in substantially their original condition, but must be exercised seasonably; and

(b) the return is at the buyer's risk and expense.

§ 2–328. Sale by Auction.

(1) In a sale by auction if goods are put up in lots each lot is the subject of a separate sale.

(2) A sale by auction is complete when the auctioneer so announces by the fall of the hammer or in other customary manner. Where a bid is made while the hammer is falling in acceptance of a prior bid the auctioneer may in his discretion reopen the bidding or declare the goods sold under the bid on which the hammer was falling.

(3) Such a sale is with reserve unless the goods are in explicit terms put up without reserve. In an auction with reserve the auctioneer may withdraw the goods at any time until he announces completion of the sale. In an auction without reserve, after the auctioneer calls for bids on an article or lot, that article or lot cannot be withdrawn unless no bid is made within a reasonable time. In either case a bidder may retract his bid until the auctioneer's announcement of completion of the sale, but a bidder's retraction does not revive any previous bid.

(4) If the auctioneer knowingly receives a bid on the seller's behalf or the seller makes or procures such a bid, and notice has not been given that liberty for such bidding is reserved, the buyer may at his option avoid the sale or take the goods at the price of the last good faith bid prior to the completion of the sale. This subsection shall not apply to any bid at a forced sale.

Part 4—Title, Creditors and Good Faith Purchasers

§ 2–401. Passing of Title; Reservation for Security; Limited Application of This Section.

Each provision of this Article with regard to the rights, obligations and remedies of the seller, the buyer, purchasers or other third parties applies irrespective of title to the goods except where the provision refers to such title. Insofar as situations are not covered by the other provisions of this Article and matters concerning title became material the following rules apply:

(1) Title to goods cannot pass under a contract for sale prior to their identification to the contract (Section 2–501), and unless otherwise explicitly agreed the buyer acquires by their identification a special property as limited by this Act. Any retention or reservation by the seller of the title (property) in goods shipped or delivered to the buyer is limited in effect to a reservation of a security interest. Subject to these provisions and to the provisions of the Article on Secured Transactions (Article 9), title to goods passes from the seller to the buyer in any manner and on any conditions explicitly agreed on by the parties.

(2) Unless otherwise explicitly agreed title passes to the buyer at the time and place at which the seller completes his performance with reference to the physical delivery of the goods, despite any reservation of a security interest and even though a document of title is to be delivered at a different time or place; and in particular and despite any reservation of a security interest by the bill of lading

    (a) if the contract requires or authorizes the seller to send the goods to the buyer but does not require him to deliver them at destination, title passes to the buyer at the time and place of shipment; but

    (b) if the contract requires delivery at destination, title passes on tender there.

(3) Unless otherwise explicitly agreed where delivery is to be made without moving the goods,

    (a) if the seller is to deliver a document of title, title passes at the time when and the place where he delivers such documents; or

    (b) if the goods are at the time of contracting already identified and no documents are to be delivered, title passes at the time and place of contracting.

(4) A rejection or other refusal by the buyer to receive or retain the goods, whether or not justified, or a justified revocation of acceptance revests title to the goods in the seller. Such revesting occurs by operation of law and is not a "sale".

§ 2–402. Rights of Seller's Creditors Against Sold Goods.

(1) Except as provided in subsections (2) and (3), rights of unsecured creditors of the seller with respect to goods which have been identified to a contract for sale are subject to the buyer's rights to recover the goods under this Article (Sections 2–502 and 2–716).

(2) A creditor of the seller may treat a sale or an identification of goods to a contract for sale as void if as against him a retention of possession by the seller is fraudulent under any rule of law of the state where the goods are situated, except that retention of possession in good faith and current course of trade by a merchant-seller for a commercially reasonable time after a sale or identification is not fraudulent.

(3) Nothing in this Article shall be deemed to impair the rights of creditors of the seller

    (a) under the provisions of the Article on Secured Transactions (Article 9); or

    (b) where identification to the contract or delivery is made not in current course of trade but in satisfaction of or as security for a pre-existing claim for money, security or the like and is made under circumstances which under any rule of law of the state where the goods are situated would apart from this Article constitute the transaction a fraudulent transfer or voidable preference.

§ 2–403. Power to Transfer; Good Faith Purchase of Goods; "Entrusting".

(1) A purchaser of goods acquires all title which his transferor had or had power to transfer except that a purchaser of a limited interest acquires rights only to the extent of the interest purchased. A person with voidable title has power to transfer a good title to a good faith purchaser for value. When goods have been delivered under a transaction of purchase the purchaser has such power even though

(a) the transferor was deceived as to the identity of the purchaser, or

(b) the delivery was in exchange for a check which is later dishonored, or

(c) it was agreed that the transaction was to be a "cash sale", or

(d) the delivery was procured through fraud punishable as larcenous under the criminal law.

(2) Any entrusting of possession of goods to a merchant who deals in goods of that kind gives him power to transfer all rights of the entruster to a buyer in ordinary course of business.

(3) "Entrusting" includes any delivery and any acquiescence in retention of possession regardless of any condition expressed between the parties to the delivery or acquiescence and regardless of whether the procurement of the entrusting or the possessor's disposition of the goods have been such as to be larcenous under the criminal law.

(4) The rights of other purchasers of goods and of lien creditors are governed by the Articles on Secured Transactions (Article 9), Bulk Transfers (Article 6) and Documents of Title (Article 7).

Part 5—Performance

§ 2–501. Insurable Interest in Goods; Manner of Identification of Goods.

(1) The buyer obtains a special property and an insurable interest in goods by identification of existing goods as goods to which the contract refers even though the goods so identified are nonconforming and he has an option to return or reject them. Such identification can be made at any time and in any manner explicitly agreed to by the parties. In the absence of explicit agreement identification occurs

(a) when the contract is made if it is for the sale of goods already existing and identified;

(b) if the contract is for the sale of future goods other than those described in paragraph (c), when goods are shipped, marked or otherwise designated by the seller as goods to which the contract refers;

(c) when the crops are planted or otherwise become growing crops or the young are conceived if the contract is for the sale of unborn young to be born within twelve months after contracting or for the sale of crops to be harvested within twelve months or the next normal harvest season after contracting whichever is longer.

(2) The seller retains an insurable interest in goods so long as title to or any security interest in the goods remains in him and where the identification is by the seller alone he may until default or insolvency or notification to the buyer that the identification is final substitute other goods for those identified.

(3) Nothing in this section impairs any insurable interest recognized under any other statute or rule of law.

§ 2–502. Buyer's Right to Goods on Seller's Insolvency.

(1) Subject to subsection (2) and even though the goods have not been shipped a buyer who has paid a part or all of the price of goods in which he has a special property under the provisions of the immediately preceding section may on making and keeping good a tender of any unpaid portion of their price recover them from the seller if the seller becomes insolvent within ten days after receipt of the first installment on their price.

(2) If the identification creating his special property has been made by the buyer he acquires the right to recover the goods only if they conform to the contract for sale.

§ 2–503. Manner of Seller's Tender of Delivery.

(1) Tender of delivery requires that the seller put and hold conforming goods at the buyer's disposition and give the buyer any notification reasonably necessary to enable him to take delivery. The manner, time and place for tender are determined by the agreement and this Article, and in particular

(a) tender must be at a reasonable hour, and if it is of goods they must be kept available for the period reasonably necessary to enable the buyer to take possession; but

(b) unless otherwise agreed the buyer must furnish facilities reasonably suited to the receipt of the goods.

(2) Where the case is within the next section respecting shipment tender requires that the seller comply with its provisions.

(3) Where the seller is required to deliver at a particular destination tender requires that he comply with subsection (1) and also in any appropriate case tender documents as described in subsections (4) and (5) of this section.

(4) Where goods are in the possession of a bailee and are to be delivered without being moved

(a) tender requires that the seller either tender a negotiable document of title covering such goods or procure acknowledgment by the bailee of the buyer's right to possession of the goods; but

(b) tender to the buyer of a non-negotiable document of title or of a written direction to the bailee to deliver is sufficient tender unless the buyer seasonably objects, and receipt by the bailee of notification of the buyer's rights fixes those rights as against the bailee and all third persons; but risk of loss of the goods and of any failure by the bailee to honor the non-negotiable document of title or to obey the direction remains on the seller until the buyer has had a reasonable time to present the document or direction, and a refusal by the bailee to honor the document or to obey the direction defeats the tender.

(5) Where the contract requires the seller to deliver documents

(a) he must tender all such documents in correct form, except as provided in this Article with respect to bills of lading in a set (subsection (2) of Section 2–323); and

(b) tender through customary banking channels is sufficient and dishonor of a draft accompanying the documents constitutes non-acceptance or rejection.

§ 2–504. Shipment by Seller.

Where the seller is required or authorized to send the goods to the buyer and the contract does not require him to deliver them at a particular destination, then unless otherwise agreed he must

(a) put the goods in the possession of such a carrier and make such a contract for their transportation as may be reasonable having regard to the nature of the goods and other circumstances of the case; and

(b) obtain and promptly deliver or tender in due form any document necessary to enable the buyer to obtain possession of the goods or otherwise required by the agreement or by usage of trade; and

(c) promptly notify the buyer of the shipment.

Failure to notify the buyer under paragraph (c) or to make a proper contract under paragraph (a) is a ground for rejection only if material delay or loss ensues.

§ 2–505. Seller's Shipment Under Reservation.

(1) Where the seller has identified goods to the contract by or before shipment:

(a) his procurement of a negotiable bill of lading to his own order or otherwise reserves in him a security interest in the goods. His procurement of the bill to the order of a financing agency or of the buyer indicates in addition only the seller's expectation of transferring that interest to the person named.

(b) a non-negotiable bill of lading to himself or his nominee reserves possession of the goods as security but except in a case of conditional delivery (subsection (2) of Section 2–507) a non-negotiable bill of lading naming the buyer as consignee reserves no security interest even though the seller retains possession of the bill of lading.

(2) When shipment by the seller with reservation of a security interest is in violation of the contract for sale it

constitutes an improper contract for transportation within the preceding section but impairs neither the rights given to the buyer by shipment and identification of the goods to the contract nor the seller's powers as a holder of a negotiable document.

§ 2–506. Rights of Financing Agency.

(1) A financing agency by paying or purchasing for value a draft which relates to a shipment of goods acquires to the extent of the payment or purchase and in addition to its own rights under the draft and any document of title securing it any rights of the shipper in the goods including the right to stop delivery and the shipper's right to have the draft honored by the buyer.

(2) The right to reimbursement of a financing agency which has in good faith honored or purchased the draft under commitment to or authority from the buyer is not impaired by subsequent discovery of defects with reference to any relevant document which was apparently regular on its face.

§ 2–507. Effect of Seller's Tender; Delivery on Condition.

(1) Tender of delivery is a condition to the buyer's duty to accept the goods and, unless otherwise agreed, to his duty to pay for them. Tender entitles the seller to acceptance of the goods and to payment according to the contract.

(2) Where payment is due and demanded on the delivery to the buyer of goods or documents of title, his right as against the seller to retain or dispose of them is conditional upon his making the payment due.

§ 2–508. Cure by Seller of Improper Tender or Delivery; Replacement.

(1) Where any tender or delivery by the seller is rejected because non-conforming and the time for performance has not yet expired, the seller may seasonably notify the buyer of his intention to cure and may then within the contract time make a conforming delivery.

(2) Where the buyer rejects a non-conforming tender which the seller had reasonable grounds to believe would be acceptable with or without money allowance the seller may if he seasonably notifies the buyer have a further reasonable time to substitute a conforming tender.

§ 2–509. Risk of Loss in the Absence of Breach.

(1) Where the contract requires or authorizes the seller to ship the goods by carrier

(a) if it does not require him to deliver them at a particular destination, the risk of loss passes to the buyer when the goods are duly delivered to the carrier even though the shipment is under reservation (Section 2–505); but

(b) if it does require him to deliver them at a particular destination and the goods are there duly tendered while in the possession of the carrier, the risk of loss passes to the buyer when the goods are there duly so tendered as to enable the buyer to take delivery.

(2) Where the goods are held by a bailee to be delivered without being moved, the risk of loss passes to the buyer

(a) on his receipt of a negotiable document of title covering the goods; or

(b) on acknowledgment by the bailee of the buyer's right to possession of the goods; or

(c) after his receipt of a non-negotiable document of title or other written direction to deliver, as provided in subsection (4)(b) of Section 2–503.

(3) In any case not within subsection (1) or (2), the risk of loss passes to the buyer on his receipt of the goods if the seller is a merchant; otherwise, the risk passes to the buyer on tender of delivery.

(4) The provisions of this section are subject to contrary agreement of the parties and to the provisions of this Article on sale on approval (Section 2–327) and on effect of breach on risk of loss (Section 2–510).

§ 2–510. Effect of Breach on Risk of Loss.

(1) Where a tender or delivery of goods so fails to conform to the contract as to give a right of rejection the risk of their loss remains on the seller until cure or acceptance.

(2) Where the buyer rightfully revokes acceptance he may to the extent of any deficiency in his effective insurance coverage treat the risk of loss as having rested on the seller from the beginning.

(3) Where the buyer as to conforming goods already identified to the contract for sale repudiates or is otherwise in breach before risk of their loss has passed to him, the seller may to the extent of any deficiency in his effective insurance coverage treat the risk of loss as resting on the buyer for a commercially reasonable time.

§ 2–511. Tender of Payment by Buyer; Payment by Check.

(1) Unless otherwise agreed tender of payment is a condition to the seller's duty to tender and complete any delivery.

(2) Tender of payment is sufficient when made by any means or in any manner current in the ordinary course of business unless the seller demands payment in legal tender and gives any extension of time reasonably necessary to procure it.

(3) Subject to the provisions of this Act on the effect of an instrument on an obligation (Section 3–802), pay-

ment by check is conditional and is defeated as between the parties by dishonor of the check on due presentment.

§ 2–512. Payment by Buyer Before Inspection.

(1) Where the contract requires payment before inspection non-conformity of the goods does not excuse the buyer from so making payment unless

(a) the non-conformity appears without inspection; or

(b) despite tender of the required documents the circumstances would justify injunction against honor under the provisions of this Act (Section 5–114).

(2) Payment pursuant to subsection (1) does not constitute an acceptance of goods or impair the buyer's right to inspect or any of his remedies.

§ 2–513. Buyer's Right to Inspection of Goods.

(1) Unless otherwise agreed and subject to subsection (3), where goods are tendered or delivered or identified to the contract for sale, the buyer has a right before payment or acceptance to inspect them at any reasonable place and time and in any reasonable manner. When the seller is required or authorized to send the goods to the buyer, the inspection may be after their arrival.

(2) Expenses of inspection must be borne by the buyer but may be recovered from the seller if the goods do not conform and are rejected.

(3) Unless otherwise agreed and subject to the provisions of this Article on C.I.F. contracts (subsection (3) of Section 2–321), the buyer is not entitled to inspect the goods before payment of the price when the contract provides

(a) for delivery "C.O.D." or on other like terms; or

(b) for payment against documents of title, except where such payment is due only after the goods are to become available for inspection.

(4) A place or method of inspection fixed by the parties is presumed to be exclusive but unless otherwise expressly agreed it does not postpone identification or shift the place for delivery or for passing the risk of loss. If compliance becomes impossible, inspection shall be as provided in this section unless the place or method fixed was clearly intended as an indispensable condition failure of which avoids the contract.

§ 2–514. When Documents Deliverable on Acceptance; When on Payment.

Unless otherwise agreed documents against which a draft is drawn are to be delivered to the drawee on acceptance of the draft if it is payable more than three days after presentment; otherwise, only on payment.

§ 2–515. Preserving Evidence of Goods in Dispute.

In furtherance of the adjustment of any claim or dispute

(a) either party on reasonable notification to the other and for the purpose of ascertaining the facts and preserving evidence has the right to inspect, test and sample the goods including such of them as may be in the possession or control of the other; and

(b) the parties may agree to a third party inspection or survey to determine the conformity or condition of the goods and may agree that the findings shall be binding upon them in any subsequent litigation or adjustment.

Part 6—Breach, Repudiation and Excuse

§ 2–601. Buyer's Rights on Improper Delivery.

Subject to the provisions of this Article on breach in installment contracts (Section 2–612) and unless otherwise agreed under the sections on contractual limitations of remedy (Sections 2–718 and 2–719), if the goods or the tender of delivery fail in any respect to conform to the contract, the buyer may

(a) reject the whole; or

(b) accept the whole; or

(c) accept any commercial unit or units and reject the rest.

§ 2–602. Manner and Effect of Rightful Rejection.

(1) Rejection of goods must be within a reasonable time after their delivery or tender. It is ineffective unless the buyer seasonably notifies the seller.

(2) Subject to the provisions of the two following sections on rejected goods (Sections 2–603 and 2–604),

(a) after rejection any exercise of ownership by the buyer with respect to any commercial unit is wrongful as against the seller; and

(b) if the buyer has before rejection taken physical possession of goods in which he does not have a security interest under the provisions of this Article (subsection (3) of Section 2–711), he is under a duty after rejection to hold them with reasonable care at the seller's disposition for a time sufficient to permit the seller to remove them; but

(c) the buyer has no further obligations with regard to goods rightfully rejected.

(3) The seller's rights with respect to goods wrongfully rejected are governed by the provisions of this Article on seller's remedies in general (Section 2–703).

§ 2–603. Merchant Buyer's Duties as to Rightfully Rejected Goods.

(1) Subject to any security interest in the buyer (subsection (3) of Section 2–711), when the seller has no agent or place of business at the market of rejection a merchant buyer is under a duty after rejection of goods in his possession or control to follow any reasonable instructions received from the seller with respect to the goods and in the absence of such instructions to make reasonable efforts to sell them for the seller's account if they are perishable or threaten to decline in value speedily. Instructions are not reasonable if on demand indemnity for expenses is not forthcoming.

(2) When the buyer sells goods under subsection (1), he is entitled to reimbursement from the seller or out of the proceeds for reasonable expenses of caring for and selling them, and if the expenses include no selling commission then to such commission as is usual in the trade or if there is none to a reasonable sum not exceeding ten per cent on the gross proceeds.

(3) In complying with this section the buyer is held only to good faith and good faith conduct hereunder is neither acceptance nor conversion nor the basis of an action for damages.

§ 2–604. Buyer's Options as to Salvage of Rightfully Rejected Goods.

Subject to the provisions of the immediately preceding section on perishables if the seller gives no instructions within a reasonable time after notification of rejection the buyer may store the rejected goods for the seller's account or reship them to him or resell them for the seller's account with reimbursement as provided in the preceding section. Such action is not acceptance or conversion.

§ 2–605. Waiver of Buyer's Objections by Failure to Particularize.

(1) The buyer's failure to state in connection with rejection a particular defect which is ascertainable by reasonable inspection precludes him from relying on the unstated defect to justify rejection or to establish breach

(a) where the seller could have cured it if stated seasonably; or

(b) between merchants when the seller has after rejection made a request in writing for a full and final written statement of all defects on which the buyer proposes to rely.

(2) Payment against documents made without reservation of rights precludes recovery of the payment for defects apparent on the face of the documents.

§ 2–606. What Constitutes Acceptance of Goods.

(1) Acceptance of goods occurs when the buyer

(a) after a reasonable opportunity to inspect the goods signifies to the seller that the goods are conforming or that he will take or retain them in spite of their nonconformity; or

(b) fails to make an effective rejection (subsection (1) of Section 2–602), but such acceptance does not occur until the buyer has had a reasonable opportunity to inspect them; or

(c) does any act inconsistent with the seller's ownership; but if such act is wrongful as against the seller it is an acceptance only if ratified by him.

(2) Acceptance of a part of any commercial unit is acceptance of that entire unit.

§ 2–607. Effect of Acceptance; Notice of Breach; Burden of Establishing Breach After Acceptance; Notice of Claim or Litigation to Person Answerable Over.

(1) The buyer must pay at the contract rate for any goods accepted.

(2) Acceptance of goods by the buyer precludes rejection of the goods accepted and if made with knowledge of a non-conformity cannot be revoked because of it unless the acceptance was on the reasonable assumption that the non-conformity would be seasonably cured but acceptance does not of itself impair any other remedy provided by this Article for non-conformity.

(3) Where a tender has been accepted

(a) the buyer must within a reasonable time after he discovers or should have discovered any breach notify the seller of breach or be barred from any remedy; and

(b) if the claim is one for infringement or the like (subsection (3) of Section 2–312) and the buyer is sued as a result of such a breach he must so notify the seller within a reasonable time after he receives notice of the litigation or be barred from any remedy over for liability established by the litigation.

(4) The burden is on the buyer to establish any breach with respect to the goods accepted.

(5) Where the buyer is sued for breach of a warranty or other obligation for which his seller is answerable over

(a) he may give his seller written notice of the litigation. If the notice states that the seller may come in and defend and that if the seller does not do so he will be bound in any action against him by his buyer by any determination of fact common to the two litigations, then unless the seller after seasonable receipt of the notice does come in and defend he is so bound.

(b) if the claim is one for infringement or the like (subsection (3) of Section 2–312) the original seller may demand in writing that his buyer turn over to him control of the litigation including settlement or else be barred from any remedy over and if he also agrees to bear all expense and to satisfy any adverse judgment, then unless the buyer after seasonable receipt of the demand does turn over control the buyer is so barred.

(6) The provisions of subsections (3), (4) and (5) apply to any obligation of a buyer to hold the seller harmless against infringement or the like (subsection (3) of Section 2–312).

§ 2–608. Revocation of Acceptance in Whole or in Part.

(1) The buyer may revoke his acceptance of a lot or commercial unit whose non-conformity substantially impairs its value to him if he has accepted it

(a) on the reasonable assumption that its non-conformity would be cured and it has not been seasonably cured; or

(b) without discovery of such non-conformity if his acceptance was reasonably induced either by the difficulty of discovery before acceptance or by the seller's assurances.

(2) Revocation of acceptance must occur within a reasonable time after the buyer discovers or should have discovered the ground for it and before any substantial change in condition of the goods which is not caused by their own defects. It is not effective until the buyer notifies the seller of it.

(3) A buyer who so revokes has the same rights and duties with regard to the goods involved as if he had rejected them.

§ 2–609. Right to Adequate Assurance of Performance.

(1) A contract for sale imposes an obligation on each party that the other's expectation of receiving due performance will not be impaired. When reasonable grounds for insecurity arise with respect to the performance of either party the other may in writing demand adequate assurance of due performance and until he receives such assurance may if commercially reasonable suspend any performance for which he has not already received the agreed return.

(2) Between merchants the reasonableness of grounds for insecurity and the adequacy of any assurance offered shall be determined according to commercial standards.

(3) Acceptance of any improper delivery or payment does not prejudice the aggrieved party's right to demand adequate assurance of future performance.

(4) After receipt of a justified demand failure to provide within a reasonable time not exceeding thirty days such

assurance of due performance as is adequate under the circumstances of the particular case is a repudiation of the contract.

§ 2–610. Anticipatory Repudiation.

When either party repudiates the contract with respect to a performance not yet due the loss of which will substantially impair the value of the contract to the other, the aggrieved party may

(a) for a commercially reasonable time await performance by the repudiating party; or

(b) resort to any remedy for breach (Section 2–703 or Section 2–711), even though he has notified the repudiating party that he would await the latter's performance and has urged retraction; and

(c) in either case suspend his own performance or proceed in accordance with the provisions of this Article on the seller's right to identify goods to the contract notwithstanding breach or to salvage unfinished goods (Section 2–704).

§ 2–611. Retraction of Anticipatory Repudiation.

(1) Until the repudiating party's next performance is due he can retract his repudiation unless the aggrieved party has since the repudiation cancelled or materially changed his position or otherwise indicated that he considers the repudiation final.

(2) Retraction may be by any method which clearly indicates to the aggrieved party that the repudiating party intends to perform, but must include any assurance justifiably demanded under the provisions of this Article (Section 2–609).

(3) Retraction reinstates the repudiating party's rights under the contract with due excuse and allowance to the aggrieved party for any delay occasioned by the repudiation.

§ 2–612. "Installment Contract"; Breach.

(1) An "installment contract" is one which requires or authorizes the delivery of goods in separate lots to be separately accepted, even though the contract contains a clause "each delivery is a separate contract" or its equivalent.

(2) The buyer may reject any installment which is nonconforming if the non-conformity substantially impairs the value of that installment and cannot be cured or if the non-conformity is a defect in the required documents; but if the non-conformity does not fall within subsection (3) and the seller gives adequate assurance of its cure the buyer must accept that installment.

(3) Whenever non-conformity or default with respect to one or more installments substantially impairs the value of the whole contract there is a breach of the whole. But the aggrieved party reinstates the contract if

he accepts a non-conforming installment without seasonably notifying of cancellation or if he brings an action with respect only to past installments or demands performance as to future installments.

§ 2–613. Casualty to Identified Goods.

Where the contract requires for its performance goods identified when the contract is made, and the goods suffer casualty without fault of either party before the risk of loss passes to the buyer, or in a proper case under a "no arrival, no sale" term (Section 2–324) then

(a) if the loss is total the contract is avoided; and

(b) if the loss is partial or the goods have so deteriorated as no longer to conform to the contract the buyer may nevertheless demand inspection and at his option either treat the contract as avoided or accept the goods with due allowance from the contract price for the deterioration or the deficiency in quantity but without further right against the seller.

§ 2–614. Substituted Performance.

(1) Where without fault of either party the agreed berthing, loading, or unloading facilities fail or an agreed type of carrier becomes unavailable or the agreed manner of delivery otherwise becomes commercially impracticable but a commercially reasonable substitute is available, such substitute performance must be tendered and accepted.

(2) If the agreed means or manner of payment fails because of domestic or foreign governmental regulation, the seller may withhold or stop delivery unless the buyer provides a means or manner of payment which is commercially a substantial equivalent. If delivery has already been taken, payment by the means or in the manner provided by the regulation discharges the buyer's obligation unless the regulation is discriminatory, oppressive or predatory.

§ 2–615. Excuse by Failure of Presupposed Conditions.

Except so far as a seller may have assumed a greater obligation and subject to the preceding section on substituted performance:

(a) Delay in delivery or non-delivery in whole or in part by a seller who complies with paragraphs (b) and (c) is not a breach of his duty under a contract for sale if performance as agreed has been made impracticable by the occurrence of a contingency the non-occurrence of which was a basic assumption on which the contract was made or by compliance in good faith with any applicable foreign or domestic governmental regulation or order whether or not it later proves to be invalid.

(b) Where the causes mentioned in paragraph (a) affect only a part of the seller's capacity to perform, he must allocate production and deliveries among his customers but may at his option include regular customers not then under contract as well as his own requirements for further manufacture. He may so allocate in any manner which is fair and reasonable.

(c) The seller must notify the buyer seasonably that there will be delay or non-delivery and, when allocation is required under paragraph (b), of the estimated quota thus made available for the buyer.

§ 2–616. Procedure on Notice Claiming Excuse.

(1) Where the buyer receives notification of a material or indefinite delay or an allocation justified under the preceding section he may by written notification to the seller as to any delivery concerned, and where the prospective deficiency substantially impairs the value of the whole contract under the provisions of this Article relating to breach of installment contracts (Section 2–612), then also as to the whole,

(a) terminate and thereby discharge any unexecuted portion of the contract; or

(b) modify the contract by agreeing to take his available quota in substitution.

(2) If after receipt of such notification from the seller the buyer fails so to modify the contract within a reasonable time not exceeding thirty days the contract lapses with respect to any deliveries affected.

(3) The provisions of this section may not be negated by agreement except in so far as the seller has assumed a greater obligation under the preceding section.

Part 7—Remedies

§ 2–701. Remedies for Breach of Collateral Contracts Not Impaired.

Remedies for breach of any obligation or promise collateral or ancillary to a contract for sale are not impaired by the provisions of this Article.

§ 2–702. Seller's Remedies on Discovery of Buyer's Insolvency.

(1) Where the seller discovers the buyer to be insolvent he may refuse delivery except for cash including payment for all goods theretofore delivered under the contract, and stop delivery under this Article (Section 2–705).

(2) Where the seller discovers that the buyer has received goods on credit while insolvent he may reclaim the goods upon demand made within ten days after the receipt, but if misrepresentation of solvency has been made to the particular seller in writing within three months before delivery the ten day limitation does not apply. Except as provided in this subsection the seller may not base a right to reclaim goods on the buyer's fraudulent or innocent misrepresentation of solvency or of intent to pay.

(3) The seller's right to reclaim under subsection (2) is subject to the rights of a buyer in ordinary course or other good faith purchaser under this Article (Section 2–403). Successful reclamation of goods excludes all other remedies with respect to them.

§ 2–703. Seller's Remedies in General.

Where the buyer wrongfully rejects or revokes acceptance of goods or fails to make a payment due on or before delivery or repudiates with respect to a part or the whole, then with respect to any goods directly affected and, if the breach is of the whole contract (Section 2–612), then also with respect to the whole undelivered balance, the aggrieved seller may

(a) withhold delivery of such goods;

(b) stop delivery by any bailee as hereafter provided (Section 2–705);

(c) proceed under the next section respecting goods still unidentified to the contract;

(d) resell and recover damages as hereafter provided (Section 2–706);

(e) recover damages for non-acceptance (Section 2–708) or in a proper case the price (Section 2–709);

(f) cancel.

§ 2–704. Seller's Right to Identify Goods to the Contract Notwithstanding Breach or to Salvage Unfinished Goods.

(1) An aggrieved seller under the preceding section may

(a) identify to the contract conforming goods not already identified if at the time he learned of the breach they are in his possession or control;

(b) treat as the subject of resale goods which have demonstrably been intended for the particular contract even though those goods are unfinished.

(2) Where the goods are unfinished an aggrieved seller may in the exercise of reasonable commercial judgment for the purposes of avoiding loss and of effective realization either complete the manufacture and wholly identify the goods to the contract or cease manufacture and resell for scrap or salvage value or proceed in any other reasonable manner.

§ 2–705. Seller's Stoppage of Delivery in Transit or Otherwise.

(1) The seller may stop delivery of goods in the possession of a carrier or other bailee when he discovers the buyer to be insolvent (Section 2–702) and may stop delivery of carload, truckload, planeload or larger shipments of express or freight when the buyer repudiates or fails to make a payment due before delivery or if for any other reason the seller has a right to withhold or reclaim the goods.

(2) As against such buyer the seller may stop delivery until

(a) receipt of the goods by the buyer; or

(b) acknowledgment to the buyer by any bailee of the goods except a carrier that the bailee holds the goods for the buyer; or

(c) such acknowledgment to the buyer by a carrier by reshipment or as warehouseman; or

(d) negotiation to the buyer of any negotiable document of title covering the goods.

(3) (a) To stop delivery the seller must so notify as to enable the bailee by reasonable diligence to prevent delivery of the goods.

(b) After such notification the bailee must hold and deliver the goods according to the directions of the seller but the seller is liable to the bailee for any ensuing charges or damages.

(c) If a negotiable document of title has been issued for goods the bailee is not obliged to obey a notification to stop until surrender of the document.

(d) A carrier who has issued a non-negotiable bill of lading is not obliged to obey a notification to stop received from a person other than the consignor.

§ 2–706. Seller's Resale Including Contract for Resale.

(1) Under the conditions stated in Section 2–703 on seller's remedies, the seller may resell the goods concerned or the undelivered balance thereof. Where the resale is made in good faith and in a commercially reasonable manner the seller may recover the difference between the resale price and the contract price together with any incidental damages allowed under the provisions of this Article (Section 2–710), but less expenses saved in consequence of the buyer's breach.

(2) Except as otherwise provided in subsection (3) or unless otherwise agreed resale may be at public or private sale including sale by way of one or more contracts to sell or of identification to an existing contract of the seller. Sale may be as a unit or in parcels and at any time and place and on any terms but every aspect of the sale including the method, manner, time, place and terms must be commercially reasonable. The resale must be reasonably identified as referring to the broken contract, but it is not necessary that the goods be in existence or that any or all of them have been identified to the contract before the breach.

(3) Where the resale is at private sale the seller must give the buyer reasonable notification of his intention to resell.

(4) Where the resale is at public sale

(a) only identified goods can be sold except where there is a recognized market for a public sale of futures in goods of the kind; and

(b) it must be made at a usual place or market for public sale if one is reasonably available and except in the case of goods which are perishable or threaten to decline in value speedily the seller must give the buyer reasonable notice of the time and place of the resale; and

(c) if the goods are not to be within the view of those attending the sale the notification of sale must state the place where the goods are located and provide for their reasonable inspection by prospective bidders; and

(d) the seller may buy.

(5) A purchaser who buys in good faith at a resale takes the goods free of any rights of the original buyer even though the seller fails to comply with one or more of the requirements of this section.

(6) The seller is not accountable to the buyer for any profit made on any resale. A person in the position of a seller (Section 2–707) or a buyer who has rightfully rejected or justifiably revoked acceptance must account for any excess over the amount of his security interest, as hereinafter defined (subsection (3) of Section 2–711).

§ 2–707. "Person in the Position of a Seller".

(1) A "person in the position of a seller" includes as against a principal an agent who has paid or become responsible for the price of goods on behalf of his principal or anyone who otherwise holds a security interest or other right in goods similar to that of a seller.

(2) A person in the position of a seller may as provided in this Article withhold or stop delivery (Section 2–705) and resell (Section 2–706) and recover incidental damages (Section 2–710).

§ 2–708. Seller's Damages for Non-Acceptance or Repudiation.

(1) Subject to subsection (2) and to the provisions of this Article with respect to proof of market price (Section 2–723), the measure of damages for non-acceptance or repudiation by the buyer is the difference between the market price at the time and place for tender and the unpaid contract price together with any incidental damages provided in this Article (Section 2–710), but less expenses saved in consequence of the buyer's breach.

(2) If the measure of damages provided in subsection (1) is inadequate to put the seller in as good a position as performance would have done then the measure of damages is the profit (including reasonable overhead) which the seller would have made from full performance by the buyer, together with any incidental damages provided in this Article (Section 2–710), due allowance for costs reasonably incurred and due credit for payments or proceeds of resale.

§ 2–709. Action for the Price.

(1) When the buyer fails to pay the price as it becomes due the seller may recover, together with any incidental damages under the next section, the price

(a) of goods accepted or of conforming goods lost or damaged within a commercially reasonable time after risk of their loss has passed to the buyer; and

(b) of goods identified to the contract if the seller is unable after reasonable effort to resell them at a reasonable price or the circumstances reasonably indicate that such effort will be unavailing.

(2) Where the seller sues for the price he must hold for the buyer any goods which have been identified to the contract and are still in his control except that if resale becomes possible he may resell them at any time prior to the collection of the judgment. The net proceeds of any such resale must be credited to the buyer and payment of the judgment entitles him to any goods not resold.

(3) After the buyer has wrongfully rejected or revoked acceptance of the goods or has failed to make a payment due or has repudiated (Section 2–610), a seller who is held not entitled to the price under this section shall nevertheless be awarded damages for non-acceptance under the preceding section.

§ 2–710. Seller's Incidental Damages.

Incidental damages to an aggrieved seller include any commercially reasonable charges, expenses or commissions incurred in stopping delivery, in the transportation, care and custody of goods after the buyer's breach, in connection with return or resale of the goods or otherwise resulting from the breach.

§ 2–711. Buyer's Remedies in General; Buyer's Security Interest in Rejected Goods.

(1) Where the seller fails to make delivery or repudiates or the buyer rightfully rejects or justifiably revokes acceptance then with respect to any goods involved, and with respect to the whole if the breach goes to the whole contract (Section 2–612), the buyer may cancel and whether or not he has done so may in addition to recovering so much of the price as has been paid

(a) "cover" and have damages under the next section as to all the goods affected whether or not they have been identified to the contract; or

(b) recover damages for non-delivery as provided in this Article (Section 2–713).

(2) Where the seller fails to deliver or repudiates the buyer may also

(a) if the goods have been identified recover them as provided in this Article (Section 2–502); or

(b) in a proper case obtain specific performance or replevy the goods as provided in this Article (Section 2–716).

(3) On rightful rejection or justifiable revocation of acceptance a buyer has a security interest in goods in his possession or control for any payments made on their price and any expenses reasonably incurred in their inspection, receipt, transportation, care and custody and may hold such goods and resell them in like manner as an aggrieved seller (Section 2–706).

§ 2–712. "Cover"; Buyer's Procurement of Substitute Goods.

(1) After a breach within the preceding section the buyer may "cover" by making in good faith and without unreasonable delay any reasonable purchase of or contract to purchase goods in substitution for those due from the seller.

(2) The buyer may recover from the seller as damages the difference between the cost of cover and the contract price together with any incidental or consequential damages as hereinafter defined (Section 2–715), but less expenses saved in consequence of the seller's breach.

(3) Failure of the buyer to effect cover within this section does not bar him from any other remedy.

§ 2–713. Buyer's Damages for Non-Delivery or Repudiation.

(1) Subject to provisions of this Article with respect to the proof of market price (Section 2–723), the measure of damages for non-delivery or repudiation by the seller is the difference between the market price at the time when the buyer learned of the breach and the contract price together with any incidental and consequential damages provided in this Article (Section 2–715), but less expenses saved in consequence of the seller's breach.

(2) Market price is to be determined as of the place for tender or, in cases of rejection after arrival or revocation of acceptance, as of the place of arrival.

§ 2–714. Buyer's Damages for Breach in Regard to Accepted Goods.

(1) Where the buyer has accepted goods and given notification (subsection (3) of Section 2–607) he may recover as damages for any non-conformity of tender the loss resulting in the ordinary course of events from the seller's breach as determined in any manner which is reasonable.

(2) The measure of damages for breach of warranty is the difference at the time and place of acceptance between the value of the goods accepted and the value they would have had if they had been as warranted, unless special circumstances show proximate damages of a different amount.

(3) In a proper case any incidental and consequential damages under the next section may be recovered.

§ 2–715. Buyer's Incidental and Consequential Damages.

(1) Incidental damages resulting from the seller's breach include expenses reasonably incurred in inspection, receipt, transportation and care and custody of goods rightfully rejected, any commercially reasonable charges, expenses or commissions in connection with effecting cover and any other reasonable expense incident to the delay or other breach.

(2) Consequential damages resulting from the seller's breach include

(a) any loss resulting from general or particular requirements and needs of which the seller at the time of contracting had reason to know and which could not reasonably be prevented by cover or otherwise; and

(b) injury to person or property proximately resulting from any breach of warranty.

§ 2–716. Buyer's Right to Specific Performance or Replevin.

(1) Specific performance may be decreed where the goods are unique or in other proper circumstances.

(2) The decree for specific performance may include such terms and conditions as to payment of the price, damages, or other relief as the court may deem just.

(3) The buyer has a right of replevin for goods identified to the contract if after reasonable effort he is unable to effect cover for such goods or the circumstances reasonably indicate that such effort will be unavailing or if the goods have been shipped under reservation and satisfaction of the security interest in them has been made or tendered.

§ 2–717. Deduction of Damages From the Price.

The buyer on notifying the seller of his intention to do so may deduct all or any part of the damages resulting from any breach of the contract from any part of the price still due under the same contract.

§ 2–718. Liquidation or Limitation of Damages; Deposits

(1) Damages for breach by either party may be liquidated in the agreement but only at an amount which is reasonable in the light of the anticipated or actual harm caused by the breach, the difficulties of proof of loss, and the inconvenience or nonfeasibility of otherwise obtaining an adequate remedy. A term fixing unreasonably large liquidated damages is void as a penalty.

(2) Where the seller justifiably withholds delivery of goods because of the buyer's breach, the buyer is entitled to restitution of any amount by which the sum of his payments exceeds

(a) the amount to which the seller is entitled by virtue of terms liquidating the seller's damages in accordance with subsection (1), or

(b) in the absence of such terms, twenty per cent of the value of the total performance for which the buyer is obligated under the contract or $500, whichever is smaller.

(3) The buyer's right to restitution under subsection (2) is subject to offset to the extent that the seller establishes

(a) a right to recover damages under the provisions of this Article other than subsection (1), and

(b) the amount or value of any benefits received by the buyer directly or indirectly by reason of the contract.

(4) Where a seller has received payment in goods their reasonable value or the proceeds of their resale shall be treated as payments for the purposes of subsection (2); but if the seller has notice of the buyer's breach before reselling goods received in part performance, his resale is subject to the conditions laid down in this Article on resale by an aggrieved seller (Section 2–706).

§ 2–719. Contractual Modification or Limitation of Remedy.

(1) Subject to the provisions of subsection (2) and (3) of this section and of the preceding section on liquidation and limitation of damages,

(a) the agreement may provide for remedies in addition to or in substitution for those provided in this Article and may limit or alter the measure of damages recoverable under this Article, as by limiting the buyer's remedies to return of the goods and repayment of the price or to repair and replacement of non-conforming goods or parts; and

(b) resort to a remedy as provided is optional unless the remedy is expressly agreed to be exclusive, in which case it is the sole remedy.

(2) Where circumstances cause an exclusive or limited remedy to fail of its essential purpose, remedy may be had as provided in this Act.

(3) Consequential damages may be limited or excluded unless the limitation or exclusion is unconscionable. Limitation of consequential damages for injury to the person in the case of consumer goods is prima facie unconscionable but limitation of damages where the loss is commercial is not.

§ 2–720. Effect of "Cancellation" or "Rescission" on Claims for Antecedent Breach.

Unless the contrary intention clearly appears, expressions of "cancellation" or "rescission" of the contract or the like shall not be construed as a renunciation or discharge of any claim in damages for an antecedent breach.

§ 2–721. Remedies for Fraud.

Remedies for material misrepresentation or fraud include all remedies available under this Article for nonfraudulent breach. Neither rescission or a claim for rescission of the contract for sale nor rejection or return of the goods shall bar or be deemed inconsistent with a claim for damages or other remedy.

§ 2–722. Who Can Sue Third Parties for Injury to Goods.

Where a third party so deals with goods which have been identified to a contract for sale as to cause actionable injury to a party to that contract

(a) a right of action against the third party is in either party to the contract for sale who has title to or a security interest or a special property or an insurable interest in the goods; and if the goods have been destroyed or converted a right of action is also in the party who either bore the risk of loss under the contract for sale or has since the injury assumed that risk as against the other;

(b) if at the time of the injury the party plaintiff did not bear the risk of loss as against the other party to the contract for sale and there is no arrangement between them for disposition of the recovery, his suit or settlement is subject to his own interest, as a fiduciary for the other party to the contract;

(c) either party may with the consent of the other sue for the benefit of whom it may concern.

§ 2–723. Proof of Market Price: Time and Place

(1) If an action based on anticipatory repudiation comes to trial before the time for performance with respect to some or all of the goods, any damages based on market price (Section 2–708 or Section 2–713) shall be determined according to the price of such goods prevailing at the time when the aggrieved party learned of the repudiation.

(2) If evidence of a price prevailing at the times or places described in this Article is not readily available the price prevailing within any reasonable time before or after the time described or at any other place which in commercial judgment or under usage of trade would serve as a reasonable substitute for the one described may be used, making any proper allowance for the cost of transporting the goods to or from such other place.

(3) Evidence of a relevant price prevailing at a time or place other than the one described in this Article offered by one party is not admissible unless and until he has given the other party such notice as the court finds sufficient to prevent unfair surprise.

§ 2–724. Admissibility of Market Quotations.

Whenever the prevailing price or value of any goods regularly bought and sold in any established commodity market is in issue, reports in official publications or trade journals or in newspapers or periodicals of general circulation published as the reports of such market shall be admissible in evidence. The circumstances of the preparation of such a report may be shown to affect its weight but not its admissibility.

§ 2–725. Statute of Limitations in Contracts for Sale.

(1) An action for breach of any contract for sale must be commenced within four years after the cause of action has accrued. By the original agreement the parties may reduce the period of limitation to not less than one year but may not extend it.

(2) A cause of action occurs when the breach occurs, regardless of the aggrieved party's lack of knowledge of the breach. A breach of warranty occurs when tender of delivery is made, except that where a warranty explicitly extends to future performance of the goods and discovery of the breach must await the time of such performance the cause of action accrues when the breach is or should have been discovered.

(3) Where an action commenced within the time limited by subsection (1) is so terminated as to leave available a remedy by another action for the same breach such other action may be commenced after the expiration of the time limited and within six months after the termination of the first action unless the termination resulted from voluntary discontinuance or from dismissal for failure or neglect to prosecute.

(4) This section does not alter the law on tolling of the statute of limitations nor does it apply to causes of action which have accrued before this Act becomes effective.

ARTICLE 2A: LEASES

Part 1—General Provisions

§ 2A–101. Short Title.

This Article shall be known and may be cited as the Uniform Commerical Code—Leases.

§ 2A–102. Scope.

This Article applies to any transaction, regardless of form, that creates a lease.

§ 2A–103. Definitions and Index of Definitions.

(1) In this Article unless the context otherwise requires:

(a) "Buyer in ordinary course of business" means a person who in good faith and without knowledge that the sale to him [or her] is in violation of the ownership rights or security interest or leasehold interest of a third party in the goods buys in ordinary course from a person in the business of selling goods of that kind but does not include a pawnbroker. "Buying" may be for cash or by exchange of other property or on secured or unsecured credit and includes receiving goods or documents of title under a pre-existing contract for sale but does not include a transfer in bulk or as security for or in total or partial satisfaction of a money debt.

(b) "Cancellation" occurs when either party puts an end to the lease contract for default by the other party.

(c) "Commercial unit" means such a unit of goods as by commercial usage is a single whole for purposes of lease and division of which materially impairs its character or value on the market or in use. A commercial unit may be a single article, as a machine, or a set of articles, as a suite of furniture or a line of machinery, or a quantity, as a gross or carload, or any other unit treated in use or in the relevant market as a single whole.

(d) "Conforming" goods or performance under a lease contract means goods or performance that are in accordance with the obligations under the lease contract.

(e) "Consumer lease" means a lease that a lessor regularly engaged in the business of leasing or selling makes to a lessee, except an organization, who takes under the lease primarily for a personal, family, or household purpose, if the total payments to be made under the lease contract, excluding payments for options to renew or buy, do not exceed $25,000.

(f) "Fault" means wrongful act, omission, breach, or default.

(g) "Finance lease" means a lease in which (i) the lessor does not select, manufacture or supply the goods, (ii) the lessor acquires the goods or the right to possession and use of the goods in connection with the lease, and (iii) either the lessee receives a copy of the contract evidencing the lessor's purchase of the goods on or before signing the lease contract, or the lessee's approval of the contract evidencing the lessor's purchase of the goods is a condition to effectiveness of the lease contract.

(h) "Goods" means all things that are movable at the time of identification to the lease contract, or are fixtures (Section 2A–309), but the term does not include money, documents, instruments, accounts, chattel paper, general intangibles, or minerals or the like, including oil and gas, before extraction. The term also includes the unborn young of animals.

(i) "Installment lease contract" means a lease contract that authorizes or requires the delivery of goods in separate lots to be separately accepted, even though the lease contract contains a clause "each delivery is a separate lease" or its equivalent.

(j) "Lease" means a transfer of the right to possession and use of goods for a term in return for consideration, but a sale, including a sale on approval or a sale or return, or retention or creation of a security interest is not a lease. Unless the context clearly indicates otherwise, the term includes a sublease.

(k) "Lease agreement" means the bargain, with respect to the lease, of the lessor and the lessee in fact as found in their language or by implication from other circumstances including course of dealing or usage of trade or course of performance as provided in this Article. Unless the context clearly indicates otherwise, the term includes a sublease agreement.

(l) "Lease contract" means the total legal obligation that results from the lease agreement as affected by this Article and any other applicable rules of law. Unless the context clearly indicates otherwise, the term includes a sublease contract.

(m) "Leasehold interest" means the interest of the lessor or the lessee under a lease contract.

(n) "Lessee" means a person who acquires the right to possession and use of goods under a lease. Unless the context clearly indicates otherwise, the term includes a sublessee.

(o) "Lessee in ordinary course of business" means a person who in good faith and without knowledge that the lease to him [or her] is in violation of the ownership rights or security interest or leasehold interest of a third party in the goods, leases in ordinary course from a person in the business of selling or leasing goods of that kind but does not include a pawnbroker. "Leasing" may be for cash or by exchange of other property or on secured or unsecured credit and includes receiving goods or documents of title under a pre-existing lease contract but does not include a transfer in bulk or as security for or in total or partial satisfaction of a money debt.

(p) "Lessor" means a person who transfers the right to possession and use of goods under a lease. Unless the context clearly indicates otherwise, the term includes a sublessor.

(q) "Lessor's residual interest" means the lessor's interest in the goods after expiration, termination, or cancellation of the lease contract.

(r) "Lien" means a charge against or interest in goods to secure payment of a debt or performance of an obligation, but the term does not include a security interest.

(s) "Lot" means a parcel or a single article that is the subject matter of a separate lease or delivery, whether or not it is sufficient to perform the lease contract.

(t) "Merchant lessee" means a lessee that is a merchant with respect to goods of the kind subject to the lease.

(u) "Present value" means the amount as of a date certain of one or more sums payable in the future, discounted to the date certain. The discount is determined by the interest rate specified by the parties if the rate was not manifestly unreasonable at the time the transaction was entered into; otherwise, the discount is determined by a commercially reasonable rate that takes into account the facts and circumstances of each case at the time the transaction was entered into.

(v) "Purchase" includes taking by sale, lease, mortgage, security interest, pledge, gift, or any other voluntary transaction creating an interest in goods.

(w) "Sublease" means a lease of goods the right to possession and use of which was acquired by the lessor as a lessee under an existing lease.

(x) "Supplier" means a person from whom a lessor buys or leases goods to be leased under a finance lease.

(y) "Supply contract" means a contract under which a lessor buys or leases goods to be leased.

(z) "Termination" occurs when either party pursuant to a power created by agreement or law puts an end to the lease contract otherwise than for default.

(2) Other definitions applying to this Article and the sections in which they appear are:

"Accessions". Section 2A–310(1).
"Construction mortgage". Section 2A–309(1)(d).
"Encumbrance". Section 2A–309(1)(e).
"Fixtures". Section 2A–309(1)(a).
"Fixture filing". Section 2A–309(1)(b).
"Purchase money lease". Section 2A–309(1)(c).

(3) The following definitions in other Articles apply to this Article:

"Accounts". Section 9–106.
"Between merchants". Section 2–104(3).
"Buyer". Section 2–103(1)(a).
"Chattel paper". Section 9–105(1)(b).
"Consumer goods". Section 9–109(1).
"Documents". Section 9–105(1)(f).
"Entrusting". Section 2–403(3).
"General intangibles". Section 9–106.
"Good faith". Section 2–103(1)(b).
"Instruments". Section 9–105(1)(i).
"Merchant". Section 2–104(1).
"Mortgage". Section 9–105(1)(j).
"Pursuant to commitment". Section 9–105(1)(k).
"Receipt". Section 2–103(1)(c).
"Sale". Section 2–106(1).
"Sale on approval". Section 2–326.
"Sale or return". Section 2–326.
"Seller". Section 2–103(1)(d).

(4) In addition Article 1 contains general definitions and principles of construction and interpretation applicable throughout this Article.

§ 2A–104. Leases Subject to Other Statutes.

(1) A lease, although subject to this Article, is also subject to any applicable:

(a) statute of the United States;

(b) certificate of title statute of this State: (list any certificate of title statutes covering automobiles, trailers, mobile homes, boats, farm tractors, and the like);

(c) certificate of title statute of another jurisdiction (Section 2A–105); or

(d) consumer protection statute of this State.

(2) In case of conflict between the provisions of this Article, other than Sections 2A–105, 2A–304(3) and 2A–305(3), and any statute referred to in subsection (1), the provisions of that statute control.

(3) Failure to comply with any applicable statute has only the effect specified therein.

§ 2A–105. Territorial Application of Article to Goods Covered by Certificate of Title.

Subject to the provisions of Sections 2A–304(3) and 2A–305(3), with respect to goods covered by a certificate of title issued under a statute of this State or of another jurisdiction, compliance and the effect of compliance or noncompliance with a certificate of title statute are governed by the law (including the conflict of laws rules) of the jurisdiction issuing the certificate until the earlier of (a) surrender of the certificate, or (b) four months after the goods are removed from that jurisdiction and thereafter until a new certificate of title is issued by another jurisdiction.

§ 2A–106. Limitation on Power of Parties to Consumer Lease to Choose Applicable Law and Judicial Forum.

(1) If the law chosen by the parties to a consumer lease is that of a jurisdiction other than a jurisdiction in which the lessee resides at the time the lease agreement becomes enforceable or within 30 days thereafter or in which the goods are to be used, the choice is not enforceable.

(2) If the judicial forum chosen by the parties to a consumer lease is a forum that would not otherwise have jurisdiction over the lessee, the choice is not enforceable.

§ 2A–107. Waiver or Renunciation of Claim or Right After Default.

Any claim or right arising out of an alleged default or breach of warranty may be discharged in whole or in part without consideration by a written waiver or renunciation signed and delivered by the aggrieved party.

§ 2A–108. Unconscionability.

(1) If the court as a matter of law finds a lease contract or any clause of a lease contract to have been unconscio-

nable at the time it was made the court may refuse to enforce the lease contract, or it may enforce the remainder of the lease contract without the unconscionable clause, or it may so limit the application of any unconscionable clause as to avoid any unconscionable result.

(2) With respect to a consumer lease, if the court as a matter of law finds that a lease contract or any clause of a lease contract has been induced by unconscionable conduct or that unconscionable conduct has occurred in the collection of a claim arising from a lease contract, the court may grant appropriate relief.

(3) Before making a finding of unconscionability under subsection (1) or (2), the court, on its own motion or that of a party, shall afford the parties a reasonable opportunity to present evidence as to the setting, purpose, and effect of the lease contract or clause thereof, or of the conduct.

(4) In an action in which the lessee claims unconscionability with respect to a consumer lease:

(a) If the court finds unconscionability under subsection (1) or (2), the court shall award reasonable attorney's fees to the lessee.

(b) If the court does not find unconscionability and the lessee claiming unconscionability has brought or maintained an action he [or she] knew to be groundless, the court shall award reasonable attorney's fees to the party against whom the claim is made.

(c) In determining attorney's fees, the amount of the recovery on behalf of the claimant under subsections (1) and (2) is not controlling.

§ 2A–109. Option to Accelerate at Will.

(1) A term providing that one party or his [or her] successor in interest may accelerate payment or performance or require collateral or additional collateral "at will" or "when he [or she] deems himself [or herself] insecure" or in words of similar import must be construed to mean that he [or she] has power to do so only if he [or she] in good faith believes that the prospect of payment or performance is impaired.

(2) With respect to a consumer lease, the burden of establishing good faith under subsection (1) is on the party who exercised the power; otherwise the burden of establishing lack of good faith is on the party against whom the power has been exercised.

Part 2—Formation and Construction of Lease Contract

§ 2A–201. Statute of Frauds.

(1) A lease contract is not enforceable by way of action or defense unless:

(a) the total payments to be made under the lease contract, excluding payments for options to renew or buy, are less than $1,000; or

(b) there is a writing, signed by the party against whom enforcement is sought or by that party's authorized agent, sufficient to indicate that a lease contract has been made between the parties and to describe the goods leased and the lease term.

(2) Any description of leased goods or of the lease term is sufficient and satisfies subsection (1)(b), whether or not it is specific, if it reasonably identifies what is described.

(3) A writing is not insufficient because it omits or incorrectly states a term agreed upon, but the lease contract is not enforceable under subsection (1)(b) beyond the lease term and the quantity of goods shown in the writing.

(4) A lease contract that does not satisfy the requirements of subsection (1), but which is valid in other respects, is enforceable:

(a) if the goods are to be specially manufactured or obtained for the lessee and are not suitable for lease or sale to others in the ordinary course of the lessor's business, and the lessor, before notice of repudiation is received and under circumstances that reasonably indicate that the goods are for the lessee, has made either a substantial beginning of their manufacture or commitments for their procurement;

(b) if the party against whom enforcement is sought admits in that party's pleading, testimony or otherwise in court that a lease contract was made, but the lease contract is not enforceable under this provision beyond the quantity of goods admitted; or

(c) with respect to goods that have been received and accepted by the lessee.

(5) The lease term under a lease contract referred to in subsection (4) is:

(a) if there is a writing signed by the party against whom enforcement is sought or by that party's authorized agent specifying the lease term, the term so specified;

(b) if the party against whom enforcement is sought admits in that party's pleading, testimony, or otherwise in court a lease term, the term so admitted; or

(c) a reasonable lease term.

§ 2A–202. Final Written Expression: Parol or Extrinsic Evidence.

Terms with respect to which the confirmatory memoranda of the parties agree or which are otherwise set forth in a writing intended by the parties as a final expression of their agreement with respect to such terms as are included therein may not be contradicted by evidence of any prior agreement or of a contemporaneous oral agreement but may be explained or supplemented:

(a) by course of dealing or usage of trade or by course of performance; and

(b) by evidence of consistent additional terms unless the court finds the writing to have been intended also as a complete and exclusive statement of the terms of the agreement.

§ 2A–203. Seals Inoperative.

The affixing of a seal to a writing evidencing a lease contract or an offer to enter into a lease contract does not render the writing a sealed instrument and the law with respect to sealed instruments does not apply to the lease contract or offer.

§2A–204. Formation in General.

(1) A lease contract may be made in any manner sufficient to show agreement, including conduct by both parties which recognizes the existence of a lease contract.

(2) An agreement sufficient to constitute a lease contract may be found although the moment of its making is undetermined.

(3) Although one or more terms are left open, a lease contract does not fail for indefiniteness if the parties have intended to make a lease contract and there is a reasonably certain basis for giving an appropriate remedy.

§ 2A–205. Firm Offers.

An offer by a merchant to lease goods to or from another person in a signed writing that by its terms gives assurance it will be held open is not revocable, for lack of consideration, during the time stated or, if no time is stated, for a reasonable time, but in no event may the period of irrevocability exceed 3 months. Any such term of assurance on a form supplied by the offeree must be separately signed by the offeror.

§ 2A–206. Offer and Acceptance in Formation of Lease Contract.

(1) Unless otherwise unambiguously indicated by the language or circumstances, an offer to make a lease contract must be construed as inviting acceptance in any manner and by any medium reasonable in the circumstances.

(2) If the beginning of a requested performance is a reasonable mode of acceptance, an offeror who is not notified of acceptance within a reasonable time may treat the offer as having lapsed before acceptance.

§ 2A–207. Course of Performance or Practical Construction.

(1) If a lease contract involves repeated occasions for performance by either party with knowledge of the nature of the performance and opportunity for objection to it by the other, any course of performance accepted or acquiesced in without objection is relevant to determine the meaning of the lease agreement.

(2) The express terms of a lease agreement and any course of performance, as well as any course of dealing and usage of trade, must be construed whenever reasonable as consistent with each other; but if that construction is unreasonable, express terms control course of performance, course of performance controls both course of dealing and usage of trade, and course of dealing controls usage of trade.

(3) Subject to the provisions of Section 2A–208 on modification and waiver, course of performance is relevant to show a waiver or modification of any term inconsistent with the course of performance.

§ 2A–208. Modification, Rescission and Waiver.

(1) An agreement modifying a lease contract needs no consideration to be binding.

(2) A signed lease agreement that excludes modification or rescission except by a signed writing may not be otherwise modified or rescinded, but, except as between merchants, such a requirement on a form supplied by a merchant must be separately signed by the other party.

(3) Although an attempt at modification or rescission does not satisfy the requirements of subsection (2), it may operate as a waiver.

(4) A party who has made a waiver affecting an executory portion of a lease contract may retract the waiver by reasonable notification received by the other party that strict performance will be required of any term waived, unless the retraction would be unjust in view of a material change of position in reliance on the waiver.

§ 2A–209. Lessee Under Finance Lease as Beneficiary of Supply Contract.

(1) The benefit of the supplier's promises to the lessor under the supply contract and of all warranties, whether express or implied, under the supply contract, extends to the lessee to the extent of the lessee's leasehold interest under a finance lease related to the supply contract, but subject to the terms of the supply contract and all of the supplier's defenses or claims arising therefrom.

(2) The extension of the benefit of the supplier's promises and warranties to the lessee (Section 2A–209(1)) does not: (a) modify the rights and obligations of the parties to the supply contract, whether arising therefrom or otherwise, or (b) impose any duty or liability under the supply contract on the lessee.

(3) Any modification or rescission of the supply contract by the supplier and the lessor is effective against the lessee unless, prior to the modification or rescission, the supplier has received notice that the lessee has entered into a finance lease related to the supply contract. If the

supply contract is modified or rescinded after the lessee enters the finance lease, the lessee has a cause of action against the lessor, and against the supplier if the supplier has notice of the lessee's entering the finance lease when the supply contract is modified or rescinded. The lessee's recovery from such action shall put the lessee in as good a position as if the modification or rescission had not occurred.

§ 2A–210. Express Warranties.

(1) Express warranties by the lessor are created as follows:

(a) Any affirmation of fact or promise made by the lessor to the lessee which relates to the goods and becomes part of the basis of the bargain creates an express warranty that the goods will conform to the affirmation or promise.

(b) Any description of the goods which is made part of the basis of the bargain creates an express warranty that the goods will conform to the description.

(c) Any sample or model that is made part of the basis of the bargain creates an express warranty that the whole of the goods will conform to the sample or model.

(2) It is not necessary to the creation of an express warranty that the lessor use formal words, such as "warrant" or "guarantee," or that the lessor have a specific intention to make a warranty, but an affirmation merely of the value of the goods or a statement purporting to be merely the lessor's opinion or commendation of the goods does not create a warranty.

§ 2A–211. Warranties Against Interference and Against Infringement; Lessee's Obligation Against Infringement.

(1) There is in a lease contract a warranty that for the lease term no person holds a claim to or interest in the goods that arose from an act or omission of the lessor, other than a claim by way of infringement or the like, which will interfere with the lessee's enjoyment of its leasehold interest.

(2) Except in a finance lease there is in a lease contract by a lessor who is a merchant regularly dealing in goods of the kind a warranty that the goods are delivered free of the rightful claim of any person by way of infringement or the like.

(3) A lessee who furnishes specifications to a lessor or a supplier shall hold the lessor and the supplier harmless against any claim by way of infringement or the like that arises out of compliance with the specifications.

§ 2A–212. Implied Warranty of Merchantability.

(1) Except in a finance lease, a warranty that the goods will be merchantable is implied in a lease contract if the lessor is a merchant with respect to goods of that kind.

(2) Goods to be merchantable must be at least such as

(a) pass without objection in the trade under the description in the lease agreement;

(b) in the case of fungible goods, are of fair average quality within the description;

(c) are fit for the ordinary purposes for which goods of that type are used;

(d) run, within the variation permitted by the lease agreement, of even kind, quality, and quantity within each unit and among all units involved;

(e) are adequately contained, packaged, and labeled as the lease agreement may require; and

(f) conform to any promises or affirmations of fact made on the container or label.

(3) Other implied warranties may arise from course of dealing or usage of trade.

§ 2A–213. Implied Warranty of Fitness for Particular Purpose.

Except in a finance lease, if the lessor at the time the lease contract is made has reason to know of any particular purpose for which the goods are required and that the lessee is relying on the lessor's skill or judgment to select or furnish suitable goods, there is in the lease contract an implied warranty that the goods will be fit for that purpose.

§ 2A–214. Exclusion or Modification of Warranties.

(1) Words or conduct relevant to the creation of an express warranty and words or conduct tending to negate or limit a warranty must be construed wherever reasonable as consistent with each other; but, subject to the provisions of Section 2A–202 on parol or extrinsic evidence, negation or limitation is inoperative to the extent that the construction is unreasonable.

(2) Subject to subsection (3), to exclude or modify the implied warranty of merchantability or any part of it the language must mention "merchantability", be by a writing, and be conspicuous. Subject to subsection (3), to exclude or modify any implied warranty of fitness the exclusion must be by a writing and be conspicuous. Language to exclude all implied warranties of fitness is sufficient if it is in writing, is conspicuous and states, for example, "There is no warranty that the goods will be fit for a particular purpose".

(3) Notwithstanding subsection (2), but subject to subsection (4),

(a) unless the circumstances indicate otherwise, all implied warranties are excluded by expressions like "as is," or "with all faults," or by other language that in common understanding calls the lessee's attention to the exclusion of warranties and makes plain that there is no implied warranty, if in writing and conspicuous;

(b) if the lessee before entering into the lease contract has examined the goods or the sample or model as fully as desired or has refused to examine the goods, there is no implied warranty with regard to defects that an examination ought in the circumstances to have revealed; and

(c) an implied warranty may also be excluded or modified by course of dealing, course of performance, or usage of trade.

(4) To exclude or modify a warranty against interference or against infringement (Section 2A–211) or any part of it, the language must be specific, be by a writing, and be conspicuous, unless the circumstances, including course of performance, course of dealing, or usage of trade, give the lessee reason to know that the goods are being leased subject to a claim or interest of any person.

§ 2A–215. Cumulation and Conflict of Warranties Express or Implied.

Warranties, whether express or implied, must be construed as consistent with each other and as cumulative, but if that construction is unreasonable, the intention of the parties determines which warranty is dominant. In ascertaining that intention the following rules apply:

(a) Exact or technical specifications displace an inconsistent sample or model or general language of description.

(b) A sample from an existing bulk displaces inconsistent general language of description.

(c) Express warranties displace inconsistent implied warranties other than an implied warranty of fitness for a particular purpose.

§ 2A–216. Third-Party Beneficiaries of Express and Implied Warranties.

Alternative A A warranty to or for the benefit of a lessee under this Article, whether express or implied, extends to any natural person who is in the family or household of the lessee or who is a guest in the lessee's home if it is reasonable to expect that such person may use, consume, or be affected by the goods and who is injured in person by breach of the warranty. This section does not displace principles of law and equity that extend a warranty to or for the benefit of a lessee to other persons. The operation of this section may not be excluded, modified, or limited, but an exclusion, modification, or limitation of the warranty, including any with respect to rights and remedies, effective against the lessee is also effective against any beneficiary designated under this section.

Alternative B A warranty to or for the benefit of a lessee under this Article, whether express or implied,

extends to any natural person who may reasonably be expected to use, consume, or be affected by the goods and who is injured in person by breach of the warranty. This section does not displace principles of law and equity that extend a warranty to or for the benefit of a lessee to other persons. The operation of this section may not be excluded, modified, or limited, but an exclusion, modification, or limitation of the warranty, including any with respect to rights and remedies, effective against the lessee is also effective against the beneficiary designated under this section.

Alternative C A warranty to or for the benefit of a lessee under this Article, whether express or implied, extends to any person who may reasonably be expected to use, consume, or be affected by the goods and who is injured by breach of the warranty. The operation of this section may not be excluded, modified, or limited with respect to injury to the person of an individual to whom the warranty extends, but an exclusion, modification, or limitation of the warranty, including any with respect to rights and remedies, effective against the lessee is also effective against the beneficiary designated under this section.

§ 2A–217. Identification.

Identification of goods as goods to which a lease contract refers may be made at any time and in any manner explicitly agreed to by the parties. In the absence of explicit agreement, identification occurs:

(a) when the lease contract is made if the lease contract is for a lease of goods that are existing and identified;

(b) when the goods are shipped, marked, or otherwise designated by the lessor as goods to which the lease contract refers, if the lease contract is for a lease of goods that are not existing and identified; or

(c) when the young are conceived, if the lease contract is for a lease of unborn young of animals.

§ 2A–218. Insurance and Proceeds.

(1) A lessee obtains an insurable interest when existing goods are identified to the lease contract even though the goods identified are nonconforming and the lessee has an option to reject them.

(2) If a lessee has an insurable interest only by reason of the lessor's identification of the goods, the lessor, until default or insolvency or notification to the lessee that identification is final, may substitute other goods for those identified.

(3) Notwithstanding a lessee's insurable interest under subsections (1) and (2), the lessor retains an insurable interest until an option to buy has been exercised by the lessee and risk of loss has passed to the lessee.

(4) Nothing in this section impairs any insurable interest recognized under any other statute or rule of law.

(5) The parties by agreement may determine that one or more parties have an obligation to obtain and pay for insurance covering the goods and by agreement may determine the beneficiary of the proceeds of the insurance.

§ 2A–219. Risk of Loss.

(1) Except in the case of a finance lease, risk of loss is retained by the lessor and does not pass to the lessee. In the case of a finance lease, risk of loss passes to the lessee.

(2) Subject to the provisions of this Article on the effect of default on risk of loss (Section 2A–220), if risk of loss is to pass to the lessee and the time of passage is not stated, the following rules apply:

(a) If the lease contract requires or authorizes the goods to be shipped by carrier

(i) and it does not require delivery at a particular destination, the risk of loss passes to the lessee when the goods are duly delivered to the carrier; but

(ii) if it does require delivery at a particular destination and the goods are there duly tendered while in the possession of the carrier, the risk of loss passes to the lessee when the goods are there duly so tendered as to enable the lessee to take delivery.

(b) If the goods are held by a bailee to be delivered without being moved, the risk of loss passes to the lessee on acknowledgment by the bailee of the lessee's right to possession of the goods.

(c) In any case not within subsection (a) or (b), the risk of loss passes to the lessee on the lessee's receipt of the goods if the lessor, or, in the case of a finance lease, the supplier, is a merchant; otherwise the risk passes to the lessee on tender of delivery.

§ 2A–220. Effect of Default on Risk of Loss.

(1) Where risk of loss is to pass to the lessee and the time of passage is not stated:

(a) If a tender or delivery of goods so fails to conform to the lease contract as to give a right of rejection, the risk of their loss remains with the lessor, or, in the case of a finance lease, the supplier, until cure or acceptance.

(b) If the lessee rightfully revokes acceptance, he [or she], to the extent of any deficiency in his [or her] effective insurance coverage, may treat the risk of loss as having remained with the lessor from the beginning.

(2) Whether or not risk of loss is to pass to the lessee, if the lessee as to conforming goods already identified to a lease contract repudiates or is otherwise in default under the lease contract, the lessor, or, in the case of a finance lease, the supplier, to the extent of any deficiency in his [or her] effective insurance coverage may treat the risk of loss as resting on the lessee for a commercially reasonable time.

§ 2A–221. Casualty to Identified Goods.

If a lease contract requires goods identified when the lease contract is made, and the goods suffer casualty without fault of the lessee, the lessor or the supplier before delivery, or the goods suffer casualty before risk of loss passes to the lessee pursuant to the lease agreement or Section 2A–219, then:

(a) if the loss is total, the lease contract is avoided; and

(b) if the loss is partial or the goods have so deteriorated as to no longer conform to the lease contract, the lessee may nevertheless demand inspection and at his [or her] option either treat the lease contract as avoided or, except in a finance lease that is not a consumer lease, accept the goods with due allowance from the rent payable for the balance of the lease term for the deterioration or the deficiency in quantity but without further right against the lessor.

Part 3—Effect of Lease Contract

§ 2A–301. Enforceability of Lease Contract.

Except as otherwise provided in this Article, a lease contract is effective and enforceable according to its terms between the parties, against purchasers of the goods and against creditors of the parties.

§ 2A–302. Title to and Possession of Goods.

Except as otherwise provided in this Article, each provision of this Article applies whether the lessor or a third party has title to the goods, and whether the lessor, the lessee, or a third party has possession of the goods, notwithstanding any statute or rule of law that possession or the absence of possession is fraudulent.

§ 2A–303. Alienability of Party's Interest Under Lease Contract or of Lessor's Residual Interest in Goods; Delegation of Performance; Assignment of Rights.

(1) Any interest of a party under a lease contract and the lessor's residual interest in the goods may be transferred unless

(a) the transfer is voluntary and the lease contract prohibits the transfer; or

(b) the transfer materially changes the duty of or materially increases the burden or risk imposed on the other party to the lease contract, and within a reasonable time after notice of the transfer the other party demands that the transferee comply with subsection (2) and the transferee fails to comply.

(2) Within a reasonable time after demand pursuant to subsection (1)(b), the transferee shall:

(a) cure or provide adequate assurance that he [or she] will promptly cure any default other than one arising from the transfer;

(b) compensate or provide adequate assurance that he [or she] will promptly compensate the other party to the lease contract and any other person holding an interest in the lease contract, except the party whose interest is being transferred, for any loss to that party resulting from the transfer;

(c) provide adequate assurance of future due performance under the lease contract; and

(d) assume the lease contract.

(3) Demand pursuant to subsection (1)(b) is without prejudice to the other party's rights against the transferee and the party whose interest is transferred.

(4) An assignment of "the lease" or of "all my rights under the lease" or an assignment in similar general terms is a transfer of rights, and unless the language or the circumstances, as in an assignment for security, indicate the contrary, the assignment is a delegation of duties by the assignor to the assignee and acceptance by the assignee constitutes a promise by him [or her] to perform those duties. This promise is enforceable by either the assignor or the other party to the lease contract.

(5) Unless otherwise agreed by the lessor and the lessee, no delegation of performance relieves the assignor as against the other party of any duty to perform or any liability for default.

(6) A right to damages for default with respect to the whole lease contract or a right arising out of the assignor's due performance of his [or her] entire obligation can be assigned despite agreement otherwise.

(7) To prohibit the transfer of an interest of a party under a lease contract, the language of prohibition must be specific, by a writing, and conspicuous.

§ 2A–304. Subsequent Lease of Goods by Lessor.

(1) Subject to the provisions of Section 2A–303, a subsequent lessee from a lessor of goods under an existing lease contract obtains, to the extent of the leasehold interest transferred, the leasehold interest in the goods that the lessor had or had power to transfer, and except as provided in subsection (2) and Section 2A–527(4), takes subject to the existing lease contract. A lessor with voidable title has power to transfer a good leasehold interest to a good faith subsequent lessee for value, but only to the extent set forth in the preceding sentence. When goods have been delivered under a transaction of purchase the lessor has that power even though:

(a) the lessor's transferor was deceived as to the identity of the lessor;

(b) the delivery was in exchange for a check which is later dishonored;

(c) it was agreed that the transaction was to be a "cash sale"; or

(d) the delivery was procured through fraud punishable as larcenous under the criminal law.

(2) A subsequent lessee in the ordinary course of business from a lessor who is a merchant dealing in goods of that kind to whom the goods were entrusted by the existing lessee before the interest of the subsequent lessee became enforceable against the lessor obtains, to the extent of the leasehold interest transferred, all of the lessor's and the existing lessee's rights to the goods, and takes free of the existing lease contract.

(3) A subsequent lessee from the lessor of goods that are subject to an existing lease contract and are covered by a certificate of title issued under a statute of this State or of another jurisdiction takes no greater rights than those provided both by this section and by the certificate of title statute.

§ 2A–305. Sale or Sublease of Goods by Lessee.

(1) Subject to the provisions of Section 2A–303, a buyer or sublessee from the lessee of goods under an existing lease contract obtains, to the extent of the interest transferred, the leasehold interest in the goods that the lessee had or had power to transfer, and except as provided in subsection (2) and Section 2A–511(4), takes subject to the existing lease contract. A lessee with a voidable leasehold interest has power to transfer a good leasehold interest to a good faith buyer for value or a good faith sublessee for value, but only to the extent set forth in the preceding sentence. When goods have been delivered under a transaction of lease the lessee has that power even though:

(a) the lessor was deceived as to the identity of the lessee;

(b) the delivery was in exchange for a check which is later dishonored; or

(c) the delivery was procured through fraud punishable as larcenous under the criminal law.

(2) A buyer in the ordinary course of business or a sublessee in the ordinary course of business from a lessee who is a merchant dealing in goods of that kind to whom the goods were entrusted by the lessor obtains, to the extent of the interest transferred, all of the lessor's and lessee's rights to the goods, and takes free of the existing lease contract.

(3) A buyer or sublessee from the lessee of goods that are subject to an existing lease contract and are covered by a certificate of title issued under a statute of this State or of another jurisdiction takes no greater rights than those provided both by this section and by the certificate of title statute.

§ 2A–306. Priority of Certain Liens Arising by Operation of Law.

If a person in the ordinary course of his [or her] business furnishes services or materials with respect to goods subject to a lease contract, a lien upon those goods in the possession of that person given by statute or rule of law for those materials or services takes priority over any interest of the lessor or lessee under the lease contract or this Article unless the lien is created by statute and the statute provides otherwise or unless the lien is created by rule of law and the rule of law provides otherwise.

§ 2A–307. Priority of Liens Arising by Attachment or Levy on, Security Interests in, and Other Claims to Goods.

(1) Except as otherwise provided in Section 2A–306, a creditor of a lessee takes subject to the lease contract.

(2) Except as otherwise provided in subsections (3) and (4) of this section and in Sections 2A–306 and 2A–308, a creditor of a lessor takes subject to the lease contract:

(a) unless the creditor holds a lien that attached to the goods before the lease contract became enforceable, or

(b) unless the creditor holds a security interest in the goods that under the Article on Secured Transactions (Article 9) would have priority over any other security interest in the goods perfected by a filing covering the goods and made at the time the lease contract became enforceable, whether or not any other security interest existed.

(3) A lessee in the ordinary course of business takes the leasehold interest free of a security interest in the goods created by the lessor even though the security interest is perfected and the lessee knows of its existence.

(4) A lessee other than a lessee in the ordinary course of business takes the leasehold interest free of a security interest to the extent that it secures future advances made after the secured party acquires knowledge of the lease or more than 45 days after the lease contract becomes enforceable, whichever first occurs, unless the future advances are made pursuant to a commitment entered into without knowledge of the lease and before the expiration of the 45-day period.

§ 2A–308. Special Rights of Creditors.

(1) A creditor of a lessor in possession of goods subject to a lease contract may treat the lease contract as void if as against the creditor retention of possession by the lessor is fraudulent under any statute or rule of law, but retention of possession in good faith and current course of trade by the lessor for a commercially reasonable time after the lease contract becomes enforceable is not fraudulent.

(2) Nothing in this Article impairs the rights of creditors of a lessor if the lease contract (a) becomes enforceable, not in current course of trade but in satisfaction of or as security for a pre-existing claim for money, security, or the like, and (b) is made under circumstances which under any statute or rule of law apart from this Article would constitute the transaction a fraudulent transfer or voidable preference.

(3) A creditor of a seller may treat a sale or an identification of goods to a contract for sale as void if as against the creditor retention of possession by the seller is fraudulent under any statute or rule of law, but retention of possession of the goods pursuant to a lease contract entered into by the seller as lessee and the buyer as lessor in connection with the sale or identification of the goods is not fraudulent if the buyer bought for value and in good faith.

§ 2A–309. Lessor's and Lessee's Rights When Goods Become Fixtures.

(1) In this section:

(a) goods are "fixtures" when they become so related to particular real estate that an interest in them arises under real estate law;

(b) a "fixture filing" is the filing, in the office where a mortgage on the real estate would be recorded or registered, of a financing statement concerning goods that are or are to become fixtures and conforming to the requirements of subsection (5) of Section 9–402;

(c) a lease is a "purchase money lease" unless the lessee has possession or use of the goods or the right to possession or use of the goods before the lease agreement is enforceable;

(d) a mortgage is a "construction mortgage" to the extent it secures an obligation incurred for the construction of an improvement on land including the acquisition cost of the land, if the recorded writing so indicates; and

(e) "encumbrance" includes real estate mortgages and other liens on real estate and all other rights in real estate that are not ownership interests.

(2) Under this Article a lease may be of goods that are fixtures or may continue in goods that become fixtures, but no lease exists under this Article of ordinary building materials incorporated into an improvement on land.

(3) This Article does not prevent creation of a lease of fixtures pursuant to real estate law.

(4) The perfected interest of a lessor of fixtures has priority over a conflicting interest of an encumbrancer or owner of the real estate if:

(a) the lease is a purchase money lease, the conflicting interest of the encumbrancer or owner arises before the goods become fixtures, the interest of the lessor is perfected by a fixture filing before the goods become fixtures or within ten days thereafter, and the lessee has an interest of record in the real estate or is in possession of the real estate; or

(b) the interest of the lessor is perfected by a fixture filing before the interest of the encumbrancer or owner is of record, the lessor's interest has priority over any conflicting interest of a predecessor in title of the encumbrancer or owner, and the lessee has an interest of record in the real estate or is in possession of the real estate.

(5) The interest of a lessor of fixtures, whether or not perfected, has priority over the conflicting interest of an encumbrancer or owner of the real estate if:

(a) the fixtures are readily removable factory or office machines, readily removable equipment that is not primarily used or leased for use in the operation of the real estate, or readily removable replacements of domestic appliances that are goods subject to a consumer lease, and before the goods become fixtures the lease contract is enforceable; or

(b) the conflicting interest is a lien on the real estate obtained by legal or equitable proceedings after the lease contract is enforceable; or

(c) the encumbrancer or owner has consented in writing to the lease or has disclaimed an interest in the goods as fixtures; or

(d) the lessee has a right to remove the goods as against the encumbrancer or owner. If the lessee's right to remove terminates, the priority of the interest of the lessor continues for a reasonable time.

(6) Notwithstanding paragraph (a) of subsection (4) but otherwise subject to subsections (4) and (5), the interest of a lessor of fixtures is subordinate to the conflicting interest of an encumbrancer of the real estate under a construction mortgage recorded before the goods become fixtures if the goods become fixtures before the completion of the construction. To the extent given to refinance a construction mortgage, the conflicting interest of an encumbrancer of the real estate under a mortgage has this priority to the same extent as the encumbrancer of the real estate under the construction mortgage.

(7) In cases not within the preceding subsections, priority between the interest of a lessor of fixtures and the conflicting interest of an encumbrancer or owner of the real estate who is not the lessee is determined by the priority rules governing conflicting interests in real estate.

(8) If the interest of a lessor has priority over all conflicting interests of all owners and encumbrancers of the real estate, the lessor or the lessee may (a) on default, expiration, termination, or cancellation of the lease agreement by the other party but subject to the provisions of the lease agreement and this Article, or (b) if necessary to enforce his [or her] other rights and remedies under this Article, remove the goods from the real

estate, free and clear of all conflicting interests of all owners and encumbrancers of the real estate, but he [or she] must reimburse any encumbrancer or owner of the real estate who is not the lessee and who has not otherwise agreed for the cost of repair of any physical injury, but not for any diminution in value of the real estate caused by the absence of the goods removed or by any necessity of replacing them. A person entitled to reimbursement may refuse permission to remove until the party seeking removal gives adequate security for the performance of this obligation.

(9) Even though the lease agreement does not create a security interest, the interest of a lessor of fixtures is perfected by filing a financing statement as a fixture filing for leased goods that are or are to become fixtures in accordance with the relevant provisions of the Article on Secured Transactions (Article 9).

§ 2A–310. Lessor's and Lessee's Rights When Goods Become Accessions.

(1) Goods are "accessions" when they are installed in or affixed to other goods.

(2) The interest of a lessor or a lessee under a lease contract entered into before the goods became accessions is superior to all interests in the whole except as stated in subsection (4).

(3) The interest of a lessor or a lessee under a lease contract entered into at the time or after the goods became accessions is superior to all subsequently acquired interests in the whole except as stated in subsection (4) but is subordinate to interests in the whole existing at the time the lease contract was made unless the holders of such interests in the whole have in writing consented to the lease or disclaimed an interest in the goods as part of the whole.

(4) The interest of a lessor or a lessee under a lease contract described in subsection (2) or (3) is subordinate to the interest of

(a) a buyer in the ordinary course of business or a lessee in the ordinary course of business of any interest in the whole acquired after the goods became accessions; or

(b) a creditor with a security interest in the whole perfected before the lease contract was made to the extent that the creditor makes subsequent advances without knowledge of the lease contract.

(5) When under subsections (2) or (3) and (4) a lessor or a lessee of accessions holds an interest that is superior to all interests in the whole, the lessor or the lessee may (a) on default, expiration, termination, or cancellation of the lease contract by the other party but subject to the provisions of the lease contract and this Article, or (b) if necessary to enforce his [or her] other rights and remedies under this Article, remove the goods from the whole, free and clear of all interests in the whole, but he

[or she] must reimburse any holder of an interest in the whole who is not the lessee and who has not otherwise agreed for the cost of repair of any physical injury but not for any diminution in value of the whole caused by the absence of the goods removed or by any necessity for replacing them. A person entitled to reimbursement may refuse permission to remove until the party seeking removal gives adequate security for the performance of this obligation.

Part 4—Performance of Lease Contract: Repudiated, Substituted and Excused

§ 2A–401. Insecurity: Adequate Assurance of Performance.

(1) A lease contract imposes an obligation on each party that the other's expectation of receiving due performance will not be impaired.

(2) If reasonable grounds for insecurity arise with respect to the performance of either party, the insecure party may demand in writing adequate asssurance of due performance. Until the insecure party receives that assurance, if commercially reasonable the insecure party may suspend any performance for which he [or she] has not already received the agreed return.

(3) A repudiation of the lease contract occurs if assurance of due performance adequate under the circumstances of the particular case is not provided to the insecure party within a reasonable time, not to exceed 30 days after receipt of a demand by the other party.

(4) Between merchants, the reasonableness of grounds for insecurity and the adequacy of any assurance offered must be determined according to commercial standards.

(5) Acceptance of any nonconforming delivery or payment does not prejudice the aggrieved party's right to demand adequate assurance of future performance.

§ 2A–402. Anticipatory Repudiation.

If either party repudiates a lease contract with respect to a performance not yet due under the lease contract, the loss of which performance will substantially impair the value of the lease contract to the other, the aggrieved party may:

(a) for a commercially reasonable time, await retraction of repudiation and performance by the repudiating party;

(b) make demand pursuant to Section 2A–401 and await assurance of future performance adequate under the circumstances of the particular case; or

(c) resort to any right or remedy upon default under the lease contract or this Article, even though the aggrieved party has notified the repudiating party that the aggrieved party would await the repudiating party's per-

formance and assurance and has urged retraction. In addition, whether or not the aggrieved party is pursuing one of the foregoing remedies, the aggrieved party may suspend performance or, if the aggrieved party is the lessor, proceed in accordance with the provisions of this Article on the lessor's right to identify goods to the lease contract notwithstanding default or to salvage unfinished goods (Section 2A–524).

§ 2A–403. Retraction of Anticipatory Repudiation.

(1) Until the repudiating party's next performance is due, the repudiating party can retract the repudiation unless, since the repudiation, the aggrieved party has cancelled the lease contract or materially changed the aggrieved party's position or otherwise indicated that the aggrieved party considers the repudiation final.

(2) Retraction may be by any method that clearly indicates to the aggrieved party that the repudiating party intends to perform under the lease contract and includes any assurance demanded under Section 2A–401.

(3) Retraction reinstates a repudiating party's rights under a lease contract with due excuse and allowance to the aggrieved party for any delay occasioned by the repudiation.

§ 2A–404. Substituted Performance.

(1) If without fault of the lessee, the lessor and the supplier, the agreed berthing, loading, or unloading facilities fail or the agreed type of carrier becomes unavailable or the agreed manner of delivery otherwise becomes commercially impracticable, but a commercially reasonable substitute is available, the substitute performance must be tendered and accepted.

(2) If the agreed means or manner of payment fails because of domestic or foreign governmental regulation:

(a) the lessor may withhold or stop delivery or cause the supplier to withhold or stop delivery unless the lessee provides a means or manner of payment that is commercially a substantial equivalent; and

(b) if delivery has already been taken, payment by the means or in the manner provided by the regulation discharges the lessee's obligation unless the regulation is discriminatory, oppressive, or predatory.

§ 2A–405. Excused Performance.

Subject to Section 2A–404 on substituted performance, the following rules apply:

(a) Delay in delivery or nondelivery in whole or in part by a lessor or a supplier who complies with paragraphs (b) and (c) is not a default under the lease contract if performance as agreed has been made impracticable by the occurrence of a contingency the nonoccurrence of which was a basic assumption on which the lease contract was made or by compliance in good faith with any applicable foreign or domestic governmental regulation or order, whether or not the regulation or order later proves to be invalid.

(b) If the causes mentioned in paragraph (a) affect only part of the lessor's or the supplier's capacity to perform, he [or she] shall allocate production and deliveries among his [or her] customers but at his [or her] option may include regular customers not then under contract for sale or lease as well as his [or her] own requirements for further manufacture. He [or she] may so allocate in any manner that is fair and reasonable.

(c) The lessor seasonably shall notify the lessee and in the case of a finance lease the supplier seasonably shall notify the lessor and the lessee, if known, that there will be delay or nondelivery and, if allocation is required under paragraph (b), of the estimated quota thus made available for the lessee.

§ 2A–406. Procedure on Excused Performance.

(1) If the lessee receives notification of a material or indefinite delay or an allocation justified under Section 2A–405, the lessee may by written notification to the lessor as to any goods involved, and with respect to all of the goods if under an installment lease contract the value of the whole lease contract is substantially impaired (Section 2A–510):

(a) terminate the lease contract (Section 2A–505(2)); or

(b) except in a finance lease that is not a consumer lease, modify the lease contract by accepting the available quota in substitution, with due allowance from the rent payable for the balance of the lease term for the deficiency but without further right against the lessor.

(2) If, after receipt of a notification from the lessor under Section 2A–405, the lessee fails so to modify the lease agreement within a reasonable time not exceeding 30 days, the lease contract lapses with respect to any deliveries affected.

§ 2A–407. Irrevocable Promises: Finance Leases.

(1) In the case of a finance lease that is not a consumer lease the lessee's promises under the lease contract become irrevocable and independent upon the lessee's acceptance of the goods.

(2) A promise that has become irrevocable and independent under subsection (1):

(a) is effective and enforceable between the parties, and by or against third parties including assignees of the parties, and

(b) is not subject to cancellation, termination, modification, repudiation, excuse, or substitution without the consent of the party to whom the promise runs.

Part 5—Default

A. In General

§ 2A–501. Default: Procedure.

(1) Whether the lessor or the lessee is in default under a lease contract is determined by the lease agreement and this Article.

(2) If the lessor or the lessee is in default under the lease contract, the party seeking enforcement has rights and remedies as provided in this Article and, except as limited by this Article, as provided in the lease agreement.

(3) If the lessor or the lessee is in default under the lease contract, the party seeking enforcement may reduce the party's claim to judgment, or otherwise enforce the lease contract by self-help or any available judicial procedure or nonjudicial procedure, including administrative proceeding, arbitration, or the like, in accordance with this Article.

(4) Except as otherwise provided in this Article or the lease agreement, the rights and remedies referred to in subsections (2) and (3) are cumulative.

(5) If the lease agreement covers both real property and goods, the party seeking enforcement may proceed under this Part as to the goods, or under other applicable law as to both the real property and the goods in accordance with his [or her] rights and remedies in respect of the real property, in which case this Part does not apply.

§ 2A–502. Notice After Default.

Except as otherwise provided in this Article or the lease agreement, the lessor or lessee in default under the lease contract is not entitled to notice of default or notice of enforcement from the other party to the lease agreement.

§ 2A–503. Modification or Impairment of Rights and Remedies.

(1) Except as otherwise provided in this Article, the lease agreement may include rights and remedies for default in addition to or in substitution for those provided in this Article and may limit or alter the measure of damages recoverable under this Article.

(2) Resort to a remedy provided under this Article or in the lease agreement is optional unless the remedy is expressly agreed to be exclusive. If circumstances cause an exclusive or limited remedy to fail of its essential purpose, or provision for an exclusive remedy is unconscionable, remedy may be had as provided in this Article.

(3) Consequential damages may be liquidated under Section 2A–504, or may otherwise be limited, altered, or excluded unless the limitation, alteration, or exclusion is unconscionable. Limitation of consequential damages for injury to the person in the case of consumer goods is prima facie unconscionable but limitation of damages where the loss is commercial is not.

(4) Rights and remedies on default by the lessor or the lessee with respect to any obligation or promise collateral or ancillary to the lease contract are not impaired by this Article.

§ 2A–504. Liquidation of Damages.

(1) Damages payable by either party for default, or any other act or omission, including indemnity for loss or diminution of anticipated tax benefits or loss or damage to lessor's residual interest, may be liquidated in the lease agreement but only at an amount or by a formula that is reasonable in light of the then anticipated harm caused by the default or other act or omission.

(2) If the lease agreement provides for liquidation of damages, and such provision does not comply with subsection (1), or such provision is an exclusive or limited remedy that circumstances cause to fail of its essential purpose, remedy may be had as provided in this Article.

(3) If the lessor justifiably withholds or stops delivery of goods because of the lessee's default or insolvency (Section 2A–525 or 2A–526), the lessee is entitled to restitution of any amount by which the sum of his [or her] payments exceeds:

(a) the amount to which the lessor is entitled by virtue of terms liquidating the lessor's damages in accordance with subsection (1); or

(b) in the absence of those terms, 20 percent of the then present value of the total rent the lessee was obligated to pay for the balance of the lease term, or, in the case of a consumer lease, the lesser of such amount or $500.

(4) A lessee's right to restitution under subsection (3) is subject to offset to the extent the lessor establishes:

(a) a right to recover damages under the provisions of this Article other than subsection (1); and

(b) the amount or value of any benefits received by the lessee directly or indirectly by reason of the lease contract.

§ 2A–505. Cancellation and Termination and Effect of Cancellation, Termination, Rescission, or Fraud on Rights and Remedies.

(1) On cancellation of the lease contract, all obligations that are still executory on both sides are discharged, but any right based on prior default or performance survives, and the cancelling party also retains any remedy for default of the whole lease contract or any unperformed balance.

(2) On termination of the lease contract, all obligations that are still executory on both sides are discharged but any right based on prior default or performance survives.

(3) Unless the contrary intention clearly appears, expressions of "cancellation," "rescission," or the like of the lease contract may not be construed as a renunciation or discharge of any claim in damages for an antecedent default.

(4) Rights and remedies for material misrepresentation or fraud include all rights and remedies available under this Article for default.

(5) Neither rescission nor a claim for rescission of the lease contract nor rejection or return of the goods may bar or be deemed inconsistent with a claim for damages or other right or remedy.

§ 2A–506. Statute of Limitations.

(1) An action for default under a lease contract, including breach of warranty or indemnity, must be commenced within 4 years after the cause of action accrued. By the original lease contract the parties may reduce the period of limitation to not less than one year.

(2) A cause of action for default accrues when the act or omission on which the default or breach of warranty is based is or should have been discovered by the aggrieved party, or when the default occurs, whichever is later. A cause of action for indemnity accrues when the act or omission on which the claim for indemnity is based is or should have been discovered by the indemnified party, whichever is later.

(3) If an action commenced within the time limited by subsection (1) is so terminated as to leave available a remedy by another action for the same default or breach of warranty or indemnity, the other action may be commenced after the expiration of the time limited and within 6 months after the termination of the first action unless the termination resulted from voluntary discontinuance or from dismissal for failure or neglect to prosecute.

(4) This section does not alter the law on tolling of the statute of limitations nor does it apply to causes of action that have accrued before this Article becomes effective.

§ 2A–507. Proof of Market Rent: Time and Place.

(1) Damages based on market rent (Section 2A–519 or 2A–528) are determined according to the rent for the use of the goods concerned for a lease term identical to the remaining lease term of the original lease agreement and prevailing at the time of the default.

(2) If evidence of rent for the use of the goods concerned for a lease term identical to the remaining lease term of the original lease agreement and prevailing at the times or places described in this Article is not readily available, the rent prevailing within any reasonable time before or after the time described or at any other place or for a different lease term which in commercial judgment or under usage of trade would serve as a reasonable substitute for the one described may be used, making any proper allowance for the difference, including the cost of transporting the goods to or from the other place.

(3) Evidence of a relevant rent prevailing at a time or place or for a lease term other than the one described in

this Article offered by one party is not admissible unless and until he [or she] has given the other party notice the court finds sufficient to prevent unfair surprise.

(4) If the prevailing rent or value of any goods regularly leased in any established market is in issue, reports in official publications or trade journals or in newspapers or periodicals of general circulation published as the reports of that market are admissible in evidence. The circumstances of the preparation of the report may be shown to affect its weight but not its admissibility.

B. Default by Lessor

§ 2A–508. Lessee's Remedies.

(1) If a lessor fails to deliver the goods in conformity to the lease contract (Section 2A–509) or repudiates the lease contract (Section 2A–402), or a lessee rightfully rejects the goods (Section 2A–509) or justifiably revokes acceptance of the goods (Section 2A–517), then with respect to any goods involved, and with respect to all of the goods if under an installment lease contract the value of the whole lease contract is substantially impaired (Section 2A–510), the lessor is in default under the lease contract and the lessee may:

(a) cancel the lease contract (Section 2A–505(1));

(b) recover so much of the rent and security as has been paid, but in the case of an installment lease contract the recovery is that which is just under the circumstances;

(c) cover and recover damages as to all goods affected whether or not they have been identified to the lease contract (Sections 2A–518 and 2A–520), or recover damages for nondelivery (Section 2A–519 and 2A–520).

(2) If a lessor fails to deliver the goods in conformity to the lease contract or repudiates the lease contract, the lessee may also:

(a) if the goods have been identified, recover them (Section 2A–522); or

(b) in a proper case, obtain specific performance or replevy the goods (Section 2A–521).

(3) If a lessor is otherwise in default under a lease contract, the lessee may exercise the rights and remedies provided in the lease contract and this Article.

(4) If a lessor has breached a warranty, whether express or implied, the lessee may recover damages (Section 2A–519(4)).

(5) On rightful rejection or justifiable revocation of acceptance, a lessee has a security interest in goods in the lessee's possession or control for any rent and security that has been paid and any expenses reasonably incurred in their inspection, receipt, transportation, and care and custody and may hold those goods and dispose of them in good faith and in a commercially reasonable manner, subject to the provisions of Section 2A–527(5).

(6) Subject to the provisions of Section 2A–407, a lessee, on notifying the lessor of the lessee's intention to do so, may deduct all or any part of the damages resulting from any default under the lease contract from any part of the rent still due under the same lease contract.

§ 2A–509. Lessee's Rights on Improper Delivery; Rightful Rejection.

(1) Subject to the provisions of Section 2A–510 on default in installment lease contracts, if the goods or the tender or delivery fail in any respect to conform to the lease contract, the lessee may reject or accept the goods or accept any commercial unit or units and reject the rest of the goods.

(2) Rejection of goods is ineffective unless it is within a reasonable time after tender or delivery of the goods and the lessee seasonably notifies the lessor.

§ 2A–510. Installment Lease Contracts: Rejection and Default.

(1) Under an installment lease contract a lessee may reject any delivery that is nonconforming if the nonconformity substantially impairs the value of that delivery and cannot be cured or the nonconformity is a defect in the required documents; but if the nonconformity does not fall within subsection (2) and the lessor or the supplier gives adequate assurance of its cure, the lessee must accept that delivery.

(2) Whenever nonconformity or default with respect to one or more deliveries substantially impairs the value of the installment lease contract as a whole there is a default with respect to the whole. But, the aggrieved party reinstates the installment lease contract as a whole if the aggrieved party accepts a nonconforming delivery without seasonably notifying of cancellation or brings an action with respect only to past deliveries or demands performance as to future deliveries.

§ 2A–511. Merchant Lessee's Duties as to Rightfully Rejected Goods.

(1) Subject to any security interest of a lessee (Section 2A–508(5)), if a lessor or a supplier has no agent or place of business at the market of rejection, a merchant lessee, after rejection of goods in his [or her] possession or control, shall follow any reasonable instructions received from the lessor or the supplier with respect to the goods. In the absence of those instructions, a merchant lessee shall make reasonable efforts to sell, lease, or otherwise dispose of the goods for the lessor's account if they threaten to decline in value speedily. Instructions are not reasonable if on demand indemnity for expenses is not forthcoming.

(2) If a merchant lessee (subsection (1)) or any other lessee (Section 2A–512) disposes of goods, he [or she] is entitled to reimbursement either from the lessor or the supplier or out of the proceeds for reasonable expenses of

caring for and disposing of the goods and, if the expenses include no disposition commission, to such commission as is usual in the trade, or if there is none, to a reasonable sum not exceeding 10 percent of the gross proceeds.

(3) In complying with this section or Section 2A–512, the lessee is held only to good faith. Good faith conduct hereunder is neither acceptance or conversion nor the basis of an action for damages.

(4) A purchaser who purchases in good faith from a lessee pursuant to this section or Section 2A–512 takes the goods free of any rights of the lessor and the supplier even though the lessee fails to comply with one or more of the requirements of this Article.

§ 2A–512. Lessee's Duties as to Rightfully Rejected Goods.

(1) Except as otherwise provided with respect to goods that threaten to decline in value speedily (Section 2A–511) and subject to any security interest of a lessee (Section 2A–508(5));

   (a) the lessee, after rejection of goods in the lessee's possession, shall hold them with reasonable care at the lessor's or the supplier's disposition for a reasonable time after the lessee's seasonable notification of rejection;

   (b) if the lessor or the supplier gives no instructions within a reasonable time after notification of rejection, the lessee may store the rejected goods for the lessor's or the supplier's account or ship them to the lessor or the supplier or dispose of them for the lessor's or the supplier's account with reimbursement in the manner provided in Section 2A–511; but

   (c) the lessee has no further obligations with regard to goods rightfully rejected.

(2) Action by the lessee pursuant to subsection (1) is not acceptance or conversion.

§ 2A–513. Cure by Lessor of Improper Tender or Delivery; Replacement.

(1) If any tender or delivery by the lessor or the supplier is rejected because nonconforming and the time for performance has not yet expired, the lessor or the supplier may seasonably notify the lessee of the lessor's or the supplier's intention to cure and may then make a conforming delivery within the time provided in the lease contract.

(2) If the lessee rejects a nonconforming tender that the lessor or the supplier had reasonable grounds to believe would be acceptable with or without money allowance, the lessor or the supplier may have a further reasonable time to substitute a conforming tender if he [or she] seasonably notifies the lessee.

§ 2A–514. Waiver of Lessee's Objections.

(1) In rejecting goods, a lessee's failure to state a particular defect that is ascertainable by reasonable inspection precludes the lessee from relying on the defect to justify rejection or to establish default:

   (a) if, stated seasonably, the lessor or the supplier could have cured it (Section 2A–513); or

   (b) between merchants if the lessor or the supplier after rejection has made a request in writing for a full and final written statement of all defects on which the lessee proposes to rely.

(2) A lessee's failure to reserve rights when paying rent or other consideration against documents precludes recovery of the payment for defects apparent on the face of the documents.

§ 2A–515. Acceptance of Goods.

(1) Acceptance of goods occurs after the lessee has had a reasonable opportunity to inspect the goods and

   (a) the lessee signifies or acts with respect to the goods in a manner that signifies to the lessor or the supplier that the goods are conforming or that the lessee will take or retain them in spite of their nonconformity; or

   (b) the lessee fails to make an effective rejection of the goods (Section 2A–509(2)).

(2) Acceptance of a part of any commercial unit is acceptance of that entire unit.

§ 2A–516. Effect of Acceptance of Goods; Notice of Default; Burden of Establishing Default After Acceptance; Notice of Claim or Litigation to Person Answerable Over.

(1) A lessee must pay rent for any goods accepted in accordance with the lease contract, with due allowance for goods rightfully rejected or not delivered.

(2) A lessee's acceptance of goods precludes rejection of the goods accepted. In the case of a finance lease, if made with knowledge of a nonconformity, acceptance cannot be revoked because of it. In any other case, if made with knowledge of a nonconformity, acceptance cannot be revoked because of it unless the acceptance was on the reasonable assumption that the nonconformity would be seasonably cured. Acceptance does not of itself impair any other remedy provided by this Article or the lease agreement for nonconformity.

(3) If a tender has been accepted:

   (a) within a reasonable time after the lessee discovers or should have discovered any default, the lessee shall notify the lessor and the supplier, or be barred from any remedy;

(b) except in the case of a consumer lease, within a reasonable time after the lessee receives notice of litigation for infringement or the like (Section 2A–211) the lessee shall notify the lessor or be barred from any remedy over for liability established by the litigation; and

(c) the burden is on the lessee to establish any default.

(4) If a lessee is sued for breach of a warranty or other obligation for which a lessor or a supplier is answerable over:

(a) The lessee may give the lessor or the supplier written notice of the litigation. If the notice states that the lessor or the supplier may come in and defend and that if the lessor or the supplier does not do so he [or she] will be bound in any action against him [or her] by the lessee by any determination of fact common to the two litigations, then unless the lessor or the supplier after seasonable receipt of the notice does come in and defend he [or she] is so bound.

(b) The lessor or the supplier may demand in writing that the lessee turn over control of the litigation including settlement if the claim is one for infringement or the like (Section 2A–211) or else be barred from any remedy over. If the demand states that the lessor or the supplier agrees to bear all expense and to satisfy any adverse judgment, then unless the lessee after seasonable receipt of the demand does turn over control the lessee is so barred.

(5) The provisions of subsections (3) and (4) apply to any obligation of a lessee to hold the lessor or the supplier harmless against infringement or the like (Section 2A–211).

§ 2A–517. Revocation of Acceptance of Goods.

(1) A lessee may revoke acceptance of a lot or commercial unit whose nonconformity substantially impairs its value to the lessee if he [or she] has accepted it:

(a) except in the case of a finance lease, on the reasonable assumption that its nonconformity would be cured and it has not been seasonably cured; or

(b) without discovery of the nonconformity if the lessee's acceptance was reasonably induced either by the lessor's assurances or, except in the case of a finance lease, by the difficulty of discovery before acceptance.

(2) Revocation of acceptance must occur within a reasonable time after the lessee discovers or should have discovered the ground for it and before any substantial change in condition of the goods which is not caused by the nonconformity. Revocation is not effective until the lessee notifies the lessor.

(3) A lessee who so revokes has the same rights and duties with regard to the goods involved as if the lessee had rejected them.

§ 2A–518. Cover; Substitute Goods.

(1) After default by a lessor under the lease contract (Section 2A–508(1)), the lessee may cover by making any purchase or lease of or contract to purchase or lease goods in substitution for those due from the lessor.

(2) Except as otherwise provided with respect to damages liquidated in the lease agreement (Section 2A–504) or determined by agreement of the parties (Section 1–102(3)), if a lessee's cover is by lease agreement substantially similar to the original lease agreement and the lease agreement is made in good faith and in a commercially reasonable manner, the lessee may recover from the lessor as damages (a) the present value, as of the date of default, of the difference between the total rent for the lease term of the new lease agreement and the total rent for the remaining lease term of the original lease agreement and (b) any incidental or consequential damages less expenses saved in consequence of the lessor's default.

(3) If a lessee's cover is by lease agreement that for any reason does not qualify for treatment under subsection (2), or is by purchase or otherwise, the lessee may recover from the lessor as if the lessee had elected not to cover and Section 2A–519 governs.

§ 2A–519. Lessee's Damages for Non-delivery, Repudiation, Default and Breach of Warranty in Regard to Accepted Goods.

(1) Except as otherwise provided with respect to damages liquidated in the lease agreement (Section 2A–504) or determined by agreement of the parties (Section 1–102(3)), if a lessee elects not to cover or a lessee elects to cover and the cover is by lease agreement that for any reason does not qualify for treatment under Section 2A–518(2), or is by purchase or otherwise, the measure of damages for non-delivery or repudiation by the lessor or for rejection or revocation of acceptance by the lessee is the present value as of the date of the default of the difference between the then market rent and the original rent, computed for the remaining lease term of the original lease agreement together with incidental and consequential damages, less expenses saved in consequence of the lessor's default.

(2) Market rent is to be determined as of the place for tender or, in cases of rejection after arrival or revocation of acceptance, as of the place of arrival.

(3) If the lessee has accepted goods and given notification (Section 2A–516(3)), the measure of damages for non-conforming tender or delivery by a lessor is the loss resulting in the ordinary course of events from the lessor's default as determined in any manner that is rea-

sonable together with incidental and consequential damages, less expenses saved in consequence of the lessor's default.

(4) The measure of damages for breach of warranty is the present value at the time and place of acceptance of the difference between the value of the use of the goods accepted and the value if they had been as warranted for the lease term, unless special circumstances show proximate damages of a different amount, together with incidental and consequential damages, less expenses saved in consequence of the lessor's default or breach of warranty.

§ 2A–520. Lessee's Incidental and Consequential Damages.

(1) Incidental damages resulting from a lessor's default include expenses reasonably incurred in inspection, receipt, transportation, and care and custody of goods rightfully rejected or goods the acceptance of which is justifiably revoked, any commercially reasonable charges, expenses or commissions in connection with effecting cover, and any other reasonable expense incident to the default.

(2) Consequential damages resulting from a lessor's default include:

(a) any loss resulting from general or particular requirements and needs of which the lessor at the time of contracting had reason to know and which could not reasonably be prevented by cover or otherwise; and

(b) injury to person or property proximately resulting from any breach of warranty.

§ 2A–521. Lessee's Right to Specific Performance or Replevin.

(1) Specific performance may be decreed if the goods are unique or in other proper circumstances.

(2) A decree for specific performance may include any terms and conditions as to payment of the rent, damages, or other relief that the court deems just.

(3) A lessee has a right of replevin, detinue, sequestration, claim and delivery, or the like for goods identified to the lease contract if after reasonable effort the lessee is unable to effect cover for those goods or the circumstances reasonably indicate that the effort will be unavailing.

§ 2A–522. Lessee's Right to Goods on Lessor's Insolvency.

(1) Subject to subsection (2) and even though the goods have not been shipped, a lessee who has paid a part or all of the rent and security for goods identified to a lease contract (Section 2A–217) on making and keeping good a tender of any unpaid portion of the rent and security due under the lease contract may recover the goods identified from the lessor if the lessor becomes insolvent within 10 days after receipt of the first installment of rent and security.

(2) A lessee acquires the right to recover goods identified to a lease contract only if they conform to the lease contract.

C. Default by Lessee

§ 2A–523. Lessee's Remedies.

(1) If a lessee wrongfully rejects or revokes acceptance of goods or fails to make a payment when due or repudiates with respect to a part or the whole, then, with respect to any goods involved, and with respect to all of the goods if under an installment lease contract the value of the whole lease contract is substantially impaired (Section 2A–510), the lessee is in default under the lease contract and the lessor may:

(a) cancel the lease contract (Section 2A–505(1));

(b) proceed respecting goods not identified to the lease contract (Section 2A–524);

(c) withhold delivery of the goods and take possession of goods previously delivered (Section 2A–525);

(d) stop delivery of the goods by any bailee (Section 2A–526);

(e) dispose of the goods and recover damages (Section 2A–527), or retain the goods and recover damages (Section 2A–528), or in a proper case recover rent (Section 2A–529).

(2) If a lessee is otherwise in default under a lease contract, the lessor may exercise the rights and remedies provided in the lease contract and this Article.

§ 2A–524. Lessor's Right to Identify Goods to Lease Contract.

(1) A lessor aggrieved under Section 2A–523(1) may:

(a) identify to the lease contract conforming goods not already identified if at the time the lessor learned of the default they were in the lessor's or the supplier's possession or control; and

(b) dispose of goods (Section 2A–527(1)) that demonstrably have been intended for the particular lease contract even though those goods are unfinished.

(2) If the goods are unfinished, in the exercise of reasonable commercial judgment for the purposes of avoiding loss and of effective realization, an aggrieved lessor or the supplier may either complete manufacture and wholly identify the goods to the lease contract or cease manufacture and lease, sell, or otherwise dispose of the goods for scrap or salvage value or proceed in any other reasonable manner.

§ 2A–525. Lessor's Right to Possession of Goods.

(1) If a lessor discovers the lessee to be insolvent, the lessor may refuse to deliver the goods.

(2) The lessor has on default by the lessee under the lease contract the right to take possession of the goods. If the lease contract so provides, the lessor may require the lessee to assemble the goods and make them available to the lessor at a place to be designated by the lessor which is reasonably convenient to both parties. Without removal, the lessor may render unusable any goods employed in trade or business, and may dispose of goods on the lessee's premises (Section 2A–527).

(3) The lessor may proceed under subsection (2) without judicial process if that can be done without breach of the peace or the lessor may proceed by action.

§ 2A–526. Lessor's Stoppage of Delivery in Transit or Otherwise.

(1) A lessor may stop delivery of goods in the possession of a carrier or other bailee if the lessor discovers the lessee to be insolvent and may stop delivery of carload, truckload, planeload, or larger shipments of express or freight if the lessee repudiates or fails to make a payment due before delivery, whether for rent, security or otherwise under the lease contract, or for any other reason the lessor has a right to withhold or take possession of the goods.

(2) In pursuing its remedies under subsection (1), the lessor may stop delivery until

(a) receipt of the goods by the lessee;

(b) acknowledgment to the lessee by any bailee of the goods, except a carrier, that the bailee holds the goods for the lessee; or

(c) such an acknowledgment to the lessee by a carrier via reshipment or as warehouseman.

(3) (a) To stop delivery, a lessor shall so notify as to enable the bailee by reasonable diligence to prevent delivery of the goods.

(b) After notification, the bailee shall hold and deliver the goods according to the directions of the lessor, but the lessor is liable to the bailee for any ensuing charges or damages.

(c) A carrier who has issued a nonnegotiable bill of lading is not obliged to obey a notification to stop received from a person other than the consignor.

§ 2A–527. Lessor's Rights to Dispose of Goods.

(1) After a default by a lessee under the lease contract (Section 2A–523(1)) or after the lessor refuses to deliver or takes possession of goods (Section 2A–525 or 2A–526), the lessor may dispose of the goods concerned or the undelivered balance thereof by lease, sale or otherwise.

(2) Except as otherwise provided with respect to damages liquidated in the lease agreement (Section 2A–504) or determined by agreement of the parties (Section 1–102(3)), if the disposition is by lease agreement substantially similar to the original lease agreement and the lease agreement is made in good faith and in a commercially reasonable manner, the lessor may recover from the lessee as damages (a) accrued and unpaid rent as of the date of default, (b) the present value as of the date of default of the difference between the total rent for the remaining lease term of the original lease agreement and the total rent for the lease term of the new lease agreement, and (c) any incidental damages allowed under Section 2A–530, less expenses saved in consequence of the lessee's default.

(3) If the lessor's disposition is by lease agreement that for any reason does not qualify for treatment under subsection (2), or is by sale or otherwise, the lessor may recover from the lessee as if the lessor had elected not to dispose of the goods and Section 2A–528 governs.

(4) A subsequent buyer or lessee who buys or leases from the lessor in good faith for value as a result of a disposition under this section takes the goods free of the original lease contract and any rights of the original lessee even though the lessor fails to comply with one or more of the requirements of this Article.

(5) The lessor is not accountable to the lessee for any profit made on any disposition. A lessee who has rightfully rejected or justifiably revoked acceptance shall account to the lessor for any excess over the amount of the lessee's security interest (Section 2A–508(5)).

§ 2A–528. Lessor's Damages for Non-acceptance or Repudiation.

(1) Except as otherwise provided with respect to damages liquidated in the lease agreement (Section 2A–504) or determined by agreement of the parties (Section 1–102(3)), if a lessor elects to retain the goods or a lessor elects to dispose of the goods and disposition is by lease agreement that for any reason does not qualify for treatment under Section 2A–527(2), or is by sale or otherwise, the lessor may recover from the lessee as damages for non-acceptance or repudiation by the lessee (a) accrued and unpaid rent as of the date of default, (b) the present value as of the date of default of the difference between the total rent for the remaining lease term of the original lease agreement and the market rent at the time and place for tender computed for the same lease term, and (c) any incidental damages allowed under Section 2A–530, less expenses saved in consequence of the lessee's default.

(2) If the measure of damages provided in subsection (1) is inadequate to put a lessor in as good a position as performance would have, the measure of damages is the profit, including reasonable overhead, the lessor would have made from full performance by the lessee, together with any incidental damages allowed under Section 2A–530, due allowance for costs reasonably incurred and due credit for payments or proceeds of disposition.

§ 2A–529. Lessor's Action for the Rent.

(1) After default by the lessee under the lease contract (Section 2A–523(1)), if the lessor complies with subsection (2), the lessor may recover from the lessee as damages:

(a) for goods accepted by the lessee and for conforming goods lost or damaged within a commercially reasonable time after risk of loss passes to the lessee (Section 2A–219), (i) accrued and unpaid rent as of the date of default, (ii) the present value as of the date of default of the rent for the remaining lease term of the lease agreement, and (iii) any incidental damages allowed under Section 2A–530, less expenses saved in consequence of the lessee's default; and

(b) for goods identified to the lease contract if the lessor is unable after reasonable effort to dispose of them at a reasonable price or the circumstances reasonably indicate that effort will be unavailing, (i) accrued and unpaid rent as of the date of default, (ii) the present value as of the date of default of the rent for the remaining lease term of the lease agreement, and (iii) any incidental damages allowed under Section 2A–530, less expenses saved in consequence of the lessee's default.

(2) Except as provided in subsection (3), the lessor shall hold for the lessee for the remaining lease term of the lease agreement any goods that have been identified to the lease contract and are in the lessor's control.

(3) The lessor may dispose of the goods at any time before collection of the judgment for damages obtained pursuant to subsection (1). If the disposition is before the end of the remaining lease term of the lease agreement, the lessor's recovery against the lessee for damages will be governed by Section 2A–527 or Section 2A–528.

(4) Payment of the judgment for damages obtained pursuant to subsection (1) entitles the lessee to use and possession of the goods not then disposed of for the remaining lease term of the lease agreement.

(5) After a lessee has wrongfully rejected or revoked acceptance of goods, has failed to pay rent then due, or has repudiated (Section 2A–402), a lessor who is held not entitled to rent under this section must nevertheless be awarded damages for non-acceptance under Sections 2A–527 and 2A–528.

ARTICLE 3: COMMERCIAL PAPER

[The 1990 Revised Article 3 appears at the end of Appendix C.]

Part 1—Short Title, Form and Interpretation

§ 3–101. Short Title.

This Article shall be known and may be cited as Uniform Commercial Code—Commercial Paper.

§ 3–102. Definitions and Index of Definitions.

(1) In this Article unless the context otherwise requires

(a) "Issue" means the first delivery of an instrument to a holder or a remitter.

(b) An "order" is a direction to pay and must be more than an authorization or request. It must identify the person to pay with reasonable certainty. It may be addressed to one or more such persons jointly or in the alternative but not in succession.

(c) A "promise" is an undertaking to pay and must be more than an acknowledgment of an obligation.

(d) "Secondary party" means a drawer or endorser.

(e) "Instrument" means a negotiable instrument.

(2) Other definitions applying to this Article and the sections in which they appear are:

"Acceptance". Section 3–410.
"Accommodation party". Section 3–415.
"Alteration". Section 3–407.
"Certificate of deposit". Section 3–104.
"Certification". Section 3–411.
"Check". Section 3–104.
"Definite time". Section 3–109.
"Dishonor". Section 3–507.
"Draft". Section 3–104.
"Holder in due course". Section 3–302.
"Negotiation". Section 3–202.
"Note". Section 3–104.
"Notice of dishonor". Section 3–508.
"On demand". Section 3–108.
"Presentment". Section 3–504.
"Protest". Section 3–509.
"Restrictive Indorsement". Section 3–205.
"Signature". Section 3–401.

(3) The following definitions in other Articles apply to this Article:

"Account". Section 4–104.
"Banking Day". Section 4–104.
"Clearing House". Section 4–104.
"Collecting Bank". Section 4–105.
"Customer". Section 4–104.
"Depositary Bank". Section 4–105.
"Documentary Draft". Section 4–104.
"Intermediary Bank". Section 4–105.
"Item". Section 4–104.
"Midnight deadline". Section 4–104.
"Payor Bank". Section 4–105.

(4) In addition Article 1 contains general definitions and principles of construction and interpretation applicable throughout this Article.

§ 3–103. Limitations on Scope of Article.

(1) This Article does not apply to money, documents of title or investment securities.

(2) The provisions of this Article are subject to the provisions of the Article on Bank Deposits and Collections (Article 4) and Secured Transactions (Article 9).

§ 3–104. Form of Negotiable Instruments; "Draft"; "Check"; "Certificate of Deposit"; "Note".

(1) Any writing to be a negotiable instrument within this Article must

(a) be signed by the maker or drawer; and

(b) contain an unconditional promise or order to pay a sum certain in money and no other promise, order, obligation or power given by the maker or drawer except as authorized by this Article; and

(c) be payable on demand or at a definite time; and

(d) be payable to order or to bearer.

(2) A writing which complies with the requirements of this section is

(a) a "draft" ("bill of exchange") if it is an order;

(b) a "check" if it is a draft drawn on a bank and payable on demand;

(c) a "certificate of deposit" if it is an acknowledgment by a bank of receipt of money with an engagement to repay it;

(d) a "note" if it is a promise other than a certificate of deposit.

(3) As used in other Articles of this Act, and as the context may require, the terms "draft", "check", "certificate of deposit" and "note" may refer to instruments which are not negotiable within this Article as well as to instruments which are so negotiable.

§ 3–105. When Promise or Order Unconditional.

(1) A promise or order otherwise unconditional is not made conditional by the fact that the instrument

(a) is subject to implied or constructive conditions; or

(b) states its consideration, whether performed or promised, or the transaction which gave rise to the instrument, or that the promise or order is made or the instrument matures in accordance with or "as per" such transaction; or

(c) refers to or states that it arises out of a separate agreement or refers to a separate agreement for rights as to prepayment or acceleration; or

(d) states that it is drawn under a letter of credit; or

(e) states that it is secured, whether by mortgage, reservation of title or otherwise; or

(f) indicates a particular account to be debited or any other fund or source from which reimbursement is expected; or

(g) is limited to payment out of a particular fund or the proceeds of a particular source, if the instrument is issued by a government or governmental agency or unit; or

(h) is limited to payment out of the entire assets of a partnership, unincorporated association, trust or estate by or on behalf of which the instrument is issued.

(2) A promise or order is not unconditional if the instrument

(a) states that it is subject to or governed by any other agreement; or

(b) states that it is to be paid only out of a particular fund or source except as provided in this section.

§ 3–106. Sum Certain.

(1) The sum payable is a sum certain even though it is to be paid

(a) with stated interest or by stated installments; or

(b) with stated different rates of interest before and after default or a specified date; or

(c) with a stated discount or addition if paid before or after the date fixed for payment, or

(d) with exchange or less exchange, whether at a fixed rate or at the current rate; or

(e) with costs of collection or an attorney's fee or both upon default.

(2) Nothing in this section shall validate any term which is otherwise illegal.

§ 3–107. Money.

(1) An instrument is payable in money if the medium of exchange in which it is payable is money at the time the instrument is made. An instrument payable in "currency" or "current funds" is payable in money.

(2) A promise or order to pay a sum stated in a foreign currency is for a sum certain in money and, unless a different medium of payment is specified in the instrument, may be satisfied by payment of that number of dollars which the stated foreign currency will purchase at the buying sight rate for that currency on the day on which the instrument is payable or, if payable on demand, on the day of demand. If such an instrument specifies a foreign currency as the medium of payment the instrument is payable in that currency.

§ 3–108. Payable on Demand.

Instruments payable on demand include those payable at sight or on presentation and those in which no time for payment is stated.

§ 3–109. Definite Time.

(1) An instrument is payable at a definite time if by its terms it is payable

   (a) on or before a stated date or at a fixed period after a stated date; or

   (b) at a fixed period after sight; or

   (c) at a definite time subject to any acceleration; or

   (d) at a definite time subject to extension at the option of the holder, or to extension to a further definite time at the option of the maker or acceptor or automatically upon or after a specified act or event.

(2) An instrument which by its terms is otherwise payable only upon an act or event uncertain as to time of occurrence is not payable at a definite time even though the act or event has occurred.

§ 3–110. Payable to Order.

(1) An instrument is payable to order when by its terms it is payable to the order or assigns of any person therein specified with reasonable certainty, or to him or his order, or when it is conspicuously designated on its face as "exchange" or the like and names a payee. It may be payable to the order of

   (a) the maker or drawer; or

   (b) the drawee; or

   (c) a payee who is not maker, drawer or drawee; or

   (d) two or more payees together or in the alternative; or

   (e) an estate, trust or fund, in which case it is payable to the order of the representative of such estate, trust or fund or his successors; or

   (f) an office, or an officer by his title as such in which case it is payable to the principal but the incumbent of the office or his successors may act as if he or they were the holder; or

   (g) a partnership or unincorporated association, in which case it is payable to the partnership or association and may be indorsed or transferred by any person thereto authorized.

(2) An instrument not payable to order is not made so payable by such words as "payable upon return of this instrument properly indorsed."

(3) An instrument made payable both to order and to bearer is payable to order unless the bearer words are handwritten or typewritten.

§ 3–111. Payable to Bearer.

An instrument is payable to bearer when by its terms it is payable to

   (a) bearer or the order of bearer; or

   (b) a specified person or bearer; or

   (c) "cash" or the order of "cash", or any other indication which does not purport to designate a specific payee.

§ 3–112. Terms and Omissions Not Affecting Negotiability.

(1) The negotiability of an instrument is not affected by

   (a) the omission of a statement of any consideration or of the place where the instrument is drawn or payable; or

   (b) a statement that collateral has been given to secure obligations either on the instrument or otherwise of an obligor on the instrument or that in case of default on those obligations the holder may realize on or dispose of the collateral; or

   (c) a promise or power to maintain or protect collateral or to give additional collateral; or

   (d) a term authorizing a confession of judgment on the instrument if it is not paid when due; or

   (e) a term purporting to waive the benefit of any law intended for the advantage or protection of any obligor; or

   (f) a term in a draft providing that the payee by indorsing or cashing it acknowledges full satisfaction of an obligation of the drawer; or

   (g) a statement in a draft drawn in a set of parts (Section 3–801) to the effect that the order is effective only if no other part has been honored.

(2) Nothing in this section shall validate any term which is otherwise illegal.

§ 3–113. Seal.

An instrument otherwise negotiable is within this Article even though it is under a seal.

§ 3–114. Date, Antedating, Postdating.

(1) The negotiability of an instrument is not affected by the fact that it is undated, antedated or postdated.

(2) Where an instrument is antedated or postdated the time when it is payable is determined by the stated date if the instrument is payable on demand or at a fixed period after date.

(3) Where the instrument or any signature thereon is dated, the date is presumed to be correct.

§ 3–115. Incomplete Instruments.

(1) When a paper whose contents at the time of signing show that it is intended to become an instrument is signed while still incomplete in any necessary respect it cannot be enforced until completed, but when it is completed in accordance with authority given it is effective as completed.

(2) If the completion is unauthorized the rules as to material alteration apply (Section 3–407), even though the paper was not delivered by the maker or drawer; but the burden of establishing that any completion is unauthorized is on the party so asserting.

§ 3–116. Instruments Payable to Two or More Persons.

An instrument payable to the order of two or more persons

(a) if in the alternative is payable to any one of them and may be negotiated, discharged or enforced by any of them who has possession of it;

(b) if not in the alternative is payable to all of them and may be negotiated, discharged or enforced only by all of them.

§ 3–117. Instruments Payable With Words of Description.

An instrument made payable to a named person with the addition of words describing him

(a) as agent or officer of a specified person is payable to his principal but the agent or officer may act as if he were the holder;

(b) as any other fiduciary for a specified person or purpose is payable to the payee and may be negotiated, discharged or enforced by him;

(c) in any other manner is payable to the payee unconditionally and the additional words are without effect on subsequent parties.

§ 3–118. Ambiguous Terms and Rules of Construction.

The following rules apply to every instrument:

(a) Where there is doubt whether the instrument is a draft or a note the holder may treat it as either. A draft drawn on the drawer is effective as a note.

(b) Handwritten terms control typewritten and printed terms, and typewritten control printed.

(c) Words control figures except that if the words are ambiguous figures control.

(d) Unless otherwise specified a provision for interest means interest at the judgment rate at the place of payment from the date of the instrument, or if it is undated from the date of issue.

(e) Unless the instrument otherwise specifies two or more persons who sign as maker, acceptor or drawer or

indorser and as a part of the same transaction are jointly and severally liable even though the instrument contains such words as "I promise to pay."

(f) Unless otherwise specified consent to extension authorizes a single extension for not longer than the original period. A consent to extension, expressed in the instrument, is binding on secondary parties and accommodation makers. A holder may not exercise his option to extend an instrument over the objection of a maker or acceptor or other party who in accordance with Section 3–604 tenders full payment when the instrument is due.

§ 3–119. Other Writings Affecting Instrument.

(1) As between the obligor and his immediate obligee or any transferee the terms of an instrument may be modified or affected by any other written agreement executed as a part of the same transaction, except that a holder in due course is not affected by any limitation of his rights arising out of the separate written agreement if he had no notice of the limitation when he took the instrument.

(2) A separate agreement does not affect the negotiability of an instrument.

§ 3–120. Instruments "Payable Through" Bank.

An instrument which states that it is "payable through" a bank or the like designates that bank as a collecting bank to make presentment but does not of itself authorize the bank to pay the instrument.

§ 3–121. Instruments Payable at Bank.

Note: If this Act is introduced in the Congress of the United States this section should be omitted. (States to select either alternative)

Alternative A—A note or acceptance which states that it is payable at a bank is the equivalent of a draft drawn on the bank payable when it falls due out of any funds of the maker or acceptor in current account or otherwise available for such payment.

Alternative B—A note or acceptance which states that it is payable at a bank is not of itself an order or authorization to the bank to pay it.

§ 3–122. Accrual of Cause of Action.

(1) A cause of action against a maker or an acceptor accrues

(a) in the case of a time instrument on the day after maturity;

(b) in the case of a demand instrument upon its date or, if no date is stated, on the date of issue.

(2) A cause of action against the obligor of a demand or time certificate of deposit accrues upon demand, but demand on a time certificate may not be made until on or after the date of maturity.

(3) A cause of action against a drawer of a draft or an indorser of any instrument accrues upon demand following dishonor of the instrument. Notice of dishonor is a demand.

(4) Unless an instrument provides otherwise, interest runs at the rate provided by law for a judgment

(a) in the case of a maker, acceptor or other primary obligor of a demand instrument, from the date of demand;

(b) in all other cases from the date of accrual of the cause of action.

Part 2—Transfer and Negotiation

§ 3–201. Transfer: Right to Indorsement.

(1) Transfer of an instrument vests in the transferee such rights as the transferor has therein, except that a transferee who has himself been a party to any fraud or illegality affecting the instrument or who as a prior holder had notice of a defense or claim against it cannot improve his position by taking from a later holder in due course.

(2) A transfer of a security interest in an instrument vests the foregoing rights in the transferee to the extent of the interest transferred.

(3) Unless otherwise agreed any transfer for value of an instrument not then payable to bearer gives the transferee the specifically enforceable right to have the unqualified indorsement of the transferor. Negotiation takes effect only when the indorsement is made and until that time there is no presumption that the transferee is the owner.

§ 3–202. Negotiation.

(1) Negotiation is the transfer of an instrument in such form that the transferee becomes a holder. If the instrument is payable to order it is negotiated by delivery with any necessary indorsement; if payable to bearer it is negotiated by delivery.

(2) An indorsement must be written by or on behalf of the holder and on the instrument or on a paper so firmly affixed thereto as to become a part thereof.

(3) An indorsement is effective for negotiation only when it conveys the entire instrument or any unpaid residue. If it purports to be of less it operates only as a partial assignment.

(4) Words of assignment, condition, waiver, guaranty, limitation or disclaimer of liability and the like accompanying an indorsement do not affect its character as an indorsement.

§ 3–203. Wrong or Misspelled Name.

Where an instrument is made payable to a person under a misspelled name or one other than his own he may indorse in that name or his own or both; but signature in both names may be required by a person paying or giving value for the instrument.

§ 3–204. Special Indorsement; Blank Indorsement.

(1) A special indorsement specifies the person to whom or to whose order it makes the instrument payable. Any instrument specially indorsed becomes payable to the order of the special indorsee and may be further negotiated only by his indorsement.

(2) An indorsement in blank specifies no particular indorsee and may consist of a mere signature. An instrument payable to order and indorsed in blank becomes payable to bearer and may be negotiated by delivery alone until specially indorsed.

(3) The holder may convert a blank indorsement into a special indorsement by writing over the signature of the indorser in blank any contract consistent with the character of the indorsement.

§ 3–205. Restrictive Indorsements.

An indorsement is restrictive which either

(a) is conditional; or

(b) purports to prohibit further transfer of the instrument; or

(c) includes the words "for collection", "for deposit", "pay any bank", or like terms signifying a purpose of deposit or collection; or

(d) otherwise states that it is for the benefit or use of the indorser or of another person.

§ 3–206. Effect of Restrictive Indorsement.

(1) No restrictive indorsement prevents further transfer or negotiation of the instrument.

(2) An intermediary bank, or a payor bank which is not the depositary bank, is neither given notice nor otherwise affected by a restrictive indorsement of any person except the bank's immediate transferor or the person presenting for payment.

(3) Except for an intermediary bank, any transferee under an indorsement which is conditional or includes the words "for collection", "for deposit", "pay any bank", or like terms (subparagraphs (a) and (c) of Section 3–205) must pay or apply any value given by him for or on the security of the instrument consistently with the indorsement and to the extent that he does so he becomes a holder for value. In addition such transferee is a holder in due course if he otherwise complies with the requirements of Section 3–302 on what constitutes a holder in due course.

(4) The first taker under an indorsement for the benefit of the indorser or another person (subparagraph (d) of

Section 3–205) must pay or apply any value given by him for or on the security of the instrument consistently with the indorsement and to the extent that he does so he becomes a holder for value. In addition such taker is a holder in due course if he otherwise complies with the requirements of Section 3–302 on what constitutes a holder in due course. A later holder for value is neither given notice nor otherwise affected by such restrictive indorsement unless he has knowledge that a fiduciary or other person has negotiated the instrument in any transaction for his own benefit or otherwise in breach of duty (subsection (2) of Section 3–304).

§ 3–207. Negotiation Effective Although It May Be Rescinded.

(1) Negotiation is effective to transfer the instrument although the negotiation is

(a) made by an infant, a corporation exceeding its powers, or any other person without capacity; or

(b) obtained by fraud, duress or mistake of any kind; or

(c) part of an illegal transaction; or

(d) made in breach of duty.

(2) Except as against a subsequent holder in due course such negotiation is in an appropriate case subject to rescission, the declaration of a constructive trust or any other remedy permitted by law.

§ 3–208. Reacquisition.

Where an instrument is returned to or reacquired by a prior party he may cancel any indorsement which is not necessary to his title and reissue or further negotiate the instrument, but any intervening party is discharged as against the reacquiring party and subsequent holders not in due course and if his indorsement has been cancelled is discharged as against subsequent holders in due course as well.

Part 3—Rights of a Holder

§ 3–301. Rights of a Holder.

The holder of an instrument whether or not he is the owner may transfer or negotiate it and, except as otherwise provided in Section 3–603 on payment or satisfaction, discharge it or enforce payment in his own name.

§ 3–302. Holder in Due Course.

(1) A holder in due course is a holder who takes the instrument

(a) for value; and

(b) in good faith; and

(c) without notice that it is overdue or has been dishonored or of any defense against or claim to it on the part of any person.

(2) A payee may be a holder in due course.

(3) A holder does not become a holder in due course of an instrument:

(a) by purchase of it at judicial sale or by taking it under legal process; or

(b) by acquiring it in taking over an estate; or

(c) by purchasing it as part of a bulk transaction not in regular course of business of the transferor.

(4) A purchaser of a limited interest can be a holder in due course only to the extent of the interest purchased.

§ 3–303. Taking for Value.

A holder takes the instrument for value

(a) to the extent that the agreed consideration has been performed or that he acquires a security interest in or a lien on the instrument otherwise than by legal process; or

(b) when he takes the instrument in payment of or as security for an antecedent claim against any person whether or not the claim is due; or

(c) when he gives a negotiable instrument for it or makes an irrevocable commitment to a third person.

§ 3–304. Notice to Purchaser.

(1) The purchaser has notice of a claim or defense if

(a) the instrument is so incomplete, bears such visible evidence of forgery or alteration, or is otherwise so irregular as to call into question its validity, terms or ownership or to create an ambiguity as to the party to pay; or

(b) the purchaser has notice that the obligation of any party is voidable in whole or in part, or that all parties have been discharged.

(2) The purchaser has notice of a claim against the instrument when he has knowledge that a fiduciary has negotiated the instrument in payment of or as security for his own debt or in any transaction for his own benefit or otherwise in breach of duty.

(3) The purchaser has notice that an instrument is overdue if he has reason to know

(a) that any part of the principal amount is overdue or that there is an uncured default in payment of another instrument of the same series; or

(b) that acceleration of the instrument has been made; or

(c) that he is taking a demand instrument after demand has been made or more than a reasonable length of time after its issue. A reasonable time for a check drawn and payable within the states and territories of the United States and the District of Columbia is presumed to be thirty days.

(4) Knowledge of the following facts does not of itself give the purchaser notice of a defense or claim

(a) that the instrument is antedated or postdated;

(b) that it was issued or negotiated in return for an executory promise or accompanied by a separate agreement, unless the purchaser has notice that a defense or claim has arisen from the terms thereof;

(c) that any party has signed for accommodation;

(d) that an incomplete instrument has been completed, unless the purchaser has notice of any improper completion;

(e) that any person negotiating the instrument is or was a fiduciary;

(f) that there has been default in payment of interest on the instrument or in payment of any other instrument, except one of the same series.

(5) The filing or recording of a document does not of itself constitute notice within the provisions of this Article to a person who would otherwise be a holder in due course.

(6) To be effective notice must be received at such time and in such manner as to give a reasonable opportunity to act on it.

§ 3–305. Rights of a Holder in Due Course.

To the extent that a holder is a holder in due course he takes the instrument free from

(1) all claims to it on the part of any person; and

(2) all defenses of any party to the instrument with whom the holder has not dealt except

(a) infancy, to the extent that it is a defense to a simple contract; and

(b) such other incapacity, or duress, or illegality of the transaction, as renders the obligation of the party a nullity; and

(c) such misrepresentation as has induced the party to sign the instrument with neither knowledge nor reasonable opportunity to obtain knowledge of its character or its essential terms; and

(d) discharge in insolvency proceedings; and

(e) any other discharge of which the holder has notice when he takes the instrument.

§ 3–306. Rights of One Not Holder in Due Course.

Unless he has the rights of a holder in due course any person takes the instrument subject to

(a) all valid claims to it on the part of any person; and

(b) all defenses of any party which would be available in an action on a simple contract; and

(c) the defenses of want or failure of consideration, non-performance of any condition precedent, non-delivery, or delivery for a special purpose (Section 3–408); and

(d) the defense that he or a person through whom he holds the instrument acquired it by theft, or that payment or satisfaction to such holder would be inconsistent with the terms of a restrictive indorsement. The claim of any third person to the instrument is not otherwise available as a defense to any party liable thereon unless the third person himself defends the action for such party.

§ 3–307. Burden of Establishing Signatures, Defenses and Due Course.

(1) Unless specifically denied in the pleadings each signature on an instrument is admitted. When the effectiveness of a signature is put in issue

(a) the burden of establishing it is on the party claiming under the signature; but

(b) the signature is presumed to be genuine or authorized except where the action is to enforce the obligation of a purported signer who has died or become incompetent before proof is required.

(2) When signatures are admitted or established, production of the instrument entitles a holder to recover on it unless the defendant establishes a defense.

(3) After it is shown that a defense exists a person claiming the rights of a holder in due course has the burden of establishing that he or some person under whom he claims is in all respects a holder in due course.

Part 4—Liability of Parties

§ 3–401. Signature.

(1) No person is liable on an instrument unless his signature appears thereon.

(2) A signature is made by use of any name, including any trade or assumed name, upon an instrument, or by any word or mark used in lieu of a written signature.

§ 3–402. Signature in Ambiguous Capacity.

Unless the instrument clearly indicates that a signature is made in some other capacity it is an indorsement.

§ 3–403. Signature by Authorized Representative.

(1) A signature may be made by an agent or other representative, and his authority to make it may be established as in other cases of representation. No particular form of appointment is necessary to establish such authority.

(2) An authorized representative who signs his own name to an instrument

(a) is personally obligated if the instrument neither names the person represented nor shows that the representative signed in a representative capacity;

(b) except as otherwise established between the immediate parties, is personally obligated if the instrument names the person represented but does not show that the representative signed in a representative capacity, or if the instrument does not name the person represented but does show that the representative signed in a representative capacity.

(3) Except as otherwise established the name of an organization preceded or followed by the name and office of an authorized individual is a signature made in a representative capacity.

§ 3–404. Unauthorized Signatures.

(1) Any unauthorized signature is wholly inoperative as that of the person whose name is signed unless he ratifies it or is precluded from denying it; but it operates as the signature of the unauthorized signer in favor of any person who in good faith pays the instrument or takes it for value.

(2) Any unauthorized signature may be ratified for all purposes of this Article. Such ratification does not of itself affect any rights of the person ratifying against the actual signer.

§ 3–405. Impostors; Signature in Name of Payee.

(1) An indorsement by any person in the name of a named payee is effective if

(a) an imposter by use of the mails or otherwise has induced the maker or drawer to issue the instrument to him or his confederate in the name of the payee; or

(b) a person signing as or on behalf of a maker or drawer intends the payee to have no interest in the instrument; or

(c) an agent or employee of the maker or drawer has supplied him with the name of the payee intending the latter to have no such interest.

(2) Nothing in this section shall affect the criminal or civil liability of the person so indorsing.

§ 3–406. Negligence Contributing to Alteration or Unauthorized Signature.

Any person who by his negligence substantially contributes to a material alteration of the instrument or to the making of an unauthorized signature is precluded from asserting the alteration or lack of authority against a holder in due course or against a drawee or other payor who pays the instrument in good faith and in accordance with the reasonable commercial standards of the drawee's or payor's business.

§ 3–407. Alteration.

(1) Any alteration of an instrument is material which changes the contract of any party thereto in any respect, including any such change in

(a) the number or relations of the parties; or

(b) an incomplete instrument, by completing it otherwise than as authorized; or

(c) the writing as signed, by adding to it or by removing any part of it.

(2) As against any person other than a subsequent holder in due course

(a) alteration by the holder which is both fraudulent and material discharges any party whose contract is thereby changed unless that party assents or is precluded from asserting the defense;

(b) no other alteration discharges any party and the instrument may be enforced according to its original tenor, or as to incomplete instruments according to the authority given.

(3) A subsequent holder in due course may in all cases enforce the instrument according to its original tenor, and when an incomplete instrument has been completed, he may enforce it as completed.

§ 3–408. Consideration.

Want or failure of consideration is a defense as against any person not having the rights of a holder in due course (Section 3–305), except that no consideration is necessary for an instrument or obligation thereon given in payment of or as security for an antecedent obligation of any kind. Nothing in this section shall be taken to displace any statute outside this Act under which a promise is enforceable notwithstanding lack or failure of consideration. Partial failure of consideration is a defense pro tanto whether or not the failure is in an ascertained or liquidated amount.

§ 3–409. Draft Not an Assignment.

(1) A check or other draft does not of itself operate as an assignment of any funds in the hands of the drawee available for its payment, and the drawee is not liable on the instrument until he accepts it.

(2) Nothing in this section shall affect any liability in contract, tort or otherwise arising from any letter of credit or other obligation or representation which is not an acceptance.

§ 3–410. Definition and Operation of Acceptance.

(1) Acceptance is the drawee's signed engagement to honor the draft as presented. It must be written on the draft, and may consist of his signature alone. It becomes operative when completed by delivery or notification.

(2) A draft may be accepted although it has not been signed by the drawer or is otherwise incomplete or is overdue or has been dishonored.

(3) Where the draft is payable at a fixed period after sight and the acceptor fails to date his acceptance the holder may complete it by supplying a date in good faith.

§ 3–411. Certification of a Check.

(1) Certification of a check is acceptance. Where a holder procures certification the drawer and all prior indorsers are discharged.

(2) Unless otherwise agreed a bank has no obligation to certify a check.

(3) A bank may certify a check before returning it for lack of proper indorsement. If it does so the drawer is discharged.

§ 3–412. Acceptance Varying Draft.

(1) Where the drawee's proffered acceptance in any manner varies the draft as presented the holder may refuse the acceptance and treat the draft as dishonored in which case the drawee is entitled to have his acceptance cancelled.

(2) The terms of the draft are not varied by an acceptance to pay at any particular bank or place in the United States, unless the acceptance states that the draft is to be paid only at such bank or place.

(3) Where the holder assents to an acceptance varying the terms of the draft each drawer and indorser who does not affirmatively assent is discharged.

§ 3–413. Contract of Maker, Drawer and Acceptor.

(1) The maker or acceptor engages that he will pay the instrument according to its tenor at the time of his engagement or as completed pursuant to Section 3–115 on incomplete instruments.

(2) The drawer engages that upon dishonor of the draft and any necessary notice of dishonor or protest he will pay the amount of the draft to the holder or to any indorser who takes it up. The drawer may disclaim this liability by drawing without recourse.

(3) By making, drawing or accepting the party admits as against all subsequent parties including the drawee the existence of the payee and his then capacity to indorse.

§ 3–414. Contract of Indorser; Order of Liability.

(1) Unless the indorser otherwise specifies (as by such words as "without recourse") every indorser engages that upon dishonor and any necessary notice of dishonor and protest he will pay the instrument according to its tenor at the time of his indorsement to the holder or to any subsequent indorser who takes it up, even though the indorser who takes it up was not obligated to do so.

(2) Unless they otherwise agree indorsers are liable to one another in the order in which they indorse, which is presumed to be the order in which their signatures appear on the instrument.

§ 3–415. Contract of Accommodation Party.

(1) An accommodation party is one who signs the instrument in any capacity for the purpose of lending his name to another party to it.

(2) When the instrument has been taken for value before it is due the accommodation party is liable in the capacity in which he has signed even though the taker knows of the accommodation.

(3) As against a holder in due course and without notice of the accommodation oral proof of the accommodation is not admissible to give the accommodation party the benefit of discharges dependent on his character as such. In other cases the accommodation character may be shown by oral proof.

(4) An indorsement which shows that it is not in the chain of title is notice of its accommodation character.

(5) An accommodation party is not liable to the party accommodated, and if he pays the instrument has a right of recourse on the instrument against such party.

§ 3–416. Contract of Guarantor.

(1) "Payment guaranteed" or equivalent words added to a signature mean that the signer engages that if the instrument is not paid when due he will pay it according to its tenor without resort by the holder to any other party.

(2) "Collection guaranteed" or equivalent words added to a signature mean that the signer engages that if the instrument is not paid when due he will pay it according to its tenor, but only after the holder has reduced his claim against the maker or acceptor to judgment and execution has been returned unsatisfied, or after the maker or acceptor has become insolvent or it is otherwise apparent that it is useless to proceed against him.

(3) Words of guaranty which do not otherwise specify guarantee payment.

(4) No words of guaranty added to the signature of a sole maker or acceptor affect his liability on the instrument. Such words added to the signature of one of two or more makers or acceptors create a presumption that the signature is for the accommodation of the others.

(5) When words of guaranty are used presentment, notice of dishonor and protest are not necessary to charge the user.

(6) Any guaranty written on the instrument is enforceable notwithstanding any statute of frauds.

§ 3–417. Warranties on Presentment and Transfer.

(1) Any person who obtains payment or acceptance and any prior transferor warrants to a person who in good faith pays or accepts that

(a) he has a good title to the instrument or is authorized to obtain payment or acceptance on behalf of one who has a good title; and

(b) he has no knowledge that the signature of the maker or drawer is unauthorized, except that this warranty is not given by a holder in due course acting in good faith

(i) to a maker with respect to the maker's own signature; or

(ii) to a drawer with respect to the drawer's own signature, whether or not the drawer is also the drawee; or

(iii) to an acceptor of a draft if the holder in due course took the draft after the acceptance or obtained the acceptance without knowledge that the drawer's signature was unauthorized; and

(c) the instrument has not been materially altered, except that this warranty is not given by a holder in due course acting in good faith

(i) to the maker of a note; or

(ii) to the drawer of a draft whether or not the drawer is also the drawee; or

(iii) to the acceptor of a draft with respect to an alteration made prior to the acceptance if the holder in due course took the draft after the acceptance, even though the acceptance provided "payable as originally drawn" or equivalent terms; or

(iv) to the acceptor of a draft with respect to an alteration made after the acceptance.

(2) Any person who transfers an instrument and receives consideration warrants to his transferee and if the transfer is by indorsement to any subsequent holder who takes the instrument in good faith that

(a) he has a good title to the instrument or is authorized to obtain payment or acceptance on behalf of one who has a good title and the transfer is otherwise rightful; and

(b) all signatures are genuine or authorized; and

(c) the instrument has not been materially altered; and

(d) no defense of any party is good against him; and

(e) he has no knowledge of any insolvency proceeding instituted with respect to the maker or acceptor or the drawer of an unaccepted instrument.

(3) By transferring "without recourse" the transferor limits the obligation stated in subsection (2)(d) to a warranty that he has no knowledge of such a defense.

(4) A selling agent or broker who does not disclose the fact that he is acting only as such gives the warranties

provided in this section, but if he makes such disclosure warrants only his good faith and authority.

§ 3–418. Finality of Payment or Acceptance.

Except for recovery of bank payments as provided in the Article on Bank Deposits and Collections (Article 4) and except for liability for breach of warranty on presentment under the preceding section, payment or acceptance of any instrument is final in favor of a holder in due course, or a person who has in good faith changed his position in reliance on the payment.

§ 3–419. Conversion of Instrument; Innocent Representative.

(1) An instrument is converted when

(a) a drawee to whom it is delivered for acceptance refuses to return it on demand; or

(b) any person to whom it is delivered for payment refuses on demand either to pay or to return it; or

(c) it is paid on a forged indorsement.

(2) In an action against a drawee under subsection (1) the measure of the drawee's liability is the face amount of the instrument. In any other action under subsection (1) the measure of liability is presumed to be the face amount of the instrument.

(3) Subject to the provisions of this Act concerning restrictive indorsements a representative, including a depositary or collecting bank, who has in good faith and in accordance with the reasonable commercial standards applicable to the business of such representative dealt with an instrument or its proceeds on behalf of one who was not the true owner is not liable in conversion or otherwise to the true owner beyond the amount of any proceeds remaining in his hands.

(4) An intermediary bank or payor bank which is not a depositary bank is not liable in conversion solely by reason of the fact that proceeds of an item indorsed restrictively (Sections 3–205 and 3–206) are not paid or applied consistently with the restrictive indorsement of an indorser other than its immediate transferor.

Part 5—Presentment, Notice of Dishonor and Protest

§ 3–501. When Presentment, Notice of Dishonor, and Protest Necessary or Permissible.

(1) Unless excused (Section 3–511) presentment is necessary to charge secondary parties as follows:

(a) presentment for acceptance is necessary to charge the drawer and indorsers of a draft where the draft so provides, or is payable elsewhere than at the residence or place of business of the drawee, or its date of payment depends upon such presentment.

The holder may at his option present for acceptance any other draft payable at a stated date;

(b) presentment for payment is necessary to charge any indorser;

(c) in the case of any drawer, the acceptor of a draft payable at a bank or the maker of a note payable at a bank, presentment for payment is necessary, but failure to make presentment discharges such drawer, acceptor or maker only as stated in Section 3–502(1)(b).

(2) Unless excused (Section 3–511)

(a) notice of any dishonor is necessary to charge any indorser;

(b) in the case of any drawer, the acceptor of a draft payable at a bank or the maker of a note payable at a bank, notice of any dishonor is necessary, but failure to give such notice discharges such drawer, acceptor or maker only as stated in Section 3–502(1)(b).

(3) Unless excused (Section 3–511) protest of any dishonor is necessary to charge the drawer and indorsers of any draft which on its face appears to be drawn or payable outside of the states, territories, dependencies, and possessions of the United States, the District of Columbia and the Commonwealth of Puerto Rico. The holder may at his option make protest of any dishonor of any other instrument and in the case of a foreign draft may on insolvency of the acceptor before maturity make protest for better security.

(4) Notwithstanding any provision of this section, neither presentment nor notice of dishonor nor protest is necessary to charge an indorser who has indorsed an instrument after maturity.

§ 3–502. Unexcused Delay; Discharge.

(1) Where without excuse any necessary presentment or notice of dishonor is delayed beyond the time when it is due

(a) any indorser is discharged; and

(b) any drawer or the acceptor of a draft payable at a bank or the maker of a note payable at a bank who because the drawee or payor bank becomes insolvent during the delay is deprived of funds maintained with the drawee or payor bank to cover the instrument may discharge his liability by written assignment to the holder of his rights against the drawee or payor bank in respect of such funds, but such drawer, acceptor or maker is not otherwise discharged.

(2) Where without excuse a necessary protest is delayed beyond the time when it is due any drawer or indorser is discharged.

§ 3–503. Time of Presentment.

(1) Unless a different time is expressed in the instrument the time for any presentment is determined as follows:

(a) where an instrument is payable at or a fixed period after a stated date any presentment for acceptance must be made on or before the date it is payable;

(b) where an instrument is payable after sight it must either be presented for acceptance or negotiated within a reasonable time after date or issue whichever is later;

(c) where an instrument shows the date on which it is payable presentment for payment is due on that date;

(d) where an instrument is accelerated presentment for payment is due within a reasonable time after the acceleration;

(e) with respect to the liability of any secondary party presentment for acceptance or payment of any other instrument is due within a reasonable time after such party becomes liable thereon.

(2) A reasonable time for presentment is determined by the nature of the instrument, any usage of banking or trade and the facts of the particular case. In the case of an uncertified check which is drawn and payable within the United States and which is not a draft drawn by a bank the following are presumed to be reasonable periods within which to present for payment or to initiate bank collection:

(a) with respect to the liability of the drawer, thirty days after date or issue whichever is later; and

(b) with respect to the liability of an indorser, seven days after his indorsement.

(3) Where any presentment is due on a day which is not a full business day for either the person making presentment or the party to pay or accept, presentment is due on the next following day which is a full business day for both parties.

(4) Presentment to be sufficient must be made at a reasonable hour, and if at a bank during its banking day.

§ 3–504. How Presentment Made.

(1) Presentment is a demand for acceptance or payment made upon the maker, acceptor, drawee or other payor by or on behalf of the holder.

(2) Presentment may be made

(a) by mail, in which event the time of presentment is determined by the time of receipt of the mail; or

(b) through a clearing house; or

(c) at the place of acceptance or payment specified in the instrument or if there be none at the place of business or residence of the party to accept or pay. If neither the party to accept or pay nor anyone authorized to act for him is present or accessible at such place presentment is excused.

(3) It may be made

    (a) to any one of two or more makers, acceptors, drawees or other payors; or

    (b) to any person who has authority to make or refuse the acceptance or payment.

(4) A draft accepted or a note made payable at a bank in the United States must be presented at such bank.

(5) In the cases described in Section 4–210 presentment may be made in the manner and with the result stated in that section.

§ 3–505. Rights of Party to Whom Presentment Is Made.

(1) The party to whom presentment is made may without dishonor require

    (a) exhibition of the instrument; and

    (b) reasonable identification of the person making presentment and evidence of his authority to make it if made for another; and

    (c) that the instrument be produced for acceptance or payment at a place specified in it, or if there be none at any place reasonable in the circumstances; and

    (d) a signed receipt on the instrument for any partial or full payment and its surrender upon full payment.

(2) Failure to comply with any such requirement invalidates the presentment but the person presenting has a reasonable time in which to comply and the time for acceptance or payment runs from the time of compliance.

§ 3–506. Time Allowed for Acceptance or Payment.

(1) Acceptance may be deferred without dishonor until the close of the next business day following presentment. The holder may also in a good faith effort to obtain acceptance and without either dishonor of the instrument or discharge of secondary parties allow postponement of acceptance for an additional business day.

(2) Except as a longer time is allowed in the case of documentary drafts drawn under a letter of credit, and unless an earlier time is agreed to by the party to pay, payment of an instrument may be deferred without dishonor pending reasonable examination to determine whether it is properly payable, but payment must be made in any event before the close of business on the day of presentment.

§ 3–507. Dishonor; Holder's Right of Recourse; Term Allowing Re-Presentment.

(1) An instrument is dishonored when

    (a) a necessary or optional presentment is duly made and due acceptance or payment is refused or

cannot be obtained within the prescribed time or in case of bank collections the instrument is seasonably returned by the midnight deadline (Section 4–301); or

    (b) presentment is excused and the instrument is not duly accepted or paid.

(2) Subject to any necessary notice of dishonor and protest, the holder has upon dishonor an immediate right of recourse against the drawers and indorsers.

(3) Return of an instrument for lack of proper indorsement is not dishonor.

(4) A term in a draft or an indorsement thereof allowing a stated time for re-presentment in the event of any dishonor of the draft by nonacceptance if a time draft or by nonpayment if a sight draft gives the holder as against any secondary party bound by the term an option to waive the dishonor without affecting the liability of the secondary party and he may present again up to the end of the stated time.

§ 3–508. Notice of Dishonor.

(1) Notice of dishonor may be given to any person who may be liable on the instrument by or on behalf of the holder or any party who has himself received notice, or any other party who can be compelled to pay the instrument. In addition an agent or bank in whose hands the instrument is dishonored may give notice to his principal or customer or to another agent or bank from which the instrument was received.

(2) Any necessary notice must be given by a bank before its midnight deadline and by any other person before midnight of the third business day after dishonor or receipt of notice of dishonor.

(3) Notice may be given in any reasonable manner. It may be oral or written and in any terms which identify the instrument and state that it has been dishonored. A misdescription which does not mislead the party notified does not vitiate the notice. Sending the instrument bearing a stamp, ticket or writing stating that acceptance or payment has been refused or sending a notice of debit with respect to the instrument is sufficient.

(4) Written notice is given when sent although it is not received.

(5) Notice to one partner is notice to each although the firm has been dissolved.

(6) When any party is in insolvency proceedings instituted after the issue of the instrument notice may be given either to the party or to the representative of his estate.

(7) When any party is dead or incompetent notice may be sent to his last known address or given to his personal representative.

(8) Notice operates for the benefit of all parties who have rights on the instrument against the party notified.

§ 3–509. Protest; Noting for Protest.

(1) A protest is a certificate of dishonor made under the hand and seal of a United States consul or vice consul or a notary public or other person authorized to certify dishonor by the law of the place where dishonor occurs. It may be made upon information satisfactory to such person.

(2) The protest must identify the instrument and certify either that due presentment has been made or the reason why it is excused and that the instrument has been dishonored by nonacceptance or nonpayment.

(3) The protest may also certify that notice of dishonor has been given to all parties or to specified parties.

(4) Subject to subsection (5) any necessary protest is due by the time that notice of dishonor is due.

(5) If, before protest is due, an instrument has been noted for protest by the officer to make protest, the protest may be made at any time thereafter as of the date of the noting.

§ 3–510. Evidence of Dishonor and Notice of Dishonor.

The following are admissible as evidence and create a presumption of dishonor and of any notice of dishonor therein shown:

(a) a document regular in form as provided in the preceding section which purports to be a protest;

(b) the purported stamp or writing of the drawee, payor bank or presenting bank on the instrument or accompanying it stating that acceptance or payment has been refused for reasons consistent with dishonor;

(c) any book or record of the drawee, payor bank, or any collecting bank kept in the usual course of business which shows dishonor, even though there is no evidence of who made the entry.

§ 3–511. Waived or Excused Presentment, Protest or Notice of Dishonor or Delay Therein.

(1) Delay in presentment, protest or notice of dishonor is excused when the party is without notice that it is due or when the delay is caused by circumstances beyond his control and he exercises reasonable diligence after the cause of the delay ceases to operate.

(2) Presentment or notice or protest as the case may be is entirely excused when

(a) the party to be charged has waived it expressly or by implication either before or after it is due; or

(b) such party has himself dishonored the instrument or has countermanded payment or otherwise has no reason to expect or right to require that the instrument be accepted or paid; or

(c) by reasonable diligence the presentment or protest cannot be made or the notice given.

(3) Presentment is also entirely excused when

(a) the maker, acceptor or drawee of any instrument except a documentary draft is dead or in insolvency proceedings instituted after the issue of the instrument; or

(b) acceptance or payment is refused but not for want of proper presentment.

(4) Where a draft has been dishonored by nonacceptance a later presentment for payment and any notice of dishonor and protest for nonpayment are excused unless in the meantime the instrument has been accepted.

(5) A waiver of protest is also a waiver of presentment and of notice of dishonor even though protest is not required.

(6) Where a waiver of presentment or notice or protest is embodied in the instrument itself it is binding upon all parties; but where it is written above the signature of an indorser it binds him only.

Part 6—Discharge

§ 3–601. Discharge of Parties.

(1) The extent of the discharge of any party from liability on an instrument is governed by the sections on

(a) payment or satisfaction (Section 3–603); or

(b) tender of payment (Section 3–604); or

(c) cancellation or renunciation (Section 3–605); or

(d) impairment of right of recourse or of collateral (Section 3–606); or

(e) reacquisition of the instrument by a prior party (Section 3–208); or

(f) fraudulent and material alteration (Section 3–407); or

(g) certification of a check (Section 3–411); or

(h) acceptance varying a draft (Section 3–412); or

(i) unexcused delay in presentment or notice of dishonor or protest (Section 3–502).

(2) Any party is also discharged from his liability on an instrument to another party by any other act or agreement with such party which would discharge his simple contract for the payment of money.

(3) The liability of all parties is discharged when any party who has himself no right of action or recourse on the instrument.

(a) reacquires the instrument in his own right; or

(b) is discharged under any provision of this Article, except as otherwise provided with respect to discharge for impairment of recourse or of collateral (Section 3–606).

§ 3–602. Effect of Discharge Against Holder in Due Course.

No discharge of any party provided by this Article is effective against a subsequent holder in due course unless he has notice thereof when he takes the instrument.

§ 3–603. Payment or Satisfaction.

(1) The liability of any party is discharged to the extent of his payment or satisfaction to the holder even though it is made with knowledge of a claim of another person to the instrument unless prior to such payment or satisfaction the person making the claim either supplies indemnity deemed adequate by the party seeking the discharge or enjoins payment or satisfaction by order of a court of competent jurisdiction in an action in which the adverse claimant and the holder are parties. This subsection does not, however, result in the discharge of the liability

(a) of a party who in bad faith pays or satisfies a holder who acquired the instrument by theft or who (unless having the rights of a holder in due course) holds through one who so acquired it; or

(b) of a party (other than an intermediary bank or a payor bank which is not a depositary bank) who pays or satisfies the holder of an instrument which has been restrictively indorsed in a manner not consistent with the terms of such restrictive indorsement.

(2) Payment or satisfaction may be made with the consent of the holder by any person including a stranger to the instrument. Surrender of the instrument to such a person gives him the rights of a transferee (Section 3–201).

§ 3–604. Tender of Payment.

(1) Any party making tender of full payment to a holder when or after it is due is discharged to the extent of all subsequent liability for interest, costs and attorney's fees.

(2) The holder's refusal of such tender wholly discharges any party who has a right of recourse against the party making the tender.

(3) Where the maker or acceptor of an instrument payable otherwise than on demand is able and ready to pay at every place of payment specified in the instrument when it is due, it is equivalent to tender.

§ 3–605. Cancellation and Renunciation.

(1) The holder of an instrument may even without consideration discharge any party

(a) in any manner apparent on the face of the instrument or the indorsement, as by intentionally cancelling the instrument or the party's signature by destruction or mutilation, or by striking out the party's signature; or

(b) by renouncing his rights by a writing signed and delivered or by surrender of the instrument to the party to be discharged.

(2) Neither cancellation nor renunciation without surrender of the instrument affects the title thereto.

§ 3–606. Impairment of Recourse or of Collateral.

(1) The holder discharges any party to the instrument to the extent that without such party's consent the holder

(a) without express reservation of rights releases or agrees not to sue any person against whom the party has to the knowledge of the holder a right of recourse or agrees to suspend the right to enforce against such person the instrument or collateral or otherwise discharges such person, except that failure or delay in effecting any required presentment, protest or notice of dishonor with respect to any such person does not discharge any party as to whom presentment, protest or notice of dishonor is effective or unnecessary; or

(b) unjustifiably impairs any collateral for the instrument given by or on behalf of the party or any person against whom he has a right of recourse.

(2) By express reservation of rights against a party with right of recourse the holder preserves

(a) all his rights against such party as of the time when the instrument was originally due; and

(b) the right of the party to pay the instrument as of that time; and

(c) all rights of such party to recourse against others.

Part 7—Advice of International Sight Draft

§ 3–701. Letter of Advice of International Sight Draft.

(1) A "letter of advice" is a drawer's communication to the drawee that a described draft has been drawn.

(2) Unless otherwise agreed when a bank receives from another bank a letter of advice of an international sight draft the drawee bank may immediately debit the drawer's account and stop the running of interest pro tanto. Such a debit and any resulting credit to any account covering outstanding drafts leaves in the drawer full power to stop payment or otherwise dispose of the amount and creates no trust or interest in favor of the holder.

(3) Unless otherwise agreed and except where a draft is drawn under a credit issued by the drawee, the drawee of an international sight draft owes the drawer no duty to pay an unadvised draft but if it does so and the draft is genuine, may appropriately debit the drawer's account.

Part 8—Miscellaneous

§ 3–801. Drafts in a Set.

(1) Where a draft is drawn in a set of parts, each of which is numbered and expressed to be an order only if no other part has been honored, the whole of the parts constitutes one draft but a taker of any part may become a holder in due course of the draft.

(2) Any person who negotiates, indorses or accepts a single part of a draft drawn in a set thereby becomes liable to any holder in due course of that part as if it were the whole set, but as between different holders in due course to whom different parts have been negotiated the holder whose title first accrues has all rights to the draft and its proceeds.

(3) As against the drawee the first presented part of a draft drawn in a set is the part entitled to payment, or if a time draft to acceptance and payment. Acceptance of any subsequently presented part renders the drawee liable thereon under subsection (2). With respect both to a holder and to the drawer payment of a subsequently presented part of a draft payable at sight has the same effect as payment of a check notwithstanding an effective stop order (Section 4–407).

(4) Except as otherwise provided in this section, where any part of a draft in a set is discharged by payment or otherwise the whole draft is discharged.

§ 3–802. Effect of Instrument on Obligation for Which It Is Given.

(1) Unless otherwise agreed where an instrument is taken for an underlying obligation

(a) the obligation is pro tanto discharged if a bank is drawer, maker or acceptor of the instrument and there is no recourse on the instrument against the underlying obligor; and

(b) in any other case the obligation is suspended pro tanto until the instrument is due or if it is payable on demand until its presentment. If the instrument is dishonored action may be maintained on either the instrument or the obligation; discharge of the underlying obligor on the instrument also discharges him on the obligation.

(2) The taking in good faith of a check which is not postdated does not of itself so extend the time on the original obligation as to discharge a surety.

§ 3–803. Notice to Third Party.

Where a defendant is sued for breach of an obligation for which a third person is answerable over under this Article he may give the third person written notice of the litigation, and the person notified may then give similar notice to any other person who is answerable over to him under this Article. If the notice states that the person notified may come in and defend and that if the person notified does not do so he will in any action against him by the person giving the notice be bound by any determination of fact common to the two litigations, then unless after seasonable receipt of the notice the person notified does come in and defend he is so bound.

§ 3–804. Lost, Destroyed or Stolen Instruments.

The owner of an instrument which is lost, whether by destruction, theft or otherwise, may maintain an action in his own name and recover from any party liable thereon upon due proof of his ownership, the facts which prevent his production of the instrument and its terms. The court may require security indemnifying the defendant against loss by reason of further claims on the instrument.

§ 3–805. Instruments Not Payable to Order or to Bearer.

This Article applies to any instrument whose terms do not preclude transfer and which is otherwise negotiable within this Article but which is not payable to order or to bearer, except that there can be no holder in due course of such an instrument.

ARTICLE 4: BANK DEPOSITS AND COLLECTIONS

Part 1—General Provisions and Definitions

§ 4–101. Short Title.

This Article shall be known and may be cited as Uniform Commercial Code—Bank Deposits and Collections.

§ 4–102. Applicability.

(1) To the extent that items within this Article are also within the scope of Articles 3 and 8, they are subject to the provisions of those Articles. In the event of conflict the provisions of this Article govern those of Article 3 but the provisions of Article 8 govern those of this Article.

(2) The liability of a bank for action or non-action with respect to any item handled by it for purposes of presentment, payment or collection is governed by the law of the place where the bank is located. In the case of action or non-action by or at a branch or separate office of a bank, its liability is governed by the law of the place where the branch or separate office is located.

§ 4–103. Variation by Agreement; Measure of Damages; Certain Action Constituting Ordinary Care.

(1) The effect of the provisions of this Article may be varied by agreement except that no agreement can disclaim a bank's responsibility for its own lack of good

faith or failure to exercise ordinary care or can limit the measure of damages for such lack or failure; but the parties may by agreement determine the standards by which such responsibility is to be measured if such standards are not manifestly unreasonable.

(2) Federal Reserve regulations and operating letters, clearing house rules, and the like, have the effect of agreements under subsection (1), whether or not specifically assented to by all parties interested in items handled.

(3) Action or non-action approved by this Article or pursuant to Federal Reserve regulations or operating letters constitutes the exercise of ordinary care and, in the absence of special instructions, action or nonaction consistent with clearing house rules and the like or with a general banking usage not disapproved by this Article, prima facie constitutes the exercise of ordinary care.

(4) The specification or approval of certain procedures by this Article does not constitute disapproval of other procedures which may be reasonable under the circumstances.

(5) The measure of damages for failure to exercise ordinary care in handling an item is the amount of the item reduced by an amount which could not have been realized by the use of ordinary care, and where there is bad faith it includes other damages, if any, suffered by the party as a proximate consequence.

§ 4–104. Definitions and Index of Definitions.

(1) In this Article unless the context otherwise requires

(a) "Account" means any account with a bank and includes a checking, time, interest or savings account;

(b) "Afternoon" means the period of a day between noon and midnight;

(c) "Banking day" means that part of any day on which a bank is open to the public for carrying on substantially all of its banking functions;

(d) "Clearing house" means any association of banks or other payors regularly clearing items;

(e) "Customer" means any person having an account with a bank or for whom a bank has agreed to collect items and includes a bank carrying an account with another bank;

(f) "Documentary draft" means any negotiable or non-negotiable draft with accompanying documents, securities or other papers to be delivered against honor of the draft;

(g) "Item" means any instrument for the payment of money even though it is not negotiable but does not include money;

(h) "Midnight deadline" with respect to a bank is midnight on its next banking day following the banking day on which it receives the relevant item or notice or from which the time for taking action commences to run, whichever is later;

(i) "Properly payable" includes the availability of funds for payment at the time of decision to pay or dishonor;

(j) "Settle" means to pay in cash, by clearing house settlement, in a charge or credit or by remittance, or otherwise as instructed. A settlement may be either provisional or final;

(k) "Suspends payments" with respect to a bank means that it has been closed by order of the supervisory authorities, that a public officer has been appointed to take it over or that it ceases or refuses to make payments in the ordinary course of business.

(2) Other definitions applying to this Article and the sections in which they appear are:

"Collecting bank" Section 4–105.
"Depositary bank" Section 4–105.
"Intermediary bank" Section 4–105.
"Payor bank" Section 4–105.
"Presenting bank" Section 4–105.
"Remitting bank" Section 4–105.

(3) The following definitions in other Articles apply to this Article:

"Acceptance" Section 3–410.
"Certificate of deposit" Section 3–104.
"Certification" Section 3–411.
"Check" Section 3–104.
"Draft" Section 3–104.
"Holder in due course" Section 3–302.
"Notice of dishonor" Section 3–508.
"Presentment" Section 3–504.
"Protest" Section 3–509.
"Secondary party" Section 3–102.

(4) In addition Article 1 contains general definitions and principles of construction and interpretation applicable throughout this Article.

§ 4–105. "Depositary Bank"; "Intermediary Bank"; "Collecting Bank"; "Payor Bank"; "Presenting Bank"; "Remitting Bank".

In this Article unless the context otherwise requires:

(a) "Depositary bank" means the first bank to which an item is transferred for collection even though it is also the payor bank;

(b) "Payor bank" means a bank by which an item is payable as drawn or accepted;

(c) "Intermediary bank" means any bank to which an item is transferred in course of collection except the depositary or payor bank;

(d) "Collecting bank" means any bank handling the item for collection except the payor bank;

(e) "Presenting bank" means any bank presenting an item except a payor bank;

(f) "Remitting bank" means any payor or intermediary bank remitting for an item.

§ 4–106. Separate Office of a Bank.

A branch or separate office of a bank [maintaining its own deposit ledgers] is a separate bank for the purpose of computing the time within which and determining the place at or to which action may be taken or notices or orders shall be given under this Article and under Article 3.

Note: *The brackets are to make it optional with the several states whether to require a branch to maintain its own deposit ledgers in order to be considered to be a separate bank for certain purposes under Article 4. In some states "maintaining its own deposit ledgers" is a satisfactory test. In others branch banking practices are such that this test would not be suitable.*

§ 4–107. Time of Receipt of Items.

(1) For the purpose of allowing time to process items, prove balances and make the necessary entries on its books to determine its position for the day, a bank may fix an afternoon hour of two P.M. or later as a cut-off hour for the handling of money and items and the making of entries on its books.

(2) Any item or deposit of money received on any day after a cut-off hour so fixed or after the close of the banking day may be treated as being received at the opening of the next banking day.

§ 4–108. Delays.

(1) Unless otherwise instructed, a collecting bank in a good faith effort to secure payment may, in the case of specific items and with or without the approval of any person involved, waive, modify or extend time limits imposed or permitted by this Act for a period not in excess of an additional banking day without discharge of secondary parties and without liability to its transferor or any prior party.

(2) Delay by a collecting bank or payor bank beyond time limits prescribed or permitted by this Act or by instructions is excused if caused by interruption of communication facilities, suspension of payments by another bank, war, emergency conditions or other circumstances beyond the control of the bank provided it exercises such diligence as the circumstances require.

§ 4–109. Process of Posting.

The "process of posting" means the usual procedure followed by a payor bank in determining to pay an item and in recording the payment including one or more of the following or other steps as determined by the bank:

(a) verification of any signature;

(b) ascertaining that sufficient funds are available;

(c) affixing a "paid" or other stamp;

(d) entering a charge or entry to a customer's account;

(e) correcting or reversing an entry or erroneous action with respect to the item.

Part 2—Collection of Items: Depositary and Collecting Banks

§ 4–201. Presumption and Duration of Agency Status of Collecting Banks and Provisional Status of Credits; Applicability of Article; Item Indorsed "Pay Any Bank".

(1) Unless a contrary intent clearly appears and prior to the time that a settlement given by a collecting bank for an item is or becomes final (subsection (3) of Section 4–211 and Sections 4–212 and 4–213) the bank is an agent or sub-agent of the owner of the item and any settlement given for the item is provisional. This provision applies regardless of the form of indorsement or lack of indorsement and even though credit given for the item is subject to immediate withdrawal as of right or is in fact withdrawn; but the continuance of ownership of an item by its owner and any rights of the owner to proceeds of the item are subject to rights of a collecting bank such as those resulting from outstanding advances on the item and valid rights of setoff. When an item is handled by banks for purposes of presentment, payment and collection, the relevant provisions of this Article apply even though action of parties clearly establishes that a particular bank has purchased the item and is the owner of it.

(2) After an item has been indorsed with the words "pay any bank" or the like, only a bank may acquire the rights of a holder

(a) until the item has been returned to the customer initiating collection; or

(b) until the item has been specially indorsed by a bank to a person who is not a bank.

§ 4–202. Responsibility for Collection; When Action Seasonable.

(1) A collecting bank must use ordinary care in

(a) presenting an item or sending it for presentment; and

(b) sending notice of dishonor or non-payment or returning an item other than a documentary draft to the bank's transferor [or directly to the depositary bank under subsection (2) of Section 4–212] (*see note to Section 4–212*) after learning that the item has not been paid or accepted as the case may be; and

(c) settling for an item when the bank receives final settlement; and

(d) making or providing for any necessary protest; and

(e) notifying its transferor of any loss or delay in transit within a reasonable time after discovery thereof.

(2) A collecting bank taking proper action before its midnight deadline following receipt of an item, notice or payment acts seasonably; taking proper action within a reasonably longer time may be seasonable but the bank has the burden of so establishing.

(3) Subject to subsection (1)(a), a bank is not liable for the insolvency, neglect, misconduct, mistake or default of another bank or person or for loss or destruction of an item in transit or in the possession of others.

§ 4–203. Effect of Instructions.

Subject to the provisions of Article 3 concerning conversion of instruments (Section 3–419) and the provisions of both Article 3 and this Article concerning restrictive indorsements only a collecting bank's transferor can give instructions which affect the bank or constitute notice to it and a collecting bank is not liable to prior parties for any action taken pursuant to such instructions or in accordance with any agreement with its transferor.

§ 4–204. Methods of Sending and Presenting; Sending Direct to Payor Bank.

(1) A collecting bank must send items by reasonably prompt method taking into consideration any relevant instructions, the nature of the item, the number of such items on hand, and the cost of collection involved and the method generally used by it or others to present such items.

(2) A collecting bank may send

(a) any item direct to the payor bank;

(b) any item to any non-bank payor if authorized by its transferor; and

(c) any item other than documentary drafts to any non-bank payor, if authorized by Federal Reserve regulation or operating letter, clearing house rule or the like.

(3) Presentment may be made by a presenting bank at a place where the payor bank has requested that presentment be made.

§ 4–205. Supplying Missing Indorsement; No Notice from Prior Indorsement.

(1) A depositary bank which has taken an item for collection may supply any indorsement of the customer which is necessary to title unless the item contains the words "payee's indorsement required" or the like. In the absence of such a requirement a statement placed on the item by the depositary bank to the effect that the item was deposited by a customer or credited to his account is effective as the customer's indorsement.

(2) An intermediary bank, or payor bank which is not a depositary bank, is neither given notice nor otherwise affected by a restrictive indorsement of any person except the bank's immediate transferor.

§ 4–206. Transfer Between Banks.

Any agreed method which identifies the transferor bank is sufficient for the item's further transfer to another bank.

§ 4–207. Warranties of Customer and Collecting Bank on Transfer or Presentment of Items; Time for Claims.

(1) Each customer or collecting bank who obtains payment or acceptance of an item and each prior customer and collecting bank warrants to the payor bank or other payor who in good faith pays or accepts the item that

(a) he has a good title to the item or is authorized to obtain payment or acceptance on behalf of one who has a good title; and

(b) he has no knowledge that the signature of the maker or drawer is unauthorized, except that this warranty is not given by any customer or collecting bank that is a holder in due course and acts in good faith

(i) to a maker with respect to the maker's own signature; or

(ii) to a drawer with respect to the drawer's own signature, whether or not the drawer is also the drawee; or

(iii) to an acceptor of an item if the holder in due course took the item after the acceptance or obtained the acceptance without knowledge that the drawer's signature was unauthorized; and

(c) the item has not been materially altered, except that this warranty is not given by any customer or collecting bank that is a holder in due course and acts in good faith

(i) to the maker of a note; or

(ii) to the drawer of a draft whether or not the drawer is also the drawee; or

(iii) to the acceptor of an item with respect to an alteration made prior to the acceptance if the holder in due course took the item after the acceptance, even though the acceptance provided "payable as originally drawn" or equivalent terms; or

(iv) to the acceptor of an item with respect to an alteration made after the acceptance.

(2) Each customer and collecting bank who transfers an item and receives a settlement or other consideration for it warrants to his transferee and to any subsequent collecting bank who takes the item in good faith that

(a) he has a good title to the item or is authorized to obtain payment or acceptance on behalf of one who has a good title and the transfer is otherwise rightful; and

(b) all signatures are genuine or authorized; and

(c) the item has not been materially altered; and

(d) no defense of any party is good against him; and

(e) he has no knowledge of any insolvency proceeding instituted with respect to the maker or acceptor or the drawer of an unaccepted item.

In addition each customer and collecting bank so transferring an item and receiving a settlement or other consideration engages that upon dishonor and any necessary notice of dishonor and protest he will take up the item.

(3) The warranties and the engagement to honor set forth in the two preceding subsections arise notwithstanding the absence of indorsement or words of guaranty or warranty in the transfer or presentment and a collecting bank remains liable for their breach despite remittance to its transferor. Damages for breach of such warranties or engagement to honor shall not exceed the consideration received by the customer or collecting bank responsible plus finance charges and expenses related to the item, if any.

(4) Unless a claim for breach of warranty under this section is made within a reasonable time after the person claiming learns of the breach, the person liable is discharged to the extent of any loss caused by the delay in making claim.

§ 4–208. Security Interest of Collecting Bank in Items, Accompanying Documents and Proceeds.

(1) A bank has a security interest in an item and any accompanying documents or the proceeds of either

(a) in case of an item deposited in an account to the extent to which credit given for the item has been withdrawn or applied;

(b) in case of an item for which it has given credit available for withdrawal as of right, to the extent of the credit given whether or not the credit is drawn upon and whether or not there is a right of charge-back; or

(c) if it makes an advance on or against the item.

(2) When credit which has been given for several items received at one time or pursuant to a single agreement is withdrawn or applied in part the security interest remains upon all the items, any accompanying documents or the proceeds of either. For the purpose of this section, credits first given are first withdrawn.

(3) Receipt by a collecting bank of a final settlement for an item is a realization on its security interest in the item, accompanying documents and proceeds. To the extent and so long as the bank does not receive final settlement for the item or give up possession of the item or accompanying documents for purposes other than collection, the security interest continues and is subject to the provisions of Article 9 except that

(a) no security agreement is necessary to make the security interest enforceable (subsection (1)(b) of Section 9–203); and

(b) no filing is required to perfect the security interest; and

(c) the security interest has priority over conflicting perfected security interests in the item, accompanying documents or proceeds.

§ 4–209. When Bank Gives Value for Purposes of Holder in Due Course.

For purposes of determining its status as a holder in due course, the bank has given value to the extent that it has a security interest in an item provided that the bank otherwise complies with the requirements of Section 3–302 on what constitutes a holder in due course.

§ 4–210. Presentment by Notice of Item Not Payable by, Through or at a Bank; Liability of Secondary Parties.

(1) Unless otherwise instructed, a collecting bank may present an item not payable by, through or at a bank by sending to the party to accept or pay a written notice that the bank holds the item for acceptance or payment. The notice must be sent in time to be received on or before the day when presentment is due and the bank must meet any requirement of the party to accept or pay under Section 3–505 by the close of the bank's next banking day after it knows of the requirement.

(2) Where presentment is made by notice and neither honor nor request for compliance with a requirement under Section 3–505 is received by the close of business on the day after maturity or in the case of demand items by the close of business on the third banking day after notice was sent, the presenting bank may treat the item as dishonored and charge any secondary party by sending him notice of the facts.

§ 4–211. Media of Remittance; Provisional and Final Settlement in Remittance Cases.

(1) A collecting bank may take in settlement of an item

(a) a check of the remitting bank or of another bank on any bank except the remitting bank; or

(b) a cashier's check or similar primary obligation of a remitting bank which is a member of or clears through a member of the same clearing house or group as the collecting bank; or

(c) appropriate authority to charge an account of the remitting bank or of another bank with the collecting bank; or

(d) if the item is drawn upon or payable by a person other than a bank, a cashier's check, certified check or other bank check or obligation.

(2) If before its midnight deadline the collecting bank properly dishonors a remittance check or authorization to charge on itself or presents or forwards for collection a remittance instrument of or on another bank which is of a kind approved by subsection (1) or has not been authorized by it, the collecting bank is not liable to prior parties in the event of the dishonor of such check, instrument or authorization.

(3) A settlement for an item by means of a remittance instrument or authorization to charge is or becomes a final settlement as to both the person making and the person receiving the settlement

(a) if the remittance instrument or authorization to charge is of a kind approved by subsection (1) or has not been authorized by the person receiving the settlement and in either case the person receiving the settlement acts seasonably before its midnight deadline in presenting, forwarding for collection or paying the instrument or authorization,—at the time the remittance instrument or authorization is finally paid by the payor by which it is payable;

(b) if the person receiving the settlement has authorized remittance by a non-bank check or obligation or by a cashier's check or similar primary obligation of or a check upon the payor or other remitting bank which is not of a kind approved by subsection (1)(b),—at the time of the receipt of such remittance check or obligation; or

(c) if in a case not covered by sub-paragraphs (a) or (b) the person receiving the settlement fails to seasonably present, forward for collection, pay or return a remittance instrument or authorization to it to charge before its midnight deadline,—at such midnight deadline.

§ 4–212. Right of Charge-Back or Refund.

(1) If a collecting bank has made provisional settlement with its customer for an item and itself fails by reason of dishonor, suspension of payments by a bank or otherwise to receive a settlement for the item which is or becomes final, the bank may revoke the settlement given by it, charge-back the amount of any credit given for the item to its customer's account or obtain refund from its customer whether or not it is able to return the items if by its midnight deadline or within a longer reasonable time after it learns the facts it returns the item or sends notification of the facts. These rights to revoke, charge-back and obtain refund terminate if and when a settlement for the item received by the bank is or be-

comes final (subsection (3) of Section 4–211 and subsections (2) and (3) of Section 4–213).

[(2) Within the time and manner prescribed by this section and Section 4–301, an intermediary or payor bank, as the case may be, may return an unpaid item directly to the depositary bank and may send for collection a draft on the depositary bank and obtain reimbursement. In such case, if the depositary bank has received provisional settlement for the item, it must reimburse the bank drawing the draft and any provisional credits for the item between banks shall become and remain final.]

Note: *Direct returns is recognized as an innovation that is not yet established bank practice, and therefore, Paragraph 2 has been bracketed. Some lawyers have doubts whether it should be included in legislation or left to development by agreement.*

(3) A depositary bank which is also the payor may charge-back the amount of an item to its customer's account or obtain refund in accordance with the section governing return of an item received by a payor bank for credit on its books (Section 4–301).

(4) The right to charge-back is not affected by

(a) prior use of the credit given for the item; or

(b) failure by any bank to exercise ordinary care with respect to the item but any bank so failing remains liable.

(5) A failure to charge-back or claim refund does not affect other rights of the bank against the customer or any other party.

(6) If credit is given in dollars as the equivalent of the value of an item payable in a foreign currency the dollar amount of any charge-back or refund shall be calculated on the basis of the buying sight rate for the foreign currency prevailing on the day when the person entitled to the charge-back or refund learns that it will not receive payment in ordinary course.

§ 4–213. Final Payment of Item by Payor Bank; When Provisional Debits and Credits Become Final; When Certain Credits Become Available for Withdrawal.

(1) An item is finally paid by a payor bank when the bank has done any of the following, whichever happens first:

(a) paid the item in cash; or

(b) settled for the item without reserving a right to revoke the settlement and without having such right under statute, clearing house rule or agreement; or

(c) completed the process of posting the item to the indicated account of the drawer, maker or other person to be charged therewith; or

(d) made a provisional settlement for the item and failed to revoke the settlement in the time and manner permitted by statute, clearing house rule or agreement.

Upon a final payment under subparagraphs (b), (c), or (d) the payor bank shall be accountable for the amount of the item.

(2) If provisional settlement for an item between the presenting and payor banks is made through a clearing house or by debits or credits in an account between them, then to the extent that provisional debits or credits for the item are entered in accounts between the presenting and payor banks or between the presenting and successive prior collecting banks seriatim, they become final upon final payment of the item by the payor bank.

(3) If a collecting bank receives a settlement for an item which is or becomes final (subsection (3) of Section 4–211, subsection (2) of Section 4–213) the bank is accountable to its customer for the amount of the item and any provisional credit given for the item in an account with its customer becomes final.

(4) Subject to any right of the bank to apply the credit to an obligation of the customer, credit given by a bank for an item in an account with its customer becomes available for withdrawal as of right

(a) in any case where the bank has received a provisional settlement for the item,—when such settlement becomes final and the bank has had a reasonable time to learn that the settlement is final;

(b) in any case where the bank is both a depositary bank and a payor bank and the item is finally paid,—at the opening of the bank's second banking day following receipt of the item.

(5) A deposit of money in a bank is final when made but, subject to any right of the bank to apply the deposit to an obligation of the customer, the deposit becomes available for withdrawal as of right at the opening of the bank's next banking day following receipt of the deposit.

§ 4–214. Insolvency and Preference.

(1) Any item in or coming into the possession of a payor or collecting bank which suspends payment and which item is not finally paid shall be returned by the receiver, trustee or agent in charge of the closed bank to the presenting bank or the closed bank's customer.

(2) If a payor bank finally pays an item and suspends payments without making a settlement for the item with its customer or the presenting bank which settlement is or becomes final, the owner of the item has a preferred claim against the payor bank.

(3) If a payor bank gives or a collecting bank gives or receives a provisional settlement for an item and there-

after suspends payments, the suspension does not prevent or interfere with the settlement becoming final if such finality occurs automatically upon the lapse of certain time or the happening of certain events (subsection (3) of Section 4–211, subsections (1)(d), (2) and (3) of Section 4–213).

(4) If a collecting bank receives from subsequent parties settlement for an item which settlement is or becomes final and suspends payments without making a settlement for the item with its customer which is or becomes final, the owner of the item has a preferred claim against such collecting bank.

Part 3—Collection of Items: Payor Banks

§ 4–301. Deferred Posting; Recovery of Payment by Return of Items; Time of Dishonor.

(1) Where an authorized settlement for a demand item (other than a documentary draft) received by a payor bank otherwise than for immediate payment over the counter has been made before midnight of the banking day of receipt the payor bank may revoke the settlement and recover any payment if before it has made final payment (subsection (1) of Section 4–213) and before its midnight deadline it

(a) returns the item; or

(b) sends written notice of dishonor or nonpayment if the item is held for protest or is otherwise unavailable for return.

(2) If a demand item is received by a payor bank for credit on its books it may return such item or send notice of dishonor and may revoke any credit given or recover the amount thereof withdrawn by its customer, if it acts within the time limit and in the manner specified in the preceding subsection.

(3) Unless previous notice of dishonor has been sent an item is dishonored at the time when for purposes of dishonor it is returned or notice sent in accordance with this section.

(4) An item is returned:

(a) as to an item received through a clearing house when it is delivered to the presenting or last collecting bank or to the clearing house or is sent or delivered in accordance with its rules; or

(b) in all other cases, when it is sent or delivered to the bank's customer or transferor or pursuant to his instructions.

§ 4–302. Payor Bank's Responsibility for Late Return of Item.

In the absence of a valid defense such as breach of a presentment warranty (subsection (1) of Section 4–207), settlement effected or the like, if an item is presented on and received by a payor bank the bank is accountable for the amount of

(a) a demand item other than a documentary draft whether properly payable or not if the bank, in any case where it is not also the depositary bank, retains the item beyond midnight of the banking day of receipt without settling for it or, regardless of whether it is also the depositary bank, does not pay or return the item or send notice of dishonor until after its midnight deadline; or

(b) any other properly payable item unless within the time allowed for acceptance or payment of that item the bank either accepts or pays the item or returns it and accompanying documents.

§ 4–303. When Items Subject to Notice, Stop-Order, Legal Process or Setoff; Order in Which Items May Be Charged or Certified.

(1) Any knowledge, notice or stop-order received by, legal process served upon or setoff exercised by a payor bank, whether or not effective under other rules of law to terminate, suspend or modify the bank's right or duty to pay an item or to charge its customer's account for the item, comes too late to so terminate, suspend or modify such right or duty if the knowledge, notice, stop-order or legal process is received or served and a reasonable time for the bank to act thereon expires or the setoff is exercised after the bank has done any of the following:

(a) accepted or certified the item;

(b) paid the item in cash;

(c) settled for the item without reserving a right to revoke the settlement and without having such right under statute, clearing house rule or agreement;

(d) completed the process of posting the item to the indicated account of the drawer, maker, or other person to be charged therewith or otherwise has evidenced by examination of such indicated account and by action its decision to pay the item; or

(e) become accountable for the amount of the item under subsection (1)(d) of Section 4–213 and Section 4–302 dealing with the payor bank's responsibility for late return of items.

(2) Subject to the provisions of subsection (1) items may be accepted, paid, certified or charged to the indicated account of its customer in any order convenient to the bank.

Part 4—Relationship Between Payor Bank and Its Customer

§ 4–401. When Bank May Charge Customer's Account.

(1) As against its customer, a bank may charge against his account any item which is otherwise properly pay-able from that account even though the charge creates an overdraft.

(2) A bank which in good faith makes payment to a holder may charge the indicated account of its customer according to

(a) the original tenor of his altered item; or

(b) the tenor of his completed item, even though the bank knows the item has been completed unless the bank has notice that the completion was improper.

§ 4–402. Bank's Liability to Customer for Wrongful Dishonor.

A payor bank is liable to its customer for damages proximately caused by the wrongful dishonor of an item. When the dishonor occurs through mistake liability is limited to actual damages proved. If so proximately caused and proved damages may include damages for an arrest or prosecution of the customer or other consequential damages. Whether any consequential damages are proximately caused by the wrongful dishonor is a question of fact to be determined in each case.

§ 4–403. Customer's Right to Stop Payment; Burden of Proof of Loss.

(1) A customer may by order to his bank stop payment of any item payable for his account but the order must be received at such time and in such manner as to afford the bank a reasonable opportunity to act on it prior to any action by the bank with respect to the item described in Section 4–303.

(2) An oral order is binding upon the bank only for fourteen calendar days unless confirmed in writing within that period. A written order is effective for only six months unless renewed in writing.

(3) The burden of establishing the fact and amount of loss resulting from the payment of an item contrary to a binding stop payment order is on the customer.

§ 4–404. Bank Not Obligated to Pay Check More Than Six Months Old.

A bank is under no obligation to a customer having a checking account to pay a check, other than a certified check, which is presented more than six months after its date, but it may charge its customer's account for a payment made thereafter in good faith.

§ 4–405. Death or Incompetence of Customer.

(1) A payor or collecting bank's authority to accept, pay or collect an item or to account for proceeds of its collection if otherwise effective is not rendered ineffective by incompetence of a customer of either bank existing at the time the item is issued or its collection is undertaken if the bank does not know of an adjudication of incompetence. Neither death nor incompetence of a customer revokes such authority to accept, pay, collect or

account until the bank knows of the fact of death or of an adjudication of incompetence and has reasonable opportunity to act on it.

(2) Even with knowledge a bank may for ten days after the date of death pay or certify checks drawn on or prior to that date unless ordered to stop payment by a person claiming an interest in the account.

§ 4–406. Customer's Duty to Discover and Report Unauthorized Signature or Alteration.

(1) When a bank sends to its customer a statement of account accompanied by items paid in good faith in support of the debit entries or holds the statement and items pursuant to a request or instructions of its customer or otherwise in a reasonable manner makes the statement and items available to the customer, the customer must exercise reasonable care and promptness to examine the statement and items to discover his unauthorized signature or any alteration on an item and must notify the bank promptly after discovery thereof.

(2) If the bank establishes that the customer failed with respect to an item to comply with the duties imposed on the customer by subsection (1) the customer is precluded from asserting against the bank

> (a) his unauthorized signature or any alteration on the item if the bank also establishes that it suffered a loss by reason of such failure; and

> (b) an unauthorized signature or alteration by the same wrongdoer on any other item paid in good faith by the bank after the first item and statement was available to the customer for a reasonable period not exceeding fourteen calendar days and before the bank receives notification from the customer of any such unauthorized signature or alteration.

(3) The preclusion under subsection (2) does not apply if the customer establishes lack of ordinary care on the part of the bank in paying the item(s).

(4) Without regard to care or lack of care of either the customer or the bank a customer who does not within one year from the time the statement and items are made available to the customer (subsection (1)) discover and report his unauthorized signature or any alteration on the face or back of the item or does not within three years from that time discover and report any unauthorized indorsement is precluded from asserting against the bank such unauthorized signature or indorsement or such alteration.

(5) If under this section a payor bank has a valid defense against a claim of a customer upon or resulting from payment of an item and waives or fails upon request to assert the defense the bank may not assert against any collecting bank or other prior party presenting or transferring the item a claim based upon the unauthorized signature or alteration giving rise to the customer's claim.

§ 4–407. Payor Bank's Right to Subrogation on Improper Payment.

If a payor bank has paid an item over the stop payment order of the drawer or maker or otherwise under circumstances giving a basis for objection by the drawer or maker, to prevent unjust enrichment and only to the extent necessary to prevent loss to the bank by reason of its payment of the item, the payor bank shall be subrogated to the rights.

(a) of any holder in due course on the item against the drawer or maker; and

(b) of the payee or any other holder of the item against the drawer or maker either on the item or under the transaction out of which the item arose; and

(c) of the drawer or maker against the payee or any other holder of the item with respect to the transaction out of which the item arose.

Part 5—Collection of Documentary Drafts

§ 4–501. Handling of Documentary Drafts; Duty to Send for Presentment and to Notify Customer of Dishonor.

A bank which takes a documentary draft for collection must present or send the draft and accompanying documents for presentment and upon learning that the draft has not been paid or accepted in due course must seasonably notify its customer of such fact even though it may have discounted or bought the draft or extended credit available for withdrawal as of right.

§ 4–502. Presentment of "On Arrival" Drafts.

When a draft or the relevant instructions require presentment "on arrival", "when goods arrive" or the like, the collecting bank need not present until in its judgment a reasonable time for arrival of the goods has expired. Refusal to pay or accept because the goods have not arrived is not dishonor; the bank must notify its transferor of such refusal but need not present the draft again until it is instructed to do so or learns of the arrival of the goods.

§ 4–503. Responsibility of Presenting Bank for Documents and Goods; Report of Reasons for Dishonor; Referee in Case of Need.

Unless otherwise instructed and except as provided in Article 5 a bank presenting a documentary draft

(a) must deliver the documents to the drawee on acceptance of the draft if it is payable more than three days after presentment; otherwise, only on payment; and

(b) upon dishonor, either in the case of presentment for acceptance or presentment for payment, may seek and follow instructions from any referee in case of need designated in the draft or if the presenting bank does not choose to utilize his services it must use diligence and good faith to ascertain the reason for dishonor, must notify its transferor of the dishonor and of the results of its effort to ascertain the reasons therefor and must request instructions.

But the presenting bank is under no obligation with respect to goods represented by the documents except to follow any reasonable instructions seasonably received; it has a right to reimbursement for any expense incurred in following instructions and to prepayment of or indemnity for such expenses.

§ 4–504. Privilege of Presenting Bank to Deal With Goods; Security Interest for Expenses.

(1) A presenting bank which, following the dishonor of a documentary draft, has seasonably requested instructions but does not receive them within a reasonable time may store, sell, or otherwise deal with the goods in any reasonable manner.

(2) For its reasonable expenses incurred by action under subsection (1) the presenting bank has a lien upon the goods or their proceeds, which may be foreclosed in the same manner as an unpaid seller's lien.

ARTICLE 4A: FUNDS TRANSFERS

Part 1—Subject Matter and Definitions

§ 4A–101. Short Title.

This Article may be cited as Uniform Commercial Code—Funds Transfers.

§ 4A–102. Subject Matter.

Except as otherwise provided in Section 4A–108, this Article applies to funds transfers defined in Section 4A–104.

§ 4A–103. Payment Order—Definitions.

(a) In this Article:

(1) "Payment order" means an instruction of a sender to a receiving bank, transmitted orally, electronically, or in writing, to pay, or to cause another bank to pay, a fixed or determinable amount of money to a beneficiary if:

(i) the instruction does not state a condition to payment to the beneficiary other than time of payment,

(ii) the receiving bank is to be reimbursed by debiting an account of, or otherwise receiving payment from, the sender, and

(iii) the instruction is transmitted by the sender directly to the receiving bank or to an agent,

funds-transfer system, or communication system for transmittal to the receiving bank.

(2) "Beneficiary" means the person to be paid by the beneficiary's bank.

(3) "Beneficiary's bank" means the bank identified in a payment order in which an account of the beneficiary is to be credited pursuant to the order or which otherwise is to make payment to the beneficiary if the order does not provide for payment to an account.

(4) "Receiving bank" means the bank to which the sender's instruction is addressed.

(5) "Sender" means the person giving the instruction to the receiving bank.

(b) If an instruction complying with subsection (a)(1) is to make more than one payment to a beneficiary, the instruction is a separate payment order with respect to each payment.

(c) A payment order is issued when it is sent to the receiving bank.

§ 4A–104. Funds Transfer—Definitions.

In this Article:

(a) "Funds transfer" means the series of transactions, beginning with the originator's payment order, made for the purpose of making payment to the beneficiary of the order. The term includes any payment order issued by the originator's bank or an intermediary bank intended to carry out the originator's payment order. A funds transfer is completed by acceptance by the beneficiary's bank of a payment order for the benefit of the beneficiary of the originator's payment order.

(b) "Intermediary bank" means a receiving bank other than the originator's bank or the beneficiary's bank.

(c) "Originator" means the sender of the first payment order in a funds transfer.

(d) "Originator's bank" means (i) the receiving bank to which the payment order of the originator is issued if the originator is not a bank, or (ii) the originator if the originator is a bank.

§ 4A–105. Other Definitions.

(a) In this Article:

(1) "Authorized account" means a deposit account of a customer in a bank designated by the customer as a source of payment of payment orders issued by the customer to the bank. If a customer does not so designate an account, any account of the customer is an authorized account if payment of a payment order from that account is not inconsistent with a restriction on the use of that account.

(2) "Bank" means a person engaged in the business of banking and includes a savings bank, savings and loan association, credit union, and trust company. A branch or separate office of a bank is a separate bank for purposes of this Article.

(3) "Customer" means a person, including a bank, having an account with a bank or from whom a bank has agreed to receive payment orders.

(4) "Funds-transfer business day" of a receiving bank means the part of a day during which the receiving bank is open for the receipt, processing, and transmittal of payment orders and cancellations and amendments of payment orders.

(5) "Funds-transfer system" means a wire transfer network, automated clearing house, or other communication system of a clearing house or other association of banks through which a payment order by a bank may be transmitted to the bank to which the order is addressed.

(6) "Good faith" means honesty in fact and the observance of reasonable commercial standards of fair dealing.

(7) "Prove" with respect to a fact means to meet the burden of establishing the fact (Section 1–201(8)).

(b) Other definitions applying to this Article and the sections in which they appear are:

"Acceptance" Section 4A–209
"Beneficiary" Section 4A–103
"Beneficiary's bank" Section 4A–103
"Executed" Section 4A–301
"Execution date" Section 4A–301
"Funds transfer" Section 4A–104
"Funds-transfer system rule" Section 4A–501
"Intermediary bank" Section 4A–104
"Originator" Section 4A–104
"Originator's bank" Section 4A–104
"Payment by beneficiary's bank to beneficiary" Section 4A–405
"Payment by originator to beneficiary" Section 4A–406
"Payment by sender to receiving bank" Section 4A–403
"Payment date" Section 4A–401
"Payment order" Section 4A–103
"Receiving bank" Section 4A–103
"Security procedure" Section 4A–201
"Sender" Section 4A–103

(c) The following definitions in Article 4 apply to this Article:

"Clearing house" Section 4–104
"Item" Section 4–104
"Suspends payments" Section 4–104

(d) In addition Article 1 contains general definitions and principles of construction and interpretation applicable throughout this Article.

§ 4A–106. Time Payment Order Is Received.

(a) The time of receipt of a payment order or communication cancelling or amending a payment order is determined by the rules applicable to receipt of a notice stated in Section 1–201(27). A receiving bank may fix a cut-off time or times on a funds-transfer business day for the receipt and processing of payment orders and communications cancelling or amending payment orders. Different cut-off times may apply to payment orders, cancellations, or amendments, or to different categories of payment orders, cancellations, or amendments. A cut-off time may apply to senders generally or different cut-off times may apply to different senders or categories of payment orders. If a payment order or communication cancelling or amending a payment order is received after the close of a funds-transfer business day or after the appropriate cut-off time on a funds-transfer business day, the receiving bank may treat the payment order or communication as received at the opening of the next funds-transfer business day.

(b) If this Article refers to an execution date or payment date or states a day on which a receiving bank is required to take action, and the date or day does not fall on a funds-transfer business day, the next day that is a funds-transfer business day is treated as the date or day stated, unless the contrary is stated in this Article.

§ 4A–107. Federal Reserve Regulations and Operating Circulars.

Regulations of the Board of Governors of the Federal Reserve System and operating circulars of the Federal Reserve Banks supersede any inconsistent provision of this Article to the extent of the inconsistency.

§ 4A–108. Exclusion of Consumer Transactions Governed by Federal Law

This Article does not apply to a funds transfer any part of which is governed by the Electronic Fund Transfer Act of 1978 (Title XX, Public Law 95–630, 92 Stat. 3728, 15 U.S.C. § 1693 et seq.) as amended from time to time.

Part 2—Issue and Acceptance of Payment Order

§ 4A–201. Security Procedure.

"Security procedure" means a procedure established by agreement of a customer and a receiving bank for the purpose of (i) verifying that a payment order or communication amending or cancelling a payment order is that of the customer, or (ii) detecting error in the transmission or the content of the payment order or communication. A security procedure may require the use of algorithms or other codes, identifying words or numbers, encryption, callback procedures, or similar security devices. Comparison of a signature on a payment order or communication with an authorized specimen signature of the customer is not by itself a security procedure.

§ 4A–202. Authorized and Verified Payment Orders.

(a) A payment order received by the receiving bank is the authorized order of the person identified as sender if that person authorized the order or is otherwise bound by it under the law of agency.

(b) If a bank and its customer have agreed that the authenticity of payment orders issued to the bank in the name of the customer as sender will be verified pursuant to a security procedure, a payment order received by the receiving bank is effective as the order of the customer, whether or not authorized, if (i) the security procedure is a commercially reasonable method of providing security against unauthorized payment orders, and (ii) the bank proves that it accepted the payment order in good faith and in compliance with the security procedure and any written agreement or instruction of the customer restricting acceptance of payment orders issued in the name of the customer. The bank is not required to follow an instruction that violates a written agreement with the customer or notice of which is not received at a time and in a manner affording the bank a reasonable opportunity to act on it before the payment order is accepted.

(c) Commercial reasonableness of a security procedure is a question of law to be determined by considering the wishes of the customer expressed to the bank, the circumstances of the customer known to the bank, including the size, type, and frequency of payment orders normally issued by the customer to the bank, alternative security procedures offered to the customer, and security procedures in general use by customers and receiving banks similarly situated. A security procedure is deemed to be commercially reasonable if (i) the security procedure was chosen by the customer after the bank offered, and the customer refused, a security procedure that was commercially reasonable for that customer, and (ii) the customer expressly agreed in writing to be bound by any payment order, whether or not authorized, issued in its name and accepted by the bank in compliance with the security procedure chosen by the customer.

(d) The term "sender" in this Article includes the customer in whose name a payment order is issued if the order is the authorized order of the customer under subsection (a), or it is effective as the order of the customer under subsection (b).

(e) This section applies to amendments and cancellations of payment orders to the same extent it applies to payment orders.

(f) Except as provided in this section and in Section 4A–203(a)(1), rights and obligations arising under this section or Section 4A–203 may not be varied by agreement.

§ 4A–203. Unenforceability of Certain Verified Payment Orders.

(a) If an accepted payment order is not, under Section 4A–202(a), an authorized order of a customer identified as sender, but is effective as an order of the customer pursuant to Section 4A–202(b), the following rules apply:

(1) By express written agreement, the receiving bank may limit the extent to which it is entitled to enforce or retain payment of the payment order.

(2) The receiving bank is not entitled to enforce or retain payment of the payment order if the customer proves that the order was not caused, directly or indirectly, by a person (i) entrusted at any time with duties to act for the customer with respect to payment orders or the security procedure, or (ii) who obtained access to transmitting facilities of the customer or who obtained, from a source controlled by the customer and without authority of the receiving bank, information facilitating breach of the security procedure, regardless of how the information was obtained or whether the customer was at fault. Information includes any access device, computer software, or the like.

(b) This section applies to amendments of payment orders to the same extent it applies to payment orders.

§ 4A–204. Refund of Payment and Duty of Customer to Report with Respect to Unauthorized Payment Order.

(a) If a receiving bank accepts a payment order issued in the name of its customer as sender which is (i) not authorized and not effective as the order of the customer under Section 4A–202, or (ii) not enforceable, in whole or in part, against the customer under Section 4A–203, the bank shall refund any payment of the payment order received from the customer to the extent the bank is not entitled to enforce payment and shall pay interest on the refundable amount calculated from the date the bank received payment to the date of the refund. However, the customer is not entitled to interest from the bank on the amount to be refunded if the customer fails to exercise ordinary care to determine that the order was not authorized by the customer and to notify the bank of the relevant facts within a reasonable time not exceeding 90 days after the date the customer received notification from the bank that the order was accepted or that the customer's account was debited with respect to the order. The bank is not entitled to any recovery from the customer on account of a failure by the customer to give notification as stated in this section.

(b) Reasonable time under subsection (a) may be fixed by agreement as stated in Section 1–204(1), but the obligation of a receiving bank to refund payment as stated in subsection (a) may not otherwise be varied by agreement.

§ 4A–205. Erroneous Payment Orders.

(a) If an accepted payment order was transmitted pursuant to a security procedure for the detection of error and the payment order (i) erroneously instructed payment to a beneficiary not intended by the sender, (ii) erroneously instructed payment in an amount greater than the amount intended by the sender, or (iii) was an erroneously transmitted duplicate of a payment order previously sent by the sender, the following rules apply:

(1) If the sender proves that the sender or a person acting on behalf of the sender pursuant to Section 4A–206 complied with the security procedure and that the error would have been detected if the receiving bank had also complied, the sender is not obliged to pay the order to the extent stated in paragraphs (2) and (3).

(2) If the funds transfer is completed on the basis of an erroneous payment order described in clause (i) or (iii) of subsection (a), the sender is not obliged to pay the order and the receiving bank is entitled to recover from the beneficiary any amount paid to the beneficiary to the extent allowed by the law governing mistake and restitution.

(3) If the funds transfer is completed on the basis of a payment order described in clause (ii) of subsection (a), the sender is not obliged to pay the order to the extent the amount received by the beneficiary is greater than the amount intended by the sender. In that case, the receiving bank is entitled to recover from the beneficiary the excess amount received to the extent allowed by the law governing mistake and restitution.

(b) If (i) the sender of an erroneous payment order described in subsection (a) is not obliged to pay all or part of the order, and (ii) the sender receives notification from the receiving bank that the order was accepted by the bank or that the sender's account was debited with respect to the order, the sender has a duty to exercise ordinary care, on the basis of information available to the sender, to discover the error with respect to the order and to advise the bank of the relevant facts within a reasonable time, not exceeding 90 days, after the bank's notification was received by the sender. If the bank proves that the sender failed to perform that duty, the sender is liable to the bank for the loss the bank proves it incurred as a result of the failure, but the liability of the sender may not exceed the amount of the sender's order.

(c) This section applies to amendments to payment orders to the same extent it applies to payment orders.

§ 4A–206. Transmission of Payment Order Through Funds-Transfer or Other Communication System.

(a) If a payment order addressed to a receiving bank is transmitted to a funds-transfer system or other third-party communication system for transmittal to the bank, the system is deemed to be an agent of the sender for the purpose of transmitting the payment order to the bank. If there is a discrepancy between the terms of the payment order transmitted to the system and the terms of the payment order transmitted by the system to the bank, the terms of the payment order of the sender are those transmitted by the system. This section does not apply to a funds-transfer system of the Federal Reserve Banks.

(b) This section applies to cancellations and amendments of payment orders to the same extent it applies to payment orders.

§ 4A–207. Misdescription of Beneficiary.

(a) Subject to subsection (b), if, in a payment order received by the beneficiary's bank, the name, bank account number, or other identification of the beneficiary refers to a nonexistent or unidentifiable person or account, no person has rights as a beneficiary of the order and acceptance of the order cannot occur.

(b) If a payment order received by the beneficiary's bank identifies the beneficiary both by name and by an identifying or bank account number and the name and number identify different persons, the following rules apply:

(1) Except as otherwise provided in subsection (c), if the beneficiary's bank does not know that the name and number refer to different persons, it may rely on the number as the proper identification of the beneficiary of the order. The beneficiary's bank need not determine whether the name and number refer to the same person.

(2) If the beneficiary's bank pays the person identified by name or knows that the name and number identify different persons, no person has rights as beneficiary except the person paid by the beneficiary's bank if that person was entitled to receive payment from the originator of the funds transfer. If no person has rights as beneficiary, acceptance of the order cannot occur.

(c) If (i) a payment order described in subsection (b) is accepted, (ii) the originator's payment order described the beneficiary inconsistently by name and number, and (ii) the beneficiary's bank pays the person identified by number as permitted by subsection (b)(1), the following rules apply:

(1) If the originator is a bank, the originator is obliged to pay its order.

(2) If the originator is not a bank and proves that the person identified by number was not entitled to receive payment from the originator, the originator is not obliged to pay its order unless the originator's bank proves that the originator, before acceptance of the originator's order, had notice that payment of a

payment order issued by the originator might be made by the beneficiary's bank on the basis of an identifying or bank account number even if it identifies a person different from the named beneficiary. Proof of notice may be made by any admissible evidence. The originator's bank satisfies the burden of proof if it proves that the originator, before the payment order was accepted, signed a writing stating the information to which the notice relates.

(d) In a case governed by subsection (b)(1), if the beneficiary's bank rightfully pays the person identified by number and that person was not entitled to receive payment from the originator, the amount paid may be recovered from that person to the extent allowed by the law governing mistake and restitution as follows:

(1) If the originator is obliged to pay its payment order as stated in subsection (c), the originator has the right to recover.

(2) If the originator is not a bank and is not obliged to pay its payment order, the originator's bank has the right to recover.

§ 4A–208. Misdescription of Intermediary Bank or Beneficiary's Bank.

(a) This subsection applies to a payment order identifying an intermediary bank or the beneficiary's bank only by an identifying number.

(1) The receiving bank may rely on the number as the proper identification of the intermediary or beneficiary's bank and need not determine whether the number identifies a bank.

(2) The sender is obliged to compensate the receiving bank for any loss and expenses incurred by the receiving bank as a result of its reliance on the number in executing or attempting to execute the order.

(b) This subsection applies to a payment order identifying an intermediary bank or the beneficiary's bank both by name and an identifying number if the name and number identify different persons.

(1) If the sender is a bank, the receiving bank may rely on the number as the proper identification of the intermediary or beneficiary's bank if the receiving bank, when it executes the sender's order, does not know that the name and number identify different persons. The receiving bank need not determine whether the name and number refer to the same person or whether the name refers to a bank. The sender is obliged to compensate the receiving bank for any loss and expenses incurred by the receiving bank as a result of its reliance on the number in executing or attempting to execute the order.

(2) If the sender is not a bank and the receiving bank proves that the sender, before the payment order was accepted, had notice that the receiving bank might rely on the number as the proper identification of the intermediary or beneficiary's bank even if it identifies a person different from the bank identified by name, the rights and obligations of the sender and the receiving bank are governed by subsection (b)(1), as though the sender were a bank. Proof of notice may be made by any admissible evidence. The receiving bank satisfies the burden of proof if it proves that the sender, before the payment order was accepted, signed a writing stating the information to which the notice relates.

(3) Regardless of whether the sender is a bank, the receiving bank may rely on the name as the proper identification of the intermediary or beneficiary's bank if the receiving bank, at the time it executes the sender's order, does not know that the name and number identify different persons. The receiving bank need not determine whether the name and number refer to the same person.

(4) If the receiving bank knows that the name and number identify different persons, reliance on either the name or the number in executing the sender's payment order is a breach of the obligation stated in Section 4A–302(a)(1).

§ 4A–209. Acceptance of Payment Order.

(a) Subject to subsection (d), a receiving bank other than the beneficiary's bank accepts a payment order when it executes the order.

(b) Subject to subsections (c) and (d), a beneficiary's bank accepts a payment order at the earliest of the following times:

(1) when the bank (i) pays the beneficiary as stated in Section 4A–405(a) or 4A–405(b), or (ii) notifies the beneficiary of receipt of the order or that the account of the beneficiary has been credited with respect to the order unless the notice indicates that the bank is rejecting the order or that funds with respect to the order may not be withdrawn or used until receipt of payment from the sender of the order;

(2) when the bank receives payment of the entire amount of the sender's order pursuant to Section 4A–403(a)(1) or 4A–403(a)(2); or

(3) the opening of the next funds-transfer business day of the bank following the payment date of the order if, at that time, the amount of the sender's order is fully covered by a withdrawable credit balance in an authorized account of the sender or the bank has otherwise received full payment from the sender, unless the order was rejected before that time or is rejected within (i) one hour after that time, or (ii) one hour after the opening of the next business day of the sender following the payment date if that time is later. If notice of rejection is received by the sender after the payment date and the authorized

account of the sender does not bear interest, the bank is obliged to pay interest to the sender on the amount of the order for the number of days elapsing after the payment date to the day the sender receives notice or learns that the order was not accepted, counting that day as an elapsed day. If the withdrawable credit balance during that period falls below the amount of the order, the amount of interest payable is reduced accordingly.

(c) Acceptance of a payment order cannot occur before the order is received by the receiving bank. Acceptance does not occur under subsection (b)(2) or (b)(3) if the beneficiary of the payment order does not have an account with the receiving bank, the account has been closed, or the receiving bank is not permitted by law to receive credits for the beneficiary's account.

(d) A payment order issued to the originator's bank cannot be accepted until the payment date if the bank is the beneficiary's bank, or the execution date if the bank is not the beneficiary's bank. If the originator's bank executes the originator's payment order before the execution date or pays the beneficiary of the originator's payment order before the payment date and the payment order is subsequently canceled pursuant to Section 4A–211(b), the bank may recover from the beneficiary any payment received to the extent allowed by the law governing mistake and restitution.

§ 4A–210. Rejection of Payment Order.

(a) A payment order is rejected by the receiving bank by a notice of rejection transmitted to the sender orally, electronically, or in writing. A notice of rejection need not use any particular words and is sufficient if it indicates that the receiving bank is rejecting the order or will not execute or pay the order. Rejection is effective when the notice is given if transmission is by a means that is reasonable in the circumstances. If notice of rejection is given by a means that is not reasonable, rejection is effective when the notice is received. If an agreement of the sender and receiving bank establishes the means to be used to reject a payment order, (i) any means complying with the agreement is reasonable and (ii) any means not complying is not reasonable unless no significant delay in receipt of the notice resulted from the use of the noncomplying means.

(b) This subsection applies if a receiving bank other than the beneficiary's bank fails to execute a payment order despite the existence on the execution date of a withdrawable credit balance in an authorized account of the sender sufficient to cover the order. If the sender does not receive notice of rejection of the order on the execution date and the authorized account of the sender does not bear interest, the bank is obliged to pay interest to the sender on the amount of the order for the number of days elapsing after the execution date to the earlier of the day the order is canceled pursuant to Section 4A–211(d) or the day the sender receives notice or learns that the order was not executed, counting the final day of the period as an elapsed day. If the withdrawable credit balance during that period falls below the amount of the order, the amount of interest is reduced accordingly.

(c) If a receiving bank suspends payments, all unaccepted payment orders issued to it are deemed rejected at the time the bank suspends payments.

(d) Acceptance of a payment order precludes a later rejection of the order. Rejection of a payment order precludes a later acceptance of the order.

§ 4A–211. Cancellation and Amendment of Payment Order.

(a) A communication of the sender of a payment order cancelling or amending the order may be transmitted to the receiving bank orally, electronically, or in writing. If a security procedure is in effect between the sender and the receiving bank, the communication is not effective to cancel or amend the order unless the communication is verified pursuant to the security procedure or the bank agrees to the cancellation or amendment.

(b) Subject to subsection (a), a communication by the sender cancelling or amending a payment order is effective to cancel or amend the order if notice of the communication is received at a time and in a manner affording the receiving bank a reasonable opportunity to act on the communication before the bank accepts the payment order.

(c) After a payment order has been accepted, cancellation or amendment of the order is not effective unless the receiving bank agrees or a funds-transfer system rule allows cancellation or amendment without agreement of the bank.

(1) With respect to a payment order accepted by a receiving bank other than the beneficiary's bank, cancellation or amendment is not effective unless a conforming cancellation or amendment of the payment order issued by the receiving bank is also made.

(2) With respect to a payment order accepted by the beneficiary's bank, cancellation or amendment is not effective unless the order was issued in execution of an unauthorized payment order, or because of a mistake by a sender in the funds transfer which resulted in the issuance of a payment order (i) that is a duplicate of a payment order previously issued by the sender, (ii) that orders payment to a beneficiary not entitled to receive payment from the originator, or (iii) that orders payment in an amount greater than the amount the beneficiary was entitled to receive from the originator. If the payment order is canceled or amended, the beneficiary's bank is entitled to recover from the beneficiary any amount paid to the beneficiary to the extent allowed by the law governing mistake and restitution.

(d) An unaccepted payment order is canceled by operation of law at the close of the fifth funds-transfer business day of the receiving bank after the execution date or payment date of the order.

(e) A canceled payment order cannot be accepted. If an accepted payment order is canceled, the acceptance is nullified and no person has any right or obligation based on the acceptance. Amendment of a payment order is deemed to be cancellation of the original order at the time of amendment and issue of a new payment order in the amended form at the same time.

(f) Unless otherwise provided in an agreement of the parties or in a funds-transfer system rule, if the receiving bank, after accepting a payment order, agrees to cancellation or amendment of the order by the sender or is bound by a funds-transfer system rule allowing cancellation or amendment without the bank's agreement, the sender, whether or not cancellation or amendment is effective, is liable to the bank for any loss and expenses, including reasonable attorney's fees, incurred by the bank as a result of the cancellation or amendment or attempted cancellation or amendment.

(g) A payment order is not revoked by the death or legal incapacity of the sender unless the receiving bank knows of the death or of an adjudication of incapacity by a court of competent jurisdiction and has reasonable opportunity to act before acceptance of the order.

(h) A funds-transfer system rule is not effective to the extent it conflicts with subsection (c)(2).

§ 4A–212. Liability and Duty of Receiving Bank Regarding Unaccepted Payment Order.

If a receiving bank fails to accept a payment order that it is obliged by express agreement to accept, the bank is liable for breach of the agreement to the extent provided in the agreement or in this Article, but does not otherwise have any duty to accept a payment order or, before acceptance, to take any action, or refrain from taking action, with respect to the order except as provided in this Article or by express agreement. Liability based on acceptance arises only when acceptance occurs as stated in Section 4A–209, and liability is limited to that provided in this Article. A receiving bank is not the agent of the sender or beneficiary of the payment order it accepts, or of any other party to the funds transfer, and the bank owes no duty to any party to the funds transfer except as provided in this Article or by express agreement.

Part 3—Execution of Sender's Payment Order by Receiving Bank

§ 4A–301. Execution and Execution Date.

(a) A payment order is "executed" by the receiving bank when it issues a payment order intended to carry out the payment order received by the bank. A payment order received by the beneficiary's bank can be accepted but cannot be executed.

(b) "Execution date" of a payment order means the day on which the receiving bank may properly issue a payment order in execution of the sender's order. The execution date may be determined by instruction of the sender but cannot be earlier than the day the order is received and, unless otherwise determined, is the day the order is received. If the sender's instruction states a payment date, the execution date is the payment date or an earlier date on which execution is reasonably necessary to allow payment to the beneficiary on the payment date.

§ 4A–302. Obligations of Receiving Bank in Execution of Payment Order.

(a) Except as provided in subsections (b) through (d), if the receiving bank accepts a payment order pursuant to Section 4A–209(a), the bank has the following obligations in executing the order:

(1) The receiving bank is obliged to issue, on the execution date, a payment order complying with the sender's order and to follow the sender's instructions concerning (i) any intermediary bank or funds-transfer system to be used in carrying out the funds transfer, or (ii) the means by which payment orders are to be transmitted in the funds transfer. If the originator's bank issues a payment order to an intermediary bank, the originator's bank is obliged to instruct the intermediary bank according to the instruction of the originator. An intermediary bank in the funds transfer is similarly bound by an instruction given to it by the sender of the payment order it accepts.

(2) If the sender's instruction states that the funds transfer is to be carried out telephonically or by wire transfer or otherwise indicates that the funds transfer is to be carried out by the most expeditious means, the receiving bank is obliged to transmit its payment order by the most expeditious available means, and to instruct any intermediary bank accordingly. If a sender's instruction states a payment date, the receiving bank is obliged to transmit its payment order at a time and by means reasonably necessary to allow payment to the beneficiary on the payment date or as soon thereafter as is feasible.

(b) Unless otherwise instructed, a receiving bank executing a payment order may (i) use any funds-transfer system if use of that system is reasonable in the circumstances, and (ii) issue a payment order to the beneficiary's bank or to an intermediary bank through which a payment order conforming to the sender's order can expeditiously be issued to the beneficiary's bank if the receiving bank exercises ordinary care in the selection of the intermediary bank. A receiving bank is not required to follow an instruction of the sender designating a funds-transfer system to be used in carrying out the funds transfer if the receiving bank, in good faith, determines that it is not feasible to follow the instruction or that following the instruction would unduly delay completion of the funds transfer.

(c) Unless subsection (a)(2) applies or the receiving bank is otherwise instructed, the bank may execute a payment order by transmitting its payment order by first class mail or by any means reasonable in the circumstances. If the receiving bank is instructed to execute the sender's order by transmitting its payment order by a particular means, the receiving bank may issue its payment order by the means stated or by any means as expeditious as the means stated.

(d) Unless instructed by the sender, (i) the receiving bank may not obtain payment of its charges for services and expenses in connection with the execution of the sender's order by issuing a payment order in an amount equal to the amount of the sender's order less the amount of the charges, and (ii) may not instruct a subsequent receiving bank to obtain payment of its charges in the same manner.

§ 4A–303. Erroneous Execution of Payment Order.

(a) A receiving bank that (i) executes the payment order of the sender by issuing a payment order in an amount greater than the amount of the sender's order, or (ii) issues a payment order in execution of the sender's order and then issues a duplicate order, is entitled to payment of the amount of the sender's order under Section 4A–402(c) if that subsection is otherwise satisfied. The bank is entitled to recover from the beneficiary of the erroneous order the excess payment received to the extent allowed by the law governing mistake and restitution.

(b) A receiving bank that executes the payment order of the sender by issuing a payment order in an amount less than the amount of the sender's order is entitled to payment of the amount of the sender's order under Section 4A–402(c) if (i) that subsection is otherwise satisfied and (ii) the bank corrects its mistake by issuing an additional payment order for the benefit of the beneficiary of the sender's order. If the error is not corrected, the issuer of the erroneous order is entitled to receive or retain payment from the sender of the order it accepted only to the extent of the amount of the erroneous order. This subsection does not apply if the receiving bank executes the sender's payment order by issuing a payment order in an amount less than the amount of the sender's order for the purpose of obtaining payment of its charges for services and expenses pursuant to instruction of the sender.

(c) If a receiving bank executes the payment order of the sender by issuing a payment order to a beneficiary different from the beneficiary of the sender's order and the funds transfer is completed on the basis of that error, the sender of the payment order that was erroneously executed and all previous senders in the funds transfer are not obliged to pay the payment orders they issued. The issuer of the erroneous order is entitled to recover from the beneficiary of the order the payment received to the extent allowd by the law governing mistake and restitution.

§ 4A–304. Duty of Sender to Report Erroneously Executed Payment Order.

If the sender of a payment order that is erroneously executed as stated in Section 4A–303 receives notification from the receiving bank that the order was executed or that the sender's account was debited with respect to the order, the sender has a duty to exercise ordinary care to determine, on the basis of information available to the sender, that the order was erroneously executed and to notify the bank of the relevant facts within a reasonable time not exceeding 90 days after the notification from the bank was received by the sender. If the sender fails to perform that duty, the bank is not obliged to pay interest on any amount refundable to the sender under Section 4A–402(d) for the period before the bank learns of the execution error. The bank is not entitled to any recovery from the sender on account of a failure by the sender to perform the duty stated in this section.

§ 4A–305. Liability for Late or Improper Execution or Failure to Execute Payment Order.

(a) If a funds transfer is completed but execution of a payment order by the receiving bank in breach of Section 4A–302 results in delay in payment to the beneficiary, the bank is obliged to pay interest to either the originator or the beneficiary of the funds transfer for the period of delay caused by the improper execution. Except as provided in subsection (c), additional damages are not recoverable.

(b) If execution of a payment order by a receiving bank in breach of Section 4A–302 results in (i) noncompletion of the funds transfer, (ii) failure to use an intermediary bank designated by the originator, or (iii) issuance of a payment order that does not comply with the terms of the payment order of the originator, the bank is liable to the originator for its expenses in the funds transfer and for incidental expenses and interest losses, to the extent not covered by subsection (a), resulting from the improper execution. Except as provided in subsection (c), additional damages are not recoverable.

(c) In addition to the amounts payable under subsections (a) and (b), damages, including consequential damages, are recoverable to the extent provided in an express written agreement of the receiving bank.

(d) If a receiving bank fails to execute a payment order it was obliged by express agreement to execute, the receiving bank is liable to the sender for its expenses in the transaction and for incidental expenses and interest losses resulting from the failure to execute. Additional damages, including consequential damages, are recoverable to the extent provided in an express written agreement of the receiving bank, but are not otherwise recoverable.

(e) Reasonable attorney's fees are recoverable if demand for compensation under subsection (a) or (b) is made and refused before an action is brought on the claim. If a claim is made for breach of an agreement under subsection (d) and the agreement does not provide for damages, reasonable attorney's fees are recoverable if demand for compensation under subsection (d) is made and refused before an action is brought on the claim.

(f) Except as stated in this section, the liability of a receiving bank under subsections (a) and (b) may not be varied by agreement.

Part 4—Payment

§ 4A–401. Payment Date.

"Payment date" of a payment order means the day on which the amount of the order is payable to the beneficiary by the beneficiary's bank. The payment date may be determined by instruction of the sender but cannot be earlier than the day the order is received by the beneficiary's bank and, unless otherwise determined, is the day the order is received by the beneficiary's bank.

§ 4A–402. Obligation of Sender to Pay Receiving Bank.

(a) This section is subject to Sections 4A–205 and 4A–207.

(b) With respect to a payment order issued to the beneficiary's bank, acceptance of the order by the bank obliges the sender to pay the bank the amount of the order, but payment is not due until the payment date of the order.

(c) This subsection is subject to subsection (e) and to Section 4A–303. With respect to a payment order issued to a receiving bank other than the beneficiary's bank, acceptance of the order by the receiving bank obliges the sender to pay the bank the amount of the sender's order. Payment by the sender is not due until the execution date of the sender's order. The obligation of that sender to pay its payment order is excused if the funds transfer is not completed by acceptance by the beneficiary's bank of a payment order instructing payment to the beneficiary of that sender's payment order.

(d) If the sender of a payment order pays the order and was not obliged to pay all or part of the amount paid, the bank receiving payment is obliged to refund payment to the extent the sender was not obliged to pay. Except as provided in Sections 4A–204 and 4A–304, interest is payable on the refundable amount from the date of payment.

(e) If a funds transfer is not completed as stated in subsection (c) and an intermediary bank is obliged to refund payment as stated in subsection (d) but is unable to do so because not permitted by applicable law or because the bank suspends payments, a sender in the funds transfer that executed a payment order in compliance with an instruction, as stated in Section 4A–302(a)(1), to route the funds transfer through that intermediary bank is entitled to receive or retain payment from the sender of the payment order that it accepted. The first sender in the funds transfer that issued an instruction requiring routing through that intermediary bank is subrogated to the right of the bank that paid the intermediary bank to refund as stated in subsection (d).

(f) The right of the sender of a payment order to be excused from the obligation to pay the order as stated in subsection (c) or to receive refund under subsection (d) may not be varied by agreement.

§ 4A–403. Payment by Sender to Receiving Bank.

(a) Payment of the sender's obligation under Section 4A–402 to pay the receiving bank occurs as follows:

(1) If the sender is a bank, payment occurs when the receiving bank receives final settlement of the obligation through a Federal Reserve Bank or through a funds-transfer system.

(2) If the sender is a bank and the sender (i) credited an account of the receiving bank with the sender, or (ii) caused an account of the receiving bank in another bank to be credited, payment occurs when the credit is withdrawn or, if not withdrawn, at midnight of the day on which the credit is withdrawable and the receiving bank learns of that fact.

(3) If the receiving bank debits an account of the sender with the receiving bank, payment occurs when the debit is made to the extent the debit is covered by a withdrawable credit balance in the account.

(b) If the sender and receiving bank are members of a funds-transfer system that nets obligations multilaterally among participants, the receiving bank receives final settlement when settlement is complete in accordance with the rules of the system. The obligation of the sender to pay the amount of a payment order transmitted through the funds-transfer system may be satisfied, to the extent permitted by the rules of the system, by setting off and applying against the sender's obligation the right of the sender to receive payment from the receiving bank of the amount of any other payment order transmitted to the sender by the receiving bank through the funds-transfer system. The aggregate balance of obligations owed by each sender to each receiving bank in the funds-transfer system may be satisfied, to the extent permitted by the rules of the system, by setting off and applying against that balance the aggregate balance of obligations owed to the sender by other members of the system. The aggregate balance is determined after the right of setoff stated in the second sentence of this subsection has been exercised.

(c) If two banks transmit payment orders to each other under an agreement that settlement of the obligations of each bank to the other under Section 4A–402 will be made at the end of the day or other period, the total amount owed with respect to all orders transmitted by one bank shall be set off against the total amount owed with respect to all orders transmitted by the other bank. To the extent of the setoff, each bank has made payment to the other.

(d) In a case not covered by subsection (a), the time when payment of the sender's obligation under Section 4A–402(b) or 4A–402(c) occurs is governed by applicable principles of law that determine when an obligation is satisfied.

§ 4A–404. Obligation of Beneficiary's Bank to Pay and Give Notice to Beneficiary.

(a) Subject to Sections 4A–211(e), 4A–405(d), and 4A–405(e), if a beneficiary's bank accepts a payment order, the bank is obliged to pay the amount of the order to the beneficiary of the order. Payment is due on the payment date of the order, but if acceptance occurs on the payment date after the close of the funds-transfer business day of the bank, payment is due on the next funds-transfer business day. If the bank refuses to pay after demand by the beneficiary and receipt of notice of particular circumstances that will give rise to consequential damages as a result of nonpayment, the beneficiary may recover damages resulting from the refusal to pay to the extent the bank had notice of the damages, unless the bank proves that it did not pay because of a reasonable doubt concerning the right of the beneficiary to payment.

(b) If a payment order accepted by the beneficiary's bank instructs payment to an account of the beneficiary, the bank is obliged to notify the beneficiary of receipt of the order before midnight of the next funds-transfer business day following the payment date. If the payment order does not instruct payment to an account of the beneficiary, the bank is required to notify the beneficiary only if notice is required by the order. Notice may be given by first class mail or any other means reasonable in the circumstances. If the bank fails to give the required notice, the bank is obliged to pay interest to the beneficiary on the amount of the payment order from the day notice should have been given until the day the beneficiary learned of receipt of the payment order by the bank. No other damages are recoverable. Reasonable attorney's fees are also recoverable if demand for interest is made and refused before an action is brought on the claim.

(c) The right of a beneficiary to receive payment and damages as stated in subsection (a) may not be varied by agreement or a funds-transfer system rule. The right of a beneficiary to be notified as stated in subsection (b) may be varied by agreement of the beneficiary or by a funds-transfer system rule if the beneficiary is notified of the rule before initiation of the funds transfer.

§ 4A–405. Payment by Beneficiary's Bank to Beneficiary.

(a) If the beneficiary's bank credits an account of the beneficiary of a payment order, payment of the bank's obligation under Section 4A–404(a) occurs when and to the extent (i) the beneficiary is notified of the right to withdraw the credit, (ii) the bank lawfully applies the credit to a debt of the beneficiary, or (iii) funds with respect to the order are otherwise made available to the beneficiary by the bank.

(b) If the beneficiary's bank does not credit an account of the beneficiary of a payment order, the time when payment of the bank's obligation under Section 4A–404(a) occurs is governed by principles of law that determine when an obligation is satisfied.

(c) Except as stated in subsections (d) and (e), if the beneficiary's bank pays the beneficiary of a payment order under a condition to payment or agreement of the beneficiary giving the bank the right to recover payment from the beneficiary if the bank does not receive payment of the order, the condition to payment or agreement is not enforceable.

(d) A funds-transfer system rule may provide that payments made to beneficiaries of funds transfers made through the system are provisional until receipt of payment by the beneficiary's bank of the payment order it accepted. A beneficiary's bank that makes a payment that is provisional under the rule is entitled to refund from the beneficiary if (i) the rule requires that both the beneficiary and the originator be given notice of the provisional nature of the payment before the funds transfer is initiated, (ii) the beneficiary, the beneficiary's bank and the originator's bank agreed to be bound by the rule, and (iii) the beneficiary's bank did not receive payment of the payment order that it accepted. If the beneficiary is obliged to refund payment to the beneficiary's bank, acceptance of the payment order by the beneficiary's bank is nullified and no payment by the originator of the funds transfer to the beneficiary occurs under Section 4A–406.

(e) This subsection applies to a funds transfer that includes a payment order transmitted over a funds-transfer system that (i) nets obligations multilaterally among participants, and (ii) has in effect a loss-sharing agreement among participants for the purpose of providing funds necessary to complete settlement of the obligations of one or more participants that do not meet their settlement obligations. If the beneficiary's bank in the funds transfer accepts a payment order and the system fails to complete settlement pursuant to its rules with respect to any payment order in the funds transfer, (i) the acceptance by the beneficiary's bank is nullified and no person has any right or obligation based on the acceptance, (ii) the beneficiary's bank is entitled to recover payment from the beneficiary, (iii) no payment by the originator to the beneficiary occurs under Section 4A–406, and (iv) subject to Section 4A–402(e), each sender in the funds transfer is excused from its obligation to pay its payment order under Section 4A–402 (c) because the funds transfer has not been completed.

§ 4A–406. Payment by Originator to Beneficiary; Discharge of Underlying Obligation.

(a) Subject to Sections 4A–211(e), 4A–405(d), and 4A–405(e), the originator of a funds transfer pays the beneficiary of the originator's payment order (i) at the time a payment order for the benefit of the beneficiary is accepted by the beneficiary's bank in the funds transfer and (ii) in an amount equal to the amount of the order accepted by the beneficiary's bank, but not more than the amount of the originator's order.

(b) If payment under subsection (a) is made to satisfy an obligation, the obligation is discharged to the same extent discharge would result from payment to the beneficiary of the same amount in money, unless (i) the payment under subsection (a) was made by a means prohibited by the contract of the beneficiary with respect to the obligation, (ii) the beneficiary, within a reasonable time after receiving notice of receipt of the order by the beneficiary's bank, notified the originator of the beneficiary's refusal of the payment, (iii) funds with respect to the order were not withdrawn by the beneficiary or applied to a debt of the beneficiary, and (iv) the beneficiary would suffer a loss that could reasonably have been avoided if payment had been made by a means complying with the contract. If payment by the originator does not result in discharge under this section, the originator is subrogated to the rights of the beneficiary to receive payment from the beneficiary's bank under Section 4A–404(a).

(c) For the purpose of determining whether discharge of an obligation occurs under subsection (b), if the beneficiary's bank accepts a payment order in an amount equal to the amount of the originator's payment order less charges of one or more receiving banks in the funds transfer, payment to the beneficiary is deemed to be in the amount of the originator's order unless upon demand by the beneficiary the originator does not pay the beneficiary the amount of the deducted charges.

(d) Rights of the originator or of the beneficiary of a funds transfer under this section may be varied only by agreement of the originator and the beneficiary.

Part 5—Miscellaneous Provisions

§ 4A–501. Variation by Agreement and Effect of Funds-Transfer System Rule.

(a) Except as otherwise provided in this Article, the rights and obligations of a party to a funds transfer may be varied by agreement of the affected party.

(b) "Funds-transfer system rule" means a rule of an association of banks (i) governing transmission of payment orders by means of a funds-transfer system of the association or rights and obligations with respect to those orders, or (ii) to the extent the rule governs rights and obligations between banks that are parties to a funds transfer in which a Federal Reserve Bank, acting as an intermediary bank, sends a payment order to the beneficiary's bank. Except as otherwise provided in this Article, a funds-transfer system rule governing rights and obligations between participating banks using the system may be effective even if the rule conflicts with this Article and indirectly affects another party to the funds transfer who does not consent to the rule. A funds-transfer system rule may also govern rights and obligations of parties other than participating banks using the system to the extent stated in Sections 4A–404(c), 4A–405(d), and 4A–507(c).

§ 4A–502. Creditor Process Served on Receiving Bank; Setoff by Beneficiary's Bank.

(a) As used in this section, "creditor process" means levy, attachment, garnishment, notice of lien, sequestration, or similar process issued by or on behalf of a creditor or other claimant with respect to an account.

(b) This subsection applies to creditor process with respect to an authorized account of the sender of a payment order if the creditor process is served on the receiving bank. For the purpose of determining rights with respect to the creditor process, if the receiving bank accepts the payment order the balance in the authorized account is deemed to be reduced by the amount of the payment order to the extent the bank did not otherwise receive payment of the order, unless the creditor process is served at a time and in a manner affording the bank a reasonable opportunity to act on it before the bank accepts the payment order.

(c) If a beneficiary's bank has received a payment order for payment to the beneficiary's account in the bank, the following rules apply:

(1) The bank may credit the beneficiary's account. The amount credited may be set off against an obligation owed by the beneficiary to the bank or may be applied to satisfy creditor process served on the bank with respect to the account.

(2) The bank may credit the beneficiary's account and allow withdrawal of the amount credited unless creditor process with respect to the account is served at a time and in a manner affording the bank a reasonable opportunity to act to prevent withdrawal.

(3) If creditor process with respect to the beneficiary's account has been served and the bank has had a reasonable opportunity to act on it, the bank may not reject the payment order except for a reason unrelated to the service of process.

(d) Creditor process with respect to a payment by the originator to the beneficiary pursuant to a funds transfer may be served only on the beneficiary's bank with respect to the debt owed by that bank to the beneficiary. Any other bank served with the creditor process is not obliged to act with respect to the process.

§ 4A–503. Injunction or Restraining Order With Respect to Funds Transfer.

For proper cause and in compliance with applicable law, a court may restrain (i) a person from issuing a payment order to initiate a funds transfer, (ii) an originator's bank from executing the payment order of the originator, or (iii) the beneficiary's bank from releasing funds to the beneficiary or the beneficiary from withdrawing the funds. A court may not otherwise restrain a person from issuing a payment order, paying or receiving payment of a payment order, or otherwise acting with respect to a funds transfer.

§ 4A–504. Order in Which Items and Payment Orders May Be Charged to Account; Order of Withdrawals From Account.

(a) If a receiving bank has received more than one payment order of the sender or one or more payment orders and other items that are payable from the sender's account, the bank may charge the sender's account with respect to the various orders and items in any sequence.

(b) In determining whether a credit to an account has been withdrawn by the holder of the account or applied to a debt of the holder of the account, credits first made to the account are first withdrawn or applied.

§ 4A–505. Preclusion of Objection to Debit of Customer's Account.

If a receiving bank has received payment from its customer with respect to a payment order issued in the name of the customer as sender and accepted by the bank, and the customer received notification reasonably identifying the order, the customer is precluded from asserting that the bank is not entitled to retain the payment unless the customer notifies the bank of the customer's objection to the payment within one year after the notification was received by the customer.

§ 4A–506. Rate of Interest.

(a) If, under this Article, a receiving bank is obliged to pay interest with respect to a payment order issued to the bank, the amount payable may be determined (i) by agreement of the sender and receiving bank, or (ii) by a funds-transfer system rule if the payment order is transmitted through a funds-transfer system.

(b) If the amount of interest is not determined by an agreement or rule as stated in subsection (a), the amount is calculated by multiplying the applicable Federal Funds rate by the amount on which interest is payable, and then multiplying the product by the number of days for which interest is payable. The applicable Federal Funds rate is the average of the Federal Funds rates published by the Federal Reserve Bank of New York for each of the days for which interest is payable divided by 360. The Federal Funds rate for any day on which a published rate is not available is the same as the published rate for the next preceding day for which there is a published rate. If a receiving bank that accepted a payment order is required to refund payment to the sender of the order because the funds transfer was not completed, but the failure to complete was not due to any fault by the bank, the interest payable is reduced by a percentage equal to the reserve requirement on deposits of the receiving bank.

§ 4A–507. Choice of Law.

(a) The following rules apply unless the affected parties otherwise agree or subsection (c) applies:

(1) The rights and obligations between the sender of a payment order and the receiving bank are governed by the law of the jurisdiction in which the receiving bank is located.

(2) The rights and obligations between the beneficiary's bank and the beneficiary are governed by the law of the jurisdiction in which the beneficiary's bank is located.

(3) The issue of when payment is made pursuant to a funds transfer by the originator to the beneficiary is governed by the law of the jurisdiction in which the beneficiary's bank is located.

(b) If the parties described in each paragraph of subsection (a) have made an agreement selecting the law of a particular jurisdiction to govern rights and obligations between each other, the law of that jurisdiction governs those rights and obligations, whether or not the payment order or the funds transfer bears a reasonable relation to that jurisdiction.

(c) A funds-transfer system rule may select the law of a particular jurisdiction to govern (i) rights and obligations between participating banks with respect to payment orders transmitted or processed through the system, or (ii) the rights and obligations of some or all parties to a funds transfer any part of which is carried out by means of the system. A choice of law made pursuant to clause (i) is binding on participating banks. A choice of law made pursuant to clause (ii) is binding on the originator, other sender, or a receiving bank having notice that the funds-transfer system might be used in the funds transfer and of the choice of law by the system when the originator, other sender, or receiving bank issued or accepted a payment order. The beneficiary of a funds transfer is bound by the choice of law if, when the funds transfer is initiated, the beneficiary has notice that the funds-transfer system might be used in the funds transfer and of the choice of law by the system. The law of a jurisdiction selected pursuant to this subsection may govern, whether or not that law bears a reasonable relation to the matter in issue.

(d) In the event of inconsistency between an agreement under subsection (b) and a choice-of-law rule under subsection (c), the agreement under subsection (b) prevails.

(e) If a funds transfer is made by use of more than one funds-transfer system and there is inconsistency between choice-of-law rules of the systems, the matter in issue is governed by the law of the selected jurisdiction that has the most significant relationship to the matter in issue.

ARTICLE 5: LETTERS OF CREDIT

§ 5–101. Short Title.

This Article shall be known and may be cited as Uniform Commercial Code—Letters of Credit.

§ 5–102. Scope.

(1) This Article applies

(a) to a credit issued by a bank if the credit requires a documentary draft or a documentary demand for payment; and

(b) to a credit issued by a person other than a bank if the credit requires that the draft or demand for payment be accompanied by a document of title; and

(c) to a credit issued by a bank or other person if the credit is not within subparagraphs (a) or (b) but conspicuously states that it is a letter of credit or is conspicuously so entitled.

(2) Unless the engagement meets the requirements of subsection (1), this Article does not apply to engagements to make advances or to honor drafts or demands for payment, to authorities to pay or purchase, to guarantees or to general agreements.

(3) This Article deals with some but not all of the rules and concepts of letters of credit as such rules or concepts have developed prior to this act or may hereafter develop. The fact that this Article states a rule does not by itself require, imply or negate application of the same or a converse rule to a situation not provided for or to a person not specified by this Article.

§ 5–103. Definitions.

(1) In this Article unless the context otherwise requires

(a) "Credit" or "letter of credit" means an engagement by a bank or other person made at the request of a customer and of a kind within the scope of this Article (Section 5–102) that the issuer will honor drafts or other demands for payment upon compliance with the conditions specified in the credit. A credit may be either revocable or irrevocable. The engagement may be either an agreement to honor or a statement that the bank or other person is authorized to honor.

(b) A "documentary draft" or a "documentary demand for payment" is one honor of which is conditioned upon the presentation of a document or documents. "Document" means any paper including document of title, security, invoice, certificate, notice of default and the like.

(c) An "issuer" is a bank or other person issuing a credit.

(d) A "beneficiary" of a credit is a person who is entitled under its terms to draw or demand payment.

(e) An "advising bank" is a bank which gives notification of the issuance of a credit by another bank.

(f) A "confirming bank" is a bank which engages either that it will itself honor a credit already issued by another bank or that such a credit will be honored by the issuer or a third bank.

(g) A "customer" is a buyer or other person who causes an issuer to issue a credit. The term also includes a bank which procures issuance or confirmation on behalf of that bank's customer.

(2) Other definitions applying to this Article and the sections in which they appear are:

"Notation of Credit". Section 5–108.
"Presenter". Section 5–112(3).

(3) Definitions in other Articles applying to this Article and the sections in which they appear are:

"Accept" or "Acceptance". Section 3–410.
"Contract for sale". Section 2–106.
"Draft". Section 3–104.
"Holder in due course". Section 3–302.
"Midnight deadline". Section 4–104.
"Security". Section 8–102.

(4) In addition, Article 1 contains general definitions and principles of construction and interpretation applicable throughout this Article.

§ 5–104. Formal Requirements; Signing.

(1) Except as otherwise required in subsection (1)(c) of Section 5–102 on scope, no particular form of phrasing is required for a credit. A credit must be in writing and signed by the issuer and a confirmation must be in writing and signed by the confirming bank. A modification of the terms of a credit or confirmation must be signed by the issuer or confirming bank.

(2) A telegram may be a sufficient signed writing if it identifies its sender by an authorized authentication. The authentication may be in code and the authorized naming of the issuer in an advice of credit is a sufficient signing.

§ 5–105. Consideration.

No consideration is necessary to establish a credit or to enlarge or otherwise modify its terms.

§ 5–106. Time and Effect of Establishment of Credit.

(1) Unless otherwise agreed a credit is established.

(a) as regards the customer as soon as a letter of credit is sent to him or the letter of credit or an authorized written advice of its issuance is sent to the beneficiary; and

(b) as regards the beneficiary when he receives a letter of credit or an authorized written advice of its issuance.

(2) Unless otherwise agreed once an irrevocable credit is established as regards the customer it can be modified or revoked only with the consent of the customer and once it is established as regards the beneficiary it can be modified or revoked only with his consent.

(3) Unless otherwise agreed after a revocable credit is established it may be modified or revoked by the issuer without notice to or consent from the customer or beneficiary.

(4) Notwithstanding any modification or revocation of a revocable credit any person authorized to honor or negotiate under the terms of the original credit is entitled to reimbursement for or honor of any draft or demand for payment duly honored or negotiated before receipt of notice of the modification or revocation and the issuer in turn is entitled to reimbursement from its customer.

§ 5–107. Advice of Credit; Confirmation; Error in Statement of Terms.

(1) Unless otherwise specified an advising bank by advising a credit issued by another bank does not assume any obligation to honor drafts drawn or demands for payment made under the credit but it does assume obligation for the accuracy of its own statement.

(2) A confirming bank by confirming a credit becomes directly obligated on the credit to the extent of its confirmation as though it were its issuer and acquires the rights of an issuer.

(3) Even though an advising bank incorrectly advises the terms of a credit it has been authorized to advise the credit is established as against the issuer to the extent of its original terms.

(4) Unless otherwise specified the customer bears as against the issuer all risks of transmission and reasonable translation or interpretation of any message relating to a credit.

§ 5–108. "Notation Credit"; Exhaustion of Credit.

(1) A credit which specifies that any person purchasing or paying drafts drawn or demands for payment made under it must note the amount of the draft or demand on the letter or advice of credit is a "notation credit".

(2) Under a notation credit

(a) a person paying the beneficiary or purchasing a draft or demand for payment from him acquires a right to honor only if the appropriate notation is made and by transferring or forwarding for honor the documents under the credit such a person warrants to the issuer that the notation has been made; and

(b) unless the credit or a signed statement that an appropriate notation has been made accompanies the draft or demand for payment the issuer may delay honor until evidence of notation has been procured which is satisfactory to it but its obligation and that of its customer continue for a reasonable time not exceeding thirty days to obtain such evidence.

(3) If the credit is not a notation credit

(a) the issuer may honor complying drafts or demands for payment presented to it in the order in which they are presented and is discharged pro tanto by honor of any such draft or demand;

(b) as between competing good faith purchasers of complying drafts or demands the person first purchasing has priority over a subsequent purchaser even though the later purchased draft or demand has been first honored.

§ 5–109. Issuer's Obligation to Its Customer.

(1) An issuer's obligation to its customer includes good faith and observance of any general banking usage but unless otherwise agreed does not include liability or responsibility

(a) for performance of the underlying contract for sale or other transaction between the customer and the beneficiary; or

(b) for any act or omission of any person other than itself or its own branch or for loss or destruction of a draft, demand or document in transit or in the possession of others; or

(c) based on knowledge or lack of knowledge of any usage of any particular trade.

(2) An issuer must examine documents with care so as to ascertain that on their face they appear to comply with the terms of the credit but unless otherwise agreed assumes no liability or responsibility for the genuineness, falsification or effect of any document which appears on such examination to be regular on its face.

(3) A non-bank issuer is not bound by any banking usage of which it has no knowledge.

§ 5–110. Availability of Credit in Portions; Presenter's Reservation of Lien or Claim.

(1) Unless otherwise specified a credit may be used in portions in the discretion of the beneficiary.

(2) Unless otherwise specified a person by presenting a documentary draft or demand for payment under a

credit relinquishes upon its honor all claims to the documents and a person by transferring such draft or demand or causing such presentment authorizes such relinquishment. An explicit reservation of claim makes the draft or demand non-complying.

§ 5–111. Warranties on Transfer and Presentment.

(1) Unless otherwise agreed the beneficiary by transferring or presenting a documentary draft or demand for payment warrants to all interested parties that the necessary conditions of the credit have been complied with. This is in addition to any warranties arising under Articles 3, 4, 7 and 8.

(2) Unless otherwise agreed a negotiating, advising, confirming, collecting or issuing bank presenting or transferring a draft or demand for payment under a credit warrants only the matters warranted by a collecting bank under Article 4 and any such bank transferring a document warrants only the matters warranted by an intermediary under Articles 7 and 8.

§ 5–112. Time Allowed for Honor or Rejection; Withholding Honor or Rejection by Consent; "Presenter".

(1) A bank to which a documentary draft or demand for payment is presented under a credit may without dishonor of the draft, demand or credit

(a) defer honor until the close of the third banking day following receipt of the documents; and

(b) further defer honor if the presenter has expressly or impliedly consented thereto.

Failure to honor within the time here specified constitutes dishonor of the draft or demand and of the credit [except as otherwise provided in subsection (4) of Section 5–114 on conditional payment].

Note: *The bracketed language in the last sentence of subsection (1) should be included only if the optional provisions of Section 5–114(4) and (5) are included.*

(2) Upon dishonor the bank may unless otherwise instructed fulfill its duty to return the draft or demand and the documents by holding them at the disposal of the presenter and sending him an advice to that effect.

(3) "Presenter" means any person presenting a draft or demand for payment for honor under a credit even though that person is a confirming bank or other correspondent which is acting under an issuer's authorization.

§ 5–113. Indemnities.

(1) A bank seeking to obtain (whether for itself or another) honor, negotiation or reimbursement under a credit may give an indemnity to induce such honor, negotiation or reimbursement.

(2) An indemnity agreement inducing honor, negotiation or reimbursement

(a) unless otherwise explicitly agreed applies to defects in the documents but not in the goods; and

(b) unless a longer time is explicitly agreed expires at the end of ten business days following receipt of the documents by, the ultimate customer unless notice of objection is sent before such expiration date. The ultimate customer may send notice of objection to the person from whom he received the documents and any bank receiving such notice is under a duty to send notice to its transferor before its midnight deadline.

§ 5–114. Issuer's Duty and Privilege to Honor; Right to Reimbursement.

(1) An issuer must honor a draft or demand for payment which complies with the terms of the relevant credit regardless of whether the goods or documents conform to the underlying contract for sale or other contract between the customer and the beneficiary. The issuer is not excused from honor of such a draft or demand by reason of an additional general term that all documents must be satisfactory to the issuer, but an issuer may require that specified documents must be satisfactory to it.

(2) Unless otherwise agreed when documents appear on their face to comply with the terms of a credit but a required document does not in fact conform to the warranties made on negotiation or transfer of a document of title (Section 7–507) or of a certificated security (Section 8–306) or is forged or fraudulent or there is fraud in the transaction:

(a) the issuer must honor the draft or demand for payment if honor is demanded by a negotiating bank or other holder of the draft or demand which has taken the draft or demand under the credit and under circumstances which would make it a holder in due course (Section 3–302) and in an appropriate case would make it a person to whom a document of title has been duly negotiated (Section 7–502) or a bona fide purchaser of a certificated security (Section 8–302); and

(b) in all other cases as against its customer, an issuer acting in good faith may honor the draft or demand for payment despite notification from the customer of fraud, forgery or other defect not apparent on the face of the documents but a court of appropriate jurisdiction may enjoin such honor.

(3) Unless otherwise agreed an issuer which has duly honored a draft or demand for payment is entitled to immediate reimbursement of any payment made under the credit and to be put in effectively available funds not later than the day before maturity of any acceptance made under the credit.

[(4) When a credit provides for payment by the issuer on receipt of notice that the required documents are in the possession of a correspondent or other agent of the issuer

(a) any payment made on receipt of such notice is conditional; and

(b) the issuer may reject documents which do not comply with the credit if it does so within three banking days following its receipt of the documents; and

(c) in the event of such rejection, the issuer is entitled by charge back or otherwise to return of the payment made.]

[(5) In the case covered by subsection (4) failure to reject documents within the time specified in sub-paragraph (b) constitutes acceptance of the documents and makes the payment final in favor of the beneficiary.]

Amended in 1977.

Note: *Subsections (4) and (5) are bracketed as optional. If they are included the bracketed language in the last sentence of Section 5–112(1) should also be included.*

§ 5–115. Remedy for Improper Dishonor or Anticipatory Repudiation.

(1) When an issuer wrongfully dishonors a draft or demand for payment presented under a credit the person entitled to honor has with respect to any documents the rights of a person in the position of a seller (Section 2–707) and may recover from the issuer the face amount of the draft or demand together with incidental damages under Section 2–710 on seller's incidental damages and interest but less any amount realized by resale or other use or disposition of the subject matter of the transaction. In the event no resale or other utilization is made the documents, goods or other subject matter involved in the transaction must be turned over to the issuer on payment of judgment.

(2) When an issuer wrongfully cancels or otherwise repudiates a credit before presentment of a draft or demand for payment drawn under it the beneficiary has the rights of a seller after anticipatory repudiation by the buyer under Section 2–610 if he learns of the repudiation in time reasonably to avoid procurement of the required documents. Otherwise the beneficiary has an immediate right of action for wrongful dishonor.

§ 5–116. Transfer and Assignment.

(1) The right to draw under a credit can be transferred or assigned only when the credit is expressly designated as transferable or assignable.

(2) Even though the credit specifically states that it is nontransferable or nonassignable the beneficiary may before performance of the conditions of the credit assign his right to proceeds. Such an assignment is an assignment of an account under Article 9 on Secured Transactions and is governed by that Article except that

(a) the assignment is ineffective until the letter of credit or advice of credit is delivered to the assignee which delivery constitutes perfection of the security interest under Article 9; and

(b) the issuer may honor drafts or demands for payment drawn under the credit until it receives a notification of the assignment signed by the beneficiary which reasonably identifies the credit involved in the assignment and contains a request to pay the assignee; and

(c) after what reasonably appears to be such a notification has been received the issuer may without dishonor refuse to accept or pay even to a person otherwise entitled to honor until the letter of credit or advice of credit is exhibited to the issuer.

(3) Except where the beneficiary has effectively assigned his right to draw or his right to proceeds, nothing in this section limits his right to transfer or negotiate drafts or demands drawn under the credit.

§ 5–117. Insolvency of Bank Holding Funds for Documentary Credit.

(1) Where an issuer or an advising or confirming bank or a bank which has for a customer procured issuance of a credit by another bank becomes insolvent before final payment under the credit and the credit is one to which this Article is made applicable by paragraphs (a) or (b) of Section 5–102(1) on scope, the receipt or allocation of funds or collateral to secure or meet obligations under the credit shall have the following results:

(a) to the extent of any funds or collateral turned over after or before the insolvency as indemnity against or specifically for the purpose of payment of drafts or demands for payment drawn under the designated credit, the drafts or demands are entitled to payment in preference over depositors or other general creditors of the issuer or bank; and

(b) on expiration of the credit or surrender of the beneficiary's rights under it unused any person who has given such funds or collateral is similarly entitled to return thereof; and

(c) a charge to a general or current account with a bank if specifically consented to for the purpose of indemnity against or payment of drafts or demands for payment drawn under the designated credit falls under the same rules as if the funds had been drawn out in cash and then turned over with specific instructions.

(2) After honor or reimbursement under this section the customer or other person for whose account the insolvent bank has acted is entitled to receive the documents involved.

ARTICLE 6: BULK TRANSFERS

§ 6–101. Short Title.

This Article shall be known and may be cited as Uniform Commercial Code—Bulk Transfers.

§ 6–102. "Bulk Transfer"; Transfers of Equipment; Enterprises Subject to This Article; Bulk Transfers Subject to This Article.

(1) A "bulk transfer" is any transfer in bulk and not in the ordinary course of the transferor's business of a major part of the materials, supplies, merchandise or other inventory (Section 9–109) of an enterprise subject to this Article.

(2) A transfer of a substantial part of the equipment (Section 9–109) of such an enterprise is a bulk transfer if it is made in connection with a bulk transfer of inventory, but not otherwise.

(3) The enterprises subject to this Article are all those whose principal business is the sale of merchandise from stock, including those who manufacture what they sell.

(4) Except as limited by the following section all bulk transfers of goods located within this state are subject to this Article.

§ 6–103. Transfers Excepted From This Article.

The following transfers are not subject to this Article:

(1) Those made to give security for the performance of an obligation;

(2) General assignments for the benefit of all the creditors of the transferor, and subsequent transfers by the assignee thereunder;

(3) Transfers in settlement or realization of a lien or other security interest;

(4) Sales by executors, administrators, receivers, trustees in bankruptcy, or any public officer under judicial process;

(5) Sales made in the course of judicial or administrative proceedings for the dissolution or reorganization of a corporation and of which notice is sent to the creditors of the corporation pursuant to order of the court or administrative agency;

(6) Transfers to a person maintaining a known place of business in this State who becomes bound to pay the debts of the transferor in full and gives public notice of that fact, and who is solvent after becoming so bound;

(7) A transfer to a new business enterprise organized to take over and continue the business, if public notice of the transaction is given and the new enterprise assumes the debts of the transferor and he receives nothing from the transaction except an interest in the new enterprise junior to the claims of creditors;

(8) Transfers of property which is exempt from execution.

Public notice under subsection (6) or subsection (7) may be given by publishing once a week for two consecutive weeks in a newspaper of general circulation where the transferor had its principal place of business in this state an advertisement including the names and addresses of the transferor and transferee and the effective date of the transfer.

§ 6–104. Schedule of Property, List of Creditors.

(1) Except as provided with respect to auction sales (Section 6–108), a bulk transfer subject to this Article is ineffective against any creditor of the transferor unless:

(a) The transferee requires the transferor to furnish a list of his existing creditors prepared as stated in this section; and

(b) The parties prepare a schedule of the property transferred sufficient to identify it; and

(c) The transferee preserves the list and schedule for six months next following the transfer and permits inspection of either or both and copying therefrom at all reasonable hours by any creditor of the transferor, or files the list and schedule in *(a public office to be here identified)*.

(2) The list of creditors must be signed and sworn to or affirmed by the transferor or his agent. It must contain the names and business addresses of all creditors of the transferor, with the amounts when known, and also the names of all persons who are known to the transferor to assert claims against him even though such claims are disputed. If the transferor is the obligor of an outstanding issue of bonds, debentures or the like as to which there is an indenture trustee, the list of creditors need include only the name and address of the indenture trustee and the aggregate outstanding principal amount of the issue.

(3) Responsibility for the completeness and accuracy of the list of creditors rests on the transferor, and the transfer is not rendered ineffective by errors or omissions therein unless the transferee is shown to have had knowledge.

§ 6–105. Notice to Creditors.

In addition to the requirements of the preceding section, any bulk transfer subject to this Article except one made by auction sale (Section 6–108) is ineffective against any creditor of the transferor unless at least ten days before he takes possession of the goods or pays for them, whichever happens first, the transferee gives notice of the transfer in the manner and to the persons hereafter provided (Section 6–107).

§ 6–106. Application of the Proceeds.

In addition to the requirements of the two preceding sections:

(1) Upon every bulk transfer subject to this Article for which new consideration becomes payable except those made by sale at auction it is the duty of the transferee to assure that such consideration is applied so far as nec-

essary to pay those debts of the transferor which are either shown on the list furnished by the transferor (Section 6–104) or filed in writing in the place stated in the notice (Section 6–107) within thirty days after the mailing of such notice. This duty of the transferee runs to all the holders of such debts, and may be enforced by any of them for the benefit of all.

(2) If any of said debts are in dispute the necessary sum may be withheld from distribution until the dispute is settled or adjudicated.

(3) If the consideration payable is not enough to pay all of the said debts in full distribution shall be made pro rata.]

Note: *This section is bracketed to indicate division of opinion as to whether or not it is a wise provision, and to suggest that this is a point on which State enactments may differ without serious damage to the principal of uniformity. In any State where this section is omitted, the following parts of sections, also bracketed in the text, should also be omitted, namely:*

Section 6–107(2)(c).
     6–108(3)(c).
     6–109(2).

In any State where this section is enacted, these other provisions should be also.

Optional Subsection (4)

[(4) The transferee may within ten days after he takes possession of the goods pay the consideration into the (specify court) in the county where the transferor had its principal place of business in this state and thereafter may discharge his duty under this section by giving notice by registered or certified mail to all the persons to whom the duty runs that the consideration has been paid into that court and that they should file their claims there. On motion of any interested party, the court may order the distribution of the consideration to the persons entitled to it.]

Note: *Optional subsection (4) is recommended for those states which do not have a general statute providing for payment of money into court.*

§ 6–107. The Notice.

(1) The notice to creditors (Section 6–105) shall state:

(a) that a bulk transfer is about to be made; and

(b) the names and business addresses of the transferor and transferee, and all other business names and addresses used by the transferor within three years last past so far as known to the transferee; and

(c) whether or not all the debts of the transferor are to be paid in full as they fall due as a result of the transaction, and if so, the address to which creditors should send their bills.

(2) If the debts of the transferor are not to be paid in full as they fall due or if the transferee is in doubt on that point then the notice shall state further:

(a) the location and general description of the property to be transferred and the estimated total of the transferor's debts;

(b) the address where the schedule of property and list of creditors (Section 6–104) may be inspected;

(c) whether the transfer is to pay existing debts and if so the amount of such debts and to whom owing;

(d) whether the transfer is for new consideration and if so the amount of such consideration and the time and place of payment; [and]

[(e) if for new consideration the time and place where creditors of the transferor are to file their claims.]

(3) The notice in any case shall be delivered personally or sent by registered or certified mail to all the persons shown on the list of creditors furnished by the transferor (Section 6–104) and to all other persons who are known to the transferee to hold or assert claims against the transferor.

§ 6–108. Auction Sales; "Auctioneer".

(1) A bulk transfer is subject to this Article even though it is by sale at auction, but only in the manner and with the results stated in this section.

(2) The transferor shall furnish a list of his creditors and assist in the preparation of a schedule of the property to be sold, both prepared as before stated (Section 6–104).

(3) The person or persons other than the transferor who direct, control or are responsible for the auction are collectively called the "auctioneer". The auctioneer shall:

(a) receive and retain the list of creditors and prepare and retain the schedule of property for the period stated in this Article (Section 6–104);

(b) give notice of the auction personally or by registered or certified mail at least ten days before it occurs to all persons shown on the list of creditors and to all other persons who are known to him to hold or assert claims against the transferor; [and]

[(c) assure that the net proceeds of the auction are applied as provided in this Article (Section 6–106).]

(4) Failure of the auctioneer to perform any of these duties does not affect the validity of the sale or the title of the purchasers, but if the auctioneer knows that the auction constitutes a bulk transfer such failure renders the auctioneer liable to the creditors of the transferor as a class for the sums owing to them from the transferor up to but not exceeding the net proceeds of the auction. If the auctioneer consists of several persons their liability is joint and several.

§ 6–109. What Creditors Protected; [Credit for Payment to Particular Creditors].

(1) The creditors of the transferor mentioned in this Article are those holding claims based on transactions or

events occurring before the bulk transfer, but creditors who become such after notice to creditors is given (Sections 6–105 and 6–107) are not entitled to notice.

[(2) Against the aggregate obligation imposed by the provisions of this Article concerning the application of the proceeds (Section 6–106 and subsection (3)(c) of 6–108) the transferee or auctioneer is entitled to credit for sums paid to particular creditors of the transferor, not exceeding the sums believed in good faith at the time of the payment to be properly payable to such creditors.]

§ 6–110. Subsequent Transfers.

When the title of a transferee to property is subject to a defect by reason of his non-compliance with the requirements of this Article, then:

(1) a purchaser of any such property from such transferee who pays no value or who takes with notice of such non-compliance takes subject to such defect, but

(2) a purchaser for value in good faith and without such notice takes free of such defect.

§ 6–111. Limitation of Actions and Levies.

No action under this Article shall be brought nor levy made more than six months after the date on which the transferee took possession of the goods unless the transfer has been concealed. If the transfer has been concealed, actions may be brought or levies made within six months after its discovery.

Note to Article 6: *Section 6–106 is bracketed to indicate division of opinion as to whether or not it is a wise provision, and to suggest that this is a point on which State enactments may differ without serious damage to the principle of uniformity.*

In any State where Section 6–106 is not enacted, the following parts of sections, also bracketed in the text, should also be omitted, namely:

Sec.6–107(2)(e).
  6–108(3)(c).
  6–109(2).

In any State where Section 6–106 is enacted, these other provisions should be also.

ARTICLE 7: WAREHOUSE RECEIPTS, BILLS OF LADING AND OTHER DOCUMENTS OF TITLE

Part 1—General

§ 7–101. Short Title.

This Article shall be known and may be cited as Uniform Commercial Code—Documents of Title.

§ 7–102. Definitions and Index of Definitions.

(1) In this Article, unless the context otherwise requires:

(a) "Bailee" means the person who by a warehouse receipt, bill of lading or other document of title acknowledges possession of goods and contracts to deliver them.

(b) "Consignee" means the person named in a bill to whom or to whose order the bill promises delivery.

(c) "Consignor" means the person named in a bill as the person from whom the goods have been received for shipment.

(d) "Delivery order" means a written order to deliver goods directed to a warehouseman, carrier or other person who in the ordinary course of business issues warehouse receipts or bills of lading.

(e) "Document" means document of title as defined in the general definitions in Article 1 (Section 1–201).

(f) "Goods" means all things which are treated as movable for the purposes of a contract of storage or transportation.

(g) "Issuer" means a bailee who issues a document except that in relation to an unaccepted delivery order it means the person who orders the possessor of goods to deliver. Issuer includes any person for whom an agent or employee purports to act in issuing a document if the agent or employee has real or apparent authority to issue documents, notwithstanding that the issuer received no goods or that the goods were misdescribed or that in any other respect the agent or employee violated his instructions.

(h) "Warehouseman" is a person engaged in the business of storing goods for hire.

(2) Other definitions applying to this Article or to specified Parts thereof, and the sections in which they appear are:

"Duly negotiate". Section 7–501.
"Person entitled under the document". Section 7–403(4).

(3) Definitions in other Articles applying to this Article and the sections in which they appear are:

"Contract for sale". Section 2–106.
"Overseas". Section 2–323.
"Receipt" of goods. Section 2–103.

(4) In addition Article 1 contains general definitions and principles of construction and interpretation applicable throughout this Article.

§ 7–103. Relation of Article to Treaty, Statute, Tariff, Classification or Regulation.

To the extent that any treaty or statute of the United States, regulatory statute of this State or tariff, classification or regulation filed or issued pursuant thereto is applicable, the provisions of this Article are subject thereto.

§ 7–104. Negotiable and Non-Negotiable Warehouse Receipt, Bill of Lading or Other Document of Title.

(1) A warehouse receipt, bill of lading or other document of title is negotiable

(a) if by its terms the goods are to be delivered to bearer or to the order of a named person; or

(b) where recognized in overseas trade, if it runs to a named person or assigns.

(2) Any other document is non-negotiable. A bill of lading in which it is stated that the goods are consigned to a named person is not made negotiable by a provision that the goods are to be delivered only against a written order signed by the same or another named person.

§ 7–105. Construction Against Negative Implication.

The omission from either Part 2 or Part 3 of this Article of a provision corresponding to a provision made in the other Part does not imply that a corresponding rule of law is not applicable.

Part 2—Warehouse Receipts: Special Provisions

§ 7–201. Who May Issue a Warehouse Receipt; Storage Under Government Bond.

(1) A warehouse receipt may be issued by any warehouseman.

(2) Where goods including distilled spirits and agricultural commodities are stored under a statute requiring a bond against withdrawal or a license for the issuance of receipts in the nature of warehouse receipts, a receipt issued for the goods has like effect as a warehouse receipt even though issued by a person who is the owner of the goods and is not a warehouseman.

§ 7–202. Form of Warehouse Receipt; Essential Terms; Optional Terms.

(1) A warehouse receipt need not be in any particular form.

(2) Unless a warehouse receipt embodies within its written or printed terms each of the following, the warehouseman is liable for damages caused by the omission to a person injured thereby:

(a) the location of the warehouse where the goods are stored;

(b) the date of issue of the receipt;

(c) the consecutive number of the receipt;

(d) a statement whether the goods received will be delivered to the bearer, to a specified person, or to a specified person or his order;

(e) the rate of storage and handling charges, except that where goods are stored under a field warehousing arrangement a statement of that fact is sufficient on a non-negotiable receipt;

(f) a description of the goods or of the packages containing them;

(g) the signature of the warehouseman, which may be made by his authorized agent;

(h) if the receipt is issued for goods of which the warehouseman is owner, either solely or jointly or in common with others, the fact of such ownership; and

(i) a statement of the amount of advances made and of liabilities incurred for which the warehouseman claims a lien or security interest (Section 7–209). If the precise amount of such advances made or of such liabilities incurred is, at the time of the issue of the receipt, unknown to the warehouseman or to his agent who issues it, a statement of the fact that advances have been made or liabilities incurred and the purpose thereof is sufficient.

(3) A warehouseman may insert in his receipt any other terms which are not contrary to the provisions of this Act and do not impair his obligation of delivery (Section 7–403) or his duty of care (Section 7–204). Any contrary provisions shall be ineffective.

§ 7–203. Liability for Non-Receipt or Misdescription.

A party to or purchaser for value in good faith of a document of title other than a bill of lading relying in either case upon the description therein of the goods may recover from the issuer damages caused by the non-receipt or misdescription of the goods, except to the extent that the document conspicuously indicates that the issuer does not know whether any part or all of the goods in fact were received or conform to the description, as where the description is in terms of marks or labels or kind, quantity or condition, or the receipt or description is qualified by "contents, condition and quality unknown", "said to contain" or the like, if such indication be true, or the party or purchaser otherwise has notice.

§ 7–204. Duty of Care; Contractual Limitation of Warehouseman's Liability.

(1) A warehouseman is liable for damages for loss of or injury to the goods caused by his failure to exercise such care in regard to them as a reasonably careful man would exercise under like circumstances but unless otherwise agreed he is not liable for damages which could not have been avoided by the exercise of such care.

(2) Damages may be limited by a term in the warehouse receipt or storage agreement limiting the amount of liability in case of loss or damage, and setting forth a specific liability per article or item, or value per unit of weight, beyond which the warehouseman shall not be

liable; provided, however, that such liability may on written request of the bailor at the time of signing such storage agreement or within a reasonable time after receipt of the warehouse receipt be increased on part or all of the goods thereunder, in which event increased rates may be charged based on such increased valuation, but that no such increase shall be permitted contrary to a lawful limitation of liability contained in the warehouseman's tariff, if any. No such limitation is effective with respect to the warehouseman's liability for conversion to his own use.

(3) Reasonable provisions as to the time and manner of presenting claims and instituting actions based on the bailment may be included in the warehouse receipt or tariff.

(4) This section does not impair or repeal . . .

Note: *Insert in subsection (4) a reference to any statute which imposes a higher responsibility upon the warehouseman or invalidates contractual limitations which would be permissible under this Article.*

§ 7–205. Title Under Warehouse Receipt Defeated in Certain Cases.

A buyer in the ordinary course of business of fungible goods sold and delivered by a warehouseman who is also in the business of buying and selling such goods takes free of any claim under a warehouse receipt even though it has been duly negotiated.

§ 7–206. Termination of Storage at Warehouseman's Option.

(1) A warehouseman may on notifying the person on whose account the goods are held and any other person known to claim an interest in the goods require payment of any charges and removal of the goods from the warehouse at the termination of the period of storage fixed by the document, or, if no period is fixed, within a stated period not less than thirty days after the notification. If the goods are not removed before the date specified in the notification, the warehouseman may sell them in accordance with the provisions of the section on enforcement of a warehouseman's lien (Section 7–210).

(2) If a warehouseman in good faith believes that the goods are about to deteriorate or decline in value to less than the amount of his lien within the time prescribed in subsection (1) for notification, advertisement and sale, the warehouseman may specify in the notification any reasonable shorter time for removal of the goods and in case the goods are not removed, may sell them at public sale held not less than one week after a single advertisement or posting.

(3) If as a result of a quality or condition of the goods of which the warehouseman had no notice at the time of deposit the goods are a hazard to other property or to the warehouse or to persons, the warehouseman may sell the goods at public or private sale without advertisement on reasonable notification to all persons known to claim an interest in the goods. If the warehouseman after a reasonable effort is unable to sell the goods he may dispose of them in any lawful manner and shall incur no liability by reason of such disposition.

(4) The warehouseman must deliver the goods to any person entitled to them under this Article upon due demand made at any time prior to sale or other disposition under this section.

(5) The warehouseman may satisfy his lien from the proceeds of any sale or disposition under this section but must hold the balance for delivery on the demand of any person to whom he would have been bound to deliver the goods.

§ 7–207. Goods Must Be Kept Separate; Fungible Goods.

(1) Unless the warehouse receipt otherwise provides, a warehouseman must keep separate the goods covered by each receipt so as to permit at all times identification and delivery of those goods except that different lots of fungible goods may be commingled.

(2) Fungible goods so commingled are owned in common by the persons entitled thereto and the warehouseman is severally liable to each owner for that owner's share. Where because of overissue a mass of fungible goods is insufficient to meet all the receipts which the warehouseman has issued against it, the persons entitled include all holders to whom overissued receipts have been duly negotiated.

§ 7–208. Altered Warehouse Receipts.

Where a blank in a negotiable warehouse receipt has been filled in without authority, a purchaser for value and without notice of the want of authority may treat the insertion as authorized. Any other unauthorized alteration leaves any receipt enforceable against the issuer according to its original tenor.

§ 7–209. Lien of Warehouseman.

(1) A warehouseman has a lien against the bailor on the goods covered by a warehouse receipt or on the proceeds thereof in his possession for charges for storages or transportation (including demurrage and terminal charges), insurance, labor, or charges present or future in relation to the goods, and for expenses necessary for preservation of the goods or reasonably incurred in their sale pursuant to law. If the person on whose account the goods are held is liable for like charges or expenses in relation to other goods whenever deposited and it is stated in the receipt that a lien is claimed for charges and expenses in relation to other goods, the warehouseman also has a lien against him for such charges and expenses whether or not the other goods have been delivered by the warehouseman. But against a person to whom a negotiable warehouse receipt is duly negotiated

a warehouseman's lien is limited to charges in an amount or at a rate specified on the receipt or if no charges are so specified then to a reasonable charge for storage of the goods covered by the receipt subsequent to the date of the receipt.

(2) The warehouseman may also reserve a security interest against the bailor for a maximum amount specified on the receipt for charges other than those specified in subsection (1), such as for money advanced and interest. Such a security interest is governed by the Article on Secured Transactions (Article 9).

(3) (a) A warehouseman's lien for charges and expenses under subsection (1) or a security interest under subsection (2) is also effective against any person who so entrusted the bailor with possession of the goods that a pledge of them by him to a good faith purchaser for value would have been valid but is not effective against a person as to whom the document confers no right in the goods covered by it under Section 7–503.

(b) A warehouseman's lien on household goods for charges and expenses in relation to the goods under subsection (1) is also effective against all persons if the depositor was a legal possessor of the goods at the time of deposit. "Household goods" means furniture, furnishings and personal effects used by the depositor in a dwelling.

(4) A warehouseman loses his lien on any goods which he voluntarily delivers or which he unjustifiably refuses to deliver.

§ 7–210. Enforcement of Warehouseman's Lien.

(1) Except as provided in subsection (2), a warehouseman's lien may be enforced by public or private sale of the goods in bloc or in parcels, at any time or place and on any terms which are commercially reasonable, after notifying all persons known to claim an interest in the goods. Such notification must include a statement of the amount due, the nature of the proposed sale and the time and place of any public sale. The fact that a better price could have been obtained by a sale at a different time or in a different method from that selected by the warehouseman is not of itself sufficient to establish that the sale was not made in a commercially reasonable manner. If the warehouseman either sells the goods in the usual manner in any recognized market therefor, or if he sells at the price current in such market at the time of his sale, or if he has otherwise sold in conformity with commercially reasonable practices among dealers in the type of goods sold, he has sold in a commercially reasonable manner. A sale of more goods than apparently necessary to be offered to insure satisfaction of the obligation is not commercially reasonable except in cases covered by the preceding sentence.

(2) A warehouseman's lien on goods other than goods stored by a merchant in the course of his business may be enforced only as follows:

(a) All persons known to claim an interest in the goods must be notified.

(b) The notification must be delivered in person or sent by registered or certified letter to the last known address of any person to be notified.

(c) The notification must include an itemized statement of the claim, a description of the goods subject to the lien, a demand for payment within a specified time not less than ten days after receipt of the notification, and a conspicuous statement that unless the claim is paid within the time the goods will be advertised for sale and sold by auction at a specified time and place.

(d) The sale must conform to the terms of the notification.

(e) The sale must be held at the nearest suitable place to that where the goods are held or stored.

(f) After the expiration of the time given in the notification, an advertisement of the sale must be published once a week for two weeks consecutively in a newspaper of general circulation where the sale is to be held. The advertisement must include a description of the goods, the name of the person on whose account they are being held, and the time and place of the sale. The sale must take place at least fifteen days after the first publication. If there is no newspaper of general circulation where the sale is to be held, the advertisement must be posted at least ten days before the sale in not less than six conspicuous places in the neighborhood of the proposed sale.

(3) Before any sale pursuant to this section any person claiming a right in the goods may pay the amount necessary to satisfy the lien and the reasonable expenses incurred under this section. In that event the goods must not be sold, but must be retained by the warehouseman subject to the terms of the receipt and this Article.

(4) The warehouseman may buy at any public sale pursuant to this section.

(5) A purchaser in good faith of goods sold to enforce a warehouseman's lien takes the goods free of any rights of persons against whom the lien was valid, despite noncompliance by the warehouseman with the requirements of this section.

(6) The warehouseman may satisfy his lien from the proceeds of any sale pursuant to this section but must hold the balance, if any, for delivery on demand to any person to whom he would have been bound to deliver the goods.

(7) The rights provided by this section shall be in addition to all other rights allowed by law to a creditor against his debtor.

(8) Where a lien is on goods stored by a merchant in the course of his business the lien may be enforced in accordance with either subsection (1) or (2).

(9) The warehouseman is liable for damages caused by failure to comply with the requirements for sale under this section and in case of willful violation is liable for conversion.

Part 3—Bills of Lading: Special Provisions

§ 7–301. Liability for Non-Receipt or Misdescription; "Said to Contain"; "Shipper's Load and Count"; Improper Handling.

(1) A consignee of a non-negotiable bill who has given value in good faith or a holder to whom a negotiable bill has been duly negotiated relying in either case upon the description therein of the goods, or upon the date therein shown, may recover from the issuer damages caused by the misdating of the bill or the non-receipt or misdescription of the goods, except to the extent that the document indicates that the issuer does not know whether any part of all of the goods in fact were received or conform to the description, as where the description is in terms of marks or labels or kind, quantity, or condition or the receipt or description is qualified by "contents or condition of contents of packages unknown", "said to contain", "shipper's weight, load and count" or the like, if such indication be true.

(2) When goods are loaded by an issuer who is a common carrier, the issuer must count the packages of goods if package freight and ascertain the kind and quantity if bulk freight. In such cases "shipper's weight, load and count" or other words indicating that the description was made by the shipper are ineffective except as to freight concealed by packages.

(3) When bulk freight is loaded by a shipper who makes available to the issuer adequate facilities for weighing such freight, an issuer who is a common carrier must ascertain the kind and quantity within a reasonable time after receiving the written request of the shipper to do so. In such cases "shipper's weight" or other words of like purport are ineffective.

(4) The issuer may by inserting in the bill the words "shipper's weight, load and count" or other words of like purport indicate that the goods were loaded by the shipper; and if such statement be true the issuer shall not be liable for damages caused by the improper loading. But their omission does not imply liability for such damages.

(5) The shipper shall be deemed to have guaranteed to the issuer the accuracy at the time of shipment of the description, marks, labels, number, kind, quantity, condition and weight, as furnished by him; and the shipper shall indemnify the issuer against damage caused by inaccuracies in such particulars. The right of the issuer to such indemnity shall in no way limit his responsibility and liability under the contract of carriage to any person other than the shipper.

§ 7–302. Through Bills of Lading and Similar Documents.

(1) The issuer of a through bill of lading or other document embodying an undertaking to be performed in part by persons acting as its agents or by connecting carriers is liable to anyone entitled to recover on the document for any breach by such other persons or by a connecting carrier of its obligation under the document but to the extent that the bill covers an undertaking to be performed overseas or in territory not contiguous to the continental United States or an undertaking including matters other than transportation this liability may be varied by agreement of the parties.

(2) Where goods covered by a through bill of lading or other document embodying an undertaking to be performed in part by persons other than the issuer are received by any such person, he is subject with respect to his own performance while the goods are in his possession to the obligation of the issuer. His obligation is discharged by delivery of the goods to another such person pursuant to the document, and does not include liability for breach by any other such persons or by the issuer.

(3) The issuer of such through bill of lading or other document shall be entitled to recover from the connecting carrier or such other person in possession of the goods when the breach of the obligation under the document occurred, the amount it may be required to pay to anyone entitled to recover on the document therefor, as may be evidenced by any receipt, judgment, or transcript thereof, and the amount of any expense reasonably incurred by it in defending any action brought by anyone entitled to recover on the document therefor.

§ 7–303. Diversion; Reconsignment; Change of Instructions.

(1) Unless the bill of lading otherwise provides, the carrier may deliver the goods to a person or destination other than that stated in the bill or may otherwise dispose of the goods on instructions from

    (a) the holder of a negotiable bill; or

    (b) the consignor on a non-negotiable bill notwithstanding contrary instructions from the consignee; or

    (c) the consignee on a non-negotiable bill in the absence of contrary instructions from the consignor, if the goods have arrived at the billed destination or if the consignee is in possession of the bill; or

    (d) the consignee on a non-negotiable bill if he is entitled as against the consignor to dispose of them.

(2) Unless such instructions are noted on a negotiable bill of lading, a person to whom the bill is duly negotiated can hold the bailee according to the original terms.

§ 7–304. Bills of Lading in a Set.

(1) Except where customary in overseas transportation, a bill of lading must not be issued in a set of parts. The issuer is liable for damages caused by violation of this subsection.

(2) Where a bill of lading is lawfully drawn in a set of parts, each of which is numbered and expressed to be valid only if the goods have not been delivered against any other part, the whole of the parts constitute one bill.

(3) Where a bill of lading is lawfully issued in a set of parts and different parts are negotiated to different persons, the title of the holder to whom the first due negotiation is made prevails as to both the document and the goods even though any later holder may have received the goods from the carrier in good faith and discharged the carrier's obligation by surrender of his part.

(4) Any person who negotiates or transfers a single part of a bill of lading drawn in a set is liable to holders of that part as if it were the whole set.

(5) The bailee is obliged to deliver in accordance with Part 4 of this Article against the first presented part of a bill of lading lawfully drawn in a set. Such delivery discharges the bailee's obligation on the whole bill.

§ 7–305. Destination Bills.

(1) Instead of issuing a bill of lading to the consignor at the place of shipment a carrier may at the request of the consignor procure the bill to be issued at destination or at any other place designated in the request.

(2) Upon request of anyone entitled as against the carrier to control the goods while in transit and on surrender of any outstanding bill of lading or other receipt covering such goods, the issuer may procure a substitute bill to be issued at any place designated in the request.

§ 7–306. Altered Bills of Lading.

An unauthorized alteration or filling in of a blank in a bill of lading leaves the bill enforceable according to its original tenor.

§ 7–307. Lien of Carrier.

(1) A carrier has a lien on the goods covered by a bill of lading for charges subsequent to the date of its receipt of the goods for storage or transportation (including demurrage and terminal charges) and for expenses necessary for preservation of the goods incident to their transportation or reasonably incurred in their sale pursuant to law. But against a purchaser for value of a negotiable bill of lading a carrier's lien is limited to charges stated in the bill or the applicable tariffs, or if no charges are stated then to a reasonable charge.

(2) A lien for charges and expenses under subsection (1) on goods which the carrier was required by law to receive for transportation is effective against the consignor or any person entitled to the goods unless the carrier had notice that the consignor lacked authority to subject the goods to such charges and expenses. Any other lien under subsection (1) is effective against the consignor and any person who permitted the bailor to have control or possession of the goods unless the carrier had notice that the bailor lacked such authority.

(3) A carrier loses his lien on any goods which he voluntarily delivers or which he unjustifiably refuses to deliver.

§ 7–308. Enforcement of Carrier's Lien.

(1) A carrier's lien may be enforced by public or private sale of the goods, in bloc or in parcels, at any time or place and on any terms which are commercially reasonable, after notifying all persons known to claim an interest in the goods. Such notification must include a statement of the amount due, the nature of the proposed sale and the time and place of any public sale. The fact that a better price could have been obtained by a sale at a different time or in a different method from that selected by the carrier is not of itself sufficient to establish that the sale was not made in a commercially reasonable manner. If the carrier either sells the goods in the usual manner in any recognized market therefor or if he sells at the price current in such market at the time of his sale or if he has otherwise sold in conformity with commercially reasonable practices among dealers in the type of goods sold he has sold in a commercially reasonable manner. A sale of more goods than apparently necessary to be offered to ensure satisfaction of the obligation is not commercially reasonable except in cases covered by the preceding sentence.

(2) Before any sale pursuant to this section any person claiming a right in the goods may pay the amount necessary to satisfy the lien and the reasonable expenses incurred under this section. In that event the goods must not be sold, but must be retained by the carrier subject to the terms of the bill and this Article.

(3) The carrier may buy at any public sale pursuant to this section.

(4) A purchaser in good faith of goods sold to enforce a carrier's lien takes the goods free of any rights of persons against whom the lien was valid, despite noncompliance by the carrier with the requirements of this section.

(5) The carrier may satisfy his lien from the proceeds of any sale pursuant to this section but must hold the balance, if any, for delivery on demand to any person to whom he would have been bound to deliver the goods.

(6) The rights provided by this section shall be in addition to all other rights allowed by law to a creditor against his debtor.

(7) A carrier's lien may be enforced in accordance with either subsection (1) or the procedure set forth in subsection (2) of Section 7–210.

(8) The carrier is liable for damages caused by failure to comply with the requirements for sale under this section and in case of willful violation is liable for conversion.

§ 7–309. Duty of Care; Contractual Limitation of Carrier's Liability.

(1) A carrier who issues a bill of lading whether negotiable or non-negotiable must exercise the degree of care in relation to the goods which a reasonably careful man would exercise under like circumstances. This subsection does not repeal or change any law or rule of law which imposes liability upon a common carrier for damages not caused by its negligence.

(2) Damages may be limited by a provision that the carrier's liability shall not exceed a value stated in the document if the carrier's rates are dependent upon value and the consignor by the carrier's tariff is afforded an opportunity to declare a higher value or a value as lawfully provided in the tariff, or where no tariff is filed he is otherwise advised of such opportunity; but no such limitation is effective with respect to the carrier's liability for conversion to its own use.

(3) Reasonable provisions as to the time and manner of presenting claims and instituting actions based on the shipment may be included in a bill of lading or tariff.

Part 4—Warehouse Receipts and Bills of Lading: General Obligations

§ 7–401. Irregularities in Issue of Receipt or Bill or Conduct of Issuer.

The obligations imposed by this Article on an issuer apply to a document of title regardless of the fact that

(a) the document may not comply with the requirements of this Article or of any other law or regulation regarding its issue, form or content; or

(b) the issuer may have violated laws regulating the conduct of his business; or

(c) the goods covered by the document were owned by the bailee at the time the document was issued; or

(d) the person issuing the document does not come within the definition of warehouseman if it purports to be a warehouse receipt.

§ 7–402. Duplicate Receipt or Bill; Overissue.

Neither a duplicate nor any other document of title purporting to cover goods already represented by an outstanding document of the same issuer confers any right in the goods, except as provided in the case of bills in a set, overissue of documents for fungible goods and substitutes for lost, stolen or destroyed documents. But the issuer is liable for damages caused by his overissue or failure to identify a duplicate document as such by conspicuous notation on its face.

§ 7–403. Obligation of Warehouseman or Carrier to Deliver; Excuse.

(1) The bailee must deliver the goods to a person entitled under the document who complies with subsections (2) and (3), unless and to the extent that the bailee establishes any of the following:

(a) delivery of the goods to a person whose receipt was rightful as against the claimant;

(b) damage to or delay, loss or destruction of the goods for which the bailee is not liable [, but the burden of establishing negligence in such cases is on the person entitled under the document];

Note: *The brackets in (1)(b) indicate that State enactments may differ on this point without serious damage to the principle of uniformity.*

(c) previous sale or other disposition of the goods in lawful enforcement of a lien or on warehouseman's lawful termination of storage;

(d) the exercise by a seller of his right to stop delivery pursuant to the provisions of the Article on Sales (Section 2–705);

(e) a diversion, reconsignment or other disposition pursuant to the provisions of this Article (Section 7–303) or tariff regulating such right;

(f) release, satisfaction or any other fact affording a personal defense against the claimant;

(g) any other lawful excuse.

(2) A person claiming goods covered by a document of title must satisfy the bailee's lien where the bailee so requests or where the bailee is prohibited by law from delivering the goods until the charges are paid.

(3) Unless the person claiming is one against whom the document confers no right under Sec. 7–503(1), he must surrender for cancellation or notation of partial deliveries any outstanding negotiable document covering the goods, and the bailee must cancel the document or conspicuously note the partial delivery thereon or be liable to any person to whom the document is duly negotiated.

(4) "Person entitled under the document" means holder in the case of a negotiable document, or the person to whom delivery is to be made by the terms of or pursuant to written instructions under a non-negotiable document.

§ 7–404. No Liability for Good Faith Delivery Pursuant to Receipt or Bill.

A bailee who in good faith including observance of reasonable commercial standards has received goods and delivered or otherwise disposed of them according to the terms of the document of title or pursuant to this Article is not liable therefor. This rule applies even though the person from whom he received the goods had no authority to procure the document or to dispose of the goods and even though the person to whom he delivered the goods had no authority to receive them.

Part 5—Warehouse Receipts and Bills of Lading: Negotiation and Transfer

§ 7–501. Form of Negotiation and Requirements of "Due Negotiation."

(1) A negotiable document of title running to the order of a named person is negotiated by his indorsement and delivery. After his indorsement in blank or to bearer any person can negotiate it by delivery alone.

(2) (a) A negotiable document of title is also negotiated by delivery alone when by its original terms it runs to bearer.

(b) When a document running to the order of a named person is delivered to him the effect is the same as if the document had been negotiated.

(3) Negotiation of a negotiable document of title after it has been indorsed to a specified person requires indorsement by the special indorsee as well as delivery.

(4) A negotiable document of title is "duly negotiated" when it is negotiated in the manner stated in this section to a holder who purchases it in good faith without notice of any defense against or claim to it on the part of any person and for value, unless it is established that the negotiation is not in the regular course of business or financing or involves receiving the document in settlement or payment of a money obligation.

(5) Indorsement of a non-negotiable document neither makes it negotiable nor adds to the transferee's rights.

(6) The naming in a negotiable bill of a person to be notified of the arrival of the goods does not limit the negotiability of the bill nor constitute notice to a purchaser thereof of any interest of such person in the goods.

§ 7–502. Rights Acquired by Due Negotiation.

(1) Subject to the following section and to the provisions of Section 7–205 on fungible goods, a holder to whom a negotiable document of title has been duly negotiated acquires thereby:

(a) title to the document;

(b) title to the goods;

(c) all rights accruing under the law of agency or estoppel, including rights to goods delivered to the bailee after the document was issued; and

(d) the direct obligation of the issuer to hold or deliver the goods according to the terms of the document free of any defense or claim by him except

those arising under the terms of the document or under this Article. In the case of a delivery order the bailee's obligation accrues only upon acceptance and the obligation acquired by the holder is that the issuer and any indorser will procure the acceptance of the bailee.

(2) Subject to the following section, title and rights so acquired are not defeated by any stoppage of the goods represented by the document or by surrender of such goods by the bailee, and are not impaired even though the negotiation or any prior negotiation constituted a breach of duty or even though any person has been deprived of possession of the document by misrepresentation, fraud, accident, mistake, duress, loss, theft or conversion, or even though a previous sale or other transfer of the goods or document has been made to a third person.

§ 7–503. Document of Title to Goods Defeated in Certain Cases.

(1) A document of title confers no right in goods against a person who before issuance of the document had a legal interest or a perfected security interest in them and who neither

(a) delivered or entrusted them or any document of title covering them to the bailor or his nominee with actual or apparent authority to ship, store or sell or with power to obtain delivery under this Article (Section 7–403) or with power of disposition under this Act (Sections 2–403 and 9–307) or other statute or rule of law; nor

(b) acquiesced in the procurement by the bailor or his nominee of any document of title.

(2) Title to goods based upon an unaccepted delivery order is subject to the rights of anyone to whom a negotiable warehouse receipt or bill of lading covering the goods has been duly negotiated. Such a title may be defeated under the next section to the same extent as the rights of the issuer or a transferee from the issuer.

(3) Title to goods based upon a bill of lading issued to a freight forwarder is subject to the rights of anyone to whom a bill issued by the freight forwarder is duly negotiated; but delivery by the carrier in accordance with Part 4 of this Article pursuant to its own bill of lading discharges the carrier's obligation to deliver.

§ 7–504. Rights Acquired in the Absence of Due Negotiation; Effect of Diversion; Seller's Stoppage of Delivery.

(1) A transferee of a document, whether negotiable or non-negotiable, to whom the document has been delivered but not duly negotiated, acquires the title and rights which his transferor had or had actual authority to convey.

(2) In the case of a non-negotiable document, until but not after the bailee receives notification of the transfer, the rights of the transferee may be defeated

(a) by those creditors of the transferor who could treat the sale as void under Section 2–402; or

(b) by a buyer from the transferor in ordinary course of business if the bailee has delivered the goods to the buyer or received notification of his rights; or

(c) as against the bailee by good faith dealings of the bailee with the transferor.

(3) A diversion or other change of shipping instructions by the consignor in a non-negotiable bill of lading which causes the bailee not to deliver to the consignee defeats the consignee's title to the goods if they have been delivered to a buyer in ordinary course of business and in any event defeats the consignee's rights against the bailee.

(4) Delivery pursuant to a non-negotiable document may be stopped by a seller under Section 2–705, and subject to the requirement of due notification there provided. A bailee honoring the seller's instructions is entitled to be indemnified by the seller against any resulting loss or expense.

§ 7–505. Indorser Not a Guarantor for Other Parties.

The indorsement of a document of title issued by a bailee does not make the indorser liable for any default by the bailee or by previous indorsers.

§ 7–506. Delivery Without Indorsement: Right to Compel Indorsement.

The transferee of a negotiable document of title has a specifically enforceable right to have his transferor supply any necessary indorsement but the transfer becomes a negotiation only as of the time the indorsement is supplied.

§ 7–507. Warranties on Negotiation or Transfer of Receipt or Bill.

Where a person negotiates or transfers a document of title for value otherwise than as a mere intermediary under the next following section, then unless otherwise agreed he warrants to his immediate purchaser only in addition to any warranty made in selling the goods

(a) that the document is genuine; and

(b) that he has no knowledge of any fact which would impair its validity or worth; and

(c) that his negotiation or transfer is rightful and fully effective with respect to the title to the document and the goods it represents.

§ 7–508. Warranties of Collecting Bank as to Documents.

A collecting bank or other intermediary known to be entrusted with documents on behalf of another or with collection of a draft of other claim against delivery of documents warrants by such delivery of the documents only its own good faith and authority. This rule applies even though the intermediary has purchased or made advances against the claim or draft to be collected.

§ 7–509. Receipt or Bill: When Adequate Compliance With Commercial Contract.

The question whether a document is adequate to fulfill the obligations of a contract for sale or the conditions of a credit is governed by the Articles on Sales (Article 2) and on Letters of Credit (Article 5).

Part 6—Warehouse Receipts and Bills of Lading: Miscellaneous Provisions

§ 7–601. Lost and Missing Documents.

(1) If a document has been lost, stolen or destroyed, a court may order delivery of the goods or issuance of a substitute document and the bailee may without liability to any person comply with such order. If the document was negotiable the claimant must post security approved by the court to indemnify any person who may suffer loss as a result of non-surrender of the document. If the document was not negotiable, such security may be required at the discretion of the court. The court may also in its discretion order payment of the bailee's reasonable costs and counsel fees.

(2) A bailee who without court order delivers goods to a person claiming under a missing negotiable document is liable to any person injured thereby, and if the delivery is not in good faith becomes liable for conversion. Delivery in good faith is not conversion if made in accordance with a filed classification or tariff or, where no classification or tariff is filed, if the claimant posts security with the bailee in an amount at least double the value of the goods at the time of posting to indemnify any person injured by the delivery who files a notice of claim within one year after the delivery.

§ 7–602. Attachment of Goods Covered by a Negotiable Document.

Except where the document was originally issued upon delivery of the goods by a person who had no power to dispose of them, no lien attaches by virtue of any judicial process to goods in the possession of a bailee for which a negotiable document of title is outstanding unless the document be first surrendered to the bailee or its negotiation enjoined, and the bailee shall not be compelled to deliver the goods pursuant to process until the document is surrendered to him or impounded by the court. One who purchases the document for value without notice of the process or injunction takes free of the lien imposed by judicial process.

§ 7–603. Conflicting Claims; Interpleader.

If more than one person claims title or possession of the goods, the bailee is excused from delivery until he has had a reasonable time to ascertain the validity of the adverse claims or to bring an action to compel all claimants to interplead and may compel such interpleader, either in defending an action for non-delivery of the goods, or by original action, whichever is appropriate.

ARTICLE 8: INVESTMENT SECURITIES

Part 1—Short Title and General Matters

§ 8–101. Short Title.

This Article shall be known and may be cited as Uniform Commercial Code—Investment Securities.

§ 8–102. Definitions and Index of Definitions.

(1) In this Article, unless the context otherwise requires:

(a) A "certificated security" is a share, participation, or other interest in property of or an enterprise of the issuer or an obligation of the issuer which is

(i) represented by an instrument issued in bearer or registered form;

(ii) of a type commonly dealt in on securities exchanges or markets or commonly recognized in any area in which it is issued or dealt in as a medium for investment; and

(iii) either one of a class or series or by its terms divisible into a class or series of shares, participations, interests, or obligations.

(b) An "uncertificated security" is a share, participation, or other interest in property or an enterprise of the issuer or an obligation of the issuer which is

(i) not represented by an instrument and the transfer of which is registered upon books maintained for that purpose by or on behalf of the issuer;

(ii) of a type commonly dealt in on securities exchanges or markets; and

(iii) either one of a class or series or by its terms divisible into a class or series of shares, participations, interests, or obligations.

(c) A "security" is either a certificated or an uncertificated security. If a security is certificated, the terms "security" and "certificated security" may mean either the intangible interest, the instrument representing that interest, or both, as the context requires. A writing that is a certificated security is governed by this Article and not by Article 3, even though it also meets the requirements of that Article. This Article does not apply to money. If a certificated security has been retained by or surrendered to the issuer or its transfer agent for reasons other than registration of transfer, other temporary purpose, payment, exchange, or acquisition by the issuer, that security shall be treated as an uncertificated security for purposes of this Article.

(d) A certificated security is in "registered form" if

(i) it specifies a person entitled to the security or the rights it represents; and

(ii) its transfer may be registered upon books maintained for that purpose by or on behalf of the issuer, or the security so states.

(e) A certificated security is in "bearer form" if it runs to bearer according to its terms and not by reason of any indorsement.

(2) A "subsequent purchaser" is a person who takes other than by original issue.

(3) A "clearing corporation" is a corporation registered as a "clearing agency" under the federal securities laws or a corporation:

(a) at least 90 percent of whose capital stock is held by or for one or more organizations, none of which, other than a national securities exchange or association, holds in excess of 20 percent of the capital stock of the corporation, and each of which is

(i) subject to supervision or regulation pursuant to the provisions of federal or state banking laws or state insurance laws,

(ii) a broker or dealer or investment company registered under the federal securities laws, or

(iii) a national securities exchange or association registered under the federal securities laws; and

(b) any remaining capital stock of which is held by individuals who have purchased it at or prior to the time of their taking office as directors of the corporation and who have purchased only so much of the capital stock as is necessary to permit them to qualify as directors.

(4) A "custodian bank" is a bank or trust company that is supervised and examined by state or federal authority having supervision over banks and is acting as custodian for a clearing corporation.

(5) Other definitions applying to this Article or to specified Parts thereof and the sections in which they appear are:

"Adverse claim". Section 8–302.
"Bona fide purchaser". Section 8–302.
"Broker". Section 8–303.
"Debtor". Section 9–105.

"Financial intermediary". Section 8–313.
"Guarantee of the signature". Section 8–402.
"Initial transaction statement". Section 8–408.
"Instruction". Section 8–308.
"Intermediary bank". Section 4–105.
"Issuer". Section 8–201.
"Overissue". Section 8–104.
"Secured Party". Section 9–105.
"Security Agreement". Section 9–105.

(6) In addition, Article 1 contains general definitions and principles of construction and interpretation applicable throughout this Article.

Amended in 1962, 1973 and 1977.

§ 8–103. Issuer's Lien.

A lien upon a security in favor of an issuer thereof is valid against a purchaser only if:

(a) the security is certificated and the right of the issuer to the lien is noted conspicuously thereon; or

(b) the security is uncertificated and a notation of the right of the issuer to the lien is contained in the initial transaction statement sent to the purchaser or, if his interest is transferred to him other than by registration of transfer, pledge, or release, the initial transaction statement sent to the registered owner or the registered pledgee.

Amended in 1977.

§ 8–104. Effect of Overissue; "Overissue".

(1) The provisions of this Article which validate a security or compel its issue or reissue do not apply to the extent that validation, issue, or reissue would result in overissue; but if:

(a) an identical security which does not constitute an overissue is reasonably available for purchase, the person entitled to issue or validation may compel the issuer to purchase the security for him and either to deliver a certificated security or to register the transfer of an uncertificated security to him, against surrender of any certificated security he holds; or

(b) a security is not so available for purchase, the person entitled to issue or validation may recover from the issuer the price he or the last purchaser for value paid for it with interest from the date of his demand.

(2) "Overissue" means the issue of securities in excess of the amount the issuer has corporate power to issue.

Amended in 1977.

§ 8–105. Certificated Securities Negotiable; Statements and Instructions Not Negotiable; Presumptions.

(1) Certificated securities governed by this Article are negotiable instruments.

(2) Statements (Section 8–408), notices, or the like, sent by the issuer of uncertificated securities and instructions (Section 8–308) are neither negotiable instruments nor certificated securities.

(3) In any action on a security:

(a) unless specifically denied in the pleadings, each signature on a certificated security, in a necessary indorsement, on an initial transaction statement, or on an instruction, is admitted;

(b) if the effectiveness of a signature is put in issue, the burden of establishing it is on the party claiming under the signature, but the signature is presumed to be genuine or authorized;

(c) if signatures on a certificated security are admitted or established, production of the security entitles a holder to recover on it unless the defendant establishes a defense or a defect going to the validity of the security;

(d) if signatures on an initial transaction statement are admitted or established, the facts stated in the statement are presumed to be true as of the time of its issuance; and

(e) after it is shown that a defense or defect exists, the plaintiff has the burden of establishing that he or some person under whom he claims is a person against whom the defense or defect is ineffective (Section 8–202).

Amended in 1977.

§ 8–106. Applicability.

The law (including the conflict of laws rules) of the jurisdiction of organization of the issuer governs the validity of a security, the effectiveness of registration by the issuer, and the rights and duties of the issuer with respect to:

(a) registration of transfer of a certificated security;

(b) registration of transfer, pledge, or release of an uncertificated security; and

(c) sending of statements of uncertificated securities.

Amended in 1977.

§ 8–107. Securities Transferable; Action for Price.

(1) Unless otherwise agreed and subject to any applicable law or regulation respecting short sales, a person obligated to transfer securities may transfer any certificated security of the specified issue in bearer form or registered in the name of the transferee, or indorsed to him or in blank, or he may transfer an equivalent uncertificated security to the transferee or a person designated by the transferee.

(2) If the buyer fails to pay the price as it comes due under a contract of sale, the seller may recover the price of:

(a) certificated securities accepted by the buyer;

(b) uncertificated securities that have been transferred to the buyer or a person designated by the buyer; and

(c) other securities if efforts at their resale would be unduly burdensome or if there is no readily available market for their resale.

Amended in 1977.

§ 8–108. Registration of Pledge and Release of Uncertificated Securities.

A security interest in an uncertificated security may be evidenced by the registration of pledge to the secured party or a person designated by him. There can be no more than one registered pledge of an uncertificated security at any time. The registered owner of an uncertificated security is the person in whose name the security is registered, even if the security is subject to a registered pledge. The rights of a registered pledgee of an uncertificated security under this Article are terminated by the registration of release.

Added in 1977.

Part 2—Issue—Issuer

§ 8–201. "Issuer".

(1) With respect to obligations on or defenses to a security, "issuer" includes a person who:

(a) places or authorizes the placing of his name on a certificated security (otherwise than as authenticating trustee, registrar, transfer agent, or the like) to evidence that it represents a share, participation, or other interest in his property or in an enterprise, or to evidence his duty to perform an obligation represented by the certificated security;

(b) creates shares, participations, or other interests in his property or in an enterprise or undertakes obligations, which shares, participations, interests, or obligations are uncertificated securities;

(c) directly or indirectly creates fractional interests in his rights or property, which fractional interests are represented by certificated securities; or

(d) becomes responsible for or in place of any other person described as an issuer in this section.

(2) With respect to obligations on or defenses to a security, a guarantor is an issuer to the extent of his guaranty, whether or not his obligation is noted on a certificated security or on statements of uncertificated securities sent pursuant to Section 8–408.

(3) With respect to registration of transfer, pledge, or release (Part 4 of this Article), "issuer" means a person on whose behalf transfer books are maintained.

Amended in 1977.

§ 8–202. Issuer's Responsibility and Defenses; Notice of Defect or Defense.

(1) Even against a purchaser for value and without notice, the terms of a security include:

(a) if the security is certificated, those stated on the security;

(b) if the security is uncertificated, those contained in the initial transaction statement sent to such purchaser or, if his interest is transferred to him other than by registration of transfer, pledge, or release, the initial transaction statement sent to the registered owner or registered pledgee; and

(c) those made part of the security by reference, on the certificated security or in the initial transaction statement, to another instrument, indenture, or document or to a constitution, statute, ordinance, rule, regulation, order or the like, to the extent that the terms referred to do not conflict with the terms stated on the certificated security or contained in the statement. A reference under this paragraph does not of itself charge a purchaser for value with notice of a defect going to the validity of the security, even though the certificated security or statement expressly states that a person accepting it admits notice.

(2) A certificated security in the hands of a purchaser for value or an uncertificated security as to which an initial transaction statement has been sent to a purchaser for value, other than a security issued by a government or governmental agency or unit, even though issued with a defect going to its validity, is valid with respect to the purchaser if he is without notice of the particular defect unless the defect involves a violation of constitutional provisions, in which case the security is valid with respect to a subsequent purchaser for value and without notice of the defect. This subsection applies to an issuer that is a government or governmental agency or unit only if either there has been substantial compliance with the legal requirements governing the issue or the issuer has received a substantial consideration for the issue as a whole or for the particular security and a stated purpose of the issue is one for which the issuer has power to borrow money or issue the security.

(3) Except as provided in the case of certain unauthorized signatures (Section 8–205), lack of genuineness of a certificated security or an initial transaction statement is a complete defense, even against a purchaser for value and without notice.

(4) All other defenses of the issuer of a certificated or uncertificated security, including nondelivery and conditional delivery of a certificated security, are ineffective against a purchaser for value who has taken without notice of the particular defense.

(5) Nothing in this section shall be construed to affect the right of a party to a "when, as and if issued" or a "when distributed" contract to cancel the contract in the event of a material change in the character of the secu-

rity that is the subject of the contract or in the plan or arrangement pursuant to which the security is to be issued or distributed.

Amended in 1977.

§ 8–203. Staleness as Notice of Defects or Defenses.

(1) After an act or event creating a right to immediate performance of the principal obligation represented by a certificated security or that sets a date on or after which the security is to be presented or surrendered for redemption or exchange, a purchaser is charged with notice of any defect in its issue or defense of the issuer if:

(a) the act or event is one requiring the payment of money, the delivery of certificated securities, the registration of transfer of uncertificated securities, or any of these on presentation or surrender of the certificated security, the funds or securities are available on the date set for payment or exchange, and he takes the security more than one year after that date; and

(b) the act or event is not covered by paragraph (a) and he takes the security more than 2 years after the date set for surrender or presentation or the date on which performance became due.

(2) A call that has been revoked is not within subsection (1).

Amended in 1977.

§ 8–204. Effect of Issuer's Restrictions on Transfer.

A restriction on transfer of a security imposed by the issuer, even if otherwise lawful, is ineffective against any person without actual knowledge of it unless:

(a) the security is certificated and the restriction is noted conspicuously thereon; or

(b) the security is uncertificated and a notation of the restriction is contained in the initial transaction statement sent to the person or, if his interest is transferred to him other than by registration of transfer, pledge, or release, the initial transaction statement sent to the registered owner or the registered pledgee.

Amended in 1977.

§ 8–205. Effect of Unauthorized Signature on Certificated Security or Initial Transaction Statement.

An unauthorized signature placed on a certificated security prior to or in the course of issue or placed on an initial transaction statement is ineffective, but the signature is effective in favor of a purchaser for value of the certificated security or a purchaser for value of an uncertificated security to whom the initial transaction statement has been sent, if the purchaser is without notice of the lack of authority and the signing has been done by:

(a) an authenticating trustee, registrar, transfer agent, or other person entrusted by the issuer with the signing of the security, of similar securities, or of initial transaction statements or the immediate preparation for signing of any of them; or

(b) an employee of the issuer, or of any of the foregoing, entrusted with responsible handling of the security or initial transaction statement.

Amended in 1977.

§ 8–206. Completion or Alteration of Certificated Security or Initial Transaction Statement.

(1) If a certificated security contains the signatures necessary to its issue or transfer but is incomplete in any other respect:

(a) any person may complete it by filling in the blanks as authorized; and

(b) even though the blanks are incorrectly filled in, the security as completed is enforceable by a purchaser who took it for value and without notice of the incorrectness.

(2) A complete certificated security that has been improperly altered, even though fraudulently, remains enforceable, but only according to its original terms.

(3) If an initial transaction statement contains the signatures necessary to its validity, but is incomplete in any other respect:

(a) any person may complete it by filling in the blanks as authorized; and

(b) even though the blanks are incorrectly filled in, the statement as completed is effective in favor of the person to whom it is sent if he purchased the security referred to therein for value and without notice of the incorrectness.

(4) A complete initial transaction statement that has been improperly altered, even though fraudulently, is effective in favor of a purchaser to whom it has been sent, but only according to its original terms.

Amended in 1977.

§ 8–207. Rights and Duties of Issuer With Respect to Registered Owners and Registered Pledgees.

(1) Prior to due presentment for registration of transfer of a certificated security in registered form, the issuer or indenture trustee may treat the registered owner as the person exclusively entitled to vote, to receive notifications, and otherwise to exercise all the rights and powers of an owner.

(2) Subject to the provisions of subsections (3), (4), and (6), the issuer or indenture trustee may treat the registered owner of an uncertificated security as the person exclusively entitled to vote, to receive notifications, and otherwise to exercise all the rights and powers of an owner.

(3) The registered owner of an uncertificated security that is subject to a registered pledge is not entitled to registration of transfer prior to the due presentment to the issuer of a release instruction. The exercise of conversion rights with respect to a convertible uncertificated security is a transfer within the meaning of this section.

(4) Upon due presentment of a transfer instruction from the registered pledgee of an uncertificated security, the issuer shall:

(a) register the transfer of the security to the new owner free of pledge, if the instruction specifies a new owner (who may be the registered pledgee) and does not specify a pledgee;

(b) register the transfer of the security to the new owner subject to the interest of the existing pledgee, if the instruction specifies a new owner and the existing pledgee; or

(c) register the release of the security from the existing pledge and register the pledge of the security to the other pledgee, if the instruction specifies the existing owner and another pledgee.

(5) Continuity of perfection of a security interest is not broken by registration of transfer under subsection (4)(b) or by registration of release and pledge under subsection (4)(c), if the security interest is assigned.

(6) If an uncertificated security is subject to a registered pledge:

(a) any uncertificated securities issued in exchange for or distributed with respect to the pledged security shall be registered subject to the pledge;

(b) any certificated securities issued in exchange for or distributed with respect to the pledged security shall be delivered to the registered pledgee; and

(c) any money paid in exchange for or in redemption of part or all of the security shall be paid to the registered pledgee.

(7) Nothing in this Article shall be construed to affect the liability of the registered owner of a security for calls, assessments, or the like.

Amended in 1977.

§ 8–208. Effect of Signature of Authenticating Trustee, Registrar, or Transfer Agent.

(1) A person placing his signature upon a certificated security or an initial transaction statement as authenticating trustee, registrar, transfer agent, or the like, warrants to a purchaser for value of the certificated security or a purchaser for value of an uncertificated security to whom the initial transaction statement has been sent, if the purchaser is without notice of the particular defect, that:

(a) the certificated security or initial transaction statement is genuine;

(b) his own participation in the issue or registration of the transfer, pledge, or release of the security is within his capacity and within the scope of the authority received by him from the issuer; and

(c) he has reasonable grounds to believe the security is in the form and within the amount the issuer is authorized to issue.

(2) Unless otherwise agreed, a person by so placing his signature does not assume responsibility for the validity of the security in other respects.

Amended in 1962 and 1977.

Part 3—Transfer

§ 8–301. Rights Acquired by Purchaser.

(1) Upon transfer of a security to a purchaser (Section 8–313), the purchaser acquires the rights in the security which his transferor had or had actual authority to convey unless the purchaser's rights are limited by Section 8–302(4).

(2) A transferee of a limited interest acquires rights only to the extent of the interest transferred. The creation or release of a security interest in a security is the transfer of a limited interest in that security.

Amended in 1977.

§ 8–302. "Bona Fide Purchaser"; "Adverse Claim"; Title Acquired by Bona Fide Purchaser.

(1) A "bona fide purchaser" is a purchaser for value in good faith and without notice of any adverse claim:

(a) who takes delivery of a certificated security in bearer form or in registered form, issued or indorsed to him or in blank;

(b) to whom the transfer, pledge, or release of an uncertificated security is registered on the books of the issuer; or

(c) to whom a security is transferred under the provisions of paragraph (c), (d)(i), or (g) of Section 8–313(1).

(2) "Adverse claim" includes a claim that a transfer was or would be wrongful or that a particular adverse person is the owner of or has an interest in the security.

(3) A bona fide purchaser in addition to acquiring the rights of a purchaser (Section 8–301) also acquires his interest in the security free of any adverse claim.

(4) Notwithstanding Section 8–301(1), the transferee of a particular certificated security who has been a party to any fraud or illegality affecting the security, or who as a prior holder of that certificated security had notice

of an adverse claim, cannot improve his position by taking from a bona fide purchaser.

Amended in 1977.

§ 8–303. "Broker".

"Broker" means a person engaged for all or part of his time in the business of buying and selling securities, who in the transaction concerned acts for, buys a security from, or sells a security to, a customer. Nothing in this Article determines the capacity in which a person acts for purposes of any other statute or rule to which the person is subject.

§ 8–304. Notice to Purchaser of Adverse Claims.

(1) A purchaser (including a broker for the seller or buyer, but excluding an intermediary bank) of a certificated security is charged with notice of adverse claims if:

    (a) the security, whether in bearer or registered form, has been indorsed "for collection" or "for surrender" or for some other purpose not involving transfer; or

    (b) the security is in bearer form and has on it an unambiguous statement that it is the property of a person other than the transferor. The mere writing of a name on a security is not such a statement.

(2) A purchaser (including a broker for the seller or buyer, but excluding an intermediary bank) to whom the transfer, pledge, or release of an uncertificated security is registered is charged with notice of adverse claims as to which the issuer has a duty under Section 8–403(4) at the time of registration and which are noted in the initial transaction statement sent to the purchaser or, if his interest is transferred to him other than by registration of transfer, pledge, or release, the initial transaction statement sent to the registered owner or the registered pledgee.

(3) The fact that the purchaser (including a broker for the seller or buyer) of a certificated or uncertificated security has notice that the security is held for a third person or is registered in the name of or indorsed by a fiduciary does not create a duty of inquiry into the rightfulness of the transfer or constitute constructive notice of adverse claims. However, if the purchaser (excluding an intermediary bank) has knowledge that the proceeds are being used or the transaction is for the individual benefit of the fiduciary or otherwise in breach of duty, the purchaser is charged with notice of adverse claims.

Amended in 1977.

§ 8–305. Staleness as Notice of Adverse Claims.

An act or event that creates a right to immediate performance of the principal obligation represented by a certificated security or sets a date on or after which a certificated security is to be presented or surrendered for redemption or exchange does not itself constitute any notice of adverse claims except in the case of a transfer:

    (a) after one year from any date set for presentment or surrender for redemption or exchange; or

    (b) after 6 months from any date set for payment of money against presentation or surrender of the security if funds are available for payment on that date.

Amended in 1977.

§ 8–306. Warranties on Presentment and Transfer of Certificated Securities; Warranties of Originators of Instructions.

(1) A person who presents a certificated security for registration of transfer or for payment or exchange warrants to the issuer that he is entitled to the registration, payment, or exchange. But, a purchaser for value and without notice of adverse claims who receives a new, reissued, or re-registered certificated security on registration of transfer or receives an initial transaction statement confirming the registration of transfer of an equivalent uncertificated security to him warrants only that he has no knowledge of any unauthorized signature (Section 8–311) in a necessary indorsement.

(2) A person by transferring a certificated security to a purchaser for value warrants only that:

    (a) his transfer is effective and rightful;

    (b) the security is genuine and has not been materially altered; and

    (c) he knows of no fact which might impair the validity of the security.

(3) If a certificated security is delivered by an intermediary known to be entrusted with delivery of the security on behalf of another or with collection of a draft or other claim against delivery, the intermediary by delivery warrants only his own good faith and authority, even though he has purchased or made advances against the claim to be collected against the delivery.

(4) A pledgee or other holder for security who redelivers a certificated security received, or after payment and on order of the debtor delivers that security to a third person, makes only the warranties of an intermediary under subsection (3).

(5) A person who originates an instruction warrants to the issuer that:

    (a) he is an appropriate person to originate the instruction; and

    (b) at the time the instruction is presented to the issuer he will be entitled to the registration of transfer, pledge, or release.

(6) A person who originates an instruction warrants to any person specially guaranteeing his signature (subsection 8–312(8)) that:

(a) he is an appropriate person to originate the instruction; and

(b) at the time the instruction is presented to the issuer:

(i) he will be entitled to the registration of transfer, pledge, or release; and

(ii) the transfer, pledge, or release requested in the instruction will be registered by the issuer free from all liens, security interests, restrictions, and claims other than those specified in the instruction.

(7) A person who originates an instruction warrants to a purchaser for value and to any person guaranteeing the instruction (Section 8–312(6)) that:

(a) he is an appropriate person to originate the instruction;

(b) the uncertificated security referred to therein is valid; and

(c) at the time the instruction is presented to the issuer

(i) the transferor will be entitled to the registration of transfer, pledge, or release;

(ii) the transfer, pledge, or release requested in the instruction will be registered by the issuer free from all liens, security interests, restrictions, and claims other than those specified in the instruction; and

(iii) the requested transfer, pledge, or release will be rightful.

(8) If a secured party is the registered pledgee or the registered owner of an uncertificated security, a person who originates an instruction of release or transfer to the debtor or, after payment and on order of the debtor, a transfer instruction to a third person, warrants to the debtor or the third person only that he is an appropriate person to originate the instruction and, at the time the instruction is presented to the issuer, the transferor will be entitled to the registration of release or transfer. If a transfer instruction to a third person who is a purchaser for value is originated on order of the debtor, the debtor makes to the purchaser the warranties of paragraphs (b), (c)(ii) and (c)(iii) of subsection (7).

(9) A person who transfers an uncertificated security to a purchaser for value and does not originate an instruction in connection with the transfer warrants only that:

(a) his transfer is effective and rightful; and

(b) the uncertificated security is valid.

(10) A broker gives to his customer and to the issuer and a purchaser the applicable warranties provided in this section and has the rights and privileges of a purchaser under this section. The warranties of and in fa-

vor of the broker, acting as an agent are in addition to applicable warranties given by and in favor of his customer.

Amended in 1962 and 1977.

§ 8–307. Effect of Delivery Without Indorsement; Right to Compel Indorsement.

If a certificated security in registered form has been delivered to a purchaser without a necessary indorsement he may become a bona fide purchaser only as of the time the indorsement is supplied; but against the transferor, the transfer is complete upon delivery and the purchaser has a specifically enforceable right to have any necessary indorsement supplied.

Amended in 1977.

§ 8–308. Indorsements; Instructions.

(1) An indorsement of a certificated security in registered form is made when an appropriate person signs on it or on a separate document an assignment or transfer of the security or a power to assign or transfer it or his signature is written without more upon the back of the security.

(2) An indorsement may be in blank or special. An indorsement in blank includes an indorsement to bearer. A special indorsement specifies to whom the security is to be transferred, or who has power to transfer it. A holder may convert a blank indorsement into a special indorsement.

(3) An indorsement purporting to be only of part of a certificated security representing units intended by the issuer to be separately transferable is effective to the extent of the indorsement.

(4) An "instruction" is an order to the issuer of an uncertificated security requesting that the transfer, pledge, or release from pledge of the uncertificated security specified therein be registered.

(5) An instruction originated by an appropriate person is:

(a) a writing signed by an appropriate person; or

(b) a communication to the issuer in any form agreed upon in a writing signed by the issuer and an appropriate person.

If an instruction has been originated by an appropriate person but is incomplete in any other respect, any person may complete it as authorized and the issuer may rely on it as completed even though it has been completed incorrectly.

(6) "An appropriate person" in subsection (1) means the person specified by the certificated security or by special indorsement to be entitled to the security.

(7) "An appropriate person" in subsection (5) means:

(a) for an instruction to transfer or pledge an uncertificated security which is then not subject to a registered pledge, the registered owner; or

(b) for an instruction to transfer or release an uncertificated security which is then subject to a registered pledge, the registered pledgee.

(8) In addition to the persons designated in subsections (6) and (7), "an appropriate person" in subsections (1) and (5) includes:

(a) if the person designated is described as a fiduciary but is no longer serving in the described capacity, either that person or his successor;

(b) if the persons designated are described as more than one person as fiduciaries and one or more are no longer serving in the described capacity, the remaining fiduciary or fiduciaries, whether or not a successor has been appointed or qualified;

(c) if the person designated is an individual and is without capacity to act by virtue of death, incompetence, infancy, or otherwise, his executor, administrator, guardian, or like fiduciary;

(d) if the persons designated are described as more than one person as tenants by the entirety or with right of survivorship and by reason of death all cannot sign, the survivor or survivors;

(e) a person having power to sign under applicable law or controlling instrument; and

(f) to the extent that the person designated or any of the foregoing persons may act through an agent, his authorized agent.

(9) Unless otherwise agreed, the indorser of a certificated security by his indorsement or the originator of an instruction by his origination assumes no obligation that the security will be honored by the issuer but only the obligations provided in Section 8–306.

(10) Whether the person signing is appropriate is determined as of the date of signing and an indorsement made by or an instruction originated by him does not become unauthorized for the purposes of this Article by virtue of any subsequent change of circumstances.

(11) Failure of a fiduciary to comply with a controlling instrument or with the law of the state having jurisdiction of the fiduciary relationship, including any law requiring the fiduciary to obtain court approval of the transfer, pledge, or release, does not render his indorsement or an instruction originated by him unauthorized for the purposes of this Article.

Amended in 1962 and 1977.

§ 8–309. Effect of Indorsement Without Delivery.

An indorsement of a certificated security, whether special or in blank, does not constitute a transfer until delivery of the certificated security on which it appears or, if the indorsement is on a separate document, until delivery of both the document and the certificated security.
Amended in 1977.

§ 8–310. Indorsement of Certificated Security in Bearer Form.

An indorsement of a certificated security in bearer form may give notice of adverse claims (Section 8–304) but does not otherwise affect any right to registration the holder possesses.
Amended in 1977.

§ 8–311. Effect of Unauthorized Indorsement or Instruction.

Unless the owner or pledgee has ratified an unauthorized indorsement or instruction or is otherwise precluded from asserting its ineffectiveness:

(a) he may assert its ineffectiveness against the issuer or any purchaser, other than a purchaser for value and without notice of adverse claims, who has in good faith received a new, reissued, or re-registered certificated security on registration of transfer or received an initial transaction statement confirming the registration of transfer, pledge, or release of an equivalent uncertificated security to him; and

(b) an issuer who registers the transfer of a certificated security upon the unauthorized indorsement or who registers the transfer, pledge, or release of an uncertificated security upon the unauthorized instruction is subject to liability for improper registration (Section 8–404).

Amended in 1977.

§ 8–312. Effect of Guaranteeing Signature, Indorsement or Instruction.

(1) Any person guaranteeing a signature of an indorser of a certificated security warrants that at the time of signing:

(a) the signature was genuine;

(b) the signer was an appropriate person to indorse (Section 8–308); and

(c) the signer had legal capacity to sign.

(2) Any person guaranteeing a signature of the originator of an instruction warrants that at the time of signing:

(a) the signature was genuine;

(b) the signer was an appropriate person to originate the instruction (Section 8–308) if the person specified in the instruction as the registered owner or registered pledgee of the uncertificated security was, in fact, the registered owner or registered pledgee of the security, as to which fact the signature guarantor makes no warranty;

(c) the signer had legal capacity to sign; and

(d) the taxpayer identification number, if any, appearing on the instruction as that of the registered owner or registered pledgee was the taxpayer identification number of the signer or of the owner or pledgee for whom the signer was acting.

(3) Any person specially guaranteeing the signature of the originator of an instruction makes not only the warranties of a signature guarantor (subsection (2)) but also warrants that at the time the instruction is presented to the issuer:

(a) the person specified in the instruction as the registered owner or registered pledgee of the uncertificated security will be the registered owner or registered pledgee; and

(b) the transfer, pledge, or release of the uncertificated security requested in the instruction will be registered by the issuer free from all liens, security interests, restrictions, and claims other than those specified in the instruction.

(4) The guarantor under subsections (1) and (2) or the special guarantor under subsection (3) does not otherwise warrant the rightfulness of the particular transfer, pledge, or release.

(5) Any person guaranteeing an indorsement of a certificated security makes not only the warranties of a signature guarantor under subsection (1) but also warrants the rightfulness of the particular transfer in all respects.

(6) Any person guaranteeing an instruction requesting the transfer, pledge, or release of an uncertificated security makes not only the warranties of a special signature guarantor under subsection (3) but also warrants the rightfulness of the particular transfer, pledge, or release in all respects.

(7) No issuer may require a special guarantee of signature (subsection (3)), a guarantee of indorsement (subsection (5)), or a guarantee of instruction (subsection (6)) as a condition to registration of transfer, pledge, or release.

(8) The foregoing warranties are made to any person taking or dealing with the security in reliance on the guarantee, and the guarantor is liable to the person for any loss resulting from breach of the warranties.

Amended in 1977.

§ 8–313. When Transfer to Purchaser Occurs; Financial Intermediary as Bona Fide Purchaser; "Financial Intermediary".

(1) Transfer of a security or a limited interest (including a security interest) therein to a purchaser occurs only:

(a) at the time he or a person designated by him acquires possession of a certificated security;

(b) at the time the transfer, pledge, or release of an uncertificated security is registered to him or a person designated by him;

(c) at the time his financial intermediary acquires possession of a certificated security specially indorsed to or issued in the name of the purchaser;

(d) at the time a financial intermediary, not a clearing corporation, sends him confirmation of the purchase and also by book entry or otherwise identifies as belonging to the purchaser

(i) a specific certificated security in the financial intermediary's possession;

(ii) a quantity of securities that constitute or are part of a fungible bulk of certificated securities in the financial intermediary's possession or of uncertificated securities registered in the name of the financial intermediary; or

(iii) a quantity of securities that constitute or are part of a fungible bulk of securities shown on the account of the financial intermediary on the books of another financial intermediary;

(e) with respect to an identified certificated security to be delivered while still in the possession of a third person, not a financial intermediary, at the time that person acknowledges that he holds for the purchaser;

(f) with respect to a specific uncertificated security the pledge or transfer of which has been registered to a third person, not a financial intermediary, at the time that person acknowledges that he holds for the purchaser;

(g) at the time appropriate entries to the account of the purchaser or a person designated by him on the books of a clearing corporation are made under Section 8–320;

(h) with respect to the transfer of a security interest where the debtor has signed a security agreement containing a description of the security, at the time a written notification, which, in the case of the creation of the security interest, is signed by the debtor (which may be a copy of the security agreement) or which, in the case of the release or assignment of the security interest created pursuant to this paragraph, is signed by the secured party, is received by

(i) a financial intermediary on whose books the interest of the transferor in the security appears;

(ii) a third person, not a financial intermediary, in possession of the security, if it is certificated;

(iii) a third person, not a financial intermediary, who is the registered owner of the security, if it is uncertificated and not subject to a registered pledge; or

(iv) a third person, not a financial intermediary, who is the registered pledgee of the security, if it is uncertificated and subject to a registered pledge;

(i) with respect to the transfer of a security interest where the transferor has signed a security agreement containing a description of the security, at the time new value is given by the secured party; or

(j) with respect to the transfer of a security interest where the secured party is a financial intermediary and the security has already been transferred to the financial intermediary under paragraphs (a), (b), (c), (d), or (g), at the time the transferor has signed a security agreement containing a description of the security and value is given by the secured party.

(2) The purchaser is the owner of a security held for him by a financial intermediary, but cannot be a bona fide purchaser of a security so held except in the circumstances specified in paragraphs (c), (d)(i), and (g) of subsection (1). If a security so held is part of a fungible bulk, as in the circumstances specified in paragraphs (d)(ii) and (d)(iii) of subsection (1), the purchaser is the owner of a proportionate property interest in the fungible bulk.

(3) Notice of an adverse claim received by the financial intermediary or by the purchaser after the financial intermediary takes delivery of a certificated security as a holder for value or after the transfer, pledge, or release of an uncertificated security has been registered free of the claim to a financial intermediary who has given value is not effective either as to the financial intermediary or as to the purchaser. However, as between the financial intermediary and the purchaser the purchaser may demand transfer of an equivalent security as to which no notice of adverse claim has been received.

(4) A "financial intermediary" is a bank, broker, clearing corporation, or other person (or the nominee of any of them) which in the ordinary course of its business maintains security accounts for its customers and is acting in that capacity. A financial intermediary may have a security interest in securities held in account for its customer.

Amended in 1962 and 1977.

§ 8–314. Duty to Transfer, When Completed.

(1) Unless otherwise agreed, if a sale of a security is made on an exchange or otherwise through brokers:

(a) the selling customer fulfills his duty to transfer at the time he:

(i) places a certificated security in the possession of the selling broker or a person designated by the broker;

(ii) causes an uncertificated security to be registered in the name of the selling broker or a person designated by the broker;

(iii) if requested, causes an acknowledgment to be made to the selling broker that a certificated or uncertificated security is held for the broker; or

(iv) places in the possession of the selling broker or of a person designated by the broker a transfer instruction for an uncertificated security, providing the issuer does not refuse to register the requested transfer if the instruction is presented to the issuer for registration within 30 days thereafter; and

(b) the selling broker, including a correspondent broker acting for a selling customer, fulfills his duty to transfer at the time he:

(i) places a certificated security in the possession of the buying broker or a person designated by the buying broker;

(ii) causes an uncertificated security to be registered in the name of the buying broker or a person designated by the buying broker;

(iii) places in the possession of the buying broker or of a person designated by the buying broker a transfer instruction for an uncertificated security, providing the issuer does not refuse to register the requested transfer if the instruction is presented to the issuer for registration within 30 days thereafter; or

(iv) effects clearance of the sale in accordance with the rules of the exchange on which the transaction took place.

(2) Except as provided in this section or unless otherwise agreed, a transferor's duty to transfer a security under a contract of purchase is not fulfilled until he:

(a) places a certificated security in form to be negotiated by the purchaser in the possession of the purchaser or of a person designated by the purchaser;

(b) causes an uncertificated security to be registered in the name of the purchaser or a person designated by the purchaser; or

(c) if the purchaser requests, causes an acknowledgment to be made to the purchaser that a certificated or uncertificated security is held for the purchaser.

(3) Unless made on an exchange, a sale to a broker purchasing for his own account is within subsection (2) and not within subsection (1).

Amended in 1977.

§ 8–315. Action Against Transferee Based Upon Wrongful Transfer.

(1) Any person against whom the transfer of a security is wrongful for any reason, including his incapacity, as against anyone except a bona fide purchaser, may:

(a) reclaim possession of the certificated security wrongfully transferred;

(b) obtain possession of any new certificated security representing all or part of the same rights;

(c) compel the origination of an instruction to transfer to him or a person designated by him an uncertificated security constituting all or part of the same rights; or

(d) have damages.

(2) If the transfer is wrongful because of an unauthorized indorsement of a certificated security, the owner may also reclaim or obtain possession of the security or a new certificated security, even from a bona fide purchaser, if the ineffectiveness of the purported indorsement can be asserted against him under the provisions of this Article on unauthorized indorsements (Section 8–311).

(3) The right to obtain or reclaim possession of a certificated security or to compel the origination of a transfer instruction may be specifically enforced and the transfer of a certificated or uncertificated security enjoined and a certificated security impounded pending the litigation.

Amended in 1977.

§ 8–316. Purchaser's Right to Requisites for Registration of Transfer, Pledge, or Release on Books.

Unless otherwise agreed, the transferor of a certificated security or the transferor, pledgor, or pledgee of an uncertificated security on due demand must supply his purchaser with any proof of his authority to transfer, pledge, or release or with any other requisite necessary to obtain registration of the transfer, pledge, or release of the security; but if the transfer, pledge, or release is not for value, a transferor, pledgor, or pledgee need not do so unless the purchaser furnishes the necessary expenses. Failure within a reasonable time to comply with a demand made gives the purchaser the right to reject or rescind the transfer, pledge, or release.
Amended in 1977.

§ 8–317. Creditors' Rights.

(1) Subject to the exceptions in subsections (3) and (4), no attachment or levy upon a certificated security or any share or other interest represented thereby which is outstanding is valid until the security is actually seized by the officer making the attachment or levy, but a certificated security which has been surrendered to the issuer may be reached by a creditor by legal process at the issuer's chief executive office in the United States.

(2) An uncertificated security registered in the name of the debtor may not be reached by a creditor except by legal process at the issuer's chief executive office in the United States.

(3) The interest of a debtor in a certificated security that is in the possession of a secured party not a financial intermediary or in an uncertificated security registered in the name of a secured party not a financial intermediary (or in the name of a nominee of the secured party) may be reached by a creditor by legal process upon the secured party.

(4) The interest of a debtor in a certificated security that is in the possession of or registered in the name of a financial intermediary or in an uncertificated security registered in the name of a financial intermediary may be reached by a creditor by legal process upon the financial intermediary on whose books the interest of the debtor appears.

(5) Unless otherwise provided by law, a creditor's lien upon the interest of a debtor in a security obtained pursuant to subsection (3) or (4) is not a restraint on the transfer of the security, free of the lien, to a third party for new value; but in the event of a transfer, the lien applies to the proceeds of the transfer in the hands of the secured party or financial intermediary, subject to any claims having priority.

(6) A creditor whose debtor is the owner of a security is entitled to aid from courts of appropriate jurisdiction, by injunction or otherwise, in reaching the security or in satisfying the claim by means allowed at law or in equity in regard to property that cannot readily be reached by ordinary legal process.

Amended in 1977.

§ 8–318. No Conversion by Good Faith Conduct.

An agent or bailee who in good faith (including observance of reasonable commercial standards if he is in the business of buying, selling, or otherwise dealing with securities) has received certificated securities and sold, pledged, or delivered them or has sold or caused the transfer or pledge of uncertificated securities over which he had control according to the instructions of his principal, is not liable for conversion or for participation in breach of fiduciary duty although the principal had no right so to deal with the securities.
Amended in 1977.

§ 8–319. Statute of Frauds.

A contract for the sale of securities is not enforceable by way of action or defense unless:

(a) there is some writing signed by the party against whom enforcement is sought or by his authorized agent or broker, sufficient to indicate that a contract has been made for sale of a stated quantity of described securities at a defined or stated price;

(b) delivery of a certificated security or transfer instruction has been accepted, or transfer of an uncertificated security has been registered and the transferee has failed to send written objection to the issuer within 10 days after receipt of the initial transaction statement confirming the registration, or payment has been made, but the contract is enforceable under this provision only to the extent of the delivery, registration, or payment;

(c) within a reasonable time a writing in confirmation of the sale or purchase and sufficient against the sender under paragraph (a) has been received by the party against whom enforcement is sought and he has failed to send written objection to its contents within 10 days after its receipt; or

(d) the party against whom enforcement is sought admits in his pleading, testimony, or otherwise in court that a contract was made for the sale of a stated quantity of described securities at a defined or stated price.

Amended in 1977.

§ 8–320. Transfer or Pledge Within Central Depository System.

(1) In addition to other methods, a transfer, pledge, or release of a security or any interest therein may be effected by the making of appropriate entries on the books of a clearing corporation reducing the account of the transferor, pledgor, or pledgee and increasing the account of the transferee, pledgee, or pledgor by the amount of the obligation or the number of shares or rights transferred, pledged, or released, if the security is shown on the account of a transferor, pledgor, or pledgee on the books of the clearing corporation; is subject to the control of the clearing corporation; and

(a) if certificated,

(i) is in the custody of the clearing corporation, another clearing corporation, a custodian bank, or a nominee of any of them; and

(ii) is in bearer form or indorsed in blank by an appropriate person or registered in the name of the clearing corporation, a custodian bank, or a nominee of any of them; or

(b) if uncertificated, is registered in the name of the clearing corporation, another clearing corporation, a custodian bank, or a nominee of any of them.

(2) Under this section entries may be made with respect to like securities or interests therein as a part of a fungible bulk and may refer merely to a quantity of a particular security without reference to the name of the registered owner, certificate or bond number, or the like, and, in appropriate cases, may be on a net basis taking into account other transfers, pledges, or releases of the same security.

(3) A transfer under this section is effective (Section 8–313) and the purchaser acquires the rights of the transferor (Section 8–301). A pledge or release under this section is the transfer of a limited interest. If a pledge or the creation of a security interest is intended, the security interest is perfected at the time when both value is given by the pledgee and the appropriate entries are made (Section 8–321). A transferee or pledgee under this section may be a bona fide purchaser (Section 8–302).

(4) A transfer or pledge under this section is not a registration of transfer under Part 4.

(5) That entries made on the books of the clearing corporation as provided in subsection (1) are not appropriate does not affect the validity or effect of the entries or the liabilities or obligations of the clearing corporation to any person adversely affected thereby.

Added in 1962; amended in 1977.

§ 8–321. Enforceability, Attachment, Perfection and Termination of Security Interests.

(1) A security interest in a security is enforceable and can attach only if it is transferred to the secured party or a person designated by him pursuant to a provision of Section 8–313(1).

(2) A security interest so transferred pursuant to agreement by a transferor who has rights in the security to a transferee who has given value is a perfected security interest, but a security interest that has been transferred solely under paragraph (i) of Section 8–313(1) becomes unperfected after 21 days unless, within that time, the requirements for transfer under any other provision of Section 8–313(1) are satisfied.

(3) A security interest in a security is subject to the provisions of Article 9, but:

(a) no filing is required to perfect the security interest; and

(b) no written security agreement signed by the debtor is necessary to make the security interest enforceable, except as provided in paragraph (h), (i), or (j) of Section 8–313(1). The secured party has the rights and duties provided under Section 9–207, to the extent they are applicable, whether or not the security is certificated, and, if certificated, whether or not it is in his possession.

(4) Unless otherwise agreed, a security interest in a security is terminated by transfer to the debtor or a person designated by him pursuant to a provision of Section 8–313(1). If a security is thus transferred, the security interest, if not terminated, becomes unperfected unless the security is certificated and is delivered to the debtor for the purpose of ultimate sale or exchange or presentation, collection, renewal, or registration of transfer. In that case, the security interest becomes unperfected after 21 days unless, within that time, the security (or securities for which it has been exchanged) is transferred to the secured party or a person designated by him pursuant to a provision of Section 8–313(1).

Added in 1977.

Part 4—Registration

§ 8–401. Duty of Issuer to Register Transfer, Pledge, or Release.

(1) If a certificated security in registered form is presented to the issuer with a request to register transfer or

an instruction is presented to the issuer with a request to register transfer, pledge, or release, the issuer shall register the transfer, pledge, or release as requested if:

(a) the security is indorsed or the instruction was originated by the appropriate person or persons (Section 8–308);

(b) reasonable assurance is given that those indorsements or instructions are genuine and effective (Section 8–402);

(c) the issuer has no duty as to adverse claims or has discharged the duty (Section 8–403);

(d) any applicable law relating to the collection of taxes has been complied with; and

(e) the transfer, pledge, or release is in fact rightful or is to a bona fide purchaser.

(2) If an issuer is under a duty to register a transfer, pledge, or release of a security, the issuer is also liable to the person presenting a certificated security or an instruction for registration or his principal for loss resulting from any unreasonable delay in registration or from failure or refusal to register the transfer, pledge, or release.

Amended in 1977.

§ 8–402. Assurance that Indorsements and Instructions Are Effective.

(1) The issuer may require the following assurance that each necessary indorsement of a certificated security or each instruction (Section 8–308) is genuine and effective:

(a) in all cases, a guarantee of the signature (Section 8–312(1) or (2)) of the person indorsing a certificated security or originating an instruction including, in the case of an instruction, a warranty of the taxpayer identification number or, in the absence thereof, other reasonable assurance of identity;

(b) if the indorsement is made or the instruction is originated by an agent, appropriate assurance of authority to sign;

(c) if the indorsement is made or the instruction is originated by a fiduciary, appropriate evidence of appointment or incumbency;

(d) if there is more than one fiduciary, reasonable assurance that all who are required to sign have done so; and

(e) if the indorsement is made or the instruction is originated by a person not covered by any of the foregoing, assurance appropriate to the case corresponding as nearly as may be to the foregoing.

(2) A "guarantee of the signature" in subsection (1) means a guarantee signed by or on behalf of a person reasonably believed by the issuer to be responsible. The issuer may adopt standards with respect to responsibility if they are not manifestly unreasonable.

(3) "Appropriate evidence of appointment or incumbency" in subsection (1) means:

(a) in the case of a fiduciary appointed or qualified by a court, a certificate issued by or under the direction or supervision of that court or an officer thereof and dated within 60 days before the date of presentation for transfer, pledge, or release; or

(b) in any other case, a copy of a document showing the appointment or a certificate issued by or on behalf of a person reasonably believed by the issuer to be responsible or, in the absence of that document or certificate, other evidence reasonably deemed by the issuer to be appropriate. The issuer may adopt standards with respect to the evidence if they are not manifestly unreasonable. The issuer is not charged with notice of the contents of any document obtained pursuant to this paragraph (b) except to the extent that the contents relate directly to the appointment or incumbency.

(4) The issuer may elect to require reasonable assurance beyond that specified in this section, but if it does so and, for a purpose other than that specified in subsection (3)(b), both requires and obtains a copy of a will, trust, indenture, articles of co-partnership, by-laws, or other controlling instrument, it is charged with notice of all matters contained therein affecting the transfer, pledge, or release.

Amended in 1977.

§ 8–403. Issuer's Duty as to Adverse Claims.

(1) An issuer to whom a certificated security is presented for registration shall inquire into adverse claims if:

(a) a written notification of an adverse claim is received at a time and in a manner affording the issuer a reasonable opportunity to act on it prior to the issuance of a new, reissued, or re-registered certificated security, and the notification identifies the claimant, the registered owner, and the issue of which the security is a part, and provides an address for communications directed to the claimant; or

(b) the issuer is charged with notice of an adverse claim from a controlling instrument it has elected to require under Section 8–402(4).

(2) The issuer may discharge any duty of inquiry by any reasonable means, including notifying an adverse claimant by registered or certified mail at the address furnished by him or, if there be no such address, at his residence or regular place of business that the certificated security has been presented for registration of transfer by a named person, and that the transfer will be registered unless within 30 days from the date of mailing the notification, either:

(a) an appropriate restraining order, injunction, or other process issues from a court of competent jurisdiction; or

(b) there is filed with the issuer an indemnity bond, sufficient in the issuer's judgment to protect the issuer and any transfer agent, registrar, or other agent of the issuer involved from any loss it or they may suffer by complying with the adverse claim.

(3) Unless an issuer is charged with notice of an adverse claim from a controlling instrument which it has elected to require under Section 8–402(4) or receives notification of an adverse claim under subsection (1), if a certificated security presented for registration is indorsed by the appropriate person or persons the issuer is under no duty to inquire into adverse claims. In particular:

(a) an issuer registering a certificated security in the name of a person who is a fiduciary or who is described as a fiduciary is not bound to inquire into the existence, extent, or correct description of the fiduciary relationship; and thereafter the issuer may assume without inquiry that the newly registered owner continues to be the fiduciary until the issuer receives written notice that the fiduciary is no longer acting as such with respect to the particular security;

(b) an issuer registering transfer on an indorsement by a fiduciary is not bound to inquire whether the transfer is made in compliance with a controlling instrument or with the law of the state having jurisdiction of the fiduciary relationship, including any law requiring the fiduciary to obtain court approval of the transfer; and

(c) the issuer is not charged with notice of the contents of any court record or file or other recorded or unrecorded document even though the document is in its possession and even though the transfer is made on the indorsement of a fiduciary to the fiduciary himself or to his nominee.

(4) An issuer is under no duty as to adverse claims with respect to an uncertificated security except:

(a) claims embodied in a restraining order, injunction, or other legal process served upon the issuer if the process was served at a time and in a manner affording the issuer a reasonable opportunity to act on it in accordance with the requirements of subsection (5);

(b) claims of which the issuer has received a written notification from the registered owner or the registered pledgee if the notification was received at a time and in a manner affording the issuer a reasonable opportunity to act on it in accordance with the requirements of subsection (5);

(c) claims (including restrictions on transfer not imposed by the issuer) to which the registration of

transfer to the present registered owner was subject and were so noted in the initial transaction statement sent to him; and

(d) claims as to which an issuer is charged with notice from a controlling instrument it has elected to require under Section 8–402(4).

(5) If the issuer of an uncertificated security is under a duty as to an adverse claim, he discharges that duty by:

(a) including a notation of the claim in any statements sent with respect to the security under Sections 8– 408(3), (6), and (7); and

(b) refusing to register the transfer or pledge of the security unless the nature of the claim does not preclude transfer or pledge subject thereto.

(6) If the transfer or pledge of the security is registered subject to an adverse claim, a notation of the claim must be included in the initial transaction statement and all subsequent statements sent to the transferee and pledgee under Section 8–408.

(7) Notwithstanding subsections (4) and (5), if an uncertificated security was subject to a registered pledge at the time the issuer first came under a duty as to a particular adverse claim, the issuer has no duty as to that claim if transfer of the security is requested by the registered pledgee or an appropriate person acting for the registered pledgee unless:

(a) the claim was embodied in legal process which expressly provides otherwise;

(b) the claim was asserted in a written notification from the registered pledgee;

(c) the claim was one as to which the issuer was charged with notice from a controlling instrument it required under Section 8–402(4) in connection with the pledgee's request for transfer; or

(d) the transfer requested is to the registered owner.

Amended in 1977.

§ 8–404. Liability and Non-Liability for Registration.

(1) Except as provided in any law relating to the collection of taxes, the issuer is not liable to the owner, pledgee, or any other person suffering loss as a result of the registration of a transfer, pledge, or release of a security if:

(a) there were on or with a certificated security the necessary indorsements or the issuer had received an instruction originated by an appropriate person (Section 8–308); and

(b) the issuer had no duty as to adverse claims or has discharged the duty (Section 8–403).

(2) If an issuer has registered a transfer of a certificated security to a person not entitled to it, the issuer on de-

mand shall deliver a like security to the true owner unless:

(a) the registration was pursuant to subsection (1);

(b) the owner is precluded from asserting any claim for registering the transfer under Section 8–405(1); or

(c) the delivery would result in overissue, in which case the issuer's liability is governed by Section 8–104.

(3) If an issuer has improperly registered a transfer, pledge, or release of an uncertificated security, the issuer on demand from the injured party shall restore the records as to the injured party to the condition that would have obtained if the improper registration had not been made unless:

(a) the registration was pursuant to subsection (1); or

(b) the registration would result in overissue, in which case the issuer's liability is governed by Section 8–104.

Amended in 1977.

§ 8–405. Lost, Destroyed, and Stolen Certificated Securities.

(1) If a certificated security has been lost, apparently destroyed, or wrongfully taken, and the owner fails to notify the issuer of that fact within a reasonable time after he has notice of it and the issuer registers a transfer of the security before receiving notification, the owner is precluded from asserting against the issuer any claim for registering the transfer under Section 8–404 or any claim to a new security under this section.

(2) If the owner of a certificated security claims that the security has been lost, destroyed, or wrongfully taken, the issuer shall issue a new certificated security or, at the option of the issuer, an equivalent uncertificated security in place of the original security if the owner:

(a) so requests before the issuer has notice that the security has been acquired by a bona fide purchaser;

(b) files with the issuer a sufficient indemnity bond; and

(c) satisfies any other reasonable requirements imposed by the issuer.

(3) If, after the issue of a new certificated or uncertificated security, a bona fide purchaser of the original certificated security presents it for registration of transfer, the issuer shall register the transfer unless registration would result in overissue, in which event the issuer's liability is governed by Section 8–104. In addition to any rights on the indemnity bond, the issuer may recover the new certificated security from the person to whom it was issued or any person taking under him

except a bona fide purchaser or may cancel the uncertificated security unless a bona fide purchaser or any person taking under a bona fide purchaser is then the registered owner or registered pledgee thereof.

Amended in 1977.

§ 8–406. Duty of Authenticating Trustee, Transfer Agent, or Registrar.

(1) If a person acts as authenticating trustee, transfer agent, registrar, or other agent for an issuer in the registration of transfers of its certificated securities or in the registration of transfers, pledges, and releases of its uncertificated securities, in the issue of new securities, or in the cancellation of surrendered securities:

(a) he is under a duty to the issuer to exercise good faith and due diligence in performing his functions; and

(b) with regard to the particular functions he performs, he has the same obligation to the holder or owner of a certificated security or to the owner or pledgee of an uncertificated security and has the same rights and privileges as the issuer has in regard to those functions.

(2) Notice to an authenticating trustee, transfer agent, registrar or other agent is notice to the issuer with respect to the functions performed by the agent.

Amended in 1977.

§ 8–407. Exchangeability of Securities.

(1) No issuer is subject to the requirements of this section unless it regularly maintains a system for issuing the class of securities involved under which both certificated and uncertificated securities are regularly issued to the category of owners, which includes the person in whose name the new security is to be registered.

(2) Upon surrender of a certificated security with all necessary indorsements and presentation of a written request by the person surrendering the security, the issuer, if he has no duty as to adverse claims or has discharged the duty (Section 8–403), shall issue to the person or a person designated by him an equivalent uncertificated security subject to all liens, restrictions, and claims that were noted on the certificated security.

(3) Upon receipt of a transfer instruction originated by an appropriate person who so requests, the issuer of an uncertificated security shall cancel the uncertificated security and issue an equivalent certificated security on which must be noted conspicuously any liens and restrictions of the issuer and any adverse claims (as to which the issuer has a duty under Section 8–403(4)) to which the uncertificated security was subject. The certificated security shall be registered in the name of and delivered to:

(a) the registered owner, if the uncertificated security was not subject to a registered pledge; or

(b) the registered pledgee, if the uncertificated security was subject to a registered pledge.

Added in 1977.

§ 8–408. Statements of Uncertificated Securities.

(1) Within 2 business days after the transfer of an uncertificated security has been registered, the issuer shall send to the new registered owner and, if the security has been transferred subject to a registered pledge, to the registered pledgee a written statement containing:

(a) a description of the issue of which the uncertificated security is a part;

(b) the number of shares or units transferred;

(c) the name and address and any taxpayer identification number of the new registered owner and, if the security has been transferred subject to a registered pledge, the name and address and any taxpayer identification number of the registered pledgee;

(d) a notation of any liens and restrictions of the issuer and any adverse claims (as to which the issuer has a duty under Section 8–403(4)) to which the uncertificated security is or may be subject at the time of registration or a statement that there are none of those liens, restrictions, or adverse claims; and

(e) the date the transfer was registered.

(2) Within 2 business days after the pledge of an uncertificated security has been registered, the issuer shall send to the registered owner and the registered pledgee a written statement containing:

(a) a description of the issue of which the uncertificated security is a part;

(b) the number of shares or units pledged;

(c) the name and address and any taxpayer identification number of the registered owner and the registered pledgee;

(d) a notation of any liens and restrictions of the issuer and any adverse claims (as to which the issuer has a duty under Section 8–403(4)) to which the uncertificated security is or may be subject at the time of registration or a statement that there are none of those liens, restrictions, or adverse claims; and

(e) the date the pledge was registered.

(3) Within 2 business days after the release from pledge of an uncertificated security has been registered, the issuer shall send to the registered owner and the pledgee whose interest was released a written statement containing:

(a) a description of the issue of which the uncertificated security is a part;

(b) the number of shares or units released from pledge;

(c) the name and address and any taxpayer identification number of the registered owner and the pledgee whose interest was released;

(d) a notation of any liens and restrictions of the issuer and any adverse claims (as to which the issuer has a duty under Section 8–403(4)) to which the uncertificated security is or may be subject at the time of registration or a statement that there are none of those liens, restrictions, or adverse claims; and

(e) the date the release was registered.

(4) An "initial transaction statement" is the statement sent to:

(a) the new registered owner and, if applicable, to the registered pledgee pursuant to subsection (1);

(b) the registered pledgee pursuant to subsection (2); or

(c) the registered owner pursuant to subsection (3).

Each initial transaction statement shall be signed by or on behalf of the issuer and must be identified as "Initial Transaction Statement".

(5) Within 2 business days after the transfer of an uncertificated security has been registered, the issuer shall send to the former registered owner and the former registered pledgee, if any, a written statement containing:

(a) a description of the issue of which the uncertificated security is a part;

(b) the number of shares or units transferred;

(c) the name and address and any taxpayer identification number of the former registered owner and of any former registered pledgee; and

(d) the date the transfer was registered.

(6) At periodic intervals no less frequent than annually and at any time upon the reasonable written request of the registered owner, the issuer shall send to the registered owner of each uncertificated security a dated written statement containing:

(a) a description of the issue of which the uncertificated security is a part;

(b) the name and address and any taxpayer identification number of the registered owner;

(c) the number of shares or units of the uncertificated security registered in the name of the registered owner on the date of the statement;

(d) the name and address and any taxpayer identification number of any registered pledgee and the number of shares or units subject to the pledge; and

(e) a notation of any liens and restrictions of the issuer and any adverse claims (as to which the issuer has a duty under Section 8–403(4)) to which the uncertificated security is or may be subject or a statement that there are none of those liens, restrictions, or adverse claims.

(7) At periodic intervals no less frequent than annually and at any time upon the reasonable written request of the registered pledgee, the issuer shall send to the registered pledgee of each uncertificated security a dated written statement containing:

(a) a description of the issue of which the uncertificated security is a part;

(b) the name and address and any taxpayer identification number of the registered owner;

(c) the name and address and any taxpayer identification number of the registered pledgee;

(d) the number of shares or units subject to the pledge; and

(e) a notation of any liens and restrictions of the issuer and any adverse claims (as to which the issuer has a duty under Section 8–403(4)) to which the uncertificated security is or may be subject or a statement that there are none of those liens, restrictions, or adverse claims.

(8) If the issuer sends the statements described in subsections (6) and (7) at periodic intervals no less frequent than quarterly, the issuer is not obliged to send additional statements upon request unless the owner or pledgee requesting them pays to the issuer the reasonable cost of furnishing them.

(9) Each statement sent pursuant to this section must bear a conspicuous legend reading substantially as follows: "This statement is merely a record of the rights of the addressee as of the time of its issuance.

Delivery of this statement, of itself, confers no rights on the recipient. This statement is neither a negotiable instrument nor a security."

Added in 1977.

ARTICLE 9: SECURED TRANSACTIONS; SALES OF ACCOUNTS AND CHATTEL PAPER

Note: *The adoption of this Article should be accompanied by the repeal of existing statutes dealing with conditional sales, trust receipts, factor's liens where the factor is given a non-possessory lien, chattel mortgages, crop mortgages, mortgages on railroad equipment, assignment of accounts and generally statutes regulating security interests in personal property.*

Where the state has a retail installment selling act or small loan act, that legislation should be carefully exam-

ined to determine what changes in those acts are needed to conform them to this Article. This Article primarily sets out rules defining rights of a secured party against persons dealing with the debtor; it does not prescribe regulations and controls which may be necessary to curb abuses arising in the small loan business or in the financing of consumer purchases on credit. Accordingly there is no intention to repeal existing regulatory acts in those fields by enactment or re-enactment of Article 9. See Section 9–203(4) and the Note thereto.

Part 1—Short Title, Applicability and Definitions

§ 9–101. Short Title.

This Article shall be known and may be cited as Uniform Commercial Code—Secured Transactions.

§ 9–102. Policy and Subject Matter of Article.

(1) Except as otherwise provided in Section 9–104 on excluded transactions, this Article applies

(a) to any transaction (regardless of its form) which is intended to create a security interest in personal property or fixtures including goods, documents, instruments, general intangibles, chattel paper or accounts; and also

(b) to any sale of accounts or chattel paper.

(2) This Article applies to security interests created by contract including pledge, assignment, chattel mortgage, chattel trust, trust deed, factor's lien, equipment trust, conditional sale, trust receipt, other lien or title retention contract and lease or consignment intended as security. This Article does not apply to statutory liens except as provided in Section 9–310.

(3) The application of this Article to a security interest in a secured obligation is not affected by the fact that the obligation is itself secured by a transaction or interest to which this Article does not apply.

Amended in 1972.

§ 9–103. Perfection of Security Interest in Multiple State Transactions.

(1) Documents, instruments and ordinary goods.

(a) This subsection applies to documents and instruments and to goods other than those covered by a certificate of title described in subsection (2), mobile goods described in subsection (3), and minerals described in subsection (5).

(b) Except as otherwise provided in this subsection, perfection and the effect of perfection or nonperfection of a security interest in collateral are governed by the law of the jurisdiction where the collateral is when the last event occurs on which is based the assertion that the security interest is perfected or unperfected.

(c) If the parties to a transaction creating a purchase money security interest in goods in one jurisdiction understand at the time that the security interest attaches that the goods will be kept in another jurisdiction, then the law of the other jurisdiction governs the perfection and the effect of perfection or non-perfection of the security interest from the time it attaches until thirty days after the debtor receives possession of the goods and thereafter if the goods are taken to the other jurisdiction before the end of the thirty-day period.

(d) When collateral is brought into and kept in this state while subject to a security interest perfected under the law of the jurisdiction from which the collateral was removed, the security interest remains perfected, but if action is required by Part 3 of this Article to perfect the security interest,

(i) if the action is not taken before the expiration of the period of perfection in the other jurisdiction or the end of four months after the collateral is brought into this state, whichever period first expires, the security interest becomes unperfected at the end of that period and is thereafter deemed to have been unperfected as against a person who became a purchaser after removal;

(ii) if the action is taken before the expiration of the period specified in subparagraph (i), the security interest continues perfected thereafter;

(iii) for the purpose of priority over a buyer of consumer goods (subsection (2) of Section 9–307), the period of the effectiveness of a filing in the jurisdiction from which the collateral is removed is governed by the rules with respect to perfection in subparagraphs (i) and (ii).

(2) Certificate of title.

(a) This subsection applies to goods covered by a certificate of title issued under a statute of this state or of another jurisdiction under the law of which indication of a security interest on the certificate is required as a condition of perfection.

(b) Except as otherwise provided in this subsection, perfection and the effect of perfection or non-perfection of the security interest are governed by the law (including the conflict of laws rules) of the jurisdiction issuing the certificate until four months after the goods are removed from that jurisdiction and thereafter until the goods are registered in another jurisdiction, but in any event not beyond surrender of the certificate. After the expiration of that period, the goods are not covered by the certificate of title within the meaning of this section.

(c) Except with respect to the rights of a buyer described in the next paragraph, a security interest, perfected in another jurisdiction otherwise than by notation on a certificate of title, in goods brought into this state and thereafter covered by a certificate of title issued by this state is subject to the rules stated in paragraph (d) of subsection (1).

(d) If goods are brought into this state while a security interest therein is perfected in any manner under the law of the jurisdiction from which the goods are removed and a certificate of title is issued by this state and the certificate does not show that the goods are subject to the security interest or that they may be subject to security interests not shown on the certificate, the security interest is subordinate to the rights of a buyer of the goods who is not in the business of selling goods of that kind to the extent that he gives value and receives delivery of the goods after issuance of the certificate and without knowledge of the security interest.

(3) Accounts, general intangibles and mobile goods.

(a) This subsection applies to accounts (other than an account described in subsection (5) on minerals) and general intangibles (other than uncertificated securities) and to goods which are mobile and which are of a type normally used in more than one jurisdiction, such as motor vehicles, trailers, rolling stock, airplanes, shipping containers, road building and construction machinery and commercial harvesting machinery and the like, if the goods are equipment or are inventory leased or held for lease by the debtor to others, and are not covered by a certificate of title described in subsection (2).

(b) The law (including the conflict of laws rules) of the jurisdiction in which the debtor is located governs the perfection and the effect of perfection or non-perfection of the security interest.

(c) If, however, the debtor is located in a jurisdiction which is not a part of the United States, and which does not provide for perfection of the security interest by filing or recording in that jurisdiction, the law of the jurisdiction in the United States in which the debtor has its major executive office in the United States governs the perfection and the effect of perfection or non-perfection of the security interest through filing. In the alternative, if the debtor is located in a jurisdiction which is not a part of the United States or Canada and the collateral is accounts or general intangibles for money due or to become due, the security interest may be perfected by notification to the account debtor. As used in this paragraph, "United States" includes its territories and possessions and the Commonwealth of Puerto Rico.

(d) A debtor shall be deemed located at his place of business if he has one, at his chief executive office if he has more than one place of business, otherwise at his residence. If, however, the debtor is a foreign air carrier under the Federal Aviation Act of 1958, as amended, it shall be deemed located at the designated office of the agent upon whom service of process may be made on behalf of the foreign air carrier.

(e) A security interest perfected under the law of the jurisdiction of the location of the debtor is perfected until the expiration of four months after a change of the debtor's location to another jurisdiction, or until perfection would have ceased by the law of the first jurisdiction, whichever period first expires. Unless perfected in the new jurisdiction before the end of that period, it becomes unperfected thereafter and is deemed to have been unperfected as against a person who became a purchaser after the change.

(4) Chattel paper.

The rules stated for goods in subsection (1) apply to a possessory security interest in chattel paper. The rules stated for accounts in subsection (3) apply to a nonpossessory security interest in chattel paper, but the security interest may not be perfected by notification to the account debtor.

(5) Minerals.

Perfection and the effect of perfection or nonperfection of a security interest which is created by a debtor who has an interest in minerals or the like (including oil and gas) before extraction and which attaches thereto as extracted, or which attaches to an account resulting from the sale thereof at the wellhead or minehead are governed by the law (including the conflict of laws rules) of the jurisdiction wherein the wellhead or minehead is located.

(6) Uncertificated securities.

The law (including the conflict of laws rules) of the jurisdiction of organization of the issuer governs the perfection and the effect of perfection or non-perfection of a security interest in uncertificated securities.

Amended in 1972 and 1977.

§ 9–104. Transactions Excluded From Article.

This Article does not apply

(a) to a security interest subject to any statute of the United States, to the extent that such statute governs the rights of parties to and third parties affected by transactions in particular types of property; or

(b) to a landlord's lien; or

(c) to a lien given by statute or other rule of law for services or materials except as provided in Section 9–310 on priority of such liens; or

(d) to a transfer of a claim for wages, salary or other compensation of an employee; or

(e) to a transfer by a government or governmental subdivision or agency; or

(f) to a sale of accounts or chattel paper as part of a sale of the business out of which they arose, or an assignment of accounts or chattel paper which is for the purpose of collection only, or a transfer of a right to payment under a contract to an assignee who is also to do the performance under the contract or a transfer of a single account to an assignee in whole or partial satisfaction of a preexisting indebtedness; or

(g) to a transfer of an interest in or claim in or under any policy of insurance, except as provided with respect to proceeds (Section 9–306) and priorities in proceeds (Section 9–312); or

(h) to a right represented by a judgment (other than a judgment taken on a right to payment which was collateral); or

(i) to any right of set-off; or

(j) except to the extent that provision is made for fixtures in Section 9–313, to the creation or transfer of an interest in or lien on real estate, including a lease or rents thereunder; or

(k) to a transfer in whole or in part of any claim arising out of tort; or

(l) to a transfer of an interest in any deposit account (subsection (1) of Section 9–105), except as provided with respect to proceeds (Section 9–306) and priorities in proceeds (Section 9–312).

Amended in 1972.

§ 9–105. Definitions and Index of Definitions.

(1) In this Article unless the context otherwise requires:

(a) "Account debtor" means the person who is obligated on an account, chattel paper or general intangible;

(b) "Chattel paper" means a writing or writings which evidence both a monetary obligation and a security interest in or a lease of specific goods, but a charter or other contract involving the use or hire of a vessel is not chattel paper. When a transaction is evidenced both by such a security agreement or a lease and by an instrument or a series of instruments, the group of writings taken together constitutes chattel paper;

(c) "Collateral" means the property subject to a security interest, and includes accounts and chattel paper which have been sold;

(d) "Debtor" means the person who owes payment or other performance of the obligation secured, whether or not he owns or has rights in the collateral, and includes the seller of accounts or chattel paper. Where the debtor and the owner of the collateral are not the same person, the term "debtor" means the owner of the collateral in any provision of the Article dealing with the collateral, the obligor in any provision dealing with the obligation, and may include both where the context so requires;

(e) "Deposit account" means a demand, time, savings, passbook or like account maintained with a bank, savings and loan association, credit union or like organization, other than an account evidenced by a certificate of deposit;

(f) "Document" means document of title as defined in the general definitions of Article 1 (Section 1–201), and a receipt of the kind described in subsection (2) of Section 7–201;

(g) "Encumbrance" includes real estate mortgages and other liens on real estate and all other rights in real estate that are not ownership interests;

(h) "Goods" includes all things which are movable at the time the security interest attaches or which are fixtures (Section 9–313), but does not include money, documents, instruments, accounts, chattel paper, general intangibles, or minerals or the like (including oil and gas) before extraction. "Goods" also includes standing timber which is to be cut and removed under a conveyance or contract for sale, the unborn young of animals, and growing crops;

(i) "Instrument" means a negotiable instrument (defined in Section 3–104), or a certificated security (defined in Section 8–102) or any other writing which evidences a right to the payment of money and is not itself a security agreement or lease and is of a type which is in ordinary course of business transferred by delivery with any necessary indorsement or assignment;

(j) "Mortgage" means a consensual interest created by a real estate mortgage, a trust deed on real estate, or the like;

(k) An advance is made "pursuant to commitment" if the secured party has bound himself to make it, whether or not a subsequent event of default or other event not within his control has relieved or may relieve him from his obligation;

(l) "Security agreement" means an agreement which creates or provides for a security interest;

(m) "Secured party" means a lender, seller or other person in whose favor there is a security interest, including a person to whom accounts or chattel paper have been sold. When the holders of obligations issued under an indenture of trust, equipment trust agreement or the like are represented by a trustee or other person, the representative is the secured party;

(n) "Transmitting utility" means any person primarily engaged in the railroad, street railway or trolley bus business, the electric or electronics communications transmission business, the transmission of goods by pipeline, or the transmission or the production and transmission of electricity, steam, gas or water, or the provision of sewer service.

(2) Other definitions applying to this Article and the sections in which they appear are:

> "Account". Section 9–106.
> "Attach". Section 9–203.
> "Construction mortgage". Section 9–313(1).
> "Consumer goods". Section 9–109(1).
> "Equipment". Section 9–109(2).
> "Farm products". Section 9–109(3).
> "Fixture". Section 9–313(1).
> "Fixture filing". Section 9–313(1).
> "General intangibles". Section 9–106.
> "Inventory". Section 9–109(4).
> "Lien creditor". Section 9–301(3).
> "Proceeds". Section 9–306(1).
> "Purchase money security interest". Section 9–107.
> "United States". Section 9–103.

(3) The following definitions in other Articles apply to this Article:

> "Check". Section 3–104.
> "Contract for sale". Section 2–106.
> "Holder in due course". Section 3–302.
> "Note". Section 3–104.
> "Sale". Section 2–106.

(4) In addition Article 1 contains general definitions and principles of construction and interpretation applicable throughout this Article.

Amended in 1966, 1972 and 1977.

§ 9–106. Definitions: "Account"; "General Intangibles".

"Account" means any right to payment for goods sold or leased or for services rendered which is not evidenced by an instrument or chattel paper, whether or not it has been earned by performance. "General intangibles" means any personal property (including things in action) other than goods, accounts, chattel paper, documents, instruments, and money. All rights to payment earned or unearned under a charter or other contract involving the use or hire of a vessel and all rights incident to the charter or contract are accounts.

Amended in 1966, 1972.

§ 9–107. Definitions: "Purchase Money Security Interest".

A security interest is a "purchase money security interest" to the extent that it is

(a) taken or retained by the seller of the collateral to secure all or part of its price; or

(b) taken by a person who by making advances or incurring an obligation gives value to enable the debtor to acquire rights in or the use of collateral if such value is in fact so used.

§ 9–108. When After-Acquired Collateral Not Security for Antecedent Debt.

Where a secured party makes an advance, incurs an obligation, releases a perfected security interest, or otherwise gives new value which is to be secured in whole or in part by after-acquired property his security interest in the after-acquired collateral shall be deemed to be taken for new value and not as security for an antecedent debt if the debtor acquires his rights in such collateral either in the ordinary course of his business or under a contract of purchase made pursuant to the security agreement within a reasonable time after new value is given.

§ 9–109. Classification of Goods; "Consumer Goods"; "Equipment"; "Farm Products"; "Inventory".

Goods are

(1) "consumer goods" if they are used or bought for use primarily for personal, family or household purposes;

(2) "equipment" if they are used or bought for use primarily in business (including farming or a profession) or by a debtor who is a non-profit organization or a governmental subdivision or agency or if the goods are not included in the definitions of inventory, farm products or consumer goods;

(3) "farm products" if they are crops or livestock or supplies used or produced in farming operations or if they are products of crops or livestock in their unmanufactured states (such as ginned cotton, wool-clip, maple syrup, milk and eggs), and if they are in the possession of a debtor engaged in raising, fattening, grazing or other farming operations. If goods are farm products they are neither equipment nor inventory;

(4) "inventory" if they are held by a person who holds them for sale or lease or to be furnished under contracts of service or if he has so furnished them, or if they are raw materials, work in process or materials used or consumed in a business. Inventory of a person is not to be classified as his equipment.

§ 9–110. Sufficiency of Description.

For purposes of this Article any description of personal property or real estate is sufficient whether or not it is specific if it reasonably identifies what is described.

§ 9–111. Applicability of Bulk Transfer Laws.

The creation of a security interest is not a bulk transfer under Article 6 (see Section 6–103).

§ 9–112. Where Collateral Is Not Owned by Debtor.

Unless otherwise agreed, when a secured party knows that collateral is owned by a person who is not the debtor, the owner of the collateral is entitled to receive from the secured party any surplus under Section 9–502(2) or under Section 9–504(1), and is not liable for the debt or for any deficiency after resale, and he has the same right as the debtor.

(a) to receive statements under Section 9–208;

(b) to receive notice of and to object to a secured party's proposal to retain the collateral in satisfaction of the indebtedness under Section 9–505;

(c) to redeem the collateral under Section 9–506;

(d) to obtain injunctive or other relief under Section 9–507(1); and

(e) to recover losses caused to him under Section 9–208(2).

§ 9–113. Security Interests Arising Under Article on Sales.

A security interest arising solely under the Article on Sales (Article 2) is subject to the provisions of this Article except that to the extent that and so long as the debtor does not have or does not lawfully obtain possession of the goods

(a) no security agreement is necessary to make the security interest enforceable; and

(b) no filing is required to perfect the security interest; and

(c) the rights of the secured party on default by the debtor are governed by the Article on Sales (Article 2).

§ 9–114. Consignment.

(1) A person who delivers goods under a consignment which is not a security interest and who would be required to file under this Article by paragraph (3)(c) of Section 2–326 has priority over a secured party who is or becomes a creditor of the consignee and who would have a perfected security interest in the goods if they were the property of the consignee, and also has priority with respect to identifiable cash proceeds received on or before delivery of the goods to a buyer, if

(a) the consignor complies with the filing provision of the Article on Sales with respect to consignments (paragraph (3)(c) of Section 2–326) before the consignee receives possession of the goods; and

(b) the consignor gives notification in writing to the holder of the security interest if the holder has filed a financing statement covering the same types of goods before the date of the filing made by the consignor; and

(c) the holder of the security interest receives the notification within five years before the consignee receives possession of the goods; and

(d) the notification states that the consignor expects to deliver goods on consignment to the consignee, describing the goods by item or type.

(2) In the case of a consignment which is not a security interest and in which the requirements of the preceding subsection have not been met, a person who delivers goods to another is subordinate to a person who would have a perfected security interest in the goods if they were the property of the debtor.

Added in 1972.

Part 2—Validity of Security Agreement and Rights of Parties Thereto

§ 9–201. General Validity of Security Agreement.

Except as otherwise provided by this Act a security agreement is effective according to its terms between the parties, against purchasers of the collateral and against creditors. Nothing in this Article validates any charge or practice illegal under any statute or regulation thereunder governing usury, small loans, retail installment sales, or the like, or extends the application of any such statute or regulation to any transaction not otherwise subject thereto.

§ 9–202. Title to Collateral Immaterial.

Each provision of this Article with regard to rights, obligations and remedies applies whether title to collateral is in the secured party or in the debtor.

§ 9–203. Attachment and Enforceability of Security Interest; Proceeds; Formal Requisites.

(1) Subject to the provisions of Section 4–208 on the security interest of a collecting bank, Section 8–321 on security interests in securities and Section 9–113 on a security interest arising under the Article on Sales, a security interest is not enforceable against the debtor or third parties with respect to the collateral and does not attach unless:

(a) the collateral is in the possession of the secured party pursuant to agreement, or the debtor has signed a security agreement which contains a description of the collateral and in addition, when the security interest covers crops growing or to be grown or timber to be cut, a description of the land concerned;

(b) value has been given; and

(c) the debtor has rights in the collateral.

(2) A security interest attaches when it becomes enforceable against the debtor with respect to the collateral. Attachment occurs as soon as all of the events specified in subsection (1) have taken place unless explicit agreement postpones the time of attaching.

(3) Unless otherwise agreed a security agreement gives the secured party the rights to proceeds provided by Section 9–306.

(4) A transaction, although subject to this Article, is also subject to . . .*, and in the case of conflict between the provisions of this Article and any such statute, the provisions of such statute control. Failure to comply with any applicable statute has only the effect which is specified therein.

Amended in 1972 and 1977.

Note: *At * in subsection (4) insert reference to any local statute regulating small loans, retail installment sales and the like.*

The foregoing subsection (4) is designed to make it clear that certain transactions, although subject to this Article, must also comply with other applicable legislation.

This Article is designed to regulate all the "security" aspects of transactions within its scope. There is, however, much regulatory legislation, particularly in the consumer field, which supplements this Article and should not be repealed by its enactment. Examples are small loan acts, retail installment selling acts and the like. Such acts may provide for licensing and rate regulation and may prescribe particular forms of contract. Such provisions should remain in force despite the enactment of this Article. On the other hand if a retail installment selling act contains provisions on filing, rights on default, etc., such provisions should be repealed as inconsistent with this Article except that inconsistent provisions as to deficiencies, penalties, etc., in the Uniform Consumer Credit Code and other recent related legislation should remain because those statutes were drafted after the substantial enactment of the Article and with the intention of modifying certain provisions of this Article as to consumer credit.

§ 9–204. After-Acquired Property; Future Advances.

(1) Except as provided in subsection (2), a security agreement may provide that any or all obligations covered by the security agreement are to be secured by after-acquired collateral.

(2) No security interest attaches under an after-acquired property clause to consumer goods other than accessions (Section 9–314) when given as additional security unless the debtor acquires rights in them within ten days after the secured party gives value.

(3) Obligations covered by a security agreement may include future advances or other value whether or not the advances or value are given pursuant to commitment (subsection (1) of Section 9–105).

Amended in 1972.

§ 9–205. Use or Disposition of Collateral Without Accounting Permissible.

A security interest is not invalid or fraudulent against creditors by reason of liberty in the debtor to use, commingle or dispose of all or part of the collateral (including returned or repossessed goods) or to collect or compromise accounts or chattel paper, or to accept the return of goods or make repossessions, or to use, commingle or dispose of proceeds, or by reason of the failure of the secured party to require the debtor to account for proceeds or replace collateral. This section does not relax the requirements of possession where perfection of a security interest depends upon possession of the collateral by the secured party or by a bailee.

Amended in 1972.

§ 9–206. Agreement Not to Assert Defenses Against Assignee; Modification of Sales Warranties Where Security Agreement Exists.

(1) Subject to any statute or decision which establishes a different rule for buyers or lessees of consumer goods, an agreement by a buyer or lessee that he will not assert against an assignee any claim or defense which he may have against the seller or lessor is enforceable by an assignee who takes his assignment for value, in good faith and without notice of a claim or defense, except as to defenses of a type which may be asserted against a holder in due course of a negotiable instrument under the Article on Commercial Paper (Article 3). A buyer who as part of one transaction signs both a negotiable instrument and a security agreement makes such an agreement.

(2) When a seller retains a purchase money security interest in goods the Article on Sales (Article 2) governs the sale and any disclaimer, limitation or modification of the seller's warranties.

Amended in 1962.

§ 9–207. Rights and Duties When Collateral is in Secured Party's Possession.

(1) A secured party must use reasonable care in the custody and preservation of collateral in his possession. In the case of an instrument or chattel paper reasonable care includes taking necessary steps to preserve rights against prior parties unless otherwise agreed.

(2) Unless otherwise agreed, when collateral is in the secured party's possession

(a) reasonable expenses (including the cost of any insurance and payment of taxes or other charges) incurred in the custody, preservation, use or operation of the collateral are chargeable to the debtor and are secured by the collateral;

(b) the risk of accidental loss or damage is on the debtor to the extent of any deficiency in any effective insurance coverage;

(c) the secured party may hold as additional security any increase or profits (except money) received from the collateral, but money so received, unless remitted to the debtor, shall be applied in reduction of the secured obligation;

(d) the secured party must keep the collateral identifiable but fungible collateral may be commingled;

(e) the secured party may repledge the collateral upon terms which do not impair the debtor's right to redeem it.

(3) A secured party is liable for any loss caused by his failure to meet any obligation imposed by the preceding subsections but does not lose his security interest.

(4) A secured party may use or operate the collateral for the purpose of preserving the collateral or its value or pursuant to the order of a court of appropriate jurisdiction or, except in the case of consumer goods, in the manner and to the extent provided in the security agreement.

§ 9–208. Request for Statement of Account or List of Collateral.

(1) A debtor may sign a statement indicating what he believes to be the aggregate amount of unpaid indebtedness as of a specified date and may send it to the secured party with a request that the statement be approved or corrected and returned to the debtor. When the security agreement or any other record kept by the secured party identifies the collateral a debtor may similarly request the secured party to approve or correct a list of the collateral.

(2) The secured party must comply with such a request within two weeks after receipt by sending a written correction or approval. If the secured party claims a security interest in all of a particular type of collateral owned by the debtor he may indicate that fact in his reply and need not approve or correct an itemized list of such collateral. If the secured party without reasonable excuse fails to comply he is liable for any loss caused to the debtor thereby; and if the debtor has properly included in his request a good faith statement of the obligation or a list of the collateral or both the secured party may claim a security interest only as shown in the statement against persons misled by his failure to comply. If he no longer has an interest in the obligation or collateral at the time the request is received he must disclose the name and address of any successor in interest known to him and he is liable for any loss caused to the debtor as a result of failure to disclose. A successor in interest is not subject to this section until a request is received by him.

(3) A debtor is entitled to such a statement once every six months without charge. The secured party may require payment of a charge not exceeding $10 for each additional statement furnished.

Part 3—Rights of Third Parties; Perfected and Unperfected Security Interests; Rules of Priority

§ 9–301. Persons Who Take Priority Over Unperfected Security Interests; Rights of "Lien Creditor".

(1) Except as otherwise provided in subsection (2), an unperfected security interest is subordinate to the rights of

(a) persons entitled to priority under Section 9–312;

(b) a person who becomes a lien creditor before the security interest is perfected;

(c) in the case of goods, instruments, documents, and chattel paper, a person who is not a secured party and who is a transferee in bulk or other buyer not in ordinary course of business or is a buyer of farm products in ordinary course of business, to the extent that he gives value and receives delivery of the collateral without knowledge of the security interest and before it is perfected;

(d) in the case of accounts and general intangibles, a person who is not a secured party and who is a transferee to the extent that he gives value without knowledge of the security interest and before it is perfected.

(2) If the secured party files with respect to a purchase money security interest before or within ten days after the debtor receives possession of the collateral, he takes priority over the rights of a transferee in bulk or of a lien creditor which arise between the time the security interest attaches and the time of filing.

(3) A "lien creditor" means a creditor who has acquired a lien on the property involved by attachment, levy or the like and includes an assignee for benefit of creditors from the time of assignment, and a trustee in bankruptcy from the date of the filing of the petition or a receiver in equity from the time of appointment.

(4) A person who becomes a lien creditor while a security interest is perfected takes subject to the security interest only to the extent that it secures advances made before he becomes a lien creditor or within 45 days thereafter or made without knowledge of the lien or pursuant to a commitment entered into without knowledge of the lien.

Amended in 1972.

§ 9–302. When Filing Is Required to Perfect Security Interest; Security Interests to Which Filing Provisions of This Article Do Not Apply.

(1) A financing statement must be filed to perfect all security interests except the following:

(a) a security interest in collateral in possession of the secured party under Section 9–305;

(b) a security interest temporarily perfected in instruments or documents without delivery under Section 9–304 or in proceeds for a 10 day period under Section 9–306;

(c) a security interest created by an assignment of a beneficial interest in a trust or a decedent's estate;

(d) a purchase money security interest in consumer goods; but filing is required for a motor vehicle required to be registered; and fixture filing is required for priority over conflicting interests in fixtures to the extent provided in Section 9–313;

(e) an assignment of accounts which does not alone or in conjunction with other assignments to the same assignee transfer a significant part of the outstanding accounts of the assignor;

(f) a security interest of a collecting bank (Section 4–208) or in securities (Section 8–321) or arising under the Article on Sales (see Section 9–113) or covered in subsection (3) of this section;

(g) an assignment for the benefit of all the creditors of the transferor, and subsequent transfers by the assignee thereunder.

(2) If a secured party assigns a perfected security interest, no filing under this Article is required in order to continue the perfected status of the security interest against creditors of and transferees from the original debtor.

(3) The filing of a financing statement otherwise required by this Article is not necessary or effective to perfect a security interest in property subject to

(a) a statute or treaty of the United States which provides for a national or international registration or a national or international certificate of title or which specifies a place of filing different from that specified in this Article for filing of the security interest; or

(b) the following statutes of this state; [list any certificate of title statute covering automobiles, trailers, mobile homes, boats, farm tractors, or the like, and any central filing statute]; but during any period in which collateral is inventory held for sale by a person who is in the business of selling goods of that kind, the filing provisions of this Article (Part 4) apply to a security interest in that collateral created by him as debtor; or

(c) a certificate of title statute of another jurisdiction under the law of which indication of a security interest on the certificate is required as a condition of perfection (subsection (2) of Section 9–103).

(4) Compliance with a statute or treaty described in subsection (3) is equivalent to the filing of a financing statement under this Article, and a security interest in

property subject to the statute or treaty can be perfected only by compliance therewith except as provided in Section 9–103 on multiple state transactions. Duration and renewal of perfection of a security interest perfected by compliance with the statute or treaty are governed by the provisions of the statute or treaty; in other respects the security interest is subject to this Article.

Amended in 1972 and 1977.

§ 9–303. When Security Interest Is Perfected; Continuity of Perfection.

(1) A security interest is perfected when it has attached and when all of the applicable steps required for perfection have been taken. Such steps are specified in Sections 9–302, 9–304, 9–305 and 9–306. If such steps are taken before the security interest attaches, it is perfected at the time when it attaches.

(2) If a security interest is originally perfected in any way permitted under this Article and is subsequently perfected in some other way under this Article, without an intermediate period when it was unperfected, the security interest shall be deemed to be perfected continuously for the purposes of this Article.

§ 9–304. Perfection of Security Interest in Instruments, Documents, and Goods Covered by Documents; Perfection by Permissive Filing; Temporary Perfection Without Filing or Transfer of Possession.

(1) A security interest in chattel paper or negotiable documents may be perfected by filing. A security interest in money or instruments (other than certificated securities or instruments which constitute part of chattel paper) can be perfected only by the secured party's taking possession, except as provided in subsections (4) and (5) of this section and subsections (2) and (3) of Section 9–306 on proceeds.

(2) During the period that goods are in the possession of the issuer of a negotiable document therefor, a security interest in the goods is perfected by perfecting a security interest in the document, and any security interest in the goods otherwise perfected during such period is subject thereto.

(3) A security interest in goods in the possession of a bailee other than one who has issued a negotiable document therefor is perfected by issuance of a document in the name of the secured party or by the bailee's receipt of notification of the secured party's interest or by filing as to the goods.

(4) A security interest in instruments (other than certificated securities) or negotiable documents is perfected without filing or the taking of possession for a period of 21 days from the time it attaches to the extent that it arises for new value given under a written security agreement.

(5) A security interest remains perfected for a period of 21 days without filing where a secured party having a perfected security interest in an instrument (other than a certificated security), a negotiable document or goods in possession of a bailee other than one who has issued a negotiable document therefor

(a) makes available to the debtor the goods or documents representing the goods for the purpose of ultimate sale or exchange or for the purpose of loading, unloading, storing, shipping, transshipping, manufacturing, processing or otherwise dealing with them in a manner preliminary to their sale or exchange, but priority between conflicting security interests in the goods is subject to subsection (3) of Section 9–312; or

(b) delivers the instrument to the debtor for the purpose of ultimate sale or exchange or of presentation, collection, renewal or registration of transfer.

(6) After the 21 day period in subsections (4) and (5) perfection depends upon compliance with applicable provisions of this Article.

Amended in 1972 and 1977.

§ 9–305. When Possession by Secured Party Perfects Security Interest Without Filing.

A security interest in letters of credit and advices of credit (subsection (2)(a) of Section 5–116), goods, instruments (other than certificated securities), money, negotiable documents, or chattel paper may be perfected by the secured party's taking possession of the collateral. If such collateral other than goods covered by a negotiable document is held by a bailee, the secured party is deemed to have possession from the time the bailee receives notification of the secured party's interest. A security interest is perfected by possession from the time possession is taken without a relation back and continues only so long as possession is retained, unless otherwise specified in this Article. The security interest may be otherwise perfected as provided in this Article before or after the period of possession by the secured party.

Amended in 1972 and 1977.

§ 9–306. "Proceeds"; Secured Party's Rights on Disposition of Collateral.

(1) "Proceeds" includes whatever is received upon the sale, exchange, collection or other disposition of collateral or proceeds. Insurance payable by reason of loss or damage to the collateral is proceeds, except to the extent that it is payable to a person other than a party to the security agreement. Money, checks, deposit accounts, and the like are "cash proceeds". All other proceeds are "non-cash proceeds".

(2) Except where this Article otherwise provides, a security interest continues in collateral notwithstanding sale, exchange or other disposition thereof unless the disposition was authorized by the secured party in the

security agreement or otherwise, and also continues in any identifiable proceeds including collections received by the debtor.

(3) The security interest in proceeds is a continuously perfected security interest if the interest in the original collateral was perfected but it ceases to be a perfected security interest and becomes unperfected ten days after receipt of the proceeds by the debtor unless

(a) a filed financing statement covers the original collateral and the proceeds are collateral in which a security interest may be perfected by filing in the office or offices where the financing statement has been filed and, if the proceeds are acquired with cash proceeds, the description of collateral in the financing statement indicates the types of property constituting the proceeds; or

(b) a filed financing statement covers the original collateral and the proceeds are identifiable cash proceeds; or

(c) the security interest in the proceeds is perfected before the expiration of the ten day period.

Except as provided in this section, a security interest in proceeds can be perfected only by the methods or under the circumstances permitted in this Article for original collateral of the same type.

(4) In the event of insolvency proceedings instituted by or against a debtor, a secured party with a perfected security interest in proceeds has a perfected security interest only in the following proceeds:

(a) in identifiable non-cash proceeds and in separate deposit accounts containing only proceeds;

(b) in identifiable cash proceeds in the form of money which is neither commingled with other money nor deposited in a deposit account prior to the insolvency proceedings;

(c) in identifiable cash proceeds in the form of checks and the like which are not deposited in a deposit account prior to the insolvency proceedings; and

(d) in all cash and deposit accounts of the debtor in which proceeds have been commingled with other funds, but the perfected security interest under this paragraph (d) is

(i) subject to any right to set-off; and

(ii) limited to an amount not greater than the amount of any cash proceeds received by the debtor within ten days before the institution of the insolvency proceedings less the sum of (I) the payments to the secured party on account of cash proceeds received by the debtor during such period and (II) the cash proceeds received by the debtor during such period to which the secured party is entitled under paragraphs (a) through (c) of this subsection (4).

(5) If a sale of goods results in an account or chattel paper which is transferred by the seller to a secured party, and if the goods are returned to or are repossessed by the seller or the secured party, the following rules determine priorities:

(a) If the goods were collateral at the time of sale, for an indebtedness of the seller which is still unpaid, the original security interest attaches again to the goods and continues as a perfected security interest if it was perfected at the time when the goods were sold. If the security interest was originally perfected by a filing which is still effective, nothing further is required to continue the perfected status; in any other case, the secured party must take possession of the returned or repossessed goods or must file.

(b) An unpaid transferee of the chattel paper has a security interest in the goods against the transferor. Such security interest is prior to a security interest asserted under paragraph (a) to the extent that the transferee of the chattel paper was entitled to priority under Section 9–308.

(c) An unpaid transferee of the account has a security interest in the goods against the transferor. Such security interest is subordinate to a security interest asserted under paragraph (a).

(d) A security interest of an unpaid transferee asserted under paragraph (b) or (c) must be perfected for protection against creditors of the transferor and purchasers of the returned or repossessed goods.

Amended in 1972.

§ 9–307. Protection of Buyers of Goods.

(1) A buyer in ordinary course of business (subsection (9) of Section 1–201) other than a person buying farm products from a person engaged in farming operations takes free of a security interest created by his seller even though the security interest is perfected and even though the buyer knows of its existence.

(2) In the case of consumer goods, a buyer takes free of a security interest even though perfected if he buys without knowledge of the security interest, for value and for his own personal, family or household purposes unless prior to the purchase the secured party has filed a financing statement covering such goods.

(3) A buyer other than a buyer in ordinary course of business (subsection (1) of this section) takes free of a security interest to the extent that it secures future advances made after the secured party acquires knowledge of the purchase, or more than 45 days after the purchase, whichever first occurs, unless made pursuant to a commitment entered into without knowledge of the purchase and before the expiration of the 45 day period.

Amended in 1972.

§ 9–308. Purchase of Chattel Paper and Instruments.

A purchaser of chattel paper or an instrument who gives new value and takes possession of it in the ordinary course of his business has priority over a security interest in the chattel paper or instrument.

(a) which is perfected under Section 9–304 (permissive filing and temporary perfection) or under Section 9–306 (perfection as to proceeds) if he acts without knowledge that the specific paper or instrument is subject to a security interest; or

(b) which is claimed merely as proceeds of inventory subject to a security interest (Section 9–306) even though he knows that the specific paper or instrument is subject to the security interest.

Amended in 1972.

§ 9–309. Protection of Purchasers of Instruments, Documents and Securities.

Nothing in this Article limits the rights of a holder in due course of a negotiable instrument (Section 3–302) or a holder to whom a negotiable document of title has been duly negotiated (Section 7–501) or a bona fide purchaser of a security (Section 8–302) and the holders or purchasers take priority over an earlier security interest even though perfected. Filing under this Article does not constitute notice of the security interest to such holders or purchasers.

Amended in 1977.

§ 9–310. Priority of Certain Liens Arising by Operation of Law.

When a person in the ordinary course of his business furnishes services or materials with respect to goods subject to a security interest, a lien upon goods in the possession of such person given by statute or rule of law for such materials or services takes priority over a perfected security interest unless the lien is statutory and the statute expressly provides otherwise.

§ 9–311. Alienability of Debtor's Rights: Judicial Process.

The debtor's rights in collateral may be voluntarily or involuntarily transferred (by way of sale, creation of a security interest, attachment, levy, garnishment or other judicial process) notwithstanding a provision in the security agreement prohibiting any transfer or making the transfer constitute a default.

§ 9–312. Priorities Among Conflicting Security Interests in the Same Collateral.

(1) The rules of priority stated in other sections of this Part and in the following sections shall govern when applicable: Section 4–208 with respect to the security interests of collecting banks in items being collected, accompanying documents and proceeds; Section 9–103 on security interests related to other jurisdictions; Section 9–114 on consignments.

(2) A perfected security interest in crops for new value given to enable the debtor to produce the crops during the production season and given not more than three months before the crops become growing crops by planting or otherwise takes priority over an earlier perfected security interest to the extent that such earlier interest secures obligations due more than six months before the crops become growing crops by planting or otherwise, even though the person giving new value had knowledge of the earlier security interest.

(3) A perfected purchase money security interest in inventory has priority over a conflicting security interest in the same inventory and also has priority in identifiable cash proceeds received on or before the delivery of the inventory to a buyer if

(a) the purchase money security interest is perfected at the time the debtor receives possession of the inventory; and

(b) the purchase money secured party gives notification in writing to the holder of the conflicting security interest if the holder had filed a financing statement covering the same types of inventory (i) before the date of the filing made by the purchase money secured party, or (ii) before the beginning of the 21 day period where the purchase money security interest is temporarily perfected without filing or possession (subsection (5) of Section 9–304); and

(c) the holder of the conflicting security interest receives the notification within five years before the debtor receives possession of the inventory; and

(d) the notification states that the person giving the notice has or expects to acquire a purchase money security interest in inventory of the debtor, describing such inventory by item or type.

(4) A purchase money security interest in collateral other than inventory has priority over a conflicting security interest in the same collateral or its proceeds if the purchase money security interest is perfected at the time the debtor receives possession of the collateral or within ten days thereafter.

(5) In all cases not governed by other rules stated in this section (including cases of purchase money security interests which do not qualify for the special priorities set forth in subsections (3) and (4) of this section), priority between conflicting security interests in the same collateral shall be determined according to the following rules:

(a) Conflicting security interests rank according to priority in time of filing or perfection. Priority dates from the time a filing is first made covering the collateral or the time the security interest is first perfected, whichever is earlier, provided that there is no period thereafter when there is neither filing nor perfection.

(b) So long as conflicting security interests are un-perfected, the first to attach has priority.

(6) For the purposes of subsection (5) a date of filing or perfection as to collateral is also a date of filing or perfection as to proceeds.

(7) If future advances are made while a security interest is perfected by filing, the taking of possession, or under Section 8–321 on securities, the security interest has the same priority for the purposes of subsection (5) with respect to the future advances as it does with respect to the first advance. If a commitment is made before or while the security interest is so perfected, the security interest has the same priority with respect to advances made pursuant thereto. In other cases a perfected security interest has priority from the date the advance is made.

Amended in 1972 and 1977.

§ 9–313. Priority of Security Interests in Fixtures.

(1) In this section and in the provisions of Part 4 of this Article referring to fixture filing, unless the context otherwise requires

(a) goods are "fixtures" when they become so related to particular real estate that an interest in them arises under real estate law

(b) a "fixture filing" is the filing in the office where a mortgage on the real estate would be filed or recorded of a financing statement covering goods which are or are to become fixtures and conforming to the requirements of subsection (5) of Section 9–402

(c) a mortgage is a "construction mortgage" to the extent that it secures an obligation incurred for the construction of an improvement on land including the acquisition cost of the land, if the recorded writing so indicates.

(2) A security interest under this Article may be created in goods which are fixtures or may continue in goods which become fixtures, but no security interest exists under this Article in ordinary building materials incorporated into an improvement on land.

(3) This Article does not prevent creation of an encumbrance upon fixtures pursuant to real estate law.

(4) A perfected security interest in fixtures has priority over the conflicting interest of an encumbrancer or owner of the real estate where

(a) the security interest is a purchase money security interest, the interest of the encumbrancer or owner arises before the goods become fixtures, the security interest is perfected by a fixture filing before the goods become fixtures or within ten days thereafter, and the debtor has an interest of record in the real estate or is in possession of the real estate; or

(b) the security interest is perfected by a fixture filing before the interest of the encumbrancer or owner is of record, the security interest has priority over any conflicting interest of a predecessor in title of the encumbrancer or owner, and the debtor has an interest of record in the real estate or is in possession of the real estate; or

(c) the fixtures are readily removable factory or office machines or readily removable replacements of domestic appliances which are consumer goods, and before the goods become fixtures the security interest is perfected by any method permitted by this Article; or

(d) the conflicting interest is a lien on the real estate obtained by legal or equitable proceedings after the security interest was perfected by any method permitted by this Article.

(5) A security interest in fixtures, whether or not perfected, has priority over the conflicting interest of an encumbrancer or owner of the real estate where

(a) the encumbrancer or owner has consented in writing to the security interest or has disclaimed an interest in the goods as fixtures; or

(b) the debtor has a right to remove the goods as against the encumbrancer or owner. If the debtor's right terminates, the priority of the security interest continues for a reasonable time.

(6) Notwithstanding paragraph (a) of subsection (4) but otherwise subject to subsections (4) and (5), a security interest in fixtures is subordinate to a construction mortgage recorded before the goods become fixtures if the goods become fixtures before the completion of the construction. To the extent that it is given to refinance a construction mortgage, a mortgage has this priority to the same extent as the construction mortgage.

(7) In cases not within the preceding subsections, a security interest in fixtures is subordinate to the conflicting interest of an encumbrancer or owner of the related real estate who is not the debtor.

(8) When the secured party has priority over all owners and encumbrancers of the real estate, he may, on default, subject to the provisions of Part 5, remove his collateral from the real estate but he must reimburse any encumbrancer or owner of the real estate who is not the debtor and who has not otherwise agreed for the cost of repair of any physical injury, but not for any diminution in value of the real estate caused by the absence of the goods removed or by any necessity of replacing them. A person entitled to reimbursement may refuse permission to remove until the secured party gives adequate security for the performance of this obligation.

Amended in 1972.

§ 9–314. Accessions.

(1) A security interest in goods which attaches before they are installed in or affixed to other goods takes priority as to the goods installed or affixed (called in this section "accessions") over the claims of all persons to the whole except as stated in subsection (3) and subject to Section 9–315(1).

(2) A security interest which attaches to goods after they become part of a whole is valid against all persons subsequently acquiring interests in the whole except as stated in subsection (3) but is invalid against any person with an interest in the whole at the time the security interest attaches to the goods who has not in writing consented to the security interest or disclaimed an interest in the goods as part of the whole.

(3) The security interests described in subsections (1) and (2) do not take priority over

(a) a subsequent purchaser for value of any interest in the whole; or

(b) a creditor with a lien on the whole subsequently obtained by judicial proceedings; or

(c) a creditor with a prior perfected security interest in the whole to the extent that he makes subsequent advances

if the subsequent purchase is made, the lien by judicial proceedings obtained or the subsequent advance under the prior perfected security interest is made or contracted for without knowledge of the security interest and before it is perfected. A purchaser of the whole at a foreclosure sale other than the holder of a perfected security interest purchasing at his own foreclosure sale is a subsequent purchaser within this section.

(4) When under subsections (1) or (2) and (3) a secured party has an interest in accessions which has priority over the claims of all persons who have interests in the whole, he may on default subject to the provisions of Part 5 remove his collateral from the whole but he must reimburse any encumbrancer or owner of the whole who is not the debtor and who has not otherwise agreed for the cost of repair of any physical injury but not for any diminution in value of the whole caused by the absence of the goods removed or by any necessity for replacing them. A person entitled to reimbursement may refuse permission to remove until the secured party gives adequate security for the performance of this obligation.

§ 9–315. Priority When Goods Are Commingled or Processed.

(1) If a security interest in goods was perfected and subsequently the goods or a part thereof have become part of a product or mass, the security interest continues in the product or mass if

(a) the goods are so manufactured, processed, assembled or commingled that their identity is lost in the product or mass; or

(b) a financing statement covering the original goods also covers the product into which the goods have been manufactured, processed or assembled.

In a case to which paragraph (b) applies, no separate security interest in that part of the original goods which has been manufactured, processed or assembled into the product may be claimed under Section 9–314.

(2) When under subsection (1) more than one security interest attaches to the product or mass, they rank equally according to the ratio that the cost of the goods to which each interest originally attached bears to the cost of the total product or mass.

§ 9–316. Priority Subject to Subordination.

Nothing in this Article prevents subordination by agreement by any person entitled to priority.

§ 9–317. Secured Party Not Obligated on Contract of Debtor.

The mere existence of a security interest or authority given to the debtor to dispose of or use collateral does not impose contract or tort liability upon the secured party for the debtor's acts or omissions.

§ 9–318. Defenses Against Assignee; Modification of Contract After Notification of Assignment; Term Prohibiting Assignment Ineffective; Identification and Proof of Assignment.

(1) Unless an account debtor has made an enforceable agreement not to assert defenses or claims arising out of a sale as provided in Section 9–206 the rights of an assignee are subject to

(a) all the terms of the contract between the account debtor and assignor and any defense or claim arising therefrom; and

(b) any other defense or claim of the account debtor against the assignor which accrues before the account debtor receives notification of the assignment.

(2) So far as the right to payment or a part thereof under an assigned contract has not been fully earned by performance, and notwithstanding notification of the assignment, any modification of or substitution for the contract made in good faith and in accordance with reasonable commercial standards is effective against an assignee unless the account debtor has otherwise agreed but the assignee acquires corresponding rights under the modified or substituted contract. The assignment may provide that such modification or substitution is a breach by the assignor.

(3) The account debtor is authorized to pay the assignor until the account debtor receives notification that the amount due or to become due has been assigned and that payment is to be made to the assignee. A notification which does not reasonably identify the rights assigned is ineffective. If requested by the account debtor,

the assignee must seasonably furnish reasonable proof that the assignment has been made and unless he does so the account debtor may pay the assignor.

(4) A term in any contract between an account debtor and an assignor is ineffective if it prohibits assignment of an account or prohibits creation of a security interest in a general intangible for money due or to become due or requires the account debtor's consent to such assignment or security interest.

Amended in 1972.

Part 4—Filing

§ 9–401. Place of Filing; Erroneous Filing; Removal of Collateral.

First Alternative Subsection (1)

(1) The proper place to file in order to perfect a security interest is as follows:

(a) when the collateral is timber to be cut or is minerals or the like (including oil and gas) or accounts subject to subsection (5) of Section 9–103, or when the financing statement is filed as a fixture filing (Section 9–313) and the collateral is goods which are or are to become fixtures, then in the office where a mortgage on the real estate would be filed or recorded;

(b) in all other cases, in the office of the [Secretary of State].

Second Alternative Subsection (1)

(1) The proper place to file in order to perfect a security interest is as follows:

(a) when the collateral is equipment used in farming operations, or farm products, or accounts or general intangibles arising from or relating to the sale of farm products by a farmer, or consumer goods, then in the office of the _____ in the county of the debtor's residence or if the debtor is not a resident of this state then in the office of the _____ in the county where the goods are kept, and in addition when the collateral is crops growing or to be grown in the office of the _____ in the county where the land is located;

(b) when the collateral is timber to be cut or is minerals or the like (including oil and gas) or accounts subject to subsection (5) of Section 9–103, or when the financing statement is filed as a fixture filing (Section 9–313) and the collateral is goods which are or are to become fixtures, then in the office where a mortgage on the real estate would be filed or recorded;

(c) in all other cases, in the office of the [Secretary of State].

Third Alternative Subsection (1)

(1) The proper place to file in order to perfect a security interest is as follows:

(a) when the collateral is equipment used in farming operations, or farm products, or accounts or general intangibles arising from or relating to the sale of farm products by a farmer, or consumer goods, then in the office of the _____ in the county of the debtor's residence or if the debtor is not a resident of this state then in the office of the _____ in the county where the goods are kept, and in addition when the collateral is crops growing or to be grown in the office of the _____ in the county where the land is located;

(b) when the collateral is timber to be cut or is minerals or the like (including oil and gas) or accounts subject to subsection (5) of Section 9–103, or when the financing statement is filed as a fixture filing (Section 9–313) and the collateral is goods which are or are to become fixtures, then in the office where a mortgage on the real estate would be filed or recorded;

(c) in all other cases, in the office of the [Secretary of State] and in addition, if the debtor has a place of business in only one county of this state, also in the office of _____ of such county, or, if the debtor has no place of business in this state, but resides in the state, also in the office of _____ of the county in which he resides.

Note: *One of the three alternatives should be selected as subsection (1).*

(2) A filing which is made in good faith in an improper place or not in all of the places required by this section is nevertheless effective with regard to any collateral as to which the filing complied with the requirements of this Article and is also effective with regard to collateral covered by the financing statement against any person who has knowledge of the contents of such financing statement.

(3) A filing which is made in the proper place in this state continues effective even though the debtor's residence or place of business or the location of the collateral or its use, whichever controlled the original filing, is thereafter changed.

Alternative Subsection (3)

[(3) A filing which is made in the proper county continues effective for four months after a change to another county of the debtor's residence or place of business or the location of the collateral, whichever controlled the original filing. It becomes ineffective thereafter unless a copy of the financing statement signed by the secured party is filed in the new county within said period. The security interest may also be perfected in the new county after the expiration of the four-month period; in such case perfection dates from the time of perfection in the new county. A change in the use of the collateral does not impair the effectiveness of the original filing.]

(4) The rules stated in Section 9–103 determine whether filing is necessary in this state.

(5) Notwithstanding the preceding subsections, and subject to subsection (3) of Section 9–302, the proper place to file in order to perfect a security interest in collateral, including fixtures, of a transmitting utility is the office of the [Secretary of State]. This filing constitutes a fixture filing (Section 9–313) as to the collateral described therein which is or is to become fixtures.

(6) For the purposes of this section, the residence of an organization is its place of business if it has one or its chief executive office if it has more than one place of business.

Amended in 1962 and 1972.

Note: *Subsection (6) should be used only if the state chooses the Second or Third Alternative Subsection (1).*

§ 9–402. Formal Requisites of Financing Statement; Amendments; Mortgage as Financing Statement.

(1) A financing statement is sufficient if it gives the names of the debtor and the secured party, is signed by the debtor, gives an address of the secured party from which information concerning the security interest may be obtained, gives a mailing address of the debtor and contains a statement indicating the types, or describing the items, of collateral. A financing statement may be filed before a security agreement is made or a security interest otherwise attaches. When the financing statement covers crops growing or to be grown, the statement must also contain a description of the real estate concerned. When the financing statement covers timber to be cut or covers minerals or the like (including oil and gas) or accounts subject to subsection (5) of Section 9–103, or when the financing statement is filed as a fixture filing (Section 9–313) and the collateral is goods which are or are to become fixtures, the statement must also comply with subsection (5). A copy of the security agreement is sufficient as a financing statement if it contains the above information and is signed by the debtor. A carbon, photographic or other reproduction of a security agreement or a financing statement is sufficient as a financing statement if the security agreement so provides or if the original has been filed in this state.

(2) A financing statement which otherwise complies with subsection (1) is sufficient when it is signed by the secured party instead of the debtor if it is filed to perfect a security interest in

(a) collateral already subject to a security interest in another jurisdiction when it is brought into this state, or when the debtor's location is changed to this state. Such a financing statement must state

that the collateral was brought into this state or that the debtor's location was changed to this state under such circumstances; or

(b) proceeds under Section 9–306 if the security interest in the original collateral was perfected. Such a financing statement must describe the original collateral; or

(c) collateral as to which the filing has lapsed; or

(d) collateral acquired after a change of name, identity or corporate structure of the debtor (subsection (7)).

(3) A form substantially as follows is sufficient to comply with subsection (1):

Name of debtor (or assignor) _____
Address _____
Name of secured party (or assignee) _____
Address _____
1. This financing statement covers the following types (or items) of property:
   (Describe) _____
2. (If collateral is crops) The above described crops are growing or are to be grown on:
   (Describe Real Estate) _____
3. (If applicable) The above goods are to become fixtures on*
*Where appropriate substitute either "The above timber is standing on _____" or "The above minerals or the like (including oil and gas) or accounts will be financed at the wellhead or minehead of the well or mine located on _____"
(Describe Real Estate) _____ and this financing statement is to be filed [for record] in the real estate records. (If the debtor does not have an interest of record) The name of a record owner is _____
4. (If products of collateral are claimed) Products of the collateral are also covered.

(use ....
whichever   Signature of Debtor (or Assignor)
   is   ....
applicable)   Signature of Secured Party
                       (or Assignee)

(4) A financing statement may be amended by filing a writing signed by both the debtor and the secured party. An amendment does not extend the period of effectiveness of a financing statement. If any amendment adds collateral, it is effective as to the added collateral only from the filing date of the amendment. In this Article, unless the context otherwise requires, the term "financing statement" means the original financing statement and any amendments.

(5) A financing statement covering timber to be cut or covering minerals or the like (including oil and gas) or accounts subject to subsection (5) of Section 9–103, or a financing statement filed as a fixture filing (Section 9–313) where the debtor is not a transmitting utility, must

show that it covers this type of collateral, must recite that it is to be filed [for record] in the real estate records, and the financing statement must contain a description of the real estate [sufficient if it were contained in a mortgage of the real estate to give constructive notice of the mortgage under the law of this state]. If the debtor does not have an interest of record in the real estate, the financing statement must show the name of a record owner.

(6) A mortgage is effective as a financing statement filed as a fixture filing from the date of its recording if

(a) the goods are described in the mortgage by item or type; and

(b) the goods are or are to become fixtures related to the real estate described in the mortgage; and

(c) the mortgage complies with the requirements for a financing statement in this section other than a recital that it is to be filed in the real estate records; and

(d) the mortgage is duly recorded.

No fee with reference to the financing statement is required other than the regular recording and satisfaction fees with respect to the mortgage.

(7) A financing statement sufficiently shows the name of the debtor if it gives the individual, partnership or corporate name of the debtor, whether or not it adds other trade names or names of partners. Where the debtor so changes his name or in the case of an organization its name, identity or corporate structure that a filed financing statement becomes seriously misleading, the filing is not effective to perfect a security interest in collateral acquired by the debtor more than four months after the change, unless a new appropriate financing statement is filed before the expiration of that time. A filed financing statement remains effective with respect to collateral transferred by the debtor even though the secured party knows of or consents to the transfer.

(8) A financing statement substantially complying with the requirements of this section is effective even though it contains minor errors which are not seriously misleading.

Amended in 1972.

Note: *Language in brackets is optional.*

Note: *Where the state has any special recording system for real estate other than the usual grantor-grantee index (as, for instance, a tract system or a title registration or Torrens system) local adaptations of subsection (5) and Section 9–403(7) may be necessary. See Mass. Gen.Laws Chapter 106, Section 9–409.*

§ 9–403. What Constitutes Filing; Duration of Filing; Effect of Lapsed Filing; Duties of Filing Officer.

(1) Presentation for filing of a financing statement and tender of the filing fee or acceptance of the statement by the filing officer constitutes filing under this Article.

(2) Except as provided in subsection (6) a filed financing statement is effective for a period of five years from the date of filing. The effectiveness of a filed financing statement lapses on the expiration of the five year period unless a continuation statement is filed prior to the lapse. If a security interest perfected by filing exists at the time insolvency proceedings are commenced by or against the debtor, the security interest remains perfected until termination of the insolvency proceedings and thereafter for a period of sixty days or until expiration of the five year period, whichever occurs later. Upon lapse the security interest becomes unperfected, unless it is perfected without filing. If the security interest becomes unperfected upon lapse, it is deemed to have been unperfected as against a person who became a purchaser or lien creditor before lapse.

(3) A continuation statement may be filed by the secured party within six months prior to the expiration of the five year period specified in subsection (2). Any such continuation statement must be signed by the secured party, identify the original statement by file number and state that the original statement is still effective. A continuation statement signed by a person other than the secured party of record must be accompanied by a separate written statement of assignment signed by the secured party of record and complying with subsection (2) of Section 9–405, including payment of the required fee. Upon timely filing of the continuation statement, the effectiveness of the original statement is continued for five years after the last date to which the filing was effective whereupon it lapses in the same manner as provided in subsection (2) unless another continuation statement is filed prior to such lapse. Succeeding continuation statements may be filed in the same manner to continue the effectiveness of the original statement. Unless a statute on disposition of public records provides otherwise, the filing officer may remove a lapsed statement from the files and destroy it immediately if he has retained a microfilm or other photographic record, or in other cases after one year after the lapse. The filing officer shall so arrange matters by physical annexation of financing statements to continuation statements or other related filings, or by other means, that if he physically destroys the financing statements of a period more than five years past, those which have been continued by a continuation statement or which are still effective under subsection (6) shall be retained.

(4) Except as provided in subsection (7) a filing officer shall mark each statement with a file number and with the date and hour of filing and shall hold the statement or a microfilm or other photographic copy thereof for public inspection. In addition the filing officer shall index the statement according to the name of the debtor and shall note in the index the file number and the address of the debtor given in the statement.

(5) The uniform fee for filing and indexing and for stamping a copy furnished by the secured party to show

the date and place of filing for an original financing statement or for a continuation statement shall be $_____ if the statement is in the standard form prescribed by the [Secretary of State] and otherwise shall be $_____, plus in each case, if the financing statement is subject to subsection (5) of Section 9–402, $_____. The uniform fee for each name more than one required to be indexed shall be $_____. The secured party may at his option show a trade name for any person and an extra uniform indexing fee of $_____ shall be paid with respect thereto.

(6) If the debtor is a transmitting utility (subsection (5) of Section 9–401) and a filed financing statement so states, it is effective until a termination statement is filed. A real estate mortgage which is effective as a fixture filing under subsection (6) of Section 9–402 remains effective as a fixture filing until the mortgage is released or satisfied of record or its effectiveness otherwise terminates as to the real estate.

(7) When a financing statement covers timber to be cut or covers minerals or the like (including oil and gas) or accounts subject to subsection (5) of Section 9–103, or is filed as a fixture filing, [it shall be filed for record and] the filing officer shall index it under the names of the debtor and any owner of record shown on the financing statement in the same fashion as if they were the mortgagors in a mortgage of the real estate described, and, to the extent that the law of this state provides for indexing of mortgages under the name of the mortgagee, under the name of the secured party as if he were the mortgagee thereunder, or where indexing is by description in the same fashion as if the financing statement were a mortgage of the real estate described.

Amended in 1972.
Note: *In states in which writings will not appear in the real estate records and indices unless actually recorded the bracketed language in subsection (7) should be used.*

§ 9–404. Termination Statement.

(1) If a financing statement covering consumer goods is filed on or after _____, then within one month or within ten days following written demand by the debtor after there is no outstanding secured obligation and no commitment to make advances, incur obligations or otherwise give value, the secured party must file with each filing officer with whom the financing statement was filed, a termination statement to the effect that he no longer claims a security interest under the financing statement, which shall be identified by file number. In other cases whenever there is no outstanding secured obligation and no commitment to make advances, incur obligations or otherwise give value, the secured party must on written demand by the debtor send the debtor, for each filing officer with whom the financing statement was filed, a termination statement to the effect that he no longer claims a security interest under the financing statement, which shall be identified by file

number. A termination statement signed by a person other than the secured party of record must be accompanied by a separate written statement of assignment signed by the secured party of record complying with subsection (2) of Section 9–405, including payment of the required fee. If the affected secured party fails to file such a termination statement as required by this subsection, or to send such a termination statement within ten days after proper demand therefor, he shall be liable to the debtor for one hundred dollars, and in addition for any loss caused to the debtor by such failure.

(2) On presentation to the filing officer of such a termination statement he must note it in the index. If he has received the termination statement in duplicate, he shall return one copy of the termination statement to the secured party stamped to show the time of receipt thereof. If the filing officer has a microfilm or other photographic record of the financing statement, and of any related continuation statement, statement of assignment and statement of release, he may remove the originals from the files at any time after receipt of the termination statement, or if he has no such record, he may remove them from the files at any time after one year after receipt of the termination statement.

(3) If the termination statement is in the standard form prescribed by the [Secretary of State], the uniform fee for filing and indexing the termination statement shall be $_____, and otherwise shall be $_____, plus in each case an additional fee of $_____ for each name more than one against which the termination statement is required to be indexed.

Amended in 1972.
Note: *The date to be inserted should be the effective date of the revised Article 9.*

§ 9–405. Assignment of Security Interest; Duties of Filing Officer; Fees.

(1) A financing statement may disclose an assignment of a security interest in the collateral described in the financing statement by indication in the financing statement of the name and address of the assignee or by an assignment itself or a copy thereof on the face or back of the statement. On presentation to the filing officer of such a financing statement the filing officer shall mark the same as provided in Section 9–403(4). The uniform fee for filing, indexing and furnishing filing data for a financing statement so indicating an assignment shall be $_____ if the statement is in the standard form prescribed by the [Secretary of State] and otherwise shall be $_____, plus in each case an additional fee of $_____ for each name more than one against which the financing statement is required to be indexed.

(2) A secured party may assign of record all or part of his rights under a financing statement by the filing in the place where the original financing statement was filed of a separate written statement of assignment signed by the secured party of record and setting forth

the name of the secured party of record and the debtor, the file number and the date of filing of the financing statement and the name and address of the assignee and containing a description of the collateral assigned. A copy of the assignment is sufficient as a separate statement if it complies with the preceding sentence. On presentation to the filing officer of such a separate statement, the filing officer shall mark such separate statement with the date and hour of the filing. He shall note the assignment on the index of the financing statement, or in the case of a fixture filing, or a filing covering timber to be cut, or covering minerals or the like (including oil and gas) or accounts subject to subsection (5) of Section 9–103, he shall index the assignment under the name of the assignor as grantor and, to the extent that the law of this state provides for indexing the assignment of a mortgage under the name of the assignee, he shall index the assignment of the financing statement under the name of the assignee. The uniform fee for filing, indexing and furnishing filing data about such a separate statement of assignment shall be $_____ if the statement is in the standard form prescribed by the [Secretary of State] and otherwise shall be $_____, plus in each case an additional fee of $_____ for each name more than one against which the statement of assignment is required to be indexed. Notwithstanding the provisions of this subsection, an assignment of record of a security interest in a fixture contained in a mortgage effective as a fixture filing (subsection (6) of Section 9–402) may be made only by an assignment of the mortgage in the manner provided by the law of this state other than this Act.

(3) After the disclosure or filing of an assignment under this section, the assignee is the secured party of record.

Amended in 1972.

§ 9–406. Release of Collateral; Duties of Filing Officer; Fees.

A secured party of record may by his signed statement release all or a part of any collateral described in a filed financing statement. The statement of release is sufficient if it contains a description of the collateral being released, the name and address of the debtor, the name and address of the secured party, and the file number of the financing statement. A statement of release signed by a person other than the secured party of record must be accompanied by a separate written statement of assignment signed by the secured party of record and complying with subsection (2) of Section 9–405, including payment of the required fee. Upon presentation of such a statement of release to the filing officer he shall mark the statement with the hour and date of filing and shall note the same upon the margin of the index of the filing of the financing statement. The uniform fee for filing and noting such a statement of release shall be $_____ if the statement is in the standard form prescribed by the [Secretary of State] and otherwise shall be $_____, plus in each case an additional fee of $_____ for each name

more than one against which the statement of release is required to be indexed.

Amended in 1972.

[§ 9–407. Information From Filing Officer].

[(1) If the person filing any financing statement, termination statement, statement of assignment, or statement of release, furnishes the filing officer a copy thereof, the filing officer shall upon request note upon the copy the file number and date and hour of the filing of the original and deliver or send the copy to such person.]

[(2) Upon request of any person, the filing officer shall issue his certificate showing whether there is on file on the date and hour stated therein, any presently effective financing statement naming a particular debtor and any statement of assignment thereof and if there is, giving the date and hour of filing of each such statement and the names and addresses of each secured party therein. The uniform fee for such a certificate shall be $_____ if the request for the certificate is in the standard form prescribed by the [Secretary of State] and otherwise shall be $_____. Upon request the filing officer shall furnish a copy of any filed financing statement or statement of assignment for a uniform fee of $_____ per page.]

Amended in 1972.

Note: *This section is proposed as an optional provision to require filing officers to furnish certificates. Local law and practices should be consulted with regard to the advisability of adoption.*

§ 9–408. Financing Statements Covering Consigned or Leased Goods.

A consignor or lessor of goods may file a financing statement using the terms "consignor," "consignee," "lessor," "lessee" or the like instead of the terms specified in Section 9–402. The provisions of this Part shall apply as appropriate to such a financing statement but its filing shall not of itself be a factor in determining whether or not the consignment or lease is intended as security (Section 1–201(37)). However, if it is determined for other reasons that the consignment or lease is so intended, a security interest of the consignor or lessor which attaches to the consigned or leased goods is perfected by such filing.

Added in 1972.

Part 5—Default

§ 9–501. Default; Procedure When Security Agreement Covers Both Real and Personal Property.

(1) When a debtor is in default under a security agreement, a secured party has the rights and remedies provided in this Part and except as limited by subsection (3) those provided in the security agreement. He may re-

duce his claim to judgment, foreclose or otherwise enforce the security interest by any available judicial procedure. If the collateral is documents the secured party may proceed either as to the documents or as to the goods covered thereby. A secured party in possession has the rights, remedies and duties provided in Section 9–207. The rights and remedies referred to in this subsection are cumulative.

(2) After default, the debtor has the rights and remedies provided in this Part, those provided in the security agreement and those provided in Section 9–207.

(3) To the extent that they give rights to the debtor and impose duties on the secured party, the rules stated in the subsections referred to below may not be waived or varied except as provided with respect to compulsory disposition of collateral (subsection (3) of Section 9–504 and Section 9–505) and with respect to redemption of collateral (Section 9–506) but the parties may by agreement determine the standards by which the fulfillment of these rights and duties is to be measured if such standards are not manifestly unreasonable:

    (a) subsection (2) of Section 9–502 and subsection (2) of Section 9–504 insofar as they require accounting for surplus proceeds of collateral;

    (b) subsection (3) of Section 9–504 and subsection (1) of Section 9–505 which deal with disposition of collateral;

    (c) subsection (2) of Section 9–505 which deals with acceptance of collateral as discharge of obligation;

    (d) Section 9–506 which deals with redemption of collateral; and

    (e) subsection (1) of Section 9–507 which deals with the secured party's liability for failure to comply with this Part.

(4) If the security agreement covers both real and personal property, the secured party may proceed under this Part as to the personal property or he may proceed as to both the real and the personal property in accordance with his rights and remedies in respect of the real property in which case the provisions of this Part do not apply.

(5) When a secured party has reduced his claim to judgment the lien of any levy which may be made upon his collateral by virtue of any execution based upon the judgment shall relate back to the date of the perfection of the security interest in such collateral. A judicial sale, pursuant to such execution, is a foreclosure of the security interest by judicial procedure within the meaning of this section, and the secured party may purchase at the sale and thereafter hold the collateral free of any other requirements of this Article.

Amended in 1972.

§ 9–502. Collection Rights of Secured Party.

(1) When so agreed and in any event on default the secured party is entitled to notify an account debtor or the obligor on an instrument to make payment to him whether or not the assignor was theretofore making collections on the collateral, and also to take control of any proceeds to which he is entitled under Section 9–306.

(2) A secured party who by agreement is entitled to charge back uncollected collateral or otherwise to full or limited recourse against the debtor and who undertakes to collect from the account debtors or obligors must proceed in a commercially reasonable manner and may deduct his reasonable expenses of realization from the collections. If the security agreement secures an indebtedness, the secured party must account to the debtor for any surplus, and unless otherwise agreed, the debtor is liable for any deficiency. But, if the underlying transaction was a sale of accounts or chattel paper, the debtor is entitled to any surplus or is liable for any deficiency only if the security agreement so provides.

Amended in 1972.

§ 9–503. Secured Party's Right to Take Possession After Default.

Unless otherwise agreed a secured party has on default the right to take possession of the collateral. In taking possession a secured party may proceed without judicial process if this can be done without breach of the peace or may proceed by action. If the security agreement so provides the secured party may require the debtor to assemble the collateral and make it available to the secured party at a place to be designated by the secured party which is reasonably convenient to both parties. Without removal a secured party may render equipment unusable, and may dispose of collateral on the debtor's premises under Section 9–504.

§ 9–504. Secured Party's Right to Dispose of Collateral After Default; Effect of Disposition.

(1) A secured party after default may sell, lease or otherwise dispose of any or all of the collateral in its then condition or following any commercially reasonable preparation or processing. Any sale of goods is subject to the Article on Sales (Article 2). The proceeds of disposition shall be applied in the order following to

    (a) the reasonable expenses of retaking, holding, preparing for sale or lease, selling, leasing and the like and, to the extent provided for in the agreement and not prohibited by law, the reasonable attorneys' fees and legal expenses incurred by the secured party;

    (b) the satisfaction of indebtedness secured by the security interest under which the disposition is made;

(c) the satisfaction of indebtedness secured by any subordinate security interest in the collateral if written notification of demand therefor is received before distribution of the proceeds is completed. If requested by the secured party, the holder of a subordinate security interest must seasonably furnish reasonable proof of his interest, and unless he does so, the secured party need not comply with his demand.

(2) If the security interest secures an indebtedness, the secured party must account to the debtor for any surplus, and, unless otherwise agreed, the debtor is liable for any deficiency. But if the underlying transaction was a sale of accounts or chattel paper, the debtor is entitled to any surplus or is liable for any deficiency only if the security agreement so provides.

(3) Disposition of the collateral may be by public or private proceedings and may be made by way of one or more contracts. Sale or other disposition may be as a unit or in parcels and at any time and place and on any terms but every aspect of the disposition including the method, manner, time, place and terms must be commercially reasonable. Unless collateral is perishable or threatens to decline speedily in value or is of a type customarily sold on a recognized market, reasonable notification of the time and place of any public sale or reasonable notification of the time after which any private sale or other intended disposition is to be made shall be sent by the secured party to the debtor, if he has not signed after default a statement renouncing or modifying his right to notification of sale. In the case of consumer goods no other notification need be sent. In other cases notification shall be sent to any other secured party from whom the secured party has received (before sending his notification to the debtor or before the debtor's renunciation of his rights) written notice of a claim of an interest in the collateral. The secured party may buy at any public sale and if the collateral is of a type customarily sold in a recognized market or is of a type which is the subject of widely distributed standard price quotations he may buy at private sale.

(4) When collateral is disposed of by a secured party after default, the disposition transfers to a purchaser for value all of the debtor's rights therein, discharges the security interest under which it is made and any security interest or lien subordinate thereto. The purchaser takes free of all such rights and interests even though the secured party fails to comply with the requirements of this Part or of any judicial proceedings

(a) in the case of a public sale, if the purchaser has no knowledge of any defects in the sale and if he does not buy in collusion with the secured party, other bidders or the person conducting the sale; or

(b) in any other case, if the purchaser acts in good faith.

(5) A person who is liable to a secured party under a guaranty, indorsement, repurchase agreement or the like and who receives a transfer of collateral from the secured party or is subrogated to his rights has thereafter the rights and duties of the secured party. Such a transfer of collateral is not a sale or disposition of the collateral under this Article.

Amended in 1972.

§ 9–505. Compulsory Disposition of Collateral; Acceptance of the Collateral as Discharge of Obligation.

(1) If the debtor has paid sixty per cent of the cash price in the case of a purchase money security interest in consumer goods or sixty per cent of the loan in the case of another security interest in consumer goods, and has not signed after default a statement renouncing or modifying his rights under this Part a secured party who has taken possession of collateral must dispose of it under Section 9–504 and if he fails to do so within ninety days after he takes possession the debtor at his option may recover in conversion or under Section 9–507(1) on secured party's liability.

(2) In any other case involving consumer goods or any other collateral a secured party in possession may, after default, propose to retain the collateral in satisfaction of the obligation. Written notice of such proposal shall be sent to the debtor if he has not signed after default a statement renouncing or modifying his rights under this subsection. In the case of consumer goods no other notice need be given. In other cases notice shall be sent to any other secured party from whom the secured party has received (before sending his notice to the debtor or before the debtor's renunciation of his rights) written notice of a claim of an interest in the collateral. If the secured party receives objection in writing from a person entitled to receive notification within twenty-one days after the notice was sent, the secured party must dispose of the collateral under Section 9–504. In the absence of such written objection the secured party may retain the collateral in satisfaction of the debtor's obligation.

Amended in 1972.

§ 9–506. Debtor's Right to Redeem Collateral.

At any time before the secured party has disposed of collateral or entered into a contract for its disposition under Section 9–504 or before the obligation has been discharged under Section 9–505(2) the debtor or any other secured party may unless otherwise agreed in writing after default redeem the collateral by tendering fulfillment of all obligations secured by the collateral as well as the expenses reasonably incurred by the secured party in retaking, holding and preparing the collateral for disposition, in arranging for the sale, and to the extent provided in the agreement and not prohibited by law, his reasonable attorneys' fees and legal expenses.

§ 9–507. Secured Party's Liability for Failure to Comply With This Part.

(1) If it is established that the secured party is not proceeding in accordance with the provisions of this Part disposition may be ordered or restrained on appropriate terms and conditions. If the disposition has occurred the debtor or any person entitled to notification or whose security interest has been made known to the secured party prior to the disposition has a right to recover from the secured party any loss caused by a failure to comply with the provisions of this Part. If the collateral is consumer goods, the debtor has a right to recover in any event an amount not less than the credit service charge plus ten per cent of the principal amount of the debt or the time price differential plus 10 per cent of the cash price.

(2) The fact that a better price could have been obtained by a sale at a different time or in a different method from that selected by the secured party is not of itself sufficient to establish that the sale was not made in a commercially reasonable manner. If the secured party either sells the collateral in the usual manner in any recognized market therefor or if he sells at the price current in such market at the time of his sale or if he has otherwise sold in conformity with reasonable commercial practices among dealers in the type of property sold he has sold in a commercially reasonable manner. The principles stated in the two preceding sentences with respect to sales also apply as may be appropriate to other types of disposition. A disposition which has been approved in any judicial proceeding or by any bona fide creditors' committee or representative of creditors shall conclusively be deemed to be commercially reasonable, but this sentence does not indicate that any such approval must be obtained in any case nor does it indicate that any disposition not so approved is not commercially reasonable.

ARTICLE 10: EFFECTIVE DATE AND REPEALER

§ 10–101. Effective Date.

This Act shall become effective at midnight on December 31st following its enactment. It applies to transactions entered into and events occurring after that date.

§ 10–102. Specific Repealer; Provision for Transition.

(1) The following acts and all other acts and parts of acts inconsistent herewith are hereby repealed: (Here should follow the acts to be specifically repealed including the following:

Uniform Negotiable Instruments Act
Uniform Warehouse Receipts Act
Uniform Sales Act
Uniform Bills of Lading Act
Uniform Stock Transfer Act
Uniform Conditional Sales Act
Uniform Trust Receipts Act
   Also any acts regulating:
Bank collections
Bulk sales
Chattel mortgages
Conditional sales
Factor's lien acts
Farm storage of grain and similar acts
Assignment of accounts receivable)

(2) Transactions validly entered into before the effective date specified in Section 10–101 and the rights, duties and interests flowing from them remain valid thereafter and may be terminated, completed, consummated or enforced as required or permitted by any statute or other law amended or repealed by this Act as though such repeal or amendment had not occurred.

Note: *Subsection (1) should be separately prepared for each state. The foregoing is a list of statutes to be checked.*

§ 10–103. General Repealer.

Except as provided in the following section, all acts and parts of acts inconsistent with this Act are hereby repealed.

§ 10–104. Laws Not Repealed.

(1) The Article on Documents of Title (Article 7) does not repeal or modify any laws prescribing the form or contents of documents of title or the services or facilities to be afforded by bailees, or otherwise regulating bailees' businesses in respects not specifically dealt with herein; but the fact that such laws are violated does not affect the status of a document of title which otherwise complies with the definition of a document of title (Section 1–201).

[(2) This Act does not repeal _____*, cited as the Uniform Act for the Simplification of Fiduciary Security Transfers, and if in any respect there is any inconsistency between that Act and the Article of this Act on investment securities (Article 8) the provisions of the former Act shall control.]

Note: *At * in subsection (2) insert the statutory reference to the Uniform Act for the Simplification of Fiduciary Security Transfers if such Act has previously been enacted. If it has not been enacted, omit subsection (2).*

ARTICLE 11: (REPORTERS' DRAFT) EFFECTIVE DATE AND TRANSITION PROVISIONS

This material has been numbered Article 11 to distinguish it from Article 10, the transition provision of the 1962 Code, which may still remain in effect in some states to cover transition problems from pre-Code law to the original Uniform Commercial Code. Adaptation may be necessary in particular states. The terms "[old Code]" and "[new Code]" and "[old U.C.C.]" and "[new U.C.C.]" are used herein, and should be suitably changed in each state.

Note: *This draft was prepared by the Reporters and has not been passed upon by the Review Committee, the Permanent Editorial Board, the American Law Institute, or the National Conference of Commissioners on Uniform State Laws. It is submitted as a working draft which may be adapted as appropriate in each state.*

§ 11–101. Effective Date.

This Act shall become effective at 12:01 A.M. on ____, 19__.

§ 11–102. Preservation of Old Transition Provision.

The provisions of [here insert reference to the original transition provision in the particular state] shall continue to apply to [the new U.C.C.] and for this purpose the [old U.C.C. and new U.C.C.] shall be considered one continuous statute.

§ 11–103. Transition to [New Code]—General Rule.

Transactions validly entered into after [effective date of old U.C.C.] and before [effective date of new U.C.C.], and which were subject to the provisions of [old U.C.C.] and which would be subject to this Act as amended if they had been entered into after the effective date of [new U.C.C.] and the rights, duties and interests flowing from such transactions remain valid after the latter date and may be terminated, completed, consummated or enforced as required or permitted by the [new U.C.C.]. Security interests arising out of such transactions which are perfected when [new U.C.C.] becomes effective shall remain perfected until they lapse as provided in [new U.C.C.], and may be continued as permitted by [new U.C.C.], except as stated in Section 11–105.

§ 11–104. Transition Provision on Change of Requirement of Filing.

A security interest for the perfection of which filing or the taking of possession was required under [old U.C.C.] and which attached prior to the effective date of [new U.C.C.] but was not perfected shall be deemed perfected on the effective date of [new U.C.C.] if [new U.C.C.] permits perfection without filing or authorizes filing in the office or offices where a prior ineffective filing was made.

§ 11–105. Transition Provision on Change of Place of Filing.

(1) A financing statement or continuation statement filed prior to [effective date of new U.C.C.] which shall not have lapsed prior to [the effective date of new U.C.C.] which shall remain effective for the period provided in the [old Code], but not less than five years after the filing.

(2) With respect to any collateral acquired by the debtor subsequent to the effective date of [new U.C.C.], any effective financing statement or continuation statement described in this section shall apply only if the filing or filings are in the office or offices that would be appropriate to perfect the security interests in the new collateral under [new U.C.C.].

(3) The effectiveness of any financing statement or continuation statement filed prior to [effective date of new U.C.C.] may be continued by a continuation statement as permitted by [new U.C.C.], except that if [new U.C.C.] requires a filing in an office where there was no previous financing statement, a new financing statement conforming to Section 11–106 shall be filed in that office.

(4) If the record of a mortgage of real estate would have been effective as a fixture filing of goods described therein if [new U.C.C.] had been in effect on the date of recording the mortgage, the mortgage shall be deemed effective as a fixture filing as to such goods under subsection (6) of Section 9–402 of the [new U.C.C.] on the effective date of [new U.C.C.].

§ 11–106. Required Refilings.

(1) If a security interest is perfected or has priority when this Act takes effect as to all persons or as to certain persons without any filing or recording, and if the filing of a financing statement would be required for the perfection or priority of the security interest against those persons under [new U.C.C.], the perfection and priority rights of the security interest continue until 3 years after the effective date of [new U.C.C.]. The perfection will then lapse unless a financing statement is filed as provided in subsection (4) or unless the security interest is perfected otherwise than by filing.

(2) If a security interest is perfected when [new U.C.C.] takes effect under a law other than [U.C.C.] which requires no further filing, refiling or recording to continue its perfection, perfection continues until and will lapse 3 years after [new U.C.C.] takes effect, unless a financing statement is filed as provided in subsection (4) or unless the security interest is perfected otherwise than by filing, or unless under subsection (3) of Section 9–302 the other law continues to govern filing.

(3) If a security interest is perfected by a filing, refiling or recording under a law repealed by this Act which required further filing, refiling or recording to continue its perfection, perfection continues and will lapse on the date provided by the law so repealed for such further filing, refiling, or recording unless a financing statement is filed as provided in subsection (4) or unless the security interest is perfected otherwise than by filing.

(4) A financing statement may be filed within six months before the perfection of a security interest would otherwise lapse. Any such financing statement may be signed by either the debtor or the secured party. It must identify the security agreement, statement or notice (however denominated in any statute or other law repealed or modified by this Act), state the office where and the date when the last filing, refiling or recording, if any, was made with respect thereto, and the filing number, if any, or book and page, if any, of recording and further state that the security agreement, statement or notice, however denominated, in another filing office under the [U.C.C.] or under any statute or other law repealed or modified by this Act is still effective. Section 9–401 and Section 9–103 determine the proper place to file such a financing statement. Except as specified in this subsection, the provisions of Section 9–403(3) for continuation statements apply to such a financing statement.

§ 11–107. Transition Provisions as to Priorities.

Except as otherwise provided in [Article 11], [old U.C.C.] shall apply to any questions of priority if the positions of the parties were fixed prior to the effective date of [new U.C.C.]. In other cases questions of priority shall be determined by [new U.C.C.].

§ 11–108. Presumption that Rule of Law Continues Unchanged.

Unless a change in law has clearly been made, the provisions of [new U.C.C.] shall be deemed declaratory of the meaning of the [old U.C.C.].

REVISED ARTICLE 3: NEGOTIABLE INSTRUMENTS

Part 1—General Provisions and Definitions

§ 3–101. Short Title

This Article may be cited as Uniform Commercial Code—Negotiable Instruments.

§ 3–102. Subject Matter

(a) This Article applies to negotiable instruments. It does not apply to money or to payment orders governed by Article 4A. A negotiable instrument that is also a certificated security under Section 8–102(1)(a) is subject to Article 8 and to this Article.

(b) In the event of conflict between the provisions of this Article and those of Article 4, Article 8, or Article 9, the provisions of Article 4, Article 8 and Article 9 prevail over those of this Article.

(c) Regulations of the Board of Governors of the Federal Reserve System and operating circulars of the Federal Reserve Banks supersede any inconsistent provision of this Article to the extent of the inconsistency.

§ 3–103. Definitions

(a) In this Article:

(1) "Acceptor" means a drawee that has accepted a draft.

(2) "Drawee" means a person ordered in a draft to make payment.

(3) "Drawer" means a person that signs a draft as a person ordering payment.

(4) "Good faith" means honesty in fact and the observance of reasonable commercial standards of fair dealing.

(5) "Maker" means a person that signs a note as promisor of payment.

(6) "Order" means a written instruction to pay money signed by the person giving the instruction. The instruction may be addressed to any person, including the person giving the instruction, or to one or more persons jointly or in the alternative but not in succession. An authorization to pay is not an order unless the person authorized to pay is also instructed to pay.

(7) "Ordinary care" in the case of a person engaged in business means observance of reasonable commercial standards, prevailing in the area in which that person is located, with respect to the business in which that person is engaged. In the case of a bank that takes an instrument for processing for collection or payment by automated means, reasonable commercial standards do not require the bank to examine the instrument if the failure to examine does not violate the bank's prescribed procedures and the bank's procedures do not vary unreasonably from general banking usage not disapproved by this Article or Article 4.

(8) "Party" means party to an instrument.

(9) "Promise" means a written undertaking to pay money signed by the person undertaking to pay. An acknowledgment of an obligation by the obligor is not a promise unless the obligor also undertakes to pay the obligation.

(10) "Prove" with respect to a fact means to meet the burden of establishing the fact (Section 1–201(8)).

(11) "Remitter" means a person that purchases an instrument from its issuer if the instrument is payable to an identified person other than the purchaser.

(b) Other definitions applying to this Article and the sections in which they appear are:

"Acceptance" Section 3–409.
"Accommodated party" Section 3–419.

"Accommodation indorsement" Section 3–205.
"Accommodation party" Section 3–419.
"Alteration" Section 3–407.
"Blank indorsement" Section 3–205.
"Cashier's check" Section 3–104.
"Certificate of deposit" Section 3–104.
"Certified check" Section 3–409.
"Check" Section 3–104.
"Consideration" Section 3–303.
"Draft" Section 3–104.
"Fiduciary" Section 3–307.
"Guarantor" Section 3–417.
"Holder in due course" Section 3–302.
"Incomplete instrument" Section 3–115.
"Indorsement" Section 3–204.
"Indorser" Section 3–204.
"Instrument" Section 3–104.
"Issue" Section 3–105.
"Issuer" Section 3–105.
"Negotiable instrument" Section 3–104.
"Negotiation" Section 3–201.
"Note" Section 3–104.
"Payable at a definite time" Section 3–108.
"Payable on demand" Section 3–108.
"Payable to bearer" Section 3–109.
"Payable to order" Section 3–110.
"Payment" Section 3–603.
"Person entitled to enforce" Section 3–301.
"Presentment" Section 3–501.
"Reacquisition" Section 3–207.
"Represented person" Section 3–307.
"Special indorsement" Section 3–205.
"Teller's check" Section 3–104.
"Traveler's check" Section 3–104.
"Value" Section 3–303.

(c) The following definitions in other Articles apply to this Article:

"Bank" Section 4–105.
"Banking day" Section 4–104.
"Clearing house" Section 4–104.
"Collecting bank" Section 4–105.
"Customer" Section 4–104.
"Depositary bank" Section 4–105.
"Documentary draft" Section 4–104.
"Intermediary bank" Section 4–105.
"Item" Section 4–104.
"Midnight deadline" Section 4–104.
"Payor bank" Section 4–105.
"Suspends payments" Section 4–104.

(d) In addition, Article 1 contains general definitions and principles of construction and interpretation applicable throughout this Article.

§ 3–104. Negotiable Instrument

(a) "Negotiable instrument" means an unconditional promise or order to pay a fixed amount of money, with or without interest or other charges described in the promise or order, if it:

(1) is payable to bearer or to order at the time it is issued or first comes into possession of a holder;

(2) is payable on demand or at a definite time; and

(3) does not state any other undertaking or instruction by the person promising or ordering payment to do any act in addition to the payment of money except that the promise or order may contain (i) an undertaking or power to give, maintain, or protect collateral to secure payment, (ii) an authorization or power to the holder to confess judgment or realize on or dispose of collateral, or (iii) a waiver of the benefit of any law intended for the advantage or protection of any obligor.

(b) "Instrument" means negotiable instrument.

(c) An order that meets all of the requirements of subsection (a) except subparagraph (1) and otherwise falls within the definition of "check" in subsection (f) is a negotiable instrument and a check.

(d) Notwithstanding subsection (a), a promise or order other than a check is not an instrument if, at the time it is issued or first comes into possession of a holder, it contains a conspicuous statement, however expressed, indicating that the writing is not an instrument governed by this Article.

(e) An instrument is a "note" if it is a promise, and is a "draft" if it is an order. If an instrument falls within the definition of both "note" and "draft," the person entitled to enforce the instrument may treat it as either.

(f) "Check" means (i) a draft, other than a documentary draft, payable on demand and drawn on a bank or (ii) a cashier's check or teller's check. An instrument may be a check even though it is described on its face by another term such as "money order."

(g) "Cashier's check" means a draft with respect to which the drawer and drawee are the same bank or branches of the same bank.

(h) "Teller's check" means a draft drawn by a bank (i) on another bank, or (ii) payable at or through a bank.

(i) "Traveler's check" means an instrument that (i) is payable on demand, (ii) is drawn on or payable at or through a bank, (iii) is designated by the term "traveler's check" or by a substantially similar term, and (iv) requires, as a condition to payment, a countersignature by a person whose specimen signature appears on the instrument.

(j) "Certificate of deposit" means an instrument containing an acknowledgment by a bank that a sum of money has been received by the bank, and a promise by the bank to repay the sum of money. A certificate of deposit is a note of the bank.

§ 3–105. Issue of Instrument

(a) "Issue" means the first delivery of an instrument by the maker or drawer, whether to a holder or nonholder, for the purpose of giving rights on the instrument to any person.

(b) An unissued instrument, or an unissued incomplete instrument (Section 3–115) that is completed, is binding on the maker or drawer, but nonissuance is a defense. An instrument that is conditionally issued or is issued for a special purpose is binding on the maker or drawer, but failure of the condition or special purpose to be fulfilled is a defense.

(c) "Issuer" applies to issued and unissued instruments and means any person that signs an instrument as maker or drawer.

§ 3–106. Unconditional Promise or Order

(a) Except as provided in subsections (b) and (c), for the purposes of Section 3–104(a), a promise or order is unconditional unless it states (i) an express condition to payment or (ii) that the promise or order is subject to or governed by another writing, or that rights or obligations with respect to the promise or order are stated in another writing; however, a mere reference to another writing does not make the promise or order conditional.

(b) A promise or order is not made conditional (i) by a reference to another writing for a statement of rights with respect to collateral, prepayment, or acceleration, or (ii) because payment is limited to resort to a particular fund or source.

(c) If a promise or order requires, as a condition to payment, a countersignature by a person whose specimen signature appears on the promise or order, the condition does not make the promise or order conditional for the purposes of Section 3–104(a). If the person whose specimen signature appears on an instrument fails to countersign the instrument, the failure to countersign is a defense to the obligation of the issuer, but the failure does not prevent a transferee of the instrument from becoming a holder of the instrument.

(d) If a promise or order at the time it is issued or first comes into possession of a holder contains a statement, required by applicable statutory or administrative law, to the effect that the rights of a holder or transferee are subject to claims or defenses that the issuer could assert against the original payee, the promise or order is not thereby made conditional for the purposes of Section 3–104(a), but there cannot be a holder in due course of the promise or order.

§ 3–107. Instrument Payable in Foreign Money

Unless the instrument otherwise provides, an instrument that states the amount payable in foreign money may be paid in the foreign money or in an equivalent amount in dollars calculated by using the current bank-offered spot rate at the place of payment for the purchase of dollars on the day on which the instrument is paid.

§ 3–108. Payable on Demand or at a Definite Time

(a) A promise or order is "payable on demand" if (i) it states that it is payable on demand or at sight, or otherwise indicates that it is payable at the will of the holder, or (ii) it does not state any time of payment.

(b) A promise or order is "payable at a definite time" if it is payable on elapse of a definite period of time after sight or acceptance or at a fixed date or dates or at a time or times readily ascertainable at the time the promise or order is issued, subject to rights of (i) prepayment, (ii) acceleration, or (iii) extension at the option of the holder or (iv) extension to a further definite time at the option of the maker or acceptor or automatically upon or after a specified act or event.

(c) If an instrument, payable at a fixed date, is also payable upon demand made before the fixed date, the instrument is payable on demand until the fixed date and, if demand for payment is not made before that date, becomes payable at a definite time on the fixed date.

§ 3–109. Payable to Bearer or to Order

(a) A promise or order is payable to bearer if it:

(1) states that it is payable to bearer or to the order of bearer or otherwise indicates that the person in possession of the promise or order is entitled to payment,

(2) does not state a payee, or

(3) states that it is payable to or to the order of cash or otherwise indicates that it is not payable to an identified person.

(b) A promise or order that is not payable to bearer is payable to order if it is payable (i) to the order of an identified person or (ii) to an identified person or order. A promise or order that is payable to order is payable to the identified person.

(c) An instrument payable to bearer may become payable to an identified person if it is specially indorsed as stated in Section 3–205(a). An instrument payable to an identified person may become payable to bearer if it is indorsed in blank as stated in Section 3–205(b).

§ 3–110. Identification of Person to Whom Instrument is Payable

(a) A person to whom an instrument is payable is determined by the intent of the person, whether or not authorized, signing as, or in the name or behalf of, the maker or drawer. The instrument is payable to the person intended by the signer even if that person is identified in the instrument by a name or other identification that is not that of the intended person. If more than one person signs in the name or behalf of the maker or drawer and all the signers do not intend the same person as payee, the instrument is payable to any person intended by one or more of the signers.

(b) If the signature of the maker or drawer of an instrument is made by automated means such as a check-writing machine, the payee of the instrument is determined by the intent of the person who supplied the name or identification of the payee, whether or not authorized to do so.

(c) A person to whom an instrument is payable may be identified in any way including by name, identifying number, office, or account number. For the purpose of determining the holder of an instrument, the following rules apply:

(1) If an instrument is payable to an account and the account is identified only by number, the instrument is payable to the person to whom the account is payable. If an instrument is payable to an account identified by number and by the name of a person, the instrument is payable to the named person, whether or not that person is the owner of the account identified by number.

(2) If an instrument is payable to:

(i) a trust, estate, or a person described as trustee or representative of a trust or estate, the instrument is payable to the trustee, the representative, or a successor of either, whether or not the beneficiary or estate is also named;

(ii) a person described as agent or similar representative of a named or identified person, the instrument is payable either to the represented person, the representative, or a successor of the representative;

(iii) a fund or organization that is not a legal entity, the instrument is payable to a representative of the members of the fund or organization; or

(iv) an office or to a person described as holding an office, the instrument is payable to the named person, the incumbent of the office, or a successor to the incumbent.

(d) If an instrument is payable to two or more persons alternatively, it is payable to any of them and may be negotiated, discharged, or enforced by any of them in possession of the instrument. If an instrument is payable to two or more persons not alternatively, it is payable to all of them and may be negotiated, discharged, or enforced only by all of them. If an instrument payable to two or more persons is ambiguous as to whether it is payable to the persons alternatively, the instrument is payable to the persons alternatively.

§ 3–111. Place of Payment

Except as otherwise provided for items in Article 4, an instrument is payable at the place of payment stated in the instrument. If no place of payment is stated, an instrument is payable at the address of the drawee or maker stated in the instrument. If no address is stated, the place of payment is the place of business of the drawee or maker. If a drawee or maker has more than one place of business, the place of payment is any place of business of the drawee or maker chosen by the person entitled to enforce the instrument. If the drawee or maker has no place of business, the place of payment is the residence of the drawee or maker.

§ 3–112. Interest

(a) Unless otherwise provided in the instrument, (i) an instrument is not payable with interest, and (ii) interest on an interest-bearing instrument is payable from the date of the instrument.

(b) Interest may be stated in an instrument as a fixed or variable amount of money or it may be expressed as a fixed or variable rate or rates. The amount or rate of interest may be stated or described in the instrument in any manner and may require reference to information not contained in the instrument. If an instrument provides for interest but the amount of interest payable cannot be ascertained from the description, interest is payable at the judgment rate in effect at the place of payment of the instrument and at the time interest first accrues.

§ 3–113. Date of Instrument

(a) An instrument may be antedated or postdated. The date stated determines the time of payment if the instrument is payable at a fixed period after date. Except as provided in Section 4–401(3), an instrument payable on demand is not payable before the date of the instrument.

(b) If an instrument is undated, its date is the date of its issue or, in the case of an unissued instrument, the date it first comes into possession of a holder.

§ 3–114. Contradictory Terms of Instrument

If an instrument contains contradictory terms, typewritten terms prevail over printed terms, handwritten terms prevail over both, and words prevail over numbers.

§ 3–115. Incomplete Instrument

(a) "Incomplete instrument" means a signed writing, whether or not issued by the signer, the contents of which show at the time of signing that it is incomplete but that the signer intended it to be completed by the addition of words or numbers.

(b) Subject to subsection (c), if an incomplete instrument is an instrument under Section 3–104, it may be enforced (i) according to its terms if it is not completed, or

(ii) according to its terms as augmented by completion. If an incomplete instrument is not an instrument under Section 3–104 but, after completion, the requirements of Section 3–104 are met, the instrument may be enforced according to its terms as augmented by completion.

(c) If words or numbers are added to an incomplete instrument without authority of the signer, there is an alteration of the incomplete instrument governed by Section 3–407.

(d) The burden of establishing that words or numbers were added to an incomplete instrument without authority of the signer is on the person asserting the lack of authority.

§ 3–116. Joint and Several Liability; Contribution

(a) Except as otherwise provided in the instrument, two or more persons who have the same liability on an instrument as makers, drawers, acceptors, indorsers who are indorsing joint payees, or anomalous indorsers, are jointly and severally liable in the capacity in which they sign.

(b) Except as provided in Section 3–417(e) or by agreement of the affected parties, a party with joint and several liability that pays the instrument is entitled to receive from any party with the same joint and several liability contribution in accordance with applicable law.

(c) Discharge of one party with joint and several liability by a person entitled to enforce the instrument does not affect the right under subsection (b) of a party with the same joint and several liability to receive contribution from the party discharged.

§ 3–117. Other Agreements Affecting an Instrument

Subject to applicable law regarding exclusion of proof of contemporaneous or prior agreements, the obligation of a party to an instrument to pay the instrument may be modified, supplemented, or nullified by a separate agreement of the obligor and a person entitled to enforce the instrument if the instrument is issued or the obligation is incurred in reliance on the agreement or as part of the same transaction giving rise to the agreement. To the extent an obligation is modified, supplemented, or nullified by an agreement under this section, the agreement is a defense to the obligation.

§ 3–118. Statute of Limitations

(a) Except as provided in subsection (e), an action to enforce the obligation of a party to pay a note payable at a definite time must be commenced within six years after the payment date or dates stated in the note or, if a payment date is accelerated, within six years after the accelerated payment date.

(b) Except as provided in subsection (d) or (e), if demand for payment is made to the maker of a note payable on demand, an action to enforce the obligation of a party to pay the note must be commenced within six years after the demand. If no demand for payment is made to the maker, an action to enforce the note is barred if neither principal nor interest on the note has been paid for a continuous period of 10 years.

(c) Except as provided in subsection (d), an action to enforce the obligation of a party to an unaccepted draft to pay the draft must be commenced within six years after dishonor of the draft or 10 years after the date of the draft, whichever period expires first.

(d) An action to enforce the obligation of the acceptor of a certified check or the issuer of a teller's check, cashier's check, or traveler's check must be commenced within six years after demand for payment is made to the acceptor or issuer, as the case may be.

(e) An action to enforce the obligation of a party to a certificate of deposit to pay the instrument must be commenced within six years after demand for payment is made to the maker, but if the instrument states a maturity date and the maker is not required to pay before that date, the six-year period begins when a demand for payment is in effect and the maturity date has passed.

(f) This subsection applies to an action to enforce the obligation of a party to pay an accepted draft, other than a certified check. If the obligation of the acceptor is payable at a definite time, the action must be commenced within six years after the payment date or dates stated in the draft or acceptance. If the obligation of the acceptor is payable on demand, the action must be commenced within six years after the date of the acceptance.

(g) Unless governed by other law regarding claims for indemnity or contribution, an action (i) for conversion of an instrument, for money had and received, or like action based on conversion, (ii) for breach of warranty, or (iii) to enforce an obligation, duty, or right arising under this Article and not governed by this section must be commenced within three years after the cause of action accrues.

§ 3–119. Notice of Right to Defend Action

In an action for breach of an obligation for which a third person is answerable over pursuant to this Article or Article 4, the defendant may give the third person written notice of the litigation, and the person notified may then give similar notice to any other person who is answerable over. If the notice states (i) that the person notified may come in and defend and (ii) that failure to do so will bind the person notified in an action later brought by the person giving the notice as to any determination of fact common to the two litigations, the person notified is so bound unless after seasonable receipt of the notice the person notified does come in and defend.

Part 2—Negotiation, Transfer and Indorsement

§ 3–201. Negotiation

(a) "Negotiation" means a transfer of possession, whether voluntary or involuntary, of an instrument to a person who thereby becomes its holder if possession is obtained from a person other than the issuer of the instrument.

(b) Except for a negotiation by a remitter, if an instrument is payable to an identified person, negotiation requires transfer of possession of the instrument and its indorsement by the holder. If an instrument is payable to bearer, it may be negotiated by transfer of possession alone.

§ 3–202. Negotiation Subject to Rescission

(a) Negotiation is effective even if obtained (i) from an infant, a corporation exceeding its powers, or a person without capacity, or (ii) by fraud, duress, or mistake, or in breach of duty or as part of an illegal transaction.

(b) To the extent permitted by law, negotiation may be rescinded or may be subject to other remedies, but those remedies may not be asserted against a subsequent holder in due course or a person paying the instrument in good faith and without knowledge of facts that are a basis for rescission or other remedy.

§ 3–203. Rights Acquired by Transfer

(a) An instrument is transferred when it is delivered by a person other than its issuer for the purpose of giving to the person receiving delivery the right to enforce the instrument.

(b) Transfer of an instrument, regardless of whether the transfer is a negotiation, vests in the transferee any right of the transferor to enforce the instrument, including any right as a holder in due course, but the transferee cannot acquire rights of a holder in due course by a transfer, directly or indirectly, from a holder in due course if the purchaser engaged in fraud or illegality affecting the instrument.

(c) Unless otherwise agreed, if an instrument is transferred for value and the transferee does not become a holder because of lack of indorsement by the transferor, the transferee has a specifically enforceable right to the unqualified indorsement of the transferor, but negotiation of the instrument does not occur until the indorsement is made.

(d) If a transferor purports to transfer less than the entire instrument, negotiation of the instrument does not occur. The transferee obtains no rights under this Article and has only the rights of a partial assignee.

§ 3–204. Indorsement

(a) "Indorsement" means a signature, other than that of a maker, drawer, or acceptor, that alone or accompanied by other words, is made on an instrument for the purpose of (i) negotiating the instrument, (ii) restricting payment of the instrument, or (iii) incurring indorser's liability on the instrument, but regardless of the intent of the signer, a signature and its accompanying words is an indorsement unless the accompanying words, the terms of the instrument, the place of the signature, or other circumstances unambiguously indicate that the signature was made for a purpose other than indorsement. For the purpose of determining whether a signature is made on an instrument, a paper affixed to the instrument is a part of the instrument.

(b) "Indorser" means a person who makes an indorsement.

(c) For the purpose of determining whether the transferee of an instrument is a holder, an indorsement that transfers a security interest in the instrument is effective as an unqualified indorsement of the instrument.

(d) If an instrument is payable to a holder under a name that is not the name of the holder, indorsement may be made by the holder in the name stated in the instrument or in the holder's name or both, but signature in both names may be required by a person paying or taking the instrument for value or collection.

§ 3–205. Special Indorsement; Blank Indorsement; Anomalous Indorsement

(a) If an indorsement is made by the holder of an instrument, whether payable to an identified person or payable to bearer, and the indorsement identifies a person to whom it makes the instrument payable, it is a "special indorsement." When specially indorsed, an instrument becomes payable to the identified person and may be negotiated only by the indorsement of that person. The principles stated in Section 3–110 applies to special indorsements.

(b) If an indorsement is made by the holder of an instrument and it is not a special indorsement, it is a "blank indorsement." When indorsed in blank, an instrument becomes payable to bearer and may be negotiated by transfer of possession alone until specially indorsed.

(c) The holder may convert a blank indorsement that consists only of a signature into a special indorsement by writing, above the signature of the indorser, words identifying the person to whom the instrument is made payable.

(d) "Anomalous indorsement" means an indorsement made by a person that is not the holder of the instrument. An anomalous indorsement does not affect the manner in which the instrument may be negotiated.

§ 3–206. Restrictive Indorsement

(a) An indorsement limiting payment to a particular person or otherwise prohibiting further transfer or negotiation of the instrument is not effective to prevent further transfer or negotiation of the instrument.

(b) An indorsement stating a condition to the right of the indorsee to receive payment does not affect the right of the indorsee to enforce the instrument. A person paying the instrument or taking it for value or collection may disregard the condition, and the rights and liabilities of that person are not affected by whether the condition has been fulfilled.

(c) The following rules apply to an instrument bearing an indorsement (i) described in Section 4–201(2), or (ii) in blank or to a particular bank using the words "for deposit," "for collection," or other words indicating a purpose of having the instrument collected for the indorser or for a particular account:

(1) A person, other than a bank, that purchases the instrument when so indorsed converts the instrument unless the proceeds of the instrument are received by the indorser or are applied consistently with the indorsement.

(2) A depositary bank that purchases the instrument or takes it for collection when so indorsed converts the instrument unless the proceeds of the instrument are received by the indorser or applied consistently with the indorsement.

(3) A payor bank that is also the depositary bank or that takes the instrument for immediate payment over the counter from a person other than a collecting bank converts the instrument unless the proceeds of the instrument are received by the indorser or applied consistently with the indorsement.

(4) Except as otherwise provided in paragraph (3), a payor bank or intermediary bank may disregard the indorsement and is not liable if the proceeds of the instrument are not received by the indorser or applied consistently with the indorsement.

(d) Except for an indorsement covered by subsection (c), the following rules apply to an instrument bearing an indorsement using words to the effect that payment is to be made to the indorsee as agent, trustee, or other fiduciary for the benefit of the indorser or another person:

(1) Unless there is notice of breach of fiduciary duty as provided in Section 3–307, a person that purchases the instrument from the indorsee or takes the instrument from the indorsee for collection or payment may pay the proceeds of payment or the value given for the instrument to the indorsee without regard to whether the indorsee violates a fiduciary duty to the indorser.

(2) A later transferee of the instrument or person that pays the instrument is neither given notice nor otherwise affected by the restriction in the indorsement unless the transferee or payor knows that the fiduciary dealt with the instrument or its proceeds in breach of fiduciary duty.

(e) Purchase of an instrument bearing an indorsement to which this section applies does not prevent the purchaser from becoming a holder in due course of the instrument unless the purchaser is a converter under subsection (c).

(f) In an action to enforce the obligation of a party to pay the instrument, the obligor has a defense if payment would violate an indorsement to which this section applies and the payment is not permitted by this section.

§ 3–207. Reacquisition

Reacquisition of an instrument occurs if it is transferred, by negotiation or otherwise, to a former holder. A former holder that reacquires the instrument may cancel indorsements made after the reacquirer first became a holder of the instrument. If the cancellation causes the instrument to be payable to the reacquirer or to bearer, the reacquirer may negotiate the instrument. An indorser whose indorsement is canceled is discharged, and the discharge is effective against any later holder.

Part 3—Enforcement of Instruments

§ 3–301. Person Entitled to Enforce Instrument

"Person entitled to enforce" an instrument means (i) the holder of the instrument, (ii) a nonholder in possession of the instrument who has the rights of a holder, or (iii) a person not in possession of the instrument who is entitled to enforce the instrument pursuant to Section 3–309. A person may be a person entitled to enforce the instrument even though the person is not the owner of the instrument or is in wrongful possession of the instrument.

§ 3–302. Holder in Due Course

(a) Subject to subsection (c) and Section 3–106(d), "holder in due course" means the holder of an instrument if:

(1) the instrument when issued or negotiated to the holder does not bear such apparent evidence of forgery or alteration or is not otherwise so irregular or incomplete as to call into question its authenticity, and

(2) the holder took the instrument (i) for value, (ii) in good faith, (iii) without notice that the instru-

ment is overdue or has been dishonored or that there is an uncured default with respect to payment of another instrument issued as part of the same series, (iv) without notice that the instrument contains an unauthorized signature or has been altered, (v) without notice of any claim to the instrument stated in Section 3–306, and (vi) without notice that any party to the instrument has any defense or claim in recoupment stated in Section 3–305(a).

(b) Notice of discharge of a party to the instrument, other than discharge in an insolvency proceeding, is not notice of a defense under subsection (a), but discharge is effective against a person who became a holder in due course with notice of the discharge. Public filing or recording of a document does not of itself constitute notice of a defense, claim in recoupment, or claim to the instrument.

(c) Except to the extent a transferor or predecessor in interest has rights as a holder in due course, a person does not acquire rights of a holder in due course of an instrument taken (i) by legal process or by purchase at an execution, bankruptcy, or creditor's sale or similar proceeding, (ii) by purchase as part of a bulk transaction not in ordinary course of business of the transferor, or (iii) as the successor in interest to an estate or other organization.

(d) If, under Section 3–303(a)(1), the promise of performance that is the consideration for an instrument has been partially performed, the holder may assert rights as a holder in due course of the instrument only to the fraction of the amount payable under the instrument equal to the value of the partial performance divided by the value of the promised performance.

(e) If (i) the person entitled to enforce an instrument has only a security interest in the instrument and (ii) the person obliged to pay the instrument has a defense, claim in recoupment or claim to the instrument that may be asserted against the person who granted the security interest, the person entitled to enforce the instrument may assert rights as a holder in due course only to an amount payable under the instrument which, at the time of enforcement of the instrument, does not exceed the amount of the unpaid obligation secured.

(f) To be effective, notice must be received at such time and in such manner as to give a reasonable opportunity to act on it.

(g) This section is subject to any law limiting status as a holder in due course in particular classes of transactions.

§ 3–303. Value and Consideration

(a) An instrument is issued or transferred for value if:

(1) the instrument is issued or transferred for a promise of performance, to the extent the promise has been performed;

(2) the transferee acquires a security interest or other lien in the instrument other than a lien obtained by judicial proceedings;

(3) the instrument is issued or transferred as payment of, or as security for, an existing obligation of any person, whether or not the obligation is due;

(4) the instrument is issued or transferred in exchange for a negotiable instrument; or

(5) the instrument is issued or transferred in exchange for the incurring of an irrevocable obligation to a third party by the person taking the instrument.

(b) "Consideration" means any consideration sufficient to support a simple contract. The drawer or maker of an instrument has a defense if the instrument is issued without consideration. If an instrument is issued for a promise of performance, the drawer or maker has a defense to the extent performance of the promise is due and the promise has not been performed. If an instrument is issued for value as stated in subsection (a), the instrument is also issued for consideration.

§ 3–304. Overdue Instrument

(a) An instrument payable on demand becomes overdue at the earliest of the following times:

(1) on the day after the day demand for payment is duly made;

(2) if the instrument is a check, 90 days after its date; or

(3) if the instrument is not a check, when the instrument has been outstanding for a period of time after its date which is unreasonably long under the circumstances of the particular case in light of the nature of the instrument and trade usage.

(b) With respect to an instrument payable at a definite time the following rules apply: (1) If the principal is payable in installments and a due date has not been accelerated, the instrument becomes overdue upon default under the instrument for nonpayment of an installment, and the instrument remains overdue until the default is cured. (2) If the principal is not payable in installments and the due date has not been accelerated, the instrument becomes overdue on the day after the due date. (3) If a due date with respect to principal has been accelerated, the instrument becomes overdue on the day after the accelerated due date.

(c) Unless the due date of principal has been accelerated, an instrument does not become overdue if there is default in payment of interest but no default in payment of principal.

§ 3–305. Defenses and Claims in Recoupment

(a) Except as stated in subsection (b), the right to enforce the obligation of a party to pay the instrument is subject to the following:

(1) A defense of the obligor based on (i) infancy of the obligor to the extent it is a defense to a simple contract, (ii) duress, lack of legal capacity, or illegality of the transaction that nullifies the obligation of the obligor, (iii) fraud that induced the obligor to sign the instrument with neither knowledge nor reasonable opportunity to learn of its character or its essential terms, or (iv) discharge of the obligor in insolvency proceedings.

(2) A defense of the obligor stated in another section of this Article or a defense of the obligor that would be available if the person entitled to enforce the instrument were enforcing a right to payment under a simple contract.

(3) A claim in recoupment of the obligor against the original payee of the instrument if the claim arose from the transaction that gave rise to the instrument. The claim of the obligor may be asserted against a transferee of the instrument only to reduce the amount owing on the instrument at the time the action is brought.

(b) The right of a holder in due course to enforce the obligation of a party to pay the instrument is subject to defenses of the obligor stated in subsection (a)(1), but is not subject to defenses of the obligor stated in subsection (a)(2) or claims in recoupment stated in subsection (a)(3) against a person other than the holder.

(c) Except as stated in subsection (d), in an action to enforce the obligation of a party to pay the instrument, the obligor may not assert against the person entitled to enforce the instrument a defense, claim in recoupment, or claim to the instrument (Section 3–306) of another person, but the other person's claim to the instrument may be asserted by the obligor if the other person is joined in the action and personally asserts the claim against the person entitled to enforce the instrument. An obligor is not obliged to pay the instrument if the person seeking enforcement of the instrument does not have rights of a holder in due course and the obligor proves that the instrument is a lost or stolen instrument.

(d) In an action to enforce the obligation of an accommodation party to pay an instrument, the accommodation party may assert against the person entitled to enforce the instrument any defense or claim in recoupment under subsection (a) that the accommodated party could assert against the person entitled to enforce the instrument, except the defenses of discharge in insolvency proceedings, infancy, or lack of legal capacity.

§ 3–306. Claims to an Instrument

A person taking an instrument, other than a person having rights of a holder in due course, is subject to a claim of a property or possessory right in the instrument or its proceeds, including a claim to rescind a negotiation and to recover the instrument or its proceeds. A person having rights of a holder in due course takes free of the claim to the instrument.

§ 3–307. Notice of Breach of Fiduciary Duty

(a) This section applies if (i) an instrument is taken from a fiduciary for payment or collection or for value, (ii) the taker has knowledge of the fiduciary status of the fiduciary, and (iii) the represented person makes a claim to the instrument or its proceeds on the basis that the transaction of the fiduciary is a breach of fiduciary duty. Notice of breach of fiduciary duty by the fiduciary is notice of the claim of the represented person. "Fiduciary" means an agent, trustee, partner, corporation officer or director, or other representative owing a fiduciary duty with respect to the instrument. "Represented person" means the principal, beneficiary, partnership, corporation, or other person to whom the duty is owed.

(b) If the instrument is payable to the fiduciary, as such, or to the represented person, the taker has notice of the breach of fiduciary duty if the instrument is (i) taken in payment of or as security for a debt known by the taker to be the personal debt of the fiduciary, (ii) taken in a transaction known by the taker to be for the personal benefit of the fiduciary, or (iii) deposited to an account other than an account of the fiduciary, as such, or an account of the represented person.

(c) If the instrument is made or drawn by the fiduciary, as such, payable to the fiduciary personally, the taker does not have notice of the breach of fiduciary duty unless the taker knows of the breach of fiduciary duty.

(d) If the instrument is made or drawn by or on behalf of the represented person to the taker as payee, the taker has notice of the breach of fiduciary duty if the instrument is (i) taken in payment of or as security for a debt known by the taker to be the personal debt of the fiduciary, (ii) taken in a transaction known by the taker to be for the personal benefit of the fiduciary, or (iii) deposited to an account other than an account of the fiduciary, as such, or an account of the represented person.

§ 3–308. Proof of Signatures and Status as Holder in Due Course

(a) In an action with respect to an instrument, the authenticity of, and authority to make, each signature on the instrument is admitted unless specifically denied in the pleadings. If the validity of a signature is denied in the pleadings, the burden of establishing validity is on the person claiming validity, but the signature is presumed to be authentic and authorized unless the action is to enforce the liability of the purported signer and the signer is dead or incompetent at the time of trial of the issue of validity of the signature. If an action to enforce the instrument is brought against a person as the undisclosed principal of a person who signed the instrument as a party to the instrument, the plaintiff has the burden of establishing that the defendant is liable on the instrument as a represented person pursuant to Section 3–402(a).

(b) If the validity of signatures is admitted or proved and there is compliance with subsection (a), a plaintiff producing the instrument is entitled to payment if the plaintiff proves entitlement to enforce the instrument under Section 3–301, unless the defendant proves a defense or claim in recoupment. If a defense or claim in recoupment is proved, the right to payment of the plaintiff is subject to the defense or claim except to the extent the plaintiff proves that the plaintiff has rights of a holder in due course which are not subject to the defense or claim.

§ 3–309. Enforcement of Lost, Destroyed, or Stolen Instrument

(a) A person not in possession of an instrument is entitled to enforce the instrument if (i) that person was in rightful possession of the instrument and entitled to enforce it when loss of possession occurred, (ii) the loss of possession was not the result of a voluntary transfer by that person or a lawful seizure, and (iii) that person cannot reasonably obtain possession of the instrument because the instrument was destroyed, its whereabouts cannot be determined, or it is in the wrongful possession of an unknown person or a person that cannot be found or is not amenable to service of process.

(b) A person seeking enforcement of an instrument pursuant to subsection (a) must prove the terms of the instrument and the person's right to enforce the instrument. If that proof is made, Section 3–308 applies to the case as though the person seeking enforcement had produced the instrument. The court may not enter judgment in favor of the person seeking enforcement unless it finds that the person required to pay the instrument is adequately protected against loss that might occur by reason of a claim by another person to enforce the instrument. Adequate protection may be provided by any reasonable means.

§ 3–310. Effect of Instrument on Obligation for Which Taken

(a) Unless otherwise agreed, if a certified check, cashier's check, or teller's check is taken for an obligation, the obligation is discharged to the same extent discharge would result if an amount of money equal to the amount of the instrument were taken in payment of the obligation. Discharge of the obligation does not affect any liability that the obligor may have as an indorser of the instrument.

(b) Unless otherwise agreed and except as provided in subsection (a), if a note or an uncertified check is taken for an obligation, the obligation is suspended to the same extent the obligation would be discharged if an amount of money equal to the amount of the instrument were taken.

(1) In the case of an uncertified check, suspension of the obligation continues until dishonor of the check or until it is paid or certified. Payment or certification of the check results in discharge of the obligation to the extent of the amount of the check.

(2) In the case of a note, suspension of the obligation continues until dishonor of the note or until it is paid. Payment of the note results in discharge of the obligation to the extent of the payment.

(3) If the check or note is dishonored and the obligee of the obligation for which the instrument was taken has possession of the instrument, the obligee may enforce either the instrument or the obligation. In the case of an instrument of a third person which is negotiated to the obligee by the obligor, discharge of the obligor on the instrument also discharges the obligation.

(4) If the person entitled to enforce the instrument taken for an obligation is a person other than the obligee, the obligee may not enforce the obligation to the extent the obligation is suspended. If the obligee is the person entitled to enforce the instrument but no longer has possession of it because it was lost, stolen, or destroyed, the obligation may not be enforced to the extent of the amount payable on the instrument, and to that extent the obligee's rights against the obligor are limited to enforcement of the instrument.

(c) If an instrument other than one described in subsection (a) or (b) is taken for an obligation, the effect is (i) that stated in subsection (a) if the instrument is one on which a bank is liable as maker or acceptor, or (ii) that stated in subsection (b) in any other case.

§ 3–311. Accord and Satisfaction by Use of Instrument

(a) This section applies if a person against whom a claim is asserted proves that (i) that person in good faith tendered an instrument to the claimant as full satisfaction of the claim, (ii) the amount of the claim was unliquidated or subject to a bona fide dispute, and (iii) the claimant obtained payment of the instrument.

(b) Unless subsection (c) applies, the claim is discharged if the person against whom the claim is asserted proves that the instrument or an accompanying written communication contained a conspicuous statement to the effect that the instrument was tendered as full satisfaction of the claim.

(c) Subject to subsection (d), a claim is not discharged under subsection (b) if the claimant is an organization and proves that within a reasonable time before the tender, the claimant sent a conspicuous statement to the person against whom the claim is asserted that communications concerning disputed debts, including an instrument tendered as full satisfaction of a debt, are to be sent to a designated person, office or place, and the instrument or accompanying communication was not received by that designated person, office, or place.

(d) Notwithstanding subsection (c), a claim is discharged under subsection (b) if the person against whom the claim is asserted proves that within a reasonable time before collection of the instrument was initiated, an agent of the claimant having direct responsibility with respect to the disputed obligation knew that the instrument was tendered in full satisfaction of the claim, or received the instrument and any accompanying written communication.

Part 4—Liability of Parties

§ 3–401. Signature

(a) A person is not liable on an instrument unless (i) the person signed the instrument, or (ii) the person is represented by an agent or representative who signed the instrument and the signature is binding on the represented person under Section 3–402.

(b) A signature may be made (i) manually or by means of a device or machine, and (ii) by the use of any name, including any trade or assumed name, or by any word, mark, or symbol executed or adopted by a person with present intention to authenticate a writing.

§ 3–402. Signature by Representative

(a) If a person acting, or purporting to act, as a representative signs an instrument by signing either the name of the represented person or the name of the signer, the represented person is bound by the signature to the same extent the represented person would be bound if the signature were on a simple contract. If the represented person is bound, the signature of the representative is the "authorized signature of the represented person" and the represented person is liable on the instrument, whether or not identified in the instrument.

(b) If a representative signs the name of the representative to an instrument and that signature is an authorized signature of the represented person, the following rules apply:

> (1) If the form of the signature shows unambiguously that the signature is made on behalf of the represented person who is identified in the instrument, the representative is not liable on the instrument.

> (2) Subject to subsection (c), if (i) the form of the signature does not show unambiguously that the signature is made in a representative capacity or (ii) the represented person is not identified in the instrument, the representative is liable on the instrument to a holder in due course that took the instrument without notice that the representative was not intended to be liable on the instrument. With respect to any other person, the representative is liable on the instrument unless the representative proves that the original parties to the instrument did not intend the representative to be liable on the instrument.

(c) If a representative signs the name of the representative as drawer of a check without indication of the representative status and the check is payable from an account of the represented person who is identified on the check, the signer is not liable on the check if the signature is an authorized signature of the represented person.

§ 3–403. Unauthorized Signature

(a) Except as otherwise provided in this Article, an unauthorized signature is ineffective except as the signature of the unauthorized signer in favor of a person who in good faith pays the instrument or takes it for value. An unauthorized signature may be ratified for all purposes of this Article.

(b) If the signature of more than one person is required to constitute the authorized signature of an organization, the signature of the organization is unauthorized if one of the required signatures is missing.

(c) The civil or criminal liability of a person who makes an unauthorized signature is not affected by any provision of this Article that makes the unauthorized signature effective for the purposes of this Article.

§ 3–404. Impostors; Fictitious Payees

(a) If an impostor by use of the mails or otherwise induces the maker or drawer of an instrument to issue the instrument to the impostor, or to a person acting in concert with the impostor, by impersonating the payee of the instrument or a person authorized to act for the payee, an indorsement of the instrument by any person in the name of the payee is effective as the indorsement of the payee in favor of any person that in good faith pays the instrument or takes it for value or for collection.

(b) If (i) a person whose intent determines to whom an instrument is payable (Section 3–110(a) or (b)) does not intend the person identified as payee to have any interest in the instrument, or (ii) the person identified as payee of the instrument is a fictitious person, the following rules apply until the instrument is negotiated by special indorsement:

> (1) Any person in possession of the instrument is its holder.

> (2) An indorsement by any person in the name of the payee stated in the instrument is effective as the indorsement of the payee in favor of any person that in good faith pays the instrument or takes it for value or for collection.

(c) Under subsection (a) or (b) an indorsement is made in the name of a payee if (i) it is made in a name substantially similar to that of the payee or (ii) the instrument, whether or not indorsed, is deposited in a depositary bank to an account in a name substantially similar to that of the payee.

(d) With respect to an instrument to which subsection (a) or (b) applies, if a person paying the instrument or taking it for value or for collection fails to exercise ordinary care in paying or taking the instrument and that failure substantially contributes to loss resulting from payment of the instrument, the person bearing the loss may recover from the person failing to exercise ordinary care to the extent the failure to exercise ordinary care contributed to the loss.

§ 3–405. Employer Responsibility for Fraudulent Indorsement by Employee

(a) This section applies to fraudulent indorsements of instruments with respect to which an employer has entrusted an employee with responsibility as part of the employee's duties. The following definitions apply to this section:

(1) "Employee" includes, in addition to an employee of an employer, an independent contractor and employee of an independent contractor retained by the employer.

(2) "Fraudulent indorsement" means (i) in the case of an instrument payable to the employer, a forged indorsement purporting to be that of the employer, or (ii) in the case of an instrument with respect to which the employer is drawer or maker, a forged indorsement purporting to be that of the person identified as payee.

(3) "Responsibility" with respect to instruments means authority (i) to sign or indorse instruments on behalf of the employer, (ii) to process instruments received by the employer for bookkeeping purposes, for deposit to an account, or for other disposition, (iii) to prepare or process instruments for issue in the name of the employer, (iv) to supply information determining the names or addresses of payees of instruments to be issued in the name of the employer, (v) to control the disposition of instruments to be issued in the name of the employer, or (vi) to otherwise act with respect to instruments in a responsible capacity. "Responsibility" does not include the assignment of duties that merely allow an employee to have access to instruments or blank or incomplete instrument forms that are being stored or transported or are part of incoming or outgoing mail, or similar access.

(b) For the purpose of determining the rights and liabilities of a person who, in good faith, pays an instrument or takes it for value or for collection, if an employee entrusted with responsibility with respect to the instrument or a person acting in concert with the employee makes a fraudulent indorsement to the instrument, the indorsement is effective as the indorsement of the person to whom the instrument is payable if it is made in the name of that person. If the person paying the instrument or taking it for value or for collection fails to exercise ordinary care in paying or taking the instrument and that failure substantially contributes to loss resulting from the fraud, the person bearing the loss may recover from the person failing to exercise ordinary

care to the extent the failure to exercise ordinary care contributed to the loss.

(c) Under subsection (b) an indorsement is made in the name of the person to whom an instrument is payable if (i) it is made in a name substantially similar to the name of that person or (ii) the instrument, whether or not indorsed, is deposited in a depositary bank to an account in a name substantially similar to the name of that person.

§ 3–406. Negligence Contributing to Forged Signature or Alteration of Instrument

(a) A person whose failure to exercise ordinary care substantially contributes to an alteration of an instrument or to the making of a forged signature on an instrument is precluded from asserting the alteration or the forgery against a person that, in good faith, pays the instrument or takes it for value.

(b) If the person asserting the preclusion fails to exercise ordinary care in paying or taking the instrument and that failure substantially contributes to loss, the loss is allocated between the person precluded and the person asserting the preclusion according to the extent to which the failure of each to exercise ordinary care contributed to the loss.

(c) Under subsection (a) the burden of proving failure to exercise ordinary care is on the person asserting the preclusion. Under subsection (b) the burden of proving failure to exercise ordinary care is on the person precluded.

§ 3–407. Alteration

(a) "Alteration" means (i) an unauthorized change in an instrument that purports to modify in any respect the obligation of a party to the instrument, or (ii) an unauthorized addition of words or numbers or other change to an incomplete instrument relating to the obligation of any party to the instrument.

(b) Except as provided in subsection (c), an alteration fraudulently made by the holder discharges any party to whose obligation the alteration applies unless that party assents or is precluded from asserting the alteration. No other alteration discharges any party, and the instrument may be enforced according to its original terms.

(c) If an instrument that has been fraudulently altered is acquired by a person having rights of a holder in due course, it may be enforced by that person according to its original terms. If an incomplete instrument is completed and is then acquired by a person having rights of a holder in due course, it may be enforced by that person as completed, whether or not the completion is a fraudulent alteration.

§ 3–408. Drawee Not Liable on Unaccepted Draft

A check or other draft does not of itself operate as an assignment of funds in the hands of the drawee available for its payment, and the drawee is not liable on the instrument until the drawee accepts it.

§ 3–409. Acceptance of Draft; Certified Check

(a) "Acceptance" means the drawee's signed agreement to pay a draft as presented. It must be written on the draft and may consist of the drawee's signature alone. Acceptance may be made at any time and becomes effective when notification pursuant to instructions is given or the accepted draft is delivered for the purpose of giving rights on the acceptance to any person.

(b) A draft may be accepted although it has not been signed by the drawer, is otherwise incomplete, is overdue, or has been dishonored.

(c) If a draft is payable at a fixed period after sight and the acceptor fails to date the acceptance, the holder may complete the acceptance by supplying a date in good faith.

(d) "Certified check" means a check accepted by the bank on which it is drawn. Acceptance may be made as stated in subsection (a) or by a writing on the check which indicates that the check is certified. The drawee of a check has no obligation to certify the check, and refusal to certify is not dishonor of the check.

§ 3–410. Acceptance Varying Draft

(a) If the terms of a drawee's acceptance vary from the terms of the draft as presented, the holder may refuse the acceptance and treat the draft as dishonored. In that case, the drawee may cancel the acceptance.

(b) The terms of a draft are not varied by an acceptance to pay at a particular bank or place in the United States, unless the acceptance states that the draft is to be paid only at that bank or place.

(c) If the holder assents to an acceptance varying the terms of a draft, the obligation of each drawer and indorser that does not expressly assent to the acceptance is discharged.

§ 3–411. Refusal to Pay Cashier's Checks, Teller's Checks, and Certified Checks

(a) In this section, "obligated bank" means the acceptor of a certified check or the issuer of a cashier's check or teller's check bought from the issuer.

(b) If the obligated bank wrongfully (i) refuses to pay a cashier's check or certified check, (ii) stops payment of a teller's check, or (iii) refuses to pay a dishonored teller's check, the person asserting the right to enforce the check is entitled to compensation for expenses and loss of interest resulting from the nonpayment and may recover consequential damages if the obligated bank refused to pay after receiving notice of particular circumstances giving rise to the damages.

(c) Expenses or consequential damages under subsection (b) are not recoverable if the refusal of the obligated bank to pay occurs because (i) the bank suspends payments, (ii) the obligated bank is asserting a claim or defense of the bank that it has reasonable grounds to believe is available against the person entitled to enforce the instrument, (iii) the obligated bank has a reasonable doubt whether the person demanding payment is the person entitled to enforce the instrument, or (iv) payment is prohibited by law.

§ 3–412. Obligation of Maker

A maker of a note is obliged to pay the note (i) according to its terms at the time it was issued or, if not issued, at the time it first came into possession of a holder, or (ii) if the maker signed an incomplete instrument, according to its terms when completed as stated in Sections 3–115 and 3–407. The obligation is owed to a person entitled to enforce the note or to an indorser that paid the note pursuant to Section 3–415.

§ 3–413. Obligation of Acceptor

(a) An acceptor of a draft is obliged to pay the draft (i) according to its terms at the time it was accepted, even though the acceptance states that the draft is payable "as originally drawn" or equivalent terms, (ii) if the acceptance varies the terms of the draft, according to the terms of the draft as varied, or (iii) if the acceptance is of a draft that is an incomplete instrument, according to its terms when completed as stated in Sections 3–115 and 3–407. The obligation is owed to a person entitled to enforce the draft or to the drawer or an indorser that paid the draft pursuant to Section 3–414 or 3–415.

(b) If the certification of a check or other acceptance of a draft states the amount certified or accepted, the obligation of the acceptor is that amount. If (i) the certification or acceptance does not state an amount, (ii) the instrument is subsequently altered by raising its amount, and (iii) the instrument is then negotiated to a holder in due course, the obligation of the acceptor is the amount of the instrument at the time it was negotiated to the holder in due course.

§ 3–414. Obligation of Drawer

(a) If an unaccepted draft is dishonored, the drawer is obliged to pay the draft (i) according to its terms at the time it was issued or, if not issued, at the time it first came into possession of a holder, or (ii) if the drawer signed an incomplete instrument, according to its terms when completed as stated in Sections 3–115 and 3–407. The obligation is owed to a person entitled to enforce the draft or to an indorser that paid the draft pursuant to Section 3–415.

(b) If a draft is accepted by a bank and the acceptor dishonors the draft, the drawer has no obligation to pay the draft because of the dishonor, regardless of when or by whom acceptance was obtained.

(c) If a draft is accepted and the acceptor is not a bank, the obligation of the drawer to pay the draft if the draft is dishonored by the acceptor is the same as the obligation of an indorser stated in Section 3–415(a) and (c).

(d) Words in a draft indicating that the draft is drawn without recourse are effective to disclaim all liability of the drawer to pay the draft if the draft is not a check or a teller's check, but they are not effective to disclaim the obligation stated in subsection (a) if the draft is a check or a teller's check.

(e) If (i) a check is not presented for payment or given to a depositary bank for collection within 30 days after its date, (ii) the drawee suspends payments after expiration of the 30-day period without paying the check, and (iii) because of the suspension of payments the drawer is deprived of funds maintained with the drawee to cover payment of the check, the drawer to the extent deprived of funds may discharge its obligation to pay the check by assigning to the person entitled to enforce the check the rights of the drawer against the drawee with respect to the funds.

§ 3–415. Obligation of Indorser

(a) Subject to subsections (b), (c) and (d) and to Section 3–419(d), if an instrument is dishonored, an indorser is obliged to pay the amount due on the instrument (i) according to the terms of the instrument at the time it was indorsed, or (ii) if the indorser indorsed an incomplete instrument, according to its terms when completed as stated in Sections 3–115 and 3–407. The obligation of the indorser is owed to a person entitled to enforce the instrument or to a subsequent indorser that paid the instrument pursuant to this section.

(b) If an indorsement states that it is made "without recourse" or otherwise disclaims liability of the indorser, the indorser is not liable under subsection (a) to pay the instrument.

(c) If notice of dishonor of an instrument is required by Section 3–503 and notice of dishonor complying with that section is not given to an indorser, the liability of the indorser under subsection (a) is discharged.

(d) If a draft is accepted by a bank after an indorsement was made and the acceptor dishonors the draft, the indorser is not liable under subsection (a) to pay the instrument.

(e) If an indorser of a check is liable under subsection (a) and the check is not presented for payment, or given to a depositary bank for collection, within 30 days after the day the indorsement was made, the liability of the indorser under subsection (a) is discharged.

§ 3–416. Transfer Warranties

(a) A person that transfers an instrument for consideration warrants to the transferee and, if the transfer is by indorsement, to any subsequent transferee that:

(1) the warrantor is a person entitled to enforce the instrument,

(2) all signatures on the instrument are authentic and authorized,

(3) the instrument has not been altered,

(4) the instrument is not subject to a defense or claim in recoupment stated in Section 3–305(a) of any party that can be asserted against the warrantor, and

(5) the warrantor has no knowledge of any insolvency proceeding commenced with respect to the maker or acceptor or, in the case of an unaccepted draft, the drawer.

(b) A person to whom the warranties under subsection (a) are made and who took the instrument in good faith may recover from the warrantor as damages for breach of warranty an amount equal to the loss suffered as a result of the breach, but not more than the amount of the instrument plus expenses and loss of interest incurred as a result of the breach.

(c) The warranties stated in subsection (a) cannot be disclaimed with respect to checks. Unless notice of a claim for breach of warranty is given to the warrantor within 30 days after the claimant has reason to know of the breach and the identity of the warrantor, the warrantor is discharged to the extent of any loss caused by the delay in giving notice of the claim.

(d) A cause of action for breach of warranty under this section accrues when the claimant has reason to know of the breach.

§ 3–417. Presentment Warranties

(a) If an unaccepted draft is presented to the drawee for payment or acceptance and the drawee pays or accepts the draft, (i) the person obtaining payment or acceptance, at the time of presentment, and (ii) a previous transferor of the draft, at the time of transfer, warrant to the drawee making payment or accepting the draft in good faith that:

(1) the warrantor is or was, at the time the warrantor transferred the draft, a person entitled to enforce the draft or authorized to obtain payment or acceptance of the draft on behalf of a person entitled to enforce the draft;

(2) the draft has not been altered; and

(3) the warrantor has no knowledge that the signature of the purported drawer of the draft is unauthorized.

(b) A drawee making payment may recover from any warrantor damages for breach of warranty equal to the amount paid by the drawee less the amount the drawee received or is entitled to receive from the drawer because of payment of the draft. In addition the drawee is entitled to compensation for expenses and loss of interest resulting from the breach. The right of the drawee to recover damages under this subsection is not affected by any failure of the drawee to exercise ordinary care in making payment. If the drawee accepts the draft (i) breach of warranty is a defense to the obligation of the acceptor, and (ii) if the acceptor makes payment with respect to the draft, the acceptor is entitled to recover from any warrantor for breach of warranty the amounts stated in the first two sentences of this subsection.

(c) If a drawee asserts a claim for breach of warranty under subsection (a) based on an unauthorized indorsement of the draft or an alteration of the draft, the warrantor may defend by proving that the indorsement is effective under Section 3–404 or 3–405 or the drawer is precluded under Section 3–406 or 4–406 from asserting against the drawee the unauthorized indorsement or alteration.

(d) This subsection applies if (i) a dishonored draft is presented for payment to the drawer or an indorser or (ii) any other instrument is presented for payment to a party obliged to pay the instrument, and payment is received. The person obtaining payment and a prior transferor of the instrument warrant to the person making payment in good faith that the warrantor is or was, at the time the warrantor transferred the instrument, a person entitled to enforce the instrument or authorized to obtain payment on behalf of a person entitled to enforce the instrument. The person making payment may recover from any warrantor for breach of warranty an amount equal to the amount paid plus expenses and loss of interest resulting from the breach.

(e) The warranties stated in subsections (a) and (d) cannot be disclaimed with respect to checks. Unless notice of a claim for breach of warranty is given to the warrantor within 30 days after the claimant has reason to know of the breach and the identity of the warrantor, the warrantor is discharged to the extent of any loss caused by the delay in giving notice of the claim.

(f) A cause of action for breach of warranty under this section accrues when the claimant has reason to know of the breach.

§ 3–418. Payment or Acceptance by Mistake

(a) Except as provided in subsection (c), if the drawee of a draft pays or accepts the draft and the drawee acted on the mistaken belief that (i) payment of the draft had not been stopped under Section 4–403, (ii) the signature of the purported drawer of the draft was authorized, or (iii) the balance in the drawer's account with the drawee represented available funds, the drawee may recover the amount paid from the person to whom or for whose benefit payment was made or, in the case of acceptance, may revoke the acceptance. Rights of the drawee under this subsection are not affected by failure of the drawee to exercise ordinary care in paying or accepting the draft.

(b) Except as provided in subsection (c), if an instrument has been paid or accepted by mistake and the case is not covered by subsection (a), the person paying or accepting may recover the amount paid or revoke acceptance to the extent allowed by the law governing mistake and restitution.

(c) The remedies provided by subsection (a) or (b) may not be asserted against a person who took the instrument in good faith and for value. This subsection does not limit remedies provided by Section 3–417 for breach of warranty.

§ 3–419. Instruments Signed for Accommodation

(a) If an instrument is issued for value given for the benefit of a party to the instrument ("accommodated party") and another party to the instrument ("accommodation party") signs the instrument for the purpose of incurring liability on the instrument without being a direct beneficiary of the value given for the instrument, the instrument is signed by the accommodation party "for accommodation."

(b) An accommodation party may sign the instrument as maker, drawer, acceptor, or indorser and, subject to subsection (d), is obliged to pay the instrument in the capacity in which the accommodation party signs. The obligation of an accommodation party may be enforced notwithstanding any statute of frauds and regardless of whether the accommodation party receives consideration for the accommodation.

(c) A person signing an instrument is presumed to be an accommodation party and there is notice that the instrument is signed for accommodation if the signature is an anomalous indorsement or is accompanied by words indicating that the signer is acting as surety or guarantor with respect to the obligation of another party to the instrument. Except as provided in Section 3–606, the obligation of an accommodation party to pay the instrument is not affected by the fact that the person enforcing the obligation had notice when the instrument was taken by that person that the accommodation party signed the instrument for accommodation.

(d) If the signature of a party to an instrument is accompanied by words indicating unambiguously that the party is guaranteeing collection rather than payment of the obligation of another party to the instrument, the signer is obliged to pay the amount due on the instrument to a person entitled to enforce the instrument only if (i) execution of judgment against the other party has been returned unsatisfied, (ii) the other party is insolvent or in an insolvency proceeding, (iii) the other party cannot be served with process, or (iv) it is otherwise apparent that payment cannot be obtained from the party whose obligation is guaranteed.

(e) An accommodation party that pays the instrument is entitled to reimbursement from the accommodated party and is entitled to enforce the instrument against the accommodated party. An accommodated party that pays the instrument has no right of recourse against, and is not entitled to contribution from, an accommodation party.

§ 3–420. Conversion of Instrument

(a) The law applicable to conversion of personal property applies to instruments. An instrument is also converted if the instrument lacks an indorsement necessary for negotiation and it is purchased or taken for collection or the drawee takes the instrument and makes payment to a person not entitled to receive payment. An action for conversion of an instrument may not be brought by (i) the maker, drawer, or acceptor of the instrument or (ii) a payee or indorsee who did not receive delivery of the instrument either directly or through delivery to an agent or a co-payee.

(b) In an action under subsection (a), the measure of liability is presumed to be the amount payable on the instrument, but recovery may not exceed the amount of the plaintiff's interest in the instrument.

(c) A representative, other than a depositary bank, that has in good faith dealt with an instrument or its proceeds on behalf of one who was not the person entitled to enforce the instrument is not liable in conversion to that person beyond the amount of any proceeds that it has not paid out.

Part 5—Dishonor

§ 3–501. Presentment

(a) "Presentment" means a demand (i) to pay an instrument made to the maker, drawee, or acceptor or, in the case of a note or accepted draft payable at a bank, to the bank, or (ii) to accept a draft made to the drawee, by a person entitled to enforce the instrument.

(b) Subject to Article 4, agreement of the parties, clearing house rules and the like,

(1) presentment may be made at the place of payment of the instrument and must be made at the place of payment if the instrument is payable at a bank in the United States; may be made by any commercially reasonable means, including an oral, written, or electronic communication; is effective when the demand for payment or acceptance is received by the person to whom presentment is made; is effective if made to any one of two or more makers, acceptors, drawees or other payors; and

(2) without dishonoring the instrument, the party to whom presentment is made may (i) treat presentment as occurring on the next business day after the day of presentment if the party to whom presentment is made has established a cut-off hour not earlier than 2 p.m. for the receipt and processing of instruments presented for payment or acceptance and presentment is made after the cut-off hour, (ii)

require exhibition of the instrument, (iii) require reasonable identification of the person making presentment and evidence of authority to make it if made on behalf of another person, (iv) require a signed receipt on the instrument for any payment made or surrender of the instrument if full payment is made, (v) return the instrument for lack of a necessary indorsement, or (vi) refuse payment or acceptance for failure of the presentment to comply with the terms of the instrument, an agreement of the parties, or other law or applicable rule.

§ 3–502. Dishonor

(a) Dishonor of a note is governed by the following rules:

(1) If the note is payable on demand, the note is dishonored if presentment is duly made and the note is not paid on the day of presentment.

(2) If the note is not payable on demand and is payable at or through a bank or the terms of the note require presentment, the note is dishonored if presentment is duly made and the note is not paid on the day it becomes payable or the day of presentment, whichever is later.

(3) If the note is not payable on demand and subparagraph (2) does not apply, the note is dishonored if it is not paid on the day it becomes payable.

(b) Dishonor of an unaccepted draft other than a documentary draft is governed by the following rules:

(1) If a check is presented for payment otherwise than for immediate payment over the counter, the check is dishonored if the payor bank makes timely return of the check or sends timely notice of dishonor or nonpayment under Section 4–301 or 4–302, or becomes accountable for the amount of the check under Section 4–302.

(2) If the draft is payable on demand and subparagraph (1) does not apply, the draft is dishonored if presentment for payment is duly made and the draft is not paid on the day of presentment.

(3) If the draft is payable on a date stated in the draft, the draft is dishonored if (i) presentment for payment is duly made and payment is not made on the day the draft becomes payable or the day of presentment, whichever is later, or (ii) presentment for acceptance is duly made before the day the draft becomes payable and the draft is not accepted on the day of presentment.

(4) If the draft is payable on elapse of a period of time after sight or acceptance, the draft is dishonored if presentment for acceptance is duly made and the draft is not accepted on the day of presentment.

(c) Dishonor of an unaccepted documentary draft occurs according to the rules stated in subparagraphs (2), (3), and (4) of subsection (b) except that payment or acceptance may be delayed without dishonor until no later than the close of the third business day of the drawee following the day on which payment or acceptance is required by those subparagraphs.

(d) Dishonor of an accepted draft is governed by the following rules:

(1) If the draft is payable on demand, the draft is dishonored if presentment for payment is duly made and the draft is not paid on the day of presentment.

(2) If the draft is not payable on demand, the draft is dishonored if presentment for payment is duly made and payment is not made on the day it becomes payable or the day of presentment, whichever is later.

(e) In any case in which presentment is otherwise required for dishonor under this section and presentment is excused under Section 3–504, dishonor occurs without presentment if the instrument is not duly accepted or paid.

(f) If a draft is dishonored because timely acceptance of the draft was not made and the person entitled to demand acceptance consents to a late acceptance, from the time of acceptance the draft is treated as never having been dishonored.

§ 3–503. Notice of Dishonor

(a) The obligation of an indorser stated in Section 3–415(a) and the obligation of a drawer stated in Section 3–414(c) may not be enforced unless (i) the indorser or drawer is given notice of dishonor of the instrument complying with this section or (ii) notice of dishonor is excused under Section 3–504(c).

(b) Notice of dishonor may be given by any person; may be given by any commercially reasonable means including an oral, written, or electronic communication; is sufficient if it reasonably identifies the instrument and indicates that the instrument has been dishonored or has not been paid or accepted. Return of an instrument given to a bank for collection is a sufficient notice of dishonor.

(c) Subject to Section 3–504(d), with respect to an instrument taken for collection by a collecting bank, notice of dishonor must be given (i) by the bank before midnight of the next banking day following the banking day on which the bank receives notice of dishonor of the instrument, and (ii) by any other person within 30 days following the day on which the person receives notice of dishonor. With respect to any other instrument, notice of dishonor must be given within 30 days following the day on which dishonor occurs.

§ 3–504. Excused Presentment and Notice of Dishonor

(a) Presentment for payment or acceptance of an instrument is excused if (i) the person entitled to present the instrument cannot with reasonable diligence make presentment, (ii) the maker or acceptor has repudiated

an obligation to pay the instrument or is dead or in insolvency proceedings, (iii) by the terms of the instrument presentment is not necessary to enforce the obligation of indorsers or the drawer, or (iv) the drawer or indorser whose obligation is being enforced waived presentment or otherwise had no reason to expect or right to require that the instrument be paid or accepted.

(b) Presentment for payment or acceptance of a draft is also excused if the drawer instructed the drawee not to pay or accept the draft or the drawee was not obligated to the drawer to pay the draft.

(c) Notice of dishonor is excused if (i) by the terms of the instrument notice of dishonor is not necessary to enforce the obligation of a party to pay the instrument, or (ii) the party whose obligation is being enforced waived notice of dishonor. A waiver of presentment is also a waiver of notice of dishonor.

(d) Delay in giving notice of dishonor is excused if the delay was caused by circumstances beyond the control of the person giving the notice and the person giving the notice exercised reasonable diligence after the cause of the delay ceased to operate.

§ 3–505. Evidence of Dishonor

(a) The following are admissible as evidence and create a presumption of dishonor and of any notice of dishonor stated:

(1) a document regular in form as provided in subsection (b) which purports to be a protest;

(2) a purported stamp or writing of the drawee, payor bank, or presenting bank on or accompanying the instrument stating that acceptance or payment has been refused unless reasons for the refusal are stated and the reasons are not consistent with dishonor;

(3) a book or record of the drawee, payor bank, or collecting bank, kept in the usual course of business which shows dishonor, even if there is no evidence of who made the entry.

(b) A protest is a certificate of dishonor made by a United States consul or vice consul, or a notary public or other person authorized to administer oaths by the law of the place where dishonor occurs. It may be made upon information satisfactory to that person. The protest must identify the instrument and certify either that presentment has been made or, if not made, the reason why it was not made, and that the instrument has been dishonored by nonacceptance or nonpayment. The protest may also certify that notice of dishonor has been given to some or all parties.

Part 6—Discharge and Payment

§ 3–601. Discharge and Effect of Discharge

(a) The obligation of a party to pay the instrument is discharged as stated in this Article or by an act or agreement with the party which would discharge an obligation to pay money under a simple contract.

(b) Discharge of the obligation of a party is not effective against a person acquiring rights of a holder in due course of the instrument without notice of the discharge.

§ 3–602. Payment

(a) Subject to subsection (b), an instrument is paid to the extent payment is made (i) by or on behalf of a party obliged to pay the instrument, and (ii) to a person entitled to enforce the instrument. To the extent of the payment, the obligation of the party obliged to pay the instrument is discharged even though payment is made with knowledge of a claim to the instrument under Section 3–306 by another person.

(b) The obligation of a party to pay the instrument is not discharged under subsection (a) if:

(1) a claim to the instrument under Section 3–306 is enforceable against the party receiving payment and (i) payment is made with knowledge by the payor that payment is prohibited by injunction or similar process of a court of competent jurisdiction, or (ii) in the case of an instrument other than a cashier's check, teller's check, or certified check, the party making payment accepted, from the person having a claim to the instrument, indemnity against loss resulting from refusal to pay the person entitled to enforce the instrument, or

(2) the person making payment knows that the instrument is a stolen instrument and pays a person that it knows is in wrongful possession of the instrument.

§ 3–603. Tender of Payment

(a) If tender of payment of an obligation of a party to an instrument is made to a person entitled to enforce the obligation, the effect of tender is governed by principles of law applicable to tender of payment of an obligation under a simple contract.

(b) If tender of payment of an obligation to pay the instrument is made to a person entitled to enforce the instrument and the tender is refused, there is discharge, to the extent of the amount of the tender, of the obligation of an indorser or accommodation party having a right of recourse against the obligor making the tender.

(c) If tender of payment of an amount due on an instrument is made by or on behalf of the obligor to the person entitled to enforce the instrument, the obligation of the obligor to pay interest after the due date on the amount tendered is discharged. If presentment is required with respect to an instrument and the obligor is able and ready to pay on the due date at every place of payment stated in the instrument, the obligor is deemed to have made tender of payment on the due date to the person entitled to enforce the instrument.

§ 3–604. Discharge by Cancellation or Renunciation

(a) A person entitled to enforce an instrument may, with or without consideration, discharge the obligation of a party to pay the instrument (i) by an intentional voluntary act such as surrender of the instrument to the party, destruction, mutilation, or cancellation of the instrument, cancellation or striking out of the party's signature, or the addition of words to the instrument indicating discharge, or (ii) by agreeing not to sue or otherwise renouncing rights against the party by a signed writing.

(b) Cancellation or striking out of an indorsement pursuant to subsection (a) does not affect the status and rights of a party derived from the indorsement.

§ 3–605. Discharge of Indorsers and Accommodation Parties

(a) For the purposes of this section, the term "indorser" includes a drawer having the obligation stated in Section 3–414(c).

(b) Discharge of the obligation of a party to the instrument under Section 3–605 does not discharge the obligation of an indorser or accommodation party having a right of recourse against the discharged party.

(c) If a person entitled to enforce an instrument agrees, with or without consideration, to a material modification of the obligation of a party to the instrument, including an extension of the due date, there is discharge of the obligation of an indorser or accommodation party having a right of recourse against the person whose obligation is modified to the extent the modification causes loss to the indorser or accommodation party with respect to the right of recourse. The indorser or accommodation party is deemed to have suffered loss as a result of the modification equal to the amount of the right of recourse unless the person enforcing the instrument proves that no loss was caused by the modification or that the loss caused by the modification was less than the amount of the right of recourse.

(d) If the obligation of a party to an instrument is secured by an interest in collateral and impairment of the value of the interest is caused by a person entitled to enforce the instrument, there is discharge of the obligation of an indorser or accommodation party having a right of recourse against the obligor to the extent of the impairment. The value of an interest in collateral is impaired to the extent (i) the value of the interest is reduced to an amount less than the amount of the right of recourse of the party asserting discharge, or (ii) the reduction in value of the interest causes an increase in the amount by which the amount of the right of recourse exceeds the value of the interest. The burden of proving impairment is on the party asserting discharge.

(e) If the obligation of a party to an instrument is secured by an interest in collateral not provided by an accommodation party and the value of the interest is impaired by a person entitled to enforce the instrument, the obligation of any party who is jointly and severally liable with respect to the secured obligation is discharged to the extent the impairment causes the party asserting discharge to pay more than that party would have been obliged to pay, taking into account rights of contribution, if impairment had not occurred. If the party asserting discharge is an accommodation party not entitled to discharge under subsection (d), the party is deemed to have a right to contribution based on joint and several liability rather than a right to reimbursement. The burden of proving impairment is on the party asserting discharge.

(f) Under subsection (d) or (e) causation of impairment includes (i) failure to obtain or maintain perfection or recordation of the interest in collateral, (ii) release of collateral without substitution of collateral of equal value, (iii) failure to perform a duty to preserve the value of collateral owed, under Article 9 or other law, to a debtor or surety or other person secondarily liable, or (iv) failure to comply with applicable law in disposing of collateral.

(g) An accommodation party is not discharged under subsection (c) or (d) unless the person agreeing to the modification or causing the impairment knows of the accommodation or has notice under Section 3–419(c) that the instrument was signed for accommodation. There is no discharge of any party under subsection (c), (d), or (e) if (i) the party asserting discharge consents to the event or conduct that is the basis of the discharge, or (ii) the instrument or a separate agreement of the party provides for waiver of discharge under this section either specifically or by general language indicating that parties to the instrument waive defenses based on suretyship or impairment of collateral.

Appendix D

UNIFORM PARTNERSHIP ACT

The Act consists of seven Parts as follows:
I. Preliminary Provisions
II. Nature of Partnership
III. Relations of Partners to Persons Dealing with the Partnership
IV. Relations of Partners to One Another
V. Property Rights of a Partner
VI. Dissolution and Winding Up
VII. Miscellaneous Provisions

An Act to make uniform the Law of Partnerships
  Be it enacted, etc.:

Part I. Preliminary Provisions

§ 1. Name of Act

This act may be cited as Uniform Partnership Act.

§ 2. Definition of Terms

In this act, "Court" includes every court and judge having jurisdiction in the case.
"Business" includes every trade, occupation, or profession.
"Person" includes individuals, partnerships, corporations, and other associations.
"Bankrupt" includes bankrupt under the Federal Bankruptcy Act or insolvent under any state insolvent act.
"Conveyance" includes every assignment, lease, mortgage, or encumbrance.
"Real property" includes land and any interest or estate in land.

§ 3. Interpretation of Knowledge and Notice

(1) A person has "knowledge" of a fact within the meaning of this act not only when he has actual knowledge thereof, but also when he has knowledge of such other facts as in the circumstances shows bad faith.

(2) A person has "notice" of a fact within the meaning of this act when the person who claims the benefit of the notice

  (a) States the fact to such person, or

  (b) Delivers through the mail, or by other means of communication, a written statement of the fact to such person or to a proper person at his place of business or residence.

§ 4. Rules of Construction

(1) The rule that statutes in derogation of the common law are to be strictly construed shall have no application to this act.

(2) The law of estoppel shall apply under this act.

(3) The law of agency shall apply under this act.

(4) This act shall be so interpreted and construed as to effect its general purpose to make uniform the law of those states which enact it.

(5) This act shall not be construed so as to impair the obligations of any contract existing when the act goes into effect, nor to affect any action or proceedings begun or right accrued before this act takes effect.

§ 5. Rules for Cases Not Provided for in This Act

In any case not provided for in this act the rules of law and equity, including the law merchant, shall govern.

Part II. Nature of Partnership

§ 6. Partnership Defined

(1) A partnership is an association of two or more persons to carry on as co-owners a business for profit.

(2) But any association formed under any other statute of this state, or any statute adopted by authority, other than the authority of this state, is not a partnership under this act, unless such association would have been a partnership in this state prior to the adoption of this act; but this act shall apply to limited partnerships except in so far as the statutes relating to such partnerships are inconsistent herewith.

§ 7. Rules for Determining the Existence of a Partnership

In determining whether a partnership exists, these rules shall apply:

(1) Except as provided by Section 16 persons who are not partners as to each other are not partners as to third persons.

(2) Joint tenancy, tenancy in common, tenancy by the entireties, joint property, common property, or part ownership does not of itself establish a partnership, whether such co-owners do or do not share any profits made by the use of the property.

(3) The sharing of gross returns does not of itself establish a partnership, whether or not the persons sharing them have a joint or common right or interest in any property from which the returns are derived.

(4) The receipt by a person of a share of the profits of a business is prima facie evidence that he is a partner in the business, but no such inference shall be drawn if such profits were received in payment:

(a) As a debt by installments or otherwise,

(b) As wages of an employee or rent to a landlord,

(c) As an annuity to a widow or representative of a deceased partner,

(d) As interest on a loan, though the amount of payment vary with the profits of the business.

(e) As the consideration for the sale of a good-will of a business or other property by installments or otherwise.

§ 8. Partnership Property

(1) All property originally brought into the partnership stock or subsequently acquired by purchase or otherwise, on account of the partnership, is partnership property.

(2) Unless the contrary intention appears, property acquired with partnership funds is partnership property.

(3) Any estate in real property may be acquired in the partnership name. Title so acquired can be conveyed only in the partnership name.

(4) A conveyance to a partnership in the partnership name, though without words of inheritance, passes the entire estate of the grantor unless a contrary intent appears.

Part III. Relations of Partners to Persons Dealing with the Partnership

§ 9. Partner Agent of Partnership as to Partnership Business

(1) Every partner is an agent of the partnership for the purpose of its business, and the act of every partner, including the execution in the partnership name of any instrument, for apparently carrying on in the usual way the business of the partnership of which he is a member binds the partnership, unless the partner so acting has in fact no authority to act for the partnership in the particular matter, and the person with whom he is dealing has knowledge of the fact that he has no such authority.

(2) An act of a partner which is not apparently for the carrying on of the business of the partnership in the usual way does not bind the partnership unless authorized by the other partners.

(3) Unless authorized by the other partners or unless they have abandoned the business, one or more but less than all the partners have no authority to:

(a) Assign the partnership property in trust for creditors or on the assignee's promise to pay the debts of the partnership,

(b) Dispose of the good-will of the business,

(c) Do any other act which would make it impossible to carry on the ordinary business of a partnership,

(d) Confess a judgment,

(e) Submit a partnership claim or liability to arbitration or reference.

(4) No act of a partner in contravention of a restriction on authority shall bind the partnership to persons having knowledge of the restriction.

§ 10. Conveyance of Real Property of the Partnership

(1) Where title to real property is in the partnership name, any partner may convey title to such property by a conveyance executed in the partnership name; but the partnership may recover such property unless the partner's act binds the partnership under the provisions of

paragraph (1) of section 9 or unless such property has been conveyed by the grantee or a person claiming through such grantee to a holder for value without knowledge that the partner, in making the conveyance, has exceeded his authority.

(2) Where title to real property is in the name of the partnership, a conveyance executed by a partner, in his own name, passes the equitable interest of the partnership, provided the act is one within the authority of the partner under the provisions of paragraph (1) of section 9.

(3) Where title to real property is in the name of one or more but not all the partners, and the record does not disclose the right of the partnership, the partners in whose name the title stands may convey title to such property, but the partnership may recover such property if the partners' act does not bind the partnership under the provisions of paragraph (1) of section 9, unless the purchaser or his assignee, is a holder for value, without knowledge.

(4) Where the title to real property is in the name of one or more or all the partners, or in a third person in trust for the partnership, a conveyance executed by a partner in the partnership name, or in his own name, passes the equitable interest of the partnership, provided the act is one within the authority of the partner under the provisions of paragraph (1) of section 9.

(5) Where the title to real property is in the names of all the partners a conveyance executed by all the partners passes all their rights in such property.

§ 11. Partnership Bound by Admission of Partner

An admission or representation made by any partner concerning partnership affairs within the scope of his authority as conferred by this act is evidence against the partnership.

§ 12. Partnership Charged with Knowledge of or Notice to Partner

Notice to any partner of any matter relating to partnership affairs, and the knowledge of the partner acting in the particular matter, acquired while a partner or then present to his mind, and the knowledge of any other partner who reasonably could and should have communicated it to the acting partner, operate as notice to or knowledge of the partnership, except in the case of a fraud on the partnership committed by or with the consent of that partner.

§ 13. Partnership Bound by Partner's Wrongful Act

Where, by any wrongful act or omission of any partner acting in the ordinary course of the business of the partnership or with the authority of his co-partners, loss or injury is caused to any person, not being a partner in the partnership, or any penalty is incurred, the partnership is liable therefor to the same extent as the partner so acting or omitting to act.

§ 14. Partnership Bound by Partner's Breach of Trust

The partnership is bound to make good the loss:

(a) Where one partner acting within the scope of his apparent authority receives money or property of a third person and misapplies it; and

(b) Where the partnership in the course of its business receives money or property of a third person and the money or property so received is misapplied by any partner while it is in the custody of the partnership.

§ 15. Nature of Partner's Liability

All partners are liable

(a) Jointly and severally for everything chargeable to the partnership under sections 13 and 14.

(b) Jointly for all other debts and obligations of the partnership; but any partner may enter into a separate obligation to perform a partnership contract.

§ 16. Partner by Estoppel

(1) When a person, by words spoken or written or by conduct, represents himself, or consents to another representing him to any one, as a partner in an existing partnership or with one or more persons not actual partners, he is liable to any such person to whom such representation has been made, who has, on the faith of such representation, given credit to the actual or apparent partnership, and if he has made such representation or consented to its being made in a public manner he is liable to such person, whether the representation has or has not been made or communicated to such person so giving credit by or with the knowledge of the apparent partner making the representation or consenting to its being made.

(a) When a partnership liability results, he is liable as though he were an actual member of the partnership.

(b) When no partnership liability results, he is liable jointly with the other persons, if any, so consenting to the contract or representation as to incur liability, otherwise separately.

(2) When a person has been thus represented to be a partner in an existing partnership, or with one or more persons not actual partners, he is an agent of the persons consenting to such representation to bind them to the same extent and in the same manner as though he were a partner in fact, with respect to persons who rely upon the representation. Where all the members of the existing partnership consent to the representation, a partnership act or obligation results; but in all other cases it is the joint act or obligation of the person acting and the persons consenting to the representation.

§ 17. Liability of Incoming Partner

A person admitted as a partner into an existing partnership is liable for all the obligations of the partnership arising before his admission as though he had been a partner when such obligations were incurred, except that this liability shall be satisfied only out of partnership property.

Part IV. Relations of Partners to One Another

§ 18. Rules Determining Rights and Duties of Partners

The rights and duties of the partners in relation to the partnership shall be determined, subject to any agreement between them, by the following rules:

(a) Each partner shall be repaid his contributions, whether by way of capital or advances to the partnership property and share equally in the profits and surplus remaining after all liabilities, including those to partners, are satisfied; and must contribute towards the losses, whether of capital or otherwise, sustained by the partnership according to his share in the profits.

(b) The partnership must indemnify every partner in respect of payments made and personal liabilities reasonably incurred by him in the ordinary and proper conduct of its business, or for the preservation of its business or property.

(c) A partner, who in aid of the partnership makes any payment or advance beyond the amount of capital which he agreed to contribute, shall be paid interest from the date of the payment or advance.

(d) A partner shall receive interest on the capital contributed by him only from the date when repayment should be made.

(e) All partners have equal rights in the management and conduct of the partnership business.

(f) No partner is entitled to remuneration for acting in the partnership business, except that a surviving partner is entitled to reasonable compensation for his services in winding up the partnership affairs.

(g) No person can become a member of a partnership without the consent of all the partners.

(h) Any difference arising as to ordinary matters connected with the partnership business may be decided by a majority of the partners; but no act in contravention of any agreement between the partners may be done rightfully without the consent of all the partners.

§ 19. Partnership Books

The partnership books shall be kept, subject to any agreement between the partners, at the principal place of business of the partnership, and every partner shall at all times have access to and may inspect and copy any of them.

§ 20. Duty of Partners to Render Information

Partners shall render on demand true and full information of all things affecting the partnership to any partner or the legal representative of any deceased partner or partner under legal disability.

§ 21. Partner Accountable as a Fiduciary

(1) Every partner must account to the partnership for any benefit, and hold as trustee for it any profits derived by him without the consent of the other partners from any transaction connected with the formation, conduct, or liquidation of the partnership or from any use by him of its property.

(2) This section applies also to the representatives of a deceased partner engaged in the liquidation of the affairs of the partnership as the personal representatives of the last surviving partner.

§ 22. Right to an Account

Any partner shall have the right to a formal account as to partnership affairs:

(a) If he is wrongfully excluded from the partnership business or possession of its property by his co-partners,

(b) If the right exists under the terms of any agreement,

(c) As provided by section 21,

(d) Whenever other circumstances render it just and reasonable.

§ 23. Continuation of Partnership Beyond Fixed Term

(1) When a partnership for a fixed term or particular undertaking is continued after the termination of such term or particular undertaking without any express agreement, the rights and duties of the partners remain the same as they were at such termination, so far as is consistent with a partnership at will.

(2) A continuation of the business by the partners or such of them as habitually acted therein during the term, without any settlement or liquidation of the partnership affairs, is prima facie evidence of a continuation of the partnership.

Part V. Property Rights of a Partner

§ 24. Extent of Property Rights of a Partner

The property rights of a partner are (1) his rights in specific partnership property, (2) his interest in the partnership, and (3) his right to participate in the management.

§ 25. Nature of a Partner's Right in Specific Partnership Property

(1) A partner is co-owner with his partners of specific partnership property holding as a tenant in partnership.

(2) The incidents of this tenancy are such that:

(a) A partner, subject to the provisions of this act and to any agreement between the partners, has an equal right with his partners to possess specific partnership property for partnership purposes; but he has no right to possess such property for any other purpose without the consent of his partners.

(b) A partner's right in specific partnership property is not assignable except in connection with the assignment of rights of all the partners in the same property.

(c) A partner's right in specific partnership property is not subject to attachment or execution, except on a claim against the partnership. When partnership property is attached for a partnership debt the partners, or any of them, or the representatives of a deceased partner, cannot claim any right under the homestead or exemption laws.

(d) On the death of a partner his right in specific partnership property vests in the surviving partner or partners, except where the deceased was the last surviving partner, when his right in such property vests in his legal representative. Such surviving partner or partners, or the legal representative of the last surviving partner, has no right to possess the partnership property for any but a partnership purpose.

(e) A partner's right in specific partnership property is not subject to dower, curtesy, or allowances to widows, heirs, or next of kin.

§ 26. Nature of Partner's Interest in the Partnership

A partner's interest in the partnership is his share of the profits and surplus, and the same is personal property.

§ 27. Assignment of Partner's Interest

(1) A conveyance by a partner of his interest in the partnership does not of itself dissolve the partnership, nor, as against the other partners in the absence of agreement, entitle the assignee, during the continuance of the partnership to interfere in the management or administration of the partnership business or affairs, or to require any information or account of partnership transactions, or to inspect the partnership books; but it merely entitles the assignee to receive in accordance with his contract the profits to which the assigning partner would otherwise be entitled.

(2) In case of a dissolution of the partnership, the assignee is entitled to receive his assignor's interest and may require an account from the date only of the last account agreed to by all the partners.

§ 28. Partner's Interest Subject to Charging Order

(1) On due application to a competent court by any judgment creditor of a partner, the court which entered the judgment, order, or decree, or any other court, may charge the interest of the debtor partner with payment of the unsatisfied amount of such judgment debt with interest thereon; and may then or later appoint a receiver of his share of the profits, and of any other money due or to fall due to him in respect of the partnership, and make all other orders, directions, accounts and inquiries which the debtor partner might have made, or which the circumstances of the case may require.

(2) The interest charged may be redeemed at any time before foreclosure, or in case of a sale being directed by the court may be purchased without thereby causing a dissolution:

(a) With separate property, by any one or more of the partners, or

(b) With partnership property, by any one or more of the partners with the consent of all the partners whose interests are not so charged or sold.

(3) Nothing in this act shall be held to deprive a partner of his right, if any, under the exemption laws, as regards his interest in the partnership.

Part VI. Dissolution and Winding Up

§ 29. Dissolution Defined

The dissolution of a partnership is the change in the relation of the partners caused by any partner ceasing to be associated in the carrying on as distinguished from the winding up of the business.

§ 30. Partnership Not Terminated by Dissolution

On dissolution the partnership is not terminated, but continues until the winding up of partnership affairs is completed.

§ 31. Causes of Dissolution

Dissolution is caused:

(1) Without violation of the agreement between the partners,

(a) By the termination of the definite term or particular undertaking specified in the agreement,

(b) By the express will of any partner when no definite term or particular undertaking is specified,

(c) By the express will of all the partners who have not assigned their interests or suffered them to be charged for their separate debts, either before or after the termination of any specified term or particular undertaking,

(d) By the expulsion of any partner from the business bona fide in accordance with such a power conferred by the agreement between the partners;

(2) In contravention of the agreement between the partners, where the circumstances do not permit a dissolution under any other provision of this section, by the express will of any partner at any time;

(3) By any event which makes it unlawful for the business of the partnership to be carried on or for the members to carry it on in partnership;

(4) By the death of any partner;

(5) By the bankruptcy of any partner or the partnership;

(6) By decree of court under section 32.

§ 32. Dissolution by Decree of Court

(1) On application by or for a partner the court shall decree a dissolution whenever:

(a) A partner has been declared a lunatic in any judicial proceeding or is shown to be of unsound mind,

(b) A partner becomes in any other way incapable of performing his part of the partnership contract,

(c) A partner has been guilty of such conduct as tends to affect prejudicially the carrying on of the business,

(d) A partner wilfully or persistently commits a breach of the partnership agreement, or otherwise so conducts himself in matters relating to the partnership business that it is not reasonably practicable to carry on the business in partnership with him,

(e) The business of the partnership can only be carried on at a loss,

(f) Other circumstances render a dissolution equitable.

(2) On the application of the purchaser of a partner's interest under sections 27 or 28:

(a) After the termination of the specified term or particular undertaking,

(b) At any time if the partnership was a partnership at will when the interest was assigned or when the charging order was issued.

§ 33. General Effect of Dissolution on Authority of Partner

Except so far as may be necessary to wind up partnership affairs or to complete transactions begun but not then finished, dissolution terminates all authority of any partner to act for the partnership,

(1) With respect to the partners,

(a) When the dissolution is not by the act, bankruptcy or death of a partner; or

(b) When the dissolution is by such act, bankruptcy or death of a partner, in cases where section 34 so requires.

(2) With respect to persons not partners, as declared in section 35.

§ 34. Right of Partner to Contribution from Copartners after Dissolution

Where the dissolution is caused by the act, death or bankruptcy of a partner, each partner is liable to his copartners for his share of any liability created by any partner acting for the partnership as if the partnership had not been dissolved unless

(a) The dissolution being by act of any partner, the partner acting for the partnership had knowledge of the dissolution, or

(b) The dissolution being by the death or bankruptcy of a partner, the partner acting for the partnership had knowledge or notice of the death or bankruptcy.

§ 35. Power of Partner to Bind Partnership to Third Persons after Dissolution

(1) After dissolution a partner can bind the partnership except as provided in Paragraph (3)

(a) By any act appropriate for winding up partnership affairs or completing transactions unfinished at dissolution;

(b) By any transaction which would bind the partnership if dissolution had not taken place, provided the other party to the transaction

(I) Had extended credit to the partnership prior to dissolution and had no knowledge or notice of the dissolution; or

(II) Though he had not so extended credit, had nevertheless known of the partnership prior to dissolution, and, having no knowledge or notice of dissolution, the fact of dissolution had not been advertised in a newspaper of general circulation in the place (or in each place if more than one) at which the partnership business was regularly carried on.

(2) The liability of a partner under paragraph (1b) shall be satisfied out of partnership assets alone when such partner had been prior to dissolution

(a) Unknown as a partner to the person with whom the contract is made; and

(b) So far unknown and inactive in partnership affairs that the business reputation of the partnership could not be said to have been in any degree due to his connection with it.

(3) The partnership is in no case bound by any act of a partner after dissolution

(a) Where the partnership is dissolved because it is unlawful to carry on the business, unless the act is appropriate for winding up partnership affairs; or

(b) Where the partner has become bankrupt; or

(c) Where the partner has no authority to wind up partnership affairs; except by a transaction with one who

(I) Had extended credit to the partnership prior to dissolution and had no knowledge or notice of his want of authority; or

(II) Had not extended credit to the partnership prior to dissolution, and, having no knowledge or notice of his want of authority, the fact of his want of authority has not been advertised in the manner provided for advertising the fact of dissolution in paragraph (1bII).

(4) Nothing in this section shall affect the liability under section 16 of any person who after dissolution represents himself or consents to another representing him as a partner in a partnership engaged in carrying on business.

§ 36. Effect of Dissolution on Partner's Existing Liability

(1) The dissolution of the partnership does not of itself discharge the existing liability of any partner.

(2) A partner is discharged from any existing liability upon dissolution of the partnership by an agreement to that effect between himself, the partnership creditor and the person or partnership continuing the business; and such agreement may be inferred from the course of dealing between the creditor having knowledge of the dissolution and the person or partnership continuing the business.

(3) Where a person agrees to assume the existing obligations of a dissolved partnership, the partners whose obligations have been assumed shall be discharged from any liability to any creditor of the partnership who, knowing of the agreement, consents to a material alteration in the nature or time of payment of such obligations.

(4) The individual property of a deceased partner shall be liable for all obligations of the partnership incurred while he was a partner but subject to the prior payment of his separate debts.

§ 37. Right to Wind Up

Unless otherwise agreed the partners who have not wrongfully dissolved the partnership or the legal representative of the last surviving partner, not bankrupt, has the right to wind up the partnership affairs; provided, however, that any partner, his legal representative or his assignee, upon cause shown, may obtain winding up by the court.

§ 38. Rights of Partners to Application of Partnership Property

(1) When dissolution is caused in any way, except in contravention of the partnership agreement, each partner as against his co-partners and all persons claiming through them in respect of their interests in the partnership, unless otherwise agreed, may have the partnership property applied to discharge its liabilities, and the surplus applied to pay in cash the net amount owing to the respective partners. But if dissolution is caused by expulsion of a partner, bona fide under the partnership agreement and if the expelled partner is discharged from all partnership liabilities, either by payment or agreement under section 36(2), he shall receive in cash only the net amount due him from the partnership.

(2) When dissolution is caused in contravention of the partnership agreement the rights of the partners shall be as follows:

(a) Each partner who has not caused dissolution wrongfully shall have,

(I) All the rights specified in paragraph (1) of this section, and

(II) The right, as against each partner who has caused the dissolution wrongfully, to damages for breach of the agreement.

(b) The partners who have not caused the dissolution wrongfully, if they all desire to continue the business in the same name, either by themselves or jointly with others, may do so, during the agreed term for the partnership and for that purpose may possess the partnership property, provided they secure the payment by bond approved by the court, or pay to any partner who has caused the dissolution wrongfully, the value of his interest in the partnership at the dissolution, less any damages recoverable under clause (2aII) of the section, and in like manner indemnify him against all present or future partnership liabilities.

(c) A partner who has caused the dissolution wrongfully shall have:

(I) If the business is not continued under the provisions of paragraph (2b) all the rights of a partner under paragraph (1), subject to clause (2aII), of this section,

(II) If the business is continued under paragraph (2b) of this section the right as against his co-partners and all claiming through them in respect of their interests in the partnership, to have the value of his interest in the partnership, less any damages caused to his co-partners by the dissolution, ascertained and paid to him in cash, or the payment secured by bond approved by the court, and to be released from all existing liabilities of the partnership; but in ascertaining the value of the partner's interest the value of the good-will of the business shall not be considered.

§ 39. Rights Where Partnership is Dissolved for Fraud or Misrepresentation

Where a partnership contract is rescinded on the ground of the fraud or misrepresentation of one of the parties thereto, the party entitled to rescind is, without prejudice to any other right, entitled,

(a) To a lien on, or right of retention of, the surplus of the partnership property after satisfying the partnership liabilities to third persons for any sum of money paid by him for the purchase of an interest in the partnership and for any capital or advances contributed by him; and

(b) To stand, after all liabilities to third persons have been satisfied, in the place of the creditors of the partnership for any payments made by him in respect of the partnership liabilities; and

(c) To be indemnified by the person guilty of the fraud or making the representation against all debts and liabilities of the partnership.

§ 40. Rules for Distribution

In settling accounts between the partners after dissolution, the following rules shall be observed, subject to any agreement to the contrary:

(a) The assets of the partnership are:

(I) The partnership property,

(II) The contributions of the partners necessary for the payment of all the liabilities specified in clause (b) of this paragraph.

(b) The liabilities of the partnership shall rank in order of payment, as follows:

(I) Those owing to creditors other than partners,

(II) Those owing to partners other than for capital and profits,

(III) Those owing to partners in respect of capital,

(IV) Those owing to partners in respect of profits.

(c) The assets shall be applied in the order of their declaration in clause (a) of this paragraph to the satisfaction of the liabilities.

(d) The partners shall contribute, as provided by section 18(a) the amount necessary to satisfy the liabilities; but if any, but not all, of the partners are insolvent, or, not being subject to process, refuse to contribute, the other parties shall contribute their share of the liabilities, and, in the relative proportions in which they share the profits, the additional amount necessary to pay the liabilities.

(e) An assignee for the benefit of creditors or any person appointed by the court shall have the right to enforce the contributions specified in clause (d) of this paragraph.

(f) Any partner or his legal representative shall have the right to enforce the contributions specified in clause (d) of this paragraph, to the extent of the amount which he has paid in excess of his share of the liability.

(g) The individual property of a deceased partner shall be liable for the contributions specified in clause (d) of this paragraph.

(h) When partnership property and the individual properties of the partners are in possession of a court for distribution, partnership creditors shall have priority on partnership property and separate creditors on individual property, saving the rights of lien or secured creditors as heretofore.

(i) Where a partner has become bankrupt or his estate is insolvent the claims against his separate property shall rank in the following order:

(I) Those owing to separate creditors,

(II) Those owing to partnership creditors,

(III) Those owing to partners by way of contribution.

§ 41. Liability of Persons Continuing the Business in Certain Cases

(1) When any new partner is admitted into an existing partnership, or when any partner retires and assigns (or the representative of the deceased partner assigns) his rights in partnership property to two or more of the partners, or to one or more of the partners and one or more third persons, if the business is continued without liquidation of the partnership affairs, creditors of the first or dissolved partnership are also creditors of the person or partnership so continuing the business.

(2) When all but one partner retire and assign (or the representative of a deceased partner assigns) their rights in partnership property to the remaining partner, who continues the business without liquidation of partnership affairs, either alone or with others, creditors of the dissolved partnership are also creditors of the person or partnership so continuing the business.

(3) When any partner retires or dies and the business of the dissolved partnership is continued as set forth in paragraphs (1) and (2) of this section, with the consent of the retired partners or the representative of the deceased partner, but without any assignment of his right in partnership property, rights of creditors of the dissolved partnership and of the creditors of the person or partnership continuing the business shall be as if such assignment had been made.

(4) When all the partners or their representatives assign their rights in partnership property to one or more third persons who promise to pay the debts and who continue the business of the dissolved partnership, creditors of the dissolved partnership are also creditors of the person or partnership continuing the business.

(5) When any partner wrongfully causes a dissolution and the remaining partners continue the business under the provisions of section 38(2b), either alone or with others, and without liquidation of the partnership affairs, creditors of the dissolved partnership are also creditors of the person or partnership continuing the business.

(6) When a partner is expelled and the remaining partners continue the business either alone or with others, without liquidation of the partnership affairs, creditors of the dissolved partnership are also creditors of the person or partnership continuing the business.

(7) The liability of a third person becoming a partner in the partnership continuing the business, under this section, to the creditors of the dissolved partnership shall be satisfied out of partnership property only.

(8) When the business of a partnership after dissolution is continued under any conditions set forth in this section the creditors of the dissolved partnership, as against the separate creditors of the retiring or deceased partner or the representative of the deceased partner, have a prior right to any claim of the retired partner or the representative of the deceased partner against the person or partnership continuing the business, on account of the retired or deceased partner's interest in the dissolved partnership or on account of any consideration promised for such interest or for his right in partnership property.

(9) Nothing in this section shall be held to modify any right of creditors to set aside any assignment on the ground of fraud.

(10) The use by the person or partnership continuing the business of the partnership name, or the name of a deceased partner as part thereof, shall not of itself make the individual property of the deceased partner liable for any debts contracted by such person or partnership.

§ 42. Rights of Retiring or Estate of Deceased Partner When the Business is Continued

When any partner retires or dies, and the business is continued under any of the conditions set forth in section 41(1, 2, 3, 5, 6), or section 38(2b), without any settlement of accounts as between him or his estate and the person or partnership continuing the business, unless otherwise agreed, he or his legal representative as against such persons or partnership may have the value of his interest at the date of dissolution ascertained, and shall receive as an ordinary creditor an amount equal to the value of his interest in the dissolved partnership with interest, or, at his option or at the option of his legal representative, in lieu of interest, the profits attributable to the use of his right in the property of the dissolved partnership; provided that the creditors of the dissolved partnership as against the separate creditors, or the representative of the retired or deceased partner, shall have priority on any claim arising under this section, as provided by section 41(8) of this act.

§ 43. Accrual of Actions

The right to an account of his interest shall accrue to any partner, or his legal representative, as against the winding up partners or the surviving partners or the person or partnership continuing the business, at the date of dissolution, in the absence of any agreement to the contrary.

Part VII. Miscellaneous Provisions

§ 44. When Act Takes Effect

This act shall take effect on the _____ day of _____ one thousand nine hundred and _____.

§ 45. Legislation Repealed

All acts or parts of acts inconsistent with this act are hereby repealed.

REVISED UNIFORM LIMITED PARTNERSHIP ACT

The Act consists of eleven Articles as follows:
1. General Provisions
2. Formation; Certificate of Limited Partnership
3. Limited Partners
4. General Partners
5. Finance
6. Distributions and Withdrawal
7. Assignment of Partnership Interests
8. Dissolution
9. Foreign Limited Partnerships
10. Derivative Actions
11. Miscellaneous

ARTICLE 1. GENERAL PROVISIONS

§ 101. Definitions

As used in this Act, unless the context otherwise requires:

(1) "Certificate of limited partnership" means the certificate referred to in Section 201, as that certificate is amended from time to time.

(2) "Contribution" means any cash, property, or services rendered, or a promissory note or other binding obligation to contribute cash or property or to perform services, which a partner contributes to a limited partnership in his capacity as a partner.

(3) "Event of withdrawal of a general partner" means an event that causes a person to cease to be a general partner as provided in Section 402.

(4) "Foreign limited partnership" means a partnership formed under the laws of any state other than this State and having as partners one or more general partners and one or more limited partners.

(5) "General partner" means a person who has been admitted to a limited partnership as a general partner in accordance with the partnership agreement and who is named in the certificate of limited partnership as a general partner.

(6) "Limited partner" means a person who has been admitted to a limited partnership as a limited partner in accordance with the partnership agreement and who is named in the certificate of limited partnership as a limited partner.

(7) "Limited partnership" and "domestic limited partnership" mean a partnership formed by 2 or more persons under the laws of this State and having one or more general partners and one or more limited partners.

(8) "Partner" means any limited partner or general partner.

(9) "Partnership agreement" means the agreement, written or, to the extent not prohibited by law, oral or both, of the partners as to the affairs of a limited partnership and the conduct of its business.

(10) "Partnership interest" has the meaning specified in Section 701.

(11) "Person" means a natural person, partnership, limited partnership (domestic or foreign), trust, estate, association, or corporation.

(12) "State" means a state, territory, or possession of the United States, the District of Columbia, or the Commonwealth of Puerto Rico.

§ 102. Name

The name of each limited partnership as set forth in its certificate of limited partnership:

(1) shall contain the words "limited partnership" in full;

(2) may not contain the name of a limited partner unless

> (i) it is also the name of a general partner or (ii) the business of the limited partnership had been carried on under that name before the admission of that limited partner;

(3) may not contain any word or phrase indicating or implying that it is organized other than for a purpose stated in its certificate of limited partnership;

(4) may not be the same as, or deceptively similar to, the name of any corporation or limited partnership organized under the laws of this State or licensed or registered as a foreign corporation or limited partnership in this State; and

(5) may not contain the following words [here insert prohibited words].

§ 103. Reservation of Name

(a) The exclusive right to the use of a name may be reserved by:

> (1) any person intending to organize a limited partnership under this Act and to adopt that name;

> (2) any domestic limited partnership or any foreign limited partnership registered in this State which, in either case, intends to adopt that name;

> (3) any foreign limited partnership intending to register in this State and to adopt that name; and

> (4) any person intending to organize a foreign limited partnership and intending to have it registered in this State and to adopt that name.

(b) The reservation shall be made by filing with the Secretary of State an application, executed by the applicant, to reserve a specified name. If the Secretary of State finds that the name is available for use by a domestic or foreign limited partnership, he shall reserve the name for the exclusive use of the applicant for a period of 120 days. Once having reserved a name, the same applicant may not again reserve the same name until more than 60 days after the expiration of the last 120-day period for which that applicant had reserved that name. The right to the exclusive use of a name so reserved may be transferred to any other person by filing in the office of the Secretary of State a notice of the transfer, executed by the applicant for whom the name was reserved and specifying the name and address of the transferee.

§ 104. Specified Office and Agent

Each limited partnership shall continuously maintain in this State:

(1) an office, which may but need not be a place of its business in this State, at which shall be kept the records required to be maintained by Section 105; and

(2) an agent for service of process on the limited partnership, which agent must be an individual resident of this State, a domestic corporation, or a foreign corporation authorized to do business in this State.

§ 105. Records to Be Kept

Each limited partnership shall keep at the office referred to in Section 104(1) the following: (1) a current list of the full name and last-known business address of each partner set forth in alphabetical order, (2) a copy of the certificate of limited partnership and all certificates of amendment thereto, together with executed copies of any powers of attorney pursuant to which any certificate has been executed, (3) copies of the limited partnership's federal, state, and local income tax returns and reports, if any, for the 3 most recent years, and (4) copies of any then effective written partnership agreements and of any financial statements of the limited partnership for the 3 most recent years. These records shall be available for inspection and copying at the reasonable request, and at the expense, of any partner during ordinary business hours.

§ 106. Nature of Business

A limited partnership may carry on any business that a partnership without limited partners may carry on except [here designate prohibited activities].

§ 107. Business Transactions of Partner with the Partnership

Except as otherwise provided in the partnership agreement, a partner may lend money to and transact other business with the limited partnership and, subject to other applicable provisions of law, has the same rights and obligations with respect thereto as a person who is not a partner.

ARTICLE 2. FORMATION; CERTIFICATE OF LIMITED PARTNERSHIP

§ 201. Certificate of Limited Partnership

(a) Two or more persons desiring to form a limited partnership shall execute a certificate of limited partnership. The certificate shall be filed in the office of the Secretary of State and shall set forth:

(1) the name of the limited partnership;

(2) the general character of its business;

(3) the address of the office and the name and address of the agent for service of process required to be maintained by Section 104;

(4) the name and the business address of each partner (specifying the general partners and limited partners separately);

(5) the amount of cash and a description and statement of the agreed value of the other property or services contributed by each partner and which each partner has agreed to contribute in the future;

(6) the times at which or events on the happening of which any additional contributions agreed to be made by each partner are to be made;

(7) any power of a limited partner to grant an assignee of any part of his partnership interest the right to become a limited partner, and the terms and conditions of the power;

(8) if agreed upon, the time at which or the events on the happening of which a partner may terminate his membership in the limited partnership and the amount of, or the method of determining, the distribution to which he may be entitled respecting his partnership interest, and the terms and conditions of the termination and distribution;

(9) any right of a partner to receive distributions of property including cash from the limited partnership;

(10) any right of a partner to receive, or of a general partner to make, distributions to a partner which include a return of all or any part of the partner's contribution;

(11) any time at which or events upon the happening of which the limited partnership is to be dissolved and its affairs wound up;

(12) any right of the remaining general partners to continue the business on the happening of an event of withdrawal of a general partner; and

(13) any other matters the partners, their sole discretion, determine to include therein.

(b) A limited partnership is formed at the time of the filing of the certificate of limited partnership in the office of the Secretary of State or at any later time specified in the certificate of limited partnership if, in each case, there has been substantial compliance with the requirements of this section.

§ 202. Amendments to Certificate

(a) A certificate of limited partnership is amended by filing a certificate of amendment thereto in the office of the Secretary of State. The certificate shall set forth:

(1) the name of the limited partnership;

(2) the date of filing of the certificate; and

(3) the amendments to the certificate.

(b) Within 30 days after the happening of any of the following events an amendment to a certificate of limited partnership reflecting the occurrence of the event or events shall be filed:

(1) a change in the amount or character of the contribution of any partner, or in any partner's obligation to make a contribution;

(2) the admission of a new partner;

(3) the withdrawal of a partner; and

(4) the continuation of the business under Section 801 after an event of withdrawal of a general partner.

(c) A certificate of limited partnership must be amended promptly by any general partner upon becoming aware that any statement therein was false when made or that any arrangements or other facts described have changed, making the certificate inaccurate in any respect, but amendments to show changes of addresses of limited partners need be filed only once every 12 months.

(d) A certificate of limited partnership may be amended at any time for any other proper purpose the general partners may determine.

(e) No person shall have any liability because an amendment to a certificate of limited partnership has not been filed to reflect the occurrence of any event referred to in subsection (b) of this section if the amendment is filed within the 30-day period specified in subsection (b).

§ 203. Cancellation of Certificate

A certificate of limited partnership shall be cancelled upon the dissolution and the commencement of winding up of the limited partnership and at any other time there are no remaining limited partners. A certificate of cancellation shall be filed in the office of the Secretary of State and shall set forth:

(1) the name of the limited partnership;

(2) the date of filing of its certificate of limited partnership;

(3) the reason for filing the certificate of cancellation;

(4) the effective date (which shall be a date certain) of cancellation if it is not to be effective upon the filing of the certificate; and

(5) any other information the general partners filing the certificate may determine.

§ 204. Execution of Certificates

(a) Each certificate required by this Article to be filed in the office of the Secretary of State shall be executed in the following manner:

(1) each original certificate of limited partnership must be signed by each partner named therein;

(2) each certificate of amendment must be signed by at least one general partner and by each other partner who is designated in the certificate as a new partner or whose contribution is described as having been increased; and

(3) each certificate of cancellation must be signed by each general partner.

(b) Any person may sign a certificate by an attorney-in-fact, but any power of attorney to sign a certificate relating to the admission or increased contribution of a partner must specifically describe the admission or increase.

(c) The execution of a certificate by a general partner constitutes an affirmation under the penalties of perjury that the facts stated therein are true.

§ 205. Amendment or Cancellation by Judicial Act

If the persons required by Section 204 to execute any certificate of amendment or cancellation fail or refuse to do so, any other partner, and any assignee of a partnership interest, who is adversely affected by the failure or refusal, may petition the [here designate the proper court] to direct the amendment or cancellation. If the court finds that the amendment or cancellation is proper and that the persons so designated have failed or refused to execute the certificate, it shall order the Secretary of State to record an appropriate certificate of amendment or cancellation.

§ 206. Filing in the Office of the Secretary of State

(a) Two signed copies of the certificate of limited partnership and of any certificates of amendment or cancellation (or of any judicial decree of amendment or cancellation) shall be delivered to the Secretary of State. A person who executes a certificate as an agent or fiduciary need not exhibit evidence of his authority as a prerequisite to filing. Unless the Secretary of State finds that any certificate does not conform to law, upon receipt of all filing fees required by law the Secretary of State shall:

(1) endorse on each duplicate original the word "Filed" and the day, month, and year of the filing thereof;

(2) file one duplicate original in his office; and

(3) return the other duplicate original to the person who filed it or his representative.

(b) Upon the filing of a certificate of amendment (or judicial decree of amendment) in the office of the Secretary of State, the certificate of limited partnership shall be amended as set forth therein, and upon the effective date of a certificate of cancellation (or a judicial decree thereof), the certificate of limited partnership shall be cancelled.

§ 207. Liability for False Statement in Certificate

If any certificate of limited partnership or certificate of amendment or cancellation contains a false statement, one who suffers loss by reliance on the statement may recover damages for the loss from:

(1) any person actually executing, or causing another to execute on his behalf, the certificate who knew, and any general partner who knew or should have known, the statement to be false at the time the certificate was executed; and

(2) any general partner who thereafter knew or should have known that any arrangements or other facts described in the certificate have changed, making the statement inaccurate in any respect, within a sufficient time before the statement was relied upon to have reasonably enabled that general partner to cancel or amend the certificate, or to file a petition for its cancellation or amendment under Section 205.

§ 208. Constructive Notice

The fact that a certificate of limited partnership is on file in the office of the Secretary of State is constructive notice that the partnership is a limited partnership and that the persons designated therein as limited partners are limited partners, but is not constructive notice of any other fact.

§ 209. Delivery of Certificates to Limited Partners

Upon the return by the Secretary of State pursuant to Section 206 of any certificate marked "Filed," the general partners shall promptly deliver or mail a copy of the certificate to each limited partner unless the partnership agreement provides otherwise.

ARTICLE 3. LIMITED PARTNERS

§ 301. Admission of Additional Limited Partners

(a) After the filing of a limited partnership's original certificate of limited partnership, a person may be admitted as a new limited partner:

(1) in the case of a person acquiring a partnership interest directly from the limited partnership, upon compliance with the partnership agreement or, if the partnership agreement does not so provide, upon the written consent of all partners; and

(2) in the case of an assignee of a partnership interest of a partner who has the power, as provided in Section 704, to grant the assignee the right to become a limited partner, upon the exercise of that power and compliance with any conditions limiting the grant or exercise of the power.

(b) In each case under subsection (a), the person acquiring the partnership interest becomes a limited partner only upon amendment of the certificate of limited partnership reflecting that fact.

§ 302. Voting

Subject to the provisions of Section 303, the partnership agreement may grant to all or a specified group of the limited partners the right to vote (on a per capita or any other basis) upon any matter.

§ 303. Liability to Third Parties

(a) Except as provided in subsection (d), a limited partner as such is not liable for the obligations of a limited partnership unless, in addition to the exercise of his rights and powers as a limited partner, he takes part in the control of the business. But the limited partner's participation in the control of the business is not substantially the same as the exercise of the powers of a general partner, he is liable only to persons who transact business with the limited partnership with actual knowledge of his participation in control.

(b) A limited partner does not participate in the control of the business within the meaning of subsection (a) solely by doing one or more of the following:

(1) being a contractor for or an agent or employee of the limited partnership or of a general partner;

(2) consulting with and advising a general partner with respect to the business of the limited partnership;

(3) acting as surety for the limited partnership;

(4) approving or disapproving an amendment to the partnership agreement; and

(5) voting on one or more of the following matters:

(i) the dissolution and winding up of the limited partnership;

(ii) the sale, exchange, lease, mortgage, pledge, or other transfer of all or substantially all of the assets of the limited partnership other than in the ordinary course of its business;

(iii) the incurrence of indebtedness by the limited partnership other than in the ordinary course of its business;

(iv) a change in the nature of the business; or

(v) the removal of a general partner.

(c) The enumeration in subsection (b) shall not be construed to mean that the possession or exercise of any other powers by a limited partner constitutes participation by him in the business of the limited partnership.

(d) A limited partner who knowingly permits his name to be used in the name of the limited partnership, except under circumstances permitted by Section 102(2)(i), is liable to creditors who extend credit to the limited partnership without actual knowledge that the limited partner is not a general partner.

§ 304. Person Erroneously Believing Himself a Limited Partner

(a) Except as provided in subsection (b) a person who makes a contribution to a business enterprise and erroneously and in good faith believes that he has become a limited partner in the enterprise is not a general partner in the enterprise and is not bound by its obligations by reason of making the contribution, receiving distributions from the enterprise, or exercising any rights of a limited partner, if, on ascertaining the mistake, he:

(1) causes an appropriate certificate of limited partnership or a certificate of amendment to be executed and filed; or

(2) withdraws from future equity participation in the enterprise.

(b) Any person who makes a contribution of the kind described in subsection (a) is liable as a general partner to any third party who transacts business with the enterprise (i) before the person withdraws and an appropriate certificate if any is filed to show the withdrawal, or (ii) before an appropriate certificate is filed to show his status as a limited partner and, in the case of an amendment, after expiration of the 30-day period for filing an amendment relating to the person as a limited partner under Section 202, but in each case only if the third party actually believed in good faith that the person was a general partner at the time of the transaction.

§ 305. Information

Each limited partner has the right to:

(1) inspect and copy any of the partnership records required to be maintained by Section 105; and

(2) obtain from the general partners from time to time upon reasonable demand (i) true and full information regarding the state of the business and financial condition of the limited partnership, (ii) promptly after becoming available, a copy of the limited partnership's federal, state, and local income tax return for each year, and (iii) any other information regarding the affairs of the limited partnership as is just and reasonable.

ARTICLE 4. GENERAL PARTNERS

§ 401. Admission

After the filing of a limited partnership's original certificate of limited partnership, new general partners may be admitted only with the specific written consent of each partner.

§ 402. Events of Withdrawal

Except as otherwise approved by the specific written consent at the time of all partners, a person ceases to be general partner of a limited partnership upon the happening of any of the following events:

(1) the general partner withdraws from the limited partnership as provided in Section 602;

(2) the general partner ceases to be a member of the limited partnership as provided in Section 702;

(3) the general partner is removed as a general partner in accordance with the partnership agreement;

(4) unless otherwise provided in the certificate of limited partnership, the general partner: makes an assignment for the benefit of creditors; files a voluntary petition in bankruptcy; is adjudicated a bankrupt or insolvent; files any petition or answer seeking for himself any reorganization, arrangement, composition, readjustment, liquidation, dissolution, or similar relief under any statute, law, or regulation; files any answer or other pleading admitting or failing to contest the material allegations of a petition filed against him in any proceeding of this nature; or seeks, consents to, or acquiesces in the appointment of any trustee, receiver, or liquidator of the general partner or of all or any substantial part of his properties;

(5) unless otherwise provided in the certificate of limited partnership, [120] days after the commencement of any proceeding against the general partner seeking any reorganization, arrangement, composition, readjustment, liquidation, dissolution, or similar relief under any statute, law, or regulation, the proceeding has not been dismissed, or if, within [90] days after the appointment without his consent or acquiescence of any trustee, receiver, or liquidator of the general partner or of all or any substantial part of his properties, the appointment is not vacated or stayed, or if, within [90] days after the expiration of any stay, the appointment is not vacated;

(6) in the case of a general partner who is a natural person

(i) his death; or

(ii) the entry by a court of competent jurisdiction adjudicating him incompetent to manage his person or his property;

(7) in the case of a general partner who is acting as such in the capacity of a trustee of a trust, the termination of the trust (but not merely the substitution of a new trustee);

(8) in the case of a general partner that is a partnership, the dissolution and commencement of winding up of the partnership;

(9) in the case of a general partner that is a corporation, the filing of a certificate of dissolution, or its equivalent, for the corporation or the revocation of its charter; and

(10) in the case of an estate, the distribution by the fiduciary of all the estate's interest in the partnership.

§ 403. General Powers and Liabilities

Except as otherwise provided in this Act and in the partnership agreement, a general partner of a limited partnership has all the rights and powers and is subject to all the restrictions and liabilities of a partner in a partnership without limited partners.

§ 404. Contributions by a General Partner

A general partner may make contributions to a limited partnership and share in the profits and losses of, and in distributions from, the limited partnership as a general partner. A general partner may also make contributions to and share in profits, losses, and distributions as a limited partner. A person who is both a general partner and a limited partner has all the rights and powers, and is subject to all the restrictions and liabilities, of a general partner and also has, except as otherwise provided in the partnership agreement, all powers, and is subject to the restrictions, of a limited partner to the extent he is participating in the partnership as a limited partner.

§ 405. Voting

The partnership agreement may grant to all or a specified group of general partners the right to vote (on a per capita or any other basis), separately or with all or any class of the limited partners, on any matter.

ARTICLE 5. FINANCE

§ 501. Form of Contributions

The contribution of a partner may be in cash, property, or services rendered, or a promissory note or other obligation to contribute cash or property or to perform services.

§ 502. Liability for Contributions

(a) Except as otherwise provided in the certificate of limited partnership, a partner is obligated to the limited partnership to perform any promise to contribute cash or property or to perform services regardless of whether he is unable to perform because of death, disability or any other reason. If a partner does not make the required contribution of property or services, he is obligated at the option of the limited partnership to contribute cash equal to that portion of the value (as stated in the certificate of limited partnership) of the stated contribution that has not been made.

(b) Unless otherwise provided in the partnership agreement, the obligation of a partner to make a contribution or return money or other property paid or distributed in violation of this Act may be compromised only by consent of all of the partners. Notwithstanding a compromise so authorized, a creditor of a limited partnership who extends credit, or whose claim arises, after the filing of the certificate of limited partnership or an amendment thereto which, in either case, reflects the obligation and before the amendment or cancellation thereof to reflect the compromise may enforce the precompromise obligation.

§ 503. Sharing of Profits and Losses

The profits and losses of a limited partnership shall be allocated among the partners, and among classes of partners, in the manner provided in the partnership agreement. If the partnership agreement does not so provide, profits and losses shall be allocated on the basis of the value (as stated in the certificate of limited partnership) of the contributions actually made by each partner to the extent they have not been returned.

§ 504. Sharing of Distributions

Distributions of cash or other assets of a limited partnership shall be allocated among the partners, and among classes of partners, in the manner provided in the partnership agreement. If the partnership agreement does not so provide, distributions shall be made on the basis of the value (as stated in the certificate of limited partnership) of the contributions actually made by each partner to the extent they have not been returned.

ARTICLE 6. DISTRIBUTIONS AND WITHDRAWAL

§ 601. Interim Distributions

Except as otherwise provided in this Article, a partner is entitled to receive distributions from a limited partnership before his withdrawal from the limited partnership and before the dissolution and winding up thereof:

(1) to the extent and at the times or upon the happening of the events specified in the partnership agreement; and

(2) if any distribution constitutes a return of any part of his contribution under Section 608(b), to the extent and at the times or upon the happening of the events specified in the certificate of limited partnership.

§ 602. Withdrawal of General Partner

A general partner may withdraw from a limited partnership at any time by giving written notice to the other partners, but if the withdrawal violates the partnership agreement, the limited partnership may recover from the withdrawing general partner damages for breach of the partnership agreement and offset the damages against the amount otherwise distributable to him.

§ 603. Withdrawal of Limited Partner

A limited partner may withdraw from a limited partnership at the time or upon the happening of the events specified in the certificate of limited partnership and in accordance with any procedures provided in the partnership agreement. If the certificate of limited partnership does not specify the time or the events upon the happening of which a limited partner may withdraw from the limited partnership or a definite time for the dissolution and winding up of the limited partnership, a limited partner may withdraw from the limited partnership upon not less than 6 months' prior written notice to each general partner at his address on the books of the limited partnership at its office in this State.

§ 604. Distributions Upon Withdrawal

Except as provided in this Article, upon withdrawal any withdrawing partner is entitled to receive any distributions to which he is entitled under the partnership agreement and, if not provided, he is entitled to receive, within a reasonable time after withdrawal, the fair value of his interest in the limited partnership as of the date of withdrawal, based upon his right to share in distributions from the limited partnership.

§ 605. Distributions in Kind

Except as provided in the certificate of limited partnership, a partner, regardless of the nature of his contribution, has no right to demand and receive any distribution from a limited partnership in any form other than cash. Except as provided in the partnership agreement, a partner may not be compelled to accept a distribution of any asset in kind from a limited partnership to the extent that the percentage of the asset distributed to him exceeds a percentage of that asset which is equal to the percentage in which he shares in distributions from the limited partnership.

§ 606. Right to Distributions

At the time a partner becomes entitled to receive a distribution, he has the status of, and is entitled to all of the remedies available to, a creditor of the limited partnership with respect to the distribution.

§ 607. Limitations on Distributions

A partner may not receive a distribution from a limited partnership to the extent that, after giving effect to the distribution, all liabilities of the limited partnership other than liabilities to partners on account of their partnership interests, exceed the fair value of the partnership's assets.

§ 608. Liability Upon Return of Contributions

(a) If a partner has received the return of any part of his contribution without violation of the partnership agreement or this Act, for a period of one year thereafter he is liable to the limited partnership for the amount of his contribution returned, but only to the extent necessary to discharge the limited partnership's liabilities to creditors who extended credit to the limited partnership during the period the contribution was held by the partnership.

(b) If a partner has received the return of any part of his contribution in violation of the partnership agreement or this Act, for a period of 6 years thereafter he is liable to the limited partnership for the amount of the contribution wrongfully returned.

(c) A partner has received a return of his contribution to the extent that a distribution to him reduces his share of the fair value of the net assets of the limited partnership below the value (as set forth in the certificate of limited partnership) of his contributions which have not theretofore been distributed to him.

ARTICLE 7. ASSIGNMENT OF PARTNERSHIP INTERESTS

§ 701. Nature of Partnership Interest

A partnership interest is a partner's share of the profits and losses of a limited partnership and the right to receive distributions of partnership assets. A partnership interest is personal property.

§ 702. Assignment of Partnership Interest

Except as otherwise provided in the partnership agreement, a partnership interest is assignable in whole or in part. An assignment of a partnership interest does not dissolve a limited partnership nor entitle the assignee to become a partner or to exercise any of the rights thereof. An assignment only entitles the assignee to receive, to the extent assigned, any distributions to which the assignor would be entitled. Except as otherwise provided in the partnership agreement, a partner ceases to be a partner upon assignment of all his partnership interest.

§ 703. Rights of Creditors

On due application to a court of competent jurisdiction by any judgment creditor of a partner, the court may charge the partnership interest of the partner with payment of the unsatisfied amount of the judgment debt with interest thereon. To the extent so charged, the judgment creditor has only the rights of an assignee of the partnership interest. This Act shall not be construed to deprive any partner of the benefit of any exemption laws applicable to his partnership interest.

§ 704. Right of Assignee to Become Limited Partner

(a) An assignee of a partnership interest, including an assignee of a general partner, may become a limited partner if and to the extent that (1) the assignor gives the assignee that right in accordance with authority described in the certificate of limited partnership or, (2) in the absence of that authority, all other partners consent.

(b) An assignee who has become a limited partner has, to the extent assigned, all the rights and powers, and is subject to all the restrictions and liabilities, of a limited partner under the partnership agreement and this Act. An assignee who becomes a limited partner is also liable for the obligations of his assignor to make and return contributions as provided in Article 6, but the assignee is not obligated for liabilities unknown to the assignee at the time he became a limited partner and which could not be ascertained from the certificate of limited partnership.

(c) If an assignee of a partnership interest becomes a limited partner, the assignor is not released from the liability to the limited partnership under Sections 207 and 502.

§ 705. Power of Estate of Deceased or Incompetent Partner

If a partner who is a natural person dies or a court of competent jurisdiction adjudges him to be incompetent to manage his person or his property, the partner's executor, administrator, guardian, conservator, or other legal representative may exercise all of the partner's rights for the purpose of settling his estate or administering his property, including any power the partner had to give an assignee the right to become a limited partner. If a partner that is a corporation, trust, or other entity other than a natural person is dissolved or terminated, those powers may be exercised by the legal representative or successor of the partner.

ARTICLE 8. DISSOLUTION

§ 801. Nonjudicial Dissolution

A limited partnership is dissolved and its affairs shall be wound up upon the happening of the first to occur of the following:

(1) at the time or upon the happening of the events specified in the certificate of limited partnership;

(2) upon the unanimous written consent of all partners;

(3) upon the happening of an event of withdrawal of a general partner unless at the time there is at least one other general partner and the certificate of limited partnership permits the business of the limited partnership to be carried on by the remaining general partner and he does so, but the limited partnership shall not be dissolved or wound up by reason of any event of withdrawal if, within 90 days after the withdrawal, all partners agree in writing to continue the business of the limited partnership and to the appointment of one or more new general partners if necessary or desired; or

(4) upon entry of a decree of judicial dissolution in accordance with Section 802.

§ 802. Dissolution by Decree of Court

On application by or for a partner the [here designate the proper court] court may decree a dissolution of a limited partnership whenever it is not reasonably practicable to carry on the business in conformity with the partnership agreement.

§ 803. Winding Up

Unless otherwise provided in the partnership agreement, the general partners who have not wrongfully dissolved the limited partnership or, if none, the limited partners, may wind up the limited partnership's affairs; but any partner, his legal representative or his assignee, upon cause shown, may obtain winding up by the [here designate the proper court] court.

§ 804. Distribution of Assets

Upon the winding up of a limited partnership, the assets shall be distributed as follows:

(1) to creditors, including partners who are creditors (to the extent otherwise permitted by law), in satisfaction of liabilities of the limited partnership other than liabilities for distributions to partners pursuant to Section 601 or 604;

(2) except as otherwise provided in the partnership agreement, to partners and ex-partners in satisfaction of liabilities for distributions pursuant to Section 601 or 604; and

(3) except as otherwise provided in the partnership agreement, to partners *first* for the return of their contributions and *second* respecting their partnership interests, in the proportions in which the partners share in distributions.

ARTICLE 9. FOREIGN LIMITED PARTNERSHIPS

§ 901. Law Governing

Subject to the constitution and public policy of this State, the laws of the state under which a foreign limited partnership is organized govern its organization and internal affairs and the liability of its limited partners, and a foreign limited partnership may not be denied registration by reason of any difference between those laws and the laws of this State.

§ 902. Registration

Before transacting business in this State, a foreign limited partnership shall register with the Secretary of State. In order to register, a foreign limited partnership shall submit to the Secretary of State in duplicate an application for registration as a foreign limited partnership, signed and sworn to by a general partner and setting forth:

(1) the name of the foreign limited partnership and, if different, the name under which it proposes to transact business and register in this State;

(2) the state and date of its formation;

(3) the general character of the business it proposes to transact in this State;

(4) the name and address of any agent for service of process on the foreign limited partnership whom the foreign limited partnership desires to appoint, which agent must be an individual resident of this State, a domestic corporation, or a foreign corporation authorized to do business in this State; and with a place of business in this State;

(5) a statement that the Secretary of State is appointed the agent of the foreign limited partnership for service of process if no agent has been appointed pursuant to paragraph (4) or, if appointed the agent's authority has been revoked or the agent cannot be found or served with the exercise of reasonable diligence;

(6) the address of the office required to be maintained in the state of its organization by the laws of that state or, if not so required, of the principal office of the foreign limited partnership; and

(7) if the certificate of limited partnership filed in the foreign limited partnership's state of organization is not required to include the names and business addresses of the partners, a list of the names and addresses.

§ 903. Issuance of Registration

(a) If the Secretary of State finds that an application for registration conforms to law and all requisite fees have been paid, he shall:

(1) endorse on the application the word "Filed", and the month, day, and year of the filing thereof;

(2) file in his office one of the duplicate originals of application; and

(3) issue a certificate of registration to transact business in this State.

(b) The certificate of registration, together with one duplicate original of the application, shall be returned to the person who filed the application or his representative.

§ 904. Name

A foreign limited partnership may register with the Secretary of State under any name (whether or not it is the name under which it is registered in its state of organization) that includes the words "limited partnership" and that could be registered by a domestic limited partnership.

§ 905. Changes and Amendments

If any statement in a foreign limited partnership's application for registration was false when made or any arrangements or other facts described have changed, making the application inaccurate in any respect, the foreign limited partnership shall promptly file in the office of the Secretary of State a certificate, signed and sworn to by a general partner, correcting the statement.

§ 906. Cancellation of Registration

A foreign limited partnership may cancel its registration by filing with the Secretary of State a certificate of cancellation signed and sworn to by a general partner. A cancellation does not terminate the authority of the Secretary of State to accept service of process on the foreign limited partnership with respect to [claims for relief] [causes of action] arising out of the transaction of business in this State.

§ 907. Transaction of Business Without Registration

(a) A foreign limited partnership transacting business in this State without registration may not maintain any action, suit, or proceeding in any court of this State until it has registered.

(b) The failure of a foreign limited partnership to register in this State does not impair the validity of any contract or act of the foreign limited partnership, and does not prevent the foreign limited partnership from defending any action, suit, or proceeding in any court of this State.

(c) A limited partner of a foreign limited partnership is not liable as a general partner of the foreign limited partnership solely by reason of the foreign limited partnership's transacting business in this State without registration.

(d) A foreign limited partnership, by transacting business in this State without registration, appoints the Secretary of State as its agent for service of process with respect to [claims for relief] [causes of action] arising out of the transaction of business in this State.

§ 908. Action by [Appropriate Official]

The [appropriate official] may bring an action to restrain a foreign limited partnership from transacting business in this State in violation of this Article.

ARTICLE 10. DERIVATIVE ACTIONS

§ 1001. Right of Action

A limited partner may bring an action in the right of a limited partnership to recover a judgment in its favor if the general partners having authority to do so have refused to bring the action or an effort to cause those general partners to bring the action is not likely to succeed.

§ 1002. Proper Plaintiff

In a derivative action, the plaintiff must be a partner at (1) the time of bringing the action, and (2) at the time of the transaction of which he complains or his status as a partner must have devolved upon him by operation of law or pursuant to the terms of the partnership agreement from a person who was a partner at the time of the transaction.

§ 1003. Pleading

In any derivative action, the complaint shall set forth with particularity the effort of the plaintiff to secure initiation of the action by a general partner having authority to do so or the reasons for not making the effort.

§ 1004. Expenses

If a derivative action is successful, in whole or in part, or anything is received by the plaintiff as a result of a judgment, compromise, or settlement of an action or claim, the court may award the plaintiff reasonable expenses, including reasonable attorney's fees, and shall direct him to account to the limited partnership for the remainder of the proceeds so received by him.

ARTICLE 11. MISCELLANEOUS

§ 1101. Savings Clause

§ 1102. Name of Act

This Act may be cited as the Uniform Limited Partnership Act.

§ 1103. Construction and Application

This Act shall be so construed and applied to effect its general purpose to make uniform the law with respect to the subject of this Act among states enacting it.

§ 1104. Rules for Cases Not Provided for in This Act

In any case not provided for in this Act the provisions of the Uniform Partnership Act govern.

§ 1105. Act Repealed

Except as affecting existing limited partnerships to the extent set forth in Section _____, the Act of [here designate the existing limited partnership act or acts] is hereby repealed.

SELECTED PROVISIONS OF THE 1985 AMENDMENTS TO THE REVISED UNIFORM LIMITED PARTNERSHIP ACT

* * *

§ 201. Certificate of Limited Partnership

(a) In order to form a limited partnership, a certificate of limited partnership must be executed and filed in the office of the Secretary of State. The certificate shall set forth:

(1) the name of the limited partnership;

(2) the address of the office and the name and address of the agent for service of process required to be maintained by Section 104;

(3) the name and the business address of each general partner;

(4) the latest date upon which the limited partnership is to dissolve; and

(5) any other matters the general partners determine to include therein.

(b) A limited partnership is formed at the time of the filing of the certificate of limited partnership in the office of the Secretary of State or at any later time specified in the certificate of limited partnership if, in either case, there has been substantial compliance with the requirements of this section.

§ 202. Amendment to Certificate

(a) A certificate of limited partnership is amended by filing a certificate of amendment thereto in the office of the Secretary of State. The certificate shall set forth:

(1) the name of the limited partnership;

(2) the date of filing the certificate; and

(3) the amendment to the certificate.

(b) Within 30 days after the happening of any of the following events, an amendment to a certificate of limited partnership reflecting the occurrence of the event or events shall be filed:

(1) the admission of a new general partner;

(2) the withdrawal of a general partner; or

(3) the continuance of the business under Section 801 after an event of withdrawal of a general partner.

(c) A general partner who becomes aware that any statement in a certificate of limited partnership was false when made or that any arrangements or other facts described have changed, making the certificate inaccurate in any respect, shall promptly amend the certificate.

(d) A certificate of limited partnership may be amended at any time for any other proper purpose the general partners determine.

(e) No person has any liability because an amendment to a certificate of limited partnership has not been filed to reflect the occurrence of any event referred to in subsection (b) of this section if the amendment is filed within the 30–day period specified in subsection (b).

(f) A restated certificate of limited partnership may be executed and filed in the same manner as a certificate of amendment.

* * *

§ 303. Liability to Third Parties

(a) Except as provided in subsection (d), a limited partner is not liable for the obligations of a limited partnership unless he [or she] is also a general partner or, in addition to the exercise of his [or her] rights and powers as a limited partner, he [or she] participates in the control of the business. However, if the limited partner participates in the control of the business, he [or she] is liable only to persons who transact business with the limited partnership reasonably believing, based upon the limited partner's conduct, that the limited partner is a general partner.

(b) A limited partner does not participate in the control of the business within the meaning of subsection (a) solely by doing one or more of the following:

(1) being a contractor for or an agent or employee of the limited partnership or of a general partner or being an officer, director, or shareholder of a general partner that is a corporation;

(2) consulting with and advising a general partner with respect to the business of the limited partnership;

(3) acting as surety for the limited partnership or guaranteeing or assuming one or more specific obligations of the limited partnership;

(4) taking any action required or permitted by law to bring or pursue a derivative action in the right of the limited partnership;

(5) requesting or attending a meeting of partners;

(6) proposing, approving, or disapproving, by voting or otherwise, one or more of the following matters:

(i) the dissolution and winding up of the limited partnership;

(ii) the sale, exchange, lease, mortgage, pledge, or other transfer of all or substantially all of the assets of the limited partnership;

(iii) the incurrence of indebtedness by the limited partnership other than in the ordinary course of its business;

(iv) a change in the nature of the business;

(v) the admission or removal of a general partner;

(vi) the admission or removal of a limited partner;

(vii) a transaction involving an actual or potential conflict of interest between a general partner and the limited partnership or the limited partners;

(viii) an amendment to the partnership agreement or certificate of limited partnership; or

(ix) matters related to the business of the limited partnership not otherwise enumerated in this subsection (b), which the partnership agreement states in writing may be subject to the approval or disapproval of limited partners;

(7) winding up the limited partnership pursuant to Section 803; or

(8) exercising any right or power permitted to limited partners under this [Act] and not specifically enumerated in this subsection (b).

(c) The enumeration in subsection (b) does not mean that the possession or exercise of any other powers by a limited partner constitutes participation by him [or her] in the business of the limited partnership.

(d) A limited partner who knowingly permits his [or her] name to be used in the name of the limited partnership, except under circumstances permitted by Section 102(2), is liable to creditors who extend credit to the limited partnership without actual knowledge that the limited partner is not a general partner.

§ 304. Person Erroneously Believing Himself [or Herself] Limited Partner

(a) Except as provided in subsection (b), a person who makes a contribution to a business enterprise and erroneously but in good faith believes that he [or she] has become a limited partner in the enterprise is not a general partner in the enterprise and is not bound by its obligations by reason of making the contribution, receiving distributions from the enterprise, or exercising any rights of a limited partner, if, on ascertaining the mistake, he [or she]:

(1) causes an appropriate certificate of limited partnership or a certificate of amendment to be executed and filed; or

(2) withdraws from future equity participation in the enterprise by executing and filing in the office of the Secretary of State a certificate declaring withdrawal under this section.

(b) A person who makes a contribution of the kind described in subsection (a) is liable as a general partner to any third party who transacts business with the enterprise (i) before the person withdraws and an appropriate certificate is filed to show withdrawal, or (ii) before an appropriate certificate is filed to show that he [or she] is not a general partner, but in either case only if the third party actually believed in good faith that the person was a general partner at the time of the transaction.

* * *

§ 401. Admission of Additional General Partners

After the filing of a limited partnership's original certificate of limited partnership, additional general partners may be admitted as provided in writing in the partnership agreement or, if the partnership agreement does not provide in writing for the admission of additional general partners, with the written consent of all partners.

* * *

§ 502. Liability for Contribution

(a) A promise by a limited partner to contribute to the limited partnership is not enforceable unless set out in a writing signed by the limited partner.

(b) Except as provided in the partnership agreement, a partner is obligated to the limited partnership to perform any enforceable promise to contribute cash or property or to perform services, even if he [or she] is unable to perform because of death, disability, or any other reason. If a partner does not make the required contribution of property or services, he [or she] is obligated at the option of the limited partnership to contribute cash equal to that portion of the value, as stated in the partnership records required to be kept pursuant to Section 105, of the stated contribution which has not been made.

(c) Unless otherwise provided in the partnership agreement, the obligation of a partner to make a contribution or return money or other property paid or distributed in violation of this [Act] may be compromised only by consent of all partners. Notwithstanding the compromise, a creditor of a limited partnership who extends credit, or, otherwise acts in reliance on that obligation after the partner signs a writing which reflects the obligation and before the amendment or cancellation thereof to reflect the compromise may enforce the original obligation.

§ 503. Sharing of Profits and Losses

The profits and losses of a limited partnership shall be allocated among the partners, and among classes of partners, in the manner provided in writing in the partnership agreement. If the partnership agreement does not so provide in writing, profits and losses shall be allocated on the basis of the value, as stated in the partnership records required to be kept pursuant to Section 105, of the contributions made by each partner to the extent they have been received by the partnership and have not been returned.

§ 504. Sharing of Distributions

Distributions of cash or other assets of a limited partnership shall be allocated among the partners and among classes of partners in the manner provided in

writing in the partnership agreement. If the partnership agreement does not so provide in writing, distributions shall be made on the basis of the value, as stated in the partnership records required to be kept pursuant to Section 105, of the contributions made by each partner to the extent they have been received by the partnership and have not been returned.

* * *

§ 603. Withdrawal of Limited Partner

A limited partner may withdraw from a limited partnership at the time or upon the happening of events specified in writing in the partnership agreement. If the agreement does not specify in writing the time or the events upon the happening of which a limited partner may withdraw or a definite time for the dissolution and winding up of the limited partnership, a limited partner may withdraw upon not less than six months' prior written notice to each general partner at his [other] address on the books of the limited partnership at its office in this State.

* * *

§ 704. Right of Assignee to Become Limited Partner

(a) An assignee of a partnership interest, including an assignee of a general partner, may become a limited partner if and to the extent that (i) the assignor gives the assignee that right in accordance with authority described in the partnership agreement, or (ii) all other partners consent.

(b) An assignee who has become a limited partner has, to the extent assigned, the rights and powers, and is subject to the restrictions and liabilities, of a limited partner under the partnership agreement and this [Act]. An assignee who becomes a limited partner also is liable for the obligations of his [or her] assignor to make and return contributions as provided in Articles 5 and 6. However, the assignee is not obligated for liabilities unknown to the assignee at the time he [or she] became a limited partner.

(c) If an assignee of a partnership interest becomes a limited partner, the assignor is not released from his [or her] liability to the limited partnership under Sections 207 and 502.

* * *

Appendix G

REVISED MODEL BUSINESS CORPORATION ACT (AS AMENDED THROUGH 1989)

CHAPTER 1: GENERAL PROVISIONS

Subchapter A. Short Title and Reservation of Power

§ 1.01 Short Title

This Act shall be known and may be cited as the "[name of state] Business Corporation Act."

§ 1.02 Reservation of Power to Amend or Repeal

The [name of state legislature] has power to amend or repeal all or part of this Act at any time and all domestic and foreign corporations subject to this Act are governed by the amendment or repeal.

Subchapter B. Filing Documents

§ 1.20 Filing Requirements

(a) A document must satisfy the requirements of this section, and of any other section that adds to or varies these requirements, to be entitled to filing by the secretary of state.

(b) This Act must require or permit filing the document in the office of the secretary of state.

(c) The document must contain the information required by this Act. It may contain other information as well.

(d) The document must be typewritten or printed.

(e) The document must be in the English language. A corporate name need not be in English if written in English letters or Arabic or Roman numerals, and the certificate of existence required of foreign corporations need not be in English if accompanied by a reasonably authenticated English translation.

(f) The document must be executed:

(1) by the chairman of the board of directors of a domestic or foreign corporation, by its president, or by another of its officers;

(2) if directors have not been selected or the corporation has not been formed, by an incorporator; or

(3) if the corporation is in the hands of a receiver, trustee, or other court-appointed fiduciary, by that fiduciary.

(g) The person executing the document shall sign it and state beneath or opposite his signature his name and the capacity in which he signs. The document may but need not contain: (1) the corporate seal, (2) an attestation by the secretary or an assistant secretary, (3) an acknowledgement, verification, or proof.

(h) If the secretary of state has prescribed a mandatory form for the document under section 1.21, the document must be in or on the prescribed form.

(i) The document must be delivered to the office of the secretary of state for filing and must be accompanied by one exact or conformed copy (except as provided in sections 5.03 and 15.09), the correct filing fee, and any franchise tax, license fee, or penalty required by this Act or other law.

[205]

§ 1.21 Forms

(a) The secretary of state may prescribe and furnish on request forms for: (1) an application for a certificate of existence, (2) a foreign corporation's application for a certificate of authority to transact business in this state, (3) a foreign corporation's application for a certificate of withdrawal, and (4) the annual report. If the secretary of state so requires, use of these forms is mandatory.

(b) The secretary of state may prescribe and furnish on request forms for other documents required or permitted to be filed by this Act but their use is not mandatory.

§ 1.22 Filing, Service and Copying Fees

[Text omitted.]

§ 1.23 Effective Time and Date of Document

(a) Except as provided in subsection (b) and section 1.24(c), a document accepted for filing is effective:

(1) at the time of filing on the date it is filed, as evidenced by the secretary of state's date and time endorsement on the original document; or

(2) at the time specified in the document as its effective time on the date it is filed.

(b) A document may specify a delayed effective time and date, and if it does so the document becomes effective at the time and date specified. If a delayed effective date but no time is specified, the document is effective at the close of business on that date. A delayed effective date for a document may not be later than the 90th day after the date it is filed.

§ 1.24 Correcting Filed Document

(a) A domestic or foreign corporation may correct a document filed by the secretary of state if the document (1) contains an incorrect statement or (2) was defectively executed, attested, sealed, verified, or acknowledged.

(b) A document is corrected:

(1) by preparing articles of correction that (i) describe the document (including its filing date) or attach a copy of it to the articles, (ii) specify the incorrect statement and the reason it is incorrect or the manner in which the execution was defective, and (iii) correct the incorrect statement or defective execution; and

(2) by delivering the articles to the secretary of state for filing.

(c) Articles of correction are effective on the effective date of the document they correct except as to persons relying on the uncorrected document and adversely affected by the correction. As to those persons, articles of correction are effective when filed.

§ 1.25 Filing Duty of Secretary of State

(a) If a document delivered to the office of the secretary of state for filing satisfies the requirements of section 1.20, the secretary of state shall file it.

(b) The secretary of state files a document by stamping or otherwise endorsing "Filed," together with his name and official title and the date and time of receipt, on both the original and the document copy and on the receipt for the filing fee. After filing a document, except as provided in sections 5.03 and 15.10, the secretary of state shall deliver the document copy, with the filing fee receipt (or acknowledgement of receipt if no fee is required) attached, to the domestic or foreign corporation or its representative.

(c) If the secretary of state refuses to file a document, he shall return it to the domestic or foreign corporation or its representative within five days after the document was delivered, together with a brief, written explanation of the reason for his refusal.

(d) The secretary of state's duty to file documents under this section is ministerial. His filing or refusing to file a document does not:

(1) affect the validity or invalidity of the document in whole or part;

(2) relate to the correctness or incorrectness of information contained in the document;

(3) create a presumption that the document is valid or invalid or that information contained in the document is correct or incorrect.

§ 1.26 Appeal From Secretary of State's Refusal to File Document

(a) If the secretary of state refuses to file a document delivered to his office for filing, the domestic or foreign corporation may appeal the refusal to the [name or describe] court [of the county where the corporation's principal office (or, if none in this state, its registered office) is or will be located] [of $_____county]. The appeal is commenced by petitioning the court to compel filing the document and by attaching to the petition the document and the secretary of state's explanation of his refusal to file.

(b) The court may summarily order the secretary of state to file the document or take other action the court considers appropriate.

(c) The court's final decision may be appealed as in other civil proceedings.

§ 1.27 Evidentiary Effect of Copy of Filed Document

A certificate attached to a copy of the document filed by the secretary of state, bearing his signature (which may be in facsimile) and the seal of this state, is conclusive evidence that the original document is on file with the secretary of state.

§ 1.28 Certificate of Existence

(a) Anyone may apply to the secretary of state to furnish a certificate of existence for a domestic corporation or a certificate of authorization for a foreign corporation.

(b) A certificate of existence or authorization sets forth:

(1) the domestic corporation's corporate name or the foreign corporation's corporate name used in this state;

(2) that (i) the domestic corporation is duly incorporated under the law of this state, the date of its incorporation, and the period of its duration if less than perpetual; or (ii) that the foreign corporation is authorized to transact business in this state;

(3) that all fees, taxes, and penalties owed to this state have been paid, if (i) payment is reflected in the records of the secretary of state and (ii) nonpayment affects the existence or authorization of the domestic or foreign corporation;

(4) that its most recent annual report required by section 16.22 has been delivered to the secretary of state;

(5) that articles of dissolution have not been filed; and

(6) other facts of record in the office of the secretary of state that may be requested by the applicant.

(c) Subject to any qualification stated in the certificate, a certificate of existence or authorization issued by the secretary of state may be relied upon as conclusive evidence that the domestic or foreign corporation is in existence or is authorized to transact business in this state.

§ 1.29 Penalty for Signing False Document

(a) A person commits an offense if he signs a document he knows is false in any material respect with intent that the document be delivered to the secretary of state for filing.

(b) An offense under this section is a [_____] misdemeanor [punishable by a fine of not to exceed $_____].

Subchapter C. Secretary of State

§ 1.30 Powers

The secretary of state has the power reasonably necessary to perform the duties required of him by this Act.

Subchapter D. Definitions

§ 1.40 Act Definitions

In this Act:

(1) "Articles of incorporation" include amended and restated articles of incorporation and articles of merger.

(2) "Authorized shares" means the shares of all classes a domestic or foreign corporation is authorized to issue.

(3) "Conspicuous" means so written that a reasonable person against whom the writing is to operate should have noticed it. For example, printing in italics or boldface or contrasting color, or typing in capitals or underlined, is conspicuous.

(4) "Corporation" or "domestic corporation" means a corporation for profit, which is not a foreign corporation, incorporated under or subject to the provisions of this Act.

(5) "Deliver" includes mail.

(6) "Distribution" means a direct or indirect transfer of money or other property (except its own shares) or incurrence of indebtedness by a corporation to or for the benefit of its shareholders in respect of any of its shares. A distribution may be in the form of a declaration or payment of a dividend; a purchase, redemption, or other acquisition of shares; a distribution of indebtedness; or otherwise.

(7) "Effective date of notice" is defined in section 1.41.

(8) "Employee" includes an officer but not a director. A director may accept duties that make him also an employee.

(9) "Entity" includes corporation and foreign corporation; not-for-profit corporation; profit and not-for-profit unincorporated association; business trust, estate, partnership, trust, and two or more persons having a joint or common economic interest; and state, United States, and foreign government.

(10) "Foreign corporation" means a corporation for profit incorporated under a law other than the law of this state.

(11) "Governmental subdivision" includes authority, county, district, and municipality.

(12) "Includes" denotes a partial definition.

(13) "Individual" includes the estate of an incompetent or deceased individual.

(14) "Means" denotes an exhaustive definition.

(15) "Notice" is defined in section 1.41.

(16) "Person" includes individual and entity.

(17) "Principal office" means the office (in or out of this state) so designated in the annual report where the principal executive offices of a domestic or foreign corporation are located.

(18) "Proceeding" includes civil suit and criminal, administrative, and investigatory action.

(19) "Record date" means the date established under chapter 6 or 7 on which a corporation determines the identity of its shareholders for purposes of this Act.

(20) "Secretary" means the corporate officer to whom the board of directors has delegated responsibility under section 8.40(c) for custody of the minutes of the meetings of the board of directors and of the shareholders and for authenticating records of the corporation.

(21) "Share" means the unit into which the proprietary interests in a corporation are divided.

(22) "Shareholder" means the person in whose name shares are registered in the records of a corporation or the beneficial owner of shares to the extent of the rights granted by a nominee certificate on file with a corporation.

(23) "State," when referring to a part of the United States, includes a state and commonwealth (and their agencies and governmental subdivisions) and a territory, and insular possession (and their agencies and governmental subdivisions) of the United States.

(24) "Subscriber" means a person who subscribes for shares in a corporation, whether before or after incorporation.

(25) "United States" includes district, authority, bureau, commission, department, and any other agency of the United States.

(26) "Voting group" means all shares of one or more classes or series that under the articles of incorporation or this Act are entitled to vote and be counted together collectively on a matter at a meeting of shareholders. All shares entitled by the articles of incorporation or this Act to vote generally on the matter are for that purpose a single voting group.

§ 1.41 Notice

(a) Notice under this Act shall be in writing unless oral notice is reasonable under the circumstances.

(b) Notice may be communicated in person; by telephone, telegraph, teletype, or other form of wire or wireless communication; or by mail or private carrier. If these forms of personal notice are impracticable, notice may be communicated by a newspaper of general circulation in the area where published; or by radio, television, or other form of public broadcast communication.

(c) Written notice by a domestic or foreign corporation to its shareholder, if in a comprehensible form, is effective when mailed, if mailed postpaid and correctly addressed to the shareholder's address shown in the corporation's current record of shareholders.

(d) Written notice to a domestic or foreign corporation (authorized to transact business in this state) may be addressed to its registered agent at its registered office or to the corporation or its secretary at its principal office shown in its most recent annual report or, in the case of a foreign corporation that has not yet delivered an annual report, in its application for a certificate of authority.

(e) Except as provided in subsections (c) and (d) written notice, if in a comprehensible form, is effective at the earliest of the following:

(1) when received;

(2) five days after its deposit in the United States Mail, as evidenced by the postmark, if mailed postpaid and correctly addressed;

(3) on the date shown on the return receipt, if sent by registered or certified mail, return receipt requested, and the receipt is signed by or on behalf of the addressee.

(f) Oral notice is effective when communicated if communicated in a comprehensible manner.

(g) If this Act prescribes notice requirements for particular circumstances, those requirements govern. If articles of incorporation or bylaws prescribe notice requirements, not inconsistent with this section or other provisions of this Act, those requirements govern.

§ 1.42 Number of Shareholders

(a) For purposes of this Act, the following identified as a shareholder in a corporation's current record of shareholders constitutes one shareholder:

(1) three or fewer co-owners;

(2) a corporation, partnership, trust, estate, or other entity;

(3) the trustees, guardians, custodians, or other fiduciaries of a single trust, estate, or account.

(b) For purposes of this Act, shareholdings registered in substantially similar names constitute one shareholder if it is reasonable to believe that the names represent the same person.

CHAPTER 2: INCORPORATION

§ 2.01 Incorporators

One or more persons may act as the incorporator or incorporators of a corporation by delivering articles of incorporation to the secretary of state for filing.

§ 2.02 Articles of Incorporation

(a) The articles of incorporation must set forth:

(1) a corporate name for the corporation that satisfies the requirements of section 4.01;

(2) the number of shares the corporation is authorized to issue;

(3) the street address of the corporation's initial registered office and the name of its initial registered agent at that office; and

(4) the name and address of each incorporator.

(b) The articles of incorporation may set forth:

(1) the names and addresses of the individuals who are to serve as the initial directors;

(2) provisions not inconsistent with law regarding:

(i) the purpose or purposes for which the corporation is organized;

(ii) managing the business and regulating the affairs of the corporation;

(iii) defining, limiting, and regulating the powers of the corporation, its board of directors, and shareholders;

(iv) a par value for authorized shares or classes of shares;

(v) the imposition of personal liability on shareholders for the debts of the corporation to a specified extent and upon specified conditions; and

(3) any provision that under this Act is required or permitted to be set forth in the bylaws.

(c) The articles of incorporation need not set forth any of the corporate powers enumerated in this Act.

§ 2.03 Incorporation

(a) Unless a delayed effective date is specified, the corporate existence begins when the articles of incorporation are filed.

(b) The secretary of state's filing of the articles of incorporation is conclusive proof that the incorporators satisfied all conditions precedent to incorporation except in a proceeding by the state to cancel or revoke the incorporation or involuntarily dissolve the corporation.

§ 2.04 Liability for Preincorporation Transactions

All persons purporting to act as or on behalf of a corporation, knowing there was no incorporation under this Act, are jointly and severally liable for all liabilities created while so acting.

§ 2.05 Organization of Corporation

(a) After incorporation:

(1) if initial directors are named in the articles of incorporation, the initial directors shall hold an organizational meeting, at the call of a majority of the directors, to complete the organization of the corporation by appointing officers, adopting bylaws, and carrying on any other business brought before the meeting;

(2) if initial directors are not named in the articles, the incorporator or incorporators shall hold an organizational meeting at the call of a majority of the incorporators:

(i) to elect directors and complete the organization of the corporation; or

(ii) to elect a board of directors who shall complete the organization of the corporation.

(b) Action required or permitted by this Act to be taken by incorporators at an organizational meeting may be taken without a meeting if the action taken is evidenced by one or more written consents describing the action taken and signed by each incorporator.

(c) An organizational meeting may be held in or out of this state.

§ 2.06 Bylaws

(a) The incorporators or board of directors of a corporation shall adopt initial bylaws for the corporation.

(b) The bylaws of a corporation may contain any provision for managing the business and regulating the affairs of the corporation that is not inconsistent with law or the articles of incorporation.

§ 2.07 Emergency Bylaws

(a) Unless the articles of incorporation provide otherwise, the board of directors of a corporation may adopt bylaws to be effective only in an emergency defined in subsection (d). The emergency bylaws, which are subject to amendment or repeal by the shareholders, may make all provisions necessary for managing the corporation during the emergency, including:

(1) procedures for calling a meeting of the board of directors;

(2) quorum requirements for the meeting; and

(3) designation of additional or substitute directors.

(b) All provisions of the regular bylaws consistent with the emergency bylaws remain effective during the emergency. The emergency bylaws are not effective after the emergency ends.

(c) Corporate action taken in good faith in accordance with the emergency bylaws:

(1) binds the corporation; and

(2) may not be used to impose liability on a corporate director, officer, employee, or agent.

(d) An emergency exists for purposes of this section if a quorum of the corporation's directors cannot readily be assembled because of some catastrophic event.

CHAPTER 3: PURPOSES AND POWERS

§ 3.01 Purposes

(a) Every corporation incorporated under this Act has the purpose of engaging in any lawful business unless a more limited purpose is set forth in the articles of incorporation.

(b) A corporation engaging in a business that is subject to regulation under another statute of this state may incorporate under this Act only if permitted by, and subject to all limitations of, the other statute.

§ 3.02 General Powers

Unless its articles of incorporation provide otherwise, every corporation has perpetual duration and succession in its corporate name and has the same powers as an individual to do all things necessary or convenient to carry out its business and affairs, including without limitation power:

(1) to sue and be sued, complain and defend in its corporate name;

(2) to have a corporate seal, which may be altered at will, and to use it, or a facsimile of it, by impressing or affixing it or in any other manner reproducing it;

(3) to make and amend bylaws, not inconsistent with its articles of incorporation or with the laws of this state, for managing the business and regulating the affairs of the corporation;

(4) to purchase, receive, lease, or otherwise acquire, and own, hold, improve, use, and otherwise deal with, real or personal property, or any legal or equitable interest in property, wherever located;

(5) to sell, convey, mortgage, pledge, lease, exchange, and otherwise dispose of all or any part of its property;

(6) to purchase, receive, subscribe for, or otherwise acquire; own, hold, vote, use, sell, mortgage, lend, pledge, or otherwise dispose of; and deal in and with shares or other interests in, or obligations of, any other entity;

(7) to make contracts and guarantees, incur liabilities, borrow money, issue its notes, bonds, and other obligations, (which may be convertible into or include the option to purchase other securities of the corporation), and secure any of its obligations by mortgage or pledge of any of its property, franchises, or income;

(8) to lend money, invest and reinvest its funds, and receive and hold real and personal property as security for repayment;

(9) to be a promoter, partner, member, associate, or manager of any partnership, joint venture, trust, or other entity;

(10) to conduct its business, locate offices, and exercise the powers granted by this Act within or without this state;

(11) to elect directors and appoint officers, employees, and agents of the corporation, define their duties, fix their compensation, and lend them money and credit;

(12) to pay pensions and establish pension plans, pension trusts, profit sharing plans, share bonus plans, share option plans, and benefit or incentive plans for any or all of its current or former directors, officers, employees, and agents;

(13) to make donations for the public welfare or for charitable, scientific, or educational purposes;

(14) to transact any lawful business that will aid governmental policy;

(15) to make payments or donations, or do any other act, not inconsistent with law, that furthers the business and affairs of the corporation.

§ 3.03 Emergency Powers

(a) In anticipation of or during an emergency defined in subsection (d), the board of directors of a corporation may:

(1) modify lines of succession to accommodate the incapacity of any director, officer, employee, or agent; and

(2) relocate the principal office, designate alternative principal offices or regional offices, or authorize the officers to do so.

(b) During an emergency defined in subsection (d), unless emergency bylaws provide otherwise:

(1) notice of a meeting of the board of directors need be given only to those directors whom it is practicable to reach and may be given in any practicable manner, including by publication and radio; and

(2) one or more officers of the corporation present at a meeting of the board of directors may be deemed to be directors for the meeting, in order of rank and within the same rank in order of seniority, as necessary to achieve a quorum.

(c) Corporate action taken in good faith during an emergency under this section to further the ordinary business affairs of the corporation:

(1) binds the corporation; and

(2) may not be used to impose liability on a corporate director, officer, employee, or agent.

(d) An emergency exists for purposes of this section if a quorum of the corporation's directors cannot readily be assembled because of some catastrophic event.

§ 3.04 Ultra Vires

(a) Except as provided in subsection (b), the validity of corporate action may not be challenged on the ground that the corporation lacks or lacked power to act.

(b) A corporation's power to act may be challenged:

(1) in a proceeding by a shareholder against the corporation to enjoin the act;

(2) in a proceeding by the corporation, directly, derivatively, or through a receiver, trustee, or other

legal representative, against an incumbent or former director, officer, employee, or agent of the corporation; or

(3) in a proceeding by the Attorney General under section 14.30.

(c) In a shareholder's proceeding under subsection (b)(1) to enjoin an unauthorized corporate act, the court may enjoin or set aside the act, if equitable and if all affected persons are parties to the proceeding, and may award damages for loss (other than anticipated profits) suffered by the corporation or another party because of enjoining the unauthorized act.

CHAPTER 4: NAME

§ 4.01 Corporate Name

(a) A corporate name:

(1) must contain the word "corporation," "incorporated," "company," or "limited," or the abbreviation "corp.," "inc.," "co.," or "ltd.", or words or abbreviations of like import in another language; and

(2) may not contain language stating or implying that the corporation is organized for a purpose other than that permitted by section 3.01 and its articles of incorporation.

(b) Except as authorized by subsections (c) and (d), a corporate name must be distinguishable upon the records of the secretary of state from:

(1) the corporate name of a corporation incorporated or authorized to transact business in this state;

(2) a corporate name reserved or registered under section 4.02 or 4.03;

(3) the fictitious name adopted by a foreign corporation authorized to transact business in this state because its real name is unavailable; and

(4) the corporate name of a not-for-profit corporation incorporated or authorized to transact business in this state.

(c) A corporation may apply to the secretary of state for authorization to use a name that is not distinguishable upon his records from one or more of the names described in subsection (b). The secretary of state shall authorize use of the name applied for if:

(1) the other corporation consents to the use in writing and submits an undertaking in form satisfactory to the secretary of state to change its name to a name that is distinguishable upon the records of the secretary of state from the name of the applying corporation; or

(2) the applicant delivers to the secretary of state a certified copy of the final judgment of a court of com-

petent jurisdiction establishing the applicant's right to use the name applied for in this state.

(d) A corporation may use the name (including the fictitious name) of another domestic or foreign corporation that is used in this state if the other corporation is incorporated or authorized to transact business in this state and the proposed user corporation:

(1) has merged with the other corporation;

(2) has been formed by reorganization of the other corporation; or

(3) has acquired all or substantially all of the assets, including the corporate name, of the other corporation.

(e) This Act does not control the use of fictitious names.

§ 4.02 Reserved Name

(a) A person may reserve the exclusive use of a corporate name, including a fictitious name for a foreign corporation whose corporate name is not available, by delivering an application to the secretary of state for filing. The application must set forth the name and address of the applicant and the name proposed to be reserved. If the secretary of state finds that the corporate name applied for is available, he shall reserve the name for the applicant's exclusive use for a nonrenewable 120-day period.

(b) The owner of a reserved corporate name may transfer the reservation to another person by delivering to the secretary of state a signed notice of the transfer that states the name and address of the transferee.

§ 4.03 Registered Name

(a) A foreign corporation may register its corporate name, or its corporate name with any addition required by section 15.06, if the name is distinguishable upon the records of the secretary of state from the corporate names that are not available under section 4.01(b)(3).

(b) A foreign corporation registers its corporate name, or its corporate name with any addition required by section 15.06, by delivering to the secretary of state for filing an application:

(1) setting forth its corporate name, or its corporate name with any addition required by section 15.06, the state or country and date of its incorporation, and a brief description of the nature of the business in which it is engaged; and

(2) accompanied by a certificate of existence (or a document of similar import) from the state or country of incorporation.

(c) The name is registered for the applicant's exclusive use upon the effective date of the application.

(d) A foreign corporation whose registration is effective may renew it for successive years by delivering to the secretary of state for filing a renewal application, which complies with the requirements of subsection (b), between October 1 and December 31 of the preceding year. The renewal application renews the registration for the following calendar year.

(e) A foreign corporation whose registration is effective may thereafter qualify as a foreign corporation under that name or consent in writing to the use of that name by a corporation thereafter incorporated under this Act or by another foreign corporation thereafter authorized to transact business in this state. The registration terminates when the domestic corporation is incorporated or the foreign corporation qualifies or consents to the qualification of another foreign corporation under the registered name.

CHAPTER 5: OFFICE AND AGENT

§ 5.01 Registered Office and Registered Agent

Each corporation must continuously maintain in this state:

(1) a registered office that may be the same as any of its places of business; and

(2) a registered agent, who may be:

(i) an individual who resides in this state and whose business office is identical with the registered office;

(ii) a domestic corporation or not-for-profit domestic corporation whose business office is identical with the registered office; or

(iii) a foreign corporation or not-for-profit foreign corporation authorized to transact business in this state whose business office is identical with the registered office.

§ 5.02 Change of Registered Office or Registered Agent

(a) A corporation may change its registered office or registered agent by delivering to the secretary of state for filing a statement of change that sets forth:

(1) the name of the corporation,

(2) the street address of its current registered office;

(3) if the current registered office is to be changed, the street address of the new registered office;

(4) the name of its current registered agent;

(5) if the current registered agent is to be changed, the name of the new registered agent and the new agent's written consent (either on the statement or attached to it) to the appointment; and

(6) that after the change or changes are made, the street addresses of its registered office and the business office of its registered agent will be identical.

(b) If a registered agent changes the street address of his business office, he may change the street address of the registered office of any corporation for which he is the registered agent by notifying the corporation in writing of the change and signing (either manually or in facsimile) and delivering to the secretary of state for filing a statement that complies with the requirements of subsection (a) and recites that the corporation has been notified of the change.

§ 5.03 Resignation of Registered Agent

(a) A registered agent may resign his agency appointment by signing and delivering to the secretary of state for filing the signed original and two exact or conformed copies of a statement of resignation. The statement may include a statement that the registered office is also discontinued.

(b) After filing the statement the secretary of state shall mail one copy to the registered office (if not discontinued) and the other copy to the corporation at its principal office.

(c) The agency appointment is terminated, and the registered office discontinued if so provided, on the 31st day after the date on which the statement was filed.

§ 5.04 Service on Corporation

(a) A corporation's registered agent is the corporation's agent for service of process, notice, or demand required or permitted by law to be served on the corporation.

(b) If a corporation has no registered agent, or the agent cannot with reasonable diligence be served, the corporation may be served by registered or certified mail, return receipt requested, addressed to the secretary of the corporation at its principal office. Service is perfected under this subsection at the earliest of:

(1) the date the corporation receives the mail;

(2) the date shown on the return receipt, if signed on behalf of the corporation; or

(3) five days after its deposit in the United States Mail, if mailed postpaid and correctly addressed.

(c) This section does not prescribe the only means, or necessarily the required means, of serving a corporation.

CHAPTER 6: SHARES AND DISTRIBUTIONS

Subchapter A. Shares

§ 6.01 Authorized Shares

(a) The articles of incorporation must prescribe the classes of shares and the number of shares of each class that the corporation is authorized to issue. If more than one class of shares is authorized, the articles of incorporation must prescribe a distinguishing designation for each class, and prior to the issuance of shares of a class the preferences, limitations, and relative rights of that class must be described in the articles of incorporation. All shares of a class must have preferences, limitations, and relative rights identical with those of other shares of the same class except to the extent otherwise permitted by section 6.02.

(b) The articles of incorporation must authorize (1) one or more classes of shares that together have unlimited voting rights, and (2) one or more classes of shares (which may be the same class or classes as those with voting rights) that together are entitled to receive the net assets of the corporation upon dissolution.

(c) The articles of incorporation may authorize one or more classes of shares that:

(1) have special, conditional, or limited voting rights, or no right to vote, except to the extent prohibited by this Act;

(2) are redeemable or convertible as specified in the articles of incorporation (i) at the option of the corporation, the shareholder, or another person or upon the occurrence of a designated event; (ii) for cash, indebtedness, securities, or other property; (iii) in a designated amount or in an amount determined in accordance with a designated formula or by reference to extrinsic data or events;

(3) entitle the holders to distributions calculated in any manner, including dividends that may be cumulative, noncumulative, or partially cumulative;

(4) have preference over any other class of shares with respect to distributions, including dividends and distributions upon the dissolution of the corporation.

(d) The description of the designations, preferences, limitations, and relative rights of share classes in subsection (c) is not exhaustive.

§ 6.02 Terms of Class or Series Determined by Board of Directors

(a) If the articles of incorporation so provide, the board of directors may determine, in whole or part, the preferences, limitations, and relative rights (within the limits set forth in section 6.01) of (1) any class of shares before the issuance of any shares of that class or (2) one or more series within a class before the issuance of any shares of that series.

(b) Each series of a class must be given a distinguishing designation.

(c) All shares of a series must have preferences, limitations, and relative rights identical with those of other shares of the same series and, except to the extent otherwise provided in the description of the series, of those of other series of the same class.

(d) Before issuing any shares of a class or series created under this section, the corporation must deliver to the secretary of state for filing articles of amendment, which are effective without shareholder action, that set forth:

(1) the name of the corporation;

(2) the text of the amendment determining the terms of the class or series of shares;

(3) the date it was adopted; and

(4) a statement that the amendment was duly adopted by the board of directors.

§ 6.03 Issued and Outstanding Shares

(a) A corporation may issue the number of shares of each class or series authorized by the articles of incorporation. Shares that are issued are outstanding shares until they are reacquired, redeemed, converted, or cancelled.

(b) The reacquisition, redemption, or conversion of outstanding shares is subject to the limitations of subsection (c) of this section and to section 6.40.

(c) At all times that shares of the corporation are outstanding, one or more shares that together have unlimited voting rights and one or more shares that together are entitled to receive the net assets of the corporation upon dissolution must be outstanding.

§ 6.04 Fractional Shares

(a) A corporation may:

(1) issue fractions of a share or pay in money the value of fractions of a share;

(2) arrange for disposition of fractional shares by the shareholders;

(3) issue scrip in registered or bearer form entitling the holder to receive a full share upon surrendering enough scrip to equal a full share.

(b) Each certificate representing scrip must be conspicuously labeled "scrip" and must contain the information required by section 6.25(b).

(c) The holder of a fractional share is entitled to exercise the rights of a shareholder, including the right to vote, to receive dividends, and to participate in the assets of the corporation upon liquidation. The holder of scrip is not entitled to any of these rights unless the scrip provides for them.

(d) The board of directors may authorize the issuance of scrip subject to any condition considered desirable, including:

(1) that the scrip will become void if not exchanged for full shares before a specified date; and

(2) that the shares for which the scrip is exchangeable may be sold and the proceeds paid to the scripholders.

Subchapter B. Issuance of Shares

§ 6.20 Subscription for Shares Before Incorporation

(a) A subscription for shares entered into before incorporation is irrevocable for six months unless the subscription agreement provides a longer or shorter period or all the subscribers agree to revocation.

(b) The board of directors may determine the payment terms of subscriptions for shares that were entered into before incorporation, unless the subscription agreement specifies them. A call for payment by the board of directors must be uniform so far as practicable as to all shares of the same class or series, unless the subscription agreement specifies otherwise.

(c) Shares issued pursuant to subscriptions entered into before incorporation are fully paid and nonassessable when the corporation receives the consideration specified in the subscription agreement.

(d) If a subscriber defaults in payment of money or property under a subscription agreement entered into before incorporation, the corporation may collect the amount owed as any other debt. Alternatively, unless the subscription agreement provides otherwise, the corporation may rescind the agreement and may sell the shares if the debt remains unpaid more than 20 days after the corporation sends written demand for payment to the subscriber.

(e) A subscription agreement entered into after incorporation is a contract between the subscriber and the corporation subject to section 6.21.

§ 6.21 Issuance of Shares

(a) The powers granted in this section to the board of directors may be reserved to the shareholders by the articles of incorporation.

(b) The board of directors may authorize shares to be issued for consideration consisting of any tangible or intangible property or benefit to the corporation, including cash, promissory notes, services performed, contracts for services to be performed, or other securities of the corporation.

(c) Before the corporation issues shares, the board of directors must determine that the consideration received or to be received for shares to be issued is adequate. That determination by the board of directors is conclusive insofar as the adequacy of consideration for the issuance of shares relates to whether the shares are validly issued, fully paid, and nonassessable.

(d) When the corporation receives the consideration for which the board of directors authorized the issuance of shares, the shares issued therefor are fully paid and nonassessable.

(e) The corporation may place in escrow shares issued for a contract for future services or benefits or a promissory note, or make other arrangements to restrict the transfer of the shares, and may credit distributions in respect of the shares against their purchase price, until the services are performed, the note is paid, or the benefits received. If the services are not performed, the note is not paid, or the benefits are not received, the shares escrowed or restricted and the distributions credited may be cancelled in whole or part.

§ 6.22 Liability of Shareholders

(a) A purchaser from a corporation of its own shares is not liable to the corporation or its creditors with respect to the shares except to pay the consideration for which the shares were authorized to be issued (section 6.21) or specified in the subscription agreement (section 6.20).

(b) Unless otherwise provided in the articles of incorporation, a shareholder of a corporation is not personally liable for the acts or debts of the corporation except that he may become personally liable by reason of his own acts or conduct.

§ 6.23 Share Dividends

(a) Unless the articles of incorporation provide otherwise, shares may be issued pro rata and without consideration to the corporation's shareholders or to the shareholders of one or more classes or series. An issuance of shares under this subsection is a share dividend.

(b) Shares of one class or series may not be issued as a share dividend in respect of shares of another class or series unless (1) the articles of incorporation so authorize, (2) a majority of the votes entitled to be cast by the class or series to be issued approve the issue, or (3) there are no outstanding shares of the class or series to be issued.

(c) If the board of directors does not fix the record date for determining shareholders entitled to a share dividend, it is the date the board of directors authorizes the share dividend.

§ 6.24 Share Options

A corporation may issue rights, options, or warrants for the purchase of shares of the corporation. The board of directors shall determine the terms upon which the rights, options, or warrants are issued, their form and content, and the consideration for which the shares are to be issued.

§ 6.25 Form and Content of Certificates

(a) Shares may but need not be represented by certificates. Unless this Act or another statute expressly provides otherwise, the rights and obligations of shareholders are identical whether or not their shares are represented by certificates.

(b) At a minimum each share certificate must state on its face:

(1) the name of the issuing corporation and that it is organized under the law of this state;

(2) the name of the person to whom issued; and

(3) the number and class of shares and the designation of the series, if any, the certificate represents.

(c) If the issuing corporation is authorized to issue different classes of shares or different series within a class, the designations, relative rights, preferences, and limitations applicable to each class and the variations in rights, preferences, and limitations determined for each series (and the authority of the board of directors to determine variations for future series) must be summarized on the front or back of each certificate. Alternatively, each certificate may state conspicuously on its front or back that the corporation will furnish the shareholder this information on request in writing and without charge.

(d) Each share certificate (1) must be signed (either manually or in facsimile) by two officers designated in the bylaws or by the board of directors and (2) may bear the corporate seal or its facsimile.

(e) If the person who signed (either manually or in facsimile) a share certificate no longer holds office when the certificate is issued, the certificate is nevertheless valid.

§ 6.26 Shares Without Certificates

(a) Unless the articles of incorporation or bylaws provide otherwise, the board of directors of a corporation may authorize the issue of some or all of the shares of any or all of its classes or series without certificates. The authorization does not affect shares already represented by certificates until they are surrendered to the corporation.

(b) Within a reasonable time after the issue or transfer of shares without certificates, the corporation shall send the shareholder a written statement of the information required on certificates by section 6.25(b) and (c), and, if applicable, section 6.27.

§ 6.27 Restriction on Transfer of Shares and Other Securities

(a) The articles of incorporation, bylaws, an agreement among shareholders, or an agreement between shareholders and the corporation may impose restrictions on the transfer or registration of transfer of shares of the corporation. A restriction does not affect shares issued before the restriction was adopted unless the holders of the shares are parties to the restriction agreement or voted in favor of the restriction.

(b) A restriction on the transfer or registration of transfer of shares is valid and enforceable against the holder or a transferee of the holder if the restriction is authorized by this section and its existence is noted conspicuously on the front or back of the certificate or is con-

tained in the information statement required by section 6.26(b). Unless so noted, a restriction is not enforceable against a person without knowledge of the restriction.

(c) A restriction on the transfer or registration of transfer of shares is authorized:

(1) to maintain the corporation's status when it is dependent on the number or identity of its shareholders;

(2) to preserve exemptions under federal or state securities law;

(3) for any other reasonable purpose.

(d) A restriction on the transfer or registration of transfer of shares may:

(1) obligate the shareholder first to offer the corporation or other persons (separately, consecutively, or simultaneously) an opportunity to acquire the restricted shares;

(2) obligate the corporation or other persons (separately, consecutively, or simultaneously) to acquire the restricted shares;

(3) require the corporation, the holders of any class of its shares, or another person to approve the transfer of the restricted shares, if the requirement is not manifestly unreasonable;

(4) prohibit the transfer of the restricted shares to designated persons or classes of persons, if the prohibition is not manifestly unreasonable.

(e) For purposes of this section, "shares" includes a security convertible into or carrying a right to subscribe for or acquire shares.

§ 6.28 Expense of Issue

A corporation may pay the expenses of selling or underwriting its shares, and of organizing or reorganizing the corporation, from the consideration received for shares.

Subchapter C. Subsequent Acquisition of Shares by Shareholders and Corporation

§ 6.30 Shareholders' Preemptive Rights

(a) The shareholders of a corporation do not have a preemptive right to acquire the corporation's unissued shares except to the extent the articles of incorporation so provide.

(b) A statement included in the articles of incorporation that "the corporation elects to have preemptive rights" (or words of similar import) means that the following principles apply except to the extent the articles of incorporation expressly provide otherwise:

(1) The shareholders of the corporation have a preemptive right, granted on uniform terms and condi-

tions prescribed by the board of directors to provide a fair and reasonable opportunity to exercise the right, to acquire proportional amounts of the corporation's unissued shares upon the decision of the board of directors to issue them.

(2) A shareholder may waive his preemptive right. A waiver evidenced by a writing is irrevocable even though it is not supported by consideration.

(3) There is no preemptive right with respect to:

(i) shares issued as compensation to directors, officers, agents, or employees of the corporation, its subsidiaries or affiliates;

(ii) shares issued to satisfy conversion or option rights created to provide compensation to directors, officers, agents, or employees of the corporation, its subsidiaries or affiliates;

(iii) shares authorized in articles of incorporation that are issued within six months from the effective date of incorporation;

(iv) shares sold otherwise than for money.

(4) Holders of shares of any class without general voting rights but with preferential rights to distributions or assets have no preemptive rights with respect to shares of any class.

(5) Holders of shares of any class with general voting rights but without preferential rights to distributions or assets have no preemptive rights with respect to shares of any class with preferential rights to distributions or assets unless the shares with preferential rights are convertible into or carry a right to subscribe for or acquire shares without preferential rights.

(6) Shares subject to preemptive rights that are not acquired by shareholders may be issued to any person for a period of one year after being offered to shareholders at a consideration set by the board of directors that is not lower than the consideration set for the exercise of preemptive rights. An offer at a lower consideration or after the expiration of one year is subject to the shareholders' preemptive rights.

(c) For purposes of this section, "shares" includes a security convertible into or carrying a right to subscribe for or acquire shares.

§ 6.31 Corporation's Acquisition of Its Own Shares

(a) A corporation may acquire its own shares and shares so acquired constitute authorized but unissued shares.

(b) If the articles of incorporation prohibit the reissue of acquired shares, the number of authorized shares is reduced by the number of shares acquired, effective upon amendment of the articles of incorporation.

(c) Articles of amendment may be adopted by the board of directors without shareholder action, shall be delivered to the secretary of state for filing, and shall set forth:

(1) the name of the corporation;

(2) the reduction in the number of authorized shares, itemized by class and series; and

(3) the total number of authorized shares, itemized by class and series, remaining after reduction of the shares.

Subchapter D. Distributions

§ 6.40 Distributions to Shareholders

(a) A board of directors may authorize and the corporation may make distributions to its shareholders subject to restriction by the articles of incorporation and the limitation in subsection (c).

(b) If the board of directors does not fix the record date for determining shareholders entitled to a distribution (other than one involving a purchase, redemption, or other acquisition of the corporation's shares), it is the date the board of directors authorizes the distribution.

(c) No distribution may be made if, after giving it effect:

(1) the corporation would not be able to pay its debts as they become due in the usual course of business; or

(2) the corporation's total assets would be less than the sum of its total liabilities plus (unless the articles of incorporation permit otherwise) the amount that would be needed, if the corporation were to be dissolved at the time of the distribution, to satisfy the preferential rights upon dissolution of shareholders whose preferential rights are superior to those receiving the distribution.

(d) The board of directors may base a determination that a distribution is not prohibited under subsection (c) either on financial statements prepared on the basis of accounting practices and principles that are reasonable in the circumstances or on a fair valuation or other method that is reasonable in the circumstances.

(e) Except as provided in subsection (g), the effect of a distribution under subsection (c) is measured:

(1) in the case of distribution by purchase, redemption, or other acquisition of the corporation's shares, as of the earlier of (i) the date money or other property is transferred or debt incurred by the corporation or (ii) the date the shareholder ceases to be a shareholder with respect to the acquired shares;

(2) in the case of any other distribution of indebtedness, as of the date the indebtedness is distributed; and

(3) in all other cases, as of (i) the date the distribution is authorized if the payment occurs within 120 days after the date of authorization or (ii) the date the payment is made if it occurs more than 120 days after the date of authorization.

(f) A corporation's indebtedness to a shareholder incurred by reason of a distribution made in accordance with this section is at parity with the corporation's indebtedness to its general, unsecured creditors except to the extent subordinated by agreement.

(g) Indebtedness of a corporation, including indebtedness issued as a distribution, is not considered a liability for purposes of determinations under subsection (c) if its terms provide that payment of principal and interest are made only if and to the extent that payment of a distribution to shareholders could then be made under this section. If the indebtedness is issued as a distribution, each payment of principal or interest is treated as a distribution, the effect of which is measured on the date the payment is actually made.

CHAPTER 7: SHAREHOLDERS

Subchapter A. Meetings

§ 7.01 Annual Meeting

(a) A corporation shall hold annually at a time stated in or fixed in accordance with the bylaws a meeting of shareholders.

(b) Annual shareholders' meetings may be held in or out of this state at the place stated in or fixed in accordance with the bylaws. If no place is stated in or fixed in accordance with the bylaws, annual meetings shall be held at the corporation's principal office.

(c) The failure to hold an annual meeting at the time stated in or fixed in accordance with a corporation's bylaws does not affect the validity of any corporate action.

§ 7.02 Special Meeting

(a) A corporation shall hold a special meeting of shareholders:

(1) on call of its board of directors or the person or persons authorized to do so by the articles of incorporation or bylaws; or

(2) if the holders of at least 10 percent of all the votes entitled to be cast on any issue proposed to be considered at the proposed special meeting sign, date, and deliver to the corporation's secretary one or more written demands for the meeting describing the purpose or purposes for which it is to be held.

(b) If not otherwise fixed under sections 7.03 or 7.07, the record date for determining shareholders entitled to demand a special meeting is the date the first shareholder signs the demand.

(c) Special shareholders' meetings may be held in or out of this state at the place stated in or fixed in accordance with the bylaws. If no place is stated or fixed in accordance with the bylaws, special meetings shall be held at the corporation's principal office.

(d) Only business within the purpose or purposes described in the meeting notice required by section 7.05(c) may be conducted at a special shareholders' meeting.

§ 7.03 Court-Ordered Meeting

(a) The [name or describe] court of the county where a corporation's principal office (or, if none in this state, its registered office) is located may summarily order a meeting to be held:

(1) on application of any shareholder of the corporation entitled to participate in an annual meeting if an annual meeting was not held within the earlier of 6 months after the end of the corporation's fiscal year or 15 months after its last annual meeting; or

(2) on application of a shareholder who signed a demand for a special meeting valid under section 7.02 if:

(i) notice of the special meeting was not given within 30 days after the date the demand was delivered to the corporation's secretary; or

(ii) the special meeting was not held in accordance with the notice.

(b) The court may fix the time and place of the meeting, determine the shares entitled to participate in the meeting, specify a record date for determining shareholders entitled to notice of and to vote at the meeting, prescribe the form and content of the meeting notice, fix the quorum required for specific matters to be considered at the meeting (or direct that the votes represented at the meeting constitute a quorum for action on those matters), and enter other orders necessary to accomplish the purpose or purposes of the meeting.

§ 7.04 Action Without Meeting

(a) Action required or permitted by this Act to be taken at a shareholders' meeting may be taken without a meeting if the action is taken by all the shareholders entitled to vote on the action. The action must be evidenced by one or more written consents describing the action taken, signed by all the shareholders entitled to vote on the action, and delivered to the corporation for inclusion in the minutes or filing with the corporate records.

(b) If not otherwise determined under sections 7.03 or 7.07, the record date for determining shareholders entitled to take action without a meeting is the date the first shareholder signs the consent under subsection (a).

(c) A consent signed under this section has the effect of a meeting vote and may be described as such in any document.

(d) If this Act requires that notice of proposed action be given to nonvoting shareholders and the action is to be taken by unanimous consent of the voting shareholders, the corporation must give its nonvoting shareholders written notice of the proposed action at least 10 days before the action is taken. The notice must contain or be accompanied by the same material that, under this Act, would have been required to be sent to nonvoting share-holders in a notice of meeting at which the proposed action would have been submitted to the shareholders for action.

§ 7.05 Notice of Meeting

(a) A corporation shall notify shareholders of the date, time, and place of each annual and special shareholders' meeting no fewer than 10 nor more than 60 days before the meeting date. Unless this Act or the articles of in-corporation require otherwise, the corporation is re-quired to give notice only to shareholders entitled to vote at the meeting.

(b) Unless this Act or the articles of incorporation re-quire otherwise, notice of an annual meeting need not include a description of the purpose or purposes for which the meeting is called.

(c) Notice of a special meeting must include a descrip-tion of the purpose or purposes for which the meeting is called.

(d) If not otherwise fixed under sections 7.03 or 7.07, the record date for determining shareholders entitled to no-tice of and to vote at an annual or special shareholders' meeting is the close of business on the day before the first notice is delivered to shareholders.

(e) Unless the bylaws require otherwise, if an annual or special shareholders' meeting is adjourned to a different date, time, or place, notice need not be given of the new date, time, or place if the new date, time, or place is announced at the meeting before adjournment. If a new record date for the adjourned meeting is or must be fixed under section 7.07, however, notice of the adjourned meeting must be given under this section to persons who are shareholders as of the new record date.

§ 7.06 Waiver of Notice

(a) A shareholder may waive any notice required by this Act, the articles of incorporation, or bylaws before or after the date and time stated in the notice. The waiver must be in writing, be signed by the shareholder entitled to the notice, and be delivered to the corpora-tion for inclusion in the minutes or filing with the cor-porate records.

(b) A shareholder's attendance at a meeting:

(1) waives objection to lack of notice or defective notice of the meeting, unless the shareholder at the beginning of the meeting objects to holding the meeting or transacting business at the meeting;

(2) waives objection to consideration of a particular matter at the meeting that is not within the purpose or purposes described in the meeting notice, unless the shareholder objects to considering the matter when it is presented.

§ 7.07 Record Date

(a) The bylaws may fix or provide the manner of fixing the record date for one or more voting groups in order to determine the shareholders entitled to notice of a shareholders' meeting, to demand a special meeting, to vote, or to take any other action. If the bylaws do not fix or provide for fixing a record date, the board of directors of the corporation may fix a future date as the record date.

(b) A record date fixed under this section may not be more than 70 days before the meeting or action requir-ing a determination of shareholders.

(c) A determination of shareholders entitled to notice of or to vote at a shareholders' meeting is effective for any adjournment of the meeting unless the board of direc-tors fixes a new record date, which it must do if the meeting is adjourned to a date more than 120 days after the date fixed for the original meeting.

(d) If a court orders a meeting adjourned to a date more than 120 days after the date fixed for the original meet-ing, it may provide that the original record date contin-ues in effect or it may fix a new record date.

Subchapter B. Voting

§ 7.20 Shareholders' List for Meeting

(a) After fixing a record date for a meeting, a corpora-tion shall prepare an alphabetical list of the names of all its shareholders who are entitled to notice of a share-holders' meeting. The list must be arranged by voting group (and within each voting group by class or series of shares) and show the address of and number of shares held by each shareholder.

(b) The shareholders' list must be available for inspec-tion by any shareholder, beginning two business days after notice of the meeting is given for which the list was prepared and continuing through the meeting, at the corporation's principal office or at a place identified in the meeting notice in the city where the meeting will be held. A shareholder, his agent, or attorney is entitled on written demand to inspect and, subject to the require-ments of section 16.02(c), to copy the list, during regular business hours and at his expense, during the period it is available for inspection.

(c) The corporation shall make the shareholders' list available at the meeting, and any shareholder, his agent, or attorney is entitled to inspect the list at any time during the meeting or any adjournment.

(d) If the corporation refuses to allow a shareholder, his agent, or attorney to inspect the shareholders' list before or at the meeting (or copy the list as permitted by subsection (b)), the [name or describe] court of the county where a corporation's principal office (or, if none in this state, its registered office) is located, on application of the shareholder, may summarily order the inspection or copying at the corporation's expense and may postpone the meeting for which the list was prepared until the inspection or copying is complete.

(e) Refusal or failure to prepare or make available the shareholders' list does not affect the validity of action taken at the meeting.

§ 7.21 Voting Entitlement of Shares

(a) Except as provided in subsections (b) and (c) or unless the articles of incorporation provide otherwise, each outstanding share, regardless of class, is entitled to one vote on each matter voted on at a shareholders' meeting. Only shares are entitled to vote.

(b) Absent special circumstances, the shares of a corporation are not entitled to vote if they are owned, directly or indirectly, by a second corporation, domestic or foreign, and the first corporation owns, directly or indirectly, a majority of the shares entitled to vote for directors of the second corporation.

(c) Subsection (b) does not limit the power of a corporation to vote any shares, including its own shares, held by it in a fiduciary capacity.

(d) Redeemable shares are not entitled to vote after notice of redemption is mailed to the holders and a sum sufficient to redeem the shares has been deposited with a bank, trust company, or other financial institution under an irrevocable obligation to pay the holders the redemption price on surrender of the shares.

§ 7.22 Proxies

(a) A shareholder may vote his shares in person or by proxy.

(b) A shareholder may appoint a proxy to vote or otherwise act for him by signing an appointment form, either personally or by his attorney-in-fact.

(c) An appointment of a proxy is effective when received by the secretary or other officer or agent authorized to tabulate votes. An appointment is valid for 11 months unless a longer period is expressly provided in the appointment form.

(d) An appointment of a proxy is revocable by the shareholder unless the appointment form conspicuously states that it is irrevocable and the appointment is cou-

pled with an interest. Appointments coupled with an interest include the appointment of:

(1) a pledgee;

(2) a person who purchased or agreed to purchase the shares;

(3) a creditor of the corporation who extended it credit under terms requiring the appointment;

(4) an employee of the corporation whose employment contract requires the appointment; or

(5) a party to a voting agreement created under section 7.31.

(e) The death or incapacity of the shareholder appointing a proxy does not affect the right of the corporation to accept the proxy's authority unless notice of the death or incapacity is received by the secretary or other officer or agent authorized to tabulate votes before the proxy exercises his authority under the appointment.

(f) An appointment made irrevocable under subsection (d) is revoked when the interest with which it is coupled is extinguished.

(g) A transferee for value of shares subject to an irrevocable appointment may revoke the appointment if he did not know of its existence when he acquired the shares and the existence of the irrevocable appointment was not noted conspicuously on the certificate representing the shares or on the information statement for shares without certificates.

(h) Subject to section 7.24 and to any express limitation on the proxy's authority appearing on the face of the appointment form, a corporation is entitled to accept the proxy's vote or other action as that of the shareholder making the appointment.

§ 7.23 Shares Held by Nominees

(a) A corporation may establish a procedure by which the beneficial owner of shares that are registered in the name of a nominee is recognized by the corporation as the shareholder. The extent of this recognition may be determined in the procedure.

(b) The procedure may set forth:

(1) the types of nominees to which it applies;

(2) the rights or privileges that the corporation recognizes in a beneficial owner;

(3) the manner in which the procedure is selected by the nominee;

(4) the information that must be provided when the procedure is selected;

(5) the period for which selection of the procedure is effective; and

(6) other aspects of the rights and duties created.

§ 7.24 Corporation's Acceptance of Votes

(a) If the name signed on a vote, consent, waiver, or proxy appointment corresponds to the name of a shareholder, the corporation if acting in good faith is entitled to accept the vote, consent, waiver, or proxy appointment and give it effect as the act of the shareholder.

(b) If the name signed on a vote, consent, waiver, or proxy appointment does not correspond to the name of its shareholder, the corporation if acting in good faith is nevertheless entitled to accept the vote, consent, waiver, or proxy appointment and give it effect as the act of the shareholder if:

(1) the shareholder is an entity and the name signed purports to be that of an officer or agent of the entity;

(2) the name signed purports to be that of an administrator, executor, guardian, or conservator representing the shareholder and, if the corporation requests, evidence of fiduciary status acceptable to the corporation has been presented with respect to the vote, consent, waiver, or proxy appointment;

(3) the name signed purports to be that of a receiver or trustee in bankruptcy of the shareholder and, if the corporation requests, evidence of this status acceptable to the corporation has been presented with respect to the vote, consent, waiver, or proxy appointment;

(4) the name signed purports to be that of a pledgee, beneficial owner, or attorney-in-fact of the shareholder and, if the corporation requests, evidence acceptable to the corporation of the signatory's authority to sign for the shareholder has been presented with respect to the vote, consent, waiver, or proxy appointment;

(5) two or more persons are the shareholder as cotenants or fiduciaries and the name signed purports to be the name of at least one of the coowners and the person signing appears to be acting on behalf of all the coowners.

(c) The corporation is entitled to reject a vote, consent, waiver, or proxy appointment if the secretary or other officer or agent authorized to tabulate votes, acting in good faith, has reasonable basis for doubt about the validity of the signature on it or about the signatory's authority to sign for the shareholder.

(d) The corporation and its officer or agent who accepts or rejects a vote, consent, waiver, or proxy appointment in good faith and in accordance with the standards of this section are not liable in damages to the shareholder for the consequences of the acceptance or rejection.

(e) Corporate action based on the acceptance or rejection of a vote, consent, waiver, or proxy appointment under this section is valid unless a court of competent jurisdiction determines otherwise.

§ 7.25 Quorum and Voting Requirements for Voting Groups

(a) Shares entitled to vote as a separate voting group may take action on a matter at a meeting only if a quorum of those shares exists with respect to that matter. Unless the articles of incorporation or this Act provide otherwise, a majority of the votes entitled to be cast on the matter by the voting group constitutes a quorum of that voting group for action on that matter.

(b) Once a share is represented for any purpose at a meeting, it is deemed present for quorum purposes for the remainder of the meeting and for any adjournment of that meeting unless a new record date is or must be set for that adjourned meeting.

(c) If a quorum exists, action on a matter (other than the election of directors) by a voting group is approved if the votes cast within the voting group favoring the action exceed the votes cast opposing the action, unless the articles of incorporation or this Act require a greater number of affirmative votes.

(d) An amendment of articles of incorporation adding, changing, or deleting a quorum or voting requirement for a voting group greater than specified in subsection (b) or (c) is governed by section 7.27.

(e) The election of directors is governed by section 7.28.

§ 7.26 Action by Single and Multiple Voting Groups

(a) If the articles of incorporation or this Act provide for voting by a single voting group on a matter, action on that matter is taken when voted upon by that voting group as provided in section 7.25.

(b) If the articles of incorporation or this Act provide for voting by two or more voting groups on a matter, action on that matter is taken only when voted upon by each of those voting groups counted separately as provided in section 7.25. Action may be taken by one voting group on a matter even though no action is taken by another voting group entitled to vote on the matter.

§ 7.27 Greater Quorum or Voting Requirements

(a) The articles of incorporation may provide for a greater quorum or voting requirement for shareholders (or voting groups of shareholders) than is provided for by this Act.

(b) An amendment to the articles of incorporation that adds, changes, or deletes a greater quorum or voting requirement must meet the same quorum requirement and be adopted by the same vote and voting groups required to take action under the quorum and voting requirements then in effect or proposed to be adopted, whichever is greater.

§ 7.28 Voting for Directors; Cumulative Voting

(a) Unless otherwise provided in the articles of incorporation, directors are elected by a plurality of the votes cast by the shares entitled to vote in the election at a meeting at which a quorum is present.

(b) Shareholders do not have a right to cumulate their votes for directors unless the articles of incorporation so provide.

(c) A statement included in the articles of incorporation that "[all] [a designated voting group of] shareholders are entitled to cumulate their votes for directors" (or words of similar import) means that the shareholders designated are entitled to multiply the number of votes they are entitled to cast by the number of directors for whom they are entitled to vote and cast the product for a single candidate or distribute the product among two or more candidates.

(d) Shares otherwise entitled to vote cumulatively may not be voted cumulatively at a particular meeting unless:

> (1) the meeting notice or proxy statement accompanying the notice states conspicuously that cumulative voting is authorized; or

> (2) a shareholder who has the right to cumulate his votes gives notice to the corporation not less than 48 hours before the time set for the meeting of his intent to cumulate his votes during the meeting, and if one shareholder gives this notice all other shareholders in the same voting group participating in the election are entitled to cumulate their votes without giving further notice.

Subchapter C. Voting Trusts and Agreements

§ 7.30 Voting Trusts

(a) One or more shareholders may create a voting trust, conferring on a trustee the right to vote or otherwise act for them, by signing an agreement setting out the provisions of the trust (which may include anything consistent with its purpose) and transferring their shares to the trustee. When a voting trust agreement is signed, the trustee shall prepare a list of the names and addresses of all owners of beneficial interests in the trust, together with the number and class of shares each transferred to the trust, and deliver copies of the list and agreement to the corporation's principal office.

(b) A voting trust becomes effective on the date the first shares subject to the trust are registered in the trustee's name. A voting trust is valid for not more than 10 years after its effective date unless extended under subsection (c).

(c) All or some of the parties to a voting trust may extend it for additional terms of not more than 10 years each by signing an extension agreement and obtaining the voting trustee's written consent to the extension. An extension is valid for 10 years from the date the first shareholder signs the extension agreement. The voting trustee must deliver copies of the extension agreement and list of beneficial owners to the corporation's principal office. An extension agreement binds only those parties signing it.

§ 7.31 Voting Agreements

(a) Two or more shareholders may provide for the manner in which they will vote their shares by signing an agreement for that purpose. A voting agreement created under this section is not subject to the provisions of section 7.30.

(b) A voting agreement created under this section is specifically enforceable.

Subchapter D. Derivative Proceedings

§ 7.40 Subchapter Definitions

In this subchapter:

(1) "Derivative proceeding" means a civil suit in the right of a domestic corporation or, to the extent provided in section 7.47, in the right of a foreign corporation.

(2) "Shareholder" includes a beneficial owner whose shares are held in a voting trust or held by a nominee on the beneficial owner's behalf.

§ 7.41 Standing

A shareholder may not commence or maintain a derivative proceeding unless the shareholder:

(1) was a shareholder of the corporation at the time of the act or omission complained of or became a shareholder through transfer by operation of law from one who was a shareholder at that time; and

(2) fairly and adequately represents the interests of the corporation in enforcing the right of the corporation.

§ 7.42 Demand

No shareholder may commence a derivative proceeding until:

(1) a written demand has been made upon the corporation to take suitable action; and

(2) 90 days have expired from the date the demand was made unless the shareholder has earlier been notified that the demand has been rejected by the corporation or unless irreparable injury to the corporation would result by waiting for the expiration of the 90 day period.

§ 7.43 Stay of Proceedings

If the corporation commences an inquiry into the allegations made in the demand or complaint, the court may stay any derivative proceeding for such period as the court deems appropriate.

§ 7.44 Dismissal

(a) A derivative proceeding shall be dismissed by the court on motion by the corporation if one of the groups specified in subsections (b) or (f) has determined in good faith after conducting a reasonable inquiry upon which its conclusions are based that the maintenance of the derivative proceeding is not in the best interests of the corporation.

(b) Unless a panel is appointed pursuant to subsection (f), the determination in subsection (a) shall be made by:

(1) a majority vote of independent directors present at a meeting of the board of directors if the independent directors constitute a quorum; or

(2) a majority vote of a committee consisting of two or more independent directors appointed by majority vote of independent directors present at a meeting of the board of directors, whether or not such independent directors constituted a quorum.

(c) None of the following shall by itself cause a director to be considered not independent for purposes of this section:

(1) the nomination or election of the director by persons who are defendants in the derivative proceeding or against whom action is demanded;

(2) the naming of the director as a defendant in the derivative proceeding or as a person against whom action is demanded; or

(3) the approval by the director of the act being challenged in the derivative proceeding or demand if the act resulted in no personal benefit to the director.

(d) If a derivative proceeding is commenced after a determination has been made rejecting a demand by a shareholder, the complaint shall allege with particularity facts establishing either (1) that a majority of the board of directors did not consist of independent directors at the time the determination was made or (2) that the requirements of subsection (a) have not been met.

(e) If a majority of the board of directors does not consist of independent directors at the time the determination is made, the corporation shall have the burden of proving that the requirements of subsection (a) have been met. If a majority of the board of directors consists of independent directors at the time the determination is made, the plaintiff shall have the burden of proving that the requirements of subsection (a) have not been met.

(f) The court may appoint a panel of one or more independent persons upon motion by the corporation to make a determination whether the maintenance of the derivative proceeding is in the best interests of the corporation. In such case, the plaintiff shall have the burden of proving that the requirements of subsection (a) have not been met.

§ 7.45 Discontinuance or Settlement

A derivative proceeding may not be discontinued or settled without the court's approval. If the court determines that a proposed discontinuance or settlement will substantially affect the interests of the corporation's shareholders or a class of shareholders, the court shall direct that notice be given to the shareholders affected.

§ 7.46 Payment of Expenses

On termination of the derivative proceeding the court may:

(1) order the corporation to pay the plaintiff's reasonable expenses (including counsel fees) incurred in the proceeding if it finds that the proceeding has resulted in a substantial benefit to the corporation;

(2) order the plaintiff to pay any defendant's reasonable expenses (including counsel fees) incurred in defending the proceeding if it finds that the proceeding was commenced or maintained without reasonable cause or for an improper purpose; or

(3) order a party to pay an opposing party's reasonable expenses (including counsel fees) incurred because of the filing of a pleading, motion or other paper, if it finds that the pleading, motion or other paper was not well grounded in fact, after reasonable inquiry, or warranted by existing law or a good faith argument for the extension, modification or reversal of existing law and was interposed for an improper purpose, such as to harass or to cause unnecessary delay or needless increase in the cost of litigation.

§ 7.47 Applicability to Foreign Corporations

In any derivative proceeding in the right of a foreign corporation, the matters covered by this subchapter shall be governed by the laws of the jurisdiction of incorporation of the foreign corporation except for sections 7.43, 7.45 and 7.46.

CHAPTER 8: DIRECTORS AND OFFICERS

Subchapter A. Board of Directors

§ 8.01 Requirement for and Duties of Board of Directors

(a) Except as provided in subsection (c), each corporation must have a board of directors.

(b) All corporate powers shall be exercised by or under the authority of, and the business and affairs of the corporation managed under the direction of, its board of directors, subject to any limitation set forth in the articles of incorporation.

(c) A corporation having 50 or fewer shareholders may dispense with or limit the authority of a board of directors by describing in its articles of incorporation who will perform some or all of the duties of a board of directors.

§ 8.02 Qualifications of Directors

The articles of incorporation or bylaws may prescribe qualifications for directors. A director need not be a resident of this state or a shareholder of the corporation unless the articles of incorporation or bylaws so prescribe.

§ 8.03 Number and Election of Directors

(a) A board of directors must consist of one or more individuals, with the number specified in or fixed in accordance with the articles of incorporation or bylaws.

(b) If a board of directors has power to fix or change the number of directors, the board may increase or decrease by 30 percent or less the number of directors last approved by the shareholders, but only the shareholders may increase or decrease by more than 30 percent the number of directors last approved by the shareholders.

(c) The articles of incorporation or bylaws may establish a variable range for the size of the board of directors by fixing a minimum and maximum number of directors. If a variable range is established, the number of directors may be fixed or changed from time to time, within the minimum and maximum, by the shareholders or the board of directors. After shares are issued, only the shareholders may change the range for the size of the board or change from a fixed to a variable-range size board or vice versa.

(d) Directors are elected at the first annual shareholders' meeting and at each annual meeting thereafter unless their terms are staggered under section 8.06.

§ 8.04 Election of Directors by Certain Classes of Shareholders

If the articles of incorporation authorize dividing the shares into classes, the articles may also authorize the election of all or a specified number of directors by the holders of one or more authorized classes of shares. Each class (or classes) of shares entitled to elect one or more directors is a separate voting group for purposes of the election of directors.

§ 8.05 Terms of Directors Generally

(a) The terms of the initial directors of a corporation expire at the first shareholders' meeting at which directors are elected.

(b) The terms of all other directors expire at the next annual shareholders' meeting following their election unless their terms are staggered under section 8.06.

(c) A decrease in the number of directors does not shorten an incumbent director's term.

(d) The term of a director elected to fill a vacancy expires at the next shareholders' meeting at which directors are elected.

(e) Despite the expiration of a director's term, he continues to serve until his successor is elected and qualifies or until there is a decrease in the number of directors.

§ 8.06 Staggered Terms for Directors

If there are nine or more directors, the articles of incorporation may provide for staggering their terms by dividing the total number of directors into two or three groups, with each group containing one-half or one-third of the total, as near as may be. In that event, the terms of directors in the first group expire at the first annual shareholders' meeting after their election, the terms of the second group expire at the second annual shareholders' meeting after their election, and the terms of the third group, if any, expire at the third annual shareholders' meeting after their election. At each annual shareholders' meeting held thereafter, directors shall be chosen for a term of two years or three years, as the case may be, to succeed those whose terms expire.

§ 8.07 Resignation of Directors

(a) A director may resign at any time by delivering written notice to the board of directors, its chairman, or to the corporation.

(b) A resignation is effective when the notice is delivered unless the notice specifies a later effective date.

§ 8.08 Removal of Directors by Shareholders

(a) The shareholders may remove one or more directors with or without cause unless the articles of incorporation provide that directors may be removed only for cause.

(b) If a director is elected by a voting group of shareholders, only the shareholders of that voting group may participate in the vote to remove him.

(c) If cumulative voting is authorized, a director may not be removed if the number of votes sufficient to elect him under cumulative voting is voted against his removal. If cumulative voting is not authorized, a director may be removed only if the number of votes cast to remove him exceeds the number of votes cast not to remove him.

(d) A director may be removed by the shareholders only at a meeting called for the purpose of removing him and the meeting notice must state that the purpose, or one of the purposes, of the meeting is removal of the director.

§ 8.09 Removal of Directors by Judicial Proceeding

(a) The [name or describe] court of the county where a corporation's principal office (or, if none in this state, its registered office) is located may remove a director of the corporation from office in a proceeding commenced either by the corporation or by its shareholders holding at least 10 percent of the outstanding shares of any class if the court finds that (1) the director engaged in fraudulent or dishonest conduct, or gross abuse of authority or discretion, with respect to the corporation and (2) removal is in the best interest of the corporation.

(b) The court that removes a director may bar the director from reelection for a period prescribed by the court.

(c) If shareholders commence a proceeding under subsection (a), they shall make the corporation a party defendant.

§ 8.10 Vacancy on Board

(a) Unless the articles of incorporation provide otherwise, if a vacancy occurs on a board of directors, including a vacancy resulting from an increase in the number of directors:

    (1) the shareholders may fill the vacancy;

    (2) the board of directors may fill the vacancy; or

    (3) if the directors remaining in office constitute fewer than a quorum of the board, they may fill the vacancy by the affirmative vote of a majority of all the directors remaining in office.

(b) If the vacant office was held by a director elected by a voting group of shareholders, only the holders of shares of that voting group are entitled to vote to fill the vacancy if it is filled by the shareholders.

(c) A vacancy that will occur at a specific later date (by reason of a resignation effective at a later date under section 8.07(b) or otherwise) may be filled before the vacancy occurs but the new director may not take office until the vacancy occurs.

§ 8.11 Compensation of Directors

Unless the articles of incorporation or bylaws provide otherwise, the board of directors may fix the compensation of directors.

Subchapter B. Meetings and Action of Directors

§ 8.20 Meetings

(a) The board of directors may hold regular or special meetings in or out of this state.

(b) Unless the articles of incorporation or bylaws provide otherwise, the board of directors may permit any or all directors to participate in a regular or special meeting by, or conduct the meeting through the use of, any means of communication by which all directors participating may simultaneously hear each other during the meeting. A director participating in a meeting by this means is deemed to be present in person at the meeting.

§ 8.21 Action Without Meeting

(a) Unless the articles of incorporation or bylaws provide otherwise, action required or permitted by this Act to be taken at a board of directors' meeting may be taken without a meeting if the action is taken by all members of the board. The action must be evidenced by one or more written consents describing the action taken, signed by each director, and included in the minutes or filed with the corporate records reflecting the action taken.

(b) Action taken under this section is effective when the last director signs the consent, unless the consent specifies a different effective date.

(c) A consent signed under this section has the effect of a meeting vote and may be described as such in any document.

§ 8.22 Notice of Meeting

(a) Unless the articles of incorporation or bylaws provide otherwise, regular meetings of the board of directors may be held without notice of the date, time, place, or purpose of the meeting.

(b) Unless the articles of incorporation or bylaws provide for a longer or shorter period, special meetings of the board of directors must be preceded by at least two days' notice of the date, time, and place of the meeting. The notice need not describe the purpose of the special meeting unless required by the articles of incorporation or bylaws.

§ 8.23 Waiver of Notice

(a) A director may waive any notice required by this Act, the articles of incorporation, or bylaws before or after the date and time stated in the notice. Except as provided by subsection (b), the waiver must be in writing, signed by the director entitled to the notice, and filed with the minutes or corporate records.

(b) A director's attendance at or participation in a meeting waives any required notice to him of the meeting unless the director at the beginning of the meeting (or promptly upon his arrival) objects to holding the meeting or transacting business at the meeting and does not thereafter vote for or assent to action taken at the meeting.

§ 8.24 Quorum and Voting

(a) Unless the articles of incorporation or bylaws require a greater number, a quorum of a board of directors consists of:

(1) a majority of the fixed number of directors if the corporation has a fixed board size; or

(2) a majority of the number of directors prescribed, or if no number is prescribed the number in office immediately before the meeting begins, if the corporation has a variable-range size board.

(b) The articles of incorporation or bylaws may authorize a quorum of a board of directors to consist of no fewer than one-third of the fixed or prescribed number of directors determined under subsection (a).

(c) If a quorum is present when a vote is taken, the affirmative vote of a majority of directors present is the act of the board of directors unless the articles of incorporation or bylaws require the vote of a greater number of directors.

(d) A director who is present at a meeting of the board of directors or a committee of the board of directors when corporate action is taken is deemed to have assented to the action taken unless: (1) he objects at the beginning of the meeting (or promptly upon his arrival) to holding it or transacting business at the meeting; (2) his dissent or abstention from the action taken is entered in the minutes of the meeting; or (3) he delivers written notice of his dissent or abstention to the presiding officer of the meeting before its adjournment or to the corporation immediately after adjournment of the meeting. The right of dissent or abstention is not available to a director who votes in favor of the action taken.

§ 8.25 Committees

(a) Unless the articles of incorporation or bylaws provide otherwise, a board of directors may create one or more committees and appoint members of the board of directors to serve on them. Each committee may have two or more members, who serve at the pleasure of the board of directors.

(b) The creation of a committee and appointment of members to it must be approved by the greater of (1) a majority of all the directors in office when the action is taken or (2) the number of directors required by the articles of incorporation or bylaws to take action under section 8.24.

(c) Sections 8.20 through 8.24, which govern meetings, action without meetings, notice and waiver of notice, and quorum and voting requirements of the board of directors, apply to committees and their members as well.

(d) To the extent specified by the board of directors or in the articles of incorporation or bylaws, each committee may exercise the authority of the board of directors under section 8.01.

(e) A committee may not, however:

(1) authorize distributions;

(2) approve or propose to shareholders action that this Act requires to be approved by shareholders;

(3) fill vacancies on the board of directors or on any of its committees;

(4) amend articles of incorporation pursuant to section 10.02;

(5) adopt, amend, or repeal bylaws;

(6) approve a plan of merger not requiring shareholder approval;

(7) authorize or approve reacquisition of shares, except according to a formula or method prescribed by the board of directors; or

(8) authorize or approve the issuance or sale or contract for sale of shares, or determine the designation and relative rights, preferences, and limitations of a class or series of shares, except that the board of directors may authorize a committee (or a senior executive officer of the corporation) to do so within limits specifically prescribed by the board of directors.

(f) The creation of, delegation of authority to, or action by a committee does not alone constitute compliance by a director with the standards of conduct described in section 8.30.

Subchapter C. Standards of Conduct

§ 8.30 General Standards for Directors

(a) A director shall discharge his duties as a director, including his duties as a member of a committee:

(1) in good faith;

(2) with the care an ordinarily prudent person in a like position would exercise under similar circumstances; and

(3) in a manner he reasonably believes to be in the best interests of the corporation.

(b) In discharging his duties a director is entitled to rely on information, opinions, reports, or statements, including financial statements and other financial data, if prepared or presented by:

(1) one or more officers or employees of the corporation whom the director reasonably believes to be reliable and competent in the matters presented;

(2) legal counsel, public accountants, or other persons as to matters the director reasonably believes

are within the person's professional or expert competence; or

(3) a committee of the board of directors of which he is not a member if the director reasonably believes the committee merits confidence.

(c) A director is not acting in good faith if he has knowledge concerning the matter in question that makes reliance otherwise permitted by subsection (b) unwarranted.

(d) A director is not liable for any action taken as a director, or any failure to take any action, if he performed the duties of his office in compliance with this section.

§ 8.31 Director Conflict of Interest [deleted in 1988]

(a) A conflict of interest transaction is a transaction with the corporation in which a director of the corporation has a direct or indirect interest. A conflict of interest transaction is not voidable by the corporation solely because of the director's interest in the transaction if any one of the following is true:

(1) the material facts of the transaction and the director's interest were disclosed or known to the board of directors or a committee of the board of directors and the board of directors or committee authorized, approved, or ratified the transaction;

(2) the material facts of the transaction and the director's interest were disclosed or known to the shareholders entitled to vote and they authorized, approved, or ratified the transaction; or

(3) the transaction was fair to the corporation.

(b) For purposes of this section, a director of the corporation has an indirect interest in a transaction if (1) another entity in which he has a material financial interest or in which he is a general partner is a party to the transaction or (2) another entity of which he is a director, officer, or trustee is a party to the transaction and the transaction is or should be considered by the board of directors of the corporation.

(c) For purposes of subsection (a)(1), a conflict of interest transaction is authorized, approved, or ratified if it receives the affirmative vote of a majority of the directors on the board of directors (or on the committee) who have no direct or indirect interest in the transaction, but a transaction may not be authorized, approved, or ratified under this section by a single director. If a majority of the directors who have no direct or indirect interest in the transaction vote to authorize, approve, or ratify the transaction, a quorum is present for the purpose of taking action under this section. The presence of, or a vote cast by, a director with a direct or indirect interest in the transaction does not affect the validity of any action taken under subsection (a)(1) if the transaction is otherwise authorized, approved, or ratified as provided in that subsection.

(d) For purposes of subsection (a)(2), a conflict of interest transaction is authorized, approved, or ratified if it receives the vote of a majority of the shares entitled to be counted under this subsection. Shares owned by or voted under the control of a director who has a direct or indirect interest in the transaction, and shares owned by or voted under the control of an entity described in subsection (b)(1), may not be counted in a vote of shareholders to determine whether to authorize, approve, or ratify a conflict of interest transaction under subsection (a)(2). The vote of those shares, however, shall be counted in determining whether the transaction is approved under other sections of this Act. A majority of the shares, whether or not present, that are entitled to be counted in a vote on the transaction under this subsection constitutes a quorum for the purpose of taking action under this section.

§ 8.32 Loans to Directors [deleted in 1988]

(a) Except as provided by subsection (c), a corporation may not lend money to or guarantee the obligation of a director of the corporation unless:

(1) the particular loan or guarantee is approved by a majority of the votes represented by the outstanding voting shares of all classes, voting as a single voting group, except the votes of shares owned by or voted under the control of the benefited director; or

(2) the corporation's board of directors determines that the loan or guarantee benefits the corporation and either approves the specific loan or guarantee or a general plan authorizing loans and guarantees.

(b) The fact that a loan or guarantee is made in violation of this section does not affect the borrower's liability on the loan.

(c) This section does not apply to loans and guarantees authorized by statute regulating any special class of corporations.

§ 8.33 Liability for Unlawful Distributions

(a) A director who votes for or assents to a distribution made in violation of section 6.40 or the articles of incorporation is personally liable to the corporation for the amount of the distribution that exceeds what could have been distributed without violating section 6.40 or the articles of incorporation if it is established that he did not perform his duties in compliance with section 8.30. In any proceeding commenced under this section, a director has all of the defenses ordinarily available to a director.

(b) A director held liable under subsection (a) for an unlawful distribution is entitled to contribution:

(1) from every other director who could be held liable under subsection (a) for the unlawful distribution; and

(2) from each shareholder for the amount the shareholder accepted knowing the distribution was made in violation of section 6.40 or the articles of incorporation.

(c) A proceeding under this section is barred unless it is commenced within two years after the date on which the effect of the distribution was measured under section 6.40(e) or (g).

Subchapter D. Officers

§ 8.40 Required Officers

(a) A corporation has the officers described in its bylaws or appointed by the board of directors in accordance with the bylaws.

(b) A duly appointed officer may appoint one or more officers or assistant officers if authorized by the bylaws or the board of directors.

(c) The bylaws or the board of directors shall delegate to one of the officers responsibility for preparing minutes of the directors' and shareholders' meetings and for authenticating records of the corporation.

(d) The same individual may simultaneously hold more than one office in a corporation.

§ 8.41 Duties of Officers

Each officer has the authority and shall perform the duties set forth in the bylaws or, to the extent consistent with the bylaws, the duties prescribed by the board of directors or by direction of an officer authorized by the board of directors to prescribe the duties of other officers.

§ 8.42 Standards of Conduct for Officers

(a) An officer with discretionary authority shall discharge his duties under that authority:

(1) in good faith;

(2) with the care an ordinarily prudent person in a like position would exercise under similar circumstances; and

(3) in a manner he reasonably believes to be in the best interests of the corporation.

(b) In discharging his duties an officer is entitled to rely on information, opinions, reports, or statements, including financial statements and other financial data, if prepared or presented by:

(1) one or more officers or employees of the corporation whom the officer reasonably believes to be reliable and competent in the matters presented; or

(2) legal counsel, public accountants, or other persons as to matters the officer reasonably believes are within the person's professional or expert competence.

(c) An officer is not acting in good faith if he has knowledge concerning the matter in question that makes reliance otherwise permitted by subsection (b) unwarranted.

(d) An officer is not liable for any action taken as an officer, or any failure to take any action, if he performed the duties of his office in compliance with this section.

§ 8.43 Resignation and Removal of Officers

(a) An officer may resign at any time by delivering notice to the corporation. A resignation is effective when the notice is delivered unless the notice specifies a later effective date. If a resignation is made effective at a later date and the corporation accepts the future effective date, its board of directors may fill the pending vacancy before the effective date if the board of directors provides that the successor does not take office until the effective date.

(b) A board of directors may remove any officer at any time with or without cause.

§ 8.44 Contract Rights of Officers

(a) The appointment of an officer does not itself create contract rights.

(b) An officer's removal does not affect the officer's contract rights, if any, with the corporation. An officer's resignation does not affect the corporation's contract rights, if any, with the officer.

Subchapter E. Indemnification

§ 8.50 Subchapter Definitions

In this subchapter:

(1) "Corporation" includes any domestic or foreign predecessor entity of a corporation in a merger or other transaction in which the predecessor's existence ceased upon consummation of the transaction.

(2) "Director" means an individual who is or was a director of a corporation or an individual who, while a director of a corporation, is or was serving at the corporation's request as a director, officer, partner, trustee, employee, or agent of another foreign or domestic corporation, partnership, joint venture, trust, employee benefit plan, or other enterprise. A director is considered to be serving an employee benefit plan at the corporation's request if his duties to the corporation also impose duties on, or otherwise involve services by, him to the plan or to participants in or beneficiaries of the plan. "Director" includes, unless the context requires otherwise, the estate or personal representative of a director.

(3) "Expenses" include counsel fees.

(4) "Liability" means the obligation to pay a judgment, settlement, penalty, fine (including an excise tax as-

sessed with respect to an employee benefit plan), or reasonable expenses incurred with respect to a proceeding.

(5) "Official capacity" means: (i) when used with respect to a director, the office of director in a corporation; and (ii) when used with respect to an individual other than a director, as contemplated in section 8.56, the office in a corporation held by the officer or the employment or agency relationship undertaken by the employee or agent on behalf of the corporation. "Official capacity" does not include service for any other foreign or domestic corporation or any partnership, joint venture, trust, employee benefit plan, or other enterprise.

(6) "Party" includes an individual who was, is, or is threatened to be made a named defendant or respondent in a proceeding.

(7) "Proceeding" means any threatened, pending, or completed action, suit, or proceeding, whether civil, criminal, administrative, or investigative and whether formal or informal.

§ 8.51 Authority to Indemnify

(a) Except as provided in subsection (d), a corporation may indemnify an individual made a party to a proceeding because he is or was a director against liability incurred in the proceeding if:

(1) he conducted himself in good faith; and

(2) he reasonably believed:

(i) in the case of conduct in his official capacity with the corporation, that his conduct was in its best interests; and

(ii) in all other cases, that his conduct was at least not opposed to its best interests; and

(3) in the case of any criminal proceeding, he had no reasonable cause to believe his conduct was unlawful.

(b) A director's conduct with respect to an employee benefit plan for a purpose he reasonably believed to be in the interests of the participants in and beneficiaries of the plan is conduct that satisfies the requirement of subsection (a)(2)(ii).

(c) The termination of a proceeding by judgment, order, settlement, conviction, or upon a plea of nolo contendere or its equivalent is not, of itself, determinative that the director did not meet the standard of conduct described in this section.

(d) A corporation may not indemnify a director under this section:

(1) in connection with a proceeding by or in the right of the corporation in which the director was adjudged liable to the corporation; or

(2) in connection with any other proceeding charging improper personal benefit to him, whether or not

involving action in his official capacity, in which he was adjudged liable on the basis that personal benefit was improperly received by him.

(e) Indemnification permitted under this section in connection with a proceeding by or in the right of the corporation is limited to reasonable expenses incurred in connection with the proceeding.

§ 8.52 Mandatory Indemnification

Unless limited by its articles of incorporation, a corporation shall indemnify a director who was wholly successful, on the merits or otherwise, in the defense of any proceeding to which he was a party because he is or was a director of the corporation against reasonable expenses incurred by him in connection with the proceeding.

§ 8.53 Advance for Expenses

(a) A corporation may pay for or reimburse the reasonable expenses incurred by a director who is a party to a proceeding in advance of final disposition of the proceeding if:

(1) the director furnishes the corporation a written affirmation of his good faith belief that he has met the standard of conduct described in section 8.51;

(2) the director furnishes the corporation a written undertaking, executed personally or on his behalf, to repay the advance if it is ultimately determined that he did not meet the standard of conduct; and

(3) a determination is made that the facts then known to those making the determination would not preclude indemnification under this subchapter.

(b) The undertaking required by subsection (a)(2) must be an unlimited general obligation of the director but need not be secured and may be accepted without reference to financial ability to make repayment.

(c) Determinations and authorizations of payments under this section shall be made in the manner specified in section 8.55.

§ 8.54 Court-Ordered Indemnification

Unless a corporation's articles of incorporation provide otherwise, a director of the corporation who is a party to a proceeding may apply for indemnification to the court conducting the proceeding or to another court of competent jurisdiction. On receipt of an application, the court after giving any notice the court considers necessary may order indemnification if it determines:

(1) the director is entitled to mandatory indemnification under section 8.52, in which case the court shall also order the corporation to pay the director's reasonable expenses incurred to obtain court-ordered indemnification; or

(2) the director is fairly and reasonably entitled to indemnification in view of all the relevant circumstances,

whether or not he met the standard of conduct set forth in section 8.51 or was adjudged liable as described in section 8.51(d), but if he was adjudged so liable his indemnification is limited to reasonable expenses incurred.

§ 8.55 Determination and Authorization of Indemnification

(a) A corporation may not indemnify a director under section 8.51 unless authorized in the specific case after a determination has been made that indemnification of the director is permissible in the circumstances because he has met the standard of conduct set forth in section 8.51.

(b) The determination shall be made:

(1) by the board of directors by majority vote of a quorum consisting of directors not at the time parties to the proceeding;

(2) if a quorum cannot be obtained under subdivision (1), by majority vote of a committee duly designated by the board of directors (in which designation directors who are parties may participate), consisting solely of two or more directors not at the time parties to the proceeding;

(3) by special legal counsel:

(i) selected by the board of directors or its committee in the manner prescribed in subdivision (1) or (2); or

(ii) if a quorum of the board of directors cannot be obtained under subdivision (1) and a committee cannot be designated under subdivision (2), selected by majority vote of the full board of directors (in which selection directors who are parties may participate); or

(4) by the shareholders, but shares owned by or voted under the control of directors who are at the time parties to the proceeding may not be voted on the determination.

(c) Authorization of indemnification and evaluation as to reasonableness of expenses shall be made in the same manner as the determination that indemnification is permissible, except that if the determination is made by special legal counsel, authorization of indemnification and evaluation as to reasonableness of expenses shall be made by those entitled under subsection (b)(3) to select counsel.

§ 8.56 Indemnification of Officers, Employees, and Agents

Unless a corporation's articles of incorporation provide otherwise:

(1) an officer of the corporation who is not a director is entitled to mandatory indemnification under section 8.52, and is entitled to apply for court-ordered indemnification under section 8.54, in each case to the same extent as a director;

(2) the corporation may indemnify and advance expenses under this subchapter to an officer, employee, or agent of the corporation who is not a director to the same extent as to a director; and

(3) a corporation may also indemnify and advance expenses to an officer, employee, or agent who is not a director to the extent, consistent with public policy, that may be provided by its articles of incorporation, bylaws, general or specific action of its board of directors, or contract.

§ 8.57 Insurance

A corporation may purchase and maintain insurance on behalf of an individual who is or was a director, officer, employee, or agent of the corporation, or who, while a director, officer, employee, or agent of the corporation, is or was serving at the request of the corporation as a director, officer, partner, trustee, employee, or agent of another foreign or domestic corporation, partnership, joint venture, trust, employee benefit plan, or other enterprise, against liability asserted against or incurred by him in that capacity or arising from his status as director, officer, employee, or agent, whether or not the corporation would have power to indemnify him against the same liability under section 8.51 or 8.52.

§ 8.58 Application of Subchapter

(a) A provision treating a corporation's indemnification of or advance for expenses to directors that is contained in its articles of incorporation, bylaws, a resolution of its shareholders or board of directors, or in a contract or otherwise, is valid only if and to the extent the provision is consistent with this subchapter. If articles of incorporation limit indemnification or advance for expenses, indemnification and advance for expenses are valid only to the extent consistent with the articles.

(b) This subchapter does not limit a corporation's power to pay or reimburse expenses incurred by a director in connection with his appearance as a witness in a proceeding at a time when he has not been made a named defendant or respondent to the proceeding.

Subchapter F. Directors' Conflicting Interest Transactions

§ 8.60 Subchapter Definitions

In this subchapter:

(1) "Conflicting interest" with respect to a corporation means the interest a director of the corporation has respecting a transaction effected or proposed to be effected by the corporation (or by a subsidiary of the corporation or any other entity in which the corporation has a controlling interest) if

(i) whether or not the transaction is brought before the board of directors of the corporation for action, the director knows at the time of commitment that he or a related person is a party to the transaction or has a beneficial financial interest in or so closely linked to the transaction and of such financial significance to the director or a related person that the interest would reasonably be expected to exert an influence on the director's judgment if he were called upon to vote on the transaction; or

(ii) the transaction is brought (or is of such character and significance to the corporation that it would in the normal course be brought) before the board of directors of the corporation for action, and the director knows at the time of commitment that any of the following persons is either a party to the transaction or has a beneficial financial interest in or so closely linked to the transaction and of such financial significance to the person that the interest would reasonably be expected to exert an influence on the director's judgment if he were called upon to vote on the transaction: (A) an entity (other than the corporation) of which the director is a director, general partner, agent, or employee; (B) a person that controls one or more of the entities specified in subclause (A) or an entity that is controlled by, or is under common control with, one or more of the entities specified in subclause (A); or (C) an individual who is a general partner, principal, or employer of the director.

(2) "Director's conflicting interest transaction" with respect to a corporation means a transaction effected or proposed to be effected by the corporation (or by a subsidiary of the corporation or any other entity in which the corporation has a controlling interest) respecting which a director of the corporation has a conflicting interest.

(3) "Related person" of a director means (i) the spouse (or a parent or sibling thereof) of the director, or a child, grandchild, sibling, parent (or spouse of any thereof) of the director, or an individual having the same home as the director, or a trust or estate of which an individual specified in this clause (i) is a substantial beneficiary; or (ii) a trust, estate, incompetent, conservatee, or minor of which the director is a fiduciary.

(4) "Required disclosure" means disclosure by the director who has a conflicting interest of (i) the existence and nature of his conflicting interest, and (ii) all facts known to him respecting the subject matter of the transaction that an ordinarily prudent person would reasonably believe to be material to a judgment about whether or not to proceed with the transaction.

(5) "Time of commitment" respecting a transaction means the time when the transaction is consummated or, if made pursuant to contract, the time when the corporation (or its subsidiary or the entity in which it has a controlling interest) becomes contractually obligated so that its unilateral withdrawal from the transaction would entail significant loss, liability, or other damage.

§ 8.61 Judicial Action

(a) A transaction effected or proposed to be effected by a corporation (or by a subsidiary of the corporation or any other entity in which the corporation has a controlling interest) that is not a director's conflicting interest transaction may not be enjoined, set aside, or give rise to an award of damages or other sanctions, in a proceeding by a shareholder or by or in the right of the corporation, because a director of the corporation, or any person with whom or which he has a personal, economic, or other association, has an interest in the transaction.

(b) A director's conflicting interest transaction may not be enjoined, set aside, or give rise to an award of damages or other sanctions, in a proceeding by a shareholder or by or in the right of the corporation, because the director, or any person with whom or which he has a personal, economic, or other association, has an interest in the transaction, if:

(1) directors' action respecting the transaction was at any time taken in compliance with section 8.62;

(2) shareholders' action respecting the transaction was at any time taken in compliance with section 8.63;

(3) the transaction, judged according to the circumstances at the time of commitment, is established to have been fair to the corporation.

§ 8.62 Directors' Action

(a) Directors' action respecting a transaction is effective for purposes of section 8.61(b)(1) if the transaction received the affirmative vote of a majority (but no fewer than two) of those qualified directors on the board of directors or on a duly empowered committee of the board who voted on the transaction after either required disclosure to them (to the extent the information was not known by them) or compliance with subsection (b); provided that action by a committee is so effective only if (1) all its members are qualified directors, and (2) its members are either all the qualified directors on the board or are appointed by the affirmative vote of a majority of the qualified directors on the board.

(b) If a director has a conflicting interest respecting a transaction, but neither he nor a related person of the director specified in section 8.60(3)(i) is a party to the transaction, and if the director has a duty under law or professional canon, or a duty of confidentiality to another person, respecting information relating to the transaction such that the director may not make the disclosure described in section 8.60(4)(ii), then disclosure is sufficient for purposes of subsection (a) if the director (1) discloses to the directors voting on the transaction the existence and nature of his conflicting interest and informs them of the character and limitations imposed by that duty before their vote on the transaction, and (2) plays no part, directly or indirectly, in their deliberations or vote.

(c) A majority (but no fewer than two) of all the qualified directors on the board of directors, or on the committee, constitutes a quorum for purposes of action that complies with this section. Directors' action that otherwise complies with this section is not affected by the presence or vote of a director who is not a qualified director.

(d) For purposes of this section, "qualified director" means, with respect to a director's conflicting interest transaction, any director who does not have either (1) a conflicting interest respecting the transaction, or (2) a familial, financial, professional, or employment relationship with a second director who does have a conflicting interest respecting the transaction, which relationship would, in the circumstances, reasonably be expected to exert an influence on the first director's judgment when voting on the transaction.

§ 8.63 Shareholders' Action

(a) Shareholders' action respecting a transaction is effective for purposes of section 8.61(b)(2) if a majority of the votes entitled to be cast by the holders of all qualified shares were cast in favor of the transaction after (1) notice to shareholders describing the director's conflicting interest transaction, (2) provision of the information referred to in subsection (d), and (3) required disclosure to the shareholders who voted on the transaction (to the extent the information was not known by them).

(b) For purposes of this section, "qualified shares" means any shares entitled to vote with respect to the director's conflicting interest transaction except shares that, to the knowledge, before the vote, of the secretary (or other officer or agent of the corporation authorized to tabulate votes), are beneficially owned (or the voting of which is controlled) by a director who has a conflicting interest respecting the transaction or by a related person of the director, or both.

(c) A majority of the votes entitled to be cast by the holders of all qualified shares constitutes a quorum for purposes of action that complies with this section. Subject to the provisions of subsections (d) and (e), shareholders' action that otherwise complies with this section is not affected by the presence of holders, or the voting, of shares that are not qualified shares.

(d) For purposes of compliance with subsection (a), a director who has a conflicting interest respecting the transaction shall, before the shareholders' vote, inform the secretary (or other office or agent of the corporation authorized to tabulate votes) of the number, and the identity of persons holding or controlling the vote, of all shares that the director knows are beneficially owned (or the voting of which is controlled) by the director or by a related person of the director, or both.

(e) If a shareholders' vote does not comply with subsection (a) solely because of a failure of a director to comply with subsection (d), and if the director estab-

lishes that his failure did not determine and was not intended by him to influence the outcome of the vote, the court may, with or without further proceedings respecting section 8.61(b)(3), take such action respecting the transaction and the director, and give such effect, if any, to the shareholders' vote, as it considers appropriate in the circumstances.

CHAPTER 9: [RESERVED]

CHAPTER 10: AMENDMENT OF ARTICLES OF INCORPORATION AND BYLAWS

Subchapter A. Amendment of Articles of Incorporation

§ 10.01 Authority to Amend

(a) A corporation may amend its articles of incorporation at any time to add or change a provision that is required or permitted in the articles of incorporation or to delete a provision not required in the articles of incorporation. Whether a provision is required or permitted in the articles of incorporation is determined as of the effective date of the amendment.

(b) A shareholder of the corporation does not have a vested property right resulting from any provision in the articles of incorporation, including provisions relating to management, control, capital structure, dividend entitlement, or purpose or duration of the corporation.

§ 10.02 Amendment by Board of Directors

Unless the articles of incorporation provide otherwise, a corporation's board of directors may adopt one or more amendments to the corporation's articles of incorporation without shareholder action:

(1) to extend the duration of the corporation if it was incorporated at a time when limited duration was required by law;

(2) to delete the names and addresses of the initial directors;

(3) to delete the name and address of the initial registered agent or registered office, if a statement of change is on file with the secretary of state;

(4) to change each issued and unissued authorized share of an outstanding class into a greater number of whole shares if the corporation has only shares of that class outstanding;

(5) to change the corporate name by substituting the word "corporation," "incorporated," "company," "limited," or the abbreviation "corp.," "inc.," "co.," or "ltd.," for a

similar word or abbreviation in the name, or by adding, deleting, or changing a geographical attribution for the name; or

(6) to make any other change expressly permitted by this Act to be made without shareholder action.

§ 10.03 Amendment by Board of Directors and Shareholders

(a) A corporation's board of directors may propose one or more amendments to the articles of incorporation for submission to the shareholders.

(b) For the amendment to be adopted:

(1) the board of directors must recommend the amendment to the shareholders unless the board of directors determines that because of conflict of interest or other special circumstances it should make no recommendation and communicates the basis for its determination to the shareholders with the amendment; and

(2) the shareholders entitled to vote on the amendment must approve the amendment as provided in subsection (e).

(c) The board of directors may condition its submission of the proposed amendment on any basis.

(d) The corporation shall notify each shareholder, whether or not entitled to vote, of the proposed shareholders' meeting in accordance with section 7.05. The notice of meeting must also state that the purpose, or one of the purposes, of the meeting is to consider the proposed amendment and contain or be accompanied by a copy or summary of the amendment.

(e) Unless this Act, the articles of incorporation, or the board of directors (acting pursuant to subsection (c)) require a greater vote or a vote by voting groups, the amendment to be adopted must be approved by:

(1) a majority of the votes entitled to be cast on the amendment by any voting group with respect to which the amendment would create dissenters' rights; and

(2) the votes required by sections 7.25 and 7.26 by every other voting group entitled to vote on the amendment.

§ 10.04 Voting on Amendments by Voting Groups

(a) The holders of the outstanding shares of a class are entitled to vote as a separate voting group (if shareholder voting is otherwise required by this Act) on a proposed amendment if the amendment would:

(1) increase or decrease the aggregate number of authorized shares of the class;

(2) effect an exchange or reclassification of all or part of the shares of the class into shares of another class;

(3) effect an exchange or reclassification, or create the right of exchange, of all or part of the shares of another class into shares of the class;

(4) change the designation, rights, preferences, or limitations of all or part of the shares of the class;

(5) change the shares of all or part of the class into a different number of shares of the same class;

(6) create a new class of shares having rights or preferences with respect to distributions or to dissolution that are prior, superior, or substantially equal to the shares of the class;

(7) increase the rights, preferences, or number of authorized shares of any class that, after giving effect to the amendment, have rights or preferences with respect to distributions or to dissolution that are prior, superior, or substantially equal to the shares of the class;

(8) limit or deny an existing preemptive right of all or part of the shares of the class; or

(9) cancel or otherwise affect rights to distributions or dividends that have accumulated but not yet been declared on all or part of the shares of the class.

(b) If a proposed amendment would affect a series of a class of shares in one or more of the ways described in subsection (a), the shares of that series are entitled to vote as a separate voting group on the proposed amendment.

(c) If a proposed amendment that entitles two or more series of shares to vote as separate voting groups under this section would affect those two or more series in the same or a substantially similar way, the shares of all the series so affected must vote together as a single voting group on the proposed amendment.

(d) A class or series of shares is entitled to the voting rights granted by this section although the articles of incorporation provide that the shares are nonvoting shares.

§ 10.05 Amendment Before Issuance of Shares

If a corporation has not yet issued shares, its incorporators or board of directors may adopt one or more amendments to the corporation's articles of incorporation.

§ 10.06 Articles of Amendment

A corporation amending its articles of incorporation shall deliver to the secretary of state for filing articles of amendment setting forth:

(1) the name of the corporation;

(2) the text of each amendment adopted;

(3) if an amendment provides for an exchange, reclassification, or cancellation of issued shares, provisions for implementing the amendment if not contained in the amendment itself;

(4) the date of each amendment's adoption;

(5) if an amendment was adopted by the incorporators or board of directors without shareholder action, a statement to that effect and that shareholder action was not required;

(6) if an amendment was approved by the shareholders:

(i) the designation, number of outstanding shares, number of votes entitled to be cast by each voting group entitled to vote separately on the amendment, and number of votes of each voting group indisputably represented at the meeting;

(ii) either the total number of votes cast for and against the amendment by each voting group entitled to vote separately on the amendment or the total number of undisputed votes cast for the amendment by each voting group and a statement that the number cast for the amendment by each voting group was sufficient for approval by that voting group.

§ 10.07 Restated Articles of Incorporation

(a) A corporation's board of directors may restate its articles of incorporation at any time with or without shareholder action.

(b) The restatement may include one or more amendments to the articles. If the restatement includes an amendment requiring shareholder approval, it must be adopted as provided in section 10.03.

(c) If the board of directors submits a restatement for shareholder action, the corporation shall notify each shareholder, whether or not entitled to vote, of the proposed shareholders' meeting in accordance with section 7.05. The notice must also state that the purpose, or one of the purposes, of the meeting is to consider the proposed restatement and contain or be accompanied by a copy of the restatement that identifies any amendment or other change it would make in the articles.

(d) A corporation restating its articles of incorporation shall deliver to the secretary of state for filing articles of restatement setting forth the name of the corporation and the text of the restated articles of incorporation together with a certificate setting forth:

(1) whether the restatement contains an amendment to the articles requiring shareholder approval and, if it does not, that the board of directors adopted the restatement; or

(2) if the restatement contains an amendment to the articles requiring shareholder approval, the information required by section 10.06.

(e) Duly adopted restated articles of incorporation supersede the original articles of incorporation and all amendments to them.

(f) The secretary of state may certify restated articles of incorporation, as the articles of incorporation currently in effect, without including the certificate information required by subsection (d).

§ 10.08 Amendment Pursuant to Reorganization

(a) A corporation's articles of incorporation may be amended without action by the board of directors or shareholders to carry out a plan of reorganization ordered or decreed by a court of competent jurisdiction under federal statute if the articles of incorporation after amendment contain only provisions required or permitted by section 2.02.

(b) The individual or individuals designated by the court shall deliver to the secretary of state for filing articles of amendment setting forth:

(1) the name of the corporation;

(2) the text of each amendment approved by the court;

(3) the date of the court's order or decree approving the articles of amendment;

(4) the title of the reorganization proceeding in which the order or decree was entered; and

(5) a statement that the court had jurisdiction of the proceeding under federal statute.

(c) Shareholders of a corporation undergoing reorganization do not have dissenters' rights except as and to the extent provided in the reorganization plan.

(d) This section does not apply after entry of a final decree in the reorganization proceeding even though the court retains jurisdiction of the proceeding for limited purposes unrelated to consummation of the reorganization plan.

§ 10.09 Effect of Amendment

An amendment to articles of incorporation does not affect a cause of action existing against or in favor of the corporation, a proceeding to which the corporation is a party, or the existing rights of persons other than shareholders of the corporation. An amendment changing a corporation's name does not abate a proceeding brought by or against the corporation in its former name.

Subchapter B. Amendment of Bylaws

§ 10.20 Amendment by Board of Directors or Shareholders

(a) A corporation's board of directors may amend or repeal the corporation's bylaws unless:

(1) the articles of incorporation or this Act reserve this power exclusively to the shareholders in whole or part; or

(2) the shareholders in amending or repealing a particular bylaw provide expressly that the board of directors may not amend or repeal that bylaw.

(b) A corporation's shareholders may amend or repeal the corporation's bylaws even though the bylaws may also be amended or repealed by its board of directors.

§ 10.21 Bylaw Increasing Quorum or Voting Requirement for Shareholders

(a) If expressly authorized by the articles of incorporation, the shareholders may adopt or amend a bylaw that fixes a greater quorum or voting requirement for shareholders (or voting groups of shareholders) than is required by this Act. The adoption or amendment of a bylaw that adds, changes, or deletes a greater quorum or voting requirement for shareholders must meet the same quorum requirement and be adopted by the same vote and voting groups required to take action under the quorum and voting requirement then in effect or proposed to be adopted, whichever is greater.

(b) A bylaw that fixes a greater quorum or voting requirement for shareholders under subsection (a) may not be adopted, amended, or repealed by the board of directors.

§ 10.22 Bylaw Increasing Quorum or Voting Requirement for Directors

(a) A bylaw that fixes a greater quorum or voting requirement for the board of directors may be amended or repealed:

(1) if originally adopted by the shareholders, only by the shareholders;

(2) if originally adopted by the board of directors, either by the shareholders or by the board of directors.

(b) A bylaw adopted or amended by the shareholders that fixes a greater quorum or voting requirement for the board of directors may provide that it may be amended or repealed only by a specified vote of either the shareholders or the board of directors.

(c) Action by the board of directors under subsection (a)(2) to adopt or amend a bylaw that changes the quorum or voting requirement for the board of directors must meet the same quorum requirement and be adopted by the same vote required to take action under the quorum and voting requirement then in effect or proposed to be adopted, whichever is greater.

CHAPTER 11: MERGER AND SHARE EXCHANGE

§ 11.01 Merger

(a) One or more corporations may merge into another corporation if the board of directors of each corporation adopts and its shareholders (if required by section 11.03) approve a plan of merger.

(b) The plan of merger must set forth:

(1) the name of each corporation planning to merge and the name of the surviving corporation into which each other corporation plans to merge;

(2) the terms and conditions of the merger; and

(3) the manner and basis of converting the shares of each corporation into shares, obligations, or other securities of the surviving or any other corporation or into cash or other property in whole or part.

(c) The plan of merger may set forth:

(1) amendments to the articles of incorporation of the surviving corporation; and

(2) other provisions relating to the merger.

§ 11.02 Share Exchange

(a) A corporation may acquire all of the outstanding shares of one or more classes or series of another corporation if the board of directors of each corporation adopts and its shareholders (if required by section 11.03) approve the exchange.

(b) The plan of exchange must set forth:

(1) the name of the corporation whose shares will be acquired and the name of the acquiring corporation;

(2) the terms and conditions of the exchange;

(3) the manner and basis of exchanging the shares to be acquired for shares, obligations, or other securities of the acquiring or any other corporation or for cash or other property in whole or part.

(c) The plan of exchange may set forth other provisions relating to the exchange.

(d) This section does not limit the power of a corporation to acquire all or part of the shares of one or more classes or series of another corporation through a voluntary exchange or otherwise.

§ 11.03 Action on Plan

(a) After adopting a plan of merger or share exchange, the board of directors of each corporation party to the merger, and the board of directors of the corporation whose shares will be acquired in the share exchange, shall submit the plan of merger (except as provided in subsection (g)) or share exchange for approval by its shareholders.

(b) For a plan of merger or share exchange to be approved:

(1) the board of directors must recommend the plan of merger or share exchange to the shareholders, unless the board of directors determines that because of conflict of interest or other special circumstances it should make no recommendation and communicates the basis for its determination to the shareholders with the plan; and

(2) the shareholders entitled to vote must approve the plan.

(c) The board of directors may condition its submission of the proposed merger or share exchange on any basis.

(d) The corporation shall notify each shareholder, whether or not entitled to vote, of the proposed shareholders' meeting in accordance with section 7.05. The notice must also state that the purpose, or one of the purposes, of the meeting is to consider the plan of merger or share exchange and contain or be accompanied by a copy or summary of the plan.

(e) Unless this Act, the articles of incorporation, or the board of directors (acting pursuant to subsection (c)) require a greater vote or a vote by voting groups, the plan of merger or share exchange to be authorized must be approved by each voting group entitled to vote separately on the plan by a majority of all the votes entitled to be cast on the plan by that voting group.

(f) Separate voting by voting groups is required:

(1) on a plan of merger if the plan contains a provision that, if contained in a proposed amendment to articles of incorporation, would require action by one or more separate voting groups on the proposed amendment under section 10.04;

(2) on a plan of share exchange by each class or series of shares included in the exchange, with each class or series constituting a separate voting group.

(g) Action by the shareholders of the surviving corporation on a plan of merger is not required if:

(1) the articles of incorporation of the surviving corporation will not differ (except for amendments enumerated in section 10.02) from its articles before the merger;

(2) each shareholder of the surviving corporation whose shares were outstanding immediately before the effective date of the merger will hold the same number of shares, with identical designations, preferences, limitations, and relative rights, immediately after;

(3) the number of voting shares outstanding immediately after the merger, plus the number of voting shares issuable as a result of the merger (either by the conversion of securities issued pursuant to the merger or the exercise of rights and warrants issued pursuant to the merger), will not exceed by more than 20 percent the total number of voting shares of the surviving corporation outstanding immediately before the merger; and

(4) the number of participating shares outstanding immediately after the merger, plus the number of participating shares issuable as a result of the merger (either by the conversion of securities issued pursuant to the merger or the exercise of rights and warrants issued pursuant to the merger), will not exceed by more than 20 percent the total number of participating shares outstanding immediately before the merger.

(h) As used in subsection (g):

(1) "Participating shares" means shares that entitle their holders to participate without limitation in distributions.

(2) "Voting shares" means shares that entitle their holders to vote unconditionally in elections of directors.

(i) After a merger or share exchange is authorized, and at any time before articles of merger or share exchange are filed, the planned merger or share exchange may be abandoned (subject to any contractual rights), without further shareholder action, in accordance with the procedure set forth in the plan of merger or share exchange or, if none is set forth, in the manner determined by the board of directors.

§ 11.04 Merger of Subsidiary

(a) A parent corporation owning at least 90 percent of the outstanding shares of each class of a subsidiary corporation may merge the subsidiary into itself without approval of the shareholders of the parent or subsidiary.

(b) The board of directors of the parent shall adopt a plan of merger that sets forth:

(1) the names of the parent and subsidiary; and

(2) the manner and basis of converting the shares of the subsidiary into shares, obligations, or other securities of the parent or any other corporation or into cash or other property in whole or part.

(c) The parent shall mail a copy or summary of the plan of merger to each shareholder of the subsidiary who does not waive the mailing requirement in writing.

(d) The parent may not deliver articles of merger to the secretary of state for filing until at least 30 days after the date it mailed a copy of the plan of merger to each shareholder of the subsidiary who did not waive the mailing requirement.

(e) Articles of merger under this section may not contain amendments to the articles of incorporation of the parent corporation (except for amendments enumerated in section 10.02).

§ 11.05 Articles of Merger or Share Exchange

(a) After a plan of merger or share exchange is approved by the shareholders, or adopted by the board of directors if shareholder approval is not required, the surviving or acquiring corporation shall deliver to the secretary of state for filing articles of merger or share exchange setting forth:

(1) the plan of merger or share exchange;

(2) if shareholder approval was not required, a statement to that effect;

(3) if approval of the shareholders of one or more corporations party to the merger or share exchange was required:

(i) the designation, number of outstanding shares, and number of votes entitled to be cast by each voting group entitled to vote separately on the plan as to each corporation; and

(ii) either the total number of votes cast for and against the plan by each voting group entitled to vote separately on the plan or the total number of undisputed votes cast for the plan separately by each voting group and a statement that the number cast for the plan by each voting group was sufficient for approval by that voting group.

(b) Unless a delayed effective date is specified, a merger or share exchange takes effect when the articles of merger or share exchange are filed.

§ 11.06 Effect of Merger or Share Exchange

(a) When a merger takes effect:

(1) every other corporation party to the merger merges into the surviving corporation and the separate existence of every corporation except the surviving corporation ceases;

(2) the title to all real estate and other property owned by each corporation party to the merger is vested in the surviving corporation without reversion or impairment;

(3) the surviving corporation has all liabilities of each corporation party to the merger;

(4) a proceeding pending against any corporation party to the merger may be continued as if the merger did not occur or the surviving corporation may be substituted in the proceeding for the corporation whose existence ceased;

(5) the articles of incorporation of the surviving corporation are amended to the extent provided in the plan of merger; and

(6) the shares of each corporation party to the merger that are to be converted into shares, obligations, or other securities of the surviving or any other corporation or into cash or other property are converted and the former holders of the shares are entitled only to the rights provided in the articles of merger or to their rights under chapter 13.

(b) When a share exchange takes effect, the shares of each acquired corporation are exchanged as provided in the plan, and the former holders of the shares are entitled only to the exchange rights provided in the articles of share exchange or to their rights under chapter 13.

§ 11.07 Merger of Share Exchange With Foreign Corporation

(a) One or more foreign corporations may merge or enter into a share exchange with one or more domestic corporations if:

(1) in a merger, the merger is permitted by the law of the state or country under whose law each foreign corporation is incorporated and each foreign corporation complies with that law in effecting the merger;

(2) in a share exchange, the corporation whose shares will be acquired is a domestic corporation, whether or not a share exchange is permitted by the law of the state or country under whose law the acquiring corporation is incorporated;

(3) the foreign corporation complies with section 11.05 if it is the surviving corporation of the merger or acquiring corporation of the share exchange; and

(4) each domestic corporation complies with the applicable provisions of sections 11.01 through 11.04 and, if it is the surviving corporation of the merger or acquiring corporation of the share exchange, with section 11.05.

(b) Upon the merger or share exchange taking effect, the surviving foreign corporation of a merger and the acquiring foreign corporation of a share exchange is deemed:

(1) to appoint the secretary of state as its agent for service of process in a proceeding to enforce any obligation or the rights of dissenting shareholders of each domestic corporation party to the merger or share exchange; and

(2) to agree that it will promptly pay to the dissenting shareholders of each domestic corporation party to the merger or share exchange the amount, if any, to which they are entitled under chapter 13.

(c) This section does not limit the power of a foreign corporation to acquire all or part of the shares of one or more classes or series of a domestic corporation through a voluntary exchange or otherwise.

CHAPTER 12: SALE OF ASSETS

§ 12.01 Sale of Assets in Regular Course of Business and Mortgage of Assets

(a) A corporation may, on the terms and conditions and for the consideration determined by the board of directors:

(1) sell, lease, exchange, or otherwise dispose of all, or substantially all, of its property in the usual and regular course of business,

(2) mortgage, pledge, dedicate to the repayment of indebtedness (whether with or without recourse), or otherwise encumber any or all of its property whether or not in the usual and regular course of business, or

(3) transfer any or all of its property to a corporation all the shares of which are owned by the corporation.

(b) Unless the articles of incorporation require it, approval by the shareholders of a transaction described in subsection (a) is not required.

§ 12.02 Sale of Assets Other Than in Regular Course of Business

(a) A corporation may sell, lease, exchange, or otherwise dispose of all, or substantially all, of its property (with or without the good will), otherwise than in the usual and regular course of business, on the terms and conditions and for the consideration determined by the corporation's board of directors, if the board of directors proposes and its shareholders approve the proposed transaction.

(b) For a transaction to be authorized:

(1) the board of directors must recommend the proposed transaction to the shareholders unless the board of directors determines that because of conflict of interest or other special circumstances it should make no recommendation and communicates the basis for its determination to the shareholders with the submission of the proposed transaction; and

(2) the shareholders entitled to vote must approve the transaction.

(c) The board of directors may condition its submission of the proposed transaction on any basis.

(d) The corporation shall notify each shareholder, whether or not entitled to vote, of the proposed shareholders' meeting in accordance with section 7.05. The notice must also state that the purpose, or one of the purposes, of the meeting is to consider the sale, lease, exchange, or other disposition of all, or substantially all, the property of the corporation and contain or be accompanied by a description of the transaction.

(e) Unless the articles of incorporation or the board of directors (acting pursuant to subsection (c)) require a greater vote or a vote by voting groups, the transaction to be authorized must be approved by a majority of all the votes entitled to be cast on the transaction.

(f) After a sale, lease, exchange, or other disposition of property is authorized, the transaction may be abandoned (subject to any contractual rights) without further shareholder action.

(g) A transaction that constitutes a distribution is governed by section 6.40 and not by this section.

CHAPTER 13: DISSENTERS' RIGHTS

Subchapter A. Right to Dissent and Obtain Payment for Shares

§ 13.01 Definitions

In this chapter:

(1) "Corporation" means the issuer of the shares held by a dissenter before the corporate action, or the surviving or acquiring corporation by merger or share exchange of that issuer.

(2) "Dissenter" means a shareholder who is entitled to dissent from corporate action under section 13.02 and who exercises that right when and in the manner required by sections 13.20 through 13.28.

(3) "Fair value," with respect to a dissenter's shares, means the value of the shares immediately before the effectuation of the corporate action to which the dissenter objects, excluding any appreciation or depreciation in anticipation of the corporate action unless exclusion would be inequitable.

(4) "Interest" means interest from the effective date of the corporate action until the date of payment, at the average rate currently paid by the corporation on its principal bank loans or, if none, at a rate that is fair and equitable under all the circumstances.

(5) "Record shareholder" means the person in whose name shares are registered in the records of a corporation or the beneficial owner of shares to the extent of the rights granted by a nominee certificate on file with a corporation.

(6) "Beneficial shareholder" means the person who is a beneficial owner of shares held by a nominee as the record shareholder.

(7) "Shareholder" means the record shareholder or the beneficial shareholder.

§ 13.02 Right to Dissent

(a) A shareholder is entitled to dissent from, and obtain payment of the fair value of his shares in the event of, any of the following corporate actions:

(1) consummation of a plan of merger to which the corporation is a party (i) if shareholder approval is required for the merger by section 11.03 or the articles of incorporation and the shareholder is entitled to vote on the merger or (ii) if the corporation is a subsidiary that is merged with its parent under section 11.04;

(2) consummation of a plan of share exchange to which the corporation is a party as the corporation whose shares will be acquired, if the shareholder is entitled to vote on the plan;

(3) consummation of a sale or exchange of all, or substantially all, of the property of the corporation other than in the usual and regular course of business, if the shareholder is entitled to vote on the sale or exchange, including a sale in dissolution, but not including a sale pursuant to court order or a sale for cash pursuant to a plan by which all or substantially all of the net proceeds of the sale will be distributed to the shareholders within one year after the date of sale;

(4) an amendment of the articles of incorporation that materially and adversely affects rights in respect of a dissenter's shares because it:

(i) alters or abolishes a preferential right of the shares;

(ii) creates, alters, or abolishes a right in respect of redemption, including a provision respecting a sinking fund for the redemption or repurchase, of the shares;

(iii) alters or abolishes a preemptive right of the holder of the shares to acquire shares or other securities;

(iv) excludes or limits the right of the shares to vote on any matter, or to cumulate votes, other than a limitation by dilution through issuance of shares or other securities with similar voting rights; or

(v) reduces the number of shares owned by the shareholder to a fraction of a share if the fractional share so created is to be acquired for cash under section 6.04; or

(5) any corporate action taken pursuant to a shareholder vote to the extent the articles of incorporation, bylaws, or a resolution of the board of directors provides that voting or nonvoting shareholders are entitled to dissent and obtain payment for their shares.

(b) A shareholder entitled to dissent and obtain payment for his shares under this chapter may not challenge the corporate action creating his entitlement unless the action is unlawful or fraudulent with respect to the shareholder or the corporation.

§ 13.03 Dissent by Nominees and Beneficial Owners

(a) A record shareholder may assert dissenters' rights as to fewer than all the shares registered in his name only if he dissents with respect to all shares beneficially owned by any one person and notifies the corporation in writing of the name and address of each person on whose behalf he asserts dissenters' rights. The rights of a partial dissenter under this subsection are determined as if the shares as to which he dissents and his other shares were registered in the names of different shareholders.

(b) A beneficial shareholder may assert dissenters' rights as to shares held on his behalf only if:

(1) he submits to the corporation and the record shareholder's written consent to the dissent not later than the time the beneficial shareholder asserts dissenters' rights; and

(2) he does so with respect to all shares of which he is the beneficial shareholder or over which he has power to direct the vote.

Subchapter B. Procedure for Exercise of Dissenters' Rights

§ 13.20 Notice of Dissenters' Rights

(a) If proposed corporate action creating dissenters' rights under section 13.02 is submitted to a vote at a shareholders' meeting, the meeting notice must state that shareholders are or may be entitled to assert dissenters' rights under this chapter and be accompanied by a copy of this chapter.

(b) If corporate action creating dissenters' rights under section 13.02 is taken without a vote of shareholders, the corporation shall notify in writing all shareholders entitled to assert dissenters' rights that the action was taken and send them the dissenters' notice described in section 13.22.

§ 13.21 Notice of Intent to Demand Payment

(a) If proposed corporate action creating dissenters' rights under section 13.02 is submitted to a vote at a shareholders' meeting, a shareholder who wishes to assert dissenters' rights (1) must deliver to the corporation before the vote is taken written notice of his intent to demand payment for his shares if the proposed action is effectuated and (2) must not vote his shares in favor of the proposed action.

(b) A shareholder who does not satisfy the requirements of subsection (a) is not entitled to payment for his shares under this chapter.

§ 13.22 Dissenters' Notice

(a) If proposed corporate action creating dissenters' rights under section 13.02 is authorized at a shareholders' meeting, the corporation shall deliver a written dissenters' notice to all shareholders who satisfied the requirements of section 13.21.

(b) The dissenters' notice must be sent no later than 10 days after the corporate action was taken, and must:

(1) state where the payment demand must be sent and where and when certificates for certificated shares must be deposited;

(2) inform holders of uncertificated shares to what extent transfer of the shares will be restricted after the payment demand is received;

(3) supply a form for demanding payment that includes the date of the first announcement to news media or to shareholders of the terms of the proposed corporate action and requires that the person asserting dissenters' rights certify whether or not he acquired beneficial ownership of the shares before that date;

(4) set a date by which the corporation must receive the payment demand, which date may not be fewer than 30 nor more than 60 days after the date the subsection (a) notice is delivered; and

(5) be accompanied by a copy of this chapter.

§ 13.23 Duty to Demand Payment

(a) A shareholder sent a dissenters' notice described in section 13.22 must demand payment, certify whether he acquired beneficial ownership of the shares before the date required to be set forth in the dissenter's notice pursuant to section 13.22(b)(3), and deposit his certificates in accordance with the terms of the notice.

(b) The shareholder who demands payment and deposits his shares under section (a) retains all other rights of a shareholder until these rights are cancelled or modified by the taking of the proposed corporate action.

(c) A shareholder who does not demand payment or deposit his share certificates where required, each by the date set in the dissenters' notice, is not entitled to payment for his shares under this chapter.

§ 13.24 Share Restrictions

(a) The corporation may restrict the transfer of uncertificated shares from the date the demand for their payment is received until the proposed corporate action is taken or the restrictions released under section 13.26.

(b) The person for whom dissenters' rights are asserted as to uncertificated shares retains all other rights of a shareholder until these rights are cancelled or modified by the taking of the proposed corporate action.

§ 13.25 Payment

(a) Except as provided in section 13.27, as soon as the proposed corporate action is taken, or upon receipt of a payment demand, the corporation shall pay each dissenter who complied with section 13.23 the amount the corporation estimates to be the fair value of his shares, plus accrued interest.

(b) The payment must be accompanied by:

(1) the corporation's balance sheet as of the end of a fiscal year ending not more than 16 months before the date of payment, an income statement for that year, a statement of changes in shareholders' equity for that year, and the latest available interim financial statements, if any;

(2) a statement of the corporation's estimate of the fair value of the shares;

(3) an explanation of how the interest was calculated;

(4) a statement of the dissenter's right to demand payment under section 13.28; and

(5) a copy of this chapter.

§ 13.26 Failure to Take Action

(a) If the corporation does not take the proposed action within 60 days after the date set for demanding payment and depositing share certificates, the corporation shall return the deposited certificates and release the transfer restrictions imposed on uncertificated shares.

(b) If after returning deposited certificates and releasing transfer restrictions, the corporation takes the proposed action, it must send a new dissenters' notice under section 13.22 and repeat the payment demand procedure.

§ 13.27 After-Acquired Shares

(a) A corporation may elect to withhold payment required by section 13.25 from a dissenter unless he was the beneficial owner of the shares before the date set forth in the dissenters' notice as the date of the first announcement to news media or to shareholders of the terms of the proposed corporate action.

(b) To the extent the corporation elects to withhold payment under subsection (a), after taking the proposed corporate action, it shall estimate the fair value of the shares, plus accrued interest, and shall pay this amount to each dissenter who agrees to accept it in full satisfaction of his demand. The corporation shall send with its offer a statement of its estimate of the fair value of the shares, an explanation of how the interest was calculated, and a statement of the dissenter's right to demand payment under section 13.28.

§ 13.28 Procedure if Shareholder Dissatisfied With Payment or Offer

(a) A dissenter may notify the corporation in writing of his own estimate of the fair value of his shares and amount of interest due, and demand payment of his estimate (less any payment under section 13.25), or reject the corporation's offer under section 13.27 and demand payment of the fair value of his shares and interest due, if:

(1) the dissenter believes that the amount paid under section 13.25 or offered under section 13.27 is less than the fair value of his shares or that the interest due is incorrectly calculated;

(2) the corporation fails to make payment under section 13.25 within 60 days after the date set for demanding payment; or

(3) the corporation, having failed to take the proposed action, does not return the deposited certifi-

cates or release the transfer restrictions imposed on uncertificated shares within 60 days after the date set for demanding payment.

(b) A dissenter waives his right to demand payment under this section unless he notifies the corporation of his demand in writing under subsection (a) within 30 days after the corporation made or offered payment for his shares.

Subchapter C. Judicial Appraisal of Shares

§ 13.30 Court Action

(a) If a demand for payment under section 13.28 remains unsettled, the corporation shall commence a proceeding within 60 days after receiving the payment demand and petition the court to determine the fair value of the shares and accrued interest. If the corporation does not commence the proceeding within the 60-day period, it shall pay each dissenter whose demand remains unsettled the amount demanded.

(b) The corporation shall commence the proceeding in the [name or describe] court of the county where a corporation's principal office (or, if none in this state, its registered office) is located. If the corporation is a foreign corporation without a registered office in this state, it shall commence the proceeding in the county in this state where the registered office of the domestic corporation merged with or whose shares were acquired by the foreign corporation was located.

(c) The corporation shall make all dissenters (whether or not residents of this state) whose demands remain unsettled parties to the proceeding as in an action against their shares and all parties must be served with a copy of the petition. Nonresidents may be served by registered or certified mail or by publication as provided by law.

(d) The jurisdiction of the court in which the proceeding is commenced under subsection (b) is plenary and exclusive. The court may appoint one or more persons as appraisers to receive evidence and recommend decision on the question of fair value. The appraisers have the powers described in the order appointing them, or in any amendment to it. The dissenters are entitled to the same discovery rights as parties in other civil proceedings.

(e) Each dissenter made a party to the proceeding is entitled to judgment (1) for the amount, if any, by which the court finds the fair value of his shares, plus interest, exceeds the amount paid by the corporation or (2) for the fair value, plus accrued interest, of his after-acquired shares for which the corporation elected to withhold payment under section 13.27.

§ 13.31 Court Costs and Counsel Fees

(a) The court in an appraisal proceeding commenced under section 13.30 shall determine all costs of the pro-

ceeding, including the reasonable compensation and expenses of appraisers appointed by the court. The court shall assess the costs against the corporation, except that the court may assess costs against all or some of the dissenters, in amounts the court finds equitable, to the extent the court finds the dissenters acted arbitrarily, vexatiously, or not in good faith in demanding payment under section 13.28.

(b) The court may also assess the fees and expenses of counsel and experts for the respective parties, in amounts the court finds equitable:

> (1) against the corporation and in favor of any or all dissenters if the court finds the corporation did not substantially comply with the requirements of sections 13.20 through 13.28; or

> (2) against either the corporation or a dissenter, in favor of any other party, if the court finds that the party against whom the fees and expenses are assessed acted arbitrarily, vexatiously, or not in good faith with respect to the rights provided by this chapter.

(c) If the court finds that the services of counsel for any dissenter were of substantial benefit to other dissenters similarly situated, and that the fees for those services should not be assessed against the corporation, the court may award to these counsel reasonable fees to be paid out of the amounts awarded the dissenters who were benefited.

CHAPTER 14: DISSOLUTION

Subchapter A. Voluntary Dissolution

§ 14.01 Dissolution by Incorporators or Initial Directors

A majority of the incorporators or initial directors of a corporation that has not issued shares or has not commenced business may dissolve the corporation by delivering to the secretary of state for filing articles of dissolution that set forth:

(1) the name of the corporation;

(2) the date of its incorporation;

(3) either (i) that none of the corporation's shares has been issued or (ii) that the corporation has not commenced business;

(4) that no debt of the corporation remains unpaid;

(5) that the net assets of the corporation remaining after winding up have been distributed to the shareholders, if shares were issued; and

(6) that a majority of the incorporators or initial directors authorized the dissolution.

§ 14.02 Dissolution by Board of Directors and Shareholders

(a) A corporation's board of directors may propose dissolution for submission to the shareholders.

(b) For a proposal to dissolve to be adopted:

(1) the board of directors must recommend dissolution to the shareholders unless the board of directors determines that because of conflict of interest or other special circumstances it should make no recommendation and communicates the basis for its determination to the shareholders; and

(2) the shareholders entitled to vote must approve the proposal to dissolve as provided in subsection (e).

(c) The board of directors may condition its submission of the proposal for dissolution on any basis.

(d) The corporation shall notify each shareholder, whether or not entitled to vote, of the proposed shareholders' meeting in accordance with section 7.05. The notice must also state that the purpose, or one of the purposes, of the meeting is to consider dissolving the corporation.

(e) Unless the articles of incorporation or the board of directors (acting pursuant to subsection (c)) require a greater vote or a vote by voting groups, the proposal to dissolve to be adopted must be approved by a majority of all the votes entitled to be cast on that proposal.

§ 14.03 Articles of Dissolution

(a) At any time after dissolution is authorized, the corporation may dissolve by delivering to the secretary of state for filing articles of dissolution setting forth:

(1) the name of the corporation;

(2) the date dissolution was authorized;

(3) if dissolution was approved by the shareholders:

(i) the number of votes entitled to be cast on the proposal to dissolve; and

(ii) either the total number of votes cast for and against dissolution or the total number of undisputed votes cast for dissolution and a statement that the number cast for dissolution was sufficient for approval.

(4) If voting by voting groups is required, the information required by subparagraph (3) shall be separately provided for each voting group entitled to vote separately on the plan to dissolve.

(b) A corporation is dissolved upon the effective date of its articles of dissolution.

§ 14.04 Revocation of Dissolution

(a) A corporation may revoke its dissolution within 120 days of its effective date.

(b) Revocation of dissolution must be authorized in the same manner as the dissolution was authorized unless that authorization permitted revocation by action by the board of directors alone, in which event the board of directors may revoke the dissolution without shareholder action.

(c) After the revocation of dissolution is authorized, the corporation may revoke the dissolution by delivering to the secretary of state for filing articles of revocation of dissolution, together with a copy of its articles of dissolution, that set forth:

(1) the name of the corporation;

(2) the effective date of the dissolution that was revoked;

(3) the date that the revocation of dissolution was authorized;

(4) if the corporation's board of directors (or incorporators) revoked the dissolution, a statement to that effect;

(5) if the corporation's board of directors revoked a dissolution authorized by the shareholders, a statement that revocation was permitted by action by the board of directors alone pursuant to that authorization; and

(6) if shareholder action was required to revoke the dissolution, the information required by section 14.03(3) or (4).

(d) Unless a delayed effective date is specified, revocation of dissolution is effective when articles of revocation of dissolution are filed.

(e) When the revocation of dissolution is effective, it relates back to and takes effect as of the effective date of the dissolution and the corporation resumes carrying on its business as if dissolution had never occurred.

§ 14.05 Effect of Dissolution

(a) A dissolved corporation continues its corporate existence but may not carry on any business except that appropriate to wind up and liquidate its business and affairs, including:

(1) collecting its assets;

(2) disposing of its properties that will not be distributed in kind to its shareholders;

(3) discharging or making provision for discharging its liabilities;

(4) distributing its remaining property among its shareholders according to their interests; and

(5) doing every other act necessary to wind up and liquidate its business and affairs.

(b) Dissolution of a corporation does not:

(1) transfer title to the corporation's property;

(2) prevent transfer of its shares or securities, although the authorization to dissolve may provide for closing the corporation's share transfer records;

(3) subject its directors or officers to standards of conduct different from those prescribed in chapter 8;

(4) change quorum or voting requirements for its board of directors or shareholders; change provisions for selection, resignation, or removal of its directors or officers or both; or change provisions for amending its bylaws;

(5) prevent commencement of a proceeding by or against the corporation in its corporate name;

(6) abate or suspend a proceeding pending by or against the corporation on the effective date of dissolution; or

(7) terminate the authority of the registered agent of the corporation.

§ 14.06 Known Claims Against Dissolved Corporation

(a) A dissolved corporation may dispose of the known claims against it by following the procedure described in this section.

(b) The dissolved corporation shall notify its known claimants in writing of the dissolution at any time after its effective date. The written notice must:

(1) describe information that must be included in a claim;

(2) provide a mailing address where a claim may be sent;

(3) state the deadline, which may not be fewer than 120 days from the effective date of the written notice, by which the dissolved corporation must receive the claim; and

(4) state that the claim will be barred if not received by the deadline.

(c) A claim against the dissolved corporation is barred:

(1) if a claimant who was given written notice under subsection (b) does not deliver the claim to the dissolved corporation by the deadline;

(2) if a claimant whose claim was rejected by the dissolved corporation does not commence a proceeding to enforce the claim within 90 days from the effective date of the rejection notice.

(d) For purposes of this section, "claim" does not include a contingent liability or a claim based on an event occurring after the effective date of dissolution.

§ 14.07 Unknown Claims Against Dissolved Corporation

(a) A dissolved corporation may also publish notice of its dissolution and request that persons with claims against the corporation present them in accordance with the notice.

(b) The notice must:

(1) be published one time in a newspaper of general circulation in the county where the dissolved corporation's principal office (or, if none in this state, its registered office) is or was last located;

(2) describe the information that must be included in a claim and provide a mailing address where the claim may be sent; and

(3) state that a claim against the corporation will be barred unless a proceeding to enforce the claim is commenced within five years after the publication of the notice.

(c) If the dissolved corporation publishes a newspaper notice in accordance with subsection (b), the claim of each of the following claimants is barred unless the claimant commences a proceeding to enforce the claim against the dissolved corporation within five years after the publication date of the newspaper notice:

(1) a claimant who did not receive written notice under section 14.06;

(2) a claimant whose claim was timely sent to the dissolved corporation but not acted on;

(3) a claimant whose claim is contingent or based on an event occurring after the effective date of dissolution.

(d) A claim may be enforced under this section:

(1) against the dissolved corporation, to the extent of its undistributed assets; or

(2) if the assets have been distributed in liquidation, against a shareholder of the dissolved corporation to the extent of his pro rata share of the claim or the corporate assets distributed to him in liquidation, whichever is less, but a shareholder's total liability for all claims under this section may not exceed the total amount of assets distributed to him.

Subchapter B. Administrative Dissolution

§ 14.20 Grounds for Administrative Dissolution

The secretary of state may commence a proceeding under section 14.21 to administratively dissolve a corporation if:

(1) the corporation does not pay within 60 days after they are due any franchise taxes or penalties imposed by this Act or other law;

(2) the corporation does not deliver its annual report to the secretary of state within 60 days after it is due;

(3) the corporation is without a registered agent or registered office in this state for 60 days or more;

(4) the corporation does not notify the secretary of state within 60 days that its registered agent or registered office has been changed, that its registered agent has resigned, or that its registered office has been discontinued; or

(5) the corporation's period of duration stated in its articles of incorporation expires.

§ 14.21 Procedure for and Effect of Administrative Dissolution

(a) If the secretary of state determines that one or more grounds exist under section 14.20 for dissolving a corporation, he shall serve the corporation with written notice of his determination under section 5.04.

(b) If the corporation does not correct each ground for dissolution or demonstrate to the reasonable satisfaction of the secretary of state that each ground determined by the secretary of state does not exist within 60 days after service of the notice is perfected under section 5.04, the secretary of state shall administratively dissolve the corporation by signing a certificate of dissolution that recites the ground or grounds for dissolution and its effective date. The secretary of state shall file the original of the certificate and serve a copy on the corporation under section 5.04.

(c) A corporation administratively dissolved continues its corporate existence but may not carry on any business except that necessary to wind up and liquidate its business and affairs under section 14.05 and notify claimants under sections 14.06 and 14.07.

(d) The administrative dissolution of a corporation does not terminate the authority of its registered agent.

§ 14.22 Reinstatement Following Administrative Dissolution

(a) A corporation administratively dissolved under section 14.21 may apply to the secretary of state for reinstatement within two years after the effective date of dissolution. The application must:

(1) recite the name of the corporation and the effective date of its administrative dissolution;

(2) state that the ground or grounds for dissolution either did not exist or have been eliminated;

(3) state that the corporation's name satisfies the requirements of section 4.01; and

(4) contain a certificate from the [taxing authority] reciting that all taxes owed by the corporation have been paid.

(b) If the secretary of state determines that the application contains the information required by subsection (a) and that the information is correct, he shall cancel the certificate of dissolution and prepare a certificate of reinstatement that recites his determination and the effective date of reinstatement, file the original of the certificate, and serve a copy on the corporation under section 5.04.

(c) When the reinstatement is effective, it relates back to and takes effect as of the effective date of the administrative dissolution and the corporation resumes carrying on its business as if the administrative dissolution had never occurred.

§ 14.23 Appeal From Denial of Reinstatement

(a) If the secretary of state denies a corporation's application for reinstatement following administrative dissolution, he shall serve the corporation under section 5.04 with a written notice that explains the reason or reasons for denial.

(b) The corporation may appeal the denial of reinstatement to the [name or describe] court within 30 days after service of the notice of denial is perfected. The corporation appeals by petitioning the court to set aside the dissolution and attaching to the petition copies of the secretary of state's certificate of dissolution, the corporation's application for reinstatement, and the secretary of state's notice of denial.

(c) The court may summarily order the secretary of state to reinstate the dissolved corporation or may take other action the court considers appropriate.

(d) The court's final decision may be appealed as in other civil proceedings.

Subchapter C. Judicial Dissolution

§ 14.30 Grounds for Judicial Dissolution

The [name or describe court or courts] may dissolve a corporation:

(1) in a proceeding by the attorney general if it is established that:

(i) the corporation obtained its articles of incorporation through fraud; or

(ii) the corporation has continued to exceed or abuse the authority conferred upon it by law;

(2) in a proceeding by a shareholder if it is established that:

(i) the directors are deadlocked in the management of the corporate affairs, the shareholders are unable to break the deadlock, and irreparable injury to the corporation is threatened or being suffered, or the business and affairs of the corporation can no longer be conducted to the advantage of the shareholders generally, because of the deadlock;

(ii) the directors or those in control of the corporation have acted, are acting, or will act in a manner that is illegal, oppressive, or fraudulent;

(iii) the shareholders are deadlocked in voting power and have failed, for a period that includes at least two consecutive annual meeting dates, to elect successors to directors whose terms have expired; or

(iv) the corporate assets are being misapplied or wasted;

(3) in a proceeding by a creditor if it is established that:

(i) the creditor's claim has been reduced to judgment, the execution on the judgment returned unsatisfied, and the corporation is insolvent; or

(ii) the corporation has admitted in writing that the creditor's claim is due and owing and the corporation is insolvent; or

(4) in a proceeding by the corporation to have its voluntary dissolution continued under court supervision.

§ 14.31 Procedure for Judicial Dissolution

(a) Venue for a proceeding by the attorney general to dissolve a corporation lies in [name the county or counties]. Venue for a proceeding brought by any other party named in section 14.30 lies in the county where a corporation's principal office (or, if none in this state, its registered office) is or was last located.

(b) It is not necessary to make shareholders parties to a proceeding to dissolve a corporation unless relief is sought against them individually.

(c) A court in a proceeding brought to dissolve a corporation may issue injunctions, appoint a receiver or custodian pendente lite with all powers and duties the court directs, take other action required to preserve the corporate assets wherever located, and carry on the business of the corporation until a full hearing can be held.

§ 14.32 Receivership or Custodianship

(a) A court in a judicial proceeding brought to dissolve a corporation may appoint one or more receivers to wind up and liquidate, or one or more custodians to manage, the business and affairs of the corporation. The court shall hold a hearing, after notifying all parties to the proceeding and any interested persons designated by the court, before appointing a receiver or custodian. The court appointing a receiver or custodian has exclusive jurisdiction over the corporation and all its property wherever located.

(b) The court may appoint an individual or a domestic or foreign corporation (authorized to transact business in this state) as a receiver or custodian. The court may require the receiver or custodian to post bond, with or without sureties, in an amount the court directs.

(c) The court shall describe the powers and duties of the receiver or custodian in its appointing order, which may be amended from time to time. Among other powers:

(1) the receiver (i) may dispose of all or any part of the assets of the corporation wherever located, at a public or private sale, if authorized by the court; and (ii) may sue and defend in his own name as receiver of the corporation in all courts of this state;

(2) the custodian may exercise all of the powers of the corporation, through or in place of its board of directors or officers, to the extent necessary to manage the affairs of the corporation in the best interests of its shareholders and creditors.

(d) The court during a receivership may redesignate the receiver a custodian, and during a custodianship may redesignate the custodian a receiver, if doing so is in the best interests of the corporation, its shareholders, and creditors.

(e) The court from time to time during the receivership or custodianship may order compensation paid and expense disbursements or reimbursements made to the receiver or custodian and his counsel from the assets of the corporation or proceeds from the sale of the assets.

§ 14.33 Decree of Dissolution

(a) If after a hearing the court determines that one or more grounds for judicial dissolution described in section 14.30 exist, it may enter a decree dissolving the corporation and specifying the effective date of the dissolution, and the clerk of the court shall deliver a certified copy of the decree to the secretary of state, who shall file it.

(b) After entering the decree of dissolution, the court shall direct the winding up and liquidation of the corporation's business and affairs in accordance with section 14.05 and the notification of claimants in accordance with sections 14.06 and 14.07.

Subchapter D. Miscellaneous

§ 14.40 Deposit With State Treasurer

Assets of a dissolved corporation that should be transferred to a creditor, claimant, or shareholder of the corporation who cannot be found or who is not competent to receive them shall be reduced to cash and deposited with the state treasurer or other appropriate state official for safekeeping. When the creditor, claimant, or shareholder furnishes satisfactory proof of entitlement to the amount deposited, the state treasurer or other appropriate state official shall pay him or his representative that amount.

CHAPTER 15: FOREIGN CORPORATIONS

Subchapter A. Certificate of Authority

§ 15.01 Authority to Transact Business Required

(a) A foreign corporation may not transact business in this state until it obtains a certificate of authority from the secretary of state.

(b) The following activities, among others, do not constitute transacting business within the meaning of subsection (a):

(1) maintaining, defending, or settling any proceeding;

(2) holding meetings of the board of directors or shareholders or carrying on other activities concerning internal corporate affairs;

(3) maintaining bank accounts;

(4) maintaining offices or agencies for the transfer, exchange, and registration of the corporation's own securities or maintaining trustees or depositaries with respect to those securities;

(5) selling through independent contractors;

(6) soliciting or obtaining orders, whether by mail or through employees or agents or otherwise, if the orders require acceptance outside this state before they become contracts;

(7) creating or acquiring indebtedness, mortgages, and security interests in real or personal property;

(8) securing or collecting debts or enforcing mortgages and security interests in property securing the debts;

(9) owning, without more, real or personal property;

(10) conducting an isolated transaction that is completed within 30 days and that is not one in the course of repeated transactions of a like nature;

(11) transacting business in interstate commerce.

(c) The list of activities in subsection (b) is not exhaustive.

§ 15.02 Consequences of Transacting Business Without Authority

(a) A foreign corporation transacting business in this state without a certificate of authority may not maintain a proceeding in any court in this state until it obtains a certificate of authority.

(b) The successor to a foreign corporation that transacted business in this state without a certificate of authority and the assignee of a cause of action arising out of that business may not maintain a proceeding based on that cause of action in any court in this state until the foreign corporation or its successor obtains a certificate of authority.

(c) A court may stay a proceeding commenced by a foreign corporation, its successor, or assignee until it determines whether the foreign corporation or its successor requires a certificate of authority. If it so determines, the court may further stay the proceeding until the foreign corporation or its successor obtains the certificate.

(d) A foreign corporation is liable for a civil penalty of $ _____ for each day, but not to exceed a total of $ _____

for each year, it transacts business in this state without a certificate of authority. The attorney general may collect all penalties due under this subsection.

(e) Notwithstanding subsections (a) and (b), the failure of a foreign corporation to obtain a certificate of authority does not impair the validity of its corporate acts or prevent it from defending any proceeding in this state.

§ 15.03 Application for Certificate of Authority

(a) A foreign corporation may apply for a certificate of authority to transact business in this state by delivering an application to the secretary of state for filing. The application must set forth:

(1) the name of the foreign corporation or, if its name is unavailable for use in this state, a corporate name that satisfies the requirements of section 15.06;

(2) the name of the state or country under whose law it is incorporated;

(3) its date of incorporation and period of duration;

(4) the street address of its principal office;

(5) the address of its registered office in this state and the name of its registered agent at that office; and

(6) the names and usual business addresses of its current directors and officers.

(b) The foreign corporation shall deliver with the completed application a certificate of existence (or a document of similar import) duly authenticated by the secretary of state or other official having custody of corporate records in the state or country under whose law it is incorporated.

§ 15.04 Amended Certificate of Authority

(a) A foreign corporation authorized to transact business in this state must obtain an amended certificate of authority from the secretary of state if it changes:

(1) its corporate name;

(2) the period of its duration; or

(3) the state or country of its incorporation.

(b) The requirements of section 15.03 for obtaining an original certificate of authority apply to obtaining an amended certificate under this section.

§ 15.05 Effect of Certificate of Authority

(a) A certificate of authority authorizes the foreign corporation to which it is issued to transact business in this state subject, however, to the right of the state to revoke the certificate as provided in this Act.

(b) A foreign corporation with a valid certificate of authority has the same but no greater rights and has the same but no greater privileges as, and except as otherwise provided by this Act is subject to the same duties, restrictions, penalties, and liabilities now or later imposed on, a domestic corporation of like character.

(c) This Act does not authorize this state to regulate the organization or internal affairs of a foreign corporation authorized to transact business in this state.

§ 15.06 Corporate Name of Foreign Corporation

(a) If the corporate name of a foreign corporation does not satisfy the requirements of section 4.01, the foreign corporation to obtain or maintain a certificate of authority to transact business in this state:

(1) may add the word "corporation," "incorporated," "company," or "limited," or the abbreviation "corp.," "inc.," "co.," or "ltd.," to its corporate name for use in this state; or

(2) may use a fictitious name to transact business in this state if its real name is unavailable and it delivers to the secretary of state for filing a copy of the resolution of its board of directors, certified by its secretary, adopting the fictitious name.

(b) Except as authorized by subsections (c) and (d), the corporate name (including a fictitious name) of a foreign corporation must be distinguishable upon the records of the secretary of state from:

(1) the corporate name of a corporation incorporated or authorized to transact business in this state;

(2) a corporate name reserved or registered under section 4.02 or 4.03;

(3) the fictitious name of another foreign corporation authorized to transact business in this state; and

(4) the corporate name of a not-for-profit corporation incorporated or authorized to transact business in this state.

(c) A foreign corporation may apply to the secretary of state for authorization to use in this state the name of another corporation (incorporated or authorized to transact business in this state) that is not distinguishable upon his records from the name applied for. The secretary of state shall authorize use of the name applied for if:

(1) the other corporation consents to the use in writing and submits an undertaking in form satisfactory to the secretary of state to change its name to a name that is distinguishable upon the records of the secretary of state from the name of the applying corporation; or

(2) the applicant delivers to the secretary of state a certified copy of a final judgment of a court of competent jurisdiction establishing the applicant's right to use the name applied for in this state.

(d) A foreign corporation may use in this state the name (including the fictitious name) of another domestic or foreign corporation that is used in this state if the other corporation is incorporated or authorized to transact business in this state and the foreign corporation:

(1) has merged with the other corporation;

(2) has been formed by reorganization of the other corporation; or

(3) has acquired all or substantially all of the assets, including the corporate name, of the other corporation.

(e) If a foreign corporation authorized to transact business in this state changes its corporate name to one that does not satisfy the requirements of section 4.01, it may not transact business in this state under the changed name until it adopts a name satisfying the requirements of section 4.01 and obtains an amended certificate of authority under section 15.04.

§ 15.07 Registered Office and Registered Agent of Foreign Corporation

Each foreign corporation authorized to transact business in this state must continuously maintain in this state:

(1) a registered office that may be the same as any of its places of business; and

(2) a registered agent, who may be:

(i) an individual who resides in this state and whose business office is identical with the registered office;

(ii) a domestic corporation or not-for-profit domestic corporation whose business office is identical with the registered office; or

(iii) a foreign corporation or foreign not-for-profit corporation authorized to transact business in this state whose business office is identical with the registered office.

§ 15.08 Change of Registered Office or Registered Agent of Foreign Corporation

(a) A foreign corporation authorized to transact business in this state may change its registered office or registered agent by delivering to the secretary of state for filing a statement of change that sets forth:

(1) its name;

(2) the street address of its current registered office;

(3) if the current registered office is to be changed, the street address of its new registered office;

(4) the name of its current registered agent;

(5) if the current registered agent is to be changed, the name of its new registered agent and the new agent's written consent (either on the statement or attached to it) to the appointment; and

(6) that after the change or changes are made, the street addresses of its registered office and the business office of its registered agent will be identical.

(b) If a registered agent changes the street address of his business office, he may change the street address of the registered office of any foreign corporation for which he is the registered agent by notifying the corporation in writing of the change and signing (either manually or in facsimile) and delivering to the secretary of state for filing a statement of change that complies with the requirements of subsection (a) and recites that the corporation has been notified of the change.

§ 15.09 Resignation of Registered Agent of Foreign Corporation

(a) The registered agent of a foreign corporation may resign his agency appointment by signing and delivering to the secretary of state for filing the original and two exact or conformed copies of a statement of resignation. The statement of resignation may include a statement that the registered office is also discontinued.

(b) After filing the statement, the secretary of state shall attach the filing receipt to one copy and mail the copy and receipt to the registered office if not discontinued. The secretary of state shall mail the other copy to the foreign corporation at its principal office address shown in its most recent annual report.

(c) The agency appointment is terminated, and the registered office discontinued if so provided, on the 31st day after the date on which the statement was filed.

§ 15.10 Service on Foreign Corporation

(a) The registered agent of a foreign corporation authorized to transact business in this state is the corporation's agent for service of process, notice, or demand required or permitted by law to be served on the foreign corporation.

(b) A foreign corporation may be served by registered or certified mail, return receipt requested, addressed to the secretary of the foreign corporation at its principal office shown in its application for a certificate of authority or in its most recent annual report if the foreign corporation:

(1) has no registered agent or its registered agent cannot with reasonable diligence be served;

(2) has withdrawn from transacting business in this state under section 15.20; or

(3) has had its certificate of authority revoked under section 15.31.

(c) Service is perfected under subsection (b) at the earliest of:

(1) the date the foreign corporation receives the mail;

(2) the date shown on the return receipt, if signed on behalf of the foreign corporation; or

(3) five days after its deposit in the United States Mail, as evidenced by the postmark, if mailed postpaid and correctly addressed.

(d) This section does not prescribe the only means, or necessarily the required means, of serving a foreign corporation.

Subchapter B. Withdrawal

§ 15.20 Withdrawal of Foreign Corporation

(a) A foreign corporation authorized to transact business in this state may not withdraw from this state until it obtains a certificate of withdrawal from the secretary of state.

(b) A foreign corporation authorized to transact business in this state may apply for a certificate of withdrawal by delivering an application to the secretary of state for filing. The application must set forth:

(1) the name of the foreign corporation and the name of the state or country under whose law it is incorporated;

(2) that it is not transacting business in this state and that it surrenders its authority to transact business in this state;

(3) that it revokes the authority of its registered agent to accept service on its behalf and appoints the secretary of state as its agent for service of process in any proceeding based on a cause of action arising during the time it was authorized to transact business in this state;

(4) a mailing address to which the secretary of state may mail a copy of any process served on him under subdivision (3); and

(5) a commitment to notify the secretary of state in the future of any change in its mailing address.

(c) After the withdrawal of the corporation is effective, service of process on the secretary of state under this section is service on the foreign corporation. Upon receipt of process, the secretary of state shall mail a copy of the process to the foreign corporation at the mailing address set forth under subsection (b).

Subchapter C. Revocation of Certificate of Authority

§ 15.30 Grounds for Revocation

The secretary of state may commence a proceeding under section 15.31 to revoke the certificate of authority of a foreign corporation authorized to transact business in this state if:

(1) the foreign corporation does not deliver its annual report to the secretary of state within 60 days after it is due;

(2) the foreign corporation does not pay within 60 days after they are due any franchise taxes or penalties imposed by this Act or other law;

(3) the foreign corporation is without a registered agent or registered office in this state for 60 days or more;

(4) the foreign corporation does not inform the secretary of state under section 15.08 or 15.09 that its registered agent or registered office has changed, that its registered agent has resigned, or that its registered office has been discontinued within 60 days of the change, resignation, or discontinuance;

(5) an incorporator, director, officer, or agent of the foreign corporation signed a document he knew was false in any material respect with intent that the document be delivered to the secretary of state for filing;

(6) the secretary of state receives a duly authenticated certificate from the secretary of state or other official having custody of corporate records in the state or country under whose law the foreign corporation is incorporated stating that it has been dissolved or disappeared as a result of a merger.

§ 15.31 Procedure for and Effect of Revocation

(a) If the secretary of state determines that one or more grounds exist under section 15.30 for revocation of a certificate of authority, he shall serve the foreign corporation with written notice of his determination under section 15.10.

(b) If the foreign corporation does not correct each ground for revocation or demonstrate to the reasonable satisfaction of the secretary of state that each ground determined by the secretary of state does not exist within 60 days after service of the notice is perfected under section 15.10, the secretary of state may revoke the foreign corporation's certificate of authority by signing a certificate of revocation that recites the ground or grounds for revocation and its effective date. The secretary of state shall file the original of the certificate and serve a copy on the foreign corporation under section 15.10.

(c) The authority of a foreign corporation to transact business in this state ceases on the date shown on the certificate revoking its certificate of authority.

(d) The secretary of state's revocation of a foreign corporation's certificate of authority appoints the secretary of state the foreign corporation's agent for service of process in any proceeding based on a cause of action which arose during the time the foreign corporation was authorized to transact business in this state. Service of process on the secretary of state under this subsection is service on the foreign corporation. Upon receipt of process, the secretary of state shall mail a copy of the process to the secretary of the foreign corporation at its principal office shown in its most recent annual report or in any subsequent communication received from the corporation stating the current mailing address of its principal office, or, if none are on file, in its application for a certificate of authority.

(e) Revocation of a foreign corporation's certificate of authority does not terminate the authority of the registered agent of the corporation.

§ 15.32 Appeal From Revocation

(a) A foreign corporation may appeal the secretary of state's revocation of its certificate of authority to the [name or describe] court within 30 days after service of the certificate of revocation is perfected under section 15.10. The foreign corporation appeals by petitioning the court to set aside the revocation and attaching to the petition copies of its certificate of authority and the secretary of state's certificate of revocation.

(b) The court may summarily order the secretary of state to reinstate the certificate of authority or may take any other action the court considers appropriate.

(c) The court's final decision may be appealed as in other civil proceedings.

CHAPTER 16: RECORDS AND REPORTS

Subchapter A. Records

§ 16.01 Corporate Records

(a) A corporation shall keep as permanent records minutes of all meetings of its shareholders and board of directors, a record of all actions taken by the shareholders or board of directors without a meeting, and a record of all actions taken by a committee of the board of directors in place of the board of directors on behalf of the corporation.

(b) A corporation shall maintain appropriate accounting records.

(c) A corporation or its agent shall maintain a record of its shareholders, in a form that permits preparation of a list of the names and addresses of all shareholders, in alphabetical order by class of shares showing the number and class of shares held by each.

(d) A corporation shall maintain its records in written form or in another form capable of conversion into written form within a reasonable time.

(e) A corporation shall keep a copy of the following records at its principal office:

(1) its articles or restated articles of incorporation and all amendments to them currently in effect;

(2) its bylaws or restated bylaws and all amendments to them currently in effect;

(3) resolutions adopted by its board of directors creating one or more classes or series of shares, and fixing their relative rights, preferences, and limitations, if shares issued pursuant to those resolutions are outstanding;

(4) the minutes of all shareholders' meetings, and records of all action taken by shareholders without a meeting, for the past three years;

(5) all written communications to shareholders generally within the past three years, including the financial statements furnished for the past three years under section 16.20;

(6) a list of the names and business addresses of its current directors and officers; and

(7) its most recent annual report delivered to the secretary of state under section 16.22.

§ 16.02 Inspection of Records by Shareholders

(a) Subject to section 16.03(c), a shareholder of a corporation is entitled to inspect and copy, during regular business hours at the corporation's principal office, any of the records of the corporation described in section 16.01(e) if he gives the corporation written notice of his demand at least five business days before the date on which he wishes to inspect and copy.

(b) A shareholder of a corporation is entitled to inspect and copy, during regular business hours at a reasonable location specified by the corporation, any of the following records of the corporation if the shareholder meets the requirements of subsection (c) and gives the corporation written notice of his demand at least five business days before the date on which he wishes to inspect and copy:

(1) excerpts from minutes of any meeting of the board of directors, records of any action of a committee of the board of directors while acting in place of the board of directors on behalf of the corporation, minutes of any meeting of the shareholders, and records of action taken by the shareholders or board of directors without a meeting, to the extent not subject to inspection under section 16.02(a);

(2) accounting records of the corporation; and

(3) the record of shareholders.

(c) A shareholder may inspect and copy the records identified in subsection (b) only if:

(1) his demand is made in good faith and for a proper purpose;

(2) he describes with reasonable particularity his purpose and the records he desires to inspect; and

(3) the records are directly connected with his purpose.

(d) The right of inspection granted by this section may not be abolished or limited by a corporation's articles of incorporation or bylaws.

(e) This section does not affect:

(1) the right of a shareholder to inspect records under section 7.20 or, if the shareholder is in litigation with the corporation, to the same extent as any other litigant;

(2) the power of a court, independently of this Act, to compel the production of corporate records for examination.

§ 16.03 Scope of Inspection Right

(a) A shareholder's agent or attorney has the same inspection and copying rights as the shareholder he represents.

(b) The right to copy records under section 16.02 includes, if reasonable, the right to receive copies made by photographic, xerographic, or other means.

(c) The corporation may impose a reasonable charge, covering the costs of labor and material, for copies of any documents provided to the shareholder. The charge may not exceed the estimated cost of production or reproduction of the records.

(d) The corporation may comply with a shareholder's demand to inspect the record of shareholders under section 16.02(b)(3) by providing him with a list of its shareholders that was compiled no earlier than the date of the shareholder's demand.

§ 16.04 Court-Ordered Inspection

(a) If a corporation does not allow a shareholder who complies with section 16.02(a) to inspect and copy any records required by that subsection to be available for inspection, the [name or describe court] of the county where the corporation's principal office (or, if none in this state, its registered office) is located may summarily order inspection and copying of the records demanded at the corporation's expense upon application of the shareholder.

(b) If a corporation does not within a reasonable time allow a shareholder to inspect and copy any other record, the shareholder who complies with section 16.02(b) and (c) may apply to the [name or describe court] in the county where the corporation's principal office (or, if none in this state, its registered office) is located for an order to permit inspection and copying of the records demanded. The court shall dispose of an application under this subsection on an expedited basis.

(c) If the court orders inspection and copying of the records demanded, it shall also order the corporation to pay the shareholder's costs (including reasonable counsel fees) incurred to obtain the order unless the corporation proves that it refused inspection in good faith because it had a reasonable basis for doubt about the right of the shareholder to inspect the records demanded.

(d) If the court orders inspection and copying of the records demanded, it may impose reasonable restrictions on the use or distribution of the records by the demanding shareholder.

Subchapter B. Reports

§ 16.20 Financial Statements for Shareholders

(a) A corporation shall furnish its shareholders annual financial statements, which may be consolidated or combined statements of the corporation and one or more of its subsidiaries, as appropriate, that include a balance sheet as of the end of the fiscal year, an income statement for that year, and a statement of changes in shareholders' equity for the year unless that information appears elsewhere in the financial statements. If financial statements are prepared for the corporation on the basis of generally accepted accounting principles, the annual financial statements must also be prepared on that basis.

(b) If the annual financial statements are reported upon by a public accountant, his report must accompany them. If not, the statements must be accompanied by a statement of the president or the person responsible for the corporation's accounting records:

(1) stating his reasonable belief whether the statements were prepared on the basis of generally accepted accounting principles and, if not, describing the basis of preparation; and

(2) describing any respects in which the statements were not prepared on a basis of accounting consistent with the statements prepared for the preceding year.

(c) A corporation shall mail the annual financial statements to each shareholder within 120 days after the close of each fiscal year. Thereafter, on written request from a shareholder who was not mailed the statements, the corporation shall mail him the latest financial statements.

§ 16.21 Other Reports to Shareholders

(a) If a corporation indemnifies or advances expenses to a director under section 8.51, 8.52, 8.53, or 8.54 in connection with a proceeding by or in the right of the corporation, the corporation shall report the indemnification or advance in writing to the shareholders with or before the notice of the next shareholders' meeting.

(b) If a corporation issues or authorizes the issuance of shares for promissory notes or for promises to render services in the future, the corporation shall report in writing to the shareholders the number of shares authorized or issued, and the consideration received by the corporation, with or before the notice of the next shareholders' meeting.

§ 16.22 Annual Report for Secretary of State

(a) Each domestic corporation, and each foreign corporation authorized to transact business in this state, shall deliver to the secretary of state for filing an annual report that sets forth:

(1) the name of the corporation and the state or country under whose law it is incorporated;

(2) the address of its registered office and the name of its registered agent at that office in this state;

(3) the address of its principal office;

(4) the names and business addresses of its directors and principal officers;

(5) a brief description of the nature of its business;

(6) the total number of authorized shares, itemized by class and series, if any, within each class; and

(7) the total number of issued and outstanding shares, itemized by class and series, if any, within each class.

(b) Information in the annual report must be current as of the date the annual report is executed on behalf of the corporation.

(c) The first annual report must be delivered to the secretary of state between January 1 and April 1 of the year following the calendar year in which a domestic corporation was incorporated or a foreign corporation was authorized to transact business. Subsequent annual reports must be delivered to the secretary of state between January 1 and April 1 of the following calendar years.

(d) If an annual report does not contain the information required by this section, the secretary of state shall promptly notify the reporting domestic or foreign corporation in writing and return the report to it for correction. If the report is corrected to contain the information required by this section and delivered to the secretary of state within 30 days after the effective date of notice, it is deemed to be timely filed.

CHAPTER 17: TRANSITION PROVISIONS

§ 17.01 Application to Existing Domestic Corporations

This Act applies to all domestic corporations in existence on its effective date that were incorporated under any general statute of this state providing for incorporation of corporations for profit if power to amend or repeal the statute under which the corporation was incorporated was reserved.

§ 17.02 Application to Qualified Foreign Corporations

A foreign corporation authorized to transact business in this state on the effective date of this Act is subject to this Act but is not required to obtain a new certificate of authority to transact business under this Act.

§ 17.03 Saving Provisions

(a) Except as provided in subsection (b), the repeal of a statute by this Act does not affect:

(1) the operation of the statute or any action taken under it before its repeal;

(2) any ratification, right, remedy, privilege, obligation, or liability acquired, accrued, or incurred under the statute before its repeal;

(3) any violation of the statute, or any penalty, forfeiture, or punishment incurred because of the violation, before its repeal;

(4) any proceeding, reorganization, or dissolution commenced under the statute before its repeal, and the proceeding, reorganization, or dissolution may be completed in accordance with the statute as if it had not been repealed.

(b) If a penalty or punishment imposed for violation of a statute repealed by this Act is reduced by this Act, the penalty or punishment if not already imposed shall be imposed in accordance with this Act.

§ 17.04 Severability

If any provision of this Act or its application to any person or circumstance is held invalid by a court of competent jurisdiction, the invalidity does not affect other provisions or applications of the Act that can be given effect without the invalid provision or application, and to this end the provisions of the Act are severable.

§ 17.05 Repeal

The following laws and parts of laws are repealed: [to be inserted].

§ 17.06 Effective Date

This Act takes effect _____ .

Appendix H

SELECTED PROVISIONS OF THE MODEL BUSINESS CORPORATION ACT

§ 15. Authorized Shares

Each corporation shall have power to create and issue the number of shares stated in its articles of incorporation. Such shares may be divided into one or more classes with such designations, preferences, limitations, and relative rights as shall be stated in the articles of incorporation. The articles of incorporation may limit or deny the voting rights of or provide special voting rights for the shares of any class to the extent not inconsistent with the provisions of this Act.

Without limiting the authority herein contained, a corporation, when so provided in its articles of incorporation, may issue shares of preferred or special classes:

(a) Subject to the right of the corporation to redeem any of such shares at the price fixed by the articles of incorporation for the redemption thereof.

(b) Entitling the holders thereof to cumulative, noncumulative or partially cumulative dividends.

(c) Having preference over any other class or classes of shares as to the payment of dividends.

(d) Having preference in the assets of the corporation over any other class or classes of shares upon the voluntary or involuntary liquidation of the corporation.

(e) Convertible into shares of any other class or into shares of any series of the same or any other class, except a class having prior or superior rights and preferences as to dividends or distribution of assets upon liquidation.

§ 18. Issuance for Shares

Subject to any restrictions in the articles of incorporation:

(a) Shares may be issued for such consideration as shall be authorized by the board of directors establishing a price (in money or other consideration) or a minimum price or general formula or method by which the price will be determined; and

(b) Upon authorization by the board of directors, the corporation may issue its own shares in exchange for or in conversion of its outstanding shares, or distribute its own shares, pro rata to its shareholders or the shareholders of one or more classes or series, to effectuate stock dividends or splits, and any such transaction shall not require consideration; provided, that no such issuance of shares of any class or series shall be made to the holders of shares of any other class or series unless it is either expressly provided for in the articles of incorporation, or is authorized by an affirmative vote or the written consent of the holders of at least a majority of the outstanding shares of the class or series in which the distribution is to be made.

§ 19. Payment for Shares

The consideration for the issuance of shares may be paid, in whole or in part, in cash, in other property, tangible or intangible, or in labor or services actually performed for the corporation. When payment of the consideration for which shares are to be issued shall have been received by the corporation, such shares shall be nonassessable.

Neither promissory notes nor future services shall constitute payment or part payment for the issuance of shares of a corporation.

In the absence of fraud in the transaction, the judgment of the board of directors or the shareholders, as the case may be, as to the value of the consideration received for shares shall be conclusive.

§ 25. Liability of Subscribers and Shareholders

A holder of or subscriber to shares of a corporation shall be under no obligation to the corporation or its creditors with respect to such shares other than the obligation to pay to the corporation the full consideration for which such shares were issued or to be issued.

Any person becoming an assignee or transferee of shares or of a subscription for shares in good faith and without knowledge or notice that the full consideration therefor has not been paid shall not be personally liable to the corporation or its creditors for any unpaid portion of such consideration.

An executor, administrator, conservator, guardian, trustee, assignee for the benefit of creditors, or receiver shall not be personally liable to the corporation as a holder of or subscriber to shares of a corporation but the estate and funds in his hands shall be so liable.

No pledgee or other holder of shares as collateral security shall be personally liable as a shareholder.

§ 26. Shareholders' Preemptive Rights

The shareholders of a corporation shall have no preemptive right to acquire unissued shares of the corporation, or securities of the corporation convertible into or carrying a right to subscribe to or acquire shares, except to the extent, if any, that such right is provided in the articles of incorporation.

§ 26A. Shareholders' Preemptive Rights [Alternative]

Except to the extent limited or denied by this section or by the articles of incorporation, shareholders shall have a preemptive right to acquire unissued shares or securities convertible into such shares or carrying a right to subscribe to or acquire shares.

Unless otherwise provided in the articles of incorporation,

(a) No preemptive right shall exist

(1) to acquire any shares issued to directors, officers or employees pursuant to approval by the affirmative vote of the holders of a majority of the shares entitled to vote thereon or when authorized by and consistent with a plan theretofore approved by such a vote of shareholders; or

(2) to acquire any shares sold otherwise than for money.

(b) Holders of shares of any class that is preferred or limited as to dividends or assets shall not be entitled to any preemptive right.

(c) Holders of shares of common stock shall not be entitled to any preemptive right to shares of any class that is preferred or limited as to dividends or assets or to any obligations, unless convertible into shares of common stock or carrying a right to subscribe to or acquire shares of common stock.

(d) Holders of common stock without voting power shall have no preemptive right to shares of common stock with voting power.

(e) The preemptive right shall be only an opportunity to acquire shares or other securities under such terms and conditions as the board of directors may fix for the purpose of providing a fair and reasonable opportunity for the exercise of such right.

§ 28. Meetings of Shareholders

Meetings of shareholders may be held at such place within or without this State as may be stated in or fixed in accordance with the by-laws. If no other place is stated or so fixed, meetings shall be held at the registered office of the corporation.

An annual meeting of the shareholders shall be held at such time as may be stated in or fixed in accordance with the by-laws. If the annual meeting is not held within any thirteen-month period the Court of _____ may, on the application of any shareholder, summarily order a meeting to be held.

A special meeting of the shareholders may be called by the board of directors, the holders of not less than one-tenth of all the shares entitled to vote at the meeting, or such other persons as may be authorized in the articles of incorporation or the by-laws.

§ 35. Board of Directors

All corporate powers shall be exercised by or under authority of, and the business and affairs of a corporation shall be managed under the direction of, a board of directors except as may be otherwise provided in this Act or the articles of incorporation. If any such provision is made in the articles of incorporation, the powers and duties conferred or imposed upon the board of directors by this Act shall be exercised or performed to such extent and by such person or persons as shall be provided in the articles of incorporation. Directors need not be residents of this State or shareholders of the corporation unless the articles of incorporation or by-laws so require. The articles of incorporation or by-laws may prescribe other qualifications for directors. The board of directors shall have authority to fix the compensation of directors unless otherwise provided in the articles of incorporation.

A director shall perform his duties as a director, including his duties as a member of any committee of the board upon which he may serve, in good faith, in a manner he reasonably believes to be in the best interests of the corporation, and with such care as an ordinarily prudent person in a like position would use under similar circumstances. In performing his duties, a director shall be entitled to rely on information, opinions, reports or statements, including financial statements and other financial data, in each case prepared or presented by:

(a) one or more officers or employees of the corporation whom the director reasonably believes to be reliable and competent in the matters presented,

(b) counsel, public accountants or other persons as to matters which the director reasonably believes to be within such person's professional or expert competence, or

(c) a committee of the board upon which he does not serve, duly designated in accordance with a provision of the articles of incorporation or the by-laws, as to matters within its designated authority, which committee the director reasonably believes to merit confidence,

but he shall not be considered to be acting in good faith if he has knowledge concerning the matter in question that would cause such reliance to be unwarranted. A person who so performs his duties shall have no liability by reason of being or having been a director of the corporation.

A director of a corporation who is present at a meeting of its board of directors at which action on any corporate matter is taken shall be presumed to have assented to the action taken unless his dissent shall be entered in the minutes of the meeting or unless he shall file his written dissent to such action with the secretary of the meeting before the adjournment thereof or shall forward such dissent by registered mail to the secretary of the corporation immediately after the adjournment of the meeting. Such right to dissent shall not apply to a director who voted in favor of such action.

§ 38. Vacancies

Any vacancy occurring in the board of directors may be filled by the affirmative vote of a majority of the remaining directors though less than a quorum of the board of directors. A director elected to fill a vacancy shall be elected for the unexpired term of his predecessor in office. Any directorship to be filled by reason of an increase in the number of directors may be filled by the board of directors for a term of office continuing only until the next election of directors by the shareholders.

§ 40. Quorum of Directors

A majority of the number of directors fixed by or in the manner provided in the by-laws or in the absence of a by-law fixing or providing for the number of directors, then of the number stated in the articles of incorporation, shall constitute a quorum for the transaction of business unless a greater number is required by the articles of incorporation or the by-laws. The act of the majority of the directors present at a meeting at which a quorum is present shall be the act of the board of directors, unless the act of a greater number is required by the articles of incorporation or the by-laws.

§ 41. Director Conflicts of Interest

No contract or other transaction between a corporation and one or more of its directors or any other corporation,

firm, association or entity in which one or more of its directors are directors or officers or are financially interested, shall be either void or voidable because of such relationship or interest or because such director or directors are present at the meeting of the board of directors or a committee thereof which authorizes, approves or ratifies such contract or transaction or because his or their votes are counted for such purpose, if:

(a) the fact of such relationship or interest is disclosed or known to the board of directors or committee which authorizes, approves or ratifies the contract or transaction by a vote or consent sufficient for the purpose without counting the votes or consents of such interested directors; or

(b) the fact of such relationship or interest is disclosed or known to the shareholders entitled to vote and they authorize, approve or ratify such contract or transaction by vote or written consent; or

(c) the contract or transaction is fair and reasonable to the corporation.

Common or interested directors may be counted in determining the presence of a quorum at a meeting of the board of directors or a committee thereof which authorizes, approves or ratifies such contract or transaction.

§ 45. Distributions to Shareholders

Subject to any restrictions in the articles of incorporation, the board of directors may authorize and the corporation may make distributions, except that no distribution may be made if, after giving effect thereto, either:

(a) the corporation would be unable to pay its debts as they become due in the usual course of its business; or

(b) the corporation's total assets would be less than the sum of its total liabilities and (unless the articles of incorporation otherwise permit) the maximum amount that then would be payable, in any liquidation, in respect of all outstanding shares having preferential rights in liquidation.

Determinations under subparagraph (b) may be based upon (i) financial statements prepared on the basis of accounting practices and principles that are reasonable in the circumstances, or (ii) a fair valuation or other method that is reasonable in the circumstances.

In the case of a purchase, redemption or other acquisition of a corporation's shares, the effect of a distribution shall be measured as of the date money or other property is transferred or debt is incurred by the corporation, or as of the date the shareholder ceases to be a shareholder of the corporation with respect to such shares, whichever is earlier. In all other cases, the effect of a distribution shall be measured as of the date of its authorization if payment occurs 120 days or less following the date of authorization, or as of the date of payment if payment occurs more than 120 days following the date of authorization.

Indebtedness of a corporation incurred or issued to a shareholder in a distribution in accordance with this Section shall be on a parity with the indebtedness of the corporation to its general unsecured creditors except to the extent subordinated by agreement.

§ 47. Loans to Employees and Directors

A corporation shall not lend money to or use its credit to assist its directors without authorization in the particular case by its shareholders, but may lend money to and use its credit to assist any employee of the corporation or of a subsidiary, including any such employee who is a director of the corporation, if the board of directors decides that such loan or assistance may benefit the corporation.

§ 48. Liability of Directors in Certain Cases

In addition to any other liabilities, a director who votes for or assents to any distribution contrary to the provisions of this Act or contrary to any restrictions contained in the articles of incorporation, shall, unless he complies with the standard provided in this Act for the performance of the duties of directors, be liable to the corporation, jointly and severally with all other directors so voting or assenting, for the amount of such dividend which is paid or the value of such distribution in excess of the amount of such distribution which could have been made without a violation of the provisions of this Act or the restrictions in the articles of incorporation.

Any director against whom a claim shall be asserted under or pursuant to this section for the making of a distribution and who shall be held liable thereon, shall be entitled to contribution from the shareholders who accepted or received any such distribution, knowing such distribution to have been made in violation of this Act, in proportion to the amounts received by them.

Any director against whom a claim shall be asserted under or pursuant to this section shall be entitled to contribution from any other director who voted for or assented to the action upon which the claim is asserted and who did not comply with the standard provided in this Act for the performance of the duties of directors.

§ 49. Provisions Relating to Actions by Shareholders

No action shall be brought in this State by a shareholder in the right of a domestic or foreign corporation unless the plaintiff was a holder of record of shares or of voting trust certificates therefor at the time of the transaction of which he complains, or his shares or voting trust certificates thereafter devolved upon him by operation of law from a person who was a holder of record at such time.

In any action hereafter instituted in the right of any domestic or foreign corporation by the holder or holders of record of shares of such corporation or of voting trust certificates therefor, the court having jurisdiction, upon final judgment and a finding that the action was brought without reasonable cause, may require the plaintiff or plaintiffs to pay to the parties named as defendant the reasonable expenses, including fees of attorneys, incurred by them in the defense of such action.

In any action now pending or hereafter instituted or maintained in the right of any domestic or foreign corporation by the holder or holders of record of less than five per cent of the outstanding shares of any class of such corporation or of voting trust certificates therefor, unless the shares or voting trust certificates so held have a market value in excess of twenty-five thousand dollars, the corporation in whose right such action is brought shall be entitled at any time before final judgment to require the plaintiff or plaintiffs to give security for the reasonable expenses, including fees of attorneys, that may be incurred by it in connection with such action or may be incurred by other parties named as defendant for which it may become legally liable. Market value shall be determined as of the date that the plaintiff institutes the action or, in the case of an intervenor, as of the date that he becomes a party to the action. The amount of such security may from time to time be increased or decreased, in the discretion of the court, upon showing that the security provided has or may become inadequate or is excessive. The corporation shall have recourse to such security in such amount as the court having jurisdiction shall determine upon the termination of such action, whether or not the court finds the action was brought without reasonable cause.

§ 50. Officers

The officers of a corporation shall consist of a president, one or more vice presidents as may be prescribed by the by-laws, a secretary, and a treasurer, each of whom shall be elected by the board of directors at such time and in such manner as may be prescribed by the by-laws. Such other officers and assistant officers and agents as may be deemed necessary may be elected or appointed by the board of directors or chosen in such other manner as may be prescribed by the by-laws. Any two or more offices may be held by the same person, except the offices of president and secretary.

All officers and agents of the corporation, as between themselves and the corporation, shall have such authority and perform such duties in the management of the corporation as may be provided in the by-laws, or as may be determined by resolution of the board of directors not inconsistent with the by-laws.

§ 52. Books and Records: Financial Reports to Shareholders; Examination of Records

Each corporation shall keep correct and complete books and records of account and shall keep minutes of the proceedings of its shareholders and board of directors and shall keep at its registered office or principal place of business, or at the office of its transfer agent or registrar, a record of its shareholders, giving the names and addresses of all shareholders and the number and class of the shares held by each. Any books, records and minutes may be in written form or in any form capable of being converted into written form within a reasonable time.

Any person who shall have been a holder of record of shares or of voting trust certificates therefor at least six months immediately preceding his demand or shall be the holder of record of, or the holder of record of voting trust certificates for, at least five percent of all the outstanding shares of the corporation, upon written demand stating the purpose thereof, shall have the right to examine, in person, or by agent or attorney, at any reasonable time or times, for any proper purpose its relevant books and records of accounts, minutes, and record of shareholders and to make extracts therefrom.

Any officer or agent who, or a corporation which, shall refuse to allow any such shareholder or holder of voting trust certificates, or his agent or attorney, so to examine and make extracts from its books and records of account, minutes, and record of shareholders, for any proper purpose, shall be liable to such shareholder or holder of voting trust certificates in a penalty of ten per cent of the value of the shares owned by such shareholder, or in respect of which such voting trust certificates are issued, in addition to any other damages or remedy afforded him by law. It shall be a defense to any action for penalties under this section that the person suing therefor has within two years sold or offered for sale any list of shareholders or of holders of voting trust certificates for shares of such corporation or any other corporation or has aided or abetted any person in procuring any list of shareholders or of holders of voting trust certificates for any such purpose, or has improperly used any information secured through any prior examination of the books and records of account, or minutes, or record of shareholders or of holders of voting trust certificates for shares of such corporation or any other corporation, or was not acting in good faith or for a proper purpose in making his demand.

Nothing herein contained shall impair the power of any court of competent jurisdiction, upon proof by a shareholder or holder of voting trust certificates of proper purpose, irrespective of the period of time during which such shareholder or holder of voting trust certificates shall have been a shareholder of record or a holder of record of voting trust certificates, and irrespective of the number of shares held by him or represented by voting trust certificates held by him, to compel the production for examination by such shareholder or holder of voting trust certificates of the books and records of account, minutes and record of shareholders of a corporation.

Each corporation shall furnish to its shareholders annual financial statements, including at least a balance sheet as of the end of each fiscal year and a statement of income for such fiscal year, which shall be prepared on the basis of generally accepted accounting principles, if the corporation prepares financial statements for such fiscal year on that basis for any purpose, and may consolidate statements of the corporation and one or more of its subsidiaries. The financial statements shall be mailed by the corporation to each of its shareholders within 120 days after the close of each fiscal year and, after such mailing and upon written request, shall be mailed by the corporation to any shareholder (or holder of a voting trust certificate for its shares) to whom a copy of the most recent annual financial statements has not previously been mailed. In the case of statements audited by a public accountant, each copy shall be accompanied by a report setting forth his opinion thereon; in other cases, each copy shall be accompanied by a statement of the president or the person in charge of the corporation's financial accounting records (1) stating his reasonable belief as to whether or not the financial statements were prepared in accordance with generally accepted accounting principles and, if not, describing the basis of presentation, and (2) describing any respects in which the financial statements were not prepared on a basis consistent with those prepared for the previous year.

§ 56. Effect of Issuance of Certificate of Incorporation

Upon the issuance of the certificate of incorporation, the corporate existence shall begin, and such certificate of incorporation shall be conclusive evidence that all conditions precedent required to be performed by the incorporators have been complied with and that the corporation has been incorporated under this Act, except as against this State in a proceeding to cancel or revoke the certificate of incorporation or for involuntary dissolution of the corporation.

§ 72. Procedure for Consolidation

Any two or more domestic corporations may consolidate into a new corporation pursuant to a plan of consolidation approved in the manner provided in this Act.

The board of directors of each corporation shall, by a resolution adopted by each such board, approve a plan of consolidation setting forth:

(a) The names of the corporations proposing to consolidate, and the name of the new corporation into which they propose to consolidate, which is hereinafter designated as the new corporation.

(b) The terms and conditions of the proposed consolidation.

(c) The manner and basis of converting the shares of each corporation into shares, obligations or other securities of the new corporation or of any other corporation or, in whole or in part, into cash or other property.

(d) With respect to the new corporation, all of the statements required to be set forth in articles of incorporation for corporations organized under this Act.

(e) Such other provisions with respect to the proposed consolidation as are deemed necessary or desirable.

§ 73. Approval by Shareholders

(a) The board of directors of each corporation in the case of a merger or consolidation, and the board of directors of the corporation the shares of which are to be acquired in the case of an exchange, upon approving such a plan of merger, consolidation or exchange, shall, by resolution, direct that the plan be submitted to a vote at a meeting of its shareholders, which may be either an annual or a special meeting. Written notice shall be given to each shareholder of record, whether or not entitled to vote at such meeting, not less than twenty days before such meeting, in the manner provided in this Act for the giving of notice of meetings of shareholders, and, whether the meeting be an annual or a special meeting, shall state that the purpose or one of the purposes is to consider the proposed plan of merger, consolidation or exchange. A copy or a summary of the plan of merger, consolidation or exchange, as the case may be, shall be included in or enclosed with such notice.

(b) At each such meeting, a vote of the shareholders shall be taken on the proposed plan. The plan shall be approved upon receiving the affirmative vote of the holders of a majority of the shares entitled to vote thereon of each such corporation, unless any class of shares of any such corporation is entitled to vote thereon as a class, in which event, as to such corporation, the plan shall be approved upon receiving the affirmative vote of the holders of a majority of the shares of each class of shares entitled to vote thereon.

§ 76. Effect of Merger, Consolidation or Exchange

Upon the issuance of the certificate of merger or the certificate of consolidation by the Secretary of State, the merger or consolidation shall be effected.

When such merger or consolidation has been effected:

(a) The several corporations parties to the plan of merger or consolidation shall be a single corporation, which, in the case of a merger, shall be that corporation designated in the plan of merger as the surviving corporation, and, in the case of a consolidation, shall be the new corporation provided for in the plan of consolidation.

(b) The separate existence of all corporations parties to the plan of merger or consolidation, except the surviving or new corporation, shall cease.

(c) Such surviving or new corporation shall have all the rights, privileges, immunities and powers and shall be subject to all the duties and liabilities of a corporation organized under this Act.

(d) Such surviving or new corporation shall thereupon and thereafter possess all the rights, privileges, immunities, and franchises, of a public as well as of a private nature, of each of the merging or consolidating corporations; and all property, real, personal and mixed, and all debts due on whatever account, including subscriptions to shares, and all other choses in action, and all and every other interest of or belonging to or due to each of the corporations so merged or consolidated, shall be taken and deemed to be transferred to and vested in such single corporation without further act or deed; and the title to any real estate, or any interest therein, vested in any of such corporations shall not revert or be in any way impaired by reason of such merger or consolidation.

(e) Such surviving or new corporation shall thenceforth be responsible and liable for all the liabilities and obligations of each of the corporations so merged or consolidated; and any claim existing or action or proceeding pending by or against any of such corporations may be prosecuted as if such merger or consolidation had not taken place, or such surviving or new corporation may be substituted in its place. Neither the rights of creditors nor any liens upon the property of any such corporation shall be impaired by such merger or consolidation.

(f) In the case of a merger, the articles of incorporation of the surviving corporation shall be deemed to be amended to the extent, if any, that changes in its articles of incorporation are stated in the plan of merger; and, in the case of a consolidation, the statements set forth in the articles of consolidation and which are required or permitted to be set forth in the articles of incorporation of corporations organized under this Act shall be deemed to be the original articles of incorporation of the new corporation.

§ 80. Right of Shareholders to Dissent and Obtain Payment for Shares

(a) Any shareholder of a corporation shall have the right to dissent from, and to obtain payment for his shares in the event of, any of the following corporate actions:

  (1) Any plan of merger or consolidation to which the corporation is a party, except as provided in subsection (c); * * *

§ 83. Voluntary Dissolution by Consent of Shareholders

A corporation may be voluntarily dissolved by the written consent of all of its shareholders.

Upon the execution of such written consent, a statement of intent to dissolve shall be executed in duplicate by the corporation by its president or a vice president and by its secretary or an assistant secretary, and verified by one of the officers signing such statement, which statement shall set forth:

(a) The name of the corporation.

(b) The names and respective addresses of its officers.

(c) The names and respective addresses of its directors.

(d) A copy of the written consent signed by all shareholders of the corporation.

(e) A statement that such written consent has been signed by all shareholders of the corporation or signed in their names by their attorneys thereunto duly authorized.

§ 84. Voluntary Dissolution by Act of Corporation

A corporation may be dissolved by the act of the corporation, when authorized in the following manner:

(a) The board of directors shall adopt a resolution recommending that the corporation be dissolved, and directing that the question of such dissolution be submitted to a vote at a meeting of shareholders, which may be either an annual or a special meeting.

(b) Written notice shall be given to each shareholder of record entitled to vote at such meeting within the time and in the manner provided in this Act for the giving of notice of meetings of shareholders, and, whether the meeting be an annual or special meeting, shall state that the purpose, or one of the purposes, of such meeting is to consider the advisability of dissolving the corporation.

(c) At such meeting a vote of shareholders entitled to vote thereat shall be taken on a resolution to dissolve the corporation. Such resolution shall be adopted upon receiving the affirmative vote of the holders of a majority of the shares of the corporation entitled to vote thereon, unless any class of shares is entitled to vote thereon as a class, in which event the resolution shall be adopted upon receiving the affirmative vote of the holders of a majority of the shares of each class of shares entitled to vote thereon as a class and of the total shares entitled to vote thereon.

(d) Upon the adoption of such resolution, a statement of intent to dissolve shall be executed in duplicate by the corporation by its president or a vice president and by its secretary or an assistant secretary, and verified by one of the officers signing such statement, which statement shall set forth:

(1) The name of the corporation.

(2) The names and respective addresses of its officers.

(3) The names and respective addresses of its directors.

(4) A copy of the resolution adopted by the shareholders authorizing the dissolution of the corporation.

(5) The number of shares outstanding, and, if the shares of any class are entitled to vote as a class, the designation and number of outstanding shares of each such class.

(6) The number of shares voted for and against the resolution, respectively, and, if the shares of any class are entitled to vote as a class, the number of shares of each such class voted for and against the resolution, respectively.

§ 94. Involuntary Dissolution

A corporation may be dissolved involuntarily by a decree of the _____ court in an action filed by the Attorney General when it is established that:

(a) The corporation has failed to file its annual report within the time required by this Act, or has failed to pay its franchise tax on or before the first day of August of the year in which such franchise tax becomes due and payable; or

(b) The corporation procured its articles of incorporation through fraud; or

(c) The corporation has continued to exceed or abuse the authority conferred upon it by law; or

(d) The corporation has failed for thirty days to appoint and maintain a registered agent in this State; or

(e) The corporation has failed for thirty days after change of its registered office or registered agent to file in the office of the Secretary of State a statement of such change.

§ 105. Survival of Remedy after Dissolution

The dissolution of a corporation either (1) by the issuance of a certificate of dissolution by the Secretary of State, or (2) by a decree of court when the court has not liquidated the assets and business of the corporation as provided in this Act, or (3) by expiration of its period of duration, shall not take away or impair any remedy available to or against such corporation, its directors, officers, or shareholders, for any right or claim existing, or any liability incurred, prior to such dissolution if action or other proceeding thereon is commenced within two years after the date of such dissolution. Any such action or proceeding by or against the corporation may be prosecuted or defended by the corporation in its corporate name. The shareholders, directors and officers shall have power to take such corporate or other action as shall be appropriate to protect such remedy, right or claim. If such corporation was dissolved by the expiration of its period of duration, such corporation may amend its articles of incorporation at any time during such period of two years so as to extend its period of duration.

§ 146. Unauthorized Assumption of Corporate Powers

All persons who assume to act as a corporation without authority so to do shall be jointly and severally liable for all debts and liabilities incurred or arising as a result thereof.

Appendix I

DICTIONARY OF LEGAL TERMS*

A

abatement Reduction or elimination of gifts by category upon the reduction in value of the estate.

absolute surety Surety liable to a creditor immediately upon the default of the principal debtor.

acceptance *Commercial paper* Acceptance is the drawee's signed engagement to honor the draft as presented. It becomes operative when completed by delivery or notification. U.C.C. § 3–410.

Contracts Compliance by offeree with terms and conditions of offer.

Sale of goods U.C.C. § 2–606 provides three ways a buyer can accept goods: (1) by signifying to the seller that the goods are conforming or that he will accept them in spite of their nonconformity, (2) by failing to make an effective rejection, and (3) by doing an act inconsistent with the seller's ownership.

acceptor Drawee who has accepted an instrument.

accession An addition to one's property by increase of the original property or by production from such property. E.g., A innocently converts

*Many of the definitions are abridged and adapted from *Black's Law Dictionary*, 5th edition, West Publishing Company, 1979.

the wheat of B into bread. U.C.C. § 9–315 changes the common law where a perfected security interest is involved.

accident and health insurance Provides protection from losses due to accident or sickness.

accommodation An arrangement made as a favor to another, usually involving a loan of money or commercial paper. While a party's intent may be to aid a maker of note by lending his credit, if he seeks to accomplish thereby legitimate objects of his own, and not simply to aid the maker, the act is not for accommodation.

accommodation indorser Signer not in the chain of title.

accommodation party A person who signs commercial paper in any capacity for the purpose of lending his name to another party to an instrument. U.C.C. § 3–415.

accord and satisfaction A method of discharging a claim whereby the parties agree to accept something in settlement, the "accord" being the agreement and the "satisfaction" its execution or performance. It is a new contract that is substituted for an old contract, which is thereby discharged, or for an obligation or cause of action and that must have all of the elements of a valid contract.

account Any account with a bank, including a checking, time, interest or savings account. U.C.C. § 4–194. Also, any right to payment, for goods or services, that is not evidenced by an instrument or chattel paper. E.g., account receivable.

accounting Equitable proceeding for a complete settlement of all partnership affairs.

act of state doctrine Rule that a court should not question the validity of actions taken by a foreign government in its own country.

actual authority Power conferred upon agent by actual consent given by principal.

actual express authority Actual authority derived from written or spoken words of principal.

actual implied authority Actual authority inferred from words or conduct manifested to agent by principal.

actual notice Knowledge actually and expressly communicated.

actus reas Wrongful or overt act.

ademption The removal or extinction of a devise by act of the testator.

adequacy of consideration Not required where parties have freely agreed to the exchange.

adhesion contract Standard "form" contract, usually between a large retailer and a consumer, in which the weaker party has no realistic choice or opportunity to bargain.

adjudication The giving or pronouncing of a judgment in a case; also the judgment given.

administrative agency Governmental entity (other than courts and legislatures) having authority to affect the rights of private parties.

administrative law Law dealing with the establishment, duties and powers of agencies in the executive branch of government.

administrative process Entire set of activities engaged in by administrative agencies while carrying out their rulemaking, enforcement, and adjudicative functions.

administrator A person appointed by the court to manage the assets and liabilities of an intestate (person dying without a will). A person who is named in the will by testator (person dying with a will) is called the executor. Female designations are administratrix and executrix.

adversary system System in which opposing parties initiate and present their case.

adverse possession A method of acquisition of title to real property by possession for a statutory period under certain conditions. There may be different periods of time, depending on whether the adverse possessor has color of title.

affidavit A written statement of facts, made voluntarily, confirmed by oath or affirmation of party making it, and taken before an authorized officer.

affiliate Person who controls, is controlled by, or is under common control with the issuer.

affirm Uphold the lower court's judgment.

affirmative action Active recruitment of minority applicants.

affirmative defense A response that attacks the plaintiff's legal right to bring an action as opposed to attacking the truth of the claim. E.g., accord and satisfaction; assumption of risk; contributory negligence; duress; estoppel.

affirmative disclosure Requirement that an advertiser include certain information in its advertisement so that it is not deceptive.

after acquired property Property the debtor may acquire at some time after the security interest attaches.

agency Relation in which one person acts for or represents another by the latter's authority.
   Actual agency Exists where the agent is really employed by the principal.
   Agency by estoppel One created by operation of law and established by proof of such acts of the principal as reasonably lead to the conclusion of its existence.
   Implied agency One created by acts of parties and deduced from proof of other facts.

agent Person authorized to act on another's behalf.

allegation A statement of a party setting out what he expects to prove.

allonge Piece of paper firmly affixed to the instrument.

annuity contract Agreement to pay periodic sums to insured upon reaching a designated age.

annul To annul a judgment or judicial proceeding is to deprive it of all force and operation.

answer The answer is the formal written statement made by a defendant setting forth the ground of his defense.

antecedent debt Preexisting obligation.

anticipatory breach of contract (or **anticipatory repudiation**) The unjustified assertion by a party that he will not perform an obligation that he is contractually obligated to perform at a future time. See U.C.C. §§ 610 & 611.

apparent authority Such principal power that a reasonable person would assume an agent has in light of the principal's conduct.

appeal Resort to a superior (appellate) court to review the decision of an inferior (trial) court or administrative agency.

appeal by right Mandatory review by a higher court.

appellant A party who takes an appeal from one court to another. He may be either the plaintiff or defendant in the original court proceeding.

appellee The party in a cause against whom an appeal is taken; that is, the party who has an interest adverse to setting aside or reversing the judgment. Sometimes also called the "respondent."

appropriation Unauthorized use of another person's name or likeness for one's own benefit.

appurtenances Things appurtenant pass as incident to the principal thing. Sometimes an easement consisting of a right of way over one piece of land will pass with another piece of land as being appurtenant to it.

APR Annual percentage rate.

arbitration The reference of a dispute to an impartial (third) person chosen by the parties who agree in advance to abide by the arbitrator's award issued after a hearing at which both parties have an opportunity to be heard.

arraignment Accused is informed of the crime against him and enters a plea.

articles of incorporation (or **certificate of incorporation**) The instrument under which a corporation is formed. The contents are prescribed in the particular state's general incorporation statute.

articles of partnership A written agreement by which parties enter into a partnership, to be governed by the terms set forth therein.

as is Disclaimer of implied warranties.

assault Unlawful attempted battery; intentional infliction of apprehension of immediate bodily harm or offensive contact.

assignee Party to whom contract rights are assigned.

assignment A transfer of the rights to real or personal property, usually intangible property such as rights in a lease, mortgage, sale agreement or partnership.

assignment of rights Voluntary transfer to a third party of the rights arising from a contract.

assignor Party making an assignment.

assumes Delegatee agrees to perform the contractual obligation of the delegator.

assumes the mortgage Purchaser of mortgaged property becomes personally liable to pay the debt.

assumption of risk Plaintiff's express or implied consent to encounter a known danger.

attachment The process of seizing property, by virtue of a writ, summons, or other judicial order, and bringing the same into the custody of the court for the purpose of securing satisfaction of the judgment ultimately to be entered in the action. While formerly the main objective was to coerce the defendant debtor to appear in court, today the writ of attachment is used primarily to seize the debtor's property in the event a judgment is rendered.
  Distinguished from execution See **execution.**
  Also, the process by which a security interest becomes enforceable. Attachment may occur upon the taking of possession or upon the signing of a security agreement by the person who is pledging the property as collateral.

authority Power of an agent to change the legal status of his principal.

authorized means Any reasonable means of communication.

automatic perfection Perfection upon attachment.

award The decision of an arbitrator.

B

bad checks Issuing a check with insufficient funds to cover the check.

bailee The party to whom personal property is delivered under a contract of bailment.
  Extraordinary bailee Absolutely liable for the safety of the bailed property without regard to the cause of the loss.
  Ordinary bailee Must exercise due care.

bailment A delivery of personal property in trust for the execution of a special object in relation to such goods, beneficial either to the bailor or bailee or both, and upon a contract to either redeliver the goods to the bailor or otherwise dispose of the same in conformity with the purpose of the trust.

bailor The party who delivers goods to another in the contract of bailment.

Bankruptcy Code A Federal law for the benefit and relief of creditors and their debtors in cases in which the latter are unable or unwilling to pay their debts. Straight bankruptcy is in the nature of a liquidation proceeding and involves the collection and distribution to creditors of all the bankrupt's non-exempt property by the trustee in the manner provided by the Code. The debtor rehabilitation provisions of the Code (Chapters 11, 12, and 13) differ however from straight bankruptcy in that the debtor looks to rehabilitation and reorganization, rather than liquidation, and the creditor looks to future earnings of the bankrupt, rather than property held by the bankrupt to satisfy their claims.

bargain Negotiated exchange.

bargained exchange Mutually agreed upon exchange.

basis of the bargain Part of the buyer's assumption underlying the sale.

battery Unlawful touching of another; intentional infliction of harmful or offensive bodily contact.

bearer Person in possession of an instrument.

bearer paper Payable to holder of the instrument.

beneficiary One who benefits from act of another. See also **third party beneficiary.**

Incidental A person who may derive benefit from performance of a contract, though he is neither the promisee nor the one to whom performance is to be rendered. Since the incidental beneficiary is not a donee or creditor beneficiary (see **third party beneficiary**), he has no right to enforce the contract.

Intended beneficiary Third party intended by the two contracted parties to receive a benefit from their contract.

Trust As it relates to trust beneficiaries, includes a person who has any present or future interest, vested or contingent, and also includes the owner of an interest by assignment or other transfer and, as it relates to a charitable trust, includes any person entitled to enforce the trust.

beyond a reasonable doubt Proof that is entirely convincing, satisfied to a moral certainty; criminal law standard.

bilateral contract Contract in which both parties exchange promises.

bill of lading Document evidencing receipt of goods for shipment issued by person engaged in business of transporting or forwarding goods and it includes airbill. U.C.C. § 1–201(6).

Through bill of lading A bill of lading which specifies at least one connecting carrier.

bill of sale A written agreement, formerly limited to one under seal, by which one person assigns or transfers his right to or interest in goods to another.

binder A written memorandum of the important terms of contract of insurance which gives temporary protection to insured pending investigation of risk by insurance company or until a formal policy is issued.

blue law Prohibition of certain types of commercial activity on Sunday.

blue sky laws A popular name for State statutes providing for the regulation and supervision of securities offerings and sales, for the protection of citizen-investors from investing in fraudulent companies.

bona fide Latin. In good faith.

bond A certificate or evidence of a debt on which the issuing company or governmental body promises to pay the bondholders a specified amount of interest for a specified length of time, and to repay the loan on the expiration date. In every case a bond represents debt—its holder is a creditor of the corporation and not a part owner as is the shareholder.

boycott Agreement among parties not to deal with a third party.

breach Wrongful failure to perform the terms of a contract.

Material breach Nonperformance which significantly impairs the aggrieved party's rights under the contract.

bribery Offering property to a public official to influence the official's decision.

bulk transfer Transfer not in the ordinary course of the transferor's business of a major part of his inventory.

burglary Breaking and entering the home of another at night with intent to commit a felony.

business judgment rule Protects directors from liability for honest mistakes of judgment.

business trust A trust (managed by a trustee for the benefit of a beneficiary) established to conduct a business for a profit.

but for rule Conduct is a cause of an event if the event would not have occurred in the absence of the person's negligent conduct.

buyer in ordinary course of business Person who buys in ordinary course, in good faith, and without knowledge that the sale to him is in violation of anyone's ownership rights or of a security interest.

by-laws Regulations, ordinances, rules of laws adopted by an association or corporation for its government.

C

callable bond Bond that is subject to redemption (reacquisition) by the corporation.

cancellation Putting an end to a contract by one party because of a breach by other party.

capital Accumulated goods, possessions, and assets, used for the production of profits and wealth. Owners' equity in a business. Often used equally correctly to mean the total assets of a business. Sometimes used to mean capital assets.

capital surplus Surplus other than earned surplus.

carrier Transporter of goods.

casualty insurance Covers property loss due to causes other than fire or the elements.

cause of action The ground on which an action may be sustained.

caveat emptor Latin. Let the buyer beware. This maxim is more applicable to judicial sales, auctions, and the like, than to sales of consumer goods where strict liability, warranty, and other laws protect.

certificate of deposit A written acknowledgment by a bank or banker of a deposit with promise to pay to depositor, to his order, or to some other person or to his order. U.C.C. § 3–104(2)(c).

certificate of title Official representation of ownership.

certification Acceptance of a check by a drawee bank.

certification of incorporation See **articles of incorporation.**

certification mark Distinctive symbol, word, or design used with goods or services to certify specific characteristics.

certiorari Latin. To be informed of. A writ of common law origin issued by a superior to an inferior court requiring the latter to produce a certified record of a particular case tried therein. It is most commonly used to refer to the Supreme Court of the United States, which uses the writ of certiorari as a discretionary device to choose the cases it wishes to hear.

chancery Equity; equitable jurisdiction; a court of equity; the system of jurisprudence administered in courts of equity.

charging order Judicial lien against a partner's interest in the partnership.

charter An instrument emanating from the sovereign power, in the nature of a grant. A charter differs from a constitution in that the former is granted by the sovereign, while the latter is established by the people themselves.

Corporate law An act of a legislature creating a corporation, or creating and defining the franchise of a corporation. Also a corporation's constitution or organic law; that is to say, the articles of incorporation taken in connection with the law under which the corporation was organized.

chattel mortgage A pre-Uniform Commercial Code security device whereby a security interest was taken by the mortgagee in personal property of the mortgagor. Such security device has generally been superseded by other types of security agreements under U.C.C. Article 9 (Secured Transactions).

chattel paper Writings that evidence both a debt and a security interest.

check A draft drawn upon a bank and payable on demand, signed by the maker or drawer, containing an unconditional promise to pay a sum certain in money to the order of the payee. U.C.C. § 3–104(2)(b).

Cashier's check A bank's own check drawn on itself and signed by the cashier or other authorized official. It is a direct obligation of the bank.

C. & F. Cost and freight; a shipping contract.

C.I.F. Cost, insurance, and freight; a shipping contract.

civil law Laws concerned with civil or private rights and remedies, as contrasted with criminal laws.

The system of jurisprudence administered in the Roman empire, particularly as set forth in the compilation of Justinian and his successors, as distinguished from the common law of England and the canon law. The civil law (Civil Code) is followed by Louisiana.

claim   A right to payment.

clearing house   An association of banks for the purpose of settling accounts on a daily basis.

close corporation   See **corporation**.

closed-ended credit   Credit extended to debtor for a specific period of time.

closed shop   Employer can only hire union members.

C.O.D.   Collect on delivery; generally a shipping contract.

code   A compilation of all permanent laws in force consolidated and classified according to subject matter. Many States have published official codes of all laws in force, including the common law and statutes as judicially interpreted, which have been compiled by code commissions and enacted by the legislatures.

codicil   A supplement or an addition to a will; it may explain, modify, add to, subtract from, qualify, alter, restrain or revoke provisions in existing will. It must be executed with the same formalities as a will.

cognovit judgment   Written authority by debtor for entry of judgment against him in the event he defaults in payment. Such provision in a debt instrument on default confers judgment against the debtor.

collateral   Secondarily liable, only liable if the party with primary liability does not perform.

collateral (security)   Personal property subject to a security interest.
  Banking   Some form of security in addition to the personal obligation of the borrower.

collateral promise   Undertaking to be secondarily liable, that is, liable if the principal debtor does not perform.

collecting bank   Any bank handling the item for collection except the payor bank. U.C.C.§ 4–105(d).

collective mark   Distinctive symbol used to indicate membership in an organization.

collision insurance   Protects the owner of an automobile against damage due to contact with other vehicles or objects.

commerce power   Exclusive power granted by the U.S. Constitution to the Federal government to regulate commerce with foreign countries and among the States.

commercial bailment   Bailment in which both parties derive a mutual benefit.

commercial impracticability   Performance can only be accomplished with unforeseen and unjust hardship.

commercial law   A phrase used to designate the whole body of substantive jurisprudence (*e.g.*, Uniform Commercial Code; Truth in Lending Act) applicable to the rights, intercourse, and relations of persons engaged in commerce, trade, or mercantile pursuits. See **Uniform Commercial Code.**

commercial paper   Bills of exchange (*i.e.*, drafts), promissory notes, bank-checks, and other negotiable instruments for the payment of money, which, by their form and on their face, purport to be such instruments. U.C.C. Article 3 is the general law governing commercial paper.

commercial reasonableness   Judgment of reasonable persons familiar with the business transaction.

commercial speech   Expression related to the economic interests of the speaker and its audience.

common carrier   Carrier open to the general public.

common law   Body of law originating in England and derived from judicial decisions. As distinguished from statutory law created by the enactment of legislatures, the common law comprises the judgments and decrees of the courts recognizing, affirming, and enforcing usages and customs of immemorial antiquity.

community property   Rights by spouses in property acquired by the other during marriage.

comparable worth   Equal pay for jobs of equal value to the employer.

comparative negligence   Under comparative negligence statutes or doctrines, negligence is measured in terms of percentage, and any damages allowed shall be diminished in proportion to amount of negligence attributable to the person for whose injury, damage or death recovery is sought.

complainant   One who applies to the courts for legal redress by filing complaint (*i.e.*, plaintiff).

complaint The pleading which sets forth a claim for relief. Such complaint (whether it be the original claim, counterclaim, cross-claim, or third-party claim) shall contain: (1) a short and plain statement of the grounds upon which the court's jurisdiction depends, unless the court already has jurisdiction and the claim needs no new grounds of jurisdiction to support it, (2) a short and plain statement of the claim showing that the pleader is entitled to relief, and (3) a demand for judgment for the relief to which he deems himself entitled. The complaint, together with the summons, is required to be served on the defendant.

composition Agreement between debtor and two or more of her creditors that each will take a portion of his claim as full payment.

compulsory arbitration Arbitration required by statute for specific types of disputes.

computer crime Crime by, with, or at a computer.

concealment Fraudulent failure to disclose a material fact.

conciliation Nonbinding process in which a third party acts as an intermediary between the disputing parties.

concurrent jurisdiction Authority of more than one court to hear the same case.

condition An uncertain event which affects the duty of performance.
Concurrent conditions Performance by the parties are to occur simultaneously.
Express condition Performance is contingent on the happening or nonhappening of a stated event.

condition precedent An event which must occur or not occur before performance is due; event or events (presentment, dishonor, notice of dishonor) which must occur to hold a secondary party liable to commercial paper.

condition subsequent An event which terminates a duty of performance.

conditional acceptance An acceptance of an offer contingent upon the acceptance of an additional or different term.

conditional contract Obligations are contingent upon a stated event.

conditional guarantor of collection Surety liable to creditor only after creditor exhausts his legal remedies against the principal debtor.

confession of judgment Written agreement by debtor authorizing creditor to obtain a court judgment in the event debtor defaults. See also **cognovit judgment.**

confiscation Governmental taking of foreign-owned property without payment.

conflict of laws That branch of jurisprudence, arising from the diversity of the laws of different nations, States or jurisdictions, that reconciles the inconsistency, or decides which law is to govern in the particular case.

confusion Results when goods belonging to two or more owners become intermixed to the point where the property of any of them no longer can be identified except as part of a mass of like goods.

consanguinity Kinship; blood relationship; the connection or relation of persons descended from the same stock or common ancestor.

consensual arbitration Arbitration voluntarily entered into by the parties.

consent Voluntary and knowing willingness that an act should be done.

conservator Appointed by court to manage affairs of incompetent or to liquidate business.

consideration The cause, motive, price, or impelling influence which induces a contracting party to enter into a contract. Some right, interest, profit or benefit accruing to one party, or some forbearance, detriment, loss, or responsibility, given, suffered, or undertaken by the other.

consignee One to whom a consignment is made. Person named in bill of lading to whom or to whose order the bill promises delivery. U.C.C. § 7–102(b).

consignment Ordinarily implies an agency and denotes that property is committed to the consignee for care or sale.

consignor One who sends or makes a consignment; a shipper of goods. The person named in a bill of lading as the person from whom the goods have been received for shipment. U.C.C.§ 7–102(c).

consolidation In *corporate law,* the combination of two or more corporations into a newly created corporation. Thus, A Corporation and B Corporation combine to form C Corporation.

constitution Fundamental law of a government establishing its powers and limitations.

constructive That which is established by the mind of the law in its act of *construing* facts, conduct, circumstances, or instruments. That which has not the character assigned to it in its own essential nature, but acquires such character in consequence of the way in which it is regarded by a rule or policy of law; hence, inferred, implied, or made out by legal interpretation; the word "legal" being sometimes used here in lieu of "constructive."

constructive assent An assent or consent imputed to a party from a construction or interpretation of his conduct; as distinguished from one which he actually expresses.

constructive conditions Conditions in contracts which are neither expressed nor implied but are rather imposed by law to meet the ends of justice.

constructive delivery Term comprehending all those acts which, although not truly conferring a real possession of the vendee, have been held by construction of law to be the equivalent to acts of real delivery.

constructive eviction Failure by the landlord in any obligation under the lease that causes a substantial and lasting injury to the tenant's enjoyment of the premises.

constructive notice Knowledge imputed by law.

constructive trust Arising by operation of law to prevent unjust enrichment. See also **trustee**.

consumer goods Goods bought or used for personal, family, or household purposes.

consumer product Tangible personal property normally used for family, household, or personal purposes.

contingent remainder Remainder interest, conditional upon the happening of an event in addition to the termination of the preceding estate.

contract An agreement between two or more persons which creates an obligation to do or not to do a particular thing. Its essentials are competent parties, subject matter, a legal consideration, mutuality of agreement, and mutuality of obligation.

Destination contract Seller is required to tender delivery of the goods at a particular destination; seller bears the expense and risk of loss.

Executed contract Fully performed by all of the parties.

Executory contract Contract partially or entirely unperformed by one or more of the parties.

Express contract Agreement of parties that is expressed in words either in writing or orally.

Formal contract Agreement which is legally binding because of its particular form or mode of expression.

Implied in fact contract Contract where agreement of the parties is inferred from their conduct.

Informal contract All oral or written contracts other than formal contracts.

Installment contract Goods are delivered in separate lots.

Integrated contract Complete and total agreement.

Output contract A contract in which one party agrees to sell his entire output and the other agrees to buy it; it is not illusory, though it may be indefinite.

Quasi contract Obligation not based upon contract that is imposed to avoid injustice.

Requirements contract A contract in which one party agrees to purchase his total requirements from the other party and hence it is binding and not illusory.

Substituted contract An agreement between the parties to rescind their old contract and replace it with a new contract.

Unconscionable contract One which no sensible man not under delusion, duress, or in distress would make, and such as no honest and fair man would accept. A contract the terms of which are excessively unreasonable, overreaching and one-sided.

Unenforceable contract Contract for the breach of which the law does not provide a remedy.

Unilateral and bilateral A unilateral contract is one in which one party makes an express engagement or undertakes a performance, without receiving in return any express engagement or promise of performance from the other. Bilateral (or reciprocal) contracts are those by which the parties expressly enter into mutual engagements.

contract clause Prohibition against the States' retroactively modifying public and private contracts.

contractual liability Obligation on a negotiable instrument, based upon signing the instrument.

contribution Payment from cosureties of their proportionate share.

contributory negligence The act or omission amounting to want of ordinary care on part of complaining party, which, concurring with defendant's negligence, is proximate cause of injury.

The defense of contributory negligence is an absolute bar to any recovery in some States; because of this, it has been replaced by the doctrine of comparative negligence in many other States.

conversion Unauthorized and wrongful exercise of dominion and control over another's personal property, to exclusion of or inconsistent with rights of the owner.

convertible bond Bond that may be exchanged for other securities of the corporation.

copyright Exclusive right granted by Federal government to authors of original works including literary, musical, dramatic, pictorial, graphic, sculptural, and film works.

corporation A legal entity ordinarily consisting of an association of numerous individuals. Such entity is regarded as having a personality and existence distinct from that of its several members and is vested with the capacity of continuous succession, irrespective of changes in its membership, either in perpetuity or for a limited term of years.

Closely held or *close corporation* Corporation that is owned by few shareholders and whose shares are not actively traded.

Corporation de facto One existing under color of law and in pursuance of an effort made in good faith to organize a corporation under the statute. Such a corporation is not subject to collateral attack.

Corporation de jure That which exists by reason of full compliance with requirements of an existing law permitting organization of such corporation.

Domestic corporation Corporation created under the laws of a given State.

Foreign corporation Corporation created under the laws of any other State, government, or country.

Subchapter S corporation A small business corporation which, under certain conditions, may elect to have its undistributed taxable income taxed to its shareholders. I.R.C. § 1371 *et seq.* Of major significance is the fact that Subchapter S status usually avoids the corporate income tax, and corporate losses can be claimed by the shareholders.

Subsidiary and parent corporation Subsidiary corporation is one in which another corporation (called parent corporation) owns at least a majority of the shares, and thus has control.

corrective advertising Disclosure in an advertisement that previous ads were deceptive.

costs A pecuniary allowance, made to the successful party (and recoverable from the losing party), for his expenses in prosecuting or defending an action or a distinct proceeding within an action. Generally, "costs" do not include attorney fees unless such fees are by a statute denominated costs or are by statute allowed to be recovered as costs in the case.

cosureties Two or more sureties bound for the same debt of a principal debtor.

co-tenants Persons who hold title concurrently.

counter offer A statement by the offeree which has the legal effect of rejecting the offer and of proposing a new offer to the offeror. However, the provisions of U.C.C. § 2–207(2) modifies this principle by providing that the "additional terms are to be construed as proposals for addition to the contract."

counterclaim A claim presented by a defendant in opposition to or deduction from the claim of the plaintiff.

course of dealing A sequence of previous acts and conduct between the parties to a particular transaction which is fairly to be regarded as establishing a common basis of understanding for interpreting their expressions and other conduct. U.C.C. § 1–205(1).

course of performance Conduct between the parties concerning performance of the particular contract.

court above—court below In appellate practice, the "court above" is the one to which a cause is removed for review, whether by appeal, writ of error, or certiorari; while the "court below" is the one from which the case is being removed.

covenant Used primarily with respect to promises in conveyances or other instruments dealing with real estate.

Covenants against encumbrances A stipulation against all rights to or interests in the land which may subsist in third persons to the diminution of the value of the estate granted.

Covenant appurtenant A covenant which is connected with land of the grantor, and not in gross. A covenant running with the land and binding heirs, executors and assigns of the immediate parties.

Covenant for further assurance An undertaking, in the form of a covenant, on the part of the vendor of real estate to do such further acts for the purpose of perfecting the purchaser's title as the latter may reasonably require.

Covenant for possession A covenant by which the grantee or lessee is granted possession.

Covenant for quiet enjoyment An assurance against the consequences of a defective title, and of any disturbances thereupon.

Covenants for title Covenants usually inserted in a conveyance of land, on the part of the grantor, and binding him for the completeness, security, and continuance of the title transferred to the grantee. They comprise covenants for seisin, for right to convey, against encumbrances, or quiet enjoyment, sometimes for further assurance, and almost always of warranty.

Covenant in gross Such as do not run with the land.

Covenant of right to convey An assurance by the covenantor that the grantor has sufficient capacity and title to convey the *estate* which he by his deed undertakes to convey.

Covenant of seisin An assurance to the purchaser that the grantor has the very estate in quantity and quality which he purports to convey.

Covenant of warranty An assurance by the grantor of an estate that the grantee shall enjoy the same without interruption by virtue of paramount title.

Covenant running with land A covenant which goes with the land, as being annexed to the estate, and which cannot be separated from the land, and transferred without it. A covenant is said to run with the land when not only the original parties or their representatives, but each successive owner of the land, will be entitled to its benefit, or be liable (as the case may be) to its obligation. Such a covenant is said to be one which "touches and concerns" the land itself, so that its benefit or obligation passes with the ownership. Essentials are that the grantor and grantee must have intended that the covenant run with the land, the covenant must affect or concern the land with which it runs, and there must be privity of estate between party claiming the benefit and the party who rests under the burden.

covenant not to compete Agreement to refrain from entering into a competing trade, profession, or business.

cover Buyer's purchase of goods in substitution for those not delivered by breaching seller.

credit beneficiary See **third party beneficiary.**

creditor Any entity having a claim against the debtor.

crime An act or omission in violation of a public law and punishable by the government.

criminal duress Coercion by threat of serious bodily injury.

criminal intent Desired or virtually certain consequences of one's conduct.

criminal law The law that involves offenses against the entire community.

cure The right of a seller under U.C.C. to correct a non-conforming delivery of goods to buyer within the contract period. U.C.C. § 2–508.

curtsey Husband's estate in the real property of his wife.

cy-pres As near as (possible). Rule for the construction of instruments in equity, by which the intention of the party is carried out *as near as may be,* when it would be impossible or illegal to give it literal effect.

D

damage Loss, injury, or deterioration, caused by the negligence, design, or accident of one person to another, in respect of the latter's person or property. The word is to be distinguished from its plural, "damages," which means a compensation in money for a loss or damage.

damages Money sought as a remedy for breach of contract or for tortious acts.

Actual damages Real, substantial and just damages, or the amount awarded to a complainant in compensation for his actual and real loss or injury, as opposed on the one hand to "nominal" damages, and on the other to "exemplary" or "punitive" damages. Synonymous with "compensatory damages" and with "general damages."

Benefit-of-the-bargain damages Difference between the value received and the value of the fraudulent party's performance as represented.

Compensatory damages Compensatory damages are such as will compensate the injured party for the injury sustained, and nothing more; such as will simply make good or replace the loss caused by the wrong or injury.

Consequential damages Such damage, loss or injury as does not flow directly and immediately from the act of the party, but only from some of the consequences or results of such act. Consequential damages resulting from a seller's breach of contract include any loss resulting from general or particular requirements and needs of which the seller at the time of contracting had reason to know and which could not reasonably be prevented by cover or otherwise, and injury to person or property proximately resulting from any breach of warranty. U.C.C. § 2–715(2).

Exemplary or punitive damages Damages other than compensatory damages which may be awarded against person to punish him for outrageous conduct.

Expectancy damages Calculable by subtracting the injured party's actual dollar position as a result of the breach from that party's projected dollar position had performance occurred.

Foreseeable damages Loss that the party in breach had reason to know of when the contract was made.

Incidental damages Under U.C.C. § 2–710, such damages include any commercially reasonable charges, expenses or commissions incurred in stopping delivery, in the transportation, care and custody of goods after the buyer's breach, in connection with the return or resale of the goods or otherwise resulting from the breach. Also, such damages, resulting from a seller's breach of contract, include expenses reasonably incurred in inspection, receipt, transportation and care and custody of goods rightfully rejected, any commercially reasonable charges, expenses or commissions in connection with effecting cover and any other reasonable expense incident to the delay or other breach. U.C.C. § 2–715(1).

Irreparable damages In the law pertaining to injunctions, damages for which no certain pecuniary standard exists for measurement.

Liquidated damages and penalties Damages for breach by either party may be liquidated in the agreement but only at an amount which is reasonable in the light of the anticipated or actual harm caused by the breach, the difficulties of proof of loss, and the inconvenience or nonfeasibility of otherwise obtaining an adequate remedy. A term fixing unreasonably large liquidated damages is void as a penalty. U.C.C. § 2–718(1).

Mitigation of damages A plaintiff may not recover damages for the effects of an injury which reasonably could have been avoided or substantially ameliorated. This limitation on recovery is generally denominated as "mitigation of damages" or "avoidance of consequences."

Nominal damages A small sum awarded where a contract has been breached but the loss is negligible or unproven.

Out-of-pocket damages Difference between the value received and the value given.

Reliance damages Contract damages placing the injured party in as good a position as he would have been in had the contract not been made.

Treble damages Three times actual loss.

de facto In fact, in deed, actually. This phrase is used to characterize an officer, a government, a past action, or a state of affairs which must be accepted for all practical purposes, but is illegal or illegitimate. See also **corporation,** *corporation de facto.*

de jure Descriptive of a condition in which there has been total compliance with all requirements of law. In this sense it is the contrary of *de facto.* See also **corporation,** *corporation de jure.*

de novo Anew; afresh; a second time.

debenture Unsecured bond.

debt security Any form of corporate security reflected as debt on the books of the corporation in contrast to equity securities such as stock; *e.g.,* bonds, notes, and debentures are debt securities.

debtor Person who owes payment or performance of an obligation.

deceit A fraudulent and cheating misrepresentation, artifice, or device, used to deceive and trick one who is ignorant of the true facts, to the prejudice and damage of the party imposed upon. See also **fraud; misrepresentation.**

decree Decision of a court of equity.

deed A conveyance of realty; a writing signed by grantor, whereby title to realty is transferred from one to another.

deed of trust Interest in real property which is conveyed to a third person as trustee for the creditor.

defamation Injury of a person's reputation by publication of false statements.

default judgment Judgment against a defendant who fails to respond to a complaint.

defendant The party against whom legal action is sought.

definite term Lease that automatically expires at end of the term.

delectus personae Partner's right to choose who may become a member of the partnership.

delegatee Third party to whom the delegator's duty is delegated.

delegation of duties Transferring all or part of one's duties arising under a contract to another.

delegator Party delegating his duty to a third party.

delivery The physical or constructive transfer of an instrument or of goods from the hands of one person to those of another. See also **constructive delivery.**

demand Request for payment made by the holder of the instrument.

demand paper Payable on request.

demurrer An allegation of a defendant that, even if the facts as stated in the pleading to which objection is taken be true, yet their legal consequences are not such as to put the demurring party to the necessity of answering them or proceeding further with the cause.

deposition The testimony of a witness taken upon interrogatories, not in court, but intended to be used in court. See also **discovery.**

depository bank The first bank to which an item is transferred for collection even though it may also be the payor bank. U.C.C. § 4–105(a).

descent Succession to the ownership of an estate by inheritance, or by any act of law, as distinguished from "purchase."

Descents are of two sorts, *lineal* and *collateral.* Lineal descent is descent in a direct or right line, as from father or grandfather to son or grandson. Collateral descent is descent in a collateral or oblique line, that is, up to the common ancestor and then down from him, as from brother to brother, or between cousins.

design defect Inadequate plans or specifications to insure the products' safety.

devise A testamentary disposition of land or realty; a gift of real property by the last will and testament of the donor. When used as a noun, means a testamentary disposition of real or personal property and when used as a verb, means to dispose of real or personal property by will.

dictum Generally used as an abbreviated form of *obiter dictum,* "a remark by the way;" that is, an observation or remark made by a judge which does not embody the resolution or determination of the court and which is made without argument or full consideration of the point.

directed verdict In a case in which the party with the burden of proof has failed to present a prima facie case for jury consideration, the trial judge may order the entry of a verdict without allowing the jury to consider it, because, as a matter of law, there can be only one such verdict.

disaffirmance Avoidance of the contract.

discharge Termination of certain allowed claims against a debtor.

disclaimer Negation of warranty.

discount A discount by a bank means a drawback or deduction made upon its advances or loans of money, upon negotiable paper or other evidences of debt payable at a future day, which are transferred to the bank.

discovery The pre-trial devices that can be used by one party to obtain facts and information about the case from the other party in order to assist the party's preparation for trial. Discovery includes: depositions upon oral and written questions, written interrogatories, production of documents or things, permission to enter upon land or other property, physical and mental examinations and requests for admission.

dishonor To refuse to accept or pay a draft or to pay a promissory note when duly presented. U.C.C. § 3–507(1); § 4–210. See also **protest.**

disparagement Publication of false statements resulting in harm to another's monetary interests.

disputed debt Obligation whose existence or amount is contested.

dissenting shareholder One who opposes a fundamental change and has the right to receive the fair value of her shares.

dissolution The dissolution of a partnership is the change in the relation of the partners caused by any partner ceasing to be associated in the carrying on as distinguished from the winding up of the business. See also **winding up.**

distribution Transfer of partnership property from the partnership to a partner; transfer of property from a corporation to any of its shareholders.

dividend The payment designated by the board of directors of a corporation to be distributed pro rata among a class or classes of the shares outstanding.

document Document of title.

document of title Instrument evidencing ownership of the document and the goods it covers.

domicile That place where a person has his true, fixed, and permanent home and principal establishment, and to which whenever he is absent he has the intention of returning.

dominant Land whose owner has rights in other land.

donee Recipient of a gift.

donee beneficiary See **third party beneficiary.**

donor Maker of a gift.

dormant partner One who is both a silent and a secret partner.

dower A species of life-estate which a woman is, by law, entitled to claim on the death of her husband, in the lands and tenements of which he was seised in fee during the marriage, and which her issue, if any, might by possibility have inherited.

Dower has been abolished in the majority of the states and materially altered in most of the others.

draft A written order by the first party, called the drawer, instructing a second party, called the drawee (such as a bank) to pay a third party, called the payee. An order to pay a sum certain in money, signed by a drawer, payable on demand or at a definite time, and to order or bearer. U.C.C. § 3–104.

drawee A person to whom a bill of exchange or draft is directed, and who is requested to pay the amount of money therein mentioned. The drawee of a check is the bank on which it is drawn.

When drawee accepts, he engages that he will pay the instrument according to its tenor at the time of his engagement or as completed. U.C.C. § 3–413(1).

drawer The person who draws a bill or draft. The drawer of a check is the person who signs it.

The drawer engages that upon dishonor of the draft and any necessary notice of dishonor or protest, he will pay the amount of the draft to the holder or to any indorser who takes it up. The drawer may disclaim this liability by drawing without recourse, U.C.C. § 3–413(2).

due negotiation Transfer of a negotiable document in the regular course of business to a holder, who takes in good faith, without notice of any defense or claim, and for value.

duress Unlawful constraint exercised upon a person, whereby he is forced to do some act against his will.

Physical duress Coercion involving physical force or the threat of physical force.

duty Legal obligation requiring a person to perform or refrain from performing an act.

E

earned surplus Undistributed net profits, income, gains and losses.

earnest The payment of a part of the price of goods sold, or the delivery of part of such goods, for the purpose of binding the contract.

easement A right in the owner of one parcel of land, by reason of such ownership, to use the land of another for a special purpose not inconsistent with a general property in the owner. This right is distinguishable from a "license" which merely confers personal privilege to do some act on the land.

Affirmative easement One where the servient estate must permit something to be done thereon, as to pass over it, or to discharge water on it.

Appurtenant easement An incorporeal right which is attached to a superior right and inheres in land to which it is attached and is in the nature of a covenant running with the land.

Easement by necessity Such arises by operation of law when land conveyed is completely shut off from access to any road by land retained by grantor or by land of grantor and that of a stranger.

Easement by prescription A mode of acquiring title to property by immemorial or long-continued enjoyment, and refers to personal usage restricted to claimant and his ancestors or grantors.

Easement in gross An easement in gross is not appurtenant to any estate in land or does not belong to any person by virtue of ownership of estate in other land but is mere personal interest in or right to use land of another; it is purely personal and usually ends with death of grantee.

Easement of access Right of ingress and egress to and from the premises of a lot owner to a street appurtenant to the land of the lot owner.

ejectment An action of which the purpose is to determine whether the title to certain land is in the plaintiff or is in the defendant.

electronic fund transfer A transaction with a financial institution by means of computer, telephone, or electronic instrument.

emancipation The act by which an infant is set at liberty from the control of parent or guardian and made his own master.

embezzlement The taking in violation of a trust the property of one's employer.

emergency Sudden, unexpected event calling for immediate action.

eminent domain   Right of the people or government to take private property for public use upon giving of a fair consideration.

employment discrimination   Hiring, firing, compensating, promoting, or training of employees based on race, color, sex, religion, or national origin.

employment relationship   One in which employer has right to control the physical conduct of employee.

endowment contract   Agreement to pay insured a lump sum upon reaching a specified age or in event of death.

entirety   Used to designate that which the law considers as one whole, and not capable of being divided into parts.

entrapment   Induced into committing a crime by a government official.

entrusting   Transfer of possession of goods to a merchant who deals in goods of that kind and who may in turn transfer valid title to a buyer in the ordinary course of business.

equal pay   Equivalent pay for the same work.

equal protection   Requirement that similarly situated persons be treated similarly by government action.

equipment   Goods used primarily in business.

equitable   Just, fair, and right. Existing in equity; available or sustainable only in equity, or only upon the rules and principles of equity.

equity   Justice administered according to fairness as contrasted with the strictly formulated rules of common law. It is based on a system of rules and principles which originated in England as an alternative to the harsh rules of common law and which were based on what was fair in a particular situation.

equity of redemption   The right of the mortgagor of an estate to redeem the same after it has been forfeited, at law, by a breach of the condition of the mortgage, upon paying the amount of debt, interest, and costs.

equity securities   Stock or similar security, in contrast to debt securities such as bonds, notes, and debentures.

error   A mistake of law, or false or irregular application of it, such as vitiates the proceedings and warrants the reversal of the judgment.

Harmless error   In appellate practice, an error committed in the progress of the trial below which was not prejudicial to the rights of the party assigning it and for which, therefore, the court will not reverse the judgment.

Reversible error   In appellate practice, such an error as warrants the appellate court in reversing the judgment before it.

escrow   A system of document transfer in which a deed, bond, or funds is delivered to a third person to hold until all conditions in a contract are fulfilled; *e.g.,* delivery of deed to escrow agent under installment land sale contract until full payment for land is made.

estate   The degree, quantity, nature, and extent of interest which a person has in real and personal property. An estate in lands, tenements, and hereditaments signifies such interest as the tenant has therein.

Also, the total property of whatever kind that is owned by a decedent prior to the distribution of that property in accordance with the terms of a will, or, when there is no will, by the laws of inheritance in the State of domicile of the decedent.

Future estate   An estate limited to commence in possession at a future day, either without the intervention of a precedent estate, or on the determination by lapse of time, or otherwise, of a precedent estate created at the same time. Examples include reversions and remainders.

estoppel   A bar or impediment raised by the law, which precludes a man from alleging or from denying a certain fact or state of facts, in consequence of his previous allegation or denial or conduct or admission, or in consequence of a final adjudication of the matter in a court of law. See also **waiver**.

eviction   Dispossession by process of law; the act of depriving a person of the possession of lands which he has held, in pursuance of the judgment of a court.

evidence   Any species of proof, or probative matter, legally presented at the trial of an issue, by the act of the parties and through the medium of witnesses, records, documents, concrete objects, etc., for the purpose of inducing belief in the minds of the court or jury as to their contention.

exception   A formal objection to the action of the court, during the trial of a cause, in refusing a request or overruling an objection; implying that the party excepting does not acquiesce in the decision of the court, but will seek to procure its reversal, and that he means to save the benefit of his request or objection in some future proceeding.

exclusionary rule Prohibition of illegally obtained evidence.

exclusive dealing Sole right to sell goods in a defined market.

exclusive jurisdiction Such jurisdiction that permits only one court (State or Federal) to hear a case.

exculpatory clause Excusing oneself from fault or liability.

execution *Execution of contract* includes performance of all acts necessary to render it complete as an instrument and imports idea that nothing remains to be done to make a complete and effective contract.
Execution upon a money judgment is the legal process of enforcing the judgment, usually by seizing and selling property of the debtor.

executive order Legislation issued by the President or a governor.

executor A person appointed by a testator to carry out the directions and requests in his will, and to dispose of the property according to his testamentary provisions after his decease. The female designation is executrix. A person appointed by the court in an intestacy situation is called the administrator(rix).

executory That which is yet to be executed or performed; that which remains to be carried into operation or effect; incomplete; depending upon a future performance or event. The opposite of executed.

executory contract See **contracts.**

executory promise Unperformed obligation.

exemplary damages See **damages.**

exoneration Relieved of liability.

express Manifested by direct and appropriate language, as distinguished from that which is inferred from conduct. The word is usually contrasted with "implied."

express warranty Explicitly made contractual promise regarding property or contract rights transferred; in a sale of goods affirmation of fact or promise about the goods or a description, including sample, of goods which becomes part of the basis of the bargain.

expropriation Governmental taking of foreign-owned property for a public purpose and with payment.

ex-ship Risk of loss passes to buyer upon the goods leaving the ship. See U.C.C. § 2–322. See also **F.A.S.**

extortion Making threats to obtain property.

F

fact An event that took place or a thing that exists.

false imprisonment Intentional interference with a person's freedom of movement by unlawful confinement.

false light Offensive publicity placing another in a false light.

false pretenses Intentional misrepresentation of fact for purpose to cheat.

farm products Crops, livestock, or stock used or produced in farming.

F.A.S. Free alongside. Term used in sales price quotations, indicating that the price includes all costs of transportation and delivery of the goods alongside the ship. See U.C.C. § 2–319(2).

Federal preemption First right of the Federal government to regulate matters within its powers to the possible exclusion of State regulation.

Federal question Any case arising under the Constitution, statutes, or treaties of the United States.

fee simple An estate of inheritance.
Absolute A fee simple absolute is an estate that is unlimited as to duration, disposition, and descendibility. It is the largest estate and most extensive interest that can be enjoyed in land.
Conditional Type of transfer in which grantor conveys fee simple on condition that something be done or not done.
Defeasible Type of fee grant which may be defeated on the happening of an event. An estate which may last forever, but which may end upon the happening of a specified event, is a "fee simple defeasible."
Determinable Created by conveyance which contains words effective to create a fee simple and, in addition, a provision for automatic expiration of estate on occurrence of stated event.

fee tail An estate of inheritance, descending only to a certain class or classes or heirs; *e.g.,* an estate is conveyed or devised "to A. and the heirs of his body," or "to A. and the heirs male of his body," or "to A., and the heirs female of his body." State statutes have dealt variously with estates tail, some converting them into estates in fee simple.

fellow servant rule Common law defense relieving employer for liability to an employee for injuries caused by negligence of fellow employee.

felony Serious crime.

fiduciary A person or institution who manages money or property for another and who must exercise a standard of care in such management activity imposed by law or contract; *e.g.*, executor of estate; receiver in bankruptcy; trustee.

fiduciary duty Duty of utmost loyalty and good faith owed by a fiduciary such as an agent owes to her principal.

field warehouse Secured party takes possession of the goods but the debtor has access to the goods.

final credit Payment of the instrument by the payor bank.

financing statement Under the Uniform Commercial Code, a financing statement is used under Article 9 to reflect a public record that there is a security interest or claim to the goods in question to secure a debt. The financing statement is filed by the security holder with the Secretary of State, or similar public body, and as such becomes public record. See also **secured transaction.**

fire (property) insurance Provides protection against loss due to fire or other related perils.

firm offer Irrevocable offer to sell or buy goods by a merchant in a signed writing which gives assurance that it will not be rescinded for up to three months.

fitness for a particular purpose Goods are fit for a stated purpose provided the seller selects the product knowing the buyer's intended use and that the buyer is relying on the seller's judgment.

fixture An article in the nature of personal property which has been so annexed to realty that it is regarded as a part of the land. Examples include a furnace affixed to a house or other building, counters permanently affixed to the floor of a store, a sprinkler system installed in a building. U.C.C. § 9–313(1)(a).
Trade fixtures Such chattels as merchants usually possess and annex to the premises occupied by them to enable them to store, handle, and display their goods, which are generally removable without material injury to the premises.

F.O.B. Free on board some location (for example, F.O.B. shipping point; F.O.B. destination); the invoice price includes delivery at seller's expense to that location. Title to goods usually passes from seller to buyer at the F.O.B. location. U.C.C. § 2–319(1).

foreclosure Procedure by which mortgaged property is sold on default of mortgagor in satisfaction of mortgage debt.

forgery Intentional falsification of a document with intent to defraud.

four unities Time, title, interest, and possession.

franchise A privilege granted or sold, such as to use a name or to sell products or services. The right given by a manufacturer or supplier to a retailer to use his products and name on terms and conditions mutually agreed upon.

fraud Elements include: false representation; of a present or past fact; made by defendant; action in reliance thereon by plaintiff; damage resulting to plaintiff from such misrepresentation.

fraud in the execution Misrepresentation that deceives the other party as to the nature of a document evidencing the contract.

fraud in the inducement Misrepresentation regarding the subject matter of a contract and inducing the other party to enter into it.

fraudulent misrepresentation False statement made with knowledge of its falsity and intent to mislead.

freehold An estate for life or in fee. It must possess two qualities: (1) immobility, that is, the property must be either land or some interest issuing out of or annexed to land; and (2) indeterminate duration.

friendly fire Fire contained where it is intended to be.

frustration of purpose doctrine Excuses a promisor in certain situations when the objectives of contract have been utterly defeated by circumstances arising after formation of agreement, and performance is excused under this rule even though there is no impediment to actual performance.

full warranty One under which warrantor will repair the product and, if unsuccessful, will replace or refund.

fungibles With respect to goods or securities, those of which any unit is, by nature or usage of trade, the equivalent of any other like unit. U.C.C. § 1–201(17); *e.g.,* a bushel of wheat or other grain.

future estate See **estate.**

G

garnishment A statutory proceeding whereby a person's property, money, or credits in the possession or control of another are applied to payment of the former's debt to a third person.

general intangible Catchall category of collateral not otherwise covered.

general partner Member of either a general or limited partnership with unlimited liability for its debts, full management powers, and a right to share in the profits.

gift A voluntary transfer of property to another made gratuitously and without consideration. Essential requisites of "gift" are capacity of donor, intention of donor to make gift, completed delivery to or for donee, and acceptance of gift by donee.

gift causa mortis A gift in view of death is one which is made in contemplation, fear, or peril of death, and with intent that it shall take effect only in case of the death of the giver.

good faith Honesty in fact in conduct or a transaction.

good faith purchaser Buyer who acts honestly, gives value, and takes the goods without notice or knowledge of any defect in the title of his transferor.

goods A term of variable content and meaning. It may include every species of personal property or it may be given a very restricted meaning. Sometimes the meaning of "goods" is extended to include all tangible items, as in the phrase "goods and services."

All things (including specially manufactured goods) which are movable at the time of identification to the contract for sale other than the money in which the price is to be paid, investment securities and things in action. U.C.C. § 2–105(1).

grantee Transferee of property.

grantor A transferor of property. The creator of a trust is usually designated as the grantor of the trust.

gratuitous promise Promise made without consideration.

group insurance Covers a number of individuals.

guaranty A promise to answer for the payment of some debt, or the performance of some duty, in case of the failure of another person, who, in the first instance, is liable to such payment or performance.

The terms *guaranty* and *suretyship* are sometimes used interchangeably; but they should not be confounded. The distinction between contract of suretyship and contract of guaranty is whether or not the undertaking is a joint undertaking with the principal or a separate and distinct contract; if it is the former it is one of "suretyship", and if the latter, it is one of "guaranty." See also **surety.**

guardianship The relationship under which a person (the guardian) is appointed by a court to preserve and control the property of another (the ward).

H

heir A person who succeeds, by the rules of law, to an estate in lands, tenements, or hereditaments, upon the death of his ancestor, by descent and right of relationship.

holder Person who is in possession of a document of title or an instrument or an investment security drawn, issued or endorsed to him or to his order, or to bearer or in blank. U.C.C. § 1–201(20).

holder in due course A holder who takes an instrument for value, in good faith, and without notice that it is overdue or has been dishonored or of any defense against or claim to it on the part of any person.

holograph A will or deed written entirely by the testator or grantor with his own hand and not witnessed (attested). State laws vary with respect to the validity of the holographic will.

homicide Unlawful taking of another's life.

horizontal restraints Agreements among competitors.

horizontal privity Who may bring a cause of action.

hostile fire Any fire outside its intended or usual place.

I

identified goods Designated goods as part of a particular contract.

illegal per se Conclusively presumed unreasonable and therefore illegal.

illusory promise Promise imposing no obligation on the promisor.

implied-in-fact condition Contingencies understood but not expressed by the parties.

implied-in-law condition Contingency that arises from operation of law.

implied warranty Obligation imposed by law upon the transferor of property or contract rights; implicit in the sale arising out of certain circumstances.

implied warranty of habitability Leased premises are fit for ordinary residential purposes.

impossibility Performance that cannot be done.

in personam Against the person. Action seeking judgment against a person involving his personal rights and based on jurisdiction of his person, as distinguished from a judgment against property (*i.e.,* in rem).

in personam jurisdiction Jurisdiction based on claims against a person in contrast to jurisdiction over his property.

in re In the affair; in the matter of; concerning; regarding. This is the usual method of entitling a judicial proceeding in which there are not adversary parties, but merely some *res* concerning which judicial action is to be taken, such as a bankrupt's estate, an estate in the probate court, a proposed public highway, etc.

in rem A technical term used to designate proceedings or actions instituted *against the thing,* in contradistinction to personal actions, which are said to be *in personam.*

   Quasi in rem A term applied to proceedings which are not strictly and purely *in rem,* but are brought against the defendant personally, though the real object is to deal with particular property or subject property to the discharge of claims asserted; for example, foreign attachment, or proceedings to foreclose a mortgage, remove a cloud from title, or effect a partition.

in rem jurisdiction Jurisdiction based on claims against property.

incidental beneficiary Third party whom the two parties to a contract have no intention of benefitting by their contract.

income bond Bond that conditions payment of interest on corporate earnings.

incontestability clause The prohibition of an insurer to avoid an insurance policy after a specified period of time.

indemnification Duty owed by principal to agent to pay agent for losses incurred while acting as directed by principal.

indemnify To reimburse one for a loss already incurred.

indenture A written agreement under which bonds and debentures are issued, setting forth maturity date, interest rate, and other terms.

independent contractor Person who contracts with another to do a particular job and is not subject to the control of the other.

indicia Signs; indications. Circumstances which point to the existence of a given fact as probable, but not certain.

indictment Grand jury charge that the defendant should stand trial.

indispensable paper Chattel paper, instruments, and documents.

indorsee The person to whom a negotiable instrument, promissory note, bill of lading, etc., is assigned by indorsement.

indorsement The act of a payee, drawee, accommodation indorser, or holder of a bill, note, check, or other negotiable instrument, in writing his name upon the back of the same, with or without further or qualifying words, whereby the property in the same is assigned and transferred to another. U.C.C. § 3–202 *et seq.*

   Blank indorsement No indorsee is specified.

   Qualified indorsement Without recourse, limiting one's liability of the instrument.

   Restrictive indorsement Limits the rights of the indorser in some manner.

   Special indorsement Designates an indorsee to be paid.

infliction of emotional distress Extreme and outrageous conduct intentionally or recklessly causing severe emotional distress.

information Formal accusation of a crime brought by a prosecutor.

infringement Unauthorized use.

injunction An equitable remedy forbidding the party defendant from doing some act which he is threatening or attempting to commit, or restraining him in the continuance thereof, such act being unjust and inequitable, injurious to the plaintiff, and not such as can be adequately redressed by an action at law.

innkeeper Hotel or motel operator.

inquisitorial system System in which the judiciary initiates, conducts and decides cases.

insider Relative or general partner of debtor, partnership in which debtor is a partner, or corporation in which debtor is an officer, director, or controlling person.

insiders Directors, officers, employees, and agents of the issuer as well as those the issuer has entrusted with information solely for corporate purposes.

insolvency Under U.C.C., a person is insolvent who either has ceased to pay his debts in the ordinary course of business or cannot pay his debts as they fall due or is insolvent within the meaning of the Federal Bankruptcy Law. U.C.C. § 1–201(23).

Insolvency (bankruptcy) Total liabilities exceed total value of assets.

Insolvency (equity) Inability to pay debts in ordinary course of business or as they become due.

inspection Examination of the goods to determine whether they conform to the contract.

instrument Negotiable instruments, stocks, bonds, and other investment securities.

insurable interest Exists where insured derives pecuniary benefit or advantage by preservation and continued existence of property or would sustain pecuniary loss from its destruction.

insurance A contract whereby, for a stipulated consideration, one party undertakes to compensate the other for loss on a specified subject by specified perils. The party agreeing to make the compensation is usually called the "insurer" or "underwriter"; the other, the "insured" or "assured"; the written contract, a "policy"; the events insured against, "risks" or "perils"; and the subject, right, or interest to be protected, the "insurable interest." Insurance is a contract whereby one undertakes to indemnify another against loss, damage, or liability arising from an unknown or contingent event.

Co-insurance A form of insurance in which a person insures property for less than its full or stated value and agrees to share the risk of loss.

Life insurance Payment of a specific sum of money to a designated beneficiary upon the death of the insured.

Ordinary life Life insurance with a savings component that runs for the life of the insured.

Term life Life insurance issued for a limited number of years that does not have a savings component.

intangible property Protected interests that are not physical.

intangibles Accounts and general intangibles.

intent Desire to cause the consequences of an act or knowledge that the consequences are substantially certain to result from the act.

inter alia Among other things.

inter se or **inter sese** Latin. Among or between themselves; used to distinguish rights or duties between two or more parties from their rights or duties to others.

interest in land Any right, privilege, power, or immunity in real property.

interest in partnership Partner's share in the partnership's profits and surplus.

interference with contractual relations Intentionally causing one of the parties to a contract not to perform the contract.

intermediary bank Any bank to which an item is transferred in the course of collection except the depositary or payor bank. U.C.C. § 4–105(c).

intermediate test Requirement that legislation have a substantial relationship to an important governmental objective.

international law Deals with the conduct and relations of nation-states and international organizations.

interpretation Construction or meaning of the contract.

interpretative rules Statements issued by an administrative agency indicating its construction of its governing statute.

intestate A person is said to die intestate when he dies without making a will. The word is also often used to signify the person himself. *Compare* **testator.**

intrusion Unreasonable and highly offensive interference with the seclusion of another.

inventory Goods held for sale or lease or consumed in a business.

invitee A person is an "invitee" on land of another if (1) he enters by invitation, express or implied, (2) his entry is connected with the owner's business or with an activity the owner conducts or permits to be conducted on his land and (3) there is mutuality of benefit or benefit to the owner.

J

joint and several liability Liability where creditor may sue partners jointly as a group or separately as individuals.

joint liability Liability where creditor must sue all of the partners as a group.

joint stock company A general partnership with some corporate attributes.

joint tenancy See **tenancy.**

joint venture An association of two or more persons to carry on a single business transaction for profit.

judgment The official and authentic decision of a court of justice upon the respective rights and claims of the parties to an action or suit therein litigated and submitted to its determination.

judgment in personam A judgment against a particular person, as distinguished from a judgment against a thing or a right or *status.*

judgment in rem An adjudication pronounced upon the status of some particular thing or subject matter, by a tribunal having competent authority.

judgment n. o. v. Judgment non obstante verdicto in its broadest sense is a judgment rendered in favor of one party notwithstanding the finding of a verdict in favor of the other party.

judgment notwithstanding the verdict A final binding determination on the merits made by the judge after and contrary to the jury's verdict.

judgment on the pleadings Final binding determination on the merits made by the judge after the pleadings.

judicial lien Interest in property that is obtained by court action to secure payment of a debt.

judicial review Power of the courts to determine the constitutionality of legislative and executive acts.

jurisdiction The right and power of a court to adjudicate concerning the subject matter in a given case.

jurisdiction over the parties Power of a court to bind the parties to a suit.

jury (From the Latin jurare, to swear.) A body of persons selected and summoned by law and sworn to try the facts of a case and to find according to the law and the evidence. In general, the province of the jury is to find the facts in a case, while the judge passes upon pure questions of law. As a matter of fact, however, the jury must often pass upon mixed questions of law and fact in determining the case, and in all such cases the instructions of the judge as to the law become very important.

justifiable reliance Reasonably influenced by the misrepresentation.

L

labor dispute Any controversy concerning terms or conditions of employment or union representation.

laches Based upon maxim that equity aids the vigilant and not those who slumber on their rights. It is defined as neglect to assert right or claim which, taken together with lapse of time and other circumstances causing prejudice to adverse party, operates as bar in court of equity.

landlord The owner of an estate in land, or a rental property, who has leased it to another person, called the "tenant." Also called "lessor."

larceny Trespassory taking and carrying away the goods of another with the intent to permanently deprive.

last clear chance Final opportunity to avoid an injury.

lease Any agreement which gives rise to relationship of landlord and tenant (real property) or lessor and lessee (real or personal property).

The person who conveys is termed the "lessor," and the person to whom conveyed, the "lessee;" and when the lessor conveys land or tenements to a lessee, he is said to lease, demise, or let them.

Sublease, or underlease One executed by the lessee of an estate to a third person, conveying the same estate for a shorter term than that for which the lessee holds it.

leasehold An estate in realty held under a lease. The four principal types of leasehold estates are the estate for years, periodic tenancy, tenancy at will, and tenancy at sufferance.

leasehold estate Right to possess real property.

legacy "Legacy" is a gift or bequest by will of personal property, whereas a "devise" is a testamentary disposition of real estate.

Demonstrative legacy A bequest of a certain sum of money, with a direction that it shall be paid out of a particular fund. It differs from a specific legacy in this respect: that, if the fund out of which it is payable fails for any cause, it is nevertheless entitled to come on the estate as a general legacy. And it differs from a general legacy in this: that it does not abate in that class, but in the class of specific legacies.

General legacy A pecuniary legacy, payable out of the general assets of a testator.

Residuary legacy A bequest of all the testator's personal estate not otherwise effectually disposed of by his will.

Specific legacy One which operates on property particularly designated. A legacy or gift by will of a particular specified thing, as of a horse, a piece of furniture, a term of years, and the like.

legal aggregate A group of individuals not having a legal existence separate from its members.

legal benefit Obtaining something one had no legal right to.

legal detriment Doing an act not legally obligated to do or not doing an act which one has a legal right to do.

legal entity An organization having a separate legal existence from its members.

legal sufficiency Benefit to promisor or detriment to promisee.

legislative rules Substantive rules issued by an administrative agency under the authority delegated to it by the legislature.

letter of credit An engagement by a bank or other person made at the request of a customer that the issuer will honor drafts or other demands for payment upon compliance with the conditions specified in the credit.

letters of administration Formal document issued by probate court appointing one an administrator of an estate.

letters testamentary The formal instrument of authority and appointment given to an executor by the proper court, empowering him to enter upon the discharge of his office as executor. It corresponds to letters of administration granted to an administrator.

levy To assess; raise; execute; exact; tax; collect; gather; take up; seize. Thus, to levy (assess, exact, raise, or collect) a tax; to levy an execution, *i.e.,* to levy or collect a sum of money on an execution.

liability insurance Covers liability to others by reason of damage resulting from injuries to another's person or property.

liability without fault Crime to do a specific act or cause a certain result without regard to the care exercised.

libel Defamation communicated by writing, television, radio, or the like.

liberty Ability of individuals to engage in freedom of action and choice regarding their personal lives.

license License with respect to real property is a privilege to go on premises for a certain purpose, but does not operate to confer on, or vest in, licensee any title, interest, or estate in such property.

licensee Person privileged to enter or remain on land by virtue of the consent of the lawful possessor.

lien A qualified right of property which a creditor has in or over specific property of his debtor, as security for the debt or charge or for performance of some act.

lien creditor A creditor who has acquired a lien on the property by attachment.

life estate An estate whose duration is limited to the life of the party holding it, or some other person. Upon the death of the life tenant, the property will go to the holder of the remainder interest or to the grantor by reversion.

limited liability Liability limited to amount invested in a business enterprise.

limited partner Member of a limited partnership with liability for its debts only to the extent of her capital contribution.

limited partnership See **partnership.**

limited partnership association A partnership which closely resembles a corporation.

liquidated Ascertained; determined; fixed; settled; made clear or manifest. Cleared away; paid; discharged.

liquidated damages See **damages.**

liquidated debt Obligation that is certain in amount.

liquidation The settling of financial affairs of a business or individual, usually by liquidating (turning to cash) all assets for distribution to creditors, heirs, etc. It is to be distinguished from dissolution.

loss of value Value of promised performance minus value of actual performance.

lost property Property which the owner has involuntarily parted with and does not know where to find or recover it, not including property which he has intentionally concealed or deposited in a secret place for safekeeping. Distinguishable from mislaid property which has been deliberately placed somewhere and forgotten.

M

McNaughton test Right/wrong test for criminal insanity.

main purpose rule Where object of promisor/surety is to provide an economic benefit for herself, the promise is considered outside of the statute of frauds.

maker One who makes or executes; as the maker of a promissory note. One who signs a check; in this context, synonymous with drawer. See **draft.**

mala in se Morally wrong.

mala prohibita Wrong by law.

mandamus Latin, we command. A legal writ compelling the defendant to do an official duty.

manslaughter Unlawful taking of another's life without malice.

Involuntary manslaughter Taking the life of another by criminal negligence or during the course of a misdemeanor.

Voluntary manslaughter Intentional killing of another under extenuating circumstances.

manufacturing defect Not produced according to specifications.

mark Trade symbol.

market allocations Division of market by customers, geographic location, or products.

marketable title Free from any defects, encumbrances or reasonable objections to one's ownership.

marshaling of assets Segregating the assets and liabilities of the partnership separately from the assets and liabilities of the individual partners.

master See **principal.**

material Matters to which a reasonable investor would attach importance in deciding whether to purchase a security.

material alteration Any change that changes the contract of any party to the instrument.

maturity The date at which an obligation, such as the principal of a bond or a note, becomes due.

maxim A general legal principle.

mechanic's lien A claim created by State statutes for the purpose of securing priority of payment of the price or value of work performed and materials furnished in erecting or repairing a building or other structure, and as such attaches to the land as well as buildings and improvements erected thereon.

mediation Nonbinding process in which a third party acts as an intermediary between the disputing parties and proposes solutions for them to consider.

mens rea Criminal intent.

mentally incompetent Unable to understand the nature and effect of one's acts.

mercantile law An expression substantially equivalent to commercial law. It designates the system of rules, customs, and usages generally recognized and adopted by merchants and traders, and which, either in its simplicity or as modified by common law or statutes, constitutes the law for the regulation of their transactions and the solution of their controversies. The Uniform Commercial Code is the general body of law governing commercial or mercantile transactions.

merchant A person who deals in goods of the kind or otherwise by his occupation holds himself out as having knowledge or skill peculiar to the practices or goods involved in the transaction or to whom such knowledge or skill may be attributed by his employment of an agent or broker or other intermediary who by his occupation holds himself out as having such knowledge or skill. U.C.C. § 2–104(1).

merchantability Merchant seller guarantees that the goods are fit for their ordinary purpose.

merger The fusion or absorption of one thing or right into another. In corporate law, the absorption of one company by another, latter retaining its own name and identity and acquiring assets, liabilities, franchises, and powers of former, and absorbed company ceasing to exist as separate business entity. It differs from a consolidation wherein all the corporations terminate their existence and become parties to a new one.

Conglomerate merger An acquisition by one company of another which is not horizontal or vertical.

Horizontal merger Merger between business competitors, such as manufacturers of the same type products or distributors selling competing products in the same market area.

Short-form merger Merger of a 90 percent subsidiary into its parent.

Vertical merger Union with corporate customer or supplier.

midnight deadline Midnight of the next banking day after receiving an item.

mining partnership A specific type of partnership for the purpose of extracting raw minerals.

minor Under full legal age (usually eighteen).

mirror image rule An acceptance cannot deviate from the terms of the offer.

misdemeanor Less serious crime.

mislaid property Property which an owner has put deliberately in a certain place but owner is unable to remember where he put it, as distinguished from lost property which the owner leaves unwittingly in a place, forgetting its location. See also **lost property.**

misrepresentation Any manifestation by words or other conduct by one person to another that, under the circumstances, amounts to an assertion not in accordance with the facts. A "misrepresentation" that justifies the rescission of a contract is a false statement of a substantive fact, or any conduct which leads to a belief of a substantive fact material to proper understanding of the matter in hand. See also **deceit; fraud.**

Fraudulent misrepresentation False statement made with knowledge of its falsity and intent to mislead.

Innocent misrepresentation Misrepresentation made without knowledge of its falsity but with due care.

Negligent misrepresentation Misrepresentation made without due care in ascertaining its falsity.

modify Change the lower court's judgment.

money Medium of exchange issued by government body.

monopoly Ability to control price or exclude others from the marketplace.

mortgage A mortgage is an interest in land created by a written instrument providing security for the performance of a duty or the payment of a debt.

mortgagor Debtor who uses real estate to secure an obligation.

multinational enterprise Business that engages in transactions involving the movement of goods, information, money, people, or services across national borders.

multiple product order Order requiring an advertiser to cease and desist from deceptive statements on all products it sells.

murder Unlawful and premeditated taking of another's life.

mutual mistake Where both parties have a common but erroneous belief forming the basis of a contract.

N

necessary Items needed to maintain a person's station in life.

negligence The omission to do something which a reasonable man, guided by those ordinary considerations which ordinarily regulate human affairs, would do, or the doing of something which a reasonable and prudent man would not do.

Culpable negligence Greater than ordinary negligence but less than gross negligence.

negligence per se Conclusive on the issue of negligence (duty of care and breach).

negotiable Legally capable of being transferred by endorsement or delivery. Usually said of checks and notes and sometimes of stocks and bearer bonds.

negotiable instrument Signed document (such as a check or promissory note) containing an unconditional promise to pay a "sum certain" of money at a definite time to order or bearer.

negotiation Transferee becomes a holder.

net assets Total assets minus total debts.

no arrival, no sale A destination contract, but if goods do not arrive, seller is excused from liability unless it is due to the seller's fault.

no-fault insurance Compensates victims of automobile accidents regardless of fault.

nonconforming use Pre-existing use not in accordance with the zoning ordinance.

nonprofit corporation One whose profits must be used exclusively for the charitable, educational, or scientific purpose for which it was formed.

nonsuit Action in form of a judgment taken against a plaintiff who has failed to appear to prosecute his action or failed to prove his case.

note See **promissory note.**

novation A novation substitutes a new party and discharges one of the original parties to a contract by agreement of all three parties. A new contract is created with the same terms as the original one but only the parties are changed.

nuisance Nuisance is that activity which arises from unreasonable, unwarranted or unlawful use by a person of his own property, working obstruction or injury to right of another, or to the public, and producing such material annoyance, inconvenience and discomfort that law will presume resulting damage.

O

obiter dictum See **dictum.**

objective fault Gross deviation from reasonable conduct.

objective manifestation What a reasonable man under the circumstances would believe.

objective satisfaction Approval based upon whether a reasonable person would be satisfied.

objective standard What a reasonable man under the circumstances would reasonably believe or do.

obligee Party to whom a duty of performance is owed (by delegator and delegatee).

obligor Party owing a duty (to the assignor).

offer A manifestation of willingness to enter into a bargain, so made as to justify another person in understanding that his assent to that bargain is invited and will conclude it. Restatement, Second, Contracts, § 24.

offeree Recipient of the offer.

offeror Person making the offer.

open-ended credit Credit arrangement under which debtor has rights to enter into a series of credit transactions.

opinion Belief in the existence of a fact or a judgment as to value.

option Contract that provides that an offer will stay open for a specified period of time.

order A final disposition made by an agency.

order paper Payable to a named person or anyone designated by that person.

order to pay Direction or command to pay.

original promise Promise to become primarily liable.

output contract See **contracts.**

P

palpable unilateral mistake Erroneous belief by one party that is recognized by the other.

parent corporation Corporation which controls another corporation.

parol evidence Literally oral evidence, but now includes prior to and contemporaneous, oral and written evidence.

parol evidence rule Under this rule, when parties put their agreement in writing, all previous oral agreements merge in the writing and a contract as written cannot be modified or changed by parol evidence, in the absence of a plea of mistake or fraud in the preparation of the writing. But rule does not forbid a resort to parol evidence not inconsistent with the matters stated in the writing. Also, as regards sales of goods, such written agreement may be explained or supplemented by course of dealing or usage of trade or by course of conduct, and by evidence of consistent additional terms unless the court finds the writing to have been intended also as a complete and exclusive statement of the terms of the agreement. U.C.C. § 2–202.

part performance In order to establish part performance taking an oral contract for the sale of realty out of the statute of frauds, the acts relied upon as part performance must be of such a character that they can reasonably be naturally accounted for in no other way than that they were performed in pursuance of the contract, and they must be in conformity with its provisions. See U.C.C. § 2–201(3).

partial assignment Transfer of a portion of contractual rights to one or more assignees.

partition The dividing of lands held by joint tenants, copartners, or tenants in common, into distinct portions, so that they may hold them in severalty.

partnership An association of two or more persons to carry on, as co-owners, a business for profit.

Partnerships are treated as a conduit and are, therefore, not subject to taxation. The various items of partnership income, gains, and losses, etc., flow through to the individual partners and are reported on their personal income tax returns.

Limited partnership Type of partnership comprised of one or more general partners who manage business and who are personally liable for partnership debts, and one or more limited partners who contribute capital and share in profits but who take no part in running business and incur no liability with respect to partnership obligations beyond contribution.

Partnership at will One with no definite term or specific undertaking.

partnership capital Total money and property contributed by partners for permanent use by the partnership.

partnership property Sum of all of the partnership's assets.

past consideration An act done before the contract is made.

patent Exclusive right to an invention.

payee The person in whose favor a bill of exchange, promissory note, or check is made or drawn.

payer, or **payor** One who pays, or who is to make a payment; particularly the person who is to make payment of a check, bill or note. Correlative to "payee."

payor bank A bank by which an item is payable as drawn or accepted. U.C.C. § 4–105(b). Drawee bank.

per capita This term, derived from the civil law, is much used in the law of descent and distribution, and denotes that method of dividing an intestate estate by which an equal share is given to each of a number of persons, all of whom stand in equal degree to the decedent, without reference to their stocks or the right of representation. It is the opposite of *per stirpes*.

per stirpes This term, derived from the civil law, is much used in the law of descents and distribution, and denotes that method of dividing an intestate estate where a class or group of distributees take the share which their deceased would have been entitled to, taking thus by their right of representing such ancestor, and not as so many individuals. It is the opposite of *per capita*.

perfect tender rule Seller's tender of delivery must conform exactly to the contract.

perfection of security interest Acts required of a secured party in the way of giving at least constructive notice so as to make his security interest effective at least against lien creditors of the debtor. See U.C.C. §§ 9–302 through 9–306. In most cases, the secured party may obtain perfection either by filing with Secretary of State or by taking possession of the collateral.

performance Fulfillment of one's contractual obligations. See also **part performance; specific performance.**

periodic tenancy Lease with a definite term that is to be continued.

personal defenses Contractual defenses which are good against holders but not holders in due course.

personal property Any property other than an interest in land.

petty crime Misdemeanor punishable by imprisonment of six months or less.

plaintiff The party who initiates a civil suit.

pleadings The formal allegations by the parties of their respective claims and defenses. Under rules of civil procedure the pleadings consist of a complaint, an answer, a reply to a counterclaim, an answer to a cross-claim, a third party complaint, and a third party answer.

pledge A bailment of goods to a creditor as security for some debt or engagement.
   Much of the law of pledges has been replaced by the provisions for secured transactions in Article 9 of the U.C.C.

possibility of reverter The interest which remains in a grantor or testator after the conveyance or devise of a fee simple determinable and which permits the grantor to be revested automatically of his estate on breach of the condition.

possibility test Under the statute of frauds the one year test is satisfied if performance possibly could be completed within one year.

power of appointment A power of authority conferred by one person by deed or will upon another (called the "donee") to appoint, that is, to select and nominate, the person or persons who are to receive and enjoy an estate or an income therefrom or from a fund, after the testator's death, or the donee's death, or after the termination of an existing right or interest.

power of attorney An instrument authorizing a person to act as the agent or attorney of the person granting it.

power of termination The interest left in the grantor or testator after the conveyance or devise of a fee simple on condition subsequent or conditional fee.

precatory Expressing a wish.

precedent An adjudged case or decision of a court, considered as furnishing an example or authority for an identical or similar case afterwards arising or a similar question of law. See also **stare decisis.**

preemptive right The privilege of a stockholder to maintain a proportionate share of ownership by purchasing a proportionate share of any new stock issues.

preference The act of an insolvent debtor who, in distributing his property or in assigning it for the benefit of his creditors, pays or secures to one or more creditors the full amount of their claims or a larger amount than they would be entitled to receive on a *pro rata* distribution.

preliminary hearing Determine whether there is probable cause.

premium The price for insurance protection for a specified period of exposure.

preponderance of the evidence Greater weight of the evidence; standard used in civil cases.

prescription Acquisition of a personal right to use a way, water, light, and air by reason of continuous usage. See also **easement.**

presenter's warranty Warranties given to any payor or acceptor of an instrument.

presentment The production of a negotiable instrument to the drawee for his acceptance, or to the drawer or acceptor for payment; or of a promissory note to the party liable, for payment of the same. U.C.C. § 3–504(1).

presumption A presumption is a rule of law, statutory or judicial, by which finding of a basic fact gives rise to existence of presumed fact, until presumption is rebutted. A presumption imposes on the party against whom it is directed the burden of going forward with evidence to rebut or meet the presumption, but does not shift to such party the burden of proof in the sense of the risk of nonpersuasion, which remains throughout the trial upon the party on whom it was originally cast.

price discrimination Price differential.

price fixing Any agreement for the purpose and effect of raising, depressing, fixing, pegging, or stabilizing prices.

prima facie Latin. At first sight; on the first appearance; on the face of it; so far as can be judged from the first disclosure; presumably; a fact presumed to be true unless disproved by some evidence to the contrary.

primary liability Absolute obligation to pay the negotiable instrument.

principal *Law of agency* The term "principal" describes one who has permitted or directed another (*i.e.*, agent or servant) to act for his benefit and subject to his direction and control. Principal includes in its meaning the term "master" or employer, a species of principal who, in addition to other control, has a right to control the physical conduct of the species of agents known as servants or employees, as to whom special rules are applicable with reference to harm caused by their physical acts.

Disclosed principal One whose existence and identity is known.

Partially disclosed principal One whose existence is known but whose identity is not known.

Undisclosed principal One whose existence and identity are not known.

principal debtor Person whose debt is being supported by a surety.

priority Precedence in order of right.

private carrier Carrier which limits its service and is not open to the general public.

private corporation One organized to conduct either a privately owned business enterprise for profit or a nonprofit corporation.

private law The law involving relationships among individuals and legal entities.

privilege Immunity from tort liability.

privity Contractual relationship.

privity of contract That connection or relationship which exists between two or more contracting parties. The absence of privity as a defense in actions for damages in contract and tort actions is generally no longer viable with the enactment of warranty statutes (*e.g.*, U.C.C. § 2–318), acceptance by States of doctrine of strict liability and court decisions which have extended the right to sue to third party beneficiaries and even innocent bystanders.

probable cause Reasonable belief of the offense charged.

probate Court procedure by which a will is proved to be valid or invalid; though in current usage this term has been expanded to generally include all matters and proceedings pertaining to administration of estates, guardianships, etc.

procedural due process Requirement that governmental action depriving a person of life, liberty, or property be done through a fair procedure.

procedural law Rules for enforcing substantive law.

procedural rules Rules issued by an administrative agency establishing its organization, method of operation, and rules of conduct for practice before it.

procedural unconscionability Unfair or irregular bargaining.

proceeds Consideration for the sale, exchange or other disposition of the collateral.

process *Judicial process* In a wide sense, this term may include all the acts of a court from the beginning to the end of its proceedings in a given cause; but more specifically it means the writ, summons, mandate, or other process which is used to inform the defendant of the institution of proceedings against him and to compel his appearance, in either civil or criminal cases.

Legal process This term is sometimes used as equivalent to "lawful process." Thus, it is said that legal process means process not merely fair on its face, but in fact valid. But properly it means a summons, writ, warrant, mandate, or other process issuing from a court.

profit corporation One founded for the purpose of operating a business for profit.

profit à prendre Right to make some use of the soil of another, such as a right to mine metals, and it carries with it the right of entry and the right to remove.

promise to pay Undertaking to pay an existing obligation.

promisee Person to whom a promise is made.

promisor Person making a promise.

promissory estoppel Arises where there is a promise which promisor should reasonably expect to induce action or forbearance on part of promisee and which does induce such action or forbearance, and where injustice can be avoided only by enforcement of the promise.

promissory note An unconditional written promise to pay a specified sum of money on demand or at a specified date. Such a note is negotiable if signed by the maker and containing an unconditional promise to pay a sum certain in money either on demand or at a definite time and payable to order or bearer. U.C.C. § 3–104.

promoters In the law relating to corporations, those persons are called the "promoters" of a company who first associate themselves together for the purpose of organizing the company, issuing its prospectus, procuring subscriptions to the stock, securing a charter, etc.

property Interest that is legally protected.

Abandoned property Intentionally disposed of by the owner.

Lost property Unintentionally left by the owner.

Mislaid property Intentionally placed by the owner but unintentionally left.

prosecute To bring a criminal proceeding.

protest A formal declaration made by a person interested or concerned in some act about to be done, or already performed, whereby he expresses his dissent or disapproval, or affirms the act against his will. The object of such a declaration is generally to save some right which would be lost to him if his implied assent could be made out, or to exonerate himself from some responsibility which would attach to him unless he expressly negatived his assent.

Notice of protest A notice given by the holder of a bill or note to the drawer or indorser that the bill has been protested for refusal of payment or acceptance. U.C.C. § 3–509.

provisional credit Tentative credit for the deposit of an instrument until final credit is given.

proximate cause Where the act or omission played a substantial part in bringing about or actually causing the injury or damage and where the injury or damage was either a direct result or a reasonably probable consequence of the act or omission.

proxy (Contracted from procuracy.) Written authorization given by one person to another so that the second person can act for the first, such as that given by a shareholder to someone else to represent him and vote his shares at a shareholders' meeting.

public corporation One created to administer a unit of local civil government or one created by the United States to conduct public business.

public disclosure of private facts Offensive publicity given to private information about another person.

public law The law dealing with the relationship between government and individuals.

puffery Sales talk that is considered general bragging or overstatement.

punitive damages Damages awarded in excess of normal compensation to punish a defendant for a serious civil wrong.

purchase money security interest A seller of goods who retains a security interest in goods purchased with the loaned money.

Q

qualified fee Ownership subject to its being taken away upon the happening of an event.

quantum meruit Expression "quantum meruit" means "as much as he deserves" and it is an expression that describes the extent of liability on a contract implied by law. Essential elements of recovery under quantum meruit are: (1) valuable services were rendered or materials furnished, (2) for person sought to be charged, (3) which services and materials were accepted by person sought to be charged, used and enjoyed by him, and (4) under such circumstances as reasonably notified person sought to be charged that plaintiff, in performing such services, was expected to be paid by person sought to be charged.

quasi Latin. As if; almost as it were; analogous to. It negatives idea of identity, but points out that the conceptions are sufficiently similar for one to be classed as the equal of the other.

quasi contract Legal fiction invented by common law courts to permit recovery by contractual remedy in cases where, in fact, there is no contract, but where circumstances are such that justice warrants a recovery as though there had been a promise.

quasi in rem See **in rem.**

quasi in rem jurisdiction Jurisdiction over property not based on claims against it.

quiet enjoyment Right of a tenant not to have his physical possession of premises interfered with by the landlord.

quitclaim deed A deed of conveyance operating by way of release; that is, intended to pass any title, interest, or claim which the grantor may have in the premises, but not professing that such title is valid, nor containing any warranty or covenants for title.

quorum When a committee, board of directors, meeting of shareholders, legislature, or other body of persons cannot act unless a certain number at least of them are present.

R

rape Unlawful and unconsented to sexual intercourse.

ratification In a broad sense, the confirmation of a previous act done either by the party himself or by another; as, confirmation of a voidable act.

In the law of principal and agent, the adoption and confirmation by one person with knowledge of all material facts, of an act or contract performed or entered into in his behalf by another who at the time assumed without authority to act as his agent.

rational relationship test Requirement that legislation bear a rational relationship to a legitimate governmental interest.

real defenses Defenses that are valid against all holders, including holders in due course.

real property Land, and generally whatever is erected or growing upon or affixed to land. Also rights issuing out of, annexed to, and exercisable within or about land. See also **fixture.**

reasonable man standard Duty of care required to avoid being negligent; one who is careful, diligent, and prudent.

receiver A fiduciary of the court, appointed as an incident to other proceedings wherein certain ultimate relief is prayed. He is a trustee or ministerial officer representing court, and all parties in interest in litigation, and property or fund intrusted to him.

recognizance Formal acknowledgment of indebtedness made in court.

redemption The realization of a right to have the title of property restored free and clear of the mortgage; performance of the mortgage obligation being essential for that purpose.

Repurchase by corporation of its own shares.

reformation Equitable remedy used to reframe written contracts to reflect accurately real agreement between contracting parties when, either through mutual mistake or unilateral mistake coupled with actual or equitable fraud by other party, the writing does not embody contract as actually made.

regulatory license Requirement to protect the public interest.

reimbursement Duty owed by principal to pay back authorized payments agent has made on principal's behalf. Duty owed by a principal debtor to repay surety who pays principal debtor's obligation.

rejection The refusal to accept an offer; manifestation of an unwillingness to accept the goods (sales).

release The relinquishment, concession, or giving up of a right, claim, or privilege, by the person in whom it exists or to whom it accrues, to the person against whom it might have been demanded or enforced.

remainder An estate limited to take effect and be enjoyed after another estate is determined.

remand To send back. The sending by the appellate court of the cause back to the same court out of which it came, for purpose of having some further action taken on it there.

remedy The means by which the violation of a right is prevented, redressed, or compensated. Though a remedy may be by the act of the party injured, by operation of law, or by agreement between the injurer and the injured, we are chiefly concerned with one kind of remedy, the judicial remedy, which is by action or suit.

rent Consideration paid for use or occupation of property. In a broader sense, it is the compensation or fee paid, usually periodically, for the use of any property, land, buildings, equipment, etc.

replevin An action whereby the owner or person entitled to repossession of goods or chattels may recover those goods or chattels from one who has wrongfully taken or who wrongfully detains such goods or chattels.

reply Plaintiff's pleading in response to the defendant's answer.

repudiation Repudiation of a contract means refusal to perform duty or obligation owed to other party.

requirements contract See **contracts.**

res ipsa loquitur "The thing speaks for itself"; permits the jury to infer both negligent conduct and causation.

rescission An equitable action in which a party seeks to be relieved of his obligations under a contract on the grounds of mutual mistake, fraud, impossibility, etc.

residuary Pertaining to the residue; constituting the residue; giving or bequeathing the residue; receiving or entitled to the residue. See also **legacy,** *residuary legacy.*

respondeat superior Latin. Let the master answer. This maxim means that a master or employer is liable in certain cases for the wrongful acts of his servant or employee, and a principal for those of his agent.

respondent In equity practice, the party who makes an answer to a bill or other proceeding in equity. In appellate practice, the party who contends against an appeal; *i.e.,* the appellee. The party who appeals is called the "appellant."

restitution An equitable remedy under which a person who has rendered services to another seeks to be reimbursed for the costs of his acts (but not his profits) even though there was never a contract between the parties.

restraint on alienation A provision in an instrument of conveyance which prohibits the grantee from selling or transferring the property which is the subject of the conveyance. Many such restraints are unenforceable as against public policy and the law's policy of free alienability of land.

restraint of trade Agreement that eliminates or tends to eliminate competition.

restrictive covenant Private restriction on property contained in a conveyance.

revenue license Measure to raise money.

reverse An appellate court uses the term "reversed" to indicate that it annuls or avoids the judgment, or vacates the decree, of the trial court.

reverse discrimination Employment decisions taking into account race or gender in order to remedy past discrimination.

reversion The term reversion has two meanings, first, as designating the estate left in the grantor during the continuance of a particular estate and also the residue left in grantor or his heirs after termination of particular estate. It differs from a remainder in that it arises by act of the law, whereas a remainder is by act of the parties. A reversion, moreover, is the remnant left in the grantor, while a remainder is the remnant of the whole estate disposed of, after a preceding part of the same has been given away.

revocation The recall of some power, authority, or thing granted, or a destroying or making void of some deed that had existence until the act of revocation made it void.

revocation of acceptance Rescission of one's acceptance of goods based upon the nonconformity of the goods which substantially impairs their value.

right Legal capacity to require another person to perform or refrain from performing an act.

right of entry The right of taking or resuming possession of land by entering on it in a peaceable manner.

right of redemption The right (granted by statute only) to free property from the encumbrance of a foreclosure or other judicial sale, or to recover the title passing thereby, by paying what is due, with interest, costs, etc. Not to be confounded with the "equity of redemption," which exists independently of statute but must be exercised before sale. See also **equity of redemption.**

right to work law State statute that prohibits union shop contracts.

rights in collateral Personal property the debtor owns, possesses, or is in the process of acquiring.

risk of loss Allocation of loss between seller and buyer where the goods have been damaged, destroyed, or lost.

robbery Larceny from a person by force or threat of force.

rule Agency statement of general or particular applicability designed to implement, interpret, or process law or policy.

rule against perpetuities Principle that no interest in property is good unless it must vest, if at all, not later than 21 years, plus period of gestation, after some life or lives in being at time of creation of interest.

rule of reason Balancing the anticompetitive effects against procompetitive effects of the restraint.

S

sale Transfer of title to goods from seller to buyer for a price.

sale on approval Transfer of possession without title to buyer for trial period.

sale or return Sale where buyer has option to return goods to seller.

sanction Means of enforcing legal judgments.

satisfaction The discharge of an obligation by paying a party what is due to him (as on a mortgage, lien, or contract) or what is awarded to him, by the judgment of a court or otherwise. Thus, a judgment is satisfied by the payment of the amount due to the party who has recovered such judgment, or by his levying the amount. See also **accord and satisfaction.**

scienter Latin. Knowingly.

seal Symbol that authenticates a document.

secondary liability Obligation to pay is subject to the conditions of presentment, dishonor, notice of dishonor, and sometimes protest.

secret partner Partner whose membership in the partnership is not disclosed.

Section 402A Strict liability in tort.

secured bond A bond having a lien on specific property.

secured claim Claim with a lien on property of the debtor.

secured party Creditor who possesses a security interest in collateral.

secured transaction A transaction which is founded on a security agreement. Such agreement creates or provides for a security interest. U.C.C. § 9–105(h).

securities Stocks, bonds, notes, convertible debentures, warrants, or other documents that represent a share in a company or a debt owed by a company.
  Certificated security Security represented by a certificate.
  Exempt security Security not subject to registration requirements of 1933 Act.
  Exempt transaction Issuance of securities not subject to the registration requirements of 1933 Act.
  Restricted securities Securities issued under an exempt transaction.
  Uncertificated security Security not represented by a certificate.

security agreement Agreement that grants a security interest.

security interest Right in personal property securing payment or performance of an obligation.

seisin Possession with an intent on the part of him who holds it to claim a freehold interest.

self-defense Force to protect oneself against attack.

separation of powers Allocation of powers among the legislative, executive, and judicial branches of government.

service mark Distinctive symbol, word, or design that is used to identify the services of a provider.

servient Land subject to an easement.

set-off A counterclaim demand which defendant holds against plaintiff, arising out of a transaction extrinsic of plaintiff's cause of action.

settlor Creator of the trust.

severance The destruction of any one of the unities of a joint tenancy. It is so called because the estate is no longer a joint tenancy, but is severed.

Term may also refer to cutting of the crops, such as corn, wheat, etc., or the separating of anything from the realty.

share A proportionate ownership interest in a corporation.

Shelley's case, rule in Where a person takes an estate of freehold, legally, or equitably, under a deed, will, or other writing, and in the same instrument there is a limitation by way of remainder of any interest of the same legal or equitable quality to his heirs, or heirs of his body, as a class of persons to take in succession from generation to generation, the limitation to the heirs entitles the ancestor to the whole estate.

The rule was adopted as a part of the common law of this country, though it has long since been abolished by most States.

shelter rule Transferee gets rights of transferor.

shipment contract Seller is authorized or required only to bear the expense of placing goods with the common carrier and bears the risk of loss only up to such point.

short swing profits Profits made by insider through sale or other disposition of the corporate stock within six months after purchase.

sight draft An instrument payable on presentment.

signature Any symbol executed with intent to validate a writing.

silent partner Partner takes no part in the partnership business.

slander Oral defamation.

small claims courts Inferior civil courts with jurisdiction limited by dollar amount.

social security Measures by which the government provides economic assistance to disabled or retired employees and their dependents.

sole proprietorship A form of business in which one person owns all the assets of the business in contrast to a partnership and corporation.

sovereign immunity Foreign country's freedom from the host country's laws.

special warranty deed Seller promises that he has not impaired title.

specific performance The doctrine of specific performance is that, where damages would be an inadequate compensation for the breach of an agreement, the contractor or vendor will be compelled to perform specifically what he has agreed to do; *e.g.*, ordered to execute a specific conveyance of land.

With respect to sale of goods, specific performance may be decreed where the goods are unique or in other proper circumstances. The decree for specific performance may include such terms and conditions as to payment of the price, damages, or other relief as the court may deem just. U.C.C. §§ 2–711(2)(b), 2–716.

standardized business form A preprinted contract.

stare decisis Doctrine that, when court has once laid down a principle of law as applicable to a certain state of facts, it will adhere to that principle, and apply it to all future cases, where facts are substantially the same; regardless of whether the parties and property are the same.

state action Actions by governments as opposed to actions taken by private individuals.

state of the art Made in accordance with the level of technology at the time the product is made.

stated capital Consideration received for issued stock other than that allocated to capital surplus.

statute of frauds A celebrated English statute, passed in 1677, and which has been adopted, in a more or less modified form, in nearly all of the United States. Its chief characteristic is the provision that no action shall be brought on certain contracts unless there be a note or memorandum thereof in writing, signed by the party to be charged or by his authorized agent.

statute of limitation A statute prescribing limitations to the right of action on certain described causes of action; that is, declaring that no suit shall be maintained on such causes of action unless brought within a specified period after the right accrued.

statutory lien Interest in property to secure payment of a debt that arises solely by statute.

stock "Stock" is distinguished from "bonds" and, ordinarily, from "debentures," in that it gives right of ownership in part of assets of corporation and right to interest in any surplus after payment of debt. "Stock" in a corporation is an equity, and it represents an ownership interest, and it is to be distinguished from obligations such as notes or bonds which are not equities and represent no ownership interest.

Capital stock See **capital.**

Common stock Securities which represent an ownership interest in a corporation. If the company has also issued preferred stock, both common and preferred have ownership rights. Claims of both common and preferred stockholders are junior to claims of bondholders or other creditors of the company. Common stockholders assume the greater risk, but generally exercise the greater control and may gain the greater reward in the form of dividends and capital appreciation.

Convertible stock Stock which may be changed or converted into common stock.

Cumulative preferred A stock having a provision that if one or more dividends are omitted, the omitted dividends must be paid before dividends may be paid on the company's common stock.

Preferred stock is a separate portion or class of the stock of a corporation, which is accorded, by the charter or by-laws, a preference or priority in respect to dividends, over the remainder of the stock of the corporation, which in that case is called *common stock.*

Stock warrant A certificate entitling the owner to buy a specified amount of stock at a specified time(s) for a specified price. Differs from a stock option only in that options are granted to employees and warrants are sold to the public.

Treasury stock Shares reacquired by a corporation.

stock option Contractual right to purchase stock from a corporation.

stop payment Order for a drawee not to pay an instrument.

strict liability A concept applied by the courts in product liability cases in which a seller is liable for any and all defective or hazardous products which unduly threaten a consumer's personal safety. This concept applies to all members involved in the manufacturing and selling of any facet of the product.

strict scrutiny test Requirement that legislation be necessary to promote a compelling governmental interest.

subagent Person appointed by agent to perform agent's duties.

subject matter jurisdiction Authority of a court to decide a particular kind of case.

subject to the mortgage Purchaser is not personally obligated to pay the debt, but the property remains subject to the mortgage.

subjective fault Desired or virtually certain consequences of one's conduct.

subjective satisfaction Approval based upon a party's honestly held opinion.

sublease Transfer of less than all of the tenant's interest in the leasehold.

subpoena A subpoena is a command to appear at a certain time and place to give testimony upon a certain matter. A subpoena duces tecum requires production of books, papers, and other things.

subrogation The substitution of one thing for another, or of one person into the place of another with respect to rights, claims, or securities.

Subrogation denotes the putting a third person who has paid a debt in the place of the creditor to whom he has paid it, so that he may exercise against the debtor all the rights which the creditor, if unpaid, might have done.

subscribe Literally to write underneath, as one's name. To sign at the end of a document. Also, to agree in writing to furnish money or its equivalent, or to agree to purchase some initial stock in a corporation.

subscriber Person who agrees to purchase initial stock in a corporation.

subsidiary corporation Corporation controlled by another corporation.

substantial performance Equitable doctrine protects against forfeiture for technical inadvertence or trivial variations or omissions in performance.

substantive due process Requirement that governmental action be compatible with individual liberties.

substantive law The basic law of rights and duties (contract law, criminal law, tort law, law of wills, etc.) as opposed to procedural law (law of pleading, law of evidence, law of jurisdiction, etc.).

substantive unconscionability Oppressive or grossly unfair contractual terms.

sue To begin a lawsuit in a court.

suit "Suit" is a generic term, of comprehensive signification, and applies to any proceeding in a court of justice in which the plaintiff pursues, in such court, the remedy which the law affords him for the redress of an injury or the recovery of a right.

Derivative suit Suit brought by a shareholder on behalf of the corporation to enforce a right belonging to the corporation.

Direct suit Suit brought by a shareholder against the corporation based upon his ownership of shares.

summary judgment Any party to a civil action may move for a summary judgment on a claim, counterclaim, or cross-claim when he believes that there is no genuine issue of material fact and that he is entitled to prevail as a matter of law.

summons Writ or process directed to the sheriff or other proper officer, requiring him to notify the person named that an action has been commenced against him in the court from where the process issues, and that he is required to appear, on a day named, and answer the complaint in such action.

superseding cause Intervening event that occurs after the defendant's negligent conduct and relieves him of liability.

supreme law Law that takes precedence over all conflicting laws.

surety One who undertakes to pay money or to do any other act in event that his principal debtor fails therein.

suretyship A guarantee of debts of another.

surplus Excess of net assets over stated capital.

T

tangible property Physical objects.

tariff Duty or tax imposed on goods moving into or out of the country.

tenancy Possession or occupancy of land or premises under lease.

Joint tenancy Joint tenants have one and the same interest, accruing by one and the same conveyance, commencing at one and the same time, and held by one and the same undivided possession. The primary incident of joint tenancy is survivorship, by which the entire tenancy on the decease of any joint tenant remains to the survivors, and at length to the last survivor.

Tenancy at sufferance Only naked possession which continues after tenant's right of possession has terminated.

Tenancy at will Possession of premises by permission of owner or landlord, but without a fixed term.

Tenancy by the entirety A tenancy which is created between a husband and wife and by which together they hold title to the whole with right of survivorship so that, upon death of either, other takes whole to exclusion of deceased heirs. It is essentially a "joint tenancy," modified by the common law theory that husband and wife are one person.

Tenancy for a period A tenancy for years or for some fixed period.

Tenancy in common A form of ownership whereby each tenant (*i.e.,* owner) holds an undivided interest in property. Unlike a joint tenancy or a tenancy by the entirety, the interest of a tenant in common does not terminate upon his or her prior death (*i.e.,* there is no right of survivorship).

tenancy in partnership Type of joint ownership that determines partners' rights in specific partnership property.

tenant Possessor of the leasehold interest.

tender An offer of money; the act by which one produces and offers to a person holding a claim or demand against him the amount of money which he considers and admits to be due, in satisfaction of such claim or demand, without any stipulation or condition.

Also, there may be a tender of performance of a duty other than the payment of money.

tender of delivery Seller makes available to buyer goods conforming to the contract and so notifies the buyer.

tender offer General invitation to all shareholders to purchase their shares at a specified price.

testament Will.

testator One who makes or has made a testament or will; one who dies leaving a will.

third party beneficiary One for whose benefit a promise is made in a contract but who is not a party to the contract.

Creditor beneficiary Where performance of a promise in a contract will benefit a person other than the promisee, that person is a creditor beneficiary if no purpose to make a gift appears from the terms of the promise in view of the accompanying circumstances and performance of the promise will satisfy an actual or supposed or asserted duty of the promisee to the beneficiary.

Donee beneficiary The person who takes the benefit of the contract even though there is no privity between him and the contracting parties. A third party beneficiary who is not a creditor beneficiary. See also **beneficiary.**

time paper Payable at definite time.

time-price doctrine Permits sellers to have different prices for cash sales and credit sales.

title The means whereby the owner of lands or of personalty has the just possession of his property.

title insurance Provides protection against defect in title to real property.

tort A private or civil wrong or injury, other than breach of contract, for which the court will provide a remedy in the form of an action for damages.

Three elements of every tort action are: Existence of legal duty from defendant to plaintiff, breach of duty, and damage as proximate result.

tort-feasor One who commits a tort.

trade acceptance A draft drawn by a seller which is presented for signature (acceptance) to the buyer at the time goods are purchased and which then becomes the equivalent of a note receivable of the seller and the note payable of the buyer.

trade name Name used in trade or business to identify a particular business or manufacturer.

trade secrets Private business information.

trademark Distinctive insignia, word, or design of a good that is used to identify the manufacturer.

transferor's warranty Warranties given by any person who transfers an instrument and receives consideration.

treaty An agreement between or among independent nations.

treble damages Three times actual loss.

trespass At common law, trespass was a form of action brought to recover damages for any injury to one's person or property or relationship with another.

Trespass to chattels or personal property An unlawful and serious interference with the possessory rights of another to personal property.

Trespass to land At common law, every unauthorized and direct breach of the boundaries of another's land was an actionable trespass. The present prevailing position of the courts finds liability for trespass only in the case of intentional intrusion, or negligence, or some "abnormally dangerous activity" on the part of the defendant. Compare **nuisance.**

trespasser Person who enters or remains on the land of another without permission or privilege to do so.

trust Any arrangement whereby property is transferred with intention that it be administered by trustee for another's benefit.

Charitable trust To benefit humankind.

Constructive trust Wherever the circumstances of a transaction are such that the person who takes the legal estate in property cannot also enjoy the beneficial interest without necessarily violating some established principle of equity, the court will immediately raise a *constructive trust,* and fasten it upon the conscience of the legal owner, so as to convert him into a trustee for the parties who in equity are entitled to the beneficial enjoyment.

Intervivos trust Established during the settlor's lifetime.

Resulting trust One that arises by implication of law, where the legal estate in property is disposed of, conveyed, or transferred, but the intent appears or is inferred from the terms of the disposition, or from the accompanying facts and circumstances, that the beneficial interest is not to go or be enjoyed with the legal title.

Spendthrift trust Removal of the trust's estate from the beneficiary's control.

Testamentary trust Established by a will.

Totten trust A tentative trust which is a joint bank account opened by the settlor.

Voting trust A trust which holds the voting rights to stock in a corporation. It is a useful device when a majority of the shareholders in a corporation cannot agree on corporate policy.

trustee In a strict sense, a "trustee" is one who holds the legal title to property for the benefit of another, while, in a broad sense, the term is sometimes applied to anyone standing in a fiduciary or confidential relation to another, such as agent, attorney, bailee, etc.

trustee in bankruptcy Representative of the estate in bankruptcy who is responsible for collecting, liquidating, and distributing the debtor's assets.

tying arrangements   Conditioning a sale of a desired product (tying product) on the buyer's purchasing a second product (tied product).

U

ultra vires   Acts beyond the scope of the powers of a corporation, as defined by its charter or laws of state of incorporation. By doctrine of ultra vires a contract made by a corporation beyond the scope of its corporate powers is unlawful.

unconscionable   Unfair or unduly harsh.

unconscionable contract   See **contracts**.

underwriter   Any person, banker, or syndicate that guarantees to furnish a definite sum of money by a definite date to a business or government in return for an issue of bonds or stock. In insurance, the one assuming a risk in return for the payment of a premium.

undisputed debt   Obligation whose existence and amount is not contested.

undue influence   Term refers to conduct by which a person, through his power over mind of testator, makes the latter's desires conform to his own, thereby overmastering the volition of the testator.

unemployment compensation   Compensation awarded to workers who have lost their jobs and cannot find other employment.

unenforceable   Neither party can recover under the contract.

unfair employer practice   Conduct in which an employer is prohibited from engaging.

unfair labor practice   Conduct in which an employer or union is prohibited from engaging.

unfair union practice   Conduct in which a union is prohibited from engaging.

Uniform Commercial Code   One of the Uniform Laws drafted by the National Conference of Commissioners on Uniform State Laws governing commercial transactions (sales of goods, commercial paper, bank deposits and collections, letters of credit, bulk transfers, warehouse receipts, bills of lading, investment securities, and secured transactions).

unilateral mistake   Erroneous belief on the part of only one of the parties to a contract.

union shop   Employer can hire nonunion members, but the employee must join the union.

universal life   Ordinary life divided into two components, a renewable term insurance policy and an investment portfolio.

unliquidated debt   Obligation that is uncertain or contested in amount.

unqualified indorsement (see **Indorsement**) One that imposes liability upon the indorser.

unreasonably dangerous   Danger beyond that which the ordinary consumer contemplates.

unrestrictive indorsement (see **Indorsement**) One that does not attempt to restrict the rights of the indorsee.

usage of trade   A usage of trade is any practice or method of dealing having such regularity of observance in a place, vocation, or trade as to justify an expectation that it will be observed with respect to the transaction in question.

usury   Collectively, the laws of a jurisdiction regulating the charging of interest rates. A usurious loan is one whose interest rates are determined to be in excess of those permitted by the usury laws.

V

value   The performance of legal consideration, the forgiveness of an antecedent debt, the giving of a negotiable instrument, or the giving of an irrevocable commitment to a third party. U.C.C. § 1–201(44).

variance   A use differing from that provided in the zoning ordinance in order to avoid undue hardship.

vendee   A purchaser or buyer; one to whom anything is sold. See also **vendor**.

vendor   The person who transfers property by sale, particularly real estate; "seller" being more commonly used for one who sells personalty. See also **vendee**.

venue   "Jurisdiction" of the court means the inherent power to decide a case, whereas "venue" designates the particular county or city in which a court with jurisdiction may hear and determine the case.

verdict   The formal and unanimous decision or finding of a jury, impaneled and sworn for the trial of a cause, upon the matters or questions duly submitted to them upon the trial.

vertical privity   Who is liable to the plaintiff.

vertical restraints Agreements among parties at different levels of the distribution chain.

vested Fixed; accrued; settled; absolute. To be "vested," a right must be more than a mere expectation based on an anticipation of the continuance of an existing law; it must have become a title, legal or equitable, to the present or future enforcement of a demand, or a legal exemption from the demand of another.

vested remainder Unconditional remainder that is a fixed, present interest to be enjoyed in the future.

vicarious liability Indirect legal responsibility; for example, the liability of an employer for the acts of an employee, or, a principal for torts and contracts of an agent.

void Null; ineffectual; nugatory; having no legal force or binding effect; unable, in law, to support the purpose for which it was intended.

There is this difference between the two words "void" and "voidable": *void* in the strict sense means that an instrument or transaction is nugatory and ineffectual so that nothing can cure it; *voidable* exists when an imperfection or defect can be cured by the act or confirmation of him who could take advantage of it.

Frequently the word "void" is used and construed as having the more liberal meaning of "voidable."

voidable Capable of being made void. See also **void.**

voir dire Preliminary examination of potential jurors.

voluntary Resulting from free choice. The word, especially in statutes, often implies knowledge of essential facts.

voting trust Transfer of corporate shares voting rights to a trustee.

W

wager (gambling) Agreement that one party will win or lose depending upon the outcome of an event in which the only interest is the gain or loss.

waiver Terms "estoppel" and "waiver" are not synonymous; "waiver" means the voluntary, intentional relinquishment of a known right, and "estoppel" rests upon principle that, where anyone has done an act, or made a statement, which would be a fraud on his part to controvert or impair, because other party has acted upon it in belief that what was done or said was true, conscience and honest dealing require that he not be permitted to repudiate his act or gainsay his statement. See also **estoppel.**

ward An infant or insane person placed by authority of law under the care of a guardian.

warehouse receipt Receipt issued by a person storing goods.

warehouser Storer of goods for compensation.

warrant, *v.* In contracts, to engage or promise that a certain fact or state of facts, in relation to the subject-matter, is, or shall be, as it is represented to be.

In conveyancing, to assure the title to property sold, by an express covenant to that effect in the deed of conveyance.

warranty A warranty is a statement or representation made by seller of goods, contemporaneously with and as a part of contract of sale, having reference to character, quality, or title of goods, and by which seller promises or undertakes to insure that certain facts are or shall be as he then represents them.

The general statutory law governing warranties on sales of goods is provided in U.C.C. § 2–312 *et seq.* The three main types of warranties are: (1) express warranty; (2) implied warranty of fitness; (3) implied warranty of merchantability.

warranty deed Deed in which grantor warrants good clear title. The usual covenants of title are warranties of seisin, quiet enjoyment, right to convey, freedom from encumbrances and defense of title as to all claims.

Special warranty deed Seller warrants that he has not impaired title.

warranty liability Applies to persons who transfer an instrument or receive payment or acceptance.

warranty of title Obligation to convey the right to ownership without any lien.

waste Any act or omission that does permanent injury to the realty or unreasonably changes its value.

white collar crime Corporate crime.

will A written instrument executed with the formalities required by statutes, whereby a person makes a disposition of his property to take effect after his death.

winding up To settle the accounts and liquidate the assets of a partnership or corporation, for the purpose of making distribution and terminating the concern.

without reserve Auctioneer may not withdraw the goods from the auction.

workers' compensation Compensation awarded to an employee who is injured when the injury arose out of and in the course of his employment.

writ of certiorari Discretionary review by a higher court. See also **certiorari.**

writ of execution Order served by sheriff upon debtor demanding payment of a court judgment against debtor.

Z

zoning Public control over land use.

Index

(Page numbers in italics denote illustrations.)